AMERICAN HORTICULTURAL SOCIETY

ENCYCLOPEDIA *of* PLANTS AND FLOWERS

AMERICAN HORTICULTURAL SOCIETY

ENCYCLOPEDIA of PLANTS AND FLOWERS

DK Publishing

LONDON, NEW YORK, MUNICH, MELBOURNE, DELHI

DK Publishing
Publisher Chuck Lang
Creative Director Tina Vaughan
Editorial Director Chuck Wills
Project Director Valerie Buckingham
US Editor Ray Rogers
Production Manager Chris Avgherinos
DTP Coordinator Milos Orlovic

American Horticultural Society
would like to thank:
Arabella S. Dane, for the use of her interactive horticultural database program "Showtime©"
Dr. H. Marc Cathey, for researching and coordinating the plant codes for heat and hardiness

DK Publishing
would also like to thank the team on the original edition
Senior Editor Joanna Chisholm
Project Editors Alison Copland, Marion Dent, Angeles Gavira, Jacqueline Jackson, Stella Martin, Lesley Riley
Additional editorial assistance from Polly Boyd, Lynn Bresler, Michèle Clarke, Peter Kirkham, Maggie O'Hanlon, Jane Parker, Nichola Thomasson, Sarah Widdicombe
Senior Art Editor Ina Stradins
DTP Project Manager Robert Campbell
Picture Research Neale Chamberlaine, Sue Hadley, Sean Hunter, Hugh Thompson
Senior Managing Editor Jonathan Metcalf
Senior Managing Art Editor Bryn Walls

Editor-in-chief for Canadian Edition Trevor Cole

Design and page make-up Schermuly Design Co. (Jenny Buzzard, Nick Buzzard, Masumi Higo, Hugh Schermuly)

Photographers Clive Boursnell, Deni Bown, Jonathan Buckley, Andrew Butler, Eric Crichton, Christine M. Douglas, John Fielding, Neil Fletcher, Nancy Gardiner, John Glover, Jerry Harpur, Sunniva Harte, Neil Holmes, Jacqui Hurst, Andrew Lawson, Andrew de Lory, Howard Rice, Matthew Ward, Steve Wooster

Illustrators Vanessa Luff, Amanda Lunn, Eric Thomas, Janos Marffy

Advisors and consultants In addition to the contributors listed on the Contents page, DK Publishing would like to thank Barry Ambrose, John Bond, Tony Clements, Steven Davis, Sheila Ecklin, Barbara Ellis, the late Thomas Everett, Jim Gardiner, Ralph Gould, David Kerly, David Pycraft, Piers Trehane, Dr. Simon Thornton-Wood, Adrian Whiteley, and the staff of the Royal Horticultural Society at Vincent Square and Wisley Garden.

First American edition published by Macmillan Publishing Company in 1989
This fully revised and updated edition first published in America in 2002
00 01 02 03 04 05 10 9 8 7 6 5 4 3 2 1

Published in the United States by
DK Publishing, Inc.
375 Hudson Street
New York, New York 10014

A catalog record for this book is available from the Library of Congress

ISBN 0-7894-8993-7

Printed and bound in Germany by Mohndruck GmbH

See our complete product line at
www.dk.com

Preface

Gardening in the 21st Century

Gardening, no matter how informally it is approached, involves the gardener working with plant selections, garden design, and the environment to create sustainable growth systems within a controlled space. The good gardener anticipates the requirements of the plants and provides water, nutrients, organic matter, and cultural practices based on his or her judgment and experiences. Good gardeners also assume that they must become active architects of their environment and, along with their successes, they accept losses due to uncontrollable events such as cold, heat, drought, flooding, and wind well as the ravages of pests and diseases. The one overarching concept for successful gardening, "the right plant for the right location," guides the gardener through that journey through success and loss.

For most gardeners, the USDA Plant Hardiness Zone Map is an indispensable tool. Published in 1960, it has allowed us to select plants appropriate for our sites based on cold tolerance. Between 1983 and 1990, while serving as the fourth director of the United States National Arboretum, I coordinated the updating of the map with data collected from 8,000 weather stations throughout America from 1974 to 1986. As a result of this update, a new USDA plant hardiness zone was added to the map, increasing the number of zones representing gardening in America from 10 to 11. We are updating again. Under my direction as president emeritus of the American Horticultural Society, the USDA Plant Hardiness Map has again been updated, and now, in 2002, the number of plant hardiness zones has increased from 11 to 15. This allows for more accurate coding of plants in our more southerly regions and includes plants not previously coded, vegetables and many grasses.

But as we all know, cold is not the only factor that influences the survival and performance of garden plants. In 1997, I coordinated the creation of the American Horticultural Society Plant Heat Zone Map that gives American gardeners a new tool for assessing the potential performance of plants in regard to another major criterion—the average number of hot summer days in their region. This map closes the circle of information on a plant's temperature tolerances and is most effective when used in conjunction with the USDA Plant Hardiness Map.

With the help of this book, I am convinced that you will be able to select exactly the right plant for the right place in your garden. Armed with this valuable information and inspiration, I hope you will be able to create a beautiful and environmentally sustainable garden—and have fun doing it, too!

Forever in green,

Dr. H. Marc Cathey
President Emeritus
AMERICAN HORICULTURAL SOCIETY

Contributors

Susyn Andrews	*Hollies*
Larry Barlow (with W.B. Wade)	*Chrysanthemums*
Kenneth A. Beckett	*Shrubs, Climbers, Bromeliads*
(with David Pycraft)	*The Plant Selector*
John Brookes (with Linden Hawthorne)	*Creating a Garden*
Eric Catterall (with Richard Gilbert)	*Begonias*
Allen J. Coombes	*Plant Origins and Names, Trees, Shrubs, Glossary of Terms*
Philip Damp (with Roger Aylett)	*Dahlias*
Kate Donald	*Peonies, Daffodils*
Kath Dryden	*Rock plants*
Raymond Evison	*Clematis*
Diana Grenfell	*Hostas*
Peter Harkness	*Roses*
Linden Hawthorne	*Chapter introductions in Plant Catalogue*
Terry Hewitt	*Cacti and other Succulents*
David Hitchcock	*Carnations and Pinks*
Hazel Key	*Pelargoniums (Geraniums)*
Sidney Linnegar	*Irises*
Brian Mathew	*Irises, Bulbs*
Victoria Matthews	*Climbers, Lilies, Tulips*
David McClintock	*Grasses, Bamboos, Rushes and Sedges*
Diana Miller (with Richard Gilbert)	*Perennials African violets*
John Paton	*Perennials*
Charles Puddle	*Camellias*
Wilma Rittershausen (with Sabina Knees)	*Orchids*
Peter Q. Rose (with Hazel Key)	*Ivies*
Keith Rushforth	*Conifers*
A.D. Schilling	*Rhododendrons and Azaleas*
Arthur Smith	*Gladiolus*
Philip Swindells (with Peter Barnes)	*Ferns*
(with Kath Dryden and Jack Wemyss-Cooke)	*Primulas*
(with Peter Robinson)	*Water plants and Waterlilies*
John Thirkell	*Delphiniums*
Alan Toogood	*Annuals and Biennials*
Major General Patrick Turpin (with David Small)	*Heathers*
Michael Upward	*Perennials*
John Wright (with Nancy Darnley)	*Fuchsias*

Contents

THE PLANT DICTIONARY

How to Use this Book

The American Horticultural Society Encyclopedia of Plants and Flowers is the ideal reference when planning a garden, selecting plants, or identifying specimens; it provides a wealth of information on the appearance and cultivation of thousands of individual plants.

The Encyclopedia is divided into several sections. Plant Names and Origins explains the international system for classifying and naming plants, while Creating a Garden offers advice on garden styles, how to position and group plants, and the use of color and texture. The Plant Selector helps you select suitable species and varieties, while the heart of the book, The Plant Catalog and The Plant Dictionary, provide detailed photographs, descriptions, and cultivation information.

Size categories

Within most groups in The Plant Catalog, plants are arranged by size (then subsequently by season of interest). Size categories range from large to small, but are defined differently from group to group. Sizes are based on plant heights. The specific height ranges for large, medium, and small can be found in the introductory section for the relevant plant group.

The color order

Within each group, plants are arranged by the color of their main feature. Colors are arranged in the same order: from white through reds, purples and blues to greens, yellows, and oranges.

Variegated plants are categorized by the color of their foliage variegation (i.e. white or yellow); succulents are arranged by the color of their flowers, if produced.

The symbols

- ☼ Prefers sun
- Prefers partial shade
- Tolerates full shade
- pH Needs acidic soil
- Prefers well-drained soil
- Prefers moist soil
- Prefers wet soil
- (!) Toxic plant

Cold hardiness and heat zones

These indicate the zone(s) in which the plant can be expected to survive (see zone maps on endpapers)

The Plant Selector

The Plant Selector recommends plants for a particular site, soil, or purpose, making it easy to find one to suit your needs. The list is divided into 24 useful categories, ranging from plants for hedges and windbreaks to those suitable for containers. Cross-references to The Plant Catalog lead you to a photograph and description of the plant you choose.

Photographic reference Garden themes and uses are illustrated, together with photographs of selected plants.

Top choices Recommended plants are arranged by group, then listed alphabetically.

The Plant Catalog

This section brings together plant portraits and descriptions in a colorful catalog that is divided into groups: Trees (including conifers), Shrubs, Roses, Climbers, Perennials (including grasses, bamboos, rushes, sedges, and ferns), Annuals and Biennials, Rock plants, Bulbs, Water plants, and Cacti and other succulents.

Each group is introduced by a four-page section that provides valuable information for growing and designing with plants in the group. This is followed by a catalog of plants arranged by size, season of interest, and color. Also included are a number of feature panels on plants of special interest, such as camellias, hollies, and African violets.

Catalog page ▼

If you know a plant but cannot recall its name, have a specimen that you want to identify, or simply wish to choose plants for your garden based on their size or coloring, The Plant Catalog will provide the answer.

Color boxes These show the color range of plants featured on each page. (See also chart, left.)

Page headings The headings on each page reflect the way in which each plant group is subdivided – usually by size and main season of interest. (See also Size categories, left.)

Plant portraits Color photographs assist in the identification and selection of plants.

Plant names The botanical name is given for each plant, along with synonyms (syn.) and common names where appropriate.

Captions Captions describe the plants in detail and draw attention to any special uses they may have.

Size and shape For most plants the approximate height (H) and spread (S) are given at the end of each caption. (The height of a trailing plant is the length of its stems, either hanging or spreading.) For Trees, Conifers, and Shrubs a scale drawing shows the size and shape of each plant at maturity.

Cultivation and cold hardiness and heat tolerance Symbols show the plant's preferred growing conditions and tolerance of cold and heat. However, the climatic and soil conditions of your particular site should also be taken into account as they also influence a plant's growth. (See also key, left.)

Cotoneaster simonsii
Deciduous or semi-evergreen, upright shrub, suitable for hedging. Has oval, glossy, dark green leaves, shallowly cup-shaped white flowers in early summer, and long-lasting orange-red fruits in autumn.

☼ ◊ (!) Z6–8 H8–6

Toxic plants This symbol indicates that the plant can be toxic. Details are given in the genus introductions in The Plant Dictionary.

◄ GROUP OPENER

Each new group begins with a photograph featuring an inspiring display of plants in the group.

▼ DESIGN ADVICE

Group openers are followed by more detailed descriptions of the characteristics of plants in the group, together with ideas for how to use these plants to best effect in your garden.

TABS

Color-coded tabs make it easy to find each plant group.

CROSS-REFERENCES ▼

Plants featured elsewhere in the book but similar in type, size, season of interest, and color to those illustrated are listed for consideration.

Chaenomeles speciosa
HEATHERS, illus. pp.178–9
HOLLIES, illus. pp.98–9
Nicotiana glauca

FEATURE PANELS ►

Plant types or genera of special interest to the gardener are presented in separate feature panels within the appropriate group.

KEY CHARACTERISTICS
The introduction outlines the features of that type of plant and gives guidance on cultivation and planting.

FLOWER FORMS
Detailed descriptions of forms and horticultural classifications within a genus are given where appropriate and often supported by line drawings.

PLANT NAMES
The botanical name is given and the Group or classification where appropriate. Plant descriptions appear in The Plant Dictionary.

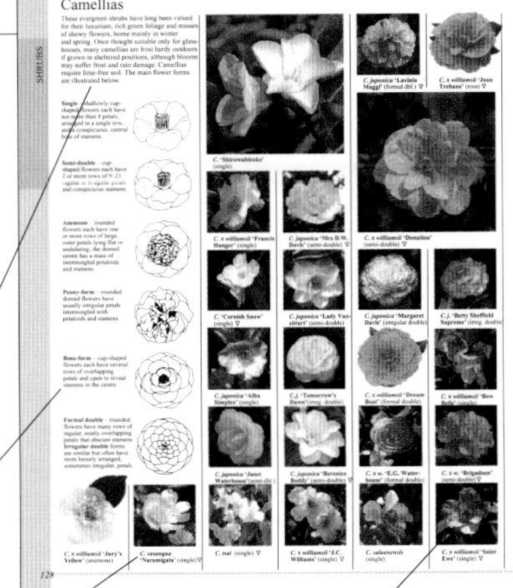

PLANT PORTRAITS
Close-up photographs of individual flowers or plants allow quick identification or selection.

The Plant Dictionary

The Plant Dictionary contains entries for every genus in the Encyclopedia and includes over 4,000 recommended plants not featured in The Plant Catalog. It also functions as the index to The Plant Catalog.

GENUS NAMES
The genus name is followed by common names, where appropriate, and family names.

GENUS ENTRIES
A concise introduction covers the distinctive characteristics and hardiness range of plants in the genus, as well as advice on siting, cultivation, propagation, and, if relevant, pruning, pests and diseases, and toxicity.

SYNONYMS
Synonyms cross-refer to the correct botanical name.

ILLUSTRATED PLANTS
Descriptions for illustrated plants appear in The Plant Catalog, unless part of a feature panel (see below left).

PLANT NAMES
Botanical names, synonyms, and common names are given as appropriate. The genus name is abbreviated; specific epithets (e.g. *sagittifolia*) are abbreviated only if previously given in full.

PLANT DESCRIPTIONS
Key characteristics of the plant are described. Hardiness and cultivation needs are included only if specific to the plant. Cultivar entries run on from the species entry, with the binomial omitted.

CROSS-REFERENCES
Common name and synonym cross-references are listed alphabetically.

> SAGITTARIA
> *Arrowhead*
>
> ALISMATACEAE
>
> Genus of deciduous, perennial, submerged and marginal water plants grown for their foliage and flowers. Some species are suitable for ponds, others for aquariums. All require full sun. Remove fading foliage as necessary. Propagate by division in spring or summer or by breaking off turions (scaly young shoots) in spring.
>
> ***S. japonica.*** See *S. sagittifolia* 'Flore Pleno'.
>
> ***S. latifolia*** illus. p.446.
>
> ***S. sagittifolia*** (Common arrowhead). Deciduous, perennial, marginal water plant. H 18in (45cm), S 12in (30cm). Upright, midgreen leaves are acutely arrow-shaped. In summer produces 3-petaled white flowers with dark purple centers. May be grown in up to 9in (23cm) depth of water. Z5–11 H12–3. **'Flore Pleno'** (syn. *S. japonica*; Japanese arrowhead) has double flowers.
>
> ***Scindapsus aureus*** **'Marble Queen'.** See *Epipremnum aureum* 'Marble Queen'.

COMMON NAMES
A comprehensive list of common names appears on pages 693-717.

Abbreviations

cv(s)	cultivar(s)	illus.	illustrated	subsp.	subspecies
f.	forma	min.	minimum	subspp.	subspecies (pl.)
H	height (or length of trailing stems)	p(p).	page(s)	syn.	synonym(s)
		pl.	plural	var.	varietas
		S	spread		

Plant Hardiness Zones

A given plant's growth and survival is determined by its interaction with many soil and climatic factors over the life of the plant. Among the most important aspects of climate is temperature, and a plant's ability to withstand relative low and high temperatures is referred to as cold hardiness and heat tolerance, respectively. To help gardeners select plants for their gardens based on these factors, the US Department of Agriculture and the American Horticultural Society have developed maps that divide the United States into recognizable zones. Based on information gathered at thousands of locations over many years, the maps and the individual cold-hardiness and heat-zone range codes that are based on them serve as a reliable guide for choosing plants for your garden. The zone maps appear on the endpapers of this book.

The individual codes for cold hardiness and heat tolerance presented in this book are offered as approximate guides and should not be considered as absolute. Practicing horticultural techniques such as mulching and winter protection will alter a plant's interaction with its environment and may enable it to survive beyond the zones given in this or other publications.

Plant Names and Origins

People have always given names to plants, but once they began to travel extensively they discovered that the same plant was often called by a different name in various parts of the world. To overcome this problem, a common naming system was devised.

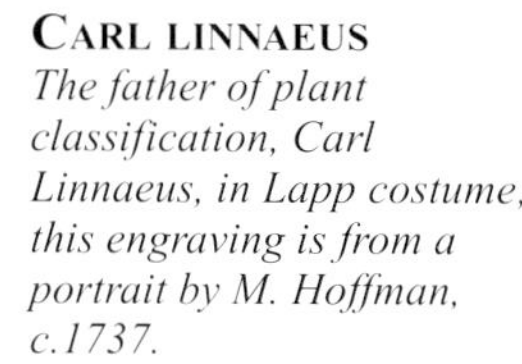

Carl Linnaeus
The father of plant classification, Carl Linnaeus, in Lapp costume; this engraving is from a portrait by M. Hoffman, c.1737.

The binomial system

Greek and Roman scholars laid the foundations of our method of naming plants, and their practice of observing and describing nature in detail was continued in the monasteries and universities of Europe, where classical Latin remained the common language. However, the binomial system in use today was established largely under the influence of the famous eighteenth-century Swedish botanist, Carl Linnaeus (1707–78). In his definitive works *Genera plantarum* and *Species plantarum*, Linnaeus classified each plant by using two words in Latin form, instead of adopting the descriptive phrases that had been in common usage among the botanists and herbalists of his day. The first word was the name of the genus (e.g. *Ilex*) and the second the specific epithet (e.g. *aquifolium*). Together they provided a name by which a particular plant (species) could be universally known (*Ilex aquifolium*, English or common holly). Other species in the same genus were then given different epithets (*Ilex crenata*, *Ilex pernyi*, *Ilex serrata* and so on).

Wild origins
Below: Rhododendron rupicola *var:* chryseum *grows wild in northwestern Yunnan, China, from where it was introduced into British gardens early in the nineteenth century.*

The meaning of plant names

A greater appreciation of botanical names may be gained by knowing something of their meaning. A name may be commemorative: the *Fuchsia* is a tribute to Leonhart Fuchs, a German physician and herbalist. It may tell us where a plant comes from, as with *Parrotia persica* (of Persia, now Iran). A plant may bear the name of the collector who introduced it: *Primula forrestii* was brought into cultivation by George Forrest. Or the name may tell us something about its physical character: *Pelargonium* derives from the Greek word *pelargos* (a stork), an appropriate description of the fruits of these plants, which resemble storks' bills; *quinquefolia*, the epithet of *Parthenocissus quinquefolia*, means with foliage made up of five leaflets, from the Latin *quinque* ("five") and *folium* ("leaf").

Common names

Although many have familiar common names, plants are usually listed under their botanical names. There are a number of reasons for this. Many plants either do not possess a common name, or they share a common name with others. Even more confusingly, the same common name may be used in different regions to describe different plants: in Scotland "plane" refers to *Acer pseudoplatanus* and in England to the London plane (*Platanus* x *hispanica*), while in North America the native *Platanus occidentalis* may be called plane tree or sycamore. Unlike botanical names, which bring related plants together by grouping them in a genus (all true hollies belong to the genus *Ilex*), with common names the same word is often used for quite unrelated plants, such as sea holly (*Eryngium*), hollyhock (*Alcea*) and summer holly (*Arctostaphylos diversifolia*), none of which is related to the true holly. Conversely, one plant may have several common names: heartsease, love-in-idleness, and Johnny-jump-up are all charming titles for *Viola tricolor*. Even greater confusion arises when a vernacular common name is in Malay, Chinese, or Arabic. In botany, as in other scientific disciplines, the universal use of Latin has therefore been found to be a convenient and precise basis for the naming of plants.

International codes

Since its instigation, the Linnaean system of plant classification has been developed by scientists so that the entire plant kingdom is divided into a multibranched "family tree" (see p.13). International cooperation has been essential to ensure that the system is reliable for scientific, commercial, and horticultural use. To this end, there are now rules laid down in the *International Code of Nomenclature for Cultivated Plants* (1995) and the *International Code of Botanical Nomenclature* (1994).

Plant introductions

Just as the origins of plant names may be traced to Classical civilization, so can the first plant introductions. The Roman Empire at its peak covered a vast area, from western Europe to Asia, and as the Romans traveled they brought with them plants they used for food or ornament, such as the Spanish chestnut, peach, fig, and many herbs. During the thirteenth century, returning Crusaders brought the Damask rose from Damascus. Centuries later, cultivated plants such as Persian lilac and the apricot were brought home from the sophisticated Turkish and Moorish gardens along the shores of the Mediterranean.

Plant hunting became more systematic when intrepid private collectors such as the two John Tradescants (father and son) made trips specifically to look for plants on the eastern coasts of North America, particularly Virginia. As the world was mapped and colonized in the eighteenth century, an explosion of botanical interest brought many plants from the New World, notably the western coasts of the American continent, South Africa, Australia, and New Zealand. In the twentieth century, the greatest rewards for the determined plant collector were to be found in the diverse flora of eastern Asia. Although not an easy region for Westerners to explore, thousands of plants, particularly trees and shrubs, were introduced from China, the Himalayan region, and Japan.

GENTIANA SINO-ORNATA
George Forrest had a special interest in gentians, collecting hundreds of specimens during his trips to China. He first discovered this plant in 1904, during a hazardous expedition high in the mountain ranges of northwestern Yunnan.

Genetics and hybridization

Natural mutations in plants have been observed for centuries, but only in the twentieth century has plant breeding developed into a science used throughout the world. Although Thomas Knight carried out some pioneering plant-breeding experiments in the nineteenth century, and the word "hybrid" was used by Darwin, it was not until Gregor Mendel's work with sweet peas in 1899 that the process was understood and could therefore be exploited commercially. Once the mysteries of recessive genes and chromosomes were revealed, it became clear that plants could be bred to be more vigorous and produce more flowers, as well as be altered in other ways. Today, breeders can produce hybrids of a certain shape, color, and habit. One result of this is that certain successful plant "cultivars" (**culti**vated **var**ieties) need to be legally protected (see Coded cultivar names, p.12).

Understanding botanical divisions

The plant kingdom may be broadly divided into vascular plants and nonvascular plants. Vascular plants are of most interest to the gardener and have specialized conducting tissue that enables them to grow in a wider range of habitats and reach a larger size than the nonvascular plants such as algae,

Plant Hunters

A desire to see the world was the original incentive for the earliest botanists, but, as interest in new and rare plants developed, private collectors began to bring back plants with them. These exotic novelties proved extremely popular, especially in fashionable gardens, and fueled the demand for further new plants for garden adornment. To encourage this new market, commercial and scientific organizations began to sponsor the plant hunters. David Douglas was employed in 1824 by the Royal Horticultural Society to travel to America's western coast, where he gathered vast quantities of seed from hitherto unknown species, including the Douglas fir. Access to China was restricted until 1842, but in the following year Robert Fortune began an expedition, again sponsored by the Royal Horticultural Society, that was to yield many ornamental garden plants. In his wake went French botanist-missionaries Father Jean Pierre Armand David, who discovered the lovely *Davidia* tree and after whom *Buddleja davidii* is named, and Father Jean Marie Delavay, who found the blue poppy (*Meconopsis betonicifolia*). Japan was also the source of hundreds of garden plants – many being introduced to Europe by the German plant hunter Philipp von Siebold in the nineteenth century.

The early twentieth century was the golden age of plant hunting. E.H. Wilson, one of the most famous plant hunters (see above right), discovered *Magnolia wilsonii* in 1904, and, in the same period, George Forrest introduced many rhododendrons and other plants from China and Tibet. In the 1920s and 1930s, Frank Kingdon Ward collected unusual primroses, rhododendrons, lilies, and gentians from the Himalayas.

Today, plant-hunting expeditions are still sponsored and new plants introduced, although in smaller quantities than before. However, the impetus for plant discovery has shifted from garden adornment and novelty to plant conservation and breeding.

Magnolia wilsonii

ERNEST HENRY WILSON
Above: E.H. Wilson, who collected in Asia for the English nursery Messrs Veitch and for the Arnold Arboretum, in Boston, discovered more than 900 new plants species and varieties, including Magnolia wilsonii.

Cotoneaster lancasteri

RECENT FINDS
Roy Lancaster (above) is a modern-day plant hunter who has introduced many new species to gardens. Among them are Hypericum lancasteri *and* Cotoneaster lancasteri *(left), both from China.*

Rose hybrids
To create a new hybrid that inherits the best features of both parents, roses are pollinated manually.

mosses, and liverworts. Vascular plants are classified into many groups, mainly according to the way they bear their seeds. For example conifers, part of the Gymnosperm group, are distinct because they bear their naked seeds in conelike fruits. The basic division within these groups is the family.

The family

Plants are grouped in particular families according to the structure of their flowers, fruits, and other organs. This means that families may consist of clearly related and specialized plants such as the orchids (family Orchidaceae) and the bromeliads (family Bromeliaceae), or embrace plants as diverse (in terms of what they offer the gardener) as those in the family Rosaceae: *Alchemilla*, *Cotoneaster*, *Crataegus*, *Geum*, *Malus*, *Prunus*, *Pyracantha*, *Sorbus*, and *Spiraea*.

The genus and its species

A family may contain one genus (for example, *Eucryphia* is the only genus in the family Eucryphiaceae) or many (the daisy family Asteraceae contains more than 1,000 genera). Each genus consists of related plants, such as oaks (genus *Quercus*), maples (genus *Acer*), and lilies (genus *Lilium*), with several features in common. A genus may contain one or many species. Thus a reference to a member of the genus *Lilium* could be to any of the lilies, but one to *Lilium candidum* would denote one particular lily (in this case the Madonna lily). Certain genera form separate horticultural groups within families. An example of this would be the heaths or heathers (including *Calluna*, *Daboecia*, and *Erica*) within the family Ericaceae, which also includes *Kalmia*, *Rhododendron*, and *Vaccinium* (see visual key, opposite).

A species is a group of plants that consistently and naturally reproduces itself, generating a plant population that shares similar characteristics and which is distinguishable from other natural populations.

Subspecies, varieties, and forms

In the wild, even plants of the same species can exhibit slight differences, and on the basis of these are often split into three botanically recognized but occasionally overlapping subdivisions. The subspecies (subsp.) is a distinct variant, usually as a result of the plant's particular geographical distribution; the variety (botanical *varietas*, abbreviated to "var.") differs slightly in its botanical structure; and the form (*forma*, f.) has only minor variations, such as habit or color of leaf, flower, or fruit.

Cultivars

Many plants grown in today's gardens may be adequately described by their botanical names, but numerous variants exist in cultivation that differ slightly from the wild form of the species. These forms may be of considerable horticultural interest, such as for their variegated leaves. They may be found as individuals in the wild and introduced to cultivation, be selected from a batch of seedlings, or occur as a mutation; all are known as cultivars – a contraction of "cultivated varieties." To come true to type, many cultivars need to be propagated vegetatively (by cuttings, grafting, or division) or grown annually from specially selected seed.

Cultivars named since 1959 must be given vernacular names printed in Roman type within single quotes (e.g. *Phygelius aequalis* 'Yellow Trumpet'); this distinguishes them from wild varieties, which are described by a Latin name in italic type.

Hybrids

Sexual crosses between botanically distinct species or genera are known as hybrids and are indicated by a multiplication sign. If the cross is between species in different genera, the result is called an intergeneric hybrid and, when two (occasionally three or more) genera are concerned, the name given is a condensed form of the names of the genera involved: X *Cupressocyparis* covers hybrids between all species of *Chamaecyparis* and *Cupressus*. If more than three genera are involved, then the hybrids are named after a person and given the ending *-ara*. Thus X *Potinara*, covering hybrids of *Brassavola*, *Cattleya*, *Laelia*, and *Sophronitis*, commemorates M. Potin of the French Orchid Society. Most common, however, are hybrids between species in the same genus. These are known as interspecific hybrids and are given a collective name similar to a species name but preceded by a multiplication sign; for example, *Epimedium* x *rubrum* covers hybrids between *E. alpinum* and *E. grandiflorum*.

When one plant is grafted onto another, a new plant may occasionally arise at the point of grafting, which contains the tissues of both parents. For naming purposes, these graft chimaeras or graft hybrids are treated in the same way as sexual hybrids, except that they are denoted by a plus sign, as in +*Laburnocytisus adamii*, which is a graft hybrid between species of *Laburnum* and *Chamaecytisus*.

Cultivars of hybrids should be listed under a botanical name if one is available or, if the parentage is complex or obscure, by giving the generic name followed solely by the cultivar name (e.g. *Rosa* 'Buff Beauty').

Name changes

It is often confusing and frustrating to come across name changes in new publications. Long-established names disappear, only to be replaced by unfamiliar ones. But there are good reasons for such changes: a plant may originally have been incorrectly identified; the same plant may already have been given a different, earlier name; a name may be found to apply to two different plants; or new scientific knowledge may cause a plant's classification to be changed. In this Encyclopedia, numerous synonyms have been given in order to minimize the problems of identifying or purchasing renamed plants.

Davidia involucrata
This lovely tree from China is named after its discoverer, Father Jean Pierre Armand David. It has several common names, including dove tree, ghost tree, and handkerchief tree.

Coded cultivar names
When plant breeders produce a new cultivar, it is given a code name to ensure its formal identification; this may be different from the name under which the plant is sold. For example, the rose selling under the name Casino also has the code name of 'Macca'; in this Encyclopedia, both names are cited and styled thus; *Rosa* CASINO ('Macca'). To safeguard their ownership of the cultivar, plant breeders may apply for plant breeder's rights, granted using the code name.

Visual Key to Plant Classification

In horticulture, as in other areas of botany, plants are classified according to a hierarchical system (taxonomy) and named primarily on the basis of Linnaeus's binomial approach (genus followed by species epithet). For a better understanding of this system, part of the family Ericaceae has been set out below, showing all levels from family through genera and species down to cultivars, groups, and hybrids.

Family

A group of several genera that share a set of underlying natural characteristics. Family names usually end in -aceae. Family limits are often controversial.

Ericaceae

Genus (pl. genera)

A group of one or more plants that share a range of distinctive characteristics. Several (rarely one) genera are classified into one family. Each genus contains one or more species, and its name is printed in italic type with an initial capital letter.

Daboecia

Calluna

Erica

Vaccinium

Kalmia

Rhododendron

Species

A group of plants that breeds naturally to produce offspring with similar characteristics; these keep it distinct from other populations in nature. Each species has a two-part name printed in italic type.

Daboecia cantabrica

Daboecia azorica

Erica arborea

Rhododendron cinnabarinum

Rhododendron yakushimanum

Hybrid

Sexual crosses between species within a genus give rise to interspecific hybrids (see also box below).

Daboecia x *scotica*

Forma

A minor variant of a species, often differing in flower color or habit from others in the species. Indicated by "f." in Roman type and an epithet printed in italic type.

Daboecia cantabrica f. *alba*

Varietas

A minor species subdivision, differing slightly in botanical structure. Indicated by "var." *(short for* varietas*) in Roman type and an epithet in italic type.*

Erica arborea var. *alpina*

Subspecies

A naturally occurring, distinct variant of a species, differing in one or more characteristics. Indicated by "subsp." *in Roman type and an epithet in italic type.*

Rhododendron cinnabarinum subsp. *xanthocodon*

Group (Cultivar Group)

An assemblage of cultivars with similar characteristics within a genus, species, or hybrid. They may be designated with a name in a modern language or in some cases be in Latin form.

Rhododendron cinnabarinum Concatenans Group

Rhododendron cinnabarinum Purpurellum Group

Cultivar

Selected or artificially raised, distinct variant of a species, subspecies, varietas, forma, or hybrid. Indicated by a vernacular name printed in Roman type within single quotation marks.

Daboecia cantabrica 'Alba Globosa'

Daboecia x *scotica* 'William Buchanan'

Daboecia x *scotica* 'Jack Drake'

Daboecia x *scotica* 'Silverwells'

Rhododendron cinnabarinum 'Copper'

Rhododendron cinnabarinum 'Amber'

Rhododendron yakushimanum 'Koichiro Wada'

Rhododendron 'Ken Janeck'

Hybrids

A graft hybrid is a nonsexual plant created through the merging of plant tissue at the point of graft between a rootstock and its scion. For example, when *Laburnum* and *Chamaecytisus* species are combined they form +*Laburnocytisus adamii*.

Laburnum anagyroides + *Chamaecytisus purpureus* = +*Laburnocytisus adamii*

A more common type of hybrid is a sexual cross between botanically distinct species or genera. If the resulting hybrids are fertile, several generations of plants may be produced, all sharing characters of both parents. Here two species of viburnum have cross-fertilized to create *Viburnum* x *bodnantense*.

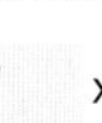

Viburnum farreri x *Viburnum grandiflorum* = *Viburnum* x *bodnantense*

Creating a Garden

Inspiration and information are essential if you want to create a garden that is attractive and also a joy in which to spend time. In this section, the basics are explained: how to plan and structure your design, how to group plants for impact, and how to use the color, light, and texture of plants to enhance their natural beauty.

Style

Gardens, like homes, have many different atmospheres or styles. Some are instantly familiar, such as the haphazard abundance of an English cottage garden or the sparse elegance of a Japanese garden, while others, such as a *jardin sauvage*, are harder to define.

Design influences

Styles of garden design may have historical associations and show, for example, the influence of the formal, stepped stone terraces of Renaissance Italy, the elegant grandeur of classical French gardens, such as Versailles, or the showy, colorful and exotic plantings of Edwardian and Victorian England.

Different styles have also developed as a result of regional cultures. This is particularly true of the United States, where East-coast picket gardens of wooden decks and open white fences contrast with glamorous West-coast gardens with their patios and pools, or the sleepy gardens of the South with their magnolias and oaks shading the veranda.

These examples may seem too ambitious for the average gardener, but they can provide the source of inspiration and be adapted to a particular site. It may be impossible to reproduce a classical French layout or an elegant Italian hillside landscape in a small city garden, but a sense of classical formality is within the reach of everyone with the use of just a few stone steps, a small fountain, and a handsome stone container filled with annuals, or perhaps an architectural, evergreen shrub or clipped tree. When choosing a style, bear in mind the climate, space, and soil type.

Proportion

To create a style in your own garden, be sensitive to the scale and mood of the surrounding landscape and buildings. A classical-style house, for instance, may well require a garden with a formal layout; the proportions between the windows and doors could suggest the pattern made in the garden by paths, pools, terraces, borders, and lawn areas. Take care with the relationships of these elements to each other and the garden as well as to the house. Whereas broad sweeps of color and grand paths are elegant in a large garden with open views, narrow borders of small flowers and winding paths would be lost in so large a space but would be ideally suited to a small, informal cottage garden.

Perspective

You can alter the apparent shape of your garden by creating false perspective in your design, using the edges of different areas

(paths, beds, or terraces) as "lines." Horizontal lines will make the site seem wider, while vertical lines will increase its length. To accentuate length even more, make vertical lines converge as they approach the bottom of the garden. Skillful placing of upright or weeping trees and shrubs enhances this effect.

Attention may be drawn to a particular spot, within or beyond the garden, by creating a dynamic, moving line, such as a curving path that leads to a focal point, perhaps a pond, arbor, specimen tree, or magnificent view. Formal or enclosed gardens with no dominant point of interest are, however, best served by static patterns, such as those created by hedges bordering geometric beds.

Materials

Paths, paved areas, fencing, and buildings should harmonize with the house and its surroundings in materials as well as in form. You may have difficulty in deciding what will be appropriate, so try determining what will not be suitable and continue by a process of elimination. For example, random paving will not enhance an eighteenth-century townhouse.

Try to make the garden a continuation of the interior in terms of color and style. This concept may be taken further, so that the view from within blends harmoniously with the internal decor and does not jolt the senses, whether you are viewing the interior from the garden, or the garden from the interior. Plants are, of course, the most important materials used to create a garden's style. Your choice will be limited by the location, soil type, and climate of the area. Bright Mediterranean flowers such as rock roses will not thrive in a shady woodland, nor will heathers and camellias flourish on open, alkaline land. Take advantage of the assets at your disposal, and do not try to fight nature. Not only will

Italian-style terrace
Above: This elegant terrace has been created on a modest scale, using terracotta pots and a small, wall-mounted fountain. The strong, horizontal lines of the pergola are softened by climbing roses, honeysuckle, and the decorative leaves of Vitis coignetiae.

Exotic garden
Left: A Japanese mood has been conjured here by combining a clear stream, cascading down stepped rocks, with a distinctive dwarf Japanese maple (Acer palmatum *'Dissectum Atropurpureum'*).

Semi-formal garden
Right: The classical pavilion sets the formal tone of this country garden. Shrubs and hedges are clipped into strong, but related, architectural shapes and lead the eye toward the austere building and to the bonsai tree, on a plinth in front of it, which provides the elegant focal point. The path has been designed with materials that harmonize with the pavilion in texture and color.

inappropriate plants never thrive, but very often when they are grown away from their natural habitat they also look out of place.

Making a style your own

Most important of all, do not forget your own relationship with the garden – let it reflect your personality. If you are a relaxed person who likes puttering around, you might allow herbaceous perennials to spill over their formal boundaries, or leave a few self-sown seedlings to interrupt a well-groomed gravel path. On the other hand, if you like everything around you to be ordered and neat, you will probably be happier with a neat, symmetrical layout, perhaps blocks of annuals or Hybrid Tea (modern) roses rather than old-fashioned (old garden) varieties.

Do not overlook any more practical requirements, either. If you have a young family, there is little point in siting an attractive lily pond in the middle of the garden, since you will need to cover it with ugly safety mesh. Instead, lay large areas of lawn and plant robust trees and shrubs. If a person using a wheelchair will be spending time in the garden, any stepped levels should be removed or replaced with gently sloping ramps or undulating banks. You might also build some raised beds; these make gardening easier for the physically challenged or for elderly gardeners.

Consider realistically how much time you are willing to spend on maintenance: some gardens are much more time-consuming than others. If time is limited, concentrate on trees, shrubs, and groundcovers; perennials and bulbs provide variety of color, form, and texture but usually demand more gardening time. For maximum commitment, grow more specialized plants, for example rock-garden plants that may have demanding cultivation requirements, or plant or sow annuals and biennials.

Keeping the planting simple

A common mistake made by gardeners is to include too many varieties of plants in a small area. There is something to be learned from a specialist's garden – the rose grower's, for example, or that of the enthusiast who cultivates only conifers and heathers. Their gardens look good because the choice of plants is restricted, giving rise to a comparatively simple design.

Cottage-style garden
Below left: A haphazard mixture of mainly perennial plants is combined with the shrub Piptanthus nepalensis, *which grows against an old stone wall, while beneath it* Corydalis ochroleuca, Hypericum *'Hidcote', and lady's mantle* (Alchemilla mollis) *intermingle happily. Note the limited color range of the planting, which makes it appear informal rather than chaotic.*

Japanese-style garden
Below right: Bamboo, stepping stones, and, in the distance, complementary foliage plants evoke a tranquil atmosphere in this Japanese-style garden. Such a style may be adapted to suit sunny or shaded sites and requires very little maintenance.

If this is too limiting, you can prevent a mixed planting from becoming overly complex and unfocused by designing within a particular color range and by grouping different varieties of plants together. This also applies to foliage, as is shown so effectively in the famous white garden at Sissinghurst in Kent, England.

Remembering the detail

Once the overall style and layout of your garden have been decided upon and the range of plants within it chosen, make sure that the furnishings do not ruin the effect. A wrought-iron bench, for instance, might be too elaborate for many gardens, whereas a simple wooden one would rarely jar. A decorated Italianate urn is probably too grand for an informal, suburban garden, even if planted with humble daisies. A period garden might be difficult to furnish economically, but on the whole, plain containers and ornaments are successful, especially in small, confined areas, and they also suit a variety of plantings. Once you have decided on the style of garden furniture, keep to your original concept: slight deviations will create a sense of clutter, and all your planning will have been in vain.

Romantic garden
Left: A circular seat is placed in the leafy shade of a country garden made romantic by rough grass and a beautiful, sprawling shrub rose.

Informal garden
Below: Even in this deceptively simple planting of herbaceous perennials, bulbs, annuals, and shrubs, each plant has been carefully selected to balance the others in form, color and texture. The barberry (Berberis) *and elegant, arching sprays of Solomon's seal* (Polygonatum x hybridum) *provide continuity and cohesion to the design.*

Structure

"Structuring" a garden does not mean physically shifting earth or laying paving slabs but developing it from a basic ground plan using elements of the planting together with manmade features, such as paths and gravel areas, to relate a garden to its setting.

Introducing different levels

Once you have decided on the style of garden you wish to create and have sketched a layout, you can start to turn your plan into three-dimensional reality. Consider the differences in height that occur or could be introduced to the site, and then decide on the plant masses and their relationship to the landscape beyond the garden and to the other elements in the garden, including each other.

Changes in ground level may already exist and can be accentuated by building steps at these points or to a pond, a vantage point, or a summerhouse. Fences and walls or structures such as pergolas, gazebos, and arbors all give a vertical emphasis or become useful screens, as can hedges, trees, or certain shrubs. Raised beds are invaluable for adding interest to a flat plot, and variety can be introduced by arranging plants of different heights.

Using structural plants
An upright tree such as a juniper may dominate too small a group of plants (A), but it may help relate that group to the scale of a wall behind it (B). The same tree may block a view (C) or, sited to one side of it, act as a counterbalance (D). By incorporating another similar group within the field of vision, a more interesting, repetitive effect may be created. Movement and progression will result from placing one juniper in front of the other (E), but sited equidistant from the viewpoint, the two plantings provide an elegant frame (F).

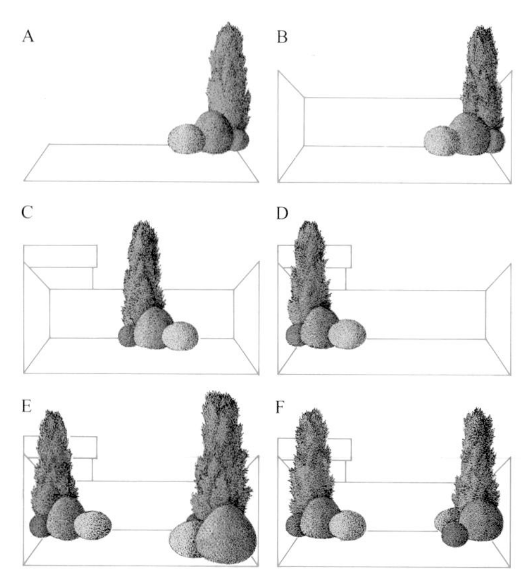

Visually reshaping a flat site
Above: The forms of trees and shrubs may be used to introduce a variety of levels to a site. Prostrate and dwarf conifers contrast with the light, horizontal branches of golden-leaved fir, the open-branched black locust (Robinia pseudoacacia), *and, in the background, the dark, upright form of a spruce.*

Changes in level
Left: Steps and a low wall serve to emphasize a change in level. The domed forms of the topiary yews (Taxus), *flanking a flowering crab-apple* (Malus), *highlight the sobriety of the former and the fresh abandon of the latter.*

Creating harmony
Purple-leaved elder helps relate the background trees to the foreground perennials, including Salvia officinalis *'Purpurascens'.*

Proportionate plantings

When planning your design, avoid crowding the basic pattern with a random or jumbled sprinkling of plants. Think instead in terms of proportionate masses, and build up the structure by adding key plants judiciously. There is much more to the look of a garden than the sum total of the individual plants that are growing within it; no matter how special a plant might be, to create a harmonious whole, it must relate to its neighbor. Moreover, each group of plants must then be in proportion to the bed in which it is situated, which in turn should relate to the entire garden.

The three-dimensional shape of the garden is largely determined by the plant masses and their siting. When you next come across a satisfying group of shrubs or perennials, analyze how the individual shapes of the plant masses are working structurally and how together they combine to form a unified whole. You will find that it is the proportionate relationship that they create with each other that makes the color masses work.

Using structural plants

No selection of plants is seen in isolation – there is always the backdrop of a garage, wall, neighbor's house, or view. The style and planting of a garden should blend rather than jar with this background. By introducing structural, or architectural, plants (those with strong outlines or forms), you can provide the bridge between the garden and what lies beyond, help to relate the garden to the house, or bind together scattered plants. Whether spiky and aggressive like a yucca, or soft and romantic like a weeping willow, the distinctive outline will add a focal point to the design. Structural plants contribute solidity and scale and, by using key plants of diminishing size, create an illusion of space.

Sensitive use of proportion
This satisfyingly mixed border is well proportioned. The strong forms of two cypresses, neatly linked to the house by a Chinese wisteria (Wisteria sinensis) *growing along the wall, encourage an easy transition from the starkly outlined mass of the house to the softer groupings of the plants. The cypresses are in turn counterbalanced by a whitebeam* (Sorbus aria *'Lutescens'*). *Shrubs and herbaceous perennials have been arranged so that the smallest are at the front of the border, yet these are all planted in sufficient quantity to make each group solid and balanced. An alternative planting* (below left) *has been devised for a hotter climate, using a Ti tree* (Cordyline fruticosa) *as the dominant feature; considerably fewer plants are used in the underplanting, but the proportions of the designs are similar.*

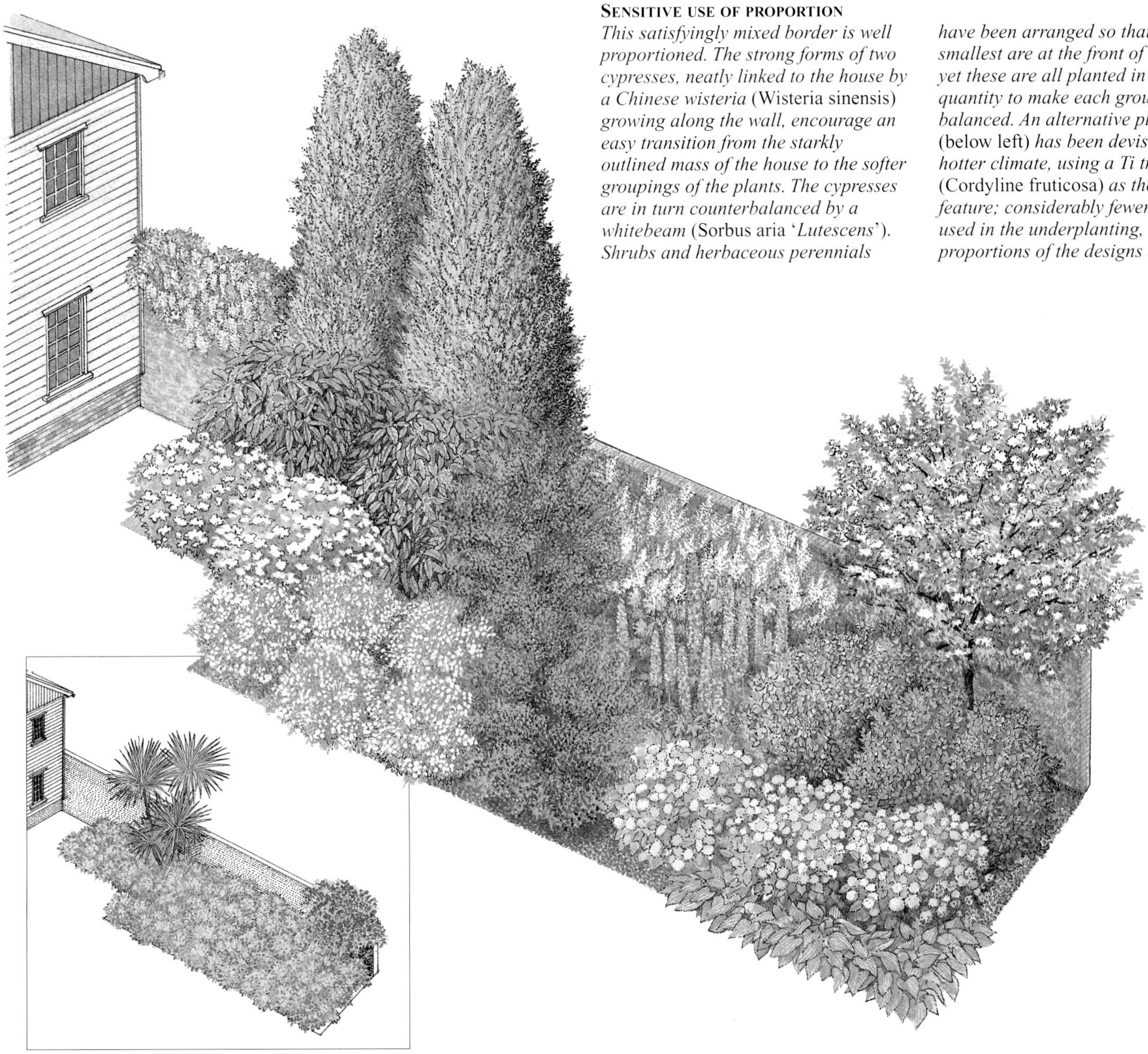

Gardening through the Year

The most successful gardens are those that provide interest throughout the year. Since no individual plant is at its peak for all 12 months, its impact in a group will alter as the year progresses. For example, a tree that is spectacular in spring when covered in blossoms may fade into the background during the rest of the year. The appearance of the group as a whole will therefore change with the seasons.

When selecting plants, remember to take into account seasonal variations in their appearance and thus ensure that each grouping sustains year-round interest. A planting of summer-flowering perennials alone may look dull in spring, autumn, and winter. Consider all the merits of each plant – its size, habit, leaf form, overall color, bark, and texture – not merely the flower color. These are the long-term plant qualities that will be on display after its main season of interest has passed.

Ideally, you should provide a succession of "feature" plants against a relatively unchanging background of shrubs and trees. In this way, when the eye-catching flowers of one plant in the bed are over, another begins to blossom. Alternatively, you might like to plan this succession in the garden as a whole, rather than just one border. In this way, the focal point will move around the garden.

SPRING
In the rock garden, Narcissus cyclamineus *nod cheerfully above* Euphorbia myrsinites.

MIDSUMMER
Above: In this cottage garden – suggestive of a wild meadow – red poppies, perhaps garish in a more dense planting, look delightful sprinkled among the cooler tones of white bellflowers and a few pale blue delphiniums.

LATE AUTUMN
Right: Evergreen and berried trees and shrubs may now be fully appreciated. Upright, dark green conifers contrast attractively with the dazzling, silvery white leaves of Elaeagnus umbellata, *while the red berries of* Cotoneaster horizontalis *provide a colorful foreground.*

Winter to spring

During winter, flower interest in the garden is likely to be minimal, and it is then that the bold shapes and foliage color provided by evergreens, such as conifers, holly, and ivy, come into their own. Less obviously, the colors and textures of twigs, branches, bark, and berries of deciduous trees and shrubs also have roles to play in providing visual interest during the winter months. The branches of the elegant willow, for instance, can look quite brilliant in winter sunlight, while white birches are especially attractive, graceful, open trees with lovely white bark that glistens on even the grayest day. The shapes of deciduous as well as evergreen plants play an important part at this time, whether silhouetted against a clear, winter sky or bearing a cloak of snow.

With the arrival of spring, the garden is soon awash with color. Some is provided by spring-flowering trees and shrubs, such as flowering cherries and magnolias, and by myriad rock plants, but most of the color comes from an abundance of flowering bulbs and corms. As these die down, they are followed by early flowering shrubs like forsythia, and the fresh green of young leaves, with scented viburnum and lilac flowers appearing in succession through late spring.

Summer to autumn

In early summer, more color is added by a profusion of perennials and biennials, often lasting until autumn. Shrub interest diminishes as the season progresses, which is when the annuals make their contribution, brightening up the heavy green face of summer. Annual flowers, although often extremely bright, may last for only short periods, so it is necessary to sow seeds and transplant seedlings successively to maintain the display. Self-seeding annuals will emerge year after year in a random way, often providing short explosions of color in unexpected places. The wealth of interesting plants that bloom in late summer, including clematis, repeat-flowering roses, and annuals and herbaceous perennials, creates a pitfall of its own: you must be selective; otherwise, the effect as a whole will be overwhelming.

As summer fades, the greenery starts to flare into the fiery colors of autumn, the intensity of the colors and their duration depending on the weather. Include trees or shrubs with spectacular autumn leaves, such as maples; they can make the garden as handsome in this season as in any other. Late-flowering perennials, such as asters and chrysanthemums, brighten up the garden until the arrival of the first frosts. When the browned leaves fall, they return us to the winter landscape.

Seasonal planting
In this small plot of about 97 square feet (9 square meters), the interplay between a group of shrubs, perennials, and bulbs can be followed throughout the seasons. Although plants will have changing roles to play at different times of year, each has been chosen to relate successfully within the whole as well as to its neighbor.

Winter
Evergreen rosemary contrasts with fleshy, purple Bergenia *leaves, variegated* Iris foetidissima *foliage, and feathery twigs of* Acer palmatum *'Sango-kaku'. Snowdrops and winter aconites* (Eranthis hyemalis) *will stud the ground by early spring.*

Spring
Bergenia *now bears its tight, red flower clusters, and the blooms of* Viburnum opulus *open. Fresh green is provided by young maple leaves and delphinium shoots.*

Summer
Blue spikes of delphinium dominate early on. Foreground interest moves from the fernlike, gray leaves of the achillea to its long-lasting, platelike, yellow flower heads.

Autumn
Yellowish maple and bronze-red viburnum foliage command the most attention, although later the viburnum berries will also become noteworthy. Iris seed pods open to reveal their orange fruits, and late-flowering chrysanthemums brighten the foreground.

Planning

A visually satisfying composition of plants consists of several elements. Look at the characteristics of the individual plants, and consider the effects those characteristics have on each other. The shapes and forms of their leaves and flowers and their color and texture are all important. Think also about the changing size of plants: a small shrub planted now may dominate the garden in five years' time.

Any combination of plants should not be seen in isolation but should be considered in relation to the overall garden plan, the house, and its surroundings. For example, a small tree or large shrub backing a small group of iris, daylilies, and meadow rue would work well, but replace the single tree or shrub with a bank of trees, and more of the smaller plants would be needed to prevent them from being "swamped." Similarly, two irises, three daylilies, and a meadow rue would probably be too few plants when sited against a two-story house.

Restricting your choice of plants

Most people tend to be shy of buying more than one or two of a particular kind of plant, or, with such a wide range of suitable subjects available, cannot resist the temptation of including yet another kind. It is just this collecting instinct that makes overall designs look fractured and detracts from the strong, simple lines of the basic concept. The plant collector and the garden designer are very often a difficult pair to reconcile!

Aim for simple, bold plant masses to begin with; later, if the effect seems too stark, widen the range of plants slightly to add a little light relief. Keep your choice of suitable plants narrow and try to see them growing, by visiting well-established gardens, before you make your final selection.

The magnificent, large-scale plantings within grand borders in the gardens of big estates that can be admired by the general public are made up of groups of perhaps twelve of this plant and eight of that; to simulate them on a domestic scale calls for an iron discipline. The same applies to planting bulbs – twos and threes tend to look messy; try groups or drifts instead. Remember, your planting is garden furnishing, and you would not cover individual chairs in the same room with contrasting fabrics if you wished to create a calm atmosphere to relax in and enjoy.

SHAPE AND SCALE
Above left: Huge-leaved Gunnera manicata, *tall giant lily* (Cardiocrinum giganteum), *bushy ferns, and yellow flag irises* (Iris pseudacorus), *although very varied in shape and scale, still form a cohesive planting for a damp site.*

COLOR RANGES
Above: The transition in color tone from the golden fronds of Juniperus x pfitzeriana *'William Pfitzer' through the orange-yellow clump of gloriosa daisies* (Rudbeckia) *to the reddish orange montbretia* (Crocosmia) *is smooth and pleasing. More varieties in smaller quantities might be difficult for the eye to absorb within this strong color range.*

SIMPLE, BOLD PLANT MASSES
Far left: Erect, silvery blue Arizona cypress (Cupressus arizonica *var.* glabra) *is balanced by the horizontal, golden foliage of* Acer shirasawanum *'Aureum'. Both trees seem stabilized by the solid-looking plants at their feet.*

STRUCTURED INFORMALITY
Left: Old stone slabs and exposed gravel punctuate the planting of lady's mantle (Alchemilla mollis), *variegated dogwood, roses, and sweet Williams, which might otherwise appear unruly.*

Siting your plants

A useful discipline when selecting and siting plants is to start with the largest and work towards the smallest. First decide on the background planting, or "chorus line." This could be either trees or shrubs, depending on the scale of the location. Forest trees may provide a link with a woodland beyond, but they can become too large for the average urban garden, whereas medium-sized trees will provide privacy, shelter, and a backdrop for your garden. Climbers may be grown around the trees or trained along garden walls or fencing. Against this background, site an occasional decorative small tree or shrub.

Think in the same way about shrubs. Use a backing group to cover a fence, to provide a screen between your garden and your neighbor's, or to camouflage unsightly buildings. Evergreens are much more suitable for this than deciduous shrubs. Many conifers are too demanding in both their shape and color for inclusion in the chorus line and make better specimen plants. Plant a group of shrubs – two or three in a small city garden, perhaps seven or eight in a larger rural one.

In front of these shrubs, plant the flowering specimens, and among the perennials and biennials introduce the smallest shrubs, including many herbs such as thyme, sage, or lavender. At this stage consider carefully the position of any feature plants.

Allowing for growth

It is essential, when planning where to site your plants, to envisage your scaled blocks of plant masses, not only as they appear now but

Creating a backdrop
Above: Climbing plants such as Clematis *'Nelly Moser', here grown through* Rosa *'American Pillar', may be used to soften or screen buildings as well as to act as a foil for other plants.*

Verdant chorus line
Left: The large shrubs Chimonanthus praecox *and* Corokia cotoneaster *form a verdant "chorus line" for smaller, more decorative flowering plants, in this case purple sage, lady's mantle* (Alchemilla mollis), *and* Campanula persicifolia. *The stone wall also makes a handsome, contrasting backdrop.*

also as they will have developed in five years' time. Site the plants to allow enough room for them to expand and merge together over that time span. Beware of selecting trees that will ultimately become far too large for the scale of your garden as a whole, even if they look delightful at the garden center or nursery.

If the planting seems too far apart initially, fill in the gaps between your groupings with bulbs, annuals, or short-lived perennials that may easily be moved later. These will then bulk out the planting design, providing a temporary source of interest and color until the larger plants have reached maturity.

Classic border planting
The striking foliage of Elaeagnus pungens *'Maculata', the rich red rose, and the golden yellow flowers of* Potentilla fruticosa *provide a classic background for a mass of low-growing perennials and violas.*

Planting for the future
It is easy to forget how quickly trees and shrubs grow, so they should be well spaced. It may help to mark out 3-foot (1-meter) sections with string. This bed has been planted for winter interest. Rosebud cherry (Prunus x subhirtella *'Autumnalis'*) *dominates the bed, while two evergreen Mexican orange blossoms* (Choisya ternata) *contrast with darker* Sarcococca humilis, *which bears fragrant flowers in late winter. Against these, the variegated* Iris foetidissima *stands out well. White-flowered* Bergenia *'Silberlicht' is placed under the cherry, and three* Helleborus argutifolius *are grouped beyond the Mexican orange blossoms.*

Year 1

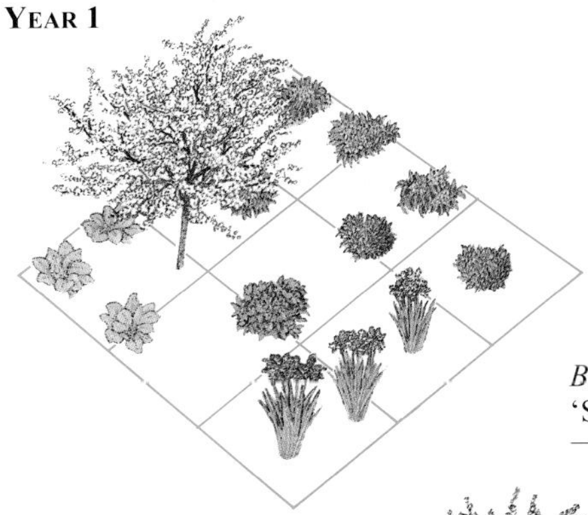

Year 3

Year 5

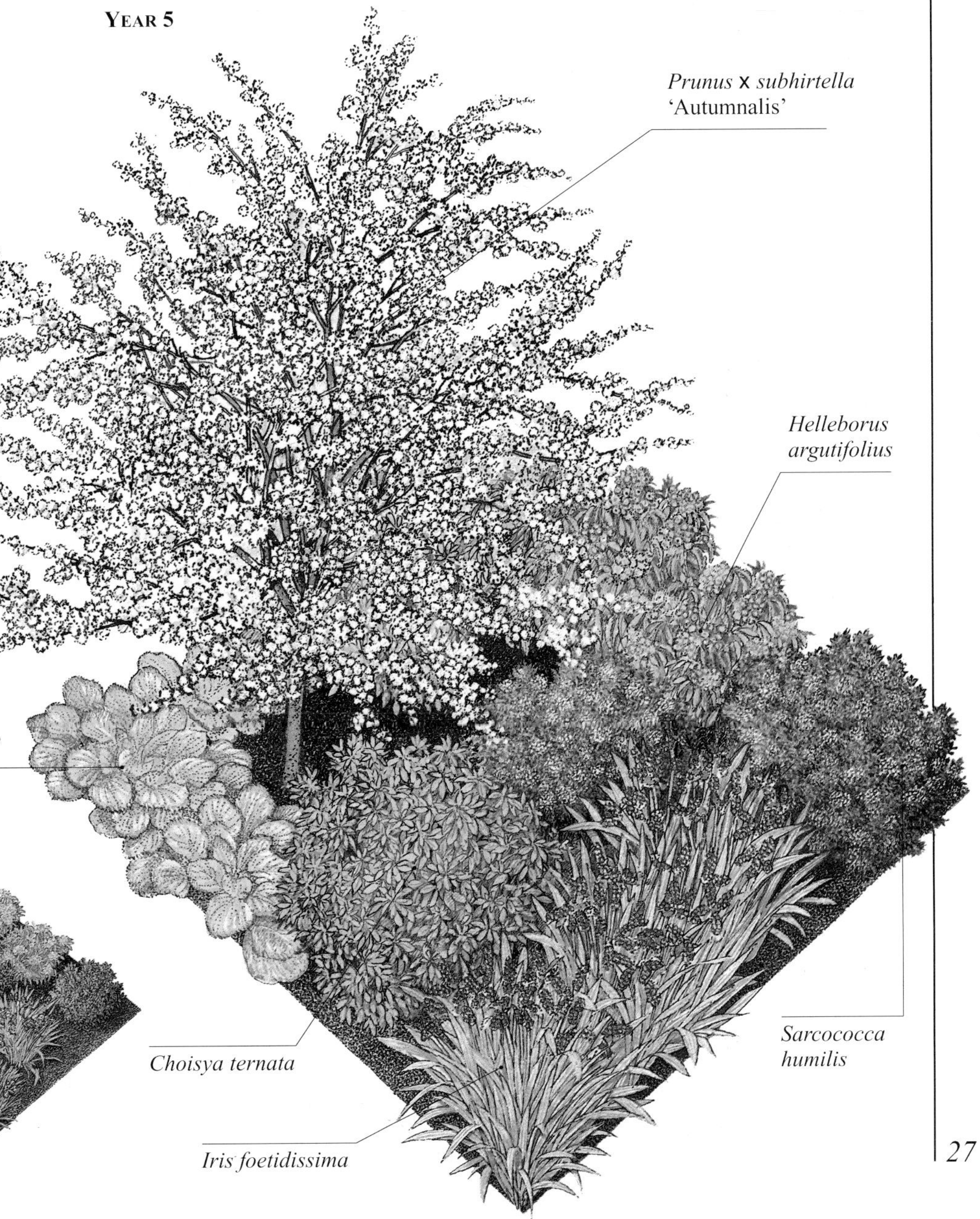

Prunus x *subhirtella* 'Autumnalis'

Helleborus argutifolius

Bergenia 'Silberlicht'

Choisya ternata

Sarcococca humilis

Iris foetidissima

Continuing care and maintenance
This bed should reach its peak of glory after about five years. Trimming may be necessary six to ten years after planting.

Using Color

Everyone interprets the moods that colors create in different ways, and many people change their minds according to the weather, the time of day, or their emotional state. Individuals with perfectly normal color vision perceive colors differently, and color blindness is a surprisingly common phenomenon.

Color choice is first and foremost about personal preferences. Although there are some fundamental design rules on how to use color, including the avoidance of such obvious clashes as hot orange with delicate pink, they really constitute only a broad guide for the use of flat planes of basic color. Often, they have little to do with the realities of a garden – the textures of living plants, the changing light, the varying hues of a color range, the season of the year, and the location.

The intricacies of color perception

The key to perceiving color is light. Soft colors look wonderful in the early morning, in the evening, and in dull or damp weather. In the Mediterranean sunshine, these colors would look blanched, and strong colors, which may be overpowering in a soft light, come into their own. Happily, nature has ensured that plants with strong-colored flowers are often native to sunny regions.

The damp light of a temperate climate is quite unlike humid, tropical light or clear, desert light; sharp, winter light is quite distinct from the hazy light of a summer noon, and both differ from misty, autumnal and dusky, evening lights. All have different effects on colors, altering our perception of them and transforming the mood of the garden. If you are going to be using your garden only at one time of day, for example the evening, bear this in mind when choosing your plants: white flowers can take on a luminous quality in fading light, but dark blue ones will be invisible.

Apart from climatic conditions, other factors determine how we notice color. The sea, for example, can alter color perception, reflecting light for some distance inland. A background building or fence will also influence color tones by reflecting or absorbing light: whether shiny or matte, made of glass, stone, brick, or wood, it will influence our view of the colors of plants grown in front of it. Colors themselves affect each other, too. The many shades of green modify any colors placed in front of them, as

Glowing pinks
Right: The pinks and purple-blues of this late summer bed set off each other excellently. The key to this success is the positioning of Artemisia ludoviciana *'Silver Queen' and agapanthus between the strong pinks of* Aster novae-angliae *'Andenken an Alma Pötschke' and ice plant* (Sedum spectabile *'Brilliant'*).

Autumnal hues
Far right: Rich bronze-red Japanese maple (Acer palmatum) *and golden-yellow* Fothergilla major *– in classic colors associated with a temperate autumn – glow even in the rather misty light typical of this season.*

SUBTLE COLORS
Far left: The pastel colors of catmint (Nepeta x faassenii) *and* Campanula lactiflora *'Loddon Anna' are used here to provide a subtle backdrop for the vivid carmine-red of the phlox.*

COLOR AND TEXTURE
Left: This planting deliberately juxtaposes extremes of color and texture, producing an almost layered effect. The sword-shaped leaves and reddish orange flowers of montbretia (Crocosmia) *contrast strongly with the yellow of feathery dill and erect, spiky verbascum; the yellow creates a link between the foreground and the background.*

STRONG COMPOSITIONS
Below: This interesting contrast of a deep yellow daylily (Hemerocallis) *set against the intense purple-blues of hydrangea and agapanthus makes a striking statement.*

do the mousy-brown colors of a wintry landscape. The individual color masses in a group influence each other, as well as affecting the whole planting. A largely white planting with a touch of purple will create one mood; but what about the reverse – a largely purple planting with a touch of white? The mood of one will be bright and sharp, the other somber and tranquil.

Considering the character of the site

In the days before the introduction of foreign species and mass hybridization, there was an indigenous range of colors in every area. To help design a harmonious garden, you might keep to this spirit of planting by analyzing the location of the garden; the particular flavor of a place is dictated by its climate and the shapes and colors of its natural plant forms.

The background color may be a dark, coniferous green with the gray of granite, or it may be deciduous green with mellower sandstone or limestone. In limestone areas, indigenous vegetation might include a proportion of gray foliage with the darker greens of yew or boxwood. Although there are some bright-colored flowers in the temperate zones, the really brilliantly colored flowers originate in hotter climates, where the intensity of the sun accentuates them. Thus the nearer the equator you go, the brighter the indigenous flowers appear.

Seasonal color associations

As well as geographical factors, there is a natural progression of dominant colors through the seasons. Pale spring colors transmute into the blues of early summer; hotter pinks of midsummer are transformed into yellows and bronzes in autumn, before turning into the browns of winter. When choosing plants for individual plant groups, it is wise to avoid certain colors against these seasonal backdrops, lest they introduce a jarring note. For example, refrain from setting soft pink against spring green, using purple in summer, or planting bright blue in autumn.

Even within the walls of a city garden with a backdrop of bricks and mortar, the seasons will still influence your color choices. For a natural look in temperate zones, try whites and pale lemon in spring; pinks, blues, and grays in

Foliage and flowers
Below right: Foliage and flower colors may be combined with equal dominance. In this planting, the huge, variegated leaves of Siberian bugloss (Brunnera macrophylla *'Dawson's White') are set off well by the surrounding, pale pink* Potentilla nepalensis *'Miss Willmott', pink astilbe flowers, and golden-leaved* Lamium maculatum *'Aureum'*

Satisfying contrasts
Below: Not only do the textures of Bowles' golden sedge (Carex elata *'Aurea') and the two hostas combine excellently, but the color and form of these plants further complement the design.*

midsummer; in late summer a little red but mainly yellows; and in autumn some bronze and purple.

Color preferences

There remain, of course, more personal preferences for certain color combinations. Strong colors are often more appreciated by the young because they are invigorating. It follows that strong colors may be more appropriate when associated with various kinds of activity – near a tennis court, for instance, or around a pool. Softer colors, such as shades of gray and pink, are more restful.

Making your personal mark

Your individual style and feelings about the moods that different colors create will be the final factors affecting the colors in your garden, just as they are in the decoration of your home. If the garden is small, the result of linking the colors with those in the room adjacent to it will have a dramatic effect on both room and garden. Where room and garden meet, avoid startling clashes such as pink roses against orange-red brick or curtains. Conversely, where the garden is larger, gradually change the colors in it so that, although those of the flowers nearest the house still link with the interior, those at the bottom of the garden work with the backdrop of the fence, hedge, or countryside beyond.

Color may be used to enhance perspective, too: hotter ranges of color (reds, oranges and pinks) look better closer to the house, while cool colors (blues and whites) introduced at a distance from it will increase the sense of space.

A sense of calm
Above: Soft colors and forms intermingle harmoniously in this shady site, where the pinkish mauve of the lacecap hydrangea is echoed in the foreground by the purple ajuga leaves and the tiny pink flowers of Lamium maculatum. *The delicate tracery of the ferns blends comfortably with the bolder, bluish leaves of* Hosta sieboldiana *var.* elegans.

Sympathetic planting
Right: This damp corner in a cottage garden contains a deliberately limited color scheme, yet with invigorating results. When set against the ferns and grasses, the yellow heads of giant cowslip (Primula florindae) *and* Ligularia przewalskii *seem natural, because they have an affinity with the character and location of the site.*

Providing Texture

A successful design is one in which the gardener has considered the entire range of an individual plant's ornamental features to create effective combinations of plants and has not relied purely on color associations. Plant texture, particularly that of foliage, plays an essential role, not only for visual impact but also because its mass and duration far outlive the more transient attractions of flowers, seed heads, or fruit, although these can also provide texture. Indeed, some of the most innovative designs depend on the variety and interplay of foliage texture to form a backcloth that is visually pleasing in its own right, while – almost incidentally – providing a foil to enhance the beauty of the flowers.

The overall effect of growing together groups of plants with markedly different textures is far greater, since the distinctive texture of each plant is emphasized and enhanced by that very contrast.

Contrasting texture

The textural variety of leaves is derived from their differing sizes, forms, and surface finishes. When considering trees, for example, it is worth noting that many of the birches and some of the smaller mountain ashes, with their small leaves and leaflets, create airy, fine-textured canopies. These can be brought into

Play on textures
Above: Spiky branches of Scotch thistle (Onopordum acanthium) *provide a most effective foil for glossy-leaved ivy, soft-leaved nicotiana, and fine-leaved lilies and marguerites. The paving slabs, the smooth terracotta pot (planted with marguerites), and the carved stone container (with* Helichrysum petiolare *'Limelight') add further variety to the scene.*

Distinctive grasses
Far left: The creamy plumes of pampas grass (Cortaderia selloana) *will help add a textural dimension to any garden, but they must be in proportion to the surrounding trees and shrubs if they are not to look out of place.*

Successful combinations
Left: This blend of flowers and leaves skillfully exploits the contrast of textures and colors between the leaves of Bowles' golden sedge (Carex elata *'Aurea'), the feathery plumes of deep red astilbes and pink candelabra primroses, and the huge leaves of* Gunnera manicata.

sharp relief by a dense coniferous backdrop of the dark-needled *Pinus peuce* or *P. nigra*. Or consider the contrasting effects to be gained from associating the fine-textured surface of small-leaved shrubs, such as boxwood (*Buxus microphylla* or *B. sempervirens*) or possibly *Osmanthus delavayi*, with the larger, glossy textures of *Viburnum tinus* or camellias; then go farther and add another dimension with the elegantly cut leaves of tree peonies or *Melianthus major*.

Perennials offer some of the most useful and distinctive plant textures. Contrast the daintily cut filigree of many artemisias, such as *Artemisia pontica* or the jagged *A. ludoviciana*, and the soft, finely divided leaves of the dicentras or ferns and the feathery pulsatillas with bolder, larger foliage, such as the huge, wrinkled leaves of the rheums and the deeply veined and architectural leaves of rodgersias. The hostas offer several textures, from the strongly ribbed, glossy leaves of *Hosta plantaginea* to the undulating, puckered leaves of *H. sieboldiana* 'Frances Williams'.

Grasses, sedges, and rushes all have more or less linear leaves that create some of the finest textures. They can be introduced in a number of planting situations to provide a range of effects, from the low, spiky, blue-green mounds of *Festuca glauca* 'Blaufuchs', through the corkscrew, hairlike leaves of *Juncus effusus* 'Spiralis', to the tall flowering plumes of *Cortaderia selloana*. Even short-lived annuals and biennials have numerous textures to offer. When used to fill gaps in a border, the filamentous leaves of *Cosmos bipinnatus* or the spiky forms of *Onopordum acanthium* will provide a visual feast.

Surface qualities

Varying foliage surfaces influence the way that light is reflected, absorbed, or diffused by the plant, so that the massed effect of matte leaves, for example, will be notably different from that of glossy leaves, which can give rise to glittering reflections in bright light. Here, too, there is a wide range of surfaces available, from the glossy-leaved hollies (*Ilex*) to matte-leaved *Phlomis russeliana*; from rough symphytums to smooth *Crinum* x *powellii*. Certain plants, among them *Allium karataviense* and *Paeonia mlokosewitschii*, have a grayish bloom to their leaves that can look exquisite when beaded with raindrops.

Leaf hairs add a further dimension when used as a foil for leaves of other textures. Hairy-leaved plants range from the bristly-hairy begonias to the almost shaggy, golden-tinted hairs of *Meconopsis napaulensis*.

The principles of texture apply equally to flowers, seed heads, and fruit, and it is also important to mention the contribution made by inanimate objects. Large stones and sea-washed pebbles, and areas of gravel and wooden decking as well as different plant pots, can all create interesting texture within a design.

Delicate touches
Below left: The spiky seed heads of Allium cristophii *contrast with the lobed leaves and satiny flowers of* Geranium x riversleaianum *'Russell Prichard'. Seed heads offer a final flourish of interest that lasts from the allium's early summer flowering until well into the autumn.*

Strong shapes
Below right: The huge, silver-downy leaves and white-woolly, yellow flower spikes of Verbascum olympicum *are a textural treat in their own right, but here their impact is lent additional weight by association with the tiny, dusky red-purple leaves of* Berberis thunbergii *f.* atropurpurea.

THE PLANT SELECTOR

CHOOSING PLANTS FOR a particular site or use, or to display specific features, is made simple with The Plant Selector. Incorporating suggestions for a variety of categories, from plants for sandy soils to those for quick cover, this unique guide will identify the ideal plant for that "problem" spot.

How to Use This Section

The following lists suggest plants that are suitable for growing in particular situations or that have special uses or characteristics. For each category the list is broadly subdivided into plant groups, following the arrangement of The Plant Catalog, pp.60–480. Plants listed here that are featured in The Plant Catalog are followed by page numbers. Refer to The Plant Dictionary if an entire genus or a plant not followed by a page number is recommended.

If a plant is listed for a particular purpose (coastal sites, shade, etc.), it should thrive there happily in normal growing conditions, even if the situation is not the plant's naturally preferred location. Bear in mind, however, that plants are not always consistent in their growing habits, and much of their success depends on climate, exposure, and available nutrients.

The following symbols occur in this section:

○ indicates evergreen or semi-evergreen plants, including those with overwintering rosettes of leaves.

△ (regarding hedges and windbreaks) the plant is moderately to fast growing.

□ (regarding clay soils) the plant tolerates slow-draining soil; all others require reasonable drainage.

▣ the plant is illustrated in this section.

Plants for Sandy Soil

Sandy soils are often termed "light" or "hungry" soils. They are usually well drained, but they dry out rapidly during drier summer periods and hold only low reserves of plant foods. Many plants have adapted to such soils by developing deeply penetrating root systems. Their leaves are also modified to reduce moisture loss: small and reflexed, evergreen and glossy, or densely covered with fine gray or silver hairs. Once established, they will usually grow steadily with little attention. To improve moisture retention, incorporate some organic matter when planting in autumn; little watering is then needed, and plants can establish well before summer.

Trees
Acacia dealbata, p.83 ○
Agonis flexuosa, p.90 ○
Amelanchier lamarckii, p.116
Betula ermanii, p.72 ▣
Betula pendula 'Dalecarlica', p.73
Castanea sativa
Celtis australis, p.67
Cercis siliquastrum, p.88
Crataegus laevigata 'Paul's Scarlet', p.91
Genista aetnensis, p.93
Nothofagus obliqua, p.68
Phoenix canariensis ○
Quercus ilex ○
Robinia pseudoacacia 'Frisia', p.81

Betula ermanii

A GARDEN ON SANDY GRAVEL
Above: Red centranthus, purple alliums, and yellow asphodeline all thrive in sandy soil.

Conifers
Abies grandis, p.104 ○
Cupressocyparis x *leylandii* and cvs ○
Juniperus ○
Larix decidua
Pinus pinaster, p.103 ○
Pinus radiata, p.104 ○
Pseudotsuga menziesii var. *glauca*, p.102 ○
Thuja occidentalis and cvs ○

Shrubs
Artemisia arborescens 'Faith Raven', p.175 ○
Berberis empetrifolia, p.157 ○
Boronia megastigma, p.156 ○
Brachyglottis Dunedin Hybrids 'Sunshine', p.140 ○

Calluna vulgaris and cvs ○
Caragana arborescens 'Lorbergii'
Ceanothus thyrsiflorus and forms ○
Chamelaucium uncinatum, pp.149, 150 ○
Chorizema ilicifolium, p.157 ○
Cistus ○
Convolvulus cneorum, p.158 ○
Cotoneaster lacteus, p.125 ○
Elaeagnus pungens 'Maculata', p.127 ○
Enkianthus cernuus f. *rubens*, p.131
Erica arborea var. *alpina*, p.178 ○
Erica cinerea and cvs ○
Gaultheria mucronata 'Mulberry Wine', p.174 ○
Gaultheria mucronata 'Wintertime', p.173 ○
Genista tinctoria, p.157
x *Halimiocistus sahucii*, p.159 ○
Halimium 'Susan', p.169 ○
Hippophäe rhamnoides, p.124
Hypericum 'Hidcote', p.170 ○
Lavandula ○
Leucospermum reflexum, p.131 ○
Olearia nummulariifolia, p.136 ○
Perovskia 'Blue Spire', p.168
Phlomis fruticosa, p.170 ○
Robinia hispida, p.141
Rosa pimpinellifolia, p.184
Rosmarinus officinalis and cvs ○
Salvia fulgens, p.166 ○
Santolina pinnata subsp. *neapolitana* 'Sulphurea', p.169 ○
Spartium junceum, p.147
Tamarix ramosissima, p.121
Teucrium fruticans 'Azureum' ○
Yucca gloriosa, p.137 ○

Climbers
Clianthus puniceus, p.204 ○
Eccremocarpus scaber, p.217 ○
Kennedia rubicunda, p.204 ○
Lapageria rosea, p.210 ○
Petrea volubilis, p.206 ○
Solanum wendlandii, p.214 ○
Streptosolen jamesonii, p.220 ○
Tropaeolum tricolorum, p.205
Vitis vinifera 'Purpurea', p.218

Perennials
Acanthus spinosus, p.251
Achillea 'Moonshine', p.291
Aphelandra squarrosa 'Louisae', p.256 ○
Artemisia absinthium 'Lambrook Silver' ○
Artemisia ludoviciana var. *albula*, p.266
Asphodeline ▣
Baptisia australis, p.252
Billbergia nutans, p.265 ○

Eryngium* x *tripartitum

Centranthus ruber, p.245 ▣
Cryptanthus zonatus ○
Echinops sphaerocephalus, p.226
Eryngium x *tripartitum*, p.253 ▣
Gaillardia x *grandiflora* cvs
Gazania rigens var. *uniflora*, p.292
Limonium latifolium 'Blue Cloud', p.286
Nepeta x *faassenii*, p.286
Oenothera fruticosa 'Fyrverkeri', p.291
Origanum vulgare 'Aureum', p.290
PELARGONIUMS, pp.246–7 ○
Phlomis russeliana, p.255 ○
Platycodon grandiflorus, p.284
Romneya coulteri, p.226
Ruellia devosiana, p.277 ○
Sansevieria trifasciata 'Laurentii', p.267 ○
Solidago 'Goldenmosa', p.255
Strelitzia reginae, p.267 ○
Verbascum dumulosum, p.359 ○

Annuals and biennials
Antirrhinum majus and cvs
Brachyscome iberidifolia, p.334
Bracteantha bracteata Monstrosum Series, p.340
Cleome hassleriana and cvs ▣
Coreopsis tinctoria, p.336
Eschscholzia californica, p.339

***Cleome hassleriana* 'Colour Fountain'**

Impatiens walleriana Novette Series, p.327 ○
Limnanthes douglasii, p.336
Limonium sinuatum, p.332
Linaria maroccana 'Fairy Lights', p.330
Mentzelia lindleyi, p.336
Papaver rhoeas Shirley Series, pp.322, 328
Portulaca grandiflora Series and cvs
Psylliostachys suworowii, p.330
Schizanthus
Senecio cineraria 'Silver Dust', p.334 ○ ▣
Tagetes
Tanacetum parthenium, p.319
Verbena x *hybrida* Series and cvs
Xanthophthalmum segetum, p.337

Rock-garden plants
Acaena caesiiglauca, p.390 ○
Achillea x *kellereri*, p.375 ○
Aethionema 'Warley Rose', p.376 ○
Andromeda polifolia 'Compacta', p.347 ○
Arenaria montana, p.374
Armeria juniperifolia, p.365 ○
Cytisus x *beanii*, p.349
Dianthus deltoides ○

***Senecio cineraria* 'Silver Dust'**

Gaultheria procumbens, p.387 ○
Gypsophila repens ○
Helianthemum ○
Maianthemum canadense, p.383
Petrorhagia saxifraga, p.375
Phlox bifida, p.381 ○
Saponaria ocymoides, p.378
Sedum ○
Sempervivum ○

Tanacetum argenteum, p.360 ○
Vaccinium vitis-idaea subsp. *minus*, p.366 ○

Bulbs, corms, and tubers
Allium ▣
Babiana rubrocyanea, p.431
Crocus
Freesia
Ipheion uniflorum 'Froyle Mill', p.431
IRISES (bulbous species), pp.234–5
Ixia
Muscari
Narcissus tazetta and Div.8 hybrids
Nerine bowdenii, p.424
Ornithogalum
Romulea bulbocodium, p.431
Scilla
Zephyranthes

Cacti and other succulents (all)

Contrasting foliage
Against a backdrop of ivy, a diversity of plants flourishes in a sunny, wall-side border, their leafy growth keeping the sandy soil shaded, cool and moist.

Plants for Clay Soils

Clay soil can be wet, sticky, and (usually) heavy, and during drier summers it sometimes shrinks and cracks, damaging plant roots. Whether establishing a new garden on clay or renovating an older one, always choose plants that will tolerate and grow satisfactorily in clay soil. Prepare the soil thoroughly, digging in the autumn, then leaving roughly dug over winter to benefit from the weathering effects of frost and/or winter rains. Dig in coarse organic matter, and work in coarse sand (not fine) to ensure the soil is well drained. Plant in early spring, at the beginning of the growing season, to avoid losses over winter.

WATERSIDE PLANTING
Above: In the rich, moist clay found at the boggy margins of pools and slow-moving streams, candelabra primroses of many colors grow and flower well in association with butterfly-like irises.

***Viburnum opulus* 'Xanthocarpum'**

Trees
Alnus glutinosa □
Castanospermum australe ○
Drimys winteri, p.78 ○
Fraxinus
Juglans nigra, p.67
Melaleuca viridiflora var. *rubriflora* ○ □
Oxydendrum arboreum, p.78 □
Populus □
Pterocarya fraxinifolia □
Quercus palustris, p.69
Quercus robur
Salix x *sepulcralis* var. *chrysocoma*, p.74 □
Salix babylonica var. *pekinensis* 'Tortuosa', p.85 □

Conifers
Cryptomeria ○ □
Metasequoia □
Taxodium distichum, p.104 □

Shrubs
Aronia arbutifolia, p.130 □
Calycanthus floridus □
Clethra alnifolia
Cornus alba 'Sibirica', p.150 □
Kalmia latifolia, p.141 ○
Ledum groenlandicum, p.154 ○ □
Magnolia virginiana ○
Salix caprea □
Salix purpurea □
Sambucus racemosa
Tetrapanax papyrifer, p.126 ○
Viburnum lentago
Viburnum opulus and cvs ⊡

Climbers
Celastrus scandens
Humulus lupulus 'Aureus', p.206
Rosa filipes 'Kiftsgate', p.196
Vitis coignetiae, p.218

Ferns
Matteuccia struthiopteris, p.312 □
Onoclea sensibilis, p.312 □
Osmunda regalis, p.312 □
Polystichum setiferum Groups, pp.311, 313 ○
Thelypteris palustris, p.312 □
Woodwardia radicans ○ □

Perennials
Aruncus dioicus, p.226 □
Cyperus papyrus, p.307 ○ □
Darmera peltata, p.238 □

***Houttuynia cordata* 'Chameleon'**

Filipendula ulmaria 'Aurea', p.290 □
Gunnera manicata, p.228 □
Helonias bullata ○ □
Houttuynia cordata 'Chameleon', p.447 □ ⊡
Iris laevigata, p.235 □
Lythrum □
Mimulus guttatus □
Primula florindae, p.273 □
Primula japonica □
Scrophularia auriculata 'Variegata' □
Trollius □

Water plants
Butomus umbellatus, p.448 □
Caltha palustris, p.451 □
Lysichiton americanus, p.451 □
Pontederia cordata, p.448 □
Ranunculus lingua, p.451 □
Sagittaria latifolia, p.446 □
Thalia dealbata □

Plants needing Neutral to Acidic Soil

Some plants, notably camellias, rhododendrons, and most heathers, grow naturally in regions such as open woodland, hillsides, or scrubland, where the soil is neutral to acidic, and so they are intolerant of alkaline soils such as those derived from limestone. These are sometimes termed "lime-haters" or "acid-lovers." Before planting, make sure the soil is suitable for these plants, and work in some acidic soil mix or organic matter. After planting, keep woody plants well mulched. In drier regions, check water needs regularly.

Embothrium coccineum

Trees

Arbutus menziesii ○
Arbutus unedo, p.93 ○
CAMELLIAS, pp.128–9 ○
Embothrium coccineum, p.93 ○ ▣
Eucryphia (most) most ○
Michelia doltsopa, p.83 ○
Nyssa sinensis, p.82
Nyssa sylvatica, p.71
Oxydendrum arboreum, p.78
Pterostyrax hispida
Stewartia
Styrax japonicus, p.77

Conifers

Abies ○
Picea (most) ○
Pinus densiflora ○
Pinus pumila ○
Pseudolarix amabilis, p.107
Pseudotsuga ○
Sciadopitys verticillata, p.106 ○
Tsuga heterophylla ○

Shrubs

Amelanchier lamarckii, p.116
Andromeda polifolia 'Compacta', p.347 ○

***Leucothöe fontanesiana* Scarletta**

Arctostaphylos (some) ○
Boronia megastigma, p.156 ○
CAMELLIAS, pp.128–9 ○
Chamaedaphne calyculata ○
Crinodendron hookerianum, p.142 ○
Cyrilla racemiflora ○
Desfontainia spinosa, p.143 ○
Enkianthus some ○
Epacris impressa, p.155 ○
Fothergilla major, p.127
Gardenia augusta ○
Gaultheria ○ ▣
Hamamelis
HEATHERS, pp.178–9, most ○ ▣
Kalmia
Ledum groenlandicum, p.154 ○
Leiophyllum buxifolium ○
Leucothöe ○ ▣
Lyonia ligustrinum
Menziesia ciliicalyx var. *purpurea*, p.155
Philesia magellanica ○
Pieris ○
Pimelea ferruginea, p.162 ○
Protea
RHODODENDRONS, pp.132–4, most ○ ▣
Styrax officinalis, p.118
Telopea speciosissima, p.142 ○
Vaccinium, most ○ ▣
Zenobia pulverulenta, p.138

Climbers

Agapetes (several) ○
Allamanda cathartica ○
Asteranthera ovata ○
Berberidopsis corallina, p.211 ○
Mitraria coccinea, p.205 ○

Perennials

Adiantum some ○
Blechnum ○
Cryptogramma crispa, p.313
Cypripedium reginae, p.296
Dianella tasmanica, p.253 ○
Drosera ○
Lilium speciosum var. *rubrum*, p.404
Lilium superbum, p.405
Nepenthes ○
Sarracenia flava, p.290
Smilacina racemosa, p.233
Tolmiea menziesii ○
Trillium
Uvularia

Rock-garden plants

Arctostaphylos ○
Cassiope ○
Cornus canadensis, p.374
Corydalis cashmeriana
Cyananthus
Epigaea ○
Galax urceolata, p.351 ○

Bilberry (*Vaccinium myrtillus*)

Gaultheria ○
Gentiana sino-ornata, p.387
Leucothöe keiskei ○
Linnaea borealis, p.375 ○
Lithodora diffusa cvs ○
Mitchella repens ○
Ourisia ○
Phlox adsurgens ○
Phlox stolonifera ○
Phyllodoce ○
Pieris nana ○
Shortia ○

Spring color
Acid-loving heathers, flanked by gaultherias and backed by two early-flowering pink rhododendrons, provide a broad strip of color to mark the end of winter.

Plants for Alkaline Soil

Regions based on limestone-derived alkaline soil are often rich in wildflowers and wildlife, and where there is a reasonable depth of topsoil, a wide range of attractive garden plants can be grown. Often, there are only a few inches of soil above bedrock, and here there is an increased risk of drought in summer. It may be necessary to excavate planting holes and to incorporate organic matter to increase levels of organic matter. On well-drained soil, plant in autumn or spring; on less than well-drained soils, defer planting until spring. Keep all young woody plants well mulched.

Malus prunifolia

Trees
Acer negundo 'Variegatum', p.79
Aesculus x *carnea* 'Briotii, p.64
Catalpa bignonioides, p.78
Cercis siliquastrum, p.88
Crataegus
Fagus sylvatica, p.68
Fraxinus ornus, p.76
Gleditsia triacanthos 'Sunburst', p.77
Ilex aquifolium cvs, pp.98–9 ○
Laurus nobilis ○
Malus ▣
Morus nigra ▣
Phillyrea latifolia ○
Prunus avium 'Plena', p.76
Robinia pseudoacacia 'Frisia', p.81
Sorbus aria and cvs
Tilia tomentosa

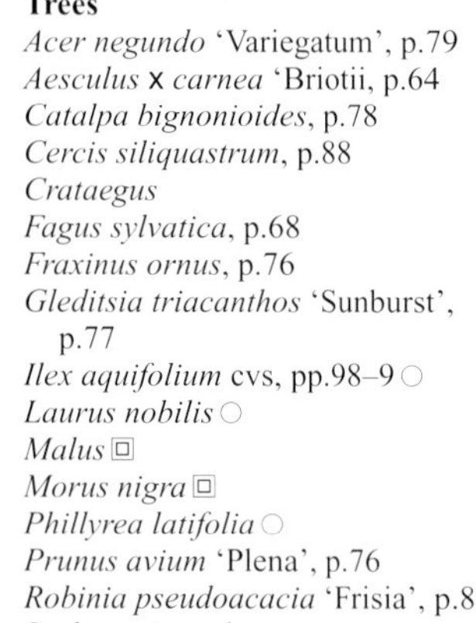

Honesty with tulips

*Below: A biennial that tolerates dry, alkaline soil, honesty (*Lunaria annua*) flowers in spring, here with* Tulipa batalinii *and forget-me-nots. The long-lasting purple flowers give way to coinlike, translucent seed pods.*

Morus nigra

Conifers
Calocedrus decurrens, p.106 ○
Cedrus libani, p.103 ○
Chamaecyparis lawsoniana and cvs ○
Cupressocyparis x *leylandii* and cvs ○
Cupressus glabra ○
Ginkgo biloba, p.103 ○
Juniperus ○
Picea omorika, p.103 ○
Pinus nigra ○
Taxus baccata and cvs ○
Thuja orientalis and cvs ○
Thuja plicata and cvs ○

Shrubs
Abutilon 'Kentish Belle', p.171 ○
Aucuba japonica 'Crotonifolia', p.152 ○
Azara microphylla, p.125 ○
Berberis darwinii, p.117 ○
Buddleja davidii and cvs
Carpenteria californica, p.138 ○
Ceanothus impressus, p.145 ○
Choisya ternata, p.127 ○
Cistus ○
Cornus mas 'Variegata', p.119
Cotoneaster, some ○ ▣
Deutzia
Forsythia suspensa, p.131
Fremontodendron 'California Glory', p.123 ○
Fuchsia 'Riccartonii', p.164
Hebe 'Great Orme', p.163 ○
Hypericum 'Hidcote', p.170 ○
LILACS, p.120
Malus sargentii, p.116
Malus sieboldii, p.130
Nerium oleander, p.121 ○

***Cotoneaster* 'Rothschildianus'**

Alkaline-loving climbers

Above: A weathered brick wall provides support for summer-flowering clematis and climbing roses. Both kinds of plant tolerate alkaline soil, but they need ample water when in growth.

Paeonia lutea var. *ludlowii*, p.237
Philadelphus
Phlomis fruticosa, p.170 ○
Photinia x *fraseri* 'Red Robin' ○
Potentilla (all shrubby species)
ROSES (most), pp.184–99, some ○ ▣
Rosmarinus officinalis 'Miss Jessopp's Upright' ○
Sambucus nigra 'Guincho Purple'
Spartium junceum, p.147
Spiraea nipponica 'Snowmound', p.139
Viburnum tinus, p.149 ○
Vitex agnus-castus
Weigela florida 'Variegata'
Yucca aloifolia, p.153 ○

Climbers
Actinidia kolomikta, p.209
Campsis radicans
Celastrus orbiculatus
CLEMATIS, pp.212–13, some ○ ▣
Eccremocarpus scaber, p.217 ○

Honeysuckle (*Lonicera*)

IVIES, p.221 ○
Jasminum officinale f. *affine*, p.208 ○
Lonicera, some ○ ⊡
Parthenocissus henryana
Passiflora caerulea, p.214 ○
Rosa 'Albéric Barbier', p.196 ○
Rosa 'Albertine', p.197 ○
Rosa banksiae 'Lutea', p.198 ○
Solanum crispum 'Glasnevin', p.214 ○
Trachelospermum jasminoides, p.207 ○
Wisteria sinensis, p.215

Ferns
Asplenium scolopendrium, p.313 ○
Asplenium trichomanes, p.313 ○
Dryopteris filix-mas, p.310
Polypodium vulgare 'Cornubiense', p.312 ○

Perennials
Acanthus spinosus, p.251
Achillea filipendulina 'Gold Plate', p.256
Aster novae-angliae and cvs
Aster novi-belgii and cvs
Bergenia ○
Doronicum
Eryngium, some ○
Gypsophila paniculata cvs ⊡
Helenium
IRISES (most), pp.234–5, some ○
Rudbeckia 'Goldquelle', p.229
Salvia nemorosa
Scabiosa caucasica 'Clive Greaves', p.285
Sidalcea
Verbascum ○
Veronica spicata

Annuals and biennials
Ageratum houstonianum and cvs
Calendula officinalis and Series and cvs
Callistephus chinensis Series and cvs
Calomeria amaranthoides, p.330
Erysimum cheiri and Series and cvs ○
Gomphrena globosa, p.331
Lavatera trimestris 'Silver Cup', p.324
Limonium sinuatum, p.322
Lobularia maritima
Lunaria annua, p.325 ⊡
Matthiola
Salvia viridis, p.331
Tagetes
Ursinia anthemoides, p.338
Xeranthemum annuum
Zinnia

***Gypsophila paniculata* 'Bristol Fairy'**

Rock-garden plants
Aethionema ○
Alyssum ○
Androsace lanuginosa, p.377 ○
Aster alpinus, p.381
Campanula (most rock-garden species), some ○
Dianthus (most rock-garden species) ○
Draba ○
Erysimum helveticum, p.373 ○
Gypsophila repens ○
Helianthemum ○ ⊡
Lathyrus vernus, p.270
Leontopodium alpinum, p.346
Linum arboreum, p.358 ○
Origanum dictamnus
Papaver burseri
Penstemon pinifolius, p.354 ○
Rhodanthemum hosmariense, p.346 ○
Saponaria ocymoides, p.378
Saxifraga (most) ○
Thymus caespititius, p.375 ○
Veronica (all rock-garden species), some ○

Bulbs, corms, and tubers
Babiana
Chionodoxa
Colchicum
Crinum x *powellii*, p.398
Crocus
Cyclamen hederifolium, p.438
DAFFODILS, pp.416–18
GLADIOLI, p.399
Hermodactylus tuberosus, p.414
Leucocoryne ixioides, p.413
Lilium regale, p.404
Muscari
Pancratium illyricum, p.419
Scilla
TULIPS, pp.410–12 ⊡
Zephyranthes

***Helianthemum* 'Rhodanthe Carneum'**

Plants for Coastal Sites

In coastal regions, and near some highways, salt from sea spray is carried a considerable distance on the wind, causing problems for many plants. Some, however, show tolerance of higher levels of salt; these frequently have hard-surfaced or high-gloss leaves with low absorbency levels, or leaves covered with fine hairs that prevent salt from reaching the surface. Coastal gardens are often exposed, so protect plants with hedges or other barriers. Prepare sandy soil by incorporating organic matter and loamy soil to encourage deep root penetration, and use dense groundcover plants to stabilize the sand and keep root areas cool.

Strawberry tree (*Arbutus unedo*)

Trees

Acer pseudoplatanus and cvs
Agonis flexuosa, p.90 ○
Alnus incana, p.66
Arbutus unedo, p.93 ○ ⊡
Castanea sativa
Cordyline australis ○
Crataegus laevigata 'Paul's Scarlet', p.91
Crataegus x *lavallei* 'Carrierei'
Eucalyptus coccifera, p.72 ○
Eucalyptus globulus ○
Eucalpytus gunnii, p.72 ○
Ficus macrophylla ○
Fraxinus excelsior
Ilex aquifolium cvs, pp.98–9 ○
Laurus nobilis ○
Melaleuca viridiflora var. *rubriflora* ○
Melia azedarach, p.76
Populus alba, p.64
Quercus ilex ○
Salix alba
Schefflera actinophylla, p.84 ○
Schinus molle ○
Sorbus aria 'Lutescens', p.78
Tabebuia chrysotricha, p.97
Thevetia peruviana, p.93 ○
Tipuana tipu

Conifers

Cupressocyparis x *leylandii* ○
Cupressus macrocarpa ○
Juniperus conferta ○
Pinus contorta var. *latifolia*, p.106 ○
Pinus nigra subsp. *nigra*, p.104 ○
Pinus radiata, p.104 ○

***Lavandula* 'Hidcote'**

Shrubs

Acacia verticillata ○
Atriplex halimus ○
Baccharis halimifolia
Berberis darwinii, p.117 ○
Brachyglottis Dunedin Hybrids 'Sunshine', p.170 ○
Buddleja globosa, p.123 ○
Bupleurum fruticosum, p.146 ○
Cassinia leptophylla subsp. *fulvida* ○
Chamaerops humilis, p.176 ○
Choisya ternata, p.127 ○
Cistus ladanifer, p.159 ○
Colutea arborescens, p.146
Corokia x *virgata* ○
Cytisus x *spachianus* ○
Duranta erecta, p.150 ○
Elaeagnus x *ebbingei* ○
Elaeagnus pungens 'Maculata', p.127 ○
Erica arborea var. *alpina*, p.178 ○
Erica cinerea 'Eden Valley', p.179 ○
Erica vagans 'Lyonesse', p.178 ○
Escallonia rubra 'Crimson Spire' ○
Euonymus japonicus ○
Euphorbia characias subspp., p.156 ○
Fabiana imbricata 'Prostrata' ○
Felicia amelloides 'Santa Anita', p.168 ○
Fuchsia magellanica, p.164
Fuchsia 'Riccartonii', p.164
Garrya elliptica 'James Roof' ○
Genista hispanica, p.170
Griselinia littoralis ○
Halimium lasianthum subsp. *formosum*, p.169 ○
Hebe x *franciscana* 'Blue Gem' ○
Hebe salicifolia ○
Hebe 'White Gem', p.158 ○
Helichrysum italicum ○
Hibiscus rosa-sinensis ○
Hippophäe rhamnoides, p.124
Hydrangea macrophylla and cvs
Lavandula 'Hidcote', p.167 ○ ⊡
Lavatera 'Rosea', p.141 ○
Leptospermum scoparium 'Red Damask', p.131 ○
Leycesteria formosa
Lonicera pileata, p.176 ○
Lycium barbarum
Malvaviscus arboreus, p.121 ○
Nerium oleander, p.121 ○
Olearia x *haastii*, p.139 ○
Olearia macrodonta ○
Ozothamnus ledifolius, p.160 ○
Parahebe perfoliata, p.286 ○
Phillyrea latifolia ○

Phlomis fruticosa, p.170 ○
Pittosporum tobira ○
Pyracantha coccinea 'Lalandei' ○
Rhamnus alaternus 'Argenteovariegata' ○
Rosa pimpinellifolia
Rosa rugosa, p.187
Rosmarinus officinalis, p.167 ○
Sambucus racemosa and cvs
Santolina chamaecyparissus ○
Spartium junceum, p.147
Tamarix ramosissima, p.121
Ulex europaeus 'Flore Pleno' ○
Viburnum tinus, p.149 ○
Yucca gloriosa, p.137 ○

Climbers

Antigonon leptopus, p.209 ○
Bougainvillea glabra, p.214 ○
Eccremocarpus scaber, p.217 ○
Ercilla volubilis ○
Euonymus fortunei 'Coloratus' ○
Fallopia baldschuanica, p.217
Ficus pumila ○
Hedera canariensis var. *algeriensis* ○
Muehlenbeckia complexa
Pandorea jasminoides, p.208 ○
Pyrostegia venusta, p.218 ○
Schisandra rubriflora, p.211
Solandra maxima, p.206 ○
Tripterygium regelii

Tropaeolum tuberosum var. *lineamaculatum* 'Ken Aslet', p.216
Wisteria sinensis, p.215

Grasses (including bamboos)
Cortaderia selloana 'Sunningdale Silver', p.306 ○
Pseudosasa japonica, p.308 ○

Perennials
Anaphalis margaritacea, p.239
Anchusa azurea 'Loddon Royalist', p.254
Anthurium andraeanum, p.264 ○

SEASIDE EXTRAVAGANZA
Left: Plants that are equipped to cope with salty sea air include tall red kniphofias as well as tender succulents, which can survive winters outdoors because of the mild coastal climate.

Argyranthemum frutescens, p.240 ○
Artemisia absinthium 'Lambrook Silver' ○
Carpobrotus edulis
Centaurea hypoleuca 'John Coutts', p.279
Centranthus ruber, p.245
Crambe maritima, p.276
Echinacea purpurea
Erigeron 'Charity', p.278
Eryngium variifolium, p.286 ○
Euphorbia griffithii 'Fireglow', p.258
Geranium sanguineum, p.354
IRISES, pp.234–5, some ○
Kniphofia, some ○ ⊡
Lampranthus aurantiacus, p.468
Myosotidium hortensia, p.287 ○
Osteospermum jucundum, p.279 ○
Peperomia obtusifolia 'Variegata', p.305 ○
Pericallis x *hybrida*
Phormium tenax ○
Pilea cadierei, p.300 ○
Romneya coulteri, p.226
Senecio cineraria 'Silver Dust', p.334 ○
Stachys byzantina, p.304 ○
Tradescantia fluminensis ○

Annuals and biennials
Antirrhinum majus and cvs
Bassia scoparia f. *trichophylla*, p.335
Calendula officinalis Series and cvs
Clarkia amoena and Series
Coreopsis tinctoria, p.336
Cynoglossum amabile 'Firmament', p.334
Dahlia 'Coltness Gem', p.329
Dianthus chinensis Series
Dorotheanthus bellidiformis
Echium ⊡
Eschscholzia californica, p.338
Gilia capitata, p.333
Impatiens walleriana Novette Series, p.327 ○
Lavatera trimestris cvs ⊡
Limnanthes douglasii, p.336
Matthiola
Portulaca grandiflora Series and cvs

***Lavatera trimestris* 'Silver Cup'**

***Tagetes* Antigua Series 'Antigua Gold'**

Rhodanthe chlorocephala subsp. *rosea*, p.321
Tagetes ⊡

Rock-garden plants
Achillea clavennae, p.373 ○
Aethionema grandiflorum, p.352 ○
Armeria maritima 'Vindictive', p.380 ○
Aubrieta deltoidea 'Argenteovariegata', p.368 ○
Dianthus deltoides ○
Draba aizoides ○
Epilobium glabellum of gardens, p.351 ○
Iberis sempervirens, p.346 ○
Origanum laevigatum, p.354
Oxalis enneaphylla
Parahebe catarractae, p.356 ○

A COASTAL ROCK GARDEN
Above: This cliffside rock garden provides sunny, sheltered conditions in beds and rock crevices for many plants, among them centranthus, dorotheanus, echium, erigeron, hebe, and phlomis.

Phlox subulata 'Marjorie', p.378 ○
Pulsatilla vulgaris, p.348
Saxifraga paniculata ○
Sedum spathulifolium 'Cape Blanco', p.391 ○
Sempervivum arachnoideum, p.389 ○
Silene schafta, p.379
Thlaspi cepaeifolium subsp. *rotundifolium*, p.365
Viola cornuta, p.349

Bulbs, corms, and tubers
Amaryllis belladonna, p.408
Crinum
Crocosmia 'Lucifer', p.401
Crocus
DAFFODILS, pp.416–18
Eucharis x *grandiflora*, p.425 ○
Freesia
Galtonia candicans, p.397
Hippeastrum
HYACINTHS, p.431
Hymenocallis
Nerine
Scilla
Sprekelia formosissima, p.413
TULIPS, pp.410–12
Veltheimia bracteata, p.425
Zantedeschia aethiopica ○

Trees and Shrubs for Exposed Sites

In very cold regions, particularly those exposed to strong winter winds, only the hardiest plants thrive without the protection of a windbreak. Where providing one is not practical, it is essential to establish a basic framework of trees, shrubs, and conifers that are fully hardy. Carefully positioned within the garden in groups, they provide sheltered situations where less hardy plants can be grown, while still retaining a degree of openness if desired.

Sorbus americana

Trees
Acer negundo
Acer rubrum, p.70
Aesculus glabra
Amelanchier laevis, p.85
Betula papyrifera, p.72
Betula pendula
Carpinus carolinianus
Celtis occidentalis
Cornus alternifolia
Crataegus x *mordenensis* 'Toba'
Fraxinus nigra 'Fallgold'
Juglans nigra, p.67
Maackia amurensis, p.90
Ostrya virginiana, p.77
Phellodendron amurensis
Populus alba, p.64
Populus nigra 'Italica', p.66
Prunus maackii, p.84
Prunus padus, p.76
Quercus alba
Salix alba 'Tristis'
Ulmus americana

Conifers
Juniperus chinensis ○
Juniperus sabina ○
Juniperus scopulorum ○
Larix decidua ○
Larix laricina ○
Picea glauca ○
Picea pungens ○
Pinus cembra, p.106 ○
Pinus contorta var. latifolia, p.106 ○
Pinus resinosa ○
Pinus strobus, p.102 ○
Pinus sylvestris ○
Thuja occidentalis ○

Shrubs
Acer tataricum ssp. ginnala, p.95
Amelanchier alnifolia
Caragana arborescens
Cornus stolonifera and cvs.
Elaeagnus angustifolius, p.122
Euonymus alatus, p.148
Hippophae rhamnoides, p.124
Hydrangea paniculata 'Grandiflora'
Lonicera tatarica
Philadelphus cvs (some), p.136
Physocarpus opulifolius
Potentilla fruticosa cvs.
Prunus cistena, p.154
Ribes alpinum
Rhus typhina
Sambucus racemosa
Shepherdia argentia
Spiraea japonica and cvs, p.163
Spiraea x *vanhouttei*, p.154
Syringa vulgaris cvs
Viburnum lantana
Viburnum trilobum

Groundcovers
Arctostaphylos uva-ursi, p.388 ○
Cornus canadensis, p.374

MAXIMUM EXPOSURE
Where it is hardy, evergreen Berberis darwinii *provides shelter for more tender plants, with the bonus of masses of spring flowers.*

Cotoneaster nanshen
Genista tinctoria, p.157
Juniperus horizontalis and cvs. ○
Microbiota decussata, p.110 ○
Pachysandra terminalis, p.388 ○
Paxistima canbyi ○

Climbers and Shrubs for Sunless Walls

Against sunless walls, it is essential to choose climbers that grow naturally in shade or semi-shade. These provide reliable and effective foliage cover, and some have attractive flowers. Climbing roses also may flower reasonably well in sunless situations and, together with shade-tolerant shrubs, add color to shaded walls and wallside borders. Shade-growing plants prefer moist, leafy, woodland-type soils; when planting, amend the soil well with organic matter, such as leaf mold.

Climbers
Akebia quinata, p.206 ○
Berberidopsis corallina, p.211 ○
Celastrus scandens
Clematis (many), some ○
Clematis alpina 'Frances Rivis', p.213 ○
Ercilla volubilis ○
Euonymus fortunei 'Coloratus' ○
Euonymus fortunei 'Silver Queen', p.151 ○
Hedera colchica 'Dentata Variegata' ○
Hedera colchica 'Sulphur Heart', p.221 ○
Hedera helix cvs ○
Hedera hibernica, p.221 ○
Hydrangea petiolaris, p.208
Lapageria rosea and forms, p.210 ○
Lonicera japonica 'Halliana', p.215 ○
Lonicera periclymenum and cvs
Lonicera tragophylla
Parthenocissus henryana
Parthenocissus quinquefolia (rough surfaces)
Parthenocissus tricuspidata and cvs
Pileostegia viburnoides, p.208
Schisandra rubriflora, p.211
Schizophragma hydrangeoides
Schizophragma integrifolium, p.208

Shrubs
Azara microphylla, p.125 ○
Camellia japonica cvs ○
Camellia x *williamsii* cvs ○
Chaenomeles speciosa 'Moerloosei', p.130
Chaenomeles x *superba* 'Rowallane', p.155
Choisya ternata, p.127 ○
Cotoneaster horizontalis, p.172
Cotoneaster lacteus, p.125 ○
Crinodendron hookerianum, p.142 ○
Drimys winteri, p.78 ○
Eucryphia x *nymansensis* 'Nymansay', p.81 ○

Lapageria rosea* var. *albiflora

x *Fatshedera lizei*, p.152 ○
Fatsia japonica ○
Forsythia suspensa, p.131
Garrya elliptica 'James Roof' ○
Itea ilicifolia, p.146 ○
Jasminum nudiflorum, p.151
Mahonia japonica, p.151 ○
Mahonia x *media* 'Charity', p.125 ○
Muehlenbeckia complexa
Osmanthus decorus ○
Pyracantha 'Orange Glow' ○
Pyracantha x *watereri*, p.136 ○
Ribes laurifolium, p.175 ○
Rosa 'Albéric Barbier', p.196 ○

COOL SECLUSION
Variegated Hedera colchica *'Sulphur Heart' and a decorative stone urn make a feature of a sunless wall.*

Rosa 'Félicité Perpétue', p.196 ○
Rosa 'Gloire de Dijon', p.196
Rosa 'Golden Showers', p.199
Rosa 'Maigold', p.199
Rosa 'Madame Alfred Carrière', p.196
Rosa 'Madame Grégoire Staechelin', p.197 ○

Deer-resistant plants

In many parts of North America, deer are becoming a major problem in gardens because they can easily gain access and browse on choice plants by jumping fences. Erecting special fences is expensive, and it is not very practical in smaller urban gardens. Other deterrents do not always work for very long and are difficult to renew in midwinter, when the garden is deep in snow. The plants on the following list are usually avoided by deer but may be eaten if they are really hungry.

Trees and shrubs
Acer negundo
Acer palmatum
Aralia elata
Arbutus menziesii ○
Berberis
Betula pendula
Buddleja davidii
Buxus ○
Ceanothus
Choisya ternata, p.127
Cotinus coggygria
Cytisus scoparius

***Choisya ternata* SUNDANCE**

Daphne mezereum, p.174
Elaeagnus angustifolius, p.122
Elaeagnus commutata
Erica, most
Euonymes japonicus
Forsythia
Fraxinus
HEATHERS, p.178, most ○
HOLLIES, p.98, except smooth-leaved species ○
Kalmia latifolia, p.141
Kerria japonica
LILACS, p.120
Liquidambar styraciflua, p.70
MAGNOLIA, p.75
Mahonia aquifolium, p.157 ○
Pieris japonica, p.116
Populus nigra 'Italica', p.66
Potentilla fruticosa
RHODODENDRON, pp.132–4, but not azalea ○
Ribes alpinum
Robinia pseudoacacia
ROSES, *especially species and many shrub types*, pp.184–8
Sambucus racemosa
Spiraea
Symphorecarpos albus
Viburnum
Yucca

Conifers
Abies ○
Juniperus, most ○
Larix decidua
Picea ○

DEER RESISTERS
*Above: The golden pampas grass (*Cortaderia selloana *'Gold Band') and summer-flowering* Agapanthus *'Loch Hope' should escape the attentions of hungry deer.*

***Syringa vulgaris* 'Decaisne'**

Pinus ○
Taxus ○

Climbers
Celastris scandens
CLEMATIS, p.212
IVIES, p.221 ○
Ipomoea
Wisteria

Perennials
Achillea
Agapanthus
Alchemilla mollis, p.290
Anemone x *hybrida*
Aquilegia
Campanula persicifolia
Centranthus ruber, p.245
DAYLILIES, p.257
DELPHINIUMS, p.230
Dicentra spectabilis, p.245
FERNS, most
Filipendual rubra, p.227
Geranium
Heleborus ○
Hesperis matrionalis, p.239
HOSTAS, pp.288–9
IRISES, pp.234–5
Leucanthemum x *superbum*
Lupinus
Lychnis coronaria, p.282
Monarda
Papaver orientale
PEONIES, pp.236–7
Perovskia atriplicifolia
Rosmarinum officinalis, p.167
Rudbeckia hirta
Salvia
Stachys byzantina, p.304

Grasses (including bamboos)
BAMBOO, most species
Cortaderia selloana
Festuca glauca
Miscanthus sinensis

Groundcovers
Ajuga reptans
Arctostaphylos uva-ursi, p.388 ○
Cerastium tomentosum, p.361
Cotoneaster horizontalis, p.172
Dicentra formosa
Epimedium
Galium odoratum, p.275
Gaultheria shallon, p.162 ○
Hypericum calycinum, p.170 ○
Lamium maculatum, p.269
Liriope ○
Vinca minor, p.176 ○

Annuals and perennials
Ageratum houstonianum
Antirrhinum majus
Calendula officinalis
Campanula medium
Catharanthus roseus, p.160
Eschscholzia californica, p.339
Impatiens walleriana
Moluccella laevis, p.335
Myosotis sylvatica
Papaver croceum
Scabiosa atropurpurea
Senecio cineria
Verbena x *hybrida*
Zinnia

Bulbs, corms, and tubers
Allium, most
Begonia x *tuberhybrida*
Crocosmia
DAFFODILS, pp.416–18
Fritillaria imperialis, p.396
Leucojum aestivum, p.396
Mirabilis jalapa, p.245
TULIPS, pp.410–12
Zantedeschia

Daffodil (*Narcissus* 'Quince')

Plants for Hedges and Windbreaks

Plants for hedging are often selected for their ornamental qualities, but there are also other aspects to consider. Boundary hedges may provide visual privacy or screen unsightly buildings; they may also be bushy or thorny to keep out animals or intruders. Make sure that plants for screening will grow to the required height, choosing conifers or evergreen shrubs for year-round effect. In exposed situations, trees and larger conifers may be used as windbreaks; two or three staggered rows are usually much more effective than a single, close-planted one.

Trees
Alnus cordata, p.66 △
Arbutus unedo, p.93 ○
Carpinus betulus
Carpinus betulus 'Fastigiata', p.100
Crataegus monogyna
Fagus sylvatica, p.68
Ilex aquifolium, p.98 ○
Ilex aquifolium 'Argentea Marginata', p.98 ○
Laurus nobilis ○
Melaleuca viridiflora var. *rubriflora* ○ △
Metrosideros excelsus, p.83 ○ △
Nothofagus dombeyi, p.68 ○ △
Nothofagus obliqua, p.68 △
Olea europaea ○
Populus x *canadensis* 'Robusta', p.65 △
Prunus lusitanica ○
Syzygium paniculatum, p.81 ○
Umbellularia californica, p.74 ○
Zelkova serrata, p.71

Conifers
Abies grandis, p.104 ○ △
Cedrus deodara
Cephalotaxus harringtonii ○
Chamaecyparis lawsoniana ○ △
Cupressocyparis x *leylandii* ○ △
Cupressus macrocarpa ○ △
Juniperus communis ○
Larix decidua △
Picea omorika, p.103 ○ △
Pinus nigra ○
Pinus radiata, p.104 ○ △
Pseudotsuga menziesii var. *glauca*, p.102 ○ △
Taxus baccata ○
Thuja plicata ○ △
Tsuga canadensis, p.107 ○ △

Shrubs
Berberis darwinii, p.117 ○
Buxus sempervirens 'Suffruticosa', p.177 ○
Choisya ternata, p.127 ○
Codiaeum variegatum var. *pictum*, p.177 ○
Cotoneaster simonsii, p.148 △
Dodonaea viscosa 'Purpurea', p.151 ○ △

Cherry laurel (*Prunus laurocerasus*)

Hydrangea hedges
Above: Parallel hedges of tall lacecap hydrangeas look spectacular in late summer, the flower colours deepening with the evening sun. Between them a gravel walk leads to an archway in a high, carefully trimmed windbreak, passing to a grassy orchard beyond.

Duranta erecta, p.150 ○ △
Elaeagnus x *ebbingei* ○ △
Escallonia 'Langleyensis', p.142 ○
Euonymus japonicus 'Macrophyllus' ○
Griselinia littoralis ○
Hibiscus rosa-sinensis ○
Hippophäe rhamnoides, p.124
Hydrangea macrophylla cvs ▣
Lavandula cvs ○
Leptospermum scoparium cvs ○ △
Ligustrum ovalifolium, p.126 ○ △
Lonicera nitida ○
Photinia x *fraseri* 'Birmingham', p.117 ○ △
Pittosporum tenuifolium, p.127 ○ △
Prunus laurocerasus ○ ▣
Prunus lusitanica ○
Pyracantha x *watereri*, p.136 ○ △
Rosmarinus officinalis and cvs ○
Tamarix ramosissima, p.121 △

Roses
Rosa californica △
Rosa 'Céleste', p.185 △
Rosa 'Felicia', p.185 △
Rosa 'Frühlingsmorgen' △
Rosa gallica var. *officinalis* △
Rosa gallica 'Versicolor', p.187 △
Rosa glauca, p.186 △
Rosa 'Great Maiden's Blush', p.185 △
Rosa 'Marguerite Hilling', p.186 △
Rosa moyesii 'Geranium', p.187 △
Rosa 'Nevada', p.185 △
Rosa 'Penelope', p.184 △
Rosa 'Président de Sèze' △

Rosa rugosa* var. *rosea

Rosa rugosa, p.187 △ ▣
Rosa 'Tuscany Superb' △

Grasses (including bamboos)
Arundo donax △
Cortaderia selloana 'Sunningdale Silver', p.306 ○
Fargesia nitida ○
Phyllostachys bambusoides, p.308 ○ △
Pseudosasa japonica, p.308 ○
Semiarundinaria fastuosa, p.308 ○
Stipa gigantea, p.307 ○

Perennials
Echinops bannaticus, p.228 △
Eupatorium purpureum, p.231 △
Filipendula camtschatica △
Helianthus atrorubens 'Monarch'
Macleaya microcarpa 'Kelway's Coral Plume', p.227 △
Phormium tenax ○
Rudbeckia 'Goldquelle', p.229 △

Architectural Plants

In gardens, plants that stand out, immediately drawing the eye with their strong, distinctive appearance, are termed "architectural" plants. Whether by chance or design, such plants give character and substance and help form the basic framework of a garden. Most are trees, conifers, and shrubs, which provide a permanent effect throughout the year. They impress by shape, as in strongly vertical, conical, or fastigiate forms of conifer, or with striking foliage – the immense leaf size of gunneras or the swordlike leaves of phormiums. In established gardens, areas attracting little attention may be improved by introducing plants with good architectural qualities.

Trees
Cordyline ○
Dracaena draco, p.100 ○
Eucalyptus (many) ○
Jacaranda mimosifolia, p.79
Kalopanax septemlobus, p.80
MAGNOLIAS, p.75, some ○
Paulownia tomentosa, p.77
Phoenix canariensis ○
Salix (several)
Trachycarpus fortunei, p.84 ○
Trochodendron aralioides, p.84 ○
Washingtonia ○

Conifers
Abies ○
Araucaria ○
Calocedrus decurrens, p.106 ○
Cedrus ○
Juniperus x *pfitzeriana* 'William Pfitzer', p.111 ○
Metasequoia glyptostroboides, p.102
Picea ○
Pseudolarix amabilis, p.107
Sciadopitys verticillata, p.106 ○
Sequoia sempervirens ○
Sequoiadendron giganteum, p.102 ○
Taxodium distichum, p.104
Tsuga heterophylla ○

Shrubs
Aesculus parviflora, p.119
Brachyglottis repanda, p.127 ○
Cycas revoluta, p.152 ○
Daphniphyllum macropodum, p.117 ○
Eriobotrya japonica ○
Fatsia japonica ○
Fatsia japonica 'Variegata', p.151 ○
Mahonia (most) ○
Parkinsonia aculeata ○
Protea ○
Rhus typhina
Rhus typhina 'Dissecta', p.124
Yucca ○ ▣

***Yucca elephantipes* 'Variegata'**

Climbers
Epipremnum aureum 'Marble Queen', p.219 ○
Hedera colchica 'Dentata', p.221 ○
Monstera deliciosa, p.220 ○
Schizophragma hydrangeoides
Schizophragma integrifolium, p.208
Vitis coignetiae, p.218

Ferns
Asplenium scolopendrium Marginatum Group, p.313 ○
Blechnum tabulare ○
Cyathea australis, p.100 ○
Dicksonia antarctica, p.310 ○
Matteuccia struthiopteris, p.312 ▣
Platycerium bifurcatum, p.310 ○
Polystichum munitum, p.316 ○
Woodwardia radicans ○

Grasses (including bamboos)
Chusquea culeou, p.308 ○
Cortaderia selloana 'Sunningdale Silver', p.306 ○

Perennials
Acanthus spinosus, p.251
Angelica archangelica, p.228
Berkheya macrocephala, p.258
Crambe cordifolia, p.226
Cynara cardunculus, p.228
Darmera peltata, p.238
Echinops bannaticus, p.228
Echium wildpretii ○
Ensete ventricosum, p.233 ○
Euphorbia characias subsp. *characias*, p.156 ○
Gunnera manicata, p.228
Heliconia ○
Hosta (many)
Kniphofia caulescens, p.263 ○
Ligularia (most)
Macleaya
Meconopsis (most), several ○
Phormium tenax and cvs ○
Puya chilensis, p.265 ○
Rheum palmatum 'Atrosanguineum'
Rodgersia
Strelitzia reginae, p.267 ○
Veratrum nigrum, p.228
Verbascum olympicum, p.229 ○

Annuals and biennials
Alcea rosea, p.321
Amaranthus tricolor cvs
Calomeria amaranthoides, p.330
Helianthus annuus and cvs
Onopordum acanthium, p.322 ▣
Silybum marianum, p.322
Verbascum densiflorum ○

Ostrich fern (*Matteuccia struthiopteris*)

Bulbs, corms, and tubers
Arisaema (most)
Arum creticum, p.415
Begonia rex and hybrids ○
Cardiocrinum giganteum, p.398
Dracunculus vulgaris, p.401
GLADIOLI, p.399 most
Sauromatum venosum, p.413
Zantedeschia aethiopica ○

Water plants
Colocasia esculenta and cvs ○
Eichhornia crassipes, p.448 ○
Lysichiton americanus, p.451
Nelumbo nucifera and cvs
Orontium aquaticum, p.451
Pontederia cordata, p.448
Sagittaria
Thalia dealbata

Cacti and other succulents
Most of the larger species, especially:
Aeonium tabuliforme, p.478 ○
Agave americana 'Striata', p.457
Aloe (most) ○
Carnegiea gigantea, p.456 ○
Cereus (most) ○
Cyphostemma juttae, p.459
Euphorbia candelabrum ○
Opuntia (most) ○

SILVER SCULPTURE
*Below: In this quiet, shady corner, the eye is immediately caught by the architectural merits of three Scotch thistles (*Onopordum acanthium*), their silvery gray stems and foliage effectively displayed against a dark background.*

CARPETING CRANESBILLS
*Left: Among the hardy herbaceous cranesbills (*Geranium*) there are several that grow rapidly, providing good groundcover and flowering attractively during summer in sun or dappled shade.*

Plants for Quick Cover

In new gardens, there are often steep banks or large spaces impractical to sod or plant, and in older gardens areas they may become neglected, or there may be little time for maintenance. Such problems may be resolved by using plants that have good ground-covering qualities – rapid, dense, low, and leafy or twiggy growth that helps to suppress weeds permanently. Always select plants that are suitable for the soil conditions and, in large areas, use vigorous ones such as ivy (*Hedera*), which may be spaced to give good cover in two or three seasons.

Conifers
Juniperus conferta ○
Juniperus sabina var. *tamariscifolia*, p.110 ○

Shrubs
Ceanothus thyrsiflorus var. *repens*, p.168 ○
Cotoneaster conspicuus ○
Cotoneaster 'Gnom' ○
Cotoneaster 'Skogholm' ○
Gaultheria shallon, p.162 ○
Hypericum calycinum, p.170 ○
Lantana camara ○
Rosa GROUSE ('Korimro'), p.189
Rosa PINK BELLS ('Poulbells'), p.190
Rubus tricolor ○
Stephanandra incisa 'Crispa'
Symphoricarpos x *chenaultii* 'Hancock'

Climbers
Hedera canariensis var. *algeriensis* 'Ravensholst' ○
Hedera colchica 'Dentata', p.221 ○
Hedera helix (small cvs) ○
Hedera hibernica, p.221 ○
Hydrangea petiolaris, p.208 ⊡
Lonicera japonica cvs ○
Pueraria lobata
Trachelospermum asiaticum ○
Trachelospermum jasminoides, p.207 ○

Ferns
Dryopteris dilatata
Polystichum aculeatum ○
Polystichum setiferum Groups, pp.311, 313 ○

Perennials
Aegopodium podagraria 'Variegatum', p.276
Alchemilla mollis, p.290
Anthemis punctata subsp. *cupaniana*, p.276 ○
Asarum europaeum, p.390 ○
Campanula portenschlagiana, p.382 ○
Cerastium tomentosum, p.361
Chelidonium majus 'Flore Pleno', p.238
Duchesnea indica ○
Euphorbia amygdaloides var. *robbiae*, p.271 ○
Geranium macrorrhizum, p.279 ○
Geranium x *oxonianum* 'Claridge Druce' ○
Glechoma hederacea 'Variegata', p.300 ○
Heterocentron elegans, p.284 ○
Lamium maculatum and cvs ○
Osteospermum jucundum, p.279 ○
Phalaris arundinacea var. *picta*, p.306 ○

Hydrangea petiolaris

Mother of thousands (*Saxifraga stolonifera*)

Prunella grandiflora 'Pink Loveliness' ○
Pulmonaria (most), some ○
Stachys byzantina, p.304 ○
Symphytum x *uplandicum* 'Variegatum', p.238

Annuals and biennials
Lathyrus odoratus 'Bijou', p.324
Portulaca grandiflora Series and cvs
Sanvitalia procumbens, p.336
Tropaeolum majus Series and cvs

Rock-garden plants
Acaena anserinifolia of gardens ○
Arabis caucasica and cvs ○
Aubrieta ○
Campanula poscharskyana, p.381
Helianthemum ○
Persicaria affinis and cvs
Persicaria vacciniifolia, p.387 ○
Phlox douglasii cvs ○
Phlox subulata ○
Phuopsis stylosa, p.352
Saxifraga stolonifera ○ ⊡
Tiarella cordifolia, p.347 ○
Waldsteinia ○

Sarcococca confusa

Groundcover Plants for Shade

An area that is shaded for some or most of the day may be regarded by some gardeners as a problem space, when in fact it should be viewed as a fortunate opportunity to experiment with a different, and often equally exciting, range of plants from those more suited to sunny positions. The following groundcover plants may be planted in any depth of shade, given reasonably fertile soil conditions.

Shrubs
Cotoneaster conspicuus ○
Cotoneaster 'Gnom' ○
Cotoneaster 'Herbstfeuer' ○
Daphne laureola subsp. *philippi*, p.156 ○
Epigaea asiatica ○
Euonymus fortunei 'Kewensis' ○
Gaultheria shallon, p.162 ○
Hypericum calycinum, p.170 ○
Leucothöe fontanesiana ○
Lonicera pileata, p.176 ○
Mahonia aquifolium, p.157 ○
Mahonia repens ○
Pachysandra terminalis, p.388 ○
Paxistima canbyi ○
Prunus laurocerasus 'Otto Luyken', p.154 ○
Rubus tricolor ○
Ruscus hypoglossum, p.176 ○
Sarcococca confusa ○ ⊡
Sarcococca humilis, p.174 ○
Vinca difformis ○
Vinca minor, p.176 ○

Climbers
Asteranthera ovata ○
Berberidopsis corallina, p.211 ○
Epipremnum aureum 'Marble Queen', p.219 ○
Ficus pumila ○
Hedera colchica 'Dentata', p.221 ○
Hedera helix 'Green Ripple', p.221 ○
Hedera helix 'Ivalace', p.221 ○
Hedera hibernica, p.221 ○
Hydrangea petiolaris, p.208
Rhoicissus capensis ○
Rhoicissus rhomboidea ○
Schizophragma hydrangeoides

Ferns
Adiantum venustum, p.313
Athyrium filix-femina
Blechnum penna-marina ○ ⊡
Blechnum spicant ○
Polypodium vulgare, p.313 ○
Polystichum setiferum Groups, pp.311, 313 ○

Blechnum penna-marina

Perennials

Acanthus spinosus, p.251
Ajuga pyramidalis ○
Ajuga reptans 'Atropurpurea', p.303 ○
Alchemilla mollis, p.290
Anemone apennina
Arisarum proboscideum
Asarum caudatum ○
Asarum europaeum, p.390 ○
Aspidistra elatior ○
Astrantia maxima, p.277
Bergenia cordifolia 'Purpurea', p.269 ○
Brunnera macrophylla
Campanula portenschlagiana, p.382 ○
Campanula poscharskyana, p.381
Ceratostigma plumbaginoides, p.360
Chelidonium majus 'Flore Pleno', p.238
Convallaria majalis, p.268
Dicentra formosa
Dicentra spectabilis, p.245
Duchesnea indica ○
Elatostema repens, p.303 ○
Epimedium perralderianum ○
Euphorbia amygdaloides var. *robbiae*, p.271 ○
Fittonia argyroneura, p.300 ○
Galax urceolata, p.351 ○
Galium odoratum, p.275
Geranium macrorrhizum, p.279 ○

Spotted deadnettle (*Lamium maculatum*)

Geranium nodosum, p.270
Geranium renardii, p.277
Geranium sanguineum, p.354
Geranium wallichianum 'Buxton's Variety', p.287
Glechoma hederacea 'Variegata', p.300 ○
HOSTAS (some), pp.288–9 ⊡
Hypsela reniformis
Iris foetidissima ○
Lamium maculatum, p.269 ○ ⊡
Liriope muscari, p.294 ○
Luzula sylvatica 'Marginata' ○
Maianthemum bifolium
Meehania urticifolia
Omphalodes cappadocica, p.349
Pachyphragma macrophyllum, p.267
Persicaria affinis 'Donald Lowndes', p.376 ○
Persicaria campanulata, p.259
Phalaris arundinacea var. *picta*, p.306 ○
Plectranthus oertendahlii ○
Pulmonaria saccharata, p.271 ○
Saxifraga x *geum*, p.347 ○
Symphytum grandiflorum of gardens
Tellima grandiflora Rubra Group, p.302 ○
Tiarella cordifolia, p.347 ○
Tolmiea menziesii ○

ORNAMENTAL GROUNDCOVER
Below: Hostas thrive in cool, shady surroundings and offer a variety of leaf texture, color, and form. Many plants grow well on the fringes of woodland, as long as conditions are not too densely shaded nor too dry.

Waldsteinia ternata

Tradescantia fluminensis 'Variegata', p.300 ○
Vancouveria hexandra, p.347
Viola riviniana 'Purpurea', p.369
Waldsteinia ternata, p.385 ○ ⊡

Rock-garden plants

Asarina procumbens, p.384
Cardamine trifolia, p.362
Cornus canadensis, p.374
Homogyne alpina ○
Mitchella repens ○
Prunella grandiflora, p.381 ○
Saxifraga stolonifera ○
Saxifraga x *urbium* ○
Tiarella cordifolia, p.347 ○

Groundcover Plants for Sun

Many plants grow naturally in dry, sunny conditions. Some have developed foliage characteristics to minimize moisture loss from their leaves; others are densely branched, keeping the soil surface shaded and cool. Most have extensive root systems that penetrate deeply to find moisture. These plants are adapted to well-drained soils; in poorly drained situations, they may not survive prolonged wet conditions. Although adapted to poorer, dry soils, young plants may have been grown in richer soil mixes and well watered, so when planting incorporate organic matter, such as leaf mold or compost, and check water needs until well established.

***Juniperus squamata* 'Blue Star'**

Conifers

Juniperus communis 'Prostrata' ○
Juniperus horizontalis 'Wiltonii' ○
Juniperus sabina var. *tamariscifolia*, p.110 ○
Juniperus squamata 'Blue Carpet' ○
Juniperus squamata 'Blue Star' ○ ◘
Microbiota decussata, p.110 ○
Picea abies 'Inversa' ○

Shrubs

Arctostaphylos nevadensis ○
Arctostaphylos nummularia ○
Arctostaphylos uva-ursi, p.388 ○
Berberis wilsoniae ○
Brachyglottis Dunedin Hybrids 'Sunshine', p.170 ○
Calluna vulgaris 'White Lawn' ○
Ceanothus thyrsiflorus var. *repens*, p.168 ○
Cotoneaster cochleatus of gardens ○
Cotoneaster 'Skogholm' ○
Cytisus x *beanii*, p.349
Cytisus scoparius subsp. *maritimus*
Ephedra gerardiana ○
Erica carnea 'Springwood White', p.178 ○
Euonymus fortunei 'Emerald Gaiety' ○
Euonymus fortunei 'Kewensis' ○
Gaultheria myrsinoides ○
Genista hispanica, p.170
x *Halimiocistus sahucii*, p.159 ○
Hebe pinguifolia 'Pagei', p.351 ○
Hebe 'Youngii' ○
Hypericum calycinum, p.170 ○
Lantana montevidensis, p.167 ○
Leiophyllum buxifolium ○
Leptospermum rupestre, p.160 ○
Potentilla fruticosa 'Abbotswood', p.158
Rosa GROUSE ('Korimro'), p.189
Rosa 'Nozomi', p.189
Rosa PINK BELLS ('Poulbells'), p.190
Rosmarinus officinalis 'Prostratus' ○
Salix repens, p.156
Santolina chamaecyparissus ○
Stephanandra incisa 'Crispa'

NATURAL SPREADERS

Several of the mat-forming acaenas provide attractive, summer-flowering groundcover in exposed, sunny sites.

Symphoricarpos x *chenaultii* 'Hancock'
Ulex europaeus 'Flore Pleno'
Vinca minor and cvs ○
Vinca major 'Variegata', p.175 ○

Climbers

Anredera cordifolia ○
Campsis radicans
Clematis armandii, p.212 ○
Clematis rehderiana, p.213
Clematis tangutica, p.213
Decumaria sinensis ○
Hardenbergia comptoniana, p.206 ○
Hedera canariensis var. *algeriensis* 'Ravensholst' ○
Hedera colchica 'Dentata Variegata' ○
Hedera hibernica, p.221 ○
Hibbertia scandens ○
Kennedia rubicunda, p.204 ○
Lathyrus latifolius, p.211
Lonicera japonica 'Halliana', p.215 ○
Parthenocissus tricuspidata, p.218
Pueraria lobata
Pyrostegia venusta, p.218 ○
Trachelospermum asiaticum ○
Vitis coignetiae, p.218

Perennials

Alchemilla mollis, p.290
Anthemis punctata subsp. *cupaniana*, p.276 ○
Artemisia alba 'Canescens' ○
Centaurea montana, p.284
Darmera peltata, p.238
Euphorbia polychroma, p.275
Geranium sanguineum, p.354
Heterocentron elegans, p.284 ○
Liriope muscari, p.294 ○
Lysimachia punctata, p.255
Nepeta x *faassenii*, p.286
Origanum vulgare 'Aureum', p.290
Osteospermum jucundum, p.279 ○

***Tropaeolum* Alaska Series**

Phlomis russeliana, p.255
Rheum palmatum 'Atrosanguineum', p.227
Stachys byzantina, p.304 ○
Veronica prostrata and cvs
Waldsteinia ternata, p.385 ○

Annuals and biennials

Any of spreading habit, such as *Tropaeolum* ◘

Rock-garden plants

Acaena microphylla, p.389 ○
Antennaria dioica var. *rosea*, p.366 ○
Arabis alpina subsp. *caucasica* 'Variegata', p.362 ○
Armeria maritima 'Vindictive', p.380 ○
Aubrieta cvs ○
Aurinia saxatilis, p.350 ○
Campanula portenschlagiana, p.382 ○
Campanula poscharskyana, p.381
Dianthus gratianopolitanus, p.377 ○
Dryas octopetala, p.375 ○
Helianthemum 'Ben More', p.354 ○
Hypericum olympicum
Iberis sempervirens, p.346 ○
Lithodora diffusa 'Heavenly Blue', p.357 ○ ◘
Nierembergia repens, p.374
Persicaria affinis and cvs
Phlox douglasii 'Crackerjack', p.379 ○
Phuopsis stylosa, p.352
Thymus serpyllum ○
Veronica prostrata 'Kapitan', p.357

***Lithodora diffusa* 'Heavenly Blue'**

Plants for Dry Shade

Dry, shady conditions persist under evergreen trees throughout the year. Under the summer leaf canopy of deciduous trees, too, very little moisture penetrates, except during prolonged rainfall. A few early-flowering bulbs, such as English bluebells (*Hyacinthoides non-scripta*), and small woodland plants grow naturally in deciduous woodlands, dying down as the trees resume growth in spring. In gardens, dry shade occurs under larger, low-branched trees or where eaves extend over borders. Planting should be done in the autumn so that roots are well established by the following spring. Fertilize regularly and monitor water needs until the plants are established.

Trees and conifers
Ilex aquifolium, p.98 ○
Taxus baccata 'Adpressa' ○
Taxus cuspidata, p.109 ○
Tsuga canadensis, p.107 ○

Shrubs
Aucuba japonica 'Crotonifolia', p.153 ○
Buxus sempervirens ○
Choisya ternata, p.127 ○
Cotoneaster horizontalis, p.172
Daphne laureola and forms ○ ◻

Daphne laureola* subsp. *philippi

Elaeagnus x *ebbingei* ○
Euonymus japonicus ○
Fatsia japonica ○
Gaultheria shallon, p.162 ○
Hedera colchica var. *algeriensis* 'Ravensholst', p.221 ○
Hedera helix ○
Hedera hibernica, p.221 ○
Hypericum calycinum, p.170 ○
Hypericum x *inodorum* 'Elstead', p.170
Hypericum x *moserianum*
Lonicera pileata, p.176 ○
Mahonia aquifolium, p.157 ○
Osmanthus decorus ○
Osmanthus delavayi, p.116 ○
Pachysandra terminalis, p.388 ○
Prunus laurocerasus 'Otto Luyken', p.154 ○
Prunus laurocerasus 'Zabeliana', p.154 ○
Prunus lusitanica ○
Rubus tricolor ○
Ruscus aculeatus ○
Ruscus hypoglossum, p.176 ○
Sambucus nigra 'Guincho Purple'
Sarcococca humilis, p.174 ○
Symphoricarpos albus var. *laevigatus*
Vaccinium angustifolium var. *laevifolium*, p.172
Viburnum rhytidophyllum, p.118 ○
Viburnum tinus, p.149 ○
Vinca major ○
Vinca minor, p.176 ○

Climbers
Berberidopsis corallina, p.211 ○
Celastrus orbiculatus
Cissus striata ○
Epipremnum aureum 'Marble Queen', p.219 ○
Euonymus fortunei 'Emerald Gaiety' ○
Hedera canariensis var. *algeriensis* ○
Lapageria rosea, p.210 ○
Lonicera japonica 'Halliana', p.215 ○
Lonicera periclymenum and cvs
Philodendron scandens, p.220 ○

Ferns
Asplenium ceterach, p.311 ○
Asplenium scolopendrium, p.313 ○
Cyrtomium falcatum, p.311 ○
Davallia canariensis
Dryopteris affinis ○
Nephrolepis exaltata, p.312 ○
Polypodium vulgare, p.313 ○
Polystichum aculeatum ○
Pteris cretica, p.311 ○

Perennials
Acanthus spinosus, p.251
Achimenes
Ajuga reptans cvs ○
Alchemilla mollis, p.290
Chelidonium majus 'Flore Pleno', p.238
Chirita ○
Corydalis lutea, p.359 ○

Bishop's hat (*Epimedium grandiflorum* 'Crimson Beauty')

A light touch
Above: The close-set, dark green leaves of Euphorbia amygdaloides *var.* robbiae, *shown here growing in association with a dark-leaved ivy, provide a good groundcover in dry shade, where soil may be poor. Rounded heads of lime green flowers add light to the clump in spring.*

Digitalis purpurea
Doronicum x *excelsum* 'Harpur Crewe'
Epimedium grandiflorum and cvs ◻
Epimedium pinnatum subsp. *colchicum* ○
Euphorbia amygdaloides var. *robbiae*, p.271 ○ ◻
Geranium macrorrhizum, p.279
Geranium phaeum, p.238
Iris foetidissima ○
Kohleria digitaliflora, p.244
Lamium maculatum, p.269 ○
Lunaria rediviva
Luzula sylvatica 'Marginata' ○
Pachysandra terminalis, p.388 ○
Polygonatum x *hybridum*, p.238
Scopolia carniolica, p.271
Sedum spathulifolium, p.389 ○
Streptocarpus saxorum, p.284 ○
Symphytum 'Goldsmith' ◻
Symphytum ibericum

***Symphytum* 'Goldsmith'**

Tellima grandiflora ○
Tolmiea menziesii ○
Tradescantia zebrina 'Quadricolor' ○
Viola riviniana 'Purpurea', p.369

Bulbs, corms, and tubers
Clivia miniata, p.419 ○
Colchicum autumnale, p.437
Haemanthus albiflos ○
Hyacinthoides hispanica, p.414
Hyacinthoides non-scripta, p.414

A COOL, MOIST CORNER
Above: Ferns and large-leaved hostas grow to perfection in moist shade at the side of a garden pool.

Plants for Moist Shade

In areas with high rainfall, the soil in parts of the garden that receive little or no sun may be cool and moist throughout the year. Low-lying gardens with a high water table or drainage problems may have shady, permanently moist areas. Similar conditions occur along the margins of natural streams or when an artificial bog is created beside a garden pond. Take advantage of these situations to grow plants such as broad-leaved hostas, ferns, and taller, moisture-loving primroses. Plant in spring, amending lighter soils with organic material. During extended dry periods, keep an eye on moisture levels.

Shrubs
Anopterus glandulosus, p.116 ○
Cassiope lycopodioides, p.363 ○
Clethra arborea ○ ⊡
Crataegus laevigata 'Punicea'
Cyathodes colensoi, p.360 ○
Danäe racemosa ○
Gaultheria procumbens, p.387 ○
Kalmia latifolia, p.141 ○
Ledum groenlandicum, p.154 ○
Leucothöe fontanesiana ○
Lindera benzoin, p.131
Lyonia ligustrina
Neillia thibetica, p.140
Paeonia lutea var. *ludlowii*, p.237
Paeonia suffruticosa subsp. *rockii*, p.236
Paxistima canbyi ○
Pieris formosa var. *forrestii* 'Wakehurst', p.142 ○
Pittosporum eugenioides ○
Prunus laurocerasus ○
RHODODENDRONS, pp.132–4, most ○
Salix magnifica
Sarcococca ruscifolia ○
Skimmia japonica, p.175 ○
Viburnum 'Pragense', p.139 ○
Xanthorhiza simplicissima

Clethra arborea

Climbers
Akebia quinata, p.206, some ○
Asteranthera ovata ○
Decumaria sinensis, p.206 ○
Dioscorea discolor, p.219 ○
Humulus lupulus 'Aureus', p.206
Hydrangea petiolaris, p.208
Lonicera tragophylla
Macleania insignis ○
Mikania scandens ○
Passiflora coccinea, p.205 ○
Pileostegia viburnoides, p.208 ○
Schizophragma integrifolium, p.208
Smilax china
Thunbergia mysorensis, p.207 ○
Trachelospermum jasminoides, p.207 ○

Ferns
Athyrium nipponicum, p.313
Blechnum tabulare ○
Cyathea australis, p.100 ○

Sword fern (*Polystichum munitum*)

Cyathea medullaris ○
Dicksonia antarctica, p.310 ○
Dryopteris goldieana
Lygodium japonicum ○
Matteuccia struthiopteris, p.312
Onoclea sensibilis, p.312
Osmunda claytoniana
Polystichum munitum, p.310 ○ ⊡
Selaginella martensii, p.311 ○
Woodwardia radicans ○

Perennials
Actaea pachypoda, p.259
Ajuga reptans 'Atropurpurea', p.303 ○
Anemone x *hybrida* cvs
Anemonella thalictroides, p.364
Anthurium scherzerianum, p.302 ○
Aruncus dioicus, p.226
Asarum europaeum, p.390 ○
Begonia rex and hybrids ○
Bergenia ○

***Helleborus* x *ballardiae* 'December Dawn'**

Brunnera macrophylla
Calathea zebrina, p.266 ○
Cardamine pentaphyllos, p.270
Cimicifuga racemosa
Convallaria majalis, p.268
Cortusa matthioli, p.354
Cyathodes colensoi, p.360 ○
Darmera peltata, p.238
Deinanthe caerulea
Dichorisandra reginae, p.252 ○
Digitalis x *mertonensis* ○
Epigaea gaultherioides, p.364 ○
Galax urceolata, p.351 ○
Geranium nodosum, p.270
Hacquetia epipactis, p.371
Hedyotis michauxii, p.383
Helleborus x *ballardiae* 'December Dawn' ⊡
Helleborus x *hybridus*, p.302 ○
HOSTAS, pp.288–9 ⊡
Isopyrum thalictroides
Jeffersonia diphylla, p.347
Kirengeshoma palmata, p.263
Lamium galeobdolon subsp. *montanum* 'Florentinum' ○
Lamium maculatum, p.269 ○
Lathraea clandestina, p.271
Lithophragma parviflorum, p.346
Maianthemum canadense, p.363
Maranta leuconeura 'Erythroneura', p.303 ○
Mitella breweri, p.384
Omphalodes cappadocica, p.349
Ourisia caespitosa, p.374 ○
Pachysandra terminalis, p.388 ○
Periscaria campanulata, p.259
Polygonatum x *hybridum*, p.238
Pratia pedunculata, p.383 ○
PRIMULAS (many), pp.272–3
Prunella grandiflora, p.381 ○
Pulmonaria, some ○
Ranzania japonica
Ruellia devosiana, p.277 ○
Tiarella cordifolia, p.347 ○
Trillium grandiflorum, p.268
Uvularia grandiflora, p.274
Vancouveria hexandra, p.347
Xanthosoma sagittifolium, p.266

Bulbs, corms, and tubers
Arisaema
Arisarum proboscideum
Arum italicum 'Marmoratum', p.434
Camassia leichtlinii, p.397
Galanthus elwesii, p.439
Galanthus nivalis and cvs
Galanthus plicatus subsp. *plicatus*
Leucojum aestivum, p.396
Leucojum vernum, p.426
Narcissus cyclamineus, p.418

Shrubs preferring Wall Protection

Walls can provide favorable growing conditions for marginally hardy often evergreen, shrubs. Some winter-flowering shrubs also flower more reliably and freely when given wall protection. The best wallside situations are warm and sunny and give good shelter from the cold winds of winter and early spring. The warmth from heat loss through house walls, and the well-drained conditions near the base of such walls, also assist the survival of less hardy shrubs.

***Fremontodendron* 'Pacific Sunset'**

Abelia floribunda ○
Abutilon megapotamicum ○
Acacia podalyriifolia, p.135 ○
Acacia pravissima, p.97 ○
Acca sellowiana, p.143 ○
Aloysia triphylla, p.143
Artemisia arborescens, p.175 ○
Azara serrata, p.135 ○
Buddleja asiatica ○
Buddleja crispa, p.143
Callistemon citrinus 'Splendens', p.143 ○
Cantua buxifolia, p.155 ○
Carpenteria californica, p.138 ○
Ceanothus impressus, p.145 ○
Chaenomeles speciosa 'Moerloosei', p.130
Chimonanthus praecox
Coronilla valentina subsp. *glauca*, p.157 ○ ⊡
Cytisus x *spachianus* ○
Daphne odora 'Aureomarginata', p.174 ○
Dendromecon rigida, p.147 ○
Drimys winteri, p.78 ○
Elsholtzia stauntonii, p.173
Escallonia 'Iveyi', p.118 ○
Fabiana imbricata f. *violacea*, p.145 ○
Fremontodendron 'California Glory', p.123 ○
Fremontodendron 'Pacific Sunset' ○ ⊡
Garrya elliptica, p.125 ○
Itea ilicifolia, p.146 ○
Jasminum mesnyi, p.207 ○
Lagerstroemia indica, p.91
Leptospermum scoparium 'Red Damask', p.131 ○

Sheltered position
Coronilla valentina *subsp.* glauca *often benefits from being grown against a warm wall.*

Lonicera fragrantissima
Luma apiculata, p.119 ○
Melianthus major ○
Myrtus communis, p.127 ○
Olearia x *scilloniensis* ○
Osteomeles schweriniae, p.138 ○
Piptanthus nepalensis, p.146 ○
Robinia hispida, p.141
Rosa banksiae 'Lutea', p.198 ○
Rosa 'Mermaid', p.198
Rosmarinus officinalis, p.167 ○
Salvia involucrata 'Bethellii', p.231
Solanum crispum 'Glasnevin', p.214 ○
Tibouchina urvilleana, p.122
Vestia foetida ○

Plants for Paving and Wall Crevices

In mountainous regions, many alpine plants grow in deep cracks and crevices in the rock. Some are clump-forming or trailing in habit; others, such as saxifrages and sempervivums, grow as rosettes, extending by means of runners. If laying irregularly shaped paving, leave crevices for small plants, but restrict planting to little-used areas, where the plants can survive. When building stone retaining walls, tilt rock slabs slightly backward to create deep pockets, planting as the wall is being constructed. Most wall plants thrive in sunny situations, but ramondas and most small ferns prefer cool, moist shade.

Floral covering
*Fleabane (*Erigeron karvinskianus*), with its daisylike flower heads in summer, is excellent in crevices.*

Annuals and biennials
Ageratum houstonianum (small cvs)
Ionopsidium acaule
Limnanthes douglasii, p.336
Lobelia erinus cvs
Lobularia maritima
Malcolmia maritima, p.323
Nemophila maculata, p.319
Nemophila menziesii, p.333
Portulaca grandiflora Series and cvs

Rock-garden plants
Acaena microphylla, p.389 ○
Acantholimon glumaceum (wall), p.377 ○
Achillea x *kellereri*, p.375 ○
Achillea x *lewisii* 'King Edward' ○
Aethionema 'Warley Rose', p.376 ○
Alyssum montanum ○
Androsace sarmentosa ○
Antennaria dioica ○
Armeria maritima 'Vindictive', p.380 ○
Artemisia pedemontana ○
Artemisia schmidtiana ○
Asplenium ceterach, p.311 ○
Aubrieta ○
Aurinia saxatilis 'Citrina', p.349 ○
Campanula cochleariifolia, p.383
Campanula poscharskyana, p.381
Cassiope 'Edinburgh', p.346 ○
Chamaemelum nobile ○
Chiastophyllum oppositifolium (wall), p.349 ○
Cyananthus microphyllus, p.383
Cymbalaria muralis
Dianthus deltoides ○ ⊡
Draba aizoides ○
Dryas octopetala, p.375 ○
Erigeron karvinskianus, p.377 ⊡
Erinus alpinus, p.366 ○
Gypsophila repens and cvs ○
Haberlea rhodopensis 'Virginalis', p.373 ○

Dianthus deltoides

Helianthemum ○
Hypericum olympicum
Lithodora diffusa 'Heavenly Blue', p.357 ○
Mazus reptans, p.368
Mentha requienii ○
Nierembergia repens, p.374
Parahebe lyallii ○
Phlox douglasii cvs ○
Physoplexis comosa (wall), p.380
Ramonda myconi (wall only), p.382 ○
Saxifraga cotyledon, p.352 ○
Sedum spathulifolium 'Cape Blanco', p.391 ○
Sempervivum montanum, p.390 ○
Thymus serpyllum and cvs ○
Vitaliana primuliflora, p.372 ○

YEAR-ROUND ATTRACTION
An informal grouping of flowering and foliage plants in separate containers allows a flexible design. Plants can be replaced when their flowering period is over, yet a pleasing air of permanence is retained for the entire arrangement.

Plants for Containers

Containers full of plants can brighten patios, courtyards, and balconies. These situations are often sheltered and sunny, so use large containers, which retain more moisture than small ones. Small trees, conifers, or shrubs in small groups, together with perennials, will give long-term interest in shape and foliage, with periods of flowering. For colorful displays, plant spring-flowering bulbs, followed by petunias and marigolds, which will flower throughout the summer.

Trees
Acer negundo
Cordyline australis and cvs ○
Crataegus laevigata and cvs
Eucalyptus (when young) ○
Ficus (most) ○
Ilex aquifolium and cvs ○
Jacaranda mimosifolia, p.79
Laurus nobilis ○ ⊡
Malus (small species and cvs)
Melia azederach, p.76
Olea europaea ○
Phoenix canariensis ○
Prunus (small species and cvs)
Sorbus (small species and cvs)
Washingtonia ○

Sweet bay (*Laurus nobilis*)

Conifers
All the small species and cvs of:
Abies ○
Chamaecyparis ○
Juniperus ○
Picea ○
Pinus ○
Thuja ○
Thujopsis dolabrata ○

Shrubs
Buxus sempervirens and cvs ○
Catharanthus roseus, p.160
Erica ○
FUCHSIAS, pp.164–5
Hebe ○
HYDRANGEAS, p.144
Lavandula ○
Myrtus communis, p.130 ○
Pittosporum ○
RHODODENDRONS (most), pp.132–4, most ○
ROSES (most), pp.184–8, some ○
Santolina ○
Senecio (shrubby species) ○
Spiraea
Viburnum tinus, p.149 ○

Climbers
Cissus antarctica, p.220 ○
CLEMATIS (small cvs), pp.212–13, some ○
Cobaea scandens, p.214 ○
Eccremocarpus scaber, p.217 ○
Hedera helix and cvs ○
Ipomoea, some ○
Jasminum (climbing species), some ○
Lathyrus (climbing species)
Lonicera (climbing species), some ○
Mandevilla ○
Passiflora ○
Stephanotis floribunda, p.204 ○
Tropaeolum (climbing species)

Ferns
Adiantum (most)
Asplenium scolopendrium Marginatum Group, p.313 ○
Athyrium niponicum, p.312
Polypodium vulgare 'Cornubiense', p.312 ○
Polystichum setiferum Divisilobum Group, p.311 ○

Perennials
Agapanthus
Bergenia ○
DAYLILIES, p.257
Geranium, some ○
Geum
HOSTAS, pp.288–9
Phormium ○
PRIMULAS (tall species and cvs), pp.272–3
Pulmonaria, some ○
Rudbeckia fulgida var. *sullivantii* 'Goldsturm', p.256
Salvia (many)
Stachys, some ○
Verbena, some ○

Annuals and biennials
Ageratum
Bassia scoparia f. *trichophylla*, p.335
Browallia speciosa, p.266
Calendula officinalis Series and cvs
Callistephus chinensis Series and cvs
Lobelia erinus cvs
Nemesia strumosa and Series
Petunia
Salpiglossis sinuata Series and cvs
Solenostemon scutellarioides Series and cvs, pp.324, 329
Tagetes
Viola x *wittrockiana* hybrids

Rock-garden plants
All rock plants are suitable, the following being particularly recommended:
Campanula (many), some ○
Dianthus (many) ○
Geranium (several), some ○
Hebe ○
Helianthemum ○
Iberis sempervirens, p.346 ○
Penstemon (many), some ○
Periscaria affinis
Phlox (several) ○
Primula auricula and hybrids
Saponaria ocymoides, p.378
Saxifraga (many) ○
Silene schafta, p.379

Bulbs, corms, and tubers
All bulbous plants are suitable, the following being particularly recommended:
CROCUSES, pp.428–9
DAFFODILS, pp.416–18
HYACINTHS, p.431
IRISES (bulbous species), pp.234–5
LILIES (most), pp.404–5
TULIPS, pp.410–12 ⊡
Zantedeschia aethiopica 'Crowborough', p.397 ○

***Tulipa* 'Keizerskroon'**

Water plants
Watertight containers are ideal for the following:
Acorus calamus 'Argenteostriatus', p.447 ○
Aponogeton distachyos, p.447
Azolla filiculoides, p.448
Eichhornia crassipes, p.448 ○
Menyanthes trifoliata, p.446
Nelumbo nucifera and cvs
Pontederia cordata, p.448
Thalia dealbata
WATERLILIES (small cvs), p.450

Trailing Plants for Walls or Baskets

Many plants grow naturally in crevices, their trailing stems covering large areas of vertical rock. In gardens, trailing alpines may be planted in pockets of soil in drystone walls. If a garden has retaining walls, climbers or low-growing conifers, trailing from the top, can soften brickwork. Smaller trailing plants, such as tender perennials or annuals, are ideal for hanging baskets. After planting, baskets may be set on large, inverted pots on a patio or old tree stump, the plants forming a conical mound of tumbling stems and flowers.

Conifers
Juniperus conferta ○
Juniperus horizontalis and cvs ○
Juniperus squamata 'Blue Carpet' ○
Microbiota decussata, p.110 ○

Shrubs
Arctostaphylos uva-ursi, p.388 ○
Ceanothus thyrsiflorus var. *repens*, p.168 ○
Chorizema ilicifolium, p.157 ○
Cotoneaster microphyllus ○
Euonymus fortunei 'Coloratus' ○
Fuchsia procumbens, p.165
Genista lydia, p.359
Hebe pinguifolia 'Pagei', p.351 ○
Helichrysum petiolare, p.175 ○ ⊡
Lantana montevidensis, p.167 ○
Leptospermum rupestre, p.160 ○
Loiseleuria procumbens, p.377 ○
Nematanthus strigillosus ○
Salix lindleyana
Salix repens, p.156

Perennials
Achimenes 'Peach Blossom'
Aeschynanthus speciosus, p.293 ○
Aporocactus flagelliformis, p.463
Campanula isophylla ○
Carpobrotus edulis
Columnea (most) ○
Convolvulus sabatius, p.356
Cyanotis kewensis ○
Elatostema repens, p.303 ○
Episcia cupreata, p.301 ○
Episcia dianthiflora, p.299 ○
Glechoma hederacea 'Variegata', p.300 ○ ⊡
Hedera colchica 'Dentata Variegata' ○
Hedera colchica 'Sulphur Heart' ○
Lampranthus spectabilis, p.463
Lotus berthelotii, p.283 ○
Pelargonium peltatum ○
Peperomia scandens ○
Plectranthus verticillatus ○
Ruellia devosiana, p.277 ○
Sarmienta repens ○
Tradescantia fluminensis and cvs ○
Tradescantia zebrina, p.301 ○
Tropaeolum polyphyllum, p.293
Verbena peruviana ○
Verbena 'Sissinghurst', p.282

Annuals and biennials
Calceolaria integrifolia ⊡
Limnanthes douglasii, p.336
Lobelia erinus cvs ⊡
Nemophila maculata, p.319
Nolana paradoxa
Petunia Cascade Series
Petunia Jamboree Series
Petunia Surfinia Series ⊡
Portulaca grandiflora Series and cvs
Sanvitalia procumbens, p.336
Tropaeolum majus Series and cvs

***Petunia* Surfinia Series 'Surfinia Purple'**

HIGH-SUMMER DISPLAY
Above: Various kinds of plant container can be attached to walls to hold colorful seasonal displays. Here fuchsias, lobelias, and petunias are planted among yellow calceolarias and trailing red and white geraniums.

Rock-garden plants
Acaena 'Blue Haze' ○ ⊡
Androsace lanuginosa, p.377 ○
Arabis caucasica ○
Campanula cochleariifolia, p.383
Cymbalaria muralis ○
Cytisus x *beanii*, p.349
Euphorbia myrsinites, p.371 ○
Gypsophila repens ○
Iberis sempervirens, p.346 ○
Lithodora diffusa cvs ○
Lysimachia nummularia, p.386 ○
Oenothera macrocarpa, p.385
Othonna cheirifolia, p.358 ○
Parahebe catarractae, p.356 ○
Parochetus communis, p.384 ○
Persicaria vacciniifolia, p.387 ○
Phlox subulata ○
Pterocephalus perennis, p.380 ○
Saxifraga stolonifera ○

SOFT HARMONY
Left: This well-filled hanging basket of pastel hues and variegated foliage includes Glechoma hederacea *'Variegata' and* Helichrysum petiolare. *It will remain attractive and fresh throughout summer.*

***Acaena* 'Blue Haze'**

Plants with Aromatic Foliage

The leaves of many plants contain essential aromatic oils, used in medicine or cooking. For gardeners, their value lies in the pleasant, pungent aromas released naturally or when bruised. Those of culinary value, such as rosemary, are often grown in herb gardens. Low-growing thymes may be planted next to paths or between paving stones to give off scent when walked on gently. The fragrance from trees may be best appreciated as it drifts through the garden on the wind.

PATH-SIDE AROMATICS
Above: Shrubby culinary herbs, such as sage and thyme, can be combined with small ornamental shrubs grown for their aromatic foliage.

Trees
Agonis flexuosa, p.90 ○
Atherosperma moschatum ○
Eucalyptus ○
Juglans regia, p.66
Laurus nobilis ○
Phellodendron chinense, p.81
Populus balsamifera
Populus trichocarpa
Sassafras albidum, p.68
Umbellularia californica, p.74 ○

Conifers
Calocedrus decurrens, p.106 ○
Chamaecyparis ○
Cupressus ○
Juniperus ○
Pseudotsuga menziesii ○
Thuja (most) ○

Shrubs
Aloysia triphylla, p.143
Artemisia abrotanum, p.176
Boronia megastigma, p.156 ○
Caryopteris x *clandonensis* 'Arthur Simmonds', p.168
Choisya ternata, p.127 ○
Cistus laurifolius ○
Elsholtzia stauntonii, p.173
Gaultheria procumbens, p.387 ○
Helichrysum italicum ○
Hyssopus officinalis, p.168

***Salvia officinalis* 'Icterina'**

Lavandula (most) ○
Lindera
Myrtus communis, p.130 ○
PELARGONIUMS (scented-leaved forms), pp.246–7 ○
Perovskia 'Blue Spire', p.168
Phlomis fruticosa, p.170 ○
Prostanthera ○
Rhododendron cinnabarinum subsp. *xanthocodon*, p.133 ○
Rhododendron rubiginosum ○
Ribes sanguineum 'Brocklebankii', p.155
Rosa rubiginosa, p.185
Rosmarinus officinalis, p.167 ○
Salvia officinalis cvs ○ ⊡
Santolina chamaecyparissus ○
Zanthoxylum piperitum, p.145

Perennials
Artemisia absinthium 'Lambrook Silver' ○
Chamaemelum nobile ○
Galium odoratum, p.275
Geranium macrorrhizum, p.279 ○
Houttuynia cordata 'Chameleon', p.447
Kaempferia pulchra, p.283
Mentha, some ○
Monarda didyma
Myrrhis odorata, p.240
Origanum vulgare
Perovskia atriplicifolia
Tanacetum parthenium, p.319

Rock-garden plants
Mentha requienii ○
Origanum laevigatum, p.354
Satureja montana
Thymus ○ ⊡

Plants with Fragrant Flowers

Fragrance is released from the flowers of numerous plants. It can be strong, pervading the air around the plant, or apparent only when you are close to individual blooms. Some plants release scent continually, but with others it is more noticeable at night. A sunny, sheltered patio is an ideal situation for small fragrant plants. Position large scented shrubs close to paths, and train fragrant climbers around doorways. Hyacinths in pots bring welcome early spring fragrance indoors.

Trees
Acacia dealbata, p.83 ○
Aesculus hippocastanum, p.64
Bauhinia variegata, p.97
Clethra arborea ○
Crataegus monogyna
Drimys winteri, p.78 ○
Eucryphia lucida, p.90 ○
Fraxinus ornus, p.76
Genista aetnensis, p.93
Laburnum x *watereri* 'Vossii', p.92
MAGNOLIAS, p.75
Malus coronaria 'Charlottae'
Malus hupehensis, p.74
Malus 'Profusion', p.77
Pittosporum tenuifolium, p.127 ○
Pittosporum undulatum ○
Plumeria rubra, p.96
Prunus mume 'Beni-chidori', p.130
Prunus padus 'Grandiflora', p.76
Prunus x *yedoensis*, p.87
Pterostyrax hispida
Robinia pseudoacacia
Styrax japonicus, p.77
Styrax obassia
Tilia x *euchlora*
Tilia 'Petiolaris', p.68
Virgilia oroboides ○

Shrubs
Abelia x *grandiflora*, p.121 ○
Abeliophyllum distichum
Azara microphylla, p.125 ○
Berberis x *stenophylla*, p.135 ○
Boronia megastigma, p.156 ○
Brugmansia arborea ○
Buddleja asiatica ○
Buddleja davidii and cvs
Camellia sasanqua 'Narumigata', p.128 ○
Chimonanthus praecox
Choisya ternata, p.127 ○
Clerodendrum bungei, p.148 ○
Clerodendrum trichotomum, p.147

Pittosporum tobira

Clethra delavayi, p.121
Colletia hystrix, p.147
Coronilla valentina subsp. *glauca*, p.157 ○
Corylopsis pauciflora, p.131
Cytisus battandieri, p.123 ○
Daphne (many), most ○
Deutzia x *elegantissima* cvs
Edgeworthia chrysantha
Elaeagnus x *ebbingei* 'Limelight', p.153 ○
Erica arborea ○
Erica lusitanica ○
Fothergilla major, p.127
Gardenia augusta 'Veitchii', p.158 ○
Hamamelis mollis
Heliotropium arborescens, p.167 ○
Itea ilicifolia, p.146 ○
Lavandula 'Hidcote', p.167 ○
Lavandula stoechas, p.167 ○
Ligustrum lucidum 'Excelsum Superbum', p.127 ○
LILACS (most), p.120
Lonicera fragrantissima
Lupinus arboreus, p.169 ○
MAGNOLIAS, p.75
Osmanthus ○
Philadelphus (many)
Pittosporum tobira ○ ⊡
ROSES (many), pp.184–8, some ○ ⊡
Sarcococca ○
Viburnum (many), some ○

Climbers
Clematis montana 'Elizabeth'
Hoya carnosa, p.208 ○
Jasminum (many), most ○
Lathyrus odoratus and cvs
Lonicera (many), some ○ ⊡
Mandevilla laxa
ROSES (many), pp.184–8, some ○
Stephanotis floribunda, p.204 ○

INTERMINGLING FRAGRANCE
*A combination of climbing roses (*Rosa*) and honeysuckles (*Lonicera*) looks delightful and emits a delicious fragrance.*

Trachelospermum ○
Wattakaka sinensis
Wisteria

Perennials
Anemone sylvestris, p.268
CARNATIONS and PINKS (most), pp.280–1 ○
Clematis heracleifolia 'Wyevale', p.213
Convallaria majalis, p.268
Cosmos atrosanguineus, p.249
Crambe cordifolia, p.226
Galium odoratum, p.275
Hedychium gardnerianum, p.232
Hemerocallis lilioasphodelus, p.257
Hesperis matronalis, p.239
HOSTAS (some), pp.288–9
Iris graminea
Iris unguicularis ○
Meehania urticifolia
Mirabilis jalapa, p.245
Myrrhis odorata, p.240
Nicotiana sylvestris, p.226
Petasites fragrans ○
Primula elatior, p.273
Primula veris, p.273
Tulbaghia natalensis
Verbena x *hybrida* Series and cvs ○
Viola odorata ○

Annuals and biennials
Amberboa moschata, p.335
Antirrhinum majus Series
Argemone mexicana, p.335
Dianthus barbatus Roundabout Series, p.326
Erysimum cheiri Series and cvs ○
Exacum affine, p.381 ○
Iberis amara, p.318
Lathyrus odoratus and cvs ⊡
Limnanthes douglasii, p.336
Matthiola incana
Mentzelia lindleyi, p.336
Nicotiana alata, p.239

Sweet pea (*Lathyrus odoratus* 'Jayne Amanda')

Primula Primrose Group
Reseda odorata, p.319
Scabiosa atropurpurea
Verbena x *hybrida* (most)

Rock-garden plants
Alyssum montanum ○
Dianthus (most) ○
Erysimum helveticum, p.373 ○
Papaver croceum
Primula auricula
Viola odorata ○

Bulbs, corms, and tubers
Amaryllis belladonna, p.408
Arisaema candidissimum, p.435
Chlidanthus fragrans, p.436
Crinum bulbispermum
Crinum x *powellii*, p.398
Crocus angustifolius
Crocus longiflorus
Cyclamen persicum, p.440
Cyclamen repandum
Eucharis x *grandiflora*, p.425 ○
Freesia (most)
Hyacinthus orientalis and cvs
Hymenocallis
LILIES (several), pp.404–5 ⊡
Muscari armeniacum, p.433
Narcissus jonquilla and Div.7 hybrids
Narcissus tazetta and Div.8 hybrids
Ornithogalum arabicum, p.420
Polianthes tuberosa

Orchids
Cattleya J.A.Carbone, p.297 ○
Coelogyne flaccida, p.296 ○

***Lilium* 'Mont Blanc'**

Cacti
Epiphyllum laui, p.461

Water plants
Aponogeton distachyos, p.449
Nymphaea 'Blue Beauty', p.450
Nymphaea 'James Brydon', p.450
Nymphaea odorata 'Sulphurea Grandiflora'

Decorative Fruits or Seed Heads

As winter approaches, dull corners of the garden or featureless borders can be brightened with the colorful fruits or berries of barberries, cotoneasters, viburnums, and other ornamental fruiting shrubs. On pergolas and trellises, *Celastrus orbiculatus* and *Clematis orientalis* provide late-season interest, with trailing skeins of yellow fruits or feathery seeds. Wall-trained pyracanthas will color drab winter walls with yellow, orange, or scarlet fruits. Hollies (*Ilex*) also provide berried material for winter decoration. The dried seed heads of many plants are used in flower arrangements to give a contrast in form and texture.

Trees
Annona reticulata
Arbutus ○
Cornus kousa
Cotoneaster frigidus ◻

Cotoneaster frigidus

Crataegus (most)
HOLLIES (most), pp.98–9, most ○
Koelreuteria paniculata, p.92
MAGNOLIAS, p.75, some ○
Malus (most)
Photinia davidiana, p.94 ○
Schinus molle ○
Sorbus (most)

Conifers
Abies (some) ○
Cedrus (some) ○
Picea (some) ○
Pinus (some) ○

Shrubs
Aucuba japonica, p.152 ○
Berberis (most), some ○
Callicarpa bodinieri var. *giraldii*, p.148
Chaenomeles
x *Citrofortunella microcarpa*, p.151 ○
Cotoneaster (most), some ○ ◻
Cyphomandra betacea, p.125 ○
Decaisnea fargesii, p.122
Euonymus (many), some ○
Gaultheria mucronata and cvs ○

ROSE HIPS AND LANTERNS
*Above: Rose hips and the inflated papery calyces that enclose the fruits of Chinese lantern (*Physalis alkekengi*) – seen here set against the crowded, deep pink flower heads of a sedum – bring warm, glowing colors to autumn mornings.*

Hippophäe rhamnoides, p.124
Hypericum x *inodorum* 'Elstead', p.170
Leycesteria formosa
Poncirus trifoliata
Pyracantha ○
ROSES (most), pp.184–8, some ○
Sambucus racemosa
Sarcococca hookeriana var. *digyna*, p.174 ○
Shepherdia argentea
Skimmia (some) ○
Symphoricarpos
Symplocos paniculata, p.138
Vaccinium vitis-idaea ○
Viburnum (several), some ○

Climbers
Actinidia deliciosa
Akebia, some ○
Billardiera longiflora, p.218 ○
Cardiospermum halicacabum
Celastrus orbiculatus
Clematis orientalis
Holboellia coriacea ○
ROSES (several), pp.184–8, some ○ ◻
Trichosanthes cucumerina var. *anguina*
Tropaeolum speciosum, p.210

Perennials
Actaea
Clintonia borealis
Disporum hookeri
Duchesnea indica ○

Iris foetidissima

Iris foetidissima ○ ◻
Ophiopogon ○
Physalis alkekengi ◻
Phytolacca
Podophyllum
Smilacina racemosa, p.233

Annuals and biennials
Briza maxima
Capsicum annuum 'Holiday Cheer'
Coix lacryma-jobi, p.308
Lagurus ovatus, p.306
Lunaria annua, p.325 ◻

Lunaria annua

Martynia annua, p.320
Nicandra physalodes
Nigella damascena and cvs
Pulsatilla vulgaris, p.348
Solanum capsicastrum ○
Zea mays

Rock-garden plants
Acaena microphylla, p.389 ○
Cornus canadensis, p.374
Dryas octopetala, p.375 ○
Gaultheria (most) ○
Maianthemum
Margyricarpus pinnatus ○
Mitchella repens ○
Nertera granadensis, p.335 ○
Pulsatilla (most)

Bulbs, corms, and tubers
Allium cristophii, p.421
Arisaema triphyllum, p.414
Arum italicum 'Marmoratum', p.434
Cardiocrinum giganteum, p.398

Water plants
Nelumbo
Nuphar lutea, p.451
Thalia dealbata

Flowers for Cutting

With careful selection, flowers can be cut from the garden at most times of the year, from the Christmas rose (*Helleborus niger*) in mid-winter to *Nerine bowdenii* in autumn. In small gardens, integrate plants for cutting into the general design, and leave some blooms for display; or plant away from the house so that the cutting is less noticeable. Fertilize regularly to counteract the weakening effects of cutting plants.

Pink (*Dianthus* 'Doris')

Shrubs
Calluna vulgaris (tall cvs) ○
Camellia japonica cvs ○
Erica ○
Forsythia
Hamamelis mollis
LILACS, p.120
Lonicera fragrantissima
Philadelphus
ROSES (some), pp.184–8, some ○
Salix caprea
Turraea obtusifolia, p.142 ○

Perennials
Alstroemeria Ligtu Hybrids, p.423
Anaphalis
Anchusa azurea
Anemone x *hybrida* cvs
Astrantia major, p.277
CARNATIONS and PINKS, pp.280–1 ○ ⊡
Cattleya (most)
CHRYSANTHEMUMS, pp.260–1
Cymbidium (most) ○
DELPHINIUMS (most), p.230
Helleborus niger, p.301
Phalaenopsis (most) ○
Phlox paniculata cvs
Rudbeckia (most)
Strelitzia reginae, p.267 ○

Annuals and biennials
Amaranthus caudatus, p.326
Amberboa moschata, p.335
Callistephus chinensis Series and cvs
Centaurea cyanus and cvs
Clarkia
Eustoma grandiflorum, p.319
Gaillardia pulchella 'Lollipops', p.338
Gypsophila elegans, p.318
Lathyrus odoratus and cvs
Malope trifida, p.324
Matthiola cvs
Moluccella laevis, p.335
Rhodanthe chlorocephala subsp. *rosea*, p.321
Xeranthemum annuum
Zinnia elegans Series and cvs (tall hybrids)

Bulbs, corms, and tubers
Allium (tall species)
Alstroemeria (tall species and cvs)
DAFFODILS (tall species and cvs), pp.416–18
DAHLIAS, pp.406–7
GLADIOLI (most), p.399
LILIES (some), pp.404–5
Nerine bowdenii, p.424
Ornithogalum thyrsoides, p.420
Polianthes tuberosa
TULIPS (tall cvs), pp.410–12
Zantedeschia aethiopica ○

CUT FLOWERS
In large gardens, a warm, sunny, sheltered border may be used to grow flowers specially for cutting.

Flowers for Drying

Many garden flowers may be dried, ideally cut just before reaching perfection. In borders, intersperse plants for drying with others that will not be cut. Groups of annuals for drying are best grown separately, away from the house, in rows to facilitate weeding and gathering; sow in well-drained, fertile soil in a sunny situation to encourage strong balanced growth and good-quality flowers.

Trees
Acacia dealbata, p.83 ○
Acacia longifolia ○
Acacia verticillata ○

Shrubs
Acacia (most) ○
Calluna vulgaris and cvs ○
Cassinia ○
Erica cinerea ○
Fothergilla major, p.127
Garrya elliptica, p.125 ○
Helichrysum (most) ○
Holodiscus discolor, p.119
Lavandula ○
LILACS, p.120
Phlomis fruticosa, p.170 ○
ROSES, pp.184–8
Rosmarinus officinalis and cvs ○

TEASEL HEADS
*The prickly, cone-shaped seed heads of teasel (*Dipsacus fullonum*) persist throughout winter. A soft pinkish purple when in bloom, teasels are best in a wild garden or at the back of a border. Cut when ripe, the heads are excellent in dried arrangements.*

Perennials
Achillea, some ○
Aconitum napellus
Alchemilla mollis, p.290
Allium x *hollandicum*, p.402
Anaphalis margaritacea, p.239
Anigozanthos flavidus, p.254
Artemisia (several), some ○
Astilbe (most)
Astrantia
Catananche caerulea 'Major', p.285
Cirsium rivulare 'Atropurpureum'
Dictamnus albus, p.240
Echinops
Eryngium, some ○
Eupatorium (some)
Gypsophila paniculata 'Bristol Fairy', p.239
Liatris spicata, p.279
Limonium (most)
Lythrum
Ranunculus asiaticus, pp.421, 423
Rodgersia
Scabiosa caucasica and cvs
Solidago (most)
Trachelium caeruleum, p.330
Typha

Annuals and biennials
Amaranthus caudatus, p.326
Bracteantha bracteata Monstrosum Series, p.340
Centaurea cyanus
Consolida ambigua Series
Dipsacus fullonum ⊡
Gilia capitata, p.333
Gomphrena globosa, p.331
Gypsophila elegans, p.318
Limonium sinuatum, p.322
Moluccella laevis, p.335
Onopordum acanthium, p.322
Psylliostachys suworowii, p.330
Rhodanthe
Salvia viridis and Series
Scabiosa atropurpurea
Tagetes erecta
Xeranthemum annuum ⊡

Xeranthemum annuum

TREES

including Conifers

TREES MAKE A USEFUL AS WELL AS decorative contribution to many garden designs. They can be grown singly as focal points, planted in a group in woodland glades, or used as street trees. Choosing the right kind and size of tree for your purpose is important if you are to get the best from it, so always check a tree's potential size before buying.

Trees

Trees are the most permanent elements in any planting plan. Fortunately, there is a wealth of ornamental trees in cultivation for the individual climate and growing conditions in your garden.

WHAT ARE TREES?

Tree are long-lived, deciduous or evergreen, perennial, woody plants that have a lifespan ranging from decades to several centuries. Most have a single stem, with a crown of branches above a clear trunk, although many species produce multiple stems, either naturally or as a result of pruning and training. Trees are diverse in size, ranging from dwarf conifers at 3ft (1m) tall, to forest giants at 300ft (90m) or more in height. They are equally variable in shape, from narrowly conical through columnar to rounded and spreading, offering strong design elements within the garden. Most conifers are evergreen and cone-bearing.

CHOOSING TREES

Since a tree is probably the most expensive of garden plants and usually the most prominent, selection and siting are the most important decisions – even more so in a small garden with room for only one or two specimens. If it is to thrive, you must consider whether a tree is suitable for your garden's climate, soil type, and degree of exposure. It is then vital to research the tree's final height and spread and to site it where it will have room to mature unimpeded by and not interfering with walls, pipes, drains, or wires.

DESIGNING WITH TREES

Trees make a strong visual impact in a planting design by virtue of their size alone; they can also contribute to the garden's structure. For example, several trees can be planted to form enclosures or define spaces, or they can be used in pairs to frame a view or in rows to form an avenue or an arch. In exposed or very large gardens, a row of trees can provide wind protection to an area five times its own height. In smaller gardens, trees that tolerate clipping, notably hornbeam (*Carpinus*), beech (*Fagus*), arborvitae (*Thuja*), Leyland cypress (X *Cupressocyparis*), and yew (*Taxus*), are ideal for a wind- and noise-filtering hedge that also affords a degree of privacy.

When a tree is grown singly as a specimen plant, it can create an interesting focal point, which is especially effective if it can be viewed from several angles. The tree's shape and ornamental qualities also influence the style of the garden. The neat, crisp outlines of the narrowly columnar *Juniperus chinensis* 'Obelisk', for example, or the flame-shaped *Carpinus betulus* 'Fastigiata' would suit a formal garden design, whereas the rounded, relaxed branch structure of a mountain ash (*Sorbus*) or a crabapple (*Malus*) provide a natural informality.

If you have room for several trees, you can develop a woodland-style garden, in the shelter of which shade-loving plants can be established. In an Oriental-style garden, Japanese maples (*Acer* species) and Japanese cherries such as *Prunus* 'Shirofugen' are ideal.

FRUIT FOR COLOR
In autumn, the mountain ashes (Sorbus) *offer berries of many colors, among them the creamy yellow fruits of* S. *'Joseph Rock' (left), the pearly white fruits of* S. cashmiriana, *and the rich scarlets of* S. aucuparia. *Many also have splendid autumn foliage.*

CONIFERS ON DISPLAY
Above: The extraordinary and exciting diversity of size, form, texture, and color to be found in dwarf conifers can be used to create a garden with year-round interest. If grouped in an island bed, as here, conifers can be viewed and enjoyed from many angles.

ALL-ROUND INTEREST
Right: Cherries (Prunus) *often have more than one season of interest and are among the most valuable of trees for smaller gardens. As well as a glorious display of blossoms in spring, many also provide fine autumn color. Some, such as* P. maackii, *also have attractive bark.*

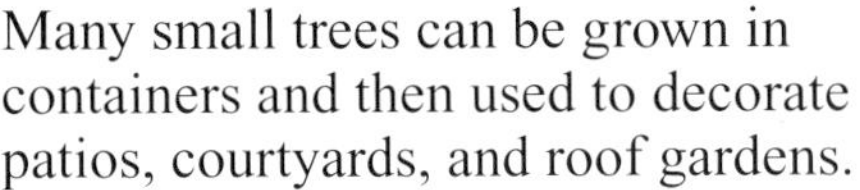

Many small trees can be grown in containers and then used to decorate patios, courtyards, and roof gardens.

Maintaining year-round interest

Broadleaved evergreens, such as hollies (*Ilex*) and some oaks (*Quercus*), provide an invaluable green backdrop throughout the year, while conifers can provide a useful contrast in shape and texture: many have a strong conical outline; others, such as *Picea breweriana*, weep gracefully. Dwarf conifers range from the neat, rounded domes of *Pinus mugo* 'Gnom' to the spreading *Juniperus* x *pfitzeriana*.

Broadleaved, deciduous trees offer a seasonally changing palette of leaf color, from the fresh, lemon yellows and lime greens of spring to the ruddy brilliance of autumn. The form of their foliage is infinitely variable: consider interesting textural contrasts such as the delicate leaves of false acacia (*Robinia pseudoacacia*) with the architectural leaves of *Catalpa bignonioides*.

Although most flowering and fruiting trees bloom in spring, some produce a welcome burst of color at other times. *Maackia amurensis*, *Sophora japonica*, and *Arbutus unedo* bear their flowers in summer and autumn, while *Magnolia campbellii* and *Prunus* x *subhirtella* 'Autumnalis' can brighten the gloomy days of winter.

Size categories used within this group		
Large	Medium	Small
over 50ft (15m)	30–50ft (10–15m)	up to 30ft (10m)

Spring benefits
Above: With the glorious Malus *'Katherine', a profusion of large double flowers in spring gives rise to tiny, red-flushed yellow fruits in autumn.*

Summer promise
Left: Acer shirasawanum *'Aureum' is noted for its elegant habit, compact size, and vibrant leaf color – the verdant greens of late spring and summer turning into peerless autumn brilliance.*

Attractive bark
Below: Many eucalyptus, such as this Eucalyptus pauciflora *subsp.* niphophila, *are renowned for their beautiful peeling and flaking bark.*

TREES large SPRING INTEREST

WHITE–YELLOW

Aesculus hippocastanum
(Horse chestnut)
Vigorous, deciduous, spreading tree. Has large leaves with 5 or 7 leaflets and spires of white flowers, flushed pink and yellow in centers, in spring. Spiny fruits contain glossy brown nuts in autumn.

Z3–8 H8–1

***Aesculus* x *carnea* 'Briotii'**
Deciduous, round-headed tree. Leaves, consisting of 5 or 7 leaflets, are glossy dark green. Panicles of red flowers are borne in late spring.

Z7–8 H8–7

Acer macrophyllum
(Oregon maple)
Deciduous, round-headed tree with large, deeply lobed, dark green leaves that turn yellow and orange in autumn. Yellowish green flowers in spring are followed by pale green fruits.

Z5–9 H9–4

OTHER RECOMMENDED PLANTS:
Acer cappadocicum 'Aureum'
Calodendrum capense
Fraxinus excelsior 'Jaspidea'

MAGNOLIAS, illus. p.75

TREES large SUMMER INTEREST

WHITE

Populus maximowiczii
Fast-growing, deciduous, conical tree. Oval, heart-shaped, bright green leaves have green-veined white undersides and turn yellow in autumn. Bears long, pendent seed heads surrounded by silky white hairs in late summer.

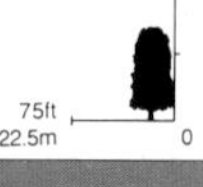

Z4–7 H7–1

Aesculus chinensis
(Chinese horse chestnut)
Slow-growing, deciduous, spreading tree. Leaves are glossy, dark green with 7 leaflets. Slender spires of white flowers are produced in mid-summer.

Z6–8 H8–6

Populus alba
(White poplar)
Deciduous, spreading tree with wavy-margined or lobed leaves, dark green above, white beneath, turning yellow in autumn.

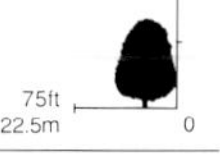

Z3–9 H9–1

OTHER RECOMMENDED PLANTS:
Acer platanoides 'Drummondii'
Aesculus indica
Castanea sativa
Ceiba pentandra
Robinia pseudoacacia
Schima wallichii

WHITE–PURPLE

***Castanea sativa* 'Albomarginata'**
Deciduous, spreading tree. Has glossy, white-edged, dark green leaves that turn yellow in autumn. Spikes of creamy yellow flowers in summer are followed by edible fruits in autumn.

Z5–7 H7–5

Liriodendron tulipifera (Tulip tree)
Vigorous, deciduous, spreading tree. Deep green leaves, with a cut-off or notched tip and lobed sides, turn yellow in autumn. Tulip-shaped, orange-marked, greenish white flowers appear in mid-summer.

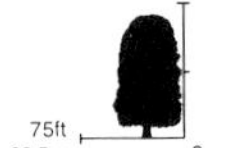

pH Z5–9 H9–1

Prunus serotina
(Black cherry, Wild rum cherry)
Deciduous, spreading tree. Spikes of fragrant white flowers appear in early summer, followed by red fruits that turn black in autumn. Glossy, dark green leaves become yellow in autumn.

Z4–8 H8–1

***Brachychiton acerifolius*,**
syn. *Sterculia acerifolia*
(Illawarra flame tree)
Deciduous tree with clusters of bright scarlet flowers in late winter, spring, or summer before 3–7-lobed, lustrous leaves develop.

pH Z12–15 H12–8

Fagus sylvatica* f. *purpurea
(Copper beech, Purple beech)
Deciduous, round-headed tree with oval, wavy-margined, purple leaves. In autumn, leaves turn a rich coppery color.

Z5–7 H7–5

Acer platanoides 'Royal Red'
Fagus sylvatica 'Dawyck Purple'
Fagus sylvatica 'Riversii'
Fagus sylvatica 'Rohanii'

Knightia excelsa
Lagerstroemia speciosa
MAGNOLIAS, illus. p.75
Toona sinensis, illus. p.79

PURPLE–GREEN

***Acer platanoides* 'Crimson King'**
Vigorous, deciduous, spreading tree. Leaves are large, lobed, and deep reddish purple, turning orange in autumn. Tiny, red-tinged, deep yellow flowers are carried in midspring.

Z4–7 H7–1

Populus* x *canescens
(Gray poplar)
Vigorous, deciduous, spreading tree with slightly lobed leaves, gray when young, glossy dark green in summer, and yellow in autumn. Usually bears grayish red catkins in spring.

Z5–9 H9–5

***Populus* x *canadensis* 'Robusta'**
Fast-growing, deciduous, conical tree with upright branches. Broadly oval, bronze young leaves mature to glossy dark green. Bears long red catkins in spring.

Z5–9 H9–5

Acer platanoides
Acer platanoides 'Emerald Queen'
Acer saccharinum
Acer velutinum

Ailanthus altissima
MAGNOLIAS, illus. p.75
Salix alba var. *caerulea*
Sorbus thibetica

TREES large SUMMER INTEREST

GREEN

***Populus* x *canadensis* 'Serotina de Selys'**, syn. *P.* x *c.* 'Serotina Erecta'
Fast-growing, deciduous, upright tree. Has broadly oval, gray-green leaves, pale green when young, and red catkins in spring.

Z4–9 H9–1

Quercus macranthera
(Caucasian oak)
Deciduous, spreading, thick-branched, handsome tree with large, deeply lobed, dark green leaves.

Z6–8 H8–6

Alnus incana (Gray alder)
Deciduous, conical tree useful for cold, wet areas and poor soils. Yellow-brown catkins are carried in late winter and early spring, followed by oval, dark green leaves.

Z2–6 H6–1

Betula maximowicziana
Castanea dentata
Celtis occidentalis
Fagus orientalis

Fagus sylvatica* f. *pendula, syn. *F.s.* 'Pendula' (Weeping beech)
Deciduous, weeping tree with oval, wavy-edged, midgreen leaves that in autumn take on rich hues of yellow and orange-brown.

Z5–7 H7–1

Quercus robur* f. *fastigiata
Deciduous, upright, columnar tree of dense habit carrying lobed, dark green leaves.

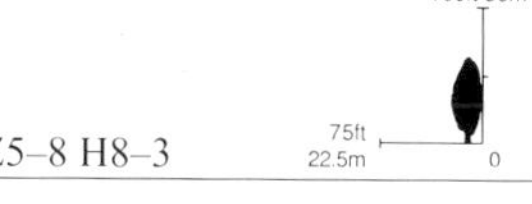

Z5–8 H8–3

Fagus sylvatica 'Dawyck'
Fagus sylvatica f. *laciniata*
Fraxinus americana
Fraxinus angustifolia

Alnus cordata (Italian alder)
Fast-growing, deciduous, conical tree. Yellow male catkins appear in late winter and early spring, followed by heart-shaped, glossy, deep green leaves. Has persistent, round, woody fruits in autumn.

Z5–7 H7–5

***Populus nigra* 'Italica'**
(Lombardy poplar)
Very fast-growing, deciduous, narrowly columnar tree with erect branches, diamond-shaped, bright green leaves, and red catkins in mid-spring.

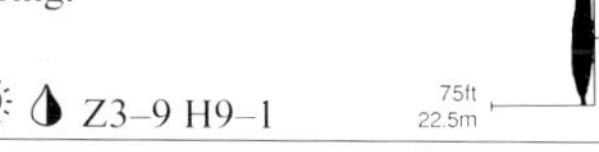

Z3–9 H9–1

Fraxinus angustifolia 'Raywood'
Fraxinus excelsior f. *diversifolia*
Fraxinus pennsylvanica
Fraxinus pennsylvanica 'Patmore'

Quercus canariensis
(Algerian oak, Mirbeck's oak)
Deciduous or semi-evergreen tree, narrow when young, broadening with age. Large, shallowly lobed, rich green leaves become yellowish brown in autumn, often persisting into late winter.

Z7–9 H9–7

Acer cappadocicum* subsp. *lobelii, syn. *A. lobelii* (Lobel's maple)
Deciduous tree of narrow, upright habit, well suited for growing in restricted space. Has wavy-edged, lobed leaves that turn yellow in autumn.

Z6–8 H8–6

Juglans regia (Walnut)
Deciduous tree with a spreading head. Aromatic leaves, usually with 5 or 7 leaflets, are bronze-purple when young and glossy midgreen when mature. Produces edible nuts.

Z3–7 H7–1

Gleditsia triacanthos 'Shademaster'
Gleditsia triacanthos 'Skyline'
Gymnocladus dioica
Juglans cathayensis

Tilia oliveri
Deciduous, spreading, open tree with pointed, heart-shaped leaves, bright green above and silvery white beneath. Produces small, fragrant, greenish yellow flowers in summer, followed by winged fruits.

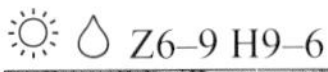
Z6–9 H9–6

Juglans nigra (Black walnut)
Fast-growing, deciduous, handsome, spreading tree with large, aromatic leaves of pointed, glossy, dark green leaflets. Produces edible nuts in autumn.

Z5–9 H9–5

Quercus muehlenbergii
Deciduous, round-headed tree with sharply toothed, bright green leaves.

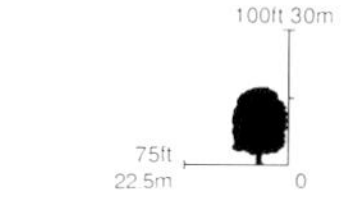
Z4–8 Z8–2

Celtis australis (Nettle tree)
Deciduous, spreading tree. Has oval, pointed, sharply toothed, dark green leaves and small, purple-black fruits.

Z6–8 H8–6

Platanus* x *hispanica, syn. *P.* x *acerifolia* (London plane)
Vigorous, deciduous, spreading tree with ornamental flaking bark. Has large, sharply lobed, bright green leaves. Spherical fruit clusters hang from shoots in autumn.

Z5–8 H8–5

Nothofagus procera, syn. *N.* x *alpina* (Rauli, Southern beech)
Fast-growing, deciduous, conical tree. Leaves, with many impressed veins, are dark green, turning orange and red in autumn.

Z8–9 H9–8

Juglans cinerea
Platanus orientalis
Populus balsamifera
Populus x *berolinensis*
Populus x *canadensis* 'Eugenei'
Populus x *candicans*
Populus deltoides
Populus lasiocarpa
Populus nigra
Populus szechuanica
Populus trichocarpa
Pterocarya fraxinifolia
Pterocarya stenoptera
Quercus cerris
Quercus imbricaria
Quercus mongolica var. *grosseserrata*

TREES large SUMMER INTEREST

GREEN

Sassafras albidum
Deciduous, upright, later spreading tree. Aromatic, glossy, dark green leaves vary from oval to deeply lobed and turn yellow or red in autumn. Produces a haze of yellowish green flowers in spring.

Z4–8 H8–3

Nothofagus obliqua
(Roblé, Southern beech)
Fast-growing, deciduous, elegant tree with slender, arching branches. Has deep green leaves that turn orange and red in autumn.

Z8–9 Z9–8

***Quercus petraea* 'Columna'**
Deciduous, upright, slender tree with large, wavy-edged, leathery, dark green leaves tinged bronze when young.

Z5–8 H8–5

Firmiana simplex,
syn. *F. platanifolia*, *Sterculia platanifolia* (Chinese parasol tree)
Robust, deciduous tree with large, lobed leaves, small, showy, lemon-yellow flowers, and papery, leaflike fruits.

Z7–15 H12–8

Quercus castaneifolia
Deciduous, spreading tree with sharply toothed leaves, glossy dark green above and gray beneath.

Z7–9 H9–7

Juglans ailantifolia* var. *cordiformis, syn. *J. cordiformis*
Deciduous, spreading tree with large, aromatic leaves consisting of many glossy, bright green leaflets. Long, yellow-green male catkins are borne in early summer. In autumn has edible nuts.

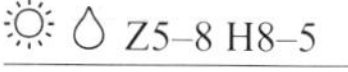

Z5–8 H8–5

Quercus nigra (Water oak)
Deciduous, spreading tree with glossy, bright green foliage retained until well into winter.

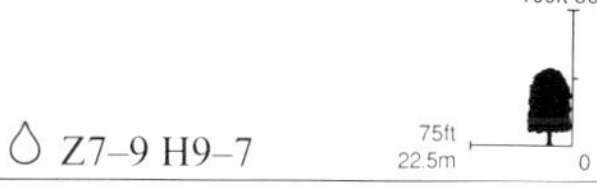

Z7–9 H9–7

***Tilia* 'Petiolaris'**, syn. *T. petiolaris* (Weeping silver linden)
Deciduous, spreading tree with pendent branches. Pointed, heart-shaped leaves, dark green above, silver beneath, shimmer in the breeze. Has fragrant, creamy yellow flowers in late summer.

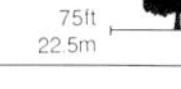

Z5–9 H9–5

Fagus sylvatica (European beech)
Deciduous, spreading tree with oval, wavy-edged leaves. These are pale green when young, mid- to dark green when mature, and turn rich yellow and orange-brown in autumn, when nuts are produced.

Z4–7 H9–4

Populus x *canadensis* 'Eugenei'
Populus x *candicans*
Populus deltoides
Populus lasiocarpa
Populus nigra
Populus szechuanica
Populus trichocarpa
Pterocarya fraxinifolia
Pterocarya stenoptera
Quercus cerris
Quercus imbricaria
Quercus mongolica var. *grosseserrata*
Tilia americana
Tilia cordata
Tilia x *euchlora*
Tilia mongolica

GREEN

Quercus frainetto (Hungarian oak)
Fast-growing, deciduous, spreading tree with a large, domed head and handsome, large, deeply lobed, dark green leaves.

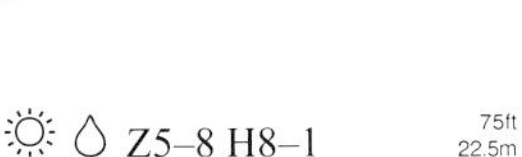
Z5–8 H8–1

Quercus palustris (Pin oak)
Fast-growing, deciduous, spreading tree with slender branches, pendulous at the tips. Deeply lobed, glossy, bright green leaves turn scarlet or red-brown in autumn.

Z5–8 H8–5

Carya ovata (Shagbark hickory)
Deciduous tree with flaking gray bark. Has dark green leaves, usually consisting of 5 slender leaflets, that turn golden yellow in autumn.

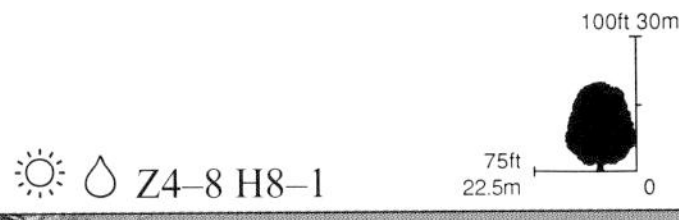

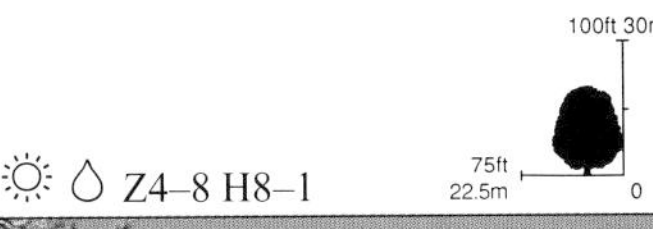
Z4–8 H8–1

GREEN–YELLOW

Quercus rubra (Red oak)
Fast-growing, deciduous, spreading tree. Attractively lobed leaves are deep green, becoming reddish or yellowish brown in autumn.

Z5–9 H9–5

***Populus alba* 'Raket'**, syn. *P.a.* 'Rocket'
Deciduous, upright, narrow tree. Leaves, often lobed, are dark green with white undersides. In autumn, foliage turns yellow.

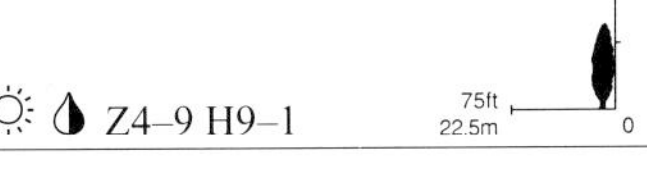
Z4–9 H9–1

Quercus laurifolia
Deciduous, round-headed tree with narrow, glossy, bright green leaves, bronze-tinged when young, that are retained until late in the year.

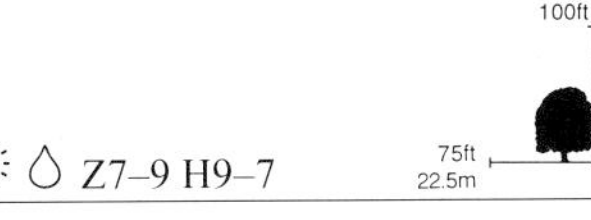
Z7–9 H9–7

***Liriodendron tulipifera* 'Aureomarginatum'**
Vigorous, deciduous tree. Deep green leaves have yellow margins, cut-off or notched tips, and lobed sides. Bears cup-shaped, greenish white flowers splashed orange in summer on mature trees.

pH Z5–9 H9–1

Pterocarya* x *rehderiana
Very fast-growing, deciduous, spreading tree. Has glossy, bright green leaves consisting of narrow, paired leaflets that turn yellow in autumn, and long catkins of winged fruits in late summer and autumn.

Z6–9 H9–6

Tilia platyphyllos
Tilia tomentosa
Ulmus americana
Ulmus glabra
Ulmus x *hollandica*
Ulmus x *hollandica* 'Vegeta'
Ulmus minor
Ulmus minor 'Sarniensis'
Ulmus procera
Zelkova carpinifolia

Alnus incana 'Aurea'
Fagus sylvatica 'Aurea Pendula'
Populus alba 'Richardii'
Robinia pseudoacacia 'Frisia', illus. p.81

TREES large AUTUMN INTEREST

PINK–RED

Chorisia speciosa (Floss silk tree)
Fast-growing, deciduous tree, the trunk and branches studded with thick, conical thorns. Pink to burgundy flowers appear as the light green leaves fall.

Z13–14 H12–10

Liquidambar styraciflua (Sweetgum)
Deciduous, conical to spreading tree. Shoots develop corky ridges. Lobed, glossy, dark green leaves turn brilliant orange, red, and purple in autumn.

Z6–9 H9–6

Quercus ellipsoidalis
Deciduous, spreading tree with deeply lobed, glossy, dark green leaves that turn dark purplish red then red in autumn.

Z4–7 H7–1

Acer pseudoplatanus* f. *erythrocarpum
Vigorous, deciduous, spreading tree with lobed, deep green leaves. Wings of young autumn fruits are bright red.

Z4–7 H7–1

***Acer rubrum* 'Scanlon'**
Deciduous, upright tree. Has lobed, dark green foliage that in autumn becomes bright red, particularly on acidic or neutral soil. Clusters of small red flowers decorate bare branches in spring.

Z3–9 H9–1

Quercus coccinea (Scarlet oak)
Deciduous, round-headed tree. Glossy, dark green leaves have deeply cut lobes ending in slender teeth. In autumn, they turn bright red, usually persisting for a few weeks on the tree.

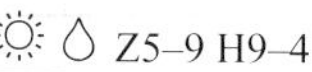

Z5–9 H9–4

***Acer rubrum* 'Schlesingeri'**
Deciduous, round-headed tree. In early autumn, dark green leaves turn deep red. Tiny red flowers appear on bare wood in spring.

Z3–9 H9–1

Acer rubrum (Red maple)
Deciduous, round-headed tree. Dark green leaves turn bright red in autumn, producing best color on acidic or neutral soil. In spring, bare gray branches are covered with tiny red flowers.

Z3–9 H9–1

OTHER RECOMMENDED PLANTS:
Acer rubrum 'Columnare', illus. p.81
Acer rubrum 'October Glory'
Acer rubrum 'Red Sunset'
Acer saccharum 'Green Mountain'
Lagerstroemia speciosa
Quercus coccinea 'Splendens'

Cercidiphyllum japonicum (Katsura tree)
Fast-growing, deciduous, spreading tree. Leaves, bronze when young, turn rich green, then yellow to purple in autumn, especially on acidic soil. Fallen leaves smell of burnt sugar.

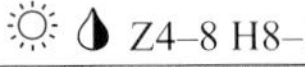

Z4–8 H8–1

Spathodea campanulata (African tulip tree, Flame-of-the-forest)
Evergreen, showy tree. Leaves have 9–19 deep green leaflets. Clusters of tulip-shaped, scarlet or orange-red flowers appear intermittently.

Z13–14 H12–10

Quercus phellos (Willow oak)
Deciduous, spreading tree of elegant habit. Narrow, willowlike, pale green leaves turn yellow then brown in autumn.

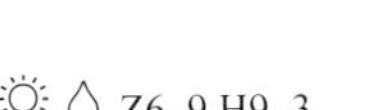

Z6–9 H9–3

Zelkova serrata
Deciduous, spreading tree with sharply toothed, finely pointed, dark green leaves that turn yellow or orange in autumn.

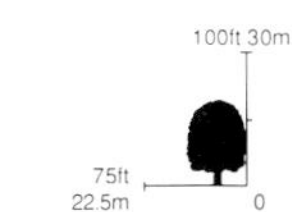

Z5–9 H9–5

Nyssa sylvatica (Black gum, Tupelo)
Deciduous, broadly conical tree with oval, glossy, dark to midgreen leaves that turn brilliant yellow, orange, and red in autumn.

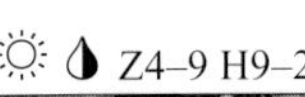

Z4–9 H9–2

Prunus avium (Gean, Bird cherry)
Deciduous, spreading tree with red-banded bark. Has sprays of white flowers in spring, deep red fruits, and dark green leaves that turn red and yellow in autumn.

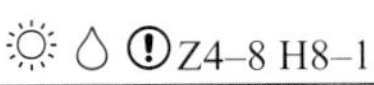

Z4–8 H8–1

Quercus alba (White oak)
Deciduous, spreading tree. Deeply lobed, glossy, dark green leaves turn reddish purple in autumn.

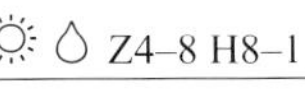

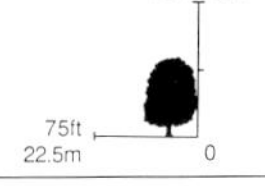

Z4–8 H8–1

***Acer platanoides* 'Palmatifidum'**, syn. *A.p.* 'Lorbergii'
Vigorous, deciduous, spreading tree. Deeply divided, pale green leaves with slender lobes turn yellow or reddish orange in autumn. Tiny yellow flowers appear in midspring.

Z3–7 H7–1

***Sophora japonica* 'Violacea'**
Fast-growing, deciduous, round-headed tree. Large sprays of pealike white flowers tinged with lilac-pink appear in late summer and early autumn.

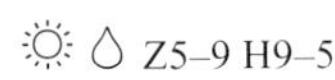

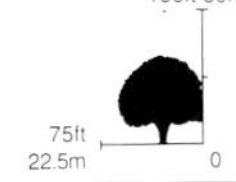

Z5–9 H9–5

Acer cappadocicum
Acer platanoides
Betula maximowicziana
Betula szechuanica
Betula utilis
Carya cordiformis
Carya glabra
Fraxinus angustifolia 'Raywood'
Gleditsia triacanthos
Gymnocladus dioica
Liquidambar styraciflua 'Lane Roberts'
Liriodendron chinense
Populus alba, illus. p.64
Populus tremula
Populus trichocarpa
Quercus velutina

TREES large WINTER/ALL YEAR INTEREST

WHITE–GREEN

Eucalyptus dalrympleana (Mountain gum)
Vigorous, evergreen tree. Creamy white young bark becomes pinkish gray, then peels. Leaves are long, narrow, and pendent. Clusters of white flowers appear in late summer and autumn.
Z9–10 H10–9

Betula papyrifera (Canoe birch, Paper birch)
Vigorous, deciduous, open-branched, round-headed tree with peeling, shiny white bark, yellowish catkins in spring, and oval, coarsely serrated leaves that turn clear yellow in autumn.
Z2-7 H7–1

Betula ermanii
Deciduous, open-branched, elegant tree that has peeling, pinkish white bark distinctively marked with large lenticels. Oval, glossy, green leaves give excellent autumn color.
Z5–8 H8–5

Eucalyptus gunnii (Cider gum)
Evergreen, conical tree with peeling cream, pinkish, and brown bark. Leaves are silver-blue when young, blue-green when mature. Clusters of white flowers with numerous stamens appear in mid-summer.
Z8–10 H10–8

***Ficus elastica* 'Doescheri'** (Rubber plant)
Strong-growing, evergreen, upright then spreading tree with oblong to oval, leathery, lustrous, deep green leaves, patterned with gray-green, yellow, and white. M
Z13–14 H12–10

GREEN

Ficus benghalensis (Banyan)
Evergreen, wide-spreading tree with trunklike prop roots. Has oval, leathery leaves, rich green with pale veins, to 8in (20cm) long, and small, figlike brown fruits.
Z13–14 H12–10

Eucalyptus coccifera (Tasmanian snow gum)
Evergreen tree with peeling, blue-gray and white bark and aromatic, pointed, gray-green leaves. Bears clusters of white flowers with numerous stamens in summer.
Z9–11 H12–10

Archontophoenix alexandrae (Alexandra palm, Northern bungalow palm)
Evergreen palm with feather-shaped, arching leaves. Mature trees bear sprays of small white or cream flowers.
Z13–14 H12–10

OTHER RECOMMENDED PLANTS:
Betula pendula
Betula utilis
Betula utilis var. *jacquemontii*, illus. p.83
Eucalyptus globulus
Ficus elastica 'Decora'
Metrosideros robustus
Tilia platyphyllos 'Prince's Street'
Archontophoenix cunninghamiana
Castanospermum australe
Ficus benjamina
Ficus lyrata
Ficus macrophylla
Ficus religiosa
Ficus rubiginosa
Nothofagus menziesii

Quercus* x *turneri
Semi-evergreen, rounded, dense tree. Lobed, leathery, dark green leaves fall just before new foliage appears in spring.

Z6–9 H9–6

Nothofagus dombeyi
Evergreen, loosely conical tree of elegant habit with shoots that droop at the tips. Leaves are sharply toothed and glossy dark green.

Z8–9 H9–8

Quercus suber (Cork oak)
Evergreen, round-headed tree with thick, corky bark. Oval, leathery leaves are glossy, dark green above and grayish beneath.

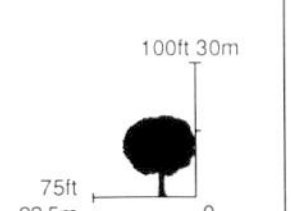

Z7–9 H9–7

***Betula pendula* 'Tristis'**
(Weeping birch)
Deciduous, slender, elegant tree with a strongly weeping habit and white bark. Oval, bright green leaves, with toothed margins, provide excellent golden color in autumn.

Z2–7 H7–1

Washingtonia robusta
(Thread palm)
Fast-growing, evergreen palm with large, fan-shaped leaves and, in summer, tiny, creamy white flowers in large, long-stalked sprays. Black berries appear in winter-spring.

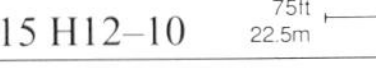

Z13–15 H12–10

Macadamia integrifolia
(Macadamia nut, Queensland nut)
Evergreen, spreading tree with edible brown nuts in autumn. Has whorls of leathery, semi-glossy leaves and panicles of small, creamy yellow flowers in spring.

Z13–15 H12–11

Syagrus romanzoffiana,
syn. *Arecastrum romanzoffianum*
(Queen palm)
Majestic, evergreen palm. Has feather-shaped leaves with lustrous green leaflets. Mature trees carry clusters of yellow flowers in summer.

Z15 H12–11

***Quercus* x *hispanica* 'Lucombeana'**,
syn. *Q.* x *lucombeana* 'William Lucombe' (Lucombe oak)
Semi-evergreen, spreading tree with toothed leaves, glossy dark green above and gray beneath.

Z7–9 H9–7

Phoenix canariensis
Quercus ilex
Roystonea regia
Salix matsudana 'Tortuosa', illus. p.85
Tamarindus indica
Terminalia catappa
Washingtonia filifera

TREES large WINTER/ALL YEAR INTEREST

GREEN

Betula albosinensis
(Chinese paper birch)
Deciduous, open-branched, elegant tree with serrated, oval to lance-shaped, pale green leaves. Peeling bark is honey-colored or reddish maroon with a gray bloom.

Z5–8 H8–5

Nothofagus betuloides
Evergreen, columnar tree with dense growth of oval, glossy, dark green leaves on bronze-red shoots.

Z8–9 H9–8

YELLOW

Umbellularia californica
(California laurel)
Evergreen, spreading tree with aromatic, leathery, glossy, dark green leaves and creamy yellow flowers in late spring. Pungent leaves may cause nausea and headache when crushed.

Z7–9 H9–7

Salix alba* var. *vitellina
(Golden willow)
Deciduous, spreading tree, usually cut back hard to promote growth of strong, young shoots that are bright orange-yellow in winter. Lance-shaped, midgreen leaves appear in spring.

Z4-9 H9–1

Salix* x *sepulcralis* var. *chrysocoma
(Golden weeping willow)
Deciduous tree with slender, yellow shoots hanging to the ground like a curtain. Yellow-green young leaves mature to midgreen.

Z6–9 H9–6

Alnus incana 'Aurea'
Alnus incana 'Ramulis Coccineis'
Betula maximowicziana
Corylus colurna

TREES medium SPRING INTEREST

WHITE

Malus hupehensis (Tea crab)
Vigorous, deciduous, spreading tree. Has deep green leaves and large, fragrant, white flowers, pink in bud, from mid- to late spring, followed by small, red-tinged yellow crabapples in late summer and autumn.

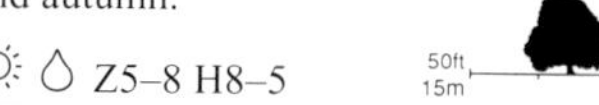

Z5–8 H8–5

Salix daphnoides (Violet willow)
Fast-growing, deciduous, spreading tree. Has lance-shaped, glossy, dark green leaves, silver male catkins in spring, and purple shoots with bluish white bloom in winter.

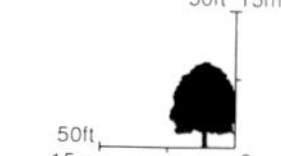

Z5–9 H9–5

Malus baccata* var. *mandschurica
Vigorous, deciduous, spreading tree with dark green leaves and a profusion of white flowers in clusters in mid-spring, followed by long-lasting, small red or yellow crabapples.

Z3–7 H7–1

OTHER RECOMMENDED PLANTS:
Dillenia indica
MAGNOLIAS, illus. p.75
Malus baccata
Malus prattii

Magnolias

A mature magnolia in full bloom is one of the most spectacular sights in the spring garden. Most magnolias are elegant in habit and, though slow-growing, eventually form imposing trees and shrubs that are valuable as focal points or as single specimens in lawns. Some species, such as *Magnolia stellata*, may be successfully grown in the smallest of gardens.

Magnolia flowers are generally saucer- or goblet-shaped and often have a subtle fragrance. The color range includes pure white or white flushed or stained with pink or purple, pink, and rich wine-purple. The genus also includes some evergreen, summer-flowering species. These often make excellent subjects for planting against a sunny wall. Some magnolias prefer acidic or neutral soil, but most tolerate any soil, provided it is organic. Plenty of compost, leaf mold, or similar amendment should be dug into the soil before planting.

***M.* 'Norman Gould'**

M. cylindrica

***M.* 'Wada's Memory'**

M. salicifolia

M. kobus

M. stellata

M.* x *wieseneri

M. wilsonii

***M. stellata* 'Water Lily'**

M. denudata

***M.* 'Charles Coates'**

***M.* 'Manchu Fan'**

M. fraseri

***M. grandiflora* 'Exmouth'**

M. tripetala

M. hypoleuca

M. sprengeri

***M.* x *veitchii* 'Peter Veitch'**

***M.* x *loebneri* 'Leonard Messel'**

M. campbellii

M. campbellii subsp. ***mollicomata***

***M.* x *s.* 'Etienne Soulange-Bodin'**

***M.* x *soulangeana* 'Rustica Rubra'**

***M. liliiflora* 'Nigra'**

***M.* 'Heaven Scent'**

***M. sprengeri* 'Wakehurst'**

***M. campbellii* 'Charles Raffill'**

***M. campbellii* 'Darjeeling'**

TREES medium SPRING INTEREST

WHITE

***Pyrus calleryana* 'Chanticleer'**
Deciduous, conical tree with glossy leaves that turn purplish in autumn. Clusters of small white flowers appear in spring. Resists fireblight.

Z5–8 H8–5

Prunus mahaleb
Deciduous, round-headed, bushy tree that bears a profusion of fragrant, cup-shaped white flowers from mid- to late spring. Rounded, glossy, dark green leaves turn yellow in autumn.

Z6–8 H8–6

Halesia monticola
(Silver bell, Snowdrop tree)
Fast-growing, deciduous, conical or spreading tree. Masses of pendent, bell-shaped white flowers appear in late spring before the leaves, followed by 4-winged fruits in autumn.

Z6–9 H9–6

Cornus nuttallii
(Mountain dogwood, Pacific dogwood)
Deciduous, conical tree. Large white bracts, surrounding tiny flowers, appear in late spring. Has oval, dark green leaves.

Z7–8 H8–7

***Prunus avium* 'Plena'**
Deciduous, spreading tree with reddish brown bark and masses of double, pure white flowers in spring. Dark green foliage turns red in autumn.

Z4–8 H8–4

Fraxinus ornus (Manna ash)
Deciduous, round-headed tree. Has deep green leaves with 5–9 leaflets. Panicles of scented, creamy white flowers appear in late spring and early summer.

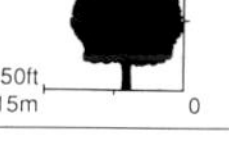

Z6–9 H9–4

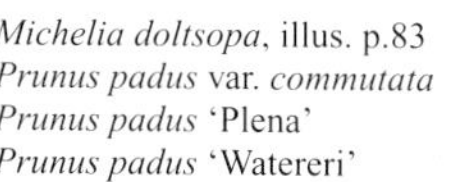

Michelia doltsopa, illus. p.83
Prunus padus var. *commutata*
Prunus padus 'Plena'
Prunus padus 'Watereri'

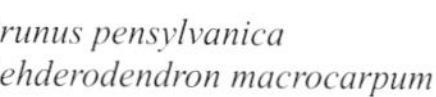

Prunus pensylvanica
Rehderodendron macrocarpum

WHITE–PINK

Prunus padus (Bird cherry)
Deciduous, spreading tree, conical when young. Bears fragrant white flowers in pendent spikes during late spring, followed by small black fruits in late summer. Dark green leaves turn yellow in autumn.

Z4–8 H8–1

Melia azedarach
(Bead tree, Chinaberry)
Deciduous, spreading tree. Has dark green leaves with many leaflets and fragrant, star-shaped, pinkish lilac flowers in spring, followed by pale orange-yellow fruits in autumn.

Z13–15 H12–10

Prunus jamasakura,
syn. *P. serrulata* var. *spontanea*
(Hill cherry)
Deciduous, spreading tree bearing cup-shaped white or pink flowers from mid- to late spring. Oval leaves, bronze when young, mature to deep green.

Z5–8 H8–5

MAGNOLIAS, illus. p.75
Malus x *robusta*
Prunus 'Spire', illus. p.87
Prunus x *yedoensis*, illus. p.87

TREES medium SUMMER INTEREST

PINK–YELLOW

***Prunus* 'Kanzan'**
Deciduous, vase-shaped tree. Large, double, pink to purple flowers are borne profusely from mid- to late spring amid bronze young leaves that mature to dark green.

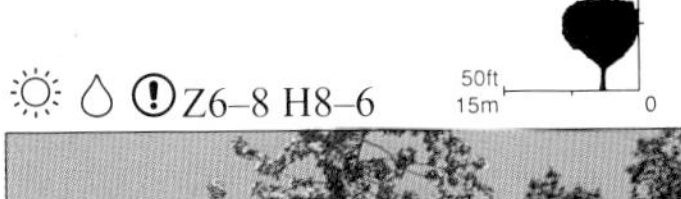

Z6–8 H8–6

***Paulownia tomentosa*,**
syn. *P. imperialis*
(Empress tree, Foxglove tree)
Deciduous, spreading tree. Has large, lobed, midgreen leaves and terminal sprays of fragrant, foxglove-like, pinkish lilac flowers in spring.

Z5–8 H8–5

***Malus* 'Profusion'**
Deciduous, spreading tree. Dark green foliage is purple when young. Cup-shaped, deep purplish pink flowers are freely borne in late spring, followed by small, reddish purple crab-apples in late summer and autumn.

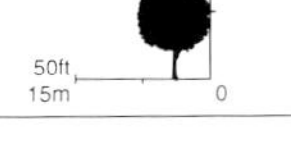

Z4–8 H8–1

***Gleditsia triacanthos* 'Sunburst'**
(Sunburst honeylocust)
Deciduous, spreading tree with fern-like, glossy foliage that is golden yellow when young and deep green in summer.

Z3–7 H7–1

Aesculus x *neglecta* 'Erythroblastos', illus. p.89
Catalpa x *erubescens* 'Purpurea'
Cercis siliquastrum, illus. p.88
MAGNOLIAS, illus. p.75
Prunus 'Okame'
Tabebuia rosea

WHITE

Styrax japonicus
(Japanese Snowbell)
Deciduous, spreading tree bearing in early summer a profusion of pendent, fragrant, bell-shaped white flowers amid glossy, dark green foliage.

pH Z6–8 H8–6

Ostrya virginiana (American hop hornbeam, Ironwood)
Deciduous, conical tree with dark brown bark and deep green leaves, yellow in autumn. Has yellowish catkins in spring, followed by greenish white fruit clusters.

Z5–9 H9–2

Davidia involucrata
(Dove tree, Ghost tree, Handkerchief tree)
Deciduous, conical tree with heart-shaped, vivid green leaves, felted beneath. Large white bracts appear on mature trees in late spring.

Z6–8 H8–6

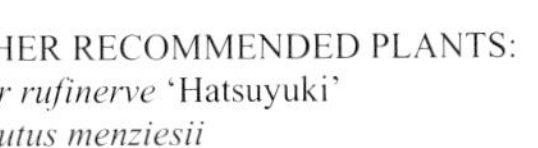

OTHER RECOMMENDED PLANTS:
Acer rufinerve 'Hatsuyuki'
Arbutus menziesii
Catalpa ovata
Cladrastis kentukea, illus. p.82
Cornus controversa
Cunonia capensis
Eucryphia cordifolia

TREES medium SUMMER INTEREST

□ WHITE

Oxydendrum arboreum
(Sorrel tree, Sourwood)
Deciduous, spreading tree with glossy, dark green foliage that turns bright red in autumn. Sprays of white flowers appear in late summer and autumn.

Z5–9 H9–3

Catalpa speciosa
Deciduous, spreading tree. Heads of large white flowers marked with yellow and purple are borne in mid-summer among glossy, midgreen leaves.

Z4–8 H8–1

Drimys winteri, syn. *Wintera aromatica* (Winter's bark)
Evergreen, conical, sometimes shrubby tree with long, glossy, pale or dark green leaves, usually bluish white beneath. Bears clusters of fragrant, star-shaped white flowers in early summer.

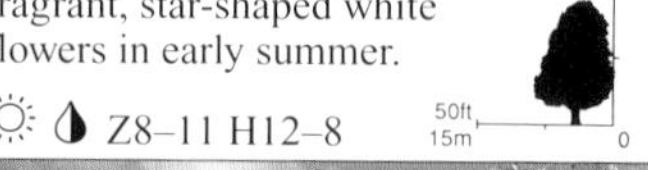

Z8–11 H12–8

***Quercus cerris* 'Argenteovariegata'**, syn. *Q.c.* 'Variegata'
Deciduous, spreading tree. Strongly toothed or lobed, glossy, dark green leaves are edged with creamy white.

Z7–9 H9–7

Sorbus vestita, syn. *S. cuspidata*
Deciduous, broadly conical tree. Has very large, veined, gray-green leaves, white-haired when young. Heads of pink-stamened white flowers in late spring or early summer are followed by russet or yellowish red fruits.

Z6–8 H8–6

Stewartia pseudocamellia
Deciduous, spreading tree with ornamental peeling bark. Bears white flowers in midsummer. Foliage is mid-green, turning orange and red in autumn.

Z5–8 H8–1

***Sorbus aria* 'Lutescens'**
Deciduous, spreading tree, upright when young. Young foliage is silvery, maturing to gray green. White flowers in late spring and early summer are followed by orange-red fruits in autumn.

Z6–8 H8–6

Catalpa bignonioides
(Indian bean tree)
Deciduous, spreading tree. Large, light green leaves are purplish when young. White flowers marked with yellow and purple appear in summer, followed by long, cylindrical, pendent pods.

Z5–9 H9–5

Cornus macrophylla
Deciduous, spreading tree. Clusters of small, creamy white flowers appear in summer. Glossy, bright green leaves are large, pointed, and oval.

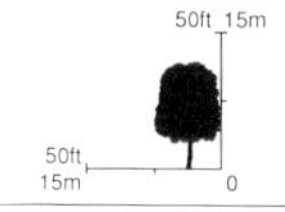

Z7–8 H8–7

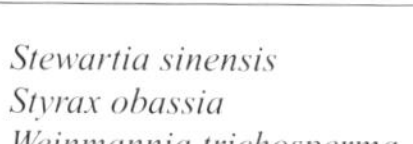

Gevuina avellana
Hoheria populnea
Lyonothamnus floribundus subsp. *aspleniifolius*
MAGNOLIAS, illus. p.75
Malus trilobata
Pterostyrax hispida
Stewartia monadelpha, illus. p.82
Stewartia sinensis
Styrax obassia
Weinmannia trichosperma

WHITE–PINK

***Acer pseudoplatanus* 'Simon Louis Frères'**
Deciduous, spreading tree. Young leaves are marked with creamy white and pink; older foliage is pale green with white markings.

Z4–7 H7–1

***Acer negundo* 'Variegatum'**
Fast-growing, deciduous, spreading tree. Has pinkish- then white-margined, bright green leaves with 3 or 5 leaflets. Inconspicuous, greenish yellow flowers appear in late spring.

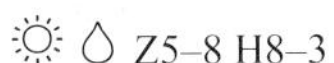
Z5–8 H8–3

***Aesculus indica* 'Sydney Pearce'**
Deciduous, spreading tree with glossy, dark green leaves, bronze when young and orange or yellow in autumn. Pinkish white flowers, marked red and yellow, appear from early to midsummer.

Z7–8 H8–1

Albizia julibrissin, illus. p.90
Clusia major
Lagunaria patersonii
Manglietia insignis
Robinia x *ambigua* 'Decaisneana'

PURPLE–GREEN

Jacaranda mimosifolia, syn. *J. acutifolia* of gardens, *J. ovalifolia*
Fast-growing, deciduous, rounded tree with fernlike leaves of many tiny, bright green leaflets. Has clusters of vivid blue to blue-purple flowers in spring and early summer.

Z13–15 H12–10

Broussonetia papyrifera
(Paper mulberry)
Deciduous, round-headed tree. Dull green leaves are large, broadly oval, toothed, and sometimes lobed. In early summer, small globes of purple flowers appear on female plants.

Z6–9 H9–6

***Sorbus thibetica* 'John Mitchell'**, syn. *S.* 'Mitchellii'
Strong-growing, deciduous, conical tree with dark green leaves, silvery beneath. Has white flowers in spring and brown fruits in late summer.

Z5–7 H7–5

Hovenia dulcis (Raisin tree)
Deciduous, spreading tree with large, glossy, dark green leaves. In summer it may bear small, greenish yellow flowers, the stalks of which become red, fleshy, and edible.

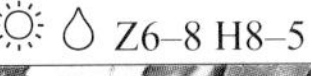
Z6–8 H8–5

Toona sinensis, syn. *Cedrela sinensis*
Deciduous, spreading tree with shaggy bark when old. Dark green leaves with many leaflets turn yellow in autumn. Bears fragrant white flowers in midsummer. Shoots are onion-scented.

Z5–8 H12–10

***Populus tremula* 'Pendula'**
(Weeping aspen)
Vigorous, deciduous, weeping tree. Leaves, reddish when young, gray-green in summer, and yellow in autumn, tremble in the wind. Has purplish catkins in late winter and spring.

Z2–8 H8–1

Acer negundo var. *violaceum*
Olea europaea
Populus tremula
Pyrus amygdaliformis
Salix alba var. *sericea*

TREES medium SUMMER INTEREST

GREEN

Quercus marilandica
(Blackjack oak)
Deciduous, spreading tree. Large leaves, 3-lobed at the apex, are glossy, dark green above, paler beneath, and turn yellow, red, or brown in autumn.

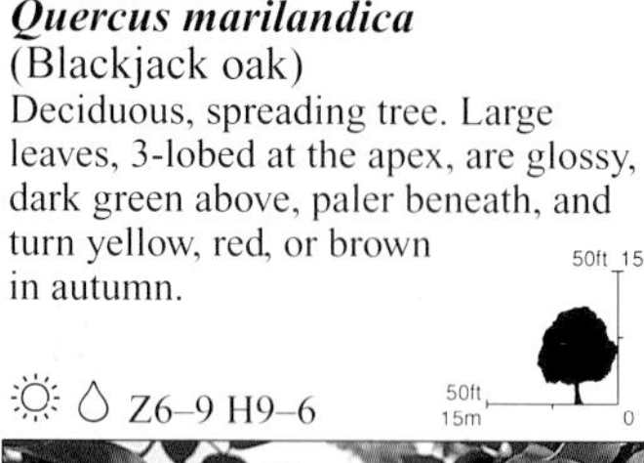

Z6–9 H9–6

Fraxinus velutina (Arizona ash)
Deciduous, spreading tree. Leaves vary but usually consist of 3 or 5 narrow, velvety, gray-green leaflets.

Z6–9 H9–6

Quercus garryana (Oregon oak)
Slow-growing, deciduous, spreading tree with deeply lobed, glossy, bright green leaves.

Z7–9 H9–7

***Tilia cordata* 'Rancho'**
Deciduous, conical, dense tree, spreading when young. Has small, oval, glossy, dark green leaves. Clusters of small, fragrant, cup-shaped yellowish flowers are borne in midsummer.

Z4–8 H8–1

Meliosma veitchiorum
Deciduous, spreading tree with thick gray shoots and large, dark green, red-stalked leaves with 9 or 11 leaflets. Small, fragrant white flowers in late spring are followed by violet fruits in autumn.

Z9–11 H12–10

Gleditsia japonica
Deciduous, conical tree with a trunk armed with spines. Shoots are purplish when young. Fernlike leaves consist of many small, midgreen leaflets.

Z8–11 H12–8

Emmenopterys henryi
Deciduous, spreading tree. Large, pointed, dark green leaves are bronze-purple when young. Clusters of white flowers (some bearing a large white bract) are rarely produced except in hot summers.

Z7–11 H12–7

Idesia polycarpa
Deciduous, spreading tree with large, heart-shaped, glossy, dark green leaves on long stalks. Small, fragrant, yellow-green flowers in midsummer are followed in autumn (on female plants) by red fruits hanging in clusters.

Z6–9 H9–6

Kalopanax septemlobus,
syn. *Acanthopanax ricinifolius*, *K. pictus*, *K. ricinifolius*
Deciduous, spreading tree with spiny stems, large, 5–7-lobed, glossy, dark green leaves, umbels of small white flowers, then black fruits in autumn.

Z5–9 H9–4

Quercus macrocarpa (Bur oak)
Slow-growing, deciduous, spreading tree. Large, oblong-oval, lobed, glossy, dark green leaves turn yellow or brown in autumn.

Z3–9 H9–1

Quercus macrolepis,
syn. *Q. aegilops*, *Q. ithaburensis* subsp. *macrolepsis*
Deciduous or semi-evergreen, spreading tree. Has gray-green leaves with angular lobes.

Z8–9 H9–8

***Quercus rubra* 'Aurea'**
Slow-growing, deciduous, spreading tree. Large, lobed leaves are clear yellow when young, becoming green by midsummer. Produces best color in an open but sheltered position.

Z5–9 H9–5

Acer giraldii
Acer monspessulanum
Aesculus glabra
Alnus glutinosa 'Imperialis'

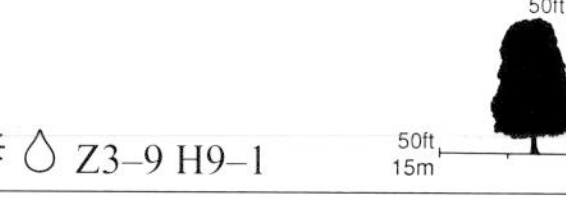

Eucommia ulmoides
Fagus grandifolia
Meliosma pinnata var. *oldhamii*
Nothofagus antarctica

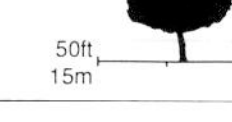

Ostrya carpinifolia
Phellodendron amurense
Platycarya strobilacea
Pyrus calleryana 'Bradford'

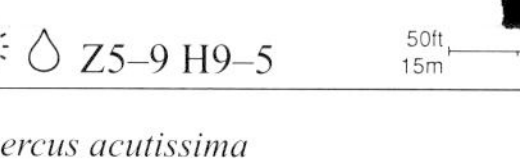

Quercus acutissima
Quercus aliena
Quercus dentata
Ulmus parvifolia

TREES medium AUTUMN INTEREST

GREEN–YELLOW

Phellodendron chinense
Deciduous, spreading tree. Aromatic leaves, with 7–13 oblong leaflets, are dark green, turning yellow in autumn. Pendent racemes of greenish flowers in early summer are followed on female trees by berry-like black fruits.

Z5–8 H8–5

***Robinia pseudoacacia* 'Frisia'**
Deciduous, spreading tree with luxuriant leaves divided into oval leaflets, golden yellow when young, greenish yellow in summer, and orange-yellow in autumn.

Z4–9 H9–4

***Ulmus minor* 'Dicksonii'**
(Dickson's golden elm)
Slow-growing, deciduous, conical tree of dense habit. Carries small, broadly oval, bright golden yellow leaves.

Z5–8 H8–5

WHITE–RED

***Eucryphia* x *nymansensis* 'Nymansay'**
Evergreen, columnar tree. Some of the leathery, glossy, dark green leaves are simple; others consist of 3 (rarely 5) leaflets. Clusters of large white flowers open in late summer or early autumn.

Z8–9 H9–8

Syzygium paniculatum
(Australian brush cherry)
Evergreen tree with glossy leaves, coppery when young. Has creamy white flowers with reddish sepals, and fragrant, rose-purple fruits.

Z10–11 H12–1

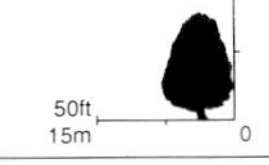

***Acer davidii* 'Madeline Spitta'**
Deciduous tree with upright branches that are striped green and white. Glossy, dark green foliage turns orange in autumn after the appearance of winged green fruits that ripen reddish brown.

Z5–7 H7–5

***Sorbus hupehensis* 'Rosea'**, syn. *S.h.* var. *obtusa*
Deciduous, spreading tree with leaves of 4–8 pairs of blue-green leaflets turning orange-red in late autumn. White flowers in spring are followed by long-lasting pink fruits.

Z6–8 H8–6

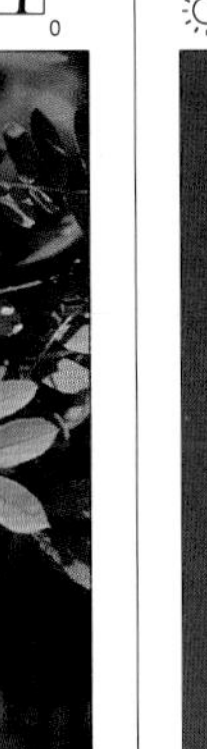

Sorbus commixta, syn. *S. discolor* of gardens
Vigorous, deciduous, spreading tree. Leaves have 6–8 pairs of glossy, deep green leaflets that turn orange and red in autumn. White flowers in spring are followed by bright red fruits.

Z6–8 H8–6

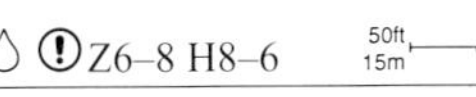

Sorbus aucuparia
(Mountain ash)
Deciduous, spreading tree. Leaves have midgreen leaflets that turn red or yellow in autumn. Bears white flowers in spring and red fruits in autumn.

Z2–7 H7–1

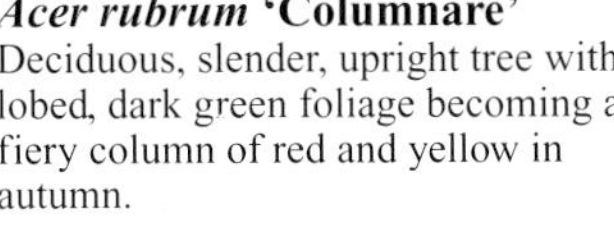

***Acer rubrum* 'Columnare'**
Deciduous, slender, upright tree with lobed, dark green foliage becoming a fiery column of red and yellow in autumn.

Z3–9 H9–1

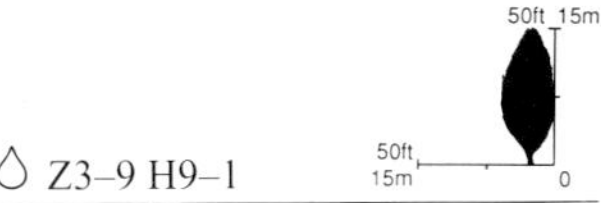

OTHER RECOMMENDED PLANTS:
Alnus glutinosa 'Aurea'
Catalpa bignonioides 'Aurea'
Quercus robur 'Concordia'
Chorisia speciosa, illus. p.70
Cornus capitata
MAGNOLIAS, illus. p.75
Rhus potaninii
Rhus verniciflua
Sorbus americana
Sorbus esserteauana
Sorbus hupehensis
Sorbus scalaris

TREES medium AUTUMN INTEREST

RED–YELLOW

Acer rufinerve
(Snakebark maple)
Deciduous tree with arching branches striped green and white. In autumn, lobed, dark green leaves turn brilliant red and orange.

Z6–9 H9–6

Aesculus flava, syn. *A. octandra*
(Sweet buckeye, Yellow buckeye)
Deciduous, spreading tree. Glossy, dark green leaves, with 5 or 7 oval leaflets, redden in autumn. Has yellow flowers in late spring and early summer followed by round fruits(buckeyes).

Z3–8 H8–1

Quercus* x *heterophylla
(Bartram's oak)
Deciduous, spreading tree with toothed, glossy, bright green leaves that turn orange-red and yellow in autumn.

Z5–8 H8–5

Stewartia monadelpha
Deciduous, spreading tree with peeling bark and glossy, dark green leaves that turn orange and red in autumn. Small, violet-anthered white flowers appear in midsummer, followed by small fruits.

Z69 H9–6

Acer henryi, syn. *A. cissifolium* subsp. *henryi*
Deciduous, spreading tree. Dark green leaves with 3 oval, toothed leaflets turn bright orange and red in autumn.

Z4–8 H8–1

Nyssa sinensis
Deciduous, spreading tree. Has long, narrow, pointed leaves that are purplish when young, dark green when mature, and brilliant scarlet in autumn.

Z7–9 H9–7

***Sorbus* 'Joseph Rock'**
Deciduous, upright tree. Bright green leaves composed of many leaflets turn orange, red, and purple in autumn. White flowers in late spring are followed by large clusters of small yellow berries in late summer and autumn.

Z7–8 H8–7

***Acer saccharum* 'Temple's Upright'**
Deciduous, columnar tree. In autumn, large, lobed leaves turn brilliant orange and red.

Z4–8 H8–1

Parrotia persica (Persian ironwood)
Deciduous, spreading, short-trunked tree with flaking gray and fawn bark. Rich green leaves turn yellow, orange, and red-purple in autumn. Small red flowers are borne on bare wood in early spring.

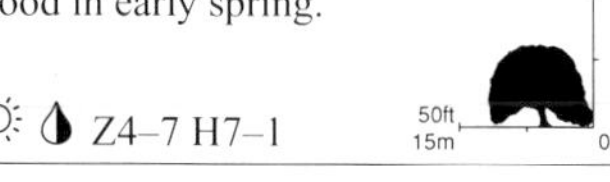

Z4–7 H7–1

Acer capillipes
(Snakebark maple)
Deciduous, spreading tree. Has lobed, bright green leaves that turn brilliant red and orange in autumn. Older branches are striped green and white.

Z5–7 H7–5

Cladrastis kentukea (Yellowwood)
Deciduous, round-headed tree. Leaves of 7 or 9 rounded-oval leaflets are dark green, turning yellow in autumn. Clusters of fragrant, pealike, yellow-marked white flowers appear in early summer.

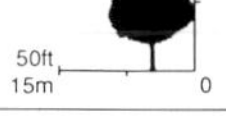

Z4–9 H9–1

Acer maximowiczianum
Diospyros kaki
Dipteronia sinensis
HOLLIES, illus. pp.98–99

Liquidambar formosana
Maclura pomifera
Malus 'Hopa'
Malus hupehensis, illus. p.74

Malus 'Profusion', illus. p.77
Malus x *robusta*
Malus x *robusta* 'Yellow Siberian'
Morus nigra

Oxydendrum arboreum, illus. p.78
Sorbus aucuparia 'Fructu Luteo'
Sorbus decora

TREES medium WINTER INTEREST

WHITE–YELLOW

Betula utilis var. ***jacquemontii***
syn. *B. jacquemontii*
(White-barked Himalayan birch)
Deciduous, open-branched, elegant tree with bright white bark. Oval, serrated, midgreen leaves turn clear yellow in autumn.

50ft 15m
50ft 15m 0
Z4–9 H9–3

Michelia doltsopa
Evergreen, rounded tree with oval, glossy, dark green leaves, paler beneath. Strongly scented, magnolia-like flowers, with white to pale yellow petals, appear in winter-spring.

50ft 15m
pH Z9–11 H12–1
50ft 15m 0

Acacia dealbata
(Mimosa, Silver wattle)
Fast-growing, evergreen, spreading tree. Has feathery, blue-green leaves with many leaflets. Racemes of globular, fragrant, bright yellow flower heads are borne in winter-spring.

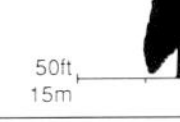

50ft 15m
Z9–11 H12–1
50ft 15m 0

OTHER RECOMMENDED PLANTS:
Bauhinia variegata
Salix daphnoides, illus. p.74
Tabebuia chrysotricha, illus. p.97

RED

Arbutus* x *andrachnoides
Evergreen, bushy, spreading tree with peeling, reddish brown bark and glossy, dark green foliage. Clusters of small white flowers in autumn to spring are followed by small, strawberry-like, orange or red fruits.

50ft 15m
Z8–9 H9–8
50ft 15m 0

Metrosideros excelsus
(New Zealand Christmas tree, Pohutukawa)
Evergreen, wide-spreading tree. Oval, gray-green leaves are white-felted beneath. Bears showy tufts of crimson stamens in winter.

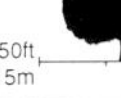

50ft 15m
Z11–15 H12–10
50ft 15m 0

TREES medium ALL YEAR INTEREST

WHITE–GREEN

***Ficus benjamina* 'Variegata'**
Evergreen, dense, round-headed, weeping tree, often with aerial roots. Has slender, pointed, lustrous leaves that are rich green with white variegation.

Z14–15 H12–10

Trochodendron aralioides
Evergreen, broadly conical tree with glossy, dark green foliage. In late spring and early summer bears clusters of unusual, petal-less, wheel-like green flowers.

Z6–11 H12–10

Schefflera actinophylla
(Queensland umbrella tree)
Evergreen, upright tree with large, spreading leaves of 5–16 leaflets. Has large sprays of small, dull red flowers in summer or autumn.

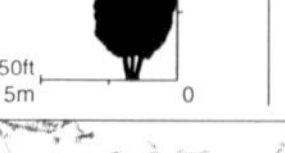

Z14–15 H12–10

Acer pensylvanicum
(Moosewood, Snakebark maple)
Deciduous, upright tree. Shoots are boldly striped green and white. Large, lobed, midgreen leaves turn bright yellow in autumn.

Z3–7 H7–1

Eucalyptus pauciflora
(White Sallee)
Evergreen, spreading tree with peeling, white, young bark and red young shoots. In summer, white flower clusters appear amid glossy, bright gray-green foliage.

Z9–11 H12–10

Trachycarpus fortunei
(Chusan palm, Windmill palm)
Evergreen palm with unbranched stem and a head of large, deeply divided, fanlike, midgreen leaves. Sprays of fragrant, creamy yellow flowers appear in early summer.

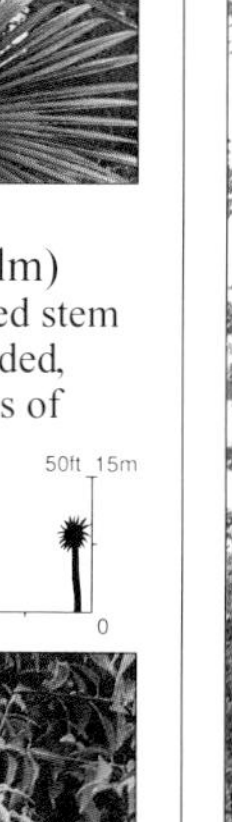

Z8–11 H12–8

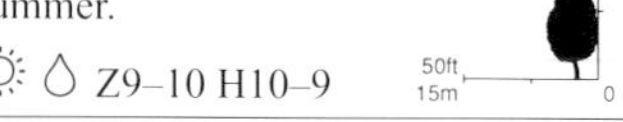

Eucalyptus pauciflora* subsp. *niphophila*, syn. *E. niphophila
(Snow gum)
Evergreen, spreading tree. Has patchworklike, flaking bark, red-rimmed, gray-green leaves, and white flowers in summer.

Z9–10 H10–9

Quercus myrsinifolia
Evergreen, rounded tree with narrow, pointed, glossy, dark green leaves, reddish purple when young.

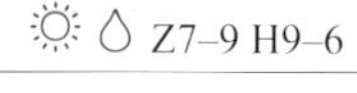

Z7–9 H9–6

Prunus maackii
Deciduous, spreading tree with peeling, yellowish brown bark. Produces spikes of small white flowers in midspring and pointed, dark green leaves that turn yellow in autumn.

Z3–7 H7–1

OTHER RECOMMENDED PLANTS:
Acer davidii
Betula 'Jermyns'
Cinnamomum camphora
Cordyline australis 'Veitchii'
Cyathea medullaris
Eucalyptus glaucescens
Ficus lyrata

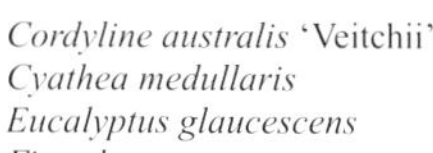

HOLLIES, illus. pp.98–9
Laurelia sempervirens
Laurus nobilis
Lithocarpus densiflorus

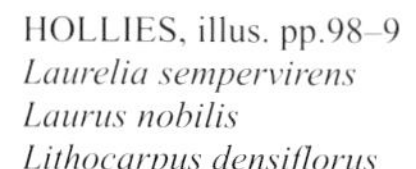

MAGNOLIAS, illus. p.75
Salix x *rubens* 'Basfordiana'

GREEN–ORANGE

Jubaea chilensis, syn. *J. spectabilis* (Chilean wine palm, Coquito)
Slow-growing, evergreen palm with a massive trunk and large, silvery green leaves. Has small maroon and yellow flowers in spring and woody yellow fruits in autumn.

50ft 15m

☼ ◊ Z8–11 H12–9

Livistona chinensis (Chinese fan palm, Chinese fountain palm)
Slow-growing, evergreen palm with a thick trunk. Has fan-shaped, glossy leaves, 3–10ft (1–3m) across. Mature trees bear loose clusters of berrylike black fruits in autumn.

50ft 15m

☼ ◊ Z11–12 H12–10

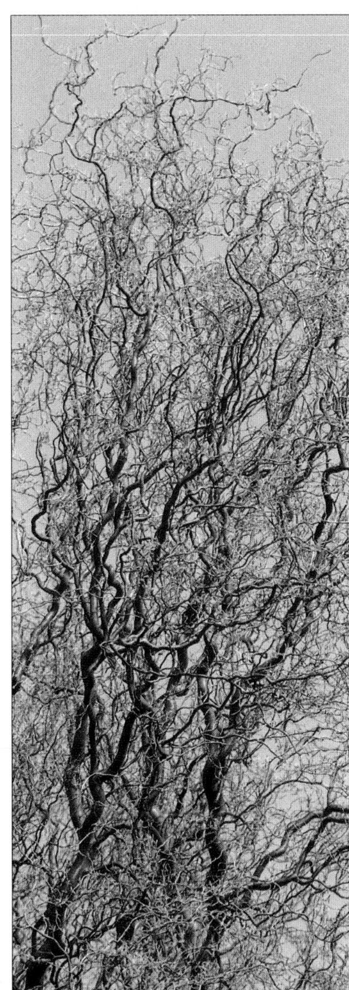

Salix babylonica var. ***pekinensis* 'Tortuosa'** (Dragon's-claw willow, Corkscrew willow)
Fast-growing, deciduous, spreading tree with curiously twisted shoots and contorted, narrow, tapering, bright green leaves.

50ft 15m

☼ ◆ Z6–9 H9–6

Quercus agrifolia (California live oak)
Evergreen, spreading tree bearing rigid, spiny-toothed, glossy, dark green leaves.

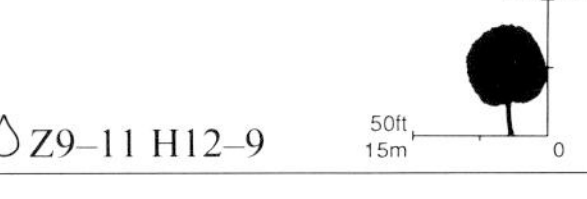

☼ ◊ Z9–11 H12–9

Corynocarpus laevigatus
Evergreen, upright tree, spreading with age. Has leathery leaves and clusters of small greenish flowers in spring-summer. Plumlike orange fruits appear in winter.

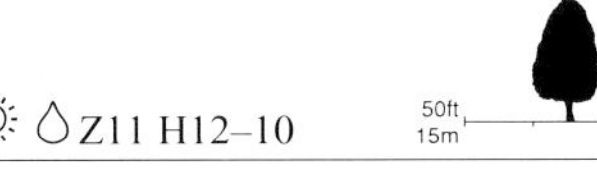

☼ ◊ Z11 H12–10

Betula alleghaniensis
HOLLIES, illus. pp.98–9
Prunus serrula
Thespesia populnea

TREES small SPRING INTEREST

WHITE

Mespilus germanica (Medlar)
Deciduous, spreading tree or shrub. Has dark green leaves that turn orange-brown in autumn, white flowers in spring-summer, and brown fruits in autumn, edible when basically half rotten.

30ft 10m

☼ ◊ Z6–9 H9–6

Crataegus laciniata, syn. *C. orientalis*
Deciduous, spreading tree with deeply lobed, hairy, dark green leaves. A profusion of white flowers in late spring or early summer is followed by red fruits tinged with yellow.

30ft 10m

☼ ◊ (!) Z6–8 H8–6

Amelanchier laevis
Deciduous, spreading tree or large shrub. Oval, bronze, young leaves turn dark green in summer, red and orange in autumn. Sprays of white flowers in spring are followed by rounded, fleshy, red fruits.

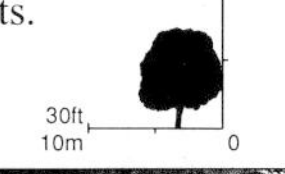

☼ ◆ Z5–9 H9–3

***Cornus florida* 'White Cloud'**
Deciduous, spreading tree. Massed flower heads, consisting of large, white bracts around tiny flowers, appear in spring. Oval, pointed, dark green leaves turn red and purple in autumn.

30ft 10m

☼ ◊ (!) Z5–8 H8–3

Aesculus californica (California buckeye)
Deciduous, spreading, sometimes shrubby tree. Dense heads of fragrant, sometimes pink-tinged white flowers appear in spring and early summer. Small, dark green leaves have 5–7 leaflets.

30ft 10m

☼ ◊ (!) Z7–8 H8–7

OTHER RECOMMENDED PLANTS:
Agonis flexuosa, illus. p.90
Amelanchier arborea
Amelanchier asiatica
Arbutus andrachne
Bauhinia variegata 'Candida', illus. p.97
Cornus 'Eddie's White Wonder', illus. p.96
Crataegus crus-galli

TREES small SPRING INTEREST

□ WHITE

Prunus 'Shogetsu', syn. *P.* 'Shimidsu'
Deciduous, round-topped tree. In late spring, pink buds open to large, double white flowers that hang in clusters from long stalks. Midgreen leaves turn orange and red in autumn.

Z6–8 H8–6

Cornus 'Porlock'
Deciduous, spreading tree. Creamy white bracts around tiny flowers turn to deep pink in summer. These are often followed by heavy crops of strawberry-like fruits in autumn.

Z5–9 H9–5

Prunus incisa (Fuji cherry)
Deciduous, spreading tree. White or pale pink flowers appear in early spring. Sharply toothed, dark green leaves are reddish when young and orange-red in autumn.

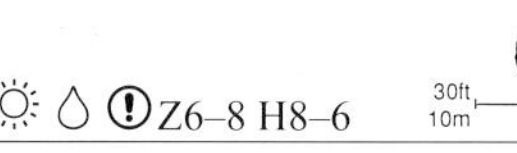

Z6–8 H8–6

Prunus 'Taihaku' (Great white cherry)
Vigorous, deciduous, spreading tree. Very large, single, pure white flowers are borne in midspring among bronze-red young leaves that mature to dark green.

Z6–8 H8–6

Prunus 'Ukon'
Vigorous, deciduous, spreading tree. Semi-double, pale greenish white flowers open from pink buds in mid-spring amid pale bronze young foliage that later turns dark green.

Z6–8 H8–6

Prunus 'Shirotae', syn. *P.* 'Mount Fuji'
Deciduous, spreading tree with slightly arching branches. Large, fragrant, single or semi-double, pure white flowers appear in mid-spring. Foliage turns orange-red in autumn.

Z6–8 H8–6

Crataegus ellwangeriana
Crataegus x *lavallei* 'Carrierei'
Docynia delavayi
Gordonia axillaris
Halesia tetraptera
MAGNOLIAS, illus. p.75
Malus 'Frettingham's Victoria'
Malus 'Golden Hornet', illus. p.97
Malus 'John Downie', illus. p.95
Malus prunifolia, illus. p.95
Malus toringoides
Malus transitoria
Malus 'Veitch's Scarlet', illus. p.94
Parrotiopsis jacquemontiana
Prunus 'Hally Jolivette'

PINK

Prunus x yedoensis
(Yoshino cherry)
Deciduous, round-headed tree with spreading, arching branches and dark green foliage. Sprays of pink buds open to white or pale pink flowers in early spring.

Z5–8 H8–5

Prunus 'Spire',
syn. *P. x hillieri* 'Spire'
Deciduous, vase-shaped tree, conical when young. Soft pink flowers appear profusely from early to midspring. Dark green leaves, bronze when young, turn brilliant orange-red in autumn.

Z6–8 H8–6

Prunus 'Hokusai',
syn. *P.* 'Uzuzakura'
Deciduous, spreading tree. Oval, bronze, young leaves mature to dark green, then turn orange and red in autumn. Semi-double, pale pink flowers are borne in midspring.

Z5–8 H8–5

Prunus x subhirtella 'Stellata'
Deciduous, spreading tree. Pink flowers with narrow, pointed petals, red in bud, open from early to mid-spring. Dark green leaves turn yellow in autumn.

Z6–8 H8–6

Prunus 'Pandora'
Deciduous tree, upright when young, later spreading. Massed, pale pink flowers appear in early spring. Leaves are bronze when young, dark green in summer, and often orange and red in autumn.

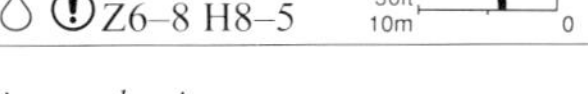

Z6–8 H8–5

Malus x arnoldiana
Deciduous, low, spreading tree with arching branches. In mid- to late spring red buds open to fragrant pink flowers that fade to white. Bears small, red-flushed yellow crabapples in autumn. Leaves are oval.

Z5–8 H8–5

Prunus 'Shirofugen'
Deciduous, spreading tree with bronze-red leaves turning orange-red in autumn. Pale pink buds open to fragrant, double white blooms that turn pink before they fade in late spring.

Z6–8 H8–6

Prunus sargentii (Sargent cherry)
Deciduous, spreading tree. Oval, dark green leaves are red when young, turning brilliant orange-red in early autumn. Clusters of blush pink flowers appear in midspring.

Z5–9 H9–5

Prunus 'Pink Perfection'
Deciduous, upright tree that bears double, pale pink flowers in late spring. Oval leaves are bronze when young, dark green in summer.

Z6–8 H8–6

Cercis canadensis
Cercis canadensis 'Forest Pansy', illus. p.91
Cornus florida 'Apple Blossom'
Cydonia oblonga 'Lusitanica'
Cydonia oblonga 'Vranja', illus. p.92
MAGNOLIAS, illus. p.75
Malus coronaria 'Charlottae'
Malus 'Katherine'
Malus 'Marshall Oyama', illus. p.96
Malus 'Professor Sprenger', illus. p.96
Malus 'Red Jade'
Melaleuca viridiflora var. *rubriflora*
Prunus davidiana
Staphylea holocarpa 'Rosea', illus. p.117

TREES small SPRING INTEREST

■ PINK

***Prunus* 'Accolade'**
Deciduous, spreading tree with clusters of deep pink buds opening to semi-double, pale pink flowers in early spring. Toothed, midgreen leaves turn orange-red in autumn.

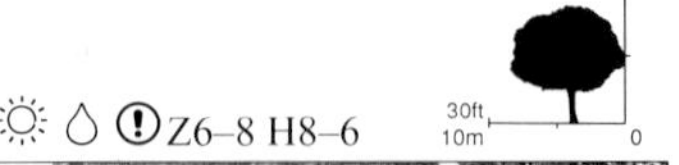

Z6–8 H8–6

***Prunus* x *subhirtella* 'Pendula Rubra'**, syn. *P. pendula* 'Pendula Rubra'
Deciduous, weeping tree that bears deep pink flowers in spring before oval, dark green leaves appear; these turn yellow in autumn.

Z4–8 H8–1

***Malus* 'Magdeburgensis'**
Deciduous, spreading tree with dark green foliage. Dense clusters of large, semi-double, deep pink flowers appear in late spring, occasionally followed by small yellow crabapples in autumn.

Z4–8 H8–1

Cercis siliquastrum (Judas tree)
Deciduous, spreading, bushy tree. Clusters of pealike, bright pink flowers appear in midspring, before or with heart-shaped leaves, followed by long, purplish red pods in late summer.

Z6–9 H9–3

***Prunus persica* 'Prince Charming'**
Deciduous, upright, bushy-headed tree with narrow, bright green leaves. Double, deep rose-pink flowers are produced in midspring.

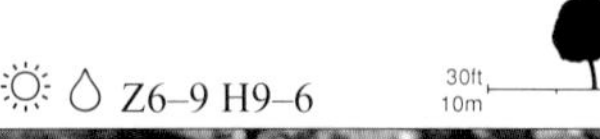

Z6–9 H9–6

***Prunus* 'Kiku-shidare-zakura'**, syn. *P.* 'Cheal's Weeping'
Deciduous, weeping tree. Has double, bright pink flowers that cover pendent branches from mid- to late spring.

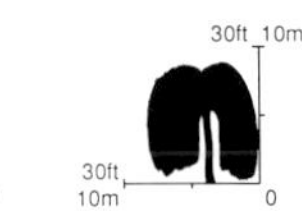

Z6–8 H8–6

Malus floribunda
Deciduous, spreading, dense-headed tree with pale pink flowers, red in bud, appearing from mid- to late spring, followed by tiny, pea-shaped yellow crabapples in autumn.

Z4–8 H8–1

Dombeya* x *cayeuxii
(Pink snowball)
Evergreen, bushy tree with rounded, toothed, hairy leaves to 8in (20cm) long. Pink flowers appear in pendent, ball-like clusters in winter or spring.

Z13–15 H12–10

***Prunus* 'Yae-murasaki'**
Deciduous, spreading tree with bright green leaves, bronze when young and orange-red in autumn. Semi-double, deep pink flowers are produced in midspring.

Z6–8 H8–6

Bauhinia variegata, illus. p.97
Cornus florida f. *rubra*
Crataegus laevigata 'Punicea'
Malus 'Almey'
Malus x *atrosanguinea*
Malus 'Chilko'
Malus 'Cowichan', illus. p.94
Malus 'Dorothea'
Malus 'Neville Copeman'
Malus 'Van Eseltine'
Prunus x *amygdalopersica* 'Pollardii'
Prunus 'Kursar'
Prunus mume 'Pendula'
Prunus persica 'Klara Meyer'
Pseudocydonia sinensis
Rhodoleia championii

RED–YELLOW

***Malus* 'Royalty'**
Deciduous, spreading tree with glossy purple foliage. Crimson-purple flowers appear from mid- to late spring, followed by dark red crabapples in autumn. Susceptible to some leaf diseases.

Z5–8 H8–5

***Acer pseudoplatanus* 'Brilliantissimum'**
Slow-growing, deciduous, spreading tree. Lobed leaves are salmon-pink when young, then turn yellow and finally dark green in summer.

Z4–7 H7–1

***Malus* 'Lemoinei'**
Deciduous, spreading tree. Oval leaves are deep reddish purple when young, later becoming tinged with bronze. Wine red flowers in late spring are followed by dark reddish purple crabapples in autumn.

Z5–8 H8–5

Michelia figo
Evergreen tree or rounded shrub. Has oval, glossy, rich green leaves and banana-scented, creamy yellow flowers edged maroon in spring-summer.

Z12–15 H12–10

***Aesculus* x *neglecta* 'Erythroblastos'**
Deciduous, spreading tree. Leaves with 5 leaflets emerge bright pink, then turn yellow, then dark green, and finally orange and yellow in autumn. May bear panicles of flowers in summer.

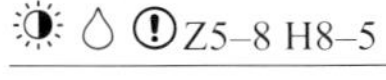
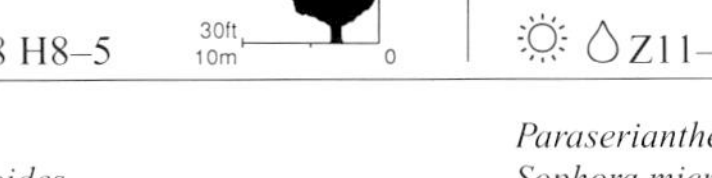

Z5–8 H8–5

Sophora tetraptera
Semi-evergreen, spreading tree or large shrub with dark green leaves composed of many tiny leaflets. Clusters of golden yellow flowers appear in late spring.

Z11–15 H12–10

Cassia fistula
Erythrina coralloides
Laburnum x *watereri* 'Vossii', illus. p.92
Malus niedzwetskyana
Paraserianthes lophantha, illus. p.93
Sophora microphylla
Thevetia peruviana, illus. p.93
Tipuana tipu

WHITE

***Cornus alternifolia* 'Argentea'**
Deciduous, spreading tree, grown for its attractive, narrowly oval, white-variegated leaves. Has small heads of white flowers in spring.

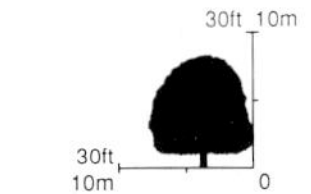

Z4–8 H8–1

***Acer crataegifolium* 'Veitchii'**
Deciduous, bushy tree with branches streaked with green and white. Small, pointed, dark green leaves, blotched with white and paler green, turn deep pink and reddish purple in autumn.

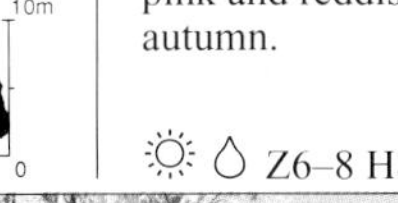

Z6–8 H8–6

***Cornus controversa* 'Variegata'**
Deciduous tree with layered branches. Clusters of small white flowers appear in summer. Leaves are bright green with broad, creamy white margins and turn yellow in autumn.

Z6–9 H9–6

OTHER RECOMMENDED PLANTS:
Aralia elata 'Variegata'
Carrierea calycina
Chionanthus virginicus, illus. p.119
Cornus kousa
Cornus kousa var. *chinensis*
Cornus mas 'Variegata', illus. p.119
Cotoneaster frigidus

TREES small SUMMER INTEREST

WHITE

Crataegus flava
(Yellow hawthorn)
Deciduous, spreading tree. Has small, dark green leaves and white flowers in late spring and early summer, followed by greenish yellow fruits.

Z7–9 H9–7

Agonis flexuosa
(Peppermint tree, Willow myrtle)
Evergreen, weeping tree. Aromatic, lance-shaped, leathery leaves are bronze-red when young. In spring-summer, mature trees bear masses of small white flowers.

Z10 H12–6

Eucryphia glutinosa
Deciduous, upright or spreading tree. Glossy, dark green leaves, consisting of 3–5 leaflets, turn orange-red in autumn. Large, fragrant, white flowers appear from mid- to late summer.

pH Z8–11 H12–8

Hoheria angustifolia
Evergreen, columnar tree with narrow, dark green leaves. Shallowly cup-shaped white flowers are borne from mid- to late summer.

Z9–11 H12–10

Hoheria lyallii
Deciduous, spreading tree with deeply toothed, gray-green leaves. Clusters of white flowers are borne in midsummer.

Z9–11 H12–10

Eucryphia lucida
Evergreen, upright, bushy tree with narrow, glossy, dark green leaves and fragrant white flowers in early or midsummer.

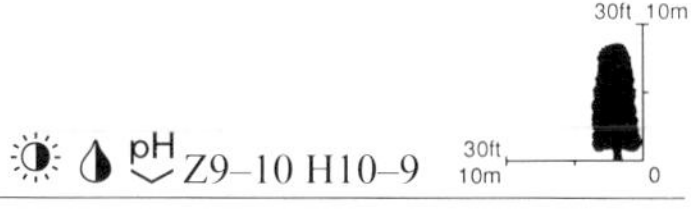

pH Z9–10 H10–9

WHITE–PINK

Maackia amurensis
Deciduous, spreading tree with deep green leaves consisting of 7–11 leaflets. Dense, upright spikes of white flowers appear from mid- to late summer.

Z5–7 H7–5

Albizia julibrissin (Mimosa)
Deciduous, spreading tree. Large leaves are light to mid-green and divided into many leaflets. Clusters of brushlike pink flowers appear from summer into autumn.

Z6–9 H9–6

***Cornus florida* 'Spring Song'**
Deciduous, spreading tree. Pink bracts, surrounding tiny flowers, appear in spring-summer. Leaves are oval, pointed, and dark green, turning red and purple in autumn.

Z5–8 H8–3

Crataegus x *prunifolia*
Crataegus tanacetifolia
Elaeocarpus cyaneus
Franklinia alatamaha

Fraxinus sieboldiana
Hoheria 'Glory of Amlwch'
Hoheria sexstylosa
MAGNOLIAS, illus. p.75

Plumeria alba
Sophora japonica 'Pendula'
Xanthoceras sorbifolium, illus. p.118

Rothmannia capensis

PINK–PURPLE

Lagerstroemia indica
(Crape myrtle)
Deciduous, rounded tree or large shrub. Has clusters of flowers with strongly waved pink, white, or purple petals in summer and early autumn.

☼ ◊ Z7–9 H9–7

***Crataegus laevigata* 'Paul's Scarlet'**
Deciduous, spreading tree. Has toothed, glossy, dark green leaves and a profusion of double red flowers in late spring and early summer.

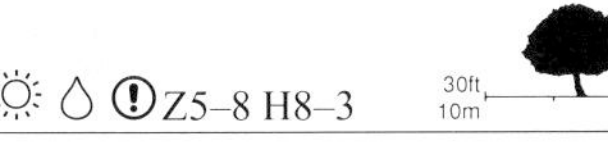

☼ ◊ ! Z5–8 H8–3

Malus yunnanensis* var. *veitchii
Deciduous, upright tree with lobed, heart-shaped leaves, covered with gray down beneath. Bears white, sometimes pink-tinged flowers in late spring and a mass of small, red-flushed brown crabapples in late summer and autumn.

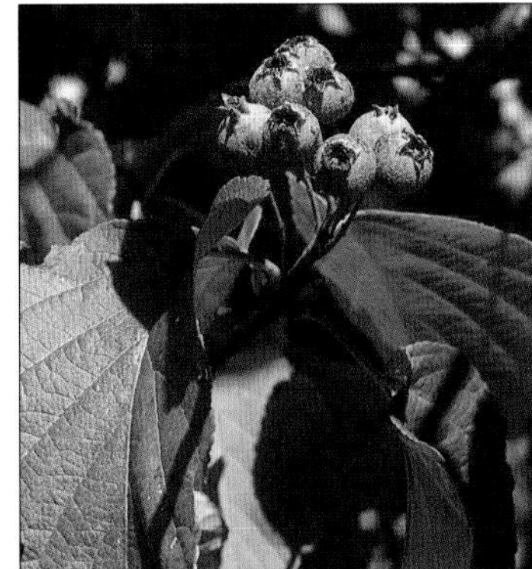

☼ ◊ Z6–8 H8–6

***Aesculus pavia* 'Atrosanguinea'**
Deciduous, round-headed, sometimes shrubby tree. In summer, panicles of deep red flowers appear among glossy, dark green leaves, which have 5 narrow leaflets.

☼ ◊ ! Z5–9 H9–5

***Cercis canadensis* 'Forest Pansy'**
Deciduous, spreading tree or shrub. In midspring has flowers that are magenta in bud, opening to pale pink, before heart-shaped, reddish purple leaves appear.

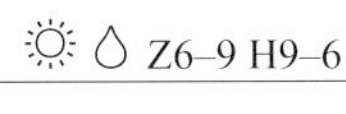

☼ ◊ Z6–9 H9–6

PURPLE–GREEN

***Prunus cerasifera* 'Nigra'**
Deciduous, round-headed tree with deep purple leaves, red when young. Pink flowers are borne in profusion from early to midspring.

☼ ◊ ! Z5–9 H9–5

Ehretia dicksonii
Deciduous, spreading tree with thick, ridged branches and large, dark green leaves. Large, flattish heads of small, fragrant white flowers are borne in midsummer.

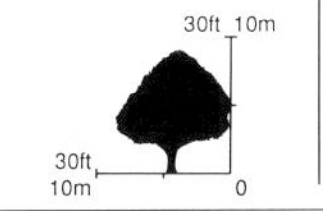

☼ ◊ Z7–11 H12–7

***Pyrus salicifolia* 'Pendula'**
Deciduous, weeping, mound-shaped tree with white flowers in midspring and narrow gray leaves.

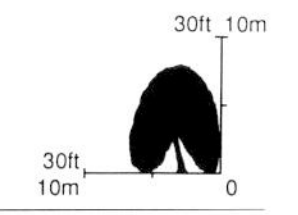

☼ ◊ Z5–9 H9–5

Acer palmatum f. *atropurpureum*, illus. p.121
Aesculus pavia
Corylus maxima 'Purpurea', illus. p.122

Erythrina coralloides
Prunus spinosa 'Purpurea', illus. p.122
Punica granatum
Virgilia oroboides

Acer platanoides 'Globosum'
Elaeagnus angustifolia, illus. p.122
Fagus sylvatica 'Purpurea Pendula'
Morus alba 'Pendula'

Pyrus elaeagrifolia
Pyrus salicifolia
Salix pentandra
Sinowilsonia henryi

TREES small SUMMER INTEREST

GREEN

Pseudopanax ferox
Evergreen, upright tree with long, narrow, rigid, sharply toothed leaves that are dark bronze-green overlaid white or gray.
Z8–11 H12–8

***Ulmus glabra* 'Camperdownii',**
syn. *U.* 'Camperdownii'
Deciduous, strongly weeping tree with sinuous branches. Leaves are rather large, rough, and dull green.

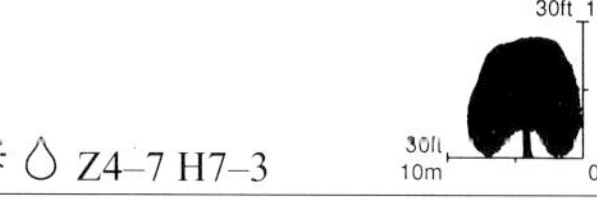

Z4–7 H7–3

***Juglans microcarpa*,**
syn. *J. rupestris*
(Little walnut, Texan walnut)
Deciduous, bushy-headed tree with large, aromatic leaves of many narrow, pointed leaflets that turn yellow in autumn.
Z6–9 H9–6

***Cydonia oblonga* 'Vranja'**
Deciduous, spreading tree. Pale green leaves, gray-felted beneath, mature to dark green and set off large white or pale pink flowers in late spring and, later, very fragrant, golden yellow fruits.
Z5–9 H9–5

***Betula pendula* 'Youngii'**
(Young's weeping birch)
Deciduous, weeping tree forming a mushroom-shaped dome of threadlike branchlets. Has triangular, serrated leaves and smooth white bark that is fissured black at maturity.
Z2–7 H7–1

Aralia elata
Celtis sinensis
Cornus alternifolia
Neolitsea sericea
Pseudopanax arboreus
Quercus pontica
Tetracentron sinense
Zelkova abelicea

GREEN–YELLOW

Acer carpinifolium
(Hornbeam maple)
Deciduous tree of elegant habit, often with several main stems. Prominently veined, hornbeamlike leaves turn golden brown in autumn.
Z4–7 H7–1

***Acer shirasawanum* 'Aureum',**
syn. *A. japonicum* 'Aureum'
Deciduous, bushy tree or large shrub. Has rounded, many-lobed, pale yellow leaves that turn darker green as the season progresses.
Z5–7 H7–5

***Morus alba* 'Laciniata'**
Deciduous, spreading tree. Has rounded, deeply lobed, glossy leaves that turn yellow in autumn and bears edible pink, red, or purple fruits in summer.

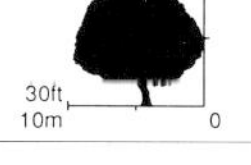

Z4–8 H8–1

Koelreuteria paniculata
(Golden rain tree, Pride of India)
Deciduous, spreading tree with mid-green leaves, turning yellow in autumn. Bears sprays of yellow flowers in summer, followed by inflated, bronze-pink fruits.
Z6–9 H9–1

***Laburnum* x *watereri* 'Vossii'**
(Voss's laburnum)
Deciduous, spreading tree. Leaves, consisting of 3 leaflets, are glossy, deep green. Pendent chains of large yellow flowers are borne in late spring and early summer.
! Z5–8 H8–3

Aralia elata 'Aureovariegata'
Laburnum anagyroides
Michelia figo, illus. p.89

TREES small AUTUMN INTEREST

YELLOW–ORANGE

Genista aetnensis
(Mount Etna broom)
Almost leafless, rounded tree with many slender, bright green branches and a profusion of fragrant, pealike, golden yellow flowers in midsummer.

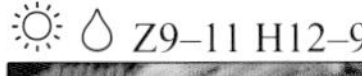
Z9–11 H12–9

Paraserianthes lophantha, syn. *Albizia distachya, A. lophantha*
Fast-growing, deciduous, spreading tree. Has fernlike, dark green leaves consisting of many leaflets. Creamy yellow flower spikes appear in spring-summer.

Z8–10 H10–8

Thevetia peruviana, syn. *T. neriifolia* (Yellow oleander)
Evergreen, erect tree with narrow, lance-shaped, rich green leaves and funnel-shaped yellow or orange-yellow flowers from winter to summer.

Z14–15 H12–10

Laburnum alpinum
(Scotch laburnum)
Deciduous, spreading tree. Leaves consist of 3 leaflets and are glossy, dark green. Long, slender chains of bright yellow flowers appear in late spring or early summer.

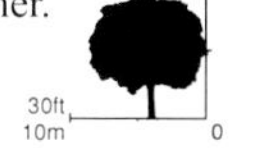
Z5–8 H8–5

Embothrium coccineum
(Chilean firebush)
Evergreen or semi-evergreen, upright, suckering tree with lance-shaped, glossy, deep green leaves. Clusters of brilliant orange-red flowers are borne in late spring and early summer.

pH Z8–11 H12–8

Caesalpinia gilliesii, illus. p.123
Plumeria rubra, illus. p.96
Tecoma stans, illus. p.96

WHITE–RED

Sorbus cashmiriana
Deciduous, spreading tree with leaves consisting of 6–9 pairs of rich green leaflets. Pink-flushed white flowers in early summer are followed by showy white fruits in autumn.

Z5–7 H7–5

***Cornus florida* 'Welchii'**
Deciduous, spreading tree. Bears a scattering of white bracts surrounding tiny flowers in spring. Midgreen leaves edged with white and pink turn red and purple in autumn.

Z5–8 H8–3

Arbutus unedo (Strawberry tree)
Evergreen, spreading tree or shrub with rough, brown bark and glossy, deep green leaves. Pendent, urn-shaped white flowers appear in autumn-winter as the previous season's strawberry-like red fruits ripen.

Z8–9 H9–6

OTHER RECOMMENDED PLANTS:
HOLLIES, illus. pp.98–9
Lagerstroemia indica, illus. p.91
Schinus molle
Schinus terebinthifolius
Sorbus insignis
Sorbus prattii

TREES small AUTUMN INTEREST

■ RED

Sorbus vilmorinii
Deciduous, spreading, arching, elegant tree. Leaves of 9–14 pairs of dark green leaflets become orange- or bronze-red in autumn. Has white blooms in late spring and small, deep pink fruits in autumn.

Z6–8 H8–6

Crataegus macrosperma* var. *acutiloba
Deciduous, spreading tree with broad, sharply toothed, dark green leaves. White flowers with red anthers in late spring are followed by bright red fruits in autumn.

Z4–8 H8–1

Photinia davidiana
Evergreen, spreading tree or large shrub with narrow, glossy, dark green leaves, older ones turning red in autumn. Sprays of white flowers in early summer are followed by clusters of bright red fruits in autumn.

Z7–9 H9–7

***Malus* 'Cowichan'**
Deciduous, spreading tree. Has dark green foliage, reddish purple when young. Pink flowers appear in midspring, followed by reddish purple crabapples.

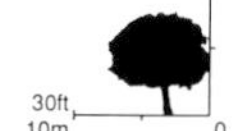

Z5–8 H8–5

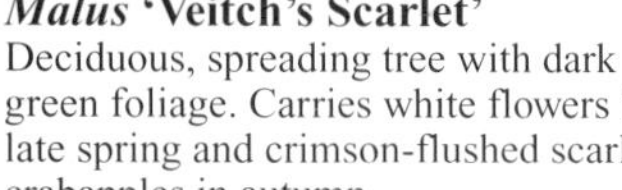

***Malus* 'Veitch's Scarlet'**
Deciduous, spreading tree with dark green foliage. Carries white flowers in late spring and crimson-flushed scarlet crabapples in autumn.

Z5–8 H8–5

Acer palmatum* var. *coreanum
Deciduous, bushy-headed tree or large shrub. Leaves are deeply lobed and midgreen, turning brilliant red in autumn. Small, reddish purple flowers are borne in spring.

Z6–8 H8–6

Cotoneaster frigidus
+ *Crataegomespilus dardarii* 'Jules d'Asnières'
Crataegus crus-galli
Crataegus ellwangeriana
Crataegus laevigata 'Punicea'
Crataegus monogyna
Crataegus phaenopyrum
HOLLIES, illus. pp.98–9
Malus 'Chilko'
Malus x *purpurea*
Malus 'Red Jade'
Rhus typhina
Sorbus sargentiana

RED

***Acer japonicum* 'Aconitifolium'**
Deciduous, bushy tree or large shrub. Deeply divided, midgreen leaves turn red in autumn. Reddish purple flowers appear in midspring.

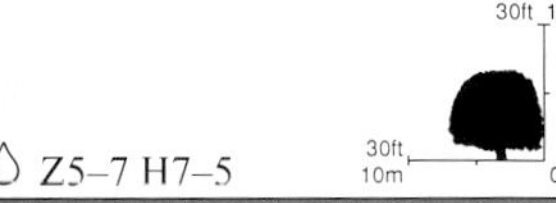

Z5–7 H7–5

***Acer japonicum* 'Vitifolium'**
Vigorous, deciduous, bushy tree or large shrub with large, rounded, lobed, midgreen leaves that turn brilliant red, orange, and purple in autumn.

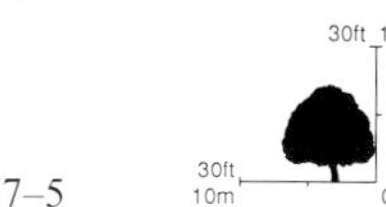

Z5–7 H7–5

Crataegus pedicellata
Deciduous, spreading tree with sharply toothed, lobed, dark green leaves that turn orange and red in autumn. White flowers with red anthers in late spring are followed by bright red fruits in autumn.

Z6–8 H8–6

***Malus* 'John Downie'**
Deciduous tree, narrow and upright when young and conical when mature. White flowers, borne amid bright green foliage in late spring, are followed by large, edible, red-flushed orange crabapples in autumn.

Z4–8 H8–1

Rhus trichocarpa
Deciduous, spreading tree. Large, ashlike leaves with 13–17 leaflets are pinkish when young, dark green in summer, and purple-red to orange in autumn. Bears pendent, bristly yellow fruits.

Z7–9 H9–7

Malus prunifolia
Deciduous, spreading tree. Has dark green leaves and fragrant white flowers in midspring. In autumn bears long-lasting, small, red or occasionally yellowish crabapples.

Z4–8 H8–1

***Acer tataricum* subsp. *ginnala*, syn. *A. ginnala* (Amur maple)**
Deciduous, spreading tree or large shrub. Clusters of fragrant, creamy white flowers are borne in early summer amid dainty, bright green leaves that turn red in autumn.

Z3–7 H7–1

TREES small AUTUMN INTEREST

RED

Acer triflorum
Slow-growing, deciduous, spreading tree with peeling, gray-brown bark. Leaves, composed of 3 leaflets, are dark green, turning brilliant orange-red in autumn. Clusters of tiny yellow-green flowers appear in late spring.

Z5–7 H7–5

***Malus* x *zumi* 'Calocarpa'**, syn. *M.* x *z.* var. *calocarpa*
Deciduous, spreading tree. Dark green leaves are sometimes deeply lobed. White flowers in late spring are followed by dense clusters of long-lasting, cherrylike, red crabapples in autumn.

Z4–8 H8–1

***Cornus* 'Eddie's White Wonder'**
Deciduous, spreading tree or shrub. Large white bracts surrounding insignificant flowers appear in late spring. Oval leaves are midgreen, turning red and purple in autumn.

Z5–8 H8–5

***Malus* 'Marshall Oyama'**
Deciduous, upright tree with dark green leaves. Pink-flushed white flowers borne in late spring are followed by a profusion of large, rounded crimson and yellow crabapples in autumn.

Z5–8 H8–5

ORANGE–YELLOW

***Malus* 'Professor Sprenger'**
Deciduous, rounded, dense tree. Dark green leaves turn yellow in late autumn. White flowers, pink in bud, open from mid- to late spring and are followed by orange-red crabapples in autumn.

Z4–8 H8–1

Plumeria rubra (Frangipani)
Deciduous, spreading tree or large shrub, sparingly branched. Has fragrant flowers in shades of yellow, orange, pink, red, and white, in summer-autumn.

Z14–15 H12–10

Tecoma stans, syn. *Bignonia stans*, *Stenolobium stans* (Yellow bells, Yellow elder)
Evergreen, rounded, upright tree or large shrub. Leaves have 5–13 leaflets. Has funnel-shaped yellow flowers from spring to autumn.

Z11–15 H12–10

Acer circinatum
Acer palmatum
Cornus florida
Crataegus x *lavallei* 'Carrierei'

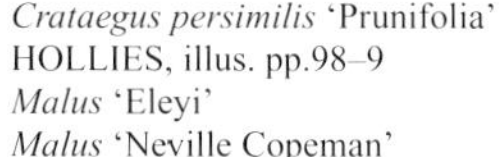

Crataegus persimilis 'Prunifolia'
HOLLIES, illus. pp.98–9
Malus 'Eleyi'
Malus 'Neville Copeman'

Malus niedzwetskyana
Malus 'Royalty', illus. p.89
Photinia nussia
Sorbus aucuparia 'Sheerwater Seedling'

Acer crataegifolium
Acer palmatum 'Sengo-kaku', illus. p.124
Annona reticulata
Malus toringoides

TREES small WINTER INTEREST

YELLOW

***Picrasma quassioides*,**
syn. *P. ailanthoides* (Quassia)
Deciduous, spreading tree with glossy, bright green leaves, composed of 9–13 leaflets, that turn brilliant yellow, orange, and red in autumn.

Z6–9 H9–6

***Malus* 'Golden Hornet',**
syn. *M.* x *zumi* 'Golden Hornet'
Deciduous, spreading tree with dark green foliage and open-cup-shaped, white flowers in late spring. In autumn, branches are weighed down by a profusion of golden yellow crabapples.

Z4–8 H8–1

Crataegus tanacetifolia
Cydonia oblonga 'Lusitanica'
Cydonia oblonga 'Vranja', illus. p.92
HOLLIES, illus. pp.98–9

WHITE–PINK

***Bauhinia variegata* 'Candida'**
Deciduous tree, rounded when young and spreading with age. Has broadly oval, deeply notched leaves and fragrant, pure white flowers, 4in (10cm) across, in winter-spring or sometimes later.

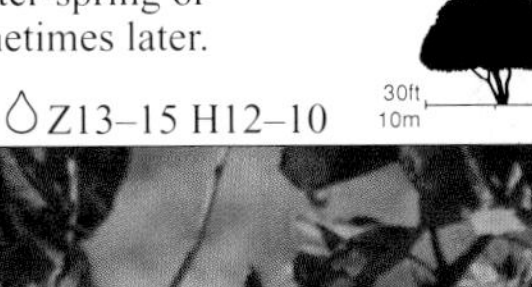

Z13–15 H12–10

Bauhinia variegata
Deciduous, rounded tree with broadly oval, deeply notched leaves. Fragrant magenta to lavender flowers, to 4in (10cm) across, appear in winter-spring, sometimes later.

Z13–15 H12–10

OTHER RECOMMENDED PLANTS:
Dombeya x *cayeuxii*, illus. p.88
Prunus incisa 'February Pink'
Prunus x *subhirtella* 'Autumnalis'

YELLOW

***Acacia pravissima* (Ovens wattle)**
Evergreen, spreading, arching tree or shrub. Has triangular, spine-tipped, silver-gray phyllodes (flat, leaflike stalks) and small heads of bright yellow flowers in late winter or early spring.

Z11–15 H12–10

Acacia baileyana
(Cootamundra wattle)
Evergreen, spreading, graceful tree with arching branches and finely divided, blue-gray leaves. Clusters of small, golden yellow flower heads appear in winter-spring.

Z10–11 H12–10

Tabebuia chrysotricha
(Golden trumpet tree)
Deciduous, round-headed tree with dark green leaves divided into 3–5 oval leaflets and rich yellow flowers, 3in (7cm) long, borne in late winter or early spring.

Z14–15 H12–10

Azara microphylla, illus. p.125

Hollies

The English holly, *Ilex aquifolium*, is one of the choicest evergreen trees, but there are many other hollies, including lesser-known *Ilex* cultivars, that make attractive garden plants. In size they range from tall specimen trees to small shrubs useful in the rock garden or for growing in containers. Hollies respond well to pruning, and many may be clipped to form good hedges. Leaves of different species and cultivars may be smooth-edged or spiny and vary considerably in color, several having gold, yellow, cream, white, or silver variegation. Small (often white) male and female flowers, borne on separate plants, are followed by attractive red, yellow, white, or black berries. In almost all cases hollies are dioecious; that is, the berries are borne only on female plants, so to obtain fruits it is usually necessary to grow plants of both sexes.

I. fargesii var. ***brevifolia*** ①

I. aquifolium **'Pyramidalis'** ①

I. aquifolium **'Argentea Marginata Pendula'** ①

I. **x *altaclerensis*** **'Camelliifolia'** ①

I. aquifolium **'Argentea Marginata'** ①

I. ciliospinosa ①

I. pernyi ①

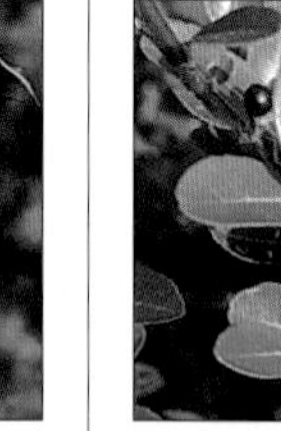

I. crenata var. ***paludosa*** ①

I. fargesii ①

I. aquifolium **'Scotica'** ①

I. **x *altaclerensis*** **'Lawsoniana'** ①

I. macrocarpa ①

I. **x *koehneana*** ①

I. crenata **'Helleri'** ①

I. **x *altaclerensis*** **'Balearica'** ①

I. aquifolium ①

I. crenata **'Latifolia'** ①

I. cornuta **'Burfordii'** ①

I. **x *altaclerensis*** **'N.F. Barnes'** ①

I. verticillata ①

I. opaca ①

I. **x *aquipernyi*** ①

I. crenata **'Convexa'** ①

I. **x *altaclerensis*** **'Belgica'** ①

I. **x *meserveae*** **'Blue Princess'** ①

I. aquifolium **'Silver Milkmaid'** ①

I. aquifolium 'Silver Queen' ⓘ

I. aquifolium **'Golden Milkboy'** ⓘ

I. aquifolium **'Madame Briot'** ⓘ

I. x *altaclerensis* **'Belgica Aurea'** ⓘ

I. aquifolium **'Crispa Aureopicta'** ⓘ

I. aquifolium **'Ovata Aurea'** ⓘ

I. aquifolium **'Aurifodina'** ⓘ

I. aquifolium **'Watereriana'** ⓘ

I. serrata f. *leucocarpa* ⓘ

I. aquifolium **'Pyramidalis Aureomarginata'** ⓘ

I.x altaclerensis **'Camelliifolia Variegata'** ⓘ

I. purpurea ⓘ

I. crenata **'Variegata'** ⓘ

I. pedunculosa ⓘ

***Pittosporum crassifolium* 'Variegatum'**

Evergreen, bushy-headed, dense tree or shrub with gray-green leaves edged with white. Clusters of small, fragrant, deep reddish purple flowers appear in spring.

Z9–11 H12–10 — 30ft 10m

Grevillea banksii

Evergreen, loosely branched tree or tall shrub. Has leaves divided into 5–11 slender leaflets, silky-downy beneath. Spiderlike red flowers appear in dense heads intermittently throughout the year.

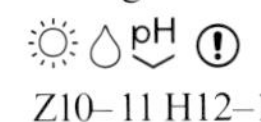

Z10–11 H12–10 — 30ft 10m

***Pittosporum eugenioides* 'Variegatum'**

Evergreen, columnar tree. Wavy-edged, glossy, dark green leaves have white margins. Honey-scented, pale yellow flowers are borne in spring.

Z9–10 H12–10 — 30ft 10m

***Dracaena marginata* 'Tricolor'**

Slow-growing, evergreen, upright tree or shrub with narrow, strap-shaped, cream-striped, rich green leaves, prominently edged with red.

Z11–12 H12–1 — 30ft 10m

Acer laxiflorum, syn. *A. pectinatum* subsp. *laxiflorum*

Deciduous, spreading tree with arching branches streaked white and green. In late summer has pale red, winged fruits. Pointed, red-stalked, dark green leaves turn orange in autumn.

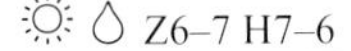

Z6–7 H7–6 — 30ft 10m

***Cordyline australis* 'Atropurpurea'**

Slow-growing, evergreen tree with purple to purplish green leaves. Has terminal clusters of white flowers in summer and small, globular white fruits in autumn.

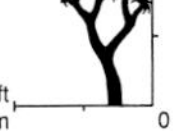

Z10–11 H12–1 — 30ft 10m

OTHER RECOMMENDED PLANTS:

Eriobotrya japonica
Kigelia africana
Pittosporum tenuifolium, illus. p.127
Polyscias guilfoylei 'Victoriae', illus. p.126

TREES small ALL YEAR INTEREST

GREY–GREEN

Leucadendron argenteum
(Silver tree)
Evergreen, conical to columnar tree, spreading with age. Leaves are covered with long, silky, white hairs. Has insignificant flowers set in silvery bracts in autumn-winter.

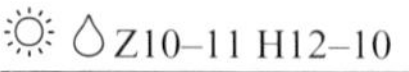
Z10–11 H12–10

Eucalyptus perriniana
(Spinning gum)
Fast-growing, evergreen, spreading tree with rounded, gray-blue young leaves joined around stems. Leaves on mature trees are long and pendulous. White flowers appear in late summer.

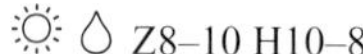
Z8–10 H10–8

Dracaena draco (Dragon tree)
Slow-growing, evergreen tree, eventually with a wide-branched head. Has stiff, lance-shaped, gray- or blue-green leaves. Mature trees bear clusters of orange berries, usually from mid- to late summer.

Z11–12 H12–1

Butia capitata,
syn. *Cocos capitata* (Jelly palm)
Slow-growing, evergreen palm. Feather-shaped leaves, composed of many leathery leaflets, are strongly arching to recurved, 6ft (2m) or more long.

Z11–12 H12–10

Meryta sinclairii (Puka, Pukanui)
Evergreen, round-headed tree with large, glossy, deep green leaves. Greenish flowers appear sporadically in spring to autumn, followed by berry-like black fruits.

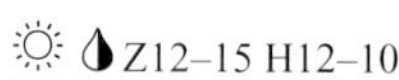
Z12–15 H12–10

Lithocarpus henryi
Slow-growing, evergreen, broadly conical tree with glossy, pale green leaves that are long, narrow, and pointed.

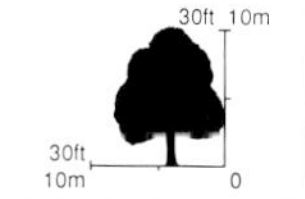

Z8–15 H12–10

***Carpinus betulus* 'Fastigiata'**,
syn. *C.b.* 'Pyramidalis'
Deciduous, erect tree with a very distinctive, flamelike outline that becomes more open with age. Oval, prominently veined, dark green leaves turn yellow and orange in autumn.

Z4–8 H8–3

Pittosporum dallii
Evergreen, rounded, dense tree or shrub. Has purplish stems and sharply toothed, deep green leaves. Clusters of small, fragrant, shallowly cup-shaped, white flowers are borne in summer.

Z9–15 H12–1

Dypsis lutescens
(Golden feather palm, Yellow palm)
Evergreen, suckering palm, forming clumps of robust, canelike stems. Has long, arching leaves of slender, yellowish green leaflets.

Z14–15 H12–1

Cyathea australis, syn. *Alsophila australis* (Australian tree fern)
Evergreen, upright tree fern with a robust, almost black trunk. Finely divided leaves, 6–12ft (2–4m) long, are light green, bluish beneath.

Z10–11 H12–7

Beaucarnea recurvata, syn. *Nolina recurvata*, *N. tuberculata*
(Elephant's foot, Pony-tail palm)
Slow-growing, evergreen tree or shrub with a sparsely branched stem. Recurving leaves, 3ft (1m) long, persist after turning brown.

Z12–15 H12–10

Acer griseum (Paperbark maple)
Deciduous, spreading tree with striking, peeling, orange-brown bark. Dark green leaves have 3 leaflets and turn red and orange in autumn.

Z4–8 H8–1

Castanopsis cuspidata
Eucalyptus ficifolia
HOLLIES, illus. pp.98–9
Howea forsteriana

Ligustrum lucidum 'Excelsum Superbum', illus. p.127
Pandanus tectorius
Pisonia umbellifera

Pittosporum crassifolium
Pittosporum tobira
Quercus alnifolia
Quercus coccifera

Ravenala madagascariensis
Sapium sebiferum
Schefflera digitata

CONIFERS large

BLUE–GREEN

***Abies concolor* 'Argentea'**, syn. *A.c.* 'Candicans'
Conical conifer with silvery foliage that contrasts well with dark gray bark. Oblong to ovoid, pale blue or green cones are 3–5in (8–12cm) long.

100ft 30m / 75ft 22.5m / 0

Z3–7 H7–1

Pinus* x *holfordiana
(Holford pine)
Broadly conical, open conifer with large cones, brown when ripe. Pendent, glaucous blue-green leaves are held in bundles of five.

100ft 30m / 75ft 22.5m / 0

Z6–7 H7–6

Cupressus cashmeriana
(Kashmir cypress)
Handsome, broadly conical conifer, spreading with age, with aromatic foliage borne in pendent, flat, glaucous blue sprays. Bears small, globose, dark brown, mature cones.

100ft 30m / 75ft 22.5m / 0

Z6–9 H9–6

x *Cupressocyparis leylandii* 'Haggerston Grey'
Vigorous, upright, columnar conifer, tapering at the apex. Has smooth bark, becoming stringy with age, flat sprays of pointed, gray-green leaves, and dark brown female cones. A popular screening plant.

100ft 30m / 75ft 22.5m / 0

Z6–9 H12–9

Cedrus atlantica* f. *glauca
(Blue Atlas cedar)
Conical conifer with silvery blue foliage that is very bright, especially in spring. Erect, cylindrical cones are produced in autumn. Widely planted as a specimen tree.

100ft 30m / 75ft 22.5m / 0

Z6–9 H9–6

Pinus peuce (Macedonian pine)
Upright conifer, forming a slender pyramid. Has dense, gray-green foliage and cylindrical green cones with white resin that ripen to brown in autumn. An attractive tree that grows consistently well in many sites.

100ft 30m / 75ft 22.5m / 0

Z5–9 H9–5

OTHER RECOMMENDED PLANTS:
Abies concolor
Abies forrestii, illus. p.105
Abies procera
Cedrus atlantica
Cedrus atlantica f. *fastigiata*
Cedrus deodara
Cedrus libani, illus. p.103
Chamaecyparis lawsoniana 'Triomf van Boskoop'
Chamaecyparis lawsoniana 'Wisselii'
Chamaecyparis nootkatensis
Cupressus lusitanica
Juniperus virginiana
Larix kaempferi
Picea pungens

CONIFERS large

GREEN

***Chamaecyparis lawsoniana* 'Intertexta'**
Elegant, weeping conifer with aromatic, gray-green foliage carried in lax, pendulous sprays. Old trees become columnar with some splayed branches.

Z5–9 H9–5 (100ft 30m; 75ft 22.5m; 0)

Pseudotsuga menziesii var. ***glauca***
(Blue Douglas fir)
Fast-growing, conical conifer with thick, grooved, corky, gray-brown bark, aromatic, glaucous blue-green leaves, and sharply pointed buds. Cones have projecting, 3-pronged bracts.

Z4–7 H7–1 (100ft 30m; 75ft 22.5m; 0)

Metasequoia glyptostroboides
(Dawn redwood)
Fast-growing, deciduous, upright conifer with fibrous, reddish bark. Soft, blue-green leaves turn yellow, pink, and red in autumn. Cones are globose to ovoid, 3/4in (2cm) long.

Z4–11 H12–1 (100ft 30m; 75ft 22.5m; 0)

Pinus strobus (Eastern white pine)
Conifer with an open, sparse, whorled crown. Has gray-green foliage and cylindrical cones. Smooth gray bark becomes fissured with age. Does not tolerate pollution.

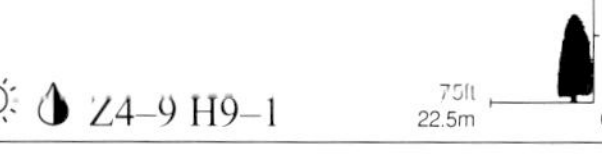

Z4–9 H9–1 (100ft 30m; 75ft 22.5m; 0)

Pinus coulteri
(Big-cone pine, Coulter pine)
Fast-growing conifer with large, broadly ovoid, prickly cones, each 2–4 1/2lb (1–2kg). Gray-green leaves in crowded clusters are sparsely set on branches. Grows in all soils, even heavy clay.

Z8–9 H9–8 (100ft 30m; 75ft 22.5m; 0)

Abies veitchii (Veitch fir)
Upright conifer with dark green leaves, silvery beneath, and cylindrical, violet-blue cones.

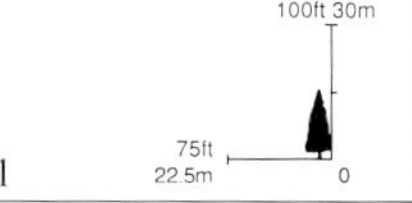

Z3–6 H6–1 (100ft 30m; 75ft 22.5m; 0)

Sequoiadendron giganteum
(Big tree, Giant redwood, Wellingtonia)
Very fast-growing, conical conifer. Has thick, fibrous, red-brown bark and sharp, bluish green leaves. It is one of the world's largest trees when mature.

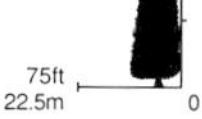

Z6–9 H9–4 (100ft 30m; 75ft 22.5m; 0)

Abies alba
Abies amabilis
Abies cephalonica
Abies homolepis
Abies nordmanniana
Araucaria heterophylla
Chamaecyparis lawsoniana 'Green Pillar', illus. p.107
Chamaecyparis obtusa
Chamaecyparis pisifera
Cryptomeria japonica
x *Cupressocyparis leylandii* 'Leighton Green'

Cedrus libani (Cedar of Lebanon)
Spreading conifer, usually with several arching stems. Branches carry flat layers of dark gray-green foliage and oblong to ovoid, grayish pink cones, 3–6in (8–15cm) long.

Z6–9 H9–3

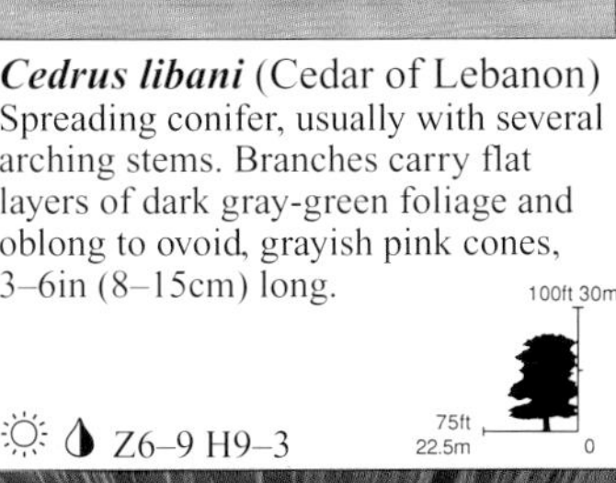

Pinus muricata (Bishop pine)
Fast-growing, often flat-topped conifer. Leaves are blue- or gray-green and held in pairs. Ovoid cones, 3–3½in (7–9cm) long, rarely open. Does particularly well in a poor, sandy soil.

Z7–9 H9–7

Picea omorika (Serbian spruce)
Narrow, conical conifer, resembling a church spire, with dark green leaves that are white below. Branches are pendulous and arch out at tips. Violet-purple cones age to glossy brown. Grows steadily in all soils.

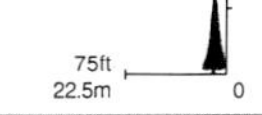

Z4–8 H8–1

Araucaria araucana
(Chile pine, Monkey puzzle)
Open, spreading conifer with gray bark, wrinkled like elephant hide. Has flattened and sharp, glossy, dark green leaves and 6in (15cm) long cones. Makes a fine specimen tree.

Z7–11 H12–6

Pinus ponderosa
(Western yellow pine)
Conical or upright conifer grown for its distinctive, deeply fissured bark, with smooth, brown plates, and bold, grayish green foliage. Bears ovoid, purplish brown cones.

Z5–8 H8–5

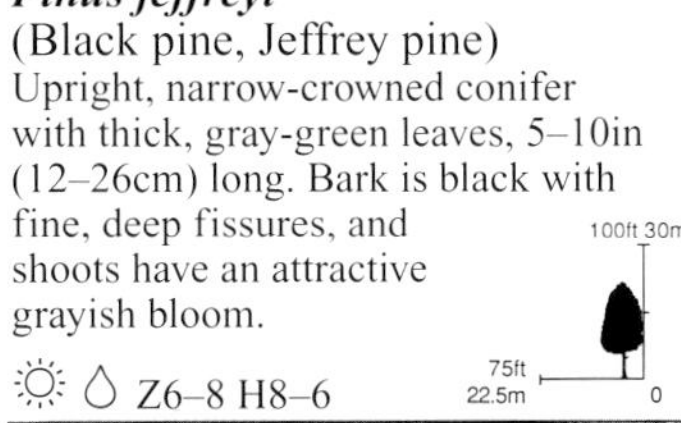

Pinus jeffreyi
(Black pine, Jeffrey pine)
Upright, narrow-crowned conifer with thick, gray-green leaves, 5–10in (12–26cm) long. Bark is black with fine, deep fissures, and shoots have an attractive grayish bloom.

Z6–8 H8–6

Ginkgo biloba (Maidenhair tree)
Long-lived, deciduous conifer, upright when young,spreading with age. Has fan-shaped, 5in (12cm) long, bright green leaves. Bears ill-smelling fruits with edible kernels in late summer and autumn if male and female plants are grown together. Fruit pulp can cause dermatitis.
(Named forms are male and don't produce fruit.)

Z5–9 H9–3

Pinus wallichiana, syn. *P. chylla, P. excelsa, P. griffithii*
(Bhutan pine, Himalayan pine)
Conical conifer with long, drooping, blue-green leaves in fives. Has smooth bark, gray-green on young trees, later fissured, and dark, cylindrical cones.

Z6–9 H9–5

Pinus pinaster
(Cluster pine, Maritime pine)
Vigorous, domed conifer with a long, branchless trunk. Has gray-green leaves and whorls of rich brown cones. Purple-brown bark is deeply fissured. Well-suited to a dry, sandy soil.

Z9–11 H12–10

Cupressus macrocarpa
Juniperus chinensis 'Keteleeri', illus. p.105
Larix decidua
Picea orientalis
Picea sitchensis
Picea smithiana
Pseudotsuga menziesii
Sequoia sempervirens
Thuja plicata
Thuja plicata 'Atrovirens'
Thujopsis dolabrata
Tsuga heterophylla

CONIFERS large

GREEN

Pinus nigra subsp. ***nigra***
(Austrian pine)
Broadly crowned conifer with well-spaced branches, often with several stems. Paired, dark green leaves are densely tufted. Tolerates exposed sites.

Z5–8 H8–4 — 100ft 30m; 75ft 22.5m; 0

Pinus radiata, syn. *P. insignis*
(Monterey pine)
Very fast-growing conifer, conical when young, domed when mature. Black bark contrasts well with soft, bright green leaves. Makes an excellent windbreak.

Z7–9 H9–7 — 100ft 30m; 75ft 22.5m; 0

Pinus heldreichii, syn.
P. heldreichii var. *leucodermis*, *P. leucodermis* (Bosnian pine)
Dense, conical conifer with dark green leaves held in pairs. Ovoid cones, 2–4in (5–10cm) long, are cobalt blue in their second summer, brown when ripe.

Z4–8 H8–1 — 100ft 30m; 75ft 22.5m; 0

GREEN–ORANGE

x ***Cupressocyparis leylandii* 'Castlewellan'**
Upright, vigorous conifer, slightly slower-growing than the species, grown for its bronze-yellow foliage.

! Z6–9 H9–3 — 100ft 30m; 75ft 22.5m; 0

***Picea orientalis* 'Skylands'**
Dense, upright, graceful conifer that retains the gold coloration of short, glossy leaves throughout the year. Narrowly oblong cones are dark purple, males turning brick-red in spring.

Z5–8 H8–5 — 100ft 30m; 75ft 22.5m; 0

Abies grandis (Giant fir, Grand fir)
Very vigorous, narrow, conical conifer with a neat habit. Midgreen leaves have an orange aroma when crushed. Cones, 3in (7–8cm) long, ripen red-brown. Makes a useful specimen tree.

Z5–6 H6–5 — 100ft 30m; 75ft 22.5m; 0

Picea abies
(Norway spruce)
Fast-growing, pyramidal conifer with dark green leaves. Narrow, pendulous, glossy, brown cones are 4–8in (10–20cm) long. Often used as a Christmas tree but less useful as an ornamental.

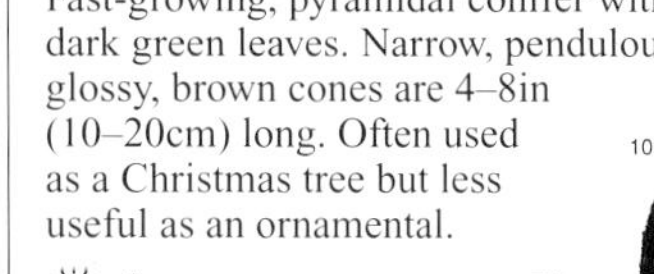

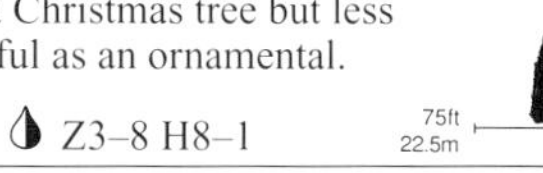

Z3–8 H8–1 — 100ft 30m; 75ft 22.5m; 0

x ***Cupressocyparis leylandii* 'Harlequin'**
(Variegated Leyland cypress)
Fast-growing, columnar conifer with a conical tip. Gray-green foliage, with patches of clear ivory-white, is held in plumelike sprays.

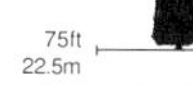

! Z6–9 H9–6 — 100ft 30m; 75ft 22.5m; 0

Taxodium distichum
(Bald cypress, Swamp cypress)
Deciduous, broadly conical conifer with small, globose to ovoid cones. Yewlike, fresh green leaves turn rich brown in late autumn. Grows in a very wet site, producing special breathing roots.

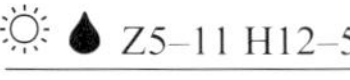

Z5–11 H12–5 — 100ft 30m; 75ft 22.5m; 0

x *Cupressocyparis leylandii* 'Robinson's Gold'
Picea orientalis 'Aurea'
Thuja plicata 'Aurea'

CONIFERS medium

BLUE–GREEN

***Picea pungens* 'Koster'**
Upright conifer with whorled branches. Has scaly gray bark and attractive, needlelike, silvery blue leaves that fade to green with age. Tends to suffer from attack by gall aphids.

Z3–8 H8–1

***Picea glauca* 'Coerulea'**
Dense, upright, conical conifer with needlelike, blue-green to silver leaves and ovoid, light brown cones.

Z3–6 H6–1

***Juniperus chinensis* 'Keteleeri'**
Dense, regular, slender, columnar conifer with scalelike, aromatic, grayish green leaves and peeling brown bark. A reliable, free-fruiting conifer for formal use.

Z3–9 H9–1

Picea breweriana
(Brewer's spruce)
Upright conifer with level branches and completely pendulous branchlets, to 6ft (2m) long. Leaves are thick and blue-green. Bears oblong purplish cones, 2½–3in (6–8cm) long.

Z6–8 H8–6

Picea engelmannii (Engelmann spruce, Mountain spruce)
Broadly conical conifer. Leaves encircle shoots and are prickly or soft, lush, and glaucous or bluish green. Bears small, cylindrical cones. Is good for a very poor site.

Z3–8 H8–1

Abies forrestii (Forrest fir)
Conical conifer with an open, whorled habit and smooth, silvery gray bark. Shoots are red-brown with spherical, white buds. Has dark green leaves, silvery white beneath, and ovoid-cylindrical, violet-blue cones.

Z5–6 H6–5

***Tsuga mertensiana* 'Glauca'**
Slow-growing, dwarf or medium-sized, columnar-conical conifer with red-brown shoots bearing spirally arranged, needlelike, flattened, glaucous, silver-gray leaves. Cones are yellow-green to purple, ripening to dark brown.

Z6–8 H8–6

***Chamaecyparis lawsoniana* 'Pembury Blue'**
Magnificent, conical conifer with aromatic, bright blue-gray foliage held in pendulous sprays.

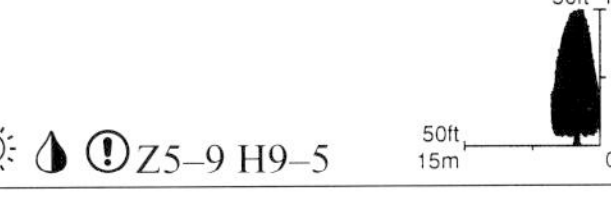

Z5–9 H9–5

Pinus parviflora
(Japanese white pine)
Slow-growing, conical or spreading conifer with fine, bluish foliage and purplish brown bark. Leaves are held in fives. Bears ovoid cones, 2–4in (5–10cm) long.

Z6–9 H9–6

OTHER RECOMMENDED PLANTS:
Abies lasiocarpa
Chamaecyparis lawsoniana 'Fletcheri'
Chamaecyparis lawsoniana 'Wisselii'
Chamaecyparis nootkatensis 'Pendula'
Chamaecyparis pisifera 'Squarrosa'
Cupressus arizonica var. *glabra*
Cupressus cashmeriana, illus. p.101
Juniperus recurva
Picea glauca
Picea likiangensis
Picea mariana
Picea pungens 'Hoopsii'
Pinus armandii
Pinus x *holfordiana*, illus. p.101
Tsuga mertensiana

CONIFERS medium

GREEN

Fitzroya cupressoides, syn. *F. patagonica* (Patagonian cypress)
Vase-shaped to sprawling conifer with red-brown bark that peels in long strips. White-lined, dark green leaves are held in open, pendulous, wiry sprays.

Z7–9 H9–7

Podocarpus salignus
Upright conifer. Leaves are willow-like, 2–4in (5–11cm) long, and glossy above. Attractive, fibrous, red-brown bark peels in strips.

Z8–11 H12–8

Pinus thunbergii
(Japanese black pine)
Rounded conifer, conical when young, with dark green leaves and gray-brown cones, 1½–2½in (4–6cm) long. Buds are covered with a silky cobweb of white hairs. Tolerates sea spray well.

Z5–8 H8–5

Pinus rigida (Northern pitch pine)
Conical conifer, often with sucker shoots from trunk. Twisted, dark green leaves are borne in threes. Ovoid to globose, red-brown cones, 1¼–3in (3–8cm) long, persist while open on the tree.

Z5–7 H7–5

Austrocedrus chilensis, syn. *Libocedrus chilensis* (Chilean incense cedar)
Conical conifer with flattened, feathery sprays of 4-ranked, small, dark green leaves, white beneath.

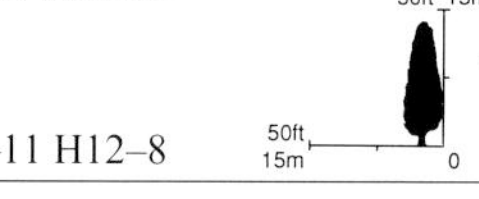

Z8–11 H12–8

Cunninghamia lanceolata
(Chinese fir)
Upright conifer, mop-headed on a dry site, with distinctive, thick and deeply furrowed, red-brown bark. Glossy green leaves are sharply pointed and lance-shaped.

Z7–9 H9–7

Phyllocladus trichomanoides
Slow-growing conifer, conical when young, developing a more rounded top with age. Leaflike, deep green, modified shoots, 4–6in (10–15cm) long, have 5–10 lobed segments.

Z12–15 H12–9

Sciadopitys verticillata
(Japanese umbrella pine)
Conical conifer with reddish brown bark. Deep green leaves, yellowish beneath, are whorled at the ends of shoots like umbrella spokes. Ovoid cones ripen over 2 years.

Z5–9 H9–4

Calocedrus decurrens, syn. *Libocedrus decurrens*
(Incense cedar)
Upright conifer with short, horizontal branches and flaky gray bark, brown beneath. Has flat sprays of aromatic, dark green leaves.

Z5–8 H8–1

Pinus cembra (Swiss stone pine)
Dense, conical conifer with dark green or bluish green leaves grouped in fives. Ovoid, bluish or purplish cones, 2½–3in (6–8cm) long, ripen brown.

Z3–7 H7–1

Pinus contorta var. ***latifolia***
(Lodgepole pine)
Conical conifer with bright green leaves, 2½–4in (6–9cm) long. Small, oval cones remain closed on the tree. Suitable for a wet or coastal site.

Z6–8 H8–6

Abies amabilis
Abies delavayi
Abies veitchii, illus. p.102
Chamaecyparis lawsoniana 'Kilmacurragh'
Juniperus chinensis
Picea omorika, illus. p.103
Pinus coulteri, illus. p.102
Pinus heldreichii, illus. p.104
Pinus wallichiana, illus. p.103
Saxegothaea conspicua
Taxus baccata
Taxus baccata 'Fastigiata'
Thuja orientalis
Tsuga caroliniana
Tsuga diversifolia

GREEN

***Pseudolarix amabilis*,**
syn. *P. kaempferi* (Golden larch)
Deciduous, open-crowned conifer, slow-growing when young. Has clusters of linear, fresh green leaves, 1–2½in (2.5–6cm) long, that gradually turn bright orange-gold in autumn.

Z5–9 H9–4

***Chamaecyparis lawsoniana* 'Green Pillar'**
Conical conifer with upright branches. Aromatic foliage is bright green and becomes tinged with gold in spring. Suitable for hedging, since it requires little clipping.

Z5–9 H9–5

Pinus banksiana (Jack pine)
Slender, conical, scrubby-looking conifer with fresh green leaves in twisted, divergent pairs. Curved cones, 1¼–2½in (3–6cm) long, point forward along shoots.

Z3–8 H8–1

Chamaecyparis thyoides
(White false cypress)
Upright conifer with aromatic, green or blue-gray leaves in rather erratic, fan-shaped sprays on very fine shoots. Cones are small, round, and glaucous blue-gray.

Z3–8 H8–1

Pinus contorta
(Beach pine, Shore pine)
Dense, conical or domed conifer. Has paired, bright green leaves and conical to ovoid cones, 1¼–3in (3–8cm) long. Well-suited to a windy, barren site, and it tolerates waterlogged ground.

Z6–8 H8–6

Picea morrisonicola
(Taiwan spruce)
Upright, conical conifer, becoming columnar with age. Needlelike, deep green leaves are pressed down on slender, pale brown shoots. Cones are cylindrical and 2–3in (5–7cm) long.

Z7–9 H9–7

Tsuga canadensis (Canada hemlock, Eastern hemlock)
Broadly conical conifer, often with several stems. Gray shoots have 2-ranked, dark green leaves, often inverted to show silver lines beneath. Cones are ovoid and light brown.

Z4–8 H8–1

Pinus halepensis (Aleppo pine)
Conical, open-crowned conifer with an open growth of bright green leaves, 2½–4½in (6–11cm) long, and ovoid, glossy, brown cones. Young trees retain glaucous juvenile needles for several years.

Z9–10 H10–9

Torreya californica
(California nutmeg)
Upright conifer with very prickly, glossy, dark green leaves, yellowish green beneath, similar to those of yew. Fruits are olivelike.

Z7–11 H12–7

***Chamaecyparis lawsoniana* 'Lanei'**
Upright conifer that forms a neat column of aromatic, golden yellow-tipped foliage.

Z5–9 H9–5

Pinus virginiana
(Scrub pine, Virginia pine)
Conifer of messy habit. Gray- to yellow-green leaves are 1½–3in (4–7cm) long. Young shoots have a pinkish white bloom. Bears oblong to conical, red-brown cones 2½in (6cm) long.

Z3–7 H7–1

Chamaecyparis obtusa 'Crippsii', illus. p.109
Chamaecyparis pisifera 'Filifera Aurea', illus. p.111
Chamaecyparis pisifera 'Plumosa'
Cupressus macrocarpa 'Goldcrest', illus. p.109
Juniperus chinensis 'Aurea'
Juniperus drupacea
Pinus densiflora
Taxus baccata 'Fastigiata Aurea'
Thuja occidentalis
Thuja occidentalis 'Fastigiata'
Thujopsis dolabrata

CONIFERS small

GREEN

***Picea mariana* 'Doumetii'**
Densely branched, globose or broadly conical conifer with short, needlelike, silvered, dark green leaves and pendulous, ovoid, purplish cones.

Z3–6 H6–1

Pinus aristata (Bristlecone pine)
Slow-growing, bushy conifer. Leaves are in bundles of 5, very dense and blue-white to gray-green, flecked with white resin. Ovoid cones, 1½–4in (4–10cm) long, have bristly prickles. Is the oldest-known living plant, over 4000 years old.

Z2–10 H9–1

Juniperus recurva
(Drooping juniper, Himalayan weeping juniper)
Slow-growing, conical conifer with aromatic, incurved, gray- or blue-green leaves and fleshy black berries. Smooth bark flakes in thin sheets.

Z7–11 H12–7

***Juniperus chinensis* 'Robust Green'**, syn. *J. virginiana* 'Robusta Green'
Slow-growing, columnlike, conical conifer, growing only 3in (7–8cm) per year, with aromatic, green foliage and small, gray-green juniper berries.

Z5–9 H9–1

***Chamaecyparis lawsoniana* 'Columnaris'**
Narrow, upright conifer that forms a neat column of aromatic, blue-gray foliage. Will tolerate poor soil and some clipping. Makes an attractive small specimen tree.

Z5–9 H9–5

***Pinus sylvestris* 'Fastigiata'**, syn. *P.s.* f. *fastigiata*
Upright conifer with erect branches forming a narrow, obelisk shape. Has flaky, red-brown bark, blue-green foliage, and conical cones. Suffers wind damage in an exposed site.

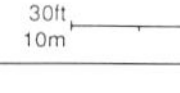

Z2–7 H7–1

Pinus bungeana (Lacebark pine)
Slow-growing, bushy conifer with dark green foliage, planted for its exquisite, gray-green bark that flakes to reveal creamy yellow patches, darkening to red or purple-brown.

Z4–7 H7–1

***Juniperus chinensis* 'Obelisk'**
Slender, irregularly columnar conifer. Has ascending branches and long, prickly, needlelike, aromatic, dark green leaves. Tolerates a wide range of soils and conditions but is particularly suited to a hot, dry site.

Z3–9 H9–1

OTHER RECOMMENDED PLANTS:
Cephalotaxus harringtonii
Chamaecyparis lawsoniana 'Ellwoodii'
Chamaecyparis lawsoniana 'Fletcheri'
Juniperus communis
Juniperus rigida
Juniperus scopulorum 'Skyrocket', illus. p.110
Juniperus squamata 'Meyeri'
Juniperus virginiana 'Hetzii'
Picea breweriana, illus. p.105
Pinus pumila
Podocarpus alpinus
Podocarpus macrophyllus
Pseudotsuga menziesii 'Fletcheri'
Taxus baccata 'Adpressa'

Pinus cembroides
(Mexican stone pine, Pinyon)
Slow-growing, bushy conifer, rarely more than 20–22ft (6–7m) high. Scaly bark is a striking silver-gray or grayish brown. Leaves, in twos and threes, are sparse and dark green to gray-green.

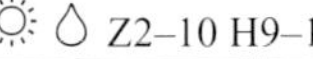

Z2–10 H9–1

***Thujopsis dolabrata* 'Variegata'**
Slow-growing, broadly conical, bushy conifer. Thick, hatchet-shaped leaves have irregular creamy patches above and are silvery beneath.

Z5–7 H7–5

Taxus cuspidata (Japanese yew)
Evergreen, spreading conifer. Leaves are dark green above, yellowish green beneath, sometimes becoming tinged red-brown in cold weather. Tolerates very dry and shady conditions.

Z4–7 H7–1

***Chamaecyparis obtusa* 'Crippsii'**
Attractive, conical conifer for the small garden, grown for its flattened sprays of aromatic, bright golden foliage. Bark is stringy and red-brown. Brown cones are round and ½in (1cm) across.

Z4–8 H8–1

Abies koreana (Korean fir)
Broadly conical conifer. Produces cylindrical, violet-blue cones when less than 3ft (1m) tall. Leaves are dark green above, silver beneath.

Z5–6 H6–5

Cryptomeria japonica
'Pyramidata'
Narrowly columnar or obelisk-shaped conifer. Foliage is blue-green when young, maturing to dark green.

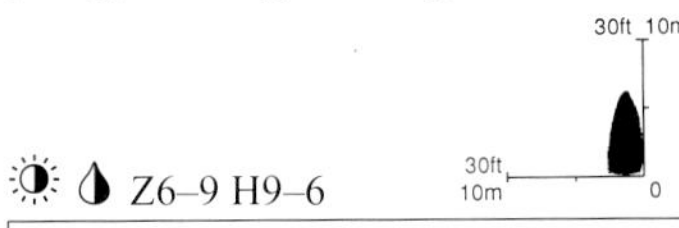

Z6–9 H9–6

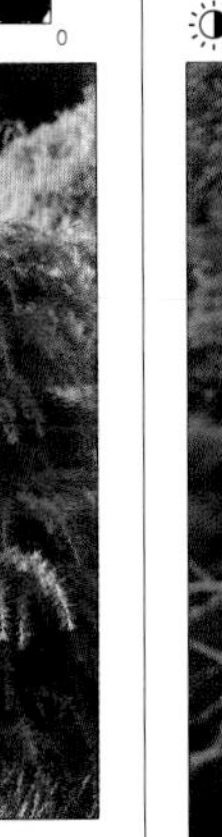

***Cedrus deodara* 'Aurea'**
Slow-growing, upright conifer with pendent branch tips and golden yellow leaves when young in spring-summer. Foliage matures to yellowish green. Makes a dramatic small specimen evergreen.

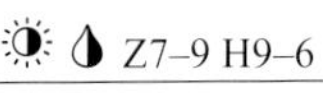

Z7–9 H9–6

***Cryptomeria japonica* 'Cristata'**
Conical conifer with twisted, curved shoots and soft, fibrous bark. Foliage is bright green, aging to brown.

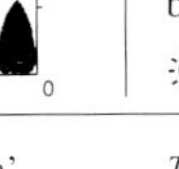

Z6–9 H9–6

Pinus pinea
(Stone pine, Umbrella pine)
Conifer with a rounded crown on a short trunk. Leaves are dark green, but blue-green, juvenile foliage is retained on young trees. Broadly ovoid cones ripen shiny brown; seeds are edible.

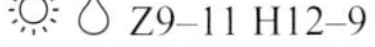

Z9–11 H12–9

Cupressus macrocarpa
'Goldcrest'
Fast-growing, conical conifer with aromatic, golden yellow foliage held in plumelike sprays that are useful in flower arrangements. Dislikes clipping.

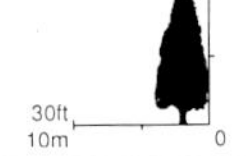

Z7–11 H12–7

Chamaecyparis obtusa 'Tetragona Aurea'
Taxus baccata Aurea Group, illus. p.111
Taxus baccata 'Semperaurea'
Thuja koraiensis
Thuja occidentalis 'Rheingold'
Tsuga canadensis 'Aurea', illus. p.111

Dwarf conifers

Dwarf conifers are valuable plants, especially for the small garden, requiring very little attention and providing year-round interest. They can be planted as features in their own right, displaying to advantage their varied shapes, habits, and often striking colors, or, in the rock garden for example, to provide scale or act as a foil for other plants such as bulbs. Several species and cultivars are spreading and good as groundcovers.

Almost all conifers are suitable for a wide range of growing conditions, although *Cedrus* and *Juniperus* do not tolerate shade, and *Juniperus* and *Pinus* are best for dry, freely drained, sandy soils. Most *Abies*, *Taxus*, *Thuja*, and *Tsuga* are particularly shade tolerant. Some species may be clipped to form a low hedge, but new growth will seldom be made if plants are cut back into wood more than 3 or 4 years old.

***Picea pungens* 'Montgomery'**

***Abies lasiocarpa* var. *arizonica* 'Compacta'**

***Juniperus squamata* 'Holger'**

***Pinus sylvestris* 'Doone Valley'**

***Picea* x *mariorika* 'Gnom'**

***Juniperus scopulorum* 'Springbank'**

***Juniperus squamata* 'Blue Star'**

***Juniperus horizontalis* 'Douglasii'**

***Juniperus squamata* 'Chinese Silver'**

***Abies concolor* 'Compacta'**

***Juniperus virginiana* 'Grey Owl'**

***Juniperus* x *pfitzeriana* 'Glauca'**

***Juniperus sabina* 'Mas'**

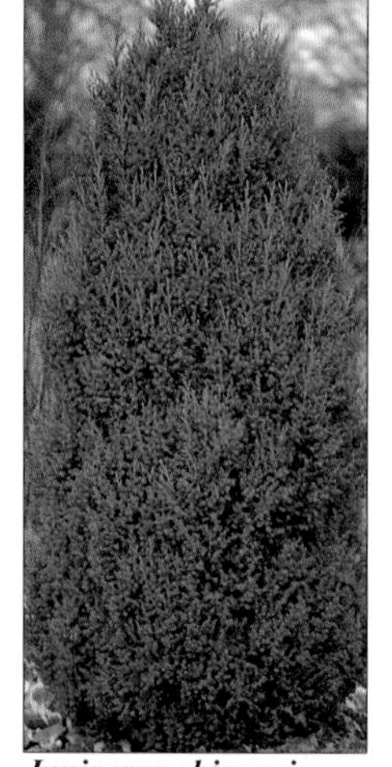
***Juniperus chinensis* 'Stricta'**

***Thuja occidentalis* 'Caespitosa'** ①

Microbiota decussata

Juniperus procumbens

***Juniperus scopulorum* 'Skyrocket'**

***Juniperus procumbens* 'Nana'**

***Juniperus horizontalis* 'Turquoise Spreader'**

***Abies balsamea* 'Nana'**

***Abies cephalonica* 'Meyer's Dwarf'**

***Pseudotsuga menziesii* 'Fretsii'**

***Abies lasiocarpa* 'Roger Watson'**

***Picea mariana* 'Nana'**

Podocarpus nivalis

***Juniperus sabina* 'Cupressifolia'**

***Juniperus recurva* 'Densa'**

Juniperus sabina* var. *tamariscifolia

***Picea abies* 'Ohlendorffii'**

***Picea abies* 'Reflexa'**

***Pinus sylvestris* 'Watereri'**

Pseudotsuga menziesii **'Oudemansii'**

Chamaecyparis lawsoniana **'Gnome'** ①

Chamaecyparis lawsoniana **'Minima'** ①

Picea abies **'Gregoryana'**

Chamaecyparis obtusa **'Intermedia'** ①

Juniperus × *pfitzeriana* **'William Pfitzer'**

Pinus heldreichii **'Smidtii'**

Chamaecyparis obtusa **'Nana Pyramidalis'** ①

Juniperus communis **'Hibernica'**

Picea glauca var. *albertiana* **'Conica'**

Cedrus libani **'Sargentii'**

Pinus heldreichii **'Compact Gem'**

Thuja orientalis **'Aurea Nana'** ①

Thuja orientalis **'Semperaurea'** ①

Thuja occidentalis **'Filiformis'** ①

Thuja plicata **'Hillieri'** ①

Juniperus chinensis **'Expansa Variegata'**

Juniperus × *pfitzeriana* **'Aurea'**

Juniperus chinensis **'Plumosa Aurea'**

Cryptomeria japonica **'Spiralis'**

Juniperus chinensis **'Blue and Gold'**

Cryptomeria japonica **'Sekkan-sugi'**

Taxus baccata **'Dovastonii Aurea'** ①

Chamaecyparis obtusa **'Nana Aurea'** ①

Chamaecyparis pisifera **'Filifera Aurea'** ①

Thuja plicata **'Collyer's Gold'** ①

Taxus baccata **Aurea Group** ①

Tsuga canadensis **'Aurea'**

Pinus sylvestris **'Aurea'**

Abies nordmanniana **'Golden Spreader'**

Thuja plicata **'Stoneham Gold'** ①

Cryptomeria japonica **'Elegans Compacta'**

Pinus sylvestris **'Gold Coin'**

SHRUBS

SHRUBS ARE AN ESSENTIAL element for year-round interest in your garden. Whether evergreen or deciduous, they provide a continuously changing but ever-present background to the more short-lived plants. While some shrubs can be left to grow unchecked, others must be trained or kept in good shape and health by regular and sometimes rigorous pruning.

Shrubs

Shrubs can form the backbone of your garden design, and with their variety of foliage, flowers, fruits, and stems, they also provide interest through the seasons.

What are shrubs?

Shrub are woody-stemmed, deciduous or evergreen plants that branch freely at or near ground level. Some shrubs grow to more than 20ft (6m) in height, although most species and cultivars attain less than half this size. There is some overlap between shrubs and other plant groups because larger shrubs, such as certain lilacs (*Syringa* species and cultivars), can be grown on a single stem and may equally well be classified as trees, while others, called subshrubs, are woody only at the base. In these, as in ceratostigma and fuchsias, softer top growth dies back annually with the onset of frost, and so they are commonly treated as herbaceous

Colorful underplanting
Above: The flowering stems of Exochorda x macrantha *'The Bride' arch gracefully above forget-me-nots* (Myosotis sylvatica), *daisies* (Bellis perennis), *and* Tulipa *'Couleur Cardinal'.*

Eye-catching impact
Above right: In a glorious design, the golds of senecio, Hypericum *'Hidcote', and violas are set against grays of santolina and* Stachys byzantina.

Contrasting foliage
Right: The golden leaves of Choisya ternata *Sundance ('Lich') provide a glowing contrast with those of* Cotinus coggygria *'Royal Purple' and* Berberis thunbergii *'Rose Glow'.*

perennials in cold climates. Some shrubs, such as *Jasminum nudiflorum*, can be wall trained, and many are grown like this because it is the neatest way to manage their sprawling growth. They also benefit from the additional warmth and shelter a wall provides, giving them some cold protection and helping their wood to mature and so improve flowering.

Choosing shrubs
When selecting a shrub, as with all garden plants, it is essential to match its hardiness and cultural requirements to the conditions in your garden. It is also vital to consider the shrub's final dimensions and to site it with sufficient room to mature. If you frequently have to prune a shrub to restrict its size, not only does this make unnecessary work but it may also weaken that shrub's resistance to disease.

Designing with shrubs
Whatever the size or style of your garden, the permanent woody structure of shrubs can form a key element in its framework. Many shrubs can be used formally or informally to create hedges, enclosures, or screens. These range in size from small, domed forms, as in *Buxus microphylla* 'Green Pillow', to almost treelike rhododendrons and amelanchiers.

The low, spreading, prostrate, or mat-forming shrubs, such as *Juniperus procumbens* or *Dryas octopetala*, or the tiered branch structure of shrubs such as *Viburnum plicatum* 'Mariesii' and *Cornus alternifolia*, provide strong horizontal lines in a composition. These can be planted so they lead the eye to contrasting rounded forms, found in many hebes or *Spiraea japonica* and its variants, or to the strong verticals of *Eucryphia* x *nymansensis* 'Nymansay' or *Viburnum dentatum*, which may also be used to make a focal point.

Certain shrubs are ideal for topiary, but they must be able to tolerate close regular clipping and preferably have small leaves that permit fine surface texture and detailed shaping. Suitable shrubs include boxwood (*Buxus*), yew (*Taxus*), and *Lonicera nitida*.

The gracefully arching or weeping shrubs, among them *Kerria japonica* 'Pleniflora', *Forsythia suspensa*, *Kolkwitzia amabilis*, and *Malus* x *arnoldiana*, can be used to link other elements in a border.

Shrubs can be planted alone in a shrub border or in a mixed border as a backdrop to the more transient bulbs, annuals, and perennials. Compact shrubs such as bay (*Laurus*) are ideal for growing in containers.

Shrubs in containers
Left: In this planting of elegant simplicity, the pink flowers of a standard fuchsia are echoed by an underplanting of pastel impatiens. After a prolonged display, the container can be moved under cover for protection during winter.

Maintaining year-round interest
Providing fragrance and color during the warmer months is relatively simple. For autumn interest, pyracanthas, cotoneasters, and *Skimmia japonica* have brilliantly colored fruits, while most species of euonymus, disanthus, and enkianthus offer vibrant foliage. In winter, the spirits can be lifted with the fragrant flowers of witch hazel (*Hamamelis*) and *Lonicera* x *purpusii* and the colored stems of *Cornus alba* 'Sibirica' and *Rubus biflorus*, while the swags of *Garrya elliptica* come into their own in the soft, pale winter sun.

Size categories used within this group		
Large	**Medium**	**Small**
over 10ft (3m)	5–10ft (1.5–3m)	up to 5ft (1.5m)

Autumn color
Top: Hamamelis x intermedia *'Diane', which bears its spidery, deep red flowers from mid- to late winter, gives added ornamental value with its vibrant autumn color.*

Winter interest
Above: The vivid red berries of a female Skimmia japonica, *produced where plants of both sexes are grown together, persist well into winter and are at their most perfect when rimed with frost.*

☐ WHITE

***Osmanthus delavayi*,**
syn. *Siphonosmanthus delavayi*
Evergreen, rounded, bushy shrub with arching branches. Has small, glossy, dark green leaves and a profusion of very fragrant, tubular white flowers from mid- to late spring.

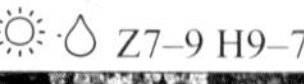
Z7–9 H9–7

Pieris japonica
Evergreen, rounded, bushy, dense shrub with glossy, dark green foliage that is bronze when young. Produces drooping racemes of white flowers during spring.

Z6–8 H8–6

Amelanchier lamarckii
Deciduous, spreading shrub. Young leaves unfold bronze as abundant sprays of star-shaped white flowers open from mid- to late spring. Foliage matures to dark green then turns brilliant red and orange in autumn.

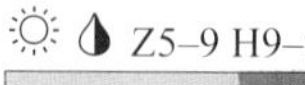
Z5–9 H9–5

***Osmanthus* x *burkwoodii*,**
syn. x *Osmarea burkwoodii*
Evergreen, rounded, dense shrub. Glossy foliage is dark green and sets off a profusion of small, very fragrant white flowers from mid- to late spring.

Z7–9 H9–7

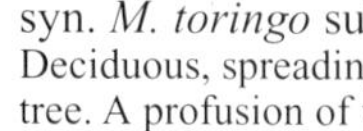

***Malus sargentii*,**
syn. *M. toringo* subsp. *sargentii*
Deciduous, spreading shrub or small tree. A profusion of white flowers in late spring is followed by long-lasting, deep red fruits. The oval, dark green leaves are sometimes lobed.

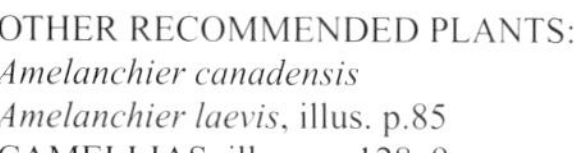
Z4–8 H8–1

Anopterus glandulosus
Evergreen, bushy shrub or, occasionally, small tree. Has narrow, glossy, dark green leaves, amid which clusters of cup-shaped white or pink flowers appear from mid- to late spring.

Z11–13 H12–11

***Viburnum plicatum* 'Mariesii'**
Deciduous, bushy, spreading shrub with tiered branches clothed in dark green leaves that turn reddish purple in autumn. Large, rounded heads of flowers with white bracts appear in late spring and early summer.

Z4–8 H8–1

Dipelta yunnanensis
Deciduous, arching shrub with peeling bark and glossy leaves. In late spring produces tubular, creamy white flowers marked orange inside.

Z7–9 H9–1

Staphylea pinnata (Bladdernut)
Deciduous, upright shrub that in late spring carries clusters of white flowers, tinted pink with age, followed by bladderlike green fruits. Foliage is divided and bright green.

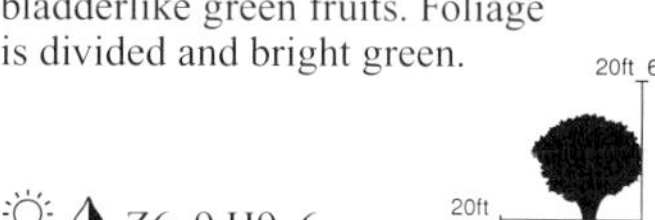

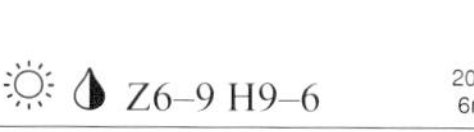
Z6–9 H9–6

OTHER RECOMMENDED PLANTS:
Amelanchier canadensis
Amelanchier laevis, illus. p.85
CAMELLIAS, illus. pp.128–9
Exochorda racemosa
Halesia tetraptera
HEATHERS, illus. pp.178–9
LILACS, illus. p.120
Lophomyrtus bullata
MAGNOLIAS, illus. p.75
Parrotiopsis jacquemontiana
Pieris formosa 'Henry Price'
Poncirus trifoliata
Prunus laurocerasus
RHODODENDRONS, illus. pp.132–4
Staphylea colchica

Dipelta floribunda
Vigorous, deciduous, upright, treelike shrub with peeling, pale brown bark. Fragrant, pale pink flowers marked yellow inside open in late spring and early summer. Has pointed, midgreen leaves.

Z6–9 H9–6

Viburnum* x *carlcephalum
Deciduous, rounded, bushy shrub. In late spring large, rounded heads of pink buds open to fragrant white flowers. These are borne amid dark green foliage that often turns red in autumn.

Z6–8 H8–5

Enkianthus campanulatus
Deciduous, bushy, spreading shrub with red shoots and tufts of dull green leaves that turn bright red in autumn. Small, bell-shaped, red-veined, creamy yellow flowers appear in late spring.

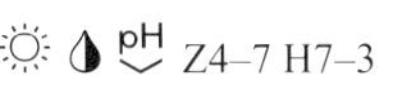
Z4–7 H7–3

***Staphylea holocarpa* 'Rosea'**
Deciduous, upright shrub or spreading, small tree. From mid- to late spring it bears pink flowers, followed by bladderlike, pale green fruits. Bronze young leaves mature to blue-green.

Z6–9 H9–6

***Photinia* x *fraseri* 'Birmingham'**
Evergreen, upright, bushy, dense shrub with glossy, dark green leaves that are bright purple-red when young. Broad heads of small white flowers are carried in late spring.

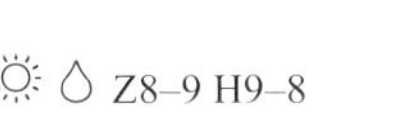
Z8–9 H9–8

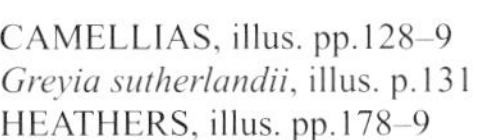
CAMELLIAS, illus. pp.128–9
Greyia sutherlandii, illus. p.131
HEATHERS, illus. pp.178–9
MAGNOLIAS, illus. p.75

Photinia x *fraseri* 'Red Robin'
Pieris 'Forest Flame'
Prunus triloba 'Multiplex'
RHODODENDRONS, illus. pp.132–4

Daphniphyllum macropodum, syn. *D. himalense* subsp. *macropodum*
Evergreen, bushy, dense shrub with thick shoots and dark green leaves. Small flowers, green on female plants and purplish on male plants, appear in late spring.

Z7–11 H12–7

Corylopsis glabrescens
Deciduous, open shrub. Oval leaves with bristlelike teeth along margins are dark green above, blue-green beneath. Drooping spikes of fragrant, bell-shaped, pale yellow flowers appear in mid-spring on bare branches.

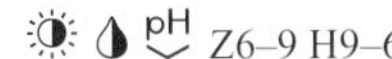
Z6–9 H9–6

Berberis darwinii
(Darwin's barberry)
Vigorous, evergreen, arching shrub. Has small, glossy, dark green leaves and a profusion of rounded, deep orange-yellow flowers from mid- to late spring, followed by bluish berries.

Z7–9 H9–7

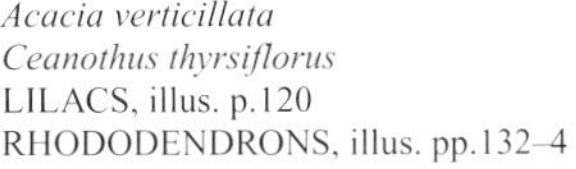
Acacia verticillata
Ceanothus thyrsiflorus
LILACS, illus. p.120
RHODODENDRONS, illus. pp.132–4

 WHITE

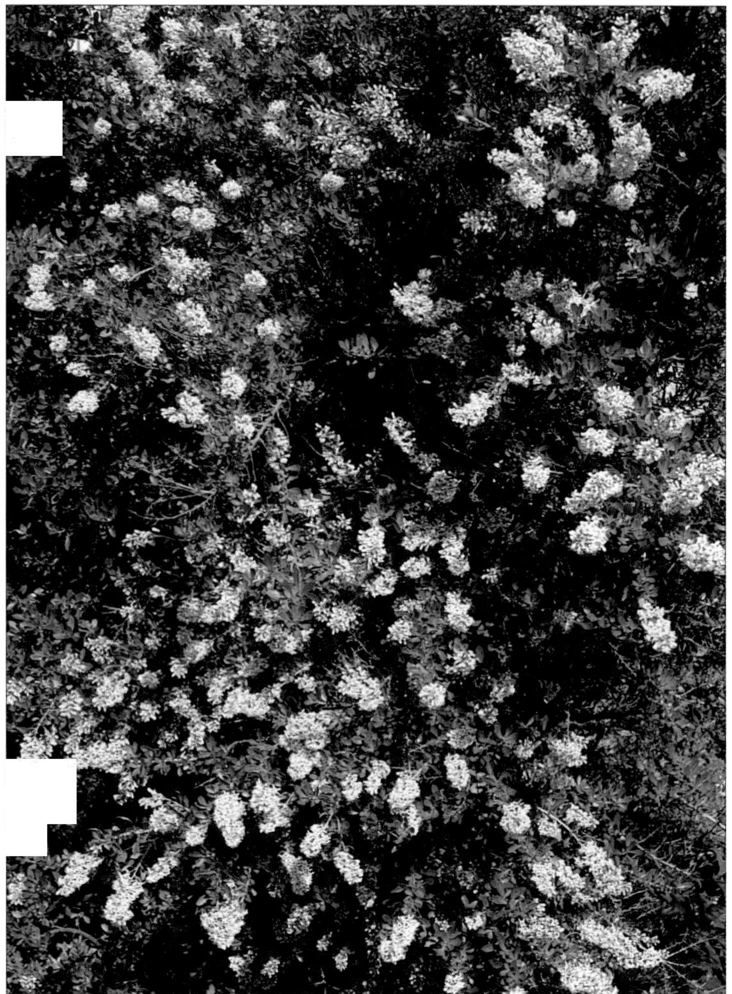

Escallonia leucantha
Evergreen, upright shrub. Narrow, oval, glossy, dark green leaves set off large racemes of small, shallowly cup-shaped white flowers in midsummer.

Z8–9 H9–8

Ligustrum sinense
Deciduous or semi-evergreen, bushy, upright shrub with oval, pale green leaves. Large panicles of fragrant, tubular white flowers are borne in midsummer, followed by small, purplish black fruits.

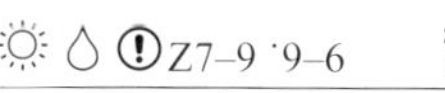 Z7–9 ’9–6

***Buddleja davidii* 'Peace'**
Vigorous, deciduous, arching shrub. Long, pointed, dark green leaves, white-felted beneath, set off long plumes of fragrant white flowers from midsummer to autumn.

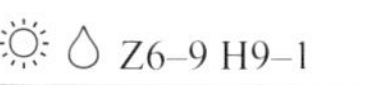 Z6–9 H9–1

Olearia virgata
Evergreen, arching, graceful shrub with very narrow, dark gray-green leaves. Produces an abundance of small, star-shaped white flower heads in early summer, arranged in small clusters along stems.

Z7–11 H12–7

Styrax officinalis
Deciduous, loose to dense shrub or small tree. Fragrant, bell-shaped white flowers appear in early summer among oval, dark green leaves with grayish white undersides.

pH Z14–15 H12–10

***Escallonia* 'Iveyi'**
Evergreen, upright shrub. Glossy, dark green foliage sets off large racemes of fragrant, tubular, pure white flowers with short lobes, borne from mid- to late summer.

Z8–9 H9–8

Viburnum rhytidophyllum
Vigorous, evergreen, open shrub with long, narrow, deep green leaves. Dense heads of small, creamy white flowers in late spring and early summer are succeeded by red fruits that mature to black.

Z5–8 H8–5

Sparrmannia africana
(African hemp)
Evergreen, erect shrub or small tree. Has large, shallowly lobed leaves and clusters of white flowers with yellow and red-purple stamens in late spring and summer.

Z12–15 ’12–10

Xanthoceras sorbifolium
Deciduous, upright shrub or small tree with bright green leaves divided into many slender leaflets. In late spring and early summer produces spikes of white flowers with red patches inside at the base of the petals.

Z5–8 H8–5

OTHER RECOMMENDED PLANTS:
Clethra arborea
Clethra barbinervis, illus. p.138
Cotoneaster lacteus, illus. p.125
Cotoneaster 'Rothschildianus'
Cotoneaster x *watereri* 'John Waterer'
Deutzia scabra, illus. p.136
Elaeocarpus cyaneus
Eucryphia milliganii, illus. p.137
HEATHERS, illus. pp.178–9
Hibiscus syriacus 'Diana'
HYDRANGEAS, illus. p.144
LILACS, illus. p.120
Lophomyrtus bullata
MAGNOLIAS, illus. p.75
Melaleuca armillaris

***Brugmansia* x *candida*,**
syn. *Datura* x *candida*
Semi-evergreen, rounded shrub or small tree. Has downy, oval leaves and strongly scented, pendulous white flowers, sometimes cream or pinkish, in summer-autumn.

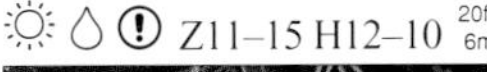

Z11–15 H12–10

***Luma apiculata*,** syn. *Amomyrtus luma, Myrceugenia apiculata, Myrtus apiculata, M. luma*
Strong-growing, evergreen shrub with peeling, golden brown and gray-white bark and cup-shaped flowers amid aromatic leaves in summer-autumn.

Z9–11 H12–10

Abutilon vitifolium* var. *album
Fast-growing, deciduous, upright shrub. Large, bowl-shaped white blooms, pink-tinged when young, are freely borne in late spring and early summer amid deeply lobed, sharply toothed, gray-green leaves.

Z8–9 H9–8

Abelia triflora
Vigorous, deciduous, upright shrub with pointed, deep green leaves. Small, extremely fragrant white flowers, tinged pale pink, appear in midsummer.

Z7–9 H9–7

Chionanthus virginicus
(Fringe tree)
Deciduous, bushy shrub or small tree. Has large, glossy, dark green leaves that turn yellow in autumn. Drooping sprays of fragrant white flowers appear in early summer.

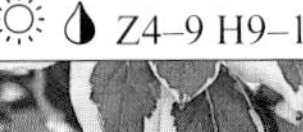

Z4–9 H9–1

***Cornus mas* 'Variegata'**
Deciduous, bushy, dense shrub or small tree. Small, star-shaped yellow flowers appear on bare branches in early spring before white-edged, dark green leaves develop.

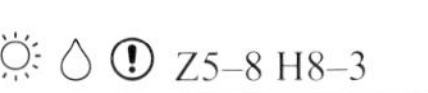

Z5–8 H8–3

Holodiscus discolor
Fast-growing, deciduous, arching shrub. Has lobed, toothed, dark green leaves and large, pendent sprays of small, creamy white flowers in midsummer.

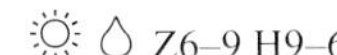

Z6–9 H9–6

Aesculus parviflora
(Bottlebrush buckeye)
Deciduous, open shrub. Leaves are bronze when young, dark green in summer, and yellow in autumn. Panicles of red-centered white flowers appear from mid- to late summer.

Z5–9 H9–4

Olearia macrodonta
Osmanthus fragrans
Philadelphus magdalenae
Prunus lusitanica
Pyracantha atalantioides
Pyracantha 'Mohave'
RHODODENDRONS, illus. pp.132–4
Rubus 'Benenden', illus. p.136
Viburnum 'Pragense', illus. p.139

Lilacs

The heady scent of the lilac (*Syringa*) epitomizes late spring. The flowers are produced in abundance and are excellent for cutting. Apart from the classic lilacs and mauves, colors include white, pink, cream, and rich red-purple; double forms are also available. Most lilacs grown in gardens are vigorous shrubs derived from *S. vulgaris*. They may eventually become treelike and are therefore best planted at the back of a shrub border or in groups in a wild garden; they may also be used as an informal hedge. Where space is restricted, choose from the smaller-growing species, some of which may be grown in containers. Spent flower heads are best removed, but care should be taken not to damage the new shoots that form below the flowers. Otherwise, little pruning is required, though older, straggly plants may be rejuvenated by hard pruning in winter.

***S. vulgaris* 'Madame Florent Stepman'**

***S. vulgaris* 'Jan van Tol'**

***S. vulgaris* 'Madame Lemoine'**

***S.* x *hyacinthiflora* 'Cora Brandt'**

***S.* x *chinensis* 'Alba'**

***S.p.* subsp. *microphylla* 'Superba'**

S. yunnanensis

***S. vulgaris* 'Michel Buchner'**

***S. vulgaris* 'Monge'**

***S. vulgaris* 'Masséna'**

***S. meyeri* 'Palibin'**

***S. vulgaris* 'Maréchal Foch'**

***S. vulgaris* 'Paul Thirion'**

***S. vulgaris* 'Charles Joly'**

S.* x *persica

***S. vulgaris* 'Madame F. Morel'**

***S. vulgaris* 'Decaisne'**

***S. vulgaris* 'Mrs. Edward Harding'**

***S.* x *hyacinthiflora* 'Clarke's Giant'**

***S. vulgaris* 'Président Grévy'**

***S. vulgaris* 'Congo'**

***S. vulgaris* 'Madame Antoine Buchner'**

***S.* x *hyacinthiflora* 'Esther Staley'**

***S.* x *hyacinthiflora* 'Blue Hyacinth'**

***S. vulgaris* 'Primrose'**

WHITE–PINK

Clethra delavayi
Deciduous, open shrub with lance-shaped, toothed, rich green leaves. Dense, spreading clusters of pink buds opening to scented white flowers appear in midsummer.

Z7–9 H9–7

Tamarix ramosissima, syn. *T. pentandra*
Deciduous, arching, graceful shrub or small tree with tiny, narrow, blue-green leaves. In late summer and early autumn bears large, upright plumes of small pink flowers.

Z3–8 H8–1

Abelia* x *grandiflora
Vigorous, semi-evergreen, arching shrub. Has glossy, dark green foliage and an abundance of fragrant, pink-tinged white flowers from midsummer to midautumn.

Z6–9 H9–1

Nerium oleander (Oleander)
Evergreen, upright, bushy shrub with leathery, deep green leaves. Clusters of pink, white, red, apricot, or yellow flowers appear from spring to autumn, often on dark red stalks.

Z13–15 H12–1

***Kolkwitzia amabilis* 'Pink Cloud'**
Deciduous, arching shrub that bears a mass of bell-shaped pink flowers amid small, oval, midgreen leaves in late spring and early summer.

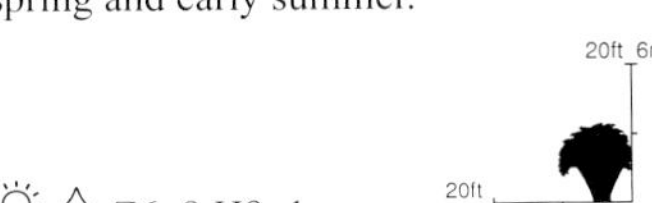

Z6–9 H9–1

RED–PURPLE

***Buddleja davidii* 'Royal Red'**
Vigorous, deciduous, arching shrub. Has long, pointed, dark green leaves with white-felted undersides, and plumes of fragrant, rich purple-red flowers from midsummer to autumn.

Z6–9 H9–6

Acer palmatum* f. *atropurpureum
Deciduous, bushy-headed shrub or small tree with lobed, reddish purple foliage that turns brilliant red in autumn. Small, reddish purple flowers are borne in midspring.

Z5–8 H8–2

***Buddleja davidii* 'Harlequin'**
Vigorous, deciduous, arching shrub. Leaves are long, pointed, and dark green with creamy white margins. Plumes of fragrant red-purple flowers appear from midsummer to autumn.

Z6–9 H9–1

Buddleja colvilei
Deciduous, arching shrub, often tree-like with age. Large, white-centered, deep pink to purplish red flowers are borne in drooping racemes amid dark green foliage during early summer.

Z8–9 H9–8

Malvaviscus arboreus
(Sleepy mallow)
Vigorous, evergreen, rounded shrub. Serrated, bright green leaves are soft-haired. Has bright red flowers with protruding stamens in summer-autumn.

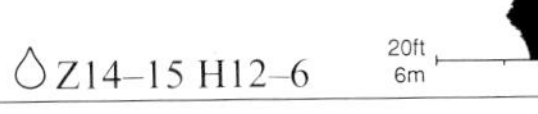

Z14–15 H12–6

***Cotinus coggygria* 'Notcutt's Variety'**
Deciduous, bushy shrub with deep reddish purple foliage. Long-lasting purplish pink plumes of massed, small flowers are produced in late summer.

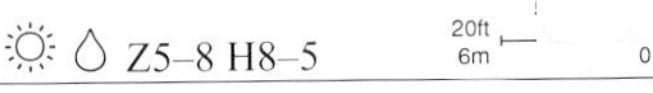

Z5–8 H8–5

Aralia elata 'Variegata'
Cornus alternifolia 'Argentea', illus. p.89
Ligustrum lucidum
LILACS, illus. p.120
MAGNOLIAS, illus. p.75
Rothmannia capensis
Sorbaria kirilowii
Viburnum cinnamomifolium

Acca sellowiana, illus. p.143
Buddleja colvilei 'Kewensis'
Callistemon viminalis
Cercis canadensis 'Forest Pansy', illus. p.91
Cotinus coggygria 'Royal Purple'
Erythrina x *bidwillii*, illus. p.143
Erythrina crista-galli, illus. p.143
HEATHERS, illus. pp.178–9

SHRUBS large SUMMER INTEREST

RED–PURPLE

***Acer palmatum* var. *heptalobum* 'Rubrum'**
Deciduous, bushy-headed shrub or small tree. Large leaves are red when young, bronze in summer, and brilliant red, orange, or yellow in autumn. Has small reddish purple flowers in midspring.

Z6–8 H8–6 20ft 6m

***Prunus spinosa* 'Purpurea'**
Deciduous, dense, spiny shrub or small tree. Bright red young leaves become deep reddish purple. Bears saucer-shaped, pale pink flowers from early to midspring, followed by blue-bloomed black fruits.

Z5–9 H9–5 20ft 6m

***Corylus maxima* 'Purpurea'**
Vigorous, deciduous, open shrub or small tree with deep purple leaves and purplish catkins with yellow anthers that hang from bare branches in late winter. Edible nuts mature in autumn.

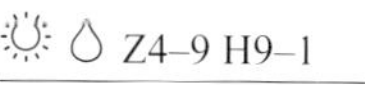

Z4–9 H9–1 20ft 6m

Buddleja alternifolia
Deciduous, arching shrub that can be trained as a weeping tree. Has slender, pendent shoots and narrow, gray-green leaves. Neat clusters of fragrant lilac-purple flowers appear in early summer.

Z6–9 H10–1 20ft 6m

Tibouchina urvilleana
(Glory bush)
Evergreen, slender-branched shrub. Velvet-haired leaves are prominently veined. Has satiny blue-purple flowers in clusters from summer to early winter.

pH Z13–15 H12–10 20ft 6m

***Acer palmatum* var. *heptalobum* 'Lutescens'**
Deciduous, bushy-headed shrub or small tree. Large, lobed leaves become clear yellow in autumn. In midspring produces small reddish purple flowers, followed by winged fruits.

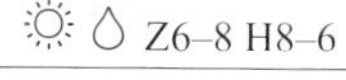

Z6–8 H8–6 20ft 6m

LILACS, illus. p.120
Melaleuca hypericifolia
RHODODENDRONS, illus. pp.132–4
Sambucus nigra 'Guincho Purple'

GREEN–YELLOW

Decaisnea fargesii
Deciduous, semi-arching, open shrub with blue-bloomed shoots and large, deep green leaves of paired leaflets. Racemes of greenish flowers in early summer are followed by pendent, sausage-shaped bluish fruits.

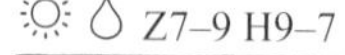

Z7–9 H9–7 20ft 6m

Elaeagnus angustifolia (Oleaster)
Deciduous, bushy shrub or spreading, small tree. Has narrow, silvery gray leaves and small, fragrant, creamy yellow flowers with spreading lobes in early summer, followed by small, oval yellow fruits.

Z2–8 H8–1 20ft 6m

Paliurus spina-christi
(Christ's thorn, Jerusalem thorn)
Deciduous, bushy shrub with slender, thorny shoots. Has oval, glossy, bright green leaves, tiny yellow flowers in summer, and curious, woody, winged fruits in autumn.

Z7–9 H9–7 20ft 6m

Acer shirasawanum 'Aureum', illus. p.92
Aralia elata 'Aureovariegata'
Buddleja x *weyeriana*
Caesalpinia pulcherrima
Colutea arborescens, illus. p.146
Dendromecon rigida, illus. p.147
Fremontodendron californicum
Fremontodendron mexicanum

***Brugmansia* x *candida* 'Grand Marnier'**
Evergreen, robust shrub with large, oval to elliptic leaves. Pendent, flared, trumpet-shaped apricot flowers open from an inflated calyx in summer.

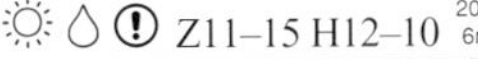

Z11–15 H12–10 20ft 6m

Brugmansia sanguinea
Semi-evergreen, erect to rounded shrub or small tree with lobed young leaves. Has large, trumpet-shaped yellow and orange-red flowers from late summer to winter.

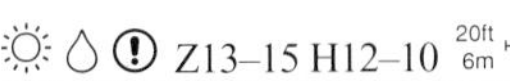

Z13–15 H12–10 20ft 6m

Crotalaria agatiflora
(Canary-bird bush)
Evergreen, loose, somewhat spreading shrub with gray-green leaves. Racemes of greenish yellow flowers appear in summer and also intermittently during the year.

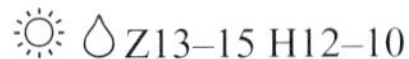

Z13–15 H12–10 20ft 6m

***Cytisus battandieri*,**
syn. *Argyrocytisus battandieri*
(Moroccan broom, Pineapple broom)
Semi-evergreen, open shrub. Leaves have 3 silver-gray leaflets. Pineapple-scented yellow flowers appear in summer.

Z7–9 H9–7 20ft 6m

***Caesalpinia gilliesii*,**
syn. *Poinciana gilliesii*
Deciduous, open shrub or small tree. Has finely divided, dark green leaves and bears short racemes of yellow flowers with long red stamens from mid- to late summer.

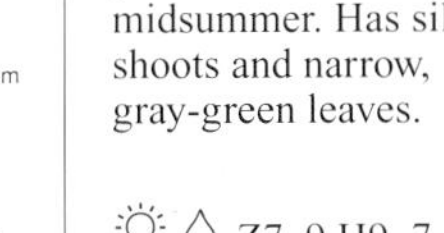

Z12–15 H12–1 20ft 6m

Genista cinerea
Deciduous, arching shrub that produces an abundance of fragrant, pealike, yellow blooms from early to midsummer. Has silky young shoots and narrow, gray-green leaves.

Z7–9 H9–7 20ft 6m

Buddleja globosa
Deciduous or semi-evergreen, open shrub with dark green foliage. Dense, rounded clusters of orange-yellow flowers are carried in early summer.

Z7–9 H9–7 20ft 6m

***Fremontodendron* 'California Glory'**
Very vigorous, evergreen or semi-evergreen, upright shrub. Has rounded, lobed, dark green leaves and large, bright yellow flowers from late spring to midautumn.

Z8–11 H12–8 20ft 6m

Ligustrum ovalifolium 'Aureum'
Luma apiculata 'Glanleam Gold'
Osmanthus fragrans f. *aurantiacus*
Sambucus canadensis 'Aurea'

Senna didymobotrya, illus. p.147
Spartium junceum, illus. p.147
Tecoma stans, illus. p.96

SHRUBS large AUTUMN INTEREST

RED–YELLOW

Cotoneaster 'Cornubia'
Vigorous, semi-evergreen, arching shrub. Clusters of white flowers, produced in early summer amid dark green foliage, are followed by large, pendent clusters of decorative, bright red fruits.

Z6–8 H8–6

Rhus typhina 'Dissecta'
Deciduous, spreading, open shrub or small tree with velvety shoots. Fernlike, dark green leaves turn brilliant orange-red in autumn, when deep red fruit clusters are also borne.

Z3–8 H8–1

Cotinus 'Flame'
Deciduous, bushy, treelike shrub with dark green leaves that turn brilliant orange-red in autumn. From late summer, showy, plumelike, purplish pink flower heads appear above the foliage.

Z5–8 H8–5

Hippophäe rhamnoides
(Sea buckthorn)
Deciduous, bushy, arching shrub or small tree with narrow silvery leaves. Tiny yellow flowers borne in midspring are followed in autumn by bright orange berries on female plants.

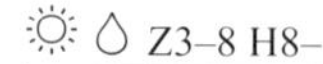

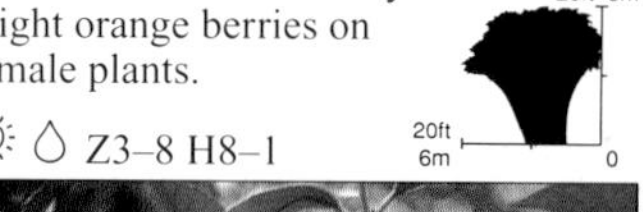

Z3–8 H8–1

Acer palmatum var. _heptalobum_
Deciduous, bushy-headed shrub or small tree with large, lobed, midgreen leaves that turn brilliant red, orange, or yellow in autumn. Bears small reddish purple flowers in midspring.

Z6–8 H8–6

Hamamelis vernalis 'Sandra'
Deciduous, upright, open shrub. Bears small, fragrant, spidery, deep yellow blooms in late winter and early spring. Oval leaves are purple when young, midgreen in summer, and purple, red, orange, and yellow in autumn.

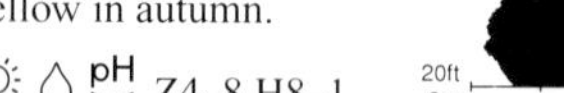

pH Z4–8 H8–1

Euonymus myrianthus
Evergreen, bushy shrub with pointed, leathery, midgreen leaves. Dense clusters of small, greenish yellow flowers in summer are followed by yellow fruits that open to show orange-red seeds.

Z7–9 H9–7

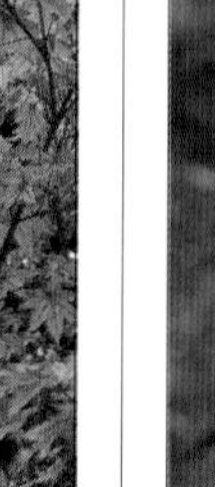

Acer palmatum 'Sango-kaku',
syn. _A.p._ 'Senkaki'
(Coralbark maple)
Deciduous, bushy-headed shrub or tree. Has coral-pink young shoots in winter. Palmate, orange-yellow leaves turn green, then pink to yellow in autumn.

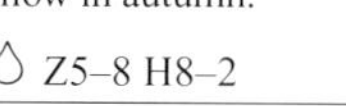

Z5–8 H8–2

Pyracantha atalantioides 'Aurea'
Vigorous, evergreen, upright, spiny shrub, arching with age. Has narrowly oval, glossy, dark green leaves and white flowers in early summer, followed by large clusters of small yellow berries in early autumn.

Z6–9 H9–6

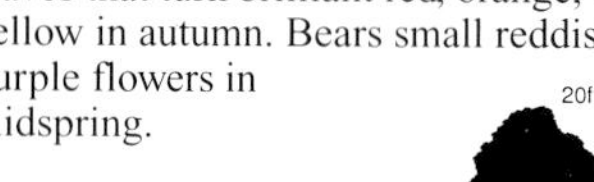

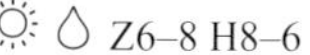

OTHER RECOMMENDED PLANTS:
Acer japonicum 'Vitifolium', illus. p.95
Acer tataricum subsp. _ginnala_, illus. p.95
Cotinus coggygria 'Royal Purple'
Cotinus obovatus
Cotoneaster x _watereri_ 'John Waterer'
Decaisnea fargesii, illus. p.122
Hibiscus mutabilis
Photinia davidiana, illus. p.94
Pyracantha 'Golden Charmer', illus. p.149
Pyracantha 'Mohave'
Sorbus aucuparia 'Fastigiata'
Tibouchina urvilleana, illus. p.122
Viburnum betulifolium, illus. p.148

YELLOW

***Mahonia* x *media* 'Charity'**
Evergreen, upright, dense shrub with large leaves composed of many spiny, dark green leaflets. Slender, upright, later spreading spikes of fragrant yellow flowers are borne from early autumn to early spring.

Z8–9 H9–8

***Mahonia* x *media* 'Buckland'**
Evergreen, upright, dense shrub. Has large leaves with many spiny, dark green leaflets. Clustered, upright then spreading, long, branched spikes of fragrant yellow flowers appear from late autumn to early spring.

Z8–9 H9–8

Hamamelis virginiana
(Common witch hazel)
Deciduous, open, upright shrub. Small, fragrant, spidery yellow flowers with 4 narrow petals open in autumn as leaves fall. Broadly oval leaves turn yellow in autumn.

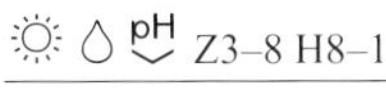
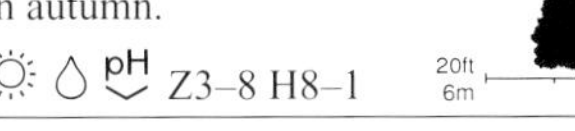

Z3–8 H8–1

Brugmansia aurea
Cotoneaster 'Rothschildianus'
HOLLIES, illus. pp.98–9
Tecoma stans, illus. p.96

RED

Cotoneaster lacteus
Evergreen, arching shrub suitable for hedging. Oval, dark green leaves set off shallowly cup-shaped white flowers from early to midsummer. Long-lasting red fruits are carried in large clusters in autumn-winter.

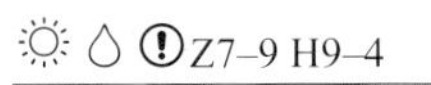

Z7–9 H9–4

***Hamamelis* x *intermedia* 'Diane'**
Deciduous, open, spreading shrub that produces fragrant, spidery, deep red flowers on bare branches from mid- to late winter. Broadly oval, midgreen leaves turn yellow and red in autumn.

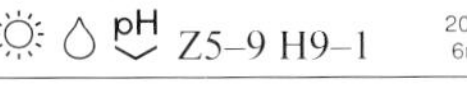

Z5–9 H9–1

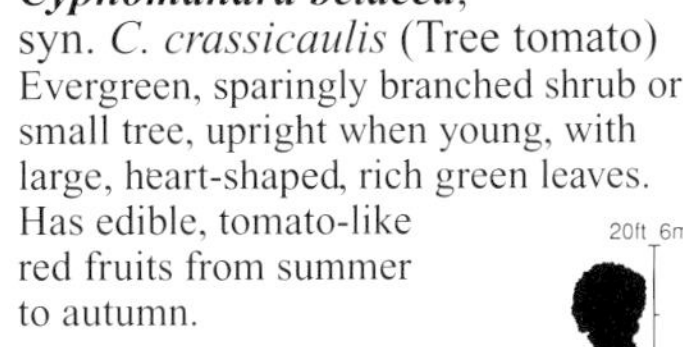

***Cyphomandra betacea*,**
syn. *C. crassicaulis* (Tree tomato)
Evergreen, sparingly branched shrub or small tree, upright when young, with large, heart-shaped, rich green leaves. Has edible, tomato-like red fruits from summer to autumn.

Z13–15 H12–10

OTHER RECOMMENDED PLANTS:
Euphorbia pulcherrima, illus. p.150
Euphorbia pulcherrima 'Paul Mikkelson'
HEATHERS, illus. pp.178–9

GREEN–YELLOW

Garrya elliptica (Silk-tassel bush)
Evergreen, bushy, dense shrub with leathery, wavy-edged, dark green leaves. Gray-green catkins, longer on male than female plants, are borne from midwinter to early spring.

Z8–11 H12–8

Azara microphylla
Elegant, evergreen shrub or small tree. Has tiny, glossy, dark green leaves and small clusters of vanilla-scented, deep yellow flowers in late winter and early spring.

Z8–11 H12–10

***Corylus avellana* 'Contorta'**
Deciduous, bushy shrub with curiously twisted shoots and broad, sharply toothed, midgreen leaves. In late winter, bare branches are covered with pendent, pale yellow catkins.

Z3–9 H9–1

Cornus mas
Hamamelis x *intermedia* 'Pallida'
Hamamelis japonica
Mahonia napaulensis

YELLOW

***Hamamelis* x *intermedia* 'Arnold Promise'**
Deciduous, open, spreading shrub. Large, fragrant, spidery yellow flowers with 4 narrow, crimped petals appear from mid- to late winter. Broadly oval, green leaves turn yellow in autumn.

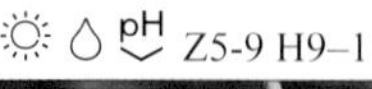
Z5-9 H9-1

***Hamamelis japonica* 'Sulphurea'**
Deciduous, upright, open shrub. In midwinter, fragrant, spidery, pale yellow flowers with 4 narrow, crimped petals are borne on leafless branches. Broadly oval, dark green leaves turn yellow in autumn.

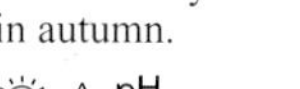
Z5-9 H9-1

***Hamamelis mollis* 'Coombe Wood'**
Deciduous, open, spreading shrub. From mid- to late winter bears very fragrant, spidery, golden yellow flowers with 4 narrow petals. Broadly oval, midgreen leaves turn yellow in autumn.

Z5-9 H9-1

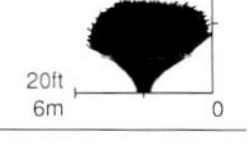

Acacia pravissima, illus. p.97
Buddleja madagascariensis
Jasminum nudiflorum, illus. p.151
Senecio grandifolius

SHRUBS large ALL YEAR INTEREST

WHITE–GREEN

***Dracaena fragrans* Deremensis Group 'Warneckei'**
Slow-growing, evergreen shrub. Erect to arching, lance-shaped leaves are banded gray-green and cream.

Z14–15 H12–1

Ligustrum ovalifolium
Vigorous, evergreen or semi-evergreen, upright, dense shrub with glossy, mid-green leaves. Dense racemes of small, rather musty-scented, tubular white flowers appear in midsummer, followed by black fruits.

Z6–8 H8–6

***Prunus lusitanica* 'Variegata'**
Slow-growing, evergreen, bushy shrub with reddish purple shoots. Has oval, glossy, dark green, white-edged leaves. Fragrant, shallowly cup-shaped, creamy white flowers in summer are followed by purple fruits.

Z7–9 H9–4

Prunus lusitanica* subsp. *azorica
Evergreen, bushy shrub with reddish purple shoots and bright green leaves, red when young. Bears spikes of small, fragrant white flowers in summer, followed by purple fruits.

Z7–9 H9–7

***Tetrapanax papyrifer*, syn. *Fatsia papyrifera* (Rice-paper plant)**
Evergreen, upright, suckering shrub. Long-stalked, circular leaves are deeply lobed. Has bold sprays of small creamy white flowers in summer and black berries in autumn-winter.

Z6–11 H12–6

***Griselinia littoralis* 'Variegata'**
Evergreen, upright shrub of dense, bushy habit. Leathery leaves are gray-green, marked with bright green and creamy white. Bears inconspicuous yellow-green flowers in late spring.

Z8–9 H9–8

***Pittosporum* 'Garnettii'**
Evergreen, columnar or conical shrub of dense, bushy habit. Rounded gray-green leaves, irregularly edged creamy white, become tinged with deep pink in cold weather. May bear small, greenish purple flowers in spring-summer.

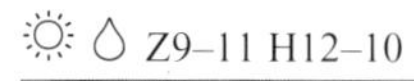
Z9–11 H12–10

***Polyscias guilfoylei* 'Victoriae' (Lace aralia)**
Slow-growing, evergreen, rounded shrub or small tree with leaves that are divided into several oval to rounded, serrated, white-margined, deep green leaflets.

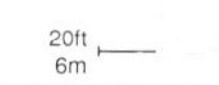
Z14–15 H12–1

OTHER RECOMMENDED PLANTS:
Cordyline fruticosa 'Imperialis'
Dracaena marginata 'Tricolor', illus. p.99
Elaeagnus x *ebbingei*
Euonymus japonicus 'Macrophyllus'
Garrya elliptica 'James Roof'
Grevillea banksii, illus. p.99
Griselinia littorális 'Dixon's Cream'
HOLLIES, illus. pp.98–9
Pittosporum crassifolium 'Variegatum', illus. p.99
Synadenium compactum var. *rubrum*

SHRUBS medium SPRING INTEREST

GREEN–YELLOW

Schefflera elegantissima, syn. *Aralia elegantissima, Dizygotheca elegantissima* (False aralia)
Evergreen, upright, open shrub. Large leaves have 7–10 coarsely toothed, lustrous, gray-green, sometimes bronze-tinted leaflets.

Z14–15 H12–1

Brachyglottis repanda
(Pukapuka, Rangiora)
Evergreen, bushy shrub or tree, upright when young, with robust, downy white stems. Has veined leaves, white beneath, and fragrant white flower heads in summer.

Z12–15 H12–10

Pittosporum tenuifolium
Evergreen, columnar, later rounded shrub or small tree with purple shoots and wavy-edged, oval, glossy, midgreen leaves. Bears honey-scented purple flowers in late spring.

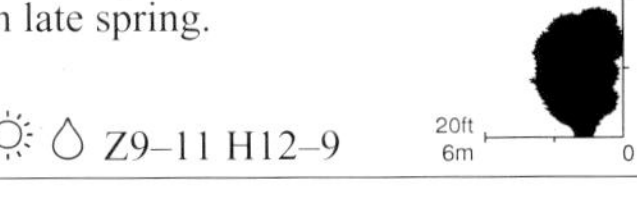

Z9–11 H12–9

***Ligustrum lucidum* 'Excelsum Superbum'**
Evergreen, upright shrub or small tree. Large, glossy, bright green leaves are marked with pale green and yellow-edged. Small, tubular white flowers open in late summer and early autumn.

Z8–11 H12–8

***Osmanthus heterophyllus* 'Aureomarginatus'**
Evergreen, upright shrub. Sharply toothed, hollylike, glossy, bright green leaves have yellow margins. Small, fragrant white flowers are produced in autumn.

Z7–9 H9–7

***Elaeagnus pungens* 'Maculata'**, syn. *E.p.* 'Aureovariegata'
Evergreen, bushy, slightly spiny shrub. Glossy dark green leaves are marked with a central, deep yellow patch. Very fragrant, urn-shaped, creamy white flowers open from mid- to late autumn.

Z7–9 H9–7

WHITE

Pieris floribunda
(Fetterbush, Mountain fetterbush)
Evergreen, bushy, dense, leafy shrub with oval, glossy, dark green leaves. Greenish white flower buds appear in winter, opening to urn-shaped white blooms from early to midspring.

Z5–8 H8–5

Fothergilla major, syn. *F. monticola*
Deciduous, upright shrub with glossy, dark green leaves, slightly bluish white beneath, that turn red, orange, and yellow in autumn. Tufts of fragrant white flowers appear in late spring.

Z4–8 H9–2

Enkianthus perulatus
Deciduous, bushy, dense shrub. Dark green leaves turn bright red in autumn. A profusion of small, pendent, urn-shaped, white flowers is borne in midspring.

Z6–8 H8–6

***Pieris japonica* 'Scarlett O'Hara'**
Evergreen, rounded, bushy, dense shrub. Young foliage and shoots are bronze-red, leaves becoming glossy, dark green. Produces sprays of white flowers in spring.

Z6–8 H8–6

Choisya ternata
(Mexican orange blossom)
Evergreen, rounded, dense shrub with aromatic, glossy, bright green leaves composed of 3 leaflets. Clusters of fragrant white blooms open in late spring and often again in autumn.

Z8–10 H10–8

Beaucarnea recurvata, illus. p.100
Castanopsis cuspidata
Cycas revoluta, illus. p.152
Elaeagnus x *ebbingei* 'Gilt Edge'
Euonymus japonicus 'Ovatus Aureus'
Pittosporum tenuifolium 'Margaret Turnbull'
Schefflera arboricola
Schefflera digitata

OTHER RECOMMENDED PLANTS:
Buddleja asiatica
CAMELLIAS, illus. pp.128–9
Gardenia thunbergia
Osmanthus x *burkwoodii*, illus. p.116
Pieris japonica Taiwanensis Group
RHODODENDRONS, illus. pp.132–4
Viburnum x *burkwoodii* 'Anne Russell'

Camellias

These evergreen shrubs have long been valued for their luxuriant, rich green foliage and masses of showy flowers borne mainly in winter and spring. Once thought suitable only for greenhouses, many camellias are hardy in marginal areas climates if grown in sheltered positions, although blooms may suffer frost and rain damage. Camellias require acidic soil. The main flower forms are illustrated below.

Single – shallowly cup-shaped flowers each have not more than 8 petals arranged in a single row, and a conspicuous, central boss of stamens.

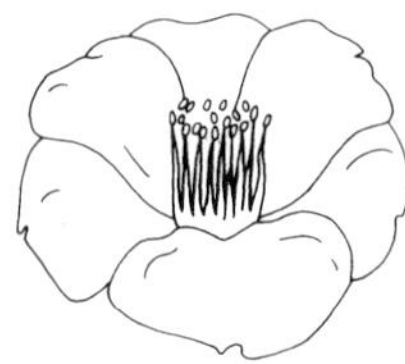

Semi-double – cup-shaped flowers each have 2 or more rows of 9–21 regular or irregular petals and conspicuous stamens.

Anemone – rounded flowers have one or more rows of large, outer petals lying flat or undulating; the domed center has a mass of intermingled petaloids and stamens.

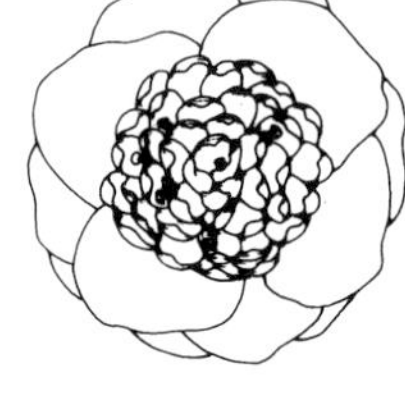

Peony-form – rounded, domed flowers have usually irregular petals intermingled with petaloids and stamens.

Rose-form – cup-shaped flowers each have several rows of overlapping petals and open to reveal stamens in the center.

Formal double – rounded flowers have many rows of regular, neatly overlapping petals that obscure stamens. **Irregular double** forms are similar but often have more loosely arranged, sometimes irregular, petals.

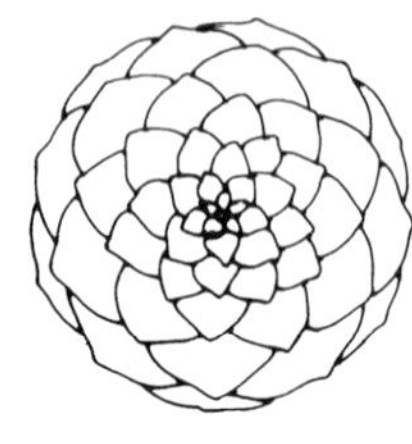

C. x *williamsii* **'Jury's Yellow'** (anemone)

C. sasanqua **'Narumigata'** (single)

C. **'Shirowabisuke'** (single)

C. x *williamsii* **'Francis Hanger'** (single)

C. japonica **'Mrs. D.W. Davis'** (semi-double)

C. **'Cornish Snow'** (single)

C. japonica **'Lady Vansittart'** (semi-double)

C. japonica **'Alba Simplex'** (single)

C.j. **'Tomorrow's Dawn'**(irreg. double)

C. japonica **'Janet Waterhouse'**(semi-dbl.)

C. japonica **'Berenice Boddy'** (semi-double)

C. tsai (single)

C. x *williamsii* **'J.C. Williams'** (single)

C. japonica **'Lavinia Maggi'** (formal dbl.)

C. x *williamsii* **'Joan Trehane'** (rose)

C. x *williamsii* **'Donation'** (semi-double)

C. japonica **'Margaret Davis'** (irregular double)

C.j. **'Betty Sheffield Supreme'** (irreg. double)

C. x *williamsii* **'Dream Boat'** (formal double)

C. x *williamsii* **'Bow Bells'** (single)

C. x *w.* **'E.G. Waterhouse'** (formal double)

C. x *w.* **'Brigadoon'** (semi-double)

C. saluenensis (single)

C. x *williamsii* **'Saint Ewe'** (single)

C. **'Inspiration'** (semi-double)

C. **'Francie L'** (semi-double)

C. reticulata **'Arch of Triumph'** (peony)

C. reticulata **'Mandalay Queen'** (semi-double)

C. **'Satan's Robe'** (semi-double)

C. japonica **'Guilio Nuccio'** (semi-double)

C. japonica **'R.L. Wheeler'** (variable)

C. reticulata **'Captain Rawes'** (semi-double)

C. japonica **'Apollo'** (semi-double)

C. japonica **'Elegans'** (anemone)

C. x williamsii **'Water Lily'** (formal double)

C. **'Innovation'** (peony)

C. **'Leonard Messel'** (semi-double)

C.j. **'Rubescens Major'** (formal double)

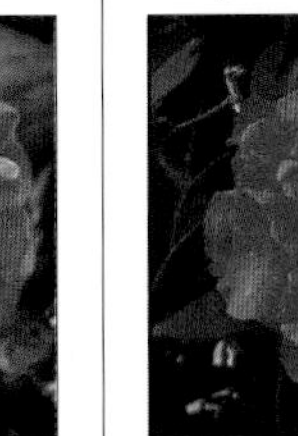
C. japonica **'Gloire de Nantes'** (semi-double)

C. japonica **'Julia Drayton'** (variable)

C. reticulata **'Houye Diechi'** (semi-double)

C. japonica **'Mathotiana'** (formal double)

C. x williamsii **'Golden Spangles'** (single)

C. x williamsii **'George Blandford'** (semi-double)

C. japonica **'Jupiter'** (single)

C. **'William Hertrich'** (semi-double)

C. **'Dr. Clifford Parks'** (variable)

C. **'Anticipation'** (peony)

C. japonica **'Adolphe Audusson'**(semi-double)

C. japonica **'Alexander Hunter'** (single)

C. japonica **'Althaeiflora'** (peony)

C. **'Black Lace'** (formal double)

C. japonica **'Bob's Tinsie'** (anemone)

C. japonica **'Coquettii'** (variable)

SHRUBS medium SPRING INTEREST

WHITE–PINK

Aronia arbutifolia
(Red chokeberry)
Deciduous shrub, upright when young, later arching. Clusters of small white flowers with red anthers appear in late spring, followed by red berries. Dark green foliage turns red in autumn.

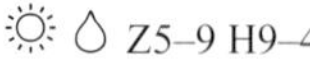
Z5–9 H9–4

Myrtus communis
(Common myrtle)
Evergreen, bushy shrub with aromatic, glossy, dark green foliage. Fragrant white flowers are borne from mid-spring to early summer, followed by purple-black berries.

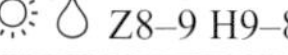
Z8–9 H9–8

Malus sieboldii
Deciduous, spreading shrub with arching branches. Bears white or pale to deep pink flowers in midspring followed by small red or yellow fruits. Dark green leaves, often lobed, turn red or yellow in autumn.

Z5–9 H9–5

***Prunus mume* 'Omoi-no-mama'**, syn. *P.m.* 'Omoi-no-wac'
Deciduous, spreading shrub with fragrant, semi-double, occasionally single, pink-flushed white flowers wreathing young growths in early spring before oval, toothed leaves appear.

Z6–8 H8–6

***Viburnum plicatum* 'Pink Beauty'**
Deciduous, bushy shrub. Dark green leaves become reddish purple in autumn. In late spring and early summer bears white, later pink, blooms, followed by red, then black, fruits.

Z4–8 H8–1

***Chaenomeles speciosa* 'Moerloosei'**
Vigorous, deciduous, bushy shrub. Has glossy, dark green leaves and pink-flushed white flowers in early spring, followed by greenish yellow fruits.

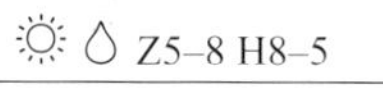
Z5–8 H8–5

PINK–RED

Cotoneaster divaricatus
Deciduous, bushy, spreading shrub. Leaves are glossy, dark green, turning red in autumn. Shallowly cup-shaped, pink-flushed white flowers in late spring and early summer are followed by deep red fruits.

Z5–7 H7–5

***Ribes sanguineum* 'Pulborough Scarlet'**
Deciduous, upright shrub that in spring bears pendent, tubular, deep red flowers amid aromatic, dark green leaves with 3–5 lobes, sometimes followed by black fruits with a white bloom.

Z6–8 H8–6

***Prunus mume* 'Beni-chidori'**, syn. *P.m.* 'Beni-shidon', *P.m.* 'Beni-shidori'
Deciduous, spreading shrub with fragrant, single carmine flowers in early spring before pointed, dark green leaves appear.

Z6–8 H8–6

***Acer palmatum* 'Corallinum'**
Very slow-growing, deciduous, bushy-headed shrub or small tree. Lobed, bright reddish pink young foliage becomes midgreen, then brilliant red, orange, or yellow in autumn. Reddish purple flowers appear in midspring.

Z6–8 H8–6

Banksia coccinea
Evergreen, dense shrub with toothed, dark green leaves, gray-green beneath. Flower heads consisting of clusters of bright red flowers with prominent styles and stigmas are borne in late winter and spring.

Z13–15 H12–10

Daphne x *burkwoodii* 'Somerset Variegaed'
MAGNOLIAS, illus. p.75
RHODODENDRONS, illus. p.132–4
Skimmia japonica, illus. p.175

Spirea 'Arguta'
Spirea prunifolia
Viburnum x *burkwoodii* 'Park Farm Hybrid'
Viburnum carlesii 'Diana'

Callistemon speciosus
CAMELLIAS, illus. pp.128–9
Chaenomeles x *superba* 'Etna'
Cytisus 'Windlesham Ruby'

HEATHERS, illus. pp.178–9
Pieris japonica 'Daisen'
Prunus tenella 'Fire Hill'
RHODODENDRONS, illus. pp.132–4

RED–PURPLE

Enkianthus cernuus* f. *rubens
Deciduous, bushy shrub with dense clusters of dull green leaves that turn deep reddish purple in autumn. Small, bell-shaped, deep red flowers appear in late spring.

Z6–8 H8–6

Greyia sutherlandii
Deciduous or semi-evergreen, rounded shrub. Coarsely serrated, leathery leaves turn red in autumn. Spikes of small, bright red flowers appear in spring with new foliage.

Z13–15 H12–10

Leucospermum reflexum
Evergreen, erect shrub with ascending branchlets. Has small, blue-gray or gray-green leaves. Slender, tubular, crimson flowers with long styles are carried in tight, rounded heads in spring-summer.

Z13–15 H12–10

***Leptospermum scoparium* 'Red Damask'**
Evergreen, upright, bushy shrub. Narrow, aromatic, dark green leaves set off sprays of double, dark red flowers in late spring and summer.

Z12–15 H12–10

Telopea truncata
(Tasmanian waratah)
Evergreen, upright shrub, bushy with age. Has deep green leaves and dense, rounded heads of small, tubular, crimson flowers in late spring and summer.

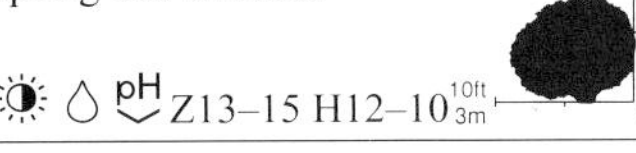

Z13–15 H12–10

Berberis thunbergii* f. *atropurpurea
Deciduous, arching, dense shrub. Reddish purple foliage turns bright red in autumn. Globose to cup-shaped, red-tinged pale yellow flowers in midspring are followed by red fruits.

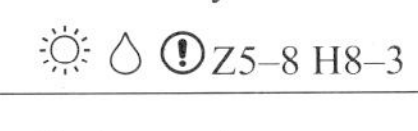

Z5–8 H8–3

Ceanothus 'Delight'
Ceanothus 'Italian Skies'
Ceanothus papillosus
Cestrum 'Newellii'

Daphne genkwa
LILACS, illus. p.120
RHODODENDRONS, illus. pp.132–4
Rosmarinus officinalis, illus. p.167

YELLOW

Corylopsis pauciflora
Deciduous, bushy, dense shrub. Oval, bright green leaves, bronze when young, have bristlelike teeth. Bears fragrant, tubular to bell-shaped, pale yellow flowers from early to midspring.

Z3–9 H9–1

Berberis gagnepainii* var. *lanceifolia
Evergreen, bushy, dense shrub. Massed, globose to cup-shaped yellow flowers appear among long, narrow, pointed, dark green leaves in late spring. Bears blue-bloomed, black berries.

Z6–9 H9–6

***Kerria japonica* 'Pleniflora'**
Vigorous, deciduous, graceful shrub. Double, golden yellow flowers are borne along green shoots from mid- to late spring. Leaves are narrowly oval, sharply toothed, and bright green.

Z5–9 H8–3

Lindera benzoin
(Spice bush)
Deciduous, bushy shrub with aromatic, bright green leaves that turn yellow in autumn. Tiny, greenish yellow flowers in midspring are followed by red berries on female plants.

Z4–9 H8–1

Forsythia suspensa
Deciduous, arching, graceful shrub with slender shoots. Nodding, narrowly trumpet-shaped, bright yellow flowers open from early to midspring before midgreen leaves appear.

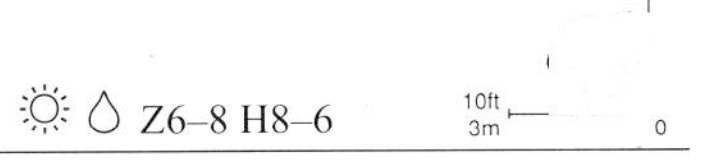

Z6–8 H8–6

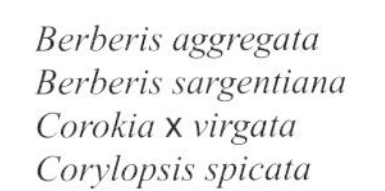

Berberis aggregata
Berberis sargentiana
Corokia x *virgata*
Corylopsis spicata

Forsythia x *intermedia* 'Spring Glory'
Lonicera morrowii
RHODODENDRONS, illus. pp.132–4

Rhododendrons and Azaleas

Rhododendrons and azaleas both belong to the huge genus *Rhododendron*, one of the largest in the plant kingdom. "Azalea" is the common name used for all the deciduous species and hybrids and many of the dwarf, small-leaved evergreens. In stature the genus ranges from alpine shrubs only a few inches high to tall, spreading trees, in the wild reaching 80ft (24m).

Rhododendrons should be grown in an acidic soil rich in organic matter but with excellent drainage. Most prefer cool, woodland conditions, although many dwarf forms will thrive in more open sites. Many will grow well in containers, in which it is often easier to provide suitable growing conditions. Once established, they require very little attention apart from an annual mulch and occasional fertilizer and will provide a colorful display for many years.

R. auriculatum (rhododendron) (!)

R. rex subsp. ***fictolacteum*** (rhododendron) (!)

***R.* 'Silver Moon'** (azalea) (!)

***R.* 'Beauty of Littleworth'** (rhododendron) (!)

***R.* 'Palestrina'** (azalea) (!)

R. occidentale (azalea) (!)

R. yakushimanum (rhododendron) (!)

R. fulvum (rhododendron) (!)

R. calophytum (rhododendron) (!)

R. racemosum (rhododendron) (!)

R. schlippenbachii (azalea) (!)

***R.* 'Seven Stars'** (rhododendron) (!)

R. souliei (rhododendron) (!)

R. argyrophyllum (rhododendron) (!)

R. sutchuenense (rhododendron) (!)

***R.* Nobleanum Group** (rhododendron) (!)

R. williamsianum (rhododendron) (!)

R. orbiculare (rhododendron) (!)

***R.* 'Mrs. G.W. Leak'** (rhododendron) (!)

R. yunnanense (rhododendron) (!)

***R.* 'Azuma-kagami'** (azalea) (!)

***R.* 'Seta'** (rhododendron) (!)

***R.* 'Strawberry Ice'** (azalea) (!)

***R.* 'Corneille'** (azalea) (!)

***R.* 'Kirin'** (azalea) (!)

***R.* 'Percy Wiseman'** (rhododendron) (!)

R. **'Pink Pearl'**
(rhododendron) ①

R. **'Elizabeth'**
(rhododendron) ①

R. davidsonianum
(rhododendron) ①

R. **'Queen Elizabeth II'**
(rhododendron) ①

R. oreotrephes
(rhododendron) ①

R. wardii
(rhododendron) ①

R. **'Rosalind'**
(rhododendron) ①

R. **'Hinode-giri'**
(azalea) ①

R. **'May Day'**
(rhododendron) ①

R. kaempferi
(azalea) ①

R. **'Blue Peter'**
(rhododendron) ①

R. calostrotum
(rhododendron) ①

R. thomsonii
(rhododendron) ①

R. cinnabarinum
(rhododendron) ①

R. hippophaeoides
(rhododendron) ①

R. lutescens
(rhododendron) ①

R. **'Hinomayo'**
(azalea) ①

R. **'President Roosevelt'**
(rhododendron) ①

R. **'John Cairns'**
(azalea) ①

R. **'Irohayama'**
(azalea) ①

R. augustinii
(rhododendron) ①

R. cinnabarinum subsp. ***xanthocodon*** (rho.) ①

R. **'Hatsugiri'**
(azalea) ①

R. arboreum
(rhododendron) ①

R. **'Cynthia'**
(rhododendron) ①

R. **'Vuyk's Scarlet'**
(azalea) ①

R. **'Homebush'**
(azalea) ①

R. **'Susan'**
(rhododendron) ①

Rhododendrons and Azaleas continued

***R.* 'Narcissiflorum'** (azalea) (!)

***R.* 'Freya'** (azalea) (!)

***R.* 'Crest'** (rhododendron) (!)

R. luteum (azalea) (!)

***R.* 'Medway'** (azalea) (!)

***R.* 'Curlew'** (rhododendron) (!)

***R.* 'George Reynolds'** (azalea) (!)

***R.* 'Fabia'** (rhododendron) (!)

***R.* 'Yellow Hammer'** (rhododendron) (!)

***R.* 'Glory of Littleworth'** (azalea x rhodo.) (!)

***R.* 'Frome'** (azalea) (!)

***R.* 'Moonshine Crescent'** (rhodo.) (!)

R. macabeanum (rhododendron) (!)

***R.* 'Gloria Mundi'** (azalea) (!)

SHRUBS medium SPRING INTEREST

□ YELLOW

Berberis verruculosa
Slow-growing, evergreen, bushy shrub. Has glossy, dark green leaves with blue-white undersides. Clusters of small, cup-shaped, bright yellow flowers in late spring and early summer are followed by blue-black fruits.

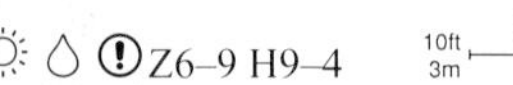

☼ ◊ (!) Z6–9 H9–4

Berberis julianae
Evergreen, bushy, dense shrub. Has glossy, dark green leaves, yellow flowers in late spring and early summer, and egg-shaped, blue-black fruits in autumn.

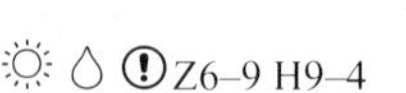

☼ ◊ (!) Z6–9 H9–4

***Forsythia* x *intermedia* 'Spectabilis'**
Vigorous, deciduous, spreading shrub with thick stems. A profusion of large, deep yellow flowers is borne from early to midspring before sharply toothed, dark green leaves appear.

10ft 3m
10ft 3m
0

☼ ◊ Z3–8 H8–4

Hibbertia cuneiformis, illus. p.146
Kerria japonica 'Pleniflora', illus. p.131
Mahonia napaulensis
Mahonia 'Undulata'
Ochna serrulata
Ribes odoratum

YELLOW–ORANGE

Azara serrata
Evergreen, upright shrub with glossy, bright green foliage and rounded bunches of fragrant yellow flowers in late spring or early summer.

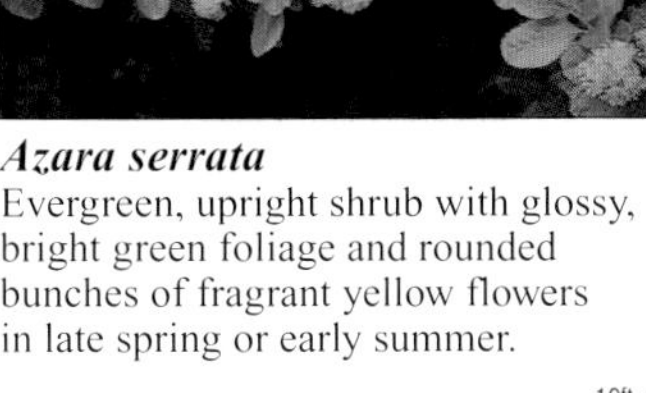

Z9–11 H12–9

Berberis* x *stenophylla
Evergreen, arching shrub with slender shoots and narrow, spine-tipped, deep green leaves, blue-gray beneath. Massed golden yellow flowers appear from mid- to late spring followed by small, blue-black fruits.

Z6–9 H9–6

***Forsythia* x *intermedia* 'Beatrix Farrand'**
Vigorous, deciduous, bushy, arching shrub with thick stems. A profusion of large, deep yellow flowers appears from early to midspring before oval, coarsely toothed, mid-green leaves emerge.

Z6–9 H9–3

***Berberis* x *lologensis* 'Stapehill'**
Vigorous, evergreen, arching shrub. Glossy, dark green foliage sets off profuse racemes of globose to cup-shaped orange flowers from mid- to late spring.

Z6–9 H9–6

Acacia podalyriifolia
(Mount Morgan wattle, Queensland silver wattle)
Evergreen, arching shrub that produces racemes of bright yellow flowers in spring. Has blue-green phyllodes (flattened, leaflike stalks).

Z11–15 H12–10

***Berberis linearifolia* 'Orange King'**
Evergreen, upright, stiff-branched shrub with narrow, rigid, dark green leaves. Bears large, globose to cup-shaped, deep orange flowers in late spring.

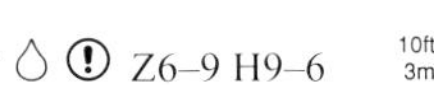

Z6–9 H9–6

WHITE

***Carissa macrocarpa* 'Tuttlei'**, syn. *C. grandiflora* 'Tuttlei'
Evergreen, compact, and spreading shrub with thorny stems and leathery leaves. Has fragrant flowers in spring-summer and edible, plum-like, red fruits in autumn.

Z10–11 H12–1

***Philadelphus* 'Beauclerk'**
Deciduous, slightly arching shrub. Large, fragrant flowers, white with a small, central, pale purple blotch, are produced from early to midsummer. Leaves are dark green.

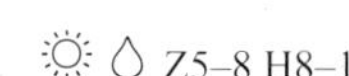

Z5–8 H8–1

***Exochorda* x *macrantha* 'The Bride'**
Deciduous, arching, dense shrub that forms a mound of pendent branches. Large white flowers are produced in abundance amid dark green foliage in late spring and early summer.

Z5–9 H9–5

OTHER RECOMMENDED PLANTS:
Acradenia frankliniae
Aronia x *prunifolia*
Brugmansia arborea
Buddleja fallowiana var. *alba*
Cistus x *cyprius*, illus. p.159
Clethra alnifolia
Cleyera japonica

Berberis x *lologensis*
Cytisus 'Firefly'
Cytisus scoparius f. *andreanus*, illus. p.171
Forsythia x *intermedia* 'Arnold Giant'

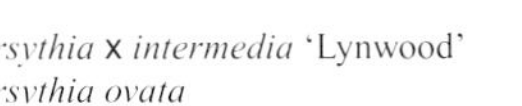

Forsythia x *intermedia* 'Lynwood'
Forsythia ovata
RHODODENDRONS, illus. pp.132–4

SHRUBS medium SUMMER INTEREST

□ WHITE

Deutzia scabra
Deciduous, upright shrub with narrowly oval, dark green leaves that, from early to midsummer, set off dense, upright clusters of 5-petaled white blooms.

Z6–8 H8–6

***Philadelphus* 'Belle Etoile'**
Deciduous, arching shrub. Very fragrant white flowers, each with a pale purple mark at the base, are borne profusely among midgreen foliage in late spring and early summer.

Z5–8 H8–5

***Pyracantha* x *watereri*,**
syn. *P.* 'Waterer's Orange'
Evergreen, upright, dense, spiny shrub with glossy, dark green foliage. Shallowly cup-shaped white flowers in early summer are succeeded by bright red berries in autumn.

Z7–9 H9–7

Spiraea canescens
Deciduous shrub with upright shoots arching at the top. Small heads of white flowers are borne in profusion amid narrowly oval, gray-green leaves from early to midsummer.

Z7–9 H9–7

Deutzia* x *magnifica
'Staphyleoides'
Vigorous, deciduous, upright shrub. Large, 5-petaled, pure white blooms, borne in dense clusters in early summer, have recurved petals. The leaves are bright green.

Z6–8 H8–6

Aronia melanocarpa
(Black chokeberry)
Deciduous, bushy shrub. White flowers appear in late spring and early summer, followed by black fruits. Has glossy, dark green leaves that turn red in autumn.

Z3–8 H8–1

Fallugia paradoxa
(Apache plume)
Deciduous, bushy shrub that bears white flowers in midsummer, followed by silky, pink- and red-tinged green fruits. Dark green leaves are finely cut and feathery.

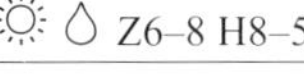
Z6–8 H8–5

***Rubus* 'Benenden',**
syn. *R.* 'Tridel'
Deciduous, arching, thornless shrub with peeling bark. Large, roselike, pure white flowers are borne among lobed, deep green leaves in late spring and early summer.

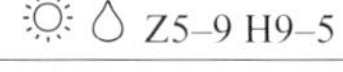
Z5–9 H9–5

Olearia nummulariifolia
Evergreen, rounded shrub with stiff, upright shoots densely covered with small, very thick, mid- to dark green leaves. Small, fragrant white flowers appear in midsummer.

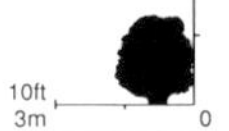
Z7–10 H10–7

Cotoneaster bullatus 'Firebird'
Cotoneaster rotundifolius
Deutzia 'Joconde'
Deutzia x *magnifica*
Deutzia setchuenensis var. *corymbiflora*
FUCHSIAS, illus. pp.164–5
Gardenia augusta 'Veitchii', illus. p.158
Hakea suaveolens
HEATHERS, illus. pp.178–9
Hebe brachysiphon
Hebe salicifolia
HYDRANGEAS, illus. p.144
Ligustrum japonicum
Ligustrum vulgare
Lyonia ligustrina
Lyonia ovalifolia

Sorbaria sorbifolia, syn. *Spiraea sorbifolia*
Deciduous, upright shrub that forms thickets by suckering. Midgreen leaves consist of many sharply toothed leaflets. Large panicles of small white flowers appear in summer.

Z2–9 H9–1

Prinsepia uniflora
Deciduous, arching, spiny shrub. From late spring to summer bears small, fragrant white flowers amid narrow, glossy, dark green leaves followed by cherrylike, deep red fruits. Grows best in heat and sun.

Z3–6 H6–1

Yucca gloriosa (Spanish dagger)
Evergreen shrub with a thick stem crowned with a tuft of long, pointed, deep green leaves, blue-green when young. Bears very long panicles of bell-shaped white flowers in summer-autumn.

Z7–11 H12–7

***Philadelphus* 'Boule d'Argent'**
Deciduous, bushy, arching shrub with dark green foliage that sets off clusters of slightly fragrant, semi-double to double, pure white flowers from early to midsummer.

Z5–8 H8–5

Eucryphia milliganii
Evergreen, upright, narrow shrub. Has tiny, dark green leaves, bluish white beneath, and small white flowers borne in midsummer.

pH Z8–9 H9–8

***Philadelphus* 'Dame Blanche'**
Deciduous, bushy, compact shrub with dark, peeling bark. Dark green foliage sets off slightly fragrant, semi-double to loosely double, pure white flowers borne in profusion from early to midsummer.

Z5–8 H8–5

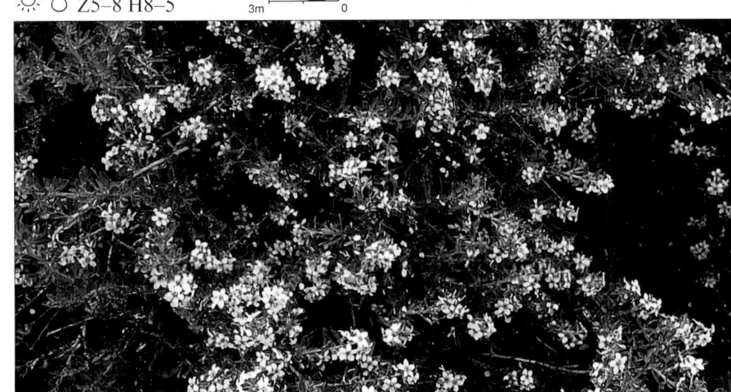

Escallonia virgata
Deciduous, spreading, graceful shrub with arching shoots and small, glossy, dark green leaves. Bears racemes of small, open cup-shaped white flowers from early to midsummer.

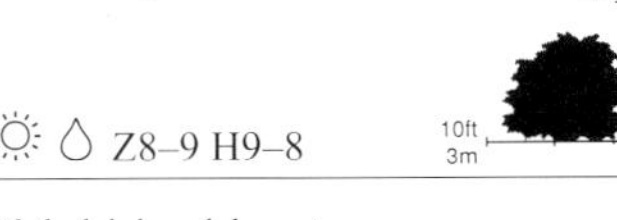

Z8–9 H9–8

Myrtus communis, illus. p.130
Myrtus communis subsp. *tarentina*
Nandina domestica
Olearia avicenniifolia
Olearia ilicifolia
Olearia phlogopappa var. *subrepanda*, illus. p.158
Olearia 'Talbot de Malahide'
Philadelphus delavayi
Philadelphus 'Virginal'
Physocarpus opulifolius
Pyracantha angustifolia
Rhaphiolepis indica
RHODODENDRONS, illus. pp.132–4
Rhodotypos scandens, illus. p.158
Sorbaria tomentosa var. *angustifolia*

□ WHITE

Osteomeles schweriniae
Evergreen, arching shrub with long, slender shoots. Leaves consisting of many small leaflets are dark green. Clusters of small white flowers in early summer are followed by red, later blue-black, fruits.

Z7–11 H12–7

Carpenteria californica
Evergreen, bushy shrub. Glossy, dark green foliage sets off fragrant, yellow-centered white flowers borne during summer.

Z8–9 H9–8

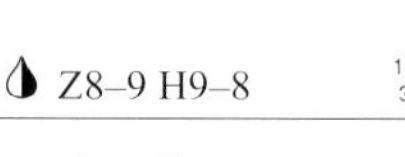

Styrax wilsonii
Deciduous, bushy shrub with slender shoots that produce an abundance of yellow-centered white flowers in early summer. Leaves are small and deep green.

pH Z7–9 H9–7

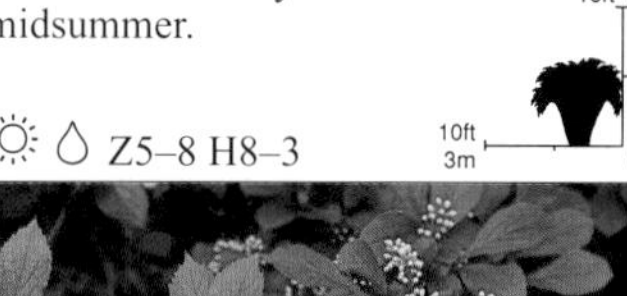

***Philadelphus* 'Lemoinei'**, syn. *P.* x *lemoinei*
Deciduous, upright, slightly arching shrub that produces profuse racemes of small, extremely fragrant white flowers from early to midsummer.

Z5–8 H8–3

Symplocos paniculata
(Sapphire berry)
Deciduous, bushy shrub or small tree. Panicles of small, fragrant white flowers in late spring and early summer are followed by small, metallic blue berries. Has dark green leaves.

Z5–8 H8–4

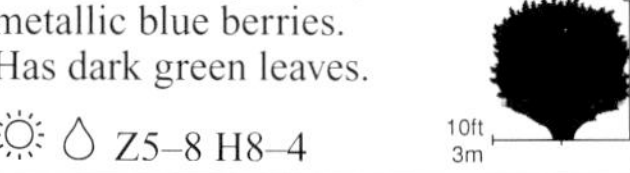

Ozothamnus rosmarinifolius, syn. *Helichrysum rosmarinifolium*
Evergreen, upright, dense shrub with woolly white shoots and narrow, dark green leaves. Clusters of fragrant white flower heads open in early summer.

Z8–9 H9–8

Clethra barbinervis
Deciduous, upright shrub with peeling bark. Has oval, toothed, dark green leaves that turn red and yellow in autumn. Racemes of fragrant white flowers are borne in late summer and early autumn.

pH Z5–8 H8–6

Ceanothus incanus
Evergreen, bushy shrub. Has spreading, spiny shoots, broad, gray-green leaves, and large racemes of white flowers in late spring and early summer.

Z8–11 H12–8

Zenobia pulverulenta
Deciduous or semi-evergreen, slightly arching shrub, often with bluish white-bloomed shoots. Glossy leaves have a bluish white reverse when young. Bears fragrant, bell-shaped white flowers from early to midsummer.

pH Z5–8 H8–5

***Cornus alba* 'Elegantissima'**
Vigorous, deciduous shrub. Young shoots are bright red in winter. Has white-edged, gray-green leaves and small, creamy white flowers in late spring and early summer, followed by white fruits.

Z2–8 H8–1

Spiraea nipponica
Spiraea 'Snow White'
Spiraea veitchii
Stachyurus praecox 'Magpie'
Viburnum dilatatum
Viburnum plicatum
Viburnum plicatum 'Nanum Semperflorens'
Weigela 'Candida'
Weigela florida 'Variegata', illus. p.160
Weigela praecox 'Variegata'

***Viburnum dilatatum* 'Catskill'**
Deciduous, low, spreading shrub with sharply toothed, dark green leaves that turn yellow, orange, and red in autumn. Flat heads of creamy white flowers in late spring and early summer are followed by bright red fruits.

Z5–8 H8–5

Olearia* x *haastii
Evergreen, bushy, dense shrub good for hedging. Has small, oval, glossy, dark green leaves and is covered with heads of fragrant, daisylike white flowers from mid- to late summer.

Z12–15 H12–10

***Spiraea nipponica* 'Snowmound',**
syn. *S.n.* var. *tosaensis* of gardens
Deciduous, spreading shrub with thick, arching, reddish branches. Small, narrow, dark green leaves set off profuse, dense clusters of small white flowers in early summer.

Z4–9 H9–1

***Leptospermum polygalifolium*,**
syn. *L. flavescens*
Evergreen, arching, graceful shrub with small, glossy, bright green leaves. Bears an abundance of small, pink-tinged white flowers in midsummer.

Z12–15 H12–10

Philadelphus delavayi
f. *melanocalyx*
Deciduous, upright shrub grown for its extremely fragrant flowers with pure white petals and deep purple sepals, opening from early to mid-summer. The leaves are dark green.

Z6–9 H9–6

Philadelphus coronarius
'Variegatus'
Deciduous, bushy shrub with racemes of very fragrant, creamy white flowers in late spring and early summer, and midgreen leaves broadly edged with white.

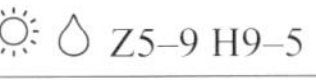

Z5–9 H9–5

Eriogonum giganteum
(St. Catherine's lace)
Evergreen, rounded shrub with oblong to oval, woolly, white leaves. Small white flowers are carried in branching clusters to 12in (30cm) or more wide in summer.

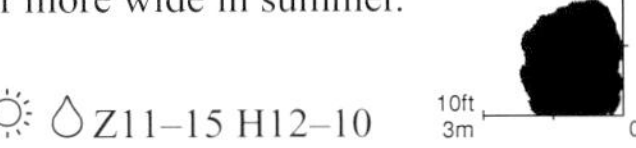

Z11–15 H12–10

***Viburnum* 'Pragense',**
syn. *V.* x *pragense*
Evergreen, rounded, bushy shrub that has dark green foliage and domed heads of white flowers opening from pink buds in late spring and early summer.

Z6–8 H8–6

***Hibiscus syriacus* 'Red Heart'**
Deciduous, upright shrub that bears large white flowers with conspicuous red centers from late summer to mid-autumn. Oval leaves are lobed and deep green.

Z5–9 H9–1

SHRUBS medium SUMMER INTEREST

WHITE–PINK

Lonicera xylosteum
(Fly honeysuckle)
Deciduous, upright, bushy, dense shrub. Creamy white flowers are produced amid gray-green leaves in late spring and early summer and are followed by red berries.

Z4–9 H9–1

***Acer palmatum* 'Butterfly'**
Slow-growing, deciduous, mounded shrub or small tree with lobed, gray-green leaves edged with cream. In midspring bears small, reddish purple flowers.

Z5–8 H8–2

Stephanandra tanakae
Deciduous, arching shrub with orange-brown shoots and sharply toothed, mid-green leaves that turn orange and yellow in autumn. Small, yellow-green buds open to white flowers from early to midsummer.

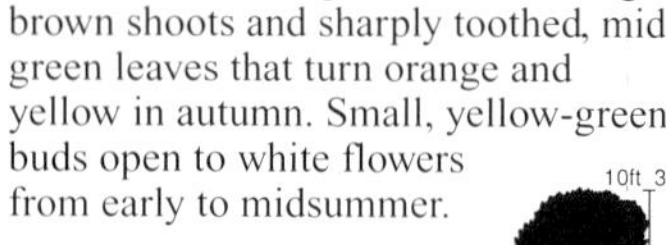

Z6–8 H8–6

Lonicera tatarica
Deciduous, bushy shrub. Tubular to trumpet-shaped, 5-lobed white, pink, or red flowers cover dark green foliage in late spring and early summer and are succeeded by red berries.

Z3–9 H9–1

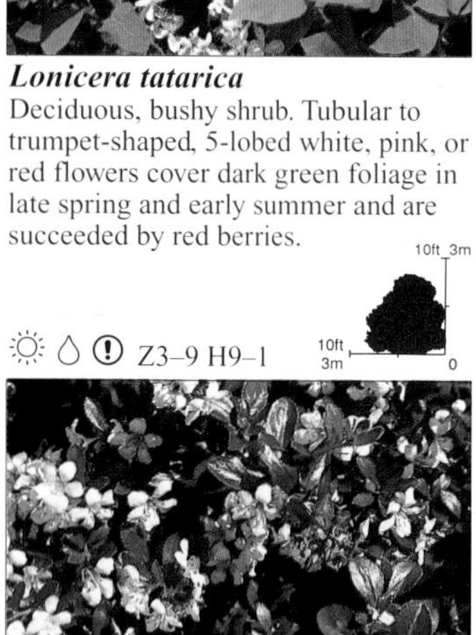

***Escallonia* 'Donard Seedling'**
Vigorous, evergreen, arching shrub with small, glossy, dark green leaves. Masses of pink flower buds open to white blooms flushed with pale pink from early to midsummer.

Z8–9 H9–8

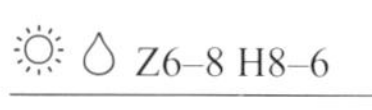

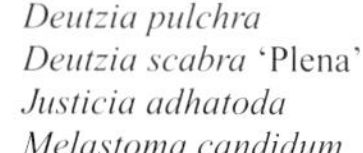

Deutzia pulchra
Deutzia scabra 'Plena'
Justicia adhatoda
Melastoma candidum

Neillia sinensis
RHODODENDRONS, illus. pp.132–4

PINK

***Deutzia longifolia* 'Veitchii'**
Deciduous, arching shrub with narrow, pointed leaves and large clusters of 5-petaled, deep pink flowers from early to midsummer.

Z7–8 H8–7

Protea neriifolia
Evergreen, bushy, upright shrub with narrow leaves. Flower heads, about 5in (13cm) long, are red, pink, or white, the bracts tipped with tufts of black hair, and appear in spring-summer.

pH Z12–15 H12–10

***Neillia thibetica*,**
syn. *N. longiracemosa*
Deciduous, arching shrub. Slender spikes of rose-pink flowers are borne profusely in late spring and early summer. Leaves are sharply toothed.

Z6–9 H9–6

Abelia x *grandiflora*, illus. p.121
Ceanothus 'Marie Simon'
Deutzia x *elegantissima* 'Fasciculata'
Grevillea rosmarinifolia

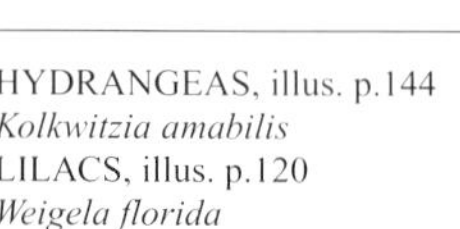

HYDRANGEAS, illus. p.144
Kolkwitzia amabilis
LILACS, illus. p.120
Weigela florida

***Escallonia* 'Apple Blossom'**
Evergreen, bushy, dense shrub. From early to midsummer, appleblossom pink flowers are borne in profusion amid glossy, dark green leaves.

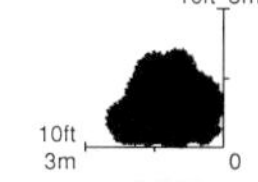

Z8–9 H9–8

Robinia hispida (Rose acacia)
Deciduous shrub of loose habit with brittle, bristly stems that carry dark green leaves composed of 7–13 leaflets. Pendent racemes of deep rose-pink blooms open in late spring and early summer.

Z6–11 H12–6

***Indigofera heterantha*,**
syn. *I. gerardiana*
Deciduous, slightly arching shrub. Has grayish green leaves consisting of many small leaflets and spikes of small, purplish pink flowers from early summer to early autumn.

Z6–9 H9–6

***Lavatera* 'Rosea',**
syn. *L. olbia* 'Rosea'
Semi-evergreen, erect shrub that produces abundant clusters of hollyhock-like, deep pink flowers throughout summer. Has lobed, sage green leaves.

Z8–11 H12–8

Kalmia latifolia (Mountain laurel)
Evergreen, bushy, dense shrub. In early summer large clusters of pink flowers open from distinctively crimped buds amid glossy, rich green foliage.

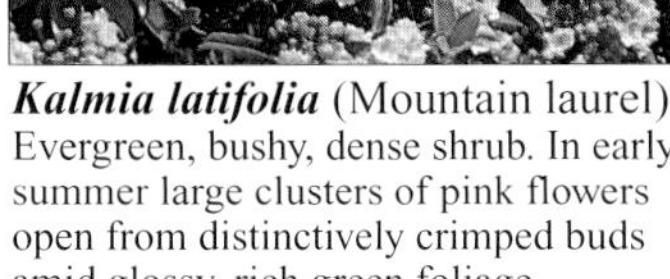

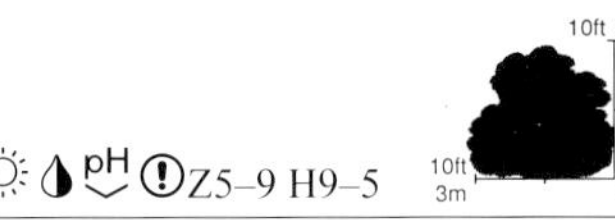

Z5–9 H9–5

Medinilla magnifica
Evergreen, upright shrub, with sparingly produced, 4-angled, robust stems and boldly veined leaves. Pink to coral-red flowers hang in long clusters beneath large pink bracts in spring-summer.

Z14–15 H12–10

***Hibiscus syriacus* 'Woodbridge'**
Deciduous, upright shrub. From late summer to midautumn large, reddish pink flowers with deeper-colored centers appear amid lobed, dark green leaves.

Z5–9 H9–5

***Hibiscus rosa-sinensis* 'The President'**
Evergreen, bushy shrub with toothed, oval, glossy, dark green leaves. In summer bears large, magenta-centered, bright pink flowers with prominent, yellow anthers.

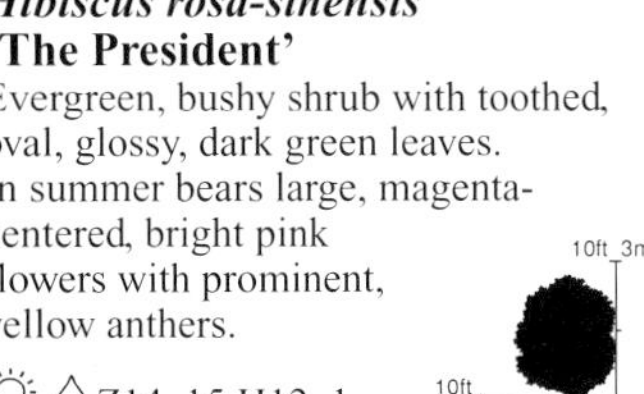

Z14–15 H12–1

Lavatera assurgentiflora
Semi-evergreen shrub with twisted gray stems. Clusters of hollyhock-like, darkly veined, deep cerise blooms open in midsummer. The palmate, midgreen leaves are white-haired beneath.

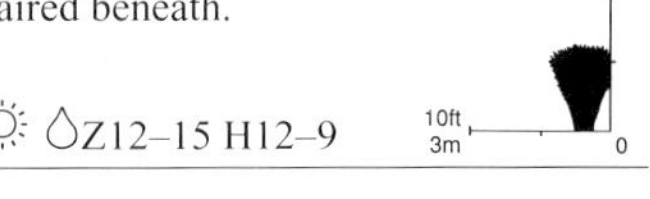

Z12–15 H12–9

Ceanothus 'Perle Rose', illus. p.163
Escallonia 'Edinensis'
FUCHSIAS, illus. pp.164–5
HEATHERS, illus. pp.178–9
HYDRANGEAS, illus. p.144
Justicia carnea, illus. p.163
Kalmia latifolia 'Ostbo Red'
LILACS, illus. p.120
RHODODENDRONS, illus. pp.132–4
Richea scoparia
Robinia hispida var. *kelseyi*
Rondeletia amoena
Rubus ulmifolius 'Bellidiflorus'
Spiraea x *billiardii*

SHRUBS medium SUMMER INTEREST

PINK–RED

Melaleuca elliptica
(Granite bottlebrush)
Evergreen, rounded shrub with long, leathery, usually grayish green leaves. Flowers, consisting of a brush of red stamens, are borne in dense, terminal spikes in spring-summer.

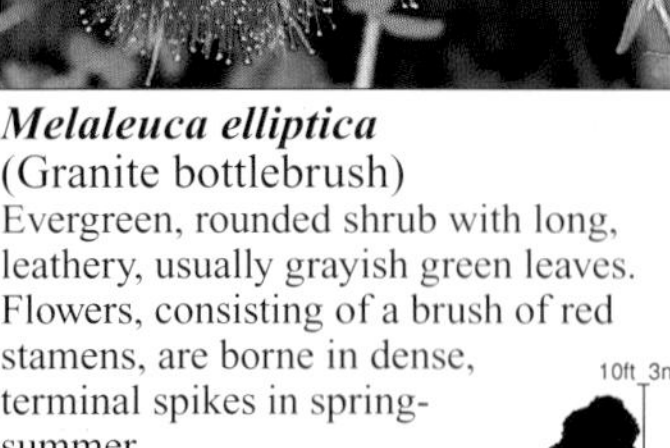

Z12–15 H12–10

Cestrum elegans
Vigorous, evergreen, arching shrub. Nodding shoots carry downy, deep green foliage. Dense racemes of tubular, purplish red flowers in late spring and summer are followed by deep red fruits.

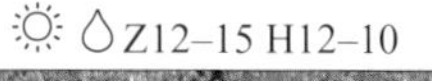

Z12–15 H12–10

***Escallonia* 'Langleyensis'**
Evergreen or semi-evergreen, arching shrub with small, glossy, bright green leaves and an abundance of rose-pink flowers from early to midsummer.

Z8–9 H9–8

Escallonia 'Donard Beauty'
Hibiscus schizopetalus
Leptospermum scoparium 'Nicholsii'
Lonicera tatarica 'Hack's Red'
Pavonia hastata
Spiraea x *billiardii* 'Triumphans'
Spiraea japonica cvs, illus. p.163
Sutherlandia frutescens, illus. p.165

RED

***Pieris formosa* var. *forrestii* 'Wakehurst'**
Evergreen, bushy, dense shrub. Young leaves are brilliant red in early summer, becoming pink, creamy yellow, and finally dark green. Bears urn-shaped white flowers in spring-summer.

pH Z7–9 H9–7

Calycanthus occidentalis
(California allspice)
Deciduous, bushy shrub. Leaves are large, aromatic, and dark green. Fragrant, purplish red flowers with many strap-shaped petals appear during summer.

Z6–9 H9–6

Crinodendron hookerianum, syn. *Tricuspidaria lanceolata*
(Lantern tree)
Evergreen, stiff-branched shrub. In late spring and early summer, lanternlike red flowers hang from shoots clothed with narrow, dark green leaves.

pH Z9–11 H12–9

Lonicera ledebourii
Deciduous, bushy shrub. Red-tinged, orange-yellow flowers are borne amid dark green foliage in late spring and early summer and are followed by black berries. As these ripen, deep red bracts enlarge around them.

Z5–9 H9–5

Bauhinia galpinii, syn. *B. punctata*
Semi-evergreen or evergreen, spreading shrub, occasionally semi-climbing. Has 2-lobed leaves and, in summer, fragrant, bright brick red flowers.

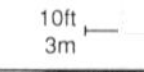

Z13–15 H12–10

Telopea speciosissima (Waratah)
Evergreen, erect, fairly bushy shrub with coarsely serrated leaves. Bears tubular red flowers in dense, globose heads surrounded by bright red bracts in spring-summer.

pH Z10–15 H12–10

Abelia floribunda
Abutilon 'Ashford Red'
Callistemon speciosus
Callistemon subulatus
Cestrum 'Newellii'
Correa 'Mannii'
Escallonia rubra 'Crimson Spire'
FUCHSIAS, illus. pp.164–5

RED

Erythrina crista-galli
(Cockspur coral-tree)
Deciduous, mainly upright shrub or small tree. Leaves have 3 oval leaflets. Has leafy racemes of crimson flowers in summer-autumn. May die back to ground level in winter.

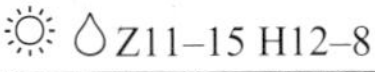
Z11–15 H12–8

Desfontainia spinosa
Evergreen, bushy, dense shrub with spiny, hollylike, glossy, dark green leaves. Long, tubular, drooping red flowers, tipped with yellow, are borne from midsummer to late autumn.

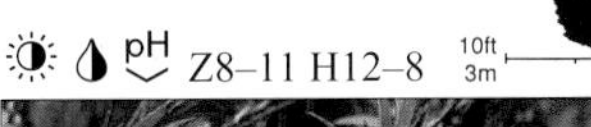
pH Z8–11 H12–8

Callistemon rigidus
Evergreen, bushy, slightly arching shrub with long, narrow, sharply pointed, dark green leaves and dense spikes of deep red flowers in late spring and early summer.

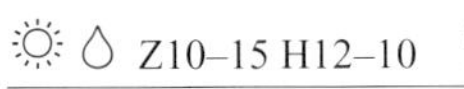
Z10–15 H12–10

Erythrina* x *bidwillii
Deciduous, upright shrub with pale to midgreen leaves divided into 3 leaflets up to 4in (10cm) long. Bright red flowers are carried in racemes in late summer or autumn.

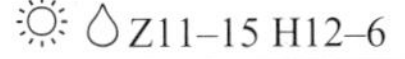
Z11–15 H12–6

***Callistemon citrinus* 'Splendens'**
Evergreen, arching shrub with broad, lemon-scented, gray-green leaves that are bronze-red when young. In early summer bright red flowers are borne in bottlebrush-like spikes.

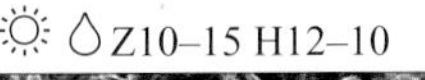
Z10–15 H12–10

Rhus glabra (Smooth sumac)
Deciduous, bushy shrub with bluish white-bloomed, reddish purple stems. Deep blue-green leaves turn red in autumn. Bears panicles of greenish red flower heads in summer, followed by red fruits on female plants.

Z2–8 H8–1

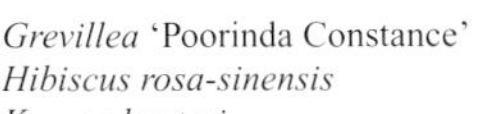

Grevillea 'Poorinda Constance'
Hibiscus rosa-sinensis
Kunzea baxteri
Macleania insignis

Phygelius capensis 'Coccineus'
Templetonia retusa
Weigela 'Bristol Ruby'

RED–PURPLE

Acca sellowiana, syn. *Feijoa sellowiana* (Pineapple guava)
Evergreen, bushy shrub or tree. Dark green leaves have white undersides. In midsummer bears large, dark red flowers with white-edged petals, followed by edible, red-tinged green fruits.

Z8–11 H12–9

***Acer palmatum* 'Bloodgood'**
Deciduous, bushy-headed shrub or small tree with deep reddish purple leaves that turn brilliant red in autumn. Small, reddish purple flowers in mid-spring are often followed by decorative, winged red fruits.

Z6–8 H8–4

Acalypha wilkesiana
(Copperleaf, Jacob's coat)
Evergreen, bushy shrub. Oval, serrated leaves are 4in (10cm) or more long, in rich copper-green variably splashed with shades of red.

Z14–15 H12–1

Aloysia triphylla, syn. *Lippia citriodora* (Lemon verbena)
Deciduous, bushy shrub. Leaves are pale green and lemon-scented. Racemes of tiny, lilac-tinged white flowers appear in early summer.

Z8–11 H12–8

Buddleja crispa
Deciduous, upright, bushy shrub that, from mid- to late summer, bears racemes of small, fragrant lilac flowers with white eyes. Has woolly white shoots and oval, grayish green leaves.

Z8–9 H9–8

***Hibiscus sinosyriacus* 'Lilac Queen'**
Deciduous, spreading, open shrub. From late summer to midautumn produces large, pale lilac flowers with red centers. Broad, lobed leaves are dark green.

Z6–9 H9–6

Buddleja fallowiana
Buddleja 'Lochinch'
Calycanthus floridus
Carmichaelia arborea

Chordospartium stevensonii
Dais cotinifolia
LILACS, illus. p.120
RHODODENDRONS, illus. pp.132–4

Hydrangeas

Valued for their late summer flowers, hydrangeas are versatile shrubs that thrive in a variety of situations. Larger-growing species, some of which may become treelike with age, are best grown in light woodland, while there is a wide range of cultivars, mostly of *H. macrophylla*, that make excellent border plants. Some may also be grown in containers. Colors range from white through pink, red, and purple to blue, but the truest blue is obtained only on acidic soil. Lacecap hydrangeas have a central corymb of small, fertile flowers surrounded by showy, large, colored bracts; mopheads (or hortensias) have domed heads of sterile bracts only. *H. paniculata* cultivars bear larger though fewer cone-shaped flower heads if pruned hard in spring. Hydrangea flower heads persist on the plants for many months and may be dried for winter decoration indoors.

***H. paniculata* 'Unique'** (!)

H. quercifolia (!)

***H. paniculata* 'Praecox'** (!)

***H. arborescens* 'Grandiflora'** (!)

***H. paniculata* 'Floribunda'** (!)

***H. macrophylla* 'Lanarth White'** (!)

***H. heteromalla* 'Bretschneideri'** (!)

***H. involucrata* 'Hortensis'** (!)

***H. paniculata* 'Brussels Lace'** (!)

***H.m.* 'Générale Vicomtesse de Vibraye'** (!)

***H. arborescens* 'Annabelle'** (!)

***H. macrophylla* 'Hamburg'** (!)

***H. paniculata* PINK DIAMOND** (!)

***H. macrophylla* 'Altona'** (!)

H. villosa (!)

***H. macrophylla* 'Lilacina'** (!)

***H. macrophylla* 'Veitchii'** (!)

***H. macrophylla* 'Blue Wave'** (!)

***H. serrata* 'Bluebird'** (!)

H. serrata (!)

***H. macrophylla* 'Blue Bonnet'** (!)

PURPLE

Prostanthera ovalifolia
Evergreen, bushy, rounded shrub with tiny, sweetly aromatic, oval, thick-textured leaves. Cup-shaped, 2-lipped purple flowers appear in short, leafy racemes in spring-summer.

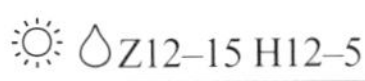

Z12–15 H12–5

Melaleuca nesophila, syn. *M. nesophylla* (Western tea-myrtle)
Evergreen, bushy shrub or small tree with oval, gray-green leaves. Flowers, consisting of a brush of lavender to rose-pink stamens, are borne in rounded, terminal heads in summer.

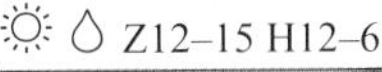

Z12–15 H12–6

***Abutilon* x *suntense* 'Violetta'**
Fast-growing, deciduous, upright, arching shrub that carries an abundance of large, bowl-shaped, deep violet flowers in late spring and early summer. Grapelike leaves are sharply toothed and dark green.

Z12–15 H12–6

Prostanthera rotundifolia
(Round-leaved mint-bush)
Evergreen, bushy, rounded shrub with tiny, sweetly aromatic, deep green leaves and short, leafy racemes of bell-shaped, lavender to purple-blue flowers in late spring or summer.

Z11–15 H12–5

Solanum rantonnetii
'Royal Robe'
Evergreen, loosely rounded shrub with smooth, bright green leaves. In summer has clusters of rich purple-blue flowers that open almost flat.

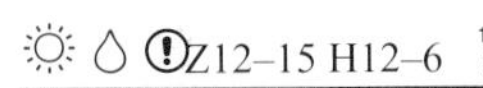

Z12–15 H12–6

Sophora davidii, syn. *S. viciifolia*
Deciduous, bushy shrub with arching shoots. Produces short racemes of small, pealike, purple and white flowers in late spring and early summer. Gray-green leaves have many leaflets.

Z6–9 H9–6

PURPLE–BLUE

Fabiana imbricata* f. *violacea, syn. *F.i.* 'Violacea'
Evergreen, upright shrub with shoots that are densely covered with tiny, heath-like, deep green leaves. Tubular lilac flowers are borne profusely in early summer.

Z9–11 H12–10

***Hibiscus syriacus* 'Oiseau Bleu'**, syn. *H.s.* 'Blue Bird'
Deciduous, upright shrub that carries large, red-centered, lilac-blue flowers from late summer to midautumn. Has lobed, deep green leaves.

Z5–9 H9–5

Ceanothus impressus
Evergreen, bushy shrub. Spreading growth is covered with small, crinkled, dark green leaves. Deep blue flowers appear in small clusters from mid-spring to early summer.

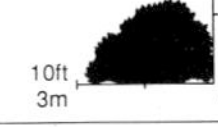

Z8–11 H12–8

Ceanothus x *veitchianus*
HYDRANGEAS, illus. p.144
Teucrium fruticans 'Azureum'
Tibouchina urvilleana, illus. p.122

GREEN

Eleutherococcus sieboldianus
Deciduous, bushy, elegant shrub. Has glossy, bright green leaves, divided into 5 leaflets, and is armed with spines. Clusters of small greenish flowers appear in early summer.

Z4–8 H9–3

Zanthoxylum piperitum
(Japan pepper)
Deciduous, bushy, spiny shrub or small tree with aromatic, glossy, dark green leaves composed of many leaflets. Small red fruits follow tiny, greenish yellow flowers in spring.

Z6–9 H9–6

***Ptelea trifoliata* 'Aurea'**
Deciduous, bushy, dense shrub or low tree. Leaves, consisting of 3 leaflets, are bright yellow when young, maturing to pale green. Bears racemes of greenish flowers in summer, followed by winged green fruits.

Z5–9 H9–5

Oplopanax horridus
Rhamnus imeretina
Ricinus communis, illus. p.335
Sambucus racemosa 'Plumosa'

GREEN–YELLOW

Itea ilicifolia
Evergreen, bushy shrub with arching shoots and oval, sharply toothed, glossy, dark green leaves. Long, catkin-like racemes of small greenish flowers appear in late summer and early autumn.

Z7–9 H9–6

***Cornus alba* 'Spaethii'**
Vigorous, deciduous shrub with bright red young shoots in winter. Bright green leaves are yellow-edged. Bears small, creamy white flowers in late spring and early summer, followed by rounded white fruits.

Z2–8 H8–1

***Piptanthus nepalensis*,**
syn. *P. laburnifolius*
Deciduous or semi-evergreen, open shrub with leaves consisting of 3 large, dark blue-green leaflets. Racemes of pealike, bright yellow flowers appear in spring-summer.

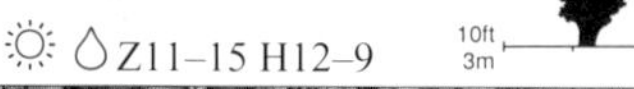

Z11–15 H12–9

***Hibbertia cuneiformis*,**
syn. *Candollea cuneiformis*
Evergreen, upright, bushy shrub with small, oval leaves, serrated at tips. Has small clusters of bright yellow flowers with spreading petals in spring-summer.

Z12–15 H12–10

Callistemon pallidus
Evergreen, arching shrub. Gray-green foliage is pink-tinged when young and in early summer is covered with dense spikes of creamy yellow flowers that resemble bottlebrushes.

Z10–15 H12–10

Bupleurum fruticosum
(Shrubby hare's ear)
Evergreen, bushy shrub with slender shoots. From midsummer to early autumn rounded heads of small yellow flowers are borne amid glossy, dark bluish green foliage.

Z7–11 H12–7

***Physocarpus opulifolius* 'Dart's Gold'**
Deciduous, compact shrub with peeling bark and oval, lobed, golden yellow leaves. Produces clusters of shallowly cup-shaped white or pale pink flowers in late spring.

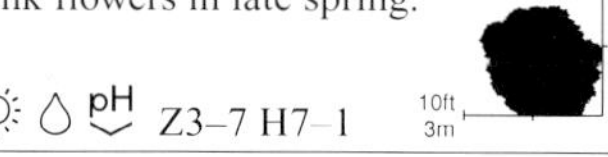

pH Z3–7 H7–1

Colutea arborescens
(Bladder senna)
Fast-growing, deciduous, open shrub. Has pale green leaves with many leaflets, pealike yellow flowers throughout summer, and bladderlike seed pods in late summer and autumn.

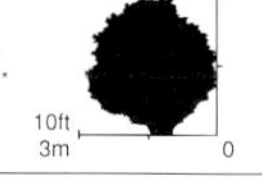

Z6–8 H8–6

Jasminum humile
(Yellow jasmine)
Evergreen, bushy shrub that bears bright yellow flowers on long, slender green shoots from early spring to late autumn. Leaves, with 5 or 7 leaflets, are bright green.

Z7–9 H9–7

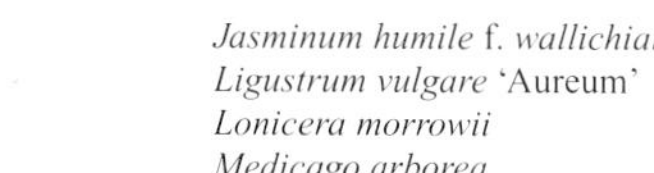

Callistemon sieberi
Cestrum parqui
Choisya ternata 'Sundance'
Cornus alba 'Gouchaultii'
Correa reflexa
Cytisus nigricans, illus. p.170
Genista tenera 'Golden Shower'
Hypericum 'Rowallane'
Jasminum humile f. *wallichianum*
Ligustrum vulgare 'Aureum'
Lonicera morrowii
Medicago arborea
Potentilla fruticosa 'Friedrichsenii', illus. p.169
Vestia foetida
Weigela 'Looymansii Aurea'

YELLOW–ORANGE

Colutea* x *media
Vigorous, deciduous, open shrub. Gray-green leaves have many leaflets. Racemes of yellow flowers tinged with copper-orange appear in summer, followed by bladderlike, papery, red-tinged seed pods.

Z6–8 H8–6

***Senna corymbosa*,**
syn. *Cassia corymbosa*
Vigorous, evergreen or semi-evergreen shrub. Leaves have 4–6 oval, bright green leaflets; sprays of bowl-shaped, rich yellow flowers appear in late summer.

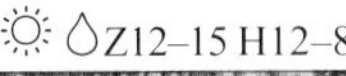

Z12–15 H12–8

Spartium junceum
(Spanish broom)
Deciduous, almost leafless, upright shrub that arches with age. Fragrant, pealike, golden yellow flowers appear from early summer to early autumn on dark green shoots.

Z8–11 H12–8

Dendromecon rigida
Vigorous, evergreen, upright shrub, best grown against a wall. Large, fragrant, golden yellow flowers appear amid gray-green foliage from spring to autumn.

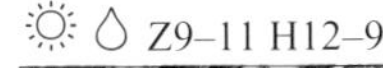

Z9–11 H12–9

Senna didymobotrya*, syn. *Cassia didymobotrya (Golden wonder)
Evergreen, rounded, sometimes spreading shrub with leaves of several leaflets. Spikes of rich yellow flowers open from glossy, blackish brown buds throughout the year.

Z14–15 H12–10

***Abutilon pictum* 'Thompsonii'**
Robust, evergreen, upright shrub with 3–5-lobed, serrated, rich green, heavily yellow-mottled leaves. Yellow-orange flowers with crimson veins are borne from summer to autumn.

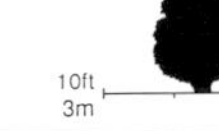

Z8–10 H12–8

Abutilon 'Golden Fleece'
Banksia baxteri
Cestrum aurantiacum
Colutea orientalis
Juanulloa mexicana, illus. p.171
Justicia spicigera, illus. p.172
Ochna serrulata
Senna x *floribunda*

WHITE–RED

Colletia hystrix*, syn. *C. armata
Almost leafless, arching, thickly branched shrub armed with rigid, gray-green spines. Pink flower buds open in late summer to fragrant, tubular white blooms that last into autumn.

Z7–11 H12–7

Clerodendrum trichotomum
Deciduous, upright, bushy-headed, treelike shrub. Clusters of deep pink and greenish white buds open to fragrant white flowers above large leaves from late summer to midautumn, followed by decorative blue berries.

Z7–9 H9–7

***Viburnum farreri*,**
syn. *V. fragrans*
Deciduous, upright shrub. In late autumn and during mild periods in winter and early spring bears fragrant white or pale pink flowers. Dark green foliage is bronze when young.

Z6–8 H8–6

Calliandra haematocephala
[pink form]
Evergreen, spreading shrub. Leaves have 16–24 narrowly oval leaflets. Flower heads consist of many pink-stamened florets from late autumn to spring.

Z12–15 H12–10

***Euonymus hamiltonianus* subsp. *sieboldianus* 'Red Elf'**
Deciduous, upright shrub with mid- to dark green foliage. Decorative, deep pink fruits, borne in profusion after tiny green flowers in early summer, open in autumn to reveal red seeds.

Z6–8 H8–6

Euonymus europaeus
'Red Cascade'
Deciduous, bushy shrub or small tree with narrowly oval, midgreen leaves that redden in autumn as red fruits open to show orange seeds. Has inconspicuous greenish flowers in early summer.

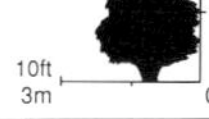

Z4–7 H7–1

OTHER RECOMMENDED PLANTS:
Berberis 'Rubrostilla', illus. p.172
Brugmansia arborea
Euonymus cornutus var. *quinquecornutus*
Eupatorium ligustrinum
Symphoricarpos albus var. *laevigatus*
Turraea obtusifolia, illus. p.172
Viburnum opulus 'Compactum', illus. p.172

RED

Viburnum betulifolium
Deciduous, upright, arching shrub. Bright green leaves are slightly glossy beneath. Heads of small white flowers in early summer are succeeded by profuse, nodding clusters of decorative, bright red fruits in autumn-winter.

Z5–8 H8–5

Euonymus latifolius
Deciduous, open shrub. Midgreen foliage turns brilliant red in late autumn. At the same time large, deep red fruits with prominent wings open to reveal orange seeds.

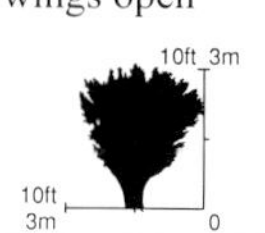
Z7–9 H9–7

Euonymus alatus (Burning bush)
Deciduous, bushy, dense shrub with shoots that develop corky wings. Dark green leaves turn brilliant red in autumn. Inconspicuous greenish flowers in summer are followed by small, purple-red fruits.

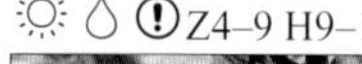
Z4–9 H9–1

Nymania capensis
Evergreen, more or less rounded, rigidly branched shrub or small tree. In spring has flowers with upright pink to rose-purple petals. Bears papery, inflated red fruits in autumn.

Z12–15 H12–10

***Cornus alba* 'Kesselringii'**
Vigorous, deciduous shrub with deep purplish stems. Dark green leaves become flushed reddish purple in autumn. Creamy white flowers in late spring and early summer are followed by white fruits.

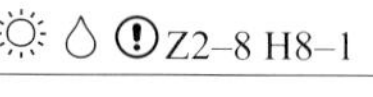
Z2–8 H8–1

Berberis x *carminea* 'Pirate King'
Cotoneaster bullatus 'Firebird'
Cotoneaster hupehensis
Cotoneaster 'Hybridus Pendulus'
Disanthus cercidifolius
Grevillea 'Poorinda Constance'
Vaccinium corymbosum 'Pioneer', illus. p.173

PURPLE–BLUE

Callicarpa bodinieri* var. *giraldii
Deciduous, bushy shrub. Leaves are pale green, often bronze-tinged when young. Tiny lilac flowers in mid-summer are followed by small violet berries.

Z4–7 H7–1

Clerodendrum bungei
Evergreen or deciduous, upright, suckering shrub or subshrub with heart-shaped, coarsely serrated leaves. Has domed clusters of small, fragrant red-purple to deep pink flowers in late summer and early autumn.

Z8–10 H12–8

***Ceanothus* 'Autumnal Blue'**
Fast-growing, evergreen, bushy shrub. Has glossy, bright green foliage and large panicles of pale to mid-blue flowers from late spring to autumn.

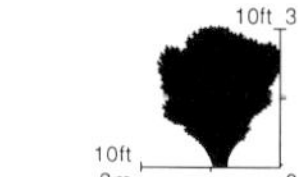
Z9–10 H10–9

Callicarpa bodinieri
Elsholtzia stauntonii, illus. p.173
HEATHERS, illus. pp.178–9
Vitex agnus-castus

ORANGE

***Berberis* x *carminea* 'Barbarossa'**
Semi-evergreen, arching shrub. Has narrowly oval, dark green leaves and racemes of rounded yellow flowers in late spring and early summer, followed by globose, orange-scarlet fruits.

Z6–9 H9–6

Zanthoxylum simulans
Deciduous, bushy shrub or small tree with thick spines. Aromatic, glossy, bright green leaves consist of 5 leaflets. Tiny, yellowish green flowers in late spring and early summer are followed by orange-red fruits.

Z6–9 H9–6

Cotoneaster simonsii
Deciduous or semi-evergreen, upright shrub suitable for hedging. Has oval, glossy, dark green leaves, shallowly cup-shaped white flowers in early summer, and long-lasting orange-red fruits in autumn.

Z6–8 H8–6

Corokia x *virgata*
Cotoneaster franchetii
Pyracantha angustifolia
Pyracantha rogersiana

ORANGE–YELLOW

Colquhounia coccinea
Evergreen or semi-evergreen, open shrub. Has aromatic, sage green leaves and whorls of scarlet or orange flowers in late summer and autumn.

Z8–9 H9–8

Cotoneaster sternianus, syn. *C. franchetii* var. *sternianus*
Evergreen or semi-evergreen, arching shrub. Leaves are gray-green, white beneath. Pink-tinged white flowers in early summer are followed by orange-red fruits.

Z7–9 H9–7

Leonotis leonurus (Lion's ear)
Semi-evergreen, sparingly branched, erect shrub. Has lance-shaped leaves and whorls of tubular, bright orange flowers in late autumn and early winter.

Z12–15 H12–6

***Pyracantha* 'Golden Charmer'**
Evergreen, bushy, arching, spiny shrub with glossy, bright green leaves. Flattish clusters of white flowers in early summer are succeeded by large, bright orange berries in early autumn.

Z7–9 H9–7

***Pyracantha* 'Golden Dome'**
Evergreen, rounded, very dense, spiny shrub. Dark green foliage sets off white flowers borne in early summer. These are followed by orange-yellow berries in early autumn.

Z7–9 H9–7

Chaenomeles speciosa
HEATHERS, illus. pp.178–9
HOLLIES, illus. pp.98–9
Nicotiana glauca

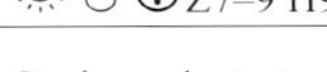

Stephanandra incisa

SHRUBS medium WINTER INTEREST

WHITE

Rubus biflorus
Deciduous, upright shrub with chalky white young shoots in winter. Leaves, consisting of 5–7 oval leaflets, are dark green above, white beneath. White flowers in late spring and early summer are followed by edible yellow fruits.

Z6–9 H9–6

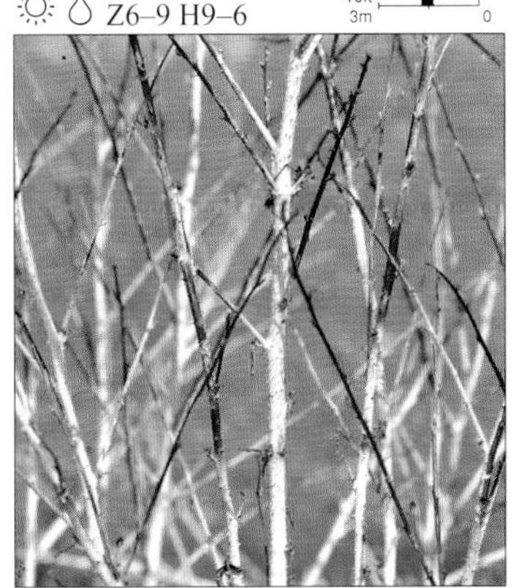

Rubus thibetanus
Deciduous, arching shrub with white-bloomed, brownish purple young shoots in winter and fernlike, glossy, dark green foliage, white beneath. Small pink flowers from mid- to late summer are followed by black fruits.

Z7–9 H9–7

Viburnum foetens, syn. *V. grandiflorum* f. *foetens*
Deciduous, bushy shrub that has aromatic, dark green leaves. Dense clusters of pink buds open to very fragrant white flowers from midwinter to early spring.

Z6–8 H8–6

Viburnum tinus (Laurustinus)
Evergreen, bushy, dense shrub with oval, dark green leaves. Freely produced flat heads of small white blooms open from pink buds during late winter and spring.

Z8–10 H10–8

Chamelaucium uncinatum (Geraldton waxflower)
Evergreen, wiry-stemmed, bushy shrub. Each needlelike leaf has a tiny, hooked tip. Flowers ranging from deep rose-purple to pink, lavender, or white appear in late winter or spring.

pH Z12–15 H12–10

Calliandra haematocephala [white form]
Evergreen, spreading shrub. Leaves have 16–24 leaflets. Flower heads consisting of many white-stamened florets appear from late autumn to spring.

Z12–15 H12–10

OTHER RECOMMENDED PLANTS:
Buddleja asiatica
Gardenia thunbergia
Lonicera fragrantissima

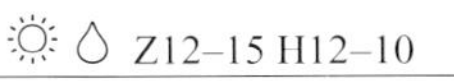

Lonicera x *purpusii*, illus. p.173
Lonicera standishii

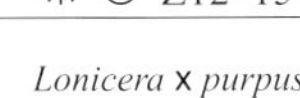

Rubus cockburnianus
Salix irrorata

SHRUBS medium WINTER INTEREST

WHITE–PINK

Dombeya burgessiae, syn. *D. mastersii*
Evergreen shrub with rounded, 3-lobed, downy leaves and dense clusters of fragrant white flowers with pink to red veins in autumn-winter.

Z12–15 H12–10

Acokanthera oblongifolia, syn. *A. spectabilis*, *Carissa spectabilis* (Wintersweet)
Evergreen, rounded shrub. Has fragrant white or pinkish flowers in late winter and spring and poisonous black fruits in autumn.

Z13–15 H12–10

Daphne bholua
Evergreen, occasionally deciduous, upright shrub with leathery, dark green foliage. Terminal clusters of richly fragrant, purplish pink and white flowers are borne in winter.

Z7–9 H9–7

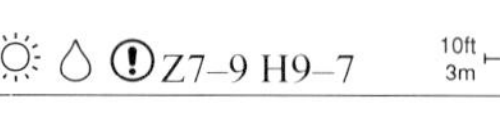

Chamelaucium uncinatum (Geraldton waxflower)
Evergreen, wiry-stemmed, bushy shrub. Each needlelike leaf has a tiny, hooked tip. Flowers ranging from deep rose-purple to pink, lavender, or white appear in late winter or spring.

pH Z12–15 H12–10

***Viburnum* x *bodnantense* 'Dawn'**
Deciduous, upright shrub with oval, bronzy young leaves that mature to dark green. Racemes of deep pink buds open to fragrant pink flowers during mild periods from late autumn to early spring.

Z7–8 H8–7

Euphorbia pulcherrima (Poinsettia)
Evergreen, sparingly branched shrub. Has small, greenish red flowers surrounded by bright red, pink, yellow, or white bracts from late autumn to spring.

Z13–15 H12–10

RED–PURPLE

***Cornus alba* 'Sibirica'**
Deciduous, upright shrub with scarlet young shoots in winter. Has dark green foliage and heads of creamy white flowers in late spring and early summer, succeeded by rounded white fruits.

Z2–8 H8–1

Ardisia crenata, syn. *A. crenulata* (Coralberry, Spiceberry)
Evergreen, upright, open shrub. Has fragrant, star-shaped white flowers in early summer, followed by long-lasting, bright red fruits.

Z113–15 H12–10

Iochroma cyanea, syn. *I. tubulosa*
Evergreen, semi-upright, slender-branched shrub. Tubular, deep purple-blue flowers with flared mouths appear in dense clusters from late autumn to early summer.

Z12–15 H12–10

YELLOW

Stachyurus praecox
Deciduous, spreading, open shrub with purplish red shoots. Drooping spikes of pale greenish yellow flowers open in late winter and early spring before pointed, deep green leaves appear.

pH Z7–9 H9–7

Duranta erecta, syn. *D. plumieri*, *D. repens* (Pigeon berry, Skyflower)
Fast-growing, usually evergreen, bushy shrub. Has spikes of lilac-blue flowers, mainly in summer, followed by yellow fruits.

Z11–12 '12–10

CAMELLIAS, illus. pp.128–9
Daphne odora
Viburnum x *bodnantense* 'Deben'
Viburnum farreri 'Candidissimum'

Viburnum grandiflorum
Viburnum tinus 'Eve Price'
Viburnum tinus 'Gwenllian'

Cornus alba
HEATHERS, illus. pp.178–9
Pachystachys coccinea
Skimmia japonica 'Rubella', illus. p.174

Chimonanthus praecox
Chimonanthus praecox 'Concolor'
Mahonia japonica 'Bealei'
Mahonia lomariifolia

YELLOW

Mahonia japonica
Evergreen, upright shrub with deep green leaves consisting of many spiny leaflets. Long, spreading sprays of fragrant yellow flowers appear from late autumn to spring, succeeded by purple-blue fruits.

Z7–9 H9–7

Jasminum nudiflorum
(Winter jasmine)
Deciduous, arching shrub with oval, dark green leaves. Bright yellow flowers appear on slender, leafless green shoots in winter and early spring.

Z6–9 H9–6

x ***Citrofortunella microcarpa***, syn. x *C. mitis*, *Citrus mitis*
(Calamondin)
Evergreen, bushy shrub with leathery leaves. Intermittently has tiny fragrant flowers followed by orange-yellow fruits.

Z13–15 H12–10

WHITE–PURPLE

***Euonymus japonicus* 'Latifolius Albomarginatus'**
Evergreen, upright, bushy and dense shrub with oval, dark green leaves broadly edged with white. Produces clusters of insignificant, greenish white flowers in late spring.

Z6–9 H9–6

***Euonymus fortunei* 'Silver Queen'**
Evergreen, bushy, sometimes scandent shrub with a dense growth of dark green leaves broadly edged with white. Produces insignificant, greenish white flowers in spring.

Z5–9 H9–5

Dracaena sanderiana
(Ribbon plant)
Evergreen, upright shrub with seldom branching, canelike stems. Lance-shaped leaves, 6–10in (15–25cm) long, are pale to gray-green with bold, creamy white edges.

Z13–15 H12–10

***Fatsia japonica* 'Variegata'**
Evergreen, rounded, bushy and dense shrub with palmate, glossy, dark green leaves, variegated marginally with creamy white, and large sprays of small white flowers in autumn.

Z8–11 H12–8

***Nandina domestica* 'Firepower'**
Evergreen or semi-evergreen, elegant, bamboolike, dwarf shrub. Leaves have dark green leaflets, purplish red when young and in autumn-winter. Bears small white flowers in summer, followed by orange-red fruits.

Z6–9 H9–1

***Dodonaea viscosa* 'Purpurea'**
Evergreen, bushy shrub or tree. Firm-textured leaves are flushed copper-purple. Has clusters of small reddish or purplish seed capsules in late summer or autumn. Makes a good hedge in a windy site.

Z12–15 H12–10

Acacia podalyriifolia, illus. p.135
Cornus stolonifera 'Flaviramea'
Cytisus x *spachianus*
Edgeworthia chrysantha
HEATHERS, illus. pp.178–9
Stachyurus chinensis

OTHER RECOMMENDED PLANTS:
Acalypha hispida
Cleyera japonica 'Tricolor'
x *Fatshedera lizei* 'Variegata'
Mackaya bella
Pandanus tectorius 'Veitchii', illus. p.175
Polyscias filicifolia 'Marginata'
Rhamnus alaternus 'Argenteovariegata'

SHRUBS medium ALL YEAR INTEREST

GREEN

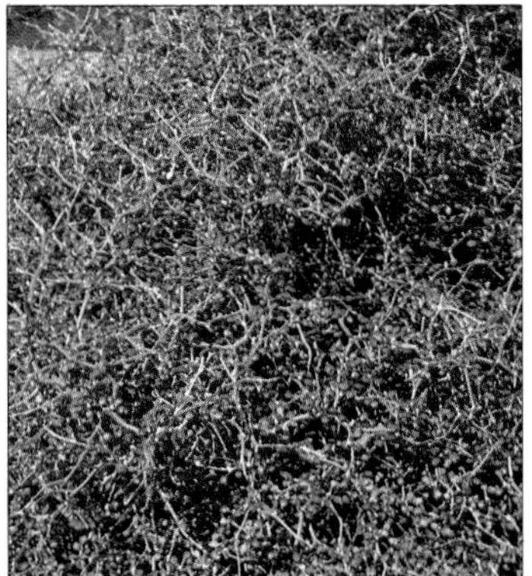

Corokia cotoneaster (Wire-netting bush)
Evergreen, bushy, open shrub with interlacing shoots. Has small, spoon-shaped, dark green leaves, fragrant yellow flowers in late spring, and red fruits in autumn.

Z9–11 H12–10

Encephalartos ferox
Slow-growing, evergreen, palmlike plant, almost trunkless for many years. Feather-shaped leaves, 2–6ft (60–180cm) long, have many serrated and spine-tipped, leathery, grayish leaflets.

Z13–15 H12–10

Cycas revoluta (Japanese sago palm)
Slow-growing, evergreen, palmlike plant that may produce several trunks. Leaves have spine-tipped leaflets with rolled margins. Bears tight clusters of reddish fruits in autumn.

Z13–15 H12–6

Aucuba japonica
Evergreen, dense, bushy shrub with stout green shoots and glossy, dark green leaves. Small purplish flowers in midspring are followed on female plants by rounded to egg-shaped, bright red berries.

Z6–15 H12–6

Arctostaphylos patula
Evergreen, rounded shrub with reddish brown bark and bright gray-green foliage. Urn-shaped white or pale pink flowers appear from mid- to late spring, followed by brown fruits.

pH Z6–9 H9–6

Rhapis excelsa (Bamboo palm, Slender lady palm)
Evergreen fan palm, eventually forming clumps. Leaves are 8–12in (20–30cm) long, composed of 20 or more narrow, glossy, deep green lobes in fans.

Z14–15 H12–1

***Buxus sempervirens* 'Handsworthensis'**
Vigorous, evergreen, bushy, upright shrub or small tree. Has broad, very dark green leaves. Its dense habit makes it ideal for hedging or screening.

Z6–8 H8–6

x *Fatshedera lizei* (Tree ivy)
Evergreen, loose-branched shrub that forms a mound of deeply lobed, glossy, deep green leaves. May also be trained as a climber. Sprays of small white flowers appear in autumn.

Z8–11 H12–8

Ficus deltoidea (Mistletoe fig)
Slow-growing, evergreen, bushy shrub with bright green leaves, red-brown-tinted beneath. Bears small greenish white fruits that mature to dull yellow.

Z14–15 H12–1

Philodendron bipinnatifidum, syn. *P. selloum*
Evergreen, unbranched shrub. Glossy leaves to 2ft (60cm) or more long are divided into many fingerlike lobes. Occasionally produces greenish white spathes.

Z14–15 H12–4

Polyscias filicifolia (Fernleaf aralia)
Evergreen, erect, sparingly branched shrub. Leaves are 12in (30cm) long and are divided into many small, serrated, bright green leaflets.

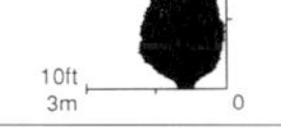

Z14–15 H12–1

Chamaedorea elegans, syn. *Neanthe bella* (Dwarf mountain palm, Parlor palm)
Evergreen, slender palm, suckering with age. Feather-shaped leaves of many glossy leaflets are 2–3ft (60–100cm) long.

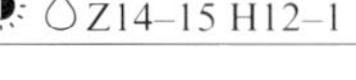

Z14–15 H12–1

Aristotelia chilensis
Buxus wallichiana
Chamaerops humilis, illus. p.176
Dioon edule
DWARF CONIFERS, illus. pp.110–11
Elaeagnus macrophylla
Eurya emarginata, illus. p.176
Fatsia japonica
HOLLIES, illus. pp.98–9
Illicium floridanum
Ligustrum japonicum 'Rotundifolium'
Lonicera nitida
Lonicera nitida 'Yunnan'
Olearia lacunosa
Phoenix roebelenii

SHRUBS small SPRING INTEREST

GREEN–YELLOW

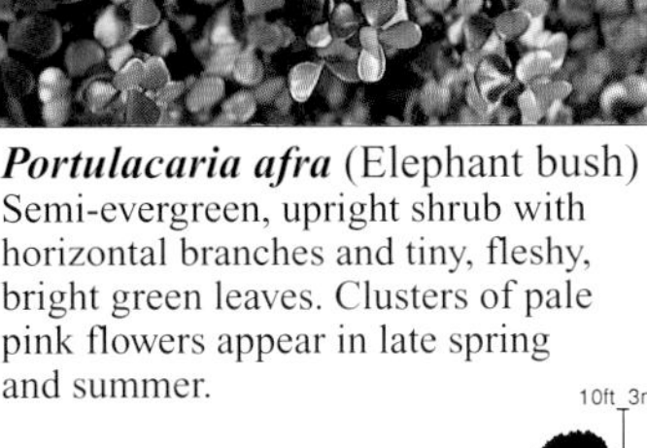

Portulacaria afra (Elephant bush)
Semi-evergreen, upright shrub with horizontal branches and tiny, fleshy, bright green leaves. Clusters of pale pink flowers appear in late spring and summer.

Z13–15 H12–10

***Elaeagnus* x *ebbingei* 'Limelight'**
Evergreen, bushy, dense shrub with glossy, dark green leaves, silver beneath, centrally marked yellow and pale green. Bears small, fragrant white flowers in autumn.

Z7–11 H12–7

Buxus balearica
(Balearic boxwood)
Evergreen, treelike shrub suitable for hedging in mild areas. Has broadly oval, bright green leaves.

Z9–11 H12–10

***Ligustrum* 'Vicaryi'**,
syn. *L.* x *vicaryi*
Semi-evergreen, bushy, dense shrub with broad, oval, golden yellow leaves. Dense racemes of small white flowers appear in midsummer.

Z4–8 H8–1

Yucca aloifolia (Spanish bayonet)
Slow-growing, evergreen shrub or small tree with few branches. Has sword-shaped, deep green leaves, 20–30in (50–75cm) long, and large panicles of purple-tinted white flowers in summer-autumn.

Z12–15 H12–1

***Aucuba japonica* 'Crotonifolia'**
Evergreen, bushy, dense shrub with thick green shoots. Large, glossy, dark green leaves are heavily mottled yellow. Small purplish flowers in midspring are followed by bright red berries.

Z6–15 H12–6

WHITE

***Salix hastata* 'Wehrhahnii'**
Deciduous, upright-branched shrub with deep purple stems that contrast with silver-gray catkins borne in early spring before foliage appears. Stems later turn yellow. Has oval, bright green leaves.

Z5–8 H8–5

Deutzia gracilis
Deciduous, upright or spreading shrub. Massed, 5-petaled, pure white flowers are borne in upright clusters amid bright green foliage in late spring and early summer.

Z5–8 H8–1

***Prunus glandulosa* 'Alba Plena'**
Deciduous, open shrub with narrowly oval, midgreen leaves and bearing racemes of double white flowers in late spring.

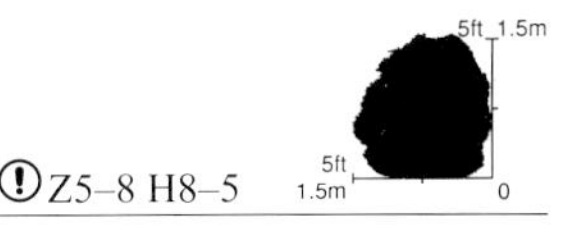

Z5–8 H8–5

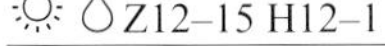

Aucuba japonica 'Gold Dust'
Aucuba japonica 'Picturata'
Cleyera japonica 'Tricolor'
Coprosma repens 'Picturata'
DWARF CONIFERS, illus. pp.110–11
Graptophyllum pictum
HOLLIES, illus. pp.98–9
Sanchezia speciosa, illus. p.177

OTHER RECOMMENDED PLANTS:
Chamaedaphne calyculata
Fothergilla gardenii
HEATHERS, illus. pp.178–9
Loropetalum chinense
Olearia x *mollis*
RHODODENDRONS, illus. pp.132–4
Westringia fruticosa, illus. p.158

SHRUBS small SPRING INTEREST

WHITE

Ledum groenlandicum
(Labrador tea)
Evergreen, bushy shrub. Foliage is dark green and aromatic. Rounded heads of small white flowers are carried from midspring to early summer.

Z2–6 H6–1

Spiraea* x *vanhouttei
(Bridal wreath)
Deciduous, compact shrub with slender, arching shoots. In late spring and early summer abundant, small, dense clusters of white flowers appear amid diamond-shaped, dark green leaves.

Z4–8 H8–1

Azorina vidalii,
syn. *Campanula vidalii*
Evergreen subshrub with erect stems. Has coarsely serrated, glossy, dark green leaves and racemes of bell-shaped white or pink flowers in spring and summer.

Z12–15 H12–10

***Prunus laurocerasus* 'Zabeliana'**
Evergreen, wide-spreading, open shrub. Leaves are very narrow and glossy, dark green. Spikes of white flowers in late spring are followed by cherrylike red, then black, fruits.

Z6–9 H9–3

***Prunus laurocerasus* 'Otto Luyken'**
Evergreen, very dense shrub. Has upright, narrow, glossy, dark green leaves and spikes of white flowers in late spring followed by cherrylike red, then black, fruits.

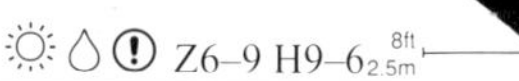

Z6–9 H9–6

 WHITE–PINK

***Gaultheria* x *wisleyensis* 'Wisley Pearl'**,
syn. x *Gaulnettya* 'Wisley Pearl'
Evergreen, bushy, dense shrub with oval, deeply veined, dark green leaves. Bears small white flowers in late spring and early summer, then purplish red fruits.

Z7–9 H9–7

Deutzia* x *rosea
Deciduous, bushy, dense shrub. In late spring and early summer produces massed, broad clusters of 5-petaled, pale pink flowers. Leaves are oval and dark green.

Z6–8 H8–6

Prunus* x *cistena
Slow-growing, deciduous, upright shrub with deep reddish purple leaves, red when young. Small pinkish white flowers from mid- to late spring may be followed by purple fruits.

Z3–8 H8–1

Viburnum* x *juddii
Deciduous, rounded, bushy shrub with dark green foliage. Rounded heads of very fragrant, pink-tinged white flowers open from pink buds from mid- to late spring.

Z5–9 H9–5

Viburnum carlesii
Deciduous, bushy, dense shrub with dark green leaves that redden in autumn. Rounded heads of very fragrant white and pink flowers, pink in bud, appear from mid- to late spring, followed by decorative black fruits.

Z5–8 H8–5

***Daphne* x *burkwoodii* 'Somerset'**
Semi-evergreen, upright shrub that bears dense clusters of very fragrant white and pink flowers in late spring and sometimes again in autumn. Leaves are lance-shaped and pale to mid-green.

Z4–7 H7–1

Bauera rubioides
Centradenia floribunda
Diosma ericoides
Gaultheria x *wisleyensis* 'Pink Pixie'
HEATHERS, illus. pp.178–9
RHODODENDRONS, illus. pp.132–4
Vinca minor 'Bowles' White'

Daphne retusa
Evergreen, densely branched, rounded shrub clothed with leathery, glossy leaves notched at the tips. In late spring and early summer deep purple buds open to very fragrant, pink-flushed white flowers borne in terminal clusters.

Z7–9 H9–7 5ft 1.5m

Prunus tenella
Deciduous, bushy shrub with upright shoots and narrowly oval, glossy leaves. Shallowly cup-shaped, bright pink flowers appear from mid- to late spring.

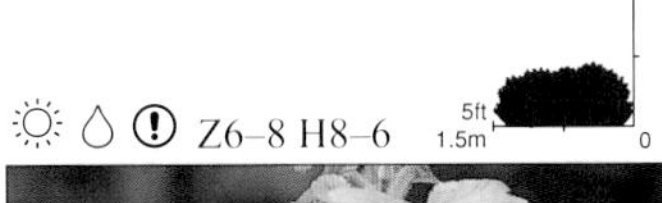
Z6–8 H8–6 5ft 1.5m

***Ribes sanguineum* 'Brocklebankii'**
Deciduous, spreading shrub. Has aromatic, pale yellow leaves and pendent clusters of small, pale pink flowers in spring, followed by white-bloomed black fruits.

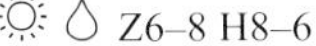
Z6–8 H8–6 5ft 1.5m

***Menziesia ciliicalyx* var. *purpurea*,** syn. *M.c.* var. *lasiophylla*
Deciduous, bushy shrub with bright green foliage and racemes of nodding, purplish pink blooms in late spring and early summer.

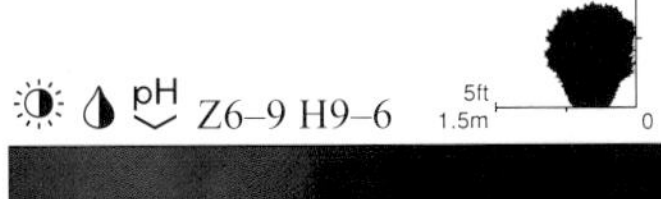
Z6–9 H9–6 5ft 1.5m

Epacris impressa
(Australian heath)
Evergreen, usually erect, fairly open, heathlike shrub with short, red-tipped leaves. Tubular pink or red flowers appear in late winter and spring.

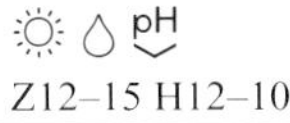
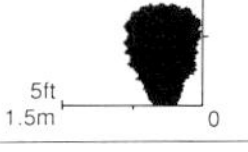
Z12–15 H12–10 5ft 1.5m

Euphorbia milii (Crown of thorns)
Fairly slow-growing, mainly evergreen, spiny, semi-succulent shrub. Clusters of tiny yellowish flowers, enclosed by 2 bright red bracts, open intermittently during the year.

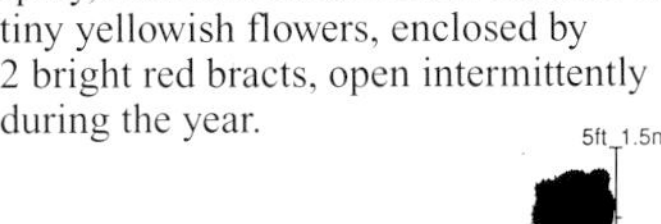
Z11–12 H12–1 5ft 1.5m

***Chaenomeles* x *superba* 'Rowallane'**
Deciduous, low, spreading shrub. Has glossy, dark green foliage and bears a profusion of large red flowers during spring.

Z5–9 H9–5 8ft 2.5m

***Cantua buxifolia*,** syn. *C. dependens*
Evergreen, arching, bushy shrub. Has gray-green foliage and drooping clusters of bright red and magenta flowers from mid- to late spring.

Z10–11 H12–10 5ft 1.5m

Chaenomeles speciosa 'Simonii'
Coleonema pulchrum
Euphorbia fulgens
Gaylussacia baccata

HEATHERS, illus. pp.178–9
Justicia rizzinii
Kalmiopsis leachiana 'La Piniec'
Protea magnifica

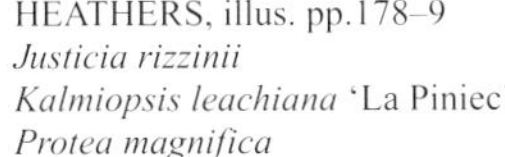

RHODODENDRONS, illus. pp.132–4

SHRUBS small SPRING INTEREST

RED–GREEN

***Chaenomeles* x *superba* 'Nicoline'**
Deciduous, bushy, dense shrub. Has glossy, dark green leaves and a profusion of large scarlet flowers in spring, followed by yellow fruits.

Z5–9 H9–5

Salix lanata (Woolly willow)
Deciduous, bushy, dense shrub with thick, woolly gray shoots and broad, silver-gray leaves. Large, yellowish green catkins appear in late spring with the foliage.

Z3–5 H5–1

Boronia megastigma
Evergreen, well branched, wiry-stemmed shrub. Small leaves have 3–5 narrow leaflets. Fragrant, bowl-shaped, brownish purple and yellow flowers hang from leaf axils in late winter and spring.

pH
Z13–15 H12–10

Euphorbia characias* subsp. *characias
Evergreen, upright shrub with clusters of narrow, gray-green leaves. During spring and early summer it bears dense spikes of pale yellowish green flowers with deep purple centers.

Z7–11 H12–7

***Arctostaphylos* 'Emerald Carpet'**
Evergreen shrub that, with a low, dense growth of oval, bright green leaves and purple stems, makes an excellent groundcover. Bears small, urn-shaped white flowers in spring.

pH Z7–9 H9–7

Daphne laureola* subsp. *philippi
Evergreen, dwarf shrub with oval, dark green leaves. Slightly fragrant, tubular, pale green flowers with short, spreading lobes appear in late winter and early spring, followed by black fruits.

Z7–8 H8–7

GREEN–YELLOW

Euphorbia characias* subsp. *wulfenii
Evergreen, upright shrub. Stems are biennial, producing clustered, gray-green leaves the first year and spikes of yellow-green blooms the following spring.

Z7–11 H12–7

Salix repens (Creeping willow)
Deciduous, prostrate or semi-upright and bushy shrub. Silky gray catkins become yellow from mid- to late spring before small, narrowly oval leaves, which are gray-green above and silvery beneath, appear.

Z5–7 H7–5

***Cytisus* x *praecox* 'Warminster'** (Warminster broom)
Deciduous, densely branched shrub. From mid- to late spring pealike, creamy yellow flowers appear in profusion amid tiny, silky, gray-green leaves with 3 leaflets.

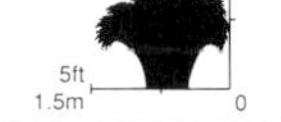

Z6–9 H9–6

Agathosma pulchella
Barleria obtusa
Brunfelsia pauciflora
HEATHERS, illus. pp.178–9
RHODODENDRONS, illus. pp.132–4
Vinca major
Xanthorhiza simplicissima

YELLOW

Mahonia aquifolium
(Oregon grape)
Evergreen, open shrub. Leaves with glossy, bright green leaflets often turn red or purple in winter. Bunches of small yellow flowers in spring are followed by blue-black berries.

Z6–9 H9–6

***Caragana arborescens* 'Nana'**
Deciduous, bushy, dwarf shrub with midgreen leaves consisting of many oval leaflets. Pealike yellow flowers are borne in late spring.

Z2–8 H8–1

Pachystachys lutea
(Lollipop plant)
Evergreen, loose, more or less rounded shrub, often grown annually from cuttings. Has tubular white flowers in tight, gold-bracted spikes in spring-summer.

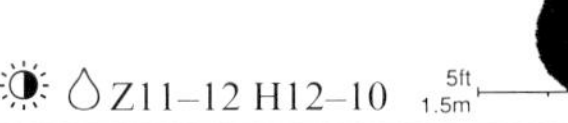

Z11–12 H12–10

***Cytisus* x *praecox* 'Allgold'**
Deciduous, densely branched shrub with silky, gray-green leaves divided into 3 leaflets, and a profusion of pealike yellow flowers from mid- to late spring.

Z6–9 H9–1

Ulex europaeus (Gorse)
Leafless or almost leafless, bushy shrub with year-round, dark green shoots and spines that make it appear evergreen. Bears massed, fragrant, pealike yellow flowers in spring.

Z6–8 H8–6

Berberis empetrifolia
Evergreen, arching, prickly shrub with narrow, gray-green leaves, globose, golden yellow flowers in late spring, and black fruits in autumn.

Z7–9 H9–7

***Coronilla valentina* subsp. *glauca*,**
syn. *C. glauca*
Evergreen, bushy, dense shrub. Has blue-gray leaves with 5 or 7 leaflets. Fragrant, pea like yellow flowers are borne from midspring to early summer.

Z8–9 H9–8

Acacia pulchella
(Western prickly Moses)
Semi-evergreen or deciduous shrub of diffuse habit, with spiny twigs and rich green foliage. Tiny, deep yellow flowers appear in dense, globular heads in spring.

Z11–15 H12–10

Acacia ulicifolia
Berberis calliantha
Caragana frutex 'Globosa'
Genista tinctoria 'Royal Gold'
Hermannia incana
Mahonia 'Heterophylla'
Mahonia repens
RHODODENDRONS, illus. pp.132–4

YELLOW–ORANGE

Genista tinctoria
(Dyers' greenweed)
Deciduous, spreading, dwarf shrub that bears dense spires of pealike, golden yellow flowers in spring and summer. Leaves are narrow and dark green.

Z2–8 H8–1

Chorizema ilicifolium
(Holly flame pea)
Evergreen, sprawling or upright shrub with spiny-toothed, leathery leaves. Has spikes of bicolored orange and pinkish red flowers in spring-summer.

Z13–15 H12–10

***Nematanthus gregarius*,** syn.
Hypocyrta radicans, *N. radicans*
Evergreen, prostrate or slightly ascending shrub with fleshy, glossy leaves. Inflated orange and yellow flowers appear mainly from spring to autumn.

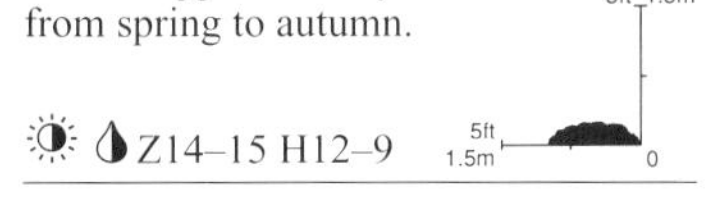

Z14–15 H12–9

Daphne giraldii
Halimium lasianthum
Lantana camara
Nematanthus strigillosus

SHRUBS small SUMMER INTEREST

□ WHITE

Deutzia monbeigii
Deciduous, arching, elegant shrub. Clusters of small, 5-petaled white flowers appear in profusion among small, dark green leaves from early to midsummer.

Z6–8 H8–6

***Hebe* 'White Gem'**,
syn. *H. brachysiphon* 'White Gem'
Evergreen, rounded shrub that produces a dense mound of small, glossy leaves, covered in early summer with tight racemes of small white flowers.

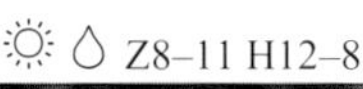

Z8–11 H12–8

Rhodotypos scandens,
syn. *R. kerrioides* (Jetbead)
Deciduous, upright or slightly arching shrub. In late spring and early summer, amid sharply toothed leaves, bears shallowly cupped white flowers followed by small, pea-shaped black fruits.

Z5–8 H8–5

Olearia phlogopappa* var. *subrepanda
Evergreen, upright, compact shrub. Heads of daisylike white flowers are borne profusely from midspring to early summer amid narrow, toothed, gray-green leaves.

Z12–15 H12–8

Cuphea hyssopifolia
(False heather)
Evergreen, rounded, dense shrub with tiny, narrowly lance-shaped, deep green leaves. Rose-purple to lilac or white flowers appear in summer-autumn.

Z12–15 H12–10

Westringia fruticosa
(Australian rosemary)
Evergreen, rounded, compact shrub. Crowded leaves, in whorls of 4, are white-felted beneath. White to palest blue flowers open in spring-summer.

Z13–15 H12–9

***Gardenia augusta* 'Veitchii'**
Fairly slow-growing, evergreen, leafy shrub with oval, glossy leaves up to 4in (10cm) long and fragrant, double white flowers from summer to winter.

pH Z14–15 H12–1

***Philadelphus* 'Manteau d'Hermine'**
Deciduous, bushy, compact shrub. Clusters of fragrant, double, creamy white flowers appear amid small, pale to mid-green leaves from early to midsummer.

Z5–8 H8–5

***Potentilla fruticosa* 'Abbotswood'**,
syn. *P.* 'Abbotswood'
Deciduous, bushy shrub. Large, pure white flowers are borne amid dark blue-green leaves, divided into 5 narrowly oval leaflets, throughout summer-autumn.

Z2–7 H7–1

***Potentilla fruticosa* 'Manchu'**
Deciduous, mound-forming shrub with reddish pink, prostrate shoots. Pure white flowers are borne amid divided, silvery gray leaves from late spring to early autumn.

Z3–7 H7–1

Convolvulus cneorum
Evergreen, rounded, bushy, dense shrub. Pink-tinged buds opening to white flowers with yellow centers are borne from late spring to late summer among narrow, silky, silvery green leaves.

Z8–11 H12–8

OTHER RECOMMENDED PLANTS:
Berzelia lanuginosa
Boenninghausenia albiflora
Cyrilla racemiflora
Cytisus albus
FUCHSIAS, illus. pp.164–5
HEATHERS, illus. pp.178–9
Hebe albicans 'Cranleigh Gem'
Hebe macrantha
Hebe ochracea
Hebe rakaiensis
Hebe vernicosa, illus. p.351
Helichrysum splendidum
RHODODENDRONS, illus. pp.132–4
Rubus tricolor

Halimium umbellatum, syn. *Helianthemum umbellatum*
Evergreen, upright shrub. Narrow, glossy, dark green leaves are white beneath. White flowers, centrally blotched with yellow, are produced in early summer from reddish buds.

Z9–11 H12–9

Cistus salviifolius
Evergreen, bushy, dense shrub with slightly wrinkled, gray-green foliage. White flowers with central yellow blotches appear in profusion during early summer.

Z8–11 H12–8

***Potentilla fruticosa* 'Farrer's White'**, syn. *P.* 'Farrer's White'
Deciduous, bushy shrub with divided, gray-green leaves. Bears an abundance of white flowers during summer-autumn.

Z3–7 H7–1

Cistus monspeliensis
Evergreen, bushy shrub with narrow, wrinkled, dark green leaves and small white flowers freely borne from early to midsummer.

Z8–12 H12–8

Cistus* x *cyprius
Evergreen, bushy shrub with sticky shoots and narrow, glossy, dark green leaves. In early summer bears large white flowers, with a red blotch at each petal base, that appear in succession for weeks but last only a day.

Z8–11 H12–8

x *Halimiocistus sahucii*, syn. *Cistus revolii* of gardens
Evergreen, bushy, dense shrub with narrow, dark green leaves that set off an abundance of pure white flowers in late spring and early summer.

Z7–9 H9–7

Cistus* x *hybridus, syn. *C.* x *corbariensis*
Evergreen, bushy, dense shrub. Has wrinkled, wavy-edged, dark green leaves and massed white flowers with central yellow blotches, carried in late spring and early summer.

Z8–11 H12–8

***Cistus* x *aguilarii* 'Maculatus'**
Evergreen, bushy shrub with narrow, wavy-edged, slightly sticky, rich green leaves. Large white flowers with a central, deep red and yellow pattern appear from early to midsummer.

Z9–11 H12–9

Cistus ladanifer, syn. *C. ladaniferus*
Evergreen, open, upright shrub. Leaves are narrow, dark green, and sticky. Bears large white flowers with red markings around the central tuft of stamens profusely in early summer.

Z7–10 H10–7

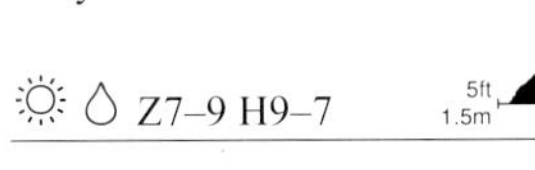
Chamaebatiaria millefolium
x *Halimiocistus wintonensis*
Sibiraea altaiensis

□ WHITE

Leptospermum rupestre
Evergreen, semi-prostrate, widely arching shrub with reddish shoots and small, dark green leaves that turn bronze-purple in winter. Small, open cup-shaped white flowers, red-flushed in bud, appear in early summer.

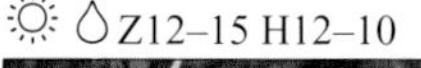
Z12–15 H12–10

Yucca whipplei,
syn. *Hesperoyucca whipplei*
Evergreen, virtually stemless shrub that forms a dense tuft of slender, pointed, blue-green leaves. Very long panicles of fragrant, greenish white flowers are produced in late spring and early summer.

Z7–9 H9–7

Vaccinium corymbosum
(Highbush blueberry)
Deciduous, upright, slightly arching shrub. Small white or pinkish flowers in late spring and early summer are followed by sweet, edible, blue-black berries. Foliage turns red in autumn.

pH Z3–7 H7–1

***Yucca flaccida* 'Ivory'**,
syn. *Y. filifera* 'Ivory'
Evergreen, very short-stemmed shrub that produces tufts of narrow, dark green leaves and long panicles of bell-shaped white flowers from mid- to late summer.

Z5–9 H9–5

Catharanthus roseus, syn. *Vinca rosea* (Rose periwinkle)
Evergreen, spreading shrub becoming messy with age. Has white to rose-pink flowers in spring to autumn, also in winter in warm areas.

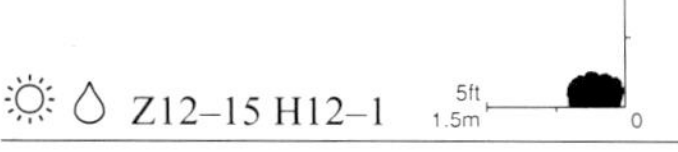
Z12–15 H12–1

Rhaphiolepis umbellata,
syn. *R. japonica, R. ovata*
Evergreen, bushy shrub with rounded, leathery, dark green leaves and clusters of fragrant white flowers in early summer.

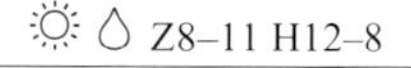
Z8–11 H12–8

***Weigela florida* 'Variegata'**
Deciduous, bushy, dense shrub. Carries a profusion of funnel-shaped pink flowers in late spring and early summer and has midgreen leaves broadly edged with creamy white.

Z5–8 H8–5

Ozothamnus ledifolius,
syn. *Helichrysum ledifolium*
Evergreen, dense shrub. Yellow shoots are covered with small, aromatic leaves, glossy, dark green above and yellow beneath. Small white flower heads are borne in early summer.

Z8–9 H9–8

Bouvardia longiflora
Cistus x *dansereaui*
FUCHSIAS, illus. pp.164–5
HEATHERS, illus. pp.178–9
Philadelphus 'Sybille'
RHODODENDRONS, illus. pp.132–4
Spiraea trilobata

Lomatia silaifolia
Evergreen, bushy shrub. Spikes of creamy white flowers, each with 4 narrow, twisted petals, are borne amid deeply divided, dark green leaves from mid- to late summer.

Z11 H12–8

Cassinia leptophylla subsp. ***vauvilliersii***, syn. *C. vauvilliersii*
Evergreen, upright shrub. Whitish shoots are covered with tiny, dark green leaves and heads of small white flowers from mid- to late summer.

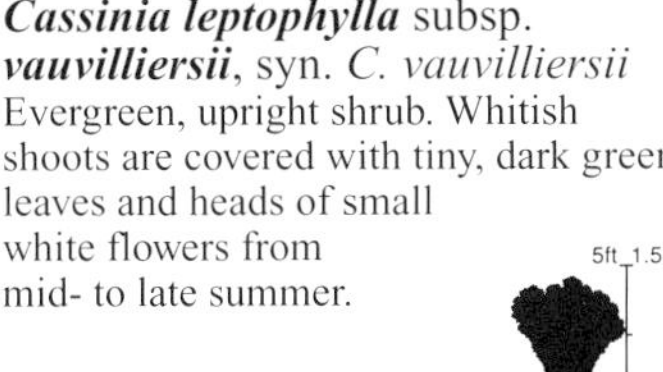

Z8–9 H9–8

Viburnum acerifolium
Deciduous, upright-branched shrub with bright green leaves that turn orange, red, and purple in autumn. Decorative red fruits, which turn purple-black, follow heads of creamy white flowers in early summer.

Z4–8 H8–1

Eriogonum arborescens
Evergreen, sparingly branched shrub. Small leaves have recurved edges and woolly white undersides. Leafy umbels of small white or pink flowers appear from spring to autumn.

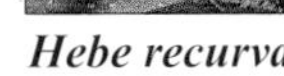

Z12–15 H12–9

Hebe recurva
Evergreen, open, spreading shrub. Leaves are narrow, curved, and blue-gray. Small spikes of white flowers appear from mid- to late summer.

Z9–11 H12–9

Hebe albicans
Evergreen shrub that forms a dense mound of blue-gray foliage covered with small, tight clusters of white flowers from early to midsummer.

Z9–11 H12–9

***Deutzia* 'Mont Rose'**
Deciduous, bushy shrub that produces clusters of pink or pinkish purple flowers in early summer with yellow anthers and occasionally white markings. Leaves are sharply toothed and dark green.

Z5–8 H8–6

***Potentilla fruticosa* 'Daydawn'**, syn. *P.* 'Daydawn'
Deciduous, bushy, rather arching shrub. Creamy yellow flowers flushed with orange-pink appear among divided, midgreen leaves from early summer to midautumn.

Z3–7 H7–1

Protea cynaroides (King protea)
Evergreen, bushy, rounded shrub. Waterlily-shaped flower heads, 5–8in (13–20cm) wide, with silky, petal-like pink to red bracts, appear in spring-summer. Leaves are oval and mid- to dark green.

Z13–15 H12–9

***Abelia* 'Edward Goucher'**
Deciduous or semi-evergreen, arching shrub. Oval, bright green leaves are bronze when young. Bears a profusion of lilac-pink flowers from midsummer to autumn.

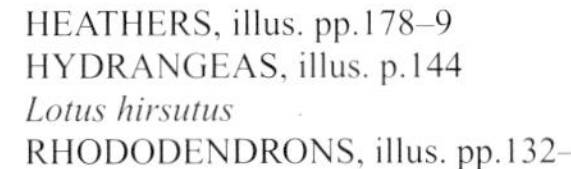

Z6–9 H9–1

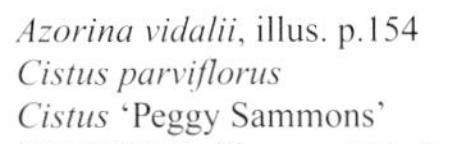

Azorina vidalii, illus. p.154
Cistus parviflorus
Cistus 'Peggy Sammons'
FUCHSIAS, illus. pp.164–5
HEATHERS, illus. pp.178–9
HYDRANGEAS, illus. p.144
Lotus hirsutus
RHODODENDRONS, illus. pp.132–4

SHRUBS small SUMMER INTEREST

PINK

Abelia schumannii
Deciduous, arching shrub. Pointed, midgreen leaves are bronze when young. Yellow-blotched rose-purple and white flowers appear from mid-summer to midautumn.

Z7–9 H9–7

Myoporum parvifolium
Evergreen, spreading to prostrate shrub with semi-succulent leaves. In summer has clusters of small honey-scented flowers, white or pink with purple spots, and tiny purple fruits in autumn.

Z11–15 H12–10

Cistus* × *skanbergii
Evergreen, bushy shrub. A profusion of pale pink flowers appears amid narrow, gray-green leaves from early to midsummer.

Z9–11 H12–9

Pimelea ferruginea
Evergreen, dense, rounded shrub with tiny, recurved, deep green leaves. Small, tubular, rich pink flowers appear in dense heads in spring or early summer.

Z12–15 H12–10

Gaultheria shallon (Shallon)
Evergreen, bushy shrub. Red shoots carry broad, sharply pointed, dark green leaves. Racemes of urn-shaped pink flowers in late spring and early summer are followed by purple berries.

Z6–8 H8–6

***Deutzia* × *elegantissima* 'Rosealind'**
Deciduous, rounded, bushy, dense shrub that produces clusters of 5-petaled, deep pink flowers from late spring to early summer.

Z6–8 H8–6

Phlomis italica
Evergreen, upright shrub. In mid-summer, whorls of lilac-pink flowers are borne at the ends of shoots amid narrow, woolly, gray-green leaves.

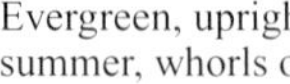

Z9–11 H12–9

Indigofera dielsiana
Deciduous, upright, open shrub. Dark green leaves consist of 7–11 oval leaflets. Slender, erect spikes of pale pink flowers are borne from early summer to early autumn.

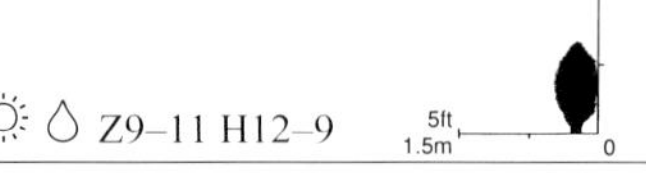

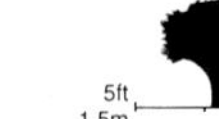

Z6–9 H9–6

***Cistus* 'Peggy Sammons'**
Evergreen, bushy shrub with oval, gray-green leaves. Saucer-shaped, pale purplish pink flowers are produced freely during early summer.

Z9–11 H12–9

Bauera rubioides
Calliandra eriophylla, illus. p.172
FUCHSIAS, illus. pp.164–5
HEATHERS, illus. pp.178–9
HYDRANGEAS, illus. p.144
Indigofera pseudotinctoria
RHODODENDRONS, illus. pp.132–4

***Weigela florida* 'Foliis Purpureis'**
Deciduous, low, bushy shrub that bears funnel-shaped flowers, deep pink outside, pale pink to white inside, in late spring and early summer. Leaves are dull purple or purplish green.

Z5–8 H8–4

***Spiraea japonica* 'Little Princess'**
Slow-growing, deciduous, mound-forming shrub that produces copious small heads of rose-pink blooms from mid- to late summer. Small, dark green leaves are bronze when young.

Z4–9 H9–1

***Spiraea japonica* 'Goldflame'**
Deciduous, upright, slightly arching shrub with orange-red young leaves turning to bright yellow and finally pale green. Bears heads of deep rose-pink flowers from mid- to late summer.

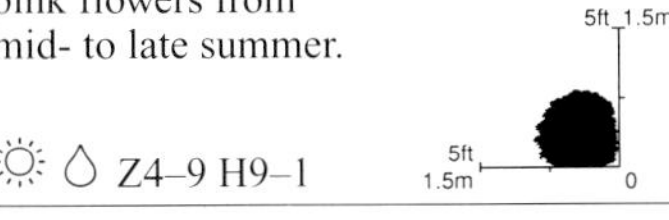

Z4–9 H9–1

***Ceanothus* 'Perle Rose'**
Deciduous, bushy shrub that from midsummer to early autumn bears dense racemes of bright carmine-pink flowers amid broad, oval, midgreen leaves.

Z8–11 H12–8

***Hebe* 'Great Orme'**
Evergreen, rounded, open shrub. Has deep purplish shoots and glossy, dark green foliage. Slender spikes of deep pink flowers that fade to white are produced from mid-summer to midautumn.

Z9–11 H12–9

***Justicia carnea*, syn. *Jacobinia carnea*, *J. pohliana* (King's crown)**
Evergreen, sparingly branched shrub with velvety-haired leaves. Has spikes of pink to rose-purple flowers in summer-autumn.

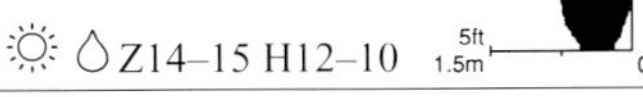

Z14–15 H12–10

Penstemon isophyllus
Slightly messy, deciduous shrub or subshrub that, from mid- to late summer, carries long sprays of large white- and red-throated, deep pink flowers above spear-shaped, glossy, midgreen leaves.

Z8–11 H12–8

***Pentas lanceolata*, syn. *P. carnea* (Egyptian star-cluster)**
Mainly evergreen, loosely rounded shrub with hairy, bright green leaves. In summer-autumn produces dense clusters of pink, lilac, red, or white flowers.

Z14–15 H12–10

***Spiraea japonica* 'Anthony Waterer'**
Deciduous, upright, compact shrub. Red young foliage matures to dark green. Heads of crimson-pink blooms appear from mid- to late summer.

Z3–9 H9–1

Cistus 'Silver Pink'
FUCHSIAS, illus. pp.164–5
HEATHERS, illus. pp.178–9
Hebe 'Eveline'
HYDRANGEAS, illus. p.144
Indigofera decora
RHODODENDRONS, illus. pp.132–4

Fuchsias

With their vividly colored blooms and long flowering season (usually throughout summer and well into autumn), fuchsias make outstanding shrubs for the greenhouse and for the garden. Single to double flowers often have flared or elegantly recurved sepals. In mild areas fuchsias may be grown outside all year; in colder climates most are best grown in a greenhouse or as summer bedding.

Fuchsias raised from cuttings are sparingly branched and often become straggly unless pruned from an early stage by pinching out the growing tips. To produce standard plants, the leader shoot is supported, and emerging side-shoots are pinched back to one pair of leaves. When the stem has reached the required height and has produced 2 or 3 pairs of leaves above this, it is then pinched out and the plant is left to develop naturally.

F. 'Jack Shahan'

F. *arborescens*

F. 'Lady Thumb'

F. 'Dollar Princess'

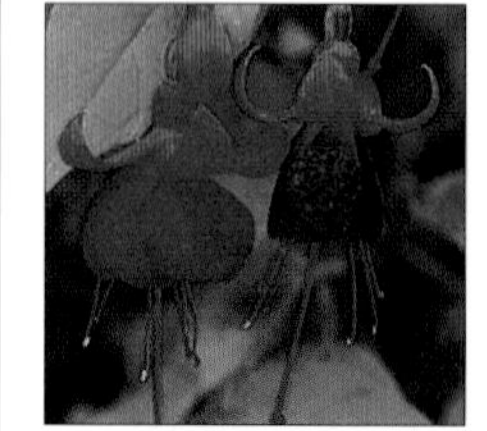
F. 'Gruss aus dem Bodethal'

F. 'Harry Gray'

F. 'Pink Galore'

F. 'Ballet Girl'

F. 'Nellie Nuttall'

F. 'Peppermint Stick'

F. 'Tom Thumb'

F. 'Annabel'

F. 'Other Fellow'

F. 'Bicentennial'

F. 'Golden Dawn'

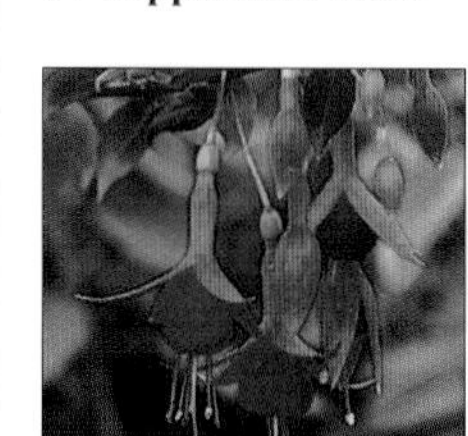
F. 'Autumnale'

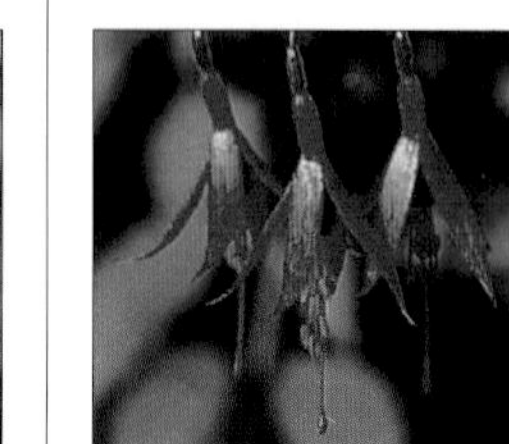
F. *magellanica*

F. 'Rufus'

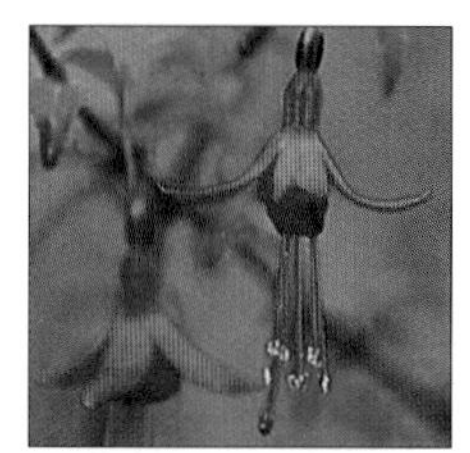
F. 'Riccartonii'

F. 'Golden Marinka'

F. 'Leonora'

F. 'Swingtime'

F. 'Heidi Weiss'

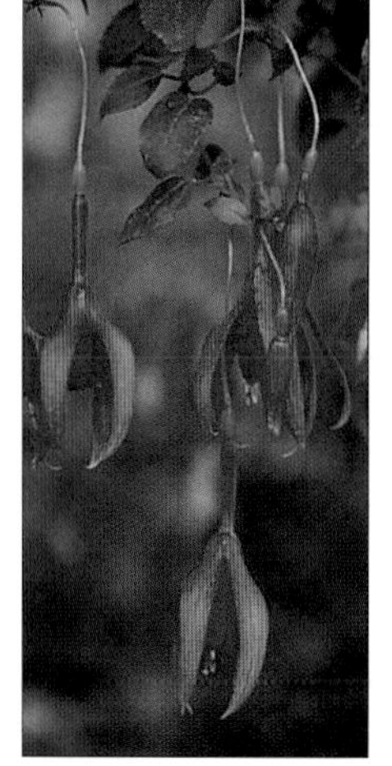
F. 'Red Spider'

F. 'Mrs. Popple'

PINK–RED

F. x *bacillaris*

F. 'Thalia'

F. 'Tom West'

F. 'Celia Smedley'

F. 'Cascade'

F. 'Estelle Marie'

F. boliviana var. ***alba***

F. 'La Campanella'

F. 'Love's Reward'

F. 'Mrs. Lovell Swisher'

F. 'Rose of Castile'

F. procumbens

F. 'Lye's Unique'

F. fulgens

F. 'Coralle'

***Cistus creticus*,**
syn. *C. incanus* subsp. *creticus*
Evergreen, bushy shrub. Pink or purplish pink flowers, each with a central yellow blotch, appear amid gray-green leaves from early to midsummer.

Z9–10 H10–9 5ft 1.5m

***Escallonia rubra* 'Woodside'**
Evergreen, bushy, dense shrub. Has small, glossy, dark green leaves and short racemes of small, tubular crimson flowers in summer-autumn.

Z8–9 H9–8 5ft 1.5m

***Kalmia angustifolia* f. *rubra*,**
syn. *K.a.* 'Rubra' (Sheep laurel)
Evergreen, bushy, mound-forming shrub with oval, dark green leaves and clusters of small, deep red flowers in early summer.

pH Z7–8 H8–7 5ft 1.5m

Sutherlandia frutescens
Evergreen, upright shrub. Has leaves of 13–21 gray-haired, deep green leaflets. Bright red flowers in late spring and summer are followed by pale green, later red-flushed, inflated seed pods.

Z13–15 H12–9 5ft 1.5m

Crossandra nilotica
Evergreen, upright to spreading, leafy shrub with oval, pointed, rich green leaves. Small, tubular apricot to pale brick-red flowers with spreading petals are carried in short spikes from spring to autumn.

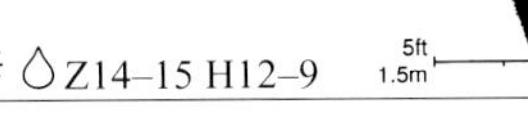

Z14–15 H12–9 5ft 1.5m

Ixora coccinea
Evergreen, rounded shrub with glossy, dark green leaves to 4in (10cm) long. Small, tubular red, pink, orange, or yellow flowers appear in dense heads in summer.

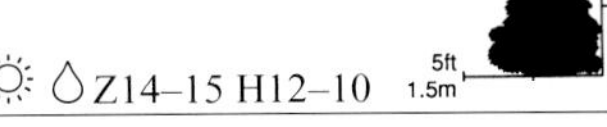

Z14–15 H12–10 5ft 1.5m

Anisodontea capensis
Cistus x *purpureus*
Coleonema pulchrum
HEATHERS, illus. pp.178–9

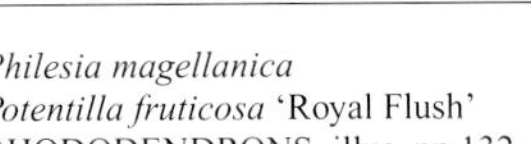

Philesia magellanica
Potentilla fruticosa 'Royal Flush'
RHODODENDRONS, illus. pp.132–4

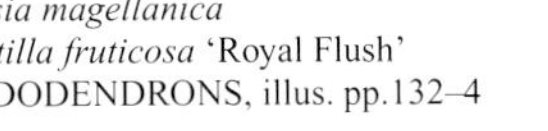

SHRUBS small SUMMER INTEREST

■ RED

***Potentilla fruticosa* 'Red Ace'**
Deciduous, spreading, bushy, dense shrub. Bright vermilion flowers, pale yellow on the backs of petals, are produced among midgreen leaves from late spring to midautumn but fade quickly in strong sun.

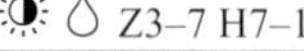
Z3–7 H7–1

Salvia microphylla* var. *neurepia
Evergreen, well-branched, upright shrub with pale to mid-green leaves. Has tubular, bright red flowers from purple-tinted green calyces in late summer and autumn.

Z12–15 H12–10

***Justicia brandegeeana*,**
syn. *Beloperone guttata*, *Drejerella guttata* (Shrimp plant)
Evergreen, rounded shrub intermittently (but mainly in summer) producing white flowers surrounded by shrimp pink bracts.

Z14–15 H12–1

***Grevillea* 'Robyn Gordon'**
Evergreen, sprawling shrub with leathery, dark green leaves. At intervals from early spring to late summer, arching stems bear racemes of crimson flowers with protruding, recurved styles.

Z13–15 H12–9

***Acer palmatum* 'Chitoseyama'**
Deciduous, arching, mound-forming shrub or small tree with lobed, mid-green foliage that gradually turns brilliant red from late summer to autumn. Produces small reddish purple flowers in midspring.

Z6–8 H8–6

Phygelius aequalis
Evergreen or semi-evergreen, upright subshrub. Clusters of tubular, pale red flowers with yellow throats appear from midsummer to early autumn. The leaves are oval and dark green.

Z7–9 H9–7

Salvia fulgens
Evergreen, upright subshrub. Oval leaves are white and woolly beneath, hairy above. Racemes of tubular, 2-lipped scarlet flowers appear in late summer.

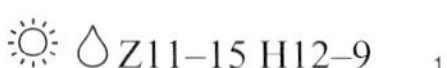
Z11–15 H12–9

***Acer palmatum* 'Dissectum Atropurpureum'**
Deciduous shrub that forms a mound of deeply divided, bronze-red or purple foliage that turns brilliant red, orange, or yellow in autumn. Has small, reddish purple flowers in midspring.

Z6–8 H8–6

Bouvardia ternifolia, illus. p.173
FUCHSIAS, illus. pp.164–5
Grevillea alpina
RHODODENDRONS, illus. pp.132–4

***Hebe hulkeana* 'Lilac Hint'**
Evergreen, upright, open-branched shrub with toothed, glossy, pale green leaves. A profusion of small, pale lilac flowers appears in large racemes in late spring and early summer.

Z9–11 H12–10

Rosmarinus officinalis (Rosemary)
Evergreen, bushy, dense shrub with aromatic, narrow leaves. Small purplish blue to blue flowers appear from mid-spring to early summer and sometimes in autumn. Used as a culinary herb.

Z8–11 H12–8

Lantana montevidensis, syn. *L. delicatissima*, *L. sellowiana*
Evergreen, trailing or mat-forming shrub with serrated leaves. Has heads of rose-purple flowers, each with a yellow eye, intermittently all year but mainly in summer.

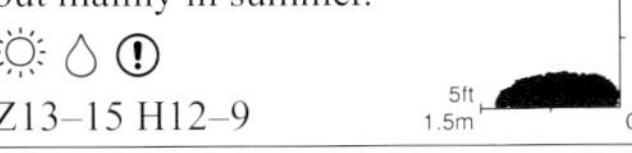

Z13–15 H12–9

Desmodium elegans, syn. *D. tiliifolium*
Deciduous, upright subshrub. Mid-green leaves consist of 3 large leaflets. Large racemes of pale lilac to deep pink flowers appear from late summer to midautumn.

Z8–11 H12–8

***Hebe* 'E.A. Bowles'**
Evergreen, rounded, bushy shrub with narrow, glossy, pale green leaves and slender spikes of lilac flowers produced from midsummer to late autumn.

Z10–11 H12–10

Heliotropium arborescens, syn. *H. peruvianum*
Evergreen, bushy shrub. Semi-glossy, dark green leaves are finely wrinkled. Purple to lavender flowers are borne in dense, flat clusters from late spring to winter.

Z12–15 H12–9

Polygala* x *dalmaisiana, syn. *P. myrtifolia* var. *grandiflora* of gardens
Evergreen, erect shrub with small, grayish green leaves. White-veined, rich purple flowers appear from late spring to autumn.

Z13–15 H12–9

***Brunfelsia pauciflora* 'Macrantha'**
Evergreen, spreading shrub with leathery leaves. Blue-purple flowers, aging to white in about 3 days, appear from winter to summer.

Z13–15 H12–10

Lavandula stoechas
(French lavender)
Evergreen, bushy, dense shrub. Heads of tiny, fragrant, deep purple flowers, topped by rose-purple bracts, appear in late spring and summer. Mature leaves are silver-gray and aromatic.

Z8–9 H9–8

***Hebe* 'Autumn Glory'**
Evergreen shrub that forms a mound of purplish red shoots and rounded, deep green leaves, over which dense racemes of deep purple-blue flowers appear from midsummer to early winter.

Z9–10 H10–9

***Lavandula* 'Hidcote'**, syn. *L. angustifolia* 'Hidcote'
Evergreen, bushy shrub with dense spikes of fragrant, deep purple flowers from mid- to late summer and narrow, aromatic, silver-gray leaves.

Z5–8 H8–3

Agathosma pulchella
Amorpha canescens
Barleria cristata
Berberis thunbergii 'Atropurpurea Nana'
Berberis thunbergii 'Rose Glow'
Carmichaelia enysii
FUCHSIAS, illus. pp.164–5
HEATHERS, illus. pp.178–9
Hebe 'Alicia Amherst'
Hebe 'La Séduisante'
HYDRANGEAS, illus. p.144
Lavandula dentata
Lavandula x *intermedia* 'Grappenhall'
Osbeckia stellata
Perovskia atriplicifolia
RHODODENDRONS, illus. pp.132–4

SHRUBS small SUMMER INTEREST

PURPLE–BLUE

***Hebe* 'Purple Queen'**, syn. *H.* 'Amy'
Evergreen, bushy, compact shrub with glossy, deep green leaves that are purple-tinged when young. Dense racemes of deep purple flowers appear from early summer to midautumn.

Z9–11 H12–9 5ft 1.5m 5ft 1.5m

Ceanothus thyrsiflorus* var. *repens (Creeping blue blossom)
Evergreen, dense shrub that forms a mound of broad, glossy, dark green leaves. Racemes of blue flowers are borne in late spring and early summer.

Z8–11 H12–8 5ft 1.5m 8ft 2.5m

***Felicia amelloides* 'Santa Anita'**
Evergreen, bushy, spreading shrub. Blue flower heads with bright yellow centers are borne on long stalks from late spring to autumn among round to oval, bright green leaves.

Z12–15 H12–9 5ft 1.5m 5ft 5m

Hyssopus officinalis (Hyssop)
Semi-evergreen or deciduous, bushy shrub with aromatic, narrowly oval, deep green leaves. Small blue flowers appear from midsummer to early autumn. Sometimes used as a culinary herb.

Z6–9 H9–6 5ft 1.5m 5ft 1.5m

***Caryopteris* x *clandonensis* 'Arthur Simmonds'**
Deciduous, bushy subshrub. Masses of blue to purplish blue flowers appear amid narrowly oval, irregularly toothed, gray-green leaves from late summer to autumn.

Z6–9 H9–6 5ft 1.5m 5ft 1.5m

***Hebe* 'Bowles' Variety'**
Evergreen, rounded shrub with ovate-oblong, slightly glossy, midgreen leaves. In summer, it bears mauve-blue flowers in compact, tapered, terminal racemes.

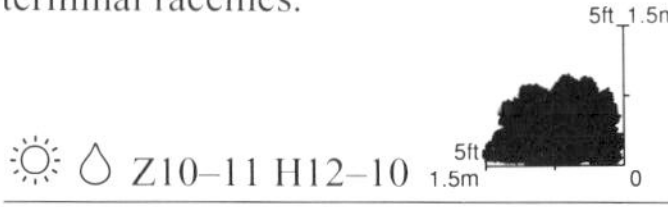

Z10–11 H12–10 5ft 1.5m 5ft 1.5m

***Ceanothus* 'Gloire de Versailles'**, syn. *C.* x *delileanus* 'Gloire de Versailles'
Vigorous, deciduous, bushy shrub. Has broad, oval, midgreen leaves and large racemes of pale blue flowers from midsummer to early autumn.

Z7–11 H12–7 5ft 1.5m 5ft 1.5m

***Perovskia* 'Blue Spire'**
Deciduous, upright subshrub with gray-white stems. Profuse spikes of violet-blue flowers appear from late summer to midautumn above aromatic, deeply cut, gray-green leaves.

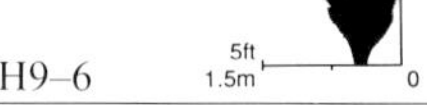

Z6–9 H9–6 5ft 1.5m 5ft 1.5m

GREEN–YELLOW

***Symphoricarpos orbiculatus* 'Foliis Variegatis'**, syn. *S.o.* 'Variegatus'
Deciduous, bushy, dense shrub with bright green leaves edged with yellow. Occasionally bears white or pink flowers in summer-autumn.

Z2–6 H6–1 5ft 1.5m 5ft 1.5m

***Justicia brandegeeana* 'Chartreuse'**
Evergreen, arching shrub producing white flowers surrounded by pale yellow-green bracts mainly in summer but also intermittently during the year.

Z14–15 H12–9 5ft 1.5m 5ft 1.5m

Weigela middendorffiana
Deciduous, bushy, arching shrub. From midspring to early summer funnel-shaped, sulfur yellow flowers spotted with orange inside are borne amid bright green foliage.

Z5–7 H7–5 5ft 1.5m 5ft 1.5m

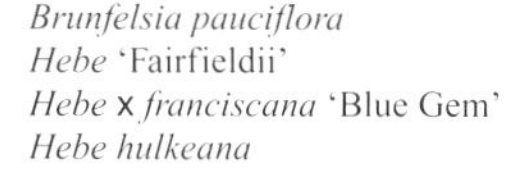

Brunfelsia pauciflora
Hebe 'Fairfieldii'
Hebe x *franciscana* 'Blue Gem'
Hebe hulkeana

HYDRANGEAS, illus. p.144
Lavandula angustifolia 'Munstead'
Perovskia 'Hybrida'
Phlomis cashmeriana

RHODODENDRONS, illus. pp.132–4

Berberis 'Parkjuweel'
Muehlenbeckia complexa
Myrsine africana

Potentilla fruticosa 'Vilmoriniana'
Deciduous, upright shrub that bears pale yellow or creamy white flowers from late spring to mid autumn. Silver-gray leaves are divided into narrow leaflets.
Z3–7 H7–1

Santolina pinnata subsp. **neapolitana 'Sulphurea'**
Evergreen, rounded, bushy shrub with aromatic, deeply cut, feathery, gray-green foliage. Produces heads of pale primrose yellow flowers in midsummer.

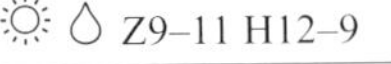

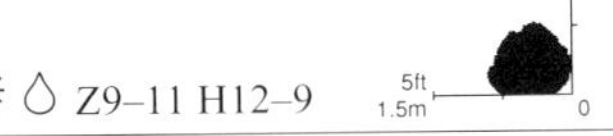

Z9–11 H12–9

Lupinus arboreus (Tree lupin)
Fast-growing, semi-evergreen, sprawling shrub that in early summer usually bears short spikes of fragrant, clear yellow flowers above hairy, pale green leaves composed of 6–9 leaflets.

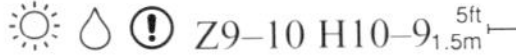

Z9–10 H10–9

Phygelius aequalis 'Yellow Trumpet'
Evergreen or semi-evergreen, upright subshrub. Bears clusters of pendent, tubular, pale creamy yellow flowers from midsummer to early autumn.
Z7–9 H9–7

Potentilla fruticosa 'Elizabeth', syn. *P.* 'Elizabeth'
Deciduous, bushy, dense shrub with small, deeply divided leaves and large, bright yellow flowers that appear from late spring to midautumn.
Z3–7 H7–1

Grevillea juniperina f. **sulphurea**, syn. *G. sulphurea*
Evergreen, rounded, bushy shrub. Has needlelike leaves, recurved and dark green above and silky-haired beneath, and groups of small, spidery, pale yellow flowers in spring-summer.

Z11–15 H12–1

Potentilla fruticosa 'Friedrichsenii'
Vigorous, deciduous, upright shrub. From late spring to midautumn, pale yellow flowers are produced amid gray-green leaves.
Z3–7 H7–1

Halimium 'Susan'
Evergreen, spreading shrub with narrow, oval, gray-green leaves. Numerous single or semi-double, bright yellow flowers with central, deep purple-red markings are borne in small clusters along branches in summer.
Z9–11 H12–9

Halimium lasianthum subsp. **formosum**, syn. *H. formosum*
Evergreen, spreading, bushy shrub. Has gray-green foliage and golden yellow flowers with central, deep red blotches, borne in late spring and early summer.

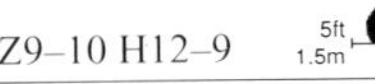

Z9–10 H12–9

Chamaecytisus supinus
Coronilla valentina subsp. *glauca*, illus. p.157
Genista tinctoria 'Royal Gold'
Helichrysum italicum
Potentilla fruticosa 'Maanelys'
RHODODENDRONS, illus. pp.132–4
Ruta graveolens 'Jackman's Blue', illus. p.177
Santolina pinnata subsp. *neapolitana*
Santolina rosmarinifolia 'Primrose Gem'
Vinca minor 'Alba Variegata'

SHRUBS small SUMMER INTEREST

□ YELLOW

Phlomis fruticosa
(Jerusalem sage)
Evergreen, spreading shrub with upright shoots. Whorls of deep golden yellow flowers are produced amid sagelike, gray-green foliage from early to midsummer.

Z8–9 H9–8

***Berberis thunbergii* 'Aurea'**
Deciduous, bushy, spiny shrub with small, golden yellow leaves. Racemes of small, red-tinged, pale yellow flowers in midspring are followed by red berries in autumn.

Z5–8 H8–5

***Cytisus nigricans*,**
syn. *Lembotropis nigricans*
Deciduous, upright shrub with dark green leaves composed of 3 leaflets. Has a long-lasting display of tall, slender spires of yellow flowers during summer.

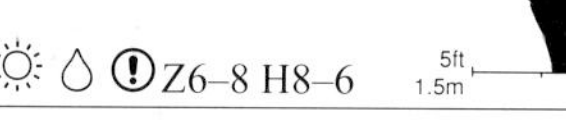

Z6–8 H8–6

Genista hispanica (Spanish gorse)
Deciduous, bushy, very spiny shrub with few leaves. Bears dense clusters of golden yellow flowers profusely in late spring and early summer.

Z7–9 H9–7

***Brachyglottis* Dunedin Hybrids 'Sunshine'**, syn. *Senecio* 'Sunshine'
Evergreen, bushy shrub that forms a mound of silvery gray young leaves, later turning dark green. Bears bright yellow flower heads on felted shoots from early to midsummer.

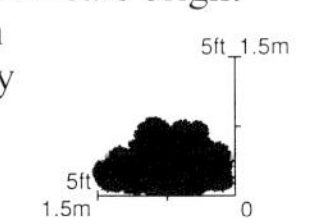

Z9–10 H10–9

Hypericum calycinum
(Aaron's beard)
Evergreen or semi-evergreen dwarf shrub that makes a good groundcover. Has large, bright yellow flowers from midsummer to midautumn and dark green leaves.

Z5–9 H9–4

***Hypericum* 'Hidcote'**
Evergreen or semi-evergreen, bushy, dense shrub. Bears an abundance of large, golden yellow flowers from midsummer to early autumn amid narrowly oval, dark green leaves.

Z6–9 H9–6

***Hypericum* x *inodorum* 'Elstead'**
Deciduous or semi-evergreen, upright shrub. Abundant, small yellow flowers borne from midsummer to early autumn are followed by ornamental, orange-red fruits. Dark green leaves are aromatic when crushed.

Z7–9 H9–7

Hypericum kouytchense
Deciduous or semi-evergreen, arching shrub. Golden yellow flowers with conspicuous stamens are borne among foliage from midsummer to early autumn and followed by decorative, bronze-red fruit capsules.

Z6–9 H9–6

***Reinwardtia indica*,**
syn. *R. trigyna* (Yellow flax)
Evergreen, upright subshrub, branching from the base. Has grayish green leaves and small clusters of yellow flowers mainly in summer but also during the year.

Z13–15 H12–10

Euryops pectinatus
Evergreen, upright shrub. Deeply cut, gray-green leaves set off large heads of daisylike, bright yellow flowers, borne in late spring and early summer and often again in winter.

Z11–15 H12–9

Brachyglottis compacta
Hermannia incana
Hypericum x *moserianum*
Lantana camara
Oxalis hedysaroides
Potentilla fruticosa
Potentilla fruticosa 'Beesii'
Potentilla fruticosa 'Elizabeth'
Potentilla fruticosa 'Gold Drop'
Santolina chamaecyparissus
Santolina rosmarinifolia

Brachyglottis monroi
Evergreen, bushy, dense shrub that makes an excellent windbreak in mild coastal areas. Has small, wavy-edged, dark green leaves with white undersides. Bears heads of bright yellow flowers in midsummer.

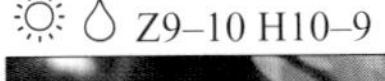

Z9–10 H10–9 5ft 1.5m 5ft 1.5m 0

***Abutilon* 'Kentish Belle'**
Semi-evergreen, arching shrub with purple shoots and deeply lobed, purple-veined, dark green leaves. Bears large, pendent, bell-shaped, orange-yellow and red flowers in summer-autumn.

Z11–15 H12–9 5ft 1.5m 5ft 1.5m 0

***Isoplexis canariensis*,**
syn. *Digitalis canariensis*
Evergreen, rounded, sparingly branched shrub. Bears open-tubular, yellow to red- or brownish orange flowers in dense, upright spikes, to 12in (30cm) tall, in summer.

Z12–15 H12–9 5ft 1.5m 5ft 1.5m 0

***Potentilla fruticosa* 'Sunset',**
syn. *P.* 'Sunset'
Deciduous shrub, bushy at first, later arching. Deep orange flowers, fading in strong sun, appear from early summer to midautumn. Mid-green leaves are divided into narrowly oval leaflets.

Z3–7 H7–1 5ft 1.5m 5ft 1.5m 0

***Grindelia chiloensis*,**
syn. *G. speciosa*
Mainly evergreen, bushy shrub with sticky stems. Sticky, lance-shaped, serrated leaves are up to 5in (12cm) long. Has large, daisylike yellow flower heads in summer.

Z11–15 H12–9 5ft 1.5m 5ft 1.5m 0

Cytisus scoparius* f. *andreanus
Deciduous, arching shrub with narrow, dark green leaves that are divided into 3 leaflets. Bears a profusion of bright yellow and red flowers along elegant green branchlets in late spring and early summer.

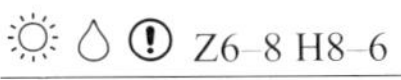

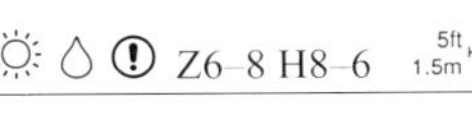

Z6–8 H8–6 5ft 1.5m 5ft 1.5m 0

***Mimulus aurantiacus*, syn.**
Diplacus glutinosus, *M. glutinosus*
Evergreen, domed to rounded shrub with sticky, lance-shaped, glossy, rich green leaves. Has tubular orange, yellow, or red-purple flowers from late spring to autumn.

Z7–11 H12–7 5ft 1.5m 5ft 1.5m 0

***Juanulloa mexicana*,**
syn. *J. aurantiaca*
Evergreen, upright, sparingly branched shrub. Leaves are felted beneath. Has orange flowers, each with a ribbed calyx, in short, nodding clusters in summer.

Z13–15 H12–9 5ft 1.5m 5ft 1.5m 0

***Lantana* 'Spreading Sunset'**
Evergreen, rounded to spreading shrub with finely wrinkled, deep green leaves. Has tiny, tubular flowers in a range of colors, carried in dense, rounded heads from spring to autumn.

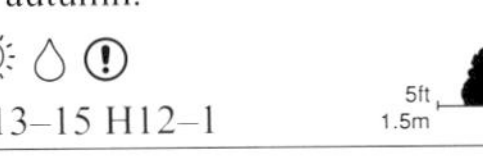

Z13–15 H12–1 5ft 1.5m 5ft 1.5m 0

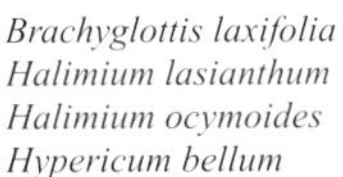

Brachyglottis laxifolia
Halimium lasianthum
Halimium ocymoides
Hypericum bellum
Hypericum x *cyathiflorum* 'Gold Cup'
Hypericum patulum
Nematanthus gregarius, illus. p.157
Nematanthus strigillosus
Phlomis chrysophylla
Phlomis longifolia var. *bailanica*
Potentilla fruticosa 'Goldfinger'
Potentilla fruticosa 'Jackman's Variety'
RHODODENDRONS, illus. pp.132–4

ORANGE

Cuphea ignea, syn. *C. platycentra* (Cigar flower)
Evergreen, spreading, bushy subshrub with bright green leaves. From spring to autumn has tubular, dark orange-red flowers, each with a dark band and white ring at the mouth.

Z10–11 H12–6

Cuphea cyanea
Evergreen, rounded subshrub with narrowly oval, sticky-haired leaves. Tubular flowers in orange-red, yellow, and violet-blue are carried in summer.

Z13–15 H12–10

Justicia spicigera, syn. *J. ghiesbreghtiana* of gardens, *Jacobinia spicigera*
Evergreen, well-branched shrub with spikes of tubular orange or red flowers in summer and occasionally other seasons.

Z14–15 H12–10

Potentilla fruticosa 'Tangerine'

SHRUBS small AUTUMN INTEREST

WHITE–RED

Turraea obtusifolia
Evergreen, rounded, bushy, arching shrub with oval to lance-shaped leaves. Bears fragrant white flowers from autumn to spring, followed by orange-yellow fruits like tiny, peeled tangerines.

Z10–11 H12–10

Calliandra eriophylla (Fairy duster)
Evergreen, stiff, dense shrub. Leaves have numerous tiny leaflets. From late spring to autumn has pompons of tiny, pink-anthered white florets, followed by brown seed pods.

Z14–15 H12–10

***Berberis* 'Rubrostilla'**
Deciduous, arching shrub. Globose to cup-shaped, pale yellow flowers, appearing in early summer, are followed by a profusion of large, coral-red fruits. Gray-green leaves turn brilliant red in late autumn.

Z7–9 H9–7

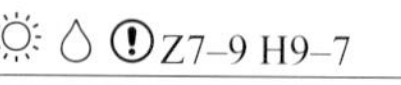

Cotoneaster horizontalis (Wall-spray)
Deciduous, stiff-branched, spreading shrub. Glossy, dark green leaves redden in late autumn. Bears pinkish white flowers from late spring to early summer, followed by red fruits.

Z4–7 H7–3

***Viburnum opulus* 'Compactum'**
Deciduous, dense shrub. Has deep green leaves, red in autumn, and profuse white flowers in spring and early summer, followed by bunches of bright red berries.

Z4–8 H8–1

Vaccinium angustifolium* var. *laevifolium (Lowbush blueberry)
Deciduous, bushy shrub with bright green leaves that redden in autumn. Edible blue fruits follow white, sometimes pinkish, spring-blooming flowers.

pH Z2–8 H8–1

OTHER RECOMMENDED PLANTS:
Anisodontea capensis
Bouvardia longiflora
Cuphea hyssopifolia, illus. p.158
Cyrilla racemiflora
HEATHERS, illus. pp.178–9
Pentas lanceolata, illus. p.163
Salvia leucantha

■ RED

***Bouvardia ternifolia*,**
syn. *B. triphylla* (Scarlet trompetilla)
Mainly evergreen, bushy, upright shrub with leaves in whorls of 3. Has tubular, bright scarlet flowers from summer to early winter.

Z13–15 H12–10

***Vaccinium corymbosum* 'Pioneer'**
Deciduous, upright, slightly arching shrub. Dark green leaves turn bright red in autumn. Small white or pinkish flowers in late spring are followed by sweet, edible, blue-black berries.

pH Z3–7 H7–1

Vaccinium parvifolium
Deciduous, upright shrub. Has small, dark green leaves that become bright red in autumn. Edible, bright red fruits are produced after small, pinkish white flowers borne in late spring and early summer.

pH Z5–8 H8–5

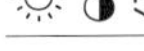

PURPLE–YELLOW

Elsholtzia stauntonii (Mint bush)
Deciduous, open subshrub. Sharply toothed, mint-scented, dark green leaves turn red in autumn. Slender spires of pale purplish flowers appear during late summer and autumn.

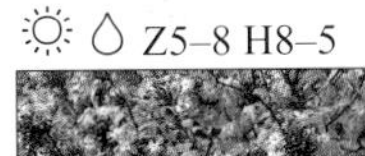

Z5–8 H8–5

Ceratostigma willmottianum
Deciduous, open shrub. Has leaves that turn red in late autumn and bright, rich blue flowers from late summer until well into autumn.

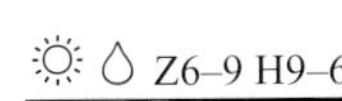

Z6–9 H9–6

Coriaria terminalis* var. *xanthocarpa
Deciduous, arching subshrub. Leaves have oval leaflets and turn red in autumn. Greenish flowers in late spring are followed by decorative, succulent yellow fruits in late summer and autumn.

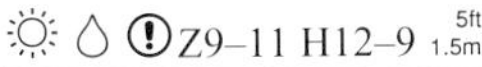

Z9–11 H12–9

□ WHITE

***Skimmia japonica* 'Fructo Albo'**
Evergreen, bushy, dense, dwarf shrub. Has aromatic, dark green leaves and dense clusters of small white flowers from mid- to late spring, succeeded by white berries.

Z7–9 H9–7

***Gaultheria mucronata* 'Wintertime'**
Evergreen, bushy, dense shrub. Has prickly, glossy, dark green leaves and white flowers in late spring and early summer, followed by large, long-lasting white berries.

pH Z8–9 H9–8

Lonicera* x *purpusii
Semi-evergreen, bushy, dense shrub with oval, dark green leaves. Small clusters of fragrant, short-tubed white flowers with spreading petal lobes and yellow anthers appear in winter and early spring.

Z7–9 H9–7

Cotoneaster adpressus
Cotoneaster microphyllus
Crossandra infundibuliformis
Salvia microphylla var. *microphylla*

Ceratostigma griffithii
HEATHERS, illus. pp.178–9
Heliotropium arborescens, illus. p.167
Rosmarinus officinalis 'Severn Sea'

OTHER RECOMMENDED PLANTS:
Daphne mezereum f. *alba*
HEATHERS, illus. pp.178–9
Sarcococca confusa
Sarcococca hookeriana
Sarcococca ruscifolia
Turraea obtusifolia, illus. p.172

SHRUBS small WINTER INTEREST

WHITE–PINK

Sarcococca humilis, syn. *S. hookeriana* var. *humilis*
Evergreen, low, clump-forming shrub. Tiny, fragrant white flowers with pink anthers appear amid glossy, dark green foliage in late winter and are followed by spherical black fruits.

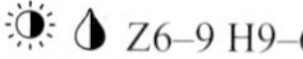

Z6–9 H9–6

Sarcococca hookeriana var. ***digyna***
Evergreen, clump-forming, suckering, dense shrub with narrow, bright green leaves. Tiny, fragrant white flowers with pink anthers open in winter and are followed by spherical black fruits.

Z6–9 H9–6

***Gaultheria mucronata* 'Mulberry Wine'**
Evergreen, bushy, dense shrub with large, globose magenta berries that mature to deep purple. These follow white flowers borne in spring–summer. Leaves are glossy dark green.

Z8–9 H9–8

***Daphne odora* 'Aureomarginata'**
Evergreen, bushy shrub with glossy, dark green leaves narrowly edged with yellow. Clusters of very fragrant, deep purplish pink and white flowers appear from midwinter to early spring.

Z7–9 H9–7

Daphne mezereum (Mezereon)
Deciduous, upright shrub. Very fragrant purple or pink blooms clothe the bare stems in late winter and early spring, followed by red fruits. Mature leaves are narrowly oval and dull gray-green.

Z5–8 H8–5

Abeliophyllum distichum
Centradenia floribunda
Diosma ericoides
HEATHERS, illus. pp.178–9

Symphoricarpos x *chenaultii* 'Hancock'

RED

***Skimmia japonica* 'Rubella'**
Evergreen, upright, dense shrub with aromatic, red-rimmed, bright green foliage. Deep red flower buds in autumn and winter open to dense clusters of small white flowers in spring.

Z7–9 H9–7

Correa pulchella
Evergreen, fairly bushy, slender-stemmed shrub with oval leaves. Small, pendent, tubular, rose-red flowers appear from summer to winter, sometimes at other seasons.

Z11–15 H12–10

Skimmia japonica subsp. ***reevesiana* 'Robert Fortune'**, syn. *S. reevesiana*
Evergreen, bushy, rather weak-growing shrub with aromatic leaves. Small white flowers in spring are followed by crimson berries.

Z7–9 H9–7

Euphorbia fulgens
Gaultheria mucronata 'Cherry Ripe'
Justicia rizzinii
Solanum pseudocapsicum 'Balloon', illus. p.341

RED–GREEN

Skimmia japonica
Evergreen, bushy, dense shrub. Has aromatic, mid- to dark green leaves and dense clusters of small white flowers from mid- to late spring, followed on female plants by bright red fruits if plants of both sexes are grown.

Z7–9 H9–7

Ribes laurifolium
Evergreen, spreading shrub. Has leathery, deep green leaves and pendent racemes of greenish yellow flowers in late winter and early spring. Produces edible black berries on female plants if plants of both sexes are grown.

Z7–9 H9–7

WHITE–GREEN

Viburnum davidii
Evergreen shrub that forms a dome of dark green foliage, over which heads of small white flowers appear in late spring. If plants of both sexes are grown, female plants bear decorative, metallic blue fruits.

Z7–9 H9–3

Breynia disticha, syn. *B. nivosa, Phyllanthus nivosus* (Snow bush)
Evergreen, well-branched shrub with slender stems. Leaves are green with white marbling. Tiny greenish flowers, borne intermittently, have no petals.

Z14–15 H12–10

***Coprosma* x *kirkii* 'Variegata'**
Evergreen, densely branched shrub, prostrate when young, later semi-erect. White-margined leaves are borne singly or in small clusters. Tiny, translucent white fruits appear in autumn on female plants if both sexes are grown.

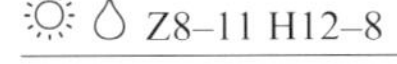

Z8–11 H12–8

***Vinca major* 'Variegata'**
Evergreen, prostrate, arching, spreading subshrub. Has bright green leaves broadly edged with creamy white and large, bright blue flowers borne from late spring to early autumn.

Z7–11 H12–1

***Pandanus tectorius* 'Veitchii'**, syn. *P. veitchii* (Veitch's screw pine)
Evergreen, upright, arching shrub with rosettes of long, light green leaves that have spiny white to cream margins.

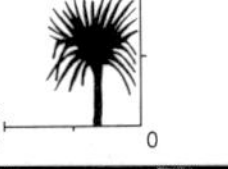

Z14–15 H12–10

Helichrysum petiolare, syn. *H. petiolatum* of gardens
Evergreen shrub with mounds of silver-green shoots and gray-felted leaves. Has yellow flower heads in summer. Often grown as an annual groundcover and edging.

Z11–15 H12–10

Leucophyta brownii
Evergreen, intricately branched shrub with velvety gray branches and tiny scalelike leaves. Clusters of flower heads, silver in bud, yellowish when expanded, appear in summer.

Z13–15 H12–10

Artemisia arborescens
Evergreen, upright shrub, grown for its finely cut, silvery white foliage. Heads of small, bright yellow flowers are borne in summer and early autumn.

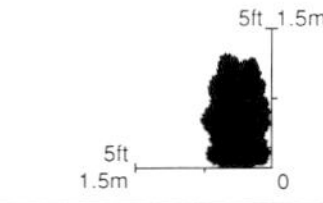

Z5–9 H9–5

Brunfelsia pauciflora 'Macrantha', illus. p.167
Eranthemum pulchellum
HEATHERS, illus. pp.178–9
Vinca difformis

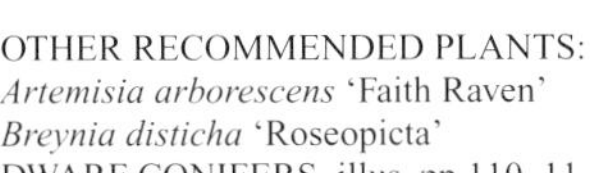

OTHER RECOMMENDED PLANTS:
Artemisia arborescens 'Faith Raven'
Breynia disticha 'Roseopicta'
DWARF CONIFERS, illus. pp.110–11
Euonymus fortunei 'Coloratus'
Euonymus fortunei 'Emerald Gaiety'
Pseuderanthemum atropurpureum
Pseudowintera colorata
Ruta graveolens 'Jackman's Blue', illus. p.177
Sideritis candicans
Ursinia sericea

GREEN

Ballota acetabulosa
Evergreen subshrub that forms a mound of rounded, gray-green leaves, felted beneath. Whorls of small pink flowers open from mid- to late summer.

Z8–9 H9–8

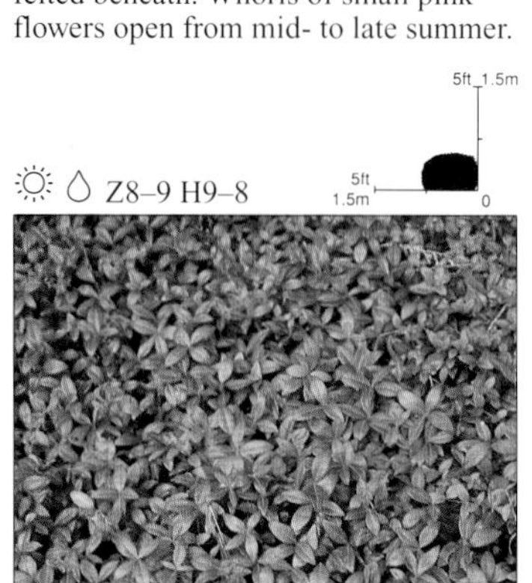

Vinca minor (Lesser periwinkle)
Evergreen, prostrate, spreading subshrub that forms extensive mats of small, glossy, dark green leaves. Bears small purple, blue, or white flowers, mainly from midspring to early summer.

Z4–9 H9–1

Chamaerops humilis (Dwarf fan palm, European fan palm)
Slow-growing, evergreen palm, suckering with age. Fan-shaped leaves, 2–3ft (60–90cm) across, have green to gray-green lobes. Has tiny yellow flowers in summer.

Z12–14 H12–10

Vaccinium glaucoalbum
Evergreen shrub with deep green leaves that, when young, are pale green above and bluish white beneath. Pink-tinged white flowers in late spring and early summer are followed by white-bloomed, blue-black fruits.

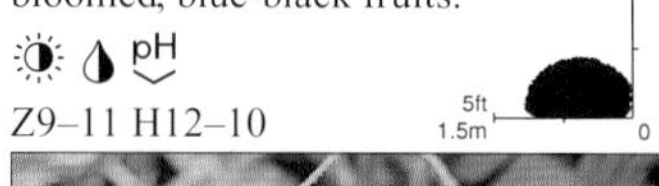

Z9–11 H12–10

Mimosa pudica
(Humble plant, Sensitive plant)
Short-lived, evergreen shrub with prickly stems; needs support. Fernlike leaves fold when touched. Has minute, pale mauve-pink flowers in summer-autumn.

Z14–15 H12–10

Artemisia abrotanum (Lad's love, Old man, Southernwood)
Deciduous or semi-evergreen, moderately bushy shrub. Aromatic, gray-green leaves have many very slender lobes. Has clusters of small yellowish flower heads in late summer.

Z5–8 H8–5

Hebe cupressoides
Evergreen, upright, dense shrub with cypresslike, gray-green foliage. On mature plants, tiny pale lilac flowers are borne from early to midsummer.

Z8–9 H9–8

Eurya emarginata
Slow-growing, evergreen, densely branched, rounded shrub with small, leathery, deep green leaves. Small greenish white flowers in late spring or summer are followed by tiny purple-black berries.

Z9–11 H12–10

***Buxus microphylla* 'Green Pillow'**
Evergreen, compact, dwarf shrub forming a dense, rounded mass of small, oval, dark green leaves. Bears insignificant flowers in late spring or early summer.

Z6–9 H9–6

Ruscus hypoglossum
Evergreen, clump-forming shrub with arching shoots. Pointed, glossy, bright green "leaves" are actually flattened shoots that bear tiny yellow flowers in spring, followed by large, bright red berries.

Z7–9 H9–7

Lonicera pileata
Evergreen, low, spreading, dense shrub with narrow, dark green leaves and tiny, short-tubed, creamy white flowers in late spring, followed by violet-purple berries. Makes a good groundcover.

Z5–9 H9–5

Sabal minor (Dwarf palmetto)
Evergreen, suckering fan palm with stems mainly underground. Has leaves of 20–30 green or gray-green lobes. Erect sprays of small white flowers are followed by shiny black berries.

Z12–15 H12–10

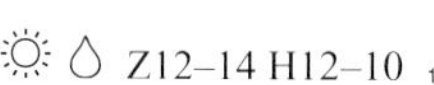

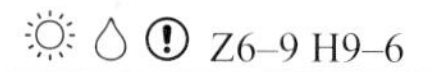

Brachyglottis rotundifolia
Buxus microphylla
Coprosma x *kirkii*
Danäe racemosa
Daphne laureola
DWARF CONIFERS, illus. pp.110–11
Ephedra gerardiana
Euonymus fortunei 'Kewensis'
Euonymus fortunei 'Sarcoxie'
Hymenanthera crassifolia
Macrozamia spiralis
Ruscus aculeatus
Salvia officinalis cvs
Serissa foetida

GREEN–YELLOW

***Buxus sempervirens* 'Suffruticosa'**
Evergreen, dwarf shrub that forms a tight, dense mass of oval, bright green leaves. Bears insignificant flowers in late spring or early summer. Trim to about 6in (15cm) if used for edging.
Z6–8 H8–6

***Ruta graveolens* 'Jackman's Blue'**
Evergreen, bushy, compact subshrub. Has aromatic, finely divided blue foliage. In summer, clusters of small mustard yellow flowers are borne.

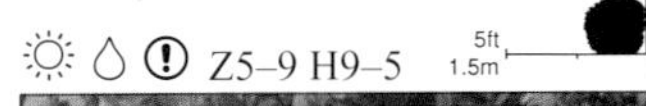

Z5–9 H9–5

***Leucothöe fontanesiana* 'Rainbow'**
Evergreen, arching shrub with sharply toothed, leathery, dark green leaves that age from pink- to cream-variegated. Racemes of white flowers open below shoots in spring.

Z5–8 H8–5

***Salvia officinalis* 'Icterina'**
Evergreen or semi-evergreen, bushy shrub used as a culinary herb. Has aromatic, gray-green leaves variegated with pale green and yellow. Occasionally bears small spikes of tubular, 2-lipped purplish flowers.
Z5–8 H8–5

***Euonymus fortunei* 'Emerald 'n' Gold'**
Evergreen, bushy shrub with bright green leaves margined with bright yellow and tinged with pink in winter.

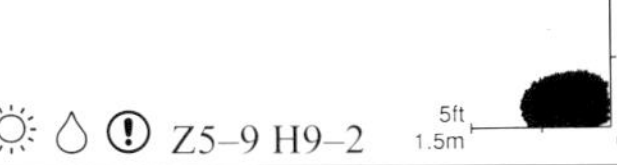

Z5–9 H9–2

***Sanchezia speciosa*, syn. *S. nobilis* of gardens**
Evergreen, erect, soft-stemmed shrub. Glossy leaves have yellow- or white-banded main veins. Tubular yellow flowers appear in axils of red bracts in summer.

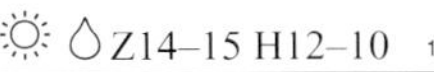

Z14–15 H12–10

DWARF CONIFERS, illus. pp.110–11

YELLOW–ORANGE

***Lonicera nitida* 'Baggesen's Gold'**
Evergreen, bushy shrub with long, arching shoots covered with tiny, bright yellow leaves. Insignificant yellowish green flowers in mid-spring are occasionally followed by mauve fruits.
Z6–9 H9–6

***Codiaeum variegatum* var. *pictum* (Croton)**
Evergreen, erect, sparingly branched shrub. Leathery, glossy leaves vary greatly in size and shape and are variegated with red, pink, orange, or yellow.
Z13–15 H12–10

***Pittosporum tenuifolium* 'Tom Thumb'**
Evergreen, rounded, dense shrub with pale green young leaves that contrast with deep reddish brown older foliage. Bears cup-shaped purplish flowers in summer.
Z9–11 H12–9

Euonymus fortunei 'Gold Tip'
Euonymus fortunei 'Sunspot'

Heaths and Heathers

As a group of plants, heaths and heathers are remarkable in that there are species and cultivars available to provide interest at all times of the year. Several are grown for their golden foliage, which often turns a deep burnt orange in winter, while others flower for a long period during summer, autumn, or winter. Flowers are in a variety of colors and are occasionally bicolored; those with double flowers may be dried for winter decoration. In habit, the plants vary from tree heaths of up to 20ft (6m) to dwarf, prostrate forms, many of which are excellent for providing groundcover.

There are three genera: *Calluna*, *Daboecia*, and *Erica*. All *Calluna* and *Daboecia* cultivars and most *Erica* species must be grown in acidic soil, but otherwise heathers require little attention. Main seasons of interest are given for each plant.

C. vulgaris **'Kinlochruel'** (sum.-aut.)

E. cinerea **'Hookstone White'** (sum.)

C. vulgaris **'Spring Cream'** (spr.-aut.)

E. mackaiana **'Dr. Ronald Gray'** (sum.)

D.* x *scotica **'Silverwells'** (spr.-aut.)

E. carnea **'Golden Starlet'** (all year)

E.* x *veitchii **'Exeter'** (win.-spr.)

E. tetralix **'Alba Mollis'** (sum.-aut.)

E. vagans **'Lyonesse'** (sum.-aut.)

E. arborea var. ***alpina*** (win.-spr.)

E. canaliculata (win.-spr.)

E.* x *darleyensis **'White Perfection'** (win.-spr.)

E.* x *darleyensis **'White Glow'** (win.-spr.)

E.* x *veitchii **'Pink Joy'** (win.-spr.)

E. ciliaris **'White Wings'** (sum.)

E. ciliaris **'David McClintock'** (sum.)

C. vulgaris **'My Dream'** (sum.-aut.)

C. vulgaris **'Anthony Davis'** (sum.-aut.)

E. carnea **'Springwood White'** (win.-spr.)

C. vulgaris **'County Wicklow'** (sum.-aut.)

C. vulgaris **'Silver Queen'** (sum.-aut.)

C. vulgaris **'Elsie Purnell'** (sum.-aut.)

E.* x *watsonii **'Dawn'** (sum.)

E.* x *darleyensis **'Darley Dale'** (win.-spr.)

E.* x *williamsii **'P.D. Williams'** (sum.)

E.* x *darleyensis **'Ghost Hills'** (win.-spr.)

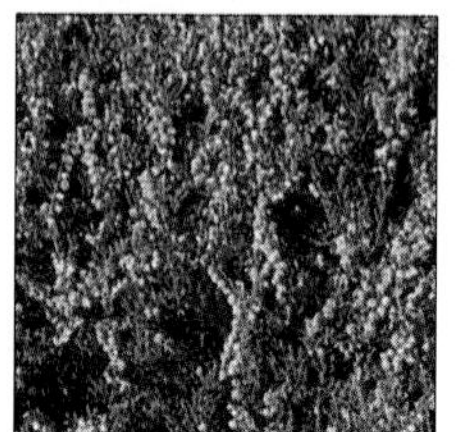
C. vulgaris **'J.H. Hamilton'** (sum.-aut.)

E.* x *darleyensis **'Archie Graham'** (win.-spr.)

E. mackaiana **'Plena'** (sum.)

D. cantabrica **'Bicolor'** (spr.-aut.)

D. x *scotica* **'William Buchanan'** (spr.-aut.)

C. vulgaris **'Alexandra'** (aut.-win.)

C. vulgaris **'Darkness'** (sum.-aut.)

E. carnea **'Rosalie'** (all year)

C. vulgaris **'Firefly'** (all year)

E. vagans **'Birch Glow'** (sum.-aut.)

E. cinerea **'Eden Valley'** (sum.)

E. cinerea **'Purple Beauty'** (sum.)

C. vulgaris **'Foxii Nana'** (all year)

E. tetralix **'Pink Star'** (sum.-aut.)

E. erigena **'Brightness'** (spr.)

E. carnea **'Vivellii'** (win.-spr.)

E. carnea **'Westwood Yellow'** (all year)

C. vulgaris **'Gold Haze'** (all year)

C. vulgaris **'Robert Chapman'** (all year)

E. ciliaris **'Corfe Castle'** (sum.)

E. cinerea **'C.D. Eason'** (sum.)

E. carnea **'December Red'** (win.)

E. erigena **'Golden Lady'** (all year)

E. cinerea **'Windlebrooke'** (all year)

C. vulgaris **'Beoley Gold'** (all year)

E. vagans **'Valerie Proudley'** (all year)

E. cinerea **'Fiddler's Gold'** (aut.-win.)

C. vulgaris **'Multicolor'** (all year)

E. tetralix **'Con Underwood'** (sum.-aut.)

C. vulgaris **'Peter Sparkes'** (sum.-aut.)

C. vulgaris **'Tib'** (sum.)

C. vulgaris **'Silver Knight'** (sum.-aut.)

E. carnea **'Ann Sparkes'** (all year)

C. vulgaris **'Golden Feather'** (all year)

C. vulgaris **'Boskoop'** (all year)

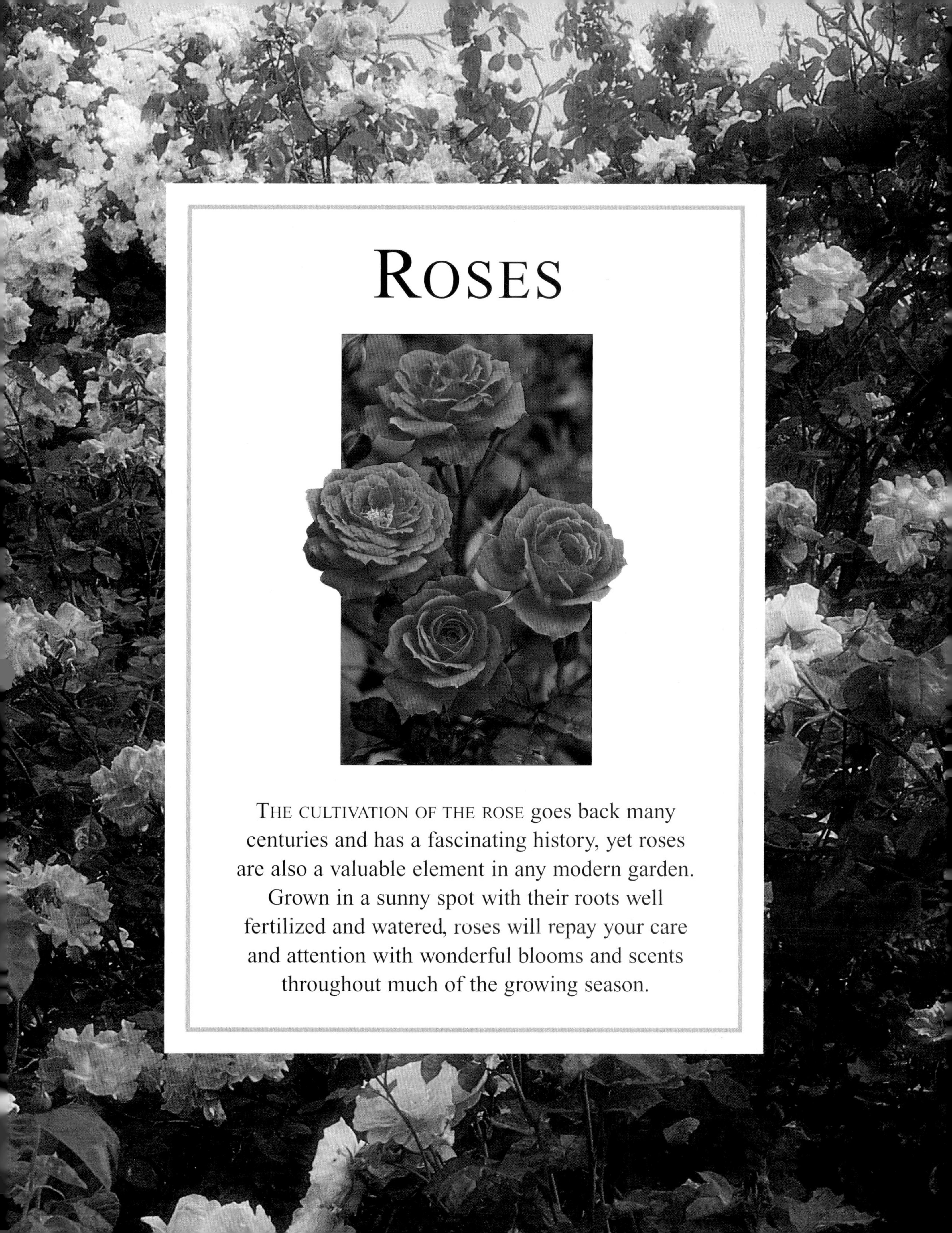

ROSES

THE CULTIVATION OF THE ROSE goes back many centuries and has a fascinating history, yet roses are also a valuable element in any modern garden. Grown in a sunny spot with their roots well fertilized and watered, roses will repay your care and attention with wonderful blooms and scents throughout much of the growing season.

Roses

These most romantic of flowers are unsurpassed in beauty and fragrance by any other single group of plants. Roses are cultivated and prized by many, and for some they are an almost indispensable element in the modern garden.

Growing roses

With some 150 species and thousands of cultivars, both ancient and modern, there are members of the genus *Rosa* for an enormous number of garden situations. They come from a wide range of habitats throughout the northern hemisphere and, because of this diversity, have a wide range of hardiness. Given attention to their cultivation needs, they will repay the gardener with a profusion of blooms.

All roses do well when grown in open, sunny sites in fertile, organic, moist but well-drained soil. However, avoid planting in soil that has grown roses before, since roses may be affected by soil sickness, caused by a buildup of harmful soil organisms.

Roses can be grown among bulbs, perennials, and other shrubs in a mixed border, provided that their fellow plants do not compete directly for moisture and nutrients. Choose companions that are shallow-rooted, such as the many herbaceous geraniums and pinks (*Dianthus* cultivars), or space plants at a sufficient distance to allow for mulching and fertilizing around the root zone.

Maintaining year-round interest

As a group, roses have a long flowering season, from the early summer blooms of 'Frühlingsmorgen' through the main flourish in midsummer to the first hard frosts, thanks to the repeat-flowering roses. Some also have attractive fruits (hips) that prolong the season, notably the tomato-like hips of the Rugosas, the flask-shaped, vibrant scarlet fruits of *R. moyesii*, and the rounded, black hips of *R. pimpinellifolia*. Regular deadheading extends the season because it redirects the expenditure of energy from seed formation into flower production.

Ornamental features

Roses embrace almost every shade of the spectrum, excluding true blue, and some have a strong fragrance that can range from the heady, sweet scent of the Damasks to that of musk or spice. A few roses have ornamental thorns, notably *R. sericea* subsp. *omeiensis* f. *pteracantha*, with its large, triangular thorns that glow blood red when backlit.

Foliage can also make an impact: the soft gray-purple leaves of *R. glauca* and the blue-green of the Alba roses are both perfect foils to crimson and purple flowers. Foliage textures range from glossy to matte, from delicately fern-like to robustly wrinkled, as in *R. rugosa*.

Designing with roses

Roses can be used for a variety of design functions in the garden, since they have a diversity of habit that

Relaxed informality
Above: In this informal planting, the profuse blooms of the gracefully arching shrub Rosa *'Cerise Bouquet' are complemented by the rounded pink heads of* Allium cristophii *and the vivid spires of foxgloves* (Digitalis purpurea).

Formal dressing
Right: Here, a sturdy arch clothed with clematis and a vigorous, free-flowering rambler lends height to the design and forms a perfect frame to draw the eye to an elegant focal point.

Summer bedfellows
Above: Alliums and bearded irises are perfect companions to roses in an early summer border, while gray-leaved artemisias lend a neutral foil to the intense colors. As a bonus, Crambe cordifolia *adds its subtle topnotes to the fragrance of the roses.*

Roses in containers
Right: Small bush roses, notably the miniatures and patio roses, are ideal for container planting. Alternatively, use trailing groundcover roses in hanging baskets.

includes the mound-forming, sometimes stem-rooting groundcover roses, the densely thorny Gallicas, and the open, gracefully arching Chinas and Damasks. Many are versatile enough to be used in more than one way.

A rose garden laid out in a formal style is perhaps the most traditional way to use roses, and geometrically ordered beds are particularly suited to the neatly upright growth of many bush roses. Roses can be used equally well as specimens, although the selection of a single favorite is difficult, with so many exquisite cultivars to choose from.

Roses range in size from the tiny Miniature bushes such as *R.* 'Rouletii', which at 8in (20cm) high are perfect for containers and windowboxes, to the most rampant of ramblers, such as *R.* 'Bobbie James', which can cover a 10m (30ft) or more in height when scrambling through large trees. Using taller cultivars of dense, thorny shrub roses, such as the Rugosa roses, you can create divisions within the garden. These may take the form of large impenetrable boundary hedges that give privacy and security or, if you use lower-growing roses, they can form garden compartments defined by low hedging or edging.

Climbing and rambling roses are extremely versatile, and can be trained on a wall to act as a colourful backdrop to foreground plantings, or on trellis to form a screen. Like all climbers, they are invaluable for lending height when grown on pillars, pergolas and arches, and can make a focal point if grown on free-standing structures such as tripods and tepee. Many of the trailing sorts are also available trained as weeping standards for elegant focal features.

The groundcover roses are ideal for clothing sunny and inaccessible banks, since most require little regular pruning.

Container-growing

Smaller roses, especially the Miniature bush roses, are perfect for containers. The smallest – Baby Masquerade ('Tanba') and Darling Flame ('Meilucca') – are suitable for windowboxes, while the trailing or spreading cultivars such as Kent ('Poulcov') are fine for baskets.

ROSES shrub and old garden

☐ WHITE

***R.* 'Madame Hardy'**
Vigorous, upright Damask rose with plentiful, leathery, matte leaves. Richly fragrant, quartered-rosette, fully double flowers, 4in (10cm) across, white with green eyes, are borne in summer. H 5ft (1.5m), S 4ft (1.2m).

Z4–9 H9–1

***R.* 'Boule de Neige'**
Upright Bourbon rose with arching stems and very fragrant, cupped to rosette, fully double flowers. White flowers, sometimes tinged with pink, 3in (8cm) across, appear in summer-autumn. Leaves are glossy and dark green. H 5ft (1.5m), S 4ft (1.2m).

Z6–9 H9–6

***R. pimpinellifolia* 'Plena'**
Dense, spreading, prickly species rose with cupped, double, creamy white flowers, 1½in (4cm) across, in early summer. Has small, fernlike, dark green leaves and blackish hips. H 3ft (1m), S 4ft (1.2m).

Z3–9 H9–1

***R.* 'Penelope'**
Dense, bushy shrub rose, with plentiful, dark green foliage, that bears many scented, cupped, double, pink-cream flowers, 3in (8cm) across, in clusters in summer-autumn. H and S 3ft (1m), more if lightly pruned.

Z6–9 H9–6

Categories of Rose

Grown for the extraordinary beauty of their flowers, roses have been in cultivation for hundreds of years. They have been widely hybridized, producing a vast number of shrubs suitable for growing as specimen plants, in the border, as hedges, and as climbers for training on walls, pergolas, and pillars. Roses are classified into three main groups:

Species

Species, or wild, roses and **species hybrids**, which share most of the characteristics of the parent species, bear flowers generally in one flush in summer and hips in autumn.

Old Garden roses

Alba – large, freely branching roses with clusters of flowers in midsummer and abundant, grayish green foliage.
Bourbon – open, remontant shrub roses that may be trained to climb. Flowers are borne, often 3 to a cluster, in summer-autumn.
China – remontant shrubs with flowers borne singly or in clusters in summer-autumn.
Damask – open shrubs bearing loose clusters of usually very fragrant flowers, mainly in summer.
Gallica – fairly dense shrubs producing richly colored flowers, often 3 to a cluster, in the summer months.
Hybrid Perpetual – vigorous, remontant shrubs with flowers borne singly or in threes in summer-autumn.
Moss – often lax shrubs with a furry, mosslike growth on stems and calyx, and flowers in summer.
Noisette – remontant climbing roses that bear large clusters of flowers, with a slight spicy fragrance, in summer-autumn.
Portland – upright, rather dense, remontant shrubs bearing loose clusters of flowers in summer-autumn.
Provence (Centifolia) – lax, thorny shrubs bearing scented flowers in summer.
Sempervirens – semi-evergreen climbing roses that bear numerous flowers in late summer.
Tea – remontant shrubs and climbers with elegant, pointed buds that open to loose flowers with a spicy fragrance.

Modern Garden roses

Shrub – a diverse group, illustrated here with the Old Garden roses because of their similar characteristics. Most are remontant and are larger than bush roses, with flowers borne singly or in sprays in summer and/or autumn.
Large-flowered bush (Hybrid Tea) – remontant shrubs with large flowers borne in summer-autumn.
Cluster-flowered bush (Floribunda) – remontant shrubs with usually large sprays of flowers in summer-autumn.
Dwarf clustered-flowered bush (Patio) – neat, remontant shrubs with sprays of flowers borne in summer-autumn.
Miniature – usually small, remontant shrubs with sprays of tiny flowers in summer-autumn.
Polyantha – tough, compact, remontant shrubs with many small flowers in summer-autumn.
Groundcover – trailing and spreading roses, some flowering in summer only, others remontant, flowering in summer-autumn.
Climbing – vigorous climbing roses, diverse in growth and flower, some flowering in summer only, others remontant, flowering in summer-autumn.
Rambler – vigorous climbing roses with flexible stems that bear clusters of flowers mostly in summer.

Flower shapes

With the mass hybridization that has occurred in recent years, roses have been developed to produce plants with a wide variety of characteristics, in particular different forms of flower, sometimes with a strong fragrance. These flower types illustrated here, give a general indication of the shape of the flower at its perfect state (which in some cases may be before it has opened fully). Growing conditions may affect the form of the flower. Flowers may be single (4–7 petals), semi-double (8–14 petals), double (15–30 petals), or fully double (over 30 petals).

Flat – open, usually single or semi-double flowers have petals that are almost flat.

Cupped – open, single to fully double flowers have petals curving outward gently from the center.

Pointed – elegant, "Hybrid Tea" shape; semi-double to fully double flowers have high, tight centers.

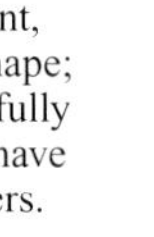
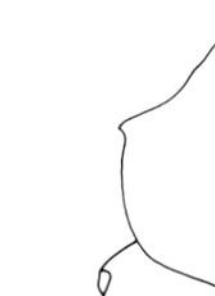

Urn-shaped – classic, curved, flat-topped, semi-double to fully double flowers are of "Hybrid Tea" type.

Rounded – usually double or fully double flowers have even-sized, overlapping petals that form a bowl-shaped or rounded outline.

Rosette – usually double or fully double flowers are rather flat with many slightly overlapping petals of uneven size.

Quartered-rosette – rather flat, usually double or fully double flowers have petals of uneven size arranged in a quartered pattern.

Pompon – small, rounded, double or fully double flowers, usually borne in clusters, have masses of small petals.

***R.* 'Dupontii'**, syn. *R. moschata* var. *nivea* (Snowbush rose)
Upright, bushy shrub rose with abundant, grayish foliage. Bears many clusters of fragrant, flat, single white flowers, tinged with blush pink, 2½in (6cm) across, in midsummer.
H and S 7ft (2.2m).

Z4–9 H9–1

***R.* 'Nevada'**
Dense, arching shrub rose with abundant, light green leaves. Scented, flat, semi-double, creamy white flowers, 4in (10cm) across, are borne freely in summer and more sparsely in autumn. H and S 7ft (2.2m).

Z4–9 H9–1

***R.* Pearl Drift ('Leggab')**
Bushy, spreading shrub rose that produces clusters of lightly scented, cupped, double, blush pink flowers, 4in (10cm) across, in summer-autumn. Leaves are plentiful and glossy.
H 3ft (1m), S 4ft (1.2m).

Z5–9 H9–5

R. 'Aimée Vibert'
R. 'Alba Semiplena'
R. 'Blanche Moreau'
R. 'Jacqueline du Pré'
R. 'Mousseline'
R. 'Noisette Carnée'
R. 'Souvenir de la Malmaison'

***R.* 'Fantin-Latour'**
Vigorous, shrubby Provence rose. Flowers appear in summer and are fragrant, cupped to flat, fully double, blush pink, with neat green button eyes, and 4in (10cm) across. Has broad, dark green leaves.
H 5ft (1.5m), S 4ft (1.2m).

Z4–9 H9–1

***R.* 'Conrad Ferdinand Meyer'**
Vigorous, arching shrub rose with cupped, fully double pink flowers, 3in (7cm) across, that are richly fragrant and borne in large numbers in summer, fewer in autumn. Foliage is leathery and prone to rust.
H 8ft (2.5m), S 4ft (1.2m).

Z4–9 H9–1

***R.* 'Great Maiden's Blush'**, syn. *R.* 'Cuisse de Nymphe', *R.* 'La Séduisante'
Vigorous, upright Alba rose. Very fragrant, rosette, fully double, pinkish white flowers, 3in (8cm) across, appear in midsummer.
H 6ft (2m), S 4 1/2ft (1.3m).

Z3–9 H9–1

***R.* 'Céleste'**, syn. *R.* 'Celestial'
Vigorous, spreading, bushy Alba rose. Fragrant, cupped, double, light pink flowers, 3in (8cm) across, appear in summer. Makes a good hedge.
H 5ft (1.5m), S 4ft (1.2m).

Z3–9 H9–1

***R.* 'Felicia'**
Vigorous shrub rose with abundant, healthy, grayish green foliage. Scented, cupped, double flowers, 3in (8cm) across, are light pink tinged with apricot and are borne in summer-autumn. H 5ft (1.5m), S 7ft (2.2m).

Z6–9 H9–6

R. rubiginosa, syn. *R. eglanteria* (Eglantine, Sweet briar)
Vigorous, arching, thorny species rose that has distinctive, apple-scented foliage. Bears cupped, single pink flowers, 1in (2.5cm) across, in midsummer and red hips in autumn.
H and S 8ft (2.4m).

Z4–9 H9–1

R. 'Cécile Brünner'
R. 'Félicité Parmentier'
R. 'Kathleen Harrop'
R. 'Omar Khayyám'

ROSES shrub and old garden

PINK

***R.* Rosy Cushion ('Interall')**
Dense, spreading shrub rose with plentiful, glossy, dark green leaves. Bears clusters of scented, cupped, semi-double flowers, 2½in (6cm) across, that are pink with ivory centers, in summer-autumn. H 3ft (1m), S 4ft (1.2m).

Z5–9 H9–5

R. glauca, syn. *R. rubrifolia*
Vigorous, arching species rose grown for its fine, grayish purple leaves and red stems. Flat, single, cerise-pink flowers, 1½in (4cm) across, with pale centers and gold stamens, appear in early summer, followed by red hips in autumn. H 6ft (2m), S 5ft (1.5m).

Z2–8 H8–1

***R.* Marguerite Hilling**, syn. *R.* 'Pink Nevada'
Dense, arching shrub rose. Many scented, flat, semi-double, rose-pink flowers, 4in (10cm) across, are borne in summer and a few in autumn. Has light green foliage. H and S 7ft (2.2m).

Z4–9 H9–1

***R.* 'Reine Victoria'**
Lax Bourbon rose with slender stems and light green leaves. Sweetly scented, rosette, double flowers, 3in (8cm) across, in shades of pink, are borne in summer-autumn. Grows well on a pillar. H 6ft (2m), S 4ft (1.2m).

Z6–9 H9–6

***R.* 'Complicata'**
Very vigorous Gallica rose with thorny, arching growth, useful as a large hedge. Slightly fragrant, cupped, single flowers, 4½in (11cm) across, are pink with pale centers and appear in midsummer. H 7ft (2.2m), S 8ft (2.5m).

Z4–9 H9–1

***R.* 'Königin von Dänemark'**, syn. *R.* 'Belle Courtisanne'
Vigorous, rather open Alba rose. Heavily scented, quartered-rosette, fully double, warm pink flowers, 3in (8cm) across and with green button eyes, appear in midsummer. H 5ft (1.5m), S 4ft (1.2m).

Z3–9 H9–1

***R.* Bonica ('Meidonomac')**, syn. *R.* 'Bonica '82'
Vigorous, spreading shrub rose bearing large sprays of slightly fragrant, cup-shaped, fully double, rose-pink flowers, 3in (7cm) across, in summer-autumn. Foliage is glossy and plentiful. H 3ft (1m), S 3½ft (1.1m).

Z4–9 H9–1

***R.* 'Pink Grootendorst'**
Upright, bushy shrub rose with plentiful, small leaves. Rosette, double flowers, 2in (5cm) across, have serrated, clear pink petals. Blooms are carried in sprays in summer-autumn. H 6ft (2m), S 5ft (1.5m).

Z3–9 H9–1

***R.* Constance Spry ('Austance')**
Shrub rose of arching habit that will climb if supported. Cupped, fully double pink flowers, 5in (12cm) across, with a spicy scent, are borne freely in summer. Leaves are large and plentiful. H 6ft (2m), S 5ft (1.5m).

Z4–9 H9–1

R. x *centifolia* 'Cristata'
R. x *centifolia* 'Muscosa'
R. 'Frühlingsmorgen'
R. 'Gloire des Mousseux'
R. 'Ispahan'
R. 'Louise Odier'
R. 'Madame Ernest Calvat'
R. 'Madame Pierre Oger'
R. 'Mary Rose'
R. 'Perle d'Or'
R. 'Saint Nicholas'
R. 'Tricolore de Flandre'

***R.* 'Mrs. John Laing'**
Bushy Hybrid Perpetual rose with plentiful, light green foliage. Produces many richly fragrant, rounded, fully double pink flowers, 5in (12cm) across, in summer and a few in autumn.
H 3ft (1m), S 2½ft (80cm).

Z5–9 H9–5

***R.* x *odorata* 'Mutabilis'**, syn. *R. chinensis* 'Mutabilis'
Open species rose with coppery young foliage. In summer-autumn bears shallowly cup-shaped, single, buff-yellow flowers, 2½in (6cm) across, that age to coppery pink or crimson. H and S 3ft (1m), to 6ft (2m) against a wall.

Z7–9 H9–7

R. rugosa
(Hedgehog rose, Japanese rose)
Vigorous, dense species rose with wrinkled leaves and large red hips. Cupped, single, white or purplish red flowers, 3½in (9cm) across, appear in good succession in summer-autumn.
H and S 3–6ft (1–2m).

Z2–9 H9–1

***R.* 'Roseraie de l'Haÿ'**
Vigorous, dense shrub rose. Bears many strongly scented, cupped to flat, double, reddish purple flowers, 4½in (11cm) across, in summer-autumn. Leaves are abundant and disease-resistant. H 7ft (2.2m), S 6ft (2m).

Z4–9 H9–1

***R.* x odorata 'Pallida'** (Old Blush China, Parson's Pink China)
Bushy China rose that may be trained as a climber on a sheltered wall. Cupped, double, pink flowers, 2½in (6cm) across, are produced freely from summer to late autumn.
H 3ft (1m), S 2½ft (80cm) or more.

Z7–9 H9–7

***R. moyesii* 'Geranium'**, syn. *R.* 'Geranium'
Vigorous, arching species rose. Flat, single flowers, 2in (5cm) across, are dusky scarlet with yellow stamens and are borne on branches in summer. Has small, dark green leaves and, in autumn, large red hips. H 10ft (3m), S 8ft (2.5m).

Z4–9 H9–1

***R. gallica* 'Versicolor'**
(Rosa Mundi)
Neat, bushy Gallica rose. In summer produces striking, slightly scented, flat, semi-double flowers, 2in (5cm) across, very pale blush pink with crimson stripes. H 2½ft (75cm), S 3ft (1m).

Z3–9 H9–1

***R.* 'Madame Isaac Pereire'**
Vigorous, arching Bourbon rose. Fragrant, cupped to quartered-rosette, fully double flowers, 6in (15cm) across, are deep purplish pink and are produced freely in summer-autumn.
H 7ft (2.2m), S 6ft (2m).

Z6–9 H9–6

***R.* 'Henri Martin'**, syn. *R.* 'Red Moss'
Vigorous, upright Moss rose. Rosette, double, purplish crimson flowers, 3½in (9cm) across, appear in summer and have a light scent and some furry green "mossing" of the calyces underneath.
H 5ft (1.5m), S 3ft (1m).

Z4–9 H9–1

R. 'Armada'
R. 'Commandant Beaurepaire'
R. 'Du Maître d'Ecole'
R. 'Fellenberg'
R. gallica var. *officinalis*
R. 'Honorine de Brabant'
R. macrophylla
R. moyesii
R. 'Président de Sèze'
R. 'Variegata di Bologna'

ROSES shrub and old garden

RED–PURPLE

R. 'Empereur du Maroc'
Compact, shrubby Hybrid Perpetual rose. Fragrant, quartered-rosette, fully double flowers, 3in (8cm) across, are rich purplish crimson and are borne freely in summer and more sparsely in autumn. H 1.2m (4ft), S 3ft (1m).

Z5–9 H9–5

R. 'Belle de Crécy'
Gallica rose of rather lax growth and few thorns. Rosette, fully double flowers, 3in (8cm) across, are pink tinged grayish purple, have green eyes and a rich, spicy fragrance, and are produced in summer.
H 4ft (1.2m), S 3ft (1m).

Z3–9 H9–1

R. CARDINAL HUME ('Harregale')
Bushy, spreading shrub rose. Cupped, fully double, reddish purple flowers, 3in (7.5cm) across, are borne in dense clusters in summer-autumn and have a musky scent. H and S 3ft (1m).

Z5–9 H9–5

R. 'William Lobb',
syn. *R.* 'Duchesse d'Istrie'
Moss rose with strong, arching, prickly stems that will climb if supported. In summer bears rosette, double, deep purplish crimson flowers, 3½in (9cm) across, that fade to lilac-gray.
H and S 6ft (2m).

Z4–9 H9–1

R. 'Cardinal de Richelieu'
Vigorous, compact Gallica rose that bears plentiful, dark green foliage and fragrant, rounded, fully double, deep burgundy-purple flowers, 3in (8cm) across, in summer.
H 4ft (1.2m), S 3ft (1m).

Z3–9 H9–1

R. 'Tour de Malakoff'
Provence rose of open habit. Scented, rosette, double flowers, 5in (12cm) across, are magenta with violet veins, fading to grayish purple, and appear in summer. H 6ft (2m), S 5ft (1.5m).

Z4–9 H9–1

R. 'Assemblage des Beautés'
R. 'Capitaine John Ingram'
R. 'Charles de Mills'
R. 'Nuits de Young'
R. 'Robert le Diable'
R. 'Souvenir d'Alphonse Lavallée'
R. 'Tuscany Superb'
R. 'Zigeunerknabe'

YELLOW

R. primula (Incense rose)
Lax, arching species rose that bears scented, cupped, single, primrose-yellow flowers, 1½in (4cm) across, in late spring. Foliage is plentiful, aromatic, and fernlike. H and S 6ft (2m).

Z5–9 H9–5

***R. foetida* 'Persiana',**
syn. *R.* 'Persian Yellow'
Upright, arching species rose with cupped, double yellow flowers, 1in (2.5cm) across, in early summer. Glossy leaves are prone to blackspot. Prune spent branches only, and shelter from cold winds. H and S 5ft (1.5m).

Z3–9 H9–1

R. ecae
Erect, wiry species rose. Cupped, single, bright yellow flowers, ¾in (2cm) across, with a musky scent, are borne close to reddish stems in late spring. Foliage is fernlike and graceful. H 5ft (1.5m), S 4ft (1.2m).

Z7–9 H9–7

R. 'Buff Beauty'
R. 'Golden Wings'

ROSES modern

YELLOW

***R. xanthina* 'Canary Bird'**
Vigorous, dense, arching species hybrid with small, fernlike leaves. Cupped, single yellow flowers, 2in (5cm) across, with a musky scent, appear in late spring and sparsely in autumn. H and S 7ft (2.1m).

Z5–9 H9–5

***R.* GRAHAM THOMAS ('Ausmas')**
Vigorous, arching shrub rose, lax in habit, with glossy, bright green leaves. In summer-autumn bears cupped, fully double yellow flowers, 4½in (11cm) across, with some scent.
H 4ft (1.2m), S 5ft (1.5m).

Z5–9 H9–5

WHITE–PINK

***R.* ICEBERG ('Korbin'),**
syn. *R.* 'Schneewittchen'
Cluster-flowered bush rose. Produces many sprays of cupped, fully double white flowers, 3in (7cm) across, in summer-autumn. Has abundant, glossy leaves. H 30in (75cm), S 26in (65cm), more if not pruned hard.

Z5–9 H9–5

***R.* MARGARET MERRIL ('Harkuly')**
Upright, cluster-flowered bush rose. Very fragrant, double, blush white or white flowers, are well-formed, urn-shaped, and 4in (10cm) across, and are borne singly or in clusters in summer-autumn. H 3ft (1m), S 2ft 60cm).

Z5–9 H9–5

***R.* GROUSE ('Korimro')**
Trailing groundcover rose with very abundant, glossy foliage and flat, single, blush pink flowers, 1½in (4cm) across, borne close to stems in summer-autumn. Has a pleasant fragrance. H 1½ft (45cm), S 10ft (3m).

Z5–9 H9–6

***R.* 'Elizabeth Harkness'**
Neat, upright, large-flowered bush rose with abundant, dark green foliage. Fragrant, pointed, fully double flowers, 5in (12cm) across, are pale, creamy pink with buff tints and are borne in summer-autumn.
H 30in (80cm), S 24in (60cm).

Z5–9 H9–5

***R.* 'The Fairy'**
Dense, cushion-forming, dwarf cluster-flowered bush rose with abundant, small, glossy leaves. Rosette, double pink flowers, 1in (2.5cm) across, are borne freely in late summer and autumn. H and S 2ft (60cm).

Z5–9 H9–5

***R.* 'Nozomi', syn.**
R. 'Heideröslein'
Creeping groundcover rose bearing flat, single, blush pink and white flowers, 1in (2.5cm) across, close to stems in summer. Has small, dark green leaves. May be used for a container. H 1½ft (45cm), S 4ft (1.2m).

Z5–9 H9–5

OTHER RECOMMENDED PLANTS:
R. 'City of London'
R. 'Elina'
R. 'English Miss'
R. 'Hannah Gordon'
R. 'Langford Light'
R. 'Len Turner'
R. 'Ophelia'
R. 'Pascali'
R. 'Yvonne Rabier'

ROSES modern

PINK

***R.* Pink Bells ('Poulbells')**
Very dense, spreading, groundcover rose with abundant, small, dark green leaves and many pompon, fully double pink flowers, 1in (2.5cm) across, borne in clusters in summer. H 2½ft (75cm), S 4ft (1.2m).

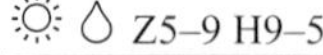 Z5–9 H9–5

***R.* 'Queen Elizabeth'**
Upright, cluster-flowered bush rose that bears long-stemmed, rounded, fully double pink flowers, 4in (10cm) across, singly or in clusters, in summer-autumn. Leaves are large and leathery. H 5ft (1.5m), S 2½ft (75cm), more if not pruned hard.

Z5–9 H9–5

***R.* 'Iced Ginger'**
Upright, cluster-flowered bush rose with sparse reddish foliage. Pointed, fully double, buff to copper-pink flowers, 4½in (11cm) across, are borne singly or in clusters in summer-autumn. H 36in (90cm), S 28in (70cm).

Z5–9 H9–5

***R.* 'Alpine Sunset'**
Compact, large-flowered bush rose with fragrant, rounded, fully double, peach-yellow flowers, 8in (20cm) across, appearing on short stems in summer-autumn. Has large, semi-glossy leaves. H and S 2ft (60cm).

Z5–9 H9–5

***R.* Sexy Rexy ('Macrexy')**
Compact, bushy, cluster-flowered bush rose. Bears clusters of slightly fragrant, cupped, camellia-like, fully double pink flowers, 3in (8cm) across, in summer-autumn. Leaves are dark green. H and S 2ft (60cm).

Z6–9 H9–5

***R.* Peek-a-boo ('Dicgrow'), syn. *R.* 'Brass Ring'**
Dense, cushion-forming, dwarf cluster-flowered bush rose with sprays of urn-shaped, double, apricot-pink flowers, 1½in (4cm) across, from summer to early winter. Leaves are narrow and dark green. H and S 18in (45cm).

Z5–9 H9–5

***R.* Rosemary Harkness ('Harrowbond')**
Vigorous, large-flowered bush rose with abundant, glossy leaves. Bears fragrant, pointed, double flowers, 4in (10cm) across, in shades of salmon-pink and orange, singly or in clusters in summer-autumn. H 3ft (1m), S 2½ft (75cm).

Z5–9 H9–5

***R.* Lovely Lady ('Dicjubell')**
Dense, rounded, large-flowered bush rose. Slightly scented, pointed, fully double, rose-pink flowers, 4in (10cm) across, are produced freely in summer-autumn. H 30in (80cm), S 28in (70cm).

 Z5–9 H9–5

***R.* 'Blessings'**
Upright, large-flowered bush rose with slightly fragrant, salmon-pink flowers that are urn-shaped and fully double, 4in (10cm) across, and are borne singly or in clusters in summer-autumn. Has large, dark green leaves. H 3ft (1m), S 2½ft (75cm).

Z5–9 H9–5

R. 'Gentle Touch'
R. 'Petit Four'
R. 'Pink Parfait'
R. 'Royal Highness'

***R.* Anisley Dickson ('Dickimono')**, syn. *R.* 'Dicky', *R.* 'Münchner Kindl'
Vigorous, cluster-flowered bush rose. Carries large clusters of slightly fragrant, pointed, double, salmon-pink flowers, 3in (8cm) across, in summer-autumn. H 3ft (1m), S 2½ft (75cm).

Z5–9 H9–5

***R.* Paul Shirville ('Harqueterwife')**
Spreading, large-flowered bush rose. Bears fragrant, pointed, fully double, rosy salmon-pink flowers, 3½in (9cm) across, in summer-autumn. Leaves are glossy, reddish, and abundant.
H and S 30in (75cm).

Z5–9 H9–5

***R.* 'Silver Jubilee'**
Dense, upright, large-flowered bush rose. Bears slightly scented, pointed, fully double, soft salmon-pink flowers, 5in (12cm) across, very freely in summer-autumn. Foliage is abundant and glossy.
H 3½ft (1.1m), S 2½ft (75cm).

Z5–9 H9–5

***R.* Keepsake ('Kormalda')**
Neat, bushy, large-flowered bush rose with plentiful, glossy leaves. Slightly scented, rounded, fully double pink flowers, 5in (12cm) across, are freely produced in summer-autumn.
H 30in (75cm), S 24in (60cm).

Z5–9 H9–5

***R.* Double Delight ('Andeli')**
Large-flowered bush rose of upright, uneven growth. Fragrant, rounded, fully double flowers, 5in (12cm) across, are creamy white edged with red, and are borne in summer-autumn. H 3ft (1m), S 2ft (60cm).

Z5–9 H9–5

R. 'Congratulations'
R. 'Fragrant Delight'
R. 'Little Woman'

R. 'Mischief'

***R.* Escapade ('Harpade')**
Dense, cluster-flowered bush rose. Fragrant, cupped, semi-double, rose-violet flowers, 3in (8cm) across, with white eyes, are borne in sprays in summer-autumn. Foliage is light green and glossy.
H 30in (75cm), S 24in (60cm).

Z5–9 H9–5

***R.* Anna Ford ('Harpiccolo')**
Dwarf cluster-flowered bush rose. Has urn-shaped (opening flat), double, orange-red flowers, 1½in (4cm) across, borne in summer-autumn, and many small, dark green leaves.
H 18in (45cm), S 15in (38cm).

Z5–9 H9–5

***R.* Trumpeter ('Mactru')**
Neat, bushy, cluster-flowered bush rose with many cupped, fully double, bright red flowers, 2½in (6cm) across, in summer-autumn. Leaves are deep green and semi-glossy.
H 24in (60cm), S 20in (50cm).

Z5–9 H9–5

R. 'Buttons'
R. 'Rose Gaujard'
R. 'Yesterday'

ROSES modern

■ RED

***R.* Royal William ('Korzaun')**, syn. *R.* 'Duftzauber '84'
Vigorous, large-flowered bush rose with large, dark green leaves. Slightly scented, pointed, fully double, deep crimson flowers, 5in (12cm) across, are carried on long stems in summer-autumn. H 3ft (1m), S 2½ft (75cm).

☼ ◊ Z5–9 H9–5

***R.* 'Precious Platinum'**, syn. *R.* 'Opa Potschke'
Vigorous, large-flowered bush rose with abundant, glossy leaves. Bears slightly scented, rounded, fully double, deep crimson-scarlet flowers, 4in (10cm) across, in summer-autumn. H 3ft (1m), S 2ft (60cm).

☼ ◊ Z5–9 H9–5

***R.* Wee Jock ('Cocabest')**
Dense, bushy, dwarf cluster-flowered bush rose. Bears rosette, fully double crimson flowers, 1½in (4cm) across, in summer-autumn. Plentiful leaves are small and dark green. H and S 18in (45cm).

☼ ◊ Z5–9 H9–5

***R.* Alexander ('Harlex')**, syn. *R.* 'Alexandra'
Vigorous, upright, large-flowered bush rose with abundant, dark green foliage. Slightly scented, pointed, double, bright red flowers, 5in (12cm) across, are borne on long stems in summer-autumn. H 5ft (1.5m), S 2½ft (75cm).

☼ ◊ Z5–9 H9–5

***R.* The Times Rose ('Korpeahn')**
Spreading, cluster-flowered bush rose. Slightly scented, cupped, double, deep crimson flowers, 3in (8cm) across, are borne in wide clusters in summer-autumn. Foliage is dark green and plentiful. H 24in (60cm), S 30in (75cm).

☼ ◊ Z5–9 H9–5

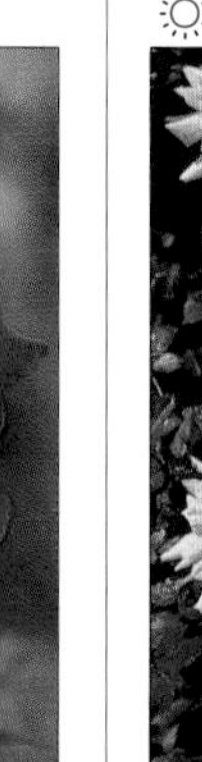

***R.* Alec's Red ('Cored')**
Vigorous, large-flowered bush rose bearing strongly fragrant, deep cherry red flowers that are pointed and fully double, 6in (15cm) across, in summer-autumn. H 3ft (1m), S 2ft (60cm).

☼ ◊ Z5–9 H9–5

□ YELLOW

***R.* Champagne Cocktail ('Horflash')**
Upright, cluster-flowered bush rose. Fragrant, cupped, double, yellow-pink flowers, 3½in (9cm) across, opening wide, are borne in summer-autumn. H 3ft (1m), S 2ft (60cm).

☼ ◊ Z5–9 H9–5

***R.* Peace ('Madame A. Meilland')**, syn. *R.* 'Gioia', *R.* 'Gloria Dei'
Vigorous, shrubby, large-flowered bush rose with scented, pointed to rounded, fully double flowers, 6in (15cm) across, borne freely in clusters in summer-autumn. Has abundant, large, glossy foliage. H 4ft (1.2m), S 3ft (1m).

☼ ◊ Z5–9 H9–5

***R.* Golden Penny ('Rugul')**, syn. *R.* 'Guletta', *R.* 'Tapis Jaune'
Compact, dense, dwarf cluster-flowered bush rose with cupped to flat, double yellow flowers, 2in (5cm) across, that are borne in summer-autumn, and rich green leaves.
H 12in (30cm), S 16in (40cm).

☼ ◊ Z5–9 H9–5

R. 'Blue Moon'
R. 'Drummer Boy'
R. 'Fragrant Cloud'
R. 'Ingrid Bergman'
R. 'Intrigue'
R. 'Invincible'
R. 'National Trust'
R. 'Shocking Blue'
R. 'Julia's Rose'
R. 'Sheila's Perfume'

***R.* 'Grandpa Dickson'**, syn. *R.* 'Irish Gold'
Neat, upright, large-flowered bush rose with sparse, pale, glossy foliage. Bears many slightly scented, pointed, fully double, light yellow flowers, 7in (18cm) across, in summer-autumn.
H 30in (80cm), S 24in (60cm).

Z5–9 H9–5

***R.* Simba ('Korbelma')**, syn. *R.* 'Goldsmith'
Upright, large-flowered bush rose with lightly fragrant, urn-shaped, fully double yellow flowers, 3½in (9cm) across, borne freely in summer-autumn. Leaves are large and dark green.
H 30in (75cm), S 24in (60cm).

Z5–9 H9–5

***R.* Mountbatten ('Harmantelle')**
Shrubby, cluster-flowered bush rose with disease-resistant foliage. Bears scented, rounded, fully double yellow flowers, 4in (10cm) across, singly or in clusters, in summer-autumn.
H 4ft (1.2m), S 2½ft (75cm).

Z5–9 H9–5

***R.* 'Korresia'**, syn. *R.* 'Friesia'
Bushy, upright, cluster-flowered bush rose. Bears open sprays of strongly scented, urn-shaped, double flowers, 3in (8cm) across, with waved yellow petals, in summer-autumn.
H 30in (75cm), S 24in (60cm).

Z5–9 H9–5

***R.* Bright Smile ('Dicdance')**
Low, bushy, cluster-flowered bush rose with bright, glossy leaves. Bears clusters of slightly scented, flat, semi-double yellow flowers, 3in (8cm) across, in summer-autumn.
H and S 18in (45cm).

Z5–9 H9–5

***R.* Freedom ('Dicjem')**
Neat, large-flowered bush rose, with many shoots and abundant, glossy foliage. Bears many lightly scented, rounded, double, bright yellow flowers, 3½in (9cm) across, in summer-autumn.
H 30in (75cm), S 24in (60cm).

Z5–9 H9–5

***R.* 'Glenfiddich'**
Upright, cluster-flowered bush rose. Slightly fragrant, urn-shaped, double, amber-yellow flowers, 4in (10cm) across, are borne singly or in clusters in summer-autumn.
H 30in (75cm), S 24in (60cm).

Z5–9 H9–5

***R.* Amber Queen ('Harroony')**
Spreading, cluster-flowered bush rose. Amber flowers are fragrant, rounded and fully double, 3in (8cm) across, and are borne in summer-autumn. Has abundant reddish foliage.
H and S 20in (50cm).

Z5–9 H9–5

R. 'Arthur Bell'
R. 'Dutch Gold'
R. 'Princess Alice'

R. 'Princess Michael of Kent'

ROSES modern

YELLOW–ORANGE

***R.* Pot o' Gold ('Dicdivine')**
Large-flowered bush rose of neat, even growth. Fragrant, rounded, fully double, golden yellow flowers, 3½in (9cm) across, are carried singly or in wide sprays in summer-autumn. H 30in (75cm), S 24in (60cm).

 Z5–9 H9–5

***R.* 'Southampton'**, syn. *R.* 'Susan Ann'
Upright, cluster-flowered bush rose. Bears fragrant, pointed, double apricot flowers, 3in (8cm) across, singly or in clusters in summer-autumn. Foliage is glossy and disease-resistant. H 3ft (1m), S 2ft (60cm).

Z5–9 H9–5

***R.* Anne Harkness ('Harkaramel')**
Upright, cluster-flowered bush rose. Urn-shaped, double amber flowers, 3in (8cm) across, are borne in sprays of many blooms in late summer and autumn. H 4ft (1.2m), S 2ft (60cm).

Z5–9 H9–5

***R.* Sweet Magic ('Dicmagic')**
Bushy, dwarf cluster-flowered bush rose. Bears sprays of lightly fragrant, urn-shaped, double, pink-flushed, golden orange flowers, 1½in (4cm) across, in summer-autumn. H 15in (38cm), S 12in (30cm).

Z5–9 H9–5

***R.* 'Doris Tysterman'**
Vigorous, upright, large-flowered bush rose with lightly scented, pointed, fully double, orange-red flowers, 4in (10cm) across, borne in summer-autumn. Leaves are large, glossy, and dark green. H 4ft (1.2m), S 2½ft (75cm).

Z5–9 H9–5

***R.* Remember Me ('Cocdestin')**
Vigorous, dense, large-flowered bush rose with pointed, fully double, copper-orange flowers, 3½in (9cm) across, freely borne in summer-autumn. Leaves are abundant and glossy. H 3ft (1m), S 2½ft (75cm).

Z5–9 H9–5

***R.* Troika ('Poumidor')**, syn. *R.* 'Royal Dane'
Vigorous, dense, large-flowered bush rose with semi-glossy leaves. Fragrant, pointed, double flowers, 6in (15cm) across, are orange-red tinged with pink and are borne in summer-autumn. H 3ft (1m), S 2½ft (75cm).

Z5–9 H9–5

***R.* Piccadilly ('Macar')**
Vigorous, bushy, large-flowered bush rose with pointed, double red and yellow flowers, 5in (12cm) across, produced freely singly or in clusters in summer-autumn. Abundant foliage is reddish and glossy. H 3ft (1m), S 2ft (60cm).

Z5–9 H9–5

***R.* 'Just Joey'**
Branching, open, large-flowered bush rose with leathery, dark green foliage. Bears rounded, fully double flowers, 5in (12cm) across, with waved, copper-pink petals and some scent, in summer-autumn. H 30in (75cm), S 24in (60cm).

Z5–7 H7–5

R. 'Clarissa'
R. 'Disco Dancer'
R. 'Matangi'
R. 'Sweet Dream'
R. 'Typhoon'
R. 'Whisky Mac'

WHITE–PINK

***R.* Snowball ('Macangeli')**, syn. *R.* 'Angelita'
Compact, creeping, miniature bush rose with pompon, fully double white flowers, 1in (2.5cm) across, that are borne in summer-autumn. Leaves are small, glossy, and plentiful.
H 8in (20cm), S 12in (30cm).

Z5–9 H9–5

***R.* 'Stacey Sue'**
Spreading, miniature bush rose with plentiful, dark green foliage and rosette, fully double pink flowers, 1in (2.5cm) across, that are borne freely in summer-autumn.
H and S 15in (38cm).

Z5–9 H9–5

***R.* Baby Masquerade ('Tanba')**, syn. *R.* 'Baby Carnival'
Dense, miniature bush rose with plentiful, leathery foliage and clusters of rosette, double, yellow-pink flowers, 1in (2.5cm) across, in summer-autumn. H and S 16in (40cm), more if not pruned.

Z5–9 H9–5

***R.* Angela Rippon ('Ocaru')** syn. *R.* 'Ocarina'
Miniature bush rose with slightly fragrant, urn-shaped, fully double, salmon-pink flowers, 1½in (4cm) across, in summer-autumn, and many small, dark green leaves.
H 18in (45cm), S 12in (30cm).

Z5–9 H9–5

***R.* 'Hula Girl'**
Wide, bushy, miniature bush rose with glossy, dark green foliage. Slightly scented, urn-shaped, fully double, salmon-orange flowers, 1in (2.5cm) across, are produced freely in summer-autumn. H 18in (45cm), S 16in (40cm).

Z5–9 H9–5

OTHER RECOMMENDED PLANTS:
R. 'Easter Morning'
R. 'Snow Carpet'

RED

***R.* Sheri Anne ('Morsherry')**
Upright, miniature bush rose with glossy, leathery foliage. Slightly scented, rosette, double, light red flowers, 1in (2.5cm) across, are borne in summer-autumn.
H 18in (45cm), S 12in (30cm).

Z5–9 H9–5

***R.* 'Fire Princess'**
Upright, miniature bush rose with small, glossy leaves. Bears sprays of rosette, fully double scarlet flowers, 1½in (4cm) across, in summer-autumn.
H 18in (45cm), S 12in (30cm).

Z5–9 H9–5

***R.* Red Ace ('Amruda')**
Compact, miniature bush rose with rosette, double, dark red flowers, 1½in (4cm) across, borne in summer-autumn.
H 14in (35cm), S 12in (30cm).

Z5–9 H9–5

RED–ORANGE

***R.* Orange Sunblaze ('Meijikitar')**, syn. *R.* 'Sunblaze' Compact, miniature bush rose. Rosette, fully double, bright orange-red flowers, 1½in (4cm) across, are freely produced in summer-autumn. Has plentiful, dark green leaves. H and S 12in (30cm).

Z5–9 H9–5

***R.* 'Rise 'n' Shine'**, syn. *R.* 'Golden Sunblaze' Bushy, upright, miniature bush rose with dark green leaves that bears rosette, fully double yellow flowers, 1in (2.5cm) across, in summer-autumn. H 16in (40cm), S 10in (25cm).

Z5–9 H9–5

***R.* Colibre '79 ('Meidanover')** Upright, rather open, miniature bush rose. Urn-shaped, double, red-veined orange flowers, 1½in (4cm) across, are borne in summer-autumn. H 15in (38cm), S 10in (25cm).

Z5–9 H9–5

R. 'Magic Carousel'

ROSES climbing

WHITE

***R.* 'Albéric Barbier'** Vigorous, semi-evergreen rambler rose. Slightly fragrant, rosette, fully double, creamy white flowers, 3in (8cm) across, appear in clusters in summer. Leaves are small and bright green. Notably shade-tolerant. H to 15ft (5m), S 10ft (3m).

Z5–9 H9–7

***R.* 'Paul's Lemon Pillar'** Stiff, upright climbing rose with large leaves and scented, pointed to rounded, fully double, lemon-white flowers, 6in (15cm) across, that appear in summer. H 15ft (5m), S 10ft (3m).

Z5–9 H9–5

***R. filipes* 'Kiftsgate'** Rampant climbing rose with abundant, glossy, light green foliage. Cupped to flat, single, creamy white flowers, 1in (2.5cm) across, appear in summer in spectacular clusters. Use to grow up a tree or in a wild garden. H and S 30ft (10m) or more.

Z6–9 H9–6

***R.* 'Félicité Perpétue'** Sempervirens climbing rose with long, slender stems. Clusters of rosette, fully double, blush-pink to white flowers, 1½in (4cm) across, appear in mid-summer. Small leaves are semi-evergreen. Prune spent wood only. H 15ft (5m), S 12ft (4m).

Z6–9 H9–6

***R.* 'Madame Alfred Carrière'** Noisette climbing rose with slender, smooth stems. Very fragrant, rounded, double flowers are creamy white tinged pink, 1½in (4cm) across, and are borne in summer-autumn. H to 18ft (5.5m), S 10ft (3m).

Z5–9 H9–5

***R.* 'Gloire de Dijon'** Stiffly branched Noisette or climbing Tea rose. Fragrant, quartered-rosette, fully double, creamy buff flowers, 4in (10cm) across, are borne in summer-autumn. H 12ft (4m), S 8ft (2.5m).

Z5–9 H9–5

OTHER RECOMMENDED PLANTS:
R. banksiae
R. 'Niphetos'
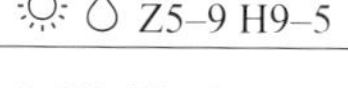
R. 'Wedding Day'
R. 'White Cockade'

R. 'New Dawn'
Vigorous, reliable climbing rose. Fragrant, cupped, double, pale pearl-pink flowers, 3in (8cm) across, are borne in clusters in summer-autumn. Tolerates more shade than many. H and S 15ft (5m).

Z5–9 H9–5

R. HANDEL ('Macha')
Stiff, upright climbing rose. Slightly scented, urn-shaped, double flowers, 3in (8cm) across, are cream edged with pinkish-red and produced in clusters in summer-autumn. Has glossy, dark green foliage.
H 10ft (3m), S 7ft (2.2m).

Z5–9 H9–5

R. 'Madame Grégoire Staechelin', syn. *R.* 'Spanish Beauty'
Vigorous, arching climbing rose with large clusters of blooms in summer. Bears rounded to cupped, fully double flowers, 5in (13cm) across, with ruffled, clear pink petals shaded carmine. H to 20ft (6m), S to 12ft (4m).

Z5–9 H9–5

R. 'Pink Perpétué'
Stiffly branched climbing rose that may be pruned to grow as a shrub. Bears clusters of cupped to rosette, double, deep pink flowers, 3in (8cm) across, in summer-autumn. Leathery foliage is plentiful.
H 9ft (2.8m), S 8ft (2.5m).

Z5–9 H9–5

R. BREATH OF LIFE ('Harquanne')
Stiff, upright climbing rose with large, lightly scented, rounded, fully double, pinkish apricot flowers, 4in (10cm) across, borne in summer-autumn. Leaves are semi-glossy.
H 9ft (2.8m), S 7ft (2.2m).

Z5–9 H9–5

R. 'Albertine'
Vigorous rambler rose with arching, thorny, reddish stems. Scented, cup-shaped, fully double, salmon-pink flowers, 3in (8cm) across, are borne in abundant clusters in summer. Is prone to mildew in a dry site.
H to 15ft (5m), S 10ft (3m).

Z5–9 H9–5

R. 'Chaplin's Pink Companion'
Vigorous climbing rose with glossy, dark green foliage and slightly scented, rounded, double, light pink flowers, 2in (5cm) across, borne freely in large clusters in summer. H and S 10ft (3m).

Z5–9 H9–5

R. 'Zéphirine Drouhin'
(Thornless rose)
Lax, arching Bourbon rose that will climb if supported. Bears fragrant, cupped, double, deep pink flowers, 3in (8cm) across, in summer-autumn. Is prone to mildew. May be grown as a hedge. H to 8ft (2.5m), S to 6ft (2m).

Z5–9 H9–5

R. 'Rosy Mantle'
Stiff, open-branched climbing rose. Very fragrant, pointed, fully double, rose-pink flowers, 4in (10cm) across, are borne in summer-autumn. Dark green foliage is rather sparse.
H 8ft (2.5m), S 6ft (2m).

Z5–9 H9–5

R. 'Aimée Vibert'
R. 'Aloha'
R. 'Belle Portugaise'
R. 'Blush Rambler'
R. 'Compassion'
R. 'François Juranville'
R. 'Kathleen Harrop'
R. 'Lady Waterlow'
R. 'Morning Jewel'
R. 'Noisette Carnée'
R. 'Paul's Himalayan Musk'
R. 'Paul Transon'

WHITE-PINK

***R.* 'Rambling Rector'**
Rampant rambler rose. Clusters of scented, cupped to flat, semi-double, creamy white flowers, 1½in (4cm) across, with golden stamens, appear in summer, followed by red hips. Arching stems are covered in grayish green foliage. H and S 20ft (6m).

Z5–9 H9–5

***R.* HIGH HOPES ('Haryup')**
Vigorous, upright and arching, long-stemmed climbing rose. Scented, urn-shaped to rounded, double, light pink flowers, 3in (8cm) across, are freely borne in summer-autumn. Has purplish green foliage. Good for high walls and pergolas. H 12ft (4m), S 7ft (2.2m).

Z5–9 H9–5

***R.* CITY GIRL ('Harzorba')**
Vigorous, free-branching climbing rose. Abundant, glossy, dark green leaves are borne on arching stems. Scented, semi-double, saucer-shaped, salmon-pink flowers, 4½in (11cm) across, appear in summer-autumn. H and S 7ft (2.2m).

Z5–9 H9–5

***R.* 'Compassion',**
syn. *R.* 'Belle de Londres'
Upright, free-branching climbing rose with glossy, dark leaves on reddish stems. Fragrant, rounded, double, pink-tinted, salmon-apricot flowers, 4in (10cm) across, are borne in summer-autumn. H 10ft (3m), S 8ft (2.5m).

Z5–9 H9–5

***R.* 'Aloha'**
Strong-growing, bushy climbing rose. Fragrant, cupped, fully double, rose- and salmon-pink flowers, 3½in (9cm) across, appear in summer-autumn. Leaves are leathery and dark green. May be grown as a shrub. H and S 8ft (2.5m).

Z5–9 H9–5

R. 'Fellenberg'
R. 'John Cabot'
R. 'Ramona'
R. 'John Davis'
R. 'Louis Jolliet'

RED

***R.* 'Danse du Feu',**
syn. *R.* 'Spectacular'
Vigorous, stiffly branched climbing rose with abundant, glossy foliage. Bears rounded, double scarlet flowers, 3in (8cm) across, in summer-autumn. H and S 8ft (2.5m).

Z5–9 H9–5

***R.* 'Dortmund'**
Upright climbing rose that may be pruned to make a shrub. Flat, single red flowers, 4in (10cm) across, with white eyes and a slight scent, are borne freely in clusters in summer-autumn. Has healthy, dark green foliage. H 10ft (3m), S 6ft (1.8m).

Z5–9 H9–5

***R.* DUBLIN BAY ('Macdub')**
Dense, shrubby climbing rose that may be pruned to grow as a shrub. Bears clusters of cupped, double, bright crimson flowers, 4in (10cm) across, in summer-autumn. Foliage is glossy, dark green, and plentiful. H and S 7ft (2.2m).

Z5–9 H9–5

***R.* 'Sympathie'**
Vigorous, free-branching climbing rose. Slightly scented, cupped, fully double, bright deep red flowers, 3in (8cm) across, are borne in summer-autumn, usually in clusters. Has plentiful, glossy, dark green foliage. H 10ft (3m), S 8ft (2.5m).

Z5–9 H9–5

R. 'Alister Stella Gray'
R. 'Emily Gray'
R. 'Henry Kelsey'
R. 'William Baffin'
R. 'Fortune's Double Yellow'
R. 'Goldfinch'
R. 'Maréchal Niel'

RED-YELLOW

R. 'Guinée'
Vigorous, stiffly branched climbing rose. Fragrant, cupped, fully double, blackish red to maroon flowers, 4½in (11cm) across, are borne in summer. Leaves are large and leathery.
H 15ft (5m), S 7ft (2.2m).

 Z5–9 H9–5

R. 'Veilchenblau',
syn. *R.* 'Blue Rambler'
Vigorous rambler rose. Rosette, double violet flowers streaked white, 1in (2.5cm) across, have a fruity scent and appear in clusters in summer.
H 12ft (4m), S 7ft (2.2m).

Z5–9 H9–5

R. 'Mermaid'
Slow-growing climbing rose that produces flat, single, primrose yellow flowers, 5in (12cm) across, in summer-autumn. Has stiff reddish stems, large, hooked thorns, and glossy, dark green leaves. H and S to 20ft (6m).

Z5–9 H9–5

R. 'Emily Gray'
Semi-evergreen rambler rose with long, lax stems. Small clusters of slightly fragrant, cupped, fully double, butter yellow flowers, 2in (5cm) across, appear in summer. Leaves are lustrous dark green. Is prone to mildew.
H 15ft (5m), S 10ft (3m).

Z5–9 H9–5

R. CASINO ('Macca'),
syn. *R.* 'Gerbe d'Or'
Upright, free-branching climbing rose. Sparse, dark green leaves appear on stiffly arching stems. Rounded, double, fragrant yellow flowers, 3½in (9cm) across, are borne in summer-autumn.
H 10ft (3m), S 7ft (2.2m).

Z5–9 H9–5

R. 'Golden Showers'
Stiff, upright climbing rose that may be pruned to grow as a shrub. In summer-autumn produces many fragrant, pointed, double yellow flowers, 4in (10cm) across, that open flat.
H 6ft (2m), S 7ft (2.2m) or more.

Z5–9 H9–5

YELLOW

R. LAURA FORD ('Chewarvel')
Upright, stiffly branching climbing rose with small, dark, glossy leaves. Sprays of scented, urn-shaped to flat, yellow flowers, 1¾in (4.5cm) across, appear in summer-autumn. Good for pillars.
H 7ft (2.2m), S 4ft (1.2m).

 Z5–9 H9–5

***R. banksiae* 'Lutea'**
(Yellow banksian)
Vigorous climbing rose bearing clusters of many scentless, rosette, fully double yellow flowers, ¾in (2cm) across, in late spring. Prune spent wood only. H and S to 30ft (10m).

Z8–9 H9–8

R. 'Maigold'
Vigorous climbing rose with prickly, arching stems that may be pruned to grow as shrub. Fragrant, cupped, semi-double, bronze-yellow flowers, 4in (10cm) across, are borne freely in early summer and sparsely in autumn.
H and S 8ft (2.5m).

Z5–9 H9–5

CLIMBERS

THIS DECORATIVE GROUP of plants provides a moving, changing part of your garden design. Trailing or twining, scrambling or clinging, these energetic plants grow upward, downward, and outward, while at the same time they provide large splashes of color and beauty in those awkward gaps in your garden that ordinary plants are unable to fill.

Climbers

One of the most versatile of plant groups, climbers are able to spread fast and trail decoratively over or through other plants and buildings and across the ground, offering enormous scope for imaginative design.

What are climbers?

Most climbers are woody, evergreen or deciduous plants, while a few are herbaceous perennials or annuals that die back with the onset of winter. They have one of several methods of climbing. They can be self-clinging or twining (with or without tendrils) or scandent, scrambling species that do not cling. It is important to identify the type, since this dictates which method of support is most appropriate.

Self-clingers such as Virginia creeper (*Parthenocissus quinquefolia*) climb by means of adhesive pads or, as in the case of ivies (*Hedera*) and the Swiss cheese plant (*Monstera deliciosa*), by aerial roots that attach themselves to any surface offering a hold such as tree trunks, cliff faces, walls, and sturdy fences. In contrast, twiners such as wisteria draw themselves up by encircling their support, while passionflowers (*Passiflora*) secure their stems with coiling tendrils. Both of these types require the support of tree branches or a system of wires, mesh, or a trellis if they are wall-trained. Self-clinging and twining climbers need initial guidance to the support but are self-supporting once established.

Scandent, scrambling plants such as winter jasmine (*Jasminum nudiflorum*) attach themselves loosely, if at all, by threading long, flexible stems through those of a host plant or by mounding their new stems over those made in previous seasons. Their stems must be tied in to their support throughout their life, but in more naturalistic plantings they can be allowed to cascade over walls or tumble down slopes as they do in the wild.

Ornamental features

Climbing plants provide a range of foliage forms, from the fine-textured, divided leaves of *Tropaeolum speciosum* to the sculptural, heart-shaped ones of *Actinidia deliciosa*.
Leaf surfaces alone provide limitless possibilities for interesting textural contrasts, from the softly downy *Vitis vinifera* to the highly glossy ivies (*Hedera* cultivars). The color range includes the golden-hued *Humulus lupulus* 'Aureus' to the deep green of many jasmines, as well as the intense purple tints of plants such as *Vitis vinifera* 'Purpurea'. Many have such attractive foliage that they make beautiful specimens in their own right – among them *Actinidia kolomikta*, with its green leaves splashed with cream and pink, or the subtle, silver-veined *Parthenocissus henryana*. Some, most notably species of *Parthenocissus* and *Vitis*, reserve their particularly brilliant foliage displays until the autumn. In winter, the architectural forms of twiners such as wisteria and celastrus come into their own.

Climbers bear some of the most beautiful flowers – as shown by the intricate blooms of the passionflowers and the elegant chains of wisteria – and many, especially the honeysuckles (*Lonicera*), sweet peas (*Lathyrus odoratus*), and jasmines, have fragrances that pervade the air over some distance. The flower colors of climbers span the spectrum, from the creamy whites of *Schizophragma integrifolium* and *Hydrangea petiolaris* to the vivid magentas of bougainvillea and somber chocolate-

Wisteria arch
A sturdy arch forms the ideal support for training climbers, such as Wisteria sinensis, *since it displays the pendent flowers to perfection. When grown around a window, as shown here, the subtle scent of the fragrant flowers can be appreciated both indoors and out.*

Fragrant pot
Graceful climbers such as this honeysuckle (Lonicera) *lend elegance and fragrance to a patio. For stability, plant in a terracotta or stoneware container in a heavy, soil-based potting mix.*

SPECTACULAR FLOWERS
Above: This passionflower (Passiflora caerulea *'Constance Elliot') produces exquisite blooms. To display them attractively, support these plants against a trellis or wires mounted on a wall or fence.*

PRETTY CLIMBER
Left: Here, the self-clinging Hydrangea petiolaris *clothes a wall, forming a superb backdrop for foreground plantings while framing a view to the garden beyond.*

AUTUMN DISPLAY
Below: The tendril-climbing ornamental grape, Vitis coignetiae, *is perfect for wall-training and equally suited to pergolas and arches. Reaching some 50ft (15m) in height, its splendid autumn color is breathtaking en masse.*

maroon of *Rhodochiton atrosanguineus*. With many climbers their season is further prolonged by decorative, silky seed heads, as in clematis, or striking berries, like the shiny blue fruits of *Ampelopsis brevipedunculata* and the orange-yellow fruits of *Celastrus orbiculatus* that split when ripe to reveal bright red seeds within.

DESIGNING WITH CLIMBERS

Growing climbers vertically to create a backdrop to other, lower, foreground plantings is one of the most obvious ways of providing height in a design, although climbers can be used in a variety of other imaginative ways. Grown on free-standing supports, they can form living screens to provide privacy and wind-filtering shelter or visual and physical barriers between areas in the garden. If grown through trees or on pillars and pyramids, climbers can form a splendid focal point, and on arches they can provide a frame for a vista. On pergolas, climbers act as a shade-forming element, linking different parts of the garden, and if you use a scented plant to clothe an arbor, it can provide both fragrance and seclusion for quiet contemplation.

When covering walls or buildings, climbers can complement the warmth of brick or stone walls or soften their hard lines, while the most vigorous are indispensable for camouflaging unsightly garden structures. If unsupported, many climbers trail along the ground and, when pegged at the nodes, will root to develop a dense carpet of groundcover. Such a strongly horizontal design element draws the eye into a design.

Some climbers look very effective when scrambling through other plants, which must be matched carefully for vigor and pruning requirements. This extends their season of interest if they flower before or after the host plant, but you can also achieve attractive associations of color and texture when they flower simultaneously.

WHITE–PINK

Beaumontia grandiflora
(Herald's trumpet)
Vigorous, evergreen, woody-stemmed, twining climber with rich green leaves that are hairy beneath. Has large, fragrant white flowers from late spring to summer.
H 25ft (8m).

Z13–15 H12–10

Decumaria sinensis
Evergreen, woody-stemmed, root climber with oval, often toothed leaves, 1–3in (2.5–8cm) long. Conical clusters of small, honey-scented cream flowers are produced in late spring and early summer. H to 6ft (2m) or more.

Z7–9 H9–7

Stephanotis floribunda
(Madagascar jasmine, Wax flower)
Moderately vigorous, evergreen, woody-stemmed, twining climber with leathery, glossy leaves. Scented, waxy white flowers appear in small clusters from spring to autumn. H 15ft (5m) or more.

Z14–15 H12–10

Clianthus puniceus* f. *albus
Evergreen or semi-evergreen, woody-stemmed, scrambling climber, grown for its drooping clusters of clawlike, creamy white flowers that open in spring and early summer. Midgreen leaves consist of many small leaflets.
H 12ft (4m).

Z7–11 H12–7

Ercilla volubilis, syn. *E. spicata*
Evergreen root climber with oval to heart-shaped, midgreen leaves, 1–2in (2.5–5cm) long. Spikes of petalless flowers, each consisting of 5 greenish or purple sepals and 6–8 white stamens, are borne in spring.
H to 30ft (10m) or more.

Z10–11 H12–10

OTHER RECOMMENDED PLANTS:
CLEMATIS, illus. pp.212–13
Decumaria sinensis, illus. p.204

PINK–RED

Mandevilla splendens,
syn. *Dipladenia splendens*
Evergreen, woody-stemmed, twining climber. Has lustrous leaves and trumpet-shaped, rose-pink flowers with yellow centers, appearing in late spring or early summer.
H 10ft (3m).

Z13–15 H12–10

Clianthus puniceus (Parrot's bill)
Evergreen or semi-evergreen, woody-stemmed, scrambling climber with leaves composed of many leaflets. In spring and early summer bears drooping clusters of unusual, clawlike, brilliant red flowers. H 12ft (4m).

Z7–11 H12–7

Distictis buccinatoria,
syn. *Phaedranthus buccinatorius*
(Mexican blood flower)
Vigorous, evergreen, woody-stemmed, tendril climber. Has trumpet-shaped, rose-crimson flowers, orange-yellow within, from early spring to summer.
H to 15ft (5m) or more.

Z9–11 H12–9

CLEMATIS, illus. pp.212–13
Pandorea jasminoides, illus. p.208
Podranea ricasoliana
Thunbergia coccinea

Kennedia rubicunda
(Dusky coral pea)
Fast-growing, evergreen, woody-stemmed, twining climber with leaves divided into 3 leaflets. Coral-red flowers are borne in small clusters in spring-summer.
H to 10ft (3m).

Z13–15 H12–10

Agapetes serpens
Evergreen, arching to pendulous, scandent shrub, best grown with support as a perennial climber. Has small, lance-shaped, lustrous leaves and pendent flowers, rose-red with darker veins, in spring.
H 6–10ft (2–3m).

pH Z12–15 H12–10

Akebia quinata (Chocolate vine)
Woody-stemmed, twining climber, semi-evergreen in mild winters or warm areas, with leaves of 5 leaflets. Vanilla-scented, brownish purple flowers appear in late spring, followed by sausage-shaped, purplish fruits.
H 30ft (10m) or more.

Z5–9 H9–5

Passiflora coccinea
(Red passionflower)
Vigorous, evergreen, woody-stemmed, tendril climber with rounded, oblong leaves. Has bright deep scarlet flowers, with red, pink, and white crowns, from spring to autumn.
H 10–12ft (3–4m).

Z14–15 H12–10

Mitraria coccinea
Evergreen, woody-stemmed, scrambling climber with oval, toothed leaves. Small, tubular, orange-red flowers are borne singly in leaf axils during late spring to summer.
H to 6ft (2m).

pH Z10–11 H12–10

Hoya macgillivrayi
Strong-growing, twining climber with thick stems and lustrous, dark green leaves. From spring to summer it bears large, cup-shaped, red-purple, purple or brownish red flowers, with dark red, occasionally white-centered coronas.
H 15–25ft (5–8m).

Z12–15 H12–10

Clytostoma callistegioides
Fast-growing, evergreen, woody-stemmed, tendril climber. Each leaf has 2 oval leaflets and a tendril. Small, nodding clusters of purple-veined lavender flowers, fading to pale pink, are borne in spring-summer.
H to 15ft (5m).

Z13–15 H12–9

Tropaeolum tricolorum
Herbaceous climber with delicate stems, small tubers, and 5–7-lobed leaves. Small orange or yellow flowers with black-tipped, reddish orange calyces are borne from early spring to early summer.
H to 3ft (1m).

Z12–15 H12–10

Manettia luteorubra,
syn. *M. bicolor*, *M. inflata*
(Brazilian firecracker)
Fast-growing, evergreen, semi-woody-stemmed, twining climber with glossy leaves. Has small, funnel-shaped red flowers with yellow tips in spring-summer. H 6ft (2m).

Z12–15 H12–10

Akebia* x *pentaphylla
Mainly deciduous, woody-stemmed, twining climber. Midgreen leaves, bronze-tinted when young, have 3 or 5 oval leaflets. Pendent racemes of small, 3-petaled purple flowers (female at base, male at apex) are borne in spring.
H to 30ft (10cm).

Z5–8 H8–5

Holboellia coriacea
Evergreen, twining climber with glossy green leaves. Clusters of tiny mauve male flowers and (lower down stems) larger, purple-tinged, green-white female flowers are borne in spring, followed by sausage-shaped purple fruits. H to 22ft (7m) or more.

Z10–11 H12–10

Agapetes 'Ludgvan Cross'
Agapetes variegata var. *rugosa*
Akebia x *pentaphylla*
Akebia trifoliata

CLEMATIS, illus. pp.212–13
Hardenbergia violacea
Kennedia nigricans

PURPLE–BLUE

Ipomoea indica, syn. *I. acuminata*, *I. learii* (Blue dawn flower)
Vigorous, perennial climber with evergreen, midgreen leaves. From late spring to autumn bears abundant, funnel-shaped, rich purple-blue to blue flowers, often maturing to purplish red. H 20ft (6m) or more.

Z12–15 H12–9

Hardenbergia comptoniana
Evergreen, woody-stemmed, twining climber with leaves of 3 or 5 lance-shaped leaflets. Has racemes of pealike, deep purple-blue flowers in spring.
H to 8ft (2.5m).

Z11–15 H12–6

Petrea volubilis
Strong-growing, evergreen, woody-stemmed, twining climber with elliptic, rough-textured leaves and deep violet and lilac-blue flowers carried in simple or branched spikes from late winter to late summer. H 20ft (6m) or more.

Z14–15 H12–6

***Hardenbergia violacea* 'Happy Wanderer'**
Evergreen, woody-stemmed, twining climber. In spring, bears pendent panicles of deep mauve-purple flowers with yellow marks on upper petals.
H to 10ft (3m).

Z12–15 H12–10

Solanum seaforthianum
(Italian jasmine, St. Vincent lilac)
Evergreen, scrambling climber with nodding clusters of star-shaped blue, purple, pink, or white flowers with yellow stamens from spring to autumn, followed by scarlet berries.
H 6–10ft (2–3m).

Z12–15 H12–10

Sollya heterophylla
Evergreen, woody-based, twining climber with narrowly lance-shaped to oval leaves, ¾-2½in (2–6cm) long. Nodding clusters of 4–9 broadly bell-shaped, sky blue flowers are carried from spring to autumn.
H to 10ft (3m).

Z10–11 H12–6

GREEN–YELLOW

Strongylodon macrobotrys
(Jade vine)
Fast-growing, evergreen, woody-stemmed, twining climber with claw-like, luminous blue-green flowers in long, pendent spikes in winter-spring. Leaves have 3 oval, glossy leaflets.
H to 70ft (20m).

Z15 H12–10

***Humulus lupulus* 'Aureus'**
Herbaceous, twining climber with rough, hairy stems and toothed, yellowish leaves divided into 3 or 5 lobes. Greenish female flower spikes are borne in pendent clusters in autumn. H to 20ft (6m).

Z4–8 H8–1

***Tecoma capensis* 'Aurea'**,
syn. *Tecomaria capensis* 'Aurea'
Erect, scrambling, evergreen shrub or climber with lustrous, mid- to dark green leaves. Racemes, to 6in (15cm) long, of slender, tubular yellow flowers, to 2in (5cm) long, are borne mainly in summer.

Z12–15 H12–10

Gelsemium sempervirens
Moderately vigorous, evergreen, twining climber with pointed, lustrous leaves. Clusters of fragrant, funnel-shaped, pale to deep yellow flowers are borne from late spring to late summer. H to 20ft (6m).

Z7–9 H9–7

Solandra maxima (Copa de oro, Golden chalice vine)
Strong-growing, evergreen, woody-stemmed, scrambling climber with glossy leaves. In spring-summer bears fragrant, pale yellow, later golden flowers. H 23–30ft (7–10m) or more.

Z11–1 H12–6

Stigmaphyllon ciliatum, illus. p.216

YELLOW

Thunbergia mysorensis
Evergreen, woody-stemmed, twining climber. Has narrow leaves and pendent spikes of flowers with yellow tubes and recurved, reddish brown lobes from spring to autumn. H 20ft (6m).

Z14–15 H12–6

Jasminum mesnyi, syn. *J. primulinum* (Primrose jasmine)
Evergreen or semi-evergreen, woody-stemmed, scrambling climber. Leaves are divided into 3 leaflets; semi-double, pale yellow flowers appear in spring. H to 10ft (3m).

Z8–11 H12–8

Canarina canariensis, illus. p.219
Macfadyena unguis-cati, illus. p.216
Pyrostegia venusta, illus. p.218
Tecoma capensis

WHITE

***Bougainvillea glabra* 'Snow White'**
Vigorous, evergreen or semi-evergreen, woody-stemmed, scrambling climber with rounded-oval leaves. In summer has clusters of white floral bracts with green veins. H to 15ft (5m).

Z13–15 H12–1

***Solanum jasminoides* 'Album'**
Semi-evergreen, woody-stemmed, scrambling climber. Oval to lance-shaped leaves are sometimes lobed or divided into leaflets. Has star-shaped white flowers, ¾–1in (2–2.5cm) across, in summer-autumn. H to 20ft (6m).

Z8–10 H10–8

Trachelospermum jasminoides
(Confederate jasmine, Star jasmine)
Evergreen, woody-stemmed, twining climber with oval leaves up to 4in (10cm) long. Very fragrant white flowers in summer, followed by pairs of pods up to 6in (15cm) long bearing tufted seeds. H to 28ft (9m).

Z8–13 H12–6

***Wisteria sinensis* 'Alba'**
Vigorous, deciduous, woody-stemmed, twining climber. Leaves are 10–12in (25–30cm) long with 11 leaflets. Has strongly scented, pealike white flowers in racemes, 8–12in (20–30cm) long, in early summer. H to 100ft (30m).

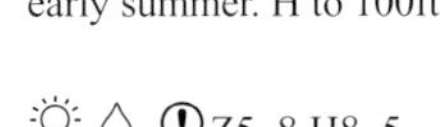

Z5–8 H8–5

Araujia sericifera (Cruel plant)
Evergreen, woody-stemmed, twining climber with leaves that are white-downy beneath. Has scented white flowers, often striped pale maroon inside, from late summer to autumn. H to 23ft (7m).

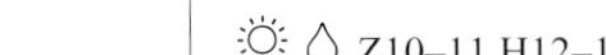

Z10–11 H12–10

***Wisteria floribunda* 'Alba'**, syn. *W.f.* 'Shiro Noda'
Deciduous, woody-stemmed, twining climber with leaves of 11–19 oval leaflets. Scented, pealike white flowers are carried in drooping racemes up to 2ft (60cm) long in early summer. H to 28ft (9m).

Z5–9 H9–5

OTHER RECOMMENDED PLANTS:
Actinidia deliciosa
Actinidia polygama
Anredera cordifolia
Beaumontia grandiflora, illus. p.204
Cionura erecta
CLEMATIS, illus. pp.212–13
Clianthus puniceus f. *albus*, illus. p.204
Cobaea scandens f. *alba*
Ipomoea alba
Jasminum angulare

WHITE

Hydrangea petiolaris, syn. *H. anomala* subsp. *petiolaris* (Climbing hydrangea)
Deciduous, woody-stemmed, root climber. Has toothed leaves and lacy heads of small white flowers in summer, only sparingly borne on young plants. H to 50ft (15m).

Z4–9 H9–1

Pileostegia viburnoides, syn. *Schizophragma viburnoides*
Slow-growing, evergreen, woody-stemmed, root climber. Tiny white or cream flowers with many prominent stamens are borne in heads from late summer to autumn. H to 20ft (6m).

Z7–11 H12–7

Clerodendrum thomsoniae
Vigorous, evergreen, woody-stemmed, scandent shrub with oval, rich green leaves. Flowers with crimson petals and bell-shaped, pure white calyces appear in clusters in summer. H 10ft (3m) or more.

Z14–15 H12–1

Schizophragma integrifolium
Deciduous, woody-stemmed, root climber with oval or heart-shaped leaves. In summer, white flowers are borne in flat heads up to 12in (30cm) across, marginal sterile flowers each having a large white bract. H to 40ft (12m).

Z5–9 H9–5

Fallopia baldschuanica, illus. p.217
Mandevilla boliviensis
Mandevilla laxa
Schizophragma hydrangeoides
Stephanotis floribunda, illus. p.204
Wisteria brachybotrys 'Shiro Kapitan'

WHITE–PINK

Hoya lanceolata subsp. ***bella***, syn. *H. bella*
Evergreen, woody-stemmed, trailing shrub with narrowly oval, pointed leaves. In summer bears tiny, star-shaped white flowers with red centers in pendulous, flattened clusters. H 18in (45cm).

Z13–15 H12–1

Pandorea jasminoides, syn. *Bignonia jasminoides* (Bower vine)
Evergreen, woody-stemmed, twining climber with leaves of 5–9 leaflets. Has clusters of funnel-shaped white flowers with pink-flushed throats from late winter to summer. H 15ft (5m).

Z11 H12–8

Jasminum officinale f. ***affine***, syn. *J. grandiflorum* of gardens
Semi-evergreen or deciduous, woody-stemmed, twining climber with leaves consisting of 7 or 9 leaflets. Clusters of fragrant 4- or 5-lobed flowers, white inside and pink outside, are borne in summer-autumn. H to 40ft (12m).

Z9–11 H12–9

Hoya australis
Moderately vigorous, evergreen, woody-stemmed, twining, root climber with fleshy, rich green leaves. Has clusters of 20–50 fragrant, star-shaped flowers, white with red-purple markings, in summer. H to 15ft (5m).

Z14–15 H12–8

Hoya carnosa (Wax plant)
Fairly vigorous, evergreen, woody-stemmed, twining, root climber. Scented, star-shaped flowers, white fading to pink with deep pink centers, are borne in dense clusters in summer-autumn. H to 15ft (5m) or more.

Z12–15 H12–8

Lathyrus odoratus **'Selana'**
Vigorous, annual, tendril climber with oval, midgreen leaves and large, fragrant, pink-flushed white flowers in summer to early autumn. H 6ft (2m).

Z10–11 H8–1

CLEMATIS, illus. pp.212–13
Dregea sinensis
Hoya coronaria
Pandorea pandorana
Passiflora x *allardii*

Actinidia kolomikta
Deciduous, woody-stemmed, twining climber with leaves 3–6in (8–16cm) long, often with areas of creamy white and pink. Has small, cup-shaped white flowers in summer, male and female on separate plants. H 12ft (4m).

 Z5–8 H8–5

***Mandevilla* x *amoena* 'Alice du Pont'**, syn. *M.* x *amabilis* 'Alice du Pont'
Vigorous, evergreen, woody-stemmed, twining climber with oval, impressed leaves. Has large clusters of trumpet-shaped, glowing pink flowers in summer. H 10ft (3m).

Z13–15 H12–2

Lathyrus grandiflorus
(Everlasting pea)
Herbaceous, tendril climber with unwinged stems and neat racemes of pink-purple and red flowers in summer. H to 5ft (1.5m).

Z6–9 H9–6

***Lonicera* x *heckrottii* 'Gold Flame'**, syn. *L.* 'Gold Flame'
Deciduous, woody-stemmed, twining climber that needs support. Leaves are oblong or oval, bluish beneath, upper ones joined into shallow cups. Scented, orange-throated pink flowers appear in clusters in summer. H to 15ft (5m).

Z6–9 H9–6

***Lathyrus odoratus* 'Xenia Field'**
Moderately fast-growing, slender, annual, tendril climber with oval, midgreen leaves. Large, fragrant, pink-and-cream flowers appear from summer to early autumn. H 6ft (2m).

Z10–11 H8–1

Antigonon leptopus (Coral vine)
Fast-growing, evergreen, woody-stemmed, tendril climber with crinkly, pale green leaves. Has dense clusters of bright pink, sometimes red or white flowers mainly in summer, but all year in tropical conditions.
H 20ft (6m).

Z14–15 H12–10

Lophospermum erubescens
Evergreen, soft-stemmed, scandent, perennial climber, sometimes woody-stemmed, often grown as an annual. Stems and leaves are downy. Rose-pink flowers, 2¾in (7cm) long, are borne in summer-autumn.
H to 10ft (3m) or more.

Z12–15 H12–10

Ipomoea horsfalliae
Strong-growing, evergreen, woody-stemmed, twining climber. Leaves have 5–7 radiating lobes or leaflets; stalked clusters of deep rose-pink or rose-purple flowers, 2½in (6cm) long, appear from summer to winter.
H 6–10ft (2–3m).

Z13–15 H12–6

CLEMATIS, illus. pp.212–13
Lathyrus sylvestris
Mandevilla splendens, illus. p.204
Mutisia oligodon
Passiflora x *exoniensis*
Passiflora mollissima
x *Philageria veitchii*
Podranea ricasoliana
Sarmienta repens

Lonicera sempervirens
(Coral honeysuckle)
Evergreen or deciduous, woody-stemmed, twining climber with oval leaves, bluish beneath, upper ones united and saucerlike. Has salmon-red to orange flowers, yellow inside, in whorls on shoot tips in summer. H to 12ft (4m).

Z4–9 H9–1

Lapageria rosea
(Chilean bellflower, Copihue)
Evergreen, woody-stemmed, twining climber with oblong to oval, leathery leaves. Has pendent, fleshy pink to red flowers, 2¾–3½in (7–9cm) long, with paler flecks, from summer to late autumn. H to 15ft (5m).

Z10–11 H12–10

***Lathyrus odoratus* 'Red Ensign'**
Vigorous, annual, tendril climber with oval, midgreen leaves and large, sweetly scented, rich scarlet flowers from summer to early autumn.
H 6ft (2m).

Z10–11 H8–1

***Lonicera* x *brownii* 'Dropmore Scarlet'**
Deciduous, woody-stemmed, twining climber with oval, blue-green leaves. Small, fragrant red flowers with orange throats are borne throughout summer.
H to 12ft (4m).

Z3–9 H9–1

***Bougainvillea* 'Miss Manila'**, syn. *B.* 'Tango'
Vigorous, mainly evergreen, woody-stemmed, scrambling climber with rounded-oval leaves. Bears clusters of pink floral bracts in summer.
H to 15ft (5m).

Z13–15 H12–1

Ipomoea lobata, syn. *I. versicolor*, *Mina lobata*, *Quamoclit lobata*
Deciduous or semi-evergreen, twining climber with 3-lobed leaves, usually grown as an annual. One-sided racemes of small, tubular, dark red flowers fade to orange then creamy yellow in summer.
H to 15ft (5m).

Z13–15 H12–10

***Bougainvillea* 'Dania'**
Vigorous, mainly evergreen, woody-stemmed, scrambling climber.
Has rounded-oval, midgreen leaves and bears clusters of deep pink floral bracts in summer. H to 15ft (5m).

Z13–15 H12–1

Ipomoea quamoclit, syn. *Quamoclit pennata* (Cypress vine)
Annual, twining climber with oval, bright green leaves cut into many threadlike segments. Slender, tubular orange or scarlet flowers are carried in summer-autumn. H 6–12ft (2–4m).

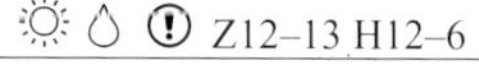

Z12–13 H12–6

Tropaeolum speciosum (Flame creeper, Flame nasturtium)
Herbaceous, twining climber with a creeping rhizome and lobed, blue-green leaves. Bears scarlet flowers in summer, followed by bright blue fruits surrounded by deep red calyces. Roots should be in shade. H to 10ft (3m).

Z8–11 H12–8

Asteranthera ovata
Bougainvillea x *buttiana* 'Scarlet Queen'
Clerodendrum splendens
Clianthus puniceus, illus. p.204
Distictis buccinatoria, illus. p.204
Gloriosa superba 'Rothschildiana', illus. p.401
Ipomoea coccinea
Ipomoea x *multifida*
Ipomoea nil 'Scarlett O'Hara'
Jasminum beesianum
Kennedia rubicunda, illus. p.205
Manettia cordifolia
Manettia luteorubra, illus. p.205
Passiflora antioquiensis
Passiflora coccinea, illus. p.205

Quisqualis indica
(Rangoon creeper)
Fairly fast-growing, deciduous or semi-evergreen, scandent shrub, often grown as an annual. From late spring to late summer has fragrant flowers varying from orange to red, sometimes pink.
H 10–15ft (3–5m).

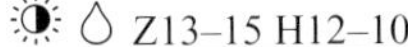
Z13–15 H12–10

Rhodochiton atrosanguineus, syn. *R. volubilis*
Evergreen, leaf-stalk climber, usually grown as an annual, with toothed leaves. Has tubular, blackish purple flowers with bell-shaped, red-purple calyces from late spring to late autumn.
H to 10ft (3m).

Z12–15 H8–2

Aristolochia littoralis, syn. *A. elegans* (Calico flower)
Fast-growing, evergreen, woody-stemmed, twining climber with heart- to kidney-shaped leaves. Heart-shaped, 5in (12cm) wide flowers, maroon with white marbling, are carried in summer.
H to 23ft (7m).

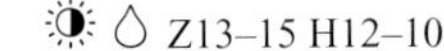
Z13–15 H12–10

Lathyrus latifolius
(Everlasting pea, Perennial pea)
Herbaceous, tendril climber with winged stems. Leaves have broad stipules and a pair of leaflets. Has small racemes of pink-purple flowers in summer and early autumn.
H 6ft (2m) or more.

Z5–9 H9–5

Schisandra rubriflora, syn. *S. grandiflora* var. *rubriflora*
Deciduous, woody-stemmed, twining climber with leathery, toothed leaves, paler beneath. Has small crimson flowers in spring or early summer and drooping red fruits in late summer.
H to 20ft (6m).

Z7–9 H9–7

Berberidopsis corallina
(Coral plant)
Evergreen, woody-stemmed, twining climber with oval to heart-shaped, leathery leaves edged with small spines. Pendent clusters of globular, deep red flowers are produced in summer to early autumn. H 14ft (4.5m).

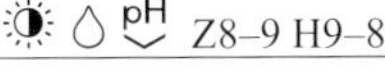
Z8–9 H9–8

Lablab purpureus, syn. *Dolichos lablab*, *D. purpureus*
(Indian bean, Hyacinth bean, Lablab)
Deciduous, woody-stemmed, twining climber, often grown as an annual. Purple, pinkish, or white flowers in summer are followed by long pods with edible seeds.
H 30ft (10m).

Z9–11 H12–9

***Bougainvillea glabra* 'Variegata'**, syn. *B.g.* 'Sanderiana'
Vigorous, mainly evergreen, woody-stemmed, scrambling climber. Rounded-oval, dark green leaves are edged with creamy white. Has many bright purple floral bracts in summer.
H to 15ft (5m).

Z13–15 H12–1

Aristolochia griffithii
Bougainvillea x *buttiana* 'Mrs Butt'
Bougainvillea spectabilis
CLEMATIS, illus. pp.212–13
Cryptostegia grandiflora
Hoya imperialis
Ipomoea horsfalliae, illus. p.209
Ipomoea horsfalliae 'Briggsii'
Lathyrus rotundifolius
Lonicera henryi
Lonicera periclymenum 'Serotina'
Mucuna pruriens var. *utilis*
Pueraria lobata

Clematis

Among the climbers, clematis are unsurpassed in their long period of flowering (with species flowering from early spring to late autumn), variety of flower shapes and colors, and tolerance of almost any exposure and climate. Some spring-flowering species and cultivars are vigorous and excellent for rapidly covering buildings, old trees, and pergolas. Other, less rampant cultivars display often large, exquisite blooms from early summer to autumn in almost every color. Clematis look attractive when trained on walls or trellises and when grown in association with other climbers, trees, or shrubs, treating them as hosts. Less vigorous cultivars may also be left unsupported to scramble at ground level, where their flowers will be clearly visible.

The various types of clematis (see the Plant Dictionary) may be divided into 3 groups, each of which has different pruning requirements. Incorrect pruning may result in cutting out the stems that will produce flowers in the current season, so the following guidelines should be followed closely.

Group 1
Early-flowering species, Alpina, Macropetala and **Montana types**
Flower stems are produced direct from the previous season's ripened stems. Prune after flowering to allow new growth to be produced and ripened for the next season. Remove dead or damaged stems and cut back other shoots that have outgrown their allotted space.

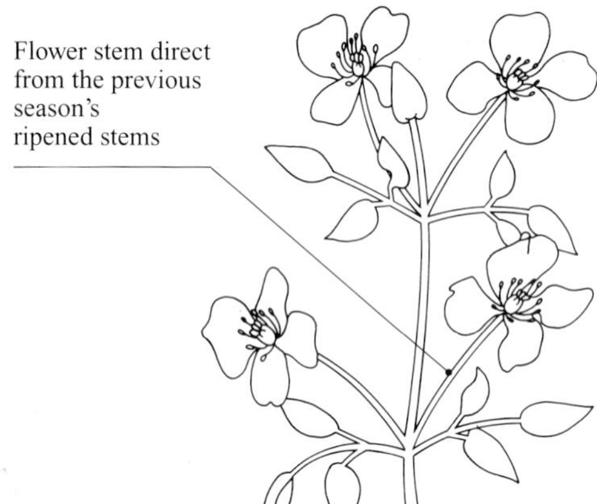

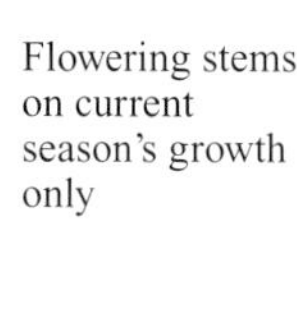

Group 2
Early, large-flowered cultivars
Flowers are produced on short, current season's stems, so prune before new growth starts, in early spring. Remove dead or damaged stems, and cut back all others to where strong, leaf-axil buds are visible. (These buds will produce the first crop of flowers.)

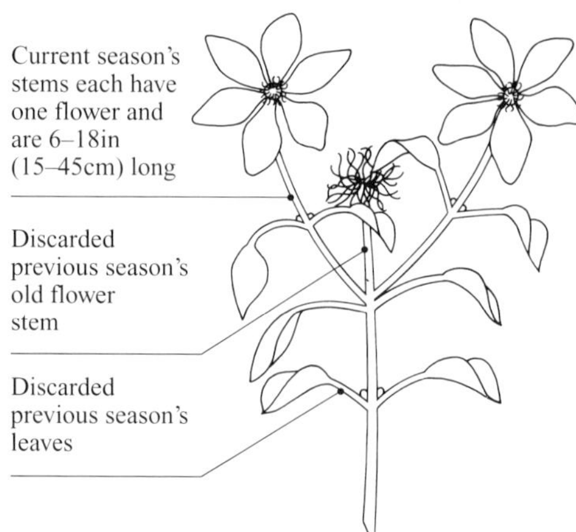

Group 3
Late, large-flowered cultivars, Late-flowering species, Small-flowered cultivars, and **Herbaceous types**
Flowers are produced on the current season's growth only, so prune before new growth commences, in early spring. Remove all of the previous season's stems down to a pair of strong, leaf-axil buds, 6–12in (15–30cm) above the soil.

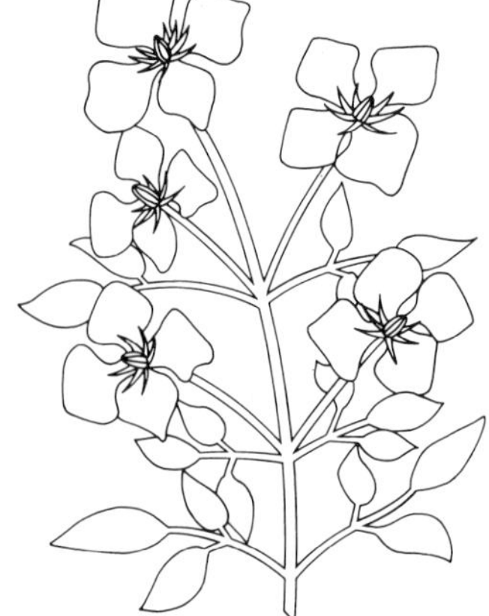

C. florida **'Sieboldii'** (3, small-fl.)

C. **'Mrs. George Jack-man'** (2, early large-fl.)

C. **'Huldine'** (3, late large-fl.)

C. flammula (3, late-fl.)

C.m. **'Mark-ham's Pink'** (1, Macrop.)

C. recta (3, herbaceous)

C. montana var. *rubens* (1, Montana)

C. **'Henryi'** (2, early large-fl.)

C. armandii (1, early-fl.)

C. montana (1, Montana)

C. Arctic Queen (2, early large-fl.)

C. montana **'Tetrarose'** (1, Montana)

C. **'Hagley Hybrid'** (3, late large-fl.)

C. 'Nelly Moser'
(2, early large-fl.)

C. Royal Velvet
(2, early large-fl.)

C. 'Vyvyan Pennell'
(2, early large-fl.)

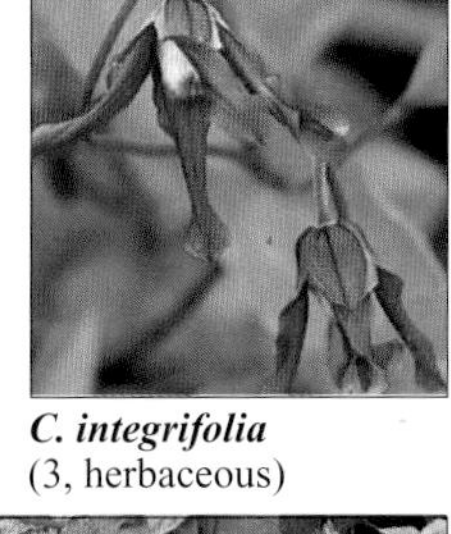
C. *integrifolia*
(3, herbaceous)

C. 'Perle d'Azur'
(3, late large-fl.)

C. 'The President'
(2, early large-fl.)

C. 'Jackmanii'
(3, late large-fl.)

C. *macropetala*
(1, Macropetala)

C. 'Lincoln Star'
(2, early large-fl.)

C. 'Madame Julia Correvon' (3, late-fl.)

C. Blue Moon
(2, early large-fl.)

C. 'Duchess of Albany'
(3, small-fl.)

C. 'Josephine'
(2, early large-fl.)

C. 'Etoile Violette'
(3, late-fl.)

C. *heracleifolia* 'Wyevale' (3, herbaceous)

C. *rehderiana*
(3, late-fl.)

C.*v.* 'Purpurea Plena Elegans' (3, late-fl.)

C. 'Ernest Markham'
(3, late large-fl.)

C. 'Elsa Spath'
(2, early large-fl.)

C. 'Lasurstern'
(2, early large-fl.)

C. Petit Faucon
(3, small-fl.)

C. *cirrhosa* (1, early-fl.)

C. 'Abundance'
(3, late-fl.)

C. Anna Louise
(2, early large-fl.)

C. 'Ascotiensis'
(3, late large-fl.)

C. *tangutica* (3, late-fl.)

C. 'Gravetye Beauty'
(3, small-fl.)

C. 'Star of India'
(3, late large-fl.)

C. 'H.F. Young'
(2, early large-fl.)

C. *alpina* 'Frances Rivis' (1, Alpina)

C. 'Bill MacKenzie'
(3, late-fl.)

PURPLE

Bougainvillea glabra
Vigorous, evergreen or semi-evergreen, woody-stemmed, scrambling climber with rounded-oval leaves. Clusters of floral bracts, in shades of cyclamen purple, appear in summer.
H to 15ft (5m).

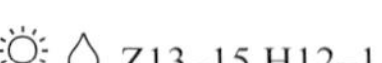
Z13–15 H12–1

***Lathyrus odoratus* 'Lady Diana'**
Moderately fast-growing, slender, annual, tendril climber with oval, mid-green leaves. Fragrant, pale violet-blue flowers are borne from summer to early autumn. H 6ft (2m).

Z10–11 H8–1

***Solanum crispum* 'Glasnevin'**
Vigorous, evergreen or semi-evergreen, woody-stemmed, scrambling climber with oval leaves. Has clusters of lilac to purple flowers, 1in (2.5cm) across, in summer. H to 20ft (6m).

Z9–15 H12–1

***Passiflora* x *caponii* 'John Innes'**
Strong-growing, evergreen, woody-stemmed, tendril climber with 3-lobed leaves. Has bowl-shaped, nodding white flowers flushed claret-purple, with purple-banded white crowns, in summer-autumn.
H 25ft (8m).

Z13–15 H12–10

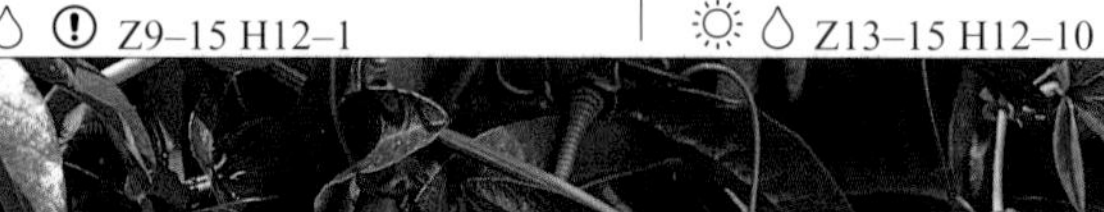

Ipomoea hederacea
(Morning glory)
Annual, twining climber with heart-shaped or 3-lobed, mid- to bright green leaves. Has funnel-shaped red, purple, pink, or blue flowers in summer to early autumn. H 10–12ft (3–4m).

Z10–15 H12–10

Codonopsis convolvulacea
Herbaceous, twining climber with 2in (5cm) long, oval or lance-shaped leaves. Widely bell- to saucer-shaped, bluish-violet flowers, 1–2in (2.5–5cm) across, are borne in summer.
H to 6ft (2m).

Z7–9 H9–7

Cobaea scandens
(Cup-and-saucer vine)
Evergreen or deciduous, woody-stemmed, tendril climber grown as an annual. From late summer to first frosts has flowers that open light yellow-green and age to purple.
H 12–15ft (4–5m).

Z11–13 H12–10

Solanum wendlandii
Robust, mainly evergreen, prickly-stemmed, scrambling climber with oblong, variably lobed leaves. Lavender flowers appear in late summer and autumn.
H 10–20ft (3–6m).

Z13–15 H12–10

Passiflora caerulea (Blue passion-flower, Common passionflower)
Fast-growing, evergreen or semi-evergreen, woody-stemmed, tendril climber. Has white flowers, sometimes pink-flushed, with blue- or purple-banded crowns, in summer-autumn.
H 30ft (10m).

Z6–9 H9–6

CLEMATIS, illus. pp.212–13
Clytostoma callistegioides, illus. p.205
Ipomoea purpurea
Lathyrus nervosus
Maurandya barclayana
Passiflora x *caeruleoracemosa*
Petrea volubilis, illus. p.206
Solanum seaforthianum, illus. p.206
Tropaeolum azureum
Vitis vinifera 'Purpurea', illus. p.218
Wisteria floribunda 'Royal Purple'

PURPLE–BLUE

Passiflora quadrangularis (Giant granadilla)
Strong-growing, evergreen, woody-stemmed climber with angled, winged stems. White, pink, red, or pale violet flowers, the crowns banded white and deep purple, appear mainly in summer. H 15–25ft (5–8m).

☼ ◊ Z13–15 H12–10

Wisteria* x *formosa
Deciduous, woody-stemmed, twining climber with leaves of 9–15 narrowly oval leaflets. Scented, pealike mauve and pale lilac flowers are carried in early summer in drooping racemes, 10in (25cm) long, followed by velvety pods. H to 80ft (25m) or more.

☼ ◊ ⓘZ6–9 H9–6

Wisteria sinensis, syn. *W. chinensis* (Chinese wisteria)
Vigorous, deciduous, woody-stemmed, twining climber. Has leaves of 11 leaflets and fragrant lilac or pale violet flowers, in racemes 8–12in (20–30cm) long, in early summer, followed by velvety pods. H to 100ft (30m).

☼ ◊ ⓘZ5–8 H8–5

***Ipomoea tricolor* 'Heavenly Blue'**, syn. *I. rubrocaerulea* 'Heavenly Blue'
Fast-growing, annual, twining climber with heart-shaped leaves and large, funnel-shaped, sky blue flowers borne from summer to early autumn.
H to 10ft (3m).

☼ ◊ ⓘ Z12–15 H12–1

Plumbago auriculata, syn. *P. capensis* (Cape leadwort)
Fast-growing, evergreen, woody-stemmed, scrambling climber. Clusters of sky blue flowers are carried from summer to early winter.
H 10–20ft (3–6m).

☼ ◊ Z12–15 H12–10

Tweedia caerulea, syn. *Oxypetalum caeruleum*
Herbaceous, twining climber with white-haired stems. Small, fleshy, pale blue flowers, maturing purple, appear in summer and early autumn.Has green fruits to 6in (15cm) long.
H to 3ft (1m).

☼ ◊ Z12–15 H12–10

CLEMATIS, illus. pp.212–13
Clitoria ternatea
Jacquemontia pentantha
Solanum jasminoides
Sollya heterophylla, illus. p.206
Thunbergia grandiflora
Wisteria floribunda 'Macrobotrys'
Wisteria sinensis 'Prolific'

YELLOW

Lonicera* x *americana, syn. *L.* x *italica* of gardens
Very free-flowering, deciduous, woody-stemmed, twining climber. Leaves are oval, upper ones united and saucerlike. Has clusters of strongly fragrant yellow flowers flushed with red-purple in summer. H to 23ft (7m).

◐ ◊ ⓘZ6–9 H9–6

***Lonicera japonica* 'Halliana'**
Evergreen or semi-evergreen, woody-stemmed, twining climber with soft-haired stems and oval, sometimes lobed, bright green leaves. Very fragrant white flowers, aging to yellow, are borne mostly in summer.
May become invasive. H to 30ft (10m).

☼ ◊ ⓘZ4–11 H12–1

***Lonicera periclymenum* 'Graham Thomas'**
Deciduous, woody-stemmed, twining climber. Oval or oblong leaves are bluish beneath Fragrant white flowers aging to yellow are borne in summer.
H to 23ft (7m).

☼ ◊ ⓘZ5–9 H9–5

Ampelopsis brevipedunculata var. *maximowiczii*
Anemopaegma chamberlaynei
Bomarea pubigera of gardens
Humulus lupulus 'Aureus', illus. p.206
Lonicera japonica 'Aureoreticulata'
Sinofranchetia chinensis
Solandra maxima, illus. p.206

YELLOW–ORANGE

***Allamanda cathartica* 'Hendersonii'**
Fast-growing, evergreen, woody-stemmed, scrambling climber. Has lance-shaped leaves in whorls and trumpet-shaped, rich bright yellow flowers in summer-autumn.
H to 15ft (5m).

Z14–15 H12–10

Thunbergia alata
(Black-eyed Susan)
Moderately fast-growing, annual, twining climber. Toothed, oval to heart-shaped leaves. Rounded, rather flat, small flowers, orange-yellow with dark brown centers. Early summer to early autumn. H 10ft (3m).

Z11–15 H12–10

Thladiantha dubia
Fast-growing, herbaceous or deciduous, tendril climber. Oval to heart-shaped midgreen leaves, 4in (10cm) long, are hairy beneath. Bell-shaped yellow flowers are carried in summer.
H 10ft (3m).

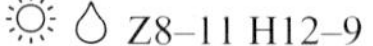

Z8–11 H12–9

Stigmaphyllon ciliatum
Fast-growing, evergreen, woody-stemmed, twining climber with heart-shaped, pale green leaves fringed with hairs. Bright yellow flowers with ruffled petals appear in spring-summer.
H 15ft (5m) or more.

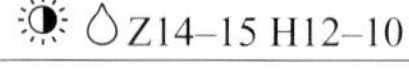

Z14–15 H12–10

Macfadyena unguis-cati
(Cat's claw)
Fast-growing, evergreen, woody-stemmed, tendril climber. Leaves have 2 leaflets and a tendril. Has yellow flowers, 4in (10cm) long, in late spring or early summer. H 25–30ft (8–10m).

Z11–15 H12–10

***Tropaeolum tuberosum* var. *lineamaculatum* 'Ken Aslet'**
Herbaceous climber with yellowish, red-streaked tubers and blue-green leaves. From midsummer to autumn has flowers with red sepals and orange petals. Where not hardy, lift and store tubers in winter. H to 8ft (2.5m).

Z8–15 H12–8

Bougainvillea x *buttiana* 'Golden Glow'
Gelsemium sempervirens
Gloriosa superba
Hibbertia scandens
Lonicera etrusca
Lonicera hildebrandiana
Lonicera tragophylla
Merremia tuberosa
Mussaenda erythrophylla
Thunbergia mysorensis, illus. p.207
Tropaeolum peregrinum
Tropaeolum tuberosum, illus. p.218
Vigna caracalla

ORANGE

Bomarea caldasii,
syn. *B. kalbreyeri* of gardens
Herbaceous, twining climber with rounded clusters of 5–40 tubular to funnel-shaped, orange-red flowers, spotted crimson within, in summer. H 10–12ft (3–4m).

Z11–15 H12–10

Lonicera* x *tellmanniana
Deciduous, woody-stemmed, twining climber with oval leaves; upper ones are joined and resemble saucers. Bright yellowish orange flowers are carried in clusters at the ends of shoots in late spring and summer. H to 15ft (5m).

Z7–9 H9–7

Eccremocarpus scaber
(Chilean glory flower, Glory vine)
Evergreen, subshrubby, tendril climber, often grown as an annual. In summer has racemes of small orange-red flowers, followed by inflated fruit pods containing many winged seeds.
H 6–10ft (2–3m).

Z11–15 H12–10

Thunbergia gregorii,
syn. *T. gibsonii*
Evergreen, woody-stemmed, twining climber, usually grown as an annual. Triangular-oval leaves have winged stalks. Glowing orange flowers are carried in summer.
H to 10ft (3m).

Z13–15 H12–10

Senecio confusus, syn.
Pseudogynoxys chenopodioides
(Mexican flame vine)
Evergreen, woody-stemmed, twining climber bearing clusters of daisylike, orange-yellow flower heads aging to orange-red, mainly in summer.
H to 10ft (3m) or more.

Z13–15 H12–10

Mutisia decurrens
Evergreen, tendril climber with narrowly oblong leaves, 2¾–5in (7–13cm) long. Flower heads, 4–5in (10–13cm) across with red or orange ray flowers, are produced in summer. Often difficult to establish but is worthwhile. H to 10ft (3m).

Z8–9 H9–8

Bignonia capreolata
Campsis radicans
Mitraria coccinea, illus. p.205
Streptosolen jamesonii, illus. p.220

Tecoma capensis

CLIMBERS AUTUMN INTEREST

WHITE–RED

Fallopia baldschuanica (Mile-a-minute plant, Russian vine)
Vigorous, deciduous, woody-stemmed, twining climber with drooping panicles of pink or white flowers in summer-autumn. H 40ft (12m) or more.

Z5–9 H9–5

***Campsis* x *tagliabuana* 'Madame Galen'**
Deciduous, woody-stemmed, root climber with leaves of 7 or more narrowly oval, toothed leaflets. Trumpet-shaped, orange-pink flowers are borne in pendent clusters from late summer to autumn. H to 30ft (10m).

Z5–9 H9–5

Passiflora manicata
Fast-growing, evergreen, woody-stemmed, tendril climber with slender, angular stems and 3-lobed leaves. Red flowers with deep purple and white crowns appear in summer-autumn.
H 10–15ft (3–5m).

Z12–15 H12–10

OTHER RECOMMENDED PLANTS:
Cobaea scandens f. *alba*
Lapageria rosea, illus. p.210
Lophospermum erubescens, illus. p.209
Pileostegia viburnoides, illus. p.208
Stephanotis floribunda, illus. p.204
Tecomanthe speciosa

RED–PURPLE

Parthenocissus tricuspidata
(Boston ivy, Japanese ivy)
Vigorous, deciduous, woody-stemmed, tendril climber. Has spectacular crimson leaf color and dull blue berries in autumn. Can cover large expanses of wall. H to 70ft (20m).

Z4–8 H8–1

***Parthenocissus tricuspidata* 'Lowii'**
Vigorous, deciduous, woody-stemmed, tendril climber with deeply cut and crinkled, 3–7-lobed leaves that turn crimson in autumn. Has insignificant flowers, followed by dull blue berries. H to 70ft (20m).

Z4–8 H8–1

Vitis coignetiae
(Crimson glory vine)
Vigorous, deciduous, woody-stemmed, tendril climber. Large leaves, brown-haired beneath, are brightly colored in autumn. Has tiny, pale green flowers in summer followed by purple-bloomed black berries. H to 50ft (15m).

Z5–9 H9–5

Parthenocissus thomsonii, syn. *Cayratia thomsonii*, *Vitis thomsonii*
Deciduous, woody-stemmed, tendril climber. Has glossy, green leaves with 5 leaflets that turn red-purple in autumn, and black berries. Provide some shade for best autumn color. H to 30ft (10m).

Z4–8 H8–1

***Vitis vinifera* 'Purpurea'**
Deciduous, woody-stemmed, tendril climber with toothed, 3- or 5-lobed, purplish leaves, white-haired when young. Has tiny, pale green flowers in summer and tiny green or purple berries. H to 23ft (7m).

Z6–9 H9–6

***Parthenocissus tricuspidata* 'Veitchii'**, syn. *Ampelopsis veitchii*
Vigorous, deciduous, woody-stemmed, tendril climber. Has spectacular red-purple leaf color and dull blue berries in autumn. Greenish flowers are insignificant. H to 70ft (20m).

Z4–8 H8–1

PURPLE–ORANGE

Billardiera longiflora
Evergreen, woody-stemmed, twining climber with narrow leaves. Small, bell-shaped, sometimes purple-tinged, green-yellow flowers are produced singly in leaf axils in summer, followed by purple-blue fruits in autumn. H to 6ft (2m).

Z8–9 H9–8

Tropaeolum tuberosum
Herbaceous, tuberous-rooted, leaf-stalk climber. Grayish green leaves have 3–5 lobes; from midsummer to late autumn has cup-shaped flowers with orange-yellow petals, orange-red sepals, and a long spur. H 6–10ft (2–3m).

Z8–15 H12–8

Pyrostegia venusta, syn. *P. ignea*
(Flame flower, Flame vine, Golden shower)
Fast-growing, evergreen, woody-stemmed, tendril climber with clusters of tubular, golden orange flowers from autumn to spring. H 30ft (10m) or more.

Z14–15 H12–10

Asarina barclayana
Cobaea scandens, illus. p.214
Ipomoea horsfalliae 'Briggsii'
Mucuna pruriens var. *utilis*
Parthenocissus henryana
Passiflora caerulea, illus. p.214
Passiflora x *caeruleoracemosa*
Passiflora vitifolia
Rhodochiton atrosanguineus, illus. p.211
Solanum seaforthianum
Solanum wendlandii, illus. p.214
Allamanda cathartica 'Hendersonii', illus. p.216
Campsis grandiflora
Senecio mikanioides

CLIMBERS WINTER INTEREST

WHITE–ORANGE

Jasminum polyanthum
Evergreen, woody-stemmed, twining climber. Dark green leaves have 5 or 7 leaflets. Large clusters of fragrant, 5-lobed white flowers, sometimes reddish on the outside, are carried from late summer to winter. H 10ft (3m) or more.

Z8–10 H10–8

Agapetes variegata* var. *macrantha
Evergreen or semi-evergreen, loose, scandent shrub that may be trained against supports. Has lance-shaped leaves and narrowly urn-shaped white or pinkish white flowers, patterned in red, in winter. H 3–6ft (1–2m).

pH Z14–15 H12–10

***Canarina canariensis*, syn. *C. campanula* (Canary Island bellflower)**
Herbaceous, tuberous, scrambling climber with triangular, serrated leaves. Has waxy orange flowers with red veins from late autumn to spring. H 6–10ft (2–3m).

Z12–15 H12–10

OTHER RECOMMENDED PLANTS:
Calochone redingii
Holmskioldia sanguinea
Pyrostegia venusta, illus. p.218
Senecio macroglossus
Senecio mikanioides
Strongylodon macrobotrys, illus. p.206
Thunbergia coccinea

CLIMBERS ALL YEAR INTEREST

WHITE–GREEN

Asparagus scandens
Evergreen, scrambling climber with lax stems and short, curved, leaflike shoots in whorls of 3. Tiny, nodding white flowers appear in clusters of 2–3 in summer, followed by red berries. H 3ft (1m) or more.

Z13–15 H12–10

***Senecio macroglossus* 'Variegatus'**
Evergreen, woody-stemmed, twining climber with triangular, fleshy leaves, bordered in white to cream and (mainly in winter) daisylike cream flower heads. H 3m (10ft).

Z12–15 H12–10

***Epipremnum aureum* 'Marble Queen', syn. *Scindapsus aureus* 'Marble Queen'**
Fairly fast-growing, evergreen, woody-stemmed, root climber. Leaves are streaked and marbled with white. Is less robust than the species. H 10–30ft (3–10m).

Z14–15 H12–10

***Epipremnum pictum* 'Argyraeum', syn. *Scindapsus pictus* 'Argyraeus' (Silver vine)**
Slow-growing, evergreen, woody-stemmed, root climber. Heart-shaped leaves are dark green with silver markings. H 6–10ft (2–3m) or more.

Z14–15 H12–10

***Syngonium podophyllum* 'Trileaf Wonder'**
Evergreen, woody-stemmed, root climber with tufted stems and arrow-head-shaped leaves when young. Mature leaves have 3 glossy leaflets with pale green or silvery gray veins. H 6ft (2m) or more.

Z14–15 H12–10

***Dioscorea discolor* (Ornamental yam)**
Evergreen, woody-stemmed, twining climber. Heart-shaped, olive green leaves are 5–6in (12–15cm) long, marbled silver, paler green, and brown, and are red beneath. H to 6ft 2m (6ft).

Z12–15 H12–10

OTHER RECOMMENDED PLANTS:
Cissus discolor
Cissus striata
Gynura aurantiaca 'Purple Passion'
IVIES, illus. p.221
Lonicera japonica 'Aureoreticulata'
Peperomia scandens
Philodendron 'Burgundy'

GREEN–ORANGE

Syngonium podophyllum, syn. *Nephthytis triphylla* of gardens
Evergreen, woody-stemmed, root climber with tufted stems and arrowhead-shaped leaves when young. Mature plants have leaves of 7–9 glossy leaflets up to 12in (30cm) long. H 6ft (2m).

Z14–15 H12–10

Tetrastigma voinierianum, syn. *Cissus voinieriana* (Chestnut vine)
Strong-growing, evergreen, woody-stemmed, tendril climber. Young stems and leaves are rust-colored and hairy; mature leaves turn lustrous, deep green above. H 30ft (10m) or more.

Z14–15 H12–10

Philodendron melanochrysum
Robust, fairly slow-growing, evergreen, woody-based, root climber. Heart-shaped leaves, to 30in (75cm) long, are lustrous, deep olive green with a coppery sheen and have pale veins. H 10ft (3m) or more.

Z14–15 H12–10

Cissus antarctica (Kangaroo vine)
Moderately vigorous, evergreen, woody-stemmed, tendril climber. Oval, pointed, coarsely serrated leaves are lustrous, rich green. H to 15ft (5m).

Z12–15 H12–10

Philodendron scandens (Heart leaf)
Fairly fast-growing, evergreen, woody-based, root climber. Rich green leaves are 4–6in (10–15cm) long when young, to 12in (30cm) long on mature plants. H 12ft (4m) or more.

Z14–15 H12–10

Gynura aurantiaca (Velvet plant)
Evergreen, woody-based, soft-stemmed, semi-scrambling climber or lax shrub with purple-haired stems and leaves. Clusters of daisylike, orange-yellow flower heads are borne in winter. H 6–10ft (2–3m), less as a shrub.

Z14–15 H12–10

Monstera deliciosa (Swiss-cheese plant)
Robust, evergreen, woody-stemmed, root climber with large-lobed, holed leaves, 16–36in (40–90cm) long. Mature plants bear cream spathes followed by scented, edible fruits. H to 20ft (6m).

Z14–15 H12–10

Cissus rhombifolia, syn. *Rhoicissus rhombifolia*, *R. rhomboidea* (Grape ivy)
Moderately vigorous, evergreen, woody-stemmed, tendril climber with lustrous leaves divided into 3 coarsely toothed leaflets. H 10ft (3m) or more. .

Z12–15 H12–10

Streptosolen jamesonii (Marmalade bush)
Evergreen or semi-evergreen, loosely scrambling shrub. Has oval, finely corrugated leaves and, mainly in spring-summer, many bright orange flowers. H 6–10ft (2–3m).

Z12–15 H12–10

Ercilla volubilis
Ficus pumila
Holboellia coriacea
Lardizabala biternata
Monstera acuminata
Philodendron cordatum
Philodendron domesticum
Philodendron pedatum
Philodendron pinnatifidum
Philodendron sagittifolium
Rhoicissus capensis
Rubus henryi var. *bambusarum*
Syngonium auritum
Syngonium erythrophyllum

Ivies

Ivies (*Hedera*) are evergreen, climbing and trailing plants suitable for growing up walls and fences or as groundcover, especially so in shade por morning sun. Plants take a year or so to establish, but thereafter growth is rapid. With time, support, and access to more light, the leaf shape and, sometimes, color will change as the plant matures from its juvenile climbing phase into the adult shrublike and flowering form.

***H. helix* 'Erecta'** ①

***H. colchica* 'Dentata'** ①

***H. helix* 'Telecurl'** ①

***H. helix* 'Pedata'** ①

***H. hibernica* 'Deltoidea'** ①

***H. helix* 'Green Ripple'** ①

H. hibernica ①

***H. helix* 'Pittsburgh'** ①

***H. hibernica* 'Gracilis'** ①

***H. helix* 'Merion Beauty'** ①

***H. helix* 'Ivalace'** ①

***H. helix* 'Lobata Major'** ①

***H. hibernica* 'Sulphurea'** ①

***H. cana.* var. *algeriensis* 'Ravensholst'** ①

***H. helix* 'Parsley Crested'** ①

***H. hibernica* 'Digitata'** ①

***H. helix* 'Nigra'** ①

***H. helix* 'Woeneri'** ①

***H. helix* 'Glymii'** ①

***H. helix* 'Adam'** ①

***H. helix* 'Heise'** ①

***H. helix* 'Glacier'** ①

***H. helix* 'Anne Marie'** ①

***H. helix* 'Manda's Crested'** ①

***H. helix* 'Atropurpurea'** ①

***H. helix* 'Eva'** ①

***H. helix* 'Angularis Aurea'** ①

***H. helix* 'Goldheart'** ①

***H. helix* 'Buttercup'** ①

***H. colchica* 'Sulphur Heart'** ①

PERENNIALS

including Grasses, Bamboos, Rushes, Sedges, and Ferns

PERENNIALS FORM the core of many garden designs because they provide such a vast range of colors, shapes, textures, and scents. Whether they are used in traditional borders or contemporary color schemes, perennials can offer a superb display that lasts for several years and so are highly prized by every kind of gardener.

Perennials

One of the largest and most versatile of plant groups, perennials offer a large, seasonally changing diversity of color, fragrance, form, and texture to the designer and a wealth of plants for every size and style of garden.

What are perennials?

Perennials are nonwoody plants that live for two or more years and, when mature, produce flowers annually. In gardens, the term is also applied to woody-based subshrubs, like lavender or artemisia, and often encompasses the grasses and ferns. Although some perennials are evergreen, most are herbaceous and die back each autumn. While this leaves borders bare in winter, many gardeners value this characteristic because it reflects the turning of the seasons: the new growth heralds spring and anticipates the glories of the forthcoming summer.

Choosing perennials

All successful plantings reflect the care taken in selecting plants good for the climate, soil type, and light levels in the garden, and this is especially true when designing with perennials. A plant that is struggling in unsuitable conditions will not fulfill its intended purpose if it fails to flower or grow well enough to fill its allotted space. The best results are usually gained by grouping plants with similar cultivation needs. Most ferns, for example, do well in shady borders in moist, organic soil, as do bamboos such as *Phyllostachys nigra*, which thrive in similar soil conditions. When perennials are massed together in borders, it is vital to consider their eventual height and spread if the robust and vigorous are not to swamp more delicate specimens.

Ornamental features

The form of perennial flowers includes strong contrasts, from the vertical spires of delphiniums or verbascums to the more horizontal shapes provided by the dense, flat flower heads of achillea. Those with arching flowers include *Polygonatum* x *hybridum*.

Because foliage is such a large textural mass, it has great impact on a

Spiky heads
Above: The sculptural forms of biennial teasels (Dipsacus fullonum) *add height and contrast to perennials in high summer, while the seed heads that follow provide interest well into winter.*

Summer border
Right: In this mixed border, drifts of Alstroemeria *Ligtu Hybrids lead the eye to a strong focal point formed by the architectural spikes of verbascum, which are cleverly echoed by the purple spires of* Salvia x superba *in the foreground.*

CONTRASTING FOLIAGE
Left: In damp, dappled shade, elegant contrasts of foliage form and texture create an atmosphere of lush abundance, but it is important to choose plants that thrive in similar conditions.

COLOR AND MOOD
Below: Use color to influence the mood of a planting design. While red, yellow, and orange suggest warmth and vitality, soft pastels and cool blues provide an air of restful charm.

WINTER IMPACT
Bottom: The strong verticals provided by the silky plumes of pampas grass (Cortaderia selloana) *take on an added aspect of beauty when rimed with frost.*

border design. Fortunately, leaf forms of perennials span a vast range: from the boldly pleated foliage of veratrum to the delicate pinnate leaves of *Polemonium caeruleum* and *Matteuccia struthiopteris*. Textural contrasts in the foliage also abound: from silky *Stachys byzantina* to the glossy foliage of *Acanthus mollis*.

DESIGNING WITH PERENNIALS
The traditional herbaceous border – a long rectangle flanked by turf and backed by a wall or well-tended hedge – has long been considered the ideal context for displaying perennials. Its width – often 10ft (3m) or more – allows for banked effects from front to back so that small plants are not obscured by taller neighbors. While only the largest of gardens have space for such grand effects, the principles used can be adapted to more modest plantings.

SIZE CATEGORIES USED WITHIN THIS GROUP

Large	Medium	Small
over 4ft (1.2m)	2–4ft (60cm–1.2m)	up to 2ft (60cm)

Low groundcover perennials such as *Cerastium tomentosum* and *Tiarella cordifolia* are ideal for the front of a border and, for greatest impact, small and medium-sized plants are best massed in odd-numbered groups. Superb effects can then be created by using single large specimens as focal points, especially those of architectural form such as *Cynara cardunculus*, *Rheum palmatum*, *Rodgersia aesculifolia*, or a tall grass such as *Stipa gigantea*. Variety of shape and texture can be introduced by combining, for example, the rounded form of *Sedum spectabile* with the upright spires of *Kniphofia*, or the lacy foliage of dicentras with the bolder outlines of hostas.

The disadvantage of planting herbaceous perennials on their own in a border is that, when they fade in autumn, only bare soil will show until the new growing season. A border mixed with shrubs to provide structure, plus annuals, biennials and bulbs, will prolong interest.

PATIO PLANTING
Pleasing arrangements of complementary colors and differing textures can be created in containers, as shown here with purple Heuchera micrantha *var.* diversifolia *'Palace Purple',* Houttuynia cordata *'Chameleon', and* Tolmiea menziesii.

□ WHITE

Epilobium angustifolium* f. *album
(White rosebay)
Vigorous, upright perennial bearing sprays of pure white flowers along wandlike stems in late summer. Leaves are small and lance-shaped. May spread rapidly. H 4–5ft (1.2–1.5m), S 20in (50cm) or more.

☼ ◊ Z3–7 H7–1

Crambe cordifolia
Robust perennial with clouds of small, fragrant white flowers borne in branching sprays in summer above mounds of large, crinkled and lobed, dark green leaves.
H to 6ft (2m), S 4ft (1.2m).

☼ ◊ Z6–9 H9–6

Eremurus himalaicus
Upright perennial with strap-shaped, basal leaves. In early summer has huge, dense racemes of open cup-shaped, pure white blooms with long stamens. Cover crowns in winter with leafmold or straw. Needs staking.
H 6–8ft (2–2.5m), S 3ft (1m).

☼ ◊ Z5–8 H8–5

Sanguisorba canadensis
(Canadian burnet)
Clump-forming perennial. In late summer bears slightly pendent spikes of bottlebrush-like white flowers on stems that arise from toothed, divided, midgreen leaves.
H 4–6ft (1.2–2m), S 2ft (60cm).

☼ ◐ Z3–8 H8–1

Nicotiana sylvestris
(Flowering tobacco)
Branching perennial, often grown as an annual, carrying panicles of fragrant, tubular white flowers at the ends of stems in late summer. Has long, rough, midgreen leaves.
H 5ft (1.5m), S 2½ft (75cm)

☼ ◊ ⓘ Z10–11 H12–1

***Eryngium eburneum*,**
syn. *E. paniculatum*
Evergreen, arching perennial bearing heads of thistlelike green flowers with white stamens on branched stems in late summer. Has arching, spiny, grasslike leaves.
H 5–6ft (1.5–2m), S 2ft (60cm).

☼ ◊ Z9–11 H12–10

Romneya coulteri
(Tree poppy)
Vigorous, bushy, subshrubby perennial grown for its large, fragrant white flowers, with prominent centers of golden stamens, that appear in late summer. Has deeply divided gray leaves. H and S 6ft (2m).

☼ ◊ Z8–10 H9–2

Echinops sphaerocephalus
Massive, bushy perennial with deeply cut, midgreen leaves, pale gray beneath, and gray stems bearing round, grayish white flower heads in late summer. H 6ft (2m), S 3ft (1m).

☼ ◊ Z3–9 H9–1

Aruncus dioicus*, syn. *A. sylvester*, *Spiraea aruncus (Goat's beard)
Hummock-forming perennial carrying large leaves with lance-shaped leaflets on tall stems and above them, in mid-summer, branching plumes of tiny, creamy white flowers.
H 6ft (2m), S 4ft (1.2m).

☼ ◊ Z3–7 H7–1

OTHER RECOMMENDED PLANTS:
Aconitum 'Ivorine'
Aconitum napellus 'Albidum'
Campanula pyramidalis
Cimicifuga racemosa
Filipendula camtschatica
Macleaya cordata
Selinum wallichianum
Veratrum album

Artemisia lactiflora
(White mugwort)
Vigorous, erect perennial. Many sprays of creamy white buds open to off-white flower heads in summer. Dark green leaves are jagged-toothed. Needs staking and is best as a foil to stronger colors.
H 4–5ft (1.2–1.5m), S 20in (50cm).

Z5–8 H8–5

Alpinia zerumbet, syn. *A. nutans* of gardens, *A. speciosa*
(Shell flower, Shell ginger)
Evergreen, clump-forming perennial. Has racemes of white flowers, with yellow lips and pink- or red-marked throats, mainly in summer.
H 10ft (3m), S 3ft (1m).

Z14–15 H12–10

***Campanula lactiflora* 'Loddon Anna'**
Upright, branching perennial with narrowly oval leaves. In summer, slender stems bear racemes of large, nodding, bell-shaped, soft dusty pink flowers. Needs staking in a windy site.
H 4ft (1.2m), S 2ft (60cm).

Z4–8 H8–1

***Macleaya microcarpa* 'Kelway's Coral Plume'**
Clump-forming perennial that in summer produces branching spikes of rich pink-buff flowers. Large, rounded, lobed leaves are gray-green above, gray-white beneath.
H 6–8ft (2–2.5m), S 3–4ft (1–1.2m).

Z4–9 H9–1

Eremurus robustus
Upright perennial with straplike leaves that die back during summer as huge racemes of cup-shaped pink blooms appear. Cover crowns in winter with leafmold or straw. Needs staking.
H 7ft (2.2m), S 3ft (1m).

Z5–8 H8–5

Anemone x *hybrida* 'Max Vogel'
Eremurus Shelford Hybrids
Kitaibela vitifolia
Lupinus 'The Chatelaine', illus. p.244

PINK–RED

Lavatera cachemiriana, syn. *L. cachemirica*
Semi-evergreen, woody-based perennial or subshrub with wiry stems bearing panicles of trumpet-shaped, silky, clear pink flowers in summer. Has ivy-shaped, downy, midgreen leaves. H 5–6ft (1.5–2m), S 3ft (1m).

Z4–9 H9–1

Filipendula rubra
Vigorous, upright perennial with large, jagged leaves and feathery plumes of tiny, soft pink flowers on tall, branching stems in midsummer. Will rapidly colonize a boggy site.
H 6–8ft (2–2.5m), S 4ft (1.2m).

Z3–9 H9–1

***Rheum palmatum* 'Atrosanguineum'**
Clump-forming perennial with very large, lobed, deeply cut leaves that are deep red-purple when young. Bears large, fluffy panicles of crimson flowers in early summer.
H and S 6ft (2m).

Z5–9 H9–5

Filipendula purpurea, illus. p.245
Kniphofia uvaria 'Nobilis'
Lobelia tupa
PHLOX, illus. p.242

PERENNIALS large SUMMER INTEREST

PURPLE–BLUE

Veratrum nigrum
(Black false hellebore)
Erect, stately perennial that from late summer onward bears long spikes of chocolate-purple flowers at the ends of thick, upright stems. Stems are clothed with ribbed, oval to narrowly oval leaves. H 6ft (2m), S 2ft (60cm).

Z6–9 H9–6

Verbena bonariensis,
syn. *V. patagonica*
Perennial often grown as an annual with a basal clump of dark green leaves. Upright, wiry stems carry tufts of tiny, purplish blue flowers in summer-autumn.
H 5ft (1.5m), S 2ft (60cm).

Z7–11 H12–7

Cynara cardunculus (Cardoon)
Stately perennial with large clumps of arching, pointed, divided, silver-gray leaves, above which rise large, thistle-like, blue-purple flower heads borne singly on thick gray stems in summer. Flower heads dry well.
H 6ft (2m), S 3ft (1m).

Z7–9 H9–7

Campanula lactiflora
'Prichard's Variety'
Upright perennial with slender stems carrying branching heads of large, nodding, bell-shaped, violet-blue flowers from early summer to late autumn. May need staking.
H 4–5ft (1.2–1.5m), S 2ft (60cm).

Z5–7 H7–5

Echinops bannaticus
Upright perennial with narrow, deeply cut leaves and globose, pale to mid-blue heads of flowers borne on branching stems in late summer. Flower heads dry well.
H 4–5ft (1.2–1.5m), S 2½ft (75cm).

Z5–9 H9–5

***Galega* 'Lady Wilson'**
Vigorous, upright perennial with spikes of small, pealike blue and pinkish white flowers in summer above bold leaves divided into oval leaflets. Needs staking. H to 5ft (1.5m), S 3ft (1m).

Z5–11 H12–5

Acanthus spinosus, illus. p.251
Aconitum napellus
Agapanthus inapertus
Campanula pyramidalis
Cicerbita bourgaei
DELPHINIUMS, illus. p.230
Echinops ritro 'Veitch's Blue', illus. p.252
Galega 'His Majesty'
Meconopsis x *sheldonii*
Thalictrum chelidonii
Thalictrum delavayi 'Hewitt's Double'

GREEN–YELLOW

Gunnera manicata
Architectural perennial with rounded, prickly-edged leaves, to 5ft (1.5m) across. Has conical, light green flower spikes in early summer, followed by orange-brown seed pods. May need a mulch cover for crowns in winter and a sheltered site. H 6ft (2m), S 7ft (2.2m).

Z7–11 H12–7

Angelica archangelica (Angelica)
Upright perennial, usually grown as a biennial, with deeply divided, bright green leaves and white or green flowers in late summer. Stems have culinary usage and when crystallized may be used for confectionery decoration.
H 6ft (2m), S 3ft (1m).

Z4–9 H9–1

Ferula communis (Giant fennel)
Upright perennial. Large multiple umbels of yellow flowers are borne from late spring to summer on the tops of stems that arise from a mound of finely cut, midgreen foliage.
H 6–7ft (2–2.3m), S 3–4ft (1–1.2m).

Z6–9 H9–6

Cephalaria gigantea
Eryngium agavifolium
Thalictrum flavum 'Illuminator'

YELLOW

Verbascum olympicum
Semi-evergreen, rosette-forming biennial or short-lived perennial. Branching stems, arising from felt-like gray foliage at the plant base, bear sprays of 5-lobed, bright golden flowers from midsummer onward. H 6ft (2m), S 3ft (1m).

Z5–9 H9–5

Ligularia przewalskii ,
syn. *Senecio przewalskii*
Loosely clump-forming perennial with stems clothed in deeply cut, round, dark green leaves. Narrow spires of small, daisylike yellow flower heads appear from mid- to late summer. H 4–6ft (1.2–2m), S 3ft (1m).

Z5–8 H8–1

***Rudbeckia* 'Goldquelle'**
Erect perennial. In late summer and autumn, daisylike, double, bright yellow flower heads with green centers are borne singly on thick stems. Has deeply divided, midgreen foliage. H 5–6ft (1.5–2m), S 2–2½ft (60–75cm).

Z3–9 H9–1

Inula magnifica
Robust, clump-forming, upright perennial with a mass of lance-shaped to elliptic, rough leaves. Leafy stems bear terminal heads of large, daisylike yellow flower heads in late summer. Needs staking. H 6ft (1.8m), S 3ft (1m).

Z5–8 H8–5

Ligularia stenocephala
Loosely clump-forming perennial with jagged-edged, round, midgreen leaves. Large heads of daisylike yellow-orange flowers open on purplish stems from mid- to late summer. H 4ft (1.2m) or more, S 2ft (60cm).

Z4–8 H8–1

Achillea filipendulina 'Gold Plate', illus. p.258
CHRYSANTHEMUMS, illus. pp.260–61
Helianthus atrorubens 'Monarch'
Helianthus x *multiflorus* 'Loddon Gold', illus. p.232
Ligularia 'Gregynog Gold'
Meconopsis paniculata
Rudbeckia 'Herbstsonne', illus. p.232
Silphium laciniatum
Telekia speciosa
Thalictrum flavum

 ORANGE

Heliopsis helianthoides subsp. ***scabra* 'Light of Loddon'**,
syn. *H.* 'Light of Loddon'
Upright perennial bearing dahlia-like, double, bright orange flower heads on strong stems in late summer. Dark green leaves are coarse and serrated. H 4–5ft (1.2–1.5m), S 2ft (60cm).

Z3–9 H9–1

Hedychium densiflorum
Clump-forming, rhizomatous perennial bearing a profusion of short-lived, fragrant orange or yellow flowers in dense spikes during late summer. Broadly lance-shaped leaves are a glossy midgreen. H 4–6ft (1.2–2m), S 2ft (60cm).

Z8–11 H12–8

Heliconia psittacorum
(Parrot flower, Parrot plantain)
Tufted perennial with long-stalked, lance-shaped leaves. In summer, mature plants carry green-tipped orange flowers with narrow, glossy, orange-red bracts. H to 6ft (2m), S 3ft (1m).

Z14–15 H12–10

Heliopsis helianthoides 'Incomparabilis'
Heliopsis helianthoides subsp. *scabra*
Kniphofia 'Samuel's Sensation'
Wachendorfia thyrsiflora

Delphiniums

Delphiniums are among the most attractive of the tall perennials, with their showy spires of flowers making a spectacular display in the summer herbaceous border. In addition to the classic blues, hybrids are available in a broad range of colors, from white through the pastel shades of dusky pink and lilac to the richer mauves and violet-purples. Plants should be securely staked to support the heavy flower spikes.

***D.* 'Butterball'** ⓘ

***D.* 'Emily Hawkins'** ⓘ

***D.* 'Bruce'** ⓘ

***D.* 'Cliveden Beauty'** ⓘ

***D.* 'Loch Leven'** ⓘ

***D.* 'Fanfare'** ⓘ

***D.* 'Gillian Dallas'** ⓘ

***D.* 'Lord Butler'** ⓘ

***D.* 'Blue Nile'** ⓘ

***D.* 'Sandpiper'** ⓘ

***D.* 'Strawberry Fair'** ⓘ

***D.* 'Mighty Atom'** ⓘ

***D.* 'Spindrift'** ⓘ

***D. grandiflorum* 'Blue Butterfly'** ⓘ

***D.* 'Chelsea Star'** ⓘ

***D.* 'Olive Poppleton'** ⓘ

***D.* 'Langdon's Royal Flush'** ⓘ

***D.* 'Blue Dawn'** ⓘ

***D.* 'Sungleam'** ⓘ

WHITE–PINK

Cimicifuga simplex
Upright perennial with arching spikes of tiny, slightly fragrant, star-shaped white flowers in autumn. Leaves are glossy and divided. Needs staking.
H 4–5ft (1.2–1.5m), S 2ft (60cm).

Z4–8 H12–1

***Anemone* x *hybrida* 'Honorine Jobert'**
Vigorous, branching perennial. Slightly cupped white flowers with contrasting yellow stamens are carried on wiry stems in late summer and early autumn above deeply divided, dark green leaves. H 5ft (1.5m), S 2ft (60cm).

Z4–8 H8–1

***Anemone hupehensis* 'September Charm'**
Vigorous, branching perennial. In late summer and early autumn bears slightly cupped, clear pink flowers on wiry stems. Leaves are deeply divided and dark green.
H 30in (75cm), S 20in (50cm).

Z4–8 H8–1

PINK–PURPLE

Eupatorium purpureum
(Joe Pye weed)
Stately, upright perennial with terminal heads of tubular, pinkish purple flowers borne in late summer and early autumn. Coarse, oval leaves are arranged in whorls along purplish stems.
H to 7ft (2.2m), S to 3ft (1m).

Z3–9 H9–1

***Salvia involucrata* 'Bethellii'**
Subshrubby perennial that produces long racemes of large, cerise-crimson blooms with pink bracts in late summer and autumn. Leaves are oval to heart-shaped. H 4–5ft (1.2–1.5m), S 3ft (1m).

Z11–15 H12–10

***Anemone hupehensis* var. *japonica* 'Bressingham Glow'**
Vigorous, branching perennial with slightly cupped, rose-purple flowers borne on wiry stems in late summer and early autumn over clumps of deeply divided, dark green leaves.
H 4–5ft (1.2–1.5m), S 2ft (60cm).

Z4–8 H8–1

OTHER RECOMMENDED PLANTS:
Anemone hupehensis var. *japonica* 'Prinz Heinrich'
Anemone x *hybrida* 'Max Vogel'
CHRYSANTHEMUMS, illus. pp.260–61
Cimicifuga simplex 'Prichard's Giant'
Leucanthemella serotina
LATE-BLOOMING ASTERS, illus. p.262
Aconitum carmichaelii 'Arendsii'
Campanula lactiflora 'Prichard's Variety', illus. p.228
Helenium 'Riverton Gem'
LATE-BLOOMING ASTERS, illus. p.262
Phytolacca americana
Salvia uliginosa
Verbena bonariensis, illus. p.228

PERENNIALS large AUTUMN INTEREST

GREEN–YELLOW

Gomphocarpus physocarpus, syn. *Asclepias physocarpa*
Deciduous, erect, hairy subshrub, leaves lance-shaped. 4in (10cm) long. Umbels of 5-horned, creamy white flowers in summer. Large, inflated, globose seed pods with soft bristles. H to 6ft (2m), S to 2ft (60cm).

Z12–15 H12–10

***Helianthus* x *multiflorus* 'Loddon Gold'**
Upright perennial bearing showy, large, vivid deep yellow flower heads with rounded, double centers in late summer and early autumn. Needs staking and may spread quickly. H 5ft (1.5m), S 2ft (60cm).

Z5–9 H9–5

Hedychium gardnerianum
Upright, rhizomatous perennial. In late summer and early autumn has many spikes of short-lived, fragrant, lemon yellow and red flowers. Lance-shaped leaves are grayish green, most markedly when young. H 5–6ft (1.5–2m), S 2½ft (75cm).

Z8–10 H12–9

***Rudbeckia* 'Herbstsonne'**
Erect perennial bearing daisylike yellow flower heads with conical green centers that are carried singly on tall stems in late summer and autumn. Midgreen leaves are shallowly lobed. H 5–7ft (1.5–2.3m), S 2–2½ft (60–75cm).

Z3–9 H9–1

Helianthus* x *multiflorus
Upright perennial. Has large yellow flower heads, with double centers surrounded by larger, rayed segments, that are borne in late summer and early autumn. Needs staking and may spread rapidly. H 5ft (1.5m), S 2ft (60cm).

Z5–9 H9–5

CHRYSANTHEMUMS, illus. pp.260–61
Helianthus salicifolius
Kniphofia caulescens, illus. p.263
Rudbeckia laciniata 'Golden Glow'
Solidago 'Golden Wings'

PERENNIALS large WINTER/ALL YEAR

PINK–PURPLE

Musa ornata (Flowering banana)
Evergreen, palmlike, suckering perennial with oblong, waxy, bluish green leaves to 6ft (2m) long. In summer has erect, yellow-orange flowers with pinkish bracts and greenish yellow fruits. H to 10ft (3m), S 7ft (2.2m).

Z14–15 H12–10

Strelitzia nicolai
Evergreen, palmlike perennial with a thick trunk. Has leaves, 5ft (1.5m) or more long, on very long stalks and intermittently bears beaklike white and pale blue flowers in boat-shaped, dark purple bracts. H 25ft (8m), S 15ft (5m).

Z12–15 H12–10

Calathea sanderiana
Evergreen, clump-forming perennial. Broadly oval, leathery, glossy leaves, to 2ft (60cm) long, are dark green with pink to white lines above, and purple beneath. Intermittently has short spikes of white to mauve flowers. H 4–5ft (1.2– 1.5m), S 3ft (1m).

Z14–15 H12–11

Doryanthes palmeri
Evergreen perennial with a rosette of arching, ribbed leaves to 6ft (2m) long. Intermittently bears panicles of small, red-bracted, orange-red flowers, white within. Flowers are often replaced by bulbils. H 6–8ft (2–2.5m), S 8ft (2.5m).

Z13–15 H12–10

***Phormium tenax* Purpureum Group**
Evergreen, upright perennial with bold, stiff, pointed leaves that are rich reddish purple to dark copper. In summer, panicles of reddish flowers appear on purplish blue stems. H 6–8ft (2–2.5m), S 3ft (1m).

Z9–11 H12–6

OTHER RECOMMENDED PLANTS:
Calathea majestica 'Roseolineata'
Costus speciosus
Impatiens sodenii
ORCHIDS, illus. pp.296–9

BLUE–GREEN

Pycnostachys dawei
Strong-growing, bushy perennial with toothed, oblong leaves, 5–12in (12–30cm) long, that are reddish below. Has compact spikes of tubular, 2-lipped, bright blue flowers in winter-spring. H 4–5ft (1.2–1.5m), S 1–3ft (30–90cm).

Z14–15 H12–10

Musa basjoo, syn. *M. japonica*
(Japanese banana)
Evergreen, palmlike, suckering perennial with arching leaves to 3ft (1m) long. Has drooping, pale yellow flowers with brownish bracts in summer followed by green fruits. H 10–15ft (3–5m), S 6–8ft (2–2.5m).

Z8–11 H12–8

Ensete ventricosum,
syn. *Musa arnoldiana*, *M. ensete*
Evergreen, palmlike perennial with small, banana-like fruits. Has 20ft (6m) long leaves with reddish midribs and, intermittently, reddish green flowers with dark red bracts. H 20ft (6m), S 10ft (3m) or more.

Z10–11 H12–1

Aciphylla scott-thomsonii
Artemisia ludoviciana var. *albula*, illus. p.266
Nepenthes rafflesiana
Phormium cookianum
Phormium cookianum subsp. *hookeri* 'Tricolor'
Phormium cookianum 'Variegatum'
Phormium tenax

WHITE

***Ranunculus aconitifolius* 'Flore Pleno'**
(Fair maids of France)
Clump-forming perennial with deeply divided, dark green leaves. Double, pure white flowers are borne on strong, branched stems in spring-summer. H 24–30in (60–75cm), S 20in (50cm).

Z5–9 H9–5

Ranunculus aconitifolius
Vigorous, clump-forming perennial with deeply divided, dark green leaves. Single white flowers, about 1in (3cm) across, are borne in spring and early summer. H and S 3ft (1m).

Z5–9 H9–5

Smilacina racemosa
(False Solomon's seal)
Arching perennial. Has oval, light green leaves terminating in feathery sprays of white flowers that appear from spring to midsummer and are followed by fleshy reddish fruits. H 30–36in (75–90cm), S 18in (45cm).

pH Z4–9 H9–1

OTHER RECOMMENDED PLANTS:
Asphodelus aestivus
Asphodelus albus, illus. p.239
Dicentra spectabilis f. *alba*, illus. p.239
IRISES, illus. pp.234–5
PEONIES, illus. pp.236–7
Polygonatum hirtum
Polygonatum multiflorum 'Flore Pleno'

Irises

These beautiful flowers were originally named after Iris, the Greek goddess of the rainbow, because their colors are reminiscent of those of the rainbow. Their distinctive flowers often have "beards" (made of short hairs) or crests along the centers of the falls.

The genus is classified into many divisions, some of which are used horticulturally for irises with similar characteristics or cultural requirements. Of these, the easiest to grow are the bearded, crested, Xiphium, and dwarf Reticulata groups. Siberian and Japanese types are excellent in a bog garden or by water, but they also tolerate drier conditions. Others, such as Juno, Oncocyclus, and Regelia irises, may be less easy to cultivate, though their flowers are among the most beautiful. Full details of all groups and guidance on their cultivation are given in the Plant Dictionary.

***I.* 'Wisley White'** (Siberian) ①

I. iberica (Oncocyclus) ①

***I.* 'Dreaming Yellow'** (Siberian) ①

***I.* 'Geisha Gown'** (Japanese) ①

I. bucharica (Juno) ①

I. magnifica (Juno) ①

I. missouriensis (Pacific Coast) ①

I. cristata (Evansia) ①

***I.* 'Rippling Rose'** (bearded) ①

I. rosenbachiana (Juno) ①

I. latifolia (Xiphium) ①

***I.* 'Bold Print'** (bearded) ①

***I.* 'Krasnia'** (bearded) ①

***I.* 'Mary Frances'** (bearded) ①

I.* × *fulvala (beardless) ①

I. douglasiana (Pacific Coast) ①

***I. pallida* 'Variegata'** (bearded) ①

***I.* 'Ruffled Velvet'** (Siberian) ①

***I.* 'Magic Man'** (bearded) ①

***I.* 'Joette'** (bearded) ①

I. tenax (Pacific Coast) ①

***I.* 'Annabel Jane'** (bearded) ①

I. versicolor (beardless) ①

I. chrysographes (Siberian) ①

***I.* 'Paradise Bird'** (bearded) ①

I. tectorum (Evansia) ①

***I.* 'Matinata'** (bearded) ①

***I.* 'Lady of Quality'** (Siberian) ①

I. japonica
(Evansia) ⓘ

I. histrioides 'Major'
(Reticulata) ⓘ

I. 'Harmony'
(Reticulata) ⓘ

I. winogradowii
(Reticulata) ⓘ

I. innominata
(Pacific Coast) ⓘ

I. danfordiae
(Reticulata) ⓘ

I. 'Peach Frost'
(bearded) ⓘ

I. 'Carnaby'
(bearded) ⓘ

I. 'Sapphire Star'
(Japanese) ⓘ

I. laevigata
(Japanese) ⓘ

I. 'Joyce'
(Reticulata) ⓘ

I. pseudacorus
(beardless) ⓘ

I. hoogiana
(Regelia) ⓘ

I. 'Katharine Hodgkin'
(Reticulata) ⓘ

I. xiphium 'Wedgwood'
(Xiphium) ⓘ

I. setosa
(beardless) ⓘ

I. 'Early Light'
(bearded) ⓘ

I. 'Sun Miracle'
(bearded) ⓘ

I. fulva (beardless) ⓘ

I. reticulata 'Cantab'
(Reticulata) ⓘ

I. ensata 'Galathea'
(Japanese) ⓘ

I. 'Bronze Queen'
(Xiphium) ⓘ

I. variegata
(bearded) ⓘ

I. 'Eyebright'
(bearded) ⓘ

I. 'Blue-eyed Brunette'
(bearded) ⓘ

I. 'Mountain Lake'
(Siberian) ⓘ

I. 'Lavender Royal'
(Pacific Coast) ⓘ

I. 'Butter and Sugar'
(Siberian) ⓘ

I. forrestii
(Siberian) ⓘ

I. 'Shepherd's Delight'
(bearded) ⓘ

I. 'Flamenco'
(bearded) ⓘ

Peonies

Peonies (*Paeonia* species and cultivars) have long been valued for their showy blooms, filling the border with subtle shades of mainly whites, pinks, and reds in late spring and early to midsummer. Peony flowers vary from single to double or anemone form (with broad, outer petals and a mass of petaloids in the center) and are often heavily scented. The flowers are also good for cutting. Peony foliage is also striking, often tinged bronze when young and assuming rich reddish tints in autumn. Besides the wide variety of border hybrids available, there are many attractive species. Tree peonies (cultivars of *P. suffruticosa*) are shrubs that rarely grow to 6ft (2m) high.

Peonies are long-lived plants that should (if possible) be left undisturbed, since they resent transplanting. If it is necessary to divide the clumps, lift and divide them in late summer or early autumn.

P. emodi (single) (!)

***P. suffruticosa* 'Godaishu'** (double) (!)

P. suffruticosa subsp. ***rockii*** (semi-dbl.) (!)

***P.* 'Krinkled White'** (single) (!)

P. obovata var. ***alba*** (single) (!)

***P.* 'White Wings'** (single) (!)

***P.* 'Whitleyi Major'** (single) (!)

***P.* 'Baroness Schroeder'** (double) (!)

***P. officinalis* 'Alba Plena'** (double) (!)

***P.* 'Duchesse de Nemours'** (dbl.) (!)

***P.* 'Alice Harding'** (double) (!)

***P.* 'Cornelia Shaylor'** (double) (!)

***P.* 'Shirley Temple'** (double) (!)

***P.* 'Mother of Pearl'** (single) (!)

***P.* 'Kelway's Supreme'** (double) (!)

***P. suffruticosa* 'Hana-kisoi'** (double) (!)

***P.* 'Avant Garde'** (single) (!)

***P. suffruticosa* 'Reine Elizabeth'** (double) (!)

***P.* 'Sarah Bernhardt'** (double) (!)

***P.* 'Ballerina'** (double) (!)

***P.* 'Bowl of Beauty'** (anemone) (!)

P. mascula subsp. ***mascula*** (single) (!)

***P.* 'Globe of Light'** (anemone) (!)

***P.* 'Evening World'** (anemone) (!)

P. cambessedesii (single) (!)

P. suffruticosa **'Kamadu-nishiki'** (double) ①

P. veitchii (single) ①

P. **'Magic Orb'** (double) ①

P. suffruticosa **'Cardinal Vaughan'** (semi-double) ①

P. **'Kelway's Gorgeous'** (single) ①

P. officinalis **'China Rose'** (single) ①

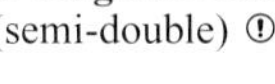

P. **'Auguste Dessert'** (semi-double) ①

P. **'Silver Flare'** (single) ①

P. **'Instituteur Doriat'** (anemone) ①

P. x ***smouthii*** (single) ①

P. **'Defender'** (single) ①

P. suffruticosa **'Hana-daijin'** (double) ①

P. peregrina **'Otto Froebel'** (single) ①

P. **'Knighthood'** (double) ①

P. tenuifolia (single) ①

P. **'Chocolate Soldier'** (semi-double) ①

P. **'Sir Edward Elgar'** (single) ①

P. delavayi (single) ①

P. officinalis **'Rubra Plena'** (double) ①

P. wittmanniana (single) ①

P. **'Laura Dessert'** (double) ①

P. **'L'Espérance'** (single) ①

P. potaninii var. ***trollioides*** (single) ①

P. mlokosewitschii (single) ①

P. **'Argosy'** (single) ①

P. lutea var. ***ludlowii*** (single) ①

P. **'Souvenir de Maxime Cornu'** (double) ①

P. **'Madame Louis Henri'** (semi-double) ①

WHITE–BLUE

Polygonatum* x *hybridum
(Solomon's seal)
Arching, leafy perennial with fleshy rhizomes. In late spring, clusters of small, pendent, tubular, greenish white flowers are produced in axils of neat, oval leaves. H 4ft (1.2m), S 3ft (1m).

Z6–9 H9–6

Geranium phaeum
(Mourning widow)
Clump-forming perennial with lobed, soft green leaves and maroon-purple flowers with reflexed petals, borne on rather lax stems in late spring.
H 30in (75cm), S 18in (45cm).

Z4–8 H8–1

***Darmera peltata*,**
syn. *Peltiphyllum peltatum*
(Umbrella plant)
Spreading perennial with large, rounded leaves. Has clusters of white or pale pink flowers in spring on white-haired stems before foliage appears.
H 3–4ft (1–1.2m), S 2ft (60cm).

Z5–9 H9–5

Symphytum caucasicum
Clump-forming perennial carrying clusters of pendent, azure blue flowers in spring above rough, hairy, mid-green foliage. Is best grown in a wild garden. H and S 24–36in (60–90cm).

Z3–9 H9–1

***Tanacetum coccineum* 'Brenda'**,
syn. *Pyrethrum* 'Brenda'
Erect perennial with somewhat aromatic, feathery leaves. Daisylike, single, magenta-pink flower heads are borne in late spring and early summer.
H 24in (60cm), S 18in (45cm) or more.

Z5–9 H9–5

BLUE–YELLOW

***Symphytum* x *uplandicum* 'Variegatum'**
Perennial with large, hairy, gray-green leaves that have broad cream margins. In late spring and early summer, pink or blue buds open to tubular blue or purplish blue flowers.
H 3ft (1m), S 2ft (60cm).

Z5–9 H9–4

***Doronicum columnae* 'Miss Mason'**
Clump-forming, rhizomatous perennial with heart-shaped leaves. Slender stems bear daisylike, bright yellow flower heads, 3in (8cm) across, held well above the foliage, in mid- and late spring. H and S 24in (60cm).

Z4–8 H8–1

***Chelidonium majus* 'Flore Pleno'**
Upright perennial with divided, bright green leaves and many cup-shaped, double yellow flowers borne on branching sprays in late spring and early summer. Seeds freely and so is best in a wild garden.
H 24–30in (60–90cm), S 12in (30cm).

Z5–8 H8–5

Aciphylla aurea
(Golden Spaniard)
Evergreen, rosette-forming perennial with long, bayonet-like, yellow-green leaves. Bears spikes of golden flowers up to 6ft (2m) tall from late spring to early summer.
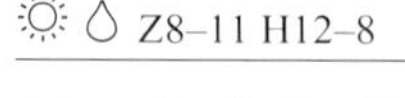
H and S in leaf 24–30in (60–75cm)

Z8–11 H12–8

Asphodeline lutea
(Yellow asphodel)
Neat, clump-forming perennial that bears dense spikes of star-shaped, yellow flowers amid narrow, gray-green leaves in late spring.
H 3–4ft (1–1.2m), S 2–3ft (60cm–1m).

Z6–9 H6–6

Anigozanthos manglesii, illus. p.250
Anigozanthos rufus
Columnea gloriosa
Dicentra spectabilis, illus. p.245
Erysimum 'Bowles Mauve'
Geranium maculatum
Meconopsis betonicifolia, illus. p.253
Salvia x *superba* 'Mainacht', illus. p.252
Anigozanthos flavidus, illus. p.254
DAYLILIES, illus. p.257
Doronicum x *excelsum* 'Harpur Crewe'
Euphorbia palustris
Trollius x *cultorum* 'Alabaster', illus. p.274
Trollius x *cultorum* 'Orange Princess'
Trollius europaeus, illus. p.275

□ WHITE

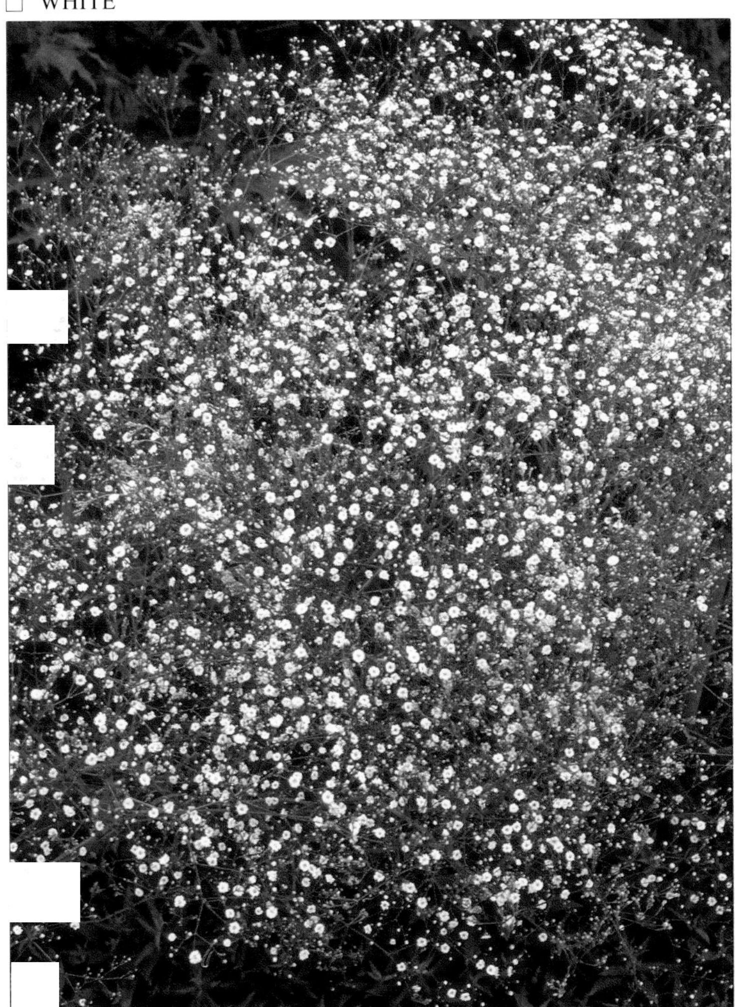

***Gypsophila paniculata* 'Bristol Fairy'**
Perennial with small, dark green leaves and wiry, branching stems bearing panicles of tiny, double white flowers in summer.
H 2–2½ft (60–75cm), S 3ft (1m).

Z5–9 H9–1

Libertia grandiflora
(New Zealand satin flower)
Loosely clump-forming, rhizomatous perennial that in early summer produces spikes of white flowers above grasslike, dark green leaves that turn brown at the tips. Has decorative seed pods in autumn. H 30in (75cm), S 24in (60cm).

Z8–11 H12–8

Asphodelus albus
(White asphodel)
Upright perennial with clusters of star-shaped white flowers borne in late spring and early summer. Has narrow, basal tufts of midgreen leaves.
H 3ft (1m), S 1½ft (45cm).

Z7–11 H12–7

Hesperis matronalis
(Dame's violet, Sweet rocket)
Upright perennial with long spikes of many 4-petaled white or violet flowers borne in summer. Flowers have a strong fragrance in the evening. Leaves are smooth and narrowly oval.
H 30in (75cm), S 24in (60cm).

Z4–9 H9–1

Anaphalis margaritacea
(Pearl everlasting)
Bushy perennial that has lance-shaped, gray-green or silvery gray leaves with white margins and many heads of small white flowers borne on erect stems in late summer. Flower heads dry well.
H 24–30in (60–75cm), S 24in (60cm).

Z4–8 H8–1

***Achillea ptarmica* 'The Pearl'**
Upright perennial with large heads of small, pomponlike white flowers in summer and tapering, glossy, dark green leaves. May spread rapidly.
H and S 30in (75cm).

Z3–8 H8–1

Nicotiana alata*, syn. *N. affinis
Rosette-forming perennial, often grown as an annual, that in late summer bears clusters of tubular, creamy white flowers, pale brownish violet externally that are fragrant at night. Has oval, midgreen leaves.
H 30in (75cm), S 12in (30cm).

Z10–11 H12–1

Dicentra spectabilis* f. *alba
Leafy perennial forming a hummock of fernlike, deeply cut, light green foliage with arching sprays of pendent, heart-shaped, pure white flowers in late spring and summer.
H 24–30in (60–75cm), S 24in (60cm).

Z3–9 H9–1

OTHER RECOMMENDED PLANTS:
Anemone narcissiflora, illus. p.275
Anemone rivularis, illus. p.275
Caladium bicolor 'Candidum'
Campanula alliariifolia, illus. p.275
Crambe maritima, illus. p.276
DELPHINIUMS, illus. p.230
Echinacea purpurea 'White Lustre'
Eupatorium rugosum
Filipendula vulgaris 'Multiplex'
Heuchera 'Pearl Drops'
IRISES, illus. pp.234–5
Lysimachia ephemerum
Physostegia virginiana 'Summer Snow'
Ranunculus aconitifolius, illus. p.233
Smilacina racemosa, illus. p.233

□ WHITE

Eupatorium rugosum, syn. *E. ageratoides, E. urticifolium* (Hardy age, Mist flower, White snakeroot)
Erect perennial with nettlelike, gray-green leaves. In late summer bears dense, flat, white flower heads. H 4ft (1.2m), S 1½ft (45cm).

Z4–8 H8–2

Dictamnus albus, syn. *D. fraxinella* (Gasplant)
Upright perennial bearing, in early summer, spikes of fragrant, star-shaped white flowers with long stamens. Light green leaves are divided into oval leaflets. Dislikes disturbance. H 3ft (1m), S 2ft (60cm).

Z3–8 H8–1

Myrrhis odorata (Sweet Cicely)
Graceful perennial that resembles cow parsley. Has aromatic, fernlike, mid-green foliage and fragrant, bright creamy white flowers in early summer. H 24–36in (60–90cm), S 24in (60cm).

Z3–7 H7–1

***Thalictrum aquilegiifolium* 'White Cloud'**
Perennial with divided, grayish green leaves. In summer produces terminal sprays of delicate, fluffy white flowers. H 3–4ft (1–1.2m), S 1ft (30cm).

Z5–9 H9–5

***Leucanthemum* x *superbum* 'Elizabeth'**, syn. *Chrysanthemum maximum* of gardens 'Elizabeth', *C.* x *superbum* 'Elizabeth'
Robust perennial with large, daisylike, single, pure white flower heads borne singly in summer. Divide and replant every 2 years. H 3ft (1m), S 2ft (60cm).

Z5–8 H8–5

Argyranthemum frutescens, syn. *Chrysanthemum frutescens* (Marguerite)
Evergreen, woody-based, bushy perennial that bears many daisylike white, yellow, or pink flower heads throughout summer. Attractive leaves are fresh green. H and S 3ft (1m).

Z10–11 H12–1

Rodgersia podophylla
Clump-forming, rhizomatous perennial with large, many-veined leaves that are bronze when young and later become midgreen, then copper-tinted. Panicles of creamy white flowers are borne well above foliage in summer. H 4ft (1.2m), S 3ft (1m).

Z5–8 H8–5

Rodgersia sambucifolia
Clump-forming, rhizomatous perennial with emerald green, sometimes bronze-tinged leaves composed of large leaflets. Sprays of creamy white flowers appear above foliage in summer. H 3–4ft (1–1.2m), S 3ft (1m).

Z5–8 H8–5

***Aruncus dioicus* 'Kneiffii'**
Hummock-forming perennial that has deeply cut, feathery leaves with lance-shaped leaflets on elegant stems and bears branching plumes of tiny, star-shaped, creamy white flowers in mid-summer. H 3ft (90cm), S 20in (50cm).

Z3–7 H7–1

Rodgersia aesculifolia
Clump-forming, rhizomatous perennial that is excellent for a bog garden or by a pond. In midsummer, plumes of fragrant, pinkish white flowers rise from crinkled bronze foliage like that of a horse chestnut tree.
H and S 3ft (1m).

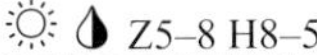
Z5–8 H8–5

***Papaver orientale* 'Perry's White'**
Hairy-leaved perennial with deep, fleshy roots. Satiny white flowers with purple centers appear on strong stems in early summer. May need support.
H 32in (80cm), S 24in (60cm).

Digitalis ferruginea
Perennial, best treated as a biennial, with long, slender spikes bearing many funnel-shaped, pale orange-brown and white flowers in midsummer above basal rosettes of oval, rough leaves. Propagate from seed.
H 3–4ft (1–1.2m), S 1ft (30cm).

Z4–9 H9–1

Lysimachia clethroides
Vigorously spreading perennial carrying spikes of small white flowers above midgreen foliage in late summer.
H 3ft (1m), S 2–3ft (60cm–1m).

Z4–9 H9–1

Morina longifolia
Evergreen perennial that produces rosettes of large, spiny, thistlelike, rich green leaves. Whorls of hooded, tubular white flowers, flushed pink within, are borne well above foliage in midsummer.
H 2–2½ft (60–75cm), S 1ft (30cm).

Z6–9 H9–6

Gillenia trifoliata
Upright perennial with many wiry, branching stems carrying clusters of dainty white flowers with reddish brown calyces in summer. Leaves are dark green and lance-shaped. May need staking. Thrives in most situations.
H 3–4ft (1–1.2m), S 2ft (60cm).

Z5–9 H9–5

Veronicastrum virginicum* f. *album
Upright perennial. In late summer, spires of small white flowers with pink-flushed bases and pink anthers crown stems clothed with whorls of narrow, dark green leaves.
H 4ft (1.2m), S 1½ft (45cm).

Z3–8 H8–1

Valeriana officinalis
(Cat's valerian, Common valerian)
Clump-forming, fleshy perennial that bears spikes of white to deep pink flowers in summer. Leaves are deeply toothed and midgreen. May attract cats.
H 3–4ft (1–1.2m), S 3ft (1m).

Z4–9 H9–1

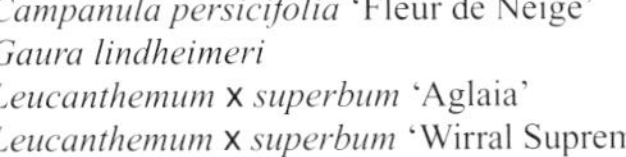

Campanula persicifolia 'Fleur de Neige'
Gaura lindheimeri
Leucanthemum x *superbum* 'Aglaia'
Leucanthemum x *superbum* 'Wirral Supreme'
PHLOX, illus. p.242
Ranunculus aconitifolius 'Flore Pleno', illus. p.233
Smilacina racemosa, illus. p.233
Xerophyllum tenax

PERENNIALS

Phlox

Border phlox (cultivars of *Phlox maculata* and *P. paniculata*) are considered to be some of the most elegant and stately of garden plants and are a mainstay of the herbaceous border in mid- to late summer. Their dome-shaped or conical panicles of flowers, which are often delicately scented, are produced in shades that include white, pink, red, and purple. Many of the flowers have attractive contrasting eyes. Some cultivars have strikingly variegated foliage that makes a bold feature before the flowers appear.

Phlox thrive in sun or partial shade and in organic, well-drained soil. Taller varieties may need staking. If larger flowers are desired, reduce the number of stems in spring, when the plant is about a quarter to a third of its eventual height, by pinching out or cutting back the weakest shoots. To prolong the flowering season, cutting back the central part of the flower head as the blooms fade will encourage the sideshoots to flower. Once the plants have finished flowering in autumn they should be cut back to the ground.

Border phlox are particularly susceptible to nematodes; to avoid infestation, plant only young, healthy stock propagated from root cuttings taken from clean stock. Any plants that show signs of disease should be dug up and discarded. It is advisable not to replant infested soil with phlox for at least two seasons.

P. paniculata **'Fujiyama'**

P. paniculata **'Mia Ruys'**

P. paniculata **'White Admiral'**

P. maculata **'Omega'**

P. paniculata **'Mother of Pearl'**

P. paniculata **'Eva Cullum'**

P. paniculata **'Brigadier'**

P. paniculata **'Eventide'**

P. paniculata **'Norah Leigh'**

P. paniculata **'Graf Zeppelin'**

P. paniculata **'Balmoral'**

P. maculata **'Alpha'**

P. paniculata **'Windsor'**

P. paniculata **'Sandringham'**

P. paniculata **'Harlequin'**

P. paniculata **'Le Mahdi'**

P. paniculata **'Prince of Orange'**

P. paniculata **'Amethyst'**

P. paniculata **'Hampton Court'**

PERENNIALS

PINK

***Linaria purpurea* 'Canon J. Went'**
Upright perennial bearing spikes of snapdragon-like pink blooms with orange-tinged throats from mid- to late summer. Has narrow, gray-green leaves.
H 2–3ft (60cm–1m), S 2ft (60cm).

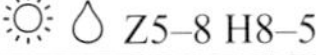
Z5–8 H8–5

***Geranium* x *oxonianum* 'Winscombe'**
Semi-evergreen, carpeting perennial with dense, dainty, lobed leaves and cup-shaped, deep pink flowers that fade to pale pink, borne throughout summer.
H 24–30in (60–75cm), S 18in (45cm).

Z4–8 H8–1

Malva moschata
Bushy, branching perennial producing successive spikes of saucer-shaped, rose-pink flowers during early summer. Narrow, lobed, divided leaves are slightly scented.
H 2–3ft (60cm–1m), S 2ft (60cm).

Z4–8 H8–1

Dictamnus albus* var. *purpureus
Upright perennial. In early summer bears stiff spikes of fragrant, star-shaped, purplish pink, sometimes paler flowers with long stamens. Has light green leaves divided into oval leaflets. Dislikes disturbance.
H 3ft (1m), S 2ft (60cm).

Z3–8 H8–1

***Persicaria bistorta* 'Superba'**, syn. *Polygonum bistorta* 'Superbum'
Vigorous, clump-forming perennial that from early to late summer produces spikes of soft pink flowers above oval leaves.
H 24–30in (60–75cm), S 24in (60cm).

Z4–8 H8–1

***Monarda* 'Croftway Pink'**
Clump-forming perennial carrying whorls of hooded, soft pink blooms throughout summer above neat mounds of aromatic foliage.
H 3ft (1m), S 1½ft (45cm).

Z4–9 H9–2

***Argyranthemum* 'Mary Wootton'**, syn. *Chrysanthemum frutescens* 'Mary Wootton'
Evergreen, woody-based, bushy perennial bearing daisylike pink flower heads throughout summer. Has attractive, fernlike, pale green foliage. H and S to 3ft (1m).

Z10–11 H12–1

***Sidalcea* 'Oberon'**
Upright perennial with rounded, deeply cut leaves divided into narrowly oblong segments. In summer, produces racemes of shallowly cup-shaped, clear pink flowers. H 24in (60cm), S 18in (45cm).

Z5–7 H8–5

Anemone hupehensis 'Hadspen Abundance', illus. p.259
Astrantia major, illus. p.277
Astrantia maxima, illus. p.277
Campanula lactiflora 'Loddon Anna'
Chelone obliqua, illus. p.259
Lythrum virgatum 'Rose Queen'
PELARGONIUMS, illus. pp.246–7
PEONIES, illus. pp.236–7
Sidalcea 'Loveliness'
Sidalcea 'Oberon'
Tanacetum coccineum 'Brenda', illus. p.238
Tanacetum coccineum 'Eileen May Robinson'
Tanacetum coccineum 'James Kelway'

PINK

***Astilbe* 'Venus'**
Leafy perennial bearing feathery, tapering plumes of tiny, pale pink flowers in summer. Foliage is broad and divided into leaflets; flowers remain on the plant, dried and brown, well into winter. Prefers organic soil. H and S to 3ft (1m).

Z3–8 H8–2

***Astilbe* 'Straussenfeder'**
Leafy perennial with handsome, divided foliage and arching, feathery, tapering plumes of tiny, coral-pink flowers in summer. Dry brown flowers remain on the plant well into winter. Prefers organic soil. H and S to 3ft (1m).

Z3–8 H8–2

***Echinacea purpurea* 'Robert Bloom'**
Upright perennial. Has lance-shaped, dark green leaves and large, daisylike, deep crimson-pink flower heads with conical, brown centers, borne singly on strong stems in summer. H 4ft (1.2m), S 20in (50cm).

Z3–9 H9–1

***Lupinus* 'The Chatelaine'**
Clump-forming perennial carrying spikes of pink-and-white flowers above divided, midgreen foliage in early summer. H 4ft (1.2m), S 1½ft (45cm).

Z4–7 H7–1

Centaurea pulcherrima
Upright perennial with deeply cut, silvery leaves. Rose-pink flower heads, with thistlelike centers paler than surrounding star-shaped ray petals, are borne singly on slender stems in summer. H 2½ft (75cm), S 2ft (60cm).

Z4–8 H8–1

***Physostegia virginiana* 'Variegata'**
Erect perennial. In late summer produces spikes of tubular, purplish pink blooms that can be moved into position. Toothed, midgreen leaves are white-variegated. H 3–4ft (1–1.2m), S 2ft (60cm).

Z4–8 H8–1

***Rehmannia elata*, syn. *R. angulata* of gardens**
Straggling perennial bearing foxglove-like, yellow-throated, rose-purple flowers in leaf axils of notched, stem-clasping, soft leaves from early to midsummer. H 3ft (1m), S 1½ft (45cm).

Z12–15 H12–10

Kohleria digitaliflora
Erect, bushy, rhizomatous perennial with white-haired stems. Has scalloped, hairy leaves and stalked clusters of tubular, very hairy, pink-and-white flowers with purple-spotted, green lobes in summer-autumn. H 24in (60cm) or more, S 18in (45cm).

Z14–15 H12–10

Caladium x *bicolor* 'Pink Cloud'
Chrysanthemum 'Clara Curtis', illus. p.259
DAYLILIES, illus. p.257

Dierama dracomontanum
Erigeron 'Foerster's Liebling'
Heuchera 'Coral Cloud'
Heuchera 'Scintillation'

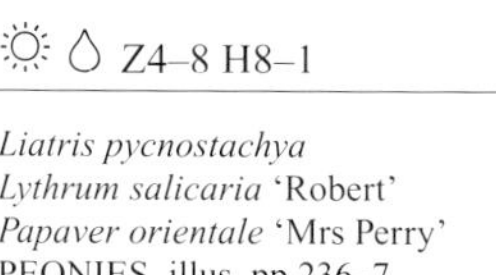

Liatris pycnostachya
Lythrum salicaria 'Robert'
Papaver orientale 'Mrs Perry'
PEONIES, illus. pp.236–7

PHLOX, illus. p.242
Rodgersia pinnata 'Superba'
Verbascum 'Pink Domino'

PINK

Dicentra spectabilis
(Bleeding heart)
Leafy perennial forming a mound of fernlike, deeply cut, midgreen foliage, above which rise arching stems carrying pendent, heart-shaped, pinkish red and white flowers in late spring and summer. H 30in (75cm), S 20in (50cm).

Z3–9 H9–1

***Lythrum salicaria* 'Feuerkerze'**, syn. *L.s.* 'Firecandle'
Clump-forming perennial for a waterside or bog garden. Bears spikes of intense rose-red blooms from mid- to late summer. Cultivation may be prohibited near wetlands. H 3ft (1m), S 1½ft (45cm).

Z4–9 H9–1

Mirabilis jalapa (Four o'clock, Marvel of Peru)
Bushy, tuberous perennial. Fragrant, trumpet-shaped crimson, pink, white, or yellow flowers, opening in evening, cover midgreen foliage in summer. H 2–4ft (60cm–1.2m), S 2–2½ft (60–75cm).

Z11-15 H12–9

***Lythrum virgatum* 'The Rocket'**
Clump-forming perennial that carries slender spikes of rose-red flowers above midgreen foliage during summer. Cultivation may be prohibited near wetlands. H 3ft (1m), S 1½ft (45cm).

Z4–9 H9–1

Geranium psilostemon, syn. *G. armenum*
Clump-forming perennial that has broad, deeply cut leaves with good autumn color and many cup-shaped, single, black-centered magenta flowers in midsummer. H and S 4ft (1.2m).

Z5–8 H8–5

RED

***Lupinus* 'Inverewe Red'**
Upright perennial with divided, bright green leaves. In early summer bears tall, upright racemes of red flowers. Cut back after flowering. May be short-lived. H 3–4ft (1–1.2m), S 2ft (60cm).

Z4–9 H9–1

Filipendula purpurea
Upright perennial with deeply divided leaves. Produces large, terminal heads of masses of tiny, rich reddish purple flowers in summer. Makes a good waterside plant.
H 4ft (1.2m), S 2ft (60cm).

Z4–9 H9–1

Centranthus ruber (Red valerian)
Perennial forming spreading colonies of fleshy leaves. Branching heads of small, star-shaped, deep reddish pink or white flowers are borne above foliage from late spring to autumn. Thrives in poor, exposed sites. H 24–36in (60–90cm), S 18–24in (45–60cm) or more.

Z5–8 H8–5

Asclepias hallii
Centaurea dealbata 'Steenbergii'
Centaurea hypoleuca 'John Coutts', illus. p.279
Francoa sonchifolia
Liatris spicata, illus. p.279
Mimulus lewisii, illus. p.279
PELARGONIUMS, illus. pp.246–7
PENSTEMONS, illus. p.248
PEONIES, illus. pp.236–7
PHLOX, illus. p.242
Sidalcea 'Puck'
Sidalcea 'Sussex Beauty'

Pelargoniums

Pelargoniums are cultivated for their colorful flowers as well as their often attractive foliage. They grow happily in containers or beds and flower almost continuously in warm climates or in a greenhouse. They need sunshine and well-drained soil; some thrive in cool temperatures.

Zonal – the common "geranium": plants with rounded leaves, distinctively marked with a zone, and single to double flowers. Foliage is often best in cool weather. **Regal** – shrubby plants with deeply serrated leaves and exotic, broadly trumpet-shaped flowers that are prone to weather damage in the open. Grow cool. **Ivy-leaved** – trailing plants, ideal for hanging baskets, with lobed, somewhat fleshy leaves and single to double flowers. Newer cultivars tolerate heat well. **Scented-leaved** and **species** – plants with small, often irregularly star-shaped flowers; scented-leaved forms are grown mainly for their fragrant leaves. **Unique** – tall-growing subshrubs with regal-like, brightly colored flowers that are borne continuously through the season. Leaves, which may be scented, vary in shape.Grow cool.

***P.* 'Dale Queen'**
(zonal) ①

***P.* 'Purple Emperor'**
(regal) ①

***P.* 'Fragrans'**
(scented-leaved) ①

***P.* 'Butterfly Lorelei'**
(zonal) ①

***P.* 'Apple Blossom Rosebud'** (zonal) ①

***P.* 'Timothy Clifford'**
(zonal) ①

***P.* 'Ivalo'** (zonal) ①

***P.* 'Clorinda'**
(scented-leaved) ①

***P.* 'Mauritania'**
(zonal) ①

***P.* 'Golden Lilac Mist'**
(zonal) ①

***P.* 'Autumn Festival'**
(regal) ①

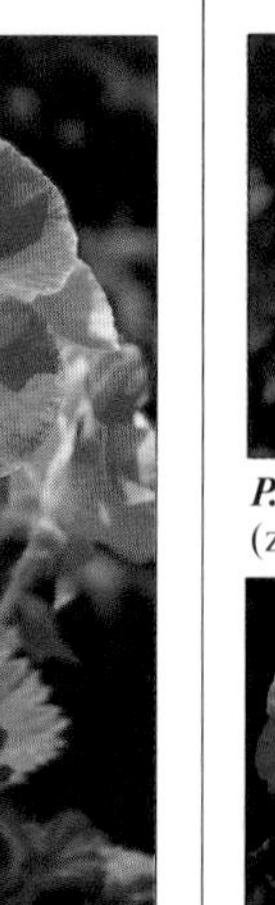
***P.* 'Cherry Blossom'**
(zonal) ①

***P.* 'Francis Parrett'**
(zonal) ①

***P.* 'Rica'**
(zonal) ①

***P.* 'Fraiche Beauté'**
(zonal) ①

***P.* 'Fair Ellen'**
(scented-leaved) ①

P. acetosum
(species) ①

***P.* 'Mr. Henry Cox'**
(zonal) ①

***P.* 'Schöne Helena'**
(zonal) ①

***P.* 'Leslie Judd'**
(regal) ①

***P.* 'Mr Everaarts'**
(zonal) ①

***P.* 'Manx Maid'**
(regal) ①

***P.* 'Brookside Primrose'** (zonal) ①

***P.* 'The Boar'**
(species) ①

***P.* 'Lachskönigin'**
(ivy-leaved) ①

***P.* 'Lachsball'**
(zonal) ①

***P.* 'Alberta'**
(zonal) ①

***P.* 'Amethyst'**
(ivy-leaved) ①

P. 'Mini Cascade' (ivy-leaved) ⓣ

P. 'Madame Fournier' (zonal) ⓣ

P. 'Caligula' (zonal) ⓣ

P. 'Bredon' (regal) ⓣ

P. 'Gustav Emich' (zonal) ⓣ

P. 'L'Elégante' (ivy-leaved) ⓣ

P. 'Paton's Unique' (unique) ⓣ

P. 'Rouletta' (ivy-leaved) ⓣ

P. 'Dolly Varden' (zonal) ⓣ

P. 'Voodoo' (unique) ⓣ

P. 'Royal Oak' (scented-leaved) ⓣ

P. 'Tip Top Duet' (regal) ⓣ

P. 'Paul Humphries' (zonal) ⓣ

P. 'Flower of Spring' (zonal) ⓣ

P. 'Robe' (zonal) ⓣ

P. capitatum (scented-leaved) ⓣ

P. tomentosum (scented-leaved) ⓣ

P. 'Friesdorf' (zonal) ⓣ

P. 'Irene' (zonal) ⓣ

P. 'Mrs. Pollock' (zonal) ⓣ

P. 'Polka' (unique) ⓣ

P. 'Purple Unique' (unique) ⓣ

P. crispum 'Variegatum' (scented-leaved) ⓣ

P. 'Tavira' (ivy-leaved) ⓣ

P. 'Purple Wonder' (zonal) ⓣ

P. 'Orange Ricard' (zonal) ⓣ

P. 'Mabel Grey' (scented-leaved) ⓣ

P. 'Rollisson's Unique' (unique) ⓣ

P. 'Capen' (zonal) ⓣ

P. 'Prince of Orange' (scented-leaved) ⓣ

P. 'Mrs. Quilter' (zonal) ⓣ

Penstemons

Increasingly valued by gardeners for their long racemes of foxglovelike flowers, penstemons are among the most elegant of border perennials. A large number of excellent cultivars is available, in a subtle range of colors that includes white, pastel and deep pink, warm cherry red, clear blue, and dusky purple. Many penstemon flowers have contrasting white throats or are attractively streaked with other colors.

Penstemons flower most prolifically in summer, but the display can be prolonged into autumn provided the plants are regularly deadheaded throughout the season. Some taller cultivars may benefit from being staked.

Penstemons thrive in well-drained soil, preferably with full sun. Where winters are expected to be severe, the plants should be lifted after flowering and before the first frosts and overwintered in a cool basement. Plants are more likely to survive freezing if they are grown in a sheltered spot in free-draining soil.

Penstemons are generally not long-lived plants and tend to become woody at the base after a few seasons; they should be regularly replaced with younger plants propagated from softwood cuttings of nonflowering shoots taken in mid- to late summer.

P. 'Apple Blossom'

P. 'Pennington Gem'

P. 'Schoenholzeri'

P. 'Alice Hindley'

P. 'Rubicundus'

P. *cardwellii*

P. 'Maurice Gibbs'

P. 'Chester Scarlet'

P. 'Burgundy'

P. 'Stapleford Gem'

P. fruticosus subsp. ***scouleri*** f. ***albus***

P. 'Evelyn'

P. 'Countess of Dalkeith'

P. *heterophyllus*

P. 'White Bedder'

P. 'Beech Park'

P. 'Andenken an Friedrich Hahn'

P. 'Sour Grapes'

■ RED

***Aquilegia vulgaris* 'Nora Barlow'**
Leafy perennial that in summer has several short-spurred, funnel-shaped, double red flowers, pale green at the tips, on long stems. Leaves are gray-green, rounded, and deeply divided.
H 24–30in (60–75cm), S 20in (50cm).

Z4–7 H7–1

***Persicaria amplexicaulis* 'Firetail'**, syn. *Polygonum amplexicaule* 'Firetail'
Clump-forming perennial that carries slender spikes of bright red flowers above heart-shaped leaves in summer-autumn. H and S 3–4ft (1–1.2m).

Z3–8 H8–1

Lychnis chalcedonica
(Maltese cross)
Neat, clump-forming perennial that bears flat heads of small vermilion flowers at the tips of thick stems in early summer. Foliage is midgreen.
H 3–4ft (1–1.2m), S 1–1½ft (30–45cm).

Z4–8 H8–1

***Lobelia* 'Cherry Ripe'**
Clump-forming perennial bearing spikes of cerise-scarlet flowers from mid- to late summer. Leaves, usually fresh green, are often tinged red-bronze. H 3ft (1m), S 9in (23cm).

Z3–8 H8–1

***Astilbe* 'Montgomery'**
Leafy perennial bearing feathery, tapering plumes of tiny, deep salmon-red flowers in summer. Foliage is broad and divided into leaflets. Flowers, brown when dried, remain on the plant well into winter. Prefers organic soil.
H 2½ft (75cm), S to 3ft (1m).

Z3–8 H8–2

***Knautia macedonica*,**
syn. *Scabiosa rumelica*
Upright perennial with deeply divided leaves and many rather lax, branching stems bearing double, almost globular, bright crimson flower heads in summer. Needs support.
H 30in (75cm), S 24in (60cm).

Z5–9 H9–5

***Cosmos atrosanguineus*,**
syn. *Bidens atrosanguinea*
(Chocolate cosmos)
Upright, tuberous perennial with chocolate-scented, maroon-crimson flower heads in late summer. In warm areas tubers may overwinter if protected.
H 24in (60cm) or more, S 18in (45cm).

Z8–11 H12–8

***Lobelia* 'Queen Victoria'**
Clump-forming perennial. From late summer to midautumn, spikes of blazing red flowers on branching stems arise from basal, deep red-purple foliage. H 3ft (1m), S 1ft (30cm).

Z3–9 H9–1

Ruellia graecizans*, syn. *R. amoena
Evergreen, bushy subshrub with wide-spreading stems. Oval, pointed leaves are 4in (10cm) long. Intermittently bears clusters of small, tubular scarlet flowers on stalks to 4in (10cm) long.
H and S 24in (60cm) or more.

Z14–15 H12–10

DAYLILIES, illus. p.257
Lobelia cardinalis
Lobelia splendens
Lobelia 'Will Scarlet'
ORCHIDS, illus. pp.296–9
Papaver orientale 'Indian Chief'
PELARGONIUMS, illus. pp.246–7
PENSTEMONS, illus. p.248
PEONIES, illus. pp.236–7
Persicaria amplexicaulis
Potentilla 'Etna'
PRIMROSES, illus. pp.272–3
Salvia involucrata
Smithiantha zebrina
Xeronema callistemon

■ RED

Hedysarum coronarium
(French honeysuckle)
Spreading, shrubby perennial or biennial. Spikes of pealike, bright red flowers are produced in summer above divided, midgreen leaves.
H and S 3ft (1m).

Z4–9 H9–1

Russelia equisetiformis,
syn. *R. juncea* (Coral plant)
Evergreen, branching, bushy subshrub with rushlike stems and tiny leaves. Showy, pendent clusters of tubular scarlet flowers appear in summer-autumn. H to 3ft (1m) or more, S 2ft (60cm).

Z11–12 H12–1

Anigozanthos manglesii
(Red-and-green kangaroo paw)
Vigorous, bushy perennial that bears racemes of large, tubular, woolly, red-and-green flowers in spring and early summer. Has long, narrow, gray-green leaves. H 3ft (1m), S 1½ft (45cm).

pH Z10–11 H12–10

***Monarda* 'Cambridge Scarlet'**
Clump-forming perennial that throughout summer bears whorls of hooded, rich red flowers above neat mounds of aromatic, hairy foliage.
H 3ft (1m), S 1½ft (45cm).

Z4–9 H9–1

Columnea* x *banksii
Evergreen, trailing perennial with oval, fleshy leaves, glossy above, purplish red below. Tubular, hooded, brilliant red flowers, to 3in (8cm) long, appear from spring to winter. Makes a useful plant for a hanging basket. H 3ft (1m), S indefinite.

Z14–15 H12–10

***Papaver orientale* 'Allegro'**,
syn. *P.o.* 'Allegro Viva'
Hairy-leaved perennial with very deep, fleshy roots. Papery, bright scarlet flowers are borne in summer on strong stems. H 24–30in (60–75cm), S 18in (45cm).

Z4–9 H9–1

■ RED–PURPLE

Kohleria eriantha
Robust, bushy, rhizomatous perennial with reddish-haired stems. Oval leaves, to 5in (13cm) long, are edged with red hairs. Has tubular red flowers with yellow-spotted lobes in nodding clusters in summer. H and S 3ft (1m) or more.

Z14–15 H12–10

***Papaver orientale* 'Beauty of Livermere'**
Hairy-leaved perennial with deep, fleshy roots. Large, solitary, cup-shaped, crimson-scarlet flowers, with a black mark at the base of each petal, are borne from late spring to mid-summer. H 3–4ft (1–1.2m), S 3ft (1m).

Z4–9 H9–1

Glycyrrhiza glabra (Licorice)
Upright perennial that has pealike, purple-blue and white flowers borne in short spikes on erect stems in late summer, and large leaves divided into oval leaflets. Grown commercially for production of licorice.
H 4ft (1.2m), S 3ft (1m).

Z9–11 H12–10

Asclepias curassavica
Calceolaria integrifolia
Gaillardia x *grandiflora* 'Dazzler', illus. p.283

Geum 'Fire Opal'
Geum 'Mrs J. Bradshaw'
ORCHIDS, illus. pp.296–9
Papaver orientale

Smithiantha zebrina

PELARGONIUMS, illus. pp.246–7

***Acanthus hungaricus*,**
syn. *A. balcanicus*, *A. longifolius*
Perennial with long, deeply cut, basal, dark green leaves. Spikes of white or pink-flushed flowers, set in spiny, red-purple bracts, are carried in summer. H 2–3ft (60cm–1m), S 3ft (1m).

Z6–9 H9–5

Linaria triornithophora
(Three birds toadflax)
Upright perennial that from early to late summer produces spikes of snapdragon-like purple and yellow flowers above narrow, gray-green leaves. H 3ft (1m), S 2ft (60cm).

Z7–9 H9–7

Monarda fistulosa
Clump-forming perennial that produces small heads of lilac-purple flowers from mid- to late summer. H 4ft (1.2m), S 1½ft (45cm).

Z3–9 H9–1

***Campanula glomerata* 'Superba'**
Vigorous, clump-forming perennial with dense, rounded heads of large, bell-shaped purple flowers borne in summer. Bears oval leaves in basal rosettes and on flower stems. Must be divided and replanted regularly. H 2½ft (75cm), S 3ft (1m) or more.

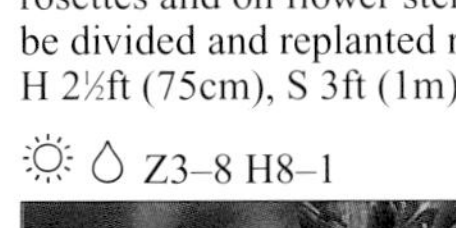

Z3–8 H8–1

Acanthus spinosus
Stately perennial that has very large, arching, deeply cut and spiny-pointed, glossy, dark green leaves. Spires of funnel-shaped, soft mauve and white flowers are borne freely in summer. H 4ft (1.2m), S 2ft (60cm) or more.

Z5–9 H9–5

***Geranium sylvaticum* 'Mayflower'**
Upright perennial with a basal clump of deeply lobed leaves, above which rise branching stems of cup-shaped, violet-blue flowers in early summer. H 3ft (1m), S 2ft (60cm).

Z4–8 H8–1

Thalictrum aquilegiifolium
Clump-forming perennial with a mass of finely divided, gray-green leaves resembling those of maidenhair fern. Bunched heads of fluffy, lilac-purple flowers are borne on strong stems in summer.
H 3–4ft (1–1.2m), S 1½ft (45cm).

Z5–9 H9–5

***Veronica spicata* 'Romiley Purple'**
Clump-forming perennial that in summer freely produces large spikes of purple flowers above whorled, midgreen leaves.
H 3–4ft (1–1.2m), S 1–2ft (30–60cm).

Z3–8 H8–1

Campanula 'Burghaltii', illus. p.286
Centaurea dealbata
DELPHINIUMS, illus. p.230
Digitalis x *mertonensis*
Erigeron 'Quakeress'
Erysimum 'Bowles Mauve'
Hesperis matronalis, illus. p.239
Monarda 'Prairie Night'
ORCHIDS, illus. pp.296–9
PHLOX, illus. p.242
Polemonium foliosissimum
Thalictrum diffusiflorum
Tricyrtis hirta

PURPLE

Campanula trachelium (Nettle-leaved bellflower)
Upright perennial with rough, serrated, oval, pointed, basal leaves. Wide, bell-shaped, blue or purple-blue flowers are spaced along erect stems in summer. H 2–3ft (60cm–1m), S 1ft (30cm).

Z5–8 H8–5

Dichorisandra reginae
Evergreen, erect, clump-forming perennial. Glossy, often silver-banded and flecked leaves are purple-red beneath. Has small spikes of densely set, purple-blue flowers in summer-autumn. H 24–30in (60–75cm), S to 12in (30cm).

Z15 H12-10

***Echinops ritro* 'Veitch's Blue'**
Upright perennial with round, thistle-like, purplish blue heads of flowers carried in late summer on silvery stems. Sharply divided leaves have pale down beneath.
H 4ft (1.2m), S 2½ft (75cm).

Z3–9 H12–10

Galega orientalis
Vigorous, upright but compact perennial that in summer bears spikes of pealike, blue-tinged violet flowers above delicate leaves divided into oval leaflets. Needs staking. Spreads freely.
H 4ft (1.2m), S 2ft (60cm).

Z5–8 H8–5

***Salvia* x *superba* 'Mainacht'**, syn. *S.* x *s.* 'May Night'
Neat, clump-forming perennial with narrow, wrinkled, midgreen leaves. In late spring and summer bears stiff racemes of violet-blue flowers.
H 3ft (1m), S 1½ft (45cm).

Z5–9 H9–4

***Campanula trachelium* 'Bernice'**
Upright perennial that has wide, bell-shaped, double, purple-violet flowers carried along erect stems in summer. Leaves are mostly basal and are rough, serrated, oval, and pointed.
H 30in (75cm), S 12in (30cm).

Z5–8 H8–5

***Aconitum* x *cammarum* 'Bicolor'**, syn. *A.* x *bicolor*
Compact, tuberous perennial with violet-blue and white flowers borne in summer along upright stems. Has deeply cut, divided, glossy, dark green leaves and poisonous roots.
H 4ft (1.2m), S 20in (50cm).

Z3–8 H8–3

Baptisia australis (False indigo)
Upright perennial bearing spikes of pealike, violet-blue flowers in summer. Bright green leaves are divided into oval leaflets. Dark gray seed pods may be used for winter decoration.
H 30in (75cm), S 24in (60cm).

Z3–9 H9–1

Campanula latifolia 'Brantwood'
DELPHINIUMS, illus. p.230
Erigeron 'Dunkelste Aller'
Erigeron 'Serenity', illus. p.284
IRISES, illus. pp.234–5
Lobelia x *gerardii* 'Vedrariensis'
ORCHIDS, illus. pp.296–9
PEONIES, illus. pp.236–7
Strobilanthes atropurpureus, illus. p.263
Sutera grandiflora

Dianella tasmanica
Upright perennial with nodding, star-shaped, bright blue or purple-blue flowers carried in branching sprays in summer, followed by deep blue berries in autumn. Has messy, evergreen, strap-shaped leaves. H 4ft (1.2m), S 20in (50cm).

pH Z12–15 H12–10

Eryngium alpinum
Upright perennial with basal rosettes of heart-shaped, deeply toothed, glossy foliage, above which rise thick stems bearing, in summer, heads of conical, purplish blue flower heads, surrounded by blue bracts and soft spines. H 2½–3ft (75cm–1m), S 2ft (60cm).

Z6–9 H9–6

Eryngium* x *oliverianum
Upright perennial that produces large, rounded heads of thistlelike blue to lavender-blue flowers in late summer. Has heart-shaped, jagged-edged, basal, midgreen leaves. H 2–3ft (60cm–1m), S 1½–2ft (45–60cm).

Z5–8 H8–5

Eryngium* x *tripartitum
Perennial with wiry stems above a basal rosette of coarsely toothed, gray-green leaves. Conical, metallic blue flower heads on blue stems are borne in summer-autumn and may be dried for winter decoration.
H 3–4ft (1–1.2m), S 20in (50cm).

Z5–8 H8–5

***Campanula persicifolia* 'Telham Beauty'**
Perennial with basal rosettes of narrow, bright green leaves. In summer, large, nodding, cup-shaped, light blue flowers are borne on slender spikes.
H 3ft (1m), S 1ft (30cm).

Z3–8 H8–1

Cichorium intybus (Chicory)
Clump-forming perennial with basal rosettes of light green leaves and daisy-like, bright blue flower heads borne along upper parts of willowy stems in summer. Flowers are at their best before noon.
H 4ft (1.2m), S 1½ft (45cm).

Z4–8 H8–1

Meconopsis grandis (Blue poppy)
Erect perennial with oblong, slightly toothed, hairy, midgreen leaves produced in rosettes at the base. Thick stems bear slightly nodding, cup-shaped, deep blue flowers in early summer. Divide every 2–3 years.
H 3–5ft (1–1.5m), S 1ft (30cm).

pH Z5–8 H8–5

Meconopsis betonicifolia
(Blue poppy)
Clump-forming perennial that bears blue flowers in late spring and early summer. Oblong, midgreen leaves are produced in basal rosettes and in decreasing size up flowering stems.
H 3–4ft (1–1.2m), S 1½ft (45cm).

pH Z7–8 H8–7

***Agapanthus* 'Dorothy Palmer'**
Clump-forming perennial bearing rounded heads of rich blue flowers, fading to reddish mauve, on erect stems in late summer. Leaves are narrow and grayish green. H 3ft (1m), S 20in (50cm).

Z9–11 H12–7

Campanula lactiflora
Campanula latiloba
Campanula latiloba 'Percy Piper'
Campanula persicifolia 'Pride of Exmouth'
DELPHINIUMS, illus. p.230
Dianella caerulea
Eryngium giganteum
Eryngium x *zabelii* 'Violetta'
Geranium pratense
Geranium pratense 'Plenum Violaceum'
Linaria purpurea
LATE-BLOOMING ASTERS, illus. p.262
Salvia pratensis Haematodes Group
Trachelium caeruleum, illus. p.330

BLUE

Agapanthus praecox subsp. orientalis, syn. *A. orientalis*
Perennial with large, dense umbels of sky blue flowers borne on strong stems in late summer over clumps of broad, almost evergreen, dark green leaves. Good plant for pots. H 3ft (1m), S 2ft (60cm).

Z12–15 H12–7

Nepeta sibirica, syn. *Dracocephalum sibiricum,* *N. macrantha*
Erect, leafy perennial that bears long, whorled cymes of blue to lavender-blue flowers in mid- and late summer. Leaves are dark green and aromatic. H 36in (90cm), S 18in (45cm).

Z3–8 H8–1

***Anchusa azurea* 'Loddon Royalist'**
Upright perennial that bears flat, single, deep blue flowers on branching spikes in early summer. Most of the lance-shaped, coarse, hairy leaves are at the base of plant. Needs support. H 4ft (1.2m), S 2ft (60cm).

Z3–8 H8–1

DELPHINIUMS, illus. p.230
Echinops bannaticus 'Taplow Blue'
Gentiana asclepiadea, illus. p.263
IRISES, illus. pp.234–5
Meconopsis grandis
Salvia nemorosa
Veronica exaltata
Veronica longifolia

GREEN–YELLOW

Euphorbia schillingii
Robust, clump-forming perennial that produces long-lasting, yellow cyathia and rounded, greenish yellow bracts from midsummer to midautumn. Stems are erect and leaves are dark green with pale green or white veins. H 3ft (1m), S 1ft (30cm).

Z7–9 H9–7

Euphorbia sikkimensis
Spreading, upright perennial bearing yellow cyathia cupped by pale to greenish yellow involucres in mid- to late summer. Young shoots are bright pink and the leaves deep green. H 4ft (1.2m), S 1½ft (45cm).

Z6–9 H9–6

Anigozanthos flavidus
(Yellow kangaroo paw)
Bushy perennial. Large, woolly, tubular racemes of sometimes red-tinged, yellowish green flowers with reddish anthers are borne in spring-summer. H 4ft (1.2m), S 1½ft (45cm).

pH Z12–15 H12–10

***Verbascum* 'Gainsborough'**
Semi-evergreen, rosette-forming, short-lived perennial bearing branched racemes of 5-lobed, pale sulfur yellow flowers throughout summer above oval, midgreen leaves borne on flower stems. H 2–4ft (60cm–1.2m), S 1–2ft (30–60cm).

Z5–9 H9–3

Thalictrum lucidum
Perennial with glossy leaves composed of numerous leaflets. Strong stems bear loose panicles of fluffy, greenish yellow flowers in summer. H 3–4ft (1–1.2m), S 20in (50cm).

Z5–9 H9–5

Artemisia pontica, illus. p.290
Euphorbia nicaeensis
HOSTAS, illus. pp.288–9
ORCHIDS, illus. pp.296–9
Paris polyphylla
Polygonum virginianum 'Painter's Palette', illus. p.290

***Argyranthemum* 'Jamaica Primrose', *syn.* *Chrysanthemum frutescens* 'Jamaica Primrose'**
Evergreen, woody-based perennial with fernlike, pale green leaves. Daisylike, single, soft yellow flower heads are borne in summer. Take stem cuttings in early autumn. H and S to 3ft (1m).

Z7–11 H12–1

Aconitum lycoctonum subsp. vulparia*, *syn. A. orientale* of gardens, *A. vulparia (Wolf's bane)
Upright, fibrous perennial that has hooded, straw yellow flowers in summer. Leaves are dark green and deeply divided. Needs support. H 3–4ft (1–1.2m), S 1–2ft (30–60cm).

Z5–8 H8–5

Gentiana lutea
(Great yellow gentian)
Erect, unbranched perennial with oval, stalkless leaves to 1ft (30cm) long. In summer has dense whorls of tubular yellow flowers in axils of greenish bracts. H 3–4ft (1–1.2m), S 2ft (60cm).

Z7–8 H8–7

Phlomis russeliana
Evergreen perennial, forming an excellent groundcover, with large, rough, heart-shaped leaves. Thick flower stems bear whorls of hooded, butter yellow flowers in summer.
H 3ft (1m), S 2ft (60cm) or more.

Z4–9 H9–1

***Anthemis tinctoria* 'E.C. Buxton'**
Clump-forming perennial with a mass of daisy like, lemon yellow flower heads borne singly in summer on slim stems. Cut back hard after flowering to promote good clumps of leaves for winter. H and S 3ft (1m).

Z3–8 H8–3

Lysimachia punctata
(Garden loosestrife)
Vigorous clump-forming perennial that in summer produces spikes of bright yellow flowers above midgreen leaves.
H 24–30in (60–75cm), S 24in (60cm).

Z4–8 H8–1

***Solidago* 'Goldenmosa'**
Clump-forming perennial. Sprays of tufted, mimosa-like yellow flower heads are carried in late summer and autumn above lance-shaped, toothed, hairy, yellowish green leaves.
H 3ft (1m), S 2ft (60cm).

Z5–9 H9–5

***Achillea* 'Schwellenberg'**
Low-growing, spreading perennial with branched stems and gray-green foliage. Silvery buds are followed by lemon yellow flower heads from early summer to early autumn.
H 18in (45cm), S 24in (60cm).

Z3–8 H8–1

Aciphylla squarrosa, illus. p.266
Chelidonium majus 'Flore Pleno', illus. p.238
CHRYSANTHEMUMS, illus. pp.260–61
DAYLILIES, illus. p.257
Digitalis lutea
Helianthus x *multiflorus* 'Capenoch Star'
IRISES, illus. pp.234–5
Kirengeshoma palmata, illus. p.263
Kniphofia 'Little Maid', illus. p.290
Linaria genistifolia
PRIMROSES, illus. pp.272–3
Rudbeckia fulgida var. *deamii*
x *Solidaster luteus*, illus. p.291
Thermopsis villosa
Verbascum chaixii

YELLOW

Thermopsis rhombifolia, syn. *T. montana*
Upright perennial bearing spikes of bright yellow flowers above divided, midgreen leaves in summer.
H 2–3ft (60cm–1m), S 2ft (60cm).

Z3–8 H8–1

Inula hookeri
Clump-forming perennial with lance-shaped to elliptic, hairy leaves and a mass of slightly scented, daisylike, greenish yellow flower heads borne in summer.
H 30in (75cm), S 18in (45cm).

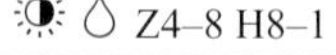

Z4–8 H8–1

***Aphelandra squarrosa* 'Louisae'**
Evergreen, erect perennial. Long, oval, glossy, slightly wrinkled, dark green leaves have white veins and midribs. Bears dense spikes of golden yellow flowers from axils of yellow bracts in late summer to autumn. H to 3ft (1m), S 2ft (60cm).

Z14–15 H12–10

***Solidago* 'Laurin'**
Compact perennial bearing spikes of deep yellow flowers in late summer. Foliage is midgreen.
H 24–30in (60–75cm), S 18in (45cm).

Z5–8 H8–5

***Rudbeckia fulgida* var. *sullivantii* 'Goldsturm'**
Erect perennial. In late summer and autumn, daisylike golden flower heads with conical black centers are borne at the ends of strong stems. Has narrow, rough, midgreen leaves. H 30in (75cm), S 12in (30cm) or more.

Z4–9 H9–1

Verbascum nigrum
Semi-evergreen, clump-forming perennial bearing narrow spikes of small, 5-lobed, purple-centered yellow flowers during summer and autumn. Oblong, midgreen leaves are downy beneath. H 2–3ft (60cm–1m), S 2ft (60cm).

Z3–8 H8–1

***Achillea* 'Coronation Gold'**
Upright perennial with feathery, silvery leaves. Bears large, flat heads of small golden flower heads in summer that dry well for winter decoration. Should be divided and replanted every third year. H 3ft (1m), S 2ft (60cm).

Z3–9 H9–1

Inula royleana, syn. *I. macrocephala* of gardens
Upright, clump-forming perennial with dark green stems and ovate, hairy leaves. Bears solitary, orange-yellow flower heads, 4–5in (10–12cm) across, from midsummer to early autumn.
H 18–24in (45–60cm), S 18in (45cm).

Z4–8 H8–1

Achillea 'Moonshine', illus. p.291
Achillea 'Taygetea', illus. p.291
Aciphylla aurea, illus. p.238
Centaurea macrocephala
CHRYSANTHEMUMS, illus. pp.260–1
DAYLILIES, illus. p.257
Gaillardia aristata, illus. p.291
HOSTAS, illus. pp.288–9
IRISES, illus. pp.234–5
Isatis tinctoria
Mirabilis jalapa, illus. p.245
ORCHIDS, illus. pp.296–9
PEONIES, illus. pp.236–7
Potentilla 'Yellow Queen', illus. p.292
PRIMROSES, illus. pp.272–3
Scabiosa ochroleuca

Daylilies

Although they belong to the lily family (Liliaceae), daylilies (*Hemerocallis*) are not true lilies; their common name comes from the lily-like flowers that generally last only a day. Daylilies range in size from compact plants that grow only to 12–15in (30–38cm) tall, to large plants that may reach 5ft (1.5m). Modern cultivars are available in a wide range of colors, from creamy white through shades of yellow, orange, red, pink, and purple to almost black; some flowers have differently colored bands on the petals. The flower forms are usually classified as single, double, or spider. Some species and a few cultivars are strongly fragrant. Most daylilies flower for three to six weeks; they thrive in almost any soil, except poorly drained clay, in sun or shade, but bloom best if they are in sun for at least half the day.
The clumps may be divided in early spring, after bloom, or in early autumn.

***H.* 'Joan Senior'**

***H.* 'Jolyene Nichole'**

***H.* 'Gentle Shepherd'**

***H.* 'Chorus Line'**

***H.* 'Millie Schlumpf'**

***H.* 'Siloam Virginia Henson'**

***H.* 'Scarlet Orbit'**

***H.* 'Super Purple'**

***H.* 'Solano Bull's Eye'**

***H.* 'Prairie Blue Eyes'**

***H.* 'Lady Fingers'**

***H.* 'Golden Chimes'**

H. lilioasphodelus

***H.* 'Real Wind'**

***H.* 'Betty Woods'**

***H.* 'Cat's Cradle'**

***H.* 'Ruffled Apricot'**

***H.* 'Marion Vaughn'**

***H.* 'Hyperion'**

***H.* 'Mauna Loa'**

***H.* 'Brocaded Gown'**

***H.* 'Eenie Weenie'**

H. citrina

***H.* 'Corky'**

***H. fulva* 'Flore Pleno'**

YELLOW

Berkheya macrocephala
Upright perennial bearing large, daisylike yellow flower heads on branched, spiny-leaved stems throughout summer. Prefers rich soil and a warm, sheltered position. H and S 3ft (1m).

Z12–15 H12–10

***Achillea filipendulina* 'Gold Plate'**
Upright perennial with sturdy, leafy stems carrying broad, flat, terminal heads of yellow flowers in summer above filigree foliage. Flower heads retain color when dried. Divide plants regularly. H 4ft (1.2m) or more, S 2ft (60cm).

Z3–9 H9–1

***Heliopsis* 'Ballet Dancer'**
Upright perennial flowering freely in late summer and bearing double yellow flower heads with frilled petals. Dark green leaves are coarse and serrated. H 3–4ft (1–1.2m), S 2ft (60cm).

Z4–9 H9–1

YELLOW–ORANGE

***Kniphofia* 'Royal Standard'**
Upright perennial with grasslike, basal tufts of leaves and terminal spikes of scarlet buds opening to lemon yellow flowers borne on erect stems in late summer. Protect crowns with winter mulch. H 1–1.2m (3–4ft), S 2ft (60cm).

Z5–8 H9–4

Kniphofia thomsonii* var. *snowdenii
Upright perennial with grasslike, basal foliage. In summer bears coral-pink flowers with yellowish interiors, spaced widely along terminal spikes. Protect crowns with winter mulch. H 3ft (1m), S 20in (50cm).

Z7–9 H9–7

Sphaeralcea ambigua
Branching, shrubby perennial. Broadly funnel-shaped, orange-coral blooms are produced singly in leaf axils from summer until the onset of cold weather. Leaves are soft, hairy, and midgreen. H and S 30–36in (75–90cm).

Z6–10 H12–8

Asclepias tuberosa
(Butterfly weed)
Erect, tuberous perennial with long, lance-shaped leaves. Small, 5-horned, bright orange-red flowers are borne in summer and followed by narrow, pointed pods, to 6in (15cm) long. H to 30in (75cm), S 18in (45cm).

Z4–9 H9–2

***Euphorbia griffithii* 'Fireglow'**
Bushy perennial that bears orange-red flowers in terminal umbels in early summer. Leaves are lance-shaped, midgreen, and have pale red midribs. H to 1m (3ft), S 50cm (20in).

Z4–9 H9–1

Buphthalmum salicifolium, illus. p.292
Chelidonium majus 'Flore Pleno', illus. p.238
CHRYSANTHEMUMS, illus. pp.260–1
Eremurus spectabilis
IRISES, illus. pp.234–5
Linaria genistifolia var. *dalmatica*
ORCHIDS, illus. pp.296–9
PRIMROSES, illus. pp.272–3
DAYLILIES, illus. p.257
Helenium 'Wyndley', illus. p.263
Kniphofia 'Atlanta'
Ligularia dentata 'Desdemona'
Papaver orientale 'May Queen'

Actaea pachypoda, syn. *A. alba* (Doll's eyes, White baneberry)
Compact, clump-forming perennial with spikes of small, fluffy white flowers in summer and clusters of white berries borne on stiff, fleshy scarlet stalks in autumn.
H 3ft (1m), S 20in (50cm).

Z3–8 H8–1

Persicaria campanulata, syn. *Polygonum campanulatum*
Compact, mat-forming perennial bearing elegant, branching heads of bell-shaped pink or white flowers from midsummer to early autumn. Has oval leaves, brown-felted beneath.
H and S 3ft (1m).

Z5–8 H8–5

Chelone obliqua (Turtlehead)
Upright perennial that bears terminal spikes of hooded, lilac-pink flowers in late summer and autumn. Leaves are dark green and lance-shaped.
H 3ft (1m), S 20in (50cm).

Z3–9 H9–3

Tricyrtis formosana, syn. *T. stolonifera*
Upright, rhizomatous perennial. In early autumn bears spurred flowers, heavily spotted with purplish pink and with yellow-tinged throats. Glossy, dark green leaves clasp stems.
H 2–3ft (60cm–1m), S 1½ft (45cm).

Z6–9 H9–6

***Anemone hupehensis* 'Hadspen Abundance'**
Erect, branching perennial that bears pink flowers with rounded, dark reddish pink outer tepals from summer to autumn. Leaves are dark green and deeply divided, with toothed leaflets.
H 2–4ft (60cm–1.2m), S 1½ft (45cm).

Z5–7 H7–5

***Chrysanthemum* 'Clara Curtis'**, syn. *C. rubellum* 'Clara Curtis'
Bushy perennial producing many clusters of flat, daisylike, clear pink flower heads throughout summer and autumn. Divide plants every other spring. H 30in (75cm), S 18in (45cm).

Z5–9 H9–1

OTHER RECOMMENDED PLANTS:
Centranthus ruber, illus. p.245
CHRYSANTHEMUMS, illus. pp.260–61
Cimicifuga simplex 'Elstead'
Kohleria digitaliflora, illus. p.244
LATE-BLOOMING ASTERS, illus. p.262
PELARGONIUMS, illus. pp.246–7
Schizostylis coccinea 'Sunrise', illus. p.294

Chrysanthemums

Florists' chrysanthemum hybrids (botanically now classified under the genus *Dendranthema*) are grouped according to their differing flower forms, approximate flowering season (early, mid- or late autumn), and habit (see also the Plant Dictionary under *Chrysanthemum*). The best groups for garden decoration are the sprays, pompons, and early reflexed chrysanthemums. The chushion mums, which produce a dense, dome-shaped mass of flowers, look most attractive displayed in pots. Most groups have only one large flower per stem, although the sprays, cushions, and pompons have several. The various flower forms are described below.

Incurved – fully double, dense, spherical flowers have incurved petals arising from the base of the flower and closing tightly over the crown.

Fully reflexed – fully double flowers have curved, pointed petals reflexing outward and downward from the crown, back to touch the stem.

Reflexed – fully double flowers are similar to those of fully reflexed forms, except that the petals are less strongly reflexed and form an umbrella-like or spiky outline.

Intermediate – fully double, roughly spherical flowers have loosely incurving petals, which may close at the crown or may reflex for the bottom half of each flower.

Anemone – single flowers each have a central, dome-shaped disk, up to half the diameter of the bloom, and up to 5 rows of flat, or occasionally spoon-type, ray petals at right angles to the stem.

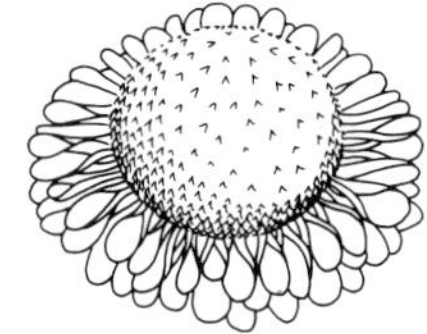

Single – flowers each have about 5 rows of flat petals, borne at right angles to the stem, that may incurve or reflex at the tips; the prominent, central disk is golden throughout or has a small green center.

Pompon – fully double, dense, spherical, or occasionally hemispherical, flowers have tubular petals with flat, rounded tips, growing outward from the crown.

Spoon – flowers are similar to those of single forms except that the ray petals are tubular and open out at their tips to form a spoon shape.

Spider – double flower heads with long, thin ray-florets; the outer ray-florets are more or less pendent, the inner ones curling upward.

Quill – double flower heads with tubular ray-florets that open out at their tips to form spoon shapes.

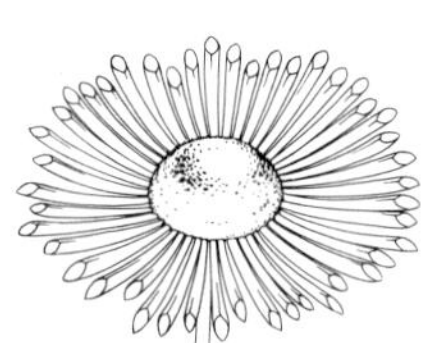

C. **'Enbee Wedding'** (spray, single, early)

C. **'Senkyo Emiaki'** (spider-form, early)

C. **'Keith Luxford'** (incurved, late)

C. **'Marian Gosling'** (reflexed, early)

C. **'Elsie Prosser'** (reflexed, late)

C. **'Madeleine'** (spray, reflexed, early)

C. **'Brietner'** (reflexed, early)

C. **'Woking Rose'** (intermediate, late)

C. **'Pennine Flute'** (quill-shaped, early)

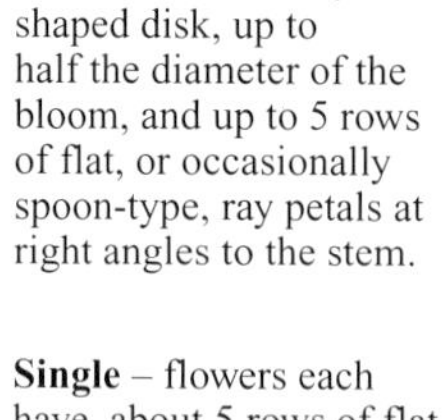

C. **'Bill Wade'** (intermediate, early)

C. **'Pennine Oriel'** (spray, anemone, early)

C. **'Lundy'** (reflexed, late)

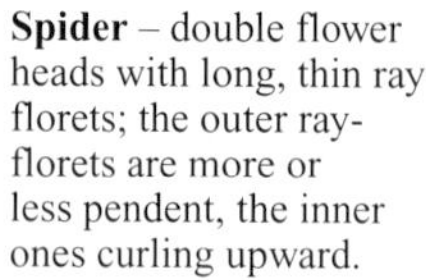

C. **'John Wingfield'** (reflexed, late)

C. **'Alison Kirk'** (incurved, early)

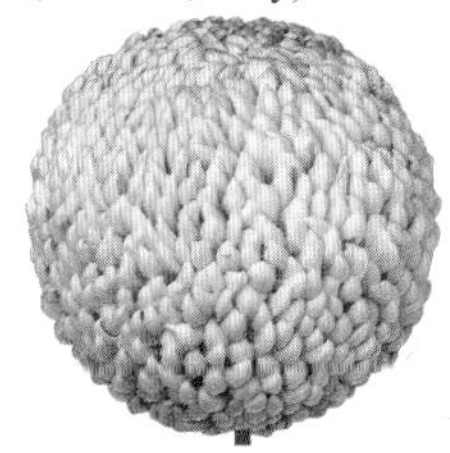

C. **'Fairweather'** (incurved, late)

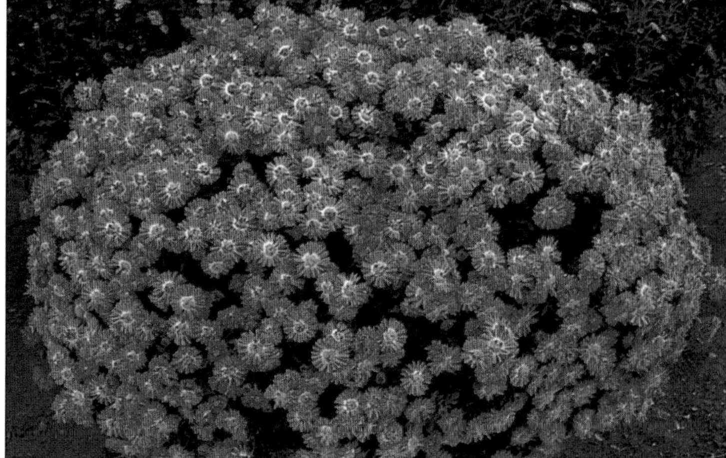

C. **'Ringdove'** (charm, late)

C. **'Rose Yvonne Arnaud'** (reflexed, early)

C. **'Yellow Brietner'** (reflexed, early)

C. **'Robeam'** (spray, reflexed, late)

C. **'Majestic'** (reflexed, late)

C. **'Golden Woolman's Glory'** (single, late)

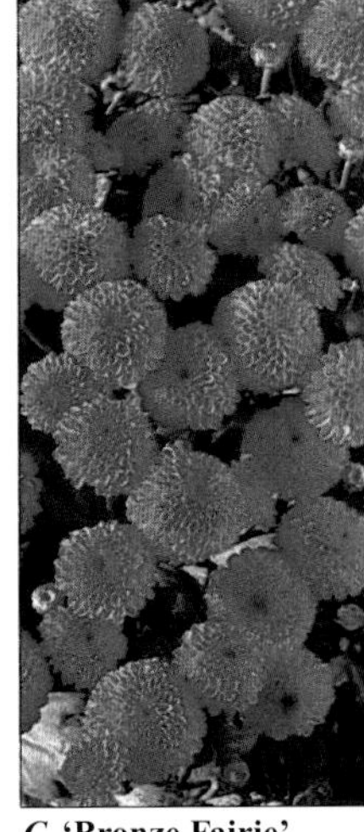
C. **'Bronze Fairie'** (pompon, early)

C. **'Salmon Fairie'** (pompon, late)

C. **'Bronze Hedgerow'** (single, late)

C. **'Yvonne Arnaud'** (reflexed, early)

C. **'Green Satin'** (intermediate, late)

C. **'Peach Brietner'** (reflexed, early)

C. **'George Griffiths'** (reflexed, early)

C. **'Marion'** (spray, reflexed, early)

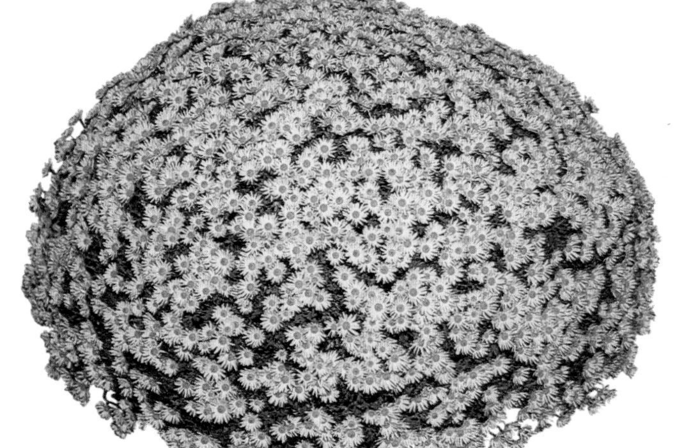
C. **'Golden Chalice'** (cushion, late)

C. **'Salmon Margaret'** (spray, reflexed, early)

C. **'Maria'** (pompon, early)

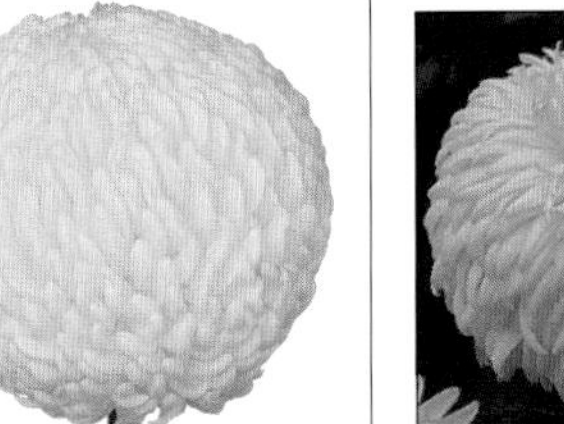
C. **'Primrose John Hughes'** (incurved, late)

C. **'Primrose West Bromwich'** (rflxd, mid)

C. **'Wendy'** (spray, reflexed, early)

C. **'Beacon'** (intermediate, late)

C. **'Autumn Days'** (intermediate, early)

C. **'Idris'** (incurved, late)

C. **'Nancye Furneaux'** (reflexed, late)

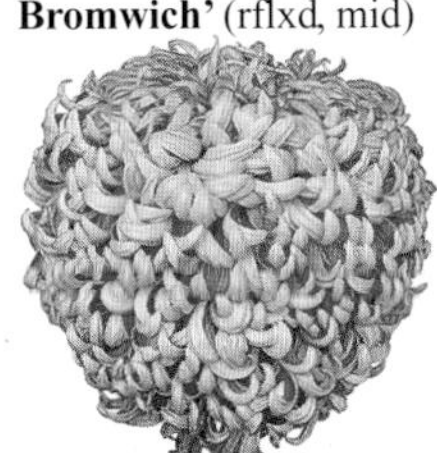
C. **'Golden Gigantic'** (incurved, late)

C. **'Gigantic'** (incurved, late)

C. **'Bronze Yvonne Arnaud'** (rflxd, early)

C. **'Oracle'** (intermediate, early)

C. **'Purple Pennine Wine'** (spray, reflexed, early)

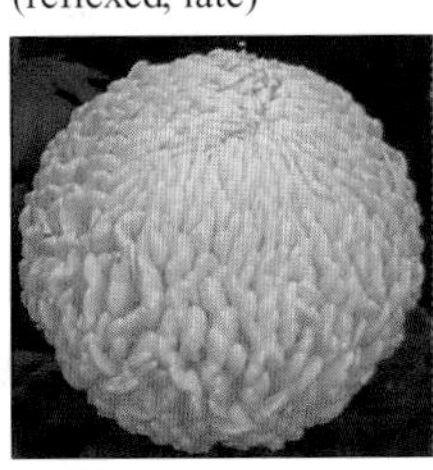
C. **'Yellow John Hughes'** (incurved, late)

C. **'Roy Coopland'** (intermediate, late)

C. **'Pennine Alfie'** (spray, spoon-type, early)

C. **'Buff Margaret'** (spray, reflexed, early)

Late-blooming Asters

Late-blooming asters (*Aster* species and cultivars, mostly of *A. novae-angliae* and *A. novi-belgii*) are invaluable border plants, since they flower later than most other perennials and continue the display until late autumn. The daisylike, single or double flowers, usually with yellow centers, range in color from white through pink and red to purple and blue and are excellent for cutting. For larger flowers pinch out or cut back weaker shoots in spring; pinching out the top 1–2in (2.5–5cm) of the remaining shoots produces bushier plants that will bear a greater quantity of smaller flowers. Tall cultivars may need staking. Late-blooming asters thrive in sun or partial shade in well-drained soil; many are susceptible to mildew, so in areas where this is a problem, treat the plants regularly with a fungicide or choose from the resistant varieties available.

***A. ericoides* 'White Heather'**

***A. novae-angliae* 'Herbstschnee'**

***A. novi-belgii* 'Sandford White Swan'**

***A. novi-belgii* 'Kristina'**

***A. ericoides* 'Golden Spray'**

***A. lateriflorus* 'Horizontalis'**

***A. cordifolius* 'Silver Spray'**

***A. novi-belgii* 'Apple Blossom'**

***A. novae-angliae* 'Harrington's Pink'**

***A. novi-belgii* 'Lassie'**

***A. novi-belgii* 'Fellowship'**

***A. novae-angliae* 'Barr's Pink'**

***A. novi-belgii* 'Patricia Ballard'**

***A. novi-belgii* 'Carnival'**

***A. novi-belgii* 'Orlando'**

***A. novi-belgii* 'Royal Ruby'**

***A. novi-belgii* 'Freda Ballard'**

***A. n.-a.* 'Andenken an Alma Pötschke'**

***A. novi-belgii* 'Chequers'**

***A. novi-belgii* 'Royal Velvet'**

***A. novi-belgii* 'Peace'**

***A. thomsonii* 'Nanus'**

***A.* 'Professor Anton Kippenburg'**

***A. amellus* 'Nocturne'**

***A. amellus* 'King George'**

***A. frikartii* 'Wunder von Stäfa'**

***A. frikartii* 'Mönch'**

***A. novi-belgii* 'Marie Ballard'**

A. linosyris

PURPLE–YELLOW

Strobilanthes atropurpureus
Upright, branching perennial with oval, toothed leaves. Spikes of numerous, violet-blue to purple flowers appear in summer-autumn. H to 4ft (1.2m), S to 2ft (60cm).

Z5–9 H9–5

Gentiana asclepiadea
(Willow gentian)
Arching perennial with narrow, oval leaves to 3in (8cm) long. In late summer to autumn has arching sprays of trumpet-shaped, deep blue flowers, spotted and striped inside.
H to 36in (90cm), S to 24in (60cm).

Z6–9 H9–6

***Kniphofia* 'Percy's Pride'**
Upright perennial with large, terminal spikes of creamy flowers, tinged green and yellow, borne on erect stems in autumn. Protect crowns with winter mulch. H 3ft (1m), S 20in (50cm).

Z6–9 H9–6

YELLOW–ORANGE

Kirengeshoma palmata
Upright perennial with rounded, lobed, bright green leaves, above which strong stems bearing clusters of narrowly funnel-shaped, creamy yellow flowers appear in late summer to autumn.
H 3ft (1m), S 2ft (60cm).

pH Z5–8 H8–5

***Helenium* 'Wyndley'**
Bushy perennial with branching stems bearing sprays of daisylike, orange-yellow flower heads for a long period in late summer and autumn. Foliage is dark green. Needs regular division in spring or autumn.
H 30in (80cm), S 20in (50cm).

Z4–8 H8–1

Kniphofia caulescens
Stately, evergreen, upright perennial with basal tufts of narrow, blue-green leaves and smooth, thick stems bearing terminal spikes of reddish salmon flowers in autumn.
H 4ft (1.2m), S 2ft (60cm).

Z6–9 H9–4

Kniphofia rooperi,
syn. *K.* 'C.M. Prichard' of gardens
Robust, evergreen perennial with arching, linear, dark green leaves. From early to late autumn produces broadly ellipsoid racemes of orange-red flowers, becoming orange-yellow.
H 4ft (1.2m), S 2ft (60cm).

Z6–9 H9–4

***Helenium* 'Moerheim Beauty'**
Upright perennial with strong, branching stems bearing sprays of daisylike, rich reddish orange flower heads in early autumn above dark green foliage. Needs regular division in spring or autumn.
H 3ft (1m), S 2ft (60cm).

Z4–8 H8–1

Chirita lavandulacea, illus. p.294
CHRYSANTHEMUMS, illus. pp.260–61
Dichorisandra reginae, illus. p.252
Eryngium x *tripartitum*, illus. p.253
Lobelia siphilitica
ORCHIDS, illus. pp.296–9
Rudbeckia fulgida var. *deamii*

Aphelandra squarrosa 'Dania'
Aphelandra squarrosa 'Louisae', illus. p.256
CHRYSANTHEMUMS, illus. pp.260–61
Helenium 'Bressingham Gold'
Helenium 'Butterpat'
Solidago 'Goldenmosa', illus. p.255
Verbascum nigrum, illus. p.256

WHITE–PINK

***Ctenanthe oppenheimiana* 'Tricolor'**
Robust, evergreen, bushy perennial. Has leathery, lance-shaped leaves, to over 12in (30cm) long, splashed with large cream blotches, and, intermittently, spikes of 3-petaled white flowers. H and S 3ft (1m).

Z14–15 H12–10

***Plectranthus forsteri* 'Marginatus'**
Evergreen, bushy perennial. Oval leaves to 2½in (6cm) long are grayish green with scalloped white margins. Irregularly has tubular white to pale mauve flowers. H and S 24in (60cm) or more.

Z13–15 H12–1

***Dieffenbachia seguine* 'Exotica',**
syn. *D.* 'Exotica', *D. maculata* 'Exotica'
Evergreen, tufted perennial, sometimes woody at the base. Broadly lance-shaped leaves, to 18in (45cm) long, are blotched with creamy white. H and S 3ft (1m) or more.

Z13-15 H12–1

Anthurium crystallinum
(Crystal anthurium)
Evergreen, erect perennial. Long, velvety, dark green leaves are distinctively pale green- to white-veined. Has long-lasting red-tinged green spathes. H to 30in (75cm), S to 24in (60cm).

Z14-15 H12–10

***Hypoestes phyllostachya*,**
syn. *H. sanguinolenta* of gardens
(Freckle face, Polka-dot plant)
Evergreen, bush perennial or sub-shrub. Dark green leaves are covered with irregular pink spots. Bears small, tubular lavender flowers intermittently. H and S 30in (75cm).

Z13–15 H12–1

***Caladium bicolor* 'Pink Beauty'**
Tufted, tuberous perennial. Has long-stalked, triangular, pink-mottled green leaves, to 18in (45cm) long, with darker pink veins. Nonshowy white spathes appear in summer. H and S 3ft (90cm).

Z15 H12–4

RED

Anthurium andraeanum
(Flamingo flower)
Evergreen, erect perennial. Long-stalked, oval leaves, with a heart-shaped base, are 8in (20cm) long. Has long-lasting, bright red spathes with yellow spadices. H 24–30in (60–75cm), S 20in (50cm).

Z14–15 H12–10

Nepenthes* x *hookeriana
Evergreen, epiphytic, insectivorous perennial with oval, leathery leaves to 12in (30cm) long and pendent, pale green pitchers with reddish purple markings and a spurred lid, to 5in (13cm) long. H 24–30in (60–75cm).

Z14–15 H12–10

***Phormium* 'Dazzler'**
Evergreen, upright perennial with tufts of bold, stiff, pointed leaves in tones of yellow, salmon-pink, orange-red, and bronze. Bluish purple stems carry panicles of reddish flowers in summer. H 6–8ft (2–2.5m) in flower, S 3ft (1m).

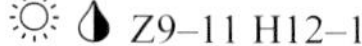
Z9–11 H12–1

OTHER RECOMMENDED PLANTS:
Alpinia calcarata
Anthurium veitchii
BROMELIADS, illus. p.265
Dieffenbachia seguine 'Memoria Corsii'
Hypoestes aristata
ORCHIDS, illus. pp.296–9
Gerbera jamesonii, illus. p.302
Tellima grandiflora Rubra Group, illus. p.302

Bromeliads

Bromeliads, or plants that belong to the family Bromeliaceae, are distinguished by their bold, usually rosetted foliage and showy flowers. Although many are epiphytes, or air plants (absorbing their food through moisture in the atmosphere and not from the host on which they grow) and are suitable for growing outdoors only in tropical regions, they will grow happily indoors in cooler climates.

Aechmea fasciata

Billbergia nutans

Bromelia balansae

Tillandsia lindenii

Cryptanthus zonatus **'Zebrinus'**

Puya alpestris

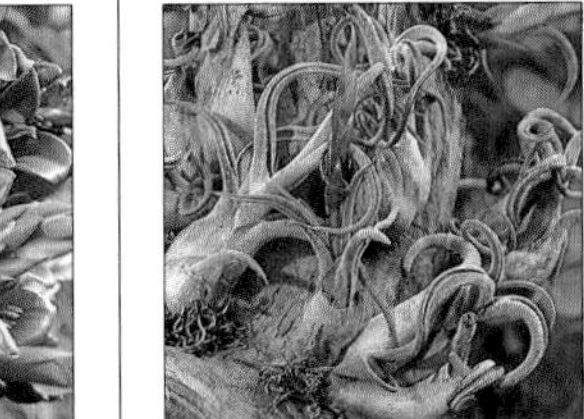
Tillandsia caput-medusae

Ananas bracteatus **'Tricolor'**

Aechmea distichantha

Neoregelia carolinae **'Tricolor'**

Guzmania monostachya

Dyckia remotiflora

Tillandsia argentea

Aechmea **Foster's Favorite Group**

Guzmania lingulata var. *minor*

Cryptanthus **'Pink Starlight'**

Aechmea recurvata

Guzmania lingulata

Tillandsia fasciculata

Cryptanthus bivittatus

Tillandsia usneoides

Tillandsia stricta

Vriesea splendens

Neoregelia concentrica

Tillandsia cyanea

Puya chilensis

PURPLE–GREEN

Browallia speciosa (Bush violet)
Bushy perennial, usually grown as an annual, propagated by seed each year. Has oval leaves to 4in (10cm) long and showy violet-blue flowers with white eyes, the season depending when sown. H 24–30in (60–75cm), S 18in (45cm).

Z14–15 H12–1

Artemisia ludoviciana var. ***albula***
Bushy perennial grown for its aromatic, lance-shaped leaves that are silvery white and woolly on both surfaces and have jagged margins. Bears slender plumes of tiny, grayish white flower heads in summer. H 4ft (1.2m), S 2ft (60cm).

Z4–9 H9–1

Aciphylla squarrosa
(Bayonet plant)
Evergreen, clump-forming perennial with tufts of pointed, divided leaves. In summer bears spiky yellow flowers in compound umbels with male and female flowers often mixed. H and S 3–4ft (1–1.2m).

Z9–15 H12–1

Asparagus densiflorus
Evergreen, trailing perennial with clusters of narrow, bright green, leaf-like stems. In summer has pink-tinged white flowers, followed by red berries. Good in a hanging basket. H to 3ft (1m), S 20in (50cm).

Z13–15 H12–1

Alocasia cuprea
Evergreen, tufted perennial. Oval leaves are 12in (30cm) long, with a metallic sheen and darker, impressed veins above, purple below; leaf stalks arise from the lower surface. Purplish spathes appear intermittently. H and S to 3ft (1m).

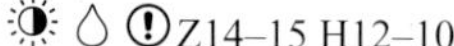
Z14–15 H12–10

Xanthosoma sagittifolium
Spreading, tufted perennial with thick stems. Broadly arrow-shaped leaves, 2ft (60cm) or more long, on long leaf stalks, are green with a grayish bloom. Has green spathes intermittently during the year. H to 6ft (2m) in flower, S 6ft (2m) or more.

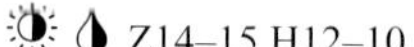
Z14–15 H12–10

***Columnea microphylla* 'Variegata'**
Evergreen, trailing perennial. Has rounded leaves narrowly bordered with cream and tubular, hooded scarlet flowers with yellow throats in winter-spring. H 3ft (1m) or more, S indefinite.

Z14–15 H12–10

Calathea zebrina (Zebra plant)
Robust, evergreen, clump-forming perennial with long-stalked, velvety, dark green leaves to 2ft (60cm) long (less if pot-grown) with paler veins, margins, and midribs. Bears short spikes of white to pale purple flowers. H and S to 3ft (90cm).

Z11-12 H12–1

Aglaonema pictum, illus. p.304
Alocasia veitchii
Calathea lindeniana
Calathea makoyana, illus. p.304
Helleborus argutifolius, illus. p.304
Musa uranoscopus
Nephthytis afzelii
ORCHIDS, illus. pp.296–9
Peperomia scandens
Xanthorrhoea australis
Xanthosoma violaceum

GREEN–ORANGE

***Asparagus densiflorus* 'Myersii'**, syn. *A. meyeri*, *A.* 'Myers' (Foxtail fern)
Evergreen, erect perennial with spikes of tight, feathery clusters of leaflike stems and pinkish white flowers in summer, then red berries. H to 3ft (1m), S 20in (50cm).

Z13–15 H12–1

***Dieffenbachia seguine* 'Rudolph Roehrs'**, syn. *D. maculata* 'Rudolph Roehrs', *D.s.* 'Roehrsii'
Evergreen, tufted perennial, sometimes woody at the base. Leaves, to 18in (45cm) long, are yellowish green or white with green midribs and margins. H and S 3ft (1m).

Z14-15 H12–1

***Sansevieria trifasciata* 'Laurentii'**
Evergreen, stemless perennial with a rosette of about 5 stiff, erect, lance-shaped and pointed leaves with yellow margins. Occasionally has pale green flowers. Propagate by division to avoid reversion. H 1½–4ft (45cm–1.2m), S 4in (10cm).

Z14–15 H12–1

Globba winitii
Evergreen, clump-forming perennial with lance-shaped leaves to 8in (20cm) long. Intermittently has pendent racemes of tubular yellow flowers with large, reddish purple, reflexed bracts. H 3ft (1m), S 1ft (30cm).

Z14–15 H12–8

***Peristrophe hyssopifolia* 'Aureovariegata'**
Evergreen, bushy perennial. Small leaves are broadly lance-shaped with long, pointed tips and central, creamy yellow blotches. Has tubular rose-pink flowers in winter. H to 2ft (60cm) or more, S 4ft (1.2m).

Z14–15 H12–1

Strelitzia reginae
(Bird of paradise)
Evergreen, clump-forming perennial with long-stalked, bluish green leaves. Has beaklike orange-and-blue flowers in boat-shaped, red-edged bracts mainly in spring. H over 3ft (1m), S 2½ft (75cm).

Z13–15 H12–1

Astilbe 'Straussenfeder', illus. p.244
Astilbe 'Venus', illus. p.244
BROMELIADS, illus. p.265
Ctenanthe lubbersiana
Dasylirion texanum
Dieffenbachia seguine
Sansevieria cylindrica
Sansevieria trifasciata

WHITE

***Epimedium* x *youngianum* 'Niveum'**
Compact groundcover perennial with heart-shaped, serrated, bronze-tinted leaflets that turn green in late spring, when small, cup-shaped, snow white flowers are borne.
H 6–12in (15–30cm), S 12in (30cm).

Z5–9 H9–5

***Lamium maculatum* 'White Nancy'**
Semi-evergreen, mat-forming perennial with white-variegated, mid-green foliage and spikes of hooded white flowers in late spring and summer. H 6in (15cm), S 3ft (1m).

Z4–8 H8–1

***Pulmonaria officinalis* 'Sissinghurst White'**
Semi-evergreen, clump-forming perennial that bears funnel-shaped white flowers in spring above long, elliptic, midgreen, spotted leaves. H 12in (30cm), S 18–24in (45–60cm).

Z6–8 H8–6

Pachyphragma macrophyllum, syn. *Thlaspi macrophyllum*
Creeping, mat-forming perennial with rosettes of rounded, long-stalked, glossy, bright green leaves, each to 4in (10cm) long. Bears many racemes of tiny white flowers in spring.
H to 12in (30cm), S indefinite.

Trillium cernuum
Clump-forming perennial with nodding, maroon-centered white flowers borne in spring beneath luxuriant, 3-parted, midgreen leaves.
H 12–18in (30–45cm), S 12in (30cm).

Z3–7 H8–1

***Lamium maculatum* 'Album'**
Semi-evergreen, mat-forming perennial that has dark green leaves with central white stripes. Bears clusters of hooded, white flowers in spring-summer.
H 8in (20cm), S 3ft (1m).

Z4–8 H8–1

OTHER RECOMMENDED PLANTS:
Convallaria majalis 'Fortin's Giant'
Helleborus x *hybridus* [white form], illus. p.300
Helleborus niger, illus. p.301
PRIMROSES, illus. pp.272–3
Sanguinaria canadensis 'Plena'
Trillium grandiflorum 'Flore Pleno'

□ WHITE

Convallaria majalis
(Lily-of-the-valley)
Low-growing, rhizomatous perennial with narrowly oval, mid- to dark green leaves and sprays of small, very fragrant, pendulous, bell-shaped white flowers. Likes organic soil. H 6in (15cm), S indefinite.

Z2–7 H7–1

Trillium ovatum
Clump-forming perennial with white flowers, later turning pink, that are carried singly in spring just above red-stalked, 3-parted, dark green foliage. H 10–15in (25–38cm), S 8in (20cm).

Z5–8 H8–5

Adonis brevistyla
Clump-forming perennial. Buttercup-like flowers, borne singly at tips of stems in early spring, are white tinged blue on the outside. Has finely cut, midgreen leaves. H and S 6–9in (15–23cm).

Z4–9 H9–7

Trillium chloropetalum
Clump-forming perennial with reddish green stems carrying 3-parted, gray-marbled, dark green leaves. Flowers vary from purplish pink to white and appear above foliage in spring. H and S 12–18in (30–45cm).

Z6–9 H9–6

Trillium grandiflorum
(Wake robin)
Clump-forming perennial. Large, pure white flowers that turn pink with age are borne singly in spring just above large, 3-parted, dark green leaves. H 15in (38cm), S 12in (30cm).

Z4–7 H7–3

Podophyllum hexandrum, syn. *P. emodi*
(Himalayan Mayapple)
Perennial with pairs of 3-lobed, brown-mottled leaves followed by white or pink flowers in spring and fleshy red fruits in summer. H 12–18in (30–45cm), S 12in (30cm).

Z5–8 H8–4

Epimedium pubigerum
Evergreen, carpeting perennial, grown for its dense, smooth, heart-shaped, divided foliage and clusters of cup-shaped, creamy white or pink flowers in spring. H and S 18in (45cm).

Z5–9 H9–4

Anemone sylvestris
(Snowdrop windflower)
Carpeting perennial that may be invasive. Fragrant, semi-pendent white flowers with yellow centers are borne in spring and early summer. Has divided, midgreen leaves. H and S 12in (30cm).

Z3–9 H9–1

***Bergenia* 'Silberlicht'**, syn. *B.* 'Silver Light'
Evergreen, clump-forming perennial that has flat, oval, midgreen leaves with toothed margins. Clusters of white flowers sometimes suffused with pink are borne on erect stems in spring. H 12in (30cm), S 20in (50cm).

Z3–8 H8–1

Bergenia ciliata
Evergreen, clump-forming perennial with attractive, large, rounded, hairy leaves. In spring bears clusters of white flowers that age to pink. Leaves are often damaged in winter, although fresh ones will appear in spring.
H 12in (30cm), S 20in (50cm).

Z5–8 H8–1

***Geranium macrorrhizum* 'Ingwersen's Variety'**
Compact, carpeting perennial, useful as a weed-suppressing groundcover. Small, soft rose-pink flowers appear in late spring and early summer. Aromatic leaves turn bronze- and scarlet-tinted in autumn. H 12in (30cm), S 24in (60cm).

Z4–8 H8–1

Heloniopsis orientalis
Clump-forming perennial with basal rosettes of narrowly lance-shaped leaves, above which rise nodding, rose-pink flowers in spring.
H and S 12in (30cm).

Z7–9 H9–7

***Bergenia cordifolia* 'Purpurea'**
Evergreen, clump-forming perennial, useful as a groundcover, with large, rounded, purple-tinged, deep green leaves. Clusters of bell-shaped, rose-pink flowers are carried on red stems from late winter to early spring.
H and S 20in (50cm).

Z3–8 H8–1

***Epimedium grandiflorum* 'Rose Queen'**
Carpeting perennial with dense, heart-shaped, divided leaves tinged with copper, and wiry stems bearing clusters of cup-shaped, spurred, deep pink flowers in spring. H and S 12in (30cm).

Z4–8 H8–2

Lamium maculatum
Semi-evergreen, mat-forming perennial with mauve-tinged, often pink-flushed leaves that have central silvery stripes. Clusters of hooded, mauve-pink flowers are borne in mid-spring. H 6in (15cm), S 36in (90cm).

Z4–8 H8–1

RED

Epimedium* x *rubrum
Carpeting perennial with dense, heart-shaped, divided leaves that are dark brownish red in spring, when clusters of cup-shaped crimson flowers with yellow spurs appear.
H 12in (30cm), S 8in (20cm).

Z4–8 H8–1

Trillium erectum
(Birthroot, Squawroot)
Clump-forming perennial with 3-lobed, midgreen leaves and bright maroon-purple flowers in spring.
H 12–18in (30–45cm), S 12in (30cm).

Z4–9 H9–1

Trillium sessile
(Toadshade, Wake robin)
Clump-forming perennial that in spring bears red-brown flowers nestling in a collar of 3-lobed leaves marked white, pale green, or bronze. H 12–15in (30–38cm), S 12–18in (30–45cm).

Z4–8 H8–1

Bergenia 'Abendglut'
Bergenia cordifolia
Bergenia 'Morgenröte'
Bergenia x *schmidtii*
Bergenia stracheyi
Bergenia 'Sunningdale'
Dicentra 'Adrian Bloom'
Dicentra 'Spring Morning', illus. p.278
Dicentra 'Stuart Boothman', illus. p.278
Helleborus x *hybridus* [pink form], illus. p.301
PRIMROSES, illus. pp.272–3
Rehmannia glutinosa

Epimedium alpinum
Pulmonaria rubra

■ PURPLE

***Anemone nemorosa* 'Allenii'**
Carpeting perennial with many large, cup-shaped, single, rich lavender-blue flowers appearing in spring over deeply divided, midgreen leaves.
H 6in (15cm), S 12in (30cm) or more.

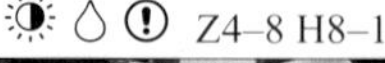
Z4–8 H8–1

Glaucidium palmatum
Leafy perennial that has large, lobed leaves and, in spring, large, delicate, cup-shaped lavender flowers.
A woodland plant, it requires organic soil and a sheltered position.
H and S 20in (50cm).

Z6–9 H9–6

Geranium nodosum
Clump-forming perennial with lobed, glossy leaves and delicate, cup-shaped lilac or lilac-pink flowers borne in spring-summer. Thrives in deep shade.
H and S 18in (45cm).

Z4–8 H8–1

Lathyrus vernus
Clump-forming perennial bearing in spring small, pealike, bright purple and blue flowers veined with red, several on each slender stem. Leaves are soft and fernlike. Often difficult to transplant successfully.
H and S 12in (30cm).

Z5–9 H9–3

***Anemone nemorosa* 'Robinsoniana'**
Carpeting perennial with flat, star-shaped, lavender-blue flowers, pale creamy gray beneath, borne singly on maroon stems. Leaves are deeply divided into lance-shaped segments.
H 6in (15cm), S 12in (30cm).

Z4–8 H8–1

***Cardamine pentaphyllos*,**
syn. *Dentaria pentaphyllos*
Upright perennial spreading by fleshy, horizontal rootstocks. Produces clusters of large white or pale purple flowers in spring. H 12–24in (30–60cm), S 18–24in (45–60cm).

Z5–9 H9–5

Cardamine pratensis 'Flore Pleno'
Chirita lavandulacea, illus. p.294
Helleborus x *hybridus* [purple form], illus. p.302
Helonias bullata
IRISES, illus. pp.234–5
ORCHIDS, illus. pp.296–9
PEONIES, illus. pp.236–7
PRIMROSES, illus. pp.272–3
Sarracenia purpurea

Pulmonaria saccharata
Semi-evergreen, clump-forming perennial. In spring bears funnel-shaped flowers opening pink and turning to blue. Long, elliptic leaves are variably spotted with creamy white. H 12in (30cm), S 24in (60cm).

 Z4–8 H8–1

Lamium orvala
Clump-forming perennial that forms a mound of midgreen leaves, sometimes with central white stripes. Clusters of pink or purple-pink flowers open in late spring to early summer.
H and S 12in (30cm).

Z4–8 H8–1

Scopolia carniolica
Clump-forming perennial that carries spikes of nodding, purple-brown flowers, yellow inside, in early spring.
H and S 24in (60cm).

Z5–8 H8–5

Lathraea clandestina (Toothwort)
Spreading perennial that grows as a parasite on willow or poplar roots. Fleshy, underground stems have colorless scales instead of leaves. Bears bunches of hooded purple flowers from late winter to early spring.
H 4in (10cm), S indefinite.

Z5–9 H9–5

***Pulmonaria* 'Mawson's Blue'**
Clump-forming perennial that in early spring bears clusters of funnel-shaped blue flowers, tinged red with age, above narrow leaves.
H and S 9in (23cm).

Z5–8 H8–5

***Mertensia pulmonarioides*,**
syn. *M. virginica*
Elegant perennial with rich blue flowers hanging in clusters in spring. Leaves are soft blue-green. Dies down in summer. Crowns are prone to slug damage. H 12–24in (30–60cm), S 12–18in (30–45cm).

Z3–7 H7–1

***Brunnera macrophylla* 'Dawson's White'**, syn. *B.m.* 'Variegata'
Groundcover perennial with heart-shaped leaves marked creamy white. In spring bears delicate sprays of small, bright blue flowers. Shelter from wind to prevent leaf damage.
H 18in (45cm), S 24in (60cm).

Z3–7 H7–1

Meconopsis quintuplinervia
(Harebell poppy)
Mat-forming perennial. Lavender-blue flowers, deepening to purple at the bases, are carried singly on hairy stems in late spring and early summer above a dense mat of large, midgreen leaves.
H 12–18in (30–45cm), S 12in (30cm).

pH Z7–8 H8–7

Euphorbia amygdaloides
var. ***robbiae***, syn. *E. robbiae*
Evergreen, spreading perennial with rosettes of dark green leaves, useful as a groundcover even in poor, dry soil and semi-shade. Bears open, rounded heads of lime green flowers in spring.
H 18–24in (45–60cm), S 24in (60cm).

Z6–9 H9–6

Euphorbia seguieriana
Bushy perennial with large, terminal clusters of yellowish green flowers in late spring and narrow, lance-shaped, glaucous leaves on slender stems.
H and S 18in (45cm).

Z8–11 H12–8

Euphorbia cyparissias
Rounded, leafy perennial with a mass of slender, gray-green leaves and umbels of small, bright lime green flowers in late spring. May become invasive. H and S 12in (30cm).

Z4–9 H9–1

Ajuga pyramidalis
Brunnera macrophylla
Cyanotis somaliensis, illus. p.303
IRISES, illus. pp.234–5

Meehania urticifolia
Pulmonaria angustifolia
Pulmonaria longifolia
Symphytum 'Hidcote Blue'

Chirita sinensis
Helleborus argutifolius, illus. p.304
Helleborus cyclophyllus
Helleborus foetidus, illus. p.305

Helleborus viridis, illus. p.305
IRISES, illus. pp.234–5
Linum narbonense, illus. p.287
Sarracenia flava, illus. p.290

Primroses

There are primroses (genus *Primula*) for almost every kind of garden situation, ranging from the pondside to the dry rock garden, but most have particular needs, and care should be taken with their cultivation. Among the various groups, Candelabra and Auricula primulas are the most widely known and have a distinctive arrangement of their flowers. (For fuller details, see the Plant Dictionary.)

P. allionii

P. polyneura

P. pulverulenta (Candelabra)

P. sonchifolia

P. frondosa

P. vulgaris **'Gigha White'**

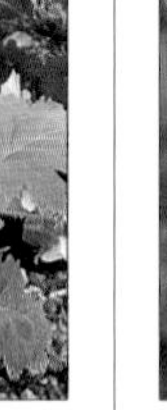
P. sinensis

P. sieboldii **'Wine Lady'**

P. **'Craddock White'**

P. malacoides [single]

P. warshenewskiana

P. secundiflora

P. petiolaris

P. denticulata var. *alba*

P. farinosa

P. malacoides [double]

P. melanops

P. japonica **'Miller's Crimson'** (Candelabra)

P. modesta var. *fauriae*

P. japonica **'Postford White'** (Candelabra)

P. vulgaris subsp. *sibthorpii*

P. x *scapeosa*

P. clusiana

P. gracilipes

P. pulverulenta **'Bartley'** (Candelabra)

P. clarkei

P. hirsuta

P. vialii

P. **'Mrs. J.H. Wilson'** (Auricula)

P. rosea

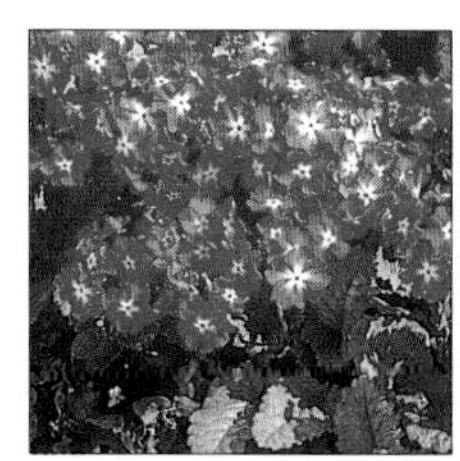
P. sieboldii

P. nana

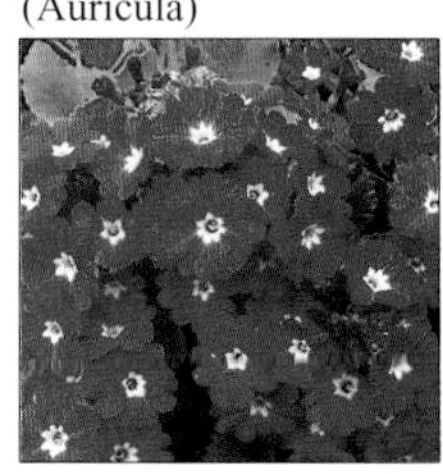
P. **'Janet'**

***P.* 'Mark'** (Auricula)

***P.* 'Linda Pope'**

P. aureata

P. florindae

P. bulleyana (Candelabra)

***P.* 'Adrian'** (Auricula)

P. reidii* var. *williamsii

P. alpicola* var. *alpicola

P. denticulata

P. vulgaris

P. sikkimensis

P. forrestii

***P.* 'Janie Hill'** (Auricula)

***P.* 'Moonstone'** (Auricula)

P. elatior

P. veris

***P.* 'Blossom'** (Auricula)

***P. marginata* 'Prichard's Variety'**

P. bhutanica

P. prolifera (Candelabra)

***P.* 'Blairside Yellow'** (Auricula)

P. chungensis (Candelabra)

***P.* 'Inverewe'** (Candelabra)

P. flaccida

***P.* 'Margaret Martin'** (Auricula)

P.* × *kewensis

P. marginata

***P.* 'Chloë'** (Auricula)

P. palinuri

P. verticillata

***P.* Gold Laced Group**

YELLOW

***Valeriana phu* 'Aurea'**
Perennial with rosettes of lemon to butter yellow young foliage that turns midgreen by summer, when heads of insignificant white flowers appear. H 15in (38cm), S 30–38cm (12–15in).

Z5–9 H9–5

Petasites japonicus
Spreading, invasive perennial that in early spring produces dense cones of small, daisylike, yellowish white flowers before large, light green leaves appear. H 2ft (60cm), S 5ft (1.5m).

Z5–9 H9–5

***Cardamine enneaphyllos*,** syn. *Dentaria enneaphyllos*
Lax perennial spreading by fleshy, horizontal rootstocks. In spring, nodding, pale yellow or white flowers open at the ends of shoots arising from deeply divided leaves. H 12–24in (30–60cm), S 18–24in (45–60cm).

Z5–8 H8–5

***Epimedium* x *versicolor* 'Neosulphureum'**
Carpeting perennial with dense, heart-shaped,, divided leaves tinted reddish purple in spring, when it bears cup-shaped, pale yellow flowers in small, pendent clusters on wiry stems. H and S 12in (30cm).

Z5–9 H9–4

***Trollius* x *cultorum* 'Alabaster'**
Clump-forming perennial producing rounded, yellowish white flowers in spring. These emerge from a basal mass of rounded, deeply divided, midgreen leaves.
H 24in (60cm), S 18in (45cm).

Z5–8 H8–5

***Anemone* x *lipsiensis*,** syn. *A.* x *intermedia, A.* x *seemannii*
Prostrate, carpeting perennial that in spring has many single, pale yellow flowers with bright yellow stamens. Leaves are deeply cut with long leaflets. H 6in (15cm), S 12in (30cm).

Z5–8 H8–5

Uvularia grandiflora
(Bellwort, Merry-bells)
Clump-forming perennial. Clusters of long, bell-shaped yellow flowers hang gracefully from slender stems in spring.
H 18–24in (45–60cm), S 12in (30cm).

Z3–7 H7–1

Anemone ranunculoides
Spreading perennial for damp woodland, bearing buttercup-like, single, deep yellow flowers in spring. Divided leaves have short stalks.
H and S 8in (20cm).

Z4–8 H8–1

Asphodeline liburnica
Doronicum austriacum
Doronicum 'Frühlingspracht'
Duchesnea indica
Epimedium x *perralchicum*
Epimedium perralderianum
Epimedium pinnatum subsp. *colchicum*
Euphorbia rigida
Hylomecon japonica, illus. p.350
Meconopsis integrifolia, illus. p.292
PRIMROSES, illus. pp.272–3
Ranunculus acris 'Flore Pleno', illus. p.292
Symphytum ibericum
Trollius x *cultorum* 'Earliest of All'
Trollius europaeus 'Canary Bird'
Uvularia perfoliata

PERENNIALS small SUMMER INTEREST

YELLOW–ORANGE

Trollius europaeus (Globeflower)
Clump-forming perennial that in spring bears rounded, lemon to medium yellow flowers above deeply divided, midgreen leaves.
H 24in (60cm), S 18in (45cm).

 Z5–8 H8–5

Euphorbia polychroma, syn. *E. epithymoides*
Rounded, bushy perennial with mid-green leaves and heads of bright yellow flowers carried for several weeks in spring. H and S 20in (50cm).

Z5–9 H9–5

Adonis vernalis
Clump-forming perennial that in early spring produces buttercup-like, greenish yellow blooms singly at the tips of stems. Midgreen leaves are delicately dissected.
H and S 9–12in (23–30cm).

Z4–7 H7–1

Adonis amurensis
Clump-forming perennial that in late winter and early spring bears buttercup-like, golden blooms singly at the tips of stems.
Midgreen foliage is finely cut.
H 12in (30cm), S 9–12in (23–30cm).

Z4–7 H7–1

Meconopsis cambrica (Welsh poppy)
Spreading perennial that in late spring carries lemon yellow or rich orange blooms. Double forms are available. Has deeply divided, fernlike foliage.
H 12–18in (30–45cm), S 12in (30cm).

Z6–8 H8–6

Epimedium* x *warleyense
Carpeting perennial with heart-shaped, divided, light green leaves tinged purple-red, and cup-shaped, rich orange flowers borne in clusters on wiry stems in spring.
H and S 12in (30cm).

Z5–9 H9–5

Calceolaria 'John Innes', illus. p.293
IRISES, illus. pp.234–5
PRIMROSES, illus. pp.272–3
Trollius x *cultorum* 'Goldquelle'

WHITE

Campanula alliariifolia
Mound-forming perennial with heart-shaped leaves, above which rise nodding, bell-shaped, creamy white flowers borne along arching, wiry stems throughout summer.
H 24in (60cm), S 20in (50cm).

Z3–7 H7–1

Galium odoratum, syn. *Asperula odorata* (Woodruff)
Carpeting perennial that bears whorls of star-shaped white flowers above neat, whorled leaves in summer.
All parts of the plant are aromatic.
H 6in (15cm), S 12in (30cm) or more.

Z5–8 H8–5

Anemone rivularis
Perennial with stiff, free-branching stems bearing delicate, cup-shaped white flowers in summer above deeply divided, dark green leaves.
H 24in (60cm), S 12in (30cm).

Z6–8 H8–6

Anemone narcissiflora
Leafy perennial that in late spring and early summer produces cup-shaped, single white flowers with a blue or purplish pink stain on reverse of petals. Leaves are dark green and deeply divided.
H to 24in (60cm), S 20in (50cm).

Z5–8 H8–5

***Leucanthemum* x *superbum* 'Esther Read'**, syn. *Chrysanthemum maximum* of gardens 'Esther Read'
Robust perennial with large, daisylike, double white flower heads borne singly on strong stems in summer.
H and S 18in (45cm).

Z5–8 H8–5

OTHER RECOMMENDED PLANTS:
Lamium maculatum 'White Nancy', illus. p.267
Libertia ixioides
Ophiopogon jaburan 'Vittatus'
Paradisea liliastrum
Polygonatum multiflorum 'Striatum'
Scabiosa caucasica 'Miss Willmott'

Anthemis punctata subsp. ***cupaniana***
Evergreen, carpeting perennial with dense, finely cut silvery foliage that turns green in winter. Small, daisy-like white flower heads with yellow centers are borne singly on short stems in early summer. H and S 12in (30cm).

Z6–9 H9–6

Anthericum liliago (St. Bernard's lily)
Upright perennial that in early summer bears tall racemes of trumpet-shaped white flowers above clumps of long, narrow, gray-green leaves.
H 18–24in (45–60cm), S 12in (30cm).

Z7–9 H9–7

Anaphalis nepalensis var. ***monocephala***, syn. *A. nubigena*
Dwarf, leafy perennial that has woolly silvery stems and lance-shaped leaves. Carries dense, terminal clusters of white flower heads in late summer.
H 8–12in (20–30cm), S 6in (15cm).

Z5–8 H8–5

***Mentha suaveolens* 'Variegata'**, syn. *M. rotundifolia* of gardens 'Variegata' (Variegated apple mint)
Spreading perennial with soft, woolly, midgreen leaves, splashed with white and cream, that smell of apples. Seldom produces flowers.
H 12–18in (30–45cm), S 24in (60cm).

Z6–9 H9–5

Crambe maritima (Sea kale)
Robust perennial with a mound of wide, curved, lobed, silvery green leaves. Bears large heads of small, fragrant white flowers opening into branching sprays in summer.
H and S 24in (60cm).

Z6–9 H9–6

***Aegopodium podagraria* 'Variegatum'**
(Variegated goutweed)
Vigorous, spreading perennial, excellent as a groundcover, with lobed, creamy white-variegated leaves. Insignificant white flowers borne in summer are best removed. H 4in (10cm), S indefinite.

Z4–9 H9–1

***Astilbe* 'Irrlicht'**
Leafy perennial bearing tapering, feathery plumes of tiny white flowers in summer. Foliage is dark green, and flowers remain on the plant, dried and brown, well into winter. Prefers organic soil.
H 1½–2ft (45–60cm), S to 3ft (1m).

Z3–8 H8–2

***Heuchera cylindrica* 'Greenfinch'**
Evergreen, clump-forming perennial with rosettes of lobed, heart-shaped leaves and, in summer, graceful spikes of small, bell-shaped, pale green or greenish white flowers.
H 18–24in (45–60cm), S 20in (50cm).

Z4–8 H8–1

***Tradescantia* Andersoniana Group 'Osprey'**, syn. *T.* 'Osprey'
Clump-forming perennial with narrow, lance-shaped leaves, 6–12in (15–30cm) long. Has clusters of white flowers with purple-blue stamens, surrounded by 2 leaflike bracts, in summer.
H to 24in (60cm), S 18in (45cm).

Z5–8 H8–2

***Geranium clarkei* 'Kashmir White'**, syn. *G. pratense* 'Kashmir White'
Carpeting, rhizomatous perennial with divided leaves and loose clusters of cup-shaped flowers, white with pale lilac-pink veins, borne for a long period in summer. H and S 18–24in (45–60cm).

Z5–8 H8–5

Streptocarpus caulescens
Erect perennial with small, narrow to oval, fleshy, dark green leaves. Stalked clusters of small, tubular, violet-striped, violet, or white flowers are carried in leaf axils intermittently.
H and S to 18in (45cm) or more.

Z14–15 H12–10

Anemone sylvestris, illus. p.268
PELARGONIUMS, illus. pp.246–7
PRIMROSES, illus. pp.272–3
Tanacetum parthenium, illus. p.319
Tulbaghia natalensis

Geranium renardii
Compact, clump-forming perennial with lobed, circular, sage green leaves and purple-veined white flowers borne in early summer.
H and S 12in (30cm).

☼ ◊ Z6–8 H8–6

Diplarrhena moraea
Clump-forming perennial with fans of long, strap-shaped leaves and clusters of irislike white flowers with centers of yellow and purple, borne on wiry stems in early summer.
H 18in (45cm), S 9in (23cm).

☼ ◊ Z9–10 H10–9

***Osteospermum* 'Whirlygig'**, syn. *O.* 'Whirligig'
Evergreen, clump-forming, semi-woody perennial of lax habit that bears bluish white flower heads in great profusion during summer. Leaves are gray-green.
H 24in (60cm), S 12–18in (30–45cm).

☼ ◊ Z10–11 H6–1

Arctotis venusta
Osteospermum 'Blue Streak'
Osteospermum ecklonis

Sinningia concinna
Tricyrtis hirta var. *alba*, illus. p.294

Ruellia devosiana
Evergreen, bushy subshrub with spreading, purplish branches. Leaves are broadly lance-shaped and dark green with paler veins above and purple below. Has mauve-tinged white flowers in spring-summer. H and S to 18in (45cm) or more.

◐ ♦ Z14–15 H12–10

***Heuchera micrantha* var. *diversifolia* 'Palace Purple'**
Clump-forming perennial with persistent, heart-shaped, deep purple leaves and sprays of small white flowers in summer. Cut leaves last well in water. H and S 18in (45cm).

◐ ◊ Z4–8 H8–1

Melittis melissophyllum (Bastard balm)
Erect perennial that in early summer bears white flowers with purple lower lips in axils of rough, oval, midgreen leaves. H and S 12in (30cm).

◐ ◊ Z6–9 H9–6

Astrantia major subsp. ***involucrata***, syn. *A.m.* subsp. *carinthiaca*
Clump-forming perennial very similar to *A. major* (below) but with longer bracts surrounding centers of flower heads. H 24in (60cm), S 18in (45cm).

☼ ◊ Z4–7 H7–1

Astrantia major (Masterwort)
Clump-forming perennial producing greenish white, sometimes pink-tinged flower heads throughout summer-autumn above a dense mass of divided, midgreen leaves.
H 24in (60cm), S 18in (45cm).

☼ ◊ Z4–7 H7–1

Astrantia maxima
Clump-forming perennial that bears rose-pink flower heads during summer-autumn.
H 24in (60cm), S 12in (30cm).

☼ ◊ Z5–8 H8–1

Geranium incanum
Sedum populifolium

PINK

***Mimulus* 'Andean Nymph'**
Spreading perennial, with hairy leaves, that in summer bears snapdragon-like, rose-pink flowers tipped with creamy yellow and spotted deep pink.
H 9in (23cm), S 10in (25cm).

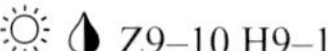

Z9–10 H9–1

***Dicentra* 'Spring Morning'**
Neat, leafy perennial with small, heart-shaped pink flowers hanging in arching sprays in late spring and summer. Attractive, fernlike foliage is gray-green and finely cut.
H and S 12in (30cm).

Z3–9 H9–1

***Dicentra* 'Stuart Boothman'**
Tufted perennial with oval, finely cut, deep gray-green leaves. In spring-summer, produces arching sprays of heart-shaped carmine flowers.
H 12in (30cm), S 16in (40cm).

Z3–9 H9–1

***Diascia* 'Blackthorn Apricot'**
Mat-forming perennial with narrowly heart-shaped, tapering leaves. From summer to autumn, produces loose racemes of apricot-pink flowers with small, narrow "windows" and almost straight, downward-pointing spurs.
H 10in (25cm), S to 20in (50cm).

Z8–9 H9–8

x *Heucherella tiarelloides*
Evergreen, groundcover perennial that has dense clusters of leaves and feathery sprays of tiny, bell-shaped pink flowers in early summer.
H and S 18in (45cm).

Z5–8 H8–5

x *Heucherella alba* 'Bridget Bloom'
Evergreen, clump-forming perennial with dense, bright green leaves and, in early summer, many feathery sprays of tiny, bell-shaped, rose-pink flowers that continue intermittently until autumn. H 18in (45cm), S 12in (30cm).

Z5–8 H8–5

***Erigeron* 'Charity'**
Clump-forming perennial with a mass of daisylike, light pink flower heads with greenish yellow centers borne for a long period in summer. May need some support. H and S to 24in (60cm).

Z5–8 H8–5

Geranium endressii
Semi-evergreen, compact, carpeting perennial with small, lobed leaves and cup-shaped, rose-pink flowers borne throughout summer.
H 18in (45cm), S 24in (60cm).

Z5–8 H8–5

Achimenes 'Peach Blossom'
Francoa appendiculata
PELARGONIUMS, illus. pp.246–7
PENSTEMONS, illus. p.248
PRIMROSES, illus. pp.272–3
Rehmannia glutinosa
Tradescantia pallida 'Purpurea', illus. p.303

***Geranium* x *oxonianum* 'Wargrave Pink'**
Semi-evergreen, carpeting perennial with dense, dainty, lobed, basal leaves acting as a weed-suppressing groundcover. Cup-shaped, bright salmon-pink flowers are borne throughout summer. H 18in (45cm), S 24in (60cm).

Z4–8 H8–1

Lychnis flos-jovis
Clump-forming perennial with rounded clusters of deep rose-pink flowers, opening in midsummer, that are set off by gray foliage.
H and S 18in (45cm).

Z4–8 H8–1

Geranium macrorrhizum
Semi-evergreen, carpeting perennial bearing magenta flowers in early summer. Rounded, divided, aromatic leaves make a good, weedproof groundcover and assume bright tints in autumn.
H 12–15in (30–38cm), S 24in (60cm).

Z4–8 H8–1

***Osteospermum jucundum*,**
syn. *O. barberae* of gardens, *Dimorphotheca barberae* of gardens
Evergreen, neat, clump-forming perennial with midgreen leaves. In late summer, soft pink flower heads, mostly dark-eyed, are borne in great abundance. H and S 12in (30cm).

Z9–11 H6–1

***Centaurea hypoleuca* 'John Coutts'**
Upright perennial. Deep rose-red flower heads, with thistlelike centers encircled by star-shaped ray petals, are borne singly on slender stems in summer. Deeply divided leaves are white-gray beneath. H 24in (60cm), S 18in (45cm).

Z3–9 H9–1

***Persicaria macrophylla*,**
syn. *P. sphaerostachya*, *Polygonum macrophyllum*, *P. sphaerostachyum*
Compact perennial carrying neat spikes of rich rose-pink blooms above narrow, lance-shaped, glaucous leaves in late summer.
H 18–24in (45–60cm), S 12in (30cm).

Z5–9 H9–5

***Erodium manescaui*,**
syn. *E. manescavii*
Mound-forming perennial with divided, fernlike, blue-green leaves. Produces loose clusters of single, deep pink, darker-blotched flowers throughout summer.
H 18in (45cm), S 24in (60cm).

Z6–8 H8–6

Incarvillea mairei
Compact, clump-forming perennial that has short stems bearing several trumpet-shaped, purplish pink flowers in early summer. Leaves are divided into oval leaflets. Protect crowns with winter mulch. H and S 12in (30cm).

Z4–8 H8–1

***Liatris spicata*,**
syn. *L. callilepis* of gardens
Clump-forming perennial. In late summer bears spikes of crowded, rose-purple flower heads on stiff stems that arise from basal tufts of grassy, midgreen foliage.
H 24in (60cm), S 12in (30cm).

Z4–9 H9–5

Mimulus lewisii
Upright perennial with downy, sticky gray leaves that provide an excellent foil for snapdragon-like, deep rose-pink flowers borne singly in summer. Tolerates dry soil.
H 24in (60cm), S 18in (45cm).

Z5–8 H8–5

***Physostegia virginiana* 'Vivid'**
(Obedient plant)
Erect, compact perennial that in late summer and early autumn bears spikes of tubular, dark lilac-pink flowers that can be placed in postion. Has toothed, midgreen leaves.
H and S 12–24in (30–60cm).

Z4–8 H8–1

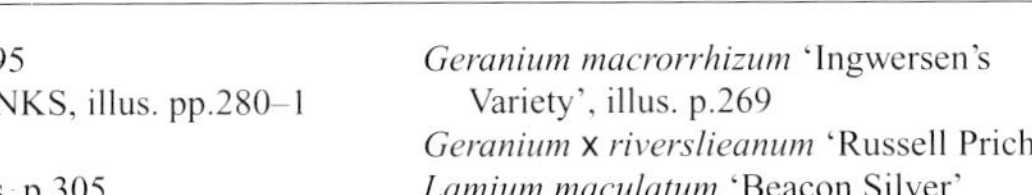

BEGONIAS, illus. p.295
CARNATIONS and PINKS, illus. pp.280–1
Dicentra formosa
Drosera spatulata, illus. p.305

Geranium macrorrhizum 'Ingwersen's Variety', illus. p.269
Geranium x *riversleaianum* 'Russell Prichard'
Lamium maculatum 'Beacon Silver'

ORCHIDS, illus. pp.296–9
Osteospermum 'Cannington Roy'
PELARGONIUMS, illus. pp.246–7
PENSTEMONS, illus. p.248

PEONIES, illus. pp.236–7
Sedum spectabile
Sphaeralcea munroana

Carnations and Pinks

Although perhaps best known for providing excellent cut flowers, carnations and pinks (*Dianthus* cultivars) are highly ornamental border subjects valued for their usually fragrant blooms (often strongly clove-scented) produced mainly in summer, and their distinctive, silvery- or gray-green foliage. Shorter-growing cultivars – the old-fashioned and modern pinks – are excellent edging plants. Many of the flowers are attractively marked or have fringed petals. Carnations and pinks need an open, sunny position, preferably in alkaline soil. Carnations and pinks are divided into the following groups:

Border carnations – plants are of upright habit and flower prolifically once in summer; each stem bears 5 or more flowers.
Perpetual-flowering carnations – similar in habit to border carnations, they are usually grown for cut flowers and bloom year-round under cover. Plants are normally disbudded, leaving one flower per stem, but spray forms have up to 5 flowers per stem.
Malmaison carnations – these produce very fragrant flowers sporadically throughout the year under cover.
Old-fashioned pinks – these have a low, spreading habit and form neat cushions of foliage; masses of fragrant flowers are produced in summer.
Modern pinks – usually more vigorous than old-fashioned pinks, they are repeat-flowering, with 2 or 3 main flushes of flowers in summer.
Alpine pinks – in early summer these plants form cushions of small, scented flowers.

***D.* 'Mrs. Sinkins'**
(old-fashioned pink)

***D.* 'Haytor'**
(modern pink)

***D.* 'White Ladies'**
(old-fashioned pink)

***D.* 'Musgrave's Pink'**
(old-fashioned pink)

***D.* 'Nives'** (perpetual-flowering carnation)

***D.* 'Eva Humphries'**
(border carnation)

***D.* 'Fair Folly'**
(modern pink)

***D.* 'Alice'**
(modern pink)

***D.* 'Gran's Favourite'**
(old-fashioned pink)

***D.* 'Dad's Favourite'**
(old-fashioned pink)

***D.* 'London Brocade'**
(modern pink)

***D.* 'Prudence'**
(old-fashioned pink)

***D.* 'Emile Paré'**
(old-fashioned pink)

***D.* 'Forest Treasure'**
(border carnation)

***D.* 'Doris'**
(modern pink)

***D.* PIERROT** (perpetual-flowering carnation)

***D.* 'Truly Yours'**
(perpetual-fl. carnation)

***D.* 'Becky Robinson'**
(modern pink)

D. **'Pink Jewel'** (alpine pink)

D. **'Joy'** (modern pink)

D. **'Astor'** (perpetual-flowering carnation)

D. **'Lavender Clove'** (border carnation)

D. **'Aldridge Yellow'** (border carnation)

D. **'Bovey Belle'** (modern pink)

D. **'Valencia'** (perpetual-flowering carnation)

D. **'Monica Wyatt'** (modern pink)

D. **'Duchess of Westminster'** (Mal. car.)

D. **'Laced Monarch'** (modern pink)

D. **'Clara'** (perpetual-flowering carnation)

D. **'Raggio di Sole'** (perpetual-fl. carnation)

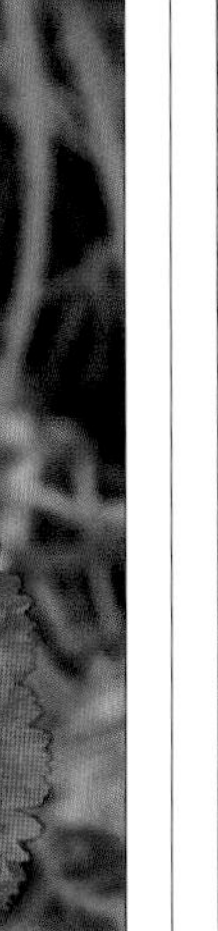
D. **'Houndspool Ruby'** (modern pink)

D. **'Nina'** (perpetual-flowering carnation)

D. **'Crompton Princess'** (perpetual-fl. carnation)

D. **'Christine Hough'** (border carnation)

D. **'Cream Sue'** (perpetual-fl. carnation)

D. **'Albisola'** (perpetual-flowering carnation)

D. **'Christopher'** (modern pink)

D. **'Bookham Perfume'** (border carnation)

D. **'Bookham Fancy'** (border carnation)

D. **'Happiness'** (border carnation)

D. **'Golden Cross'** (border carnation)

PINK

***Achimenes* 'Little Beauty'**
Bushy perennial with oval, toothed leaves. Large, funnel-shaped, deep pink flowers with yellow eyes are carried in summer. H 10in (25cm), S 12in (30cm).

Z14–15 H12–1

***Sinningia* 'Red Flicker'**
Short-stemmed, tuberous perennial with rosettes of oval, velvety leaves to 8in (20cm) long. In summer has fleshy, nodding, funnel-shaped, pinkish red flowers, pouched on lower sides. H to 12in (30cm), S 18in (45cm).

Z14–15 H12–10

Incarvillea delavayi
Clump-forming perennial with deeply divided leaves and erect stems bearing several trumpet-shaped, pinkish red flowers in early summer. Has attractive seed pods. H 18–24in (45–60cm), S 12in (30cm).

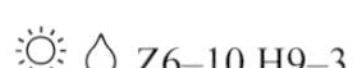
Z6–10 H9–3

***Potentilla nepalensis* 'Miss Willmott'**
Clump-forming perennial with palmate, strawberry-like, bright green leaves. Numerous slender, branching stems carry cherry red-centered pink flowers throughout summer. H 20in (50cm), S 24in (60cm).

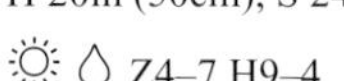
Z4–7 H9–4

***Verbena* 'Sissinghurst'**
Mat-forming perennial that throughout summer bears heads of brilliant pink flowers above midgreen foliage. Is excellent for edging a path or growing in a barrel or large pot. H 6–8in (15–20cm), S 18in (45cm).

Z7–11 H12–1

Sedum spectabile 'Brilliant', illus. p.294

RED

***Lychnis viscaria* 'Splendens Plena'**
Clump-forming perennial bearing spikes of double magenta flowers in early summer. Stems and large, oval to lance-shaped, basal leaves are covered in sticky hairs. H 12–18in (30–45cm), S 9in (23cm) or more.

Z4–8 H8–1

Lychnis coronaria
Clump-forming perennial, often grown as a biennial. From mid- to late summer, brilliant rose-crimson flowers are borne in panicles on branched gray stems that rise from neat gray leaves. H 18–24in (45–60cm), S 18in (45cm).

Z4–8 H8–1

***Sinningia* 'Switzerland'**
Short-stemmed, tuberous perennial with rosettes of oval, velvety leaves, to 8in (20cm) long. In summer has large, fleshy, trumpet-shaped, bright scarlet flowers with ruffled white borders. H to 12in (30cm), S 18in (45cm).

Z14–15 H12–10

***Astilbe* 'Fanal'**
Leafy perennial with strong stems. In summer bears neat, tapering, feathery panicles of tiny, crimson-red flowers that turn brown and keep their shape in winter. Broad leaves are divided into leaflets. Prefers organic soil. H 24in (60cm), S to 36in (90cm).

Z3–8 H8–2

***Heuchera* 'Red Spangles'**
Evergreen perennial forming clumps of heart-shaped, purplish green leaves. Bears spikes of small, bell-shaped, crimson-scarlet flowers in summer. H and S 12in (30cm).

Z3–8 H8–1

Alonsoa warscewiczii, illus. p.329
Geum 'Lionel Cox'
Lychnis viscaria
Potentilla 'Monsieur Rouillard'
Salvia blepharophylla
Stachys coccinea
Verbena peruviana

RED

Lotus berthelotii (Parrot's beak)
Semi-evergreen, straggling perennial suitable for a hanging basket or grown as a standard. Has hairy silvery branches, plus leaves and clusters of pealike scarlet flowers in spring and summer. H 12in (30cm), S indefinite.

Z12–15 H12–10

Columnea crassifolia
Evergreen, shrubby perennial with fleshy, lance-shaped leaves. Erect, tubular, hairy scarlet flowers, about 3in (8cm) long, each with a yellow throat, are carried from spring to autumn. H and S to 18in (45cm).

Z14–15 H12–10

***Smithiantha* 'Orange King'**
Strong-growing, erect, rhizomatous perennial. Large, scalloped, velvety leaves are emerald green with dark red-marked veins. In summer-autumn has tubular, orange-red flowers, red-spotted within and with yellow lips. H and S to 24in (60cm).

Z14–15 H12-10

Potentilla atrosanguinea
Clump-forming perennial with hairy, palmate, strawberry-like leaves. Loose clusters of dark red flowers are borne throughout summer.
H 18in (45cm), S 24in (60cm).

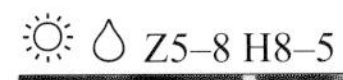
Z5–8 H8–5

***Gaillardia* x *grandiflora* 'Dazzler'**
Upright, rather open perennial bearing large, terminal, daisylike, yellow-tipped red flower heads for a long period in summer. Leaves are soft and divided. Often needs staking and may be short-lived.
H 24in (60cm), S 20in (50cm).

Z3–8 H8–1

***Mimulus* 'Royal Velvet'**
Compact perennial, often grown as an annual, producing in summer many large, snapdragon-like, mahogany-red flowers with mahogany-speckled gold throats. Leaves are midgreen.
H 12in (30cm), S 9in (23cm).

Z6–9 H9–6

PURPLE

Polemonium carneum
Clump-forming perennial that carries clusters of cup-shaped, pink or lilac-pink flowers in early summer. Foliage is finely divided. H and S 18in (45cm).

Z4–8 H8–1

Kaempferia pulchra
Tufted, rhizomatous perennial with horizontal, aromatic, dark green leaves variegated with paler green above. Short spikes of lilac-pink flowers appear from the center of clumps in summer. H 6in (15cm), S 12in (30cm).

Z14–15 H12–10

Tulbaghia violacea
Vigorous, semi-evergreen, clump-forming perennial that in summer-autumn carries umbels of lilac-purple or lilac-pink flowers above a mass of narrow, glaucous, blue-gray leaves.
H 18–24in (45–60cm), S 12in (30cm).

Z7–10 H10–7

Achimenes antirrhina
Achimenes 'Brilliant'
Aeschynanthus pulcher
Impatiens niamniamensis
Kohleria bogotensis
Lychnis x *haagena*
Potentilla 'Gibson's Scarlet'
Potentilla 'Gloire de Nancy'
Potentilla 'William Rollison'
Smithiantha cinnabarina

Geranium nodosum, illus. p.270
Ophiopogon planiscapus 'Nigrescens', illus. p.303
PELARGONIUMS, illus. pp.246–7

PURPLE

Streptocarpus saxorum
(False African violet)
Evergreen, rounded, woody-based perennial with small, oval, hairy leaves in whorls. Lilac flowers with white tubes arise from leaf axils in summer-autumn. H and S 12in (30cm) or more.

Z14–15 H12–10

Verbena rigida, syn. *V. venosa*
Neat, compact perennial bearing heads of pale violet flowers from mid-summer onward. Has lance-shaped, rough, midgreen leaves borne on flower stems.
H 18–24in (45–60cm), S 12in (30cm).

Z8–15 H12–1

Heterocentron elegans, syn. *Heeria elegans*, *Schizocentron elegans*
Evergreen, mat-forming perennial with dense, creeping, midgreen foliage. Massed, bright deep purple flowers open in summer-autumn and under cover in winter. H 2in (5cm), S indefinite.

Z12–15 H12–1

Polemonium pulcherrimum
Vigorous perennial with bright green leaves divided into leaflets. Tubular, purple-blue flowers with throats of yellow or white are borne in summer.
H 20in (50cm), S 12in (30cm).

Z4–8 H8–1

***Tradescantia* Andersoniana Group 'Purple Dome'**
Clump-forming perennial with narrow, lance-shaped leaves, 6–12in (15–30cm) long. Has clusters of rich purple flowers surrounded by 2 leaflike bracts in summer.
H to 24in (60cm), S 18in (45cm).

Z5–9 H9–5

***Erigeron* 'Serenity'**
Clump-forming perennial. Many daisy-like violet flower heads with yellow centers are borne in early and mid-summer. Needs some support.
H and S to 24in (60cm).

Z5–8 H8–5

Centaurea montana
Spreading perennial with many rather lax stems carrying, in early summer, one or more large purple, blue, white, or pink flower heads with thistlelike centers encircled by star-shaped ray petals. H 20in (50cm), S 24in (60cm).

Z3–9 H9–1

Platycodon grandiflorus
(Balloon flower)
Neat, clump-forming perennial that in summer bears clusters of large, balloon-like buds opening to bell-shaped blue or purplish flowers. Stems are clothed with bluish green leaves. H 18–24in (45–60cm), S 12–18in (30–45cm).

Z4–9 H9–1

CARNATIONS and PINKS, illus. pp.280–1
Drosera capensis, illus. p.305
Euphorbia amygdaloides 'Purpurea'
Geranium 'Ann Folkard'
Geranium clarkei 'Kashmir Purple'
Geranium palmatum
Geranium procurrens
Lamium orvala, illus. p.271
ORCHIDS, illus. pp.296–9
Osteospermum 'Nairobi Purple'
PENSTEMONS, illus. p.248
PRIMROSES, illus. pp.272–3
Ranzania japonica
Senecio pulcher, illus. p.294
Sinningia speciosa
Stachys macrantha

Stachys macrantha **'Superba'**
Clump-forming perennial with heart-shaped, soft, wrinkled, midgreen leaves, from which arise thick stems producing whorls of hooded, purple-violet flowers in summer. H 12–18in (30–45cm), S 12–24in (30–60cm).

Z4–8 H8–1

Geranium himalayense,
syn. *G. grandiflorum*, *G. meeboldii*
Clump-forming perennial with large, cup-shaped, violet-blue flowers borne on long stalks in summer over dense clumps of neatly cut leaves.
H 12in (30cm), S 24in (60cm).

Z4–7 H7–1

Geranium pratense
'Mrs. Kendall Clark'
Clump-forming perennial with hairy stems and deeply divided leaves. In early and midsummer bears erect, saucer-shaped, pearl-gray or violet-blue flowers with white or pale pink veins.
H 24–36in (60–90cm), S 24in (60cm).

Z4–8 H8–1

Scabiosa caucasica
'Clive Greaves'
Clump-forming perennial that throughout summer has violet-blue flower heads with pincushion-like centers. Basal, midgreen leaves are lance-shaped and slightly lobed on the stems. H and S 18–24in (45–60cm).

Z4–9 H9–1

Stokesia laevis
Perennial with overwintering, evergreen rosettes. In summer, cornflower-like, lavender- or purple-blue flower heads are borne freely. Leaves are narrow and midgreen.
H and S 12–18in (30–45cm).

Z5–9 H9–5

Geranium **x** ***magnificum***
Clump-forming perennial with hairy, deeply lobed leaves and cup-shaped, prominently veined, violet-blue flowers borne in small clusters in summer.
H 18in (45cm), S 24in (60cm).

Z4–8 H8–1

Geranium **'Johnson's Blue'**
Vigorous, clump-forming perennial with many divided leaves and cup-shaped, deep lavender-blue flowers borne throughout summer.
H 12in (30cm), S 24in (60cm).

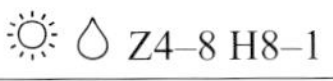

Z4–8 H8–1

Polemonium caeruleum
(Jacob's ladder)
Clump-forming perennial. Clusters of cup-shaped, lavender-blue flowers with orange-yellow stamens open in summer amid finely divided foliage.
H and S 18–24in (45–60cm).

Z4–9 H9–1

Catananche caerulea **'Major'**
Perennial forming clumps of grassy, gray-green leaves, above which rise wiry, branching stems each carrying a daisylike, lavender-blue flower head in summer. Propagate regularly by root cuttings.
H 18–24in (45–60cm), S 24in (30cm).

Z3–8 H8–1

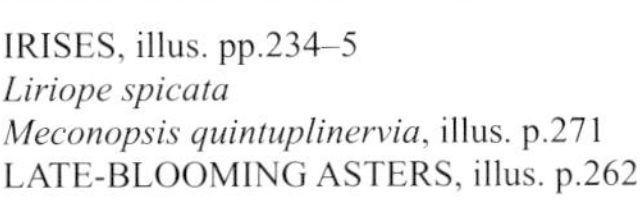

Adenophora potaninii
Chirita sinensis
Dracocephalum ruyschiana
Geranium ibericum
IRISES, illus. pp.234–5
Liriope spicata
Meconopsis quintuplinervia, illus. p.271
LATE-BLOOMING ASTERS, illus. p.262
Nierembergia caerulea 'Purple Robe', illus. p.331
Salvia farinacea 'Victoria', illus. p.332
Salvia jurisicii
Scabiosa caucasica 'Floral Queen'
Stachys officinalis
Tacca leontopetaloides

PURPLE

Limonium latifolium **'Blue Cloud'**
Clump-forming perennial. In late summer carries diffuse clusters of bluish mauve flowers that can be dried for indoor decoration. Has large, leathery, dark green leaves.
H 12in (30cm), S 18in (45cm).

Z4–9 H9–1

Campanula **'Burghaltii'**
Mound-forming perennial with long, pendent, funnel-shaped, pale lavender flowers displayed on erect, wiry stems in summer. Leaves are oval, soft, and leathery. May need staking.
H 24in (60cm), S 12in (30cm).

Z4–8 H8–1

Eryngium bourgatii
Clump-forming perennial that, from mid- to late summer, carries heads of thistlelike, blue-green then lilac-blue flowers on branched, wiry stems well above deeply cut, basal, gray-green leaves. H 18–24in (45–60cm), S 12in (30cm).

Z5–9 H9–5

Anemonopsis macrophylla
(False anemone)
Clump-forming perennial with waxy, nodding, purplish blue flowers borne on slender, branching stems in summer above fernlike leaves.
H 18–24in (45–60cm), S 20in (50cm).

Z5–8 H8–5

Nepeta* x *faassenii (Catmint)
Bushy, clump-forming perennial, useful for edging. Forms mounds of small, grayish green leaves, from which loose spikes of tubular, soft lavender-blue flowers appear in early summer. H and S 18in (45cm).

Z4–8 H8–1

BLUE

Amsonia orientalis,
syn. *Rhazya orientalis*
Neat, clump-forming perennial.
In summer, heads of small, star-shaped, gray-blue flowers open on tops of wiry stems clothed with green, sometimes grayish leaves. H 18–24in (45–60cm), 12–18in (30–45cm).

Z5–8 H8–5

Parahebe perfoliata, syn. *Veronica perfoliata* (Digger's speedwell)
Evergreen subshrub with willowy stems clasped by leathery, glaucous leaves. Elegant, long, branching sprays of blue flowers are borne in summer.
H 18–24in (45–60cm), S 18in (45cm).

Z9–11 H12–3

Eryngium variifolium
Evergreen, rosette-forming perennial with stiff stems that, in late summer, bear heads of thistlelike, gray-blue flowers, each with a collar of white bracts. Jagged-edged leaves are midgreen marbled with white.
H 18in (45cm), S 10in (25cm).

Z5–9 H9–5

Campanula isophylla
Chirita lavandulacea, illus. p.294
IRISES, illus. pp.234–5
Nepeta nervosa

Veronica gentianoides
Mat-forming perennial with spikes of very pale blue flowers opening in early summer on tops of stems that arise from glossy, basal leaves.
H and S 18in (45cm).

 Z4–7 H7–1

Amsonia tabernaemontana
Clump-forming perennial with willowy stems bearing drooping clusters of small, tubular, pale blue flowers in late spring and into summer. Midgreen leaves may turn yellow in autumn.
H 18–24in (45–60cm), S 12in (30cm).

 Z3–9 H9–1

Myosotidium hortensia
(Chatham Island forget-me-not)
Evergreen, clump-forming perennial bearing large clusters of forget-me-not-like blue flowers in summer above a basal mound of large, ribbed, glossy leaves. H 18–24in (45–60cm), S 24in (60cm).

Z12–15 H12–1

Linum narbonense
Clump-forming, short-lived perennial, best renewed frequently from seed. Has lance-shaped, grayish green leaves and heads of somewhat cup-shaped, pale to deep blue flowers in spring-summer.
H 12–24in (30–60cm), S 12in (30cm).

Z7–9 H9–7

Veronica peduncularis
Mat-forming perennial with ovate to lance-shaped, glossy, purple-tinged, midgreen leaves. Bears abundant, saucer-shaped, deep blue flowers with small white eyes over a long period from early spring to summer.
H to 4in (10cm), S 24in (60cm) or more.

Z6–8 H8–6

Geranium wallichianum
'Buxton's Variety',
syn. *G.w.* 'Buxton's Blue'
Spreading perennial with luxuriant, white-flecked leaves and large, white-centered blue or blue-purple flowers from midsummer to autumn.
H 12–18in (30–45cm), S 36in (90cm).

Z4–8 H8–1

Veronica spicata subsp. ***incana***,
syn. *V. incana*
Mat-forming perennial, densely covered with silver hairs, with linear to lance-shaped leaves. Bears spikes of small, star-shaped, clear blue flowers in summer. H and S 12in (30cm).

Z3–8 H8–1

Campanula isophylla
Kristal Hybrids 'Stella Blue'
Compact, free-flowering perennial with strong stems and small, heart-shaped, toothed, light green leaves. Large, upright, saucer-shaped, pale blue flowers in midsummer. H 6–8in (15–20cm), S to 12in (30cm).

Z13–15 H9–1

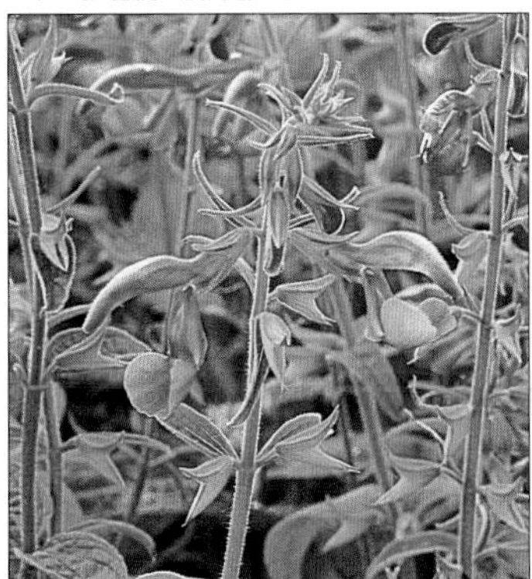

***Salvia patens* 'Cambridge Blue'**
Erect, branching perennial with ovate, midgreen leaves. From midsummer to midautumn produces loose terminal racemes of paired, pale blue flowers, 2in (5cm) long, with wide-open mouths.H 18–24in (45–60cm), S 18in (45cm).

Z8–9 H9–8

Nepeta 'Souvenir d'André Chaudron'
Orthrosanthus chimboracensis
Platycodon grandiflorus var. *mariesii*
Salvia nemorosa 'Lubecca'
Stokesia laevis 'Blue Star'
Veronica spicata

Hostas

The luxuriance of their foliage and attractive habit have made hostas, or plantain lilies, increasingly sought after as plants for every garden, large or small. Native to the East, they also add an exotic touch to any waterside or damp, shady corner.

Hosta species vary in size from plants a few inches high to vigorous forms that will make a clump of up to 5ft (1.5m) across in a few years. Their elegant leaves are diverse in shape, texture, and coloration, with subtle variegations and shadings. Many hostas also produce decorative spikes of flowers that rise gracefully above the foliage in midsummer.

Suitable for a range of situations from containers to borders and pondsides, hostas are essentially shade- and moisture-loving plants, preferring rich, well-drained soils. Leaves must be protected from slugs to avoid damage.

H. undulata
var. ***univittata***

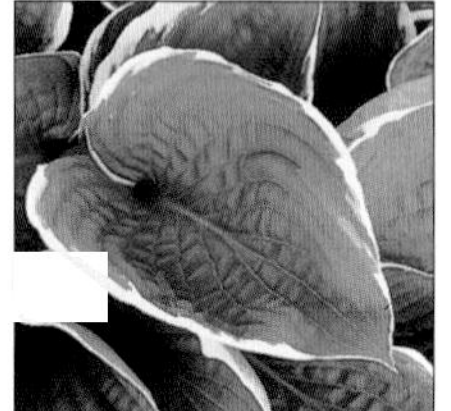

***H.* 'Francee'**

H. undulata
var. ***albomarginata***

***H.* 'Ground Master'**

H. sieboldii

***H.* 'Ginko Craig'**

***H.* 'Krossa Regal'**

***H.* 'Shade Fanfare'**

***H.* 'Snowden'**

***H.* 'Regal Splendor'**

H. tokudama
'Aureonebulosa'

H. sieboldiana

***H.* 'Love Pat'**

H. sieboldiana
var.***elegans***

H. tokudama

***H.* 'Hadspen Blue'**

***H.* 'Halcyon'**

H. tardiflora

***H.* 'Blue Wedgwood'**

H. ventricosa

H. 'Tall Boy'

H. plantaginea

H. 'Royal Standard'

H. venusta

H. sieboldiana
'Frances Williams'

H. 'Honeybells'

H. 'Yellow River'

H. fortunei 'Albopicta'

H. montana
'Aureomarginata'

H. 'Great Expectations'

H. 'Grand Tiara'

H. fortunei
'Aureomarginata'

H. 'Golden Tiara'

H. 'Zounds'

H. 'Kabitan'

H. 'Wide Brim'

H. ventricosa
'Variegata'

H. 'Gold Standard'

H. 'Piedmont Gold'

H. 'Golden Prayers'

H. 'Moonlight'

H. 'Sum and Substance'

GREEN–YELLOW

Artemisia pontica (Roman wormwood)
Vigorous, upright perennial with aromatic, feathery, silver-green foliage and tall spikes of small grayish flower heads in summer. May spread quickly. H 24in (60cm), S 8in (20cm).

Z4–8 H8–1

Alchemilla conjuncta
Clump-forming perennial that has neat, wavy, star-shaped leaves with pale margins. Loose clusters of tiny, greenish yellow flowers with conspicuous outer calyces, appearing in midsummer, may be dried for winter decoration. H and S 12in (30cm).

Z3–7 H7–1

***Persicaria virginiana* 'Painter's Palette'**
Mounded perennial grown for its attractive leaves, which are green with central brownish zones, ivory-yellow splashes and stripes, and a deep pink tinge. Flowers are insignificant. May become invasive. H and S 24in (60cm).

Z5–9 H9–5

Alchemilla mollis (Lady's mantle)
Clump-forming, groundcover perennial that has rounded, pale green leaves with crinkled edges. Bears small sprays of tiny, bright greenish yellow flowers with conspicuous outer calyces in midsummer that may be dried. H and S 20in (50cm).

Z4–7 H7–1

Sarracenia flava (Yellow pitcher plant)
Erect perennial with red-marked, yellow-green pitchers (modified leaves) that have hooded tops. From late spring to early summer bears nodding yellow or greenish yellow flowers.
H and S 18in (45cm).

Z7–10 H10–7

***Origanum vulgare* 'Aureum'**
Woody-based perennial forming a dense mat of aromatic, golden yellow, young leaves that turn pale yellow-green in midsummer. Occasionally bears tiny mauve flowers in summer.
H in leaf 3in (8cm), S indefinite.

Z5–9 H9-5

Aeschynanthus marmoratus
Clintonia borealis
Elatostema repens var. *pulchra*
Mentha x *gracilis* 'Variegata'
Mentha x *piperita* f. *citrata*
Mentha suaveolens 'Variegata', illus. p.276
Nicotiana 'Lime Green'

YELLOW

Sisyrinchium striatum
Semi-evergreen perennial that forms tufts of long, narrow, gray-green leaves. Bears slender spikes of purple-striped, straw yellow flowers in summer. Self seeds freely.
H 18–24in (45–60cm), S 12in (30cm).

Z7–8 H8–7

***Filipendula ulmaria* 'Aurea'**
Leafy perennial grown for its divided foliage, which is bright golden yellow in spring and pale green in summer. Clusters of creamy white flowers are carried in branching heads in midsummer. H and S 12in (30cm).

Z3–9 H9–1

***Kniphofia* 'Little Maid'**
Upright perennial with grasslike leaves and short, erect stems bearing terminal spikes of pale creamy yellow flowers in summer. Protect crowns with a loose, dry mulch in winter.
H 24in (60cm), S 18in (45cm).

Z6–9 H9–6

***Osteospermum* 'Buttermilk'**
Evergreen, upright, semi-woody perennial. Daisylike, pale yellow flower heads with dark eyes are borne singly amid gray-green foliage from midsummer to autumn.
H 24in (60cm), S 12in (30cm).

Z12–15 H6–1

Farfugium japonicum 'Aureomaculatum'
IRISES, illus. pp.234–5
Mimulus moschatus
PRIMROSES, illus. pp.272–3
Scrophularia auriculata 'Variegata'

***Stachys byzantina* 'Primrose Heron'**
Evergreen, mat-forming perennial with woolly, yellowish gray leaves to 4in (10cm) long. Erect stems bear spikes of pink-purple flowers from early summer to early autumn.
H 18in (45cm), S 24in (60cm).

 Z4–8 H8–1

***Achillea* 'Taygetea',**
syn. *A. aegyptica* of gardens
Perennial with erect stems bearing flat heads of lemon yellow flowers throughout summer above clumps of feathery gray leaves. Divide and replant every third year.
H 24in (60cm), S 20in (50cm).

Z3–8 H8–1

x *Solidaster luteus*,
syn. x *S. hybridus*
Clump-forming perennial. From midsummer onward, slender stems carry dense heads of bright creamy yellow flowers above narrow, midgreen leaves.
H 24in (60cm), S 30in (75cm).

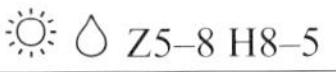 Z5–8 H8–5

***Achillea* 'Moonshine'**
Upright perennial that bears flat heads of bright yellow flowers throughout summer above a mass of small, feathery, gray-green leaves.
Divide plants regularly in spring.
H 24in (60cm), S 20in (50cm).

 Z3–9 H9–1

***Potentilla recta* 'Warrenii',**
syn. *P.r.* 'Macrantha'
Clump-forming perennial with lobed, midgreen leaves. Rich golden yellow flowers are borne on open, branched stems throughout summer.
H 20in (50cm), S 24in (60cm).

Z4–8 H8–1

***Helichrysum* 'Schwefellicht',**
syn. *H.* 'Sulphur Light'
Clump-forming perennial that bears silver-gray leaves and a mass of everlasting, fluffy, sulfur yellow flower heads from mid- to late summer.
H 16–24in (40–60cm), S 12in (30cm).

Z9–10 H10–9

***Barbarea vulgaris* 'Variegata'**
Perennial with rosettes of long, toothed, glossy leaves blotched with cream, above which rise branching heads of small, silvery yellow flowers in early summer.
H 10–18in (25–45cm), S to 9in (23cm).

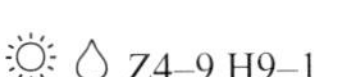 Z4–9 H9–1

***Gaillardia aristata* (Blanket flower)**
Upright, rather open perennial that has large, terminal, daisylike, single flower heads in rich yellow with red centers for a long period in summer, and soft, aromatic, divided leaves. Needs staking and may be short-lived.
H 24in (60cm), S 20in (50cm).

Z3–8 H8–1

***Oenothera fruticosa* 'Fyrverkeri',**
syn. *O.f.* 'Fireworks'
Clump-forming perennial that from mid- to late summer bears spikes of fragrant, cup-shaped flowers. Has reddish stems and glossy, midgreen foliage. H and S 12–15in (30–38cm).

Z4–8 H8–1

BEGONIAS, illus. p.295
DAYLILIES, illus. p.257
HOSTAS, illus. pp.288–9
IRISES, illus. pp.234–5
Nautilocalyx bullatus
Oenothera perennis
ORCHIDS, illus. pp.296–9
PELARGONIUMS, illus. pp.246–7
Potentilla atrosanguinea var. *argyrophylla*
PRIMROSES, illus. pp.272–3
Rhodiola rosea
Salvia bulleyana
Sedum aizoon
Ursinia chrysanthemoides

YELLOW

***Ranunculus constantinopolitanus* 'Plenus'**
Clump-forming perennial with divided, toothed leaves sometimes spotted gray and white. Neat, pomponlike, double yellow flowers appear in early summer. H 20in (50cm), S 12in (30cm).

Z7–9 H9–7

Mimulus luteus
(Yellow monkeyflower)
Spreading perennial. Throughout summer, snapdragon-like, occasionally red-spotted yellow flowers are freely produced above hairy, midgreen foliage. H and S 12in (30cm).

Z7–9 H9–7

Meconopsis integrifolia
(Lampshade poppy)
Rosette-forming biennial or short-lived perennial carrying spikes of large, pale yellow flowers in late spring and early summer. Has large, pale green leaves. H 18–24in (45–60cm), S 24in (60cm).

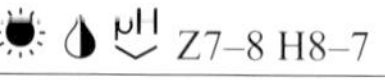
Z7–8 H8–7

***Geum* 'Lady Stratheden',**
syn. *G.* 'Goldball'
Clump-forming perennial with lobed leaves and cup-shaped, double, bright yellow flowers with prominent green stamens, borne on slender, branching stems for a long period in summer. H 18–24in (45–60cm), S 18in (45cm).

Z5–9 H9–5

Potentilla megalantha
Clump-forming perennial with large, palmate, hairy, soft green leaves. Large, rich yellow flowers are produced in summer. H 8in (20cm), S 6in (15cm).

Z5–8 H8–5

Buphthalmum salicifolium
(Yellow ox-eye)
Spreading perennial that carries daisy-like, deep yellow flower heads singly on willowy stems throughout summer. May need staking. Divide regularly; spreads on rich soil. H 24in (60cm), S 36in (90cm).

Z5–8 H8–5

Gazania rigens* var. *uniflora
Mat-forming perennial often grown as an annual. Yellow or orange-yellow flower heads, sometimes with central white spots, are borne singly in early summer above rosettes of narrow, silver-backed leaves. H 9in (23cm), S 8–12in (20–30cm).

Z8–10 H10–6

***Potentilla* 'Yellow Queen'**
Clump-forming perennial with strawberry-like, dark green leaves and bright yellow flowers in midsummer. H to 24in (60cm) or more, S 18in (45cm).

Z5–8 H8–5

***Ranunculus acris* 'Flore Pleno'**
(Double meadow buttercup)
Clump-forming perennial. Wiry stems with lobed and cut leaves act as a foil for rosetted, double, golden yellow flowers in late spring and early summer. H and S 18–24in (45–60cm).

Z4–8 H8–1

Arctotheca calendula, illus. p.294
Coreopsis 'Sunray', illus. p.337
Coreopsis tinctoria 'Golden Crown'
DAYLILIES, illus. p.257
Duchesnea indica
HOSTAS, illus. pp.288–9
IRISES, illus. pp.234–5
ORCHIDS, illus. pp.296–9
PRIMROSES, illus. pp.272–3

YELLOW

***Sedum aizoon* 'Aurantiacum'**
Erect perennial with red stems carrying fleshy, toothed, dark green leaves. In summer produces gently rounded heads of dark yellow flowers followed by red seed capsules. H and S 18in (45cm).

Z3–8 H8–1

Tropaeolum polyphyllum
Prostrate perennial with spurred, short, trumpet-shaped, rich yellow flowers, borne singly in summer above trailing, gray-green leaves and stems. May spread widely once established but is good on a bank. H 2–3in (5–8cm), S 12in (30cm) or more.

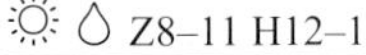

Z8–11 H12–1

Coreopsis lanceolata
Bushy perennial that in summer freely produces daisylike, bright yellow flower heads on branching stems. Lance-shaped leaves are borne on flower stems. Propagate by seed or division. H 18in (45cm), S 12in (30cm).

Z4–9 H9–1

Hieracium lanatum
Clump-forming perennial that produces mounds of broad, downy gray leaves, above which dandelion-like yellow flower heads appear on wiry stems in summer. H 12–18in (30–45cm), S 12in (30cm).

Z5–8 H8–5

Coreopsis verticillata
Bushy perennial with finely divided, dark green foliage and many tiny, star-shaped, golden flower heads borne throughout summer. Divide and replant in spring. H 16–24in (40–60cm), S 12in (30cm).

Z4–9 H9–1

Impatiens repens
Evergreen, creeping perennial with rooting stems. Has small, oval to rounded leaves and, in summer, yellow flowers, each with a large, hairy spur. H to 2in (5cm), S indefinite.

Z13–15 H12–4

Eriophyllum lanatum, syn. *Bahia lanata*
Perennial forming low cushions of divided silvery leaves. Daisylike yellow flower heads are produced freely in summer, usually singly, on gray stems. H and S 12in (30cm).

Z5–8 H8–5

Inula ensifolia
Clump-forming perennial with small, lance-shaped to elliptic leaves, bearing many daisylike yellow flower heads, singly on wiry stalks, in late summer. H and S 12in (30cm).

Z4–9 H9–1

***Calceolaria* 'John Innes'**
Vigorous, evergreen, clump-forming perennial that in spring-summer produces large, pouchlike, reddish brown-spotted, deep yellow flowers, several to each stem. Has broadly oval, basal, midgreen leaves. H 6–8in (15–20cm), S 10–12in (25–30cm).

Z8–9 H6–1

ORANGE

Aeschynanthus speciosus, syn. *A. splendens*
Evergreen, trailing perennial with waxy, narrowly oval leaves usually carried in whorls. Erect, tubular, bright orange-red flowers are borne in large clusters in summer. H and S 12–24in (30–60cm).

Z14–15 H12–1

Geum coccineum, syn. *Geum* x *borisii* of gardens
Clump-forming perennial with irregularly lobed leaves, above which in summer rise slender, branching, hairy stems bearing single orange flowers with prominent yellow stamens. H and S 12in (30cm).

Z5–8 H8–5

Rhodiola heterodonta, syn. *Sedum heterodontum*, *S. rosea* var. *heterodontum*
Clump-forming perennial with heads of yellow or red, sometimes greenish flowers from spring to early summer. Stems bear toothed, blue-green leaves. H 18in (45cm), S 10in (25cm).

Z5–9 H9–5

Coreopsis auriculata 'Superba'
Coreopsis 'Goldfink'
DAYLILIES, illus. p.257
Inula oculis-christi
IRISES, illus. pp.234–5
Mimulus guttatus
Oenothera fruticosa subsp. *glauca*
PRIMROSES, illus. pp.272–3
Wachendorfia thyrsiflora

DAYLILIES, illus. p.257
IRISES, illus. pp.234–5
PELARGONIUMS, illus. pp.246–7
PRIMROSES, illus. pp.272–3

WHITE–PINK

Tricyrtis hirta* var. *alba
Upright, rhizomatous perennial that bears clusters of large, bell-shaped, spurred white flowers, occasionally purple-spotted, in upper leaf axils of hairy, stem-clasping, dark green leaves during late summer and early autumn. H 18–24in (45–60cm), S 18in (45cm).

Z4–9 H9–1

***Sedum spectabile* 'Brilliant'**
(Ice plant)
Clump-forming perennial that from late summer to autumn produces flat heads of bright rose-pink flowers. These are borne profusely over a mass of fleshy, gray-green leaves and attract butterflies. H and S 12–18in (30–45cm).

Z49 H9–1

***Schizostylis coccinea* 'Sunrise'**
Clump-forming, rhizomatous perennial that in early autumn produces spikes of large, shallowly cup-shaped pink flowers above grassy, midgreen foliage. H 24in (60cm), S 9–12in (23–30cm).

Z7–9 H9–7

RED–YELLOW

***Schizostylis coccinea* 'Major'**, syn. *S.c.* 'Grandiflora'
Rhizomatous perennial with long, narrow, grasslike leaves. Gladiolus-like spikes of cup-shaped, bright crimson flowers appear in autumn. H 24in (60cm) or more, S 12in (30cm) or more.

Z7–9 H9–7

Liriope muscari
Evergreen, spreading perennial that in autumn carries spikes of thickly clustered, rounded-bell-shaped, lavender or purple-blue flowers among narrow, glossy, dark green leaves. H 12in (30cm), S 18in (45cm).

Z6–10 H10–6

Cautleya spicata
Upright perennial that in summer and early autumn bears spikes of light orange or soft yellow flowers in maroon-red bracts. Has handsome, long, midgreen leaves. Needs a sheltered site and rich, deep soil. H 24in (60cm), S 20in (50cm).

Z7–9 H9–7

Chirita lavandulacea
Evergreen, erect perennial with downy, pale green leaves to 8in (20cm) long. In leaf axils has clusters of lavender-blue flowers with white tubes. May be sown in succession to flower from spring to autumn. H and S 24in (60cm).

Z14–15 H12–10

Senecio pulcher
Perennial with leathery, hairy, dark green leaves. In summer-autumn produces handsome, daisylike, yellow-centered, bright purplish-pink flower heads. H 18–24in (45–60cm), S 20in (50cm).

Z11–15 H12–6

Arctotheca calendula
(Cape dandelion)
Carpeting perennial. Leaves are woolly below, rough-haired above. Heads of daisylike, bright yellow flowers with darker yellow centers appear from late spring to autumn. H 12in (30cm), S indefinite.

Z12–15 H12–10

OTHER RECOMMENDED PLANTS:
Astrantia major, illus. p.277
Astrantia major subsp. *involucrata*, illus. p.277
Astrantia maxima, illus. p.277
LATE-BLOOMING ASTERS, illus. p.262
PELARGONIUMS, illus. pp.246–7
Schizostylis coccinea 'Mrs Hegarty'
Geranium wallichianum 'Buxton's Variety', illus. p.287
Mimulus guttatus
LATE-BLOOMING ASTERS, illus. p.262
ORCHIDS, illus. pp.296–9
Osteospermum 'Buttermilk', illus. p.290
Tricyrtis macrantha

Begonias

The genus *Begonia* is one of the most versatile, providing interest year-round. Semperflorens begonias are excellent for summer bedding, while the Rex-cultorum group has distinctive and handsome foliage. Others, such as the Tuberhybrida cultivars with their large and showy blooms, are grown mainly for their flowers. Many also make attractive plants for hanging baskets.

B. 'Merry Christmas'

B. masoniana

B. prismatocarpa

B. 'Billie Langdon'

B. scharffii

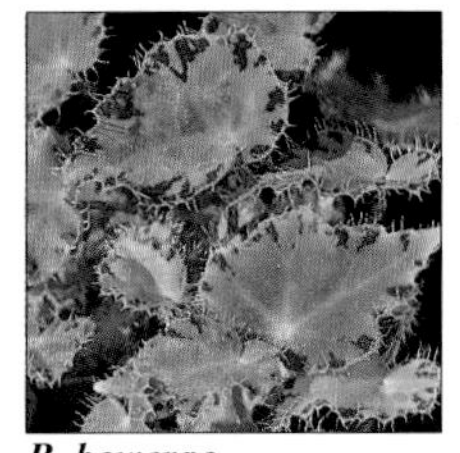
B. bowerae

B. 'Apricot Cascade'

B. albopicta

B. 'Weltoniensis'

B. 'Orpha C. Fox'

B. 'Flamboyant'

B. 'Can-Can'

B. foliosa

B. 'Ingramii'

B. 'Roy Hartley'

B. 'Helen Lewis'

B. olsoniae

B. metallica

B. 'Lucerna'

B. 'Duartei'

***B. manicata* 'Crispa'**

B. 'Orange Rubra'

B. manicata

B. serratipetala

B. 'Red Ascot'

B. 'Organdy'

B. 'Thurstonii'

***B. pustulata* 'Argentea'**

B. 'Tiger Paws'

B. 'Oliver Twist'

B. sutherlandii

Orchids

Flamboyant, exotic, even seductive, orchids are prized for their unusual flowers. Their aura of mystique and many popular misconceptions may have discouraged gardeners from growing these beautiful plants, but their cultivation is not always difficult. Indeed, some will thrive happily indoors as house plants.

There are two main groups. Terrestrials grow in a wide range of habitats in the wild. Epiphytes, the more showy of the two and mostly native to the tropics, cling to tree branches or rocks, obtaining nourishment through their leaves and aerial roots. They need special potting mixes and often must be grown under cover (see also 'Orchids', p.637).

(Key: x *Brass.* – x *Brassolaeliocattleya*; *Cym.* – *Cymbidium*; x *Oda.* – x *Odontioda*; *Odm.* – *Odontoglossum*; *Paphioped.* – *Paphiopedilum*; x *Soph.* – x *Sophrolaeliocattleya*; e – epiphyte; t – terrestrial)

Coelogyne cristata [e]

Masdevallia infracta [e]

Lemboglossum rossii [e]

Cypripedium acaule [t]

Masdevallia tovarensis [e]

Dendrobium infundibulum [e]

Coelogyne flaccida [e]

Calanthe vestita [t]

Lemboglossum cervantesii [e]

Dendrobium aphyllum [e]

***Phalaenopsis* Allegria** [e]

***Odm.* Royal Occasion** [e]

***Paphiopedilum* Freckles** [t] (!)

Angraecum sesquipedale [e]

Paphiopedilum fairrieanum [t] (!)

Oncidium ornithorrhynchum [e]

Paphiopedilum niveum [t] (!)

Coelogyne nitida [e]

***Cymbidium* Portelet Bay** [e] (!)

Paphiopedilum callosum [t] (!)

Cypripedium reginae [t]

Spiranthes cernua [t]

Odm. crispum [e]

***Miltoniopsis* Robert Strauss 'Ardingly'** [e]

***Cymbidium* Strathbraan** [e] (!)

Paphiopedilum bellatulum [t] (!)

Brassavola nodosa [e]

Paphiopedilum appletonianum [t] (!)

Lemboglossum bictoniense [e]

Dendrobium nobile [e]

Ophrys tenthredinifera [t]

Calypso bulbosa [t]

x *Laeliocattleya* Rojo 'Mont Millais' [e]

Lemboglossum cordatum [e]

x *Oda.* Mount Bingham [e]

Cymbidium Strath Kanaid [e] ①

x *Wilsonara* Hambuhren Stern 'Cheam' [e]

x *Brass.* Hetherington Horace 'Coronation' [e]

Pleione bulbocodioides [t]

Cattleya J.A. Carbone [e]

x *Vuylstekeara* Cambria 'Lensing's Favorite' [e]

Cymbidium Pontac 'Mont Millais' [e] ①

x *Oda.* Pacific Gold x *Odm. cordatum* [e]

Laelia anceps [e]

Bletilla striata [t]

x *Soph.* Trizac 'Purple Emperor' [e]

x *Brassocattleya* Mount Adams [e]

x *Brass.* St. Helier [e]

Miltoniopsis Anjou 'St. Patrick' [e]

Epidendrum ibaguense [e]

Rossioglossum grande [e]

Cattleya bowringiana [e]

Odm. Le Nez Point [e]

Cym. Strathdon 'Cooksbridge Noel' [e] ①

Paphiopedilum Maudiae [t] ①

x *Odontocidium* Artur Elle 'Colombian' [e]

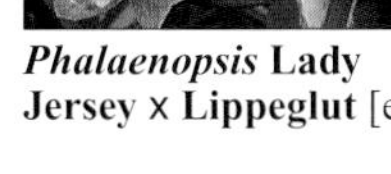
Phalaenopsis Lady Jersey x Lippeglut [e]

Masdevallia coccinea [e]

x *Oda.* Petit Port [e]

Phaius tankervilleae [t]

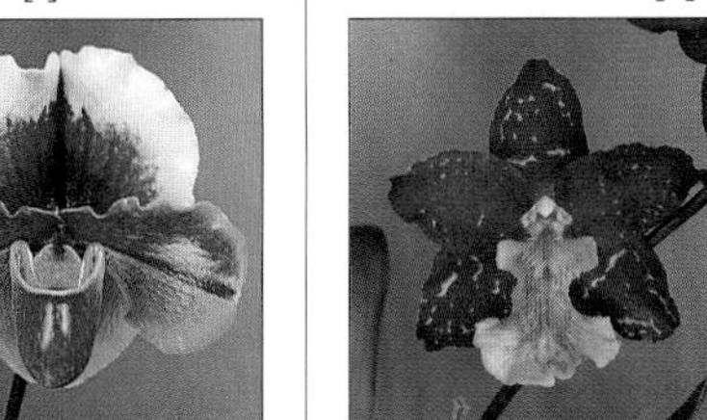
Paphiopedilum Lyric 'Glendora' [t] ①

x *Odontocidium* Tiger Butter x *Wilsonara* Wigg's 'Kay' [e]

Orchids continued

Phalaenopsis cornu-cervi [e]

Cymbidium devonianum [e] (!)

Paphiopedilum sukhakulii [t] (!)

Paphioped. Buckhurst 'Mont Millais' [t] (!)

Miltonia candida [e]

Zygopetalum mackaii [e]

Paphiopedilum haynaldianum [t] (!)

Gomesa planifolia [e]

Odm. Eric Young [e]

x *Aliceara* Dark Warrior [e]

Zygopetalum Perrenoudii [e]

Coelogyne speciosa [e]

Cymbidium King's Loch 'Cooksbridge' [e] (!)

Masdevallia wagneriana [e]

x *Odontocidium* Tigersun 'Orbec' [e]

Gongora quinquenervis [e]

Orchis morio [t]

Ophrys fusca [t]

Phalaenopsis Lundy [e]

Oncidium tigrinum [e]

Bulbophyllum careyanum [e]

Cymbidium hookerianum [e] (!)

Cymbidium Caithness Ice 'Trinity' [e] (!)

Cymbidium elegans [e] (!)

Ophrys lutea [t]

Miltonia clowesii [e]

Cymbidium tracyanum [e] (!)

Cypripedium macranthos [t]

Vanda Rothschildiana [e]

Epidendrum difforme [e]

Cypripedium calceolus [t]

□ WHITE

Maxillaria porphyrostele [e]

x *Potinara* **Cherub 'Spring Daffodil'** [e]

Laelia cinnabarina [e]

Dendrobium chrysotoxum [e]

Lycaste cruenta [e]

Psychopsis papilio [e]

x *Odontocidium* **Tiger Hambuhren** [e]

Oncidium flexuosum [e]

Ada aurantiaca [e]

Cypripedium pubescens [t]

x *Soph.* **Hazel Boyd 'Apricot Glow'** [e]

x *Oda.* **(Chantos x Marzorka)** x *Odm.* **Buttercrisp** [e]

Cymbidium **Christmas Angel 'Cooksbridge Sunburst'** [e] ①

Paphiopedilum venustum [t] ①

***Spathiphyllum* 'Mauna Loa'**
Robust, evergreen, tufted perennial with rhizomes. Has long, lance-shaped, glossy leaves. Irregularly bears fleshy white spadices of fragrant flowers enclosed in large, oval white spathes. H and S 18–24in (45–60cm).

◐ 💧 ① Z14–15 H12–6

Episcia dianthiflora, syn. *Alsobia dianthiflora* (Lace flower)
Evergreen perennial with creeping, prostrate stems. Has thick, velvety leaves with brownish midribs and, intermittently, pure white flowers with fringed petals. H 4in (10cm), S indefinite.

◐ ◊ Z14–15 H12–6

Hemigraphis repanda
Evergreen, prostrate perennial with spreading, rooting stems. Lance-shaped, toothed, purple-tinged leaves, 2in (5cm) long, are darker purple below. Has tiny, tubular white flowers intermittently. H to 6in (15cm), S indefinite.

◐ ◊ Z14–15 H12–1

OTHER RECOMMENDED PLANTS:
AFRICAN VIOLETS, illus. p.302
Aglaonema commutatum
Aglaonema 'Malay Beauty'
BROMELIADS, illus. p.265
Peperomia argyreia
Sonerila margaritacea

□ WHITE

Spathiphyllum wallisii
(Peace lily, White sails)
Evergreen, tufted, rhizomatous perennial. Has clusters of long, lance-shaped leaves. Fleshy white spadices of fragrant flowers in white spathes are irregularly produced. H and S 12in (30cm) or more.

Z14–15 H12–1

Pilea cadierei (Aluminum plant)
Evergreen, bushy perennial with broadly oval leaves, each with a sharply pointed tip and raised silvery patches that appear quilted. Has insignificant greenish flowers.
H and S 12in (30cm).

Z13–15 H12–1

***Tradescantia fluminensis* 'Variegata'**, syn. *T. albiflora* 'Variegata'
Evergreen, trailing perennial with rooting stems and leaves irregularly striped creamy white. Intermittently has clusters of white flowers. H 12in (30cm), S indefinite.

Z14–15 H12–1

***Fittonia albivenis* Argyroneura Group** (Silver net-leaf)
Evergreen, creeping perennial with small, oval, white-veined, olive green leaves. Remove flowers if they form. H to 6in (15cm), S indefinite.

Z14–15 H12–1

***Tradescantia fluminensis* 'Albovittata'**,
syn. *T. albiflora* 'Albovittata'
Strong-growing, evergreen perennial with trailing, rooting stems. Bluish green leaves have broad white stripes. Bears small white flowers. H 12in (30cm), S indefinite.

Z14–15 H12–1

***Aglaonema commutatum* 'Treubii'**
Evergreen, erect, tufted perennial. Lance-shaped leaves to 12in (30cm) long are marked with pale green or silver. Occasionally has greenish white spathes. H and S to 18in (45cm).

Z14–15 H12–1

***Glechoma hederacea* 'Variegata'**
(Variegated ground ivy)
Evergreen, carpeting perennial that has small, heart-shaped leaves, with white marbling, on trailing stems. Bears insignificant flowers in summer. Spreads rapidly but is useful for a container. H 6in (15cm), S indefinite.

Z6–9 H9–6

Helleborus* x *hybridus
(Lenten rose)
Evergreen, clump-forming perennial with dense, divided foliage, above which rise nodding, cup-shaped white, pink, or purple flowers, sometimes darker spotted, in winter or early spring. H and S 18in (45cm).

Z6–9 H9–6

Peperomia caperata
(Emerald ripple)
Evergreen, bushy perennial with pinkish leaf stalks. Has oval, fleshy, wrinkled, dark green leaves, to 2in (5cm) long, with sunken veins; spikes of white flowers appear irregularly. H and S to 6in (15cm).

Z13–15 H12–1

Sonerila margaritacea 'Argentea'
Sonerila margaritacea 'Hendersonii'
Spathiphyllum floribundum
Spathiphyllum wallisii 'Clevelandii'

***Chlorophytum comosum* 'Vittatum'**
Evergreen, tufted, rosette-forming perennial. Long, narrow, lance-shaped, creamy white leaves have green stripes and margins. Irregularly has small, star-shaped white flowers on thin stems. H and S 12in (30cm).

Z12–15 H12–1

***Aspidistra elatior* 'Variegata'**
Evergreen, rhizomatous perennial with upright, narrow, glossy, dark green leaves that are longitudinally cream-striped. Occasionally has inconspicuous cream to purple flowers near soil level. H 24in (60cm), S 18in (45cm).

Z13–15 H12–1

***Oplismenus africanus* 'Variegatus'**, syn. *O. hirtellus* 'Variegatus'
Evergreen, creeping, perennial grass with wiry, rooting stems. White-striped, wavy-edged leaves are often tinged pink. Bears inconspicuous flowers intermittently. H 8in (20cm) or more, S indefinite.

Z13–15 H12–1

Helleborus niger (Christmas rose)
Evergreen, clump-forming perennial with divided, deep green leaves and cup-shaped, nodding white flowers with golden stamens, borne in winter or early spring. H and S 12in (30cm).

Z3–8 H8–1

Helleborus* x *sternii
Evergreen, clump-forming perennial with divided leaves and cup-shaped, often pink-tinged, pale green flowers borne in terminal clusters in winter and early spring. H and S 18in (45cm).

Z6–9 H9–6

Helleborus* x *hybridus (Lenten rose)
Evergreen, clump-forming perennial with dense, divided foliage, above which rise nodding, cup-shaped white, pink, or purple flowers, sometimes darker spotted, in winter or early spring. H and S 18in (45cm).

Z6–9 H9–6

AFRICAN VIOLETS, illus. p.302
Bergenia cordifolia 'Purpurea', illus. p.269
BROMELIADS, illus. p.265
Episcia cupreata 'Metallica'
Episcia cupreata 'Tropical Topaz'
ORCHIDS, illus. pp.296–9
Peristrophe hyssopifolia
Tradescantia zebrina 'Quadricolor'

***Streptocarpus* 'Nicola'**
Evergreen, stemless perennial with a rosette of strap-shaped, wrinkled leaves. Funnel-shaped rose-pink flowers are produced intermittently in small clusters. H l0in (25cm), S 20in (50cm).

Z13–15 H12–10

Tradescantia zebrina, syn. *Zebrina pendula* (Bronze inch plant)
Evergreen, trailing or mat-forming perennial. Bluish green leaves, purple-tinged beneath, have 2 broad silver bands. Has pink or violet-blue flowers intermittently during the year. H 6in (15cm), S indefinite.

Z14–15 H12–1

Episcia cupreata (Flame violet)
Evergreen, creeping perennial. Has small, downy, wrinkled leaves, usually silver-veined or -banded, and, intermittently, scarlet flowers marked yellow within. H 4in (10cm), S indefinite.

Z14–15 H12–7

Anthurium scherzerianum 'Rothschildianum'
Bergenia 'Ballawley'
Bergenia crassifolia
BROMELIADS, illus. p.265

African violets

African violet is the common name for the genus *Saintpaulia*. These small, rosetted perennials may be grown as summer bedding in warm, humid climates but also make attractive indoor pot plants, flowering freely if kept in a draft-free, light, humid position, specially if grown under fluorescent lights. A wide range of flower colors and forms is available.

***S.* 'Rococo Anna'**

***S.* 'Garden News'**

***S.* 'Starry Trail'**

***S.* 'Pip Squeek'**

***S.* 'Colorado'**

***S.* 'Porcelain'**

***S.* 'Ice Maiden'**

***S.* 'Zoja'**

***S.* 'Bright Eyes'**

***S.* 'Delft'**

RED–PURPLE

Anthurium scherzerianum
(Flamingo flower)
Evergreen, tufted perennial with erect, leathery, dark green leaves to 8in (20cm) long. Has large, long-lasting, bright red spathes and fleshy red to orange spadices. H and S 12–24in (30–60cm).

Z11–12 H12–10

Helleborus* x *hybridus
(Lenten rose)
Evergreen, clump-forming perennial with dense, divided foliage, above which rise nodding, cup-shaped white, pink, or purple flowers, sometimes darker spotted, in winter or early spring. H and S 18in (45cm).

Z6–9 H9–6

Gerbera jamesonii
(Barberton daisy)
Evergreen, upright perennial with daisy-like, variably colored flower heads borne intermittently on long stems, and basal rosettes of large, jagged leaves. Flowers are excellent for cutting. H 24in (60cm), S 18in (45cm).

Z11 H12–6

***Phormium* 'Bronze Baby'**
Evergreen, upright perennial with tufts of bold, stiff, pointed, wine red leaves. Panicles of reddish flowers are occasionally produced on purplish stems during summer.
H and S 18–24in (45–60cm).

Z9–11 H12–6

***Tellima grandiflora* Rubra Group**, syn. *T.g.* 'Purpurea'
Semi-evergreen, clump-forming perennial with a mass of hairy, basal, reddish purple leaves underlaid dark green. In late spring, erect stems bear spikes of bell-shaped, pinkish cream flowers. H and S 24in (60cm).

Z4–8 H8–1

***Fittonia albivenis* Verschaffeltii Group**, syn. *F. verschaffeltii* (Painted net-leaf)
Evergreen, creeping perennial with small, oval, red-veined, olive green leaves. Flowers are best removed as they form. H to 6in (15cm), S indefinite.

Z14 –15 H12–1

Alternanthera ficoidea var. *amoena*
Alternanthera ficoidea 'Versicolor'
Bergenia purpurascens
Bertolonia marmorata

ORCHIDS, illus. pp.296–9

PURPLE

***Ophiopogon planiscapus* 'Nigrescens'**
Evergreen, spreading, clump-forming perennial, grown for its distinctive, grasslike black leaves. Racemes of lilac flowers in summer are followed by black fruits. H 9in (23cm), S 12in (30cm).

Z6–11 H12–1

***Tradescantia pallida* 'Purpurea'**
Evergreen, creeping perennial with dark purple stems and slightly fleshy leaves. Has pink or pink-and-white flowers in summer. H 12–16in (30–40cm), S 12in (30cm) or more.

Z11–12 H12–1

***Ajuga reptans* 'Atropurpurea'**
Evergreen, groundcover perennial, spreading freely by runners, with small rosettes of glossy, deep bronze-purple leaves. Short spikes of blue flowers appear in spring.
H 6in (15cm), S 36in (90cm).

Z3–9 H9–1

Helleborus atrorubens
Heterocentron elegans, illus. p.284
Lathraea clandestina, illus. p.271
ORCHIDS, illus. pp.296–9

Elatostema repens
(Watermelon begonia)
Evergreen, creeping perennial with rooting stems. Broadly oval, olive green leaves have purplish brown edges and paler green centers. Flowers are insignificant. H 4in (10cm), S indefinite.

Z8–10 H10–8

Tradescantia sillamontana, syn. *T. pexata*, *T. velutina*
Evergreen, erect perennial. Oval, stem-clasping leaves are densely covered with woolly white hairs. Has clusters of small, bright purplish pink flowers in summer. H and S to 12in (30cm).

Z14–15 H12–10

Streptocarpus rexii

Tetranema roseum, syn. *T. mexicanum*
(Mexican foxglove, Mexican violet)
Short-stemmed perennial with crowded, stalkless leaves, bluish green beneath. Intermittently has nodding purple flowers with paler throats. H to 8in (20cm), S 12in (30cm).

Z10–15 H12–10

***Ajuga reptans* 'Multicolor'**, syn. *A.r.* 'Rainbow'
Evergreen, mat-forming perennial. Dark green leaves, marked with cream and pink, make a good groundcover. Spikes of small blue flowers appear in spring. H 5in (12cm), S 18in (45cm).

Z3–9 H9–1

***Streptocarpus* 'Constant Nymph'**
Evergreen, stemless perennial with a rosette of strap-shaped, wrinkled leaves. Funnel-shaped, purplish blue flowers, darker veined and yellow-throated, are intermittently produced in small clusters. H 10in (25cm), S 20in (50cm).

Z13–15 H12–10

PURPLE–GREEN

Cyanotis somaliensis (Pussy ears)
Evergreen, creeping perennial. Small, narrow, glossy, dark green leaves with white hairs surround stems. Has purplish blue flowers in leaf axils in winter-spring. H 2in (5cm), S indefinite.

Z13–15 H12–10

***Maranta leuconeura* 'Erythroneura'**, syn. *M.l.* 'Erythrophylla' (Prayer plant)
Evergreen perennial. Oblong leaves have veins marked red with paler yellowish green midribs and are upright at night, flat by day. H and S to 12in (30cm).

Z14–15 H12–1

***Sansevieria trifasciata* 'Hahnii'**
Evergreen, stemless perennial with a rosette of about 5 stiff, erect, broadly lance-shaped and pointed leaves, banded horizontally with pale green or white. Occasionally has small, pale green flowers. H 6–12in (15–30cm), S 4in (10cm).

Z11 H12–10

Aeschynanthus pulcher
BROMELIADS, illus. p.265
Cyanotis kewensis
Tradescantia zebrina 'Purpusii'

GREEN

Calathea makoyana
(Peacock plant)
Evergreen, clump-forming perennial. Horizontal leaves, 12in (30cm) long, are dark and light green above, reddish purple below. Intermittently has short spikes of white flowers. H to 2ft (60cm), S to 4ft (1.2m).

Z15–15 H12–1

Aglaonema pictum
Evergreen, erect, tufted perennial. Oval leaves, to 6in (15cm) long, are irregularly marked with grayish white or gray-green. Has creamy white spathes in summer. H and S to 24in (60cm).

Z14–15 H12–1

***Aglaonema* 'Silver King'**
Evergreen, erect, tufted perennial. Broadly lance-shaped, midgreen leaves to 12in (30cm) long are marked with dark and light green. Has greenish white spathes in summer. H and S to 18in (45cm).

Z14–15 H12–6

Maranta leuconeura var. ***kerchoviana*** (Rabbit tracks)
Evergreen perennial that intermittently bears white to mauve flowers. Oblong leaves with dark brown blotches become greener with age and are upright at night, flat by day. H and S to 12in (30cm).

Z14–15 H12–1

Welwitschia mirabilis, syn. *W. bainesii*
Evergreen perennial with a short, woody trunk. Has 2 strap-shaped leaves, to 8ft 2.5m (8ft) long, with tips splitting to form many tendril-like strips. Bears small, reddish brown cones. Rare and difficult. H to 12in (30cm), S indefinite.

Z13–15 H12–10

Peperomia marmorata
(Silver heart)
Evergreen, bushy perennial with insignificant flowers. Has oval, long-pointed, fleshy, dull green leaves, marked with grayish white and quilted above, reddish below. H and S to 8in (20cm).

Z13–15 H12–1

Stachys byzantina, syn. *S. lanata*, *S. olympica*
(Lambs' ears, Woolly betony)
Evergreen, mat-forming perennial with woolly gray foliage that is excellent for a border front or as a groundcover. Bears mauve-pink flowers in summer. H 12–15in (30–38cm), S 24in (60cm).

Z4–8 H8–1

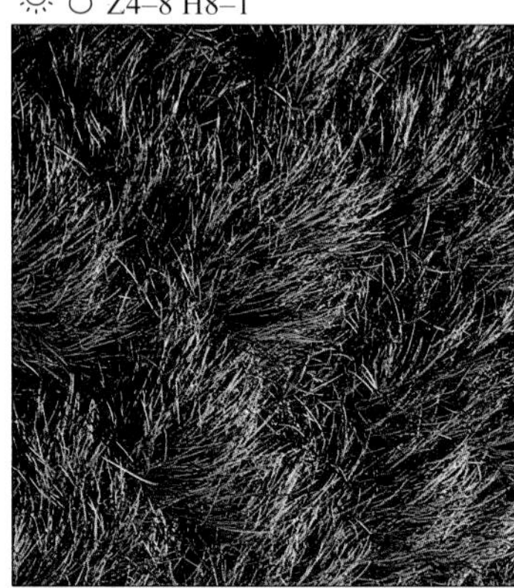

Ophiopogon japonicus
Evergreen, clump or mat-forming perennial with grasslike, glossy, dark green foliage. Spikes of lilac flowers in late summer are followed by blue-black berries. H 12in (30cm), S indefinite.

Z7–10 H12–1

Helleborus argutifolius
Clump-forming perennial with evergreen, divided, spiny, dark green leaves and cup-shaped, pale green flowers borne in large clusters in winter-spring.
H 24in (60cm), S 18in (45cm).

Z6–9 H9–6

Soleirolia soleirolii, syn. *Helxine soleirolii* (Baby's tears)
Usually evergreen, invasive, prostrate perennial with small, round, vivid green leaves that form a carpet. May choke other plants if not controlled.
H 2in (5cm), S indefinite.

Z10–15 H12–10

Callisia repens
Evergreen, creeping perennial with rooting stems and densely packed leaves, sometimes white-banded and often purplish beneath. Rarely has inconspicuous white flowers in winter.
H 4in (10cm), S indefinite.

Z14–15 H12–10

Ajuga pyramidalis 'Metallica Crispa'
Ajuga reptans 'Jungle Beauty'
Aspidistra elatior
Callisia navicularis
Chamaemelum nobile
Chamaemelum nobile 'Treneague'
Chlorophytum comosum
Peperomia clusiifolia
Peperomia griseoargentea
Peperomia metallica
Peperomia obtusifolia
Peperomia rubella
Plectranthus oertendahlii
Plectranthus verticillatus
Tradescantia fluminensis

GREEN

Drosera spatulata
Evergreen, insectivorous perennial with rosettes of spoon-shaped leaves that have sensitive red, glandular hairs. Has many small pink or white flowers on leafless stems in summer. H and S to 3in (8cm).

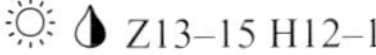 Z13–15 H12–1

Peperomia glabella (Wax privet)
Evergreen perennial with wide-spreading red stems. Has broadly oval, fleshy, glossy, bright green leaves to 2in (5cm) long and insignificant flowers. H to 6in (15cm), S 12in (30cm).

Z13–15 H12–1

Helleborus viridis
(Green hellebore)
Clump-forming perennial with deciduous, divided, dark green leaves. Bears cup-shaped green flowers in late winter or early spring.
H and S 12in (30cm).

Z6–8 H8–1

Drosera capensis (Cape sundew)
Evergreen, insectivorous perennial. Rosettes of narrow leaves have sensitive, red, glandular hairs. Many small purple flowers are borne on leafless stems in summer. H and S to 6in (15cm).

Z8–10 H10–8

***Peperomia obtusifolia* 'Variegata'**
Evergreen, bushy perennial with spade-shaped, fleshy leaves to 8in (20cm) long that have irregular, yellowish green to creamy white margins and usually grayish centers. Flowers are insignificant. H and S to 6in (15cm).

Z13–15 H12–10

Pilea nummulariifolia
(Creeping Charlie)
Evergreen, mat-forming perennial with creeping, rooting reddish stems. Rounded, pale green leaves, about ¾in (2cm) wide, have a corrugated surface. Flowers are insignificant. H to 2in (5cm), S 12in (30cm).

Z13–15 H12–1

BROMELIADS, illus. p.265
Helleborus lividus
ORCHIDS, illus. pp.296–9
Tolmiea menziesii

GREEN–YELLOW

***Iresine herbstii* 'Aureoreticulata'**
Evergreen, bushy perennial with red stems and inconspicuous flowers. Rounded, midgreen leaves, 4in (10cm) long, have yellow or red veins and notched tips.
H to 24in (60cm), S 18in (45cm).

Z11–12 h12–1

Dionaea muscipula (Venus flytrap)
Evergreen, insectivorous perennial with rosettes of 6 or more spreading, hinged leaves, pink-flushed inside, edged with stiff bristles. Clusters of tiny white flowers are carried in summer.
H 4in (10cm), S 12in (30cm).

Z12–15 H12–1

Helleborus foetidus
(Stinking hellebore)
Evergreen, clump-forming perennial with deeply divided, dark green leaves and, in late winter and early spring, panicles of cup-shaped, red-margined, pale green flowers.
H and S 18in (45cm).

Z6–9 H9–6

***Sansevieria trifasciata* 'Golden Hahnii'**
Evergreen, stemless perennial with a rosette of about 5 stiff, erect, broadly lance-shaped leaves with wide yellow borders. Sometimes bears small, pale green flowers. H 6–12in (15–30cm), S 4in (10cm).

Z14–15 H12–1

Nautilocalyx lynchii
Robust, evergreen, erect, bushy perennial. Broadly lance-shaped, slightly wrinkled leaves are glossy, greenish red above, reddish beneath.
In summer has tubular, red-haired, pale yellow flowers with red calyces.
H and S to 24in (60cm).

Z14–15 H12–1

Adonis amurensis, illus. p.275
BROMELIADS, illus. p.265
ORCHIDS, illus. pp.296–9
Peperomia obtusifolia 'Greengold'
Pilea involucrata
Tradescantia spathacea 'Vittata'

GRASSES, BAMBOOS, RUSHES, *and* SEDGES

WHITE–GREEN

***Cortaderia selloana* 'Silver Comet'**
Evergreen, clump-forming, perennial grass with very narrow, sharp-edged, recurved leaves, 3ft (1m) long, that have silver margins. Carries plumelike panicles of spikelets from late summer. H 4–5ft (1.2–1.5m), S 3ft (1m).

Z7–11 H12–7

***Phalaris arundinacea* var. *picta*,** syn. *P.a.* 'Picta' (Gardener's garters)
Evergreen, spreading, perennial grass with broad, white-striped leaves. Produces narrow panicles of spikelets in summer. Normally invasive. H 3ft (1m), S indefinite.

Z4–9 H9–1

***Holcus mollis* 'Albovariegatus',** syn. *H.m.* 'Variegatus' (Variegated creeping soft grass)
Evergreen, spreading, perennial grass with white-striped leaves and hairy nodes. In summer carries purplish white flower spikes. H 12–18in (30–45cm), S indefinite.

Z5–9 H9–5

***Pleioblastus variegatus*,** syn. *Arundinaria fortunei*, *A. variegata* (Dwarf white-stripe bamboo)
Evergreen, slow-spreading bamboo with narrow, slightly downy, white-striped leaves. Stems are branched near the base. H 30in (80cm), S indefinite.

Z6–11 H12–6

***Arundo donax* var. *versicolor*,** syn. *A.d.* 'Variegata'
Herbaceous, rhizomatous, perennial grass with strong stems bearing broad, creamy-white-striped leaves. May bear dense, erect panicles of whitish yellow spikelets in late summer. H 8–10ft (2.5–3m), S 2ft (60cm).

Z7–15 H12–1

***Sasa veitchii*,** syn. *S. albomarginata*
Evergreen, slow-spreading bamboo. Leaves, 10in (25cm) long, soon develop white edges. Stems, often purple, produce a single branch at each node. White powder appears beneath nodes. H to 5ft (1.5m), S indefinite.

Z6–15 H12–1

Lagurus ovatus (Hare's-tail grass)
Tuft-forming, annual grass that in early summer bears dense, egg-shaped, soft panicles of white flower spikes with golden stamens, lasting well into autumn. Leaves are long, narrow, and flat. Self-seeds readily. H 18in (45cm), S 6in (15cm).

H12–1

***Cortaderia selloana* 'Sunningdale Silver'**
Evergreen, clump-forming, perennial grass with narrow, sharp-edged, recurved leaves, 5ft (1.5m) long. Bears long-lasting, feathery panicles of creamy white spikelets in late summer. H 7ft (2.1m), S 4ft (1.2m).

Z7–11 H12–7

***Glyceria maxima* 'Variegata',** syn. *G. aquatica* 'Variegata'
Herbaceous, spreading, perennial grass with cream-striped leaves often tinged pink at the base. Bears open panicles of greenish spikelets in summer. H 30in (80cm), S indefinite.

Z4–9 H10–3

***Miscanthus sinensis* 'Zebrinus'**
Herbaceous, clump-forming, perennial grass. Leaves, hairy beneath, have transverse, yellowish white ring markings. May carry awned, hairy white spikelets in fan-shaped panicles in autumn. H 4ft (1.2m), S 3ft (1m).

Z4–9 H9–1

***Schoenoplectus lacustris* subsp. *tabernaemontani* 'Zebrinus'**
Evergreen, spreading, perennial sedge with leafless stems, striped horizontally with white, and brown spikelets in summer. Withstands brackish water. H 5ft (1.5m), S indefinite.

 Z6–9 H9–6

OTHER RECOMMENDED PLANTS:
Arrhenatherum elatius subsp. *bulbosum* 'Variegatum'
Arundo donax
Carex riparia 'Variegata'
Chionochloa conspicua
Cortaderia selloana
Cyperus albostriatus 'Variegatus'
Dactylis glomerata 'Variegata'
Luzula sylvatica 'Marginata'
Scirpoides holoschoenus 'Variegatus'
Stenotaphrum secundatum 'Variegatum'

Luzula nivea (Snowy woodrush)
Evergreen, slow-spreading, perennial rush with fairly dense clusters of shining white flower spikes in early summer. Leaves are edged with white hairs.
H 24in (60cm), S 18–24in (45–60cm).

 Z4–9 H9–1

Hordeum jubatum
(Foxtail barley, Squirrel-tail grass)
Tufted, short-lived perennial or annual grass. In summer to early autumn has flat, arching, feathery, plumelike flower spikes with silky awns.
H 12–24in (30–60cm), S 12in (30cm).

Z4–8 H8–1

Pennisetum villosum,
syn. *P. longistylum* (Feather-top)
Herbaceous, tuft-forming, perennial grass with long-haired stems. In autumn has panicles of creamy pink spikelets, fading to pale brown, with very long, bearded bristles.
H to 3ft (1m), S 20in (50cm).

Z9–15 H12–1

Stipa gigantea (Golden oats)
Evergreen, tuft-forming, perennial grass with narrow leaves, 18in (45cm) or more long. In summer carries elegant, open panicles of silvery spikelets, with long awns and dangling golden anthers, that persist well into winter. H 8ft (2.5m), S 3ft (1m).

Z8–15 H12–1

Cyperus papyrus
(Paper reed, Papyrus)
Evergreen, clump-forming, perennial sedge with stout, triangular, leafless stems, each carrying huge umbels of spikelets with up to 100 rays in summer. Grows in water. H to 10–15ft (3–5m), S 3ft (1m).

Z13–15 H12–6

Helictotrichon sempervirens, syn. *Avena candida*, *A. sempervirens*
(Blue oat grass)
Evergreen, tufted, perennial grass with stiff, silvery blue leaves up to 12in (30cm) or more long. Produces erect panicles of straw-colored flower spikes in summer. H 3ft (1m), S 2ft (60cm).

Z4–9 H9–1

Bambusa multiplex, syn.
B. glaucescens (Hedge bamboo)
Evergreen, clump-forming bamboo with narrow leaves, 4–6in (10–15cm) long. Useful for hedges and windbreaks. H to 50ft (15m), S indefinite.

Z8–15 H12–1

Bouteloua gracilis,
syn. *B. oligostachya*
(Blue grama, Mosquito grass)
Semi-evergreen, tuft-forming, narrow-leaved, perennial grass. In summer bears comblike flower spikes, 1½in (4cm) long, held at right angles to stems. H 20in (50cm), S 8in (20cm).

Z5–9 H9–5

***Melica altissima* 'Atropurpurea'**
Evergreen, tuft-forming, perennial grass with broad leaves, short-haired beneath. Purple spikelets in narrow panicles, 4in (10cm) long, hang from the tops of stems during summer.
H and S 24in (60cm).

Z5–8 H8–5

Briza maxima
Briza media
Bromus ramosus
Carex buchananii
Fargesia nitida
Molinia caerulea subsp. *arundinacea*
Pennisetum alopecuroides
Pennisetum setaceum
Stipa arundinacea

GRASSES, BAMBOOS, RUSHES, *and* SEDGES

GREEN

Yushania anceps, syn. *Arundinaria anceps*, *A. jaunsarensis*, *Sinarundinaria jaunsarensis* (Anceps bamboo)
Evergreen, spreading bamboo with erect, later arching stems bearing several branches at each node. H 6–10ft (2–3m), S indefinite.
Z8–13 H12–8

Semiarundinaria fastuosa, syn. *Arundinaria fastuosa* (Narihira bamboo)
Evergreen, clump-forming bamboo with 6in (15cm) long leaves and short, tufted branches at each node. Culm sheaths open to reveal polished purplish interiors. H 20ft (6m), S indefinite.
Z6–9 H9–6

Shibataea kumasasa
Evergreen, clump-forming bamboo with stubby side branches on greenish brown stems. Leaves are broad, 2–4in (5–10cm) long. H 3–5ft (1–1.5m), S 1ft (30cm).
Z6–15 H12–1

Panicum capillare (Witch grass)
Tuft-forming, annual grass with broad leaves and hairy stems. Top half of each stem carries a dense panicle of numerous, minute, greenish brown spikelets on delicate stalks in summer. H 2–3ft (60cm–1m), S 1ft (30cm).
H12–1

Phyllostachys nigra var. ***henonis***, syn. *P.* 'Henonis'
Evergreen, clump-forming bamboo with bristled auricles on culm sheaths and a profusion of leaves. H 30ft (10m), S 6–10ft (2–3m).
Z7–11 H12–7

***Juncus effusus* 'Spiralis'**, syn. *J.e.* f. *spiralis*, *Scirpus lacustris* 'Spiralis' (Corkscrew rush)
Evergreen, tuft-forming, perennial rush with leafless stems that twist and curl and are often prostrate. Fairly dense, greenish brown flower panicles form in summer. H 3ft (1m), S 2ft (60cm).
Z6–9 H9–6

Chusquea culeou (Chilean bamboo)
Slow-growing, evergreen, clump-forming bamboo. Bears long-lasting culm sheaths, shining white when young, at the swollen nodes of thick, solid stems. H to 15ft (5m), S 8ft (2.5m) or more.
Z8–13 H12–10

Cyperus involucratus, syn. *C. alternifolius* of gardens, *C. flabelliformis*
Evergreen, tuft-forming, perennial sedge with leaflike bracts forming a whorl beneath the clustered flower spikes in summer. H to 3ft (1m), S 1ft (30cm).
Z13–15 H12–10

Pseudosasa japonica, syn. *Arundinaria japonica* (Arrow bamboo, Metake)
Evergreen, clump-forming bamboo that may run. Has long-persistent, roughly pubescent brown sheaths and broad leaves, 14in (35cm) long. H 15ft (5m), S indefinite.
Z7–11 H12–1

Phyllostachys bambusoides (Timber bamboo)
Evergreen, clump-forming bamboo with thick, erect green stems. Bears leaf sheaths with prominent bristles, and large, broad leaves. H 20–25ft (6–8m), S indefinite.
Z7–10 H10–7

Coix lacryma-jobi (Job's tears)
Tuft-forming grass, often grown as an annual, with broad leaves and insignificant spikelets followed by hard, beadlike green fruits turning shiny, grayish mauve in autumn. H 18–36in (45cm–90cm), S 4–6in (10–15cm).
Z7–15 H12–1

Phyllostachys flexuosa (Zigzag bamboo)
Evergreen, clump-forming bamboo with slender, markedly zigzag stems that turn black with age. Leaf sheaths have no bristles. Leaves often stay fresh green all winter. H 20–25ft (6–8m), S indefinite.
Z6–15 H12–1

Arundo donax
Carex elata
Cyperus longus
Deschampsia cespitosa
Festuca glauca
Leymus arenarius
Sesleria heufleriana
Stipa calamagrostis

***Miscanthus sinensis* 'Gracillimus'**
Herbaceous, clump-forming, perennial grass with very narrow leaves, hairy beneath, often turning bronze. May bear fan-shaped panicles of awned, hairy white spikelets in early autumn. H 4ft (1.2m), S 1½ft (45cm).

Z5–9 H9–1

***Spartina pectinata* 'Aureomarginata',**
syn. *S.p.* 'Aureovariegata'
Herbaceous, spreading, rhizomatous grass with long, arching, yellow-striped leaves that turn orange-brown in late autumn to winter.
H to 6ft (2m), S indefinite.

Z8–11 H12–8

***Pleioblastus auricomus*,**
syn. *Arundinaria auricoma*, *A. viridistriata*, *P. viridistriatus*
Evergreen, slow-spreading bamboo with purple stems and broad, softly downy, bright yellow leaves with green stripes. H 5ft (1.5m), S indefinite.

Z7–15 H12–1

***Alopecurus pratensis* 'Aureovariegatus',**
syn. *A.p.* 'Aureomarginatus' (Golden foxtail)
Herbaceous, tuft-forming, perennial grass with yellow or yellow-green-streaked leaves and dense flower spikes in summer. H and S 9–12in (23–30cm).

Z5–8 H–5

Carex pendula
(Pendulous sedge)
Evergreen, tuft-forming, graceful, perennial sedge with narrow green leaves, 18in (45cm) long. Solid, triangular stems freely produce pendent, greenish brown flower spikes in summer. H 3ft (1m), S 1ft (30cm).

Z5–9 H9–5

***Carex hachijoensis* 'Evergold',**
syn. *C. oshimensis* 'Evergold'
Evergreen, tuft-forming, perennial sedge with narrow, yellow-striped leaves, 8in (20cm) long. Solid, triangular stems may carry insignificant flower spikes in summer.
H 8in (20cm), S 6–8in (15–20cm).

Z6–9 H9–6

Phyllostachys viridiglaucescens
Evergreen, clump-forming bamboo with greenish brown stems that arch at the base. Has white powder beneath nodes. H 20–25ft (6–8m), S indefinite.

Z7–15 H12–1

***Carex elata* 'Aurea',**
syn. *C. stricta* 'Aurea'
(Bowles' golden sedge)
Evergreen, tuft-forming, perennial sedge with golden yellow leaves. Solid, triangular stems bear blackish brown flower spikes in summer.
H to 16in (40cm), S 6in (15cm).

Z5–9 H9–3

***Hakonechloa macra* 'Aureola'**
Slow-growing, herbaceous, shortly rhizomatous grass with purple stems and green-striped yellow leaves that age to reddish brown. Open panicles of reddish brown flower spikes appear in early autumn and last into winter.
H 16in (40cm), S 18–24in (45–60cm).

Z5–9 H9–5

Eleocharis acicularis
Isolepis setaceus
Lamarckia aurea
Melica altissima
Melinis repens
Milium effusum 'Aureum'
Molinia caerulea 'Variegata'
Phyllostachys aurea
Phyllostachys aureosulcata
Sasa palmata
Stipa arundinacea

GREEN

***Phlebodium aureum* 'Mandaianum'**
Evergreen fern with creeping rhizomes. Has arching, deeply lobed, glaucous fronds with attractive orange-yellow sporangia on reverses; pinnae are deeply cut and wavy. H 3–5ft (1–1.5m), S 2ft (60cm).

Z13–15 H12–10

Dryopteris filix-mas (Male fern)
Deciduous or semi-evergreen fern with "shuttlecocks" of elegantly arching, upright, broadly lance-shaped, mid-green fronds that arise from crowns of large, upright, brown-scaled rhizomes. H 4ft (1.2m), S 3ft (1m).

Z4–8 H8–1

Platycerium bifurcatum
(Common staghorn fern)
Evergreen, epiphytic fern with broad, platelike sterile fronds and long, arching or pendent, forked, gray-green fertile fronds bearing velvety brownish spore patches beneath.
H and S 3ft (1m).

Z12–15 H12–10

Dicksonia antarctica
(Australian tree fern)
Evergreen, treelike fern. Thick trunks are covered with brown fibers and crowned by spreading, somewhat arching, broadly lance-shaped, much-divided, palmlike fronds. H 30ft (10m) or more, S 12ft (4m).

Z12–15 H12–10

***Polystichum aculeatum* 'Pulcherrimum'**
Evergreen or semi-evergreen fern with broadly lance-shaped, daintily cut, sharp-edged fronds that are yellowish green in spring and mature to a glossy, rich dark green.
H 24in (60cm), S 30in (75cm).

Z3–8 H8–1

Blechnum penna-marina, syn. *B. alpinum*
Fast-growing, evergreen, carpeting fern. Has narrow, ladderlike, dark green fronds, red-tinged when young. Outer sterile fronds are spreading; inner fertile ones erect. H 6–12in (15–30cm), S 12–18in (30–45cm).

pH Z10–11 H12–10

Polystichum munitum
(Giant holly fern)
Evergreen fern with erect, leathery, lance-shaped, dark green fronds that consist of small, spiny-margined pinnae. H 4ft (1.2m), S 1ft (30cm).

Z3–8 H8–1

Polypodium glycyrrhiza
(Licorice fern)
Deciduous fern. Has oblong-triangular to narrowly oval, divided, midgreen fronds with lance-shaped to oblong pinnae, arising from a licorice-scented rootstock. H and S 45cm (18in).

Z4–9 H9–1

Microlepia speluncae
Large, terrestrial fern with a spreading rhizome and triangular, divided, softly hairy fronds consisting of triangular to lance-shaped pinnae. H to 4ft (1.2m), S to 6ft (2m).

Z12–15 H12–10

OTHER RECOMMENDED PLANTS:
Asplenium bulbiferum
Blechnum penna-marina
Blechnum spicant
Cyrtomium fortunei
Dicksonia fibrosa
Dicksonia squarrosa
Dryopteris marginalis
Nephrolepis cordifolia
Pellaea atropurpurea
Polystichum acrostichoides
Polystichum aculeatum
Polystichum tsussimense
Pteris ensiformis
Pteris ensiformis 'Arguta'

Polypodium scouleri
Evergreen, creeping fern with triangular to oval, leathery, divided fronds that arise from a spreading rootstock. H and S 12–16in (30–40cm).

Z12–15 H12–10

***Pteris cretica* 'Wimsettii'**
Evergreen or semi-evergreen fern with broadly ovate fronds divided into narrow pinnae, each with an incised margin and crested tip. H 18in (45cm), S 12in (30cm).

Z12–15 H12–10

Adiantum aleuticum
Semi-evergreen fern with a short rootstock. Has glossy, dark brown or blackish stems and dainty, divided, fingerlike fronds with blue-green pinnae that are more crowded than those of *A. pedatum*. Grows well in alkaline soils. H and S to 18in (45cm).

Z3–8 H8–1

***Phlebodium aureum*,**
syn. *Polypodium aureum*
Evergreen fern with creeping, golden-scaled rhizomes. Has arching, deeply lobed, midgreen or glaucous fronds with attractive orange-yellow sporangia on reverses. H 3–5ft (90cm–1.5m), S 2ft (60cm).

Z12–15 H12–10

Selaginella martensii
Evergreen, mosslike perennial with dense, much-branched, frondlike sprays of glossy, rich green foliage. H and S 9in (23cm).

Z12–15 H12–1

Asplenium ceterach
(Rusty-back fern)
Semi-evergreen fern with lance-shaped, leathery, dark green fronds divided into alternate, bluntly rounded lobes. Backs of young fronds are covered with silvery scales that mature to reddish brown. H and S 6in (15cm).

Z5–8 H8–3

Polystichum setiferum
Divisilobum Group
Evergreen or semi-evergreen fern. Broadly lance-shaped or oval, soft-textured, much-divided, spreading fronds are clothed with white scales as they unfurl. H 24in (60cm), S 18in (45cm).

Z6–9 H9–6

Cyrtomium falcatum
(Fishtail fern, Holly fern)
Evergreen fern. Fronds are lance-shaped and have hollylike, glossy, dark green pinnae; young fronds are often covered with whitish or brown scales. H 12–24in (30–60cm), S 12–18in (30–45cm).

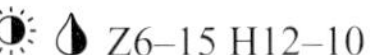

Z6–15 H12–10

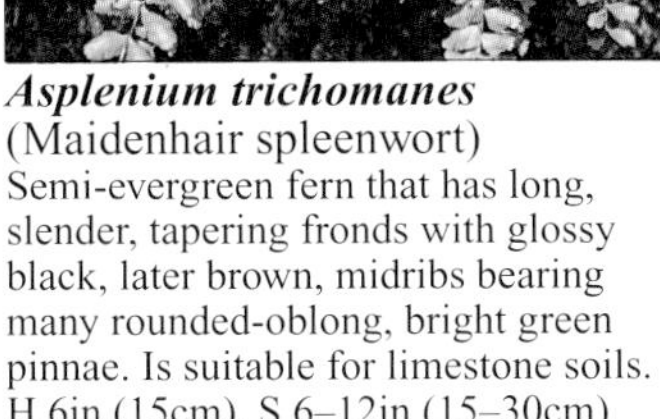

Asplenium trichomanes
(Maidenhair spleenwort)
Semi-evergreen fern that has long, slender, tapering fronds with glossy black, later brown, midribs bearing many rounded-oblong, bright green pinnae. Is suitable for limestone soils. H 6in (15cm), S 6–12in (15–30cm).

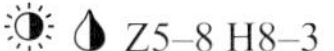

Z5–8 H8–3

Adiantum raddianum 'Fritz-Luthi'
Adiantum tenerum
Blechnum tabulare
Cheilanthes tomentosa
Davallia canariensis
Davallia mariesii
Didymochlaena truncata
Dryopteris carthusiana
Dryopteris cycadina
Dryopteris dilatata
Dryopteris filix-mas 'Grandiceps Wills'
Dryopteris wallichiana
Lygodium japonicum
Matteuccia orientalis
Oreopteris limbosperma
Phegopteris connectilis

FERNS

GREEN

Thelypteris palustris
(Marsh buckler fern, Marsh fern)
Deciduous fern. Has strong, erect, lance-shaped, pale green fronds with widely separated, deeply cut pinnae, produced from wiry, creeping blackish rhizomes. Grows well beside a pond or stream. H 30in (75cm), S 12in (30cm).

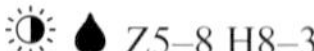 Z5–8 H8–3

Nephrolepis exaltata (Sword fern)
Evergreen fern. Has erect, sometimes spreading, lance-shaped, divided, pale green fronds borne on wiry stems. H and S 36in (90cm) or more.

 Z13–15 H12–1

Osmunda regalis (Royal fern)
Deciduous fern with elegant, broadly oval to oblong, divided, bright green fronds, pinkish when young. Mature plants bear tassel-like, rust brown fertile flower spikes at ends of taller fronds. H 6ft (2m), S 3ft (1m).

Z2–10 H9–1

Selaginella kraussiana
Evergreen, trailing, more or less prostrate, mosslike perennial with bright green foliage. H ½in (1cm). S indefinite.

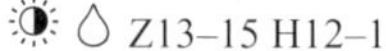 Z13–15 H12–1

***Polypodium vulgare* 'Cornubiense'**
Evergreen fern with narrow, lance-shaped, divided, fresh green fronds; segments are further subdivided to give an overall lacy effect. H and S 10–12in (25–30cm).

Z6–8 H8–6

Onoclea sensibilis (Sensitive fern)
Deciduous, creeping fern with handsome, arching, almost triangular, divided, fresh pale green fronds often suffused pinkish brown in spring. In autumn, fronds turn an attractive yellowish brown. H and S 18in (45cm).

Z4–9 H9–1

Adiantum pedatum
(Northern maidenhair fern)
Semi-evergreen fern with a thick, creeping rootstock. Dainty, divided, fingerlike, midgreen fronds are produced on glossy, dark brown or blackish stems. H and S to 18in (45cm)

pH Z3–8 H8–1

Matteuccia struthiopteris
(Ostrich fern)
Deciduous, rhizomatous fern. Lance-shaped, erect, divided fronds are arranged like a shuttlecock; outermost, fresh green sterile fronds surround denser, dark brown fertile fronds. H 3ft (1m), S 1½ft (45cm).

Z3–8 H8–1

Polypodium cambricum
Polypodium vulgare 'Cristatum'
Polystichum braunii
Polystichum rigens
Selaginella lepidophylla
Woodsia polystichoides
Woodwardia radicans
Woodwardia unigemmata

***Polystichum setiferum* Plumosodivisilobum Group**
Evergreen fern that produces a "shuttlecock" of lance-shaped, divided fronds with segments narrowed towards the frond tips; lower pinnae often overlap. H 4ft (1.2m), S 3ft (1m).

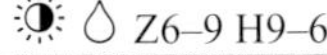 Z6–9 H9–6

Polypodium vulgare
(Common polypody, Polypody)
Evergreen fern with narrow, lance-shaped, divided, herringbone-like, midgreen fronds arising from creeping rhizomes covered with copper-brown scales. H and S 10–12in (25–30cm).

Z6–8 H8–6

Asplenium scolopendrium, syn. *Phyllitis scolopendrium*, *Scolopendrium vulgare*
(Hart's-tongue fern)
Evergreen fern with stocky rhizomes and tongue-shaped, leathery, bright green fronds. Is good in alkaline soils. H 18–30in (45–75cm), S to 18in (45cm).

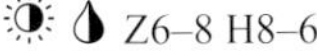 Z6–8 H8–6

Asplenium nidus (Bird's-nest fern)
Evergreen fern. Produces broadly lance-shaped, glossy, bright green fronds in a shuttlecock-like arrangement. H 2–4ft (60cm–1.2m), S 1–2ft (30–60cm).

Z13–15 H12–3

***Asplenium scolopendrium* Marginatum Group**
Evergreen fern with stocky, upright rhizomes and lobed, slightly frilled, tongue-shaped fronds that are leathery and bright green. Is good in alkaline soils. H and S 12in (30cm) or more.

Z6–8 H8–6

Athyrium niponicum, syn. *A. goeringianum, A. nipponicum* (Japanese painted fern)
Deciduous fern. Broad, triangular, divided, purple-tinged, grayish green fronds arise from a scaly, creeping brownish or reddish rootstock.
H and S 12in (30cm).

 Z5–8 H8–1

Adiantum venustum
Deciduous fern. Bears delicate, pale green fronds, tinged brown when young, consisting of many small, triangular pinnae on glossy stems.
H 9in (23cm), S 12in (30cm).

pH Z5–8 H8–5

Cryptogramma crispa
(Parsley fern)
Deciduous fern with broadly oval to triangular, finely divided, bright pale green fronds that resemble parsley.
In autumn, fronds turn bright rusty brown and persist during winter. H 6–9in (15–23cm), S 6–12in (15–30cm).

pH Z5–8 H8–5

Adiantum capillus-veneris
Adiantum raddianum
Adiantum raddianum 'Grandiceps'
Athyrium filix-femina
Athyrium otophorum
Cystopteris bulbifera
Cystopteris dickieana
Dryopteris affinis
Dryopteris erythrosora
Dryopteris goldieana
Osmunda cinnamomea
Osmunda claytoniana
Pityrogramma triangularis
Pteris cretica 'Albolineata'
Pteris cretica 'Mayi'
Selaginella kraussiana 'Variegata'

ANNUALS *and* BIENNIALS

VIGOROUS, FREELY FLOWERING growers, often with a lengthy season and yet inexpensive, most annuals and biennials are used to fill in small areas around more permanent plants or in informal or wildflower plantings. Many gardeners exploit their extensive color spectrum to daub fresh areas of color on their garden canvas.

Annuals and Biennials

The rapid growth and relatively low cost of annuals and biennials make them ideal for providing immediate color in new gardens until more permanent plantings of trees, shrubs, and perennials are established. They are also invaluable in formal settings as bedding plants to fill gaps or create specific effects, as well as in informal situations, especially natural areas and wildflower meadows.

What are annuals and biennials?

Annuals are plants that grow, bloom, set seed, and die in a single growing season. Biennials complete their life cycle in two seasons: most are sown in summer and make leafy growth in the first year, then flower, set seed, and die in the next.

Growing annuals and biennials

Hardy annuals withstand some frost and so can be sown *in situ* in early autumn or spring. Semi-hardy and tender annuals are sown under cover between late winter and early spring and are planted out when all danger of frost has passed. Gardeners often use other types of plants in the same way as annuals, in particular tender perennials, such as *Pelargonium (*geraniums) or *Impatiens*, which grow vigorously and flower freely in their first year from seed. Like annuals, tender perennials are cleared away at the end of the season.

Ornamental features

Annuals and biennials are available in an enormous range of sizes and habits, from the lowest hummock-forming cultivars of *Ageratum houstonianum* and trailing nasturtiums (*Tropaeolum majus*) to the tall spires of foxgloves (*Digitalis purpurea*) or the grandeur of the Scotch thistle (*Onopordum acanthium*). They include climbers such as Canary creeper (*Tropaeolum peregrinum)* and fragrant sweet peas (*Lathyrus odoratus*), as well as a number grown primarily for foliage effects, for instance the feathery-leaved *Bassia scoparia* f. *trichophylla,* or *Senecio cineraria* with its gray foliage. The flower range, in all colors and tones, is also huge and presents a bewildering choice. Colors extend from the opalescent whites of *Lavatera trimestris* 'Mont Blanc' to the vibrant scarlets of pelargoniums or the intense magentas and purples of petunias, as well as the more subtle pastel shades exhibited by plants such as China aster (*Callistephus chinensis*).

Maintaining year-round color

The long and prolific season of annuals and biennials has traditionally been exploited in formal beds devoted entirely to achieving brilliant, seasonally changing displays. Spring displays of

Multipurpose pot marigolds
Above: Forming a strong edging in a potager, the edible flowers of pot marigolds (Calendula officinalis) *attract beneficial insects such as hoverflies to prey pests, especially aphids.*

Early-season scents
Right: Self-sown Dame's violet (Hesperis matronalis) *and poached-egg plant* (Limnanthes douglasii) *add scents and a natural informality.*

primroses and forget-me-nots (*Myosotis*) are sometimes used as a carpet beneath spring bulbs, then lifted to make way for a summer design juxtaposing, for example, the exotic foliage of *Ricinus communis* with swaths of hot color provided by zinnias or pelargoniums. As summer fades, the entire display may be replaced with winter-flowering pansies (*Viola* x *wittrockiana*) or spring wallflowers (*Erysimum cheiri*).

This potential for year-round color can also be employed in more domestic situations, albeit scaled down to suit modest yards. While the uniformity of habit and color of many modern annuals are perfect where formality or complex patternwork is needed, they are equally adaptable to more informal plantings. Sinuous drifts of graduated height suggest a cottage-garden style, while yet more naturalistic effects are possible by using "old-fashioned" annuals such as corncockle (*Agrostemma githago*), cornflower (*Centaurea cyanus*) or field poppy (*Papaver rhoeas*).

If there is room, annuals and biennials can be grown in a border for cutting, especially stocks (*Matthiola incana*), *Cleome hassleriana*, and China asters (*Callistephus*) for flower arrangements, and everlastings such as *Bracteantha bracteata* and *Limonium sinuatum* for dried arrangements. In a mixed border annuals and biennials are invaluable, whether used to add textural qualities or color highlights among more permanent plants, or as fillers to mask gaps left by the foliage of perennials that die back after flowering.

SUMMER HARMONIES
Above: Opium poppies (Papaver somniferum) *and foxgloves* (Digitalis purpurea) *are used here to add subtle color to a mixed border.*

ANNUALS IN POTS
Right: Use annuals in pots to bring summer-long color to patio plantings. Here, these vivid nasturtiums (Tropaeolum majus) *will flower continuously, well into early autumn.*

WILD-LOOKING GARDEN
Below: Sown en masse, corn marigold (Xanthophthalmum segetum), *field poppies* (Papaver rhoeas), *and cornflowers* (Centaurea cyanus) *look entirely natural.*

PLANTING IN CONTAINERS

Annuals and biennials can create eye-catching features in pots, barrels, and hanging baskets. Use them alone in compositions in which trailers, such as the ivy-leaved geraniums or cascading lobelias, surround mound-forming verbenas or impatiens, and link them with the airy foliage of brachyscome or felicia. Or add color to container-grown dwarf conifers, such as *Juniperus communis* 'Compressa', or to a trailing or more fomally grown evergreen ivy (*Hedera* cultivars).

WHITE

***Digitalis purpurea* f. *albiflora*,**
syn. *D.p.* f. *alba*
Slow-growing, short-lived perennial grown as a biennial. Has a rosette of large, pointed-oval leaves and erect stems carrying tubular white flowers in summer.
H 3–5ft (1–1.5m), S 1–1½ft (30–45cm).

Z5–9 H10–1

Omphalodes linifolia
(Venus's navelwort)
Fairly fast-growing, slender, erect annual with lance-shaped, gray-green leaves. Tiny, slightly scented, rounded white flowers, rarely tinged blue, are carried in summer.
H 6–12in (15–30cm), S 6in (15cm).

Z7–9 H9–7

Gypsophila elegans
Fast-growing, erect, bushy annual. Has lance-shaped, grayish green leaves and clouds of tiny white flowers in branching heads from summer to early autumn.
H 24in (60cm), S 30cm (12in) or more.

Z5–9 H9–1

***Lavatera trimestris* 'Mont Blanc'**
Moderately fast-growing, erect, branching annual with oval, lobed leaves. Shallowly trumpet-shaped, brilliant white flowers appear from summer to early autumn.
H to 24in (60cm), S 18in (45cm).

Z11 H12–1

Iberis amara
Fast-growing, erect, bushy annual with lance-shaped, midgreen leaves. Has flattish heads of small, scented, 4-petaled white flowers in summer.
H 12in (30cm), S 6in (15cm).

Z11 H12–1

***Lobularia maritima* 'Little Dorrit'**, syn. *Alyssum maritimum* 'Little Dorrit'
Fast-growing, compact annual with lance-shaped, grayish green leaves and heads of scented, 4-petaled white flowers in summer and early autumn.
H 3–6in (8–15cm), S 8–12in (20–30cm).

Z10–11 H12–1

***Matthiola* 'Giant Imperial'**
Fast-growing, erect, bushy biennial, grown as an annual. Has lance-shaped, grayish green leaves and long spikes of highly scented white to creamy-yellow flowers in summer. Produces excellent flowers for cutting.
H to 24in (60cm), S 12in (30cm).

Z8–9 H9–1

***Petunia* Recoverer Series** [white]
Moderately fast-growing, branching, bushy perennial, grown as an annual. Has oval, mid- to deep green leaves and large, flared, trumpet-shaped white flowers in summer-autumn.
H 6–12in (15–30cm), S 12in (30cm).

Z9–11 H12–1

OTHER RECOMMENDED PLANTS:
Adlumia fungosa
Antirrhinum majus and cvs
Bracteantha bracteata cvs
Callistephus chinensis and cvs
Campanula medium and cvs
Centaurea cyanus
Consolida ajacis Dwarf Hyacinth Series
Dianthus chinensis and cvs
Eustoma grandiflorum Heidi Series
Iberis umbellata
Lobelia erinus 'Color Cascade'
Lobularia maritima

Dimorphotheca pluvialis, syn. *D. annua* (Rain daisy)
Branching annual with oval, hairy, deep green leaves. In summer has small, daisylike flower heads, the rays purple beneath and white above, with brownish purple centers.
H 8–12in (20–30cm), S 6in (15cm).

Z9–11 H12–6

Nemophila maculata (Five-spot)
Fast-growing, spreading annual with lobed leaves. Small, bowl-shaped white flowers with purple-tipped petals are carried in summer.
H and S 6in (15cm).

Z9–10 H7–1

Tanacetum parthenium, syn. *Chrysanthemum parthenium*, *Pyrethrum parthenium* (Feverfew)
Moderately fast-growing, short-lived, bushy perennial, grown as an annual. Has aromatic leaves and small white flower heads in summer and early autumn. H and S 8–18in (20–45cm).

Z4–9 H9–1

Euphorbia marginata (Snow-on-the-mountain)
Moderately fast-growing, upright, bushy annual. Has pointed-oval, bright green leaves; upper leaves are white-margined. Broad, petal-like white bracts surround insignificant flowers in summer. H 24in (60cm), S 12in (30cm).

Z13–15 H12–1

Nicotiana* x *sanderae
Domino Series
Fairly slow-growing, bushy annual with pointed-oval leaves. Somewhat trumpet-shaped flowers, to 3in (8cm) long, appear in a wide range of colors in summer and early autumn.
H and S 12in (30cm).

Z10–15 H12–1

Reseda odorata (Mignonette)
Moderately fast-growing, erect, branching annual with oval leaves. Conical heads of small, very fragrant, somewhat star-shaped white flowers with orange-brown stamens are carried in summer and early autumn.
H 12–24in (30–60cm), S 12in (30cm).

Z10–11 H6–1

Viola* x *wittrockiana
Floral Dance Series [white]
Bushy perennial, grown as an annual or biennial. Has oval, midgreen leaves and rounded, 5-petaled white flowers in cool and cold weather.
H 6–8in (15–20cm), S 8in (20cm).

Z8–11 H12–1

Eustoma grandiflorum
Slow-growing, upright annual with lance-shaped, deep green leaves. Poppylike pink, purple, blue, or white flowers, 2in (5cm) wide, are carried in summer.
H 24in (60cm), S 12in (30cm).

Z8–11 H12–1

Lobularia maritima
Matthiola cvs
Myosotis sylvatica 'White Ball'
Nemesia strumosa
Nigella damascena
Papaver somniferum 'White Cloud'
PELARGONIUMS, illus. pp.246–7
Pericallis x *hybrida*
Petunia cvs
Phlox drummondii cvs
Portulaca grandiflora
Salvia farinacea f. *alba*
Salvia viridis cvs
Verbascum lychnitis
Viola x *wittrockiana* cvs
Zinnia cvs

WHITE–PINK

Hibiscus trionum
(Flower-of-an-hour)
Fairly fast-growing, upright annual with oval, serrated leaves. Trumpet-shaped, creamy white or pale yellow flowers with purplish brown centers are borne from late summer to early autumn.
H 24in (60cm), S 12in (30cm).

Z10–11 H12–10

Martynia annua
(Unicorn plant)
Fairly fast-growing, upright annual with long-stalked leaves. Has foxglove-like, lobed, creamy white flowers marked red, pink, and yellow in summer, followed by horned green, then brown, fruits. H 24in (60cm), S 12in (30cm).

H12–6

***Lathyrus odoratus* 'Knee Hi'**
Fast-growing annual with oval, divided, midgreen leaves and large, fragrant flowers in shades of pink, red, blue, or white that are borne in summer or early autumn. H and S 3ft (90cm).

Z9–10 H8–1

Crepis rubra
Fairly fast-growing, rosette-forming annual with lance-shaped, serrated leaves. In summer bears dandelion-like pink, occasionally red or white, flower heads. H 12in (30cm), S 6in (15cm).

Z5–7 H7–4

***Zea mays* 'Gracillima Variegata'**
Fairly fast-growing, erect annual with lance-shaped leaves striped green and creamy white. Has tassel-like silvery flower heads and large, bright yellow ears.
H 3ft (90cm), S 1–1½ft (30–45cm).

H12–1

Impatiens balsamina (Balsam)
Fairly fast-growing, erect, compact, bushy annual with lance-shaped leaves. Small, cup-shaped, spurred pink or white flowers are borne in summer and early autumn.
H to 30in (75cm), S 18in (45cm).

H12–1

***Ismelia carinata* 'Monarch Court Jesters'**
Fast-growing, erect, branching annual. Has feathery, gray-green leaves and, in summer, daisylike, zoned flower heads, to 3in (8cm) wide, in various color combinations.
H 24in (60cm), S 12in (30cm).

H9–1

Silene coeli-rosa, syn. *Agrostemma coeli-rosa*, *Lychnis coeli-rosa*, *Viscaria elegans*
Moderately fast-growing, erect annual with lance-shaped, grayish green leaves. Has 5-petaled, pinkish purple flowers with white centers in summer.
H 18in (45cm), S 6in (15cm).

H9–1

Cleome hassleriana

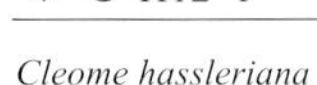
Impatiens balsamina 'Blackberry Ice'

Rhodanthe chlorocephala subsp. ***rosea***
Moderately fast-growing, erect annual. Lance-shaped leaves are grayish green; small, daisylike, papery, semi-double pink flower heads appear in summer. Flowers dry well.
H 12in (30cm), S 6in (15cm).

H12–1

***Matthiola* 'Giant Excelsior'**
Fast-growing, erect, bushy biennial, grown as an annual. Lance-shaped leaves are grayish green; long spikes of highly scented flowers in shades of pink, red, pale blue, or white appear in summer.
H to 30in (75cm), S 12in (30cm).

Z8–9 H9–1

Antirrhinum majus
Coronette Series (Snapdragon)
Erect, bushy, compact perennial, grown as an annual, with lance-shaped leaves. Spikes of tubular, 2-lipped flowers in a wide range of colors are produced from spring to autumn.
H 24in (60cm), S 12in (30cm).

Z9–11 H12–1

***Primula* 'Dreamer'**
(Primrose Group)
Rosette-forming perennial, normally grown as a biennial, with oval leaves. In spring, has flat flowers in cream, apricot, pink, or rose-pink; all bicolors have darker eyes and yellow centers.
H 3–4in (8–10cm), S 6–8in (15–20cm).

Z6–8 H8–6

Rhodanthe manglesii,
syn. *Helipterum manglesii*
Moderately fast-growing, erect annual. Has pointed-oval, grayish green leaves and daisylike, papery red, pink, or white flower heads in summer and early autumn. Flowers dry well.
H 12in (30cm), S 6in (15cm).

Z11–12 H9–1

Papaver somniferum
'Peony Flowered'
Fast-growing, erect annual with lobed, pale grayish green leaves. Has large, rounded, often cup-shaped, double flowers in a mixture of colors – red, pink, purple, or white – in summer.
H 30in (75cm), S 12in (30cm).

Z3–8 H8–1

***Matthiola* Brompton Group**
Fast-growing, erect, bushy biennial, grown as an annual. Lance-shaped leaves are grayish green; long spikes of highly scented flowers in shades of pink, red, purple, yellow, or white are borne in summer.
H 18in (45cm), S 12in (30cm).

Z8–9 H9–1

***Pelargonium* Orbit Series**
[salmon]
Slow-growing, evergreen, branching, bushy perennial, grown as an annual, with lobed leaves zoned with bronze or red. Has large, rounded heads of salmon-pink flowers in summer-autumn. H and S 12–24in (30–60cm).

Z10–11 H12–1

Alcea rosea, syn. *Althaea rosea*
(Hollyhock)
Biennial with tall, erect stems and lobed, rough-textured leaves. Spikes of single flowers, in a range of colors including pink, yellow, and cream, appear in summer and early autumn.
H 5–6ft (1.5–2m), S to 2ft (60cm).

Z3–9 H9–1

Salvia splendens
Cleopatra Series [salmon]
Slow-growing, bushy perennial, grown as an annual. Oval, serrated leaves are fresh green; dense racemes of tubular, salmon-pink flowers are carried in summer and early autumn.
H to 12in (30cm), S 8–12in (20–30cm).

Z11–13 H12–1

***Impatiens walleriana* Swirl Series**
Subshrubby perennial, usually grown as an annual, with light green to red-flushed stems and leaves. In summer bears flattened, slender-spurred, pink-and-orange flowers margined in rose-red. H 6–8in (15–20cm), S to 24in (60cm).

Z10–15 H12–1

Ageratum houstonianum 'Swing Pink'
Silene pendula

PINK

***Petunia* Aladdin Series**
Fairly fast-growing, branching, bushy perennial, grown as an annual. Has oval leaves and in summer-autumn produces flowers in a range of colors, including strong shades of red and salmon-pink. H to 12in (30cm), S 12–36in (30–90cm).

Z9–11 H12–1

***Papaver rhoeas* Shirley Series** [double]
Fast-growing, slender, erect annual with lobed, light green leaves. Rounded, often cup-shaped, double flowers, in shades of red, pink, or white, including bicolors, are borne in summer. H 24in (60cm), S 12in (30cm).

H12–1

***Cleome hassleriana* 'Colour Fountain'**
Fast-growing, bushy annual with hairy stems and divided leaves. In summer has heads of narrow-petaled flowers, with long, protruding stamens, in shades of pink, mauve, purple, or white. H 3–4ft (1–1.2m), S 1½–2ft (45–60cm).

H12–1

***Lobularia maritima* 'Wonderland'**, syn. *Alyssum maritimum* 'Wonderland'
Fast-growing, compact annual with lance-shaped leaves. Bears heads of tiny, scented, deep purplish pink flowers in summer and early autumn. H to 6in (15cm), S to 12in (30cm).

Z10–11 H12–1

***Zinnia elegans* Thumbelina Series**
Moderately fast-growing, sturdy, erect annual with oval to lance-shaped leaves. In summer and early autumn has large, daisylike, double and semi-double flower heads in a range of colors. H 6in (15cm), S 12in (30cm).

H12–1

***Schizanthus* 'Hit Parade'**
Moderately fast-growing, erect, bushy annual with deeply divided leaves. Tubular flowers, in a mixture of rich colors including pink, red, purple, or white, often with contrasting markings inside, appear in summer-autumn. H and S 12in (30cm).

Z12–13 H7–1

Centaurea cyanus [tall, rose] (Cornflower)
Fast-growing, erect, branching annual with lance-shaped, gray-green leaves. Branching heads of daisylike, rose-pink flower heads are carried in summer and early autumn. H to 3ft (90cm), S 1ft (30cm).

H7–1

Limonium sinuatum
Fairly slow-growing, bushy, upright perennial, grown as an annual. Has lance-shaped, lobed, deep green leaves and, in summer and early autumn, tiny blue, pink, white, yellow, or salmon flowers borne in clusters on winged stems. H 18in (45cm), S 12in (30cm).

H9–3

***Eschscholzia californica* Ballerina Series**
Fast-growing, slender, erect annual. Has feathery, bluish green leaves and cup-shaped, 4-petaled, frilled, double flowers in shades of red, yellow, pink, or orange in summer-autumn. H 12in (30cm), S 6in (15cm).

Z11 H9–1

Onopordum acanthium (Cotton thistle, Scotch thistle)
Slow-growing, erect, branching biennial. Large, lobed, spiny leaves are hairy and bright silvery gray. Winged, branching flower stems bear deep purplish pink flower heads in summer. H 6ft (1.8m), S 3ft (90cm).

Z6–8 H12–7

Silybum marianum (Mary's thistle)
Biennial with a basal rosette of deeply lobed, very spiny, heavily white-marbled, deep green leaves. Has thistle-like, dark purplish pink flower heads on erect stems in summer and early autumn. H 4ft (1.2m), S 2ft (60cm).

Z6–9 H6–1

***Iberis umbellata* Fairy Series**
Fast-growing, upright, bushy annual with lance-shaped, midgreen leaves. Heads of small, 4-petaled flowers in shades of pink, red, purple, or white are carried in summer and early autumn. H and S 8in (20cm).

Z11 H12–1

Agrostemma githago
Alcea rosea 'Majorette'
Bellis perennis cvs
Campanula medium and cvs
Clarkia amoena
Consolida ajacis Dwarf Hyacinth Series
Eustoma grandiflorum Heidi Series
Impatiens cvs
Matthiola cvs
Salvia viridis cvs

***Petunia* Primetime Series**
Moderately fast-growing perennial, grown as an annual. In summer-autumn it bears flowers in a very wide range of colors, including white, blue, pink, or red, some with dark veins or central stars or picotee margins.
H to 14in (35cm), S 12–36in (30–90cm).

Z9–11 H12–1

***Agrostemma githago* 'Milas'**
Fast-growing, slender, upright, thin-stemmed annual. Has lance-shaped leaves and 5-petaled, purplish pink flowers, 3in (8cm) wide, in summer.
H 2–3ft (60–90cm), S 1ft (30cm).

H9–1

Malcolmia maritima
(Virginian stock)
Fast-growing, slim, erect annual with oval, grayish green leaves. Carries tiny, fragrant, 4-petaled pink, red, green, or white flowers from spring to autumn. Sow in succession for a longer flowering season. H 8in (20cm), S 2–3in (5–8cm).

Z8–9 H9–1

***Matthiola* Brompton Group**
[pink]
Fast-growing, erect, bushy biennial, grown as an annual, with lance-shaped, grayish green leaves. Long spikes of highly scented pink flowers are carried in summer.
H 18in (45cm), S 12in (30cm).

Z8–9 H9–1

***Lunaria annua* 'Variegata'**
Fast-growing, erect biennial with pointed-oval, serrated, white-variegated leaves. Heads of small, scented, 4-petaled, deep purplish pink flowers are borne in spring and early summer followed by rounded silvery seed pods.
H 30in (75cm), S 12in (30cm).

Z5–9 H9–1

***Silene armeria* 'Electra'**
Moderately fast-growing, erect annual with oval, grayish green leaves. Heads of 5-petaled, bright rose-pink flowers are carried in summer and early autumn. H 12in (30cm), S 6in (15cm).

H8–1

PINK

***Clarkia amoena* 'Sybil Sherwood'**
Erect annual with lance-shaped, sometimes toothed leaves. Single, fluted, salmon-pink flowers, fading to white at the margins, are borne at the tips of long, leafy shoots in summer.
H to 18in (45cm), S 12in (30cm).

H7–1

***Brassica oleracea* forms**
(Ornamental cabbage)
Moderately fast-growing, evergreen, rounded biennial, grown as an annual. Has heads of large, often crinkled leaves in combinations of red/green, white/pink, or pink/green.
H and S 12–18in (30–45cm).

Z8–9 H9–1

Solenostemon scutellarioides*, syn. *Coleus blumei* var. *verschaffeltii
Fast-growing, bushy perennial, grown as an annual. Leaves are a mixture of colors, including pink, red, green, or yellow. Flower spikes should be removed. H to 18in (45cm), S 12in (30cm) or more.

Z13–15 H12–1

Malope trifida
Moderately fast-growing, erect, branching annual with rounded, lobed leaves. Flared, trumpet-shaped, reddish purple flowers, to 3in (8cm) wide and with deep pink veins, are carried in summer and early autumn.
H 3ft (90cm), S 1ft (30cm).

H8–1

***Lavatera trimestris* 'Silver Cup'**
Moderately fast-growing, erect, branching annual with oval, lobed leaves. Shallowly trumpet-shaped, rose-pink flowers are carried in summer and early autumn.
H 24in (60cm), S 18in (45cm).

Z9–11 H12–1

***Dianthus chinensis* Baby Doll Series**
Neat, bushy annual or biennial, grown as an annual. Light or midgreen leaves are lance-shaped; small, single, zoned flowers in various colors are carried in summer and early autumn.
H 6in (15cm), S 6–12in (15–30cm).

Z8–9 H9–1

***Lathyrus odoratus* 'Bijou'**
Fast-growing annual with oval, divided, midgreen leaves and large, fragrant flowers in shades of pink, red, or blue that are carried in summer or early autumn. H and S 18in (45cm).

Z9–10 H8–1

***Clarkia* 'Brilliant'**
Fast-growing, erect, bushy annual with oval leaves. Large, rosettelike, double, bright reddish pink flowers are carried in long spikes in summer and early autumn.
H to 24in (60cm), S 12in (30cm).

H8–1

***Callistephus chinensis* Milady Super Series [rose]**
Moderately fast-growing, erect, bushy annual with oval, toothed leaves. Has large, daisylike, double, rose-pink flower heads in summer and early autumn. H 10–12in (25–30cm), S 12–18in (30–45cm).

H9–1

Antirrhinum majus
Arctotis Harlequin Hybrids 'China Rose'
Bracteantha bracteata cvs
Callistephus chinensis and cvs
Cleome hassleriana 'Rose Queen'
Dianthus chinensis
Digitalis purpurea
Papaver somniferum
PELARGONIUMS, illus. pp.246–7
Pericallis x *hybrida* cvs
Petunia cvs
Phlox drummondii cvs
Portulaca grandiflora
Schizanthus cvs
Zinnia cvs

Matthiola **Ten-week Group**[dwarf]
Fast-growing, erect, bushy biennial, grown as an annual. Lance-shaped leaves are grayish green; long spikes of highly scented, single to double flowers in shades of pink, red, or white appear in summer. H and S 12in (30cm).

Z8–9 H9–1

Lunaria annua, syn. *L. biennis* (Honesty)
Fast-growing, erect biennial with pointed-oval, serrated leaves. Heads of scented, 4-petaled white to deep purple flowers in spring and early summer are followed by rounded silvery seed pods. H 30in (75cm), S 12in (30cm).

Z3–9 H9–1

Silene coeli-rosa **'Rose Angel'**
Moderately fast-growing, slim, erect annual. Has lance-shaped, grayish green leaves and 5-petaled, deep rose-pink flowers in summer.
H 12in (30cm), S 6in (15cm).

H9–1

Dorotheanthus bellidiformis **'Magic Carpet'**
Carpeting annual with succulent, lance-shaped, pale green leaves. Daisylike flower heads in bright shades of red, pink, yellow, or white open only in summer sunshine.
H 6in (15cm), S 12in (30cm).

Z11 H9–1

Petunia **Resisto Series** [rose-pink]
Moderately fast-growing, branching, bushy perennial, grown as an annual. Has oval leaves and rain-resistant, flared, trumpet-shaped, rose-pink flowers in summer-autumn.
H 6–12in (15–30cm), S 12in (30cm).

Z9–11 H12–1

Antirrhinum majus **Princess Series** [white with purple eye]
Erect perennial, grown as an annual, branching from the base. Has lance-shaped leaves and spikes of tubular, 2-lipped white and pinkish purple flowers borne from spring to autumn. H and S 18in (45cms).

Z9–11 H12–1

Xeranthemum annuum [double]
Erect annual with lance-shaped silvery leaves and branching heads of daisy-like, papery, double flower heads in shades of pink, mauve, purple, or white in summer. Produces good dried flowers. H 24in (60cm), S 18in (45cm).

H9–1

Cosmos bipinnatus **Sensation Series**
Moderately fast-growing, bushy, erect annual. Has feathery, midgreen leaves and daisylike flower heads, to 4in (10cm) wide, in shades of red, pink, or white, from early summer to early autumn. H 3ft (90cm), S 2ft (60cm).

H12–1

Impatiens balsamina **Tom Thumb Series**
Dwarf, sparsely branched, slightly hairy annual with toothed leaves. From summer to early autumn bears double pink, scarlet, violet, or white flowers. H to 12in (30cm), S 18in (45cm).

H12–1

***Phlox drummondii* 'Chanal'**
Erect to spreading but compact, bushy, hairy annual with very variable, stem-clasping leaves. In late spring bears cymes of double, almost roselike pink flowers. H 4–18in (10–45cm), S to 10in (25cm) or more.

☼ ◊ H12–1

***Verbena* x *hybrida* 'Showtime'**
Fairly slow-growing, bushy perennial, grown as an annual. Has lance-shaped, serrated, mid- to deep green leaves and clusters of small, tubular flowers in a range of colors in summer-autumn. H 8in (20cm), S 12in (30cm).

☼ ◊ Z9–11 H12–1

Dianthus barbatus
Roundabout Series [dwarf]
Slow-growing, upright, bushy biennial with lance-shaped leaves. In early summer has flat heads of zoned and eyed flowers in shades of pink, red, or white.
H 6in (15cm), S 8–12in (20–30cm).

☼ ◊ Z3–9 H9–1

Impatiens walleriana
Super Elfin Series 'Lipstick'
Fast-growing, evergreen, bushy perennial, grown as an annual. Has pointed-oval, fresh green leaves and small, flat, spurred, rose-red flowers from spring to autumn.
H and S 8in (20cm).

◐ ◑ Z10–15 H12–1

Portulaca grandiflora
Sundance Hybrids
Slow-growing, semi-trailing annual with lance-shaped, succulent, bright green leaves. Cup-shaped flowers with conspicuous stamens appear in a mixture of colors in summer and early autumn. H to 8in (20cm), S 6in (15cm).

☼ ◊ Z9–11 H12–1

Amaranthus caudatus
(Love-lies-bleeding, Tassel flower)
Bushy annual with oval, pale green leaves. Pendulous panicles of tassel-like red flowers, 18in (45cm) long, are carried in summer-autumn.
H to 4ft (1.2m), S 1½ft (45cm).

☼ ◊ Z10–15 H12–1

***Petunia* Picotee Series**
'Picotee Rose'
Fairly fast-growing, compact perennial, grown as an annual, with oval leaves. In summer-autumn it has large, deep rose-pink flowers with white margins.
H to 8in (20cm), S 18in (45cm).

☼ ◊ Z9–11 H12–1

Nicotiana* x *sanderae
Starship Series
Upright, woody-based, sticky annual or short-lived perennial that bears open racemes or panicles of tubular pink, red, rose-pink, white, or lime green flowers in summer.
H 12in (30cm), S 12–16in (30–40cm).

◐ ◊ Z10–15 H12–1

***Petunia* 'Mirage Velvet'**
Branching, bushy perennial, grown as an annual, with oval, dark green leaves. Large, flared, trumpet-shaped, rich red flowers, with almost black centers, appear in summer-autumn.
H 10in (25cm), S 12in (30cm).

☼ ◊ Z9–11 H12–1

Phlox drummondii
'Sternenzauber'
Moderately fast-growing, slim, erect annual. Lance-shaped leaves are pale green; heads of star-shaped flowers in a bright mixture of colors, some with contrasting centers, are carried in summer. H 6in (15cm), S 4in (10cm).

☼ ◊ H12–1

Bellis perennis cvs
Celosia argentea var. *cristata*
PELARGONIUMS, illus. pp.246–7
Pericallis x *hybrida* cvs
Zinnia cvs

***Alcea rosea* 'Chater's Double'**
Erect biennial with lobed, rough-textured leaves. Spikes of rosettelike, double flowers in several different colors are carried on upright stems in summer and early autumn.
H 6–8ft (1.8–2.4m), S to 2ft (60cm).

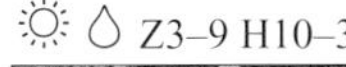
Z3–9 H10–3

***Viola* x *wittrockiana* Imperial Series 'Imperial Frosty Rose'**
Erect, bushy perennial, grown as an annual or biennial, with oval leaves. In spring it bears large, rose-purple flowers fading to pink and white.
H 6–9in (16–23cm),
S 9–12in (23–30cm).

Z8–11 H9–1

***Impatiens walleriana* Novette Series 'Red Star'**
Fast-growing, evergreen, bushy perennial, grown as an annual. Has pointed-oval, fresh green leaves and from spring to autumn small, flat, spurred red flowers with star-shaped white markings. H and S 6in (15cm).

Z10–15 H12–1

***Impatiens* Confection Series**

Fast-growing, evergreen, bushy perennial, grown as an annual. Has fresh green leaves and small, flat, spurred, double or semi-double flowers in shades of red or pink from spring to autumn. H and S 8–12in (20–30cm).

Z10–15 H12–1

***Salvia splendens* Sizzler Series**
Slow-growing, bushy perennials, grown as annuals, with flowers in bright shades of cerise-red, lavender-blue, salmon-pink, purple, scarlet, or white, available as single colors, borne in early summer. H 10–12in (25–30cm),
S 9–14in (23–35cm).

Z11–12 H12–1

***Bellis perennis* Pomponette Series**
Slow-growing, carpeting perennial, grown as a biennial. Has oval leaves and small, daisylike, double flower heads in red, pink, or white in spring.
H and S 4–6in (10–15cm).

Z4–8 H8–1

***Linum grandiflorum* 'Rubrum'**
Fairly fast-growing, slim, erect annual. Lance-shaped leaves are gray-green; small, rounded, flattish, deep red flowers are carried in summer.
H 18in (45cm), S 6in (15cm).

H8–1

***Dianthus chinensis* 'Fire Carpet'**
Slow-growing, bushy annual or biennial, grown as an annual. Lance-shaped leaves are light or midgreen. Small, rounded, single, bright red flowers are carried in summer and early autumn.
H 8in (20cm), S 6–12in (15–30cm).

Z4–8 H8–1

***Phlox drummondii* 'African Sunset'**
Erect to spreading, bushy, hairy annual with very variable, stem-clasping leaves. In late spring produces tubular, hairy, dusky to deep red flowers.
H 4–18in (10–45cm),
S to 10in (25cm) or more.

H12–1

■ RED

***Zinnia elegans* Ruffles Series** [scarlet]
Moderately fast-growing, sturdy, upright annual with oval to lance-shaped leaves. Ruffled, daisylike, double scarlet flower heads are carried in summer and early autumn.
H 24in (60cm), S 12in (30cm).

☼ ◊ H12–1

***Salvia splendens* 'Scarlet King'**
Slow-growing, compact, bushy perennial, usually grown as an annual, with oval, toothed, dark green leaves. Produces long-tubed, bright scarlet flowers in dense, terminal spikes in early summer. H to 10in (25cm), S 9–14in (23–35cm).

☼ ◊ Z11–12 H12–1

***Pelargonium* Multibloom Series**
Erect, bushy, evergreen perennials, grown as annuals. Abundant flowers in white or shades of pink or red are borne in clusters over a long period throughout summer.
H 10–12in (25–30cm), S 12in (30cm).

☼ ◊ ! Z12–15 H12–1

***Petunia* Carpet Series**
Moderately fast-growing, compact, spreading perennial, grown as an annual, with oval leaves. In summer-autumn it bears flowers in a color range that includes strong reds and oranges.
H 8–10in (20–25cm),
S 12–36in (30–90cm).

☼ ◊ Z8–11 H12–1

Papaver rhoeas
Shirley Series [single]
Fast-growing, slender, erect annual with lobed, light green leaves. Rounded, often cup-shaped, single flowers in shades of red, pink, salmon, or white appear in summer.
H 24in (60cm), S 12in (30cm).

☼ ◊ Z11 H9–1

Nemesia strumosa
Carnival Series
Fairly fast-growing, bushy annual with serrated, pale green leaves. In summer has small, somewhat trumpet-shaped flowers in a range of colors, including yellow, red, orange, purple, and white.
H 8–12in (20–30cm), S 6in (15cm).

☼ ◊ H7–1

***Petunia* Picotee Series** [red]
Fairly fast-growing, branching, bushy perennial, grown as an annual, with oval leaves. Has flared, somewhat trumpet-shaped red flowers edged with white in summer-autumn.
H 6–12in (15–30cm), S 12in (30cm).

☼ ◊ Z9–11 H12–1

***Verbena* x *hybrida* Sandy Series**
Compact, erect, bushy perennial, grown as an annual. Has lance-shaped, serrated, mid- to deep green leaves. In summer and autumn produces clusters of small flowers in rose-pink, rose-pink with white eyes, magenta, scarlet, or white. H 8in (20cm), S 12in (30cm).

☼ ◊ Z9–11 H12–1

***Primula* Pacific Series** [dwarf]
Rosette-forming perennial, normally grown as a biennial, with lance-shaped leaves. Has heads of large, fragrant, flat flowers in shades of blue, yellow, red, pink, or white in spring.
H 4–6in (10–15cm), S 8in (20cm).

☼ ◊ Z6–8 H8–1

Antirrhinum majus
Bracteantha bracteata cvs
Calceolaria Anytime Series
Calceolaria 'Monarch'
Capsicum annuum 'Holiday Cheer'
Erysimum cheiri
Gaillardia pulchella [double, mixed]
Impatiens balsamina Tom Thumb Series
Impatiens walleriana
Ipomoea coccinea
Ipomoea x *multifida*
Ipomoea nil 'Scarlett O'Hara'
Ipomoea quamoclit, illus. p.210
Ipomopsis aggregata
Ismelia carinata Tricolor Series
Papaver commutatum

Zinnia elegans
Ruffles Series [mixed]
Moderately fast-growing, sturdy, upright annual with pale or midgreen leaves. Ruffled, pompon, double flower heads in a mixture of colors are carried in summer and early autumn.
H 24in (60cm), S 12in (30cm).

☼ ◊ H12–1

***Salpiglossis sinuata* Casino Series**
Erect, compact annual with slender, freely branching stems. From summer to autumn has broadly funnel-shaped, 5-lobed flowers in blue, purple, red, yellow, or orange, often heavily veined.
H to 24in (60cm), S to 12in (30cm).

☼ ◊ Z10–11 H12–1

Ismelia carinata
'Monarch Court Jesters'
Fast-growing, erect, branching annual. In summer has feathery, gray-green leaves and daisylike, zoned flower heads, to 3in (8cm) wide, in various color combinations.
H 24in (60cm), S 12in (30cm).

☼ ◊ H9–1

Viola x *wittrockiana*
Floral Dance Series
Fairly fast-growing, bushy perennial, grown as an annual or biennial. Has oval, midgreen leaves and rounded, 5-petaled flowers in a wide range of colors in cool and cold weather.
H 6–8in (15–20cm), S 8in (20cm).

☼ ◊ Z8–11 H12–1

Alonsoa warscewiczii
(Mask flower)
Perennial, grown as an annual, with slender, branching red stems carrying oval, toothed, deep green leaves. Spurred, bright scarlet flowers are produced during summer-autumn.
H 12–24in (30–60cm), S 12in (30cm).

☼ ◊ Z10–11 H12–10

***Dahlia* 'Coltness Gem'**
Well-branched, erect, bushy, tuberous perennial, grown as an annual. Has deeply lobed leaves and daisylike, single flower heads in many colors throughout summer until autumn frosts.
H and S 18in (45cm).

☼ ◊ Z9–11 H12–1

***Tagetes* 'Cinnabar'**
Fast-growing, bushy annual with aromatic, very feathery, deep green leaves. Heads of rounded, daisylike, single, rich rust-red flowers, yellow-red beneath, are carried in summer and early autumn. H and S 12in (30cm).

☼ ◊ (!) H12–1

Solenostemon scutellarioides
'Brightness', syn. *Coleus blumei* var. *verschaffeltii* 'Brightness'
Fast-growing, bushy perennial, grown as an annual. Has rust-red leaves edged with green. Flower spikes should be removed. H to 18in (45cm), S 12in (30cm) or more.

☼ ◊ Z13–15 H12–1

Petunia cvs
Portulaca grandiflora
Salpiglossis sinuata cvs
Salvia splendens
Solanum capsicastrum
Solanum pseudocapsicum 'Fancy'
Solenostemon scutellarioides, illus. p.324
Tagetes patula
Tropaeolum majus

ANNUALS *and* BIENNIALS

■ RED

Amaranthus hypochondriacus
(Prince's feather)
Bushy annual with upright, sometimes flattened panicles, 6in (15cm) or more long, of dark red flowers in summer-autumn. Leaves are heavily suffused purple. H to 4ft (1.2m), S 1½ft (45cm).

H12–1

***Ricinus communis* 'Impala'**
Fast-growing, evergreen, erect shrub, usually grown as an annual. Has deeply lobed bronze leaves to 12in (30cm) wide (sometimes more) and clusters of small red flowers in summer, followed by globular, prickly red seed heads. H 5ft (1.5m), S 3ft (90cm).

Z11–14 H12–1

Calomeria amaranthoides
(Incense plant)
Erect, branching biennial with a strong fragrance of incense. Has lance-shaped leaves and heads of tiny pink, brownish red, or crimson flowers in summer-autumn. H to 6ft (1.8m), S 3ft (90cm).

Z12–15 H12–10

Amaranthus tricolor 'Joseph's Coat'
Atriplex hortensis var. *rubra*
Nicotiana x *sanderae* 'Crimson Rock'
Scabiosa atropurpurea

■ PURPLE

Trachelium caeruleum
(Throatwort)
Moderately fast-growing, erect perennial, grown as an annual. Has oval, serrated leaves and clustered heads of small, tubular, lilac-blue or white flowers in summer.
H 2–3ft (60–90cm), S 1ft (30cm).

Z9–13 H12–1

Salvia sclarea* var. *turkestanica
Moderately fast-growing, erect biennial, grown as an annual. Has aromatic, oval, hairy leaves and panicles of tubular white and lavender-purple flowers with prominent, lavender-purple bracts in summer.
H 30in (75cm), S 12in (30cm).

Z8-9 H12-1

***Linaria maroccana* 'Fairy Lights'**
Fast-growing, erect, bushy annual with lance-shaped, pale green leaves. Tiny, snapdragon-like flowers in shades of red, pink, purple, yellow, or white are borne in summer.
H 8in (20cm), S 6in (15cm).

H9–1

***Psylliostachys suworowii*, (Statice)**
Fairly slow-growing, erect, branching annual with lance-shaped leaves. Bears branching spikes of small, tubular pink to purple flowers in summer and early autumn. Flowers are good for drying.
H 18in (45cm), S 12in (30cm).

H12–6

Schizanthus pinnatus
Moderately fast-growing, upright, bushy annual with feathery, light green leaves. In summer-autumn has rounded, lobed, multicolored flowers in shades of pink, purple, white, or yellow.
H 1–4ft (30cm–1.2m), S 1ft (30cm).

Z12–15 H8–1

Antirrhinum majus
Centaurea cyanus
Consolida ajacis Dwarf Hyacinth Series
Iberis umbellata

Impatiens balsamina Tom Thumb Series
Ionopsidium acaule
Lobelia erinus 'Color Cascade'
Matthiola cvs

Nemesia strumosa
Proboscidea fragrans
Xeranthemum annuum

■ PURPLE

Exacum affine (Persian violet)
Evergreen, bushy biennial, usually grown as an annual. Has oval, glossy leaves and masses of tiny, scented, saucer-shaped purple flowers with yellow stamens in summer and early autumn. H and S 8–12in (20–30cm).

 H7–1

Collinsia grandiflora
Moderately fast-growing, slender-stemmed annual. Upper leaves are lance-shaped; lower are oval. Whorls of pale purple flowers with purplish blue lips are carried in spring-summer. H and S 6–12in (15–30cm).

Z10–11 H11–1

***Campanula medium* 'Bells of Holland'**
Slow-growing, evergreen, clump-forming, erect biennial with lance-shaped, toothed leaves. In spring and early summer has bell-shaped flowers in a mixture of blue, lilac, pink, or white. H to 24in (60cm), S 12in (30cm).

Z5–8 H8–5

Echium vulgare [dwarf]
Moderately fast-growing, erect, bushy annual or biennial with lance-shaped, dark green leaves. Spikes of tubular flowers in shades of white, pink, blue, or purple appear in summer. H 12in (30cm), S 8in (20cm).

 Z3–8 H8–1

***Nierembergia caerulea* 'Purple Robe'**
Moderately fast-growing, rounded, branching perennial, grown as an annual, with narrow, lance-shaped leaves. Has cup-shaped, dark bluish purple flowers in summer and early autumn. H and S 6–8in (15–20cm).

Z11 H12–1

Salvia viridis, syn. *S. horminum*
Moderately fast-growing, upright, branching annual with oval leaves. Tubular, lipped flowers, enclosed by purple, pink, or white bracts, are carried in spikes at tops of stems in summer and early autumn. H 18in (45cm), S 8in (20cm).

H9–1

Orychophragmus violaceus
Moderately fast-growing, upright annual or biennial with branching flower stems and pointed-oval, pale green leaves. Heads of 4-petaled, purple-blue flowers are borne in spring. H 12–24in (30–60cm), S 12in (30cm).

Z10–13 H8–1

***Callistephus chinensis* Ostrich Plume Series**
Fast-growing, bushy annual with long, branching stems. From late summer to late autumn it produces spreading, feathery, reflexed, double flower heads, mainly in pinks and crimsons. H to 2ft (60cm), S 1ft (30cm).

H9–1

Gomphrena globosa
(Globe amaranth)
Moderately fast-growing, upright, bushy annual with oval, hairy leaves. Has oval, cloverlike flower heads in pink, yellow, orange, purple, or white in summer and early autumn. H 12in (30cm), S 8in (20cm).

Z11–12 H12–1

***Petunia* Daddy Series 'Sugar Daddy'**
Fairly fast-growing, branching, bushy perennial, grown as an annual, with oval leaves. In early summer to autumn has large purple flowers with dark veins. H to 14in (35cm), S 12–36in (30–90cm).

Z9–13 H12–1

***Salvia splendens* Cleopatra Series** [violet]
Slow-growing, bushy perennial, grown as an annual. Oval, serrated leaves are dark green; dense racemes of tubular, deep violet-purple flowers are carried in summer and early autumn. H to 12in (30cm), S 8–12in (20–30cm).

Z11–13 H12–1

***Cerinthe major* 'Purpurascens'**
Annual of lax habit with oval to spoon-shaped leaves to 2½in (6cm) long. Bears terminal sprays of nodding, tubular, pale to midyellow flowers with violet-tinged tips. Bracts around flowers are strongly suffused purple. H and S 2ft (60cm).

H12–8

Amaranthus tricolor 'Molten Fire'
Arctotis Harlequin Hybrids 'Bacchus'
Papaver somniferum
Perilla frutescens
Petunia cvs
Phlox drummondii cvs
Schizanthus cvs
Senecio elegans
Viola x *wittrockiana* cvs
Zinnia cvs

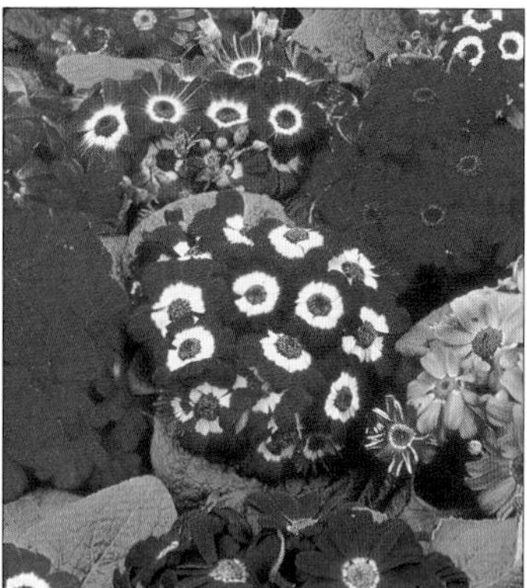

Pericallis **x** ***hybrida*** **'Spring Glory'** (Cineraria)
Slow-growing, evergreen, mound- or dome-shaped perennial, grown as a biennial, with large, oval, serrated leaves. Bears heads of large flowers in a mixture of colors in spring.
H 8in (20cm), S 12in (30cm).

Z12–13 H7–1

Callistephus chinensis **Milady Super Series** [blue]
Moderately fast-growing, erect, bushy annual with oval, toothed leaves. Has large, daisylike, double, purplish blue flower heads in summer and early autumn. H 10–12in (25–30cm), S 12–18in (30–45cm).

H9–1

Petunia **Resisto Series** [blue]
Moderately fast-growing, branching, bushy perennial, grown as an annual. Has oval leaves and rain-resistant, flared, trumpet-shaped, intense blue flowers in summer-autumn.
H 6–12in (15–30cm), S 12in (30cm).

Z9–11 H12–1

Lobelia erinus **'Sapphire'**
Slow-growing, pendulous, spreading annual or occasionally perennial. Oval to lance-shaped leaves are pale green; small, sapphire blue flowers with white centers are produced continuously in summer and early autumn.
H 8in (20cm), S 6in (15cm).

Z9–10 H8–1

Consolida ajacis **Giant Imperial Series** (Giant larkspur)
Fast-growing, upright, branching annual with feathery leaves. Long spikes of rounded, spurred, double flowers in pink, blue, or white are carried in summer.
H 4ft (1.2m), S 1ft (30cm).

Z7–9 H9–1

Convolvulus tricolor **'Blue Flash'**
Moderately fast-growing, upright, bushy annual with oval to lance-shaped leaves. Has small, saucer-shaped, intense blue flowers with cream and yellow centers in summer.
H 8–12in (20–30cm), S 8in (20cm).

Z9–10 H10–1

Salvia farinacea **'Victoria'**
Moderately fast-growing perennial, grown as an annual, with many erect stems. Has oval or lance-shaped leaves and spikes of tubular, violet-blue flowers in summer.
H 18in (45cm), S 12in (30cm).

Z8–11 H12–1

Viola **x** ***wittrockiana*** **Joker Series**
Bushy, spreading perennial, usually grown as an annual or biennial. Large, rounded, 5-petaled, purplish blue flowers with black and white "faces" and yellow eyes appear in spring.
H and S 15cm (6in).

Z8–11 H9–1

Primula **Super Giants Series** [blue]
Rosette-forming perennial, usually grown as a biennial, with lance-shaped leaves. Heads of large, fragrant, flat blue flowers appear in spring.
H and S to 12in (30cm).

Z6–8 H8–1

Browallia speciosa, illus. p.266
Ipomoea purpurea

Torenia fournieri
(Wishbone flower)
Moderately fast-growing, erect, branching annual with serrated, light green leaves. Dark blue-purple flowers, paler and yellow within, are carried in summer and early autumn. H 12in (30cm), S 8in (20cm).

Z12–13 H6–1

Gilia capitata
Erect, branching annual. Has very feathery, midgreen leaves and tiny, dense, rounded heads of soft lavender-blue flowers in summer and early autumn. Is good for cut flowers.
H 18in (45cm), S 8in (20cm).

H12–1

Nigella damascena
Persian Jewels Series
Fast-growing, erect annual with feathery leaves. Small, semi-double flowers in shades of blue, pink, or white appear in summer, followed by inflated seed pods that can be cut and dried.
H 18in (45cm), S 8in (20cm).

H10–1

Ageratum houstonianum
'Blue Mink'
Moderately fast-growing, hummock-forming annual. Has pointed-oval leaves and clusters of feathery, brush-like, pastel blue flower heads in summer-autumn. Makes a useful edging plant. H and S 8–12in (20–30cm).

Z10–13 H12–1

Ageratum houstonianum
'Blue Danube'
Moderately fast-growing, hummock-forming annual with pointed-oval leaves. Has clusters of feathery, brush-like, lavender-blue flower heads in summer-autumn. Makes a useful edging plant. H and S 6in (15cm).

Z10–13 H12–1

Sedum caeruleum
Moderately fast-growing annual with branching flower stems. Oval, light green leaves become red-tinged when clusters of small, star-shaped, light blue flowers with white centers are borne in summer. H and S 4-6in (10-15cm).

H9–1

***Nigella damascena* 'Miss Jekyll'**
Fast-growing, slender, erect annual. Feathery leaves are bright green; small, rounded, many-petaled, semi-double blue flowers are carried in summer, followed by inflated seed pods that can be cut and dried.
H 18in (45cm), S 8in (8in).

H12–1

***Nemophila menziesii*,**
syn. *N. insignis* (Baby blue-eyes)
Fast-growing, spreading annual with serrated, gray-green leaves. Small, bowl-shaped blue flowers with white centers are carried in summer.
H 8in (20cm), S 6in (15cm).

H12–2

***Viola* x *wittrockiana* 'True Blue'**
Erect, bushy perennial, grown as an annual or biennial, with spreading stems and oval leaves. In cold or cool weather it bears large, clear sky blue flowers, each with a small yellow eye.
H 6–9in (16–23cm),
S 9–12in (23–30cm).

Z4–8 H9–1

Callistephus chinensis
Consolida ajacis Dwarf Hyacinth Series
Lobelia erinus 'Blue Cascade'
Nolana paradoxa
Petunia cvs
Phacelia tanacetifolia
Phlox drummondii cvs
Salvia viridis cvs
Trachymene coerulea
Viola x *wittrockiana* cvs

BLUE

Centaurea cyanus [tall, blue] (Cornflower)
Fast-growing, erect, branching annual. Has lance-shaped, gray-green leaves and branching heads of daisylike blue flowers in summer and early autumn. H to 3ft (90cm), S 1ft (30cm).

☼ ◊ H7–1

Brachyscome iberidifolia (Swan River daisy)
Moderately fast-growing, thin-stemmed, bushy annual with deeply cut leaves. Has small, fragrant, daisylike flower heads, usually blue but also pink, mauve, purple, or white, in summer and early autumn. H and S to 18in (45cm).

☼ ◊ Z5–8 H9–3

Felicia bergeriana (Kingfisher daisy)
Fairly fast-growing, mat-forming annual. Has lance-shaped, hairy, gray-green leaves. Small, daisylike blue flower heads with yellow centers open only in sunshine in summer and early autumn. H and S 6in (15cm).

☼ ◊ Z11–12 H12–1

***Myosotis sylvatica* 'Blue Ball'**
Slow-growing, bushy, compact perennial, often grown as a biennial. Has lance-shaped leaves and, in spring and early summer, spikes of tiny, 5-lobed, deep blue flowers.
H to 8in (20cm), S 6in (15cm).

◐ ◊ Z5–9 H7–1

***Cynoglossum amabile* 'Firmament'**
Slow-growing, upright, bushy annual or biennial with lance-shaped, hairy, gray-green leaves. Pendulous, tubular, pure sky blue flowers are carried in summer. H 18in (45cm), S 12in (30cm).

☼ ◊ Z5–8 H8–5

Commelina coelestis (Day flower)
Fairly fast-growing, upright perennial, usually grown as an annual, with lance-shaped, midgreen leaves. Small, 3-petaled, bright pure blue flowers are freely produced from late summer to midautumn.
H to 18in (45cm), S 12in (30cm).

☼ ◊ Z9–10 H12–9

Phacelia campanularia (California bluebell)
Moderately fast-growing, branching, bushy annual with oval, serrated, deep green leaves. Bell-shaped, pure blue flowers, 1in (2.5cm) wide, are carried in summer and early autumn.
H 8in (20cm), S 6in (15cm).

☼ ◊ ! Z5–10 H9–1

***Anchusa capensis* 'Blue Angel'**
Bushy biennial, grown as an annual. Has lance-shaped, bristly leaves. Heads of shallowly bowl-shaped, brilliant blue flowers are borne in summer.
H and S 8in (20cm).

☼ ◊ Z7–9 H9–7

Borago officinalis (Borage)
Spreading, clump-forming, annual herb. Has oval, crinkled, rough-haired leaves and sprays of star-shaped blue flowers in summer and early autumn. Young leaves are sometimes used as a cooler in drinks. Self seeds prolifically.
H 3ft (90cm), S 1ft (30cm).

☼ ◊ H12–1

BLUE–GREEN

***Lobelia erinus* 'Crystal Palace'**
Slow-growing, spreading, compact, bushy annual or occasionally perennial. Bronzed leaves are oval to lance-shaped; small, deep blue flowers are produced continuously in summer and early autumn. H 4–8in (10–20cm), S 4–6in (10–15cm).

☼ ◊ Z2–8 H8–1

***Senecio cineraria* 'Silver Dust'**, syn. *S. maritimus* 'Silver Dust'
Moderately fast-growing, evergreen, bushy subshrub, usually grown as an annual, with deeply lobed silver leaves. Small, daisylike yellow flower heads appear in summer but are best removed. H and S 12in (30cm).

☼ ◊ ! Z8–11 H12–8

Nicotiana langsdorffii
Fairly slow-growing, erect, branching perennial, grown as an annual, with oval to lance-shaped leaves. Slightly pendent, bell-shaped, pale green to yellow-green flowers with blue stamens appear in summer.
H 3–5ft (1–1.5m), S 1ft (30cm).

☼ ◊ ! Z10–11 H12–1

Anchusa capensis 'Blue Bird'
Browallia americana
Campanula medium
Convolvulus tricolor 'Flying Saucers'
Eustoma grandiflorum Heidi Series
Gilia achilleifolia
Lobelia erinus 'Cambridge Blue'
Lobelia erinus 'Color Cascade'
Nigella damascena
Senecio cineraria

GREEN–YELLOW

Moluccella laevis
(Bells of Ireland)
Fairly fast-growing, erect, branching annual. Rounded leaves are pale green; spikes of small, tubular white flowers, each surrounded by a conspicuous, pale green calyx, appear in summer.
H 24in (60cm), S 8in (20cm).

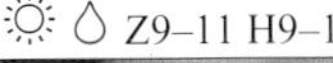
Z9–11 H9–1

***Zinnia elegans* 'Envy'**
Moderately fast-growing, sturdy, erect annual. Has oval to lance-shaped, pale or midgreen leaves and large, daisy-like, double green flower heads in summer and early autumn. Color is best when grown out of strong sun.
H 24in (60cm), S 12in (30cm).

H12–1

***Bassia scoparia* f. *trichophylla*,**
syn. *Kochia scoparia* f. *trichophylla*
(Burning bush, Summer cypress)
Moderately fast-growing, erect, very bushy annual. Narrow, lance-shaped, light green leaves, 2–3in (5–8cm) long, turn red in autumn. Has insignificant flowers. H 3ft (90cm), S 2ft (60cm).

Z9–11 H9–2

Ricinus communis
(Castor bean)
Fast-growing, evergreen, erect shrub, usually grown as an annual. Has large, deeply lobed, midgreen leaves and heads of green and red flowers in summer, followed by globular, prickly seed pods. H 5ft (1.5m), S 3ft (90cm).

Z11–14 H12–1

***Amberboa moschata*, syn.**
Centaurea moschata (Sweet sultan)
Fast-growing, upright, slender-stemmed annual with lance-shaped, grayish green leaves. Large, fragrant, cornflower-like flower heads in a range of colors are carried in summer and early autumn.
H 18in (45cm), S 8in (20cm).

H12–1

Platystemon californicus
(Cream cups)
Moderately fast-growing, upright, compact annual with lance-shaped, grayish green leaves. Saucer-shaped, cream or pale yellow flowers, about 1in (2.5cm) across, appear in summer.
H 12in (30cm), S 4in (10cm).

H12–7

Angelica archangelica, illus. p.228
Nicandra physalodes
Nicotiana 'Lime Green'
Solenostemon scutellarioides, illus. p.324
Tanacetum parthenium 'Aureum'

YELLOW

Smyrnium perfoliatum
Slow-growing, upright biennial. Upper leaves, rounded and yellow-green, encircle stems that bear heads of yellowish green flowers in summer.
H 2–3ft (60cm–1m), S 2ft (60cm).

Z6–10 H8–1

Argemone mexicana
(Devil's fig, Prickly poppy)
Spreading perennial, grown as an annual, with leaves divided into white-marked, grayish green leaflets.
In summer has fragrant, poppylike yellow or orange flowers, 3in (8cm) wide. H to 24in (60cm), S 12in (30cm).

H12–7

Glaucium flavum (Horned poppy)
Slow-growing, erect biennial with oval, lobed, light grayish green leaves. Poppylike, vivid yellow flowers, 3in (8cm) wide, appear in summer and early autumn.
H 12–24in (30–60cm), S 18in (45cm).

Z6–9 H9–6

Calendula officinalis 'Fiesta Gitana'
Tagetes Gem Series 'Lemon Gem'
Xanthophthalmum coronarium

□ YELLOW

Viola* x *wittrockiana
'Clear Sky Primrose'
Erect, bushy perennial, grown as an annual or biennial, with oval leaves. In cool and cold weather it produces primrose yellow flowers brushed in canary yellow. H 6–9in (16–23cm), S 9–12in (23–30cm).

Z4–8 H9–1

Limnanthes douglasii (Meadow foam, Poached-egg flower)
Fast-growing, slender, erect annual. Feathery leaves are glossy, light green; slightly fragrant, cup-shaped white flowers with yellow centers are carried from early to late summer.
H 6in (15cm), S 4in (10cm).

H9–1

Eschscholzia caespitosa
Fast-growing, slender, erect annual with feathery, bluish green leaves. Cup-shaped, 4-petaled yellow flowers, 1in (2.5cm) wide, appear in summer and early autumn. H and S 6in (15cm).

Z8–10 H9–2

***Antirrhinum majus* Tahiti Series**
Erect perennial, grown as an annual, branching from the base, with lance-shaped leaves. In summer and autumn it bears 2-lipped flowers in red, orange, rose-pink, and bronze, plus a pink and white bicolor. Rust resistant.
H 8–12in (20–30cm), S 12in (30cm).

Z8–11 H12–1

***Helianthus annuus* 'Music Box'**
Fast-growing, free-flowering, many-branched, hairy-stemmed annual. Bears daisylike flower heads, 4–5in (10–12cm) across, with ray florets ranging from creamy yellow to dark red, and black disk florets, in summer.
H 28in (70cm), S to 24in (60cm).

H12–1

Lindheimera texana (Star daisy)
Moderately fast-growing, erect, branching annual with hairy stems and oval, serrated, hairy leaves. Daisy-like yellow flower heads appear in late summer and early autumn.
H 12–24in (30–60cm), S 12in (30cm).

H12–7

Viola* x *wittrockiana
'Super Chalon Giants'
Fairly fast-growing, bushy perennial, grown as an annual or biennial.
Has oval, serrated leaves and, in cool weather, 5-petaled, ruffled and waved, bicolored flowers.
H 6–8in (15–20cm), S 8in (20cm).

Z8–11 H9–1

Calendula officinalis
Kablouna Series
Fast-growing, bushy annual with strongly aromatic, lance-shaped leaves. From spring to autumn has crested, daisylike orange, gold, or yellow flower heads. H 24in (60cm),
S 12–24in (30–60cm).

H6–1

Mentzelia lindleyi,
syn. *Bartonia aurea*
Fairly fast-growing, bushy annual with fleshy stems and lance-shaped, serrated leaves. Has fragrant, cup-shaped, deep yellow flowers with conspicuous stamens in summer.
H 18in (45cm), S 8in (20cm).

H9–1

***Tagetes* 'Gold Coins'**
[Erecta Group]
Fast-growing, erect, bushy annual. Has aromatic, feathery, glossy, deep green leaves and large, daisylike, double flower heads in shades of yellow and orange in summer and early autumn.
H 3ft (90cm), S 1–1½ft (30–45cm).

H12–1

Sanvitalia procumbens
(Creeping zinnia)
Moderately fast-growing, prostrate annual with pointed-oval leaves. Daisy-like yellow flower heads, 1in (2.5cm) wide, with black centers, are borne in summer. H 6in (15cm), S 12in (30cm).

H12–1

Amaranthus tricolor 'Joseph's Coat'
Antirrhinum majus
Arctotis Harlequin Hybrids 'Sunshine'
Bracteantha bracteata cvs

Calceolaria Anytime Series
Calceolaria 'Monarch'
Cosmos bipinnatus 'Sea Shells'
Erysimum cheiri

Gaillardia pulchella [double, mixed]
Gazania Daybreak Series
Helianthus annuus 'Russian Giant'
Helianthus annuus 'Teddy Bear', illus. p.337

Hunnemannia fumariifolia 'Sunlite'
Ismelia carinata Tricolor Series
Layia platyglossa
Nemesia strumosa

Coreopsis tinctoria (Tickseed)
Fast-growing, erect, bushy annual with lance-shaped leaves. Large, daisylike, bright yellow flower heads with red centers are carried in summer and early autumn.
H 2–3ft (60–90cm), S 8in (20cm).

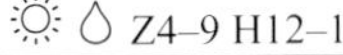
Z4–9 H12–1

Viola* x *wittrockiana
Clear Crystals Series
[yellow]
Bushy perennial, grown as an annual or biennial. Has oval, midgreen leaves and rounded, 5-petaled yellow flowers in spring.
H 6–8in (15–20cm), S 8in (20cm).

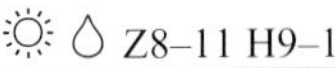
Z8–11 H9–1

Viola* x *wittrockiana
Crystal Bowl Series
[yellow]
Bushy, spreading perennial, usually grown as an annual or biennial, with oval, midgreen leaves. Large, rounded, 5-petaled yellow flowers are carried in spring. H and S 6in (15cm).

Z8–11 H9–1

Xanthophthalmum segetum
Moderately fast-growing, erect annual with lance-shaped, gray-green leaves. Daisylike, single flower heads, to 3in (8cm) wide, in shades of yellow, are carried in summer and early autumn. Excellent for cut flowers.
H 18in (45cm), S 12in (30cm).

H9–1

Cladanthus arabicus
Moderately fast-growing, hummock-forming annual with aromatic, feathery, light green leaves. Has fragrant, daisy-like, single, deep yellow flower heads, 2in (5cm) wide, in summer and early autumn. H 24in (60cm), S 12in (30cm).

H12–1

***Antirrhinum majus* Sonnet Series**
Erect, bushy, early flowering perennial, grown as an annual, branching from the base, with lance-shaped leaves. From spring to autumn it freely produces 2-lipped flowers in bronze, pink, carmine-red, crimson, burgundy, white, and yellow. H and S 18in (45cm).

Z8–11 H12–1

***Coreopsis* 'Sunray'**
Spreading, clump-forming perennial, grown as an annual by sowing under cover in early spring. Has lance-shaped, serrated leaves and daisylike, double, bright yellow flower heads in summer.
H 18in (45cm), S 12–18in (30–45cm).

Z4–9 H9–1

Helianthus annuus
Fast-growing, erect annual with oval, serrated, midgreen leaves. Daisylike yellow flower heads to 12in (30cm) or more wide, with brown or purplish centers, appear in summer.
H 3–10ft (1–3m), S 3ft (1m).

H12–1

***Helianthus annuus* 'Teddy Bear'**
Fast-growing, compact, hairy-stemmed annual with toothed, roughly hairy leaves. Produces daisylike, double, deep yellow flower heads, to 5in (13cm) across, in summer.
H 36in (90cm), S to 24in (60cm).

H12–1

Portulaca grandiflora
Salpiglossis sinuata Bolero Hybrids
Schizanthus cvs
Solenostemon scutellarioides, illus. p.324
Tolpis barbata
Tropaeolum majus
Tuberaria guttata
Viola x *wittrockiana* cvs
Zinnia cvs

☐ YELLOW

***Zinnia elegans* 'Belvedere'**
Moderately fast-growing, sturdy, erect annual with oval to lance-shaped, pale or midgreen leaves. Large, daisylike, double flower heads in a mixture of colors appear in summer and early autumn. H and S 12in (30cm).

H12–1

Ursinia anthemoides
Moderately fast-growing, bushy annual with feathery, pale green leaves. Small, daisylike, purple-centered flower heads with orange-yellow rays, purple beneath, appear in summer and early autumn. H 12in (30cm), S 8in (20cm).

H12–6

***Gaillardia pulchella* 'Lollipops'**
Moderately fast-growing, upright annual with lance-shaped, hairy, grayish green leaves. Daisylike, double, red-and-yellow flower heads, 2in (5cm) wide, are carried in summer.
H and S 12in (30cm).

Z10–11 H12–1

***Calceolaria* 'Bright Bikinis'**
Compact, bushy annual or biennial. Has oval, slightly hairy, midgreen leaves and heads of small, rounded, pouched flowers in shades of yellow, orange, or red in summer.
H and S 8in (20cm).

Z8–9 H6–1

***Tagetes* Solar Series**
Bushy annual bearing large, densely double flower heads, in colors including orange with red flecking, sulfur yellow, and golden yellow, some with crested centers, from late spring to early autumn.
H 14in (35cm), S 12–16in (30–40cm).

H12–1

***Tagetes* 'Naughty Marietta'**
Fast-growing, bushy annual with aromatic, deeply cut, deep green leaves. Heads of daisylike, bicolored flowers in deep yellow and maroon are carried in summer and early autumn.
H and S 12in (30cm).

H12–1

***Calendula officinalis* Pacific Beauty Series 'Lemon Queen'**
Fast-growing, erect annual with softly hairy, aromatic leaves. Daisylike, double, lemon yellow flower heads, with red-brown disk florets, are borne from summer to autumn. H to 18in (45cm), S 12–18in (30–45cm).

H6–1

***Viola* x *wittrockiana* Forerunner Series**
Erect, bushy perennials, grown as annuals or biennials, with oval leaves. In cool and cold weather it bears midsized flowers in a range of bright, single colors and bicolors. H 6–9in (16–23cm), S 9–12in (23–30cm).

Z8–11 H12–1

***Eschscholzia californica* [mixed]**
Fast-growing, slender, erect annual. Feathery leaves are bluish green; cup-shaped, 4-petaled, single flowers, in shades of red, orange, yellow, or cream, are borne in summer-autumn.
H 12in (30cm), S 6in (15cm).

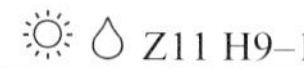

Z11 H9–1

Rudbeckia hirta
Rudbeckia hirta 'Irish Eyes'
Tagetes patula

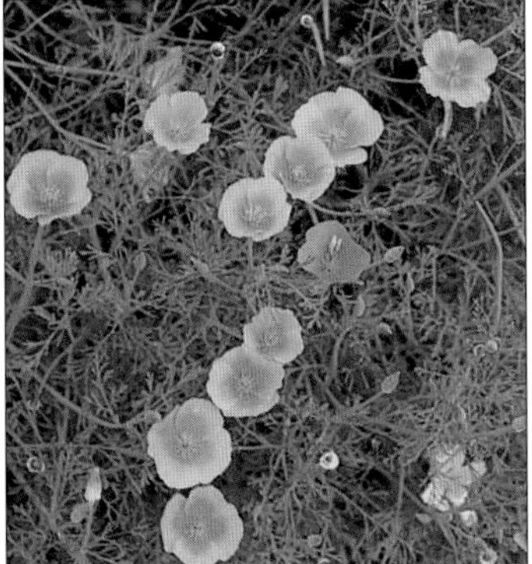

Eschscholzia californica
Fast-growing, slender, erect annual with feathery, bluish green leaves. Cup-shaped, 4-petaled, vivid orange-yellow flowers are borne in summer-autumn. H 12in (30cm), S 6in (15cm).

 Z11 H9–1

***Eschscholzia* californica**
Thai Silk Series
Fast-growing, compact, slender, erect annual with feathery, bluish green leaves. In summer-autumn it produces single or semi-double, fluted, bronze-tinged flowers in red, pink, or orange. H 8–10in (20–25cm), S 6in (15cm).

☼ ◊ Z8–10 H9–2

***Tropaeolum* Alaska Series**
Fast-growing, bushy annual with rounded, variegated leaves. Spurred, trumpet-shaped flowers in shades of red or yellow appear in summer and early autumn. H and S 12in (30cm).

☼ ◊ Z10–11 H9–1

***Primula* Pacific Series**
(Polyanthus primrose)
Rosette-forming perennial, normally grown as a biennial, with lance-shaped leaves. Has heads of large, fragrant, flat flowers in shades of blue, yellow, red, pink, or white in spring.
H and S 8–9in (20–22cm).

☼ ◊ Z6–8 H8–1

Nemesia strumosa
Triumph Series
Fairly fast-growing, bushy, compact annual with lance-shaped, serrated, pale green leaves. Small, somewhat trumpet-shaped flowers, in a range of bright colors, are borne in summer.
H 8in (20cm), S 6in (15cm).

☼ ◊ Z9–11 H6–1

Viola* x *wittrockiana
Universal Series [apricot]
Bushy, spreading perennial, usually grown as a biennial. Large, rounded, 5-petaled, deep apricot flowers are borne in winter-spring.
H and S 6–8in (15–20cm).

☼ ◊ Z8–11 H9–1

***Calceolaria* 'Sunshine'**
Evergreen, compact, bushy perennial, grown as an annual. Has oval, mid-green leaves and heads of small, rounded, pouched, bright golden yellow flowers in late spring and summer.
H and S 8in (20cm).

☼ ◊ Z8–9 H6–1

Calendula officinalis
'Fiesta Gitana'
Fast-growing, bushy annual with strongly aromatic, lance-shaped, pale green leaves. Daisylike, double flower heads, ranging from cream to orange, are carried from spring to autumn.
H and S 12in (30cm).

☼ ◊ H6–1

Calceolaria Anytime Series
Calceolaria 'Monarch'

ORANGE

***Rudbeckia hirta* 'Marmalade'**
Moderately fast-growing, erect, branching perennial, grown as an annual, with lance-shaped leaves. In summer-autumn bears daisylike, deep golden orange flower heads, 3in (8cm) wide, with black centers.
H 18in (45cm), S 12in (30cm).

☼ ◊ Z3–7 H7–1

***Rudbeckia hirta* 'Goldilocks'**
Moderately fast-growing, erect, branching perennial, grown as an annual. Has lance-shaped leaves and daisylike, double or semi-double, golden orange flower heads, 3in (8cm) across, in summer-autumn.
H 24in (60cm), S 12in (30cm).

☼ ◊ Z3–7 H7–1

***Tagetes* 'Tangerine Gem'**
Fast-growing, bushy annual with aromatic, feathery leaves. Small, single, deep orange flower heads appear in summer and early autumn.
H 8in (20cm), S 12in (30cm).

☼ ◊ (!) H12–1

***Rudbeckia hirta* 'Rustic Dwarfs'**
Moderately fast-growing, erect, branching perennial, grown as an annual, with lance-shaped, midgreen leaves. Bears daisylike yellow, mahogany, or bronze flower heads, 3in (8cm) wide, in summer-autumn.
H 24in (60cm), S 12in (30cm).

☼ ◊ Z3–7 H7–1

***Tithonia rotundifolia* 'Torch'**
Slow-growing, erect annual with rounded, lobed leaves. Has daisylike, bright orange or scarlet flower heads, 2–3in (5–8cm) wide, in summer and early autumn.
H 3ft (90cm), S 1ft (30cm).

☼ ◊ Z10–11 H12–1

***Tagetes* 'Orange Winner'**
Fast-growing, bushy annual with aromatic, feathery, deep green leaves. Crested, daisylike, double, bright orange flower heads are carried in summer and early autumn.
H 6in (15cm), S to 12in (30cm).

☼ ◊ (!) H12–1

***Tagetes* Boy Series**
Compact annual that bears double, crested flower heads in a range of colors, including shades of golden yellow, yellow, orange, or reddish brown, with deep orange or yellow crests, in late spring and early summer.
H to 6in (15cm), S to 12in (30cm).

☼ ◊ (!) H12–1

***Erysimum* x *allionii* 'Orange Bedder'**
Slow-growing, short-lived, evergreen, bushy perennial, grown as a biennial. Has lance-shaped, midgreen leaves. Heads of scented, 4-petaled, brilliant orange flowers appear in spring.
H and S 12in (30cm).

☼ ◊ Z3–7 H7–1

***Bracteantha bracteata* Monstrosum Series**
Moderately fast-growing, erect, branching annual. Has daisylike, papery, double flower heads in pink, red, orange, yellow, or white in summer and early autumn. Flowers dry well.
H 3ft (90cm), S 1ft (30cm).

☼ ◊ Z7–11 H12–1

Antirrhinum majus
Arctotis Harlequin Hybrids 'Tangerine'
Arctotis Harlequin Hybrids 'Torch'
Erysimum cheiri
Gazania Daybreak Series
Portulaca grandiflora
Salpiglossis sinuata Bolero Hybrids
Tagetes patula
Tropaeolum majus

***Zinnia haageana* 'Orange Star'**, syn. *Z. angustifolia* 'Orange Star', *Z. haageana* 'Classic'
Dwarf, bushy annual with daisylike, broad-petaled orange flower heads borne in summer. Is mildew-resistant and good as a groundcover.
H to 10in (25cm), S to 12in (30cm).

H12–1

***Tropaeolum* Jewel Series**
Fast-growing, bushy annual with rounded leaves. Spurred, trumpet-shaped flowers in shades of red, yellow, or orange are held well above leaves from early summer to early autumn.
H and S 12in (30cm).

Z11 H12–1

***Calendula officinalis* 'Geisha Girl'**
Fast-growing, bushy annual with strongly aromatic, lance-shaped, pale green leaves. Heads of double orange flowers with incurved petals are borne from late spring to autumn.
H 24in (60cm), S 12–24in (30–60cm).

H6–1

***Erysimum cheiri* 'Fire King'**, syn. *Cheiranthus cheiri* 'Fire King'
Moderately fast-growing, evergreen, bushy perennial, grown as a biennial. Lance-shaped leaves are mid- to deep green; heads of 4-petaled, reddish orange flowers are carried in spring.
H 15in (38cm), S 12–15in (30–38cm).

Z3–7 H7–1

Emilia coccinea (Tassel flower)
Moderately fast-growing, upright annual with lance-shaped, grayish green leaves and double red or yellow flower heads in summer.
H 12–24in (30–60cm),
S 12in (30cm) or more.

H9–1

***Solanum pseudocapsicum* 'Balloon'**
Evergreen, bushy shrub, grown as an annual. Has lance-shaped leaves and, in summer, small, star-shaped white flowers. Large cream fruits turn orange in winter. H 12in (30cm), S 12–18in (30–45cm).

Z12–14 H12–1

***Solanum pseudocapsicum* 'Red Giant'**
Fairly slow-growing, evergreen, bushy shrub, usually grown as an annual. Has lance-shaped, deep green leaves, small white flowers in summer, and large, round, orange-red fruits in winter.
H and S 12in (30cm).

Z12–14 H12–1

***Clarkia amoena* Princess Series** [salmon]
Fast-growing annual with slender, upright stems and lance-shaped, mid-green leaves. Spikes of frilled, salmon-pink flowers are carried in summer.
H and S 12in (30cm).

H7–1

***Sanvitalia procumbens* 'Mandarin Orange'**
Moderately fast-growing, prostrate annual. Has pointed-oval, midgreen leaves and daisylike orange flower heads, 1in (2.5cm) wide, in summer.
H 6in (15cm), S 12in (30cm).

H12–1

***Dahlia* 'Dandy'**
Well-branched, erect, bushy, tuberous perennial, grown as an annual. Has pointed-oval, serrated leaves and heads of daisylike flowers, with contrasting central collars of quilled petals, in shades of red, yellow, or orange in summer. H and S 2ft (60cm).

Z9–11 H12–1

***Celosia argentea* 'Fairy Fountains'**
Moderately fast-growing, erect, bushy perennial, grown as an annual. Has pointed-oval leaves and conical, feathery flower heads, to 6in (15cm) tall, in a wide range of colors in summer-autumn. H and S 12in (30cm).

H9–2

ROCK PLANTS

WHEN SPACE is at a premium, many gardeners turn to rock plants, because most of this group of dwarf trees, shrubs, bulbs, and perennials can be grown in very confined spots. Rock plants also grow in dry conditions yet produce some of the most attractive flowers – characteristics that endear them to gardeners with difficult sites and climates.

Rock Plants

Noted for their natural charm and simple, clear-colored, abundant flowers in spring and early summer, rock plants are good choices for almost every situation, from the tiniest trough to the grandest rock garden.

What are rock plants?

The term rock plants includes bulbs and mat- and cushion-forming perennials (many of which are evergreen) as well as dwarf, evergreen, coniferous, and deciduous trees and shrubs. They may be true alpines or simply plants of small stature that are suitable for rock garden plantings. While many of the alpines have specialized needs, the group includes many species and cultivars, such as aubrieta and *Aurinia saxatilis*, that are undemanding in cultivation and thrive in any well-drained site of suitable exposure.

True alpines grow at high altitudes above the treeline, on scree slopes, in rock crevices, or in short grass, while subalpine plants live below the treeline on rocky slopes or in high pastures or meadowland. Most alpines are compact in habit and frequently deep-rooting, usually with small leaves that are leathery, fleshy, or covered in fine hair. These adaptations help them survive the drying high-velocity winds, brilliant burning sun, and extreme temperature fluctuations of their natural habitat.

Most rock plants grow in areas characterized by stony soils with rapid drainage and so cannot withstand the combination of constant wetness at the roots and winter cold that is experienced in some regions. Such species also dislike warm, humid summers, which may be the main limiting factor. In the wild, plants are insulated from winter cold by a blanket of snow, beneath which they remain dormant until spring, conditions that occur in many parts of the United States. Those environments that mimic conditions in the wild, such as rock gardens, scree beds, troughs, raised beds, open frames, and alpine houses, are therefore best for cultivating rock plants, which must have sharp drainage and, usually, protection from excessive winter moisture.

Woodland plants
Above: Natives of mountain woodlands, such as the trilliums seen here, generally need moist, neutral to acidic soil and are perfectly at home in a good loamy soil in dappled shade.

Planning a rock garden
Right: Siting a rock garden on a gentle slope assists rapid drainage, while carefully placed rocks form a niche, where penetrating roots can be kept cool and moist during the summer.

Designing with rock plants

One of the major attractions of this group is their diminutive size, which can satisfy the gardener's hunger for diversity because many different plants can be grown in a relatively confined space. In a rock garden – as in larger-scale plantings – small shrubs, such as the highly fragrant *Daphne cneorum* and *D. retusa,* or berried shrubs like *Cotoneaster horizontalis*, can be used to form the structural framework of a design. Miniature conifers, such as *Juniperus communis* 'Compressa', can create vertical emphasis and year-round color, in contrast to plants of rounded habit, such as the evergreen *Hebe cupressoides* 'Boughton Dome'.

This structure can then be filled in with mat- and cushion-forming plants, such as sandworts (*Arenaria*) or *Dianthus deltoides*, at the feet of taller, feathery-leaved pulsatillas or the airy *Linum narbonense*. There are also tight, dome-forming saxifrages, rosette-forming sedums, and fleshy-leaved sempervivums, whose surfaces contrast perfectly with the white-haired leaves of edelweiss (*Leontopodium*) or the silky, silver leaves of the celmisias.

Container planting
Troughs are ideal for creating landscapes in miniature, but to provide perfect drainage they must be filled with gritty soil mix. Here, the flowers of an alpine poppy, a campanula, and a lewisia lend color to the neat, lime-encrusted rosettes of high-alpine saxifrages.

MAINTAINING YEAR-ROUND INTEREST
Evergreen and structural plantings are more important in rock gardens than in other styles of garden, because most alpines bloom in one burst between spring and early summer. The season can be extended, however, by planting early spring bulbs, such as alpine narcissus or crocuses, by using later-flowering rock plants, such as helianthemums, phlox, or veronicas, and by planting the autumn-flowering *Persicaria vacciniifolia* and cyclamen or the berry-bearing gaultherias.

MINIATURE LANDSCAPES
In courtyards or tiny gardens, or where the soil in the open garden is too heavy or drainage is inadequate, rock plants can be grown in troughs or raised beds to create landscapes in miniature. The latter also bring small plants closer to eye level and are ideal for gardeners of reduced mobility.

Drystone walls are also potential planting sites for many crevice-lovers, such as lewisias or ramonda, while the tops of the walls are ideal planting positions for cascading specimens, such as *Saxifraga* 'Tumbling Waters'.

SIZE CATEGORIES USED WITHIN THIS GROUP		
Large	Medium	Small
over 6in (15cm)	—	up to 6in (15cm)

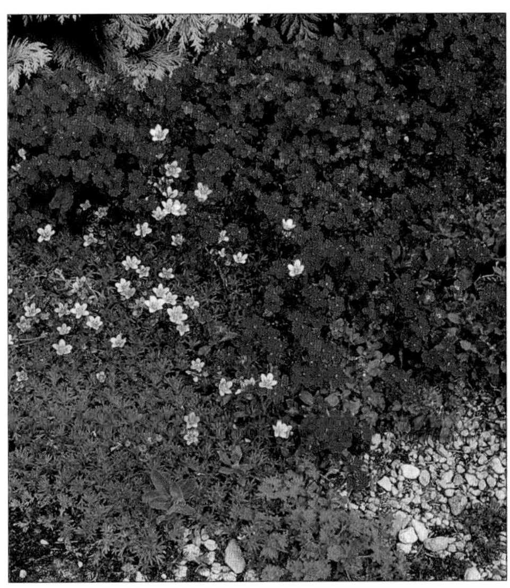

ROCK PLANTS FOR EDGING
Above: Robust, low-growing mat-formers such as aubrieta and mossy saxifrages make excellent edging plants at the front of a rock garden.

A PERFECT PARTNERSHIP
Left: In an open site in full sun, dwarf shrubs and conifers provide a permanent structural framework for the profuse spring and early summer flowers that are typical of alpine plants.

□ WHITE

Leontopodium alpinum (Edelweiss)
Short-lived perennial with tufts of lance-shaped, woolly leaves. Clusters of small, silvery white flower heads, borne in spring or early summer, are surrounded by petal-like, thick, felted bracts that form a star shape. Dislikes winter and summer wet. H and S 6–8in (15–20cm).

Z4–6 H6–1

Lithophragma parviflorum
Clump-forming, tuberous perennial that has small, open clusters of campion-like white or pink flowers in spring above a basal cluster of deeply toothed, kidney-shaped leaves. Lies dormant in summer.
H 6–8in (5–20cm), S to 8in (20cm).

Z4–6 H6–1

Saxifraga granulata (Fair maids of France, Meadow saxifrage)
Clump-forming perennial that loses its kidney-shaped, crumpled, glossy leaves in summer. Sticky stems carry loose panicles of rounded white flowers in late spring. H 9–15in (23–38cm), S 6in (15cm) or more.

Z7–8 H8–7

Iberis sempervirens, syn. *I. commutata*
Evergreen, spreading subshrub with narrow, oblong, dark green leaves bearing dense, rounded heads of white flowers in late spring and early summer. Trim after flowering. H 6–12in (15–30cm), S 18–24in (45–60cm).

Z5–9 H9–3

Pulsatilla alpina (Alpine anemone)
Tufted perennial with feathery leaves that bears upright or somewhat nodding, cup-shaped white, sometimes blue- or pink-flushed flowers singly in spring and early summer, followed by feathery seed heads.
H 6–12in (15–30cm), S to 4in (10cm).

Z5–7 H7–5

Rhodanthemum hosmariense
Evergreen, shrubby perennial with finely cut, bright silvery green leaves that clothe lax, woody stems. From late spring to early autumn, white flower heads are borne singly above foliage.
H 6in (15cm) or more, S 12in (30cm).

Z9 11 H12–7

***Andromeda polifolia* 'Alba'**
Evergreen, open, twiggy shrub bearing terminal clusters of pitcher-shaped white flowers in spring and early summer. Glossy, dark green leaves are leathery and lance-shaped.
H 18in (45cm), S 24in (60cm).

pH Z2–6 H6–1

***Cassiope* 'Muirhead'**
Evergreen, loose, bushy shrub with scalelike, dark green leaves on upright branches. In spring, these bear tiny, virtually stemless, bell-shaped white flowers along their length.
H and S 8in (20cm).

pH Z4–6 H6–1

***Cassiope* 'Edinburgh'**
Evergreen, dwarf shrub with tiny, dark green leaves tightly pressed to upright stems. In spring, many small, bell-shaped white flowers are borne singly in leaf axils. H and S 8in (20cm).

pH Z2–6 H6–1

OTHER RECOMMENDED PLANTS:
Achillea clavennae, illus. p.373
Cassiope fastigiata
Cassiope mertensiana, illus. p.364
Cassiope selaginoides
Corydalis ochroleuca, illus. p.351
Cyathodes colensoi, illus. p.360
DAFFODILS, illus. pp.416–18
Daphne alpina
Galax urceolata, illus. p.351
x *Halimiocistus wintonensis*
Hebe carnosula
Hebe pinguifolia 'Pagei', illus. p.351
Houttuynia cordata 'Flore Pleno'
Iberis sempervirens 'Schneeflocke'
IRISES, illus. pp.234–5

WHITE

Saxifraga hirsuta
Evergreen, mound-forming perennial with rosettes of round, hairy leaves and loose panicles of tiny, star-shaped white flowers, often yellow-spotted at the base of petals, in late spring and early summer.
H 6–8in (15–20cm), S 8in (20cm).

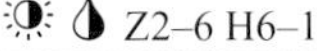
Z2–6 H6–1

Jeffersonia diphylla
Slow-growing, tufted perennial with distinctive, 2-lobed, light to midgreen leaves. Bears solitary, cup-shaped white flowers with prominent yellow stamens in late spring. Do not disturb roots.
H 6–9in (15–23cm), S to 9in (23cm).

Z5–7 H7–5

Daphne blagayana
Evergreen, prostrate shrub with trailing branches, each bearing a terminal cluster of oval, leathery leaves and, in early spring, dense clusters of fragrant, tubular white flowers. Likes organic soil. H 12–16in (30–40cm), S 24–32in (60–80cm) or more.

Z7–9 H9–7

Tiarella cordifolia (Foamflower)
Vigorous, evergreen, spreading perennial. Lobed, pale green leaves sometimes have darker marks; veins turn bronze-red in winter. Bears many spikes of profuse white flowers in late spring and early summer. H 6–8in (15–20cm), S to 12in (30cm) or more.

Z3–8 H7–1

***Saxifraga* 'Tumbling Waters'**
Slow-growing, evergreen, mat-forming perennial with a tight rosette of narrow, lime-encrusted leaves. After several years produces arching sprays of white flowers in conical heads; main rosette then dies but small offsets survive.
H to 24in (60cm), S to 8in (20cm).

Z6–7 H7–6

Vancouveria hexandra
Vigorous, spreading perennial with open sprays of many tiny white flowers in late spring and early summer. Leathery leaves are divided into almost hexagonal leaflets. Makes a good woodland groundcover.
H 8in (20cm), S indefinite.

Z5–8 H8–5

WHITE–PINK

Dodecatheon meadia* f. *album
Clump-forming perennial with basal rosettes of oval, pale green leaves. In spring, strong stems bear several white flowers with dark centers and reflexed petals. Lies dormant in summer.
H 8in (20cm), S 6in (15cm).

Z4–8 H8–1

Saxifraga* x *geum
Evergreen, mat-forming perennial with shallow-rooted rosettes of spoon-shaped, hairy leaves. In summer, star-shaped, pink-spotted white flowers, deep pink in bud, are borne on loose panicles on slender stems.
H 6–8in (15–20cm), S 12in (30cm).

Z6–8 H8–6

Andromeda polifolia
Evergreen, open, twiggy shrub with narrow, leathery, glossy, midgreen leaves. Bears terminal clusters of pitcher-shaped pink flowers in spring and early summer.
H 12–18in (30–45cm), S 24in (60cm).

pH Z2–6 H6–1

***Andromeda polifolia* 'Compacta'**
Evergreen, compact, twiggy shrub that bears delicate, terminal clusters of pitcher-shaped, coral-pink flowers with white undertones in spring and early summer. Leaves are lance-shaped and glossy, dark green.
H 6–9in (15–23cm), S 12in (30cm).

pH Z2–6 H6–1

***Dodecatheon hendersonii*,**
syn. *D. latifolium*
Clump-forming perennial with a flat rosette of kidney-shaped leaves, above which deep pink flowers with reflexed petals appear in late spring. Needs a dry, dormant summer period.
H 12in (30cm), S 3in (8cm).

Z5–7 H7–5

***Phyllodoce* x *intermedia* 'Drummondii'**
Evergreen, bushy, dwarf shrub with narrow, heathlike, glossy leaves. From late spring to early summer bears terminal clusters of pitcher-shaped, rich pink flowers on slender red stalks. H and S 9in (23cm).

pH Z2–5 H5–1

Leiophyllum buxifolium
Ourisia macrocarpa
Parnassia palustris, illus. p.350
PEONIES, illus. pp.236–7
Phyllodoce nipponica
PRIMROSES, illus. pp.272–3
Saxifraga cuneifolia, illus. p.351
Anthyllis montana, illus. p.352
Anthyllis montana 'Rubra'
Arabis alpina subsp. *caucasica* 'Variegata', illus. p.362
Dodecatheon meadia
Saxifraga cotyledon, illus. p.352
Saxifraga 'Southside Seedling', illus. p.352
Shortia galacifolia, illus. p.364

PINK–PURPLE

Daphne cneorum
Evergreen, low-growing shrub with trailing branches clothed in small, oval, leathery, dark green leaves. Fragrant, deep rose-pink flowers are borne in terminal clusters in late spring. Prefers organic soil.
H 9in (23cm), S to 6ft (2m).

Z5–7 H7–1

***Dodecatheon* 'Red Wings'**
Clump-forming perennial with a basal cluster of oblong, soft, pale green leaves. In late spring and early summer bears small, loose clusters of deep magenta flowers with reflexed petals on strong stems. Lies dormant in summer. H 8in (20cm), S 4in (10cm).

Z5–7 H7–5

Phyllodoce empetriformis
Evergreen, mat-forming shrub with fine, narrow, heathlike leaves and terminal clusters of bell-shaped, purplish pink flowers in late spring and early summer.
H 6–9in (15–23cm), S 8in (20cm).

pH Z3–6 H6–1

Phyllodoce caerulea,
syn. *P. taxifolia*
Evergreen, dwarf shrub with fine, narrow, heathlike leaves. Bears bell-shaped purple to purplish pink flowers, singly or in clusters, in late spring and summer.
H and S to 12in (30cm).

pH Z2–5 H5–1

Pulsatilla vulgaris (Pasque flower)
Tufted perennial with feathery, light green leaves. In spring bears nodding, cup-shaped flowers in shades of purple, red, pink, or white, all with bright yellow centers. Flower stems rapidly elongate as feathery seeds mature.
H and S 6–9in (15–23cm).

Z5–7 H7–5

Cortusa matthioli, illus. p.354
Daphne collina
Dicentra 'Spring Morning', illus. p.278
Kalmiopsis leachiana 'La Piniec'

x *Phylliopsis hillieri* 'Pinocchio'
Phyllodoce x *intermedia* 'Fred Stoker'
PRIMROSES, illus. pp.272–3
Rhodothamnus chamaecistus, illus. p.352

PURPLE–BLUE

Erinacea anthyllis,
syn. *E. pungens* (Hedgehog broom)
Slow growing, evergreen subshrub with hard, blue-green spines. Pealike, soft lavender flowers appear in axils of spines in late spring to early summer.
H and S 6–10in (15–25cm).

Z7–8 H8–7

Pulsatilla halleri
Tufted perennial, intensely hairy in all parts, that in spring bears nodding, later erect, cup-shaped flowers in shades of purple. Has feathery leaves and seed heads. H 6–15in (15–38cm), S 6–8in (15–20cm).

Z5–7 H7–5

Aquilegia alpina
(Alpine columbine)
Short-lived, upright perennial with spurred, clear blue or violet-blue flowers on slender stems in spring and early summer. Has basal rosettes of rounded, finely divided leaves. Needs rich soil. H 18in (45cm), S 6in (15cm)

Z4–7 H7–1

IRISES, illus. pp.234–5
Olsynium douglasii
Sisyrinchium graminoides, illus. p.356

Viola cornuta (Horned violet)
Rhizomatous perennial with oval, toothed leaves and flat-faced, rather angular, spurred, pale to deep purplish blue, occasionally white flowers in spring and much of summer. H 8in (12–20cm), S to 8in (20cm) or more.

Z6–9 H9–1

Omphalodes verna
Semi-evergreen, clump-forming perennial that in spring bears long, loose sprays of flat, bright blue flowers with white eyes. Leaves are oval and midgreen.
H and S 8in (20cm) or more.

Z6–9 H9–6

Omphalodes cappadocica
Spreading perennial with creeping underground stems and many loose sprays of flat, bright blue flowers in spring-summer above tufts of oval, hairy, basal leaves.
H 6–8in (15–20cm),
S 10in (25cm) or more.

Z6–8 H8–6

IRISES, illus. pp.234–5
Lithodora zahnii
Pulsatilla halleri subsp. *grandis*

Salix helvetica
Deciduous, spreading, much-branched, dwarf shrub that has small, oval, glossy leaves, white-haired beneath. In spring bears short-stalked, silky gray then yellow catkins.
H 24in (60cm), S 12in (30cm).

Z5–8 H8–5

Betula nana (Arctic birch)
Deciduous, bushy, dwarf shrub with small, toothed leaves that turn bright yellow in autumn. Has tiny, yellowish brown catkins in spring.
H 12in (30cm), S 18in (45cm).

pH Z2–5 H5–1

Corydalis cheilanthifolia
Evergreen perennial with fleshy roots. Produces spreading rosettes of fernlike, near-prostrate, sometimes bronze-tinted, midgreen leaves. Dense spikes of short-spurred yellow flowers are borne in late spring and early summer. H 8–12in (20–30cm), S 6–8in (15–20cm).

Z5–7 H7–3

DAFFODILS, illus. pp.416–18
IRISES, illus. pp.234–5
Paeonia mlokosewitschii, illus. p.237
PRIMROSES, illus. pp.272–3

Corydalis wilsonii
Evergreen perennial with a fleshy rootstock. Forms rosettes of near-prostrate, divided, bluish green leaves. Loose racemes of spurred, green-tipped yellow flowers are produced in spring.
H and S 4–10in (10–25cm).

Z6–7 H7–6

***Aurinia saxatilis* 'Citrina'**,
syn. *Alyssum saxatile* 'Citrinum'
Evergreen, clump-forming perennial with oval, hairy, gray-green leaves. Bears racemes of many small, pale lemon yellow flowers in late spring and early summer.
H 9in (23cm), S 12in (30cm).

Z4–8 H8–1

Chiastophyllum oppositifolium,
syn. *Cotyledon simplicifolia*
Evergreen, trailing perennial with large, oblong, serrated, succulent leaves. In late spring and early summer bears many tiny yellow flowers in arching sprays.
H 6–8in (15–20cm), S 6in (15cm).

Z6–9 H9–6

Cytisus* x *beanii
Deciduous, low-growing shrub with arching sprays of pealike, golden yellow flowers that appear in late spring and early summer on previous year's wood. Leaves, divided into 3 leaflets, are small, linear, and hairy. H 6–16in (5–40cm), S 12–30in (30–75cm).

Z7–8 H8–7

***Aurinia saxatilis* 'Variegata'**,
syn. *Alyssum saxatile* 'Variegatum'
Evergreen perennial that bears racemes of many small yellow flowers in spring above a mat of large, oval, soft gray-green leaves with cream margins.
H 9in (23cm), S 12in (30cm).

Z4–10 H9–1

Pulsatilla alpina subsp. *apiifolia*
Salix arbuscula

ROCK PLANTS large SPRING INTEREST

YELLOW–ORANGE

Hylomecon japonica
Vigorous, spreading perennial with large, cup-shaped, bright yellow flowers that are borne singly on slender stems in spring. Soft, dark green leaves are divided into 4 unequal lobes. H to 12in (30cm), S 8in (20cm).

Z5–8 H8–5

Stylophorum diphyllum
Perennial with basal rosettes of large, lobed, hairy leaves. Bears open cup-shaped, golden yellow flowers in spring on upright, branched stems. Prefers rich, woodland conditions.
H and S to 12in (30cm) or more.

Z5–8 H8–1

Aurinia saxatilis,
syn. *Alyssum saxatile* (Gold dust)
Evergreen perennial forming low clumps of oval, hairy, gray-green leaves. Has substantial spikes of small, chrome yellow flowers in spring.
H 9in (23cm), S 12in (30cm).

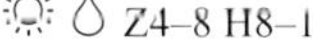

Z4–8 H8–1

***Erysimum* 'Bredon'**,
syn. *Cheiranthus* 'Bredon'
Semi-evergreen, rounded, woody perennial clothed in oval, dark green leaves. In late spring bears dense spikes of flat, bright mustard yellow flowers.
H 12–18in (30–45cm), S 18in (45cm).

Z5–8 H8–5

***Erysimum* x *kewense* 'Harpur Crewe'**
Evergreen, shrubby perennial with stiff stems and narrow leaves. Fragrant, double, deep yellow flowers open in succession from late spring to mid-summer. Grows best in poor soil and a sheltered site. H and S 12in (30cm).

Z5–8 H8–5

***Berberis* x *stenophylla* 'Corallina Compacta'**
Evergreen, neat, dwarf shrub with spiny stems clothed in small, narrowly oval leaves. In late spring bears many tiny, bright orange flowers. Is slow-growing and difficult to propagate.
H and S to 10in (25cm).

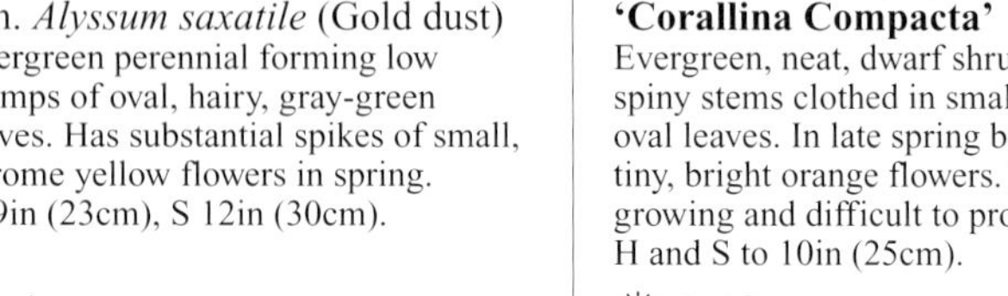

Z6–9 H9–6

Alyssoides utriculata
Corydalis lutea, illus. p.359
DAFFODILS, illus. pp.416–18
Euryops acraeus, illus. p.358
Euryops pectinatus, illus. p.170
Genista lydia, illus. p.359
IRISES, illus. pp.234–5

ROCK PLANTS large SUMMER INTEREST

WHITE

Parnassia palustris
(Grass of Parnassus)
Perennial with low, basal tufts of heart-shaped, pale to midgreen leaves. Bears saucer-shaped white flowers with dark green or purplish green veins on erect stems in late spring and early summer. H 8in (20cm), S 2½in (6cm) or more.

Z4–11 H12–1

Armeria pseudarmeria,
syn. *A. latifolia*
Evergreen, clump-forming perennial with large, spherical heads of white flowers occasionally suffused pink; these are borne in summer on stiff stems above long, narrow, glaucous leaves. H and S 12in (30cm).

Z6–7 H7–6

Celmisia walkeri,
syn. *C. webbiana*
Evergreen, loose, spreading perennial with long, oval or lance-shaped leaves, glossy and green above and hairy and white beneath. Has large, daisylike white flower heads in summer.
H 9in (23cm), S to 6ft (2m).

pH Z9–10 H10–9

OTHER RECOMMENDED PLANTS:
Andromeda polifolia 'Alba', illus. p.346
Artemisia caucasica
Artemisia frigida
Artemisia stelleriana 'Boughton Silver'
Boykinia aconitifolia
CARNATIONS and PINKS, illus. pp.280–1
Cotoneaster congestus

Helianthemum apenninum
Evergreen, spreading, much-branched shrub that bears saucer-shaped, pure white flowers in midsummer. Stems and small, linear leaves are covered in white down. H and S 18in (45cm).

Z6–8 H8–5

Saxifraga cuneifolia
Evergreen, carpeting perennial with neat rosettes of rounded leaves. In late spring and early summer bears panicles of tiny white flowers, frequently with yellow, pink, or red spots, on slender stems. H 6–8in (15–20cm), S 12in (30cm) or more.

Z5–7 H7–5

***Chamaecytisus purpureus* f. *albus*,** syn. *Cytisus purpureus* f. *albus*
Deciduous, low-growing shrub with semi-erect stems clothed in leaves, divided into 3 leaflets. A profusion of pealike white flowers appear in early summer on previous year's wood. H 18in (45cm), S 24in (60cm).

Z6–9 H9–6

***Helianthemum* 'Wisley White'**
Evergreen, spreading shrub with oblong, gray-green leaves bearing saucer-shaped white flowers for a long period in summer. H 9in (23cm), S 12in (30cm) or more.

Z6–8 H8–6

Galax urceolata, syn. *G. aphylla*
Evergreen, clump-forming perennial. Large, round, leathery, midgreen leaves on slender stems turn bronze in autumn-winter. Has dense spikes of small white flowers in late spring and early summer. H 6–8in (15–20cm), S to 12in (30cm).

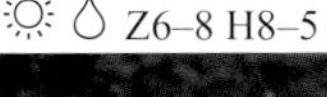
pH Z5–8 H8–5

Epilobium glabellum of gardens
Semi-evergreen, clump-forming perennial. Bears outward-facing, cup-shaped white flowers singly on slender stems in summer above oval, midgreen leaves. Makes a useful groundcover. H to 8in (20cm), S 6in (15cm).

Z5–8 H8–5

Hebe vernicosa
Evergreen, bushy, compact shrub with small, oval, glossy, dark green leaves densely packed on stems. In early and midsummer, spikes of small, 4-lobed white flowers are freely produced. H 2ft (60cm), S 4ft (1.2m).

Z9–10 H10–9

***Hebe pinguifolia* 'Pagei'**
Evergreen, semi-prostrate shrub with small, oblong, slightly cupped, intensely glaucous leaves. Bears short spikes of small, pure white flowers in late spring or early summer. Excellent groundcover. H 6–12in (15–30cm), S 24–36in (60cm–1m).

Z8–10 H10–8

Corydalis ochroleuca, syn. *Pseudofumaria ochroleuca*
Evergreen, clump-forming perennial with fleshy, fibrous roots and much divided, basal, gray-green leaves. Bears slender, yellow-tipped, creamy white flowers in late spring and summer. H and S 8–12in (20–30cm).

Z6–8 H8–6

Deinanthe bifida
Eomecon chionantha
Fabiana imbricata 'Prostrata'
x *Halimiocistus wintonensis*
Hebe buchananii
HOSTAS, illus. pp.288–9
Iberis sempervirens 'Schneeflocke'
IRISES, illus. pp.234–5
Leontopodium alpinum, illus. p.346
Luetkea pectinata
Papaver burseri
Phyllodoce nipponica
PRIMROSES, illus. pp.272–3
Rhodanthemum hosmariense, illus. p.346
Stephanandra incisa 'Crispa'
Tiarella cordifolia, illus. p.347

WHITE–PINK

Saxifraga cotyledon
Evergreen perennial with large, pale green rosettes of leaves, dying after flowering. In late spring and early summer produces arching, conical panicles of cup-shaped white flowers, sometimes strongly marked red internally. H and S to 12in (30cm).

 Z4–6 H6–1

Aethionema grandiflorum, syn. *A. pulchellum* (Persian stone cress)
Short-lived, evergreen or semi-evergreen, lax shrub. Bears tiny, pale to deep rose-pink flowers in loose sprays in spring-summer. Blue-green leaves are narrow and lance-shaped.
H 12in (30cm), S 9in (23cm).

Z5–7 H9–7

Onosma alborosea
Semi-evergreen, clump-forming perennial covered in fine hairs that may irritate skin. Clusters of long, pendent, tubular flowers, borne for a long period in summer, open white and then turn pink.
H 6–12in (15–30cm), S 8in (20cm).

Z7–9 H9–7

***Saxifraga* 'Southside Seedling'**
Evergreen, mat-forming perennial, with large, pale green rosettes of leaves, dying after flowering. In late spring and early summer bears arching panicles of open cup-shaped white flowers, strongly red-banded within.
H and S to 12in (30cm).

Z4–6 H6–1

Rhodothamnus chamaecistus
Evergreen, low-growing, dwarf shrub with narrow, oval leaves edged with bristles. In late spring and early summer bears cup-shaped, rose- to lilac-pink flowers, with dark stamens, in leaf axils.
H 6–8in (15–20cm), S to 10in (25cm).

pH Z7–9 H9–7

PINK

Anthyllis montana
Rounded, bushy or somewhat spreading perennial with loose branches and finely cut foliage. Heads of cloverlike, pale pink flowers with red markings are borne in late spring and early summer.
H and S 12in (30cm).

Z6–8 H8–6

Phuopsis stylosa, syn. *Crucianella stylosa*
Low-growing perennial with whorls of pungent, pale green leaves and rounded heads of small, tubular pink flowers in summer. Is good grown over a bank or large rock.
H 12in (30cm), S 12in (30cm) or more.

Z5–8 H8–5

***Lewisia* 'George Henley'**
Evergreen, clump-forming perennial with rosettes of narrow, fleshy, dark green leaves. Bears dense sprays of open cup-shaped, deep pink flowers with magenta veins from late spring to late summer.
H 6in (15cm) or more, S 4in (10cm).

pH Z3–7 H7–1

Achillea x *kellereri*, illus. p.375
Diascia vigilis
Gaultheria miqueliana
Lotus hirsutus

Alyssum spinosum
Saxifraga granulata 'Plena'
Saxifraga longifolia
Saxifraga x *urbium*

Aethionema armenum, illus. p.377
Aethionema 'Warley Rose', illus. p.376
CARNATIONS and PINKS, illus. pp.280–1
Crepis incana

Dianthus superbus
Erigeron glaucus 'Elstead Pink'
Erodium foetidum
Incarvillea mairei, illus. p.279

***Origanum* 'Kent Beauty'**
Prostrate perennial with trailing stems clothed in aromatic, rounded-oval leaves. In summer bears short spikes of tubular, pale pink flowers with darker bracts. Is suitable for a wall or ledge. H 6–8in (15–20cm), S 12in (30cm).

Z5–8 H8–5

***Helianthemum* 'Rhodanthe Carneum'**, syn. *H.* 'Wisley Pink'
Evergreen, lax shrub with saucer-shaped, soft, pale pink flowers with orange centers borne for a long period in summer. Has oblong, gray-green leaves. H and S 12in (30cm) or more.

Z6–8 H8–6

Oxalis tetraphylla, syn. *O. deppei*
Tuft-forming, tuberous perennial with brown-marked, basal leaves, usually divided into 4 leaflets. Produces loose sprays of widely funnel-shaped, deep pink flowers in late spring and summer. Needs a sheltered site. H 6–10in (15–30cm), S 4–6in (10–15cm).

Z8–9 H9–8

***Astilbe* 'Perkeo'**,
syn. *A.* x *crispa* 'Perkeo'
Erect, compact perennial bearing small plumes of tiny, salmon-pink flowers from mid- to late summer on thin stems. Has stiff, deeply cut, crinkled leaves. H 6–8in (15–20cm), S 4in (10cm).

Z3–8 H8–2

Diascia cordata of gardens
Prostrate perennial with stems clothed in heart-shaped, pale green leaves. Bears terminal clusters of spurred, flat-faced, bright pink flowers in summer and early autumn.
H 6–8in (15–20cm), S 8in (20cm).

Z8–9 H9–8

Diascia rigescens
Trailing perennial with semi-erect stems covered in heart-shaped, midgreen leaves. Spurred, flat-faced, salmon-pink flowers are borne along the stems in summer and early autumn.
H 9in (23cm), S to 12in (30cm).

Z7–9 H9–7

Crassula sarcocaulis
Evergreen or semi-evergreen, bushy subshrub with tiny, oval, succulent leaves. Bears terminal clusters of tiny red buds opening to pale pink flowers in summer.
H and S 12in (30cm).

Z12–14 H9–1

Ononis fruticosa
(Shrubby restharrow)
Deciduous shrub that in summer bears pendent clusters of large, pea-like, purplish pink blooms with darker streaks. Leaves are divided into 3 serrated leaflets that are hairy when young. H and S 12–24in (30–60cm).

Z7–10 H10–7

Geranium orientalitibeticum
Perennial spreading by tuberous, underground runners. Has cup-shaped pink flowers with white centers in summer. Leaves are deeply cut and marbled in shades of green. May be invasive. H in flower 6–10in (15–25cm), S indefinite.

Z5–7 H78–5

Incarvillea mairei 'Frank Ludlow'
Ononis rotundifolia
Ourisia 'Loch Ewe'
PEONIES, illus. pp.236–7
Potentilla nitida
PRIMROSES, illus. pp.272–3
Teucrium polium, illus. p.379

PINK

Cortusa matthioli
Clump-forming perennial with a basal rosette of rounded, dull green leaves and, in late spring and early summer, one-sided racemes of small, pendent, bell-shaped, reddish- or pinkish purple flowers.
H 6–10in (15–20cm), S 4in (10cm).

Z5–8 H8–5

Geranium sanguineum
(Bloody cranesbill)
Hummock-forming, spreading perennial with many cup-shaped, deep magenta-pink flowers borne in summer above round, deeply divided, dark green leaves. Makes a good groundcover. H to 10in (25cm), S 12in (30cm) or more.

Z3–8 H8–1

Origanum laevigatum
Deciduous, mat-forming subshrub with small, aromatic, dark green leaves, branching red stems, and a profusion of tiny, tubular, cerise-pink flowers surrounded by red-purple bracts in summer. H 9–12in (23–30cm), S 8in (20cm) or more.

Z7–11 H12–1

***Lewisia* Cotyledon Hybrids**
Evergreen, clump-forming perennials with rosettes of large, thick, toothed leaves. In early summer bear clusters of flowers in various shades of pink to purple on erect stems. Good for a rock crevice or an alpine house.
H to 12in (30cm), S 6in (15cm) or more.

pH Z5–8 H8–1

Dianthus carthusianorum
Evergreen perennial carrying rounded, upward-facing, cherry red or deep pink flowers on slender stems in summer above small tufts of grasslike leaves.
H 8in (20cm), S 2½in (6cm).

Z5–9 H9–3

RED

Penstemon newberryi* f. *humilior
Evergreen, mat-forming shrub with arching branches clothed in small, leathery, dark green leaves. Bears short sprays of tubular, lipped, cherry red to deep pink flowers in early summer.
H 6–8in (15–20cm), S 12in (30cm).

Z7–10 H10–7

***Helianthemum* 'Ben More'**
Evergreen, spreading, twiggy shrub that bears a succession of saucer-shaped, reddish orange flowers in loose, terminal clusters in late spring and summer. Has small, glossy, dark green leaves.
H 9–12in (23–30cm), S 12in (30cm).

Z6–8 H8–6

***Helianthemum* 'Raspberry Ripple'**
Evergreen, spreading shrub with saucer-shaped, red-centered white flowers that are borne in midsummer. Has small, linear, gray-green leaves.
H 6–9in (15–23cm),
S 9–12in (23–30cm).

Z6–8 H8–6

Penstemon pinifolius
Evergreen, bushy shrub with branched stems clothed in fine, dark green leaves. In summer, very narrow, tubular, orange-red flowers are borne in loose, terminal spikes.
H 4–8in (10–20cm), S 6in (15cm).

Z7–8 H12–1

***Helianthemum* 'Fire Dragon'**
Evergreen, spreading shrub with saucer-shaped, orange-scarlet flowers in late spring and summer. Leaves are linear and gray-green.
H 9–12in (23–30cm), S 18in (45cm).

Z6–8 H8–6

Anthyllis montana 'Rubra'
Astilbe chinensis var. *pumila*
Dianthus armeria
Micromeria juliana
Origanum rotundifolium
Phyllodoce caerulea, illus. p.348
Phyllodoce x *intermedia* 'Drummondii', illus. p.347

Armeria 'Bees Ruby'
Helianthemum 'Ben Hope'
PEONIES, illus. pp.236–7
Phyllodoce x *intermedia* 'Fred Stoker'
PRIMROSES, illus. pp.272–3
Zauschneria californica
Zauschneria californica subsp. *cana*

■ RED

Zauschneria californica subsp. ***cana* 'Dublin'**, syn. *Z.c.* 'Glasnevin'
Clump-forming, woody-based perennial with lance-shaped, gray-green leaves. From late summer to early autumn bears terminal clusters of tubular, deep orange-scarlet flowers. H 12in (30cm), S 18in (45cm).

☼ ◊ Z8–11 H12–8

Punica granatum var. ***nana***
(Dwarf pomegranate)
Slow-growing, deciduous, rounded shrub that, in summer, bears funnel-shaped red flowers with somewhat crumpled petals, followed by small, rounded, orange-red fruits.
H and S 12–36in (30–90cm).

☼ ◊ Z7–11 H12–7

Delphinium nudicaule
Short-lived, upright perennial with erect stems bearing deeply divided, basal leaves and, in summer, spikes of hooded red or occasionally yellow flowers with contrasting stamens.
H 8in (20cm), S 2–4in (5–10cm).

☼ ◊ ! Z5–7 H7–5

■ PURPLE

Calceolaria arachnoidea
Evergreen, clump-forming perennial with a basal rosette of wrinkled leaves covered in white down. Upright stems carry spikes of many pouch-shaped, dull purple flowers in summer.
Is best treated as a biennial.
H 10in (25cm), S 5in (12cm).

☼ ♦ Z8–9 H6–1

Erodium cheilanthifolium
Compact, mound-forming perennial with pink flowers, veined and marked with purple-red, borne on stiff stems in late spring and summer. Grayish green leaves are crinkled and deeply cut.
H 6–8in (15–20cm),
S 8in (20cm) or more.

☼ ◊ Z5–8 H8–5

Scabiosa lucida
Clump-forming perennial with tufts of oval leaves and rounded heads of pale lilac to deep mauve flowers, borne on erect stems in summer.
H 8in (20cm), S 6in (15cm).

☼ ◊ Z4–9 H9–1

Penstemon serrulatus,
syn. *P. diffusus*
Semi-evergreen subshrub, deciduous in severe climates, that has small, elliptic, dark green leaves and tubular blue to purple flowers borne in loose spikes in summer. Soil should not be too dry. H 24in (60cm), S 12in (30cm).

☼ ◊ Z3–9 H9–1

Erigeron alpinus
(Alpine fleabane)
Clump-forming perennial of variable size that bears daisylike, lilac-pink flower heads on erect stems in summer. Leaves are long, oval, and hairy. Good for a sunny border, bank, or large rock garden. H 10in (25cm), S 8in (20cm).

☼ ◊ Z5–8 H8–5

Semiaquilegia ecalcarata
Short-lived, upright perennial with narrow, lobed leaves. In summer each slender stem bears several pendent, open bell-shaped, dusky pink to purple flowers with no spurs.
H 8in (20cm), S 2½in (6cm).

☼ ◊ Z4–7 H8–1

Chamaecytisus purpureus
Geranium procurrens
IRISES, illus. pp.234–5
Oxalis hirta
PEONIES, illus. pp.236–7
Scabiosa graminifolia

Parahebe catarractae
Evergreen subshrub with oval, toothed, midgreen leaves and, in summer, loose sprays of small, open funnel-shaped white flowers heavily zoned and veined pinkish-purple.
H and S 12in (30cm).

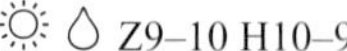
Z9–10 H10–9

Campanula barbata
(Bearded bellflower)
Evergreen perennial with a basal rosette of oval, hairy, gray-green leaves. In summer it bears one-sided racemes of bell-shaped, white to lavender-blue flowers. Is short lived but sets seed freely. H 8in (20cm), S 5in (12cm).

Z5–8 H8–5

Sisyrinchium graminoides, syn. *S. angustifolium*, *S. bermudiana*
Semi-evergreen, erect perennial with tufts of grasslike leaves. Small; pale to dark purplish blue flowers with yellow bases are borne in terminal clusters in late spring and early summer.
H to 12in (30cm), S 3in (8cm).

Z5–8 H8–5

Phlox divaricata subsp. ***laphamii***
Semi-evergreen, creeping perennial with oval leaves and upright stems bearing loose clusters of saucer-shaped, pale to deep violet-blue flowers in summer.
H 12in (30cm) or more, S 8in (20cm).

Z4–8 H8–1

Lithodora oleifolia, syn. *Lithospermum oleifolium*
Evergreen shrub with oval, pointed, silky, midgreen leaves. Curving stems carry loose sprays of several small, funnel-shaped, light blue flowers in early summer.
H 6–8in (15–20cm), S to 3ft (1m).

Z7–8 H8–7

Wulfenia amherstiana
Evergreen perennial with rosettes of narrowly spoon-shaped, toothed leaves. Erect stems bear loose clusters of small, tubular purple or pinkish purple flowers in summer.
H 6–12in (15–30cm), S to 12in (30cm).

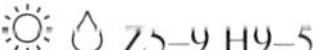
Z5–9 H9–5

Phlox divaricata subsp. ***laphamii* 'Chatahoochee'**
Short-lived, clump-forming perennial that has saucer-shaped, red-eyed, bright lavender flowers throughout summer-autumn. Narrow, pointed leaves are dark reddish purple when young.
H 6–8in (15–20cm), S 12in (30cm).

Z4–8 H8–1

Convolvulus sabatius, syn. *C. mauritanicus*
Trailing perennial with slender stems clothed in small, oval leaves and open trumpet-shaped, vibrant blue-purple flowers in summer and early autumn.
H 6–8in (15–20cm), S 12in (30cm).

Z7–9 H9–7

Linum perenne
Upright perennial with slender stems, clothed in grasslike leaves, that bear terminal clusters of open funnel-shaped, clear blue flowers in succession throughout summer.
H 12in (30cm), S to 6in (15cm).

Z5–8 H8–5

Aster alpinus, illus. p.381
Carmichaelia enysii
CARNATIONS and PINKS, illus. pp.280–1
Deinanthe caerulea
Dracocephalum ruyschiana
Erinacea anthyllis, illus. p.348
Erysimum linifolium
Horminum pyrenaicum
IRISES, illus. pp.234–5
Moltkia petraea
Penstemon hirsutus
Penstemon procerus
Phlox divaricata
Satureja montana
Viola cornuta, illus. p.349
Wulfenia carinthiaca

***Veronica prostrata*, syn. *V. rupestris* (Prostrate speedwell)**
Dense, mat-forming perennial that has upright spikes of small, saucer-shaped, brilliant blue flowers in early summer. Foliage is narrow, oval, and toothed.
H to 12in (30cm), S indefinite.

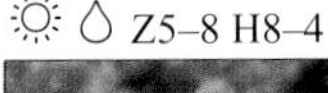
Z5–8 H8–4

Moltkia suffruticosa
Deciduous, upright subshrub that in summer bears clusters of funnel-shaped, bright blue flowers, pink in bud, on hairy stems. Leaves are long, pointed, and hairy.
H 6–16in (15–40cm), S 12in (30cm).

Z7–9 H9–7

***Veronica prostrata* 'Trehane'**
Dense, mat-forming perennial bearing upright spikes of small, saucer-shaped, deep violet-blue flowers in early summer above narrow, toothed yellow or yellowish-green leaves.
H in flower 6–8in (15–20cm), S indefinite.

Z5–8 H8–5

***Veronica prostrata* 'Kapitan'**
Dense, mat-forming perennial bearing erect spikes of small, saucer-shaped, bright deep blue flowers in early summer. Foliage is narrow, oval, and toothed. H to 12in (30cm), S indefinite.

Z5–8 H8–5

Mertensia echioides
Clump-forming perennial with basal rosettes of long, oval, hairy, blue-green leaves. Slender stems carry many open funnel-shaped, dark blue flowers in summer.
H 6–9in (15–23cm), S 6in (15cm).

Z6–9 H9–6

Phyteuma scheuchzeri
Tufted perennial with narrow, dark green leaves and terminal heads of spiky blue flowers that are borne in summer. Seeds freely; dislikes winter wet. H 6–8in (15–20cm), S 4in (10cm).

Z5–7 H7–5

Symphyandra wanneri
Clump-forming perennial with branching stems and hairy, oval leaves. In summer bears pendent, bell-shaped, blue to violet-blue flowers in loose, terminal spikes.
H 6–9in (15–23cm), S 10in (25cm).

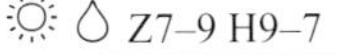
Z7–9 H9–7

***Lithodora diffusa* 'Heavenly Blue'**
Evergreen, prostrate shrub with trailing stems bearing pointed, oblong, hairy leaves and, in summer, a profusion of open funnel-shaped, deep blue flowers in leaf axils. Trim stems hard after flowering. H 6–12in (15–30cm), S to 18in (45cm).

pH Z6–8 H8–6

Aphyllanthes monspeliensis
Ceratostigma plumbaginoides, illus. p.360
Delphinium tatsienense
Gentiana septemfida, illus. p.360
IRISES, illus. pp.234–5
Lithodora diffusa 'Grace Ward'
Lithodora zahnii
Moltkia x *intermedia*
Omphalodes cappadocica, illus. p.349
Penstemon heterophyllus 'True Blue'
Rosmarinus officinalis 'Prostratus'
Symphyandra armena
Veronica austriaca subsp. *teucrium* 'Royal Blue'
Veronica pectinata
Veronica prostrata 'Spode Blue'

BLUE–YELLOW

Veronica austriaca
subsp. ***teucrium***, syn. *V. teucrium*
Spreading perennial with narrow spikes of small, flat, outward-facing, bright blue flowers in summer. Leaves are small, divided, hairy, and grayish green. H and S 10–24in (25–60cm).

Z4–8 H8–2

Erodium chrysanthum
Mound-forming perennial grown for its dense silvery stems and finely cut, fernlike leaves. Has small sprays of cup-shaped, sulfur- or creamy yellow flowers in late spring and summer.
H and S 9in (23cm).

Z7–8 H8–7

Hypericum olympicum
f. ***uniflorum* 'Citrinum'**
Deciduous, dense, rounded subshrub with tufts of upright stems clothed in small, oval, gray-green leaves. Bears terminal clusters of lemon yellow flowers throughout summer.
H and S 6–12in (15–30cm).

Z6–8 H8–6

YELLOW

***Verbascum* 'Letitia'**
Evergreen, stiff-branched shrub with toothed gray leaves. Bears outward-facing, 5-lobed, bright yellow flowers with reddish orange centers continuously from late spring to mid-autumn. Hates winter wet; is good in an alpine house. H and S to 10in (25cm).

Z5–9 H9–5

***Helianthemum* 'Wisley Primrose'**
Fast-growing, evergreen, compact shrub with saucer-shaped, pale yellow flowers in summer. Has oblong, gray-green leaves.
H 9in (23cm), S 12in (30cm) or more.

Z6–8 H8–6

Othonna cheirifolia,
syn. *Othonnopsis cheirifolia*
Evergreen shrub with narrow, somewhat fleshy gray leaves. In early summer bears daisylike yellow flower heads singly on upright stems.
H 8–12in (20–30cm), S 12in (30cm) or more.

Z8–9 H9–8

Linum arboreum
Evergreen, compact shrub with blue-green leaves. In summer has a succession of funnel-shaped, bright yellow flowers opening in sunny weather and borne in terminal clusters.
H to 12in (30cm), S 12in (30cm).

Z6–9 H9–6

Euryops acraeus,
syn. *E. evansii* of gardens
Evergreen, dome-shaped shrub with stems clothed in toothed, silvery blue leaves. Bears solitary daisylike, bright yellow flower heads in late spring and early summer.
H and S 12in (30cm).

Z9–11 H12–9

Eriogonum umbellatum
Evergreen, prostrate to upright perennial with mats of green leaves, white and woolly beneath. In summer carries heads of tiny yellow flowers that later turn copper. Dwarf forms are available. H 3–12in (8–30cm), S 6–12in (15–30cm).

Z3–8 H12–1

Helianthemum 'Jubilee'
HOSTAS, illus. pp.288–9
Meum athamanticum

Anthyllis hermanniae
Arnebia pulchra
Arnica montana
Aurinia saxatilis 'Citrina', illus. p.349

Chiastophyllum oppositifolium, illus. p.349
Corydalis cheilanthifolia, illus. p.349
Craspedia incana
Cremanthodium reniforme

Cytisus x *beanii*, illus. p.349
Erysimum x *kewense* 'Harpur Crewe', illus. p.350
Euryops pectinatus, illus. p.170

Corydalis lutea,
syn. *Pseudofumaria lutea*
Evergreen, clump-forming perennial with fleshy, fibrous roots and semi-erect, basal, gray-green leaves. Bears racemes of slender yellow flowers with short spurs in late spring and summer. H and S 8–12in (20–30cm).

Z5–8 H8–4

Verbascum dumulosum
Evergreen, mat-forming, shrubby perennial with hairy gray or gray-green leaves. In late spring and early summer bears a succession of 5-lobed, bright yellow flowers in short racemes. Dislikes winter wet. H 6in (15cm) or more, S 9–12in (23–30cm) or more.

Z6–9 H9–6

Chrysogonum virginianum
Mat-forming perennial with daisylike yellow flower heads borne on short stems in summer-autumn and oval, toothed, midgreen leaves. Although plant spreads by underground runners, it is not invasive. H 6–8in (15–20cm), S 4–6in (10–15cm) or more.

Z5–9 H9–2

Sedum rupestre, syn. *S. reflexum*
(Reflexed stonecrop)
Evergreen perennial with loose mats of rooting stems bearing narrow, fleshy leaves. Carries flat, terminal heads of tiny, bright yellow flowers in summer. Makes a good groundcover.
H 6–8in (15–20cm), S indefinite.

Z6–9 H9–6

Ranunculus gramineus
Erect, slender perennial with grasslike, blue-green leaves. Bears several cup-shaped, bright yellow flowers in late spring and early summer. Prefers rich soil. Seedlings will vary in height and flower size. H 16–20in (40–50cm), S 3–4in (8–10cm).

Z6–8 H8–6

Ononis natrix
(Large yellow restharrow)
Deciduous, compact, erect shrub with pealike, red-streaked yellow flowers in pendent clusters in summer. Hairy leaves are divided into 3 leaflets. H and S 12in (30cm) or more.

Z7–10 H10–7

Genista lydia
Deciduous, domed shrub with slender, arching branches and blue-green leaves. Massed terminal clusters of pealike, bright yellow flowers appear in late spring and early summer. Will trail over a large rock or wall. H 18–24in (45–60cm), S 24in (60cm) or more.

Z6–9 H9–3

Crepis aurea
Clump-forming perennial with a basal cluster of oblong, light green leaves. In summer produces dandelion-like orange flower heads singly on stems covered with black and white hairs. H 4–12in (10–30cm), S 6in (15cm).

Z5–7 H7–4

Genista pilosa
Helianthemum 'Golden Queen'
HOSTAS, illus. pp.288–9
Hypericum balearicum
Hypericum coris
Hypericum olympicum
IRISES, illus. pp.234–5
Linum flavum
PEONIES, illus. pp.236–7
PRIMROSES, illus. pp.272–3
Tanacetum haradjanii
Helianthemum 'Ben Nevis'
IRISES, illus. pp.234–5
PRIMROSES, illus. pp.272–3

ROCK PLANTS large AUTUMN INTEREST

WHITE–BLUE

Gaultheria cuneata
Evergreen, compact shrub with stiff stems clothed in leathery, oval leaves. In summer bears nodding, urn-shaped white flowers in leaf axils, followed by white berries in autumn.
H and S 12in (30cm).

pH Z4 H7–1

Ceratostigma plumbaginoides
Bushy perennial that bears small, terminal clusters of single, brilliant blue flowers on reddish, branched stems in late summer and autumn. Oval leaves turn rich red in autumn.
H 18in (45cm), S 8in (20cm).

Z5–9 H9–4

Sorbus reducta
Deciduous shrub forming a low thicket of upright branches. Small, gray-green leaves divided into leaflets turn bronze-red in late autumn. In early summer bears loose clusters of flat white flowers followed by pink berries. H and S to 12in (30cm) or more.

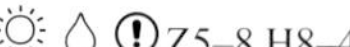
Z5–8 H8–4

Gentiana septemfida
Evergreen perennial with many upright then arching stems clothed with oval leaves. Bears heads of trumpet-shaped, midblue flowers in summer-autumn. Likes organic soil but tolerates reasonably drained, heavy clay.
H 6–8in (15–20cm), S 12in (30cm).

Z6–8 H8–6

OTHER RECOMMENDED PLANTS:
Chrysogonum virginianum, illus. p.359
Convolvulus sabatius, illus. p.356
Diascia rigescens, illus. p.353
Gaultheria miqueliana
Persicaria affinis 'Darjeeling Red'
Rhodanthemum hosmariense, illus. p.346

ROCK PLANTS large WINTER/ALL YEAR

WHITE–GRAY

Ranunculus calandrinioides
Clump-forming perennial that loses its long, oval, blue-green leaves in summer; in a reasonable winter it will bear a succession of cup-shaped, pink-flushed white flowers for many weeks. Needs very sharp drainage.
H and S to 8in (20cm).

Z7–8 H8–7

Cyathodes colensoi
Evergreen, low-growing shrub with stiff stems clothed in tiny, gray-green leaves. Bears clusters of small, tubular white flowers in spring at the ends of new growth. Red or white berries in late summer are rare in cultivation.
H and S 12in (30cm).

Z8–9 H9–8

Celmisia semicordata,
syn. *C. coriacea* of gardens
Evergreen perennial with swordlike silver leaves in large clumps and, in summer, daisylike white flower heads borne singly on hairy stems.
H and S 12in (30cm).

pH Z8–9 H9–8

Tanacetum argenteum,
syn. *Achillea argentea*
Mat-forming perennial, usually evergreen, grown for its finely cut, bright silver leaves. Has a profusion of small, daisylike white flower heads in summer. H in flower 6–9in (15–23cm), S 8in (20cm).

Z5–7 H7–5

OTHER RECOMMENDED PLANTS:
Eriogonum crocatum
Eriogonum ovalifolium
Euonymus fortunei 'Emerald Gaiety'
Persicaria affinis

GRAY–GREEN

Tanacetum densum subsp. ***amani***, syn. *Chrysanthemum densum*
Clump-forming perennial retaining fernlike, hairy gray leaves in winter in mild climates. Bears daisylike yellow flower heads with woolly bracts in summer. Dislikes winter wet. H and S 8in (20cm).

 Z6–8 H8–6

Ozothamnus coralloides, syn. *Helichrysum coralloides*
Evergreen, upright shrub with gray stems clothed in neat, dark green leaves marked silver. Occasionally bears fluffy yellow flower heads. Good for a cold frame or an alpine house. Hates winter wet. H 6–9in (15–23cm), S 6in (15cm).

Z8–9 H9–8

Salix* x *boydii
Very slow-growing, deciduous, upright shrub forming a gnarled, branched bush. Has oval, rough-textured leaves; catkins are rarely produced. Will tolerate light shade. H to 6–9in (15–23cm), S to 12in (30cm).

 Z4–7 H7–1

***Hebe cupressoides* 'Boughton Dome'**
Slow-growing, evergreen, dome-shaped shrub with scalelike, stem-clasping, dark gray-green leaves. Has terminal clusters of small, 4-lobed, blue-tinged white flowers in summer.
H 12in (30cm), S to 24in (60cm).

Z8–9 H9–8

Ozothamnus selago, syn. *Helichrysum selago*
Evergreen, upright shrub with stiff stems covered in scalelike leaves. Intermittently bears fluffy, creamy white flower heads. Makes a good foil for spring bulbs.
H and S 6–9in (15–23cm).

Z9–10 H10–9

Ballota pseudodictamnus
Evergreen, mound-forming subshrub with rounded, gray-green leaves and stems covered with woolly white hairs. In summer bears whorls of small pink flowers with conspicuous, enlarged, pale green calyces.
H 2ft (60cm), S 3ft (90cm).

Z7–9 H9–7

Arctostaphylos 'Emerald Carpet', illus. p.156
Buxus microphylla 'Green Pillow', illus. p.176
Euonymus fortunei 'Golden Prince'
Myrsine africana
Pachysandra axillaris
Paxistima canbyi
Rubus tricolor

ROCK PLANTS small SPRING INTEREST

WHITE

Cerastium tomentosum
(Snow in summer)
Very vigorous, groundcover perennial, good on a hot, dry bank, with prostrate stems covered by tiny gray leaves.
In late spring and summer bears star-shaped white flowers above foliage.
H 3in (8cm), S indefinite.

Z3–7 H7–1

Androsace pyrenaica
Evergreen perennial with small rosettes of tiny, hairy leaves, tightly packed to form hard cushions. Minute, stemless, single white flowers appear in spring. H 1½in (4cm), S to 4in (10cm).

Z6–7 H7–6

Arenaria tetraquetra
Evergreen perennial that forms a hard, gray-green cushion of small leaves. Stemless, star-shaped white flowers appear in late spring. Is well suited to a trough or an alpine house.
H 1in (2.5cm), S 6in (15cm) or more.

Z3–5 H5–1

OTHER RECOMMENDED PLANTS:
Androsace chamaejasme
Androsace cylindrica
Androsace hirtella
Arabis procurrens 'Variegata', illus. p.388
Callianthemum coriandrifolium
Cassiope wardii
Claytonia megarhiza

□ WHITE

Cardamine trifolia
Groundcover perennial with creeping stems clothed in rounded, toothed, 3-parted leaves. In late spring and early summer bears loose heads of open cup-shaped white flowers on bare stems.
H 4–6in (10–15cm), S 12in (30cm).

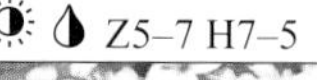
Z5–7 H7–5

***Androsace vandellii*,**
syn. *A. imbricata*
Evergreen, dense, cushion-forming perennial with narrow gray leaves and a profusion of stemless white flowers in spring. Needs careful cultivation with a deep collar of grit under the cushion.
H 1in (2.5cm), S to 4in (10cm).

pH Z5–7 H7–5

***Arabis alpina* subsp. *caucasica* 'Variegata'**
Evergreen, mat-forming perennial with rosettes of oval, cream-splashed, midgreen leaves. Bears bunches of single, sometimes pink-flushed white flowers from early spring to summer.
H and S 6in (15cm).

Z4–8 H8–1

Saxifraga scardica
Slow-growing, evergreen perennial with hard cushions composed of blue-green rosettes of leaves. In spring bears small clusters of upward-facing, cup-shaped white flowers. Does best in an alpine house or sheltered scree.
H 1in (2.5cm), S 3in (8cm).

Z7–8 H8–7

Weldenia candida
Perennial with rosettes of strap-shaped, wavy-margined leaves growing from tuberous roots. Bears a succession of upright, cup-shaped, pure white flowers in late spring and early summer. H and S 3–6in (8–15cm).

Z9–10 H10–9

Arenaria balearica
Prostrate perennial that is evergreen in all but the most severe winters. Will form a green film over a wet, porous rock face. Minute white flowers stud mats of foliage in late spring and early summer.
H less than ½in (1cm), S indefinite.

Z4–7 H7–1

Dicentra cucullaria
(Dutchman's breeches)
Compact perennial with fernlike foliage and arching stems, each bearing a few small, yellow-tipped white flowers like tiny, inflated trousers in spring. Lies dormant in summer.
H 6in (15cm), S to 12in (30cm).

Z4–8 H8–1

Celmisia ramulosa, illus. p.374
Clintonia uniflora
Cornus canadensis, illus. p.374
DAFFODILS, illus. pp.416–18
Dodecatheon dentatum
Epigaea asiatica
Haberlea rhodopensis 'Virginalis', illus. p.373
Iberis saxatilis, illus. p.374
IRISES, illus. pp.234–5
Leontopodium stracheyi
Lewisia rediviva [white form], illus. p.373
Ourisia caespitosa, illus. p.374
Pieris nana
Pratia angulata
PRIMROSES, illus. pp.272–3

Maianthemum canadense
Vigorous, groundcover, rhizomatous perennial with large, upright, oval, wavy-edged, glossy leaves. Slender stems bear sprays of small white flowers in late spring and early summer, followed by red berries.
H 4in (10cm), S indefinite.

Z4–7 H7–1

Sanguinaria canadensis
(Bloodroot)
Rhizomatous perennial with fleshy, underground stems that exude red sap when cut. In spring bears white flowers, sometimes pink-flushed or slate-blue on reverses, as blue-gray leaves unfurl.
H 4–6in (10–15cm), S 12in (30cm).

Z3–9 H8–1

Ranunculus alpestris
(Alpine buttercup)
Short-lived, evergreen, clump-forming perennial that bears cup-shaped white flowers on erect stems from late spring to midsummer. Glossy, dark green leaves are rounded and serrated.
H 1–5in (2.5–12cm), S 4in (10cm).

Z5–8 H8–5

Cassiope lycopodioides
Evergreen, prostrate, mat-forming shrub with slender stems densely set with minute, scalelike, dark green leaves. In spring, short reddish stems carry tiny, bell-shaped white flowers, in red calyces, singly in leaf axils.
H 3in (8cm), S 12in (30cm).

Z7–8 H8–7

Saxifraga burseriana
Slow-growing, evergreen perennial with hard cushions of spiky, gray-green leaves. In spring bears open cup-shaped white flowers on short stems.
H 1–2in (2.5–5cm), S to 4in (10cm).

Z6–8 H8–6

Pulsatilla vernalis
Tufted perennial with rosettes of feathery leaves. Densely hairy brown flower buds appear in late winter and open in early spring to somewhat nodding, open cup-shaped, pearl white flowers. Buds dislike winter wet.
H 2–4in (5–10cm), S 4in (10cm).

Z4–7 H7–1

Androsace villosa
Evergreen, mat-forming perennial with very hairy rosettes of tiny leaves. Bears umbels of small white flowers, with yellow centers that turn red, in spring. H 1in (2.5cm), S 8in (20cm).

Z5–7 H7–5

Salix apoda
Slow-growing, deciduous, prostrate shrub. In early spring, male forms bear fat, silky silver catkins with orange to pale yellow stamens and bracts. Oval, leathery leaves are hairy when young, becoming dark green later.
H to 6in (15cm), S 12–24in (30–60cm).

Z7–9 H9–1

***Ranunculus ficaria* 'Albus'**
Mat-forming perennial bearing in early spring cup-shaped, single, creamy white flowers with glossy petals. Leaves are heart-shaped and dark green. Can spread rapidly; is good for a wild garden.
H 2in (5cm), S 8in (20cm).

Z4–8 H8–1

Saxifraga burseriana 'Crenata'
Saxifraga burseriana 'Gloria'
Silene alpestris, illus. p.373
Tanakaea radicans

Thlaspi alpinum

WHITE–PINK

Cassiope mertensiana
Evergreen, dwarf shrub with scale-like, dark green leaves tightly pressed to stems. In early spring carries bell-shaped, creamy white flowers, with green or red calyces, in leaf axils. H 6in (15cm), S 8in (20cm).

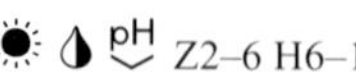
Z2–6 H6–1

Scoliopus bigelowii, syn. *S. bigelovii*
Compact perennial with basal, veined leaves, sometimes marked brown. In early spring bears flowers with purple inner petals and greenish white outer petals with deep purple lines. H 3–4in (8–10cm), S 4–6in (10–15cm).

Z6–8 H8–6

Gypsophila cerastioides
Prostrate perennial with a profusion of small, saucer-shaped, purple-veined white flowers borne in late spring and early summer above mats of rounded, velvety, midgreen foliage. H ¾in (2cm), S to 4in (10cm) or more.

Z5–8 H8–5

Paraquilegia anemonoides, syn. *P. grandiflora*
Tufted perennial with fernlike, blue-green leaves. In spring, pale lavender-blue buds open to pendent, cup-shaped, almost white flowers borne singly on arching stems. May be difficult to establish. H and S 4–6in (10–15cm).

Z5–8 H8–5

Corydalis popovii
Tuberous perennial with leaves divided into 3–6 bluish green leaflets. In spring bears loose racemes of deep red-purple and white flowers, each with a long spur. Keep dry when dormant. H and S 4–6in (10–15cm).

Z7–8 H8–7

Leptinella atrata* subsp. *luteola
Evergreen, mat-forming perennial that in late spring and early summer bears blackish red flower heads with creamy yellow stamens. Leaves are small, finely cut, and dark green. Needs adequate moisture; best in an alpine house. H 1in (2.5cm), S to 10in (25cm).

Z8–9 H9–8

Anemonella thalictroides
Perennial with delicate, fernlike leaves growing from a cluster of small tubers. From spring to early summer bears small, cup-shaped white or pink flowers on finely branched stems. Needs organic soil. H 4in (10cm), S 1½in (4cm) or more.

Z4–7 H7–1

Lewisia tweedyi
Evergreen, rosetted perennial with large, fleshy leaves and thick, branched stems that bear open cup-shaped, many-petaled white to pink flowers in spring. Best grown in an alpine house. H 6in (15cm), S 5–6in (12–15cm).

Z4–7 H7–1

Shortia galacifolia (Oconee bells)
Evergreen, clump-forming, dwarf perennial with round, toothed, leathery, glossy leaves. In late spring bears cup- to trumpet-shaped, often pink-flushed white flowers with deeply serrated petals. H to 6in (15cm), S 6–9in (15–23cm).

Z6–9 H9–6

Daphne jasminea
Evergreen, compact shrub. Bears small white flowers, pink-flushed externally, in late spring and early summer and again in autumn. Brittle stems are clothed in gray-green leaves. Good for an alpine house or a dry wall. H 3–4in (8–10cm), S to 12in (30cm).

Z7–9 H9–7

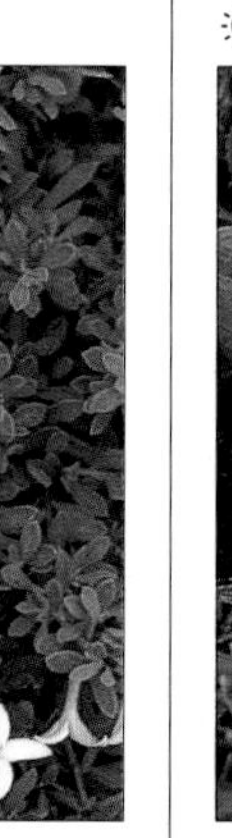

Epigaea gaultherioides, syn. *Orphanidesia gaultherioides*
Evergreen, prostrate subshrub with cup-shaped, shell pink flowers borne in terminal clusters in spring. Hairy stems carry heart-shaped, dark green leaves. Is difficult to grow and propagate. H to 4in (10cm), S to 10in (25cm) or more.

Z8–9 H9–8

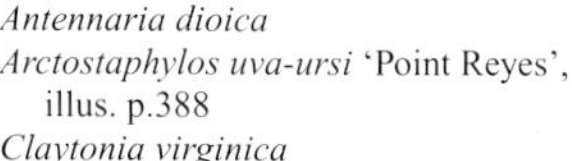

Antennaria dioica
Arctostaphylos uva-ursi 'Point Reyes', illus. p.388
Claytonia virginica
Dryas octopetala, illus. p.375
Epigaea repens
Hypsela reniformis
Kelseya uniflora
Ranunculus glacialis
Shortia uniflora 'Grandiflora'

Trillium rivale
Perennial with oval leaves divided into 3 leaflets. In spring bears open cup-shaped white or pale pink flowers with dark-spotted, heart-shaped petals, singly on upright, later arching stems. H to 6in (15cm), S 4in (10cm).

Z5–8 H8–5

***Saxifraga* x *irvingii* 'Jenkinsiae'**, syn. *S.* 'Jenkinsiae'
Slow-growing perennial with very tight, gray-green cushions of foliage. Carries a profusion of open cup-shaped, lilac-pink flowers on slender stems in early spring. H 3–4in (8–10cm), S to 6in (15cm).

Z6–7 H7–6

Androsace carnea
Evergreen, cushion-forming perennial that has small rosettes of pointed leaves with hairy margins. In spring, two or more stems rise above each rosette, bearing tiny, single pink flowers. Good in a trough. H and S 2in (5cm).

Z4–7 H7–1

Thlaspi cepaeifolium subsp. ***rotundifolium***
Clump-forming perennial with dense tufts of round leaves and small, open cup-shaped, pale to deep purplish- or lilac-pink flowers in spring. Needs cool conditions. May be short-lived. H 2–3in (5–8cm), S 4in (10cm).

Z6–9 H9–6

Arenaria purpurascens
Evergreen, mat-forming perennial with sharp-pointed, glossy leaves, above which rise many small clusters of star-shaped, pale to deep purplish pink flowers in early spring. H ½in (1cm), S to 6in (15cm).

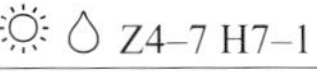

Z4–7 H7–1

Oxalis acetosella var. ***subpurpurascens***
Creeping, rhizomatous perennial forming mats of 3-lobed leaves. Cup-shaped, soft pink flowers, each ½in (1cm) across, with 5 darker-veined petals, are produced in spring. H 2in (5cm), S indefinite.

Z3–8 H8–1

Silene acaulis (Moss campion)
Evergreen, cushion-forming perennial with minute, bright green leaves studded with tiny, stemless, 5-petaled pink flowers in spring. May be difficult to bring into flower; prefers a cool climate. H to 1in (2.5cm), S 6in (15cm).

Z3–5 H5–1

Armeria juniperifolia, syn. *A. caespitosa*
Evergreen, cushion-forming perennial composed of loose rosettes of sharp-pointed, mid- to gray-green leaves. Pale pink flowers are borne in spherical umbels in late spring and early summer. H 2–3in (5–8cm), S 6in (15cm).

Z5–7 H8–4

***Arabis* x *arendsii* 'Rosabella'**, syn. *A. caucasica* 'Rosabella'
Evergreen, mat-forming perennial with a profusion of single, deep pink flowers in spring and early summer and large rosettes of small, oval, soft green leaves. H 6in (15cm), S 12in (30cm).

Z5–8 H8–5

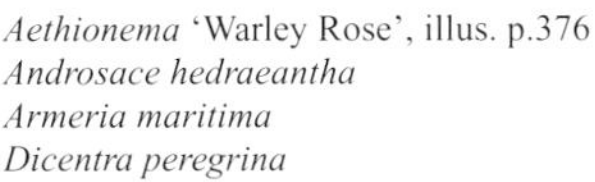

Aethionema 'Warley Rose', illus. p.376
Androsace hedraeantha
Armeria maritima
Dicentra peregrina
Erodium corsicum, illus. p.376
Ourisia microphylla, illus. p.376
x *Phyllothamnus erectus*
PRIMROSES, illus. pp.272–3
Rhodohypoxis 'Margaret Rose', illus. p.376

PINK

Oxalis adenophylla
Mat-forming, fibrous-rooted, tuberous perennial with gray-green leaves divided into narrow, fingerlike, wavy lobes. In spring bears rounded, purplish pink flowers, each 1–1½in (2.5–4cm) across, with darker purple eyes.
H to 2in (5cm), S 3–4in (8–10cm).

Z6–8 H8–6

Shortia soldanelloides
Evergreen, mat-forming perennial with rounded, toothed leaves and small, pendent, bell-shaped and fringed, deep pink flowers in late spring.
H 2–4in (5–10cm), S 4–6in (10–15cm).

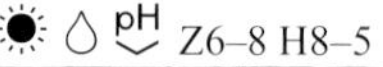
Z6–8 H8–5

Erinus alpinus
Semi-evergreen, short-lived perennial with rosettes of soft, midgreen leaves covered in late spring and summer with small purple, pink, or white flowers. Self seeds freely.
H and S 2–3in (5–8cm).

Z4–7 H7–1

Antennaria dioica* var. *rosea
Semi-evergreen perennial forming a spreading mat of tiny, oval, woolly leaves. Bears fluffy, rose-pink flower heads in small, terminal clusters in late spring and early summer. Is good as a groundcover with small bulbs.
H 1in (2.5cm), S to 16in (40cm).

Z5–9 H9–4

Daphne arbuscula
Evergreen, prostrate shrub. In late spring bears many very fragrant, tubular, deep pink flowers in terminal clusters. Narrow, leathery, dark green leaves are crowded at the ends of the branches. Likes organic soil.
H 4–6in (10–15cm), S 20in (50cm).

Z5–7 H7–5

Saxifraga oppositifolia
(Purple mountain saxifrage)
Evergreen, prostrate perennial with clusters of tiny, white-flecked leaves. Has open cup-shaped, dark purple, purplish pink, or, rarely, white flowers in early spring. Likes an open position.
H 1–2in (2.5–5cm), S 6in (15cm).

Z1–7 H7–1

***Daphne petraea* 'Grandiflora'**
Slow-growing, evergreen, compact shrub that bears terminal clusters of fragrant, rich pink flowers in late spring and tiny, glossy leaves. Good in an alpine house, a sheltered rock garden with organic soil, or a trough.
H to 6in (15cm), S to 10in (25cm).

Z5–7 H7–3

Claytonia megarhiza* var. *nivalis
Evergreen perennial with a rosette of spoon-shaped, succulent leaves. Bears small heads of tiny, deep pink flowers in spring. Grows best in a deep pot of gritty soil mix in an alpine house.
H ½in (1cm), S 3in (8cm).

Z5–7 H7–5

Vaccinium vitis-idaea
subsp. ***minus***, syn. *V. v.-i.* 'Minus'
Evergreen, mat-forming subshrub with tiny, oval, leathery leaves. In late spring produces small, erect racemes of many tiny, bell-shaped, deep pink or deep pink and white flowers.
H 2–3in (5–8cm), S 4–6in (10–15cm).

Z2–6 H6–1

Androsace sarmentosa
Anemonella thalictroides 'Oscar Schoaf'
Antennaria dioica 'Nyewoods'
Arabis blepharophylla
Erinus alpinus 'Dr Hähnle'
Geranium cinereum 'Ballerina', illus. p.379
Lewisia rediviva [pink form], illus. p.379
PRIMROSES, illus. pp.272–3
Salix lindleyana
Saxifraga x *irvingii* 'Walter Irving'
Shortia soldanelloides var. *ilicifolia*
Shortia soldanelloides var. *magna*
Viola cazorlensis

***Anagallis tenella* 'Studland'**
Short-lived perennial that forms prostrate mats of tiny, bright green leaves studded in spring with honey-scented, star-shaped, bright pink flowers.
H ½in (1cm), S 6in (15cm) or more.

Z5–7 H7–5

Androsace carnea* subsp. *laggeri
Evergreen, cushion-forming perennial composed of small, tight rosettes of pointed leaves. Cup-shaped, deep pink flowers are borne in small clusters above cushions in spring.
H and S 2in (5cm).

Z4–7 H7–1

***Corydalis solida* 'George Baker'**, syn. *C.s.* 'G.P. Baker'
Tuberous perennial with fernlike, divided leaves and dense racemes of spurred, rich deep rose-red flowers in spring. H and S 4–6in (10–15cm).

Z5–7 H7–5

***Saxifraga frederici-augustii* subsp. *grisebachii* 'Wisley Variety'**, syn. *S. grisebachii* 'Wisley Variety'
Evergreen perennial with rosettes of lime-encrusted leaves. Crozier-shaped stems with pale pink to bright red hairs bear dense racemes of dark red flowers in spring. H 4in (10cm), S 6in (15cm).

Z6–8 H8–6

Saxifraga sempervivum
Evergreen, hummock-forming perennial with tight rosettes of tufted, silvery green leaves. Crozier-shaped flower stems, covered in silvery hairs and emerging from rosettes, bear racemes of dark red flowers in early spring. H and S 4–6in (10–15cm).

Z6–7 H7–6

Leptinella atrata, syn. *Cotula atrata*
Evergreen, mat-forming perennial with small, finely cut, grayish green leaves and blackish red flower heads in late spring and early summer. Not easy to grow successfully.
H 1in (2.5cm), S to 10in (25cm).

Z8–9 H9–8

Aethionema 'Warley Ruber'
Androsace sempervivoides
Armeria juniperifolia 'Bevan's Variety'
Dodecatheon pulchellum
Penstemon davidsonii
PRIMROSES, illus. pp.272–3
Rhodohypoxis 'Albrighton', illus. p.380
Rhodohypoxis 'Douglas', illus. p.380

PURPLE

Corydalis diphylla
Tuberous perennial with semi-erect, basal leaves divided into narrow leaflets, and loose racemes of purple-lipped flowers with white spurs in spring. Protect tubers from excess moisture in summer.
H 4–6in (10–15cm), S 3–4in (8–10cm).

Z5–8 H8–5

Polygonatum hookeri
Slow-growing, dense, rhizomatous perennial that bears loose spikes of several small, bell-shaped, lilac-pink flowers in late spring and early summer. Leaves are tiny and lance-shaped. Good in peaty soil.
H to 2in (5cm), S to 12in (30cm).

Z6–9 H9–6

***Aubrieta* 'Joy'**
Vigorous, evergreen, trailing perennial that forms mounds of soft green leaves. In spring bears double, pale mauve flowers on short stems.
H 4in (10cm), S 8in (20cm).

Z5–7 H7–5

PRIMROSES, illus. pp.272–3
Ramonda nathaliae
Ramonda serbica
Viola 'Nellie Britton', illus. p.381

■ PURPLE

***Aubrieta deltoidea* 'Argenteovariegata'**
Evergreen, compact perennial, grown for its trailing green leaves, which are heavily splashed with creamy white. Produces pinkish lavender flowers in spring. H 2in (5cm), S 6in (15cm).

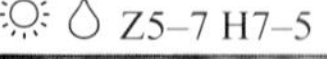

Z5–7 H7–5

Mazus reptans
Prostrate perennial that has tubular purple or purplish pink flowers, with protruding white lips, spotted red and yellow, borne singly on short stems in spring. Narrow, toothed leaves are in pairs along the stems.
H to 2in (5cm), S 12in (30cm) or more.

Z5–8 H8–5

Soldanella villosa
Evergreen, clump-forming perennial with round, leathery, hairy-stalked leaves and nodding, bell-shaped, fringed, purplish lavender flowers borne on erect stems in early spring. Dislikes winter wet.
H 4in (10cm), S 4–6in (10–15cm).

Z4–7 H7–1

***Aubrieta* 'Hartswood Purple',**
syn. *A.* 'Carnival'
Vigorous, evergreen, mound-forming perennial that carries many short spikes of large, single, violet-purple flowers in spring above small, soft green leaves.
H 4in (10cm), S 12in (30cm).

Z5–7 H7–5

Soldanella alpina
(Alpine snowbell)
Evergreen, clump-forming perennial with tufts of leaves and short, bell-shaped, fringed, pinkish lavender or purplish pink flowers in early spring. Can be difficult to flower well.
H to 3in (8cm), S 3–4in (8–10cm).

Z4–7 H7–1

Saxifraga stribrnyi
Evergreen, mound-forming perennial with small, lime-encrusted rosettes of leaves. Crozier-shaped stems covered in pinkish buff hairs bear racemes of deep maroon flowers above leaves in late spring and early summer.
H 3in (8cm), S 4–5in (10–12cm).

Z6–7 H7–6

Polygala chamaebuxus* var. *grandiflora
Evergreen, woody-based perennial that bears terminal clusters of pealike, reddish purple and yellow flowers in late spring and early summer. Leaves are small, oval, leathery, and dark green.
H to 6in (15cm), S to 12in (30cm).

Z6–9 H9–6

***Aubrieta* 'J.S. Baker'**
Evergreen perennial with single purple flowers in spring borne above mounds of small, soft green leaves.
H 4in (10cm), S 8in (20cm).

Z5–7 H7–5

Viola calcarata
Clump-forming perennial, with oval leaves, that bears flat, outward-facing, single white, lavender, or purple flowers for a long period from late spring to summer. Prefers rich soil.
H 4–6in (10–15cm), S to 8in (20cm).

Z

Aubrieta 'Doctor Mules'
IRISES, illus. pp.234–5
Polygala vayredae
Saxifraga x *arco-valleyi* 'Arco'
Saxifraga oppositifolia 'Ruth Draper'
Soldanella minima
Soldanella montana
Viola obliqua
Viola odorata
Viola palmata

***Aubrieta* 'Cobalt Violet'**
Evergreen, mound-forming perennial with single, blue-violet flowers carried in short, terminal spikes in spring above a mat of small, soft green leaves. H 4in (10cm), S 8in (20cm).

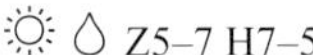
Z5–7 H7–5

Viola tricolor
(Heartsease, Wild pansy)
Short-lived perennial or annual with neat, flat-faced flowers in combinations of white, yellow, and shades of purple from spring to autumn. Self seeds profusely. H 2–6in (5–15cm), S 2–6in (5–15cm) or more.

Z3–9 H12–1

Hepatica nobilis* var. *japonica
Slow-growing perennial with leathery, lobed leaves, semi-evergreen in all but very cold or arid climates. Bears slightly cupped, lilac-mauve, pink, or white flowers in spring.
H to 3in (8cm), S to 5in (12cm).

Z5–8 H8–5

***Viola riviniana* 'Purpurea',**
syn. *V. labradorica* 'Purpurea'
Clump-forming perennial with tiny, flat-faced purple flowers in spring-summer. Leaves are kidney-shaped and dark purple-green. Invasive but is good for a bank, woodland, or wild garden.
H 1–2in (2.5–5cm), S indefinite.

Z5–8 H8–5

***Jeffersonia dubia*,**
syn. *Plagiorhegma dubia*
Tufted perennial with 2-lobed, blue-green leaves, sometimes flushed pink when unfolding. Bears cup-shaped, pale lilac to purplish blue flowers singly in spring.
H 4–6in (10–15cm), S to 9in (23cm).

Z5–8 H8–5

Jancaea heldreichii
Perennial with rosettes of thick, hairy, silver-green leaves, above which rise slender stems bearing clusters of tiny, lavender-blue flowers in late spring. Is rare and difficult to grow and is best in an alpine house. H and S to 3in (8cm).

Z5–7 H7–5

Viola pedata (Bird's-foot violet)
Clump-forming perennial with finely divided foliage and yellow-centered, pale violet, rarely white flowers borne singly on slender stems in late spring and early summer. Needs well-drained soil or soil mix.
H 2in (5cm) S 3in (8cm).

pH Z4–8 H8–1

Mertensia maritima
Prostrate perennial with oval, fleshy, bright silver-blue or silver-gray leaves. Thick stems carry clusters of pendent, funnel-shaped, sky blue flowers in spring. Prone to slug damageand needs very good drainage.
H 4–6in (10–15cm), S 5in (12cm).

Z3–7 H7–1

Synthyris stellata
Evergreen, mounded, rhizomatous perennial that bears dense spikes of small, violet-blue flowers in spring above rounded, deeply toothed leaves. Tolerates sun if soil remains moist.
H 4–6in (10–15cm), S 6in (15cm).

Z7–9 H9–7

Aubrieta 'Gurgedyke'
Haberlea ferdinandi-coburgii
Haberlea rhodopensis
Hedyotis michauxii, illus. p.383
IRISES, illus. pp.234–5
Omphalogramma vinciflorum
Phlox 'Emerald Cushion', illus. p.381
Thalictrum orientale

■ BLUE

Myosotis alpestris, syn. *M. rupicola* (Alpine forget-me-not)
Short-lived, clump-forming perennial producing dense clusters of tiny, bright blue flowers with creamy yellow eyes in late spring and early summer, just above tufts of hairy leaves. Prefers gritty soil. H and S 4–6in (10–15cm).

Z4–8 H8–1

Anchusa cespitosa
Evergreen, mound-forming perennial with rosettes of lance-shaped, dark green leaves. In spring, stemless, white-centered blue flowers appear in centers of rosettes. Old plants do not flower well; take early-summer cuttings.
H 1–2in (2.5–5cm), S to 9in (23cm).

Z5–7 H7–5

Gentiana verna (Spring gentian)
Evergreen perennial, often short-lived, with small rosettes of oval, dark green leaves. In early spring, tubular, bright blue flowers with white throats are held upright on short stems.
H and S to 2in (5cm).

Z4–7 H7–1

■ BLUE–GREEN

Gentiana acaulis, syn. *G. excisa, G. kochiana* (Stemless gentian)
Evergreen, clump-forming perennial with narrowly oval, glossy leaves. Bears trumpet-shaped, deep blue flowers with green-spotted throats on short stems in spring and often in autumn. H in leaf ¾in (2cm), S to 4in (10cm) or more.

Z5–8 H8–5

***Viola tricolor* 'Bowles' Black'**
Clump-forming perennial with flat-faced, very dark violet, almost black flowers borne continuously from spring to autumn. Oval leaves are sometimes lobed and toothed. Is short-lived; treat as biennial.
H 2–6in (5–15cm), S 2–3in (5–8cm).

Z4–8 H8–1

Salix reticulata
(Net-veined willow)
Deciduous, spreading, mat-forming shrub. Carries plump, reddish brown then yellow catkins on male plants in spring and rounded, slightly crinkled leaves. Likes cool, peaty soil.
H 2–3in (5–8cm), S 8in (20cm) or more.

Z2–6 H6–1

Eritrichium nanum, illus. p.383
Hepatica x *media* 'Ballardii'
IRISES, illus. pp.234–5
Omphalodes luciliae
Polygala calcarea, illus. p.384
Polygala calcarea 'Bulley's Form', illus. p.384
Synthyris reniformis
Hepatica nobilis
Hepatica transsilvanica

GREEN–YELLOW

Mandragora officinarum
Rosetted, fleshy-rooted perennial with coarse, wavy-edged leaves. Bears funnel-shaped, yellowish- or purplish white flowers in spring, followed by large, tomato-like, shiny yellow fruits. H 2in (5cm), S 12in (30cm).

Z5–8 H8–5

Hacquetia epipactis
Clump-forming perennial spreading by short rhizomes. In late winter and early spring bears yellow or yellow-green flower heads, encircled by apple green bracts, before rounded, 3-parted leaves appear.
H 2½in (6cm), S 6–9in (15–23cm).

Z5–7 H7–5

Euphorbia myrsinites
Evergreen, prostrate perennial with terminal clusters of bright yellow-green flowers in spring. Woody stems are clothed in small, pointed, fleshy gray leaves. Is good on a wall or ledge.
H 2–3in (5–8cm),
S to 8in (20cm) or more.

Z5–8 H8–5

Corydalis wilsonii, illus. p.349

YELLOW

Saxifraga* x *boydii
'Hindhead Seedling'
Evergreen perennial that forms a hard dome of small, tufted, spiny, blue-green leaves. In spring bears upward-facing, open, cup-shaped, pale yellow flowers, 2 or 3 to each short stem.
H 1in (2.5cm), S 3in (8cm).

Z6–8 H8–6

Saxifraga* x *apiculata
'Gregor Mendel'
Evergreen perennial with a tight cushion of bright green foliage. Bears clusters of open, cup-shaped, pale yellow flowers in early spring.
H 4–6in (10–15cm), S 6in (15cm) or more.

Z6–8 H8–6

***Saxifraga* 'Elizabethae'**,
syn. *S.* x *elizabethae*
Evergreen, cushion-forming perennial composed of densely packed, tiny rosettes of spiny leaves. In spring, upward-facing, bright yellow flowers are carried on tops of red-based stems.
H 1in (2.5cm), S 4–6in (10–15cm).

Z5–7 H7–5

Calceolaria uniflora var. *darwinii*
Cytisus ardoinoi, illus. p.386
DAFFODILS, illus. pp.416–18

Viola aetolica
Clump-forming perennial bearing flat-faced yellow flowers singly on upright stems in late spring and early summer. Leaves are oval and midgreen.
H 2–3in (5–8cm), S 6in (15cm).

Z8–9 H9–8

Draba rigida
Evergreen perennial with tight hummocks of minute, dark green leaves. Tiny clusters of bright yellow flowers on fine stems cover hummocks in spring. Good in a scree garden or alpine house. Dislikes winter wet.
H 1½in (4cm), S 2½in (6cm).

Z4–6 H6–1

Dionysia aretioides
Evergreen perennial forming cushions of soft, hairy, grayish green leaves that are covered in early spring by scented, stemless, round, bright yellow flowers.
H 2–4in (5–10cm),
S 6–12in (15–30cm).

Z5–7 H7–5

Draba aizoides
Draba hispanica
Draba polytricha
Draba rigida var. *bryoides*

Draba longisiliqua
Semi-evergreen, cushion-forming perennial composed of firm rosettes of tiny silvery leaves. Bears sprays of small yellow flowers on long stalks in spring. Needs plenty of water in growth; is best grown in an alpine house. H 2–3in (5–8cm), S 6in (15cm).

Z4–6 H6–1

Saxifraga sancta
Evergreen, mat-forming perennial with tufts of bright green leaves. Bears short racemes of upward-facing, open cup-shaped, bright yellow flowers in spring. H 2in (5cm), S 6in (15cm).

Z7–8 H8–7

IRISES, illus. pp.234–5
Onosma stellulata
Polygala chamaebuxus, illus. p.385
PRIMROSES, illus. pp.272–3

ROCK PLANTS small SPRING INTEREST

□ YELLOW

Draba mollissima
Semi-evergreen, cushion-forming perennial covered in spring with clusters of tiny yellow flowers on slender stems. Minute leaves form a soft green dome, which should be packed beneath with small stones. Grow in an alpine house.
H 1½in (4cm), S 6in (15cm) or more.

Z4–6 H6–1

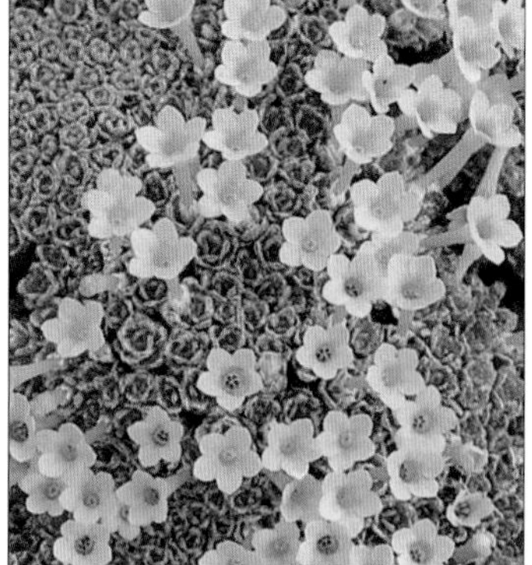

Dionysia tapetodes
Evergreen, prostrate perennial producing a tight mat of tiny, gray-green leaves. Bears small, upward-facing yellow flowers in early spring.
H ½in (1cm), S to 6in (15cm).

Z5–7 H7–5

Morisia monanthos, syn. *M. hypogaea*
Prostrate perennial with flat rosettes of divided, leathery, dark green leaves. Bears stemless, flat, bright yellow flowers in late spring and early summer. Needs very good drainage.
H 1in (2.5cm), S to 3in (8cm).

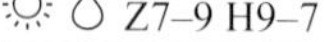

Z7–9 H9–7

***Ranunculus ficaria* 'Flore Pleno'**
Mat-forming perrennial with heart-shaped, dark green leaves and, in early spring, double, bright yellow flowers with glossy petals. May spread rapidly. Is good for a wild garden.
H 1–2in (2.5–5cm), S 8in (20cm).

Z4–8 H8–1

Vitaliana primuliflora, syn. *Douglasia vitaliana*
Evergreen, prostrate perennial with a mat of rosetted, midgreen leaves that are covered in spring with many small clusters of stemless, tubular, bright yellow flowers.
H 1in (2.5cm), S 8in (20cm).

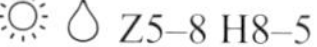

Z5–8 H8–5

***Viola* 'Jackanapes'**
Clump-forming perennial with oval, toothed leaves. Produces flat-faced flowers with reddish brown upper petals and yellow lower ones throughout late spring and summer.
H 3–5in (8–12cm), S to 8in (20cm) or more.

Z4–8 H8–1

Ranunculus ficaria 'Brazen Hussy'
Salix herbacea
Sarcocapnos enneaphylla
Saxifraga aizoides
Saxifraga brunonis
Saxifraga burseriana 'Brookside'
Saxifraga ferdinandi-coburgi
Saxifraga 'Valerie Finnis'
Sedum acre 'Aureum', illus. p.385
Townsendia parryi
Viola glabella
Viola lutea
Waldsteinia ternata, illus. p.385

ROCK PLANTS small SUMMER INTEREST

YELLOW

Trollius pumilus
Tufted perennial with leaves divided into 5 segments, each further lobed. Carries solitary cup-shaped, bright yellow flowers in late spring and early summer.
H 6in (15cm), S 6in (15cm) or more.

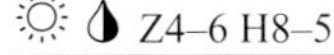
Z4–6 H8–5

Erysimum helveticum,
syn. *E. pumilum*
Semi-evergreen, clump-forming perennial with closely-packed tufts of long, narrow leaves and many fragrant, bright yellow flowers borne in flat heads in late spring and early summer.
H 4in (10cm), S 6in (15cm).

Z5–8 H8–5

***Ranunculus ficaria* 'Aurantiacus'**
Mat-forming perennial bearing in early spring cup-shaped, single orange flowers with glossy petals. Leaves are heart-shaped and midgreen. May spread rapidly. Is good for a wild garden. H 2in (5cm), S 8in (20cm).

Z4–8 H8–1

WHITE

Silene alpestris,
syn. *Heliosperma alpestris*
Perennial with branching stems and narrow leaves. Bears small, rounded, fringed white, occasionally pink-flushed flowers in late spring and early summer. Self seeds freely.
H 4–6in (10–15cm), S 8in (20cm).

Z4–7 H7–1

***Phlox stolonifera* 'Ariane'**
Evergreen, low-growing perennial with flowering shoots that bear heads of open, saucer-shaped white blooms in early summer. Has oval, pale green leaves. Cut back flowered shoots by half after flowering.
H to 6in (15cm), S 12in (30cm).

pH Z4–8 H8–1

Achillea clavennae
Semi-evergreen, carpeting perennial that bears loose clusters of white flower heads with gold centers from summer to midautumn. Leaves are narrowly oval, many-lobed, and covered with fine white hairs. Dislikes winter wet.
H 6in (15cm), S 9in (23cm) or more.

Z3–8 H8–1

***Haberlea rhodopensis* 'Virginalis'**
Evergreen perennial with small, arching sprays of funnel-shaped, pure white flowers borne in late spring and early summer above neat rosettes of oval, toothed, dark green leaves.
H and S in flower 4–6in (10–15cm).

Z5–7 H7–5

Potentilla alba
Vigorous mat-forming perennial bearing loose sprays of flat, single white flowers in summer. Leaves are divided into oval leaflets and are silvery beneath.
H 2–3in (5–8cm), S 3in (8cm).

Z5–8 H8–3

Lewisia rediviva [white form]
(Bitter root)
Tufted, rosetted perennial with clusters of fine, narrow leaves that are summer-deciduous. Bears large white flowers that open in bright weather in late spring and early summer.
H ½–1½in (1–4cm), S to 2in (5cm).

pH Z4–7 H7–1

Cyananthus lobatus* f. *albus
Prostrate perennial with branched stems clothed in small, wedge-shaped, dull green leaves. Bears funnel-shaped, single white flowers with spreading lobes in late summer.
H 3in (8cm), S 12in (30cm).

Z6–7 H7–6

***Campanula carpatica* 'Bressingham White'**
Clump-forming perennial bearing open cup-shaped white flowers, singly on unbranched stems, in summer. Has abundant, rounded, bright green leaves.
H 4–6in (10–15cm), S 6in (15cm).

Z4–7 H7–1

DAFFODILS, illus. pp.416–18
Hypericum cerastioides
IRISES, illus. pp.234–5
Leucogenes grandiceps, illus. p.389

OTHER RECOMMENDED PLANTS:
Aethionema iberideum
Arabis alpina subsp. *caucasica*
Arabis alpina subsp. *caucasica* 'Flore Pleno'
Arabis alpina subsp. *caucasica* 'Variegata', illus. p.362
Arctostaphylos nevadensis
Arenaria balearica, illus. p.362
Artemisia schmidtiana 'Nana', illus. p.389
Cardamine trifolia, illus. p.362
Celmisia bellidioides
Celmisia traversii

ROCK PLANTS small SUMMER INTEREST

☐ WHITE

Arenaria montana
Prostrate perennial that forms loose mats of small, narrowly oval leaves and bears large, round white flowers in summer. Good for a wall or rock crevice. Must have adequate moisture. H 2in (5cm), S 5in (12cm).

Z3–5 H5–1

Celmisia ramulosa
Evergreen, shrubby perennial with small, hairy, gray-green leaves. Daisy-like white flower heads are borne singly on short stems in late spring and early summer. H and S 4in (10cm).

pH Z7–8 H8–7

Anacyclus pyrethrum
var. ***depressus***, syn. *A. depressus*
Short-lived, prostrate perennial that has white flower heads with red reverses to ray petals in summer. Flowers close in dull light. Stems are clothed in fine leaves. Dislikes wet. H 1–2in (2.5–5cm) or more, S 4in (10cm).

Z6–8 H8–6

Epilobium chlorifolium
var. ***kaikourense***
Clump-forming, woody-based perennial with deciduous but persistent, oval, hairy bronze and dark green leaves. In summer has short spikes of funnel-shaped white to pink flowers. H 4in (10cm), S 6in (15cm).

Z4–6 H6–1

Iberis saxatilis
Evergreen, dwarf subshrub that in late spring and early summer produces large heads of numerous small white flowers that become tinged violet with age. Glossy, dark leaves are linear and cylindrical. Trim after flowering. H 3–5in (8–12cm), S 12in (30cm).

Z7–9 H9–7

Ourisia caespitosa
Evergreen, prostrate perennial with creeping rootstocks and stems bearing tiny, oval leaves and many outward-facing, open cup-shaped white flowers in late spring and early summer. H 1in (2.5cm), S 4in (10cm).

Z5–7 H7–5

Petrocosmea kerrii
Evergreen perennial with compact rosettes of oval, pointed, hairy, rich green leaves. In summer bears clusters of short, outward-facing, tubular, open-mouthed white flowers. Good in an alpine house. H to 3in (8cm), S 5–6in (12–15cm).

Z10–11 H12–9

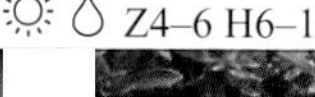

Gentiana saxosa
Evergreen, hummock-forming perennial clothed in small, spoon-shaped, fleshy, dark green leaves. Produces small, upturned, bell-shaped white flowers in early summer. Is a short-lived scree plant. H 2in (5cm), S 6in (15cm).

Z4–8 H8–1

Cornus canadensis
(Creeping dogwood)
Groundcover subshrub with whorls of oval leaves. In late spring and early summer bears green, sometimes purple-tinged flowers, within white bracts, followed by red berries. H 4–6in (10–15cm), S 12in (30cm) or more.

pH ! Z2–7 H7–1

Nierembergia repens
Mat-forming perennial with upright, open bell-shaped, yellow-centered white flowers, occasionally flushed pink with age, borne for a long period in summer. Leaves are small, oval, and light green. Useful for cracks in paving. H 2in (5cm), S 8in (20cm) or more.

Z7–11 H12–7

Cerastium tomentosum, illus. p.361
Cymbalaria muralis
Diapensia lapponica
Dryas drummondii
Dryas x *suendermannii*
Helichrysum bellidioides
Leucanthemopsis alpina
Lewisia nevadensis
Maianthemum bifolium
Pentachondra pumila
Petrophytum caespitosum
Petrophytum hendersonii
Phlox douglasii 'May Snow'
Ranunculus alpestris, illus. p.363
Satureja montana 'Prostrate White'
Weldenia candida, illus. p.362

Dryas octopetala
Evergreen, prostrate perennial forming mats of oval, lobed, leathery, dark green leaves on thick stems. In late spring and early summer, cup-shaped, creamy white flowers are borne just above foliage, followed by attractive, feathery seeds. H 2½in (6cm), S indefinite.

Z3–6 H6–1

Achillea* x *kellereri
Semi-evergreen perennial that bears daisylike white flower heads in loose clusters in summer. Leaves are feathery and gray-green. Good for a wall or bank. Dislikes winter wet and must have perfect drainage.
H 6in (15cm), S 9in (23cm) or more.

Z5–7 H7–5

Carlina acaulis (Alpine thistle)
Clump-forming perennial that in summer-autumn bears large, stemless, thistlelike, single, off-white or pale brown flower heads with papery bracts on rosettes of long, spiny-margined, deeply cut leaves.
H 3–4in (8–10cm), S 6–9in (15–23cm).

Z5–7 H7–5

Linnaea borealis (Twinflower)
Evergreen, mat-forming, subshrubby perennial with rooting stems bearing small, oval leaves, above which in summer rise threadlike stems bearing pairs of small, fragrant, tubular, pale pink and white flowers.
H ¾in (2cm), S 12in (30cm) or more.

pH Z2–6 H6–1

Dianthus pavonius,
syn. *D. neglectus*
Evergreen, prostrate perennial with comparatively large, rounded, pale to deep pink flowers, buff on reverses, borne on short stems in summer above low mats of spiky leaves.
H 2in (5cm), S 3in (8cm).

pH Z3–8 H8–1

***Gypsophila repens* 'Dorothy Teacher'**
Semi-evergreen, prostrate perennial. Sprays of small, rounded white flowers, which age to deep pink, cover mats of narrow, bluish green leaves in summer. trim stems after flowering. H 1–2in (2.5–5cm), S 12in (30cm) or more.

Z4–7 H7–1

Petrorhagia saxifraga, syn. *Tunica saxifraga* (Tunic flower)
Mat-forming perennial with tufts of grasslike leaves. In summer bears a profusion of small, pale pink flowers, veined deeper pink, on slender stems. Grows best on poor soil. Self-seeds easily. H 4in (10cm), S 6in (15cm).

Z5–7 H7–5

Thymus caespititius,
syn. *T. azoricus, T. micans*
Evergreen, mat-forming, aromatic subshrub with slender, woody stems covered in minute, hairy, midgreen leaves. Bears tiny, pale lilac or lilac-pink flowers in small clusters in summer. H 1in (2.5cm), S 8in (20cm).

Z4–9 H9–1

Convolvulus althaeoides
Vigorous perennial with long, trailing stems clothed in heart-shaped, cut, mid-green leaves overlaid silver. Bears large, open trumpet-shaped pink flowers in summer. May be invasive in a mild climate.
H 2in (5cm), S indefinite.

Z6–8 H8–1

Anemonella thalictroides, illus. p.364
Daphne jasminea, illus. p.364
Erodium reichardii
Geranium cinereum

Gypsophila cerastoides, illus. p.364
Lewisia columbiana
Oenothera acaulis
Ranunculus glacialis

Antennaria dioica
Arctostaphylos uva-ursi, illus. p.388
Arctostaphylos uva-ursi 'Point Reyes', illus. p.388

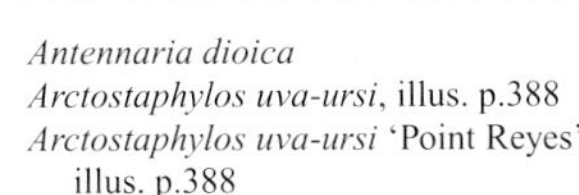

CARNATIONS and PINKS, illus. pp.280–1
Diascia barberae 'Ruby Field'
Dicentra peregrina
Gaultheria trichophylla

PINK

Geranium sanguineum var. ***striatum***
Hummock-forming, spreading perennial that has cup-shaped pink flowers with darker veins, borne singly in summer above round, deeply divided, dark green leaves. H 4–6in (10–15cm), S 12in (30cm) or more.

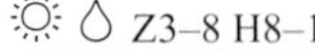
Z3–8 H8–1

Erodium corsicum
Compact, clump-forming perennial that has soft, gray-green leaves with wavy margins. Bears flat-faced pink flowers with darker veins on stiff, slender stems in late spring and summer. Grows best in an alpine house. H 3in (8cm), S 6in (15cm).

Z4–7 H7–1

Saponaria* x *olivana
Compact perennial with a firm cushion of narrow leaves. Flowering stems, produced around edges of the cushion, bear flat, single, pale pink flowers in summer. Needs very good drainage. H 3in (8cm), S 4in (10cm).

Z4–8 H8–1

***Aethionema* 'Warley Rose'**
Short-lived, evergreen or semi-evergreen, compact subshrub with tiny, linear, bluish green leaves. Bears racemes of small pink flowers on short stems in profusion in spring-summer. H and S 6in (15cm).

Z6–8 H8–6

Ourisia microphylla
Semi-evergreen, mat-forming perennial with neat, scalelike, pale green leaves and bearing a profusion of small pink flowers in late spring and early summer. Is difficult to grow in an arid climate. H 2–4in (5–10cm), S 6in (15cm).

Z7–9 H9–7

***Phlox adsurgens* 'Wagon Wheel'**
Evergreen, prostrate perennial forming wide mats of woody stems clothed in oval leaves. Bears heads of wheel-shaped pink flowers with narrow petals in summer. Needs organic soil. H 4in (10cm), S 12in (30cm).

pH Z4–8 H8–1

Asperula suberosa
Clump-forming perennial with a mound of loose stems bearing tiny, hairy gray leaves and, in early summer, many tubular, pale pink flowers. Dislikes winter wet but needs moist soil in summer. Is best in an alpine house. H 3in (8cm), S to 12in (30cm).

Z5–7 H7–5

***Rhodohypoxis* 'Margaret Rose'**
Perennial with a tuberlike rootstock and an erect, basal tuft of narrowly lance-shaped, hairy leaves. Bears a succession of upright, flattish, pale pink flowers on slender stems in spring and early summer. H 2–4in (5–10cm), S 1–2in (2.5–5cm).

Z9–10 H10–9

Persicaria affinis
'Donald Lowndes'
Evergreen, mat-forming perennial that has thick, branching, spreading stems clothed with pointed leaves. In summer bears dense spikes of small red flowers that become paler with age. H 3–6in (8–15cm), S to 6in (15cm).

Z3–8 H8–1

Geranium traversii var. *elegans*
Lychnis alpina
Origanum amanum
Petrorhagia saxifraga 'Rosette'
PRIMROSES, illus. pp.272–3
Sedum spurium
Silene hookeri
Vaccinium myrtillus

Geranium dalmaticum
Prostrate, spreading perennial with outward-facing, almost flat, shell pink flowers borne in summer above divided, dark green leaves. Will grow taller in partial shade. H 3–4in (8–10cm) or more, S 5–8in (12–20cm).

Z5–7 H7–5

Erigeron karvinskianus,
syn. *E. mucronatus*
Spreading perennial with lax stems bearing narrow, lance-shaped, hairy leaves and, in summer-autumn, daisy-like flower heads that open white, turn pink, then fade to purple.
H 4–6in (10–15cm), S indefinite.

Z5–7 H7–5

Aethionema armenum
Short-lived, evergreen or semi-evergreen, dense subshrub with narrow, blue-green leaves. Carries loose sprays of tiny, pale to deep pink flowers in summer. H and S 6in (15cm).

Z7–9 H9–7

Androsace lanuginosa
Evergreen, trailing perennial with loose stems covered in silky hairs and carrying deep green leaves and, in summer, clusters of small, flat, lilac-pink or pale pink flowers with dark pink or yellow eyes. H 1½in (4cm), S to 7in (18cm).

Z5–7 H7–3

***Dianthus* 'Little Jock'**
Evergreen, compact, clump-forming perennial with spiky, silvery green foliage. In summer produces strongly fragrant, rounded, semi-double pink flowers with darker eyes.
H and S 4in (10cm).

Z5–9 H9–5

Dianthus gratianopolitanus,
syn. *D. caesius* (Cheddar pink)
Evergreen perennial with loose mats of narrow, gray-green leaves. In summer it produces very fragrant, flat, pale pink flowers on slender stems.
H to 6in (15cm), S to 12in (30cm).

Z3–9 H9–1

Loiseleuria procumbens
(Alpine azalea, Trailing azalea)
Evergreen, prostrate shrub with small, oval leaves, hairy and beige beneath. Has terminal clusters of open funnel-shaped, rose-pink to white flowers in early summer.
H to 3in (8cm), S 4–6in (10–15cm).

pH Z2–5 H5–1

Acantholimon glumaceum
Evergreen, cushion-forming perennial with hard, spiny, dark green leaves and short spikes of small, star-shaped pink flowers in summer.
H 4in (10cm), S 8in (20cm).

Z7–9 H9–7

Acantholimon venustum
Antennaria dioica var. *rosea*, illus. p.366
Arabis x *arendsii* 'Rosabella', illus. p.365
Armeria juniperifolia, illus. p.365
Armeria maritima
Astilbe simplicifolia 'Gnom'
CARNATIONS and PINKS, illus. pp.280–1
Dianthus deltoides
Epilobium obcordatum
Erica spiculifolia
Erodium x *variabile* 'Ken Aslet'
Geranium farreri
Gypsophila repens
Penstemon rupicola
Persicaria capitata
Phlox adsurgens

PINK

***Dianthus* 'Pike's Pink'**
Evergreen, compact, cushion-forming perennial with spiky, gray-green foliage that bears fragrant, rounded, double pink flowers in summer.
H and S 4in (10cm).

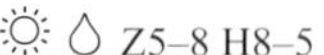
Z5–8 H8–5

Saponaria caespitosa
Mat-forming perennial with small, lance-shaped leaves. Tiny, flat, single pink to purple flowers are borne in small heads in summer. Needs very good drainage.
H 3in (8cm), S 4in (10cm).

Z4–8 H8–1

Oxalis depressa, syn. *O. inops*
Tuberous perennial with 3-lobed leaves and short-stemmed, widely funnel-shaped, bright rose-pink flowers, ¾in (2cm) across, in summer. Often benefits from a sheltered site or cool greenhouse.
H 2in (5cm), S 3–4in (8–10cm).

Z7–10 H10–7

Androsace villosa* var. *jacquemontii
Evergreen, mat-forming perennial with small rosettes of hairy, gray-green leaves. Bears tiny, pinkish purple flowers on red stems in late spring and early summer. Good in an alpine house.
H ½–1½in (1–4cm), S 8in (20cm).

Z5–7 H7–5

Dianthus microlepis
Evergreen perennial with tiny tufts of minute, fine, grasslike leaves, above which rise numerous small, rounded pink flowers in early summer.
Does well in a trough.
H 2in (5cm), S 8in (20cm).

Z5–9 H8–1

Saponaria ocymoides
(Tumbling Ted)
Perennial with compact or loose, sprawling mats of hairy, oval leaves, above which a profusion of tiny, flat, pale pink to crimson flowers is carried in summer. Excellent on a dry bank.
H 1–3in (2.5–8cm), S 16in (40cm).

Z4–8 H8–1

Dianthus myrtinervius
Evergreen, spreading perennial with numerous small, rounded pink flowers that appear in summer above tiny, grasslike leaves.
H 2in (5cm), S 8in (20cm).

Z4–9 H9–1

***Dianthus* 'La Bourboule'**, syn. *D.* 'La Bourbille'
Evergreen perennial with small clumps of tufted, spiky foliage. Bears a profusion of strongly fragrant, small, single pink flowers in summer.
H 2in (5cm), S 3in (8cm).

Z5–9 H9–1

Dianthus alpinus (Alpine pink)
Evergreen, compact perennial that bears comparatively large, rounded, rose-pink to crimson flowers singly in summer above mats of narrow, dark green foliage. Likes organic soil.
H 2in (5cm), S 3in (8cm).

Z4–8 H8–1

***Phlox subulata* 'Marjorie'**
Evergreen, mound-forming perennial with fine leaves and a profusion of flat, star-shaped, bright rose-pink flowers in early summer. Trim after flowering.
H 4in (10cm), S 8in (20cm).

Z5–8 H8–1

PRIMROSES, illus. pp.272–3
Prunella grandiflora 'Pink Loveliness'
Vaccinium nummularia

ROCK PLANTS

***Dianthus* 'Annabelle'**
Evergreen, compact, clump-forming perennial with spiky, gray-green foliage. In summer it bears fragrant, rounded, semi-double, cerise-pink flowers, singly on slender stems.
H and S 4in (10cm).

Z5–9 H8–1

***Phlox* 'Camla'**
Evergreen mound-forming perennial with wiry, arching stems and fine leaves. Has a profusion of open saucer-shaped, rich pink flowers in early summer. Trim after flowering.
Needs organic soil.
H 5in (12cm), S 12in (30cm).

Z4–8 H8–1

***Geranium cinereum* 'Ballerina'**
Spreading, rosetted perennial that bears cup-shaped, purplish pink flowers, with deep purple veins, on lax stems in late spring and summer. Basal leaves are round, deeply divided, and soft. H 4in (10cm), S 12in (30cm).

Z4–9 H9–3

Teucrium polium
Deciduous, dome-shaped subshrub that has much-branched, woolly white or yellowish stems and leaves with scalloped margins. Bears yellowish white or pinkish purple flowers in flat heads in summer. Requires very good drainage. H and S 6in (15cm).

Z5–9 H9–5

Lewisia rediviva [pink form]
(Bitter root)
Tufted, rosetted perennial. Clusters of narrow leaves are summer-deciduous. Large, many-petaled pink flowers open in bright weather in late spring and early summer. Good in an alpine house.
H ½–1½in (1–4cm), S to 2in (5cm).

pH Z4–7 H7–1

***Phlox douglasii* 'Crackerjack'**
Evergreen, compact, mound-forming perennial. Has a profusion of saucer-shaped, bright crimson or magenta flowers in early summer. Leaves are lance-shaped and midgreen.
Cut back after flowering.
H to 3in (8cm), S 8in (20cm).

Z5–7 H7–5

Silene schafta
Spreading perennial with tufts of narrow, oval leaves. Bears sprays of 5-petaled, rose-magenta flowers from late spring to late autumn.
H 4–6in (10–15cm), S 3–4in (8–10cm).

Z4–8 H9–3

Geranium cinereum
var. ***subcaulescens***,
syn. *G. subcaulescens*
Spreading perennial with round, deeply divided, soft leaves. In summer bears brilliant purple-magenta flowers with striking black eyes and stamens on lax stems. H 4in (10cm), S 12in (30cm).

Z4–9 H9–3

Aethionema 'Warley Ruber'
Anemonella thalictroides 'Oscar Schoaf'
Antennaria dioica 'Nyewoods'
Armeria juniperifolia 'Bevan's Variety'
Erinus alpinus 'Dr Hähnle'
Phlox x *procumbens* 'Millstream'
Saponaria 'Bressingham'
Saxifraga x *primulaize*
Silene elisabethae

PINK

***Rhodohypoxis* 'Albrighton'**
Perennial with tuberlike rootstock and an erect, basal tuft of narrowly lance-shaped, hairy leaves. Bears a succession of erect, deep pink flowers singly on slender stems in spring and early summer.
H 2–4in (5–10cm), S 1–2in (2.5–5cm).

Z9–10 H10–9

***Armeria maritima* 'Vindictive'**
Evergreen, clump-forming perennial with grasslike, dark blue-green leaves, above which rise stiff stems bearing spherical heads of small, deep rose-pink flowers for a long period in summer. H 4in (10cm), S 6in (15cm).

Z3–9 H6–1

***Dianthus deltoides* 'Leuchtfunk'**, syn. *D.d.* 'Flashing Light'
Evergreen, mat-forming perennial. Many small, flat, upward-facing, brilliant cerise flowers are borne singly above tiny, oblong, pointed leaves.
H 4–6in (10–15cm), S 8in (20cm).

Z3–10 H12–1

RED–PURPLE

***Rhodohypoxis* 'Douglas'**
Perennial with a tuberlike rootstock and an erect, basal tuft of narrowly lance-shaped, hairy leaves. Bears a succession of upright, flattish, rich deep red flowers singly on slender stems in spring and early summer.
H 2–4in (5–10cm), S 1–2in (2.5–5cm).

Z9–10 H10–9

Penstemon hirsutus* var. *pygmaeus
Short-lived, evergreen, compact subshrub that bears tubular, lipped, hairy, purple- or blue-flushed white flowers in summer. Has tightly packed, dark green leaves and is suitable for a trough.
H and S 3in (8cm).

Z3–9 H9–1

Pterocephalus perennis, syn. *P. parnassi*
Semi-evergreen, mat-forming perennial with crinkled, hairy leaves. Bears tight, rounded heads of tubular, pinkish lavender flowers, singly on short stems in summer, followed by feathery seed heads. H 2in (5cm), S 10cm (4in).

Z5–7 H7–5

Dianthus 'Hidcote'
Dianthus 'Mars'
Erinus alpinus, illus. p.366
Geranium orientalitibeticum
Penstemon menziesii
Phlox douglasii 'Red Admiral'
Sedum sempervivoides
Viola cenisia

PURPLE

***Phlox douglasii* 'Boothman's Variety'**
Evergreen, mound-forming perennial with lance-shaped leaves and masses of pale lavender-blue flowers with violet-blue markings around eyes in early summer. Cut back after flowering.
H to 2in (5cm), S 8in (20cm).

Z5–7 H7–5

Physoplexis comosa, syn. *Phyteuma comosum*
Tufted perennial with deeply cut leaves and round heads of bottle-shaped, violet-blue, rarely white flowers in summer. Good in crevices but dislikes winter wet. H 3in (8cm), S 4in (10cm).

Z5–7 H7–5

Globularia meridionalis, syn. *G. bellidifolia, G. cordifolia* subsp. *bellidifolia, G. pygmaea*
Evergreen, dome-shaped subshrub. In summer, globular, fluffy, lavender to lavender-purple flower heads are borne singly just above glossy leaves.
H to 4in (10cm), S to 8in (20cm).

Z5–7 H7–5

IRISES, illus. pp.234–5
Leptinella atrata, illus. p.367
Linaria alpina
Mentha requienii

Thymus leucotrichus
Evergreen, aromatic, mound-forming subshrub with fine, twiggy stems and narrow leaves fringed with white hairs. Bears dense heads of small, pinkish-purple flowers with purple bracts in summer.
H 4–5in (10–12cm), S 6in (15cm).

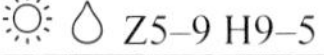 Z5–9 H9–5

***Phlox* 'Emerald Cushion'**
Evergreen perennial with emerald green mounds of fine leaves, studded in late spring and early summer with large, saucer-shaped, bright violet-blue flowers. Trim after flowering.
H 3in (8cm), S 6in (15cm).

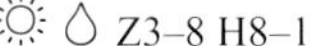 Z3–8 H8–1

Phlox bifida (Sand phlox)
Evergreen, mound-forming perennial with lance-shaped leaves. Bears a profusion of small heads of star-shaped lilac or white flowers with deeply cleft petals in summer. Cut back stems by half after flowering.
H 4–6in (10–15cm), S 6in (15cm).

 Z4–8 H8–1

***Viola* 'Nellie Britton',**
syn. *V.* 'Haslemere'
Clump-forming perennial with small, oval, toothed leaves and flat-faced, lavender-pink flowers borne from late spring to late summer. Soil should not be too dry.
H 3–6in (8–15cm), S to 8in (20cm).

Z5–7 H7–1

Campanula poscharskyana
Rampant, spreading perennial with bell-shaped violet flowers borne on leafy stems in summer. Leaves are round with serrated edges. Vigorous runners make it suitable for a bank or a wild garden.
H 4–6in (10–15cm), S indefinite.

Z3–9 H9–1

***Prunella grandiflora* 'Loveliness',**
syn. *P.* x *webbiana* 'Loveliness'
Semi-evergreen, basal-rosetted, ground-cover perennial. Bears whorls of pale purple flowers in terminal spikes on leafy stems in summer. May be invasive; cut old flower stems before they seed.
H 4–6in (10–15cm), S 12in (30cm).

Z5–8 H8–5

Aster alpinus
Clump-forming, spreading perennial with lance-shaped, dark green leaves. Bears daisylike, purplish blue or pinkish purple flower heads with yellow centers from mid- to late summer.
H 6in (15cm), S 12–18in (30–45cm).

Z4–8 H8–1

Thymus herba-barona
(Caraway thyme)
Evergreen subshrub with a loose mat of tiny, caraway-scented, dark green leaves. In summer, small lilac flowers are borne in terminal clusters.
H in flower 2–4in (5–10cm), S to 8in (20cm).

Z6–9 H9–6

***Edraianthus serpyllifolius*,**
syn. *Wahlenbergia serpyllifolia*
Evergreen, prostrate perennial with tight mats of tiny leaves and small, bell-shaped, deep violet flowers borne on short stems in early summer. Is uncommon and seldom sets seed in gardens. H ½in (1cm), S to 2in (5cm).

Z7–9 H9–7

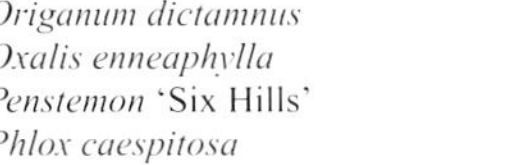
Origanum dictamnus
Oxalis enneaphylla
Penstemon 'Six Hills'
Phlox caespitosa
Polygala vayredae
Polygonatum hookeri, illus. p.367
Saxifraga stribrnyi, illus. p.368
Sedum anacampseros
Viola calcarata, illus. p.368
Viola hederacea
Viola pedata, illus. p.369
Viola tricolor, illus. p.369

PURPLE

Prunella grandiflora, syn. *P.* x *webbiana* (Large self-heal)
Semi-evergreen, spreading, mat-forming perennial with basal rosettes of leaves. In midsummer it bears short spikes of funnel-shaped purple flowers in whorls.
H 4–6in (10–15cm), S 12in (30cm).

Z5–7 H8–5

***Campanula* 'Birch Hybrid'**
Vigorous, evergreen perennial with tough, arching, prostrate stems and ivy-shaped, bright green leaves. Bears many open bell-shaped, deep violet flowers in summer.
H 4in (10cm), S 12in (30cm) or more.

Z4–7 H7–1

Campanula portenschlagiana
Vigorous, evergreen, prostrate perennial with dense mats of small, ivy-shaped leaves and large clusters of erect, open bell-shaped violet flowers in summer. H 6in (15cm), S indefinite.

Z4–7 H7–1

Ramonda myconi, syn. *R. pyrenaica*
Evergreen, rosette-forming perennial with hairy, crinkled leaves and, in late spring and early summer, flat, blue-mauve, pink, or white flowers borne on branched stems.
H 3in (8cm), S to 4in (10cm).

Z5–7 H7–5

***Viola* 'Huntercombe Purple'**
Perennial forming wide clumps of neat, oval, toothed leaves. Has a profusion of flat-faced, rich violet flowers from spring to late summer. Divide clumps every three years.
H 4–6in (10–15cm), S 6–12in (15–30cm) or more.

Z5–7 H7–1

Pinguicula grandiflora
Clump-forming perennial with a basal rosette of sticky, oval, pale green leaves. In summer it bears spurred, open funnel-shaped, violet-blue to purple flowers singly on upright, slender stems.
H 5–6in (12–15cm), S 2in (5cm).

Z3–5 H5–1

***Campanula* 'G.F. Wilson'**
Neat, mound-forming perennial with large, upturned, bell-shaped violet flowers in summer. Has rounded, pale yellow-green leaves.
H 3–4in (8–10cm), S 5–6in (12–15cm).

Z4–7 H7–1

Edraianthus pumilio
Short-lived perennial with low tufts of fine, grasslike leaves. In early summer, upturned, bell-shaped, pale to deep lavender flowers on very short stems appear amid foliage.
H 1in (2.5cm), S 3in (8cm).

Z6–8 H8–6

Delphinium brunonianum
IRISES, illus. pp.234–5
Polygala chamaebuxus var. *grandiflora*, illus. p.368
Scutellaria scordiifolia
Thalictrum kiusianum

Cyananthus microphyllus
Mat-forming perennial with very fine red stems clothed in tiny leaves. Bears funnel-shaped, violet-blue flowers at the end of each stem in late summer. Likes organic soil.
H ¾in (2cm), S 8in (20cm).

Z5–7 H7–5

Townsendia grandiflora
Short-lived, evergreen perennial with basal rosettes of small, spoon-shaped leaves. Upright stems carry solitary daisylike violet or violet-blue flower heads in late spring and early summer.
H to 6in (15cm), S 4in (10cm).

Z4–7 H7–1

Sisyrinchium idahoense
Semi-evergreen, upright, clump-forming perennial that for a long period in summer and early autumn has many flowering stems carrying tiny tufts of blue to violet-blue flowers. Foliage is grasslike. Self seeds readily.
H to 5in (12cm), S 4in (10cm).

Z7–8 H8–7

Aquilegia jonesii
Compact perennial that bears short-spurred, violet-blue flowers in summer, a few to each slender stem. Has small rosettes of finely divided, blue-gray or gray-green leaves. An uncommon plant suitable for an alpine house.
H 1in (2.5cm), S to 2in (5cm).

Z4–8 H8–1

Pratia pedunculata
Vigorous, evergreen, creeping perennial with small leaves and a profusion of star-shaped, pale to mid-blue or occasionally purplish blue flowers borne in summer. Makes a good groundcover in a moist site.
H ½in (1cm), S indefinite.

Z5–7 H7–5

Hedyotis michauxii**,**
syn. *Houstonia serpyllifolia* (Creeping bluets)
Vigorous perennial with rooting stems. Produces mats of midgreen foliage studded with star-shaped, violet-blue flowers in late spring and early summer. H 3in (8cm), S 12in (30cm).

Z3–8 H8–1

Globularia cordifolia
Evergreen, mat-forming, dwarf shrub with creeping, woody stems clothed in tiny, oval leaves. Bears stemless, round, fluffy blue to pale lavender-blue flower heads in summer.
H 1–2in (2.5–5cm), S to 8in (20cm).

Z5–7 H7–5

Campanula cochleariifolia**,**
syn. *C. pusilla* (Fairy thimbles)
Spreading perennial. Runners produce mats of rosetted, tiny, round leaves. Bears small clusters of white, lavender, or pale blue flowers in summer on many thin stems above foliage.
H 3in (8cm), S indefinite.

Z5–7 H7–1

Trachelium asperuloides**,**
syn. *Diosphaera asperuloides*
Mat-forming perennial with threadlike stems clothed in minute, midgreen leaves, above which rise many tiny, upright, tubular, pale blue flowers in summer. Do not remove old stems in winter. H 3in (8cm), S to 6in (15cm).

Z8–13 H12–6

Eritrichium nanum
Clump-forming perennial with tufts of hairy, gray-green leaves. Bears small, stemless, flat, pale blue flowers in late spring and early summer. Requires good drainage. Is usually at its best an alpine house.
H ¾in (2cm), S 1in (2.5cm).

Z5–7 H7–5

Campanula carpatica 'Jewel'
Campanula carpatica 'Turbinata'
Campanula garganica 'W.H. Paine'
Campanula x *haylodgensis* 'Plena'

Campanula 'Joe Elliott'
Campanula pulla
Campanula raineri
Campanula zoysii

Cyananthus lobatus
Edraianthus serpyllifolius 'Major'
Haberlea ferdinandi-coburgii
Haberlea rhodopensis

Myosotis alpestris, illus. p.370
Omphalodes luciliae
Phlox stolonifera 'Blue Ridge'
Wahlenbergia congesta

ROCK PLANTS small SUMMER INTEREST

BLUE

Parochetus communis
(Shamrock pea)
Evergreen, prostrate perennial with cloverlike leaves and pealike, brilliant blue flowers that are borne almost continuously. Grows best in an alpine house.
H 1–2in (2.5–5cm), S indefinite.

Z8–11 H12–8

***Polygala calcarea* 'Bulley's Form'**
Evergreen, prostrate perennial with rosettes of small, narrowly oval leaves and loose heads of deep blue flowers in late spring and early summer. Likes organic soil. Good in a trough.
H 1in (2.5cm), S 3–4in (8–10cm).

Z7–9 H9–7

Polygala calcarea
Evergreen, prostrate, occasionally upright, perennial. Has small, narrowly oval leaves and pale to dark blue flowers in loose heads in late spring and early summer. Likes orgganic soil. Good in a trough. May be difficult to establish.
H 1in (2.5cm), S to 6in (15cm).

Z7–9H9–7

Gentiana clusii
Gentiana gracilipes
Wahlenbergia albomarginata

GREEN–YELLOW

Gunnera magellanica
Mat-forming perennial grown for its rounded, toothed leaves, often bronze-tinged when young, on short, creeping stems. Small green flowers with reddish bracts are borne on male and female plants. Likes peaty soil.
H 1in (2.5cm), S to 12in (30cm).

Z8–9 H9–8

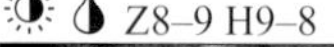

Mitella breweri
Neat, clump-forming, rhizomatous perennial with slender, hairy stems bearing small, pendent, tubular, greenish white flowers with flared mouths in summer. Has lobed, kidney-shaped, basal leaves.
H and S 6in (15cm).

Z5–7 H7–5

Sedum acre (Common stonecrop)
Evergreen, mat-forming perennial with dense, spreading shoots, clothed in tiny, fleshy, pale green leaves. Bears flat, terminal heads of tiny yellow flowers in summer. Is invasive but easily controlled.
H 1–2in (2.5–5cm), S indefinite.

Z3–8 H8–1

Alchemilla alpina
Arctostaphylos alpina
Salix lindleyana
Satureja montana 'Prostrate White'

YELLOW

Asarina procumbens,
syn. *Antirrhinum asarina*
Semi-evergreen perennial with trailing stems bearing soft, hairy leaves and tubular, pale cream flowers with yellow "palates" throughout summer. Dislikes winter wet. Self seeds freely. H ½–1in (1–2.5cm), S 9–12in (23–30cm).

Z6–9 H9–6

Papaver fauriei,
syn. *P. miyabeanum* of gardens
Short-lived, clump-forming perennial with basal rosettes of finely cut, hairy, soft gray leaves. Bears pendent, open cup-shaped, pale yellow flowers in summer. Dislikes winter wet.
H and S 2–4in (5–10cm).

Z5–7 H7–5

Alyssum montanum
Alyssum wulfenianum
Calceolaria fothergillii
Calceolaria polyrrhiza

Polygala chamaebuxus
Evergreen, woody-based perennial with tiny, hard, dark green leaves. In late spring and early summer bears many racemes of small, pealike, white-and-yellow flowers, sometimes marked brown. Needs organic soil.
H 2in (5cm), S 8in (20cm).

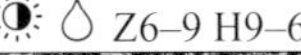
Z6–9 H9–6

***Sedum acre* 'Aureum'**
Evergreen, dense, mat-forming perennial with spreading shoots, yellow-tipped in spring and early summer, and clothed in tiny, fleshy yellow leaves. Bears flat heads of tiny, bright yellow flowers in summer. Is invasive but easy to control.
H 1–2in (2.5–5cm), S indefinite.

Z3–8 H8–1

Scutellaria orientalis
Rhizomatous perennial with hairy gray, rooting stems. Has terminal spikes of tubular yellow flowers with brownish purple lips in summer. Leaves are toothed and oval. May be invasive in a small space.
H 2–4in (5–10cm), S to 9in (23cm).

Z5–8 H8–5

***Waldsteinia ternata*,**
syn. *W. trifolia*
Semi-evergreen perennial with loose, spreading mats of toothed, 3-parted leaves. Bears saucer-shaped yellow flowers in late spring and early summer. Is good on a bank.
H 4in (10cm), S 8–12in (20–30cm).

Z3–8 H8–1

***Oenothera macrocarpa*,**
syn. *O. missouriensis*
Spreading perennial with thick stems and oval leaves. Throughout summer it bears a succession of wide, bell-shaped yellow flowers, sometimes spotted red, that open at sundown. H to 4in (10cm), S to 16in (40cm) or more.

Z5–9 H12–1

***Linum flavum* 'Compactum'**
Shrubby perennial with narrow leaves and terminal clusters of many upward-facing, open funnel-shaped, single, bright yellow flowers in summer. Provide a sunny, sheltered position and protection from winter wet.
H and S 6in (15cm).

Z5–7 H7–5

Potentilla eriocarpa
Clump-forming perennial with tufts of oval, dark green leaves divided into leaflets. Flat, single, pale yellow flowers are borne throughout summer just above the leaves.
H 2–3in (5–8cm), S 4–6in (10–15cm).

Z6–8 H8–1

Calceolaria tenella
Vigorous, evergreen, prostrate perennial with creeping reddish stems and oval, midgreen leaves, above which rise small spikes of pouch-shaped, red-spotted yellow flowers in summer.
H 4in (10cm), S indefinite.

Z7–8 H6–1

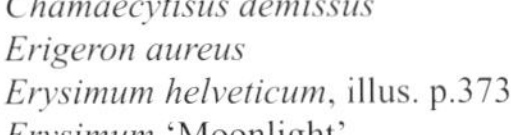

Chamaecytisus demissus
Erigeron aureus
Erysimum helveticum, illus. p.373
Erysimum 'Moonlight'
Genista delphinensis
Helianthemum oelandicum subsp. *alpestre*
Hippocrepis comosa 'E.R. Janes'
Hypericum reptans
IRISES, illus. pp.234–5
Jasminum parkeri
Jovibarba hirta, illus. p.388
Linum 'Gemmell's Hybrid'
Morisia monanthos, illus. p.372
Onosma stellulata
Oxalis chrysantha
Oxalis lobata, illus. p.387

ROCK PLANTS small SUMMER INTEREST

YELLOW

Genista sagittalis, syn. *Chamaespartium sagittale*
Deciduous, semi-prostrate shrub with winged stems bearing a few oval, dark green leaves. Pealike yellow flowers appear in dense, terminal clusters in early summer, followed by hairy seed pods. H 3in (8cm), S 12in (30cm) or more.

Z5–8 H8–5

Cytisus ardoinoi, syn. *C. ardoinii*
Deciduous, hummock-forming, dwarf shrub with arching stems. In late spring and early summer, pealike, bright yellow flowers are produced in pairs in leaf axils. Leaves are divided into three leaflets. H 4in (10cm), S 6in (15cm).

Z6–8 H8–6

Potentilla aurea
Rounded perennial, with a woody base, that in late summer bears loose sprays of flat, single, yellow flowers with slightly darker eyes. Leaves are divided into oval, slightly silvered leaflets. H 4in (10cm), S 8in (20cm).

Z5–8 H8–5

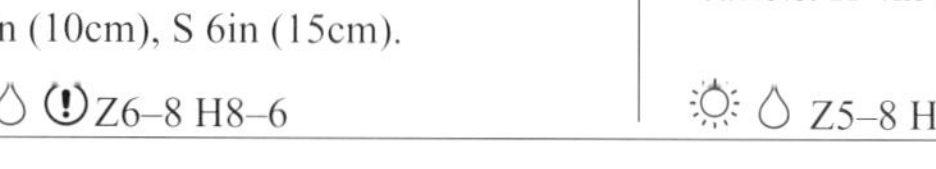

YELLOW–ORANGE

***Lysimachia nummularia* 'Aurea'**
(Golden creeping Jenny)
Prostrate perennial. Creeping, rooting stems bear pairs of round, soft yellow leaves that later turn greenish yellow or green in dense shade. Has bright yellow flowers in leaf axils in summer. H 1–2in (2.5–5cm), S indefinite.

Z4–8 H8–1

Hypericum empetrifolium var. ***prostratum*** of gardens
Evergreen, prostrate shrub with angled branches and bright green leaves that have curled margins. Bears flat heads of small, bright yellow flowers in summer. Needs winter protection. H ¾in (2cm), S 12in (30cm).

Z4–7 H7–1

Hippocrepis comosa
(Horseshoe vetch)
Vigorous perennial with prostrate, rooting stems bearing small, open spikes of pealike yellow flowers in summer and leaves divided into leaflets. Self seeds freely and may spread rapidly. H 2–3in (5–8cm), S indefinite.

Z5–7 H7–5

***Calceolaria* 'Walter Shrimpton'**
Evergreen, mound-forming perennial with glossy, dark green leaves. In early summer bears short spikes of many pouch-shaped, bronze-yellow flowers spotted rich brown, with white bands across centers. H 4in (10cm), S 9in (23cm).

Z8–9 H6–1

Alstroemeria hookeri
Tuberous perennial with narrow leaves and loose heads of widely flared, orange-suffused pink flowers in summer; upper petals are spotted and blotched red and yellow. H 4–6in (10–15cm), S 18–24in (45–60cm).

Z8–10 H10–8

PRIMROSES, illus. pp.272–3
Ranunculus montanus 'Molten Gold'
Saxifraga aizoides
Trollius pumilus, illus. p.373
Viola aetolica, illus. p.371
Viola biflora
Viola 'Jackanapes', illus. p.372
Viola lutea

Achillea x *lewisii* 'King Edward'
Crepis aurea, illus. p.359
Erigeron aurantiacus
Geum montanum
Helianthemum nummularium 'Amy Baring'
Hypericum cerastioides
Inula acaulis
Potentilla x *tonguei*

PINK–BLUE

***Persicaria vacciniifolia*,**
syn. *Polygonum vacciniifolium*
Evergreen, perennial with woody red stems. Leaves are tinged red in autumn. Bears deep pink or rose-red flowers in late summer and autumn.
H 4–6in (10–15cm), S to 12in (30cm).

Z8–11 H12–3

Gaultheria procumbens
Vigorous, evergreen subshrub with prostrate stems carrying clusters of oval, leathery leaves that turn red in winter. In summer, solitary bell-shaped, pink-flushed white flowers appear in leaf axils, followed by scarlet berries.
H 2–6in (5–15cm), S indefinite.

Z3–8 H8–1

***Gentiana* × *macaulayi* 'Wells's Variety'**, syn. *G.* 'Wellsii'
Evergreen, prostrate perennial with trumpet-shaped, midblue flowers in late summer and autumn. Spreading stems are clothed in narrow, midgreen leaves. Soil should be quite moist.
H in flower 2in (5cm), S 8in (20cm).

Z5–7 H7–5

OTHER RECOMMENDED PLANTS:
Arctostaphylos nevadensis
Cornus canadensis
Sedum cauticola
Sedum ewersii

BLUE–ORANGE

Gentiana sino-ornata
Evergreen, prostrate, spreading perennial that, in autumn, bears trumpet-shaped, rich blue flowers singly at the ends of stems. Leaves are narrow. Lift and divide every 3 years. Needs moist soil. H in flower 2in (5cm), S to 12in (30cm).

Z5–7 H7–5

Oxalis lobata
Clump-forming perennial with woolly-coated tubers. Midgreen leaves have up to five rounded lobes. Produces racemes of widely funnel-shaped, bright yellow flowers, ½–¾in (1–2cm) across, in late summer and autumn.
H 2in (5cm), S 3–4in (8–10cm).

Z8–9 H9–8

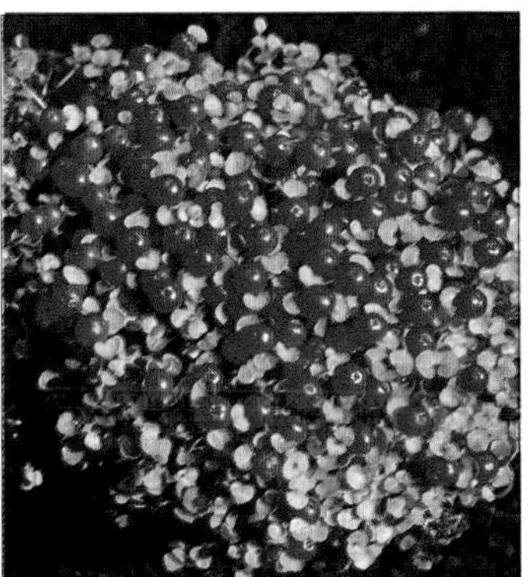

***Nertera granadensis*,**
syn. *N. depressa* (Bead plant)
Prostrate perennial, dense mats of tiny, bright green leaves. In early summer bears minute, greenish white flowers, then many shiny orange berries. Needs ample moisture in summer. H to ½in (1cm), S 4in (10cm).

Z12–13 H6–1

Carlina acaulis, illus. p.375
Gentiana ornata
Gentiana 'Susan Jane'
Sedum kamtschaticum
Sedum kamtschaticum 'Variegatum', illus. p.391
Solidago virgaurea subsp. *minuta*
Vaccinium nummularia

ROCK PLANTS small WINTER/ALL YEAR INTEREST

WHITE–RED

***Arabis procurrens* 'Variegata'**
Evergreen, mat-forming perennial with small, oval green leaves splashed with cream. Bears small white flowers in spring and early summer. May revert to type, with plain green leaves.
H ¾in (2cm), S 12in (30cm).

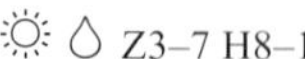
Z3–7 H8–1

***Arctostaphylos uva-ursi* 'Point Reyes'**
Evergreen, prostrate shrub with long shoots and glossy leaves. In late spring and early summer bears terminal clusters of urn-shaped, pale pink to white flowers, followed by red berries.
H 4in (10cm), S 20in (50cm).

Z2–6 H6–1

Pachysandra terminalis
Evergreen, creeping perennial that has smooth leaves clustered at the ends of short stems. Bears spikes of tiny white flowers, sometimes flushed purple, in early summer. Makes an excellent groundcover in a moist or dry site.
H 4in (10cm), S 8in (20cm).

Z4–8 H8–1

Sedum lydium
Evergreen, mat-forming perennial with reddish stems and narrow, fleshy, often red-flushed leaves. Bears flat-topped, terminal clusters of tiny white flowers in summer.
H 2in (5cm), S to 6in (15cm).

Z5–8 H8–5

Jovibarba hirta*, syn. *Sempervivum hirtum
Evergreen, mat-forming perennial with rosettes of hairy, midgreen leaves, often suffused red, and terminal clusters of star-shaped, pale yellow flowers in summer. Dislikes winter wet.
H 3–6in (8–15cm), S 4in (10cm).

Z5–8 H8–5

Arctostaphylos uva-ursi
Evergreen, low-growing shrub with arching, intertwining stems clothed in small, oval, bright green leaves. Bears urn-shaped, pinkish white flowers in summer, followed by scarlet berries.
H 4in (10cm), S 20in (50cm).

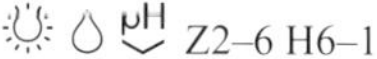
Z2–6 H6–1

Sedum obtusatum
Evergreen, prostrate perennial with small, fat, succulent leaves that turn bronze-red in summer. Loose, flat sprays of tiny, bright yellow flowers are borne in summer. Dislikes summer wet.
H 2in (5cm), S 4–6in (10–15cm).

Z5–9 H9–5

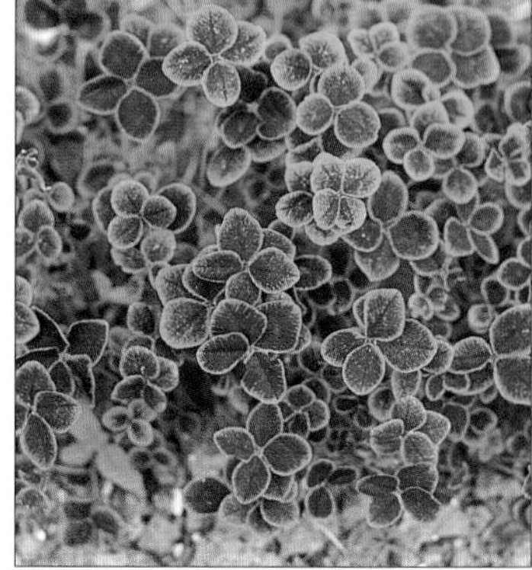

***Trifolium repens* 'Purpurascens'**
Vigorous, semi-evergreen, groundcover perennial grown for its divided, bronze-green foliage, variably edged bright green. Produces heads of small, pea-like white blooms throughout summer.
H in flower 3–5in (8–12cm), S 8–12in (20–30cm) or more.

Z4–8 H8–1

OTHER RECOMMENDED PLANTS:
Ajuga reptans 'Multicolor', illus. p.303
Briggsia muscicola
Pachysandra terminalis 'Variegata'
Paronychia capitata

Acaena microphylla
Compact, mat-forming perennial, usually evergreen, with leaves divided into tiny leaflets, bronze-tinged when young. Heads of small flowers with spiny, dull red bracts are borne in summer and develop into decorative burrs. H 2in (5cm), S 6in (15cm).

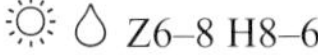 Z6–8 H8–6

Raoulia hookeri* var. *albo-sericea
Evergreen, prostrate perennial with tiny rosettes of silver leaves. Flower heads appear briefly in summer as fragrant, yellow fluff. Is best in poor, gritty soil in an alpine house. Dislikes winter wet.
H to ½in (1cm), S 10in (25cm).

☼ ◊ Z8–9 H9–8

***Artemisia schmidtiana* 'Nana'**
Prostrate perennial with fernlike, silver foliage. Has insignificant sprays of daisylike yellow flowers in summer. Suitable for a wall or bank.
H 3in (8cm), S 8in (20cm).

☼ ◊ Z5–8 H8–5

Sempervivum tectorum
(Houseleek, Hen and chicks)
Vigorous, evergreen perennial with purple-tipped leaves, sometimes suffused deep red. In summer has clusters of star-shaped, reddish purple flowers on stems 12in (30cm) tall.
H 4–6in (10–15cm), S to 8in (20cm).

☼ ◊ Z4–8 H8–1

Sempervivum arachnoideum
(Cobweb hen and chicks)
Evergreen, mat-forming perennial. Rosettes of oval, fleshy leaves are covered in a web of white hairs. Bears loose clusters of star-shaped, rose-red flowers in summer. H 2–5in 5–12cm (2–5in), S to 4in (10cm) or more.

☼ ◊ Z5–8 H8–5

Sedum spathulifolium
Evergreen, mat-forming perennial with rosettes of fleshy green or silver leaves, usually strongly suffused bronze-red, and small clusters of tiny yellow flowers borne just above foliage in summer. Tolerates shade.
H 2in (5cm), S indefinite.

☼ ◊ (!) Z5–9 H9–5

Leucogenes grandiceps
Evergreen, dense, woody-based perennial with neat rosettes of downy silver leaves. Yellow flower heads within woolly white bracts are borne singly in spring or early summer.
H and S 4–6in (10–15cm).

☼ ◊ Z7–8 H8–7

Sempervivum ciliosum
Evergreen, mat-forming perennial with rosettes of hairy, gray-green leaves and, in summer, heads of small, star-shaped yellow flowers. Dislikes winter wet; is best grown in an alpine house.
H 3–4in (8–10cm), S 4in (10cm).

☼ ◊ Z7–11 H12–7

Acaena 'Blue Haze'
Acaena buchananii
Acaena novae-zelandiae
Acantholimon venustum
Ajuga reptans 'Atropurpurea', illus. p.303
Raoulia eximia
Saxifraga stolonifera 'Tricolor'
Sempervivum 'Commander Hay'
Sempervivum grandiflorum
Thymus pseudolanuginosus
Tiarella wherryi
Viola odorata

GREEN

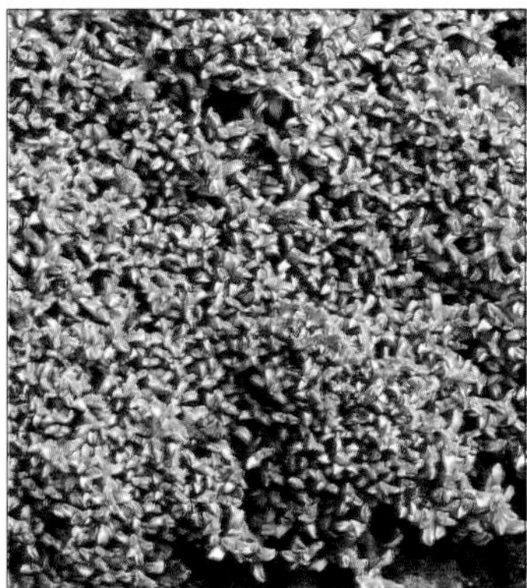

Raoulia australis
Evergreen, carpeting perennial forming a hard mat of gray-green leaves. Bears tiny, fluffy, sulfur yellow flower heads in summer.
H to ½in (1cm), S 10in (25cm).

Z8–9 H9–8

Acaena caesiiglauca
Vigorous, groundcover perennial, usually evergreen. Has hairy, glaucous blue leaves divided into leaflets. Heads of small flowers with spiny, brownish green bracts, borne in summer, develop into brownish red burrs.
H 2in (5cm), S 30in (75cm) or more.

Z6–9 H9–6

Sempervivum montanum
Evergreen, mat-forming perennial with dark green rosettes of fleshy, hairy leaves. Star-shaped, wine red flowers are borne in terminal clusters in summer. Is a variable plant that hybridizes freely.
H 3–6in (10–15cm), S 4in (10cm).

Z5–8 H8–5

Azorella trifurcata, syn. *A. nivalis*
Evergreen perennial forming tight, hard cushions of tiny, leathery, oval leaves in rosettes. Bears many small, stalkless umbels of yellow flowers in summer.
H to 4in (10cm), S 6in (15cm).

Z7–11 H12–1

Asarum europaeum (Asarabacca, European wild ginger)
Vigorous, evergreen, prostrate, rhizomatous perennial with kidney-shaped, leathery, glossy leaves that hide tiny brown flowers appearing in spring.
H 6in (15cm), S indefinite.

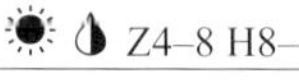
Z4–8 H8–1

Sagina boydii
Evergreen perennial with hard cushions of minute, stiff, bottle-green leaves in small rosettes. Bears insignificant flowers in summer. Is difficult and slow-growing.
H ½in (1cm), S to 8in (20cm).

Z5–7 H7–5

Acantholimon glumaceum, illus. p.377
Arctostaphylos hookeri 'Monterey Carpet'
Asarum caudatum
Asarum hartwegii
Asarum shuttleworthii
Euonymus fortunei 'Kewensis'
Homogyne alpina
Jovibarba sobolifera
Mitchella repens
Thymus 'Porlock'
Thymus serpyllum
Thymus serpyllum 'Annie Hall'
Thymus serpyllum 'Elfin'

Sempervivum giuseppii
Vigorous, evergreen, prostrate perennial. Leaves are hairy, especially in spring, and have dark spots at tips. Produces terminal clusters of star-shaped, deep pink or red flowers in summer. H in flower 3–4in (8–10cm), S 4in (10cm).

Z7–9 H9–7

Bolax gummifera
Very slow-growing, evergreen perennial with neat rosettes of small, blue-green leaves forming extremely hard cushions. Insignificant yellow flowers are rarely produced.
H 1in (2.5cm), S 4in (10cm).

Z5–6 H6–5

Plantago nivalis
Evergreen perennial with neat rosettes of thick, silver-haired green leaves. Bears spikes of insignificant, dull gray flowers in summer. Dislikes winter wet. H in leaf 1in (2.5cm), S 2in (5cm).

Z6–7 H7–6

Raoulia haastii
Evergreen perennial forming low, irregular hummocks of minute leaves that are apple green in spring, dark green in autumn, and chocolate brown in winter. Occasionally has small, fluffy, sulfur yellow flower heads in summer. H to ½in (1cm), S 10in (25cm).

Z7–8 H8–7

Paronychia kapela* subsp. *serpyllifolia
Evergreen, very compact, mat-forming perennial with minute silver leaves. Inconspicuous flowers, borne in summer, are surrounded by papery silver bracts. H to ½in (1cm), S 8in (20cm).

Z8–10 H10–8

***Sedum kamtschaticum* 'Variegatum'**
Semi-evergreen, prostrate perennial with fleshy leaves edged with cream. Has a tracery of fleshy stems and leaf buds in winter and terminal clusters of orange-flushed yellow flowers in early autumn. H 2–3in (5–8cm), S 8in (20cm).

Z4–8 H9–1

***Sedum spathulifolium* 'Cape Blanco'**
Evergreen perennial with rosettes of fleshy leaves, frequently suffused purple. Tiny yellow flowers appear above foliage in summer. Tolerates shade. H 2in (5cm), S indefinite.

Z5–9 H9–5

***Saxifraga exarata* subsp. *moschata* 'Cloth of Gold'**
Evergreen hummock-forming perennial, grown for its small, soft rosettes of bright golden foliage; produces best color in shade. Has star-shaped white flowers on slender stems in summer. H 4–6in (10–15cm), S 6in (15cm).

Z5–7 H7–5

Leucogenes leontopodium
Thymus x *citriodorus* 'Aureus'

BULBS

including Corms and Tubers

A BULB OR CORM is a small pocket of energy that, given the right soil and conditions, will burst into foliage or flower with exuberant color exactly when and where you want it. Although its contribution to the flower bed or container may often be brief, you can be sure of what you are going to get, and few other plants are so easy and so rewarding to grow.

Bulbs

Bulbous plants are found throughout the world in habitats as varied as woodland and scrub, meadows, the sides of rivers and streams, and on rocky hills and mountains. They provide some of the loveliest of flowers in the plant kingdom.

What are bulbs?

The term bulb can be used to describe all swollen, underground, food-storage organs and includes true bulbs as well as corms, rhizomes, and tubers. True bulbs have fleshy scales – modified leaves or leaf bases – that are tightly overlapping and can be enclosed in a papery tunic, as in the daffodil, or be naked and loosely arranged, as in the lily. Corms are compressed and enlarged stem bases, usually enclosed in a fibrous or papery tunic, as in the crocus. Each corm lasts one year and is replaced by a new one after flowering. Tubers, seen in plants such as cyclamen or dahlia, are solid, underground sections of modified stem or root and they seldom possess scales or tunics. Rhizomes are modified stems that creep at or just below soil level; they may be thin and wiry, as in lily-of-the-valley, (*Convallaria*), or swollen and fleshy, as in bearded irises.

Although a few bulbs are evergreen, most grow and bloom during a fairly short season then die back to below ground level. Although they are then described as dormant, bulbs are far from quiescent, since they are developing the following year's flowers. This is why the siting of bulbs is often crucial to their continued success. Those bulbs that originated in dry, summer climates usually need warm, dry conditions when dormant to aid maturation and flower formation, while those bulbs from woodland or other damp, shaded habitats require a cool and slightly moist position. Since their leaves produce the food storage for the following year, it is vital to leave bulb foliage in place until it has died down naturally.

Designing with bulbs

There are bulbs for almost every garden site and design, from the tiny *Iris danfordiae* or the autumn daffodil (*Sternbergia lutea*) for the rock garden to the carpeting erythroniums or the towering *Cardiocrinum giganteum* for the dappled shade of woodland gardens.

Bulbs are extremely versatile when used to define a garden style. The strongly upright habit and sculptural flower forms of many hybrid tulips, the precise formation of the dahlias, or the flamboyant spires of gladioli are ideal in formal beds. Amaryllis, lilies, and agapanthus, often grown in containers to add formal elegance to patio plantings, are equally at home among perennials and roses. Many bulbs thrive in pots, whether indoors or outside. Bulbs can be planted in informal groups in a

Container combination
Left: Planting two different tulip bulbs together can highlight the beauty of both. Site the container where it can be appreciated at close quarters.

Naturalized bulbs
Above: Short grass sprinkled with naturalized early crocuses (here, cultivars of Crocus chrysanthus*) confirm the onset of spring.*

Summer colour
Right: From midsummer to early autumn, the robust, vibrantly colored flower spikes of cormous perennial Crocosmia *'Lucifer' lend height and arching grace to the mixed border.*

SPRING BEAUTY
Left: As spring eases into summer, the crown imperials (Fritillaria imperialis) *raise their majestic heads above a carpet of late-flowering daffodils and grape hyacinths.*

AUTUMN HIGHLIGHTS
Below: Autumn-flowering colchicums flowering with scarlet-flowered Stachys coccinea *provide a startling finale to the season .*

border with annuals, shrubs, and perennials for year-round interest. In a woodland setting, drifts of great white trillium (*Trillium grandiflorum*) and erythroniums look natural, while short grass spangled with crocuses or snake's-head fritillaries (*Fritillaria meleagris*) mimics their wild habitat to perfection.

MAINTAINING YEAR-ROUND INTEREST
Most bulbs have a distinct flowering season, which might be considered a disadvantage, yet with careful planning it is possible to extend or enhance this period of interest.

The first snowdrops (*Galanthus*) and early narcissus mark the onset of spring and begin the gardening year. Most bulbs bloom in spring and early summer, producing splashes of color before the summer-flowering shrubs and perennials reach their peak. The combination of certain genera, notably *Narcissus* and *Tulipa*, can provide constant color from spring to summer. Summer-flowering species, such as *Galtonia candicans* and many alliums, offer colorful highlights or allow subtle associations of contrasting form in the border. As summer draws to an end, the crinums, nerines, and crocosmias are at their best and often continue to bloom into autumn.

The autumn-flowering crocuses, colchicums, and cyclamen give their best displays with the onset of autumn rains, when much else in the garden is fading quietly. Some bulbs, for example *Arum italicum* 'Marmoratum' or *Cyclamen hederifolium*, have pretty marbled foliage that persists through winter. These and early-flowering bulbs, such as winter aconites (*Eranthis*), *Anemone blanda*, and dwarf narcissus (*Narcissus* 'February Gold', for example), brighten the garden before most shrubs come into leaf. Grape hyacinths, chionodoxas, scillas, and dwarf irises can create complementary carpets of blue beneath flowering shrubs such as corylopsis, forsythia, and witch hazel (*Hamamelis*).

Many bulbs, notably lilies, also offer an intense fragrance and are ideal for blending with other highly scented plants, such as roses or philadelphus.

SIZE CATEGORIES USED WITHIN THIS GROUP		
Large	Medium	Small
over 2ft (60cm)	9in–2ft (23cm–60cm)	up to 9in (23cm)

WHITE

Leucojum aestivum
(Summer snowflake)
Spring-flowering bulb with long, strap-shaped, semi-erect, basal leaves. Bears heads of pendent, long-stalked, bell-shaped, green-tipped white flowers on leafless stems. H 1½–3ft (50cm–1m), S 4–5in (10–12cm).

Z3–9 H9–1

Fritillaria raddeana
Robust, spring-flowering bulb with lance-shaped leaves in whorls on lower half of stem. Has a head of up to 20 widely conical, pale yellow or greenish yellow flowers, 1¼–1½in (3–4cm) long, topped by a scrown of small leaves. H to 3ft (1m), S 6–9in (15–23cm).

Z6–9 H9–6

Fritillaria verticillata
Spring-flowering bulb with slender leaves in whorls up stem that bears a loose spike of 1–15 bell-shaped white flowers, ¾–1½in (2–4cm) long and checkered green or brown. H to 3ft (1m), S 3–4in (8–10cm).

Z6–8 H8–6

OTHER RECOMMENDED PLANTS:
Albuca canadensis
Canna iridiflora, illus. p.403
Chasmanthe aethiopica
Fritillaria imperialis 'Lutea'
Fritillaria imperialis 'Rubra Maxima'
Hymenocallis x *festalis*
Phaedranassa carmioli, illus. p.400

PURPLE–ORANGE

Fritillaria persica
Spring-flowering bulb with narrow, lance-shaped, gray-green leaves along stem. Produces a spike of 10–20 or more narrow, bell-shaped, blackish- or brownish purple flowers, ⅝–¾in (1.5–2cm) long. H to 5ft (1.5m), S 4in (10cm).

Z6–8 H8–6

Fritillaria recurva
(Scarlet fritillary)
Spring-flowering bulb with whorls of narrow, lance-shaped, gray-green leaves. Bears a spike of up to 10 narrow, yellow-checkered orange or red flowers with flared tips. H to 3ft (1m), S 3–4in (8–10cm).

Z6–9 H9–6

Fritillaria imperialis
(Crown imperial)
Spring-flowering bulb with glossy, pale green leaves carried in whorls on leafy stems. Has up to 5 widely bell-shaped orange flowers crowned by small, leaflike bracts. H to 3ft (1m), S 9–12in (23–30cm).

Z4–9 H8–2

□ WHITE

***Crinum* x *powellii* 'Album'**
Late summer- or autumn-flowering bulb with a long neck, producing a group of semi-erect, strap-shaped leaves. Leafless flower stems carry heads of fragrant, widely funnel-shaped white flowers.
H to 3ft (1m), S 2ft (60cm).

☼ ◊ ⓘ Z7–11 H12–8

Hymenocallis* x *macrostephana
Evergreen, spring- or summer-flowering bulb with strap-shaped, semi-erect, basal leaves. Bears fragrant white or cream- to greenish yellow flowers, 6–8in (15–20cm) wide.
H 32in (80cm), S 12–18in (30–45cm).

◑ ◊ Z14–15 H12–1

Eucomis pallidiflora
(Giant pineapple lily)
Summer-flowering bulb with sword-shaped, crinkly-edged, semi-erect, basal leaves. Bears a dense spike of star-shaped, greenish white flowers crowned with a cluster of leaflike bracts.
H to 30in (75cm), S 12–24in (30–60cm).

☼ ◊ Z8–11 H12–8

***Zantedeschia aethiopica* 'Green Goddess'**
Very robust, summer-flowering tuber with arrow-shaped, semi-erect, basal, deep green leaves. Bears a succession of green spathes, each with a large, central, green-splashed white area. H 1½–3ft (45cm–1m), S 1½–2ft (45–60cm).

☼ ◊ ⓘ Z6–10 H10–4

Galtonia candicans
(Summer hyacinth)
Late summer- or autumn-flowering bulb with widely strap-shaped, fleshy, semi-erect, basal, gray-green leaves. Leafless stem has a spike of up to 30 pendent, short-tubed white flowers.
H 3–4ft (1–1.2m), S 7–9in (18–23cm).

☼ ◊ Z7–10 H10–7

***Zantedeschia aethiopica* 'Crowborough'**
Early to mid-summer-flowering tuber with arrow-shaped, semi-erect, basal, deep green leaves. Produces a succession of white spathes, each with a yellow spadix.
H 1½–3ft (45cm–1m), S 1½ft (45cm).

☼ ◊ ⓘ Z8–10 H10–8

Camassia leichtlinii
Tuft-forming bulb with long, narrow, erect, basal leaves. Each leafless stem bears a dense spike of 6-petaled, star-shaped, bluish violet or white flowers, 1½–3in (4–8cm) across, in summer.
H 3–5ft (1–1.5m), S 8–12in (20–30cm).

☼ ◆ Z4–11 H12–1

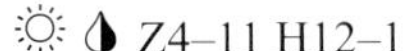

***Camassia leichtlinii* 'Semiplena'**
Tuft-forming bulb with long, narrow, erect, basal leaves. Each leafless stem carries a dense spike of narrow-petaled, double, creamy white flowers, 1½–3in (4–8cm) across, in summer.
H 3–5ft (1–1.5m), S 8–12in (20–30cm).

◑ ◆ Z4–10 H10–1

OTHER RECOMMENDED PLANTS:
Camassia quamash
Cardiocrinum giganteum, illus. p.398
Chlorogalum pomeridianum
DAHLIAS, illus. pp.406–407
GLADIOLI, illus. p.399
LILIES, illus. pp.404–405
Polianthes tuberosa
Nomocharis saluenensis

Crinum moorei
Summer-flowering bulb, long neck, up to 3ft (1m) tall, and strap-shaped, semi-erect, gray-green leaves. Leafless flower stems bear heads of long-tubed, funnel-shaped white to deep pink flowers. H 20–28in (50–70cm), S 24in (60cm).

Z7–11 H12–7

Nectaroscordum siculum subsp. ***bulgaricum***, syn. *N. dioscoridis*
Late spring- to early summer-flowering bulb with pendent, bell-shaped white flowers flushed purple-red and green. In seed, stalks bend upward, holding dry seed pods erect. H to 4ft (1.2m), S 1–1½ft (30–45cm).

Z6–10 H10–6

Cardiocrinum giganteum
(Giant lily)
Robust, leafy-stemmed bulb. In summer has long spikes of fragrant, slightly pendent cream flowers, 6in (15cm) long, with purple-red streaks inside, then brown seed pods. H to 10ft (3m), S 2½–3½ft (75cm–1.1m).

Z7–9 H9–7

Eucomis comosa
Clump-forming bulb with strap-shaped, wavy-margined leaves spotted purple beneath. Purple-spotted stem bears a spike of white or greenish white, sometimes pink-tinted flowers with purple ovaries. H to 28in (70cm), S 12–24in (30–60cm).

Z8–11 H10–8

Nomocharis pardanthina, syn. *N. mairei*
Summer-flowering bulb with stems bearing whorls of lance-shaped leaves and up to 15 outward-facing white or pale pink flowers, each with purple blotches and a dark purple eye. H to 3ft (1m), S 5–6in (12–15cm).

Z7–9 H9–7

Crinum* x *powellii
Late summer- or autumn-flowering bulb producing a group of strap-shaped, semi-erect leaves. Leafless flower stems bear heads of fragrant, widely funnel-shaped pink flowers. H to 3ft (1m), S 2ft (60cm).

Z7–11 H12–8

Crinum bulbispermum
DAHLIAS, illus. pp.406–407
GLADIOLI, illus. p.399
LILIES, illus. pp.404–405

Gladiolus hybrids

Gladiolus hybrids produce excellent flowers for garden decoration, flower arrangements, and exhibition. They are divided into the Grandiflorus Group, with long, densely packed flower spikes and categorized as miniature, small, medium-sized, large, or giant according to the width of the lowest flowers, and the Primulinus and Nanus Groups, with loose spikes of small flowers. (See also the Plant Dictionary.)

***G.* 'Inca Queen'**
(large)

***G.* 'Pink Lady'**
(large)

***G.* 'Stardust'**
(miniature)

***G.* 'Melodie'**
(small)

***G.* 'Ice Cap'**
(large)

***G.* 'White Ice'**
(medium)

***G.* 'The Bride'**
(Nanus Group)

***G.* 'Halley'**
(Nanus Group)

***G.* 'Amanda Mahy'**
(Nanus Group)

***G.* 'Rose Supreme'**
(giant)

***G.* 'Miss America'**
(medium)

***G.* 'Anna Leorah'**
(large)

***G.* 'Pulchritude'**
(medium)

***G.* 'Mi Mi'** (small)

***G.* 'Drama'**
(large)

***G.* 'Black Lash'**
(small)

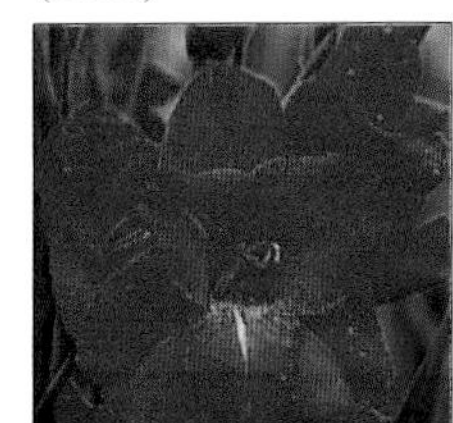

***G.* 'Victor Borge'**
(large)

***G.* 'Vaucluse'**
(giant)

***G.* 'Green Woodpecker'**
(medium)

***G.* 'Tesoro'**
(medium)

***G.* 'Esta Bonita'**
(giant)

***G.* 'Peter Pears'**
(large)

***G.* 'Little Darling'**
(Primulinus Group)

Notholirion campanulatum
Early summer-flowering bulb with long, narrow leaves in a basal tuft. Leafy stem bears a spike of 10–40 pendent, funnel-shaped flowers, each 1½–2in (4–5cm) long, with green-tipped, deep rose-purple petals. H to 3ft (1m), S 3–4in (8–10cm).

Z7–10 H10–7

Watsonia borbonica
Very robust, summer-flowering corm with narrowly sword-shaped leaves both at base and on stem. Produces a loose, branched spike of rich pink flowers with 6 spreading, pointed, rose-red lobes. H 3–5ft (1–1.5m), S 1½–2ft (45–60cm).

Z11–13 H12–6

Dierama pulcherrimum
Upright, summer-flowering corm with long, narrow, straplike, evergreen leaves, above which rise elegant, arching, wiry stems bearing funnel-shaped, deep pink flowers. Prefers deep, rich soil. H 5ft (1.5m), S 1ft (30cm).

Z8–10 H10–8

Watsonia pillansii, syn. *W. beatricis*
Summer-flowering corm with long, sword-shaped, erect leaves, some basal and some on stem. Stem carries a dense, branched spike of tubular, orange-red flowers, each 2½–3in (6–8cm) long, with 6 short lobes. H to 3ft (1m), S 1–1½ft (30–45cm).

Z11–13 H12–6

Gladiolus italicus, syn. *G. segetum*
Early summer-flowering corm with a fan of erect, sword-shaped leaves from the basal part of stem. Carries a loose spike of up to 20 pinkish purple flowers, 1½–2in (4–5cm) long. H to 3ft (1m), S 4–6in (10–15cm).

Z8–10 H9–1

Gladiolus communis* subsp. *byzantinus, syn. *G. byzantinus*
Early summer-flowering corm with a dense spike of up to 20 deep purplish red or purplish pink flowers, 1½–2½in (4–6cm) long. Produces a fan of sword-shaped, erect, basal leaves. H to 28in (70cm), S 4–6in (10–15cm).

Z8–10 H9–1

Phaedranassa carmioli
Spring- and summer-flowering bulb with upright, elliptic or lance-shaped, basal leaves. Bears a head of 6–10 pendent, pinkish red flowers with green bases and yellow-edged green lobes at each apex. H 20–28in (50–70cm), S 12–18in (30–45cm).

Z12–14 H12–9

***Alstroemeria* MARGARET (‘Stacova’)**
Mid- to late summer-flowering tuber with narrow, lance-shaped, twisted, bright green leaves. Thick, leafy stems bear widely flared, funnel-shaped, deep red flowers. H 3ft (1m), S 2–3ft (60cm–1m).

(!) Z8–11 H12–7

x *Amarcrinum memoria-corsii*, illus. p.408
DAHLIAS, illus. pp.406–407
LILIES, illus. pp.404–405
*Watsonia meriana*e

■ RED

Dracunculus vulgaris, syn. *Arum dracunculus* (Dragon's arum)
Spring- and summer-flowering tuber with deeply divided leaves at apex of thick, blotched stem. A blackish maroon spadix protrudes from a deep maroon-purple spathe, 14in (35cm) long.
H to 3ft (1m), S 1½–2ft (45–60cm).

Z8–10 H10–8

***Gloriosa superba* 'Rothschildiana'** (Glory lily)
Deciduous, summer-flowering, tuberous, tendril climber. Upper leaf axils each bear a large flower that has 6 reflexed red petals with scalloped yellow edges. H to 6ft (2m), S 1–1½ft (30–45cm).

Z11–12 H12–7

***Crocosmia* 'Bressingham Blaze'**
Clump-forming, late summer-flowering corm with sword-shaped, pleated, basal, erect leaves. Branched stem bears widely funnel-shaped, fiery red flowers.
H 30in (75cm), S 6–8in (15–20cm).

Z6–9 H9–6

***Crocosmia* 'Lucifer'**
Robust, clump-forming corm with sword-shaped, erect, basal, bright green leaves. Bears funnel-shaped, deep rich red flowers in dense, branching spikes in midsummer.
H to 3ft (1m), S 8–10in (20–25cm).

Z6–9 H9–2

***Canna* 'Assaut'**, syn. *C.* 'Assault'
Summer-flowering, rhizomatous perennial with thick, leafy stems bearing wide, purple-green leaves. Has a spike of scarlet flowers surrounded by purple bracts. H to 4ft (1.2m), S 1½–2ft (45–60cm).

Z8–11 H12–8

Crocosmia masoniorum
Robust, clump-forming corm with erect, basal, deep green leaves, pleated lengthwise. Erect, branched stem has a horizontal, upper part that carries upright, reddish orange flowers in summer-autumn.
H to 5ft (1.5m), S 1–1½ft (30–45cm).

Z6–9 H9–2

■ RED–PURPLE

Scadoxus multiflorus* subsp. *katherinae, syn. *Haemanthus katherinae* (Blood flower)
Very robust, clump-forming bulb with lance-shaped, wavy-edged leaves. Bears an umbel of up to 200 red flowers in summer. H to 4ft (1.2m), S 1–1½ft (30–45cm).

Z14–15 H12–10

Allium stipitatum
Summer-flowering bulb with thick stems and straplike, semi-erect, basal leaves. Carries 50 or more star-shaped, purplish pink flowers in a spherical umbel, 3–5in (8–12cm) across. H to 3–4ft (1–1.5m), S 6–8in (15–20cm).

Z4–9 H9–1

Dierama pendulum, syn. *D. ensifolium* (Angel's fishing rod)
Clump-forming, late summer-flowering corm with arching, basal leaves. Bears pendulous, loose racemes of bell-shaped, pinkish purple flowers, 1in (2.5cm) long.
H to 5ft (1.5m), S 6–8in (15–20cm).

Z7–9 H9–7

Canna 'Lucifer'
Chasmanthe aethiopica
Chasmanthe floribunda
DAHLIAS, illus. pp.406–407
Dichelostemma ida-maia
GLADIOLI, illus. p.399
LILIES, illus. pp.404–405
Scadoxus multiflorus
Watsonia fourcadei
DAHLIAS, illus. pp.406–407

PURPLE–BLUE

Allium giganteum
Robust, summer-flowering bulb with long, wide, semi-erect, basal leaves. Produces a thick stem with a dense, spherical umbel, 5in (12cm) across, of numerous star-shaped purple flowers. H to 6ft (2m), S 12–14in (30–35cm).

Z3–9 H9–5

***Allium* x *hollandicum*,**
syn. *A. aflatunense* of gardens
Summer-flowering bulb with mid-green, basal leaves dying away by flowering time. Carries numerous star-shaped, purplish pink flowers in a dense, spherical umbel, 4in (10cm) across. H 3ft (1m), S 4in (10cm).

Z4–8 H8–1

***Dichelostemma congestum*,**
syn. *Brodiaea congesta*
Early summer-flowering bulb with semi-erect, basal leaves dying away when a dense head of funnel-shaped, purple flowers, each ⅝–¾in (1.5–2cm) long, appears.
H to 3ft (1m), S 3–4ft (8–10cm).

Z6–10 H10–6

***Aristea major*,** syn. *A. thyrsiflora*
Robust, evergreen, clump-forming rhizome with sword-shaped, erect leaves, to 1in (2.5cm) across, and dense spikes of purple-blue flowers on short stalks in summer. H to 3ft (1m), S 1½–2ft (45–60cm).

Z11–13 H12–1

Neomarica caerulea
Summer-flowering rhizome with sword-shaped, semi-erect leaves in basal fans. Stems each bear a leaflike bract and a succession of irislike blue flowers with white, yellow, and brown central marks. H to 3ft (1m), S 3–5ft (1–1.5m).

Z13–15 H12–10

GREEN–YELLOW

Dietes bicolor
Evergreen, tuft-forming, summer-flowering rhizome. Tough, long, narrow, erect, basal leaves. Branching stems each bear a succession of flattish, irislike, pale to midyellow flowers; each large petal has a brown patch. H to 3ft (1m), S 1–2ft (30–60cm).

Z8–10 H10–8

Galtonia viridiflora
Clump-forming, summer-flowering bulb with widely strap-shaped, fleshy, semi-erect, basal, gray-green leaves. Leafless stem bears a spike of up to 30 pendent, short-tubed, funnel-shaped, pale green flowers.
H 3–4ft (1–1.2m), S 7–9in (18–23cm).

Z8–10 H10–8

Arisaema consanguineum
Summer-flowering tuber with robust, spotted stems and erect, umbrella-like leaves with narrow leaflets. Produces purplish white- or white-striped green spathes, 6–8in (15–20cm) long, and bright red berries.
H to 3ft (1m), S 1–1½ft (30–45cm)

Z5–9 H9–7

Fritillaria chitralensis
Spring- to early summer-flowering bulb with ovate, mid- to light green leaves and open umbels of 4 or 5 conical, pendent, bright yellow flowers. Similar to *F. imperialis*.
H 20–32in (50–80cm), S 4in (10cm).

Z6–8 H8–6

Moraea ramosissima
Late spring- to early summer-flowering corm with numerous, semi-erect, narrowly linear, channeled, basal leaves. Yellow flowers, with deeper yellow marks on the inner petals, appear on many-branched stems. H 20–48in (50–120cm), S 4in (10cm).

Z11–13 H12–6

Zantedeschia elliottiana
(Golden calla lily)
Summer-flowering tuber with heart-shaped, semi-erect, basal leaves with transparent marks. Bears a 6in (15cm) long yellow spathe surrounding a yellow spadix. H 2–3ft (60cm–1m), S 1½–2ft (45–60cm).

Z8–10 H10–4

Allium caeruleum, illus. p.422
Arisaema tortuosum
Camassia quamash
DAHLIAS, illus. pp.406–407

GLADIOLI, illus. p.399
IRISES, illus. pp.234–5

Bowiea volubilis, illus. p.460
Stenanthium gramineum

***Crocosmia* 'Golden Fleece'**, syn. *C.* 'Citronella' of gardens
Clump-forming, late summer-flowering corm with sword-shaped, erect, basal, gray-green leaves. Flowers are funnel-shaped and clear golden yellow. H 24–30in (60–75cm), S 6–8in (15–20cm).

☼ ◊ Z6–9 H10–9

Moraea huttonii
Summer-flowering corm with long, narrow, semi-erect, basal leaves. Tough stem bears a succession of iris-like yellow flowers, 2–3in (5–7cm) across, with brown marks near the center. H 2½–3ft (75cm–1m), S 6–10in (15–25cm).

☼ ◊ Z9–10 H10–9

***Crocosmia* 'Star of the East'**
Late summer-flowering corm with sword-shaped, erect, basal, midgreen leaves. Bears horizontal-facing, funnel-shaped, clear orange flowers, each with a paler orange center, on branched stems. H 28in (70cm), S 3in (8cm).

☼ ◊ Z6–9 H9–6

Alstroemeria 'Walter Fleming'
DAHLIAS, illus. pp.406–407
GLADIOLI, illus. p.399
Gladiolus papilio, illus. p.408
Gloriosa superba
Moraea spathulata

Alstroemeria aurea, syn. *A. aurantiaca*
Summer-flowering, tuberous perennial with narrow, lance-shaped, twisted leaves and loose heads of orange flowers tipped with green and streaked dark red.
H to 3ft (1m), S 2–3ft (60cm–1m).

☼ ◊ (!) Z7–10 H10–7

Littonia modesta
Deciduous, summer-flowering, tuberous, scandent climber. Has slender stems bearing lance-shaped leaves with tendrils at apex. Leaf axils bear pendent, bell-shaped orange flowers, 1½–2in (4–5cm) across. H 3–6ft (1–2m), S 4–6in (10–15cm).

☼ ◊ Z14–15 H12–10

Canna iridiflora
Very robust, spring- or summer-flowering, rhizomatous perennial with broad, oblong leaves and spikes of pendent, long-tubed, reddish pink or orange flowers, each 4–6in (10–15cm) long, with reflexed petals. H 10ft (3m), S 1½–2ft (45–60cm).

☼ ♦ Z8–11 H12–8

Belamcanda chinensis
Canna 'Orange Perfection'
Crocosmia aurea
Crocosmia paniculata
DAHLIAS, illus. pp.406–407
GLADIOLI, illus. p.399

Lilies

Lilies (*Lilium* species and cultivars) are graceful plants that bring elegance to the summer border. Their attractive, flamboyant flowers are in various shapes, some nodding, others upright or trumpet-shaped, and others in the distinctive turkscap form (with recurving petals). Most are borne usually several per stem. Many have a distinctive, powerful fragrance, though a few species are unpleasantly scented. Most widely grown are the numerous hybrids, available in a dazzling array of colors – white, pink, red, and rich shades of yellow and orange – but among the species are several that have been undeservedly neglected. Lily flowers are often attractively spotted with a darker or contrasting color or have conspicuous stamens or pollen. Lilies thrive in sun and well-drained soil. Once established, they are best left undisturbed, since the bulbs are easily damaged.

***L.* 'Mont Blanc'**

***L.* 'Bronwen North'**

L. 'Star Gazer'

***L.* 'Sterling Star'**

L. martagon

***L.* 'Casa Blanca'**

L. martagon
var. ***album***

***L.* 'Bright Star'**

L. rubellum

***L.* 'Côte d'Azur'**

L. candidum

***L.* Olympic Hybrids**

***L.* 'Black Magic'**

***L.* Imperial Gold Group**

L. mackliniae

***L.* 'Corsage'**

***L.* 'Montreux'**

***L.* 'Journey's End'**

L. longiflorum

L. duchartrei

L. regale

L. auratum
var. ***platyphyllum***

***L.* 'Magic Pink'**

L. speciosum
var. ***rubrum***

***L.* 'Angela North'**

L.* x *dalhansonii

L. **'Black Beauty'**

*L. **nepalense***

L. **'Rosemary North'**

L. **'Amber Gold'**

*L. **lancifolium***
var. ***splendens***

L. **'Lady Bowes Lyon'**

L. **Golden Splendor Group**

*L. **hansonii***

L. **'Brushmarks'**

*L. **tsingtauense***

L. **'Karen North'**

*L. **canadense***

*L. **bulbiferum***
var. ***croceum***

*L. **pyrenaicum***
var. ***rubrum***

L. **'Roma'**

*L. **monadelphum***

L. **'Apollo'**

L. **Golden Clarion Group**

L. **'Destiny'**

*L. **pyrenaicum***

L. **'Enchantment'**

L. **'Harmony'**

*L. **chalcedonicum***

*L. **pardalinum***

L. **'Connecticut King'**

*L. **superbum***

*L. **medeoloides***

*L. **davidii***
var. ***willmottiae***

Dahlias

The variety of border hybrids offers a dazzling display of color and form to every gardener, and no special skills are required to cultivate or propagate them. In color the flowers range from deep reds, crimsons, purples, hues of mauve, and vibrant pinks to whites, apricots, oranges, bronzes, and brilliant scarlets, in size from the tiny pompons of 2in (5cm) to huge exhibition blooms greater than 10in (25cm) across.

Dahlias provide excellent cut flowers and will bloom vigorously throughout summer until the first frosts – in the right conditions, a single plant may produce up to 100 blooms. Their various flower types (shown below) form the basis of the recognized groups.

Single – each flower usually has 8–10 broad petals surrounding an open, central disk.

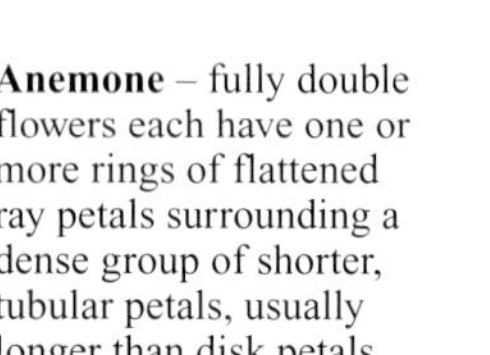

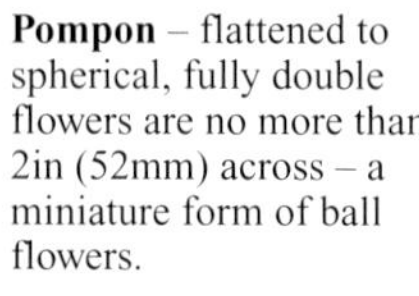

Anemone – fully double flowers each have one or more rings of flattened ray petals surrounding a dense group of shorter, tubular petals, usually longer than disk petals found in single dahlias.

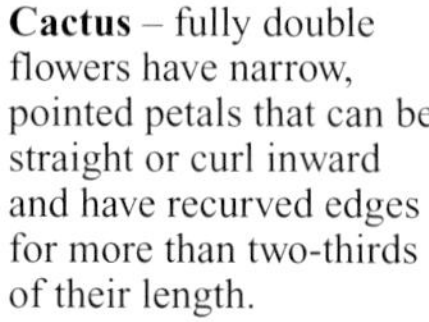

Collarette – single flowers each have broad, outer petals, usually 8–10, and an inner collar of smaller petals surrounding an open, central disk.

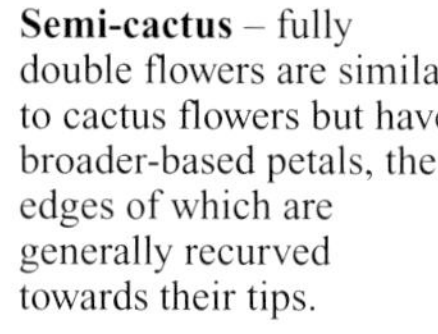

Waterlily – fully double flowers have large, generally sparse ray petals, which are flat or with slightly incurved or recurved margins, giving the flower a flat appearance.

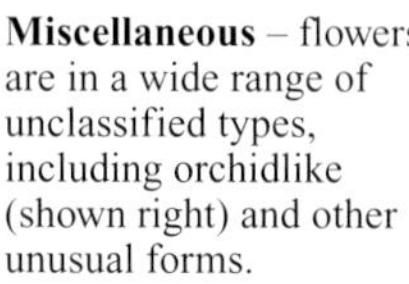

Decorative – fully double flowers have broad, flat petals that incurve slightly at their margins and usually reflex to the stem.

Ball – flattened to spherical, fully double flowers have densely packed, almost tubular petals.

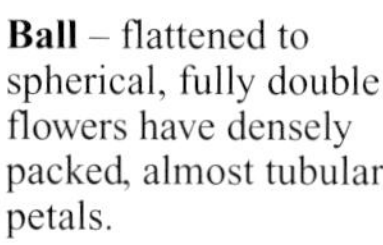

Pompon – flattened to spherical, fully double flowers are no more than 2in (52mm) across – a miniature form of ball flowers.

Cactus – fully double flowers have narrow, pointed petals that can be straight or curl inward and have recurved edges for more than two-thirds of their length.

Semi-cactus – fully double flowers are similar to cactus flowers but have broader-based petals, the edges of which are generally recurved towards their tips.

Miscellaneous – flowers are in a wide range of unclassified types, including orchidlike (shown right) and other unusual forms.

***D.* 'Rhonda'** (pompon)

***D.* 'Gay Princess'** (decorative)

***D.* 'Vicky Crutchfield'** (waterlily)

***D.* 'Mi Wong'** (pompon)

***D.* 'Pearl of Heemstede'** (waterlily)

***D.* 'Pontiac'** (cactus)

***D.* 'Noreen'** (pompon)

***D.* 'Fascination'** (miscellaneous)

***D.* 'Pink Symbol'** (semi-cactus)

***D.* 'Pink Shirley Alliance'** (cactus)

***D.* 'White Alva's'** (decorative)

***D.* 'White Ballet'** (waterlily)

***D.* 'Easter Sunday'** (collarette)

***D.* 'White Klankstad'** (cactus)

***D.* 'Small World'** (pompon)

***D.* 'Wootton Cupid'** (ball)

D. 'Hayley Jayne' (semi-cactus)

D. 'Zorro' (decorative)

D. 'Moor Place' (pompon)

D. 'Butterball' (decorative)

D. 'Wootton Impact' (semi-cactus)

D. 'Grenidor Pastelle' (semi-cactus)

D. 'Pink Jupiter' (semi-cactus)

D. 'Comet' (anemone)

D. 'Hamari Katrina' (semi-cactus)

D. 'Mark Hardwick' (decorative)

D. 'East Anglian' (decorative)

D. 'Yelno Firelight' (waterlily)

D. 'Lavender Athalie' (cactus)

D. 'Bishop of Llandaff' (miscellaneous)

D. 'Davenport Sunlight' (semi-cact.)

D. 'Yellow Hammer' (single)

D. 'Wanda's Capella' (decorative)

D. 'Hamari Gold' (decorative)

D. 'Hillcrest Royal' (cactus)

D. 'Clair de Lune' (collarette)

D. 'Jeanette Carter' (decorative)

D. 'So Dainty' (semi-cactus)

D. 'Jescot Julie' (miscellaneous)

D. 'Jim Branigan' (semi-cactus)

D. 'Preston Park' (single)

D. 'Whale's Rhonda' (pompon)

D. 'Chimborazo' (collarette)

D. 'Hamari Accord' (semi-cactus)

D. 'Shandy' (semi-cactus)

D. 'Kathryn's Cupid' (ball)

D. 'Shirley Alliance' (cactus)

D. 'Biddenham Sunset' (decorative)

BULBS large AUTUMN INTEREST

WHITE–PURPLE

***Amaryllis belladonna* 'Hathor'**
Autumn-flowering bulb with a thick purple stem bearing fragrant, pure white flowers, 4in (10cm) long, with yellow throats. Strap-shaped, semi-erect, basal leaves appear in late winter or spring. H 20–32in (50–80cm), S 12–18in (30–45cm).

Z7–11 H12–7

x *Amarcrinum memoria-corsii*,
syn. x *A. howardii*,
x *Crinodonna corsii*
Evergreen, clump-forming bulb with wide, semi-erect, basal leaves. Thick stems carry fragrant, rose-pink flowers in loose heads in late summer and autumn. H and S to 3ft (1m).

Z13–15 H12–9

Amaryllis belladonna
(Belladonna lily)
Autumn-flowering bulb with a thick purple stem bearing fragrant, funnel-shaped, pink flowers, 4in (10cm) long. Forms strap-shaped, semi-erect, basal leaves after flowering. H 20–32in (50–80cm), S 12–18in (30–45cm).

Z7–11 H12–7

x *Amarygia parkeri*,
syn. x *Brunsdonna parkeri*
Early autumn-flowering bulb. Thick stem carries a large head of funnel-shaped, deep rose flowers with yellow and white throats. Produces strap-shaped, semi-erect, basal leaves after flowering. H to 3ft (1m), S 2–3ft (60cm–1m).

Z9–11 H12–9

***Gladiolus papilio*,**
syn. *G. purpureoauratus*
Clump-forming, summer- or autumn-flowering corm with stolons. Bears up to 10 yellow or white flowers suffused violet, with hooded upper petals and darker yellow patches on lower petals. H to 3ft (1m), S 6in (15cm).

Z8–10 H9–1

OTHER RECOMMENDED PLANTS:
Crinum macowanii
Crinum x *powellii*, illus. p.398
Crinum x *powellii* 'Album', illus. p.397
Crocosmia masoniorum, illus. p.401
Galtonia candicans, illus. p.397
Urginea maritima
Worsleya rayneri

BULBS medium SPRING INTEREST

WHITE

Erythronium oregonum
Clump-forming, spring-flowering tuber with 2 semi-erect, mottled, basal leaves. Has up to 3 pendent white flowers with yellow eyes and often brown rings near center; petals reflex as flowers open. Increases rapidly by offsets.
H to 14in (35cm), S 5in (12cm).

Z3–9 H9–1

***Allium neapolitanum*,**
syn. *A. cowanii*
Spring-flowering bulb with narrow, semi-erect leaves on the lower quarter of flower stems. Stems each develop an umbel, 2–4in (5–10cm) across, of up to 40 white flowers. H 8–20in (20–50cm), S 4–5in (10–12cm).

Z7–9 H9–7

Calochortus venustus
Late spring-flowering bulb with 1 or 2 narrow, erect leaves near the base of the branched stem. Bears 1–4 white, yellow, purple, or red flowers with a dark red, yellow-margined blotch on each large petal. H 8–24in (20–60cm), S 2–4in (5–10cm).

Z6–10 H10–6

OTHER RECOMMENDED PLANTS:
Crinum asiaticum, illus. p.419
DAFFODILS, illus. pp.416–18
Freesia 'White Swan'
Hippeastrum 'White Dazzler'
Hymenocallis narcissiflora, illus. p.420
Leucojum aestivum, illus. p.396
Ornithogalum umbellatum

□ WHITE

***Erythronium californicum* 'White Beauty'**
Vigorous, clump-forming tuber with basal, mottled leaves. In spring has a loose spike of 1–10 reflexed white flowers, each with a brown ring near the center. Spreads rapidly. H 8–12in (20–30cm), S 4–5in (10–12cm).

◑ ◊ Z3–9 H9–1

Calochortus albus
(Fairy lantern, Globe lily)
Spring-flowering bulb with long, narrow, erect, gray-green leaves near the base of the loosely branched stem. Each branch carries a pendent, globose white or pink flower. H 8–20in (20–50cm), S 2–4in (5–10cm).

☼ ◊ Z6–10 H10–6

Pamianthe peruviana
Evergreen, spring-flowering bulb with a stemlike neck and semi-erect leaves with drooping tips. Stem has a head of 2–4 fragrant white flowers, each with a bell-shaped cup and 6 spreading petals. H 20in (50cm), S 18–24in (45–60cm).

◑ ◊ Z13–15 H12–8

□ PINK

Erythronium hendersonii
Spring-flowering tuber with 2 semi-erect, basal brown- and green-mottled leaves. Flower stem carries up to 10 lavender or lavender-pink flowers with reflexed petals and deep purple central eyes. H 8–12in (20–30cm), S 4–5in (10–12cm).

◑ ◊ Z3–9 H9–1

Allium unifolium
Late spring-flowering bulb with one semi-erect, basal, gray-green leaf. Each flower stem carries a domed umbel, 2in (5cm) across, of up to 30 purplish pink flowers. H to 12in (30cm), S 3–4in (8–10cm).

☼ ◊ ⓘ Z4–9 H9–1

Erythronium revolutum
Freesia corymbosa
Hippeastrum 'Apple Blossom', illus. p.425
Hippeastrum 'Bouquet'
Rhodophiala advena, illus. p.421

Tulips

Tulips are good for a wide range of plantings and are excellent in the rock garden, in formal bedding, as elegant cut flowers, and for containers. Their bold flowers are generally simple in outline and held upright, with colors that are often bright and strong. Many of the species deserve to be more widely grown, alongside the large variety of hybrids now available. *Tulipa* is classified in 15 divisions.

Div.1 Single early – cup-shaped, single flowers, often opening wide in the sun, are borne from early to midspring.

Div.2 Double early – long-lasting, double flowers open wide in early and midspring.

Div.3 Triumph – sturdy stems bear rather conical, single flowers, becoming more rounded, in mid- and late spring.

Div.4 Darwin hybrids – large, single flowers are borne on strong stems from mid- to late spring.

Div.5 Single late – single flowers, variable but usually with pointed petals, are borne in late spring and very early summer.

Div.6 Lily-flowered – strong stems bear narrow-waisted, single flowers, with long, pointed, often reflexed petals, in late spring.

Div.7 Fringed – flowers are similar to those in Div.6 but have fringed petals.

Div.8 Viridiflora – variable, single flowers, with partly greenish petals, are borne in late spring.

Div.9 Rembrandt – flowers are similar to those in Div.6, but have striped or feathered patterns caused by virus and appear in late spring.

Div.10 Parrot – has large, variable, single flowers, with frilled or fringed and usually twisted petals, in late spring.

Div.11 Double late (peony-flowered) – usually bowl-shaped, double flowers appear in late spring.

Div.12 Kaufmanniana hybrids – single flowers are usually bicolored, open flat in the sun, and appear in early spring. Leaves are usually mottled or striped.

Div.13 Fosteriana hybrids – large, single flowers open wide in the sun from early to midspring. Leaves are often mottled or striped.

Div.14 Greigii hybrids – large, single flowers appear in mid- and late spring. Mottled or striped leaves are often wavy-edged.

Div.15 Miscellaneous – a diverse category of other species and their cultivars and hybrids. Flowers appear in spring and early summer.

T. **'White Triumphator'** (Div.6) ①

T. **'White Parrot'** (Div.10) ①

T. **'White Dream'** (Div.3) ①

T. biflora (Div.15) ①

T. turkestanica (Div.15) ①

T. **'Diana'** (Div.1) ①

T. **'Angélique'** (Div.11) ①

T. **'Don Quichotte'** (Div.3) ①

T. **'Purissima'** (Div.13) ①

T. **'Groenland'** (Div.8) ①

T. saxatilis (Div.15) ①

T. **'Page Polka'** (Div.3) ①

T. **'Spring Green'** (Div.8) ①

T. **'Ballade'** (Div.6) ①

T. **'Carnaval de Nice'** (Div.11) ①

T. **'Menton'** (Div.5) ①

T. **'Fancy Frills'** (Div.10) ①

T. **'New Design'** (Div.3) ①

T. **'China Pink'** (Div.6) ①

T. **'Gordon Cooper'** (Div.4) ①

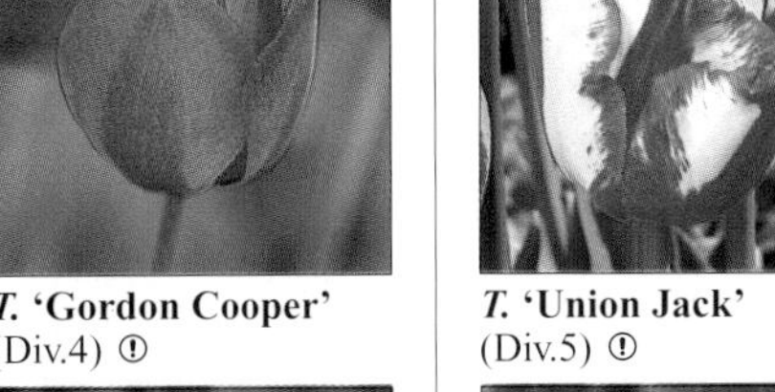
T. **'Union Jack'** (Div.5) ①

T. **'Ad Rem'** (Div.4) ①

T. **'Red Riding Hood'** (Div.14) ①

T. **'Juan'** (Div.13) ①

T. **'Peer Gynt'** (Div.3) ①

T. **'Garden Party'** (Div.3) ①

T. **'Bing Crosby'** (Div.3) ①

T. **'Dreamland'** (Div.5) ①

T. **'Red Parrot'** (Div.10) ①

T. **'Uncle Tom'** (Div.11) ①

T. **'Oranje Nassau'** (Div.2) ①

T. undulatifolia (Div.15) ①

T. **'Keizerskroon'** (Div.1) ①

T. **'Attila'** (Div.3) ①

T. **'Madame Lefèber'** (Div.13) ①

T. **'Plaisir'** (Div.14) ①

T. acuminata (Div.15) ①

T. **'Bird of Paradise'** (Div.10) ①

T. sprengeri (Div.15) ①

T. **'Kingsblood'** (Div.5) ①

T. **'Margot Fonteyn'** (Div.3) ①

T. **'Apeldoorn's Elite'** (Div.4) ①

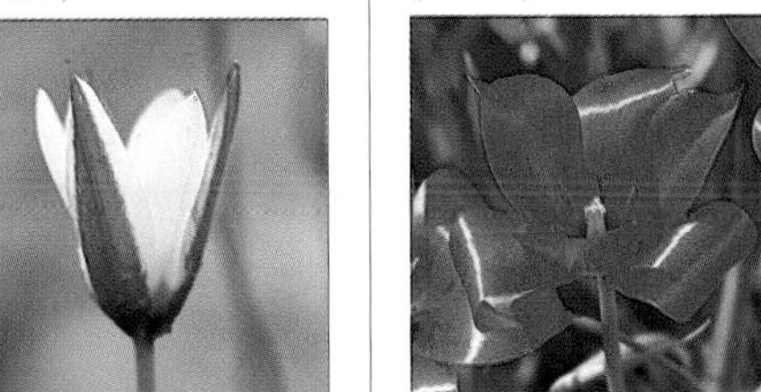
T. clusiana (Div.15) ①

T. linifolia (Div.15) ①

T. **'Lustige Witwe'** (Div.3) ①

T. **'Balalaika'** (Div.5) ①

T. **'Glück'** (Div.12) ①

T. **'Estella Rijnveld'** (Div.10) ①

T. hageri (Div.15) ①

T. praestans **'Unicum'** (Div.15) ①

T. **'Fringed Beauty'** (Div.7) ①

T. marjollettii (Div.15) ①

T. **'Dreaming Maid'** (Div.3) ①

T. batalinii (Div.15) ①

T. **'West Point'** (Div.6) ①

T. sylvestris (Div.15) ①

T. **'Candela'** (Div.13) ①

T. **'Dreamboat'** (Div.14) ①

T. **'Greuze'** (Div.5) ①

T. urumiensis (Div.15) ①

T. clusiana var. *chrysantha* (Div.15) ①

T. **'Artist'** (Div.8) ①

T. **'Shakespeare'** (Div.12) ①

T. violacea (Div.15) ①

T. kaufmanniana (Div.15) ①

T. **'Golden Apeldoorn'** (Div.4) ①

T. **'Dillenburg'** (Div.5) ①

T. orphanidea (Div.15) ①

T. humilis (Div.15) ①

T. tarda (Div.15) ①

T. **'Prinses Irene'** (Div.1) ①

T. praestans **'Van Tubergen's Variety'** (Div.15) ①

T. **'Blue Parrot'** (Div.10) ①

T. **'Maja'** (Div.7) ①

T. **'Yokohama'** (Div.1) ①

T. **'Cape Cod'** (Div.14) ①

T. whittallii (Div.15) ①

T. **'Queen of Night'** (Div.5) ①

T. **'Bellona'** (Div.1) ①

T. **'Golden Artist'** (Div.8) ①

T. **'Apricot Beauty'** (Div.1) ①

BULBS

RED–PURPLE

Anemone pavonina
Leafy tuber with cup-shaped, single, dark-centered scarlet, purple, or blue flowers rising above divided, frilly leaves in early spring. H 16in (40cm), S 8in (20cm).

Z8–10 H10–8

Sprekelia formosissima
(Aztec lily, Jacobean lily)
Clump-forming, spring-flowering bulb with semi-erect, basal leaves. Stem bears a deep red flower, 5in (12cm) wide, that has 6 narrow petals with green-striped bases. H 6–14in (15–35cm), S 5–6in (12–15cm).

Z13–15 H12–10

Sauromatum venosum, syn. *S. guttatum*
(Monarch-of-the-East, Voodoo lily)
Early spring-flowering tuber. Bears a large, acrid, purple-spotted spathe, then a lobed leaf on a long, spotted stalk. H 12–18in (30–45cm), S 12–14in (30–35cm).

Z7–10 H12–10

Fritillaria meleagris
(Snake's-head fritillary)
Spring-flowering bulb with slender stems producing scattered, narrow, gray-green leaves. Has solitary bell-shaped, prominently checkered flowers in shades of pinkish purple or white. H to 12in (30cm), S 2–3in (5–8cm).

Z4–9 H8–2

Fritillaria pyrenaica
Spring-flowering bulb with scattered, lance-shaped leaves, often rather narrow. Develops 1 or rarely 2 broadly bell-shaped flowers with flared-tipped, checkered, deep brownish- or blackish purple petals. H 6–12in (15–30cm), S 2–3in (5–8cm).

Z6–8 H8–6

PURPLE

Muscari latifolium
Spring-flowering bulb with one strap-shaped, semi-erect, basal, gray-green leaf. Has a dense spike of tiny, bell-shaped, blackish violet to blue flowers with constricted mouths; upper ones are paler and smaller. H to 10in (25cm), S 2–3in (5–8cm).

Z4–8 H8–1

Fritillaria camschatcensis
(Black sarana)
Spring-flowering bulb. Thick stems carry lance-shaped, glossy leaves, mostly in whorls. Bears up to 8 deep blackish purple or brown flowers. Needs organic soil. H 6–24in (15–60cm), S 3–4in (8–10cm).

Z4–9 H8–2

Leucocoryne ixioides
(Glory-of-the-sun)
Spring-flowering bulb with long, narrow, semi-erect, basal leaves that are withered by flowering time. Wiry, slender flower stem has a loose head of up to 10 lilac-blue flowers. H 12–16in (30–40cm), S 3–4in (8–10cm).

Z12–14 H8–1

Anemone x *fulgens*, illus. p.430
Arum dioscoridis
Freesia 'Romany'
Fritillaria tubiformis
Hippeastrum 'Red Lion', illus. p.425
Scadoxus puniceus
TULIPS, illus. pp.410–12

BLUE

Hyacinthoides hispanica, syn. *Endymion hispanicus*, *Scilla campanulata*, *S. hispanica* (Spanish bluebell)
Spring-flowering bulb with strap-shaped, glossy leaves and pendent, bell-shaped blue, white, or pink flowers. H to 12in (30cm), S 4–6in (10–15cm).
Z4–10 H9–1

Hyacinthoides non-scripta, syn. *Endymion non-scriptus*, *Scilla non-scripta*, *S. nutans* (English bluebell)
Clump-forming, spring-flowering bulb with strap-shaped leaves. An erect stem, arching at the apex, bears fragrant blue, pink, or white flowers. H 8–16in (20–40cm), S 3–4in (8–10cm).
Z4–10 H9–1

Ixiolirion tataricum, syn. *I. montanum*
Spring- to early summer-flowering bulb with long, narrow, semi-erect leaves on the lower part of stem. Has a loose cluster of blue flowers with a darker, central line along each petal. H to 16in (40cm), S 3–4in (8–10cm).
Z10–11 H12–7

Aristea ecklonii
IRISES, illus. pp.234–5
Moraea polystachya

GREEN

Fritillaria acmopetala
Spring-flowering bulb with slender stems that bear narrowly lance-shaped, scattered leaves, and 1 or 2 broadly bell-shaped green flowers with brown-stained petals flaring outward at the tips. H 6–16in (15–40cm), S 2–3in (5–8cm).
Z6–8 H8–6

Fritillaria pontica
Spring-flowering bulb with stems carrying lance-shaped, gray-green leaves, the topmost in a whorl of 3. Has solitary, broadly bell-shaped green flowers, 1¼–1¾in (3–4.5cm) long, often suffused brown. H 6–18in (15–45cm), S 2–3in (5–8cm).
Z7–8 H8–7

Arisaema triphyllum, syn. *A. atrorubens* (Jack-in-the-pulpit)
Spring-flowering tuber with 3-lobed, erect leaves. Produces green or purple-brown-striped green spathes, hooded at tips, followed by bright red berries. H 16–20in (40–50cm), S 12–18in (30–45cm).
Z4–9 H9–1

Ixia viridiflora
Spring- to early summer-flowering corm with very narrow, erect leaves mostly at stem base. Carries a spike of flattish, jade green flowers, 1–2in (2.5–5cm) across, with purple-black eyes. H 12–24in (30–60cm), S 1–2in (2.5–5cm).
Z10–11 H12–7

Hermodactylus tuberosus, syn. *Iris tuberosa* (Widow iris)
Spring-flowering perennial with finger-like tubers. Very long, narrow, gray-green leaves are square in cross-section. Has a fragrant, yellowish green flower with large, blackish brown-tipped petals. H 8–16in (20–40cm), S 2–3in (5–8cm).
Z7–9 H9–7

Fritillaria cirrhosa
Spring-flowering bulb with slender stems and narrow, whorled leaves; upper leaves have tendril-like tips. Produces up to 4 widely bell-shaped flowers, purple or yellowish-green with dark purple checkered patterns. H to 24in (60cm), S 2–3in (5–8cm).
Z6–8 H8–6

Bellevalia pycnantha

Fritillaria pallidiflora
Robust, spring-flowering bulb with broadly lance-shaped, gray-green leaves, scattered or in pairs on stem. Has 1–5 widely bell-shaped yellow to greenish yellow flowers, usually faintly checkered brownish red within. H 6–28in (15–70cm), S 3–4in (8–10cm).

Z4–9 H8–2

Arum creticum
Spring-flowering tuber that bears white or yellow spathes, each bottle-shaped at the base, slightly reflexed at the apex and with a protruding yellow spadix. Has arrow-shaped, semi-erect, deep green leaves in autumn. H 12–20in (30–50cm), S 8–12in (20–30cm).

Z8–10 H10–8

Ferraria crispa, syn. *F. undulata*
Spring-flowering corm, leafy stem with a succession of upward-facing brown or yellowish brown flowers, 1½–2in (4–5cm) across, with 6 wavy-edged, spreading petals that are conspicuously lined and blotched. H 8–16in (20–40cm), S 3–4in (8–10cm).

Z10–13 H12–8

***Gladiolus* 'Christabel'**
Spring-flowering corm with a wiry stem producing a loose spike of fragrant, widely funnel-shaped, primrose yellow flowers, 2½–3in (6–8cm) across, with purple-brown-veined, upper petals. H to 18in (45cm), S 3–4in (8–10cm).

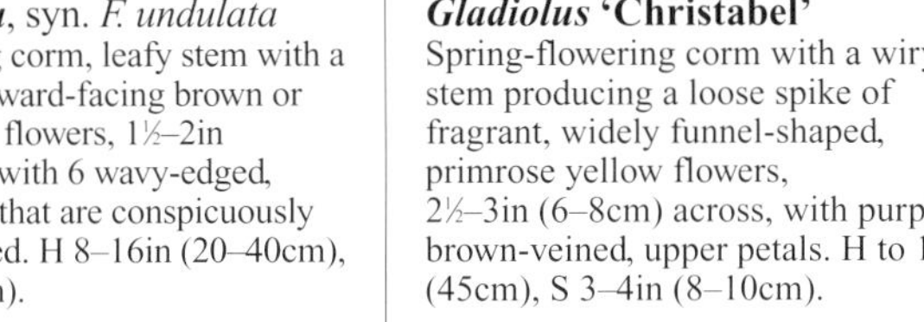

Z8–10 H9–1

***Erythronium* 'Pagoda'**
Robust, spring-flowering tuber with 2 semi-erect, basal, faintly mottled, glossy leaves. Flower stem produces up to 10 pendent, pale yellow flowers with reflexed petals. H 10–14in (25–35cm), S 6–8in (15–20cm).

Z4–9 H9–1

Calochortus luteus
(Yellow mariposa)
Late spring-flowering bulb with long, narrow, erect leaves near the base of the loosely branched stem. Each branch bears a 3-petaled yellow flower with central brown blotches. H 8–18in (20–45cm), S 2–4in (5–10cm).

Z5–10 H10–5

Bloomeria crocea
Calochortus amabilis, illus. p.434
DAFFODILS, illus. pp.416–18
Erythronium grandiflorum
Erythronium tuolumnense
Fritillaria acmopetala
Homeria ochroleuca
Hymenocallis 'Sulphur Queen'
IRISES, illus. pp.234–5
TULIPS, illus. pp.410–12

Daffodils

The charm and beauty of the daffodil (botanically known as *Narcissus*) grace the garden early in the year. The diversity of its flowers provides infinite variation, from the tiny Cyclamineus daffodil, with its swept-back petals, to the stately trumpet daffodil. Many may be naturalized, forming a golden carpet in grass or a wild garden, but dwarf forms are best in rock gardens or troughs, brightening the landscape before most other plants emerge.

The genus is classified in 13 divisions. Their flower forms are illustrated below, with the exception of Div.12, miscellaneous, and Div.13, mostly wild species. Both have varying flowers, including hoop-petticoat forms, produced between autumn and early summer.

Div.1 Trumpet – usually solitary flowers each have a trumpet that is as long as, or longer, than the petals. Early to late spring-flowering.

Div.2 Large-cupped – solitary flowers each have a cup at least one-third the length of, but shorter than, the petals. Spring-flowering.

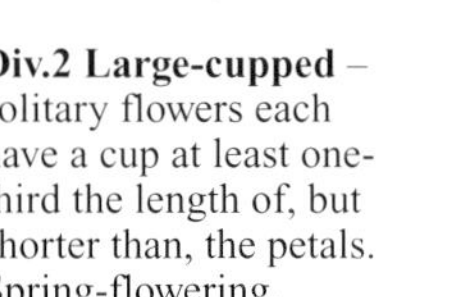

Div.3 Small-cupped – flowers are often borne singly; each has a cup not more than one-third the length of the petals. Spring- or early summer-flowering.

Div.4 Double – most have solitary large, fully or semi-double flowers with the cup and petals, or just the cup, replaced by petaloid structures. Some have smaller flowers in clusters of 4 or more. Spring- or early summer-flowering.

Div.5 Triandrus – nodding flowers, with short, sometimes straight-sided cups and narrow, reflexed petals, are borne 2–6 per stem. Spring-flowering.

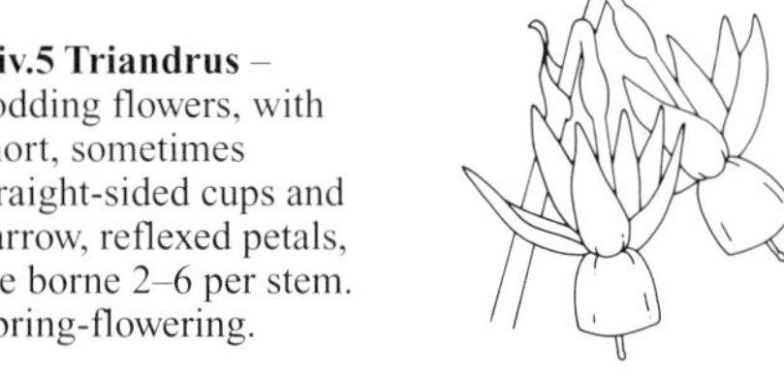

Div.6 Cyclamineus – flowers are borne usually 1 or 2 per stem with cups that are sometimes flanged and often longer than those of Div.5. Petals are narrow, pointed, and reflexed. Early to mid-spring flowering.

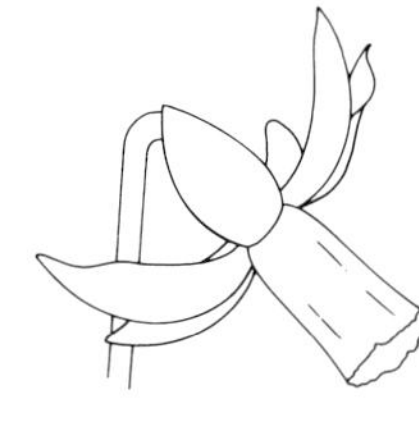

Div.7 Jonquil – sweetly scented flowers are borne usually 2 or more per stem. Cups are short, sometimes flanged; petals are often flat, fairly broad, and rounded. Spring-flowering.

Div.8 Tazetta – flowers are borne in clusters of either 12 or more small, fragrant flowers per stem or 3 or 4 large ones. Cups are small and often straight-sided, petals broad and mostly pointed. Late autumn- to mid-spring-flowering.

Div.9 Poeticus – flowers each have a small, colored cup and glistening white petals. They are borne usually 1 but sometimes 2 per stem and may be sweetly fragrant. Late spring- or early summer-flowering.

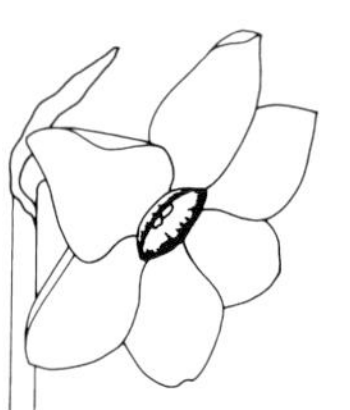

Div.10 Bulbocodium – flowers usually borne singly on very short stems, with insignificant petals and large, widely flaring cups. Winter- to spring-flowering.

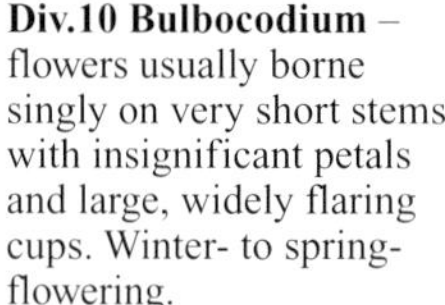

Div.11 Split-cupped – usually solitary flowers that have cups split for more than half their length. Spring-flowering.

(a) Collar – wide cup segments lie back on the petals.

(b) Papillon – narrower cup segments have tips arranged at the margin of the petals.

N. cantabricus (Div.13) ①

***N.* 'Irene Copeland'** (Div.4) ①

***N.* 'Aircastle'** (Div.3) ①

***N.* 'Canisp'** (Div.2) ①

***N.* 'Ice Follies'** (Div.2) ①

***N.* 'Trousseau'** (Div.1) ①

***N.* 'Cheerfulness'** (Div.4) ①

N. rupicola subsp. ***watieri*** (Div.10) ①

***N.* 'Portrush'** (Div.3) ①

***N.* 'White Lady'** (Div.3) ①

N.* x *medioluteus (Div.13) ①

***N.* 'Thalia'** (Div.5) ①

N. **'Silver Chimes'** (Div.8) ①

N. **'Empress of Ireland'** (Div.1) ①

N. **'Merlin'** (Div.3) ①

N. **'Passionale'** (Div.2) ①

N. **'Woodland Star'** (Div 3)

N. **'Satin Pink'** (Div.2) ①

N. **'Pride of Cornwall'** (Div.8) ①

N. **'Actaea'** (Div.9) ①

N. **'Kilworth'** (Div.2) ①

N. **'Cantabile'** (Div.9) ①

N. **'Bridal Crown'** (Div.4) ①

N. **'Rockall'** (Div.3) ①

N. **'Rainbow'** (Div.2) ①

N. **'Dove Wings'** (Div.6) ①

N. **'Broadway Star'** (Div.11b) ①

N. **'Bravoure'** (Div.1) ①

N. **'Acropolis'** (Div.4) ①

N. **'February Silver'** (Div.6) ①

N. poeticus var. ***recurvus*** (Div.13) ①

N. **'Jack Snipe'** (Div.6) ①

N. triandrus (Div.13) ①

N. **'Canaliculatus'** (Div.8) ①

N. **'Cassata'** (Div.11a) ①

N. **'Belcanto'** (Div.11a) ①

N. **'Spellbinder'** (Div.1) ①

N. **'Avalanche'** (Div.8) ①

N. **'Minnow'** (Div.8) ①

N. romieuxii (Div.13) ①

N. **'Honeybird'** (Div.1) ①

N. **'Binkie'** (Div.2) ①

N. pseudonarcissus (Div.13) (!)

N. **'Rip van Winkle'** (Div.4) (!)

N. **'Sweetness'** (Div.7) (!)

N. **'Stratosphere'** (Div.7) (!)

N. **'Ambergate'** (Div.2) (!)

N. **'Suzy'** (Div.7) (!)

N. rupicola (Div.13) (!)

N. **'February Gold'** (Div.6) (!)

N. **'Liberty Bells'** (Div.5) (!)

N. jonquilla (Div.13) (!)

N. cyclamineus (Div.13) (!)

N. **'Saint Keverne'** (Div.11b) (!)

N. **'Jetfire'** (Div.6) (!)

N. **'Home Fires'** (Div.2) (!)

N. **'Pipit'** (Div.7) (!)

N. minor (Div.13) (!)

N. **'Pencrebar'** (Div.4) (!)

N. **'Golden Ducat'** (Div.4) (!)

N. **'Tahiti'** (Div.4) (!)

N. **'Hawera'** (Div.5) (!)

N. **'Fortune'** (Div.2) (!)

N. **'Tête-à-Tête'** (Div.12) (!)

N. **'Bartley'** (Div.6) (!)

N. **'Shining Light'** (Div.2) (!)

N. **'Scarlet Gem'** (Div.8) (!)

N. **'Charity May'** (Div.6) (!)

N. x *odorus* **'Rugulosus'** (Div.7) (!)

N. **'Jumblie'** (Div.12) (!)

N. **'Kingscourt'** (Div.1) (!)

N. **'Grand Soleil d'Or'** (Div.8) (!)

N. **'Altruist'** (Div.3) (!)

ORANGE

Stenomesson variegatum, syn. *S. incarnatum*
Clump-forming bulb. Bears reddish yellow, pink, or white flowers with 6 green lobes at the apex in winter or spring. H 12–24in (30–60cm), S 12in (30cm).

Z12–15 H12–10

Stenomesson miniatum, syn. *Urceolina peruviana*
Late spring-flowering bulb with strap-shaped, semi-erect, basal leaves. Bears a head of red or orange flowers, ¾–1½in (2–4cm) long, with yellow anthers. H 8–12in (20–30cm), S 4–6in (10–15cm).

Z11–15 H12–10

Clivia miniata
Evergreen, tuft-forming rhizome with strap-shaped, semi-erect, basal, dark green leaves, 16–24in (40–60cm) long. Stems each produce a head of 10–20 orange or red flowers in spring or summer. H 16in (40cm), S 12–24in (30–60cm).

(!) Z9–11 H12–1

DAFFODILS, illus. pp.416–18
Dipcadi serotinum, illus. p.434
Hippeastrum 'Orange Sovereign', illus. p.425
Ixia maculata
Tritonia crocata
TULIPS, illus. pp.410–12

WHITE

Crinum asiaticum
Clump-forming bulb with strap-shaped, semi-erect, basal, dark green leaves, 3ft (1m) long. Leafless flower stems produce heads of long-tubed white flowers with narrow petals in spring or summer. H 1½–2ft (45–60cm), S 2–3ft (60cm–1m).

(!) Z8–11 H12–8

Pancratium illyricum
Summer-flowering bulb with strap-shaped, semi-erect, basal, grayish green leaves. Leafless stem has a head of 5–12 fragrant, 6-petaled white flowers, 3in (8cm) across. H to 18in (45cm), S 10–12in (25–30cm).

Z8–11 H12–8

Ornithogalum narbonense
Clump-forming, late spring- to summer-flowering bulb with long, narrow, semi-erect, basal, gray-green leaves. Leafless stem produces a spike of star-shaped white flowers, ¾in (2cm) wide. H 12–16in (30–40cm), S 4–6in (10–15cm).

(!) Z7–10 H10–7

Triteleia hyacinthina, syn. *Brodiaea hyacinthina*, *B. lactea*
Late spring- to early summer-flowering corm with long, narrow, semi-erect or spreading, basal leaves. Heads of white, sometimes purple-tinged flowers are borne on wiry stems. H 12–20in (30–50cm), S 3–4in (8–10cm).

Z7–13 H12–7

Arisaema sikokianum
Early summer-flowering tuber with erect leaves divided into 3–5 leaflets. Produces deep brownish purple and white spathes, 6in (15cm) long, with clublike white spadices protruding from the mouths. H 12–20in (30–50cm), S 12–18in (30–45cm).

Z4–9 H9–3

OTHER RECOMMENDED PLANTS:
BEGONIAS, illus. p.295
Cyrtanthus mackenii
Dietes iridioides
Haemanthus albiflos
Hesperocallis undulata
LILIES, illus. pp.404–405
Pancratium maritimum

□ WHITE

Ornithogalum thyrsoides (Chincherinchee)
Summer-flowering bulb with strap-shaped, semi-erect, basal leaves. Bears a dense, conical spike of cup-shaped white flowers, ¾–1¼in (2–3cm) across. H 12–18in (30–45cm), S 4–6in (10–15cm).

☼ ◊ ⓘ Z7–10 H10–7

Zigadenus fremontii
Clump-forming, early summer-flowering bulb with long, strap-shaped, semi-erect, basal leaves. Stem produces a spike of star-shaped, pale creamy green flowers with darker green nectaries on petal bases. H 12–20in (30–50cm), S 4–6in (10–15cm).

☼ ◊ ⓘ Z8–9 H9–8

Hymenocallis narcissiflora, syn. *H. calathina, Ismene calathina* (Peruvian daffodil)
Spring- or summer-flowering bulb with semi-erect, basal leaves, dying in winter. Bears a loose head of 2–5 fragrant white flowers. H to 24in (60cm), S 12–18in (30–45cm).

◑ ◊ Z12–15 H12–10

WHITE–RED

Ornithogalum arabicum
Early summer-flowering bulb with strap-shaped, semi-erect leaves in a basal cluster. Has a flattish head of up to 15 scented white or creamy white flowers, 1½–2in (4–5cm) across, with black ovaries in centers. H 12–18in (30–45cm), S 4–6in (10–15cm).

☼ ◊ ⓘ Z9–11 H12–9

Allium cernuum
Clump-forming, summer-flowering bulb with narrow, semi-erect, basal leaves. Each stem produces up to 30 cup-shaped pink or white flowers in a loose, nodding umbel, ¾–1½in (2–4cm) across. H 12–28in (30–70cm), S 3–5in (8–12cm).

☼ ◊ ⓘ Z3–9 H9–5

Allium senescens subsp. ***montanum***
Vigorous, clump-forming, summer-flowering bulb with strap-shaped, often twisted, gray-green leaves. Has dense umbels, ¾in (2cm) across, of up to 30 long-lasting, cup-shaped pink flowers. H 18in (45cm), S 24in (60cm).

☼ ◊ ⓘ Z5–9 H9–5

Alstroemeria pelegrina, syn. *A. gayana*
Summer-flowering tuber with narrow, lance-shaped leaves. Each leafy stem has 1–3 white flowers stained pinkish mauve and spotted yellow and brownish purple. H 1–2ft (30–60cm), S 2–3ft (60cm–1m).

☼ ◊ ⓘ Z8–10 H10–8

Tritonia disticha subsp. ***rubrolucens***, syn. *T. rosea, T. rubrolucens*
Late summer-flowering corm with narrowly sword-shaped, erect leaves in a flattish, basal fan. Has pink flowers in a loose, one-sided spike. H 12–20in (30–50cm), S 3–4in (8–10cm).

☼ ◊ Z9–10 H10–9

Lycoris radiata (Red spider lily)
Late summer-flowering bulb with a head of 5 or 6 bright rose-red flowers with narrow, wavy-margined, reflexed petals and conspicuous anthers. Has strap-shaped, semi-erect, basal leaves after flowering time. H 12–16in (30–40cm), S 4–6in (10–15cm).

☼ ◊ Z7–10 H10–7

Allium campanulatum
LILIES, illus. pp.404–405

BEGONIAS, illus. p.295
Bessera elegans
GLADIOLI, illus. p.399
Haemanthus coccineus, illus. p.435

Haemanthus sanguineus
Zantedeschia rehmannii
Zephyranthes grandiflora, illus. p.424

Rhodophiala advena,
syn. *Hippeastrum advenum*
Clump-forming, spring- to summer-flowering bulb with basal, gray-green leaves. Leafless stem carries a head of 2–8 narrowly funnel-shaped red flowers, 2in (5cm) long. H to 16in (40cm), S 6–8in (15–20cm).

Z9–10 H10–9

Ranunculus asiaticus
(Persian buttercup)
Early summer-flowering perennial with clawlike tubers and long-stalked leaves both at the base and on the stem. Has single or double flowers in red, white, pink, yellow, or orange. H 18–22in (45–55cm), S 4in (10cm).

Z7–11 H12–7

Allium schubertii
Early summer-flowering bulb with widely strap-shaped, semi-erect, basal leaves. Bears large umbels of 40 or more star-shaped pink or purple flowers on very unequal stalks, followed by brown seed capsules. H 12–24in (30–60cm), S 6–8in (15–20cm).

Z4–10 H10–1

Allium beesianum
Allium cyaneum
Allium macranthum
Allium narcissiflorum, illus. p.436
Cyrtanthus obliquus
Cyrtanthus sanguineus
DAHLIAS, illus. pp.406–407
Dichelostemma pulchellum

Allium cristophii,
syn. *A. albopilosum*, *A. christophii*
Summer-flowering bulb with semi-erect, hairy gray leaves that droop at tips. Has a large, spherical umbel of 50 or more star-shaped, purplish violet flowers that dry well. H 6–16in (15–40cm), S 6–8in (15–20cm).

Z3–9 H9–5

Patersonia umbrosa
Evergreen, clump-forming, spring- and early summer-flowering rhizome with erect, basal leaves. Tough flower stems each carry a succession of irislike, purple-blue flowers, 1¼–1½in (3–4cm) across. H 12–18in (30–45cm), S 12–24in (30–60cm).

Z11–15 H12–6

Gloxinia perennis
Late summer- to autumn-flowering rhizome with heart-shaped, toothed, hairy leaves on spotted stems. Has bell-shaped, lavender-blue flowers with rounded lobes and purple-blotched throats. H to 24in (60cm), S 12–14in (30–35cm).

Z13–15 H12–10

Oxalis bowiei
Roscoea purpurea

BLUE

Allium caeruleum, syn. *A. azureum*
Clump-forming, summer-flowering bulb with narrow, erect leaves on the lower third of slender flower stems that bear 30–50 star-shaped blue flowers in a dense, spherical umbel, 1¼–1½in (3–4cm) across. H 8–32in (20–80cm), S 4–6in (10–15cm).

Z4–10 H10–1

Triteleia laxa, syn. *Brodiaea laxa*
Early summer-flowering corm with narrow, semi-erect, basal leaves. Stem carries a large, loose umbel of funnel-shaped, deep to pale purple-blue flowers, ¾–2in (2–5cm) long, mostly held upright. H 4–20in (10–50cm), S 3–4in (8–10cm).

Z6–10 H10–6

Aristea ecklonii
Ixiolirion tataricum, illus. p.414

GREEN–YELLOW

Arisaema griffithii
Summer-flowering tuber with large, erect leaves above a green or purple spathe, 8–10in (20–25cm) long, strongly netted with paler veins and expanded like a cobra's hood. H to 24in (60cm), S 18–24in (45–60cm).

Z7–9 H9–7

Arisaema jacquemontii
Summer-flowering tuber with 1 or 2 erect leaves divided into wavy-edged leaflets. Produces slender, white-lined green spathes that are hooded at tips and drawn out into long points. H 12–20in (30–50cm), S 12–15in (30–38cm).

Z7–9 H9–7

Eucomis bicolor
Summer-flowering bulb with wavy-margined, semi-erect, basal leaves. Stem, often spotted purple, bears a spike of green or greenish white flowers, with 6 purple-edged petals topped by a cluster of leaflike bracts. H 12–20in (30–50cm), S 12–24in (30–60cm).

Z8–10 H10–8

Cyrtanthus breviflorus
Hymenocallis 'Sulphur Queen'
Ixia viridiflora, p.414
Lycoris aurea

Allium flavum
Clump-forming, summer-flowering bulb. Leaves are linear and semi-erect on lower half of slender flower stem. Produces a loose umbel of up to 60 small, bell-shaped yellow flowers on thin, arching stalks. H 4–14in (10–35cm), S 2–3in (5–8cm).

Z4–10 H10–1

Cyrtanthus mackenii var. ***cooperi***
Clump-forming, summer-flowering bulb with long, narrow, semi-erect, basal leaves. Leafless stems each carry a head of up to 10 fragrant, tubular, cream or yellow flowers, 2in (5cm) long and slightly curved. H 12–16in (30–40cm), S 3–4in (8–10cm).

Z11–13 H12–6

Calochortus barbatus, syn. *Cyclobothra lutea*
Summer-flowering bulb with narrow, erect leaves near the base of the loosely branched stem. Each branch bears a pendent yellow or greenish yellow flower that is hairy inside. H 12–24in (30–60cm), S 2–4in (5–10cm).

Z6–10 H10–6

Triteleia ixioides

Ranunculus asiaticus
(Persian buttercup)
Early summer-flowering perennial with clawlike tubers and long-stalked, palmate leaves at base and on stem. Has single or double flowers in yellow, white, pink, red, or orange. H 18–22in (45–55cm), S 3–4in (8–10cm).

Z7–11 H12–7

Cypella herbertii
Summer-flowering bulb with a fan of narrow, sword-shaped, erect, basal leaves. Branched flower stem carries a succession of short-lived, irislike, orange-yellow flowers with spotted purple centers. H 12–20in (30–50cm), S 3–4in (8–10cm).

Z11–13 H12–1

***Alstroemeria* 'Parigo Charm'**
Summer-flowering tuber with narrow, twisted, mid- to gray-green leaves and umbels of salmon-pink flowers. The inner tepals are primrose yellow, marked carmine.
H 3ft (1m), S 24in (60cm).

Z8–10 H10–8

***Polianthes geminiflora*,**
syn. *Bravoa geminiflora*
Summer-flowering tuber with strap-shaped, narrow, semi-erect leaves in a basal tuft. Stems carry long spikes of downward-curving, tubular red or orange flowers in pairs. H 8–16in (20–40cm), S 4–6in (10–15cm).

Z14–15 H12–1

***Alstroemeria* Ligtu Hybrids**
Summer-flowering tuber with narrow, twisted leaves and heads of widely flared flowers in shades of pink, yellow, or orange, often spotted or streaked with contrasting colors. H 1½–2ft (45–60cm), S 2–3ft (60cm–1m).

Z8–11 H12–7

Sandersonia aurantiaca
(Chinese-lantern lily)
Deciduous, summer-flowering, tuberous climber. Slender stem bearing scattered, lance-shaped leaves, some tendril-tipped. Orange flowers are produced in axils of upper leaves. H 24in (60cm), S 10–12in (25–30cm).

Z11–14 H12–10

***Crocosmia* 'Jackanapes'**
Clump-forming, late summer-flowering corm with sword-shaped, erect, basal leaves. Produces striking bicolored yellow and orange-red flowers. H 16–24in (40–60cm), S 6–8in (15–20cm).

Z6–9 H9–6

Tigridia pavonia
(Peacock flower, Tiger flower)
Summer-flowering bulb with sword-shaped, pleated, erect leaves near stem base. Succession of short-lived flowers from white to orange, red, or yellow, often with contrasting spots. H to 18in (45cm), S 4–6in (12–15cm).

Z8–10 H12–3

Clivia miniata, illus. p.419
Crocosmia 'Emily McKenzie'
LILIES, illus. pp.404–405

WHITE–PINK

Nerine bowdenii* f. *alba
Autumn-flowering bulb with a thick stem and strap-shaped, semi-erect, basal leaves. Produces a head of 5–10 white, often pink-flushed flowers; petals widen slightly toward wavy-margined, recurved tips. H 18–24in (45–60cm), S 5–6in (12–15cm).

Z8–10 H10–8

Nerine undulata*, syn. *N crispa
Autumn-flowering bulb with narrowly strap-shaped, semi-erect, basal leaves. Flower stem carries a head of pink flowers with very narrow petals crinkled for their entire length. H 12–18in (30–45cm), S 4–5in (10–12cm).

Z8–10 H10–8

***Nerine* 'Orion'**
Autumn-flowering bulb with strap-shaped, semi-erect, basal leaves. Thick, leafless stem bears a head of pale pink flowers with very wavy-margined petals that have recurved tips. H 12–20in (30–50cm), S 8–10in (20–25cm).

Z8–10 H10–8

Nerine bowdenii
Autumn-flowering bulb with a thick stem and strap-shaped, semi-erect, basal leaves. Carries a head of 5–10 glistening pink flowers with petals that widen slightly toward wavy-margined, recurved tips. H 18–24in (45–60cm), S 5–6in (12–15cm).

Z8–10 H10–5

Scilla scilloides*, syn. *S. chinensis*, *S. japonica
Late summer- and autumn-flowering bulb with 2–4 narrowly strap-shaped, semi-erect, basal leaves. Stem bears a slender, dense spike of up to 30 flattish pink flowers, ¼–½in (0.5–1cm) across. H to 12in (30cm), S 2in (5cm).

Z4–8 H8–1

PINK–ORANGE

Zephyranthes grandiflora
Late summer- to early autumn-flowering bulb with narrowly strap-shaped, semi-erect, basal leaves. Each stem bears a funnel-shaped pink flower, held almost erect. H 8–12in (20–30cm), S 3–4in (8–10cm).

Z8–11 H12–9

***Nerine* 'Brian Doe'**
Autumn-flowering bulb with strap-shaped, semi-erect, basal leaves. Thick, leafless stem bears a head of salmon flowers with 6 reflexed, wavy-margined petals. H 12–20in (30–50cm), S 8–10in (20–25cm).

Z8–10 H10–8

***Nerine sarniensis* (Guernsey lily)**
Autumn-flowering bulb with strap-shaped, semi-erect, basal leaves. Leafless stem carries a spherical head of up to 20 deep orange-pink flowers, 2½–3in (6–8cm) across, with wavy-margined petals. H 18–24in (45–60cm), S 5–6in (12–15cm).

Z8–10 H10–8

OTHER RECOMMENDED PLANTS:
Amaryllis belladonna, illus. p.408
Crinum macowanii
Habranthus robustus, illus. p.437
Nerine 'Blanchefleur'
Nerine filifolia
Nerine flexuosa

Brunsvigia josephinae
Eucomis autumnalis
Gloxinia perennis, illus. p.421
Nerine 'Bagdad'
Nerine 'Corusca Major'
Nerine 'Fothergillii Major'

WHITE–RED

***Eucharis* x *grandiflora*,**
syn. *E. amazonica* of gardens
Evergreen, clump-forming bulb with strap-shaped, semi-erect, basal leaves. Bears a head of up to 6 fragrant, slightly pendent white flowers at almost any season. H 16–24in (40–60cm), S 2–3ft (60cm–1m).

Z14–15 H12–10

Veltheimia bracteata
Clump-forming, winter-flowering bulb with semi-erect, strap-shaped, basal, glossy leaves and dense spikes of pendent, tubular pink, red, or yellowish red flowers. H 12–18in (30–45cm), S 10–15in (25–38cm).

Z13–15 H12–10

***Hippeastrum* 'Red Lion'**
Tuft-forming, winter- and spring-flowering bulb with a thick stem bearing a head of 2–6 dark red flowers with yellow anthers. Strap-shaped leaves appear with or just after flowers. H 12–20in (30–50cm), S 12in (30cm).

Z14–15 H12–10

***Hippeastrum* 'Apple Blossom'**
Winter- to spring-flowering bulb with strap-shaped, semi-erect, basal leaves produced as, or just after, flowers form. Thick stem has a head of 2–6 white flowers becoming pink at petal tips. H 12–20in (30–50cm), S 12in (30cm).

Z14–15 H12–10

***Hippeastrum* 'Striped'**
Winter- to spring-flowering bulb with strap-shaped, semi-erect, basal leaves produced with or just after flowers. Thick stem has a head of 2–6 widely funnel-shaped flowers striped white and red. H 20in (50cm), S 12in (30cm).

Z14–15 H12–10

***Hippeastrum aulicum*,**
syn. *H. morelianum*
Winter- and spring-flowering bulb with a basal cluster of strap-shaped, semi-erect leaves. Thick stem bears two red flowers with green-striped petals and green throats. H 12–20in (30–50cm), S 12in (30cm).

Z14–15 H12–10

RED–YELLOW

***Hippeastrum* 'Orange Sovereign'**
Winter- to spring-flowering bulb with strap-shaped, semi-erect, basal, gray-green leaves produced as, or just after, flowers form. Thick stem carries a head of 2–6 rich orange-red flowers. H 12–20in (30–50cm), S 12in (30cm).

Z14–15 H12–10

Lachenalia orchioides
var. ***glaucina***, syn. *L. glaucina*
Late winter- and early spring-flowering bulb with 2 strap-shaped, semi-erect, basal leaves, usually spotted purple. Has a spike of fragrant, whitish blue or pale lilac flowers. H to 12in (30cm), S 2–3in (5–8cm).

Z11–14 H12–6

***Freesia* 'Oberon'**
Winter- and spring-flowering corm with narrow, erect, basal leaves. Produces yellow flowers, 1½–2in (4–5cm) long, light blood red inside; the throats are lemon yellow with small red veins. H to 16in (40cm), S 1½–2½in (4–6cm).

Z10–11 H12–6

OTHER RECOMMENDED PLANTS:
Freesia lactea
Freesia corymbosa
Hippeastrum 'Belinda'
Hippeastrum 'Bouquet'
Hippeastrum 'White Dazzler'
Hymenocallis speciosa
Lachenalia rubida
Stenomesson variegatum, illus. p.419
Veltheimia capensis
Freesia 'Romany'
Lachenalia mutabilis
Moraea polystachya

☐ WHITE

Anemone blanda
'White Splendour'
Knobby tuber with semi-erect leaves that have 3 deeply toothed lobes. Bears upright, flattish white flowers, 1½–2in (4–5cm) across, with 9–14 narrow petals, in early spring. H 2–4in (5–10cm), S 4–6in (10–15cm).

Z4–8 H8–1

Puschkinia scilloides
var. ***libanotica*** **'Alba'**
Spring-flowering bulb with usually 2 strap-shaped, semi-erect, basal leaves. Produces a dense spike of star-shaped white flowers, ⅝–¾in (1.5–2cm) across. H 6in (15cm), S 1–2in (2.5–5cm).

Z3–9 H9–1

Ornithogalum balansae,
syn. *O. oligophyllum* of gardens
Spring-flowering bulb with 2 almost prostrate, inversely lance-shaped, mid-green basal leaves. Has a broad head of 2–5 flowers, glistening white inside, bright green outside, that open wide. H 2–6in (5–15cm), S 2–3in (5–8cm).

Z7–10 H10–7

Leucojum vernum
(Spring snowflake)
Spring-flowering bulb with strap-shaped, semi-erect, basal leaves. Leafless stem carries 1 or 2 pendent, bell-shaped flowers, ⅝–¾in (1.5–2cm) long, with 6 green-tipped white petals. H 4–6in (10–15cm), S 3–4in (8–10cm).

Z4–8 H8–1

Sternbergia candida
Spring-flowering bulb. Strap-shaped, semi-erect, basal, grayish green leaves appear together with a fragrant, funnel-shaped white flower, 1½–2in (4–5cm) long, borne on a leafless stem. H 4–8in (10–20cm), S 3–4in (8–10cm).

Z8–10 H10–8

Ornithogalum montanum
Clump-forming, spring-flowering bulb with strap-shaped, semi-erect, basal, gray-green leaves. Leafless stem produces a head of star-shaped white flowers, 1¼–1½in (3–4cm) across, striped green outside. H and S 4–6in (10–15cm).

Z6–10 H10–6

Ornithogalum lanceolatum
Spring-flowering, dwarf bulb with a flattish rosette of prostrate, lance-shaped, basal leaves. Carries a head of flattish, star-shaped white flowers, 1¼–1½in (3–4cm) across, broadly striped green outside. H 2–4in (5–10cm), S 4–6in (10–15cm).

Z5–10 H10–1

OTHER RECOMMENDED PLANTS:
CROCUSES, illus. pp.428–9
Cyclamen creticum
DAFFODILS, illus. pp.416–18
Fritillaria bucharica
Gagea graeca
Galanthus 'Atkinsii', illus. p.439
Galanthus elwesii, illus. p.439
Galanthus gracilis, illus. p.439
Galanthus ikariae, illus. p.440
Galanthus nivalis 'Flore Pleno', illus. p.439
Galanthus nivalis 'Pusey Green Tip', illus. p.439
Galanthus nivalis 'Sandersii', illus. p.440
Galanthus nivalis 'Scharlockii', illus. p.440

Erythronium californicum
Clump-forming, spring-flowering tuber. Bears 2 semi-erect, basal, mottled leaves. Up to 3 white or creamy white flowers, sometimes red-brown externally, have reflexed petals, yellow eyes, and often brown rings near centers. H 6–14in (15–35cm), S 4–5in (10–12cm).

Z3–9 H9–1

Allium akaka
Spring-flowering bulb with 1–3 broad, prostrate and basal, gray-green leaves and an almost stemless, spherical umbel, 2–3in (5–7cm) across of 30–40 star-shaped white to pinkish white flowers with red centers. H 6–8in (15–20cm), S 5–6in (12–15cm).

Z4–9 H9–1

Allium karataviense
Late spring-flowering bulb with narrowly elliptic to elliptic, prostrate, basal, grayish purple leaves. Stem bears 50 or more star-shaped, pale purplish pink flowers in a spherical umbel, 6in (15cm) or more across.
H to 8in (20cm), S 10–12in (25–30cm).

Z3–9 H9–5

Galanthus plicatus subsp. *byzantinus*, illus. p.440
Galanthus rizehensis, illus. p.439
HYACINTHS, illus. p.431
Hypoxis capensis
IRISES, illus. pp.234–5
Ornithogalum nutans
TULIPS, illus. pp.410–12

***Chionodoxa forbesii* 'Pink Giant'**
Early spring-flowering bulb with 2 narrow, semi-erect, basal leaves. Leafless stem produces a spike of 5–10 flattish, white-eyed pink flowers, ¾–1in (2–2.5cm) across. H 4–10in (10–25cm), S 1–2in (2.5–5cm).

Z3–9 H9–1

Cyclamen libanoticum
Spring-flowering tuber with ivy-shaped, dull green leaves with lighter patterns and purplish green undersides. Flowers are musty-scented, clear pink, each with deep carmine marks at the mouth. Grows best in an alpine house. H to 4in (10cm), S 4–6in (10–15cm).

Z11–13 H7–1

Anemone tschaernjaewii
Spring-flowering tuber with 3-palmate, oval, midgreen leaves, the leaflets shallowly lobed. Bears 5-petaled, saucer-shaped, purple-centered white or pink flowers, ¾–1¾in (2–4.5cm) across. Needs warm, dry summer dormancy. H 2–4in (5–10cm), S 2–3in (5–8cm).

Z5–8 H8–5

Cyclamen persicum, illus. p.440
Cyclamen persicum 'Pearl Wave', illus. p.440
Merendera robusta
TULIPS, illus. pp.410–12

Crocuses

Crocuses (*Crocus* species and cultivars) are possibly the most versatile and reliable of dwarf cormous plants, most flowering in late winter or early spring, though some species flower in autumn. A wide color range is available, from white through pinkish lilac to rich purples, creams, and yellows. Many are also attractively striped or feathered with other colors. Their usually goblet-shaped flowers, sometimes produced before the leaves, open wide in full sun, in some cases to reveal contrasting centers or conspicuous stamens. Most crocuses are also fragrant. To appreciate their scent to the fullest, plant in bowls or shallow pans for indoor display; start them into growth in a bulb frame outside, then bring them inside a week or two before they would normally bloom in the garden, so that the warmth stimulates them into flower.

Outside, crocuses may be used in rock gardens in association with other early-flowering dwarf bulbs or perennials, or planted *en masse* in drifts or beneath deciduous trees and shrubs, where they will rapidly colonize large areas and provide pleasure for many years. To promote vigor, fertilize the plants once the flowers have faded and while the leaves are in full growth. If naturalized in grass, delay mowing until the leaves have died down. Congested clumps may be dug up after flowering and divided.

***C.* 'Eyecatcher'**

***C.* 'Blue Bird'**

C. hadriaticus

C. tommasinianus* f. *albus

C. kotschyanus

C. dalmaticus

C. minimus

C. vernus* subsp. *albiflorus

***C. sieberi* 'Bowles' White'**

C. laevigatus

C. pulchellus

C. sieberi* subsp. *sublimis* f. *tricolor

***C. etruscus* 'Zwanenburg'**

C. malyi

C. boryi

***C.* 'Snow Bunting'**

C. goulimyi

***C. imperati* 'De Jager'**

***C.* 'Blue Pearl'**

C. medius

C. nudiflorus

C. banaticus

C. etruscus

C. longiflorus

C. baytopiorum

C. speciosus 'Conqueror'

C. vernus 'Queen of the Blues'

C. biflorus

C. 'Advance'

C. vernus

C. tommasinianus 'Ruby Giant'

C. vernus 'Prinses Juliana'

C. vernus 'Pickwick'

C. 'Dorothy'

C. 'Ladykiller'

C. cvijicii

C. tommasinianus 'Whitewell Purple'

C. speciosus

C. vernus 'Purpureus Grandiflorus'

C. cartwrightianus

C. 'Cream Beauty'

C. vernus 'Remembrance'

C. speciosus 'Oxonian'

C. 'E. A. Bowles'

C. gargaricus

PINK

Erythronium dens-canis
(Dog's-tooth violet)
Spring-flowering tuber with 2 basal, mottled leaves. Stem has a pendent pink, purple, or white flower, with bands of brown, purple, and yellow near the center, and reflexed petals. H 6–10in (15–25cm), S 3–4in (8–10cm).

Z3–9 H9–1

Allium acuminatum
Spring-flowering bulb with 2–4 long, narrow, semi-erect, basal leaves. Stem bears an umbel, 2in (5cm) across, of up to 30 small, purplish pink flowers. H 4–12in (10–30cm), S 2–3in (5–8cm).

Z4–9 H9–1

Allium oreophilum,
syn. *A. ostrowskianum*
Spring- and summer-flowering, dwarf bulb with 2 narrow, semi-erect, basal leaves. Has loose, domed umbels of up to 10 widely bell-shaped, deep rose-pink flowers, ⅝–¾in (1.5–2cm) across. H 2–4in (5–10cm), S 3–4in (8–10cm).

Z4–9 H9–1

***Anemone blanda* 'Radar'**
Knobby tuber with semi-erect, deep green leaves with 3 deeply toothed lobes. In early spring, stems each bear an upright, flattish, white-centered, bright red-violet flower with 9–14 narrow petals. H 2–4in (5–10cm), S 4–6in (10–15cm).

Z4–8 H8–1

Cyclamen persicum 'Renown', illus. p.441
Cyclamen trochopteranthum
Erythronium hendersonii, illus. p.409
HYACINTHS, illus. p.431
TULIPS, illus. pp.410–12

RED–PURPLE

Anemone* x *fulgens
Spring- or early summer-flowering tuber with deeply divided, semi-erect, basal leaves. Thick stems each carry an upright, bright red flower, 2–3in (5–7cm) across, with 10–15 petals. H 4–12in (10–30cm), S 3–4in (8–10cm).

Z8–11 H12–8

Sparaxis tricolor
Spring-flowering corm, with lance-shaped, erect leaves in a basal fan. Stem has a loose spike of up to 5 flattish orange, red, purple, pink, or white flowers, 2–2½in (5–6cm) across, with black or red centers. H 4–12in (10–30cm), S 3–5in (8–12cm).

Z7–10 H10–7

Bulbocodium vernum
Spring-flowering corm with stemless, widely funnel-shaped, reddish purple flowers. Narrow, semi-erect, basal leaves appear with flowers but do not elongate until later. Dies down in summer. H 1¼–1½in (3–4cm), S 1¼–2in (3–5cm).

Z7–9 H9–7

Anemone coronaria
Arisarum proboscideum
Corydalis cava
CROCUSES, illus. pp.428–9

Babiana rubrocyanea (Winecups)
Spring-flowering corm with lance-shaped, erect, folded leaves in a basal fan. Carries short spikes of 5–10 flowers, each with 6 petals, purple-blue at the top and red at the base. H 6–8in (15–20cm), S 2–3in (5–8cm).

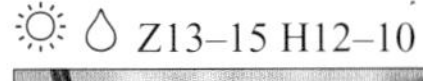 Z13–15 H12–10

***Ipheion uniflorum* 'Froyle Mill'**
Spring-flowering bulb with narrow, semi-erect, basal, pale green leaves that smell of onions if crushed. Each leafless stem carries a star-shaped, violet-blue flower, 1¼–1½in (3–4cm) across. H 4–6in (10–15cm), S 2–3in (5–8cm).

Z6–9 H9–6

Romulea bulbocodium
Spring-flowering corm with long, semi-erect, threadlike leaves in a basal tuft. Slender flower stems each carry 1–6 upward-facing flowers, usually pale lilac-purple with yellow or white centers. H 2–4in (5–10cm). S 1–2in (2.5–5cm).

Z5–9 H9–5

Hyacinths

Grown for their sweet, penetrating scent, hyacinths (*Hyacinthus*) are deservedly popular spring bulbs. The most widely offered for sale are showy cultivars derived from *H. orientalis* and are available in an increasingly wide color range: white, many shades of pink, lilac, blue, purple, yellow, and warm salmon-orange. In the garden they are most effective if planted *en masse* in blocks of a single color, or in containers positioned near the house where their fragrance can be appreciated to the fullest. They are also excellent for growing in bowls indoors; the bulbs may later be planted out in the garden. Specially treated bulbs for indoor culture are available that flower in midwinter. (For details see the Plant Dictionary.) These forced bulbs may afterward be planted outdoors in a sheltered spot, where they should flower again in later years. To keep the bulbs healthy and productive, fertilize them after the flower spikes have faded.

***H. orientalis* 'Delft Blue'** ①

***H. orientalis* 'White Pearl'** ①

***H. orientalis* 'Lady Derby'** ①

***H. orientalis* 'Ostara'** ①

***H.o.* 'Queen of the Pinks'** ①

***H. orientalis* 'Jan Bos'** ①

***H. orientalis* 'Blue Jacket'** ①

***H. orientalis* 'City of Haarlem'** ①

***H. orientalis* 'Distinction'** ①

***H. orientalis* 'Violet Pearl'** ①

***H. orientalis* 'Princess Maria Christina'** ①

PURPLE–BLUE

Gynandriris sisyrinchium
Spring-flowering corm with 1 or 2 semi-erect, narrow, basal leaves. Wiry stems each carry a succession of lavender- to violet-blue flowers, 1¼–1½in (3–4cm) across, with white or orange patches on the 3 larger petals. H 4–8in (10–20cm), S 3–4in (8–10cm).

Z9–10 H10–9

***Muscari comosum* 'Plumosum'**, syn. *M.c.* 'Monstrosum' (Feather grape hyacinth)
Spring-flowering bulb with up to 5 strap-shaped, semi-erect, basal, gray-green leaves. Normal flowers are replaced by a fluffy mass of purple threads. H to 10in (25cm), S 4–5in (10–12cm).

Z4–8 H8–1

Puschkinia scilloides* var. *libanotica (Striped squill)
Spring-flowering bulb with usually 2 strap-shaped, semi-erect, basal leaves. Carries a dense spike of star-shaped, pale blue flowers with a darker blue stripe down each petal center. H 6in (15cm), S 1–2in (2.5–5cm).

Z3–9 H9–1

Hyacinthella leucophaea
Spring-flowering bulb with 2 narrowly strap-shaped, semi-erect, basal leaves and a thin, wiry, leafless flower stem. Carries a short spike of tiny, bell-shaped, very pale blue, almost white flowers. H 4in (10cm), S 1–2in (2.5–5cm).

Z7–9 H9–7

Brimeura amethystina, syn. *Hyacinthus amethystinus*
Late spring-flowering bulb with very narrow, semi-erect, basal leaves. Each leafless stem bears a spike of up to 15 pendent, tubular blue flowers. H 4–10in (10–25cm), S 1–2in (2.5–5cm).

Z5–9 H9–5

Bellevalia hyacinthoides, syn. *Strangweja spicata*
Spring-flowering bulb with prostrate, narrow leaves in a basal cluster. Bears a dense spike of up to 20 bell-shaped, pale lavender-blue, almost white flowers with darker, central veins. H 2–6in (5–15cm), S 2in (5cm).

Z7–9 H9–7

Scilla mischtschenkoana, syn. *S. tubergeniana*, *S.* 'Tubergeniana'
Early spring-flowering bulb with 2 or 3 strap-shaped, semi-erect, basal, mid-green leaves. Stems elongate as cup-shaped or flattish, pale blue flowers, with darker blue veins, open. H 2–4in (5–10cm), S 2in (5cm).

Z4–7 H9–6

Tecophilaea cyanocrocus* var. *leichtlinii, syn. *T.c.* 'Leichtlinii'
Spring-flowering corm with 1 or 2 narrowly lance-shaped, semi-erect, basal leaves and solitary upward-facing, widely funnel-shaped, pale blue flowers with large white centers. H 3–4in (8–10cm), S 2–3in (5–8cm).

Z7–9 H9–7

***Scilla siberica* 'Atrocoerulea'**
Early spring-flowering bulb with 2–4 strap-shaped, semi-erect, basal, glossy leaves, widening toward tips. Bell-shaped, deep rich blue flowers, ½–⅝in (1–1.5cm) long, are borne in a short spike. H 4–6in (10–15cm), S 2in (5cm).

Z5–8 H8–5

Anemone apennina
Anemone blanda
Babiana plicata
Babiana stricta
Brodiaea coronaria
Chionodoxa sardensis
Corydalis fumariifolia
CROCUSES, illus. pp.428–9
Hyacinthoides italica
Ipheion uniflorum 'Wisley Blue'
IRISES, illlus. pp.234–5
Muscari armeniacum 'Blue Spike'
Muscari azureum
Muscari botryoides
Muscari comosum

***Muscari aucheri*,**
syn. *M. lingulatum*
Spring-flowering bulb with 2 strap-shaped, grayish green leaves. Bears small, almost spherical, bright blue flowers with white-rimmed mouths; upper flowers are often paler. H 2–6in (5–15cm), S 2–3in (5–8cm).

Z6–9 H9–5

***Chionodoxa luciliae*,**
syn. *C. gigantea*
Early spring-flowering bulb with 2 somewhat curved, semi-erect, basal leaves. Leafless stem bears 1–3 upward-facing blue flowers with white eyes. H 2–4in (5–10cm), S 1–2in (2.5–5cm).

Z3–9 H9–1

***Chionodoxa forbesii*,**
syn. *C. luciliae* of gardens, *C. siehei*, *C. tmolusii*
Early spring-flowering bulb with 2 semi-erect, narrow, basal leaves. Bears a spike of 5–10 outward-facing, rich blue-lilac flowers with white eyes. H 4–10in (10–25cm), S 1–2in (2.5–5cm).

Z3-9 H9-1

Tecophilaea cyanocrocus
(Chilean blue crocus)
Spring-flowering corm with 1 or 2 lance-shaped, semi-erect, basal leaves. Carries upward-facing, funnel-shaped, deep gentian blue flowers, 1½–2in (4–5cm) across, with white throats. H 3–4in (8–10cm), S 2–3in (5–8cm).

Z7–9 H9–7

Muscari armeniacum
Spring-flowering bulb with 3–6 long, narrow, semi-erect, basal leaves. Carries a dense spike of small, fragrant, bell-shaped, deep blue flowers with constricted mouths that have a rim of small, paler blue or white "teeth." H 6–8in (15–20cm), S 3–4in (8–10cm).

Z4–8 H8–1

***Muscari neglectum*,**
syn. *M. racemosum*
Spring-flowering bulb. Bears 4–6 often prostrate leaves from autumn to early summer. Has small, ovoid, deep blue or blackish blue flowers with white-rimmed mouths. Increases rapidly. H 4–8in (10–20cm), S 3–4in (8–10cm).

Z4–8 H8–1

***Anemone blanda* 'Atrocaerulea'**
Knobby tuber with semi-erect, dark green leaves that have 3 deeply toothed lobes. In early spring, stems each bear an upright, flattish, bright blue flower, 1½–2in (4–5cm) across, with 9–14 narrow petals. H 2–4in (5–10cm), S 4–6in (10–15cm).

(!) Z4–8 H8–1

x *Chionoscilla allenii*
Early spring-flowering bulb with 2 narrow, semi-erect, basal, dark green leaves and flattish, star-shaped, deep blue flowers, ½–¾in (1–2cm) across, in a loose spike. H 4–6in (10–15cm), S 1–2in (2.5–5cm).

Z3–9 H9–1

HYACINTHS, illus. p.431

GREEN–YELLOW

***Ledebouria socialis*,**
syn. *Scilla socialis, S. violacea*
Evergreen, spring-flowering bulb with lance-shaped, semi-erect, basal, dark-spotted gray or green leaves. Produces a short spike of bell-shaped, purplish green flowers. H 2–4in (5–10cm), S 3–4in (8–10cm).

Z11–13 H12–6

Muscari macrocarpum
Spring-flowering bulb with 3–5 semi-erect, basal, grayish green leaves. Carries a dense spike of fragrant, brown-rimmed, bright yellow flowers. Upper flowers may initially be brownish purple. H 4–8in (10–20cm), S 4–6in (10–15cm).

Z7–9 H9–7

***Arum italicum* 'Marmoratum'**
Late spring-flowering tuber. Produces semi-erect leaves with cream or white veins in autumn, followed by pale green or creamy white spathes, then red berries in autumn. Is good for flower arrangements. H 6–10in (15–25cm), S 8–12in (20–30cm).

Z7–9 H9–3

YELLOW–ORANGE

Calochortus amabilis (Golden fairy lantern, Golden globe tulip)
Spring-flowering bulb with one long, narrow, erect leaf near the base of the loosely branched stem. A fringed, deep yellow, sometimes green-tinged flower hangs from each branch. H 4–12in (10–30cm), S 2–4in (5–10cm).

Z6–10 H10–6

Colchicum luteum
Spring-flowering corm with wineglass-shaped yellow flowers – the only yellow *Colchicum* known. Semi-erect, basal leaves are short at flowering time but later expand. H 2–4in (5–10cm), S 2–3in (5–8cm).

(!) Z4–9 H9–1

Erythronium americanum
Spring-flowering tuber with 2 semi-erect, basal leaves mottled green and brown, and a pendent yellow flower, often bronze outside, with petals reflexing in sunlight. Forms clumps by stolons. H 2–10in (5–25cm), S 2–3in (5–8cm).

Z3–9 H9–1

Fritillaria pudica
(Yellow fritillary)
Spring-flowering bulb with stems bearing scattered, narrowly lance-shaped, gray-green leaves. Has 1 or 2 deep yellow, sometimes red-tinged flowers, ½–1in (1–2.5cm) long. H 2–8in (5–20cm), S 2in (5cm).

Z2–9 H9–1

Dipcadi serotinum
Spring-flowering bulb with 2–5 very narrow, semi-erect, basal leaves. Leafless stem has a loose spike of nodding, tubular brown or dull orange flowers, ½–⅝in (1–1.5cm) long. H 4–12in (10–30cm), S 2–3in (5–8cm).

Z8–10 H10–8

Albuca canadensis
CROCUSES, illus. pp.428–9
Eranthis hyemalis, illus. p.441
Erythronium grandiflorum
Fritillaria pallidiflora, illus. p.415
Gagea peduncularis
HYACINTHS, illus. p.431
TULIPS, illus. pp.410–12
CROCUSES, illus. pp.428–9
Sparaxis elegans
TULIPS, illus. pp.410–12

WHITE–PINK

Lloydia serotina
Early summer-flowering bulb with wiry stems bearing scattered, threadlike, semi-erect leaves near the stem base. Carries 1 or 2 bell-shaped white flowers, ½–⅝in (1–1.5cm) long, with purple or purple-red veins. H 2–6in (5–15cm), S 1–2in (2.5–5cm).

Z6–9 H9–6

Arisaema candidissimum
Early summer-flowering tuber with large, cowl-like, pink-striped white spathes, enclosing tiny, fragrant flowers on spadices, followed by broad, 3-palmate, semi-erect leaves, 12in (30cm) long. H 4–6in (10–15cm), S 12–18in (30–45cm).

Z7–9 H9–7

Albuca humilis
Summer-flowering, dwarf bulb with very narrow, basal, dark green leaves. Carries a loose head of 1–3 cup-shaped white flowers, ½in (1cm) long, striped green, later reddish, outside. H 2–4in (5–10cm), S 2–3in (5–8cm).

Z11–12 H12–10

Allium schoenoprasum (Chives)
Clump-forming, summer-flowering bulb with narrow, hollow, erect, dark green leaves at base. Stems each carry up to 20 tiny, bell-shaped, pale purple or pink flowers in a dense umbel up to 2in (5cm) across. H 5–10in (12–25cm), S 2–4in (5–10cm).

Z5–11 H9–1

Cyclamen purpurascens,
syn. *C. europaeum, C. fatrense*
Summer- and autumn-flowering tuber with rounded, silver-patterned leaves. Bears very fragrant, lilac-pink to reddish purple flowers. H to 4in (10cm), S 4–6in (10–15cm).

Z5–9 H9–4

RED

Hippeastrum striatum,
syn. *H. rutilum*
Spring- and summer-flowering bulb with strap-shaped, semi-erect, basal, bright green leaves. Funnel-shaped flowers have pointed scarlet petals with central green stripes. H 12in (30cm), S 8–10in (20–25cm).

Z14–15 H12–10

Cyrtanthus brachyscyphus
Clump-forming, summer-flowering bulb with strap-shaped, semi-erect, basal, bright green leaves. Leafless stem bears a head of 6–12 tubular orange or brilliant red flowers with 6 lobes. H 8–12in (20–30cm), S 4–6in (10–15cm).

Z12–15 H12–10

Haemanthus coccineus (Blood lily)
Summer-flowering bulb with 2 elliptic leaves, hairy beneath, that lie flat on the ground. Spotted stem, forming before leaves, bears a cluster of tiny red flowers with prominent stamens within fleshy red or pink bracts. H to 12in (30cm), S 8–12in (20–30cm).

Z13–15 H12–10

OTHER RECOMMENDED PLANTS:
Allium campanulatum
Allium oreophilum, illus. p.430
Caloscordum neriniflorum
Habranthus robustus, illus. p.437
Triteleia peduncularis
Zephyranthes atamasco

Anomatheca laxa
BEGONIAS, illus. p.295
Habranthus tubispathus

PURPLE

Allium narcissiflorum, syn. *A. pedemontanum* of gardens
Clump-forming, summer-flowering bulb with very narrow, erect, gray-green leaves on the lower part of the flower stem. Has an umbel of up to 15 bell-shaped, pinkish purple flowers. H 6–12in (15–30cm), S 3–4in (8–10cm).

Z5–8 H8–5

Allium cyathophorum* var. *farreri
Clump-forming, summer-flowering bulb with tufts of narrow, erect, basal leaves. Each stem bears a small, loose umbel, ⅝–1½in (1.5–4cm) wide, of up to 30 bell-shaped, dark reddish purple flowers with sharply pointed petals. H 6–12in (15–30cm), S 4–6in (10–15cm).

Z4–9 H9–1

Roscoea humeana
Summer-flowering tuber. Erect, broadly lance-shaped, rich green leaves form a stemlike sheath at base. Carries up to 10 long-tubed purple flowers, each with a hooded, upper petal, a wide, pendent lip, and 2 narrower petals. H 6–10in (15–25cm), S 6–8in (15–20cm).

Z7–9 H9–7

Allium cristophii, illus. p.421
Biarum tenuifolium, illus. p.439
Ledebouria cooperi
Scilla litardierei
Triteleia laxa, illus. p.422

BLUE–YELLOW

Scilla peruviana
Early summer-flowering bulb with a basal cluster of up to 10 lance-shaped, semi-erect leaves. Stem bears a broadly conical head of up to 50 flattish, violet-blue flowers, ⅝–1¼in (1.5–3cm) across. H 4–10in (10–25cm), S 6–8in (15–20cm).

Z8–9 H9–8

Chlidanthus fragrans
Summer-flowering bulb with narrow, semi-erect leaves in a basal tuft. Leafless stem carries a head of 3–5 fragrant, funnel-shaped,yellow flowers, 1½–2¾in (4–7cm) long. H 4–12in (10–30cm), S 3–4in (8–10cm).

Z12–15 H12–7

Roscoea cautleyoides
Summer-flowering tuber. Erect, lance-shaped leaves form a stemlike sheath at the base. Has up to 5 long-tubed yellow flowers, each with a hooded, upper petal, a broad, 2-lobed, lower lip, and 2 narrower petals. H 6–10in (15–25cm), S 4–6in (10–15cm).

Z6–9 H9–6

Allium moly
Clump-forming, summer-flowering bulb with 1–3 broad, semi-erect, basal, gray-green leaves. Stems each bear up to 40 star-shaped yellow flowers in a fairly dense umbel, 1½–3in (4–8cm) across. H 4–14in (10–35cm), S 4–5in (10–12cm).

Z3–9 H9–1

Calochortus monophyllus
Summer-flowering bulb with an erect, branched stem with 1–3 slender leaves and one long, narrow basal leaf. Bears cup-shaped, deep yellow flowers, often with a reddish mark on the claws. Petals are fringed and densely bearded. H 3–8in (8–20cm), S 2in (5cm).

Z6–10 H10–6

Hypoxis angustifolia
Summer-flowering corm with slender, hairy, semi-erect, basal leaves. Stems each carry 3–7 star-shaped yellow flowers, ⅝–¾in (1.5–2cm) across. H 4–8in (10–20cm), S 2–3in (5–8cm).

Z11–14 H12–8

Allium cyaneum
Allium flavum
Allium sikkimense
BEGONIAS, illus. p.295
Pinellia ternata
Romulea macowanii var. *alticola*

☐ WHITE

Cyclamen hederifolium* f. *albiflorum
Autumn-flowering tuber. Pure white flowers with reflexed petals appear before or with variable leaves that are often ivy-shaped with silvery green patterns. H to 4in (10cm), S 4–6in (10–15cm).

Z8–9 H9–7

***Colchicum speciosum* 'Album'**
Vigorous, autumn-flowering corm with large, semi-erect, basal leaves in late winter or spring. Cup-shaped white flowers withstand bad weather. H and S 6–8in (15–20cm).

Z4–9 H9–1

Leucojum autumnale
(Autumn snowflake)
Autumn-flowering bulb with thread-like, erect, basal leaves appearing with or just after the flowers. Slender stems produce a head of up to 14 bell-shaped white flowers tinged pink at bases. H 4–6in (10–15cm), S 1–2in (2.5–5cm).

Z5–9 H9–1

OTHER RECOMMENDED PLANTS:
Colchicum autumnale 'Alboplenum'
Cyclamen cyprium
Galanthus reginae-olgae

 WHITE–PINK

Zephyranthes candida
Autumn-flowering bulb with narrow, erect, basal leaves forming tufts. Each leafless stem carries crocuslike white flowers to 2½in (6cm) across. H 6–10in (15–25cm), S 2–3in (5–8cm).

Z7–9 H9–6

Habranthus robustus
Late summer- to early autumn-flowering bulb with narrowly strap-shaped, semi-erect, basal leaves. Leafless flower stems each bear a funnel-shaped pink flower. H 8–12in (20–30cm), S 3–4in (8–10cm).

Z7–10 H10–7

Cyclamen africanum
Autumn-flowering tuber with ivy-shaped, deep green leaves with lighter patterns. Bears pendent white or pink flowers with reflexed petals and darker stains around mouths as or just before leaves appear. H to 4in (10cm), S 4–6in (10–15cm).

Z8–9 H9–8

Colchicum autumnale
(Autumn crocus, Meadow saffron)
Autumn-flowering corm with up to 8 long-tubed, wineglass-shaped purple, pink, or white flowers, followed by 3–5 large, strap-shaped, semi-erect, basal, glossy leaves in spring. H and S 4–6in (10–15cm).

Z4–9 H9–1

Cyclamen mirabile
Autumn-flowering tuber with pale pink flowers with toothed petals and dark purple-stained mouths. Heart-shaped, patterned leaves, purplish green beneath, are minutely toothed on margins. H to 4in (10cm), S 2–3in (5–8cm).

Z8–9 H9–8

Colchicum byzantinum
Robust, autumn-flowering corm with up to 20 large, funnel-shaped, pale purplish pink flowers, 4–6in (10–15cm) long. In spring produces very broad, semi-erect, basal leaves ribbed lengthwise. H and S 6–8in (15–20cm).

Z4–9 H9–1

Allium mairei
Leucojum roseum

PINK

Cyclamen graecum
Autumn-flowering tuber with heart-shaped, toothed, velvety, dark green leaves patterned silver or light green. Flowers are pink or white with purple stains around mouths. Grows best in an alpine house. H to 4in (10cm), S 4–6in (10–15cm).

Z5–9 H9–5

Cyclamen rohlfsianum
Autumn-flowering tuber with coarsely toothed leaves zoned with light and dark green patterns, and pale pink-lilac flowers stained darker at mouths. H to 4in (10cm), S 4–6in (10–15cm).

Z8–9 H9–8

Cyclamen cilicium
Autumn-flowering tuber with broadly heart-shaped leaves that have light and dark green zones. Has white or pink flowers, each with a dark purple stain at the mouth, just before or with leaves. H to 4in (10cm), S 2–4in (5–10cm).

Z5–9 H9–3

Colchicum cilicicum
Autumn-flowering corm with large, cup-shaped, pale pink to deep rose-purple flowers, sometimes slightly checkered. Very broad, semi-erect, basal leaves, ribbed lengthwise, appear soon after flowers have faded. H and S 6–8in (15–20cm).

Z4–9 H9–5

Cyclamen hederifolium,
syn. *C. neapolitanum*
Autumn-flowering tuber. Pale to deep pink flowers, stained darker at mouths, appear before or with foliage. Leaves vary but are often ivy-shaped with silvery green patterns. H to 4in (10cm), S 4–6in (10–15cm).

Z5–7 H9–7

Colchicum bivonae,
syn. *C. bowlesianum*, *C. sibthorpii*
Autumn-flowering corm with large, funnel-shaped, pinkish purple flowers, strongly checkered darker purple and with purple anthers. Produces 8–10 erect leaves in spring. H 4–6in (10–15cm), S 6–8in (15–20cm).

Z4–9 H9–1

PINK–PURPLE

Colchicum agrippinum
Early autumn-flowering corm. Narrow, slightly waved, semi-erect, basal leaves develop in spring. Bears erect, funnel-shaped, bright purplish pink flowers with a darker checkered pattern and pointed petals. H 4–6in (10–15cm), S 3–4in (8–10cm).

Z4–9 H9–1

***Colchicum* 'Waterlily'**
Autumn-flowering corm with rather broad, semi-erect, basal leaves in winter or spring. Tightly double flowers have 20–40 pinkish lilac petals. H 4–6in (10–15cm), S 6–8in (15–20cm).

Z4–9 H9–1

***Merendera montana*,**
syn. *M. bulbocodium*
Autumn-flowering corm with narrowly strap-shaped, semi-erect, basal leaves, produced just after upright, broad-petaled, funnel-shaped, rose- or purple-lilac flowers appear. H to 2in (5cm), S 2–3in (5–8cm).

Z6–9 H9–6

Biarum eximium
Colchicum 'The Giant'
CROCUSES, illus. pp.428–9
Cyclamen purpurascens, illus. p.435

PURPLE–YELLOW

Biarum tenuifolium
Late summer- or autumn-flowering tuber producing clusters of acrid, narrow, erect, basal leaves after stemless, upright and often twisted, blackish purple spathes appear. H to 8in (20cm), S 3–4in (8–10cm).

Z7–9 H9–7

Arum pictum
Autumn-flowering tuber. Arrow-shaped, semi-erect, glossy leaves with cream veins appear at the same time as a cowl-like, deep purple-brown spathe and dark purple spadix. H 6–10in (15–25cm), S 6–8in (15–20cm).

Z6–9 H9–6

Sternbergia lutea
Autumn-flowering bulb with strap-shaped, semi-erect, basal, deep green leaves appearing together with a funnel-shaped, bright yellow flower, 1–2½in (2.5–6cm) long, on a leafless stem. H 1–6in (2.5–15cm), S 3–4in (8–10cm).

Z7–9 H9–6

CROCUSES, illus. pp.428–9
Sternbergia clusiana
Sternbergia sicula
Zephyranthes citrina

WHITE

***Galanthus nivalis* 'Flore Pleno'**
(Double common snowdrop)
Late winter- and early spring-flowering bulb with semi-erect, basal, gray-green leaves. Bears rosetted, many-petaled, double white flowers, some inner petals having a green mark at the apex. H 4–6in (10–15cm), S 2–3in (5–8cm).

Z3–9 H9–1

***Galanthus nivalis* 'Pusey Green Tip'**
Late winter- and early spring-flowering bulb with narrowly strap-shaped, semi-erect, basal, gray-green leaves. Each stem bears a white flower with many mostly green-tipped petals. H 4–6in (10–15cm), S 2–3in (5–8cm).

Z3–9 H9–1

Galanthus gracilis
Late winter- and early spring-flowering bulb with slightly twisted, strap-shaped, semi-erect, basal, gray-green leaves. Bears white flowers with 3 inner petals, each marked with a green blotch at the apex and base. H 4–6in (10–15cm), S 2–3in (5–8cm).

Z3–9 H9–1

Galanthus rizehensis
Late winter- and early spring-flowering bulb with very narrow, strap-shaped, semi-erect, basal, dark green leaves. Produces white flowers, ⅝–¾in (1.5–2cm) long, with a green patch at the apex of each inner petal. H 4–8in (10–20cm), S 2in (5cm).

Z3–9 H9–1

Galanthus elwesii
Late winter- and early spring-flowering bulb with semi-erect, basal, gray-green leaves that widen gradually toward tips. Each inner petal of the white flowers bears green marks at the apex and base, which may merge. H 4–12in (10–30cm), S 2–3in (5–8cm).

Z3–8 H8–1

***Galanthus* 'Atkinsii'**
Vigorous, late winter- and early spring-flowering bulb with strap-shaped, semi-erect, basal, gray-green leaves. Each stem carries a slender white flower with a green mark at the apex of each inner petal. H 4–10in (10–25cm), S 2–3½in (5–9cm).

Z3–9 H9–1

OTHER RECOMMENDED PLANTS:
Galanthus nivalis
Galanthus plicatus subsp. *plicatus*

WHITE

***Galanthus nivalis* 'Sandersii'**, syn. *G.n.* 'Lutescens'
Late winter- and early spring-flowering bulb with narrowly strap-shaped, semi-erect, basal, gray-green leaves. Flowers, ⅝–¾in (1.5–2cm) long, are white with yellow patches at the apex of each inner petal. H 4in (10cm), S 1–2in (2.5–5cm).

Z3–9 H9–1

Galanthus ikariae
Late winter- and early spring-flowering bulb with strap-shaped, semi-erect, basal, glossy, bright green leaves. Produces one white flower, ⅝–1in (1.5–2.5cm) long, marked with a green patch at the apex of each inner petal. H 4–10in (10–25cm), S 2–3in (5–8cm).

Z3–9 H9–1

***Galanthus nivalis* 'Scharlockii'**
Vigorous, late winter- and early spring-flowering bulb with semi-erect, basal, gray-green leaves. Has white flowers with green marks at the apex of inner petals, topped by 2 narrow spathes that resemble donkeys' ears. H 4–6in (10–15cm), S 2–3in (5–8cm).

Z3–9 H9–1

Galanthus plicatus* subsp. *byzantinus
Late winter- and early spring-flowering bulb. Semi-erect, basal, deep green leaves have a gray bloom and reflexed margins. White flowers have green marks at bases and tips of inner petals. H 4–8in (10–20cm), S 2–3in (5–8cm).

Z3–9 H9–1

Cyclamen coum* f. *albissimum, syn. *C.c.* 'Album'
Winter-flowering tuber with rounded, deep green leaves, sometimes silver-patterned. Carries white flowers, each with a maroon mark at the mouth. H to 4in (10cm), S 2–4in (5–10cm).

Z5–9 H9–5

PINK

Cyclamen persicum
Winter- or spring-flowering tuber with heart-shaped leaves marked light and dark green and silver. Bears fragrant, slender white or pink flowers, 1¼–1½in (3–4cm) long and stained carmine at mouths. H 4–8in (10–20cm), S 4–6in (10–15cm).

Z13–15 H6–1

***Cyclamen persicum* 'Pearl Wave'**
Winter- and spring-flowering tuber with heart-shaped leaves marked light and dark green and silver. Produces fragrant, slender, deep pink flowers, with 2–2½in (5–6cm) long, frilly-edged petals. H 4–8in (10–20cm), S 4–6in (10–15cm).

Z13–15 H6–1

Cyclamen coum
Winter-flowering tuber with rounded leaves, plain deep green or silver-patterned. Produces bright carmine flowers with dark stains at mouths. H to 4in (10cm), S 2–4in (5–10cm).

Z5–9 H9–5

Cyclamen coum subsp. *caucasicum*
HYACINTHS, illus. p.431

RED

***Cyclamen persicum* 'Esmeralda'**
Winter-flowering tuber with heart-shaped, silver-patterned leaves and broad-petaled, carmine-red flowers.
H 4–8in (10–20cm), S 6–8in (15–20cm).

Z13–15 H6–1

***Cyclamen persicum* 'Renown'**
Winter- and spring-flowering tuber with heart-shaped, bright silver-green leaves, each with a central, dark green mark. Carries fragrant, slender scarlet flowers, 2–2½in (5–6cm) long.
H 4–8in (10–20cm), S 4–6in (10–15cm).

Z13–15 H6–1

***Cyclamen persicum* Kaori Series**
Winter-flowering tuber with neat, heart-shaped, silver-marbled leaves. Produces fragrant flowers, 1½in (4cm) long, in a wide range of colors.
H 4–8in (10–20cm),
S 4–6in (10–15cm).

Z13–15 H6–1

HYACINTHS, illus. p.431
Lachenalia aloides
Lachenalia rubida

YELLOW

Lachenalia aloides
var. *quadricolor*
Winter- to spring-flowering bulb with 2 strap-shaped, semi-erect, basal leaves. Has a spike of 10–20 purplish red buds opening to greenish yellow or orange flowers. H 6–10in (15–25cm), S 2–3in (5–8cm).

Z12–14 H12–6

***Lachenalia aloides* 'Nelsonii',**
syn. *L.* 'Nelsonii'
Winter- to spring-flowering bulb. Has 2 strap-shaped, purple-spotted, semi-erect, basal leaves and a spike of 10–20 pendent, tubular, green-tinted, bright yellow flowers, (1¼in) 3cm long.
H 6–10in (15–25cm), S 2–3in (5–8cm).

Z12–14 H12–6

Eranthis hyemalis
(Winter aconite)
Clump-forming tuber. Bears stalkless, cup-shaped yellow flowers, ¾–1in (2–2.5cm) across, from late winter to early spring. A dissected, leaflike bract forms a ruff beneath each bloom.
H 2–4in (5–10cm), S 3–4in (8–10cm).

Z4–9 H9–1

Eranthis x *tubergenii* 'Guinea Gold'
HYACINTHS, illus. p.431

Water Plants

Many water plants are extremely attractive in their own right; others have the additional benefit of keeping the water clean and healthy. This wide-ranging group of plants will do well in all kinds of water feature, from the constantly moist bog garden to the small ornamental barrel and deep-water pond.

Water Plants

The sound-producing and light-reflecting qualities of water have long been used to bring vitality to garden designs. For many, still or moving water is the soul of the garden, and it also greatly extends the range of plants that can be grown.

What are water plants?
The broad definition of water plants includes all plants that grow rooted, submerged, or floating in water. They may be further subdivided into deep-water, surface-floating, marginal, bog, or moisture-loving plants, depending on the depth of water that is required for them to thrive.

Why cultivate water plants?
Water plants differ from other plant groups in that they are seldom grown for ornament alone. Nearly all are important for the creation of the healthy ecosystem that is essential if you wish to maintain a water feature's beauty. To do this you need to introduce a balanced range of water plants to regulate the light, oxygen, and nutrient levels, thus producing conditions in which plants and animals alike can thrive.

Submerged plants, such as water milfoil (*Myriophyllum*), act as "oxygenators," providing the dissolved oxygen that is vital for all pond life. They also remove excess nutrients from the water and help keep it clear by controlling algal growth, which causes cloudy, green water and blocks out the light necessary for healthy aquatic plant and pond life. Surface-floaters, such as the fairy moss (*Azolla filiculoides*) or water hyacinth (*Eichhornia crassipes*), also reduce dissolved nutrients by absorbing them through their slender roots. Apart from being very attractive in themselves, deep-water plants, such as *Nuphar* and waterlilies (*Nymphaea*), with their roots at the pond bottom and flowers and foliage floating at the surface, provide shelter for pond life and also shade out algal growth.

Ornamental water features
Whether tiny or large, formal or informal, every garden has room for a water feature and its associated plants. In restricted spaces, aquatics such as the dwarf waterlily *Nymphaea tetragona* 'Helvola' or slender water irises (*Iris laevigata*) can be grown, while in larger

Formal feature
Above: This formal, split-level pool not only makes an elegant focal point within the garden, but it also cleverly provides different water depths to accommodate the needs of various types of water plant, from deep-water perennials like waterlilies to the shallow-water marginals such as Houttuynia cordata.

Marginal planting
Below: The curving edges of an informal pond offer perfect conditions for marginals, such as pickerel weed (Pontederia cordata) *and arrowhead* (Sagittaria latifolia), *which root in water up to 6in (15cm) deep. Marginals disguise and soften pool edges and provide invaluable shelter for wildlife.*

areas *Typha latifolia* will look effective. In a sunken or raised formal pool, using those plants with an architectural outline, such as *Pontederia cordata* or *Zantedeschia aethiopica*, can provide an elegant focal point and emphasize the formal style. The advantage of an informal pond is that it offers great versatility: its sinuous margins are longer than straight-sided ponds of similar size, and its sloping banks can provide a range of planting depths, greatly increasing your choice of marginal plants. With its sloping and possibly boggy banks, it is also much easier to attract wildlife into the garden. This lends an extra dimension of interest and also benefits both gardener and plants, because many amphibians, birds, and small mammals actively prey on garden pests.

Waterlilies
Waterlilies (Nymphaea), *which need still water to thrive, perform a dual function: they are incomparably ornamental, and their floating leaves shade out algal growth and provide shelter for fish and their fry.*

Designing with water plants

A water feature should be designed following the same principles that apply to other plant groups, using contrasting and complementary colors, textures, and forms. Water plants can offer a wide succession of interest if you choose those that provide diversity in foliage, flower color and shape, and seed heads.

To accommodate a range of water plants, however, it is essential to provide differing depths of water. Deep-water plants, such as Cape pondweed (*Aponogeton distachyos*), with its very fragrant white flowers at the water surface, and the floating water soldier (*Stratiotes aloides*), with its spiky, aloe-like leaves, require a depth of about 3ft (1m). Waterlilies (*Nymphaea*), with their pristine flowers in colors ranging from pure white to deepest red, need to root at depths of ½–3ft (15–100cm), depending on the species or cultivar.

Marginal plants, which thrive in conditions ranging from pure mud to water that is 1–1½ft (30–45cm) deep, are the most diverse of aquatics. They are invaluable for disguising edges of artificial and natural ponds, for creating interesting reflections, and for providing wildlife cover. Marginals have a range of habits: from bog bean (*Menyanthes trifoliata*), with its dainty clusters of white flowers in spring and glossy leaves that spill out across the water surface, to the flowering rush (*Butomus umbellatus*), with its upright stems bearing umbels of small pink flowers, and the substantial skunk cabbages (*Lysichiton*), with their large calla lily-like blooms and handsome foliage.

In a bog garden, constantly moist to saturated soil provides perfect conditions for many bog natives and moisture-lovers, including the robust candelabra primroses, the globeflower (*Trollius europaeus*), with its deeply divided foliage, and the elegant ostrich fern, *Matteuccia struthiopteris*.

Streamside planting
Above right: The damp soil of a stream bank makes an ideal home for moisture-loving perennials like the candelabra primroses, while water crowfoot (Ranunculus aquatilis), *which thrives in fast-moving water, is a good choice for planting in the stream bed.*

Contrasting foliage
Right: A lush profusion of foliage makes a strong design statement if plants of contrasting form are set side by side. Here, the horizontal, flat shapes of waterlilies bring into high relief the vertical heart-shaped foliage of pickerel weed.

□ WHITE

Menyanthes trifoliata
(Bog bean, Buckbean)
Deciduous, perennial, marginal water plant that has 3-parted, midgreen leaves and fringed white flowers borne in spring. H 9in (23cm), S 12in (30cm).

☼ ● Z4–8 H8–1

Alisma plantago-aquatica
(Water plantain)
Deciduous, perennial, marginal water plant with upright, oval, bright green leaves that emerge well above the water. Loose, conical panicles of small pinkish to white flowers appear in summer. H 30in (75cm), S 18in (45cm).

☼ ● Z5–8 H8–5

Lysichiton camtschatcensis
(White skunk cabbage)
Vigorous, deciduous, perennial, marginal water or bog plant. Pure white spathes surrounding spikes of insignificant, small flowers are borne in spring before oblong to oval, bright green leaves emerge. H 30in (75cm), S 24in (60cm).

☼ ● Z5–9 H9–1

Hydrocharis morsus-ranae
(Frogbit)
Deciduous, perennial, floating water plant with rosettes of kidney-shaped, olive green leaves and small white flowers during summer. S 4in (10cm), but young plantlets remain attached to form a mass up to 3ft (1m) across.

☼ ● Z6–11 H12–7

Calla palustris (Bog arum)
Deciduous or semi-evergreen, perennial, spreading, marginal water plant with heart-shaped, glossy, mid- to dark green leaves. In spring it produces large white spathes, usually followed by red or orange fruits. H 10in (25cm), S 12in (30cm).

☼ ● ⓘ Z4–8 H8–1

Sagittaria latifolia
(Duck potato)
Deciduous, perennial, marginal water plant with curved, soft green leaves and sprays of white flowers in summer. H 5ft (1.5m), S 2ft (60cm).

☼ ● Z5–11 H12–5

OTHER RECOMMENDED PLANTS:
Luronium natans
Nelumbo nucifera 'Alba Grandiflora'
Sagittaria sagittifolia
Sagittaria sagittifolia 'Flore Pleno'
WATERLILIES, illus. p.450

Saururus cernuus (Lizard's tail, Swamp lily, Water dragon)
Deciduous, perennial, marginal water or bog plant. Has clumps of heart-shaped, midgreen leaves and racemes of creamy flowers in summer.
H 9in (23cm), S 12in (30cm).

Z5–11 H12–5

Hottonia palustris (Water violet)
Deciduous, perennial, submerged water plant. Dense whorls of much-divided, light green leaves form a spreading mass of foliage. Lilac or whitish flowers appear above water surface in summer. S indefinite.

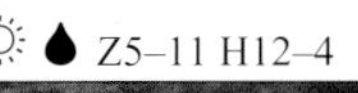

Z5–11 H12–4

***Acorus gramineus* 'Variegatus'**
Semi-evergreen, perennial, marginal or submerged water plant. Narrow, stiff, grasslike leaves are dark green with cream variegation.
H 10in (25cm), S 6in (15cm).

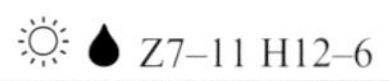

Z7–11 H12–6

Stratiotes aloides (Water soldier)
Semi-evergreen, perennial, submerged, free-floating water plant. Spiny, olive green leaves are arranged in rosettes. Produces cup-shaped white, sometimes pink-tinged flowers in summer. Increases by producing small buds that can be detached. S 12in (30cm).

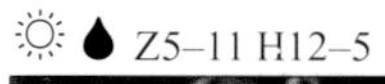

Z5–11 H12–5

Aponogeton distachyos
(Cape pondweed, Water hawthorn)
Deciduous, perennial, deep-water plant with floating, oblong, mid- to dark green leaves, often splashed with purple. Very fragrant, forked white flowers with black stamens are produced throughout summer. S 4ft (1.2m).

Z9–10 H12–10

***Acorus calamus* 'Argenteostriatus'**, syn. *A.c.* 'Variegatus'
Semi-evergreen, perennial, marginal water plant. Swordlike, tangerine-scented, midgreen leaves have cream variegation and are flushed rose-pink in spring.
H 30in (75cm), S 24in (60cm).

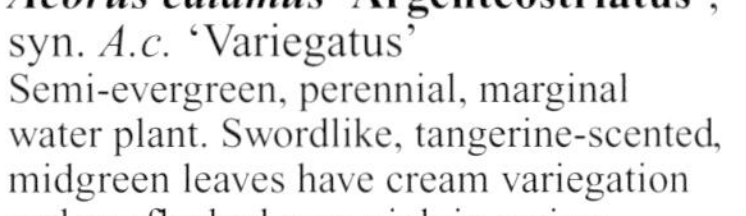

Z10–11 H12–2

***Houttuynia cordata* 'Chameleon'**, syn. *H.c.* 'Variegata'
Vigorous, deciduous, perennial, ground-cover, marginal water plant. Aromatic, leathery leaves are splashed yellow and red. Has small sprays of white flowers in summer. Needs some sun to enhance variegation. H 4in (10cm), S indefinite.

Z5–11 H12–1

Caltha leptosepala
(Alpine marsh marigold)
Deciduous, perennial, marginal water plant with heart-shaped, dark green leaves and buttercup-like white flowers produced in spring.
H and S 12in (30cm).

Z5–8 H8–5

Nelumbo nucifera (Sacred lotus)
Vigorous, deciduous, perennial, marginal water plant. Sturdy stems carry very large, platelike, blue-green leaves and, in summer, large, vivid rose-pink flowers maturing to flesh pink. H 3–5ft (1–1.5m) above water surface, S 4ft (1.2m).

Z4–11 H12–3

Nelumbo nucifera 'Alba Striata'
Nelumbo nucifera 'Rosea Plena'
WATERLILIES, illus. p.450

PINK–BLUE

Butomus umbellatus
(Flowering rush)
Deciduous, perennial, rushlike, marginal water plant with narrow, twisted, midgreen leaves and umbels of pink to rose-red flowers in summer. H 3ft (1m), S 1½ft (45cm).

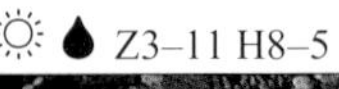
Z3–11 H8–5

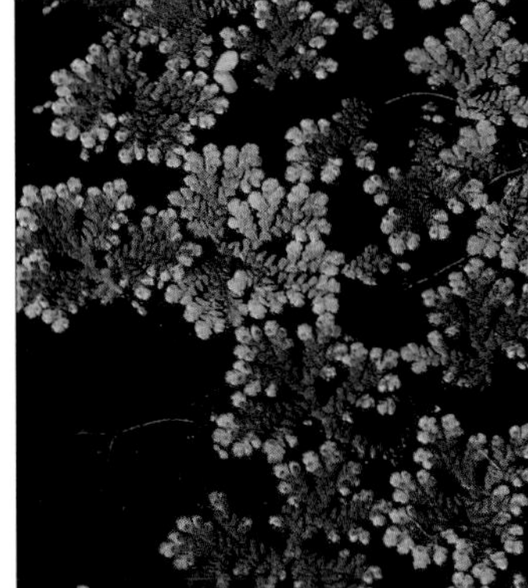

Azolla filiculoides,
syn. *A. caroliniana*
(Fairy moss, Water fern)
Deciduous, perennial, floating water fern with divided fronds that vary from red to purple in full sun and from pale green to blue-green in shade. Helps reduce algae. S indefinite.

Z7–11 H12–1

Pontederia cordata
(Pickerel weed)
Deciduous, perennial, marginal water plant. In late summer, dense spikes of blue flowers emerge between lance-shaped, glossy, dark green leaves. H 30in (75cm), S 18in (45cm).

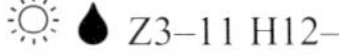
Z3–11 H12–1

Colocasia esculenta 'Illustris'
Cryptocoryne spiralis
Thalia dealbata
Thalia geniculata

WATERLILIES, illus. p.450

BLUE–GREEN

***Myosotis scorpioides* 'Mermaid'**
Deciduous, perennial, marginal water plant for mud or very shallow water. Narrow, midgreen leaves form sprawling mounds. Bears small blue forget-me-not flowers throughout summer. H 6in (15cm), S 12in (30cm).

Z5–9 H9–5

Typha latifolia (Cattail)
Deciduous, perennial, marginal water plant with large clumps of midgreen foliage. Produces spikes of beige flowers in late summer, followed by decorative, cylindrical, dark brown seed heads. Is invasive.
H to 8ft (2.5m), S 2ft (60cm).

Z2–11 H12–1

Eichhornia crassipes,
syn. *E. speciosa* (Water hyacinth)
Evergreen or semi-evergreen, perennial water plant with glossy leaves, floating on air-filled leaf stalks. Bears spikes of blue-and-lilac flowers in summer. Is invasive in warmer areas.
H and S 9in (23cm).

Z9–11 H12–1

Myriophyllum aquaticum,
syn. *M. proserpinacoides*
(Parrot feather)
Deciduous, perennial, partially or completely submerged water plant. Spreading, finely divided, blue-green foliage turns reddish in autumn if it surfaces. S indefinite.

Z6–11 H12–6

Colocasia esculenta (Taro)
Deciduous, perennial, marginal water plant with large, bold, mid- to dark green leaves, often with prominent white veins. Bears insignificant spathes in summer. May be grown in wet soil in a pot. H 3½ft (1.1m), S 2ft (60cm).

Z10–11 H12–4

Potamogeton crispus
(Curled pondweed)
Deciduous, perennial, submerged water plant that produces spreading colonies of seaweedlike bronze- or midgreen foliage. Insignificant reddish flowers are borne in summer. Prefers cool water. S indefinite.

Z7–11 H12–7

WATERLILIES, illus. p.450

GREEN

Pistia stratiotes (Water lettuce)
Deciduous, perennial, floating water plant for a pool or aquarium, evergreen in tropical conditions. Hairy, soft green foliage is lettucelike in arrangement. Produces tiny greenish flowers at varying times. H and S 4in (10cm).

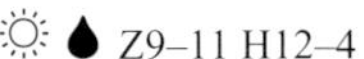 Z9–11 H12–4

Salvinia auriculata
Deciduous, perennial, floating water plant, evergreen in tropical conditions, that forms spreading colonies. Has rounded, pale to midgreen leaves, sometimes suffused purplish brown, in pairs on branching stems. S indefinite.

Z14–15 H12–1

Trapa natans
(Jesuit's nut, Water chestnut)
Annual, floating water plant with diamond-shaped, midgreen leaves, often marked purple, arranged in neat rosettes. Bears white flowers in summer. S 9in (23cm).

Z14–15 H12–1

Lagarosiphon major,
syn. *Elodea crispa* of gardens
Semi-evergreen, perennial, spreading, submerged water plant that forms dense, underwater swards of foliage. Ascending stems are covered in narrow, reflexed, dark green leaves. Bears insignificant flowers in summer. S indefinite.

Z8–11 H12–6

Typha minima (Dwarf cattail)
Deciduous, perennial, marginal water plant with grasslike leaves. Spikes of rust brown flowers in late summer are succeeded by decorative, cylindrical seed heads. H 18–24in (45–60cm), S 12in (30cm).

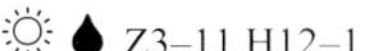 Z3–11 H12–1

Euryale ferox
Annual, deep-water plant. Has floating, rounded, spiny, olive green leaves with rich purple undersides and bears small, violet-purple flowers in summer. Suitable for a tropical pond.
S 5ft (1.5m).

Z12–15 H12–6

GREEN–YELLOW

Sparganium erectum, syn.
S. ramosum (Branched burr reed)
Vigorous, deciduous or semi-evergreen, perennial, marginal water plant with narrow, midgreen leaves. Bears small, greenish brown burrs in summer.
H 3ft (1m), S 2ft (60cm).

Z5–9 H9–5

Myriophyllum verticillatum
(Whorled water milfoil)
Deciduous, perennial, spreading, submerged water plant, overwintering by club-shaped winter buds. Slender stems are covered with whorls of finely divided, olive green leaves.
S indefinite.

Z3–11 H12–1

Hydrocleys nymphoides
(Water poppy)
Deciduous, perennial, deep-water plant, evergreen in tropical conditions, with floating, oval, midgreen leaves. Poppy-like yellow flowers are held above foliage during summer.
S to 2ft (60cm).

Z9–10 H10–7

Baldellia ranunculoides
Cabomba caroliniana
Ceratophyllum demersum
Colocasia esculenta 'Fontanesii'
Cryptocoryne ciliata
Egeria densa
Fontinalis antipyretica
Myriophyllum hippuroides
Salvinia natans
Sparganium natans
Vallisneria spiralis

Waterlilies

The serene beauty of a waterlily (*Nymphaea*) will add a focal point and color to any water garden. Neat, small-leaved plants will grow in only 3in (8cm) of water, but more vigorous plants may need up to 3ft (1m). Their large, platelike leaves provide shelter for fish and also reduce the spread of algae. Waterlilies make few demands, although they prefer an open, sunny site and still water.

N. **'Virginia'**

N. tetragona **'Alba'**

N. **'Gladstoneana'**

N. **Marliacea Group 'Albida'**

N. **'General Pershing'**

N. **'Rose Arey'**

N. **'American Star'**

N. **'Attraction'**

N. **'Firecrest'**

N. **'Froebelii'**

N. **'Escarboucle'**

N. **'Lucida'**

N. **'James Brydon'**

N. **Laydekeri Group 'Fulgens'**

N. **'Blue Beauty'**

N. tetragona **'Helvola'**

N. **Marliacea Group 'Chromatella'**

N. **'Sunrise'**

YELLOW

Lysichiton americanus, syn. *L. americanum*
(Yellow skunk cabbage)
Vigorous, deciduous, perennial, marginal or bog plant. Before large, fresh green leaves appear in spring, it produces showy, bright yellow spathes. H 3ft (1m), S 2½ft (75cm).

Z7–9 H9–7

***Caltha palustris* 'Flore Pleno'**
Deciduous, perennial, marginal water plant with rounded, dark green leaves. Bears clusters of double, bright golden yellow flowers in spring. H and S 10in (25cm).

 Z3–7 H7–1

Nymphoides peltata
(Fringed waterlily, Water fringe)
Deciduous, perennial, deep-water plant with floating, small, round, midgreen leaves, often spotted and splashed with brown. Produces small, fringed yellow flowers throughout summer. S 24in (60cm).

Z6–11 H12–6

Caltha palustris
(Kingcup, Marsh marigold)
Deciduous, perennial, marginal water plant that has rounded, dark green leaves and bears clusters of cup-shaped, bright golden yellow flowers in spring. H 24in (60cm), S 18in (45cm).

Z3–7 H7–1

Ranunculus lingua
(Greater spearwort)
Deciduous, perennial, marginal water plant with thick stems and lance-shaped glaucous leaves. Clusters of yellow flowers are borne in late spring. H 3ft (90cm), S 1½ft (45cm).

 Z4–9 H9–1

Nuphar lutea
(Spatterdock, Yellow pond lily)
Vigorous, deciduous, perennial, deep-water plant for a large pool. Midgreen leaves are leathery. Small, sickly-smelling, bottle-shaped yellow flowers open in summer and are followed by decorative seed heads. S 5ft (1.5m).

Z3–9 H9–1

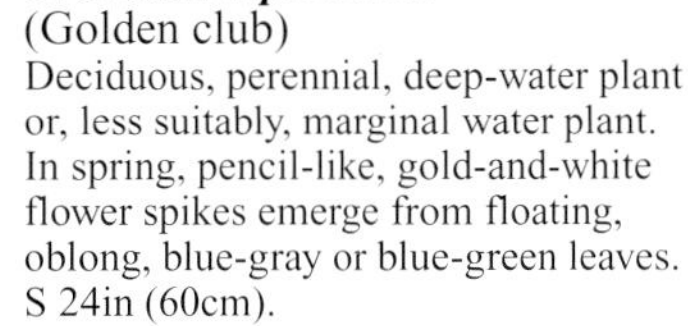

Orontium aquaticum
(Golden club)
Deciduous, perennial, deep-water plant or, less suitably, marginal water plant. In spring, pencil-like, gold-and-white flower spikes emerge from floating, oblong, blue-gray or blue-green leaves. S 24in (60cm).

 Z6–10 H10–4

Cotula coronopifolia
Nelumbo lutea
Nuphar advena
Ranunculus lingua 'Grandiflorus'
Utricularia gibba
Utricularia vulgaris

CACTI *and other* SUCCULENTS

CACTI AND OTHER SUCCULENTS are very adaptable and will grow in a range of extreme climates. These fascinating plants also offer the gardener great diversity of form, texture, and size and, while some flower constantly, others provide rare but spectacular flower displays, made all the more special by the wait.

Cacti and other Succulents

The world's harshest climates have imposed evolutionary pressures on the plant life that survives in them, and these have resulted in a group of plants unrivaled in the strangeness and diversity of their forms.

What are cacti and succulents?
Succulents are plants in which the leaves, stems, or roots have become adapted for water storage, enabling them to sustain life during seasons of drought. Cacti differ from other succulents in that they have areoles, which are cushion-like growths on their stems.

Since their leaves are primary sites of water loss, many succulents either drop them during periods of drought or do without them altogether. Their surfaces have also developed to conserve moisture and be protected from harsh light and extreme heat, ranging from the waxy, blue-gray-bloomed leaves of *Pachyphytum* and the leathery gasterias to the densely hairy *Oreocereus celsianus* or fiercely spiny *Echinocactus*. Spines, which are prized by gardeners as an ornamental feature, in fact protect plants from predators and also condense droplets of atmospheric moisture, which then fall onto the roots.

Choosing succulents
In order to grow succulents successfully, it is important to understand and imitate their natural environments as closely as possible. The most familiar cacti and other succulents are native to arid desert and semi-desert conditions, but some originate from cold, high-alpine habitats – the sempervivums for instance – while others, such as the epiphyllums, come from subtropical and tropical rainforests.

Displaying small succulents
Here, neat architectural forms of parodias and astrophytums provide strong contrasts with the more globose mammillarias.

Gardeners who live in frost-free, dry climates can therefore grow desert cacti and other succulents outside, in large, architectural compositions in a border. In such areas, rainfall is often highly seasonal, but when it does occur it stimulates spectacular floral displays.

In frost-free, humid regions, conditions are perfect for the rainforest cacti and other succulents such as *Selenicereus*, *Schlumbergera*, and *Epiphyllum*. These need a little shade and can be sited where they will cascade from the branches of a host tree. Meanwhile, their often nocturnal and sometimes highly fragrant flowers may scent the air over some distance.

In colder, frost-prone regions, tender species must be grown indoors or in a greenhouse or conservatory. Most need a minimum temperature of 50–59°F (10–15°C), while some tropical species require at least 68°F (20°C).

Borders in open ground or raised beds provide a home for hardier genera such as *Sempervivum*, *Jovibarba*, *Sedum*, and some of the euphorbias. Most require excellent drainage and grow well with true alpines, which have similar drainage, light, and moisture needs.

Designing with succulents
Succulent textures and shapes range from the tight cushions of fleshy, rosetted leaves of the echeverias to the spiny, cylindrical, branching desert cacti *Cereus* and *Cleistocactus* to the gracefully pendent, rainforest tree-clingers (epiphytes) *Rhipsalis* and *Schlumbergera*. There are also globose and ribbed forms, as in *Mammillaria*, *Haageocereus*, and the very small, pebble-like *Lithops*.

Such a distinctive range has many decorative uses. The majestic, highly sculptural globes, cylinders, and branching, candelabra-shaped types, for example, offer scope for exciting designs when contrasted with the basal-rosetted aloes, agaves, and yuccas, with their spiky leaves.

Hanging beauty
Left: Rainforest cacti such as Aporocactus *and epiphyllums and their hybrids often flower along the length of trailing stems. Here,* x Aporophyllum *'Sussex Pink' is shown to perfection in a hanging basket.*

Growing in containers
Most cacti and other succulents adapt successfully to container cultivation, and impressive displays can be created to decorate outdoor patios and terraces during the warmer months. In winter they will need a sunny windowsill or a greenhouse. The most important rule for effective compositions of different species in containers is to group plants of similar growth rates and

Glorious flowers
Above: The brilliant, hot shades of the summer-flowering Echinopsis *'Glorious', which are typical of many cactus flowers, add vibrant color to a display of sculptural forms.*

In a natural setting
*Left: In their native hot, dry climates, cacti and other succulents can be grouped to produce living sculpture gardens, as here, where the rosettes of agaves are used as a foil to the columns of the saguaro cactus (*Carnegiea gigantea*) and pad-forming opuntias.*

Greenhouse cultivation
Below: In cool temperate climates, most cacti and other succulents need protection from frost, cold, and excessive moisture, and some require shade. The greenhouse and the home provide the ideal conditions for the cultivation and display of their many and varied forms.

cultivation needs together, so that they will thrive without outgrowing their allotted space and overwhelming their companions.

Many cacti and other succulents, such as the jade tree (*Crassula ovata)*, *Aeonium arboreum*, and many agaves, make splendid specimens when grown alone in attractive containers. These, along with plants such as sansevierias, *Senecio rowleyanus*, or *Ceropegia linearis* subsp. *woodii*, are often so long-lived, easily propagated, and extraordinarily tolerant of neglect that specimens and their offspring have been passed from generation to generation between families and friends.

Be careful where you site cacti with spines, because they are capable of inflicting injury. They must be placed well away from eye-level and out of reach of children and pets.

Size categories used within this group		
Large	**Medium**	**Small**
over 3ft (1m)	9in–3ft (23cm–1m)	up to 9in (23cm)

□ WHITE

Selenicereus grandiflorus
(Queen-of-the-night)
Climbing cactus. Has 7-ribbed, ½–¾in (1–2cm) wide green stems with yellow spines. White flowers, 7–12in (18–30cm) across, open at night in summer. H 10ft (3m), S indefinite.

Z12–15 H12–7

Echinopsis lageniformis, syn. *E. bridgesii, Trichocereus bridgesii*
Columnar cactus with 4–8-ribbed stems branching at base. Areoles each produce up to 6 spines. Scented, funnel-shaped white flowers open at night in summer. H to 15ft (5m), S 3ft (1m).

Z14–15 H12–10

Cereus validus, syn. *C. forbesii*
Columnar cactus with a branching, blue-green stem bearing dark spines on 4–7 prominent ribs. Has 10in (25cm) long, cup-shaped white flowers at night in summer, followed by red fruits. H 22ft (7m), S 10ft (3m).

Z12–15 H12–10

Myrtillocactus geometrizans
(Blue candle)
Columnar cactus with a much-branched, 5- or 6-ribbed, blue-green stem. Bears short black spines on plants over 1ft (30cm) tall, and white flowers at night in summer. H to 12ft (4m), S 6ft (2m).

Z13–15 H12–10

Cereus uruguayansus
Columnar cactus. Has a branching, silvery blue stem with golden spines on 4–8 sharply indented ribs. Carries cup-shaped white flowers, 4in (10cm) across, at night in summer, followed by pear-shaped red fruits. H 15ft (5m), S 12ft (4m).

Z11 H12–10

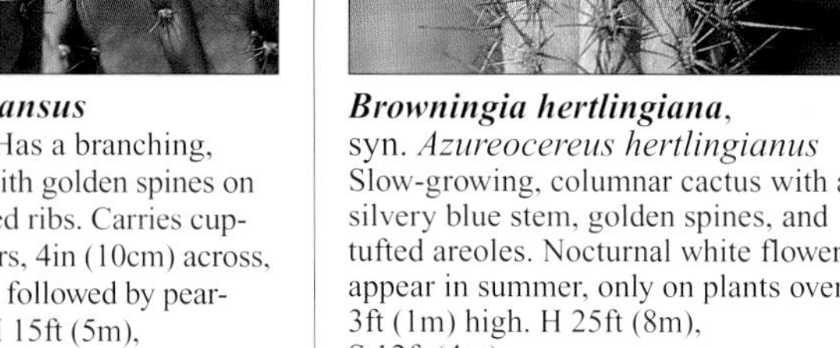

Browningia hertlingiana, syn. *Azureocereus hertlingianus*
Slow-growing, columnar cactus with a silvery blue stem, golden spines, and tufted areoles. Nocturnal white flowers appear in summer, only on plants over 3ft (1m) high. H 25ft (8m), S 12ft (4m).

Z12–15 H12–10

Pachypodium lamerei
Tree-like succulent with a spiny, pale green stem crowned by linear leaves. Has fragrant, trumpet-shaped, creamy white flowers in summer on plants over 5ft (1.5m) tall. Stems branch after each flowering. H 20ft (6m), S 6ft (2m).

Z13–15 H12–6

Carnegiea gigantea (Saguaro)
Very slow-growing cactus with a thick, 12–24-ribbed, spiny, green stem. Tends to branch and bears short, funnel-shaped, fleshy white flowers at stem tips in summer, only when over 12ft (4m) high. H to 40ft (12m), S 10ft (3m).

Z12–15 H12–10

OTHER RECOMMENDED PLANTS:
Agave americana
Echinopsis candicans, illus. p.461
Epiphyllum anguliger, illus. p.461
Lepismium warmingianum, illus. p.461
Rhipsalis floccosa, illus. p.461

Pachycereus marginatus
(Organ-pipe cactus)
Columnar cactus with a 5- or 6-ribbed, branching, shiny stem. Areoles bear minute spines. Produces funnel-shaped white flowers in summer. H 22ft (7m), S 10ft (3m).

Z13–15 H12–10

Agave parviflora
Basal-rosetted succulent. Has narrow, white-marked, dark green leaves with white fibers peeling from edges. Produces white flowers in summer. H 5ft (1.5m), S 20in (50cm).

Z12–15 H12–10

Stetsonia coryne
Tree-like cactus with a short, swollen trunk bearing 8- or 9-ribbed, blue-green stems. Black spines fade with age to white with black tips. Funnel-shaped white flowers appear at night in summer. H 25ft (8m), S 12ft (4m).

Z13–15 H12–10

Crassula ovata (Friendship tree, Jade tree, Money tree)
Succulent with a swollen stem crowned by glossy green leaves, at times red-edged. Bears 5-petaled white flowers in autumn-winter. H 12ft (4m), S 6ft (2m).

Z11–12 H12–1

Echinopsis spachiana
(Torch cactus)
Clump-forming cactus with glossy green stems bearing 10–15 ribs and pale golden spines. Fragrant, funnel-shaped white flowers open at night in summer. H and S 6ft (2m).

Z14–15 H12–10

Espostoa lanata (Cotton ball, Peruvian old-man cactus)
Very slow-growing, columnar cactus with a branching, woolly green stem. Foul-smelling white flowers appear in summer, only on plants over 3ft (1m) high. H to 12ft (4m), S 6ft (2m).

Z14–15 H12–10

Pereskia aculeata (Barbados gooseberry, Lemon vine)
Fast-growing, deciduous, climbing cactus with broad, glossy leaves. Orange-centered, creamy white flowers appear in autumn, only on plants over 3ft (1m) high. H to 30ft (10m), S 15ft (5m).

Z12–15 H12–10

***Agave americana* 'Striata'**
Basal-rosetted succulent with sharply pointed, sword-shaped, blue-green leaves with yellow edges. Stem carries white flowers, each 3½in (9cm) long, in spring-summer.Offsets freely. H and S 6ft (2m).

Z12–15 H12–10

Agave americana 'Mediopicta'
Ceropegia haygarthii
Epiphyllum crenatum
Epiphyllum oxypetalum
Neobuxbaumia euphorbioides
Pereskia aculeata 'Godseffiana'

CACTI *and other* SUCCULENTS large

WHITE–PINK

Haageocereus versicolor
Columnar cactus. Dense radial spines, golden, red, or brown, at times form colored bands around a longer central spine up the green stem. Long-tubed white flowers appear near crown of plant in summer. H to 6ft (2m), S 3ft (1m).

☼ ◊ Z13–15 H12–10

Crassula arborescens
(Silver jade plant)
Succulent with a thick, robust stem crowned by branches bearing rounded, silvery blue leaves, often with red edges. Has 5-petaled pink flowers in autumn-winter. H 12ft (4m), S 6ft (2m).

☼ ◊ Z11–12 H12–1

Pereskia grandifolia, syn. *Rhodocactus grandifolius*
(Rose cactus)
Deciduous, bushy cactus with black spines. Single roselike pink flowers form in summer-autumn only on plants over 1ft (30cm) high. H 15ft (5m), S 10ft (3m).

☼ ◊ Z13–15 H12–10

Adenium obesum
Treelike succulent with a fleshy, tapering, green trunk and stems crowned by oval, glossy green leaves, dull green beneath. Carries funnel-shaped pink to pinkish red flowers, white inside, in summer. H 6ft (2m), S 20in (50cm).

◑ ◊ ! Z11 H12–10

Pachycereus schottii, syn. *Lophocereus schottii*
Columnar cactus, branching with age. Olive to dark green stem, covered with small white spines, bears 4–15 ribs. Funnel-shaped pink flowers are produced at night in summer. H 22ft (7m), S 6ft (2m).

☼ ◊ Z13–15 H12–10

Pilosocereus leucocephalus, syn. *P. palmeri*
Columnar cactus with a 10–12-ribbed stem and white-haired crown. Bears tubular pink flowers with cream anthers at night in summer, on plants over 5ft (1.5m) tall. H to 20ft (6m), S 3ft (1m).

☼ ◊ Z13–15 H12–10

Ceropegia linearis subsp. *woodii*, illus. p.462
Haageocereus chosicensis
Oreocerus celsianus, illus. p.462
Pachycereus schottii 'Monstrosus'
Senecio rowleyanus, illus. p.462

***Aloe arborescens* 'Variegata'**
Evergreen, bushy, succulent-leaved shrub. Each stem is crowned by rosettes of long, slender, blue-green leaves with toothed edges and cream stripes. Produces numerous spikes of red flowers in late winter and spring. H and S 6ft (2m).

☼ 💧 Z12–15 H12–10

Aloe ferox
Evergreen tree with a woody stem crowned by a dense rosette of sword-shaped, blue-green leaves that have spined margins. Carries an erect spike of bell-shaped, orange-scarlet flowers in spring. H to 10ft (3m), S 5–6ft (1.5–2m).

☼ 💧 Z10–11 H12–10

Cyphostemma juttae*, syn. *Cissus juttae
Succulent. Swollen stem has peeling bark and deciduous, scandent branches with broad leaves. Bears inconspicuous, yellow-green flowers in summer. Green fruits turn yellow or red. H and S 6ft (2m).

☼ 💧 Z13–15 H12–10

***Pedilanthus tithymaloides* 'Variegata'** (Devil's backbone)
Bushy succulent with stems angled at each node. Leaves have white or pink marks. Stem tips carry small greenish flowers in red to yellowish green bracts in summer. H to 10ft (3m), S 1ft (30cm).

◑ 💧 ⓘ Z11 H12–1

Aloe ciliaris
Climbing succulent with a slender stem crowned by a rosette of narrow green leaves. Has white teeth where leaf base joins stem. Bears bell-shaped scarlet flowers with yellow and green mouths in spring. H 15ft (5m), S 1ft (30cm).

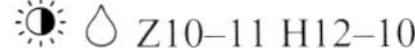

◑ 💧 Z10–11 H12–10

Neobuxbaumia euphorbioides
Columnar cactus. Has gray-green to dark green stems, 4in (10cm) across, with 8–10 ribs and 1 or 2 black spines per areole. Funnel-shaped, wine red flowers appear in summer. H to 10ft (3m), S 3ft (1m).

☼ 💧 Z14–15 H12–10

Cleistocactus strausii (Silver torch)
Fast-growing, columnarcactus with 3in (8cm) wide stems carrying short, dense white spines. Masses of long, tubular red flowers appear in spring, only on plants over 2ft (60cm) high. H 10ft (3m), S 3–6ft (1–2m).

☼ 💧 Z12–15 H12–10

Aloe arborescens
Cereus uruguayanus 'Monstrosus'
Crassula perfoliata var. *minor*, illus. p.464
Opuntia cylindrica
Pedilanthus tithymaloides
Tylecodon paniculatus

GREEN–YELLOW

Cephalocereus senilis
(Old-man cactus)
Very slow-growing, columnar cactus with a green stem covered in long white hairs masking short white spines. Is unlikely to flower in cultivation. H 50ft (15m), S 6in (15cm).

Z12–15 H12–10

***Furcraea foetida* 'Mediopicta'**
Basal-rosetted succulent with broad, sword-shaped green leaves striped with creamy white, to 8ft (2.5m) long. Has bell-shaped green flowers with white interiors in summer. H 10ft (3m), S 15ft (5m).

Z12–15 H12–10

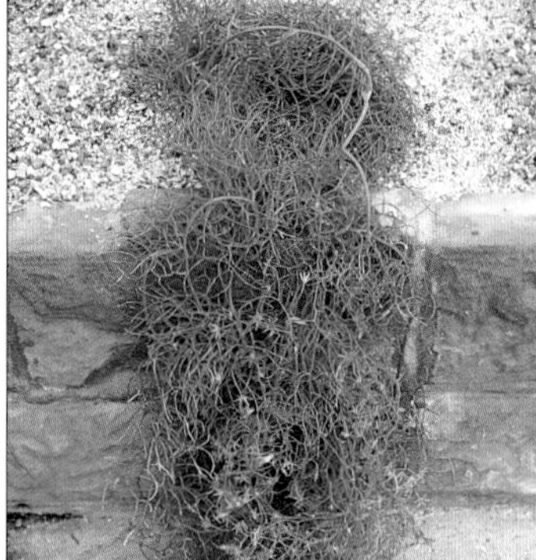

Bowiea volubilis
Bulbous succulent with climbing, much-branched, slender stems and no proper leaves. Produces small, star-shaped green flowers at tips of stems in summer. Provide support. H 3–6ft (1–2m), S 1½–2ft (45–60cm).

Z13–15 H12–10

Kalanchoe beharensis
Bushy succulent with triangular to lance-shaped, olive green leaves covered with fine brown hairs. Bell-shaped yellow flowers appear in late winter, only on plants over 6ft (2m) high. H and S to 12ft (4m).

Z11–12 H12–1

Pachycereus pringlei
Slow-growing, columnar cactus with a branched, bluish green stem that has 10–15 ribs. Large areoles each have 15–25 black-tipped white spines. Unlikely to flower in cultivation. H 35ft (11m), S 10ft (3m).

Z11 H12–10

Echinocactus grusonii (Golden barrel cactus, Mother-in-law's seat)
Slow-growing, spherical cactus. Spined green stem has 30 ribs. Woolly crown bears a ring of straw-colored flowers in summer, only on stems over 15in (38cm) wide. H and S to 6ft (2m).

Z9–10 H10–8

Ferocactus cylindraceus
Slow-growing, columnar cactus, spherical when young. Green, 10–20-ribbed stem is covered with large, hooked red or yellow spines. Funnel-shaped yellow flowers form in summer on plants over 10in (25cm) across. H 10ft (3m), S 32in (80cm).

Z13–15 H12–10

Opuntia robusta
Bushy cactus. Silvery blue stem has flattened, oval segments with either no spines or 8–12 white ones, to 2in (5cm) long, per areole. Saucer-shaped yellow flowers, 3in (7cm) across, appear in spring-summer. H and S 15ft (5m).

(!) Z12–15 H12–10

Agave attenuata, illus. p.467
Agave filifera, illus. p.465
Ceropegia sandersonii
Cleistocactus smaragdiflorus
Echinocactus platyacanthus
Euphorbia candelabrum
Ferocactus wislizenii
Furcraea foetida
Opuntia brasiliensis
Opuntia ficus-indica
Pachycereus pecten-aboriginum
Parodia leninghausii, illus. p.468

☐ WHITE

Gymnocalycium gibbosum
Spherical to columnar cactus that has a dark green stem with 12–19 rounded ribs, pale yellow spines darkening with age, and white flowers to 3in (7cm) long in summer. H 12in (30cm), S 8in (20cm).

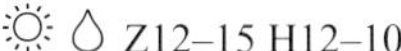 Z12–15 H12–10

Agave victoriae-reginae
(Royal agave)
Very slow-growing, domed succulent with a basal rosette of spineless, white-striped and -edged leaves. Has cream flowers on a 12ft (4m) tall stem in spring-summer after 20–30 years. H and S 2ft (60cm).

☼ ◊ Z9–11 H12–5

Epiphyllum anguliger
(Fishbone cactus)
Erect then pendent cactus. Has strap-shaped, flattened green stems with indented margins. Produces tubular, 4in (10cm) wide white flowers in summer. H 3ft (1m), S 16in (40cm).

☼ ◊ Z11–12 H12–1

Echinopsis candicans,
syn. *Trichocereus candicans*
Clump-forming, branching cactus with up to 11 ribs. Areoles each have 10–15 radial spines and 4 central ones. Fragrant, funnel-shaped white flowers open at night in summer. H 3ft (1m), S indefinite.

☼ ◊ Z12–15 H12–10

Lepismium warmingianum
Erect then pendent cactus with slender, notched, cylindrical green branches, sometimes tinged red or brown, with 2–4 angles. Has green-white flowers in winter-spring, followed by violet berries. H 3ft (1m), S 20in (50cm).

◑ ◊ Z13–15 H12–10

Echinopsis oxygona,
syn. *E. multiplex*
Spherical to columnar cactus with a 13–15-ribbed green stem and long spines. Has 4in (10cm) wide, tubular white to lavender flowers to 8in (20cm) long in spring-summer.
H and S 12in (30cm).

☼ ◊ Z12–15 H12–10

Rhipsalis cereuscula (Coral cactus)
Pendent cactus with 4- or 5-angled or cylindrical green stems and branches to 1¼in (3cm) long in whorls. Stem tips each bear bell-shaped white flowers in winter-spring. H 24in (60cm), S 20in (50cm).

◑ ◊ Z13–15 H12–10

Epiphyllum laui
Bushy cactus, usually with strap-shaped, red-tinged, glossy stems that may also be spiny, cylindrical, or 4-angled. Has fragrant white flowers with brown sepals in spring-summer. H 12in (30cm), S 20in (50cm).

◑ ◊ Z13–15 H12–10

Rhipsalis floccosa
Pendent cactus with cylindrical green stems to 1cm (½in) across branching less than many other *Rhipsalis* species. Has masses of very pale pink flowers in early summer, then pinkish white berries. H 3ft (1m), S 20in (50cm).

◑ ◊ Z13–15 H12–10

OTHER RECOMMENDED PLANTS:
Echinopsis eyriesii
Haageocereus decumbens
Hatiora clavata
Hylocereus undatus
Neoporteria chilensis
Rhipsalis capilliformis
Rhipsalis crispata
Rhipsalis paradoxa
Ruschia crassa

WHITE–PINK

Senecio rowleyanus
(String of beads)
Pendent succulent. Very slender green stems bear spherical green leaves. Has heads of fragrant, tubular white flowers from spring to autumn. Good in a hanging pot. H 3ft (1m), S indefinite.

Z12–15 H12–10

Ceropegia linearis* subsp. *woodii, syn. *C. woodii* (Heart vine, Rosary vine, String of hearts)
Semi-evergreen, trailing, succulent subshrub with tuberous roots. Leaves redden in sun. Has hairy, pinkish green flowers from spring to autumn. H 3ft (1m), S indefinite.

Z12–15 H12–10

***Kalanchoe fedtschenkoi* 'Variegata'**
Bushy succulent. Blue-green and cream leaves also color red. Bears a new plantlet in each leaf notch. Has brownish pink flowers in late winter. H and S to 3ft (1m).

Z11 H12–1

Echinocereus schmollii, syn. *Wilcoxia schmollii* (Lamb's-tail cactus)
Erect to prostrate, tuberous cactus with 8–10-ribbed, purplish green stems and mostly white spines. Has pinkish purple flowers in spring-summer. H and S 12in (30cm).

Z12–15 H12–10

PINK

***Senecio articulatus* 'Variegatus'**
Deciduous, spreading succulent with gray-marked stems. Has cream- and pink-marked, blue-green leaves in summer and yellow flower heads from autumn to spring. H 2ft (60cm), S indefinite.

Z13–15 H12–10

Hesperaloe parviflora, syn. *Yucca parviflora*
Basal-rosetted succulent, often with peeling white fibers at leaf edges. Flower stems each bear a raceme of bell-shaped pink to red flowers in summer-autumn. H 3ft (1m) or more, S 6ft (2m).

Z6–11 H12–6

***Nopalxochia phyllanthoides* 'Deutsche Kaiserin'**
Pendent, epiphytic cactus with flattened, toothed, glossy green stems, each 2in (5cm) across. Stem margins each bear pink flowers, to 4in (10cm) across, in spring. H 2ft (60cm), S 3ft (1m).

Z13–15 H12–10

Oreocereus celsianus, syn. *Borzicactus celsianus, Cleistocactus celsianus* (Old man of the Andes)
Slow-growing cactus. Has both thick and wispy spines. Mature plants bear pink flowers in summer. H 3ft (1m), S 1ft (30cm).

Z13–15 H12–10

Kalanchoe daigremontiana
(Mexican hat plant)
Erect succulent with a stem bearing fleshy, boat-shaped, toothed leaves. Produces a plantlet in each leaf notch. Umbels of pink flowers appear at stem tops in winter. H to 3ft (1m), S 1ft (30cm).

Z11 H12–1

Echinocereus reichenbachii* var. *baileyi, syn. *E. baileyi*
Columnar cactus with a slightly branched stem bearing 12–23 ribs and yellowish white, 1¼in (3cm) long spines. Produces pink flowers with darker bases in spring. H 12in (30cm), S 8in (20cm).

Z8–10 H10–7

Echinopsis rhodotricha

***Kalanchoe* 'Wendy'**
Semi-erect succulent with narrowly oval, glossy green leaves, 3in (7cm) long. In late winter bears bell-shaped, pinkish red flowers, ¾in (2cm) long, with yellow tips. Ideal for a hanging basket. H and S 12in (30cm).

Z13–15 H12–10

Aporocactus flagelliformis
(Rat's-tail cactus)
Pendent cactus with pencil-thick green stems bearing short golden spines. Has cerise flowers along stems in spring. Is good for a hanging basket. H 3ft (1m), S indefinite.

Z13–15 H12–10

***Nopalxochia* 'Gloria'**
Erect then pendent cactus. Strap-shaped, flattened green stems have toothed edges. Produces pinkish red flowers, 4in 10cm (4in) across, in spring. H 1ft (30cm), S 3ft (1m).

Z13–15 H12–10

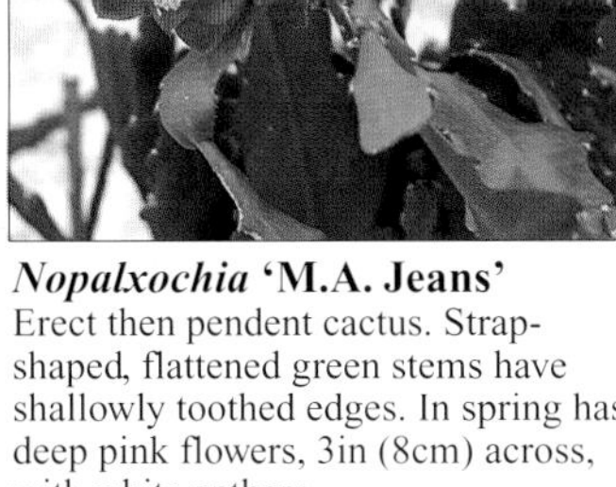

***Nopalxochia* 'M.A. Jeans'**
Erect then pendent cactus. Strap-shaped, flattened green stems have shallowly toothed edges. In spring has deep pink flowers, 3in (8cm) across, with white anthers.
H 12in (30cm), S 20in (50cm).

Z13–15 H12–10

Echinocereus pentalophus
Clump-forming cactus with spined green stems, 1¼–1½in (3–4cm) wide, that have 4–8 ribs, later rounded. Has trumpet-shaped, bright pink flowers, paler at base, to 5in (12cm) across, in spring. H 2ft (60cm), S 3ft (1m).

Z12–15 H12–10

Lampranthus spectabilis
Spreading succulent with erect stems and narrow, cylindrical, gray-green leaves. In summer produces daisylike flowers, cerise with yellow centers or golden yellow throughout.
H 1ft (30cm), S indefinite.

Z12–15 H12–10

Echinocereus cinerascens
Echinocereus pectinatus
Echinocereus reichenbachii
Kalanchoe fedtschenkoi
Lampranthus haworthii
Neoporteria chilensis
Oreocereus trollii

CACTI *and other* SUCCULENTS medium

PINK–RED

***Kalanchoe blossfeldiana* Hybrids**
Bushy succulent with oval to oblong, toothed, glossy green leaves. Produces clusters of yellow, orange, pink, red, or purple flowers year-round. Makes an excellent house plant.
H and S 1ft (30cm).

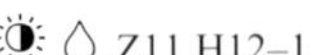

Z11 H12–1

***Gymnocalycium mihanovichii* 'Red Head'**
Cactus with a red stem, 8 angular ribs, and curved spines. Must be grafted on to any fast-growing stock since it contains no chlorophyll. Has pink flowers in spring-summer. H and S as per graft stock.

Z13–15 H12–10

Aloe variegata, syn. *A. punctata* (Partridge-breasted aloe)
Clustered succulent. Has triangular, white-marked, dark green leaves with pronounced keels beneath. Bears a spike of pinkish red flowers in spring. Is a good house plant. H 12in (30cm), S 4in (10cm).

Z10–11 H12–3

Echeveria pulvinata (Plush plant)
Bushy succulent with brown-haired stems, each crowned by a rosette of thick, rounded green leaves that become red-edged in autumn. Leaves have short white hairs. Bears red flowers in spring. H 12in (30cm), S 20in (50cm).

Z12–15 H12–10

Oroya peruviana
Spherical cactus with a much-ribbed stem covered in yellow spines, ⅝in (1.5cm) long, with darker bases. Pink flowers with yellow bases open in spring-summer. H 10in (25cm), S 8in (20cm).

Z13–15 H12–10

***Kalanchoe* 'Tessa'**
Prostrate to pendent succulent with narrowly oval green leaves, 1¼in (3cm) long. Bears tubular, orange-red flowers in late winter. H 1ft (30cm), S 2ft (60cm).

Z13–15 H12–10

Ferocactus hamatacanthus, syn. *Hamatocactus hamatacanthus*
Slow-growing, spherical to columnar cactus with a 13-ribbed stem that bears hooked red spines to 5in (12cm) long. Has yellow blooms in summer, then spherical red fruits. H and S 2ft (60cm).

Z12–15 H12–10

Dudleya pulverulenta
Basal-rosetted succulent with strap-shaped, pointed, silvery gray leaves. Bears masses of star-shaped red flowers in spring-summer. H 60cm (2ft), S 1ft (30cm).

Z12–15 H12–10

Crassula perfoliata* var. *minor, syn. *C. falcata* (Propeller plant)
Bushy, perennial succulent that branches freely. Long leaves each twist like a propeller. Has large clusters of fragrant red flowers in late summer. H and S 1m (3ft).

Z12–15 H12–10

Echeveria gibbiflora
Mammillaria magnimamma
Neoporteria subgibbosa
Oreocereus haynei
Pachypodium succulentum

Mammillaria hahniana (Old lady cactus, Old woman cactus)
Spherical to columnar cactus with a green stem bearing long, woolly white hairs. Carries cerise flowers in spring and spherical red fruits in autumn.
H 16in (40cm), S 6in (15cm).

Z12–15 H12–10

Opuntia erinacea
Bushy cactus with a green stem consisting of 6in (15cm) long, flattened segments. Areoles bear 6–15 flattened, 8in (20cm) long, hairlike spines. Has masses of saucer-shaped red or yellow flowers in summer. H 20in (50cm), S 6ft (2m).

Z12–15 H12–10

Beschorneria yuccoides
Clump-forming succulent with a basal rosette of up to 20 rough, grayish-green leaves to 3ft (1m) long and 2in (5cm) across. Produces pendent, tubular, bright red flowers in summer in spikes over 6ft (2m) tall. H 3ft (1m), S 10ft (3m).

Z12–15 H12–10

Tylecodon reticulatus, syn. *Cotyledon reticulata* (Barbed-wire plant)
Deciduous, bushy, succulent shrub. Swollen branches bear cylindrical leaves in winter. Has tubular, green-yellow flowers on a woody stem in autumn.
H and S 1ft (30cm).

Z12–15 H12–10

Mammillaria geminispina
Clump-forming cactus. Has a spherical green stem densely covered with short white radial spines and very long white central spines. Has red flowers, ½–¾in (1–2cm) across, in spring. H 10in (25cm), S 20in (50cm).

Z12–15 H12–10

Agave filifera (Thread agave)
Basal-rosetted succulent with narrow green leaves, each spined at the tip. White leaf margins gradually break away, leaving long white fibers. Carries yellow-green flowers on a 8ft (2.5m) tall stem in summer. Offsets freely.
H 3ft (1m), S 6ft (2m).

Z13–15 H12–10

Crassula coccinea
Drosanthemum hispidum
Echeveria gibbiflora
Echinocereus triglochidiatus
Hoodia gordonii
Kalanchoe blossfeldiana
Mammillaria elegans of gardens
Mammillaria rhodantha
Nopalxochia ackermannii
Tylecodon wallichii

CACTI *and other* SUCCULENTS medium

□ YELLOW

Aloe vera, syn. *A. barbadensis*
Clump-forming succulent with basal rosettes of tapering, thick leaves mottled green, later gray-green. Flower stems carry bell-shaped yellow flowers in summer. Propagate by offsets, since plant is sterile. H 2ft (60cm), S indefinite.

☼ ◊ Z10–11 H12–3

x *Pachyveria glauca*
Clump-forming succulent with a dense, basal rosette of fleshy, incurved, oval, silvery blue leaves, to 2½in (6cm) long, with darker marks. Bears star-shaped, yellow flowers, each with a red tip, in spring. H and S 12in (30cm).

☼ ◊ Z10–11 H12–3

Agave parryi
Basal-rosetted succulent with stiff, broad, gray-green leaves, each to 12in (30cm) long with a solitary dark spine at its pointed tip. Flower stems to 12ft (4m) long bear creamy yellow flowers in summer. H 20in (50cm), S 3ft (1m).

☼ ◊ Z9–11 H12–5

Leuchtenbergia principis
Basal-rosetted cactus with narrow, angular, dull gray-green tubercles, each 4in (10cm) long and crowned by papery spines to 4in (10cm) long. Crown bears yellow flowers to 3in (7cm) across in summer. H and S 12in (30cm).

☼ ◊ Z12–15 H12–10

Astrophytum myriostigma
(Bishop's cap, Bishop's miter)
Slow-growing, spherical to slightly elongated cactus. A fleshy stem has 4–6 ribs and is flecked with tiny tufts of white spines. Bears yellow flowers in summer. H 12in (30cm), S 8in (20cm).

☼ ◊ Z12–15 H12–10

Aeonium haworthii (Pinwheel)
Bushy succulent. Freely branching stems bear rosettes, 5in (12cm) across, of blue-green leaves, often with red margins. Has a terminal spike of star-shaped, pink-tinged, pale yellow flowers in spring. H 2ft (60cm), S 3ft (1m).

◑ ◊ Z12–15 H12–10

Copiapoa cinerea
Very slow-growing, clump-forming cactus. Blue-green stem bears up to 25 ribs and black spines. Has a woolly, white-gray crown and, on plants over 10cm (4in) across, yellow flowers in spring-summer. H 50cm (20in), S 2m (6ft).

◑ ◊ Z13–15 H12–10

Copiapoa marginata
Graptopetalum amethystinum
Pelargonium carnosum
Senecio articulatus

Opuntia microdasys var. ***alpispina***
Bushy cactus with green, flattened, oval segments. Spineless areoles with slender, barbed white hairs are set in diagonal rows. Funnel-shaped yellow flowers appear in summer.
H 2ft (60cm), S 1ft (30cm).

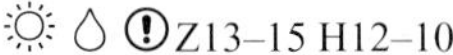
Z13–15 H12–10

Dioscorea elephantipes,
syn. *Testudinaria elephantipes*
(Elephant's foot)
Very slow-growing, deciduous succulent with a domed, woody trunk, annual, climbing stems, and yellow flowers in autumn. H 20in (50cm), S 3ft (1m).
Z13–15 H12–10

Kalanchoe tomentosa
(Panda plant, Pussy ears)
Bushy succulent with thick, oval gray leaves, covered with velvety bristles and often edged with brown at tips. Has yellowish purple flowers in winter.
H 20in (50cm), S 12in (30cm).

Z11 H12–1

Thelocactus setispinus
Slow-growing cactus with a 13-ribbed stem and yellow or white spines. Fragrant yellow flowers with red throats appear in summer, only on plants over 2in (5cm) across.
H and S 12in (30cm).

Z12–15 H12–10

Lobivia haageana
Columnar cactus with a 20–25-ribbed, bluish- to dark green stem that has yellow radial spines with longer, darker central ones. In summer produces yellow flowers, 3in (7cm) across, with red throats. H 12in (30cm), S 6in (15cm).

Z12–15 H12–6

Agave attenuata
Succulent with a thick stem crowned by a rosette of sword-shaped, spineless, pale green leaves. Arching flower stem to 5ft (1.5m) long is densely covered with yellow flowers in spring-summer.
H 3ft (1m), S 6ft (2m).

Z9–11 H12–5

***Nopalxochia* 'Jennifer Ann'**
Erect then pendent cactus. Has strap-shaped, flattened green stems with toothed margins. Bears yellow flowers, 6in (15cm) across, in spring.
H 12in (30cm), S 20in (50cm).

Z13–15 H12–10

Aeonium arboreum
Copiapoa coquimbana
Cyphostemma bainesii
Ferocactus chrysacanthus
Hoodia bainii
Opuntia microdasys
Parodia scopa

YELLOW–ORANGE

Parodia chrysacanthion
Spherical cactus with a much-ribbed green stem densely covered with bristlelike golden spines, each ½–¾in (1–2cm) long. Crown bears yellow flowers in spring and, often, pale yellow wool. H and S 1ft (30cm).

Z13–15 H12–10

***Aeonium* 'Zwartkop',**
syn. *A. arboreum* 'Schwarzkopf'
Bushy succulent with stems each crowned by a rosette, to 6in (15cm) across, of blackish purple leaves. Bears golden pyramids of flowers in spring on 2–3-year-old stems, which then die. H to 2ft (60cm), S 3ft (1m).

Z9–11 H9–4

Aloe striata
Basal-rosetted succulent. Has broad, blue-green leaves, with white margins and marks, that become suffused red in full sun. Has a panicle of reddish orange flowers in spring. Makes a good house plant. H and S 3ft (1m).

Z10–11 H12–10

Hatiora salicornioides
(Bottle plant, Drunkard's dream)
Bushy, epiphytic cactus with freely branching, 1¼in (3cm) long stems. Has joints with expanded tips and terminal, bell-shaped, golden yellow flowers in spring. H and S 1ft (30cm).

Z13–15 H12–10

Cotyledon orbiculata* var. *oblonga
Evergreen, upright, succulent subshrub with a swollen stem bearing oval green leaves, densely coated in white wax, with flat, wavy tips. Each 28in (70cm) long flower stem bears a bell-shaped orange flower in autumn. H and S 20in (50cm).

Z12–15 H12–10

***Parodia leninghausii*,**
syn. *Notocactus leninghausii*
(Golden ball cactus)
Clump-forming cactus. Woolly crown always slopes toward sun. Yellow blooms open flat in summer on plants over 4in (10cm) tall. H 3ft (1m), S 1ft (30cm).

Z13–15 H12–10

Opuntia tunicata
Mounded cactus. Has cylindrical green stem segments densely covered with 2in (5cm) long golden spines that are enclosed in a silver papery sheath. Bears shallowly saucer-shaped yellow flowers in spring-summer. H 2ft (60cm), S 3ft (1m).

Z13–15 H12–10

Kalanchoe delagoensis
Erect succulent with long, almost cylindrical, gray-green leaves with reddish brown mottling and flattened, notched tips that form plantlets. Bears an umbel of orange-yellow flowers in late winter. H to 3ft (1m), S 1ft (30cm).

Z11 H12–1

Lampranthus aurantiacus
Erect, then prostrate, sparse-branching succulent with short, cylindrical, tapering, gray-green leaves. Masses of daisylike, bright orange flowers, 2in (5cm) wide, open in summer sun. H 20in (50cm), S 28in (70cm).

Z12–15 H12–10

Cleistocactus baumannii
Cotyledon orbiculata
Drosanthemum speciosum

☐ WHITE

Mammillaria plumosa
Clump-forming cactus. Has a spherical green stem completely covered with feathery white spines. Carries cream flowers in midwinter. Is challenging to grow well. Add calcium to soil.
H 5in (12cm), S 16in (40cm).

☼ ◊ Z13–15 H12–10

Gibbaeum velutinum
Clump-forming succulent with paired, fingerlike, velvety, bluish gray-green leaves to 2½in (6cm) long. Produces daisylike pink, lilac, or white flowers, 2in (5cm) across, in spring.
H 3in (8cm), S 12in (30cm).

☼ ◊ Z12–15 H12–10

Haworthia truncata
Clump-forming succulent with a basal fan of broad, erect, rough, blue-gray leaves with pale gray lines and flat ends. Produces small, tubular white flowers with spreading petals from spring to autumn. H ¾in (2cm), S 4in (10cm).

◑ ◊ Z13–15 H12–10

Lithops marmorata
Egg-shaped succulent divided into 2 unequal-sized, swollen, pale gray leaves with dark gray marks on convex upper surfaces. Bears a white flower in late summer or early autumn.
H ¾–1¼in (2–3cm), S 2in (5cm).

☼ ◊ Z12–15 H12–10

Lithops karasmontana
Egg-shaped succulent, divided into 2 unequal-sized gray leaves that have pink upper surfaces with sunken, darker pink marks. Bears a white flower in late summer or early autumn.
H to 1½in (4cm), S 2in (5cm).

☼ ◊ Z12–15 H12–10

Adromischus maculatus
Clump-forming succulent with rounded, glossy green leaves with purple marks. Leaf tips are often wavy. Carries tubular, purplish white flowers on a 12in (30cm) tall stem in summer.
H 2½in (6cm), S 4–6in (10–15cm).

◑ ◊ Z12–15 H12–10

Echinocereus leucanthus, syn. *Wilcoxia albiflora*
Clump-forming, tuberous cactus with spined, 6- or 7-ribbed, prostrate stems. In spring bears often terminal, dark-throated white flowers, softly streaked purple, with green stigmas.
H 8in (20cm), S 12in (30cm).

☼ ◊ Z12–15 H12–10

Trichodiadema mirabile
Bushy to prostrate succulent with cylindrical, dark green leaves tipped with dark brown bristles and covered in papillae. Stem tip bears white flowers, 1½in (4cm) across, from spring to autumn. H 6in (15cm), S 12in (30cm).

☼ ◊ Z12–15 H12–10

Haworthia attenuata f. ***clariperla***
Clump-forming succulent with a basal rosette of triangular, 1¼in (3cm) long, dark green leaves that have pronounced white dots. Has tubular white flowers with spreading petals from spring to autumn. H 3in (7cm), S 10in (25cm).

◑ ◊ Z12–15 H12–10

OTHER RECOMMENDED PLANTS:
Cheiridopsis denticulata
Gymnocalycium quehlianum
Lithops fulleri
Lithops julii
Orostachys chanetii

☐ WHITE

Crassula socialis
Spreading succulent with short, dense rosettes, to ½in(1cm) across, of fleshy, triangular green leaves. Produces clusters of star-shaped white flowers on 1¼in (3cm) tall stems in spring. H 2in (5cm), S indefinite.

Z12–15 H12–10

Oophytum nanum
Clump-forming succulent with 2 united, very fleshy, bright green leaves. Has daisylike white flowers, ½in (1cm) across, in autumn. Is covered in a dry, paperlike sheath, except in spring. H ¾in (2cm), S ½in (1cm).

Z12–15 H12–10

***Haworthia arachnoidea*,**
syn. *H. setata*
Slow-growing, clump-forming succulent with a basal rosette of triangular leaves. Bears soft white teeth along leaf margins. Has white flowers from spring to autumn. H 2in (5cm), S 4in (10cm).

Z12–15 H12–10

Strombocactus disciformis
Very slow-growing, hemispherical cactus with a gray-green to brown stem set with a spiral of blunt tubercles. Woolly crown has bristlelike spines that soon fall off, and cream flowers in summer. H 1¼in (3cm), S 4in (10cm).

Z12–15 H12–10

Lithops lesliei* var. *albinica
Egg-shaped succulent, divided into 2 unequal-sized leaves; convex, pale green upper surfaces have dark green and yellow marks. Bears a white flower in late summer or early autumn. H ¾–1¼in (2–3cm), S 2in (5cm).

Z12–15 H12–10

Conophytum truncatum
Slow-growing, clump-forming succulent with pea-shaped, dark spotted, blue-green leaves, each with a sunken fissure at the tip. Produces cream flowers, ⅝in (1.5cm) across, in autumn. H ⅝in (1.5cm), S 6in (15cm).

Z12–15 H12–10

Mammillaria schiedeana
Clump-forming cactus. Green stem is covered with short, feathery yellow spines that turn white. Produces cream flowers and narrow red seed pods in late summer. H 4in (10cm), S 12in (30cm).

Z13–15 H12–10

Neoporteria villosa
Clump-forming cactus with a branched green to dark gray-green stem. Has dense, sometimes curved gray spines, 1¼in (3cm) long. Produces tubular pink or white flowers in spring or autumn. H 6in (15cm), S 4in (10cm).

Z12–15 H12–10

Mammillaria elongata
(Lace cactus)
Clump-forming cactus. Has columnar green stems, 1¼in (3cm) across, densely covered with yellow, golden, or brown spines. Bears cream flowers in summer. H 6in (15cm), S 12in (30cm).

Z12–15 H12–10

Aptenia cordifolia 'Variegata'
Crassula lactea
Haworthia attenuata
Haworthia x *cuspidata*
Haworthia fasciata
Lithops bella
Mammillaria gracilis
Mammillaria gracilis var. *fragilis*
Mammillaria prolifera
Ophthalmophyllum maughanii

WHITE–PINK

Mammillaria bocasana
(Powderpuff cactus)
Clump-forming cactus. Long white hairs cover hemispherical stems. Has cream or rose-pink flowers in summer and red seed pods the following spring-summer. H 4in (10cm), S 12in (30cm).

Z12–15 H12–10

Crassula multicava
Bushy succulent with oval, gray-green leaves, 3in (8cm) across. Carries numerous clusters of small, star-shaped pink flowers on elongated stems in spring, followed by small plantlets. H 6in (15cm), S 3ft (1m).

Z12–15 H12–10

Neoporteria napina
Flattened-spherical cactus with very short gray spines pressed flat against a greenish brown stem. Produces white, pink, carmine, or brown flowers, 2in (5cm) across, in summer. H ¾in (2cm), S 1½in (3.5cm).

Z12–15 H12–10

Lampranthus deltoides
Spreading succulent. Has chunky, triangular, blue-green leaves, to ½in (1cm)long, with small-toothed, often reddened leaf margins. Fragrant pink flowers, ½–¾in (1–2cm) wide, appear in early summer. H 6in (15cm), S 3ft (1m).

Z12–15 H12–10

Lophophora williamsii
(Dumpling cactus, Mescal button)
Very slow-growing, clump-forming cactus with an 8-ribbed, blue-green stem. Masses of pink flowers appear in summer on plants over 1¼in (3cm) high. H 2in (5cm), S 3in (8cm).

Z13–15 H12–10

Epithelantha micromeris
Slow-growing, spherical cactus with a green stem completely obscured by close-set areoles bearing tiny white spines. Bears funnel-shaped, pale pinkish red flowers, ¼in (0.5cm) across, on a woolly crown in summer. H and S 1½in (4cm).

Z13–15 H12–10

Crassula exilis subsp. *cooperi*
Gymnocalycium schickendantzii
Mammillaria candida
Ophthalmophyllum longum

Schlumbergera 'Wintermärchen'

PINK

Parodia rutilans,
syn. *Notocactus rutilans*
Columnar cactus. Areoles each have about 15 radial spines and 2 upward- or downward-pointing central spines. Has cream-centered pink flowers in summer. H 4in (10cm), S 2in (5cm).

Z13–15 H12–10

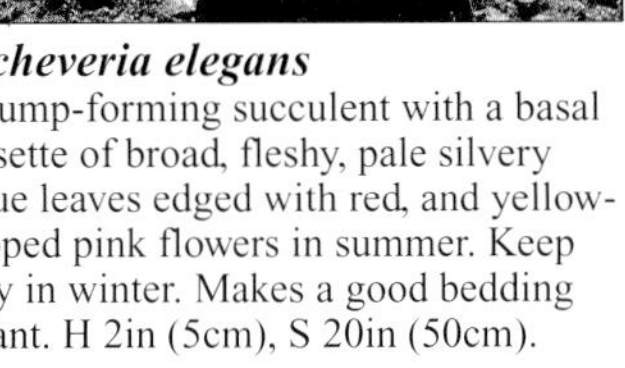

Echeveria elegans
Clump-forming succulent with a basal rosette of broad, fleshy, pale silvery blue leaves edged with red, and yellow-tipped pink flowers in summer. Keep dry in winter. Makes a good bedding plant. H 2in (5cm), S 20in (50cm).

Z12–15 H12–10

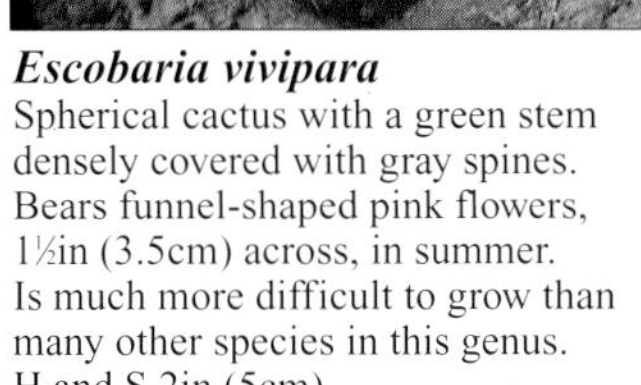

Escobaria vivipara
Spherical cactus with a green stem densely covered with gray spines. Bears funnel-shaped pink flowers, 1½in (3.5cm) across, in summer. Is much more difficult to grow than many other species in this genus. H and S 2in (5cm).

Z12–15 H12–10

Ruschia acuminata
Stenocactus lamellosus

PINK

***Schlumbergera* 'Gold Charm'**
Erect then pendent cactus. Has flattened, oblong green stem segments with toothed margins. Flowers, yellow in early autumn, are pinkish orange in winter. H 6in (15cm), S 12in (30cm).

Z13–15 H12–10

Mammillaria sempervivi
Slow-growing, spherical cactus. Has a dark green stem with short white spines. Has white wool between short, angular tubercles on plants over 1½in (4cm) high. Bears a ring of cerise flowers in spring. H and S 3in (7cm).

Z12–15 H12–10

Melocactus intortus, syn. *M. communis* (Melon cactus)
Flattened-spherical cactus. Has an 18–20-ribbed stem with yellow-brown spines. Crown matures to a white column with fine brown spines. Bears pink flowers in summer. H 8in (20cm), S 10in (25cm).

Z14–15 H12–10

Ariocarpus fissuratus
Very slow-growing, flattened-spherical cactus. Gray stem is covered with rough, triangular tubercles each producing a tuft of wool. Has 1½in (4cm) wide, pink-red flowers in autumn. H 4in (10cm), S 6in (15cm).

Z12–15 H12–10

Stenocactus obvallatus, syn. *S. pentacanthus, S. violaciflorus*
Spherical cactus with wavy-margined ribs. White areoles each bear 5–12 grayish brown spines. In spring, has pale yellow to pale pink flowers with a purplish-red stripe on each petal. H and S 3in (8cm).

Z12–15 H12–10

Aptenia cordifolia, syn. *Mesembryanthemum cordifolium*
Fast-growing, prostrate succulent with oval, glossy green leaves and, in summer, daisylike, bright pink flowers. Is ideal as a groundcover. H 2in (5cm), S indefinite.

Z12–15 H12–10

Hatiora rosea
Bushy cactus with slender, 3- or 4-angled, bristly green stem segments, usually tinged purple, to 2in (5cm) long. Has masses of bell-shaped pink flowers, to 1½in (4cm) across, in spring. H and S 4in (10cm).

Z13–15 H12–10

Ophthalmophyllum villetii
Clump-forming succulent with 2 fleshy, gray-green leaves that are broad, erect, and united for most of their length but have distinctly divided upper lobes. Pale pink flowers appear in late summer. H 1in (2.5cm), S ½in (1cm).

Z12–15 H12–10

Thelocactus bicolor
Spherical to columnar cactus with an 8–13-ribbed stem. Areoles each have 4 usually flattened, yellow central spines, sometimes bicolored yellow and red, and numerous shorter, radial spines. Flowers are purple-pink. H and S 8in (20cm).

Z12–15 H12–10

Rebutia minuscula
Clump-forming cactus with a tuberculate, dark green stem. Areoles each produce 15–20 brown spines, to ¼in (0.5cm) long. Has trumpet-shaped, deep pink to violet flowers, to ¾in (2cm) across, in spring. H 2in (5cm), S 6in (15cm).

Z12–15 H12–10

Aptenia cordifolia 'Variegata'
Carpobrotus edulis
Kalanchoe pumila
Melocactus bahiensis
Melocactus matanzanus
Rebutia pygmaea
Rebutia senilis
Ruschia macowanii

PINK

Mammillaria zeilmanniana
(Rose pincushion)
Clump-forming cactus with a spherical green stem that has hooked spines and bears a ring of deep pink to purple flowers in spring. H 6in (15cm), S 12in (30cm).

Z13–15 H12–10

Echinopsis backebergii, syn. *Lobivia backebergii*
Clump-forming, almost spherical cactus with a 10–15-ribbed, spined, dark green stem. Has funnel-shaped pink, red, or purple flowers with paler throats in summer. H 4in (10cm), S 6in (15cm).

Z12–15 H12–10

Echinopsis pentlandii, syn. *Lobivia pentlandii*
Clump-forming or solitary, variable cactus with a 10–20-ribbed stem and 6–20 spined aeroles. Has white, pink, purple, or orange flowers with paler throats in summer. H 3in (8cm), S 4in (10cm).

Z12–15 H12–10

Melocactus oaxacensis

PINK–RED

Frithia pulchra
Basal-rosetted succulent with erect, rough gray leaves, cylindrical with flattened tips. Produces masses of stemless, daisylike, bright pink flowers with paler centers in summer. H 1¼in (3cm), S 2½in (6cm).

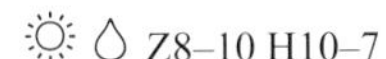

Z8–10 H10–7

Graptopetalum bellum, syn. *Tacitus bellus*
Basal-rosetted succulent with triangular to oval gray leaves, 2in (5cm) long. Has clusters of deep pink to red flowers, ¾in (2cm) across, in spring-summer. H 1¼in (3cm), S 6in (15cm).

Z13–15 H12–10

Crassula schmidtii
Carpeting succulent with dense rosettes of linear, dark green leaves, pitted and marked, each 1¼–1½in (3–4cm) long. Bears masses of star-shaped, bright pinkish red flowers in clusters in winter. H 4in (10cm), S 12in (30cm).

Z12–15 H12–10

Argyroderma pearsonii, syn. *A. schlechteri*
Prostrate, egg-shaped succulent. A united pair of very fleshy, silvery gray leaves has a deep fissure in which a red flower, 1¼in (3cm) across, appears in summer. H 1¼in (3cm), S 2in (5cm).

Z12–15 H12–10

Echeveria secunda
Clump-forming succulent with short stems, each crowned by a rosette of broad, fleshy, light green to gray leaves, reddened toward tips. Bears cup-shaped, red-and-yellow flowers in spring-summer. H 1½in (4cm), S 12in (30cm).

Z12–15 H12–10

Schlumbergera truncata, syn. *Zygocactus truncatus*
(Crab cactus, Holiday cactus)
Erect then pendent cactus. Oblong stem segments have toothed margins. Bears purple-red flowers in early autumn and winter. H 6in (15cm), S 12in (30cm).

Z13–15 H12–10

Cheiridopsis purpurea
Echinopsis cinnabarina
Gibbaeum petrense
Huernia pillansii
Lampranthus roseus
Neoporteria nidus
Trichodiadema densum

RED

Cephalophyllum alstonii
(Red spike)
Prostrate succulent with cylindrical, gray-green leaves to 3in (7cm) long. Carries daisylike, dark red flowers, 3in (8cm) across, in summer. H 4in (10cm), S 3ft (1m).

Z12–15 H12–10

Parodia microsperma
Clump-forming cactus. Has a much-ribbed green stem densely covered with brown radial spines and red central spines, some of which are hooked. Bears blood red, occasionally yellow flowers in spring. H 3in (8cm), S 12in (30cm).

Z13–15 H12–10

Rebutia krainziana
Clump-forming cactus with a tuberculate, dark green stem. Bears prominent white areoles with very short white spines. Trumpet-shaped, bright red flowers, to 2in (5cm) across, appear at stem base in spring. H 2in (5cm), S 8in (20cm).

Z12–15 H12–10

Parodia nivosa
Ovoid cactus that has a much-ribbed green stem with stiff white spines, each ½–¾in (1–2cm) long. Has a woolly white crown and bright red flowers, to 2in (5cm) across, in summer. H to 6in (15cm), S 4in (10cm).

Z13–15 H12–10

Rebutia tiraquensis,
syn. *Sulcorebutia tiraquensis*
Variable cactus with a green stem. Elongated areoles bear spines of gold or bicolored red and white. Has dark pink- or orange-red flowers in spring. H 6in (15cm), S 4in (10cm).

Z13–15 H12–10

Argyroderma fissum,
syn. *A. brevipes*
Clump-forming succulent with finger-shaped, fleshy leaves, 2–4in (5–10cm) long and often reddish at the tip. Has light red flowers between leaves in summer. H 6in (15cm), S 4in (10cm).

Z12–15 H12–10

Cotyledon ladismithensis
Evergreen, freely branching, later prostrate, succulent subshrub with fleshy green leaves, swollen and blunt at tips and covered with short, golden brown hairs. Clusters of tubular, brownish red flowers appear in autumn. H and S 8in (20cm).

Z12–15 H12–10

Opuntia verschaffeltii
Clump-forming cactus with cylindrical, usually spineless stems, to 10in (25cm) long. Stem tips each bear short-lived, cylindrical leaves from spring to autumn. Has orange-red flowers in spring. H 6in (15cm), S 3–6ft (1–2m).

Z11–12 H12–9

Echeveria agavoides
Basal-rosetted succulent with tapering, light green leaves, often red-margined. Carries cup-shaped red flowers, ½in (1cm) long, in summer. H 6in (15cm), S 12in (30cm).

Z10–11 H12–1

Aloe brevifolia
Ferocactus latispinus
Rebutia minuscula
Rebutia senilis

■ RED

Rebutia spegazziniana
Clump-forming cactus with a spherical, spined green stem, to 1½in (4cm) across, becoming columnar with age. Bears masses of slender-tubed, orange-red flowers at base in late spring. H 4in (10cm), S 8in (20cm).

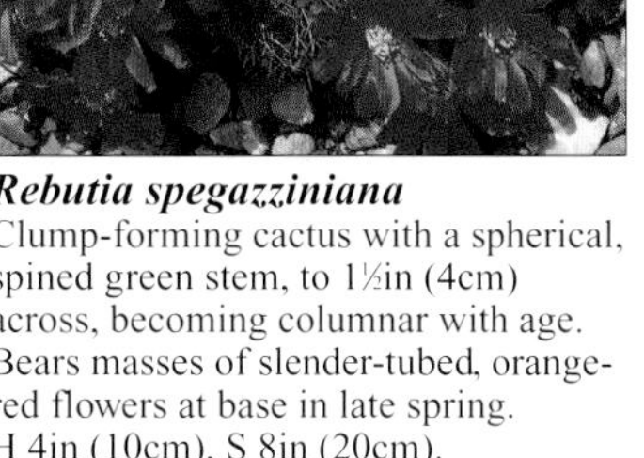

☼ 💧 Z12–15 H12–10

Echinopsis chamaecereus
(Peanut cactus)
Clump-forming cactus with spined stems, initially erect then prostrate. Has funnel-shaped, orange-red flowers in late spring. H 4in (10cm), S indefinite.

☼ 💧 Z11 H12–7

Hatiora gaertneri
(Easter cactus)
Bushy cactus with flat, oblong, glossy green stem segments, each to 2in (5cm) long, often tinged red at edges. Segment ends each bear orange-red flowers in spring. H 6in (15cm), S 13in (20cm).

◑ 💧 Z11–12 H12–1

Parodia haselbergii,
syn. *Notocactus haselbergii*
(Scarlet ball cactus)
Slow-growing cactus with a stem covered in white spines. Slightly sunken crown bears red flowers with yellow stigmas in spring. H 4in (10cm), S 10in (25cm).

◑ 💧 Z13–15 H12–10

Pachyphytum oviferum
(Moonstones)
Clump-forming succulent with a basal rosette of oval, pinkish blue leaves. Stem bears 10–15 bell-shaped flowers with powder blue calyces and orange-red petals in spring. H 4in (10cm), S 12in (30cm).

☼ 💧 Z13–15 H12–10

Echinocereus triglochidiatus
var. ***paucispinus***
Clump-forming cactus with a 4in (10cm) wide, dark green stem that has 6 or 7 ribs, and 4–6 spines, 1¼–1½in (3–4cm) long, per areole. Has orange-red flowers in spring. H 8in (20cm), S 20in (50cm).

☼ 💧 Z11–12 H12–9

■ PURPLE

***Schlumbergera* 'Bristol Beauty'**
Erect then pendent cactus with flattened green stem segments with toothed margins. Bears reddish purple flowers with silvery white tubes in early autumn and winter. H 6in (15cm), S 12in (30cm).

◑ 💧 Z13–15 H12–10

Neolloydia conoidea
Clump-forming cactus. Has a columnar, blue-green stem densely covered with white radial spines and longer, black central spines. Bears funnel-shaped, purple-violet flowers in summer. H 4in (10cm), S 6in (15cm).

☼ 💧 Z13–15 H12–10

Caralluma joannis
Clump-forming succulent with blue-gray stems and rudimentary leaves on stem edges. Bears clusters of star-shaped purple flowers, with short, fine hairs on petal tips, in late summer near stem tips. H 8in (20cm), S 3ft (1m).

☼ 💧 Z13–15 H12–10

Echeveria harmsii
Echeveria setosa
Schlumbergera 'Zara'

Schlumbergera x *buckleyi*
Thelocactus macdowellii

■ PURPLE

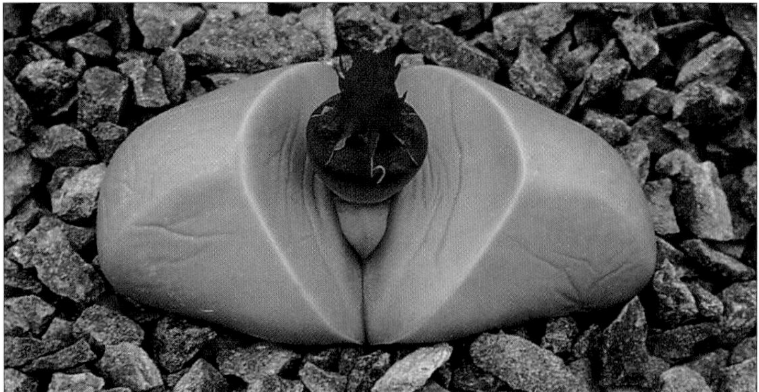

Argyroderma delaetii, syn. *A. aureum*, *A. blandum*
Prostrate, egg-shaped succulent with 2 very fleshy, silvery green leaves between which daisylike, pink-purple flowers, 2in (5cm) across, appear in late summer. H 1½in (3cm), S 2in (5cm).

Z12–15 H12–10

Stenocactus coptonogonus
Spherical cactus. White areoles each have 3–5 flat, upward-curving, pale brownish red spines. Bears purple to white flowers with pink-purple or violet-purple stripes in spring. H 4in (10cm), S 6in (16cm).

Z12–15 H12–10

Orbea variegata, syn. *Stapelia variegata* (Star flower)
Clump-forming, branching succulent with 4-angled, indented stems. Flowers, variable in color and blotched yellow or purple- or red-brown, appear in summer-autumn. H to 4in (10cm), S indefinite.

Z11–12 H12–9

Huernia macrocarpa* var. *arabica
Clump-forming succulent with finger-shaped, 4- or 5-sided green stems. Produces short-lived, deciduous leaves and, in autumn, bell-shaped, white-haired, dark purple flowers with recurved petal tips. H and S 4in (10cm).

Z13–15 H12–10

Stapelia grandiflora
Clump-forming succulent with 4-angled, hairy, toothed green stems. In summer-autumn carries star-shaped, purple-brown flowers, to 4in (10cm) across, ridged with white or purple hairs. H to 8in (20cm), S indefinite.

Z13–15 H12–10

Rebutia rauschii

GREEN–YELLOW

Duvalia corderoyi
Clump-forming succulent. Has a prostrate, leafless stem with 6 often purple, indistinct ribs. Bears star-shaped, dull green flowers, ½in (1cm) across and covered in purple hairs, in summer-autumn. H 2in (5cm), S 24in (60cm).

Z13–15 H12–10

Crassula deceptor, syn. *C. deceptrix*
Slow-growing, clump-forming succulent with branching stems surrounded by fleshy gray leaves set in 4 rows. Each leaf has minute lines around raised dots. Bears insignificant flowers in spring. H and S 4in (10cm).

Z12–15 H12–10

Stapelia gigantea
Clump-forming succulent. In summer-autumn bears star-shaped, red-marked, yellow-brown flowers, 12in (30cm) across, with white-haired, recurved edges. H to 8in (20cm), S indefinite.

Z13–15 H12–10

Huernia zebrina
Parodia graessneri
Sclerocactus scheeri

Sclerocactus scheeri
Spherical to columnar cactus. Stem bears spines and, in spring, funnel-shaped, straw-colored flowers. Lowest and longest spines are darker and hooked. H 4in (10cm), S 2½in (6cm).

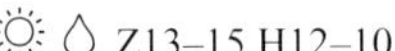

Z13–15 H12–10

Maihuenia poeppigii
Slow-growing, clump-forming cactus. Has a cylindrical, branched, spiny, green-brown stem. Most branches produce a spike of cylindrical green leaves at the tip, crowned by funnel-shaped yellow flowers in summer. H 2½in (6cm), S 12in (30cm).

Z11–15 H12–6

***Aichryson* x *domesticum* 'Variegatum'**
Prostrate succulent with stems crowned by rosettes of hairy, cream-marked green leaves, sometimes pure cream. Has star-shaped yellow flowers in spring. H 6in (15cm), S 16in (40cm).

Z12–15 H12–10

Frailea pygmaea
Columnar cactus with a much-ribbed, dark green stem bearing white to light brown spines. Buds, which rarely open to flattish yellow flowers in summer, become tufts of spherical, spiny seed pods. H to 2in (5cm), S ¾in (2cm).

Z12–15 H12–10

Aloinopsis schooneesii
Dwarf, mounded succulent with tuberous roots and fleshy, almost spherical, blue-green leaves arranged tightly in tufts. Produces flattish yellow flowers in winter-spring. H 1½in (3cm), S to 3in (7cm).

Z13–15 H12–10

Parodia mammulosa,
syn. *Notocactus mammulosus*
Spherical cactus. Green stem has about 20 ribs and straight, stiff, yellow-brown to white spines to ½in (1cm) long. Woolly crown produces masses of golden flowers in summer. H and S 4in (10cm).

Z13–15 H12–10

Astrophytum ornatum
Elongated, spherical cactus with a very fleshy, 8-ribbed stem. Crown of each rib bears 2–4½in (5–11cm) long spines on each raised areole. Has yellow flowers, 3in (8cm) across, in summer. H 6in (15cm), S 5in (12cm).

Z12–15 H12–10

Gymnocalycium andreae
Clump-forming, spherical cactus with a glossy, dark green stem bearing 8 rounded ribs and up to 8 pale yellow-white spines per areole. Has 2in (5cm) wide yellow flowers in spring-summer. H 2½in (6cm), S 4in (10cm).

Z11–12 H12–10

Euphorbia obesa
(Baseball cactus, plaid cactus)
Spherical succulent. Spineless green stem, often checkered with brown, has 8 low ribs. Crown bears rounded heads of cupped yellow flowers in summer. H 5in (12cm), S 6in (15cm).

Z13–15 H12–10

Carpobrotus edulis
Copiapoa echinoides
Dudleya brittonii
Echinopsis aurea
Ferocactus latispinus
Huernia macrocarpa
Huernia thurettii var. *primulina*
Mammillaria densispina
Neoporteria napina
Stomatium agninum
Stomatium patulum
Titanopsis schwantesii

□ YELLOW

Rhombophyllum rhomboideum
Clump-forming succulent. Linear, glossy, gray-green leaves have expanded middles and white margins. Stems, ¾–2in (2–5cm) long, bear 3–7 yellow flowers, to 1½in (4cm) across, in summer. H 2in (5cm), S 6in (15cm).

Z12–15 H12–10

Schwantesia ruedebuschii
Mat-forming succulent with cylindrical, bluish green leaves, 1–2in (3–5cm) long, with expanded tips. Leaf edges each produce 3–7 minute blue teeth with brown tips. Has yellow flowers in summer. H 2in (5cm), S 8in (20cm).

Z12–15 H12–10

Pleiospilos compactus
Clump-forming succulent with 1 or 2 pairs of thick gray leaves, to 3in (8cm) long. Bears coconut-scented yellow flowers in early autumn. H 4in (10cm), S 12in (30cm).

Z13–15 H12–10

Lithops pseudotruncatella* var. *pulmonuncula
Egg-shaped succulent, divided into 2 unequal-sized gray leaves with dark green and red marks on upper surfaces. Bears a yellow flower in summer or autumn. H ¾–1¼in (2–3cm), S 1½in (4cm).

Z12–15 H12–10

Aeonium tabuliforme
Prostrate, almost stemless, short-lived succulent with a basal rosette, to 12in (30cm) across, like a flat, bright green plate. Has star-shaped yellow flowers in spring, then dies. Propagate from seed. H 2in (5cm), S 12in (30cm).

Z9–11 H9–4

Lithops schwantesii*, syn. *L. schwantesii* var. *kuibisensis
Egg-shaped succulent divided into 2 unequal-sized leaves with blue or red marks on upper surface. Has a yellow flower in late summer or autumn. H ¾–1¼in (2–3cm), S 1¼in (3cm).

Z12–15 H12–10

Lithops dorotheae
Egg-shaped succulent divided into 2 unequal-sized leaves in pale pink-yellow to green with darker marks and red dots and lines on upper surfaces. Produces a daisylike yellow flower in summer or autumn. H ¾–1¼in (2–3cm), S 2in (5cm).

Z12–15 H12–10

Mammillaria microhelia
Columnar cactus with a 2in (5cm) wide green stem bearing cream or brown spines, discoloring with age. Has ⅝in (1.5cm) wide yellow or pink flowers in spring. Offsets slowly with age. H 8in (20cm), S 16in (40cm).

Z12–15 H12–10

Opuntia compressa
Prostrate cactus. Each areole bears up to 3 spines 1¼in (3cm long). Has flat, rounded to oval, purple-tinged, dark green stem segments, 3–7in (7–18cm) long. Bears 3in (8cm) wide yellow flowers in spring-summer. Keep dry in winter. H 6in (15cm), S 3ft (1m).

Z11–12 H12–9

Agave utahensis
Basal-rosetted succulent with rigid, blue-gray leaves, each with spines up margins and a long, dark spine at tip. Flower stem, to 5ft (1.5m) long, carries yellow flowers in summer. H 9in (23cm) or more, S 6ft (2m).

Z13–15 H12–10

***Graptopetalum paraguayense* (Ghost plant)**
Clump-forming succulent with a basal rosette, 6in (15cm) across, of gray-green leaves often tinged pink. Bears star-shaped, yellow-and-red flowers in summer. H 4in (10cm), S 3ft (1m).

Z12–15 H12–10

Astrophytum asterias
Caralluma europaea
Cephalophyllum pillansii
Crassula muscosa
Euphorbia gorgonis
Lithops aucampiae
Lithops insularis
Lithops lesliei
Lithops olivacea
Lithops otzeniana
Lithops pseudotruncatella
Lithops schwantesii
Lithops turbiniformis

Coryphantha cornifera, syn. *C. radians*
Spherical to columnar cactus with angular tubercles, each bearing a curved, dark central spine and shorter radial spines. Has funnel-shaped yellow flowers in summer. H 6in (15cm), S 4in (10cm).

☼ ◊ Z12–15 H12–10

Conophytum bilobum
Slow-growing, clump-forming succulent with 2-lobed, fleshy green leaves, each 1½in (4cm) long and ¾in (2cm) wide. Has a flared yellow flower, 1¼in (3cm) across, in autumn. H 1½in (4cm), S 6in (15cm).

☼ ◊ Z12–15 H12–10

Faucaria tigrina (Tiger jaws)
Clump-forming, stemless succulent. Fleshy green leaves, 2in (5cm) long, have 9 or 10 teeth along each margin. Bears daisylike yellow flowers, 2in (5cm) across, in autumn. H 4in (10cm), S 20in (50cm).

☼ ◊ Z12–15 H12–10

Parodia erinacea
(Colombian ball cactus)
Slow-growing, flattened-spherical cactus with a glossy stemwith up to 20 wartlike ribs bearing yellow-white spines and yellow blooms in summer. H 3in (8cm), S 3½in (9cm).

☼ ◊ Z13–15 H12–10

Glottiphyllum nelii
Clump-forming succulent with semi-cylindrical, fleshy green leaves to 2in (5cm) long. Carries daisylike, golden yellow flowers, 1½in (4cm) across, in spring-summer. H 2in (5cm), S 12in (30cm).

☼ ◊ Z12–15 H12–10

Lobivia shaferi
Columnar cactus. Has narrow, much-ribbed green stems covered with pale radial spines, often surrounded by 1–3 very thick central spines to 1in (2.5cm) long. Produces yellow flowers in summer. H and S 4in (10cm).

☼ ◊ Z12–15 H12–10

Fenestraria aurantiaca
(Baby's toes)
Clump-forming succulent with a basal rosette of glossy leaves. Has yellow flowers in late summer and autumn. H 2in (5cm), S 12in (30cm).

☼ ◊ Z12–15 H12–10

Titanopsis calcarea
Clump-forming succulent with a basal rosette of very fleshy, triangular, blue-gray leaves covered in wartlike, gray-white and beige tubercles. Has yellow flowers from autumn to spring. H 1¼in (3cm), S 4in (10cm).

☼ ◊ Z13–15 H12–10

Pleiospilos bolusii
(Living rock)
Clump-forming succulent with 1 or 2 pairs of gray leaves, often wider than long and narrowing at incurved tips. Has golden yellow flowers in early autumn. H 4in (10cm), S 8in (20cm).

☼ ◊ Z13–15 H12–10

Glottiphyllum semicylindricum
Parodia concinna
Parodia ottonis
Thelocactus leucacanthus

YELLOW–ORANGE

***Rebutia arenacea*,**
syn. *Sulcorebutia arenacea*
Sphericalcactus. Has a brown-green stem with white spines on spirally arranged tubercles. Has golden yellow blooms, to 1¼in (3cm) across, in spring. H 2in (5cm), S 2½in (6cm).

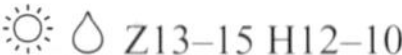
Z13–15 H12–10

***Gasteria bicolor* var. *liliputana*,**
syn. *G. liliputana*
Succulent that forms rosettes of dark green leaves blotched with white. Flower stems to 6in (15cm) long bear spikes of bell-shaped, orange/green flowers in spring. H 3in (7cm), S 4in (10cm).

Z12–15 H12–10

Pachyphytum compactum
Clump-forming succulent with a basal rosette of green leaves, each narrowing to a blunt point, with angular, paler edges. Stems each bear 3–10 flowers with green to pink calyces and orange petals in spring. H 6in (15cm), S indefinite.

Z12–15 H12–10

Conophytum notabile
Slow-growing, spherical succulent forming clumps of 2-lobed, very fleshy, gray-green leaves, often with a red spot on the edge of the fissure between the lobes. Carries copper-orange flowers in autumn. H 1¼in (3cm). S indefinite.

Z12–15 H12–10

Malephora crocea
Erect or spreading succulent with semi-cylindrical, blue-green leaves on short shoots. Carries solitary daisylike, orange-yellow flowers, reddened on outsides, in spring-summer. H 8in (20cm), S 3ft (1m).

Z12–15 H12–10

***Oreocereus aurantiacus*,**
syn. *Borzicactus aurantiacus*, *Matucana aurantiaca*
Spherical cactus with a 15–17-ribbed stem. Elongated areoles each bear up to 30 spines. Has orange-yellow flowers in summer. H 5in (12cm), S 16in (40cm).

Z13–15 H12–10

Aloe aristata
(Lace aloe, Torch plant)
Clump-forming succulent that has a basal rosette of pointed, dark green leaves with white spots and soft-toothed edges. Has orange flowers in spring. Offsets freely. H 4in (10cm), S 12in (30cm).

Z13–15 H12–10

Rebutia aureiflora
Clump-forming cactus with a dark green stem, often tinged violet-red, that has stiff radial spines and longer, soft central spines. Has masses of yellow, violet, or red flowers in late spring. H 4in (10cm), S 8in (20cm).

Z12–15 H12–10

***Gasteria carinata* var. *verrucosa*,**
syn. *G. verrucosa*
Clump-forming succulent with stiff, dark green leaves with raised white dots and incurved edges. Has spikes of bell-shaped, orange/green flowers in spring. H 4in (10cm), S 12in (30cm).

Z12–15 H12–10

Rebutia fiebrigii*, syn. *R. muscula
Clump-forming cactus. Has a dark green stem densely covered with soft white spines to ¼in (0.5cm) long. Bears bright orange flowers, ¾–1¼in (2–3cm) across, in late spring. H 4in (10cm), S 6in (15cm).

Z12–15 H12–10

Aloe humilis
Echeveria derenbergii
Gasteria caespitosa
Rebutia neocumingii
Rebutia senilis

The Plant Dictionary

A complete listing of more than 8,000 plants, suitable for growing in temperate gardens worldwide. Includes full descriptions of the characteristics and cultivation of 4,000 plants not already described in The Plant Catalog.

INDEX OF PLANT NAMES

ABELIA

CAPRIFOLIACEAE

Genus of deciduous, semi-evergreen or evergreen shrubs grown for their foliage and freely borne flowers. Does best against a south- or west-facing wall at the limits of hardiness. Requires a sheltered, sunny position and fertile, well-drained soil. Remove dead wood in late spring and prune out older branches after flowering to restrict growth, if required. Propagate by softwood cuttings in summer.

***A.* 'Edward Goucher'** illus. p.161.

A. floribunda. Evergreen, arching shrub. H 10ft (3m), S 12ft (4m). Has oval, glossy, dark green leaves and, in early summer, drooping, tubular, bright red flowers. Z8–11 H12–8.

A.* x *grandiflora illus. p.121. **'Francis Mason'** is a vigorous, semi-evergreen, arching shrub. H 6ft (2m), S 10ft (3m). Has coppery yellow young shoots and oval, yellowish green leaves, darker in centers. Bears a profusion of fragrant, bell-shaped white flowers tinged with pink from midsummer to midautumn. Z6–9 H9–1.

A. schumannii illus. p.162.

A. triflora illus. p.119.

ABELIOPHYLLUM

OLEACEAE

Genus of one species of deciduous shrub grown for its winter flowers. In marginal areas grow against a south- or west-facing wall. Requires plenty of sun and fertile, well-drained soil. Thin out excess older shoots after flowering each year to encourage vigorous, young growth. Propagate by softwood cuttings in summer.

A. distichum. Deciduous, open shrub. H and S 4ft (1.2m). In late winter produces fragrant, star-shaped white flowers tinged with pink on bare stems; flowers may be damaged by hard frosts. Leaves are oval and dark green. Z5–9 H9–1.

ABIES

Fir

PINACEAE

Genus of tall conifers with whorled branches. Spirally arranged leaves are needlelike, flattened, usually soft, and often have silvery bands beneath. Bears erect cones that ripen in their first autumn to release seeds and scales. See also CONIFERS.

A. alba. Fast-growing, conical conifer. H 50–80ft (15–25m), S 15–25ft (5–8m). Has silvery gray bark and dull green leaves, silvery beneath. Cylindrical cones, 4–6in (10–15cm) long, ripen to red-brown. Z5–8 H8–5.

A. amabilis (Pacific fir). Conical conifer. H 50ft (15m), S 12–15ft (4–5m). Dense, notched, square-tipped, glossy, dark green leaves, banded with white beneath, are borne on hairy gray shoots. Oblong, violet-blue cones are 3½–6in (9–15cm) long. Z6–8 H8–6. **'Spreading Star'**, H 20in (50cm), S 12–15ft (4–5m), is a procumbent form suitable as a groundcover.

A. balsamea (Balsam fir). Z3–6 H6–1. f. ***hudsonia*** is a dense, dwarf conifer of flattened to globose habit. H and S 2–3ft (60cm–1m). Has smooth gray bark and gray-green leaves that are semi-spirally arranged. **'Nana'** (illus. p.110) is another dwarf form that makes a dense, globose mound with spirally arranged leaves.

A. cephalonica (Greek fir). Upright conifer with a conical crown; old trees have massive, spreading, erect branches. H 70–100ft (20–30m), S 15–30ft (5–10m). Sharp, stiff, glossy, deep green leaves are whitish green beneath. Cylindrical, tapered cones, 4–6in (10–15cm) long, are brown when ripe. Z5–6 H6–5. **'Meyer's Dwarf'** (syn. *A.c.* 'Nana'; illus. p.110), H 20in (50cm), S 5ft (1.5m), has short leaves and forms a spreading, flat-topped mound.

A. concolor (White fir). Upright conifer. H 50–100ft (15–30m), S 15–25ft (5–8m). Has widely spreading, blue-green or gray leaves and cylindrical green or pale blue cones, 3–5in (8–12cm) long. Z3–7 H7–1. **'Argentea'** (syn. *A.c.* 'Candicans'; illus. p.101). **'Compacta'** (syn. *A.c.* 'Glauca Compacta'; illus. p.110), H to 6ft (2m), S 6–10ft (2–3m), is a cultivar with steel blue foliage. Z3–7 H7–2.

A. delavayi (Delavay's fir). Upright conifer producing tiered, spreading branches. H 30–50ft (10–15m), S 12–20ft (4–6m). Has maroon shoots and curved, bright deep green leaves, spirally arranged, with vivid silver bands beneath and rolled margins. Cones are narrowly cylindrical, 2½–6in (6–15cm) long, and violet-blue. Z8–9 H9–8.

A. forrestii illus. p.105.

A. grandis illus. p.104.

A. homolepis (Nikko fir). Conifer that is conical when young, later columnar. H 50ft (15m), S 20ft (6m). Pink-gray bark peels in fine flakes. Has pale green leaves, silver beneath, and cylindrical, violet-blue cones, 3–5in (8–12cm) long. Tolerates urban conditions. Z4–6 H6–4.

A. koreana illus. p.109.

A. lasiocarpa (Subalpine fir). Narrowly conical conifer. H 30–50ft (10–15m), S 10–12ft (3–4m). Has gray or blue-green leaves and cylindrical, violet-blue cones, 2½–4in (6–10cm) long. Z5–6 H6–5. Var. ***arizonica*** **'Compacta'** (illus. p.110), H 12–15ft (4–5m), S 5–6ft (1.5–2m), is a slow-growing, ovoid to conical tree with corky bark and blue foliage. **'Roger Watson'** (illus. p.110), H and S 2½ft (75cm), is dwarf and conical, with silvery gray leaves.

A. nordmanniana (Caucasian fir). Columnar, dense conifer. H 50–80ft (15–25m), S 15ft (5m). Luxuriant foliage is rich green. Cylindrical cones, 4–6in (10–15cm) long, are green-brown, ripening to brown. Z4–6 H6–4. **'Golden Spreader'** (illus. p.111), H and S 3ft (1m), is a dwarf form with a spreading habit and bright golden yellow leaves.

A. procera (Noble fir). Narrowly conical conifer. H 50ft (15m), S 15ft (5m). Has attractive, smooth, silvery gray bark and gray-green or bright blue-gray leaves. Produces thickly cylindrical green cones, 6–10in (15–25cm) long, that ripen to brown. Z5–6 H6–5.

A. veitchii illus. p.102.

ABUTILON

MALVACEAE

Genus of evergreen, semi-evergreen or deciduous shrubs, perennials and annuals grown for their flowers and foliage. Needs full sun or partial shade and fertile, well-drained soil. Water containerized specimens freely when in full growth, less at other times. In the growing season, young plants may need tip pruning to promote bushy growth. Mature specimens may have previous season's stems cut back hard annually in early spring. Tie lax-growing species to a support if necessary. Propagate by seed in spring or by softwood, greenwood, or semi-ripe cuttings in summer. Whitefly and spider mite may attack.

***A.* 'Ashford Red'.** Strong-growing, evergreen, erect to spreading shrub. H and S 6–10ft (2–3m). Has maple- to heart-shaped, serrated, pale to mid-green leaves. Pendent, bell-shaped crimson flowers are carried from spring to autumn. Z9–10 H10–1.

***A.* 'Golden Fleece'.** Strong-growing, evergreen, rounded shrub. H and S 6–10ft (2–3m). Has maple- to heart-shaped, serrated, rich green leaves. Pendent, bell-shaped yellow flowers are carried from spring to autumn. Z10–11 H12–1.

***A.* 'Kentish Belle'** illus. p.171.

A. megapotamicum. Evergreen shrub with long, slender branches normally trained against a wall. H and S to 10ft (3m). Pendent, bell-shaped, yellow-and-red flowers appear from late spring to autumn. Leaves are oval, with heart-shaped bases, and dark green. Z8–10 H12–1.

A. pictum, syn. *A. striatum* of gardens. **'Thompsonii'** illus. p.147.

A. striatum of gardens. See *A. pictum*.

A.* x *suntense. Fast-growing, deciduous, upright, arching shrub. H 15ft (5m), S 10ft (3m). Has oval, lobed, toothed, dark green leaves. Produces an abundance of large, bowl-shaped, pale to deep purple, occasionally white flowers from late spring to early summer. Z12–15 H12–6. **'Violetta'** illus. p.145.

A. vitifolium. Fast-growing, deciduous, upright shrub. H 12ft (4m), S 8ft (2.5m). Masses of large, bowl-shaped, purplish blue flowers are produced in late spring and early summer. Has oval, lobed, sharply toothed, gray-green leaves. Z8–9 H9–8. var. ***album*** illus. p.119.

ACACIA

Mimosa

LEGUMINOSAE/MIMOSACEAE

Genus of evergreen, semi-evergreen, or deciduous trees and shrubs grown for their tiny flowers composed of massed stamens, and for their foliage. Many species have phyllodes instead of true leaves. Requires full sun and well-drained soil. Propagate by seed in spring. Spider mite and mealy bug may be problematic.

A. baileyana illus. p.97.

A. dealbata illus. p.83.

A. juniperina. See *A. ulicifolia.*

A. longifolia (Sydney golden wattle). Evergreen, spreading tree. H and S 20ft (6m). Has narrowly oblong, dark green phyllodes. Bears cylindrical clusters of golden yellow flowers in early spring. Z9–11 H12–1.

A. podalyriifolia illus. p.135.

A. pravissima illus. p.97.

A. pulchella illus. p.157.

A. ulicifolia, syn. *A. juniperina.* Evergreen, bushy shrub. H 3ft (1m), S 5ft (1.5m). Has very narrow, cylindrical, spinelike, rich green phyllodes and, in midspring, globular clusters of pale yellow flowers. Z11–15 H12–10.

A. verticillata (Prickly Moses). Evergreen, spreading tree or bushy shrub. H and S 28ft (9m). Has needle-like, dark green phyllodes and, in spring, dense, bottlebrush-like spikes of bright yellow flowers. Z11-15 H12-10.

ACAENA

ROSACEAE

Genus of mainly summer-flowering subshrubs and perennials grown for their leaves and colored burrs and as a groundcover. Has tight, rounded heads of small flowers. Is good for a rock garden, but some species may be invasive. Needs sun or partial shade and

well-drained soil. Propagate by division in early spring or by seed in autumn.
A. anserinifolia of gardens. See *A. novae-zelandiae*.
***A.* 'Blue Haze'**, syn. *A.* 'Pewter'. Vigorous, evergreen, prostrate perennial. H 4in (10cm), S 30in (75cm) or more. Leaves are divided into 9–15 oval, toothed, steel blue leaflets. Produces spherical, brownish red flower heads that develop in autumn to dark red burrs with pinkish red spines. Z7–9 H9–7.
A. buchananii. Vigorous, evergreen, prostrate perennial. H ¾in (2cm), S 30in (75cm) or more. Bears glaucous leaves composed of 11–17 oval, toothed leaflets. Globose green flower heads are borne in summer and develop into spiny, yellow-green burrs. Z6–8 H8–6.
A. caerulea. See *A. caesiiglauca*.
A. caesiiglauca, syn. *A. caerulea*, illus. p.390.
A. microphylla illus. p.389
A. novae-zelandiae, syn. *A. anserinifolia* of gardens. Vigorous, evergreen, prostrate subshrub. H 4in (10cm), S 30in (75cm) or more. Has brown-green leaves divided into 9–13 oval, toothed leaflets. In summer, red-spined, brownish burrs develop from spherical heads of greenish brown flowers. Z6–8 H8–6.
***A.* 'Pewter'.** See *A.* 'Blue Haze'.

ACALYPHA

EUPHORBIACEAE

Genus of evergreen shrubs and perennials grown for their flowers and foliage. Needs partial shade and organic, well-drained soil. Water containerized plants freely when in full growth, much less at other times and in low temperatures. Stem tips may be removed in growing season to promote branching of young plants. Propagate by softwood, greenwood, ,or semi-ripe cuttings in summer. Spider mite, whitefly, and mealy bug may attack.
A. hispida (Red-hot cat's tail). Evergreen, upright, soft-stemmed shrub. H 6ft (2m) or more, S 3–6ft (1–2m). Has oval, toothed, lustrous, deep green leaves. Tiny crimson flowers hang in long, dense, catkinlike spikes, intermittently year-round. May be grown as a short-lived cordon. Z11 H12–6.
A. wilkesiana illus. p.143.

ACANTHOLIMON

PLUMBAGINACEAE

Genus of evergreen perennials grown for their flowers and tight cushions of spiny leaves. Suitable for rock gardens and walls. Prefers sun and well-drained soil. Dislikes damp winters. Seed is rarely set in cultivation. Propagate by softwood cuttings in late spring.
A. glumaceum illus. p.377.
A. venustum. Evergreen, cushion-forming perennial. H and S 4in (10cm). Small spikes of star-shaped pink flowers on 1¼in (3cm) stems are produced from late spring to early summer amid rosetted, spear-shaped, spiny, blue-green leaves that are edged with silver. Needs a very hot, well-drained site. Makes an excellent alpine-house plant. Z7–9 H9–7.

Acanthopanax. Reclassified as *Eleutherococcus*, except for ***A. ricinifolius***, for which see *Kalopanax septemlobus*.

ACANTHUS

Bear's breeches

ACANTHACEAE

Genus of perennials, some of which are semi-evergreen, grown for their large, deeply cut leaves and their spikes of flowers. Prefers full sun, warm conditions, and well-drained soil but will tolerate shade. Protect crowns in first winter after planting. Long, thong-like roots make plants difficult to eradicate if wrongly placed. Propagate by seed or division in early autumn or spring or by root cuttings in winter.
A. balcanicus. See *A. hungaricus*.
A. dioscoridis. Upright, architectural perennial. H to 3ft (1m), S 18in (45cm). Has oval, deeply cut, rigid, basal leaves and hairy stems. Dense spikes of small, funnel-shaped, purple-and-white flowers are produced in summer.
A. hungaricus, syn. *A. balcanicus*, *A. longifolius*, illus. p.251.
A. longifolius. See *A. hungaricus*.
A. mollis. Semi-evergreen, stately, upright perennial. H 4ft (1.2m), S 18in (45cm). Has long, oval, deeply cut, bright green leaves and, in summer, produces many spikes of funnel-shaped, mauve-and-white flowers. Z7–11 H12–7.
A. spinosus illus. p.251.

ACCA,

syn. FEIJOA

MYRTACEAE

Genus of evergreen, opposite-leaved shrubs grown for their shallowly cup-shaped flowers. Needs a sheltered, sunny site and light, well-drained soil. Propagate by seed sown as soon as ripe or by semi-ripe cuttings in summer.
A. sellowiana illus. p.143.

ACER

Maple

ACERACEAE

Genus of deciduous or evergreen trees and shrubs grown for their foliage that often colors brilliantly in autumn and, in some cases, for their ornamental bark or stems. Small but often attractive flowers are followed by 2-winged fruits. Requires sun or semi-shade and fertile, moist but well-drained soil. Many maples produce their best autumn color on neutral to acidic soil. Propagate species by seed as soon as ripe or in autumn; cultivars by various grafting methods in late winter or early spring, or by budding in summer. Leaf-eating caterpillars or aphids sometimes infest plants, and maple tar spot and leaf galls may affect some species.
A. buergerianum (Trident maple). Deciduous, spreading tree. H 30ft (10m) or more, S 25ft (8m). Has 3-lobed, glossy, dark green leaves, usually providing an attractive, long-lasting display of red, orange, and purple in autumn. Z5–9 H9–5.
A. capillipes illus. p.82.
A. cappadocicum (Cappadocian maple). Deciduous, spreading tree. H 70ft (20m), S 50ft (15m). Has 5-lobed, bright green leaves that turn yellow in autumn. Z5–7 H7–5. **'Aureum'** has bright yellow young leaves that turn light green in summer and assume yellow autumn tints. Z6–8 H8–6. subsp. ***lobelii*** (syn. *A. lobelii*) illus. p.66.
A. carpinifolium illus. p.92.
A. circinatum (Vine maple). Deciduous, spreading, bushy tree or shrub. H 15ft (5m) or more, S 20ft (6m). Rounded, 7–9-lobed, midgreen leaves turn brilliant orange and red in autumn. Bears clusters of small, purple-and-white flowers in spring. Z6–9 H9–4.
A. cissifolium. Deciduous, spreading tree. H 25ft (8m), S 40ft (12m). Leaves consist of 3 oval, toothed leaflets, bronze-tinged when young, dark green in summer, turning red and yellow in autumn. Does best in semi-shade and on neutral to acidic soil. Z4–8 H8–1. subsp. ***henryi*** see *A. henryi*.
A. crataegifolium (Hawthorn maple). Deciduous, arching tree. H and S 30ft (10m). Branches are streaked green and white. Small, oval, midgreen leaves turn orange in autumn. Z6–8 H8–6. **'Veitchii'** illus. p.89.
A. davidii (Père David's maple, Snake-bark maple). Deciduous tree with upright branches. H and S 50ft (15m). Branches are striped green and white. Oval, glossy, dark green leaves often turn yellow or orange in autumn. Z5–7 H7–5. Subsp. ***grosseri*** (syn. *A. grosseri*, *A.g.* var. *hersii*, *A. hersii*; Hers's maple, Snakebark maple) is a deciduous, upright and spreading tree. H and S 30ft (10m). Has white-striped trunk and branches. Broadly oval, deeply lobed, bright green leaves turn red in autumn. Z6–8 H8–5. **'Madeline Spitta'** illus. p.81.
A.* x *freemanii. A hybrid between *A. rubrum* and *A. saccharinum*. 'Autumn Blaze'. Fast growing, oval-headed, deciduous tree. H 50ft (15m) S 40ft (12m). Has deeply lobed, midgreen leaves that turn orange in fall and keep their color for several weeks. **'Celebration'**. Upright, deciduous tree. H 45ft (14m) S 25ft (8m). Leaves turn red then gold in autumn. Does not have fruit.
A. ginnala. See *A. tataricum* subsp. *ginnala*.
A. giraldii. Deciduous, spreading tree. H and S 30ft (10m). Shoots have a blue-gray bloom. Large, shallowly lobed leaves with long pink stalks are dark green above, blue-white beneath. Z7–9 H9–7.
A. grandidentatum. See *A. saccharum* subsp. *grandidentatum*.
A. griseum illus. p.100.
A. grosseri. See *A. davidii* subsp. *grosseri*. var. ***hersii*** see *A. davidii* subsp. *grosseri*.
A. henryi, syn. *A. cissifolium* subsp. *henryi*, illus. p.82.
A. hersii. See *A. davidii* subsp. *grosseri*.
A. japonicum (Full-moon maple, Japanese maple). Deciduous, bushy tree or shrub. H and S 30ft (10m). Rounded, lobed leaves are midgreen, turning red in autumn. Clusters of small, reddish purple flowers open in midspring. Shelter from strong winds. Z5–7 H8–3. **'Aconitifolium'** illus. p.95. **'Aureum'** see *A. shirasawanum* 'Aureum'. **'Vitifolium'** illus. p.95.
A. laxiflorum, syn. *A. pectinatum* subsp. *laxiflorum*, illus. p.99.
A. lobelii. See *A. cappadocicum* subsp. *lobelii*.
A. macrophyllum illus. p.64.
A. maximowiczianum, syn. *A. nikoense* (Nikko maple). Slow-growing, deciduous, round-headed tree. H and S 40ft (12m). Leaves have 3 oval, bluish green leaflets that turn brilliant red and yellow in autumn. Z6–9 H9–6.
A. monspessulanum (Montpelier maple). Deciduous, usually compact, round-headed tree or shrub. H and S 40ft (12m). Small, 3-lobed, glossy, dark green leaves remain on tree until late autumn. Z5–9 H9–5.
A. negundo (Box elder). Fast-growing, deciduous, spreading tree. H 50ft (15m), S 25ft (8m). Bright green leaves have 3–5 oval leaflets. Clusters of inconspicuous, greenish yellow flowers are borne in late spring. Z5–8 H8–3. **'Variegatum'** illus. p.79. Var. ***violaceum*** has purplish branchlets covered in a glaucous bloom and prominent clusters of tassel-like, purplish pink flowers.
A. nikoense. See *A. maximowiczianum*.
A. opalus (Italian maple). Deciduous, round-headed tree. H and S 50ft (15m). Clusters of small yellow flowers emerge from early to midspring before foliage. Leaves are broad, 5-lobed, and dark green, turning yellow in autumn. Z5–8 H8–5.
A. palmatum (Japanese maple). Deciduous, bushy-headed shrub or tree. H and S 20ft (6m) or more. Palmate, deeply lobed, midgreen leaves turn brilliant orange, red, or yellow in autumn. Clusters of small, reddish purple flowers are borne in midspring. Z5–8 H8–2. f. ***atropurpureum*** illus. p121. **'Bloodgood'** illus. p.143. **'Butterfly'** illus. p.140. **'Chitoseyama'** illus. p.166. **'Corallinum'** illus. p.130. var. ***coreanum*** illus. p.94. **'Dissectum Atropurpureum'** illus. p.166. var. ***heptalobum*** illus. p.124. var. ***heptalobum* 'Lutescens'** illus.

p.122. var. ***heptalobum* 'Rubrum'** illus. p.122. **'Osakazuki'** has larger leaves, with 7 lobes, that turn brilliant scarlet in autumn. **'Sango-kaku'** (syn. *A.p.* 'Senkaki') illus. p.124.
A. pectinatum subsp. ***laxiflorum***. See *A. laxiflorum*.
A. pensylvanicum (Snakebark maple. Moosewood) illus. p.84. **'Erythrocladum'** is a deciduous, upright tree. H 30ft (10m), S 20ft (6m). Has brilliant candy pink young shoots in winter and large, boldly lobed, mid-green leaves that turn bright yellow in autumn. Z3–7 H7–1.
A. platanoides (Norway maple). Vigorous, deciduous, spreading tree. H 80ft (25m), S 50ft (15m). Has large, broad, sharply lobed, bright green leaves that turn yellow or orange in autumn. Clusters of yellow flowers borne in midspring before the leaves appear. Z3–7 H7–1. **'Columnare'**, H 40ft (12m), S 25ft (8m), is dense and columnar. **'Crimson King'** illus. p.65. **'Drummondii'** has leaves broadly edged with creamy white. **'Emerald Queen'** is upright when young. **'Globosum'**, H 25ft (8m), S 30ft (10m), has a dense, round crown. **'Lorbergii'** see *A.p.*'Palmatifidum'. **'Palmatifidum'** (syn. *A.p.* 'Lorbergii') illus. p.71. **'Royal Red'** has deep reddish purple leaves. Those of **'Schwedleri'** are bright red when young, maturing to purplish green in summer and turning orange-red in autumn. **'Summershade'** has dark green leaves.
A. pseudoplatanus (Sycamore maple). Fast-growing, deciduous, spreading tree. H 100ft (30m), S 50ft (15m). Has broadly 5-lobed, dark green leaves. Makes a fine specimen tree and is good for an exposed position. Z4–7 H7–1. **'Brilliantissimum'** illus. p.89. f. ***erythrocarpum*** illus. p.70. **'Simon Louis Frères'** illus. p.79.
A. rubrum (Red maple) illus. p.70. **'Columnare'** illus. p.81. **'Morgan.'** See **'Red Sunset'**. **'October Glory'** is a deciduous, spreading tree. H 70ft (20m), S 40ft (12m). Has 3- or 5-lobed, glossy, dark green leaves that become intense red in autumn, particularly on neutral to acidic soil. In spring, bare branches are covered with clusters of tiny red flowers. Z3–9 H9–1. **'Red Sunset'** (syn. **'Morgan'**) has dense growth that also turns brilliant red in autumn. Z 4–9 H9–1. **'Scanlon'** and **'Schlesingeri'** illus. p.70.
A. rufinerve (Snakebark maple) illus. p.82. **'Hatsuyuki'** (syn. *A.r.* f. *albolimbatum*) is a deciduous, arching tree. H 30ft (10m), S 25ft (8m). Branches are striped green and white. Has 3-lobed, midgreen leaves, mottled and edged with white, that turn orange and red in autumn.
A. saccharinum (Silver maple). Fast-growing, deciduous, spreading tree. H 80ft (25m), S 50ft (15m). Deeply lobed, midgreen leaves with silver undersides turn yellow in autumn. Z4–8 H8–1. f. ***laciniatum* 'Wieri'** (syn. *A.s.* 'Laciniatum Wieri') has pendent lower branches and deeply lobed leaves.
A. saccharum (Sugar maple). subsp. ***grandidentatum*** (syn. *A. grandidentatum)* is a deciduous, spreading tree. H and S 30ft (10m) or more. Broad 3- or 5-lobed, bright green leaves turn bright orange-red in early autumn. Z3–8 H8–1. **'Green Mountain'**, H 70ft (20m), S 40ft (12m), is upright. Large, 5-lobed leaves turn brilliant scarlet in autumn. Z3–8 H8–1. **'Temple's Upright'** illus. p.82.
***A. shirasawanum* 'Aureum'**, syn. *A. japonicum* 'Aureum', illus. p.92.
A. tataricum subsp. ***ginnala***, syn. *A. ginnala*, illus. p.95.
A. triflorum illus. p.96.
A. velutinum. Deciduous, spreading tree. H 70ft (20m), S 50ft (15m). Produces large, lobed, dark green leaves with undersides covered with pale brown down. var. ***vanvolxemii*** (Van Volxem's maple) has even larger leaves, slightly glaucous and smooth beneath. Z7–9 H9–1.

ACHILLEA
Yarrow

ASTERACEAE/COMPOSITAE

Genus of mainly upright perennials, some of which are semi-evergreen, suitable for borders and rock gardens. Has fernlike foliage and large, usually platelike flower heads, mainly in summer. Flower heads may be dried for winter decoration. Tolerates most soils but does best in a sunny, well-drained site. Tall species and cultivars need staking. Propagate by division in early spring or autumn or by softwood cuttings in early summer. Contact with foliage may aggravate skin allergies.
A. aegyptica of gardens. See *A.* 'Taygetea'.
A. argentea. See *Tanacetum argenteum*.
A. argentea of gardens. See *A. clavennae*.
A. clavennae, syn. *A. argentea* of gardens, illus. p.373.
A. clypeolata. Semi-evergreen, upright perennial. H 18in (45cm), S 12in (30cm). Has divided, hairy silver leaves and dense, flat heads of small yellow flowers in summer. Divide plants regularly in spring. Z3–9 H9–1.
***A.* 'Coronation Gold'** illus. p.256.
***A. filipendulina* 'Gold Plate'** illus. p.258.
A.* x *kellereri illus. p.375.
***A.* x *lewisii* 'King Edward'**. Semi-evergreen, rounded, compact, woody-based perennial. H 4in (10cm), S 9in (23cm) or more. Has feathery, soft, gray-green leaves. Bears compact heads of minute, buff-yellow flower heads in summer. Is suitable for a rock garden, wall, or bank.
A. millefolium (Yarrow). **'Fire King'** is a vigorous, upright perennial. H and S 24in (60cm). Has a mass of feathery, dark green leaves and flat heads of rich red flowers in summer. Z3–9 H9–1.
***A.* 'Moonshine'** illus. p.291.
***A. ptarmica* 'The Pearl'** illus. p.239.
***A.* 'Schwellenberg'** illus. p.255.
***A.* 'Taygetea'**, syn. *A. aegyptica* of gardens, illus. p.291.

ACHIMENES
Hot-water plant

GESNERIACEAE

Genus of erect or trailing perennials with small rhizomes and showy flowers. Prefers bright light, but not direct sunlight, and well-drained soil. Use tepid water for watering pot-grown plants. Allow plants to dry out after flowering and store rhizomes in a frost-free place over winter. Propagate by division of rhizomes or by seed (if available) in spring, or by stem cuttings in summer. All of the following are Z14–15 H12–1.
A. antirrhina. Erect perennial. H and S 14in (35cm) or more. Has oval, toothed leaves, to 2in (5cm) or more long and of unequal size in each opposite pair. In summer bears funnel-shaped, red-orange flowers to 1½in (4cm) long, with yellow throats.
***A.* 'Brilliant'**. Erect, compact perennial. H and S 12in (30cm). Has oval, toothed leaves and, in summer, large, funnel-shaped scarlet flowers.
A. coccinea. See *A. erecta*.
A. erecta, syn. *A. coccinea*, *A. pulchella*. Erect, bushy, branching perennial. H and S 18in (45cm). Has narrowly oval, toothed leaves, often arranged in whorls of 3. Tubular scarlet flowers with yellow eyes are produced in summer.
A. grandiflora. Erect perennial. H and S to 24in (60cm). Oval, toothed leaves are often reddish below. In summer has tubular, dark pink to purple flowers with white eyes.
***A.* 'Little Beauty'** illus. p.282.
***A.* 'Paul Arnold'**. Erect, compact, free-flowering perennial. H and S 12in (30cm). Has oval, toothed leaves. Bears large, funnel-shaped purple flowers in summer.
***A.* 'Peach Blossom'**. Trailing perennial. H and S to 10in (25cm). Has oval, toothed leaves and large, funnel-shaped, peach-colored flowers in summer.
A. pulchella. See *A. erecta*.

Achnatherum calamagrostis. See *Stipa calamagrostis*.
Acidanthera bicolor var. ***murieliae***. See *Gladiolus callianthus*.
Acidanthera murieliae. See *Gladiolus callianthus*.

ACIPHYLLA

APIACEAE/UMBELLIFERAE

Genus of evergreen perennials grown mainly for the architectural value of their spiky foliage but also for their flowers, which are produced more freely on male plants. Requires sun and well-drained soil. Protect neck of plant from winter wet with a deep layer of stone chips. Propagate by seed when fresh (in late summer) or in early spring.
A. aurea illus. p.238.
A. scott-thomsonii (Giant Spaniard). Evergreen, rosette-forming perennial. H to 14ft (4.5m), S 2–3ft (60cm–1m). Much-dissected, spiny foliage is bronze when young, maturing to silver-gray. Prickly spikes of tiny, creamy yellow flowers are rarely produced. Prefers a moist but well-drained site. Z8–11 H12–8.
A. squarrosa illus. p.266.

ACOKANTHERA

APOCYNACEAE

Genus of evergreen shrubs and trees, grown for their flowers and overall appearance. Requires full light and good drainage. Water containerized plants moderately, less when not in full growth. Propagate by seed in spring or autumn or by semi-ripe cuttings in summer. The sap and small, plumlike fruits that follow the flowers are highly toxic if ingested.
A. oblongifolia, syn. *A. spectabilis*, *Carissa spectabilis*, illus. p.150.
A. spectabilis. See *A. oblongifolia*.

ACONITUM
Aconite, Monkshood, Wolf's bane

RANUNCULACEAE

Genus of perennials with poisonous, tuberous or fibrous roots and upright, sometimes scandent stems bearing curious, hooded flowers in summer. Leaves are mostly rounded in outline. Good in rock gardens and borders. Prefers a position in sun but tolerates some shade, which may enhance flower color. Requires fertile, well-drained soil. Propagate by division in autumn, every 2–3 years, or by seed in autumn. Contact with the foliage may irritate skin; all parts are highly toxic if ingested.
A. anthora. Compact, tuberous perennial. H 24in (60cm), S 20in (50cm). Has erect, leafy stems that bear several hooded yellow flowers in summer. Leaves are divided and dark green. Z5–8 H8–5.
A.* x *bicolor. See *A.* x *cammarum* 'Bicolor'.
***A.* 'Bressingham Spire'**. Compact, upright, tuberous perennial. H 3ft (1m), S 20in (50cm). Erect spikes of hooded, violet-blue flowers are produced in summer. Bears deeply divided leaves that are glossy and dark green. Z3–8 H8–3.
***A.* x *cammarum* 'Bicolor'**, syn. *A.* x *bicolor*, illus. p.252.
***A. carmichaelii* 'Arendsii'**, syn. *A.c.* 'Arends'. Erect, tuberous perennial. H 5ft (1.5m), S 1ft (30cm). Has divided, rich green leaves and, in autumn, spikes of hooded, rich deep blue flowers. Upright stems may need staking, particularly if planted in a shady site. Z3–8 H8–3.
A. hemsleyanum, syn. *A. volubile* of gardens. Wiry, scandent, fibrous perennial. H 6–8ft (2–2.5m), S 3–4ft (1–1.2m). Hooded lilac flowers are produced in drooping clusters in late

summer. Leaves are divided and midgreen. Is best grown where it can scramble through a shrub or be supported. Z5–8 H8–5.
***A.* 'Ivorine'.** Upright, tuberous perennial. H 5ft (1.5m), S 20in (50cm). Bears hooded, creamy white flowers in erect spikes in early summer. Strong stems bear deeply divided, glossy green leaves. Z3–8 H8–3.
A. lycoctonum subsp. ***vulparia***, syn. *A. orientale* of gardens, *A. vulparia*, illus. p.255.
A. napellus (Helmet flower, Monkshood). Upright, tuberous perennial. H 5ft (1.5m), S 1ft (30cm). Bears tall, slender spires of hooded, light indigo blue flowers in late summer and deeply cut, midgreen leaves. Z3–8 H8–3. **'Albidum'** (syn. *A.n.* f. *album*) has white flowers.
***A.* 'Newry Blue'.** Upright, tuberous perennial. H 4ft (1.2m), S 20in (50cm). Produces hooded, dark blue flowers on erect stems in summer and has deeply divided, glossy, dark green leaves. Z5–8 H8–5.
A. orientale of gardens. See *A. lycoctonum* subsp. *vulparia*.
***A.* 'Sparks' Variety'.** Upright, tuberous perennial. H 4ft (1.2m), S 20in (50cm). Bears violet-blue flowers on branching stems in summer and has deeply divided, glossy, dark green leaves. Z5–8 H8–5.
A. volubile of gardens. See *A. hemsleyanum*.
A. vulparia. See *A. lycoctonum* subsp. *vulparia*.

ACORUS

ARACEAE

Genus of semi-evergreen, perennial, marginal and submerged water plants grown for their frequently aromatic foliage. Needs an open, sunny position. *A. calamus* requires up to 10in (25cm) depth of water. Clean up fading foliage in autumn, and lift and divide plants every 3 or 4 years in spring as clumps become congested.
***A. calamus* 'Argenteostriatus'**, syn. *A.c.* 'Variegatus', illus. p.447.
***A. gramineus* 'Pusillus'.** Semi-evergreen, perennial, marginal water plant or submerged aquarium plant. H and S 4in (10cm). Has narrow, grass-like, stiff leaves. Rarely, insignificant greenish flower spikes are produced in summer. Z10–11 H12–2. **'Variegatus'** illus. p.447.

Acroclinium. Reclassified as *Rhodanthe*.

ACTAEA
Baneberry

RANUNCULACEAE

Genus of clump-forming perennials grown for their colorful, poisonous berries. Likes woodland conditions – moist, peaty soil and shade. Propagate by division in spring or by seed in autumn. The berries are highly toxic if ingested.
A. alba. See *A. pachypoda*.
A. erythrocarpa of gardens. See *A. rubra*.
A. pachypoda, syn. *A. alba*, illus. p.259.
A. rubra, syn. *A. erythrocarpa* of gardens (Red baneberry). Clump-forming perennial. H 20in (50cm), S 12in (30cm). Small, fluffy white flowers are followed in autumn by clusters of poisonous, rounded scarlet berries borne above oval, divided, bright green leaves. Z4–8 H8–1.

ACTINIDIA

ACTINIDIACEAE

Genus of mainly deciduous, woody-stemmed, twining climbers. Grows in partial shade but needs sun for fruit to form and ripen. Grow in any well-drained soil that does not dry out. Prune in winter if necessary. Propagate by seed in spring or autumn, by semi-ripe cuttings in midsummer or by layering in winter.
A. chinensis of gardens. See *A. deliciosa*.
A. deliciosa, syn. *A. chinensis* of gardens (Chinese gooseberry, Kiwi fruit). Vigorous, mainly deciduous, woody-stemmed, twining climber. H 28–30ft (9–10m). Heart-shaped leaves are 5–8in (13–20cm) long. In summer bears clusters of cup-shaped white flowers that later turn yellowish, followed by edible, hairy brown fruits. To obtain fruits, both male and female plants must usually be grown. Z7–9 H9–7.
A. kolomikta illus. p.209.
A. polygama (Silver vine). Mainly deciduous, woody-stemmed, twining climber. H 12–20ft (4–6m). Heart-shaped leaves, 3–5in (7–13cm) long, are bronze when young and sometimes have creamy upper sections. In summer has scented, cup-shaped white flowers, usually arranged in groups of 3 male, female, or bisexual, followed by edible but not very palatable, egg-shaped, bright yellow fruits. Z4–9 H9–7.

ADA

See also ORCHIDS.
A. aurantiaca (illus. p.299). Evergreen, epiphytic orchid for a cool greenhouse. H 9in (23cm). Bears sprays of tubular orange flowers, 1in (2.5cm) long, in early spring. Has narrowly oval leaves, 4in (10cm) long. Needs shade in summer. Z14–15 H12–6.

ADANSONIA
Baobab

BOMBACACEAE

Genus of deciduous or semi-evergreen, mainly spring-flowering trees grown for their characteristically swollen trunks, their foliage, and for shade. Has flowers only on large, mature specimens. Requires full light and sharply drained soil. Allow soil of containerized specimens to almost dry out between waterings. Propagate by seed sown in spring. Pot specimens kept under glass are susceptible to spider mite.
A. digitata. Slow-growing, semi-evergreen, rounded tree. H and S 50ft (15m) or more. Has palmate leaves of 5–7 lustrous green leaflets. Produces fragrant, pendent, long-stalked white flowers with 5 reflexed petals in spring, followed by edible, sausage-shaped brown fruits. Z11 H12–10.

ADENIUM
Desert rose

APOCYNACEAE

Genus of succulents with fleshy, swollen trunks. Needs sun or partial shade and well-drained soil; plants are very prone to rotting. Propagate by seed sown in spring or summer. The milky sap that exudes from broken stems may irritate skin and cause severe discomfort if ingested.
A. obesum illus. p.458.

ADENOPHORA
Gland bellflower

CAMPANULACEAE

Genus of summer-flowering, fleshy-rooted perennials. Requires a site in full sun and rich, well-drained but not overly dry soil. May sometimes become invasive, but resents disturbance. Propagate by basal cuttings taken in early spring or by seed sown in autumn.
A. potaninii. Rosette-forming perennial. H 18in (45cm) or more, S 24in (60cm). Arching sprays of bell-shaped, pale bluish lavender flowers are produced in late summer. Has oval to lance-shaped, basal, midgreen leaves. Z4–8 H8–1.

Adhatoda duvernoia. See *Justicia adhatoda*.

ADIANTUM

ADIANTACEAE/PTERIDACEAE

Genus of deciduous, semi-evergreen or evergreen ferns. Prefers semi-shade and moist, neutral to acidic soil (*A. aleuticum* prefers alkaline soil). Remove fading fronds regularly. Propagate by spores in summer.
A. aleuticum, syn. *A. pedatum* var. *aleuticum*, illus. p.311.
A. capillus-veneris (Maidenhair fern). Semi-evergreen or evergreen fern. H and S 12in (30cm). Has dainty, triangular to oval, segmented, arching, light green fronds borne on black stems. Z7–11 H9–3.
A. cuneatum. See *A. raddianum*.
A. pedatum illus. p.312. var. ***aleuticum.*** See *A. aleuticum*.
A. raddianum, syn. *A. cuneatum* (Delta maidenhair). H and S 12in (30cm). Semi-evergreen or evergreen fern. Triangular, divided, pale green segments are borne on finely dissected fronds that have purplish black stems. Z11 H12–10. **'Fritz-Luthi'** has bright green fronds. **'Grandiceps'** (Tassel maidenhair) has elegant, tasselled fronds.
A. tenerum. Semi-evergreen or evergreen fern. H 1–3ft (30cm–1m), S 2–3ft (60cm–1m). Broadly lance-shaped, much-divided, spreading, midgreen fronds consist of rounded or diamond-shaped pinnae. Z11 H12–9.
A. venustum illus. p.313.

ADLUMIA

FUMARIACEAE/PAPAVERACEAE

Genus of one species of herbaceous, biennial, leaf-stalk climber grown for its leaves and flowers. Grow in semi-shade in any soil. Propagate by seed in spring.
A. cirrhosa. See *A. fungosa*.
A. fungosa, syn. *A. cirrhosa* (Allegheny vine, Climbing fumitory). Herbaceous, biennial, leaf-stalk climber. H 10–12ft (3–4m). Delicate leaves have numerous leaflets. Tiny, tubular, spurred white or purplish flowers are carried in drooping panicles in summer. Z4–8 H8–1.

ADONIS

RANUNCULACEAE

Genus of spring-flowering perennials grown for their foliage and flowers. Some thrive in semi-shade; others need an open, well-drained site. Propagate by seed when fresh (in late summer) or by division after flowering.
A. amurensis illus. p.275.
A. brevistyla illus. p.268.
A. vernalis illus. p.275.

ADROMISCHUS

CRASSULACEAE

Genus of succulents and evergreen subshrubs with rounded, thin or fat leaves. Needs partial shade and very well-drained soil. Propagate by leaf or stem cuttings in spring or summer.
A. clavifolius. See *A. cooperi*.
A. cooperi, syn. *A. clavifolius*, *Cotyledon cooperi*, *Echeveria cooperi*. Freely branching perennial succulent. H 4in (10cm), S to 6in (15cm). Has grayish brown stems and inversely lance-shaped, glossy, gray-green leaves, to 2in (5cm) long, often purple-marked above. In summer produces tubular, green-and-red flowers with white-margined pink or purple lobes on a stem 10in (25cm) or more long. Z12–15 H12–10.
A. maculatus illus. p.469.

AECHMEA

BROMELIACEAE

Genus of evergreen, rosette-forming, epiphytic perennials cultivated for their foliage, flowers, and fruits. May be grown in full light or a semi-shaded site. Provide a rooting medium of equal parts organic soil and either sphagnum moss or bark or plastic chips used for orchid culture. Using soft water, water moderately in summer, sparingly at all other times, and keep cuplike, rosette centers filled with water from spring through to autumn. Propagate by

offsets in late spring.
A. distichantha (illus. p.265). Evergreen, basal-rosetted, epiphytic perennial. H and S to 3ft (1m). Forms dense rosettes of narrowly oblong, round-tipped, arching leaves that are dull green above, gray and scaly beneath. Has panicles of small, tubular purple or blue flowers among white-felted pink bracts, usually in summer. Z14–15 H12–1.
A. fasciata, syn. *Billbergia rhodocyanea* (Silver vase plant, Urn plant; illus. p.265). Evergreen, tubular-rosetted, epiphytic perennial. H 16–24in (40–60cm), S 12–20in (30–50cm). Has loose rosettes of broadly oblong, round-tipped, incurved, arching leaves with dense gray scales and silver cross-banding. Bears dense, pyramidal panicles of tubular, blue-purple flowers among pink bracts, just above foliage, from spring to autumn. Z14–15 H12–1.
***A.* Foster's Favorite Group** (Lacquered wine-cup; illus. p.265). Evergreen, basal-rosetted, epiphytic perennial. H and S 12–24in (30–60cm). Has loose rosettes of strap-shaped, arching, lustrous, wine red leaves. Drooping spikes of small, tubular, deep purple-blue flowers are borne in summer, followed later by pear-shaped red fruits. Z14–15 H12–1.
A. fulgens (Coral berry). Evergreen, basal-rosetted, epiphytic perennial. H and S 16–30in (40–75cm). Forms loose rosettes of broadly oblong, arching, glossy, midgreen leaves with gray scales beneath and rounded or pointed tips. In summer produces erect panicles of small, tubular, violet-purple flowers that turn red with age. These are succeeded by small, rounded to ovoid red fruits on red stalks. Z14–15 H12–1.
A. nudicaulis. Evergreen, basal-rosetted, epiphytic perennial. H and S 16–30in (40–75cm). Produces loose rosettes of a few broadly strap-shaped, arching, olive green leaves with spiny edges and usually banded with gray scales beneath. Spikes of small, tubular yellow flowers open above large red bracts in summer. Z9–15 H12–10.
A. recurvata (illus. p.265). Evergreen, basal-rosetted, epiphytic perennial. H and S 6–8in (15–20cm). Narrowly triangular, tapered, spiny-edged, arching, red-flushed, midgreen leaves are produced in dense rosettes. In summer bears a short, dense spike of tubular, red-and-white flowers with red bracts, just above leaves. Z9–15 H12–1.

AEGOPODIUM

Goutweed, Ground elder

APIACEAE/UMBELLIFERAE

Genus of invasive, rhizomatous perennials, most of which are weeds, although *A. podagraria* 'Variegatum' makes an excellent groundcover. Tolerates sun or shade and any well-drained soil. Propagate by division of rhizomes in spring or autumn.
***A. podagraria* 'Variegatum'** illus. p.276.

AEONIUM

CRASSULACEAE

Genus of succulents, some of which are short-lived, and evergreen, succulent shrubs grown for their rosettes of bright green or blue-green, occasionally purple leaves. Prefers partial shade and very well-drained soil. Most species grow from autumn to spring and are semi-dormant in midsummer. Propagate by seed in summer or, for branching species, by stem cuttings in spring or summer.
A. arboreum. Bushy, perennial succulent. H to 2ft (60cm), S 3ft (1m). Branched stems are each crowned by a rosette, up to 6in (15cm) across, of broadly lance-shaped, glossy, bright green leaves. In spring produces cones of small, star-shaped golden flowers on 2–3-year-old stems, which then die back. **Z9–11 H9–4???. 'Schwarzkopf'** see *A.* 'Zwartkop'.
A. haworthii illus. p.466.
A. tabuliforme illus. p.478.
***A.* 'Zwartkop'**, syn. *A. arboreum* 'Schwarzkopf', illus. p.468.

AESCHYNANTHUS

GESNERIACEAE

Genus of evergreen, climbing, trailing or creeping perennials useful for growing in hanging baskets. Needs a fairly humid atmosphere and a position out of direct sun. Water sparingly in low temperatures. Propagate by tip cuttings in spring or summer.
***A.* 'Black Pagoda'.** Semi-trailing perennial. H 24in (60cm), S to 18in (45cm). Has elliptic leaves, to 4in (10cm) long, pale green with dark brown marbling above, and purple beneath. Bears terminal clusters of deep burnt orange flowers with green calyces from summer to winter. Z14-15 H12–10.
A. marmoratus, syn. *A. zebrinus*. Evergreen, trailing perennial. H and S to 24in (60cm). Oval, waxy leaves are dark green, veined yellowish green above, purplish below. Produces tubular greenish flowers with dark brown markings, borne in terminal clusters in summer. Z14–15 H12–10.
A. pulcher (Lipstick plant, Royal red bugler). Evergreen, climbing or trailing perennial. H and S indefinite. Produces thick, oval leaves and small, tubular, hooded, bright red flowers with yellow throats, borne in terminal clusters from summer to winter. Z14–15 H12–10.
A. speciosus, syn. *A. splendens*, illus. p.293.
A. splendens. See *A. speciosus*.
A. zebrinus. See *A. marmoratus*.

AESCULUS

Buckeye, Horse chestnut

HIPPOCASTANACEAE

Genus of deciduous trees and shrubs grown for their bold, divided leaves and conspicuous, upright panicles or clusters of flowers, followed by fruits (horse chestnuts), sometimes with spiny outer casings. Requires sun or semi-shade and fertile, well-drained soil. Propagate species by sowing seed in autumn; cultivars by budding in late summer or by grafting in late winter. Leaf spot may affect young foliage. All parts of these plants may cause mild stomach upset if ingested.
A. californica illus. p.85.
A. x carnea (Red horse chestnut). **'Briotii'** illus. p.64.
A. chinensis illus. p.64.
A. flava, syn. *A. octandra*, illus. p.82.
A. glabra (Ohio buckeye). Deciduous, round-headed, sometimes shrubby tree. H and S 30ft (10m). Leaves, usually composed of 5 narrowly oval leaflets, are dark green. Bears 4-petaled, greenish yellow flowers in upright clusters in late spring and early summer. Z3–7 H7–1.
A. hippocastanum (Horse chestnut) illus. p.64. **'Baumannii'** is a vigorous, deciduous, spreading tree. H 100ft (30m), S 15m (50ft). Large, dark green leaves, consisting of 5 or 7 narrowly oval leaflets, turn yellow in autumn. Has large panicles of long-lasting, double, yellow- or red-marked white flowers from mid- to late spring. Z3–8 H8–4.
A. indica (Indian horse chestnut). Deciduous, spreading, elegant tree. H 70ft (20m), S 40ft (12m). Glossy, dark green leaves with usually 7 narrowly oval leaflets are bronze when young, orange or yellow in autumn. Upright panicles of 4-petaled, pink-tinged white flowers marked with red or yellow appear in midsummer. Z7–8 H8–7. **'Sydney Pearce'** illus. p.79.
A. x neglecta (Sunrise horse-chestnut). **'Erythroblastos'** illus. p.89.
A. octandra. See *A. flava*.
A. parviflora illus. p.119.
A. pavia (Red buckeye). Deciduous, round-headed, sometimes shrubby tree. H 15ft (5m), S 10ft (3m). Glossy, dark green leaves consist of 5 narrowly oval leaflets. Has panicles of 4-petaled red flowers in early summer. Z5–9 H9–5. **'Atrosanguinea'** illus. p.91.
A. turbinata (Japanese horse chestnut). Deciduous, spreading, thick-branched tree. H 70ft (20m), S 40ft (12m). Large, dark green leaves consist of 5 or 7 narrowly oval leaflets. Panicles of creamy white flowers appear in late spring and early summer. Z6–8 H8–6.

AETHIONEMA

BRASSICACEAE/CRUCIFERAE

Genus of short-lived, evergreen or semi-evergreen shrubs, subshrubs, and perennials grown for their prolific flowers. Needs sun and well-drained soil. Propagate by softwood cuttings in spring or by seed in autumn. Most species self seed readily.
A. armenum illus. p.377.
A. grandiflorum, syn. *A. pulchellum*, illus. p.352.
A. iberideum. Evergreen or semi-evergreen, rounded, compact shrub. H and S 6in (15cm). Bears small, lance-shaped, gray-green leaves and, in summer, ¾in (2cm) stems each bear a raceme of small, saucer-shaped white flowers. Z6–8 H8–6.
A. pulchellum. See *A. grandiflorum*.
***A.* 'Warley Rose'** illus. p.376.
***A.* 'Warley Ruber'.** Evergreen or semi-evergreen, rounded, compact subshrub. H and S 6in (15cm). Has tiny, linear, bluish green leaves. Racemes of small, deep rose pink flowers appear on ¾–1¼in (2–3cm) stems in spring-summer. Z6–8 H8–6.

AGAPANTHUS

AGAPANTHACEAE/LILIACEAE

Genus of clump-forming perennials, some of which are evergreen, with erect stems that carry large umbels of bell- to tubular-bell-shaped or trumpet-shaped flowers, usually blue and often fading to purple with age. Leaves are strap-shaped. Grow in full sun and in moist but well-drained soil. Protect crowns in winter with mulch where marginally hardy. Plants increase slowly but may be propagated by division in spring; may also be raised from seed in autumn or spring. Named cultivars will not come true from seed.
A. africanus (African lily). Evergreen, clump-forming perennial. H 3ft (1m), S 20in (50cm). In late summer has rounded umbels of deep blue flowers on upright stems, above broad, dark green leaves. Z7–10 H12–1.
***A.* 'Alice Gloucester'.** Clump-forming perennial. H 3ft (1m), S 20in (50cm). Produces large, dense, rounded umbels of white flowers in summer, above narrow, midgreen leaves. Z7–10 H10–7.
***A.* 'Ben Hope'.** Clump-forming perennial. H 3–4ft (1–1.2m), S 20in (50cm). Erect stems support dense, rounded umbels of deep blue flowers in late summer and early autumn, borne over narrow, grayish green leaves. Z7–10 H10–7.
A. campanulatus. Clump-forming perennial. H 2–4ft (60cm–1.2m), S 20in (50cm). Rounded umbels of blue flowers are borne on strong stems in summer, above narrow, grayish green leaves. Z7–11 H12–7.
***A.* 'Cherry Holley'.** Clump-forming perennial. H 3ft (1m), S 20in (50cm). Rounded umbels of dark blue flowers, carried in summer above narrow leaves, do not fade to purple with age. Z7–10 H10–7.
***A.* 'Dorothy Palmer'** illus. p.253.
A. inapertus. Clump-forming perennial. H 5ft (1.5m), S 2ft (60cm). Pendent, narrowly tubular blue flowers are borne on very erect stems, above narrow, bluish green leaves in late summer and autumn. Z9–11 H12–7.
***A.* 'Lilliput'.** Compact, clump-forming perennial. H 32in (80cm), S 20in (50cm). Has small, rounded umbels of dark blue flowers that are produced in summer. Leaves are narrow and midgreen. Z6–9 H9–4.
***A.* 'Loch Hope'.** Clump-forming perennial. H 3–4ft (1–1.2m), S 20in (50cm). Bears large, rounded umbels of deep blue flowers in late summer and early autumn above narrow,

grayish green leaves. Z8–11 H12–1.
A. orientalis. See *A. praecox* subsp. *orientalis*.
A. praecox subsp. ***orientalis***, syn. *A. orientalis*, illus. p.254.

AGAPETES, syn. PENTAPTERYGIUM

ERICACEAE

Genus of evergreen or deciduous, scandent shrubs and semi-scrambling climbers grown for their flowers. Provide full light or partial shade and a organic, well-drained but not dry, neutral to acidic soil. Water potted specimens freely when in full growth, but moderately at other times. Overly long stems may be cut back to promote branching, but they are best tied to supports. Propagate by seed sown in spring or by semi-ripe cuttings taken in late summer.
***A.* 'Ludgvan Cross'.** Evergreen, scandent shrub with arching or pendulous stems. H and S 6–10ft (2–3m). Lance-shaped leaves are dark green. Urn-shaped red flowers with darker patterning are produced in spring. Z10–11 H12–7.
A. macrantha. See *A. variegata* var. *macrantha*.
A. rugosa. See *A. variegata* var. *rugosa*.
A. serpens illus. p.205.
A. variegata var. ***macrantha***, syn. *A. macrantha*, illus. p.219. var. ***rugosa*** (syn. *A. rugosa*) is an evergreen, loose shrub with arching or spreading stems. H and S to 10ft (3m). Leaves are lance-shaped, wrinkled, and bright green. In spring, clusters of pendent, urn-shaped white flowers patterned with purple-red are borne from leaf axils. Z15–15 H12–10.

AGASTACHE

Mexican giant hyssop

LABIATAE/LAMIACEAE

Genus of summer-flowering perennials with aromatic leaves. Needs full sun and fertile, well-drained soil. Plants are short-lived and should be propagated each year by softwood or semi-ripe cuttings taken in late summer.
A. mexicana, syn. *Brittonastrum mexicanum*, *Cedronella mexicana*. Upright perennial with aromatic leaves. H to 3ft (1m), S to 1ft (30cm). In summer bears whorls of small, tubular flowers in shades of pink to crimson. Leaves are oval, pointed, toothed, and midgreen. Z7–11 H12–7.

Agathaea. Reclassified as *Felicia*.

AGAVE

AGAVACEAE

Genus of rosetted succulents with sword-shaped, sharp-toothed leaves. Small species, to 1ft (30cm) high, flower after 5–10 years; tall species, to 15ft (5m) high, may take 20–40 years to flower. Agaves need full sun and well-drained soil. Propagate by seed or offsets in spring or summer.
A. americana (Century plant). Basal-rosetted succulent. H 3–6ft (1–2m), S 6–10ft (2–3m) or more. Has sharply pointed, toothed leaves to 5–6ft (1.5–2m) long. Branched flower stem to 25ft (8m) high bears dense, tapering spikes of bell-shaped white to pale creamy yellow flowers, each 3½in (9cm) long, in spring-summer. Offsets freely. Z9–11 H12–5. **'Mediopicta'**, H and S 6ft (2m), has central yellow stripes along leaves. Z12–15 H12-10. **'Striata'** illus. p.457.
A. attenuata illus. p.467.
A. filifera illus. p.465.
A. parryi illus. p.466.
A. parviflora illus. p.457.
A. utahensis illus. p.478.
A. victoriae-reginae illus. p.461.

Ageratina ligustrina. See *Eupatorium ligustrinum*

AGERATUM

Floss flower

ASTERACEAE/COMPOSITAE

Genus of annuals and biennials. Grow in sun and in fertile, well-drained soil, which should not be allowed to dry out; otherwise, growth and flowering will be poor. Plants must be deadheaded regularly to ensure continuous flowering. Propagate by seed sown outdoors in late spring.
A. houstonianum. Moderately fast-growing, hummock-forming annual. Tall cultivars, H and S 12in (30cm); medium, H and S 8in (20cm); dwarf, H and S 6in (15cm). All have oval, midgreen leaves and clusters of feathery, brushlike flower heads throughout summer and into autumn. Useful for bedding. Z10–13 H12–1. **'Blue Danube'** (dwarf) and **'Blue Mink'** (tall) illus. p.333. **Hawaii Series** includes uniform, compact plants with deep to pale blue or white flower heads. **'Pacific'** (medium) is neat, with tight clusters of deep violet-blue flower heads. **'Swing Pink'** (dwarf) has attractive pink flower heads.

AGLAONEMA

Chinese evergreen

ARACEAE

Genus of evergreen, erect, tufted perennials grown mainly for their foliage. Tolerates shade, although the variegated forms need more light, and prefers moist but well-drained soil. Water moderately when in full growth, less in winter. Propagate by division or stem cuttings in summer. Mealy bug may be a problem.
A. commutatum. Evergreen, erect, tufted perennial. H and S to 18in (45cm) or more. Broadly lance-shaped leaves are 12in (30cm) long and dark green with irregular, grayish white patches along lateral veins. Has greenish white spathes produced in summer. Z14–15 H12–1. **'Malay Beauty'** (syn. *A.c.* 'Pewter') bears very dark green leaves mottled greenish white and cream. **'Pewter'** see *A.c.* 'Malay Beauty'. **'Treubii'** illus. p.300.
A. pictum illus. p.304.
***A.* 'Silver King'** illus. p.304.

AGONIS

Willow myrtle

MYRTACEAE

Genus of evergreen, mainly spring-flowering shrubs and trees grown for their foliage, flowers, and graceful appearance. Needs full light and well-drained but moisture-retentive soil. Water containerized specimens moderately, scarcely at all in winter. Pruning is tolerated when necessary. Propagate by seed in spring or by semi-ripe cuttings in summer.
A. flexuosa illus. p.90.

AGROSTEMMA

Corn cockle

CARYOPHYLLACEAE

Genus of summer-flowering annuals. Grow in sun; flowers best in very well-drained soil that is not very fertile. Support with sticks and deadhead to prolong flowering. Propagate by seed sown *in situ* in spring or early autumn. Seeds may cause severe discomfort if ingested.
A. coeli-rosa. See *Silene coeli-rosa*.
A. githago. Fast-growing, erect annual with thin stems. H 2–3ft (60cm–1m), S 1ft (30cm). Has lance-shaped, midgreen leaves and, in summer, 5-petaled, open trumpet-shaped pink flowers, 3in (8cm) wide. Seeds are tiny, rounded, dark brown, and poisonous. H9-1. **'Milas'** illus. p.323.

AICHRYSON

CRASSULACEAE

Genus of annual and perennial succulents, often shrublike, grown for their fleshy, spoon-shaped to rounded, hairy leaves. Most species are short-lived, dying after flowering. Needs full sun or partial shade and very well-drained soil. Propagate by seed or stem cuttings in spring or summer.
***A.* x *domesticum* 'Variegatum'** illus. p.477.

AILANTHUS

SIMAROUBACEAE

Genus of deciduous trees grown for their foliage and 3–5-winged fruits; they can be particularly useful since they are extremely tolerant of urban pollution. Needs sun or semi-shade and deep, fertile, well-drained soil. To grow as shrubs, cut back hard in spring, after which vigorous shoots bearing very large leaves are produced. Propagate by seed sown in autumn or by suckers or root cuttings taken in winter. Male flowers are unpleasantly scented; the pollen may cause an allergic reaction.
A. altissima (Tree of heaven). Fast-growing, deciduous, spreading tree. H 80ft (25m), S 50ft (15m). Large, dark green leaves consist of 15–30 paired, oval leaflets. Large clusters of small green flowers in midsummer are followed by attractive, winged green, then reddish brown, fruits. Z4–8 H8–1.

AJUGA

LABIATAE/LAMIACEAE

Genus of annuals and perennials, some of which are semi-evergreen or evergreen and excellent as a groundcover. Tolerates sun or shade and any soil but grows more vigorously in moist conditions. Propagate by division in spring.
A. pyramidalis (Pyramidal bugle). Semi-evergreen perennial. H 6in (15cm), S 18in (45cm). Forms a creeping carpet of oblong to spoon-shaped, deep green leaves, above which appear spikes of whorled, 2-lipped blue flowers in spring. Z3–9 H8–2. **'Metallica Crispa'** has curled leaves with a metallic-bronze luster and dark blue flowers. Z5–9 H9–5.
***A. reptans* 'Atropurpurea'** illus. p.303. **'Jungle Beauty'** is a semi-evergreen, mat-forming perennial. H 15in (38cm), S 24in (60cm). Has large, oval, toothed or slightly lobed, dark green leaves, sometimes suffused purple and, in spring, spikes of whorled, 2-lipped blue flowers. **'Multicolor'** (syn. *A.r.* 'Rainbow') illus. p.303. **'Rainbow'** see *A.r.* 'Multicolor'. Both Z3–9 H9–1.

AKEBIA

LARDIZABALACEAE

Genus of deciduous or semi-evergreen, woody-stemmed, twining climbers grown for their leaves and flowers. Individual plants seldom produce fruits; cross-pollination between two individuals is required for fruit formation. Prefers a position in full sun and any good, well-drained soil. Tolerates an east- or north-facing position. Dislikes disturbance. May be propagated in a number of ways: by seed sown in autumn or spring, by semi-ripe cutings taken in summer, or by layering in winter.
A. lobata. See *A. trifoliata*.
A.* x *pentaphylla illus. p.205.
A. quinata illus. p.205.
A. trifoliata, syn. *A. lobata*. Deciduous, woody-stemmed, twining climber. H to 30ft (10m) or more. Midgreen leaves, bronze-tinted when young, have 3 oval leaflets; drooping racemes of 3-petaled purple flowers appear in spring, followed by sausage-shaped purplish fruits. Z5–8 H8–5.

ALBIZIA

LEGUMINOSAE/MIMOSACEAE

Genus of deciduous or semi-evergreen trees grown for their feathery foliage and unusual flower heads composed of numerous stamens and resembling bottlebrushes. Requires full sun and well-drained soil. May be short-lived,

and its seedlings may become a nuisance. *A. julibrissin* may be grown as a summer bedding plant for its foliage. Propagate by seed in autumn.
A. distachya. See *Paraserianthes lophantha*.
A. julibrissin illus. p.90.
A. lophantha. See *Paraserianthes lophantha*.

ALBUCA

HYACINTHACEAE/LILIACEAE

Genus of spring- or summer-flowering bulbs. Needs an open, sunny position and well-drained soil. Dies down in spring or late summer after flowering. Propagate by seed in spring or by offsets when dormant.
A. canadensis, syn. *A. major*, *A. minor*. Spring-flowering bulb. H 6in (15cm), S 3–4in (8–10cm). Has 3–6 narrowly lance-shaped, erect, basal leaves. Produces a loose spike of tubular yellow flowers, ⅝–¾in (1.5–2cm) long, with a green stripe on each petal. Z11–13 H12–7.
A. humilis illus. p.435.
A. major. See *A. canadensis*.
A. minor. See *A. canadensis*.

ALCEA
Hollyhock

MALVACEAE

Genus of biennials and short-lived perennials grown for their tall spikes of flowers. Needs full sun and well-drained soil. Propagate by seed in late summer or spring. Rust may be a problem.
A. rosea, syn. *Althaea rosea* (biennial), illus. p.321. **'Chater's Double'** (biennial), illus. p.327. **'Majorette'** is an erect biennial grown as an annual. H 24in (60cm), S to 12in (30cm). Rounded, lobed, pale green leaves have a rough texture. Spikes of rosettelike, double flowers in several different colors are produced during summer and early autumn. **'Summer Carnival'** (annual or biennial), H 6–8ft (1.8–2.4m), S to 2ft (60cm), has double flowers in mixed colors. Both Z3–9 H10–3.

ALCHEMILLA
Lady's mantle

ROSACEAE

Genus of perennials that produce sprays of tiny, greenish yellow flowers with conspicuous outer calyces in summer. Some are good for groundcover. Grow in sun or partial shade, in all but boggy soils. Propagate by seed or division in spring or autumn.
A. alpina (Alpine lady's mantle). Mound-forming perennial. H 6in (15cm), S 24in (60cm) or more. Rounded, lobed, pale green leaves are covered in silky hairs. Bears upright spikes of tiny, greenish yellow flowers with conspicuous green outer calyces in summer. Is suitable as a groundcover and on a dry bank. Z3–8 H8–1.
A. conjuncta illus. p.290.
A. mollis illus. p.290.

x ALICEARA

See also ORCHIDS.
x ***A.*** **Dark Warrior** (illus. p.298). Evergreen, epiphytic orchid for a cool greenhouse. H 10in (25cm). Produces sprays of wispy, mauve-brown, cream-yellow, or green flowers, 1½in (4cm) across; flowering season varies. Leaves, 4in (10cm) long, are narrowly oval. Grow in semi-shade in summer. Z14–15 H12–6.

ALISMA

ALISMATACEAE

Genus of deciduous, perennial, marginal water plants grown for their foliage and flowers. Requires an open, sunny position in mud or up to 10in (25cm) depth of water. Clean up fading foliage in autumn, and remove dying flower spikes before ripening seeds are dispersed. May be propagated by division in spring or by seed in late summer. Contact with sap may irritate skin; all parts may cause mild stomach upset if ingested.
A. natans. See *Luronium natans*.
A. plantago-aquatica illus. p.446.
A. ranunculoides. See *Baldellia ranunculoides*.

ALLAMANDA

APOCYNACEAE

Genus of evergreen, woody-stemmed, scrambling climbers grown for their trumpet-shaped flowers. Prefers partial shade in summer and organic, well-drained, neutral to acidic soil. Water regularly, less when not in full growth. Stems must be tied to supports. Prune previous season's growth back to 1 or 2 nodes in spring. Propagate by softwood cuttings in spring or summer. Whitefly and spider mite may be troublesome. Contact with sap may irritate skin; all parts may cause mild stomach upset if ingested.
A. cathartica (Golden trumpet). **'Hendersonii'** illus. p.216.

ALLIUM
Onion

ALLIACEAE/LILIACEAE

Genus of perennials, some of which are edible, with bulbs, rhizomes, or fibrous rootstocks. Nearly all have narrow, basal leaves smelling of onions when crushed, and most have small flowers packed together in a loose to dense, spherical or roughly oval umbel. Dried umbels of tall border species are good for winter decoration. Requires an open, sunny situation and well-drained soil; is best left undisturbed to form clumps. Plant in autumn. Propagate by seed in autumn or by division of clumps – spring-flowering varieties in late summer and summer-flowering ones in spring. Contact with the bulbs may irritate skin or aggravate skin allergies.
A. acuminatum, syn. *A. murrayanum*, illus. p.430.
A. aflatunense of gardens. See *A.* x *hollandicum*.
A. akaka illus. p.427.
A. albopilosum. See *A. cristophii*.
A. azureum. See *A. caeruleum*.
A. beesianum. Clump-forming, late summer-flowering bulb. H 8–12in (20–30cm), S 2–4in (5–10cm). Has linear, gray-green leaves and, in late summer, pendent heads of bell-shaped, blue flowers. Z6–10 H10–6.
A. caeruleum, syn. *A. azureum*, illus. p.422.
A. campanulatum. Clump-forming, summer-flowering bulb. H 4–12in (10–30cm), S 5–10cm (2–4in). Linear, semi-erect, basal leaves die away before flowering time. Bears a domed umbel, 1–3in (2.5–7cm) wide, of up to 30 small, star-shaped, pale pink or white flowers. Z9–10 H10–9
A. carinatum subsp. ***pulchellum***, syn. *A. pulchellum*. Clump-forming, summer-flowering bulb. H 12–24in (30–60cm), S 3–4in (8–10cm). Linear, semi-erect leaves sheath lower two-thirds of stem. Has an umbel of pendent, cup-shaped purple flowers. Z6–9 H9–6.
A. cernuum illus. p.420.
A. christophii. See *A. cristophii*.
A. cowanii. See *A. neapolitanum*.
A. cristophii, syn. *A. albopilosum*, *A. christophii*, illus. p.421.
A. cyaneum. Tuft-forming, summer-flowering bulb. H 4–12in (10–30cm), S 2–3in (5–8cm). Leaves are threadlike and erect. Stems each bear a small, dense umbel of 5 or more pendent, cup-shaped blue or violet-blue flowers, ¼in (0.5cm) long. Z5–9 H9–5.
A. cyathophorum var. ***farreri*** illus. p.436.
A. flavum illus. p.422.
A. giganteum illus. p.402.
A. x ***hollandicum***, syn. *A. aflatunense* of gardens, illus. p.402.
A. kansuense. See *A. sikkimense*.
A. karataviense illus. p.427.
A. macranthum. Tuft-forming, summer-flowering bulb. H 8–12in (20–30cm), S 4–5in (10–12cm). Has linear leaves on lower part of flower stem, which bears a loose umbel of up to 20 bell-shaped, deep purple flowers, each ½in (1cm) long, on slender stalks. Z4–10 H10–1.
A. mairei. Clump-forming, late summer- to autumn-flowering bulb. H 4–8in (10–20cm), S 4–5in (10–12cm). Leaves are erect, threadlike, and basal. Wiry stems each carry a small umbel of up to 20 upright, bell-shaped pink flowers, each ½in (1cm) long. Z4–10 H10–1.
A. moly illus. p.436.
A. murrayanum. See *A. acuminatum*.
A. narcissiflorum, syn. *A. pedemontanum* of gardens, illus. p.436.
A. neapolitanum, syn. *A. cowanii*, illus. p.408.
A. oreophilum, syn. *A. ostrowskianum*, illus. p.430.
A. ostrowskianum. See *A. oreophilum*.
A. pedemontanum of gardens. See *A. narcissiflorum*.
A. pulchellum. See *A. carinatum* subsp. *pulchellum*.
A. schoenoprasum illus. p.435.
A. schubertii illus. p.421.
A. senescens var. ***calcareum.*** See *A.s.* subsp. *montanum*.
subsp. ***montanum*** (syn. *A.s.* var. *calcareum*) illus. p.420.
A. sikkimense, syn. *A. kansuense*. Tuft-forming, summer-flowering bulb. H 4–10in (10–25cm), S 2–4in (5–10cm). Leaves are linear, erect, and basal. Up to 15 bell-shaped blue flowers, ¼–½in (0.5–1cm) long, are borne in a small, pendent umbel. Z6–10 H10–6.
A. sphaerocephalon. Clump-forming, summer-flowering bulb. H to 24in (60cm), S 3–4in (8–10cm). Has linear, semi-erect leaves on basal third of slender, wiry stems and a very dense umbel, ¾–1½in (2–4cm) across, of up to 40 small, bell-shaped, pinkish purple flowers. Z4–8 H8–1.
A. stipitatum illus. p.401.
A. unifolium illus. p.409.

ALNUS
Alder

BETULACEAE

Genus of deciduous trees and shrubs grown mainly for their ability to thrive in wet situations. Flowers are borne in catkins in late winter or early spring, the males conspicuous and attractive, the females forming persistent, woody, conelike fruits. Most do best in sun and any moist or even waterlogged soil, but *A. cordata* will also grow well on poor, dry soils. Propagate species by seed sown in autumn, and cultivars by budding in late summer or by hardwood cuttings taken in early winter.
A. cordata illus. p.66.
A. glutinosa (Black alder). **'Aurea'** is a slow-growing, deciduous, conical tree. H to 80ft (25m), S 30ft (10m). Has rounded leaves, bright yellow until midsummer, later becoming pale green. Produces yellow-brown catkins in early spring. Useful grown in a boggy area. Z3–7 H7–1. **'Imperialis'**, H 30ft (10m), S 12ft (4m), is slow-growing and has deeply cut, lobed leaves.
A. incana (Gray alder) illus. p.66. **'Aurea'** is a deciduous, conical tree. H 70ft (20m), S 25ft (8m). Has reddish yellow or orange shoots in winter and broadly oval yellow leaves. Reddish yellow or orange catkins are borne in late winter and early spring. Useful for cold, wet areas and poor soils. **'Ramulis Coccineis'** has red winter shoots and buds and orange catkins. Both Z2–6 H6–1.

ALOCASIA

ARACEAE

Genus of evergreen perennials, with underground rhizomes, grown for their attractive foliage. Produces tiny flowers on a spadix enclosed in a leaflike

spathe. Needs high humidity, partial shade, and well-drained soil. Propagate by seed, stem cuttings, or division of rhizomes in spring. Contact with sap may irritate skin; all parts may cause mild stomach upset if ingested.
A. cuprea illus. p.266.
A. lowii var. ***veitchii.*** See *A. veitchii.*
A. macrorrhiza (Giant elephant's ear, Taro). Evergreen, tufted perennial with a thick, trunklike stem. H to 10ft (3m) or more, S 6ft (2m). Broad, arrow-shaped, glossy green leaves to 3ft (1m) long are carried on stalks 3ft (1m) long. Has yellowish green spathes to 8in (20cm) high. Z11 H12–10.
A. picta. See *A. veitchii.*
A. veitchii, syn. *A. lowii* var. *veitchii*, *A. picta.* Evergreen, tufted perennial. H 3ft (1m) or more, S 30in (75cm). Narrow, triangular leaves with arrow-shaped bases are 18in (45cm) long and green with grayish midribs, veins, and margins, purple below. Greenish spathes. Z14–15 H12–10.

ALOE

ALOEACEAE/LILIACEAE

Genus of evergreen, rosetted trees, shrubs, perennials, and scandent climbers with succulent foliage and tubular to bell-shaped flowers. Tree aloes and shrubs with a spread over 1ft (30cm) prefer full sun; most smaller species prefer partial shade. Needs very well-drained soil. Propagate by seed, stem cuttings,or offsets in spring or summer.
A. arborescens. Evergreen, bushy, succulent-leaved shrub. H and S 6ft (2m). Stems are crowned by rosettes of widely spreading, long, slender, curved, dull blue-green leaves with toothed margins. Long flower stems produce masses of tubular to bell-shaped red flowers in late winter and spring. Z11 H12–10. **'Variegata'** illus. p.459.
A. aristata illus. p.480.
A. barbadensis. See *A. vera.*
A. brevifolia. Basal-rosetted succulent producing many offsets. H 6in (15cm), S 12in (30cm). Has broadly sword-shaped, fleshy, blue-green leaves with a few teeth along edges. In spring, flower stems, 20in (50cm) long, carry narrowly bell-shaped, bright red flowers. Z10–11 H12–3.
A. ciliaris illus. p.459.
A. ferox illus. p.459.
A. humilis. Rosetted succulent. H 4in (10cm), S 12in (30cm). Has a dense, basal rosette of narrowly sword-shaped, spine-edged, fleshy, blue-green leaves, often erect, with incurving tips. Produces flower stems 12in (30cm) long, each bearing a spike of narrowly bell-shaped orange flowers in spring. Offsets freely. Z10–11 H12–10.
A. punctata. See *A. variegata.*
A. striata illus. p.468.
A. variegata, syn. *A. punctata*, illus. p.464.
A. vera, syn. *A. barbadensis*, illus. p.466.

ALOINOPSIS

AIZOACEAE

Genus of dwarf, tuberous succulents with daisylike flowers from late summer to early spring. Requires a sunny site and very well-drained soil. Very susceptible to overwatering. Propagate by seed in summer.
A. schooneesii illus. p.477.

ALONSOA

SCROPHULARIACEAE

Genus of perennials grown as annuals. May be used for cut flowers. Grow in sun and in rich, well-drained soil. Flowering may be poor outdoors in a wet summer. Young plants should have growing shoots pinched out to encourage bushy growth. Propagate by seed sown outdoors in late spring. Aphids may be troublesome, particularly under cover.
A. warscewiczii illus. p.329.

ALOPECURUS

GRAMINEAE/POACEAE

See also GRASSES, BAMBOOS, RUSHES and SEDGES.
A. pratensis **'Aureovariegatus'**, syn. *A.p.* 'Aureomarginatus', illus. p.309.

ALOYSIA

VERBENACEAE

Genus of deciduous or evergreen, summer-flowering shrubs grown for their aromatic foliage and sprays of tiny flowers. Needs full sun and well-drained soil. Cut out any dead wood in early summer. Propagate by softwood cuttings in summer.
A. triphylla, syn. *Lippia citriodora*, illus. p.143.

ALPINIA

ZINGIBERACEAE

Genus of mainly evergreen perennials, with fleshy rhizomes, grown for their flowers in well-drained soil with plenty of organic matter, a moist atmosphere, and partial shade. Not successful in containers. Propagate by division in late spring or early summer. Spider mite may be a problem.
A. calcarata (Indian ginger). Evergreen, upright, clump-forming perennial. H and S to 3ft (1m). Has stalkless, aromatic, lance-shaped leaves to 1ft (30cm) long. At any time of year may bear horizontal spikes of whitish flowers with 1in (2.5cm) long yellow lips marked reddish purple. Z14–15 H12–10
A. nutans of gardens. See *A. zerumbet.*
A. speciosa. See *A. zerumbet.*
A. zerumbet, syn. *A. nutans* of gardens, *A. speciosa*, illus. p.227.

Alsobia dianthiflora. See *Episcia dianthiflora.*
Alsophila. Reclassified as *Cyathea.*

ALSTROEMERIA

ALSTROEMERIACEAE

Genus of mostly summer-flowering, tuberous perennials with showy, multicolored flowers. Flowers are good for cutting because they last well. Where marginally hardy, protect by covering dormant tubers with a loose, dry mulch. Needs sun and well-drained soil. Propagate by seed or division in early spring. Contact with foliage may aggravate skin allergies.
A. aurantiaca. See *A. aurea.*
A. aurea, syn. *A. aurantiaca*, illus. p.403.
A. gayana. See *A. pelegrina.*
A. hookeri illus. p.386.
***A.* Ligtu Hybrids** illus. p.423.
***A.* MARGARET ('Stacova')** illus. p.400
***A.* 'Parigo Charm'** illus. p.423
A. pelegrina, syn. *A. gayana*, illus. p.420.
***A.* 'Stacova'.** See *A.* MARGARET.
***A.* 'Walter Fleming'.** Summer-flowering, tuberous perennial. H to 3ft (1m), S 2–3ft (60cm–1m). Each leafy stem produces narrowly lance-shaped, twisted leaves and widely funnel-shaped, deep yellow flowers, 2–2½in (5–6cm) across, flushed purple with reddish purple spots. Z8–11 H12–7.

ALTERNANTHERA

AMARANTHACEAE

Genus of bushy perennials grown for their attractive colored foliage. Useful for carpeting or bedding. Needs sun or partial shade and moist but well-drained soil. Propagate by tip cuttings or division in spring.
A. amoena. See *A. ficoidea* var. *amoena.*
A. ficoidea (Parrot leaf). var. ***amoena*** (syn. *A. amoena*) is a mat-forming perennial. H 2in (5cm), S indefinite. Has narrowly oval green leaves marked red, yellow, and orange, with wavy margins. Z11–12 H12–1. **'Versicolor'** (syn. *A. versicolor*) is an erect form, H and S to 12in (30cm), with rounded to spoon-shaped leaves shaded brown, red, and yellow.
A. versicolor. See *A. ficoidea* 'Versicolor'.

Althaea rosea. See *Alcea rosea*

ALYSSUM

BRASSICACEAE/CRUCIFERAE

Genus of perennials (some of which are evergreen) and annuals grown for their flowers. Requires a sunny site and well-drained soil. Cut back lightly after flowering. Propagate either by softwood cuttings taken in late spring or by seed sown in autumn.
A. maritimum. See *Lobularia maritima.*
A. montanum. Evergreen, prostrate perennial. H and S 6in (15cm). Leaves are small, oval, hairy, and gray. Flower stems, 6in (15cm) long, each bear an open, spherical raceme carrying small, highly fragrant, soft yellow flowers in summer. Is a good plant for a rock garden. Z4–9 H9–1.
A. saxatile. See *Aurinia saxatilis.*
A. spinosum, syn. *Ptilotrichum spinosum.* Semi-evergreen, rounded, compact shrub. H 8in (20cm) or more, S 12in (30cm). Intricate branches bear spines and narrowly oval to linear silver leaves. Spherical heads of tiny, 4-petaled white to purple-pink flowers appear in early summer. Z5–9 H9–5.
A. wulfenianum. Prostrate perennial. H ¾in (2cm), S 8in (20cm). Loose heads of small, bright yellow flowers appear in summer above small, oval gray leaves. Z6–9 H9–6.

AMARANTHUS

AMARANTHACEAE

Genus of annuals grown for their dense panicles of tiny flowers or their colorful foliage. Grow in a sunny position in rich or fertile, well-drained soil. Propagate from seed sown outdoors in late spring. Aphids may be a problem.
A. caudatus illus. p.326.
A. hypochondriacus illus. p.330.
A. tricolor **'Joseph's Coat'.** Bushy annual. H to 3ft (1m), S 1½ft (45cm) or more. Has oval scarlet, green, and yellow leaves, to 8in (20cm) long, and produces small panicles of tiny red flowers in summer. Leaves of **'Molten Fire'** are crimson, bronze, and purple. Both H12–5.

x AMARCRINUM

AMARYLLIDACEAE

Hybrid genus (*Amaryllis* x *Crinum*) of one robust, evergreen bulb grown for its large, funnel-shaped flowers. Needs a sunny position and well-drained soil. Plant with neck just covered by soil. Propagate by division in spring.
x ***A. howardii.*** See x *A. memoria-corsii.*
x ***A. memoria-corsii***, syn. x *A. howardii*, x *Crinodonna corsii*, illus. p.408.

x AMARYGIA

AMARYLLIDACEAE

Hybrid genus (*Amaryllis* x *Brunsvigia*) of thick, autumn-flowering bulbs that are cultivated for their large, showy flowers. Needs full sun and benefits from the shelter of a wall where marginally hardy. Plant bulbs just beneath the surface of well-drained soil. Propagate by division in spring.
x ***A. parkeri***, syn. x *Brunsdonna parkeri*, illus. p.408.

AMARYLLIS

AMARYLLIDACEAE

Genus of autumn-flowering bulbs grown for their funnel-shaped flowers. Grow in a sheltered, sunny situation and in well-drained soil. Plant bulbs

under at least 3in (8cm) of soil. Propagate by division in late spring as leaves die down, or in late summer before growth recommences.
A. belladonna and **'Hathor'** illus. p.408.

AMBERBOA
Sweet sultan

ASTERACEAE/COMPOSITAE

Genus of erect annuals or biennials grown for their attractive, cornflower-like flower heads that are borne from spring to autumn. Needs full sun and moderately fertile, well-drained soil. Deadhead to prolong flowering. Propagate by seed in spring or autumn.
A. moschata, syn. *Centaurea moschata*, illus. p.335.

AMELANCHIER
Juneberry, Serviceberry, Shadbush

ROSACEAE

Genus of deciduous, spring-flowering trees and shrubs grown primarily for their profuse flowers and their foliage, which is frequently brightly colored in autumn. Requires sun or semi-shade and well-drained but not too dry, preferably neutral to acidic soil. Propagate in autumn by seed, in late autumn to early spring by layering, or, in the case of suckering species, by division. Fireblight may sometimes be troublesome.
A. alnifolia. Deciduous, upright, suckering shrub. H 12ft (4m) or more, S 10ft (3m) or more. Leaves are oval to rounded and dark green. Erect spikes of star-shaped, creamy white flowers are borne in late spring, followed by small, edible, juicy, rounded, purple-black fruits. Z4–9 H8–3.
A. arborea. Deciduous, spreading, sometimes shrubby tree. H 30ft (10m), S 40ft (12m). Clusters of star-shaped white flowers appear in midspring as oval, white-haired, young leaves unfold. Foliage matures to dark green, turning to red or yellow in autumn. Rounded fruits are small, dry, and reddish purple. Z4–9 H9–4.
A. asiatica. Deciduous, spreading tree or shrub of elegant habit. H 25ft (8m), S 30ft (10m). Leaves are oval and dark green, usually woolly when young and turning yellow or red in autumn. Star-shaped white flowers are borne profusely in late spring, followed by edible, juicy, rounded, black-purple fruits. Z5–7 H7–5.
A. canadensis. Deciduous, upright, dense shrub. H 20ft (6m), S 10ft (3m). Star-shaped white flowers are borne from mid- to late spring amid unfolding, oval, white-haired leaves that mature to dark green and turn orange-red in autumn. Fruits are edible, rounded, blackish purple, sweet, and juicy. Z3–7 H7–1.
A. laevis illus. p.85.
A. lamarckii illus. p.116.
Amomyrtus luma. See *Luma apiculata*.
***Amomyrtus luma* 'Glanleam Gold'.** See *Luma apiculata* 'Glanleam Gold'.

AMORPHA

LEGUMINOSAE/PAPILIONACEAE

Genus of deciduous shrubs and subshrubs grown for their flowers and foliage. Is a useful plant for cold, dry, exposed positions. Requires full sun and well-drained soil. May be propagated by softwood cuttings taken in summer or by seed sown in autumn.
A. canescens (Lead plant). Deciduous, open subshrub. H 3ft (1m), S 5ft (1.5m). Dense spikes of tiny, pealike purple flowers with orange anthers are produced in late summer and early autumn amid oval, gray-haired leaves divided into many narrowly oval leaflets. Z2–8 H8–1.

AMPELOPSIS

VITACEAE

Genus of deciduous, woody-stemmed, tendril climbers, some of which are twining, grown for their leaves. Grow in a sheltered position in sun or partial shade in any soil. Need plenty of room since they grow quickly and can cover a large area. Propagate by greenwood or semi-ripe cuttings in midsummer.
A. aconitifolia, syn. *Vitis aconitifolia.* Fast-growing, deciduous, woody-stemmed, twining, tendril climber. H to 40ft (12m). Rounded leaves have 3 or 5 toothed, lobed, dark green leaflets; inconspicuous greenish flowers appear in late summer, followed later by orange berries. Z.
A. brevipedunculata var. ***maximowiczii***, syn. *A. glandulosa* var. *brevipedunculata*, *A. heterophylla*, *Vitis heterophylla*. Vigorous, deciduous, woody-stemmed, twining, tendril climber with hairy, young stems. H to 15ft (5m) or more. Has dark green leaves that vary in size and shape and are almost hairless beneath. Inconspicuous greenish flowers are produced in summer, followed by bright blue berries. Z5–8 H8–2.
A. glandulosa var. ***brevipedunculata.*** See *A. brevipedunculata* var. *maximowiczii*.
A. heterophylla. See *A. brevipedunculata* var. *maximowiczii*.
A. sempervirens. See *Cissus striata.*
A. veitchii. See *Parthenocissus tricuspidata* 'Veitchii'.

AMSONIA
Blue star

APOCYNACEAE

Genus of slow-growing, clump-forming, summer-flowering perennials. Grow in full sun and in well-drained soil. Is best left undisturbed for some years. May be propagated by division in spring, by softwood cuttings in summer, or by seed in autumn. Contact with the milky sap may irritate skin.
A. orientalis, syn. *Rhazya orientalis*, illus. p.286.
A. tabernaemontana illus. p.287.

Anacharis densa. See *Egeria densa.*

ANACYCLUS

ASTERACEAE/COMPOSITAE

Genus of summer-flowering, prostrate perennials with stems radiating from a central rootstock. Needs full sun and well-drained soil. Propagate by softwood cuttings in spring or by seed in autumn.
A. depressus. See *A. pyrethrum* var. *depressus*.
A. pyrethrum var. ***depressus***, syn. *A. depressus*, illus. p.374.

ANAGALLIS

PRIMULACEAE

Genus of annuals and creeping perennials grown for their flowers. Plant in an open, sunny site in fertile, moist soil. Propagate by seed or division in spring. Raise *A. tenella* by soft tip cuttings in spring or early summer.
A. tenella (Bog pimpernel). **'Studland'** illus. p.367.

ANANAS

BROMELIACEAE

Genus of evergreen, rosette-forming perennials grown for their foliage and edible fruits (pineapples). Prefers full light, but tolerates some shade. Needs fertile, well-drained soil. Water moderately during growing season, sparingly at other times. Propagate by suckers or cuttings of "leafy" fruit tops in spring or summer.
A. bracteatus (Red pineapple, Wild pineapple). **'Tricolor'** (syn. *A.b.* 'Striatus', *A.b.* var. *tricolor*; illus. p.265) is an evergreen, basal-rosetted perennial. H and S 3ft (1m). Forms dense rosettes of strap-shaped, spiny-edged, arching, deep green leaves, longitudinally yellow-striped and often with marginal red spines. Dense spikes of small, tubular, lavender-violet flowers with prominent, reddish pink bracts appear usually in summer. These are followed by brownish orange-red fruits that are 6in (15cm) or more long. Z14–15 H12–1.
***A. comosus* 'Variegatus'**, syn *A.c.* var *variegatus*. Evergreen, basal-rosetted perennial. H and S 24in (60cm) or more. Produces very narrowly strap-shaped, channeled, rigid, gray-green leaves that are suffused pink, have cream margins, are gray-scaled beneath, and sometimes have spiny edges. Produces tubular, purple-blue flowers with inconspicuous green bracts; fruits are the edible pineapples grown commercially but are much smaller on pot-grown plants. Z11-12 H12–1.

ANAPHALIS
Pearly everlasting

ASTERACEAE/COMPOSITAE

Genus of perennials with heads of small, papery flowers used dried for winter decoration. Prefers sun but will grow in semi-shade. Soil should be well-drained but not too dry. Propagate by seed in autumn or by division in winter or spring.
A. margaritacea illus. p.239.
A. nepalensis var. ***monocephala***, syn. *A. nubigena*, illus. p.276.
A. nubigena. See *A. nepalensis* var. *monocephala*.

ANCHUSA
Alkanet

BORAGINACEAE

Genus of annuals, biennials and perennials, some of which are evergreen, with usually blue flowers. Needs sun and well-drained soil; resents too much winter wet. Tall perennial species may need to be staked and allowed room to spread. Propagate perennials by root cuttings in winter, annuals and biennials by seed in autumn or spring.
A. azurea, syn. *A. italica*. Z3–8 H8–1. **'Little John'** is a clump-forming perennial. H 20in (50cm), S 24in (60cm). Mainly basal leaves are narrowly oval and hairy. Bears branching racemes of large, open cup-shaped, dark blue flowers in early summer. **'Loddon Royalist'** illus. p.254. **'Opal'**, H 1.2m (4ft), has paler blue flowers.
A. caespitosa. See *A. cespitosa*.
***A. capensis* 'Blue Angel'** illus. p.334. **'Blue Bird'** is a bushy biennial grown as an annual. H to 18in (45cm), S 8in (20cm). Has lance-shaped, bristly, midgreen leaves and, in summer, heads of shallowly bowl-shaped, sky blue flowers. Z7–9 H9–7.
A. cespitosa, syn. *A. caespitosa*, illus. p.370.
A. italica. See *A. azurea*.

Ancistrocactus megarhizus. See *Sclerocactus scheeri*.
Ancistrocactus scheeri. See *Sclerocactus scheeri*.
Ancistrocactus uncinatus. See *Sclerocactus uncinatus*.

ANDROMEDA
Bog rosemary

ERICACEAE

Genus of evergreen shrubs with an open, twiggy habit. Needs full light and organic, moist, acidic soil. Propagate by semi-ripe cuttings taken in late summer or by seed sown in spring.
A. polifolia illus. p.347. **'Alba'** illus. p.346. **'Compacta'** illus. p.347.

ANDROSACE
Rock jasmine

PRIMULACEAE

Genus of annuals and evergreen perennials, usually compact cushion-forming and often with soft, hairy leaves. Many species are suitable for cold greenhouses and troughs with winter snow cover. Needs sun and very well-drained soil; some species prefer acidic soil. Resents wet foliage in winter. Propagate by tip cuttings in summer or by seed in autumn. Is prone to botrytis and attack by aphids.
A. carnea illus. p.365. subsp ***laggeri*** illus. p.367.
A. chamaejasme. Evergreen, basal-rosetted, variable perennial with easily rooted stolons. H 1¼–2½in (3–6cm), S to 6in (5cm). Has open, hairy rosettes of oval leaves. In spring bears clusters of 2–8 flattish white flowers, each with a yellow eye that sometimes turns red with age. Z4–7 H7–1.
A. cylindrica. Evergreen, basal-rosetted perennial. H ½–¾in (1–2cm), S 4in (10cm). Leaves are linear and glossy. Flower stems each carry up to 10 small, flattish white flowers, each with a yellow-green eye, in early spring. Is suitable for a cold greenhouse. Z6–7 H7–6.
A. hedraeantha. Evergreen, tight cushion-forming perennial. H ½–¾in (1–2cm), S to 4in (10cm). Bears loose rosettes of narrowly oval, glossy leaves. Umbels of 5–10 flattish, yellow-throated pink flowers are produced in spring. Is best in a cold greenhouse. Z6–7 H7–6.
A. hirtella. Evergreen, tight cushion-forming perennial. H ½in (1cm), S to 4in (10cm). Produces rosettes of small, thick, linear to oblong, hairy leaves. Almond-scented, flattish white flowers are borne in spring on very short stems, 1 or 2 per rosette. Z6–8 H8–6.
A. imbricata. See *A. vandellii.*
A. lanuginosa illus. p.377.
A. pyrenaica illus. p.361.
A. sarmentosa. Evergreen, mat-forming perennial spreading by runners. H 1½–4in (4–10cm), S 12in (30cm). Has open rosettes of small, narrowly elliptic, hairy leaves. Large clusters of flattish, yellow-eyed, bright pink flowers open in spring. Is a good rock plant in all but extremely wet areas. Z5–7 H7–5.
A. sempervivoides. Evergreen, mat-forming, rosetted perennial with stolons. H ½–3in (1–7cm), S 12in (30cm). Has leathery, oblong or spoon-shaped leaves. In spring produces small heads of 4–10 flattish pink flowers, with yellow then red eyes. Is a good rock plant. Z5–7 H7–5.
A. vandellii, syn. *A. imbricata*, illus. p.362.
A. villosa illus. p.363. var. ***jacquemontii*** illus. p.378.

ANEMONE
Windflower

RANUNCULACEAE

Genus of spring-, summer- and autumn-flowering perennials, sometimes tuberous or rhizomatous, with mainly rounded, shallowly cup-shaped flowers. Leaves are rounded to oval, often divided into 3–15 leaflets. Most species thrive in full light or semi-shade in organic, well-drained soil. Propagate by division in spring, by seed sown in late summer when fresh, or by root cuttings in winter. Contact with the sap may irritate skin.
A. apennina (Apennine anemone). Spreading, spring-flowering, rhizomatous perennial. H and S 6–8in (15–20cm). Fernlike leaves have 3 deeply toothed lobes. Each stem carries a large, upright, flattish blue, white, or pink flower with 10–20 narrow petals. Z5–9 H9–3.
A. blanda. Spreading, early spring-flowering perennial with a knobby tuber. H 2–4in (5–10cm), S 4–6in (10–15cm). Leaves are broadly oval and semi-erect, with 3 deeply toothed lobes. Each stem bears an upright, flattish blue, white, or pink flower, 1½–2in (4–5cm) across, with 9–14 narrow petals. Z4–8 H8–1. **'Atrocaerulea'** illus. p.433. **'Ingramii'** bears purple-backed, deep blue flowers. **'Radar'** illus. p.430. **'White Splendour'** illus. p.426.
A. coronaria. Spring-flowering perennial with a misshapen tuber. H 2–10in (5–25cm), S 4–6in (10–15cm). Produces parsleylike, divided, semi-erect leaves. Each stiff stem carries a large, 5–8-petaled, shallowly cup-shaped flower in shades of red, pink, blue, or purple. Z8–11 H12–8. Garden groups include **De Caen Group** and **St. Brigid Group**, which have larger flowers varying in color from white through red to blue.
A. x fulgens illus. p.430.
A. hepatica. See *Hepatica nobilis.*
A. hupehensis **'Hadspen Abundance'** illus. p.259. var. ***japonica*** **'Bressingham Glow'** (syn. *A* x *hybrida* 'Bressingham Glow'; semi-double) illus. p.231. Var. ***japonica*** **'Prinz Heinrich'** (syn. *A.* x *hybrida* 'Prince Henry') has single, deep pink flowers on slender stems. Z4–8 H8–1. **'September Charm'** (single) illus. p.231.
A. x hybrida, syn. *A. japonica* of gardens (Japanese anemone). Group of vigorous, branching, perennials. H 5ft (1.5m), S 2ft (60cm). Bears shallowly cup-shaped, single, semi-double or double flowers in late summer and early autumn. Leaves are deeply divided and dark green. Z4–8 H8–5. **'Bressingham Glow'** see *A. hupehensis* var. *japonica* 'Bressingham Glow'. **'Honorine Jobert'** (single) illus. p.231. **'Max Vogel'** has semi-double, pinkish mauve flowers on wiry stems. Z4–8 H8–1. **'Prince Henry'** see *A. hupehensis* var. *japonica* 'Prinz Heinrich'.
A. x intermedia. See *A.* x *lipsiensis.*
A. japonica of gardens. See *A.* x *hybrida.*
A. x lipsiensis, syn. *A.* x *intermedia, A.* x *seemannii*, illus. p.274.
A. narcissiflora illus. p.275.
A. nemorosa (Wood anemone). Vigorous, carpeting, rhizomatous perennial. H 6in (15cm), S 12in (30cm). Produces masses of star-shaped, single white flowers with prominent yellow stamens in spring and early summer, above deeply cut, midgreen leaves. Likes woodland conditions. Z4–8 H8–1. **'Allenii'** and **'Robinsoniana'** illus. p.270. **'Vestal'** has anemone-centered, double white flowers. **'Wilks' Giant'** (syn. *A.n.* 'Wilk's Giant') has larger, single white flowers.
A. pavonina illus. p.413.
A. ranunculoides illus. p.274. **'Pleniflora'** (syn *A.r.* 'Flore Pleno') is a spreading, rhizomatous perennial. H and S 8in (20cm). Bears buttercup-like, double yellow flowers in spring. Leaves are divided. Likes damp, woodland conditions. Z4–8 H8–1.
A. rivularis illus. p.275.
A. x seemannii. See *A.* x *lipsiensis.*
A. sylvestris illus. p.268. **'Macrantha'** is a clump-forming perennial that can be invasive. H and S 12in (30cm). Large, fragrant, semi-pendent, shallowly cup-shaped white flowers are produced in spring and early summer. Leaves are divided and midgreen. Z3–9 H9–1.
A. tschaernjaewii illus. p.427.
A. vitifolia. Branching, clump-forming perennial. H 4ft (1.2m), S 20in (50cm). In summer bears open cup-shaped, occasionally pink-flushed white flowers with yellow stamens. Grapelike leaves are woolly beneath. Z5–8 H8–5.

ANEMONELLA

RANUNCULACEAE

Genus of one species of tuberous perennial grown for its flowers. Needs shade and organic, moist soil. Propagate by seed when fresh or by division every 3–5 years in autumn.
A. thalictroides illus. p.364. **'Oscar Schoaf'** (syn. *A.t.* 'Schoaf's Double') is a slow-growing, tuberous perennial. H 4in (10cm), S 1½in (4cm) or more. Has delicate, fernlike leaves. From spring to early summer bears small, cup-shaped, double, strawberry-pink flowers, singly on finely branched, slender stems. Z4–7 H7–1.

ANEMONOPSIS
False anemone

RANUNCULACEAE

Genus of one species of perennial, related to *Anemone*. Likes a sheltered, semi-shaded position and organic, moist but well-drained soil. Propagate by division in spring or by seed sown in late summer when fresh.
A. macrophylla illus. p.286.

ANGELICA

APIACEAE/UMBELLIFERAE

Genus of summer-flowering, often short-lived perennials, some of which have culinary and medicinal uses. Grows in sun or shade and in any well-drained soil. Remove seed heads when produced; otherwise, plants may die. Propagate by seed when ripe.
A. archangelica illus. p.228.
A. gigas. Upright, short-lived perennial with leaves divided into three parts and 12-16in (30-40cm) long. H 3-6ft (1-2m), S 4ft (1.2m). In summer has very showy inflated reddish leaf bases and flat umbels of purple flowers up to 6in (15cm) across with purple bracts and stems. An attractive border plant. Z4–9 H8–2.

ANGRAECUM

See also ORCHIDS.
A. sesquipedale, syn. *Macroplectrum sesquipedale* (Star-of-Bethlehem orchid; illus. p.296). Evergreen, epiphytic orchid for an intermediate greenhouse. H 12in (30cm) or more. Waxy white flowers, 3in (8cm) across, each with a 12in (30cm) long spur, are borne, usually 2 to a stem, in winter. Has narrowly oval, semi-rigid, horizontal leaves, 6in (15cm) long. Needs shade in summer. Z14–15 H12–10.

ANGULOA

See also ORCHIDS.
A. clowesii (Cradle orchid). Deciduous, epiphytic orchid for a cool greenhouse. H 24in (60cm). Fragrant, erect, cup-shaped, lemon yellow flowers, 4in (10cm) long, each with a loosely hinged yellow lip, are produced singly in early summer. Broadly oval, ribbed leaves are 18in (45cm) long. Grow in semi-shade in summer. Z13–15 H12–10.

ANIGOZANTHOS
Kangaroo paw

HAEMODORACEAE

Genus of perennials with thick rootstocks and fans of sword-shaped leaves, grown for their curious flowers. Needs an open, sunny position and does best in well-drained, peaty or leafy, acidic soil. Propagate by division in spring or by seed when fresh, in late summer.
A. flavidus illus. p.254.
A. manglesii illus. p.250.

ANISODONTEA

MALVACEAE

Genus of evergreen shrubs and perennials grown for their flowers. Needs full light and well-drained soil. Water containerized plants freely when in full growth, very little at other times. In growing season, young plants may need tip pruning to promote a bushy habit. Propagate by seed in spring or by greenwood or semi-ripe cuttings in late summer.
A. capensis, syn. *Malvastrum capensis.* Evergreen, erect, bushy shrub. H to 3ft (1m), S 2ft (60cm) or more. Each oval leaf has 3–5 deep lobes. Bowl-shaped, 5-petaled, rose-magenta flowers with darker veins appear from spring to autumn. Z8–9 H9–8.

ANNONA

Cherimoya, Custard apple, Sweet sop

ANNONACEAE

Genus of deciduous or evergreen shrubs and trees grown for their edible fruits and ornamental appearance. Needs full light or partial shade and fertile, moisture-retentive but well-drained soil. Water containerized specimens moderately when in full growth, sparingly in winter. Propagate by seed in spring or by semi-ripe cuttings in late summer. Spider mite may be a nuisance.

A. reticulata (Bullock's heart, Custard apple). Mainly deciduous, rounded tree. H 20ft (6m) or more, S 10–15ft (3–5m). Has oblong to lance-shaped, 5–10in (13–25cm) long leaves. Cup-shaped, olive green flowers, often flushed purple, appear in summer, followed by edible, heart-shaped, red-flushed, greenish brown fruits, each 5in (13cm) long. Z14–15 H12–10.

Anoiganthus breviflorus. See *Cyrtanthus breviflorus*.
Anoiganthus luteus. See *Cyrtanthus breviflorus*.

ANOPTERUS

ESCALLONIACEAE

Genus of evergreen shrubs or small trees grown for their foliage and flowers. Needs shade or semi-shade and moist but well-drained, lime-free soil. Propagate by semi-ripe cuttings in summer.

A. glandulosus illus. p.116.

ANREDERA

Madeira vine, Mignonette vine

BASELLACEAE

Genus of evergreen, tuberous, twining climbers grown for their luxuriant foliage and small, scented flowers. If grown in cool areas will die down in winter. Requires a position in full light and well-drained soil. Water moderately during the growing season, but sparingly at other times. Provide support. Cut back the previous season's growth by half or to just above ground level in spring. Propagate by tubers produced at stem bases in spring or by softwood cuttings in summer.

A. cordifolia, syn. *Boussingaultia baselloides* of gardens. Fast-growing, evergreen, tuberous, twining climber. H to 20ft (6m). Has oval to lance-shaped, fleshy leaves and tiny, fragrant white flowers borne in clusters from upper leaf axils in summer. Z10–11 H12–1.

ANTENNARIA

Cat's ears, Pussy-toes

ASTERACEAE/COMPOSITAE

Genus of evergreen or semi-evergreen perennials grown for their almost stemless flower heads and mats of often woolly leaves. Makes a good groundcover. Needs sun and well-drained soil. Propagate by seed or division in spring.

A. dioica. Semi-evergreen, mat-forming, dense perennial. H 1in (2.5cm), S 10in (25cm). Leaves are tiny, oval, usually woolly and greenish white. Short stems carry fluffy white or pale pink flower heads in late spring and early summer. Good grown in a rock garden. Z5–9 H9–4. Compact **'Nyewoods'** has very deep rose pink flowers. **'Rosea'** see *A.d.* var. *rosea*.

Var. ***rosea*** (syn. *A.d.* 'Rosea', *A. rosea*) illus. p.366.

A. rosea. See *A. dioica* var. *rosea*.

ANTHEMIS

Dog's fennel

ASTERACEAE/COMPOSITAE

Genus of carpeting and clump-forming perennials, some of which are evergreen, grown for their daisylike flower heads and fernlike foliage. Prefers a position in sun and well-drained soil. May need staking for support. Cut to ground level after flowering to produce good leaf rosettes in winter. Propagate by division in spring or, for some species, by basal cuttings in late summer, autumn, or spring.

A. nobilis. See *Chamaemelum nobile*.

A. punctata subsp. ***cupaniana*** illus. p.276.

A. sancti-johannis. Evergreen, spreading, bushy perennial. H and S 24in (60cm). In summer bears many daisylike, bright orange flower heads among fernlike, shaggy, midgreen leaves. Z3–8 H8–3.

A. tinctoria. Evergreen, clump-forming perennial. H and S 3ft (1m). Produces a mass of daisylike yellow flower heads in midsummer, borne singly above a basal clump of fernlike, crinkled, midgreen leaves. Propagate by basal cuttings in spring or late summer. Z3–8 H8–3.**'E.C. Buxton'** illus. p.255.

ANTHERICUM

Spider plant

ANTHERICACEAE/LILIACEAE

Genus of upright perennials with saucer- or trumpet-shaped flowers rising in spikelike racemes from clumps of leaves. Likes a sunny site and fertile, well-drained soil that does not dry out in summer. Propagate by division in spring or by seed in autumn.

A. graminifolium. See *A. ramosum*.

A. liliago illus. p.276.

A. ramosum, syn. *A. graminifolium*. Upright perennial. H 3ft (1m), S 1ft (30cm). Erect racemes of small, saucer-shaped white flowers are borne in summer above a clump of grasslike, grayish green leaves. Z5–8 H8–5.

Antholyza paniculata. See *Crocosmia paniculata*.

ANTHURIUM

Flamingo flower

ARACEAE

Genus of evergreen, erect, climbing or trailing perennials, some grown for their foliage and others for their bright flower spathes. Prefers bright light in winter and indirect sun in summer; needs a fairly moist atmosphere and moist, but not waterlogged, peaty soil. Propagate by division in spring. If ingested, all parts may cause mild stomach disorder; contact with sap may irritate skin.

A. andraeanum illus. p.264.

A. crystallinum illus. p.264.

A. scherzerianum illus. p.302.

'Rothschildianum' is an evergreen, erect, short-stemmed perennial. H and S 12in (30cm). Produces upright, oblong leaves, to 8in (20cm) long. Intermittently bears a long-lasting red spathe, spotted with white, that surrounds a yellow spadix. Z11–12 H12–10.

A. veitchii (King anthurium). Evergreen, erect, short-stemmed perennial. H 3ft (1m) or more, S to 3ft (1m). Glossy, corrugated leaves, to 3ft (1m) long, are oval, with heart-shaped bases on 2–3ft (60cm–1m) long leaf stalks. Intermittently bears a long-lasting, leathery green to white spathe that surrounds a cream spadix. Z11 H12–10.

ANTHYLLIS

PAPILIONACEAE

Genus of rounded, bushy perennials grown for their flowers and finely divided leaves. Needs sun and well-drained soil. Propagate by softwood cuttings in summer or by seed in autumn.

A. hermanniae. Rounded, bushy perennial. H and S to 24in (60cm). Spiny, tangled stems bear simple or 3-parted, bright green leaves. Has small, pea-like yellow flowers in summer. Good for a rock garden.

A. montana illus. p.352.

'Rubra' is a rounded or spreading, woody-based perennial. H and S 12in (30cm). Divided leaves consist of 17–41 narrowly oval leaflets. Heads of cloverlike, bright pink flowers are borne in late spring and early summer. Is good for a rock garden. Z6–8 H8–6.

ANTIGONON

Coral vine

POLYGONACEAE

Genus of evergreen, woody-stemmed, tendril climbers grown for their foliage and profuse clusters of small flowers. Grow in full light and any fertile, well-drained soil. Water freely in the growing season, sparingly at other times. Needs tropical conditions to flower well. Provide support. Thin out congested growth in early spring. Propagate by seed in spring or by softwood cuttings in summer.

A. leptopus illus. p.209.

ANTIRRHINUM

Snapdragon

SCROPHULARIACEAE

Genus of perennials and semi-evergreen subshrubs usually grown as annuals, flowering from spring to autumn. Needs sun and rich, well-drained soil. Deadhead to prolong flowering season. Propagate by seed sown outdoors in late spring or by stem cuttings in early autumn or spring. Rust disease may be a problem with *A. majus*, but rust-resistant cultivars are available.

A. asarina. See *Asarina procumbens*.

A. majus. Erect perennial that branches from the base. Cultivars are grown as annuals and are grouped according to size and flower type: tall, H 2–3ft (60cm–1m), S 12–18in (30–45cm); intermediate, H and S 18in (45cm); dwarf, H 8–12in (20–30cm), S 12in (30cm); the regular, familiarly shaped flowers that can be "snapped"; peloric, trumpet-shaped flowers; double; and irregular tubular-shaped flowers. All have lance-shaped leaves and, from spring to autumn, carry spikes of usually 2-lipped, sometimes double flowers in a variety of colors, including white, pink, red, purple, yellow, and orange. Z7–11 H12–1.

Bells Series (dwarf, regular) is early-flowering, with long-lasting flowers in purple, purple and white, red, rose pink, pink, bronze, yellow, or white. **Bells Series 'Pink Bells'** has pink flowers. **'Chimes'** (dwarf, regular) is very compact, producing flowers in a wide color range including several bicolors. **Coronette Series** (tall, regular) illus. p.321. **'Floral Showers** (dwarf, regular) is early-flowering, bearing flowers in up to 10 colors, including some bicolors; tolerates wet weather. **Kim Series** (intermediate, regular) has flowers in scarlet, deep rose, deep orange, primrose yellow, and white as well as orange bicolor. **Madame Butterfly Series** (tall, peloric) is available in a mixture of colors. **Princess Series** (intermediate, regular) has flowers in a mixture of colors (white with purple eye, illus. p.325). **Rocket Series** (tall, regular) is vigorous, with flowers in a broad color range; they are excellent for cut flowers. **Sonnet Series** (intermediate, regular) illus. p.337. **Tahiti Series** (dwarf, regular) illus. p.336. **'Trumpet Serenade'** (dwarf, peloric) has bicolored flowers in a mixture of pastel shades.

APHELANDRA

ACANTHACEAE

Genus of evergreen shrubs and perennials with showy flowers. Grows best in bright light but out of direct sun in summer. Use soft water and keep soil moist but not waterlogged. Benefits from fertilizing when flower spikes are forming. Propagate by seed or tip cuttings from young stems in spring.

A. squarrosa (Zebra plant). **'Dania'** is an evergreen, compact perennial. H 3ft (1m), S slightly less. Oval, glossy, dark green leaves with white veins and midribs are nearly 1ft (30cm) long. Has dense, 4-sided spikes, to 6in (15cm) long, of 2-lipped, bright yellow flowers in axils of yellow bracts in autumn. Z14–15 H12–10. **'Louisae'** illus. p.256.

APHYLLANTHES

APHYLLANTHACEAE/LILIACEAE

Genus of one species of summer-flowering perennial. Often best grown in a sunny, warm, sheltered corner, preferably in an alpine house, and in well-drained, sandy, peaty soil. Resents disturbance. Propagate by seed in autumn or spring.

A. monspeliensis. Tuft-forming perennial. H 6–8in (15–20cm), S 2in (5cm). Star-shaped, pale to deep blue flowers are borne singly or in small groups at tops of wiry, glaucous green stems from early to midsummer. Leaves are reduced to red-brown sheaths surrounding stems. Z9–10 H12–10.

APONOGETON

APONOGETONACEAE

Genus of deciduous, perennial, deep-water plants grown for their floating foliage and often heavily scented flowers. Requires an open, sunny position. Clean up fading foliage in autumn. Propagate by division in spring or by seed while still fresh.

A. distachyos illus. p.447.

APOROCACTUS

CACTACEAE

Genus of cacti grown for their pendent, slender, fleshy stems and bright flowers. Is suitable for hanging baskets. Needs partial shade and very well-drained soil. Occasional light watering in winter will prevent stems dying back. Propagate by stem cuttings in spring or summer.

A. flagelliformis illus. p.463.

AQUILEGIA
Columbine

RANUNCULACEAE

Genus of graceful, clump-forming, short-lived perennials grown for their mainly bell-shaped, spurred flowers in spring and summer. Many are suitable for rock gardens. Prefers an open, sunny site and well-drained soil. Propagate species by seed in autumn or spring. Selected forms only occasionally come true from seed (e.g. *A. vulgaris* 'Nora Barlow') as they cross freely; they should be widely segregated. Prone to aphid and leaf miner attack. Contact with sap may irritate skin.

A. akitensis. See *A. flabellata.*

A. alpina illus. p.348.

A. canadensis (Canada columbine). Clump-forming, leafy perennial. H 24in (60cm), S 12in (30cm). In early summer bears semi-pendent, bell-shaped flowers with yellow sepals and red spurs, several per slender stem, above fernlike, dark green foliage. Z3–8 H8–1.

A. chrysantha. Vigorous, clump-forming perennial. H 4ft (1.2m), S 2ft (60cm). Bears semi-pendent, bell-shaped, soft yellow flowers with long spurs, several per stem, in early summer. Has fernlike, divided, mid-green leaves. Z3–8 H8–1.

A. flabellata, syn. *A. akitensis*. Clump-forming perennial. H 10in (25cm), S 4in (10cm). Bell-shaped, soft blue flowers, each with fluted petals and a short spur, are produced in summer. Rounded, finely divided leaves form an open, basal rosette. Needs semi-shade and moist soil. Z4–9 H9–1. Var. ***pumila*** f. ***alba*** (syn. *A.f.* 'Nana Alba'), H 4in (10cm), is compact with white flowers.

A. jonesii illus. p.383.

A. longissima. Clump-forming, leafy perennial. H 24in (60cm), S 20in (50cm). Bell-shaped, pale yellow flowers with very long, bright yellow spurs are borne, several per stem, in early summer, above fernlike, divided, midgreen leaves. Z4–9 H9–1.

***A.* 'Mrs. Scott Elliott'.** See *A.* Mrs. Scott Elliott Hybrids.

***A.* Mrs. Scott Elliott Hybrids**, syn. *A.* 'Mrs. Scott Elliott'. Clump-forming, leafy perennial. H 3ft (1m), S 20in (50cm). Bell-shaped flowers of various colors, often bicolored, have long spurs and appear in early summer on branching, wiry stems. Has fernlike, divided, bluish green leaves. Z4–7 H7–1

A. scopulorum. Clump-forming perennial. H 2½in (6cm), S 3½in (9cm). In summer produces bell-shaped, fluted, pale blue or rarely pink flowers, each with a cream center and very long spurs. Leaves are divided into 9 oval, glaucous leaflets. Z4–8 H8–1.

A. vulgaris (Granny's bonnets). Clump-forming, leafy perennial. H 3ft (1m), S 20in (50cm). Many funnel-shaped, short-spurred flowers in shades of pink, crimson, purple, and white are borne, several per long stem, in early summer. Leaves are gray-green, rounded, and divided into leaflets. Z3–8 H8–1. **'Nora Barlow'** illus. p.249.

ARABIS
Rock cress

BRASSICACEAE/CRUCIFERAE

Genus of robust, evergreen perennials. Excellent groundcover in a rock garden. Needs sun and well-drained soil. Propagate by softwood cuttings in summer or by seed in autumn.

A. albida. See *A. alpina* subsp. *caucasica.*

A. alpina subsp. ***caucasica***, syn. *A. albida, A. caucasica.* Evergreen, mat-forming perennial. H 6in (15cm), S 20in (50cm). Bears loose rosettes of obovate, toothed, midgreen leaves and, in late spring and summer, fragrant, 4-petaled white, occasionally pink flowers. Is excellent on a dry bank. Trim back after flowering. Z3–7 H8–1. **'Flore Pleno'** (syn. *A. caucasica* 'Plena') has double white flowers. **'Variegata'** (syn. *A. caucasica* 'Variegata') illus. p.362.

***A.* x *arendsii* 'Rosabella'**, syn. *A. caucasica* 'Rosabella', illus. p.365.

A. blepharophylla. Short-lived, evergreen, mat-forming perennial. H 5in (12cm), S 8in (20cm). Dislikes winter wet. Has oval, toothed, dark green leaves, with hairy, gray margins, borne in loose rosettes. Fragrant, 4-petaled, bright pink to white flowers are produced in spring. Z5–8 H8–5.

A. caucasica. See *A. alpina* subsp. *caucasica*. **'Plena'** see *A. alpina* subsp. *caucasica* 'Flore Pleno'. **'Rosabella'** see *A.* x *arendsii* 'Rosabella'. **'Variegata'** see *A. alpina* subsp. *caucasica* 'Variegata'.

***A. ferdinandi-coburgi* 'Variegata'.** See *A. procurrens* 'Variegata'.

***A. procurrens* 'Variegata'**, syn. *A. ferdinandi-coburgi* 'Variegata', illus. p.388.

ARALIA

ARALIACEAE

Genus of deciduous trees, shrubs, and perennials grown for their bold leaves and small but profusely borne flowers. Requires sun or semi-shade, some shelter, and fertile, well-drained soil. Propagate those listed below by seed in autumn or by suckers or root cuttings in late winter.

A. elata (Japanese angelica tree). Deciduous tree or suckering shrub with sparse, thick, prickly stems. H and S 30ft (10m). Has large, dark green leaves with numerous oval, paired leaflets. Billowing heads of tiny white flowers, forming a large panicle 12–24in (30–60cm) wide, are borne in late summer and autumn. Z4–9 H9–1. **'Albomarginata'** see *A.e.* 'Variegata'. **'Aureovariegata'** has leaflets broadly edged with yellow. Leaflets of **'Variegata'** (syn. *A.e.* 'Albomarginata') have creamy white margins.

A. elegantissima. See *Schefflera elegantissima.*

A. japonica. See *Fatsia japonica.*

A. sieboldii. See *Fatsia japonica.*

ARAUCARIA

ARAUCARIACEAE

See also CONIFERS.

A. araucana illus. p.103.

A. excelsa of gardens. See *A. heterophylla.*

A. heterophylla, syn. *A. excelsa* of gardens (Norfolk Island pine). Upright conifer. H 100ft (30m), S 15–25ft (5–8m). Has spirally set, needlelike, incurved, fresh green leaves. Cones are seldom produced in cultivation. Is often grown as a shade-tolerant house plant. Z9–11 H12–9.

ARAUJIA

ASCLEPIADACEAE

Genus of evergreen, twining climbers with woody stems that exude milky juice when cut. Needs sun and fertile, well-drained soil. Propagate by seed in spring or by stem cuttings in late summer or early autumn.

A. sericifera illus. p.207.

ARBUTUS

ERICACEAE

Genus of evergreen trees and shrubs grown for their leaves, clusters of small, urn-shaped flowers, ornamental bark, and strawberry-like fruits, which are edible but insipid. Must be protected from strong, cold winds when young. Prefers a position in full sun and needs fertile, well-drained soil; *A. menziesii* requires acidic soil. May be propagated by semi-ripe cuttings in late summer or by seed sown in autumn.

A. andrachne (Grecian strawberry tree). Evergreen, spreading tree or shrub. H and S 20ft (6m). Has oval, glossy, dark green leaves and peeling, reddish brown bark. Panicles of urn-shaped white flowers in late spring are followed by orange-red fruits. Prefers a sheltered position. Z7–9 H9–7.

A.* x *andrachnoides illus. p.83.

A. menziesii (Madroña, Madroñe). Evergreen, spreading tree. H and S 50ft (15m). Has smooth, peeling reddish bark and oval, dark green leaves. Large, upright, terminal panicles of urn-shaped white flowers in early summer are followed by orange or red fruits. Z7–9 H9–7.

A. unedo illus. p.93.

ARCHONTOPHOENIX
King palm

ARECACEAE/PALMAE

Genus of evergreen palms grown for their majestic appearance. Needs full light or partial shade and organic, well-drained soil. Water containerized specimens moderately, much less when temperatures are low. Propagate by seed in spring at not less than 75°F (24°C). Spider mite may be troublesome.

A. alexandrae illus. p.72.

A. cunninghamiana (Illawarra palm, Piccabeen palm). Evergreen palm. H 50–70ft (15–20m), S 6–15ft (2–5m). Has long, arching, feather-shaped leaves. Mature trees produce large clusters of small lavender or lilac flowers in summer, followed by large, egg-shaped red fruits. Z10–11 H12–9.

Arcterica nana. See *Pieris nana.*

ARCTOSTAPHYLOS
Manzanita, Bearberry

ERICACEAE

Genus of evergreen trees and shrubs grown for their foliage, flowers, and fruits. Some species are also grown

for their bark, others as groundcover. Does best in full sun and well-drained, acidic soil. Propagate by semi-ripe cuttings in summer or by seed in autumn.
A. alpina, syn. *Arctous alpinus.* Deciduous, creeping shrub. H 2in (5cm), S to 5in (12cm). Has drooping, terminal clusters of tiny, urn-shaped, pink-flushed white flowers in late spring, followed by rounded, purple-black berries. Leaves are oval, toothed, glossy, and bright green. Z2–7 H7–1.
A. diversifolia, syn. *Comarostaphylis diversifolia* (Summer holly). Evergreen, upright shrub or tree. H 15ft (5m), S 10ft (3m). Leaves are oblong, glossy, and dark green. Terminal racemes of fragrant, urn-shaped white flowers appear from early to mid-spring, followed by spherical red fruits. Z7–9 H9–7.
***A.* 'Emerald Carpet'** illus. p.156.
***A. hookeri* 'Monterey Carpet'**, syn. A. *uva-ursi* subsp. *hookeri* 'Monterey Carpet'. Evergreen, open shrub. H 4–6in (10–15cm), S 16in (40cm) or more. Has hairy branchlets bearing glossy, pale green leaves and, in early summer, urn-shaped white flowers, sometimes flushed pink, that are followed by globose red fruits. Z8–9 H9–8.
A. manzanita. Evergreen, upright shrub. H and S 6ft (2m) or more. Has peeling, reddish brown bark and oval, leathery, gray-green leaves. From early to midspring produces small, urn-shaped, deep pink flowers. Z8–9 H9–8.
A. nevadensis (Pine-mat manzanita). Evergreen, prostrate shrub. H 4in (10cm), S 3ft (1m). Has small, oval leaves. In summer, pendent, urn-shaped white flowers are borne in clusters in leaf axils, followed by globose, brownish red fruits. Is useful as a groundcover. Z7–9 H9–7.
A. nummularia. Evergreen, erect to prostrate shrub. H 1ft (30cm) or more, S 3ft (1m). Leaves are small, rounded, leathery, and toothed. Pendent, urn-shaped white flowers are borne in clusters from leaf axils in summer, followed by globose green fruits. Makes a good ground cover. Z7–9 H9–7.
A. patula illus. p.152.
A. stanfordiana (Stanford manzanita). Evergreen, erect shrub. H and S 5ft (1.5m). Bark is smooth and reddish brown. Has narrowly oval, glossy, bright green leaves. Bears drooping clusters of urn-shaped pink flowers from early to midspring. Z6–9 H9–6.
A. uva-ursi illus. p.388. subsp. ***hookeri* 'Monterey Carpet'** see *A. hookeri* 'Monterey Carpet'. **'Point Reyes'** illus. p.388. **'Vancouver Jade'** is an evergreen, trailing, sometimes arching shrub. H 4in (10cm), S 20in (50cm). Has small, oval, bright green leaves and bears urn-shaped white flowers in summer. Z2–6 H6–1.

ARCTOTHECA

ASTERACEAE/COMPOSITAE

Genus of creeping perennials. Needs bright light and fertile, well-drained soil; dislikes humid conditions. Propagate by seed or division in spring.
A. calendula, syn. *Cryptostemma calendulaceum*, illus. p.294.

ARCTOTIS, syn. X VENIDIOARCTOTIS

ASTERACEAE/COMPOSITAE

Genus of annuals and perennials grown for their flower heads and foliage. Requires full sun and leafy soil with sharp sand added. Propagate by seed in autumn or spring or by stem cuttings year-round.
***A.* Harlequin Hybrids**, syn. *A.* x *hybrida*, x *Venidioarctotis*. Fairly slow-growing, upright, branching perennial usually grown as an annual. H and S 18in (45cm). Lance-shaped, lobed leaves are grayish green above, white below. In summer has large, daisylike flower heads in many shades, including yellow, orange, bronze, purple, pink, cream, and red. Z13–15 H12–10. **'Bacchus'** has purple flower heads; **'China Rose'** deep pink; **'Sunshine'** yellow; **'Tangerine'** orange-yellow; and **'Torch'** bronze.
A.* x *hybrida. See *A.* Harlequin Hybrids.
A. stoechadifolia. See *A. venusta.*
A. venusta, syn. *A. stoechadifolia* (African daisy). Compact perennial, often grown as an annual. H 20in (50cm) or more, S 16in (40cm). Daisy-like, creamy white flower heads with blue centers are borne singly throughout summer and into autumn. Chrysanthemum-like leaves are dark green above, gray beneath.

Arctous alpinus. See *Arctostaphylos alpina.*

ARDISIA

MYRSINACEAE

Genus of evergreen shrubs and trees grown for their fruits and foliage. Needs partial shade and organic, well-drained but not dry soil. Water potted plants freely when in full growth, moderately at other times. Cut back old plants in early spring if required. Propagate by seed in spring or by semi-ripe cuttings in summer.
A. crenata, syn. *A. crenulata*, illus. p.150.
A. crenulata. See *A. crenata*.

Areca lutescens. See *Dypsis lutescens.*
Arecastrum romanozoffianum. See *Syagrus romanozoffiana.*
Aregelia carolinae. See *Neoregelia carolinae.*

ARENARIA
Sandwort

CAROPHYLLACEAE

Genus of spring- and summer-flowering annuals and perennials, some of which are evergreen. Most need sun and well-drained, sandy soil. Propagate by division or softwood cuttings in early summer or by seed in autumn or spring.
A. balearica illus. p.362.
A. montana illus. p.374.
A. purpurascens illus. p.365.
A. tetraquetra illus. p.361.

ARGEMONE

PAPAVERACEAE

Genus of robust perennials, most of which are best treated as annuals. Grow in sun and in very well-drained soil without supports. Deadhead plants to prolong the flowering season. Propagate by seed sown outdoors in late spring.
A. mexicana illus. p.335.

ARGYRANTHEMUM

ASTERACEAE/COMPOSITAE

Genus of evergreen subshrubs, grown for their daisylike flowers. Needs full sun and moderately fertile, well-drained soil. Propagate by semi-ripe cuttings in summer or root greenwood cuttings in spring.
A. frutescens, syn. *Chrysanthemum frutescens* (Marguerite), illus. p.240.
***A.* 'Jamaica Primrose'**, syn. *Chrysanthemum frutescens* 'Jamaica Primrose', illus. p255.
***A.* 'Mary Wootton'**, syn. *Chrysanthemum frutescens* 'Mary Wootton', illus. p.243.

Argyrocytisus battandieri. See *Cytisus battandieri.*

ARGYRODERMA

AIZOACEAE

Genus of succulents grown for their very fleshy, gray-green leaves united in a prostrate egg shape. In summer, daisylike flowers appear in central split between leaves. Needs full sun and very well-drained soil. Overwatering causes leaves to split or plant to rot. Propagate by seed in summer.
A. aureum. See *A. delaetii.*
A. blandum. See *A. delaetii.*
A. brevipes. See *A. fissum.*
A. delaetii, syn. *A. aureum*, *A. blandum*, illus. p.476.
A. fissum, syn. *A. brevipes*, illus. p.474.
A. pearsonii, syn. *A. schlechteri*, illus. p.473.
A. schlechteri. See *A. pearsonii.*

ARIOCARPUS
Living rock

CACTACEAE

Genus of extremely slow-growing cacti with large, swollen roots. Produces flattened, spherical green stems with angular tubercles and tufts of wool. Prefers full sun and extremely well-drained, lime-rich soil. Is very prone to rotting. Propagate by seed in spring or summer.
A. fissuratus illus. p.472.

ARISAEMA

ARACEAE

Genus of tuberous perennials grown for their large, curious, hooded spathes, each enclosing a pencil-shaped spadix. Forms spikes of fleshy red fruits in autumn before dying down. Needs sun or partial shade and moist but well-drained organic soil. Plant tubers 6in (15cm) deep in spring or autumn. Propagate by seed in autumn or spring or by offsets in spring.
A. atrorubens. See *A. triphyllum.*
A. candidissimum illus. p.435.
A. consanguineum illus. p.402.
A. griffithii illus. p.422.
A. jacquemontii illus. p.422.
A. ringens. Early spring-flowering, tuberous perennial. H 10–12in (25–30cm), S 12–18in (30–45cm). Bears 2 erect leaves, each with 3 long-pointed lobes, and a widely hooded green spathe, enclosing the spadix, that has paler green stripes and is edged with dark brown-purple. Z6–9 H9–6.
A. sikokianum illus. p.419.
A. tortuosum. Summer-flowering, tuberous perennial. H 1–3ft (30cm–1m), S 1–1½ft (30–45cm). Each dark green-mottled, pale green stem bears 2–3 erect leaves divided into several oval leaflets. A hooded green or purple spathe with a protruding, S-shaped spadix overtops leaves. Produces spikes of attractive, fleshy red fruits in autumn. Z8–9 H9–7.
A. triphyllum, syn. *A. atrorubens*, illus. p.414.

ARISARUM

ARACEAE

Genus of tuberous perennials grown mainly for their curious, hooded spathes enclosing spadices with minute flowers. Needs partial shade and organic, well-drained soil. Propagate in autumn by division of an established clump of tubers, which produce offsets freely.
A. proboscideum (Mouse plant). Clump-forming, spring-flowering, tuberous perennial. H to 4in (10cm), S 8–12in (20–30cm). Leaves are arrow-shaped and prostrate. Produces a spadix of minute flowers concealed in a hooded, dark brown spathe that is drawn out into a tail up to 6in (15cm) long, giving a mouselike effect. Z7–9 H9–7.

ARISTOLOCHIA
Dutchman's pipe

ARISTOLOCHIACEAE

Genus of evergreen or deciduous, woody-stemmed, twining and scrambling climbers grown for their foliage and flowers. Requires partial shade in summer and well-drained soil. Water regularly, less when not in full growth. Provide support. Cut back previous season's growth to 2 or 3 nodes in spring.Propagate by seed in spring or by semi-ripe cuttings in summer. Spider mite and whitefly may be a nuisance.
A. durior. See *A. macrophylla.*
A. elegans. See *A. littoralis.*
A. gigas. See *A. grandiflora.*
A. grandiflora, syn. *A. gigas* (Pelican

flower, Swan flower). Fast-growing, evergreen, woody-stemmed, twining climber. H 22ft (7m) or more. Leaves are broadly oval, 6–10in (15–25cm) long. In summer bears large, unpleasant-smelling, tubular, purple-veined white flowers, each with a long tail and expanding at the mouth into a heart-shaped lip. Z13–15 H12–10.
A. littoralis, syn. *A. elegans*, illus. p.211.
A. macrophylla, syn. *A. durior, A. sipho*. Vigorous, deciduous twining vine. H 25-30ft (8-10m). Has large, heart-shaped leaves 4-12in (10-30cm) long that are dark green above and lighter beneath. Small greenish flowers mottled with purple and brown produced in midsummer. Z5–8 H8–4.
A. sipho. See *A. macrophylla.*

ARMERIA

PLUMBAGINACEAE

Genus of evergreen perennials and occasionally subshrubs grown for their tuftlike clumps or rosettes of leaves and their flower heads. Requires sun and well-drained soil. Propagate by semi-ripe cuttings in summer or by seed in autumn.
***A.* 'Bees Ruby'**, syn. *A. pseudarmeria* 'Bees Ruby'. Evergreen, clump-forming, dwarf subshrub. H and S 12in (30cm). Round heads of many small, ruby red flowers are produced in summer on stiff stems above narrow, grasslike, dark green leaves. Z5–7 H9–4.
A. caespitosa. See *A. juniperifolia.*
A. juniperifolia, syn. *A. caespitosa*, illus. p.365. **'Bevans Variety'** is an evergreen, densely cushioned subshrub. H 2–3in (5–8cm), S 6in (15cm). Has narrow, pointed, mid- to gray-green leaves in loose rosettes. Round heads of small, deep pink flowers are borne in late spring and early summer. Z5–7 H8–4.
A. latifolia. See *A. pseudarmeria.*
A. maritima (Sea pink, Thrift). Evergreen, clump-forming perennial or dwarf subshrub. H 4in (10cm), S 6in (15cm). Leaves are narrow, grasslike, and dark green. Stiff stems carry round heads of many small white to pink flowers in summer. Makes a good edging plant. Z3–9 H9–1. **'Vindictive'** illus. p.380.
A. pseudarmeria, syn. *A. latifolia*, illus. p.350. **'Bees Ruby'** see *A.* 'Bees Ruby'.

ARNICA

ASTERACEAE/COMPOSITAE

Genus of rhizomatous perennials grown for their large, daisylike flower heads. Is suitable for large rock gardens. Prefers sun and organic, well-drained soil. Propagate by division or seed in spring. All parts may cause severe discomfort if ingested, and contact with sap may aggravate skin allergies.
A. montana. Tufted, rhizomatous perennial. H 12in (30cm), S 6in (15cm). Bears narrowly oval to oval, hairy, gray-green leaves and, in summer, solitary, daisylike golden flower heads, 5cm (2in) wide. Prefers acidic soil. Z5–8 H8–5.

ARONIA

Chokeberry

ROSACEAE

Genus of deciduous shrubs cultivated for their flowers, fruits, and colorful autumn foliage. Needs sun (for autumn color at its best) or semi-shade and fertile, well-drained soil. May be propagated in several ways: by softwood or semi-ripe cuttings taken in summer, by seed sown in autumn, or by division from early autumn to spring.
A. arbutifolia illus. p.130.
A. melanocarpa illus. p.136.
A.* x *prunifolia. Deciduous, upright shrub. H 10ft (3m), S 8ft (2.5m). Oval, glossy, dark green leaves redden in autumn. Produces star-shaped white flowers in late spring and early summer, followed by spherical, purplish black fruits. Z5–9 H9–5.

ARRHENATHERUM

GRAMINAE/POACEAE

See also GRASSES, BAMBOOS, RUSHES and SEDGES.
A. elatius (False oat grass). subsp. ***bulbosum* 'Variegatum'** is a loosely tuft-forming, herbaceous, perennial grass. H 20in (50cm), S 8in (20cm). Has a basal stem swelling, hairless gray-green leaves with white margins, and open panicles of brownish spikelets in summer. Z5–8 H8–5.

ARTEMISIA

Wormwood

ASTERACEAE/COMPOSITAE

Genus of perennials and spreading, dwarf subshrubs and shrubs, some of which are evergreen or semi-evergreen, grown mainly for their fernlike silvery foliage that is sometimes aromatic. Prefers an open, sunny, well-drained site; dwarf types benefit from a winter protection of very coarse sand or gravel. Trim lightly in spring. Propagate by division in spring or autumn or by softwood or semi-ripe cuttings in summer.
A. abrotanum illus. p.176.
***A. absinthium* 'Lambrook Silver'.** Evergreen, bushy perennial, woody at base. H 32in (80cm), S 20in (50cm). Has a mass of finely divided, aromatic, silvery gray leaves. Produces tiny, insignificant gray flower heads borne in long panicles in summer. Needs protection in an exposed site. Z5–11 H12–8.
***A. alba* 'Canescens'**, syn. *A. canescens, A. splendens*. Semi-evergreen, bushy perennial. H 20in (50cm), S 12in (30cm). Has delicate, finely cut, curling, silvery gray leaves. In summer, insignificant yellow flower heads are borne on erect silver stems. Makes a good groundcover. Z4–8 H8–1.
A. arborescens illus. p.175. **'Brass Band'** see *A.* 'Powis Castle'. **'Faith Raven'** is an evergreen, upright shrub. H 4ft (1.2m), S 3ft (1m). Differs from the species in that it is hardier. Has finely cut, aromatic, silvery white foliage and, in summer and early autumn, rounded heads of small, bright yellow flowers. Z6–9 H9–6.
A. assoana. See *A. caucasica.*
A. canescens. See *A. alba* 'Canescens'.
A. caucasica, syn. *A. assoana, A. lanata, A. pedemontana*. Evergreen or semi-evergreen, prostrate perennial. H and S 12in (30cm). Fernlike foliage is densely covered with silvery white hairs. Small clusters of small, rounded yellow flower heads are borne in summer. Good in a rock garden or wall. Z5–9 H9–1.
A. lactiflora illus. p.227.
A. lanata. See *A. caucasica.*
A. ludoviciana var. ***albula*** illus. p.266. **'Silver Queen'** is a semi-evergreen, clump-forming perennial. H 30in (75cm), S 24in (60cm) or more. Has large, lance-shaped, downy, silvery white leaves that become greener with age. From midsummer to autumn bears densely white-woolly panicles of brownish yellow flower heads. Z5–11 H12–8.
A. pedemontana. See *A. caucasica.*
A. pontica illus. p.290.
***A.* 'Powis Castle'**, syn. *A. arborescens* 'Brass Band'. Vigorous, evergreen subshrub. H 3ft (1m), S 4ft (1.2m). Has abundant, finely cut, aromatic, silvery gray foliage and sprays of insignificant, yellowish gray flower heads in summer.
A. schmidtiana. Semi-evergreen, hummock-forming perennial with creeping stems. H 3–12in (8–30cm), S 24in (60cm). Has fernlike, very finely and deeply cut silver leaves and, in summer, produces short racemes of small, rounded, pale yellow flower heads. Is good for a large rock garden, wall, or bank. Needs sandy, peaty soil. Z5–8 H8–5. **'Nana'** illus. p.389.
A. splendens. See *A. alba* 'Canescens'.
A. stelleriana. Evergreen, rounded, rhizomatous perennial with a woody base. H 1–2ft (30–60cm), S 2–3ft (60cm–1m). White-haired silver leaves are deeply lobed or toothed. Bears slender sprays of small yellow flower heads in summer. Needs light soil. Z7–7 H7–1. **'Boughton Silver'** (syn. *A.s.* 'Mori', *A.s.* 'Silver Brocade'), S 3ft (1m), is vigorous and arching in habit. **'Mori'** see *A.s.* 'Boughton Silver'. **'Silver Brocade'** see *A.s.* 'Boughton Silver'.

ARUM

Cuckoo pint, Lords and ladies

ARACEAE

Genus of tuberous perennials grown for their leaves and spathes, each enclosing a pencil-shaped spadix of tiny flowers. Requires sun or partial shade and moist but well-drained soil. Propagate by seed in autumn or by division in early autumn.
A. creticum illus. p.415.
A. dioscoridis. Spring-flowering, tuberous perennial. H 8–14in (20–35cm), S 12–18in (30–45cm). Has a sail-like green or purple spathe, blotched dark purple, surrounding a blackish purple spadix. Arrow-shaped, semi-erect leaves appear in autumn. Z7–9 H9–7.
A. dracunculus. See *Dracunculus vulgaris.*
***A. italicum* 'Marmoratum'**, syn. *A.i.* 'Pictum', illus. p.434.
A. pictum illus. p.439.

ARUNCUS

ROSACEAE

Genus of perennials, grown for their hummocks of broad, fernlike leaves and their plumes of white flowers in summer. Thrives in full light and any well-drained soil. Propagate by seed in autumn or by division in spring or autumn.
A. dioicus, syn. *A. sylvester, Spiraea aruncus*, illus. p.226. **'Kneiffii'** illus. p.240.

A. sylvester. See *A. dioicus.*
Arundinaria anceps. See *Yushania anceps.*
Arundinaria auricoma. See *Pleioblastus auricomus.*
Arundinaria falconeri. See *Himalayacalamus falconeri.*
Arundinaria fastuosa. See *Semiarundinaria fastuosa.*
Arundinaria fortunei. See *Pleioblastus variegatus.*
Arundinaria japonica. See *Pseudosasa japonica.*
Arundinaria jaunsarensis. See *Yushania anceps.*
Arundinaria murieliae. See *Fargesia murieliae.*
Arundinaria nitida. See *Fargesia nitida.*
Arundinaria variegata. See *Pleioblastus variegatus.*
Arundinaria viridistriata. See *Pleioblastus auricomus.*

ARUNDO

GRAMINAE/POACEAE

See also GRASSES, BAMBOOS, RUSHES and SEDGES.
A. donax (Giant reed). Herbaceous, rhizomatous, perennial grass. H to 20ft (6m), S 3ft (1m). Has thick stems that bear broad, floppy, blue-green leaves. Produces dense, erect panicles of whitish yellow spikelets in summer. Can be grown in moist soil. Var. ***versicolor*** (syn. *A.d.* 'Variegata') illus. p.306. **'Variegata'** see *A.d.* var. ***versicolor***.

ASARINA

SCROPHULARIACEAE

Genus of evergreen climbers and perennials, often with scandent stems, grown for their flowers. Is herbaceous in cold climates. Grow in a position with full light and in any well-drained

soil. Propagate by seed in spring.
A. barclayana. See *Maurandya barclayana.*
A. erubescens. *See Lophospermum erubescens.*
A. procumbens, syn. *Antirrhinum asarina*, illus. p.384.

Asarum,
syn. HEXASTYLIS
Wild ginger

ARISTOLOCHIACEAE

Genus of rhizomatous perennials, some of which are evergreen, with pitcher-shaped flowers carried under kidney- or heart-shaped leaves. Makes a good groundcover, although leaves may become damaged in severe weather. Prefers shade and organic, moist but well-drained soil. Propagate by division in spring. Self seeds readily.
A. caudatum. Evergreen, prostrate, rhizomatous perennial. H 3in (8cm), S 10in (25cm) or more. Heart-shaped, leathery, glossy, dark green leaves, 2–4in (5–10cm) across, conceal small, pitcher-shaped, reddish brown or brownish purple flowers with tail-like lobes in early summer. Z4–8 H8–1.
A. europaeum illus. p.390.
A. hartwegii. Evergreen, prostrate, rhizomatous perennial. H 3in (8cm), S 10in (25cm) or more. Pitcher-shaped, very dark brown, almost black flowers with tail-like lobes appear in early summer beneath heart-shaped, silver-marked, midgreen leaves, 2–4in (5–10cm) wide. Z6–8 H8–6.
A. shuttleworthii. Evergreen, prostrate, rhizomatous perennial. H 3in (8cm), S 10in (25cm) or more. Has broadly heart-shaped, usually silver-marked, midgreen leaves, 3in (8cm) across. Bears pitcher-shaped, dark brown flowers, mottled violet inside, in early summer. Z5–9 H9–1.

Asclepias
Milkweed, Silkweed

ASCLEPIADACEAE

Genus of tuberous perennials or subshrubs, some of which are evergreen, grown for their flowers. Stems exude milky white latex when cut. Hardy species prefer a position in sun and a organic, well-drained soil. Propagate by division or seed in spring. Tender species require sun and a moist atmosphere; cut back during periods of growth. Water very sparingly in low temperatures. Propagate by tip cuttings or seed in spring. Contact with the milky sap may irritate skin.
A. hallii. Upright, tuberous perennial. H to 3ft (1m), S 2ft (60cm). Has oblong leaves, to 5in (13cm) long. Umbels of small, 5-horned, dark pink flowers are carried in summer; tightly packed silky seeds are enclosed in narrowly ovoid fruits to 6in (15cm) long.
Z9–11 H12–10.
A. physocarpa. See *Gomphocarpus physocarpus.*
A. syriaca. Upright, tuberous perennial. H and S 3ft (1m) or more. Bears oval leaves to 8in (20cm) long. Produces umbels of small, 5-horned, purplish pink flowers carried on drooping flower stalks in summer, followed by narrowly ovoid fruits to 6in (15cm) long and filled with silky seeds. Z3–9 H9–2.
A. tuberosa illus. p.258.

Asimina

ANNONACEAE

Genus of deciduous or evergreen shrubs and trees grown for their foliage and flowers. Prefers full sun and fertile, deep, moist but well-drained soil. Propagate by seed in autumn or by layering or root cuttings in winter.
A. triloba (Pawpaw). Deciduous, open shrub. H and S 12ft (4m). Large, oval, midgreen leaves emerge in late spring or early summer, just after or at the same time as 6-petaled, purplish brown flowers. Later it produces small, globular brownish fruits. Z6–8 H8–6.

Asparagus

ASPARAGACEAE

Genus of perennials and scrambling climbers and shrubs, some of which are evergreen, grown for their foliage. Grow in partial shade or bright light, but not direct sun, in any fertile, well-drained soil. Propagate by seed or division in spring.
A. densiflorus illus. p.266.
'Myersii' (syn. *A. meyeri*, *A.* 'Myers') illus. p.267.
A. meyeri. See *A. densiflorus* 'Myersii'.
***A.* 'Myers'.** See *A. densiflorus* 'Myersii'.
A. scandens illus. p.219.

Asperula

RUBIACEAE

Genus of annuals and perennials; some species make good alpine house plants. Most species need sun and well-drained soil with moisture at roots. Dislikes winter wet on the crown. Propagate by softwood cuttings or seed in early summer.
A. athoa of gardens. See *A. suberosa.*
A. odorata. See *Galium odoratum.*
A. suberosa, syn. *A. athoa* of gardens, illus. p.376.

Asphodeline

ASPHODELACEAE/LILIACEAE

Genus of perennials with thick, fleshy roots. Requires sun and not overly rich soil. Propagate by division in early spring, taking care not to damage roots, or by seed in autumn or spring.
A. liburnica. Neat, clump-forming perennial. H 10–24in (25–60cm), S 12in (30cm). In spring produces racemes of shallowly cup-shaped yellow flowers on slender stems above linear, gray-green leaves. Z6–9 H9–6.
A. lutea illus. p.238.

Asphodelus

ASPHODELACEAE

Genus of spring- or summer-flowering annuals and perennials. Requires sun; most prefer fertile, well-drained soil. *A. albus* prefers light, well-drained soil. Propagate by division in spring or by seed in autumn.
A. acaulis. Prostrate perennial. H 2in (5cm), S 9in (23cm). In spring or early summer, stemless, funnel-shaped, flesh pink flowers appear in the center of each cluster of grasslike, midgreen leaves. Is suitable for an alpine house. Z9–10 H10–9.
A. aestivus, syn. *A. microcarpus* (Asphodel). Upright perennial. H 3ft (1m), S 1ft (30cm). Dense panicles of star-shaped white flowers are borne in late spring. Has basal rosettes of uright then spreading, grasslike, channeled, leathery, midgreen leaves. Z7–10 H10–7.
A. albus illus. p.239.
A. microcarpus. See *A. aestivus.*

Aspidistra

CONVALLARIACEAE/LILIACEAE

Genus of evergreen, rhizomatous perennials that spread slowly, grown mainly for their glossy foliage. Very tolerant, but is best grown in a cool, shady position away from direct sun-light and in well-drained soil. Water frequently when in full growth, less at other times. Propagate by division of rhizomes in spring.
A. elatior (Cast-iron plant). Evergreen, rhizomatous perennial. H 24in (60cm), S 18in (45cm). Has upright, narrow, pointed-oval leaves, to 24in (60cm) long; inconspicuous cream to purple flowers are occasionally produced on short stalks near soil level.
Z7–11 H12–4.
'Variegata' illus. p.301.

Asplenium

ASPLENIACEAE

Genus of evergreen or semi-evergreen ferns. Plants described prefer partial shade, but *A. trichomanes* tolerates nearly full sun. Grow in any moist soil, although containerized plants should be grown in a mix including chopped sphagnum moss or coarse peat. Remove fading fronds regularly. Propagate by spores or bulbils, if produced, in late summer.
A. bulbiferum (Hen-and-chicken fern, Mother spleenwort). Semi-evergreen or evergreen fern. H 6–12in (15–30cm), S 12in (30cm). Lance-shaped, finely divided, dark green fronds produce bulbils, from which young plants develop. Z9–11 H12–8.
A. ceterach, syn. *Ceterach officinarum*, illus. p.311.
A. nidus illus. p.313.
A. scolopendrium, syn. *Phyllitis scolopendrium*, *Scolopendrium vulgare*, illus. p.313. **Marginatum Group** (syn. *Phyllitis scolopendrium* 'Marginatum') illus. p.313.
A. trichomanes illus. p.311.

Aster

ASTERACEAE/COMPOSITAE

Genus of perennials and deciduous or evergreen subshrubs with daisylike flower heads borne in summer-autumn. Prefers sun or partial shade and fertile, well-drained soil, with adequate moisture all summer. Tall asters require staking. Propagate by softwood cuttings in spring or by division in spring or autumn. Spray modern forms of *A. novi-belgii* against mildew and insect attack. Other species may suffer too. See also feature panel p.262.
A. acris. See *A. sedifolius.*
A. albescens, syn. *Microglossa albescens.* Deciduous, upright, slender-stemmed subshrub. H 3ft (1m), S 5ft (1.5m). Has narrowly lance-shaped, gray-green leaves and flattish sprays of lavender-blue flower heads with yellow centers in midsummer.
A. alpinus illus. p.381. **'Dark Beauty'** see *A.a.* 'Dunkle Schöne'. **'Dunkle Schöne'** (syn. *A.a.* 'Dark Beauty') is a clump-forming perennial. H 10in (25cm), S 18in (45cm). Leaves are lance-shaped and dark green. Deep purple flower heads are borne from mid- to late summer. Is suitable for a rock garden. Z4–8 H8–1.
***A. amellus* 'King George'** (illus. p.262). Bushy perennial. H and S 20in (50cm). In autumn, carries many large, terminal, daisylike, deep blue-violet flower heads with yellow centers. Leaves are oval and rough. **'Mauve Beauty'** bears clusters of large, violet flower heads with yellow centers in autumn. Leaves are lance-shaped, coarse, and midgreen. **'Nocturne'** (illus. p.262), H 75cm (30in), has deep lilac flower heads with yellow centers. **'Rudolph Goethe'** with large, violet-blue flower heads, **'Sonia'** with pink flower heads, and **'Veilchenkönigin'** (syn. *A.a.* 'Violet Queen') with deep violet flower heads are other good cultivars. **'Violet Queen'** see *A.a.* 'Veilchenkönigin'. All Z4–8 H8–1.
A. capensis. See *Felicia amelloides.*
***A. cordifolius* 'Silver Spray'** (illus. p.262). Bushy perennial. H 4ft (1.2m), S 3ft (1m). Dense, arching stems carry sprays of small, pink-tinged white flower heads in autumn. Midgreen leaves are lance-shaped. Needs staking. Z4–8 H8–1.
A. diffusus. See *A. lateriflorus.*
***A. ericoides* 'Golden Spray'** (illus. p.262). Bushy perennial. H 3ft (1m), S 1ft (30cm). Produces daisylike, pink-tinged white flower heads with bold, golden yellow centers from late summer to late autumn. Has small, lance-shaped, midgreen leaves and slender, freely branched stems. **'White Heather'** (illus. p.262) has long-lasting, neat white flower heads in late autumn and wiry stems that may need support. Both Z4–8 H8–1.
***A. frikartii* 'Mönch'** (illus. p262). Bushy perennial. H 30in (75cm), S 18in (45cm). Bears daisylike, single, soft lavender-blue flower heads with

yellowish green centers continuously from midsummer to late autumn. Leaves are oval and rough. May need staking. **'Wunder von Stäfa'** (illus. p.262) is similar but has lavender flowers. Both Z4–8 H8–1.
A. lateriflorus, syn. *A. diffusus*. Branching perennial. H 24in (60cm), S 20in (50cm). Bears sprays of tiny mauve flower heads with pinkish brown centers in autumn. Lance-shaped leaves are small and dark green. Z4–8 H8–1.**'Horizontalis'** (illus. p.262) has flowers heads that are sometimes tinged pink, with darker pink centers.
A. linosyris (Goldilocks; illus. p.262). Upright, unbranched perennial. H 24in (60cm), S 12in (30cm). Bears many small, dense, single, golden yellow flower heads in late summer-autumn. Leaves are narrowly lance-shaped. Z4–8 H8–1.
A. novae-angliae **'Andenken an Alma Pötschke'**, syn. *A.n.-a.* 'Alma Pötschke' (illus. p.262). Vigorous, upright perennial. H 30in (75cm), S to 24in (60cm). In autumn produces clusters of single pink flower heads on stiff stems. Has lance-shaped, rough leaves. May need staking. **'Autumn Snow'** see *A.n.-a.* 'Herbstschnee'. **'Barr's Pink'** (illus. p.262) bears semi-double, bright rose pink flower heads in summer-autumn. **'Harrington's Pink'** (illus. p.262), H 4–5ft (1.2–1.5m), has single, clear pink flower heads with yellow centers. Those of **'Herbstschnee'** (syn. *A.n.-a.* 'Autumn Snow'; illus. p.262), H 2½–3½ft (75cm–1.1m), are white with yellow centers. All Z4–8 H8–1.
A. novi-belgii **'Apple Blossom'** (illus. p.262). Vigorous, spreading perennial. H 36in (90cm), S 24–30in (60–75cm). Panicles of single, pale soft pink flowers are borne in autumn amid lance-shaped, midgreen leaves. **'Carnival'** (illus. p.262), H 30in (75cm), S to 45cm (18in), bears double, cerise-red flower heads with yellow centers. Leaves are dark green. Is prone to mildew. **'Chequers'** (illus. p.262), H 36in (90cm), S 24–30in (60–75cm), has single purple flowers. **'Climax'**, H 5ft (1.5m), S 2ft (60cm), bears single, light blue flowers. Is mildew-resistant. The flower heads of **'Fellowship'** (illus. p.262), H 4ft (1.2m), S 20in (50cm), are large, double, and clear, deep pink; those of **'Freda Ballard'** (illus. p.262) are semi-double and rich rose-red. **'Kristina'** (illus. p.262), H 12in (30cm), S 18in (45cm), has large, semi-double white flower heads with yellow centers. **'Lassie'** (illus. p.262), H 4ft (1.2m), S 30in (75cm), produces large, single, clear pink flowers. **'Little Pink Beauty'**, H 18in (45cm), S 20in (50cm), is a good dwarf semi-double pink cultivar. **'Marie Ballard'** (illus. p.262), H to 3ft (1m), S to 18in (45cm), has double, midblue flowers. Is prone to mildew. **'Orlando'** (illus. p.262), H 3ft (1m), S to 18in (45cm), has large, single, bright pink flower heads with golden centers. Leaves are dark green. Mildew may be a problem. **'Patricia Ballard'** (illus. p.262), H 4ft (1.2m), S 30in (75cm), produces semi-double pink flowers. Large, single flowers of **'Peace'** (illus. p.262) are mauve; those of **'Raspberry Ripple'**, H 30in (75cm), S 24in (60cm), are smaller and reddish violet. **'Royal Ruby'** (illus. p.262), H and S to 18in (45cm), bears semi-double, rich red flower heads with yellow centers. Is prone to mildew. **'Royal Velvet'** (illus. p.262), H 4ft (1.2m), S 30in (75cm), has single deep violet flowers. **'Sandford White Swan'** (illus. p.262), H 36in (90cm), S 24in (60cm), bears white flower heads. All Z4–8 H8–1.
A. pilosus var. ***demotus***, syn. *A. tradescantii* of gardens. Erect perennial. H 4ft (1.2m), S 20in (50cm). Has lance-shaped, midgreen leaves. In autumn, clusters of small white flower heads appear on wiry, leafy stems and provide a good foil to bright autumn leaf colors. Z4–8 H8–1.
A. **'Professor Anton Kippenburg'** (illus. p.262) is a compact, bushy perennial. H 12in (30cm), S to 18in (45cm). Carries large clusters of daisy-like, yellow-centered, clear blue flower heads in autumn. Z4–8 H8–1.
A. sedifolius, syn. *A. acris*. Bushy perennial. H 3ft (1m), S 2ft (60cm). Produces clusters of almost star-shaped, lavender-blue flower heads with yellow centers in autumn. Has small, narrowly oval, bright green leaves. Z4–8 H8–1.**'Nanus'**, H and S 20in (50cm), makes a compact dome of blooms.
A. thomsonii. Upright perennial. H 3ft (1m), S 20in (50cm). Produces long-petaled, pale lilac flower heads freely in autumn. Leaves are slightly heart-shaped. Z4–8 H8–1. **'Nanus'** (illus. p.262) is more compact, H 18in (45cm), S 9in (23cm).
A. tongolensis. Mat-forming perennial. H 20in (50cm), S 12in (30cm). Large, lavender-blue flower heads with orange centers are borne singly in early summer. Has lance-shaped, hairy, dark green leaves. Z4–8 H8–1.
A. tradescantii of gardens. See *A. pilosus* var. *demotus*.

ASTILBE

SAXIFRAGACEAE

Genus of summer-flowering perennials grown for their panicles of flowers that remain handsome even when dry brown in winter. Is suitable for borders and rock gardens. Needs partial shade in most species, and a rich, moist soil. Leave undisturbed if possible, and give an annual spring mulch of well-rotted compost. Propagate species by seed sown in autumn, others by division in spring or autumn.
A. **'Bressingham Beauty'.** Leafy, clump-forming perennial. H and S to 3ft (1m). In summer bears feathery, tapering panicles of small, star-shaped, rich pink flowers on strong stems. Broad leaves are divided into oblong to oval, toothed leaflets. Z3–8 H8–2.
A. chinensis var. ***pumila.*** Clump-forming perennial. H 12in (30cm), S 8in (20cm). Lower two-thirds of flower stem bears deeply dissected, coarse, toothed, hairy, dark green leaves. Dense, fluffy spikes of tiny, star-shaped, deep raspberry red flowers appear in summer. Is good for a shaded, moist rock garden. Z4–8 H8–1.
A. x ***crispa*** **'Perkeo'.** See *A.* 'Perkeo'.
A. **'Fanal'** illus. p.282.
A. **'Gnom'**, syn. *A. simplicifolia* 'Gnom'. Arching, clump-forming, slender-stemmed perennial. H 6in (15cm), S 4in (10cm). Has oval, deeply lobed or cut, crimped, reddish green leaves in a basal rosette. Produces dense racemes of tiny, star-shaped pink flowers in summer. Is good for a shaded, moist rock garden. Self seeds in damp places but will not come true. Z5–8 H8–2.
A. **'Granat'.** Clump-forming, leafy perennial. H 2ft (60cm), S to 3ft (1m). Produces pyramidal trusses of tiny, star-shaped, deep red flowers in summer above broad, bronze-flushed, rich green leaves that sare divided into oblong to oval, toothed leaflets. Z3–8 H8–2.
A. **'Irrlicht'** illus. p.276.
A. **'Montgomery'** illus. p.249.
A. **'Ostrich Plume'.** See *A.* 'Straussenfeder'.
A. **'Perkeo'**, syn. *A.* x *crispa* 'Perkeo', illus. p.353.
A. simplicifolia **'Gnom'.** See *A.* 'Gnom'.
A. **'Sprite'.** Clump-forming, dwarf, leafy perennial. H 20in (50cm), S to 3ft (1m). Has feathery, tapering panicles of tiny, star-shaped, shell pink flowers in summer, borne above broad leaves divided into narrowly oval, toothed leaflets. Z4–8 H8–1.
A. **'Straussenfeder'**, syn *A.* 'Ostrich Plume', illus. p.244.
A. **'Venus'** illus. p.244.

ASTRANTIA

Masterwort

APIACEAE/UMBELLIFERAE

Genus of perennials. Needs sun or semi-shade and well-drained soil. Propagate by division in spring or by seed when fresh, in late summer.
A. major illus. p.277. subsp. ***carinthiaca*** see *A.m.* subsp. *involucrata*. **'Hadspen Blood'** has dark red bracts and flowers. subsp. ***involucrata*** (syn. *A.m.* subsp. *carinthiaca*) illus. p.277.
A. maxima illus. p.277.

ASTROPHYTUM

CACTACEAE

Genus of slow-growing cacti grown for their attractive form and freely produced, flattish yellow flowers, some with red centers. Prefers sun and very well-drained, lime-rich soil. Allow to dry completely in winter. Is prone to rot if wet. Propagate by seed sown in spring or summer.
A. asterias, syn. *Echinocactus asterias* (Sea urchin cactus, Silver dollar cactus). Slow-growing, slightly domed cactus. H 3–4in (8–10cm), S 4in (10cm). Spineless stem has about 8 low ribs bearing small, tufted areoles. Produces bright yellow flowers to 3in (8cm) across in summer. Z13–15 H12–10.
A. myriostigma, syn. *Echinocactus myriostigma*, illus. p.466.
A. ornatum, syn. *Echinocactus ornatus*, illus. p.477.

Asystasia bella. See *Mackaya bella*.

ATHROTAXIS

TAXODIACEAE

Genus of conifers with awl-shaped leaves that clasp stems. See also CONIFERS.
A. selaginoides (King William pine). Irregularly conical conifer. H 50ft (15m) or more, S 15ft (5m). Has tiny, thick-textured, loosely overlapping, dark green leaves and insignificant, globular cones. Z8–9 H9–8.

ATHYRIUM

ATHYRIACEAE/WOODSIACEAE

Genus of deciduous or, occasionally, semi-evergreen ferns. Needs shade and organic, moist soil. Remove fading fronds regularly. Propagate by spores in late summer or by division in autumn or winter.
A. filix-femina (Lady fern). Deciduous fern. H 2–4ft (60cm–1.2m), S 1–3ft (30cm–1m). Dainty, lance-shaped, much-divided, arching fronds are pale green. Has very variable frond dissection. Z4–9 H9–1.
A. goeringianum. See *A. niponicum*.
A. niponicum, syn. *A. goeringianum*, A. *nipponicum*, illus. p.313.
A. *nipponicum*. See *A. niponicum*.
A. otophorum. Semi-evergreen fern. H and S to 30in (75cm). Has arching, broadly ovate, midgreen or purple-tinged, divided fronds, 18–30in (45–75cm) long. Stalk and midrib are a contrasting deep wine purple. Z5–8 H8–2.

ATRIPLEX

CHENOPODIACEAE

Genus of annuals, perennials, and evergreen or semi-evergreen shrubs grown for their foliage. Grows well by the coast. Needs full sun and well-drained soil. Propagate by softwood cuttings taken in summer or by seed sown in autumn.
A. halimus (Tree purslane). Semi-evergreen, bushy shrub. H 6ft (2m), S 10ft (3m). Oval leaves are silvery gray. Produces flowers very rarely. Z7–9 H9–7.
A. hortensis var. ***rubra*** (Red mountain spinach, Red orach). Fast-growing, erect annual. H 4ft (1.2m), S 1ft (30cm). Triangular, deep red leaves to 6in (15cm) long are edible. Bears insignificant flowers in summer. Z7–9 H9–7.

AUBRIETA

BRASSICACEAE/CRUCIFERAE

Genus of evergreen, trailing and mound-forming perennials. Is useful on dry banks, walls, and in rock gardens. Thrives in sun and in any well-drained soil. To maintain a compact shape, cut back hard after flowering. Propagate by greenwood cuttings in summer or by semi-ripe cuttings in late summer or autumn.

***A.* 'Carnival'.** See *A.* 'Hartswood Purple'.

***A.* 'Cobalt Violet'** illus. p.369.

***A. deltoidea* 'Argenteovariegata'** illus. p.368.

***A.* 'Doctor Mules'.** Vigorous, evergreen, mound-forming perennial. H 2–3in (5–8cm), S 12in (30cm). Has rounded, toothed, soft green leaves and, in spring, large, single, rich purple flowers on short spikes. Z5–7 H7–5.

***A.* 'Gurgedyke'.** Evergreen, mound-forming perennial. H 4in (10cm), S 8in (20cm). Bears rounded, toothed, soft green leaves. Produces 4-petaled, deep purple flowers in spring. Z5–7 H7–5.

***A.* 'Hartswood Purple'**, syn. *A.* 'Carnival', illus. p.368.

***A.* 'Joy'** illus. p.367.

***A.* 'J.S. Baker'** illus. p.368.

AUCUBA

CORNACEAE

Genus of evergreen shrubs grown for their foliage and fruits. To obtain fruits, grow both male and female plants. Makes good house plants when kept in a cool, shaded position. Tolerates full sun through to dense shade. Grow in any but waterlogged soil. To restrict growth, cut old shoots back hard in spring. Propagate by semi-ripe cuttings taken in summer.

A. japonica illus. p.152. **'Crotonifolia'** (male) illus. p.153. **'Gold Dust'** is an evergreen, bushy, dense, female shrub. H and S 8ft (2.5m). Has thick green shoots and oval, glossy, gold-speckled, dark green leaves. Small, star-shaped purple flowers in midspring are followed by egg-shaped, bright red fruits. Bright green leaves of **'Picturata'** (male) each have a central golden blotch. Some plants of 'Crotonifolia' and 'Picturata' are known to be female and have produced fruits. Both Z6–15 H12–6.

AURINIA

BRASSICACEAE/CRUCIFERAE

Genus of evergreen perennials, grown for their gray-green foliage and showy flower sprays. Is suitable for rock gardens, walls, and banks. Needs sun and well-drained soil. Propagate by softwood or greenwood cuttings in early summer or by seed in autumn.

A. saxatilis, syn. *Alyssum saxatile*, illus. p.350. **'Citrina'** illus. p.349. **'Dudley Nevill'** is an evergreen, clump-forming perennial. H 9in (23cm), S 12in (30cm). Has oval, hairy, gray-green leaves and, in late spring and early summer, produces racemes of many small, 4-petaled, buff-yellow flowers. Z4–10 H9–1. **'Variegata'** illus. p.349.

AUSTROCEDRUS

CUPRESSACEAE

Genus of conifers with flattish sprays of scalelike leaves. See also CONIFERS.

A. chilensis, syn. *Libocedrus chilensis*, illus. p.106.

Avena candida. See *Helictotrichon sempervirens.*

Avena sempervirens. See *Helicto-trichon sempervirens.*

AZARA

FLACOURTIACEAE

Genus of evergreen shrubs and trees grown for their foliage and also for their yellow flowers that are composed of a mass of stamens. Where marginally hardy, plants are best grown situated against a south- or west-facing wall for added protection. Grows in sun or shade, and in fertile, well-drained soil. Propagate by semi-ripe cuttings in summer.

A. lanceolata. Evergreen, bushy shrub or spreading tree. H and S 20ft (6m). Has narrowly oval, sharply toothed, bright green leaves. Small, rounded clusters of pale yellow flowers are carried in late spring or early summer. Z8–11 H12–10.

A. microphylla illus. p.125.

A. serrata illus. p.135.

AZOLLA

AZOLLACEAE

Genus of deciduous, perennial, floating water ferns grown for their decorative foliage and also to control algal growth by reducing light in water beneath. Grows in sun or shade. If not kept in check may be invasive; reduce spread by removing portions with a net. Propagate by redistributing clusters of plantlets when they appear.

A. caroliniana. See *A. filiculoides.*

A. filiculoides, syn *A. caroliniana*, illus. p.448.

AZORELLA

APIACEAE/UMBELLIFERAE

Genus of evergreen, tufted or spreading perennials grown for their flowers and neat, rosetted foliage. Is useful as alpine house plants. Thrives in full light and well-drained soil. Propagate by division in spring.

A. nivalis. See *A. trifurcata.*

A. trifurcata, syn. *A. nivalis*, illus. p.390.

AZORINA

CAMPANULACEAE

Genus of one species of erect evergreen shrub with bell-shaped flowers. Needs full light and fertile, moist but well-drained soil. Propagate by seed in spring or take softwood or semi-ripe cuttings in summer.

Azorina vidalii, syn. *Campanula vidalii*, illus. p.154.

Azureocereus hertlingianus. See *Browningia hertlingiana.*

B

BABIANA

IRIDACEAE

Genus of spring- and early summer-flowering corms valued for their brightly colored flowers, which are somewhat like freesias. Requires a position in sun and well-drained soil. Propagate in autumn by seed or natural division of corms.

B. disticha. See *B. plicata.*

B. plicata, syn. *B. disticha.* Spring-flowering corm. H 4–8in (10–20cm), S 2–3in (5–8cm). Has a fan of lance-shaped, erect, basal leaves and short spikes of funnel-shaped, violet-blue flowers, 1½–2in (4–5cm) long, with yellow-patched petals. Z13–15 H12–10.

B. rubrocyanea illus. p.431.

B. stricta. Spring-flowering corm. H 4–8in (10–20cm), S 2–3in (5–8cm). Produces a fan of narrowly lance-shaped, erect, basal leaves and short spikes of up to 10 funnel-shaped purple, blue, cream, or pale yellow flowers, 1–1½in (2.5–4cm) long and sometimes red-centered. Z13–15 H12–10

BACCHARIS

ASTERACEAE/COMPOSITAE

Genus of evergreen or deciduous, mainly autumn-flowering shrubs grown for their foliage and fruits. Is useful for exposed, coastal gardens and dry soil. Requires a position in full sun and well-drained soil. Propagate by softwood cuttings in summer.

B. halimifolia (Bush groundsel). Vigorous, deciduous, bushy shrub. H and S 12ft (4m). Has gray-green, sharply toothed, oval leaves. Large clusters of tiny white flower heads in midautumn are followed by fluffy white heads of tiny fruits. Z3–7 H7–1.

Bahia lanata. See *Eriophyllum lanatum.*

BALDELLIA

ALISMATACEAE

Genus of deciduous or evergreen, perennial, bog plants and submerged water plants grown for their foliage. Prefers a position in sun but tolerates shade. Remove fading foliage and excess growth as required. Propagate by division in spring or summer.

B. ranunculoides, syn. *Alisma ranunculoides*, *Echinodorus ranunculoides*. Deciduous, perennial, bog plant or submerged water plant. H 9in (23cm), S 6in (15cm). Has lance-shaped, midgreen leaves and, in summer, umbels of small, 3-parted pink or white flowers with basal yellow marks. Z5–8 H8–5

BALLOTA

LABIATAE/LAMIACEAE

Genus of perennials and evergreen or deciduous subshrubs grown for their foliage and flowers. Requires very well-drained soil and full sun. Cut back in spring before growth starts. Propagate by semi-ripe cuttings in summer.

B. acetabulosa illus. p.176.

B. pseudodictamnus illus. p.361..

BAMBUSA

GRAMINEAE/POACEAE

See also GRASSES, BAMBOOS, RUSHES, and SEDGES.

B. glaucescens. See *B. multiplex.*

B. multiplex, syn. *B. glaucescens*, illus. p.307.

BANKSIA

PROTEACEAE

Genus of evergreen shrubs and trees grown for their flowers and foliage. Requires full light and well- drained, sandy soil containing little phosphates or nitrates. Water containerized plants moderately when in full growth, sparingly at other times. Freely ventilate plants grown under cover. Propagate by seed in spring.

B. baxteri. Evergreen, spreading, open shrub. H and S 6–10ft (2–3m). Leathery, midgreen leaves are strap-shaped, cut from the midrib into triangular, sharply pointed lobes. Produces dense, spherical heads of small, tubular yellow flowers in summer. Z10–11 H12–10.

B. coccinea illus. p.130.

B. ericifolia (Heath banksia). Evergreen, irregularly rounded, wiry, freely branching shrub. H and S to 10ft (3m). Has small, needlelike leaves and dense, upright, bottlebrush-like spikes, each 4–6in (10–15cm) long, of small, tubular, bronze-red or yellow flowers in late winter and spring. Z10–13 H12–10.

B. serrata. Evergreen, bushy, upright shrub or tree. H 10–30ft (3–10m), S 5–10ft (1.5–3m). Oblong to lance-shaped, saw-toothed, leathery leaves are mid- to deep green. Small, tubular, reddish-budded cream flowers appear in dense, upright, bottlebrush-like spikes, each 4–6in (10–15cm) long, from spring to late summer. Z10–13 H12–10.

BAPTISIA

LEGUMINOSAE/PAPILIONACEAE

Genus of summer-flowering perennials grown for their flowers. Requires full sun and deep, well-drained, preferably neutral to acidic soil. Is best not disturbed once planted. Propagate by division in early spring or by seed in autumn.

B. australis illus. p.252.

Barbacenia elegans. See *Vellozia elegans*.

BARBAREA

BRASSICACEAE/CRUCIFERAE

Genus of summer-flowering perennials, biennials, and annuals. Most species are weeds or winter salad plants, but the variegated form of *B. vulgaris* is grown for decorative purposes. Grows in a sunny or shady position and in any well-drained but not very dry soil. Propagate by seed or division in spring.

B. vulgaris (Winter cress, Yellow rocket). **'Variegata'** illus. p.291.

BARLERIA

ACANTHACEAE

Genus of evergreen shrubs and perennials grown for their flowers. Needs full light or partial shade and fertile soil. Water potted plants well when in full growth, moderately at other times. In the growing season, prune tips of young plants to encourage branching. For a more compact habit, shorten long stems after flowering. May be propagated by seed in spring or by greenwood or semi-ripe cuttings in summer.

B. cristata (Philippine violet). Evergreen, semi-erect shrub. H and S 2–4ft (60cm–1.2m). Has elliptic, coarsely haired leaves. Tubular, light violet flowers, sometimes pale pink or white, are produced from upper leaf axils in summer. Z10–11 H12–10.

B. obtusa. Evergreen, erect, spreading shrub. H and S to 3ft (1m). Leaves are elliptic. Tubular mauve flowers are produced from upper leaf axils during winter-spring. Z113 15 H12–10.

Barosma pulchella. See *Agathosma pulchella*.

Bartonia aurea. See *Mentzelia lindleyi*.

BASSIA, syn. KOCHIA

CHENOPODIACEAE

Genus of annuals and perennials grown for their habit, the feathery effect of their leaves, and their autumn tints. Does best in sun and in fertile, well-drained soil. May require support in very windy areas. Propagate by seed sown under cover in early to midspring, or outdoors in late spring.

B. scoparia f. ***trichophylla*** illus. p.335.

BAUERA

CUNONIACEAE

Genus of evergreen shrubs grown mainly for their flowers. Needs full sun and organic, well-drained, neutral to acidic soil. Water potted plants moderately, less when not in full growth. Remove straggly stems after flowering. May be propagated by seed sown in spring or by semi-ripe cuttings taken in late summer.

B. rubioides. Evergreen, bushy, wiry-stemmed shrub, usually of spreading habit. H and S 1–2ft (30–60cm). Leaves each have 3 oval to lance-shaped, glossy leaflets. Bowl-shaped pink or white flowers appear in early spring and summer. Z13–15 H12–1.

BAUHINIA

LEGUMINOSAE/PAPILIONACEAE

Genus of evergreen, semi-evergreen or deciduous trees, shrubs, and scandent climbers grown for their flowers. Requires full light and fertile, well-drained soil. Water containerized specimens freely when in full growth, less in winter. Thin out congested growth after flowering. Propagate by seed in spring.

B. galpinii, syn. *B. punctata*, illus. p.142.

B. punctata. See *B. galpinii*.

B. variegata and **'Candida'** illus. p.97.

BEAUCARNEA

AGAVACEAE/DRACAENACEAE

Genus of evergreen shrubs and trees grown mainly for their intriguing, overall appearance. Needs full light and well- drained, fertile soil; drought conditions are tolerated. Water potted specimens moderately; allow soil mix to almost dry out between waterings. Propagate by seed or suckers in spring or by stem-tip cuttings in summer.

B. recurvata, syn. *Nolina recurvata*, ***N. tuberculata,*** illus. p.100.

BEAUMONTIA

APOCYNACEAE

Genus of evergreen, woody-stemmed, twining climbers grown for their large, fragrant flowers and handsome leaves. Requires fertile, well-drained soil and full light. Water freely in growing season, sparingly otherwise. Provide support. Thin out previous season's growth after flowering. Propagate by semi-ripe cuttings in late summer.

B. grandiflora illus. p.204.

BEGONIA

BEGONIACEAE

Genus of evergreen or deciduous shrubs and small, treelike perennials and annuals grown for their colorful flowers and/or ornamental leaves. Prefers slightly acidic soil. Susceptible to powdery mildew and botrytis from late spring to early autumn. Commonly cultivated begonias are divided into the following groupings, each with varying cultivation requirements. See also feature panel p.295.

Cane-stemmed begonias
Evergreen, woody perennials, many known as "Angelwings," with usually erect, canelike stems bearing regularly spaced, swollen nodes and flowers in large, pendulous panicles. Encourage branching by pinching out growing tips. New growth develops from base of plant. Grow under cover in good light but not direct sun (poor light reduces quantity of flowers) and in free-draining, soil-based mix. Stake tall plants. Propagate in spring by seed or tip cuttings.

Rex-cultorum (Rex) begonias
Mostly evergreen, rhizomatous perennials of variable habit derived from crosses of *B. rex* and related species. They are grown for their brilliantly colored, oval to lance-shaped leaves, 3–12in (8–30cm) long, that are sometimes spirally twisted. Prefer 40–75% relative humidity. Grow under cover in cool climates, in partial shade and in well-drained soil; water only sparingly. Do not allow water to remain on the leaves; otherwise, they become susceptible to botrytis. Propagate in spring by seed, leaf cuttings, or division of rhizomes.

Rhizomatous begonias
Variable, mostly evergreen, rhizomatous perennials grown for their foliage and small, single flowers. Smooth, crested or puckered green or brown leaves, 3–12in (8–30cm) long, often marked silver, are sometimes spirally twisted. Creeping cultivars are more freely branched than erect ones and are useful for hanging baskets. Prefer 40–75% relative humidity. Grow under cover in cool climates, in partial shade and in well-drained soil; water only sparingly. Do not allow water to remain on the leaves; otherwise, they become susceptible to botrytis. Propagate in spring by seed, leaf cuttings, or division of rhizomes.

Semperflorens begonias
Evergreen, bushy perennials derived from *B. cucullata* var. *hookeri*, *B. schmidtiana*, and other species, often grown as bedding annuals. Stems are soft, succulent, and branch freely, bearing generally rounded green, bronze, or variegated, highly shiny leaves, 2in (5cm) long. Flowers are single or double. Pinch out growing tips to produce bushy plants. Requires sun or partial shade and well-drained soil. Propagate in spring by seed or stem cuttings.

Shrublike begonias
Evergreen, multistemmed, bushy perennials, usually freely branched with flexible, erect or pendent stems, often hairy. Leaves may be hairy or glabrous and up to 6in (15cm) across, 4–12in (10–30cm) long. Single flowers are pink, cream, or white. Prefer 55% relative humidity. Grow under cover in good light and moist but well-drained soil. Propagate in spring by seed or stem cuttings.

Tuberous begonias (including the Tuberhybrida, Multiflora, and Pendula begonias)
Mostly upright, bushy, tuberous, winter-dormant perennials grown for their foliage and flowers. Tuberhybrida begonias, H and S 30in (75cm), vary from pendent to erect, with sparsely branched, succulent stems and oval, pointed, glossy, bright to dark green leaves, 8in (20cm) long. Most are summer flowering and mainly double-flowered. Multiflora cultivars, H and S 12in (30cm), are more bushy and have 3in (8cm) long leaves and single, semi-double, or double flowers, each 1½ 2in (4–5cm) across, in summer; tolerates full sun. Pendula cultivars, H to 3ft (1m), have long, thin, trailing stems; leaves are 2½–3in (6–8cm) long. Masses of single or double flowers are borne in summer. Outdoors, grow in dappled shade and moist conditions; under cover, plant in cool shade with 65–70% relative humidity. Tubers are dormant in winter. Start into growth in spring for midsummer to early autumn flowering. Remove all flower buds until stems show at least 3 pairs of leaves; with large-flowered types allow only central male bud to flower, so remove flanking buds. Plants may require staking. Propagate in spring by seed, by stem or basal cuttings, or by division of tubers.

Winter-flowering begonias
Evergreen, low-growing, very compact perennials, with succulent, thin stems, that are often included in the tuberous group. Two main groups are recognized: the single-flowered, usually pink or white Lorraine, Cheimantha, or Christmas begonias; and the single, semi-double or double Elatior and Rieger begonias that occur in a wide range of colors. Leaves are green or bronze, 2in (5cm) long. Flowers are borne mainly from late autumn to mid-spring. Prefer 40% relative humidity. Indirect sun and moist soil are preferred. Cut back old stems to 4in (10cm) after flowering. Propagate in spring by seed or stem cuttings.

All of the following begonias are Z13–15 H12–1.

B. albopicta (illus. p.295). Fast-growing, evergreen, cane-stemmed begonia. H to 3ft (1m), S 1ft (30cm). Freely branched green stems turn brown-green when mature. Narrowly oval to lance-chaped, wavy-edged green leaves are silver-spotted. Has clusters of single, green-white flowers in summer-autumn.

B. angularis. See *B. stipulacea*.

***B.* 'Apricot Cascade'** (illus. p.295). Pendent Tuberhybrida begonia. H and S 2ft (60cm). Has emerald green leaves and, from early summer to midautumn, double, orange-apricot flowers. Other cascades are **'Bridal Cascade'** (pink-edged white petals), **'Crimson Cascade'**, **'Gold Cascade'** and **'Orange Cascade'**.
***B.* 'Beatrice Haddrell'.** Evergreen, creeping, rhizomatous begonia. H 8–12in (20–30cm), S 10–12in (25–30cm). Oval leaves are deeply cleft, 3–6in (8–15cm) long, and dark green with paler veins. Produces single pink flowers above foliage in winter and early spring.
***B.* 'Bethlehem Star'.** Evergreen, creeping, rhizomatous begonia. H 8–12in (20–30cm), S 10–12in (25–30cm). Oval, slightly indented, almost black leaves, less than 3in (8cm) long, each have a central, creamy green star. Bears masses of single, pale pink flowers with darker pink spots from late winter to early spring.
***B.* 'Billie Langdon'** (illus. p.295). Upright Tuberhybrida begonia. H 2ft (60cm), S 18in (45cm). In summer has masses of heavily veined, double white flowers, each 7in (18cm) across, with a perfect rosebud center.
***B.* 'Bokit'.** Evergreen, erect, rhizomatous begonia. H 8–12in (20–30cm), S 10–14in (25–35cm). Has oval, spirally twisted, yellow-green leaves with brown tiger stripes. Bears masses of single white flowers flecked with pink in winter.
B. bowerae (Eyelash begonia; illus. p.295). Evergreen, creeping, rhizomatous begonia. H 10–12in (25–30cm), S 8–10in (20–25cm). Has oval, bright green leaves, 1in (2.5cm) long, with chocolate marks and bristles around edges. Bears single, pink-tinted white flowers freely in winter.
***B.* 'Bridal Cascade'.** See *B.* 'Apricot Cascade'.
***B.* 'Can-Can'** (illus. p.295). Upright Tuberhybrida begonia. H 3ft (1m), S 18in (45cm). Has double yellow flowers, each 8in (20cm) wide, with rough-edged red petals in summer. Produces few side shoots.
***B.* 'City of Ballarat'.** Vigorous, upright Tuberhybrida begonia. H 2ft (60cm), S 18in (45cm). Leaves are rich dark green. Carries double, glowing orange flowers, each 7in (18cm) across, with broad petals and a formal center, in summer.
B. coccinea (Angelwing begonia). Evergreen, cane-stemmed begonia. H 4ft (1.2m), S 1ft (30cm). Produces narrowly oval, glossy green leaves, buff-colored beneath, and, in spring, profuse, single pink or coral-red flowers.
***B.* 'Cocktail'.** Semperflorens begonia. H and S 8–12in (20–30cm). Produces rounded, wavy, green-bronze leaves and pink, red, or white flowers from summer until autumn frosts.
***B.* 'Corallina de Lucerna'.** See *B.* 'Lucerna'.
***B.* 'Crimson Cascade'.** See *B.* 'Apricot Cascade'.
***B.* 'Curly Merry Christmas'.** Rex-cultorum begonia. H 10in (25cm), S 12in (30cm). Is a sport of *B.* 'Merry Christmas' with spirally twisted leaves.
B. dichroa. Evergreen, cane-stemmed begonia. H 14in (35cm), S 10in (25cm). Oval leaves are midgreen, 5in (12cm) long; occasionally new leaves bear silver spots. Produces small, single orange flowers, each with a white ovary, in summer.
B. disticha. See *B. stipulacea.*
B. dregei (Mapleleaf begonia). Semi-tuberous begonia. H 30in (75cm), S 14in (35cm). Has small, maplelike, lobed, purple-veined bronze leaves, with red beneath and occasionally silver-speckled when young. Profuse, pendent, single white flowers are borne in summer. Needs winter rest.
***B.* 'Duartei'** (illus. p.295). Rex-cultorum begonia. H and S 18–24in (45–60cm). Has spirally twisted, red-haired, very dark green leaves, over 6in (15cm) long, with silver-gray streaks and almost black edges. Is difficult to grow to maturity.
B.* x *erythrophylla. See *B.* 'Erythrophylla'.
***B.* 'Erythrophylla'**, syn. *B.* x *erythrophylla*, *B.* 'Feastii'. Evergreen, creeping, rhizomatous begonia. H 8in (20cm), S 9–12in (23–30cm). Thick, midgreen leaves, 3–6in (8–15cm) long, are almost rounded, with leaf stalks attached to center of red undersides; slightly wavy margins have white hairs. Produces single, light pink flowers well above foliage in early spring.
***B.* 'Feastii'.** See *B.* 'Erythrophylla'.
***B.* 'Flamboyant'** (illus. p.295). Upright Tuberhybrida begonia. H 7in (17cm), S 6in (15cm). Leaves are slender and bright green. Has single scarlet flowers in profusion in summer.
B. foliosa (illus. p.295). Evergreen, shrublike begonia. H 12–20in (30–50cm), S 12–14in (30–35cm). Bears erect then arching stems and oval, toothed, dark green leaves, ½in (1cm) long. Has very small, single white flowers in spring and autumn. Is susceptible to whitefly. var. ***miniata*** see *B. fuchsioides*.
B. fuchsioides, syn. *B. foliosa* var. *miniata* (Fuchsia begonia). Evergreen, shrublike begonia. H to 4ft (1.2m), S 1ft (30cm). Oval, toothed leaves are numerous and dark green, 1½in (4cm) long. Pendent, single, bright red flowers are borne in winter.
***B.* 'Gloire de Lorraine'** (Christmas begonia, Lorraine begonia). Evergreen, winter-flowering, Cheimantha begonia. H 12in (30cm), S 12–14in (30–35cm). Is well-branched with rounded, bright green leaves and single white to pale pink flowers.
***B.* 'Gold Cascade'.** See *B.* 'Apricot Cascade'.
B. gracilis var. ***martiana***, syn. *B. martiana*. Tuberous begonia. H 24–30in (60–75cm), S 16in (40cm). Has small, oval to lance-shaped, lobed, pale green or brown-green leaves with tapering tips and large, fragrant, single pink flowers, 1in (2.5cm) across, in summer.
B. haageana. See *B. scharffii.*
***B.* 'Helen Lewis'** (illus. p.295). Rex-cultorum begonia. H and S 18–24in (45–60cm). Has an erect rhizome and silky, deep royal purple leaves, 6–8in (15–20cm) long, with silver bands. Slightly hairy, single cream flowers are produced in early summer.
***B.* 'Ingramii'** (illus. p.295). Evergreen, shrublike begonia. H 28in (70cm), S 18in (45cm). Produces elliptic, toothed, bright green leaves, 3in (8cm) long, and, intermittently from spring to autumn, masses of single pink flowers on spreading branches.
***B.* 'Iron Cross'.** See *B. masoniana.*
***B.* 'Krefeld'.** Evergreen, winter-flowering, Rieger begonia. H 10in (25cm), S 12in (30cm). Is semi-tuberous with succulent stems, oval, midgreen leaves, and masses of single, vivid orange or bright crimson flowers. Is very susceptible to botrytis and mildew at base of stems, so water by pot immersion.
***B.* 'Lucerna'**, syn. *B.* 'Corallina de Lucerna' (illus. p.295). Vigorous, evergreen, cane-stemmed begonia. H 6–7ft (2–2.2m), S 1½–2ft (45–60cm). Has oval, silver-spotted, bronze-green leaves, 10–14in (25–35cm) long, with tapered tips and year-round, large panicles of single, deep pink flowers; male flowers remain almost closed.
***B.* 'Mac's Gold'.** Evergreen, creeping, rhizomatous begonia. H and S 8–10in (20–25cm). Star-shaped, lobed yellow leaves, 3–6in (8–15cm) long, have chocolate-brown marks. Has single pink flowers intermittently in spring-summer in moderate quantity.
***B.* 'Madame Richard Galle'.** Upright Tuberhybrida begonia. H 10in (25cm), S 8in (20cm). Has masses of small, double, soft apricot flowers in summer.
B. manicata (illus. p.295). Evergreen, erect, rhizomatous begonia. H 24in (60cm), S 12–16in (30–40cm). Bears large, oval, brown-mottled green leaves and, below each leaf base, a collar of stiff red hairs around the leaf stalk. Produces single, pale pink flowers in very early spring. Propagate by plantlets during growing season. **'Crispa'** (syn *B.m.* 'Cristata'; illus. p.295) has deeper pink flowers and light green leaves with crested margins. **'Cristata'** see *B.m.* 'Crispa'.
B. martiana. See *B. gracilis* var. *martiana.*
B. masoniana, syn. *B.* 'Iron Cross' (Iron cross begonia; illus. p.295). Evergreen, creeping, rhizomatous begonia. H 18–24in (45–60cm), S 12–18in (30–45cm). Bears oval, toothed, rough, bright green leaves, 6in (5cm) long, with tapering tips and cross-shaped black or dark brown centers. Has single, pink-flushed white flowers during summer.
B. mazae. Evergreen, trailing, rhizomatous begonia. H to 9in (23cm), S indefinite. Bears rounded, red-veined, bronze-green leaves and in early spring fragrant, single, red-spotted pink flowers. Is good for a hanging basket.
***B.* 'Merry Christmas'** (syn. *B.* 'Ruhrtal'; illus. p.295). Rex-cultorum begonia. H and S 10–12in (25–30cm). Has satiny red leaves, 6–8in (15–20cm) long, each with an outer, broad band of emerald green and a deep velvety red center, sometimes edged with gray.
B. metallica (Metal-leaf begonia; illus. p.295). Evergreen, shrublike begonia. H 20in–4ft (50cm–1.2m), S 18in (45cm). Bears white-haired stems and oval, toothed, silver-haired, bronze-green leaves, 7in (18cm) long, with dark green veins, red beneath. Has single pink flowers, with red bristles in summer-autumn.
***B.* 'Oliver Twist'** (illus. p.295). Evergreen, creeping, rhizomatous begonia. H 18–24in (45–60cm), S 10–18in (25–45cm). Oval leaves are pale to midgreen, to 12in (30cm) long, with heavily crested edges. Has single pink flowers in early spring.
B. olsoniae (illus. p.295). Evergreen, compact, shrublike begonia. H 9–12in (23–30cm), S 12in (30cm). Rounded, satiny, bronze-green leaves have cream veins. Bears single, very pale pink flowers year-round on arching, 12in (30cm) long stems.
***B.* 'Orange Cascade'.** See *B.* 'Apricot Cascade'.
***B.* 'Orange Rubra'** (illus. p.295). Slow-growing, evergreen, cane-stemmed begonia. H 20in (50cm), S 18in (45cm). Oval leaves are light green. Produces abundant clusters of single orange flowers all year.
***B.* 'Organdy'** (illus. p.295). Weather-resistant Semperflorens begonia. H and S 6in (15cm). Has rounded, waxy, green-bronze leaves and pink, red, or white flowers throughout summer until autumn frosts.
***B.* 'Orpha C. Fox'** (illus. p.295). Evergreen, cane-stemmed begonia. H 3ft (1m), S 1ft (30cm). Oval, silver-spotted, olive green leaves, 6in (15cm) long, are maroon beneath. Produces large clusters of single, bright pink flowers year-round.
B. paulensis. Evergreen, creeping, rhizomatous begonia. H and S 10–12in (25–30cm). Erect stems bear rounded, midgreen leaves, 6in (15cm) long, with "seersucker" surfaces criss-crossed with a spider's web of veins. Produces single, cream-white flowers with wine-colored hairs in late spring.
***B.* 'Président Carnot'.** Vigorous, evergreen, cane-stemmed begonia. H to 7ft (2.2m), S 1½ft (45cm). Erect stems bear 11in (28cm) long, "angelwing," green leaves with lighter spots. Produces large panicles of single pink flowers, each 1½in (4cm) across, year-round.
***B.* 'Princess of Hanover'.** Rex-cultorum begonia. H and S 10–12in (25–30cm). Has spirally twisted, deep green leaves, 8in (20cm) long, with bands of silver edged with ruby red; entire leaf surfaces are covered with fine pink hairs.
B. prismatocarpa (illus. p.295). Evergreen, creeping, rhizomatous

begonia. H 6–8in (15–20cm), S 8–10in (20–25cm). Leaves are oval, lobed, light green, and less than 3in (8cm) long. Produces single, bright yellow flowers year-round. Needs 60–65% relative humidity.
B. pustulata. Evergreen, creeping, rhizomatous begonia. H 6–8in (15–20cm), S 8–10in (20–25cm). Bears oval, fine-haired, dark green leaves with small blisters or pustules, and single, rose pink flowers in summer. Prefers 70–75% relative humidity. **'Argentea'** (syn. *B.* 'Silver'; illus. p.295) has silver-splashed leaves and creamy white flowers.
***B.* 'Red Ascot'** (illus. p.295). Semperflorens begonia. H and S 6in (15cm). Has rounded, emerald green leaves and masses of crimson-red flowers in summer.
B. rex. Rhizomatous begonia, the parent of the Rex-cultorum begonias. H 10in (25cm), S 12in (30cm). Has 8–10in (20–25cm) long, heart-shaped, deep green leaves with a metallic sheen and zoned silvery white above. Produces pink flowers in winter.
***B.* 'Roy Hartley'** (illus. p.295). Upright Tuberhybrida begonia. H 2ft (60cm), S 18in (45cm). In summer bears double, salmon-colored flowers with soft pink tinge. Color depth depends on light intensity. Produces few side shoots.
***B.* 'Ruhrtal'.** See *B.* 'Merry Christmas'.
B. scharffii, syn. *B. haageana* (illus. p.295). Evergreen, shrublike begonia. H 2–4ft (60cm–1.2m), S 2ft (60cm). Stems are often covered with white hairs. Has oval, fine-haired, dark metallic green leaves, 11in (28cm) long, with very tapered tips and reddish green undersides. Produces single, pinkish white flowers, each with a pink beard, from autumn to summer.
***B.* 'Scherzo'.** Evergreen, creeping, rhizomatous begonia. H 10–12in (), S 12–14in (30–35cm). Oval leaves are small, highly serrated, and yellow with black marks. Bears single white flowers in early spring.
B. serratipetala (illus. p.295). Evergreen, trailing, shrublike begonia. H and S 18in (45cm). Obliquely oval leaves are highly serrated and bronze-green with raised, deep pink spots. Produces mostly female, single, deep pink flowers intermittently throughout the year. Prefers 60% relative humidity, but with fairly dry roots.
***B.* 'Silver'.** See *B. pustulata* 'Argentea'.
***B.* 'Silver Helen Teupel'.** Rex-cultorum begonia. H and S 12–14in (30–35cm). Has long, deeply cut silver leaves, each with a glowing pink center, giving a feathered effect.
B. stipulacea, syn. *B. angularis*, *B. disticha*, *B. zebrina*. Evergreen, cane-stemmed begonia. H 2–4ft (60cm–1.2m), S 1ft (30cm). Bears well-branched, angular stems and oval, wavy-edged, 8in (20cm) long, gray-green leaves with silver-gray veins, pale green beneath. Single white flowers are produced in winter-spring.
***B.* 'Sugar Candy'.** Tuberhybrida begonia. H 24in (60cm), S 18in (45cm). Leaves are midgreen. Produces double, clear pink flowers in summer.
B. sutherlandii (illus. p.295). Trailing, tuberous begonia. H 3ft (1m), S indefinite. Slender stems carry small, lance-shaped, lobed, bright green leaves with red veins and, in summer, loose clusters of single orange flowers in profusion. In late autumn, leaves and stems collapse prior to winter dormancy. Makes an excellent hanging-basket plant. Is particularly susceptible to mildew.
***B.* 'Thurstonii'** (illus. p.295). Evergreen, shrublike begonia. H to 4ft (1.2m), S 1½ft (45cm). Has rounded to oval, smooth, glossy, bronze-green leaves with dark red veins and, in summer, bears single pink flowers.
***B.* 'Tiger Paws'** (illus. p.295). Evergreen, creeping, rhizomatous begonia. H 6in (15cm), S 10–12in (25–30cm). Small, rounded, striking bright green leaves with yellow and brown splashes have bristly white hairs on the margins. Many clusters of small white flowers are carried well above the foliage in spring.
B. versicolor. Evergreen, creeping, rhizomatous begonia. H 6in (15cm), S 6–12in (15–30cm). Produces broadly oval or oblong, velvety leaves, 3in (8cm) long, in shades of mahogany, apple green, and maroon, and, in spring-summer, single, salmon-pink flowers. Provide 65–70% relative humidity.
B.* x *weltoniensis. See *B.* 'Weltoniensis'.
***B.* 'Weltoniensis'**, syn. *B.* x *weltoniensis.* (Mapleleaf begonia; illus. p.295). Semi-tuberous begonia with a shrublike habit. H 12–20in (30–50cm), S 12in (30cm). Has small, oval, long-pointed, toothed, dark green leaves. Heads of 5–8 single pink or white flowers appear from leaf axils in summer.
B. xanthina. Evergreen, bushy, creeping, rhizomatous begonia. H 10–12in (25–30cm), S 12–14in (30–35cm). Bears oval, dark green leaves, 6–9in (15–23cm) long, with yellow veins and purple and hairy beneath. Pendent, single, orange-yellow flowers are borne in summer. Provide 75% relative humidity.
B. zebrina. See *B. stipulacea.*

BELAMCANDA

IRIDACEAE

Genus of summer-flowering bulbs grown for their irislike flowers. Needs sun and well-drained, organic soil. Propagate by seed in spring.
B. chinensis (Blackberry lily). Summer-flowering bulb. H 1½–3ft (45cm–1m), S 6–10in (15–25cm). Carries a fan of sword-shaped, semi-erect leaves. A loosely branched stem bears a succession of flattish, orange-red flowers, 1½–2in (4–5cm) across, with darker blotches. Seed heads are shiny and blackberry-like. Z5–9 H9–5.

BELLEVALIA

HYACINTHACEAE/LILIACEAE

Genus of spring-flowering bulbs similar to *Muscari*, but with longer, more tubular flowers. Some species have ornamental value, but most are uninteresting horticulturally. Needs an open, sunny position and well-drained soil that dries out in summer. Propagate by seed, preferably in autumn.
B. hyacinthoides, syn. *Strangweja spicata*, illus. p.432.
B. paradoxa of gardens. See *B. pycnantha.*
B. pycnantha, syn. *B. paradoxa* of gardens, *Muscari paradoxum* of gardens, *M. pycnantha.* Spring-flowering bulb. H to 16in (40cm), S 2–3in (5–8cm). Has strap-shaped, semi-erect, basal, grayish green leaves. Tubular, deep dusky blue flowers, ¼in (0.5cm)long and with yellow tips, appear in a dense, conical spike. Z7–9 H9–7.

BELLIS

English daisy

ASTERACEAE/COMPOSITAE

Genus of perennials, some grown as biennials for spring bedding. Grow in sun or semi-shade and in fertile, very well-drained soil. Deadhead regularly. Propagate by seed in early summer or by division after flowering.
B. perennis (English daisy). Stoloniferous, carpeting perennial. Cultivars are grown as biennials. H and S 6–8in (15–20cm). All have inversely lance-shaped to spoon-shaped, midgreen leaves and semi-double to fully double flower heads in spring. Large-flowered (flower heads to 3in/8cm wide) and miniature-flowered (flower heads to 1in/2½cm wide) cultivars are available. Z4–8 H8–1. **Habanera Series** cultivars bear long-petaled pink, white, or red flower heads, to 2.5in (6cm) across, in early summer. **Pomponette Series** (illus. p.327) cultivars bear double pink, white, or red flower heads, to 1½in (4cm) across, with quilled petals. **Roggli Series** cultivars flower early and prolifically, with semi-double red, rose pink, salmon-pink, or white flower heads, to 1¼in (3cm) across. **Tasso Series** cultivars have double pink, white, or red flower heads, to 2½in (6cm) across, with quilled petals.

Beloperone guttata. See *Justicia brandegeeana.*

BERBERIDOPSIS

FLACOURTIACEAE

Genus of one species of evergreen, woody-stemmed, twining climber. Dislikes strong winds and strong sun . Soil, preferably lime-free, should be moist but well-drained. Cut out dead growth in spring; train to required shape. Propagate by seed in spring or by stem cuttings or layering in late summer or autumn.
B. corallina illus. p.211.

BERBERIS

Barberry

BERBERIDACEAE

Genus of deciduous, semi-evergreen or evergreen, spiny shrubs grown mainly for their rounded to cup-shaped flowers, with usually yellow sepals and petals, and for their fruits. The evergreens are also cultivated for their leaves, and the deciduous shrubs for their colorful autumn foliage. Requires sun or semi-shade and any but water-logged soil. Propagate species by seed in autumn, deciduous hybrids and cultivars by softwood or semi-ripe cuttings in summer, and evergreen hybrids and cultivars by semi-ripe cuttings in summer. All parts may cause mild stomach upset if ingested; contact with the spines may irritate skin. Many *Berberis* are an alternate host of wheat rust. Their cultivation is prohibited in some states.
B. aggregata. Deciduous, bushy shrub. H and S 5ft (1.5m). Oblong to oval, midgreen leaves redden in autumn. Dense clusters of pale yellow flowers appear in late spring or early summer and are followed by egg-shaped, white-bloomed red fruits. Z6–9 H9–6.
B. buxifolia. Semi-evergreen or deciduous, arching shrub. H 8ft (2.5m), S 10ft (3m). Has oblong to oval, spine-tipped, leathery, dark green leaves. Deep orange-yellow flowers appear from early to midspring and are followed by spherical black fruits with a white bloom. Z6–9 H9–6.
B. calliantha. Evergreen, bushy shrub. H and S 3–5ft (1–1.5m). Has oblong, sharply spiny, glossy green leaves, white beneath, and large, pale yellow flowers in late spring, followed by egg-shaped black fruits with a white bloom. Z7–9 H9–7.
B. candidula. Evergreen, bushy, compact shrub. H and S 3ft (1m). Leaves are narrowly oblong, glossy, dark green, and white beneath. Has bright yellow flowers in late spring, then egg-shaped, blue-purple fruits. Z6–9 H9–6.
***B.* x *carminea* 'Barbarossa'** illus. p.148. **'Pirate King'** is a deciduous, arching shrub. H 6ft (2m), S 10ft (3m). Bears oblong, dark green leaves. In late spring and early summer produces clusters of yellow flowers followed by spherical, pale red fruits. Z6–9 H9–6.
***B.* 'Chenault'.** See *B.* 'Chenaultii'.
***B.* 'Chenaultii'**, syn. *B.* 'Chenault'. Evergreen, bushy shrub. H 5ft (1.5m), S 6ft (2m). Narrowly oblong, wavy-edged, glossy, dark green leaves set off golden yellow flowers in late spring and early summer. Bears egg-shaped, blue-black fruits. Z6–9 H9–6.
B. coxii. Evergreen, bushy, dense shrub. H 6ft (2m), S 10ft (3m). Produces narrowly oval, glossy, dark

green leaves with white undersides and, in late spring, yellow flowers. Egg-shaped, blue-black fruits have a gray-blue bloom.
B. darwinii illus. p.117.
B. empetrifolia illus. p.157.
B. gagnepainii var. ***lanceifolia*** illus. p.131.
B. jamesiana. Vigorous, deciduous, arching shrub. H and S 12ft (4m). Yellow flowers in late spring are followed by pendent racemes of spherical red berries. Oval, dark green leaves redden in autumn. Z7–9 H9–7.
B. julianae illus. p.134.
B. linearifolia **'Orange King'** illus. p.135.
B.* x *lologensis. Vigorous, evergreen, arching shrub. H 10ft (3m), S 15ft (5m). Has broadly oblong, glossy, dark green leaves. Profuse clusters of orange flowers are borne from mid- to late spring. Z6–9 H9–6. **'Stapehill'** illus. p.135.
B.* x *ottawensis **'Purpurea'.** See *B.* x *o.* 'Superba'. **'Superba'** (syn. *B.* x *o.* 'Purpurea') is a deciduous, arching shrub. H and S 8ft (2.5m). Produces rounded to oval, deep reddish purple leaves. Bears small, red-tinged yellow flowers in late spring, then egg-shaped red fruits in autumn. Z4–8 H8–3.
B. **'Park Jewel'.** See *B.* 'Parkjuweel'.
B. **'Parkjuweel'**, syn. *B.* 'Park Jewel'. Semi-evergreen, bushy, rounded shrub. H and S 3ft (1m). Leaves are oval, glossy, and bright green; some turn red in autumn. Flowers are of little value. Z6–9 H9–6.
B. polyantha of gardens. See *B. prattii*.
B. prattii, syn. *B. polyantha* of gardens. Deciduous, bushy shrub. H and S 10ft (3m). Has oblong, glossy, dark green leaves. Large clusters of small yellow flowers in late summer are followed by a profusion of long-lasting, egg-shaped, coral-pink fruits. Z6–9 H9–6.
B.* x *rubrostilla. See *B.* 'Rubrostilla'.
B. **'Rubrostilla'**, syn. *B.* x *rubrostilla*, illus. p.172.
B. sargentiana. Evergreen, bushy shrub. H and S 6ft (2m). Leaves are oblong, glossy, bright green. Yellow flowers produced in late spring and early summer are succeeded by egg-shaped, blue-black fruits. Z5–8 H8–5.
B.* x *stenophylla illus. p.135. **'Corallina Compacta'** illus. p.350.
B. thunbergii. Deciduous, arching, dense shrub. H 6ft (2m), S 10ft (3m). Broadly oval, pale to midgreen leaves turn brilliant orange-red in autumn. Small, red-tinged, pale yellow flowers appear in midspring, followed by egg-shaped, bright red fruits. Z5–8 H8–5. f. ***atropurpurea*** illus. p.131. **'Atropurpurea Nana'** (syn. *B.t.* 'Crimson Pygmy'), H and S 24in (60cm), bears reddish purple foliage. **'Aurea'** illus. p.170. **'Crimson Pygmy'** see *B.t.* 'Atropurpurea Nana'. Upright branches of **'Erecta'** spread with age. **'Golden Ring'** has purple leaves narrowly margined with golden yellow, turning red in autumn, and produces red fruit. **'Rose Glow'** has reddish purple leaves marbled pink and white.
B. verruculosa illus. p.134.
B. wilsoniae. Deciduous or semi-evergreen, bushy shrub. H 3ft (1m), S 5ft (1.5m). Narrowly oblong, gray-green leaves turn bright orange-red in autumn. In late spring and early summer has yellow flowers, then showy, spherical, coral-red fruits. Z6–9 H9–4.

BERCHEMIA

RHAMNACEAE

Genus of deciduous, twining climbers grown for their leaves and fruit. Is useful for covering walls, fences, and tree stumps. Grow in sun or shade, in any well-drained soil. Propagate by seed in autumn or spring, by semi-ripe cuttings in summer, or by layering or root cuttings in winter.
B. racemosa **'Variegata'.** Deciduous, twining climber. H 15ft (5m) or more. Has heart-shaped, green leaves, 1¼–3in (3–8cm) long and paler beneath, that are variegated creamy white. Small, bell-shaped, greenish white flowers in summer are followed by rounded, green fruits that turn red then black. Z6–9 H9–6.

BERGENIA,

syn. MEGASEA
Elephant's ears, pigsqueak

SAXIFRAGACEAE

Genus of evergreen perennials with thick, usually large, rounded to oval or spoon-shaped, leathery leaves, with indented veins, that make an ideal groundcover. Tolerates sun or shade and any well-drained soil, but leaf color is best on relatively poor soil and in full sun. Propagate by division in spring after flowering.
B. **'Abendglut'**, syn. *B.* 'Evening Glow'. Evergreen, clump-forming perennial. H 9in (23cm), S 12in (30cm). Bears rosettes of oval, crinkled, short-stemmed maroon leaves, from which arise racemes of open cup-shaped, semi-double, deep magenta flowers in spring. Z6–9 H9–6.
B. **'Ballawley'.** Evergreen, clump-forming perennial. H and S 24in (60cm). Large, rounded to oval, flat, deep green leaves turn red in winter. Racemes of cup-shaped, bright crimson flowers are borne on red stems in spring. Shelter from cold winds. Z6–9 H9–6.
B. beesiana. See *B. purpurascens*.
B. ciliata illus. p.269.
B. cordifolia. Evergreen, clump-forming perennial. H 18in (45cm), S 24in (60cm). Leaves are rounded, puckered, and crinkle-edged. Produces racemes of open cup-shaped, light pink flowers in spring. Z3–8 H8–1. **'Purpurea'** illus. p.269.
B. crassifolia. Evergreen, clump-forming perennial. H 12in (30cm), S 18in (45cm). Has oval- or spoon-shaped, fleshy, flat leaves that turn mahogany in winter. Bears spikes of open cup-shaped, lavender-pink flowers in spring. Z3–8 H8–1.
B. **'Evening Glow'.** See *B.* 'Abendglut'.
B. **'Morgenröte'**, syn. *B.* 'Morning Red'. Evergreen, clump-forming perennial. H 18in (45cm), S 12in (30cm). Leaves are rounded, crinkled, and deep green. Spikes of open cup-shaped, deep carmine flowers in spring are often followed by a second crop in summer. Z4–9 H9–2.
B. **'Morning Red'.** See *B.* 'Morgenröte'.
B. purpurascens, syn. *B. beesiana*. Evergreen, clump-forming perennial. H 18in (45cm), S 12in (30cm). Oval to spoon-shaped, flat, dark green leaves turn beet red in late autumn. In spring bears racemes of open cup-shaped, rich red flowers. Z3–8 H8–1.
B.* x *schmidtii. Evergreen, clump-forming perennial. H 12in (30cm) S 24in (60cm). Oval, flat leaves have toothed margins. Sprays of open cup-shaped, soft pink flowers are borne in early spring on short stems. Z4–8 H8–1.
B. **'Silberlicht'**, syn. *B.* 'Silver Light', illus. p.268.
B. **'Silver Light'.** See *B.* 'Silberlicht'.
B. stracheyi. Evergreen, clump-forming perennial. H 9in (23cm), S 12in (30cm). Small, rounded, flat leaves form neat rosettes, among which nestle heads of open cup-shaped white or pink flowers in spring. Z4–8 H8–1.
B. **'Sunningdale'.** Evergreen, clump-forming perennial. H 24in (60cm), S 12in (30cm). Rounded, slightly crinkled, deep green leaves are mahogany beneath. Bears racemes of open cup-shaped, lilac-carmine flowers on red stalks in spring. Z3–8 H8–1.

BERKHEYA

ASTERACEAE/COMPOSITAE

Genus of summer-flowering perennials. Where marginally hardy, grow most species against a south- or west-facing wall. Needs full sun and fertile, well-drained soil. Sow seed in autumn or divide in spring.
B. macrocephala illus. p.258.

BERTOLONIA

MELASTOMATACEAE

Genus of evergreen perennials grown for their foliage. Requires a fairly shaded position and high humidity, although soil should not be water-logged. Propagate by tip or leaf cuttings in spring or summer.
B. marmorata. Evergreen, rosette-forming perennial. H 6in (15cm) or more in flower, S 18in (45cm). Broadly oval, slightly fleshy leaves have heart-shaped bases, silvery midribs, and puckered surfaces and are reddish purple below, velvety green above. Intermittently produces spikes of saucer-shaped, pinkish purple flowers.

BERZELIA

BRUNIACEAE

Genus of evergreen, heatherlike, summer-flowering shrubs grown for their flowers. Requires full sun and well-drained, neutral to acidic soil. Water containerized plants moderately, less when not in full growth. Plants may be cut back lightly after flowering. Propagate by seed in spring or by semi-ripe cuttings in late summer.
B. lanuginosa. Evergreen, erect shrub with soft-haired young shoots. H and S to 3ft (1m). Has small, heatherlike leaves. Compact, spherical heads of tiny, creamy white flowers are carried in dense, terminal clusters in summer. Z14–15 H12–10.

BESCHORNERIA

AGAVACEAE

Genus of perennial succulents with narrowly lance-shaped leaves forming erect, almost stemless, basal rosettes. Needs full sun and very well-drained soil. Propagate by seed or division in spring or summer.
B. yuccoides illus. p.465.

BESSERA

ALLIACEAE/LILIACEAE

Genus of summer-flowering bulbs grown for their striking, brightly colored flowers. Needs an open, sunny situation and well-drained soil. Propagate by seed in spring. Overwinter indoors.
B. elegans (Coral drops). Summer-flowering bulb. H to 24in (60cm), S 3–4in (8–10cm). Has long, narrow, erect, basal leaves. Each leafless stem bears pendent, bell-shaped, bright red flowers on long, slender stalks. Z12–15 H12–10

BETULA

Birch

BETULACEAE

Genus of deciduous trees and shrubs grown for their bark and autumn color. Needs sun and moist but well-drained soil; some species prefer acidic soil. Transplant young trees in autumn. Propagate by grafting in late winter or by softwood cuttings in early summer. May be subject to leaf miner, borer, and crown dieback.
B. albosinensis illus. p.74.
B. alleghaniensis, syn. *B. lutea* (Yellow birch). Deciduous, upright, open tree, often multistemmed. H 40ft (12m) or more, S 10ft (3m). Smooth, glossy, golden brown bark peels in thin shreds. Oval, mid- to pale green leaves rapidly turn gold in autumn. Bears yellow-green catkins in spring. Z4–7 H7–1.
B. ermanii illus. p.72.
B. jacquemontii. See *B. utilis* var. *jacquemontii*.
B. lutea. See *B. alleghaniensis*.
B. maximowicziana (Monarch birch). Fast-growing, deciduous, broad-headed tree. H 60ft (18m), S 10ft (3m). Has orange-brown or pink bark and racemes of yellowish catkins in spring. Large, oval, midgreen leaves turn bright butter yellow in autumn. Z6–8 H8–6.
B. nana illus. p.349.
B. nigra (River birch). Conical tree that grows well in wetter soils. H 60ft

(18m). Cinnamon brown bark peels in layers, even on young trees. Yellow fall color. Z4–9 H9–1. **'Heritage'** has white to pale salmon young bark that darkens to a rusty brown with age. Resistant to leaf miners and bronze birch borer.
B. papyrifera illus. p.72.
B. pendula (European white birch). Deciduous, broadly columnar or conical, graceful tree. H 80ft (25m) or more, S 30ft (10m). Has slender, drooping shoots and silver-white bark that becomes black and rugged at base of trunk with age. Yellow-brown catkins appear in spring. Oval, bright green leaves turn yellow in autumn. Z2–7 H7–1. **'Dalecarlica'** has a more upright habit with pendant, shorter shoots at the end of the branches, and much more deeply cut leaves. **'Laciniata'** has a narrow crown. **'Tristis'** illus. p.73. **'Youngii'** illus. p.92.
B. platyphylla var. ***szechuanica.*** See *B. szechuanica.*
B. szechuanica, syn. *B. platyphylla* var. *szechuanica* (Szechuan birch). Vigorous, deciduous, open tree with stiff branches. H 46ft (14m), S 8ft (2.5m). Bark is strikingly chalky white when mature. Has triangular to oval, serrated, leathery, deep green leaves that turn brilliant gold in autumn. Bears yellow-green catkins in spring. Z5–7 H7–5.
B. utilis (Himalayan birch). Deciduous, upright, open tree. H 60ft (18m), S 30ft (10m). Paper-thin, peeling bark varies from creamy white to dark copper-brown. Yellow-brown catkins are borne in spring. Oval, midgreen leaves, hairy beneath when young, turn golden yellow in autumn. Z5–7 H7–5. var. ***jacquemontii*** (syn *B. jacquemontii*) illus. p.83.

BIARUM

ARACEAE

Genus of mainly autumn-flowering, tuberous perennials with tiny flowers carried on a pencil-shaped spadix enclosed within a tubular spathe. Upper part of spathe is hooded or flattened out and showy. In winter protect in a cold frame or greenhouse. Needs a sunny position and well-drained soil. Dry out tubers when dormant in summer. Propagate in autumn by seed or offsets.
B. eximium. Early autumn-flowering, tuberous perennial. H and S 3–4in (8–10cm). Lance-shaped, semi-erect, basal leaves follow stemless, tubular, velvety, blackish maroon spathe, up to 6in (15cm) long and often lying flat on ground. Upper part is flattened out. Spadix is upright and black. Z7–9 H9–7.
B. tenuifolium illus. p.439.

BIDENS

ASTERACEAE/COMPOSITAEE

Genus of annuals, perennials, and shrubs grown for their spreading habit and summer flowers. Requires fertile, well drained soil in full sun. Propagate by seed in spring or stem cuttings in fall or early spring from plants over-wintered indoors.
B. atrosanguinea. See *Cosmos atrosanguinea.*
B. ferulifera. Spreading, short-lived perennial usually treated as an annual. H 12in (30cm) S indefinite. Grown for its finely divided bright green foliage and golden yellow, single flowers freely produced. Good for baskets and planters. Z8–11 H12–8.

BIGNONIA

Cross vine

BIGNONIACEAE

Genus of one species of evergreen, tendril climber. In colder areas may lose its leaves in winter. Needs sun and fertile soil to flower well. If necessary, prune in spring. Propagate by stem cuttings in summer or autumn or by layering in winter.
B. capensis. See *Tecoma capensis.*
B. capreolata, syn. *Doxantha capreolata* (Cross vine, Trumpet flower). Evergreen, tendril climber. H 30ft (10m) or more. Each leaf has 2 narrowly oblong leaflets and a branched tendril. In summer, funnel-shaped, reddish orange flowers appear in clusters in leaf axils. Pea-pod-shaped fruits, to 6in (15cm) long, are produced in autumn. Z6–9 H9–5.
B. grandiflora. See *Campsis grandiflora.*
B. jasminoides. See *Pandorea jasminoides.*
B. pandorana. See *Pandorea pandorana.*
B. radicans. See *Campsis radicans.*
B. stans. See *Tecoma stans.*

Bilderdykia. Reclassified as *Fallopia.*

BILLARDIERA

PITTOSPORACEAE

Genus of evergreen, woody-stemmed, twining climbers grown mainly for their fruits. Grow in any well-drained soil in a sheltered position and partial shade. Propagate by seed in spring or stem cuttings in summer or autumn.
B. longiflora illus. p.218.

BILLBERGIA

BROMELIACEAE

Genus of evergreen, rosette-forming perennials grown for their flowers and foliage. Requires semi-shade and well-drained soil, ideally adding sphagnum moss or plastic chips used for orchid culture. Water moderately when in full growth, sparingly at other times. Propagate by division or offsets after flowering or in late spring.
B. nutans (Queen's tears; illus. p.265). Evergreen, clump-forming, tubular-rosetted perennial. H and S to 16in (40cm). Strap-shaped leaves are usually dark green. In spring, pendent clusters of tubular, purple-blue-edged, lime green flowers emerge from pink bracts. Z9–15 H12–1.
B. rhodocyanea. See *Aechmea fasciata.*
B.* x *windii (Angel's tears). Evergreen, clump-forming, tubular-rosetted perennial. H and S to 16in (40cm). Similar to *B. nutans* but produces broader, spreading, gray-green leaves and larger bracts. Flowers intermittently from spring to autumn. Z9–15 H12–10

Biota orientalis. See *Thuja orientalis.*

BLECHNUM

Hard fern

BLECHNACEAE

Genus of evergreen or semi-evergreen ferns. Most species prefer semi-shade. Requires moist, neutral to acidic soil. Remove fading fronds regularly. Propagate *B. penna-marina* by division in spring, other species by spores in late summer.
B. alpinum. See *B. penna-marina.*
B. chilense of gardens. See *B. tabulare.*
B. magellanicum. See *B. tabulare.*
B. penna-marina, syn. *B. alpinum*, illus. p.310.
B. spicant (Hard fern). Evergreen fern. H 12–30in (30–75cm), S 12–18in (30–45cm). Bears narrowly lance-shaped, indented, leathery, spreading, dark green fronds. Prefers shade and peaty or leafy soil. Z10–11 H12–10.
B. tabulare, syn. *B. chilense* of gardens, *B. magellanicum*. Evergreen or semi-evergreen fern. H 1–3ft (30cm–1m), S 1–2ft (30–60cm). Outer, midgreen, sterile fronds are broadly lance-shaped, heavily indented, and arranged symmetrically. Inner fertile fronds are brown and fringed. Z10–11 H12–10.

BLETILLA

See also ORCHIDS.
B. hyacinthina. See *B. striata.*
B. striata, syn. *B. hyacinthina* (illus. p.297). Deciduous, terrestrial orchid. H to 24in (60cm). In late spring or early summer bears magenta or white flowers, 1¼in (3cm) long, and broadly lance-shaped leaves, 20in (50cm) long. Needs shade in summer. Z5–8 H8–5.

BLOOMERIA

ALLIACEAE/LILIACEAE

Genus of onionlike, spring-flowering bulbs, with spherical flower heads on leafless stems, which die down in summer. Needs a sheltered, sunny situation and well-drained soil. Propagate by seed in autumn or by division in late summer or autumn.
B. crocea. Late spring-flowering bulb. H to 12in (30cm), S to 4in (10cm). Long, narrow, semi-erect, basal leaves die at flowering time. Each leafless stem carries a loose, spherical head, 4–6in (10–15cm) across, of star-shaped, dark-striped yellow flowers. Z8–9 H9–8

Bocconia cordata. See *Macleaya cordata.*

BOENNINGHAUSENIA

RUTACEAE

Genus of one species of deciduous sub-shrub usually with soft, herbaceous stems, grown for its foliage and flowers. Cut back nearly to the groung in spring. Needs full sun and fertile, well-drained but not too dry soil. Propagate by softwood cuttings in summer or by seed in autumn.
B. albiflora. Deciduous, bushy sub-shrub. H and S 3ft (1m). Has pungent, midgreen leaves divided into oval leaflets. Loose panicles of small, cup-shaped white flowers appear from midsummer to early autumn. Z6–10 H10–6.

BOLAX

APIACEAE/UMBELLIFERAE

Genus of evergreen, hummock- and cushion-forming perennials, often included in *Azorella*. Is grown for its symmetrical rosettes of small, thick, tough leaves. Flowers only rarely in cultivation. Is suitable for gritty screes, troughs, and alpine houses. Needs sun and organic, well-drained soil. Propagate by rooting rosettes in summer.
B. gummifera illus. p.391.

BOMAREA

ALSTROEMERIACEAE/LILIACEAE

Genus of herbaceous or evergreen, tuberous-rooted, scrambling and twining climbers grown for their tubular or bell-shaped flowers. Grow in any well-drained soil and in full light. Water regularly in growing season, sparingly when dormant. Provide support. Cut out old flowering stems at ground level when leaves turn yellow. Propagate by seed or division in early spring.
B. andimarcana, syn. *B. pubigera* of gardens. Evergreen, scrambling climber with straight, slender stems. H 6–10ft (2–3m). Has lance-shaped leaves, white and hairy beneath. Bears nodding, tubular, green-tipped, pale yellow flowers suffused pink from early summer to autumn. Z9–10 H10–9.
B. caldasii, syn. *B. kalbreyeri* of gardens, illus. p.217.
B. kalbreyeri of gardens. See *B. caldasii.*
B. pubigera of gardens. See *B. andimarcana.*

BORAGO

Borage

BORAGINACEAE

Genus of annuals and perennials grown for culinary use as well as for their flowers. Requires sun and fertile, well-drained soil. For culinary use gather only young leaves. Propagate by seed sown outdoors in spring. Some species will self seed prolifically and may become invasive.
B. officinalis illus. p.334.

BORONIA

RUTACEAE

Genus of evergreen shrubs grown primarily for their flowers. Requires full light and sandy, neutral to acidic soil. Water potted specimens moderately, less when not in full growth. For a compact habit, shorten long stems after flowering. Propagate by seed in spring or by semi-ripe cuttings in late summer. Spider mite may be a problem.
B. megastigma illus. p.156.

Borzicactus. Reclassified as *Oreocereus*.

BOUGAINVILLEA

NYCTAGINACEAE

Genus of deciduous or evergreen, woody-stemmed, scrambling climbers grown for their showy floral bracts. Grow in fertile, well-drained soil and in full light. Water moderately in the growing season; keep containerized plants almost dry when dormant. Tie to a support. Cut back previous season's lateral growths in spring, leaving ¾–1¼in (2–3cm) long spurs. Propagate by semi-ripe cuttings in summer or by hardwood cuttings when dormant. Whitefly and mealy bug may attack.
B.* x *buttiana. Vigorous, evergreen, woody-stemmed, scrambling climber. H 25–40ft (8–12m). Has ovate, mid-green leaves, to 3in (8cm) long, lighter below. Bears large clusters of golden yellow, purple, or red floral bracts from summer to autumn. Z13–15 H12–1. **'California Gold'** see *B.* x *b.* 'Golden Glow'. **'Crimson Lake'** see *B.* x *b.* 'Mrs. Butt'. Floral bracts of **'Golden Glow'** (syn. *B.* x *b.* 'California Gold') are orange-yellow; those of **'Mrs. Butt'** (syn. *B.* x *b.*'Crimson Lake') are crimson-magenta; and those of **'Scarlet Queen'** are scarlet.
***B.* 'Dania'** illus. p.210.
B. glabra illus. p.214. **'Sanderiana'** see *B.g.* 'Variegata'. **'Snow White'** illus. p.207. **'Variegata'** (syn *B.g.* 'Sanderiana') illus. p.211.
***B.* 'Miss Manila'**, syn. *B.* 'Tango', illus. p.210.
B. spectabilis. Strong-growing, mainly evergreen, woody-stemmed, scrambling climber; stems usually have a few spines. H to 22ft (7m). Has elliptic to oval leaves and, in summer, large clusters of red-purple bracts. Z9–11 H12–1.
***B.* 'Tango'.** See *B.* 'Miss Manila'.

Boussingaultia baselloides **of gardens.** See *Anredera cordifolia*.

BOUTELOUA

GRAMINEAE/POACEAE

See also GRASSES, BAMBOOS, RUSHES, and SEDGES.
B. gracilis, syn. *B. oligostachya*, illus. p.307.
B. oligostachya. See *B. gracilis*.

BOUVARDIA

RUBIACEAE

Genus of deciduous, semi-evergreen or evergreen shrubs and perennials grown for their flowers. Prefers full light and fertile, well-drained soil. Water freely when in full growth, moderately at other times. Cut back stems by half to three-quarters after flowering. Propagate by softwood cuttings in spring or by greenwood or semi-ripe cuttings in summer. Whitefly and mealy bug may be troublesome.
B. humboldtii. See *B. longiflora*.
B. longiflora, syn. *B. humboldtii*. Semi-evergreen, spreading shrub. H and S 3ft (1m) or more. Has lance-shaped leaves, and terminal clusters of fragrant white flowers with slender tubes and 4 petal lobes from summer to early winter. Z12–15 H12–10.
B. ternifolia, syn. *B. triphylla*, illus. p.173.
B. triphylla. See *B. ternifolia*.

BOWIEA

HYACINTHACEAE/LILIACEAE

Genus of summer-flowering, bulbous succulents with scrambling, branched, green stems that produce no true leaves. Needs sun and well-drained soil; plant with half of bulb above soil level. Support with stakes or a small trellis. Propagate by seed sown under cover in winter or spring. Gradually produces offsets.
B. volubilis illus. p.460.

BOYKINIA

SAXIFRAGACEAE

Genus of mound-forming perennials. Most species require shade and organic, moist but well-drained, acidic soil. Propagate by division in spring or by seed in autumn.
B. aconitifolia. Mound-forming perennial. H 3ft (1m), S 6in (15cm). Has rounded to kidney-shaped, lobed leaves. In summer, flower stems carry very small, bell-shaped white flowers. Z5–9 H9–5.
B. jamesii, syn. *Telesonix jamesii*. Mound-forming, rhizomatous perennial. H and S 6in (15cm). Each woody stem bears a rosette of kidney-shaped leaves with lacerated edges. In early summer bears open bell-shaped, frilled pink flowers with green centers. Z5–9 H9–5.

Brachychilum horsfieldii. See *Hedychium horsfieldii*.

BRACHYCHITON

STERCULIACEAE

Genus of evergreen or deciduous, mainly spring- and summer-flowering trees grown for their flowers and overall appearance. Needs full light and organic, well-drained, preferably acidic soil. Water containerized plants moderately, much less in winter. Prune if needed. Propagate by seed in spring. Spider mite may be a nuisance.
B. acerifolius, syn. *Sterculia acerifolia*, illus. p.65.
B. populneus, syn. *Sterculia diversifolia* (Kurrajong). Evergreen, conical tree, pyramidal when young. H and S 50–70ft (15–20m). Pointed or 3–5-lobed, glossy, deep green leaves are chartreuse when young. In spring-summer has panicles of saucer-shaped, cream or greenish white flowers with red, purple, or yellow throats. Z9–11 H12–10.

BRACHYGLOTTIS

ASTERACEAE/COMPOSITAE

Genus of evergreen shrubs and trees grown for their bold foliage and daisy-like flower heads. Needs full light or partial shade and well-drained soil. Water plants in containers freely in summer. Take semi-ripe cuttings in late summer.
B. compacta, syn. *Senecio compactus*. Evergreen, bushy, dense shrub. H 3ft (1m), S 6ft (2m). Bears small, oval, white-edged, dark green leaves, white below, and daisylike, bright yellow flowers in clustered heads from mid- to late summer. Feltlike white hairs cover the shoots. Z9–10 H10–9.
***B.* Dunedin Hybrids**, syn. *Senecio* Dunedin Hybrids, *S. greyi* of gardens, *S. laxifolius* of gardens. Spreading, bushy, mound-forming shrubs. H 5ft (1.5m), S 6ft (2m) or more. Leaves are obovate to elliptic, often wavy-margined, white-hairy, later hairless, and mid- to dark green. Loose, terminal panicles of bright yellow flower heads with conspicuous ray florets are produced from summer to autumn. Z9–10 H10–9. **'Sunshine'** (syn. *Senecio* 'Sunshine') illus. p.170.
B. laxifolia, syn. *Senecio laxifolius*. Evergreen, bushy, spreading shrub. H 3ft (1m), S 6ft (2m). Oval, gray-white leaves become dark green. Has large clusters of daisylike, golden yellow flower heads in summer.
B. monroi, syn. *Senecio monroi*, illus. p.171.
B. repanda illus. p.127.
B. rotundifolia, syn. *Senecio reinholdii*, *S. rotundifolius*. Evergreen, rounded, dense shrub. H and S 3ft (1m). Has rounded, leathery, glossy leaves, dark green above, white-felted below, and tiny yellow flower heads from early to midsummer. Withstands salt winds in mild coastal areas. Z.

BRACHYSCOME

ASTERACEAE/COMPOSITAE

Genus of annuals and perennials grown for their daisylike flower heads and very variable, often finely divided foliage. Requires sun, a sheltered position, and rich, well-drained soil. Pinch out growing shoots of young plants to encourage a bushy habit. Propagate by seed sown under cover in spring or outdoors in late spring.
B. iberidifolia illus. p.334.

BRACTEANTHA

ASTERACEAE/COMPOSITAE

Genus of herbaceous perennials and annuals grown for their daisylike flower heads with papery bracts. Stalkless, hairy leaves are borne on erect, branching stems. Needs full sun and moderately fertile, moist but well-drained soil. Propagate by seed sown in spring. *B. bracteata* is often grown for cutting and drying.
B. bracteata (Everlasting flower, Immortelle, Strawflower). Z10–11 H12–3. **'Bright Bikini'** is a moderately fast-growing, upright, branching annual. H and S 12in (30cm). Has lance-shaped, mid-green leaves. From summer to early autumn produces papery, daisylike flower heads in many colors, including red, pink, orange, yellow, and white. **Monstrosum Series** illus. p.340.

Brassaia. Reclassified as *Schefflera*.

BRASSAVOLA

See also ORCHIDS.
B. nodosa (Lady-of-the-night; illus. p.296). Evergreen, epiphytic orchid for an intermediate greenhouse. H 9in (23cm). Narrow-petaled, pale green flowers, 2in (5cm) across and each with a white lip, are produced, 1–3 to a stem, in spring; they are fragrant at night. Leaves, 3–4in (8–10cm) long, are thick and cylindrical. Is best grown on a bark slab. Provide good light in summer. Z14–15 H12–10.

BRASSICA

BRASSICACEAE/CRUCIFERAE

Genus of annuals and evergreen biennials and perennials. Most are edible vegetables, e.g. cabbages and kales, but forms of *B. oleracea* are grown for their ornamental foliage. Grow in sun and in fertile, well-drained soil. Lime-rich soil is recommended, though not essential. Propagate by seed sown outdoors in spring or under cover in early spring. Is susceptible to clubroot.
B. oleracea forms illus. p.324.

x BRASSOCATTLEYA

See also ORCHIDS.
x ***B.* Mount Adams** (illus. p.297). Evergreen, epiphytic orchid for an intermediate greenhouse. H 18in (45cm). Intermittently produces lavender-pink flowers, to 6in (15cm) across, each with a darker lip marked yellow and red, up to 4 per stem. Has oval, stiff leaves, 4–6in (10–15cm) long. Needs good light in summer. Z14–15 H12–9.

x BRASSOLAELIO-CATTLEYA

See also ORCHIDS.
x ***B.* Hetherington Horace 'Coronation'** (illus. p.297). Evergreen,

epiphytic orchid for an intermediate greenhouse. H 18in (45cm). Bears stiff, oval leaves, 4–6in (10–15cm) long, and fragrant, light pink flowers, 4in (10cm) across, each with a deep pink-yellow lip, up to 4 to a stem, mainly in spring. Provide good light in summer. Z14–15 H12–9.
x ***B.* St. Helier** (illus. p.297). Evergreen, epiphytic orchid for an intermediate greenhouse. H 18in (45cm). Produces oval, stiff leaves, 4–6in (10–15cm) long. Pinkish purple flowers, to 4in (10cm) across, each with a yellow-marked, rich red lip, are borne 1–4 to a stem, mainly in spring. Grow in good light in summer. Z14–15 H12–9.

***Bravoa geminiflora*.** See *Polianthes geminiflora*.

BREYNIA

EUPHORBIACEAE

Genus of evergreen shrubs and trees grown for their foliage. Needs full light or partial shade and fertile, well-drained soil. Water containerized plants freely when in full growth, moderately at other times. Large bushes should be cut back hard after flowering. Propagate by greenwood or semi-ripe cuttings in summer. Whitefly, spider mite, and mealy bug may be troublesome.
B. disticha, syn. *B. nivosa*, *Phyllanthus nivosus*, illus. p.175. **'Roseopicta'** is an evergreen, rounded, well-branched shrub with slender stems. H and S to 3ft (1m). Has broadly oval green leaves variably bordered and splashed with white and flushed pink. Insignificant, petalless flowers are borne in spring-summer. Z14–15 H12–10.
***B. nivosa*.** See *B. disticha*.

BRIGGSIA

GESNERIACEAE

Genus of evergreen perennials grown for their rosettes of hairy leaves. Needs shade and peaty soil with plenty of moisture in summer and good air circulation in winter. Protect against moisture in winter. Propagate by seed in spring.
***B. muscicola*.** Evergreen, basal-rosetted perennial. H 3–4in (8–10cm), S 9in (23cm). Leaves are oval, silver-haired, and pale green. Arching flower stems bear loose clusters of tubular, pale yellow flowers with protruding tips in early summer. Is best grown in an alpine house. Z12–15 H12–10.

BRIMEURA

HYACINTHACEAE

Genus of spring-flowering bulbs, similar to miniature bluebells, cultivated for their attractive flowers. Is suitable for rock gardens and shrub borders. Requires partial shade and prefers organic, well-drained soil. Propagate by sowing seed in autumn or by division in late summer.
B. amethystina, syn. *Hyacinthus amethystinus*, illus. p.432.
***Brittonastrum mexicanum*.** See *Agastache mexicana*.

BRIZA

Quaking grass

GRAMINEAE/POACEAE

See also GRASSES, BAMBOOS, RUSHES, and SEDGES.
B. maxima (Greater quaking grass). Robust, tuft-forming, annual grass. H to 20in (50cm), S 3–4in (8–10cm). Midgreen leaves are mainly basal. Produces loose panicles of up to 10 pendent, purplish green spikelets, in early summer, that dry particularly well for winter decoration. Self seeds readily. H12–1.
B. media (Common quaking grass). Evergreen, tuft-forming, rhizomatous, perennial grass. H 12–24in (30–60cm), S 3–4in (8–10cm). Midgreen leaves are mainly basal. In summer produces open panicles of up to 30 pendent, purplish brown spikelets that dry well for winter decoration. Z4–11 H12–1.

BRODIAEA

ALLIACEAE/LILIACEAE

Genus of mainly spring-flowering bulbs with colorful flowers produced in loose heads on leafless stems. Needs a sheltered, sunny situation and light, well-drained soil. Dies down in summer. Propagate in autumn by seed or in late summer and autumn by freely produced offsets.
***B. capitata*.** See *Dichelostemma pulchellum*.
***B. congesta*.** See *Dichelostemma congestum*.
B. coronaria, syn. *B. grandiflora*. Late spring- to early summer-flowering bulb. H 4–10in (10–25cm), S 3–4in (8–10cm). Long, narrow, semi-erect, basal leaves die down by flowering time. Leafless stems each carry a loose head of erect, funnel-shaped, violet-blue flowers on long, slender stalks. Z8–10 H10–8.
***B. grandiflora*.** See *B. coronaria*.
***B. hyacinthina*.** See *Triteleia hyacinthina*.
***B. ida-maia*.** See *Dichelostemma ida-maia*.
***B. ixioides*.** See *Triteleia ixioides*.
***B. lactea*.** See *Triteleia hyacinthina*.
***B. laxa*.** See *Triteleia laxa*.
***B. lutea*.** See *Triteleia ixioides*.
***B. peduncularis*.** See *Triteleia peduncularis*.
***B. pulchella*.** See *Dichelostemma pulchellum*.

BROMELIA

BROMELIACEAE

Genus of evergreen, rosette-forming perennials grown for their overall appearance. Needs full light and well-drained soil. Water moderately in summer, sparingly at other times. Propagate by suckers in spring.
B. balansae (Heart of flame; illus. p.265). Evergreen, clump-forming, basal-rosetted perennial. H 3ft (1m), S 5ft (1.5m). Produces narrowly strap-shaped, arching, mid- to gray-green leaves with large, hooked spines. Club-shaped panicles of tubular, red- or violet-purple flowers with long, bright red bracts are borne in spring-summer or sometimes later. Z14–15 H12–1.

BROMUS

GRAMINEAE/POACEAE

See also GRASSES, BAMBOOS, RUSHES, and SEDGES.
B. ramosus (Hairy brome grass). Evergreen, tuft-forming, perennial grass. H to 6ft (2m), S 1ft (30cm). Midgreen leaves are lax and hairy. Produces long, arching panicles of nodding, gray-green spikelets in summer. Prefers shade. H12–1.

BROUSSONETIA

MORACEAE

Genus of deciduous trees and shrubs grown for their foliage and unusual flowers. Male and female flowers are produced on different plants. Requires a position in full sun and well-drained soil. Propagate by softwood cuttings in summer or by seed in autumn.
B. papyrifera illus. p.79.

BROWALLIA

SOLANACEAE

Genus of shrubby perennials, usually grown as annuals, with showy, open trumpet-shaped flowers. Grows best in sun or partial shade and in fertile, well-drained soil that should not dry out completely. Feed when flowering if pot-grown and pinch out young shoots to encourage bushiness. Propagate by seed in spring; for winter flowers, sow in late summer.
B. americana, syn. *B. elata*. Moderately fast-growing, bushy perennial, usually grown as an annual. H 12in (30cm), S 6in (15cm). Has oval, midgreen leaves and, in summer, trumpet-shaped blue flowers, 1½in (4cm) wide. Z10–11 H8–1.
***B. elata*.** See *B. americana*.
B. speciosa illus. p.266.

BROWNINGIA

CACTACEAE

Genus of slow-growing, eventually treelike cacti. Spiny, silvery- or green-blue stems with up to 20 or more ribs are crowned by stiff, erect, green-blue branches. Requires a position in full sun and very well-drained soil. Propagate by seed in spring or summer.
B. hertlingiana, syn. *Azureocereus hertlingianus*, illus. p.456.

BRUGMANSIA,

syn. DATURA
Angels' trumpets

SOLANACEAE

Genus of evergreen or semi-evergreen shrubs, trees, and annuals cultivated for their flowers borne mainly in summer-autumn. Prefers full light and fertile, well-drained soil. Water containerized specimens freely in full growth, moderately at other times. May be pruned hard in early spring. Propagate by seed sown in spring or by greenwood or semi-ripe cuttings in early summer or later. Whitefly and spider mite may be troublesome. All parts are highly toxic if ingested.
B. arborea, syn. *B. versicolor* of gardens. Evergreen or semi-evergreen, rounded, robust shrub. H and S to 10ft (3m). Bears narrowly oval leaves, each 8in (20cm) or more long. Bears strongly fragrant, pendent, trumpet-shaped white flowers, each 6–8in (16–20cm) long with a spathelike calyx in summer-autumn. Z11–15 H12–10.
***B. aurea*.** Evergreen, rounded shrub or tree. H and S 20–35ft (6–11m). Has oval leaves, 6in (15cm) long, and, in summer-autumn, pendent, trumpet-shaped white or yellow flowers, 6–10in (15–25cm) long. Z11–15 H12–10.
B.* x *candida illus. p.119. **'Grand Marnier'** (syn. *B.* 'Grand Marnier') illus. p.123.
***B.* 'Grand Marnier'.** See *B.* x *candida* 'Grand Marnier'.
***B. rosei* of gardens.** See *B. sanguinea*.
B. sanguinea, syn. *B. rosei* of gardens, illus. p.123.
***B. versicolor* of gardens.** See *B. arborea*.

BRUNFELSIA

SOLANACEAE

Genus of evergreen shrubs grown for their flowers. Needs semi-shade and organic, well-drained soil. Water containerized plants moderately, much less in low temperatures. Remove stem tips to promote branching in growing season. Propagate by semi-ripe cuttings in summer. Mealy bug and whitefly may be a problem.
***B. calycina*.** See *B. pauciflora*.
***B. eximia*.** See *B. pauciflora*.
B. pauciflora, syn. *B. calycina*, *B. eximia* (Yesterday-today-and-tomorrow). Evergreen, spreading shrub. H and S 2ft (60cm) or more. Bears oblong to lance-shaped, leathery, glossy leaves. Blue-purple flowers, each with a tubular base and 5 overlapping, wavy-edged petals, are carried from winter to summer. Z12–15 H12–10.**'Macrantha'** illus. p.167.

BRUNNERA

BORAGINACEAE

Genus of spring-flowering perennials. Prefers light shade and moist soil. Propagate by division in spring or autumn or by seed in autumn.
B. macrophylla (Siberian bugloss).

Clump-forming perennial. H 18in (45cm), S 24in (60cm). Delicate sprays of small, star-shaped, forget-me-not-like, bright blue flowers in early spring are followed by heart-shaped, rough, long-stalked leaves. Makes a good groundcover. Z3–7 H7–1. **'Dawson's White'** (syn. *B.m.* 'Variegata') illus. p.271.

x ***Brunsdonna parkeri.*** See x *Amarygia parkeri*.

BRUNSVIGIA

AMARYLLIDACEAE

Genus of autumn-flowering bulbs with heads of showy flowers. Requires sun and well-drained soil. Water in autumn to encourage bulbs into growth and continue watering until summer, when the leaves will die away. Dormant bulbs should be kept fairly dry and warm. Propagate by seed sown in autumn or by offsets in late summer.
B. josephinae (Josephine's lily). Autumn-flowering bulb. H to 18in (45cm), S 18–24in (45–60cm). Bears a thick, leafless stem with a spherical head of 20–30 funnel-shaped red flowers, 3–3½in (7–9cm) long, with recurved petal tips. Semi-erect, oblong leaves appear after flowering. Z12–15 H12–10.

Bryophyllum. Reclassified as *Kalanchoe*.

BUDDLEJA

BUDDLEJACEAE

Genus of deciduous, semi-evergreen or evergreen shrubs and trees grown for their clusters of small, often fragrant flowers. Requires full sun and fertile, well-drained soil. *B. crispa*, *B. davidii*, *B. fallowiana*, *B.* 'Lochinch', and *B.* x *weyeriana* should be cut back hard in spring. Prune *B. alternifolia* by removing shoots that have flowered. Other species may be cut back lightly after flowering. Propagate by semi-ripe cuttings in summer.
B. alternifolia illus. p.122.
B. asiatica. Evergreen, arching shrub. H and S 10ft (3m). Long plumes of very fragrant, tubular white flowers appear amid long, narrow, dark green leaves in late winter and early spring. Z8–9 H9–8.
B. colvilei illus. p.121. **'Kewensis'** is a deciduous, arching shrub, often tree-like with age. H and S 15ft (5m). Has lance-shaped, dark green leaves. Large, tubular, white-throated, deep red flowers hang in drooping clusters in early summer. Z8–9 H9–8.
B. crispa illus. p.143.
B. davidii (Butterfly bush). Z6–9 H9–1. **'Black Knight'** is a vigorous, deciduous, arching shrub. H and S 15ft (5m). Leaves are long, lance-shaped, and dark green with white-felted undersides. Dense clusters of fragrant, tubular, dark violet-purple flowers are borne from midsummer to autumn. Flowers of **'Empire Blue'** are rich violet-blue. **'Harlequin'** illus. p.121. **'Peace'** illus. p.118. **'Pink Pearl'** produces pale lilac-pink flowers. **'Royal Red'** illus. p.121.
B. fallowiana. Deciduous, arching shrub. H 6ft (2m), S 10ft (3m). Shoots and lance-shaped leaves are covered with white hairs when young; foliage then becomes dark gray-green. Has fragrant, tubular, lavender-purple flowers in late summer and early autumn. var. ***alba*** has white flowers. Both Z8–9 H9–8.
B. globosa illus. p.123.
***B.* 'Lochinch'.** Deciduous, arching shrub. H and S 10ft (3m). Long plumes of fragrant, tubular, lilac-blue flowers are borne above lance-shaped, gray-green leaves in late summer and autumn. Z6–9 H9–1.
B. madagascariensis, syn. *Nicodemia madagascariensis*. Evergreen, arching shrub. H and S 12ft (4m) or more. Has narrowly lance-shaped, dark green leaves, white beneath and, in late winter and spring, long clusters of tubular, orange-yellow flowers.
B.* x *weyeriana. Deciduous, arching shrub. H and S 12ft (4m). Bears lance-shaped, dark green leaves and loose, rounded clusters of tubular, orange-yellow flowers, often tinged purple, from midsummer to autumn. Z6–8 H8–6.

BULBOCODIUM

COLCHICACEAE/LILIACEAE

Genus of spring-flowering corms, related to *Colchicum* and with funnel-shaped flowers. Is particularly suitable for rock gardens and cool greenhouses. Requires an open, sunny site and well-drained soil. Propagate by seed sown in autumn or by division in late summer and early autumn.
B. vernum illus. p.430.

BULBOPHYLLUM

See also ORCHIDS.
B. careyanum (illus. p.298). Evergreen, epiphytic orchid for an intermediate greenhouse. H 3in (8cm). Oval leaves are 3–4in (8–10cm) long. In spring produces tight sprays of many slightly fragrant brown flowers, ¼in (0.5cm) across. Grows best in a hanging basket. Needs semi-shade in summer. Z13–15 H12–10

BUPHTHALMUM

ASTERACEAE/COMPOSITAE

Genus of summer-flowering perennials. Requires full sun; grows well in any but rich soil. Propagate by seed in spring or autumn or by division in autumn. Needs frequent division to curb invasiveness.
B. salicifolium illus. p.292.
B. speciosum. See *Telekia speciosa*.

BUPLEURUM

APIACEAE/UMBELLIFERAE

Genus of perennials and evergreen shrubs grown for their foliage and flowers. Grows well in coastal gardens. Needs full sun and well-drained soil. Propagate by semi-ripe cuttings in summer.
B. fruticosum illus. p.146.

BUTIA

Yatay palm

ARECACEAE/PALMAE

Genus of evergreen palms grown for their overall appearance. Grow in any fertile, well-drained soil and in full light or partial shade. Water regularly, less in winter. Propagate by seed in spring at not less than 75°F (24°C). Spider mite may be a problem.
B. capitata, syn. *Cocos capitata*, illus. p.100.

BUTOMUS

BUTOMACEAE

Genus of one species of deciduous, perennial, rushlike, marginal water plant grown for its fragrant, cup-shaped flowers. Requires an open, sunny situation in up to 10in (25cm) depth of water. Propagate by division in spring or by seed in spring or late summer.
B. umbellatus illus. p.448.

BUXUS

Boxwood

BUXACEAE

Genus of evergreen shrubs and trees grown for their foliage and habit. Is excellent for edging, hedging, and topiary work. Flowers are often fragrant but insignificant. Requires sun or semi-shade and any but waterlogged soil. Trim hedges in summer. Promote new growth by cutting back stems to 12in (30cm) or less in late spring. Propagate by semi-ripe cuttings in summer. Contact with boxwood sap may irritate skin.
B. balearica illus. p.153.
B. microphylla (Small-leaved boxwood). Evergreen, bushy shrub. H 3ft (1m), S 5ft (1.5m). Forms a dense, rounded mass of small, oblong, dark green leaves. Z6–9 H9–6. **'Green Pillow'** illus. p.176.var. *koreana* is hardier, as are hybrids between this and *B. sempervirens*, such as **'Green Gem'** and **'Green Velvet'**.
B. sempervirens (Common boxwood). Evergreen, bushy shrub or tree. H and S 15ft (5m). Produces leaves that are oblong, glossy, and dark green. Useful for hedging and screening. Z6-8 H8–6. **'Handsworthensis'** illus. p.152. **'Suffruticosa'** illus. p.177.

CABOMBA

CABOMBACEAE

Genus of deciduous or semi-evergreen, perennial, submerged water plants with finely divided foliage. Is suitable for aquariums. Prefers partial shade. Propagate by stem cuttings in spring summer.
C. caroliniana (Fanwort, Carolina water shield). Deciduous or semi-evergreen, perennial, submerged water plant. S indefinite. Forms dense, spreading hummocks of fan-shaped, coarsely cut, bright green leaves. Useful as an oxygenating plant. Z6–11 H12–6.

CAESALPINIA

CAESALPINIACEAE/LEGUMINOSAE

Genus of deciduous or evergreen shrubs, trees, and scrambling climbers grown for their foliage and flowers. Needs full sun and fertile, well-drained soil. Propagate by softwood cuttings in summer or by seed in autumn or spring.
C. gilliesii, syn. *Poinciana gilliesii*, illus. p.123.
C. pulcherrima, syn. *Poinciana pulcherrima* (Barbados pride). Evergreen shrub or tree of erect to spreading habit. H and S 10–20ft (3–6m). Has fernlike leaves composed of many small, midgreen leaflets. In summer bears cup-shaped yellow flowers, 1¼in (3cm) wide, with very long red anthers, in short, dense, erect racemes. Z9–11 H12–9.

CALADIUM

ARACEAE

Genus of perennials with tubers from which arise long-stalked, ornamental leaves. Requires partial shade and moist, organic soil. After leaves die down, store tubers in a frost-free, dark place. Propagate by separating small tubers when planting in spring. Contact with all parts may irritate skin, and ingestion may cause mild stomach upset.
C. bicolor (Angels' wings). **'Candidum'** is a tufted perennial. All Z15 H12–4. H and S to 36in (90cm). Triangular, green-veined white leaves, to 18in (45cm) long, have arrow-shaped bases and long leaf stalks. Intermittently bears white spathes; small flowers clustered on spadix sometimes produce whitish berries. **'John Peed'** has purple stems and waxy green leaves with metallic orange-red centers and scarlet veins. **'Pink Beauty'** illus. p.264. **'Pink Cloud'** has large, dark green leaves with mottled pink centers, and pink to white areas along the veins.

CALANTHE

See also ORCHIDS.
C. vestita (illus. p.296). Deciduous, terrestrial orchid. H 24in (60cm). In winter bears sprays of many white flowers, 1½in (4cm) across, each with a large, red-marked lip. Has broadly oval, ribbed, soft leaves, 12in (30cm) long. In summer requires semi-shade and regular feeding. Z14–15 H12–10.

CALATHEA

MARANTACEAE

Genus of evergreen perennials with brightly colored and patterned leaves. Prefers a shaded, humid position without fluctuations of temperature in organic, well-drained soil. Water with soft water, sparingly in low temper-atures, but do not allow to dry out completely. Propagate by division in spring.
C. lindeniana. Evergreen, clump-forming perennial. H 3ft (1m), S 2ft (60cm). Lance-shaped, long-stalked, more or less upright leaves, over 1ft (30cm) long, are dark green with paler green, feathered midribs above and marked with reddish purple below. Intermittently bears short, erect spikes of 3-petaled, pale yellow flowers. Z14–15 H12–10.
***C. majestica* 'Roseolineata'**, syn. *C. ornata* 'Roseolineata'. Evergreen, clump-forming, stemless perennial. H to 6ft (2m), S to 5ft (1.5m). Narrowly oval, leathery leaves, to 2ft (60cm) long, are dark green with close-set, fine pink stripes along the lateral veins and reddish purple below. Intermittently bears short, erect spikes of 3-petaled white to mauve flowers. Z14–15 H12–1.**'Sanderiana'** see *C. sanderiana*.
C. makoyana illus. p.304.
C. oppenheimiana. See *Ctenanthe oppenheimiana*.
***C. ornata* 'Roseolineata'.** See *C. majestica* 'Roseolineata'.
C. sanderiana, syn. *C. majestica* 'Sanderiana', illus. p.232.
C. zebrina illus. p.266.

CALCEOLARIA

Pouch flower, Slipper flower

SCROPHULARIACEAE

Genus of annuals, biennials and evergreen perennials, subshrubs, and scandent climbers, some of which are grown as annuals. Most prefer sun but some like a shady, cool site and moist but well-drained soil, incor-porating coarse sand and compost, and dislike wet conditions in winter. Propagate by softwood cuttings in late spring or summer or by seed in autumn.
C. acutifolia. See *C. polyrrhiza*.
***C.* Anytime Series.** Compact, bushy annuals or biennials. H 8in (20cm), S 6in (15cm). Has oval, slightly hairy, midgreen leaves and, in spring-summer, heads of 2in (5cm) long, rounded, pouched flowers in red and yellow shades, including bicolors. Z8–9 H6–1.
C. arachnoidea illus. p.355.
***C.* 'Bright Bikinis'** illus. p.338.
C. darwinii. See *C. uniflora* var. *darwinii*.
C. fothergillii. Evergreen, clump-forming, short-lived perennial. H and S 5in (12cm). Has a rosette of rounded, light green leaves with hairy edges and, in summer, solitary pouch-shaped, sulfur yellow flowers with crimson spots. Is good for a sheltered rock ledge or trough or in an alpine house. Needs gritty, peaty soil. Is prone to aphid attack. Z8–9 H6–1.
C. integrifolia. Evergreen, upright subshrub sometimes grown as an annu-al. H to 4ft (1.2m), S 2ft (60cm). In summer bears crowded clusters of pouch-shaped yellow to red-brown flowers above oblong to elliptic, midgreen leaves, sometimes rust-colored beneath. Z8–9 H6–1
***C.* 'John Innes'** illus. p.293.
***C.* 'Monarch'.** Group of bushy annuals or biennials. H and S 12in (30cm). Has oval, lightly hairy, midgreen leaves and, in spring-summer, bears heads of large, rounded, pouched flowers, 2in (5cm) long, in a wide range of colors. Z8–9 H6–1.
C. pavonii. Robust, evergreen, scandent climber. H 6ft (2m) or more. Has oval, serrated, soft-haired leaves with winged stalks. Pouched yellow flowers with brown marks appear in large clusters from late summer to winter. Z8–9 H6–1.
C. polyrrhiza, syn. *C. acutifolia*. Evergreen, prostrate perennial. H 1in (2.5cm), S 6in (15cm). Has rounded, hairy, midgreen leaves along flower stem, which bears pouch-shaped, purple-spotted yellow flowers in summer. Is good for a shady rock garden. May also be propagated by division in autumn or spring. Z8–9 H6–1.
***C.* 'Sunshine'** illus. p.339.
C. tenella illus. p.385.
C. uniflora* var. *darwinii, syn. *C. darwinii*. Evergreen, clump-forming, short-lived perennial. H 3in (8cm), S 4in (10cm). Bears rounded, wrinkled, glossy, dark green leaves. In late spring, flower stems carry pendent, pouch-shaped yellow flowers with dark brown spots on lower lips and central white bands. Is difficult to grow. Needs a sheltered, sunny site in moist, gritty, peaty soil. Is prone to attack by aphids. Z8–9 H6–1.
***C.* 'Walter Shrimpton'** illus. p.386.

CALENDULA

Pot marigold

ASTERACEAE/COMPOSITAE

Genus of annuals and evergreen shrubs. Grow in sun or partial shade and in any well-drained soil. Deadhead regularly to prolong flowering. Propagate annuals by seed sown outdoors in spring or autumn, shrubs by stem cuttings in summer. Annuals may self-seed. Cucumber mosaic virus and powdery mildew may cause problems.
C. officinalis (Pot marigold). Fast-growing, bushy annual. Tall cultivars, H and S 24in (60cm); dwarf forms, H and S 12in (30cm). All have lance-shaped, strongly aromatic, pale green leaves. Daisylike, single or double flower heads in a wide range of yellow and orange shades are produced from spring to autumn. H6–1. **'Fiesta Gitana'** illus. p.339. **'Geisha Girl'** (tall) illus. p.341. **Kablouna Series** (tall) illus. p.336. **Pacific Beauty Series 'Lemon Queen'** illus. p.338.

CALLA

ARACEAE

Genus of one species of deciduous or semi-evergreen, perennial, spreading, marginal water plant grown for its foliage and showy spathes that surround insignificant flower clusters. Requires a sunny position, in mud or in water to 10in (25cm) deep. Propagate by division in spring or by seed in late summer. Contact with the foliage may aggravate skin allergies.
C. palustris illus. p.446.

CALLIANDRA

LEGUMINOSAE/MIMOSACEAE

Genus of evergreen trees, shrubs and scandent semi-climbers grown for their flowers and overall appearance. Requires full light or partial shade and well-drained soil. Water containerized plants freely when in full growth, much less when temperatures are low. To restrict growth, cut back stems by one-half to two-thirds after flowering. Propagate by seed sown indoors in spring. Whitefly and mealy bug may be troublesome.
C. eriophylla illus. p.172.
C. haematocephala [pink form] illus. p.147, [white form] illus. p.149.

CALLIANTHEMUM

RANUNCULACEAE

Genus of perennials grown for their daisylike flowers and thick, dissected leaves. Is excellent for rock gardens and alpine houses. Needs sun and moist but well-drained soil. Propagate by seed when fresh.
C. coriandrifolium, syn. *C. rutifolium*. Prostrate perennial with upright flower stems. H 3in (8cm), S 8in (20cm). Leaves, forming open rosettes, are long-stalked, very dissected, and blue-green. In spring has short-stemmed, many-petaled white flowers with yellow centers. Susceptible to slugs. Z4–7 H7–1.
C. rutifolium. See *C. coriandrifolium*.

CALLICARPA

VERBENACEAE

Genus of deciduous, summer-flowering shrubs grown for their small but striking, clustered fruits. Does best in full sun and fertile, well-drained soil. Propagate by softwood cuttings in summer.
C. bodinieri. Deciduous, bushy shrub. H 10ft (3m), S 8ft (2.5m). Has oval, dark green leaves. Tiny, star-shaped lilac flowers in midsummer are followed by dense clusters of spherical, violet fruits. Z4–7 H7–1. var. ***giraldii*** illus. p.148.

CALLISIA

COMMELINACEAE

Genus of evergreen, prostrate perennials grown for their ornamental foliage and trailing habit. Grow in full light, but out of direct sunlight, in fertile, well-drained soil. Propagate by tip cuttings in spring, either annually or when plants become straggly.
C. navicularis, syn. *Tradescantia navicularis*. Evergreen, low-growing perennial with creeping, rooting shoots, 20in (50cm) or more long. H 2–3in (5–8cm), S indefinite. Has 2 rows of oval, keeled leaves, 1in (2.5cm) long, sheathing the stem, and stalkless clusters of small, 3-petaled, pinkish purple flowers in leaf axils in summer-autumn. Z6–8 H8–6.
C. repens illus. p.304.

CALLISTEMON

Bottlebrush

MYRTACEAE

Genus of evergreen shrubs, usually with narrow, pointed leaves, grown for their clustered flowers that, with their profusion of long stamens, resemble bottlebrushes. Where marginally hardy, grow against a south- or west-facing wall or in a cool greenhouse. Requires full sun and fertile, well-drained soil. Propagate by semi-ripe cuttings in summer or by seed in autumn or spring.
***C. citrinus* 'Splendens'** illus. p.143.
C. pallidus illus. p.146.
C. paludosus. See *C. sieberi*.
C. pityoides. Evergreen, compact, upright shrub. H 5ft (1.5m), S 3ft (1m). Is densely covered with sharply pointed, dark green leaves and has short spikes of yellow flowers in mid and late summer. Z12–15 H12–10.
C. rigidus illus. p.143.
C. sieberi, syn. *C. paludosus*. Evergreen, bushy, dense shrub. H 5ft (1.5m), S 3ft (1m). Has short, narrowly lance-shaped, rigid, midgreen leaves and, from mid to late summer, small clusters of pale yellow flowers. Z10–15 H12–10.
C. speciosus (Albany bottlebrush). Evergreen, bushy shrub. H and S 10ft (3m). Produces long, narrow, gray-green leaves. Cylindrical clusters of bright red flowers appear in late spring and early summer. Z10–15 H12–10.
C. subulatus. Evergreen, arching shrub. H and S 5ft (1.5m). Leaves are narrowly oblong and bright green. Dense spikes of crimson flowers are produced in summer. Z8–15 H12–10
C. viminalis. Evergreen, arching shrub. H and S 15ft (5m). Narrowly oblong, bronze, young leaves mature to dark

green. Bears clusters of bright red flowers in summer. Z9–15 H12–10.

CALLISTEPHUS

China aster

ASTERACEAE/COMPOSITAE

Genus of one species of annual. Requires sun, a sheltered position, and fertile, well-drained soil. Tall cultivars need support; all should be dead-headed. Propagate by seed sown under cover in spring; seed may also be sown outdoors in midspring. Aster yellows, virus diseases, foot rot, root rot, and aphids may be a problem.

C. chinensis. Moderately fast-growing, erect, bushy annual. Tall cultivars, H 24in (60cm), S 18in (45cm); intermediate, H 18in (45cm), S 12in (30cm); dwarf, H 10–12in (25–30cm), S 12–18in (30–45cm); very dwarf, H 8in (20cm), S 12in (30cm). All have oval, toothed, midgreen leaves and flower in summer and early autumn. Different forms are available in a wide color range, including pink, red, blue, and white. H9–1. **Duchesse Series** (tall) has incurved, chrysanthemum-like flower heads. **Milady Super Series** (dwarf) has incurved, fully double flower heads available either in mixed or single colors (blue, illus. p.332; rose, illus. p.324). **Ostrich Plume Series** (tall) illus. p.331. **Pompon Series** (tall) has small, double flower heads. **Princess Series** (tall) has double flower heads with quilled petals.

CALLUNA

ERICACEAE

See also HEATHERS.

C. vulgaris (Ling, Scotch heather). Evergreen, bushy shrub. H to 24in (60cm), S 18in (45cm). Slightly fleshy, linear leaves, in opposite and overlapping pairs, may range in color from bright green to shades of gray, yellow, orange, and red. Spikes of bell- to urn-shaped, single or double flowers are produced from midsummer to late autumn.

Unlike *Erica*, most of the flower color derives from the sepals. The following cultivars are H 18in (45cm), have midgreen leaves, and bear single flowers in late summer and early autumn, unless otherwise stated. Z5–7 H7–5.
'Alba Plena', H 12–18in (30–45cm), bears double white flowers.
'Alexandra' (illus. p.179), H 12in (30cm), S 16in (40cm), has an upright habit, dark green foliage, and deep crimson buds until early winter.
'Alicia', H 12in (30cm), S 16in (40cm), has white buds until early winter and a neat, compact habit. **'Allegro'**, H 24in (60cm), is compact in habit and produces purple-red flowers. **'Alportii'**, H 24–36in (60–90cm), has purple-red flowers. **'Anette'**, H 14in (35cm), S 16in (40cm), has clear pink buds until early winter. **'Annemarie'**, H 20in (50cm), S 24in (60cm), has outstanding, double, rose pink flowers ideal for cutting. **'Anthony Davis'** (illus. p.178) has gray leaves and white flowers. **'Beoley Gold'** (illus. p.179), S 20in (50cm), has golden foliage and white flowers. **'Beoley Silver'**, H 16in (40cm), has silver foliage and white flowers. **'Blazeaway'**, H 14in (35cm), S 24in (60cm), has gold foliage in summer that turns orange then fiery red in winter. **'Bonfire Brilliance'**, H 12in (30cm), has bright, flame-colored foliage and mauve-pink flowers.
'Boskoop' (illus. p.179), H 12in (30cm), is compact, with golden foliage that turns deep orange in winter and lilac-pink flowers.
'County Wicklow' (illus. p.178), H 12in (30cm), S 14in (35cm), is compact with double, shell pink flowers. **'Dark Beauty'**, H 8in (20cm), S 14in (35cm), is neat and compact and bears bright, semi-double crimson flowers. **'Darkness'** (illus. p.179), H 16in (40cm), S 14in (35cm), is compact with crimson flowers. **'Elsie Purnell'** (illus. p.178) is a spreading cultivar with grayish green leaves and double, pale pink flowers. **'Finale'** bears dark pink flowers from late autumn to early winter. **'Firefly'** (illus. p.179), S 20in (50cm), with deep mauve flowers, has foliage that is terracotta in summer and brick-red in winter. **'Foxii Nana'** (illus. p.179), H 6in (15cm), forms low mounds of bright green foliage and produces a few mauve-pink flowers. **'Fred J. Chapple'** has bright pink- and coral-tipped foliage in spring; mauve-pink flowers are borne on long stems. **'Gold Haze'** (illus. p.179) has bright golden foliage and white flowers. **'Golden Feather'** (illus. p.179) has bright yellow foliage turning orange in winter, and mauve-pink flowers. **'Hammondii Aureifolia'**, H 12in (30cm), S 16in (40cm), has white flowers. Foliage is light green tipped yellow in spring and early summer. **'H.E. Beale'**, H 20in (50cm), is one of the best double-flowered heathers, with pale pink flowers on long stems. **'J.H. Hamilton'** (illus. p.178), H 8in (20cm), S 16in (40cm), is compact with double, salmon-pink flowers. **'Joy Vanstone'** has golden foliage turning to orange and bronze, and mauve-pink flowers. **'Kerstin'**, H 12in (30cm), produces mauve flowers and has downy, deep lilac-gray foliage in winter, tipped pale yellow and red in spring. **'Kinlochruel'** (illus. p.178), H 12in (30cm), S 14in (35cm), bears an abundance of large, double white flowers. **'Loch Turret'**, H 12in (30cm), has emerald green foliage and produces white flowers in early summer. **'Mair's Variety'**, an old cultivar, has white flowers on long spikes. **'Marleen'** is unusual in that its long-lasting, dark mauve flower buds, borne from early to late autumn, do not open fully. **'Mullion'** H 10in (25cm), S 20in (50cm), is a spreading cultivar with rich mauve-pink flowers.
'Multicolor' (illus. p.179), H 8in (20cm), is compact with foliage in shades of yellow, orange, red, and green year-round; flowers are mauve-pink.
'My Dream' (syn. *C.v.* 'Snowball'; illus. p.178), H 20in (50cm), produces double white flowers that are borne on long, tapering stems. **'Peter Sparkes'** (illus. p.179), H 20in (50cm), S 22in (55cm), bears double, deep pink flowers. **'Robert Chapman'** (illus. p.179) is a spreading cultivar and grown mainly for its foliage, which is golden yellow in summer, turning orange and brilliant red in winter; flowers are mauve-pink. **'Ruth Sparkes'**, H 10in (25cm), has golden foliage and white flowers. **'Silver Knight'** (illus. p.179), H 12in (30cm), is of upright habit with gray leaves and mauve-pink flowers. **'Silver Queen'** (illus. p.178), H 16in (40cm), S 22in (55cm), is a spreading cultivar with dark mauve-pink flowers. **'Sir John Charrington'** has bright-colored foliage, varying from golden yellow in summer to orange and red in winter, and dark mauve-pink flowers. **'Sister Anne'**, H 6in (15cm), has gray leaves and pale mauve-pink flowers.
'Snowball' see *C.v.* 'My Dream'.
'Spring Cream' (illus. p.178) has bright green leaves, which have cream tips in spring, and white flowers.
'Spring Torch', H 16in (40cm), S 24in (60cm), has mauve flowers with cream, orange, and red tips in spring.
'Sunset', H 10in (25cm), has brightly colored foliage changing from golden yellow in spring to orange in summer and fiery red in winter; flowers are mauve-pink. **'Tib'** (illus. p.179), H 12in (30cm), S 16in (40cm), is the earliest-flowering double cultivar, producing small, double, deep pink flowers in early summer.
'White Lawn', H 4in (10cm), is a creeping cultivar with bright green foliage and white flowers on long stems; is suitable for a rock garden.
'Wickwar Flame' is primarily a foliage plant with leaves in shades of yellow, orange, and red that are particularly effective in winter; flowers are mauve-pink.

CALOCEDRUS

CUPRESSACEAE

See also CONIFERS.

C. decurrens, syn. *Libocedrus decurrens*, illus. p.106.

Calocephalus brownii. See *Leucophyta brownii.*

CALOCHONE

RUBIACEAE

Genus of evergreen, scrambling climbers grown for their showy flowers. Requires full light and organic, well-drained soil. Water regularly, less in cold weather. Needs tying to a support. Thin out crowded stems after flowering. Prop-agate by semi-ripe cuttings in summer.

C. redingii. Moderately vigorous, evergreen, scrambling climber. H 10–15ft (3–5m). Has oval, pointed, hairy leaves, 3–5in (7–12cm) long. Clusters of primrose-shaped red to orange-pink flowers appear in winter. Z14–15 H12–10.

CALOCHORTUS

Cat's ears, Fairy lantern, Mariposa lily, Mariposa tulip

LILIACEAE

Genus of bulbs grown for their spring and summer flowers. Needs a sheltered, sunny position and well-drained soil. In cold, damp climates, cover or lift spring-flowering species when dormant (in summer), or grow in a cold frame or cold greenhouse. After flowering, remove bulbils formed in leaf axils for propagation. Propagate by seed or bulbils – spring-flowering species in autumn, summer-flowering species in spring.

C. albus illus. p.409.
C. amabilis illus. p.434.
C. barbatus, syn. *Cyclobothra lutea*, illus. p.422.
C. luteus illus. p.415.
C. monophyllus illus. p.436.
C. splendens. Late spring-flowering bulb. H 8–24in (20–60cm), S 2–4in (5–10cm). Bears 1 or 2 linear, erect leaves near base of branched stem and 1–4 upward-facing, saucer-shaped, pale purple flowers, 2–3in (5–7cm) across, with a darker blotch at the base of each of the 3 large petals. Z6–10 H10–6.
C. superbus. Late spring-flowering bulb. H 8–24in (20–60cm), S 2–4in (5–10cm). Is similar to *C. splendens*, but flowers are white, cream, or pale lilac, with a brown mark near the base of each of the 3 large petals. Z5–10 H10–6.
C. venustus illus. p.408.
C. vestae. Late spring-flowering bulb. H 8–24in (20–60cm), S 2–4in (5–10cm). Is similar to *C. splendens*, but flowers are white or purple, with a rust-brown mark near the base of each of the 3 large petals. Z5–10 H10–5.
C. weedii. Summer-flowering bulb. H 12–24in (30–60cm), S 2–4in (5–10cm). Has a linear, erect leaf near base of stem. Carries usually 2 upright, saucer-shaped flowers, 1½–2in (4–5cm) across, that are orange-yellow with brown lines and flecks and hairy inside. Z6–10 H10–6.

CALODENDRUM

RUTACEAE

Genus of evergreen trees, grown for their flowers that are produced mainly in spring-summer. Needs full light and fertile, well-drained but moisture-retentive soil. Water containerized specimens freely when in full growth, less at other times. Tolerates some pruning. Propagate by seed in spring or by semi-ripe cuttings in summer.

C. capense (Cape chestnut). Fairly fast-growing, evergreen, rounded tree. H and S to 15m (50ft) or more. Has oval leaves patterned with translucent dots. Terminal panicles of 5-petaled, light pink to deep mauve flowers appear from spring to early summer. Z12–15 H12–10.

CALOMERIA, syn. HUMEA

ASTERACEAE/COMPOSITAE

Genus of perennials and evergreen shrubs. Only *C. amaranthoides* is cultivated, usually as a biennial. Needs sun and fertile, well-drained soil. Propagate by seed sown under cover in midsummer.

C. amaranthoides, syn. *C. elegans*, illus. p.330.

C. elegans. See *C. amaranthoides*.

Calonyction aculeatum. See *Ipomoea alba*.

CALOSCORDUM

ALLIACEAE/LILIACEAE

Genus of one species of summer-flowering bulb, related and similar to *Allium*. Is suitable for a rock garden. Needs an open, sunny situation and well-drained soil. Lies dormant in winter. Propagate in early spring by seed or division before growth starts.

C. neriniflorum, syn. *Nothoscordum neriniflorum*. Clump-forming bulb. H 10–25cm (4–10in), S 8–10cm (3–4in). Threadlike, semi-erect, basal leaves die down at flowering time. Each leafless stem produces a loose head of 10–20 small, funnel-shaped, pinkish red flowers in late summer. Z5–10 H10–5.

CALOTHAMNUS

MYRTACEAE

Genus of evergreen, summer-flowering shrubs, grown for their flowers and overall appearance. Thrives in a dryish, airy environment. Requires full sun and well-drained, sandy soil. Water containerized plants moderately when in full growth, less at other times. Propagate by seed or semi-ripe cuttings in summer.

C. quadrifidus (Common net bush). Erect to spreading, evergreen shrub. H 6–12ft (2–4m), S 6–15ft (2–5m). Has linear, grayish to dark green or gray leaves. Irregular, axillary, one-sided spikes of rich red, feathery flowers, 1in (2.5cm) long, are produced from late spring to autumn, often forming clusters, 8in (20cm) or more across, around the stems. Z12–15 H12–10.

CALTHA

RANUNCULACEAE

Genus of deciduous, perennial, marginal water plants, bog plants, and rock garden plants grown for their attractive flowers. Most prefer an open, sunny position. Smaller-growing species are suitable for rock gardens, troughs, and alpine houses and require moist but well-drained soil; larger species are best in marginal conditions. Propagate species by seed in autumn or by division in autumn or early spring, selected forms by division in autumn or early spring.

C. leptosepala illus. p.447.

C. palustris illus. p.451. var. ***alba*** (syn. *C.p.* 'Alba') is a compact, deciduous, perennial, marginal water plant. H 9in (22cm), S 12in (30cm). Has rounded, glossy, dark green leaves and bears solitary white flowers with yellow stamens in early spring, often before the foliage develops. Z3–7 H7–1. **'Flore Pleno'** illus. p.451.

CALYCANTHUS

CALYCANTHACEAE

Genus of deciduous, summer-flowering shrubs grown for their purplish- or brownish red flowers with strap-shaped petals. Requires sun or light shade and fertile, deep, moist but well-drained soil. Propagate by softwood cuttings in summer or by seed in autumn.

C. floridus (Carolina allspice). Deciduous, bushy shrub. H and S 6ft (2m). Has oval, aromatic, dark green leaves and, from early to midsummer, fragrant, brownish red flowers with masses of spreading petals. Z5–9 H9–1.

C. occidentalis illus. p.142.

CALYPSO

See also ORCHIDS.

C. bulbosa (illus. p.297). Deciduous, terrestrial orchid. H 2–8in (5–20cm). Cormlike stem produces a single, oval, pleated leaf, 1¼–4in (3–10cm) long. Purplish pink flowers, ⅝–¾in (1.5–2cm) long, with hairy, purple-blotched white or pale pink lips, are produced singly in late spring or early summer. Requires a damp, semi-shaded position, preferably with a mulch of leaf mold. Z6–9 H9–6.

CAMASSIA

HYACINTHACEAE/LILIACEAE

Genus of summer-flowering bulbs suitable for borders and pond margins. Requires sun or partial shade and deep, moist soil. Plant bulbs in autumn, 4in (10cm) deep. Propagate by seed in autumn or by division in late summer. If seed is not desired, cut off stems after flowering.

C. esculenta. See *C. quamash*.

C. leichtlinii illus. p.397. **'Semiplena'** illus. p.397.

C. quamash, syn. *C. esculenta* (Common camassia, Quamash). Clump-forming, summer-flowering bulb. H 8–32in (20–80cm), S 8–12in (20–30cm). Produces long, narrow, erect, basal leaves. Leafless stems each bear a dense spike of star-shaped blue, violet, or white flowers to 3in (7cm) across. Z4–11 H12–1.

CAMELLIA

THEACEAE

Genus of evergreen shrubs and trees grown for their flowers and foliage. Flowers are classified according to the following types: single, semi-double, anemone-form, peony-form, rose-form, formal double, and irregular double. See feature panel pp.128–9 for illustrations and descriptions. Grows well against walls and in containers. Most prefer a sheltered position and semi-shade. Well-drained, neutral to acidic soil is essential. Prune to shape after flowering. Propagate by semi-ripe or hardwood cuttings from midsummer to early winter or by grafting in late winter or early spring. Aphids, thrips, and scale insects may cause problems under cover.

Virtually all camellias are Z7–8 H8–7, except where noted.

***C.* 'Anticipation'** (illus. p.129). Robust, evergreen, upright shrub. H 10ft (3m), S 5ft (1.5m). Has lance-shaped, dark green leaves. Large, peony-form, deep rose pink blooms are freely produced in spring.

***C.* 'Black Lace'** (illus. p.129). Slow-growing, dense, upright shrub. H 5–8ft (1.5–2.5m), S 3–8ft (1–2.5m). Has ovate, dark green leaves, 3in (8cm) long, and large, formal double, deep velvety red flowers from early to late spring.

C. chrysantha. See *C. nitidissima*.

***C.* 'Cornish Snow'** (illus. p.128). Fast-growing, evergreen, upright, bushy shrub. H 10ft (3m), S 5ft (1.5m). Has lance-shaped leaves, bronze when young, maturing to dark green. In early spring bears a profusion of small, cup-shaped, single white flowers.

C. cuspidata. Evergreen, upright shrub becoming bushy with age. H 10ft (3m), S 5ft (1.5m). Has small, lance-shaped leaves, bronze when young, maturing to purplish green. Small, cup-shaped, single, pure white flowers are freely produced from leaf axils in early spring.

***C.* 'Dr. Clifford Parks'** (illus. p.129). Evergreen, spreading shrub. H 12ft (4m), S 8ft (2.5m). In midspring has large, flame red flowers, often semi-double, peony-, and anemone-form on the same plant. Leaves are large, oval and dark green.

***C.* 'Francie L.'** (illus. p.129). Vigorous shrub with long, fan-shaped branches. H 15ft (5m), S 20ft (6m). Leaves are lance-shaped and dark green, 2½–4in (6–10cm) long. Has large, semi-double, salmon-red to deep rose-red flowers from late winter to late spring.

C. granthamiana. Evergreen, open shrub. H to 10ft (3m), S 6ft (2m). Oval, leathery leaves are crinkly and glossy, deep green. In late autumn bears large, saucer-shaped, single white flowers, to 7in (18cm) across, with up to 8 broad petals.

C. hiemalis. Evergreen, upright, bushy shrub. H 6–10ft (2–3m), S 1 5ft (5m). Has small, lance-shaped leaves and fragrant, single, cup-shaped, semi- or irregular double white, pink, or red flowers borne in late autumn and winter. Is good for hedging.

C. hongkongensis. Evergreen, bushy shrub or tree. H to 10ft (3m), S 6ft (2m). Lance-shaped leaves, 4in (10cm) long, are dark red when young, maturing to dark green. Bears cup-shaped, single, deep crimson flowers, velvety beneath, in late spring.

***C.* 'Innovation'** (illus. p.129). Evergreen, open, spreading shrub. H 15ft (5m), S 10ft (3m). Has large, oval, leathery leaves and, in spring, produces large, peony-form, lavender-shaded, claret red flowers with twisted petals.

***C.* 'Inspiration'** (illus. p.129). Evergreen, upright shrub. H 12ft (4m), S 6ft (2m). Leaves are oval and leathery. Saucer-shaped, semi-double, phlox pink flowers are freely produced in spring.

C. japonica (Common camellia). Evergreen shrub that is very variable in habit, foliage, and floral form. H 30ft x (30ft), S 25ft (8m). Numerous cultivars are available; they are spring-flowering unless otherwise stated.

'Adolphe Audusson' (illus. p.129) is a very reliable, old cultivar that is suitable for all areas and will withstand lower temperatures than most other variants. Produces large, saucer-shaped, semi-double, dark red flowers with prominent yellow stamens. Leaves are broadly lance-shaped and dark green.

'Alba Simplex' (illus. p.128) is bushy in habit with broadly lance-shaped, mid- to yellow-green leaves and cup-shaped, single white flowers in early spring.

'Alexander Hunter' (illus. p.129), an upright, compact shrub, has flattish, single, deep crimson flowers with some petaloids, and lance-shaped, dark green leaves. H10–7.

'Althaeiflora' (illus. p.129) has a vigorous, bushy habit, large, peony-form, dark red flowers. and broadly oval, very dark green leaves.

'Apollo' (syn. *C.j.* 'Paul's Apollo'; illus. p.129) is a vigorous, branching shrub that produces semi-double red flowers sometimes blotched with white. Leaves are glossy, dark green.

'Berenice Boddy' (illus. p.128) is a vigorous shrub that bears semi-double, light pink flowers amid lance-shaped, dark green leaves. H10–7.

'Betty Sheffield Supreme' (illus. p.128) is upright in habit with lance-shaped, midgreen leaves. Irregular double flowers have white petals bordered with shades of rose pink.

'Bob's Tinsie' (illus. p.129) has a dense, upright habit and bears miniature, anemone-form, brilliant red flowers from early to late spring.

'Coquettii' (syn. *C.j.* 'Glen 40'; illus. p.129) is a slow-growing, erect shrub. In early and midspring bears profuse, medium to large, deep red flowers, sometimes formal double, sometimes peony-form. H10–7.

'Donckelaeri' see *C.j.* 'Masayoshi'.

'Elegans' (illus. p.129) has a spreading habit and anemone-form, deep rose pink flowers with central petaloids often variegated white. Leaves are broadly lance-shaped and dark green. H10–7.

'Glen 40' see *C.j.* 'Coquettii'.

'Gloire de Nantes' (illus. p.129) is an upright shrub, becoming bushy with age, that bears flattish to cup-shaped, semi-double, bright rose pink flowers over a long period. Has oval to lance-shaped, glossy, dark green leaves.

'Guilio Nuccio' (illus. p.129) is an upright, free-flowering cultivar that spreads with age. Produces large, cup-shaped, semi-double, rose-red flowers with wavy petals and often a "confused" center of petaloids and golden stamens. Dark green leaves are lance-shaped and occasionally have "fish-tail" tips.

'Hagoromo' (syn. *C.j.* 'Magnoliiflora') has a bushy habit and flattish to cup-shaped, semi-double, blush-pink flowers. Twisted, light green leaves point downward. H10–7.

'Janet Waterhouse' (illus. p.128) is strong-growing and has semi-double white flowers with golden anthers borne amid dark green foliage.

'Julia Drayton' (illus. p.129) has an upright habit and large crimson flowers varying from formal double to rose-form. Dark green leaves are oval to lance-shaped and slightly twisted.

'Jupiter' (illus. p.129) is an upright shrub that bears lance-shaped, dark green leaves and large, saucer-shaped, single, pinkish red flowers with golden stamens.

'Kumasaka' (syn. *C.j.* 'Lady Marion') has an upright habit with narrowly lance-shaped, midgreen leaves. Produces formal double, or occasionally peony-form, deep rose pink flowers. H10–7.

'Lady Marion' see *C.j.* 'Kumasaka'.

'Lady Vansittart' (illus. p.128) is upright, with unusual, hollylike, twisted, midgreen foliage. Saucer-shaped, semi-double white flowers are flushed rose pink; flower color is variable, and often self-colored mutations appear.

'Lavinia Maggi' (illus. p.128) has an upright habit and formal double white flowers striped with pink and carmine. Sometimes sports red flowers.

'Magnoliiflora' see *C.j.* 'Hagoromo'.

'Margaret Davis' (illus. p.128) is a spreading cultivar with oval to lance-shaped, dark green leaves. Has irregular double blooms with ruffled, creamy white petals often lined with pink. Edges of each petal are bright rose-red.

'Masayoshi' (syn. *C.j.* 'Donckelaeri') is slow-growing, bushy and pendulous with saucer-shaped, semi-double, red flowers, often white-marbled. Has lance-shaped, dark green leaves.

'Mathotiana' (illus. p.129) is of spreading habit. Very large, formal double, velvety, dark crimson flowers become purplish with age and in warm climates often have rose-form centers. Leaves are lance-shaped to oval, slightly twisted, and dark green. H10–7.

'Mrs. D.W. Davis' (illus. p.128) is a dense, spreading cultivar that bears very large, pendulous, cup-shaped, semi-double, delicate pink flowers that are backed by oval to lance-shaped, dark green leaves. H10–7.

'Paul's Apollo' see *C.j.* 'Apollo'.

'R.L. Wheeler' (illus. p.129) has a robust, upright growth, large, broadly oval, leathery, very dark green leaves and very large, flattish, anemone-form to semi-double, rose pink flowers with distinctive rings of golden stamens, often including some petaloids.

'Rubescens Major' (illus. p.129) is an upright cultivar, becoming bushy with age, with oval to lance-shaped, dark green leaves. Bears formal double, crimson-veined, rose-red flowers.

'Sieboldii' see *C.j.* 'Tricolor'.

'Tomorrow Park Hill', one of the best of many mutations of 'Tomorrow', is of vigorous, upright habit. Has lance-shaped, midgreen leaves and bears irregular double flowers with deep pink outer petals gradually fading to soft pink centers that are often variegated with white.

'Tomorrow's Dawn' (illus. p.128) is similar to 'Tomorrow Park Hill' but produces pale pink flowers, each with a white border and frequently red-streaked.

'Tricolor' (syn. *C.j.* 'Sieboldii') has bright green, crinkled, hollylike leaves and bears medium, single or semi-double red flowers striped pink and white in early spring.

***C.* 'Leonard Messel'** (illus. p.129). Evergreen, open shrub. H 12ft (4m), S 8ft (2.5m). Has large, oval, leathery, dark green leaves. In spring bears a profusion of large, flattish to cup-shaped, semi-double, rose pink flowers.

C.* x *maliflora. Evergreen, upright, bushy shrub. H 6ft (2m), S 3ft (1m). Has small, lance-shaped, thin-textured, light green leaves and, in spring, produces flattish to cup-shaped, semi-double, pale pink- or white-centered flowers with rose pink margins.

C. nitidissima, syn. *C. chrysantha.* Fast-growing, evergreen, open shrub or tree. H 20ft (6m) or more, S 10ft (3m). Has large, oval, leathery, veined leaves. Small, stalked, cup-shaped, single, clear yellow flowers are produced from leaf axils in spring.

C. oleifera. Evergreen, bushy shrub. H 6ft (2m), S 5ft (1.5m). Leaves are oval and dull green. Has cup-shaped, single white (sometimes pinkish) flowers in early spring. Z6–9 H9–5.

C. reticulata. Evergreen, open, treelike shrub. H 30ft (10m) or more, S 15ft (5m). Has large, oval, leathery leaves; large, saucer-shaped, single, rose pink and salmon-red flowers are borne in spring. **'Arch of Triumph'** (illus. p.129) bears very large, loose peony-form, orange-tinted, crimson-pink flowers. **'Butterfly Wings'** see *C.r.* 'Houye Diechi'. **'Captain Rawes'** (illus. p.129) has a profusion of large, semi-double, carmine-rose blooms. **'Houye Diechi'** (syn. *C.r.* 'Butterfly Wings'; illus. p.129) produces very large, flattish to cup-shaped, semi-double, rose pink flowers with wavy, central petals. **'Mandalay Queen'** (illus. p.129) has large, semi-double, deep rose pink flowers. **'Robert Fortune'** see *C.r.* 'Songzilin'. **'Songzilin'** (syn. *C.r.* 'Robert Fortune') is upright and has large, formal double, deep red flowers.

C. rosiflora. Evergreen, spreading shrub. H and S 3ft (1m). Leaves are oval and dark green. In spring bears small, saucer-shaped, single, rose pink flowers.

C. saluenensis (illus. p.128). Fast-growing, evergreen, bushy shrub. H to 12ft (4m), S to 8ft (2.5m). Has lance-shaped, stiff, dull green leaves. Cup-shaped, single white to rose-red flowers are freely produced in early spring. Some forms may withstand lower temperatures.

C. sasanqua. Fast-growing, evergreen, dense, upright shrub. H 10ft (3m), S 5ft (1.5m). Has lance-shaped, glossy, bright green leaves. In autumn bears a profusion of fragrant, flattish to cup-shaped, single, rarely semi-double white flowers; they may occasionally be pink or red. **'Narumigata'** (illus. p.128) has large, cup-shaped, single white flowers, sometimes pink-flushed. **'Shishigashira'** has small, semi-double to rose-form double, pinkish red flowers.

***C.* 'Satan's Robe'** (illus. p.129). Vigorous, erect shrub. H 10–15ft (3–5m), S 6–10ft (2–3m). Leaves are broadly elliptic, glossy, and dark green, 5–6in (12–16cm) long. From early to late spring produces large, semi-double, bright carmine-red flowers with yellow stamens.

***C.* 'Shirowabisuke'** (illus. p.128). Slow-growing, compact shrub. H 8ft (2.5m), S 5ft (1.5m). Has narrow, mid-green leaves. From midwinter to early spring produces small, single, bell-shaped white flowers.

C. tsai (illus. p.128). Evergreen, bushy shrub. H 12ft (4m), S 10ft (3m). Small, lance-shaped, light green leaves turn bronze with age. Small, cup-shaped, single white flowers are freely produced in spring.

C.* x *vernalis. Fast-growing, evergreen, upright shrub. H to 10ft (3m), S 5ft (1.5m). Has lance-shaped, bright green leaves and, in late winter, fragrant, flattish to cup-shaped, single white, pink, or red flowers. Some forms produce irregular double flowers.

***C.* 'William Hertrich'** (illus. p.129). Strong-growing, evergreen, open shrub. H 15ft (5m), S 10ft (3m). Is free-flowering with large, flattish to cup-shaped, semi-double blooms of a bright cherry red in spring. Petal formation is very irregular, and petals often form a "confused" center with only a few golden stamens. Leaves are large, oval and deep green.

***C.* x *williamsii* 'Bow Bells'** (illus. p.128). Evergreen, upright, spreading shrub. H 12ft (4m), S 8ft (2.5m). Has small, lance-shaped, midgreen leaves and, in early spring, masses of cup-shaped, single, rose pink flowers with deeper pink centers and veins. **'Brigadoon'** (illus. p.128) is a bushy shrub bearing semi-double, rose pink flowers with broad, downward-curving petals. **'Donation'** (illus. p.128) is a compact, upright plant that is very floriferous, with large, cup-shaped, semi-double pink flowers. **'Dream Boat'** (illus. p.128) has a spreading habit and bears medium, formal double, pale purplish pink flowers with incurved petals in midspring. **'E.G. Waterhouse'** (illus. p.128) is an upright, free-flowering cultivar bearing formal double pink flowers among pale green foliage. **'Elizabeth de Rothschild'** is vigorous and upright; cup-shaped, semi-double, rose pink flowers appear among glossy foliage. **'Francis Hanger'** (illus. p.128) has an upright habit and carries single white flowers with gold stamens. **'George Blandford'** (illus. p.129) is spreading and bears semi-double, bright crimson-pink flowers in early spring. **'Golden Spangles'** (illus. p.129) is a cup-shaped, single, deep pink cultivar with unusual variegated foliage, yellowish in centers of leaves with dark green margins. **'J.C. Willams'** (illus. p.128) is of pendulous habit when mature and bears cup-shaped, single pink flowers from early winter to late spring. **'Joan Trehane'** (illus. p.128) has strong, upright growth and large, rose-form double, rose pink flowers. **'Jury's Yellow'** (illus. p.128) is narrow and erect, bearing medium, anemone-form white flowers with centers of yellow petaloids. **'Saint Ewe'** (syn. *C.* x *w.* 'St. Ewe'; illus. p.128) has glossy, light green foliage and funnel-shaped, single, deep pink flowers. **'Water Lily'** (illus. p.129) is an upright, compact cultivar with dark green leaves that bears formal double, midpink flowers with incurving petals in mid to late spring.

CAMPANULA

Bellflower

CAMPANULACEAE

Genus of spring- and summer-flowering annuals, biennials, and perennials, some of which are evergreen. Grows in sun or shade, but delicate flower colors are preserved best in shade. Most forms prefer moist but well-drained soil. Propagate by softwood or basal cuttings in summer or by seed or division in autumn or spring. Is prone to slug attack, and rust may be a problem in autumn.

C. alliariifolia illus. p.275.

C. barbata illus. p.356.

C. betulifolia. Prostrate, slender-stemmed perennial. H ¾in (2cm), S 12in (30cm). In summer, long, branching flower stems each carry a cluster of open bell-shaped, single white to pink flowers, deep pink outside. Leaves are wedge-shaped. Z5–8 H8–5.

***C.* 'Birch Hybrid'** illus. p.382.

C.* x *burghaltii. See *C.* 'Burghaltii'.

***C.* 'Burghaltii'**, syn. *C.* x *burghaltii*, illus. p.286.

C. carpatica. Clump-forming perennial. H 3–4in (8–10cm), S to 12in (30cm). Leafy, branching stems bear

rounded to oval, toothed leaves and, in summer, broadly bell-shaped blue or white flowers. Z4–7 H7–1. **'Bressingham White'** illus. p.373. **'Jewel'** has deep violet flowers. Flowers of **'Turbinata'** (syn. *C.c.* var. *turbinata*) are pale lavender.
C. cochleariifolia, syn. *C. pusilla*, illus. p.383.
C. garganica. Spreading perennial. H 2in (5cm), S 12in (30cm). Has small, ivy-shaped leaves along stems. Clusters of star-shaped, single, pale lavender flowers are produced from leaf axils in summer. Makes an excellent wall or bank plant. Z4–7 H7–1 **'W.H. Paine'** has bright lavender-blue flowers, each with a white eye.
***C.* 'G.F. Wilson'** illus. p.382.
***C. glomerata* 'Superba'** illus. p.251.
C.* x *haylodgensis. See *C.* x *haylodgensis* 'Plena'.
***C.* x *haylodgensis* 'Plena'**, syn. *C.* x *haylodgensis*. Spreading perennial. H 2in (5cm), S 8in (20cm). Has small, heart-shaped leaves and, in summer, bears pomponlike, double, deep lavender-blue flowers. Is suitable for a rock garden or wall. Z5–8 H8–5.
C. isophylla. Evergreen, dwarf, trailing perennial often grown as an annual. H 4in (10cm), S 12in (30cm). In summer, star-shaped blue or white flowers are borne above small, heart-shaped, toothed leaves. Is ideal for a hanging basket. Z13–15 H9–1. **Kristal Hybrids 'Stella Blue'** illus. p.287.
***C.* 'Joe Elliott'.** Mound-forming perennial. H 3in (8cm), S 5in (12cm). In summer, large, funnel-shaped, mid-lavender-blue flowers almost obscure small, heart-shaped, downy, gray-green leaves. Is good for an alpine house, trough, or rock garden. Needs well-drained, alkaline soil. Protect from winter wet. Is prone to slug attack. Z5–8 H8–5.
C. lactiflora. Upright, branching perennial. H 4ft (1.2m), S 2ft (60cm). In summer, slender stems bear racemes of large, nodding, bell-shaped blue, occasionally pink or white flowers. Leaves are narrowly oval. Needs staking in a windy site. Z5–7 H7–5. **'Loddon Anna'** illus. p.227. **'Prichard's Variety'** illus. p.228.
***C. latifolia* 'Brantwood'.** Clump-forming, spreading perennial. H 4ft (1.2m), S 2ft (60cm). Strong stems are clothed with bell-shaped, rich violet-purple flowers in summer. Oval leaves are rough-textured. Z5–7 H7–5.
C. latiloba. Rosette-forming perennial. H 3ft (1m), S 1½ft (45cm). Leaves are oval. Widely cup-shaped flowers, in shades of blue, occasionally white, are borne in summer. Z5–7 H7–5. **'Percy Piper'** has lavender flowers. Z4–8 H8–1.
C. medium (Canterbury bells). Slow-growing, evergreen, erect, clump-forming biennial. Tall cultivars, H 3ft (1m), S 1ft (30cm); dwarf, H 2ft (60cm), S 1ft (30cm). All have lance-shaped, toothed, fresh green leaves. Bell-shaped, single or double flowers, white or in shades of blue and pink, are produced in spring and early summer. Z5–8 H8–5. **'Bells of Holland'** illus. p.331.
C. morettiana. Tuft-forming perennial. H 1in (2.5cm), S 3in (7cm). Leaves are ivy-shaped with fine hairs. Arching flower stems each carry a solitary erect, bell-shaped, violet-blue flower in late spring and early summer. Needs gritty, alkaline soil and a dry but not arid winter climate. Spider mite may be troublesome. Z5–7 H7–5.
C. persicifolia. Rosette-forming, spreading perennial. H 3ft (1m), S 1ft (30cm). In summer, nodding, bell-shaped white or blue flowers are borne above narrowly lance-shaped, bright green leaves. Z3–8 H8–1. **'Fleur de Neige'** has double white flowers. **'Pride of Exmouth'** bears double, powder blue flowers. **'Telham Beauty'** illus. p.253.
C. portenschlagiana illus. p.382.
C. poscharskyana illus. p.381.
C. pulla. Often short-lived perennial that spreads by underground runners. H 1in (2.5cm), S 4in (10cm). Tiny, rounded leaves form ½in (1cm) wide rosettes, each bearing a flower stem with a solitary, pendent, bell-shaped, deep violet flower from late spring to early summer. Is good for a scree or rock garden. Needs gritty, alkaline soil that is not too dry. Slugs may prove troublesome. Z5–7 H7–5.
C. pusilla. See *C. cochleariifolia.*
C. pyramidalis (Chimney bellflower). Erect, branching biennial. H 6ft (2m), S 2ft (60cm). Produces long racemes of star-shaped blue or white flowers in summer. Leaves are heart-shaped. Needs staking. Z6–8 H8–6.
C. raineri. Perennial that spreads by underground runners. H 1½in (4cm), S 3in (8cm). Leaves are oval, toothed, and gray-green. Flower stems each carry a large, upturned, bell-shaped, pale lavender flower in summer. Is suitable for an alpine house or trough that is protected from winter wet. Requires semi-shade. Z5–7 H7–5.
C. trachelium and **'Bernice'** illus. p.252.
C. vidalii. See *Azorina vidalii.*
C. zoysii. Tuft-forming perennial. H 2in (5cm), S 4in (10cm). Has tiny, rounded, glossy green leaves. In summer, flower stems each bear a bottle-shaped lavender flower held horizontally. Needs gritty, alkaline soil. Is difficult to grow and flower well, dislikes winter wet, and is prone to slug attack. Z5–7 H7–5.

CAMPSIS

BIGNONIACEAE

Genus of deciduous, woody-stemmed, root climbers grown for their flowers. Grow in sun in fertile, well-drained soil, and water regularly in summer. Prune in spring. Propagate by semi-ripe cuttings in summer or by layering in winter.
C. chinensis. See *C. grandiflora.*
C. grandiflora, syn. *Bignonia grandiflora*, *Campsis chinensis*, *Tecoma grandiflora* (Chinese trumpet creeper, Chinese trumpet vine). Deciduous, woody-stemmed, root climber. H 22–30ft (7–10m). Leaves have 7 or 9 oval, toothed leaflets, hairless beneath. Drooping clusters of trumpet-shaped, deep orange or red flowers, 2–3in (5–8cm) long, are produced in late summer and autumn. Z7–9 H9–7.
C. radicans, syn. *Bignonia radicans*, *Tecoma radicans* (Trumpet creeper, Trumpet vine). Deciduous, woody-stemmed, root climber. H to 40ft (12m). Leaves of 7–11 oval, toothed leaflets are downy beneath. Small clusters of trumpet-shaped orange, scarlet, or yellow flowers, 2½–3in (6–8cm) long, open in late summer and early autumn. Z5–9 H9–3.
***C.* x *tagliabuana* 'Madame Galen'** illus. p.217.

CANARINA

CAMPANULACEAE

Genus of herbaceous, tuberous, scrambling climbers grown for their flowers. Grow in full light and in any fertile, well-drained soil. Water moderately from early autumn to late spring, then keep dry. Needs tying to a support. Remove dead stems when dormant. Propagate by basal cuttings or seed sown in spring or autumn.
C. campanula. See *C. canariensis.*
C. canariensis, syn. *C. campanula*, illus. p.219.

Candollea cuneiformis. See *Hibbertia cuneiformis.*

CANNA

CANNACEAE

Genus of robust, showy, rhizomatous perennials grown for their striking flowers and ornamental foliage. Is generally used for summer-bedding displays and container growing. Requires a warm, sunny position and organic, moist soil. If grown under cover or for summer bedding, encourage into growth in spring at 61°F (16°C), and store rhizomes in slightly damp soil or peat in winter. Propagate in spring by division or in winter by seed sown at 68°F (20°C) or more.
***C.* 'Assault'.** See *C.* 'Assaut'.
***C.* 'Assaut'**, syn. *C.* 'Assault', illus. p.401.
***C.* 'Black Knight'.** Rhizomatous perennial. H 6ft (1.8m), S 1½–2ft (45–60cm). Thick stems bear broadly lance-shaped, bronze-green leaves. From midsummer to early autumn has large racemes of gladiolus-like, very dark red flowers, 3in (7cm) across, with wavy petals. Z8–11 H12–8.
C. iridiflora illus. p.403.
***C.* 'Lucifer'.** Rhizomatous perennial. H 3ft (1m), S 1½–2ft (45–60cm). Has broadly lance-shaped, midgreen leaves, and profuse racemes of yellow-edged red flowers from midsummer to early autumn. Z8–11 H12–8.

CANTUA

POLEMONIACEAE

Genus of evergreen shrubs grown for their showy flowers in spring. Only one species is in general cultivation and often benefits from being grown against a south- or west-facing wall. Requires full sun and fertile, well-drained soil. Propagate by semi-ripe cuttings in summer.
C. buxifolia, syn. *C. dependens*, illus. p.155.
C. dependens. See *C. buxifolia.*

CAPSICUM

SOLANACEAE

Genus of evergreen shrubs, subshrubs, and short-lived perennials usually grown as annuals. Some species produce edible fruits (e.g. sweet peppers), others small, ornamental ones. Grow in sun and in fertile, well-drained soil. Spray flowers with water to encourage fruit to set. Propagate by seed sown under cover in spring. Spider mite may cause problems.
C. annuum (Ornamental pepper). **'Holiday Cheer'** is a moderately fast-growing, evergreen, bushy perennial grown as an annual. H and S 8–12in (20–30cm). Has oval, midgreen leaves. Bears small, star-shaped white flowers in summer and, in autumn-winter, spherical green fruits maturing to red. Z9–11 H12–1.

CARAGANA

LEGUMINOSAE/PAPILIONACEAE

Genus of deciduous shrubs grown for their foliage and flowers. Needs full sun and fertile but not overly rich, well-drained soil. Propagate species by softwood cuttings in summer or by seed in autumn, and cultivars by softwood or semi-ripe cuttings or budding in summer or by grafting in winter.
C. arborescens. Fast-growing, deciduous, upright shrub. H 20ft (6m), S 12ft (4m). Has spine-tipped, dark green leaves, each composed of 8–12 oblong leaflets. Produces clusters of pealike yellow flowers in late spring. Z2–8 H8–1. Arching **'Lorbergii'**, H 10ft (3m), S 8ft (2.5m), has very narrow leaflets and smaller flowers and is often grown as a tree by top-grafting. **'Nana'** illus. p.157. **'Walker'**, H 1ft (30cm), S 6–10ft (2–3m), is prostrate but is usually top-grafted to form a weeping tree, H 6ft (2m), S 2½ft (75cm).
***C. frutex* 'Globosa'.** Slow-growing, deciduous, upright shrub. H and S 1ft (30cm). Midgreen leaves each have 4 oblong leaflets. Pealike, bright yellow flowers are borne only rarely in late spring. Z2–8 H8–1.

CARALLUMA

ASCLEPIADACEAE

Genus of succulents with 4–6-ribbed, fingerlike, blue-gray or blue-green to

purple stems. Needs sun and extremely well-drained soil. Water sparingly, and only in the growing season. May be difficult to grow. Propagate by seed or stem cuttings in summer.
C. europaea, syn. *Stapelia europaea*. Clump-forming succulent. H 8in (20cm), S 3ft (1m). Rough, 4-angled, erect to procumbent gray stems often arch over and root. Has clusters of small, star-shaped yellow and brownish purple flowers near stem crown from mid- to late summer, then twin-horned gray seed pods. Flowers smell faintly of rotten meat. Is one of the easier species to grow. Z13–15 H12–10.
C. joannis illus. p.475.

CARDAMINE
Bitter cress

BRASSICACEAE/CRUCIFERAE

Genus of spring-flowering annuals and perennials. Some are weeds, but others are suitable for informal and woodland gardens. Requires sun or semi-shade and moist soil. Propagate by seed or division in autumn.
C. enneaphyllos, syn. *Dentaria enneaphyllos*, illus. p.274.
C. pentaphyllos, syn. *Dentaria pentaphyllos*, illus. p.270.
C. pratensis (Cuckoo flower, Lady's smock). **'Flore Pleno'** is a neat, clump-forming perennial. H 18in (45cm), S 12in (30cm). Bears dense sheaves of double lilac flowers in spring. Mid-green leaves are divided into rounded leaflets. May also be propagated by leaf-tip cuttings in midsummer. Prefers moist to wet conditions. Z5–8 H8–5.
C. trifolia illus. p.362.

CARDIOCRINUM

LILIACEAE

Genus of summer-flowering, lilylike bulbs grown for their spectacular flowers. Needs partial shade and deep, organic, moist soil. Plant bulbs just below the soil surface in autumn. Water well in summer and mulch with leaf mold. Provide a deep mulch in winter. After flowering the main bulb dies, but it produces offsets. To produce flowers in up to 5 years, propagate by offsets in autumn; may also be propagated by seed in autumn or winter and will then flower in 7 years.
C. giganteum (Giant lily) illus. p.398. var. ***yunnanense*** is a large, leafy-stemmed bulb. H 5–6ft (1.5–2m), S 2½–3ft (75cm–1m). Has bold, heart-shaped, bronze-green leaves. Fragrant, pendent, trumpet-shaped cream flowers, 6in (15cm) long, with purple-red streaks inside, are borne in long spikes in summer and are followed by decorative seed heads. Z7–9 H9–7.

CARDIOSPERMUM

SAPINDACEAE

Genus of herbaceous or deciduous, shrubby climbers grown mainly for their attractive fruits. Is useful for covering bushes or trellises. Grow in full light and any soil. Propagate by seed in spring.
C. halicacabum (Balloon vine, Heart pea, Heart seed). Deciduous, shrubby, scandent, perennial climber usually grown as an annual or biennial. H to 10ft (3m). Has toothed leaves of 2 oblong leaflets. Inconspicuous whitish flowers are produced in summer, followed by downy, spherical, inflated, 3-angled, light green becoming straw-colored fruits containing black seeds, each with a heart-shaped white spot. Z10–15 H12–1.

CAREX

CYPERACEAE

See also GRASSES, BAMBOOS, RUSHES, and SEDGES.
C. buchananii (Leatherleaf sedge). Evergreen, tuft-forming, perennial sedge. H to 24in (60cm), S 8in (20cm). Very narrow, copper-colored leaves turn red toward base. Solid, triangular stems bear insignificant brown spikelets in summer.
C. elata, syn. *C. stricta* (Tufted sedge). Evergreen, tuft-forming, perennial sedge. H to 3ft (1m), S 6in (15cm). Leaves are somewhat glaucous. Solid, triangular stems bear blackish brown spikelets in summer. Z5–9 H9–3.
'Aurea' illus. p.309.
C. grayi (Mace sedge). Evergreen, tuft-forming, perennial sedge. H to 24in (60cm), S 8in (20cm). Has bright green leaves. Large, female spikelets, borne in summer, mature to pointed, knobby, greenish brown fruits. Z3–8 H8–1.
***C. hachijoensis* 'Evergold'**, syn. *C. oshimensis* 'Evergold', illus. p.309.
C. morrowii of gardens. See *C. oshimensis*.
C. oshimensis, syn. *C. morrowii* of gardens. Evergreen, tuft-forming, perennial sedge. H 8–20in (20–50cm), S 8–10in (20–25cm). Has narrow, mid-green leaves. Solid, triangular stems bear insignificant spikelets in summer. Z4–8 H8–1. **'Evergold'** see *C. hachijoensis* 'Evergold'.
C. pendula illus. p.309.
C. riparia (Greater pond sedge). **'Variegata'** is a vigorous, evergreen, perennial sedge. H 2–3ft (60cm–1m), S indefinite. Has broad, white-striped, midgreen leaves and solid, triangular stems that bear narrow, bristle-tipped, dark brown spikelets in summer.
C. stricta. See *C. elata*.

CARISSA

APOCYNACEAE

Genus of evergreen, spring- to summer-flowering shrubs grown for their flowers and overall appearance. Needs partial shade and well-drained soil. Water containerized specimens moderately, less when temperatures are low. Propagate by seed when ripe or in spring or by semi-ripe cuttings in summer. The seeds are poisonous.
C. grandiflora. See *C. macrocarpa*.
C. macrocarpa, syn. *C. grandiflora* (Natal plum). **'Tuttlei'** illus. p.135.
C. spectabilis. See *Acokanthera oblongifolia*.

CARLINA
Thistle

ASTERACEAE/COMPOSITAE

Genus of annuals, biennials, and perennials grown for their ornamental flower heads. Requires a sunny position and well-drained soil. Propagate by seed: annuals in spring, perennials in autumn.
C. acaulis illus. p.375.

CARMICHAELIA

LEGUMINOSAE/PAPILIONACEAE

Genus of deciduous, usually leafless shrubs grown for their profusion of tiny flowers in summer. Flattened green shoots assume function of leaves. Needs full sun and well-drained soil. Cut out dead wood in spring. Propagate by semi-ripe cuttings in summer or by seed in autumn or spring.
C. arborea, syn. *C. australis*. Deciduous, upright shrub. H 6ft (2m), S 5ft (1.5m). Small clusters of pealike, pale lilac flowers appear from early to midsummer. May need staking when mature. Z9–10 H10–9.
C. australis. See. *C. arborea*.
C. enysii. Deciduous, mound-forming, dense shrub. H and S 1ft (30cm). Shoots are rigid. Pealike violet flowers are borne in midsummer. Is best grown in a rock garden. Z9–10 H10–9.

CARNEGIEA

CACTACEAE

Genus of one species of very slow-growing cactus with thick, 12–24-ribbed, spiny stems. Is unlikely to flower or branch at less than 12ft (4m) high. Requires full sun and very well-drained soil. Propagate by seed in spring or summer.
C. gigantea illus. p.456.

CARPENTERIA

HYDRANGEACEAE/PHILADELPHACEAE

Genus of one species of evergreen, summer-flowering shrub cultivated for its flowers and foliage. Grows well against a south- or west-facing wall, especially where marginally hardy. Prefers full sun and fairly moist but well-drained soil. Propagate by greenwood cuttings in summer or by seed in autumn.
C. californica illus. p.138.

CARPINUS
Hornbeam

CORYLACEAE

Genus of deciduous trees grown for their foliage, autumn color, and clusters of small, winged nuts. Needs sun or semi-shade and fertile, well-drained soil. Propagate species by seed in autumn, cultivars by budding in late summer.
C. betulus (European hornbeam). Deciduous, round-headed tree. H 80ft (25m), S 70ft (20m). Has a fluted trunk and oval, prominently veined, dark green leaves that turn yellow and orange in autumn. Bears green catkins from late spring to autumn, when clusters of winged nuts appear. Z4–8 H8–1. **'Fastigiata'** (syn. *C.b.* 'Pyramidalis'; illus. p.100).
'Pyramidalis' see *C.b.* 'Fastigiata'.
C. caroliniana (American hornbeam, Blue beech). Deciduous, spreading tree with branches that droop at tips. H and S 30ft (10m). Has a fluted, gray trunk, green catkins in spring and oval, bright green leaves that turn orange and red in autumn, when clusters of winged nuts appear. Z3–9 H9–1.
C. tschonoskii. Deciduous, rounded tree of elegant habit, with branches drooping at tips. H and S 40ft (12m). Has oval, sharply toothed, glossy, dark green leaves. Green catkins are carried in spring and clusters of small, winged nuts appear in autumnn. Z6–9 H9–1.
C. turczaninowii. Deciduous, spreading tree of graceful habit. H 40ft (12m), S 30ft (10m). Green catkins are borne in spring. Produces clusters of small, winged nuts in autumn, when small, oval, glossy, deep green leaves turn orange. Z6–9 H9–1.

CARPOBROTUS

AIZOACEAE

Genus of mat-forming succulents with triangular, fleshy, dark green leaves and daisylike flowers. Is excellent for binding sandy soils. Needs full sun and well-drained soil. Propagate by seed or stem cuttings in spring or summer.
C. edulis (Hottentot fig, Kaffir fig). Carpeting succulent. H 6in (15cm), S indefinite. Prostrate, rooting branches bear leaves ⅝in (1.5cm) thick and 5in (12cm) long. Yellow, purple or pink flowers, 5in (12cm) across, open in spring-summer from about noon in sun. Bears edible, figlike brownish fruits in late summer and autumn.

CARRIEREA

FLACOURTIACEAE

Genus of deciduous trees. Only *C. calycina,* grown for its flowers, is in general cultivation. Requires full sun and fertile, well-drained soil. Propagate by softwood cuttings in summer.
C. calycina. Deciduous, spreading tree. H 25ft (8m), S 30ft (10m). Oval, glossy, midgreen leaves set off upright clusters of cup-shaped, creamy white or greenish white flowers borne in early summer. Z13–15 H12–10.

CARYA
Hickory

JUGLANDACEAE

Genus of deciduous trees grown for their stately habit, divided leaves, autumn color, and, in some cases, edible nuts. Has insignificant flowers in spring. Requires sun or semi-shade

and deep, fertile soil. Plant young seedlings in a permanent position during their first year, since older plants resent transplanting. Propagate by seed in autumn.
C. cordiformis (Bitternut, Bitternut hickory). Vigorous, deciduous, spreading tree. H 80ft (25m), S 50ft (15m). Bark is smooth at first, later fissured. Bright yellow, winter leaf buds develop into large, dark green leaves, with usually 7 oval to oblong leaflets; these turn yellow in autumn. Nuts are pear-shaped or rounded, ¾–1½in (2–4cm) long, each with a bitter kernel. Z4–9 H9–1.
C. glabra (Pignut, Pignut hickory). Deciduous, spreading tree. H 80ft (25m), S 70ft (20m). Dark green leaves, with usually 5 narrowly oval leaflets, turn bright yellow and orange in autumn. Pear-shaped or rounded nuts, ¾–1½in (2–4cm) long, each have a bitter kernel. Z5–8 H8–1.
C. ovata illus. p.69.

CARYOPTERIS

VERBENACEAE

Genus of deciduous subshrubs,grown for their foliage and small but freely produced blue flowers. Prefers full sun and light, well-drained soil. Cut back hard in spring. Propagate species by greenwood or semi-ripe cuttings in summer or by seed in autumn; propagate cultivars by cuttings only, in summer.
***C.* x *clandonensis* 'Arthur Simmonds'** illus. p.168. **'Heavenly Blue'** is a deciduous, bushy subshrub. H and S 3ft (1m). Forms an upright, compact mass of lance-shaped, gray-green leaves. Dense clusters of tubular blue to purplish blue flowers with prominent stamens are borne from late summer to autumn. Z6–9 H9–4.
C. incana, syn. *C. mastacanthus*. Deciduous, bushy subshrub. H and S 4ft (1.2m). Bears tubular, violet-blue flowers with prominent stamens amid lance-shaped, gray-green leaves from late summer to early autumn. Z6–9 H9–1.
C. mastacanthus. See *C. incana*.

CASSIA

CAESALPINIACEAE/LEGUMINOSAE

Genus of annuals, perennials, and evergreen or deciduous trees and shrubs grown for their flowers produced mainly from winter to summer. Needs full light and fertile, well-drained soil. Water containerized specimens freely when in full growth, moderately to sparingly in winter. Pruning is tolerated, severe if need be, but trees are best left to grow naturally. Propagate by seed in spring.
C. artemisioides. See *Senna artemisioides*.
C. corymbosa. See *Senna corymbosa*. var. ***plurijuga*** of gardens. See *Senna* x *floribunda*.
C. didymobotrya. See *Senna didymobotrya*.
C. fistula (Golden shower, Indian laburnum, Pudding pipe-tree). Fast-growing, almost deciduous, ovoid tree. H 25–30ft (8–10m), S 12–20ft (4–6m). Has 12–18in (30–45cm) long leaves, each with 4–8 pairs of oval leaflets, coppery when young. In spring produces racemes of small, fragrant, 5-petaled, cup-shaped, bright yellow flowers. Cylindrical, dark brown pods, to 24in (60cm) long, yield cassia pulp. Z11–12 H12–10.
C.* x *floribunda. See *Senna* x *floribunda*.
C. siamea. See *Senna siamea*.

CASSINIA

ASTERACEAE/COMPOSITAE

Genus of evergreen shrubs grown for their foliage and flowers. Where marginally hardy, avoid cold, exposed positions. Needs full sun and fertile, well-drained soil. Propagate by softwood cuttings in summer.
C. fulvida. See *C. leptophylla* subsp. *fulvida*.
C. leptophylla subsp. ***fulvida***, syn. *C. fulvida*. Evergreen, bushy shrub. H and S 6ft (2m). Has yellow shoots, small, oblong, dark green leaves, and, in midsummer, clustered heads of minute white flowers. Is useful as a coastal hedging plant. Z8–9 H9–8. subsp. ***vauvilliersii*** (syn. *C. vauvilliersii*) illus. p.161.
C. vauvilliersii. See *C. leptophylla* subsp. *vauvilliersii*.

CASSIOPE

ERICACEAE

Genus of evergreen, spring-flowering shrubs suitable for walls and for rock gardens. Needs a sheltered, shaded or semi-shaded site and moist, peaty, acidic soil. Propagate by semi-ripe or greenwood cuttings in summer or by seed in autumn or spring.
***C.* 'Edinburgh'** illus. p.346.
C. fastigiata. Evergreen, upright, loose shrub. H 12in (30cm), S 6–8in (15–20cm). In spring, bell-shaped, creamy white flowers resting in green or red calyces are borne on short stalks in leaf axils. Leaves are tiny and scale-like. Needs semi-shade. Z2–6 H6–1.
C. lycopodioides illus. p.363.
C. mertensiana illus. p.364.
***C.* 'Muirhead'** illus. p.346.
C. selaginoides. Evergreen, spreading shrub. H 10in (25cm), S 6in (15cm). Stem is hidden by dense, scalelike, midgreen leaves. Bears solitary relatively large, pendent, bell-shaped white flowers in spring. Needs a shaded site.
C. tetragona. Evergreen, upright shrub. H 4–10in (10–25cm), S 4–6in (10–15cm). Dense, scalelike, dark green leaves conceal branched stems. In spring, leaf axils bear solitary pendent, bell-shaped white flowers in red calyces. Needs a semi-shaded site. Z2–7 H7–1.
C. wardii. Evergreen, upright to spreading, loose shrub. H 6in (15cm), S 8in (20cm). Semi-upright stems are densely clothed with scalelike, dark green leaves that give them a squared appearance. Bell-shaped white flowers, set close to stems, open in spring. Needs shade in all but cool areas. May also be propagated by division of runners in spring. Z4–6 H6–1.

CASTANEA

Chestnut

FAGACEAE

Genus of deciduous, summer-flowering trees and shrubs grown for their foliage, stately habit, flowers, and edible fruits (chestnuts). Requires sun or semi-shade; does particularly well in hot, dry areas. Needs fertile, well-drained soil; grows poorly on shallow, alkaline soil. Propagate species by seed in autumn, cultivars by budding in summer or by grafting in late winter.
C. mollissima (Chinese chestnut). Deciduous, spreading tree with attractive bark. H and S 70ft (20m). Leaves are oblong to oval, midgreen, and up to 8in (20cm) long. Pale yellow, unpleasantly scented flowers appear in early summer. Edible fruit in very prickly husks are produced in fall. Resistant to chestnut blight. Z4–8 H8–1.
C. sativa (Spanish chestnut, Sweet chestnut). Deciduous, spreading tree. H 100ft (30m), S 50ft (15m). Bark becomes spirally ridged with age. Oblong, glossy, dark green leaves turn yellow in autumn. Spikes of small, creamy yellow flowers in summer are followed by edible fruits in rounded, spiny husks. Z5–7 H7–5. **'Albomarginata'** illus. p.65.

CASTANOPSIS

FAGACEAE

Genus of evergreen shrubs and trees grown for their habit and foliage. Flowers are insignificant. Needs a sheltered position in sun or semi-shade and fertile, well-drained but not too dry, acidic soil. Propagate by seed when ripe, in autumn.
C. cuspidata. Evergreen, bushy, spreading shrub or tree with drooping shoots. H and S 25ft (8m) or more. Bears long, oval, slender-tipped, leathery leaves that are glossy, dark green above and bronze beneath. Z9–11 H12–10.

CASTANOSPERMUM

Black bean tree, Moreton Bay chestnut

LEGUMINOSAE/PAPILIONACEAE

Genus of one species of evergreen tree grown for its overall ornamental appearance and for shade. Requires full light and fertile, moisture-retentive but well-drained soil. Water containerized specimens freely when in full growth, moderately at other times. Propagate by seed in spring.
C. australe. Strong-growing, evergreen, rounded tree. H 50ft (15m) or more, S 25ft (8m) or more. Has 18in (45cm) long leaves of 8–17 oval leaflets. Racemes of large, pealike yellow flowers that age to orange and red are produced in autumn, but only on mature trees and are succeeded by cylindrical, reddish brown pods, each 10in (25cm) long, containing large, chestnutlike seeds. Z11 H12–10.

CATALPA

BIGNONIACEAE

Genus of deciduous, summer-flowering trees and shrubs, extremely resistant to urban pollution, grown for their foliage and bell- or trumpet-shaped flowers with frilly lobes. Trees are best grown as isolated specimens. Prefers full sun and does best in hot summers. Needs deep, fertile, well-drained but not too dry soil. Propagate species by seed in autumn, cultivars by softwood cuttings in summer or by budding in late summer.
C. bignonioides (Indian bean tree) illus. p.78. **'Aurea'** is a deciduous, spreading tree. H and S 30ft (10m). Has broadly oval, bright yellow leaves, bronze when young. Bell-shaped white flowers, marked with yellow and purple, appear in summer, followed by long, pendent, cylindrical pods, often persisting after leaf fall. Z5–9 H9–3.
***C.* x *erubescens* 'Purpurea'**. Deciduous, spreading tree. H and S 50ft (15m). Broadly oval or 3-lobed, very dark purple, young leaves mature to dark green. Fragrant, bell-shaped white flowers marked with yellow and purple appear from mid to late summer. Z5–9 H9–5.
C. ovata. Deciduous, spreading tree. H and S 30ft (10m). Bears 3-lobed purplish leaves when young, maturing to pale green. Large clusters of bell-shaped white flowers spotted with red and yellow bloom from mid- to late summer. Z4–8 H8–1.
C. speciosa illus. p.78.

CATANANCHE

Blue cupidone, Cupid's dart

ASTERACEAE/COMPOSITAE

Genus of perennials with daisylike flower heads that may be successfully dried for winter flower arrangements. Needs sun and light, well-drained soil. Propagate by seed in spring or by root cuttings in winter.
***C. caerulea* 'Major'** illus. p.285.

CATHARANTHUS

APOCYNACEAE

Genus of evergreen shrubs grown for their flowers. *C. roseus* is often grown annually from seed or cuttings and used as a summer bedding plant. Needs full light and well-drained soil. Water potted specimens moderately, less when temperatures are low. Prune long or straggly stems in early spring to promote a more bushy habit. Propagate by seed in spring or by greenwood or semi-ripe cuttings in summer.
C. roseus, syn. *Vinca rosea*, illus. p.160.

CATTLEYA

See also ORCHIDS.
C. bowringiana (illus. p.297). Evergreen, epiphytic orchid for a cool greenhouse. H 18in (45cm). In autumn bears large heads of rose-purple-lipped magenta flowers, 3in (8cm) across. Has oval, stiff leaves, 3–4in (8–10cm) long. Grow in semi-shade during summer, and do not spray overhead. Z14–15 H12–6.
***C.* J.A. Carbone** (illus. p.297). Evergreen, epiphytic orchid for an intermediate greenhouse. H 18in (45cm). Large heads of fragrant, pinkish mauve flowers, 4in (10cm) across and each with a yellow-marked, deep pink lip, open in early summer. Has oval, stiff leaves, 4–6in (10–15cm) long. Avoid spraying from above. Z12–15 H12–6.

CAUTLEYA

ZINGIBERACEAE

Genus of summer- and autumn-flowering perennials. Grow in a sunny, wind-free position and in deep, rich, moist but well-drained soil. Propagate by seed or division in spring.
C. spicata illus. p.294.

Cayratia thomsonii. See *Parthenocissus thomsonii.*

CEANOTHUS

RHAMNACEAE

Genus of evergreen or deciduous shrubs and small trees grown for their small but densely clustered, mainly blue flowers. At the edge of their hardiness plant against a south- or west-facing wall. Needs a sheltered site in full sun and light, well-drained soil. Cut dead wood from evergreens in spring and trim their side-shoots after flowering. Cut back shoots of deciduous species to basal framework in early spring. Propagate by semi-ripe cuttings in summer.
***C.* 'Autumnal Blue'** illus. p148.
***C.* 'Blue Mound'.** Evergreen, bushy, dense shrub. H 5ft (1.5m), S 6ft (2m). Forms a mound of oblong, glossy, dark green leaves, covered in late spring with rounded clusters of deep blue flowers. Z9–10 H10–8.
***C.* 'Burkwoodii'.** Evergreen, bushy, dense shrub. H 5ft (1.5m), S 6ft (2m). Has oval, glossy, dark green leaves, downy and gray beneath. Produces dense panicles of bright blue flowers from midsummer to midautumn.
***C.* 'Burtonensis'.** Evergreen, bushy, spreading shrub. H 6ft (2m) or more, S 12ft (4m). Has small, rounded, almost spherical, crinkled leaves that are lustrous and dark green. Small, deep blue flowers appear in clusters, ¾in (2cm) wide, from midspring to early summer. Z9–10 H10–8.
***C.* 'Cascade'.** Vigorous, evergreen, arching shrub. H and S 12ft (4m). Leaves are narrowly oblong, glossy, and dark green. Large panicles of powder blue flowers open in late spring and early summer. Z9–11 H12–9.
***C.* 'Delight'.** Fast-growing, evergreen, bushy shrub. H 10ft (3m), S 15ft (5m). Bears oblong, glossy, deep green leaves. Long clusters of rich blue flowers appear in late spring. Z9–10 H10–9
***C.* x *delileanus* 'Gloire de Versailles'.** See *C.* 'Gloire de Versailles'.
C. dentatus. Evergreen, bushy, dense shrub. H 1 5ft. (5m), S 6ft (2m). Produces small, oblong, glossy, dark green leaves and is covered in late spring with rounded clusters of bright blue flowers. Z9–10 H10–9.
C. dentatus of gardens. See *C.* x *lobbianus.*
***C.* 'Gloire de Versailles'**, syn. *C.* x *delileanus* 'Gloire de Versailles', illus. p.168.
C. gloriosus. Evergreen, prostrate shrub. H 1ft (30cm), S 6ft (2m). Leaves are oval and dark green. Rounded clusters of deep blue or purplish blue flowers appear from mid- to late spring. May suffer from chlorosis on alkaline soils. Z7–9 H9–7.
C. impressus illus. p.145.
C. incanus illus. p.138.
***C.* 'Italian Skies'.** Evergreen, bushy, spreading shrub. H 5ft (1.5m), S 10ft (3m). Has small, oval, glossy, dark green leaves. Produces dense, conical clusters of bright blue flowers during late spring. Z9–10 H10–9.
C.* x *lobbianus, syn. *C. dentatus* of gardens. Evergreen, bushy, dense shrub. H and S 6ft (2m). Rounded clusters of bright deep blue flowers are borne in late spring and early summer amid oval, dark green leaves.
***C.* 'Marie Simon'.** Deciduous, bushy shrub. H and S 5ft (1.5m). Has broadly oval, midgreen leaves. Conical clusters of soft pink flowers are carried in profusion from midsummer to early autumn. Z8–10 H10–8.
C. papillosus. Evergreen, arching shrub. H 10ft (3m), S 15ft (5m). Leaves are narrowly oblong, glossy, dark green and sticky. Produces dense racemes of blue or purplish blue flowers during late spring. Z9–10 H10–9.
***C.* 'Perle Rose'** illus. p.163.
C. rigidus (Monterey ceanothus). Evergreen, bushy shrub of dense, spreading habit. H 4ft (1.2m), S 8ft (2.5m). Bears oblong to rounded, glossy, dark green leaves and, from midspring to early summer, produces rounded clusters of deep purplish blue flowers. Z9–10 H10–9.
***C.* 'Southmead'.** Evergreen, bushy, dense shrub. H and S 5ft (1.5m). Has small, oblong, glossy, dark green leaves. Deep blue flowers are produced in rounded clusters in late spring and early summer. Z9–10 H10–9.
C. thyrsiflorus. Evergreen, bushy shrub or spreading tree. H and S 20ft (6m). Has broadly oval, glossy, midgreen leaves and, in late spring and early summer, bears rounded clusters of pale blue flowers. Z7–11 H10–3. var. ***repens*** illus. p.168.
***C.* 'Trewithen Blue'.** Vigorous, evergreen, bushy, spreading shrub. H 20ft (6m), S 25ft (8m) or more. In spring and early summer, large, pyramidal clusters of rich blue flowers are borne amid broadly oval to rounded, dark green leaves. Z9–10 H10–9.
C.* x *veitchianus. Vigorous, evergreen, bushy shrub. H and S 10ft (3m). Dense, oblong clusters of deep blue flowers are borne in late spring and early summer amid oblong, glossy, dark green leaves. Z9–10 H10–9.

Cedrela sinensis. See *Toona sinensis.*
Cedronella mexicana. See *Agastache mexicana.*

CEDRUS
Cedar

PINACEAE

See also CONIFERS.
C. atlantica, syn. *C. libani* subsp. *atlantica* (Atlas cedar). Conifer that is conical when young, broadening with age. H 50–80ft (15–25m), S 15–30ft (5–10m). Leaves are spirally arranged, needlelike, and dull green or bright blue-gray. Has ovoid cones, males pale brown, females pale green, ripening to brown. Z6–9 H9–6. f. ***fastigiata*** (syn. *C.a.* Fastigiata Group), S 12–15ft (4–5m), has a narrower, more upright habit. f. ***glauca*** (syn. *C.a.* Glauca Group) illus. p.101.
C. deodara (Deodar). Fast-growing conifer, densely conical with weeping tips when young, broader when mature. H 50–80ft (15–25m), S 15–30ft (5–10m). Has spirally arranged, needlelike, gray-green leaves and barrel-shaped, glaucous cones, 3–5in (8–12cm) long, ripening to brown. Z6–9 H9–6. **'Aurea'** illus. p.109.
C. libani (Cedar of Lebanon; illus. p.103). Open conifer with tiered, arching branches. H 80ft (25m), S 50ft (15m). Spirally arranged, needlelike, gray-green foliage is produced in dense, flat layers. Has grayish pink cones. Z6–9 H9–3. subsp. ***atlantica*** see *C. atlantica.* **'Comte de Dijon'**, H 3–6ft (1–2m), S 2–4ft (60cm–1.2m), is a dwarf form that grows only 2in (5cm) per year. Z7–9 H9–7 **'Sargentii'** (illus. p.111), H and S 1–1.5m (3–5ft), has horizontal then weeping branches and makes a bush that is rounded in shape. Z7–9 H9–7.

CEIBA

BOMBACACEAE

Genus of evergreen, semi-evergreen, or deciduous trees grown for their overall appearance and for shade. Requires full light or light shade and fertile, moisture-retentive but well-drained soil. Water potted specimens freely while in full growth, less at other times. Pruning is tolerated if necessary. Propagate by seed in spring or by semi-ripe cuttings in summer.
C. pentandra (Kapok, Silk cotton tree). Fast-growing, semi-evergreen tree with a spine-covered trunk. H and S 80ft (25m) or more. Hand-shaped leaves have 5–9 elliptic leaflets, red when young, becoming midgreen. Bears clusters of 5-petaled white, yellow, or pink flowers in summer, followed by woody brownish seed pods containing silky kapok fiber. Z14–15 H12–10.

CELASTRUS

CELASTRACEAE

Genus of deciduous shrubs and twining climbers grown for their attractive fruits. Most species bear male and female flowers on separate plants, so both sexes must be grown to obtain fruits; hermaphrodite forms of *C. orbiculatus* are available. Grow in any soil and in full or partial shade. Prune in spring to cut out old wood and maintain shape. Propagate by seed in autumn or spring or by semi-ripe cuttings in summer.
C. articulatus. See *C. orbiculatus.*
C. orbiculatus, syn. *C. articulatus* (Oriental bittersweet, Staff vine). Vigorous, deciduous, twining climber. H to 46ft (14m). Has small, rounded, toothed leaves. Clusters of 2–4 small green flowers are produced in summer; tiny, long-lasting, spherical fruits begin green, turn dark in autumn, then split and show yellow insides and red seeds. Z4–8 H8–1.
C. scandens (American bittersweet). Deciduous, twining climber. H to 30ft (10m). Oval leaves are 2–4in (5–10cm) long. Tiny greenish flowers are borne in small clusters in leaf axils in summer. Long-lasting, spherical fruits are produced in bunches, 2–3in (5–8cm) long; each fruit splits to show an orange interior and scarlet seeds. Z3–8 H8–1.

CELMISIA

ASTERACEAE/COMPOSITAE

Genus of evergreen, late spring- and summer-flowering perennials grown for their foliage and daisylike flower heads. Is suitable for rock gardens but may be difficult to grow in hot, dry climates. Needs a sheltered, sunny site and organic, moist but well-drained, sandy, acidic soil. Propagate by division in early summer or by seed when fresh.
C. bellidioides. Evergreen, mat-forming perennial. H ¾in (2cm), S to 6in (15cm). Dark green leaves are rounded and leathery. Bears almost stemless, ½in (1cm) wide, daisylike white flower heads in early summer. Z8–9 H9–8.
C. coriacea of gardens. See

C. semicordata.
C. ramulosa illus. p.374.
C. semicordata, syn. *C. coriacea* of gardens, illus. p.360.
C. traversii. Slow-growing, evergreen, clump-forming perennial. H 6in (15cm), S 8in (20cm). Sword-shaped, dark green leaves have reddish brown margins and cream undersides. In summer carries 2½–3in (6–7cm) wide, daisylike,white flower heads. Is difficult to establish.
C. walkeri, syn. *C. webbiana*, illus. p.350.
C. webbiana. See *C. walkeri.*

CELOSIA

AMARANTHACEAE

Genus of erect perennials grown as annuals. Grows best in a sunny, sheltered position and in fertile, well-drained soil. Propagate by seed sown under cover in spring.
C. argentea. Moderately fast-growing, erect, bushy perennial grown as an annual. H 12–24in (30–60cm), S to 18in (45cm). Has oval to lance-shaped, pale to midgreen leaves and, in summer, silvery white, pyramid-shaped, feathery flower heads, to 4in (10cm) long. Cultivars are available in red, orange, yellow, and cream. H 9–2. Dwarf cultivars, H 12in (30cm), include **'Fairy Fountains'**, illus. p.341, and **Olympia Series**, which has crested, coral-like heads of tightly clustered flowers, 3–5in (8–12cm) across, in colors such as golden yellow, scarlet, light red, deep cerise, and purple.

CELTIS

Hackberry, Nettle tree

ULMACEAE

Genus of deciduous trees, with inconspicuous flowers in spring, grown for their foliage and small fruits. Needs full sun and fertile, well-drained soil. Propagate by seed in autumn.
C. australis illus. p.67.
C. occidentalis (Common hackberry). Deciduous, spreading tree. H and S 70ft (20m). Oval, sharply toothed, glossy, bright green leaves turn yellow in autumn, when they are accompanied by globose, yellowish red then red-purple fruits. Z2–9 H9–1.
C. sinensis. Deciduous, rounded tree. H and S 30ft (10m). Has oval, glossy, dark green leaves with fine teeth, and small, globose orange fruits. Z7–9 H9–7.

CENTAUREA

Knapweed

ASTERACEAE/COMPOSITAE

Genus of annuals and perennials grown for their flower heads that each have a thistlelike center surrounded by a ring of slender ray petals. Requires sun; grows in any well-drained soil, even poor soil. Propagate by seed or division in autumn or spring.
C. cyanus (Bluebottle, Cornflower, Bachelor's buttons). Fast-growing, upright, branching annual. H 1–3ft (30cm–1m), S 1ft (30cm). Has lance-shaped, gray-green leaves and, in summer and early autumn, branching stems with usually double, daisylike flower heads in shades of blue, pink, red, purple, or white. Flowers are excellent for cutting. Tall (blue, illus. p.334; rose, illus. p.322) and dwarf cultivars are available. H7–1. **Baby Series** (dwarf), H to 1ft (30cm), has blue, white, or pink flower heads.
C. dealbata. Erect perennial. H 3ft (1m), S 2ft (60cm). Lilac-purple flower heads are borne freely in summer, one or more to each stem. Has narrowly oval, finely cut, light green leaves. Z3–9 H9–1. **'Steenbergii'**, H 2ft (60cm), has carmine-lilac flowers. Z3–7 H9–1.
***C. hypoleuca* 'John Coutts'** illus. p.279.
C. macrocephala. Robust, clump-forming perennial. H 3ft (1m), S 2ft (60cm). In summer, thick stems bear large yellow flower heads enclosed in papery, silvery brown bracts. Midgreen leaves are narrowly oval and deeply cut. Z3–7 H7–1.
C. montana illus. p.284.
C. moschata. See *Amberboa moschata.*
C. pulcherrima illus. p.244.

CENTRADENIA

MELASTOMATACEAE

Genus of evergreen perennials and shrubs grown for their flowers and foliage. Needs light shade and fertile, well-drained soil. Water containerized plants freely when in full growth, moderately at other times. Tip prune young plants to promote a bushy habit; old plants become straggly unless trimmed each spring. Propagate from early spring to early summer by seed or by softwood or greenwood cuttings. If grown as pot plants, propagate annually.
C. floribunda. Evergreen, loosely rounded, soft-stemmed shrub. H and S to 24in (60cm). Lance-shaped leaves are prominently veined and glossy green above, bluish green beneath. Large, terminal clusters of 4-petaled pink or white flowers develop from pink buds in late winter and spring.

CENTRANTHUS

VALERIANACEAE

Genus of late spring- to autumn-flowering perennials. Requires sun. Thrives in an exposed position and in poor, alkaline soil. Propagate by seed in autumn or spring.
C. ruber illus. p.245.

CEPHALARIA

DIPSACACEAE

Genus of coarse, summer-flowering perennials good for large borders and wild gardens. Prefers sun and well-drained soil. Propagate by division in spring or by seed in autumn.
C. gigantea, syn. *C. tatarica* (Giant scabious, Yellow scabious). Robust, branching perennial. H 6ft (2m), S 4ft (1.2m). In early summer, wiry stems bear pincushion-like heads of primrose yellow flowers well above lance-shaped, deeply cut, dark green leaves. Z3–7 H7–1.
C. tatarica. See *C. gigantea.*

CEPHALOCEREUS

CACTACEAE

Genus of slow-growing, columnar cacti with 20–30-ribbed, green stems. Prefers full sun and extremely well-drained, lime-rich soil. Is prone to rot if overwatered. Propagate by seed in spring or summer.
C. senilis illus. p.460.

CEPHALOPHYLLUM

AIZOACEAE

Genus of clump-forming, bushy succulents with semi-cylindrical to cylindrical green leaves. Flowers are borne after 1 or 2 years. Requires sun and well-drained soil. Propagate by seed in spring or summer.
C. alstonii illus. p.474.
C. pillansii. Clump-forming succulent. H 3in (8cm), S 24in (60cm). Leaves are cylindrical, 2½in (6cm) long, dark green, and covered in darker dots. Short flower stems produce daisylike, red-centered yellow flowers, 2½in (6cm) across, from spring to autumn. Z13–15 H12–10.

CEPHALOTAXUS

CEPHALOTAXACEAE

See also CONIFERS.
C. harringtonii (Cow's-tail pine, Plum yew). Bushy, spreading conifer. H 15ft (5m), S 10ft (3m). Needlelike, flattened leaves are glossy, dark green, grayish beneath, radiating around erect shoots. Bears ovoid, fleshy green fruits that ripen to brown. Z6–9 H9–3.

CERASTIUM

CAROPHYLLACEAE

Genus of annuals and perennials with star-shaped flowers. Some species are useful as groundcovers. Needs sun and well-drained soil. Propagate by division in spring.
C. alpinum (Alpine mouse-ear). Prostrate perennial. H 3in (8cm), S 16in (40cm). Tiny, oval gray leaves cover stems. Flower stems carry solitary ½in (1cm) wide, star-shaped white flowers throughout summer. Z3–7 H7–1.
C. tomentosum illus. p.361.

CERATOPHYLLUM

CERATOPHYLLACEAE

Genus of deciduous, perennial, submerged water plants grown for their foliage. Is suitable for ponds and cold-water aquariums. Prefers an open, sunny position but tolerates shade better than most submerged plants. Propagation occurs naturally when scaly, young shoots or winter buds separate from main plants. Or, take stem cuttings in the growing season.
C. demersum (Hornwort). Deciduous, perennial, spreading, submerged water plant that occasionally floats. S indefinite. Has small, dark green leaves with 3 linear lobes. Does best in a cool-water pond.

CERATOPTERIS

PARKERIACEAE

Genus of deciduous or semi-evergreen, perennial, floating water ferns grown for their attractive foliage. Is suitable for aquariums. Prefers a sunny position. Remove fading fronds regularly. Propagate in summer by division or by buds that develop on the leaves.
C. thalictroides (Water fern). Semi-evergreen, perennial, spreading, floating water fern that sometimes roots and becomes submerged. S indefinite. Lance- or heart-shaped, soft green fronds are wavy-edged. Z13–15 H12–10.

CERATOSTIGMA

PLUMBAGINACEAE

Genus of deciduous, semi-evergreen or evergreen shrubs and perennials grown for their blue flowers and autumn color. Requires a sunny position with well-drained soil. Cut out old, dead wood from shrubs in spring. Propagate shrubs by softwood cuttings in summer, perennials by division in spring.
C. griffithii. Evergreen or semi-evergreen, bushy, dense shrub. H 3ft (1m), S 5ft (1.5m). Spoon-shaped, bristly, purple-edged, dull green leaves redden in autumn. Clusters of tubular, bright blue flowers with spreading petal lobes appear in late summer and autumn. Z8–10 H10–8.
C. plumbaginoides illus. p.360.
C. willmottianum illus. p.173.

CERCIDIPHYLLUM

CERCIDIPHYLLACEAE

Genus of deciduous trees grown for their foliage and often spectacular autumn color. Late frosts may damage young foliage but do not usually cause lasting harm. Requires sun or semi-shade and fertile, moist but well-drained soil. Propagate by seed in autumn.
C. japonicum illus. p.71.

CERCIS

Judas tree, Redbud

LEGUMINOSAE/PAPILIONACEAE

Genus of deciduous shrubs and trees with sometimes shrubby growth, cultivated for their foliage and small, pealike flowers borne profusely in spring. Requires a position in full sun with deep, fertile, well-drained soil. Plant out as young specimens. Resents transplanting. Propagate species by seed sown in autumn, cultivars by budding in summer.

C. canadensis (Eastern redbud). Deciduous, spreading tree or shrub. H and S 30ft (10m). Heart-shaped, dark green leaves turn yellow in autumn. Pealike flowers are magenta in bud, opening to midpink in midspring before leaves emerge. Z4–9 H9–2. **'Forest Pansy'** illus. p.91.
C. siliquastrum illus. p.88.

CEREUS

CACTACEAE

Genus of columnar cacti with spiny stems, most having 4–10 pronounced ribs. Cup-shaped flowers usually open at night. Needs full sun and very well-drained soil. Propagate in spring by seed or, for branching species, by stem cuttings.
C. forbesii. See *C. validus*.
C. peruvianus of gardens. See *C. uruguayanus*.
C. spachianus. See *Echinopsis spachiana*.
C. uruguayanus, syn. *C. peruvianus* of gardens, illus. p.456. **'Monstrosus'** is a columnar cactus. H 15ft (5m), S 12ft (4m). Swollen, occasionally fan-shaped, silvery blue stems bear golden spines on 4–8 (or more) uneven ribs. Unlikely to flower in cultivation. Z11 H12–10
C. validus, syn. *C. forbesii*, illus. p.456.

CERINTHE

BORAGINACEAE

Genus of annuals, biennials, and perennials with somewhat fleshy stems and leaves. Requires a site in full sun, with dry to moist, but well-drained soil. Propagate by seed sown in autumn or spring.
***C. major* 'Purpurascens'** illus. p.331.

CEROPEGIA

ASCLEPIADACEAE

Genus of semi-evergreen, succulent shrubs and subshrubs, most with slender, climbing or pendent stems, grown for their unusual flowers. Needs partial shade and very well-drained soil. Propagate by seed or stem cuttings in spring or summer. *C. woodii* is often used as grafting stock for difficult plants in the Asclepiadaceae.
C. distincta subsp. ***haygarthii.*** See *C. haygarthii*.
C. haygarthii, syn. *C. distincta* subsp. *haygarthii*. Semi-evergreen, climbing, succulent subshrub. H 6ft (2m) or more, S indefinite. Bears oval or rounded, dark green leaves, ½–¾in (1–2cm) long. In summer, produces masses of small white or pinkish white flowers, each with a pitcher-shaped tube, widening toward the top and then united at the tip by purplish spotted petals that form a short stem ending in 5 knobs edged with fine hairs. The whole resembles an insect hovering over a flower. Z12–15 H12–10.
C. linearis subsp. ***woodii***, syn. *C. woodii*, illus. p.462.
C. sandersoniae. See *C. sandersonii*.
C. sandersonii, syn. *C. sandersoniae* (Fountain flower, Parachute plant). Semi-evergreen, scrambling, succulent subshrub. H 6ft (2m), S indefinite. Leaves are triangular to oval, fleshy and ¾in (2cm) long. In summer-autumn has tubular green flowers, 2in (5cm) long, with paler green to white marks; the petals are flared widely at tips to form "parachutes." Z12–15 H12–10.
C. woodii. See *C. linearis* subsp. *woodii*.

CESTRUM

SOLANACEAE

Genus of deciduous or evergreen shrubs and semi-scrambling climbers grown for their showy flowers. Foliage has an unpleasant scent. Requires fertile, well-drained soil. Water containerized specimens freely when in full growth, moderately at other times. Support is needed for scrambling species. Propagate hardy species by softwood cuttings in summer, tender species by seed in spring or by semi-ripe cuttings in summer.
C. aurantiacum. Mainly evergreen semi-scrambler that remains a rounded shrub if cut back annually. H and S to 6ft (2m). Deciduous at low temperatures. Bears oval, bright green leaves. Tubular, bright orange flowers are carried in large, terminal clusters in summer and may be followed by spherical white fruits. Prune annually, cutting out old stems to near base after flowering. Z11–12 H12–10.
C. elegans, syn. *C. purpureum*, illus. p.142.
C. 'Newellii'. Evergreen, arching shrub. H and S 10ft (3m). Bears clusters of tubular crimson flowers in late spring and summer. Leaves are large, broadly lance-shaped and dark green. Z8–11 H12–1.
C. parqui. Deciduous, open shrub. H and S 6ft (2m). Large clusters of tubular, yellowish green flowers, fragrant at night, are borne in profusion in summer amid narrowly lance-shaped, midgreen leaves. Z8–11 H12–8.
C. purpureum. See *C. elegans*.

Ceterach officinarum. See *Asplenium ceterach*.

CHAENOMELES

Flowering quince, Japonica

ROSACEAE

Genus of deciduous, usually thorny, spring-flowering shrubs grown for their showy spring flowers and fragrant fruits produced in autumn and used for preserves. Prefers sun and well-drained soil. On wall-trained shrubs cut back side-shoots after flowering to 2 or 3 buds and shorten shoots growing away from wall during growing season. Propagate species by softwood or greenwood cuttings in summer or by seed in autumn, cultivars by cuttings only in summer. Fireblight and (on alkaline soils) chlorosis are common problems.
C. cathayensis. Deciduous, spreading, open shrub with thorns. H and S 10ft (3m) or more. Produces long, narrow, pointed, midgreen leaves. Small, 5-petaled, pink-flushed white flowers appear from early to midspring, followed by large, egg-shaped, yellow-green fruits. Z7–9 H9–7.
C. japonica (Japanese quince, Japonica). Deciduous, bushy, spreading shrub with thorns. H 3ft (1m), S 6ft (2m). Has oval, midgreen leaves and, in spring, a profusion of 5-petaled red or orange-red flowers, then spherical, yellow fruits. Z5–9 H9–1.
C. speciosa. Vigorous, deciduous, bushy shrub with thorns. H 8ft (2.5m), S 15ft (5m). Leaves are oval, glossy and dark green. Clustered, 5-petaled red flowers are borne from early to midspring and are followed by spherical, greenish yellow fruits. Z5–9 H9–1. **'Moerloosei'** illus. p.130. Flowers of **'Nivalis'** are pure white. **'Simonii'**, H 3ft (1m), S 6ft (2m), bears masses of semi-double, deep red flowers.
***C. x superba* 'Crimson and Gold'.** Deciduous, bushy, dense shrub with thorns. H 3ft (1m), S 6ft (2m). Has oval, glossy, dark green leaves. Bears masses of 5-petaled, deep red flowers with conspicuous, golden yellow anthers in spring, followed by round yellow fruits. Flowers of **'Etna'**, H 5ft (1.5m), S 10ft (3m), are scarlet. **'Knap Hill Scarlet'**, H 5ft (1.5m), S 10ft (3m), produces large, brilliant red flowers. **'Nicoline'** illus. p.156. **'Rowallane'** illus. p.155. All of the above Z5–9 H9–5.

Chamaecereus silvestrii. See *Echinopsis chamaecereus*.

CHAMAEBATIARIA

ROSACEAE

Genus of one species of deciduous shrub grown for its foliage and summer flowers. Needs a sheltered, sunny position and well-drained soil. Propagate by semi-ripe cuttings in summer.
C. millefolium. Deciduous, upright, open shrub. H and S 3ft (1m). Has finely divided, aromatic, gray-green leaves. Shallowly cup-shaped white flowers with yellow stamens are borne in terminal, branching panicles from mid- to late summer. Z6–9 H9–5.

CHAMAECYPARIS

False cypress

CUPRESSACEAE

Contact with the foliage may aggravate skin allergies. See also CONIFERS.
C. lawsoniana (Lawson False cypress). Upright, columnar conifer with branches drooping at tips. H 150–80ft (5–25m), S 10–12ft (3–4m). Bears flattened sprays of scalelike, aromatic, dark green leaves and globular cones, the males brick red, the females insignificant and green. Z5–9 H9–5. **'Columnaris'** illus. p.108. **'Ellwoodii'**, H 10ft (3m), S 5ft (1.5m), is erect with incurved, blue-gray leaves. **'Fletcheri'**, H 15–40ft (5–12m), S 6–10ft (2–3m), has gray leaves that are incurved. **'Gnome'** (illus. p.111), H and S 20in (50cm), is a dwarf, bun-shaped form with blue foliage. **'Green Pillar'** illus. p.107. **'Intertexta'** illus. p.102. c **'Kilmacurragh'**, H 30–50ft (10–15m), S 3ft (1m), has very bright green foliage. **'Lanei'** illus. p.107. **'Minima'** (illus. p.111), H and S 3ft x (3ft), is dwarf and globular and has light green foliage. **'Pembury Blue'** illus. p.105. **'Tamariscifolia'** (syn. *C.l.* Tamariscifolia Group), H 10ft (3m), S 12ft (4m), is a dwarf, spreading form. **'Triomf van Boskoop'**, H 70ft (20m), is broadly columnar, with gray-blue foliage. **'Wisselii'**, H 50ft (15m), S 6–10ft (2–3m), is fast-growing, with erect branches and blue-green leaves.
C. nootkatensis (Nootka False cypress). Almost geometrically conical conifer. H 150ft (5m), S 20ft (6m). Bears long, pendent sprays of scalelike, aromatic, gray-green leaves and globular, hooked, dark blue and green cones that ripen to brown. Z4–7 H7–1. **'Pendula'** has a gaunt crown of arching, weeping foliage.
C. obtusa (Hinoki False cypress). Conical conifer. H 50–70ft (15–20m), S 15ft (5m). Has stringy, red-brown bark and scalelike, aromatic, dark green leaves with bright silver lines at sides and incurving tips. Small, rounded cones ripen to yellow-brown. Z4–8 H8–1. **'Coralliformis'**, H to 20in (50cm), S 3ft (1m), is dwarf, with threadlike shoots. **'Crippsii'** illus. p.109. **'Intermedia'** (illus. p.111), H to 12in (30cm), S 16in (40cm), is a globular, open, dwarf shrub with downward-spreading, light green foliage. **'Kosteri'**, H 3–6ft (1–2m), S 6–10ft (2–3m), forms a sprawling bush with twisted, lustrous foliage. Extremely slow-growing **'Nana'**, eventual H 3ft (1m), S 5–6ft (1.5–2m), makes a flat-topped bush. **'Nana Aurea'** (illus. p.111), H and S 6ft (2m), is a form with golden yellow leaves.**'Nana Gracilis'**, H 6ft (2m), S 5–6ft (1.5–2m), is a form with glossy foliage. **'Nana Pyramidalis'** (illus. p.111), H and S to 2ft (60cm), is a slow-growing, dense, conical, dwarf cultivar with horizontal, cup-shaped leaves. **'Tetragona Aurea'**, H 30ft (10m), S 6–10ft (2–3m), produces golden- or bronze-yellow leaves.
C. pisifera (Sawara False cypress). Conical conifer with horizontal branches. H 50ft (15m), S 15ft (5m). Has ridged, peeling, red-brown bark, scalelike, aromatic, fresh green leaves, white at sides and beneath, and angular, yellow-brown cones. Z4–8 H8–1 . **'Boulevard'** has silver-blue foliage. **'Filifera'** has whiplike, hanging shoots, and dark green foliage. **'Filifera Aurea'** (illus. p.111), H 40ft (12m),

S 10–15ft (3–5m), also has whiplike shoots, but with golden yellow leaves. **'Filifera Nana'**, H 2ft (60cm), S 3ft (1m), is a dwarf form with whiplike branches. **'Nana'**, H and S 20in (50cm), is also dwarf, with dark bluish green foliage. **'Plumosa'** is broadly conical to columnar, with yellowish gray-green leaves. **'Plumosa Rogersii'**, H 6ft (2m), S 3ft (1m), has yellow foliage. Slow-growing **'Squarrosa'**, H to 70ft (20m), has a broad crown and soft, blue-gray foliage.
C. thyoides illus. p.107. **'Andelyensis'** is a slow-growing, conical, dwarf conifer. H 10ft (3m), S 3ft (1m). Has wedge-shaped tufts of scalelike, aromatic, blue-green leaves. Globular cones are glaucous blue-gray. Z3–8 H8–1.

CHAMAECYTISUS

LEGUMINOSAE/PAPILIONACEAE

Genus of evergreen and deciduous trees, shrubs, and subshrubs grown for their pealike flowers. Best in full sun and moderately fertile, well-drained soil. Propagate by seed in autumn or spring or by semi-ripe cuttings in summer.
C. albus. See *Cytisus albus*.
C. demissus, syn. *C. hirsutus* var. *demissus*, *Cytisus demissus*. Slow-growing, deciduous, prostrate shrub. H 3in (8cm), S 8–12in (20–30cm). Densely hairy stems bear tiny, bright green leaves with 3-palmate, obovate leaflets. Produces axillary clusters of 2–4 bright yellow flowers, each with a brown keel, in early summer. Good for a rock garden or trough. Z6–9 H9–6.
C. hirsutus var. ***demissus***. See *C. demissus*.
C. purpureus, syn. *Cytisus purpureus* (Purple broom). Deciduous, arching shrub. H 18in (45cm), S 60cm (24in). Semi-erect stems are clothed with leaves of 3-palmate, obovate leaflets. Clusters of 2–3 pale lilac to purple flowers open in early summer on previous year's wood. Is good for a bank or sunny border. Z6–9 H9–6. f. ***albus*** illus. p.351.
C. supinus, syn. *Cytisus supinus*. Deciduous, bushy, rounded shrub. H and S 3ft (1m). Dense, terminal heads of large yellow flowers are borne from midsummer to autumn amid gray-green leaves with 3-palmate, oblong-elliptic leaflets. Z5–9 H9–5.

CHAMAEDAPHNE

ERICACEAE

Genus of one species of evergreen shrub grown for its white flowers. Needs sun or semi-shade and moist, peaty, acidic soil. Propagate by semi-ripe cuttings in summer.
C. calyculata (Leatherleaf). Evergreen, arching, open shrub. H 2½ft (75cm), S 3ft (1m). Leaves are small, oblong, leathery, and dark green. Leafy racemes of small, urn-shaped flowers appear on slender branches in mid to late spring. Z3–6 H6–1.

CHAMAEDOREA

ARECACEAE/PALMAE

Genus of evergreen palms grown for their overall appearance. Needs shade or semi-shade and organic, well-drained soil. Water containerized plants moderately, less when temperatures are low. Propagate by seed in spring at not less than 77°F (25°C). Spider mite may be troublesome.
C. elegans, syn. *Neanthe bella*, illus. p.152.

CHAMAEMELUM

ASTERACEAE/COMPOSITAE

Genus of evergreen perennials suitable as a groundcover or for a specialized lawn. Flowers may be used to make tea. Needs sun and well-drained soil. Propagate by division in spring or by seed in autumn.
C. nobile, syn. *Anthemis nobilis* (Chamomile). Evergreen, mat-forming, invasive perennial. H 4in (10cm), S 18in (45cm). Has finely divided, aromatic leaves and daisylike heads of white flowers with yellow centers borne in late spring or summer. Z6–9 H9–6. **'Treneague'** is a non-flowering, less invasive cultivar that, requiring less mowing, is easier to maintain.

Chamaenerion. Reclassified as *Epilobium*.
Chamaepericlymenum canadense. See *Cornus canadensis*.

CHAMAEROPS

ARECACEAE/PALMAE

Genus of evergreen palms cultivated for their overall appearance. Needs full light and fertile, well-drained soil. Water containerized plants moderately, less when not in full growth. Propagate by seed in spring at not less than 72°F (22°C) or by suckers in late spring. Spider mite may be a nuisance.
C. humilis illus. p.176.

Chamaespartium sagittale. See *Genista sagittalis*.
Chamaespartium sagittale subsp. ***delphinense.*** See *Genista delphinensis*.

CHAMELAUCIUM

MYRTACEAE

Genus of evergreen shrubs grown for their flowers and overall appearance. Requires full sun and well-drained, sandy, neutral to acidic soil. Water containerized specimens moderately, sparingly when not in full growth. To maintain a more compact habit, cut back flowered stems by half when the last bloom falls. Propagate by seed in spring or by semi-ripe cuttings in summer.
C. uncinatum [pink form] illus. p.150, [white form] illus. p.149.

CHASMANTHE

IRIDACEAE

Genus of corms grown for their showy flowers. Requires a site in full sun or partial shade and well-drained soil, with plenty of water in growing season (late winter and early spring). Reduce watering in summer-autumn. Propagate by division in autumn.
C. aethiopica. Spring- and early summer-flowering corm. H to 32in (80cm), S 15–7in (2–18cm). Has narrowly sword-shaped, erect, basal leaves in a flat fan. Produces a spike of scarlet flowers, all facing one way, with yellow tubes, 2–2½in (5–6cm) long, and hooded, upper lips. Z8–10 H10–8.
C. floribunda. Summer-flowering corm. H to 32in (80cm), S 5–7in (12–18cm). Is similar to *C. aethiopica*, but the leaves are much wider, and the longer orange or scarlet flowers do not all face in the same direction. Z9–10 H10–9.

CHEILANTHES

ADIANTACEAE

Genus of evergreen ferns. Needs full light and organic, well-drained soil. Do not overwater containerized plants or splash water on fronds. Remove fading foliage regularly. Propagate by spores in summer.
C. lanosa of gardens. See *C. tomentosa*.
C. tomentosa, syn. *C. lanosa* of gardens. Evergreen fern. H and S 6–9in (15–23cm). Leaves are triangular or lance-shaped and have much divided, soft green fronds on hairy black stems. Z6–9 H9–6.

Cheiranthus. Reclassified as *Erysimum*.

CHEIRIDOPSIS

AIZOACEAE

Genus of clump-forming succulents with pairs of semi-cylindrical leaves. Needs sun and well-drained soil. Water in autumn to encourage flowers. Propagate by seed or stem cuttings in spring or summer.
C. candidissima. See *C. denticulata*.
C. denticulata, syn. *C. candidissima*. Clump-forming succulent. H 4in (10cm), S 8in (20cm). Has semi-cylindrical, slender, fleshy, blue-gray leaves, each 4in (10cm) long with a flat top, joined in pairs for almost half their length. Bears daisylike, shiny white flowers, to 2½in (6cm) across, in spring. Z9–11 H12–10.
C. purpurata. See *C. purpurea*.
C. purpurea, syn. *C. purpurata*. Carpeting succulent. H 4in (10cm), S 12in (30cm). Has semi-cylindrical, thick, short, glaucous green leaves, each with a flat top. In early spring produces daisylike, purple-pink flowers, 1½in (4cm) across. Z13–15 H12–10.

CHELIDONIUM

Celandine, Greater celandine

PAPAVERACEAE

Genus of one species of perennial that rapidly forms a groundcover. Grows in sun or shade and in any but very wet soil. Propagate by seed or division in autumn. Contact with the sap may cause skin blisters.
C. majus **'Flore Pleno'** illus. p.238.

CHELONE

Turtlehead

SCROPHULARIACEAE

Genus of summer- and autumn-flowering perennials. Needs semi-shade and moist soil. Propagate by soft-tip cuttings in summer or by division or seed in autumn or spring.
C. barbata. See *Penstemon barbatus*.
C. obliqua illus. p.259.

CHIASTOPHYLLUM

CRASSULACEAE

Genus of one species of evergreen perennial grown for its succulent leaves and attractive sprays of small yellow flowers. Thrives in rock crevices. Needs shade and well-drained soil that is not too dry. Propagate by side-shoot cuttings in early summer or by seed in autumn.
C. oppositifolium, syn. *Cotyledon simplicifolia*, illus. p.349.

CHIMONANTHUS

CALYCANTHACEAE

Genus of deciduous or evergreen, winter-flowering shrubs grown for their flowers. At limits of hardiness reduce susceptibility of flowers to frost and cold by training plants against a south- or west-facing wall. Needs full sun and fertile, well-drained soil. Propagate species by seed when ripe (in late spring and early summer), cultivars by softwood cuttings in summer.
C. fragrans. See *C. praecox*.
C. praecox, syn. *C. fragrans* (Wintersweet). Deciduous, bushy shrub. H 8ft (2.5m) or more, S 10ft (3m). Has oval, rough, glossy, dark green leaves. Bears very fragrant, many-petaled, cup-shaped yellow flowers with purple centers on bare branches in mild periods during winter. Z7–9 H9–7. **'Concolor'** (syn. *C.p.* var. *concolor*, *C.p.* 'Luteus', *C.p.* var. *luteus*) has pure yellow flowers.

CHIONANTHUS

OLEACEAE

Genus of deciduous shrubs grown for their profuse white flowers. Flowers more freely in areas with hot summers. Prefers full sun and fertile, well-drained but not too dry soil. Propagate by seed in autumn.
C. retusus (Chinese fringe tree). Deciduous, often treelike, arching shrub. H and S 10ft (3m). From early

to midsummer, star-shaped, pure white flowers appear in large clusters amid oval, bright green leaves. Z5–9 H9–3.
C. virginicus illus. p.119.

CHIONOCHLOA

GRAMINEAE/POACEAE

See also GRASSES, BAMBOOS, RUSHES, and SEDGES.
C. conspicua (Hunangemoho grass). Evergreen, tussock-forming, perennial grass. H 4–5ft (1.2–1.5m), S 3ft (1m). Very long, midgreen leaves are tinged reddish brown. Has thick, arching stems with long, loose, open panicles of cream spikelets in summer. Z7–10 H10–7.

CHIONODOXA

Glory-of-the-snow

HYACINTHACEAE/LILIACEAE

Genus of spring-flowering bulbs related to *Scilla*. Is suitable for rock gardens and for naturalizing under shrubs, in sun or partial shade. Requires well-drained soil, top dressed with leaf mold or compost in autumn. Propagate by seed in autumn or by division in late summer or autumn.
C. forbesii, syn. *C. luciliae* of gardens, *C. siehei*, *C. tmolusii*, illus. p.433. **'Pink Giant'** illus. p.427.
C. gigantea. See *C. luciliae*.
C. luciliae, syn. *C. gigantea*, illus. p.433.
C. luciliae of gardens. See *C. forbesii*.
C. sardensis. Early spring-flowering bulb. H 4–8in (10–20cm), S 1–2in (2.5–5cm). Has 2 narrowly lance-shaped, semi-erect, basal leaves. Leafless stem produces 5–10 flattish, slightly pendent or outward-facing, deep rich blue flowers, ⅝–¾in (1.5–2cm) across and without white eyes. Z3–9 H9–1.
C. siehei. See *C. forbesii*.
C. tmolusii. See *C. forbesii*.

x CHIONOSCILLA

HYACINTHACEAE/LILIACEAE

Hybrid genus (*Chionodoxa* x *Scilla*) of spring-flowering bulbs suitable for rock gardens. Needs full sun or partial shade and organic, well-drained soil. Propagate by division in late summer or autumn.
x ***C. allenii*** illus. p.433.

CHIRITA

GESNERIACEAE

Genus of evergreen perennials or subshrubs grown for their attractive foliage and sometimes their flowers. Requires well-drained soil, a fairly humid atmosphere, and a light position out of direct sunlight. Propagate by tip cuttings in summer or, if available, seed in late winter or spring.
C. lavandulacea illus. p.294.
C. sinensis. Evergreen, stemless, rosetted perennial. H to 6in (15cm), S 10in (25cm) or more. Has oval, almost fleshy leaves, the corrugated, hairy surfaces usually patterned with silver marks. In spring-summer, clusters of tubular lavender flowers are held above leaves. Z14–15 H12–10.

CHLIDANTHUS

AMARYLLIDACEAE

Genus of one species of summer-flowering bulb grown for its showy, funnel-shaped flowers. Needs a sunny site and well-drained soil. Plant in the open in spring. After flowering, if necessary, lift and dry off for winter. Propagate by offsets in spring.
C. fragrans illus. p.436.

CHLOROGALUM

HYACINTHACEAE/LILIACEAE

Genus of summer-flowering bulbs grown more for botanical interest than for floral display. Requires sun and well-drained soil. Propagate by seed in autumn or spring.
C. pomeridianum. Summer-flowering bulb. H to 8ft (2.5m). S 6–8in (15–20cm). Semi-erect, basal leaves are long, narrow, and gray-green with wavy margins. Carries a large, loosely branched head of small, saucer-shaped white flowers, with a central green or purple stripe on each petal, that open after midday.

CHLOROPHYTUM

ANTHERICACEAE/LILIACEAE

Genus of evergreen, stemless perennials with short rhizomes, grown for their foliage. Grow in a light position, away from direct sun, in fertile, well-drained soil. Water freely in growing season but sparingly at other times if pot-grown. Propagate by seed, division, or plantlets (produced on flower stems of some species) at any time except early winter.
C. capense. Evergreen, tufted perennial. H 12in (30cm), S indefinite. Forms rosettes of lance- or strap-shaped, bright green leaves, to 24in (60cm) long. Tiny white flowers in racemes to 24in (60cm) long are borne in summer. Does not produce plantlets. Z13–15 H12–10.
C. capense of gardens. See *C. comosum*.
C. comosum, syn. *C. capense* of gardens (Spider plant). Evergreen, tufted perennial. H 12in (30cm), S indefinite. Very narrow leaves to 18in (45cm) long spread from a rosette. Racemes of many small, star-shaped white flowers are carried on thin stems, 24in (60cm) or more long, at any time. Small rosettes of leaves may appear on flower stems, forming plantlets. Z13–15 H12–10. **'Vittatum'** illus. p.301.

CHOISYA

RUTACEAE

Genus of evergreen shrubs grown for their foliage and flowers. Requires full sun and fertile, well-drained soil. Propagate by semi-ripe cuttings in late summer.
C. ternata (Mexican orange blossom) illus. p.127. **SUNDANCE ('Lich')** is an evergreen, rounded, dense shrub. H and S 8ft (2.5m). Aromatic, glossy, bright yellow leaves each consist of 3 oblong leaflets. Fragrant, star-shaped white flowers are produced in clusters in late spring and often again in autumn. Z8–10 H10–8.

CHORDOSPARTIUM

LEGUMINOSAE/PAPILIONACEAE

Genus of one species of deciduous, almost leafless shrub grown for its habit and flowers. Slender green shoots assume function of leaves. Requires a sheltered, sunny position and fertile, well-drained soil. Propagate by seed in autumn.
C. stevensonii. Deciduous, almost leafless, arching shrub. H 10ft (3m), S 6ft (2m). Produces small, pealike, purplish pink flowers in cylindrical racemes in midsummer. Z9–10 H10–9.

CHORISIA

BOMBACACEAE

Genus of deciduous trees, usually with spine-covered trunks, grown mainly for their flowers in autumn and winter and their overall appearance. Needs full light and well-drained soil. Water containerized specimens freely when in full growth, very little when leafless. Pruning is tolerated if necessary. Propagate by seed in spring. Spider mite may be troublesome.
C. speciosa illus. p.70.

CHORIZEMA

LEGUMINOSAE/PAPILIONACEAE

Genus of evergreen subshrubs, shrubs, and scandent climbers grown mainly for their flowers. Requires full light and organic, well-drained, sandy soil, preferably neutral to acidic. Water potted plants moderately, less when not in full growth. Tie climbers to supports, or grow in hanging baskets. Propagate by seed in spring or by semi-ripe cuttings in summer.
C. ilicifolium illus. p.157.

Chrysalidocarpus lutescens. See *Dypsis lutescens*.

CHRYSANTHEMUM

ASTERACEAE/COMPOSITAE

Genus of annuals, perennials (some of which are evergreen), and evergreen subshrubs grown for their flowers. Each flower head is referred to horticulturally as a flower, even though it does in fact consist of a large number of individual flowers or florets; this horticultural usage has been followed in the descriptions below. Leaves are usually deeply lobed or cut, often feathery, oval to lance-shaped.
Florists' chrysanthemums (nowadays considered to belong to the genus *Dendranthema*) consist of the vast majority of chrysanthemums now cultivated and are perennials grown for garden decoration, cutting, and exhibition. Florists' chrysanthemums (and the other chrysanthemums treated here) generally perform well in Z5–9 H9–1; for extra protection, crowns should be lifted and stored in a frost-free place over winter. Provide a sunny site and reasonably fertile, well-drained soil. Plants grown for exhibition will require regular feeding. Pinch out growing tips to encourage lateral growths on which flowers will be borne, and stake tall plants. Propagate annuals by seed sown in position in spring; thin out, but do not transplant. Propagate perennials by division in autumn, after flowering, or in early spring. Florists' chrysanthemums are best propagated from basal softwood cuttings in spring. Spray regularly to control aphids, plant bugs, spitbugs, earwigs, mildew, and white rust. Other pests and diseases can occur and should be monitored.

Florists' chrysanthemums
Florists' chrysanthemums are grouped according to their widely varying flower forms, approximate flowering season (early, mid- or late autumn), and habit. They are divided into disbudded and non-disbudded types. For descriptions and illustrations of flower forms see feature panel pp.260–61.

Disbudded types – single, anemone, incurved, intermediate, and reflexed – are so called because all buds, except the one that is to flower, are removed from each stem. To produce exhibition flowers, incurved, intermediate, and reflexed chrysanthemums may be restricted to only 2 blooms per plant by removing all except the 2 most vigorous lateral growths. In gardens, allow 4 or 5 blooms per plant to develop. Single and anemone flowers should be reduced to 4–8 blooms per plant for exhibition, according to their vigor, and 10 or more for garden decoration or cutting.

Non-disbudded types – cushion, pompon, and spray chrysanthemums – have several flowers per stem.
Cushion chrysanthemums are dwarf plants that produce hundreds of star-shaped, single flowers, usually 1in (2.5cm) across, densely covering each plant to form a hemispherical to almost spherical head. For exhibition, finish growing in at least 12in (30cm) pots. Plants for indoor decoration are grown in smaller pots and have smaller, though equally dense, heads of blooms.
Pompon chrysanthemums are also dwarf. Each plant has 50 or more dense, spherical or occasionally hemispherical, fully double flowers that have tubular petals (for illustrations see p.261). They are excellent for growing in borders.
Spray chrysanthemums have a variety of flower forms: single, anemone,

intermediate, reflexed, pompon, spoon (in which each straight, tubular floret opens out like a spoon at its tip), quill, and spider. Each plant should be allowed to develop 4 or 5 stems with at least 5 flowers per stem. Grow late-flowering sprays on up to 3 stems per plant. With controlled daylength (to regulate flowering dates for exhibition purposes), late sprays should be allowed to develop at least 12 flowers per stem; without daylength control, 6 or 7 flowers per stem.

Those most suitable for garden decoration are sprays, pompons, and early reflexed chrysanthemums. All are suitable for cutting, except for cushions. Late-flowering chrysanthemums are only suitable for growing under cover since flowers need protection from poor weather; they should be grown in pots and placed in a greenhouse in early autumn, when the flower buds have developed. Intermediate cultivars are also less suitable for garden decoration since florets may collect and retain rain and thus become damaged. Those cultivars suitable for exhibition are noted below. Measurements of flowers given are the greatest normally achieved and may vary considerably depending on growing conditions.

***C.* 'Alison Kirk'** (illus. p.260). Incurved florists' chrysanthemum. H 4ft (1.2m), S 1–2ft (30–60cm). Produces white flowers, to 5–6in (12–15cm) across, in early autumn. Is more suitable for exhibition than for garden use.
***C. alpinum*.** See *Leucanthemopsis alpina*.
***C.* 'Amber Yvonne Arnaud'.** Reflexed florists' chrysanthemum. H 4ft (1.2m), S 2–2½ft (60–75cm). Is a sport of *C.* 'Yvonne Arnaud' with fully reflexed amber flowers in early autumn.
***C.* 'Autumn Days'** (illus. p.261). Intermediate florists' chrysanthemum. H 3½–4ft (1–1.2m), S to 2½ft (75cm). Bears loosely incurving bronze flowers, 5in (12cm) across, in early autumn.
***C.* 'Beacon'** (illus. p.261). Intermediate florists' chrysanthemum. H 4ft (1.2m), S 2ft (60cm). Tender. Bears red, sometimes bronze flowers, to 7in (18cm) wide, in late autumn. Is good for exhibition.
***C.* 'Bill Wade'** (illus. p.260). Intermediate florists' chrysanthemum. H 4½ft (1.35m), S 2ft (60cm). Loosely incurving white flowers, 7–8in (18–20cm) across, are produced in early autumn. Is more suitable for exhibition than for garden use.
***C.* 'Brietner'** (illus. p.260). Reflexed florists' chrysanthemum. H 3½–4ft (1.1–1.2m), S 2½ft (75cm). Fully reflexed pink flowers, to 5in (12cm) wide, appear in early autumn.
***C.* 'Bronze Fairie'** (illus. p.261). Pompon florists' chrysanthemum. H 1–2ft (30–60cm), S 2ft (60cm). Has bronze flowers, 1½in (4cm) across, in early autumn.
***C.* 'Bronze Hedgerow'** (illus. p.261). Single florists' chrysanthemum. H 5ft (1.5m), S 2½–3ft (75cm–1m). Tender. Produces bronze flowers, 5in (12cm) across, in late autumn.
***C.* 'Bronze Yvonne Arnaud'** (illus. p.261). Reflexed florists' chrysanthemum. H 4ft (1.2m), S 2–2½ft (60–75cm). Is a sport of *C.* 'Yvonne Arnaud' with fully reflexed bronze flowers in early autumn.
***C.* 'Buff Margaret'** (illus. p.261). Spray florists' chrysanthemum. H 4ft (1.2m), S to 2½ft (75cm). Has reflexed, pale bronze flowers to 3½in (9cm) wide in early autumn.
***C. carinatum*.** See *Ismelia carinata*.
***C.* 'Chessington'.** Intermediate florists' chrysanthemum. H 6–7ft (2–2.2m), S 2½ft (75cm). Produces fairly tightly incurving white flowers, 7–8in (18–20cm) across, in early autumn. Is more suitable for exhibition than for garden use.
***C.* 'Christina'.** Intermediate florists' chrysanthemum. H 4½–5ft (1.35–1.5m), S 2–2½ft (60–75cm). Bears loosely incurving, white flowers, to 5½in (14cm) wide, in early autumn. Is suitable for exhibition.
***C.* 'Claire Louise'.** Reflexed florists' chrysanthemum. H 4–4½ft (1.2–1.35m), S 2½ft (75cm). Produces fully reflexed bronze flowers, to 6in (15cm) across, in early autumn. Is ideal for exhibition.
***C.* 'Clara Curtis'**, syn. *C. rubellum* 'Clara Curtis', illus. p.259.
***C. coccineum*.** See *Tanacetum coccineum*.
***C. coronarium*.** See *Xanthophthalmum coronarium*.
***C. densum*.** See *Tanacetum densum* subsp. *amani*.
***C.* 'Elsie Prosser'** (illus. p.260). Fully reflexed florists' chrysanthemum. H 4½–5ft (1.3–1.5m), S 1ft (30cm). Tender. Bears pink flowers, 10in (25cm) wide, in late autumn. Is good for exhibition.
***C.* 'Enbee Wedding'** (illus. p.260). Spray florists' chrysanthemum. H 4ft (1.2m), S 2½ft (75cm). Has single, light pink flowers to 3in (8cm) wide in early autumn. Is good for exhibition.
***C.* 'Fairweather'** (illus. p.260). Incurved florists' chrysanthemum. H 3½ft (1.1m), S 2ft (60cm). Tender. Bears pale purplish pink flowers, 5½in (14cm) wide, in late autumn. Is good for exhibition.
***C.* 'Fiona Lynn'.** Reflexed florists' chrysanthemum. H 5ft (1.5m), S 2½ft (75cm). Fully reflexed pink flowers to 8in (20cm) across appear in early autumn. Is ideal for exhibition.
***C. frutescens*.** See *Argyranthemum frutescens*. **'Jamaica Primrose'** see *A.* 'Jamaica Primrose'. **'Mary Wootton'** see *A.* 'Mary Wootton'.
***C.* 'George Griffiths'** (illus. p.261). Reflexed florists' chrysanthemum. H 4–4½ft (1.2–1.35m), S 2½ft (75cm). Produces fully reflexed, deep red flowers to 5½in (14cm) wide in early autumn. Is excellent for exhibition.
***C.* 'Gigantic'** (illus. p.261). Tightly incurved or loosely reflexed florists' chrysanthemum, its form depending on the amount of warmth provided. H 4½ft (1.3m), S 1ft (30cm). Tender. Has salmon-pink flowers, 10–11in (25–27cm) wide, in late autumn. Is good for exhibition.
***C.* 'Ginger Nut'.** Intermediate florists' chrysanthemum. H 4ft (1.2m), S 2–2½ft (60–75cm). Bears tightly incurving, light bronze flowers, to 5½in (14cm) across, occasionally closing at top to form a true incurved flower, in early autumn. Is good for exhibition.
***C.* 'Golden Chalice'** (illus. p.261). Cushion florists' chrysanthemum. H and S 3ft (1m). Tender. Bears single yellow flowers, 1in (2.5cm) wide, in late autumn. Is good for exhibition.
***C.* 'Golden Gigantic'** (illus. p.261). Tightly incurved or loosely reflexed florists' chrysanthemum. H 4½ft (1.3m), S 1ft (30cm). Tender. Produces large gold flowers, 10–11in (25–27cm) wide, in late autumn. Is good for exhibition.
***C.* 'Golden Woolman's Glory'** (illus. p.261). Single florists' chrysanthemum. H 5ft (1.5m), S 3ft (1m). Tender. Golden flowers, to 7in (18cm) across, appear in late autumn. Is excellent for exhibition.
***C.* 'Green Satin'** (illus. p.261). Intermediate florists' chrysanthemum. H 4ft (1.2m), S 2ft (60cm). Tender. Produces loosely incurving, green flowers to 5in (12cm) wide in late autumn.
***C. haradjanii*.** See *Tanacetum haradjanii*.
***C. hosmariense*.** See *Rhodanthemum hosmariense*.
***C.* 'Idris'** (illus. p.261). Incurved florists' chrysanthemum. H 4½ft(1.3m), S 1½ft (45cm). Tender. Has salmon-pink flowers, 8–10in (21–25cm) wide, in late autumn.
***C.* 'John Wingfield'** (illus. p.260). Reflexed florists' chrysanthemum. H 5ft (1.5m), S 1½–2ft (45–60cm). Tender. Produces white, often pink-flushed flowers, 5in (12cm) wide, in late autumn. Is good for exhibition.
***C.* 'Keith Luxford'** (illus. p.260). Incurved florists' chrysanthemum. H 5ft (1.5m), S 1½ft (45cm). Tender. Bears pink flowers, 8–10in (21–25cm) wide, in late autumn. Is good for exhibition.
***C.* 'Lundy'** (illus. p.260). Fully reflexed florists' chrysanthemum. H 5ft (1.5m), S 1½ft (45cm). Tender. Bears white flowers, 8–10in (21–25cm) wide, often broader than they are deep, in late autumn. Is good for exhibition.
***C.* 'Madeleine'** (illus. p.260). Spray florists' chrysanthemum. H 4ft (1.2m), S 2½ft (75cm). Has reflexed pink flowers to 3in (8cm) across in early autumn. Is good for exhibition.
***C.* 'Majestic'** (illus. p.261). Fully reflexed florists' chrysanthemum. H 4½ft (1.3m), S 1½ft (45cm). Tender. Has light bronze flowers, 8–10in (21–25cm) wide, in late autumn. Is good for exhibition.
***C.* 'Maria'** (illus. p.261). Pompon florists' chrysanthemum. H 1½ft (45cm), S 1–2ft (30–60cm). Bears masses of pink flowers, to 1½in (4cm) across, in early autumn.
***C.* 'Marian Gosling'** (illus. p.260). Reflexed florists' chrysanthemum. H 4–4½ft (1.2–1.35m), S 2ft (60cm). Fully reflexed, pale pink flowers, to 5½in (14cm) wide, appear in early autumn. Is good for exhibition.
***C.* 'Marion'** (illus. p.261). Spray florists' chrysanthemum. H 4ft (1.2m), S 2½ft (75cm). Produces reflexed, pale yellow flowers to 3in (8cm) wide from late summer.
***C.* 'Mason's Bronze'.** Single florists' chrysanthemum. H 4½–5ft (1.35–1.5m), S to 3ft (1m). Tender. Has bronze flowers to 5in (12cm) wide in late autumn. Is excellent for exhibition.
C. maximum of gardens. See *Leucanthemum* x *superbum*.
***C.* 'Nancye Furneaux'** (illus. p.261). Reflexed florists' chrysanthemum. H 5ft (1.5m), S 1½ft (45cm). Tender. Has yellow flowers, 8–10in (21–25cm) wide, in late autumn. Is good for exhibition.
***C.* 'Oracle'** (illus. p.261). Intermediate florists' chrysanthemum. H 4ft (1.2m), S 2–2½ft (60–75cm). Produces loosely incurving, pale bronze flowers to 5in (13cm) wide in early autumn. Is useful for exhibition.
***C. parthenium*.** See *Tanacetum parthenium*.
***C.* 'Peach Brietner'** (illus. p.261). Reflexed florists' chrysanthemum. H 3½–4ft (1.1–1.2m), S 2½ft (75cm). Is a sport of *C.* 'Brietner' with fully reflexed, peach-colored flowers.
***C.* 'Pennine Alfie'** (illus. p.261). Spray florists' chrysanthemum. H 4ft (1.2m), S 2–2½ft (60–75cm). Spoon, pale bronze flowers to 2½–3in (6–8cm) wide appear in early autumn. Is suitable for exhibition.
***C.* 'Pennine Flute'** (illus. p.260). Quill florists' chrysanthemum. H 4ft (1.2m), S 2–2½ft (60–75cm). Is similar to *C.* 'Pennine Alfie' but has pink flowers.
***C.* 'Pennine Oriel'** (illus. p.260). Spray florists' chrysanthemum. H 4ft (1.2m), S 2–2½ft (60–75cm). Anemone-centered white flowers to 3½in (9cm) across are produced in early autumn. Is very good for exhibition.
***C.* 'Peter Rowe'.** Incurved florists' chrysanthemum. H 4½ft (1.35m), S 2–2½ft (60–75cm). Produces yellow flowers to 5½in (14cm) across in early autumn. Is ideal for exhibition.
***C.* 'Primrose Fairweather'.** Incurved florists' chrysanthemum. H 3–3½ft (1–1.1m), S to 2½ft (75cm). Produces pale yellow flowers to 5½–6in (14–15cm) wide in late autumn. Is good for exhibition.
***C.* 'Primrose John Hughes'** (illus. p.261). Perfectly incurved florists' chrysanthemum. H 4ft (1.2m), S 2–2½ft (60–75cm). Tender. Bears primrose yellow flowers, 5–5½in (12–14cm) wide, in late autumn. Is good for exhibition.
***C.* 'Primrose West Bromwich'** (illus. p.261). Reflexed florists'

chrysanthemum. H 7ft (2.2m), S 1½–2ft (45–60cm). Fully reflexed, pale yellow flowers to 7in (18cm) or more wide appear in midautumn. Use only for exhibition.
***C.* 'Purple Pennine Wine'** (illus. p.261). Spray florists' chrysanthemum. H 4ft (1.2m), S 2–2½ft 60–75cm. Bears reflexed, purplish red flowers to 3in (8cm) wide in early autumn. Is very good for exhibition.
***C.* 'Ringdove'** (illus. p.260). Cushion florists' chrysanthemum. H and S 3ft (1m). Tender. Has masses of pink flowers, 1in (2.5cm) across, in late autumn. Is excellent for exhibition.
***C.* 'Robeam'** (illus. p.261). Spray florists' chrysanthemum. H 5ft (1.5m), S 2½–3ft (75–100cm). Tender. Produces reflexed yellow flowers to 3in (8cm) wide in late autumn. Is good for exhibition.
***C.* 'Rose Yvonne Arnaud'** (illus. p.261). Reflexed florists' chrysanthemum. H 4ft (1.2m), S 2–2½ft (60–75cm). Is a sport of *C.* 'Yvonne Arnaud', producing fully reflexed red flowers in early autumn.
***C.* 'Roy Coopland'** (illus. p.261). Intermediate to loosely incurved florists' chrysanthemum. H 4½ft (1.3m), S 2ft (60cm). Tender. Produces bronze flowers, 6in (15cm) wide, in late autumn. Is good for exhibition.
***C. rubellum* 'Clara Curtis'.** See *C.* 'Clara Curtis'.
***C.* 'Salmon Fairie'** (illus. p.261). Pompon florists' chrysanthemum. H 1–2ft (30–60cm), S 2ft (60cm). Similar to *C.* 'Bronze Fairie', but with salmon flowers.
***C.* 'Salmon Margaret'** (illus. p.261). Spray florists' chrysanthemum. H 4ft (1.2m), S to 2½ft (75cm). Is similar to *C.* 'Buff Margaret', but has salmon flowers.
***C. segetum*.** See *Xanthophthalmum segetum*.
***C.* 'Senkyo Emiaki'** (illus. p.260). Spider florists' chrysanthemum. H 1–2ft (30–60cm), S to 2ft (60cm). Tender. Bears light pink flowers, 6in (15cm) wide, in early autumn. Is good for exhibition.
***C. serotinum*.** See *Leucanthemella serotina*.
***C.* x *superbum*.** See *Leucanthemum* x *superbum*.
***C. tricolor*.** See *Ismelia carinata*.
***C. uliginosum*.** See *Leucanthemella serotina*.
***C.* 'Venice'.** Reflexed florists' chrysanthemum. H 4ft (1.2m), S 2–2½ft (60–75cm). Reflexed pink flowers to 6in (15cm) wide are produced in early autumn. Is good for exhibition.
***C.* 'Wendy'** (illus. p.261). Spray florists' chrysanthemum. H 4ft (1.2m), S 2–2½ft (60–75cm). Produces reflexed, pale bronze flowers to 3in (8cm) wide in early autumn. Is excellent for exhibition.
***C.* 'Woking Rose'** (illus. p.260). Intermediate florists' chrysanthemum. H 5ft (1.5m), S 1½ft (45cm). Tender. Has rose pink flowers to 8in (21cm) wide in late autumn. Is good for exhibition.
***C.* 'Yellow Brietner'** (illus. p.261). Reflexed florists' chrysanthemum. H 3½–4ft(1.1–1.2m), S 2½ft (75cm). Is a sport of *C.* 'Brietner' with fully reflexed yellow flowers in early autumn.
***C.* 'Yellow John Hughes'** (illus. p.261). Incurved florists' chrysanthemum. H 4ft (1.2m), S 2–2½ft (60–75cm). Tender. Yellow flowers to 5–5½in (12–14cm) wide appear in late autumn. Is excellent for exhibition.
***C.* 'Yvonne Arnaud'** (illus. p.261). Reflexed florists' chrysanthemum. H 4ft (1.2m), S 2–2½ft (60–75cm). Fully reflexed purple flowers to 5in (12cm) wide are produced in early autumn.

CHRYSOGONUM

ASTERACEAE/COMPOSITAE

Genus of one species of summer- to autumn-flowering perennial. Good in a rock garden. Needs partial shade and moist but well-drained, peaty, sandy soil. Propagate by division in spring or by seed when fresh.
C. virginianum illus. p.359.

CHUSQUEA

GRAMINEAE/POACEAE

See also GRASSES, BAMBOOS, RUSHES, and SEDGES.
C. culeou illus. p.308.

CICERBITA,
syn. MULGEDIUM

ASTERACEAE/COMPOSITAE

Genus of perennials grown for their attractive flower heads. Requires shade and damp but well-drained soil. Propagate by division in spring or by seed in autumn. Some species may be invasive.
C. alpina, syn. *Lactuca alpina* (Mountain sow thistle). Branching, upright perennial. H to 6ft (2m), S 2ft (60cm). Midgreen leaves are lobed, with a large, terminal lobe. Elongated panicles of thistlelike, pale blue flower heads are produced in summer. Z5–9 H9–5.
C. bourgaei, syn. *Lactuca bourgaei*. Rampant, erect perennial. H to 6ft (2m), S 2ft (60cm). Leaves are oblong to lance-shaped, toothed, and light green. Many-branched panicles of thistlelike, mauve-blue or purplish blue flower heads appear in summer. Z5–9 H9–5.

CICHORIUM
Chicory

ASTERACEAE/COMPOSITAE

Genus of annuals, biennials, and perennials grown mainly as ornamental plants (*C. intybus* has edible leaves). Needs full sun and well-drained soil. Propagate by seed in autumn or spring. Contact with all parts of the plants may irritate skin or aggravate skin allergies.
C. intybus illus. p.253.

CIMICIFUGA
Bugbane

RANUNCULACEAE

Genus of perennials grown for their flowers, which have an unusual, slightly unpleasant smell. Grow in light shade and moist soil. Needs staking. Propagate by seed when fresh or by division in spring.
C. racemosa*.** Clump-forming perennial. H 1–5ft (30–150cm), S 2ft (60cm). Spikes of bottlebrush-like, pure white flowers are borne in midsummer above broadly oval, divided, fresh green leaves. Z3–8 H12–1. var. ***cordifolia see *C. rubifolia*.
C. rubifolia, syn. *C. racemosa* var. *cordifolia*. Clump-forming perennial. H 5ft (1.5m), S 2ft (60cm). Feathery plumes of star-shaped, creamy white flowers are produced in midsummer above broadly oval to lance-shaped, dissected, light green leaves. Z4–8 H12–1.
C. simplex illus. p.231.
'Elstead' is an upright perennial. H 4ft (1.2m), S 2ft (60cm). Purple stems bear arching racemes of fragrant, bottlebrush-like white flowers in autumn. Has broadly oval to lance-shaped, divided, glossy leaves.
'Prichard's Giant', H 7ft (2.2m), has large, much-divided leaves and produces white flowers on arching panicles.Both Z4–8 H12–1.

Cineraria cruentus of gardens. See *Pericallis* x *hybrida*.
***Cineraria* x *hybridus*.** See *Pericallis* x *hybrida*.

CINNAMOMUM

LAURACEAE

Genus of evergreen trees grown for their foliage and to provide shade. Requires full light or partial shade and fertile, moisture-retentive but well-drained soil. Water containerized specimens freely when in full growth but less at other times. May be pruned if necessary. Propagate by seed in spring or by semi-ripe cuttings in summer.
***C. camphora*.** Moderately fast-growing, evergreen, rounded tree. H and S 40ft (12m) or more. Oval, lustrous, rich green leaves, tinted blue-gray beneath and reddish or coppery when young, are camphor-scented when bruised. Has insignificant flowers in spring. Z8–10 H10–8.

CIONURA

ASCLEPIADACEAE

Genus of one species of deciduous, twining climber grown for its flowers. Grow in any soil and in full sun. Prune after flowering. Propagate by seed in spring or by stem cuttings in late summer or early autumn. Contact with the latex exuded by cut leaves and stems may irritate skin or cause blisters and may cause severe discomfort if ingested.
C. erecta, syn. *Marsdenia erecta*. Deciduous, twining climber. H 10ft (3m) or more. Heart-shaped, grayish green leaves are 1¼–2½in (3–6cm) long. In summer, clusters of fragrant white flowers with 5 spreading petals are borne in leaf axils, followed by 3in (7cm) long fruits, containing many silky seeds, in autumn. Z9–10 H11–10.

CIRSIUM

ASTERACEAE/COMPOSITAE

Genus of annuals, biennials, and perennials. Most species are not cultivated – indeed some are pernicious weeds – but *C. rivulare* has decorative flower heads. Tolerates sun or shade and any but wet soil. Propagate by division in spring or by seed in autumn.
***C. rivulare* 'Atropurpureum'.** Erect perennial. H 4ft (1.2m), S 2ft (60cm). Heads of pincushion-like, deep crimson flowers are borne on erect stems in summer. Leaves are narrowly oval to oblong or lance-shaped and deeply cut, with weakly spiny margins. Z4–8 H8–1.

CISSUS

VITACEAE

Genus of evergreen, woody-stemmed, mainly tendril climbers grown for their attractive foliage. Bears insignificant greenish flowers, mainly in summer. Provide fertile, well-drained soil with semi-shade in summer. Water regularly, less in cold weather. Needs tying to supports. Thin out crowded stems in spring. Propagate by semi-ripe cuttings in summer.
C. antarctica illus. p.220.
***C. bainesii*.** See *Cyphostemma bainesii*.
C. discolor (Rex begonia vine). Moderately vigorous, evergreen, tendril climber with slender, woody stems. H to 10ft (3m). Has oval, pointed leaves, 4–6in (10–15cm) long, that are deep green with silver bands above, maroon beneath. Z11 H12–10.
***C. hypoglauca*.** Evergreen, woody-stemmed, scrambling climber. H 6–10ft (2–3m). Leaves are divided into 4 or 5 oval leaflets that are pale green above and blue-gray beneath. Z13–15 H12–10.
***C. juttae*.** See *Cyphostemma juttae*.
C. rhombifolia, syn. *Rhoicissus rhombifolia*, *R. rhomboidea*, illus. p.220.
C. striata, syn. *Ampelopsis sempervirens*, *Parthenocissus striata*, *Vitis striata* (Ivy of Uruguay, Miniature grape ivy). Fast-growing, evergreen, woody-stemmed, tendril climber. H 30ft (10m) or more. Has leaves of 3–5 oval, serrated, lustrous green leaflets. Mature plants may produce pea-shaped, glossy, black berries in autumn. Z12–15 H12–10.
***C. voinieriana*.** See *Tetrastigma voinierianum*.

CISTUS

Rock rose

CISTACEAE

Genus of evergreen shrubs grown for a succession of freely borne, short-lived, showy flowers. Is good in coastal areas, withstanding sea winds well. Does best in full sun and light, well-drained soil. Resents being transplanted. Cut out any dead wood in spring, but do not prune hard. Propagate species by softwood or greenwood cuttings in summer or by seed in autumn, hybrids and cultivars by cuttings only in summer.

***C.* x *aguilarii* 'Maculatus'** illus. p.159.

C. albidus. Evergreen, bushy shrub. H and S 3ft (1m). Leaves are oblong and white-felted. Saucer-shaped, pale rose pink flowers, each with a central, yellow blotch, open in early summer. Z8–10 H10–8.

C. algarvensis. See *Halimium ocymoides*.

C.* x *corbariensis. See *C.* x *hybridus*.

C. creticus, syn. *C. incanus* subsp. *creticus*, illus. p.165.

C.* x *cyprius illus. p.159.

C.* x *dansereaui, syn. *C.* x *lusitanicus* of gardens. Evergreen, bushy, compact shrub. H and S 3ft (1m). Leaves are narrowly oblong and dark green. Saucer-shaped white flowers, each with a central, deep red blotch, appear from early to midsummer.

C.* x *hybridus, syn. *C.* x *corbariensis*, illus. p.159.

***C. incanus* subsp. *creticus*.** See *C. creticus*.

C. ladanifer, syn. *C. ladaniferus*, illus. p.159.

C. ladaniferus. See *C. ladanifer*.

C. laurifolius. Evergreen, bushy, dense shrub. H and S 6ft (2m). Has oval, aromatic, dark green leaves and, in summer, saucer-shaped white flowers, each with a central yellow blotch. Z8–10 H10–8.

C.* x *lusitanicus of gardens. See *C.* x *dansereaui*.

C. monspeliensis illus. p.159.

C. parviflorus. Evergreen, bushy, dense shrub. H and S 3ft (1m). Small, saucer-shaped, pale pink flowers appear among oval, gray-green leaves in early summer. Z8–10 H10–8.

***C.* 'Peggy Sammons'** illus. p.162.

C.* x *purpureus. Evergreen, bushy, rounded shrub. H and S 3ft (1m). Produces saucer-shaped, deep purplish pink flowers, each blotched with deep red, from early to midsummer. Leaves are narrowly lance-shaped and gray-green. Z9–10 H10–8.

C. revolii of gardens. See x *Halimiocistus sahucii*.

C. salviifolius illus. p.159.

***C.* 'Silver Pink'.** Evergreen, bushy shrub. H 2ft (60cm), S 3ft (1m). Oval, dark green leaves set off large, saucer-shaped, clear pink flowers, each with conspicuous yellow stamens, from early to midsummer. Z8–10 H10–8.

C.* x *skanbergii illus. p.162.

x CITROFORTUNELLA

RUTACEAE

Hybrid genus (*Citrus* x *Fortunella*) of evergreen shrubs and trees grown for their flowers, fruits, and overall appearance. Requires full light and fertile, well-drained but not dry soil. Water containerized specimens freely when in full growth, moderately at other times. Propagate by seed when ripe or by greenwood or semi-ripe cuttings in summer. Whitefly, spider mite, mealy bug, and lime-induced and magnesium-deficiency chlorosis may be troublesome.

x ***C. microcarpa***, syn. x *C. mitis*, *Citrus mitis*, illus. p.151.

x ***C. mitis.*** See x *C. microcarpa*.

Citrus mitis. See x *Citrofortunella microcarpa*.

CLADANTHUS

ASTERACEAE/COMPOSITAE

Genus of one species of annual grown for its fragrant foliage and daisylike flower heads. Grow in sun and in reasonably fertile, very well-drained soil. Deadhead to prolong flowering. Propagate by seed sown outdoors in midspring.

C. arabicus illus. p.337.

CLADRASTIS

LEGUMINOSAE/PAPILIONACEAE

Genus of deciduous, summer-flowering trees grown for their pendent, wisteria-like flower clusters and autumn foliage. Requires full sun and fertile, well-drained soil. Propagate by seed in autumn or by root cuttings in late winter. The wood is brittle: older trees are prone to damage by strong winds.

C. kentukea, syn. *C. lutea*, illus. p.82.

C. lutea. See *C. kentukea*.

CLARKIA,
syn. GODETIA

ONAGRACEAE

Genus of annuals grown for their flowers, which are good for cutting. Grow in sun and in reasonably fertile, well-drained soil. Avoid rich soil, since it encourages vegetative growth at the expense of flowers. Propagate by seed sown outdoors in spring, or in early autumn in mild areas. Botrytis may be troublesome.

C. amoena. Fast-growing annual with upright, thin stems. H to 24in (60cm), S 12in (30cm). Has lance-shaped, mid-green leaves. Spikes of 5-petaled, single or double flowers in shades of lilac to pink are produced in summer. Tall forms, H 24in (60cm), have double flowers in shades of pink or red. H7–1. **Grace Series**, intermediate, H to 20in (50cm), has single, lavender-pink, red, salmon-pink, or pink flowers with contrasting centers. **Princess Series**, dwarf, H 12in (30cm), has frilled flowers in shades of pink, including salmon (illus. p.341). **Satin Series**, dwarf, H to 8in (20cm), has single flowers in various colors, many with white margins or contrasting centers. **'Sybil Sherwood'** illus. p.324.

***C.* 'Brilliant'** illus. p.324.

CLAYTONIA

PORTULACACEAE

Genus of mainly evergreen perennials with succulent leaves; is related to *Lewisia*. Grows best in alpine houses. Tolerates sun or shade and prefers well-drained soil. Propagate by seed or division in autumn. May be difficult to grow.

C. megarhiza, syn. *Calandrinia megarhiza*. Evergreen, basal-rosetted perennial with a long taproot. H ½in (1cm), S 3in (8cm). Leaves are spoon-shaped and fleshy. Bears small heads of tiny, bowl-shaped white flowers in spring. Prefers sun and gritty soil. Is prone to aphid attack. Z5–7 H7–5. var. ***nivalis*** illus. p.366.

C. virginica (Spring beauty). Clump-forming perennial with flat, black tubers. H 4in (10cm), S 8in (20cm) or more. Narrowly spoon-shaped leaves, reddish when young, later turn green and glossy. Branched stems bear cup-shaped white or pink flowers, striped deep pink, in early spring. Needs shade. Z4–9 H6–1.

CLEISTOCACTUS,
syn. BORZICACTUS

CACTACEAE

Genus of columnar cacti with branched, cylindrical, much-ribbed stems with spines. Is one of the faster-growing cacti, some reaching 6ft (2m) in 5 years or less. Tubular flowers contain plenty of nectar and are pollinated by hummingbirds. Needs full sun and very well-drained soil. Propagate by seed or stem cuttings in spring or summer.

C. baumannii. Erect then prostrate cactus. H 3ft (1m) or more, S 15ft (5m). Thick stems produce long, uneven, variable-colored spines. Has S-shaped, tubular, bright orange-red flowers in spring-summer. Z13–15 H12-10.

C. celsianus. See *Oreocereus celsianus*.

C. smaragdiflorus. Erect, then prostrate cactus. H 5ft (1.5m), S 20ft (6m). Similar to *C. baumannii*, but it has straight, tubular flowers with green-tipped petals. Z13–15 H12–10.

C. strausii illus. p.459.

C. trollii. See *Oreocereus trollii*.

CLEMATIS

Old man's beard, Travelers' joy

RANUNCULACEAE

Genus of evergreen or deciduous, mainly twining climbers and herbaceous perennials cultivated for their mass of flowers, often followed by decorative seed heads, and grown on walls and trellises and together with trees, shrubs, and other host plants. Only early-flowering species are evergreen, although some later-flowering species are semi-evergreen. Most species have nodding, bell-shaped flowers, with 4 petals (botanically known as perianth segments), or flattish flowers, each usually with 4–6 generally pointed petals. Large-flowered cultivars also bear flattish flowers, but with 4–10 petals. May be grown in partial shade or full sun, but prefers rich, well-drained soil with roots shaded. Propagate cultivars in early summer by softwood or semi-ripe cuttings or layering, species from seed sown in autumn. Aphids, mildew, and clematis wilt may cause problems.

Clematis may be divided into groups according to their approximate flowering seasons, habit, and pruning needs. See also feature panel pp.212–13.

Group 1

Early-flowering species preferring a sheltered, sunny site with well-drained soil. Small, single flowers, either bell-shaped or open-bell-shaped, ¾–2in (2–5cm) long, or saucer-shaped, 1½–2in (4–5cm) across, are borne on the previous season's shoots in spring or, occasionally, in late winter. Leaves are evergreen and glossy, or deciduous, and usually divided into 3 lance-shaped, 5in (12cm) long leaflets or into 3 fernlike, 2in (5cm) long leaflets.

***C. alpina*, *C. macropetala*, and their cultivars** tolerate cold, exposed positions. Small, bell-shaped to open bell-shaped, single, semi-double, or double flowers, 1¼–3in (3–7cm) across, are borne on the previous season's shoots in spring, occasionally also on the current season's shoots in summer. Deciduous, pale to midgreen leaves are divided into 3–5 lance-shaped to broadly oblong, toothed leaflets, 1¼in (3cm) long.

***C. montana* and its cultivars** are vigorous, deciduous climbers suitable for growing over large buildings and trees. Small, flat to saucer-shaped, usually single flowers, 2–3in (5–7cm) across, are borne on the previous season's shoots in late spring. Leaves are mid- to purplish green and divided into 3 lance-shaped to broadly oval, serrated leaflets, 3in (8cm) long with pointed tips.

Prune all group 1 clematis after flowering to allow new growth to be produced and ripened for the following season. Remove dead or damaged stems and cut back other shoots that have outgrown their allotted space. This will encourage production of new growth to bear flowers in the following season.

Group 2

Early- to midseason, large-flowered cultivars bearing mostly saucer-shaped, single, semi-double, or fully double flowers, 4–8in (10–20cm) across, that are borne on the previous season's shoots, in late spring and early summer, and on new shoots in mid- and

CLEMATIS

late summer. Generally the second flush of flowers on semi-double and double forms produces single flowers. Deciduous, pale to mid-green leaves are usually 4–6in (10–15cm) long and divided into 3 ovate or lance-shaped leaflets, or are simple and ovate and to 4in (10cm) long.

Prune before new growth starts in early spring. Remove any dead or damaged stems and cut back all remaining shoots to where strong buds are visible. These buds provide a framework of second-year shoots which, in turn, produce sideshoots that flower in late spring and early summer. The flowers may then be removed. Young shoots bear more flowers later in the summer.

Group 3
Late, large-flowered cultivars producing outward-facing, usually saucer-shaped, single flowers, 3–6in (7–15cm) across, borne on new shoots in summer or early autumn. Leaves are deciduous and similar to those of early cultivars (group 2), described above. **Late-flowering species** and **small-flowered cultivars** that bear small, single or double flowers on the current season's shoots in summer-autumn. Flowers vary in shape and may be star-shaped, tubular, bell-shaped, flattish, or resembling nodding lanterns; they vary in size from ½in (1cm) to 4in (10cm) across. Have generally deciduous, pale to dark green or gray-green leaves divided into 3 lance-shaped to broadly oval leaflets, each ½in (1cm) long, or hairy and/or toothed leaves divided into 5 or more lance-shaped to broadly oval leaflets, each ½–4in (1–10cm) long. **Herbaceous species and cultivars** producing single flowers that are either saucer-shaped, ½–¾in (1–2cm) wide, or bell-shaped or tubular, ½–1½in (1–4cm) long, and are produced on the current season's shoots in summer. Mid- to dark green or gray-green leaves are simple and lance-shaped to elliptic, 1–6in (2.5–15cm) long, or are divided into 3–5 lance-shaped to ovate, serrated leaflets, each 4–6in (10–15cm) long with a pointed tip.

Prune all group 3 clematis before new growth begins, in early spring. Cut back all the previous season's stems to a pair of strong buds, 15–20cm (6–8in) above soil level.

The following clematis spread about 3 ft (1m) unless otherwise noted.

***C.* 'Abundance'**, syn. *C. viticella* 'Abundance' (illus. p.213). Late-flowering clematis (group 3). H 6–10ft (2–3m). Produces flattish, deep purplish red flowers, 2in (5cm) across, with cream anthers, in summer. Z5–9 H9–5.
***C.* 'Aljonushka'.** Semi-herbaceous, non-clinging clematis (group 3). H 3–4ft (1–1.2m). In midsummer to early autumn produces single, rich mauvish pink flowers, 2½–3in (6–8cm) wide, with a satin sheen when young, with deep ridges on the reverse, and crumpled edges; the petal tips recurve and twist as they age. Z5-9 H9–5.
C. alpina. Alpina clematis (group 1). H 6–10ft (2–3m), S 5ft (1.5m). Has lantern-shaped, single blue flowers, 1½–3in (4–7cm) long, in spring and, occasionally, summer. Forms attractive, fluffy, silvery seed heads in summer. Is ideal for a north-facing or very exposed site. Z6–9 H9–6. **'Columbine'** has 2in (5cm) long, pale blue petals. **'Constance'** has semi-double, deep purplish pink flowers. **'Frances Rivis'** (illus. p.213) is free-flowering, with slightly twisted, 3in (7cm) long, midblue petals. **'Frankie'** has light to midblue flowers with cream petaloid stamens tipped pale blue.
***C.* Anna Louise** ('Evithree') (illus. p.213). Compact, early, large-flowered clematis (group 2). H 3–4ft (1-1.2m). Freely produces single flowers with violet petals with a contrasting red-purple central bar and striking brown anthers in late spring to early summer, and again in late summer to early autumn. Z4–9 H9–1.
***C.* Arctic Queen** ('Evitwo') (illus. p.212). Early, large-flowered clematis (group 2). H 10ft (3m). From early summer to early autumn it freely produces double, clear creamy white flowers, 4–7in (10–18cm) across, with yellow anthers. Z7–9 H9–7.
C. armandii (illus. p.212). Strong-growing, evergreen, early-flowering clematis (group 1). H 10–15ft (3–5m), S 6–10ft (2–3m). Bears scented, flattish, single white flowers, 1½in (4cm) across, in early spring. May benefit from a sheltered, south- or south-west-facing site. Z7–9 H9–7.
***C.* 'Ascotiensis'** (illus. p.213). Vigorous, late, large-flowered clematis (group 3). H 10–12ft (3–4m). Single, bright violet-blue flowers, 3½–5in (9–12cm) across, with pointed petals and brownish green anthers, are produced in summer. Z4–9 H9–1.
***C.* 'Bees Jubilee'.** Compact, early, large-flowered clematis (group 2). H 8ft (2.5m). In early summer bears a profusion of single, deep pink flowers, 4–5in (10–12cm) across, with brown anthers and a central, rose madder stripe on each petal. Prefers partial shade. Z4–9 H9–1.
***C.* 'Bill MacKenzie'** (illus. p.213). Vigorous, late-flowering clematis (group 3). H 22ft (7m), S 10–12ft (3–4m). Has dark green leaves. Flowers are yellow and 2½–3in (6–7cm) wide. Z6–9 H9–6.
***C.* Blue Moon ('Evirin')** (illus. p.213). Compact, free-flowering, early, large-flowered clematis (group 2). H 8–10ft (2–3m). Bears single white flowers, 6–7in (15–18cm) wide, suffused with pale lilac becoming darker at the wavy petal edges, in late spring to early summer. In late summer to early autumn, flowers are slightly smaller and darker. Z7–9 H9–7.
C. calycina. See *C. cirrhosa*.
***C.* 'Carnaby'.** Compact, early, large-flowered clematis (group 2). H 8ft (2.5m). In early summer has a profusion of single, deep pink flowers, 8–10cm (3–4in) across, with a darker stripe on each petal and red anthers. Prefers partial shade. Z4–9 H9–5.
***C.* 'Charissima'.** Free-flowering, early, large-flowered clematis (group 2). H 8–10ft (2–3m). In late spring to early summer produces single flowers, 6–7in (15–18cm) across, with pointed, cerise-pink petals, a deeper pink bar and veins throughout the flower, and dark maroon anthers. Z7–9 H9–7.
C. cirrhosa, syn. *C. calycina* (illus. p.213). Evergreen, early-flowering clematis (group 1). H 6–10ft (2–3m), S 3–6ft (1–2m). Produces bell-shaped, cream flowers, 1¼in (3cm) across and spotted red inside, in late winter and early spring during frost-free weather. Z7–9 H9–7.
***C.* 'Comtesse de Bouchaud'.** Strong-growing, late, large-flowered clematis (group 3). H 6–10ft (2–3m). In summer has masses of single, bright mauve-pink flowers, 3–4in (8–10cm) across, with yellow anthers. Z4–9 H9–1.
***C.* 'Daniel Deronda'.** Vigorous, early, large-flowered clematis (group 2). H 10ft (3m). Has double and semi-double, deep purple-blue flowers, 4–5½in (10–14cm) across, with cream anthers, then single flowers in late summer. Z7–9 H9–7.
***C.* 'Doctor Ruppel'.** Early, large-flowered clematis (group 2). H 8ft (2.5m). Single flowers, 4–6in (10–15cm) across, with deep rose pink petals with darker central bands and light chocolate anthers, are freely produced throughout summer. Z4–8 H8–1.
***C.* 'Duchess of Albany'** (illus. p.213). Vigorous, small-flowered clematis (group 3). H 8ft (2.5m). In summer and early autumn has masses of small, tuliplike, single, soft pink flowers, 2½in (6cm) long, with brown anthers and a deeper pink stripe inside each petal. Z4–9 H9–1.
***C.* 'Duchess of Edinburgh'.** Early, large-flowered clematis (group 2). H 6–10ft (2–3m). In summer produces double white flowers, 3–4in (8–10cm) across, with yellow anthers and green outer petals. May be weak-growing. Z4–9 H9–1.
***C.* x *durandii*.** Semi-herbaceous, late-flowering clematis (group 3). H 3–6ft (1–2m), S 1½–5ft (45cm–1.5m). In summer has flattish, single, deep blue flowers, 2½–3in (6–8cm) across, with 4 petals and yellow anthers. Leaves are elliptic. Z4–9 H9–5.
***C.* 'Elsa Spath'** (illus. p.213). Early, large-flowered clematis (group 2). H 6–10ft (2–3m). Bears masses of single, 5in (12cm) wide flowers, with overlapping, rich mauve-blue petals and red anthers throughout summer. Z4–9 H9–1.
***C.* 'Ernest Markham'** (illus. p.213). Vigorous, late, large-flowered clematis (group 3). H 10–12ft (3–4m). In summer bears 10cm (4in) wide, single flowers with blunt-tipped, vivid magenta petals and chocolate anthers. Thrives in full sun. Z4–9 H9–1.
***C.* 'Etoile Violette'**, syn. *C. viticella* 'Etoile Violette' (illus. p.213). Vigorous, late-flowering clematis (group 3). H 10–15ft (3–5m), S 5ft (1.5m). Produces masses of flattish, single, violet-purple flowers, 1½–2½in (4–6cm) wide, with yellow anthers, in summer. Z4–9 H9–1.
***C.* 'Evifour'.** See *C.* Royal Velvet.
***C.* 'Evirin'.** See *C.* Blue Moon.
***C.* 'Evisix'.** See *C.* Petit Faucon.
***C.* 'Evithree'.** See *C.* Anna Louise.
***C.* 'Evitwo'.** See *C.* Arctic Queen.
C. flammula (illus. p.212). Vigorous, late-flowering clematis; may be semi-evergreen (group 3). H 10–15ft (3–5m), S 6ft (2m). Produces masses of almond-scented, flattish, single white flowers, ¾in (2cm) across, in summer and early autumn. Z7–9 H9–7.
***C. florida* 'Sieboldii'**, syn. *C. florida* 'Bicolor' (illus. p.212). Weak-growing, small-flowered clematis (group 3). H 6–10ft (2–3m). In summer has passionflower-like, single blooms, each 3in (8cm) wide with creamy white petals and a domed boss of petal-like, rich purple stamens. Needs a sheltered aspect. Z6–9 H9–6.
***C.* 'Général Sikorski'.** Early, large-flowered clematis (group 2). H 10ft (3m). Has numerous 4in (10cm) wide, single flowers with large, overlapping blue petals and cream anthers in summer. Z4–9 H9–1.
***C.* 'Gipsy Queen'.** Vigorous, late, large-flowered clematis (group 3). H 10ft (3m). Bears single, 4in (10cm) wide flowers with velvety, violet-purple petals and red anthers in summer. Z4–9 H9–1.
***C.* 'Gravetye Beauty'** (illus. p.213). Vigorous, small-flowered clematis (group 3). H 8ft (2.5m). In summer and early autumn has masses of small, tuliplike, single, bright red flowers, 2½in (6cm) long, with brown anthers. Is similar to *C.* 'Duchess of Albany', but flowers are more open. Z5–9 H9–5.
***C.* 'Guernsey Cream'.** Early, large-flowered clematis (group 2). H 8ft (2.5m). Bears single flowers, 5in (12cm) across, with creamy yellow petals and anthers in early summer. Flowers are smaller and creamy white in late summer. Fades in full sun. Z5–9 H9–5.
***C.* 'Hagley Hybrid'** (illus. p.212). Vigorous, late, large-flowered clematis (group 3). H 8ft (2.5m). Produces 3–4in (8–10cm) wide, single flowers with boat-shaped, rose-mauve petals and red anthers in summer. Prefers partial shade. Z4–9 H9–1.
***C.* 'Henryi'** (illus. p.212). Vigorous, early, large-flowered clematis (group 2). H 10ft (3m). Has 5in (12cm) wide, single flowers with white petals and dark chocolate anthers in summer. Z4–9 H9–1.
***C. heracleifolia* var. *davidiana*.** Herbaceous clematis (group 3). H 3ft

(1m), S 2½ft (75cm). In summer, thick stems bear axillary clusters of scented, tubular, single, pale blue flowers, ¾–1¼in (2–3cm) long, with reflexed petal tips. **'Wyevale'** (illus. p.213) has strongly scented, dark blue flowers. Z3–8 H8–1.
***C.* 'H.F. Young'** (illus. p.213). Compact, early, large-flowered clematis (group 2). H 8ft (2.5m). Bears 4in (10cm) wide, single flowers with violet-tinged blue petals and cream anthers in summer. Is ideal for a container or patio garden. Z4–9 H9–1.
***C.* 'Huldine'** (illus. p.212). Very vigorous, late, large-flowered clematis (group 3). H 10–12ft (3–4m), S 6ft (2m). In summer has 2½in (6cm) wide, single white flowers, mauve beneath and with cream anthers. Is ideal for an archway or pergola. Z4–9 H9–1.
C. integrifolia (illus. p.213). Herbaceous clematis (group 3). H and S 30in (75cm). Leaves are narrowly lance-shaped. In summer bears bell-shaped, single, deep blue flowers, 1¼in (3cm) long, with cream anthers, followed by attractive, gray-brown seed heads. Z3–7 H7–1.
***C.* 'Jackmanii'** (illus. p.213). Vigorous, late, large-flowered clematis (group 3). H 10ft (3m). Bears masses of velvety, single, dark purple flowers fading to violet, 3–4in (8–10cm) across, with light brown anthers, in midsummer. Z4–9 H9–1.
***C.* 'Jackmanii Superba'.** Vigorous, late, large-flowered clematis (group 3). Is similar to *C.* 'Jackmanii' but has more rounded, darker flowers. Z4–9 H9–1.
***C.* 'John Huxtable'.** Late, large-flowered clematis (group 3). H 6–10ft (2–3m). Bears masses of 3in (8cm) wide, single white flowers with cream anthers in midsummer. Z7–9 H9–1.
***C.* 'Josephine'** (illus. p.213). Early, large-flowered clematis (group 2). H 8ft (2.5m). From early summer to early autumn bears double flowers, 5in (12cm) across, with almost bronze, green-tinged petals with a darker central bar; the petals become lilac with a pink bar in midsummer. Best color in sun. Z4–9 H9–1.
C.* x *jouiniana. Sprawling, sub-shrubby, late-flowering clematis (group 3). H 3ft (1m), S 10ft (3m). Has coarse foliage and, in summer, masses of tubular, single, soft lavender or off-white flowers, ¾in (2cm) wide, with reflexed petal tips. Is non-clinging. H3–8 H8–1. **'Praecox'** has slightly darker flowers 2 weeks earlier. .
***C.* 'Kathleen Wheeler'.** Early, large-flowered clematis (group 2). H 8–10ft (2–3m). Has single, plum-mauve flowers, 5–5½in (12–14cm) across with yellow anthers, in early summer. Z4–9 H9–1.
***C.* 'Lasurstern'** (illus. p.213). Vigorous, early, large-flowered clematis (group 2). H 6–10ft (2–3m). In summer bears single blue flowers, 4–5in (10–12cm) across, with overlapping, wavy-edged petals and cream anthers. Z4–9 H9–1.
***C.* 'Lincoln Star'** (illus. p.213). Early, large-flowered clematis (group 2). H 6–10ft (2–3m). Has 4–5in (10–12cm) wide, single, raspberry pink flowers with red anthers in early summer. Early flowers are darker than late ones, which have very pale pink petal edges. Prefers partial shade. Z4–9 H9–1.
C. macropetala (illus. p.213). Macropetala clematis (group 1). H 10ft (3m), S 5ft (1.5m). During late spring and summer has masses of semi-double, mauve-blue flowers, 5cm (2in) long and lightening in color toward the center, followed by fluffy, silvery seed heads. Z6–9 H9–3.**'Markham's Pink'** (illus. p.212) has pink flowers. Z6–9 H9–3
***C.* 'Madame Edouard André'.** Late, large-flowered clematis (group 3). H 8ft (2.5m). Freely produces single, deep red flowers, 3–4in (8–10cm) across, with silver undersides, pointed petals, and yellow anthers, in midsummer. Z4–9 H9–1.
***C.* 'Madame Julia Correvon'**, syn. *C. viticella* 'Madame Julia Correvon' (illus. p.213). Late-flowering clematis (group 3). H 8–11ft (2.5–3.5m). Has flattish, single, wine red flowers, 2–3in (5–7cm) wide, with twisted petals, in summer. Z6–9 H9–6.
***C.* 'Madame Le Coultre'**. See *C.* 'Marie Boisselot'.
***C.* 'Marie Boisselot'**, syn. *C.* 'Madame Le Coultre'. Vigorous, early, large-flowered clematis (group 2). H 10ft (3m). Bears single flowers, 5in (12cm) across, with overlapping white petals and cream anthers in summer. Z4–9 H9–1.
***C.* 'Miss Bateman'.** Compact, early, large-flowered clematis (group 2). H 8ft (2.5m). Masses of single white flowers, 3–4in (8–10cm) across with red anthers, are produced in summer. Is good for a container or patio garden. Z4–9 H9–1.
C. montana (illus. p.212). Vigorous, Montana clematis (group 1). H 22–40ft (7–12m), S 6–10ft (2–3m). In late spring bears masses of single white flowers, 1½–2in (4–5cm) across, with yellow anthers. Z6–9 H9–3. **'Broughton Star'**, H 12–15ft (4–5m), bears semi-double to fully double, cup-shaped, dusty pink flowers with slightly darker veins. **'Elizabeth'**, H 30–40ft (10–12m), has scented, soft pink flowers with widely spaced petals. Flowers of var. ***rubens*** (illus. p.212) are pale pink. **'Tetrarose'** (illus. p.212), H 22–25ft (7–8m), has coarse, 3in (8cm) long leaflets and 2½–3in (6–7cm) wide, deep satin pink flowers.
***C.* 'Mrs. Cholmondeley'.** Early, large-flowered clematis (group 2). H 6–10ft (2–3m). In summer has single, light bluish lavender flowers, 4–5in (10–12cm) across with widely spaced petals and light chocolate anthers. Z4–9 H9–1.
***C.* 'Mrs. George Jackman'** (illus. p.212). Early, large-flowered clematis (group 2). H 6–10ft (2–3m). Bears 4in (10cm) wide, semi-double flowers with creamy white petals and light brown anthers in early summer. Z4–9 H9–1.
***C.* 'Mrs. N. Thompson'.** Compact, early, large-flowered clematis (group 2). H 8ft (2.5m). Produces masses of 3–4in (8–10cm) wide, single magenta flowers, with a central, slightly darker stripe on each bluish purple-edged petal and red anthers, in summer. Is good for a container or patio garden. Z4–9 H9–1.
***C.* 'Nelly Moser'** (illus. p.213). Early, large-flowered clematis (group 2). H 11ft (3.5m). In early summer has 5–6½in (12–16cm) wide, single, rose-mauve flowers with reddish purple anthers and, on each petal, a carmine stripe that fades in strong sun. Prefers a shaded situation. Z4–9 H9–1.
***C.* 'Niobe'.** Early, large-flowered clematis (group 2). H 6–10ft (2–3m). Throughout summer produces masses of single, rich deep red flowers, 4–5½in (10–14cm) across with yellow anthers. Z4–9 H9–1.
C. orientalis. Late-flowering clematis (group 3). H 10–12ft (3–4m), S 5ft (1.5m). Leaves are gray- to dark green. In summer lantern-shaped, single, greenish yellow flowers, 1¼in (3cm) wide with recurved petal tips, are followed by feathery seed heads. Z6–9 H9–6.
***C.* 'Perle d'Azur'** (illus. p.213). Late, large-flowered clematis (group 3). H 10ft (3m). Single, azure-blue flowers, 3in (8cm) across, with recurved petal tips and creamy green anthers, open in summer. Z4–9 H9–1.
***C.* Petit Faucon ('Evisix')** (illus. p.213). Non-clinging, midseason, small-flowered clematis (group 3). H 5ft (1.5m). From midsummer to midautumn it freely produces nodding, single, deep blue flowers, 3–3½in (7–9cm) across, with orange-yellow stamens that become creamy white with age. Z4–9 H9–1.
***C.* 'Purpurea Plena Elegans'.** See *C. viticella* 'Purpurea Plena Elegans'.
***C.* 'Ramona'.** Early, large-flowered clematis (group 2). H 10ft (3m), . Has coarse, dark green leaves offset in summer by single, pale blue flowers, 4–5in (10–12cm) across with red anthers. Z4–9 H9–1.
C. recta (illus. p.212). Clump-forming, herbaceous clematis (group 3). H 3–6ft (1–2m), S 20in (50cm). Leaves are dark or gray-green. Bears masses of sweetly scented, flattish, single white flowers, ¾in (2cm) across, in midsummer. Z3–7 H7–1.
C. rehderiana (illus. p.213). Vigorous, late-flowering clematis (group 3). H 20–22ft (6–7m), S 6–10ft (2–3m). Bears loose clusters of fragrant, tubular, single yellow flowers, ½–¾in (1–2cm) long, in late summer and early autumn. Leaves are coarse-textured. Z6–9 H9–6.
***C.* 'Rhapsody'.** Compact, early, large-flowered clematis (group 2). H 8ft (2.5m). From early summer to early autumn bears single, sapphire blue flowers, 4–5in (10–13cm) across, with splayed, creamy yellow anthers. Color deepens with age. Z4–9 H9-1.
***C.* 'Richard Pennell'.** Early, large-flowered clematis (group 2). H 6–10ft (2–3m). Produces 4–5in (10–12cm) wide, single flowers with rich purple-blue petals and golden yellow anthers in summer. Z6–9 H9–6.
***C.* 'Rouge Cardinal'.** Early, large-flowered clematis (group 3). H 6–10ft (2–3m). In summer has single, velvety crimson flowers, 3–4in (8–10cm) across, with red anthers. Z4–9 H9–1.
***C.* Royal Velvet ('Evifour')** (illus. p.213). Early, large-flowered clematis (group 2). H 6–8ft (2–2.5m). In early and midsummer bears single flowers, 4–6in (10–15cm) wide, with bluish, rich velvet-purple petals with darker central bands and red anthers. Z4–9 H9–1.
***C.* 'Souvenir du Capitaine Thuilleaux'.** Compact, early, large-flowered clematis (group 2). H 8ft (2.5m). In early summer bears 3–4in (8–10cm) wide, single flowers with red anthers and deep pink-striped, cream-pink petals. Is ideal for a container or patio garden. Z4–9 H9–1.
***C.* 'Star of India'** (illus. p.213). Vigorous, late, large-flowered clematis (group 3). H 10ft (3m). Bears masses of 3–4in (8–10cm) wide, single, deep purple-blue flowers with light brown anthers in midsummer; each petal has a deep carmine-red stripe. Z4–9 H9–1.
C. tangutica (illus. p.213). Vigorous, late-flowering clematis (group 3). H 15–20ft (5–6m), S 6–10ft (2–3m). Has lantern-shaped, single yellow flowers, 1½in (4cm) long, throughout summer and early autumn, followed by fluffy silvery seed heads. Z6–9 H9–6.
***C.* 'The President'** (illus. p.213). Early, large-flowered clematis (group 2). H 6–10ft (2–3m). In early summer bears masses of single, rich purple flowers, silver beneath, 4in (10cm) wide, with red anthers. Z4–9 H9–1.
***C.* 'Ville de Lyon'.** Late, large-flowered clematis (group 3). H 6–10ft (2–3m). In midsummer has single, bright carmine-red flowers, 3–4in (8–10cm) across, with darker petal edges and yellow anthers. Lower foliage tends to become scorched by late summer. Z4–9 H9–1.
C. viticella. Late-flowering clematis (group 3). H 6–10ft (2–3m). Produces nodding, open bell-shaped, single, purple-mauve flowers, 1½in (3.5cm) long, in summer. Z5–9 H9–1. **'Abundance'** see *C.* 'Abundance'. **'Etoile Violette'** see *C.* 'Etoile Violette'. **'Madame Julia Correvon'** see *C.* 'Madame Julia Correvon'. **'Purpurea Plena Elegans'** (syn *C.* 'Purpurea Plena Elegans'; illus. p.213) bears abundant, double flowers with many purplish mauve sepals, occasionally green outer sepals, and no anthers from midsummer to late autumn.
***C.* 'Vyvyan Pennell'** (illus. p.213). Early, large-flowered clematis (group

2). H 6–10ft (2–3m). Has double lilac flowers, 4–5in (10–12cm) wide, with a central, lavender-blue rosette of petals and golden yellow anthers in early summer, then single, blue-mauve flowers. Z4–9 H9–1.
***C.* 'W.E. Gladstone'.** Vigorous, early, large-flowered clematis (group 2). H 10–12ft (3–4m). Produces single lavender flowers, 6in (15cm) wide with red anthers, in summer. Z4–9 H9–1.
***C.* 'William Kennett'.** Early, large-flowered clematis (group 2). H 6–10ft (2–3m). In summer has masses of single flowers, 4–5in (10–12cm) across, with red anthers and tough, lavender-blue petals, each bearing a central, darker stripe that fades as the flower matures. Z4–9 H9–1.

CLEOME
Spider flower

CAPPARACEAE

Genus of annuals and a few evergreen shrubs grown for their unusual, spidery flowers. Grow in sun and in fertile, well-drained soil. Remove dead flowers. Propagate by seed sown outdoors in late spring. Aphids may be a problem.
C. hassleriana, syn. *C. spinosa*. Fast-growing, bushy annual. H to 4ft (1.2m), S 1½ft (45cm). Has hairy, spiny stems and midgreen leaves divided into lance-shaped leaflets. Large, rounded heads of narrow-petaled, pink-flushed white flowers with long, protruding stamens, appear in summer. Z11 H12–1.
'Colour Fountain' illus. p.322.
'Rose Queen' has rose pink flowers.
C. spinosa. See *C. hassleriana*.

CLERODENDRUM

VERBENACEAE

Genus of evergreen or deciduous, small trees, shrubs, subshrubs and woody-stemmed, twining climbers grown for their showy flowers. Needs organic, well-drained soil and full sun, with partial shade in summer. Water freely in growing season, less at other times. Stems require support. Thin out crowded growth in spring. Propagate by seed in spring, by softwood cuttings in late spring or by semi-ripe cuttings in summer. Whitefly, spider mite, and mealy bug may be a problem.
C. bungei illus. p.148.
***C. chinense* 'Pleniflorum'**, syn. *C. fragrans* 'Pleniflorum', *C. philippinum*. Evergreen or deciduous, bushy shrub. H and S to 8ft (2.5m). Leaves are broadly oval, coarsely and shallowly toothed, and downy. Fragrant, double pink or white flowers are borne in domed, terminal clusters in summer. Z10–11 H12–1.
C. fallax. See *C. speciosissimum*.
***C. fragrans* 'Pleniflorum'.** See *C. chinense* 'Pleniflorum'.
C. philippinum. See *C. chinense* 'Pleniflorum'.
C. speciosissimum, syn. *C. fallax*. Evergreen, erect to spreading, sparingly branched shrub. H and S to 10ft (3m). Bears broadly heart-shaped, wavy-edged leaves, each to 1ft (30cm) across, on long stalks and, from late spring to autumn, tubular scarlet flowers with spreading petal lobes in 1ft (30cm) long, terminal clusters. Makes a good pot plant. Z13–15 H12–10.
C. splendens. Vigorous, evergreen, woody-stemmed, twining climber. H 10ft (3m) or more. Has oval to elliptic, rich green leaves. Clusters of 5-petaled, tubular scarlet flowers, 1in (2.5cm) wide, are produced in summer.
C. thomsoniae illus. p.208.
C. trichotomum illus. p.147.

CLETHRA

CLETHRACEAE

Genus of deciduous or evergreen shrubs and trees grown for their fragrant white flowers. Needs semi-shade and moist, peaty, acidic soil. Propagate by softwood cuttings in summer or by seed in autumn.
C. alnifolia (Sweet pepperbush). Deciduous, bushy shrub. H and S 8ft (2.5m). Has oval, toothed, midgreen leaves and, in late summer and early autumn, slender spires of small, bell-shaped flowers. Z3–9 H9–1.
C. arborea (Lily-of-the-valley tree). Evergreen, bushy, dense shrub or tree. H 25ft (8m), S 20ft (6m). Bears long, nodding clusters of small, strongly fragrant, bell-shaped flowers among oval, toothed, rich green leaves from late summer to midautumn. Z8–9 H9–8.
C. barbinervis illus. p.138.
C. delavayi illus. p.121.

CLEYERA

THEACEAE

Genus of evergreen, summer-flowering shrubs and trees grown for their foliage and flowers. Requires a sheltered position in sun or semi-shade and moist, acidic soil. Propagate by semi-ripe cuttings in summer.
***C. fortunei* 'Variegata'.** See *C. japonica* **'Tricolor'**.
C. japonica. Evergreen, bushy shrub. H and S 10ft (3m). Small, fragrant, bowl-shaped, creamy white flowers are borne in summer and narrowly oblong to oval-oblong, glossy, dark green leaves. Occasionally has small, spherical red fruits ripening to black. Z8–11 H12–7. **'Tricolor'** (syn. *C. fortunei* 'Variegata', *Eurya japonica* 'Variegata' of gardens), H and S 6ft (2m), produces pink-flushed young leaves, later green edged with creamy white.

CLIANTHUS

LEGUMINOSAE/PAPILIONACEAE

Genus of evergreen or semi-evergreen, woody-stemmed, scrambling climbers grown for their attractive flowers. Grow in well-drained soil and full sun. In spring prune out growing tips to give a bushier habit and cut out any dead wood. Propagate by seed in spring or stem cuttings in late summer.
C. puniceus and f. ***albus*** illus. p.204.

CLINTONIA

CONVALLARIACEAE/LILIACEAE

Genus of late spring- or summer-flowering, rhizomatous perennials. Prefers shade and moist but well-drained, peaty, neutral to acidic soil. Propagate by division in spring or by seed in autumn.
C. andrewsiana. Clump-forming, rhizomatous perennial. H 24in (60cm), S 12in (24cm). In early summer produces clusters of small, bell-shaped, pinkish purple flowers at tops of stems above sparse, broadly oval, glossy, rich green leaves. Bears globose blue fruits in autumn. Z8–9 H9–1.
C. borealis. (Corn lily). Clump-forming, rhizomatous perennial. H and S 12in (24cm). Is similar to *C. andrewsiana* but has nodding, yellowish green flowers and small, globose blackish fruits. Z2–7 H8–1.
C. uniflora (Queencup). Spreading, rhizomatous perennial. H 6in (15cm), S 12in (24cm). Has oval, glossy green leaves. Slender stems bear solitary star-shaped white flowers in late spring, then large, globose, blue-black fruits. Z4–8 H8–1.

CLITORIA

LEGUMINOSAE/PAPILIONACEAE

Genus of perennials and evergreen shrubs and twining climbers grown for their large, pealike flowers. Grow in full light and in any fertile, well-drained soil. Water moderately, less when not in full growth. Provide support for stems. Thin out crowded stems in spring. Propagate by seed in spring or by softwood cuttings in summer. Whitefly and spider mite may be a problem.
C. ternatea. Evergreen, twining climber with slender stems. H 10–15ft (3–5m). Leaves are divided into 3 or 5 oval leaflets. Clear bright blue flowers, 3–5in (7–12cm) wide, are carried in summer. Z11 H12–10.

CLIVIA

AMARYLLIDACEAE

Genus of robust, evergreen, rhizomatous perennials cultivated for their funnel-shaped flowers. Good in borders and large containers. Needs partial shade and well-drained soil. Water well in summer, less in winter. Propagate by seed in winter or spring or by division in spring or summer after flowering. Mealy bugs may cause problems. All parts of *C. miniata* may cause mild stomach upset if ingested, and the sap may irritate skin.
C. miniata illus. p.419.
C. nobilis. Evergreen, spring- or summer-flowering, rhizomatous perennial. H 12–16in (30–40cm), S 12–24in (30–60cm). Has strap-shaped, semi-erect, basal leaves, 16–24in (40–60cm) long. Each leafless stem bears a dense, semi-pendent head of over 20 narrowly funnel-shaped red flowers with green tips and yellow margins on petals. Z12–15 H12–10.

CLUSIA

CLUSIACEAE

Genus of evergreen, mainly summer-flowering climbers, shrubs, and trees grown for their foliage and flowers.. Needs partial shade and well-drained soil. Water potted specimens moderately, very little when temperatures are low. Pruning is tolerated if necessary. Propagate by layering in spring or by semi-ripe cuttings in summer. Whitefly and spider mite may be a problem.
C. major, syn. *C. rosea* (Autograph tree, Copey, Fat pork tree, Pitch apple). Slow-growing, evergreen, rounded tree or shrub. H and S to 50ft (50m). Bears oval, lustrous, deep green leaves. Cup-shaped pink flowers, 2in (5cm) wide, are produced in summer, followed by globose greenish fruits that yield a sticky resin. Z14–15 H12–10.

CLYTOSTOMA

BIGNONIACEAE

Genus of evergreen, woody-stemmed, tendril climbers grown for their flowers. Grow in well-drained soil with partial shade in summer. Water freely in summer, less at other times. Provide support for stems. Thin out congested growth after flowering or in spring. Propagate by semi-ripe cuttings in summer.
C. callistegioides, syn. *Pandorea lindleyana*, illus. p.205.

COBAEA

COBAEACEAE/POLEMONIACEAE

Genus of evergreen or deciduous, woody-stemmed, tendril climbers. Only one species, *C. scandens*, is generally cultivated. Grow outdoors in warm areas in full light and in any well-drained soil. In colder regions may be grown under cover or treated as an annual. Propagate by seed in spring.
C. scandens illus. p.214.
f. ***alba*** is an evergreen, woody-stemmed, tendril climber. H 12–15ft (4–5m). Has long-stalked, bell-shaped green then white flowers from late summer until first frosts. Leaves have 4 or 6 oval leaflets. Z11–13 H12–10.

Cocos capitata. See *Butia capitata*.

CODIAEUM

EUPHORBIACEAE

Genus of evergreen shrubs grown for their foliage. Prefers partial shade and fertile, moist but well-drained soil. Remove tips from young plants to promote a branched habit. Propagate

by greenwood cuttings from firm stem tips in spring or summer. Mealy bug and soft scale may be a nuisance. Contact with the foliage may aggravate skin allergies.
C. variegatum var. ***pictum*** illus. p.177.

CODONOPSIS

CAMPANULACEAE

Genus of perennials and mostly herbaceous, twining climbers grown for their bell- or saucer-shaped flowers. Requires a position in semi-shade, with light, well-drained soil. Train over supports or allow to scramble through other, larger plants. Propagate by seed sown in autumn or spring.
C. clematidea. Herbaceous, twining climber. H to 5ft (1.5m). Has small, oval, midgreen leaves. In summer produces nodding, bell-shaped flowers, 1in (2.5cm) long; they are white tinged with blue and marked inside with darker veining and 2 purple rings. Z7–9 H9–7.
C. convolvulacea illus. p.214.
C. ovata. Upright perennial with scarcely twining stems. H to 12in (24cm). Has small, oval leaves and, in summer, small, bell-shaped, pale blue flowers, often with darker veins.

COELOGYNE

See also ORCHIDS.
C. cristata (illus. p.296). Evergreen, epiphytic orchid for a cool greenhouse. H 6in (15cm). In winter produces sprays of white flowers, 2in (5cm) across and marked orange on each lip. Narrowly oval leaves are 3–4in (8–10cm) long. Needs a position in good light in summer. Z14–15 H12–6.
C. flaccida (illus. p.296). Evergreen, epiphytic orchid for a cool greenhouse. H 6in (15cm). During spring bears drooping spikes of fragrant, star-shaped, light buff flowers, 1½in (4cm) across, with yellow and brown marks on each lip. Has narrowly oval, semi-rigid leaves, 3–4in (8–10cm) long. Grow in semi-shade in summer. Z14–15 H12–6.
C. nitida, syn. *C. ochracea* (illus. p.296). Evergreen, epiphytic orchid for a cool greenhouse. H 5in (12cm). In spring produces sprays of very fragrant white flowers, 1in (2.5cm) across and with a yellow mark on each lip. Narrowly oval, semi-rigid leaves are 3–4in (8–10cm) long. Requires semi-shade in summer. Z14–15 H12–6.
C. ochracea. See *C. nitida*.
C. speciosa (illus. p.298). Vigorous, evergreen, epiphytic orchid for an intermediate greenhouse. H 10in (25cm). In summer produces pendent, light green flowers, 2½in (6cm) across, with brown- and white-marked lips, that open in succession along stems. Has broadly oval leaves, 9–10in (23–5cm) long. Grow in good light in summer. Z14–15 H12–6.

COIX

GRAMINEAE/POACEAE

See also GRASSES, BAMBOOS, RUSHES, and SEDGES.
C. lacryma-jobi illus. p.308.

COLCHICUM

COLCHICACEAE/LILIACEAE

Genus of spring- and autumn-flowering corms grown for their mainly goblet-shaped blooms, up to 8in (20cm) long, most of which emerge before leaves. Each corm bears 2–7 narrowly strap-shaped to broadly elliptic, basal leaves. Needs an open, sunny situation and well-drained soil. Propagate by seed or division in autumn. All parts are highly toxic if ingested and, if in contact with skin, may cause irritation.
C. agrippinum illus. p.439.
C. autumnale illus. p.437. **'Alboplenum'** is an autumn-flowering corm. H and S 4–6in (10–15cm). In spring has 3–5 large, semi-erect, basal, glossy, green leaves. Produces a bunch of up to 8 long-tubed, rounded, double white flowers with 15–30 narrow petals. Z4–9 H9–1.
***C.* 'Beaconsfield'.** Robust, autumn-flowering corm. H and S 6–8in (15–20cm). Bears large, goblet-shaped, rich pinkish purple flowers, faintly checkered and white in centers. Large, semi-erect, basal leaves appear in spring. 4–9 H9–1.
C. bivonae, syn. *C. bowlesianum*, *C. sibthorpii*, illus. p.438.
C. bowlesianum. See *C. bivonae*.
C. byzantinum illus. p.437.
C. cilicicum illus. p.438.
***C.* 'Lilac Wonder'.** Vigorous, autumn-flowering corm. H and S 6–8in (15–20cm). Produces goblet-shaped, deep lilac-pink flowers, 6–8in (15–20cm) long. Broad, semi-erect, basal leaves appear in spring. Z4–9 H9–1.
C. luteum illus. p.434
C. sibthorpii. See *C. bivonae*.
C. speciosum. Vigorous, autumn-flowering corm. H and S 6–8in (15–20cm). Bears goblet-shaped, pale to deep pinkish purple flowers, 6–8in (15–20cm) long, often with white throats. Large, semi-erect, basal leaves develop in winter or spring. Z4–9 H9–1. **'Album'** illus. p.437.
***C.* 'The Giant'.** Robust, autumn-flowering corm. H and S 6–8in (15–20cm). Produces up to 5 funnel-shaped, deep mauve-pink flowers, each 6–8in (15–20cm) long and fading to white in the center. Broad, semi-erect, basal leaves emerge in winter or spring. Z4–9 H9–1.
C. variegatum. Autumn-flowering corm. H 4–6in (10–15cm), S 3–4in (8–10cm). Bears widely funnel-shaped, reddish purple flowers with strong checkered patterns. More or less horizontal, basal leaves with wavy margins appear in spring. Benefits from a hot, sunny site. 4–9 H9–1.
***C.* 'Waterlily'** illus. p.439.

COLEONEMA

RUTACEAE

Genus of evergreen, heathlike shrubs grown for their flowers and overall appearance. Requires a position in full sun and well-drained, neutral to acidic soil. Water potted plants moderately when in full growth, sparingly at other times. For a more compact habit, prune after flowering. Propagate by seed sown in spring or by semi-ripe cuttings in late summer.
C. pulchrum. Evergreen, spreading to domed shrub with wiry stems. H 2–4ft (60cm–1.2m), S 3–5ft (1–1.5m). Has soft, needlelike, bright green leaves. Carries 5-petaled, pale pink to red flowers in spring-summer. Z8–11 H12–8.

Coleus. Reclassified as *Solenostemon* except for:
C. thyrsoideus for which see *Plectranthus thyrsoideus*.

COLLETIA

RHAMNACEAE

Genus of deciduous, usually leafless shrubs grown for their curious, spiny shoots and profuse, small flowers. Shoots assume function of leaves. Requires a sheltered, sunny site and well-drained soil. Propagate by semi-ripe cuttings in late summer.
C. armata. See *C. hystrix*.
C. cruciata. See *C. paradoxa*.
C. hystrix, syn. *C. armata*, illus. p.147. **'Rosea'** is a deciduous, thickly branched shrub. H 8ft (2.5m), S 15ft (5m). Shoots have rigid, gray-green spines. Bears fragrant, tubular pink flowers in late summer and early autumn. Z7–11 H12–7.
C. paradoxa, syn. *C. cruciata*. Deciduous, arching shrub with stiff branches. H 10ft (3m), S 15ft (5m). Has thick, flattened, blue-green spines. Fragrant, tubular white flowers are borne in late summer and early autumn. Z7–11 H12–7.

COLLINSIA

SCROPHULARIACEAE

Genus of spring- to summer-flowering annuals. Grow in partial shade and in fertile, well-drained soil. Support with thin sticks. Propagate by seed sown outdoors in spring or early autumn.
C. grandiflora illus. p.331.

COLOCASIA

ARACEAE

Genus of deciduous or evergreen, perennial, marginal water plants grown for their foliage. Has edible tubers, known as "taros," for which it is widely cultivated. Is suitable for the edges of ponds; may also be grown in wet soil in pots. Grows in sun or light shade and in mud or shallow water. Propagate by division in spring. All parts may cause mild stomach upset if ingested without cooking, and contact with the sap may irritate the skin.
C. antiquorum. See *C. esculenta*.
C. esculenta, syn. *C. antiquorum*, illus. p.448. **'Fontanesii'** is a deciduous, perennial, marginal water plant. H 3½ft (1.1m), S 2ft (60cm). Has large, bold, oval, midgreen leaves with dark green veins and margins and blackish violet leaf stalks and spathe tubes. Z9–11 H12–8. **'Illustris'** has brownish purple leaf stalks and dark green leaf blades with purple spots.

COLQUHOUNIA

LABIATAE/LAMIACEAE

Genus of evergreen or semi-evergreen shrubs grown for their flowers in late summer and autumn. Needs well-drained soil. Propagate by softwood cuttings in summer.
C. coccinea illus. p.149.

COLUMNEA

GESNERIACEAE

Genus of evergreen, creeping or trailing perennials or subshrubs grown for their showy flowers. Trailing species are useful for hanging baskets. Needs bright but indirect light, a fairly humid atmosphere, and moist soil, except in winter. Propagate by tip cuttings after flowering.
C. x banksii illus. p.250.
C. crassifolia illus. p.283.
C. gloriosa (Goldfish plant). Evergreen, trailing perennial with more or less unbranched stems. H or S to 3ft (90cm). Oval leaves have reddish hairs. Has tubular, hooded scarlet flowers to 3in (8cm) long with yellow throats in winter-spring. Z14–15 H12–10.
C. microphylla. Evergreen perennial, sparsely branched on each trailing stem. H or S 3ft (1m) or more. Has small, rounded leaves with brown hairs. Hooded, tubular scarlet flowers to 3in (8cm) long with yellow throats appear in winter-spring. Z14–15 H12–10. **'Variegata'** illus. p.266.

COLUTEA

LEGUMINOSAE/PAPILIONACEAE

Genus of deciduous, summer-flowering shrubs grown for their foliage, pealike flowers, and bladder-shaped seed pods. Grow in full sun and any but water-logged soil. Propagate by softwood cuttings in summer or by seed in autumn. Seeds may cause mild stomach upset if ingested.
C. arborescens illus. p.146.
C. x media illus. p.147.
C. orientalis. Deciduous, bushy shrub. H and S 6ft (2m). Has blue-gray leaves consisting of 7 or 9 oval leaflets. Clusters of yellow-marked, coppery red flowers produced in summer are followed by inflated green then pale brown seed pods. Z6–9 H9–6.

Comarostaphylis diversifolia. See *Arctostaphylos diversifolia*.

COMBRETUM

COMBRETACEAE

Genus of evergreen trees, shrubs, and scandent to twining climbers grown for their small, showy flowers. Provide organic, well-drained soil, with partial shade in summer. Water freely in summer, less at other times. Support for stems is necessary. Thin out and cut back congested growth after flowering. Propagate by semi-ripe cutting in summer. Spider mite may be a problem.
C. grandiflorum. Moderately vigorous, evergreen, scandent to twining climber. H to 20ft (6m). Has oblong to elliptic, pointed leaves, 4–8in (10–20cm) long. Tubular, bright red flowers with long stamens are borne in summer in one-sided spikes, 4–5in (10–13cm) long. Z11 H12–10.

COMMELINA

COMMELINACEAE

Genus of perennials usually grown as annuals. Grow in a sunny, sheltered position and in fertile, well-drained soil. Crowns should be lifted before frosts and overwintered in slightly moist, frost-free conditions. Propagate by seed sown under cover or by division of the crown in spring.
C. coelestis, syn. *C. tuberosa* Coelestis Group, illus. p.334.
***C. tuberosa* Coelestis Group.** See *C. coelestis*.

CONANDRON

GESNERIACEAE

Genus of one species of tuberous perennial grown for its fleshy leaves and drooping flower clusters. Grow in alpine houses. Needs shade and organic, well-drained soil. Keep containerized plants moist in summer, dry when dormant in winter. Propagate by division or seed in spring.
C. ramondioides. Hummock-forming, tuberous perennial. H 12in (24cm), S 8in (20cm). Bears broadly oval, fleshy, wrinkled, midgreen leaves with toothed edges. In midsummer, each flower stem carries 5–25 tubular flowers, usually lilac, but white, purple, or pink forms also occur. Z7–8 H8–7.

CONIFERS

Group of trees and shrubs distinguished botanically from others by producing seeds exposed or uncovered on the scales of fruits. Most conifers are evergreen, have needlelike leaves, and bear woody fruits (cones). All genera in the Cupressaceae family, however, have needlelike juvenile leaves and, excepting many junipers and some other selected forms, scalelike adult leaves. Conifers described in this book are evergreen unless otherwise stated.

Conifers are excellent garden plants. Most provide year-round foliage, which may be green, blue, gray, bronze, gold, or silver. They range in height from trees 100ft (30m) or more tall to dwarf shrubs that grow less than 2in (5cm) every 10 years. Tall conifers may be planted as specimen trees or to provide shelter, screening, or hedging. Dwarf conifers make good features in their own right as well as in groups; they also associate well with heathers, add variety to rock gardens, and provide excellent groundcover. They may also be grown in containers.

Position and soil

x *Cupressocyparis*, *Cupressus*, *Larix*, and *Pinus* need full sun. *Cedrus*, *Juniperus*, and *Pseudolarix* do not tolerate shade. All other conifers will thrive in sun or shade, and most *Abies* and all *Cephalotaxus*, *Podocarpus*, *Taxus*, *Thuja*, *Torreya*, and *Tsuga* will grow in deep shade once established.

Conifers grow well on most soils, but certain genera and species will not do well on soils over limestone. In this book such conifers are: *Abies*, *Pseudolarix*, *Pseudotsuga*, and *Tsuga*; also *Picea*, except *P. likiangesis*, *P. omorika*, and *P. pungens*; and *Pinus*, except *P. aristata*, *P. armandii*, *P. cembroides*, *P. halepensis*, *P. heldreichii*, *P. nigra*, *P. peuce*, and *P. wallichiana*.

Certain conifers tolerate extreme conditions. *Abies alba*, *A. homolepis*, *A. nordmanniana*, *Cryptomeria*, *Cunninghamia*, *Metasequoia*, *Pinus coulteri*, *P. peuce*, *P. ponderosa*, *Sciadopitys*, *Sequoia*, *Sequoiadendron*, and *Taxodium* will grow on heavy clay soils. *Picea omorika*, *P. sitchensis*, *Pinus contorta*, *Sciadopitys verticillata*, and *Thuja plicata* are all happy on wet soil, and *Metasequoia* and *Taxodium* thrive in waterlogged conditions. *Cupressus*, *Juniperus*, and *Pinus* grow well on dry, sandy soil.

Pruning

If a conifer produces more than one leader, remove all but one. Bear in mind when trimming hedges that most conifers will not make new growth when cut back into old wood or from branches that have turned brown. This does not, however, apply to *Cephalotaxus*, *Cryptomeria*, *Cunninghamia*, *Sequoia*, *Taxus*, and *Torreya*, and these conifers may be kept to a reasonable size in the garden by cutting back the main stem, which will later coppice (make new growth). Young specimens of *Araucaria*, *Ginkgo*, *Metasequoia*, and *Taxodium* will sometimes do the same.

Propagation

Seed is the easiest method of propagation, but forms selected for leaf color (other than blue in some species) do not come true. Sow in autumn or spring. All genera apart from *Abies*, *Cedrus*, *Picea* (except young plants or dwarf forms), *Pinus*, *Pseudolarix*, *Pseudotsuga*, and *Tsuga* (except young plants or dwarf forms) may be raised fairly easily from cuttings: current growth from autumn to spring for evergreens, softwood cuttings in summer for deciduous conifers. Tall-growing forms of Pinaceae (*Abies*, *Cedrus*, *Picea*, *Pinus*, *Pseudolarix*, *Pseudotsuga*, and *Tsuga*) are usually propagated by grafting in late summer, winter, or early spring. Layering may be possible for some dwarf conifers.

Conifers are illustrated on pp.101–109, dwarf forms on pp.110–111. See also *Abies*, *Araucaria*, *Athrotaxis*, *Austrocedrus*, *Calocedrus*, *Cedrus*, *Cephalotaxus*, *Chamaecyparis*, *Cryptomeria*, *Cunninghamia*, x *Cupressocyparis*, *Cupressus*, *Fitzroya*, *Ginkgo*, *Juniperus*, *Larix*, *Metasequoia*, *Microbiota*, *Phyllocladus*, *Picea*, *Pinus*, *Podocarpus*, *Pseudolarix*, *Pseudotsuga*, *Saxegothaea*, *Sciadopitys*, *Sequoia*, *Sequoiadendron*, *Taxodium*, *Taxus*, *Thuja*, *Thujopsis*, *Torreya*, and *Tsuga*.

CONOPHYTUM

AIZOACEAE

Genus of slow-growing, clump-forming succulents with spherical or 2-eared leaves that grow for only 2 months each year, after flowering. In early summer, old leaves gradually shrivel to papery sheaths from which new leaves and flowers emerge in late summer. Needs full sun and well-drained soil. Keep dry in winter. Propagate by seed from spring to autumn or by division in late summer.
C. bilobum illus. p.479.
C. longum. See *Ophthalmophyllum longum*.
C. notabile illus. p.480.
C. truncatum illus. p.470.

CONSOLIDA

Larkspur

RANUNCULACEAE

Genus of annuals providing excellent cut flowers. Needs sun and fertile, well-drained soil. Support stems of tall-growing plants with sticks. Propagate by seed sown outdoors in spring, or in early autumn in mild areas. Protect young plants from slugs and snails. The seeds are poisonous.
C. ajacis, syn. *C. ambigua*, *Delphinium consolida*. Fast-growing, upright, branching annual. Giant forms, H to 4ft (1.2m), S 1ft (30cm); dwarf, H and S 1ft (30cm). All have feathery, mid-green leaves and, throughout summer, spikes of rounded, spurred flowers. H9–1. **Dwarf Hyacinth Series** has spikes of tubular flowers in shades of pink, mauve, blue, or white. **Giant Imperial Series** illus. p.332.
C. ambigua. See *C. ajacis*.

CONVALLARIA

Lily-of-the-valley

CONVALLARIACEAE/LILIACEAE

Genus of spring-flowering, rhizomatous perennials. Prefers partial shade and does best in organic, moist soil. Propagate by division after flowering or in autumn. The seeds of *C. majalis* may cause mild stomach upset if ingested.
C. majalis illus. p.268. **'Flore Pleno'** is a low-growing, rhizomatous perennial. H 9–12in (23–30cm), S indefinite. Sprays of small, very fragrant, pendent, bell-shaped flowers that are double and white open in spring. Narrowly oval leaves are mid- to dark green. **'Fortin's Giant'**, H 45cm (18in), has larger flowers and leaves that appear a little earlier. Both 2–7 H7–1.

CONVOLVULUS

CONVOLVULACEAE

Genus of dwarf, bushy and climbing annuals, perennials, and evergreen shrubs and subshrubs. Grow in sun and in poor to fertile, well-drained soil. Dead-head to prolong flowering. Propagate by seed sown outdoors in midspring for hardy plants or under cover in spring for tender plants, perennials and subshrubs by softwood cuttings in late spring or summer.
C. althaeoides illus. p.375.
C. cneorum illus. p.158.
C. mauritanicus. See *C. sabatius*.
C. minor. See *C. tricolor*.
C. purpureus. See *Ipomoea purpurea*.
C. sabatius, syn. *C. mauritanicus*, illus. p.356.
C. tricolor, syn. *C. minor*. Moderately fast-growing, upright, bushy or climbing annual. H 8–12in (20–30cm), S 8in (20cm). Has oval to lance-shaped, midgreen leaves. In summer bears saucer-shaped blue or white flowers, 1in (2.5cm) wide, with yellowish white throats. Tall, climbing forms, H to 10ft (3m) have flowers to 4in (10cm) wide. Z9–11 H12–1. **'Blue Flash'** (bushy) illus. p.332. **'Flying Saucers'** (climber) has blue-and-white-striped flowers.

COPIAPOA

CACTACEAE

Genus of slow-growing cacti with funnel-shaped, yellow flowers. Many species have large taproots. Needs partial shade and very well-drained soil. Propagate by seed or grafting in spring or summer.
C. cinerea illus. p.466.
C. coquimbana. Clump-forming, spherical then columnar cactus. H to 1ft (30cm), S 3ft (1m). Dark gray-green stem has 10–17 ribs. Areoles each bear 8–10 dark brown radial spines and 1 or 2 thicker central spines. Yellow flowers, 1¼in (3cm) across, appear in summer. Is slow to form clumps. Z113–15 H12–10.
C. echinoides. Flattened spherical cactus, ribbed like a sea urchin. H 6in (15cm), S 4in (10cm). Solitary gray-green stem bears dark brown spines, 1¼in (3cm) long, which soon fade to gray. In summer produces pale yellow flowers, 1½in (4cm) across. Z13–15 H12–10.
C. marginata. Clump-forming cactus. H 2ft (60cm), S 1ft (30cm). Gray-green

stem bears very close-set areoles with dark-tipped, pale brown spines, to 1¼in (3cm) long. Has yellow flowers, ¾–2in (2–5cm) across, in spring-summer. Z13–15 H12–10.

COPROSMA

RUBIACEAE

Genus of evergreen shrubs and trees grown for their foliage and fruits. Separate male and female plants are needed to obtain fruits. Prefers full light and well-drained soil. Water containerized specimens freely in summer, moderately at other times. Propagate by seed in spring or by semi-ripe cuttings in late summer.

C. baueri. See *C. repens*.

C. baueriana. See *C. repens*.

***C.* x *kirkii*.** Evergreen, prostrate then semi-erect, densely branched shrub. H to 3ft (1m), S 4–6ft (1.2–2m). Narrowly oblong to lance-shaped, leathery, glossy leaves are borne singly or in small clusters. In late spring has insignificant flowers, followed on female plants by tiny, egg-shaped, translucent white fruits with red speckles. Z8–11 H12–8. **'Variegata'** illus. p.175.

C. repens, syn. *C. baueri*, *C. baueriana*. Evergreen, spreading then erect shrub. H and S to 6ft (2m). Has broadly oval, leathery, lustrous, rich green leaves. Carries insignificant flowers in late spring, followed on female plants by egg-shaped, orange-red fruits from late summer to autumn. Z8–10 H10–8. Leaves of **'Picturata'** each have a central cream blotch.

CORDYLINE

AGAVACEAE

Genus of evergreen shrubs and trees grown primarily for their foliage, although some also have decorative flowers. Provide fertile, well-drained soil and full light or partial shade. Water potted plants moderately, less in winter. Propagate by seed or suckers in spring or by stem cuttings in summer. Spider mite may be a nuisance.

C. australis, syn. *Dracaena australis* (New Zealand cabbage palm). Slow-growing, evergreen, sparsely branched tree. H 50ft (50m) or more, S 15ft (5m) or more. Each stem is crowned by a rosette of strap-shaped, 1–3ft (30cm–1m) long leaves. Has small, scented white flowers in large, open panicles in summer and, in autumn, globose white fruits. Z10–11 H12–10. **'Atropurpurea'** illus. p.99. Long, sword-shaped leaves of **'Veitchii'** have red bases and midribs.

C. fruticosa, syn. *C. terminalis* (Good-luck plant, Ti tree). Slow-growing, evergreen, upright shrub, sparingly branched and suckering. H 6–12ft (2–4m), S 3–6ft (1–2m). Broadly lance-shaped, glossy, deep green leaves are 1–2ft (30–60cm) long. Produces branched panicles of small white, purplish, or reddish flowers in summer. Z11 H12–7. Foliage of **'Baptisii'** is deep green with pink and yellow stripes and spots. **'Imperialis'** has red- or pink-marked, deep green leaves.

C. indivisa, syn. *Dracaena indivisa*. Slow-growing, evergreen, erect tree or shrub. H 10ft (3m) or more, S 6ft (2m). Bears lance-shaped, 2–6ft (60cm–2m) long, green leaves, orange-brown veined above, blue-gray tinted beneath. In summer tiny, star-shaped white flowers in dense clusters, 2ft (60cm) or more long, are followed by tiny, spherical, blue-purple fruits. Z9–10 H12–1.

C. terminalis. See *C. fruticosa*.

COREOPSIS
Tickseed

ASTERACEAE/COMPOSITAE

Genus of annuals and perennials grown for their daisylike flower heads. Needs full sun and fertile, well-drained soil. Propagate annuals by seed in spring; *C. lanceolata* by seed or division in spring; *C. auriculata* 'Superba', *C.* 'Goldfink', and *C. grandiflora* 'Badengold' by softwood cuttings or division in spring or summer; and *C. verticillata* by division in spring.

***C. auriculata* 'Superba'.** Bushy perennial. H and S 18in (45cm). Daisylike, rich yellow flower heads with central purple blotches are borne in summer. Oval to lance-shaped leaves are lobed and light green. Some plants grown as *C. auriculata* are the closely related annual *C. basalis*. Z4–9 H9–1.

***C.* 'Goldfink'.** Short-lived, dwarf, bushy perennial. H and S 12in (24cm). Sprays of daisylike, deep yellow flower heads appear in summer above narrowly oval, deep green leaves. Z4–9 H9–1.

***C. grandiflora* 'Badengold'.** Short-lived, erect perennial with lax stems. H 30in (75cm), S 24in (60cm). Bears large, daisylike, rich buttercup yellow flower heads in summer and broadly lance-shaped, divided, bright green leaves. Z4–9 H9–1.

C. lanceolata illus. p.293.

***C.* 'Sunray'** illus. p.337.

C. tinctoria illus. p.337. **'Golden Crown'** is a fast-growing, upright, bushy annual. H 24in (60cm), S 8in (20cm). Has lance-shaped, deep green leaves and, in summer and early autumn, large, daisylike, deep yellow flower heads with brown centers. Z4–9 H12–1.

C. verticillata illus. p.293.

CORIARIA

CORIARIACEAE

Genus of deciduous, spring- or summer-flowering shrubs and sub-shrubs grown for their habit, foliage, and fruits. Needs full sun and fertile, well-drained soil. Propagate by softwood cuttings in summer or by seed in autumn. The leaves and fruits of some species may cause severe stomach upset if ingested; in other species, the fruits are edible, although the seeds are thought to be poisonous.

C. terminalis. Deciduous, arching sub-shrub. H 3ft (1m), S 6ft (2m). Broadly lance-shaped, fernlike, midgreen leaves turn red in autumn. Minute green flowers in late spring are succeeded by small, spherical black fruits. Z9–11 H12–1. var. ***xanthocarpa*** illus. p.173.

CORNUS
Dogwood

CORNACEAE

Genus of deciduous shrubs and deciduous or evergreen trees grown for their flowers, foliage, or brightly colored winter stems. Needs sun or semi-shade and fertile, well-drained soil. Those grown for winter stem color do best in full sun. *C. florida*, *C. kousa*, and *C. nuttallii* dislike shallow, alkaline soil. *C. canadensis* prefers acidic soil. Plants grown for their stems should be cut back almost to ground level each year in early spring. Propagate *C. alba* and *C. stolonifera* 'Flaviramea' by softwood cuttings in summer or by hardwood cuttings in autumn or winter; variegated forms of *C. alternifolia* and *C. controversa* by grafting in winter; *C. canadensis* by division in spring or autumn; *C. capitata*, *C. florida*, and *C. kousa* by seed in autumn or by softwood cuttings in summer; *C. nuttallii* by seed in autumn; all others described here by softwood cuttings in summer. The fruits of some species may cause mild stomach upset if ingested; contact with the leaf hairs may irritate skin.

C. alba (Redtwig dogwood). Vigorous, deciduous, upright, then spreading shrub. H and S 10ft (3m). Young shoots are bright red in winter. Has oval, dark green leaves, often red or orange in autumn. Bears flattened heads of star-shaped, creamy white flowers in late spring and early summer, followed by spherical, sometimes blue-tinted white fruits. Z2–8 H8–1. **'Elegantissima'** illus. p.138. **'Gouchaultii'** has pink-flushed leaves broadly edged with yellow. **'Kesselringii'** illus. p.148. **'Sibirica'** illus. p.150. **'Spaethii'** illus. p.146.

C. alternifolia. Deciduous, spreading tree or bushy shrub, with tiered branches. H and S 20ft (6m). Oval, bright green leaves, which each taper to a point, often turn red in autumn. Clusters of tiny, star-shaped, creamy white flowers in early summer are followed by small, rounded, blue black fruits. Z4–8 H8–1. **'Argentea'** illus. p.89.

C. canadensis, syn. *Chamaepericlymenum canadense*, illus. p.374.

C. capitata, syn. *Dendrobenthamia capitata* (Bentham's cornel). Evergreen or semi-evergreen, spreading tree. H and S up to 40ft (12m). Pale yellow bracts surrounding insignificant flowers appear in early summer, followed by large, strawberry-like red fruits. Has oval, gray-green leaves. Is good for mild coastal areas. Z8–9 H9–8.

C. controversa. Deciduous tree with layered branches. H and S 50ft (50m). Clusters of small, star-shaped white flowers appear in summer. Leaves are oval, pointed, and bright green, turning purple in autumn. Z6–9 H9–6. **'Variegata'** illus. p.89.

***C.* 'Eddie's White Wonder'** illus. p.96.

C. florida (Flowering dogwood). Deciduous, spreading tree. H 20ft (6m), S 25ft (8m). In late spring bears white or pinkish white bracts surrounding tiny, insignificant flowers. Oval, pointed, dark green leaves turn red and purple in autumn. Z5–8 H8–3. **'Apple Blossom'** has pale pink bracts. f. ***rubra*** bears pink or red bracts. **'Spring Song'** illus. p.90. **'Welchii'** illus. p.93. **'White Cloud'** illus. p.85.

C. kousa. Deciduous, vase-shaped tree or shrub. H 22ft (7m), S 15ft (5m). Flower heads of large white bracts surrounding insignificant flowers appear in early summer, followed by strawberry-like fruits. Oval, glossy, dark green leaves turn bright red-purple in autumn. Z5–8 H8–5. var. ***chinensis*** has larger flower heads and more narrowly pointed bracts.

C. macrophylla illus. p.78.

C. mas (Cornelian cherry). Deciduous, spreading, open shrub or tree. H and S 15ft (5m). Oval, dark green leaves change to reddish purple in autumn. Produces small, star-shaped yellow flowers on bare shoots in late winter and early spring, then edible, oblong, bright red fruits. Z5–8 H8–5. **'Aureoelegantissima'** (syn. *C.m.* 'Elegantissima'), H 6ft (2m), S 10ft (3m), has pink-tinged leaves edged with yellow. **'Elegantissima'** see *C.m.* 'Aureoelegantissima'. **'Variegata'** illus. p.119.

***C.* 'Norman Hadden'.** Deciduous, spreading tree. H and S 25ft (8m). Creamy white bracts around tiny flowers turn to deep pink in summer. These are often followed by strawberry-like fruits in autumn. Z8–9 H9–8.

C. nuttallii illus. p.76

***C.* 'Porlock'** illus. p.86.

***C. stolonifera* 'Flaviramea'.** Vigorous, deciduous, spreading shrub with creeping, underground stems. H 6ft (2m), S 4m (12ft). Has bright greenish yellow young shoots in winter and oval, dark green leaves. Small, star-shaped white flowers appear in late spring and early summer and are followed by spherical white fruits. Z3–8 H8–1.

COROKIA

ESCALLONIACEAE

Genus of evergreen shrubs grown for their habit, foliage, flowers, and fruits. Is good in mild, coastal areas, where it is very wind-tolerant. Protect from strong winds at limits of hardiness. Needs full sun and fertile, well-drained soil. Propagate by softwood cuttings in summer.

C. buddlejoides. Evergreen, upright shrub. H 10ft (3m), S 6ft (2m). Has slender gray shoots and narrowly oblong, glossy, dark green leaves. Produces panicles of star-shaped yellow

flowers in late spring, followed by spherical, blackish red fruits. Z9–10 H10–9.
C. cotoneaster illus. p.152.
***C.* x *virgata*.** Evergreen, upright, dense shrub. H and S 10ft (3m). Leaves are oblong and glossy, dark green above, white beneath. Produces star-shaped yellow flowers in midspring, then egg-shaped, bright orange fruits. Makes a good hedge, especially in coastal areas. Z8–10 H10–8.

CORONILLA

LEGUMINOSAE/PAPILIONACEAE

Genus of deciduous or evergreen shrubs and perennials grown for their foliage and flowers. Requires full sun and light, well-drained soil. Propagate by softwood cuttings in summer.
C. glauca. See *C. valentina* subsp. *glauca*.
C. valentina subsp. ***glauca***, syn. *C. glauca*, illus. p.157.

CORREA

RUTACEAE

Genus of evergreen shrubs grown for their flowers. Prefers full light or partial shade and fertile, well-drained, neutral to acidic soil. Water potted specimens moderately, less when not in flower. Propagate by seed in spring or by semi-ripe cuttings in late summer.
***C. backhouseana*.** Evergreen, rounded, well-branched shrub. H and S 6ft (2m). Leaves are oval to elliptic and dark green, with dense, pale buff down beneath. Tubular, pale yellow-green to white flowers appear in spring and intermittently until autumn. Z9–10 H10–8
***C.* x *harrisii*.** See *C.* 'Mannii'.
***C.* 'Harrisii'.** See *C.* 'Mannii'.
***C.* 'Mannii'**, syn. *C.* x *harrisii*, *C.* 'Harrisii'. Evergreen, bushy, slender-stemmed shrub. H and S 6ft (2m). Has narrowly oval leaves with short hairs beneath. Tubular scarlet flowers are carried in summer-autumn, sometimes in other seasons. Z9–10 H10–9.
C. pulchella illus. p.174.
C. reflexa, syn. *C. speciosa*. Evergreen, bushy, slender-stemmed shrub. H and S to 6ft (2m). Oval leaves have thick down beneath. Bears tubular, greenish yellow to crimson or rose flowers with greenish white petal tips in summer-autumn, sometimes in other seasons. Z9–10 H10–9.
***C. speciosa*.** See *C. reflexa*.

CORTADERIA

GRAMINEAE/POACEAE

See also GRASSES, BAMBOOS, RUSHES, and SEDGES.
C. selloana (Pampas grass). Evergreen, clump-forming, stately, perennial grass. H to 8ft (2.5m), S 4ft (1.2m). Has narrow, very sharp-edged, outward-curving leaves, 5ft (1.5m) long. In late summer, erect, plumelike silvery panicles, up to 2ft (60cm) long, are borne above midgreen leaves. Male and female flowers are produced on separate plants; females, with long, silky hairs, are more decorative. Z7–11 H12–7. **'Aureolineata'** (syn. *C.s.* 'Gold Band'), H to 7ft (2.2m), is compact and has leaves with rich yellow margins aging to dark golden yellow. **'Gold Band'** see *C.s.* 'Aureolineata'. **'Silver Comet'** and **'Sunningdale Silver'** illus. p.306.

CORTUSA

PRIMULACEAE

Genus of clump-forming, spring- and summer-flowering perennials, related to *Primula*, with one-sided racemes of bell-shaped flowers. Is not suited to hot, dry climates, since it needs shade and organic, moist soil. Propagate by seed when fresh or by division in autumn.
C. matthioli illus. p.354.

CORYDALIS

PAPAVERACEAE

Genus of spring- and summer-flowering annuals and tuberous or fibrous-rooted perennials, some of which are evergreen, grown for their tubular, spurred, 2-lipped flowers or for their fernlike leaves. Needs full sun or partial shade and well-drained soil; some require organic soil and cool growing conditions. Propagate by seed in autumn or by division when dormant: autumn for spring-flowering species, spring for summer-flowering species.
C. ambigua of gardens. See *C. fumariifolia*.
C. bulbosa of gardens. See *C. cava*.
***C. cashmeriana*.** Tuft-forming, fibrous-rooted perennial. H 4–10in (10–25cm), S 3–4in (8–10cm). Has divided, semi-erect, basal leaves and, in summer, dense spikes of 2-lipped, brilliant blue flowers. Needs cool, partially shaded, organic, neutral to acidic soil. Is good for a rock garden. Dies down in winter. Z6–8 H8–6.
C. cava, syn. *C. bulbosa* of gardens. Spring-flowering, tuberous perennial. H 4–8in (10–20cm), S 3–4in (8–10cm). Leaves are semi-erect, basal, and much divided. Carries dense spikes of tubular, dull purple flowers. Dies down in summer. Z6-8 H8–6.
C. cheilanthifolia illus. p.349.
C. diphylla illus. p.367.
C. fumariifolia, syn. *C. ambigua* of gardens. Tuberous perennial, flowering from spring to early summer. H to 6in (15cm), S to 4in (10cm). Stem bears much-divided leaves and a short spike of 2-lipped, azure blue or purplish blue flowers, with flattened, triangular spurs. Dies down in summer.
***C. halleri*.** See *C. solida*.
C. lutea, syn. *Pseudofumaria lutea*, illus. p.359.
***C. nobilis*.** Perennial with long, fleshy, fibrous roots. H and S 8–14in (20–35cm). Bears much-divided leaves on lower part of flower stems, each of which carries a dense spike of long-spurred, pale yellow flowers, with lips tipped green or brown, in spring. Z5–8 H8–5.
C. ochroleuca, syn. *Pseudofumaria ochroleuca*, illus. p.351.
C. popovii illus. p.364.
C. solida, syn. *C. halleri*. Tuft-forming, tuberous perennial. H 4–8in (10–20cm), S 3–5in (8–12cm). Leaves alternate on flower stems, each of which carries a dense spike of dull purplish red flowers in spring. Dies down in summer. Z5–7 H7–3. **'George Baker'** (syn. *C.s.* 'G.P. Baker') illus. p.367.
C. wilsonii illus. p.349.

CORYLOPSIS

HAMAMELIDACEAE

Genus of deciduous shrubs and trees grown for their fragrant yellow flowers, which are produced before hazel-like leaves emerge. Late frosts may damage flowers. Prefers semi-shade and fertile, moist but well-drained, acidic soil. Propagate by softwood cuttings in summer or by seed in autumn.
C. glabrescens illus. p.117.
C. pauciflora illus. p.131.
C. sinensis, syn. *C. willmottiae*. Vigorous, deciduous, spreading, open shrub. H and S 12ft (4m). Leaves are bright green above, blue-green beneath. Clusters of bell-shaped, pale yellow flowers open from early to midspring. Z5–9 H9–2.**'Spring Purple'** has deep plumpurple, young leaves.
***C. spicata*.** Deciduous, spreading, open shrub. H 6ft (2m), S 10ft (3m). Bristle-toothed leaves are dull, pale green above, blue-green beneath. Drooping clusters of bell-shaped, pale yellow flowers are borne in midspring. Z5–8 H8–5.
***C. willmottiae*.** See *C. sinensis*.

CORYLUS
Hazel

CORYLACEAE

Genus of deciduous trees and shrubs grown for their habit, catkins, and often edible fruits (nuts). Prefers sun or semi-shade and fertile, well-drained soil. Cut out suckers as they arise. Propagate species by seed in autumn, and cultivars by grafting in late summer or by suckers or layering in late autumn to early spring. Mildew may cause defoliation; other fungi and insects may spoil nuts.
C. avellana (Cobnut). **'Contorta'** illus. p.125.
C. colurna (Turkish hazel). Deciduous, conical tree. H 70ft (20m), S 22ft (7m). Has broadly oval, strongly toothed, almost lobed, dark green leaves. Long yellow catkins are borne in late winter. Clusters of nuts are set in fringed husks. Z5–7 H7–5.
C. maxima (Filbert). Vigorous, deciduous, bushy, open shrub or tree. H 20ft (6m), S 15ft (5m). Bears oval, toothed, midgreen leaves, long yellow catkins in late winter, and edible, egg-shaped brown nuts. Z4–9 H9–1. **'Purpurea'** illus. p.122.

CORYNOCARPUS

CORYNOCARPACEAE

Genus of evergreen trees grown for their foliage and overall appearance. Needs full light or partial shade and fertile, moisture-retentive but well-drained soil. Water containerized specimens moderately, less when temperatures are low. Pruning is tolerated if necessary. Propagate by seed when ripe or by semi-ripe cuttings in summer.
C. laevigatus illus. p.85.

CORYPHANTHA

CACTACEAE

Genus of cacti with roughly spherical, spiny green stems. Stems have elongated areoles in grooves running along upper sides of tubercles; many species show this groove only on very old plants. Funnel-shaped flowers are produced in summer, followed by cylindrical green seed pods. Needs a site in full sun with very well-drained soil. Propagate by seed in spring or summer.
C. cornifera, syn. *C. radians*, illus. p.479.
***C. radians*.** See *C. cornifera*.
***C. vivipara*.** See *Escobaria vivipara*.

COSMOS

ASTERACEAE/COMPOSITAE

Genus of summer- and early autumn-flowering annuals and tuberous perennials. Needs sun and does best in moist but well-drained soil. In milder areas, tubers of *C. atrosanguineus* may be overwintered in ground if protected with a deep mulch. Propagate perennial species by basal cuttings in spring, annuals by seed in autumn or spring.
C. atrosanguineus, syn. *Bidens atrosanguinea*, illus. p.249.
***C. bipinnatus*.** Upright, bushy annual. H to 5ft (1.5m), S 1½ft (45cm). Has feathery, midgreen leaves, and, throughout summer, produces solitary, bowl- or saucer-shaped flower heads in white, pink, or crimson, with yellow centers. H12–1. **'Candy Stripe'**, H to 3ft (90cm), has white flower heads edged and flecked with crimson. **'Sea Shells'**, H to 3ft (90cm), produces carmine-red, pink, or white flower heads with tubular florets. **Sensation Series** illus. p.325.
C. sulphureus **Ladybird Series**. Group of upright, bushy annuals. H 12–16in (30–40cm), S 8in (20cm). Has feathery, midgreen leaves and in summer produces clusters of semi-double, bowl-shaped flower heads in yellow, orange, or scarlet, with black centers. H12–1.

COSTUS

ZINGIBERACEAE

Genus of mostly clump-forming, rhizomatous perennials grown for their showy, solitary or paired, tubular flowers with basal bracts. Grow in a humid atmosphere, out of direct sunlight, in organic soil. Propagate by division in spring. Pot-grown plants may be attacked by spider mite.
C. speciosus (Malay ginger). Clump-forming, rhizomatous perennial. H 6ft (2m) or more, S 3ft (1m). Has narrowly oval, downy leaves, to 10in (25cm) long. Reddish bracts are spine-tipped, each surrounding one white or pink-flushed flower to 4in (10cm) wide with a broad, yellow-centered lip; flowers are produced intermittently throughout the year. Z11–12 H12–9.

COTINUS

ANACARDIACEAE

Genus of deciduous shrubs and trees grown for their foliage, flower heads, and autumn color. Individual flowers are inconspicuous. Requires a position in full sun or semi-shade, with fertile but not overly rich soil. Purple-leaved forms need full sun to bring out their best colors. Propagate species by softwood or greenwood cuttings in summer or by seed in autumn, cultivars by cuttings only in summer.
C. americanus. See *C. obovatus*.
C. coggygria, syn. *Rhus cotinus* (Smoke tree, Venetian sumac). Deciduous, bushy shrub. H and S 15ft (5m). Leaves are rounded or oval and light green, becoming yellow or red in autumn. From late summer, as insignificant fruits develop, masses of tiny flower stalks form showy, light brown, later gray, plumelike clusters. Z5–9 H9–3. **'Flame'** see *C.* 'Flame'. **'Notcutt's Variety'** illus. p.121. **'Royal Purple'** has deep pink plumes and deep purplish red leaves.
***C.* 'Flame'**, syn. *C. coggygria* 'Flame', illus. p.124
C. obovatus, syn. *C. americanus*, *Rhus cotinoides*. Vigorous, deciduous, bushy shrub or tree. H 10m (30ft), S 25ft (8m). Has large, oval leaves that are bronze-pink when young, maturing to midgreen and turning orange, red, and purple in autumn. Z4–8 H8–1.

COTONEASTER

ROSACEAE

Genus of deciduous, semi-evergreen or evergreen shrubs and trees grown for their foliage, flowers, and fruits. Some species make fine specimen plants; others may be used for hedging or as groundcover. Deciduous species and cultivars prefer full sun, but evergreens do well in either sun or semi-shade. All resent waterlogged soil and are particularly useful for dry sites. Propagate species by cuttings in summer or by seed in autumn, hybrids and cultivars by cuttings only, in summer. Take semi-ripe cuttings for evergreens and semi-evergreens, softwood cuttings for deciduous plants. Fireblight is a common problem. The seeds may cause mild stomach upset if ingested.
C. adpressus. Deciduous, arching shrub. H 1ft (30cm), S 6ft (2m). Rounded, wavy-edged, dark green leaves redden in autumn. Produces small, 5-petaled pink flowers in early summer, then spherical red fruits. Z5–7 H7–1. var. *praecox* see *C. nanshen*.
***C.* 'Autumn Fire'**. See *C.* 'Herbstfeuer'.
C. bullatus* 'Firebird'**, syn. *C.* 'Firebird'. Deciduous, bushy, open shrub. H and S 10ft (3m). Large, oval, deeply veined, dark green leaves redden in autumn. Small, 5-petaled white flowers in early summer are followed by masses of spherical, bright red fruits. Z6–8 H8–6. var. ***macrophyllus see *C. rehderi*.
C. cashmiriensis, syn. *C. cochleatus* of gardens, *C. microphyllus* var. *cochleatus* of gardens. Evergreen, prostrate shrub. H to 1½ft (45cm), S 6ft (2m). Has small, oval, notched, dark green leaves. Small white flowers are produced in late spring, followed by spherical red fruits. Z6–8 H8–6.
C. cochleatus of gardens. See *C. cashmiriensis*.
C. congestus. Evergreen, prostrate shrub. H 8in (20cm), S 6ft (2m). Forms dense mounds of oval, dull green leaves. Produces small, 5-petaled, pinkish white flowers in early summer, followed by spherical, bright red fruits. Is excellent for a rock garden. Z7–8 H8–7.
C. conspicuus, syn. *C.c.* var. *decorus*. Evergreen, prostrate, arching shrub. H 1ft (30cm), S 6–10ft (2–3m). Leaves are oblong and glossy, very dark green. Small, 5-petaled white flowers in late spring are succeeded by large, spherical, scarlet or orange-red fruits. Z6–8 H8–6.
***C.* 'Coral Beauty'.** Evergreen, arching, dense shrub. H 3ft (1m), S 6ft (2m). Has small, oval, glossy, dark green leaves and, in early summer, produces small, 5-petaled white flowers. Fruits are spherical and bright orange-red. Z7–8 H8–7.
***C.* 'Cornubia'** illus. p.124.
C. dielsianus. Deciduous, arching shrub. H and S 8ft (2.5m). Slender shoots are clothed in oval, dark green leaves. Produces small, 5-petaled pink flowers in early summer, followed by spherical, glossy red fruits. Z6–8 H8–6.
C. divaricatus illus. p.130.
***C.* 'Firebird'.** See *C. bullatus* 'Firebird'.
C. franchetii. Evergreen or semi-evergreen, arching shrub. H and S 10ft (3m). Oval, gray-green leaves are white beneath. Bears small, 5-petaled, pink-tinged white flowers in early summer, then a profusion of oblong, bright orange-red fruits. Z7–9 H9–7. var. ***sternianus*** see *C. sternianus*.
C. frigidus (Tree cotoneaster). Vigorous, deciduous tree, upright when young, arching when mature. H and S 10m (30ft). Has large, broadly oval, wavy-edged, dull green leaves and broad heads of small, 5-petaled white flowers borne in early summer, followed by large clusters of long-lasting, small, spherical, bright red fruits. Z7–8 H8–7.
C. glaucophyllus. Evergreen, arching, open shrub. H and S 10ft (3m). Leaves are oval, dark green, bluish white beneath. Produces small, 5-petaled white flowers in midsummer, followed by small, spherical, deep red fruits in autumn. Z7–8 H8–7. var. ***serotinus*** see *C. serotinus*.
***C.* 'Gnom'**, syn. *C.* 'Gnome', *C. salicifolius* 'Gnom'. Evergreen, prostrate shrub. H 8in (20cm), S 6ft (2m). Bears narrowly lance-shaped, dark green leaves, small, 5-petaled white flowers in early summer, then clusters of small, spherical red fruits. Makes a good groundcover. Z7–8 H8–7.
***C.* 'Gnome'.** See *C.* 'Gnom'.
***C.* 'Herbstfeuer'**, syn. *C.* 'Autumn Fire'. Evergreen, prostrate or arching shrub. H 1ft (30cm), S 6ft (2m). Has lance-shaped, bright green leaves. Small, 5-petaled white flowers in early summer are followed by spherical, bright red fruits. May be grown as groundcover or as a weeping standard. Z5–8 H8–5.
C. horizontalis illus. p.172.
C. hupehensis. Deciduous, arching shrub. H 6ft (2m), S 10ft (3m). Oval, bright green leaves become yellow in autumn. Masses of small, 5-petaled white flowers in late spring are succeeded by large, spherical, bright red fruits. Z5–8 H8–5.
***C.* 'Hybridus Pendulus'.** Evergreen, prostrate shrub, almost always grown as a weeping standard. H 6ft (2m), S 5ft (1.5m). Has oblong, dark green leaves. Small, 5-petaled white flowers in early summer are followed by spherical, deep red fruits. Z6–8 H8–6.
C. lacteus illus. p.125.
C. linearifolius, syn. *C. microphyllus* var. *thymifolius* of gardens. Evergreen, prostrate shrub. H 2ft (60cm), S 6ft (2m). Rigid branches bear tiny, narrow, blunt-ended, glossy leaves. Produces small white flowers in late spring, followed by spherical red fruits. Z6–8 H8–6.
C. lucidus (Hedge cotoneaster). Upright growth produces a rounded shrub. H and S 2-3m (6-10ft). Shiny, dark green leaves are hairy beneath. Small clusters of pale pink flowers in late spring and shiny black fruit in fall. Often used for hedging. Z3–7 H7–1.
C. microphyllus. Evergreen, spreading, dense shrub. H 3ft (1m), S 6ft (2m). Rigid shoots are clothed in small, oval, dark green leaves. Small, 5-petaled white flowers in late spring are followed by spherical red fruits. Z6–8 H8–6. var. ***cochleatus*** of gardens see *C. cashmiriensis*. var. ***thymifolius*** of gardens see *C. linearifolius*.
C. nanshen syn. *C. adpressus* var. *praecox*. A low, creeping, deciduous plant that is a good groundcover for stabilizing banks and slopes. H 18in (45cm) S 4ft (1.2m). Rounded foliage is midgreen, turning red in fall. Pink flowers in late spring produce persistent bright red fruits. Z5–8 H8–5. **'Boer'** has larger, earlier fruits.
C. prostratus of gardens. See *C. rotundifolius*.
C. rehderi, syn. *C. bullatus* var. *macrophyllus*. Deciduous, bushy, open shrub. H 15ft (5m), S 10ft (3m). Very large, oval, deeply veined, dark green leaves change to red in autumn. Clusters of small, 5-petaled pink flowers appear in late spring and early summer, succeeded by spherical, bright red fruits. Z6–8 H8–6.
***C.* 'Rothschildianus'.** Evergreen or semi-evergreen, arching shrub. H and S 15ft (5m). Has narrowly oval, bright green leaves, small, 5-petaled white flowers in early summer, and large clusters of spherical, golden yellow fruits. Z6–8 H8–6.
C. rotundifolius, syn. *C. prostratus* of gardens. Evergreen, arching shrub. H 5ft (1.5m), S 8ft (2.5m). Has small, oval, glossy, dark green leaves. Produces small, 5-petaled white flowers in early summer, followed by spherical, deep red fruits. Z7–8 H8–7.
C. salicifolius. Vigorous, evergreen, arching shrub. H and S 15ft (5m). Has narrowly lance-shaped, dark green leaves. Small, 5-petaled white flowers in early summer, are followed by clusters of small, spherical red fruits. Z6–8 H8–6. **'Gnom'** see *C.* 'Gnom'.
C. serotinus, syn. *C. glaucophyllus* var. *serotinus*. Evergreen, arching, open shrub. H and S 20ft (6m). Has oval, dark green leaves. Small white flowers are borne from mid to late summer and the fruits last until spring. Z7–8 H8–7.
C. simonsii illus. p.148
***C.* 'Skogholm'**, syn. *C.* 'Skogsholmen'. Evergreen, arching, wide-spreading shrub. H 2ft (60cm), S 10ft (3m). Leaves are small, oval, and glossy, dark green. Bears small, 5-petaled white flowers during early summer, then rather sparse, spherical red fruits. Makes a good groundcover. Z6–8 H8–6.
***C.* 'Skogsholmen'.** See *C.* 'Skogholm'.
C. sternianus, syn. *C. franchetii* var. *sternianus*, illus. p.149.
***C.* x *watereri* 'John Waterer'.** Vigorous, evergreen or semi-evergreen, arching shrub. H and S 15ft (5m). Has lance-shaped, dark green leaves. Bears small, 5-petaled white flowers in early summer and produces a profusion of spherical red fruits in large clusters. Z6–8 H8–6.

COTULA

ASTERACEAE/COMPOSITAE

Genus of perennials and a few marginal water plants, most of which are evergreen, grown for their neat foliage and buttonlike flower heads. Many species are useful for cracks in paving stones but may be invasive. Most need a position in full sun, with well-drained soil that is not too dry. Propagate by division in spring.
C. atrata. See *Leptinella atrata*.
C. coronopifolia (Brass buttons). Short-lived, deciduous, perennial, marginal water plant. H 6in (15cm),

S 12in (24cm). Has fleshy stems, small, lance-shaped, midgreen leaves, and, in summer, buttonlike yellow flower heads. Z7–9 H9–7.

COTYLEDON

CRASSULACEAE

Genus of evergreen, succulent shrubs and subshrubs grown for their diverse foliage that ranges from large, oval, gray leaves to small, cylindrical, midgreen leaves. Likes a sunny or partially shaded site and very well-drained soil. Propagate by seed or stem cuttings in spring or summer.

C. cooperi. See *Adromischus cooperi.*
C. ladismithensis illus. p.474.
C. orbiculata. Evergreen, upright, succulent shrub. H and S 20in (50cm) or more. Swollen stem bears thin, oval, midgreen leaves densely coated in white wax and sometimes red-edged. Flower stems, to 28in (70cm) long, have pendent, tubular orange flowers in autumn. Z12–15 H12–10.
var. ***oblonga*** (syn. *C. undulata*) illus. p.468.
C. paniculata. See *Tylecodon paniculatus.*
C. reticulata. See *Tylecodon reticulatus.*
C. simplicifolia. See *Chiastophyllum oppositifolium.*
C. undulata. See *C. orbiculata* var. *oblonga.*
C. wallichii. See *Tylecodon papillaris* subsp. *wallichii.*

CRAMBE

BRASSICACEAE/CRUCIFERAE

Genus of annuals and perennials grown for their bold leaves and large sprays of white flowers in summer. Leaf shoots of *C. maritima* (Sea kale) are eaten as a spring vegetable. Will grow in any well-drained soil; prefers an open position in full sun but tolerates some shade. Propagate by division in spring or by seed in autumn or spring.

C. cordifolia illus. p.226.
C. maritima illus. p.276.

CRASPEDIA

ASTERACEAE/COMPOSITAE

Genus of basal-rosetted, summer-flowering perennials, some of which are best treated as annuals. Needs a site in sun and well-drained soil. Propagate by seed sown when very fresh in summer.

C. incana. Basal-rosetted perennials. H 8–12in (20–30cm), S 4in (10cm). Has narrowly oval, basal leaves with dense, woolly white hairs beneath, and smaller leaves on the flower stems. In summer, many domed heads of 3–10 tiny, tubular yellow flowers are produced in large, terminal clusters. Z9–10 H10–9.

CRASSULA

CRASSULACEAE

Genus of succulents and evergreen, succulent shrubs and subshrubs, ranging from ¾in (2cm) high, very succulent-leaved species to 15ft (5m) shrubby ones. Most are easy to grow. Most prefer full sun; others like partial shade. Needs very well-drained soil and a little water in winter. Propagate by seed or stem cuttings in spring or autumn.

C. arborescens illus. p.458.
C. argentea of gardens. See *C. ovata.*
C. coccinea, syn. *Rochea coccinea.* Evergreen, erect, succulent shrub. H to 24in (60cm), S 12in (24cm) or more. Alternate pairs of fleshy, oval to oblong-oval, hairy-margined, dull green leaves, each united at the base, are arranged at right angles in 4 rows up the woody green stems. Produces umbels of tubular, bright red flowers in summer or autumn. Z12–15 H12–10.
C. cooperi. See *C. exilis* subsp. *cooperi.*
C. deceptor, syn. *C. deceptrix*, illus. p.476.
C. deceptrix. See *C. deceptor.*
C. exilis subsp. ***cooperi***, syn. *C. cooperi.* Carpeting succulent. H ¾in (2cm), S 12in (24cm). Has small, spoon- to lance-shaped, light green leaves pitted with darker green or blackish green marks. Produces clusters of minute, 5-petaled white to pale pink flowers in winter. Z12–15 H12–10.
C. falcata. See *C. perfoliata* var. *minor.*
C. lactea. Prostrate to semi-erect succulent. H 8in (20cm), S 3ft (1m). Leaves are triangular-oval, glossy, and dark green. In winter produces masses of small, 5-petaled white flowers in terminal clusters. Likes partial shade. Z12–15 H12–10.
C. lycopodioides. See *C. muscosa.*
C. muscosa, syn. *C. lycopodioides.* Dense, bushy, woody-based succulent. H 6in (15cm), S 12in (24cm). Bears small, scalelike, neatly overlapping, midgreen leaves arranged in 4 rows around erect stems. In spring, produces tiny, 5-petaled, greenish yellow flowers. Likes partial shade. Z12–15 H12–10.
C. multicava illus. p.471.
C. ovata, syn. *C. argentea* of gardens, *C. portulacea*, illus. p.457.
C. perfoliata var. ***minor***, syn. *C. falcata*, illus. p.464.
C. portulacea. See *C. ovata.*
C. sarcocaulis illus. p.353.
C. schmidtii illus. p.473.
C. socialis illus. p.470.

+ CRATAEGOMESPILUS

ROSACEAE

Botanically curious and extremely rarely grown group of grafted, hybrid, deciduous trees (*Crataegus* and *Mespilus*) grown for their flowers, foliage, and fruits. Requires sun or semi-shade and fertile, well-drained soil. Propagate by grafting in late summer.

+ ***C. dardarII*** (Bronvaux medlar). **'Jules d'Asnières'** is a deciduous, spreading tree. H and S 20ft (6m). Has drooping branches and spiny shoots. Variable, oval or deeply lobed, dark green leaves, gray when young, turn orange and yellow in autumn. Clusters of saucer-shaped white, sometimes rose-tinted flowers in late spring or early summer are followed by small, rounded, red-brown fruits. Z7–9 H9–7.

CRATAEGUS

Hawthorn

ROSACEAE

Genus of deciduous, or more rarely semi-evergreen, spiny, often spreading trees and shrubs grown for their clustered, 5-petaled, occasionally double flowers in spring-summer, ornamental fruits, and, in some cases, autumn color. Prefers full sun but is suitable for most sites and may be grown in any but very wet soil. Is useful for growing in polluted urban areas, exposed sites, and coastal gardens. Propagate species by seed in autumn, cultivars by budding in late summer. Fireblight is sometimes a problem. The seeds may cause mild stomach upset if ingested.

C. cordata. See *C. phaenopyrum.*
C. crus-galli (Cockspur hawthorn). Deciduous, flat-topped tree. H 25ft (8m), S 10m (30ft). Has shoots armed with long, curved thorns and oval, glossy, dark green leaves that turn bright crimson in autumn. Clusters of white flowers with pink anthers in late spring are followed by long-lasting, rounded, bright red fruits. Z4–7 H7–1.
C. crus-galli of gardens. See ***C. flava*** illus. p.90.
C. laciniata, syn. *C. orientalis*, illus. p.85.
C. laevigata, syn. *C. oxyacantha* of gardens (Hawthorn, May tree). **'Paul's Scarlet'** illus. p.91. **'Punicea'** is a deciduous, spreading tree. H and S 20ft (6m). In late spring and early summer, oval, lobed, toothed, glossy, dark green leaves set off clusters of crimson flowers, which are followed by rounded red fruits. Z5–8 H8–3..
C. x ***lavallei*** **'Carrierei'.** Vigorous, deciduous, spreading tree. H 22ft (7m), S 10m (30ft). Oval, glossy, dark green leaves turn red in late autumn. Has clusters of white flowers in late spring, followed by long-lasting, rounded, orange-red fruits. Z5–7 H7–4.
C. macrosperma var. ***acutiloba*** illus. p.94.
C. mollis. Deciduous, spreading tree. H 30ft (10m), S 40ft (12m). Large, broadly oval, lobed, dark green leaves have white-haired undersides when young. Bears heads of large white flowers in late spring, followed by short-lived, rounded red fruits. Z3–6 H6–1.
C. monogyna (Singleseed hawthorn). Deciduous, round-headed tree. H 30ft (10m), S 25ft (8m). Has broadly oval, deeply lobed, glossy, dark green leaves. Clusters of fragrant white flowers are borne from late spring to early summer, followed by rounded red fruits. Makes a dense hedge. Z5–7 H7–4. **'Biflora'** (Glastonbury thorn) has flowers and leaves in mild winters as well as in spring. Z5–7 H7–5.
C. x mordenensis. A rounded, deciduous tree with very few thorns. H and S 20ft (6m). Foliage is dark green and turns bronze in fall. Double flowers are freely produced in late spring and followed by sparse, spherical red fruit that persist into winter. Z3–1 H8–1. **'Toba'** has pale pink flowers that darken with age; **'Snowbird'** is white.
C. orientalis. See *C. laciniata.*
C. oxyacantha of gardens. See *C. laevigata.*
C. pedicellata illus. p.95.
C. persimilis **'Prunifolia'**, syn. *C. crus-galli* of gardens, *C.* x *prunifolia.* Deciduous, spreading, thorny tree. H 25ft (8m), S 30ft (10m). Oval, glossy, dark green leaves turn red or orange in autumn. Has clusters of white flowers with pink anthers in early summer, then rounded, dark red fruits. Z6–7
C. phaenopyrum, syn. *C. cordata* (Washington thorn). Deciduous, round-headed tree. H and S 30ft (10m). Broadly oval leaves are sharply lobed, glossy, and dark green. Clusters of white flowers with pink anthers are produced from early to midsummer, followed by rounded, glossy red fruits that last through winter. Z4–8.
C. x ***prunifolia.*** See *C. persimilis* 'Prunifolia'.
C. viridis 'Winter King'. A round-headed tree with slender thorns and attractive green new bark. H 20ft (6m) S 15ft (5m). Foliage is glossy, midgreen, turning red in fall. White flowers (with yellow anthers) produce masses of showy bright red fruit that last well into winter. Older bark flakes off in plates, giving winter interest. Z5–7 H7–5.

CREMANTHODIUM

ASTERACEAE/COMPOSITAE

Genus of basal-rosetted perennials grown for their pendent, half-closed, daisylike flower heads. Is often very difficult to grow in all but cold areas with snow cover. Dislikes winter wet. Needs shade and organic, moist but well-drained soil. Propagate by seed when fresh.

C. reniforme. Basal-rosetted perennial. H and S 8in (20cm). Leaves are large and kidney-shaped. Thick stems each carry a large, daisylike yellow flower head in summer.

CREPIS

Hawk's beard

ASTERACEAE/COMPOSITAE

Genus of summer-flowering annuals, biennials, and perennials, some of which are evergreen, with long taproots and leaves in flat rosettes. Many species are persistent weeds, but some are grown for their many-petaled, dandelion-like flower heads. Tolerates sun or shade and prefers well-drained soil. Propagate annuals and biennials by seed in autumn, perennials by root cuttings (not from taproot) in late winter, although most species self-seed freely.

C. aurea illus. p.359.
C. incana (Pink dandelion). Basal-

rosetted perennial. H 8in (20cm), S 4in (10cm). Bears oblong, divided, hairy, grayish green leaves. Uneven disks of ragged pink flower heads are produced on stiff stems in summer. Is good for a sunny rock garden or border. Z5–7 H7–4.
C. rubra illus. p.320.

CRINODENDRON

ELAEOCARPACEAE

Genus of evergreen shrubs and trees grown for their flowers and foliage. Requires shade or semi-shade, with plant base in cool shade. Soil should be fertile, moist but well-drained, and acidic. Propagate by softwood cuttings in summer or by seed in autumn.
C. hookerianum, syn. *Tricuspidaria lanceolata*, illus. p.142.

x ***Crinodonna corsii.*** See x *Amarcrinum memoria-corsii.*

CRINUM

AMARYLLIDACEAE

Genus of robust bulbs grown for their often fragrant, funnel-shaped flowers. Needs full sun, shelter and rich, well-drained soil. Propagate by offsets in spring or by seed when fresh or in spring. All parts may cause severe discomfort if ingested; contact with the sap may irritate skin.
C. americanum. Tuft-forming, spring- and summer-flowering bulb. H 16–30in (40–75cm), S 24in (60cm). Has 6–10 strap-shaped, semi-erect, basal leaves. Leafless stem bears a head of up to 6 fragrant, long-tubed white flowers with narrow petals. Z8–11 H12–8.
C. asiaticum illus. p.419.
C. bulbispermum, syn. *C. longifolium*. Summer-flowering bulb. H to 3ft (1m), S 2ft (60cm). Leafless flower stem has a head of fragrant, long-tubed white or pinkish red flowers with darker red stripes. Bears long, strap-shaped, semi-erect leaves grouped in a tuft on a short stalk. Z7–11 H12–8.
C. longifolium. See *C. bulbispermum*.
C. macowanii. Autumn-flowering bulb. H and S 2ft (60cm) or more. Similar to *C. bulbispermum*, but leaves are wavy-edged. Z10–11 H12–10.
C. moorei illus. p.398.
C. x ***powellii*** illus. p.398. **'Album'** illus. p.397.

CROCOSMIA

Montbretia

IRIDACEAE

Genus of corms grown for their brightly colored flowers produced mainly in summer. Forms dense clumps of sword-shaped, erect leaves. Requires well-drained soil and an open, sunny site. In cold areas, plant in a sheltered position or lift and store corms over winter. Propagate by division as growth commences in spring.
C. aurea. Tuft-forming, summer-flowering corm. H 20–30in (50–75cm), S 6–8in (15–20cm). Erect, basal leaves are long, narrow, and sword-shaped. Carries a loosely branched spike of tubular orange or yellow flowers, each 1–2in (3–5cm) long and with 6 spreading petals.
***C.* 'Bressingham Blaze'** illus. p.401.
***C.* 'Citronella'** of gardens. See *C.* 'Golden Fleece'.
***C.* 'Emily McKenzie'.** Compact, late summer-flowering corm. H to 24in (60cm), S 6–8in (15–20cm). Leaves are erect, basal, and sword-shaped. Bears a dense spike of widely funnel-shaped, deep orange flowers, each with a dark mahogany throat. Z6–9 H9–2.
***C.* 'Golden Fleece'**, syn. *C.* 'Citronella' of gardens, illus. p.403.
***C.* 'Jackanapes'** illus. p.423.
***C.* 'Lucifer'** illus. p.401
C. masoniorum, syn. *C. masonorum*, illus. p.401.
C. masonorum. See *C. masoniorum*.
C. paniculata, syn. *Antholyza paniculata*, *Curtonus paniculatus*. Summer-flowering corm. H to 5ft (1.5m), S 1–1½ft (30–45cm). Has sword-shaped, erect, basal leaves, pleated lengthwise. Carries long-tubed orange flowers on branched stems, which are strongly zig-zag in shape. Z6–9 H9–2.
***C.* 'Star of the East'** illus. p.403.

CROCUS

IRIDACEAE

Genus of mainly spring- or autumn-flowering corms with funnel-shaped to rounded, long-tubed flowers. Has long, very narrow, semi-erect, basal leaves, (usually 1–5 per corm), each with a white line along the center. Some autumn-flowering species have no leaves at flowering time, these appearing in winter or spring. Most species are less than 4in (10cm) tall when in flower and have a spread of 1–3in (2.5–8cm). Ideal for rock gardens and for forcing in bowls for an early indoor display. Most require well-drained soil and a sunny situation; *C. banaticus* prefers moist soil and semi-shade. Plant 2–2½in (5–6cm) deep in late summer or early autumn. Propagate in early autumn by seed or division if clumps of corms have formed. See also feature panel pp.428–9.
***C.* 'Advance'** (illus. p.429). Late winter- to midspring flowering corm. Funnel-shaped flowers are buttercup yellow inside and paler yellow outside, suffused violet-bronze. Z3–8 H8–1.
C. aerius of gardens. See *C. biflorus* subsp. *pulchricolor*.
C. ancyrensis. Spring-flowering corm. Produces up to 7 fragrant, bright orange-yellow flowers, 2–2½in (5–6cm) long. Z3–8 H8–1.
C. angustifolius, syn. *C. susianus* (Cloth-of-gold crocus). Spring-flowering corm. Fragrant flowers are bright golden yellow, striped or stained bronze outside. Z3–8 H8–1.
C. aureus. See *C. flavus*.
C. balansae. See *C. olivieri* subsp. *balansae*.
C. banaticus, syn. *C. iridiflorus* (illus. p.429). Autumn-flowering corm. Usually has one long-tubed, pale violet flower; outer 3 petals are much larger than inner 3. Very narrow, semi-erect, basal leaves, each with a paler line along the center, appear in spring. Z3–8 H8–1.
C. baytopiorum (illus. p.429). Spring-flowering corm. Each corm bears 1 or 2 rounded, clear turquoise blue, slightly darker-veined flowers. Z3–8 H8–1.
C. biflorus (illus. p.429). Early spring-flowering corm. Has narrow, semi-erect, basal leaves, each with a white line along the center. Bears fragrant white or purplish white flowers with yellow throats, vertically striped purple outside. Z3–8 H8–1. subsp. ***alexandri*** has fragrant, deep violet flowers with white insides. subsp. ***pulchricolor*** (syn. *C. aerius* of gardens) has rich deep blue flowers with golden yellow centers.
***C.* 'Blue Bird'** (illus. p.428). Late winter- to midspring-flowering corm. Funnel-shaped flowers are white inside with deep yellow throats and violet margined with white outside.
***C.* 'Blue Pearl'** (illus. p.428). Early spring-flowering corm. Produces narrow, semi-erect, basal leaves with white lines along the centers. Fragrant, long-tubed, funnel-shaped, soft lavender-blue flowers, bluish white within, have golden yellow throats. Z3–8 H8–1.
C. boryi (illus. p.428). Autumn-flowering corm. Flowers are ivory-white, sometimes veined or flushed with mauve outside. Z4–8 H8–1.
C. cancellatus. Autumn-flowering corm. Slender flowers are pale blue, slightly striped outside. Leaves appear in spring. Z5–8 H8–5.
C. cartwrightianus (illus. p.429). Autumn-flowering corm. Produces leaves at same time as strongly veined, violet or white flowers, each 1½–2½in (4–6cm) across and with 3 long, bright red stigmas, similar to those of *C. sativus*. Z6–8 H8–6.
C. chrysanthus. Spring-flowering corm. Scented flowers are orange-yellow throughout with deeper orange-red stigmas. Z3–8 H8–1.
***C.* 'Cream Beauty'** (illus. p.429). Spring-flowering corm. Scented rich cream flowers with deep yellow throats, are stained purplish brown outside at base. Bears very narrow, semi-erect, basal, dark green leaves, each with a white, central line. Z3–8 H8–1.
C. cvijicii (illus. p.429). Spring-flowering corm. Usually has one funnel-shaped yellow flower. Produces very narrow, semi-erect, basal leaves, each with a white line along the center, which scarcely show at flowering time. Z3–8 H8–1.
C. dalmaticus (illus. p.428). Spring-flowering corm. Very narrow, semi-erect leaves have central white lines. Bears 1-3 purple-veined, pale violet flowers, with yellow centers, overlaid with silver or yellow outside. Z3–8 H8–1
***C.* 'Dorothy'** (illus. p.429). Spring-flowering corm. Scented flowers are pale lemon yellow. Z3–8 H8–1
***C.* 'Dutch Yellow'.** See *C.* 'Golden Yellow'.
***C.* 'E.A. Bowles'** (illus. p.429). Early spring-flowering corm. Has scented, funnel-shaped, deep yellow flowers stained bronze near base on outside. Has narrow, semi-erect leaves, each with a central white line. Increases well by offsets. Z3–8 H8–1.
C. etruscus (illus. p.429). Spring-flowering corm. Has very narrow, semi-erect, basal, dark green leaves with central white lines. Bears long-tubed, funnel-shaped, pale purple-blue flowers washed silver outside and with violet veining. Z3–8 H8–1. **'Zwanenburg'** (illus. p.428) has pale purple-blue flowers washed with warm brown and flecked violet outside.
***C.* 'Eyecatcher'** (illus. p.428). Late winter- to midspring-flowering corm. Produces funnel-shaped, gray-white, yellow-throated flowers with white-edged, deep purple outer segments. Z3–8 H8–1.
C. flavus, syn. *C. aureus*. Spring-flowering corm. Fragrant flowers are bright yellow or orange-yellow throughout; often several flowers are produced together or in quick succession. Z5–8 H8–5.
C. gargaricus (illus. p.429). Spring-flowering corm. Bears yellow flowers, 1½–2in (4–5cm) long. Increases by stolons. Tolerates slightly damper conditions than most crocuses.
***C.* 'Golden Yellow'**, syn. *C.* 'Dutch Yellow', *C.* x *luteus* 'Golden Yellow'. Very vigorous, clump-forming, spring-flowering corm. Bears yellow flowers, 3–4in (8–10cm) long and faintly striped outside at bases. Naturalizes well in grass. Z3–8 H8–1.
C. goulimyi (illus. p.428). Autumn-flowering corm. Usually has one long-tubed, pale lilac to pinkish lilac flower with a white throat and 3 inner petals usually paler than the 3 outer ones. Leaves and flowers appear together. Needs a warm site. Z3–8 H8–1.
C. hadriaticus (illus. p.428). Autumn-flowering corm. Leaves appear with the white flowers, which usually have yellow throats and may be lilac-feathered at the base. Z3–8 H8–1.
C. imperati. Strikingly bicolored, spring-flowering corm. Develops 1 or 2 scented, purple flowers, 2½–3in (6–8cm) long, light brown with purple striping outside and with yellow throats. Z3–8 H8–1. In **'De Jager'** (illus. p.428), flowers are rich violet-purple inside and warm brown with violet feathering outside.
C. iridiflorus. See *C. banaticus*.
C. korolkowii (Celandine crocus). Spring-flowering corm. Produces up to 20 narrow leaves. Carries fragrant yellow flowers that are speckled or stained brown or purple outside. When open in sun, petals reveal glossy surfaces.
C. kotschyanus, syn. *C. zonatus* (illus.

p.428). Autumn-flowering corm. Pinkish lilac or purplish blue flowers have yellow centers and white anthers. Narrow, semi-erect, basal leaves with white lines along centers appear in winter-spring. Z3–8 H8–1.
var. ***leucopharynx*** has pale lilac-blue flowers with white centers and white anthers. Leaves appear in winter-spring.
C. 'Ladykiller' (illus. p.429). Late winter- to midspring-flowering corm. Has funnel-shaped flowers, white or pale lilac within and deep violet-purple with white margins outside. Z3–8 H8–1.
C. laevigatus (illus. p.428). Very variable corm, flowering intermittently for a month or more in autumn or winter, depending on the form. Fragrant flowers appear with leaves and are usually lilac-purple with bold stripes on outside; inside each has a yellow eye and cream-white anthers. Z3–8 H8–1.
C. longiflorus. (illus. p.429). Autumn-flowering corm. Produces fragrant, slender purple flowers, which are striped darker purple outside, at the same time as leaves. Flowers have yellow centers and anthers and red stigmas. Z5–8 H8–5.
***C.* x *luteus* 'Golden Yellow'.** See *C.* 'Golden Yellow'.
C. malyi (illus. p.428). Spring-flowering corm. Has 1 or 2 funnel-shaped white flowers with yellow throats, brown or purple tubes, and showy, bright orange stigmas. Leaves are very narrow, semi-erect and basal with central white lines. Z3–8 H8–1.
C. medius (illus. p.428). Autumn-flowering corm. Has 1 or 2 funnel-shaped, uniform rich purple flowers with yellow anthers and red stigmas cut into many threadlike branches. Linear, basal leaves appear in winter-spring, after flowering. Z3–8 H8–1.
C. minimus (illus. p.428). Late spring-flowering corm. Has very narrow, semi-erect, basal, dark green leaves that have central white lines. Bears 1 or 2 flowers, purple inside and stained darker violet or sometimes darker striped on outside. Z3–8 H8–1.
C. niveus. Autumn-flowering corm. Produces 1 or 2 white or pale lavender flowers, 4–6in (10–15cm) long, with conspicuous yellow throats. Leaves appear with flowers or just afterward. Needs a warm, sunny site. Z3–8 H8-1.
C. nudiflorus (Autumn crocus; illus. p.428). Autumn-flowering corm. Has linear, basal leaves in winter-spring. Usually bears one slender, long-tubed, rich purple flower with a frilly, bright orange or yellow stigma. Naturalizes in grass.
C. olivieri. Spring-flowering corm. Bears rounded, bright orange flowers. Z5–8 H8–5. Flowers of subsp. ***balansae*** (syn. *C. balansae*) are stained or striped bronze-brown outside.
C. pulchellus (illus. p.428). Autumn-flowering corm. Bears long-tubed, pale lilac-blue flowers with darker veins, conspicuous yellow throats, and white anthers. Leaves are very narrow, semi-erect, and basal, with white lines along centers. Z3–8 H8–1.
C. salzmannii. See *C. serotinus* subsp. *salzmannii*.
C. sativus, syn. *C.s.* var. *cashmirianus* (Saffron crocus). Autumn-flowering corm. Leaves appear with saucer-shaped, dark-veined, purple flowers, 2–3in (5–7cm) across, each with 3 long, bright red stigmas that yield saffron. Z5–8 H8–1.
C. serotinus subsp. ***salzmannii***, syn. *C. salzmannii*. Autumn-flowering corm. Lilac-blue flowers to 4in (10cm) long, sometimes with yellow throats, appear with leaves. Z5–8 H8–1.
C. sieberi. Spring-flowering corm. Has white flowers with yellow throats and purple staining outside, either in horizontal bands or vertical stripes. Z3–8 H8–1. **'Albus'** see *C.s.* 'Bowles' White'. subsp. ***atticus*** has pale lilac to violet-blue flowers with frilly orange stigmas. **'Bowles' White'** (syn. *C.s.* 'Albus'; illus. p.428) produces pure white flowers with large, deep yellow areas in the throats. **'Hubert Edelsten'** has yellow-throated, pale lilac flowers, the outer segments of which are white and tipped, centrally marked, and feathered with rich purple. subsp. ***sublimis*** f. ***tricolor*** (illus. p.428) has unusual flowers divided into 3 distinct bands of lilac, white, and golden yellow.
***C.* 'Snow Bunting'** (illus. p.428). Spring-flowering corm. Fragrant, long-tubed, funnel-shaped white flowers have mustard yellow centers and orange stigmas. Very narrow, semi-erect, basal leaves are dark green with white, central lines. Z3–8 H8–1.
C. speciosus (illus. p.429). Autumn-flowering corm. Produces lilac-blue to deep purple-blue flowers, usually with a network of darker veins and a much-divided orange stigma. Leaves appear in winter-spring. Z3–8 H8–1. **'Conqueror'** (illus. p.429) has large, deep sky-blue flowers. **'Oxonian'** (illus. p.429) produces dark violet-blue flowers with prominent darker veining externally.
C. susianus. See *C. angustifolius*.
C. tommasinianus. Spring-flowering corm. H to 4in (10cm), S 1–3in (2.5–8cm). Bears slender, long-tubed, funnel-shaped flowers, varying in color from lilac or purple to violet, sometimes with darker tips to petals and occasionally silver outside. Naturalizes well. Z3–8 H8–1. f. ***albus*** (illus. p.428) has white flowers. **'Ruby Giant'** (illus. p.429) bears clusters of large, rich reddish purple flowers. **'Whitewell Purple'** (illus. p.429) has slender, reddish purple flowers.
C. tournefortii. Autumn-flowering corm. Leaves appear at same time as 1 or 2 pale lilac-blue flowers that open flattish to reveal a much-divided orange stigma and white anthers. Requires a warm, sunny site. Z5–8 H8–5.
C. vernus (Dutch crocus, Spring crocus; illus. p.429). Spring-flowering corm. H to 4in (10cm), S 1–3in (2.5–8cm). Variable in color from white to purple or violet, and often striped and feathered. Stigmas are large, frilly, and orange or yellow. Is suitable for naturalizing. Z3–8 H8–1. subsp. ***albiflorus*** (illus. p.428) has small white flowers sometimes slightly marked or striped purple. **'Jeanne d'Arc'** has white flowers with a deep purple base. **'Pickwick'** (illus. p.429) has pale, grayish white flowers with dark violet stripes and purplish bases. **'Prinses Juliana'** (illus. p.429) has midpurple flowers with darker veins. **'Purpureus Grandiflorus'** (illus. p.429) has shiny, violet-purple flowers. **'Queen of the Blues'** (illus. p.429) has rich blue flowers that have higher margins and a darker base. **'Remembrance'** (illus. p.429) has shiny violet flowers. **'Vanguard'**, a very early cultivar, has bluish lilac flowers, paler and silvered outside.
***C.* 'Zephyr'.** Autumn-flowering corm. Bears very pale silver-blue flowers veined darker, each with a conspicuous yellow throat and white anthers. Z3–8 H8–1.
C. zonatus. See *C. kotschyanus*.
***C.* 'Zwanenburg Bronze'.** Spring-flowering corm. H to 4in (10cm), S 1–3in (2.5–8cm). Has bicolored flowers, rich yellow inside and stained bronze outside. Z3–8 H8–1.

CROSSANDRA

ACANTHACEAE

Genus of evergreen perennials, subshrubs and shrubs grown mainly for their flowers. Needs partial shade or full light and organic, well-drained soil. Water potted plants freely when in full growth, moderately at other times. For a strong branch system, cut back flowered growth by at least half in late winter. Propagate by seed in spring or by greenwood cuttings in late spring or summer. Whitefly may be troublesome.
C. infundibuliformis, syn. *C. undulifolia*. Evergreen, erect to spreading, soft-stemmed shrub or subshrub. H to 3ft (1m), S 2ft (60cm). Has oval to lance-shaped, glossy, deep green leaves and, in summer-autumn or earlier, fan-shaped, salmon-red flowers in conical spikes, each 4in (10cm) long. Z14–15 H12–1.
C. nilotica illus. p.165.
C. undulifolia. See *C. infundibuliformis*.

CROTALARIA

LEGUMINOSAE/PAPILIONACEAE

Genus of evergreen shrubs, perennials, and annuals grown mainly for their flowers. Requires full light and well-drained soil. Water containerized specimens freely when in full growth, less at other times. For a more compact habit, cut back old stems by half after flowering. Propagate by seed in spring or by semi-ripe cuttings in summer. Spider mite may be troublesome.
C. agatiflora illus. p.123.

Crucianella stylosa. See *Phuopsis stylosa*.

CRYPTANTHUS

BROMELIACEAE

Genus of evergreen, rosette-forming perennials grown for their attractive foliage. Needs semi-shade and well-drained soil, preferably mixed with sphagnum moss. Water moderately during the growing season, sparingly at other times. Propagate by offsets or suckers in late spring.
C. acaulis (Green earth star). Evergreen, clump-forming, basal-rosetted perennial. H to 4in (10cm), S 6–12in (15–30cm). Loose, flat rosettes of lance-shaped to narrowly triangular, wavy, midgreen leaves have serrated edges. A cluster of fragrant, tubular white flowers appears in each rosette center, usually in summer. Z15 H12–10. **'Ruber'** has red-flushed foliage.
C. bivittatus (illus. p.265). Evergreen, clump-forming, basal-rosetted perennial. H to 6in (15cm), S 10–15in (25–38cm). Loose, flat rosettes of broadly lance-shaped, wavy, mid- to yellowish green leaves have finely toothed margins and are striped lengthwise with 2 coppery beige to buff bands. Small clusters of tubular white flowers appear from center of each rosette, usually in summer. Z15 H12–10.
C. bromelioides (Rainbow star). Evergreen, spreading, basal-rosetted perennial. H 8in (20cm) or more, S 14in (35cm) or more. Strap-shaped, wavy, finely toothed, arching, mid- to bright green leaves are produced in dense rosettes. Occasionally bears clusters of tubular white flowers in center of each rosette, usually in summer. Z15 H12–10. **'Tricolor'** has carmine-suffused, white-striped foliage.
***C.* 'Pink Starlight'** (illus. p.265). Vigorous, evergreen, spreading, basal-rosetted perennial. H 8in (20cm) or more, S 14in (35cm) or more. Strap-shaped, wavy, finely toothed, arching green leaves are striped yellowish green and heavily suffused deep pink. Clusters of tubular white flowers occasionally appear from each rosette center in summer. Z15 H12–10.
C. zonatus. Evergreen, basal-rosetted perennial. H 4–6in (10–15cm), S 12–16in (30–40cm). Forms loose, flat rosettes of strap-shaped, wavy, finely toothed, sepia-green leaves cross-banded with gray-buff and with grayish white scales beneath. A cluster of tubular white flowers opens in each rosette, usually in summer. Z15 H12–10. **'Zebrinus'** (illus. p.265) has silver-banded foliage.

x CRYPTBERGIA

BROMELIACEAE

Hybrid genus (*Cryptanthus* x *Billbergia*) of evergreen, rosette-forming perennials, grown for their foliage. Needs semi-shade and fertile, well-drained soil. Water moderately during growing season, sparingly in winter. Propagate by suckers or offsets in spring.
x ***C.* 'Rubra'.** Evergreen, clump-forming, basal-rosetted perennials. H and S 6–12in (15–30cm). Loose rosettes consist of strap-shaped, pointed, bronze-red leaves. Rarely, small, tubular white flowers are produced in rosette centers in summer. Z14-15 H12-10.

CRYPTOCORYNE

ARACEAE

Genus of semi-evergreen, perennial, submerged water plants and marsh plants grown for their foliage. Is suitable for tropical aquariums. Needs sun and rich soil. Remove fading foliage, and divide plants periodically. Propagate by division in spring or summer.
C. beckettii var. ***ciliata***. See *C. ciliata*.
C. ciliata, syn. *C. beckettii* var. *ciliata*. Semi-evergreen, perennial, submerged water plant. S 6in (15cm). Lance-shaped, deep green leaves have paler midribs. Small, hooded, fringed purplish spathes appear intermittently at base of plant. Z10–11 H12–10
C. spiralis. Semi-evergreen, perennial, submerged water plant. S 6in (15cm). Small, hooded purplish spathes are borne intermittently among lance-shaped, purplish green leaves. Z10–11 H12–10.

CRYPTOGRAMMA

CRYPTOGRAMMACEAE

Genus of deciduous or semi-evergreen ferns. Needs partial shade and moist but well-drained, neutral or acidic soil. Remove fading fronds. Propagate by spores in late summer.
C. crispa illus. p.313.

CRYPTOMERIA

TAXODIACEAE

See also CONIFERS.
C. japonica (Japanese cedar). Fast-growing, columnar to conical, open conifer. H 50–70ft (15–20m), S 15–25ft (5–8m). Has soft, fibrous, red-brown bark, needlelike, incurved, spirally arranged, mid- to dark green leaves, and globular brown cones. Z6–9 H9–6. **'Bandai-sugi'**, H and S 6ft (2m), makes an irregularly rounded shrub with foliage that turns bronze in winter. **'Cristata'** illus. p.109. **'Elegans Compacta'** (illus. p.111), H 6–15ft (2–5m), S 6ft (2m), is a dwarf form. **'Pyramidata'** illus. p.109. **'Sekkan-sugi'** (illus. p.111), H 30ft (10m), S 10–12ft (3–4m), has semi-pendulous branches and light golden cream foliage. **'Spiralis'** (illus. p.111), H and S 6–10ft (2–3m), forms a tree or dense shrub with spirally twisted foliage and is very slow-growing. **'Vilmoriniana'**, H and S 3ft (1m), forms a globular mound of yellow-green foliage that turns bronze in winter.

CRYPTOSTEGIA

ASCLEPIADACEAE

Genus of evergreen, twining climbers grown for their flowers. Provide fertile, well-drained soil and full light. Water regularly, less when not in full growth. Stems require support. Cut back previous season's old flowering stems in spring. Propagate by seed in spring or by softwood cuttings in summer.
C. grandiflora (Rubber vine). Strong-growing, evergreen, twining climber. H 30ft (10m) or more. Has thick-textured, oval, glossy leaves. Funnel-shaped, reddish to lilac-purple flowers appear in summer. Stems produce a poisonous latex that may cause severe discomfort if ingested. Z11 H12–10.

***Cryptostemma calendulaceum*.** See *Arctotheca calendula*.

CTENANTHE

MARANTACEAE

Genus of evergreen, bushy perennials grown for their ornamental foliage. Requires a humid atmosphere, even temperature, and partial shade. Prefers moist but well-drained soil and soft water; do not allow to dry completely. Propagate by division in spring.
***C. lubbersiana*.** Evergreen, clump-forming, bushy perennial. H and S to 30in (75cm) or more. Long-stalked, lance-shaped, sharply pointed leaves are 10in (25cm) long, green above, irregularly marked and striped with pale yellowish green, and pale greenish yellow below. Intermittently bears dense, one-sided spikes of many small, 3-petaled white flowers. Z15 H12–10.
C. oppenheimiana, syn. *Calathea oppenheimiana*. Robust, evergreen, bushy perennial. H and S 3ft (1m) or more. Lance-shaped, leathery leaves are over 1ft (30cm) long, red below, dark green above, and with pale green or white bands along veins on either side of midribs. Dense, one-sided spikes of many small, 3-petaled white flowers are produced intermittently. Z14–15 H12–10. **'Tricolor'** illus. p.264.

***Cudrania tricuspidata*.** See *Maclura tricuspidata*.

CUNNINGHAMIA

TAXODIACEAE

See also CONIFERS.
C. lanceolata illus. p.106.

CUNONIA

CUNONIACEAE

Genus of evergreen, summer-flowering trees grown for their foliage, flowers, and overall appearance. Requires full light and well-drained soil. Water potted plants moderately, less in winter. Pruning is tolerated. Propagate by seed in spring or by semi-ripe cuttings in summer.
C. capensis (African red alder). Moderately fast-growing, evergreen, rounded tree. H and S 30–50ft (10–15m), more in rich soil. Has lustrous, dark green leaves divided into pairs of lance-shaped, serrated leaflets. Tiny, long-stamened white flowers appear in dense, bottlebrush-like spikes, each 4–5in (10–13cm) long, in late summer.

CUPHEA

LYTHRACEAE

Genus of annuals, perennials, and evergreen shrubs and subshrubs, grown for their flowers. Prefers full sun and fertile, well-drained soil. Water freely when in full growth, moderately at other times. Remove flowered shoots after flowering to maintain a bushy habit. Propagate by seed in spring or by greenwood cuttings in spring or summer. Spider mite may be troublesome.
C. cyanea illus. p.172.
C. hyssopifolia illus. p.158.
C. ignea, syn. *C. platycentra*, illus. p.172.
***C. platycentra*.** See *C. ignea*.

x CUPRESSOCYPARIS

CUPRESSACEAE

Contact with the foliage may aggravate skin allergies. See also CONIFERS.
x ***C. leylandii* 'Castlewellan'** illus. p.104. **'Haggerston Grey'** illus. p.101. **'Harlequin'** illus. p.104. **'Leighton Green'** is a very fast-growing, columnar conifer with a conical tip. H 80–120ft (25–35m), S 12–15ft (4–5m). Bears flattened sprays of paired, scalelike, rich green leaves and globular, glossy, dark brown cones. **'Robinson's Gold'**, H 50–70ft (15–20m), has bright golden leaves. Z6–9 H9–6.

CUPRESSUS

Cypress

CUPRESSACEAE

See also CONIFERS.
C. arizonica var. ***glabra***, syn. *C. glabra* (Arizona cypress, Smooth cypress). Conical conifer. H 30–50ft (10–15m), S 10–15ft (3–5m). Has smooth, flaking, reddish purple bark and upright, spirally arranged sprays of scalelike, aromatic, glaucous blue-gray leaves that are flecked with white resin. Globular cones are chocolate brown. Z6–9 H9–2.
C. cashmeriana, syn. *C. torulosa* 'Cashmeriana', illus. p.101.
C. glabra. See *C. arizonica* var. *glabra*.
C. lusitanica (Cedar of Goa, Mexican cypress). Conical conifer. H 70ft (20m), S 15–25ft (5–8m). Has fissured bark and spreading, spirally arranged sprays of scalelike, aromatic, gray-green leaves. Bears small, globular cones that are glaucous blue when young, ripening to glossy brown. Z9–10 H10–8.
C. macrocarpa (Monterey cypress). Fast-growing, evergreen conifer, columnar when young, often wide-spreading with age. H 70ft (20m), S 20–80ft (6–25m). Bark is shallowly fissured. Scalelike, aromatic, bright to dark green leaves are borne in plume-like sprays. Globular cones are glossy and brown. Z7–11 H12–7.
'Goldcrest' illus. p.109.
***C. torulosa* 'Cashmeriana'.** See *C. cashmeriana*.

***Curtonus paniculatus*.** See *Crocosmia paniculata*.

CYANANTHUS

CAMPANULACEAE

Genus of late summer-flowering perennials suitable for rock gardens, walls, and troughs. Needs partial shade and organic, moist but well-drained soil. Propagate by softwood cuttings in spring or by seed in autumn.
C. lobatus*.** Prostrate perennial. H ¾in (2cm), S 8in (20cm). Branched stems are clothed in small, wedge-shaped, dull green leaves. In late summer, each stem carries a funnel-shaped blue flower. Z6–7 H7–6. f. ***albus illus. p.373.
C. microphyllus illus. p.383.

CYANOTIS

COMMELINACEAE

Genus of evergreen, creeping perennials grown for their foliage. Prefers a position in sun or partial shade, with organic, well-drained soil. Propagate by tip cuttings from spring to autumn.
C. kewensis (Teddy-bear vine). Evergreen perennial forming rosettes with trailing stems. H 2in (5cm), S 12in (24cm). Clasping the stem are 2 rows of overlapping, oval leaves, to 2in (5cm) long, dark green above, purple with velvety brown hairs below. Stalkless clusters of 3-petaled, purplish pink flowers are produced in axils of leaflike bracts almost all year round. Z13–15 H12–10
C. somaliensis illus. p.303.

CYATHEA,
syn. ALSOPHILA, SPHAEROPTERIS

CYATHEACEAE

Genus of evergreen tree ferns grown for their foliage and overall appearance. Needs a humid atmosphere, sun or partial shade, and organic, moisture-retentive but well-drained soil. Water potted plants freely in summer, moderately at other times. Propagate by spores in spring.

C. australis illus. p.100.
C. medullaris (Black tree fern, Mamaku). Evergreen, upright tree fern with a slender, black trunk. H 22–52ft (7–16m), S 20–40ft (6–12m). Has arching fronds, each to 22ft (7m) long, divided into small, oblong, glossy, dark green leaflets, paler beneath. Z10–11 H12–10.

CYATHODES

EPACRIDACEAE

Genus of evergreen, heathlike shrubs suitable for rock gardens. Needs a sheltered, shaded site and gritty, moist, peaty soil. Propagate in summer by seed or semi-ripe cuttings.
C. colensoi, syn. *Leucopogon colensoi*, illus. p.360.

CYBISTAX

BIGNONIACEAE

Genus of deciduous trees grown for their spring flowers and for shade. Needs full light and fertile, moisture-retentive but well-drained soil. Will not bloom when confined to a container. Young plants may be pruned to shape when leafless; otherwise, pruning is not required. Propagate by seed or air-layering in spring or by semi-ripe cuttings in summer.
C. donnell-smithii, syn. *Tabebuia donnell-smithii*. Fairly fast-growing, deciduous, rounded tree. H and S 30ft (10m) or more. Leaves have 5–7 oval, 2–8in (5–20cm) long leaflets. Bell-shaped, 5-lobed, bright yellow flowers appear in spring before the leaves, often in great profusion. Z14–15 H12–10.

CYCAS

CYCADACEAE

Genus of slow-growing, evergreen, woody-stemmed perennials grown for their palmlike appearance. Prefers a position in full light and organic, well-drained soil. Water potted specimens moderately, less when not in full growth. Propagate in spring by seed or suckers taken from mature plants.
C. revoluta illus. p.152.

CYCLAMEN

PRIMULACEAE

Genus of tuberous perennials, some of which are occasionally evergreen, grown for their pendent flowers, each with 5 reflexed petals and a mouth often stained with a darker color. Grow in sun or partial shade, and in organic, well-drained soil. If grown in containers, in summer dry off tubers of all except *C. purpurascens* (which is evergreen and flowers in summer); repot in autumn and water to restart growth. Propagate by seed in late summer or autumn. *C. persicum* and its cultivars are susceptible to black root rot. All parts may cause severe discomfort if ingested.
C. africanum illus. p.437.
C. alpinum. See *C. trochopteranthum*.
C. caucasicum. See *C. coum* subsp. *caucasicum*.
C. cilicium illus. p.438.
C. coum and f. ***albissimum*** (syn. *C.c.* 'Album') illus. p.440. subsp. ***caucasicum*** (syn. *C. caucasicum*) is a winter-flowering, tuberous perennial. H to 4in (10cm), S 2–4in (5–10cm). Has heart-shaped, silver-patterned leaves and produces a succession of bright carmine flowers, each with a dark stain at the mouth. Z5–9 H9–5.
C. creticum. Spring-flowering, tuberous perennial. H to 4in (10cm), S 2–4in (5–10cm). Produces heart-shaped, dark green leaves, sometimes silver-patterned, and fragrant white flowers. Z6–9 H9–7.
C. cyprium. Autumn-flowering, tuberous perennial. H to 4in (10cm), S 2–4in (5–10cm). Heart-shaped, toothed, dark green leaves patterned with lighter green appear with or just after fragrant white flowers, each with carmine marks around the mouth. Z7–9 H9–7.
C. europaeum. See *C. purpurascens*.
C. fatrense. See *C. purpurascens*.
C. graecum illus. p.438.
C. hederifolium, syn. *C. neapolitanum*, illus. p.438. f. ***albiflorum*** illus. p.437.
C. libanoticum illus. p.427.
C. mirabile illus. p.437.
C. neapolitanum. See *C. hederifolium*.
C. persicum illus. p.440. **'Esmeralda'** illus. p.441. **Halios Series** is a late summer- or autumn-flowering, tuberous perennial. H 12in (24cm), S 7in (18cm). Tender. Blunt-toothed, heart-shaped, dark green leaves have silver marbling. Produces a succession of white, pink, scarlet, lilac, or purple flowers. **Kaori Series** illus. p.441. **'Pearl Wave'** illus. p.440. **'Renown'** illus. p.441. **'Scentsation'**, H 6in (15cm), bears strongly scented flowers in pink, carmine-red, or crimson from early winter to early spring. All Z13–15 H6–1.
C. pseudibericum. Spring-flowering, tuberous perennial. H to 4in (10cm), S 4–6in (10–15cm). Has heart-shaped, toothed leaves patterned with silvery and dark green zones. Flowers are deep carmine-purple with darker, basal stains and white-rimmed mouths. Z8–9 H9–8.
C. purpurascens, syn. *C. europaeum*, *C. fatrense*, illus. p.435.
C. repandum. Spring-flowering, tuberous perennial. H to 4in (10cm), S 4–6in (10–15cm). Has heart-shaped, jagged-toothed, dark green leaves with lighter patterns. Bears fragrant, slender, reddish purple flowers. Z7–9 H9–7.
C. rohlfsianum illus. p.438.
C. trochopteranthum, syn. *C. alpinum*. Spring-flowering, tuberous perennial. H 4in (10cm), S 2–4in (5–10cm). Bears rounded or heart-shaped leaves zoned with silver. Produces musty-scented, pale carmine or white flowers stained dark carmine at mouths; petals are twisted and propeller-shaped. Z8–9 H9–8.

Cyclobothra lutea. See *Calochortus barbatus*.

CYDONIA

ROSACEAE

Genus of one species of deciduous, spring-flowering tree grown for its flowers and fruits, which are used as a flavoring and for preserves. Grow against a south- or west-facing wall at the limits of hardiness. Requires sun and fertile, well-drained soil. Propagate species by seed in autumn, cultivars by softwood cuttings in summer. Mildew, brown rot, and fireblight are sometimes a problem.
C. oblonga (Quince). **Portugal ('Lusitanica')** is a deciduous, spreading tree. H and S 15ft (5m). Broadly oval, dark green leaves are gray-felted beneath. Has a profusion of large, 5-petaled, pale pink flowers in late spring, followed by fragrant, pear-shaped, deep yellow fruits. Z5–9 H9–3. **'Vranja'** illus. p.92.
C. sinensis. See *Pseudocydonia sinensis*.

CYMBALARIA

SCROPHULARIACEAE

Genus of annuals, biennials, and short-lived perennials related to *Linaria*, grown for their tiny flowers on slender stems. Is good for rock gardens, walls, and banks, but it may be invasive. Needs shade and moist soil. Propagate by seed in autumn. Self-seeds readily.
C. muralis (Ivy-leaved toadflax, Kenilworth ivy). Spreading perennial. H 2in (5cm), S 5in (12cm). Bears small, ivy-shaped, midgreen leaves and, in summer, masses of tiny, tubular, spurred, sometimes purple-tinted white flowers. Z4–8 H8–1.

CYMBIDIUM

Contact with the foliage may aggravate skin allergies. See also ORCHIDS. All of the following are Z14–15 H12–6 except where noted.
***C.* Caithness Ice 'Trinity'** (illus. p.298). Evergreen, epiphytic orchid for a cool greenhouse. H 30in (75cm). Sprays of green flowers, 4in (10cm) across, each with a red-marked white lip, are borne in early spring. Has narrowly oval leaves to 24in (60cm) long. Needs a position in semi-shade in summer.
***C.* Christmas Angel 'Cooksbridge Sunburst'** (illus. p.299). Evergreen, epiphytic orchid for a cool greenhouse. H 30in (75cm). In winter produces sprays of yellow flowers, 4in (10cm) across and with red-spotted lips. Narrowly oval leaves are up to 24in (60cm) long. Grow in semi-shade in summer.
C. devonianum (illus. p.298). Evergreen, epiphytic orchid for a cool greenhouse. H 24in (60cm). In early summer bears pendent spikes of 1in (2.5cm) wide, olive green flowers overlaid with purple and with purple lips. Has broadly oval, semi-rigid leaves to 12in (24cm) long. Needs semi-shade in summer.
C. elegans, syn. *Cyperorchis elegans* (illus. p.298). Evergreen, epiphytic orchid for a cool greenhouse. H 30in (75cm). Dense, pendent sprays of fragrant, tubular yellow flowers, 1½in (4cm) across, appear in early summer. Has narrowly oval leaves to 24in (60cm) long. Requires semi-shade in summer. Z12–15 H12–6.
C. grandiflorum. See *C. hookerianum*.
C. hookerianum, syn. *C. grandiflorum* (illus. p.298). Evergreen, epiphytic orchid for a cool greenhouse. H 30in (75cm). In winter produces sprays of deep green flowers, 3in (8cm) across, each with a hairy, brown-spotted, creamy white lip. Narrowly oval leaves are up to 24in (60cm) long. Grow in semi-shade in summer.
***C.* King's Loch 'Cooksbridge'** (illus. p.298). Evergreen, epiphytic orchid for a cool greenhouse. H 24in (60cm). Sprays of green flowers, 2in (5cm) across and each with a purple-marked white lip, open in spring. Leaves are narrowly oval and up to 24in (60cm) long. Provide semi-shade in summer. Z12–15 H12–6.
***C.* Pontac 'Mont Millais'** (illus. p.297). Evergreen, epiphytic orchid for a cool greenhouse. H 30in (75cm). Bears sprays of 3in (8cm) wide, rich deep red flowers edged and marked with white in spring. Has narrowly oval leaves to 24in (60cm) long. Grow in semi-shade in summer.
***C.* Portelet Bay** (illus. p.296). Evergreen, epiphytic orchid for a cool greenhouse. H 30in (75cm). Red-lipped white flowers, 4in (10cm) across, are borne in sprays in spring. Has narrowly oval leaves to 24in (60cm) long. Provide semi-shade in summer.
***C.* Strath Kanaid** (illus. p.297). Evergreen, epiphytic orchid for a cool greenhouse. H 24in (60cm). In spring bears arching spikes of deep red flowers, 2in (5cm) across. Lips are white, marked deep red. Narrowly oval leaves are up to 24in (60cm) long. Requires semi-shade in summer.
***C.* Strathbraan** (illus. p.296). Evergreen, epiphytic orchid for a cool greenhouse. H 24in (60cm). In spring produces slightly arching spikes of off-white flowers, 2in (5cm) across, with red marks on each lip. Leaves are narrowly oval, to 24in (60cm) long. Requires semi-shade in summer.
***C.* Strathdon 'Cooksbridge Noel'** (illus. p.297). Evergreen, epiphytic orchid for a cool greenhouse. H 3ft (1m). Sprays of rich pink flowers, 2in (5cm) across, with red-spotted, yellow-tinged lips, appear in winter. Has narrowly oval leaves up to 24in (60cm) long. Needs

semi-shade in summer.
C. tracyanum (illus. p.298). Evergreen, epiphytic orchid for a cool greenhouse. H 30in (75cm). In autumn produces long spikes of fragrant, olive green flowers, 3in (8cm) across, overlaid with reddish dots and dashes. Has narrowly oval leaves to 24in (60cm) long. Grow in semi-shade in summer.

CYNARA

ASTERACEAE/COMPOSITAE

Genus of architectural perennials grown for their large heads of flowers. The plant described is grown both as a vegetable and as a decorative border plant. Requires sun and fertile, well-drained soil. Propagate by seed or division in spring.
C. cardunculus illus. p.228.

CYNOGLOSSUM
Hound's tongue

BORAGINACEAE

Genus of annuals, biennials, and perennials grown for their long flowering period from late spring to early autumn. Needs sun and fertile but not overly rich soil. Propagate by division in spring or by seed in autumn or spring.
***C. amabile* 'Firmament'** illus. p.334.

CYPELLA

IRIDACEAE

Genus of summer-flowering bulbs grown for their short-lived, irislike flowers that have 3 large, spreading outer petals and 3 small, incurved inner ones. May survive outdoors in marginal areas if planted near a sunny wall. Needs full sun and well-drained soil. Lift bulbs when dormant; partially dry off in winter. Propagate by seed in spring.
C. herbertii illus. p.423.

Cyperorchis elegans. See *Cymbidium elegans*.

CYPERUS

CYPERACEAE

See also GRASSES, BAMBOOS, RUSHES, and SEDGES.
C. albostriatus, syn. *C. diffusus* of gardens, *C. elegans* of gardens. Evergreen, perennial sedge. H 24in (60cm), S indefinite. Stem has prominently veined, midgreen leaves and up to 8 leaflike green bracts surrounding a well-branched umbel of brown spikelets produced in summer. Z10–11 H12–4. **'Variegatus'** has white-striped leaves and bracts.
C. alternifolius of gardens. See *C. involucratus*.
C. diffusus of gardens. See *C. albostriatus*.
C. elegans of gardens. See *C. albostriatus*.
C. flabelliformis. See *C. involucratus*.
C. involucratus, syn. *C. alternifolius* of gardens, *C. flabelliformis*, illus. p.308.
C. isocladus of gardens. See *C. papyrus* 'Nanus'.
C. longus (Galingale). Deciduous, spreading, perennial sedge. H 5ft (1.5m), S indefinite. Bears rough-edged, glossy, dark green leaves and, in summer, attractive umbels of narrow, flattened, milk-chocolate-colored spikelets that keep their color well. Tolerates its roots in water. Z3–11 H12–1.
C. papyrus illus. p.307. **'Nanus'** (syn. *C. isocladus* of gardens) is an evergreen, spreading, perennial sedge with a red rhizome; it is a dwarf variant of the species, sometimes considered distinct and is often grown under misapplied names. H 32in (80cm), S indefinite. Triangular, leafless stems bear umbels of brown spikelets on 3–4in (8–10cm) stalks in summer. Z13–15 H12–6.

CYPHOMANDRA

SOLANACEAE

Genus of evergreen shrubs and trees grown for their fruits and foliage. Grow in full light or partial shade and in well-drained soil. Water containerized specimens freely when in growth, sparingly at other times, when some leaves may fall. Tip prune at intervals while young to promote branching. Propagate by seed in spring. Whitefly and spider mite may cause problems.
C. betacea, syn. *C. crassicaulis*, illus. p.125.
C. crassicaulis. See *C. betacea*.

CYPHOSTEMMA

VITACEAE

Genus of deciduous succulents with very thick, fleshy, almost woody caudices and branches. Leaf undersides often exude droplets of resin. Needs full sun and very well-drained soil. Keep dry in winter. Is difficult to grow. Propagate by seed in spring.
C. bainesii, syn. *Cissus bainesii*. Deciduous succulent. H and S 24in (60cm). Has a thick, swollen, bottle-shaped trunk, often unbranched, covered in peeling, papery yellow bark. Fleshy, silvery green leaves with deeply serrated edges are divided into 3 oval leaflets, silver-haired when young. Bears tiny, cup-shaped, yellow-green flowers in summer, then grapelike red fruits. Z13–15 H12–10.
C. juttae, syn. *Cissus juttae*, illus. p.459.

CYPRIPEDIUM
Slipper orchid

See also ORCHIDS.
C. acaule (Moccasin flower; illus. p.296). Deciduous, terrestrial orchid. H to 16in (40cm). Yellowish green or purple flowers, 1½–2½in (4–6cm) long, each with a pouched pink or white lip, are borne singly in spring-summer. Leaves are broadly lance-shaped, pleated and 4–12in (10–30cm) long. Does best in partial shade. Z3–7 H7–1.
C. calceolus (Lady's slipper orchid, Yellow lady's slipper orchid; illus. p.298). Deciduous, terrestrial orchid. H 30in (75cm). In spring-summer bears paired or solitary yellow-pouched purple-brown flowers, 1¼–3in (3–7cm) long. Broadly lance-shaped leaves, 2–8in (5–20cm) long, are arranged in a spiral up stem. Stems and leaves are slightly hairy. Prefers partial shade. Z3–7 H7–1. var. ***pubescens*** see *C. pubescens*.
C. macranthon. See *C. macranthos*.
C. macranthos, syn. *C. macranthon* (illus. p.298). Deciduous, terrestrial orchid. H 20in (50cm). Pouched violet or purplish red flowers, 1½–2½in (4–6cm) long, usually borne singly, open in spring-summer. Stems and oval leaves, 1½–3in (4–7cm) long, are slightly hairy. Prefers partial shade. Z3–7 H7–1.
C. pubescens, syn. *C. calceolus* var. *pubescens* (illus. p.299). Deciduous, terrestrial orchid. H 30in (75cm). Has large, purple-marked, greenish yellow flowers, 3–4in (8–10cm) long, in spring-summer. Large, broadly lance-shaped leaves, 6–8in (15–20cm) long, are arranged in a spiral up the stem. Stems and leaves are hairy. Prefers partial shade. Z3–7 H7–1.
C. reginae (Showy lady's slipper orchid; illus. p.296). Deciduous, terrestrial orchid. H to 3ft (1m). In spring-summer, white flowers, ¾–2in (2–5cm) long, each with a pouched, white-streaked pink lip, are borne singly or in groups of 2 or 3. Stem and oval leaves, 4–10in (10–25cm) long, are hairy. Does best in partial shade. Z2–7 H7–1.

CYRILLA

CYRILLACEAE

Genus of one very variable species of deciduous or evergreen shrub grown for its flowers in late summer and autumn. Prefers full sun and needs peaty, acidic soil. Propagate by semi-ripe cuttings in summer.
C. racemiflora (Leatherwood). Deciduous or evergreen, bushy shrub. H and S 4ft (1.2m). Oblong, glossy, dark green leaves redden in autumn. Slender spires of small, 5-petaled white flowers are borne in late summer and autumn. Z6–9 H9–4.

CYRTANTHUS

AMARYLLIDACEAE

Genus of bulbs with brightly colored flowers, usually in summer. Requires full sun and free-draining, light soil. In frost-free areas may flower for much of the year. Plant in spring. Water freely in the growing season. Propagate by seed or offsets in spring.
C. brachyscyphus, syn. *C. parviflorus*, illus. p.435.
C. breviflorus, syn. *Anoiganthus breviflorus*, *A. luteus*. Clump-forming summer-flowering bulb. H 8–12in (20–30cm), S 3–4in (8–10cm). Has narrowly strap-shaped, semi-erect, basal leaves. Leafless flower stem bears up to 6 funnel-shaped yellow flowers, ¾–1¼in (2–3cm) long. Prefers a warm, sheltered situation. Z10–15 H12–10.
C. elatus, syn. *C. purpureus*, *Vallota speciosa*. Clump-forming, summer-flowering bulb. H 12–20in (30–50cm), S 5–6in (12–15cm). Bears widely strap-shaped, semi-erect, basal, bright green leaves. Thick stem produces a head of up to 5 widely funnel-shaped scarlet flowers, 3–4in (8–10cm) long. Makes an excellent house plant. Z8–10 H10–8.
C. mackenii. Clump-forming, summer-flowering bulb. H 12–16in (30–40cm), S 3–4in (8–10cm). Bears strap-shaped, semi-erect, basal leaves. Leafless stems each carry an umbel of up to 10 fragrant, tubular white flowers, 2in (5cm) long and slightly curved. Z11–13 H12–6. var. ***cooperi*** illus. p.422.
C. obliquus. Clump-forming, summer-flowering bulb. H 8–24in (20–60cm), S 15–6in (2–15cm). Bears widely strap-shaped, semi-erect, basal, grayish green leaves, twisted lengthwise. Carries a head of up to 12 pendent, tubular, red-and-yellow flowers, each 3in (7cm) long. Z10–11 H12–10.
C. parviflorus. See *C. brachyscyphus*.
C. purpureus. See *C. elatus*.
C. sanguineus. Clump-forming, summer-flowering bulb. H 12–20in (30–50cm), S 5–6in (12–15cm). Has strap-shaped, semi-erect, basal, bright green leaves. Thick stem bears 1 or 2 long-tubed scarlet flowers, 3–4in (8–10cm) long. Z10–11 H12–10.

CYRTOMIUM

AMARYLLIDACEAE

Genus of evergreen ferns. Does best in semi-shade and organic, moist soil. Remove fading fronds. Propagate by division in spring or summer or by spores in summer.
C. falcatum illus. p.311.
C. fortunei, syn. *Phanerophlebia fortunei*. Evergreen fern. H 24in (60cm). S 16in (40cm). Has erect, dull, pale green fronds, 12–24in (30–60cm) long, with broadly sickle-shaped pinnae, 1–2in (2.5–5cm) long. Z7–10 H10–7.

CYSTOPTERIS

WOODSIACEAE

Genus of deciduous ferns suitable for rock gardens. Does best in semi-shade and in soil that is never allowed to dry out. Remove fronds as they fade. Propagate by division in spring, by spores in summer, or by bulbils when available.
C. bulbifera (Berry bladder fern). Deciduous fern. H 6in (15cm), S 9in (23cm). Broadly lance-shaped, much-divided, dainty, pale green fronds produce tiny bulbils along their length. Propagate by bulbils as soon as mature. Z4–8 H8–1.
C. dickieana. Deciduous fern. H 6in

(15cm), S 9in (23cm). Has broadly lance-shaped, divided, delicate, pale green fronds, with oblong, blunt, indented pinnae that arch downward. Z2–7 H7–1.
C. fragilis (Brittle bladder fern). Deciduous fern. H 6in (15cm), S 9in (23cm). Broadly lance-shaped, pale green fronds are delicate and much divided into oblong, pointed, indented pinnae. Z4–8 H8–1.

CYTISUS
Broom

LEGUMINOSAE/PAPILIONACEAE

Genus of deciduous or evergreen shrubs grown for their abundant, pea-like flowers. Prefers full sun and fertile, but not overly rich, well-drained soil. Resents being transplanted. Propagate species by semi-ripe cuttings in summer or by seed in autumn, hybrids and cultivars by semi-ripe cuttings in late summer. All parts, especially the seeds, may cause mild stomach upset if ingested.
C. albus, syn. *Chamaecytisus albus*, *Cytisus leucanthus*. Deciduous, spreading shrub. H 1ft (30cm), S 3ft (1m). Has oval leaves, each with 3 tiny leaflets and, from early to midsummer, creamy white flowers borne in dense clusters. Z7–8 H8–7.
C. ardoinii. See *C. ardoinoi*.
C. ardoinoi, syn. *C. ardoinii*, illus. p.386.
C. battandieri, syn. *Argyrocytisus battandieri*, illus. p.123.
C.* x *beanii illus. p.349.
C. canariensis of gardens. See *C.* x *spachianus*.
C. demissus. See *Chamaecytisus demissus*.
***C.* 'Firefly'.** Deciduous, bushy shrub with slender, arching shoots. H and S 5–6ft (1.5–2m). Small, midgreen leaves are oblong and have 3 tiny leaflets. Produces masses of yellow flowers marked with red from late spring to early summer. Z6–9 H9–6.
C.* x *kewensis. Deciduous, arching shrub. H 1ft (30cm), S to 6ft (2m). Has leaves, each composed of 3 tiny leaflets, along downy stems. In late spring bears creamy white flowers. Is good for a bank or large rock garden. Z6–8 H8–6.
C. leucanthus. See *C. albus*.
C. nigricans, syn. *Lembotropis nigricans*, illus. p.170.
***C.* x *praecox* 'Allgold'** illus. p.157. **'Warminster'** illus. p.156.
C. purpureus. See *Chamaecytisus purpureus*.
C. racemosus of gardens. See *C.* x *spachianus*.
C. scoparius (Common broom). f. ***andreanus*** illus. p.171. subsp. ***maritimus*** (syn. *C.s.* var. *prostratus*) is a deciduous, prostrate shrub forming dense mounds of interlocking shoots. H 8in (20cm), S 4–6ft (1.2–2m). Small, gray-green leaves usually have 3 oblong leaflets but may be reduced to a single leaflet. Has masses of golden yellow flowers in late spring and early summer. Z6–8 H8–6. var. ***prostratus*** *see C.s.* subsp. *maritimus*.
C.* x *spachianus, syn. *C. canariensis* of gardens, *C. racemosus* of gardens, *Genista fragrans* of gardens, *G.* x *spachiana*. Vigorous, evergreen, arching shrub. H and S 10ft (3m). Has dark green leaves with 3 oval leaflets. Produces long, slender clusters of fragrant, golden yellow flowers in winter and early spring. Is often grown as a houseplant. Z9–11 H12–9.
C. supinus. See *Chamaecytisus supinus*.
***C.* 'Windlesham Ruby'.** Deciduous, bushy shrub with slender, arching shoots. H and S 5–6ft (1.5–2m). Small, midgreen leaves have 3 oblong leaflets. Large, rich red flowers are borne in profusion in late spring and early summer. Z7–9 H9–7.
***C.* 'Zeelandia'.** Deciduous, bushy shrub with slender, arching shoots. H and S 5–6ft (1.5–2m). Small, mid-green leaves have 3 oblong leaflets. Has masses of bicolored, creamy white and lilac-pink flowers from late spring to early summer. Z6–9

DABOECIA

ERICACEAE

See also HEATHERS.
D. azorica. Evergreen, compact shrub. H to 6in (15cm), S to 24in (60cm). Lance-shaped leaves are dark green above, silver-gray beneath. Urn-to bell-shaped flowers are vivid red and open in late spring or early summer. Z6–8 H8–6.
D. cantabrica (St. Daboec's heath). Evergreen, straggling shrub. H to 18in (45cm), S 24in (60cm). Top growth may be damaged by frost and cold winds, but plants respond well to hard pruning and produce new growth from base. Leaves are lance-shaped to oval, dark green above, silver-gray beneath. Bears bell- to urn-shaped, single or double white, purple, or mauve flowers from late spring to midautumn. Z6–8 H8–6. **'Bicolor'** (illus. p.178) bears white, purple, and striped flowers on the same plant. **'Praegerae'**, H 14in (35cm), has glowing deep pink flowers. **'Snowdrift'** has bright green foliage and long racemes of large white flowers.
D.* x *scotica. Evergreen, compact shrub. H to 6in (15cm), S to 2ft (60cm). Lance-shaped to oval leaves are dark green above, silver-gray beneath. Bears bell- to urn-shaped white, purple, or mauve flowers from late spring to midautumn. Z6–8 H8–6. **'Jack Drake'**, H 8in (20cm), has small, dark green leaves and ruby-colored flowers. **'Silverwells'** (illus. p.178) has small, bright green leaves and large white flowers. **'William Buchanan'** (illus. p.179), H 18in (45cm), is a vigorous cultivar with dark green leaves and deep purple flowers.

DACTYLIS

GRAMINAE/POACEAE

See also GRASSES, BAMBOOS, RUSHES, and SEDGES.
D. glomerata (Cock's-foot, Orchard grass). **'Variegata'** is an evergreen, tuft-forming, perennial grass. H 3ft (1m), S 8–10in (20–25cm). Silver-striped, gray-green leaves arise from tufted rootstock. In summer bears panicles of densely clustered, awned, purplish green spikelets. Z5–9 H9–5.

DACTYLORHIZA

See also ORCHIDS.
D. elata, syn. *Orchis elata*. Deciduous, terrestrial orchid. H 3½ft (1.1m). Spikes of pink or purple flowers, ½–¾in (1–2cm) long, open in spring-summer. Lance-shaped leaves, 6–10in (15–25cm) long, are spotted with brownish purple and arranged spirally on stem. Requires shade outdoors; keep pot plants semi-shaded in summer. Z6–8 H8–6.
D. foliosa, syn. *D. maderensis*, *Orchis maderensis*. Deciduous, terrestrial orchid. H 28in (70cm). Spikes of bright purple or pink flowers, ½–¾in (1–2cm) long, are borne in spring-summer. Has lance-shaped or triangular leaves, 4–8in (10–20cm) long, arranged spirally on stem. Cultivate as for *D. elata*. Z7–8 H8–7.
D. maderensis. See *D. foliosa*.

DAHLIA

ASTERACEAE/COMPOSITAE

Genus of bushy, summer- and autumn-flowering, tuberous perennials grown as bedding plants or for their flower heads, which are good for cutting or exhibition. Dwarf forms are used for mass planting and are also suitable for containers. Needs a sunny position and well-drained soil. All apart from dwarf forms require staking. After flowering, lift tubers and store in a frost-free place; replant once all frost danger has passed. Where hardy (Z9–11 H12–1), plants may be left in the ground as normal herbaceous perennials, but they benefit from regular propagation to maintain vigor. Propagate dwarf forms by seed sown under cover in late winter, others in spring by seed, basal shoot cuttings, or division of tubers. Dahlias may be subject to attack by aphids, spider mite, and thrips, among other insects. Powdery mildew has become a problem in some areas. Dahlias also succumb quickly to virus infection. See also feature panel, pp.406–407.

Border dahlias
Prolific and long-flowering, various species of *Dahlia* have been hybridized and, with constant breeding and selection, have developed into many forms and have a wide color range (although there is no blue). Shoots may be stopped, or pinched out, to promote vigorous growth and a bushy shape. Spread measurements depend on the amount of stopping carried out and the time at which it is done: early stopping encourages a broader shape, stopping later in the growing season results in a taller plant with much less spread, even in the same cultivar. Leaves are generally midgreen and divided into oval leaflets, some with rounded tips and some with toothed margins. Each flower head is referred to horticulturally as a flower, even though it does in fact consist of a large number of individual flowers. This horticultural usage has been followed in the descriptions below. All forms with flower heads to 6in (15cm) across are suitable for cutting; those suitable for exhibition are so noted.

Groups and flower sizes
Dahlias are divided into groups, according to the size and type of their flower heads, although the latter may vary in color and shape depending on soil and weather conditions. The groups are: (1) single; (2) anemone; (3) collerette; (4) waterlily; (5) decorative; (6) ball; (7) pompon; (8) cactus; (9) semi-cactus; (10) miscellaneous. For illustrations and descriptions, see p.406.

Flower sizes are as follows:

Giant-flowered; usually over 10in (25cm) in diameter.

Large-flowered; usually 8–10in (20–25cm) in diameter.

Medium-flowered; usually 6–8in (15–20cm) in diameter.

Small-flowered; usually 4–6in (10–15cm) in diameter.

Miniature-flowered; usually not exceeding 4in (10cm) in diameter.

Pompon dahlias; not exceeding 2in (5cm) in diameter.

***D.* 'Alloway Cottage'.** Medium-flowered decorative dahlia. H 4ft (1.2m), S 2ft (60cm). Bears very full, formal, soft yellow flowers, with a touch of lavender-blue on the tip of each petal, in summer-autumn. Is good for exhibition.
***D.* 'Alva's Doris'.** Small-flowered cactus dahlia. H 4ft (1.2m), S 2ft (60cm). Freely produces blood red flowers on strong stems in summer-autumn. Is good for exhibition.
***D.* 'Alva's Supreme'.** Giant-flowered decorative dahlia. H 3½ft (1.1m), S 2ft (60cm). In summer-autumn bears pale yellow flowers. Is good for exhibition.
***D.* 'Apricot Honeymoon Dress'.** Small-flowered decorative dahlia. H 4ft (1.2m), S 2ft (60cm). In summer-

autumn bears apricot flowers. Is good for exhibition.
***D.* 'Banker'.** Small-flowered cactus dahlia. H 4ft (1.2m), S 2ft (60cm). In summer-autumn produces red flowers that are good for exhibition.
***D.* 'Biddenham Sunset'** (illus. p.407). Small-flowered decorative dahlia. H 3½ft (1.1m), S 2ft (60cm). Orange-red flowers are borne in midsummer to autumn.
***D.* 'Bishop of Llandaff'** (illus. p.407). Miscellaneous dahlia. H 3ft (1m), S 18in (45cm). Has bronze-green leaves and single, open-centered, dark red flowers, 3in (7cm) across, in summer-autumn. It is excellent as a bedding plant.
***D.* 'Black Monarch'.** Giant-flowered decorative dahlia. H 4ft (1.2m), S 2ft (60cm). Produces oxblood red flowers, shading to crimson, in summer-autumn.
***D.* 'Butterball'** (illus. p.407). Miniature-flowered decorative dahlia. H 2ft (60cm), S 1ft (30cm). Produces bright yellow flowers in early summer.
***D.* 'Candy Cupid'.** Miniature ball dahlia. H 3½ft (1.1m), S 2ft (60cm). In summer-autumn bears lavender-pink flowers that are good for exhibition.
***D.* 'Chimborazo'** (illus. p.407). Collerette dahlia. H 3½ft (1.1m), S 2ft (60cm). Leaves are glossy, dark green. Has 4in (10cm) wide flowers with red outer petals and yellow inner petals in summer-autumn. Flowers are good for exhibition.
***D.* 'Clair de Lune'** (illus. p.407). Collerette dahlia. H 3½ft (1.1m), S 2ft (60cm). Has 4in (10cm) wide flowers with lemon yellow outer petals and paler yellow inner petals in summer-autumn. Good for exhibition.
***D.* 'Coltness Gem'** illus. p.329.
***D.* 'Comet'** (illus. p.407). Anemone dahlia. H 3½ft (1.1m), S 2ft (60cm). Leaves are glossy, dark green. Dark red flowers, 4–6in (10–15cm) across, are produced in summer-autumn.
***D.* 'Cryfield Bryn'.** Small-flowered semi-cactus dahlia. H 3½ft (1.1m), S 2ft (60cm). In summer-autumn has butter-yellow flowers that are excellent for exhibition.
***D.* 'Daddy's Choice'.** Small-flowered semi-cactus dahlia. H 4½ft (1.3m), S 2ft (60cm). In summer-autumn bears pale lemonyellow flowers with a pale lilac tinge.
***D.* 'Dana Iris'.** Small-flowered cactus dahlia. H 4½ft (1.3m), S 2ft (60cm). Bears outstanding red flowers in summer-autumn. Good for exhibition.
***D.* 'Dandy'** illus. p.341.
***D.* 'Davenport Honey'.** Miniature-flowered decorative dahlia. H 4ft (1.2m), S 2ft (60cm). In summer-autumn has amber flowers that are good for exhibition.
***D.* 'Davenport Sunlight'** (illus. p.407). Medium-flowered semi-cactus dahlia. H 4ft (1.2m), S 2ft (60cm). Has bright yellow flowers in summer-autumn that are good for exhibition.
***D.* 'David Howard'.** Miniature-flowered decorative dahlia. H 3ft (1m), S 2ft (60cm). Dark, bronze-colored foliage offsets orange-bronze flowers produced in summer-autumn.
***D.* 'Debra Ann Craven'.** Giant-flowered semi-cactus dahlia. H 4½ft (1.3m), S 2ft (60cm). Deep red flowers are held well above the foliage on strong stems in summer-autumn. Is good for exhibition.
***D.* Disco Series.** Group of well-branched, erect dahlias grown as annuals. H and S 18in (45cm). Leaves are divided into oval leaflets. Daisylike, semi-double and double flower heads, with quilled florets in a wide color range, appear throughout summer and until autumn frosts.
***D.* 'East Anglian'** (illus. p.407). Small-flowered decorative dahlia. H 3ft (1m), S 2ft (60cm). Has orange-yellow flowers in summer-autumn.
***D.* 'Easter Sunday'** (illus. p.406). Collerette dahlia. H 3ft (1m), S 2ft (60cm). Leaves are glossy, dark green. Produces 4in (10cm) wide flowers with white inner and outer petals and dark yellow centers,in summer-autumn. Is good for exhibition.
***D.* 'Eastwood Moonlight'.** Medium-flowered semi-cactus dahlia. H 3½ft (1.1m), S 2ft (60cm). Bears bright yellow flowers in summer-autumn. Is a very good exhibition cultivar.
***D.* 'Fascination'** (illus. p.406). Dwarf miscellaneous dahlia. H 18in (45cm), S 12in (30cm). Has single, light purple flowers, 3in (7cm) across, in summer-autumn. Is useful for bedding.
***D.* 'Gateshead Festival'.** Small-flowered decorative dahlia. H 4ft (1.2m), S 2ft (60cm). In summer-autumn bears peach to orange flowers with lemon yellow petal bases. Good for exhibition.
***D.* 'Gay Princess'** (illus. p.406). Small-flowered decorative dahlia. H 4ft (1.2m), S 2ft (60cm). Produces lilac-lavender flowers in summer-autumn.
***D.* 'Geerling's Indian Summer'**, syn. *D.* 'Indian Summer'. Small-flowered cactus dahlia. H 4ft (1.2m), S 2ft (60cm). Has red flowers in summer-autumn. Very free-flowering.
***D.* 'Gerrie Hoek'.** Small-flowered waterlily dahlia. H 3½ft (1.1m), S 2ft (60cm). Flowers have pale pink outer petals and dark pink inner petals and are borne in summer-autumn.
***D.* 'Grenidor Pastelle'** (illus. p.407). Medium-flowered semi-cactus dahlia. H 4½ft (1.3m), S 2ft (60cm). Bears salmon-pink flowers with cream petal bases in summer-autumn. Good for exhibition.
***D.* 'Hallmark'.** Pompon dahlia. H 3½ft (1.1m), S 2ft (60cm). Has spherical pink flowers in summer-autumn. Is good for exhibition.
***D.* 'Hamari Accord'** (illus. p.407). Large-flowered semi-cactus dahlia. H 4ft (1.2m), S 2ft (60cm). Has pale, clear yellow flowers held well above the foliage on strong stems in summer-autumn. Good for exhibition.
***D.* 'Hamari Bride'.** Medium-flowered semi-cactus dahlia. H 4ft (1.2m), S 2ft (60cm). Bears clear white flowers in summer-autumn. A good exhibition cultivar.
***D.* 'Hamari Gold'** (illus. p.407). Giant-flowered decorative dahlia. H 3½ft (1.1m), S 2ft (60cm). Has golden orange-bronze flowers in summer-autumn. Is suitable for exhibition.
***D.* 'Hamari Katrina'** (illus. p.407). Large-flowered semi-cactus dahlia. H 4ft (1.2m), S 2ft (60cm). Bears deep butter yellow flowers in summer-autumn that are good for exhibition.
***D.* 'Hayley Jane'** (illus. p.407). Small-flowered semi-cactus dahlia. H 3½ft (1.1m), S 2ft (60cm). Produces white flowers evenly tipped purple-red in summer-autumn. Is good for exhibition.
***D.* 'Hillcrest Hillton'.** Large-flowered semi-cactus dahlia. H 4ft (1.2m), S 2ft (60cm). In summer-autumn produces weather-resistant, deep rich yellow flowers. Is good for exhibition.
***D.* 'Hillcrest Royal'** (illus. p.407). Medium-flowered cactus dahlia. H 3½ft (1.1m), S 2ft (60cm). In summer-autumn, has rich purple flowers with incurving petals.
***D.* 'Indian Summer'.** See *D.* 'Geerling's Indian Summer'.
***D.* 'Jeanette Carter'** (illus. p.407). Miniature-flowered decorative dahlia. H 3½ft (1.1m), S 2ft (60cm). Bears pale yellow flowers, sometimes flushed pink in the centers, in summer-autumn.
***D.* 'Jescot Julie'** (illus. p.407). Miscellaneous dahlia. H 24in (60cm), S 18in (45cm). Has sparse, midgreen foliage and orchidlike, double, orange-purple flowers, 3in (7cm) across, with purple-backed petals, in summer-autumn.
***D.* 'Jim Branigan'** (illus. p.407). Large-flowered semi-cactus dahlia. H 4½ft (1.3m), S 2ft (60cm). Bright red flowers are held well above the foliage in summer-autumn. Is good for exhibition.
***D.* 'Kathryn's Cupid'** (illus. p.407). Miniature ball dahlia. H 4ft (1.2m), S 2ft (60cm). In summer-autumn produces peach flowers that are good for exhibition.
***D.* 'Klankstad Kerkrade'.** Small-flowered cactus dahlia. H 4ft (1.2m), S 2ft (60cm). Has glossy, dark green leaves and bears soft sulfur yellow flowers in summer-autumn that are good for exhibition.
***D.* 'Lady Linda'.** Small-flowered decorative dahlia. H 4ft (1.2m), S 2ft (60cm). Well-formed, primrose yellow flowers are held well above the foliage in summer-autumn. Very vigorous and free-flowering. Is good for exhibition.
***D.* 'Lavender Athalie'** (illus. p.407). Small-flowered cactus dahlia. H 4ft (1.2m), S 2ft (60cm). Is a sport of *D.* 'Athalie'. Bears soft lilac-lavender flowers in summer-autumn.
***D.* 'Linda's Chester'.** Small-flowered cactus dahlia. H 4ft (1.2m), S 2ft (60cm). In summer-autumn produces yellow flowers overlaid with bronze at the petal tips. Is good for exhibition.
***D.* 'Mariposa'.** Collerette dahlia. H 3ft (1m), S 2ft (60cm). In summer-autumn has white flowers; outer petals are tinged with lilac. Is good for exhibition.
***D.* 'Mark Damp'.** Large-flowered semi-cactus dahlia. H 3–4ft (1–1.2m), S 2ft (60cm). Bears bronze-orange flowers tinged with peach in summer-autumn. Is suitable for exhibition.
***D.* 'Mark Hardwick'** (illus. p.407). Giant-flowered decorative dahlia. H 3½ft (1.1m), S 2ft (60cm). Compact plant bearing bright, deep yellow flowers on strong stems in summer-autumn. Is good for exhibition.
***D.* 'Mi Wong'** (illus. p.406). Pompon dahlia. H 3½ft (1.1m), S 2ft (60cm). Bears white flowers suffused pink in summer-autumn. Is good for exhibition.
***D.* 'Moor Place'** (illus. p.407). Pompon dahlia. H 3ft (1m), S 2ft (60cm). Leaves are glossy, dark green. Has royal purple flowers in summer-autumn. Is a good exhibition cultivar.
***D.* 'Nationwide'.** Small-flowered decorative dahlia. H 3–4ft (1–1.2m), S 2ft (60cm). Bears yellowish orange flowers in summer-autumn.
***D.* 'Noreen'** (illus. p.406). Pompon dahlia. H 3ft (1m) S 2ft (60cm). In summer-autumn produces dark pinkish purple flowers that are good for exhibition.
***D.* 'Pearl of Heemstede'** (illus. p.406). Small-flowered waterlily dahlia. H 3ft (1m), S 18in (45cm). Low-growing, very free-flowering dahlia that produce pale silvery pink flowers on long, thin stems in summer-autumn.
***D.* 'Pink Jupiter'** (illus. p.407). Giant-flowered semi-cactus dahlia. H 4½ft (1.3m), S 2ft (60cm). In summer-autumn produces deep pinkish mauve flowers. Is good for exhibition.
***D.* 'Pink Shirley Alliance'** (illus. p.406). Small-flowered cactus dahlia. H 4ft (1.2m), S 2ft (60cm). Has soft lilac-pink flowers in summer-autumn.
***D.* 'Pink Symbol'** (illus. p.406). Medium-flowered semi-cactus dahlia. H 3–4ft (1–1.2m), S 2ft (60cm). Bears pink flowers in summer-autumn. Is good for exhibition.
***D.* 'Pontiac'** (illus. p.406). Small-flowered cactus dahlia. H 3ft (1m), S 2ft (60cm). Leaves are glossy, dark green. Bears dark pinkish purple flowers in summer-autumn.
***D.* 'Porcelain'.** Small-flowered waterlily dahlia. H 3ft (1m), S 2ft (60cm). Produces whitish lilac flowers in summer-autumn. Useful for exhibition.
***D.* 'Preston Park'** (illus. p.407). Dwarf single dahlia. H 18in (45cm), S 12in (30cm). Bedding plant with nearly black foliage. In summer-autumn bears bright scarlet flowers, to 3in (7cm) across, with prominent yellow anthers in the center, on short stems.
***D.* 'Redskin'.** Well-branched dahlia grown as an annual. H and S 12in (30cm). Has bronze-green to maroon leaves divided into oval leaflets. Throughout summer and until autumn frosts it bears daisylike, double flower heads in many colors.
***D.* 'Reginald Keene'.** Large-flowered semi-cactus dahlia. H 3½–4ft

(1.1–1.2m), S 2ft (60cm). In summer-autumn has orange-flame flowers. Is good for exhibition.
***D.* 'Rhonda'** (illus. p.406). Pompon dahlia. H 3ft (1m), S 2ft (60cm). In summer-autumn produces whitish lilac flowers that are suitable for exhibition.
***D.* 'Ruby Wedding'.** Miniature-flowered decorative dahlia. H 3ft (1m), S 2ft (60cm). Bears deep purple flowers in summer-autumn. Is suitable for exhibition.
***D.* 'Scottish Relation'.** Small-flowered semi-cactus dahlia. H 3½ft (1.1m), S 2ft (60cm). Bears vivid purple flowers with cream petal bases in summer-autumn. Good for exhibition.
***D.* 'Shandy'** (illus. p.407). Small-flowered semi-cactus dahlia. H 3ft (1m), S 2ft (60cm). Produces light brown flowers in summer-autumn.
***D.* 'Sherwood Standard'.** Medium-flowered decorative dahlia. H 4ft (1.2m), S 2ft (60cm). Has orange flowers in summer-autumn. Is suitable for exhibition.
***D.* 'Shirley Alliance'** (illus. p.407). Small-flowered cactus dahlia. H 4½ft (1.3m), S 2ft (60cm). In summer-autumn bears soft orange flowers with a gold base to each petal. Is good for exhibition.
***D.* 'Small World'** (illus. p.406). Pompon dahlia. H 3ft (1m), S 2ft (60cm). Leaves are glossy, dark green. Has white flowers in summer-autumn. Is suitable for exhibition.
***D.* 'So Dainty'** (illus. p.407). Miniature-flowered semi-cactus dahlia. H 3½ft (1.1m), S 2ft (60cm). Produces bronze-colored flowers in summer-autumn that are suitable for exhibition.
***D.* 'Trengrove Jill'.** Medium-flowered decorative dahlia. H 4½ft (1.3m), S 2ft (60cm). Deep bronze flowers are held well above the foliage on strong stems in summer-autumn.
***D.* 'Vicky Crutchfield'** (illus. p.406). Small-flowered waterlily dahlia. H 3ft (1m), S 2ft (60cm). Bears pink flowers in summer-autumn. Is suitable for exhibition.
***D.* 'Wanda's Capella'** (illus. p.407). Giant-flowered decorative dahlia. H 4ft (1.2m), S 2ft (60cm). Has bright yellow flowers in summer-autumn. Is good for exhibition.
***D.* 'Whale's Rhonda'** (illus. p.407). Pompon dahlia. H 3ft (1m), S 2ft (60cm). Leaves are glossy, very dark green. In summer-autumn has purple flowers that are good for exhibition.
***D.* 'White Alva's'** (illus. p.406). Giant-flowered decorative dahlia. H 4ft (1.2m), S 2ft (60cm). Produces pure white flowers, held well above the foliage on strong stems, in summer-autumn. Is good for exhibition.
***D.* 'White Ballet'** (illus. p.406). Small-flowered waterlily dahlia. H 3ft (1m), S 2ft (60cm). Produces pure white flowers in summer-autumn.
***D.* 'White Klankstad'** (illus. p.406). Small-flowered cactus dahlia. H 3½–4ft (1.1–1.2m), S 2ft (60cm). Is a sport of *D.* 'Klankstad Kerkrade' Has white flowers in summer-autumn.
***D.* 'White Moonlight'.** Medium-flowered semi-cactus dahlia. H 4ft (1.2m), S 2ft (60cm). Produces white flowers in summer-autumn. Is good for exhibition.
***D.* 'Willo's Violet'.** Pompon dahlia. H 3ft (1m), S 2ft (60cm). Has glossy, dark green leaves and bears violet-purple flowers in summer-autumn. Is suitable for exhibition.
***D.* 'Wootton Cupid'** (illus. p.406). Miniature ball dahlia. H 3½–4ft (1.1–1.2m), S 2ft (60cm). Produces pink flowers in summer-autumn. Is good for exhibition.
***D.* 'Wootton Impact'** (illus. p.407). Medium-flowered semi-cactus dahlia. H 4ft (1.2m), S 2ft (60cm). Has flowers in shades of bronze, held well above the foliage on strong stems, in summer-autumn. Is good for exhibition.
***D.* 'Yellow Hammer'** (illus. p.407). Dwarf, single dahlia. H 18in (45cm), S 12in (30cm). Has rich yellow flowers, 3in (7cm) across, in summer-autumn.
***D.* 'Yelno Firelight'** (illus. p.407). Small-flowered waterlily dahlia. H 4ft (1.2m), S 2ft (60cm). In summer-autumn has red and yellow flowers with a neat petal formation, held on strong stems.
***D.* 'Yelno Velvena'.** Small-flowered waterlily dahlia. H 4ft (1.2m), S 2ft (60cm). Deep maroon flowers are held on strong stems in summer-autumn.
***D.* 'Zorro'** (illus. p.407). Giant-flowered decorative dahlia. H 4ft (1.2m), S 2ft (60cm). Produces bright blood red flowers in summer-autumn Good for exhibition.

Daiswa polyphylla. See *Paris polyphylla.*

DANÄE

LILACEAE/RUSCACEAE

Genus of one species of evergreen shrub with inconspicuous flowers, grown for its attractive, flattened, leaflike shoots. Grows in sun or shade and in moist soil. Propagate by seed in autumn or by division from autumn to spring.
D. racemosa (Alexandrian laurel). Evergreen, arching, dense shrub. H and S 3ft (1m). Has slender stems, lance-shaped, leaflike, glossy green shoots and pointed, glossy, bright green "leaves." Occasionally bears spherical red berries. Z6–9 H9–2.

DAPHNE

THYMELAEACEAE

Genus of evergreen, semi-evergreen, or deciduous shrubs grown for their usually fragrant, tubular flowers, each with 4 spreading lobes, and, in some species, for their foliage or fruits (seeds are poisonous). Dwarf species and cultivars are good for rock gardens. Most need full sun (although *D. alpina, D. arbuscula,* and *D. blagayana* may be grown in semi-shade, and *D. laureola* tolerates deep shade) and fertile, well-drained but not overly dry soil. Resents being transplanted. Propagate species by seed when fresh or by semi-ripe cuttings in summer, cultivars by cuttings only. Is susceptible to viruses that cause leaf mottling, and some may die suddenly for no apparent reason. All parts, including the seed, are highly toxic if ingested, and contact with the sap may irritate skin.
D. alpina. Deciduous, erect shrub. H 20in (50cm), S 16in (40cm). Leaves are oval, downy, and gray-green. Carries terminal clusters of fragrant white flowers in late spring. Is suitable for a rock garden. Z6–8.
D. arbuscula illus. p.366.
D. bholua illus. p.150.
D. blagayana illus. p.347.
***D.* x *burkwoodii* 'Somerset'** illus. p.154. **'Somerset Variegated'** is a semi-evergreen, upright shrub. H 5ft (1.5m), S 3ft (1m). Bears dense clusters of very fragrant, white-throated pink flowers in late spring, sometimes again in autumn. Narrowly oblong, gray-green leaves are edged with creamy white or pale yellow. Z4–7 H7–1.
D. cneorum illus. p.348. **'Eximia'** is an evergreen, prostrate shrub. H 4in (10cm), S to 20in (50cm) or more. Has small, oval, leathery, dark green leaves and, in late spring, terminal clusters of fragrant white flowers, crimson outside and often pink-flushed within. Z5–7 H7–5.
D. collina. Evergreen, domed, compact shrub. H and S 20in (50cm). Oval, dark green leaves densely cover upright branches. Has terminal clusters of small, fragrant, purple-rose flowers in late spring. Is good for a rock garden. Z7–8 H8–7.
D. genkwa. Deciduous, upright, open shrub. H and S 5ft (1.5m). Oval, dark green leaves are bronze when young. Large, faintly scented lilac flowers are borne from mid- to late spring. Z6–9 H9–6.
D. giraldii. Deciduous, upright shrub. H and S 2ft (60cm). Clusters of fragrant, golden yellow flowers are produced amid oblong, pale blue-green leaves in late spring and early summer and are followed by egg-shaped red fruits. Z4–8.
D. jasminea illus. p.364.
D. laureola (Spurge laurel). Evergreen, bushy shrub. H 3ft (1m), S 5ft (1.5m). Has oblong, dark green leaves. Slightly fragrant, pale green flowers are borne from late winter to early spring, followed by spherical black fruits. Z7–8 H8–7. subsp. ***philippi*** illus. p.156.
D. mezereum illus. p.174. f. ***alba*** is a deciduous, upright to spreading shrub. H and S 4ft (1.2m). Bears very fragrant white or creamy white flowers that clothe bare stems in late winter and early spring. Has spherical yellow fruits. Leaves are oblong and dull gray-green. Z5–8 H8–5..
D. odora. Evergreen, bushy shrub. H and S 5ft (1.5m). Has oval, glossy, dark green leaves and, from midwinter to early spring, very fragrant, deep purplish pink-and-white flowers. Z7–9 H9–7. **'Aureomarginata'** illus. p.174.
***D. petraea* 'Grandiflora'** illus. p.366.
D. retusa illus. p.155.
D. tangutica. Evergreen, bushy shrub with thick shoots. H and S 3ft (1m). Narrowly oval, leathery leaves are dark green. Bears clusters of fragrant, white-flushed, purple-pink flowers in mid- to late spring. Z7–9 H9–7.

DAPHNIPHYLLUM

DAPHNIPHYLLACEAE

Genus of evergreen trees and shrubs grown for their habit and foliage. Male and female flowers are borne on separate plants. Needs a sheltered position in sun or semi-shade and deep, fertile, well-drained but not too dry soil. Propagate by semi-ripe cuttings in summer.
D. himalense subsp. ***macropodum.*** See *D. macropodum.*
D. macropodum, syn. *D. himalense* subsp. *macropodum*, illus. p.117.

DARMERA, syn. PELTIPHYLLUM

Umbrella plant

SAXIFRAGACEAE

Genus of one species of perennial grown for its unusual foliage. Makes fine marginal water plants. Grows in sun or shade and requires moist soil. Propagate by division in spring or by seed in autumn or spring.
D. peltata illus. p.238.

DASYLIRION

Bear grass

DRACAENACEAE

Genus of evergreen, palmlike perennials grown for their foliage and flowers. Male and female flowers are produced on separate plants. Requires well-drained soil and a sunny position. Water freely when in full growth, sparingly at other times. Propagate by seed in spring.
D. texanum. Evergreen, palmlike perennial with a 30in (75cm) high trunk. H over 3ft (1m), S 10ft (3m). Has a rosette of narrow, drooping, green leaves, each 2–3ft (60–90cm) long, with yellowish prickles along margins. Stems, 15ft (5m) long, emerge from center of plant carrying dense, narrow panicles of small, bell-shaped whitish flowers in summer. Dry, 3-winged fruits appear in autumn. Z11–12 H12–1.

Datura. Reclassified as *Brugmansia.*

DAVALLIA

DAVALLIACEAE

Genus of evergreen or semi-evergreen, often epiphytic ferns best suited to growing in pots and hanging baskets. Requires semi-shade and very fibrous,

moist, peaty soil. Remove fading fronds regularly. Propagate by division in spring or summer or by spores in summer.
D. canariensis (Hare's-foot fern). Semi-evergreen fern. H and S 12in (30cm). Broadly lance-shaped, leathery, midgreen fronds with numerous triangular pinnae arise from a scaly, brown rootstock. Z10-11 H12–10.
D. mariesii (Squirrel's-foot fern). Evergreen fern. H 6in (15cm), S 9in (23cm). Broadly triangular, delicately divided, leathery, midgreen fronds arise from a creeping, scaly, brown rootstock. Z9–11 H12–9.

DAVIDIA

CORNACEAE/DAVIDIACEAE

Genus of one species of deciduous, spring- and summer-flowering tree grown for its habit and showy white bracts surrounding insignificant flower heads. Needs shelter from strong winds. Requires sun or semi-shade and fertile, well-drained but preferably moist soil. Propagate by semi-ripe cuttings in spring or by seed when ripe in autumn.
D. involucrata illus. p.77.

DECAISNEA

LARDIZABALACEAE

Genus of deciduous, summer-flowering shrubs grown for their foliage, flowers, and sausage-shaped fruits. Requires a sheltered, sunny situation and fertile soil that is not too dry. Propagate by seed in autumn.
D. fargesii illus. p.122.

DECUMARIA

HYDRANGEACEAE

Genus of evergreen or deciduous, woody-stemmed, root climbers. Prefers sun and loamy, well-drained soil that does not dry out. Prune, if necessary, after flowering. Propagate by stem cuttings in late summer or early autumn.
D. sinensis illus. illus. p.204.

DEINANTHE

HYDRANGEACEAE

Genus of slow-growing perennials with creeping, underground rootstocks. Is useful for rock gardens. Needs shaded, moist soil. Propagate by division in spring or by seed when fresh.
D. bifida. Slow-growing, mound-forming perennial. H 8in (20cm), S 4–8in (10–20cm). Nodding, star-shaped white flowers are produced in summer amid rounded, crinkled leaves with 2-lobed, lacerated tips. Z4–8. H8–1.
D. caerulea. Slow-growing, mound-forming perennial. H 8in (20cm), S to 6in (15cm). Stems, each carrying a cluster of nodding, bowl-shaped, pale violet-blue flowers, rise above 3–4 oval, toothed leaves in summer. Z5–9 H9–5.

Delairea odorata. See *Senecio mikanioides.*

DELOSPERMA

AIZOACEAE

Genus of densely branched, trailing, perennials, sometimes shrubby succulents, some with tuberous roots. Requires full sun and very well-drained soil. Propagate by seed or stem cuttings in spring or summer.
D. cooperi. Spreading, mat-forming succulent. H 2in (5cm), S indefinite. Has cylindrical, fleshy, light green leaves, 2in (5cm) long, and, in mid- to late summer, solitary, daisylike magenta flowers. Z8–10 H10–8.

DELPHINIUM

RANUNCULACEAE

Genus of perennials, biennials, and annuals grown for their spikes of irregularly cup-shaped, sometimes hooded, spurred flowers. Needs an open, sunny position and fertile or rich, well-drained soil. Tall cultivars need staking and ample feeding and watering in spring and early summer. In spring remove thin growths from well-established plants, leaving 5–7 strong shoots. If flower spikes are removed after they fade, a second flush may be produced in late summer, provided plants are fertilized and watered well. Propagate species by seed in autumn or spring; Belladonna Group cultivars by division or basal cuttings of young shoots in spring; Elatum Group cultivars by cuttings only. All parts may cause severe discomfort if ingested, and contact with foliage may irritate skin. See also feature panel, p.230.

For ease of reference, delphinium cultivars have been grouped as follows:

Belladonna Group. Upright, branched perennials with palmately lobed leaves. H 3–4ft (1–1.2m), S to 18in (45cm). Wiry stems bear loose, branched spikes, 12in (30cm) long, of elf-cap-shaped, single flowers, ¾in (2cm) or more across, with spurs up to 1¼in (3cm) long, in early and late summer.
Elatum Group. Erect perennials with large, palmate leaves. H 5–6ft (1.5–2m), S 24–36in (60–90cm). In summer, produce closely packed spikes, 16in–4ft (40cm–1.2m) long, of regularly spaced, semi-double, rarely fully double flowers, 3–4in (8–10cm) wide, in a range of colors from white to blue and purple, sometimes red-pink, usually with contrasting eyes.
Pacific Hybrids. Similar to Elatum Group cultivars, but grown as annuals or biennials. They produce short-lived, large, semi-double flowers on spikes in early and midsummer.

Delphiniums are good in Z3–7 H7–1 except where otherwise noted.

***D.* 'Balkleid'.** Belladonna Group perennial. H 3–4ft (1–1.2m). Bears spikes of widely spaced, midblue flowers on spikes 12in (30cm) long.
***D.* 'Blue Dawn'** (illus. p.230). Elatum Group perennial. H 6–7ft (2–2.2m). Bears pinkish purple-flushed, pale blue flowers with dark brown eyes on spikes to 4ft (1.2m) long.
***D.* 'Blue Nile'** (illus. p.230). Elatum Group perennial. H 5–5½ft (1.5–1.7m). Has rich blue flowers with lightly blue-streaked white eyes on spikes to 27in (68cm) long.
***D.* 'Bruce'** (illus. p.230). Elatum Group perennial. H 5½–7ft (1.7–2.2m). Bears deep violet-purple flowers, silver-flushed toward centers and with gray-brown eyes, on spikes to 4ft (1.2m) long.
D. brunonianum. Upright perennial. H and S to 8in (20cm). Hairy stems bear rounded, 3- or 5-lobed leaves. In early summer, flower stems each produce a spike, to 6in (15cm) long, of hooded, single, pale blue to purple flowers, 1½in (4cm) wide, with short black spurs. Is good for a rock garden.
***D.* 'Butterball'** (illus. p.230). Elatum Group perennial. H 5–5½ft (1.5–1.7m). Produces cream-eyed white flowers, overlaid with very pale greenish yellow, on spikes to 20in (50cm) long.
D. cardinale. Short-lived, upright perennial. H 3–6ft (1–2m), S 2ft (60cm). In summer has single scarlet flowers, 1½in (4cm) wide, with yellow eyes, on spikes, 12–18in (30–45cm) long, above palmate, finely divided leaves.
***D.* 'Chelsea Star'** (illus. p.230). Elatum Group perennial. H 6ft (2m). Has rich deep violet flowers with white eyes on spikes to 3½ft (1.1m) long.
D. chinense. See *D. grandiflorum.*
***D.* 'Cliveden Beauty'** (illus. p.230). Belladonna Group perennial. H 3–4ft (1–1.2m). Produces sky blue flowers on spikes 12in (30cm) long. Z3–7 H6–1.
D. consolida. See *Consolida ajacis.*
***D.* 'Emily Hawkins'** (illus. p.230). Elatum Group perennial. H 6–7ft (2–2.2m). Has lilac-flushed, pale blue flowers with light brown eyes on spikes to 32in (80cm) long.
***D.* 'Fanfare'** (illus. p.230). Elatum Group perennial. H 6–7ft (2–2.2m). Bears pale blue to silvery mauve flowers with white-and-violet eyes on spikes 2–2½ft (60–75cm) long.
***D.* 'Fenella'.** Elatum Group perennial. H 3½–5ft (1.1–1.5m). Bears purple-flushed, gentian blue flowers with black eyes on spikes to 3ft (1m) long.
***D.* 'Gillian Dallas'** (illus. p.230). Elatum Group perennial. H 6ft (2m). Has spikes, to 32in (80cm) long, of white-eyed, pale lilac flowers, shading to even paler lilac on outer edges.
D. grandiflorum, syn. *D. chinense.* **'Blue Butterfly'** (illus. p.230) is a short-lived, erect perennial usually grown as an annual. H 1½ft (45cm), S 1ft (30cm). Has palmate, divided leaves. In summer produces loose, branching spikes, to 6in (15cm) long, of single, deep blue flowers, 1½in (3.5cm) wide. Is useful as a bedding plant. Z3–8 H8–1.
***D.* 'Langdon's Royal Flush'** (illus. p.230). Elatum Group perennial. H 6ft (2m). Has cream-eyed, pinkish purple flowers on spikes to 34in (85cm) long; upper petals are a darker shade than lower ones.
***D.* 'Loch Leven'** (illus. p.230). Elatum Group perennial. H 5½ft (1.7m). Bears midblue flowers with white eyes on spikes to 3ft (1m) long. Z3–7 H8–1.
***D.* 'Loch Nevis'.** Elatum Group perennial. H 6ft (2m). Has midblue flowers with white eyes on spikes to 3½ft (1.1m) long.
***D.* 'Lord Butler'** (illus. p.230). Elatum Group perennial. H 5–5½ft (1.5–1.7m). Produces midblue flowers, lightly flushed with pale lilac and with blue-marked white eyes, on spikes to 30in (75cm) long. Z3–7 H9–1.
***D.* 'Mighty Atom'** (illus. p.230). Elatum Group perennial. H 5–6ft (1.5–2m). Has midviolet flowers with violet-marked, yellowish brown eyes on spikes to 2½ft (75cm) long.
D. nudicaule illus. p.355. Z3–7 H9–1.
***D.* 'Olive Poppleton'** (illus. p.230). Elatum Group perennial. H 6–8ft (2–2.5m). Produces white flowers, with fawn eyes, on spikes to 3ft (1m) long.
***D.* Pacific Hybrids.** Perennials, often grown as annuals, and available in single colors and as a mixture. Seedlings may not come true. Flowers are produced in spikes, 1½–3ft (45cm–1m) long. Z3–8 H6–1.
***D.* 'Sandpiper'** (illus. p.230). Elatum Group perennial. H 3–4½ft 1–1.35m. Has white flowers with creamy brown eyes on spikes to 2½ft (75cm) long.
***D.* 'Spindrift'** (illus. p.230). Elatum Group perennial. H 5½–6ft (1.7–2m). Produces spikes, to 3ft (1m) long, of pinkish purple flowers overlaid with pale blue and with creamy white eyes; toward centers, the pinkish purple becomes paler and the blue darker. Flower color varies with different types of soil; on acidic soil, flowers are greenish.
***D.* 'Strawberry Fair'** (illus. p.230). Elatum Group perennial. H 5½ft (1.7m). Has white-eyed, mulberry pink flowers on spikes to 31in (78cm) long.
***D.* 'Sungleam'** (illus. p.230). Elatum Group perennial. H 5½–6ft (1.7–2m). Produces spikes, 16–30in (40–75cm) long, of white flowers overlaid with pale yellow and with yellow eyes.
D. tatsienense. Short-lived, upright perennial. H 12in (30cm), S 2–4in (5–10cm). Loose spikes, to 6in (15cm) long, of small-spurred, single, bright blue flowers, 1in (2.5cm) long, are borne in summer. Leaves are rounded to oval and deeply cut. Good in a rock garden. Needs gritty soil.
***D.* 'Völkerfrieden'.** Belladonna Group perennial. H 3–4ft (1–1.2m). Produces deep blue flowers on spikes 12in (30cm) long. Z3–8 H6–1.

Dendrobenthamia capitata. See *Cornus capitata.*

DENDROBIUM

See also ORCHIDS.
D. aphyllum, syn. *D. pierardii* (illus. p.296). Deciduous, epiphytic orchid for an intermediate greenhouse. H to 24in (60cm). In early spring produces pairs of soft pink flowers, 1½in 4cm across and each with a large cream lip. Has oval leaves, 2–3in (5–8cm) long. Requires semi-shade in summer. Is best grown hanging from a bark slab. Z12–15 H12–10.
D. chrysotoxum (illus. p.299). Deciduous, epiphytic orchid for an intermediate greenhouse. H 24in (60cm). Clusters of cup-shaped, deep yellow flowers, ¾in (2cm) across and with hairy, red-marked lips, are borne in spring. Oval leaves are 2–3in (5–8cm) long. Provide good light in summer. Z14–15 H12–6.
D. infundibulum (illus. p.296). Evergreen, epiphytic orchid for a cool greenhouse. H 12in (30cm). In spring, stems each produce up to 6 pure white flowers, 3in (8cm) wide and each with a yellow-marked lip. Has oval leaves, 2–3in (5–8cm) long. Grow in semi-shade in summer. Z14–15 H12–6.
D. nobile (illus. p.297). Deciduous, epiphytic orchid (often evergreen in cultivation) for a cool greenhouse. H 12in (30cm). Clusters of delicate, rose-pink flowers, 2in (5cm) across and each with a prominent maroon lip, are borne along stems in spring. Oval leaves are 2–3in (5–8cm) long. Requires semi-shade in summer. Z14–15 H12–6.
D. pierardii. See *D. aphyllum*.

DENDROCHILUM

See also ORCHIDS.
D. glumaceum (Silver chain). Evergreen, epiphytic orchid for a cool greenhouse. H 4in (10cm). Pendent sprays of fragrant, pointed, orange-lipped, creamy white flowers, ½in (1cm) long, are produced in autumn. Narrowly oval leaves are 6in (15cm) long. Requires semi-shade in summer. Z14–15 H12–10.

DENDROMECON

PAPAVERACEAE

Genus of evergreen shrubs grown for their foliage and showy flowers. Plant against a south- or west-facing wall where marginally hardy. Requires full sun and very well-drained soil. Propagate by softwood cuttings in summer, by seed in autumn or spring or by root cuttings in winter.
D. rigida illus. p.147.

Dentaria enneaphyllos. See *Cardamine enneaphyllos*.
Dentaria pentaphyllos. See *Cardamine pentaphyllos*.

DESCHAMPSIA

GRAMINEAE/POACEAE

See also GRASSES, BAMBOOS, RUSHES, and SEDGES.
D. cespitosa (Tufted hair grass). Evergreen, tuft-forming, perennial grass. H to 3ft (1m), S 10–12in (25–30cm). Has dense, narrow, rough-edged, dark green leaves. In summer produces dainty, open panicles of minute, pale brown spikelets that last well into winter. Tolerates sun or shade. Z4–8 H8–1.

DESFONTAINIA

DESFONTAINIACEAE/LOGANIACEAE

Genus of evergreen shrubs grown for their foliage and showy, tubular flowers. Provide shelter in cold areas. Needs some shade, particularly in dry regions, and moist, peaty, preferably acidic soil. Propagate by semi-ripe cuttings in summer.
D. spinosa illus. p.143.

DESMODIUM

LEGUMINOSAE/PAPILIONACEAE

Genus of perennials and deciduous shrubs and subshrubs grown for their flowers. Needs full sun and well-drained soil. Propagate by softwood cuttings in late spring or by seed in autumn. May also be divided in spring.
D. elegans, syn. *D. tiliifolium*, illus. p.167.
D. tiliifolium. See *D. elegans*.

DEUTZIA

HYDRANGEACEAE

Genus of deciduous shrubs grown for their profuse, 5-petaled flowers. Needs full sun and fertile, well-drained soil. Plants benefit from regular thinning out of old shoots after flowering. Propagate by softwood cuttings in summer.
***D. x elegantissima* 'Fasciculata'.** Deciduous, upright shrub. H 6ft (2m), S 5ft (1.5m). From late spring to early summer produces large clusters of 5-petaled, pale pink flowers. Leaves are oval, toothed, and midgreen. Z6–8 H8–6. **'Rosealind'** illus. p.162.
D. gracilis illus. p.153.
***D.* 'Joconde'.** Deciduous, upright shrub. H and S 5ft (1.5m). Bears 5-petaled white flowers, striped purple outside, in early summer. Oval, mid-green leaves are long-pointed. Z6–8 H8–6.
D. longifolia. Deciduous, arching shrub. H 6ft (2m), S 10ft (3m). Large clusters of 5-petaled, deep pink flowers are produced from early to mid-summer. Narrowly lance-shaped leaves are gray-green. Z7–8 H8–7. **'Veitchii'** illus. p.140.
D. x magnifica. Vigorous, deciduous, upright shrub. H 8ft (2.5m), S 6ft (2m). Produces dense clusters of 5-petaled, pure white flowers in early summer. Leaves are narrowly oval and bright green. Z6–8 H8–5. **'Staphyleoides'** illus. p.136.
D. monbeigii illus. p.158.
***D.* 'Mont Rose'** illus. p.161.
D. pulchra. Vigorous, deciduous, upright shrub. H 8ft (2.5m), S 6ft (2m). Has peeling, orange-brown bark and lance-shaped, dark green leaves. Slender, pendulous panicles of 5-petaled, pink-tinged white flowers appear in late spring and early summer. Z7–8 H8–7.
D. x rosea illus. p.154.
D. scabra illus. p.136. **'Plena'** (syn. *D.s.* 'Flore Pleno') is a deciduous, upright shrub. H 10ft (3m), S 6ft (2m). Narrowly oval, dark green leaves set off dense, upright clusters of double white flowers, purplish pink outside, from early to midsummer. Z6–8 H8–6.
D. setchuenensis* var. *corymbiflora. Deciduous, upright shrub with peeling, pale brown bark when mature. H 6ft (2m), S 5ft (1.5m). Small, 5-petaled white flowers are borne in broad clusters in early and midsummer. Produces lance-shaped, long-pointed, gray-green leaves. Z6–8 H8–6.

DIANELLA

Flax lily

LILIACEAE/PHORMIACEAE

Genus of evergreen, summer-flowering perennials. Is suitable outdoors only in mild areas and elsewhere requires a cold greenhouse or frame. Needs sun and well-drained, neutral to acidic soil. Propagate by division or seed in spring.
D. caerulea. Evergreen, tuft-forming perennial. H 30in (75cm), S 12in (30cm). In summer has panicles of small, star-shaped blue flowers above grasslike leaves, followed by blue berries. Z9–10 H10–9.
D. tasmanica illus. p.253.

DIANTHUS

Carnation, Pink

CARYOPHYLLACEAE

Genus of evergreen or semi-evergreen, mainly summer-flowering perennials, annuals, and biennials grown for their mass of flowers, often scented, some of which are excellent for cutting. Carnations and pinks (see below) are excellent for cut flowers and border decoration, the biennial *D. barbatus* (Sweet William) is suitable for bedding, and smaller, tuft-forming species and cultivars are good for rock gardens. Needs an open, sunny position and well-drained, slightly alkaline soil, except for *D. pavonius*, which prefers acidic soil. Deadheading of repeat-flowering types is beneficial. Tall forms of carnations and pinks have a loose habit and need staking. Propagate border carnations by layering in late summer, other named forms by softwood cuttings in early to midsummer, and species by seed at any time. Is susceptible to rust, spider mite, and virus infection through aphids, but many cultivars are available from virus-free stock.

Carnations and pinks have narrowly lance-shaped, silvery- or gray-green leaves scattered up the flower stems, which may coil outward on carnations. They are divided into the following groups, all with self-colored and bicolored cultivars. See also feature panel, pp.280–81.

Carnations
Border carnations are annuals or evergreen perennials that flower prolifically once in midsummer and are good for border decoration and cutting. Each stem bears 5 or more often scented, semi-double or double flowers to 3in (8cm) across; picotee forms (with petals outlined in a darker color) are available. H 2½–3½ft (75cm–1.1m), S to 1ft (30cm).
Perpetual-flowering carnations are evergreen perennials that flower year-round if grown in a greenhouse, but more prolifically in summer. They are normally grown for cut flowers: flower stems should be disbudded, leaving one terminal bud per stem. Fully double flowers, to 4in (10cm) across, are usually unscented and are often flecked or streaked. H 3–5ft (1–1.5m), S 1ft (30cm) or more.

Spray forms are not disbudded so have 5 or more flowers per stem, each 2–2½in (5–6cm) across. H 2–3ft (60cm–1m), S to 1ft (30cm).
Malmaison carnations are evergreen perennials, derived from *D.* 'Souvenir de la Malmaison'. Grown under cover, they bear large, double, scented flowers sporadically during the year. The flowers can reach up to 5in (13cm) across. They are mostly self-colored, and they tend to split their calyces. H 20–28in (50–70cm), S 16in (40cm).

Pinks
Evergreen, clump-forming perennials grown for border decoration and cutting, that in summer produce a succession of basal shoots, each bearing 4–6 fragrant, single to fully double flowers, 1½–2½in (3.5–6cm) across. H 12–18in (30–45cm), S 9–12in (23–30cm) or more.
Old-fashioned pinks have a low, spreading habit and produce masses of flowers in one flowering period in mid-summer. Mule types (a border carnation crossed with a Sweet William) and laced types (in which the central color extends as a loop around each petal) are available.
Modern pinks, obtained by crossing an old-fashioned pink with a perpetual-flowering carnation, are more vigorous than old-fashioned pinks and are repeat-flowering with two or three main flushes of flowers in summer.
Alpine pinks are evergreen species and cultivars forming neat mat or cushion plants. They will grow at the edge of a border or in a rock garden, trough, or alpine house. In early summer they bear single, semi-double, or double, often scented flowers. Foliage is

gray-green. H 3–4in (8–10cm), S 8in (20cm).

The following do well in Z5–9 H8–1 except where otherwise noted.

***D.* 'A.J. MacSelf'.** See *D.* 'Dad's Favourite'.
***D.* 'Albisola'** (illus. p.281). Perpetual-flowering carnation. Fully double flowers are clear tangerine-orange.
***D.* 'Aldridge Yellow'** (illus. p.281). Border carnation. Semi-double flowers are clear yellow.
***D.* 'Alice'** (illus. p.280). Modern pink. Has clove-scented, semi-double, ivory-white flowers, each with a bold crimson eye.
D. alpinus illus. p.378.
***D.* 'Annabelle'** illus. p.379.
***D.* 'Arctic'.** Perpetual-flowering, spray carnation. Fully double flowers are white with pink flecks.
D. armeria (Deptford pink). Evergreen, tuft-forming perennial sometimes grown as an annual. H 12in (30cm), S 18in (45cm). Has narrowly lance-shaped, dark green leaves. In summer, tall stems each carry small, 5-petaled, cerise-pink flowers in small bunches. Is good for a rock garden or bank. Z3–9 H9–1.
***D.* 'Astor'** (illus. p.281). Perpetual-flowering carnation. Produces fully double scarlet flowers; is one of the few scented, perpetual-flowering cultivars.
D. barbatus (Sweet William). **Roundabout Series** (dwarf) illus. p.326.
***D.* 'Becky Robinson'** (illus. p.280). Modern pink. Bears clove-scented, fully double, rose-pink flowers with ruby red lacing. Is good for exhibition.
***D.* 'Bombardier'.** Evergreen, tuft-forming perennial. H and S 4in (10cm). Has a basal tuft of linear, gray-green leaves and, in summer, small, double scarlet flowers. Is good for a rock garden.
***D.* 'Bookham Fancy'** (illus. p.281). Border carnation. Produces bright yellow flowers, edged and flecked carmine-purple, on short, stiff stems.
***D.* 'Bookham Perfume'** (illus. p.281). Perennial border carnation. Has scented, semi-double crimson flowers.
***D.* 'Bovey Belle'** (illus. p.281). Modern pink. Has clove-scented, fully double, bright purple flowers that are excellent for cutting.
***D.* 'Brympton Red'.** Old-fashioned pink. Flowers are single, bright crimson with deeper shading.
D. caesius. See *D. gratianopolitanus*.
D. carthusianorum illus. p.354.
***D.* 'Charles Musgrave'.** See *D.* 'Musgrave's Pink'.
D. chinensis (Indian pink). Slow-growing, bushy annual. H and S 6–12in (15–30cm). Lance-shaped leaves are pale or midgreen. Tubular, single or double flowers, 1in (2.5cm) or more wide and with open, spreading petals, in shades of pink, red, or white, are produced in summer and early autumn. Z9–11 H12–1. **Baby Doll Series** illus. p.324; **'Fire Carpet'** illus. p.327; **Heddewigii Group**, H 12in (30cm), has flowers in mixed colors.
***D.* 'Christine Hough'** (illus. p.281). Perennial border carnation. Semi-double flowers are apricot overlaid and streaked with rose-pink.
***D.* 'Christopher'** (illus. p.281). Modern pink. Produces lightly scented, fully double, bright salmon-red flowers.
***D.* 'Clara'** (illus. p.281). Perpetual-flowering carnation. Fully double flowers are yellow with salmon flecks.
***D.* 'Constance Finnis'.** See *D.* 'Fair Folly'.
***D.* 'Cream Sue'** (illus. p.281). Perpetual-flowering carnation. Flowers are cream. Is a sport of *D.* 'Apricot Sue'.
***D.* 'Crompton Princess'** (illus. p.281). Perpetual-flowering carnation. Flowers are pure white.
***D.* 'Dad's Favourite'**, syn. *D.* 'A.J. MacSelf' (illus. p.280). Old-fashioned pink. Bears scented, semi-double white flowers with chocolate brown lacing.
D. deltoides (Maiden pink). Evergreen, mat-forming, basal-tufted perennial. H 6in (15cm), S 12in (30cm). In summer, small, 5-petaled white, pink, or cerise flowers are borne singly above tiny, lance-shaped leaves. Good for a rock garden or bank. Trim back after flowering.Z3–10 H10–1. **'Leuchtfunk'** (syn. *D.d.* 'Flashing Light') illus. p.380.
***D.* 'Denis'.** Modern pink. Strongly clove-scented, fully double magenta flowers are freely produced.
***D.* 'Doris'** (illus. p.280). Modern pink. Has compact growth and an abundance of fragrant, semi-double, pale pink flowers, each with a salmon-red ring towards base of the flower. Is one of the most widely grown cultivars and provides excellent flowers for cutting.
***D.* 'Duchess of Westminster'** (illus. p.281). Vigorous Malmaison carnation. Produces salmon-pink flowers with stronger calyces than most Malmaison carnations.
***D.* 'Edenside'.** Perennial border carnation. Semi-double flowers are clear white.
***D.* 'Emile Paré'** (illus. p.280). Old-fashioned, mule pink. Has clusters of semi-double, salmon-pink flowers and, unusually for a pink, midgreen foliage.
***D.* 'Eva Humphries'** (illus. p.280). Perennial border carnation. Has fragrant, semi-double flowers with white petals outlined in purple.
***D.* 'Fair Folly'**, syn. *D.* 'Constance Finnis' (illus. p.280). Modern pink. Flowers are single and of variable color, usually dusky pink to dusky purple with 2 white splashes on each petal.
***D.* 'Forest Treasure'** (illus. p.280). Perennial border carnation. Has double white flowers with reddish purple splashes on each petal.
***D.* 'Freckles'.** Modern pink. A compact cultivar, it has fully double flowers that are red-speckled and dusky pink.
***D.* 'Golden Cross'** (illus. p.281). Border carnation. Produces bright yellow flowers on short, stiff stems.
***D.* 'Gran's Favourite'** (illus. p.280). Old-fashioned pink. Bears fragrant, semi-double white flowers with deep raspberry lacing.
D. gratianopolitanus, syn. *D. caesius*, illus. p.377.
***D.* 'Green Eyes'.** See *D.* 'Musgrave's Pink'.
D. haematocalyx. Evergreen, tuft-forming perennial. H 12cm (5in), S 4in (10cm). Leaves are lance-shaped and usually glaucous. Bears 5-petaled, toothed, beige-backed, deep pink flowers on slender stems in summer. Good in a rock garden or scree. Z5–9 H9–5.
***D.* 'Happiness'** (illus. p.281). Perennial border carnation. Semi-double flowers are yellow, striped scarlet-orange.
***D.* 'Haytor'**, syn. *D.* 'Haytor White' (illus. p.280). Modern pink. Fully double white flowers, borne on strong stems, have a good scent. Is widely grown, especially to provide cut flowers.
***D.* 'Haytor White'.** See *D.* 'Haytor'.
***D.* 'Hidcote'.** Evergreen, tufted, compact perennial. H and S 4in (10cm). Bears a basal tuft of linear, spiky, gray-green leaves and, in summer, double red flowers. Good in a rock garden.
***D.* 'Houndspool Ruby'**, syn. *D.* 'Ruby', *D.* 'Ruby Doris' (illus. p.281). Modern pink. Sport of *D.* 'Doris' with strongly scented, ruby-pink flowers that each have a deeper eye.
***D.* 'Ibiza'.** Perpetual-flowering, spray carnation. Fully double flowers are shell pink.
***D.* 'Iceberg'.** Modern pink. Fragrant flowers are semi-double and pure white. Has a somewhat looser habit than *D.* 'Haytor'.
***D.* 'Joy'** (illus. p.281). Modern pink. Bears semi-double, pink flowers that are strongly scented and good for cutting.
***D.* 'Kobusa'.** See *D.* PIERROT.
***D.* 'La Bourbille'.** See *D.* 'La Bourboule'.
***D.* 'La Bourboule'**, syn. *D.* 'La Bourbille', illus. p.378.
***D.* 'Laced Monarch'** (illus. p.281). Modern pink. Double flowers are pink, laced with maroon.
***D.* 'Laced Prudence'.** See *D.* 'Prudence'.
***D.* 'Lavender Clove'** (illus. p.281). Vigorous border carnation. Bears lavender-gray flowers on long stems.
***D.* 'Little Jock'** illus. p.377.
***D.* 'London Brocade'** (illus. p.280). Modern pink. Has clove-scented, crimson-laced, pink flowers.
***D.* 'London Delight'.** Old-fashioned pink. Fragrant flowers are semi-double and lavender, laced with purple.
***D.* 'Manon'.** Perpetual-flowering carnation. Is one of the best deep pink cultivars with fully double flowers.
***D.* 'Mars'.** Evergreen, tuft-forming perennial. H and S 4in (10cm). Has small, double, cherry red flowers in summer. Bears a basal tuft of linear, gray-green leaves. Is good in a rock garden.
***D.* 'Master Stuart'.** Perennial border carnation. Has striking, semi-double flowers that are white with scarlet stripes.
D. microlepis illus. p.378.
***D.* 'Monica Wyatt'** illus. p.281. Modern pink. Very fragrant, fully double flowers are cyclamen pink, each with a magenta eye. Is very free-flowering and provides excellent cut flowers.
D. monspessulanus. Evergreen, mat-forming perennial. H 12in (30cm), S 4–6in (10–15cm). In summer, masses of strongly fragrant, 5-petaled, deeply fringed, pale lavender flowers rise on slender stems above short tufts of fine, grasslike leaves. Is good for a rock garden. Needs gritty soil.
***D.* 'Mrs. Sinkins'** (illus. p.280). Old-fashioned pink. Flowers are heavily scented, fringed, fully double, and white.
***D.* 'Murcia'.** Perpetual-flowering carnation. Has fully double, deep golden yellow flowers.
***D.* 'Musgrave's Pink'**, syn. *D.* 'Charles Musgrave', *D.* 'Green Eyes' (illus. p.280). Old-fashioned pink. An old cultivar, it bears single white flowers with green eyes.
D. myrtinervius illus. p.378.
D. neglectus. See *D. pavonius*.
***D.* 'Nina'** (illus. p.281). Perpetual-flowering carnation. Is one of the best crimson cultivars. Fully double flowers have smooth-edged petals.
***D.* 'Nives'** (illus. p.280). Perpetual-flowering carnation. Fully double flowers are clear white and are borne on short stems.
D. pavonius, syn. *D. neglectus*, illus. p.375.
***D.* PIERROT ('Kobusa')** (illus. p.280). Perpetual-flowering carnation. Bears fully double, light rose-lavender flowers with purple-edged petals.
***D.* 'Pike's Pink'** illus. p.378.
***D.* 'Pink Calypso'.** See *D.* 'Truly Yours'.
***D.* 'Pink Jewel'** (illus. p.281). Alpine pink. Has strongly scented, semi-double pink flowers.
***D.* 'Prudence'**, syn. *D.* 'Laced Prudence' (illus. p.280). Old-fashioned pink. Fragrant flowers are semi-double and pinkish white with purple lacing. Has a spreading habit.
***D.* 'Raggio di Sole'** (illus. p.281). Perpetual-flowering carnation. Fully double flowers are bright orange.
***D.* 'Red Barrow'.** Perpetual-flowering, spray carnation. Fully double, bright scarlet flowers are borne in abundance.
***D.* 'Ruby'.** See *D.* 'Houndspool Ruby'.
***D.* 'Ruby Doris'.** See *D.* 'Houndspool Ruby'.
***D.* 'Sam Barlow'.** Old-fashioned pink. Bears very fragrant, frilly, fully double white flowers with chocolate brown centers.
***D.* 'Show Ideal'.** Modern pink. Flat-petaled, semi-double flowers are white with red eyes and are strongly scented. Is excellent for exhibition.
***D.* 'Sops-in-Wine'.** Old-fashioned

pink. Bears fragrant, single maroon flowers with white markings.
D. superbus. Evergreen, mat-forming perennial. H to 8in (20cm), S 6in (15cm). Has narrowly lance-shaped, pale green leaves. In summer, slender stems bear very fragrant, 5-petaled, deeply fringed pink flowers with darker centers. Good in a rock garden. Z3–8 H8–1.
***D.* 'Tigré'.** Perpetual-flowering carnation. Has fully double yellow flowers with a uniform, pinkish purple stripe and edging to each petal.
***D.* 'Tony'.** Perpetual-flowering, spray carnation. Fully double flowers are yellow with red stripes.
***D.* 'Truly Yours'**, syn. *D.* 'Pink Calypso' (illus. p.280). Perpetual-flowering carnation. Fully double flowers are a good pink.
***D.* 'Valda Wyatt'.** Modern pink. Flowers are very fragrant, fully double, and rose-lavender.
***D.* 'Valencia'** (illus. p.281). Perpetual-flowering carnation. Has fully double, golden orange flowers.
***D.* 'White Ladies'** (illus. p.280). Old-fashioned pink. Bears very fragrant, fully double white flowers with greenish centers.
***D.* 'Widecombe Fair'.** Modern pink. Semi-double flowers borne on strong stems are of unusual coloring – peach-apricot opening to blush-pink.

DIAPENSIA

DIAPENSIACEAE

Genus of evergreen, spreading subshrubs suitable for rock gardens and troughs. Needs partial shade and peaty, sandy, acidic soil. Is very difficult to grow in hot, dry climates at low altitudes. Propagate by seed in spring or by semi-ripe cuttings in summer.
D. lapponica. Evergreen, spreading subshrub. H and S 3in (7cm). Has tufts of small, rounded, leathery leaves. Carries solitary tiny, bowl-shaped white flowers in early summer.

DIASCIA

SCROPHULARIACEAE

Genus of summer- and autumn-flowering annuals and perennials, some of which are semi-evergreen, grown for their tubular pink flowers. Is suitable for banks and borders. Needs sun and organic, well-drained soil that is not too dry. Cut back old stems in spring. Propagate by softwood cuttings in late spring, by semi-ripe cuttings in summer, or by seed in autumn.
***D. barberae* 'Ruby Field'.** Mat-forming perennial. H 3in (8cm), S 6in (15cm). Heart-shaped, pale green leaves clothe short, wiry stems. Produces tubular, wide-lipped, salmon-pink flowers throughout summer. Z8–9 H9–8.
***D.* 'Blackthorn Apricot'** illus. p.278.
D. cordata of gardens illus. p.353.
D. rigescens illus. p.353.
D. vigilis. Prostrate perennial. H 12–16in (30–40cm), S 24in (60cm). Leaves are small, rounded, toothed, and pale green. Upright branchlets carry loose spikes of flattish, outward-facing, pale pink flowers in summer. Z7–9 H9–7.

DICENTRA

PAPAVERACEAE

Genus of perennials, grown for their elegant sprays of pendent flowers. Most do best in semi-shade and organic, moist but well-drained soil. Propagate by division when dormant in late winter, species also by seed in autumn. Contact with the foliage may aggravate skin allergies.
***D.* 'Adrian Bloom'.** Spreading, tuft-forming perennial. H 18in (45cm), S 12in (30cm). Produces sprays of pendent, heart-shaped, rich carmine-pink flowers above oval, gray-green leaves. Z4–8 H10–1.
D. cucullaria illus. p.362.
D. eximia of gardens. See *D. formosa.*
D. formosa, syn. *D. eximia* of gardens. Spreading, tufted perennial. H 18in (45cm), S 12in (30cm). In spring-summer bears slender, arching sprays of pendent, heart-shaped pink or dull red flowers above oval, finely cut, gray-green leaves. Z4–8 H8–1.
D. peregrina. Tuft-forming perennial. H 3in (8cm), S to 2in (5cm). Locket-shaped pink flowers appear in spring-summer above fernlike, blue-green leaves. Needs gritty soil. Is suitable for an alpine house. Z4–8 H8–1.
D. spectabilis illus. p.245.
f. ***alba*** illus. p.239.
***D.* 'Spring Morning'** illus. p.278.
***D.* 'Stuart Boothman'** illus. p.278.

DICHELOSTEMMA

ALLIACEAE/LILIACEAE

Genus of summer-flowering bulbs grown for their dense flower heads on leafless stems. Is related to *Brodiaea* and is similar to *Allium* in appearance. Where marginally hardy, grow in a sheltered position. Needs a sunny site and well-drained soil. Water freely in spring, but allow to dry out after flowering. Propagate by seed in autumn or spring or by offsets in autumn before growth commences.
D. congestum, syn. *Brodiaea congesta*, illus. p.402.
D. ida-maia, syn. *Brodiaea ida-maia.* Early summer-flowering bulb. H to 3ft (1m), S 3–4in (8–10cm). Long, narrow leaves are semi-erect and basal. Leafless stem carries a dense head of ¾–1in (2–2.5cm) long flowers, each with a red tube and 6 green petals. Z5–8 H8–5.
D. pulchellum, syn. *Brodiaea capitata, B. pulchella.* Early summer-flowering bulb. H 12–24in (30–60cm), S 3–4in (8–10cm). Long, narrow leaves are semi-erect and basal. Leafless stem produces a dense head of narrowly funnel-shaped, pale to deep violet flowers, ½–¾in (1–2cm long), with violet bracts. Z6–10 H10–6.

DICHORISANDRA

COMMELINACEAE

Genus of erect, clump-forming, evergreen perennials, grown for their ornamental foliage. Prefers fertile, moist but well-drained soil, humid conditions, and partial shade. Propagate by division in spring or by stem cuttings in summer.
D. reginae illus. p.252.

DICKSONIA

DICKSONIACEAE

Genus of evergreen or semi-evergreen, treelike ferns that resemble palms and that are sometimes used to provide height in fern plantings. Needs semi-shade and organic, moist soil. Remove faded fronds regularly. Propagate by spores in summer.
D. antarctica illus. p.310.
D. fibrosa. Evergreen, treelike fern (deciduous in cold climates). H to 6m (20ft), S to 12ft (4m). Thick trunks are crowned by a rosette of spreading, divided, lance-shaped, dark green fronds, to 6ft (2m) long. Z9–10 H10–9.
D. squarrosa. Evergreen, treelike fern (deciduous in cold climates). H to 20ft (6m), S to 12ft (4m). Slender trunks are crowned by a rosette of spreading, divided, lance-shaped, midgreen fronds, to 6ft (2m) long, with blackish stalks and midribs. Z9–10 H10–9.

DICTAMNUS

RUTACEAE

Genus of summer-flowering perennials. Requires full sun and fertile, well-drained soil. Resents disturbance. Propagate by seed sown in late summer when fresh. The foliage, roots, and seeds of *D. albus* may cause mild stomach upset if ingested, and contact with the foliage may cause photodermatitis.
D. albus, syn. *D. fraxinella*, illus. p.240. var. ***purpureus*** illus. p.243.
D. fraxinella. See *D. albus.*

Didiscus coeruleus. See *Trachymene coerulea.*

DIEFFENBACHIA

Dumb cane, Leopard lily

ARACEAE

Genus of evergreen, tufted perennials grown for their foliage. Grow in fertile, well-drained soil and in partial shade. Propagate in spring or summer by stem cuttings or pieces of leafless stem placed horizontally in soil mix. Scale insects or spider mite may be troublesome. All parts may cause severe discomfort if ingested, and contact with sap may irritate skin.
D. amoena of gardens. See *D. seguine* 'Amoena'.
***D.* 'Exotica'**. See. *D. seguine* 'Exotica'.
***D. maculata* 'Exotica'.** See *D. seguine* 'Exotica'. **'Rudolph Roehrs'** see *D. seguine* 'Rudolph Roehrs'.
***D.* 'Memoria'.** See *D. seguine* 'Memoria Corsii'.
D. seguine. Evergreen, tufted perennial. H and S 3ft (1m) or more. Broadly lance-shaped leaves, to 18in (45cm) long, are glossy and dark green. Insignificant, tiny, greenish white flowers clustered on the spadix are surrounded by a narrow, leaflike spathe that appears intermittently. **'Amoena'** (syn *D. amoena* of gardens) is robust, H to 6ft (2m), with creamy white bars along lateral veins on the leaves. Z14–15 H12–1. **'Exotica'** (syn. *D.* 'Exotica', *D. maculata* 'Exotica') illus. p.264. **'Memoria Corsii'** (syn. *D.* 'Memoria') has gray-green leaves marked dark green and spotted white. **'Rudolph Roehrs'** (syn. *D. maculata* 'Rudolph Roehrs', *D.s.* 'Roehrs') illus. p.267.

DIERAMA

Angel's fishing rod, Wandflower

IRIDACEAE

Genus of evergreen, clump-forming, summer-flowering corms with pendent, funnel- or bell-shaped flowers on long, arching, wiry stems. Flourishes near pools. Prefers a warm, sheltered, sunny site and well-drained soil that should be kept moist in summer when in growth. Dies down partially in winter. Propagate by division of corms in spring or by seed in autumn or spring. Resents disturbance, and divisions take a year or more to settle and start flowering again.
***D.* 'Blackbird'.** Evergreen, upright perennial. H 5ft (1.5m), S 1ft (30cm). Produces cascades of nodding, funnel-shaped, violet-mauve flowers on wiry, pendulous stems in summer above grasslike leaves. Z7–9 H9–7.
D. dracomontanum, syn. *D. pumilum* of gardens. Vigorous, evergreen, upright perennial. H 30in (75cm), S 12in (30cm). In summer freely produces nodding, funnel-shaped flowers in shades of pink and violet on wiry stems. Leaves are grasslike.
D. ensifolium. See *D. pendulum.*
D. pendulum, syn. *D. ensifolium*, illus. p.401.
D. pulcherrimum illus. p.400.
D. pumilum of gardens. See *D. dracomontanum.*

DIERVILLA

CAPRIFOLIACEAE

Genus of deciduous, summer-flowering shrubs grown for their overall appearance. Is similar to *Weigela*. Tolerates partial shade or full light and moderately fertile, well-drained soil. For a more shapely shrub remove 2- and 3-year-old stems in winter or after flowering. Propagate by semi-ripe cuttings in late summer or by hardwood cuttings in autumn.
D. sessilifolia. Deciduous, spreading shrub. H and S 3–5ft (1–1.5m). Narrowly oval, pointed, serrated green leaves are often copper-tinted

when young. Has terminal and lateral clusters of tubular, pale yellow flowers in summer. To treat as a herbaceous perennial, cut back to ground level each spring and apply a mulch and a fertilizer. Z4–8 H8–1.

DIETES

IRIDACEAE

Genus of evergreen, irislike, rhizomatous perennials grown for their attractive flowers in spring or summer. Needs sun or partial shade and organic, well-drained soil that does not dry out excessively. Propagate by seed in autumn or spring or by division in spring (although divisions do not become re-established very readily).
D. bicolor illus. p.402.
D. iridioides, syn. *D. vegeta* of gardens. Evergreen, spring- and summer-flowering, rhizomatous perennial. H to 2ft (60cm), S 1–2ft (30–60cm). Bears sword-shaped, semi-erect, basal leaves in a spreading fan. Branching, wiry stems bear irislike white flowers, 2½–3in (6–8cm) across. Each of the 3 large petals has a central yellow mark. Z8–11 H12–8.
D. vegeta of gardens. See *D. iridioides*.

DIGITALIS

Foxglove

SCROPHULARIACEAE

Genus of biennials and perennials, some of which are evergreen, grown for their flower spikes in summer. Species mentioned grow in most conditions, even dry, exposed sites, but do best in semi-shade and moist but well-drained soil. Propagate by seed in autumn. All parts may cause severe discomfort if ingested. Contact with foliage may irritate skin.
D. ambigua. See *D. grandiflora*.
D. canariensis. See *Isoplexis canariensis*.
D. eriostachya. See *D. lutea*.
D. ferruginea illus. p.241.
D. grandiflora, syn. *D. ambigua* (Yellow foxglove). Evergreen, clump-forming perennial. H 30in (75cm), S 12in (30cm). Racemes of downward-pointing, tubular, creamy yellow flowers appear in summer above a rosette of oval to oblong, smooth, strongly veined leaves. Z3–8 H8–1.
D. lutea, syn. *D. eriostachya*. Upright perennial. H 30in (75cm), S 12in (30cm). In summer, delicate spires of downward-pointing, narrowly tubular, creamy yellow flowers are borne above a rosette of oval, smooth, midgreen leaves. Z3–8 H8–1.
D. x mertonensis. Clump-forming perennial. H 30in (75cm), S 12in (30cm). Produces spikes of downward-pointing, tubular, rose-mauve to coppery flowers in summer above a rosette of oval, hairy, soft leaves. Divide after flowering. Z3–8 H8–1.
D. purpurea. Upright, short-lived perennial, grown as a biennial. H 3–5ft (1–1.5m), S 2ft (60cm). Has a rosette of oval, rough, deep green leaves and, in summer, tall spikes of tubular flowers in shades of pink, red, purple, or white. Z4–8 H9–1. f. ***albiflora*** (syn. *D.p.* f. *alba*) illus. p.318.

DILLENIA

DILLENIACEAE

Genus of evergreen or briefly deciduous, spring-flowering trees grown for their flowers and foliage and for shade. Needs moisture-retentive, fertile soil and full light. Water potted plants freely while in full growth, less in winter. Propagate by seed in spring.
D. indica (Elephant apple). Briefly deciduous, spreading tree. H and S 8–12m (25–40ft). Has oval, serrated, boldly parallel-veined, glossy leaves, each 1ft (30cm) long. Nodding, cup-shaped white flowers, each 10in (25cm) wide, are produced in spring, followed by edible, globular greenish fruits. Z14–15 H12–1.

DIMORPHOTHECA

African daisy, Cape marigold

ASTERACEAE/COMPOSITAE

Genus of annuals, perennials, and evergreen subshrubs. Grow in sun and in fertile, very well-drained soil. Deadhead to prolong flowering. Propagate annuals by seed sown under cover in midspring, perennials by semi-ripe cuttings in summer. Is susceptible to botrytis in wet summers.
D. annua. See *D. pluvialis*.
D. barberae of gardens. See *Osteospermum jucundum*.
D. pluvialis, syn. *D. annua*, illus. p.319.

DIONAEA

DROSERACEAE

Genus of evergreen, insectivorous, rosette-forming perennials. Needs partial shade and a humid atmosphere; grow in a very peaty mix kept constantly moist. Propagate by seed or division in spring.
D. muscipula illus. p.305.

DIONYSIA

PRIMULACEAE

Genus of evergreen, cushion forming perennials. Grow in an alpine house in sun and very gritty, well-drained soil. Position adeep collar of grit under the cushion and ensure good ventilation at all times. Dislikes winter wet. Propagate by softwood cuttings in summer. Plants are susceptible to botrytis.
D. aretioides illus. p.371.
D. microphylla. Evergreen perennial. H 2in (5cm), S 6in (15cm). Rosettes of oval to rounded, often sharply pointed, gray-green leaves, with a mealy yellow coating beneath, form tight cushions. Small, short-stemmed, 5-petaled, white-eyed, pale to deep violet-yellow flowers with darker petal bases, appear in early spring. Z5–7 H7–5.
D. tapetodes illus. p.372.

DIOSCOREA

DIOSCOREACEAE

Genus of tuberous perennials, some of which are succulent, and herbaceous or evergreen, twining climbers grown mainly for their decorative leaves. Insignificant flowers are generally yellow. Prefers full sun or partial shade and fertile, well-drained soil. Propagate by division or by cutting off sections of tuber in spring or autumn, or by seed in spring.
D. discolor illus. p.219.
D. elephantipes, syn. *Testudinaria elephantipes*, illus. p.467.

DIOSMA

RUTACEAE

Genus of evergreen, wiry-stemmed shrubs grown for their flowers and overall appearance. Needs full light and well-drained, neutral to acidic soil. Water potted specimens moderately, less when not in full growth. To create a compact habit, shorten flowered stems after flowering. Propagate by seed in spring or by semi-ripe cuttings in late summer.
D. ericoides (Breath of heaven). Fast-growing, evergreen, loosely rounded shrub. H and S 1–2ft (30–60cm). Aromatic, needlelike leaves are crowded on stems. In winter-spring carries a profusion of small, fragrant, 5-petaled white flowers, sometimes tinted red. Z13–15 H12–10.

Diosphaera. Reclassified as *Trachelium*.

DIOSPYROS

EBENACEAE

Genus of deciduous or evergreen trees and shrubs grown for their foliage and fruits. Needs full sun and does best in hot summers. Requires fertile, well-drained soil. To obtain fruits, plants of both sexes must be grown. Propagate by seed in autumn.
D. kaki (Chinese persimmon, Kaki, Persimmon). Deciduous, spreading tree. H 10m (30ft), S 22ft (7m). Oval, glossy, dark green leaves turn orange, red, and purple in autumn. Tiny, yellowish white flowers in summer are followed on female trees by large, edible, rounded yellow or orange fruits. Z7–10 H10–7.
D. lotus (Date plum). Deciduous, spreading tree. H 30ft (10m), S 20ft (6m). Has oval, glossy, dark green leaves, tiny, red-tinged green flowers from mid- to late summer, and, on female trees, unpalatable, rounded purple or yellow fruits. Z6–10 H10–6.

DIPCADI

HYACINTHACEAE/LILIACEAE

Genus of spring-flowering bulbs grown mainly for botanical interest. Will not tolerate cold, wet winters, so is best grown in a cold frame or alpine house. Needs a warm, sunny situation and light, well-drained soil. Is dormant in summer. Propagate by seed in autumn.
D. serotinum illus. p.434.

DIPELTA

CAPRIFOLIACEAE

Genus of deciduous shrubs, with bold, long-pointed leaves, grown for their showy, tubular flowers and peeling bark. After flowering, bracts beneath flowers enlarge and become papery and brown, surrounding the fruits. Requires sun or semi-shade and fertile, well-drained soil. Benefits from the occasional removal of old shoots after flowering. Propagate by softwood cuttings in summer.
D. floribunda illus. p.117.
D. yunnanensis illus. p.116.

DIPHYLLEIA

BERBERIDACEAE

Genus of perennials with creeping rootstocks and umbrella-like leaves. Is best suited to woodland gardens. Needs semi-shade and moist soil. Propagate by division in spring or by seed in autumn.
D. cymosa (Umbrella leaf). Rounded perennial. H 24in (60cm), S 12in (30cm). Has large, rounded, 2-lobed leaves. In spring bears loose heads of inconspicuous white flowers followed by indigo blue berries on red stalks. Z7–10 H10–7.

Dipidax. Reclassified as *Onixotis*.
Diplacus glutinosus. See *Mimulus aurantiacus*.
Dipladenia. Reclassified as *Mandevilla*.

DIPLARRHENA

IRIDACEAE

Genus of one species of summer-flowering perennial. Needs sun and well-drained soil. Propagate by seed or division in spring.
D. moraea illus. p.277.

DIPSACUS

Teasel

DIPSACACEAE

Genus of biennials or short-lived perennials grown for their flower heads, which are good for drying. Requires sun or partial shade and any fertile soil, including heavy clay. Propagate by seed in autumn or spring.
D. fullonum. Prickly biennial. H 5–6ft (1.5–2m), S 12–32in (30–80cm). In the first year produces a basal rosette of toothed, dark green leaves covered in spiny pustules. Thistlelike, pinkish purple or white flower heads with stiff, prickly bracts are borne terminally on upright stems with paired leaves in mid- and late summer of the second year. Z5-8 H8–5.

DIPTERONIA

ACERACEAE

Genus of deciduous trees grown for their foliage and fruits. Needs full sun

and fertile, well-drained soil. Propagate by softwood cuttings in summer or by seed in autumn.
D. sinensis. Deciduous, spreading, sometimes shrubby tree. H 30ft (10m), S 20ft (6m). Large, midgreen leaves have 7–11 oval to lance-shaped leaflets. Inconspicuous, greenish white flowers in summer are followed by large clusters of winged red fruits. Z8–10 H10–8.

DISA

See also ORCHIDS.
D. uniflora. Deciduous, terrestrial orchid. H 1½–2ft (45–60cm). Has narrowly lance-shaped, glossy, dark green leaves, to 9in (22cm) long, that clasp stems. In early summer each stem bears up to 7 hooded scarlet flowers, 3–4in (8–10cm) long, that have darker veins and are suffused yellow. Needs partial shade and continually moist soil. Raise from seed or propagate by division of offsets when dormant. Z13-15 H12–10.

DISANTHUS

HAMAMELIDACEAE

Genus of one species of deciduous, autumn-flowering shrub grown for its overall appearance and autumn color. Needs partial shade and organic, moist but not wet, neutral to acidic soil. Propagate by layering in spring or by seed when ripe or in spring.
D. cercidifolius. Deciduous, rounded shrub. H and S to 10ft (3m). Bears broadly oval to almost circular, bluish green leaves that turn yellow, orange, red, or purple in autumn. Has small, dark red flowers in autumn as the leaves fall, or later. Z5–8 H8–5.

DISCARIA

RHAMNACEAE

Genus of deciduous or almost leafless shrubs and trees grown for their habit and flowers. Spiny green shoots assume function of leaves. Needs a sheltered, sunny site and fertile, well-drained soil. Propagate by softwood cuttings in summer.
D. toumatou (Wild Irishman). Deciduous or almost leafless, bushy shrub. H and S 6ft (2m). Shoots have sharp, rigid spines. Tiny, star-shaped, greenish white flowers are borne in dense clusters in late spring. Z8–9 H9–8.

DISPORUM

Fairy bells

CONVALLARIACEAE/LILIACEAE

Genus of spring- or early summer-flowering perennials. Is best suited to woodland gardens. Requires a cool, semi-shaded position and organic soil. Propagate by division in spring or by seed in autumn.
D. hookeri. Clump-forming perennial. H 30in (75cm), S 12in (30cm). Leaves are narrowly oval and midgreen. Orange-red berries in autumn follow clusters of drooping, open bell-shaped, greenish white flowers in spring. Z4–9 H9–1.
***D. sessile* 'Variegatum'.** Rapidly spreading, clump-forming perennial. H 18in (45cm), S 12in (30cm). Solitary tubular-bell-shaped to bell-shaped, creamy white flowers are produced in spring. Narrowly oval, pleated leaves are irregularly striped with white. Z4–9 H9–1.

DISTICTIS

BIGNONIACEAE

Genus of evergreen, woody-stemmed, tendril climbers grown for their colorful, trumpet-shaped flowers. Well-drained soil is suitable with full light. Water freely in summer, less at other times. Support for stems is necessary. Thin out congested growth in spring. Propagate by softwood cuttings in early summer or by semi-ripe cuttings in late summer.
D. buccinatoria, syn. *Phaedranthus buccinatorius*, illus. p.204.

DISTYLIUM

HAMAMELIDACEAE

Genus of evergreen shrubs and trees grown for their foliage and flowers. Prefers a sheltered, partially shaded position and moist, peaty soil. Propagate by semi-ripe cuttings in summer.
D. racemosum. Evergreen, arching shrub. H 6ft (2m), S 10ft (3m). Leaves are oblong, leathery, glossy, and dark green. Small flowers with red calyces and purple anthers are borne in late spring and early summer. Z11 H12–10.

Dizygotheca elegantissima. See *Schefflera elegantissima*.

DOCYNIA

ROSACEAE

Genus of evergreen or semi-evergreen, spring-flowering trees grown for their flowers and foliage; is related to *Cydonia*. Requires full light and well-drained soil. Other than shaping while young, pruning is not necessary. Propagate by seed in spring or autumn, by budding in summer, or by grafting in winter. Is usually trouble-free, though caterpillars may be troublesome.
D. delavayi. Evergreen or semi-evergreen, spreading tree. H and S 25ft (8m) or more. Oval to lance-shaped leaves are white-felted beneath. In spring has fragrant, 5-petaled white flowers, pink in bud, followed by ovoid, downy yellow fruits in autumn. Z8–10 H10–8.

DODECATHEON

Shooting stars

PRIMULACEAE

Genus of spring- and summer-flowering perennials grown for their distinctive flowers with reflexed petals and prominent stamens. Once fertilized, flowers turn skyward – hence their common name. Is dormant after flowering. Prefers sun or partial shade and moist but well-drained soil. Propagate by seed in autumn or by division in winter.
D. dentatum. Clump-forming perennial. H 3in (7cm), S 10in (25cm). Leaves are long, oval, and toothed. In late spring, frail stems bear white flowers with prominent, dark stamens and reflexed petals. Prefers a partially shaded position. Z4–8 H8–2.
D. hendersonii, syn. *D. latifolium*, illus. p.347.
D. latifolium. See *D. hendersonii.*
D. meadia. Clump-forming perennial. H 8in (20cm), S 6in (15cm). Leaves are oval and pale green. In spring, strong stems carry pale pink flowers with reflexed petals above foliage. Prefers a partially shaded position. Z4–8 H8–1.
f. ***album*** illus. p.347.
D. pauciflorum of gardens. See *D. pulchellum*.
D. pulchellum, syn. *D. pauciflorum* of gardens. Clump-forming perennial. H 6in (15cm), S 4in (10cm). Is similar to *D. meadia*, but flowers are usually deep cerise. Z4–7 H8–2.
***D.* 'Red Wings'** illus. p.348.

DODONAEA

SAPINDACEAE

Genus of evergreen trees and shrubs grown mainly for their foliage and overall appearance. Prefers full sun and well-drained soil. Water potted plants freely when in full growth, less at other times. Cut back in late summer and in spring, if needed, to maintain a balanced shape. Propagate by seed in spring or by semi-ripe cuttings in late summer.
***D. viscosa* 'Purpurea'** illus. p.151.

Dolichos lablab. See *Lablab purpureus*.
Dolichos purpureus. See *Lablab purpureus*.

DOMBEYA

STERCULIACEAE

Genus of evergreen shrubs and trees grown for their flowers. Needs full light or partial shade and fertile, well-drained soil. Water potted specimens freely when in full growth, less at low temperatures. May be cut back after flowering. Propagate by seed in spring or by semi-ripe cuttings in summer. Whitefly and spider mite may be a nuisance.
D. burgessiae, syn. *D. mastersii*, illus. p.150.
D. × cayeuxii illus. p.88.
D. mastersii. See *D. burgessiae*.

Dondia. Reclassified as *Hacquetia*.

DORONICUM

Leopard's bane

ASTERACEAE/COMPOSITAE

Genus of perennials grown for their daisylike flower heads, which are good for cutting. Most prefer full light or shade and moist, well-drained soil. Propagate by division in autumn.
D. austriacum. Clump-forming perennial. H 18in (45cm), S 12in (30cm). Daisylike, pure yellow flower heads are produced singly on slender stems in spring. Heart-shaped, bright green leaves are hairy and wavy-edged. Z5–8 H8–5.
D. columnae, syn. *D. cordatum.* **'Miss Mason'** illus. p.238.
D. cordatum. See *D. columnae*.
***D. × excelsum* 'Harpur Crewe'**, syn. *D. plantagineum* 'Excelsum'. Elegant, clump-forming perennial. H 3ft (1m), S 2ft (60cm). Large, daisylike, buttercup yellow flower heads are borne 3 or 4 to a stem in spring. Leaves are heart-shaped and bright green. Is good for a dry, shaded site.
***D.* 'Frühlingspracht'**, syn *D.* 'Spring Beauty'. Clump-forming perennial. H 18in (45cm), S 12in (30cm). Produces daisylike, double, bright yellow flower heads in spring. Bears heart-shaped, bright green leaves. Z5–8 H8–5.
***D. plantagineum* 'Excelsum'.** See *D. × excelsum* 'Harpur Crewe'.
***D.* 'Spring Beauty'.** See *D.* 'Frühlingspracht'.

DOROTHEANTHUS

AIZOACEAE

Genus of succulent annuals suitable for hot, dry places such as rock gardens, banks, and gaps in paving. Needs sun and grows well in poor, very well-drained soil. Deadhead to prolong flowering. Propagate by seed sown under cover in early spring, or outdoors in mid-spring. Protect from slugs and snails.
D. bellidiformis, syn. *Mesembryanthemum criniflorum* (Ice-plant, Livingstone daisy). **'Magic Carpet'** illus. p.325.

DORYANTHES

DORYANTHACEAE/LILIACEAE

Genus of evergreen, rosette-forming perennials grown for their flowers. Needs a sunny position and organic, well-drained soil. Propagate by mature bulbils, by seed in spring or by suckers after flowering.
D. palmeri illus. p.232.

Dorycnium hirsutum. See *Lotus hirsutus*.
Douglasia vitaliana. See *Vitaliana*

primuliflora.
Doxantha. Reclassified as *Macfadyena* except for:
D. capreolata for which see *Bignonia capreolata*.

DRABA

BRASSICACEAE/CRUCIFERAE

Genus of spring-flowering annuals and evergreen or semi-evergreen, cushion- or mat-forming perennials with extensive root systems. Some species form soft, green cushions that in winter turn brown except at the tips, appearing almost dead. Is suitable for alpine houses. Needs sun and gritty, well-drained soil. Dislikes winter wet. Propagate by softwood cuttings of the rosettes in late spring or by seed in autumn.
D. aizoides (Yellow whitlow grass). Semi-evergreen, mat-forming perennial. H 1in (2.5cm), S 6in (15cm). Has lance-shaped, stiff-bristled leaves in rosettes and, in spring, 4-petaled, bright yellow flowers. Best in a scree garden. Z4–6 H6–1.
D. bryoides. See *D. rigida* var. *bryoides*.
D. hispanica. Semi-evergreen, cushion-forming perennial. H 2in (5cm), S 4in (10cm). Leaves are oval, soft, fragile, and pale green. Clusters of flat, 4-petaled, pale yellow flowers are borne in spring. Z4–6 H6–1.
D. longisiliqua illus. p.371.
D. mollissima illus. p.372.
D. polytricha. Semi-evergreen, cushion-forming perennial. H 2½in (6cm), S 6in (15cm). Has minute, rounded leaves in neat, symmetrical rosettes. Frail stems carry flat, 4-petaled, golden yellow flowers in spring. Difficult to grow. Keep stones under cushion at all times. Remove dead rosettes at once. Z4–6 H6–1.
D. rigida illus. p.371. var. ***bryoides*** (syn. *D. bryoides*) is an evergreen, tight hummock-forming perennial. H 1½in (4cm), S 2½in (6cm). Leaves are tiny, rounded, hard, and dark green. Produces small clusters of almost stemless, 4-petaled, bright yellow flowers that cover hummocks in spring. Good in a trough or scree. Z4–6 H6–1.

DRACAENA

AGAVACEAE/DRACAENACEAE

Genus of evergreen trees and shrubs grown for their foliage and overall appearance. Needs full light or partial shade and well-drained soil. Water containerized plants moderately, much less in low temperatures. Rejuvenate leggy plants by cutting back to near soil level in spring. Propagate by seed or air-layering in spring or by tip or stem cuttings in summer. Mealy bug may be a nuisance.
D. australis. See *Cordyline australis*.
D. deremensis. See *D. fragrans* Deremensis Group. **'Souvenir de Schrijver'** see *D. fragrans* Deremenis Group 'Warneckei'. **'Warneckei'** see *D. fragrans* Deremensis Group 'Warneckei'.
D. draco illus. p.100.
D. fragrans (Corn plant). **Deremensis Group**, syn. *D. deremensis*, is a slow-growing, evergreen, erect, sparsely branched shrub. H 6ft (2m) or more, S 3ft (1m) or more. Has lance-shaped, erect to arching, glossy, deep green leaves to 18in (45cm) long. Mature plants may occasionally bear large panicles of small, red-and-white flowers in summer. Z14–15 H12–1. **Deremensis Group 'Warneckei'** (syn. *D. deremensis* 'Souvenir de Schrijver', *D.d.* 'Warneckei') illus. p.126. **'Massangeana'.** Evergreen, erect, sparsely branched shrub. H 10–20ft (3–6m), S 3–10ft (1–3m). Has strap-shaped, arching leaves, to 2ft (60cm) long, with longitudinal bands of yellow and pale green. In early summer, fragrant, star-shaped yellow flowers, rarely produced, are followed by rounded-oblong, orange-red fruits. Z13–15 12–10.
D. indivisa. See *Cordyline indivisa*.
D. marginata (Madagascar dragon tree). Slow-growing, evergreen, erect shrub or tree. H 10ft (3m) or more, S 3–6ft (1–2m) or more. Leaves are narrowly strap-shaped and rich green with red margins. Flowers are rarely produced. Z11–12 H12–1. **'Tricolor'** illus. p.99.
D. sanderiana illus. p.151.

DRACOCEPHALUM

Dragon's head

LABIATAE/LAMIACEAE

Genus of summer-flowering annuals and perennials suitable for rock gardens and borders. Prefers sun and fertile, well-drained soil. Propagate by seed or division in spring or autumn or by basal cuttings of young growth in spring.
D. ruyschiana. Erect perennial. H 18–24in (45–60cm), S 12in (30cm). Freely bears whorled spikes of 2-lipped, violet-blue flowers from early to mid-summer. Midgreen leaves are linear to lance-shaped. Z3–7 H7–1.
D. sibiricum. See *Nepeta sibirica*.

DRACUNCULUS

ARACEAE

Genus of robust, tuberous perennials that produce roughly triangular, foul-smelling spathes. Where marginally hardy, protect dormant tubers with a heavy mulch. Needs sun and well-drained soil that dries out in summer. Propagate by freely borne offsets in late summer or by seed in autumn.
D. vulgaris, syn. *Arum dracunculus*, illus. p.401.

DREGEA

ASCLEPIADACEAE

Genus of evergreen, woody-stemmed, twining climbers grown for botanical interest. Grow in sun and in any well-drained soil. Propagate by seed in spring or by stem cuttings in summer or autumn.
D. corrugata. See *D. sinensis*.
D. sinensis, syn. *D. corrugata*, *Wattakaka sinensis*. Evergreen, woody-stemmed, twining climber. H to 10ft (3m). Oval, midgreen leaves, heart-shaped at base, 1¼–4in (3–10cm) long, are grayish beneath. In summer has clusters of 10–25 small, fragrant, star-shaped flowers, white or cream with red dots and streaks, followed by pairs of slender pods, 2–3in (5–7cm) long. Z8–10 H10–8.

Drejerella guttata. See *Justicia brandegeeana*.
Drepanostachyum falconeri. See *Himalayacalamus falconeri*.

DRIMYS

WINTERACEAE

Genus of evergreen trees and shrubs grown for their foliage and star-shaped flowers. Where marginally hardy, grow against a south- or west-facing wall. Needs sun or semi-shade and fertile, moist but well-drained soil. Propagate by semi-ripe cuttings in summer or by seed in autumn.
D. aromatica. See *D. lanceolata*.
D. axillaris. See *Pseudowintera axillaris*.
D. colorata. See *Pseudowintera colorata*.
D. lanceolata, syn. *D. aromatica* (Mountain pepper). Evergreen, upright, dense shrub or tree. H 12ft (4m), S 8ft (2.5m). Has deep red shoots and oblong, dark green leaves. Produces clusters of star-shaped white flowers in spring. Z9–10.
D. winteri, syn. *Wintera aromatica*, illus. p.78.

DROSANTHEMUM

AIZOACEAE

Genus of erect or prostrate, succulent shrubs with slender stems and masses of flowers in summer. Leaves are finely covered in papillae. Needs full sun and very well-drained soil. Propagate by seed or stem cuttings in spring or summer.
D. hispidum. Succulent shrub with arching or spreading branches that root down. H 2ft (60cm), S 3ft (1m). Has cylindrical, light green leaves, ⅝–1in (1.5–2.5cm) long. In summer, masses of shiny, daisylike purple flowers, to 1cm (2.5cm) across, are borne. Z12–15 H12–10.
D. speciosum. Erect, shrubby succulent. H 2ft (60cm), S 3ft (1m). Has semi-cylindrical leaves, ½–¾in (1–2cm) long. Masses of daisylike, green-centered, orange-red flowers, to 2in (5cm) across, appear in summer. Z12–15 H12–10.

DROSERA

Sundew

DROSERACEAE

Genus of evergreen, insectivorous perennials. Grow in sun, in a very peaty mix that is not allowed to dry out. Propagate by seed or division in spring.
D. capensis illus. p.305.
D. spatulata illus. p.305.

DRYANDRA

PROTEACEAE

Genus of evergreen, spring- to summer-flowering shrubs and trees grown for their flowers, foliage, and overall appearance. Needs full light and well-drained, sandy soil that contains few nitrates or phosphates. Is difficult to grow. Water containerized specimens moderately, less in low temperatures. Plants under cover must be freely ventilated. Propagate by seed in spring.
D. formosa. Evergreen, bushy shrub. H 6–15ft (2–5m), S 5–10ft (1.5–3m). Strap-shaped leaves are divided into triangular, closely set lobes, creating a saw-blade effect. In spring carries small, scented, tubular, orange-yellow flowers in domed, terminal heads. Z10–11 H12–10.

DRYAS

Mountain avens

ROSACEAE

Genus of evergreen, prostrate, woody-based perennials with oaklike leaves and cup-shaped flowers. Is useful on banks and walls, in rock gardens ,and as a groundcover. Prefers sun and gritty, well-drained, peaty soil. Propagate by seed when fresh or by semi-ripe cuttings in summer.
D. drummondii. Evergreen, prostrate, woody-based perennial. H 2in (5cm), S indefinite. Thick stems are clothed in small, oval, lobed, leathery, dark green leaves. Nodding, creamy white flowers are borne in early summer but never open fully. Z2–6 H6–1.
D. octopetala illus. p.375.
D. x suendermannii. Evergreen, prostrate, woody-based perennial. H 2in (5cm), S indefinite. Is similar to *D. drummondii* but has slightly nodding, pale cream flowers that open horizontally. Z3–6 H6–1.

DRYOPTERIS

ASPIDIACEAE/DRYOPTERIDACEAE

Genus of deciduous or semi-evergreen ferns, many of which form regular, shuttlecock-like crowns. Requires shade and moist soil. Regularly remove fading fronds. Propagate by spores in summer or by division in autumn or winter.
D. affinis, syn. *D. borreri*, *D. pseudomas* (Golden male fern). Virtually evergreen fern. H and S to 3ft (1m). Produces a "shuttlecock" of lance-shaped, divided fronds, 8–32in (20–80cm) tall, from an erect rhizome. Fronds are pale green as they unfurl in spring, in contrast to the scaly, golden brown midribs; they mature to dark green and often remain green through winter. Distinguished from *D. filix-mas*

by a dark spot where each pinna joins the midrib. Z6–8 H8–6.
D. atrata of gardens. See *D. cycadina*.
D. austriaca. See *D. dilatata*.
D. borreri. See *D. affinis*.
D. carthusiana (Narrow buckler fern). Deciduous or semi-evergreen, creeping, rhizomatous fern. H 3ft (1m), S 18in (45cm). Produces lance-shaped, much-divided, midgreen fronds with triangular to oval pinnae. Z6–8 H8–6.
D. cycadina, syn. *D. atrata* of gardens, *D. hirtipes*. Deciduous fern. H 24in (60cm), S 18in (45cm). Has an erect rhizome producing a "shuttlecock" of lance-shaped, divided, bright green fronds, 18in (45cm) tall, with green midribs. Z6–9 H9–6.
D. dilatata, syn. *D. austriaca* (Broad buckler fern). Deciduous or semi-evergreen fern. H 3ft (1m), S 18in (45cm). Has much-divided, arching, midgreen fronds with triangular to oval pinnae on thick, dark brown stems. Z6–8 H8–5.
D. erythrosora (Japanese shield fern). Deciduous fern. H 18in (45cm), S 12in (30cm). Broadly triangular, coppery pink fronds divided into triangular to oval pinnae persist until midwinter. Z5–9 H9–1.
D. filix-mas illus. p.310. **'Grandiceps Wills'** is a deciduous fern. H and S 3ft (90cm). Has "shuttlecocks" of broadly lance-shaped, tasselled, elegantly arching, midgreen fronds arising from crowns of large, upright, brown-scaled rhizomes. The tip of each frond has a heavy crest, and the pinnae are also finely crested. Z4–8 H8–1.
D. goldieana (Giant wood fern). Deciduous fern. H 3ft (1m), S 2ft (60cm). Has broadly oval, light green fronds divided into numerous oblong, indented pinnae. Z6–8 H8–5.
D. hirtipes. See *D. cycadina*.
D. marginalis. Deciduous fern. H 24in (60cm), S 12in (30cm). Fronds are lance-shaped, dark green, and divided into numerous oblong, slightly indented pinnae. Z3–8 H8–1.
D. pseudomas. See *D. affinis*.
D. sieboldii. Semi-evergreen, tufted fern. H and S 1–2ft (30–60cm). Produces long-stalked, erect or arching, yellowish green fronds, 8–20in (20–50cm) long, with up to 6 pairs of narrowly lance-shaped pinnae, 6–12in (15–30cm) long. Z6-8 H8–6.
D. wallichiana (Wallich's wood fern). Deciduous fern. H 3–6ft (1–1.8m), S 30in (75cm). Produces an erect rhizome and a "shuttlecock" of lance-shaped, divided, dark green fronds, yellow-green when young, 3ft (1m) or more long. Midribs are covered with dark brown or black scales, providing attractive color contrasts in spring. Z5–7 H12-10.

DUCHESNEA

ROSACEAE

Genus of perennials, some of which are semi-evergreen, grown as groundcover as well as for their flowers. May be used in hanging baskets. Grow in well-drained soil and in sun or partial shade. Propagate by division in spring, by rooting plantlets formed at ends of runners in summer, or by seed in autumn.
D. indica, syn. *Fragaria indica*. Semi-evergreen, trailing perennial. H to 4in (10cm), S indefinite. Dark green leaves have 3 toothed leaflets like those of strawberries. Solitary, 5-petaled, bright yellow flowers, to 1in (2.5cm) wide and with leafy green frills of sepals, appear from spring to early summer. Strawberry-like, tasteless red fruits appear in late summer. Z6–8 H8–6.

DUDLEYA

CRASSULACEAE

Genus of basal-rosetted succulents closely related to *Echeveria*. Requires full sun and very well-drained soil. Water sparingly when plants are semi-dormant in midsummer. Propagate by seed or division in spring or summer.
D. brittonii. Basal-rosetted succulent. H 8–24in (20–60cm) or more when in flower, S 20in (50cm). Has narrowly lance-shaped, tapering, fleshy, silvery white leaves. Masses of star-shaped, pale yellow flowers are produced in spring-summer. Z13–15 H12-10.
D. pulverulenta illus. p.464.

DURANTA

VERBENACEAE

Genus of fast-growing, evergreen or partially deciduous trees and shrubs grown for their flowers and overall appearance. Needs full light and fertile, well-drained soil. Water potted plants freely when in full growth, moderately at other times. Prune as necessary to curb vigor. Propagate by seed in spring or by semi-ripe cuttings in summer. Whitefly may be troublesome.
D. erecta, syn. *D. plumieri*, *D. repens*, illus. p.150.
D. plumieri. See *D. erecta*.
D. repens. See *D. erecta*.

DUVALIA

ASCLEPIADACEAE

Genus of clump-forming or carpeting succulents with short, thick, leafless stems; is closely related to *Stapelia*. Star-shaped flowers have thick, fleshy petals recurved at tips. Requires partial shade and very well-drained soil. Propagate by seed or stem cuttings in spring or summer.
D. corderoyi illus. p.476.

Duvernoia adhatodoides. See *Justicia adhatoda*.

DYCKIA

BROMELIACEAE

Genus of evergreen, rosette-forming perennials grown for their overall appearance. Requires full light and well-drained soil containing coarse sand or grit. Water moderately in summer, scarcely or not at all in winter, and sparingly at other times. Propagate by offsets or division in spring.
D. remotiflora (illus. p.265). Evergreen, basal-rosetted perennial. H and S 12–20in (30–50cm). Has dense rosettes of very narrowly triangular, pointed, thick-textured, arching, dull green leaves with hooked spines and gray scales beneath. Woolly spikes of tubular, orange-yellow flowers appear above foliage in summer-autumn. Z113–15 H12–1.

DYPSIS

ARECACEAE/PALMAE

Genus of evergreen palms grown for their elegant appearance. Needs full light or partial shade and fertile, well-drained soil. Water potted specimens moderately, much less when temperatures are low. Propagate by seed in spring at not less than 79°F (26°C). Spider mite may sometimes be a nuisance.
D. lutescens, syn. *Areca lutescens*, *Chrysalidocarpus lutescens*, illus. p.100.

ECCREMOCARPUS

BIGNONIACEAE

Genus of evergreen, subshrubby, tendril climbers grown for their attractive flowers produced over a long season. One species only is commonly grown. Usually treated as an annual. Grow in full light and in any well-drained soil. Propagate by seed in early spring.
E. scaber illus. p.217.

ECHEVERIA

CRASSULACEAE

Genus of rosetted succulents with long-lasting flowers. Leaves take on their brightest colors from autumn to spring. Needs sun, good ventilation, and very well-drained soil. Propagate by seed, stem or leaf cuttings, division, or offsets in spring or summer.
E. agavoides illus. p.474.
E. cooperi. See *Adromischus cooperi*.
E. derenbergii. Clump-forming succulent. H 1½in (4cm), S 12in (30cm). Produces a short-stemmed rosette of rounded, gray-green leaves. Flower stem, 3in (8cm) long, produces cup-shaped, yellow-and-red or orange flowers in spring. Offsets freely. Is often used as a parent in breeding. Z13–15 H12–10.
E. elegans illus. p.471.
E. gibbiflora. Rosetted succulent. H 4–10in (10–25cm), S 12in (30cm). Rosettes of spoon-shaped, pointed, gray-green leaves, often tinged red-brown, are stemless or borne on short stems. Cup-shaped red flowers, yellow within, are borne on stems, 3ft (90cm) long, in autumn-winter. Z13–15 H12–10. **'Metallica'** (syn. *E.g.* var. *metallica*) has white- or red-margined, purple-green leaves that mature to green-bronze.
E. harmsii, syn. *Oliveranthus elegans*. Bushy succulent. H 8in (20cm), S 12in (30cm). Erect stems are each crowned by a 2½in (6cm) wide rosette of short, narrowly lance-shaped, pale green leaves covered in short hairs. In spring bears cup-shaped, orange-tipped red flowers, yellow within. Z13–15 H12–10.
E. pulvinata illus. p.464.
E. secunda illus. p.473.
E. setosa (Mexican firecracker). Basal-rosetted succulent. H 1½in (4cm), S 12in (30cm). Has long, narrow, midgreen leaves covered in short, thick white hairs. Bears cup-shaped, red-and-yellow flowers in spring. Is prone to rotting: do not water foliage. Z13–15 H12–10.

ECHINACEA

Coneflower

ASTERACEAE/COMPOSITAE

Genus of summer-flowering perennials. Prefers sun and organic, moist but well-drained soil. Propagate by division or root cuttings in spring. May seed freely.
E. purpurea, syn. *Rudbeckia purpurea*. **'Robert Bloom'** illus. p.244. **'White Lustre'** is a vigorous, upright perennial. H 4ft (1.2m), S 1½ft (45cm). Large, daisylike white flower heads, each with a prominent, central, orange-brown cone, are borne singly on strong stems in summer. Has lance-shaped, dark green leaves. Z3–9 H12-1.

ECHINOCACTUS

CACTACEAE

Genus of slow-growing, hemispherical cacti. Cold temperatures cause yellow patches on *E. grusonii*. Requires full sun and very well-drained soil. Yellow-flowered species are easy to grow. Propagate by seed in spring.
E. asterias. See *Astrophytum asterias*.
E. chilensis. See *Neoporteria chilensis*.
E. eyriesii. See *Echinopsis eyriesii*.
E. grusonii illus. p.460.
E. ingens. See *E. platyacanthus*.
E. myriostigma. See *Astrophytum myriostigma*.
E. ornatus. See *Astrophytum ornatum*.
E. platyacanthus, syn. *E. ingens*. Slow-growing, hemispherical cactus. H 10ft (3m), S 6ft (2m). Gray-blue stem has a woolly crown and up to 50 ribs. Funnel-shaped yellow flowers, 1¼in (3cm) across, appear in summer only on plants over 16in (40cm) in diameter. Z12–15 H12–10.
E. scheeri. See *Sclerocactus scheeri*.
E. uncinatus. See *Sclerocactus uncinatus*.

ECHINOCEREUS

CACTACEAE

Genus of spherical to columnar cacti, freely branching with age, some with tuberous rootstocks. Buds, formed inside spiny stem, burst through skin, producing long-lasting flowers with reflexed petal tips and prominent green stigmas, followed by pear-shaped, spiny seed pods. Some species tolerate light frost if dry. Needs full sun and very well-drained soil. Propagate by seed or stem cuttings in spring or summer.

E. baileyi. See *E. reichenbachii* var. *baileyi*.

E. cinerascens. Clump-forming cactus. H 1ft (30cm), S 3ft (1m). Has 3in (7cm) wide stems, each with 5–12 ribs. Areoles each bear 8–15 yellowish white spines. Mature plants produce masses of trumpet-shaped, bright pink or purple flowers, 5in (12cm) across and with paler petal bases, in spring. Z12–15 H12–10.

E. leucanthus, syn. *Wilcoxia albiflora*, illus. p.469.

E. pectinatus. Columnar cactus. H 14in (35cm), S 8in (20cm). Has sparsely branched, green stems with 12–23 ribs and short, comblike spines, often variably colored. In spring produces trumpet-shaped purple, pink, or yellow flowers, 5in (12cm) across, with paler petal bases. Z12–15 H12–10.

E. pentalophus, syn. *E. procumbens*, illus. p.463.

E. procumbens. See *E. pentalophus*.

E. reichenbachii. Columnar cactus. H 14in (35cm), S 8in (20cm). Has a slightly branched, multicolored stem with 12–23 ribs and comblike spines, ⅝in (1.5cm) long. Carries trumpet-shaped pink or purple flowers, 5in (12cm) across, with darker petal bases, in spring. Z13–15 H12–10. var. ***baileyi*** (syn. *E. baileyi*) illus. p.462.

E. schmollii, syn. *Wilcoxia schmollii*, illus. p.462.

E. triglochidiatus. Clump-forming cactus. H 12in (30cm), S 6in (15cm). Has a short, thick, dark green stem with 3–5 spines, each to 1in (2.5cm) long, per areole. In spring bears funnel-shaped, bright red flowers, 3in (7cm) across, with prominent red stamens and green stigmas. Z11–12 H12–9. var. ***paucispinus*** illus. p.475.

Echinodorus ranunculoides. See *Baldellia ranunculoides*.

Echinofossulocactus. Reclassified as *Stenocactus*.

Echinomastus macdowellii. See *Thelocactus macdowellii*.

ECHINOPS

Globe thistle

ASTERACEAE/COMPOSITAE

Genus of summer-flowering perennials grown for their globelike, spiky flower heads. Does best in full sun and in poor soil. Propagate by division or seed in autumn or by root cuttings in winter.

E. bannaticus illus. p.228. **'Taplow Blue'** is an erect perennial, H 4ft (1.2m), S 3ft (1m). Wiry stems produce thistlelike, rounded heads of powder blue flowers in summer. Narrowly oval leaves are divided and grayish green. Z3–9 H12–1.

***E. ritro* 'Veitch's Blue'** illus. p.252.

E. sphaerocephalus illus. p.226.

ECHINOPSIS

CACTACEAE

Genus of spherical to columnar cacti, mostly freely branching; it is sometimes held to include *Trichocereus*. Requires full sun and well-drained soil. Tolerates long periods of neglect. Propagate by seed or offsets in spring or summer.

E. aurea, syn. *Lobivia aurea*, *L. cylindrica*, *Pseudolobivia aurea*. Clump-forming cactus. H 5in (12cm), S 8in (20cm). Green stem with 14 or 15 ribs is densely covered with white radial spines and a longer, darker central spine. Produces funnel-shaped to flattish yellow flowers, 3in (8cm) across, in summer. Z12–15 H12–10.

E. backebergii, syn. *Lobivia backebergii*, illus. p.473.

E. bridgesii. See *E. lageniformis*.

E. candicans, syn. *Trichocereus candicans*, illus. p.461.

E. chamaecereus, syn. *Chamaecereus silvestrii*, *Lobivia silvestrii*, illus. p.475.

E. cinnabarina, syn. *Lobivia cinnabarina*. Spherical cactus. H and S 6in (15cm). Glossy, dark green stem has about 20 warty ribs and mostly curved, dark spines. In summer bears funnel-shaped to flattish, carmine-red flowers, 3in (8cm) across.

E. eyriesii, syn. *Echinocactus eyriesii*. Flattened spherical cactus. H 12in (30cm), S 20in (50cm). Has slowly branching, midgreen stems with 11–18 ribs and very short spines. Tubular white flowers appear in spring-summer. Z13–15 H12–10.

E. lageniformis, syn. *E. bridgesii*, *Trichocereus bridgesii*, illus. p.456.

E. multiplex. See *E. oxygona*.

E. oxygona, syn. *E. multiplex*, illus. p.461.

E. pentlandii, syn. *Lobivia pentlandii*, illus. p.473.

E. rhodotricha. Spherical to columnar cactus. H 2ft (60cm), S 8in (20cm). Produces branching, dark green stems, 3½in (9cm) across, with 8–13 ribs. Curved, dark spines, ¾in (2cm) long, later turn pale. Has tubular white to pink flowers in spring-summer. Z13–15 H12–10.

E. spachiana, syn. *Cereus spachianus*, *Trichocereus spachianus*, illus. p.457.

Echioides longiflorum. See *Arnebia pulchra*.

ECHIUM

BORAGINACEAE

Genus of annuals and evergreen shrubs, biennials, and perennials grown for their flowers. Needs full sun and fertile, well-drained soil. Water containerized specimens freely in summer, moderately at other times. Propagate by seed in spring or by greenwood or semi-ripe cuttings in summer. Whitefly may sometimes be troublesome. All parts may cause mild stomach upset if ingested; contact with the foliage may irritate skin.

E. bourgaeanum. See *E. wildpretii*.

E. vulgare [dwarf] illus. p.331.

E. wildpretii, syn. *E. bourgaeanum*. Evergreen, erect, unbranched biennial that dies after fruiting. H 8ft (2.5m) or more, S 2ft (60cm). Narrowly lance-shaped, silver-haired leaves, 1ft (30cm) long, form a dense rosette. Has compact spires, 3–5ft (1–1.5m) long, of small, funnel-shaped red flowers in late spring and early summer. Z9-10 H10–9.

EDGEWORTHIA

THYMELAEACEAE

Genus of deciduous shrubs grown for their flowers in late winter and early spring. Is best grown against a south- or west-facing wall where marginally hardy. Requires full sun and well-drained soil. Dislikes being transplanted. Propagate by semi-ripe cuttings in summer or by seed in autumn.

E. chrysantha, syn. *E. papyrifera*. Deciduous, rounded, open shrub. H and S 5ft (1.5m). Very supple shoots produce terminal, rounded heads of fragrant, tubular yellow flowers in late winter and early spring. Has oval, dark green leaves. Z8–10 H10–8.

E. papyrifera. See *E. chrysantha*.

EDRAIANTHUS

CAMPANULACEAE

Genus of short-lived perennials, some of which are evergreen, usually growing from central rootstocks. In winter, a small, resting bud is just visible from each rootstock. In spring, prostrate stems radiate to carry leaves and flowers. Is suitable for rock gardens, screes, and troughs. Needs sun and well-drained soil. Propagate by softwood cuttings from side shoots in early summer or by seed in autumn.

E. dalmaticus. Upright, then arching perennial. H 4in (10cm), S 6in (15cm). Bears narrowly lance-shaped, pale green leaves and, in early summer, terminal clusters of bell-shaped, violet-blue flowers, 1in (2.5cm) across. Z8–9 H9–8.

E. pumilio illus. p.382.

E. serpyllifolius, syn. *Wahlenbergia serpyllifolia*, illus. p.381. Z7–9 H9–7. **'Major'** is an evergreen, prostrate perennial. H ½in (1cm), S to 2in (5cm). Has tight mats of tiny, oval, dark green leaves. In early summer, bell-shaped, deep violet flowers, ⅝in (1.5cm) wide, are borne on very short stems. Often benefits from a sheltered site. Seldom sets seed.

Edwardsia microphylla. See *Sophora microphylla*.

EGERIA

HYDROCHARITACEAE

Genus of semi-evergreen or evergreen, perennial, floating, or submerged water plants grown for their foliage. Is similar to *Elodea* but has more conspicuous flowers, held above water surface. Needs a sunny position. Propagate by stem cuttings in spring or summer.

E. densa, syn. *Anacharis densa*, *Elodea densa*. Semi-evergreen, perennial, spreading, submerged water plant. S indefinite. Forms a dense mass of whorled, small, lance-shaped, dark green leaves borne on long, wiry stems. Small, 3-parted white flowers appear in summer. Z6–15 H12–6.

EHRETIA

BORAGINACEAE

Genus of deciduous, summer-flowering trees grown for their foliage and star-shaped flowers. May suffer cold damage when young. Requires sun or semi-shade and fertile, well-drained soil. Propagate by softwood cuttings in summer.

E. dicksonii illus. p.91.

EICHHORNIA

PONTEDERIACEAE

Genus of evergreen or semi-evergreen, perennial, floating and marginal water plants. Needs an open, sunny position in warm water. Grows prolifically and requires regular thinning year-round. Propagate by detaching young plants as required.

E. crassipes, syn. *E. speciosa*, illus. p.448.

E. speciosa. See *E. crassipes*.

ELAEAGNUS

ELAEAGNACEAE

Genus of deciduous or evergreen shrubs and trees grown for their foliage and small, usually very fragrant flowers, often followed by ornamental fruits. Evergreen species are good for providing shelter or for hedging, particularly in coastal areas. Most evergreen species thrive in sun or shade, but those with silver leaves and deciduous species prefer full sun. Needs fertile, well-drained soil. Trim hedges in late summer. Propagate species by seed in autumn, evergreen forms also by semi-ripe cuttings in summer, and deciduous forms by softwood or semi-ripe cuttings in summer.

E. angustifolia illus. p.122.

E. commutata (Silverberry). Dense, deciduous shrub that spreads by suckers and is good for stabilizing slopes and on poor soils. H 12ft (4m)

S 6ft (2m). Both shoots and leaves are covered with silvery scales. Fragrant, pale yellow flowers in spring become silvery red, mealy fruits in late autumn. Z2–6 H6–1.
***E.* x *ebbingei*.** Evergreen, bushy, dense shrub. H and S 15ft (5m). Has oblong to oval, glossy, dark green leaves, silvery beneath. Fragrant, bell-shaped, silvery white flowers are borne from mid- to late autumn. Z7–11 H12–7. Leaves of **'Gilt Edge'** have golden yellow margins. Z7–10 H10–7. **'Limelight'** illus. p.153.
***E. macrophylla*.** Evergreen, bushy, dense shrub. H and S 10ft (3m). Broadly oval leaves are silvery gray when young, becoming glossy, dark green above, but remaining silvery gray beneath when mature. Fragrant, bell-shaped, creamy yellow flowers, silvery outside, appear from mid- to late autumn, followed by egg-shaped red fruits. Z7–9 H9–7.
***E. pungens* 'Maculata'**, syn. *E. pungens* 'Aureovariegata', illus. p.127.
***E. umbellata*.** Vigorous, deciduous, bushy shrub. H and S 15ft (5m). Oblong, wavy-edged, bright green leaves are silvery when young. Has fragrant, bell-shaped, creamy yellow flowers in late spring and early summer, then egg-shaped red fruits. Z4–8 H8–1.

ELATOSTEMA, syn. PELLIONIA

URTICACEAE

Genus of evergreen, creeping perennials and subshrubs with attractive foliage that often tends to lie flat, making useful groundcover. Requires a humid atmosphere away from drafts, indirect light, and moist soil. Propagate from stem cuttings in spring or summer.
E. pulchra, syn. *E. repens* var. *pulchra*. Evergreen, slightly fleshy perennial with rooting, creeping stems. H 3–4in (8–10cm), S 2ft (60cm) or more. Broadly oval leaves, 2in (5cm) long, are blackish green with dark green veins above, purple below. Flowers are insignificant.
E. repens, syn. *Pellionia daveauana, P. repens*, illus. p.303. var. ***pulchra*** see *E. pulchra*.

ELEOCHARIS

CYPERACEAE

See also GRASSES, BAMBOOS, RUSHES, and SEDGES.
E. acicularis (Needle spike-rush). Evergreen, spreading, rhizomatous, perennial sedge. H to 4in (10cm), S indefinite. Basal, midgreen leaves are very narrow. Hairless, unbranched, square stems bear solitary, minute brown spikelets in summer. Z9–11 H12-9.

ELEUTHEROCOCCUS, syn. ACANTHOPANAX

ARALIACEAE

Genus of deciduous shrubs and trees grown for their foliage and fruits. Produces tiny, usually greenish white flowers. Prefers full sun and needs well-drained soil. Propagate by seed in spring or by root cuttings in late winter.
E. sieboldianus illus. p.145.

***Elliottia paniculata*.** See *Tripetaleia paniculata*.
Elodea crispa of gardens. See *Lagarosiphon major*.
***Elodea densa*.** See *Egeria densa*.

ELSHOLTZIA

LABIATAE/LAMIACEAE

Genus of perennials and deciduous shrubs and subshrubs grown for their flowers, generally blooming in autumn. Needs full sun and fertile, well-drained soil. Cut back old shoots hard in early spring. Propagate by softwood cuttings in summer.
E. stauntonii illus. p.173.

***Elymus arenarius*.** See *Leymus arenarius*.

EMBOTHRIUM

PROTEACEAE

Genus of evergreen or semi-evergreen trees grown for their flowers. Provide shelter from cold winds. Needs semi-shade and moist but well-drained, lime-free soil. Propagate by suckers in spring or autumn or by seed in autumn.
E. coccineum illus. p.93.

EMILIA, syn. CACALIA

ASTERACEAE/COMPOSITAE

Genus of annuals and perennials with flower heads that are good for cutting. Is ideal for hot, dry areas and coastal soils. Requires sun and very well-drained soil. Propagate by seed sown under cover in spring, or outdoors in late spring.
E. coccinea, syn. *E. flammea, E. javanica* of gardens, illus. p.341.
***E. flammea*.** See *E. coccinea*.
E. javanica of gardens. See *E. coccinea*.

EMMENOPTERYS

RUBIACEAE

Genus of deciduous trees grown for their foliage and sometimes flowers. Even where reliably hardy, young growths may be damaged by late frosts. Needs partial shade and deep, fertile, moist but well-drained soil. Propagate by softwood cuttings in summer.
E. henryi illus. p.80.

ENCEPHALARTOS

ZAMIACEAE

Genus of evergreen shrubs and trees grown for their palmlike appearance. Needs full light and well-drained soil. Water potted plants moderately when in full growth, less at other times. Propagate by seed in spring.
E. ferox illus. p.152.
***E. longifolius*.** Slow-growing, evergreen, palmlike tree, sometimes branched with age. H 10ft (3m) or more, S 5–8ft (1.5–2.5m). Has feather-shaped leaves, each 2–5ft (60cm–1.5m) long, divided into narrowly lance-shaped to oval, blue-green leaflets, usually with hook-tipped teeth. Conelike, brownish flower heads appear intermittently. Z11 H12–10.

ENCYCLIA

See also ORCHIDS.
***E. cochleata*.** Evergreen, epiphytic orchid for a cool greenhouse. H 12in (30cm). Upright spikes of green flowers, 2in (5cm) long, with dark purple lips at the top and ribbonlike sepals and petals, are produced in summer and, on mature plants, intermittently throughout the year. Leaves are narrowly oval and 6in (15cm) long. Requires semi-shade in summer. Z14–15 H12–10.
***E. radiata*.** Evergreen, epiphytic orchid for a cool greenhouse. H 10in (25cm). Bears upright spikes of very fragrant, well-rounded, creamy white flowers, ½in (1cm) across, with red-lined white lips, in summer. Narrowly oval leaves are 4–6in (10–15cm) long. Needs semi-shade in summer. Z14–15 H12–10.

***Endymion*.** Reclassified as *Hyacinthoides*.

ENKIANTHUS

ERICACEAE

Genus of deciduous or semi-evergreen, spring-flowering shrubs and trees grown for their mass of small, bell- or urn-shaped flowers and their autumn color. Needs sun or semi-shade and moist, peaty, acidic soil. Propagate by semi-ripe cuttings in summer or by seed in autumn.
E. campanulatus illus. p.117.
E. cernuus* f. *rubens illus. p.131.
E. perulatus illus. p.127.

ENSETE

MUSACEAE

Genus of evergreen perennials grown for their foliage (that resembles that of bananas) and fruits. Has false stems made of overlapping leaf sheaths that die after flowering. Grow in sun or partial shade and organic soil. Propagate by seed in spring or by division year-round.
E. ventricosum, syn. *Musa arnoldiana, M. ensete*, illus. p.233.

EOMECON

PAPAVERACEAE

Genus of one species of perennial that spreads rapidly and deeply underground. Is suitable for large rock gardens. Needs sun and well-drained soil. Propagate by seed or runners in spring.
E. chionantha (Snow poppy). Vigorous, spreading perennial. H to 16in (40cm), S indefinite. Leaves are large, palmate, and gray. Erect stems each carry a long panicle of small, poppylike white flowers in summer. Z7–9 H9–7.

EPACRIS

EPACRIDACEAE

Genus of evergreen, heathlike shrubs grown for their flowers. Needs full sun and organic, well-drained, neutral to acidic soil. Water potted plants moderately when in full growth, less at other times. Flowered stems may be shortened after flowering to maintain a neat habit. Propagate by seed in spring or semi-ripe cuttings in late summer.
E. impressa illus. p.155.

EPHEDRA

EPHEDRACEAE

Genus of evergreen shrubs grown for their habit and green shoots. Makes a good groundcover in dry soil. Grow male and female plants together in order to obtain fruits. Requires full sun and well-drained soil. Propagate by seed in autumn or by division in autumn or spring.
***E. gerardiana*.** Evergreen, spreading shrub with slender, erect, rushlike green shoots. H 2ft (60cm), S 6ft (2m). Leaves and flowers are inconspicuous. Bears small, spherical red fruits. Z5–9 H9–5.

EPIDENDRUM

See also ORCHIDS.
E. difforme (illus. p.298). Evergreen, epiphytic orchid for an intermediate greenhouse. H 9in (23cm). Large heads of semi-translucent green flowers, ¼in (0.5cm) across, open in autumn. Has oval, rigid leaves, 1–2in (2.5–5cm) long. Requires shade in summer. Avoid spraying, which can cause spotting of leaves. Propagate by division in spring. Z14–15 H12–10.
E. ibaguense, syn. *E. radicans* (illus. p.297). Evergreen, epiphytic orchid for a cool greenhouse. H 6ft (2m) or more. Flowers more or less constantly, bearing a succession of feathery-lipped, deep red blooms, ¼in (0.5cm) across. Leaves, 1–2in (2.5–5cm) long, are oval and rigid. Grow in semi-shade during summer. Propagate by tip cuttings in spring. Z14 H12–6.
***E. radicans*.** See *E. ibaguense*.

EPIGAEA

ERICACEAE

Genus of evergreen, prostrate, spring-flowering subshrubs. Needs shade and organic, moist, acidic soil. Most are difficult to cultivate. Propagate by seed in spring or by softwood cuttings in early summer.
***E. asiatica*.** Evergreen, creeping subshrub. H to 4in (10cm), S to 8in (20cm). Stems and heart-shaped, deep green leaves are covered with brown hairs. Bears terminal clusters of 3–6 tiny, slightly fragrant, urn-shaped white or pink flowers in spring. Z5–7 H7–5.

E. gaultherioides, syn. *Orphanidesia gaultherioides*, illus. p.364.
E. repens (Mayflower, Trailing arbutus). Evergreen, creeping subshrub. H 4in (10cm), S 12in (30cm). Hairy stems, bearing heart-shaped, leathery leaves, root at intervals. In spring produces terminal clusters of 4–6 cup-shaped white flowers, sometimes flushed pink. Is relatively easy to grow. Z3–9 H9–1.

EPILOBIUM,

syn. CHAMAENERION
Willow herb

ONAGRACEAE

Genus of annuals, biennials, perennials, and deciduous subshrubs grown for their deep pink to white flowers in summer. Is useful on dry banks; many species are invasive. Tolerates sun or shade and prefers moist but well-drained soil. Propagate species by seed in autumn, selected forms by softwood cuttings from side-shoots in spring.
E. angustifolium f. ***album*** illus. p.226.
E. californicum. See *Zauschneria californica*.
E. canum. See *Zauschneria californica* subsp. *cana*.
E. chlorifolium var. ***kaikourense*** illus. p.374.
E. glabellum of gardens illus. p.351.
E. obcordatum. Clump-forming perennial. H 6in (15cm), S 4in (10cm). Oval leaves are glossy green. Spikes of open cup-shaped, deep rose-pink flowers are borne in summer. Is good for a rock garden or alpine house. Needs a sheltered site and full sun. In cultivation may not retain character, especially in mild climates. Z5–8 H8–5.
E. septentrionale. See *Zauschneria septentrionalis*.

EPIMEDIUM

Barrenwort

BERBERIDACEAE

Genus of spring-flowering perennials, some of which are evergreen. Flowers are cup-shaped with long or short spurs. Makes a good groundcover. Does best in partial shade and organic, moist but well-drained soil. Cut back just before new growth appears in spring. Propagate by division in spring or autumn.
E. alpinum. Evergreen, clump-forming perennial. H 9in (23cm), S to 12in (30cm). Racemes of pendent, short-spurred flowers with crimson sepals and yellow petals appear in spring. Has finely toothed, glossy leaves divided into oval, angled, midgreen leaflets, bronze when young. Z4–9 H9–4.
E. grandiflorum* 'Crimson Beauty'** (illus. p.51). Clump-forming perennial. H and S 12in (30cm). Racemes of pendent, long-spurred, copper-crimson flowers are produced in spring at the same time as heart-shaped, copper-marked, light green leaves, divided into oval leaflets, which mature to midgreen. Z5–8 H8-5. **'Rose Queen'** illus. p.269. f. ***violaceum has young leaves that are flushed bronze and produces purple-and-white flowers. Z5–8 H8–5.
E. × perralchicum. Evergreen, carpeting perennial. H 45cm (18in), S 12in (30cm). Short spires of pendent yellow flowers with short spurs are borne on slender stems in spring. Leaves, divided into rounded to oval leaflets, are dark green. Z5–8 H8–5.
E. perralderianum. Semi-evergreen, carpeting perennial. H 12in (30cm), S 18in (45cm). Clusters of small, pendent, short-spurred, bright yellow flowers are borne in spring. Has large, toothed, glossy, deep green leaves divided into rounded to oval leaflets.
E. pinnatum subsp. ***colchicum.*** Evergreen, carpeting perennial. H and S 12in (30cm). In spring, clusters of small, pendent, bright yellow flowers with short spurs are produced above dark green leaves, divided into rounded to oval leaflets, that are hairy when young. Z5–9 H9–4.
E. pubigerum illus. p.268.
E. × rubrum illus. p.269.
E. × versicolor. Clump-forming perennial. H and S 12in (30cm). Small, pendent clusters of yellow flowers with long, red-tinged spurs appear in spring. Heart-shaped, fresh green leaves are divided into oval leaflets that are tinted reddish purple. Z5–9 H9–4. **'Neosulphureum'** illus. p.274.
E. × warleyense illus. p.275.
***E. × youngianum* 'Niveum'** illus. p.267.

EPIPHYLLUM

Orchid cactus, Strap cactus

CACTACEAE

Genus of cacti with strap-shaped, flattened green stems that have notched edges. Flowers are produced at notches. Grow in sun or partial shade and in rich, well-drained soil. Propagate by stem cuttings in spring or summer.
E. ackermannii. See *Nopalxochia ackermannii*.
E. anguliger illus. p.461.
E. crenatum. Erect, then pendent cactus. H and S 10ft (3m). Has a flattened stem. Bears lightly perfumed, funnel-shaped, broad-petaled white flowers, 8in (20cm) across, in spring-summer. Is often used as a parent for breeding. Z11–12 H12–1.
E. laui illus. p.461.
E. oxypetalum. Erect, then pendent cactus. H 10ft (3m), S 3ft (1m). Produces freely branching, flattened stems, 5in (12cm) across. In spring-summer bears nocturnal, tubular, white flowers, 10in (25cm) long. Makes a good house plant. Z11–12 H12–1.

EPIPREMNUM,

syn. POTHOS

ARACEAE

Genus of evergreen, woody-stemmed, root climbers, including *Pothos*, grown for their handsome leaves. Grow in light shade away from direct sun; any well-drained, moisture-retentive soil is suitable. Water regularly, less in cold weather. Stems need good supports. Remove shoot tips to induce branching at any time. Propagate by leaf-bud or stem-tip cuttings in late spring or by layering in summer. All parts may cause severe discomfort if ingested, and contact with the sap of *E. aureum* may irritate skin.
***E. aureum* 'Marble Queen'**, syn. *Scindapsus aureus* 'Marble Queen', illus. p.219.
***E. pictum* 'Argyraeum'**, syn. *Scindapsus pictus* 'Argyraeus', illus. p.219.

EPISCIA

GESNERIACEAE

Genus of evergreen, low-growing and creeping perennials grown for their ornamental leaves and colorful flowers. Is useful as a groundcover or in hanging baskets. Requires high humidity and a fairly shaded position in organic, well-drained soil. Keep well watered, but avoid waterlogging. Propagate in summer by stem cuttings, division, or removing rooted runners.
E. cupreata (Flame violet) illus. p.301. **'Metallica'** is an evergreen, creeping perennial. H 4in (10cm), S indefinite. Has oval, downy, wrinkled leaves, tinged pink to copper and with broad, silvery bands along midribs. Funnel-shaped, orange-red flowers marked yellow within are borne intermittently. Z14–15 H9–1. **'Tropical Topaz'** has yellow flowers.
E. dianthiflora, syn. *Alsobia dianthiflora*, illus. p.299.
E. lilacina. Evergreen, low-growing perennial with runners bearing plantlets. H 4in (10cm), S indefinite. Has oval, hairy, pale green leaves to 3in (8cm) long. Funnel-shaped white flowers, tinged mauve and with yellow eyes, are produced in small clusters from autumn to spring. Z14–15 H12–1. Leaves of **'Cuprea'** are bronze-tinged.

EPITHELANTHA

CACTACEAE

Genus of very slow-growing, spherical cacti densely covered with very short spines. Needs full sun and well-drained soil, and is prone to rot if overwatered. Is usually easier to cultivate if grafted. Propagate by seed or stem cuttings in spring or summer.
E. micromeris illus. p.471

ERANTHEMUM

ACANTHACEAE

Genus of perennials and evergreen shrubs grown for their flowers. Requires full light or partial shade and fertile, well-drained soil. Water containerized plants freely when in full growth, moderately at other times. In spring or after flowering remove at least half of each spent flowering stem to encourage a bushier habit. Propagate by softwood cuttings in late spring. Whitefly may be a nuisance.
E. atropurpureum. See *Pseuderanthemum atropurpureum*.
E. nervosum. See *E. pulchellum*.
E. pulchellum, syn. *E. nervosum*. Evergreen, erect shrub. H 3–4ft (1–1.2m), S 2ft (60cm) or more. Produces elliptic to oval, prominently veined, deep green leaves. Blue flowers, each with a 1¼in (3cm) long tube and rounded petal lobes, are produced in winter-spring. Z13–15 H12–10.

ERANTHIS

RANUNCULACEAE

Genus of clump-forming perennials, with knobby tubers, grown for their cup-shaped flowers surrounded by leaf-like ruffs of bracts. Prefers partial shade and organic soil, well-drained but not drying out excessively. Dies down in summer. Propagate by seed in autumn or by division of clumps immediately after flowering while still in leaf. All parts may cause mild stomach upset if ingested, and contact with the sap may irritate skin.
E. hyemalis illus. p.441.
***E. × tubergenii* 'Guinea Gold'.** Late winter- or early spring-flowering, tuberous perennial. H 3–4in (8–10cm), S 1½–2½in (4–6cm). Stems each bear a stalkless, deep golden yellow flower, 1¼–1½in (3–4cm) across, surrounded by a bronze-green bract cut into narrow lobes. Rounded leaves are divided into finger-shaped lobes. Z4–9 H9–1.

ERCILLA,

syn. BRIDGESIA

PHYTOLACCACEAE

Genus of evergreen, root climbers grown for their neat green leaves and green and purple flower spikes. Grow in sun or partial shade and in any well-drained soil. Prune after flowering, if required. Propagate by stem cuttings in late summer or autumn.
E. spicata. See *E. volubilis*.
E. volubilis, syn. *E. spicata*, illus. p.204.

EREMURUS

Foxtail lily, King's spear

ASPHODELACEAE/LILIACEAE

Genus of perennials, with fleshy, finger-like roots, grown for their stately spires of shallowly cup-shaped flowers in summer. Requires a sunny, warm position and well-drained soil. Tends to come into growth very early, and young shoots may be frosted. Provide a covering of dry mulch in late winter to protect the crowns when shoots are first developing. Stake tall species and hybrids. Propagate by division in spring or early autumn or by seed in autumn.
E. himalaicus illus. p.226.
E. robustus illus. p.227.
***E.* Shelford Hybrids.** Group of perennials of varying habit and flower color. H 5ft (1.5m), S 2ft (60cm). Long racemes of orange, buff, pink, or white flowers are borne freely in midsummer.

Leaves are strap-shaped and in basal rosettes. Z6–9 H9–4.
E. spectabilis. Erect perennial. H 4ft (1.2m), S 2ft (60cm). Bears long racemes of pale yellow flowers with brick red anthers in early summer. Leaves are strap-shaped and in basal rosettes. Z7–9 H9–7.

ERIA

See also ORCHIDS.
E. coronaria, syn. *Trichosma suavis*. Evergreen, epiphytic orchid for a cool greenhouse. H 9in (23cm). Sprays of fragrant, rounded, creamy white flowers, 1cm (½in) across, each with a red- and yellow-marked lip, open in autumn. Has broadly oval, glossy leaves, 4in (10cm) long. Needs semi-shade in summer and moist potting medium year-round. Z6–8 H8–6.

ERICA

ERICACEAE

See also HEATHERS.
E. arborea (Tree heath). Evergreen, upright, shrublike tree heath. H 6m (20ft), S 5ft (1.5m). Liable to damage from frost and cold winds. Has needlelike, bright green leaves in whorls of 3 or 4 and bears scented, bell-shaped white flowers from late winter to late spring. May tolerate slightly alkaline soil. Z9–10 H10–9. **'Albert's Gold'**, H 6ft (2m), retains its golden foliage year-round. var. ***alpina*** (illus. p.178) has vivid green foliage that contrasts well with compact racemes of white flowers. May be pruned hard to keep its shape and to encourage new growth.
E. australis (Spanish heath, Spanish tree heath). Evergreen, shrublike tree heath. H to 7ft (2.2m), S 3ft (1m). Stems may be damaged by snow and frost. Has needlelike leaves in whorls of 4 and tubular to bell-shaped, white or purplish pink flowers in spring. May tolerate slightly alkaline soil. Z9–10 H10–9. **'Mr. Robert'** has white flowers. **'Riverslea'** has bright purple-pink flowers, mostly in clusters of 4.
E. canaliculata (Channeled heath; illus. p.178). Evergreen, erect shrub. H to 10ft (3m), S 3ft (1m). Dark green leaves are narrow and needlelike in whorls of 3. Cup-shaped, pearl white flowers, sometimes rose-tinted, with dark brown, almost black anthers, are borne in winter (under cover) or early spring (in the open). Requires acidic soil. Z9–10 H10–9.
E. carnea, syn. *E. herbacea* (Alpine heath, Winter heath). Evergreen, spreading shrub. H to 12in (30cm), S to 18in (45cm) or more. Produces whorls of needlelike, mid- to dark green leaves and bears tubular to bell-shaped flowers that are in shades of pink and red, occasionally white, from early winter to late spring. Tolerates limestone and some shade. Makes a good groundcover. Z5–7 H7–5. **'Altadena'** has golden foliage and pale pink flowers. **'Ann Sparkes'** (illus. p.179), H 6in (15cm), has golden foliage, turning to bronze in winter, and rose-pink flowers. **'Bell's Extra Special'**, H 6in (15cm), S 16in (40cm), has a neat habit, with crimson flowers borne on distinctive, whisky-colored foliage, flecked with tints of orange and gold. **'Cecilia M. Beale'**, H 6in (15cm), bears an abundance of white flowers from mid-winter to early spring. **'December Red'** (illus. p.178) has a spreading habit and vigorous growth. Deep rose-pink flowers are borne in winter. **'Foxhollow'**, a vigorous, spreading cultivar, has foliage that is golden yellow in summer, with orange tips in spring, and a few pale pink flowers. **'Golden Starlet'** (illus. p.178), H 6in (15cm), S 16in (40cm), bears white flowers set on lime green foliage that turns a glowing yellow in summer. **'Ice Princess'**, H 6in (15cm), S 14in (35cm), has white flowers held erect on bright green foliage. **'Isabell'**, H 6in (15cm), S 14in (35cm), has large white flowers on bright green foliage, and an erect but spreading habit. **'King George'**, H 8in (20cm), has dark green foliage and deep rose-pink flowers from early winter to midspring. **'Loughrigg'**, H 6in (15cm), produces dark purplish red flowers from late winter to spring. **'March Seedling'** has a spreading habit, dark green foliage and rich, rose-purple flowers. **'Myretoun Ruby'**, H 8in (20cm), is vigorous but compact with brilliant deep purple-red flowers in late winter and early spring. **'Nathalie'**, H 6in (15cm), S 16in (40cm), the deepest and brightest of the *E. carnea* cultivars, has purple flowers, neat, dark green foliage, and a compact, upright habit. **'Pink Spangles'**, H 6in (15cm), is vigorous with flowers that have shell pink sepals and deeper pink corollas. **'Pirbright Rose'** is very floriferous with bright pink flowers from early winter to early spring. **'R.B. Cooke'**, H 8in (20cm), bears clear pink flowers from early winter to early spring. **'Rosalie'** (illus. p.179), H 6in (15cm), S 14in (35cm), has bright pink flowers, bronze-green foliage, and a low, upright but spreading habit. **'Springwood White'** (illus. p.178), H 6in (15cm), the most vigorous white cultivar, is excellent as a groundcover and bears large white flowers with brown anthers from late winter to spring. **'Vivellii'** (illus. p.179), H 6in (15cm), has dark bronze-green foliage and bears deep purple-pink flowers from late winter to spring. **'Westwood Yellow'** (illus. p.179) is compact with golden yellow foliage and deep pink flowers. **'Winter Sun'** see *E.c.* 'Wintersonne'. **'Wintersonne'** (syn. *E.c.* 'Winter Sun'), H 6in (15cm), S 14in (35cm), has magenta flowers and red-brown foliage.
E. ciliaris (Dorset heath). Evergreen, loose shrub. H to 12in (30cm), S 16in (40cm). May be damaged in severe weather. Has needlelike, dark green leaves in whorls of 3. Bears long racemes of bell-shaped, bright pink flowers in tiers of 3 or 4 in summer. Requires acidic soil and prefers warm, moist conditions. Z8–9 H9–8. **'Aurea'** has somewhat straggly growth, with golden foliage and clear pink flowers. **'Corfe Castle'** (illus. p.179) produces salmon-pink flowers from summer to early autumn. **'David McClintock'** (illus. p.178) has light gray-green foliage and bears white flowers with deep pink tips from summer to early autumn. **'Mrs. C.H. Gill'** has dark gray-green foliage and clear red flowers. **'White Wings'** (illus. p.178), a sport of 'Mrs. C.H. Gill', has dark gray-green foliage and white flowers.
E. cinerea (Bell heather). Evergreen, compact shrub. H 12in (30cm), S 18–24in (45–60cm). Has needlelike, mid- to deep green leaves and bears bell-shaped flowers that are in shades of pink and dark red, occasionally white, from early summer to early autumn. Prefers a warm, dry position. Requires acidic soil. Z6–8 H8–6. **'Atropurpurea'** has deep purple flowers in long racemes. **'C.D. Eason'** (illus. p.179) has distinctive, dark green foliage and bright red flowers. **'Cevennes'** is upright in habit and bears a profusion of mauve flowers. **'C.G. Best'** has midgreen foliage and rose-pink flowers. **'Domino'** produces white flowers that contrast with dark brown stems and sepals and almost black stigmas. **'Eden Valley'** (illus. p.179), H 8in (20cm), bears white flowers with lavender-mauve tips. **'Fiddler's Gold'** (illus. p.179), H 10in (25cm), has golden yellow foliage, deepening to red in winter, and lilac-pink flowers. **'Golden Hue'**, H 14in (35cm), has amethyst flowers set on pale yellow foliage tipped orange in winter. **'Hookstone White'** (illus. p.178), H 14in (35cm), has bright green foliage and bears long racemes of large white flowers. **'Lime Soda'**, H 14in (35cm), produces soft lavender flowers in profusion on attractive, lime green foliage. **'Pentreath'** has rich purple flowers. **'Pink Ice'**, H 8in (20cm), is compact with soft pink flowers. **'P.S. Patrick'** is a vigorous cultivar with purple flowers and dark green foliage. **'Purple Beauty'** (illus. p.179) has purple flowers and dark foliage. **'Stephen Davis'**, H 10in (25cm), has brilliant, almost fluorescent red flowers. **'Velvet Night'**, H 10in (25cm), produces very dark purple, almost black flowers. **'Windlebrooke'** (illus. p.179), H 10in (25cm), is vigorous, with golden foliage turning bright orange-red in winter, and mauve flowers.
E. x darleyensis. Evergreen, bushy shrub. H 18in (45cm), S 3ft (1m) or more. Has needlelike, midgreen foliage with cream, pink, or red young growth in late spring. Bell-shaped white, pink, or purple flowers are borne in racemes from early winter to late spring. Tolerates limestone. Z7–8 H8–7. **'Archie Graham'** (illus. p.178), H 20in (50cm), is vigorous, with mauve-pink flowers. **'Arthur Johnson'**, H 3ft (1m), has young foliage with cream and pink tips in spring and long racemes of mauve-pink flowers from midwinter to spring. **'Darley Dale'** (illus. p.178) bears pale mauve flowers from midwinter to spring. **'George Rendall'** carries deep pink flowers from early winter to early spring. **'Ghost Hills'** (illus. p.178) has cream-tipped foliage in spring and a profusion of pink flowers from midwinter to spring. **'Jack H. Brummage'**, H 12in (30cm), has golden foliage with yellow and orange tints, and mauve flowers. **'J.W. Porter'**, H 12in (30cm), has reddish young shoots in spring and mauve-pink flowers from midwinter to late spring. **'Kramer's Rote'** (syn. *E.* x *d.* 'Kramer's Red') has dark bronze-green foliage with deep purple-red flowers from late autumn to late spring. Spring foliage does not have cream or red tips. **'Molten Silver'** see *E.* x *d.* 'Silberschmelze'. **'Silberschmelze'** (syn. *E.* x *d.* 'Molten Silver') is vigorous and produces young shoots with creamy pink tips in spring and white flowers. **'White Glow'** (illus. p.178), H 12in (30cm), bears white flowers. **'White Perfection'** (illus. p.178) has bright green foliage and white flowers.
E. erigena, syn. *E. hibernica*, *E. mediterranea*. Evergreen, upright shrub. H to 8ft (2.5m), S to 3ft (1m). Top growth may be damaged in severe weather, but plant recovers well from the base. Has needlelike, midgreen leaves and, usually, bell-shaped, mauve-pink flowers from early winter to late spring. Tolerates lime. Flowers of some cultivars have a pronounced honey scent. Z8–9 H9–8. **'Brightness'** (illus. p.179), H 18in (45cm), has bronze-green foliage and mauve-pink flowers in spring. **'Golden Lady'** (illus. p.179), H 12in (30cm), has a neat, compact habit with year-round golden foliage and white flowers in late spring. **'Irish Dusk'**, H 18in (45cm), has dark green foliage and salmon-pink flowers from midwinter to early spring. **'Superba'**, H 6ft (2m), bears strongly scented, rose-pink flowers during spring. **'W.T. Rackliff'**, H 2ft (60cm), has dark green foliage and produces thick clusters of white flowers from late winter to late spring.
E. gracilis. Evergreen, compact shrub. H and S to 12in (30cm). Has needle-like, midgreen leaves and clusters of small, bell-shaped cerise flowers from early autumn to early spring. Is usually grown as a pot plant; may be planted outdoors in summer in a sheltered site. Z10–11 H12–10.
E. herbacea. See *E. carnea*.
E. hibernica. See *E. erigena*.
E. x hiemalis. Evergreen, bushy shrub. H and S 12in (30cm). Tender. Has needlelike, midgreen foliage and racemes of tubular to bell-shaped, pink-tinged, white flowers from late autumn

to midwinter. Z7–8 H8–7.
E. lusitanica (Portuguese heath). Evergreen, upright, bushy, tree heath. H to 10ft (3m), S 3ft (1m). Has feathery, bright green leaves and, from late autumn to late spring, bears tubular to bell-shaped flowers that are pink in bud but pure white when fully open. Z8–10 H10–8. **'George Hunt'** has golden foliage.
E. mackaiana, syn. *E. mackayana* (Mackay's heath). Evergreen, spreading shrub. H to 10in (25cm), S 16in (40cm). Has needlelike, midgreen leaves and bears umbels of rounded pink, mauve-pink, or white flowers from midsummer to early autumn. Likes damp, acidic soil. Z5–7 H7–5. **'Dr. Ronald Gray'** (illus. p.178), H 6in (15cm), has dark green foliage and pure white flowers. **'Plena'** (illus. p.178), H 6in (15cm), has double, deep pink flowers shading to white in centers.
E. mackayana. See *E. mackaiana.*
E. mediterranea. See *E. erigena.*
E. pageana. Evergreen, bushy shrub. H to 2ft (60cm), S 1ft (30cm). Has needlelike, midgreen leaves and, from late spring to early summer, bell-shaped, rich yellow flowers. Z10 H12–10.
E.* x *praegeri. See *E.* x *stuartii.*
E. scoparia (Besom heath). Evergreen, bushy shrub. H to 10ft (3m), S 3ft (1m). Has needlelike, dark green leaves. Clusters of rounded, bell-shaped, greenish brown flowers appear in late spring and early summer. Requires acidic soil. Z8–9 H9–8. **'Minima'**, H 12in (30cm), has bright green foliage.
E. spiculifolia, syn. *Bruckenthalia spiculifolia* (Spike heath). Evergreen, heathlike shrub. H and S 6in (15cm). Tiny, needlelike, glossy, dark green leaves clothe stiff stems. Terminal clusters of tiny pink flowers appear in summer. Z5–7 H7–5.
E. stricta. See *E. terminalis.*
E.* x *stuartii, syn. *E.* x *praegeri.* Evergreen, compact shrub. H 6in (15cm), S 12in (30cm). Has needlelike, dark green leaves. Numerous umbels of bell-shaped pink flowers are produced in late spring and summer. Prefers moist, acidic soil. Z5–7 H7–5. **'Irish Lemon'** produces young foliage with lemon-yellow tips in spring and bright pink flowers. **'Irish Orange'** has orange-tipped young foliage and dark pink flowers.
E. terminalis, syn. *E. stricta* (Corsican heath). Evergreen, shrublike tree heath with stiff, upright growth. H and S to 8ft (2.5m). Has needlelike, midgreen foliage. Bell-shaped, mauve-pink flowers, borne from early summer to early autumn, turn russet as they fade in winter. Tolerates lime. Z5–7 H7–5.
E. tetralix (Cross-leaved heath). Evergreen, spreading shrub. H to 12in (30cm), S 18in (45cm). Has needlelike, gray-green leaves in whorls of 4. Large umbels of bell-shaped pink flowers appear from summer to early autumn. Requires acidic, preferably moist soil. Z5–7 H7–5. **'Alba Mollis'** (illus. p.178) has silver-gray foliage and bears white flowers from early summer to late autumn. **'Con Underwood'** (illus. p.179) has dark red flowers. **'Hookstone Pink'** has silver-gray foliage and bears rose-pink flowers from late spring to early autumn. **'Pink Star'** (illus. p.179) produces pink flowers held upright in a starlike pattern.
E. umbellata. Evergreen, bushy shrub. H and S 2ft (60cm). Has needlelike, midgreen foliage and bell-shaped mauve flowers with chocolate-brown anthers in late spring.
E. vagans (Cornish heath). Vigorous, evergreen, bushy shrub. H and S 30in (75cm). Leaves are needlelike and midgreen. Rounded, bell-shaped pink, mauve, or white flowers appear from midsummer to late autumn. Tolerates some lime. Responds well to hard pruning. Z5–7 H7–5. **'Birch Glow'** (illus. p.179), H 18in (45cm), has bright green foliage and glowing rose-pink flowers. **'Lyonesse'** (illus. p.178), H 18in (45cm), has dark green foliage and long, tapering spikes of white flowers with brown anthers. **'Mrs. D.F. Maxwell'**, H 18in (45cm), has dark green foliage and glowing deep pink flowers. **'St. Keverne'**, H 18in (45cm), is a neat, bushy shrub with rose-pink flowers; may be used for a low hedge. **'Valerie Proudley'** (illus. p.179), H 18in (45cm), has golden foliage year-round when grown in full light, and bears sparse white flowers in late summer and autumn.
E.* x *veitchii. Evergreen, bushy, shrub-like tree heath. H to 6ft (2m), S 3ft (1m). Has needlelike, midgreen leaves. Scented, tubular to bell-shaped white flowers are produced in dense clusters from midwinter to spring. Z8–9 H9–8. **'Exeter'** (illus. p.178) has a profusion of white flowers almost obscuring the foliage. **'Gold Tips'** is similar to 'Exeter', but young foliage has golden tips in spring. **'Pink Joy'** (illus. p.178) has pink flower buds that open to clear white.
E. verticillata. Evergreen, erect shrub. H to 2ft (60cm), S 1ft (30cm). Has a very unusual and attractive arrangement of flowers tightly packed in whorls at intervals along an otherwise almost bare stem. Bears tubular, pale mauve-pink flowers, ½in (1.5cm) long, intermittently throughout the year.
E.* x *watsonii. Evergreen, compact shrub. H 12in (30cm), S 15in (38cm). Needlelike, midgreen leaves often have bright-colored tips in spring. Bears rounded, bell-shaped pink flowers from mid- to late summer. Z5–7 H7–5. **'Cherry Turpin'** has long racemes of pale pink flowers from midsummer to mid-autumn. **'Dawn'** (illus. p.178) produces young foliage with orange-yellow tips and bears deep mauve-pink flowers in compact clusters all summer.
E.* x *williamsii. Evergreen, spreading shrub. H 12in (30cm), S 24in (60cm). Has needlelike, dark green leaves with bright yellow tips when young in spring. Bears bell-shaped mauve or pink flowers in midsummer. Prefers acidic soil. Z5–7 H7–5. **'Gwavas'** has pale pink flowers on a neat, compact plant from midsummer to autumn. **'P.D. Williams'** (illus. p.178), H 18in (45cm), has dark mauve-pink flowers; it sometimes keeps its golden foliage tips all summer.

ERIGERON
Fleabane

ASTERACEAE/COMPOSITAE

Genus of mainly spring- and summer-flowering annuals, biennials, and perennials grown for their daisylike flower heads. Is good for rock gardens or herbaceous borders. Prefers sun and well-drained soil but should not be allowed to dry out during growing season. Resents winter wet. Propagate by division in spring or early autumn or by seed in autumn, selected forms by softwood cuttings in early summer.
E. alpinus illus. p.355.
E. aurantiacus. Clump-forming perennial. H 6in (15cm), S 12in (30cm). Has long, oval, gray-green leaves and produces daisylike, brilliant orange flower heads in summer. Propagate by seed or division in spring. Z5–8 H8–5.
E. aureus. Short-lived, clump-forming perennial. H 2–4in (5–10cm), S 6in (15cm). Bears small, spoon-shaped to oval, hairy leaves. Slender stems each bear a relatively large, daisylike, golden yellow flower head in summer. Dislikes winter wet with no snow cover. Is excellent for a scree, trough, or alpine house; is prone to aphid attack. Z5–8 H8–5. **'Canary Bird'**, H to 4in (10cm), is longer lived and bears bright canary yellow flower heads.
***E.* 'Charity'** illus. p.278.
***E.* 'Darkest of All'.** See *E.* 'Dunkelste Aller'.
***E.* 'Dunkelste Aller'**, syn. *E.* 'Darkest of All'. Clump-forming perennial. H 32in (80cm), S 24in (60cm) or more. Produces a mass of daisylike, deep purple flower heads with yellow centers in summer. Has narrowly oval, grayish green leaves. Z5–8 H8–5.
***E.* 'Foerster's Liebling'.** Clump-forming perennial. H 32in (80cm), S 24in (60cm). In summer daisylike, semi-double pink flower heads with yellow centers are borne above narrowly oval, grayish green leaves. Z5–8 H8–5.
***E. glaucus* 'Elstead Pink'.** Tufted perennial. H 12in (30cm), S 6in (15cm). Daisylike, dark lilac-pink flower heads appear throughout summer above oval, gray-green leaves. Z5–8 H8–5.
E. karvinskianus, syn. *E. mucronatus*, illus. p.377.
E. mucronatus. See *E. karvinskianus.*
***E.* 'Quakeress'.** Clump-forming perennial. H 32in (80cm), S 24in (60cm). Produces a mass of daisylike, delicate lilac-pink flower heads with yellow centers in summer. Narrowly oval leaves are grayish green. Z5–8 H8–5.
***E.* 'Serenity'** illus. p.284.

ERINACEA

LEGUMINOSAE/PAPILIONACEAE

Genus of one species of slow-growing, evergreen subshrub with hard, sharp, blue-green spines and pealike flowers. In spring produces short-lived, soft leaves. Needs a sheltered position with full sun and deep, gritty, well-drained soil. Propagate by seed when available or by softwood cuttings in late spring or summer.
E. anthyllis, syn. *E. pungens*, illus. p.348.
E. pungens. See *E. anthyllis.*

ERINUS
Fairy foxglove

SCROPHULARIACEAE

Genus of short-lived, semi-evergreen perennials suitable for rock gardens, walls, and troughs. Needs sun and well-drained soil. Propagate species by seed in autumn (but seedlings will vary considerably), and selected forms by softwood cuttings in early summer. Self-seeds freely.
E. alpinus illus. p.366. **'Dr. Hähnle'** (syn. *E.a.* 'Dr. Haenele') is a semi-evergreen, basal-rosetted perennial. H and S 2–3in (5–8cm). Small, flat, 2-lipped, deep pink flowers open in late spring and summer. Leaves are small, oval, and midgreen. Z4–7 H7–1.

ERIOBOTRYA

ROSACEAE

Genus of evergreen, autumn-flowering trees and shrubs grown for their foliage, flowers, and edible fruits. Where marginally hardy, it is best grown against a south- or west-facing wall. Fruits, which ripen in spring, may be damaged by hard frosts. Requires sunny, fertile, well-drained soil. Propagate by seed in autumn or spring.
E. japonica (Loquat). Evergreen, bushy shrub or spreading tree. H and S 25ft (8m). Has thick shoots and large, oblong, prominently veined, glossy, dark green leaves. Fragrant, 5-petaled white flowers are borne in large clusters in early autumn, followed by pear-shaped, orange-yellow fruits. Z8–11 H12–8.

ERIOGONUM
Wild buckwheat

POLYGONACEAE

Genus of annuals, biennials, and evergreen perennials, subshrubs, and shrubs grown for their rosetted, hairy, often silver or white leaves. Needs full sun and well-drained, even poor soil. In colder, wet-winter areas protect shrubby species and hairy-leaved perennials. Water potted plants moderately in summer, less in spring and autumn, and very little in winter. Remove flower heads after flowering unless seed is required. Propagate by

seed in spring or autumn or by semi-ripe cuttings in summer. Divide perennial root clumps in spring.
E. arborescens illus. p.161.
E. crocatum. Evergreen, subshrubby perennial. H to 8in (20cm), S 6in (15cm). Oval, hairy leaves have woolly white undersides. Heads of minute, sulfur yellow flowers are borne in summer. Is a good alpine-house plant. Z9–10 H10.
E. giganteum illus. p.139.
E. ovalifolium. Evergreen, domed perennial. H 12in (30cm), S 4in (10cm). In summer carries tiny, bright yellow flowers in umbels above branched stems bearing tiny, spoon-shaped, hairy gray leaves. Is excellent for an alpine house. Z4–8 H8–1.
E. umbellatum illus. p.358.

ERIOPHYLLUM

ASTERACEAE/COMPOSITAE

Genus of summer-flowering perennials and evergreen subshrubs with (usually) silvery foliage and attractive, daisylike flower heads. Suitable for rock gardens and front of borders. Needs sun and well-drained soil. Propagate by division in spring or by seed in autumn.
E. lanatum, syn. *Bahia lanata*, illus. p.293.

ERITRICHIUM

BORAGINACEAE

Genus of short-lived perennials with soft, gray-green leaves and forget-me-not-like flowers. Is suitable for rock gardens and alpine houses. Needs sun and well-drained, peaty, sandy soil with a deep collar of grit; dislikes damp conditions. Is extremely difficult to grow. Propagate by seed when available or by softwood cuttings in summer.
E. elongatum. Tuft-forming perennial. H ¾in (2cm), S 1¼in (3cm). Leaves are oval, hairy, and gray-green. Short flower stems each carry small, rounded, flat blue flowers in early summer. Z5–7 H7–5
E. nanum illus. p.383.

ERODIUM

GERANIACEAE

Genus of mound-forming perennials suitable for rock gardens. Needs sun and well-drained soil. Propagate by semi-ripe cuttings in summer or by seed when available.
E. chamaedryoides. See *E. reichardii*.
E. cheilanthifolium, syn. *E. petraeum* subsp. *crispum*, illus. p.355.
E. chrysanthum illus. p.358.
E. corsicum illus. p.376.
E. foetidum, syn. *E. petraeum*. Compact, mound-forming perennial. H 6–8in (15–20cm), S 8in (20cm). Produces saucer-shaped, single, red-veined pink flowers in summer. Oval gray leaves have deeply cut edges. Z6–8 H8–6
E. manescaui, syn. *E. manescavii*, illus. p.279.
E. manescavii. See *E. manescaui*.
E. petraeum. See *E. foetidum*. subsp. ***crispum*** see *E. cheilanthifolium*.
E. reichardii, syn. *E. chamaedryoides*. Mound-forming perennial. H 1in (2.5cm), S 2½–3in (6–8cm). In summer saucer-shaped, single flowers, either white or pink with darker veins, are borne above tiny, oaklike leaves. Is good for a rock garden or trough. Z8–9 H9–8 .
***E. x variabile* 'Flore Pleno'.** Variable, cushion-forming or spreading perennial. H 4in (10cm), S 12in (30cm). Has oval to narrowly oval, dark to gray-green leaves with scalloped edges and long stalks. From spring to autumn, flower stems each bear 1 or 2 rounded, double pink flowers with darker veins; outer petals are rounded, inner petals narrower. **'Ken Aslet'** has prostrate stems, midgreen leaves and single, deep pink flowers. Both Z5–8 H8–5.

Erpetion reniforme. See *Viola hederacea*.

ERYNGIUM
Sea holly

APIACEAE/UMBELLIFERAE

Genus of biennals and perennials, some of which are evergreen, grown for their flowers, foliage, and habit. Thrives in sun and fertile, well-drained soil. Propagate species by seed in autumn, and selected forms by division in spring or by root cuttings in winter.
E. agavifolium, syn. *E. bromeliifolium* of gardens. Evergreen, clump-forming perennial. H 5ft (1.5m), S 2ft (60cm). Forms rosettes of sword-shaped, sharply toothed, rich green leaves. Thistlelike, greenish white flower heads are produced on branched stems in summer. Z6–9 H9–6.
E. alpinum illus. p.253.
E. amethystinum. Rosette-forming perennial. H and S 24in (60cm). Oval leaves are divided, spiny, and mid-green. Produces much-branched stems that in summer bear heads of small, thistlelike blue flowers surrounded by spiky, darker blue bracts. Z3–8 H8–1.
E. bourgatii illus. p.286.
E. bromeliifolium of gardens. See *E. agavifolium*.
E. eburneum, syn. *E. paniculatum*, illus. p.226.
E. giganteum. Clump-forming biennial or short-lived perennial that dies after flowering. H 3–4ft (1–1.2m), S 2½ft (75cm). Heart-shaped, basal leaves are midgreen. Large, rounded heads of thistlelike blue flowers, surrounded by broad, spiny silvery bracts, are produced in late summer. Z4–9 H12–1.
E. x oliverianum illus. p.253.
E. paniculatum. See *E. eburneum*.
E. x tripartitum illus. p.253.
E. variifolium illus. p.286.
***E. x zabelii* 'Violetta'.** Upright perennial. H 30in (75cm), S 24in (60cm). Has rounded, midgreen leaves divided into 3–5 segments. Loose heads of thistlelike, deep violet flowers, surrounded by narrow, spiny, silvery blue bracts, appear in late summer. Z5–8 H8–5.

ERYSIMUM

BRASSICACEAE/CRUCIFERAE

Genus of annuals, biennials, and evergreen or semi-evergreen, short-lived perennials and subshrubs grown for their flowers. Is closely related to *Cheiranthus* and is suitable for borders, banks, and rock gardens. Needs sun and well-drained soil. Propagate by seed in spring or autumn or by softwood cuttings in summer.
E. x allionii, syn. *Cheiranthus x allionii* (Siberian wallflower). **'Orange Bedder'** illus. p.340.
***E.* 'Bowles Mauve'**, syn. *Cheiranthus* 'Bowles Mauve', *E.* 'E.A. Bowles'. Bushy perennial. H to 30in (75cm), S 18in (45cm). Narrowly lance-shaped, dark green leaves are 2in (5cm) long. Many clusters of small, rich mauve flowers, each with 4 spreading petals, are borne in spring and early summer. Z5–8 H8–5.
***E.* 'Bredon'**, syn. *Cheiranthus* 'Bredon', illus. p.350.
E. cheiri, syn. *Cheiranthus cheiri*. Moderately fast-growing, evergreen, bushy perennial grown as a biennial. H 10–32in (25–80cm), S 12–16in (30–40cm). Has lance-shaped, mid- to deep green leaves. Heads of fragrant, 4-petaled flowers in many colors, including red, yellow, bronze, white, and orange, are produced in spring. Z3–7 H7–1. **Bedder Series** is dwarf and has golden yellow, primrose yellow, orange, or scarlet flowers. **Fair Lady Series** bears flowers in pale pink, yellow, and creamy white, with some reds. **'Fire King'** illus. p.341. Flowers of **'Ivory White'** are creamy white.
***E.* 'E.A. Bowles'.** See *E.* 'Bowles' Mauve'.
E. helveticum, syn. *E. pumilum*, illus. p.373.
***E. x kewense* 'Harpur Crewe'**, syn. *Cheiranthus cheiri* 'Harpur Crewe', illus. p.350.
E. linifolium. Short-lived, semi-evergreen, open, dome-shaped subshrub. H to 12in (30cm), S 8in (20cm) or more. Leaves are narrowly lance-shaped and blue-gray. Tight heads of small, 4-petaled, pale violet flowers appear in early summer. Z7–9 H9–7.
***E.* 'Moonlight'**, syn. *Cheiranthus* 'Moonlight'. Evergreen, mat-forming perennial. H 2in (5cm), S 8in (20cm) or more. Leaves are small and narrowly oval. Leafy stems each carry clusters of 4-petaled, pale yellow flowers, opening in succession during summer. Makes a good rock garden plant. Needs a sheltered, sunny site and poor, gritty soil. 6–8 H8–6.
E. pumilum. See *E. helveticum*.

ERYTHRINA

LEGUMINOSAE/PAPILIONACEAE

Genus of deciduous or semi-evergreen trees, shrubs, and perennials grown for their flowers from spring to autumn. Requires full light and well-drained soil. Water containerized plants moderately, very little in winter or when leafless. Propagate by seed in spring or by semi-ripe cuttings in summer. Spider mite may be troublesome.
E. americana. See *E. coralloides*.
E. x bidwillii illus. p.143.
E. coralloides, syn. *E. americana* (Flame coral tree, Naked coral tree). Deciduous, irregularly rounded shrub or tree with somewhat prickly stems. H and S 10–20ft (3–6m). Has leaves of 3 triangular leaflets, the largest central one 4½in (11cm) long. Racemes of pealike red flowers are borne on leafless stems in early spring and summer.
E. crista-galli illus. p.143.

ERYTHRONIUM

LILIACEAE

Genus of spring-flowering, tuberous perennials grown for their pendent flowers and in some cases attractively mottled leaves. Requires partial shade and organic, well-drained soil, where tubers will not become too hot and dry in summer while dormant. Prefers cool climates. Propagate by seed in autumn. Some species increase by offsets, which should be divided in late summer. Do not allow tubers to dry out before replanting, 6in (15cm) deep.
E. americanum illus. p.434.
E. californicum illus. p.427.
'White Beauty' illus. p.409.
E. dens-canis illus. p.430.
E. grandiflorum. Spring-flowering, tuberous perennial. H 4–12in (10–30cm), S 2–3in (5–8cm). Has 2 lance-shaped, semi-erect, basal, plain bright green leaves. Stem carries 1–3 pendent, bright yellow flowers with reflexed petals. Z4–9 H9–1.
E. hendersonii illus. p.409.
E. oregonum illus. p.408.
***E.* 'Pagoda'** illus. p.415.
E. revolutum. Spring-flowering, tuberous perennial. H 8–12in (20–30cm), S 6in (15cm). Produces 2 lance-shaped, semi-erect, basal, brown-mottled green leaves and a loose spike of 1–4 pendent, pale to deep pink flowers with reflexed petals. Z5–8 H8-5.
E. tuolumnense. Spring-flowering, tuberous perennial. H to 12in (30cm), S 5–6in (12–15cm). Has 2 lance-shaped, semi-erect, basal, glossy, plain green leaves. Carries a spike of up to 10 pendent, bright yellow flowers with reflexed petals. Increases rapidly by offsets. Z3–9 H9–1.

ESCALLONIA

ESCALLONIACEAE/GROSSULARIACEAE

Genus of evergreen, semi-evergreen, or deciduous shrubs and trees grown for

their profuse, 5-petaled flowers and glossy foliage. Thrives in mild areas, where *Escallonia* is wind-resistant and ideal for hedging in coastal gardens. At the limits of hardiness, protect from strong winds and grow against a south- or west-facing wall. Requires full sun and fertile, well-drained soil. Trim hedges and wall-trained plants after flowering. Propagate by softwood cuttings in summer.
***E.* 'Apple Blossom'** illus. p.141.
***E.* 'Donard Beauty'.** Evergreen, arching shrub with slender shoots. H and S 5ft (1.5m). Bears deep pink flowers from early to midsummer among small, oval, dark green leaves. Z8–9 H9–8.
***E.* 'Donard Seedling'** illus. p.140.
***E.* 'Edinensis'.** Vigorous, evergreen, arching shrub. H 6ft (2m), S 10ft (3m). Bears small, oblong, bright green leaves. Small pink flowers are produced from early to midsummer. Is one of the hardier escallonias. Z8–9 H9–8.
***E.* 'Iveyi'** illus. p.118.
***E.* 'Langleyensis'** illus. p.142.
E. leucantha illus. p.118.
***E. rubra* 'Crimson Spire'.** Very vigorous, evergreen, upright shrub. H and S 10ft (3m). Has oval, rich green leaves and, throughout summer, tubular, deep red flowers. Z8–9 H9–8. **'Woodside'** illus. p.165.
E. virgata illus. p.137.

ESCHSCHOLZIA
Califorinia poppy

PAPAVERACEAE

Genus of annuals grown for their bright, poppylike flowers. Is suitable for rock gardens and gaps in paving. Requires sun and grows well in poor, very well-drained soil. Deadhead regularly to ensure a long flowering period. Propagate by seed sown outdoors in spring or early autumn.
E. caespitosa illus. p.336.
E. californica illus. p.339, [mixed] illus. p.338. **Ballerina Series** illus. p.322. **Thai Silk Series** illus. p.339.

ESCOBARIA

CACTACEAE

Genus of mainly spherical to columnar cacti. The stems are studded with tubercles (each with a furrow immediately above it) and very spiny, generally white aeroles. Needs full sun and poor to moderately fertile, well-drained soil. Propagate by seed in spring or by offsets in summer.
E. vivipara, syn. *Coryphantha vivipara*, illus. p.471.

ESPOSTOA

CACTACEAE

Genus of columnar cacti, each with a 10–30-ribbed stem, eventually becoming bushy or treelike with age. Most species are densely covered in woolly white hairs masking short, sharp spines. Bears cup-shaped flowers, as well as extra wool down the side of stems facing the sun, only after about 30 years. Needs full sun and very well-drained soil. Propagate by seed in spring or summer.
E. lanata illus. p.457.

EUCALYPTUS
Gum tree

MYRTACEAE

Genus of evergreen trees and shrubs grown for their bark, flowers, and aromatic foliage. Needs full sun, shelter from strong, cold winds, and fertile, well-drained soil. Plant smallest obtainable trees. Water potted plants moderately, less in winter. Attractive, young foliage of some species, normally lost with age, may be retained by cutting growth back hard in spring. Propagate by seed in spring or autumn.
E. camaldulensis (Murray red gum, River red gum). Fast-growing, evergreen, irregularly rounded tree. H 100ft (30m) or more, S 70ft (20m) or more. Young bark is gray, brown, and cream; leaves are lance-shaped, slender green or blue-green. Has umbels of small cream flowers in summer. Is a drought-resistant tree. Z9–10 H10–9.
E. coccifera illus. p.72.
E. dalrympleana illus. p.72.
E. ficifolia (Flowering gum). Moderately fast-growing, evergreen, rounded tree. H and S to 25ft (8m). Has broadly lance-shaped, glossy, deep green leaves and, in spring-summer, large panicles of many-stamened, pale to deep red flowers. Is best in acidic soil. Z9–10 H10–9.
E. glaucescens (Tingiringi gum). Evergreen, spreading tree. H 40ft (12m), S 25ft (8m). Young bark is white. Leaves are silvery blue and rounded when young, and long, narrow, and blue-gray when mature. In autumn bears clusters of many-stamened white flowers. Z9–10 H10–9.
E. globulus (Blue gum, Tasmanian blue gum). Very fast-growing, evergreen, spreading tree. H 100ft (30m), S 40ft (12m). Bark peels in ribbons. Large, oval to oblong, silvery blue leaves are long, narrow, and glossy, midgreen when mature. White flowers, consisting of tufts of stamens, appear in summer-autumn, often year-round. Z9–10 H10–9.
E. gunnii illus. p.72.
E. niphophila. See *E. pauciflora* subsp. *niphophila*.
E. pauciflora illus. p.84. subsp. ***niphophila*** (syn. *E. niphophila*) illus. p.84.
E. perriniana illus. p.100.
E. viminalis (Manna gum, Ribbon gum). Vigorous, evergreen, spreading tree. H 100ft (30m), S 50ft (15m). Bark peels on upper trunk. Lance-shaped, dark green leaves become very long, narrow, and pale green when mature. Bears clusters of stamened white flowers in summer. Z8–10 H10–8.

EUCHARIS

AMARYLLIDACEAE

Genus of evergreen bulbs grown for their fragrant white flowers that resemble large white daffodils, with a cup and 6 spreading petals. Prefers at least 50% relative humidity. Needs partial shade and organic soil. Water freely in summer. Propagate by seed when ripe or by offsets in spring.
E. amazonica of gardens. See *E.* x *grandiflora*.
E.* x *grandiflora, syn. *E. amazonica* of gardens, illus. p.425.

EUCOMIS
Pineapple flower

HYACINTHACEAE/LILIACEAE

Genus of summer- and autumn-flowering bulbs, grown for their dense spikes of flowers, which are overtopped by a tuft of small, leaflike bracts, as in a pineapple. Where not hardy, lift in autumn and overwinter indoors. Needs full sun and well-drained soil. Plant in spring and water freely in summer. Propagate by seed or division of clumps in spring.
E. autumnalis, syn. *E. undulata*. Late summer- to autumn-flowering bulb. H 8–12in (20–30cm), S 24–30in (60–75cm). Has strap-shaped, wavy-edged leaves in a semi-erect, basal tuft. Leafless stem bears small, star-shaped, pale green or white flowers in a dense spike, with cluster of leaflike bracts at apex. Z7–10.
E. bicolor illus. p.422.
E. comosa illus. p.398.
E. pallidiflora illus. p.397.
E. undulata. See *E. autumnalis*.

EUCOMMIA

EUCOMMIACEAE

Genus of one species of deciduous tree grown for its attractive foliage and tolerance of atmospheric conditions. Needs full sun and fertile, well-drained soil. Propagate by softwood cuttings in summer.
E. ulmoides (Hardy rubber tree). Deciduous, spreading tree. H 40ft (12m), S 25ft (8m). Drooping, oval leaves are pointed and glossy, dark green; when carefully pulled apart, leaf pieces stay joined by rubbery threads. Inconspicuous flowers appear in late spring before leaves. Z4–7 H7–1..

EUCRYPHIA

EUCRYPHIACEAE

Genus of evergreen, semi-evergreen or deciduous trees and shrubs grown for their foliage and often fragrant white flowers. Needs a sheltered, semi-shaded position in all but mild, wet areas, where it will withstand more exposure. Does best with roots in a cool, moist, shaded position and the crown in sun. Requires fertile, well-drained, lime-free soil, except in the case of *E. cordifolia* and *E.* x *nymansensis*. Propagate by semi-ripe cuttings in late summer.
E. cordifolia (Ulmo). Evergreen, columnar tree. H 50ft (15m), S 25ft (8m). Has oblong, wavy-edged, dull green leaves with gray down beneath. Large, roselike white flowers are borne in late summer and autumn. Z8–12 H12–7.
E. glutinosa illus. p.90.
E. lucida illus. p.90.
E. milliganii illus. p.137.
***E.* x *nymansensis* 'Nymansay'** illus. p.81.

Eugenia australis of gardens. See *Syzygium paniculatum*.
Eugenia paniculata. See *Syzygium paniculatum*.
Eugenia ugni. See *Ugni molinae*.
Euodia. Reclassified as *Tetradium*.

EUONYMUS

CELASTRACEAE

Genus of evergreen or deciduous shrubs and trees, sometimes climbing, grown for their foliage, autumn color, and fruits. Needs sun or semi-shade and any well-drained soil, although, for evergreen species in full sun, soil should not be very dry. Propagate by semi-ripe cuttings in summer or by seed in autumn. Many are prone to infestation by scale insects, *E. europaeus* and *E. japonicus* may be attacked by caterpillars; *E. japonicus* is susceptible to mildew. All parts may cause mild stomach upset if ingested.
E. alatus illus. p.148. **'Compactus'** is a deciduous, bushy, dense shrub. H 3ft (1m), S 10ft (3m). Shoots have corky wings. Oval, dark green leaves turn brilliant red in autumn. Bears inconspicuous, greenish white flowers in summer, followed by small, 4-lobed purple or red fruits. Z3–9 H9–1.
E. europaeus (Spindle tree). **'Red Cascade'** illus. p.147.
E. fortunei. Evergreen shrub, grown only as var. ***radicans*** and its cultivars, which are climbing or creeping and prostrate. H 15ft (5m) if supported, S indefinite. Bears oval, dark green leaves and inconspicuous, greenish white flowers from early to midsummer. Makes a good groundcover. Z5–9 H9–2. Foliage of **'Coloratus'** turns reddish purple in autumn-winter. **'Emerald Gaiety'**, H 3ft (1m), S 5ft (1.5m), is bushy, with rounded, white-edged, deep green leaves. **'Emerald 'n' Gold'** illus. p.177. **'Gold Tip'** see *E.f.* 'Golden Prince'. Young, rounded leaves of **'Golden Prince'** (syn. *E.f.* 'Gold Tip') are edged bright yellow, aging to creamy white. **'Kewensis'**, H 4in (10cm) or more, has slender stems and tiny leaves and forms dense mats of growth. **'Sarcoxie'**, H and S 4ft (1.2m), is vigorous, upright, and bushy, with glossy, dark green leaves. **'Silver Queen'** illus. p.151. **'Sunspot'** bears deep green leaves, each marked in center with golden yellow.
E. hamiltonianus subsp. ***sieboldianus***, syn. *E. yedoensis*. Deciduous, treelike shrub. H and S 6m (20ft) or more. Oval, midgreen leaves often turn pink and red in autumn. Tiny green flowers in late spring and early summer are followed by 4-lobed pink fruits. Z6–8 H8–6. subsp. ***sieboldianus* 'Red Elf'** illus. p.147.
E. japonicus (Japanese euonymus).

'Latifolius Albomarginatus' (syn. *E.j.* 'Macrophyllus Albus') illus. p.151. **'Macrophyllus'** is an evergreen, upright, dense shrub. H 12ft (4m), S 6ft (2m). Has very large, oval, glossy, dark green leaves and, in summer, small, star-shaped green flowers, sometimes succeeded by spherical pink fruits with orange seeds. Is good for hedging, particularly in coastal areas. Z6–8 H8–6. **'Macrophyllus Albus'** see *E.j.* 'Latifolius Albomarginatus'. Leaves of **'Ovatus Aureus'** are broadly edged with golden yellow.
E. latifolius illus. p.148.
E. myrianthus illus. p.124.
E. nanus (Dwarf burning bush). Dwarf, slightly spreading, deciduous shrub H 3ft (1m) S 4ft (1.2m). Leaves are dark green, toothed, and turn brilliant red in fall; they may be alternate or in whorls. Fruits are pink with red to orange seeds. Z2–7 H7–1. var. *turkestanicus* is more upright and most readily available.
E. oxyphyllus. Deciduous, upright shrub or tree. H and S 8ft (2.5m). Oval, dull green leaves become purplish red in autumn. Produces tiny, greenish white flowers in late spring, followed by globose, 4- or 5-lobed, deep red fruits.
E. planipes, syn. *E. sachalinensis* of gardens. Deciduous, upright, open shrub. H and S 10ft (3m). Bears oval, midgreen leaves that turn to brilliant red in autumn as large, 4- or 5-lobed red fruits open to reveal bright orange seeds. Star-shaped green flowers open in late spring. Z5–9 H9–5.
E. sachalinensis of gardens. See *E. planipes*.
E. yedoensis. See *E. hamiltonianus* var. *sieboldianus*.

EUPATORIUM

ASTERACEAE/COMPOSITAE

Genus of perennials, subshrubs, and shrubs, many of which are evergreen, grown mainly for their flowers, some also for their architectural foliage. Requires full light or partial shade. Will grow in any conditions, although most species prefer moist but well-drained soil. Water containerized plants freely when in full growth, moderately at other times. Prune shrubs lightly after flowering or in spring. Propagate by seed in spring; shrubs and subshrubs may also be propagated by softwood or greenwood cuttings in summer, and perennials by division in early spring or autumn. Spider mite and whitefly may be troublesome.
E. ageratoides. See *E. rugosum*.
E. ligustrinum, syn. *Ageratina ligustrina*, *E. micranthum*, *E. weinmannianum*. Evergreen, rounded shrub. H and S 6–12ft (2–4m). Has elliptic to lance-shaped, bright green leaves and, in autumn, fragrant white or pink flowers are produced in flattened clusters, 10–20cm (4–8in) wide.
E. maculatum (Joe Pye weed). Upright perennial with lance-shaped foliage in whorls. H 7ft (2.2m) S 3ft (1m). Flat-topped corymbs of purple flowers in late summer. Grows best on moist, alkaline soils. Z5–11 H9–1. **'Atropurpureum'** has purple tinged leaves and dark purple flower heads. Z3–7 H7–1.
E. micranthum. See *E. ligustrinum*.
E. purpureum illus. p.231.
E. rugosum, syn. *E. ageratoides*, *E. urticifolium*, illus. p.240.
E. urticifolium. See *E. rugosum*.
E. weinmannianum. See *E. ligustrinum*.

EUPHORBIA

Milkweed, Spurge

EUPHORBIACEAE

Genus of shrubs, succulents,and perennials, some of which are semi-evergreen or evergreen, and annuals. Flower heads consist of cup-shaped bracts in various colors and usually each containing several flowers lacking typical sepals and petals. Does best in sun or partial shade and in moist but well-drained soil. Propagate by basal cuttings in spring or summer, by division in spring or early autumn, or by seed in autumn or spring. All parts may cause severe discomfort if ingested; contact with their milky sap may irritate skin.
E. amygdaloides (Wood spurge). **'Purpurea'** is a semi-evergreen, erect perennial. H and S 1ft (30cm). Stems and narrowly oval leaves are green, heavily suffused purple-red. Has flower heads of cup-shaped yellow bracts in spring. Is susceptible to mildew. Z6–10 H10–2. var. ***robbiae*** (syn. *E. robbiae*) illus. p.271.
E. biglandulosa. See *E. rigida*.
E. candelabrum. Deciduous, treelike succulent. H 30ft (10m), S 15ft (5m). Erect, 3–5-angled, deeply indented, glossy, dark green stems, often marbled white, branch and rebranch in candelabra fashion. Has short-lived, spear-shaped leaves. Rounded heads of small flowers with cup-shaped, yellow bracts are produced in spring.
E. characias subsp. ***characias*** and subsp. ***wulfenii*** illus. p.156.
E. cyparissias illus. p.271.
E. epithymoides. See *E. polychroma*.
E. fulgens (Scarlet plume). Evergreen shrub of erect and arching habit. H 3–5ft (1–1.5m), S 2–3ft (60–90cm). Has elliptic to lance-shaped, mid- to deep green leaves to 4in (10cm) long. From winter to spring, bears leafy, wandlike sprays of small flowers, each cluster surrounded by 5 petal-like, bright scarlet bracts, ¾–1¼in (2–3cm) across. Z14–15 H12-10.
E. gorgonis (Gorgon's head). Deciduous, hemispherical succulent. H 3in (8cm), S 4in (10cm). Has a much-ribbed green main stem crowned by 3–5 rows of prostrate, ½in (1cm) wide stems that are gradually shed. In spring, crown also bears rounded heads of small, fragrant flowers with cup-shaped yellow bracts. Z14–15 H12-10.
E. griffithii **'Fireglow'** illus. p.258.
E. marginata illus. p.319.
E. milii illus. p.155. var. ***splendens*** (syn. *E. splendens*) is a slow-growing, mainly evergreen, spreading, spiny, semi-succulent shrub. H to 6ft (2m), S to 3ft (1m). Has oblong to oval leaves and, intermittently year-round but especially in spring, clusters of tiny flowers enclosed in large, petal-like red bracts. Z11–12 H12-1.
E. myrsinites illus. p.371.
E. nicaeensis. Clump-forming perennial with a woody base. H 30in (75cm), S 18in (45cm). Has narrowly oval, fleshy, gray-green leaves. Umbels of greenish yellow flower heads with cup-shaped bracts are borne throughout summer. Z5–8 H8–5.
E. obesa illus. p.477.
E. palustris. Bushy perennial. H and S 3ft (1m). Clusters of yellow-green flower heads with cup-shaped bracts appear in spring above oblong to lance-shaped, yellowish green leaves. Z7–9 H7–6.
E. polychroma, syn. *E. epithymoides*, illus. p.275.
E. pulcherrima illus. p.150. **'Paul Mikkelson'** is a mainly evergreen, erect, freely branching shrub. H and S 10–12ft (3–4m). Bears oval to lance-shaped, shallowly lobed leaves. From late autumn to spring has flattened heads of small, greenish white flowers with large, leaflike, bright red bracts. Z13–15 H12–1.
E. rigida, syn. *E. biglandulosa*. Evergreen, erect perennial. H and S 18in (45cm). In early spring produces terminal heads of yellow flowers with cup-shaped bracts above oblong to oval, pointed, gray-green leaves. Z7–11 H12–7.
E. robbiae. See *E. amygdaloides* var. *robbiae*.
E. schillingii illus. p.254.
E. seguieriana illus. p.271.
E. sikkimensis illus. p.254.
E. splendens. See *E. milii* var. *splendens*.

EURYA

THEACEAE

Genus of evergreen shrubs and trees grown for their foliage. Insignificant flowers are produced from spring to summer. Tolerates partial shade or full light and needs fertile, well-drained soil. Water containerized specimens freely when in full growth, less at other times. Propagate by seed when ripe or in spring or by semi-ripe cuttings in late summer.
E. emarginata illus. p.176.
E. japonica. Evergreen, bushy shrub or small tree. H and S 30ft (10m). Has elliptic to lance-shaped, bluntly toothed, leathery, dark green leaves. Inconspicuous green flowers borne from spring to summer are followed on female plants by tiny, spherical, purple-black fruits. Z8–10 H10–8. **'Variegata'** of gardens see *Cleyera japonica* 'Tricolor'.

EURYALE

NYMPHAEACEAE

Genus of one species of annual, deep-water plant grown for its floating foliage; is suitable only for a warm pond. Needs full light, constant warmth and heavy feeding. Propagate by seed in spring.
E. ferox illus. p.449.

EURYOPS

ASTERACEAE/COMPOSITAE

Genus of evergreen shrubs and subshrubs grown for their attractive leaves and showy, daisylike flower heads. Is suitable for borders and rock gardens. Needs sun and moist but well-drained soil. May not tolerate root disturbance. Propagate by softwood cuttings in summer.
E. acraeus, syn. *E. evansii* of gardens, illus. p.358.
E. evansii of gardens. See *E. acraeus*.
E. pectinatus illus. p.170.

EUSTOMA

GENTIANACEAE

Genus of annuals and perennials with poppylike flowers that are good for cutting. Makes good pot plants. Needs sun and well-drained soil. Propagate by seed sown under cover in late winter.
E. grandiflorum, syn. *E. russellianum*, *Lisianthus russellianus*, illus. p.319. **Heidi Series** has flowers in shades of rose-pink, blue, white and bicolors.
E. russellianum. See *E. grandiflorum*.

Evodia. Reclassified as *Tetradium*.

EXACUM

GENTIANACEAE

Genus of annuals, biennials and perennials, grown for their profusion of flowers, that are excellent as pot plants. Grow in sun and in well-drained soil. Propagate by seed sown in early spring for flowering the same year or in late summer for the following year.
E. affine illus. p.331.

EXOCHORDA

ROSACEAE

Genus of deciduous shrubs grown for their abundant, showy white flowers. Does best in full sun and fertile, well-drained soil. Improve vigor and flowering by thinning out old shoots after flowering. Propagate by softwood cuttings in summer or by seed in autumn. Chlorosis may be a problem on shallow, alkaline soil.
E. giraldii. Deciduous, widely arching shrub. H and S 10ft (3m). Has pinkish green young growths

and oblong leaves. Bears upright racemes of large, 5-petaled white flowers in late spring. Z6–9 H9–6.
***E. x macrantha* 'The Bride'** illus. p.135.
E. racemosa. Deciduous, arching shrub. H and S 12ft (4m). Has upright clusters of 5-petaled white flowers in late spring. Leaves are oblong and deep blue-green. Prefers acidic soil. Z5–9 H9–5.

FABIANA

SOLANACEAE

Genus of evergreen shrubs grown for their foliage and flowers. Even where hardy may need a sheltered position. Requires full sun and fertile, well-drained soil. Propagate by softwood cuttings in summer.
F. imbricata* 'Prostrata'.** Evergreen, mound-forming, very dense shrub. H 3ft (1m), S 6ft (2m). Shoots are densely covered with tiny, heathlike, deep green leaves. Bears a profusion of tubular white flowers in early summer. Z9-11 H12-10. f. ***violacea, syn. *F.i.* 'Violacea', illus. p.145.

FAGUS
Beech

FAGACEAE

Genus of deciduous trees grown for their habit, foliage, and autumn color. Insignificant flowers appear in late spring, and hairy fruits ripen in autumn to release edible, triangular beechnuts. Requires sun or semi-shade; purple-leaved forms prefer full sun, yellow-leaved forms a little shade. Grows well in any but waterlogged soil. *F. sylvatica*, when used as hedging, should be trimmed in summer. Propagate species by seed sown in autumn, and selected forms by budding in late summer. Problems may be caused by bracket fungi, canker-causing fungi, and aphids, among others.
F. americana. See *F. grandifolia*.
F. grandifolia, syn. *F. americana* (American beech). Deciduous, spreading tree. H and S 30ft (10m). Oval, silky, pale green young leaves mature to dark green in summer, then turn golden brown in autumn. Z3–9 H9–1.
F. orientalis (Oriental beech). Deciduous, spreading tree. H 70ft (20m), S 15m (50ft). Has large, oval, wavy-edged, dark green leaves that turn yellow in autumn. Z4–7 H7-1.
F. sylvatica (European beech) illus. p.68. f. ***atropunicea*** see *F.s.* f. *purpurea*. **'Aurea Pendula'** is a deciduous, slender tree with pendulous branches. H 100ft (30m), S 80ft (25m). Oval, wavy-edged leaves are bright yellow and become rich yellow and orange-brown in autumn. **'Dawyck'**, S 22ft (7m), is columnar, with erect branches; pale green leaves mature to mid- to dark green then turn rich yellow and orange-brown in autumn. **'Dawyck Purple'** is similar but has deep purple foliage. Leaves of f. ***laciniata*** are deeply cut. f. ***pendula*** (syn. *F.s.* 'Pendula') illus. p.66. f. ***purpurea*** (syn. *F.s.* f. *atropunicea*) illus. p.65. **'Purpurea Pendula'**, H and S 10ft (3m), has stiff, weeping branches and blackish purple foliage. Leaves of **'Riversii'** are very dark purple. Those of **'Rohanii'** are deeply cut and reddish purple. **'Zlatia'** produces yellow, young foliage that later becomes mid- to dark green. All cultivars above Z5–7 H7–5.

FALLOPIA,
syn. BILDERDYKIA, REYNOUTRIA

POLYGONACEAE

Genus of rhizomatous, climbing or scrambling, woody-based perennials that are good for training on pergolas and deciduous trees or for covering unsightly structures. Grow in full sun or partial shade and moist but well-drained soil. Propagate by seed sown as soon as ripe or in spring or by semi-ripe cuttings in summer or hardwood cuttings in autumn.
F. aubertii, syn. *Polygonum aubertii* (Mile-a-minute plant, Russian vine). Vigorous, deciduous, woody-stemmed, twining climber. H to 40ft (12m) or more. Leaves are broadly heart-shaped. Panicles of small white or greenish flowers aging to pink are carried in summer-autumn; they are followed by angled, pinkish white fruits. Is often confused with *F. baldschuanica*. Z5–9 H9–3.
F. aubertii of gardens. See *Fallopia baldschuanica*.
F. baldschuanica, syn. *F. aubertii* of gardens, *Polygonum baldschuanicum*, illus. p.217.

FALLUGIA

ROSACEAE

Genus of one species of deciduous shrub grown for its flowers and showy fruit clusters. Needs a hot, sunny position and well-drained soil. Propagate by softwood cuttings taken in summer or by seed sown in autumn.
F. paradoxa illus. p.136.

FARFUGIUM

ASTERACEAE/COMPOSITAE

Genus of perennials grown for their foliage and daisylike flower heads. Grow in sun or semi-shade and in moist but well-drained soil; can be grown in shallow standing water if grown in containers. Propagate by division in spring or by seed in autumn or spring.
F. japonicum, syn. *Ligularia tussilaginea*. Loosely clump-forming perennial. H and S 24in (60cm). Has large, rounded, toothed, basal, midgreen leaves, above which rise woolly, branched stems bearing clusters of daisylike, pale yellow flower heads in late summer. Z7–9 H9–7. **'Aureomaculatum'** (Leopard plant) has variegated, gold-and-white leaves and is less hardy.

FARGESIA

GRAMINEAE/POACEAE

See also GRASSES, BAMBOOS, RUSHES, and SEDGES.
F. murieliae, syn. *Arundinaria murieliae*, *Fargesia spathacea* of gardens, *Sinarundinaria murieliae*, *Thamnocalamus murieliae*, *T. spathaceus* of gardens (Muriel bamboo). Evergreen, clump-forming bamboo. H 12ft (4m), S indefinite. Has attractive gray young culms with loose, light brown sheaths and broad, apple green leaves, each one very long and drawn-out at its tip. Flower spikes are unimportant. Z5–9 H9–4.
F. nitida, syn. *Arundinaria nitida*, *Sinarundinaria nitida*. Evergreen, clump-forming bamboo. H 15ft (5m), S indefinite. Has small, pointed, mid-green leaves on dark purple stalks and several branches at each node. Stems are often purple with close sheaths. Z5–9 H9–5.
F. spathacea of gardens. See *F. murieliae*.

x FATSHEDERA

ARALIACEAE

Hybrid genus (*Fatsia japonica* 'Moseri' x *Hedera helix* 'Hibernica') of one evergreen, autumn-flowering shrub grown for its foliage. Is good trained against a wall or pillar or, if supported by stakes, grown as a house plant. Thrives in sun or shade and in fertile, well-drained soil. Propagate by semi-ripe cuttings in summer.
x *F. lizei* illus. p.152. **'Variegata'** is an evergreen, mound-forming, loose-branched shrub. H 5ft (1.5m), or more if trained as a climber, S 10ft (3m). Has rounded, deeply lobed, glossy, deep green leaves narrowly edged with creamy white. From mid- to late autumn bears sprays of small white flowers. Z8–11 H12–8.

FATSIA

ARALIACEAE

Genus of one species of evergreen, autumn-flowering shrub grown for its foliage, flowers, and fruits. Is excellent for conservatories. At limits of hardiness, provide shelter from strong winds. Tolerates sun or shade and requires fertile, well-drained soil. May be propagated by semi-ripe cuttings taken in summer or by seed sown in autumn or spring.
F. japonica, syn. *Aralia japonica*, *A. sieboldii* (Japanese aralia). Evergreen, rounded, dense shrub. H and S 10ft (3m). Has thick shoots and very large, rounded, deeply lobed, glossy, dark green leaves. In midautumn, produces dense clusters of tiny white flowers, followed by rounded black fruits. Z8–11 H12–8. **'Variegata'** illus. p.151.
F. papyrifera. See *Tetrapanax papyrifer*.

FAUCARIA

AIZOACEAE

Genus of clump-forming, stemless, perennial succulents with semi-cylindrical or 3-angled, fleshy, bright green leaves and yellow flowers that open in late afternoons in autumn. Buds and dead flowers may appear orange or red. Needs full sun and well-drained soil. Keep dry in winter and water sparingly in spring. Propagate by seed or stem cuttings in spring or summer.
F. tigrina illus. p.479.

Feijoa. Reclassified as *Acca*.

FELICIA,
syn. AGATHAEA

ASTERACEAE/COMPOSITAE

Genus of annuals, evergreen subshrubs, and (rarely) shrubs grown for their daisylike, mainly blue flower heads. Requires a position in full sun and well-drained soil. Water potted plants moderately, less when not in full growth. Dislikes wet conditions, particularly in low temperatures. Cut off dead flowering stems and cut back straggly shoots regularly. Propagate by seed in spring or by greenwood cuttings in summer or early autumn.
F. amelloides, syn. *Aster capensis* (Blue marguerite). Bushy subshrub often grown as an annual. Bears deep green leaves, to 1¼in (3cm) long, and light to deep blue flowers from summer to autumn. Z12–15 H12–1.
'Santa Anita' illus. p.168.
F. bergeriana illus. p.334.

FENESTRARIA

AIZOACEAE

Genus of clump-forming succulents with basal rosettes of fleshy leaves that have gray "windows" in their flattened tips. Needs sun and very well-drained soil. Keep nearly bone dry in winter. Propagate by seed in spring or summer.
F. aurantiaca illus. p.479.
f. ***rhopalophylla*** is a clump-forming, perennial succulent. H 2in (5cm), S 8in (20cm). Forms open cushions of erect, club-shaped, glossy glaucous to midgreen leaves, each with a flattened tip. Bears daisylike white flowers on long stems in late summer and autumn. Z13–15 H12–10.

FEROCACTUS
Barrel cactus

CACTACEAE

Genus of slow-growing, spherical cacti, becoming columnar after many years. Needs full sun and very well-drained soil. Propagate by seed in spring or summer. Treat blackened areoles with

systemic fungicide and ensure plants have good ventilation.
F. acanthodes of gardens. See *F. cylindraceus*.
F. chrysacanthus. Slow-growing, spherical cactus. H 3ft (1m), S 2ft (60cm). Green stem with 15–20 ribs is fairly densely covered with curved, yellow-white spines. In summer bears funnel-shaped yellow, rarely red, flowers, 2in (5cm) across, only on plants 10in (25cm) or more in diameter. Z12–15 H12-10.
F. cylindraceus, syn. *F. acanthodes* of gardens, illus. p.460.
F. hamatacanthus, syn. *Hamatocactus hamatacanthus*, illus. p.464.
F. latispinus. Slow-growing, flattened spherical cactus. H 8in (20cm), S 16in (40cm). Green stem with 15–20 ribs bears broad, hooked red or yellow spines. Funnel-shaped, pale yellow or red flowers appear in summer on plants over 4in (10cm) wide. Z13–15 H12-10.
F. setispinus. See *Thelocactus setispinus*.
F. wislizenii. Slow-growing, spherical cactus. H 6ft (2m), S 3ft (1m). Green stem with up to 25 ribs is covered in flattened, fish-hook, usually reddish brown spines to 2in (5cm) long. Funnel-shaped orange or yellow flowers, 2½in (6cm) across, appear in late summer, on plants over 10in (25cm) wide, which should attain this size 10–15 years after raising from seed. Z13–15 H12–10.

FERRARIA

IRIDACEAE

Genus of spring-flowering corms grown for their curious flowers with 3 large outer petals and 3 small inner ones, with very wavy edges. Is unpleasant-smelling to attract flies, which pollinate flowers. Requires full sun and well-drained soil. Plant in autumn, water during winter, and dry off after flowering. Dies down in summer. Propagate by division in late summer or by seed in autumn.
F. crispa, syn. *F. undulata*, illus. p.415.
F. undulata. See *F. crispa*.

FERULA

Giant fennel

APIACEAE/UMBELLIFERAE

Genus of mainly summer-flowering perennials grown for their bold, architectural form. Should not be confused with culinary fennel, *Foeniculum*. Requires sun and well-drained soil. Propagate by seed when fresh, in late summer.
F. communis illus. p.228.

FESTUCA

GRAMINEAE/POACEAE

See also GRASSES, BAMBOOS, RUSHES, and SEDGES.
F. glauca, syn. *F. ovina* var. *glauca* (Blue fescue). Group of evergreen, tuft-forming, perennial grasses. H and S 4in (10cm). Bears narrow leaves in various shades of blue-green to silvery white. Produces unimportant panicles of spikelets in summer. Is good for bed edging. Divide every 2–3 years in spring. Z4–8 H8–1.
F. ovina var. ***glauca.*** See *F. glauca*.

FICUS

MORACEAE

Genus of evergreen or deciduous trees, shrubs, and scrambling or root climbers grown for their foliage and for shade; a few species also for fruit. All bear insignificant clusters of flowers in spring or summer. Prefers full light or partial shade and fertile, well-drained soil. Water potted specimens moderately, very little when temperatures are low. Propagate by seed in spring or by leaf-bud or stem-tip cuttings or air-layering in summer. Spider mite and scale insects may be nuisances. The foliage may cause mild stomach upset if ingested; the sap may irritate skin or aggravate allergies.
F. benghalensis illus. p.72.
F. benjamina (Weeping fig). Evergreen, weeping tree, often with aerial roots. H and S 60–70ft (18–20m). Has slender, oval leaves, 3–5in (7–13cm) long, in lustrous, rich green. Z10–11 H12–10. **'Variegata'** illus. p.84.
F. deltoidea illus. p.152.
F. elastica (India rubber tree, Rubber plant). **'Decora'** is a strong-growing, evergreen, irregularly ovoid tree. H to 100ft (30m), S 50–70ft (15–20m). Has broadly oval, leathery, lustrous, deep green leaves, pinkish bronze when young. Z11 H12–10. **'Doescheri'** illus. p.72. Leaves of **'Variegata'** are cream-edged, mottled with gray-green.
F. lyrata (Fiddleleaf fig). Evergreen, ovoid, robust-stemmed tree. H 50ft (15m) or more, S to 30ft (10m). Fiddle-shaped leaves, 1ft (30cm) or more long, are lustrous, deep green. Z11–12 H12–7.
F. macrophylla (Australian banyan, Moreton Bay fig). Evergreen, wide-spreading, dense tree with a buttressed trunk when mature. H 70–100ft (20–30m), S 100–130ft (30–40m). Oval leaves, to 8in (20cm) long, are leathery, glossy, deep green. Z11–12 H12–7.
F. pumila, syn. *F. repens* (Creeping fig). Evergreen, root climber. H 25ft (8m); 5ft (1.5m) as a pot-grown plant. Bright green leaves are heart-shaped and ¾–1¼in (2–3cm) long when young, 1¼–3in (3–8cm) long, leathery and oval when mature. Unpalatable fruits are 2½in (6cm) long, orange at first, then flushed red-purple. Reaches adult stage only in warm regions or under cover. Pinch out branch tips to encourage branching. Z9–11 H12–1. Young leaves of **'Minima'** are shorter and narrower.
F. religiosa (Bo, Peepul, Sacred fig tree). Mainly evergreen, rounded to wide-spreading tree with prop roots from branches. H and S 70–100ft (20–30m). Leaves, 4–6in (10–15cm) long, are broadly oval to almost triangular with long, threadlike tips, pink-flushed when expanding. Z14–15 H12–10.
F. repens. See *F. pumila*.
F. rubiginosa (Port Jackson fig, Rusty-leaved fig). Evergreen, dense-headed tree with a buttressed trunk. H and S 70–100ft (20–30m) or more. Elliptic, blunt-pointed leaves, to 4in (10cm) long, are glossy, dark green above, usually with rust-colored down beneath. Z14–15 H12–10.

FILIPENDULA

Meadowsweet

ROSACEAE

Genus of spring- and summer-flowering perennials. Most grow in full sun or partial shade in moist but well-drained, leafy soil; some species, forexample *F. rubra*, will thrive in boggy sites. *F. vulgaris* needs a drier site in full sun. Propagate by seed in autumn or bydivision in autumn or winter.
F. camtschatica, syn. *F. kamtschatica*. Clump-forming perennial. H to 5ft (1.5m), S 3ft (1m). In midsummer it produces frothy, flat heads of scented, star-shaped white or pale pink flowers above large, lance-shaped, divided and cut leaves. Z3–9 H9–1.
F. hexapetala. See *F. vulgaris*. **'Flore Pleno'** see *F. vulgaris* 'Multiplex'.
F. kamtschatica. See *F. camtschatica*.
F. purpurea illus. p.245.
F. rubra illus. p.227.
F. ulmaria, syn. *Spiraea ulmaria*. **'Aurea'** illus. p.290.
F. vulgaris, syn. *F. hexapetala* (Dropwort). **'Multiplex'** (syn. *F. hexapetala* 'Flore Pleno') is an upright, rosette-forming perennial with fleshy, swollen roots. H 3ft (1m), S 1½ft (45cm). In summer produces flat panicles of rounded, double white flowers, sometimes flushed pink, above fernlike, finely divided, toothed, hairless, dark green leaves. Z4–7 H8–1.

FIRMIANA

STERCULIACEAE

Genus of mainly deciduous trees and shrubs grown for their foliage and to provide shade. Requires well-drained but moisture-retentive, fertile soil and full light or partial shade. Water containerized specimens freely when in full growth, less in winter. Pruning is tolerated if necessary. Propagate by seed when ripe or in spring.
F. platanifolia. See *F. simplex*.
F. simplex, syn. *F. platanifolia*, *Sterculia platanifolia*, illus. p.68.

FITTONIA

ACANTHACEAE

Genus of evergreen, creeping perennials grown mainly for their foliage. Is useful as a groundcover. Needs a fairly humid atmosphere. Grow in a shaded position and in well-drained soil; keep well watered but avoid waterlogging, especially in winter. If it becomes too straggly, cut back in spring. Propagate in spring or summer, with extra heat, by division or stem cuttings.
F. albivenis **Argyroneura Group**, syn. *F. argyroneura*, *F. verschaffeltii* var. *argyroneura*, illus. p.300.
Verschaffeltii Group (syn. *F. verschaffeltii*) illus. p.302.
F. argyroneura. See *F. albivenis* Argyroneura Group.
F. verschaffeltii. See *F. albivenis* Verschaffeltii Group. var. ***argyroneura*** see *F. albivenis* Argyroneura Group.

FITZROYA

CUPRESSACEAE

See also CONIFERS.
F. cupressoides, syn. *F. patagonica*, illus. p.106.
F. patagonica. See *F. cupressoides*.

FOENICULUM

APIACEAE/UMBELLIFERAE

Genus of summer-flowering biennials and perennials, some of which are grown for their umbels of yellow flowers. Is also grown for its leaves, which are both decorative in borders and used for culinary flavoring. Grow in an open, sunny position and in fertile, well-drained soil. Remove flower heads after fading to prevent self seeding. Propagate by seed in autumn.
F. vulgare (Fennel). **'Purpureum'** is an erect, branching perennial. H 6ft (2m), S 1½ft (45cm). Has very finely divided, hairlike bronze leaves and, in summer, large, flat umbels of small yellow flowers. Z6–9 H9–6.

FONTINALIS

FONTINALACEAE

Genus of evergreen, perennial, submerged water plants grown for their foliage, which provides dense cover for fish and a good site for the deposit of spawn. Grows in sun or semi-shade in streams and other running water; tolerates still water if cool, but then does not grow to full size. Propagate by division in spring.
F. antipyretica (Water moss, Willow moss). Evergreen, perennial, submerged water plant. H 1in (2.5cm), S indefinite. Forms spreading colonies of mosslike, dark olive green leaves.

FORSYTHIA

OLEACEAE

Genus of deciduous, spring-flowering shrubs grown for their usually profuse yellow flowers, which are produced before the leaves emerge. *F.* x *intermedia* 'Beatrix Farrand' and *F.* x *i.* 'Lynwood' make attractive, flowering hedges. Prefers a position in full sun and in fertile, well-drained soil. Many older varieties fail to flower well because the flower buds are not as hardy as the rest of the plant and are killed above the snow line. Thin out old

shoots and trim hedges immediately after flowering. Propagate by softwood cuttings in summer or by hardwood cuttings in autumn or winter.
***F.* x *intermedia* 'Beatrix Farrand'** illus. p.135. **'Lynwood'**, H 10ft (3m), is very free-flowering, vigorous, and upright. Z6–9 H9–6. **'Minigold'**, H and S 6ft (2m), has oblong, midgreen leaves and produces masses of small, 4-lobed yellow flowers from early to midspring. **'Spectabilis'** illus. p.134. **'Spring Glory'**, H 6ft (2m), S 5ft (1.5m), has clusters of large, 4-lobed, pale yellow flowers borne in midspring and oblong, toothed, bright green leaves.
***F.* 'Northern Gold'**, **'Northern Sun'**, and **'Vermont Sun'**have improved flower bud hardiness. Z3–9 H9–1.
F. ovata. Deciduous, bushy shrub. H and S 5ft (1.5m). Bears broadly oval, toothed, dark green leaves. Produces small, 4-lobed, bright yellow flowers in early spring. Z5–7 H7–5. **'Ottawa'** was selected for its bud hardiness as was**'Tetragold'**, with larger flowers.
F. suspensa illus. p.131.

FOTHERGILLA

HAMAMELIDACEAE

Genus of deciduous, spring-flowering shrubs grown for their autumn color and fragrant flowers, each with a dense, bottlebrush-like cluster of stamens, which open before or as leaves emerge. Grows in sun or semi-shade but colors best in full sun. Requires moist, peaty, acidic soil. Propagate by softwood cuttings taken in summer.
F. gardenii (Witch alder). Deciduous, bushy, dense shrub. H and S 3ft (1m). Produces dense clusters of tiny, fragrant white flowers that appear from mid- to late spring, usually before broadly oval, dark blue-green leaves emerge. Leaves turn brilliant red in autumn. Z4–8 H8–1.
F. major, syn. *F. monticola*, illus. p.127.
F. monticola. See *F. major*.

Fragaria indica. See *Duchesnea indica*.

FRAILEA

CACTACEAE

Genus of spherical to columnar cacti with tuberculate ribs. Bears short spines, mostly bristlelike. In summer produces masses of buds, most of which develop into small, spherical, shiny pods without opening. Needs partial shade and very well-drained soil. Is not well-adapted to long periods of drought. Propagate by seed in spring or summer.
F. pulcherrima. See *F. pygmaea*.
F. pygmaea, syn. *F. pulcherrima*, illus. p.477.

FRANCOA

SAXIFRAGACEAE

Genus of summer- and early autumn-flowering perennials. Needs full sun and fertile, well-drained soil. Propagate by seed or division in spring.
F. appendiculata (Bridal wreath). Clump-forming perennial. H 24in (60cm), S 18in (45cm). Racemes of small, bell-shaped, pale pink flowers spotted with deep pink at base appear on graceful, erect stems from summer to early autumn above oblong to oval, lobed, hairy, crinkled, dark green leaves.
F. sonchifolia. Clump-forming perennial. H 30in (75cm), S 18in (45cm). Bears racemes of cup-shaped, red-marked pink flowers from summer to early autumn. Lobed leaves each have a large, terminal lobe. Z7–9 H9–7.

FRANKLINIA

THEACEAE

Genus of one species of deciduous tree or shrub grown for its flowers and autumn color. Needs full sun and moist but well-drained, neutral to acidic soil. Propagate by softwood cuttings in summer, by seed in autumn or by hardwood cuttings in early winter.
F. alatamaha. Deciduous, upright tree or shrub. H and S 15ft (5m) or more. Large, shallowly cup-shaped white flowers with yellow stamens open in late summer and early autumn. Oblong, glossy, bright green leaves turn red in autumn. Z6–9 H9–6.

FRAXINUS
Ash

OLEACEAE

Genus of deciduous trees and shrubs grown mainly for their foliage of paired leaflets; flowers are usually insignificant. Requires a position in sun and fertile, well-drained but not too dry soil. Propagate species by seed in autumn, selected forms by budding in summer.
F. americana (White ash). Fast-growing, deciduous, spreading tree. H 80ft (25m), S 50ft (15m). Leaves are dark green with 5–9 oval to lance-shaped leaflets that yellow or purple in autumn. Z6–9 H9–6. **'Autumn Blaze'** and **'Autumn Purple'** were selected for their reddish purple fall color. **'Skyline'** has a more upright form and turns orange-red in autumn.
F. angustifolia, syn. *F. oxycarpa* (Narrow-leaved ash). Deciduous, spreading, elegant tree. H 80ft (25m), S 40ft (12m). Leaves usually consist of 9–11 slender, lance-shaped, glossy, dark green leaflets that are golden yellow in autumn. Z6–9 H9–6. **'Raywood'** (Claret ash) is vigorous, H 70ft (20m), S 50ft (15m). Leaves have 5–7 narrowly oval leaflets that turn bright reddish purple in autumn.
F. excelsior (European ash). Vigorous, deciduous, spreading tree. H 100ft (30m), S 70ft (20m). Dark green leaves, with usually 9–11 oval leaflets, sometimes become yellow in autumn. Black leaf buds are conspicuous in winter. Z5–8 H8–5. f. ***diversifolia*** has leaves that are simple or with only 3 leaflets. Leaves of **'Jaspidea'** are yellow in spring and turn golden in autumn; shoots are yellow in winter. **'Pendula'**, H 50ft (15m), S 25–30ft (8–10m), has branches weeping to the ground.
F. nigra (Black ash). Fast-growing, upright, deciduous tree. H 50ft (15m) S 25ft (8m). Leaves have 11 tapering, dark green leaflets and turn yellow in fall. Z3–8 H8–1. **'Fallgold'** is a sterile selection with long-lasting golden autumn color.
F. ornus illus. p.76.
F. oxycarpa. See *F. angustifolia*.
F. pennsylvanica (Green ash, Red ash). Fast-growing, deciduous, spreading tree. H and S 70ft (20m). Leaves of usually 7 or 9 narrowly oval, dull green leaflets are often velvety beneath, like the shoots, and turn yellow in autumn. Z3–9 H9–4. **'Patmore'** is disease-resistant, with long-lasting, glossy leaves, but it does not bear fruit.
F. velutina illus. p.80.

FREESIA

IRIDACEAE

Genus of winter- and spring-flowering corms grown for their usually fragrant, funnel-shaped flowers, which are popular for cutting. Requires full sun and well-drained soil. Plant in autumn and water throughout winter. Support with twigs or small stakes. Dry off corms after flowering. Plant specially prepared corms outdoors in spring for flowering in summer. Propagate by offsets in autumn or by seed in spring.
F. alba of gardens. See *F. lactea*.
F. armstrongii. See *F. corymbosa*.
F. corymbosa, syn. *F. armstrongii*. Late winter- and spring-flowering corm. H to 12in (30cm), S 1½–2½in (4–6cm). Has narrowly sword-shaped, erect, basal leaves. Flower stem bends horizontally near the top and bears a spike of unscented, upright pink flowers, 1¼–1½in (3–3.5cm) long, with yellow bases. Z10–11 H12–6.
***F.* 'Golden Melody'.** Winter- and spring-flowering corm. H to 12in (30cm), S 1½–2½in (4–6cm). Is similar to *F. corymbosa* but has larger, fragrant flowers, yellow throughout. Z10–11 H12–6.
F. lactea, syn. *F. alba* of gardens, *F. refracta* var. *alba*. Late winter- and spring-flowering corm. H 8–12in (20–30cm), S 1½–2½in(4–6cm). Has narrowly sword-shaped, erect leaves in a basal fan. Leafless stems bear loose spikes of very fragrant white flowers, each 2–3in (5–8cm) long. Z10–11 H12–6.
***F.* 'Oberon'** illus. p. 425.
***F. refracta* var. *alba*.** See *F. lactea*.
***F.* 'Romany'.** Winter- and spring-flowering corm. H to 12in (30cm), S 1½–2½in (4–6cm). Is similar to *F. corymbosa* but has fragrant, double, pale mauve flowers. Z10–11 H12–6.
***F.* 'White Swan'.** Winter- and spring-flowering corm. H to 12in (30cm), S 1½–2½in (4–6cm). Is similar to *F. corymbosa* but has very fragrant white flowers with cream throats. Z10–11 H12–6.

Fremontia. Reclassified as *Fremontodendron*.

FREMONTODENDRON,
syn. FREMONTIA
Flannel flower

STERCULIACEAE

Genus of vigorous, evergreen or semi-evergreen shrubs grown for their large, very showy flowers. At the limits of hardiness, plant against a south- or west-facing wall. Needs full sun and light, not too rich, well-drained soil. In mild areas may be grown as a spreading shrub, but it needs firm staking when young. Resents being transplanted. Propagate by semi-ripe cuttings in summer or by seed in autumn or spring. Contact with the foliage and shoots may irritate skin.
***F.* 'California Glory'** illus. p.123.
F. californicum. Vigorous, evergreen or semi-evergreen, upright shrub. H 20ft (6m), S 12ft (4m), when grown against a wall. Large, saucer-shaped, bright yellow flowers are borne amid dark green leaves, each with 3 rounded lobes, from late spring to midautumn. Z8–10 H10–8.
F. mexicanum. Vigorous, evergreen or semi-evergreen, upright shrub. H 20ft (6m), S 12ft (4m) when grown against a wall. Dark green leaves have 5 deep, rounded lobes. Bears a profusion of large, saucer-shaped, deep golden yellow flowers from late spring to midautumn. Z9–10 H10–9.
***F.* 'Pacific Sunset'** (illus. p.53). Upright, evergreen shrub. H 15ft (5m), S 10–12ft (3–4m). Rounded, strongly lobed leaves are dark green. In summer produces saucer-shaped, bright yellow flowers, to 2½in (6cm) across, with long, slender-pointed lobes. Z9–10 H10–9.

FRITHIA

AIZOACEAE

Genus of one species of rosette-forming succulent. Needs sun and well-drained soil. Propagate by seed in spring or summer.
F. pulchra illus. p.473.

FRITILLARIA

LILIACEAE

Genus of spring-flowering bulbs grown for their pendent, mainly bell-shaped flowers on leafy stems. Protect smaller, 2–6in (5–15cm) high species in cold frames or cold greenhouses. Needs full sun or partial shade and well-drained soil that dries out slightly in summer when bulbs are dormant but that does not become sunbaked. Grow *F. meleagris*, which is good for naturalizing in grass, in moisture-retentive soil. Propagate by offsets in summer or by seed in autumn or winter.
F. acmopetala illus. p.414.
F. bucharica. Spring-flowering bulb. H 4–14in (10–35cm), S 2in (5cm).

Stems each bear scattered, lance-shaped, gray-green leaves and a raceme of up to 10 cup-shaped, green-tinged white flowers, ⅝–¾in (1.5–2cm) long.
F. camschatcensis illus. p.413.
F. chitralensis illus. p.402.
F. cirrhosa illus. p.414.
F. crassifolia. Spring-flowering bulb. H 4–8in (10–20cm), S 2in (5cm). Has scattered, lance-shaped gray leaves. Stems each produce 1–3 bell-shaped green flowers, ¾–1in (2–2.5cm) long and checkered with brown. Z8–6 H6–8.
F. delphinensis. See *F. tubiformis*.
F. imperialis illus. p.396. **'Lutea'** is a spring-flowering bulb. H to 5ft (1.5m), S 9–12in (23–30cm). Leafy stems each bear lance-shaped, glossy, pale green leaves in whorls and a head of up to 5 widely bell-shaped yellow flowers, 2in (5cm) long, crowned by small, leaflike bracts. **'Rubra Maxima'** is very robust with red flowers. Both Z5–9 H9–4.
F. meleagris illus. p.413.
F. michailovskyi. Spring-flowering bulb. H 4–8in (10–20cm), S 2in (5cm). Has lance-shaped gray leaves scattered on stem. Bears 1–4 bell-shaped, ¾–1¼in (2–3cm) long flowers colored purplish brown with upper third of petals bright yellow. Z5–8 H8–5.
F. pallidiflora illus. p.415.
F. persica illus. p.396. **'Adiyaman'** is a spring-flowering bulb. H to 5ft (1.5m), S 4in (10cm). Has narrowly lance-shaped gray leaves along stem. Produces a spike of 10–20 or more narrowly bell-shaped, deep blackish purple flowers, ⅝–¾in (1.5–2cm) long. Z6–8 H8–6.
F. pontica illus. p.414.
F. pudica illus. p.434.
F. pyrenaica illus. p.413.
F. raddeana illus. p.396.
F. recurva illus. p.396.
F. sewerzowii, syn. *Korolkowia sewerzowii*. Spring-flowering bulb. H 6–10in (15–25cm), S 3–4in (8–10cm). Stems bear scattered, broadly lance-shaped leaves. Produces a spike of up to 10 narrowly bell-shaped green or metallic purplish blue flowers, 1–1½in (2.5–3.5cm) long, with flared mouths.
F. tubiformis, syn. *F. delphinensis*. Spring-flowering bulb. H 6–14in (15–35cm), S 2–3in (5–8cm). Stems carry scattered, narrowly lance-shaped gray leaves and a solitary, broadly bell-shaped, purplish pink flower, 1½–2in (3.5–5cm) long, conspicuously checkered and suffused gray outside. Z7–9 H9–7.
F. verticillata illus. p.396.

FUCHSIA

ONAGRACEAE

Genus of deciduous or evergreen shrubs and trees grown for their flowers, usually borne from early summer to early autumn. If temperatures remains above 39°F (4°C), deciduous plants are evergreen, but temperatures above 90°F (32°C) should be avoided. Prolonged low temperatures cause loss of top growth. If top growth dies in winter, cut back to ground level in spring. Needs a sheltered, partially shaded position, except where stated otherwise, and fertile, moist but well-drained soil. When grown as pot plants in a greenhouse, fuchsias also need high-nitrogen fertilizer and, when flowering, plenty of potassium. Propagate by softwood cuttings in any season.

Tubular flowers are almost always pendulous and often bicolored, with petals of one hue and a tube and 4 sepals of another. Leaves are oval and midgreen unless otherwise stated. Spherical to cylindrical, usually blackish purple fruits are edible, but mostly poorly flavored. Upright types may be trained as compact bushes or standards or, with more difficulty, as pyramids. Lax or trailing plants are good for hanging baskets but may be trained on trellises; if they are used for summer bedding, they require staking.

Heights given in descriptions below are of plants grown in frost-free conditions. See also feature panel pp.164–5.

Fuchsias do well in Z9–11 H12–9 except where otherwise indicated.

***F.* 'Alice Hoffman'.** Deciduous, compact shrub. H and S 2½ft (75cm). Has bronze foliage and small, semi-double flowers with rose-red tubes and sepals and rose-veined white petals.
***F.* 'Annabel'** (illus. p.164). Deciduous, upright shrub. H 3ft (1m), S 2½ft (75cm). Produces large, double, pink-tinged, creamy white flowers amid pale green leaves. Makes an excellent standard.
***F.* 'Applause'.** Deciduous, lax, upright shrub. H 12–18in (30–40cm), S 18–24in (45–60cm). Bears very large, double flowers with short, thick, pale carmine tubes, very broad carmine sepals with a pale central streak, and many, spreading, deep orange-red petals. Produces best color in shade. Needs staking as a bush but will trail with weights.
F. arborea. See *F. arborescens*.
F. arborescens, syn. *F. arborea* (Tree fuchsia; illus. p.164). Evergreen, upright tree. H 25ft (8m), S 8ft (2.5m). Tender. Foliage is mid- to dark green. Erect heads of tiny, pale mauve to pink flowers borne year-round are followed by black fruits with gray-blue bloom. May also be grown as a pot plant.
***F.* 'Auntie Jinks'.** Deciduous, trailing shrub. H 6–8in (15–20cm), S 8–16in (20–40cm). Bears small, single flowers with pink-red tubes, cerise-margined white sepals, and white-shaded purple petals.
***F.* 'Autumnale'**, syn. *F.* 'Burning Bush' (illus. p.164). Deciduous, lax shrub grown mainly for its foliage. H 6ft (2m), S 20in (50cm). Bears variegated red, gold, and bronze leaves. Flowers have red tubes and sepals with reddish purple petals. Is suitable for a hanging basket or for training as a weeping standard.
F. x bacillaris, syn. *F. parviflora* of gardens (illus. p.165). Group of deciduous, lax shrubs. H and S 2½ft (75cm). Small leaves are mid- to dark green. Bears minute white, pink, or crimson flowers (color varying according to sun), sometimes followed by glossy black fruits. Is suitable for a rock garden or hanging basket.
***F.* 'Ballet Girl'** (illus. p.164). Deciduous, upright shrub. H 12–18in (30–45cm), S 18–30in (45–75cm). Produces large, double flowers with bright cerise tubes and sepals, and white petals with cerise veins at the base.
***F.* 'Bicentennial'** (illus. p.164). Deciduous, lax shrub. H 12–18in (30–45cm), S 18–24in (45–60cm). Bears medium, double flowers with thin white tubes, orange sepals, and double corollas with magenta centers surrounded by orange petals.
F. boliviana. Fast-growing, deciduous, upright shrub. H 10ft (3m), S 3ft (1m). Tender. Has large, soft, gray-green leaves with reddish midribs. Long-tubed scarlet flowers, bunched at ends of branches, are followed by pleasantly flavored black fruits. Needs a large pot and plenty of space to grow well. Resents being pinched back. Is very susceptible to whitefly. var. ***alba*** (syn. *F.b.* var. *luxurians* 'Alba', *F. corymbiflora* 'Alba'; illus. p.165) has flowers with white tubes and sepals and scarlet petals, followed by green fruits. Z13–15 H12–9.
***F.* 'Bon Accorde'.** Vigorous, deciduous, upright shrub. H 5ft (1.5m), S 20in (50cm). Small, erect flowers have white tubes and sepals and pale purple petals.
***F.* 'Brookwood Belle'.** Deciduous, lax, bushy shrub with strong, short-jointed stems. H and S 18–24in (45–60cm). Medium, double flowers have deep cerise tubes and sepals and white petals flushed pink and veined deep rose-pink.
***F.* 'Brutus'.** Vigorous, deciduous, upright shrub. H 5ft (1.5m), S 3ft (1m). Single or semi-double flowers have crimson-red tubes and sepals and deep purple petals.
***F.* 'Burning Bush'.** See *F.* 'Autumnale'.
***F.* 'Cascade'** (illus. p.165). Deciduous, trailing shrub. H 6ft (2m), S indefinite. Bears red-tinged white tubes and sepals and deep carmine petals. Is excellent grown in a hanging basket.
***F.* 'Celia Smedley'** (illus. p.165). Vigorous, deciduous, upright shrub. H 5ft (1.5m), S 3ft (1m). Large, single or semi-double flowers have greenish white tubes, pale pinkish white sepals, and currant red petals. Is best when trained as a standard.
***F.* 'Checkerboard'.** Vigorous, deciduous, upright shrub with strong stems. H 30–36in (75–90cm), S 18–30in (45–75cm). Produces medium, single flowers with slightly recurved, long red tubes, red sepals turning white, and white-based, dark red petals.
***F.* 'Cloverdale Pearl'.** Deciduous, upright shrub. H 3ft (1m), S 2½ft (75cm). Foliage is midgreen with crimson midribs. Flowers have pinkish white tubes, pink-veined white petals, and green-tipped pink sepals. Is readily trained as a standard.
***F.* 'Coquet Bell'.** Vigorous, deciduous, upright shrub. H 5ft (1.5m), S 3ft (1m). Has a profusion of single or semi-double flowers with pinkish red tubes and sepals and red-veined, pale mauve petals.
***F.* 'Coralle'**, syn. *F.* 'Koralle' (illus. p.165). Deciduous, upright shrub. H and S 3ft (1m). Tender. Foliage is velvety and deep green. Salmon-orange flowers with long, narrow tubes and small sepals and petals are bunched at branch ends. Is useful for summer bedding and as a specimen plant. Prefers sun. Z13–15 H12–9.
***F. corymbiflora* 'Alba'.** See *F. boliviana* var. *alba*.
***F.* 'Dark Eyes'.** Deciduous, bushy, upright shrub. H 18–24in (45–60cm), S 24–30in (60–75cm). Bears medium, double flowers that hold their shape for a long period. The tubes and upturned sepals are deep red, and the petals are deep violet-blue.
F. denticulata. Deciduous, straggling shrub. H 12ft (4m), S indefinite. Tender. Leaves are glossy, dark green above and reddish green beneath. Flowers have long, crimson tubes, green-tipped, pale pink sepals, and vermilion petals. With good cultivation under cover, flowers appear throughout autumn and winter.
***F.* 'Display'.** Deciduous, upright shrub. H 3ft (1m), S 2½ft (75cm). Bears saucer-shaped flowers in shades of pink.
***F.* 'Dollar Princess'** (illus. p.164). Deciduous, upright shrub. H 3ft (1m), S 2½ft (75cm). Small, double flowers have cerise-red tubes and sepals and purple petals.
***F.* 'Estelle Marie'** (illus. p.165). Deciduous, upright shrub. H 3ft (1m), S 20in (50cm). Flowers with white tubes, green-tipped white sepals, and mauve petals are borne above foliage. Is excellent for summer bedding.
***F.* 'Flash'.** Fast-growing, deciduous, stiffly erect shrub. H 8ft (2.5m), S 20in (50cm). Produces small red flowers amid small leaves.
***F.* 'Flirtation Waltz'.** Vigorous, deciduous, upright shrub. H 3ft (1m), S 2½ft (75cm). Has large, double flowers with petals in shades of pink, and white tubes and sepals.
F. fulgens (illus. p.165). Deciduous, upright shrub with tubers. H 6ft (2m), S 3ft (1m). Tender. Long-tubed orange flowers hang in short clusters amid large, pale green leaves and are followed by edible but acidic green fruits. Tubers may be stored dry for winter. May also be propagated by division of tubers in spring. Is highly susceptible to whitefly. Z13–15 H12–9.
***F.* 'Garden News'.** Deciduous, upright shrub with strong stems. H and S 18–24in (45–60cm). Medium, double flowers have short, thick pink tubes,

FUCHSIA

frost pink sepals, and magenta-rose petals becoming rose-pink at the base.

***F.* 'Genii'.** Deciduous, erect shrub. H 5ft (1.5m), S 2½ft (75cm). Has golden green foliage. Produces small flowers with cerise-red tubes and sepals and reddish purple petals. Makes a good standard.

***F.* 'Golden Dawn'** (illus. p.164). Deciduous, upright shrub. H 5ft (1.5m), S 2½ft (75cm). Flowers are salmon-pink. Is good for training as a standard.

***F.* 'Golden Marinka'** (illus. p.164). Deciduous, trailing shrub. H 6ft (2m), S indefinite. Has red flowers and variegated golden yellow leaves with red veins. Is excellent for a hanging basket.

***F.* 'Gruss aus dem Bodethal'** (illus. p.164). Deciduous, upright shrub. H 3ft (1m), S 2½ft (75cm). Small, single or semi-doubles crimson flowers open almost black, becoming larger and paler with age.

***F.* 'Harry Gray'** (illus. p.164). Deciduous, lax shrub. H 6ft (2m), S indefinite. Bears a profusion of double flowers with pale pink tubes, green-tipped white sepals, and white to pale pink petals. Is excellent in a hanging basket.

***F.* 'Heidi Weiss'**, syn. *F.* 'White Ann' of gardens, *F.* 'White Heidi Ann' of gardens (illus. p.164). Deciduous, upright shrub. H 3ft (1m), S 2½ft (75cm). Has double flowers with red tubes and sepals and cerise-veined white petals. Is good for training as a standard.

***F.* 'Hula Girl'.** Deciduous, trailing shrub. H 6ft (2m), S indefinite. Bears large, double flowers with deep rose-pink tubes and sepals and pink-flushed white petals. Does best in a large hanging basket or when trained against a trellis.

***F.* 'Jack Shahan'** (illus. p.164). Vigorous, deciduous, trailing shrub. H 6ft (2m), S indefinite. Has large, pale to deep pink flowers. Is excellent for a hanging basket or for training into a weeping standard or upright against a trellis.

***F.* 'Joy Patmore'.** Vigorous, deciduous, upright shrub. H 5ft (1.5m), S 3ft (1m). Flowers have white tubes, green-tipped white sepals, and cerise petals with white bases. Makes a good standard.

***F.* 'Koralle'.** See *F.* 'Coralle'.

***F.* 'La Campanella'** (illus. p.165). Deciduous, trailing shrub. H 5ft (1.5m), S indefinite. Has small, semi-double flowers with white tubes, pink-flushed white sepals, and cerise-purple petals. Does best in a hanging basket or trained against a trellis.

***F.* 'Lady Thumb'** (illus. p.164). Deciduous, upright, dwarf shrub. H and S 20in (50cm). Has small, semi-double flowers with reddish pink tubes and sepals and pink-veined white petals. May be trained as a miniature standard.

***F.* 'Lena'.** Deciduous, lax shrub. H and S 3ft (1m). Bears double flowers with pale pink sepals and tubes and pink-flushed purple petals. Makes a good standard.

***F.* 'Leonora'** (illus. p.164). Vigorous, deciduous, upright shrub. H 5ft (1.5m), S 3ft (1m). Flowers are pink with green-tipped sepals. Is good for training as a standard.

***F.* 'Love's Reward'** (illus. p.165). Deciduous, upright, short-jointed shrub. H and S 12–18in (30–45cm). Small to medium, single flowers have white to pale pink tubes and sepals and violet-blue petals.

***F.* 'Lye's Unique'** (illus. p.165). Vigorous, deciduous, upright shrub. H 5ft (1.5m), S 3ft (1m). Has small flowers with long white tubes and sepals and orange-red petals. Excellent for training as a large pyramid.

F. magellanica (Lady's eardrops; illus. p.164). Deciduous, upright shrub. H 10ft (3m), S 6ft (2m). Small flowers with red tubes, long red sepals, and purple petals are followed by black fruits. **'Alba'** see *F.m.* var. *molinae*. var. ***molinae*** (syn. *F.m.* 'Alba') has very pale pink flowers. Z6 (with extensive protection)–9 H9–6.var. ***molinae* 'Enstone'** has gold and green variegated foliage. var. ***molinae* 'Sharpitor'** produces cream and pale green variegated leaves.

***F.* 'Margaret Brown'** (illus. p.45). Deciduous, free-flowering, upright shrub. H and S 2–3ft (60–90cm). Has strong stems and light green foliage and bears small, single, 2-tone pink flowers in summer.

***F.* 'Marinka'.** Deciduous, trailing shrub. H 6ft (2m), S indefinite. Red flowers with darker petals that are folded at outer edges are produced amid dark green leaves with crimson midribs. Foliage becomes discolored in full sun or cold winds. Is excellent in a hanging basket.

***F.* 'Micky Goult'.** Vigorous, deciduous, upright shrub. H 3ft (1m), S 2½ft (75cm). Small flowers with white tubes, pink-tinged white sepals, and pale purple petals are produced amid pale green foliage.

***F.* 'Mieke Meursing'.** Deciduous, upright shrub. H 3ft (1m), S 2½ft (75cm). Single to semi-double flowers have red tubes and sepals and pale pink petals with cerise veins.

***F.* 'Mrs. Lovell Swisher'** (illus. p.165). Deciduous, upright shrub. H 18–24in (45–60cm), S 12–24in (30–60cm). Produces masses of small, single flowers with flesh-pink tubes, pinkish white sepals, and deep rose-pink petals.

***F.* 'Mrs. Popple'** (illus. p.164). Vigorous, deciduous, upright shrub. H 5ft (1.5m), S 2½ft (75cm). Has flowers with red tubes, overhanging red sepals, and purple petals. Where completely hardy it makes an attractive hedge.

***F.* 'Mrs. Rundle'.** Vigorous, deciduous, lax shrub. H and S 2½ft (75cm). Tender. Produces large flowers with long pink tubes, green-tipped pink sepals, and vermilion petals. Is good for training as a standard or growing in a large hanging basket.

***F.* 'Nancy Lou'.** Vigorous, deciduous, upright shrub. H and S 3ft (1m). Large, double flowers have pink tubes, upright, green-tipped pink sepals, and bright white petals.

***F.* 'Nellie Nuttall'** (illus. p.164). Vigorous, deciduous, upright shrub. H 3ft (1m), S 2½ft (75cm). Flowers with rose-red tubes and sepals and white petals are borne well above foliage. Is especially suitable for summer bedding; is also good as a standard.

***F.* 'Other Fellow'** (illus. p.164). Deciduous, upright shrub. H 5ft (1.5m), S2½ft (75cm). Has small flowers with white tubes and sepals and pink petals.

***F.* 'Pacquesa'.** Vigorous, deciduous, upright shrub. H 3ft (1m), S 2½ft (75cm). Has flowers with deep red tubes and sepals and red-veined white petals. Is good for training as a standard.

F. parviflora **of gardens.** See *F.* x *bacillaris*.

***F.* 'Peppermint Stick'** (illus. p.164). Deciduous, upright shrub. H 5ft (1.5m), S 3ft (1m). Large, double flowers have carmine-red tubes and sepals and pink-splashed purple petals. Makes a good standard.

***F.* 'Phyllis'.** Deciduous, upright shrub. H 6ft (2m), S 3ft (1m). Single to semi-double flowers with rose-red tubes and sepals and crimson petals are followed by masses of black fruits. It makes an attractive hedge.

***F.* 'Pink Fantasia'.** Deciduous, stiff, upright shrub. H 12–18in (30–40cm), S 18–24in (45–60cm). Bears single, upward-looking flowers in profusion, with white tubes and sepals blushed dark pink, and dark purple petals veined pink with white bases. Excellent for borders or pots.

***F.* 'Pink Galore'** (illus. p.164). Deciduous, trailing shrub. H 5ft (1.5m), S indefinite. Has large, double, pale pink flowers. Grows best in a large hanging basket or when trained against a trellis.

F. procumbens (illus. p.165). Deciduous, prostrate shrub. H 4in (10cm), S indefinite. Produces tiny, erect, petalless, yellow-tubed flowers with purple sepals and bright blue pollen. Has small, dark green leaves and large red fruits. Good in a rock garden as well as a hanging basket. Encourage flowering by root restriction or growing in poor, sandy soil.

***F.* 'Red Spider'** (illus. p.164). Deciduous, trailing shrub. H 5ft (1.5m), S indefinite. Has long red flowers with long, narrow, spreading sepals and darker petals. Is best in a large hanging basket or when trained against a trellis.

***F.* 'Riccartonii'** (illus. p.164). Deciduous, stiff, upright shrub. H 6ft (2m), S 5ft (1.5m). Has small flowers with red tubes, broad, overhanging red sepals, and purple petals. Where completely hardy it makes an attractive hedge. Many plants sold under name of *F.* 'Riccartonii' are lax hybrids of *F. magellanica*.

***F.* 'Rose Fantasia'.** Deciduous, stiff, upright shrub. H 12–18in (30–40cm), S 18–24in (45–60cm). Produces single, upward-looking flowers in profusion, with rose-pink tubes, dark rose-pink sepals with green tips, and red-purple petals veined rose-pink. Excellent plant for either borders or pots.

***F.* 'Rose of Castile'** (illus. p.165). Vigorous, deciduous, upright shrub. H 5ft (1.5m), S 3ft (1m). Produces small flowers with white tubes, green-tipped white sepals, and purple-flushed pink petals. Makes a good standard.

***F.* 'Rough Silk'.** Vigorous, deciduous, trailing shrub. H 6ft (2m), S indefinite. Bears large flowers with pink tubes, long, spreading pink sepals, and wine red petals. Grows best in a large hanging basket or when trained against a trellis.

***F.* 'Royal Velvet'.** Vigorous, deciduous, upright shrub. H 5ft (1.5m), S 2½ft (75cm). Has large, double flowers with red tubes and sepals and deep purple petals, splashed deep pink. Is an excellent standard.

***F.* 'Rufus'** (illus. p.164). Vigorous, deciduous, upright shrub. H 5ft (1.5m), S 2½ft (75cm). Has a profusion of small, bright red flowers. Is easily trained as a standard.

***F.* 'Shellford'.** Deciduous, upright, short-jointed shrub. H 14–20in (35–50cm), S 18–24in (45–60cm). Bears masses of medium-sized, single flowers with slightly fluted, baby pink tubes, long, narrow, baby pink sepals, and white petals with slight pink veining at the base. Suitable for all forms of training.

F. splendens. Deciduous, upright shrub. H 6ft (2m), S 3ft (1m). Small flowers, with broad orange tubes pinched in their middles and short green sepals and petals, appear in spring amid pale green foliage. Is very susceptible to whitefly.

***F.* 'Strawberry Delight'.** Deciduous, lax shrub. H and S 3ft (1m). Leaves are yellowish green and slightly bronzed. Large, double flowers have red tubes and sepals and pink-flushed white petals. Is excellent as a standard or hanging basket plant.

***F.* 'Swingtime'** (illus. p.164). Vigorous, deciduous, lax shrub. H and S 3ft (1m). Has large, double flowers with red tubes and sepals and red-veined, creamy white petals. Makes a good standard or hanging basket plant.

***F.* 'Texas Longhorn'.** Deciduous, lax shrub. H and S 2½ft (75cm). Very large, double flowers have red tubes, long, spreading red sepals, and cerise-veined white petals. Grow as a standard or in a hanging basket.

***F.* 'Thalia'** (illus. p.165). Deciduous, upright shrub. H and S 3ft (1m). Tender. Foliage is dark maroon and velvety. Long, slender flowers with long red tubes, small red sepals, and small, orange-red petals are bunched at ends of branches. Makes an excellent specimen plant in summer bedding schemes. Prefers full sun.

F. thymifolia. Deciduous, lax shrub. H and S 3ft (1m). Has pale green foliage and a few minute, greenish

white flowers that age to purplish pink. Bears black fruits on female plants if pollen-bearing plants of this species or of *F.* x *bacillaris* are also grown.
***F.* 'Tom Thumb'** (illus. p.164). Deciduous, upright shrub. H and S 20in (50cm). Bears small flowers with red tubes and sepals and mauve-purple petals. May be trained as a miniature standard.
***F.* 'Tom West'** (illus. p.165). Deciduous, upright, lax shrub. H and S 12–24in (30–60cm). Has green and cream variegated foliage and small, single flowers with red tubes and sepals and purple petals.
F. triphylla. Deciduous, upright shrub, sometimes confused with *F.* 'Thalia'. H and S 20in (50cm). Tender. Spikes of narrow, long-tubed, bright reddish orange flowers with small petals and sepals are borne above dark bronze-green leaves that are purple beneath. Is very difficult to grow.
***F.* 'White Ann'** of gardens. See *F.* 'Heidi Weiss'.
***F.* 'White Heidi Ann'** of gardens. See *F.* 'Heidi Weiss'.

FURCRAEA

AGAVACEAE

Genus of succulents with basal rosettes of sword-shaped, fleshy, toothed leaves; rosettes die after flowering. Resembles *Agave* but has short-tubed flowers. Requires a sunny position and well-drained soil. Propagate by bulbils, borne on lower stems, when developed.
F. foetida, syn. *F. gigantea*. Basal-rosetted succulent. H 10ft (3m), S 15ft (5m). Has broadly sword-shaped, fleshy, midgreen leaves to 8ft (2.5m) long, with edges toothed only at the base. Flower stems to 25ft (8m) bear scented, bell-shaped green flowers, white within, in summer. Z13–15 H12–10. **'Mediopicta'** (syn. *F.f.* var. *mediopicta*, *F.f.* 'Variegata') illus. p.460.
F. gigantea. See *F. foetida*.

G

GAGEA

LILIACEAE

Genus of spring-flowering bulbs grown for their clusters of funnel- or star-shaped white or yellow flowers. Is suitable for rock gardens. Prefers full light and well-drained soil that does not become too hot and dry. Dies down in summer. Propagate by division in spring or autumn or by seed in autumn.
G. graeca, syn. *Lloydia graeca*. Spring-flowering bulb. H 2–4in (5–10cm), S 1¼–2in (3–5cm). Threadlike, semi-erect leaves form at ground level and on wiry stems. Bears up to 5 widely funnel-shaped, purple-veined white flowers, ½–⅝in (1–1.5cm) long. Z7–9 H9–7.
G. peduncularis. Spring-flowering bulb. H 2–6in (5–15cm), S 1–2in (2.5–5cm). Has threadlike, semi-erect leaves at base and on stem. Produces a loose head of flat, star-shaped yellow flowers, each ⅝–1¼in (1.5–3cm) across, with green stripes outside. Z6–9 H9–6.

GAILLARDIA

Blanket flower

ASTERACEAE/COMPOSITAE

Genus of summer-flowering annuals and perennials that tend to be short-lived. Requires sun and prefers well-drained soil. May need staking. Propagate species by seed in autumn or spring, selected forms by root cuttings in winter.
G. aristata illus. p.291.
***G.* x *grandiflora* 'Dazzler'** illus. p.283. **'Wirral Flame'** is a clump-forming, short-lived perennial. H 24in (60cm), S 20in (50cm). Produces large, terminal, daisylike, deep cardinal red flower heads during summer. Leaves are lance-shaped, lobed, and soft green. Z3–8 H8–1.
G. pulchella. Moderately fast-growing, upright annual or short-lived perennial. H 18in (45cm), S 12in (30cm). Has lance-shaped, hairy, grayish green leaves and, in summer, daisylike, double, crimson-zoned yellow, pink, or red flower heads. Z10–11 H12–1. **'Lollipops'** illus. p.338.

GALANTHUS

Snowdrop

AMARYLLIDACEAE

Genus of bulbs grown for their pendent white flowers, one on each slender stem between 2 basal leaves. Is easily recognized by its 3 large outer petals and 3 small inner ones forming a green-marked cup. Needs a cool, partially shaded position and organic, moist soil. Do not allow bulbs to dry out excessively. Propagate by division in spring after flowering or in late summer or autumn when bulbs are dormant. All parts may cause mild stomach upset if ingested; contact with the bulbs may irritate skin.
***G.* 'Atkinsii'** illus. p.439.
G. elwesii illus. p.4309.
G. gracilis, syn. *G. graecus* of gardens, illus. p.439.
G. graecus of gardens. See *G. gracilis*.
G. ikariae, syn. *G. latifolius* of gardens, illus. p.440.
G. latifolius of gardens. See *G. ikariae*.
G. nivalis (Common snowdrop). Late winter- and early spring-flowering bulb. H 4–6in (10–15cm), S 2–3in (5–8cm). Produces narrowly strap-shaped, semi-erect, basal, gray-green leaves. Flowers are ¾–1in (2–2.5cm) long with a green mark at the tip of each inner petal. Z3–8 H8–1.
'Flore Pleno' illus. p.439.
'Lutescens' see *G.n. 'Sandersii'*.
'Pusey Green Tip' illus. p.439.
'Sandersii' (syn. *G.n.* 'Lutescens') and **'Scharlockii'** illus. p.440.
G. plicatus subsp. ***plicatus.*** Late winter- and early spring-flowering bulb. H 4–8in (10–20cm), S 2–3in (5–8cm). Bears broadly strap-shaped, semi-erect, basal, deep green leaves that have gray bands along the centers and reflexed margins. White flowers, ¾–1¼in (2–3cm) long, have a green patch at the tip of each inner petal. Z3–9 H9–1. subsp. ***byzantinus*** illus. p.440.
G. reginae-olgae (Autumn snowdrop). Autumn-flowering bulb. H 4–8in (10–20cm), S 2in (5cm). Has ⅝–1in (1.5–2.5cm) long flowers with a green patch at the apex of each inner petal, before or just as narrowly strap-shaped, deep green leaves, each with a central, gray stripe, appear. Z7–9 H9–7.
G. rizehensis illus. p.439.

GALAX

DIAPENSIACEAE

Genus of one species of evergreen perennial grown for its foliage and for its flowers borne in late spring and summer. Is useful for underplanting shrubs. Needs shade and moist, peaty, acidic soil. Propagate by division of rooted runners in spring.
G. aphylla. See *G. urceolata.*
G. urceolata, syn. *G. aphylla*, illus. p.351.

GALEGA

Goat's rue

LEGUMINOSAE/PAPILIONACEAE

Genus of summer-flowering perennials. Grow in an open, sunny position and in any well-drained soil. Requires support. Propagate by seed in autumn or by division in winter.
***G.* 'Her Majesty'.** See *G.* 'His Majesty'.
***G.* 'His Majesty'**, syn. *G.* 'Her Majesty'. Vigorous, upright perennial. H to 5ft (1.5m), S 3ft (1m). In summer produces spikes of small, pealike, clear lilac-mauve and white flowers. Bold, oblong to lance-shaped leaves consist of oval leaflets. Z5–11 H12–5.
***G.* 'Lady Wilson'** illus. p.228.
G. orientalis illus. p.252.

GALIUM

Bedstraw

RUBIACEAE

Genus of spring- and summer-flowering perennials, many of which are weeds; *G. odoratum* is cultivated as a groundcover. Grows well in partial shade but tolerates sun and thrives in any well-drained soil. Propagate by division in early spring or autumn.
G. odoratum, syn. *Asperula odorata*, illus. p.275.

GALTONIA

HYACINTHACEAE/LILIACEAE

Genus of summer- and autumn-flowering bulbs grown for their elegant spikes of pendent, funnel-shaped white or green flowers. Needs a sheltered, sunny site and fertile, well-drained soil that does not dry out in summer. Dies down in winter. May be lifted for replanting in spring. Propagate by seed in spring or by offsets in autumn or spring.
G. candicans illus. p.397.
G. viridiflora illus. p.402.

GARDENIA

RUBIACEAE

Genus of evergreen shrubs and trees grown for their flowers and foliage. Prefers partial shade and organic, well-drained, neutral to acidic soil. Water containerized specimens freely when in full growth, moderately at other times. After flowering, shorten strong shoots to maintain a shapely habit. Propagate by greenwood cuttings in spring or by semi-ripe cuttings in summer. Whitefly and mealy bug may cause problems.
G. augusta, syn. *G. florida*, *G. grandiflora*, *G. jasminoides* (Cape jasmine, Common gardenia). **'Veitchii'** illus. p.158.
G. capensis. See *Rothmannia capensis.*
G. florida. See *G. augusta.*
G. grandiflora. See *G. augusta.*
G. jasminoides. See *G. augusta.*
G. rothmannia. See *Rothmannia capensis.*
G. thunbergia. Evergreen, bushy shrub with white stems. H and S to 6ft (2m) or more. Has elliptic, glossy, deep green leaves. Fragrant, 7–9-petaled, white flowers, 2½–4in (6–10cm) wide, are borne in winter-spring. Z8–11 H12–8.

GARRYA

GARRYACEAE

Genus of evergreen shrubs and trees grown for their catkins in winter and spring, which are longer and more attractive on male plants. Hard frosts may damage catkins. Requires a sheltered, sunny site and tolerates any poor soil. Is suitable for a south- or west-facing wall. Dislikes being transplanted. Propagate by semi-ripe cuttings in summer.
G. elliptica illus. p.125. **'James Roof'** is an evergreen, bushy, dense shrub. H and S 12ft (4m). Has oval, wavy-edged, leathery, dark green leaves. Very long, gray-green catkins with yellow anthers are borne from mid- or late winter to early spring. Z8–10 H10–8.

GASTERIA

ALOEACEAE/LILIACEAE

Genus of succulents with thick, fleshy leaves, usually arranged in a fan, later becoming a tight rosette. Is easy to grow, needing sun or partial shade and very well-drained soil. Propagate by seed or leaf cuttings or division in spring or summer.
G. bicolor var. ***liliputana***, syn. *G. liliputana*, illus. p.480.
G. caespitosa. Fan-shaped succulent. H 6in (15cm), S 12in (30cm). Produces triangular, thick, dark green leaves, 6in

(15cm) long, with horny borders. Upper leaf surfaces have numerous white or pale green dots, usually in diagonal rows. Bears spikes of bell-shaped, orange/green flowers in spring. Z12–15 H12–10.
G. carinata var. ***verrucosa***, syn. *G. verrucosa*, illus. p.480.
G. liliputana. See *G. bicolor* var. *liliputana*.
G. verrucosa. See *G. carinata* var. *verrucosa*.

x ***Gaulnettya* 'Pink Pixie'.** See *Gaultheria* x *wisleyensis* 'Pink Pixie'.
x ***Gaulnettya* 'Wisley Pearl'.** See *Gaultheria* x *wisleyensis* 'Wisley Pearl'.

GAULTHERIA

ERICACEAE

Genus of evergreen shrubs and sub-shrubs grown for their foliage, flowers, and fruits. Grows best in shade or semi-shade and requires moist, peaty, acidic soil. Will tolerate sun, provided soil is permanently moist. Propagate by semi-ripe cuttings in summer or by seed in autumn; for *G. shallon* and *G. trichophylla* propagate by division in autumn or spring. All parts may cause mild stomach upset if ingested except the fruits, which are edible.
G. cuneata illus. p.360.
G. forrestii. Evergreen, rounded shrub. H and S 5ft (1.5m). Has oblong, glossy, dark green leaves and racemes of small, fragrant, rounded white flowers in spring, followed by rounded blue fruits. Z7–8 H8–7.
G. miqueliana. Evergreen, compact shrub. H and S 10in (25cm). Has oval, leathery leaves clothing stiff stems. In late spring produces bell-shaped, pink-tinged white flowers, up to 6 per stem, followed by rounded white or pink fruits. Z6–8 H8–6.
G. mucronata, syn. *Pernettya mucronata.* Evergreen, bushy, dense shrub, spreading by underground stems. H and S 4ft (1.2m). Oval, prickly, glossy, dark green leaves set off tiny, urn-shaped white flowers in late spring and early summer. Has spherical, fleshy fruit varying in color between cultivars. Sprays of fruit are good for indoor display. Z8–9 H9–8. Fruits of **'Cherry Ripe'** (female) are large and bright cherry red. **'Edward Balls'** (male) bears thick, upright red shoots and sharply spined, bright green leaves. **'Mulberry Wine'** (female) illus. p.174. **'Wintertime'** (female) illus. p.173.
G. myrsinoides, syn. *G. prostrata*, *Pernettya prostrata.* Evergreen, spreading shrub. H 6–12in (15–30cm), S 12in (30cm) or more. Bears oval, leathery, dark green leaves. Urn-shaped white flowers are produced in early summer and are followed by large, rounded, blue-purple fruits. Is suitable for a rock garden. Z7–8 H8–7.
G. nummularioides. Evergreen, compact shrub. H 4–6in (10–15cm), S 8in (20cm). Leaves are oval to heart-shaped and leathery. Egg-shaped, pink-flushed white flowers are produced from the upper leaf axils in late spring or summer. Produces rounded, blue-black fruits, but only rarely. Z7–8 H8–7.
G. procumbens illus. p.387.
G. prostrata. See *G. myrsinoides.*
G. pumila, syn. *Pernettya pumila.* Evergreen, mat-forming, creeping shrub. H 2in (5cm), S 12–24in (30–60cm). Prostrate branches bear tiny, bell-shaped white flowers in early summer among tiny, rounded, leathery leaves. Rounded fruits are pink or white. Is good for a rock garden. Z7–8H8–7.
G. shallon illus. p.162.
G. tasmanica, syn. *Pernettya tasmanica.* Evergreen, mat-forming shrub. H 2–3in (5–8cm), S 8in (20cm). Has oval, toothed, leathery leaves with wavy edges. Bell-shaped white flowers in early summer are followed by rounded red fruits. Is good for a rock garden. Z8–9 H9–8.
G. trichophylla. Evergreen, compact shrub with creeping, underground stems. H 3–6in (7–15cm), S 8in (20cm). Bell-shaped pink flowers in early summer are followed by egg-shaped blue fruits produced from leaf axils. Leaves are small and oval. Z6–8 H8–6.
***G.* x *wisleyensis* 'Pink Pixie'**, syn. x *Gaulnettya* 'Pink Pixie'. Evergreen, dense, bushy shrub. H and S 3ft (1m). Bears broadly oval, deeply veined, dark green leaves. Small, urn-shaped, pale pink flowers, produced in late spring and early summer, are followed by spherical, purplish red fruits. Z7–9 H9–7. **'Wisley Pearl'**, syn. x *Gaulnettya* 'Wisley Pearl', illus. p.154.

GAURA

ONAGRACEAE

Genus of summer-flowering annuals and perennials that are sometimes short-lived. Prefers full sun and light, well-drained soil. Propagate by softwood or semi-ripe cuttings in summer or by seed in autumn or spring.
G. lindheimeri. Bushy perennial. H 4ft (1.2m), S 3ft (1m). In summer produces racemes of tubular, pink-suffused white flowers. Leaves are lance-shaped and midgreen. Z6–8 H9–6

GAYLUSSACIA

Huckleberry

ERICACEAE

Genus of deciduous, occasionally evergreen shrubs grown for their flowers, fruits, and autumn color. Needs sun or semi-shade and moist, peaty, acidic soil. Propagate by softwood cuttings in summer or by seed in autumn.
G. baccata (Black huckleberry). Deciduous, bushy shrub. H and S 3ft (1m). Oval, sticky, dark green leaves redden in autumn. Produces clusters of small, urn-shaped, dull red flowers in late spring, then edible, spherical black fruits. Z3–7 H7–1.

GAZANIA

ASTERACEAE/COMPOSITAE

Genus of evergreen perennials often grown as annuals and useful for summer bedding, pots, and barrels. Requires sun and sandy soil. Propagate by seed in spring or by heel cuttings in spring or summer.
***G.* Daybreak Series.** Carpeting perennial, grown as an annual. H and S 8in (20cm). Has lance-shaped leaves and, in summer, large, daisylike flower heads in a mixture of orange, yellow, pink, bronze, and white. Flowers remain open in dull weather. Z8–10 H10–8.
G. pinnata. Mat-forming perennial. H 6in (15cm), S 12in (30cm). Daisy-like, orange-red flower heads with central black rings appear singly in early summer above oval, finely cut, hairy, bluish gray leaves. Z8–10 H10–8.
G. rigens var. ***uniflora***, syn. *G. uniflora*, illus. p.292.
***G.* Talent Series.** Vigorous perennials. H and S to 10in (25cm). Produce solitary yellow, orange, pink, or brown flower heads on short stems just above the leaves in summer. Z8–10 H10–8.
G. uniflora. See *G. rigens* var. *uniflora*.

GELSEMIUM

LOGANIACEAE

Genus of evergreen, twining climbers grown for their fragrant, jasminelike flowers. In cool climates best grown under cover. Provide full light and fertile, well-drained soil. Water regularly, less in cold weather. Stems require support and should be thinned out after flowering or in spring. Propagate by seed in spring or by semi-ripe cuttings in summer.
G. sempervirens illus. p.206.

GENISTA

Broom

LEGUMINOSAE/PAPILIONACEAE

Genus of deciduous, sometimes almost leafless, shrubs, and trees grown for their mass of small, pealike flowers. Does best in full sun and not overly rich, well-drained soil. Resents being transplanted. Propagate species by softwood or semi-ripe cuttings in summer or by seed in autumn, selected forms by softwood cuttings only in summer.
G. aetnensis illus. p.93.
G. cinerea illus. p.123.
G. delphinensis, syn. *Chamaespartium sagittale* subsp. *delphinense*, *G. sagittalis* subsp. *delphinensis.* Deciduous, prostrate shrub. H ½in (1cm), S 8in (20cm). Has tangled, winged branches, covered with minute, oval, dark green leaves. Masses of golden yellow flowers are produced along stems in early summer. Suitable for a rock garden or wall. Z5–8 H8–5.
G. fragrans of gardens. See *Cytisus* x *spachianus.*
G. hispanica illus. p.170.
G. lydia illus. p.359.
G. monosperma, syn. *Retama monosperma*. Deciduous, almost leafless, graceful, arching shrub. H 1m (3ft), S 5ft (1.5m). Slender, silky-gray shoots bear clusters of very fragrant white flowers in early spring. Has a few inconspicuous leaves.
G. pilosa. Deciduous, domed shrub. H and S 12in (30cm). Narrowly oval leaves are silky-haired beneath. Bright yellow flowers on short stalks are borne in leaf axils in summer. Is useful on a bank or as a groundcover. Propagate by semi-ripe cuttings in summer. Z9–11 H12–9. **'Vancouver Gold'** is more mounded, H 18in (45cm), with golden yellow flowers.
G. sagittalis, syn. *Chamaespartium sagittale*, illus. p.386. subsp. ***delphinensis.*** See *G. delphinensis.*
G.* x *spachiana. See *Cytisus* x *spachianus.*
***G. tenera* 'Golden Shower'.** Vigorous, deciduous, arching shrub. H 10ft (3m), S 15ft (5m). Narrowly oblong leaves are gray-green. Bears racemes of fragrant, golden yellow flowers in early to midsummer. Z6–9 H9–6.
G. tinctoria illus. p.157. **'Royal Gold'** is a deciduous, upright shrub. H and S 3ft (1m). Produces long, conical panicles of golden yellow flowers in spring-summer and leaves that are narrowly lance-shaped and dark green. Z4–8 H8–1.

GENTIANA

Gentian

GENTIANACEAE

Genus of annuals, biennials, and perennials, some of which are semi-evergreen or evergreen, grown for their usually blue flowers. Is excellent for rock gardens. Prefers sun or semi-shade and organic, well-drained, moist, neutral to acidic soil. Some species grow naturally on alkaline soils. Propagate by division or offshoots in spring or by seed in autumn. Divide autumn-flowering species and *G. clusii* every 3 years in early spring and replant in fresh soil.
G. acaulis, syn. *G. excisa*, *G. kochiana*, illus. p.370.
G. angustifolia. Evergreen, clump-forming perennial. H 4in (10cm), S 8in (20cm). Has rosettes of oblong, dull green leaves and, in summer, solitary, tubular, sky blue flowers on 3in (7cm) stems. Tolerates alkaline soils. Z6–8 H8–6.
G. asclepiadea illus. p.263.
G. clusii (Trumpet gentian). Evergreen, clump-forming perennial. H 2in (5cm), S 6–9in (15–23cm). Has rosettes of oval, glossy, dark green leaves. Trumpet-shaped, azure blue flowers with green-spotted, paler throats are borne on 1–4in (2.5–10cm) stems in early summer. Tolerates alkaline soils. Z7–9 H9–7.

G. excisa. See *G. acaulis.*
G. gracilipes. Semi-evergreen, tufted perennial with arching stems. H 6in (15cm), S 8in (20cm). Forms a central rosette of long, strap-shaped, dark green leaves from which lax flower stems bearing tubular, dark purplish blue flowers, greenish within, are produced in summer. Tolerates some shade. Z6–8 H8–6.
G. kochiana. See *G. acaulis.*
G. lutea illus. p.255.
***G.* x *macaulayi* 'Wells's Variety'**, syn. *G.* 'Wellsii', illus. p.387.
G. ornata. Semi-evergreen, clump-forming perennial with small, overwintering rosettes. H 2in (5cm), S 4in (10cm). Forms a central rosette of grasslike leaves. In autumn, each stem tip carries an upright, bell-shaped, midblue flower with a white throat and deep blue stripes shading to creamy white outside. Requires acidic soil and a moist atmosphere. Z5–7 H7–5.
G. saxosa illus. p.374.
G. septemfida illus. p.360.
G. sino-ornata illus. p.387.
***G.* 'Susan Jane'.** Vigorous, semi-evergreen, spreading perennial with small, overwintering rosettes. H 2in (5cm), S 12in (30cm). Prostrate stems bear grasslike leaves. Large, trumpet-shaped, white-throated, deep blue flowers, greenish within, appear in autumn. Requires acidic soil. Z5–7 H7–5.
G. verna illus. p.370.
***G.* 'Wellsii'.** See *G.* x *macaulayi* 'Wells's Variety'.

GERANIUM
Cranesbill

GERANIACEAE

Genus of perennials, some of which are semi-evergreen, grown for their flowers and often as a groundcover. Compact species are suitable for rock gardens. Most species prefer sun, but some do better in shade. Will grow in all but waterlogged soils. Propagate by semi-ripe cuttings in summer or by seed or division in autumn or spring. Cultivars should be propagated by division or cuttings only.
G. anemonifolium. See *G. palmatum.*
***G.* 'Ann Folkard'.** Spreading perennial. H 20in (50cm), S 36in (1m). Has rounded, deeply cut, yellowish green leaves and, in summer-autumn, masses of shallowly cup-shaped, rich magenta flowers with black veins. Z5–9 H9–3.
G. armenum. See *G. psilostemon.*
G. cinereum. Semi-evergreen, rosetted perennial with spreading flowering stems. H 6in (15cm), S 12in (30cm). Has cup-shaped flowers, either white to pale pink strongly veined with purple, or pure white, on lax stems in late spring and summer. Basal leaves are rounded, deeply divided, soft, and gray-green. Is good for a large rock garden. Z5–9 H9–5. **'Ballerina'** and var. ***subcaulescens*** (syn. *G. subcaulescens*) illus. p.379.
***G. clarkei* 'Kashmir Purple'**, syn. *G. pratense* 'Kashmir Purple'. Carpeting, rhizomatous perennial. H and S 18–24in (45–60cm). Bears loose clusters of cup-shaped, deep purple flowers in summer. Rounded leaves are deeply divided and finely veined. Z5–8 H8–5. **'Kashmir White'** (syn. *G. pratense* 'Kashmir White') illus. p.276.
G. dalmaticum illus. p.377.
G. endressii illus. p.278.
'Wargrave Pink' see *G.* x *oxonianum* 'Wargrave Pink'.
G. farreri. Rosetted perennial with a taproot. H 4in (10cm), S 4–6in (10–15cm) or more. Outward-facing, flattish, very pale mauve-pink flowers set off blue-black anthers in early summer. Has kidney-shaped, matte green leaves. Both flower and leaf stems are red. Z4–7 H7–1.
G. grandiflorum. See *G. himalayense.*
G. himalayense, syn. *G. grandiflorum, G. meeboldii,* illus. p.285.
G. ibericum. Clump-forming perennial. H and S 24in (60cm). In summer produces sprays of 5-petaled, saucer-shaped, violet-blue flowers. Has heart-shaped, lobed or cut, hairy leaves. Z5–8 H8–5.
G. incanum. Semi-evergreen, spreading, mounded perennial. H 12–15in (30–38cm), S 24–36in (60–90cm). Shallowly cup-shaped flowers are variable but usually deep pink, borne singly in summer above aromatic, deeply divided, gray-green leaves with linear segments. Z5–8 H8–5.
***G.* 'Johnson's Blue'** illus. p.285.
G. macrorrhizum illus. p.279. **'Ingwersen's Variety'** illus. p.269.
G. maculatum. Clump-forming perennial. H 30in (75cm), S 18in (45cm). In spring bears heads of flattish, pinkish lilac flowers above rounded, lobed or scalloped, midgreen leaves that turn fawn and red in autumn. Z4–8 H8–1.
G. maderense. Vigorous, semi-evergreen, bushy perennial with a woody base. H and S 3ft (1m). Produces large sprays of shallowly cup-shaped, deep magenta flowers in summer above palmate, finely cut, dark green leaves. Z8–9 H9–8.
G.* x *magnificum illus. p.285.
G. meeboldii. See *G. himalayense.*
G. nodosum illus. p.270.
G. orientalitibeticum, syn. *G. stapfianum* var. *roseum* of gardens, illus. p.353.
***G.* x *oxonianum* 'Claridge Druce'.** Vigorous, semi-evergreen, carpeting perennial. H and S 60–75cm (24–30in). Bears clusters of cup-shaped, darker-veined, mauve-pink flowers throughout summer. Has dainty, rounded, lobed leaves. Z4–8 H8–1. **'Wargrave Pink'** (syn. *G. endressii* 'Wargrave Pink') illus. p.279. **'Winscombe'** illus. p.243.
G. palmatum, syn. *G. anemonifolium.* Vigorous, semi-evergreen, bushy perennial with a woody base. H 18in (45cm), S 24in (60cm). Has palmate, deeply lobed, dark green leaves and, in late summer, large sprays of shallowly cup-shaped, purplish red flowers. Z7–9 H9–7.
G. phaeum illus. p.238.
G. pratense (Meadow cranesbill). Clump-forming perennial. H 30in (75cm), S 24in (60cm). Bears 5-petaled, saucer-shaped, violet-blue flowers on branching stems in summer. Rounded, lobed to deeply divided, midgreen leaves become bronze in autumn. Z4–8 H8–1. **'Kashmir Purple'** see *G. clarkei* 'Kashmir Purple'. **'Kashmir White'** see *G. clarkei* 'Kashmir White'. **'Mrs. Kendall Clark'** illus. p.285. **'Plenum Violaceum'** is more compact than the species with double, deep violet flowers. Z5–7 H8–1.
G. procurrens. Carpeting perennial. H 12in (30cm), S 24in (60cm). Has rounded, lobed, glossy leaves and, in summer, clusters of saucer-shaped, deep rose-purple flowers.
G. psilostemon, syn. *G. armenum*, illus. p.245.
G. pylzowianum. Spreading perennial with underground runners and tiny tubers. H 5–10in (12–25cm), S 10in (25cm) or more. Bears semi-circular, deeply cut, dark green leaves and, in late spring and summer, trumpet-shaped, green-centered, deep rose-pink flowers. May be invasive. Z5–8 H8–5.
G. renardii illus. p.277.
***G.* x *riversleaianum* 'Russell Prichard'.** Semi-evergreen, clump-forming perennial. H 1ft (30cm), S 3ft (1m). Saucer-shaped, clear pink flowers are borne singly or in small clusters from early summer to autumn. Rounded leaves are lobed and gray-green. Z6–8 H8–6.
G. sanguineum illus. p.354. var. ***striatum*** (syn. *G.s.* var. *lancastriense*) illus. p.376.
G. stapfianum* var. *roseum of gardens. See *G. orientalitibeticum.*
G. subcaulescens. See *G. cinereum* var. *subcaulescens.*
***G. sylvaticum* 'Mayflower'** illus. p.251.
G. traversii* var. *elegans. Semi-evergreen, rosetted perennial with spreading stems. H 4in (10cm), S 10in (25cm). Large, upward-facing, saucer-shaped, pale pink flowers with darker veins rise above rounded, lobed, gray-green leaves in summer. Is suitable for a sheltered ledge or rock garden. Protect from winter wet. Needs gritty soil. Z8–9 H9–8.
***G. wallichianum* 'Buxton's Variety'**, syn. *G.w.* 'Buxton's Blue', illus. p.287.
G. wlassovianum. Clump-forming perennial. H and S 24in (60cm). Has velvety stems and rounded, lobed, dark green leaves. Saucer-shaped, deep purple flowers are borne singly or in small clusters in summer. Z4–8 H8–1.

GERBERA

ASTERACEAE/COMPOSITAE

Genus of perennials flowering from summer to winter, depending on growing conditions. Grow in full sun and in light, sandy soil. Propagate by heel cuttings from side shoots in summer or by seed in autumn or early spring.
G. jamesonii illus. p.302.

GEUM
Avens

ROSACEAE

Genus of summer-flowering perennials. Does best in sun and prefers moist but well-drained soil. Propagate by division or by seed in autumn.
G.* x *borisii of gardens. See *G. coccineum.*
G. chiloense, syn. *G. coccineum* of gardens. Clump-forming perennial. H 16–24in (40–60cm), S 24in (60cm). Saucer-shaped scarlet flowers are produced from early to late summer. Pinnate leaves are deeply lobed and toothed. Z5–9 H9–5.
G. coccineum, syn. *G.* x *borisii* of gardens, illus. p.293.
G. coccineum of gardens. See *G. chiloense.*
***G.* 'Feuerball'.** See *G.* 'Mrs. J. Bradshaw'.
***G.* 'Fire Opal'.** Clump-forming perennial. H 32in (80cm), S 18in (45cm). Rounded, double, bronze-scarlet flowers are borne in small clusters in summer above oblong to lance-shaped, lobed, fresh green leaves. Z5–9 H9–5.
***G.* 'Goldball'.** See *G.* 'Lady Stratheden'.
***G.* 'Lady Stratheden'**, syn. *G.* 'Goldball', illus. p.292.
***G.* 'Lionel Cox'.** Clump-forming perennial. H and S 12in (30cm). In early summer produces small clusters of 5-petaled, cup-shaped, shrimp red flowers above oblong to lance-shaped, lobed, fresh green leaves. Z3–7 H7–1.
G. montanum (Alpine avens). Dense, clump-forming, rhizomatous perennial that spreads slowly. H 4in (10cm), S 9in (23cm). Shallowly cup-shaped, golden yellow flowers in early summer are followed by fluffy, buff-colored seed heads. Leaves are pinnate, each with a large, rounded, terminal lobe. Suitable for a rock garden. Z4–8 H8–1.
'Mrs. J. Bradshaw', syn. *G.* 'Feuerball'. Clump-forming perennial. H 32in (80cm), S 18in (45cm). Rounded, double crimson flowers are borne in small sprays in summer. Fresh green leaves are oblong to lance-shaped and lobed. Z5–9 H9–5.

GEVUINA

PROTEACEAE

Genus of evergreen trees grown for their foliage and flowers in summer. Needs semi-shade and fertile, moist but well-drained soil. Propagate by semi-ripe cuttings in late summer or by seed in autumn.
G. avellana (Chilean hazel). Evergreen, conical tree. H and S 30ft (10m). Has large, glossy, dark green leaves divided into numerous oval, toothed leaflets. Slender spires of spidery white flowers in late summer are followed by cherry-like red then black fruits. Z9–10 H10–9.

GIBBAEUM

AIZOACEAE

Genus of clump-forming succulents with pairs of small, swollen leaves, often of unequal size. Needs full sun and very well-drained soil. Water very lightly in early winter. Propagate by seed or stem cuttings in spring or summer.

G. petrense. Carpeting succulent. H 1¼in (3cm), S 12in (30cm) or more. Each branch carries 1 or 2 pairs of thick, triangular, pale gray-green leaves, ½in (1cm) long. Bears daisy-like, pink-red flowers, ⅝in (1.5cm) across, in spring. Z12–15 H12–10.

G. velutinum illus. p.469.

GILIA

POLEMONIACEAE

Genus of summer- and autumn-flowering annuals. Grows best in sun and in fertile, very well-drained soil. Stems may need support. Propagate by seed sown outdoors in spring, or in early autumn for early flowering the following year.

G. achilleifolia. Fast-growing, upright, bushy annual. H 24in (60cm), S 8in (20cm). Finely divided, midgreen leaves are hairy and sticky. Heads of funnel-shaped blue flowers, 1in (2.5cm) wide, are produced in summer. H12–1.

G. capitata illus. p.333.

GILLENIA

ROSACEAE

Genus of summer-flowering perennials. Grow in sun or shade and any well-drained soil. Needs staking. Propagate by seed in autumn or spring.

G. trifoliata illus. p.241.

GINKGO

GINKGOACEAE

See also CONIFERS.

G. biloba illus. p.103.

GLADIOLUS

IRIDACEAE

Genus of corms, each producing a spike of funnel-shaped flowers and a fan of erect, sword-shaped leaves on the basal part of flower stem. Is suitable for cutting or for planting in mixed borders; most hybrids are also good for exhibition. Needs a sunny and fertile, well-drained site. Plant 4–6in (10–15cm) deep and the same distance apart in spring. Water well in summer and support tall cultivars with stakes. Where not hardy, lift in autumn then cut off stems and dry corms in a frost-free but cool place. Pot up spring-flowering species and cultivars in autumn and place in a cool greenhouse; after flowering, dry off corms during summer months and repot in autumn.

Propagate by seed or by removal of young cormlets from parent. Seed sown in early spring in a cool greenhouse will take 2–3 years to flower and may not breed true to type. Cormlets, removed after lifting, should be stored in frost-free conditions and then be planted out 2in (5cm) deep in spring; lift in winter as for mature corms. They will flower in 1–2 years.

While in storage, corms may be attacked by various rots and pests. Protect sound, healthy corms by treating with a combination fungicide/insecticide dust or dip; store in an airy, cool, frost-free place. Gladiolus scab causes blotches on leaves; gladiolus yellows shows as yellowing stripes on leaves, which then die; in both cases destroy affected corms. Thrips feed on buds causing streaked blooms and overwinter and feed on corms, destroying or weakening them. As a preventative measure, always plant healthy corms in a new site each year. See also feature panel p.399.

Gladiolus hybrids

Most hybrids are derived from *G.* x *hortulanus*. All have stiff leaves, 8–20in (20–50cm) long, ranging from pale willow green or steely blue-green to almost bottle green. All are good for flower arranging. They are divided into Grandiflorus, Primulinus, and Nanus Groups.

Grandiflorus Group produces long, densely packed spikes of funnel-shaped flowers with ruffled, thick-textured petals or plain-edged, thin-textured ones. Giant-flowered hybrids have a bottom flower of over 5½in (14cm) across (flower head is 26–32in (65–80cm) long); large-flowered 4½–5½in (11–14cm) across (flower head 24–36in (60cm–1m) long); medium-flowered 3½–4½in (9–11cm) across (flower head 24–32in (60–80cm) long); small-flowered 2½–3½in (6–9cm) across (flower head 20–28in (50–70cm) long); and miniature-flowered 1½–2½in (3.5–6cm) across (flower head 16–24in (40–60cm) long).

Primulinus Group has fairly loose spikes of plain-edged, funnel-shaped flowers, 2½–3in (6–8cm) across, each with a strongly hooded, upper petal over the stigma and anthers. Flower heads are 12in (30cm) long.

Nanus Group produces 2 or 3 slender spikes with loosely arranged flowers, 1½–2in (4–5cm) across. Flower heads are 9–14in (22–35cm) long.

Gladiolus are usually hardy in Z8–10 H9–1. Planting in a well-drained site and providing a deep winter mulch may extend hardiness to Z6.

***G.* 'Amanda Mahy'** (illus. p.399). Nanus Group gladiolus. H 32in (80cm), S 3–4in (8–10cm). Produces spikes of up to 7 salmon-pink flowers with lip tepals flecked violet and white in early summer.

***G.* 'Amsterdam'.** Grandiflorus Group, giant-flowered gladiolus. H 5½ft (1.7m), S 1ft (30cm). Spikes of up to 27 slightly upward-facing, finely ruffled white flowers are produced in late summer. Is good for exhibition.

***G.* 'Amy Beth'.** Grandiflorus Group, small-flowered gladiolus. H 4ft (1.2m), S 20–25cm (8–10in). Produces spikes of up to 22 heavily ruffled lavender flowers with thick, waxy, cream-lipped petals in late summer.

***G.* 'Anna Leorah'** (illus. p.399). Grandiflorus Group, large-flowered gladiolus. H 5½ft (1.6m), S 6in (15cm). In midsummer bears spikes of up to 25 strongly ruffled, midpink flowers with large white throats. Is good for exhibition.

***G.* 'Atlantis'.** Grandiflorus Group, medium-flowered gladiolus. H 5ft (1.5m), S 8–10in (20–25cm). Produces spikes of up to 20 lightly ruffled, deep violet-blue flowers with small white throats in late summer.

***G.* 'Beau Rivage'.** Grandiflorus Group, large-flowered gladiolus. H to 4ft (1.2m), S 1ft (30cm). Spikes of up to 15 ruffled, deep coral-pink flowers are produced in summer. Is good for exhibition.

***G.* 'Beauty of Holland'.** Grandiflorus Group, large-flowered gladiolus. H 5½ft (1.7m) , S 6in (15cm). Produces spikes of up to 27 ruffled, pink-margined white flowers in midsummer. Is good for exhibition.

***G.* 'Black Lash'** (illus. p.399). Grandiflorus Group, small-flowered gladiolus. H 4½ft (1.35m), S 6–8in (15–20cm). Bears spikes of up to 25 lightly ruffled, deep black-rose flowers with pointed, slightly reflexed petals from late summer to early autumn.

G. blandus. See *G. carneus*.

G. byzantinus. See *G. communis* subsp. *byzantinus*.

G. callianthus, syn. *Acidanthera bicolor* var. *murieliae*, *A. murieliae*. Late summer-flowering corm. H to 3ft (1m), S 4–6in (10–15cm). Has a loose spike of up to 10 fragrant flowers, each with a curved, 4in (10cm) long tube and 6 white petals, each with a deep purple blotch at the base.

G. cardinalis. Summer-flowering corm. H to 4ft (1.2m), S 4–6in (10–15cm). Arching stem bears a spike of up to 12 widely funnel-shaped flowers, each 3in (8cm) long and bright red with spear-shaped white marks on the lower 3 petals.

G. carneus, syn. *G. blandus*. Spring-flowering corm. H 8–16in (20–40cm), S 3–4in (8–10cm). Stem bears a loose spike of 3–12 widely funnel-shaped, white or pink flowers, 1½–2½in (4–6cm) long, marked on lower petals with darker red or yellow blotches.

***G.* 'Charmer'.** Grandiflorus Group, large-flowered gladiolus. H 5½ft (1.7m), S 6in (15cm). In early and mid-summer produces spikes of up to 27 strongly ruffled, almost translucent, light pink flowers. Is good for exhibition.

***G.* 'Christabel'** illus. p.415.

G. communis subsp. ***byzantinus***, syn. *G. byzantinus*, illus. p.400.

***G.* 'Côte d'Azur'.** Grandiflorus Group, giant-flowered gladiolus. H 5½ft (1.7m), S 6in (15cm). Bears spikes of up to 23 ruffled, midblue flowers with pale blue throats in early summer. Is good for exhibition.

G. dalenii, syn. *G. natalensis*, *G. primulinus*, *G. psittacinus*. Vigorous, summer-flowering corm. H to 5ft (1.5m), S 4–6in (10–15cm). Produces up to 14 red, yellow-orange, yellow, or greenish yellow flowers, 3–5in (8–12cm) long, each with a hooded upper petal and often flecked or streaked red.

***G.* 'Drama'** (illus. p.399). Grandiflorus Group, large-flowered gladiolus. H 5½ft (1.7m), S 10–12in (25–30cm). In late summer produces spikes of up to 26 lightly ruffled, deep watermelon pink flowers with red-marked yellow throats. Is superb for exhibition.

***G.* 'Dutch Mountain'.** Grandiflorus Group, large-flowered gladiolus. H 5½ft (1.7m), S 6in (15cm). In midsummer, produces spikes of up to 25 slightly ruffled white flowers with small green marks in the throats. Is good for exhibition.

***G.* 'Esta Bonita'** (illus. p.399). Grandiflorus Group, giant-flowered gladiolus. H 5½ft (1.7m), S 1ft (30cm). Produces spikes of up to 24 apricot-orange flowers, slightly darker toward petal edges, in late summer. Is good for exhibition.

***G.* 'Firestorm'.** Grandiflorus Group, miniature-flowered gladiolus. H 3½ft (1.1m), S 3–4in (8–10cm). Spikes of up to 22 loosely spaced, ruffled, vivid scarlet flowers with yellowish white flecks on the outer tepals are produced in early summer. Is good for exhibition.

***G.* 'Georgette'.** Grandiflorus Group, small-flowered gladiolus. H 4ft (1.2m), S 3–4in (8–10cm). Produces spikes of up to 22 slightly ruffled, yellow-suffused orange flowers, with large lemon-yellow throats in midsummer. Is good for exhibition.

***G.* 'Green Isle'.** Grandiflorus Group, medium-flowered gladiolus. H 4½ft (1.35m), S 8–10in (20–25cm). Spikes carrying up to 22 slightly informal flowers, lime green throughout with chiseled ruffling, are produced in late summer.

***G.* 'Green Woodpecker'** (illus. p.399). Grandiflorus Group, medium-flowered gladiolus. H 5ft (1.5m), S 1ft (30cm). Has spikes of up to 25 uranium green flowers with wine red throats in late summer. Is very good for exhibition.

***G.* 'Halley'** (illus. p.399). Nanus Group gladiolus. H 3ft (1m), S 3–4in (8–10cm). In early summer produces spikes carrying up to 7 white-flushed, pale yellow flowers, each with bright red marks in the throats.

***G.* 'Ice Cap'** (illus. p.399). Grandiflorus Group, large-flowered gladiolus. H 5½ft (1.7m), S 10–12in (25–30cm). Produces spikes of up to 27 heavily ruffled, ice white flowers from late summer to early autumn.

***G.* 'Inca Queen'** (illus. p.399). Grandiflorus Group, large-flowered gladiolus. H 5ft (1.5m), S 8–10in (20–25cm). Bears spikes of up to 25 heavily ruffled, waxy, deep salmon-pink flowers with lemon-yellow lip petals and throats in late summer.

G. italicus, syn. *G. segetum*, illus.

p.400.
***G.* 'Little Darling'** (illus. p.399). Primulinus Group gladiolus. H 3½ft (1.1m), S 3–4in (8–10cm). Bears spikes of up to 16 loosely spaced, salmon- to rose-pink flowers with lemon lip tepals in midsummer. Is good for exhibition.
***G.* 'Magistral'.** Grandiflorus Group, large-flowered gladiolus. H 6ft (1.8m), S 6in (15cm). Produces spikes of up to 24 ruffled, oyster white flowers with magenta lines in midsummer. Is good for exhibition.
***G.* 'Melodie'** (illus. p.399). Grandiflorus Group, small-flowered gladiolus. H 4ft (1.2m), S 6–8in (15–20cm). Produces spikes of up to 17 salmon-rose flowers with longitudinal, spearlike, red-orange marks in throats in late summer.
***G.* 'Mi Mi'** (illus. p.399). Grandiflorus Group, small-flowered gladiolus. H 4½ft (1.3m), S 3–4in (8–10cm). In midsummer bears spikes of up to 24 strongly ruffled, deep lavender-pink flowers with white throats. Is good for exhibition.
***G.* 'Miss America'** (illus. p.399). Grandiflorus Group, medium-flowered gladiolus. H 5ft (1.5m), S 1ft (30cm). In late summer produces spikes of up to 24 deep pink flowers that are heavily ruffled. Is excellent for exhibition.
G. natalensis. See *G. dalenii.*
G. papilio, syn. *G. purpureoauratus*, illus. p.408.
***G.* 'Parade'.** Grandiflorus Group, giant-flowered gladiolus. H 5½ft (1.7m), S 10–14in (25–35cm). Produces spikes of up to 27 finely ruffled, salmon-pink flowers with small cream throats in early autumn. Is superb for exhibition.
***G.* 'Peace'.** Grandiflorus Group, giant-flowered gladiolus. H 5½ft (1.7m), S 6in (15cm). Bears spikes of up to 26 strongly ruffled cream flowers with pale lemon throats and pale pink margins in midsummer. Is good for exhibition.
***G.* 'Peter Pears'** (illus. p.399). Grandiflorus Group, large-flowered gladiolus. H 5½ft (1.7m), S 14in (35cm). In late summer bears spikes of up to 26 apricot-salmon flowers with red throat marks. Is excellent for exhibition.
***G.* 'Pink Flare'.** Grandiflorus Group, small-flowered gladiolus. H 4½ft (1.3m) (4½ft), S 3–4in (8–10cm). Spikes of up to 25 ruffled, midpink flowers, each with a small white throat, are produced in midsummer. Is good for exhibition.
***G.* 'Pink Lady'** (illus. p.399). Grandiflorus Group, large-flowered gladiolus. H 5ft (1.5m), S 10–12in (25–30cm). Has spikes of up to 25 lightly ruffled, deep rose-pink flowers with large, white throats in late summer and early autumn.
G. primulinus. See *G. dalenii.*
G. psittacinus. See *G. dalenii.*
***G.* 'Pulchritude'** (illus. p.399). Grandiflorus Group, medium-flowered gladiolus. H 4½ft (1.3m), S 5in (12cm). Produces spikes of up to 27 ruffled, light lavender-pink flowers, deepening at the tepal margins, and with a magenta-red mark on each lip tepal, in midsummer. Is good for exhibition.
G. purpureoauratus. See *G. papilio.*
***G.* 'Rose Supreme'** (illus. p.399). Grandiflorus Group, giant-flowered gladiolus. H 5½ft (1.7m), S 10–12in (25–30cm). Spikes of up to 24 rose-pink flowers, flecked and streaked darker pink toward petal tips and with cream throats, are produced in late summer.
***G.* 'Royal Dutch'.** Grandiflorus Group, large-flowered gladiolus. H 5½ft (1.7m), S 10–12in (25–30cm). Produces spikes of up to 27 flowers, each pale lavender blending into a white throat, from late summer to early autumn. Is very good for exhibition.
G. segetum. See *G. italicus.*
***G.* 'Stardust'** (illus. p.399). Grandiflorus Group, miniature-flowered gladiolus. H 4ft (1.2m), S 3–4in (8–10cm). Has spikes of up to 21 ruffled, pale yellow flowers with lighter yellow throats in midsummer. Is good for exhibition.
***G.* 'Tendresse'.** Grandiflorus Group, medium-flowered gladiolus. H 5ft (1.5m), S 8–10in (20–25cm). In late summer has spikes of up to 28 slightly ruffled, dark pink flowers with small cream throats marked with longitudinal, faint rose-pink "spears."
***G.* 'Tesoro'** (illus. p.399). Grandiflorus Group, medium-flowered gladiolus. H 5ft (1.5m), S 8–10in (20–25cm). Bears spikes of up to 26 silky flowers, slightly ruffled and glistening yellow, in early autumn. Is among the top exhibition gladioli.
***G.* 'The Bride'** (illus. p.399). Nanus Group gladiolus. H 32in (80cm), S 3–4in (8–10cm). Produces spikes of up to 7 white flowers with green-marked throats in early summer.
***G.* 'Vaucluse'** (illus. p.399). Grandiflorus Group, giant-flowered gladiolus. H 6ft (1.9m), S 6in (15cm). In late summer, bears spikes of up to 27 slightly ruffled, vermilion red flowers with small, creamy white throats. Is good for exhibition.
***G.* 'Victor Borge'** (illus. p.399). Grandiflorus Group, large-flowered gladiolus. H 5½ft (1.7m), S 14in (35cm). Spikes of up to 22 vermilion-orange flowers with pale cream throat marks are produced in late summer.
***G.* 'White Ice'** (illus. p.399). Grandiflorus Group, medium-flowered gladiolus. H 5ft (1.5m), S 5in (12cm). Produces spikes of up to 25 ruffled white flowers in late summer. Is good for exhibition.
***G.* 'Zephyr'.** Grandiflorus Group, large-flowered gladiolus. H 5½ft (1.7m), S 6in (15cm). In midsummer has spikes of up to 26 light lavender-pink flowers with small ivory throats. Is good for exhibition.

Glandulicactus uncinatus. See *Sclerocactus uncinatus.*

GLAUCIDIUM

GLAUCIDIACEAE/PAEONIACEAE

Genus of one species of spring-flowering perennial. Is excellent in woodland gardens. Needs a partially shaded, sheltered position and moist, peaty soil. Propagate by seed in autumn.
G. palmatum illus. p.270.

GLAUCIUM

Horned poppy

PAPAVERACEAE

Genus of annuals, biennials, and perennials grown for their bright, poppylike flowers. Grow in sun and in fertile, well-drained soil. Propagate annuals by seed sown outdoors in spring; perennials by seed sown outdoors in spring or autumn; biennials by seed sown under cover in late spring or early summer. Roots are toxic if ingested.
G. flavum illus. p.335.

GLECHOMA

LABIATAE/LAMIACEAE

Genus of evergreen, summer-flowering perennials. Makes a good groundcover, but may be invasive. Tolerates sun or shade. Prefers moist but well-drained soil. Propagate by division in spring or autumn or by softwood cuttings in spring.
G. hederacea (Ground ivy, Creeping Charlie). **'Variegata'** illus. p.300.

GLEDITSIA

CAESALPINIACEAE/LEGUMINOSAE

Genus of deciduous, usually spiny trees grown for their foliage. Fragrant, inconspicuous flowers are followed by large seed pods. Young plants may suffer frost damage. Requires plenty of sun and fertile, well-drained soil. Propagate species by seed in autumn, selected forms by budding in late summer.
G. caspica (Caspian locust). Deciduous, spreading tree. H 40ft (12m), S 30ft (10m). Trunk is armed with long, branched spines. Has fern-like, glossy, midgreen leaves. Z7–10 H10–7.
G. japonica illus. p.80.
G. triacanthos (Honey locust). Deciduous, spreading tree. H 70ft (20m), S 15m (50ft). Trunk is very thorny. Fernlike, glossy, dark green leaves turn yellow in autumn. Z33–7 H7–1. f. ***inermis*** is thornless. **'Shademaster'** is vigorous, with long-lasting leaves. **'Skyline'** is thornless, broadly conical, and has golden yellow foliage in autumn. **'Sunburst'** illus. p.77.

GLOBBA

ZINGIBERACEAE

Genus of evergreen, aromatic, clump-forming perennials grown for their flowers. Needs partial shade, high humidity, and organic, well-drained soil. Keep plants dry when dormant in winter. Propagate by division or seed in spring or by mature bulbils that fall off plants.
G. winitii illus. p.267.

GLOBULARIA

Globe daisy

GLOBULARIACEAE

Genus of mainly evergreen, summer-flowering shrubs and subshrubs grown for their dome-shaped hummocks and usually blue or purple flower heads. Needs full sun and well-drained soil. Propagate by division in spring, by softwood or semi-ripe cuttings in summer, or by seed in autumn.
G. bellidifolia. See *G. meridionalis.*
G. cordifolia illus. p.383. subsp. ***bellidifolia*** see *G. meridionalis.*
G. meridionalis, syn. *G. bellidifolia*, *G. cordifolia* subsp. *bellidifolia*, *G. pygmaea*, illus. p.380.
G. pygmaea. See *G. meridionalis.*

GLORIOSA

COLCHICACEAE/LILIACEAE

Genus of deciduous, summer-flowering, tendril climbers with finger-like tubers. Needs full sun and rich, well-drained soil. Water freely in summer and give liquid fertilizer every 2 weeks. Provide support. Dry off tubers in winter and keep cool but frost-free. Propagate by seed or division in spring. Highly toxic if ingested; handling tubers may irritate the skin.
G. rothschildiana. See *G. superba* 'Rothschildiana'.
G. superba (Glory lily). Deciduous, tendril climber with tubers. H to 6ft (2m), S 1–1½ft (30–45cm). Slender stems bear scattered, broadly lance-shaped leaves. In summer, upper leaf axils carry large yellow or red flowers with 6 sharply reflexed, wavy-edged petals, changing to dark orange or deep red. Stamens are prominent. Z8–10 H12–7. **'Rothschildiana'** (syn. *G. rothschildiana*) illus. p.401.

GLOTTIPHYLLUM

AIZOACEAE

Genus of clump-forming succulents with semi-cylindrical leaves often broader at tips. Grow in full sun and poor, well-drained soil. Propagate by seed or stem cuttings in spring or summer.
G. nelii illus. p.479.
G. semicylindricum. Clump-forming, perennial succulent. H 3in (8cm), S 12in (30cm) or more. Has semi-cylindrical, bright green leaves, 2½in (6cm) long, with a tooth halfway along each margin. Short-stemmed, daisylike, golden yellow flowers, 1½in (4cm) across, appear in spring-summer.

GLOXINIA

GESNERIACEAE

Genus of late summer- to autumn-flowering, rhizomatous perennials. Needs partial shade and organic, well-drained soil. Dies down in late autumn or winter; then keep rhizomes nearly dry. Propagate by division or seed in spring or by stem or leaf cuttings in summer.

G. perennis illus. p.421.

G. speciosa. See *Sinningia speciosa.*

GLYCERIA

Manna grass

POACEAE

See also GRASSES, BAMBOOS, RUSHES, and SEDGES.

***G. aquatica* 'Variegata'.** See *G. maxima* 'Variegata'.

***G. maxima* 'Variegata'**, syn. *G. aquatica* 'Variegata', illus. p.306.

GLYCYRRHIZA

Licorice

LEGUMINOSAE/PAPILIONACEAE

Genus of summer-flowering perennials. Needs sun and deep, rich, well-drained soil. Propagate by division in spring or seed in autumn or spring.

G. glabra illus. p.250.

Godetia. Reclassified as *Clarkia*.

GOMESA

See also ORCHIDS.

G. planifolia (illus. p.298). Evergreen, epiphytic orchid for a cool greenhouse. H 9in (23cm). Sprays of star-shaped, pea green flowers, ¼in (0.5cm) across, are produced in autumn. Narrowly oval leaves are 6in (15cm) long. Grow in semi-shade during summer. Z14–15 H12–6.

GOMPHOCARPUS

ASCLEPIADACEAE

Genus of evergreen and deciduous subshrubs and perennials. Hooded, cup-shaped flowers are followed by seed pods that are usually inflated. Grows in sun or partial shade and in any well-drained soil. Propagate by seed or softwood cuttings in spring. Some species exude a milky sap, which may aggravate skin allergies.

G. physocarpus, syn. *Asclepias physocarpa*, illus. p.232.

GOMPHRENA

AMARANTHACEAE

Genus of annuals, biennials, and perennials. Only one species, *G. globosa*, is usually cultivated; its flower heads are good for cutting and drying. Grows best in sun and in fertile, well-drained soil. Propagate by seed sown under cover in spring.

G. globosa illus. p.331.

GONGORA

See also ORCHIDS.

G. quinquenervis (illus. p.298). Evergreen, epiphytic orchid for an intermediate greenhouse. H 10in (25cm). In summer, fragrant brown, orange, and yellow flowers, ½in (1cm) across, which resemble birds in flight, are produced in long, pendent spikes. Has oval, ribbed leaves, 5–6in (12–15cm) long. Is best grown in a hanging basket. Requires semi-shade in summer. Z14–15 H12–6.

GORDONIA

THEACEAE

Genus of evergreen shrubs and trees grown for their flowers and overall appearance. Prefers sun or partial shade and organic, acidic soil. Water potted plants moderately, less in winter. Propagate by semi-ripe cuttings in late summer or by seed when ripe, in autumn, or in spring.

G. axillaris. Evergreen, bushy shrub or tree. H and S 10–15ft (3–5m), sometimes much more. Has lance-shaped, leathery, glossy leaves, each with a blunt tip, and bears saucer-shaped white flowers from autumn to spring. Z9–10 H10–9.

G. lasianthus (Loblolly bay). Evergreen, upright tree. H to 70ft (20m), S to 30ft (10m). Lance-shaped to elliptic leaves are shallowly serrated. Has fragrant, saucer- to bowl-shaped white flowers in summer. Needs sub-tropical summer warmth to grow and flower well. Z8–11 H12–8.

GRAPTOPETALUM

CRASSULACEAE

Genus of rosetted succulents very similar to *Echeveria*, with which it hybridizes. Is easy to grow, needing sun or partial shade and very well-drained soil. Propagate by seed or by stem or leaf cuttings in spring or summer.

G. amethystinum. Clump-forming, prostrate succulent. H 16in (40cm), S 36in (90cm). Produces thick, rounded, blue-gray to red leaves, 3in (7cm) long, in terminal rosettes and star-shaped, yellow-and-red flowers, ½–¾in (1–2cm) across, in spring-summer. Z13–15 H12–10.

G. bellum, syn. *Tacitus bellus*, illus. p.473.

G. paraguayense illus. p.478.

GRAPTOPHYLLUM

ACANTHACEAE

Genus of evergreen shrubs grown mainly for their foliage. Needs partial shade and fertile, well-drained soil. Water potted plants freely when in full growth, much less when temperatures are low. Young plants need tip pruning after flowering to promote branching; leggy specimens may be cut back hard after flowering or in spring. Propagate by greenwood or semi-ripe cuttings in spring or summer.

G. pictum (Caricature plant). Evergreen, erect, loose shrub. H to 6ft (2m), S 2ft (60cm) or more. Has oval, pointed, glossy green leaves with central yellow blotches. Bears short, terminal spikes of tubular red to purple flowers in spring and early summer. Z13–15 H12–10.

GRASSES, BAMBOOS, RUSHES, AND SEDGES

Group of evergreen or herbaceous, perennial and annual grasses or grass-like plants belonging to the Gramineae (including Bambusoideae), Juncaceae, and Cyperaceae families. They are grown mainly as foliage plants, adding grace and contrast to borders and rock gardens, although several grasses have attractive flower heads in summer that may be dried for winter decoration. Dead foliage may be cut back on herbaceous perennials when dormant. Propagate species by seed in spring or autumn or by division in spring; selected forms by division only. Pests and diseases usually give little trouble. Grasses, bamboos, rushes, and sedges are illustrated on pp.306–309.

Grasses (Gramineae)
Family of evergreen, semi-evergreen, or herbaceous, sometimes creeping perennials, annuals, and marginal water plants, usually with rhizomes or stolons, that form tufts, clumps, or carpets. All have basal leaves and rounded flower stems that bear alternate, long, narrow leaves. Flowers are bisexual (males and females in same spikelet) and are arranged in panicles, racemes, or spikes. Each flower head consists of spikelets, with one or more florets, that are covered with glumes (scales), from which awns (long, slender bristles) may grow. Unless otherwise stated, grasses will tolerate a range of light conditions and flourish in any well-drained soil. Many genera, such as *Briza*, self seed readily.

See also *Alopecurus, Arrhenatherum, Arundo, Bouteloua, Briza, Bromus, Chionochloa, Coix, Cortaderia, Dactylis, Deschampsia, Festuca, Glyceria, Hakonechloa, Helictotrichon, Holcus, Hordeum, Lagurus, Lamarckia, Leymus, Melica, Melinis, Milium, Miscanthus, Molinia, Oplismenus, Panicum, Pennisetum, Phalaris, Sesleria, Setaria, Spartina, Stenotaphrum, Stipa, Zea,* and *Zizania*.

Bamboos (Bambusoideae)
Subfamily of the Gramineae, consisting of evergreen, rhizomatous perennials, sometimes grown as hedging as well as for ornamentation. Most bamboos differ from other perennial grasses in that they have woody stems (culms). These are hollow (except in *Chusquea*), mostly greenish brown, and, due to their silica content, very strong, with a circumference of up to 6in (15cm) in some tropical species. Leaves are lance-shaped with cross veins that give a checkered appearance, which may be obscured in the more tender species. Flowers are produced at varying intervals but are not decorative. After flowering, stems die down, but few plants die completely. Bamboos thrive in a sheltered, not too dry situation in sun or shade, unless otherwise stated.

See also *Bambusa, Chusquea, Fargesia, Himalayacalamus, Phyllostachys, Pleioblastus, Pseudosasa, Sasa, Semiarundinaria, Shibataea,* and *Yushania*.

Rushes (Juncaceae)
Family of evergreen, tuft-forming or creeping, mostly rhizomatous annuals and perennials. All have either rounded, leafless stems or stems bearing long, narrow, basal leaves that are flat and hairless except *Luzula* (woodrushes) which has flat leaves edged with white hairs. Rounded flower heads are generally unimportant. Most rushes prefer sun or partial shade and a moist or wet situation, but *Luzula* prefers drier conditions.

See also *Isolepis, Juncus,* and *Luzula.*

Sedges (Cyperaceae)
Family of evergreen, rhizomatous perennials that form dense tufts. Stems are triangular and bear long, narrow leaves, sometimes reduced to scales. Spikes or panicles of florets covered with glumes are produced and contain both male and female flowers, although some species of *Carex* have separate male and female flower heads on the same stem. Grow in sun or partial shade. Some sedges grow naturally in water, but many may be grown in any well-drained soil.

See also *Carex, Cyperus, Eleocharis, Schoenoplectus,* and *Scirpoides.*

GREVILLEA

PROTEACEAE

Genus of evergreen shrubs and trees, grown for their flowers and foliage. Grow in full sun and well-drained, preferably acidic soil. Water potted specimens moderately, very little in winter. Pruning is tolerated if necessary. Propagate by seed in spring or by semi-ripe cuttings in summer. All parts may aggravate skin allergies.

G. alpestris. See *G. alpina*.

G. alpina, syn. *G. alpestris*. Evergreen, rounded, wiry-stemmed shrub. H and S 1–2ft (30–60cm). Has narrowly oblong or oval leaves, dark green above, silky-haired beneath. Bears tubular red flowers in small clusters in spring-summer. Z9–10 H10–9.

G. banksii illus. p.99.

G. juniperina* f. *sulphurea, syn. *G. sulphurea*, illus. p.169.

***G.* 'Poorinda Constance'.** Evergreen, bushy, rounded shrub. H and S to 6ft (2m). Has small, lance-shaped, mid to deep green leaves with prickly toothed margins. Tubular, bright red flowers in conspicuous clusters are borne from spring to autumn, sometimes longer.

Z10–11 H12–10.
G. robusta (Silky oak). Fast-growing, evergreen, upright to conical tree. H 100ft (30m), S to 150ft (5m). Fernlike leaves are 6–10in (15–25cm) long. Mature specimens bear upturned bell-shaped, bright yellow or orange flowers in dense, one-sided spikes, 4in (10cm) or more long, in spring-summer. Z10–11 H12–3.
***G.* 'Robyn Gordon'** illus. p.166.
G. rosmarinifolia. Evergreen, rounded, well-branched shrub. H and S to 6ft (2m). Dark green leaves are needle-shaped with reflexed margins, silky-haired beneath. Has short, dense clusters of tubular red, occasionally pink or white flowers in summer.
G. sulphurea. See *G. juniperina* f. *sulphurea*.

GREYIA

GRAYIACEAE

Genus of evergreen, semi-evergreen, or deciduous, spring-flowering shrubs and trees grown for their flowers and overall appearance. Needs full light and well-drained soil. Water containerized specimens moderately, less when not in full growth. Remove or shorten flowered stems after flowering. Propagate by seed in spring or by semi-ripe cuttings in summer. Plants grown under cover need plenty of ventilation.
G. sutherlandii illus. p.131.

GRINDELIA

ASTERACEAE/COMPOSITAE

Genus of annuals, biennials, evergreen perennials, and subshrubs grown for their flower heads. Needs a warm, sheltered site. Requires sun and well-drained soil. Water potted specimens moderately, less when not in full growth. Remove spent flowering stems either as they die or in following spring. Propagate by seed in spring or by semi-ripe cuttings in late summer.
G. chiloensis, syn. *G. speciosa*, illus. p.171.
G. speciosa. See *G. chiloensis*.

GRISELINIA

CORNACEAE/GRISELINIACEAE

Genus of evergreen shrubs and trees, with inconspicuous flowers, grown for their foliage. Thrives in mild, coastal areas, where it is effective as a hedge or windbreak because it is very wind- and salt-resistant. In colder areas provide shelter. Requires sun and fertile, well-drained soil. Restrict growth and trim hedges in early summer. Propagate by semi-ripe cuttings in summer.
G. littoralis (Broadleaf). Fast-growing, evergreen, upright shrub of dense habit. H 20ft (6m), S 15ft (5m). Bears oval, leathery leaves that are bright apple green. Tiny, inconspicuous, yellow-green flowers are borne in late spring. Z7–9 H9–7. **'Dixon's Cream'**, H 10ft (3m), S 6ft (2m), is slower-growing and has central, creamy white leaf variegation. **'Variegata'** illus. p.126.
G. lucida. Fast-growing, evergreen, upright shrub. H 20ft (6m), S 15ft (5m). Is similar to *G. littoralis* but has larger, glossy, dark green leaves.

GUNNERA

GUNNERACEAE/HALORAGIDACEAE

Genus of summer-flowering perennials grown mainly for their foliage. Some are clump-forming with very large leaves; others are mat-forming with smaller leaves. Shelter from wind in summer and cover with hay or compost in winter. Some require sun, while others do best in partial shade; all need moist soil. Propagate by seed in autumn or spring; small species by division in spring.
G. brasiliensis. See *G. manicata*.
G. chilensis. See *G. tinctoria*.
G. magellanica illus. p.384.
G. manicata, syn. *G. brasiliensis*, illus. p.228.
G. scabra. See *G. tinctoria*.
G. tinctoria, syn. *G. chilensis*, *G. scabra*. Robust, rounded, clump-forming perennial. H and S 5ft (1.5m) or more. Has very large, rounded, puckered and lobed leaves, 1½–2ft (45–60cm) across. In early summer produces dense, conical clusters of tiny, dull reddish green flowers. Z9–10 H10–9.

GUZMANIA

BROMELIACEAE

Genus of evergreen, rosette-forming, epiphytic perennials, grown for their overall appearance. Needs semi-shade and a rooting medium of equal parts organic soil and either sphagnum moss, or bark or plastic chips used for orchid culture. Using soft water, water moderately during growing season, sparingly at other times, and keep rosette centers filled with water from spring to autumn. Propagate by offsets in spring or summer.
G. lingulata (illus. p.265). Evergreen, basal-rosetted, epiphytic perennial. H and S 12–18in (30–45cm). Loose rosettes of broadly strap-shaped, arching, midgreen leaves. Cluster of tubular white to yellow flowers, surrounded by a rosette of bright red bracts, usually in summer. Z14–15 H12–1. var. ***minor*** (illus. p.265), H and S 6in (15cm), has yellow-green leaves and red or yellow bracts.
G. monostachia. See *G. monostachya*.
G. monostachya, syn. *G. monostachia*, *G. tricolor* (Striped torch; illus. p.265). Evergreen, basal-rosetted, epiphytic perennial. H and S 12–16in (30–40cm). Has dense rosettes of strap-shaped, erect to arching, pale to yellowish green leaves. In summer, elongated spikes of tubular white flowers emerge from axils of oval bracts, the upper ones red, the lower ones green with purple-brown stripes. Z14–15 H12–1.
G. sanguinea. Evergreen, basal-rosetted, epiphytic perennial. H 8in (20cm), S 12–14in (30–35cm). Has dense, slightly flat rosettes of broadly strap-shaped, arching, mid- to deep green leaves. In summer, a compact cluster of tubular yellow flowers surrounded by red bracts, appears at the heart of each mature rosette. Z14–15 H12–1.
G. tricolor. See *G. monostachya*.
G. vittata. Evergreen, basal-rosetted, epiphytic perennial. H and S 14–24in (35–60cm). Produces fairly loose rosettes of strap-shaped, erect, dark green leaves with pale green cross-bands and recurved tips. Stem bears a compact, egg-shaped head of small, tubular white flowers in summer. Z14–15 H12–1.

GYMNOCALYCIUM

CACTACEAE

Genus of cacti with masses of funnel-shaped flowers in spring-summer. Crowns generally bear smooth, scaly buds. Needs full sun or partial shade and very well-drained soil. Propagate by seed or offsets in spring or summer.
G. andreae illus. p.477.
G. gibbosum illus. p.461.
***G. mihanovichii* 'Red Head'**, syn. *G.m* 'Hibotan', *G.m.* 'Red Cap', illus. p.464.
G. quehlianum. Flattened spherical cactus. H 2in (5cm), S 3in (7cm). Gray-blue to brown stem has 11 or so rounded ribs. Areoles each produce 5 curved spines. Has white flowers, 2in (5cm) across, with red throats, in spring-summer. Easy to bring into flower. Z13–15 H12–10.
G. schickendantzii. Spherical cactus. H and S 4in (10cm). Dark green stem has 7–14 deeply indented ribs and long, red-tipped, gray-brown spines. Bears greenish white to pale pink flowers, 2in (5cm) across, in summer. Z13–15 H12–10.

GYMNOCARPIUM

DRYOPTERIDACEAE/WOODSIACEAE

Genus of about 5 species of deciduous, rhizomatous, terrestrial ferns with triangular fronds, ideal for growing as a groundcover. Grow in deep shade and preferably neutral to acidic, leafy, moist soil. Propagate from spores when ripe, or divide in spring.
G. dryopteris (Oak fern). Deciduous fern. H 8in (20cm), S indefinite. Bears distinctive, divided fronds, each with a leaf-blade 4–7in (10–18cm) long and across, on a stem 4in (10cm) long. Pinnae are triangular, with oblong to ovate, toothed and scalloped segments. Pale yellowish green when young, the fronds darken to vivid rich green as they mature. Z4–8.

GYMNOCLADUS

CAESALPINIACEAE/LEGUMINOSAE

Genus of deciduous trees grown for their foliage. Needs full sun and deep, fertile, well-drained soil. Propagate by seed in autumn.
G. dioica (Kentucky coffee tree). Slow-growing, deciduous, spreading tree. H 70ft (20m), S 50ft (15m). Very large leaves with 4–7 pairs of oval leaflets are pinkish when young, dark green in summer, then yellow in autumn. Small, star-shaped white flowers are borne in early summer, followed by long, bean-like pods on female plants. Z5–9 H9–5.

GYNANDRIRIS

IRIDACEAE

Genus of irislike, spring-flowering corms grown mainly for botanical interest, with very short-lived blooms. Dormant corms require warmth and dryness, so plant in a sunny site that dries out in summer. Needs well-drained soil, but with plenty of moisture in winter-spring. Propagate by seed or by removing cormlets from the parent in autumn.
G. sisyrinchium illus. p.432.

GYNURA

ASTERACEAE/COMPOSITAE

Genus of evergreen perennials, shrubs, and semi-scrambling climbers grown for their ornamental foliage or flower heads. Needs light shade in summer and any fertile, well-drained soil. Water moderately throughout the year, less in cool conditions; do not overwater. Provide support for stems. Remove stem tips to encourage branching. Propagate by softwood or semi-ripe cuttings in spring or summer.
G. aurantiaca illus. p.220. **'Purple Passion'** (syn. *G. sarmentosa* of gardens) is an evergreen, erect, woody-based, soft-stemmed shrub or semi-scrambling climber. H 2ft (60cm) or more. Stems and lance-shaped, lobed, serrated leaves are covered with velvety purple hairs. Leaves are purple-green above, deep red-purple beneath. In winter produces clusters of daisylike, orange-yellow flower heads that become purplish as they mature. Z14–15 H12–10.
G. sarmentosa of gardens. See *G. aurantiaca* 'Purple Passion'.

GYPSOPHILA

CARYOPHYLLACEAE

Genus of spring- to autumn-flowering annuals and perennials, some of which are semi-evergreen. Needs sun. Will grow in dry, sandy, and stony soils but does best in deep, well-drained soil. Resents being disturbed. Cut back after flowering for a second flush of flowers. Propagate *G. paniculata* cultivars by grafting in winter; others by softwood cuttings in summer or by seed in autumn or spring.
G. cerastioides illus. p.364.
G. elegans illus. p.318.
***G. paniculata* 'Bristol Fairy'** illus. p.239. **'Flamingo'** is a spreading, short-lived perennial. H 2–2½ft (60–75cm), S 3ft (1m). In summer bears panicles of numerous, small, rounded, double, pale pink flowers on wiry, branching stems. Has small, linear, midgreen leaves. Z4–9 H9-2.
G. repens. Semi-evergreen, prostrate

perennial with much-branched rhizomes. H 1–2in (2.5–5cm) or more, S 12in (30cm) or more. In summer produces sprays of small, rounded white, lilac, or pink flowers on slender stems that bear narrowly oval, bluish green leaves. Is excellent for a rock garden, wall, or dry bank. May also be propagated by division in spring. Z4–7 H7–1. **'Dorothy Teacher'** illus. p.375.

HAAGEOCEREUS

CACTACEAE

Genus of cacti with ribbed, densely spiny, columnar green stems branching from the base. Requires full sun and very well-drained soil. Propagate by seed or stem cuttings in spring or summer.
H. ambiguus. See *H. decumbens*.
H. australis. See *H. decumbens*.
H. chosicensis. See. *H. multangularis*.
H. decumbens, syn. *H. ambiguus*, *H. australis*, *H. litoralis*. Prostrate cactus. H 1ft (30cm), S 3ft (1m). Stems, 2½in (6cm) across, with 20 or so ribs, have dark brown central spines, 2in (5cm) long, and shorter, dense golden radial spines. Tubular white flowers, 3in (8cm) across, are produced in summer near crowns, only on mature plants. Z13–15 H12-10.
H. litoralis. See *H. decumbens*.
H. multangularis, syn. *H. chosicensis*. Upright cactus. H 5ft (1.5m), S 3ft (1m). Green stem, 4in (10cm) across, with 19 or so ribs, bears white, golden, or red central spines and shorter, dense, bristlelike white radial ones. Has tubular white, lilac-white, or pinkish red flowers, 3in (7cm) long, near the crown in summer. Z13–15 H12-10.
H. versicolor illus. p.458.

HABERLEA

GESNERIACEAE

Genus of evergreen, rosetted perennials grown for their elegant sprays of flowers. Is useful on walls. Needs partially shaded, moist soil. Resents disturbance to roots. Propagate by seed in spring or by leaf cuttings or offsets in early summer.
H. ferdinandi-coburgii. Evergreen, dense, basal-rosetted perennial. H 4–6in (10–15cm), S 12in (30cm). Has oblong, toothed, dark green leaves, hairy below, almost glabrous above. Sprays of funnel-shaped, blue-violet flowers, each with a white throat, appear on long stems in late spring and early summer. Z5–8 H8–5.
H. rhodopensis. Evergreen, dense, basal-rosetted perennial. H 4in (10cm), S 6in (15cm) or more. Is similar to *H. ferdinandi-coburgii*, but leaves are soft-haired on both surfaces. Z5–7 H7–5. **'Virginalis'** illus. p.373.

HABRANTHUS

AMARYLLIDACEAE

Genus of summer- and autumn-flowering bulbs with funnel-shaped flowers. Needs a sheltered, sunny site and fertile soil that is well supplied with moisture in the growing season. Propagate by seed or offsets in spring.
H. andersonii. See *H. tubispathus*.
H. brachyandrus. Summer-flowering bulb. H to 12in (30cm), S 2–3in (5–8cm). Long, linear, semi-erect, narrow leaves form a basal cluster. Each flower stem bears a semi-erect, widely funnel-shaped, pinkish red flower, 3–4in (7–10cm) long. Z10–11 H12–10.
H. robustus, syn. *Zephyranthes robusta*, illus. p.437.
H. tubispathus, syn. *H. andersonii*. Summer-flowering bulb. H to 6in (15cm), S 2in (5cm). Has linear, semi-erect, basal leaves and a succession of flower stems each bearing solitary 1–1½in (2.5–3.5cm) long, funnel-shaped flowers, yellow inside, copper-red outside. Z10–11 H12–10.

HACQUETIA,
syn. DONDIA

APIACEAE/UMBELLIFERAE

Genus of one species of clump-forming, rhizomatous perennial that creeps slowly and is grown for its yellow or yellow-green flower heads borne on leafless plants in late winter and early spring. Is good in rock gardens. Prefers shade and organic, moist soil. Resents disturbance to roots. Propagate by division in spring, by seed when fresh in autumn, or by root cuttings in winter.
H. epipactis illus. p.371.

HAEMANTHUS

AMARYLLIDACEAE

Genus of summer-flowering bulbs with dense heads of small, star-shaped flowers, often brightly colored. Prefers full sun or partial shade and well-drained soil or sandy soil mix. Apply liquid fertilizer in the growing season. Leave undisturbed as long as possible before replanting. Propagate by offsets or seed before growth commences in early spring. All parts may cause mild stomach upset if ingested; contact with the sap may irritate skin.
H. albiflos (Paintbrush). Summer-flowering bulb. H 2–12in (5–30cm), S 8–12in (20–30cm). Has 2–6 almost prostrate, broadly elliptic leaves with hairy edges. Flower stem, appearing between leaves, bears a brushlike head of up to 50 white flowers with very narrow petals and protruding stamens. Z13–15 H12-10.
H. coccineus illus. p.435.
H. katherinae. See *Scadoxus multiflorus* subsp. *katherinae*.
H. magnificus. See *Scadoxus puniceus*.
H. multiflorus. See *Scadoxus multiflorus*.
H. natalensis. See *Scadoxus puniceus*.
H. puniceus. See *Scadoxus puniceus*.
H. sanguineus. Summer-flowering bulb. H to 12in (30cm), S 8–12in (20–30cm). Bears 2 prostrate, elliptic, rough, dark green leaves, hairy beneath. Brownish purple-spotted green flower stem, forming before leaves, produces a dense head of small, narrow-petaled red flowers surrounded by whorls of narrow, leaf-like red or pink bracts.

HAKEA

PROTEACEAE

Genus of evergreen shrubs and trees grown for their often needlelike leaves and their flowers. Is very wind-resistant, except in cold areas. Requires a position in full sun and fertile, well-drained soil. Water containerized specimens moderately in the growing season, but only sparingly in winter. Propagate by semi-ripe cuttings in summer or by seed in autumn.
H. lissosperma, syn. *H. sericea* of gardens. Evergreen, upright, densely branched shrub of pinelike appearance. H 15ft (5m), S 10ft (3m). Bears long, slender, sharply pointed, gray-green leaves and produces, in late spring and early summer, clusters of small, spidery white flowers. Z10–11 H12–10.
H. sericea of gardens. See *H. lissosperma*.
H. suaveolens. Evergreen, rounded shrub. H and S 6ft (2m) or more. Tender. Leaves are divided into cylindrical, needlelike leaflets or occasionally are undivided and lance-shaped. Small, fragrant, tubular white flowers, carried in short, dense clusters, are produced from summer to winter. Z10–11 H12–10.

HAKONECHLOA

GRAMINEAE/POACEAE

See also GRASSES, BAMBOOS, RUSHES, and SEDGES.
***H. macra* 'Aureola'** illus. p.309.

HALESIA
Silver bell, Snowdrop tree

STYRACACEAE

Genus of deciduous, spring-flowering trees and shrubs grown for their showy, pendent, bell-shaped flowers and their curious, winged fruits. Needs a sunny, sheltered position. Prefers moist but well-drained, neutral to acidic soil. Propagate by softwood cuttings in summer or by seed in autumn.
H. carolina, syn. *H. tetraptera*. Deciduous, spreading tree or shrub. H 25ft (8m), S 30ft (10m). Oval leaves are midgreen. Masses of bell-shaped white flowers hanging from bare shoots are produced in late spring and are followed by 4-winged green fruits. Z5–8 H8–4.
H. monticola illus. p.76.
H. tetraptera. See *H. carolina*.

x HALIMIOCISTUS

CISTACEAE

Hybrid genus (*Cistus* x *Halimium*) of evergreen shrubs grown for their flowers. Requires full sun and well-drained soil. Propagate by semi-ripe cuttings in summer.
x ***H. sahucii***, syn. *Cistus revolii* of gardens, illus. p.159.
x ***H. wintonensis***, syn. *Halimium wintonense*. Evergreen, bushy shrub. H 2ft (60cm), S 3ft (1m). Saucer-shaped white flowers, each with deep red bands and a yellow center, open amid lance-shaped, gray-green leaves in late spring and early summer. Z7–9 H9–7.

HALIMIUM

CISTACEAE

Genus of evergreen shrubs grown for their showy flowers. Is good for coastal gardens. Does best in full sun and light, well-drained soil. Propagate by semi-ripe cuttings in summer.
H. formosum. See *H. lasianthum* subsp. *formosum*.
H. lasianthum. Evergreen, bushy, spreading shrub. H 3ft (1m), S 5ft (1.5m). Leaves are oval and gray-green. In late spring and early summer bears saucer-shaped, golden yellow flowers, sometimes with small, central red blotches. Z9–11 H12–9. subsp. ***formosum*** (syn. *H. formosum*) illus. p.169.
H. ocymoides, syn. *Cistus algarvensis*. Evergreen, bushy shrub. H 2ft (60cm), S 3ft (1m). Narrowly oval leaves, covered in white hairs when young, mature to dark green. In early summer produces upright clusters of saucer-shaped, golden yellow flowers, conspicuously blotched with black or purple. Z9–11 H12–9. **'Susan'** see *H.* 'Susan'.
***H.* 'Susan'**, syn. *H. ocymoides* 'Susan', illus. p.169.
H. umbellatum, syn. *Helianthemum umbellatum*, illus. p.159.
H. wintonense. See x *Halimiocistus wintonensis*.

HAMAMELIS
Witch hazel

HAMAMELIDACEAE

Genus of deciduous, autumn- to early spring-flowering shrubs grown for their autumn color and fragrant, cold-resistant flowers, each with 4 narrowly strap-shaped petals. Flourishes in sun or semi-shade and fertile, well-drained, peaty, acidic soil. Propagate species by seed in autumn and selected forms by softwood cuttings in summer, by budding in late summer, or by grafting in winter.
***H.* x *intermedia* 'Arnold Promise'** illus. p.126. **'Diane'** illus. p.125. **'Jelena'** is a deciduous, upright shrub. H and S 12ft (4m) or more. Broadly oval, glossy, bright green leaves turn bright orange or red in autumn. Bears masses of large, fragrant orange

flowers along bare branches from early to midwinter. **'Pallida'** (syn. *H. mollis* 'Pallida'), S 10ft (3m), bears dense clusters of large, sulfur yellow flowers. All Z5–9 H9–1.
H. japonica (Japanese witch hazel). Deciduous, upright, open shrub. H and S 12ft (4m). Broadly oval, glossy, mid-green leaves turn yellow in autumn. Fragrant yellow flowers, with crinkled petals are produced on bare branches from mid- to late winter. Z5–9 H9–5. **'Sulphurea'** illus. p.126. **'Zuccariniana'** bears paler, lemon yellow flowers in early spring and orange-yellow leaves in autumn.
H. mollis (Chinese witch hazel). Deciduous, upright, open shrub. H and S 12ft (4m) or more. Broadly oval, midgreen leaves turn yellow in autumn. Produces extremely fragrant yellow flowers along bare branches in mid- and late winter. Z5–9 H9–5. **'Coombe Wood'** illus. p.126. **'Pallida'** see *H.* x *intermedia* 'Pallida'.
***H. vernalis* 'Sandra'** illus. p.124.
H. virginiana illus. p.125.

Hamatocactus hamatacanthus. See *Ferocactus hamatacanthus.*
Hamatocactus setispinus. See *Thelocactus setispinus.*
Hamatocactus uncinatus. See *Sclerocactus uncinatus.*

HARDENBERGIA

LEGUMINOSAE/PAPILIONACEAE

Genus of evergreen, woody-stemmed, twining climbers or subshrubs grown for their curtains of leaves and racemes of pealike flowers. Grows best in sun and in well-drained soil that does not dry out. Propagate by stem cuttings in late summer or autumn or by seed (soaked before sowing) in spring.
H. comptoniana illus. p.206.
H. monophylla. See *H. violacea.*
H. violacea, syn. *H. monophylla* (Australian sarsparilla, Coral pea, Vine lilac). Evergreen, woody-stemmed, twining climber. H to 10ft (3m). Narrowly oval leaves are 1–5in (2.5–12cm) long. Violet, occasionally pink or white flowers with yellow blotches on upper petals are borne in spring. Brownish pods, 1¼–1½in (3–4cm) long, are produced in autumn. Z12–15 H12–10. **'Happy Wanderer'** illus. p.206.

HATIORA

CACTACEAE

Genus of perennial, epiphytic cacti with short, jointed, cylindrical stems, each swollen at one end like a bottle. Requires partial shade and very well-drained soil. Keep damp in summer; water a little in winter. Propagate by stem cuttings in spring or summer.
H. clavata, syn. *Rhipsalis clavata*. Pendent, perennial, epiphytic cactus. H 2ft (60cm), S 3ft (1m). Multi-branched, cylindrical, dark green stems each widen toward tips. Masses of terminal, bell-shaped white flowers, ⅝in (1.5cm) wide, appear in late winter and early spring on plants over 1ft (30cm) high.
H. gaertneri, syn. *Rhipsalidopsis gaertneri*, illus. p.475.
H. rosea, syn. *Rhipsalidopsis rosea*, illus. p.472.
H. salicornioides, syn. *Rhipsalis salicornioides*, illus. p.468.

HAWORTHIA

ALOEACEA/LILIACEAE

Genus of basal-rosetted, clump-forming succulents with triangular to rounded green leaves. Roots tend to wither in winter or during long periods of drought. Needs partial shade to stay green and grow quickly; if planted in full sun many turn red or orange and grow slowly. Requires very well-drained soil. Keep dry in winter. Propagate by seed or division from spring to autumn.
H. arachnoidea, syn. *H. setata*, illus. p.470.
H. attenuata. Clump-forming succulent. H 3in (7cm), S 10in (25cm). Bears a basal rosette of triangular, dark green leaves, 3cm 1¼in (3cm) long, covered in raised white dots. Has tubular to bell-shaped white flowers on long, slender stems from spring to autumn. Z12–15 H12–10.
f. ***clariperla*** illus. p.469.
H.* x *cuspidata. Clump-forming succulent. H 2in (5cm), S 10in (25cm). Produces a basal rosette of smooth, rounded, fleshy, light green leaves covered with translucent marks. Tubular to bell-shaped white flowers appear from spring to autumn on long, slender stems. Z13–15 H12–10.
H. fasciata. Slow-growing, clump-forming succulent. H 6in (15cm), S 12in (30cm). Has raised, white dots, mostly in bands, on undersides of triangular, slightly incurved leaves, to 3in (8cm) long, which are arranged in a basal rosette. Bears tubular to bell-shaped white flowers on long, slender stems from spring to autumn. Z12–15 H12–10.
H. setata. See *H. arachnoidea.*
H. truncata illus. p.469.

HEATHERS

ERICACEAE

Heathers (otherwise known as heaths) are evergreen, woody-stemmed shrubs grown for their flowers and foliage, both of which may provide color in the garden all year round. There are 3 genera: *Calluna*, *Daboecia*, and *Erica*. *Calluna* has only one species, *C. vulgaris*, but it contains a large number of cultivars that flower mainly from midsummer to late autumn. *Daboecia* has 2 species, both of which are summer-flowering. The largest genus is *Erica*, which, although broadly divided into 2 groups (winter- and summer-flowering species) has some species also flowering in spring and autumn. They vary in height from tree heaths, which may grow to 20ft (6m), to dwarf, prostrate plants that, if planted 12–18in (30–45cm) apart, soon spread to form a thick mat of groundcover.

Heathers prefer an open, sunny position and require organic, well-drained soil. *Calluna* and *Daboecia* dislike alkalinity and must be grown in acidic soil; some species of *Erica* tolerate slightly alkaline soil but all are better grown in acidic soils. Prune lightly after flowering each year to keep plants bushy and compact. Propagate species by seed in spring or by softwood cuttings, division, or layering in summer. Seed cannot be relied on to come true. All cultivars should be vegetatively propagated. Heathers are illustrated on pp.178–9.

HEBE

SCROPHULARIACEAE

Genus of evergreen shrubs grown for their often dense spikes, panicles, or racemes of flowers and their foliage. Grows well in coastal areas. Smaller species and cultivars are suitable for rock gardens. Requires position in full sun and well-drained soil. Growth may be restricted, or leggy plants neatened, by cutting back in spring. Propagate by semi-ripe cuttings in summer.
H. albicans illus. p.161. **'Cranleigh Gem'** is an evergreen, rounded shrub. H 2ft (60cm), S 3ft (1m). Has dense spikes of small, 4-lobed white flowers, with conspicuous, black anthers, amid narrowly oval, gray-green leaves in early summer. Z9-10 H10–9.
***H.* 'Alicia Amherst'.** Fast-growing, evergreen, upright shrub. H and S 4ft (1.2m). Has large, oblong, glossy, dark green leaves and, in late summer-autumn, large spikes of small, 4-lobed, deep violet-purple flowers. Z9–10 H10–9.
***H.* 'Amy'.** See *H.* 'Purple Queen'.
***H.* 'Andersonii Variegata'.** See *H.* x *andersonii* 'Variegata'.
***H.* x *andersonii* 'Variegata'**, syn. *H.* 'Andersonii Variegata'.Evergreen, bushy shrub. H and S 6ft (2m). Leaves are oblong and dark green, each with a gray-green center and creamy white margins. Has dense spikes of small, 4-lobed lilac flowers from midsummer to autumn. Z10–11 H12-10.
***H.* 'Autumn Glory'** illus. p.167.
***H.* 'Bowles' Variety'** illus. p.168.
H. brachysiphon. Evergreen, bushy, dense shrub. H and S 6ft (2m). Has oblong, dark green leaves. Produces dense spikes of small, 4-lobed white flowers in midsummer. Z8–10 H10–8. **'White Gem'** see *H.* 'White Gem'.
H. buchananii. Evergreen, dome-shaped shrub. H and S 6in (15cm) or more. Very dark stems bear oval, bluish green leaves. In summer produces clusters of small, 4-lobed white flowers at stem tips. Z8–10 H10–8. **'Minor'**, H 2–4in (5–10cm), has smaller leaves.
H. canterburiensis, syn. *H.* 'Tom Marshall'. Evergreen, low growing, spreading shrub. H and S 1–3ft (30–90cm). Small, oval, glossy, dark green leaves are densely packed on stems. In early summer, short racemes of small white flowers are freely produced in leaf axils. Z8-10 H10–8.
***H.* 'Carl Teschner'.** See *H.* 'Youngii'.
H. carnosula. Evergreen, prostrate shrub. H 6–12in (15–30cm), S 12in (30cm) or more. Has small, oblong to oval, slightly convex, fleshy, glaucous leaves. Terminal clusters of many small white flowers with 4 pointed lobes are borne in late spring or early summer.
H. cupressoides illus. p.176. **'Boughton Dome'** illus. p.361.
***H.* 'E.A. Bowles'** illus. p.167.
***H.* 'Eveline'**, syn. *H.* 'Gauntlettii'. Evergreen, upright shrub. H and S 3ft (1m). Has long spikes of small, 4-lobed pink flowers, each with a purplish tube, amid rich green, oblong leaves from late summer to late autumn.
***H.* 'Fairfieldii'.** Evergreen, upright shrub. H and S 2ft (60cm). Oval, toothed, glossy, bright green leaves are red-margined. Large, open panicles of small, 4-lobed, pale lilac flowers are produced in late spring and early summer. Z9–10 H10–9.
***H.* x *franciscana* 'Blue Gem'.** Evergreen, spreading shrub. H 2ft (60cm), S 4ft (1.2m). Has oblong, densely arranged, midgreen leaves. Bears dense spikes of small, 4-lobed, violet-blue flowers from midsummer until early winter. Z9–10 H10–9.
***H.* 'Gauntlettii'.** See *H.* 'Eveline'.
***H.* 'Great Orme'** illus. p.163.
H. hulkeana. Evergreen, upright, open shrub. H and S 3ft (1m). Oval, toothed, glossy, dark green leaves have red margins. Has masses of small, 4-lobed, pale lilac flowers in large, open panicles in late spring and early summer. Z9–11 H12-10. **'Lilac Hint'** illus. p.167.
***H.* 'La Séduisante'**, syn. *H.* 'Ruddigore', *H. speciosa* 'Ruddigore'. Evergreen, upright shrub. H and S 3ft (1m). Oval, glossy, deep green leaves are purple beneath. Produces small, 4-lobed, deep purplish red flowers in large spikes from late summer to late autumn. Z9–11 H12–9.
H. macrantha. Evergreen, bushy shrub. H 2ft (60cm), S 3ft (1m). Has oval, toothed, fleshy, bright green leaves and produces racemes of large, 4-lobed, pure white flowers in early summer. May become bare at base. Z9–11 H12–9.
***H.* 'Midsummer Beauty'.** Evergreen, rounded, open shrub. H 6ft (2m), S 5ft (1.5m). Long, narrow, glossy, bright green leaves are reddish purple beneath. Long spikes of small, 4-lobed lilac flowers that fade to white are borne from midsummer to late autumn. Z9-11 H12–9.
H. ochracea. Evergreen, bushy, dense shrub. H and S 3ft (1m). Slender shoots are densely covered with tiny, scale-like, ochre-tinged, olive green leaves. Clusters of small, 4 lobed white flowers appear in late spring and early summer. Z8–10 H10–8.
H. pinguifolia (Disk-leaved hebe). **'Pagei'** illus. p.351.
***H.* 'Purple Queen'**, syn. *H.* 'Amy',

illus. p.168.
H. rakaiensis. Evergreen, rounded, compact shrub. H 3ft (1m), S 4ft (1.2m). Produces small, dense spikes of small, 4-lobed white flowers amid small, oblong, midgreen leaves from early to midsummer. Z8–10 H10–8.
H. recurva illus. p.161.
***H.* 'Ruddigore'.** See *H.* 'La Séduisante'.
H. salicifolia. Evergreen, upright shrub. H and S 8ft (2.5m). Has long, narrow, pointed, pale green leaves and, in summer, produces slender spikes of small, 4-lobed white or pale lilac flowers. Z9–10 H10–9.
***H. speciosa* 'Ruddigore'.** See *H.* 'La Séduisante'.
***H.* 'Tom Marshall'.** See *H. canterburiensis*.
H. vernicosa illus. p.351.
***H.* 'White Gem'**, syn. *H. brachysiphon* 'White Gem', illus. p.158.
***H.* 'Youngii'**, syn. *H.* 'Carl Teschner'. Evergreen, prostrate, becoming dome-shaped shrub. H 6in (15cm), S 12in (30cm) or more. Blackish brown stems are covered in small, oval, glossy, dark green leaves. Bears short racemes of tiny, 4-lobed, white-throated purple flowers in summer. Is excellent as a border plant. Z8–9 H9–8.

HEDERA
Ivy

ARALIACEAE

Genus of evergreen, woody-stemmed, trailing perennials and self-clinging climbers with adventitious rootlets, used for covering walls and fences and as groundcover. Takes a year or so to become established, but thereafter growth is rapid. On the ground and while climbing, it bears mostly roughly triangular, usually lobed leaves. Given extra height and access to light, leaves become less lobed and, in autumn, umbels of small, yellowish green flowers are produced, followed by globose black, occasionally yellow fruits. Ivies with green leaves are very shade tolerant and do well against a north-facing wall. Those with variegated or yellow leaves prefer more light, are usually less hardy, and often sustain cold and wind damage in severe winters. All prefer well-drained, slightly alkaline soil. Prune in spring to control height and spread, and to remove any damaged growth. Propagate in late summer by softwood cuttings or rooted layers. Spider mite may be a problem when plants are grown in dry conditions. All parts of ivy may cause severe discomfort if ingested; contact with the sap may aggravate skin allergies or irritate skin. See also feature panel p.221.
H. algeriensis. See *H. canariensis* var. *algeriensis*.
H. canariensis (Canary Island ivy). var. ***algeriensis*** (syn. *H. algeriensis*; Algerian ivy) is a fast-growing, evergreen, self-clinging climber. H to 20ft (6m), S 15ft (5m). May be damaged in severe winters but soon recovers. Has oval to triangular, unlobed, glossy, midgreen leaves and reddish purple stems. Z6–11 H12–6. **'Gloire de Marengo'** has silver-variegated leaves. **'Ravensholst'** (illus. p.221) is vigorous with large leaves; makes a good groundcover.
H. colchica (Persian ivy). Evergreen, self-clinging climber or trailing perennial. H 30ft (10m), S 15ft (5m). Has large, oval, unlobed, dark green leaves. Is suitable for growing against a wall. Z6–11 H12–1. **'Dentata'** (Elephant's ears; illus. p.221) is more vigorous and has large, light green leaves that droop, hence its common name. Is good when grown against a wall or as a groundcover. **'Dentata Variegata'**, H 15ft (5m), has variegated, cream-yellow leaves; is useful to brighten a shady corner. **'Paddy's Pride'** see 'Sulphur Heart'. **'Sulphur Heart'** (syn. *H.c.* 'Paddy's Pride'; illus. p.221), H 15ft (5m), S 10ft (3m), has leaves variegated yellow and light green.
H. helix (English ivy). Vigorous, evergreen, self-clinging climber or trailing perennial. H 30ft (10m), S 15ft (5m). Has 5-lobed, dark green leaves. Makes good ground- and wallcover but may be invasive; for a small garden, the more decorative cultivars are preferable. Z5–11 H12–6. **'Adam'** (illus. p.221), H 4ft (1.2m), S 3ft (1m), has small, light green leaves variegated cream-yellow; may suffer leaf damage in winter but will recover. **'Angularis Aurea'** (illus. p.221), H 12ft (4m), S 8ft (2.5m), has glossy, light green leaves with bright yellow variegation; is not suitable as a groundcover . **'Anne Marie'** (illus. p.221), H 4ft (1.2m), S 3ft (1m), has light green leaves with cream varie-gation, mostly at margins; may suffer leaf damage in winter. **'Atropurpurea'** (syn. *H.h.* 'Purpurea'; Purple-leaved ivy; illus. p.221), H 12ft (4m), S 8ft (2.5m), has dark green leaves that turn deep purple in winter. var. ***baltica*** (syn. *H.h.* 'Baltica'), an exceptionally hardy cultivar, has small leaves and makes a good groundcover in an exposed area. **'Buttercup'** (illus. p.221), H 6ft (2m), S 8ft (2.5m), has light green leaves that turn rich butter yellow in full sun. **'Caenwoodiana'** see *H.h.* 'Pedata'. **'Congesta'**, H 1½ft (45cm), S 2ft (60cm), is a non-climbing, erect cultivar with spirelike shoots and small leaves; is suitable for a rock garden. **'Conglomerata'** (Clustered ivy), H and S 3ft (1m), will clamber over a low wall or grow in a rock garden; has small, curly, unlobed leaves. **'Cristata'** see *H.h.* 'Parsley Crested'. **'Curly-locks'** see *H.h.* 'Manda's Crested'. **'Deltoidea'** see *H. hibernica* 'Deltoidea'. **'Digitata'** see *H. hibernica* 'Digitata'. **'Erecta'** (illus. p.221), H 3ft (1m), S 4ft (1.2m), is a non-climbing, erect cultivar similar to *H.h.* 'Congesta'. **'Eva'** (illus. p.221), H 4ft (1.2m), S 3ft (1m), has small, gray-green leaves with cream variegation; may suffer leaf damage in winter. **'Glacier'** (illus. p.221), H 10ft (3m), S 6ft (2m), has silvery gray-green leaves. **'Glymii'** (illus. p.221), H 8ft (2.5m), S 6ft (2m), has glossy, dark green leaves that turn deep purple in winter; is not suitable as a groundcover. **'Goldheart'** (syn. *H.h.* 'Jubiläum Goldherz', *H.h.* 'Jubilee Goldheart', *H.h.* 'Oro di Bogliasco'; illus. p.221), H 20ft (6m), has dark green leaves with bright yellow centers; is slow to establish, then grows rapidly; is not suitable as a groundcover. **'Gracilis'** see *H. hibernica* 'Gracilis'. **'Green Feather'** see *H.h.* Triton'. **'Green Ripple'** (illus. p.221), H and S 4ft (1.2m), has midgreen leaves with prominent, light green veins; is good as a groundcover or for growing against a low wall. **'Hahn's Self-branching'** see *H.h.* 'Pittsburgh'. **'Heise'** (illus. p.221), H 1ft (30cm), S 2ft (60cm), has small, gray-green leaves with cream varie-gation; is suitable as a groundcover for a small area. var. ***hibernica*** see *H. hibernica*. **'Ivalace'** (illus. p.221), H 3ft (1m), S 4ft (1.2m), has curled and crimped, glossy leaves; is good as a groundcover and for growing against a low wall. **'Jubiläum Goldherz'** see *H.h.* 'Goldheart'. **'Jubilee Goldheart'** see *H.h.* 'Goldheart'. **'Königers Auslese'** (syn. *H.h.* 'Sagittifolia'), H 4ft (1.2m), S 3ft (1m), has fingerlike, deeply cut leaves; is not suitable as a groundcover. **'Lobata Major'** (syn. *H. hibernica* 'Lobata Major'; illus. p.221), H 15ft (5m), is vigorous, with large, 3-lobed leaves. **'Manda's Crested'** (syn. *H.h.* 'Curlylocks'; illus. p.221), H and S 6ft (2m), has elegant, wavy-edged, midgreen leaves that turn a coppery shade in winter. **'Merion Beauty'** (illus. p.221), H 4ft (1.2m), S 3ft (1m), with delicately lobed leaves; is not suitable as a groundcover. **'Nigra'** (illus. p.221), H and S 4ft (1.2m), has small, very dark green leaves that turn purple-black in winter. **'Oro di Bogliasco'** see *H.h.* 'Goldheart'. **'Parsley Crested'** (syn. *H.h.* 'Cristata'; illus. p.221), H 6ft (2m), S 4ft (1.2m), has light green leaves, crested at margins; is not suitable as a groundcover. **'Pedata'** (syn. *H.h.* 'Caenwoodiana'; Bird's-foot ivy; illus. p.221), H 12ft (4m), S 10ft (3m), has gray-green leaves shaped like a bird's foot; is not suitable as a groundcover. **'Pittsburgh'** (syn. *H.h.* 'Hahn's Self-branching'; illus p.221), H 3ft (1m), S 4ft (1.2m), has midgreen leaves; is suitable for growing against a low wall and as a groundcover. **'Purpurea'** see *H.h.* 'Atropurpurea'. **'Sagittifolia'** see *H.h.* 'Königers Auslese'. **'Telecurl'** (illus. p.221), H and S 3ft (1m), has elegantly twisted, light green leaves. **'Triton'** (syn. *H.h.* 'Green Feather'), H 1½ft (45cm), S 3ft (1m), is a non-climbing cultivar that has leaves with deeply incised lobes that resemble whips; makes a good groundcover. **'Woeneri'** (illus. p.221), H 12ft (4m), S 10ft (3m), is a vigorous cultivar that has bluntly lobed, gray-green leaves, with lighter colored veins, that turn purple in winter.
H. hibernica, syn. *H. helix* var. *hibernica* (Irish ivy; illus. p.221). Vigorous, evergreen climber. H 15ft (5m), S 20ft (6m). Has large, midgreen leaves. Is good for covering a large area, either on the ground or against a wall. Z6–11 H12–6. **'Deltoidea'** (syn. *H. helix* 'Deltoidea'; Shield ivy, Sweetheart ivy; illus. p.221), H 15ft (5m), S 10ft (3m), has heart-shaped leaves; is suitable only for growing against a wall. **'Digitata'** (syn. *H. helix* 'Digitata'; Finger-leaved ivy; illus. p.221), H 20ft (6m), has large leaves; is not suitable as a groundcover. **'Gracilis'** (syn. *H. helix* 'Gracilis'; illus. p.221), H 15ft (5m), has sharply lobed, dark green leaves that turn bronze-purple in winter; is not suitable as a groundcover. **'Lobata Major'** see *H. helix* 'Lobata Major'. **'Sulphurea'** (illus. p.221), H and S 10ft (3m), has medium-sized leaves with sulfur yellow variegation; is suitable for growing against a wall or as a groundcover and as a foil for brightly colored plants.
H. nepalensis (Nepalese ivy). Evergreen, self-clinging climber. H 12ft (4m), S 8ft (2.5m). Young growth may suffer damage from late frosts. Has oval to triangular, toothed, olive green leaves and is suitable only for growing against a sheltered wall. Z8–11 H12–1.
H. pastuchovii. Moderately vigorous, evergreen, self-clinging climber. H 8ft (2.5m), S 6ft (2m). Has shield-shaped, glossy, dark green leaves and should only be grown against a wall. Z6–11 H12–6.
H. rhombea (Japanese ivy). Evergreen, self-clinging climber. H and S 4ft (1.2m). Has small, fairly thick, diamond-shaped, unlobed, midgreen leaves. Is suitable only for growing against a low wall. Z6–11 H12–6. **'Variegata'** has leaves with narrow white margins.

HEDYCHIUM
Garland flower, Ginger lily

ZINGIBERACEAE

Genus of perennials with thick, fleshy rhizomes. Fragrant, showy flowers are short-lived but borne profusely. Grow in sheltered borders and conservatories. Needs sun and rich, moist soil. Propagate by division in spring; should not be divided when dormant.
H. coronarium (White ginger lily). Upright, rhizomatous perennial. H 5ft (1.5m), S 2–3ft (60cm–1m). Produces dense spikes of very fragrant, butterfly-like white flowers with basal yellow blotches in midsummer. Lance-shaped, midgreen leaves are downy beneath. H7–11 H12–6.
H. densiflorum illus. p.229.
H. gardnerianum illus. p.232.
H. horsfieldii, syn. *Brachychilum horsfieldii*. Clump-forming, tufted perennial. H and S to 3ft (1m). Has short-stalked, lance-shaped, leathery leaves to 1ft (30cm) long. Produces showy, tubular, yellow-and-white flowers, to 3in (8cm) across, in

summer, followed by orange fruits that open to reveal red seeds.

HEDYOTIS,
syn. HOUSTONIA

RUBIACEAE

Genus of mat-forming, summer-flowering perennials. Thrives in shady sites on moist, sandy leaf mold. Propagate by division in spring or by seed in autumn.
H. michauxii illus. p.383.

HEDYSARUM

LEGUMINOSAE/PAPILIONACEAE

Genus of perennials, biennials, and deciduous subshrubs. Prefers sun and well-drained soil. Resents being disturbed. Propagate by seed in autumn or spring.
H. coronarium illus. p.250.

Heeria. Reclassified as *Heterocentron*.
Heimerliodendron brunonianum. See *Pisonia umbellifera*.

HELENIUM
Sneezeweed

ASTERACEAE/COMPOSITAE

Genus of late summer- and autumn-flowering perennials grown for their daisylike flower heads, each with a prominent, central disk. Needs a site in full sun and any well-drained soil. Propagate by division in spring or autumn. All parts may cause severe discomfort if ingested; contact with foliage may aggravate skin allergies.
***H.* 'Bressingham Gold'.** Erect, bushy perennial with thick stems clothed in lance-shaped, midgreen leaves. H 3ft (1m), S 2ft (60cm). Sprays of bright yellow flower heads are produced in late summer and autumn. Z4–8 H8–1.
***H.* 'Bruno'.** Erect, bushy perennial. H 4ft (1.2m), S 2½ft (75cm). Sprays of deep bronze-red flower heads are produced in late summer-autumn. Thick stems are clothed in lance-shaped leaves. Z4–8 H8-1.
***H.* 'Butterpat'.** Compact perennial. H 3ft (1m), S 2ft (60cm). Has thick stems clothed in lance-shaped leaves. Bears sprays of rich deep yellow flower heads in late summer and autumn. Z4–8 H8–1.
***H.* 'Moerheim Beauty'** illus. p.263.
***H.* 'Riverton Gem'.** Erect, bushy perennial. H 4½ft (1.4m), S 3ft (1m). Has sprays of red-and-gold flower heads in late summer-autumn. Stems are clothed in lance-shaped leaves. Z4–8 H8–1.
***H.* 'Wyndley'** illus. p.263.

HELIANTHEMUM
Rock rose

CISTACEAE

Genus of evergreen, spring- to autumn-flowering shrubs and subshrubs grown for their flowers. Is useful for rock gardens and dry banks. Needs full sun and well-drained soil. Cut back lightly after flowering. Propagate by semi-ripe cuttings in early summer.
H. apenninum illus. p.351.
***H.* 'Ben Hope'.** Evergreen, domed shrub. H 9–12in (23–30cm), S 18in (45cm). Bears small, linear gray-green leaves and saucer-shaped, carmine red flowers in midsummer. Z6–8 H8–6.
***H.* 'Ben More'** illus. p.354.
***H.* 'Ben Nevis'.** Evergreen, hummock-forming, compact shrub. H and S 6–9in (15–23cm). Has small, linear, dark green leaves and, in midsummer, saucer-shaped orange flowers with bronze centers. Z6–8 H8–6.
***H.* 'Fire Dragon'** illus. p.354.
***H.* 'Golden Queen'.** Evergreen, domed, compact shrub. H 9in (23cm), S 12in (30cm). Saucer-shaped, golden yellow flowers appear amid small, linear, dark green leaves in midsummer. Z6–8 H8–6.
H. guttatum. See *Tuberaria guttata*.
***H.* 'Jubilee'.** Evergreen, domed, compact shrub. H 6–9in (15–23cm), S 9–12in (23–30cm). Has small, linear, dark green leaves. Bears saucer-shaped, double, pale yellow flowers from spring to late summer. Z6–8 H8–6.
***H. nummularium* 'Amy Baring'.** Evergreen, spreading shrub. H 4–6in (10–15cm), S 60cm (24in). Small, oblong, light gray leaves are hairy beneath. In summer bears a succession of saucer-shaped, orange-centered, deep yellow flowers in loose, terminal clusters. Z6–8 H8–6.
H. oelandicum subsp. ***alpestre.*** Evergreen, open, twiggy shrub. H 3–5in (7–12cm), S 6in (15cm) or more. Produces terminal clusters of 3–6 saucer-shaped, bright yellow flowers from early to midsummer. Leaves are tiny, oblong, and midgreen. Is suitable for growing in a trough. Z6–8 H8–6.
***H.* 'Raspberry Ripple'** illus. p.354.
***H.* 'Rhodanthe Carneum'**, syn. *H.* 'Wisley Pink', illus. p.353.
H. umbellatum. See *Halimium umbellatum*.
***H.* 'Wisley Pink'.** See *H.* 'Rhodanthe Carneum'.
***H.* 'Wisley Primrose'** illus. p.358.
***H.* 'Wisley White'** illus. p.351.

HELIANTHUS
Sunflower

ASTERACEAE/COMPOSITAE

Genus of summer- and autumn-flowering annuals and perennials grown for their large, daisylike, usually yellow flower heads. May be invasive. All need sun and well-drained soil; some prefer moist conditions. Many need staking. Propagate by seed or division in autumn or spring. Contact with the foliage may aggravate skin allergies.
H. annuus (illus. p.337). Fast-growing, upright annual. H 3–10ft (1–3m) or more; S 12–18in (30–45cm). Has large, oval, serrated, midgreen leaves. Very large, daisylike, brown- or purplish centered, yellow flower heads, 12in (30cm) or more wide, are produced in summer. Tall, intermediate, and dwarf cultivars are available. H12–1. **'Music Box'** (dwarf) illus p.336. **'Russian Giant'** (tall), H 10ft (3m) or more, has yellow flower heads with green-brown centers. **'Teddy Bear'** (dwarf) illus. p.337.
***H. atrorubens* 'Monarch'.** Erect perennial. H 7ft (2.2m), S 3ft (1m). Bears terminal, daisylike, semi-double, golden yellow flower heads on branching stems in late summer. Has lance-shaped, coarse, midgreen leaves. Replant each spring to keep in check. Z5–9 H9–3.
H. debilis subsp. ***cucumerifolius* 'Italian White'.** Erect perennial. H 4ft (1.2m), S 1½–2ft (45–60cm). In summer has large, black-centered, creamy white flower heads. Purple-mottled stems bear coarsely hairy, sharply toothed, glossy, midgreen leaves. H12–1.
H.* x *multiflorus illus. p.232. **'Capenoch Star'** is an erect perennial. H 4ft (1.2m), S 2ft (60cm). In summer, daisylike, lemon yellow flower heads are borne terminally on branching stems. Leaves are lance-shaped, coarse, and midgreen. Z5–9 H9–5. **'Loddon Gold'** illus. p.232.
H. orgyalis. See *H. salicifolius*.
H. salicifolius, syn. *H. orgyalis* (Willow-leaved sunflower). Upright perennial. H 7ft (2.2m), S 2ft (60cm). Bears small, daisylike yellow flower heads at ends of thick, branching stems in autumn. Has narrow, willowlike, drooping, deep green leaves. Z6–9 H9–6

HELICHRYSUM

ASTERACEAE/COMPOSITAE

Genus of summer- and autumn-flowering perennials, annuals, and evergreen subshrubs and shrubs. When dried, flower heads are "everlasting." Needs sun and well-drained soil. Propagate shrubs and subshrubs by heel or semi-ripe cuttings in summer; perennials by division or seed in spring; annuals by seed in spring.
H. angustifolium. See *H. italicum*.
H. bellidioides. Evergreen, prostrate shrub. H 2in (5cm), S 9in (23cm). Has small, rounded, fleshy, dark green leaves and, in early summer, terminal clusters of daisylike white flower heads. Z7–10 H10–7.
H. coralloides. See *Ozothamnus coralloides*.
H. italicum, syn. *H. angustifolium* (Curry plant). Evergreen, bushy subshrub. H 2ft (60cm), S 3ft (1m). Has linear, aromatic, silvery gray leaves. Broad clusters of small, oblong, bright yellow flower heads are produced on long, upright white shoots during summer. Z7–11 H12–1. subsp. ***serotinum*** (syn. *H. serotinum*), H and S 6in (15cm), is dome-shaped; stems and oval leaves are densely felted with white hairs. Dislikes winter wet and cold climates. Z7–10 H10–7.
H. ledifolium. See *Ozothamnus ledifolius*.
H. marginatum of gardens. See *H. milfordiae*.
H. milfordiae, syn. *H. marginatum* of gardens. Evergreen, mat-forming, dense subshrub. H 2in (5cm), S 9in (23cm). On sunny days in early summer, large, conical red buds open into daisylike, white flower heads with red-backed petals; they close in dull or wet weather. Has basal rosettes of oval, hairy silver leaves. Prefers very gritty soil. Dislikes winter wet. Propagate in spring by rooting single rosettes. Z8–10 H10–8.
H. petiolare, syn. *H. petiolatum* of gardens, illus. p.175. **'Limelight'** is an evergreen, mound-forming shrub. H to 20in (50cm), S 6ft (2m). Trailing, silver-green shoots bear oval to heart-shaped, bright lime green leaves. In late summer and autumn has daisylike, off-white flower heads. Z10–11 H12–1.
H. petiolatum of gardens. See *H. petiolare*.
H. rosmarinifolium. See *Ozothamnus rosmarinifolius*.
***H.* 'Schwefellicht'**, syn. *H.* 'Sulphur Light', illus. p.291.
H. selago. See. *Ozothamnus selago*.
H. serotinum. See *H. italicum* subsp. *serotinum*.
H. splendidum. Evergreen, bushy, dense shrub. H and S 4ft (1.2m). Woolly white shoots are clothed in small, oblong, silvery gray leaves. Small, oblong, bright yellow flower heads are produced in clusters from midsummer to autumn or sometimes into winter. Z9–11 H12–9.
***H.* 'Sulphur Light'.** See *H.* 'Schwefellicht'.

HELICONIA
Lobster claws

HELICONIACEAE/MUSACEAE

Genus of tufted perennials, evergreen in warm climates, grown for their spikes of colorful flowers and for the attractive foliage on younger plants. Needs partial shade and organic, well-drained soil. Water generously in growing season, very sparingly when plants die down in winter. Propagate by seed or division of rootstock in spring.
H. metallica. Tufted perennial. H to 10ft (3m), S 3ft (1m). Oblong, long-stalked leaves, to 2ft (60cm) long, are velvety green above with paler veins, sometimes purple below. In summer, mature plants bear erect stems with tubular, glossy, greenish white-tipped red flowers enclosed in narrow, boat-shaped green bracts.
H. psittacorum illus. p.229.

HELICTOTRICHON

GRAMINEAE/POACEAE

See also GRASSES, BAMBOOS, RUSHES, and SEDGES.
H. sempervirens, syn. *Avena candida*, *A. sempervirens*, illus. p.307.

HELIOPSIS

ASTERACEAE/COMPOSITAE

Genus of summer-flowering perennials. Requires sun and any well-drained soil. Propagate by seed or division in

autumn or spring.
***H.* 'Ballet Dancer'** illus. p.258.
H. helianthoides* 'Incomparabilis'.** Upright perennial. H to 5ft (1.5m), S 2ft (60cm). Bears daisylike, single orange flower heads in late summer. Leaves are narrowly oval, coarsely toothed, and midgreen. Z4–9 H9–1. **'Patula'** bears flattish, semi-double, orange-yellow flower heads. Z3–9 H9–1. subsp. ***scabra (syn. *H. scabra*) has very rough stems and leaves and double, orange-yellow flower heads. Z4–9 H9–1. subsp. ***scabra* 'Light of Loddon'** (syn. *H.* 'Light of Loddon') illus. p.229.
***H.* 'Light of Loddon'.** See *H. helianthoides* subsp. *scabra* 'Light of Loddon'.
H. scabra. See *H. helianthoides* subsp. *scabra*.

Heliosperma alpestris. See *Silene alpestris*.

HELIOTROPIUM
Heliotrope

BORAGINACEAE

Genus of annuals, evergreen subshrubs, and shrubs grown for their fragrant flowers. Needs full sun and fertile, well-drained soil. Water potted plants freely when in full growth, moderately at other times. In spring, tip prune young plants to promote a bushy habit and cut leggy, older plants back hard. Propagate by seed in spring, by greenwood cuttings in summer, or by semi-ripe cuttings in early autumn.
H. arborescens, syn. *H. peruvianum*, illus. p.167.
H. peruvianum. See *H. arborescens*.

Helipterum manglesii. See *Rhodanthe manglesii*.
Helipterum roseum. See *Rhodanthe chlorocephala* subsp. *rosea*.

HELLEBORUS

RANUNCULACEAE

Genus of perennials, some of which are evergreen, grown for their winter and spring flowers. Most deciduous species retain their old leaves over winter. These should be cut off in early spring as flower buds develop. Is excellent in woodlands. Prefers semi-shade and moisture-retentive, well-drained soil. Propagate by fresh seed or division in autumn or very early spring. Is prone to aphid attack in early summer. All parts may cause severe discomfort if ingested, and the sap may irritate skin on contact.
H. argutifolius, syn. *H. corsicus*, *H. lividus* subsp. *corsicus*, illus p.304.
H. atrorubens. Clump-forming perennial. H and S 1ft (30cm). Shallowly cup-shaped, deep purple flowers are borne in late winter. Has palmate, deeply divided, toothed, glossy, dark green leaves. Z5–9 H9–5.
***H.* x *ballardiae* 'December Dawn'** (illus. p.52). Clump-forming perennial with deep bluish green leaves. H to 14in (35cm), S 12in (30cm). From mid-winter to early spring bears saucer-shaped, white flowers, 2½–3in (6–8cm) across, flushed pinkish purple, maturing to a dull metallic purple. Z6–9 H9–6.
H. corsicus. See *H. argutifolius*.
H. cyclophyllus. Clump-forming perennial. H to 60cm (24in), S 18in (45cm). In early spring produces shallowly cup-shaped, yellow-green flowers with prominent, yellowish white stamens. Leaves are palmate, deeply divided, and bright green. Z6–9 H9–6.
H. foetidus illus. p.305.
H.* x *hybridus [white form] illus. p.300, [pink form] illus. p.301, [purple form] illus. p.302.
H. lividus. Evergreen, clump-forming perennial. H and S 18in (45cm). Has 3-parted, midgreen leaves marbled pale green and purplish green below, with obliquely oval, slightly toothed or entire leaflets. Produces large clusters of cup-shaped, purple-suffused, yellow-green flowers in late winter. Z8–9 H9–8. subsp. ***corsicus*** see *H. argutifolius*.
H. niger illus. p.301.
H. purpurascens. Neat, clump-forming perennial. H and S 1ft (30cm). Small, nodding, cup-shaped, pure deep purple or green flowers splashed with deep purple on outside are produced in early spring. Dark green leaves are palmate and deeply divided into narrowly lance-shaped, toothed segments. Z5–8 H8–5.
H.* x *sternii illus. p.301.
H. viridis illus. p.305.

HELONIOPSIS

LILIACEAE/MELANTHIACEAE

Genus of spring-flowering, rosette-forming perennials. Grow in semi-shade and in moist soil. Propagate by division in autumn or by seed in autumn or spring.
H. orientalis illus. p.269.

HELWINGIA

HELWINGIACEAE

Genus of deciduous shrubs, bearing flowers and showy fruits directly on leaf surfaces, grown mainly for botanical interest. Requires separate male and female plants in order to produce fruits. Needs sun or semi-shade and moist soil. Propagate by softwood cuttings in summer.
H. japonica. Deciduous, bushy, open shrub. H and S 5ft (1.5m). Oval, bright green leaves have bristlelike teeth. In early summer, tiny, star-shaped green flowers appear at the center of each leaf and are followed by spherical black fruits.

Helxine soleirolii. See *Soleirolia soleirolii*.

HEMEROCALLIS
Daylily

HEMEROCALLIDACEAE/LILIACEAE

Genus of perennials, some of which are semi-evergreen or evergreen. Flowers, borne in succession, each last for only a day. Does best in full sun and fertile, moist soil. Propagate by division in late summer to autumn, or spring. Cultivars raised from seed will not come true to type; species may come true if grown in isolation from other daylilies. Slug and snail control is essential in early spring when young foliage first appears. See also feature panel p.257.

Daylilies grow well in Z3–10 H12–2.

***H.* 'Betty Woods'** (illus. p.257). Robust, spreading evergreen, clump-forming perennial. H 26in (65cm), S 2ft (60cm). Large, peony-like yellow flowers are borne in mid- and late summer. Leaves are arching, strap-shaped, and midgreen.
***H.* 'Brocaded Gown'** (illus. p.257). Semi-evergreen, clump-forming perennial. H and S to 2ft (60cm). In summer has rounded, ruffled creamy yellow flowers amid broad, strap-shaped, midgreen leaves.
***H.* 'Catherine Woodbery'.** Robust, clump-forming perennial. H 28in (70cm), S 30in (75cm). Fragrant, trumpet-shaped, delicate, pale lavender flowers with soft lime green throats are produced above strap-shaped, mid-green leaves in late summer.
***H.* 'Cat's Cradle'** (illus. p.257). Semi-evergreen, clump-forming perennial. H 3ft (1m), S 2½ft (75cm). In summer has large, spiderlike, bright yellow flowers amid slender grassy leaves.
***H.* 'Chorus Line'** (illus. p.257). Extended-blooming, semi-evergreen, clump-forming perennial. H 20in (50cm), S 24in (60cm). Produces remontant, triangular, slightly fragrant, bright pink flowers with pink- and yellow-marked tepals and dark green throats from early to midsummer.
H. citrina (illus. p.257). Vigorous, coarse-growing, clump-forming perennial. H and S 2½ft (75cm). Many large, very fragrant, trumpet-shaped, rich lemon yellow flowers open at night in midsummer. Strap-shaped leaves are dark green.
***H.* 'Corky'** (illus. p.257). Clump-forming perennial. H and S 18in (45cm). Bears trumpet-shaped, lemon yellow flowers, brown on outsides, in late spring and early summer above slender, strap-shaped, midgreen leaves. Flowers are borne prolifically.
H. dumortieri. Compact, clump-forming perennial. H 1½ft (45cm), S 2ft (60cm). In early summer produces fragrant, trumpet-shaped, brown-backed, golden yellow flowers. Midgreen leaves are strap-shaped, stiff, and coarse.
***H.* 'Eenie Weenie'** (illus. p.257). Clump-forming perennial. H and S 1ft (30cm). Bears an abundance of clear yellow flowers in early summer. Leaves are narrow and arching.
H. flava. See *H. lilioasphodelus*.
***H.* 'Frank Gladney'.** Robust, semi-evergreen, clump-forming perennial. In summer produces very large, rounded, vivid coral-pink flowers with golden throats; anthers are black. Broad, strap-shaped leaves are midgreen.
H. fulva (Fulvous daylily, Tawny daylily). Vigorous, clump-forming perennial. H 3ft (1m), S 2½ft (75cm). Trumpet-shaped, tawny orange flowers appear from mid- to late summer above a mound of strap-shaped, light green leaves. **'Flore Pleno'** (illus. p.257) has double flowers. **'Kwanzo Variegata'** has leaves variably marked with white.
***H.* 'Gentle Shepherd'** (illus. p.257). Semi-evergreen, clump-forming perennial. H 28in (70cm), S 24in (60cm). From early to midsummer carries ruffled, near-white flowers with green throats above light green leaves.
***H.* 'Golden Chimes'** (illus. p.257). Clump-forming perennial of graceful habit. H 2½ft (75cm), S 2ft (60cm). Bears small, delicate, trumpet-shaped, golden yellow flowers with a brown reverse from early to midsummer. Has narrow, strap-shaped, midgreen leaves.
***H.* 'Hyperion'** (illus. p.257). Clump-forming perennial. H and S 3ft (90cm). In midsummer, very fragrant, lilylike, pale lemon yellow flowers are borne above strap-shaped leaves.
***H.* 'Joan Senior'** (illus. p.257). Vigorous, semi-evergreen, clump-forming perennial. H 25in (63cm), S 3ft (1m). Open trumpet-shaped, almost pure white flowers are produced on well-branched stems from mid- to late summer. Leaves are strap-shaped and midgreen.
***H.* 'Jolyene Nichole'** (illus. p.257). Semi-evergreen, clump-forming perennial. H and S 20in (50cm). Bears rounded, ruffled, rose-pink flowers amid lush, blue-green leaves.
***H.* 'Lady Fingers'** (illus. p.257). Semi-evergreen, clump-forming perennial with narrow leaves. H 32in (80cm), S 30in (75cm). In midsummer, bears spider-shaped, pale yellow-green flowers with green throats and spoon-shaped tepals.
H. lilioasphodelus (syn. *H. flava*; illus. p.257). Robust, clump-forming, spreading perennial. H and S 2ft (60cm) or more. Very fragrant, delicate, lemon- to chrome yellow flowers, lasting sometimes 2 days, are borne in late spring and early summer. Strap-shaped leaves are midgreen.
***H.* 'Lullaby Baby'.** Vigorous, semi-evergreen, clump-forming perennial. H and S 20in (50cm). Produces very pale pink flowers with green throats in midsummer amid strap-shaped, mid-green leaves.
***H.* 'Luxury Lace'.** Compact, clump-forming perennial. H 2½ft (75cm), S 2ft (60cm). In late summer produces small, trumpet-shaped, creamy lavender-pink flowers with lime green throats and prominent anthers. Each petal is curled and ruffled and has a near-white midrib. Leaves are strap-shaped and midgreen.
***H.* 'Marion Vaughn'** (illus. p.257). Clump-forming perennial. H 3ft (1m), S 2ft (60cm). Produces fragrant, trumpet-shaped, green-throated, pale lemon yellow flowers in late summer. Each petal has a raised, near-white

midrib. Strap-shaped leaves are midgreen.
***H.* 'Mauna Loa'** (illus. p.257). Vigorous, free-flowering, evergreen, clump-forming perennial. H 22in (55cm), S 3ft (1m). Produces rounded, bright tangerine-orange flowers with chartreuse throats and contrasting black anthers in mid- to late summer.
***H.* 'Millie Schlumpf'** (illus. p.257). Vigorous, free-flowering, evergreen, clump-forming perennial. H 20in (50cm), S 24in (60cm). Triangular to rounded, pale pink flowers with deeper pink halos and green throats are borne in early to midsummer.
H. minor (Grass-leaved daylily). Compact, clump-forming perennial. H 16in (40cm), S 18in (45cm). In early summer, fragrant, trumpet-shaped, lemon yellow flowers with tawny-backed outer petals overtop narrowly strap-shaped, midgreen leaves that die back in early autumn.
***H.* 'Prairie Blue Eyes'** (illus. p.257). Semi-evergreen, clump-forming perennial. H 32in (80cm), S 36in (90cm). In midsummer produces lavender flowers, banded with blue-purple, that have green throats. Slender, strap-shaped leaves are midgreen.
***H.* 'Real Wind'** (illus. p.257). Vigorous, free-flowering, evergreen, clump-forming perennial with dense foliage. H 26in (65cm), S 3ft (1m). Produces triangular to round, pale buff to salmon-pink flowers with bold rose-pink eyes in mid- to late summer.
***H.* 'Ruffled Apricot'** (illus. p.257). Slow-growing, clump-forming perennial. Large, deep apricot flowers with lavender-pink midribs are ruffled at edges. Leaves are stiff, strap-shaped, and midgreen.
***H.* 'Scarlet Orbit'** (illus. p.257). Low-growing, semi-evergreen, clump-forming perennial. H 20in (50cm), S 26in (65cm). Scarlet flowers with green throats open flat amid lush, strap-shaped, midgreen leaves in midsummer.
***H.* 'Siloam Virginia Henson'** (illus. p.257). Clump-forming perennial. H 18in (45cm), S 26in (65cm). In early summer bears rounded, ruffled, creamy pink flowers banded with rose-pink and with green throats. Broad, strap-shaped leaves are midgreen.
***H.* 'Solano Bulls Eye'** (illus. p.257). Vigorous, free-flowering, evergreen, clump-forming perennial. H 20in (50cm), S 30in (75cm). Produces round, bright yellow flowers with deep brownish purple eyes over a long period from early to late summer.
***H.* 'Super Purple'** (illus. p.257). Clump-forming perennial. H 27in (68cm), S 26in (65cm). Bears rounded, ruffled, velvety, red-purple flowers with lime green throats in midsummer amid strap-shaped, light green leaves.

HEMIGRAPHIS

ACANTHACEAE

Genus of annuals and evergreen perennials, usually grown for their foliage. Grows well in bright but not direct sunlight and in moist but well-drained soil. Water frequently during growing season, less in winter. Regularly cut back straggly stems to neaten. Propagate by stem cuttings in spring or summer.
H. repanda illus. p.299.

HEPATICA

RANUNCULACEAE

Genus of very variable perennials, some of which are semi-evergreen. Flowers are produced in early spring before new leaves are properly formed. Needs partial shade and deep, organic, moist soil. Thick, much-branched rootstock resents disturbance. Propagate by seed when fresh or by division or removing side shoots in spring.
H. angulosa. See *H. transsilvanica.*
***H.* x *media* 'Ballardii'.** Slow-growing, dome-shaped perennial. H 4in (10cm), S 12in (30cm). Has rounded, 3-lobed, stalked, soft green leaves and, in early spring, shallowly cup-shaped, many-petaled, intense blue flowers. Fully double, colored forms are also known. Propagate by division only. Z3–8 H8–1.
H. nobilis, syn. *Anemone hepatica, H. triloba.* Slow-growing, semi-evergreen, dome-shaped perennial. H 3in (8cm), S 4–5in (10–12cm). Bears rounded, 3-lobed, fleshy, midgreen leaves. Shallowly cup-shaped, many-petaled flowers – white through pink to carmine, pale to deep blue, or purple – are produced in early spring. Fully double, colored forms are also known. Is excellent when grown in woodland or a rock garden. Z5–8 H8–4.var. ***japonica*** illus. p.369.
H. transsilvanica, syn. *H. angulosa.* Semi-evergreen, spreading perennial. H 3in (8cm), S 8in (20cm). Shallowly cup-shaped, many-petaled flowers varying from blue to white or pink are produced in early spring amid rounded, 3-lobed, hairy, green leaves. Fully double, colored forms are also known. Z5–8 H8–5.
H. triloba. See *H. nobilis.*

HEPTACODIUM

Seven-son flower

CAPRIFOLIACEAE

Genus of deciduous shrubs or small trees flowering in late summer. Needs full sun to dappled shade and a well drained soil. Propagate by seed when fresh or by stem cuttings in spring.
H. miconioides. Deciduous bushy shrub or small tree. H 20ft (6m) S 8-10ft (2.5-3m). Foliage is yellow- green in spring, darkening with age, and turning purplish in fall. Bark is tan and peeling. Clusters of fragrant white flowers appear from late summer to autumn and are followed by purple fruits in red calyces. Z5–9 H9–4.

Heptapleurum. Reclassified as *Schefflera.*

HERACLEUM

Cow parsnip

APIACEAE

Genus of tall perennials with alternate, simple, lobed leaves and compound umbels of flowers. Grow in moist, well drained soil, in full sun to light shade. Propagate by seed sown in place in spring.
H. mantegazzianum (Giant hogweed). Short-lived, large perennial with hollow, purple-blotched stems. H 10ft (3m) S 3ft (1m). Has very large umbels of white flowers. Can cause severe discomfort if ingested. Foliage can cause skin rash and photodermatitis. Z3–9 H9–1.

HERMANNIA

STERCULIACEAE

Genus of evergreen subshrubs and shrubs grown mainly for their flowers. Prefers full light and fertile, well-drained soil. Water containerized plants freely when in full growth, moderately at other times. Tip prune young plants to produce well-branched specimens. Propagate by softwood or greenwood cuttings in late spring or summer.
H. candicans. See *H. incana.*
H. incana, syn. *H. candicans.* Evergreen, bushy subshrub. H and S 24in (60cm) or more. Oval to oblong leaves are covered with white down beneath. Produces small, nodding, bell-shaped, bright yellow flowers carried in terminal clusters to 6in (15cm) long in spring-summer. Z12–15 H12–10.

HERMODACTYLUS

IRIDACEAE

Genus of one species of spring-flowering tuber, with an elongated, fingerlike rootstock, grown mainly for its attractive, irislike flowers. Requires a hot, sunny site, where tubers will mature in summer, and well-drained soil. Grows particularly successfully on hot, alkaline soils. Propagate by division in late summer.
H. tuberosus, syn. *Iris tuberosa*, illus. p.414.

HESPERALOE

AGAVACEAE

Genus of basal-rosetted succulents with very narrow, strap-shaped, grooved, dark green leaves that often have peeling, white fibers at their margins. Is closly related to *Agave* and *Yucca.* Produces offsets freely at base. Grows well in a sunny situation and in very well-drained soil. Propagate by seed or division in spring or summer.
H. parviflora, syn. *Yucca parviflora*, illus. p.462.

HESPERANTHA

IRIDACEAE

Genus of spring-flowering corms with spikes of small, funnel- or cup-shaped flowers. Needs full sun and well-drained soil. Plant in autumn, water through winter, and dry off corms after flowering. Propagate by seed in autumn or spring.
H. buhrii. See *H. cucullata.*
H. cucullata, syn. *H. buhrii.* Spring-flowering corm. H 8–12in (20–30cm), S 1¼–2in (3–5cm). Has linear, erect leaves on lower part of branched stems, each of which produces a spike of up to 7 cup-shaped white flowers, flushed pink or purple outside, that open only at evening. Z10–11 H12–10.

HESPERIS

BRASSICACEAE/CRUCIFERAE

Genus of late spring- or summer-flowering annuals and perennials. Requires a sunny site and well-drained soil. *H. matronalis* tolerates poor soil. Tends to become woody at base, so raise new stock from seed every few years. Propagate by basal cuttings in spring or by seed in autumn or spring.
H. matronalis illus. p.239.

HESPEROCALLIS

LILIACEAE

Genus of spring- to summer-flowering bulbs. Needs a sunny, well-drained site. Is difficult to cultivate in all but warm, dry areas; in cool, damp climates, protect in a cool greenhouse. Requires ample water in spring, followed by a hot, dry period during its summer dormancy. Propagate by seed in autumn.
H. undulata. Spring- to summer-flowering bulb. H 8–20in (20–50cm), S 4–6in (10–15cm). Has a cluster of long, narrow, wavy-margined leaves, semi-erect or prostrate, at base. Thick stems each bear a spike of upward-facing, funnel-shaped white flowers with a central green stripe along each of the 6 petals. Z9–10 H10–9.

Hesperoyucca. Reclassified as *Yucca.*

HETEROCENTRON, syn. HEERIA

MELASTOMATACEAE

Genus of evergreen, summer- and autumn-flowering perennials and shrubs. Requires sun and well-drained soil. Propagate by softwood or stem-tip cuttings in late winter or early spring.
H. elegans, syn. *Schizocentron elegans*, illus. p.284.

Heteromeles arbutifolia. See *Photinia arbutifolia.*

HEUCHERA

Coral bells

SAXIFRAGACEAE

Genus of evergreen, summer-flowering perennials forming large clumps of

leaves that are often tinted bronze or purple. Makes a good groundcover. Prefers semi-shaded position and moisture-retentive but well-drained soil. Propagate species by seed in autumn or by division in autumn or spring, and cultivars by division only, using young, outer portions of crown.
H. americana. Evergreen, mound forming perennial. H 18in (45cm) S 12in (30cm). New foliage has brown to copper marbling and veins. Flowers are greenish and not showy. Z4–8 H8–1. There are many named selections, such as **'Chocolate Veil'** with leaves of chocolate brown and silver; **'Pewter Veil'** with silver leaves and charcoal veins; **'Velvet Night'** with almost black leaves.
***H. cylindrica* 'Greenfinch'** illus. p.276.
***H.* 'Firebird'.** Evergreen, compact perennial. H 2ft (60cm), S 1ft (30cm). In early summer bears long, feathery sprays of small, pendent, bell-shaped, crimson-scarlet flowers. Leaves are rounded, lobed, toothed, and dark green. Z4–8 H8–1.
***H. micrantha* var. *diversifolia* 'Palace Purple'** illus. p.277.
***H.* 'Pearl Drops'.** Evergreen, clump-forming perennial. H 2ft (60cm), S 1ft (30cm). In early summer bears small, pendent, bell-shaped white flowers tinged pink. Leaves are rounded, lobed, toothed, and dark green. Z3–8 H8–1.
***H.* 'Red Spangles'** illus. p.282.
***H.* 'Scintillation'.** Evergreen, clump-forming perennial. H 18–30in (45–75cm), S 12–18in (30–45cm). In early summer produces long, feathery sprays of small, pendent, bell-shaped, deep pink flowers, each rimmed with coral-pink. Bears rounded, lobed, toothed, and dark green leaves. Z3-8 H8–1.

x HEUCHERELLA

SAXIFRAGACEAE

Hybrid genus (*Heuchera* x *Tiarella*) of evergreen, mainly late spring- and summer-flowering perennials. Prefers semi-shade and needs fertile, well-drained soil. Propagate by basal cuttings in spring or by division in spring or autumn.
x ***H. alba* 'Bridget Bloom'** illus. p.278.
x ***H. tiarelloides*** illus. p.278.

Hexastylis. Reclassified as *Asarum*.

HIBBERTIA, syn. CANDOLLEA

DILLENIACEAE

Genus of evergreen shrubs and twining climbers grown for their flowers. Grow in well-drained soil in full light or semi-shade. Water freely in summer, less at other times. Provide stems with support. Thin out congested growth in spring. Propagate by semi-ripe cuttings in summer.
H. cuneiformis illus. p.146.
H. scandens, syn. *H. volubilis*. Vigorous, evergreen, twining climber. H 20ft (6m). Has 1½–3½in (4–9cm) long, oblong to lance-shaped, glossy, deep green leaves. Saucer-shaped, bright yellow flowers, 1½in (4cm) across, are produced mainly in summer. Z12-15 H12–10.
H. volubilis. See *H. scandens*.

HIBISCUS

MALVACEAE

Genus of evergreen or deciduous shrubs, trees, perennials, and annuals grown for their flowers. Needs full sun and organic, well-drained soil. Water containerized specimens freely when in full growth, moderately at other times. Tip prune young plants to promote bushiness; cut old plants back hard in spring. Propagate by seed in spring; shrubs and trees by greenwood cuttings in late spring or by semi-ripe cuttings in summer; and perennials by division in autumn or spring. Whitefly may cause problems.
H. mutabilis (Confederate rose, Cotton rose). Evergreen, erect to spreading shrub or tree. H and S 10–15ft (3–5m). Rounded leaves have 5–7 shallow lobes. In summer-autumn bears funnel-shaped, sometimes double white or pink flowers, 3–4in (7–10cm) wide, that age from pink to deep red. Often dies back to ground level for winter. Z10–11 H12–8.
H. rosa-sinensis. Evergreen, rounded, leafy shrub. H and S 5–10ft (1.5–3m) or more. Oval, glossy leaves are coarsely serrated. Produces funnel-shaped, bright crimson flowers, 4in (10cm) wide, mainly in summer but also in spring and autumn. Z14–15 H12–1. Many color selections are grown including **'The President'** illus. p.141.
H. schizopetalus. Evergreen, upright, spreading, loose shrub. H to 10ft (3m), S 6ft (2m) or more. Has oval, serrated leaves and, in summer, pendent, long-stalked flowers, 2½in (6cm) wide, with deeply fringed, reflexed pink or red petals. May be trained as a climber. Z13–15 H12-10.
***H. sinosyriacus* 'Lilac Queen'** illus. p.143.
***H. syriacus* 'Blue Bird'.** See *H.s.* 'Oiseau Bleu'. **'Diana'** is a deciduous, upright shrub. H 10ft (3m), S 6ft (2m). Has oval, lobed, deep green leaves and bowl-shaped, pure white flowers with wavy-edged petals from late summer to midautumn. Z5–9 H9–5. **'Oiseau Bleu'** (syn. *H.s.* 'Blue Bird') illus. p.145. **'Red Heart'** illus. p.139. **'Woodbridge'** illus. p.141.
H. trionum illus. p.320.

HIDALGOA
Climbing dahlia

ASTERACEAE/COMPOSITAE

Genus of evergreen, leaf-stalk climbers grown for their single, dahlia-like flower heads. Requires full light and organic, well-drained soil. Water freely when in full growth, less at other times. Needs support. In spring thin out crowded stems or cut back all growth to ground level. Propagate by softwood cuttings in spring. Aphids, spider mite, and whitefly may be troublesome.
H. wercklei. Moderately vigorous, evergreen, leaf-stalk climber. H 15ft (5m) or more. Oval leaves are divided into 3, 5, or more coarsely serrated leaflets. In summer bears dahlia-like scarlet flower heads, yellowish in bud.

HIERACIUM
Hawkweed

ASTERACEAE/COMPOSITAE

Genus of perennials; most are weeds, but the species described is grown for its foliage. Needs sun and poor, well-drained soil. Propagate by seed or division in autumn or spring.
H. lanatum illus. p.293.

HIMALAYACALAMUS

GRAMINEAE/POACEAE

See also GRASSES, BAMBOOS, RUSHES, and SEDGES.
H. falconeri, syn. *Arundinaria falconeri*, *Drepanostachyum falconeri*, *Thamnocalamus falconeri*. Evergreen, clump-forming bamboo. H 15–30ft (5–10m), S 3ft (1m). Greenish brown stems have a dark purple ring beneath each node. Has 4–6in (10–15cm) long, yellowish green leaves without visible checkering, and unimportant flower spikes.

HIPPEASTRUM

AMARYLLIDACEAE

Genus of bulbs grown for their funnel-shaped flowers. Is often incorrectly cultivated as *Amaryllis*. Requires a position in full sun or partial shade and well-drained soil. Plant large-flowered hybrids in autumn, half burying bulb; after the leaves die away, dry off bulb until following autumn. Smaller, summer-flowering species should be kept dry while dormant in winter. Propagate by seed in spring or by offsets in spring (summer-flowering species) or autumn (large-flowered hybrids). All parts may cause mild stomach upset if ingested.
Hippeastrums grow well outdoors in Z14–15 H12–10 except where otherwise noted. Widely grown indoors in containers for winter-spring bloom.
H. advenum. See *Rhodophiala advena*.
***H.* 'Apple Blossom'** illus. p.425.
H. aulicum, syn. *H. morelianum*, illus. p.425.
***H.* 'Belinda'.** Winter- and spring-flowering bulb with a basal leaf cluster. H 12–20in (30–50cm), S 12in (30cm). Is similar to *H. aulicum*, but flowers are deep velvety-red throughout, stained darker toward centers.
***H.* 'Bouquet'.** Winter- and spring-flowering bulb with a basal leaf cluster. H 12–20in (30–50cm), S 12in (30cm). Is similar to *H. aulicum*, but has very wide, salmon-pink flowers with deep red veins and red centers.
H. morelianum. See *H. aulicum*.
***H.* 'Orange Sovereign'** illus. p.425.
H. procerum. See *Worsleya rayneri*.
***H.* 'Red Lion'** illus. p.425.
H. reginae. Summer-flowering bulb. H to 20in (50cm), S 8–10in (20–25cm). Flower stem produces a head of 2–4 scarlet flowers, each 4–6in (10–15cm) across and with a star-shaped green mark in the throat. Long, strap-shaped, semi-erect leaves develop at base after flowering has finished. Z11-12 H12–1.
H. rutilum. See *H. striatum*.
H. striatum, syn. *H. rutilum*, illus. p.435.
***H.* 'Striped'** illus. p.425.
H. vittatum. Vigorous, spring-flowering bulb. H 3ft (1m), S 1ft (30cm). Leaves are broadly strap-shaped, semi-erect, and basal. Thick, leafless stem precedes leaves and terminates in a head of 2–6 red-striped white flowers, each 5–8in (12–20cm) across. Z13–15 H12–10.
***H.* 'White Dazzler'.** Winter- and spring-flowering bulb with a basal leaf cluster. H 12–20in (30–50cm), S 12in (30cm). Is similar to *H. aulicum* but has pure white flowers.

HIPPOCREPIS
Vetch

LEGUMINOSAE/PAPILIONACEAE

Genus of annuals and perennials grown for their pealike flowers. Requires full sun and well-drained soil. Propagate by seed in spring or autumn. Self-seeds readily. May be invasive.
H. comosa (Horseshoe vetch) illus. p.386. **'E.R. Janes'** is a vigorous, prostrate, woody-based perennial. H 2–3in (5–8cm), S 6in (15cm) or more. Rooting stems bear small, loose spikes of pealike yellow flowers from late spring to late summer. Leaves are divided, with 3–8 pairs of narrowly oval leaflets. Z5–7 H7–5.

HIPPOPHÄE

ELAEAGNACEAE

Genus of deciduous shrubs and trees, with inconspicuous flowers, grown for their foliage and showy fruits. Separate male and female plants are required in order to obtain fruits. Is suitable for coastal areas, where it is wind-resistant and excellent when grown as hedging. Needs a sunny position and is particularly useful for poor, dry, or very sandy soil. Propagate by softwood cuttings in summer or by seed in autumn.
H. rhamnoides illus. p.124.

HOHERIA

MALVACEAE

Genus of deciduous, semi-evergreen or evergreen trees and shrubs grown for their flowers, produced mainly in summer. Requires sun or semi-shade and fertile, well-drained soil. Propagate by semi-ripe cuttings in summer or by seed in autumn.
H. angustifolia illus. p.90.
***H.* 'Glory of Amlwch'.** Semi-evergreen, spreading tree. H 22ft (7m), S 20ft (6m). Has long, narrowly oval,

glossy, bright green leaves and a profusion of large, 5-petaled white flowers from mid- to late summer. Z9–10 H10–9.
H. lyallii illus. p.90.
H. populnea (Lace-bark). Evergreen, spreading tree. H 40ft (12m), S 30ft (10m). Bears narrowly oval, glossy, dark green leaves and produces dense clusters of 5-petaled white flowers in late summer and early autumn. Bark on mature trees is pale brown and white and often flaky. Z9–10 H10–9.
H. sexstylosa (Ribbonwood). Fast-growing, evergreen, upright tree or shrub. H 25ft (8m), S 20ft (6m). Glossy, pale green leaves are narrowly oval and sharply toothed. Star-shaped, 5-petaled white flowers are borne in clusters from mid- to late summer. Z9–10 H10–9.

HOLBOELLIA

LARDIZABALACEAE

Genus of evergreen, twining climbers grown mainly for their fine foliage. Both male and female flowers are borne on the same plant. Grow in any well-drained soil in a position in shade or full light. Propagate by stem cuttings in late summer or autumn.
H. coriacea illus. p.205.

HOLCUS

GRAMINEAE/POACEAE

See also GRASSES, BAMBOOS, RUSHES, and SEDGES.
H. mollis (Creeping soft grass). **'Albovariegatus'** (syn. *H.m.* 'Variegatus') illus. p.306.

HOLMSKIOLDIA

VERBENACEAE

Genus of evergreen shrubs or scrambling climbers. Any fertile, well-drained soil is suitable in a position in full light. Water freely in growing season, less at other times. Requires tying to supports. Crowded growth should be thinned out in spring or after flowering has finished. Propagate by seed in spring or by softwood or semi-ripe cuttings in summer. Whitefly and spider mite may be troublesome.
H. sanguinea (Chinese hat plant, Mandarin's hat plant). Evergreen, straggly shrub. H to 15ft (5m), S 6ft (2m). Leaves are 2–4in (5–10cm) long, oval, and serrated. Produces showy red or orange flowers with saucer-shaped calyces and central, 5-lobed tubes in autumn through to winter. Z10–11 H12–10.

HOLODISCUS

ROSACEAE

Genus of deciduous shrubs grown for their flowers in summer. Needs sun or semi-shade and any but very dry soil. Propagate by softwood cuttings in summer.
H. discolor illus. p.119.

HOMERIA

IRIDACEAE

Genus of spring- or summer-flowering corms with widely funnel-shaped, cup-shaped, or flattish flowers. Needs a sunny site and well-drained soil. To produce flowers in spring, pot in autumn in a cool greenhouse, water until after flowering, then dry off for summer. To produce flowers in summer, plant in the open in spring. Propagate by seed, division or offsets in autumn. *H. collina* is toxic to livestock.
H. ochroleuca. Spring- or summer-flowering corm. H to 22in (55cm), S 2–3in (5–8cm). Slender, wiry stems each bear 1 or 2 long, narrow, semi-erect leaves on lower part of stem. Bears a succession of upright, cup-shaped to flattish yellow flowers, each sometimes with a central orange stain. Z9–10 H10–9.

HOMOGYNE

ASTERACEAE/COMPOSITAE

Genus of evergreen perennials useful as a groundcover in rock gardens and woodland. Needs shade and moist soil. Propagate by division in spring or by seed when fresh.
H. alpina (Alpine coltsfoot). Evergreen, mat-forming, rhizomatous perennial. H 3–6in (8–15cm), S 6in (15cm) or more. Has kidney-shaped, toothed, glossy leaves and, in summer, stems 3–6in (8–15cm) or more long each carry a daisylike, rose-purple flower head.

HOODIA

ASCLEPIADACEAE

Genus of branching succulents with firm, erect, green stems, generally branching from the base. Needs full sun and very well-drained soil. Is difficult to cultivate. Water sparingly at all times. Propagate by seed or grafting in spring or summer.
H. bainii. Clump-forming succulent. H 12in (30cm), S 6in (15cm). Dull green stem has spiral rows of tubercles, each terminating in a sharp thorn. Produces 5-lobed, dull yellow flowers, 3in (7cm) across, from summer to autumn. Keep dry in winter. Z13–15 H12-10.
H. gordonii. Variable, erect, clump-forming succulent. H 32in (80cm), S 12in (30cm). Green stem is covered with short, spine-tipped tubercles in distorted rows. Often branches into clumps. Produces 5-lobed, flesh-colored to brownish flowers in late summer. Z13–15 H12-10.

HORDEUM

GRAMINEAE/POACEAE

See also GRASSES, BAMBOOS, RUSHES, and SEDGES.
H. jubatum illus. p.307.

HORMINUM

LABIATAE/LAMIACEAE

Genus of one species of basal-rosetted perennial suitable for rock gardens. Needs sun and well-drained soil. Propagate by division in spring or by seed in autumn.
H. pyrenaicum (Dragon's mouth). Basal-rosetted perennial. H and S 8in (20cm). In summer carries whorls of nodding, short-stalked, funnel-shaped, blue-purple or white flowers above oval, leathery, dark green leaves, 3–4in (8–10cm) long. Z6–8 H8–6.

HOSTA

Plantain lily

HOSTACEAE/LILIACEAE

Genus of perennials grown mainly for their decorative foliage. Forms large clumps that are excellent as a groundcover (heights given are those of foliage). Most prefer shade and rich, moist but well-drained, neutral soil. Propagate by division in early spring. Seed-raised plants (except of *H. ventricosa*) very rarely come true to type. Slug and snail control is essential. See also feature panel pp.288-9.

Hostas grow well in Z3–9 H9–1.

H. albomarginata. See *H. sieboldii.*
***H.* 'Blue Moon'.** Slow-growing, compact, clump-forming perennial. H 5in (12cm), S 12in (30cm). Oval to rounded, grayish blue leaves taper to a point. In midsummer, dense clusters of trumpet-shaped mauve flowers are borne just above leaves. Is suitable for a rock garden. Prefers partial shade.
***H.* 'Blue Wedgwood'** (illus. p.288). Slow-growing, clump-forming perennial. H 1ft (30cm), S 1½ft (45cm). Has wedge-shaped, deeply quilted blue leaves and, in summer, produces lavender flowers.
***H.* 'Brim Cup'.** Slow-growing, clump-forming perennial. H 12in (30cm), S 14–16in (35–40cm). Erect, heart-shaped, slightly cupped and puckered, thick, dark green leaves are irregularly margined with cream fading to white. Bears racemes of pale lavender-blue flowers in summer.
H. decorata. Stoloniferous perennial. H 12in (30cm), S 18in (45cm). Oval to rounded, dark green leaves have white margins. Dense racemes of trumpet-shaped, deep violet or sometimes white flowers are borne in midsummer. f. ***normalis*** has plain green leaves.
***H. fluctuans* 'Sagae'**, syn. *H.f.* 'Variegated', *H.* 'Sagae'. Vigorous, clump-forming perennial. H and S 3ft (1m). Has undulate, heart-shaped, olive green leaves boldly margined creamy white. Racemes of bell-shaped, near-white flowers are produced in mid- to late summer on leafy, glaucous gray scapes. **'Variegated'** see *H.f.* 'Sagae'.
H. fortunei. Group of vigorous, clump-forming, hybrid perennials. H 2½–3ft (75cm–1m), S 3ft (1m) or more. Leaves are oval to heart-shaped. **'Albopicta'** (syn. *H.f.* var. *albopicta*; illus. p.289) has pale green leaves, with creamy yellow centers, fading to dull green from midsummer. Racemes of trumpet-shaped, pale violet flowers open above foliage in early summer. **'Aureomarginata'** (syn. *H.f.* 'Yellow Edge'; illus. p.289) has midgreen leaves with irregular, creamy yellow edges. In midsummer, trumpet-shaped violet flowers are carried in racemes above foliage. Mass planting produces effective results. Tolerates full sun. **'Yellow Edge'** see *H.f.* 'Aureomarginata'.
***H.* 'Fragrant Bouquet'.** Clump-forming perennial. H 18in (45cm), S 26in (65cm). Has oval to heart-shaped, slightly undulate, glossy, light green leaves with irregular, creamy yellow margins. Racemes of funnel-shaped, fragrant, mauvish white flowers are produced in late summer. Tolerates some sun.
***H.* 'Francee'** (illus. p.288). Vigorous, clump-forming perennial. H 22in (55cm), S 3ft (1m). Has oval to heart-shaped, slightly cupped and puckered, olive green leaves with irregular white margins. In summer, produces arching, leafy scapes bearing funnel-shaped, lavender-blue flowers. Is late to emerge.
***H.* 'Ginko Craig'** (illus. p.288). Low-growing, clump-forming perennial. H and S 1ft (30cm). Has small, narrow, dark green leaves irregularly edged with white. In summer produces spikes of bell-shaped, deep mauve flowers. Is a good edging plant.
***H.* 'Gold Standard'** (illus. p.289). Vigorous, clump-forming perennial. H 2½ft (75cm), S 3ft (1m). Oval to heart-shaped leaves are pale green, turning to gold from midsummer, with narrow, regular, dark green margins. Racemes of trumpet-shaped violet flowers are produced above leaves in midsummer. Prefers partial shade.
***H.* 'Golden Prayers'** (illus. p.289). Upright, clump-forming perennial. H 6in (15cm), S 12in (30cm). Cupped leaves are puckered and bright golden green. Flowers are white suffused with pale lavender. Good in a rock garden.
***H.* 'Golden Tiara'** (illus. p.289). Clump-forming perennial. H 6in (15cm), S 12in (30cm). Neat, broadly heart-shaped, dark green leaves have well-defined, chartreuse-yellow edges. In summer produces tall spikes of lavender-purple flowers.
***H.* 'Grand Tiara'** (illus. p.289). Vigorous perennial forming a compact mound. H 12in (30cm), S 20in (50cm). Has ovate to heart-shaped, midgreen leaves with irregular, wide yellow margins. In summer, has scapes of bell-shaped, sometimes remontant, deep purple flowers, each striped lavender-blue within.
***H.* 'Great Expectations'** (illus. p.289). Clump-forming perennial. H 22in (55cm), S 34in (85cm). Has green-

margined near-white leaf stalks bearing heart-shaped, stiff, puckered, thick leaves; they are glaucous, blue-green, and irregularly but widely splashed with yellow, fading to near-white in the centers. In early summer, bell-shaped, grayish white flowers are borne on leafy scapes.

***H.* 'Ground Master'** (illus. p.288). Vigorous, stoloniferous, prostrate perennial. H 10in (25cm), S 22in (55cm). Has ovate to lance-shaped, matte, olive green leaves with wavy, irregular creamy margins, fading to white. Straight, leafy scapes of funnel-shaped purple flowers are borne in summer.

***H.* 'Hadspen Blue'** (illus. p.288). Slow-growing, clump-forming perennial. H and S 12in (30cm). Smooth leaves are heart-shaped and deep glaucous blue. Produces short spikes of lavender flowers in summer.

***H.* 'Halcyon'** (illus. p.288). Robust, clump-forming perennial. H 1ft (30cm), S 3ft (1m). Has heart-shaped, tapering, grayish blue leaves that fade to muddy green in full sun; texture may be spoiled by heavy rain. Heavy clusters of trumpet-shaped, violet-mauve flowers open just above foliage in midsummer.

***H.* 'Honeybells'** (illus. p.289). Clump-forming perennial. H 3ft (1m), S 2ft (60cm). Light green leaves are blunt at the tips and have wavy edges. In late summer bears fragrant, pale lilac flowers.

H. hypoleuca (White-backed hosta). Clump-forming perennial. H 1½ft (45cm), S 3ft (1m). Broadly oval leaves have widely spaced veins and are pale green above, striking white beneath. In late summer bears drooping racemes of trumpet-shaped, milky violet flowers with mauve-flecked, pale green bracts. Tolerates full sun.

***H.* 'Kabitan'**, syn. *H. sieboldii* 'Kabitan' (illus. p.289). Clump-forming perennial spreading by stolons. H to 1ft (30cm), S 2ft (60cm). Lance-shaped, thin-textured, glossy leaves are yellow-centered and have narrow, undulating, dark green margins. In early summer produces a short raceme of small, trumpet-shaped, pale violet flowers. Is suitable for a shaded rock garden. Benefits from being established in a pot for the first few years.

H. kikutii. Clump-forming perennial. H 16in (40cm), S 2ft (60cm). Has oval to lance-shaped, deeply veined, dark green leaves. Racemes of bell-shaped, near-white flowers are borne in a tight bunch at the top of the raceme on conspicuously leaning scapes in mid-summer. var. ***caput-avis*** is smaller, and the flower bud resembles a bird's head. **'Kifukurin'** has larger leaves, attractively margined with cream.

***H.* 'Krossa Regal'** (illus. p.288). Vase-shaped, clump-forming perennial. H and S 3ft (1m). Arching, deeply ribbed leaves are grayish blue. Produces tall spikes of pale lilac flowers in summer. Tolerates sun.

H. lancifolia. Arching, clump-forming perennial. H 1½ft (45cm), S 2½ft (75cm). Has narrowly lance-shaped, thin-textured, glossy, midgreen leaves. Produces racemes of trumpet-shaped, deep violet flowers above foliage in late summer through to autumn.

***H.* 'Love Pat'** (illus p.288). Vigorous, clump-forming perennial. H and S to 2ft (60cm). Produces rounded, deeply puckered, deep glaucous blue leaves. Bears racemes of pale lilac flowers during summer.

H. montana. Vigorous, clump-forming perennial. H 3½ft (1.1m), S 3ft (1m). Has oval, prominently veined, glossy, dark green leaves. Racemes of trumpet-shaped, pale violet flowers open well above foliage in midsummer. Slower-growing **'Aureomarginata'** (illus. p.289) has leaves irregularly edged with golden yellow. Is often the first hosta to appear in spring.

***H.* 'Moonlight'** (illus. p.289). Clump-forming perennial. H 20in (50cm), S 28in (70cm). Has pale yellow leaves that emerge olive green narrowly margined white. Requires full shade.

H. nigrescens. Vigorous, clump-forming perennial. H 28in (70cm), S 26in (65cm). Has oval to heart-shaped, concave, puckered, glaucous gray-green leaves, and racemes of funnel-shaped, pearl gray to white flowers on 4½ft (1.4m) undulating scapes in late summer.

***H.* 'Paxton's Original'.** See *H. sieboldii.*

***H.* 'Pearl Lake'.** Vigorous, clump-forming perennial. H 14–16in (35–40cm), S 3ft (1m). Has heart-shaped, flat, glaucous gray-green leaves and racemes of bell-shaped, opalescent lavender-blue flowers on scapes towering above the leaf mound in summer.

***H.* 'Piedmont Gold'** (illus. p.289). Slow-growing, clump-forming perennial. H 2ft (60cm), S 2½ft (75cm). Smooth leaves are bright yellowish green with fluted margins. Racemes of white flowers are produced in summer. Is best in light shade.

H. plantaginea (illus. p.289). Lax, clump-forming perennial. H 2ft (60cm), S 4ft (1.2m). Leaves are oval and glossy, pale green. Rising well above these are flower stems crowned in late summer and early autumn with fragrant, trumpet-shaped white flowers that open in the evening. Prefers sunny conditions. **'Grandiflora'** (syn. *H.p.* var. *japonica*) has larger, longer-tubed flowers, to 5in (13cm) long. Prefers sun. var. ***japonica*** see *H.p.* 'Grandiflora'.

H. rectifolia. Upright, clump-forming perennial. H 3ft (1m), S 2½ft (75cm). Produces oval to lance-shaped, dark green leaves and racemes of large, trumpet-shaped violet flowers from mid- to late summer.

***H.* 'Regal Splendor'** (illus. p.288). Clump-forming perennial. H and S 3ft (1m). Arching, grayish blue leaves are suffused white or yellow at the margins. Talls spikes of lilac flowers are produced in summer.

***H.* 'Royal Standard'** (illus. p.289). Upright, clump-forming perennial. H 2ft (60cm), S 4ft (1.2m). Broadly oval leaves are glossy, pale green. Pure white, slightly fragrant, trumpet-shaped flowers are carried well above foliage and open in the evening. Prefers sun.

***H.* 'Sagae'.** See *H. fluctuans* 'Sagae'.

***H.* 'Shade Fanfare'** (illus. p.288). Vigorous, clump-forming perennial. H 1½ft (45cm), S 2½ft (75cm). Heart-shaped leaves are pale green with cream margins. In summer has an abundance of lavender flowers.

H. sieboldiana (illus. p.288). Robust, clump-forming perennial. H 3ft (1m) or more, S 5ft (1.5m). Large, heart-shaped, deeply ribbed, puckered leaves are bluish gray. Racemes of trumpet-shaped, very pale lilac flowers open in early summer, just above foliage. Makes a good groundcover. Tolerates sun, but leaves may then turn dull green. var. ***elegans*** (illus. p.288) has larger, bluer leaves. **'Frances Williams'** (illus. p.289) has yellow-edged leaves, is slower-growing and should not be grown in full sun.

H. sieboldii, syn. *H. albomarginata*, *H.* 'Paxton's Original' (illus. p.288). Vigorous, clump-forming perennial. H 1½ft (45cm), S 2ft (60cm). Lance-shaped, round-tipped leaves are mid- to dark green with narrow, irregular white edges. Racemes of trumpet-shaped violet flowers appear at tops of stems in late summer and are followed by ovoid, glossy, dark green then brown seed heads that are useful for flower arrangements. **'Kabitan'** see *H.* 'Kabitan'.

***H.* 'Snowden'** (illus. p.288). Clump-forming perennial. H and S 3ft (1m) or more. Produces large, pointed, glaucous blue leaves that age to sage green. Tall stems bear white tinged with green flowers in summer.

***H.* 'Sum and Substance'** (illus. p.289). Vigorous, clump-forming perennial. H and S to 3ft (1m). Produces large, greenish gold leaves that are thick in texture and, in midsummer, tall spikes of pale lavender flowers appear. Tolerates full sun.

***H.* 'Summer Music'.** Clump-forming perennial. H 12in (30cm), S 16in (40cm). Twisted, oval to heart-shaped white leaves of thin substance are widely and irregularly margined light green. Racemes of bell-shaped, pale lavender flowers are produced in summer.

***H.* 'Tall Boy'** (illus. p.289). Clump-forming perennial. H and S 2ft (60cm). Has large, bright green leaves ending in long points. In summer an abundance of rich lilac flowers is produced on stems 4ft (1.2m) tall or more.

H. tardiflora (illus. p.288). Slow-growing, clump-forming perennial. H 1ft (30cm), S 2½ft (75cm). Has narrowly lance-shaped, thick-textured, dark green leaves. Dense racemes of trumpet-shaped, lilac-purple flowers open just above foliage from late summer to early autumn.

***H.* 'Thomas Hogg'.** See *H. undulata* var. *albomarginata*.

H. tokudama (illus. p.288). Very slow-growing, clump-forming perennial. H 1½ft (45cm), S 2½ft (75cm). Produces cup-shaped, puckered blue leaves. Racemes of trumpet-shaped, pale lilac-gray flowers appear just above foliage in midsummer. **'Aureonebulosa'** (syn. *H.t.* 'Variegata'; illus. p.288) has irregular, cloudy-yellow centers to leaves. **'Flavocircinalis'**, often mistaken for a juvenile *H.* 'Frances Williams', has heart-shaped leaves with wide, irregular, creamy yellow margins. **'Variegata'** see *H.t.* 'Aureonebulosa'.

H. undulata var. ***albomarginata***, syn. *H.* 'Thomas Hogg' (illus. p.288). Clump-forming perennial. H 22in (55cm), S 24in (60cm). Has oval to lance-shaped, round-tipped, midgreen leaves irregularly margined cream to near-white. Racemes of trumpet-shaped, pale mauve flowers rise well above the foliage in early and mid-summer. var. ***erromena*** is robust, H 1½ft (45cm), S 2ft (60cm), and bears trumpet-shaped, pale mauve flowers high above oblong, wavy, midgreen leaves. Leaves of var. ***undulata*** have irregular white centers on the first crop of the season and white streaks on the second. Leaf stalks and flower bracts are white with narrow green margins. var. ***univittata*** (illus. p.288) is vigorous with oval, midgreen leaves that have narrow, white centers.

H. ventricosa (illus. p.289). Clump-forming perennial. H 28in (70cm), S 3ft (1m) or more. Has heart-shaped to oval, slightly wavy-edged, glossy, dark green leaves. Racemes of bell-shaped, deep purple flowers appear above foliage in late summer. Usually comes true from seed. **'Variegata'** (syn. *H.v.* 'Aureomarginata'; illus. p.289) has leaves with irregular cream margins.

H. venusta (illus. p.289). Vigorous, mat-forming perennial. H 1in (2.5cm), S to 12in (30cm). Has oval to lance-shaped, mid- to dark green leaves and abundant racemes of trumpet-shaped purple flowers borne well above the foliage in midsummer. Suitable for a rock garden.

***H.* 'Veronica Lake'.** Vigorous, clump-forming perennial. H 14–16in (35–40cm), S 3ft (1m). Has striking, cream-margined, heart-shaped, flat, glaucous gray-green leaves and racemes of bell-shaped, opalescent lavender-blue flowers in summer.

***H.* 'Wide Brim'** (illus. p.289). Vigorous, clump-forming perennial. H and S to 2½ft (75cm). Leaves are heavily puckered and dark blue-green with wide irregular, creamy white margins. Produces white or very pale lavender flowers in summer.

***H.* 'Yellow River'** (illus. p.289). Clump-forming perennial. H 22in (55cm), S 3ft (1m). Has ovate to heart-shaped, pointed, thick, dark green leaves with irregular yellow margins. Leafy scapes of funnel-shaped, very pale lavender-blue flowers are produced in early summer.

***H.* 'Zounds'** (illus. p.289). Slow-growing, clump-forming perennial. H and S to 3ft (1m). Large, bright gold leaves are heavily puckered and have metallic sheen. White or pale lavender flowers are produced in early summer.

HOTTONIA

PRIMULACEAE

Genus of deciduous, perennial, submerged water plants grown for their handsome foliage and delicate, primroselike flowers. Needs sun and clear, cool water, still or running. Periodically thin overcrowded growth. Propagate by stem cuttings in spring or summer.
H. palustris illus. p.447.

Houstonia. Reclassified as *Hedyotis*.

HOUTTUYNIA

SAURURACEAE

Genus of one species of perennial or deciduous marginal water plant with far-spreading rhizomes. Is suitable as a groundcover, although it is very invasive. Prefers position in semi-shade and moist soil, or shallow water beside streams and ponds. Propagate by runners in spring.
***H. cordata* 'Chameleon'**, syn. *H.c.* 'Variegata', illus. p.447.
'Flore Pleno' (syn. *H.c.* 'Plena') is a spreading perennial. H 6–24in (15–60cm), S indefinite. Spikes of insignificant flowers, surrounded by 8 or more oval white bracts, are produced above aromatic, fleshy, leathery, heart-shaped, pointed leaves in spring. Z6–11 H12–2. **'Plena'** see *H.c.* 'Flore Pleno'. **'Variegata'** see *H.c.* 'Chamaeleon'.

HOVENIA

RHAMNACEAE

Genus of one species of deciduous, summer-flowering tree grown for its foliage. Young, immature growth is susceptible to frost damage. Does best in a position in full sun and requires fertile, well-drained soil. Propagate by softwood cuttings in summer or by seed in autumn.
H. dulcis illus. p.79.

HOWEA,
syn. HOWEIA, KENTIA

ARECACEAE/PALMAE

Genus of evergreen palms, grown for their ornamental appearance. Needs partial shade and organic, well-drained soil. Water containerized specimens freely in summer, minimally in winter and moderately at other times. Propagate by seed in spring at not less than 79°F (26°C). Is prone to spider mite.
H. forsteriana (Paradise palm, Sentry palm, Thatch-leaf palm). Evergreen, upright palm with a slender stem. H 30ft (10m), S 10–12ft (3–4m). Has spreading, feather-shaped leaves, 5–8ft (1.5–2.5m) long, made up of strap-shaped leaflets. Branching clusters of several spikes of small, greenish brown flowers are produced in winter. Z11–12 H12–1.

Howeia. Reclassified as *Howea*.

HOYA

ASCLEPIADACEAE

Genus of evergreen, woody-stemmed, twining and/or root climbers and loose shrubs grown for their flowers and foliage. Grow in organic, well-drained soil with semi-shade in summer. Water moderately when in full growth, sparingly at other times. Stems require support. Cut back and thin out crowded stems after flowering or in spring. Propagate by semi-ripe cuttings in summer.
H. australis, syn. *H. darwinii* of gardens, illus. p.208.
H. bella. See *H. lanceolata* subsp. *bella*.
H. carnosa illus. p.208.
H. coronaria. Slow-growing, evergreen, woody-stemmed, twining and root climber. H 6–10ft (2–3m). Bears thick, leathery, oblong to oval leaves. In summer, bell-shaped yellow to white, red-spotted flowers are produced.
H. darwinii of gardens. See *H. australis*.
H. imperialis. Vigorous, evergreen, woody-stemmed, twining and root climber. H to 20ft (6m). Oval, leathery, leaves are covered with down and 4–9in (10–23cm) long. In summer produces large, star-shaped, brown-purple to deep magenta flowers, each with a cream center.
H. lanceolata* subsp. *bella, syn. *H. bella*, illus. p.208.
H. macgillivrayi illus. p.205.

HUERNIA

ASCLEPIADACEAE

Genus of clump-forming succulents with fingerlike, usually 4-angled stems. Produces minute, short-lived, deciduous leaves on new growth. Requires a position in sun or partial shade and extremely well-drained soil. Is one of easiest stapeliads to grow. Propagate by seed or stem cuttings in spring or summer.
H. macrocarpa. Deciduous, clump-forming succulent. H and S 4in (10cm). Has fingerlike, 4- or 5-sided, gray-green stems. In summer through to autumn bell-shaped yellow flowers with narrow purple bands and recurved tips are produced at base of new growth. Z13–15 H12–10.
var. ***arabica*** illus. p.476.
H. pillansii. Deciduous, clump-forming succulent. H 2in (5cm), S 4in (10cm). Has a fingerlike, light green stem that is densely covered with short tubercles with hairlike tips. Produces bell-shaped, creamy red flowers with red spots at base of new growth in summer through to autumn. Z13–15 H12-10.
H. primulina. See *H. thuretii* var. *primulina*.
H. thuretii* var. *primulina, syn. *H. primulina*. Deciduous, clump-forming succulent. H 4in (10cm), S 6in (15cm). Stems are short, thick, and gray-green. In summer through to autumn bell-shaped, dull yellow flowers, ¾in (2cm) across with reflexed blackish tips, are produced at base of new growth. Z13–15 H12-10.
H. zebrina (Owl-eyes). Deciduous, clump-forming succulent. H 4in (10cm), S 6in (15cm). Is similar to *H. thuretii* var. *primulina* but produces pale yellow-green flowers with conspicuous bands of red-brown. Z13–15 H12-10.

Humea. Reclassified as *Calomeria*.

HUMULUS
Hops

CANNABACEAE

Genus of herbaceous, twining climbers. Is useful for concealing unsightly garden sheds or tree stumps. Male and female flowers are produced on separate plants; female flower spikes become drooping clusters known as "hops." Grow in a position in sun or semi-shade and in any well-drained soil. Propagate by tip cuttings in spring.
H. lupulus (Common hops).
'Aureus' illus. p.206.

HUNNEMANNIA

PAPAVERACEAE

Genus of poppylike perennials usually grown as annuals. Grow in sun and in poor to fertile, very well-drained soil. Deadhead plants regularly. Provide support, especially in windy areas. Propagate by seed sown under cover in early spring, or outdoors in midspring.
H. fumariifolia (Mexican tulip poppy). **'Sunlite'** is a fast-growing, upright perennial, grown as an annual. H 24in (60cm), S 8in (20cm). Has oblong, very divided, bluish green leaves and, in summer and early autumn, poppy-like, semi-double, bright yellow flowers, to 3in (8cm) wide. Z10–11 H12–9.

HYACINTHELLA

HYACINTHACEAE/LILIACEAE

Genus of spring-flowering bulbs with short spikes of small, bell-shaped flowers, suitable for rock gardens and cold greenhouses. Requires an open, sunny situation and well-drained soil that partially dries out while bulbs are dormant in summer. Propagate by seed in autumn.
H. leucophaea illus. p.432.

HYACINTHOIDES,
syn. ENDYMION
Bluebell

HYACINTHACEAE/LILIACEAE

Genus of spring-flowering bulbs grown for their flowers. Is suitable for growing in borders and for naturalizing in grass beneath trees and shrubs. Requires partial shade and plenty of moisture. Prefers heavy soil. Plant bulbs in autumn 4–6in (10–15cm) deep. Propagate by division in late summer or by seed in autumn. All parts may irritate skin on contact and may cause severe discomfort if ingested.
H. hispanica, syn. *Scilla campanulata*, *S. hispanica*, illus. p.414.
H. italica, syn. *Scilla italica*. Spring-flowering bulb. H 6–8in (15–20cm), S 2–3in (5–8cm). Produces a basal cluster of narrowly strap-shaped, semi-erect leaves. Leafless stem produces a conical spike of many flattish, star-shaped blue flowers, ½in (1cm) across.
H. non-scripta, syn. *Scilla non-scripta*, *S. nutans*, illus. p.414.

HYACINTHUS
Hyacinth

HYACINTHACEAE/LILIACEAE

Genus of bulbs grown for their dense spikes of fragrant, tubular flowers; is ideal for spring bedding displays and for pot cultivation indoors. Needs an open, sunny situation or partial shade and well-drained soil. Plant in autumn. For winter flowers, force large-size, specially treated bulbs of *H. orientalis* cultivars by potting in early autumn, then keep cool and damp for several weeks to ensure adequate root systems develop. When shoot tips are visible, move into max. 50°F (10°C) at first, raising temperature as more shoot appears and giving as much light as possible. After forcing, keep in a cool place to finish growth, then plant out to recover. Propagate by offsets in late summer or early autumn. All parts may cause stomach upset if ingested; contact with the bulbs may aggravate skin allergies. See also feature panel p.431.

Hyacinths grow well in Z5–9 H9–5.

H. amethystinus. See *Brimeura amethystina*.
H. azureus. See *Muscari azureum*.
***H. orientalis* 'Amsterdam'.** Winter- or spring-flowering bulb. H 4–8in (10–20cm), S 2½–4in (6–10cm). Has strap-shaped, channeled, semi-erect, glossy, basal leaves that develop fully only after flowering. Flower stem carries a dense, cylindrical spike of fragrant, tubular, bright rose-red flowers, each with 6 recurving petals. **'Blue Jacket'** (illus. p.431) has very large spikes of navy blue flowers with purple veining. **'City of Haarlem'** (illus. p.431) bears pale yellow flowers in a dense spike. **'Delft Blue'** (illus. p.431) has violet-flushed, soft blue flowers. **'Distinction'** (illus. p.431) produces slender, open spikes of reddish purple flowers; those of **'Jan Bos'** (illus. p.431) are crimson. **'Lady Derby'** (illus. p.431) bears rose-pink flowers. **'L'Innocence'** has ivory-white flowers. **'Ostara'** (illus. p.431) has a

large spike of blue flowers with a dark stripe along each petal . **'Pink Pearl'** has a dense spike of carmine-pink flowers. Flowers of **'Princess Maria Christina'** (illus. p.431) are salmon-pink; those of **'Queen of the Pinks'** (illus. p.431) are soft pink. **'Violet Pearl'** (illus. p.431) produces spikes of violet flowers. **'White Pearl'** (illus. p.431) has pure white flowers.

HYDRANGEA

HYDRANGEACEAE

Genus of deciduous shrubs and deciduous or evergreen root climbers grown for their mainly domed or flattened flower heads. Each head usually consists of masses of small, inconspicuous, fertile flowers surrounded by or mixed with much larger, sterile flowers bearing showy, petal-like sepals. However, in some forms, all or most of the flowers are sterile. Prefers a position in full sun or semi-shade and fertile, moist but well-drained soil. Requires more shade in dry areas. Propagate by softwood cuttings in summer. All parts of hydrangeas may cause mild stomach upset if ingested; contact with the foliage may aggravate skin allergies. See also feature panel p.144.

H. anomala **subsp. *petiolaris.*** See *H. petiolaris*.

H. arborescens **'Annabelle'** (illus. p.144). Deciduous, open shrub. H and S 8ft (2.5m). Long-stalked, broadly oval leaves are glossy, dark green above, paler beneath. Very large, rounded heads of mainly sterile white flowers are borne in summer. **'Grandiflora'** (illus. p.144) has smaller flower heads but larger sterile flowers. Both Z4–9 H9–1.

H. aspera **Villosa Group.** See *H. villosa*. subsp. ***sargentiana*** see *H. sargentiana*.

H. bretschneideri. See *H. heteromalla* 'Bretschneideri'.

H. heteromalla. Deciduous, arching shrub. H 15ft (5m), S 10ft (3m). Narrowly oval, dark green leaves turn yellow in autumn. Broad, flat, open heads of white flowers are borne in mid- and late summer, the outer ones aging to deep pink. Z4–9 H9-1. **'Bretschneideri'** (syn. *H. bretschneideri*) illus. p.144.

H. involucrata. Deciduous, spreading, open shrub. H 3ft (1m), S 6ft (2m). Has broadly heart-shaped, bristly, midgreen leaves. During late summer and autumn bears heads of small blue inner flowers surrounded by large, pale blue to white outer ones. Z7–9 H9–7. **'Hortensis'** (illus. p.144) is smaller and has clusters of cream, pink, and green flowers.

H. macrophylla. Deciduous, bushy shrub. H 5–6ft (1.5–2m), S 6–8ft (2–2.5m). Has oval, toothed, glossy, light green leaves. In mid- to late summer, blue or purple flowers are produced in acidic soils with a pH of up to about 5.5. In neutral or alkaline soils above this level, flowers are pink or red. White flowers are not affected by pH. Prune older shoots back to base in spring. Trim back winter-damaged shoots to new growth and remove spent flower heads in spring. Is divided into 2 groups: Hortensias, which have domed, dense heads of mainly sterile flowers, and Lacecaps, which have flat, open heads, each with fertile flowers in the and larger, sterile flowers on the outside that are green in bud. Z6–9 H9–6. **'Altona'** (Hortensia; illus. p.144), H 3ft (1m), S 5ft (1.5m), has large heads of rich pink to deep purple-blue flowers. **'Ami Pasquier'** (Hortensia), H 2ft (60cm), S 3ft (1m), is compact, with deep crimson or blue-purple flowers. **'Blue Bonnet'** (Hortensia; illus. p.144), H 6ft (2m), S to 8ft (2.5m), produces heads of rich blue or lilac to pink flowers. **'Blue Wave'** (syn. *H.m.* 'Mariesii Perfecta', Lacecap; illus. p.144), H 6ft (2m), S to 8ft (2.5m), produces heads of rich blue or lilac to pink flowers. Flower heads of **'Générale Vicomtesse de Vibraye'** (Hortensia; illus. p.144), H and S 5ft (1.5m), are rounded and pale blue or pink. Foliage is light green. **'Hamburg'** (Hortensia; illus. p.144), H 3ft (1m), S 5ft (1.5m), is vigorous and has large, deep pink to deep blue flowers with serrated sepals. **'Lanarth White'** (Lacecap; illus. p.144), H and S 5ft (1.5m), has pink or blue fertile flowers edged with pure white sterile flowers. **'Lilacina'** (Lacecap; illus. p.144), H and S 6ft (2m), has deep lilac central flowers and pinkish purple outer flowers. **'Madame E. Mouillère'** (Hortensia) has white flowers becoming pale pink, and prefers partial shade. **'Mariesii Perfecta'** see *H.m.* 'Blue Wave'. subsp. ***serrata*** see *H. serrata*. subsp. ***serrata*** **'Preziosa'** see *H.* 'Preziosa'. **'Veitchii'** (Lacecap; illus. p.144) has lilac-blue flowers.

H. paniculata **'Brussels Lace'** (illus. p.144). Deciduous, upright, open shrub. H and S to 10ft (3m). Has large, pointed, dark green leaves. Bears delicate, open panicles of white flowers in late summer and early autumn. **'Floribunda'** (illus. p.144) has dense conical heads of small, fertile central flowers surrounded by large white ray flowers. **'Grandiflora'** has large, oval and dark green leaves. Large, conical panicles of mostly sterile white flowers turn pink or red from late summer. Prune back hard in spring to obtain largest panicles. **'Interhydia'** see *H.p.* 'Pink Diamond'. Flower heads of **'Pink Diamond'** (**'Interhydia'**) (illus. p.144) turn pink with age. **'Praecox'** (illus. p.144) flowers from midsummer. **'Tardiva'** has both fertile and sterile flowers from early to midautumn. **'Unique'** (illus. p.144) is similar to 'Grandiflora' but is more vigorous and has larger flowers. All Z3–8 H8–1.

H. petiolaris, syn. *H. anomala* subsp. *petiolaris*, illus. p.208.

H. **'Preziosa'**, syn. *H. macrophylla* subsp. *serrata* 'Preziosa', *H. serrata* 'Preziosa'. Deciduous, bushy shrub. H 5–6ft (1.5–2m), S 6–8ft (2–2.5m). Has oval, toothed, light green leaves. Bears pink flowers, becoming deep crimson. Z6–9 H9–6.

H. quercifolia (Oak-leaved hydrangea; illus. p.144). Deciduous, bushy, mound-forming shrub. H and S 6ft (2m). Deeply lobed, dark green leaves turn red and purple in autumn. Has white flower heads from midsummer to midautumn. Z5–9 H9–5.

H. sargentiana, syn. *H. aspera* subsp. *sargentiana*. Deciduous, upright, gaunt shrub. H 8ft (2.5m), S 6ft (2m). Has peeling bark, thick shoots, and very large, narrowly oval, bristly, dull green leaves with gray down beneath. In late summer to midautumn bears broad heads of flowers, the inner ones small and blue or deep purple, the outer ones larger and white, sometimes flushed purplish pink.

H. serrata, syn. *H. macrophylla* subsp. *serrata* (illus p.144). Deciduous, bushy, dense shrub. H and S 4ft (1.2m). Has slender stems and light green leaves. From mid- to late summer bears flat heads of pink, lilac, or white inner and pink or blue outer flowers. Z6–9 H9–6. '**Bluebird**' (illus. p.144) has pale pink, pale purple or blue flowers. '**Preziosa**' see *H.* 'Preziosa'.

H. villosa (syn. *H. aspera* Villosa Group; illus. p.144). Deciduous, upright shrub. H and S 10ft (3m). Has peeling bark and, from late summer to midautumn, heads of small blue or purple central flowers and larger white, sometimes flushed purplish pink outer ones. Z7–9 H9–7.

HYDROCHARIS

HYDROCHARITACEAE

Genus of one species of deciduous, perennial, floating water plant grown for its foliage and flowers. Requires an open, sunny position in still water. Propagate by detaching young plantlets as desired.

H. morsus-ranae illus. p.446.

Hydrocleis. Reclassified as *Hydrocleys*.

HYDROCLEYS, syn. HYDROCLEIS

LIMNOCHARITACEAE

Genus of deciduous or evergreen, annual or perennial, water plants grown for their floating foliage and attractive flowers. Is best grown in large aquariums and tropical pools with plenty of light. Propagate by seed when ripe or by tip cuttings year-round.

H. nymphoides illus. p.449.

HYGROPHILA

ACANTHACEAE

Genus of deciduous or evergreen, perennial, submerged water plants and marsh plants grown for their foliage. Remove fading leaves regularly. Propagate by stem cuttings in spring or summer.

H. polysperma. Deciduous, perennial, submerged water plant. S indefinite. Lance-shaped, pale green leaves are borne on woody stems. Given water above 61°F (16°C), it is evergreen. Is suitable for a tropical aquarium. Z14–15 H12-10.

HYLOCEREUS

CACTACEAE

Genus of fast-growing cacti with erect, slender, climbing stems that are jointed into sections, and many aerial roots. Makes successful grafting stock. Requires a position in sun or partial shade and very well-drained soil. Propagate by stem cuttings in spring or summer.

H. undatus (Night-blooming cereus, Queen-of-the-night). Fast-growing, climbing cactus. H 3ft (1m), S indefinite. Bears freely branching, 3-angled, weakly spined, dark green stems, 3in (7cm) wide and jointed into sections. In summer produces flattish white flowers, 12in (30cm) across, that last only one night. Z11 H12–10.

HYLOMECON

PAPAVERACEAE

Genus of one species of vigorous perennial grown for its large, cup-shaped flowers. Is good for rock gardens, borders, and woodlands but may be invasive. Prefers partial shade and organic, moist soil. Propagate by division in spring or by seed in autumn.

H. japonica illus. p.350.

Hylotelephium anacampseros. See *Sedum anacampseros*.

Hylotelephium cauticola. See *Sedum cauticola*.

Hylotelephium ewersii. See *Sedum ewersii*.

Hylotelephium populifolium. See *Sedum populifolium*.

Hylotelephium spectabile. See *Sedum spectabile*.

Hylotelephium tatarinowii. See *Sedum tatarinowii*.

Hymenanthera. Reclassified as *Melicytus*.

HYMENOCALLIS

AMARYLLIDACEAE

Genus of bulbs, some of which are evergreen, grown for their fragrant flowers, somewhat like those of large daffodils. Needs a sheltered site, full sun or partial shade, and well-drained soil. Plant in early summer, lifting for winter where not hardy. Alternatively, grow in a heated greenhouse; reduce water in winter (without drying out completely), then repot in spring. Propagate by offsets in spring or early summer.

H. calathina. See *H. narcissiflora*.

H.* x *festalis. Spring- or summer-flowering bulb with a basal leaf cluster. H to 32in (80cm), S 12–18in (30–45cm). Bears strap-shaped, semi-

erect leaves. Produces a head of 2–5 scented white flowers, each 8in (20cm) across, with a deep, central cup and 6 narrow, reflexed petals. Z8–10 H10–8.
H.* x *macrostephana illus. p.397.
H. narcissiflora, syn. *H. calathina*, *Ismene calathina*, illus. p.420.
H. speciosa. Evergreen, winter-flowering bulb. H and S 12–18in (30–45cm). Has broadly elliptic, semi-erect, basal leaves. Produces a head of 5–10 fragrant white or green-white flowers, each 8–12in (20–30cm) wide with a funnel-shaped cup and 6 long, narrow petals.
***H.* 'Sulphur Queen'.** Spring- or summer-flowering bulb. H 24in (60cm), S 12–18in (30–45cm). Produces widely strap- or lance-shaped, semi-erect, basal leaves. Has a loose head of 2–5 fragrant, yellow-green flowers, each 6–8in (16–20cm) wide with a frilly-edged cup and 6 spreading petals. Z10–11 H12–9.

HYMENOSPORUM

PITTOSPORACEAE

Genus of one species of evergreen shrub or tree grown for its flowers and overall appearance. Prefers full sun, though some shade is tolerated. Requires organic, well-drained soil, ideally neutral to acidic. Water containerized specimens freely when in full growth, less at other times. Propagate by seed when ripe, in autumn, or in spring or by semi-ripe cuttings in late summer.
H. flavum (Native Australian frangipani). Evergreen, erect shrub or tree, gradually spreading with age. H 30ft (10m) or more, S 15ft (5m) or more. Has oval to oblong, lustrous, rich green leaves. In spring-summer bears terminal panicles of very fragrant, tubular, 5-petaled cream flowers that age to deep sulfur yellow. Z9–11 H12–9.

HYPERICUM

CLUSIACEAE/GUTTIFERAE

Genus of perennials and deciduous, semi-evergreen or evergreen subshrubs and shrubs grown for their showy yellow flowers with prominent stamens. Large species and cultivars need sun or semi-shade and fertile, not too dry soil. Smaller types, which are good in rock gardens, do best in full sun and well-drained soil. Propagate species subshrubs and shrubs by softwood cuttings in summer or by seed in autumn, cultivars by softwood cuttings only in summer; perennials by seed or division in autumn or spring. Generally trouble-free, but *H.* x *inodorum* 'Elstead' is susceptible to rust, which produces orange spots on leaves, and *H.* 'Hidcote' to a virus that makes leaves narrow and variegated.
H. balearicum. Evergreen, compact shrub. H and S to 2ft (60cm). Small, oval green leaves have wavy edges and rounded tips. Solitary, large, fragrant, shallowly cup-shaped yellow flowers are produced at stem tips above foliage from early summer to autumn. Z6–9 H9–6.
***H. beanii* 'Gold Cup'.** See *H.* x *cyathiflorum* 'Gold Cup'.
H. bellum. Semi-evergreen, arching, graceful shrub. H 3ft (1m), S 5ft (1.5m). Cup-shaped, golden yellow flowers are borne from midsummer to early autumn. Shoots are red. Oval, wavy-edged, midgreen leaves redden in autumn. Z5–9 H9–5.
H. calycinum illus. p.170.
H. cerastioides, syn. *H. rhodoppeum*. Vigorous, evergreen subshrub with upright and arching branches. H 6in (15cm) or more, S 16–20in (40–50cm). Leaves are oval, hairy, and soft grayish green. In late spring and early summer produces masses of saucer-shaped, bright yellow flowers in terminal clusters. Cut back hard after flowering. Is suitable for a large rock garden. Z6–9 H9–6.
H. coris. Evergreen, open, dome-shaped, occasionally prostrate subshrub. H 6–12in (15–30cm), S 8in (20cm) or more. Bears long-stemmed whorls of 3 or 4 pointed-oval leaves. Produces panicles of shallowly cup-shaped, bright yellow flowers, streaked red, in summer. Good in a rock garden. Z7–9 H9–7.
***H.* x *cyathiflorum* 'Gold Cup'**, syn. *H. beanii* 'Gold Cup'. Semi-evergreen, arching shrub. H and S 3ft (1m). Produces pinkish brown shoots, oval, dark green leaves, and, from midsummer to early autumn, large, cup-shaped, golden yellow flowers. Z8–9 H9–8.
H. empetrifolium* subsp. *oliganthum*.** See *H.e.* var. *prostratum* of gardens. var. ***prostratum of gardens (syn. *H.e.* subsp. *oliganthum*) illus. p.386.
***H.* 'Hidcote'** illus. p.170.
***H.* x *inodorum* 'Elstead'** illus. p.170.
H. kouytchense, syn. *H. patulum* var. *grandiflorum*, illus. p.170.
***H.* x *moserianum*.** Deciduous, arching shrub. H 12in (30cm), S 24in (60cm). Small, bowl-shaped yellow flowers are produced above oval, dark green leaves from midsummer to midautumn. Z7–9 H9–7 **'Tricolor'** has leaves that are edged with white and pink. Benefits from a sheltered position.
H. olympicum. Deciduous, upright, slightly spreading, dense subshrub. H 6–12in (15–30cm), S to 6in (15cm). Tufts of upright stems are covered in small, oval, gray-green leaves. Produces terminal clusters of up to 5 cup-shap f. ***uniflorum* 'Citrinum'** (syn. *H.o.* 'Sulphureum') illus. p.358.
H. patulum. Evergreen or semi-evergreen, upright shrub. H and S 3ft (1m). Large, cup-shaped, golden yellow flowers open above oval, dark green leaves from midsummer to midautumn. Z7–9 H9–7. var. ***grandiflorum*** see *H. kouytchense*.
H. reptans. Deciduous, mat-forming shrub. H 2in (5cm), S 8in (20cm). Oval green leaves turn yellow or bright red in autumn. In summer produces flattish, golden yellow flowers, crimson-flushed outside. Good in a rock garden. Z7–9 H9–7.
H. rhodoppeum. See *H. cerastioides*.
***H.* 'Rowallane'.** Semi-evergreen, arching shrub. H and S 5ft (1.5m). Bears large, bowl-shaped, deep golden yellow flowers from midsummer to mid- or late autumn. Oval leaves are rich green. Z7–9 H9–7.

Hypocyrta radicans. See *Nematanthus gregarius*.
Hypocyrta strigillosa. See *Nematanthus strigillosus*.

HYPOESTES

ACANTHACEAE

Genus of mainly evergreen perennials, shrubs, and subshrubs grown for their flowers and foliage. Grow in bright light and in well-drained soil. Water frequently in growing season, less in winter. Straggly stems should be cut back. Propagate by stem cuttings in spring or summer. *H. phyllostachya* may be treated as an annual and propagated by seed in spring.
H. aristata. Evergreen, bushy perennial or subshrub. H to 3ft (1m), S 2ft (60cm). Has oval, midgreen leaves to 3in (8cm) long. Small, tubular, deep pink to purple flowers are produced in terminal spikes in late winter.
H. phyllostachya, syn. *H. sanguinolenta* of gardens, illus. p.264.
H. sanguinolenta of gardens. See *H. phyllostachya*.

HYPOXIS

HYPOXIDACEAE

Genus of spring- or summer-flowering corms grown for their flat, star-shaped flowers. Good in a rock garden. Requires full sun and light, well-drained soil. Propagate by seed in autumn or spring.
H. angustifolia illus. p.436.
H. capensis, syn. *H. stellata*, *Spiloxene capensis*. Spring-flowering corm with a basal leaf cluster. H 4–8in (10–20cm), S 2–3in (5–8cm). Has very slender, narrowly lance-shaped, erect leaves. Stems each produce an upward-facing flower with pointed white or yellow petals and a purple eye. Z9–10 H10–9.
H. stellata. See *H. capensis*.

HYPSELA

CAMPANULACEAE

Genus of vigorous, creeping perennials grown for their flowers and heart-shaped leaves. Good as a groundcover, especially in rock gardens. Needs shade and moist soil. Propagate by division in spring.
H. longiflora. See *H. reniformis*.
H. reniformis, syn. *H. longiflora*. Vigorous, creeping, stemless perennial. H ¾in (2cm), S indefinite. Has tiny, heart-shaped, fleshy leaves and, in spring-summer, small, star-shaped, pink-and-white flowers. Z7–9 H9–7.

HYSSOPUS

LABIATAE/LAMIACEAE

Genus of perennials and semi-evergreen or deciduous shrubs grown for their flowers, which attract bees and butterflies, and for their aromatic foliage, which has culinary and medicinal uses. May be grown as a low hedge. Requires full sun and fertile, well-drained soil. Cut back hard or, if grown as a hedge, trim lightly, in spring. Propagate by softwood cuttings in summer or by seed in autumn.
H. officinalis (Hyssop) illus. p.168. subsp. ***aristatus*** is a semi-evergreen or deciduous, upright, dense shrub. H 2ft (60cm), S 3ft (1m). Bears aromatic, narrowly lance-shaped leaves that are bright green. Produces densely clustered, small, 2-lipped, dark blue flowers from midsummer to early autumn. Z6–8 H9–2.

IBERIS

BRASSICACEAE/CRUCIFERAE

Genus of annuals, perennials, evergreen subshrubs and shrubs grown for their flowers and excellent for rock gardens. Some species are short-lived, flowering themselves to death. Requires sun and well-drained soil. Propagate by seed in spring, subshrubs and shrubs by semi-ripe cuttings in summer.
I. amara illus. p.318. **'Giant Hyacinth-flowered'** is a group of fast-growing, upright, bushy annuals. H 12in (30cm), S 15cm (6in). Has lance-shaped, midgreen leaves and, in summer, flattish heads of large, scented, 4-petaled flowers in a variety of colors. Z11 H10–1.
I. commutata. See *I. sempervirens*.
I. saxatilis illus. p.374.
I. sempervirens, syn. *I. commutata*, illus. p.346. **'Schneeflocke'** (syn. *I.s.* 'Snowflake') is an evergreen, spreading subshrub. H 6–12in (15–30cm), S 18–24in (45–60cm). Leaves are narrowly oblong, glossy, and dark green. Dense, semi-spherical heads of 4-petalled white flowers are produced in late spring and early summer. Trim after flowering. Z5–9 H9–5.
I. umbellata. Fast-growing, upright, bushy annual. H 6–12in (15–30cm), S 8in (20cm). Has lance-shaped, midgreen leaves. Heads of small, 4-petalled white or pale purple flowers, sometimes bicolored, are carried in summer and early autumn. H12–1.
Fairy Series illus. p.322.

IDESIA

FLACOURTIACEAE

Genus of one species of deciduous, summer-flowering tree grown for its foliage and fruits. Both male and female plants are required to obtain fruits. Needs sun or semi-shade and fertile, moist but well-drained soil, preferably neutral to acidic. Propagate by softwood cuttings in summer or by seed in autumn.

I. polycarpa illus. p.80.

ILEX

Holly

AQUIFOLIACEAE

Genus of evergreen or deciduous trees and shrubs grown for their foliage and fruits (berries). Mainly spherical berries, ranging in color from red through yellow to black, are produced in autumn, following insignificant, usually white flowers borne in spring. Almost all plants are unisexual, so to obtain fruits on a female plant a male also needs to be grown. All prefer well-drained soil. Grow in sun or shade, but deciduous plants and those with variegated foliage do best in sun or semi-shade. Hollies resent being transplanted but respond well to hard pruning and pollarding, which should be carried out in late spring. Propagate by seed in spring or by semi-ripe cuttings from late summer to early winter. Holly leaf miner and holly aphid may cause problems. The berries may cause mild stomach upset if ingested. See also feature panel pp.98–9.

I. × altaclerensis. Group of vigorous, evergreen shrubs and trees. Is resistant to pollution and coastal exposure. Z7–9 H9–7.

'Balearica' (illus. p.98) is an erect, female tree. H 40ft (12m), S 15ft (5m). Has green to olive green young branches. Large, broadly oval leaves are spiny- or smooth-edged and glossy, dark green. Freely produces large, bright red berries.

'Belgica' (illus. p.98) is an erect, dense, female tree. H 40ft (12m), S 15ft (5m). Young branches are green to yellowish green. Has large, lance-shaped to oblong, spiny- or smooth-edged, glossy, midgreen leaves. Large, orange-red fruits are freely produced.

'Belgica Aurea' (syn. *I.* × *a.* 'Silver Sentinel', *I. perado* 'Aurea'; illus. p.99) is an upright, female tree. H 25ft (8m), S 10ft (3m). Young branches are green with yellow streaks. Has large, lance-shaped, mainly spineless, dark green leaves mottled with gray-green and irregularly edged with yellow. Red berries are produced only rarely.

'Camelliifolia' (illus. p.98) is a narrow, pyramidal, female tree. H 46ft (14m), S 10ft (3m). Has purple young branches and large, oblong, mainly smooth-edged, glossy, dark green leaves. Reliably produces large scarlet fruits; is an excellent specimen tree.

'Camelliifolia Variegata' (illus. p.99). H 25ft (8m), S 10ft (3m). Is similar to *I.* × *a.* 'Camelliifolia', but leaves have broad yellow margins.

'Golden King' is a bushy, female shrub. H 20ft (6m), S 15ft (5m). Young branches are green with a purplish flush. Has large, oblong to oval, sometimes slightly spiny, dark green leaves, each splashed with gray-green in the center and with a bright yellow margin that turns to cream on older leaves. Is not a good fruiter, bearing only a few reddish brown berries, but it is excellent as a hedge or a specimen plant.

'Hodginsii' is a vigorous, dense, male tree. H 46ft (14m), S 30ft (10m). Shoots are purple; leaves are broadly oval, sparsely spiny, and glossy blackish green.

'Lawsoniana' (illus. p.98) is a bushy, female shrub. H 20ft (6m), S 15ft (5m). Is similar to *I.* × *a.* 'Golden King' but has leaves splashed irregularly in the center with gold and lighter green. Foliage tends to revert to plain green.

'N.F. Barnes' (illus. p.98) is a dense, female shrub. H 18ft (5.5m), S 12ft (4m). Has purple shoots and oval, mainly entire but spine-tipped, glossy, dark green leaves and red berries.

'Silver Sentinel' see *I.* × *a.* 'Belgica Aurea'.

'Wilsonii' is a vigorous, female tree. H 25ft (8m), S 15ft (5m). Has purplish green young branches and large, oblong to oval, glossy, midgreen leaves with prominent veins and large spines. Freely produces large scarlet fruits and makes a good hedging or specimen plant.

I. aquifolium (English holly; illus. p.98). Evergreen, much-branched, erect shrub or tree. H 70ft (20m), S 20ft (6m). Has variably shaped, wavy, sharply spined, glossy, dark green leaves and bright red berries. Z7–9 H9–7

'Argentea Marginata' (Silver-margined holly; illus. p.98) is a columnar, female tree. H 46ft (14m), S 15ft (5m). Young branches are green, streaked with cream. Broadly oval, spiny, dark green leaves with wide cream margins are shrimp pink when young. Bears an abundance of bright red berries. Is good for hedging.

'Argentea Marginata Pendula' (Perry's weeping silver holly; illus. p.98) is a slow-growing, weeping, female tree. H 20ft (6m), S 15ft (5m). Has purple young branches and broadly oval, spiny, dark green leaves mottled with gray-green and broadly edged with cream. Bears red fruits. Is good as a specimen plant in a small garden.

'Atlas' is an erect, male shrub. H 15ft (5m), S 10ft (3m). Has green young branches and oval, spiny, glossy, dark green leaves. Is useful for landscaping and hedging.

'Aurea Regina' see *I.a.* 'Golden Queen'.

'Aurifodina' (illus. p.99) is an erect, dense, female shrub. H 20ft (6m), S 10ft (3m). Young branches are purplish. Oval, spiny leaves are olive green with golden yellow margins that turn tawny yellow in winter. Produces a good crop of deep scarlet berries.

f. ***bacciflava*** (syn. *I.a.* 'Bacciflava') is a much-branched, usually erect shrub or tree. H 70ft (20m), S 20ft (6m). Has variably shaped, wavy, sharply spined, glossy, dark green leaves and yellow fruits.

'Crispa Aureopicta' (illus. p.99) is a male tree of open habit. H 30ft (10m), S 20ft (6m). Narrowly oval, twisted, sparsely spiny, blackish green leaves are centrally blotched with golden yellow. Foliage tends to revert to plain green.

'Ferox' (Hedgehog holly) is an open, male shrub. H 20ft (6m), S 12ft (4m). Has purple young branches and oval, dark green leaves with spines over the entire leaf surface.

'Ferox Argentea' (Silver hedgehog holly) is similar to *I.a.* 'Ferox' but has leaves with cream margins.

'Flavescens' (Moonlight holly) is a columnar, female shrub. H 20ft (6m), S 15ft (5m). Young branches are purplish red. Variably shaped leaves are dark green with a yellowish flush when young that will last year-round when grown in good light. Produces plentiful red berries.

'Golden Milkboy' (illus. p.99) is a dense, male shrub. H 20ft (6m), S 12ft (4m). Has purplish green young branches and oval, very spiny, bright green leaves with heavily blotched, bright yellow centers. Leaves tend to revert to plain green.

'Golden Queen' (syn. *I.a.* 'Aurea Regina') is a dense tree that, despite its name, is male. H 30ft (10m), S 20ft (6m). Broadly oval, very spiny, midgreen leaves are edged with golden yellow.

'Golden van Tol', a sport of *I.a.* 'J.C. van Tol', is an upright, female shrub. H 12ft (4m), S 10ft (3m). Young branches are purple. Oval, puckered, slightly spiny, dark green leaves have irregular, clear yellow margins. Produces a sparse crop of red fruits. Is good for hedging or as a specimen plant.

'Handsworth New Silver' is a dense, columnar, female shrub. H 25ft (8m), S 15ft (5m). Branches are purple. Oblong to oval, spiny, dark green leaves have broad cream margins. Bears a profusion of bright red fruits. Is excellent as a hedge or specimen plant and is good for a small garden.

'Hascombensis' is a slow-growing, dense shrub of unknown sex. H 5ft (1.5m), S 3–4ft (1–1.2m). Has purplish green young branches and small, oval, spiny, dark green leaves. Does not produce berries. Good in a rock garden.

'J.C. van Tol' is an open, female shrub that does not require cross-fertilization to produce fruits. H 20ft (6m), S 12ft (4m). Branches are dark purple when young. Oval, puckered, slightly spiny leaves are dark green. Produces a good crop of red berries. Is useful as a hedge or for a pot.

'Madame Briot' (illus. p.99) is a vigorous, bushy, female tree. H 30ft (10m), S 15ft (5m). Young branches are purplish green. Leaves are large, broadly oval, spiny and dark green with bright golden borders. Bears scarlet berries.

'Ovata Aurea' (illus. p.99) is a dense, male shrub. H 15ft (5m), S 12ft (4m). Has reddish brown young branches and oval, regularly spiny, dark green leaves with bright golden margins.

'Pyramidalis' (illus. p.98) is a dense, female tree that does not require cross-fertilization to produce fruits. H 20ft (6m), S 15ft (5m). Has green young branches and narrowly elliptic, slightly spiny, midgreen leaves. Produces masses of scarlet fruits. Is suitable for a small garden.

'Pyramidalis Aureomarginata' (illus. p.99) is an upright, female shrub. H 20ft (6m), S 15ft (5m). Young branches are green. Has narrowly elliptic, midgreen leaves with prominent golden margins and spines on upper half. Bears a large crop of red berries.

'Pyramidalis Fructu Luteo' is a conical, female shrub that broadens with age. H 20ft (6m), S 12ft (4m). Branches are green when young. Has oval, often spineless, dark green leaves and bears yellow berries. Is excellent for a small garden.

'Scotica' (illus. p.98) is a large, stiff, compact, female shrub. H 20ft (6m), S 12ft (4m). Oval, usually spineless, glossy, very dark green leaves are slightly twisted. Bears red fruits.

'Silver King' see *I.a.* 'Silver Queen'.

'Silver Milkboy' see *I.a.* 'Silver Milkmaid'.

'Silver Milkmaid' (syn. *I.a.* 'Silver Milkboy'; illus. p.98) is a dense, female shrub. H 18ft (5.5m), S 12ft (4m). Oval, wavy-edged, very spiny leaves are bronze when young, maturing to bright green, each with a central, creamy white blotch, but tend to revert to plain green. Produces an abundance of scarlet berries. Makes a very attractive specimen plant.

'Silver Queen' (syn. *I.a.* 'Silver King'; illus. p.99) is a dense shrub that, despite its name, is male. H 15ft (5m), S 12ft (4m). Has purple young branches. Oval, spiny leaves, pink when young, mature to very dark green, almost black, with broad cream edging.

'Watereriana' (syn. *I.a.* 'Waterer's Gold'; Waterer's gold holly; illus. p.99) is a dense, male bush. H and S 15ft (5m). Young branches are green streaked with yellow. Oval, spiny- or smooth-edged leaves are grayish green with broad golden margins. Is best grown as a specimen plant.

'Waterer's Gold' see *I.a.* 'Watereriana'.

I. × aquipernyi (illus. p.98). Evergreen, upright shrub. H 15ft (5m), S 10ft (3m). Has small, oval, spiny, glossy, dark green leaves with long tips. Berries are large and red. Z6–8 H8–6.

I. chinensis of gardens. See *I. purpurea.*

I. ciliospinosa (illus. p.98). Evergreen, upright shrub or tree. H 20ft (6m), S 12ft (4m). Has small, oval, weak-spined, dull green leaves and red berries. Z6–9 H9–6.
I. cornuta (Chinese holly). Evergreen, dense, rounded shrub. H 12ft (4m), S 15ft (5m). Rectangular, dull green leaves are spiny except on older bushes. Produces large red berries. Z7–9 H9–7. **'Burfordii'** (illus. p.98) is female, S 8ft (2.5m), has glossy leaves with only a terminal spine and bears a profusion of fruits. Z6–9 H9–1. **'Rotunda'**, H 6ft (2m), S 4ft (1.2m), is also female and produces a small crop of fruits; is useful for a container or small garden. Z7–9 H9–7.
I. crenata (Japanese holly). Evergreen, spreading shrub or tree. H 15ft (5m), S 10ft (3m). Has very small, oval, dark green leaves with rounded teeth. Bears glossy black fruits. Is useful for landscaping or as hedging. Z5–7 H7–5.
'Bullata' see *I.c.* 'Convexa'.
'Convexa' (syn. *I.c.* 'Bullata'; illus. p.98) is a dense, female shrub. H 8ft (2.5m), S 4–5ft (1.2–1.5m). Has purplish green young branches and oval, puckered, glossy leaves. Bears glossy black fruits.
'Helleri' (illus. p.98) is a spreading, female shrub. H 4ft (1.2m), S 3–4ft (1–1.2m). Has green young branches and oval leaves with few spines. Has glossy black fruits. Is much used for landscaping.
'Latifolia' (syn. *I.c.* f. *latifolia*; illus. p.98) is a spreading to erect, female shrub or tree. H 20ft (6m), S 10ft (3m). Young branches are green and broadly oval leaves have tiny teeth. Produces glossy black berries.
var. ***paludosa*** (illus. p.98) is a prostrate shrub or tree. H 6–12in (15–30cm), S indefinite. Has very small, oval, dark green leaves with rounded teeth. Bears glossy black fruits.
'Variegata' (illus. p.99) is an open, male shrub. H 12ft (4m), S 8ft (2.5m). Oval leaves are spotted or blotched with yellow but tend to revert to plain green.
I. dipyrena (Himalayan holly). Evergreen, dense, upright tree. H 40ft (12m), S 25ft (8m). Elliptic, dull green leaves are spiny when young, later smooth-edged. Bears large red fruits. Z7–9 H9–7.
I. fargesii (illus. p.98). Evergreen, broadly conical tree or shrub. H 20ft (6m), S 15ft (5m). Has green or purple shoots and oval, small-toothed, mid- to dark green leaves. Produces red berries. Z6–9 H9–6. Var. ***brevifolia*** (illus. p.98), H 12ft (4m), is dense and rounded.
I. georgei. Evergreen, compact shrub. H 15ft (5m), S 12ft (4m). Has small, lance-shaped or oval, weak-spined, glossy, dark green leaves with long tips. Berries are red.
I. glabra (Inkberry). Evergreen, dense, upright shrub. H 8ft (2.5m), S 6ft (2m). Small, oblong to oval, dark green leaves are smooth-edged or may have slight teeth near tips. Produces black fruits. Z5–9 H9–3.
I. insignis. See *I. kingiana*.
I. integra. Evergreen, dense, bushy shrub or tree. H 20ft (6m), S 15ft (5m). Has oval, blunt-tipped, bright green leaves with smooth edges. Bears large, deep red berries. Z7–11 H10–7.
***I.* 'Jermyns Dwarf'.** See *I. pernyi* 'Jermyns Dwarf'.
I. kingiana, syn. *I. insignis*. Evergreen, upright tree. H 20ft (6m), S 12ft (4m). Very large, oblong, leathery, dark green leaves have small spines. Berries are bright red. Z7–9 H9–7.
I. x koehneana (illus. p.98). Evergreen, conical shrub. H 20ft (6m), S 15ft (5m). Young branches are green. Has very large, oblong, spiny, midgreen leaves and red fruits. Z7–9 H9–7.
I. latifolia (Tarajo holly). Evergreen, upright shrub. H 20ft (6m), S 15ft (5m). Has thick, olive green young branches, very large, oblong, dark green leaves with short spines, and plentiful red fruits. Z7–9 H9–6.
I. macrocarpa (illus. p.98). Deciduous, upright tree. H 30ft (10m), S 20ft (6m). Has large, oval, saw-toothed, midgreen leaves and very large black berries. Z7–9 H9–7.
I. x meserveae (Blue holly). Group of vigorous, evergreen, dense shrubs. Does not thrive in a maritime climate. Has oval, glossy, greenish blue leaves. Z5–9 H9–5. **'Blue Princess'** (illus. p.98), H 10ft (3m), S 4ft (1.2m), is female and has purplish green young branches, small, oval, wavy, spiny leaves, and an abundance of red fruits.
I. opaca (American holly; illus. p.98). Evergreen, erect tree. H 46ft (14m), S 4ft (1.2m). Does not thrive in a maritime climate. Oval leaves are dull green above, yellow-green beneath, and spiny- or smooth-edged. Has red fruits. Z5–9 H9–5.
I. pedunculosa (illus. p.99). Evergreen, upright shrub or tree. H 30ft (10m), S 20ft (6m). Oval, dark green leaves are smooth-edged. Bright red berries are borne on very long stalks. Z6–9 H9–6.
***I. perado* 'Aurea'.** See *I.* x *altaclerensis* 'Belgica Aurea'.
I. pernyi (illus. p.98). Slow-growing, evergreen, stiff shrub. H 25ft (8m), S 12ft (4m). Has pale green young branches and small, oblong, spiny, dark green leaves. Produces red berries. Z6–9 H9–6. **'Jermyns Dwarf'** (syn. *I.* 'Jermyns Dwarf'), H 2ft (60cm), S 4ft (1.2m), is low-growing and female, with glossy, very spiny leaves.
I. purpurea, syn. *I. chinensis* of gardens (illus. p.99). Evergreen, upright tree. H 40ft (12m), S 20ft (6m). Oval, thin-textured, glossy, dark green leaves have rounded teeth. Lavender flowers are followed by egg-shaped, glossy scarlet fruits. Z7–9 H9–7.
I. serrata. Deciduous, bushy shrub. H 12ft (4m), S 8ft (2.5m). Small, oval, finely toothed, bright green leaves are downy when young. Pink flowers are followed by small red fruits. Z5–7 H7–5. f. ***leucocarpa*** (illus. p.99) bears white berries.
I. verticillata (Winterberry; illus. p.98). Deciduous, dense, suckering shrub. H 6ft (2m), S 4–5ft (1.2–1.5m). Young branches are purplish green. Produces oval or lance-shaped, saw-toothed, bright green leaves. Bears masses of long-lasting red berries that remain on bare branches during winter. Z5–8 H8–2.
I. yunnanensis. Evergreen, spreading to erect shrub. H 12ft (4m), S 8ft (2.5m). Branches are downy. Small, oval leaves with rounded teeth are brownish green when young and glossy, dark green in maturity. Produces red berries. Z5–8 H8–5.

ILLICIUM

ILLICIACEAE

Genus of evergreen, spring- to early summer-flowering trees and shrubs grown for their foliage and unusual flowers. Does best in semi-shade or shade and moist, neutral to acidic soil. Propagate by semi-ripe cuttings in summer.
I. anisatum (Chinese anise). Slow-growing, evergreen, conical tree or shrub. H and S 20ft (6m). Produces oval, aromatic, glossy, dark green leaves. Star-shaped, greenish yellow flowers with numerous narrow petals are carried in midspring. Z7–9 H9–7.
I. floridanum (Purple anise). Evergreen, bushy shrub. H and S 6ft (2m). Lance-shaped, leathery, deep green leaves are very aromatic. Star-shaped red or purplish red flowers with numerous, narrow petals are produced in late spring and early summer. Z7–9 H9–4.

IMPATIENS

BALSAMINACEAE

Genus of annuals and mainly tender evergreen perennials and subshrubs, often with succulent but brittle stems. Prefers sun or semi-shade and moist but not waterlogged soil. Propagate by seed or by stem cuttings in spring or summer. Spider mite, aphids, and whitefly may cause problems under cover.
I. balsamina illus. p.320. **'Blackberry Ice'** is a fast-growing, upright, bushy annual. H 28in (70cm), S 18in (45cm). Has lance-shaped, pale green leaves and, in summer and early autumn, large, double purple flowers splashed with white. H12–1. **Tom Thumb Series** illus. p.325.
***I.* Confection Series** illus. p.327.
***I.* New Guinea Group.** Hybrid subshrubby perennials usually grown as annuals from cuttings. H and S 1-2ft (30-60cm). Grown for their attractive, often multi-colored foliage and large, bright flowers. They grow best in sun or light shade. **'Tango'** has dark green leaves and orange flowers and can be raised from seed.
I. niamniamensis. Evergreen, bushy perennial. H to 3ft (90cm), S 1ft (30cm). Has reddish green stems and oval, toothed leaves to 8in (20cm) long. Showy, 5-petaled, hooded, yellowish green flowers, 1in (2.5cm) long and each with a long orange, red, crimson, or purple spur, appear in summer-autumn. **'Congo Cockatoo'** has red, green, and yellow flowers.
I. oliveri. See *I. sodenii*.
I. repens illus. p.293.
I. sodenii, syn. *I. oliveri*. Evergreen, strong-growing, bushy perennial. H 4ft (1.2m) or more, S 2ft (60cm). Narrowly oval, toothed leaves in whorls of 4–10 are 6in (15cm) or more long. Almost flat white or pale pink to mauve flowers, 2in (5cm) or more wide, are produced mainly in summer.
I. walleriana . Fast-growing, evergreen, bushy perennial very widely grown grown as an annual. H and S to 2ft (60cm). Has oval, fresh green leaves. Flattish, 5-petaled, spurred, bright red, pink, purple, violet, or white flowers appear from spring to autumn. Z 10–15 H12–1. **Novette Series 'Red Star'** illus. p.327. **Super Elfin Series**, H and S 8in (20cm), has flattish flowers in mixed colors. **Super Elfin Series 'Lipstick'** illus. p.326. **Swirl Series** illus. p.321. Flowers of **Tempo Series**, H to 9in (23cm), include shades of violet, orange, pink, and red as well as bicolors and picotees.

IMPERATA

GRAMINEA/POACEAE

See also GRASSES, BAMBOOS, RUSHES, and SEDGES
***I. cylindrica* 'Rubra'**, syn. *I.c.* 'Red Baron'. (Japanese blood grass) A slow-spreading perennial grass forming clumps of green leaves that turn bright red from the tip downward. H 20in (50cm) S infinite. Fluffy white spikes of flowers are produced in late summer. Z5–9 H9–3.

INCARVILLEA

BIGNONIACEAE

Genus of late spring- or summer-flowering perennials suitable for rock gardens and borders. Protect crowns with straw or compost in winter. Requires sun and fertile, well-drained soil. Propagate by seed in autumn or spring.
I. delavayi illus. p.282.
I. mairei illus. p.279. **'Frank Ludlow'** is a compact, clump-forming perennial. H and S 12in (30cm). Short stems bear trumpet-shaped, rich deep pink flowers in early summer. Divided leaves consist of up to 4 pairs of narrowly oval, dark green leaflets. Z4–8 H8–1.

INDIGOFERA

LEGUMINOSAE/PAPILIONACEAE

Genus of perennials and deciduous shrubs grown for their foliage and small, pealike flowers. Cold weather often cuts plants to ground, but they usually regrow from base in spring. Needs full sun and fertile, well-drained soil. Cut out dead wood in spring. Propagate by softwood cuttings in summer or by seed in autumn.
I. decora. Deciduous, bushy shrub.

H 1½ft (45cm), S 3ft (1m). Glossy, dark green leaves each have 7–13 oval leaflets. Long spikes of pink or white flowers appear from mid- to late summer. Z7–9.
I. dielsiana illus. p.162.
I. gerardiana. See *I. heterantha*.
I. heterantha, syn. *I. gerardiana*, illus. p.141.
I. pseudotinctoria. Deciduous, arching shrub. H 3ft (1m) or more, S 6ft (2m). Each dark green leaf has usually 7–9 oval leaflets. Long, dense racemes of small, pale pink flowers are borne in midsummer to early autumn. Z7–9 H9–7.

INULA

ASTERACEAE/COMPOSITAE

Genus of summer-flowering, clump-forming, sometimes rhizomatous perennials. Most need sun and moist but well-drained soil. Propagate by seed or division in spring or autumn.
I. acaulis. Tuft-forming, rhizomatous perennial. H 2–4in (5–10cm), S 6in (15cm). Has lance-shaped to elliptic, hairy leaves. Solitary, almost stemless, daisylike, golden yellow flower heads are produced in summer. Is good for a rock garden. Z4–9 H8–1.
I. ensifolia illus. p.293.
I. hookeri illus. p.256.
I. macrocephala of gardens. See *I. royleana*.
I. magnifica illus. p.229.
I. oculis-christi. Spreading, rhizomatous perennial. H 18in (45cm), S 24in (60cm). Stems each bear 2 or 3 daisylike yellow flower heads in summer. Has lance-shaped to elliptic, hairy, midgreen leaves. Z4–8 H8–1.
I. royleana, syn. *I. macrocephala* of gardens, illus. p.256.

IOCHROMA

SOLANACEAE

Genus of evergreen shrubs grown for their flowers. Needs full light or partial shade and fertile, well-drained soil. Water potted plants freely when in full growth, moderately at other times. Tip prune young plants to stimulate a bushy habit. Cut back flowered stems by half in late winter. Propagate by greenwood or semi-ripe cuttings in summer. Whitefly and spider mite are sometimes troublesome.
I. cyanea, syn. *I. tubulosa*, illus. p.150.
I. tubulosa. See *I. cyanea*.

IONOPSIDIUM

BRASSICACEAE/CRUCIFERAE

Genus of annuals. Only one species is usually cultivated for rock gardens and as edging. Grow in semi-shade and in fertile, well-drained soil. Propagate by seed sown outdoors in spring, early summer, or early autumn.
I. acaule (Violet cress). Fast-growing, upright annual. H 2–3in (5–8cm), S 1in (2.5cm). Rounded leaves are midgreen. Tiny, 4-petaled lilac or white flowers flushed with deep blue are produced in summer and early autumn.

IPHEION

ALLIACEAE/LILIACEAE

Genus of bulbs that freely produce many star-shaped blue, white, or yellow flowers in spring and make excellent pot plants in cold greenhouses. Prefers a sheltered situation in dappled sunlight and well-drained soil. Plant in autumn; after flowering, dies down for summer. Propagate by offsets in late summer or early autumn.
I. uniflorum **'Froyle Mill'** illus. p.431. **'Wisley Blue'** is a spring-flowering bulb. H 4–6in (10–15cm), S 2–3in (5–8cm). Bears linear, semi-erect, basal, pale green leaves that smell of onions if damaged. Leafless stems each produce an upward-facing, pale blue flower, 1¼–1½in (3–4cm) across. Z6–9 H9–6.

IPOMOEA,
syn. MINA, PHARBITIS

CONVOLVULACEAE

Genus of mainly evergreen shrubs, perennials, annuals, and soft- or woody-stemmed, twining climbers. Provide full light and organic, well-drained soil. Water freely when in full growth, less at other times. Support is needed. Thin out or cut back congested growth in spring. Propagate by seed in spring or by softwood or semi-ripe cuttings in summer. Whitefly and spider mite may cause problems. Seeds are highly toxic if ingested.
I. acuminata. See *I. indica*.
I. alba, syn. *Calonyction aculeatum*, *I. bona-nox* (Moon flower). Evergreen, soft-stemmed, twining climber with prickly stems that exude milky juice when cut. H 22ft (7m) or more. Oval or sometimes 3-lobed leaves are 8in (20cm) long. Fragrant, tubular white flowers, to 6in (15cm) long and expanded at the mouths to 6in (15cm) across, open at night in summer. Z12–15 H12–10.
I. bona-nox. See *I. alba*.
I. coccinea, syn. *Quamoclit coccinea* (Red morning glory, Star ipomoea). Annual, twining climber. H to 10ft (3m). Arrow- or heart-shaped leaves are long-pointed and often toothed. Fragrant, tubular scarlet flowers with yellow throats and expanded mouths are produced in late summer and autumn.
I. hederacea illus. p.214.
I. horsfalliae illus. p.209. **'Briggsii'** is a strong-growing, evergreen, woody-stemmed, twining climber. H 6–10ft (2–3m). Has leaves with 5–7 radiating lobes or leaflets. Stalked clusters of funnel-shaped, deep rose-pink or rose-purple flowers are produced from summer to winter; flowers are larger and more richly colored than those of the species. Z13–15 H12–6.
I. imperialis. See *I. nil*.
I. indica, syn. *I. acuminata*, *I. learii*, illus. p.206.
I. learii. See *I. indica*.
I. lobata, syn. *I. versicolor*, *Quamoclit lobata*, illus. p.210.
I.* x *multifida, syn. *I.* x *sloteri* (Cardinal climber, Hearts-and-honey vine). Annual, twining climber. H 10ft (3m). Triangular-oval leaves are divided into 7–15 segments. Tubular, wide-mouthed crimson flowers with white eyes appear in summer. H12–1.
I. nil, syn. *I. imperialis*. **'Early Call'** is a short-lived, soft-stemmed, perennial, twining climber with hairy stems, best grown as an annual. H to 12ft (4m). Leaves are heart-shaped or 3-lobed. From summer to early autumn bears large, funnel-shaped flowers in a range of colors with white tubes. H12–1. **'Scarlett O'Hara'** has deep red flowers.
I. purpurea, syn. *Convolvulus purpureus* (Common morning glory). Short-lived, soft-stemmed, perennial, twining climber, best grown as an annual, with hairy stems. H to 15ft (5m). Leaves are heart-shaped or 3-lobed. From summer to early autumn has funnel-shaped, deep purple to bluish purple or reddish flowers with white throats and bristly sepals.
I. quamoclit, syn. *Quamoclit pennata*, illus. p.210.
I. rubrocaerulea **'Heavenly Blue'.** See *I. tricolor* 'Heavenly Blue'.
I.* x *sloteri. See *I.* x *multifida*.
I. tricolor **'Heavenly Blue'**, syn. *I. rubrocaerulea* 'Heavenly Blue', illus. p.215.
I. tuberosa. See *Merremia tuberosa*.
I. versicolor. See *I. lobata*.

IPOMOPSIS

POLEMONIACEAE

Genus of perennials and biennials often grown as pot plants for greenhouses and conservatories. Grow in cool, airy conditions with bright light and in fertile, well-drained soil. Propagate by seed sown under cover in early spring or early summer.
I. aggregata. Slow-growing biennial with upright, slender, hairy stems. H to 3ft (1m), S 1ft (30cm). Midgreen leaves are divided into linear leaflets. Fragrant, trumpet-shaped flowers borne in summer are usually brilliant red, sometimes spotted yellow, but may be rose, yellow, or white. Z6–9 H9–6.

IRESINE

AMARANTHACEAE

Genus of perennials grown for their colorful leaves. Requires bright light to retain leaf color and a good, loamy, well-drained soil. Pinch out tips in the growing season to obtain bushy plants. Propagate by stem cuttings in spring.
I. herbstii (Beefsteak plant, Chicken gizzard). Bushy perennial. H to 24in (60cm), S 18in (45cm). Has red stems and rounded, purplish red leaves, notched at their tips and 4in (10cm) long, with paler or yellowish red veins. Flowers are insignificant. Z11–12 H12–1. **'Aureoreticulata'** illus. p.305.
I. lindenii (Blood leaf). Bushy perennial. H 24in (60cm), S 18in (45cm). Has lance-shaped, dark red leaves, 2–4in (5–10cm) long. Flowers are insignificant. Z11–12 H12–1.

IRIS

IRIDACEAE

Genus of upright, rhizomatous or bulbous (occasionally fleshy-rooted) perennials, some of which are evergreen, grown for their distinctive and colorful flowers. Each flower has 3 usually large "falls" (pendent or semi-pendent petals), which in a number of species have conspicuous beards or crests; 3 generally smaller "standards"(erect, horizontal, or pendent petals); and a 3-branched style. In some irises the style branches are petal-like. Unless otherwise stated below, flower stems are unbranched. Green then brown seed pods are ellipsoid to cylindrical and often ribbed. Irises are suitable for borders, rock gardens, woodlands, watersides, bog gardens, alpine houses, cold frames, and containers. Some groups thrive only in the specific growing conditions mentioned below. Propagate species by division of rhizomes or offsets in late summer or by seed in autumn, named cultivars by division only. Botanically, irises are divided into a number of subgenera and sections, and it is convenient for horticultural purposes to use some of these botanical names for groups of irises with similar characteristics and requiring comparable cultural treatment. All parts may cause severe discomfort if ingested; contact with the sap may irritate skin. See also feature panel pp.234–5.

Rhizomatous
These irises have rhizomes as rootstocks; leaves are sword-shaped and usually in a basal fan.

Bearded irises are rhizomatous and have "beards," consisting of numerous often colored hairs, along the center of each fall. In some irises, the end of the beard is enlarged into the shape of a horn. The group covers the vast majority of irises, including many named cultivars, grown in gardens. Bearded irises thrive in full sun in fairly rich, well-drained, preferably slightly alkaline soil. Some are very tolerant and will grow and flower reasonably in partial shade in poorer soil. For horticultural purposes, various groupings of hybrid bearded irises are recognized, based mainly on the height of the plants in flower. These include **Miniature Dwarf**, H to 8in (20cm); **Standard Dwarf**, H 8–16in (20–40cm); **Intermediate**, H 16–28in (40–70cm); and **Tall**, H 28in (70cm) or more. In general, the shorter the iris, the earlier the flowering season (from early spring to early summer).
Oncocyclus irises are rhizomatous, with very large and often bizarrely colored flowers, one to each stem, that have bearded falls. They require full sun, sharply drained but fairly rich soil, and, after flowering, a dry period

of dormancy in summer and early autumn. Difficult to cultivate successfully, they are best grown in an alpine house or covered frame in climates subject to summer rains.
Regelia irises are closely related to Oncocyclus irises, differing in having bearded standards as well as falls and in having 2 flowers to each stem. They require similar conditions of cultivation, although a few species, such as *I. hoogiana*, have proved easier to grow than Oncocyclus irises. Hybrids between the 2 groups have been raised and are known as **Regeliocyclus** irises.

Beardless irises, also rhizomatous, lack hairs on the falls; most have very similar cultural requirements to bearded irises, but some prefer heavier soil. Various groupings are recognized, of which the following are the most widely known. **Pacific Coast** irises, a group of Californian species and their hybrids, prefer acidic to neutral soil and grow well in sun or partial shade, appreciating some organic matter in the soil; they are best grown from seed as they resent being moved. **Spuria** irises (*I. spuria* and its relatives) grow in sun or semi-shade and well-drained but moist soil. A number of species and hybrids prefers moist or even waterside conditions; these include the well-known **Siberian** irises (*I. sibirica* and its relatives) and the **Japanese** water irises, such as *I. ensata* and *I. laevigata*, which may also be grown as border plants but succeed best in open, sunny, organic, moist sites.

Crested irises, also rhizomatous, have ridges, or cockscomblike crests, instead of beards. They include the **Evansia** irises, with often widely spreading, creeping stolons. Most have very similar cultivation requirements to bearded irises but some prefer damp, organic conditions.

Bulbous
These irises are distinguished by having bulbs as storage organs, sometimes with thickened, fleshy roots, and leaves that are lance-shaped and channeled, 4-sided (more or less square in cross section), or almost cylindrical – unlike the flat and usually sword-shaped leaves of the rhizomatous irises.
Xiphium irises include the Spanish, English and Dutch irises, which are excellent both for garden decoration and as cut flowers. All grow in sunny, well-drained sites, preferring slightly alkaline conditions, but also growing well on acidic soil. **Spanish** irises are derived from *I. xiphium*, which is variable in flower color, from blue and violet to yellow and white, and produces its channeled leaves in autumn. **English** irises have been produced from *I. latifolia*, which varies from blue to violet (occasionally white) and produces its channeled leaves in spring. **Dutch** irises are hybrids of *I. xiphium* and the related pale to deep blue *I. latifolia*. They are extremely variable in flower color.
Juno irises have bulbs with thickened, fleshy roots, channeled leaves, and very small standards that are sometimes only bristlelike and often horizontally placed. Although very beautiful in flower, they are mostly difficult to grow successfully, requiring the same cultivation conditions as Oncocyclus irises to thrive. Care must be taken not to damage the fleshy roots when transplanting or dividing clumps.

Reticulata irises include the dwarf, bulbous irises valuable for flowering early in the year. Unlike other bulbous irises, they have netlike bulb tunics and leaves that are 4-sided or occasionally cylindrical. With few exceptions (not described here), Reticulata irises grow well in open, sunny, well-drained sites.

I. acutiloba. Rhizomatous Oncocyclus iris. H 3–10in (8–25cm), S 12–15in (30–38cm). Has narrowly sickle-shaped, midgreen leaves. In late spring produces solitary, strongly purple-violet- or brownish purple-veined white flowers, 2–3in (5–7cm) across, with a dark brown blaze around the beard of each fall. Z13–15 H12–1
***I.* 'Annabel Jane'** (illus. p.234). Vigorous, rhizomatous, bearded iris (Tall). H 4ft (1.2m), S indefinite. Well-branched stem bears 8–12 flowers, 6–10in (15–25cm) across, with pale lilac falls and paler standards. Flowers in early summer. Z4–9 H9–1.
***I.* 'Anniversary'.** Rhizomatous, beardless Siberian iris. H 2ft (60cm), S indefinite. From late spring to early summer, branched stem bears 1–4 white flowers, 2–4in (5–10cm) across, with a creamy white stripe in the throat of each fall. Grows well in moist soil or a bog garden. Z4–9 H9–1.
I. aphylla. Rhizomatous, bearded iris. H 6–12in (15–30cm), S indefinite. Branched stem produces up to 5 pale to dark purple or blue-violet flowers, 2½–3in (6–7cm) across, in late spring and sometimes again in autumn if conditions are favorable.
I. aucheri. Bulbous Juno iris. H 6–10in (15–25cm), S 6in (15cm). Has channeled, midgreen leaves packed closely together on stem, looking somewhat leeklike. In late spring bears up to 6 blue to white flowers, 2½–3in (6–7cm) across with yellow-ridged falls, in leaf axils. Z3–9 H9–1.
I. aurea. See *I. crocea.*
I. bakeriana. Bulbous Reticulata iris. H 4in (10cm), S 2–2½in (5–6cm). In early spring bears a solitary, long-tubed, pale blue flower, 2–2½in (5–6cm) across, with each fall having a dark blue blotch at the tip and a spotted, deep blue center. Has narrow, almost cylindrical leaves that are very short at flowering time but elongate later. Z3–9 H9–1.
***I.* 'Banbury Beauty'.** Rhizomatous, beardless Pacific Coast iris. H 18in (45cm), S indefinite. In late spring and early summer, branched stem produces 2–10 light lavender flowers, 4–6in (10–15cm) across, with a purple zone on each fall. Z3–9 H9–1.
***I.* 'Bibury'.** Rhizomatous, bearded iris (Standard Dwarf). H 12in (30cm), S indefinite. Has 2–4 cream flowers, 4in (10cm) wide, on a branched stem in late spring. Z3–9 H9–1.
***I.* 'Blue-eyed Brunette'** (illus. p.235). Rhizomatous, bearded iris (Tall). H 3ft (1m), S indefinite. Well-branched stem produces 7–10 brown flowers, 4–6in (10–15cm) wide with a blue blaze and a golden beard on each fall in early summer. Z3–9 H9–1.
***I.* 'Bold Print'** (illus. p.234). Rhizomatous, bearded iris (Intermediate). H 22in (55cm), S indefinite. In late spring or early summer, branched stem bears up to 6 flowers, 5in (13cm) wide, with purple-edged white standards and white falls that are each purple-stitched at the edge and have a bronze-tipped white beard. Z3–9 H9–1.
***I.* 'Bronze Queen'** (illus. p.235). Bulbous Xiphium iris (Dutch). H to 32in (80cm), S 6in (15cm). In spring and early summer produces 1 or 2 golden brown flowers, 3–4in (8–10cm) wide, flushed bronze and purple. Lance-shaped, channeled, midgreen leaves are scattered up the flower stem. Z3–9 H9–1.
***I.* 'Brown Lasso'.** Rhizomatous, bearded iris (Intermediate). H 22in (55cm), S indefinite. In early summer, sturdy, well-branched stem bears 6–10 flowers, 4–5in (10–12cm) across, with deep butterscotch standards and brown-edged, light violet falls. Z3–9 H9–1.
I. bucharica (illus. p.234). Vigorous, bulbous Juno iris. H 8–16in (20–40cm), S 5in (12cm). In late spring produces 2–6 flowers, 2½in (6cm) across, golden yellow to white with yellow falls, from leaf axils. Has narrowly lance-shaped, channeled, glossy, midgreen leaves scattered up the flower stem. Is easier to grow than most Juno irises. Z5–9 H9–5.
***I.* 'Butter and Sugar'** (illus. p.235). Rhizomatous, beardless Siberian iris. H to 3ft (1m), S indefinite. From late spring to early summer produces large yellow and white flowers. Z4–9 H9–1.
***I.* 'Carnaby'** (illus. p.235). Rhizomatous, bearded iris (Tall). H to 3ft (1m), S indefinite. Well-branched stem bears 6–8 flowers, 6–7in (15–18cm) wide, with pale pink standards and deep rose-pink falls with orange beards in early summer. Z4–9 H9–1.
I. chamaeiris. See *I. lutescens.*
I. chrysographes (illus. p.234). Rhizomatous, beardless Siberian iris. H 16in (40cm), S indefinite. From late spring to early summer, branched stem bears 1–4 deep red-purple or purple-black flowers, 2–4in (5–10cm) across, with gold etching down falls. Prefers moist conditions. Z4–9 H9–1.
***I.* 'Clairette'**, syn. *I. reticulata* 'Clairette'. Bulbous Reticulata iris. H 4–6in (10–15cm), S 1½–2½in (4–6cm). In early spring bears a solitary, fragrant, long-tubed, pale blue flower, 1½–2½in (4–6cm) wide, with white-flecked, deep violet falls. Narrow, squared leaves elongate after flowering time. Z5–9 H8–4.
I. clarkei. Rhizomatous, beardless Siberian iris. H 2ft (60cm), S indefinite. From late spring to early summer, solid stem produces 2–3 branches each with 2 blue to red-purple flowers, 2–4in (5–10cm) across, with a violet-veined white blaze on each fall. Prefers moist conditions. Z4–9 H9–1.
I. colchica. See *I. graminea.*
I. confusa. Evergreen or semi-evergreen, rhizomatous Evansia iris with short stolons. H 1–3ft (30cm–1m), S indefinite. Bamboolike, erect stem is crowned by a fan of lax leaves. In mid-spring, widely branched flower stem produces a long succession of up to 30 white flowers, 1½–2in (4–5cm) across, with yellow and purple spots around a yellow crest on each fall. Prefers well-drained soil and often benefits from the protection of a south-facing wall. Z4–10 H12–9.
***I.* 'Conjuration'.** Rhizomatous, bearded iris (Tall). H 3ft (90cm), S indefinite. In early summer, bears 6–11 flowers with standards that are white at the edges, suffusing inward to pale violet-blue, and white falls suffusing to amethyst violet at the edges. The horned beard is white, tipped with yellow. Z3–9 H9–1.
I. cristata (illus. p.234). Evansia iris with much-branched rhizomes. H 4in (10cm), S indefinite. Has neat fans of lance-shaped leaves. In early summer produces 1 or 2 virtually stemless, long-tubed lilac, blue, lavender, or white flowers, 1¼–1½in (3–4cm) across, with a white patch and orange crest on each fall. Prefers semi-shade and moist soil. Z4–10 H10–1.
I. crocea, syn. *I. aurea*. Rhizomatous, beardless Spuria iris. H 3–4ft (1–1.2m), S indefinite. Has long leaves. Strong, erect, sparsely branched stem produces terminal clusters of 2–10 golden yellow flowers, 5–7in (12–18cm) across, with wavy-edged falls, in early summer. Resents being disturbed.
I. cuprea. See *I. fulva.*
***I.* 'Custom Design'.** Rhizomatous, beardless Spuria iris. H 3ft (1m), S indefinite. Strong, erect-branched stem produces 2–10 deep maroon-brown flowers, each 2–5in (5–12cm) wide, with a heavily veined, bright yellow blaze on each fall from early to midsummer. Z4–8 H8–1.
I. danfordiae (illus. p.235). Bulbous Reticulata iris. H 2–4in (5–10cm), S 2in (5cm). In early spring bears usually one yellow flower, 1¼–2in (3–5cm) across, with green spots on each fall. Standards are reduced to short bristles. Narrow, squared leaves are very short at flowering time but elongate later. Tends to produce masses of small bulblets and requires deeper planting than other Reticulata irises to maintain bulbs at flowering size. Z5–8 H8–4.
I. douglasiana (illus. p.234). Evergreen, rhizomatous, beardless Pacific Coast

iris. H 10–28in (25–70cm), S indefinite. Leathery, dark green leaves are stained red-purple at base. Branched stem produces 1–3 lavender to purple, occasionally white flowers, 3–5in (7–13cm) wide, with variable, central yellowish zones on the falls, in late spring and early summer. Z7–9 H9–7.

***I.* 'Dreaming Spires'.** Rhizomatous, beardless Siberian iris. H 3ft (1m), S indefinite. From late spring to early summer, branched stem produces 1–4 flowers, 2–4in (5–10cm) wide, with lavender standards and royal blue falls. Prefers moist soil. Z5–9 H9–5.

***I.* 'Dreaming Yellow'** (illus. p.234). Rhizomatous, beardless Siberian iris. H 3ft (1m), S indefinite. From late spring to early summer, branched stem produces 1–4 flowers, 2–4in (5–10cm) across. Standards are white and falls are creamy yellow fading to white with age. Prefers moist soil. Z4–9 H9–1.

***I.* 'Early Light'** (illus. p.235). Rhizomatous, bearded iris (Tall). H 3ft (1m), S indefinite. In early summer, well-branched stem bears 8–10 flowers, 6–7in (15–18cm) wide, with lemon-flushed cream standards and slightly darker falls with a yellow beard. Z3–9 H9–1.

***I.* 'Elmohr'.** Rhizomatous, bearded iris. H 3ft (1m), S indefinite. In early summer, well-branched stem produces 2–5 strongly veined, red-purple flowers, 6–8in (15–20cm) across. Z7–9 H9–7.

I. ensata, syn. *I. kaempferi* (Japanese iris). Rhizomatous, beardless Japanese iris. H 2–3ft (60–90cm), S indefinite. Branched stem produces 3–15 purple or red-purple flowers, 3–6in (8–15cm) across, with a yellow blaze on each fall, from early to midsummer. May be distinguished from the related, smooth-leaved *I. laevigata* by the prominent midrib on the leaves. Has produced many hundreds of garden forms, some with double flowers, in shades of purple, pink, lavender, and white, sometimes bicolored. Prefers partial shade and thrives in a water or bog garden. Z3–9 H9–1. **'Galathea'** (syn. *I.* 'Galathea'; illus. p.235), H 32in (80cm), has blue-purple flowers with a yellow blaze on each fall.

I. extremorientalis. See *I. sanguinea*.

***I.* 'Eyebright'** (illus. p.235). Rhizomatous, bearded iris (Standard Dwarf). H 12in (30cm), S indefinite. In late spring produces 2–4 bright yellow flowers, 3–4in (7–10cm) wide, each with a brown zone on the falls surrounding the beard, on usually an unbranched stem. Z3–9 H9–1.

***I.* 'Flamenco'** (illus. p.235). Rhizomatous, bearded iris (Tall). H 3ft (1m), S indefinite. In early summer, well-branched stem produces 6–9 flowers, 6in (15cm) wide, with gold standards infused red and white to yellow falls with red borders. Z4–9 H9–1.

I. foetidissima (Gladwin, Roast-beef plant, Stinking iris). Evergreen, rhizomatous, beardless iris. H 1–3ft (30cm–1m), S indefinite. Branched stem bears up to 9 yellow-tinged, dull purple or occasionally pure yellow flowers, 2–4in (5–10cm) wide, from early to midsummer. Cylindrical seed pods open to reveal rounded, bright scarlet fruits throughout winter. Thrives in a bog or water garden, although it tolerates drier conditions. Z4–9 H9–2.

I. forrestii (illus. p.235). Rhizomatous, beardless Siberian iris. H 6–16in (15–40cm), S indefinite. From late spring to early summer, unbranched stem produces 1 or 2 fragrant, yellow flowers, 2–2½in (5–6cm) across, with black lines on each fall and occasionally brownish flushing on standards. Has linear, glossy, midgreen leaves, gray-green below. Prefers moist, lime-free soil. Z6–9 H9–6.

I. fosteriana. Bulbous Juno iris. H 4–6in (10–15cm), S 2½in (6cm). In spring produces 1 or 2 long-tubed flowers, 1½–2in (4–5cm) wide, with downward-turned, rich purple standards, which are larger than those of most Juno irises, and creamy yellow falls. Has narrowly lance-shaped, channeled, silver-edged, midgreen leaves scattered on flower stem. Is difficult to grow and is best in an alpine house or cold frame. Z6–9 H9–6.

***I.* 'Frank Elder'.** Bulbous Reticulata iris. H 2½–4in (6–10cm), S 2–3in (5–7cm). Has a solitary, very pale blue flower, 6–7cm2½–3in wide, suffused pale yellow and veined and spotted darker blue, in early spring. Narrow, squared leaves are very short at flowering time but elongate later. Z3–9 H9–1.

I. fulva, syn. *I. cuprea* (illus. p.235). Rhizomatous, beardless iris. H 18–32in (45–80cm), S indefinite. In late spring or summer produces a slender, slightly branched stem with 4–6 (occasionally more) copper- or orange-red flowers, 2–3in (5–7cm) across, with 2 flowers per leaf axil. Thrives in a bog or water garden or in a border. Z4–9 H9–3.

I.* x *fulvala, syn. *I.* 'Fulvala' (illus. p.234). Rhizomatous, beardless iris. H 18in (45cm), S indefinite. In summer, zigzag stem produces 4–6 velvety, deep red-purple flowers, 2–5in (5–12cm) across, with 2 flowers per leaf axil. Has a yellow blaze on each fall. Thrives in a bog or water garden. Z6–9 H9–6

***I.* 'Galathea'.** See *I. ensata* 'Galathea'.

***I.* 'Geisha Gown'** (illus. p.234). Rhizomatous, beardless Japanese iris. H 32in (80cm), S indefinite. In summer, branched stem produces 3–5 double, rose-purple-veined white flowers, 6–12in (15–30cm) across, with purple styles and a gold blaze on each fall. Leaves are ridged. Prefers sun or semi-shade. Thrives in a bog or water garden. Z3–9 H9–1.

***I.* 'Golden Harvest'.** Bulbous Xiphium iris (Dutch). H to 32in (80cm), S 6in (15cm). Bears 1 or 2 deep rich yellow flowers, 2½–3in (6–8cm) wide, in spring and early summer. Has scattered, narrowly lance-shaped, channeled, midgreen leaves. Z5–9 H9–5.

I. gracilipes. Clump-forming, rhizomatous Evansia iris with short stolons. H 6–8in (15–20cm), S indefinite. In late spring and early summer, a slender, branched stem produces a succession of 4 or 5 lilac-blue flowers, each 1¼–1½in (3–4cm) across, with a violet-veined white zone surrounding a yellow and white crest. Has narrow, grasslike leaves. Prefers semi-shade and peaty soil. Z5–8 H8–5.

I. graeberiana. Bulbous Juno iris. H 6–14in (15–35cm), S 2½–3in (6–8cm). In late spring produces 4–6 bluish lavender flowers, 2½–3in (6–8cm) across, with a white crest on each fall, from leaf axils. Lance-shaped, channeled leaves are white-margined, glossy, midgreen above, grayish green below, and scattered up the flower stem. Is easier to grow than most Juno irises. Z6–9 H9–6.

I. graminea, syn. *I. colchica*. Rhizomatous, beardless Spuria iris. H 8–16in (20–40cm), S indefinite. In late spring, narrowly lance-shaped leaves partially hide up to 10 plum-scented flowers, 2–5in (5–12cm) wide, with wine-purple standards and heavily veined, violet-blue falls, borne on a flattened, angled stem. Resents being disturbed. Z6–9 H9–5.

***I.* 'Harmony'** (illus. p.235). Bulbous Reticulata iris. H 6–10cm (2½–4in), S 2½–3in (6–7cm). In early spring bears a solitary, fragrant, long-tubed, clear pale blue flower, 2–2½in (5–6cm) across, with white marks and a yellow ridge down each fall center. Narrow, squared leaves are very short at flowering time but elongate later. Z5–8 H8–5.

I. histrioides. Bulbous Reticulata iris. H 6–10cm (2½–4in), S 2½–3in (6–7cm). In early spring produces solitary flowers, 2½–3in (6–7cm) across, which vary from light to deep violet-blue. Each fall is lightly to strongly spotted with dark blue and has white marks and a yellow ridge down center. Narrow, squared leaves are very short at flowering time but elongate later. Z5–8 H8–4. **'Lady Beatrix Stanley'** has light blue flowers and heavily spotted falls. **'Major'** (illus. p.235) has darker blue-violet flowers.

***I.* 'Holden Clough'.** Rhizomatous, beardless iris. H 20–28in (50–70cm), S indefinite. In early summer, branched stem bears 6–12 yellow flowers, each 2in (5cm) wide, with very heavy, burnt sienna veining. Is excellent in a bog or water garden, but it also grows well in any rich, well-drained soil. Z5–8 H8–5.

I. hoogiana (illus. p.235). Regelia iris with thick rhizomes. H 16–24in (40–60cm), S indefinite. Produces 2 or 3 scented, delicately veined, lilac-blue flowers, 3–4in (7–10cm) across, in late spring and early summer. Is relatively easy to cultivate. Z7–9 H9–7.

I. iberica (illus. p.234). Rhizomatous Oncocyclus iris. H 6–8in (15–20cm), S indefinite. Has narrow, strongly curved, gray-green leaves. Bears solitary, bicolored flowers, 4–5in (10–12cm) across, in late spring. Standards are white, pale yellow, or pale blue with slight brownish purple veining; spoon-shaped falls are white or pale lilac, spotted and strongly veined brownish purple. Grows best in a frame or alpine house. Z7–9 H9–7

I. innominata (illus. p.235). Evergreen or semi-evergreen, rhizomatous, beardless Pacific Coast iris. H 6–10in (16–25cm), S indefinite. Stem bears 1 or 2 flowers, 2½–3in (6.5–7.5cm) across, from late spring to early summer. Varies greatly in color from cream to yellow or orange and from lilac-pink to blue or purple; falls are often veined with maroon or brown. Z7–9 H9–7.

I. japonica (illus. p.235). Vigorous, rhizomatous Evansia iris with slender stolons. H 18–32in (45–80cm), S indefinite. Has fans of broadly lance-shaped, glossy leaves. In late spring produces branched flower stem with a long succession of flattish, frilled or ruffled, pale lavender or white flowers, ½–3in (1–8cm) across, marked violet around an orange crest on each fall. Z7–9 H9–7.

***I.* 'Joette'** (illus. p.234). Rhizomatous, bearded iris (Intermediate). H 18in (45cm), S indefinite. In late spring or early summer, branched stems carry uniformly lavender-blue flowers with yellow beards. Is excellent in flower arrangements. Z3–9 H9–1.

***I.* 'Joyce'** (illus. p.235). Bulbous Reticulata iris. H 2½–4in (6–10cm), S 2½–3in (6–7cm). In early spring bears a solitary, fragrant, long-tubed, clear blue flower, 2–2½in (5–6cm) across, with white marks and a yellow ridge down each fall center. Narrow, squared leaves are very short at flowering time but elongate later. Z5–9 H8–4.

***I.* 'June Prom'.** Vigorous, rhizomatous, bearded iris (Intermediate). H 20in (50cm), S indefinite. In late spring or early summer, branched stem bears up to 6 pale blue flowers, 3–4in (8–10cm) wide, with a green tinge on each fall. Z6–9 H9–6.

I. kaempferi. See *I. ensata*.

***I.* 'Katharine Hodgkin'** (illus. p.235). Bulbous Reticulata iris. H 2½–4in (6–10cm), S 2–3in (5–7cm). Is similar to *I.* 'Frank Elder' but has yellower flowers, 2½–3in (6–7cm) wide, suffused pale blue, lined and dotted dark blue. Flowers in early spring. Z5–9 H8–4.

I. kerneriana. Rhizomatous, beardless Spuria iris. H 10in (25cm), S indefinite. Has very narrow, grasslike leaves. Strong, erect-branched stem bears 2–4 soft lemon- or creamy yellow flowers, 2–5in (5–12cm) across, from each pair of bracts, in early summer. Resents being disturbed. Z6–9 H9–6.

I. korolkowii. Regelia iris with thick rhizomes. H 16–24in (40–60cm), S indefinite. From late spring to early summer, each spathe encloses 2 or 3 delicately blackish maroon- or olive-green-veined, creamy white or light purple flowers, 2½–3in (6–8cm) across. Is best grown in a bulb frame. Z8–9 H9–8.

***I.* 'Krasnia'** (illus. p.234). Rhizomatous, bearded iris (Tall). H 3ft

(1m), S indefinite. In early summer, well-branched stem produces 8–12 flowers, 5–7in (13–18cm) wide, with purple standards and purple-edged white falls. Z3–9 H9–1.

***I.* 'Lady of Quality'** (illus. p.234). Rhizomatous, beardless Siberian iris. H to 3ft (1m), S indefinite. Flowers, produced in mid- or late spring, have light blue-violet standards and lighter blue falls. Z3–9 H9–1.

I. laevigata (illus. p.235). Rhizomatous, beardless Japanese iris. H 2–3ft (60–90cm) or more, S indefinite. Sparsely branched stem produces 2–4 blue, blue-purple, or white flowers, 2–5in (5–12cm) across, from early to midsummer. Is related to *I. ensata* but has smooth, not ridged leaves. Grows well in sun or semi-shade in moist conditions or in shallow water. Z4–9 H9–1.**'Regal'** bears single, cyclamen-red flowers. Flowers of **'Snowdrift'** are double and white. **'Variegata'**, H 10in (25cm), has white-and-green-striped leaves and often flowers a second time in early autumn. Z5–9 H9–1.

I. latifolia, syn. *I. xiphioides* (English iris; illus. p.234). Bulbous Xiphium iris (English). H 32in (80cm), S 6in (15cm). In late spring and summer, 1 or 2 blue to deep violet flowers, 3–4in (8–10cm) wide, with a yellow stripe down center of each very broad fall, are produced from the bracts. Lance-shaped, channeled, midgreen leaves are scattered up flower stem.Z5–8 H8–5. **'Duchess of York'** bears purple flowers. Flowers of **'Mont Blanc'** are pure white. **'Queen of the Blues'** has blue standards and purple-blue falls.

***I.* 'Lavender Royal'** (illus. p.235). Rhizomatous, beardless Pacific Coast iris. H 18in (45cm), S indefinite. In late spring to early summer, branched stems carry lavender flowers with darker flushes. Z5–8 H8–5.

I. lutescens, syn. *I. chamaeiris*. Fast-growing, very variable, rhizomatous, bearded iris. H 2–12in (5–30cm), S indefinite. Branched stem produces 1 or 2 yellow-bearded violet, purple, yellow, white, or bicolored flowers, 2½–3in (6–8cm) across, in early summer. Z7–9 H9–7. **'Nancy Lindsay'** has scented yellow flowers.

***I.* 'Magic Man'** (illus. p.234). Rhizomatous, bearded iris (Tall). H 3ft (1m), S indefinite. In early summer, branched stems carry flowers that have light blue standards and velvety purple falls with light blue edges; beards are orange. Z3–9 H9–1.

I. magnifica (illus. p.234). Bulbous Juno iris. H 12–24in (30–60cm), S 6in (15cm). In late spring produces 3–7 very pale lilac flowers, 2½–3in (6–8cm) across, with a central yellow area on each fall, from leaf axils. Bears scattered, lance-shaped, channeled, glossy, midgreen leaves. Z6–8 H8–6.

***I.* 'Margot Holmes'.** Rhizomatous, beardless Siberian iris. H 10in (25cm), S indefinite. In early summer produces 2 or 3 purple-red flowers, 4–6in (10–15cm) across, with yellow veining on each fall. Z6–8 H8–6.

***I.* 'Marhaba'.** Rhizomatous, bearded iris (Miniature Dwarf). H 6in (15cm), S indefinite. Bears 1, rarely 2 deep blue flowers, 2–3in (5–8cm) wide, in mid-spring. Z6–8 H8–6.

***I.* 'Mary Frances'** (illus. p.234). Rhizomatous, bearded iris (Tall). H 3ft (1m), S indefinite. In early summer, well-branched stem bears 6–9 pink-lavender flowers, 6in (15cm) wide. Z3–9 H9–1.

***I.* 'Matinata'** (illus. p.234). Rhizomatous, bearded iris (Tall). H 3ft (1m), S indefinite. In early summer, well-branched stem produces 6–9 flowers 6in (15cm) wide, that are dark purple-blue throughout. Z3–9 H9–1.

I. missouriensis, syn. *I. tolmeiana* (Missouri iris; illus. p.234). Very variable, rhizomatous, beardless Pacific Coast iris. H to 2½ft (75cm), S indefinite. Branched stem produces 2 or 3 pale blue, lavender, lilac, blue ,or white flowers, 2–3in (5–8cm) wide, in each spathe, in late spring or early summer. Falls are veined and usually have a yellow blaze. Z3–9 H9–1.

***I.* 'Mountain Lake'** (illus. p.235). Rhizomatous, beardless Siberian iris. H 3ft (1m), S indefinite. From late spring to early summer, branched stem produces 1–4 midblue flowers, 2–4in (5–10cm) across, with darker veining on falls. Prefers moist soil. Z3–8 H8–1.

***I. ochroleuca*.** See *I. orientalis*.

I. orientalis, syn. *I. ochroleuca*. Rhizomatous, beardless Spuria iris. H to 3ft (90cm), S indefinite. In late spring each stem, usually with one branch, bears 3–5 white flowers, 3–4in (8–10cm) wide. Falls are white with yellow centers. Leaves are often present over winter. Z6–9 H9–5.

I. orientalis of gardens. See *I. sanguinea*.

I. pallida (Dalmatian iris). Rhizomatous, bearded iris. H 28–36in (70–90cm) or more, S indefinite. In late spring and early summer produces 2–6 scented, lilac-blue flowers, 3–5in (8–12cm) across and with yellow beards, from silvery spathes on strong, branched stems. Z3–9 H9–1.Leaves of **'Variegata'** (syn. *I.p.* 'Aurea Variegata'; illus. p.234) are striped green and yellow.

***I.* 'Paradise Bird'** (illus. p.234). Rhizomatous, bearded iris (Tall). H 34in (85cm), S indefinite. In early summer, well-branched stem produces 8–10 flowers, 5½–6in (14–15cm) wide, with magenta falls and paler standards. Z3–9 H9–1.

***I.* 'Peach Frost'** (illus. p.235). Rhizomatous, bearded iris (Tall). H 3ft (1m), S indefinite. Well-branched stem bears 6–10 flowers, 6in (15cm) wide, in early summer. Standards are peach-pink, the falls white with peach-pink borders and tangerine beards. Z3–9 H9–1.

***I.* 'Piona'.** Rhizomatous, bearded iris (Intermediate). H 18in (45cm), S indefinite. In late spring and early summer, branched stem bears up to 6 deep violet flowers, 3–4in (8–10cm) wide, with golden beards. Midgreen leaves have purple bases. Z3–9 H9–1.

***I.* 'Professor Blaauw'.** Bulbous Xiphium iris (Dutch). H 32in (80cm), S 6in (15cm). From spring to early summer produces 1 or 2 rich violet-blue flowers, 2½–3in (6–8cm) across. Narrowly lance-shaped, channeled, midgreen leaves are arranged up the flower stem. Z3–9 H9–1.

I. pseudacorus (Yellow flag; illus. p.235). Robust, rhizomatous, beardless iris. H to 6ft (2m), S indefinite. Branched stem produces 4–12 golden yellow flowers, 2–5in (5–12cm) wide, usually with brown or violet veining and a darker yellow patch on the falls, from early to midsummer. Leaves are broad, ridged, and grayish green. Prefers semi-shade and thrives in a water garden. Z5–8 H8–3. **'Variegata'** has yellow-and-green-striped foliage in spring, often turning green before flowering.

I. pumila (Dwarf bearded iris). Rhizomatous, bearded iris. H 4–6in (10–15cm), S indefinite. In midspring has a ½in (1cm) long flower stem bearing 2 or 3 long-tubed flowers, 1–2in (2.5–5cm) wide, varying from violet-purple to white, yellow, or blue, with yellow or blue beards on the falls. Prefers very well-drained, slightly alkaline soil. Z4–9 H9–1.

***I. reticulata*.** Bulbous Reticulata iris. H 4–6in (10–15cm), S 1½–2½in (4–6cm). In early spring bears a solitary, fragrant, long-tubed, deep violet-purple flower, 1½–2½in (4–6cm) wide, with a yellow ridge down each fall center. Narrow, squared leaves elongate after flowering time. Z5–9 H8–4. **'Cantab'** (illus. p.235) has clear pale blue flowers with a deep yellow ridge on each fall. **'Clairette'** see *I.* 'Clairette'. Flowers of **'J.S. Dijt'** are reddish purple with an orange ridge on each fall. **'Violet Beauty'** see *I.* 'Violet Beauty'.

***I.* 'Rippling Rose'** (illus. p.234). Rhizomatous, bearded iris (Tall). H 3ft (1m), S indefinite. In early summer, well-branched stem has 6–10 white flowers, 6in (15cm) wide, with purple marks and lemon yellow beards. Z4–9 H9–1.

I. rosenbachiana (illus. p.234). Bulbous Juno iris. H 4–6in (10–15cm), S 2½in (6cm). In spring produces 1 or 2 long-tubed flowers, 1½–2in (4–5cm) wide, with small, downward-turned, rich purple standards and reddish purple falls, each with a yellow ridge in the center. Has lance-shaped, channeled, midgreen leaves in a basal tuft. Is difficult to grow and is best in an alpine house or cold frame. Z4–9 H9–1.

***I.* 'Ruffled Velvet'** (illus. p.234). Rhizomatous, beardless Siberian iris. H to 3ft (1m), S indefinite. In early summer produces 2 or 3 red-purple flowers marked with yellow. Z4–9 H9–1.

***I.* 'Saffron Jewel'.** Rhizomatous, bearded iris (Intermediate). H 30in (75cm), S indefinite. In early summer, branched stem produces 2–5 flowers, 2–4in (5–10cm) across, with oyster falls veined chartreuse and paler standards. Falls each have a blue blaze and beard. Z3–9 H9–1.

I. sanguinea, syn. *I. extremorientalis*, *I. orientalis* of gardens. Rhizomatous, beardless Siberian iris. H to 3ft (1m), S indefinite. From late spring to early summer, branched stem produces 2 or 3 deep purple or red-purple flowers, 2–4in (5–10cm) wide, from each set of bracts. Falls are red-purple with white throats finely veined purple. Z3–9 H9–1.

***I.* 'Sapphire Star'** (illus. p.235). Rhizomatous, beardless Japanese iris. H 4ft (1.2m), S indefinite. In summer, branched stem bears 3–5 white-veined lavender flowers, 6–12in (15–30cm) wide, pencilled with a white halo around a yellow blaze on each fall. Prefers moist soil. Z3–8 H8–1.

I. setosa (Bristle-pointed iris; illus. p.235). Rhizomatous, beardless iris, very variable in stature. H 4–36in (10–90cm), S indefinite. Bears 2–13 deep blue or purple-blue flowers, 2–3in (5–8cm) across, from each spathe in late spring and early summer. Falls have paler blue or white marks; each standard is reduced to a bristle. Z3–8 H8–1.

***I.* 'Shepherd's Delight'** (illus. p.235). Rhizomatous, bearded iris (Tall). H 3ft (1m), S indefinite. In early summer, well-branched stem produces 6–10 clear pink flowers, 6–7in (15–18cm) wide, with a yellow cast. Z3–8 H8-1.

I. sibirica (Siberian iris). Rhizomatous, beardless Siberian iris. H 20–48in (50–120cm), S indefinite. From late spring to early summer, branched stem bears 2 or 3 dark-veined blue or blue-purple flowers, 2–4in (5–10cm) across, from each spathe. Prefers moist or boggy conditions. Z3–9 H9–1.

***I.* 'Splash Down'.** Rhizomatous, beardless Siberian iris. H 3ft (1m), S indefinite. From late spring to early summer, branched stem produces 1–4 flowers, 2–4in (5–10cm) across. Standards are pale blue and falls speckled blue on a pale ground. Prefers moist soil. Z3–9 H9–1.

***I. spuria*.** Very variable, rhizomatous, beardless Spuria iris. H 20–36in (50–90cm), S indefinite. Strong, erect-branched stem produces 2–5 pale blue-purple, sky blue, violet-blue, white, or yellow flowers, 2–5in (5–12cm) across, in early summer. Prefers moist soil. Z6–9 H9–5.

***I.* 'Stepping Out'.** Rhizomatous, bearded iris (Tall). H 3ft (1m), S indefinite. Well-branched stem produces 8–11 white flowers, 5½–6in (14–15cm) wide, with deep blue-purple marks in early summer. Z3–9 H9–1.

***I. stylosa*.** See *I. unguicularis*.

***I.* 'Sun Miracle'** (illus. p.235). Rhizomatous, bearded iris (Tall). H 3ft (1m), S indefinite. Well-branched stem produces 7–10 pure yellow flowers, 6–7in (15–18cm) wide, in early summer. Z3–9 H9–1.

I. susiana (Mourning iris). Rhizomatous Oncocyclus iris. H 14–16in (35–40cm),

S indefinite. In late spring produces a solitary, grayish white flower, 3–6in (8–15cm) wide, heavily veined deep purple. Standards appear larger than incurved falls, which each carry a black blaze and a deep purple beard. Grows best in a frame or alpine house. Z7–9 H9–1.
I. tectorum (Japanese roof iris, Wall iris; illus. p.234). Evansia iris with thick rhizomes. H 10–14in (25–35cm), S indefinite. Has fans of broadly lance-shaped, ribbed leaves. In early summer, sparsely branched stem produces 2–3 darker-veined, bright lilac flowers, ½–3in (1–8cm) across with a white crest on each fall, from each spathe. Z5–9 H9–3.
I. tenax (illus. p.234). Rhizomatous, beardless Pacific Coast iris. H 6–12in (15–30cm), S indefinite. From late spring to early summer produces 1 or 2 deep purple to lavender-blue flowers, 3–5in (8–12cm) across, often with yellow and white marking on falls. White, cream, and yellow variants also occur. Narrow, dark green leaves are stained pink at base. Z5–9 H9–5.
***I.* 'Theseus'.** Rhizomatous Regeliocyclus iris. H 18in (45cm), S indefinite. From late spring to early summer produces usually 2 flowers, 4–6in (10–15cm) across, with violet standards and violet-veined cream falls. Is best in a frame or alpine house. Z7–9 H9–7.
***I.* 'Thornbird'.** Rhizomatous, bearded iris (Tall). H 3ft (90cm), S indefinite. In early summer, produces up to 7 flowers with standards that are pale greenish white and falls that are greenish brown overlaid with deep violet lines. The long, horned beard is violet, tipped with mustard yellow. Z3–9 H9–1.
I. tolmeiana. See *I. missouriensis*.
I. tuberosa. See *Hermodactylus tuberosus*.
I. unguicularis, syn. *I. stylosa* (Algerian iris, Algerian winter iris, Winter iris). Evergreen, rhizomatous, beardless iris. H to 8in (20cm), S indefinite. Has narrow, tough leaves. Almost stemless, primrose-scented, lilac flowers, 2–3in (5–8cm) across with yellow centers to the falls and with very long tubes, appear from late autumn to early spring. Buds are prone to slug attack. Is excellent for cutting. Prefers a sheltered site against a south- or west-facing wall. Z7–9 H9–7. **'Mary Barnard'** has deep violet-blue flowers. Flowers of **'Walter Butt'** are pale silvery lavender.
I. variegata (illus. p.235). Rhizomatous, bearded iris. H 12–20in (30–50cm), S indefinite. In early summer, branched stem produces 3–6 flowers, 2–3in (5–8cm) across, with bright yellow standards and white or pale yellow falls, heavily veined red-brown and appearing striped. Z5–9 H9–5.
I. verna. Rhizomatous, beardless iris. H 2in (5cm), S indefinite. In midspring bears 1, occasionally 2, lilac-blue flowers, 1–2in (2.5–5cm) across, with a narrow, orange stripe in the center of each fall. Prefers semi-shade and moist but well-drained soil. Z5–9 H9–5.
I. versicolor (Blue flag, Wild iris; illus. p.234). Robust, rhizomatous, beardless iris. H 2ft (60cm), S indefinite. Branched stem produces 3–5 or more purple-blue, reddish purple, lavender, or slate-purple flowers, 2–4in (5–10cm) across, from early to midsummer. Falls usually have a central white area veined purple. Prefers partial shade and thrives in moist soil or in shallow water. Z3–9 H9–1. **'Kermesina'** has red-purple flowers.
***I.* 'Violet Beauty'**, syn. *I. reticulata* 'Violet Beauty'. Bulbous Reticulata iris. H 4–6in (10–15cm), S 1½–2½in (4–6cm). In early spring bears a solitary, fragrant, long-tubed, deep violet-purple flower, 1½–2½in (4–6cm) wide, with an orange ridge down the center of each fall. Narrow, squared leaves elongate after flowering time. Z5–9 H8–4.
I. warleyensis. Bulbous Juno iris. H 8–18in (20–45cm), S 3in (7–8cm). In spring produces up to 5 pale lilac or violet-blue flowers, 2–3in (5–7cm) across, in leaf axils. Each fall has a darker blue apex and a yellow stain in the center. Bears scattered, lance-shaped, channeled, midgreen leaves. Z6–8 H8–6.
***I.* 'White Excelsior'.** Bulbous Xiphium iris (Dutch). H to 32in (80cm), S 6in (15cm). From spring to early summer bears 1 or 2 white flowers, 2½–3in (6–8cm) wide, with a yellow stripe down each fall center. Narrowly lance-shaped, channeled, midgreen leaves are scattered on the flower stem. Z6–8 H8–6.
I. winogradowii (illus. p.235). Bulbous Reticulata iris. H 2½–4in (6–10cm), S 2½–3in (6–7cm). Solitary pale primrose yellow flower, 2½–3in (6–7cm) wide, spotted green on falls, appears in early spring. Narrow, squared leaves are very short at flowering time but elongate later. Z6–8 H8–6.
***I.* 'Wisley White'** (illus. p.234). Rhizomatous, beardless Siberian iris. H to 3ft (1m), S indefinite. Each stem carries 2 or 3 white flowers, held well above the foliage, in early summer. Z6–8 H8–6.
I. xiphioides. See *I. latifolia*.
I. xiphium. Bulbous Xiphium iris (Spanish). H to 32in (80cm), S 6in (15cm). Has 1 or 2 blue or violet, occasionally yellow or white flowers, 2½–3in (6–8cm) across, with central orange or yellow marks on the falls, in spring and early summer. Narrowly lance-shaped, channeled, midgreen leaves are scattered on flower stem. Z5–9 H9–5. **'Blue Angel'** produces bright midblue flowers with a yellow mark in the center of each fall. Flowers of **'Lusitanica'** are pure yellow. **'Queen Wilhelmina'** produces white flowers in spring. **'Wedgwood'** (illus. p.235) has bright blue flowers.

ISATIS

BRASSICACEAE/CRUCIFERAE

Genus of summer-flowering annuals, biennials, and perennials. Needs sun and fertile, well-drained soil. Propagate by seed in autumn or spring.
I. tinctoria (Woad). Vigorous, upright biennial. H to 4ft (1.2m), S 1½ft (45cm). Has oblong to lance-shaped, glaucous leaves and, in summer, large, terminal panicles of 4-petaled yellow flowers. Z4–8 H8–1.

ISMELIA

ASTERACEAE/COMPOSITAE

Genus of one species of annuals grown for its daisylike flower heads. Needs full sun and well-drained soil. Propagate by seed in spring.
I. carinata, syn. *Chrysanthemum carinatum*, *C. tricolor*. H9–1. **'Monarch Court Jesters'** (red with yellow centers) illus. p.329, (white with red centers) illus. p.320. **Tricolor Series** is a group of fast-growing, upright, branching annuals. H 12–24in (30–60cm), S 12in (30cm). Has feathery, light green leaves and, in summer, daisylike, single or double flower heads, to 3in (8cm) wide, in many color combinations. Tall cultivars, H 24in (60cm), S 12in (30cm), and dwarf, H and S 12in (30cm), are available.

Ismene calathina. See *Hymenocallis narcissiflora*.

ISOLEPIS

CYPERACEAE

See also GRASSES, BAMBOOS, RUSHES, and SEDGES.
I. setaceus, syn. *Scirpus setaceus* (Bristle club-rush). Tuft-forming annual or short-lived perennial rush. H 4–6in (10–15cm), S 8cm (3in). Has very slender, lax, basal leaves. Very slender, unbranched stems each bear 1–3 minute, egg-shaped green spikelets in summer. Z12-15 H12–10.

ISOPLEXIS

SCROPHULARIACEAE

Genus of evergreen, mainly summer-flowering shrubs grown for their flowers. Is closely related to *Digitalis*. Tolerates full light or partial shade and prefers well-drained soil. Water potted specimens freely when in full growth, moderately at other times. Remove spent flower spikes. Propagate by seed in spring or by semi-ripe cuttings in late summer.
I. canariensis, syn. *Digitalis canariensis*, illus. p.171.

ISOPYRUM

RANUNCULACEAE

Genus of spring-flowering perennials grown for their small flowers and delicate foliage. Is suitable for woodlands and rock gardens. Requires shade and organic, moist soil. Propagate by seed when fresh or by division in autumn. Self-seeds readily.
I. thalictroides. Dainty, clump-forming perennial. H and S 10in (25cm). Central stalk bears fernlike, 3-parted leaves, each leaflet being cut into 3. Has small, nodding, cup-shaped white flowers in spring. Z5–8 H8–5.

ITEA

ESCALLONIACEAE

Genus of deciduous or evergreen trees and shrubs grown for their foliage and flowers. Needs sun or semi-shade and fertile, well-drained but not too dry soil. Propagate by softwood cuttings in summer.
I. ilicifolia illus. p.146.

IXIA

IRIDACEAE

Genus of spring- and summer-flowering corms with wiry stems and spikes of flattish flowers. Grow in an open, sunny situation and in well-drained soil. Plant in autumn for spring and early summer flowers; plant in spring for later summer display. Dry off after flowering. Propagate in autumn by seed or by offsets at replanting time.
***I.* 'Mabel'.** Spring- to early summer-flowering corm. H 16in (40cm), S 1–2in (2.5–5cm). Has linear, basal, midgreen leaves and spikes of deep pink flowers. Z10–11 H12–10.
I. maculata. Spring- to early summer-flowering corm. H 16in (40cm), S 1–2in (2.5–5cm). Leaves are linear, erect, and mostly basal. Wiry stem bears a spike of flattish, orange or yellow flowers, 1–2in (2.5–5cm) across, with brown or black centers. Z10–11 H12–10.
I. monadelpha. Spring- to early summer-flowering corm. H 12in (30cm), S 1–2in (2.5–5cm). Linear, erect leaves are mostly basal. Stem produces a dense spike of 5–10 flattish white, pink, purple, or blue flowers, 1¼–1½in (3–4cm) across, often with differently colored eyes. Z10–11 H12–10.
I. viridiflora illus. p.414.

IXIOLIRION

AMARYLLIDACEAE

Genus of bulbs grown for their funnel-shaped flowers mainly in spring. Needs a sheltered, sunny site and well-drained soil that becomes hot and dry in summer to mature the bulb. Propagate by seed or offsets in autumn.
I. montanum. See *I. tataricum*.
I. tataricum, syn. *I. montanum*, illus. p.414.

IXORA

RUBIACEAE

Genus of evergreen, summer-flowering shrubs grown primarily for their flowers, some also for their foliage. Prefers full sun and organic, well-drained soil. Water containerized specimens freely when in full growth, moderately at other times. Propagate by seed in spring or by semi-ripe cuttings in summer.
I. coccinea illus. p.165.

J

JACARANDA

BIGNONIACEAE

Genus of deciduous or evergreen trees grown for their flowers and foliage in spring-summer. Grows in any fertile, well-drained soil and in full light. Water potted specimens freely in full growth, sparingly at other times. Potted plants grown for foliage may be cut back hard in late winter. Propagate by seed in spring or semi-ripe cuttings in summer.

J. acutifolia of gardens. See *J. mimosifolia.*

J. mimosifolia, syn. *J. acutifolia* of gardens, *J. ovalifolia*, illus. p.79.

J. ovalifolia. See *J. mimosifolia.*

Jacobinia carnea. See *Justicia carnea.*

Jacobinia coccinea. See *Pachystachys coccinea.*

Jacobinia pohliana. See *Justicia carnea.*

Jacobinia spicigera. See *Justicia spicigera.*

JACQUEMONTIA

CONVOLVULACEAE

Genus of evergreen, twining climbers grown for their flowers. Any well-drained soil is suitable with full light. Water freely except in cold weather. Provide support and thin out by cutting old stems to ground level in spring. Propagate by seed in spring or by semi-ripe cuttings in summer. Spider mite and whitefly may cause problems.

J. pentantha, *syn. J. violacea*. Fast-growing, evergreen, twining climber. H 6–10ft (2–3m). Has heart-shaped, pointed leaves and 1in (2.5cm) wide, funnel-shaped, rich violet-blue or pure blue flowers in long-stalked clusters in summer-autumn.

J. violacea. See *J. pentantha.*

JAMESIA

HYDRANGEACEAE

Genus of one species of deciduous shrub, grown for its flowers. Needs full sun and fertile, well-drained soil. Propagate by softwood cuttings in summer.

J. americana. Deciduous, bushy shrub. H 5ft (1.5m), S 8ft (2.5m). Rounded, gray-green leaves are gray-white beneath. Clusters of small, slightly fragrant, star-shaped white flowers are produced during late spring. Z5–9 H12–10.

JANCAEA, syn. JANKAEA

GESNERIACEAE

Genus of one species of evergreen, rosetted perennial grown for its flowers and silver-green leaves. Makes a good alpine house plant. Is difficult to grow, since it needs shade from midday sun in high summer, a organic, gritty, moist, alkaline soil, and a collar of grit under the crown. Dislikes winter wet. Propagate by seed in spring or by leaf cuttings in midsummer. Z5–7 H7–5.

J. heldreichii illus. p.369.

Jankaea. Reclassified as *Jancaea*.

JASIONE

CAMPANULACEAE

Genus of summer-flowering annuals, biennials, and perennials grown for their attractive flower heads. Needs sun and sandy soil. Remove old stems in autumn. Propagate by seed in autumn or by division in spring.

J. laevis, syn. *J. perennis* (Sheep's bit). Tufted perennial. H 2–12in (5–30cm), S 4–8in (10–20cm). Has narrowly oblong, very hairy or glabrous, gray-green leaves and, in summer, spiky, spherical blue flower heads borne on erect stems. Is good for a rock garden. Z6–8 H8–6.

J. perennis. See *J. laevis.*

JASMINUM

Jasmine

OLEACEAE

Genus of deciduous or evergreen shrubs and woody-stemmed, scrambling or twining climbers grown for their often fragrant flowers and their foliage. Needs full sun and fertile, well-drained soil. *J. nudiflorum*, which needs supporting, benefits from having old shoots thinned out after flowering, when others may be pruned. Propagate by semi-ripe cuttings in summer.

J. angulare, syn. *J. capense*. Evergreen, woody-stemmed, scrambling climber. H 6ft (2m) or more. Dark green leaves have 3 oval leaflets. Small clusters of fragrant, tubular, 5-lobed white flowers are carried in late summer. Z10–11 H12–9.

J. beesianum. Evergreen, woody-stemmed, scrambling climber, deciduous in cool areas. H to 15ft (5m). Has lance-shaped leaves. Fragrant, tubular, usually 6-lobed, pinkish red flowers, 1–3 together, borne in early summer; then shiny black berries. Z10-11 H12–10.

J. capense. See *J. angulare.*

J. grandiflorum of gardens. See *J. officinale* f. *affine.*

J. humile (Yellow jasmine) illus. p.146. **'Revolutum'** is an evergreen, bushy shrub. H 8ft (2.5m), S 10ft (3m). Bears large, fragrant, tubular, upright, bright yellow flowers with 5 spreading lobes on long, slender, green shoots from early spring to late autumn. Glossy, bright green leaves each consist of 3–7 oval leaflets. Z7–9 H9–7.

f. ***wallichianum*** has semi-pendent flowers and 7–13 leaflets.

J. mesnyi, syn. *J. primulinum*, illus. p.207.

J. nobile subsp. ***rex***, syn. *J. rex*. Evergreen, woody-stemmed, twining climber. H 10ft (3m). Has broadly oval, leathery, deep green leaves, 4–8in (10–20cm) long. Scentless, tubular, 5-lobed, pure white flowers are pink-tinged in bud and appear intermittently all year if warm enough. Z13–15 H12–10.

J. nudiflorum illus. p.151.

J. officinale (Common jasmine, Jessamine). Semi-evergreen or deciduous, woody-stemmed, twining climber. H to 40ft (12m). Leaves consist of 7 or 9 leaflets. Has clusters of fragrant, 4- or 5-lobed white flowers in summer-autumn. Z8–11 H12–8.

f. ***affine*** (syn. *J. grandiflorum* of gardens) illus. p.208.

J. parkeri. Evergreen, domed shrub. H 6in (15cm), S 18in (38cm) or more. Produces a tangled mass of fine stems and twigs bearing minute, oval leaves. Masses of tiny, tubular, 5-lobed yellow flowers appear from leaf axils in early summer. Z7–11 H12–7.

J. polyanthum illus. p.219.

J. primulinum. See *J. mesnyi.*

J. rex. See *J. nobile* subsp. *rex*.

JEFFERSONIA

BERBERIDACEAE

Genus of spring-flowering perennials. Needs shade or partial shade and organic, moist soil. Extensive root systems resent disturbance. Top-dress crown in late autumn. Propagate by seed as soon as ripe.

J. diphylla illus. p.347.

J. dubia, syn. *Plagiorhegma dubia*, illus. p.369.

JOVIBARBA

CRASSULACEAE

Genus of evergreen perennials that spread by short stolons and are grown for their symmetrical rosettes of oval to strap-shaped, pointed, fleshy leaves. Makes ground-hugging mats suitable for rock gardens, screes, walls, banks, and alpine houses. Needs sun and gritty soil. Takes several years to reach flowering size. Rosettes die after plants have flowered, but they leave numerous offsets. Propagate by offsets in summer.

J. hirta, syn. *Sempervivum hirtum*, illus. p.388.

J. sobolifera, syn. *Sempervivum soboliferum*. Vigorous, evergreen, mat-forming perennial. H 4in (10cm), S 8in (20cm). Rounded, grayish green or olive green rosettes are often red-tinged. Flower stems bear terminal clusters of small, cup-shaped, 6-petaled (rarely 5 or 7), pale yellow flowers in summer.

JUANULLOA

SOLANACEAE

Genus of evergreen, summer-flowering shrubs, grown for their flowers. Low temperatures cause leaf drop. Prefers full light and fertile, freely draining soil. Water potted specimens moderately, less when not in full growth. To encourage a branching habit, tip prune young plants. Propagate by semi-ripe cuttings in summer. Whitefly, spider mite, and mealy bug may be troublesome.

J. aurantiaca. See J. mexicana.

J. mexicana, syn. J. aurantiaca, illus. p.171

JUBAEA

ARECACEAE

Genus of one species of evergreen palm grown for its overall appearance. Needs full light and fertile, well-drained soil. Water potted specimens moderately, less frequently in winter. Propagate by seed in spring at not less than 77°F (25°C). Spider mite may be a nuisance.

J. chilensis, syn. *J. spectabilis*, illus. p.85.

J. spectabilis. See *J. chilensis.*

JUGLANS

Walnut

JUGLANDACEAE

Genus of deciduous trees, with aromatic leaves, grown for their foliage, stately habit, and, in some species, edible nuts (walnuts). Produces greenish yellow catkins in spring and early summer. Young plants are prone to cold damage. Requires full sun and deep, fertile, well-drained soil. Propagate by seed when ripe in autumn.

J. ailantifolia, syn. *J. sieboldiana* (Japanese walnut). Deciduous, spreading tree with thick shoots. H and S 50ft (15m). Very large leaves consist of 11–17 oblong, glossy, bright green leaflets. Bears edible walnuts in autumn. Z5–8 H8–5. var. ***cordiformis*** (syn. *J. cordiformis*) illus. p.68.

J. cathayensis (Chinese walnut). Deciduous, spreading tree. H and S 70ft (20m). Has very large leaves consisting of 11–17 oval to oblong, dark green leaflets. Bears edible walnuts in autumn. Z5–8 H8–5.

J. cinerea (Butternut). Fast-growing, deciduous, spreading tree. H 80ft (25m), S 70ft (20m). Leaves are large and very aromatic, with 7–19 oval to oblong, pointed, bright green leaflets. Bears dense clusters of large, rounded nuts in autumn. Z3–9 H9–1.

J. cordiformis. See *J. ailantifolia* var. *cordiformis.*

J. microcarpa, syn. *J. rupestris*, illus. p.92.

J. nigra illus. p.67.

J. regia illus. p.66. **'Carpathian'**,

J. rupestris. See *J. microcarpa.*

J. sieboldiana. See *J. ailantifolia.*

JUNCUS

JUNCACEAE

See also GRASSES, BAMBOOS, RUSHES, AND SEDGES.

***J. effusus* 'Spiralis'**, syn. *J. effusus* f. *spiralis*, *Scirpus lacustris* 'Spiralis', illus. p.308.

JUNIPERUS
Juniper

CUPRESSACEAE

See also CONIFERS.
J. chinensis (Chinese juniper). Conical conifer, making a tree. H 50ft (15m), S 6–10ft (2–3m), or a spreading shrub, H 3–15ft (1–5m), S 10–15ft (3–5m). Has peeling bark. Both scale- and needlelike, aromatic, dark green leaves, paired or in threes, are borne on the same shoot. Globose, fleshy, berrylike fruits are glaucous white. Many cultivars commonly listed under *J. chinensis* are forms of *J.* x *pfitzeriana*. Z3–9 H9–1. **'Aurea'**, H 30–50ft (10–15m), S 10–12ft (3–4m), is a slow-growing, oval or conical form with gold foliage and abundant yellow, male cones. **'Blaauw'** (syn. *J.* x *media* 'Blaauw'), H and S 6ft (2m), is a spreading shrub with blue-green foliage. **'Blue and Gold'** (syn. *J.* x *media* 'Blue and Gold'; illus. p.111), H and S to 3ft (1m), is a spreading form with leaves variegated sky blue and gold. **'Expansa Variegata'** (syn. *J. davurica* 'Expansa Variegata'; illus. p.111) is a conifer with trailing or ascending branchlets. H 30in (75cm), S 5–6ft (1.5–2m). Bears scale- and needlelike, aromatic, yellow-variegated, bluish green leaves. **'Kaizuka'**, H 15ft (5m), S 10–15ft (3–5m), forms a sprawling, irregular bush and has a profusion of cones. **'Keteleeri'** illus. p.105. **'Obelisk'** illus. p.108. **'Plumosa Aurea'** (syn. *J.* x *media* 'Plumosa Aurea'; illus. p.111) is more erect, with green-gold foliage turning bronze in winter. **'Pyramidalis'**, H 30ft (10m), S 3–6ft (1–2m), is a columnar, dense form with ascending branches bearing needlelike, blue-green leaves. **'Robust Green'** syn. *J. virginiana* 'Robusta Green' (illus. p.108). **'Stricta'** (illus. p.110), H to 15ft (5m), S to 3ft (1m), is conical, with soft, blue-green, young foliage.
J. communis (Common juniper). Conifer, ranging from a spreading shrub to a narrow, upright tree. H 1–25ft (30cm–8m), S 3–12ft (1–4m). Has needlelike, aromatic, glossy, mid- or yellow-green leaves in threes and bears globular to ovoid, fleshy greenish berries that become glaucous blue and then ripen to black in their third year. Z2–6 H6–1. **'Compressa'**, H 30in (75cm), S 6in (15cm), is a dwarf, erect form. **'Hibernica'** (illus. p.111), H 10–15ft (3–5m), S 12in (30cm), is columnar. **'Hornibrookii'**, H 20in (50cm), S 6ft (2m), and **'Prostrata'**, H 8–12in (20–30cm), S 3–6ft (1–2m), are carpeting plants.
J. conferta, syn. *J. rigida* subsp. *conferta* (Shore juniper). Prostrate, shrubby conifer. H 6in (15cm), S 3–6ft (1–2m). Spreading branches bear dense, needle-like, aromatic, glossy, bright green leaves, glaucous beneath. Produces glaucous black berries. Tolerates salty, coastal air.
***J. davurica* 'Expansa Variegata'**. See *J. chinensis* 'Expansa Variegata'.
J. drupacea (Syrian juniper). Columnar conifer. H 30–50ft (10–15m), S 3–6ft (1–2m). Has needlelike, aromatic, light green leaves in threes and ovoid or almost globose, fleshy brown berries.
J. horizontalis (Creeping juniper). Prostrate, wide-spreading, shrubby conifer, eventually forming mats up to 20in (50cm) thick. Has scale- or needlelike, aromatic, blue-green or -gray leaves and pale blue-gray berries. Z3–9 H9–1. Leaves of **'Andorra Compact'** (syn. *J.h.* 'Plumosa Compacta') turn bronze-purple in winter. **'Douglasii'** (illus. p.110) has glaucous blue foliage that turns plum purple in winter. **'Plumosa'** is less dense than 'Andorra Compact' and has gray-green leaves becoming purple during winter. **'Plumosa Compacta'** see *J.h.* 'Andorra Compact'. **'Prince of Wales'** has bright green foliage tinged blue when young and turning purple-brown in winter. **'Turquoise Spreader'** (illus. p.110) has turquoise-green foliage. **'Wiltonii'** has bluish gray leaves that retain their color over winter.
J.* x *media. See *J.* x *pfitzeriana*. **'Blaauw'** see *J. chinensis* 'Blaauw'. **'Blue and Gold'** see *J. chinensis* 'Blue and Gold'. **'Hetzii'** see *J. virginiana* 'Hetzii'. **'Pfitzeriana'** see *J.* x *pfitzeriana* 'William Pfitzer'. **'Pfitzeriana Aurea'** see *J.* x *pfitzeriana* 'Aurea'. **'Pfitzeriana Glauca'** see *J.* x *pfitzeriana* 'Glauca'. **'Plumosa'**, H 3ft (1m), S 6–10ft (2–3m), is a spreading shrub with drooping sprays of midgreen foliage. **'Plumosa Aurea'** see *J. chinensis* 'Plumosa Aurea'.
J.* x *pfitzeriana, syn. *J.* x *media*. Group of spreading to conical conifers. H 50ft (15m), S 6–10ft (2–3m). Has peeling bark. Mainly scalelike, dark green leaves exude a fetid smell when crushed. Fruits are globose to rounded and white or blue-black. Cultivars are suitable as a groundcover or as specimen plants in a small garden. Z4–9 H9–1. Some forms are commonly listed under *J. chinensis*. **'Aurea'** (syn. *J.* x *media* 'Pfitzeriana Aurea'; illus. p.111) has golden foliage. **'Glauca'** (syn. *J.* x *media* 'Pfitzeriana Glauca'; illus. p.110) has gray-blue leaves. **'William Pfitzer'** (syn. *J.* x *media* 'Pfitzeriana'; illus. p.111), H 10ft (3m), S 10–15ft (3–5m), is a spreading, flat-topped shrub with gray-green leaves.
J. procumbens (Bonin Isles juniper; illus. p.110). Spreading, prostrate, shrubby conifer. H 30in (75cm), S 6ft (2m). Has red-brown bark. Thick branches carry needlelike, aromatic, light green or yellow-green leaves and globose, fleshy brown or black berries. Z3–9 H9–1. **'Nana'** (illus. p.110), H 6–8in (15–20cm), S 30in (75cm),is less vigorous and is mat-forming.
J. recurva (Drooping juniper, Himalayan weeping juniper) illus. p.108. var. ***coxii*** (Coffin juniper) is a slow-growing, conical conifer. H to 50ft (15m), S to 22ft (7m). Smooth bark flakes in thin sheets. Weeping sprays of long, needlelike, aromatic, incurved leaves are bright green. Globose or ovoid, fleshy berries are black. **'Densa'** (syn. *J. recurva* 'Nana'; illus. p.110), H 1ft (30cm), S 3ft (1m), is a spreading shrub with sprays of green leaves that are erect at tips. Both Z7–11 H12–7.**'Nana'** see *J.r.* 'Densa'.
J. rigida (Temple juniper). Sprawling, shrubby conifer. H and S 25ft (8m). Gray or brown bark peels in strips. Very sharp, needlelike, aromatic, bright green leaves in threes are borne in nodding sprays. Globose, fleshy fruits are purplish black. subsp. ***conferta*** see *J. conferta.*
J. sabina (Savin). Spreading, shrubby conifer. H to 12ft (4m), S 10–15ft (3–5m). Has flaking, red-brown bark. Slender shoots bear mainly scalelike, aromatic, dark green leaves that give off a fetid smell when crushed. Bears rounded, blue-black berries. Z4–7 H7–1. **'Blaue Donau'** (syn. *J.s.* 'Blue Danube'), H 6ft (2m), S 6–12ft (2–4m), is a spreading form with branch tips curved upward and gray-blue foliage. **'Blue Danube'** see *J.s.* 'Blaue Donau'. **'Cupressifolia'** (syn. *J.s.* Cupressifolia Group; illus. p.110), H 6ft (2m), S 12ft (4m), is a free-fruiting, female form with horizontal or ascending branches and blue-green leaves. **'Mas'** (illus. p.110), has ascending branches. Leaves are blue above, green below, and purplish in winter. var. ***tamariscifolia*** (syn. *J.s.* Tamariscifolia Group; illus. p.110), H 3ft (1m), S 6ft (2m), has tiered layers of mainly needlelike, bright green or blue-green leaves.
J. scopulorum (Rocky Mountain juniper). Slow-growing, round-crowned conifer. H 30ft (10m), S 12ft (4m). Reddish brown bark is furrowed into strips or squares and peels on branches. Scalelike, aromatic leaves are gray-green to dark green. Bears globose, fleshy blue berries. Z3–7 H7–1. **'Skyrocket'** (syn. *J. virginiana* 'Skyrocket'; illus. p.110), H 25ft (8m), S 2½ft (75cm), is very narrow in habit with glaucous blue foliage. **'Springbank'** (illus. p.110) is narrowly conical with drooping branch tips and intense silvery blue foliage. **'Tabletop'**, H 6ft (2m), S 15ft (5m), has a flat-topped habit and silvery blue leaves.
J. squamata (Flaky juniper). Prostrate to sprawling, shrubby conifer. H 1–12ft (30cm–4m), S 3–15ft (1–5m). Bark is red-brown and flaking. Needle-like, aromatic, fresh green or bluish green leaves spread at tips of shoots. Produces ovoid, fleshy black berries. Z4–9 H9–1. **'Blue Carpet'**, H 1ft (30cm), S 6–10ft (2–3m), is vigorous and prostrate, with glaucous blue foliage. **'Blue Star'** (illus. p.110), H 20in (50cm), S 24in (60cm), forms a dense, rounded bush and has blue foliage. **'Chinese Silver'** (illus. p.110), H and S 10–12ft (3–4m), has branches with nodding tips and bluish leaves with bright silver undersides. **'Holger'** (illus. p.110), H and S 6ft (2m), has sulfur yellow young leaves that contrast with steel blue old foliage. **'Meyeri'**, H and S 15ft (5m), sprawls and has steel-blue foliage.
J. virginiana (Pencil cedar). Slow-growing, conical or broadly columnar conifer. H 50–70ft (15–20m), S 20–25ft (6–8m). Both scale- and needlelike, aromatic, gray-green leaves are borne on same shoot. Ovoid, fleshy berries are brownish violet and very glaucous. Z3–9 H9–1. **'Grey Owl'** (illus. p.110), H 10ft (3m), S 10–15ft (3–5m), is a low, spreading cultivar with ascending branches and silvery gray foliage. **'Hetzii'** (syn. *J.* x *media* 'Hetzii'), H 10–12ft (3–4m), S 12ft (4m), has tiers of gray-green foliage. **'Robusta Green'** see *J. chinensis* 'Robust Green'. **'Skyrocket'** see *J. scopulorum* 'Skyrocket'.

JUSTICIA

ACANTHACEAE

Genus of evergreen perennials, subshrubs, and shrubs grown mainly for their flowers. Requires full light or partial shade and fertile, well-drained soil. Water containerized specimens freely when in full growth, moderately at other times. Some species need regular pruning. Propagate by softwood or greenwood cuttings in spring or early summer. Whitefly may cause problems.
J. adhatoda, syn. *Adhatoda duvernoia, Duvernoia adhatodoides* (Snake bush). Evergreen, erect shrub. H 6–10ft (2–3m), S 3–6ft (1–2m). Has elliptic, dark green leaves. Fragrant, tubular white or mauve flowers with pink, red, or purple marks appear in summer-autumn.
J. brandegeeana, syn. *Beloperone guttata, Drejerella guttata*, illus. p.166. **'Chartreuse'** illus. p.168.
J. carnea, syn. *Jacobinia carnea, J. pohliana*, illus. p.163.
J. coccinea. See *Pachystachys coccinea.*
J. floribunda. See *J. rizzinii.*
J. ghiesbreghtiana of gardens. See *J. spicigera.*
J. pauciflora. See *J. rizzinii.*
J. rizzinii, syn. *J. floribunda, J. pauciflora, Libonia floribunda*. Evergreen, rounded, freely branching shrub. H and S 1–2ft (30-60cm). Min. 59°F (15°C) to flower well in winter. Leaves are oval, and midgreen. Bears nodding clusters of tubular, yellow-tipped scarlet flowers mainly autumn-spring; best repropagated every few years.
J. spicigera, syn. *J. ghiesbreghtiana* of gardens, *Jacobinia spicigera*, illus. p.172.

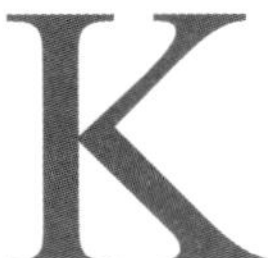

KAEMPFERIA

ZINGIBERACEAE

Genus of tufted, rhizomatous perennials grown for their aromatic leaves and their flowers. Needs a moist atmosphere, partial shade, and moist, organic soil. Allow to dry out when plants become dormant. Propagate by division in late spring.
K. pulchra illus. p.283.
K. roscoeana. Rhizomatous perennial without an obvious stem. H 2–4in (5–10cm), S 8–10in (20–25cm). Usually has only 2 almost rounded, aromatic leaves, to 4in (10cm) long, dark green with pale green marks above, reddish green below, that are held horizontally. A short spike of pure white flowers, each with a deeply lobed lip, appears from the center of leaf tuft in autumn. Z11–12 H12–10.

KALANCHOE, syn. BRYOPHYLLUM

CRASSULACEAE

Genus of succulents or shrubs with very fleshy, mainly cylindrical, oval, or linear leaves and bell-shaped to tubular flowers. Many species produce new plantlets from indented leaf margins. Needs full sun or partial shade and well-drained soil. Keep moist from spring to autumn. Water lightly and only occasionally in winter. Propagate by seed, offsets, or stem cuttings in spring or summer.
K. beharensis illus. p.460.
K. blossfeldiana (Flaming Katy). Bushy succulent. H and S 12in (30cm). s Has oval to oblong, glossy, dark green leaves with toothed edges and clusters of tubular scarlet flowers, ¼in (0.5cm) across, in spring. Prefers partial shade. Many hybrids are available in a range of colors (salmon pink is illus. p.464). Z11 H12–1.
K. daigremontiana illus. p.462.
K. delagoensis, syn. *K. tubiflora*, illus. p.468.
K. fedtschenkoi (South American air plant). Bushy succulent. H and S 3ft (1m). Produces oval, indented, blue-gray leaves with new plantlets in each notch. Bell-shaped, brownish pink flowers, ¾in (2cm) long, appear in late winter. Prefers a sunny position. Z11 H12–10. **'Variegata'** illus. p.462.
K. pumila. Creeping succulent. H 4in (10cm), S indefinite. Has oval, powdery gray-white leaves with indented margins. Tubular pink flowers, ½in (1cm) long, appear in spring. Good in a hanging basket in a sunny position. Z11 H12–1.
***K.* 'Tessa'** illus. p.464.
K. tomentosa illus. p.467.
K. tubiflora. See *K. delagoensis*.
K. uniflora, syn. *Kitchingia uniflora*. Creeping succulent. H 2½in (6cm), S indefinite. Produces rounded, midgreen leaves, ¼–1¼in (0.5–3cm) long, and bell-shaped, yellow-flushed, reddish purple flowers, ½in (1cm) long, in late winter. Prefers partial shade.
***K.* 'Wendy'** illus. p.463.

KALMIA

ERICACEAE

Genus of evergreen, summer-flowering shrubs grown for their clusters of distinctive, usually cup-shaped flowers. Needs sun or semi-shade and moist, peaty, acidic soil. Propagate species by softwood cuttings in summer or by seed in autumn, selected forms by softwood cuttings in summer. All parts may cause severe discomfort if ingested.
K. angustifolia (Sheep laurel). f. ***rubra*** (syn. *K. angustifolia* 'Rubra') illus. p.165.
K. latifolia (Calico bush) illus. p.141. **'Ostbo Red'** is an evergreen, bushy, dense shrub. H and S 10ft (3m). Has oval, glossy, rich green leaves. Large, showy clusters of deep pink flowers open in early summer from crimped, deep red buds. Prefers full sun. Z5–9 H9–5.

KALMIOPSIS

ERICACEAE

Genus of one species of evergreen, spring-flowering shrub grown for its flowers. Requires semi-shade and moist, peaty, acidic soil. Propagate by softwood or semi-ripe cuttings in summer.
***K. leachiana* 'La Piniec'**, syn. *K.l.* 'M. le Piniec'. Evergreen, bushy shrub. H and S 12in (30cm). Terminal clusters of small, widely bell-shaped, purplish pink flowers are produced from early to late spring. Has small, oval, glossy, dark green leaves. Z7–9 H9–7.

KALOPANAX

ARALIACEAE

Genus of one species of deciduous, autumn-flowering tree grown for its foliage and fruits. Unripened wood on young plants is susceptible to cold damage. Does best in sun or semi-shade and in fertile, moist but well-drained soil. Propagate by softwood cuttings in summer.
K. pictus. See *K. septemlobus*.
K. ricinifolius. See *K. septemlobus*.
K. septemlobus, syn. *Acanthopanax ricinifolius*, *K. pictus*, *K. ricinifolius*, illus. p.80.

KELSEYA

ROSACEAE

Genus of one species of extremely small, evergreen subshrub. Is difficult to grow and is best in an alpine house, since the foliage deeply resents both summer and winter wet. Needs full sun and moist, alkaline soil. Propagate by soft-tip cuttings in late spring or by seed in autumn. Is susceptible to molds, so remove any dead rosettes at once.
K. uniflora. Slow-growing, evergreen, rosetted subshrub. H ½in (1cm), S to 8in (20cm). Forms a hard mat of closely packed, small rosettes of tiny, oval, dark green leaves. In early spring carries stemless, star-shaped, occasionally pink-flushed white flowers. Z5–7 H7–5.

KENNEDIA, syn. KENNEDYA

LEGUMINOSAE/PAPILIONACEAE

Genus of evergreen, woody-stemmed, trailing and twining climbers grown for their pealike flowers. Provide full light and moderately fertile, sandy soil. Water regularly when in full growth, sparingly in cold weather. Requires support. Thin out congested growth after flowering or in spring. Propagate by seed in spring or by semi-ripe cuttings in summer.
K. nigricans (Black bean). Vigorous, evergreen, woody-stemmed, twining climber. H to 6ft (2m). Leaves are divided into 3 leaflets with notched tips. Has small clusters of pealike, velvety, black-purple flowers with yellow blazes in spring-summer. Z13–15 H12–10.
K. rubicunda illus. p.205.

Kennedya. Reclassified as *Kennedia*.
Kentia. Reclassified as *Howea*.

KERRIA

ROSACEAE

Genus of one species of deciduous shrub grown for its showy yellow flowers. Needs sun or semi-shade and fertile, well-drained soil. Thin out old shoots after flowering. Propagate by softwood cuttings in summer or by division in autumn.
K. japonica* 'Pleniflora'** illus. p.131. var. ***simplex is a deciduous, arching, graceful shrub. H and S 6ft (2m). Has bright green foliage. Single, buttercup-like, golden yellow flowers are borne from mid- to late spring. Z5–9 H9–3.

KIGELIA

BIGNONIACEAE

Genus of one species of evergreen tree grown for its flowers, curious, sausagelike fruits, and for shade. Requires full light and organic, well-drained soil. Water potted specimens moderately, very little when temperatures are low. Propagate by seed in spring at not less than 73°F (23°C).
K. africana, syn. *K. pinnata* (Sausage tree). Evergreen, spreading, fairly bushy tree. H and S 25ft (8m) or more. Leaves have 7–11 oblong to oval leaflets. Scented, bell-shaped, purplish red flowers open at night from autumn to spring. Bears inedible, cylindrical, hard-shelled brown fruits, 12–18in (30–45cm) long. Z10–11 H12–10.
K. pinnata. See *K. africana*.

KIRENGESHOMA

HYDRANGEACEAE

Genus of late summer- and autumn-flowering perennials. Grow in light shade and in deep, moist, lime-free soil. Propagate by seed or division in autumn or spring.
K. palmata illus. p.263.

KITAIBELA, syn. KITAIBELIA

MALVACEAE

Genus of one species of summer-flowering perennial. Needs full sun and fertile, preferably dry soil. Propagate by seed in autumn or spring.
K. vitifolia. Bushy, upright perennial. H to 5ft (1.5m), S 2ft (60cm). In summer bears small clusters of open cup-shaped white or rose-pink flowers. Has palmately lobed, coarsely toothed leaves. Z6–8 H8–6.

Kitaibelia. Reclassified as *Kitaibela*
Kitchingia uniflora. See *Kalanchoe uniflora*.
Kleinia articulata. See *Senecio articulatus*.

KNAUTIA

DIPSACACEAE

Genus of summer-flowering annuals and perennials. Needs sun and well-drained soil. Requires staking. Propagate by basal cuttings in spring or by seed in autumn.
K. arvensis, syn. *Scabiosa arvensis* (Scabious). Erect perennial. H 4ft (1.2m), S 1½ft (45cm). Produces heads of pincushion-like, bluish lilac flowers in summer. Stems are clothed in narrowly oval to lyre-shaped, deeply divided leaves.
K. macedonica, syn. *Scabiosa rumelica*, illus. p.249.

KNIGHTIA

PROTEACEAE

Genus of evergreen, summer-flowering trees grown for their flowers, foliage, and overall appearance. Grows in any reasonably fertile, well-drained soil and in sun or partial shade. Water potted specimens moderately, less in winter. Propagate by seed in spring.
K. excelsa (New Zealand honeysuckle, Rewa rewa). Evergreen, upright tree. H 70ft (20m) or more, S 6–12ft (2–4m). Has oblong to lance-shaped, coarsely serrated, leathery leaves, that are glossy and deep green. Dense racemes of slender, tubular, deep red flowers are produced in summer. Z10–11 H12–10.

KNIPHOFIA

Red-hot poker, Torch lily

ASPHODELACEAE/LILIACEAE

Genus of perennials, some of which are evergreen. Needs full sun and well-drained conditions, with constantly moist soil in summer. Propagate species by seed or division in spring, cultivars by division only in spring.

***K.* 'Atlanta'.** Evergreen, upright perennial. H to 3ft (1m), S 1½ft (45cm). In summer, thick stems bear dense, terminal racemes of tubular, bright orange-yellow flowers. Has thick, grasslike, channeled leaves. Does well in a coastal area. Z6–9 H9–4.

***K.* 'Bee's Lemon'.** Upright perennial. H 3ft (1m), S 1½ft (45cm). Has dense, terminal racemes of tubular, green-tinged, citron yellow flowers on thick stems in late summer and autumn. Grasslike, deep green leaves have serrated edges. Z6–9 H9–6.

K. caulescens illus. p.263.

***K.* 'C.M. Prichard'** of gardens. See *K. rooperi*.

***K.* 'Little Maid'** illus. p.290.

***K.* 'Maid of Orleans'.** Upright perennial. H 4ft (1.2m), S 1½ft (45cm). In summer, slender stems are each crowned with a dense raceme of yellow buds that open to tubular, creamy white flowers. Leaves are fresh green, basal, and strap-shaped. Z6–9 H9–6.

***K.* 'Percy's Pride'** illus. p.263.

K. rooperi, syn. *K.* 'C.M. Prichard' of gardens, illus. p.263.

***K.* 'Royal Standard'** illus. p.258.

***K.* 'Samuel's Sensation'.** Upright perennial. H 5ft (1.5m), S 2ft (60cm). In late summer, dense, terminal racemes of tubular, deep orange flowers are produced on thick stems. Has strap-shaped, basal, dark green leaves. Z6–9 H9–6.

K. snowdenii of gardens. See *K. thomsonii* var. *snowdenii*.

K. thomsonii var. ***snowdenii***, syn. *K. snowdenii* of gardens, illus. p.258.

K. uvaria (Red-hot poker). **'Nobilis'** is an upright perennial with erect then spreading leaves. H 6ft (2m), S 3ft (1m). In late summer and autumn, thick stems each bear a dense, terminal raceme of tubular, bright red flowers. Has strap-shaped, channeled, dark green leaves. Z5–9 H9–1.

Kochia. Reclassified as *Bassia*.

KOELREUTERIA

SAPINDACEAE

Genus of deciduous, summer-flowering trees, grown for their foliage, flowers, and fruits. Requires full sun, and fertile, well-drained soil. Propagate by seed in autumn or by root cuttings in late winter.

K. paniculata illus. p.92.

KOHLERIA

GESNERIACEAE

Genus of erect perennials, with scaly rhizomes, grown for their showy, tubular flowers borne mainly in summer. Grow in moist but well-drained soil and in full sun or semi-shade. Water sparingly in winter; over-watering will cause rhizomes to rot. Propagate in spring by division of rhizomes or by seed if available.

K. amabilis. Rhizomatous perennial. H 3–6in (8–16cm), S 2ft (60cm). Oval, hairy leaves, to 3in (8cm) long, are often marked with silver and brown above. Small, nodding, tubular, deep pink flowers with red-marked lobes appear in summer. Is useful for a hanging basket. Z14–15 H12–10.

K. bogotensis. Erect, rhizomatous perennial. H and S 18in (45cm) or more. Oval, velvety, green leaves, to 3in (8cm) long, are sometimes marked with paler green above. In summer has small, tubular flowers, red with a yellow base outside, red-dotted, yellow within. Z14–15 H12–10.

K. digitaliflora illus. p.244.

K. eriantha illus. p.250.

K. warscewiczii. Erect, rhizomatous perennial. H 3ft (1m), S 2ft (60cm). Oval, dark green leaves have scalloped margins. In summer and autumn has tubular, hairy, yellow-based scarlet flowers with red- or brown spotted, greenish yellow or bright yellow lobes. Z14–15 H12–10.

KOLKWITZIA

CAPRIFOLIACEAE

Genus of one species of deciduous shrub grown for its abundant flowers. Prefers full sun and fertile, well-drained soil. Cut out old shoots after flowering. Propagate by softwood cuttings in summer.

K. amabilis (Beauty bush). Deciduous, arching shrub. H and S 10ft (3m). Has peeling bark and oval, dark green leaves. Bell-shaped, yellow-throated white or pink flowers are borne in late spring and early summer. Z5–9 H9–5. **'Pink Cloud'** illus. p.121.

Korolkowia sewerzowii. See *Fritillaria sewerzowii*.

L

LABLAB

PAPILIONACEAE/LEGUMINOSAE

Genus of one species of deciduous, woody-stemmed, twining climber grown for its attractive, pealike flowers (in the tropics it is grown for green manure and animal feed and for its edible pods and seeds). Often raised as an annual. Grow in sun and in any well-drained soil. Propagate by seed in spring.

L. purpureus, syn. *Dolichos lablab*, *D. purpureus*, illus. p.211.

LABURNUM

PAPILIONACEAE/LEGUMINOSAE

Genus of deciduous trees grown for their profuse, pendent flower clusters in spring and summer. Does best in full sun; grows in any but waterlogged soil. Seeds are very poisonous. Propagate species by seed in autumn, hybrids by budding in summer. All parts are highly toxic if ingested.

L. alpinum illus. p.93.

L. anagyroides, syn. *L. vulgare* (Common laburnum, Golden chain). Deciduous, spreading tree. H and S 22ft (7m). Leaves have 3 oval leaflets and are gray-green. Short, pendent, dense clusters of pealike yellow flowers appear in late spring and early summer. Z6-8 H8–5.

L. vulgare. See *L. anagyroides*.

***L.* x *watereri* 'Vossii'** illus. p.92.

LACHENALIA

HYACINTHACEAE/LILIACEAE

Genus of winter- and spring-flowering bulbs with tubular or bell-shaped flowers; some have attractively mottled leaves. Is useful as pot plants and in open borders. Requires light, well-drained soil and a sunny site. Plant in early autumn; dry off when foliage has died down. Propagate in autumn by seed or freely produced offsets.

L. aloides, syn. *L. tricolor*, *L.* 'Tricolor'. Winter- and spring-flowering bulb. H 6–10in (15–25cm), S 2–3in (5–8cm). Produces 2 strap-shaped, semi-erect, basal, purple-spotted green leaves. Has a spike of 10–20 pendent flowers, each 1¼in (3cm) long with a yellow tube shading to red at the apex and with flared green tips. Z11 H12–10. **'Nelsonii'** (syn. *L.* 'Nelsonii') illus. p.441. var. ***quadricolor*** illus. p.441.

L. angustifolia. See *L. contaminata*.

L. contaminata, syn. *L. angustifolia*. Winter- and spring-flowering bulb. H to 8in (20cm), S 2–3in (5–8cm). Has narrowly strap-shaped, semi-erect leaves in a basal cluster. Bears a spike of bell-shaped white flowers, ¼in (0.5cm) long, suffused and tipped with red and green. Z11 H12 10.

L. glaucina. See *L. orchioides* var. *glaucina*.

L. mutabilis. Winter- and spring-flowering bulb. H to 12in (30cm), S 2–3in (5–8cm). Has 2 strap-shaped, semi-erect, basal leaves. Stem bears a loose spike of up to 25 tubular, ½in (1cm) long flowers that are purple or lilac in bud and open to reddish brown-tipped petals with a green tube base.

***L.* 'Nelsonii'.** See *L. aloides* 'Nelsonii'.

L. orchioides. Winter- and spring-flowering bulb. H 6–12in (15–30cm), S 2–3in (5–8cm). Has 2 strap-shaped, semi-erect, basal green leaves, sometimes spotted blackish- or purple-brown. Stem produces a dense spike of fragrant, semi-erect, tubular white flowers, ½in (1cm) long, blue-tinged and tipped with green. Z11–14 H12–6. var. ***glaucina*** (syn. *L. glaucina*) illus. p.425.

L. rubida. Winter-flowering bulb. H to 10in (25cm), S 2–3in (5–8cm). Bears 2 strap-shaped, purple-spotted green leaves, semi-erect and basal, and a loose spike of pendent, tubular red flowers, ¾–1¼in (2–3cm) long, shading to yellow at tips.

L. tricolor. See *L. aloides*.

***L.* 'Tricolor'.** See *L. aloides*.

Lactuca alpina. See *Cicerbita alpina*.

Lactuca bourgaei. See *Cicerbita bourgaei*.

LAELIA

See also ORCHIDS.

L. anceps (illus. p.297). Evergreen, epiphytic orchid for a cool greenhouse. H 10in (25cm). Lilac-pink flowers, 2½in (6cm) wide, each with a deep mauve lip, are carried in tall spikes in autumn. Has oval, rigid leaves, 4–6in (10–15cm) long. Needs semi-shade in summer. Z14-15 H12–6.

L. cinnabarina (illus. p.299). Evergreen, epiphytic orchid for an intermediate greenhouse. H 6in (15cm). Produces sprays of slender, orange flowers, 2in (5cm) or more across, usually in winter. Has narrowly oval, rigid leaves, 3–4in (8–10cm) long. Needs good light in summer. Z14–15 H12–6.

x LAELIOCATTLEYA

See also ORCHIDS.

x *L.* Rojo 'Mont Millais' (illus. p.297). Evergreen, epiphytic orchid for an intermediate greenhouse. H 12in (30cm). In winter-spring bears arching heads of slender, reddish orange flowers, ¾in (2cm) across. Oval leaves are up to 6in (15cm) long. Provide good light in summer. Z14–15 H12–6.

LAGAROSIPHON

HYDROCHARITACEAE

Genus of semi-evergreen, perennial, spreading, submerged water plants grown for their decorative foliage. Oxygenates water. Needs full sun. Thin regularly to keep under control. Propagate by stem cuttings in spring or summer.

L. major, syn. *Elodea crispa* of gardens, illus. p.449.

LAGERSTROEMIA

LYTHRACEAE

Genus of deciduous or evergreen, summer-flowering shrubs and trees grown for their flowers. Prefers fertile, well-drained soil and full sun. Water potted specimens freely when in full growth, less at other times. To maintain as shrubs, cut back hard the previous season's stems each spring. Propagate by seed in spring or by semi-ripe

cuttings in summer.
L. indica illus. p.91.
L. speciosa (Queen's Crape myrtle, Pride of India). Deciduous, rounded tree. H 50–70ft (15–20m), S 30–50ft (10–15m). Mid- to deep green leaves are narrowly oval, 3–7in (8–18cm) long. Has panicles of funnel-shaped, rose-pink to rose-purple flowers in summer-autumn, often when leafless. Z9–10 H10–9.

LAGUNARIA

MALVACEAE

Genus of one species of evergreen tree grown for its flowers in summer-autumn and its overall appearance. Prefers fertile, well-drained soil and full light. Water potted plants freely when in full summer growth, moderately at other times. Pruning is tolerated if required. Propagate by seed in spring or by semi-ripe cuttings in summer. Under cover, spider mite may be troublesome. Contact with the seeds may irritate skin.
L. patersonii (Norfolk Island hibiscus, Queensland pyramidal tree). Fast-growing, evergreen, upright tree, pyramidal when young. H 30–46ft (10–14m), S 15–22ft (5–7m). Oval, rough-textured leaves are matte green above, whitish green beneath. Bears hibiscus-like, rose-pink flowers, 2in (5cm) wide, in summer. Z12–15 H12–10.

LAGURUS

Hare's tail

POACEAE/GRAMINEAE

See also GRASSES, BAMBOOS, RUSHES, and SEDGES.
L. ovatus illus. p.306.

LAMARCKIA

POACEAE/GRAMINEAE

See also GRASSES, BAMBOOS, RUSHES, and SEDGES.
L. aurea (Golden top). Tuft-forming, annual grass. H and S 8in (20cm). Wiry stems bear scattered, pale green leaves and, in summer, erect, dense, one-sided golden panicles. Needs sun. H7–1.

LAMIUM

Deadnettle

LAMIACEAE/LABIATAE

Genus of spring- or summer-flowering perennials, most of which are semi-evergreen, including a number of weeds; some species make a useful groundcover. Prefers full or partial shade and moist but well-drained soil. Resents excessive winter wet. Propagate by stem-tip cuttings of non-flowering shoots in midsummer or by division in autumn or early spring.
L. galeobdolon subsp. ***montanum*** **'Florentinum'**, syn. *L.g.* 'Variegatum'. Semi-evergreen, carpeting perennial. H to 12in (30cm), S indefinite. Oval, midgreen leaves are marked with silver. Racemes of tubular, 2-lipped, lemon yellow flowers appear in summer. **'Hermann's Pride'** has leaves marked with silver. Both Z4–8 H8–1.
L. maculatum illus. p.269. **'Album'** illus. p.267. **'Aureum'** (syn. *L.m.* 'Gold Leaf') is a semi-evergreen, mat-forming perennial. H 8in (20cm), S 24in (60cm). Produces oval yellow leaves with paler white centers. Whorls of hooded pink flowers appear on short stems in summer. **'Beacon Silver'** bears mauve-tinged silver leaves, sometimes with narrow green margins, and clear pale pink flowers. Both Z4–8 H8–1. **'Gold Leaf'** see *L.m.* 'Aureum'. **'White Nancy'** illus. p.267.
L. orvala illus. p.271.

LAMPRANTHUS

AIZOACEAE

Genus of creeping, bushy succulents and subshrubs with daisylike flowers. Becomes woody after several years, when it is best replenished. Plants are good for summer bedding, particularly in arid conditions. Leaves redden in strong sun. Requires full sun and very well-drained soil. Propagate by seed or stem cuttings in spring or autumn.
L. aurantiacus illus. p.468.
L. deltoides, syn. *Oscularia deltoides*, illus. p.471.
L. haworthii. Erect to creeping succulent. H 20in (50cm), S indefinite. Blue-gray leaves are cylindrical and 2in (5cm) long. In spring bears masses of daisylike cerise flowers, 3in (7cm) across, that only open in sun. Z12–15 H12-10.
L. multiradiatus. See. *L. roseus*.
L. roseus, syn. *L. multiradiatus*, *Mesembryanthemum multiradiatum.* Creeping succulent. H 6in (15cm), S indefinite. Produces solid, 3-angled, mid- to glaucous green leaves, 2in (5cm) long. Daisylike, dark rose-red flowers, 1½in (4cm) across, open only in sun from spring to autumn. Z12–15 H12–10.
L. spectabilis illus. p.463.

LANTANA

Shrub verbena

VERBENACEAE

Genus of evergreen perennials and shrubs grown for their flowers. Needs full light and fertile, well-drained soil. Water containerized specimens freely when in full growth, moderately at other times. Tip prune young plants to promote a bushy habit. Propagate by seed in spring or by semi-ripe cuttings in summer. Spider mite and whitefly may be troublesome. All parts may cause severe discomfort if ingested, and contact with foliage may irritate skin.
L. camara. Evergreen, rounded to spreading shrub. H and S 3–6ft (1–2m). Bears oval, finely wrinkled, deep green leaves. From spring to autumn, tiny, tubular, 5-lobed flowers, in dense, domed heads, open yellow then turn red. Many color forms have been selected. Z11 H12-1.
L. delicatissima. See *L. montevidensis*.
L. montevidensis, syn. *L. delicatissima*, *L. sellowiana*, illus. p.167.
L. sellowiana. See *L. montevidensis*.
***L.* 'Spreading Sunset'** illus. p.171.

LAPAGERIA

PHILESIACEAE/LILIACEAE

Genus of one species of evergreen, woody-stemmed, twining climber grown for its large, waxy blooms. Requires organic, well-drained soil and partial shade. Water moderately, scarcely at all when not in full growth. Provide support. Thin out congested growth in spring. Propagate in spring by seed, soaked for 2 days before sowing, or in spring or autumn by layering.
L. rosea illus. p.210. var. ***albiflora*** (illus. p.44) is an evergreen, woody-stemmed, twining climber. H to 15ft (5m). Has oblong to oval, leathery, dark green leaves. From summer to late autumn bears pendent, fleshy, narrowly bell-shaped white flowers. Z10–11 H12–10.

Lapeirousia cruenta. See *Anomatheca laxa*.
Lapeirousia laxa. See *Anomatheca laxa*.

LARDIZABALA

LARDIZABALACEAE

Genus of evergreen, woody-stemmed, twining climbers grown for their foliage. Male and female flowers are produced on the same plant in late autumn to winter. Is useful for growing on trellises or pergolas. Grow in any well-drained soil and sun or partial shade. Propagate by seed in spring or by stem cuttings in late summer or autumn.
L. biternata. Evergreen, woody-stemmed, twining climber. H 10–12ft (3–4m). Rounded leaves have broadly oval, leathery, dark green leaflets. In winter produces brown flowers with tiny whitish petals, the males in drooping spikes, the females solitary. In winter-spring bears many-seeded, berrylike purple fruits, 2–3in (5–8cm) long. Z9–10 H10–9.

LARIX

PINACEAE

See also CONIFERS.
L. decidua, syn. *L. europaea* (European larch). Fast-growing, deciduous conifer with a conical crown when young, broadening on maturity, and spaced branches. H 80–100ft (25–30m), S 16–50ft (5–15m). Shoots are yellow-brown in winter. Has light green leaves and small, erect, conical cones. Z3–6 H6–1.
L. europaea. See *L. decidua*.
L. kaempferi, syn. *L. leptolepis* (Japanese larch). Fast-growing, deciduous, columnar conifer with a conical tip. H 80–100ft (25–30m), S 15–25ft (5–8m). Shoots are purplish red and leaves are needlelike, flattened, grayish green or bluish. Small cones have reflexed scales. Z5–7 H7–4.
L. leptolepis. See *L. kaempferi*.

LATHRAEA

SCROPHULARIACEAE

Genus of spreading perennials that grow as parasites on the roots of trees, in the case of *L. clandestina* on willow or poplar. True leaves are not produced. Grows in dappled shade cast by host tree and prefers moist conditions. Roots resent being disturbed. Propagate by seed when fresh in late summer.
L. clandestina illus. p.271.

LATHYRUS

PAPILIONACEAE/LEGUMINOSAE

Genus of annuals and perennials, many of them tendril climbers, grown for their racemes of attractive flowers. Flowers are followed by long, thin seed pods. Grow in organic, fertile, well-drained soil and in full light. Provide support and remove dead flowers regularly. Cut down perennials in late autumn. Propagate annuals by seed (soaked before sowing) in early spring or early autumn, perennials by seed in autumn or by division in spring. Botrytis and mildew may cause problems. Seeds may cause mild stomach upset if ingested.
L. grandiflorus illus. p.209.
L. latifolius illus. p.211.
L. magellanicus of gardens. See *L. nervosus*.
L. nervosus, syn. *L. magellanicus* of gardens (Lord Anson's blue pea). Herbaceous, tendril climber. H to 15ft (5m). Gray-green leaves each have a pair of leaflets, a 3-branched tendril, and large stipules. Fragrant, purplish blue flowers are borne in long-stalked racemes in summer. Z3-10 H10–1.
L. odoratus (Sweet pea). Moderately fast-growing, annual, tendril climber. H to 10ft (3m). Has oval, midgreen leaves with tendrils. Scented flowers are produced in shades of pink, blue, purple, or white, from summer to early autumn. Dwarf, non-climbing cultivars are available. Z9-10 H8–1. **'Bijou'** illus. p.324. **'Jayne Amanda'** (illus. p.57) bears racemes of usually 4, rarely 5 rose-pink flowers, and may be grown as a cordon or bush.
'Knee Hi' illus. p.320. **'Lady Diana'** illus. p.214. **'Red Ensign'** illus. p.210. **'Selana'** illus. p.208. **'Xenia Field'** illus. p.209.
L. rotundifolius (Persian everlasting pea). Herbaceous, tendril climber with winged stems. H to 3ft (1m). Leaves each have narrow stipules, a pair of leaflets, and a 3-branched tendril. Has small racemes of 3–8 pink to purplish flowers in summer. Z5-10 H10–1.
L. sylvestris (Everlasting pea, Perennial pea). Herbaceous, tendril climber with winged stems. H to 6ft

(2m). Leaves each have narrow stipules, a pair of leaflets, and a terminal, branched tendril. In summer and early autumn bears racemes of 4–10 rose-pink flowers marked with green and purple. Z6–9 H9–6.
L. vernus, syn. *Orobus vernus*, illus. p.270. **'Alboroseus'** is a clump-forming perennial. H and S 12in (30cm). In spring, slender stems each bear 3–5 white and deep pink flowers. Has fernlike, much-divided, soft leaves. Z5–7 H7–5.

LAURELIA
Laurel

ATHEROSPERMATACEAE/MONIMIACEAE

Genus of evergreen trees and shrubs grown for their aromatic foliage. Requires sun or semi-shade; grows in any but very dry soil. Propagate by semi-ripe cuttings in summer.
L. sempervirens, syn. *L. serrata* of gardens (Chilean laurel). Evergreen, broadly conical tree or shrub. H and S to 50ft (15m). Oval, leathery leaves are glossy, dark green and very aromatic. In summer bears inconspicuous flowers. Z9–10 H10–9.
L. serrata of gardens. See *L. sempervirens.*

LAURUS
Bay tree, Laurel

LAURACEAE

Genus of evergreen trees grown for their foliage. Foliage may be scorched by strong, cold winds. Needs a sheltered position in sun or semi-shade and fertile, well-drained soil. In tubs may be grown well as standards, which should be trimmed during summer. Propagate by semi-ripe cuttings in summer or by seed in autumn.
L. nobilis (Bay laurel, Sweet bay). Evergreen, broadly conical tree. H 40ft (12m), S 30ft (10m). Narrowly oval, leathery, glossy, dark green leaves are very aromatic and used in cooking. Has small, star-shaped, pale yellow flowers in spring, followed by globose to ovoid green then black fruits. Z8-11 H12–1.

LAVANDULA
Lavender

LAMIACEAE/LABIATAE

Genus of evergreen, mainly summer-flowering shrubs with entire or divided, often gray-green leaves, gsrown for their aromatic foliage and flowers. Makes an effective, low hedge. Needs full sun and fertile, well-drained soil. Trim hedges lightly in spring to maintain a compact habit. Propagate by semi-ripe cuttings in summer.
***L. angustifolia* 'Hidcote'** see *L.* 'Hidcote'. **'Munstead'** is an evergreen, bushy, compact shrub. H and S 2ft (60cm). Narrowly oblong, aromatic leaves are gray-green. Produces dense spikes of tiny, fragrant, tubular blue flowers from mid- to late summer. Z5–8 H8–3.
L. dentata (French lavender). Evergreen, bushy shrub. H and S 3ft (1m). Aromatic leaves are fernlike, toothed, and gray-green. Dense spikes of small, slightly fragrant, tubular, lavender-blue flowers with purple bracts are borne from mid- to late summer. Z5–9 H9–4.
***L.* 'Grappenhall'.** See *L.* x *intermedia* 'Grappenhall'.
***L.* 'Hidcote'**, syn. *L. angustifolia* 'Hidcote', illus. p.167.
L.* x *intermedia (English lavender). **'Grappenhall'**, syn. *L.* 'Grappenhall', is an evergreen, bushy shrub. H 3ft (1m), S 5ft (1.5m). Produces narrowly oblong, aromatic, gray-green leaves. Produces long-stalked spikes of tiny, slightly fragrant, tubular, blue-purple flowers in mid- and late summer. Z5–8 H8–5.
L. stoechas illus. p.167.

LAVATERA
Tree mallow

MALVACEAE

Genus of mainly summer-flowering annuals, biennials, perennials, and semi-evergreen subshrubs and shrubs. Needs sun and well-drained soil. Propagate perennials, subshrubs, and shrubs by softwood cuttings in early spring or summer, annuals and biennials by seed in spring or early autumn.
L. assurgentiflora illus. p.141.
***L.* 'Barnsley'.** Vigorous, semi-evergreen subshrub. H and S 6ft (2m). Midgreen, palmate leaves have 3–5 lobes. Throughout summer bears profuse clusters of open funnel-shaped, red-eyed white flowers, aging to soft pink, with deeply notched petals. Z7–9 H9–7.
L. cachemiriana, syn. *L. cachemirica*, illus. p.227.
L. cachemirica. See *L. cachemiriana.*
***L. olbia* 'Rosea'.** See *L.* 'Rosea'.
***L.* 'Rosea'**, syn. *L. olbia* 'Rosea', illus. p.141.
***L. trimestris* 'Mont Blanc'** illus. p.318. **'Silver Cup'** illus. p.324.

LAYIA

ASTERACEAE/COMPOSITAE

Genus of annuals useful for hot, dry places. Grow in sun and in poor to fertile, very well-drained soil. Propagate by seed sown outdoors in spring or early autumn.
L. elegans. See *L. platyglossa.*
L. platyglossa, syn. *L. elegans* (Tidy tips). Fast-growing, upright, bushy annual. H 18in (45cm), S 12in (30cm). Has lance-shaped, grayish green leaves. Daisylike flower heads, 2in (5cm) wide, with white-tipped yellow ray petals and yellow centers, are produced from early summer to early autumn. Is suitable for cutting. H12–6.

Lechenaultia. Reclassified as *Leschenaultia.*

LEDEBOURIA

HYACINTHACEAE/LILIACEAE

Genus of bulbs, some of which are evergreen, with ornamental, narrowly lance-shaped leaves. Produces very small flowers with reflexed tips. Makes good pot plants in cool greenhouses. Needs full light to allow leaf marks to develop well, and loose, open soil. Propagate by offsets in spring.
L. cooperi, syn. *Scilla adlamii, S. cooperi*. Summer-flowering bulb. H 2–4in (5–10cm), S 1–2in (2.5–5cm). Semi-erect, basal, green leaves with brownish purple stripes die away in winter. Stem carries a short spike of small, bell-shaped, greenish purple flowers. Z9–10 H10–9.
L. socialis, syn. *Scilla socialis, S. violacea*, illus. p.434.

LEDUM

ERICACEAE

Genus of evergreen shrubs grown for their aromatic foliage and small white flowers. Needs shade or semi-shade and moist, peaty, acidic soil. Benefits from deadheading. Propagate by semi-ripe cuttings in summer or by seed in autumn.
L. groenlandicum illus. p.154.

LEIOPHYLLUM

ERICACEAE

Genus of one species of evergreen shrub with an extensive, spreading root system. Prefers semi-shade and well-drained, peaty, acidic soil. Top-dress regularly with peaty soil. Propagate by seed in spring or by semi-ripe cuttings in summer.
L. buxifolium. Evergreen, dome-shaped shrub. H 10in (25cm), S 18in (45cm). Stems are covered with tiny, oval, leathery, dark green leaves. In late spring, terminal clusters of deep pink buds develop into small, star-shaped white flowers with prominent stamens. Z6–8 H8–6.

Lemaireocereus euphorbioides. See *Neobuxbaumia euphorbioides.*
Lemaireocereus marginatus. See *Pachycereus marginatus.*
Lemaireocereus thurberi. See *Stenocereus thurberi.*

LEMBOGLOSSUM

See also ORCHIDS.
L. bictoniense, syn. *Odontoglossum bictoniense* (illus. p.296). Evergreen, epiphytic orchid for a cool greenhouse. H 9in (23cm). Olive green flowers, 1½in (4cm) across, barred with dark brown and each with a sometimes pink-flushed white lip, are produced in spikes in late summer. Leaves are narrowly oval and 4–6in (10–15cm) long. Requires shade in summer. Z14–15 H12–6.
L. cervantesii, syn. *Odontoglossum cervantesii* (illus. p.296). Evergreen, epiphytic orchid for a cool greenhouse. H 3in (8cm). In winter produces sprays of papery white flowers, 1in (2.5cm) across, with cobweblike, light brown marks. Has narrowly oval leaves, 4–6in (10–15cm) long. Grow in shade in summer. Z14–15 H12–6.
L. cordatum, syn. *Odontoglossum cordatum* (illus. p.297). Evergreen, epiphytic orchid for a cool greenhouse. H 5in (12cm). Sprays of brown-marked yellow flowers, 1in (2.5cm) across, open in spring. Leaves are narrowly oval and 4–6in (10–15cm) long. Provide shade in summer and keep very dry in winter. Z14–15 H12–6.
L. rossii, syn. *Odontoglossum rossii* (illus. p.296). Evergreen, epiphytic orchid for a cool greenhouse. H 3in (8cm). In autumn-winter, white to pink flowers, 1in (2.5cm) across and speckled with beige, are borne in spikes. Narrowly oval leaves are 4–6in (10–15cm) long. Needs shade in summer. Z14–15 H12–6.

Lembotropis nigricans. See *Cytisus nigricans.*

LEONOTIS

LAMIACEAE/LABIATAE

Genus of annuals, evergreen and semi-evergreen perennials, subshrubs, and shrubs grown for their flowers and overall appearance. Needs full sun and rich, well-drained soil. Water containerized specimens freely when in full growth, much less at other times. Cut back perennials and subshrubs to within 6in (15cm) of ground in early spring. Propagate by seed in spring or by greenwood cuttings in early summer.
L. leonurus illus. p.149.

LEONTOPODIUM
Edelweiss

COMPOSITAE/ASTERACEAE

Genus of short-lived, spring-flowering, woolly perennials grown for their flower heads. Is suitable for rock gardens. Needs sun, gritty, well-drained soil, and a deep collar of grit. Shelter from prevailing, rain-bearing winds, since crowns are very intolerant of winter wet. Propagate by division in spring or by seed when fresh. Many seeds are not viable.
L. alpinum illus. p.346.
L. stracheyi. Mound-forming, spreading, woolly perennial. H and S 4in (10cm). Star-shaped, glistening white flower heads are produced among thick, oval, silver leaves in spring. Makes a good alpine house plant. Z5–7 H7–5.

Leopoldia comosa. See *Muscari comosum.*

LEPISMIUM

CACTACEAE

Genus of epiphytic and lithophytic (growing on rocks) cacti often pendulous in habit with cylindrical, ribbed, angled or flat, usually segmented stems. Small, funnel- to disc-shaped flowers are followed by spherical, often purple or red berries. Needs partial shade and rich, well-drained soil. Prefers 80% relative humidity – higher than for most cacti. Give only occasional, very light watering in winter. Propagate by seed or stem cuttings in spring or summer.
L. warmingianum, syn. *Rhipsalis warmingiana*, illus. p.461.

LEPTINELLA

ASTERACEAE/COMPOSITAE

Genus of annuals and creeping perennials that are effective as a low groundcover. Grow in full sun and moderately fertile, sharply drained soil. Propagate by seed as soon as ripe or by division in spring.
L. atrata, syn. *Cotula atrata*, illus. p.367. subsp. ***luteola*** illus. p.364.

LEPTOSPERMUM

MYRTACEAE

Genus of evergreen trees and shrubs grown for their foliage and small, often profuse flowers. Grows well in coastal areas if not too exposed. Needs full sun and fertile, well-drained soil. Propagate by semi-ripe cuttings in summer.
L. flavescens. See *L. polygalifolium.*
L. humifusum. See *L. rupestre.*
L. polygalifolium, syn. *L. flavescens*, illus. p.139.
L. rupestre, syn. *L. humifusum*, illus. p.160.
L. scoparium (Manuka, New Zealand tea-tree). **'Keatleyi'** is an evergreen, rounded shrub. H and S 10ft (3m). Narrowly lance-shaped, aromatic, gray-green leaves set off a profusion of large, star-shaped, pale pink flowers during late spring and summer. **'Nicholsii'** produces bronze-purple leaves and smaller crimson flowers. Both Z12–15 H12–10. **'Red Damask'** illus. p.131.

LESCHENAULTIA, syn. LECHENAULTIA

GOODENIACEAE

Genus of evergreen shrubs grown for their flowers. Needs full light and peaty, well-drained soil with few phosphates and nitrates. Water containerized plants moderately during growing season, sparingly at other times. Shorten overly long stems after flowering. Propagate by seed in spring or by semi-ripe cuttings in summer. Most species are not easy to grow under cover; good ventilation is essential.
L. floribunda. Evergreen, domed, wiry-stemmed shrub. H and S 12–24in (30–60cm). Has narrow, cylindrical, pointed leaves and, in spring-summer, short, tubular, pale blue flowers, each with 5 angular petals, in terminal clusters. Z12–15 H12–10.

LEUCADENDRON

PROTEACEAE

Genus of evergreen shrubs and trees grown for their flower heads from autumn to spring and for their foliage. Needs full light and sharply drained soil, mainly of sand and peat, ideally with very little nitrogen and phosphates. Water potted specimens moderately while in growth, sparingly at other times. Propagate by seed in spring.
L. argenteum illus. p.100.

LEUCANTHEMELLA

ASTERACEAE/COMPOSITAE

Genus of hairy perennials grown for their daisylike flower heads in autumn. Grow in full sun or partial shade and reliably moist soil. Propagate by division or basal cuttings in spring.
L. serotina, syn. *Chrysanthemum serotinum*, *C. uliginosum*. Erect perennial. H 5ft (1.5m), S 3ft (90cm). Lance-shaped leaves are toothed and dark green. Leafy stems carry sprays of large, green-centered white flower heads in late autumn. Z4–9 H9–1.

LEUCANTHEMOPSIS

ASTERACEAE/COMPOSITAE

Genus of dwarf, tufted, clump- or mat-forming perennials grown for their solitary, daisylike flower heads in summer. Grow in full sun and sharply drained soil. Propagate by seed as soon as ripe or by division or basal cuttings in spring.
L. alpina, syn. *Chrysanthemum alpinum*. Tuft-forming, short-lived perennial. H 4in (10cm), S 8in (20cm). Small tufts of deeply cut leaves are produced from short, rhizomatous stems. Has large white flower heads with yellow centers in summer. Is good for a rock garden or scree. Z6–9 H9–6.

LEUCANTHEMUM

ASTERACEAE/COMPOSITAE

Genus of annuals and perennials grown for their attractive flowers. Cultivars of L. x *superbum* are valued for their profusion of large daisylike summer flowers. Some species are suitable for rock gardens. Needs full sun and well-drained soil. Propagate species by seed or division, cultivars by division only.
L. x superbum, syn. *Chrysanthemum maximum* of gardens, *C.* x *superbum* (Shasta daisy). Z5–8 H8–5. **'Aglaia'** is a robust perennial. H 3ft (1m), S 2ft (60cm). Large, daisylike, semi-double white flower heads are borne singly in summer. Has spoon-shaped, coarse, lobed, toothed leaves. Divide every 2 years. **'Elizabeth'** illus. p.240. **'Esther Read'** illus. p.275 **'Wirral Supreme'** is double with short central florets.

LEUCHTENBERGIA

CACTACEAE

Genus of one species of cactus. Looks like a small *Agave* in foliage, but its flowers, seed pods, and seeds are similar to *Ferocactus*. Tubercles eventually form on short, rough, woody stems. Needs full sun and very well-drained soil. Keep completely dry in winter; water sparingly from spring to autumn. Propagate by seed in spring or summer.
L. principis illus. p.466.

LEUCOCORYNE

ALLIACEAE/LILIACEAE

Genus of spring-flowering bulbs with loose heads of flattish flowers. Needs sun and well-drained soil. Plant in autumn, water when in growth, and keep almost dry when dormant in summer. Propagate by seed or offsets in autumn.
L. ixioides illus. p.413.

LEUCOGENES

New Zealand edelweiss

ASTERACEAE/COMPOSITAE

Genus of evergreen, woody-based perennials grown mainly for their foliage. Is excellent for alpine houses in areas where summers are cool. Needs sun and gritty, well-drained, peaty soil. Resents winter wet and may be difficult to grow. Propagate by seed when fresh or by softwood cuttings in late spring or early summer.
L. grandiceps illus. p.389.
L. leontopodium, syn. *Raoulia leontopodium* (North Island edelweiss). Evergreen, rosetted perennial. H and S 5in (12cm). Has oblong to oval, overlapping, silvery white to yellowish leaves. In early summer has up to 15 small, star-shaped, woolly, silvery white flower heads surrounded by thick, felted white bracts.

LEUCOJUM

Snowflake

AMARYLLIDACEAE

Genus of bulbs grown for their pendent, bell-shaped white or pink flowers in autumn or spring. Some species prefer a moist, partially shaded site; others do best in sun and well-drained soil. Propagate by division in spring or early autumn or by seed in autumn.
L. aestivum illus. p.396.
L. autumnale illus. p.437.
L. roseum. Early autumn-flowering bulb. H to 4in (10cm), S 1–2in (2.5–5cm). Slender stems bear usually solitary, pale pink flowers, ½in (1cm) long. Threadlike, erect, basal leaves appear with or just after flowers. Prefers sun and well-drained soil. Z3–9 H9–1.
L. vernum illus. p.426.

LEUCOPHYTA

Cushion bush

ASTERACEAE/COMPOSITAE

Genus of annuals, evergreen perennials, and small shrubs, often grown annually from cuttings and used as summer bedding. Requires well-drained soil and full light. Water containerized plants moderately when in full growth, sparingly at other times. Remove stem tips of young plants to promote a bushy habit. Propagate by semi-ripe cuttings in late summer. Botrytis may be troublesome if plants are kept too cool and damp in winter.
L. brownii, syn. *Calocephalus brownii*, illus. p.175.

Leucopogon colensoi. See *Cyathodes colensoi.*

LEUCOSPERMUM

PROTEACEAE

Genus of evergreen shrubs grown for their flower heads. Requires full light and sandy, well-drained soil with few phosphates and nitrates. Water containerized specimens moderately when in growth, sparingly at other times. Propagate by seed in spring. Is not easy to cultivate long term under cover; good ventilation is essential.
L. cordifolium, syn. *L. nutans*. Evergreen, rounded to spreading, well-branched shrub. H and S 4ft (1.2m). Elongated, heart-shaped, blue-gray leaves each have a 3-toothed tip. In summer, very slender, tubular, brick red to orange flowers, each with a long style, are borne in tight heads that resemble single blooms.
L. nutans. See *L. cordifolium.*
L. reflexum illus. p.131.

LEUCOTHÖE

ERICACEAE

Genus of evergreen, semi-evergreen, or deciduous shrubs grown for their white flowers and their foliage. Needs shade or semi-shade and moist, peaty, acidic soil. Propagate by semi-ripe cuttings in summer.
L. catesbaei of gardens. See *L. fontanesiana.*
L. fontanesiana, syn. *L. catesbaei* of gardens, *L. walteri*. Evergreen, arching shrub. H 5ft (1.5m), S 10ft (3m). Lance-shaped, leathery, glossy, dark green leaves have long points and sharp teeth. Short racemes of small, urn-shaped white flowers are borne beneath shoots from mid- to late spring. Z5–8 H8–5. **'Rainbow'** illus. p.177. SCARLETTA (**'Zeblid'**) (illus. p.39) has dark red-purple young foliage that turns dark green, then bronze in winter. **'Zeblid'** see *L.f.* SCARLETTA.
L. keiskei. Evergreen shrub with erect or semi-procumbent stems. H 6–24in (15–60cm), S 12–24in (30–60cm). Oval, thin-textured, glossy, dark green leaves have a red flush when young and

a leathery appearance. Bears pendent, urn-shaped white flowers from leaf axils in summer. Is good for a rock garden or alpine house. Prefers mild, damp climates. Z6–8 H8–6..
L. walteri. See *L. fontanesiana.*

LEWISIA

PORTULACACEAE

Genus of perennials, some of which are evergreen, with rosettes of succulent leaves and deep taproots. Most species are good in alpine houses, troughs, and rock gardens. Evergreen species need semi-shaded, organic, moist or well-drained, neutral to acidic soil and resent water in their rosettes at all times. Herbaceous species shed their leaves in summer and require sun and well-drained, neutral to acidic soil; dry off after flowering. Propagate herbaceous species by seed in spring or autumn, evergreen species by seed in spring or by offsets in summer. Seed of *L.* Cotyledon Hybrids may not come true.
L. columbiana. Evergreen, basal-rosetted perennial. H 6in (15cm) or more, S 4–6in (10–15cm). Bears thick, narrowly oblong, flat, glossy green leaves and, in early summer, terminal sprays of small, cup-shaped, deeply veined white to deep pink flowers. Prefers moist soil. Z4–8 H8–3.
***L.* Cotyledon Hybrids** illus. p.354.
***L.* 'George Henley'** illus. p.352.
L. nevadensis. Loose, basal-rosetted perennial. H 1½–2½in (4–6cm), S 3in (8cm). In summer, large, almost stemless, cup-shaped white flowers appear above small clusters of strap-shaped, dark green leaves. Z3–4 H4–1.
L. rediviva [pink form] illus. p.379; [white form] illus. p.373.
L. tweedyi illus. p.364.

LEYCESTERIA

CAPRIFOLIACEAE

Genus of deciduous shrubs grown for their showy flower clusters. Suitable for a cool greenhouse. Needs full sun and fertile, well-drained soil. Propagate by softwood cuttings in summer or by seed or division in autumn.
L. formosa (Himalayan honeysuckle). Deciduous, upright shrub. H and S 6ft (2m). Has blue-green shoots and slender, oval, dark green leaves. In summer and early autumn, small, funnel-shaped white flowers are produced at tip of each pendent cluster of purplish red bracts and are followed by spherical, reddish purple fruits. Cut weak shoots to ground level in early spring. Z7–9 H9–6.

LEYMUS

POACEAE/GRAMINEAE

See also GRASSES, BAMBOOS, RUSHES, and SEDGES.
L. arenarius, syn. *Elymus arenarius* (Lyme grass). Vigorous, spreading, herbaceous, rhizomatous, perennial grass. H to 5ft (1.5m), S indefinite. Has broad, glaucous leaves. Has thick, terminal spikes of grayish green flowers on erect stems in late summer. Is useful for binding coastal dunes. Z4–10 H10–1.

LIATRIS

Gayfeather, Blazing star

ASTERACEAE/COMPOSITAE

Genus of summer-flowering perennials with thickened, cormlike rootstocks. Prefers sun and well-drained soil. Propagate by division in spring.
L. callilepis of gardens. See *L. spicata*.
L. pycnostachya (Kansas gayfeather). Clump-forming perennial. H 4ft (1.2m), S 1ft (30cm). In summer bears tall spikes of clustered, feathery, mauve-pink flower heads. Grasslike, dark green leaves form basal tufts. Z3–9 H9–2.
L. spicata, syn. *L. callilepis* of gardens, illus. p.279.

LIBERTIA

IRIDACEAE

Genus of rhizomatous perennials grown for their foliage, decorative seed pods, and flowers. Needs a sheltered, sunny or partially shaded site and well-drained soil. Propagate by division in spring or by seed in autumn or spring.
L. grandiflora illus. p.239.
L. ixioides. Clump-forming, rhizomatous perennial. H and S 24in (60cm). Produces panicles of saucer-shaped white flowers in summer. Grasslike, dark green leaves turn orange-brown during winter.

Libocedrus chilensis. See *Austrocedrus chilensis.*
Libocedrus decurrens. See *Calocedrus decurrens.*
Libonia floribunda. See *Justicia rizzinii.*

LIGULARIA

ASTERACEAE/COMPOSITAE

Genus of perennials grown for their foliage and large, daisylike flower heads. Grow in sun or semi-shade and in moist but well-drained soil. Propagate by division in spring or by seed in autumn or spring. Is prone to damage by slugs and snails.
***L. clivorum* 'Desdemona'**. See *L. dentata* 'Desdemona'.
***L. dentata* 'Desdemona'**, syn. *L. clivorum* 'Desdemona'. Compact, clump-forming perennial. H 4ft (1.2m), S 2ft (60cm). Has heart-shaped, long-stalked, leathery, basal, dark brownish green leaves, almost mahogany beneath, and bears terminal clusters of large, daisylike, vivid orange flower heads on branching stems from mid- to late summer. Z4–8 H8–1.
***L.* 'Gregynog Gold'.** Clump-forming perennial. H 6ft (2m), S 2ft (60cm). Leaves are large, heart-shaped, and deep green. Conical panicles of daisylike, orange-yellow flower heads are borne from mid- to late summer. Z6–9 H9–6.
L. przewalskii, syn. *Senecio przewalskii*, illus. p.229.
L. stenocephala illus. p.229.
L. tussilaginea. See *Farfugium japonicum.*

LIGUSTRUM

Privet

OLEACEAE

Genus of deciduous, semi-evergreen or evergreen shrubs and trees grown for their foliage and, in some species, flowers. Requires sun or semi-shade, the variegated forms doing best in full sun. Thrives on any well-drained soil, including alkaline soil. All except *L. lucidum* occasionally need cutting back in midspring to restrict growth. Propagate by semi-ripe cuttings in summer. All parts may cause severe discomfort if ingested.
L. japonicum (Japanese privet). Evergreen, bushy, dense shrub. H 10ft (3m), S 8ft (2.5m). Has oval, glossy, very dark green leaves and, from mid-summer to early autumn, large, conical panicles of small, tubular white flowers with 4 lobes. Z7–10 H10–7.
'Coriaceum' see *L.j.* 'Rotundifolium'
'Rotundifolium', syn. *L.j.* 'Coriaceum', is slow-growing, with a dense mass of rounded, leathery leaves.
L. lucidum (Chinese privet). Evergreen, upright shrub or tree. H 30ft (10m), S 25ft (8m). Bears large, oval, glossy, dark green leaves. Produces large panicles of small, tubular white flowers with 4 lobes in late summer and early autumn. Z8–10 H10–8.
'Excelsum Superbum' illus. p.127.
L. ovalifolium illus. p.126.
'Aureum' is a vigorous, evergreen or semi-evergreen, upright, dense shrub. H 12ft (4m), S 10ft (3m). Leaves are oval, glossy, and midgreen, broadly edged with bright yellow. Dense panicles of small, rather musty/sweet-scented, tubular white flowers with 4 lobes appear in midsummer and are succeeded by spherical black fruits. Cut back hedges to 1ft (30cm) after planting and prune hard for first 2 years, then trim as necessary during the growing season. Z6–10 H10–9.
L. sinense illus. p.118.
***L.* 'Vicaryi'**, syn. *L.* x *vicaryi*, illus. p.153.
***L.* x *vicaryi*.** See *L.* 'Vicaryi'.
L. vulgare. Deciduous or semi-evergreen, bushy shrub. H and S 10ft (3m). Leaves are narrowly lance-shaped and dark green. Produces panicles of small, strongly scented, tubular white flowers with 4 lobes from early to midsummer, then spherical black fruits. Cut back hedges to 1ft (30cm) after planting and prune hard for first 2 years, then trim as necessary during the growing season. Z5–8 H8–5.
'Lodense', a more compact form. H and S 4ft (1.2m). Z4–11 H12–1.

LILIUM

Lily

LILIACEAE

Genus of mainly summer-flowering bulbs grown for their colorful, often fragrant flowers. Each fleshy-scaled bulb produces one unbranched, leafy stem, in some cases with annual roots in lower part. Mostly lance-shaped or linear leaves, to 9in (22cm) long, are scattered or in whorls, sometimes with bulbils in axils. Flowers, usually several per stem, are mainly trumpet- to bowl-shaped or with the 6 petals strongly reflexed to form a turkscap shape. (Petals of *Lilium* are known botanically as perianth segments.) Each plant has a spread of up to 12in (30cm). Needs sun and any well-drained soil, unless otherwise stated. Propagate by seed in autumn or spring, by bulb scales in summer, or by stem bulbils (where present) in autumn. Virus and fungal diseases (such as botrytis) may cause problems. See also feature panel pp.404–405.

Lilies do well in Z3–8 H8–1 except where otherwise noted.

L. amabile. Summer-flowering bulb with stem roots. H 1–3ft (30cm–1m). Scattered leaves are lance-shaped. Has up to 10 unpleasant-smelling, nodding, turkscap, black-spotted red flowers; each petal is 2–2¼in (5–5.5cm) long.
***L.* 'Amber Gold'** (illus. p.405). Summer-flowering bulb. H 4–5ft (1.2–1.5m). Has nodding, turkscap, deep yellow flowers, each with maroon spots in throat.
***L.* 'Angela North'** (illus. p.404). Mid-summer flowering bulb. H to 3ft (1m). Has slightly fragrant, dark red flowers, spotted darker red, that have strongly recurved petals.
***L.* 'Apollo'** (illus. p.405). Summer-flowering bulb. H 4ft (1.2m). Has downward-facing, turkscap, pale orange flowers with strongly reflexed petals.
L. auratum (Japanese gold-band lily). Summer- and autumn-flowering bulb with stem roots. H 2–5ft (60cm–1.5m). Has long, scattered, lance-shaped leaves. Produces up to 10 fragrant, outward-facing, widely bowl-shaped white flowers; each petal is 5–7in (12–18cm) long with a central yellow or red band and often red or yellow spots. Requires semi-shade and neutral to acidic soil. var. ***platyphyllum*** (illus. p.404) has broader leaves; petals have a central yellow band and fewer spots.
***L.* 'Black Beauty'** (illus. p.405). Summer-flowering bulb. H 5–6ft (1.5–2m). Has outward-facing, flattish, green-centered, very deep red flowers with recurved, white-margined petals.
***L.* 'Black Dragon'.** Summer-flowering bulb. H 5ft (1.5m). Has outward-facing, trumpet-shaped flowers with dark purplish red outsides and white insides.
***L.* 'Black Magic'** (illus. p.404). Summer-flowering bulb. H 4–6ft (1.2–2m). Scented, outward-facing,

trumpet-shaped flowers are purplish brown outside and white inside.
***L.* 'Bonfire'.** Late summer-flowering bulb. H 4–5ft (1.2–1.5m). Produces outward-facing, bowl-shaped flowers with broad petals, white outside flushed with pink and dark crimson inside spotted paler crimson.
***L.* 'Bright Star'** (illus. p.404). Summer-flowering bulb. H 3–5ft (1–1.5m). Has flattish white flowers; petals have recurved tips and a central orange streak inside.
***L.* 'Bronwen North'** (illus. p.404). Midsummer-flowering bulb. H to 3ft (1m). In midsummer, each stem carries 7 or more slightly fragrant flowers with strongly recurving, pale mauve-pink petals, paler at the tips, and pale pink throats with dark spots and lines; nectaries are reddish black.
***L.* 'Brushmarks'** (illus. p.405). Early summer-flowering bulb. H 4½ft (1.35m). Upward-facing, cup-shaped orange flowers are green-throated. Petals each have deep red blotches and sometimes spots.
L. bulbiferum (Fire lily, Orange lily). Summer-flowering bulb with stem roots. H 16in–5ft (40cm–1.5m). Stem bears scattered, lance-shaped leaves and, usually, bulbils in leaf axils. Bears 1–5 or more upward-facing, shallowly cup-shaped, orange-red flowers. Each petal is 2½–3¼in (6–8.5cm) long and spotted black or deep red. var. ***croceum*** (illus. p.405) has orange flowers and does not normally bear bulbils.
L. canadense (Canada lily, Meadow lily, Wild yellow lily; illus. p.405). Summer-flowering bulb with stem roots. H to 5ft (1.5m). Narrowly to broadly lance-shaped leaves are mainly in whorls. Bears about 10 nodding, bell-shaped yellow or red flowers; each petal is 2–3in (5–8cm) long with dark red or purple spots in lower part. Z2–6 H6–1.
L. candidum (Madonna lily; illus. p.404). Summer-flowering bulb. H 3–6ft (1–2m). Flower stem bears scattered, lance-shaped leaves and 5–20 fragrant, outward-facing, broadly funnel-shaped white flowers. Each petal is 2–3in (5–8cm) long with a yellow base and a slightly recurved tip. In autumn bears basal leaves that remain throughout winter but die off as flowering stems mature. Prefers lime-rich soil. Z6–9 H9–6.
***L. carniolicum*.** See *L. pyrenaicum* subsp. *carniolicum*.
***L.* 'Casa Blanca'** (illus. p.404). Late summer-flowering bulb. H 3ft (90cm). Waxy white flowers have yellowish white midribs and violet-red nectaries.
***L. cernuum*.** Summer-flowering bulb with stem roots. H to 2ft (60cm). Long, linear leaves are scattered. Produces 7–15 fragrant, nodding, turkscap flowers, usually pinkish purple with purple spots. Each petal is 1½–2in (3.5–5cm) long.
L. chalcedonicum, syn. *L. heldreichii* (Scarlet turkscap lily; illus. p.405). Summer-flowering bulb with stem roots. H 20in–5ft (50cm–1.5m). Leaves are scattered and mostly lance-shaped, lower ones spreading, upper ones smaller and closer to stem. Bears up to 12 slightly scented, nodding, turkscap flowers with red or reddish orange petals, each 2–3in (5–7cm) long. Z7–9 H9–7.
***L.* 'Connecticut King'** (illus. p.405). Early to midsummer-flowering bulb. H 3ft (1m). Flowers are upward-facing, cup-shaped, and bright yellow.
***L.* 'Corsage'** (illus. p.404). Summer-flowering bulb. H 4ft (1.2m). Bears outward-facing, bowl-shaped flowers with recurved petals, pink-flushed outside and pink inside with white centers and maroon spots.
***L.* 'Côte d'Azur'** (illus. p.404). Summer-flowering bulb. H 16in (40cm). Strong stems bear deep rose-pink flowers with darker-spotted throats.
L. x dalhansonii (illus. p.404). Variable, summer-flowering bulb. H 5–6ft (1.5–2m). Has unpleasant-smelling, turkscap flowers that are chestnut brown or dark maroon with gold spots. **'Marhan'** see *L.* 'Marhan'.
L. davidii*.** Summer-flowering bulb with stem roots. H 3–4½ft (1–1.4m). Linear leaves are scattered. Produces 5–20 nodding, turkscap red or reddish orange flowers; each petal is 2–3in (5–8cm) long with dark purple spots. var. ***willmottiae (illus. p.405) differs in its slender, arching stems to 6ft (2m) and pendent flower stalks.
***L.* 'Destiny'** (illus. p.405). Early summer-flowering bulb. H 3–4ft (1–1.2m). Flowers are upward-facing, cup-shaped, and yellow with brown spots.
L. duchartrei (illus. p.404). Summer-flowering bulb. H 2–3ft (60cm–1m). Lance-shaped leaves are scattered up stems. Has up to 12 fragrant, nodding, turkscap white flowers that are flushed purple outside and spotted deep purple inside. Z7–8 H8–7.
***L.* 'Enchantment'** (illus. p.405). Early summer-flowering bulb. H 3ft (1m). Produces upward-facing, cup-shaped, orange-red flowers with black-spotted throats. Z2–8 H8–1.
***L.* Golden Clarion Group** (illus. p.405). Late spring to early summer-flowering bulb. H 3–6ft (1–2m). Has outward-facing, trumpet-shaped, pale to deep yellow flowers that may be flushed with reddish purple outside. Z5–7 H7–5.
***L.* Golden Splendor Group** (illus. p.405). Vigorous, mid to late summer-flowering bulb with stem roots. H 5–6ft (1.5–2m). Large, funnel-shaped flowers are deep golden yellow with maroon stripes on the back of each petal.
L. hansonii (illus. p.405). Summer-flowering bulb with stem roots. H 3–5ft (1–1.5m). Long leaves in whorls are lance-shaped to oval. Has 3–12 scented, nodding, turkscap, orange-yellow flowers. Each thick petal is 1¼–1½in (3–4cm) long with brown-purple spots toward the base. Z2–7 H7–1.
***L.* 'Harmony'** (illus. p.405). Summer-flowering bulb. H 1½–3ft (50cm–1m). Orange flowers are upward-facing, cup-shaped, and spotted with maroon.
***L. heldreichii*.** See *L. chalcedonicum*.
***L. henryi*.** Late summer-flowering bulb with stem roots. H 3–10ft (1–3m). Has scattered, lance-shaped leaves. Produces 5–20, sometimes up to 70, nodding, turkscap orange flowers; petals are 2½–3in (6–8cm) long with dark spots and prominent warts toward bases. Prefers lime-rich soil.
***L.* Imperial Crimson Group.** Late summer-flowering bulb. H 5ft (1.5m). Fragrant, flattish, deep crimson flowers have white throats and white-edged petals. Z5–8 H8–5.
***L.* Imperial Gold Group** (illus. p.404). Summer-flowering bulb. H 6ft (2m). Bears fragrant, flattish white flowers spotted maroon and with a yellow stripe up each petal center. Z5–8 H8–5.
***L.* 'Journey's End'** (illus. p.404). Late summer-flowering bulb. H 6ft (2m). Outward-facing, bowl-shaped, maroon-spotted, deep pink flowers have recurved petals, white at tips and edges.
***L.* 'Karen North'** (illus. p.405). Summer-flowering bulb. H to 1.4m (4½ft). Turkscap flowers are downward-facing, with orange-pink petals sparsely spotted with deep pink. Z4–8 H8–1.
***L.* 'Lady Bowes Lyon'** (illus. p.405). Summer-flowering bulb. H 3–4ft (1–1.2m). Downward-facing, black-spotted, rich red flowers have reflexed petals.
L. lancifolium, syn. *L. tigrinum* (Tiger lily). Summer- to early autumn-flowering bulb with stem roots. H 2–5ft (60cm–1.5m). Produces long, scattered, narrowly lance-shaped leaves. Produces 5–10, sometimes up to 40, nodding, turkscap, pink- to red-orange flowers; each petal is 3–4in (7–10cm) long and spotted with dark purple. Z2–7 H7–1. var. ***flaviflorum*** has yellow flowers. Vigorous var. ***splendens*** (illus. p.405) bears larger, brighter red-orange flowers.
***L. lankongense*.** Summer-flowering bulb with stem roots. H to 4ft (1.2m). Leaves are scattered and lance-shaped. Has up to 15 scented, nodding, turkscap pink flowers. Petals, each 1½–2½in (4–6.5cm) long with a central green stripe and red-purple spots mainly on edges, are often mauve-flushed. Needs partial shade in warmer areas.
***L. leichtlinii*.** Summer-flowering bulb with stem roots. H to 4ft (1.2m). Scattered leaves are linear to narrowly lance-shaped. Produces 1–6 nodding, turkscap yellow flowers; each petal is 2½–3¼in (6–8.5cm) long with dark reddish purple spots. Needs semi-shade.
***L.* 'Limelight'.** Summer-flowering bulb. H 3–5ft (1–1.5m). Flowers are outward-facing or slightly nodding, trumpet-shaped, and yellow-green.
L. longiflorum (Easter lily; illus. p.404). Summer-flowering bulb with stem roots. H 1–3ft (30cm–1m). Leaves are scattered and lance-shaped. Produces 1–6 fragrant, outward-facing, funnel-shaped white flowers. Each petal is 5–8in (13–20cm) long with slightly recurved tips. Z7–9 H9–1.
L. mackliniae (Manipur lily; illus. p.404). Late spring- to summer-flowering bulb with stem roots. H to 16in (40cm). Small, narrowly lance-shaped to narrowly oval leaves are scattered or whorled near top of stem. Has 1–6 usually nodding, broadly bell-shaped, purplish pink flowers; each petal is 1¾–2in (4.5–5cm) long. Needs semi-shade. Z7–8 H8–7.
L. maculatum, syn. *L. thunbergianum*. Summer-flowering bulb with stem roots. H to 2ft (60cm). Scattered leaves are lance-shaped or oval. Has 1–6 upward-facing, cup-shaped yellow, orange, or red flowers with darker spots; each petal is 3–4in (8–10cm) long.
***L.* 'Magic Pink'** (illus. p.404). Early summer-flowering bulb. H 3–4ft (1–1.2m). Flowers are satin pink with darker pink spots.
***L.* 'Marhan'**, syn. *L.* x *dalhansonii* 'Marhan'. Early summer-flowering bulb. H 4–6ft (1.2–2m). Nodding, turkscap, deep orange flowers are spotted red-brown.
L. martagon (Martagon lily; illus. p.404). Summer-flowering bulb with stem roots. H 3–6ft (1–2m). Has lance-shaped to oval leaves in whorls and up to 50 scented, nodding, turkscap flowers. Petals are 1¼–1¾in (3–4.5cm) long and pink or purple, often with darker spots. var. ***album*** (illus. p.404) has pure white flowers.
L. medeoloides (illus. p.405). Summer-flowering bulb. H to 2½ft (75cm). produces lance-shaped leaves and up to 10 turkscap apricot to orange-red flowers, usually with darker spots. Z3–7 H7–1.
L. monadelphum, syn. *L. szovitsianum* (illus. p.405). Summer-flowering bulb with stem roots. H 1½–6ft (50cm–2m). Has scattered, lance-shaped to oval leaves. Produces usually 1–5, sometimes up to 30, scented, nodding, turkscap yellow flowers, usually with deep red or purple spots inside. Each petal is 2½–4in (6–10cm) long. Z5–8 H8–5.
***L.* 'Mont Blanc'** (illus. p.404). Summer-flowering bulb. H 3ft (90cm). Has upward-facing, creamy white flowers spotted with brown.
***L.* 'Montreux'** (illus. p.404). Midsummer-flowering bulb. H 3ft (1m). Bears about 8 pink flowers with darker pink midribs; orange-pink throats are spotted with brown.
L. nanum, syn. *Nomocharis nana*. Late spring- or summer-flowering bulb. H 2½–18in (6–45cm). Scattered leaves are linear. Bears a usually nodding, broadly bell-shaped, purplish pink flower with 1¾–2in (4.5–5cm) long petals. Needs partial shade. var. ***flavidum*** has pale yellow flowers.
L. nepalense (illus. p.405). Summer-flowering bulb with stem roots. H 28–36in (70cm–1m). Has scattered, lance-shaped leaves. Produces often unpleasant-smelling, nodding, funnel-shaped, greenish white or greenish yellow flowers, each with a dark reddish purple base inside and petals to 6in (15cm) long. Z7–8 H8–7.

***L.* Olympic Hybrids** (illus. p.404). Summer-flowering bulb. H 4–6ft (1.2–2m). Scented, outward-facing, trumpet-shaped flowers are usually pink or purple outside with yellow throats; white, cream, yellow, or pink variants also occur.
L. pardalinum (Leopard lily, Panther lily; illus. p.405). Summer-flowering bulb. H 6–10ft (2–3m). Long, narrowly elliptic leaves are mainly in whorls. Has up to 10 often scented, nodding, turkscap flowers. Each petal is 2–3½in (5–9cm) long with red upper parts. Orange lower parts have maroon spots, some of which are encircled with yellow. Z5–8 H8–5.
L. ponticum. See *L. pyrenaicum* subsp. *ponticum*.
L. pumilum, syn. *L. tenuifolium*. Summer-flowering bulb with stem roots. H 6–36in (15cm–1m). Small, scattered leaves are linear. Produces usually up to 7 but occasionally up to 30 slightly scented, nodding, turkscap flowers; each petal is 1¼–1½in (3–3.5cm) long and scarlet with or without black basal spots.
L. pyrenaicum (Yellow turkscap lily; illus. p.405). Late spring to early summer-flowering bulb often with stem roots. H 1–4½ft (30cm–1.35m). Has scattered, linear to narrowly elliptic, hairless leaves. Produces up to 12 unpleasant-smelling, nodding, turkscap flowers. Each petal is 1½–2½in (4–6.5cm) long and yellow or green-yellow with deep purple spots and lines. Z4–7 H7–1. subsp. ***carniolicum*** (syn. *L. carniolicum*) has red- or orange-spotted flowers. Leaves may be hairless or downy. subsp. ***ponticum*** (syn. *L. ponticum*) bears deep yellow flowers, densely lined and spotted with red-brown or purple; leaves are downy beneath. var. ***rubrum*** (illus. p.405) has orange-red or dark red flowers.
L. regale (Regal lily; illus. p.404). Summer-flowering bulb with stem roots. H 20in–6ft (50cm–2m). Linear leaves are scattered. Produces up to 25 fragrant, outward-facing, funnel-shaped flowers. Petals are each 5–6in (12–15cm) long, white inside with a yellow base and pinkish purple outside.
***L.* 'Roma'** (illus. p.405). Early summer-flowering bulb. H 5ft (1.5m). Green buds open to cream flowers that sometimes age to pale greenish yellow.
***L.* 'Rosemary North'** (illus. p.405). Mid- to late summer-flowering bulb. H to 3ft (1m). Produces 12 or more slightly fragrant, rich orange flowers that sometimes have darker spots.
L. rubellum (illus. p.404). Early summer-flowering bulb with stem roots. H 12–32in (30–80cm). Has scattered, narrowly oval leaves and up to 9 scented, outward-facing, broadly funnel-shaped pink flowers with dark red spots at bases; each petal is 2½–3in (6–8cm) long. Z3–7 H7–1.
***L.* 'Shuksan'.** Summer-flowering bulb. H 4–6ft (1.2–2m). Nodding, turkscap, yellowish orange flowers are flushed red at petal tips and sparsely spotted with black.
L. speciosum. Late summer-flowering bulb with stem roots. H 3–5½ft (1–1.7m). Has long, scattered, broadly lance-shaped leaves. Produces up to 12 scented, nodding, turkscap white or pink flowers; each petal is up to 4in (10cm) long, with pink or crimson spots. Requires neutral to acidic soil. var. ***album*** has white flowers and purple stems. Flowers of var. ***rubrum*** (illus. p.404) are carmine, stems are purple.
***L.* 'Star Gazer'** (illus. p.404). Late summer-flowering bulb. H 3ft (90cm). Fragrant, rich crimson flowers are spotted maroon.
***L.* 'Sterling Star'** (illus. p.404). Summer-flowering bulb. H 3–4ft (1–1.2m). Has upward-facing, cup-shaped white flowers with tiny brown spots.
L. superbum (Swamp lily, Turkscap lily; illus. p.405). Late summer- to early autumn-flowering bulb with stem roots. H 5–10ft (1.5–3m). Lance-shaped to elliptic leaves are mainly in whorls. Bears up to 40 nodding, turkscap, orange flowers. Each petal is 2½–4in (6–10cm) long, with a green base inside and usually flushed red and spotted maroon. Requires neutral to acidic soil. Z4–8 H8–1.
L. szovitsianum. See *L. monadelphum*.
L. tenuifolium. See *L. pumilum*.
L.* x *testaceum (Nankeen lily). Summer-flowering bulb. H 3–5ft (1–1.5m). Has scattered, linear, often twisted leaves. Produces 6–12 fragrant, nodding, turkscap, light orange to brownish yellow flowers; each petal is 3in (8cm) long, usually with reddish spots inside.
L. thunbergianum. See *L. maculatum*.
L. tigrinum. See *L. lancifolium*.
L. tsingtauense (illus. p.405). Summer-flowering bulb with stem roots. H 3ft (1m). Lance-shaped leaves are mainly in whorls. Produces 1–5 upward-facing, cup-shaped orange to orange-red flowers; petals are up to 2in (5cm) long and spotted with maroon.
L. wallichianum. Late summer- to autumn-flowering bulb with stem roots. H to 6ft (2m). Long, scattered leaves are linear or lance-shaped. Bears 1–4 fragrant, outward-facing, funnel-shaped white or cream flowers that are green or yellow towards bases. Each petal is 6–12in (15–30cm) long.

Limnanthemum nymphoides. See *Nymphoides peltata*.

LIMNANTHES

LIMNANTHACEAE

Genus of annuals useful for rock gardens and for edging. Prefers a sunny situation and fertile, well-drained soil. Propagate by seed sown outdoors in spring or early autumn. Self seeds freely.
L. douglasii illus. p.336.

LIMONIUM

Sea lavender

PLUMBAGINACEAE

Genus of summer- and autumn-flowering perennials, sometimes grown as annuals, and subshrubs, some of which are evergreen. Grows in full sun and in well-drained soil. Propagate by division in spring, by seed in autumn or early spring, or by root cuttings in winter.
L. bellidifolium, syn. *L. reticulatum*. Evergreen, dome-shaped perennial with a woody base. H 6–8in (15–20cm), S 4in (10cm). Has basal rosettes of rounded, dark green leaves. Much-branched flower stems produce masses of small, "everlasting," trumpet-shaped blue flowers in summer-autumn. Is excellent for a rock garden. Z7–9 H9–7.
***L. latifolium* 'Blue Cloud'** illus. p.286.
L. perezii. Evergreen, rounded subshrub. H and S 3ft (1m) or more. Has long-stalked, oval to diamond-shaped, deep green leaves. Dense clusters, 8in (20cm) wide, of tiny, tubular, deep mauve-blue flowers are carried well above the leaves in autumn. Needs good ventilation if grown under cover. Z10–11 H12–1.
L. reticulatum. See *L. bellidifolium*.
L. sinuatum illus. p.322. **Fortress Series** is a slow-growing, upright, bushy perennial grown as an annual. H 18in (45cm), S 12in (30cm). Has lance-shaped, lobed and often wavy-margined, deep green leaves and, in summer and early autumn, clusters of small, tubular flowers in a mixture of shades such as pink, yellow, or blue. H9–3.
L. suworowii. See *Psylliostachys suworowii*.

LINARIA

Toadflax

SCROPHULARIACEAE

Genus of spring-, summer-, or autumn-flowering annuals, biennials, and perennials useful for rock gardens and borders. Prefers sun or light shade; thrives in any well-drained soil. Propagate by seed in autumn or spring. Self seeds freely.
L. alpina (Alpine toadflax). Tuft-forming, compact, annual, biennial or short-lived perennial with a sparse root system. H 6in (15cm), S 4–6in (10–15cm). Has whorls of linear to lance-shaped, fleshy, gray-green leaves. A succession of snapdragon-like, yellow-centered, purple-violet flowers is borne in loose racemes in summer. Z4–9 H9–1.
L. dalmatica. See *L. genistifolia* var. *dalmatica*.
L. genistifolia. Upright perennial. H 2–4ft (60cm–1.2m), S 9in (23cm). From midsummer to autumn produces racemes of small, snapdragon-like, orange-marked yellow flowers. Lance-shaped, glossy, midgreen leaves clasp the stems. Z5–8 H8–5. var. ***dalmatica*** (syn. *L. dalmatica*; Dalmatian toadflax), H 3–4ft (1–1.2m), S 2ft (60cm), bears much larger, golden yellow flowers from mid- to late summer and has broader, more glaucous leaves.
***L. maroccana* 'Fairy Lights'** illus. p.330.
L. purpurea (Purple toadflax). Upright perennial. H 2–3ft (60cm–1m), S 2ft (60cm). From mid- to late summer, racemes of snapdragon-like, purplish blue flowers touched with white at throats are produced above narrowly oval, gray-green leaves. Z5–8 H8–5. **'Canon J. Went'** illus. p.243.
L. triornithophora illus. p.251.

LINDERA

LAURACEAE

Genus of deciduous or evergreen shrubs and trees grown for their foliage, which is often aromatic, and their autumn color. Fruits are produced on female plants if male plants are also grown. Needs semi-shade and moist, acidic soil. Propagate by softwood cuttings in summer or by seed in autumn.
L. benzoin illus. p.131.
L. obtusiloba. Deciduous, bushy shrub. H and S 20ft (6m). Bears 3-lobed, aromatic, glossy, dark green leaves becoming butter yellow in autumn. Clusters of small, star-shaped, deep yellow flowers, borne on bare shoots from early to midspring, are followed by small, spherical black fruits. Z6–9 H9–6.

LINDHEIMERA

ASTERACEAE/COMPOSITAE

Genus of late summer- and early autumn-flowering annuals. Grow in sun and in fertile, well-drained soil. Propagate by seed sown under cover in early spring or outdoors in late spring.
L. texana illus. p.336.

LINNAEA

Twin flower

CAPRIFOLIACEAE

Genus of one species of evergreen, creeping, summer-flowering, subshrubby perennial that makes an extensive, twiggy mat. Is useful as groundcover in rock gardens. Requires partial shade and moist, peaty, acidic soil. Propagate by rooted runners in spring, by softwood cuttings in summer or by seed in autumn.
L. borealis illus. p.375.

LINUM

LINACEAE

Genus of annuals, biennials, perennials, subshrubs, and shrubs, some of which are evergreen or semi-evergreen, grown for their flowers. Is suitable for rock gardens. Prefers sun and organic, well-drained, peaty soil. Propagate subshrubs and shrubs by semi-ripe cuttings in summer or by seed in autumn, and annuals, biennials, and perennials by seed in autumn.
L. arboreum illus. p.358.
L. flavum (Golden flax, Yellow flax). Bushy perennial with a woody rootstock. H 12in (30cm), S 6in (15cm). Has narrowly oval, green leaves and, in summer, upward-facing,

funnel-shaped yellow flowers in terminal clusters. Z5–7 H7–5. **'Compactum'** illus. p.385.
***L.* 'Gemmell's Hybrid'.** Semi-evergreen, domed perennial with a woody rootstock. H 6in (15cm), S 8in (20cm). Leaves are oval and gray-green. In summer, short-stalked, broadly funnel-shaped, bright chrome yellow flowers are produced in terminal clusters. Prefers alkaline soil. Z6–9 H9–5.
***L. grandiflorum* 'Rubrum'** illus. p.327.
L. narbonense illus. p.287.
L. perenne illus. p.356.
L. salsoloides. See *L. suffruticosum* subsp. *salsoloides*.
L. suffruticosum subsp. ***salsoloides***, syn. *L. salsoloides*. Perennial with spreading, sometimes woody-based stems. H 2–8in (5–20cm), S 3in (8cm). Slender stems produce fine, heathlike, gray-green leaves and, in summer, a succession of short-lived, saucer-shaped, pearl white flowers, flushed blue or pink, in terminal clusters.

Lippia citriodora. See *Aloysia triphylla*.

LIQUIDAMBAR

HAMAMELIDACEAE

Genus of deciduous trees, with inconspicuous flowers, grown for their maplelike foliage and autumn color. Requires sun or semi-shade and fertile, moist but well-drained soil; grows poorly on shallow, alkaline soil. Propagate by softwood cuttings in summer or by seed in autumn.
L. formosana, syn. *L. monticola*. Deciduous, broadly conical tree. H 40ft (12m), S 30ft (10m). Has large, 3-lobed, toothed leaves, purple when young, dark green in summer, and turning orange, red and purple in autumn. Z7–9 H9–7.
L. monticola. See *L. formosana*.
L. orientalis (Oriental sweet gum). Slow-growing, deciduous, bushy tree. H 20ft (6m), S 12ft (4m). Small, 5-lobed, midgreen leaves turn orange in autumn. Z7–9 H9–7.
L. styraciflua (Sweet gum) illus. p.70. **'Lane Roberts'** is a deciduous, broadly conical to spreading tree. H 80ft 25m), S 40ft (12m). Shoots usually have corky ridges. Glossy green leaves, each with 5 lobes, turn deep reddish purple in autumn. Z6–9 H9–6..

LIRIODENDRON

MAGNOLIACEAE

Genus of deciduous trees grown for their foliage and flowers in summer. Flowers are not produced on young trees. Requires sun or semi-shade and deep, fertile, well-drained, preferably slightly acidic soil. Propagate species by seed in autumn and selected forms by budding in late summer.
L. chinense (Chinese tulip tree). Fast-growing, deciduous, spreading tree. H 80ft (25m), S 40ft (12m). Bears large, deep green leaves, cut off at the tips and with a deep lobe on each side; leaves become yellow in autumn. Cup-shaped, orange-based, greenish white flowers appear in midsummer. Z4–9 H9–2.
L. tulipifera illus. p.65. **'Aureomarginatum'** illus. p.69.

LIRIOPE

Lilyturf

CONVALLARIACEAE/LILIACEAE

Genus of evergreen perennials with swollen, fleshy rhizomes. Some are grown as a groundcover. Requires sun and well-drained soil. Propagate by division in spring or by seed in autumn.
L. graminifolia var. ***densiflora***. See *L. muscari*.
L. muscari, syn. *L. graminifolia* var. *densiflora*, *L. platyphylla* (illus. p.294). **'Majestic'** is an evergreen, spreading, rhizomatous perennial. H 12in (30cm), S 18in (45cm). In late autumn produces spikes of thickly clustered, rounded-bell-shaped violet flowers among linear, glossy, bright green leaves. Z6–10 H12–1.
L. platyphylla. See *L. muscari*.
L. spicata. Evergreen, spreading, rhizomatous perennial. H 12in (30cm), S 12–16in (30–40cm). Grasslike, glossy, dark green leaves make a good groundcover. Produces spikes of rounded-bell-shaped, pale lavender flowers in late summer. Z6–11 H12–1.

Lisianthus russellianus. See *Eustoma grandiflorum*.

LITHOCARPUS

FAGACEAE

Genus of evergreen trees grown for their foliage. Needs sun or semi-shade. Prefers well-drained, neutral to acidic soil. Shelter from strong winds. Propagate by seed, when ripe, in autumn.
L. densiflorus (Tanbark oak). Evergreen, spreading tree. H and S 30ft (10m). Has chestnutlike, leathery, glossy, dark green leaves and upright, pale yellow flower spikes borne in spring and often again in autumn. Z8–10 H10–8.
L. henryi illus. p.100.

LITHODORA

BORAGINACEAE

Genus of evergreen subshrubs and shrubs grown for their flowers. Is excellent in rock gardens. Needs full sun and moist, well-drained soil; some species are limestone haters and need acidic conditions. Resents root disturbance. Propagate by semi ripe cuttings in midsummer or by seed in autumn.
L. diffusa, syn. *Lithospermum diffusum*. **'Grace Ward'** is an evergreen, compact, semi-prostrate shrub. H 6–12in (15–30cm), S to 12in (30cm). Trailing stems bear lance-shaped, hairy, dull green leaves. In early summer bears masses of funnel-shaped, deep blue flowers in terminal clusters. Needs acidic soil. Plants should be trimmed back after flowering. Z6–8 H8–6. **'Heavenly Blue'** illus. p.357.
L. oleifolia, syn. *Lithospermum oleifolium*, illus. p.356.
L. zahnii, syn. *Lithospermum zahnii*. Evergreen, much-branched, upright shrub. H and S 12in (30cm) or more. Stems are covered in oval, hairy, dark green or grayish green leaves. Funnel-shaped, azure blue flowers with spreading lobes open in succession from early spring to midsummer. Sets buds and flowers intermittently until mid-autumn. Prefers alkaline soil.

LITHOPHRAGMA

SAXIFRAGACEAE

Genus of tuberous perennials grown for their campion-like flowers. Is dormant in summer. Tolerates all but deepest shade and prefers organic, moist soil. Propagate by seed or division in spring or autumn.
L. parviflorum illus. p.346.

LITHOPS

Living stones, Stone plant

AIZOACEAE

Genus of prostrate, egg-shaped succulents with almost united pairs of swollen, erect leaves that are separated on upper surface by a fissure from which a daisylike flower emerges. Each pair of old leaves splits and dries away to papery skin in spring to reveal a pair of new leaves growing at right angles to old ones. Slowly forms clumps. Needs full sun and extremely well-drained soil or gritty soil mix. Water regularly in growing season (midsummer to early autumn), not at all in winter. Propagate by seed in spring or summer.
L. aucampiae. Egg-shaped succulent. H ½in (1cm), S 1¼in (3cm). Pairs of brown leaves have flat, upper surfaces bearing darker marks. Produces a yellow flower in late summer or early autumn. Z12–15 H12–10.
L. bella, syn. *L. karasmontana* subsp. *bella*. Egg-shaped succulent. H ¾–1¼in (2–3cm), S ⅝in (1.5cm). Has pairs of brown to brown-yellow leaves with darker marks on convex, upper surfaces. Produces a white flower in late summer or early autumn. Z12–15 H12–10.
L. bromfieldii var. ***insularis.*** See *L. insularis*.
L. dorotheae illus. p.478.
L. fulleri. Egg-shaped succulent. H and S ¾in (2cm). Pairs of leaves are dove gray to brown-yellow. Convex, upper surfaces have sunken, darker marks. In late summer or early autumn bears a white flower. Z12–15 H12–10.
L. hookeri. See *L. turbiniformis*.
L. insularis, syn. *L. bromfieldii* var. *insularis*. Egg-shaped succulent. H ¾–1¼in (2–3cm), S ¾in (2cm). Slightly convex, upper surfaces of paired brown leaves have dark green windows and red dots and lines. Prduces a yellow flower in late summer or early autumn. Z12–15 H12–10.
L. julii. Egg-shaped succulent. H ¾–1¼in (2–3cm), S 2in (5cm). Has paired, pearl- to pink-gray leaves, each with a slightly convex, darker-marked, upper surface. In late summer or autumn produces a white flower. Z12–15 H12–10.
L. karasmontana illus. p.469. subsp. ***bella*** see *L. bella*.
L. lesliei. Egg-shaped succulent. H ½in (1cm), S ¾in (2cm). Is similar to *L. aucampiae*, but upper leaf surfaces are convex. Z12–15 H12–10. var. ***albinica*** illus. p.470.
L. marmorata illus. p.469.
L. olivacea. Egg-shaped succulent. H and S ¾in (2cm). Paired, dark olive green leaves have darker windows on convex, upper surfaces. Yellow flower appears in late summer or early autumn. Z12–15 H12–10.
L. otzeniana. Egg-shaped succulent. H 1¼in (3cm), S ¾in (2cm). Paired, gray-violet leaves each have a convex, upper surface with a distinctive, light border and large, semi-translucent windows. In late summer or early autumn bears a yellow flower. Z12–15 H12–10.
L. pseudotruncatella. Egg-shaped succulent. H 1¼in (3cm), S 1½in (4cm). Bears pairs of pale gray or blue to lilac leaves with darker marks on convex, upper surfaces. Fissure reaches from side to side only on mature plants. Has a yellow flower in late summer or early autumn. Z12–15 H12–10. var. ***pulmonuncula*** illus. p.478.
L. schwantesii, syn. *L.s.* var. *kuibisensis*, illus. p.478.
L. turbiniformis, syn. *L. hookeri*. Egg-shaped succulent. H 1½in (4cm), S ¾in (2cm). Has a flattish, upper surface with (usually) sunken, dark brown marks on paired brown leaves. Yellow flower appears in late summer or early autumn. Z12–15 H12–10.

Lithospermum diffusum. See *Lithodora diffusa*.
Lithospermum oleifolium. See *Lithodora oleifolia*.
Lithospermum zahnii. See *Lithodora zahnii*.
Litsia glauca. See *Neolitsia sericea*.

LITTONIA

COLCHICACEAE/LILIACEAE

Genus of deciduous, perennial, scandent, tuberous climbers grown for their pendent, bell-shaped flowers in summer. Requires full sun and rich, well-drained soil. Provide support. Dies down in winter; lift and dry off tubers and store in a frost-free place. Propagate by seed in spring; tubers sometimes will divide naturally.
L. modesta illus. p.403.

LIVISTONA

ARECACEAE/PALMAE

Genus of evergreen palms grown for their overall appearance. Has clusters of insignificant flowers in summer. Needs full light or partial shade and fertile, well-drained soil, ideally neutral to acidic. Water potted specimens moderately, less in winter. Propagate by seed in spring at not less than 73°F (23°C). Spider mite may be a nuisance on plants grown in containers.
L. australis (Australian cabbage palm, Gippsland fountain palm). Slow-growing, evergreen palm with a fairly slender trunk. H 50–70ft (15–20m), S 10–20ft (3–6m). Has fan-shaped leaves, 4–8ft (1.2–2.5m) wide, divided into narrow, slender-pointed, glossy, green leaflets. Leaf stalks are spiny. Z11–12 H12–10.
L. chinensis illus. p.85.

LLOYDIA

LILIACEAE

Genus of summer-flowering bulbs grown for their small, graceful, bell-shaped flowers. Is not easy to grow. Requires partial shade and well-drained, peaty soil; provide plenty of moisture in summer but, preferably, keep fairly dry in winter. Propagate by seed in spring.
L. graeca. See *Gagea graeca.*
L. serotina illus. p.435.

LOBELIA

CAMPANULACEAE

Genus of annuals, perennials, and deciduous or evergreen shrubs grown for their flowers. Some are suitable for wild gardens or by the waterside. Prefers sun and moist but well-drained soil. Resents wet conditions in winter; in cold areas some perennials and shrubs are therefore best lifted in autumn and placed in well-drained soil mix in frames. Propagate annuals by seed in spring, perennial species by seed or division in spring, perennial cultivars by division only, and shrubs by semi-ripe cuttings in summer. Contact with the milky sap of some species may irritate skin.
L. cardinalis (Cardinal flower). Clump-forming perennial. H 3ft (1m), S 9in (23cm). Bears racemes of 2-lipped, brilliant scarlet flowers from mid- to late summer. Lance-shaped leaves may be fresh green or red-bronze. Z2–8 H8–1.
***L.* 'Cherry Ripe'** illus. p.249.
***L.* 'Dark Crusader'.** Clump-forming perennial. H 3ft (1m), S 9in (23cm). From mid- to late summer bears racemes of 2-lipped, dark red flowers above lance-shaped, fresh green or red-bronze leaves.
***L. erinus* 'Blue Cascade'.** Slow-growing, pendulous, spreading annual, occasionally perennial. H 4–8in (10–20cm), S 4–6in (10–15cm). Oval to lance-shaped leaves are pale green. Small, 2-lipped, pale blue flowers are produced continuously in summer and early autumn. **'Cambridge Blue'** is compact and has blue flowers. **'Colour Cascade'** has flowers in a mixture of colors, such as blue, red, pink, mauve, or white. **'Crystal Palace'** illus. p.334. **'Red Cascade'** produces white-eyed, purple-red flowers. **'Sapphire'** illus. p.332. All of the above Z2–8 H8–1.
L. fulgens. See *L. splendens.*
***L.* x *gerardii* 'Vedrariensis'**, syn *L.* 'Vedrariensis'. Clump-forming perennial. H 3ft (1m), S 1ft (30cm). In late summer produces racemes of 2-lipped, purple flowers. Has lance-shaped, dark green leaves. Z8–9 H9–8.
***L.* 'Queen Victoria'** illus. p.249.
L. siphilitica. Clump-forming perennial. H 3ft (1m), S 9in (23cm). Racemes of 2-lipped blue flowers appear in late summer and autumn above narrowly oval, green leaves. Thrives in damp, heavy soil. Z4–8 H8–1.
L. splendens, syn. *L. fulgens.* Clump-forming perennial. H 3ft (1m), S 9in (23cm). Racemes of 2-lipped, brilliant scarlet flowers are produced from mid- to late summer. Lance-shaped leaves are reddish green. Z8–9 H9–8.
L. tupa. Clump-forming perennial. H 5–6ft (1.5–2m), S 3ft (1m). Bears large spikes of 2-lipped, brick red flowers in late summer, above narrowly oval, hairy, light green leaves. Often benefits from a sheltered, sunny site. Z8–10 H10–8.
***L.* 'Vedrariensis'.** See *L.* x *gerardii* 'Vedrariensis'.
***L.* 'Will Scarlet'.** Clump-forming perennial. H 3ft (1m), S 1ft (30cm). Racemes of 2-lipped, bright red flowers are borne in summer. Lance-shaped leaves are coppery green. Z4–8 H8–1.

LOBIVIA

CACTACEAE

Genus of spherical to columnar cacti, forming clumps with age, with flowers that each last only 1–2 days. Is easy to grow, requiring full sun and well-drained soil. Propagate by seed or stem cuttings from spring to autumn.
L. aurea. See *Echinopsis aurea.*
L. backebergii. See *Echinopsis bachebergii.*
L. cinnabarina. See *Echinopsis cinnabarina.*
L. cylindrica. See *Echinopsis aurea.*
L. haageana illus. p.467.
L. pentlandii. See *Echinopsis pentlandii.*
L. pygmaea. See *Rebutia pygmaea.*
L. shaferi illus. p.479.
L. silvestrii. See *Echinopsis chamaecereus.*

LOBULARIA

BRASSICACEAE/CRUCIFERAE

Genus of summer- and early autumn-flowering annuals. Grow in sun and in fertile, well-drained soil. Deadhead to encourage continuous flowering. Propagate by seed sown under cover in spring, or outdoors in late spring.
L. maritima, syn. *Alyssum maritimum* (Sweet alyssum). Fast-growing, spreading annual. H 3–6in (8–15cm), S 8–12in (20–30cm). Has lance-shaped, grayish green leaves. Rounded heads of tiny, scented, 4-petaled white flowers are produced in summer and early autumn. Z10–11 H12–1. **'Little Dorrit'** illus. p.318. **'Wonderland'** illus. p.322.

LOISELEURIA

ERICACEAE

Genus of one species of evergreen, creeping, prostrate shrub grown for its flowers. Requires full light and organic, well-drained, acidic soil. Is difficult to grow. Propagate by seed in spring or by softwood or semi-ripe cuttings in summer.
L. procumbens illus. p.377.

LOMATIA

PROTEACEAE

Genus of evergreen shrubs and trees grown for their foliage and flowers, which have 4 narrow, twisted petals. Often best in a cool greenhouse. Requires sun or semi-shade and moist but well-drained, acidic soil. Propagate by softwood or semi-ripe cuttings in summer.
L. ferruginea. Evergreen, upright shrub or tree. H 30ft (10m), S 15ft (5m). Thick, brown-felted shoots bear oblong to oval, dark green leaves, deeply cut into 6–15 oblong lobes. Racemes of yellow-and-red flowers are borne in midsummer. Z11 H12–8.
L. silaifolia illus. p.161.

LONICERA

Honeysuckle

CAPRIFOLIACEAE

Genus of deciduous, semi-evergreen or evergreen shrubs and woody-stemmed, twining climbers grown mainly for their flowers, which are often fragrant. Flowers are tubular, with spreading, 2-lipped petal lobes. Climbers may be trained into large shrubs. Grows in any fertile, well-drained soil in sun or semi-shade. Prune out flowered wood of climbers after flowering. Prune shrubs only to remove dead shoots or restrain growth. Propagate by seed in autumn or spring, by semi-ripe cuttings in summer, or by hardwood cuttings in late autumn. Aphids may be a problem, especially on *L. tatarica.* The berries may cause mild stomach upset if ingested.
L.* x *americana, syn. *L.* x *italica* of gardens, illus. p.215.
L.* x *brownii (Scarlet trumpet honeysuckle). **'Dropmore Scarlet'** illus. p.210.
L. etrusca (Etruscan honeysuckle). Deciduous or semi-evergreen, woody-stemmed, twining climber. H to 12ft (4m). Oval, midgreen leaves are blue-green beneath, the upper ones united into cups. Fragrant, long-tubed, pale yellow flowers borne in summer-autumn turn deeper yellow and become red-flushed with age. Grow in sun.
L. fragrantissima. Deciduous or semi-evergreen, bushy, spreading shrub. H 6ft (2m), S 12ft (4m). Bears oval, dark green leaves. Fragrant, short-tubed, creamy white flowers open in winter and early spring. Z4–8 H8–3.
***L.* 'Gold Flame'.** See *L.* x *heckrottii* 'Gold Flame'.
***L.* x *heckrottii*.** Deciduous or semi-evergreen, twining climber. H 15ft (5m). Oval, dark green leaves are blue-green beneath, the upper pairs united. Bears terminal whorls of fragrant pink flowers, orange-yellow inside, in summer, sometimes followed by red berries. Z6–9 H9–6. **'Gold Flame'** (syn. *L.* 'Gold Flame') illus. p.209.
L. henryi. Evergreen or semi-evergreen, woody-stemmed, twining climber. H to 30ft (10m). Narrowly oval, dark green leaves are paler beneath. Terminal clusters of long-tubed, red-purple flowers appear in summer-autumn, followed by black berries. Z3–8 H8–1.
L. hildebrandiana (Giant Burmese honeysuckle). Evergreen or semi-evergreen, woody-stemmed, twining climber. H to 70ft (20m). Oval or rounded, midgreen leaves are paler beneath. Long-tubed white or cream flowers, aging to creamy orange or brownish yellow, appear in pairs in leaf axils or at shoot tips in summer. Grow in sun. Z6–8 H8–6.
L.* x *italica of gardens. See *L.* x *americana.*
L. japonica (Japanese honeysuckle). **'Aureoreticulata'** is an evergreen or semi-evergreen, twining climber with soft-haired, woody stems. H to 30ft (10m). Oval, sometimes lobed leaves are bright green with bright yellow veins. Fragrant, long-tubed white flowers, becoming yellowish, are produced in summer-autumn. Is useful for hiding a tree stump or an unsightly wall or fence. Z4–8 H12-1. **'Halliana'** illus. p.215.
L. ledebourii illus. p.142.
L. maackii. Vigorous, deciduous, bushy shrub. H and S 15ft (5m). Leaves are oval and dark green. Fragrant, short-tubed white (later yellow) flowers in early summer are followed by spherical, bright red fruits. Z2–8 H9–4.
L. morrowii. Deciduous, spreading shrub with arching branches. H 6ft (2m), S 10ft (3m). Has oval, dark green leaves and, in late spring and early summer, small, short-tubed, creamy white flowers that age to yellow. Z4–9 H9–4.
L. nitida. Evergreen, bushy, dense shrub. H 6ft (2m), S 10ft (3m). Leaves are small, oval, glossy and dark green. Tiny, fragrant, short-tubed, creamy white flowers appear in late spring and are followed by small, spherical, purple fruits. Is good for hedging. Z6–9 H9–5. **'Baggesen's Gold'** illus. p.177. **'Yunnan'** is more upright, has thicker shoots and larger leaves and flowers more freely.
L. periclymenum (Common honeysuckle, Woodbine). **'Graham**

Thomas' illus. p.215. **'Serotina'** (Late Dutch honeysuckle) is a deciduous H to 22ft (7m). Oval or oblong, mid-green leaves are gray-green beneath. Very fragrant, long-tubed, dark purple flowers, pinkish within, are borne in mid and late summer. Grow in sun or shade. Z5–9 H9–5.
L. pileata illus. p.176.
L. x purpusii illus. p.173. **'Winter Beauty'** has red-purple shoots and freely bears very fragrant white flowers. Z7–9 H9–7.
L. sempervirens illus. p.210.
L. standishii. Evergreen, bushy shrub. H and S 6ft (2m). Has peeling bark, oblong, bristly, dark green leaves, and, in winter, fragrant, short-tubed, creamy white flowers. Z5–8 H8–4.
L. tatarica illus. p.140. **'Hack's Red'** is a deciduous, bushy shrub. H and S 8ft (2.5m). Produces short-tubed, deep pink flowers in late spring and early summer, followed by spherical red fruits. Leaves are oval and dark green. Z3–9 H9–1.
L. x tellmanniana illus. p.217.
L. tragophylla. Deciduous, woody-stemmed, twining climber. H 15–20ft (5–6m). Oval leaves are bluish green, the uppermost pair united into a cup. Produces clusters of up to 20 long-tubed, bright yellow flowers in early summer.
***L. x xylosteoides* 'Clavey's Dwarf'.** Deciduous, upright, dense shrub. H 6ft (2m), S 3ft (1m). Leaves are oval and gray-green. Bears short-tubed pink flowers in late spring, then spherical red fruits.
L. xylosteum illus. p.140.

Lophocereus schottii. See *Pachycereus schottii*.

LOPHOPHORA
Peyote

CACTACEAE

Genus of very slow-growing cacti that resemble small blue dumplings, with up to 10 ribs, each separated by an indented line. Has long taproots. Flowering areoles each produce tufts of short, white hairs. Needs sun and well-drained soil. Is very prone to rotting, so water lightly from spring to autumn. Propagate by seed in spring or summer. Some are illegal to own.
L. echinata. See *L. williamsii*.
L. lutea. See *L. williamsii*.
L. williamsii, syn. *L. echinata*, *L. lutea*, illus. p.471.

LOPHOSPERMUM

SCROPHULARIACEAE

Genus of deciduous and evergreen, perennial climbers and shrubs. Has triangular to rounded leaves and tubular to funnel-shaped flowers. Needs sun and moist but well-drained soil. Propagate by seed in spring or semi-ripe cuttings in late summer.
L. erubescens, syn. *Asarina erubescens*, *Maurandya erubescens*, illus. p.209.

LOROPETALUM

HAMAMELIDACEAE

Genus of evergreen shrubs grown for their flowers. Requires full light or semi-shade and rich, well-drained, neutral to acidic soil. Water containerized plants freely when in full growth, moderately at other times. Propagate by layering or seed in spring or by semi-ripe cuttings in late summer.
L. chinense. Evergreen, rounded, well-branched shrub. H and S 4ft (1.2m). Asymmetrically oval leaves are deep green. White flowers, each with 4 strap-shaped petals, are borne in tufted, terminal clusters, mainly in winter-spring. Z8–9 H9–8.

LOTUS

PAPILIONACEAE/LEGUMINOSAE

Genus of summer-flowering perennials, some of which are semi-evergreen, and evergreen subshrubs, grown for their foliage and flowers. Prefers sun and well-drained soil. Propagate by softwood cuttings from early to midsummer or by seed in autumn or spring.
L. berthelotii illus. p.283.
L. hirsutus, syn. *Dorycnium hirsutum*. Deciduous, upright subshrub. H and S 24in (60cm). Bears silver-gray leaves with 3 oval leaflets. Dense clusters of pealike, pink-tinged white flowers in summer and early autumn are followed by oblong to ovoid, reddish brown seed pods. Z6–9 H9–6.

LUCULIA

RUBIACEAE

Genus of evergreen shrubs grown for their flowers and foliage. Needs full light or partial shade and fertile, well-drained soil. Water potted specimens freely when in full growth, moderately at other times. Cut back flowered stems hard in spring, if container-grown. Propagate by seed in spring or by semi-ripe cuttings in summer.
L. grandifolia. Evergreen, rounded to upright, robust shrub. H and S 10–20ft (3–6m). Oval green leaves have red veins and stalks. Fragrant, tubular white flowers, each 2½in (6cm) long, with 5 rounded petal lobes, appear in terminal clusters in summer. Z7–9 H9–7.

LUETKEA

ROSACEAE

Genus of one species of deciduous subshrub grown for its fluffy flower heads. Is suitable for banks and rock gardens. Requires shade and well-drained but not too dry soil. Propagate by division or seed in spring.
L. pectinata. Deciduous, spreading, decumbent subshrub. H to 12in (30cm), S 8in (20cm). Stems are clothed in finely dissected, very dark green leaves. In summer has terminal racemes of small, fluffy, off-white flower heads.

LUMA

MYRTACEAE

Genus of evergreen shrubs and small trees grown for their aromatic leaves and cup-shaped white flowers. Grow in full sun or partial shade and fertile, ideally organic, well-drained soil. Propagate by seed in spring or by semi-ripe cuttings in late summer.
L. apiculata, syn. *Amomyrtus luma*, *Myrceugenia apiculata*, *Myrtus apiculata*, *M. luma*, illus. p.119. **'Glanleam Gold'** is a strong-growing, evergreen, upright shrub. H and S 30ft (10m). Has thick stems, peeling, brown and white bark, and oval, bright green leaves edged with creamy yellow. Slightly fragrant flowers are borne from midsummer to midautumn. Z9–10 H10–9.
L. chequen, syn. *Myrtus chequen*. Strong growing upright-shrub or small tree. H 20ft (6m) S 15ft (5m). Has broadly ovate, wavy-margined, aromatic, dark green leaves. In late summer and early-autumn bears cup-shaped white flowers, singly or in small clusters, followed by black berries. Z9–10 H10–9.

LUNARIA
Honesty

CRUCIFERAE/BRASSIACEAE

Genus of biennials and perennials grown for their flowers and silvery seed pods. Will grow in sun or shade, but prefers partial shade and well-drained soil. Propagate perennials by seed in autumn or spring or by division in spring, biennials by seed only. Self seeds prolifically.
L. annua, syn. *L. biennis*, illus. p.325. **'Variegata'** illus. p.323.
L. biennis. See *L. annua*.
L. rediviva. Rosette-forming perennial. H 24–30in (60–75cm), S 12in (30cm). Produces racemes of 4-petaled lilac or white flowers in spring, followed by elliptical silvery seed pods that are useful for indoor decoration. Has oval, coarse, sometimes maroon-tinted, mid-green leaves. Z6–9 H9–6.

LUPINUS
Lupin

PAPILIONACEAE/LEGUMINOSAE

Genus of annuals, perennials, and semi-evergreen shrubs grown for their large, imposing racemes of pealike flowers. Prefers sun and well-drained soil. Remove seed heads of most varieties to prevent self seeding. Propagate species by seed when fresh in autumn, and selected forms by cuttings from non-flowering side-shoots in spring or early summer. The seeds may cause severe discomfort if ingested.
L. arboreus illus. p.169.
L. 'Band of Nobles'. Clump-forming perennial. H to 5ft (1.5m), S 2½ft (75cm). In early and midsummer, racemes of flowers in white, yellow, pink, red, blue, or bicolors (usually white or yellow in combination with another color) arise above palmate, deeply divided, midgreen leaves. Z5–8 H8–5.
L. 'Inverewe Red' illus. p.245.
L. 'My Castle'. Clump-forming perennial. H 3ft (90cm), S 2½ft (75cm). Bears racemes of deep rose-pink flowers above palmate, deeply divided, midgreen leaves in early and midsummer. Z4–7 H7–1.
L. 'Noble Maiden'. Clump-forming perennial. H 90m (3ft), S 2½ft (75cm). In early and midsummer, racemes of creamy white flowers arise above palmate, deeply divided, midgreen leaves. Z4–7 H7–1.
L. 'The Chatelaine' illus. p.244.

LURONIUM

ALISMATACEAE

Genus of deciduous, perennial, marginal water plants and marsh plants grown for their foliage and flowers. Requires shallow water and full sun. Thin plants when overcrowded. Propagate in spring by seed or division.
L. natans, syn. *Alisma natans* (Floating water plantain). Deciduous, perennial, marginal water plant. H 1–2in (2.5–5cm), S 12in (30cm). Produces small, elliptic to lance-shaped, midgreen leaves and, in summer, small, 3-lobed, yellow-spotted white flowers. Z5–8 H8–5.

LUZULA
Woodrush

JUNCACEAE

See also GRASSES, BAMBOOS, RUSHES, and SEDGES.
L. maxima. See *L. sylvatica*.
L. nivea illus. p.307.
L. sylvatica, syn. *L. maxima* (Greater woodrush). **'Marginata'** (syn. *L.s.* 'Aureomarginata') is a slow-growing, evergreen, spreading, rhizomatous, perennial grass. H to 12in (30cm), S indefinite. Produces thick tufts of broad, hairy-edged, midgreen leaves with white margins. Leafy stems bear terminal, open brown flower spikes in summer. Tolerates shade. Z4–9 H9–4.

LYCASTE

See also ORCHIDS.
L. cruenta (illus. p.299). Vigorous, deciduous, epiphytic orchid for a cool greenhouse. H 12in (30cm). Fragrant, triangular, green-and-yellow flowers, 2in (5cm) across, are produced singly in spring. Has broadly oval, ribbed, soft leaves to 12in (30cm) long. Grow in semi-shade during summer and avoid spraying, which can mark leaves. Z14–15 H12–6.

LYCHNIS

CARYOPHYLLACEAE

Genus of summer-flowering annuals, biennials and perennials. Requires sun and well-drained soil. Propagate by division or seed in autumn or spring.

***L.* 'Abbotswood Rose'**. See *L.* x *walkeri* 'Abbotswood Rose'.
L. alpina, syn. *Viscaria alpina* (Alpine catchfly). Tuft-forming perennial. H 2–6in (5–15cm), S 4–6in (10–15cm). Has dense tufts of thick, linear, deep green leaves. In summer, sticky stems each bear a rounded head of pale to deep pink or, rarely, white flowers with spreading, frilled petals. Good in a rock garden. Z4–7 H7–1.
L. chalcedonica illus. p.249.
L. coeli-rosa. See *Silene coeli-rosa.*
L. coronaria illus. p.282.
L. flos-jovis illus. p.279.
L.* x *haageana, syn. *L.* x *haagena.* Short-lived, clump-forming perennial. H 18in (45cm), S 12in (30cm). Produces clusters of large, 5-petaled white, orange, or red flowers in summer. Oval leaves are midgreen. Best raised regularly from seed.
L.* x *haagena. See *L.* x *haageana.*
***L.* x *walkeri* 'Abbotswood Rose'**, syn. *L.* 'Abbotswood Rose'. Neat, clump-forming perennial. H 12–15in (30–38cm), S 9in (23cm). Has oval gray leaves and gray, branching stems that, from mid- to late summer, bear sprays of rounded, 5-petaled, bright rose-pink flowers.
L. viscaria. Clump-forming perennial. H 12in (30cm), S 30–45cm (12–18in). From early to midsummer, rather sticky, star-shaped, reddish purple flowers are borne in dense clusters above narrowly oval to oblong, dark green leaves. Suitable for the front of a border or a rock garden. Z3–7 H3–1. **'Splendens Plena'** illus. p.282.

Lycianthes rantonnetii. See *Solanum rantonnetii.*

LYCIUM

SOLANACEAE

Genus of deciduous shrubs, sometimes with long, scandent branches, grown for their habit, flowers, and fruits. Useful for poor, dry soil and coastal gardens. May be grown as a hedge. Prefers full sun and not too rich, well-drained soil. Remove dead wood in winter and cut back to restrict growth if necessary. Cut back hedges hard in spring. Propagate by softwood cuttings in summer, by seed in autumn, or by hardwood cuttings in winter.
L. barbarum, syn. *L. halimifolium* (Chinese box thorn, Duke of Argyll's tea-tree). Deciduous, arching, often spiny shrub. H 8ft (2.5m), S 15ft (5m). Funnel-shaped purple or pink flowers in late spring and summer are followed by spherical, orange-red berries. Leaves are lance-shaped, bright green or gray-green. Z6–9 H9–5.
L. halimifolium. See *L. barbarum.*

LYCORIS

AMARYLLIDACEAE

Genus of late summer- and early autumn-flowering bulbs with showy flower heads on leafless stems. In colder areas is best grown in pots. Needs sun, well-drained soil and a warm period in summer to ripen bulbs so they flower. Provide regular liquid fertilizer while in growth. After summer dormancy, water from early autumn until following summer, when foliage dies away. Propagate by seed when ripe or in spring or summer or by offsets in late summer.
L. aurea (Golden spider lily). Late summer- and early autumn-flowering bulb. H 12–16in (30–40cm), S 4–6in (10–15cm). Produces a head of 5 or 6 bright yellow flowers that have narrow, reflexed petals with very wavy margins, and conspicuous stamens. Strap-shaped, semi-erect, basal leaves appear after flowering. Z8–10 H10–8.
L. radiata illus. p.420.
L. squamigera (Resurrection lily). Late summer- or early autumn-flowering bulb. H 18–24in (45–60cm), S 4–6in (10–15cm). Carries a head of 6–8 fragrant, funnel-shaped, rose-pink flowers, 4in (10cm) l ong, with reflexed petal tips. Strap-shaped, semi-erect, basal leaves form after flowers. Z6–11 H12–6.

LYGODIUM

SCHIZAEACEAE

Genus of deciduous or semi-evergreen, climbing ferns, usually with 2 kinds of fronds: vegetative and fertile. Needs shade or semi-shade and organic, moist, peaty soil. Is best grown among shrubby plants that can provide support. Plants grown under cover in pots need strong, twiggy supports. Remove faded fronds regularly. Propagate by division in spring or by spores in summer.
L. japonicum (Japanese climbing fern). Deciduous, climbing fern. H 6ft (2m), S indefinite. Midgreen, vegetative fronds consist of delicate, finger-shaped pinnae; fertile fronds are broader and 3–5 lobed, with a longer, terminal lobe. Z10–11 H12–9.

LYONIA

ERICACEAE

Genus of deciduous, semi-evergreen or evergreen shrubs and trees grown for their racemes of small, urn-shaped flowers. Needs shade or semi-shade and moist, peaty, acidic soil. Propagate by semi-ripe cuttings in summer.
L. ligustrina. (Maleberry) Deciduous, bushy shrub. H and S 6ft (2m). Oval, dark green leaves set off dense racemes of globular urn-shaped white flowers from mid- to late summer. Z5–9 H9–5.
L. ovalifolia. Deciduous or semi-evergreen, bushy shrub. H and S 6ft (2m). Produces red shoots and oval, dark green leaves. Racemes of urn-shaped, white flowers appear in late spring and early summer. Z5–9 H9–5.

LYONOTHAMNUS

ROSACEAE

Genus of one species of evergreen tree grown for its foliage and flowers. Needs sun or semi-shade, a warm, sheltered position, and fertile, well-drained soil. Propagate by softwood cuttings in summer or by seed in autumn.
L. floribundus (Catalina ironwood). Evergreen tree grown only in the form subsp. ***aspleniifolius***. Slender tree, H 40ft (12m), S 6m (20ft), with rather stringy, reddish brown bark and much divided, fernlike, dark green leaves. Large, flattened heads of 5-petaled, star-shaped white flowers are produced in early summer. Z9–10 H10–9.

LYSICHITON

ARACEAE

Genus of deciduous, perennial, marginal water plants and bog plants grown for their handsome spathes and very large, glossy foliage. Prefers full sun, but tolerates semi-shade. Tolerates both still and running water. Propagate by seed when fresh, in late summer.
L. americanum. See *L. americanus.*
L. americanus, syn. *L. americanum*, illus. p.451.
L. camtschatcensis illus. p.446.

LYSIMACHIA

Loosestrife

PRIMULACEAE

Genus of summer-flowering annuals and perennials suitable for the border or rock garden. Prefers sun or semi-shade and moist but well-drained soil. Propagate by division in spring or by seed in autumn.
L. clethroides illus. p.241.
L. ephemerum. Neat, clump-forming perennial. H 3ft (1m), S 1ft (30cm). Erect, terminal racemes of star-shaped, grayish white flowers are borne on slender stems in summer, followed by light green seed heads. Lance-shaped leaves are leathery and glaucous.
L. nummularia (Moneywort). **'Aurea'** illus. p.386.
L. punctata illus. p.255.

LYTHRUM

Purple loosestrife

LYTHRACEAE

Genus of summer-flowering perennials that thrive by the waterside and in bog gardens. Grows in full sun or semi-shade and in moist or wet soil. Propagate cultivars by division in spring, species by seed or division in spring or autumn. Some species have become noxious weeds in North America and should not be grown near wetlands.
***L. salicaria* 'Feuerkerze'**, syn. *L.s.* 'Firecandle', illus. p.245.
'Firecandle' see *L.s.* 'Feuerkerze'.
'Robert' is a clump-forming perennial. H 2½ft (75cm), S 18in (45cm). Produces racemes of 4-petaled, clear pink flowers from mid- to late summer. Leaves are midgreen and lance-shaped. Z3–9 H9–1.
***L. virgatum* 'Rose Queen'.** Clump-forming perennial. H 3ft (1m), S 2ft (60cm). Racemes of 4-petaled, star-shaped, light pink flowers are produced from mid- to late summer above lance-shaped, hairless, midgreen leaves. Z4–9 H9–1. **'The Rocket'** illus. p.245.

MAACKIA

LEGUMINOSAE/PAPILIONACEAE

Genus of deciduous, summer-flowering trees grown for their foliage and flowers. Requires full sun and fertile, well-drained soil. Propagate by seed in autumn.
M. amurensis illus. p.90.

MACADAMIA

PROTEACEAE

Genus of evergreen trees grown for their foliage and fruits. Prefers full light, though some shade is tolerated. Provide organic, moisture-retentive but well-drained soil. Water freely while in full growth, moderately at other times. Pruning is not usually necessary, but it is tolerated in autumn. Propagate by seed when ripe (in autumn) or in spring.
M. integrifolia illus. p.73.

MACFADYENA,

syn. DOXANTHA

BIGNONIACEAE

Genus of evergreen, woody-stemmed, tendril climbers grown for their foxglovelike flowers. Any fertile, well-drained soil is suitable with full light. Water regularly, less when not in full growth. Stems need support. Thin out crowded shoots after flowering or in spring. Propagate by semi-ripe cuttings in summer.
M. unguis-cati, syn. *Bignonia unguis-cati*, *Doxantha unguis-cati*, illus. p.216.

MACKAYA

ACANTHACEAE

Genus of one species of evergreen shrub grown for its flowers and overall appearance. Requires full light or partial shade and fertile, well-drained soil. Water potted plants freely when in full growth, moderately at other times. Pruning is tolerated in winter if necessary. Propagate by greenwood cuttings in spring or by semi-ripe cuttings in summer.
M. bella, syn. *Asystasia bella.* Evergreen, erect, then spreading,

well-branched shrub. H to 5ft (1.5m), S 4–5ft (1.2–1.5m). Leaves are oval, pointed, glossy, and mid- to deep green. Has spikes of tubular, dark-veined lavender flowers, each with 5 large, flared petal lobes, from spring to autumn. In warm conditions, above 55°F (13°C), will flower into winter.

MACLEAYA

Plume poppy

PAPAVERACEAE

Genus of summer-flowering perennials grown for their overall appearance. Grows in sun and in well-drained soil. May spread rapidly. Propagate by division in early spring or by root cuttings in winter.

M. cordata, syn. *Bocconia cordata*. Spreading, clump-forming perennial. H 5ft (1.5m) or more, S 2ft (60cm) or more. Large, rounded, lobed, gray-green leaves, gray-white beneath, are produced at base of plant and up lower parts of stems. Large, feathery panicles of dainty, creamy white flowers are produced in summer. Z4–8 H8–1.

***M. microcarpa* 'Coral Plume'.** See *M.m.* 'Kelway's Coral Plume'. **'Kelway's Coral Plume'** (syn. *M.m.* 'Coral Plume) illus. p.227.

MACLURA

MORACEAE

Genus of deciduous trees grown for their foliage and unusual fruits. Both male and female trees need to be planted to obtain fruits. Young plants are susceptible to cold damage. Requires full sun and needs hot summers to thrive in cold areas. Grows in any but waterlogged soil. Propagate by softwood cuttings in summer, by seed in autumn, or by root cuttings in late winter.

M. aurantiaca. See *M. pomifera*.

M. pomifera, syn. *M. aurantiaca* (Osage orange). Deciduous, rounded, spreading tree. H 50ft (15m), S 40ft (12m). Has spiny shoots and oval, dark green leaves that turn yellow in autumn. Tiny, cup-shaped yellow flowers in summer are followed on female trees by large, rounded, fragrant, wrinkled, pale green fruits. Z5–9 H9–5.

M. tricuspidata, syn. *Cudrania tricuspidata*. Deciduous, spreading tree. H 22ft (7m), S 20ft (6m). Bears oval, dark green leaves that are sometimes 3-lobed. Produces small, rounded clusters of tiny green flowers in midsummer. Z5–9 H9–5.

Macroplectrum sesquipedale. See *Angraecum sesquipedale*.

Macrotomia echioides. See *Arnebia pulchra*.

MAGNOLIA

MAGNOLIACEAE

Genus of deciduous, semi-evergreen, or evergreen trees and shrubs grown for their showy, usually fragrant flowers. Leaves are mainly oval. Flowers and buds of early-flowering magnolias may be damaged by late frosts. Needs sun or semi-shade and shelter from strong winds. Does best in fertile, well-drained soil. *M. delavayi*, *M. kobus*, *M. sieboldii* and *M. wilsonii* grow on alkaline soil. Other species prefer neutral to acidic soil, but will grow in alkaline soil if deep and organic. Dry, sandy soils should be generously enriched with manure and leaf mold before planting. Propagate species by semi-ripe cuttings in summer or by seed when ripe (summer-autumn), selected forms by semi-ripe cuttings in summer, or by grafting in winter. See also feature panel p.75.

M. acuminata (Cucumber tree). Vigorous, deciduous tree, conical when young, later spreading. H 70ft (20m), S 30ft (10m). Fragrant, cup-shaped, bluish green flowers appear from early to midsummer amid large, oval, pale green leaves, followed by small, egg-shaped green, later red, fruits. Z4–8 H8–2.

***M.* 'Ann'.** Deciduous spreading shrub with dark green leaves that are slightly hairy above. H 8–10ft (2.5–3m) S 10ft (3m). Deep purple, goblet-shaped flowers with 7–9 petals, 5in (13cm) across open in spring. Z3–8 H8-1.

***M.* 'Betty'.** Deciduous shrub with a rounded habit. H and S 12ft (4m). Ovate, midgreen leaves about 6in (15cm) long. Produces 8in (20cm) cup-shaped flowers, with up to 19 petals, that are purple outside and red inside, in midspring. Z6–9 H9–6.

M. campbellii illus. p.75. Deciduous tree, upright when young, later spreading. H 50ft (15m), S 30ft (10m). Large, slightly fragrant, pale to deep pink flowers are borne on leafless branches from late winter to midspring on trees 15–20 years old or more. Z7–9 H9–7. **'Charles Raffill'** (illus. p.75) bears large, fragrant, cup-shaped, purplish pink flowers from late winter to mid-spring on trees at least 15 years old. Leaves are large, oval, and midgreen. **'Darjeeling'** (illus. p.75) is similar to the species but has large, very deep pink flowers. **'Kew's Surprise'** bears deep purplish pink flowers. subsp. ***mollicomata*** (illus. p.75) has lilac-pink flowers slightly earlier in the year.

***M.* 'Charles Coates'** (illus. p.75). Deciduous, rounded, open, spreading tree. H 70ft (19m), S 25ft (8m). Extremely fragrant, creamy white flowers with conspicuous red stamens are produced in late spring and early summer amid large, light green leaves. Z6–9 H9–8.

M. cylindrica (illus. p.75). Deciduous, spreading tree or large shrub. H and S 15ft (5m). Fragrant, upright, creamy white flowers are produced in midspring, after which the young leaves turn dark green. Z6–9 H9–6.

M. dawsoniana. Deciduous tree or shrub, with a broadly oval head. H 50ft (15m), S 30ft (10m). In early spring, large, fragrant, pendent, open cup-shaped, pale lilac-pink flowers are carried profusely on older plants (20 years from seed, 10 years from grafting). Leaves are oval, leathery, and deep green. Z7–9 H9–7.

M. denudata, syn. *M. heptapeta* (Lily tree, Yulan; illus. p.75). Deciduous, rounded, bushy shrub or spreading tree. H and S 30ft (10m). Produces masses of fragrant, cup-shaped white flowers from mid- to late spring before oval, midgreen leaves appear. Z6–9 H9–6.

M. fraseri (illus. p.75). Deciduous, spreading, open tree. H 30ft (10m), S 25ft (8m). Fragrant white or pale yellow flowers open in late spring and early summer amid large, pale green leaves. Z6–9 H9–6.

***M.* 'Galaxy'.** Deciduous, fast growing, conical tree H 40ft (12m) S 25ft (8m). It has 5in (13cm) purple-pink flowers in early spring before the leaves. Flowers at a young age. Z6–9 H9–6.

M. grandiflora (Bull bay, Southern magnolia). Evergreen, broadly conical or rounded, dense tree. H and S 30ft (10m). Bears large, very fragrant, bowl-shaped white flowers intermittently from midsummer to early autumn. Has oblong, glossy, mid- to dark green leaves. Z7–9 H9–1. **'Exmouth'** (illus. p.75) has creamy white flowers and narrow, leathery leaves. Z7–10 H10–7. **'Edith Bogue'**, one of the hardiest selections, grows well in Z6–9 H9–6. **'Ferruginea'** has dark green leaves, rust-brown beneath. Z8–9 H9–8.

***M.* 'Heaven Scent'** (illus. p.75). Vigorous, deciduous shrub or tree. H and S 30ft (10m). Fragrant, vase-shaped flowers, each with usually 9 petals that are pink outside and white within, are borne from midspring to early summer. Leaves are broadly elliptic and glossy green. Z6–9 H9–6.

M. heptapeta. See *M. denudata*.

M. hypoleuca, syn. *M. obovata* (Japanese big-leaf magnolia; illus. p.75). Vigorous, deciduous, upright tree. H 50ft (15m), S 30ft (10m). Large, fragrant, pink-flushed white or pale cream flowers with crimson stamens appear in early summer. Z5–9 H9–5.

M. insignis. See *Manglietia insignis*.

***M.* 'Jane'.** Upright deciduous shrub or small tree H 12ft (4m) S 10ft (3m). Produces fragrant flowers with 10 petals in late spring. Flowers are red-purple outside, white inside. Z6–9 H9–6.

***M.* x *kewensis* 'Wada's Memory'.** See *M.* 'Wada's Memory'.

M. kobus (illus. p.75). Deciduous, broadly conical tree. H 30ft (10m), S 25ft (8m). Bears a profusion of fragrant, pure white flowers in midspring before small, slightly aromatic, dark green leaves appear. Z5–9 H9–5..

M. liliiflora, syn. *M. quinquepeta*. Deciduous, bushy shrub. H 10ft (3m), S 4m (12ft). Has fragrant, upright, vase-shaped, purplish pink flowers that are borne amid oval, very dark green leaves from midspring to midsummer. Z4–9 H9–1.**'Nigra'** (illus. p.75) has large, deep purple flowers.

***M.* x *loebneri* 'Leonard Messel'** (illus. p.75). Deciduous, upright shrub or small tree. H 25ft (8m), S 20ft (6m). In midspring, fragrant flowers with many pale lilac-pink petals appear before and after oval, deep green leaves emerge. Z5–9 H9–5. **'Merrill'** has funnel-shaped white flowers. Z5–9 H9–1..

***M.* 'Manchu Fan'** (illus. p.75). Vigorous, deciduous shrub or tree. H 20ft (6m), S 15ft (5m). In late spring has large, goblet-shaped, creamy white flowers with usually 9 petals, the inner ones flushed purple-pink at the base. Leaves are ovate. Z6–9 H9–6.

***M.* 'Norman Gould'** (illus. p.75). Deciduous, spreading tree or bushy shrub. H and S 15ft (5m). Silky buds open into fragrant, star-shaped white flowers in midspring. Leaves are oblong and dark green. Z6–9 H9–6.

M. obovata. See *M. hypoleuca*.

M. quinquepeta. See *M. liliiflora*.

***M.* 'Ricki'.** Spreading deciduous shrub. H and S 12ft (4m). Flowers open in midspring and are pink outside, paler within, and have 15 twisted petals. Z6–9 H9-6.

M. salicifolia (Willow-leaved magnolia; illus. p.75). Deciduous, conical tree. H 30ft (10m), S 15ft (5m). Has aromatic, oval leaves, midgreen above, gray-white beneath. Fragrant, pure white flowers open in midspring before foliage appears. Z6–9 H9–6.

M. sieboldii. Deciduous, arching shrub or wide-spreading tree. H 25ft (8m), S 40ft (12m). Fragrant, cup-shaped white flowers with crimson anthers are carried above oval, dark green leaves from late spring to late summer. Z6–9 H9–6. subsp. ***sinensis*** (syn. *M. sinensis*) has slightly larger, fully pendent flowers and more rounded, oval leaves.

M. sinensis. See. *M. sieboldii* subsp. *sinensis*.

***M.* x *soulangeana* 'Alba'** see *M.* x *s.* 'Alba Superba'. **'Alba Superba'** (syn. *M.* x *s.* 'Alba') is a deciduous, rounded, spreading shrub or small tree. H and S 20ft (6m). Bears large, fragrant, tuliplike white flowers, faintly flushed with pink at the bases, from mid- to early spring, the first before mid- to dark green leaves emerge. **'Brozzonii'**, H 25ft (8m), S 20ft (6m), is treelike, with large, purple-flushed white flowers. Z6–9 H9–6. **'Etienne Soulange-Bodin'** (illus. p.75) bears purple-flushed white blooms. Z5–9 H9–5. Flowers of **'Lennei'** are large, goblet-shaped, and deep rose-purple. Z5–9 H9–6. **'Picture'**, H 25ft (8m), S 20ft (6m), is vigorous, compact and upright, with large, erect, deep reddish purple flowers. Z5–9 H9–5.**'Rubra'** of gardens see *M.* x *s.* 'Rustica Rubra'. **'Rustica Rubra'** (syn. *M.* x *s.* 'Rubra' of gardens; illus. p.75) has purplish red blooms suffused pink. Z6–9 H9–6.

M. sprengeri (illus. p.75). Deciduous, spreading tree. H 50ft (15m), S 30ft (10m). In midspring has fragrant, bowl-shaped white flowers, sometimes fringed with red or pale pink, before

oval, dark green leaves appear. Z7–9 H9–7. **'Wakehurst'** (illus. p.75) has deep purplish pink flowers.
M. stellata (Star magnolia; illus. p.75). Deciduous, bushy, dense shrub. H 10ft (3m), S 12ft (4m). Fragrant, star-shaped flowers with many narrow petals open from silky buds during early to midspring. Leaves are narrow and deep green. Z5–9 H9–5. **'Water Lily'** (illus. p.75) has large white flowers with many petals. Z6–9 H9–6.
M. tripetala (illus. p.75). Deciduous, spreading, open tree, conical when young. H 30ft (10m), S 25ft (8m). Has large, dark green leaves clustered about shoot tips, and rather unpleasantly scented, creamy white flowers with narrow petals in late spring and early summer. Z5–9 H9–5.
***M.* x *veitchii* 'Peter Veitch'** (illus. p.75). Fast-growing, deciduous, spreading tree. H 60ft (20m), S 50ft (15m). Bears large, fragrant, pale pink and white flowers in midspring, before dark green leaves emerge. Usually flowers within 10 years of planting. Z7–9 H9–7.
M. virginiana (Sweet bay). Deciduous or semi-evergreen, conical shrub or tree. H 28ft (9m), S 20ft (6m). Has very fragrant, cup-shaped, creamy white flowers from early summer to early autumn. Oblong, glossy, mid- to dark green leaves are bluish white beneath. Z6–9 H9–6.
***M.* 'Wada's Memory'**, syn. *M.* x *kewensis* 'Wada's Memory' (illus. p.75). Deciduous, conical tree. H 30ft (10m), S 15ft (5m). Has aromatic, dark green foliage and a profusion of large, fragrant white flowers borne from mid- to late spring before oval leaves appear. Z6–9 H9–6.
***M.* x *watsonii*.** See *M.* x *wieseneri*.
M.* x *wieseneri, syn. *M.* x *watsonii* (illus. p.75). Deciduous, spreading, open tree or shrub. H 25ft (8m), S 15ft (5m). Rounded white buds open in late spring to early summer to fragrant, creamy white flowers, flushed pink outside and with crimson stamens. Z5–9 H9–5.
M. wilsonii (illus. p.75). Deciduous, spreading tree or shrub. H 25ft (8m), S 22ft (7m). In late spring and early summer, fragrant, cup-shaped white flowers with crimson stamens hang from arching branches amid narrow, dark green leaves. Z7–9 H9–7.

x MAHOBERBERIS

BERBERIDACEAE

Hybrid genus (*Berberis* x *Mahonia*) of evergreen shrubs grown for their foliage, flowers, and botanical interest. Needs sun or semi-shade and fertile, well-drained soil. Propagate by semi-ripe cuttings in summer.
x ***M. aquisargentii*.** Evergreen, upright, densely leaved shrub. H and S 6ft (2m). Leaves are bright green, often with 3 leaflets, some oblong and finely toothed, others holly-shaped. Terminal clusters of barberry-like yellow flowers are sparsely produced in late spring. Z6–8 H8–6.

MAHONIA

BERBERIDACEAE

Genus of evergreen shrubs grown for their foliage, their usually short racemes of often fragrant, rounded, bell-shaped yellow flowers, and, with tall species and cultivars, for their deeply fissured bark. Large mahonias make good specimen plants; low-growing ones are excellent as a groundcover. Prefers shade or semi-shade and fertile, well-drained but not too dry soil. Propagate species by leaf-bud or semi-ripe cuttings in summer or by seed in autumn, and selected forms by leaf-bud or semi-ripe cuttings only.
***M. acanthifolia*.** See *M. napaulensis*.
M. aquifolium illus. p.157.
***M. bealei*.** See *M. japonica* 'Bealei'.
***M.* 'Heterophylla'.** Evergreen, upright shrub. H 3ft (1m), S 5ft (1.5m). Has reddish purple shoots and glossy, bright green leaves, each composed of 5 or 7 narrowly lance-shaped, wavy-edged or curled leaflets that turn reddish purple in winter. Small clusters of yellow flowers appear in spring. Z9–10 H10–9.
M. japonica illus. p.151. **'Bealei'** (syn. *M. bealei*). Bears blue-green leaves divided into broad leaflets and pale yellow flowers in shorter, upright racemes. Z7–8 H8–7.
***M. lomariifolia*.** Evergreen, very upright shrub. H 10ft (3m), S 6ft (2m). Large, dark green leaves each have 19–37 narrow, hollylike, spiny leaflets. Fragrant, bright yellow flowers are produced in dense, upright racemes during late autumn and winter. Z8–9 H9–5.
***M.* x *media*. 'Buckland'** and **'Charity'** illus. p.125.
M. napaulensis, syn. *M. acanthifolia*. Evergreen, upright, open shrub. H 8ft (2.5m), S 10ft (3m). Leaves are composed of up to 15 hollylike, spiny, dark green leaflets. Produces long, slender racemes of yellow flowers in early and midspring. Z8–9 H9–8.
***M. repens*.** Evergreen, upright shrub that spreads by underground stems. H 1ft (30cm), S 6ft (2m). Blue-green leaves each consist of 3–7 oval leaflets with bristlelike teeth. Dense clusters of deep yellow flowers are borne from mid- to late spring. Z5–8 H8–3.
***M.* 'Undulata'.** Evergreen, upright shrub. H and S 6ft (2m). Glossy, dark green leaves each have 5–9 hollylike, wavy-edged leaflets that become bronzed in winter. Bears dense clusters of deep yellow flowers in mid- and late spring. Z5–8 H8–5.

MAIANTHEMUM

May lily

CONVALLARIACEAE/LILIACEAE

Genus of perennials with extensive, spreading rhizomes. Is useful as a groundcover in woodlands and wild areas. Prefers shade and organic, moist, sandy, neutral to acidic soil. Propagate by seed in autumn or by division in any season.
***M. bifolium*.** Spreading, rhizomatous perennial. H 4in (10cm), S indefinite. Pairs of large, oval, glossy, dark green leaves with wavy edges arise directly from rhizomes. Slender stems each produce a raceme of 4-petaled white flowers in early summer, followed by small, spherical red berries. May be invasive. Z4–5 H5–1.
M. canadense illus. p.363.

MAIHUENIA

CACTACEAE

Genus of slow-growing, summer-flowering, alpine cacti, clump-forming with age, with cylindrical stems. Requires sun and well-drained soil. Protect from winter rain. Propagate by seed or stem cuttings in spring or summer.
M. poeppigii illus. p.477.

MALCOLMIA

BRASSICACEAE/CRUCIFERAE

Genus of spring- to autumn-flowering annuals. Grow in sun and in fertile, well-drained soil. Propagate by seed sown outdoors in spring, summer or early autumn. Self-seeds freely.
M. maritima illus. p.323.

MALEPHORA

AIZOACEAE

Genus of erect or spreading succulents with semi-cylindrical leaves. Needs sun and very well-drained soil. Propagate by seed or stem cuttings in spring or summer.
M. crocea illus. p.480.

MALOPE

MALVACEAE

Genus of annuals grown for their showy flowers that are ideal for cutting. Grow in sun and in fertile, well-drained soil. Propagate by seed sown outdoors in spring. Self-seeds freely.
M. trifida illus. p.324.

MALUS

Crabapple

ROSACEAE

Genus of deciduous, mainly spring-flowering trees and shrubs grown for their shallowly cup-shaped flowers, fruits, foliage, or autumn color. Crabapples may be used to make preserves. Prefers full sun but tolerates semi-shade; grows in any but waterlogged soil. In winter, cut out dead or diseased wood and prune to maintain a balanced branch system. Propagate by budding in late summer or by grafting in midwinter. Trees are sometimes attacked by aphids, caterpillars, and spider mite and are susceptible to fireblight, mildew, and apple scab.
***M.* 'American Beauty'.** Vigorous, medium-sized, spreading tree with bronze foliage. H 20–25ft (6–8m) S 25–30ft (8–10m). Flowers are double, deep red, but few fruits are produced. Susceptible to scab. Z5–8 H8–5.
M.* x *arnoldiana illus. p.87.
***M.* x *atrosanguinea*.** Deciduous, spreading tree. H and S 20ft (6m). Produces oval, glossy, dark green leaves. Red flower buds open to single, rich pink blooms in late spring. Bears small, rounded, red-flushed yellow crabapples. Z4–8 H8–1.
M. baccata (Siberian crab). Deciduous, spreading tree. H and S 50ft (15m). Has oval, dark green leaves, a profusion of single white flowers from mid- to late spring, and tiny, rounded red or yellow crabapples. Z3–7 H7-1. var. ***mandschurica*** illus. p.74.
***M.* 'Candied Apple'**, syn. 'Weeping Candied Apple'. Small weeping tree H and S 15ft (5m). Oval, textured leaves have a reddish tint. Buds are dark red and open to single pink flowers. Fruit is dark red and persistent. Z5–8 H8–5.
***M.* 'Chilko'.** Deciduous, spreading tree. H and S 25ft (8m). Oval, dark green leaves are reddish purple when young. Has single, rose-pink flowers in midspring, followed by large, rounded, bright crimson crabapples. Z5–8 H8–5.
***M. coronaria* 'Charlottae'.** Deciduous, spreading tree. H and S 28ft (9m). Broadly oval, lobed or deeply toothed leaves are dark green, turning red in autumn. Semi-double, pale pink flowers are borne in late spring and early summer. Z4–8 H8–1.
***M.* 'Cowichan'** illus. p.94.
***M.* 'Dolgo'.** Wide, spreading tree with an open habit. H and S 30ft (10m). Pink buds open to large, fragrant, white flowers. Fruit are glossy red, about ½in (1cm) in diameter. They fall early but are tasty and good for jelly. Good disease resistance but blooms well only every other year. Z4–8 H8–1.
M. floribunda illus. p.88.
***M.* 'Golden Hornet'**, syn. *M.* x *zumi* 'Golden Hornet', illus. p.97.
***M.* x *hartwigii* 'Katherine'.** See *M.* 'Katherine'.
M. hupehensis illus. p.74.
***M.* 'Indian Magic'.** Small tree with a rounded habit. H and S 20ft (6m). Buds are red and open to single, deep pink flowers. Fruit is glossy red becoming orange with age, and persisting. Susceptible to scab. Z5–8 H8–5.
***M.* 'Inglis'** see *M.* 'White Angel'.
***M.* 'John Downie'** illus. p.95.
***M.* 'Lemoinei'**, syn. *M.* x *purpurea* 'Lemoinei', illus. p.89.
***M.* 'Magdeburgensis'** illus. p.88.
***M.* 'Marshall Oyama'** illus. p.96.
***M.* x *moerlandsii* 'Profusion'.** See *M.* 'Profusion'.
M. niedzwetskyana, syn. *M. pumila* var. *niedzwetskyana*. Deciduous, spreading tree. H 20ft (6m), S 25ft (8m). Oval leaves are red when young, later purple. Produces clusters of single, deep reddish purple flowers in late spring, then very large, conical, reddish purple crabapples.
***M.* 'Pink Spires'.** An upright tree with foliage that is tinged red in spring, turning green later. H 25ft (8m) S 15ft (5m). Dark mauve buds open the same

color but fade to pale mauve as the flowers age. Fruit are dark red and last well. Moderately susceptible to scab. Z5–8 H8–5.
M. prattii. Deciduous tree, upright when young, later spreading. H and S 30ft (10m). Oval, red-stalked, glossy, midgreen leaves become orange and red in autumn. Single white flowers in late spring are followed by small, rounded or egg-shaped, white-flecked red crabapples. Z5–8 H8–5.
***M.* 'Professor Sprenger'** illus. p.96.
***M.* 'Profusion'**, syn. *M.* x *moerlandsii* 'Profusion', illus. p.77.
M. prunifolia illus. p.95.
M. pumila var. ***niedzwetskyana.*** See *M. niedzwetskyana.*
M.* x *purpurea (Purple crab). Deciduous, spreading tree. H 25ft (8m), S 30ft (10m). Oval, young leaves are reddish, maturing to green. Single, deep ruby red flowers that become paler with age are produced in late spring and are followed by rounded, reddish purple crabapples. Z5–8 H8–5. **'Lemoinei'** see *M.* 'Lemoinei'. **'Neville Copeman'** see *M.* 'Neville Copeman'.
***M.* 'Red Jade'**, syn. *M.* x *schiedeckeri* 'Red Jade'. Deciduous, weeping tree. H 12ft (4m), S 20ft (6m). In late spring has single white flowers, sometimes pale pink-flushed, then long-lasting, rounded to egg-shaped red crabapples. Leaves are dark green and oval. Z4–8 H6–1.
***M.* 'Red Splendor'.** Upright open tree. H 30ft (10m) S 20ft (6m). Foliage is dark green but turns purple in fall. Flowers are rose pink and single, and the fruit is red. Moderately susceptible to fireblight. Z4–8 H8–1.
M.* x *robusta. Vigorous, deciduous, spreading tree. H 40ft (12m), S 30ft (10m). Bears masses of single white or pink flowers above oval, dark green leaves in late spring. These are followed by long-lasting, rounded yellow or red crabapples. Z4–8 H8–1. **'Yellow Siberian'** produces white flowers, which are sometimes pink-tinged, and yellow crabapples. Z4–8 H8–4.
***M.* 'Royal Beauty'.** A small weeping tree with reddish purple leaves that turn green. H 6ft (2m) S 8ft (2.5m). Flowers are dark red-purple, and the fruit is dark red. Z5–8 H8–5.
***M.* 'Royalty'** illus. p.89.
M. sargentii, syn. *M. toringo* subsp. *sargentii*, illus. p.116.
***M.* x *schiedeckeri* 'Red Jade'.** See *M.*'Red Jade'.
M. sieboldii, syn. *M. toringo*, illus. p.130.
***M.* 'Snowdrift'.** Dense, rounded, vigorous tree with glossy, dark green foliage. H and S 20ft (6m). Abundant white flowers and persistent, orange-red fruits. Somewhat susceptible to fireblight. Z5–8 H8–5.
***M.* 'Thunderchild'.** A small, upright tree H 15ft (5m) S 10ft (3m) with single rose-pink flowers and dark red fruits. Very good disease resistance.
M. toringo. See *M. sieboldii*. subsp. ***sargentii*** see *M. sargentii.*
M. toringoides. Deciduous, spreading tree. H 25ft (8m), S 30ft (10m). Oval, deeply lobed, glossy, bright green leaves turn yellow in autumn. Bears single white flowers in late spring and rounded or egg-shaped, red-flushed yellow crabapples in autumn. Z5–8 H8–5.
M. transitoria. Deciduous, spreading, elegant tree. H 25ft (8m), S 30ft (10m). Oval, deeply lobed, midgreen leaves turn yellow in autumn. Has masses of single white flowers in late spring, followed by small, rounded, pale yellow crabapples. Z5–8 H8–5.
M. trilobata. Deciduous, conical tree. H 50ft (15m), S 22ft (7m). Has maple-like, lobed, glossy, bright green leaves that often become brightly colored in autumn. Bears single white flowers in early summer, followed by small, rounded or pear-shaped red or yellow crabapples. Z5–8 H8–5.
M. tschonoskii. Deciduous, conical tree. H 40ft (12m), S 22ft (7m). Broadly oval, glossy, midgreen leaves turn brilliant shades of orange, red, and purple in autumn. Single, pink-tinged white flowers borne in late spring are succeeded by rounded, red-flushed, yellowish green crabapples. Z5–8 H8–5.
***M.* 'Van Eseltine'.** Deciduous, upright tree. H 20ft (6m), S 12ft (4m). Bears double pink flowers in late spring and rounded yellow crabapples in autumn. Has oval, dark green leaves. Z4–8 H8–1.
***M.* 'Veitch's Scarlet'** illus. p.94.
'Weeping Candied Apple'. See **'Candied Apple'**
***M.* 'White Angel'**, syn. *M.* 'Inglis'. Rounded tree that tends to lose its shape because of its heavy fruiting. H and S 20ft (6m). Abundant white flowers open from pale pink buds. Fruit is a glossy red and persists well. Quite good disease resistance. Z5–8 H8–5.
M. yunnanensis var. ***veitchii*** illus. p.91.
M.* x *zumi* 'Calocarpa'**, syn. *M.* x *z.* var. *calocarpa*, illus. p.96. var. ***calocarpa see *M.* x *z.* 'Calocarpa'. **'Golden Hornet'** see *M.* 'Golden Hornet'.

MALVA
Mallow

MALVACEAE

Genus of annuals, biennials, and free-flowering, short-lived perennials. Requires sun and fertile, well-drained soil. Propagate species by seed in autumn, selected forms by cuttings from firm, basal shoots in late spring or summer. These shoots may be encouraged by cutting the plant back after first flowers have faded.
M. moschata illus. p.243.

Malvastrum capensis. See *Anisodontea capensis*.

MALVAVISCUS

MALVACEAE

Genus of evergreen shrubs and trees grown for their flowers. Requires a position in full light and in fertile, well-drained soil. Water containerized plants freely during growing season, moderately at other times. To maintain shape, flowered stems may be cut back hard in late winter. Propagate by seed in spring or by semi-ripe cuttings in summer. Whitefly and spider mite may be troublesome.
M. arboreus illus. p.121.

MAMMILLARIA
Pincushion cactus

CACTACEAE

Genus of hemispherical, spherical or columnar cacti grown for their rings of funnel-shaped flowers that develop near crowns. Flowers, offsets, and long, slender to spherical seed pods grow between tubercles on a spiny green stem with extended areoles. Requires full sun and very well-drained soil. Keep almost completely dry in winter; otherwise, plants rot easily. Propagate by seed in spring or summer.
M. bocasana illus. p.471.
M. candida (Snowball pincushion). Slow-growing, clump-forming cactus. H and S 6in (15cm). Columnar green stem is densely covered with short, stiff white spines. Produces cream to rose flowers, ½–¾in (1–2cm) across, in spring. Water sparingly in summer. Z12–15 H12–10.
M. centricirrha. See *M. magnimamma.*
M. conoidea. See *Neolloydia conoidea.*
M. densispina. Slow-growing, spherical cactus. H 4in (10cm), S 8in (20cm). Has a green stem densely covered with thick, golden spines and, in spring, yellow flowers, ½–¾in (1–2cm) wide. Z12–15 H12–10.
M. elegans of gardens. See *M. haageana.*
M. elongata illus. p.470.
M. geminispina illus. p.465.
M. gracilis. Clump-forming cactus. H 2in (5cm), S 8in (20cm). Produces a columnar green stem densely covered with pure white spines. In early summer carries pale cream flowers, ½–¾in (1–2cm) across. Stem is shallow-rooted and reroots readily. Z12–15 H12–10. var. ***fragilis***, H 1½in (4cm), is more fragile and has off-white spines.
M. haageana, syn. *M. elegans* of gardens. Spherical to columnar cactus. H 12in (30cm), S 8in (20cm). Bears a green stem densely covered with short, bristly spines and bright red flowers, ½in (1cm) across, in spring. Offsets occasionally. Z12–15 H12–10.
M. hahniana illus. p.465.
M. magnimamma, syn. *M. centricirrha.* Clump-forming cactus. H 1ft (30cm), S 2ft (60cm). Green stem has pronounced, angular, dark green tubercles with white spines of variable length. Bears cream, pink, or red flowers, ½–¾in (1–2cm) wide, in spring and possibly again in late summer. Z12–15 H12–10.
M. microhelia illus. p.478.
M. plumosa illus. p.469.
M. prolifera (Strawberry cactus). Clump-forming cactus. H 4in (10cm), S 12in (30cm). Green stem bears dense golden to white spines. Produces masses of cream or yellow flowers, ½–¾in (1–2cm) wide, in summer, followed by red berries that taste like strawberries. Z12–15 H12–10.
M. rhodantha. Spherical to columnar cactus. H and S 2ft (60cm). Green stem, branching from crown with age, is densely covered with brown to yellow spines, often curved. In late summer produces bright red flowers, ½–¾in (1–2cm) across. Z12–15 H12–10.
M. schiedeana illus. p.470.
M. sempervivi illus. p.472.
M. zeilmanniana illus. p.473.

MANDEVILLA,
syn. DIPLADENIA

APOCYNACEAE

Genus of evergreen, semi-evergreen or deciduous, woody-stemmed, twining climbers grown for their large, trumpet-shaped flowers. Grow in any well-drained soil, with light shade in summer. Water freely when in full growth, sparingly at other times. Provide support. Thin out and spur back congested growth in early spring. Propagate by seed in spring or by semi-ripe cuttings in summer. Whitefly and spider mite may cause problems. Contact with the sap may cause skin irritation, and all parts may cause mild stomach upset if ingested.
***M.* x *amabilis* 'Alice du Pont'.** See *M.* x *amoena* 'Alice du Pont'.
***M.* x *amoena* 'Alice du Pont'**, syn. *M.* x *amabilis* 'Alice du Pont', illus. p.209.
M. boliviensis, syn. *Dipladenia boliviensis*. Vigorous, evergreen, woody-stemmed, twining climber. Tender. H to 12ft (4m). Oblong, pointed leaves are lustrous green. Large, trumpet-shaped white flowers with gold eyes are produced in small clusters in summer.
M. laxa, syn. *M. suaveolens*, *M. tweediana* (Chilean jasmine). Fast-growing, deciduous or semi-evergreen, woody-stemmed, twining climber. H 15ft (5m) or more. Tender. Oval leaves have heart-shaped bases. Clusters of fragrant white flowers are borne in summer.
M. splendens, syn. *Dipladenia splendens*, illus. p.204.
M. suaveolens. See *M. laxa*.
M. tweediana. See *M. laxa*.

MANDRAGORA
Mandrake

SOLANACEAE

Genus of rosetted perennials with large, deep, fleshy roots. Needs sun or partial shade and deep, organic, well-drained soil. Resents being transplanted. Propagate by seed in autumn. Alkaloids

in the plant may be harmful if ingested.
M. officinarum illus. p.371.

MANETTIA

RUBIACEAE

Genus of evergreen, soft- or semi-woody-stemmed, twining climbers grown for their small but showy flowers. Grow in any organic, well-drained soil, with partial shade in summer. Water regularly, sparingly when temperatures are low. Stems need support. Cut back if required in spring. Propagate by softwood or semi-ripe cuttings in summer. Whitefly is sometimes a problem.
M. bicolor. See *M. luteorubra.*
M. cordifolia (Firecracker vine). Fast-growing, evergreen, soft-stemmed, twining climber. H 6ft (2m) or more. Has narrowly heart-shaped, glossy leaves. Funnel-shaped red flowers, sometimes yellow flushed on the lobes, appear in small clusters in summer. Z12–15 H12–10.
M. inflata. See *M. luteorubra.*
M. luteorubra, syn. *M. bicolor*, *M. inflata*, illus. p.205.

MANGLIETIA

MAGNOLIACEAE

Genus of evergreen trees grown for their foliage and flowers. Provide organic, moisture-retentive but well-drained, acidic soil and full light or partial shade. Water potted plants freely when in full growth, less at other times. Pruning is tolerated if necessary. Propagate by seed in spring.
M. insignis, syn. *Magnolia insignis*. Evergreen, broadly conical tree. H 25–40ft (8–12m) or more, S 10–15ft (3–5m) or more. Leaves are narrowly oval, lustrous, dark green above, bluish green beneath. In early summer produces solitary, magnolia-like pink to carmine flowers that are cream-flushed. Z11 H12–10.

MARANTA

MARANTACEAE

Genus of evergreen perennials grown for their distinctively patterned, colored foliage. Needs constant, high humidity and a shaded position away from draughts or wind. Grow in organic, well-drained soil. Propagate by division in spring or summer or by stem cuttings in summer.
M. leuconeura (Prayer plant). **'Erythroneura'** (syn. *M.l.* 'Erythrophylla') illus. p.303. **'Erythrophylla'.** See *M.l.* 'Erythroneura'. var. ***kerchoviana*** illus. p.304. var. ***massangeana*** is an evergreen, short-stemmed perennial, branching at the base. H and S 1ft (30cm). Each oblong, velvety, dark green leaf (often purplish green below), 6in (15cm) long, has a wide, irregular, pale midrib and white, lateral veins Leaves stand upright at night but lie flat during the day. Bears small, 3-petaled white to mauve flowers in slender, upright spikes year-round. Z14–15 H12–1.

Marginatocereus marginatus. See *Pachycereus marginatus.*

MARGYRICARPUS

ROSACEAE

Genus of evergreen shrubs grown for their fruits. Is good for rock gardens. Needs a sunny position and well-drained soil. Propagate by softwood cuttings in early summer or by seed in autumn.
M. pinnatus, syn. *M. setosus* (Pearl berry). Evergreen, prostrate shrub. H 9–12in (23–30cm), S 3ft (1m). Has dark green leaves divided into linear, silky leaflets. Has tiny, inconspicuous, green flowers in early summer, then small, globose, glossy white fruits. Z8–10 H10–8.
M. setosus. See *M. pinnatus.*

Marsdenia erecta. See *Cionura erecta.*

MARTYNIA

PEDALIACEAE

Genus of annuals grown for their flowers and horned fruits. Needs a sunny, sheltered site and fertile, well-drained soil. Propagate by seed sown under glass in early spring.
M. annua illus. p.320.
M. louisianica. See *Proboscidea louisianica.*

MASDEVALLIA

See also ORCHIDS.
M. coccinea (illus. p.297). Evergreen, epiphytic orchid for a cool greenhouse. H 6in (15cm). Narrowly oval leaves are 4in (10cm) long. Bears rich cerise flowers, 3in (8cm) long, in summer. Needs shade in summer. Z14–15 H12–6.
M. infracta (illus. p.296). Evergreen, epiphytic orchid for a cool greenhouse. H 6in (15cm). Narrowly oval leaves are 4in (10cm) long. Bears rounded, red-and-white flowers, 2in (5cm) long, with tail-like greenish sepals, in summer. Needs shade in summer. Z14–15 H12–6.
M. tovarensis (illus. p.296). Evergreen, epiphytic orchid for a cool greenhouse. H 6in (15cm). Has oval leaves, 4in (10cm) long, and in autumn milky white flowers, 1½in (4cm) long, with short-tailed sepals, singly or up to 3 to a stem. Grow in shade in summer. Z14–15 H12–6.
M. wageneriana (illus. p.298). Evergreen, epiphytic orchid for a cool greenhouse. H 3in (8cm). Narrowly oval leaves are 4in (10cm) long. Bears pale yellow flowers, 1½in (4cm) long, with long, tail-like sepals, singly or in pairs in summer. Needs summer shade. Z14–15 H12–6.

MATTEUCCIA

DRYOPTERIDACEAE/WOODSIACEAE

Genus of deciduous, rhizomatous ferns. Prefers semi-shade and wet soil. Remove faded fronds regularly and divide plants when crowded. Propagate by division in autumn or winter.
M. orientalis. Deciduous, rhizomatous fern. H and S to 3ft (1m). Produces a "shuttlecock" of sterile, arching, broadly ovate, divided fronds, to 32in (80cm) long, light green when young, becoming darker. Fertile, erect, blackish green fronds appear from the center of the plant in summer. Z3–8 H8–1.
M. struthiopteris illus. p.312.

MATTHIOLA

Stock

BRASSICACEAE/CRUCIFERAE

Genus of annuals, biennials, perennials, and evergreen subshrubs. Flowers of most annual or biennial stocks are highly scented and excellent for cutting. Grow in sun or semi-shade and in fertile, well-drained, ideally lime-rich soil. Tall cultivars may need support. If grown as biennials outdoors, provide protection during winter.
To produce flowers outdoors the same summer, sow seed of annuals under glass in early spring, or outdoors in midspring. Sow seed of perennials under glass in spring. Propagate subshrubs by semi-ripe cuttings in summer. Is prone to aphids, flea beetle, club root, downy mildew, and botrytis.
***M.* Brompton Group** (mixed) illus. p.321, (pink) illus. p.323.
***M.* East Lothian Group.** Group of fast-growing, upright, bushy biennials and short-lived perennials grown as annuals. H and S 1ft (30cm). Has lance-shaped, grayish green leaves and, in summer, spikes, 6in (15cm) or more long, of scented, 4-petaled, single or double flowers, in shades of pink, red, purple, yellow, or white. Z8–9 H9–1.
***M.* 'Giant Excelsior'** illus. p.321.
***M.* 'Giant Imperial'** illus. p.318.
M. incana (Brompton stock). Fast-growing, upright, bushy biennial or short-lived perennial grown as an annual. H 1–2ft (30–60cm), S 1ft (30cm). Has lance-shaped, grayish green leaves and, in summer, scented, 4-petaled, light purple flowers borne in spikes, 3–6in (7–15cm) long. Z5–8 H8–5.
***M.* 'Mammoth Column'.** Fast-growing, upright, bushy biennial or short-lived perennial grown as an annual. H to 2½ft (75cm), S 1ft (30cm). Has lance-shaped, grayish green leaves and, in summer, 12–15in (30–38cm) long spikes, of scented, 4-petaled flowers, available in mixed or single colors. Flowers are excellent for cutting. Z8–9 H9–1.
***M.* Park Series.** Group of fast-growing, upright, bushy biennials and short-lived perennials grown as annuals. H and S to 1ft (30cm). Lance-shaped leaves are grayish green. In summer, spikes, at least 6in (15cm) long, of scented, 4-petaled flowers are borne in a wide range of colors. Z8–9 H9–1.
***M.* Ten-week Group.** Group of fast-growing, upright, bushy biennials and short-lived perennials grown as annuals. H and S to 1ft (30cm). Has lance-shaped, grayish green leaves. Has scented, 4-petaled flowers, in spikes at least 6in (15cm) long, in a wide range of colors in summer. Dwarf (illus. p.325) and "selectable" cultivars have double flowers. Z8–9 H9–1.
***M.* 'Trysomic'.** Fast-growing, upright, bushy biennial or short-lived perennial grown as an annual. H and S to 1ft (30cm). Lance-shaped leaves are grayish green. Spikes, at least 6in (15cm) long, of scented, mostly double flowers are produced in a wide range of colors in summer. Z8–9 H9–1.

Matucana aurantiaca. See *Oreocereus aurantiacus.*
Matucana haynei. See *Oreocereus haynei.*

MAURANDYA

SCROPHULARIACEAE

Genus of twining, woody-based, perennial climbers grown against a wall or to clothe a trellis. Needs full sun and moderately fertile, moist but well-drained soil. Propagate by seed in spring or softwood cuttings in late spring.
M. barclayana, syn. *Asarina barclayana*. Evergreen, soft-stemmed, scandent climber, herbaceous in cold climates. H to 6ft (2m). Has angular, heart-shaped, hairless leaves. Trumpet-shaped white, pink, or purple flowers, each with a green or whitish throat, 2½–3in (6–7cm) long, are produced in summer-autumn. Z9–10 H10–9.
M. erubescens. See *Lophospermum erubescens.*

MAXILLARIA

See also ORCHIDS.
M. picta. Evergreen, epiphytic orchid for a cool greenhouse. H 9in (23cm). Fragrant, deep yellow to white flowers, 1in (2.5cm) across, marked purple to dark reddish brown outside, are produced singly beneath foliage in winter. Has narrowly oval leaves, 6–9in (15–23cm) long. Requires semi-shade in summer. Z14–15 H12–6.
M. porphyrostele (illus. p.299). Evergreen, epiphytic orchid for a cool greenhouse. H 3in (8cm). White- and red-lipped yellow flowers, ½in (1cm) across, are borne singly in summer-autumn. Narrowly oval leaves are 3in (8cm) long. Grow in good light during summer. Z14–15 H12–6.
M. tenuifolia. Evergreen, epiphytic orchid for a cool greenhouse. H 6in (15cm). Fragrant, white-lipped yellow flowers, 1in (2.5cm) across and heavily overlaid with red, are borne singly throughout summer. Has narrowly oval leaves, 6in (15cm) long. Needs good light in summer. Z14–15 H12–6.

MAZUS

SCROPHULARIACEAE

Genus of creeping, spring-flowering perennials. Is useful for rock gardens and in paving. Needs a sunny site and moist soil. Propagate by division in spring or by seed in autumn.
M. reptans illus. p.368.

MECONOPSIS

PAPAVERACEAE

Genus of perennials, some short-lived, others monocarpic (die after flowering), grown for their flowers. Needs shade and, in warm areas, a cool position. Most prefer organic, moist, neutral to acidic soil. All but *M.* x *sheldonii* may be propagated by seed when fresh, in late summer; *M. cambrica*, *M. grandis*, *M. quintuplinervia*, *M.* x *sheldonii* and their cultivars may also be propagated by division after flowering.
M. betonicifolia illus. p.253.
M. cambrica illus. p.275.
M. grandis illus. p.253.
M. integrifolia illus. p.292.
M. paniculata. Short-lived, clump-forming perennial that dies after flowering. H 5ft (1.5m), S 2ft (60cm). Produces racemes of nodding, shallowly cup-shaped yellow flowers in late spring or early summer. Bears large rosettes of oblong to lance-shaped, deeply lobed and cut, hairy, yellowish green leaves. Z8–9 H9–8.
M. quintuplinervia illus. p.271.
M.* x *sheldonii. Clump-forming perennial. H 4–5ft (1.2–1.5m), S 1½–2ft (45–60cm). In early summer bears clusters of cup-shaped, clear deep blue flowers. Has rosettes of oblong to oval, toothed, hairy, midgreen leaves. Divide every three years to maintain vigor. Z7–8 H8–7. **'Branklyn'** bears vivid blue flowers and coarsely toothed leaves. **'Slieve Donard'** has slightly smaller flowers and leaves with fewer teeth.

MEDICAGO

LEGUMINOSAE/PAPILIONACEAE

Genus of annuals, perennials, and evergreen shrubs grown for their flowers. Is good in mild, coastal areas as is very wind-resistant. Requires sun and well-drained soil. Cut out dead wood in spring. Propagate shrubs by semi-ripe or softwood cuttings in summer or by seed in autumn or spring, annuals and perennials by seed in autumn or spring.
M. arborea (Moon trefoil, Tree medick). Evergreen, bushy, dense shrub. H and S 6ft (2m). Bears clusters of small, pealike yellow flowers from midspring to late autumn or winter, followed by curious, flattened, snail-like green then brown seed pods. Has dark green leaves, each composed of 3 narrowly triangular leaflets that are silky-haired when young. Z7–9 H9–7.

MEDINILLA

MELASTOMATACEAE

Genus of evergreen shrubs and scrambling climbers grown for their flowers and foliage. Needs partial shade and organic, well-drained soil. Water potted plants freely when in full growth, moderately at other times. Propagate by greenwood cuttings in spring or summer.
M. magnifica illus. p.141.

MEEHANIA

LABIATAE/LAMIACEAE

Genus of perennials often with creeping stems, grown mainly as a groundcover. Prefers shade and well-drained but not dry, organic soil. May be propagated by seed, division, or stem cuttings in spring.
M. urticifolia. Trailing, hairy perennial with long, creeping, leafy stems and erect flowering stems. H to 1ft (30cm), S indefinite. Oval to triangular, toothed leaves are 4in (10cm) or more long on the creeping stems and smaller on flowering stems. Whorls of fragrant, 2-lipped, purplish blue flowers, to 2in (5cm) long, are carried in erect spikes in late spring. Z5–8 H8–5.

Megasea. Reclassified as *Bergenia*.

MELALEUCA

MYRTACEAE

Genus of evergreen, spring- and summer-flowering trees and shrubs grown for their flowers and overall appearance. Needs full light and well-drained soil, preferably without much nitrogen. Some species tolerate waterlogged soils. Water containerized specimens moderately, less in low temperatures. Propagate by seed in spring or by semi-ripe cuttings in summer.
M. armillaris (Bracelet honey myrtle). Evergreen, rounded, wiry-stemmed shrub or tree. H 10–20ft (3–6m), S 4–10ft (1.2–3m). Has needlelike, deep green leaves and, in summer, dense, bottlebrush-like clusters, 1¼–2½in (3–6cm) long, each flower consisting of a small brush of white stamens. Z12-15 H12–10.
M. elliptica illus. p.142.
M. hypericifolia. Evergreen, rounded shrub. H and S 6–15ft (2–5m). Leaves are oblong to elliptic and mid- to deep green above, paler beneath. Crimson flowers, each composed of a ¾–1in (2–2.5cm) long brush of stamens of the same color, are borne in summer, mainly in bottlebrush-like spikes, 1½–3in (4–8cm) long. Z12-15 H12–10.
M. nesophila, syn. *M. nesophylla*, illus. p.145.
M. nesophylla. See *M. nesophila*.
M. quinquenervia. See *M. viridiflora* var. *rubriflora*.
M. squarrosa (Scented paper-bark). Evergreen, erect, wiry-stemmed shrub or tree. H 10–20ft (3–6m), S 2–4m (6–12ft). Has tiny, oval, deep green leaves. Bears 1½in (4cm) long spikes of scented flowers, each consisting of a tiny brush of cream stamens, in late spring and summer.
M. viridiflora var. ***rubriflora***, syn. *M. quinquenervia* (Paper-bark tree). Strong-growing, evergreen, rounded tree. H 20–40ft (6–12m), S 10–20ft (3–6m). Leaves are elliptic and lustrous. Has peeling, papery, tan-colored bark and, in spring, small white or creamy pink flowers in bottlebrush-like clusters. Tolerates waterlogged soil. Z12-15 H12–10.

MELASPHAERULA

IRIDACEAE

Genus of one species of spring-flowering corm grown mainly for botanical interest. Needs sun and well-drained soil. Plant in autumn and keep watered until after flowering, then dry off. Propagate by seed or offsets in autumn.
M. graminea. See *M. ramosa*.
M. ramosa, syn. *M. graminea*. Spring-flowering corm. H to 24in (60cm), S 4–6in (10–15cm). Has narrowly sword-shaped, semi-erect leaves in a basal fan. Wiry, branched stem bears loose sprays of small, pendent, funnel-shaped, yellowish green flowers with pointed petals.

MELASTOMA

MELASTOMATACEAE

Genus of evergreen, mainly summer-flowering shrubs and trees grown for their flowers and foliage. Requires full light or partial shade and fertile, well-drained soil. Water containerized specimens freely when in full growth, moderately at other times. Pruning is tolerated in late winter if necessary. Propagate by softwood or greenwood cuttings in spring or summer. Spider mite and whitefly may cause problems.
M. candidum. Evergreen, rounded, bristly-stemmed shrub. H and S 3–6ft (1–2m). Bears oval, leathery, bristly leaves. Small, terminal clusters of fragrant, 5–7-petaled white or pink flowers are produced profusely in summer. Z9–10 H10–9.

MELIA

MELIACEAE

Genus of deciduous, spring-flowering trees grown for their foliage, flowers, and fruits. Is useful for very dry soil and does well in coastal gardens in mild areas. Requires a position in full sun; grows in any well-drained soil. Propagate by seed in autumn.
M. azedarach illus. p.76.

MELIANTHUS

MELIANTHACEAE

Genus of evergreen perennials and shrubs grown primarily for their foliage. Requires sun and fertile, well-drained soil. Water potted specimens freely in summer, moderately at other times. Long stems may be shortened in early spring. May be propagated by seed in spring or by greenwood cuttings in summer. Spider mite may be troublesome.
M. major (Honeybush). Evergreen, sprawling, sparingly branched shrub. H and S 6–10ft (2–3m). Leaves are 10–18in (25–45cm) long, with 7–13 oval, toothed, blue-gray leaflets. Has tubular, rich brownish red flowers in terminal spikes, 12in (30cm) long, in spring-summer. Z8–11 H12–8.

MELICA

GRAMINEAE/POACEAE

See also GRASSES, BAMBOOS, RUSHES and SEDGES.
M. altissima (Siberian melic, Tall melic). Evergreen, tuft-forming, perennial grass. H 24in (60cm), S 8in (20cm). Bears slender stems and broad, midgreen leaves, rough beneath. In summer produces pendent tawny spikelets in narrow panicles. Z5–8 H8–5.**'Atropurpurea'** illus. p.307.

MELICYTUS,
syn. HYMENANTHERA

VIOLACEAE

Genus of evergreen shrubs and trees grown for their overall appearance and ornamental fruits. Requires a position in full light or partial shade and in well-drained soil. Water pot plants moderately, less in winter. Pruning is tolerated if required. Propagate by seed when ripe (in autumn) or in spring.
M. crassifolius, syn. *Hymenanthera crassifolia*. Evergreen, densely twiggy shrub of irregular outline. H and S to 4ft (1.2m). Bears narrowly oval to oblong, leathery, midgreen leaves. Carries tiny, bell-shaped, 5-petaled yellow flowers in spring-summer, followed by egg-shaped purple fruits.
M. ramiflorus (Mahoe, Whiteywood). Evergreen, spreading shrub or tree. H and S 20–30ft (6–10m). Bark is gray-white. Bears lance-shaped, bluntly serrated, bright green leaves. Small, rounded greenish flowers are produced in axillary clusters in summer, followed by tiny violet to purple-blue berries. Z5–8 H8–5.

MELINIS

GRAMINEAE/POACEAE

See also GRASSES, BAMBOOS, RUSHES and SEDGES.
M. repens, syn. *Rhynchelytrum repens*, *R. roseum* (Natal grass, Ruby grass). Tuft-forming, annual or short-lived, perennial grass. H 4–6ft (1.2–2m), S 2–3ft (60cm–1m). Leaves are midgreen, flat, and finely pointed. Produces loose panicles of awned pink spikelets in summer.

MELIOSMA

MELIOSMACEAE

Genus of deciduous trees and shrubs grown for their habit, foliage, and

flowers, which, however, do not appear reliably. Prefers full sun and deep, fertile, well-drained soil. Propagate by seed in autumn.
M. oldhamii. See *M. pinnata* var. *oldhamii*.
M. pinnata var. ***oldhamii***, syn. *M. oldhamii.* Deciduous, thick-branched tree, upright when young, spreading when mature. H 30ft (10m), S 20ft (6m). Has very large, dark green leaves divided into 5–13 oval leaflets. Bears large clusters of small, fragrant, star-shaped white flowers in early summer. Z9–10 H10–9.
M. veitchiorum illus. p.80.

MELITTIS
Bastard balm

LABIATAE/LAMIACEAE

Genus of one species of summer-flowering perennial. Does best in light shade and requires fertile, well-drained soil. Propagate by seed in autumn or by division in spring or autumn.
M. melissophyllum illus. p.277.

MELOCACTUS
Turk's cap

CACTACEAE

Genus of spherical, ribbed cacti. On reaching flowering size, usually 6in (15cm) high, stems produce woolly crowns; then stems appear to stop growing while woolly crowns slowly develop into columns. Has funnel-shaped flowers in summer, followed by elongated or rounded red, pink, or white seed pods.. Requires a position in full sun and extremely well-drained soil. Propagate by seed in spring or summer.
M. actinacanthus. See *M. matanzanus*.
M. bahiensis. Spherical cactus. H and S 6in (15cm). Dull green stem bears 10–15 ribs. Produces thick, slightly curved, dark brown spines that become paler with age. Crown bears brown bristles and pink flowers, ½–¾in (1–2cm) across, in summer. Z14–15 H12–10.
M. communis. See *M. intortus*.
M. curvispinus, syn. *M. oaxacensis*. Spherical to columnar cactus. H 8in (20cm), S 6in (15cm). Green stem has 15 rounded ribs. Areoles each bear a straight central spine and curved radial spines. Flat, woolly crown bears deep pink flowers, ½in (1cm across, in summer. Z14–15 H12–10.
M. intortus, syn. *M. communis*, illus. p.472.
M. matanzanus, syn. *M. actinacanthus*. Spherical cactus. H and S 4in (10cm). Dark green stem has neat, short spines and develops a woolly crown about 5 years from seed. In summer produces pink flowers, ½in (1cm) across. Z14–15 H12–10.
M. oaxacensis. See *M. curvispinus*.

MENISPERMUM
Moonseed

MENISPERMACEAE

Genus of deciduous, woody or semi-woody, twining climbers grown for their attractive fruits that each contain a crescent-shaped seed – hence the common name. Male and female flowers are carried on separate plants; to produce fruits, plants of both sexes must be grown. Grow in sun and in any well-drained soil. Propagate by seed or suckers in spring. The fruits may cause severe discomfort if ingested.
M. canadense (Canada moonseed, Yellow parilla). Vigorous, deciduous, woody-stemmed, twining climber producing a dense tangle of stems and spreading by underground suckers. H to 15ft (5m). Produces oval to heart-shaped, rounded leaves that are usually 3–7-lobed. Small, cup-shaped, greenish yellow flowers are carried in summer, followed by clusters of poisonous, spherical, glossy blackish fruits. Z5–8 H8–5.

MENTHA
Mint

LABIATAE/LAMIACEAE

Genus of perennials, some of which are semi-evergreen, grown for their aromatic foliage, which is both decorative and used as a culinary herb. Plants are invasive, however, and should be used with caution. Grow in a sunny or shady position and in well-drained soil. Propagate by division in spring or autumn.
M. corsica. See *M. requienii*.
***M. x gentilis* 'Variegata'.** See *M. x gracilis* 'Variegata'.
***M. x gracilis* 'Variegata'**, syn. *M. x gentilis* 'Variegata'. Spreading perennial. H 18in (45cm), S 24in (60cm). Forms a mat of oval, dark green leaves that are speckled and striped with yellow, most conspicuously in full sun. Produces stems that carry whorls of small, 2-lipped, pale mauve flowers in summer. Z6–9 H9–6.
M. x piperita f. ***citrata*** (Eau-de-Cologne mint) is a vigorous, spreading perennial. H 12–24in (30–60cm), S 24in (60cm). Reddish green stems, bearing terminal spikes of small, 2-lipped purple flowers in summer, arise from a carpet of oval, slightly toothed, midgreen leaves that have a scent which is similar to eau de Cologne. Z3–7 H7–1.
M. requienii, syn. *M. corsica* (Corsican mint). Semi-evergreen, mat-forming, creeping perennial. H to ½in (1cm), S indefinite. When they are crushed, the rounded, bright apple green leaves exude a strong peppermint fragrance. Carries tiny, stemless, lavender-purple flowers in summer. Is suitable for a rock garden or paved path. Needs shade and moist soil. Z6–9 H9–6.
M. rotundifolia of gardens. See *M. suaveolens*.
M. suaveolens, syn. *M. rotundifolia* of gardens (Apple mint). **'Variegata'** illus. p.276.

MENTZELIA

LOASACEAE

Genus of annuals, perennials, and evergreen shrubs. Requires a position in sun and in fertile, very well-drained soil; tender species are best grown in pots under glass. Propagate by seed in spring; shrubs may also be propagated by semi-ripe cuttings in summer.
M. lindleyi, syn. *Bartonia aurea*, illus. p.336.

MENYANTHES

MENYANTHACEAE

Genus of deciduous, perennial, marginal water plants grown for their foliage and flowers. Prefers an open, sunny position. Remove fading flower heads and foliage, and divide overcrowded clumps in spring. Propagate by stem cuttings in spring.
M. trifoliata illus. p.446.

MENZIESIA

ERICACEAE

Genus of deciduous shrubs grown for their small, urn-shaped flowers. Needs semi-shade and fertile, moist, peaty, acidic soil. Propagate by softwood cuttings in summer or by seed in autumn.
M. ciliicalyx var. ***lasiophylla.*** See *M.c.* var. *purpurea*. var. ***purpurea*** (syn. *M.c.* var. *lasiophylla*) illus. p.155.

MERENDERA

COLCHICACEAE/LILIACEAE

Genus of corms similar to *Colchicum* but with less showy flowers. Needs a sunny position and well-drained soil. In cool, damp areas grow in an unheated greenhouse or frame where corms can dry out in summer. Plant in autumn and keep watered through winter and spring. Propagate by seed or offsets in autumn.
M. bulbocodium. See *M. montana*.
M. montana, syn. *M. bulbocodium*, illus. p.439.
M. robusta. Spring-flowering corm. H 3in (8cm), S 2–3in (5–8cm). Narrowly lance-shaped, semi-erect, basal leaves appear at the same time as upright, funnel-shaped flowers, 2–2½in (5–6cm) wide, with narrow, pale purplish pink or white petals. Z7–9 H9–7.

MERREMIA

CONVOLVULACEAE

Genus of evergreen, twining climbers grown for their flowers and fruits. Prefers fertile, well-drained soil and full light. Water moderately, much less when not in full growth. Provide support. Thin out congested stems during spring. Propagate by seed in spring. Spider mite may be a problem.
M. tuberosa, syn. *Ipomoea tuberosa*, *Operculina tuberosa* (Wood rose, Yellow morning glory). Fast-growing, evergreen, twining climber. H 20ft (6m) or more. Leaves have 7 radiating lobes. In summer bears funnel-shaped yellow flowers, followed by semi-woody, globose, ivory-brown fruits. Z13-15 H12–10.

MERTENSIA

BORAGINACEAE

Genus of perennials grown for their funnel-shaped flowers. Requires sun or shade and deep, well-drained soil. Propagate by division in spring or by seed in autumn.
M. echioides illus. p.357.
M. maritima illus. p.369.
M. pulmonarioides, syn. *M. virginica*, illus. p.271.
M. virginica. See *M. pulmonarioides*.

MERYTA

ARALIACEAE

Genus of evergreen trees grown for their handsome foliage. Requires full light or partial shade and organic, moisture-retentive but moderately drained soil. Freely water containerized plants in full growth, less at other times. Propagate by semi-ripe cuttings in summer or by seed when ripe in late summer.
M. sinclairii illus. p.100.

Mesembryanthemum cordifolium. See *Aptenia cordifolia*.
Mesembryanthemum criniflorum. See *Dorotheanthus bellidiformis*.
Mesembryanthemum multiradiatum. See *Lampranthus roseus*.

MESPILUS
Medlar

ROSACEAE

Genus of one species of deciduous tree or shrub grown for its habit, flowers, foliage, and edible fruits. Needs sun or semi-shade and fertile, well-drained soil. Propagate species by seed in autumn and named forms (for fruit) by budding in late summer.
M. germanica illus. p.85.

METASEQUOIA

TAXODIACEAE

See also CONIFERS.
M. glyptostroboides illus. p.102.

METROSIDEROS

MYRTACEAE

Genus of evergreen, winter-flowering shrubs, trees, and scrambling climbers grown for their flowers, the trees also for their overall appearance and for shade. Grows in fertile, well-drained soil and in full light. Freely water containerized specimens in full growth, moderately at other times. Pruning is tolerated if necessary. Propagate by seed in spring or by semi-ripe cuttings in summer.
M. excelsus, syn. *M. tomentosus*, illus. p.83.
M. robustus (Rata). Robust, evergreen,

rounded tree. H 70–80ft (20–25m) or more, S 30–50ft (10–15m). Oblong to elliptic, leathery leaves are dark green and lustrous. Produces large clusters of flowers, which are mostly composed of long, dark red stamens, during winter.
M. tomentosus. See *M. excelsus*.

MEUM

APIACEAE/UMBELLIFERAE

Genus of summer-flowering perennials grown for their aromatic leaves. Is useful on banks and in wild gardens. Needs sun and well-drained soil. Propagate by seed when fresh, in autumn.
M. athamanticum (Baldmoney, Spignel). Upright, clump-forming perennial. H 6–18in (15–45cm), S 4–6in (10–15cm). Mainly basal and deeply dissected leaves have narrowly linear leaflets. In summer produces flattish flower heads consisting of clusters of tiny white or purplish white flowers. Z10–15 H12–10.

MICHELIA

MAGNOLIACEAE

Genus of evergreen, winter- to summer-flowering shrubs and trees grown for their flowers and foliage. Provide organic, well-drained, neutral to acidic soil and full light or partial shade. Water potted specimens freely when in full growth, less in winter. Propagate by semi-ripe cuttings in summer or by seed when ripe (in autumn), or in spring.
M. doltsopa illus. p.83.
M. figo illus. p.89.

MICROBIOTA

Russian arbovitae

CUPRESSACEAE

See also CONIFERS.
M. decussata (illus. p.110). Spreading, shrubby conifer. H 20in (50cm), S 6–10ft (2–3m). Flat sprays of scalelike, yellow-green leave turn bronze in winter. Globose, yellow-brown cones have only one seed. Z3–7 H7–1.

Microglossa albescens. See *Aster albescens*.

MICROLEPIA

DENNSTAEDTIACEAE

Genus of deciduous, semi-evergreen or evergreen ferns best grown in pans and hanging baskets. Requires shade or semi-shade and moist soil. Remove faded fronds regularly. Propagate by division in spring or by spores in summer.
M. speluncae illus. p.310.

MICROMERIA

LABIATAE/LAMIACEAE

Genus of evergreen or semi-evergreen shrubs, subshrubs, and perennials suitable for rock gardens and banks. Needs sun and well-drained soil. Propagate by seed in spring or by softwood cuttings in early summer.
M. juliana. Evergreen or semi-evergreen, bushy shrub or subshrub. H and S 12in (30cm). Has small, oval, aromatic green leaves pressed close to stems. In summer, minute, tubular, bright deep pink flowers are carried in whorls on upper parts of stems. Z7–10 H10–7.

MIKANIA

ASTERACEAE/COMPOSITAE

Genus of evergreen or herbaceous, scrambling or twining climbers, shrubs, and erect perennials grown for their foliage and flower heads. Any fertile, well-drained soil is suitable, with partial shade in summer. Water regularly, less when not in full growth. Support for stems is needed, and ties may be necessary. Thin out congested growth in spring. Propagate by semi-ripe or softwood cuttings in summer. Aphids may be a problem.
M. scandens. Herbaceous, twining climber. H 10–15ft (3–5m). Oval to triangular, midgreen leaves have 2 basal lobes. Tiny pink to purple flower heads appear in compact clusters in summer-autumn. Z112–15 H12-10.

MILIUM

GRAMINEAE/POACEAE

See also GRASSES, BAMBOOS, RUSHES and SEDGES.
M. effusum (Wood millet). **'Aureum'** is an evergreen, tuft-forming, perennial grass. H 3ft (1m), S 1ft (30cm). Has flat, golden yellow leaves. Produces open, tiered panicles of greenish yellow spikelets in summer. Self seeds readily in shade. Z6–9 H9–6.

MILLA

ALLIACEAE/LILIACEAE

Genus of summer-flowering bulbs grown for their fragrant flowers, each consisting of a slender tube with 6 spreading, star-shaped petals at the tip. Needs a sunny position and well-drained soil. Plant in spring. After flowering lift bulbs and partially dry off for winter. Propagate by seed or offsets in spring.
M. biflora. Summer-flowering bulb. H 12–18in (30–45cm), S 3–4in (8–10cm). Has long, narrow, semi-erect, basal leaves. Stem bears a loose head of 2–6 erect white flowers, 1¼–2½in (3–6cm) across, each on a slender stalk to 8in (20cm) long. Z9–10 H10–9.

MILTONIA

See also ORCHIDS.
M. candida (illus. p.298). Evergreen, epiphytic orchid for a cool or intermediate greenhouse. H 8in (20cm). Cream-lipped, green-patterned brown flowers, 2in (5cm) across, are borne in spikes in autumn. Has narrowly oval leaves, 4–5in (10–12cm) long. Grow in semi-shade in summer. Z14–15 H12–6.
M. clowesii (illus. p.298). Evergreen, epiphytic orchid for an intermediate greenhouse. H 8in (20cm). In early summer produces large spikes of 1½in (4cm) wide, yellow flowers, barred with reddish brown and each with a white-and-mauve lip. Has broadly oval leaves, 12in (30cm) long. Grow in semi-shade in summer. Z14–15 H12–6.

MILTONIOPSIS

Pansy orchid

See also ORCHIDS.
***M.* Anjou 'St. Patrick'** (illus. p.297). Evergreen, epiphytic orchid for a cool greenhouse. H 6in (15cm). Has sprays of deep crimson flowers, 4in (10cm) across, with red and yellow patterns on each lip, mainly in summer. Narrowly oval, soft leaves are 4–5in (10–12cm) long. Needs shade in summer. Z14–15 H12–6.
***M.* Robert Strauss 'Ardingly'** (illus. p.296). Evergreen, epiphytic orchid for a cool greenhouse. H 6in (15cm). Bears sprays of white flowers, 4in (10cm) across, marked reddish brown and purple; flowering season varies. Narrowly oval, soft leaves are 4–5in (10–12cm) long. Requires shade in summer. Z14–15 H12–6.

MIMOSA

LEGUMINOSAE/MIMOSACEAE

Genus of annuals and evergreen perennials, shrubs, trees, and scrambling climbers, cultivated for their flowers and foliage. *M. pudica* is usually grown as an annual. Needs partial shade and fertile, well-drained soil. Water potted specimens freely when in full growth, moderately at other times. Propagate by seed in spring, shrubs also by semi-ripe cuttings in summer. Spider mite may be a nuisance.
M. pudica illus. p.176.

MIMULUS

Monkey musk

SCROPHULARIACEAE

Genus of annuals, perennials, and evergreen shrubs. Small species are good for moist pockets in rock gardens. Most prefer full sun and wet or moist soil; some, such as *M. aurantiacus*, need a dry site. Propagate perennials by division in spring, subshrubs by softwood cuttings in late summer; annuals and all species by seed in autumn or early spring.
***M.* 'Andean Nymph'** illus. p.278.
M. aurantiacus, syn. *Diplacus glutinosus*, *M. glutinosus*, illus. p.171.
M. glutinosus. See *M. aurantiacus*.
M. guttatus, syn. *M. langsdorffii*. Spreading, mat-forming perennial. H and S 24in (60cm). Snapdragon-like, bright yellow flowers, spotted with reddish brown on lower lobes, are borne in succession in summer and early autumn. Oval leaves are coarsely or sometimes deeply toothed and midgreen. Z6–9 H9–6.
M. langsdorffii. See *M. guttatus*.
M. lewisii illus. p.279.
M. luteus illus. p.292.
***M.* Magic Series.** Early-flowering perennial. H 6–8in (15–20cm). Produces small flowers, ranging from bright orange, yellow, and red to more usual pastel shades and bicolors. Z9–10 H10–9.
M. moschatus (Musk). Spreading, mat-forming perennial. H and S 6–12in (15–30cm). Bears snapdragon-like, pale yellow flowers, lightly speckled with brown, in summer-autumn. Leaves are oval, hairy, and pale green. Z7–10 H10–7.
***M.* 'Royal Velvet'** illus. p.283.
***M.* 'Whitecroft Scarlet'.** Short-lived, spreading perennial. H 8–12in (20–30cm), S 12in (30cm). Bears snapdragon-like, scarlet flowers freely from early to late summer. Has oval, toothed, midgreen leaves. Z8–9 H9–8.

MIRABILIS

Four o'clock, Marvel of Peru

NYCTAGINACEAE

Genus of summer-flowering annuals and tuberous perennials. Is best grown in fertile, well-drained soil and in full sun. Lift tubers and store over winter in frost-free conditions. Propagate by seed or division of tubers in early spring.
M. jalapa illus. p.245.

MISCANTHUS

GRAMINEAE/POACEAE

See also GRASSES, BAMBOOS, RUSHES and SEDGES.
M. sacchariflorus (Amur silver grass). Vigorous, herbaceous, slow-spreading, rhizomatous, perennial grass. H 10ft (3m), S indefinite. Hairless, midgreen leaves last into winter, often turning bronze. Has rare, open, branched panicles of hairy, purplish brown spikelets in summer. Z8–9 H9–8.
***M. sinensis* 'Gracillimus'** illus. p.309. **'Zebrinus'** illus. p.306.

MITCHELLA

RUBIACEAE

Genus of evergreen, trailing subshrubs grown for their foliage and fruits. Makes an excellent groundcover, especially in woodlands, although it is sometimes difficult to establish. Prefers shade and organic, neutral to acidic soil. Propagate by division of rooted runners in spring or by seed in autumn.
M. repens (Partridge berry). Evergreen, trailing, mat-forming subshrub. H 2in (5cm), S indefinite. Bears small, oval, white-striped green leaves with heart-shaped bases. In early summer has pairs of tiny, fragrant, tubular white flowers, sometimes purple-tinged, followed by spherical, bright red fruits. Good in a rock garden. Z4–9 H9–1.

Mitella

SAXIFRAGACEAE

Genus of clump-forming, summer-flowering, slender-stemmed, rhizomatous perennials. Requires shade and organic, moist soil. Propagate by division in spring or by seed in autumn.
M. breweri illus. p.384.

Mitraria

GESNERIACEAE

Genus of one species of evergreen, woody-stemmed, scrambling climber. Requires a position in semi-shade and in peaty, acidic soil. Propagate by seed in spring or by stem cuttings in summer.
M. coccinea illus. p.205.

Molinia

GRAMINEAE/POACEAE

See also GRASSES, BAMBOOS, RUSHES and SEDGES.
M. altissima. See *M. caerulea* subsp. *arundinacea*.
M. caerulea subsp. ***arundinacea***, syn. *M. altissima*. Tuft-forming, herbaceous, perennial grass. H 8ft (2.5m), S 2ft (60cm). Has broad, flat, gray-green leaves and spreading panicles of purple spikelets on stiff, erect stems in summer. Needs a dry, sunny position and acidic soil. Z4–8 H8–1. **'Variegata'** (Variegated purple moor grass), H 2ft (60cm), has yellow-striped, midgreen leaves and, in late summer, panicles of purplish spikelets.

Moltkia

BORAGINACEAE

Genus of deciduous, semi-evergreen or evergreen subshrubs and perennials grown for their funnel-shaped flowers in summer. Prefers sun and well-drained, neutral to acidic soil. Propagate by semi-ripe cuttings in summer or by seed in autumn.
M. x intermedia. Evergreen, open, dome-shaped subshrub. H 12in (30cm), S 20in (50cm). Stems are clothed in narrowly linear, dark green leaves. Masses of loose spikes of small, open funnel-shaped, bright blue flowers appear in summer.
M. petraea. Semi-evergreen, bushy shrub. H 12in (30cm), S 24in (60cm). Has long, narrow, hairy leaves and clusters of pinkish purple buds open into funnel-shaped, violet-blue flowers in summer. Z7–9 H9–7.
M. suffruticosa illus. p.357.

Moluccella

LABIATAE/LAMIACEAE

Genus of annuals and perennials grown for their flowers that may be dried successfully. Grow in sun and in rich, very well-drained soil. May be propagated by seed sown under cover in spring, or outdoors in late spring.
M. laevis illus. p.335.

Monarda

Bergamot

LABIATAE/LAMIACEAE

Genus of annuals and perennials grown for their aromatic foliage as well as their flowers. Requires sun and moist soil. Propagate species and cultivars by division in spring, species only by seed in spring.
***M.* 'Adam'.** Clump-forming perennial. H 2½ft (75cm), S 18in (45cm). Bears dense whorls of 2-lipped cerise flowers throughout summer. Oval, usually toothed, midgreen leaves are aromatic and hairy. Z4-9 H9-1.
M. didyma (Bee balm, Bergamot). **'Cambridge Scarlet'** illus. p.250. **'Croftway Pink'** illus. p.243.
M. fistulosa illus. p.251.
***M.* 'Prairie Night'.** See *M.* 'Prärienacht'.
***M.* 'Prärienacht'**, syn. *M.* 'Prairie Night'. Clump-forming perennial. H 4ft (1.2m), S 1½ft (45cm). Produces dense whorls of 2-lipped, rich violet-purple flowers from mid- to late summer. Oval, toothed leaves are midgreen. Z4–9 H9–1

Monstera

ARACEAE

Genus of evergreen, woody-stemmed, root climbers grown for their large, handsome leaves. Bears insignificant, creamy white flowers with hooded spathes intermittently. Provide organic, well-drained soil and light shade in summer. Water moderately, less when temperatures are low. Provide support. If necessary, shorten long stems in spring. Propagate by leaf-bud or stem-tip cuttings in summer. All parts except the fruit may cause mild stomach upset when ingested, and contact with the fruit may irritate skin.
M. acuminata (Shingle plant). Evergreen, woody-stemmed, root climber with robust stems. H 10ft (3m) or more. Has lopsided, oval, pointed, rich green leaves with a heart-shaped base, sometimes cleft into a few large lobes, to 25cm (10in) long. Z14–15 H12-10.
M. deliciosa illus. p.220.

Moraea

IRIDACEAE

Genus of corms with short-lived, irislike flowers. Divides into 2 groups: winter- and summer-growing species. Winter-growing species need full sun and well-drained soil; keep dry in summer during dormancy and start into growth by watering in autumn. Summer-growers are dormant in winter; grow in a sheltered, sunny site and well-drained soil. Propagate winter growers by seed in autumn, spring for summer growers.
M. huttonii illus. p.403.
M. polystachya. Winter-growing corm. H to 12in (30cm), S 2–3in (5–8cm). Bears long, narrow, semi-erect, basal leaves. Stem has a succession of erect, flattish, blue or lilac flowers, 3in (8cm) wide, in winter-spring. Outer petals each have a central yellow mark.
M. ramosissima illus. p.402.
M. spathacea. See *M. spathulata*.
M. spathulata, syn. *M. spathacea*. Summer-growing corm. H to 3ft (1m), S 4–6in (10–15cm). Has one long, narrow, semi-erect, basal leaf. Tough flower stem carries a succession of up to 5 upward-facing yellow flowers, 2–3in (5–7cm) wide, with reflexed outer petals, in summer. Z8–10 H10–8.

Morina

Whorlflower

MORINACEAE

Genus of evergreen perennials, only one species of which is in general cultivation: this is grown for its thistle-like foliage and its flowers. Needs protection from drying spring winds. Needs full sun and well-drained, preferably sandy soil. Propagate by division directly after flowering or by seed when fresh, in late summer.
M. longifolia illus. p.241.

Morisia

BRASSICACEAE/CRUCIFERAE

Genus of one species of rosetted perennial with a long taproot. Is good for rock gardens and alpine houses. Needs sun and gritty, well-drained soil. Propagate by seed in autumn or by root cuttings in winter.
M. hypogaea. See *M. monanthos*.
M. monanthos, syn. *M. hypogaea*, illus. p.372.

Morus

Mulberry

MORACEAE

Genus of deciduous trees grown for foliage and edible fruits. Tiny flowers appear in spring. Requires full sun and fertile, well-drained soil. Propagate by softwood cuttings in summer or by seed in autumn.
M. alba (White mulberry). **'Laciniata'** illus. p.92. **'Pendula'** is a deciduous, weeping tree. H 10ft (3m), S 15ft (5m). Rounded, sometimes lobed, glossy, deep green leaves turn yellow in autumn. Edible, oval, fleshy pink, red, or purple fruits ripen in summer. Z4–8 H8–1.
M. nigra (Black mulberry). Deciduous, round-headed tree. H 40ft (12m), S 50ft (15m). Heart-shaped, dark green leaves turn yellow in autumn. Bears edible, oval, succulent, dark purplish red fruits in late summer or early autumn. Z5–9 H9–5.

Mucuna

LEGUMINOSAE/PAPILIONACEAE

Genus of vigorous, evergreen, twining climbers grown for their large, pealike flowers. Organic, moist but well-drained soil is essential, with partial shade in summer. Water freely when in full growth, less at other times. Needs plenty of space to climb; provide support. Thin out crowded stems in spring. Propagate by seed in spring or by layering in late summer. Whitefly and spider mite may cause problems.
M. bennettii. Strong- and fast-growing, evergreen, twining climber. H 50–80ft (15–25m). Leaves are divided into 3 oval leaflets. In summer has pendent clusters of pealike, orange-scarlet flowers. Z5-9 H9–5.
M. deeringiana. See *M. pruriens* var. *utilis*.
M. pruriens var. ***utilis***, syn. *M. deeringiana*. Vigorous, evergreen, twining climber. H 50ft (15m) or more. Has pealike, both green- and red-purple flowers in long, pendent clusters in summer-autumn. Leaves, of 3 oval leaflets, are used for fodder and green manure. May be short-lived. Z14–15 H12–10.

Muehlenbeckia

POLYGONACEAE

Genus of deciduous or evergreen, slender-stemmed, summer-flowering shrubs and woody-stemmed, scrambling climbers grown for their foliage. Grow in sun or shade and in well-drained soil. Propagate by semi-ripe cuttings in summer.
M. axillaris of gardens. See *M. complexa*.
M. complexa, syn. *M. axillaris* of gardens. Deciduous, mound-forming shrub or twining climber. H 2–3ft (60cm–1m), S 3ft (1m). Slender, wiry stems bear variably shaped (oval to fiddle-shaped), dark green leaves. Produces tiny, star-shaped, greenish white flowers in midsummer that are followed by small, spherical, waxy white fruits. Z8–10 H10–8.

Mulgedium. Reclassified as *Cicerbita*.

Murraya

RUTACEAE

Genus of evergreen trees and shrubs grown for their overall appearance. Requires a position in full light or partial shade and in organic, well-drained soil. Water containerized plants freely when in full growth, moderately at other times. Pruning is tolerated in late winter if necessary. Propagate by seed in spring or by semi-ripe cuttings in summer. Whitefly may be a problem.
M. exotica. See *M. paniculata*.
M. paniculata, syn. *M. exotica* (Orange jasmine). Evergreen, rounded shrub or tree. H and S 6–12ft (2–4m). Pungently aromatic, edible, glossy, rich green leaves each have 9 or more oval leaflets. Carries fragrant, 5-petaled white flowers in terminal clusters year-round, followed by tiny, egg-shaped red fruits. Z9–11 H12–9.

MUSA
Banana

MUSACEAE

Genus of evergreen, palmlike, suckering perennials, with false stems formed from overlapping leaf sheaths, grown for their foliage, flowers, and fruits (bananas), not all of which are edible. Grow in sun or partial shade and in organic, well-drained soil. Propagate by division year-round, by offsets in summer, or by suckers after flowering.

M. arnoldiana. See *Ensete ventricosum.*

M. basjoo, syn. *M. japonica*, illus. p.233.

M. coccinea, syn. *M. uranoscopus* (Scarlet banana). Evergreen, palmlike perennial. H to 3ft (1m), S 5ft (1.5m). Bears oblong to oval, dark green leaves, to 3ft (1m) long, that are paler below. In summer produces erect spirals of tubular yellow flowers enclosed in red bracts, followed by banana-like, orange-yellow fruits, 2in (5cm) long. Z11–12 H12–5.

M. ensete. See *Ensete ventricosum.*

M. japonica. See *M. basjoo.*

M. ornata illus. p.232.

M. uranoscopus. See *M. coccinea.*

MUSCARI
Grape hyacinth

HYACINTHACEAE/LILIACEAE

Genus of spring-flowering bulbs, each with a cluster of narrowly strap-shaped, basal leaves, usually appearing in spring just before flowers. Leafless flower stems bear dense spikes of small flowers, most of which have constricted mouths. Needs sun and fairly well-drained soil. Plant in autumn. Propagate by division in late summer or by seed in autumn.

M. armeniacum illus. p.433. **'Blue Spike'** is a spring-flowering bulb. H 6–8in (15–20cm), S 3–4in (8–10cm). Produces 3–6 long, narrow, semi-erect, basal leaves. Bears dense spikes of fragrant, bell-shaped, deep blue flowers; constricted mouths have rims of paler blue or white "teeth." Z4–8 H8–1.

M. aucheri, syn. *M. lingulatum*, illus. p.433.

M. azureum, syn. *Hyacinthus azureus, Pseudomuscari azureum.* Spring-flowering bulb. H 4–6in (10–15cm), S 2–3in (5–8cm). Bears 2 or 3 narrow, semi-erect, basal, grayish green leaves, slightly wider toward the tips. Produces a very dense spike of bell-shaped, pale clear blue flowers; mouths have small "teeth" with central, dark blue stripes. May self-seed freely. Z5–9 H9–1.

M. botryoides. Spring-flowering bulb. H 6–8in (15–20cm), S 2–3in (5–8cm). Bears 2–4 narrow, semi-erect, basal leaves that widen slightly at the tips. Each tiny, nearly spherical, bright blue flower has a constricted mouth and white-toothed rim. Z2–8 H8–1.

M. comosum, syn. *Leopoldia comosa* (Tassel grape hyacinth). Late spring-flowering bulb. H 8–12in (20–30cm), S 4–5in (10–12cm). Has up to 5 strap-shaped, semi-erect, basal, gray-green leaves. Bears a loose spike of bell-shaped, fertile, brownish yellow flowers with a tuft of threadlike, sterile, purplish blue flowers at the tip. Z4–8 H8–1. **'Monstrosum'** see *M.c.* 'Plumosum'. **'Plumosum'** (syn. *M.c.* 'Monstrosum') illus. p.432.

M. latifolium illus. p.413.

M. lingulatum. See *M. aucheri.*

M. macrocarpum illus. p.434.

M. neglectum, syn. *M. racemosum*, illus. p.433.

M. paradoxum of gardens. See *Bellevalia pycnantha.*

M. pycnantha. See *Bellevalia pycnantha.*

M. racemosum. See *M. neglectum.*

MUSSAENDA

RUBIACEAE

Genus of evergreen shrubs and scrambling climbers grown for their flowers. Requires a position in full light and fertile, well-drained soil. Water freely when in full growth, less at other times. Provide support and thin out crowded stems in spring. Propagate by seed in spring or by air-layering in summer. Whitefly and spider mite may cause problems.

M. erythrophylla. Moderately vigorous, evergreen, scrambling climber. H 20–30ft (6–10m). Has broadly oval, bright green leaves and flowers in summer-autumn. Each flower has one greatly enlarged, oval, bractlike red sepal, a red tube, and yellow petal lobes. Z11 H12–7.

MUTISIA

ASTERACEAE/COMPOSITAE

Genus of evergreen, tendril climbers grown for their long-lasting flower heads. Plant with roots in shade and leafy parts in sun, in well-drained soil. Propagate by seed in spring, by stem cuttings in summer or by layering in autumn.

M. decurrens illus. p.217.

M. oligodon. Evergreen, tendril climber. H to 5ft (1.5m). Oblong, glossy, green leaves with sharply toothed margins are 1–1½in (2.5–3.5cm) long. In summer-autumn produces long-stalked, daisy-like pink flower heads with yellow centers. Grow against a low wall or through a shrub. Z9-10 H10–9.

MYOPORUM

MYOPORACEAE

Genus of evergreen shrubs and trees grown for their overall appearance and as hedges and windbreaks. Prefers full light and well-drained soil; will tolerate poor soil. Water potted specimens moderately. Propagate by seed when ripe or in spring or by semi-ripe cuttings in late summer.

M. laetum. Evergreen, rounded to upright shrub or tree. H 10–30ft (3–10m), S 6–15ft (2–5m). Has fleshy, oval, lustrous, bright green leaves and axillary clusters of small, bell-shaped white flowers dotted with purple in spring-summer, then tiny, narrowly oblong, pale to deep red-purple fruits. Z11–15 H12–10.

M. parvifolium illus. p.162.

MYOSOTIDIUM
Chatham Island forget-me-not

BORAGINACEAE

Genus of one species of evergreen perennial that is suitable for mild, coastal areas. Prefers semi-shade and moist soil. Seaweed is often recommended as a mulch. Is not easy to cultivate, and once established should not be disturbed. Propagate by division in spring, or by seed when ripe in summer or autumn.

M. hortensia, syn. *M. nobile*, illus. p.287. Bears oval to heart-shaped, glossy leaves. H and S 24in (60cm). In early summer produces bell-shaped, pale to dark blue flowers, sometimes with white-margined lobes. Z12–15 H12–1.

M. nobile. See *M. hortensia.*

MYOSOTIS
Forget-me-not

BORAGINACEAE

Genus of annuals, biennials, and perennials grown for their flowers. Most species are good for rock gardens and screes; *M. scorpioides* is best grown as a marginal water plant. Most prefer sun or semi-shade and fertile, well-drained soil. Propagate by seed in autumn.

M. alpestris, syn. *M. rupicola*, illus. p.370.

M. australis. Short-lived, tuft-forming perennial. H 5in (12cm), S 3in (8cm). Has oval, rough-textured leaves and, in summer, tight sprays of open funnel-shaped, yellow or white flowers. Is good for a scree. Z4–8 H8–1.

M. caespitosa. See *M. laxa* subsp. *caespitosa.*

M. laxa subsp. ***caespitosa***, syn. *M. caespitosa.* Clump-forming annual or short-lived perennial. H 5in (12cm), S 6in (15cm). Lance-shaped, leathery leaves are dark green. Bears rounded, bright blue flowers in summer. Z4–8 H8-1.

M. palustris. See *M. scorpioides.*

M. rupicola. See *M. alpestris.*

M. scorpioides, syn. *M. palustris* (Water forget-me-not). **'Mermaid'** illus. p.448.

M. sylvatica **'Blue Ball'** illus. p.334. **'White Ball'** is a slow-growing, short-lived, bushy, compact perennial grown as a biennial. H to 8in (20cm), S 6in (15cm). Leaves are lance-shaped. Sprays of tiny, 5-lobed, pure white flowers are produced in early summer. Z5–9 H7–1.

Myrceugenia apiculata. See *Luma apiculata.*

MYRIOPHYLLUM

HALORAGIDACEAE

Genus of deciduous, perennial, submerged water plants grown for their foliage. Most species are ideal as depositories for fish spawn. Requires full sun. Spreads widely: keep in check by removing excess growth as required. Propagate by stem cuttings in spring or summer.

M. aquaticum, syn. *M. proserpinacoides*, illus. p.448.

M. hippuroides. Deciduous, perennial, spreading, submerged water plant with thin stems. S indefinite. Produces a dense mass of small, feathery, pale green leaves. Inconspicuous, greenish cream flowers are borne from the axils of the emergent leaves in summer. Is suitable for a cold-water aquarium. Z9–11 H12–10.

M. proserpinacoides. See *M. aquaticum.*

M. verticillatum illus. p.449.

MYRRHIS
Sweet Cicely

APIACEAE/UMBELLIFERAE

Genus of one species of summer-flowering perennial. Requires a position in sun or shade and in well-drained soil. Propagate by seed in autumn or spring.

M. odorata illus. p.240.

MYRSINE

MYRSINACEAE

Genus of evergreen shrubs and trees, with inconspicuous flowers, grown mainly for their foliage. Also bears decorative fruits, for which plants of both sexes must be grown. Is suitable for rock gardens. Requires a position in sun or shade and in any fertile, well-drained soil other than a shallow, alkaline one. Propagate by semi-ripe cuttings in summer.

M. africana (Cape myrtle). Very slow-growing, evergreen, bushy, dense shrub. H and S 2½ft (75cm). Small, glossy, dark green leaves are aromatic and rounded. Tiny, yellowish brown flowers in late spring are succeeded by spherical, pale blue fruits. Z9–10 H10–9.

MYRTILLOCACTUS

CACTACEAE

Genus of branching cacti with ribbed, spiny, blue-green stems. Bears star-shaped flowers that open at night. Needs a sunny, well-drained site. Propagate by seed or stem cuttings in spring or summer.

M. geometrizans illus. p.456.

MYRTUS
Myrtle

MYRTACEAE

Genus of evergreen shrubs, sometimes treelike, grown for their flowers, fruits, and aromatic foliage. At limits of

hardiness, plant against a south- or west-facing wall. Requires full sun and fertile, well-drained soil. May be pruned in spring. Propagate by semi-ripe cuttings in late summer.
M. apiculata. See *Luma apiculata*.
M. bullata. See *Lophomyrtus bullata*.
M. chequen. See *Luma chequen*.
M. communis (Common myrtle) illus. p.130. subsp. ***tarentina*** is an evergreen, bushy shrub. H and S 6ft (2m). Bears small leaves that are narrowly oval, glossy, and dark green. Produces fragrant, saucer-shaped white flowers, each with a dense cluster of stamens, from midspring to early summer, followed by spherical white fruits. Is very wind-resistant and good for hedging in mild areas. Z8–9 H9–8.
M. luma. See *Luma apiculata*.
'Glanleam Gold' see *Luma apiculata* 'Glanleam Gold'.
M. ugni. See *Ugni molinae*.

N

NANDINA

BERBERIDACEAE

Genus of one species of evergreen or semi-evergreen, summer-flowering shrub grown for its foliage, flowers, and fruits. Prefers a sheltered, sunny site and fertile, well-drained but not too dry soil. On established plants prune old stems to base in spring. Propagate by semi-ripe cuttings in summer.
N. domestica (Heavenly bamboo, Sacred bamboo). Evergreen or semi-evergreen, upright, elegant shrub. H and S 6ft (2m). Leaves have narrowly lance-shaped, dark green leaflets, purplish red when young and in autumn-winter. Large panicles of small, star-shaped white flowers with large yellow anthers in midsummer are followed by spherical red fruits. Z6–11 H12–4. **'Firepower'** illus. p.151.

NARCISSUS

Daffodil

AMARYLLIDACEAE

Genus of bulbs grown for their ornamental flowers. Daffodils have usually linear, basal leaves and a spread of up to 8in (20cm). Each flower has a trumpet or cup (the corona) and petals (botanically known as perianth segments). Prefer sun or light shade and well-drained soil, but Div.8 cultivars (see below) prefer a sunny site and tolerate lighter soils. Deadhead flowers and remove faded foliage. Most cultivars increase naturally by offsets; dense clumps should be divided no sooner than 6 weeks after flowering every 3–5 years. Species may be propagated by fresh seed in late summer or autumn. Narcissus yellow stripe virus, basal rot, slugs, bulb fly and bulb and stem nematodes may cause problems. Contact with the sap of daffodils may irritate skin or aggravate skin allergies.

Horticulturally, *Narcissus* is split into the following divisions. See also feature panel pp.416–18:

Narcissus grow well in Z3–9 H9–1 except where otherwise indicated.

Div.1 Trumpet – usually solitary flowers each have a trumpet that is as long as, or longer than, the petals. Early to late spring-flowering.
Div.2 Large-cupped – solitary flowers each have a cup at least one-third the length of, but shorter than, the petals. Spring-flowering.
Div.3 Small-cupped – flowers are often borne singly; each has a cup not more than one-third the length of the petals. Spring-flowering.
Div.4 Double – most have solitary, large, fully or semi-double flowers, sometimes scented, with both cup and petals or cup alone replaced by petaloid structures. Some have smaller flowers, produced in clusters of 4 or more, which are often sweetly fragrant. Spring-flowering.
Div.5 Triandrus – nodding flowers with short, sometimes straight-sided cups and narrow, reflexed petals are borne 2–6 per stem. Spring-flowering.
Div.6 Cyclamineus – flowers are borne usually 1 or 2 per stem, each with a cup sometimes flanged and often longer than those of Div.5. Petals are narrow, pointed, and reflexed. Early to midspring-flowering.
Div.7 Jonquilla – sweetly scented flowers are borne usually 2 or more per stem. Cup is short, sometimes flanged; petals are often flat, fairly broad, and rounded. Spring-flowering.
Div.8 Tazetta – sweetly fragrant flowers of small-flowered cultivars are borne in clusters of 12 or more per stem; large-flowered cultivars have 3 or 4 flowers per stem. All have a small, often straight-sided cup and broad, mostly pointed petals. Late autumn- to midspring-flowering. Autumn-flowering hybrids provide valuable cut flowers; prepared bulbs may be grown in pots for midwinter flowering.
Div.9 Poeticus – flowers, sometimes borne 2 per stem, may be sweetly fragrant. Each has a small, colored cup and glistening white petals. Some *N. poeticus* hybrids are categorized as Div.3 or 8. Late spring-flowering.
Div.10 Bulbocodium – flowers usually borne singly on very short stems, showing all the hallmarks of hoop-petticoat daffodils (*N. bulbocodium* subsp. *bulbocodium*), with insignificant petals and a disproportionately large, widely flaring cup. Winter- to spring-flowering.
Div.11 Split-cupped – usually solitary flowers that have cups split for more than half their length. In (a), Collar daffodils, the overlapping segments of the cup lie against the petals, but in (b), Papillon daffodils, the segments of the cup tend to be narrower, with their tips arranged at the margin of the petals. Most flowers fall into category (a). Spring-flowering.
Div.12 Miscellaneous – a miscellaneous category containing hybrids with varying, intermediate flower shapes that cannot be satisfactorily classified elsewhere. Autumn- to spring-flowering.
Div.13 Daffodils distinguished solely by botanical name – a wide variety of flowers showing the huge range of floral characteristics of wild daffodils: from the tiny *N. cyclamineus* and the sweetly scented, many-flowered *N. tazetta* to the stately trumpet species. Flower in early autumn to late srping.

***N.* 'Acropolis'** (illus. p.417), Div.4. Mid- to late spring-flowering bulb. H 17in (42cm). Large, double flowers have white outer petals and petaloids; white inner petals are interspersed with shorter, orange-red petaloids. Is suitable for exhibition.
***N.* 'Actaea'** (illus. p.417), Div.9. Late spring-flowering bulb. H 16in (40cm). Fragrant flowers have glistening white petals and shallow, flanged, rich lemon cups with narrow, orange-red rims.
***N.* 'Aircastle'** (illus. p.416), Div.3. Midspring-flowering bulb. H 16in (40cm). Flowers have white petals that age greenish; shallow, flat, lemon yellow cups deepen in color at the rim.
***N.* 'Albus Plenus Odoratus'.** See *N. poeticus* 'Plenus'.
***N.* 'Altruist'** (illus. p.418), Div.3. Midspring-flowering bulb. H 18in (45cm). Flowers have smooth, pale orange petals and a neat, ribbed, shallow, orange-red cup.
***N.* 'Ambergate'** (illus. p.418), Div.2. Midspring-flowering bulb. H 18in (45cm). Flowers each have a shallow, widely expanded, fiery scarlet cup and soft tangerine petals.
***N.* 'Arctic Gold'**, Div.1. Midspring-flowering bulb. H 16in (40cm). Rich golden yellow flowers have broad petals and well-proportioned, flanged trumpets with neatly serrated rims. Is suitable for exhibition.
N. assoanus, syn. *N. juncifolius*, *N. requienii*, Div.13. Midspring-flowering bulb. H 6in (15cm). Is similar to *N. jonquilla* but has thin, cylindrical leaves and rounded, bright clear yellow flowers with a sweet, slightly lemony fragrance. Thrives in sunny, gritty soil.
N. asturiensis, syn. *N. minimus*, Div.13. Late winter- or early spring-flowering bulb. H 3in (8cm). Small, pale yellow flowers have waisted trumpets and slender petals. Prefers full sun.
***N.* 'Avalanche'** (illus. p.417), Div.8. Early spring-flowering bulb. H 14in (35cm). Produces 8 or more sweetly fragrant flowers, each with white petals and a primrose yellow cup that scarcely fades. May be forced.
***N.* 'Bartley'** (illus. p.418), Div.6. Early spring-flowering bulb. H 14in (35cm). Long, slender golden flowers have reflexed petals and narrow, angled trumpets. Flowers are long-lasting.
***N.* 'Belcanto'** (illus. p.417), Div.11a. Late spring-flowering bulb. H 18in (45cm). Flowers, 3–5in (8–12cm) across, have rounded perianth segments almost obscured by the flattened, pale yellow cups.
***N.* x *biflorus*.** See *N.* x *medioluteus*.
***N.* 'Binkie'** (illus. p.417), Div.2. Early spring-flowering bulb. H 12in (30cm). Flowers open clear pale lemon and cups turn sulfur-white with ruffled lemon rims.
***N.* 'Birma'**, Div.3. Midspring-flowering bulb. H 18in (45cm). Flowers have soft yellow petals and fiery orange cups with heavily ruffled rims.
***N.* 'Bravoure'** (illus. p.417), Div.1. Early to midspring-flowering bulb. H 15in (38cm). Large flowers have overlapping white petals and unusually slender, only slightly flared, lemon-yellow trumpets.
***N.* 'Bridal Crown'** (illus. p.417), Div.4. Late spring-flowering bulb. H 16in (40cm). Long-lasting, small, sweetly scented flowers are semi-double, with rounded, milk white petals and white petaloids interspersed with shorter, saffron-orange ones toward center.
***N.* 'Broadway Star'** (illus. p.417), Div.11b. Midspring-flowering bulb. H 16in (40cm). Has white flowers, 3in (8cm) across. The expanded segments of the split cups are flattened against the perianth segments; each has a narrow, orange midstripe running lengthwise.
***N.* 'Brunswick'**, Div.2. Early spring-flowering bulb. H 16in (40cm). Long-lasting flowers have white petals and long, flared, primrose cups that fade to lemon, with darker rims. Foliage is a striking bluish green.
N. bulbocodium subsp. ***bulbocodium*** (Hoop-petticoat daffodil), Div.13. Vigorous, spring-flowering bulb. H 3–6in (8–16cm). Flowers are golden yellow with conical cups and narrow, pointed petals. Thrives in moist soil in full sun, especially in rough grass. var. ***citrinus***, H 6in (15cm), has slender, dark green leaves and clear pale lemon flowers. Hybrids of this species are placed in Div.10.
N. campernelli. See *N.* x *odorus*.
***N.* 'Canaliculatus'** (illus. p.417), Div.8. Midspring-flowering bulb. H 9in (23cm). Produces a cluster of 4 or more small, fragrant flowers per stem, each with reflexed white petals and a shallow, straight-sided, dark yellow cup.
***N.* 'Canisp'** (illus. p.416), Div.2. Midspring-flowering bulb. H 16in (40cm). A robust garden and exhibition daffodil with large, milk white flowers with broad, overlapping petals, lightly reflexed at the apex, and a slightly darker, flanged, trumpetlike cup with a rolled mouth.
***N.* 'Cantabile'** (illus. p.417), Div.9. Late spring-flowering bulb. H 10in (25cm). Stiff stems bear neat, well-rounded, glistening white flowers with tiny, red-rimmed yellow cups with a prominent green eye.
N. cantabricus (illus. p.416), Div.13. Spring- and sometimes winter-flowering bulb. H 4in (10cm). Is similar in form to *N. bulbocodium*

subsp. *bulbocodium* but is less robust. Flowers are milk- or ice white. Thrives in an alpine house or greenhouse.
***N.* 'Cantatrice'**, Div.1. Midspring-flowering bulb. H 16in (40cm). Flowers have pure white petals and slender, milk white trumpets.
***N.* 'Capax Plenus'.** See *N.* 'Eystettensis'.
***N.* 'Cassata'** (illus. p.417), Div.11a. Midspring-flowering bulb. H 16in (40cm). Cups are soft primrose and distinctly split into segments with ruffled margins, while petals are broad and milk white.
***N.* 'Charity May'** (illus. p.418), Div.6. Early to midspring-flowering bulb. H 12in (30cm). Small, pale lemon flowers each have broad, reflexed petals and slightly darker cups.
***N.* 'Cheerfulness'** (illus. p.416), Div.4. Midspring-flowering bulb. H 16in (40cm). Long-lasting, small, sweetly scented, fully double flowers, 2¼in (5.5cm) across, are borne several to a stem, with milk white petals and petaloids interspersed with shorter, orange-yellow ones at the center.
N. cyclamineus (illus. p.418), Div.13. Late winter- to early spring-flowering bulb. H 6in (15cm). Slender, nodding, clear gold flowers have narrow, reflexed petals and long, slender, flanged, waisted trumpets.
***N.* 'Dove Wings'** (illus. p.417), Div.6. Midspring-flowering bulb. H 12in (30cm). Has small flowers with milk white petals and fairly long, soft primrose cups.
***N.* 'Empress of Ireland'** (illus. p.417), Div.1. Midspring-flowering bulb. H 16in (40cm). Large, robust, milk white flowers have broad, overlapping petals, reflexed at the apex, and a slightly darker, flanged trumpet with a rolled mouth.
***N.* 'Eystettensis'**, syn. *N.* 'Capax Plenus' (Queen Anne's double daffodil), Div.4. Midspring-flowering bulb. H 8in (20cm). Dainty, double flowers are composed of pointed, soft pale primrose petaloids neatly arranged in whorls.
***N.* 'February Gold'** (illus. p.418), Div.6. Early spring-flowering bulb. H 13in (32cm). Solitary, long-lasting flowers have clear golden petals and long, flanged, slightly darker trumpets. Is useful for borders and naturalizing.
***N.* 'February Silver'** (illus. p.417), Div.6. Robust, early spring-flowering bulb. H 13in (32cm). Has long-lasting flowers with milk white petals and long, sturdy, nodding trumpets that open rich lemon and age to creamy yellow.
***N.* 'Fortune'** (illus. p.418), Div.2. Early to midspring-flowering bulb. H 16in (40cm). Flowers have ribbed, dark lemon petals and bold, flared, copper-orange cups.
***N.* 'Foxfire'**, Div.2. Midspring-flowering bulb. H 14in (35cm). Has very rounded flowers with conspicuously white petals. Small, greenish cream cups each have a small, green eye zone and a coral-orange rim.
***N.* 'Golden Ducat'** (illus. p.418), Div.4. Midspring-flowering bulb. H 15in (38cm). Produces variable, sometimes poorly formed, double, rich golden flowers.
***N.* 'Grand Primo Citronière'**, Div.8. Late autumn- to early spring-flowering bulb. H 13in (32cm). Bears 8 or more fragrant flowers, each with milk white petals and a clear lemon cup that fades to cream. Treated bulbs may be forced for midwinter flowering.
***N.* 'Grand Soleil d'Or'** (illus. p.418), Div.8. Late autumn- to early spring-flowering bulb. H 14in (35cm). Flowers are sweetly scented with a dash of lemon. Each has rich golden petals and a clear tangerine cup. May be forced for midwinter flowering, but staking is needed. Z7–9 H9–7.
***N.* 'Hawera'** (illus. p.418), Div.5. Mid-spring-flowering bulb. H 8in (20cm). Nodding flowers are a delicate lemon yellow. Requires a sunny position. Good for forcing.
***N.* 'Home Fires'** (illus. p.418), Div.2. Early spring-flowering bulb. H 18in (45cm). Flowers each have pointed, rich lemon petals and an orange-scarlet cup with a lobed and frilled rim.
***N.* 'Honeybird'** (illus. p.417), Div.1. Midspring-flowering bulb. H 20in (50cm). Well-proportioned flowers, 4½in (10.5cm) across, open greenish yellow. The trumpets gradually fade almost to pure white.
***N.* 'Ice Follies'** (illus. p.416), Div.2. Early spring-flowering bulb. H 16in (40cm). Flowers have milk white petals and very wide, almost flat, primrose yellow cups, fading to cream.
***N.* 'Irene Copeland'** (illus. p.416), Div.4. Midspring-flowering bulb. H 14in (35cm). Bears large, fully double flowers of neatly arranged, milk white petaloids interspersed with shorter, pale creamy yellow ones.
***N.* 'Jack Snipe'** (illus. p.417), Div.6. Sturdy, early to midspring-flowering bulb. H 9in (23cm). Long-lasting, milk white flowers are similar to those of *N.* 'Dove Wings' but have narrower petals with incurved margins and medium-length cups of lemon yellow.
***N.* 'Jenny'**, Div.6. Early to midspring-flowering bulb. H 12in (30cm). Bears long-lasting flowers, each with milk white petals and a medium-length, flanged, soft lemon trumpet that turns creamy white.
***N.* 'Jetfire'** (illus. p.418), Div.6. Floriferous, early spring-flowering bulb. H 9in (23cm). Flowers have overlapping, reflexed, clear golden yellow petals and a cylindrical, ribbed, vibrant orange cup, slightly waisted before the rim.
N. jonquilla (Wild jonquil; illus. p.418), Div.13. Midspring-flowering bulb. H 12in (30cm). Richly fragrant flowers are borne in a cluster of 6 or more; each has tapering, yellow petals and a shallow, dark gold cup. Distinctive foliage is semi-cylindrical, dark, shining, and grooved. **'Flore Pleno'** (Queen Anne's jonquil) has loosely double flowers; broad, incurved, yellow petals are interspersed with short, darker ones.
***N.* 'Jumblie'** (illus. p.418), Div.12. Early spring-flowering bulb. H 8in (20cm). Bears 2 or 3 long-lasting flowers, each with broad golden petals and a sturdy, flanged, orange-yellow cup. Good for forcing.
N. juncifolius. See *N. assoanus*.
***N.* 'Kilworth'** (illus. p.417), Div.2. Vigorous, late spring-flowering bulb. H 15in (38cm). Flowers have pointed, milk white petals and dark reddish orange cups with green eyes.
***N.* 'Kingscourt'** (illus. p.418), Div.1. Sturdy, midspring-flowering bulb. H 42cm (17in). Flowers have flanged, flared, rich gold trumpets with broad, rounded, paler gold petals.
***N.* 'Liberty Bells'** (illus. p.418), Div.5. Sturdy, midspring-flowering bulb. H 13in (32cm). Flowers are slightly fragrant and clear lemon.
N.* x *medioluteus, syn. *N.* x *biflorus* (illus. p.416), Div.13. Mid- to late-spring-flowering bulb. H 16in (40cm). Produces neat, medium-sized, sweetly scented flowers of rounded outline, with overlapping, almost pure white petals and a small, shallow, solid primrose yellow, bowl-shaped cup. Is usually twin-headed.
***N.* 'Merlin'** (illus. p.417), Div.3. Mid-spring-flowering bulb. H 14in (35cm). Flowers have broad, rounded, glistening white petals and relatively large, almost flat, rich gold cups, each with a small, green eye and a broad, lightly ruffled, orange-red rim.
N. minimus. See *N. asturiensis*.
***N.* 'Minnow'** (illus. p.417), Div.8. Robust, early to midspring-flowering bulb. H 7in (18cm). Has a cluster of 4 or more fragrant flowers per stem, each with rounded, creamy yellow petals and a lemon cup. Increases freely and is suitable for a container or rock garden.
N. minor, syn. *N. nanus* of gardens (illus. p.418), Div.13. Early spring-flowering bulb. H 8in (20cm). Flowers have slightly overlapping, soft yellow petals and almost straight, darker yellow trumpets with frilled rims. subsp. ***pumilus*** see *N. pumilus*.
N. minor of gardens. See *N. pumilus*.
N. nanus, Div.13. Early spring-flowering bulb. H 5in (12cm). Flowers each have twisted cream petals and a thick, straight, dull yellow trumpet with a frilled rim. Leaves are broad. Is suitable for naturalizing.
N. nanus of gardens. See *N. minor*.
N. obvallaris, syn. *N. pseudonarcissus* subsp. *obvallaris* (Tenby daffodil), Div.13. Sturdy, early spring-flowering bulb. H 12in (30cm). Gold flowers, borne on stiff stems, have short petals and broad trumpets.
N.* x *odorus, syn. *N. campernelli* (Campernelle jonquil), Div.13. Robust, midspring-flowering bulb. H 8–12in (20–30cm). Has usually 2 richly fragrant, dark gold flowers. **'Rugulosus'** (illus. p.418), Div.7, H 28cm (11in), is more vigorous and produces up to 4 small-cupped, rich gold flowers.
***N.* 'Paper White Grandiflorus'**, syn. *N. papyraceus* 'Grandiflorus', *N.* 'Paper White Snowflake', Div.8. Winter- to midspring-flowering bulb. H 14in (35cm). Produces 10 or more long-lived, heavily fragrant, star-shaped, glistening white flowers, each with long, spreading petals and a small, flanged cup containing conspicuous, saffron yellow stamens. Popular for forcing in pebbles and water. Z7–9 H9–7.
***N.* 'Paper White Snowflake'.** See *N.* 'Paper White Grandiflorus'.
***N. papyraceus* 'Grandiflorus'.** See *N.* 'Paper White Grandiflorus'.
***N.* 'Passionale'** (illus. p.417), Div.2. Midspring-flowering bulb. H 16in (40cm). Each flower has milk white petals and a long, flanged, apricot-tinged pink cup.
***N.* 'Pencrebar'** (illus. p.418), Div.4. Midspring-flowering bulb. H 7in (18cm). Fragrant flowers are small, rounded, and fully double, often in pairs. Outer petaloids and large, inner ones are pale gold and are evenly interspersed with darker ones.
***N.* 'Pipit'** (illus. p.418), Div.7. Mid-spring-flowering bulb. H 10in (25cm). Bears up to 3 scented flowers per stem, slightly greenish sulfur yellow on opening. The ruffled, flared cup and the base of the overlapping petals become almost white at maturity.
N. poeticus (Poet's daffodil, Poet's narcissus), Div.13. Variable, late spring-flowering bulb. H 9–17in (22–42cm). Each fragrant flower consists of glistening white petals and a small, shallow yellow or orange cup with a red rim. Is ideal for naturalizing in grass but is slow to establish. **'Flore Pleno'** see *N.p.* 'Plenus'. **'Plenus'** (syn. *N.* 'Albus Plenus Odoratus', *N.p.* 'Flore Pleno'), H 16in (40cm), has loosely double, pure white flowers with inconspicuous, greenish yellow or orange centers, in late spring. var. ***recurvus*** (Pheasant's eye; illus. p.417), H 42cm (17in), bears larger, long-lasting flowers with strongly swept-back petals and very shallow, greenish yellow cups with crimson rims in late spring.
***N.* 'Portrush'** (illus. p.416), Div.3. Late spring- to early summer-flowering bulb. H 14in (35cm). Produces small flowers, each with green-tinged, glistening milk white petals and a small, shallow, flanged, creamy white cup with a bright green eye.
***N.* 'Pride of Cornwall'** (illus. p.417), Div.8. Midspring-flowering bulb. H 15in (38cm). Bears several large, fragrant flowers, each with milk white petals and a rich yellow cup shading to an orange-red rim outside.
N. pseudonarcissus (Lent lily, Wild daffodil; illus. p.418), Div.13. Extremely variable, early spring flowering bulb. H 6–12in (15–30cm). Nodding flowers have overlapping, straw yellow petals and large, darker yellow trumpets. Ideal for naturalizing. subsp. ***obvallaris*** see *N. obvallaris*.

N. pumilus, syn. *N. minor* of gardens, *N. minor* subsp. *pumilus*, Div.13. Early spring-flowering bulb. H 6–9in (15–23cm). Bears bright gold flowers with separated, slightly paler petals and large trumpets with lobed and frilled rims. **'Plenus'** see *N.* 'Rip van Winkle'.
***N.* 'Rainbow'** (illus. p.417), Div.2. Vigorous, midspring-flowering bulb. H 18in (45cm). White flowers have cups that are broadly banded with coppery pink at the rim.
N. requienii. See *N. assoanus*.
***N.* 'Rip van Winkle'**, syn. *N. pumilus* 'Plenus' (illus. p.418), Div.4. Early spring-flowering bulb. H 6in (15cm). Shaggy, double flowers have densely arranged, flat, tapering, greenish lemon petals with incurving tips.
***N.* 'Rockall'** (illus. p.417), Div.3. Midspring-flowering bulb. H 20in (50cm). Produces neat flowers with overlapping white petals and a shallow, ribbed, orange-red, bowl-shaped cup.
N. romieuxii (illus. p.417), Div.13. Early spring-flowering bulb. H 4in (10cm). Best grown in a frame or an alpine house. Is similar to *N. bulbocodium* subsp. *bulbocodium*, but each fragrant flower has a large, almost flat, flanged cup of glistening pale primrose.
N. rupicola (illus. p.418), Div.13. Midspring-flowering bulb. H 3in (8cm). Is similar to *N. assoanus* but has more angled, bluish green foliage and solitary, less scented lemon flowers, each with a 6-lobed cup. subsp. **watieri** (illus. p.416), H 4in (10cm), produces relatively large, fragrant, crystalline-textured white flowers with shallow, lobed cups.
***N.* 'Saint Keverne'** (illus. p.418), Div.11b. Sturdy, early to midspring-flowering bulb. H 17in (42cm). Solitary flowers have clear rich golden petals and slightly darker cups of almost trumpet proportions.
***N.* 'Satin Pink'** (illus. p.417), Div.2. Midspring-flowering bulb. H 17in (42cm). Each flower has broad, ribbed, milk white petals and a long, barely flared, flanged, soft buff-pink cup of almost trumpet proportions.
***N.* 'Scarlet Gem'** (illus. p.418), Div.8. Midspring-flowering bulb. H 14in (35cm). Produces 7–8 scented flowers with golden petals and scarlet or deep orange-red cups.
***N.* 'Shining Light'** (illus. p.418), Div.2. Midspring-flowering bulb. H 17in (42cm). Refined, well-balanced flowers have smooth, overlapping, clear, pale golden yellow petals, and the slightly ribbed, cup-shaped cup is rich orange-red. The lightly toothed rim is slightly darker. Is good for exhibition.
***N.* 'Silver Chimes'** (illus. p.417), Div.8. Sturdy, mid- to late spring-flowering bulb. H 13in (32cm). Has up to 10 fragrant flowers, each with broad, milk white petals and a straight, shallow, creamy primrose cup. Foliage is dark green. Thrives in a warm site.
***N.* 'Spellbinder'** (illus. p.417), Div.1. Early spring-flowering bulb. H 17in (42cm). Long-lasting, bright sulfur yellow flowers each have a slender, flanged trumpet, reversing to palest sulfur-white inside, except for the lobed, rolled-back rim, which is tinged with lemon.
***N.* 'Stratosphere'** (illus. p.418), Div.7. Midspring-flowering bulb. H 16in (40cm). Bears usually 3 fragrant flowers, each with rich golden petals and a darker gold cup. Is excellent for exhibition.
***N.* 'Suzy'** (illus. p.418), Div.7. Robust, midspring-flowering bulb. H 15in (38cm). Produces 3 or 4 long-lasting, large, fragrant flowers, each with clear golden petals and a large, flanged, rich tangerine cup.
***N.* 'Sweetness'** (illus. p.418), Div.7. Early spring-flowering bulb. H 15in (38cm). Sweetly fragrant flowers, occasionally borne in pairs, have intense, golden yellow petals and a darker, waved cup of strong substance.
***N.* 'Tahiti'** (illus. p.418), Div.4. Robust, midspring-flowering bulb. H 15in (38cm). Solitary, loosely double flowers have golden petals and petaloids interspersed with short, fiery orange inner petaloids.
N. tazetta (Bunch-flowered daffodil, Polyanthus daffodil), Div.13. Extremely variable, late autumn- to midspring-flowering bulb. H 12–16in (30–40cm). Bears usually 12 or more fragrant flowers, generally with slender white or yellow petals and shallow white or yellow cups. Z7–9 9–1.
***N.* 'Tête-à-Tête'** (illus. p.418), Div.12. Early spring-flowering bulb. H 6–12in (15–30cm). Produces long-lasting flowers, each with reflexed, rich golden petals and a square, flanged, warm yellowish orange cup. Should be twin-flowered. Is very susceptible to viruses.
***N.* 'Thalia'** (illus. p.416), Div.5. Vigorous, midspring-flowering bulb. H 15in (38cm). Has 3 or more long-lived, charming, milk white flowers per stem, each with irregularly formed, often propeller-shaped petals and a flanged, bold cup.
***N.* 'Tresamble'**, Div.5. Sturdy, early spring-flowering bulb. H 16in (40cm). Bears up to 6 flowers per stem, each with milk white petals and a flanged, creamy white cup, paler at the rim.
***N.* 'Trevithian'**, Div.7. Vigorous, early to midspring-flowering bulb. H 18in (45cm). Produces 2 or 3 large, fragrant flowers, rounded and soft primrose, each with broad petals and a short cup.
N. triandrus (Angel's tears; illus. p.417), Div.13. Early spring-flowering bulb. H 5in (12cm). Bears nodding, milk white flowers, each with narrow, reflexed petals and a fairly long, straight-sided cup. Makes a good container plant.
***N.* 'Trousseau'** (illus. p.416), Div.1. Early spring-flowering bulb. H 17in (42cm). Flowers each have milk white petals and a straight, flanged, soft lemon trumpet with a flared, lobed rim turning rich creamy buff tinged with pale pink.
***N.* 'Tudor Minstrel'**, Div.2. Mid-spring-flowering bulb. H 17in (42cm). Produces flowers with white, pointed petals. Chrome yellow cups are slender and flanged.
***N.* 'Waterperry'**, Div.7. Midspring-flowering bulb. H 10in (25cm). Flowers have dull creamy white petals. Lightly flanged, spreading primrose cups turn rich buff-yellow, shading to pinkish apricot rims.
***N.* 'White Lady'** (illus. p.416), Div.3. Vigorous, mid- to late-spring-flowering bulb. H 18in (45cm). Large, scented flowers have spreading, slightly overlapping, pure white petals. The small, shallow, heavily frilled cup is strong primrose yellow on opening, becoming more creamy yellow.
***N.* 'Woodland Star'** (illus. p.417), Div.3. Midspring-flowering bulb. H 20in (50cm). Large flowers have white petals and small, bowl-shaped, deep red cups.
***N.* 'W.P. Milner'**, Div.1. Early spring-flowering bulb. H 9in (23cm). Nodding flowers have slender, twisted, light creamy yellow petals and a flared, pale lemon trumpet that fades to palest sulfur.

NAUTILOCALYX

GESNERIACEAE

Genus of evergreen, erect, bushy perennials grown for their flowers and foliage. Requires high humidity, partial shade and well-drained soil; avoid water-logging, especially in winter. Propagate by stem cuttings in summer or by seed in spring.
N. bullatus, syn. *N. tessellatus*. Evergreen, erect, bushy perennial. H and S 2ft (60cm). Narrowly oval, wrinkled leaves, to 9in (23cm) long, are dark green with a bronze sheen above, reddish green beneath. Clusters of small, tubular, white-haired, pale yellow flowers are produced in the leaf axils, mainly in summer. Z14–15 H12–10.
N. lynchii illus. p.305.
N. tessellatus. See *N. bullatus*.

Neanthe bella. See *Chamaedorea elegans*.

NECTAROSCORDUM

ALLIACEAE/LILIACEAE

Genus of flowering bulbs related to *Allium*, with long, linear, erect leaves. Exudes a very strong onion smell when bruised. Stems with erect, shuttlecock-like seed heads may be dried for winter decoration. Needs partial shade. Grow in rough grass or borders in any soil that is neither too dry nor waterlogged. Propagate by freely produced offsets in late summer or by seed in autumn.
N. dioscoridis. See *N. siculum* subsp. *bulgaricum*.
N. siculum subsp. ***bulgaricum***, syn. *N. dioscoridis*, illus. p.398.

NEILLIA

ROSACEAE

Genus of deciduous shrubs grown for their graceful habit and profuse clusters of small flowers. Requires sun or semi-shade and fertile, well-drained soil. Established plants benefit from having some older shoots cut to base after flowering. Propagate by softwood cuttings in summer or by suckers in autumn.
N. longiracemosa. See *N. thibetica*.
N. sinensis. Deciduous, arching shrub. H and S 6ft (2m). Has peeling brown bark and oval, sharply toothed, mid-green leaves. Bears nodding racemes of small, tubular, pinkish white flowers in late spring and early summer. Z5–7 H7–5.
N. thibetica, syn. *N. longiracemosa*, illus. p.140.

NELUMBO

NYMPHAEACEAE

Genus of deciduous, perennial, marginal water plants grown for their foliage and flowers. Needs an open, sunny position and 24in (60cm) depth of water. Remove fading foliage; flowers may be left to develop into decorative seed pods. Divide overgrown plants in spring. Propagate species by seed in spring, selected forms by division in spring.
N. lutea (American lotus). Vigorous, deciduous, perennial, marginal water plant. H and S 3ft (1m). Rounded, blue-green leaves, prominently veined beneath, develop on thick, 1–2ft (30–60cm) long stems. Large, chalice-shaped yellow flowers open in summer. Z4-11 H12–1.
N. nucifera illus. p.447. **'Alba Grandiflora'** is a vigorous, deciduous, perennial, marginal water plant. H 4–6ft (1.2–1.8m), S 4ft (1.2m). Has very large, rounded, wavy-margined, dark green leaves on sturdy stems, with large, fragrant, chalice-shaped white flowers, 9–10in (22–25cm) across, in summer. **'Alba Striata'** bears white flowers, 6in (15cm) across, with jagged red margins. **'Rosea Plena'** has double, soft pink flowers to 12in (30cm) across. All of the above Z4–11 H12–3.

NEMATANTHUS

GESNERIACEAE

Genus of perennials and soft-stemmed, evergreen shrubs grown for their flowers and foliage. Requires partial shade and organic, moist but well-drained soil. Water potted specimens moderately, allowing soil almost to dry out between applications. Tip prune young plants to stimulate branching. Propagate by softwood or greenwood cuttings in summer.
N. gregarius, syn. *Hypocyrta radicans*, *N. radicans*, illus. p.157.
N. radicans. See *N. gregarius*.
N. strigillosus, syn. *Hypocyrta strigillosa*. Evergreen, prostrate shrub. H 6–12in (15–30cm), S 2–3ft (60cm–1m). Elliptic, slightly cupped leaves are clothed in dense down. Small, tubular orange or orange-red flowers appear in leaf axils mainly from spring to autumn.

Nemesia

SCROPHULARIACEAE

Genus of annuals, perennials, and evergreen subshrubs grown for summer bedding and as greenhouse plants. Prefers sun and fertile, well-drained soil. Cut back stems after flowering. Pinch out growing shoots of young plants to ensure a bushy habit. Propagate by seed sown under cover in early spring, or outdoors in late spring.
N. strumosa. Fast-growing, bushy annual. H 8–18in (20–45cm), S 6in (15cm). Has lance-shaped, serrated, pale green leaves and, in summer, trumpet-shaped yellow, white, or purple flowers, 1in (2.5cm) across, that are suitable for cutting. H7–1. **Carnival Series** illus. p.328. **Triumph Series** illus. p.339.

Nemophila

HYDROPHYLLACEAE

Genus of annuals useful for rock gardens and for edging. Grow in sun or semi-shade and in fertile, well-drained soil. Propagate by seed sown outdoors in spring or early autumn. Is prone to aphids.
N. insignis. See *N. menziesii.*
N. maculata illus. p.319.
N. menziesii, syn. *N. insignis*, illus. p.333.

Neobuxbaumia

CACTACEAE

Genus of columnar or treelike cacti with cylindrical stems and usually low-set ribs. Nocturnal flowers, produced in summer, are followed by angular fruits that open like stars when ripe. Requires sun and poor to moderately fertile, sharply drained, gritty soil. Propagate by seed in spring.
N. euphorbioides, syn. *Lemaireocereus euphorbioides*, *Rooksbya euphorbioides*, illus. p.459.

Neochilenia mitis of gardens. See *Neoporteria napina.*

Neolitsea

LAURACEAE

Genus of evergreen trees and shrubs grown for their foliage. Where marginally hardy it does best against a south- or west-facing wall. Requires sun or semi-shade and fertile, well-drained soil. Propagate by semi-ripe cuttings in late summer.
N. glauca. See *N. sericea.*
N. sericea, syn. *Litsea glauca*, *N. glauca*. Evergreen, broadly conical, dense tree or shrub. H and S 20ft (6m). Narrowly oval, pointed leaves are glossy, midgreen above, white beneath and, when young, are densely covered with silky, brown hairs. Small, star-shaped yellow flowers are borne in autumn.

Neolloydia

CACTACEAE

Genus of spherical to columnar cacti with dense spines and short tubercles in spirals. Most species are exceptionally difficult to cultivate unless grafted. Needs full sun and well-drained soil. Water sparingly from spring to autumn; keep dry in winter. Propagate by seed in spring or summer.
N. conoidea, syn. *Mammillaria conoidea*, illus. p.475.
N. macdowellii. See *Thelocactus macdowellii.*

Neomarica

IRIDACEAE

Genus of evergreen, summer-flowering, irislike, rhizomatous perennials with clusters of short-lived flowers. Needs partial shade and fertile, moist, preferably organic soil. Water freely in summer; reduce water in winter, but do not allow plants to dry out. Propagate by seed in spring or by division in spring or summer.
N. caerulea illus. p.402.

Neopanax. Reclassified as *Pseudopanax.*

Neoporteria

CACTACEAE

Genus of spherical to columnar cacti. Egg-shaped red, brown or green, seed pods are similar to those of *Wigginsia.* Requires full sun and very well-drained soil. Prop-agate by seed in spring or summer.
N. chilensis, syn. *Echinocactus chilensis*. Spherical, then columnar cactus. H 12in (30cm), S 4in (10cm). Pale green stem has a dense covering of thick golden spines of varying lengths. Crown bears flattish, pink-orange or white flowers to 2in (5cm) across in summer. Z12–15 H12–10.
N. litoralis. See *N. subgibbosa.*
N. mitis. See *N. napina.*
N. napina, syn. *Neochilenia mitis* of gardens, *Neoporteria mitis*, illus. p.471. Flattened spherical cactus. H 1¼in (3cm), S 2in (5cm). Has very short, black spines pressed flat against a chocolate brown stem. In summer the crown produces flattish yellow flowers, 2in (5cm) across. Z12–15 H12–10.
N. nidus. Spherical to columnar cactus. H 4in (10cm), S 3in (8cm). Long, soft gray spines completely encircle a dark greenish brown stem. During spring or autumn the crown produces tubular pink to cerise flowers that are 1¼–2in (3–5cm) long, with paler bases, and open only at the tips. Z12–15 H12–10.
N. subgibbosa, syn. *N. litoralis*. Spherical to columnar cactus. H 12in (30cm), S 4in (10cm). Light green to dark gray-green stem bears large, woolly areoles and thick, amber spines. In late summer, crown bears flattish, carmine-pink flowers, 1½in (4cm) across. Z12–15 H12–10.
N. villosa illus. p.470.

Neoregelia

BROMELIACEAE

Genus of evergreen, rosette-forming, epiphytic perennials grown for their overall appearance. Requires semi-shade and a rooting medium of equal parts organic soil and sphagnum moss or bark or plastic chips used for orchid culture. Using soft water, water moderately during growing season, sparingly at other times, and keep rosette centers filled with water from spring to autumn. Propagate by offsets in spring or summer.
N. carolinae, syn. *Aregelia carolinae*, *Nidularium carolinae* (Blushing bromeliad). Evergreen, spreading, basal-rosetted, epiphytic perennial. H 8–12in (20–30cm), S 16–24in (40–60cm). Strap-shaped, finely spine-toothed, lustrous, bright green leaves are produced in dense rosettes. A compact cluster of tubular, blue-purple flowers surrounded by red bracts is borne at the heart of each mature rosette, usually in summer. Z13–15 H12–1. f. **tricolor** see *N.c.* 'Tricolor'. **'Tricolor'** (syn. *N.c.* f. *tricolor*; illus. p.265) has leaves striped with ivory-white that flush pink with age.
N. concentrica (illus. p.265). Evergreen, spreading, basal-rosetted, epiphytic perennial. H 8–12in (20–30cm), S to 28in (70cm). Very broadly strap-shaped to oval, glossy, dark green leaves, with spiny, black teeth and usually with dark blotches, are borne in dense rosettes. In summer, a compact cluster of tubular, pale blue flowers surrounded by pinkish lilac bracts is produced at the heart of each mature rosette. Z13–15 H12–1. var. ***plutonis*** (syn. *N.c.* 'Plutonis') has bracts flushed with red. **'Plutonis'** see *N.c.* var. *plutonis.*

Nepenthes

Pitcher plant

NEPENTHACEAE

Genus of evergreen, insectivorous, mostly epiphytic perennials with leaves adapted to form pendulous, lidded, colored pitchers that trap and digest insects. Is suitable for hanging baskets. Requires a humid atmosphere, partial shade, and moist, fertile soil with added peat. Propagate by seed in spring or by stem cuttings in spring or summer.
N. x hookeriana illus. p.264.
N. rafflesiana. Evergreen, epiphytic, insectivorous perennial. H 10ft (3m), S 3–4ft (1–1.2m). Has lance-shaped, dark green leaves. Greenish yellow pitchers to 10in (25cm) long are mottled purple and brown and have spurred lids. Inconspicuous green flowers are borne in racemes and produced intermittently. Z15 H12–10.

Nepeta

Catmint

LABIATAE/LAMIACEAE

Genus of summer-flowering perennials useful for edging, particularly where they can tumble over paving. Grows in sun or partial shade and any well-drained soil. Propagate by division in spring or by stem-tip or softwood cuttings in spring or summer, species only by seed in autumn.
N. 'Blue Beauty'. See *N.* 'Souvenir d'André Chaudon'.
N. x faassenii illus. p.286.
N. grandiflora. Neat, erect perennial. H 16–32in (40–80cm), S 1½–2ft (45–60cm). Has slightly hairy stems, oval, round-toothed, light green leaves with heart-shaped bases, and, in summer, racemes of small, hooded blue flowers. Z3–8 H8–1.
N. macrantha. See *N. sibirica.*
N. nervosa. Clump-forming perennial. H 14in (35cm), S 12in (30cm). Forms a mound of narrowly oblong to lance-shaped, pointed, prominently veined, midgreen leaves. Produces dense racemes of small, tubular, pale blue flowers from early to midsummer. Z5–7 H7–5.
N. sibirica, syn. *Dracocephalum sibiricum*, *N. macrantha*, illus. p.254. **'Souvenir d'André Chaudron'** see *N.* 'Souvenir d'André Chaudron'.
***N.* 'Souvenir d'André Chaudron'**, syn. *N.* 'Blue Beauty', *N. sibirica* 'Souvenir d'André Chaudron'. Spreading, clump-forming perennial. H and S 18in (45cm). Tubular blue flowers are borne throughout summer above oval to lance-shaped, toothed gray leaves. Z3–8 H8-1.

Nephrolepis

NEPHROLEPIDACEAE/OLEANDRACEAE

Genus of evergreen or semi-evergreen ferns. Needs a shady position. Prefers moist soil but is extremely tolerant of both drought and waterlogging. Remove fading fronds and divide regularly. Propagate by division in summer or early autumn.
N. cordifolia (Ladder fern, Sword fern). Semi-evergreen fern. H 18in (45cm), S 12in (30cm). Has narrowly lance-shaped, arching, dark green fronds with rounded, finely serrated pinnae. Z9–11 H12–1.
N. exaltata illus. p.312.

Nephthytis

ARACEAE

Genus of evergreen, tufted perennials with horizontal, creeping rhizomes, grown for their foliage. Requires a humid atmosphere, moist, organic soil, and partial shade. Propagate by division in spring or summer.
N. afzelii. Evergreen, creeping, rhizomatous perennial. H to 2½ft (75cm), S indefinite. Has tufts of arrow-shaped, lobed, dark green leaves to 10in (25cm) long. Intermittently bears a hooded greenish spathe

enclosing a green spadix, followed by spherical orange fruits. Z14–15 H12-10.
N. triphylla of gardens. See *Syngonium podophyllum*.

NERINE

AMARYLLIDACEAE

Genus of bulbs, some of which are semi-evergreen, grown for their spherical heads of wavy-petaled pink to red, occasionally white flowers. Most flower in autumn before leaves appear. Needs full sun and light, sandy soil. Plant in early autumn. Dislikes being disturbed. Water until leaves die down, then dry off. Propagate by seed when fresh or divide offsets in autumn or when leaves have died down. If ingested, all parts may cause mild stomach upset.

***N.* 'Baghdad'.** Autumn-flowering bulb. H 24in (60cm), S 6–8in (15–20cm). Leaves are strap-shaped, semi-erect, and basal. Has crimson flowers, paler toward centers; long, narrow petals have recurved tips and ruffly margins. Z8–10 H10–8.

***N.* 'Blanchefleur'.** Autumn-flowering bulb. H 12–20in (30–50cm), S 6–8in (15–20cm). Produces strap-shaped, semi-erect, basal leaves and a tight head of 5–10 pure white flowers. Upper parts of petals are twisted. Z8–10 H10–8.

N. bowdenii illus. p.424. f. ***alba*** illus. p.424.

***N.* 'Brian Doe'** illus. p.424.

***N.* 'Corusca Major'**, syn. *N. sarniensis* var. *corusca* 'Major'. Autumn-flowering bulb. H 24in (60cm), S 5–6in (12–15cm). Forms strap-shaped, semi-erect, basal leaves. Thick stem bears 10–15 scarlet-red flowers with narrow petals. Is useful for cutting. Z8–10 H10–8.

N. crispa. See *N. undulata*.

N. filifolia. Autumn-flowering bulb. H to 10in (25cm), S 3–4in (8–10cm). Has threadlike, semi-erect leaves in a basal tuft. Slender stem has pale pink flowers with narrow petals. Z8–10 H10–8.

N. flexuosa. Semi-evergreen, autumn-flowering bulb. H 16–20in (40–50cm), S 5–6in (12–15cm). Bears strap-shaped, semi-erect, basal leaves and 10–15 pink flowers; each petal has a deeper pink midvein and a recurved, wavy upper half. Z8–10 H10–8.

***N.* 'Fothergillii Major'.** Late summer- to early autumn-flowering bulb. H 1½–2ft (45–60cm), S 5–6in (12–15cm). Leaves are strap-shaped, semi-erect, and basal. Very strong stem has about 10 bright scarlet-salmon flowers with recurved petals. Z8–10 H10–8.

N. masoniorum. Autumn-flowering bulb. H 6–8in (15–20cm), S 3–4in (8–10cm). Produces threadlike, semi-erect leaves in a basal tuft. Stem bears pink flowers with very ruffly petal margins. Z8–10 H10–8.

***N.* 'Orion'** illus. p.424.

N. sarniensis illus. p.424. var. ***corusca* 'Major'** see *N.* 'Corusca Major'.

N. undulata, syn. *N. crispa*, illus. p.424.

NERIUM

APOCYNACEAE

Genus of evergreen shrubs grown for their flowers. Requires full sun and well-drained soil. Water containerized plants freely when in full growth, sparingly at other times. Tip prune young plants to promote branching. Propagate by seed in spring or by semi-ripe cuttings in summer. All parts are highly toxic if ingested; contact with foliage may irritate skin.

N. oleander illus. p.121.

NERTERA

RUBIACEAE

Genus of creeping perennials grown for their mass of spherical, beadlike fruits in autumn. Makes excellent alpine house plants. Requires a sheltered, semi-shaded position in gritty, moist but well-drained, sandy soil. Resents winter wet. Propagate in spring by seed, division, or tip cuttings.

N. depressa. See *N. granadensis*.

N. granadensis, syn. *N. depressa*, illus. p.387.

NICANDRA

SOLANACEAE

Genus of one species of annual with short-lived flowers. Grow in sun and in rich, well-drained soil. Propagate by seed sown in spring.

N. physalodes (Apple of Peru, Shoo-fly). Fast-growing, upright, branching annual. H 3ft (1m), S 1ft (30cm) or more. Has oval, serrated, midgreen leaves. In summer to early autumn has bell-shaped, white-throated, light violet-blue flowers, over 1in (2.5cm) wide that last one day. Spherical green fruits, 2in (5cm) wide, are surrounded by purple and green calyces. Is thought to repel flies, hence its name. H9-1.

Nicodemia madagascariensis. See *Buddleja madagascariensis*.

NICOTIANA

SOLANACEAE

Genus of annuals, perennials that are usually grown as annuals, and semi-evergreen shrubs. Needs sun or partial shade and fertile, well-drained soil. Propagate annuals and perennials by seed in early spring, shrubs by seed in spring or by semi-ripe cuttings in summer. Contact with the foliage may irritate skin.

N. affinis. See *N. alata*.

N. alata, syn. *N. affinis*, illus. p.239.

N. glauca. Semi-evergreen, upright shrub. H and S 8–10ft (2.5–3m). Thick, blue-gray shoots bear narrowly oval, fleshy, blue-gray leaves. Showy, tubular, bright yellow flowers are produced in summer and early autumn. Z10–11 H12–1.

N. langsdorffii illus. p.334.

***N.* 'Lime Green'.** Upright annual. H 24in (60cm), S 10in (25cm). Mid-green leaves are spoon-shaped. In late summer and autumn produces racemes of open trumpet-shaped, greenish yellow flowers that are fragrant at night. Z10–11 H12–1.

***N.* x *sanderae* 'Crimson Rock'.** Fairly slow-growing, bushy annual. H 2ft (60cm), S 1ft (30cm). Oval leaves are midgreen. Evening-scented, trumpet-shaped, bright crimson flowers to 3in (8cm) long are produced throughout summer and early autumn. Z10–11 H12–1. **Domino Series** illus. p.319. **Nicki Series**, H 15in (38cm), produces fragrant flowers in an extensive color range that includes white, pink, red, and purple. **Starship Series** illus. p.326.

N. sylvestris illus. p.226.

NIDULARIUM

BROMELIACEAE

Genus of evergreen, rosette-forming, epiphytic perennials grown for their overall appearance. Requires a position in semi-shade and a rooting medium of equal parts organic soil and sphagnum moss or bark or plastic chips generally used for orchid culture. Using soft water, water moderately during the growing season, sparingly at other times, and keep centers of rosettes filled with water from spring to autumn. Propagate by offsets in spring or summer.

N. carolinae. See *Neoregelia carolinae*.

N. fulgens (Blushing bromeliad). Evergreen, spreading, basal-rosetted, epiphytic perennial. H 8in (20cm) or more, S 16–20in (40–50cm). Has dense rosettes of strap-shaped, spiny-toothed, arching, glossy, rich green leaves. Tubular, white-and-purple flowers, almost hidden in a rosette of bright scarlet bracts, are produced mainly in summer. Z14–15 H12–10.

N. innocentii (Bird's-nest bromeliad). Evergreen, spreading, basal-rosetted, epiphytic perennial. H 8–12in (20–30cm), S 24in (60cm). Has dense rosettes of strap-shaped, prickle-toothed, arching, dark green, sometimes reddish green leaves with reddish purple undersides. Tubular white flowers, partially hidden in a rosette of bright red bracts, appear mainly in summer. Z14–15 H12–10.

N. procerum. Evergreen, spreading, basal-rosetted, epiphytic perennial. H 8–12in (20–30cm), S 20–30in (50–75cm). Strap-shaped, spiny-toothed, bright green leaves are produced in dense rosettes. Clusters of small, tubular blue flowers are produced in summer. Z14–15 H12–10.

NIEREMBERGIA

SOLANACEAE

Genus of summer-flowering perennials, sometimes grown as annuals, and deciduous or semi-evergreen sub-shrubs. Prefers sun and moist but well-drained soil. Propagate by division in spring, by semi-ripe cuttings in summer, or by seed in autumn.

N. caerulea, syn. *N. hippomanica*. **'Purple Robe'** illus. p.331.

N. hippomanica. See *N. caerulea*.

N. repens, syn. *N. rivularis*, illus. p.374.

N. rivularis. See *N. repens*.

NIGELLA

RANUNCULACEAE

Genus of annuals grown for their attractive flowers, which are suitable for cutting, and their ornamental seed pods. Grows best in sun and in fertile, well-drained soil. Propagate by seed sown outdoors in spring or early autumn.

N. damascena (Love-in-a-mist). Fast-growing, upright annual. H 24in (60cm), S 8in (20cm). Has feathery, bright green leaves. Spurred, many-petaled blue or white flowers appear in summer, followed by inflated, rounded green then brown seed pods that may be cut and dried. H12–1. **'Miss Jekyll'** and **Persian Jewels Series** illus. p.333.

NOLANA

SOLANACEAE

Genus of annuals useful for growing in hot, dry sites and rock gardens and as edging. Grow in sun and in fertile, well-drained soil. Propagate by seed sown outdoors in spring.

N. atriplicifolia. See *N. paradoxa*.

N. grandiflora. See *N. paradoxa*.

N. paradoxa, syn. *N. atriplicifolia*, *N. grandiflora*. Moderately fast-growing, prostrate annual. H 3in (8cm), S 6in (15cm). Has oval, midgreen leaves and, in summer, funnel-shaped, purplish blue flowers, to 2in (5cm) wide, that have white-zoned yellow throats. Z9–11 H12–1.

Nolina recurvata. See *Beaucarnea recurvata*.

Nolina tuberculata. See *Beaucarnea recurvata*.

NOMOCHARIS

LILIACEAE

Genus of bulbs with a lilylike habit and, in summer, loose spikes of flattish flowers, often conspicuously spotted. Requires partial shade and rich, well-drained soil with a high organic content. In summer needs moist but not waterlogged soil. Is dormant throughout winter. Propagate by seed in winter or spring.

N. mairei. See *N. pardanthina*.

N. nana. See *Lilium nanum*.

N. pardanthina, syn. *N. mairei*, illus. p.398.

N. saluenensis. Summer-flowering bulb. H 34in (85cm), S 5–6in (12–15cm). Leafy stems bear lance-shaped, scattered leaves. Has a loose spike of 2–6 saucer-shaped white or pink flowers with dark purple eyes and purple spots.

Nopalxochia

CACTACEAE

Genus of epiphytic cacti with flattened, strap-shaped stems. Is closely related to *Epiphyllum*, with which it hybridizes. Spines are insignificant. Stems may die back after flowering. Needs partial shade and rich, well-drained soil. Is easy to grow. Propagate by stem cuttings in spring or summer.

N. ackermannii, syn. *Epiphyllum ackermannii* (Red orchid cactus). Erect, then pendent, epiphytic cactus. H 1ft (30cm), S 2ft (60cm).Has fleshy, toothed green stems to 3in (7cm) across and 16in (40cm) long; 6in (15cm) wide, funnel-shaped red flowers appear in spring-summer along indented edges of stems.

***N.* 'Gloria'** illus. p.463.

***N.* 'Jennifer Ann'** illus. p.467.

***N.* 'M.A. Jeans'** illus. p.463.

***N. phyllanthoides* 'Deutsche Kaiserin'**, illus. p.462.

Nothofagus

Southern beech

FAGACEAE

Genus of deciduous or evergreen trees grown for their habit, foliage, and, in the case of deciduous species, autumn color. Has inconspicuous flowers in late spring. Needs sun or semi-shade and, since it is not very resistant to strong winds, should have the shelter of other trees. Prefers deep, fertile, moist but well-drained soil; is not suitable for shallow, alkaline soil. Propagate by seed in autumn.

***N.* x *alpina*.** See *N. procera*.

N. antarctica (Antarctic beech, Nirre). Deciduous, broadly conical tree, sometimes with several main stems. H 50ft (15m), S 30ft (10m). Small, oval, crinkly-edged, glossy, dark green leaves turn yellow in autumn. Z7–10 H10–7.

N. betuloides illus. p.74.

N. dombeyi illus. p.73.

N. menziesii (Silver beech). Evergreen, conical tree. H 70ft (20m), S 40ft (12m). Has tiny, rounded, sharply toothed, glossy, dark green leaves. Z8–9 H9–8.

N. obliqua illus. p.68.

N. procera, syn. *N.* x *alpina*, illus. p.67.

Notholirion

LILIACEAE

Genus of summer-flowering bulbs related to *Lilium*, grown for their funnel-shaped flowers. Often produces early leaves, which may be damaged by spring frosts, so grow in a cool greenhouse in areas subject to alternating mild and cold periods in spring. Prefers partial shade or full sun and organic, well-drained soil. Bulb dies after flowering. Propagate in spring or autumn by offsets, which take 2–3 years to reach flowering size. Alternatively propagate by seed in winter or spring.

N. campanulatum illus. p.400.

***Nothopanax*.** Reclassified as *Pseudopanax*.

***Nothoscordum neriniflorum*.** See *Caloscordum neriniflorum*.

***Notocactus apricus*.** See *Parodia concinna*.

***Notocactus graessneri*.** See *Parodia graessneri*.

***Notocactus haselbergii*.** See *Parodia haselbergii*.

***Notocactus leninghausii*.** See *Parodia leninghausii*.

***Notocactus mammulosus*.** See *Parodia mammulosa*.

***Notocactus ottonis*.** See *Parodia ottonis*.

***Notocactus rutilans*.** See *Parodia rutilans*.

***Notocactus scopa*.** See *Parodia scopa*.

Notospartium

LEGUMINOSAE/PAPILIONACEAE

Genus of leafless, summer-flowering shrubs grown for their habit, green shoots, and flowers. Where marginally hardy it does best against a south- or west-facing wall. Requires a sheltered, sunny position and well-drained soil. Older plants may need staking. Propagate by semi-ripe cuttings in summer or by seed in autumn.

N. carmichaeliae (Pink broom). Leafless, arching shrub. H 6ft (2m), S 5ft (1.5m). Short, dense spikes of pea-like, purple-blotched pink flowers are produced in midsummer on slender, drooping green shoots. Z8–10 H10–8.

Nuphar

NYMPHAEACEAE

Genus of deciduous, perennial, deep-water plants grown for their floating foliage and spherical flowers. Grows in shade or sun and in running or still water; is often grown for a waterlily effect in conditions where true water lilies would not thrive. Remove fading foliage and flowers, and periodically divide crowded plants. Propagate by division in spring.

N. advena (American spatterdock, Yellow pond lily). Deciduous, perennial, deep-water plant. S 4ft (1.2m). Has broadly oval, floating, midgreen leaves; central ones are occasionally erect. Small, purple-tinged yellow flowers in summer are followed by decorative seed heads. Z6–11 H12–6.

N. lutea illus. p.451.

***Nutallia*.** Reclassified as *Oemleria*.

Nymania

ALTONIACEAE/MELIACEAE

Genus of one species of evergreen, spring-flowering shrub grown for its flowers and fruits. Needs full light and fertile, well-drained soil. Water potted specimens moderately, less when not in full growth. Propagate by seed in spring or by semi-ripe cuttings in summer.

N. capensis illus. p.148.

Nymphaea

Waterlily

NYMPHAEACEAE

Genus of deciduous, summer-flowering, perennial water plants grown for their floating, usually rounded leaves and brightly colored flowers. Needs an open, sunny position and still water. Remove fading foliage to prevent it from fouling water. Plants have tuberlike rhizomes and require dividing and replanting in spring or early summer every 3 or 4 years. Where not hardy, tropical waterlilies may be treated as annuals. May also be propagated by seed or by separating plantlets in spring or early summer. See also feature panel p.450.

Waterlilies indicated as Hardy grow well in Z3–11 H12–1, and those indicated as Tropical do well in Z10–11 H12–7.

***N.* 'Amabilis'.** Deciduous, perennial water plant with floating leaves. S 5–7ft (1.5–2.2m). Rounded leaves, reddish purple when young, mature to dark green with red-margined, light green undersides. In summer, has star-shaped pink flowers, 6–7in (15–19cm) across, with light pink tips and dark yellow stamens. Hardy.

***N.* 'American Star'** (illus. p.450). Deciduous, perennial water plant with floating leaves. S to 4ft (1.2m). Young leaves are purplish green or bronze, maturing to bright green. Star-shaped flowers, 4in (10cm) across, are deep pink and are held above water throughout summer. Tropical.

***N.* 'Attraction'** (illus. p.450). Deciduous, perennial water plant with floating leaves. S to 6ft (2m). Has dark green leaves. In summer bears cup-shaped, garnet red flowers 6in (15cm) across and flecked with white. Hardy.

***N.* 'Aurora'.** Deciduous, perennial water plant with floating leaves. S to 2½ft (75cm). Olive green leaves are mottled with purple. In summer has star-shaped flowers, 2in (5cm) across, cream in bud, opening to yellow, then passing through orange to blood red. Good for a small- to medium-sized pond. Tropical.

***N.* 'Blue Beauty'** (illus. p.450). Deciduous, perennial water plant with floating leaves. S to 8ft (2.5m). Leaves are brown-freckled, dark green above, purplish green beneath. Fragrant, rounded, deep blue flowers to 12in (30cm) across are produced in summer. Tropical.

N. capensis (Cape blue waterlily). Deciduous, perennial water plant with floating leaves. S to 6ft (2m). Large, midgreen leaves are often splashed with purple beneath. Star-shaped, bright blue flowers, 6–8in (15–20cm) across, appear in summer. Tropical.

***N.* 'Emily Grant Hutchings'.** Deciduous, perennial water plant with floating leaves. S to 4ft (1.2m). Has small green leaves overlaid with bronze-crimson. Cup-shaped, pinkish red flowers, 6–8in (15–20cm) across, open at night in summer. Tropical.

***N.* 'Escarboucle'** (illus. p.450). Deciduous, perennial water plant with floating leaves. S to 10ft (3m). Leaves are dark green. In summer has cup-shaped, deep crimson flowers, 4–6in (10–15cm) across, with golden centers. Hardy.

***N.* 'Fabiola'.** Deciduous, perennial water plant with floating leaves. S to 5ft (1.5m). In summer, produces fragrant, peony-shaped flowers, 6–7in (15–18cm) across, with pink-flecked petals, above midgreen leaves. Tropical.

***N.* 'Firecrest'** (illus. p.450). Deciduous, perennial water plant with floating leaves. S to 4ft (1.2m). Dark green leaves are suffused with purple. In summer bears star-shaped, deep pink flowers, 6–8in (15–20cm) across, with red-tipped stamens. Hardy.

***N.* 'Froebelii'** (illus. p.450). Deciduous, perennial water plant with floating leaves. S 3ft (90cm). Has rounded, pale green leaves, bronzed when young. In summer, produces cup-shaped, later star-shaped, burgundy red flowers, 4–5in (10–12cm) across, with orange-red stamens. Hardy.

***N.* 'General Pershing'** (illus. p.450). Deciduous, perennial water plant with floating leaves. S 5–6ft (1.5–1.8m). Leaves are rounded, wavy-margined, olive green, and marked with purple. In summer, bears day-blooming, cup-shaped, later flat, highly fragrant, lavender-pink flowers, 8–11in (20–27cm) across, with yellow stamens. Tropical.

***N.* 'Gladstoneana'** (illus. p.450). Deciduous, perennial water plant with floating leaves. S to 10ft (3m). Leaves are midgreen. Star-shaped white flowers, 6–12in (15–30cm) across, appear in summer. Hardy.

***N.* 'Gonnère'.** Deciduous, perennial water plant with floating leaves. S to 5ft (1.5m). Has bright pea-green leaves and, in summer, rounded white flowers, 6–8in (15–20cm) across. Hardy.

***N.* 'Green Smoke'.** Deciduous, perennial water plant with floating leaves. S to 6ft (2m). Bronze-green leaves have bronze speckling. Star-shaped flowers, 4–8in (10–20cm) across, are chartreuse shading to blue. Tropical.

***N.* 'James Brydon'** (illus. p.450). Deciduous, perennial water plant with floating leaves. S to 8ft (2.5m). Fragrant, peony-shaped, orange-suffused crimson flowers, 6–8in (15–20cm) across, are borne in summer above dark green leaves. Hardy.

***N.* 'Laydekeri Fulgens'.** See *N.* Laydekeri Group 'Fulgens'.

***N.* Laydekeri Group 'Fulgens'**, syn. *N.* 'Laydekeri Fulgens' (illus. p.450). Deciduous, perennial water plant with floating leaves. S to 3ft (1m). Dark green leaves have purplish green

undersides. Star-shaped, bright crimson flowers, 2–4in (5–10cm) across, appear in summer. Hardy.
***N.* 'Lucida'** (illus. p.450). Deciduous, perennial water plant with floating leaves. S 5–6ft (1.5–1.8m). Has broadly ovate, midgreen leaves, and star-shaped flowers, 5–6in (12–15cm) across, with red inner petals, pink-veined, whitish pink outer petals, and yellow stamens, in summer. Hardy.
***N.* 'Madame Wilfon Gonnère'.** Deciduous, perennial water plant with floating leaves. S to 5ft (1.5m). Has midgreen leaves and, in summer, cup-shaped white flowers, 6in (15cm) across, spotted with deep rose-pink. Tropical.
***N.* Marliacea Group 'Albida'** (illus. p.450). Deciduous, perennial water plant with floating leaves. S to 6ft (2m). Deep green leaves have red or purplish green undersides. Bears fragrant, cup-shaped, pure white flowers, 6–8in (15–20cm) across, in summer.
'Chromatella' (illus. p.450) has olivegreen leaves heavily mottled with maroon and bronze, and cup-shaped, canary yellow flowers, 6–8in (15–20cm) across. Both Hardy.
***N. odorata* 'Sulphurea Grandiflora'**, syn *N.* 'Odorata Sulphurea Grandiflora'. Deciduous, perennial water plant with floating leaves. S to 3ft (1m). Dark green leaves are heavily mottled with maroon. Bears fragrant, star-shaped yellow flowers, 4–6in (10–15cm) across, throughout summer. Z2–10 H12–1
***N.* 'Odorata Sulphurea Grandiflora'.** See *N. odorata* 'Sulphurea Grandiflora'.
***N.* 'Pink Sensation'.** Deciduous, perennial water plant with floating leaves. S 4ft (1.2m). In summer, bears cup-shaped, later star-shaped pink flowers, 5–6in (12–15cm) across, with yellow inner stamens and pink outer stamens, above rounded, midgreen leaves, purple-green when young. Hardy.
***N. pygmaea*.** See *N. tetragona*.
***N.* 'Ray Davies'.** Deciduous, perennial water plant with floating leaves. S to 5ft (1.5m). In summer, produces peony-shaped, light pink flowers, 15–18cm (6–7in) across, slightly yellow in the center, above rounded, deep green leaves. Tropical.
***N.* 'Red Flare'.** Deciduous, perennial water plant with floating leaves. S 5–6ft (1.5–1.8m). Leaves are rounded, strongly toothed, and reddish green. In summer, bears night-blooming, flat, dark red flowers, 7–10in (17–25cm) across, with light pink or yellowish stamens. Tropical.
***N.* 'Rose Arey'** (illus. p.450). Deciduous, perennial water plant with floating leaves. S to 5ft (1.5m). Leaves are reddish green, purple when young. In summer produces star-shaped, deep rose-pink flowers, 4–6in (10–15cm) across, that pale with age and have a strong anise fragrance. Hardy.
***N.* 'Saint Louis'.** Deciduous, perennial water plant with floating leaves. S to 6ft (2m). Bright green leaves are spotted with brown when young. Produces star-shaped, bright yellow flowers, 6–10in (15–25cm) across, in summer. Tropical.
***N.* 'Sunrise'** (illus. p.450). Deciduous, perennial water plant with floating leaves. S to 6ft (2m). Midgreen leaves have downy stalks and undersides. Bears star-shaped yellow flowers, 4–6in (10–15cm) across, in summer. Hardy.
N. tetragona, syn. *N. pygmaea*. **'Alba'** (illus. p.450). Deciduous, perennial water plant with floating leaves. S to 12in (30cm). Has small, dark green leaves, purplish green beneath, and, in summer, star-shaped white flowers, ¾–1¼in (2–3cm) across. Hardy.
'Helvola' (illus. p.450), S to 18in (45cm), has small, olive green leaves with heavy purple or brown mottling. Produces star-shaped yellow flowers, ¾–1½in (2–4cm) across, in summer.
***N.* 'Virginia'** (illus. p.450). Deciduous, perennial water plant with floating leaves. S to 5ft (1.5m). Has purplish green leaves and, in summer, star-shaped white flowers, 4–6in (10–15cm) across. Hardy.
***N.* 'Wood's White Knight'.** Deciduous, perennial water plant with floating leaves. S to 6ft (2m). Leaves are midgreen, dappled with darker green beneath. In summer, produces star-shaped, creamy white flowers, 4–8in (10–20cm) across and with prominent gold stamens, that open at night. Tropical.

NYMPHOIDES

MENYANTHACEAE

Genus of deciduous, perennial, deep-water plants with floating foliage, grown for their flowers. Requires an open, sunny position. Propagate by division in spring or summer.
N. peltata, syn. *Limnanthemum nymphoides*, *Villarsia nymphoides*, illus. p.451.

NYSSA

Tupelo

NYSSACEAE

Genus of deciduous trees grown for their foliage and brilliant autumn color. Needs sun or semi-shade; does best in hot summers. Requires moist, neutral to acidic soil. Resents being transplanted. Propagate by softwood cuttings in summer or by seed in autumn.
N. sinensis illus. p.82.
N. sylvatica illus. p.71.

OCHNA

OCHNACEAE

Genus of mainly evergreen trees and shrubs grown mostly for their flowers and fruits. Prefers full light and well-drained soil. Water containerized specimens moderately, less when not in full growth. Prune, if necessary, in early spring. Propagate by seed in spring or by semi-ripe cuttings in summer.
***O. multiflora*.** See *O. serrulata*.
O. serratifolia of gardens. See *O. serrulata*.
O. serrulata, syn. *O. multiflora*, *O. serratifolia* of gardens (Mickey-mouse plant). Evergreen, irregularly rounded, twiggy shrub that is semi-evergreen in low temperatures. H to 6ft (2m), S 3–6ft (1–2m) or more. Leaves are narrowly elliptic, toothed, and glossy. Has 5-petaled, bright yellow flowers in spring-summer, then oddly shaped, red fruits, each with 1–5 berry-like seeds clustered on top. Z11 H12–9.

x ODONTIODA

See also ORCHIDS.
x *O.* (*O.* Chantos x *O.* Marzorka) x *Odontoglossum* Buttercrisp (illus. p.299). Evergreen, epiphytic orchid for a cool greenhouse. H 9in (23cm). Produces arching spikes of intricately patterned red, tan, orange, and yellow flowers, 3in (8cm) across; flowering season varies. Has narrowly oval leaves, 4–6in (10–15cm) long. Needs shade in summer. Z14–15 H12–6.
x *O.* Mount Bingham (illus. p.297). Evergreen, epiphytic orchid for a cool greenhouse. H 9in (23cm). Bears pink-edged, red flowers, 3½in (9cm) across, in spikes; flowering season varies. Has narrowly oval leaves, 4–6in (10–15cm) long. Needs shade in summer. Z14–15 H12–6.
x *O.* Pacific Gold x *Odontoglossum cordatum* (illus. p.297). Evergreen, epiphytic orchid for a cool greenhouse. H 9in (23cm). Bears long spikes of yellow-striped and -marked, rich chocolate brown flowers 3in (7cm) across; flowering season varies. Leaves are narrowly oval and 4–6in (10–15cm) long. Grow in shade in summer. Z14–15 H12–6.
x *O.* Petit Port (illus. p.297). Evergreen, epiphytic orchid for a cool greenhouse. H 9in (23cm). Bears spikes of rich red flowers, 3in (8cm) across, each with a pink-and-yellow-marked lip; flowering season varies. Narrowly oval leaves are 4–6in (10–15cm) long. Needs shade in summer. Z14–15 H12–6.

x ODONTOCIDIUM

See also ORCHIDS.
x *O.* Artur Elle 'Colombian' (illus. p.297). Evergreen, epiphytic orchid for a cool greenhouse. H 9in (23cm). Produces tall spikes of pale yellow flowers, 2½in (6cm) across and intricately patterned with brown; flowering season varies. Has narrowly oval leaves, 4–6in (10–15cm) long. Requires shade in summer. Z14–15 H12–6.
x *O.* Tiger Butter x *Wilsonara* Wigg's 'Kay' (illus. p.297). Evergreen, epiphytic orchid for a cool greenhouse. H 9in (23cm). Bears spikes of mottled, deep reddish brown flowers, 2in (5cm) across, each with a rich golden yellow lip; flowering season varies. Narrowly oval leaves are 4–6in (10–15cm) long. Grow in shade in summer. Z14–15 H12–6.
x *O.* Tiger Hambuhren (illus. p.299). Evergreen, epiphytic orchid for a cool greenhouse. H 9in (23cm). Deep yellow flowers, 3in (8cm) across and heavily patterned with chestnut brown, are borne in tall spikes; flowering season varies. Has narrowly oval leaves, 4–6in (10–15cm) long. Needs shade in summer. Z14–15 H12–6.
x *O.* Tigersun 'Orbec' (illus. p.298). Evergreen, epiphytic orchid for a cool greenhouse. Is very similar to x *O.* Tiger Hambuhren, but flowers are slightly smaller and have lighter patterning. Z14–15 H12–6.

ODONTOGLOSSUM

See also ORCHIDS.
***O. bictoniense*.** See *Lemboglossum bictoniense*.
***O. cervantesii*.** See *Lemboglossum cervantesii*.
***O. cordatum*.** See *Lemboglossum cordatum*.
O. crispum (illus. p.296). Evergreen, epiphytic orchid for a cool greenhouse. H 6in (15cm). Bears long sprays of rounded flowers, 3in (8cm) across, white or spotted or flushed with pink, each with a red-and-yellow-marked lip; flowering season varies. Has narrowly oval leaves, 4–6in (10–15cm) long. Requires shade in summer. Z13–15 H12–6.
***O.* Eric Young** (illus. p.298). Evergreen, epiphytic orchid for a cool greenhouse. H 6in (15cm). Has spikes of white-lipped, pale yellow flowers, 3in (8cm) across, spotted with rich yellow; flowering season varies. Bears narrowly oval leaves, 4–6in (10–15cm) long. Grow in shade in summer. Z13–15 H12–6.
***O. grande*.** See *Rossioglossum grande*.
***O.* Le Nez Point** (illus. p.297). Evergreen, epiphytic orchid for a cool greenhouse. H 6in (15cm). Crimson flowers, 2½in (6cm) across, are borne in spikes; flowering season varies. Has narrowly oval leaves, 4–6in (10–15cm) long. Needs shade in summer. Z13–15 H12–6.
***O. rossii*.** See *Lemboglossum rossii*.
***O.* Royal Occasion** (illus. p.296). Evergreen, epiphytic orchid for a cool greenhouse. H 6in (15cm). Has spikes of white flowers, 3in (8cm) across, with deep yellow markings in the centers of the lips, in autumn-winter. Leaves are narrowly oval and 4–6in (10–15cm) long. Shade in summer. Z13–15 H12–6.

x ODONTONIA

See also ORCHIDS.
x *O.* Olga. Evergreen, epiphytic orchid

for a cool greenhouse. H 6in (15cm). Pure white flowers, 4in (10cm) across, with large, reddish brown-blotched lips, are borne in tall, arching racemes, mainly in autumn. Produces ovoid pseudobulbs and narrowly oval leaves, 5in (12cm) long. Is best grown in shade during the summer. Z14–15 H12–10.

OEMLERIA,
syn. NUTTALLIA, OSMARONIA

ROSACEAE

Genus of one species of deciduous, early spring-flowering shrub grown for its fragrant flowers and decorative fruits. Separate male and female plants are needed in order to obtain fruits. Prefers sun or semi-shade and moist soil. To restrict growth, remove suckers and cut old shoots back or down to base in late winter. Propagate by suckers in autumn.

O. cerasiformis. (Indian plum, Oso berry). Deciduous, upright then arching shrub that forms dense thickets. H 8ft (2.5m), S 12ft (4m). Leaves are narrowly oval and dark blue-green. Has nodding clusters of small, fragrant, bell-shaped white flowers in early spring, then small, plum-shaped purple fruits. Z6-10 H10–6.

OENOTHERA
Evening primrose

ONAGRACEAE

Genus of annuals, biennials, and perennials grown for their profuse but short-lived flowers in summer. Needs full sun and well-drained, sandy soil. Propagate by seed or division in autumn or spring or by softwood cuttings in late spring.

O. acaulis. Tuft-forming perennial. H 6in (15cm), S 8in (20cm). Has oblong to oval, deeply toothed or lobed leaves. Cup-shaped white flowers, turning pink, open at sunset in summer. Good in a rock garden. Z5–9 H9–5.

O. caespitosa. Clump-forming, stemless perennial. H 5in (12cm), S 8in (20cm). Has narrowly oval, entire or toothed, midgreen leaves. Flowers, opening at sunset in summer, are fragrant, cup-shaped and white, becoming pink with age. Good in a rock garden. Z4–8 H8–1.

O. fraseri. See *O. fruticosa* subsp. *glauca*.

O. fruticosa* 'Fireworks'.** See *O.f.* 'Fyrverkeri'. **'Fyrverkeri'** (syn. *O.f.* 'Fireworks') illus. p.291. subsp. ***glauca (syn. *O. fraseri*, *O. glauca*, *O. tetragona*) is a clump-forming perennial. H 1½–2ft (45–60cm), S 18in (45cm). Dense spikes of fragrant, cup-shaped, bright yellow flowers appear from mid- to late summer. Leaves, borne on reddish green stems, are narrowly oval to lance-shaped and glossy midgreen. Z4–8 H8–1.

O. glauca. See *O. fruticosa* subsp. *glauca*.

O. macrocarpa, syn. *O. missouriensis*, illus. p.385.

O. missouriensis. See *O. macrocarpa*.

O. perennis, syn. *O. pumila*. Clump-forming perennial. H 6–24in (15–60cm), S 12in (30cm). In summer, loose spikes of nodding buds open to fragrant, funnel-shaped yellow flowers above narrowly spoon-shaped, mid-green leaves. Z3–8 H8–1.

O. pumila. See *O. perennis*.

O. speciosa (White evening primrose). Often short-lived, clump-forming perennial with running rhizomes. H 18in (45cm), S 12in (30cm) or more. In summer bears spikes of fragrant, saucer-shaped, green-centered, pure white flowers that age to pink and open flat. Leaves are narrowly spoon-shaped, deeply cut, and midgreen. Z5–8 H8–1.

O. tetragona. See *O. fruticosa* subsp. *glauca*.

OLEA

OLEACEAE

Genus of evergreen trees grown for their foliage and edible fruits. Needs full sun and deep, fertile, very well-drained soil. Propagate by semi-ripe cuttings in summer or by seed in autumn.

O. europaea (Olive). Slow-growing, evergreen, spreading tree. H and S 30ft (10m). Is very long-lived. Narrowly oblong leaves are gray-green above, silvery beneath. Tiny, fragrant white flowers, borne in short racemes in late summer, are followed by edible, oval green then purple fruits. Z8–10 H10–8.

OLEARIA
Daisy bush

ASTERACEAE/COMPOSITAE

Genus of evergreen shrubs and trees grown for their foliage and daisylike flower heads. In coastal areas provides good, very wind-resistant shelter. Needs full sun and well-drained soil. Cut out dead wood in spring. Propagate by semi-ripe cuttings in summer.

O. albida of gardens. See *O.* 'Talbot de Malahide'.

O. avicenniifolia. Evergreen, rounded, dense shrub. H 10ft (3m), S 15ft (5m). Oval to lance-shaped, dark gray-green leaves are white beneath. Bears wide heads of fragrant white flowers in late summer and early autumn.

O. x haastii illus. p.139.

***O.* 'Henry Travers'**, syn. *O. semidentata* of gardens. Evergreen, rounded, compact shrub. H and S 10ft (3m). Has white shoots and narrowly lance-shaped, leathery, gray-green leaves. Large heads of purple-centered lilac flowers appear from early to midsummer.

O. ilicifolia. Evergreen, bushy, dense shrub. H and S 10ft (3m). Narrowly oblong, rigid leaves are sharply toothed, gray-green, and musk-scented. Fragrant white flower heads are borne in clusters in early summer.

O. lacunosa. Evergreen, upright, dense shrub. H and S 10ft (3m). Narrowly oblong, pointed, rigid leaves have rust brown hairs when young and mature to glossy, dark green with central white veins. Produces white flowerheads only rarely.

O. macrodonta. Vigorous, evergreen, upright shrub, often treelike. H 20ft (6m), S 15ft (5m). Has holly-shaped, sharply toothed, gray-green leaves, silvery white beneath. Large heads of fragrant white flowers appear in early summer.

O. x mollis. Evergreen, rounded, dense shrub. H 3ft (1m), S 5ft (1.5m). Has oval, wavy-edged, silvery gray leaves. Large heads of small white flowers are borne profusely in late spring. **'Zennorensis'**, H and S 6ft (2m), has narrowly oblong leaves.

O. nummulariifolia illus. p.136.

O. phlogopappa. Evergreen, upright, compact shrub. H and S 6ft (2m). Leaves are gray-green and oblong with wavy edges. Massed white flower heads are carried in late spring. Z12–15 H12–8. var. ***subrepanda*** illus. p.158.

O. x scilloniensis. Evergreen, upright, then rounded, dense shrub. H and S 6ft (2m). Narrowly oblong, wavy-edged, dark gray-green leaves set off masses of white flower heads in late spring.

O. semidentata of gardens**.** See *O.* 'Henry Travers'.

***O.* 'Talbot de Malahide'**, syn. *O. albida* of gardens. Evergreen, bushy, dense shrub. H 10ft (3m), S 15ft (5m). Oval, dark green leaves are silvery beneath. Bears broad heads of fragrant white flowers in late summer. Excellent for exposed coastal gardens. Z9–10 H10–9.

O. virgata illus. p.118.

Oliveranthus elegans. See *Echeveria harmsii*.

OLSYNIUM

IRIDACEAE

Genus of fibrous-rooted, clump-forming perennials grown for their nodding, trumpet- to bell-shaped flowers in spring. Requires partial shade and moist, organic, moderately fertile soil. Propagate by seed in autumn. Young plants take 2 or 3 years to flower.

O. biflorum, syn. *Phaiophleps biflora*, *Sisyrinchium odoratissimum*. Clump-forming, spring- to summer-flowering, rhizomatous perennial. H 10–14in (25–35cm), S 2–3in (5–8cm). Has cylindrical, rushlike, erect, basal leaves. Bears a small head of pendent white flowers that are striped and veined red. Z9–10 H10–9.

O. douglasii, syn. *Sisyrinchium douglasii*, *S. grandiflorum* (Grass widow, Spring bell). Stiff, upright, summer-deciduous perennial. H 10in (25cm), S 6in (15cm). Has grasslike leaves sheathing very short, threadlike flowering stems and, in early spring, a succession of pendent, bell-shaped, violet to red-purple or sometimes white flowers. Good in a rock garden or alpine house. Z4–9 H9–3.

OMPHALODES

BORAGINACEAE

Genus of annuals and perennials, some of which are evergreen or semi-evergreen. Makes a good groundcover, especially in rock gardens. Needs shade or semi-shade and moist but well-drained soil, except for *O. linifolia* and *O. luciliae*, which prefer sun. Propagate by seed or division in spring.

O. cappadocica illus. p.349.

O. linifolia illus. p.318.

O. luciliae. Semi-evergreen, mound-forming perennial. H 3in (7cm), S 6in (15cm). Has oval, blue-gray leaves. In spring-summer, loose sprays of pink buds develop into flattish, sky blue flowers. Resents winter wet, so plant in a sheltered site or alpine house. Prefers sun and very gritty soil. Z7–9 H9–7.

O. verna illus. p.349.

OMPHALOGRAMMA

PRIMULACEAE

Genus of perennials closely related to *Primula*, grown for their flowers. Makes good rock garden plants but is difficult to grow, especially in hot, dry areas. Needs shade and gritty, moist but well-drained, peaty soil. Propagate by seed in spring.

O. vinciflorum. Basal-rosetted perennial. H 6in (15cm), S 4in (10cm). Has oval, hairy, midgreen leaves. In spring produces nodding, funnel-shaped violet flowers, each with a deeper violet throat and a flat, flared mouth.

ONCIDIUM

See also ORCHIDS.

O. flexuosum (Dancing-doll orchid; illus. p.299). Evergreen, epiphytic orchid for a cool or intermediate greenhouse. H 9in (23cm). In autumn produces terminal sprays of many small, large-lipped, bright yellow flowers, ¼in (0.5cm) across, with red-brown markings on the sepals and petals. Bears narrowly oval leaves, 4in (10cm) long. Is best grown on a bark slab. Keep in semi-shade in summer. Z14–15 H12–6.

O. ornithorrhynchum (illus. p.296). Evergreen, epiphytic orchid for a cool greenhouse. H 6in (15cm). Dense, arching sprays of very fragrant, rose-lilac flowers, ¼in (0.5cm) across with a yellow highlight, are borne freely in autumn. Has narrowly oval leaves, 4in (10cm) long. Requires semi-shade in summer. Z14–15 H12–6.

O. papilio. See *Psychopsis papilio*.

O. tigrinum (illus. p.298). Evergreen, epiphytic orchid for a cool or intermediate greenhouse. H 9in (23cm). Branching spikes of fragrant, yellow-marked, brown flowers, 2in (5cm) across, each with a large yellow lip, open in autumn. Has oval leaves, 6in (15cm) long. Requires semi-shade in summer. Z14–15 H12–6.

ONIXOTIS,
syn. DIPIDAX

COLCHICACEAE/LILIACEAE

Genus of spring-flowering corms cultivated mainly for botanical interest. Requires sun and well-drained soil. Plant corms in early autumn and keep them watered until after flowering. Dry off in summer. Propagate by seed in autumn.

O. triquetra, syn. *Dipidax triquetrum*. Spring-flowering corm. H 8–12in (20–30cm), S 2–3in (5–8cm). Long, narrow leaves are semi-erect and basal. Carries a spike of flattish, star-shaped white flowers, each narrow petal having a basal red mark.

ONOCLEA

ATHYRIACEAE/DRYOPTERIDACEAE

Genus of one species of deciduous fern that rapidly colonizes wet areas. Grows in sun or shade and in wet soil. Remove fronds as they fade. Propagate by division in autumn or winter.

O. sensibilis illus. p.312.

ONONIS

LEGUMINOSAE/PAPILIONACEAE

Genus of summer-flowering annuals, perennials, and deciduous or semi-evergreen shrubs and subshrubs grown for their pealike flowers. Is good for rock gardens, walls, and banks. Needs a sunny position in well-drained soil. Propagate by seed in autumn or spring, shrubs also by softwood cuttings in summer.

O. fruticosa illus. p.353.

O. natrix illus. p.359.

O. rotundifolia. Deciduous or semi-evergreen, glandular, upright subshrub. H 8–24in (20–60cm), S 8–12in (20–30cm) or more. Bears small, rounded, 3-parted, toothed, hairy green leaves, with the terminal leaflet long-stalked. Flowers that are relatively large, red-streaked rose-pink appear in small clusters in summer. Z7–10 H10–7.

ONOPORDUM,
syn. ONOPORDON

ASTERACEAE/COMPOSITAE

Genus of annuals, biennials, and perennials ranging from stemless to tall, branching plants. Grow in sun or semi-shade and in rich, well-drained soil. To prevent self seeding remove dead flower heads. Propagate by seed sown outdoors in autumn or spring. Leaves are prone to slug and snail damage.

O. acanthium illus. p.322.

ONOSMA

BORAGINACEAE

Genus of summer-flowering annuals, semi-evergreen biennials, perennials and subshrubs grown for their long, pendent, tubular flowers. Is suitable for rock gardens and banks. Requires full sun and well-drained soil. Dislikes wet summers. Propagate by softwood cuttings in summer or by seed in autumn.

O. alborosea illus. p.352.

O. stellulata. Semi-evergreen, upright subshrub. H and S 6in (15cm). Leaves are oblong and covered in hairs that may irritate the skin. Clusters of yellow flowers open in late spring and summer. Z8–9 H9–8.

OOPHYTUM

AIZOACEAE

Genus of clump-forming, egg-shaped succulents with 2 united, very fleshy leaves. These are covered in dry, papery sheaths, except in spring when sheaths split open, revealing a new pair of leaves. Flowers are produced from a slight central fissure on upper surface. Is difficult to grow. Requires sun and well-drained soil. Propagate by seed or stem cuttings in spring or summer.

O. nanum illus. p.470.

Operculina tuberosa. See *Merremia tuberosa*.

OPHIOPOGON

CONVALLARIACEAE/LILIACEAE

Genus of evergreen perennials grown mainly for their grasslike foliage. Grows in sun or partial shade and in fertile, well-drained soil. Propagate by division in spring or by seed in autumn.

O. jaburan. Evergreen, clump-forming perennial. H 6in (15cm), S 12in (30cm). Has dark green foliage. In early summer produces racemes of bell-shaped white flowers, followed by deep blue berries. Z7–10 H10–7.

'Variegatus' see *O.j.* 'Vittatus'.

'Vittatus' (syn. *O.j.* 'Variegatus') has white- or yellow-striped foliage and is much less robust.

O. japonicus illus. p.304.

O. planiscapus **'Nigrescens'** illus. p.303.

OPHRYS

See also ORCHIDS.

O. aranifera. See *O. sphegodes*.

O. fuciflora. See *O. holoserica*.

O. fusca (illus. p.298). Deciduous, terrestrial orchid. H 10–40cm (4–16in). Spikes of greenish, yellow, or brown flowers, ¼in (0.5cm) long, each with a yellow-edged bluish, brown, or purple lip, are produced in spring. Has oval or lance-shaped leaves, 3–5in (8–12cm) long. Grow in shade outdoors. Containerized plants require semi-shade in summer. Z12–15 H12–6.

O. holoserica, syn. *O. fuciflora*. Deciduous, terrestrial orchid. H 6–22in (15–55cm). Spikes of flowers, ⅜in (1cm) long, from white through pink to blue and green, appear in spring-summer. Leaves are oval to oblong, 2–4in (5–10cm) long. Cultivate as for *O. fusca*. Z7–9 H9–7.

O. lutea (illus. p.298). Deciduous, terrestrial orchid. H 3–12in (8–30cm). In spring bears short spikes of flowers, ⅜in (1cm) long, with greenish sepals, yellow petals, and brown-centered, bright yellow lips. Has oval, basal leaves, 5–10cm (2–4in) long. Cultivate as for *O. fusca*. Z8–9 H9–8.

O. speculum. See *O. vernixia*.

O. sphegodes, syn. *O. aranifera* (Spider orchid). Deciduous, terrestrial orchid. H 4–18in (10–45cm). In spring-summer carries spikes of flowers, ⅜in (1cm) long, that vary from green to yellow and have spiderlike, blackish brown marks on lips. Leaves are oval to lance-shaped and 1½–3in (4–8cm) long. Cultivate as for *O. fusca*. Z7–9 H9–7.

O. tenthredinifera (Sawfly orchid; illus. p.297). Deciduous, terrestrial orchid. H 6–22in (15–55cm). In spring has spikes of flowers, ⅜in (1cm) long, in colors of white to pink, or blue and green, each with a violet or bluish lip edged with pale green. Has a basal rosette of oval to oblong leaves, 2–3½in (5–9cm) long. Cultivate as for *O. fusca*. Z7–9 H9–7.

O. vernixia, syn. *O. speculum*. Deciduous, terrestrial orchid. H 3–12in (8–30cm). In spring produces dense spikes of flowers, ⅜in (1cm) long, with greenish or yellow sepals, purple petals, brown lips. Has oblong to lance-shaped leaves, 1½–3in (4–7cm) long. Cultivate as for *O. fusca*. Z7–9 H9–7.

OPHTHALMOPHYLLUM

AIZOACEAE

Genus of clump-forming succulents related to *Lithops*. Each plant has 2 cylindrical, very fleshy leaves, erect and united for most of their length but with a fissure between them at the top. Leaves each have a rounded upper surface with a translucent window. Requires sun and well-drained soil. Water in late summer and early autumn; thereafter keep almost dry. Propagate by seed or stem cuttings in spring or summer.

O. herrei. See *O. longum*.

O. longum, syn. *Conophytum longum*, *O. herrei*. Clump-forming succulent. H 1¼in (3cm), S ⅝in (1.5cm). Has 2 almost united, cylindrical, very fleshy, erect, gray-green to brown leaves. In late summer bears daisylike white to pink flowers, ¾in (2cm) across. Z12–15 H12–10.

O. maughanii. Clump-forming succulent. H 1½in (4cm), S 4in (10cm). Produces 2 almost united, cylindrical, very fleshy, erect, yellowish green leaves with upper surface bearing ¼–½in (0.5–1cm) deep fissure. In late summer bears daisylike white flowers, ⅝in (1.5cm) across. Z12–15 H12–10.

O. villetii illus. p.472.

OPLISMENUS

GRAMINEAE/POACEAE

See also GRASSES, BAMBOOS, RUSHES and SEDGES.

O. africanus, syn. *O. hirtellus* (Basket grass). **'Variegatus'** illus. p.301.

O. hirtellus. See *O. africanus*.

OPLOPANAX

ARALIACEAE

Genus of deciduous, summer-flowering shrubs grown for their habit, fruits, and spiny foliage. Young growth may be damaged by late frosts. Does best in a cool, partially shaded position and in moist soil. Propagate by seed in autumn or by root cuttings in late winter.

O. horridus (Devil's club). Deciduous, spreading, open, sparsely branched shrub. H and S 6ft (2m). Prickly stems bear large, oval, 7–9-lobed, toothed, midgreen leaves. Bears dense umbels of small, star-shaped, greenish white flowers from mid- to late summer, then spherical red fruits. Z7–9 H9–7.

OPUNTIA
Prickly pear

CACTACEAE

Genus of cacti ranging from small, alpine, groundcover plants to large, evergreen, tropical trees, with at times insignificant glochids – short, soft, barbed spines produced on areoles. Mature plants carry masses of short-spined, pear-shaped green, yellow, red, or purple fruits (prickly pears), edible in some species. Needs sun and well-drained soil. Water containerized specimens when in full growth. Propagate by seed or stem cuttings in spring or summer. Contact with the bristles causes intense irritation to skin, and they are difficult to remove.

O. brasiliensis. Treelike cactus. H 18ft (5.5m), S 10ft (3m). Has a cylindrical green stem bearing bright green branches of flattened, oval, spiny segments. Sheds 2–3-year-old side branches. Masses of shallowly saucer-shaped yellow flowers, 1½in (4cm) across, appear in spring-summer, only on plants over 2ft (60cm) tall, and are followed by small yellow fruits. Z11–12 H12–9.

O. compressa, syn. *O. humifusa*, illus. p.478.

O. cylindrica. Bushy cactus. H 12–20ft (4–6m). S 3ft (1m). On cylindrical stems, 1½–2in (4–5cm) across, are borne short-lived, cylindrical, dark green leaves, to ¾in (2cm) long, on new growth. Areoles may lack spines or each produce 2 or 3 barbed ones. Shallowly saucer-shaped, pink-red flowers appear in spring-summer, only on plants over 6ft (2m) tall, and are followed by greenish yellow fruits. Z11–12 H12–9.

O. engelmannii. See *O. ficus-indica*.

O. erinacea illus. p.465.

O. ficus-indica, syn. *O. engelmannii*, *O. megacantha* (Edible prickly pear, Indian fig). Bushy to treelike cactus. H and S 15ft (5m). Bears flattened, oblong, blue-green stem segments, 20in (50cm) long and spineless. In spring-summer has masses of shallowly saucer-shaped yellow flowers, 4in (10cm) across, followed by edible purple fruits. Z11–12 H12–9.

O. humifusa. See *O. compressa*.

O. megacantha. See *O. ficus-indica*.
O. microdasys (Bunny ears). Bushy cactus. H and S 2ft (60cm). Has flattened, oval, green stem segments, 3–7in (8–18cm) long, that develop brown marks in low temperatures. Bears spineless areoles with white, yellow, brown, or red glochids closely set in diagonal rows. Masses of funnel-shaped yellow flowers, 2in (5cm) across, appear in summer on plants over 6in (15cm) tall, and are followed by small, dark red fruits. Z11–12 H12–9. var. ***albispina*** illus. p.467.
O. robusta illus. p.460.
O. tunicata illus. p.468.
O. verschaffeltii illus. p.474.

ORBEA

ASCLEPIADACEAE

Genus of clump-forming succulents with erect, 4-angled stems. Stem edges are often indented and may produce small leaves that drop after only a few weeks. Needs sun or partial shade and well-drained soil. Propagate by seed or stem cuttings in spring or summer.
O. variegata, syn. *Stapelia variegata*, illus. p.476.

ORCHIDS

ORCHIDACEAE

Family of perennials, some of which are evergreen or semi-evergreen, grown for their beautiful, unusual flowers. These consist of 3 outer sepals and 3 inner petals, the lowest of which, known as the lip, is usually enlarged and different from the others in shape, markings, and color. There are about 750 genera and 17,500 species, together with an even greater number of hybrids, bred partly for their vigor and ease of care. They are divided into epiphytic and terrestrial plants. (The spread of most orchids is indefinite.)

Epiphytic orchids
Epiphytes have more flamboyant flowers than terrestrial orchids and are more commonly grown. In the wild, they grow on tree branches or rocks (lithophytes), obtaining nourishment through clinging roots and moisture through aerial roots. Most consist of a horizontal rhizome, from which arise vertical, water-storing, often swollen stems known as pseudobulbs. Flowers and foliage are produced from the newest pseudobulbs. Other epiphytes consist of a continuously growing upright rhizome; on these, flower spikes appear in the axils of leaves growing from the rhizome.
In temperate climates, epiphytes need to be grown under cover.

Cultivation of epiphytes
For cultivation purposes, epiphytes, which are all tender (they cannot withstand freezing temperatures), may be divided into 3 groups: cool-greenhouse types, which require min. 50°F (10°C) and max. 75°F (24°C); intermediate-greenhouse types, needing a range of 55–80°F (13–27°C); and warm-greenhouse types, requiring 65–80°F (18–27°C). In summer, temperatures need to be controlled by shading the glass and by ventilation. Cool-greenhouse orchids may be placed outdoors in summer; this improves flowering. Other types may also be grown outdoors if the air temperature remains within these ranges.
The amount of light required in summer is given in individual plant entries. All epiphytic orchids, however, need to be kept out of direct sun in summer to avoid scorching, and they require full light in winter.
Epiphytic orchids, whether grown indoors or outside, require a special soil-free mix obtained from an orchid nursery or made by mixing 2 parts fibrous material (such as bark chips and/or peat) with 1 part porous material (such as sphagnum moss and/or expanded clay pellets). Most epiphytes may be grown in pots, although some may be successfully cultivated in a hanging basket or on a slab of bark (with moss around their roots) suspended in the greenhouse.
In summer, water plants freely and spray regularly. Those suspended on bark slabs need a constantly moist atmosphere. In winter, water moderately and, if plants are in growth, spray occasionally. Some orchids rest in winter and require scarcely any water or none at all. Orchids benefit from weak foliar fertilizing; apply as for watering. Repot plants every other year, in spring; if they are about to flower, repot after flowering.

Terrestrial orchids
Terrestrial orchids, some of which also produce pseudobulbs, grow in soil or leaf mold, sustaining themselves in the normal way through roots or tubers. Some may be grown in borders, but many in temperate climates need to be cultivated in pots and protected under cover during winter.

Cultivation of terrestrial orchids
Terrestrial orchids are hardy to tender, min. 65°F (18°C). *Cypripedium* species may be grown outdoors, preferably in neutral to acidic soil, but cannot withstand severe cold or tolerate very wet soil in winter. Other terrestrial orchids, except in very mild areas, are best grown in pots; use the same mix as for epiphytes but add 1 part coarse to 2 parts mix. Place pots outdoors in a cold frame or keep in a greenhouse during the growing season. Keep dry when dormant. Under cover, light requirements, watering, fertilizing, and repotting are as for epiphytes.

Orchid propagation
Orchids with pseudobulbs may be increased by removing and replanting old, leafless pseudobulbs when repotting in spring. Take care to retain at least 4 pseudobulbs on the parent plant. Some genera that may be propagated in this way are: *Ada*, x *Aliceara*, *Anguloa*, *Bletilla*, *Brassavola* (large plants only and retaining at least 6 pseudobulbs on the parent), x *Brassocattleya*, x *Brassolaeliocattleya*, *Bulbophyllum*, *Calanthe*, *Cattleya*, *Coelogyne*, *Cymbidium*, *Dendrobium*, *Dendrochilum*, *Encyclia*, *Gomesa*, *Gongora*, *Laelia*, x *Laeliocattleya*, *Lycaste*, *Maxillaria*, *Miltonia*, *Miltoniopsis*, x *Odontioda*, x *Odontocidium*, *Odontoglossum*, x *Odontonia*, *Oncidium*, *Phaius*, *Pleione*, x *Potinara*, x *Sophrolaeliocattleya*, *Stanhopea*, x *Vuylstekeara*, x *Wilsonara*, and *Zygopetalum*.
Some orchids without pseudobulbs produce new growth from the base. When a plant has 6 new growths, divide it in spring into 2 and repot both portions. Propagate *Disa*, *Paphiopedilum*, and *Phragmipedium* in this way. Large specimens of *Eria*, *Masdevallia*, and *Pleurothallis* may be divided in spring, leaving 4–6 stems on each portion.
Propagation of *Phalaenopsis* is by stem cuttings taken soon after flowering. *Vanda* may be increased by removing the top half of the stem once it has produced aerial roots and leaves; new growths will develop from the leafless base. With both of these methods,achieving success is difficult and not recommended for the beginner.
Propagate terrestrial orchids with tubers by division of the tubers. Genera that may be increased in this way are: *Cypripedium* (in spring), *Dactylorhiza* (spring), *Ophrys* (autumn), *Orchis* (spring), *Serapias* (autumn), and *Spiranthes* (spring). *Calypso* is rarely propagated successfully in cultivation. *Angraecum* should not be propagated in cultivation, because the parent plant is easily endangered.
The most easily increased orchids are *Cymbidium*. Propagation of *Epidendrum* may be extremely difficult; see genus for specific details.

Orchids are illustrated on pp.296–9. See also *Ada*, x *Aliceara*, *Angraecum*, *Anguloa*, *Bletilla*, *Brassavola*, x *Brassocattleya*, x *Brassolaeliocattleya*, *Bulbophyllum*, *Calanthe*, *Calypso*, *Cattleya*, *Coelogyne*, *Cymbidium*, *Cypripedium*, *Dactylorhiza*, *Dendrobium*, *Dendrochilum*, *Encyclia*, *Epidendrum*, *Eria*, *Gomesa*, *Gongora*, *Laelia*, x *Laeliocattleya*, *Lemboglossum*, *Lycaste*, *Masdevallia*, *Maxillaria*, *Miltonia*, *Miltoniopsis*, x *Odontioda*, x *Odontocidium*, *Odontoglossum*, x *Odontonia*, *Oncidium*, *Ophrys*, *Orchis*, *Paphiopedilum*, *Phaius*, *Phalaenopsis*, *Phragmipedium*, *Pleione*, *Pleurothallis*, x *Potinara*, *Psychopsis*, *Rossioglossum*, *Serapias*, x *Sophrolaeliocattleya*, *Spiranthes*, *Stanhopea*, *Vanda*, x *Vuylstekeara*, x *Wilsonara*, and *Zygopetalum*.

ORCHIS

See also ORCHIDS.
O. elata. See *Dactylorhiza elata*.
O. morio (Gandergoose, Green-veined orchid; illus. p.298). Deciduous, terrestrial orchid. H 16in (40cm). Reddish purple, mauve, or rarely white flowers, ⅜in (1cm) long, with green veins on the cupped sepals, open along stems in spring. Has a basal cluster of lance-shaped or broadly oblong, pale to midgreen leaves, 4–6in (10–16cm) long. Requires sun or semi-shade. Z12–15 H12–6.

OREOCEREUS,
syn. BORZICACTUS

CACTACEAE

Genus of mainly columnar cacti with thick, cylindrical, much-ribbed stems with spines, usually branching from the base, and, in some species, are covered in long hairs. Solitary, tubular-funnel-shaped flowers are produced near stem tips during the day in summer. Requires a position in full sun and very well-drained, slightly alkaline soil. Propagate by seed in spring or summer.
O. aurantiacus, syn. *Matucana aurantiaca*, illus. p.480.
O. celsianus, syn. *Cleistocactus celsianus*, illus. p.462.
O. haynei, syn. *Matucana haynei*. Slow-growing, spherical to columnar cactus. H 24in (60cm), S 4in (10cm). Has a cylindrical, much-ribbed, grass-green stem densely covered with short white or yellow spines. Red, orange-brown, or purple-crimson flowers appear in summer on plants over 6in (15cm) high.
O. peruviana. See *Oroya peruviana*.
O. trollii, syn. *Cleistocactus trollii* (Old man of the Andes). Slow-growing, columnar cactus. H 28in (70cm), S 4in (10cm). Cylindrical, green stem, 3–4in (7–10cm), with thick golden spines is almost hidden by long, wispy, hairlike white spines. Pink flowers, recurved at tips and 4in (10cm) long, appear in summer on mature plants.

OREOPTERIS

THELYPTERIDACEAE

Genus of deciduous ferns. Tolerates sun or semi-shade. Grow in moist or very moist soil. Remove fading fronds regularly. Propagate by division in spring.
O. limbosperma, syn. *Thelypteris oreopteris* (Mountain buckler fern, Mountain fern, Mountain wood fern). Deciduous fern. H 2–3ft (60cm–1m), S 1ft (30cm). Has mainly lance-shaped, much-divided fronds with oblong to lance-shaped, midgreen pinnae. Z12-15 H12–10.

ORIGANUM
Dittany

LABIATAE/LAMIACEAE

Genus of deciduous subshrubs and perennials, sometimes with over-

wintering leaf rosettes. Some species are grown as culinary herbs, others for their clusters of tubular, usually pink flowers. Most species have arching, prostrate stems and are useful for trailing over rocks, banks, and walls. Prefers sun and well-drained, alkaline soil. Propagate by division in spring, by cuttings of non-flowering shoots in early summer, or by seed in autumn or spring.
O. amanum. Deciduous, rounded, compact subshrub. H and S 6–8in (15–20cm). Open funnel-shaped, pale pink or white flowers are borne all summer above small, heart-shaped, pale green leaves. Makes a good alpine house plant; dislikes a humid atmosphere. Z5–8 H8–5.
O. dictamnus (Cretan dittany). Prostrate perennial. H 5–6in (12–15cm), S 16in (40cm). Arching stems are clothed in rounded, aromatic, hairy, gray-white leaves. Has pendent heads of open funnel-shaped, purplish pink flowers in summer. Z8–11 H12–8.
***O.* 'Kent Beauty'** illus. p.353.
O. laevigatum illus. p.354.
O. rotundifolium. Deciduous, prostrate subshrub. H 9–12in (23–30cm), S 12in (30cm). Throughout summer bears whorls of pendent, funnel-shaped, pale pink flowers surrounded by yellow-green bracts. Has small, rounded, midgreen leaves. Z7–9 H9–7.
O. vulgare (Wild marjoram). Mat-forming, woody-based perennial. H and S 18in (45cm). Has oval, aromatic, dark green leaves, above which branched, wiry stems bear clusters of tiny, tubular, 2-lipped mauve flowers in summer. Z4–9 H10–2.
'Aureum' illus. p.290.

ORNITHOGALUM
Star-of-Bethlehem

HYACINTHACEAE/LILIACEAE

Genus of bulbs grown for their mostly star-shaped white flowers, usually backed with green. Needs sun or partial shade and well-drained soil. Lift and dry tender species for winter, if grown outside in summer, and replant in spring. Propagate by seed or offsets in autumn for spring-flowering bulbs and in spring for summer-flowering bulbs. All parts may cause severe discomfort if ingested; the sap may irritate skin.
O. arabicum illus. p.420.
O. balansae, syn. *O. oligophyllum* of gardens, illus. p.426.
O. lanceolatum illus. p.426.
O. montanum illus. p.426.
O. narbonense illus. p.419.
O. nutans (Drooping star-of-Bethlehem). Spring-flowering bulb. H 6–14in (15–35cm), S 3–4in (8–10cm). Has a cluster of linear, channeled, semi-erect, basal leaves. Stem bears a spike of pendent, bell-shaped, translucent white flowers, ¾–1¼in (2–3cm) long with pale green outsides. Prefers partial shade. Z4–9 H9–5.
O. oligophyllum of gardens**.** See *O. balansae*.
O. saundersiae. Summer-flowering bulb. H to 3ft (1m), S 6–8in (15–20cm). Produces a basal cluster of strap- or lance-shaped, semi-erect leaves. Stem bears a flat-topped head of erect, flattish white or cream flowers, each with a blackish green ovary forming a dark eye. Z7–10 H10–7.
O. thyrsoides illus. p.420.
O. umbellatum. Spring-flowering bulb. H 4–12in (10–30cm), S 4–6in (10–15cm). Linear, channeled, semi-erect green leaves each have a white line on upper surface. Bears a loose, flat-topped head of star-shaped white flowers, backed with green. Often becomes invasive and a pest in lawns. Z6–10 H10–1.

Orobus vernus. See *Lathyrus vernus*.

ORONTIUM

ARACEAE

Genus of one species of deciduous, perennial, deep-water plant grown for its floating foliage and flower spikes. Needs full sun. Remove faded flower spikes. Propagate by seed when fresh in midsummer.
O. aquaticum illus. p.451.

OROSTACHYS

CRASSULACEAE

Genus of short-lived, basal-rosetted succulents with very fleshy, sword-shaped leaves. Produces flowers 3 years from sowing seed, then dies. Requires sun and well-drained soil. Propagate by seed or division in spring or summer.
O. chanetii. Basal-rosetted succulent. H 1½in (4cm), S 3in (8cm). Bears gray-green leaves that are shorter in rosette center. Flower stem produces a dense, tapering spike of star-shaped white or pink flowers, ½–¾in (1–2cm) across, in spring-summer. Z13–15 H12–1.

OROYA

CACTACEAE

Genus of spherical cacti. Inner flower petals form a tube and outer ones open fully. Needs a sunny, well-drained site. Propagate by seed in spring or summer.
O. neoperuviana. See *O. peruviana*.
O. peruviana, syn. *Oreocereus neoperuviana*, *O. peruviana*, illus. p.464.

Orphanidesia gaultherioides. See *Epigaea gaultheriodes*.

ORTHROSANTHUS

IRIDACEAE

Genus of perennials with short, woody rhizomes, grown for their flowers. Prefers sun and well-drained soil. Propagate by division or seed in spring.
O. chimboracensis. Tufted, rhizomatous perennial. H 2ft (60cm) in flower, S 6in (15cm). Has very narrow, grasslike, ribbed, stiff leaves, to 18in (45cm) long, with finely toothed margins. In summer, produces clusters of short-lived, long-stalked, shallowly bowl-shaped, lavender-blue flowers, each enclosed in 2 leaflike bracts. Z10–11 H12–1.

ORYCHOPHRAGMUS

BRASSICACEAE/CRUCIFERAE

Genus of late spring- to summer-flowering annuals. Grow in sun and in fertile, well-drained soil. Propagate by seed in spring.
O. violaceus illus. p.331.

OSBECKIA

MELASTOMATACEAE

Genus of evergreen, summer-flowering perennials, subshrubs, and shrubs grown for their flowers and foliage. Needs full light or partial shade and organic, well-drained soil. Water potted specimens freely when in full growth, moderately at other times. Cut back flowered stems by at least half in early spring to maintain vigor and to produce large flower clusters. Propagate by seed in spring or by greenwood cuttings in summer.
O. stellata. Evergreen, rounded, stiff-stemmed shrub. H and S 3–6ft (1–2m). Has narrowly oval, hairy, prominently veined leaves. Bears terminal clusters of 4-petaled, rose-purple flowers in late summer. Z14–15 H12–10.

Oscularia deltoides. See *Lampranthus deltoides*.

OSMANTHUS

OLEACEAE

Genus of evergreen shrubs and trees grown for their foliage and small, fragrant flowers. *O.* x *burkwoodii* and *O. heterophyllus* may be used for hedging. Tolerates sun or shade and fertile, well-drained soil. Restrict growth by cutting back after flowering; trim hedges in midsummer. Propagate by semi-ripe cuttings in summer.
O. armatus. Evergreen, bushy, dense shrub. H and S 12ft (4m). Large, oblong, dark green leaves are rigid and sharply toothed. Has tubular, 4-lobed white flowers in autumn followed by egg-shaped, dark violet fruits. Z8–9 H9–8.
O.* x *burkwoodii, syn. x *Osmarea burkwoodii*, illus. p.116.
O. decorus, syn. *Phillyrea decora*. Evergreen, upright, rounded, dense shrub. H 10ft (3m), S 15ft (5m). Has large, oblong, glossy, dark green leaves. Bears tubular, 4-lobed white flowers in midspring, then egg-shaped, blackish purple fruits. Z6–9 H9–6.
O. delavayi, syn. *Siphonosmanthus delavayi*, illus. p.116.
O. forrestii. See *O. yunnanensis*.
O. fragrans (Fragrant olive). Evergreen, upright shrub or tree. H and S 20ft (6m). Very fragrant, tubular, 4-lobed white flowers are borne amid oblong, glossy, dark green leaves from early to late summer, followed by ovoid, blue-black fruits. Z8–11 H12–8. f. ***aurantiacus*** has orange flowers. Z7–10 H10–7.
***O. heterophyllus* 'Aureomarginatus'** illus. p.127. **'Gulftide'** is an evergreen, bushy, dense shrub. H 8ft (2.5m), S 10ft (3m). Holly-shaped, sharply toothed, glossy, dark green leaves set off tubular, 4-lobed white flowers in autumn. Z7–9 H9–7.
O. yunnanensis, syn. *O. forrestii*. Evergreen, treelike, upright then spreading shrub. H and S 30ft (10m). Has large, oblong, glossy, bright green leaves, bronze when young. Produces tubular, 4-lobed, creamy white flowers in clusters in late winter or early spring. Z8–9 H9–8..

x ***Osmarea burkwoodii.*** See *Osmanthus* x *burkwoodii*.
Osmaronia. Reclassified as *Oemleria*.

OSMUNDA

OSMUNDACEAE

Genus of deciduous ferns. Requires shade, except for *O. regalis*, which also tolerates sun. *O. cinnamomea* and *O. claytoniana* need moist soil; *O. regalis* does best in very wet conditions. Remove fading fronds regularly. Propagate by division in autumn or winter or by spores as soon as ripe.
O. cinnamomea (Cinnamon fern). Deciduous fern. H 3ft (1m), S 18in (45cm). Outer, lance-shaped, divided, pale green sterile fronds with deeply cut pinnae surround brown fertile fronds, all arising from a fibrous rootstock. Z4–8 H8-1.
O. claytoniana (Interrupted fern). Deciduous fern. H 2ft (60cm), S 1ft (30cm). Has lance-shaped, pale green fronds divided into oblong, blunt pinnae; outer sterile fronds are larger than fertile ones at center of plant. Z2–10 H9–1.
O. regalis illus. p.312.

OSTEOMELES

ROSACEAE

Genus of evergreen, summer-flowering shrubs grown for their habit, foliage, and flowers. In most areas plant against a south- or west-facing wall. Requires a position in sun and fertile, well-drained soil. Propagate by semi-ripe cuttings in summer.
O. schweriniae illus. p.138.

OSTEOSPERMUM

ASTERACEAE/COMPOSITAE

Genus of evergreen, semi-woody perennials. Does best in warm areas. Requires sun and well-drained soil. Propagate by cuttings of non-flowering shoots in midsummer.
O. barberae of gardens. See *O. jucundum*.
***O.* 'Blue Streak'**, syn. *O. ecklonis* 'Blue Streak'. Evergreen, upright

perennial. H and S 18in (45cm). In summer-autumn, daisylike flower heads with dark slate blue centers and white ray florets (blue on the reverse) are borne above lance-shaped, gray-green leaves. Z10–11 H6–1.
***O.* 'Buttermilk'** illus. p.290.
***O.* 'Cannington Roy'.** Evergreen, clump-forming, prostrate perennial. H 12in (30cm), S 18in (45cm). Large, daisylike pink flower heads with darker eyes are borne profusely in summer-autumn. Leaves are linear and gray. Z10–11 H6–1.
O. ecklonis. Evergreen, upright or somewhat straggling perennial. H and S 18in (45cm). In summer-autumn, daisylike white flower heads, with dark blue centers are borne singly above lance-shaped, gray-green leaves. Z10–11 H6–1. **'Blue Streak'** see *O.* 'Blue Streak'.
O. jucundum, syn. *Dimorphotheca barberae* of gardens, *O. barberae* of gardens, illus. p.279.
***O.* 'Nairobi Purple'.** Evergreen, semi-prostrate perennial. H 12in (30cm), S 12–18in (30–45cm). Bears daisylike, velvety, deep purple-red flower heads with darker streaks on outside of ray petals in summer. Has fresh green, lance-shaped leaves. Will not flower freely in rich soils. Z10–11 H6–1.
***O.* 'Whirligig'**. See. *O.* 'Whirlygig'.
***O.* 'Whirlygig'**, syn. *O.* 'Whirligig', illus. p.277.

OSTROWSKIA

CAMPANULACEAE

Genus of one species of summer-flowering perennial. Prefers a warm, sunny situation and rich, moist but well-drained soil. May be difficult to grow since it needs a resting period after flowering, so cover with a frame until late autumn to keep dry. Propagate by seed in autumn or spring.
O. magnifica. Erect perennial. H 5ft (1.5m), S 1½ft (45cm). From early to midsummer produces very large, bell-shaped blooms of delicate light blue-purple veined with darker purple. Produces whorls of oval, blue-gray leaves. Z7–8 H8–7.

OSTRYA

BETULACEAE/CORYLACEAE

Genus of deciduous trees grown for their foliage, catkins, and fruits. Needs sun or semi-shade and fertile, well-drained soil. Propagate by seed in autumn.
O. carpinifolia (Hop hornbeam). Deciduous, rounded tree. H and S 50ft (15m). Has gray bark and oval, glossy, dark green leaves that turn yellow in autumn. Yellow catkins in midspring are followed by hoplike, greenish white fruit clusters that become brown in autumn. Z6–9 H9–6..
O. virginiana illus. p.77.

OTHONNA,
syn. OTHONNOPSIS

ASTERACEAE/COMPOSITAE

Genus of evergreen shrubs grown for their daisylike flower heads in summer. Needs sun and well-drained soil. Propagate by softwood cuttings in early summer.
O. cheirifolia illus. p.358.

Othonnopsis. Reclassified as *Othonna.*

OURISIA

SCROPHULARIACEAE

Genus of evergreen perennials with creeping rootstocks. Excellent for walls. Needs shade and moist, peaty soil. Propagate by division or seed in spring.
O. caespitosa illus. p.374.
***O.* 'Loch Ewe'.** Vigorous, evergreen, rosetted perennial. H and S 12in (30cm). Prostrate stems have heart-shaped, leathery, green leaves. Produces dense spikes of outward-facing, tubular, salmon-pink flowers in late spring and early summer. Z7–8 H8–7.
O. macrocarpa. Vigorous, evergreen, prostrate perennial. H 24in (60cm), S 8in (20cm). Has rosettes of heart-shaped, leathery, dark green leaves. Produces spikes of open cup-shaped, yellow-centered white flowers in late spring. Z7–9 H9–7.
O. magellanica. See *O. ruellioides.*
O. microphylla illus. p.376.
O. ruellioides, syn. *O. magellanica.* Evergreen, straggling perennial. H 1½in (4cm), S to 6in (15cm). In summer produces tubular scarlet flowers above broadly heart-shaped leaves. Z7–9 H9–7.

OXALIS

OXALIDACEAE

Genus of tuberous, rhizomatous ,or fibrous-rooted perennials and semi-evergreen subshrubs grown for their colorful flowers, which in bud are rolled like an umbrella, and attractive leaves. Leaves are mostly less than ¾in (2cm) across and are divided into 3 or more leaflets. Some species may be invasive; smaller species and cultivars are good in a rock garden. Needs full sun or semi-shade and well-drained soil. Propagate by division in autumn or early spring.
O. acetosella (Wood sorrel). Creeping, spring-flowering, rhizomatous perennial. H 2in (5cm), S 12–18in (30–45cm). Forms mats of cloverlike, 3-lobed leaves. Delicate stems bear cup-shaped white flowers, each ⅜in (1cm) across with 5 purple-veined petals. Prefers semi-shade. Z3–8 H8–1. var. ***purpurascens*** see *O.a.* var. *subpurpurascens*. var. ***subpurpurascens*** (syn. *O.a.* var. *purpurascens*) illus. p.365.
O. adenophylla illus. p.366.
O. bowiei, syn. *O. purpurata* var. *bowiei*. Spring- to summer-flowering, tuberous perennial. H to 12in (30cm), S 6in (15cm). Has long-stalked, clover-like, 3-lobed leaves. Stems each produce a loose head of 3–10 widely funnel-shaped, pinkish purple flowers, 1¼–1½in (3–4cm) across. Needs a sheltered, sunny site. Z8–10 H10–8.
O. chrysantha. Creeping, fibrous-rooted perennial. H 1½–2in (4–5cm), S 6–12in (15–30cm). Forms mats of cloverlike, 3-lobed leaves. Stems each produce a funnel-shaped, bright yellow flower, ¾–1¼in (2–3cm) across, in summer. Needs a sheltered site. Z8–10 H10–8.
O. deppei. See *O. tetraphylla.*
O. depressa, syn. *O. inops*, illus. p.378.
O. enneaphylla (Scurvy grass). Tuft-forming, rhizomatous perennial. H 2–3in (5–7cm), S 3–4in (8–10cm). Gray-green leaves are divided into narrowly oblong to oval leaflets. In summer, stems bear widely funnel-shaped, 1¼–1½in (3–4cm wide), lilac-pink or white flowers. Z5–9 H9–5.
O. hedysaroides. Semi-evergreen, bushy subshrub. H 3ft (1m), S 1–1½ft (30–45cm). Stems have cloverlike, 3-lobed green leaves. Leaf axils bear clusters of widely funnel-shaped yellow flowers, ¾–1¼in (2–3cm) across, in spring-summer. Z9–10 H10–9.
O. hirta. Late summer-flowering, tuberous perennial. H 12in (30cm), S 4–6in (10–15cm). Stem produces scattered leaves with 3 narrowly lance-shaped leaflets. Leaf axils each produce a widely funnel-shaped, rose-purple flower, ¾–1¼in (2–3cm) wide, with a yellow center. Z9–10 H10–9.
O. inops. See *O. depressa.*
***O.* 'Ione Hecker'.** Tuft-forming, rhizomatous perennial. H 2in (5cm), S 2–3in (5–8cm). Gray leaves are composed of narrowly oblong, wavy leaflets. In summer bears funnel-shaped, pale purple-blue flowers, 1½in (4cm) across, with darker veins. Z8–9 H9–8.
O. laciniata. Tuft-forming, rhizomatous perennial. H 2in (5cm), S 2–3in (5–8cm). Has blue-gray leaves with narrowly oblong, crinkly-edged leaflets. In summer bears wide funnel-shaped, steel blue flowers, 1½in (4cm) across, with darker veins. Z8–9 H9–8.
O. lobata illus. p.387.
O. purpurata var. ***bowiei.*** See *O. bowiei.*
O. tetraphylla, syn. *O. deppei*, illus. p.353.

OXYDENDRUM

ERICACEAE

Genus of one species of deciduous tree grown for its flowers and spectacular autumn color. For good coloring, plant in an open position in sun or semi-shade. Needs moist, acidic soil. Propagate by softwood cuttings in summer or by seed in autumn.
O. arboreum illus. p.78.

Oxypetalum caeruleum. See *Tweedia caerulea.*

OZOTHAMNUS

ASTERACEAE/COMPOSITAE

Genus of evergreen, summer-flowering shrubs grown for their foliage and small, densely clustered flower heads. Requires full sun and well-drained soil. Propagate by semi-ripe cuttings in summer.
O. coralloides, syn. *Helichrysum coralloides*, illus. p.361.
O. ledifolius, syn. *Helichrysum ledifolium*, illus. p.160.
O. rosmarinifolius, syn. *Helichrysum rosmarinifolium*, illus. p.138.
O. selago, syn. *Helichrysum selago*, illus. p.361.

P

PACHYCEREUS

CACTACEAE

Genus of slow-growing, columnar cacti, branching with age. The funnel-shaped flowers are unlikely to appear in cultivation, since they are produced only on plants over 10ft (3m) high. Requires sun and well-drained soil. Propagate by seed in spring or summer.
P. marginatus, syn. *Lemaireocereus marginatus*, *Marginatocereus marginatus*, *Stenocereus marginatus*, illus. p.457.
P. pecten-aboriginum. Columnar cactus. H 35ft (11m), S 10ft (3m). Dark green stems bear 9–11 deep ribs. Each areole has 8 radial spines, ½in (1cm) long, and longer central spines. All spines are dark brown with red bases and fade to gray. Z13-15 H12-10.
P. pringlei illus. p.460.
P. schottii, syn. *Lophocereus schottii*, illus. p.458. **'Monstrosus'** is a columnar cactus. H 22ft (7m), S 6ft (2m). Irregular, olive- to dark green stems have 4–15 ribs and no spines. Has funnel-shaped pink flowers, 1¼in (3cm) wide, at night in summer. Z13-15 H12-10.

PACHYPHRAGMA

BRASSICACEAE/CRUCIFERAE

Genus of perennials with rosettes of basal leaves, often grown as a ground-cover under shrubs. Needs sun or partial shade and moist soil. Propagate by division or stem cuttings in late spring or by seed in autumn.
P. macrophyllum, syn. *Thlaspi macrophyllum*, illus. p.267.

PACHYPHYTUM

CRASSULACEAE

Genus of rosetted succulents, closely related to *Echeveria*, with which it hybridizes. Needs sun and well-drained soil. Propagate by seed, or leaf or stem

cuttings in spring or summer.
P. compactum illus. p.480.
P. oviferum illus. p.475.

PACHYPODIUM

APOCYNACEAE

Genus of bushy or treelike succulents, mostly with swollen stems, closely related to *Adenium*, except that most species have spines. Requires full sun and very well-drained soil. May be very difficult to grow. Propagate by seed in spring or summer.
P. lamerei illus. p.456.
P. succulentum. Treelike succulent. H 2ft (60cm), S 1ft (30cm). Swollen trunk, 6in (15cm) across, has narrow, vertical green to gray-brown stems. Has trumpet-shaped, pink-crimson flowers, ¾in (2cm) across, near stem tips in summer. Z14-15 H12-10.

PACHYSANDRA

BUXACEAE

Genus of evergreen, creeping perennials and subshrubs grown for their tufted foliage. Is useful as a groundcover. Tolerates dense shade and will grow well in any but very dry soil. Propagate by division in spring.
P. procumbens (Alleghany spurge). A clump-forming semi-evergreen perennial. H 12in (30cm) S indefinite. Toothed leaves are in whorls and are a dark green, often mottled with brown. Spikes of fragrant white flowers appear with the new foliage in spring. Z5–9 H8–3.
P. terminalis illus. p.388.
'Variegata' is an evergreen, creeping perennial. H 4in (10cm), S 8in (20cm). Diamond-shaped, cream-variegated leaves are clustered at stem tips. In early summer bears spikes of tiny white flowers, sometimes flushed purple. Z4-8 H8–1.

PACHYSTACHYS

ACANTHACEAE

Genus of evergreen perennials and shrubs grown for their flowers. Needs partial shade and fertile, well-drained soil. Water potted plants freely when in full growth, moderately at other times. Cut back flowered stems in late winter to maintain a bushy habit. Propagate by greenwood cuttings in early summer. Whitefly and spider mite may cause problems.
P. cardinalis. See *P. coccinea.*
P. coccinea, syn. *Jacobinia coccinea, Justicia coccinea, P. cardinalis* (Cardinal's guard). Evergreen, erect, robust shrub. H 4–6ft (1.2–2m), S 2–3ft (60cm–1m). Leaves are oval and deep green. Has tubular, bright red flowers in tight, green-bracted spikes, 6in (15cm) long, in winter.
P. lutea illus. p.157.

Pachystima. Reclassified as *Paxistima*.

x PACHYVERIA

CRASSULACEAE

Hybrid genus (*Echeveria* x *Pachyphytum*) of clump-forming, rosetted succulents, sometimes almost stemless. Requires a position in full sun or partial shade and very well-drained soil. Propagate by leaf or stem cuttings in spring or summer.
x ***P. glauca*** illus. p.466.

PAEONIA

Peony

PAEONIACEAE

Genus of late spring-flowering perennials and deciduous shrubs (tree peonies), valued for their bold foliage, showy blooms, and, in some species, colorful seed pods. Young growth (especially on tree peonies) may be damaged by late spring frosts. Prefers sun (but tolerates light shade) and rich, well-drained soil. Tall and very large-flowered cultivars need support. Propagate all species by seed in autumn (may take up to 3 years to germinate), tuberous species by root cuttings in winter, and tree peonies by semi-ripe cuttings in late summer or by grafting in winter. Perennials may also be propagated by division in late summer. Is prone to peony wilt. All parts can cause mild stomach upset if ingested. See also feature panel pp.236–7.

Peonies grow well in Z3–8 H8–1.

Flower forms
Unless stated otherwise, peonies described below flower between late spring and early summer and have large, alternate leaves divided into oval to lance-shaped or linear leaflets. Flowers are single, semi-double, double, or anemone-form.
Single – flowers are mostly cup-shaped, with 1 or 2 rows of large, often lightly ruffled, incurving petals and a conspicuous central boss of stamens.
Semi-double – flowers are similar to single ones, but have 2 or 3 rows of petals.
Double – flowers are rounded, usually composed of 1 or 2 outer rows of large, often lightly ruffled, incurving petals, the remaining petals being smaller, usually becoming more densely arranged and diminishing in size toward the center. Stamens are few, inconspicuous, or absent.
Anemone-form (Imperial or Japanese) – flowers usually have 1 or 2 rows of broad, incurving, outer petals; the center of the flower is often filled entirely with numerous densely arranged, sometimes deeply cut, narrow petaloids derived from stamens.

***P.* 'Alice Harding'** (illus. p.236). Clump-forming perennial. H and S to 3ft (1m). Bears very large, fragrant, double, creamy white flowers.
***P.* 'America'.** Clump-forming perennial. H and S to 3ft (1m). Has large, single flowers with very broad, crimson petals, lightly ruffled at edges.
***P.* 'Argosy'** (illus. p.237). Deciduous, upright shrub (tree peony). H and S to 5ft (1.5m). Magnificent, large, single flowers are lemon yellow, each with a crimson-purple blotch at base. Is hard to propagate.
P. arietina. See *P. mascula* subsp. *arietina.*
***P.* 'Auguste Dessert'** (illus. p.237). Clump-forming perennial. H and S to 30in (75cm). Foliage provides rich autumn color. Has masses of fragrant, semi-double flowers; carmine petals are tinged salmon-pink and have slightly ruffled, striking silvery white margins.
***P.* 'Avant Garde'** (illus. p.236). Clump-forming perennial. H and S to 3ft (1m). Has luxuriant foliage. Medium-sized to large, fragrant, single flowers are pale rose pink with darker veins and bright golden anthers that have yellow-red filaments. Flowers are borne on stiff, straight stems in midspring and are ideal for cutting.
***P.* 'Ballerina'** (illus. p.236). Clump-forming perennial. H and S 3ft (1m). Foliage provides autumn color. Fragrant, double flowers are soft blush pink, tinged lilac at first, later fading to white. Outer rows of petals are loosely arranged, very broad and incurving; inner petals are also incurving but are more densely arranged, narrower, more uneven in size, and often have slightly ruffled margins.
***P.* 'Baroness Schroeder'** (illus. p.236). Vigorous, clump-forming perennial. H and S to 3ft (1m). Is very free-flowering with large, fragrant, globe-shaped, double flowers, tinged with pale flesh pink on opening but fading to almost pure white. Has several rows of nearly flat, outer petals; inner petals are incurving, ruffled, and very tightly arranged. Is one of the best peonies for cutting.
***P.* 'Barrymore'.** Clump-forming perennial. H and S to 34in (85cm). Has very large, anemone-form flowers with broad, outer petals that are palest blush pink on opening, later white. Clear pale golden yellow petaloids are very narrow, relatively short, and are neatly and densely arranged.
***P.* 'Bowl of Beauty'** (illus. p.236). Clump-forming perennial. H and S to 3ft (1m). Has very large, striking, anemone-form flowers with pale carmine-pink outer petals and numerous narrow, densely arranged, ivory-white petaloids.
P. cambessedesii (Majorcan peony; illus. p.236). Clump-forming perennial. H and S 18in (45cm). Has especially attractive foliage, dark green above with veins, stalks, and undersurfaces suffused purple-red. Single, deep rose-pink flowers are borne in midspring.
***P.* 'Cheddar Cheese'.** Clump-forming perennial. H and S to 3ft (1m). Produces well-formed, large, double flowers in midsummer. Neatly and densely arranged, slightly ruffled, ivory-white petals, the inner ones incurving, are interspersed with shorter yellow petals.
***P.* 'Chocolate Soldier'** (illus. p.237). Clump-forming perennial. H and S to 3ft (1m). Has mid- to dark green leaves that are often tinged bronze-red when young. Semi-double, purple-red flowers, borne in early summer, have yellow-mottled centers.
***P.* 'Colonel Heneage'.** Clump-forming perennial of upright habit. H and S to 34in (85cm). Has masses of anemone-form flowers with both outer petals and inner petaloids of dark rose-crimson.
P. corallina. See *P. mascula* subsp. *mascula.*
***P.* 'Cornelia Shaylor'** (illus. p.236). Erect, clump-forming perennial. H and S to 34in (85cm). Fragrant, double flowers, flushed rose pink on opening and gradually fading to blush white, are borne freely from early to mid-summer. Ruffled petals are neatly and densely arranged.
***P.* 'Dayspring'.** Clump-forming perennial. H and S to 28in (70cm). Has an abundance of fragrant, single, clear pink flowers borne in clusters.
P. decora. See *P. peregrina.*
***P.* 'Defender'** (illus. p.237). Clump-forming, vigorous perennial. H and S to 3ft (1m). Single, satiny crimson flowers, to 6in (15cm) across with a central boss of golden anthers are carried on strong stems.
P. delavayi (illus. p.237). Deciduous, upright, open shrub (tree peony). H to 6ft (2m), S to 4ft (1.2m). Leaves are divided into pointed-oval leaflets, often with reddish stalks. Single flowers are small, bowl-shaped and rich dark red, with conspicuous, leafy bracts below flowers. var. ***ludlowii*** see *P. lutea* var. *ludlowii*. var. ***lutea*** see *P. lutea*.
***P.* 'Dresden'.** Robust, clump-forming perennial. H and S to 34in (85cm). Foliage provides autumn color. Single flowers are ivory white tinged with soft rose pink.
***P.* 'Duchesse de Nemours'**, syn. *P.* 'Mrs. Gwyn Lewis' (illus. p.236). Vigorous, clump-forming perennial. H and S to 28in (70cm). Produces masses of richly fragrant, double flowers with very large, incurving, outer petals, tinged palest green at first, soon fading to pure white; inner petals with irregular margins are densely arranged toward the center and are creamy yellow at their base.
P. emodi (illus. p.236). Clump-forming perennial. H to 4ft (1.2m), S to 3ft (1m). Glossy green foliage is topped by tall stems bearing several large, fragrant, single, pure white flowers with golden yellow anthers.
***P.* 'Evening World'** (illus. p.236). Clump-forming perennial. H and S to 3ft (1m). Has abundant, large, anemone-form flowers with soft blush pink outer petals and very tightly arranged, pale flesh pink petaloids.
***P.* 'Félix Crousse'**, syn. *P.* 'Victor Hugo'. Vigorous, clump-forming perennial. H and S to 30in (75cm). Bears a profusion of fragrant, double, rich carmine-pink flowers with darker red centers. Petals are ruffled, very

numerous, and tightly arranged, with edges sometimes tipped silvery white.
P. 'Festiva Maxima'. Clump-forming perennial. H and S to 3ft (1m). Has dense, spreading foliage and huge, fragrant, double flowers borne on strong stems. Rather loosely arranged petals are large with irregular margins; outer petals are pure white, inner ones each have a basal crimson blotch.
P. 'Flamingo'. Clump-forming perennial. H and S to 34in (85cm). Foliage provides autumn color. Double flowers are large and clear pale salmon-pink.
P. 'Globe of Light' (illus. p.236). Clump-forming perennial. H and S to 3ft (1m). Has large, fragrant, anemone-form flowers. Outer petals are pure rose pink, petaloids clear golden yellow.
P. 'Heirloom'. Compact, clump-forming perennial. H and S to 28in (70cm). Bears masses of large, fragrant, double, pale lilac-pink flowers.
P. 'Instituteur Doriat' (illus. p.237). Clump-forming perennial. H and S to 3ft (1m). Foliage provides autumn color. Has abundant, large, anemone-form flowers with reddish carmine outer petals and densely arranged, relatively broad petaloids, paler and more pink than outer petals, with ruffled, silvery white margins.
P. 'Kelway's Gorgeous' (illus. p.237). Clump-forming perennial. H and S to 34in (85cm). Single, intense clear carmine flowers with a hint of salmon-pink are borne very freely.
P. 'Kelway's Majestic'. Clump-forming perennial. H and S to 3ft (1m). Freely borne, large, fragrant, anemone-form flowers have bright rose pink outer petals and lilac-pink petaloids flecked with silver or pale gold.
P. 'Kelway's Supreme' (illus. p.236). Clump-forming perennial. H and S to 3ft (1m). Foliage provides autumn color. Has large, strongly fragrant, double flowers produced over a long period, sometimes borne in clusters on well-established plants. Petals are broad, incurving, soft blush pink, fading to milk white. Single or semi-double axillary flowers are often produced.
P. 'Knighthood' (illus. p.237). Clump-forming perennial. H and S to 30in (75cm). Double flowers have densely arranged, rather narrow, ruffled petals of unusually rich burgundy red.
P. 'Krinkled White' (illus. p.236). Robust, clump-forming perennial. H and S to 32in (80cm). Large, bowl-shaped, single, milk white flowers are sometimes flushed palest pink. Petals are large with ruffled margins.
P. 'Laura Dessert' (illus. p.237). Clump-forming perennial. H and S to 30in (75cm). Produces fragrant, double flowers with creamy blush pink outer petals. Densely arranged, incurving inner petals are flushed rich lemon yellow, their margins sometimes deeply cut.
P. 'L'Espérance', syn. *P.* x *lemoinei* 'L'Espérance' (illus. p.237). Has very large, single, primrose yellow flowers with a carmine blotch at the base of each petal.
***P.* x *lemoinei* 'L'Espérance'.** See *P.* 'L'Espérance'.
P. lobata. See *P. peregrina.*
P. lutea, syn. *P. delavayi* var. *lutea*. Deciduous, upright shrub (tree peony). H and S to 5ft (1.5m). Single flowers are usually vivid yellow; brownish- or purplish yellow forms also occur. var. ***ludlowii*** (syn. *P. delavayi* var. *ludlowii*; illus. p.237), H and S to 8ft (2.5m), is grown as much for its large, bright green leaves divided into deeply cut, pointed leaflets as for its bowl-shaped, golden yellow flowers.
P. 'Madame Louis Henri' (illus. p.237). Deciduous, upright shrub (tree peony). H and S to 5ft (1.5m). Has loosely semi-double, whitish yellow flowers with large, incurving, outer petals very heavily suffused with rust-red. Smaller, often darker, inner petals each have a basal, dull red blotch.
P. 'Magic Orb' (illus. p.237). Clump-forming perennial. H and S to 3ft (1m). Foliage provides autumn color. Bears masses of large, strongly fragrant, double flowers, each with several outer whorls of fairly broad, ruffled, intense cherry pink petals and a center of densely arranged, smaller, incurving petals. Outermost rows of central petals are blush white, heavily shaded with rose-carmine; the innermost petals are mostly creamy white.
P. mascula subsp. ***arietina***, syn. *P. arietina*. Tuberous perennial. H and S to 30in (75cm). Foliage is hairy underneath and dark green; stems are dark red. Has single, reddish pink flowers. Seed capsules with 2–5 boat-shaped sections split to reveal purplish black seeds. subsp. ***mascula*** (syn. *P. corallina*; illus. p.236) is clump-forming, H and S to 3ft (1m), with hairless leaflets. Produces purple- or carmine-red, occasionally pink or white flowers with bosses of golden yellow anthers on purple filaments.
P. mlokosewitschii (illus. p.237). Clump-forming perennial. H and S to 30in (75cm). Soft bluish green foliage, sometimes edged reddish purple, is topped by large, single, lemon yellow flowers.
P. 'Mother of Pearl' (illus p.236). Clump-forming perennial. H to 30in (75cm) and S to 24in (60cm). Grayish green leaves provide an attractive foil for the single, rose pink flowers.
P. 'Mrs Gwyn Lewis'. See *P.* 'Duchesse de Nemours'.
P. obovata var. ***alba*** (illus. p.236). Clump-forming perennial. H and S 28–36in (70–90cm). Has erect stems and large, deep green leaves, each with 9 uneven, broadly elliptic leaflets, pale gray-green and slightly hairy beneath. Bears single, cup-shaped white flowers with purple filaments.
P. officinalis. Clump-forming, tuberous perennial. H and S to 24in (60cm). The single, red apothecaries' peony has long been in cultivation, but is seldom seen today, having been superseded by larger, often double-flowered hybrids, such as the following. **'Alba Plena'** (illus. p.236), H and S to 30in (75cm), has double white flowers that are sometimes tinged with pink. **'China Rose'** (illus. p.237), H and S to 18in (45cm), has handsome, dark green foliage and single flowers with incurving, clear dark salmon-rose petals contrasting with central bosses of orange-yellow anthers. **'Rubra Plena'** (illus. p.237), H and S to 30in (75cm), is long-lived and has distinctive foliage divided into broadly oval leaflets, and double, vivid pinkish crimson flowers with ruffled petals.
P. peregrina, syn. *P. decora*, *P. lobata*. Clump-forming, tuberous perennial. H and S to 3ft (1m). Produces bowl-shaped, single, ruby red flowers. **'Otto Froebel'** (syn. *P.p.* 'Sunshine'; illus. p.237) has glossy, bright green leaves and bears large, single vermilion flowers, tinged with salmon-rose.
P. potaninii. Deciduous, rhizomatous shrub (tree peony). H to 24in (60cm), S indefinite. Has deeply divided leaves with narrowly oval, irregularly cut or lobed leaflets and small, single, deep maroon-red or occasionally white flowers. Is similar to *P. delavayi* but is more invasive and has less conspicuous, leafy bracts below the flowers. var. ***trollioides*** (illus. p.237) has finely divided leaves and yellow flowers.
P. 'Président Poincaré'. Clump-forming perennial. H and S to 1m (3ft). Foliage provides autumn color. Fragrant, double, clear rich ruby-crimson flowers are borne very freely.
P. rockii. See *P. suffruticosa* subsp. *rockii.*
P. 'Sarah Bernhardt' (illus. p.236). Vigorous, erect, clump-forming perennial. H and S to 3ft (1m). Produces an abundance of huge, fragrant, fully double flowers with large, ruffled, slightly dull rose pink petals, fading to silvery blush-white at margins.
P. 'Shirley Temple' (illus. p.236). Clump-forming perennial. H and S to 34in (85cm). Profuse, soft rose-pink flowers, fading to palest buff-white, are fully double, with broad petals arranged in whorls; innermost petals are smaller and more loosely packed.
P. 'Silver Flare' (illus. p.237). Clump-forming perennial. H and S to 3ft (1m). Foliage gives autumn color. Stems are flushed dull reddish brown. Produces masses of fragrant, single flowers with rather long, slender, rich carmine-pink petals, each feathering to a striking silvery white margin.
P. 'Sir Edward Elgar' (illus. p.237). Clump-forming perennial. H and S to 30in (75cm). Foliage provides autumn color. Has an abundance of single, chocolate brown-tinged, rich crimson flowers with bosses of loosely arranged, clear lemon yellow anthers.
P.* x *smouthii (illus. p.237). Clump-forming perennial. H and S to 24in (60cm). Produces an abundance of fragrant, single, glistening, dark crimson flowers, to 4in (10cm) across, with conspicuous yellow stamens, although both flowers and foliage may vary in color.
P. 'Souvenir de Maxime Cornu' (illus. p.237). Deciduous, upright shrub (tree peony). H and S to 5ft (1.5m). Large, richly fragrant flowers are fully double with warm golden yellow petals densely arranged toward centers; ruffled margins are dull reddish orange.
P. suffruticosa (Moutan). Deciduous, upright shrub (tree peony). H and S to 7ft (2.2m). Bears variable, large, cup-shaped flowers, single or semi-double, with incurving, rose-pink or white petals, each sometimes with a basal, usually chocolate-maroon blotch. Has given rise to many cultivars with semi-double and double flowers. **'Cardinal Vaughan'** (illus. p.237) has semi-double, ruby-purple flowers. **'Godaishu'** ('large globe'; illus. p.236) bears semi- or fully double white flowers with yellow centers amid light green leaves that are fringed and twisted. **'Hana-daijin'** ("Magnificent Flower"; illus. p.237), H and S 6ft (2m) or more, is a vigorous cultivar that bears masses of double purple flowers. **'Hana-kisoi'** ("Floral Rivalry"; illus. p.236) has double, pale cerise-pink flowers. **JEWEL IN THE LOTUS ('Tama-fuyo')** is vigorous and freely produces double pink flowers earlier than most other cultivars. **'Joseph Rock'** see *P.s.* subsp. *rockii.* **'Kamadu-nishiki'** ("Kamada Brocade"; illus. p.237), H and S to 4ft (1.2m), produces large, double flowers, to 8in (20cm) across, that are lilac-pink striped white at the edge of each petal. **'Reine Elizabeth'** (illus. p.236), H and S to 6ft (2m), has large, fully double flowers with broad, salmon-pink petals flushed with bright copper-red and lightly ruffled at margins. **'Renkaku'** ("Flight of Cranes"), H and S to 3ft (1m), bears double flowers, each with broad, incurving, slightly ruffled, ivory-white petals, loosely arranged in 3 or more whorls, that surround a large boss of long, golden yellow anthers. subsp. ***rockii*** (syn. *P. rockii*, *P.s.* 'Joseph Rock', *P.s.* 'Rock's Variety'; illus. p.236) has large, spreading, semi-double white flowers; inner petals each have a basal, dark maroon blotch. Is difficult to propagate. **'Rock's Variety'** see *P.s.* subsp. *rockii*. **'Tama-fuyo'** see *P.s.* JEWEL IN THE LOTUS.
P. tenuifolia (illus. p.237). Clump-forming perennial. H and S to 18in (45cm). Elegant leaves are finely divided into many linear segments. Has single, dark crimson flowers with golden yellow anthers.
P. veitchii (illus. p.237). Clump-forming perennial. H and S to 30in (75cm). Shiny, bright green leaves are divided into oblong to elliptic leaflets. In early summer produces nodding, cup-shaped, single, purple-pink flowers.
P. 'Victor Hugo'. See *P.* 'Félix Crousse'.

***P.* 'White Wings'** (illus. p.236). Clump-forming perennial. H and S to 34in (85cm). Glossy, dark green foliage also provides autumn color. In midsummer produces masses of large, fragrant, single flowers with broad white petals, sometimes tinged sulfur yellow, that are each slightly ruffled at the apex.
***P.* 'Whitleyi Major'** (illus. p.236). Clump-forming perennial. H to 3ft (1m), S to 2ft (60cm). Foliage and stems are flushed rich reddish brown. Large, single, ivory-white flowers have a satin sheen and central bosses of clear yellow anthers.
P. wittmanniana (illus. p.237). Clump-forming perennial. H and S to 3ft (1m). Has large, single, pale primrose yellow flowers, each with a large, central boss of yellow anthers on purple-red filaments. Leaves are divided into broadly oval leaflets, shiny dark green above, paler beneath.

PALIURUS

RHAMNACEAE

Genus of deciduous, spiny, summer-flowering shrubs and trees grown for their foliage and flowers. *P. spina-christi* is also grown for its religious association, reputedly being the plant from which Christ's crown of thorns was made. Requires full sun and well-drained soil. Propagate by softwood cuttings in summer or by seed in autumn.
P. spina-christi illus. p.122.

PAMIANTHE

AMARYLLIDACEAE

Genus of one species of evergreen, spring-flowering bulb grown for its large, strongly fragrant, showy flowers. Needs partial shade and rich, well-drained soil. Fertilize with high-potassium liquid fertilizer in summer. Reduce watering in winter, but do not allow to dry out. Propagate by seed in spring or by offsets in late winter.
P. peruviana illus. p.409.

PANCRATIUM

AMARYLLIDACEAE

Genus of bulbs with large, fragrant, daffodil-like flowers in summer. Needs sun and well-drained soil that is warm and dry in summer when bulbs are dormant. Plant at least 6in (15cm) deep. Feed with a high-potassium liquid fertilizer every 2 weeks from autumn to spring. Propagate by seed in autumn or by offsets detached in early autumn.
P. illyricum illus. p.419.
P. maritimum (Sea daffodil, Sea lily). Late summer-flowering bulb. H 18in (45cm), S 10–12in (25–30cm). Has strap-shaped, erect, basal, grayish green leaves. Produces a head of 5–12 white flowers, each with a large, deep cup in the center and 6 spreading petals. Can be shy-flowering in cultivation.

PANDANUS
Screw pine

PANDANACEAE

Genus of evergreen trees, shrubs, and scramblers grown for their foliage and overall appearance. Flowers and fruits only appear on large, mature specimens. Requires full light or partial shade and fertile, well-drained soil. Water containerized plants freely when in full growth, moderately at other times. Propagate by seed or suckers in spring or by cuttings of lateral shoots in summer. Spider mite may attack.
P. odoratissimus. See *P. tectorius*.
P. tectorius, syn. *P. odoratissimus*. Evergreen, rounded tree. H to 20ft (6m), S 10ft (3m) or more. Has rosettes of strap-shaped, deep green leaves, each 3–5ft (1–1.5m) long, with spiny margins and a spiny midrib beneath. Small flowers, the males in clusters, each with a lance-shaped white bract, appear mainly in summer. Fruits are like round pineapples. Z14-15 H12-10.**'Veitchii'** (syn. *P. veitchii*) illus. p.175.
P. veitchii. See *P. tectorius* 'Veitchii'.

PANDOREA

BIGNONIACEAE

Genus of evergreen, woody-stemmed, twining climbers grown for their handsome flowers and attractive leaves. Grow in sun and in any well-drained soil. Prune after flowering to restrain growth. Propagate by seed sown in spring or by stem cuttings or layering in summer.
P. jasminoides, syn. *Bignonia jasminoides*, illus. p.208.
P. lindleyana. See *Clytostoma callistegioides*.
P. pandorana, syn. *Bignonia pandorana*, *Tecoma australis* (Wonga-wonga vine). Fast-growing, evergreen, woody-stemmed, twining climber. H 20ft (6m) or more. Leaves have 3–9 scalloped leaflets. Small, funnel-shaped cream flowers, streaked and often spotted with red, brown, or purple, are borne in clusters in summer.
P. ricasoliana. See *Podranea ricasoliana*.

PANICUM

GRAMINEAE/POACEAE

See also GRASSES, BAMBOOS, RUSHES, and SEDGES.
P. capillare illus. p.308.

PAPAVER
Poppy

PAPAVERACEAE

Genus of annuals, biennials, and perennials, some of which are semi-evergreen, grown for their cup-shaped flowers. Needs sun or semi-shade and prefers moist but well-drained soil. Propagate by seed in autumn or spring. *P. orientale* and its cultivars are best propagated by root cuttings in late autumn. Self-seeds readily.
P. alpinum subsp. ***burseri.*** See *P. burseri*.
P. atlanticum. Clump-forming, short-lived perennial. H and S 4in (10cm). Has oval, toothed, hairy leaves and, in summer, single, dull orange flowers. Is good for a rock garden. Z5–7 H7–4.
P. burseri, syn. *P. alpinum* subsp. *burseri* (Alpine poppy). Semi-evergreen, tuft-forming, short-lived perennial, best treated as an annual or biennial. H 6–8in (15–20cm), S 4in (10cm). Has finely cut gray leaves. Carries single white flowers throughout summer. Good in a rock garden, wall, or bank. Z5–8 H8–5.
P. commutatum, syn. *P.c.* 'Ladybird'. Fast-growing, erect, branching annual. H and S 18in (45cm). Has elliptic, deeply lobed, midgreen leaves and, in summer, single red flowers, each with a black blotch in center. H8–1.
'Ladybird' see *P. commutatum*.
P. croceum, syn. *P. nudicaule* of gardens (Iceland poppy). Tuft-forming perennial. H to 12in (30cm), S 4in (10cm). Hairy stems each produce a fragrant, single white and yellow flower, sometimes marked green outside, in summer. Many color forms have been selected. Leaves are oval, toothed, and soft green. Needs partial shade. Is good for a rock garden. Z2–7 H9–2.
P. fauriei, syn. *P. miyabeanum* of gardens, illus. p.384.
P. miyabeanum of gardens. See *P. fauriei*.
P. nudicaule of gardens. See *P. croceum*.
P. orientale (Oriental poppy). Rosetted perennial. H 3ft (1m), S 1–3ft (30cm–1m). Single, brilliant vermilion flowers, with dark blotches at bases of petals, are borne in early summer. Has broadly lance-shaped, toothed or cut, rough, midgreen leaves. Flowering stems need support. Z4–9 H9–1 **'Allegro'** (syn. *P.o.* 'Allegro Viva') illus. p.250. **'Allegro Viva'** see *P.o.* 'Allegro'. **'Beauty of Livermere'** illus. p.250. **'Indian Chief'** has deep mahogany-red flowers. **'May Queen'** bears double orange flowers. **'Mrs. Perry'** has large, salmon-pink flowers. **'Perry's White'** illus. p.241.
P. rhoeas (Corn poppy, Field poppy). **Shirley Series** (double) illus. p.322; (single) illus. p.328.
P. somniferum (Opium poppy). Fast-growing, upright annual. H 30in (75cm), S 12in (30cm). Has oblong, lobed, light grayish green leaves. Large, single flowers, to 4in (10cm) wide, in shades of red, pink, purple, or white, are produced in summer. Z3–8 H8–1. Several double-flowered forms are available, including **Carnation-flowered Series**, with fringed flowers in mixed colors; **'Peony Flowered'** illus. p.321; **'Pink Beauty'**, which has salmon-pink flowers; and **'White Cloud'**, which produces large white flowers.

PAPHIOPEDILUM
Slipper orchid

Contact with foliage may aggravate skin allergies. See also ORCHIDS.
P. appletonianum (illus. p.296). Evergreen, terrestrial orchid. H 3in (8cm). In spring, green flowers, 2½in (6cm) across and each with a pouched brownish lip and pink-flushed petals, are borne singly on tall, slender stems. Has oval, mottled leaves, 4in (10cm) long. Needs shade in summer. Z12–15 H12–6.
P. bellatulum (illus. p.296). Evergreen, terrestrial orchid. H 2in (5cm). Bears almost stemless, rounded, pouch-lipped white flowers, 3in (8cm) across, spotted with dark maroon, singly in spring. Oval, marbled leaves are 3in (8cm) long. Grow in shade in summer. Z12–15 H12–6.
***P.* Buckhurst 'Mont Millais'** (illus. p.298). Evergreen, terrestrial orchid. H 4in (10cm). Rounded, yellow-and-white flowers, to 5in (12cm) across and lined and spotted with red, are produced singly in winter. Has oval leaves, 4in (10cm) long. Requires shade in summer. Z12–15 H12–6.
P. callosum (illus. p.296). Evergreen, terrestrial orchid. H 3in (8cm). Purple- and green-veined white flowers, 3in (8cm) across, are borne on tall stems in spring-summer. Has oval, mottled leaves, 4in (10cm) long. Needs shade in summer. Z12–15 H12–6.
P. fairrieanum (illus. p.296). Evergreen, terrestrial orchid. H 3in (8cm). Rich purple- and green-veined flowers, 2in (5cm) across, with curved petals and orange-brown pouches, are borne singly in autumn. Oval leaves are 3in (8cm) long. Grow in shade in summer. Z12–15 H12–6.
***P.* Freckles** (illus. p.296). Evergreen, terrestrial orchid. H 4in (10cm). Rounded, reddish brown-spotted and pouched white flowers, 4in (10cm) across, are produced singly in winter. Has oval leaves, 4in (10cm) long. Grow in shade in summer. Z12–15 H12–6.
P. haynaldianum (illus. p.296). Evergreen, terrestrial orchid. H 5in (12cm). In summer, long-petaled, brown-marked flowers in green, pink, and white, to 6in (15cm) across, are produced singly. Has oval leaves, 8–9in (20–23cm) long. Requires shade in summer. Z12–15 H12–6.
***P.* Lyric 'Glendora'** (illus. p.297). Evergreen, terrestrial orchid. H 4in (10cm). Rounded, glossy flowers in white, red, and green, 4in (10cm) across, appear singly in winter. Has oval leaves, 6in (15cm) long. Needs shade in summer. Z12–15 H12–6.
***P.* Maudiae** (illus. p.297). Evergreen, terrestrial orchid. H 4in (10cm). Clear apple green or deep reddish purple flowers, 4in (10cm) across, appear singly on long stems in spring or early summer. Has oval, mottled leaves, 4in (10cm) long. Requires shade in summer. Z12–15 H12–6.
P. niveum (illus. p.296). Evergreen,

terrestrial orchid. H 2in (5cm). White flowers, 1½in (4cm) across, are produced singly, mainly in spring. Oval, marbled leaves are 3in (8cm) long. Needs shade in summer. Z12–15 H12–6.
P. sukhakulii (illus. p.298). Evergreen, terrestrial orchid. H 3in (8cm). In spring-summer, purple-pouched, black-spotted green flowers, 3in (8cm) across, appear singly on tall stems. Has oval, mottled leaves, 4in (10cm) long. Grow in shade in summer. Z12–15 H12–6.
P. venustum (illus. p.299). Evergreen, terrestrial orchid. H 4in (10cm). Variably colored flowers, ranging from pink to orange with green veins and darker spots, are 2½in (6cm) across and borne singly in autumn. Has oval, mottled leaves, 4in (10cm) long. Needs shade in summer. Z12–15 H12–6.

PARAHEBE

SCROPHULARIACEAE

Genus of evergreen or semi-evergreen, summer-flowering perennials, subshrubs and shrubs, similar to *Hebe* and *Veronica*. Is suitable for rock gardens. Needs sun and well-drained, peaty, sandy soil. Propagate by semi-ripe cuttings in early summer.
P. catarractae illus. p.356.
P. lyallii. Semi-evergreen, prostrate shrub. H 6in (15cm), S 8–10in (20–25cm). Has oval, toothed, leathery leaves and, in early summer, erect stems bearing loose sprays of flattish, pink-veined white flowers. Z8–9 H9–8.
P. perfoliata, syn. *Veronica perfoliata*, illus. p.286.

PARAQUILEGIA

RANUNCULACEAE

Genus of tufted perennials grown for their cup-shaped flowers and fernlike foliage. Is difficult to cultivate and flower successfully. Prefers dry winters and cool climates. Is good in alpine houses and troughs. Needs sun and gritty, well-drained, alkaline soil. Propagate by seed in autumn.
P. anemonoides, syn. *P. grandiflora*, illus. p.364.
P. grandiflora. See *P. anemonoides*.

PARASERIANTHES

LEGUMINOSAE/MIMOSACEAE

Genus of deciduous or semi-evergreen trees grown for their feathery foliage and unusual flower heads composed of numerous stamens and resembling bottlebrushes. Where marginally hardy, do not plant out until late spring. Requires full sun and well-drained soil. Propagate by seed in spring.
P. lophantha, syn. *Albizia distachya*, *A. lophantha*, illus. p.93.

PARNASSIA

PARNASSIACEAE

Genus of rosetted, mainly summer-flowering perennials grown for their saucer-shaped flowers. Is good for rock gardens. Needs sun and wet soil. Propagate by seed in autumn.
P. palustris illus. p.350.

PAROCHETUS

LEGUMINOSAE/PAPILIONACEAE

Genus of one species of evergreen perennial. Grows best in alpine houses. Needs semi-shade and gritty, moist soil. Propagate by division of rooted runners in any season.
P. communis illus. p.384.

PARODIA

CACTACEAE

Genus of rounded cacti with tubercles arranged in ribs that often spiral around green stems. Crown forms woolly buds, then funnel-shaped flowers. Requires full sun or partial shade and very well-drained soil. Water very lightly in winter; tends to lose roots during a long period of drought. Propagate by seed in spring or summer.
P. aprica. See *P. concinna*.
P. chrysacanthion illus. p.468.
P. concinna, syn. *Notocactus apricus*, *P. aprica*. Flattened spherical cactus. H 3in (7cm), S 4in (10cm). Much-ribbed, pale green stem is densely covered with short, soft, golden brown spines. In summer, crown produces flattish, glossy, bright yellow flowers, 3in (8cm) across, with purple stigmas. Prefers partial shade.
P. erinacea, syn. *Wigginsia vorwerkiana*, illus. p.479.
P. graessneri, syn. *Notocactus graessneri*. Slow-growing, flattened spherical cactus. H 4in (10cm), S 10in (25cm). Bristlelike golden spines completely cover much-ribbed green stem. Slightly sunken crown bears funnel-shaped, glossy, greenish yellow flowers with yellow stigmas in early spring. Prefers partial shade.
P. haselbergii, syn. *Notocactus haselbergii*, illus. p.475.
P. leninghausii, syn. *Notocactus leninghausii*, illus. p.468.
P. mammulosa, syn. *Notocactus mammulosus*, illus. p.477.
P. microsperma, syn. *P. sanguiniflora*, illus. p.474.
P. nivosa illus. p.474.
P. ottonis, syn. *Notocactus ottonis*. Variable, spherical cactus. H and S 4in (10cm). Has pale to dark green stem with 8–12 rounded ribs bearing stiff golden radial spines and longer, soft red central spines. In summer, crown bears flattish, glossy golden flowers, 3in (8cm) across, with purple stigmas. Offsets freely from stolons. Prefers sun.
P. rutilans, syn. *Notocactus rutilans*, illus. p.471.
P. sanguiniflora. See *P. microsperma*.
P. scopa, syn. *Notocactus scopa* (Silver ball cactus). Spherical to columnar cactus. H 10in (25cm), S 6in (15cm). Stem, with 30–35 ribs, is densely covered with white radial spines and longer red central spines, 3 or 4 per areole. Crown bears funnel-shaped, glossy yellow flowers, 1½in (4cm) across, with purple stigmas, in summer. Prefers a sunny position.

PARONYCHIA

CARYOPHYLLACEAE/ILLECEBRACEAE

Genus of evergreen perennials making loose mats of prostrate stems. Is useful for rock gardens and walls. Needs sun and well-drained soil. Propagate by division in spring.
P. capitata. Vigorous, evergreen, mat-forming perennial. H ½in (1cm), S 16in (40cm). Silvery leaves are small and oval. In summer produces inconspicuous flowers surrounded by papery bracts. Makes a good groundcover.
P. kapela subsp. ***serpyllifolia*** illus. p.391.

PARROTIA

HAMAMELIDACEAE

Genus of one species of deciduous tree grown for its flowers and autumn color. Flower buds may be killed by hard frosts. Requires full sun and grows best in fertile, moist but well-drained soil. Is lime-tolerant but usually colors best in acidic soil. Propagate by softwood cuttings in summer or by seed in autumn.
P. persica illus. p.82.

PARTHENOCISSUS

VITACEAE

Genus of deciduous, woody-stemmed, tendril climbers grown for their leaves, which often turn beautiful colors in autumn. Broad tips of tendrils have suckerlike pads that cling to supports. Has insignificant greenish flowers in summer. Will quickly cover north- or east-facing walls or fences and may be grown up large trees. Grow in semi-shade or shade and in well-drained soil. Propagate by softwood or greenwood cuttings in summer or by hardwood cuttings in early spring. The berries may cause mild stomach upset if ingested.
P. henryana, syn. *Vitis henryana*. Deciduous, tendril climber with 4-angled, woody stems. H to 30ft (10m) or more. Leaves have 3–5 toothed, oval leaflets, each 1½–5in (4–13cm) long, and are velvety, deep green or bronze with white or pinkish veins. Small, dark blue berries are produced in autumn. Leaf color is best with a northern or eastern exposure. Z8–9 H9–1.
P. quinquefolia, syn. *Vitis quinquefolia* (Five-leaved ivy, Virginia creeper). Deciduous, woody-stemmed, tendril climber. H 50ft (15m) or more. Leaves have 5 oval, toothed, dull green leaflets, paler beneath, that turn a beautiful crimson in autumn. Blue-black berries are produced in autumn. Is ideal for covering a high wall or building. Z7–9 H9–1.
P. striata. See *Cissus striata*.
P. thomsonii, syn. *Cayratia thomsonii*, *Vitis thomsonii*, illus. p.218.
P. tricuspidata, illus. p.218. **'Lowii'** and **'Veitchii'** (syn. *Ampelopsis veitchii*) illus. p.218.

PASSIFLORA

Passionflower

PASSIFLORACEAE

Genus of evergreen or semi-evergreen, woody-stemmed, tendril climbers grown for their unique flowers, each one with a central corona of filaments. Produces egg-shaped to rounded, fleshy, edible fruits that mature to orange or yellow in autumn. Grow in full sun or partial shade and in any fertile, well-drained soil. Water freely in full growth, less at other times. Stems need support. Thin out and spur back crowded growth in spring. Propagate by seed in spring or by semi-ripe cuttings in summer.
P. x allardii, syn. *P.* 'Allardii'. Strong-growing, evergreen, woody-stemmed, tendril climber. H 22–30ft (7–10m). Has 3-lobed leaves. Flowers, 3–4in (7–10cm) wide, are white, tinted pink, with purple-banded crowns, and are carried in summer-autumn. Z7–9 H9–7.
***P.* 'Allardii'.** See *P.* x *allardii*.
P. antioquiensis, syn. *Tacsonia van-volxemii* (Banana passionfruit). Fast-growing, evergreen, woody-stemmed, tendril climber. H 15ft (5m) or more. Has downy leaves, with 3 deep lobes. Produces long-tubed, rose-red flowers, 4–5in (10–12cm) across, with purplish blue centers, in summer-autumn. Z12–15 H12–10.
P. caerulea illus. p.214. **'Constance Elliot'** is a fast-growing, evergreen or semi-evergreen, woody-stemmed, tendril climber. H 30ft (10m) or more. Has rich green leaves and, in summer-autumn, produces bowl-shaped, fragrant white flowers with pale blue or white filaments. Z6–9 H9–6.
P. x caeruleoracemosa. See *P.* x *violacea*.
***P. x caponii* 'John Innes'** illus. p.214.
P. coccinea illus. p.205.
P. x exoniensis. Fast-growing, evergreen, woody-stemmed, tendril climber. H 25ft (8m) or more. Leaves have 3 deep lobes and are softly downy. Rose-pink flowers, 3in (8cm) across, with purplish blue crowns, are produced in summer-autumn. Z13–15 H12–10.
P. manicata illus. p.217.
P. mollissima, syn. *Tacsonia mollissima*. Fast-growing, evergreen, woody-stemmed, tendril climber. H 15ft (5m) or more. Softly downy leaves have 3 deep lobes. Long-tubed pink flowers, to 3in (8cm) wide, each with a purplish blue crown, appear in summer-autumn.
P. quadrangularis illus. p.215.
P. racemosa (Red passionflower). Fast-growing, evergreen, tendril climber with slender, woody stems. H 15ft (5m). Has wavy, leathery leaves with 3 deep lobes. In summer-autumn bears terminal racemes of pendent crimson flowers, 3–4in (8–10cm) across, with white- and purple-banded crowns. Z13–15 H12–10.
P. sanguinea. See *P. vitifolia*.
P. x violacea, syn. *P.* x *caeruleoracemosa*. Vigorous, evergreen, woody-stemmed, tendril climber. H 30ft

(10m). Has 3-lobed leaves. Purple flowers, 3in (8cm) across, appear in summer-autumn. Z12-15 H12-10.
P. vitifolia, syn. *P. sanguinea*. Evergreen, woody-stemmed, tendril climber; slender stems have fine brown hairs. H to 15ft (5m). Has 3-lobed, lustrous leaves. In summer-autumn bears bright scarlet flowers, 5in (13cm) wide, each with a short crown banded red, yellow, and white. Z10-11 H12–10.

PATERSONIA

IRIDACEAE

Genus of evergreen, clump-forming, spring- and early summer-flowering, rhizomatous perennials. Needs full sun and light, well-drained soil. Leave undisturbed once planted. Propagate by seed in autumn.
P. umbrosa illus. p.421.

PATRINIA

VALERIANACEAE

Genus of perennials, with neat clumps, grown for their flowers. Is suitable for rock gardens. Needs a site in partial shade with moist soil. Propagate by division in spring or by seed in autumn. Self-seeds freely.
P. triloba. Clump-forming perennial. H 8–20in (20–50cm), S 6–12in (15–30cm). Neat heads of small, golden yellow flowers are borne throughout summer. Rounded, 3- to 5-lobed green leaves turn gold in autumn. Z5–8 H8–4.

PAULOWNIA

SCROPHULARIACEAE

Genus of deciduous trees grown for their large leaves and foxglovelike flowers borne before the foliage emerges. Flower buds and young growth of small plants may be damaged by very hard frosts. Requires full sun and fertile, moist but well-drained soil. In cold areas may be grown for foliage only by cutting back young shoots hard in spring and cutting out all but one of the subsequent shoots; this results in very large leaves. Propagate by seed in autumn or spring or by root cuttings in winter.
P. fortunei. Deciduous, spreading tree. H and S 25ft (8m). Has large, oval, midgreen leaves. In late spring bears large, fragrant flowers, purple-spotted and white inside, pale purple outside. Z5–8 H8–4.
P. imperialis. See *P. tomentosa*.
P. tomentosa, syn. *P. imperialis*, illus. p.77.

PAXISTIMA, syn. PACHYSTIMA

CELASTRACEAE

Genus of evergreen, spreading shrubs and subshrubs grown for their foliage. Is suitable as a groundcover. Prefers shade and organic, moist soil. Propagate by division in spring or by semi-ripe cuttings in summer.
P. canbyi. (Cliff green, ratstripper). Evergreen, spreading subshrub. H 6–12in (15–30cm), S 8in (20cm). Leaves are linear or oblong. Short, pendent spikes of tiny, greenish white flowers are produced in summer. Z3–7 H7–1.

PEDILANTHUS

EUPHORBIACEAE

Genus of bushy, summer-flowering succulents. Produces small, yellowish green, pink, red, or brown bracts that are shaped like a bird's head. Needs sun or partial shade and well-drained soil. Propagate by seed or stem cuttings in spring or summer. The stems and leaves contain a milky sap that may cause stomach upset if ingested.
P. tithymaloides. (Devil's backbone). Bushy succulent. H 10ft (3m), S 1ft (30cm). Has thin, erect stems zigzagging at each node. Leaves are midgreen and boat-shaped, with prominent ribs beneath. Red to yellowish green bracts are produced at each of the stem tips in summer. Prefers partial shade. Z11 H12–1. **'Variegata'** illus. p.459.

PELARGONIUM
Geranium

GERANIACEAE

Genus of mainly summer-flowering perennials, most of which are evergreen, often cultivated as annuals. Is grown for its colorful flowers and is useful in pots or as bedding plants; in warm conditions flowers are borne almost continuously. A sunny site with 12 hours of daylight is required for good flowering. Prefers well-drained, neutral to alkaline soil. Dislikes very hot, humid conditions. Deadhead frequently and fertilize regularly if grown in pots; do not overwater. Plants may be kept through winter in the greenhouse by cutting back in autumn-winter to 5in (12cm) and repotting. Propagate by softwood cuttings from spring to autumn. Contact with the foliage may occasionally aggravate skin allergies.

Geraniums are hardy in Z12–15 H12–1, although the protection of a wall and a deep, dry mulch may extend hardiness to Zone7.

Geraniums may be divided into 5 groups; all flower in summer-autumn unless stated otherwise. See also feature panel pp.246–7.

Zonal – plants with rounded leaves, distinctively marked with a darker zone, and single (5-petaled), semi-double or fully double flowers.
Regal (Martha Washington)– shrubby plants with rounded to oval, deeply serrated leaves and broadly trumpet-shaped, often richly colored flowers that are prone to weather-damage in the open. Prefer cooler weather.
Ivy-leaved – trailing plants, ideal for hanging baskets, with rounded, lobed leaves and flowers similar to those of zonal geraniums.
Scented-leaved and **species** – plants with small, often irregularly star-shaped flowers; scented-leaved forms are grown for their fragrance.
Unique – Tall-growing subshrubs with regal-like, single, brightly colored flowers that are borne continuously through the season. Leaves, which may be scented, vary in shape.

P. acetosum (illus. p.246). Species geranium. H 20–24in (50–60cm), S 8–10in (20–25cm). Stems are succulent with fleshy, gray-green leaves that are often margined red. Bears single, salmon-pink flowers. Is good as a pot plant in a greenhouse.
***P.* 'Alberta'** (illus. p.246). Evergreen zonal geranium. H 18in (45cm), S 12in (30cm). Bears clusters of small, single, crimson-and-white flowers. Is best grown as a bedding plant.
***P.* 'Amethyst'** (illus. p.246). Evergreen, trailing ivy-leaved geranium. H and S to 5ft (1.5m). Leaves are fleshy with pointed lobes. Bears fully double, light mauve-purple flowers.
***P.* 'Apple Blossom Rosebud'** (illus. p.246). Evergreen zonal geranium. H 12in (30cm), S 9in (23cm). Fully double, pinkish white flowers edged with red look like miniature rosebuds.
***P.* 'Autumn Festival'** (illus. p.246). Evergreen, bushy regal geranium. H and S 12in (30cm). Salmon-pink flowers have pronounced, white throats.
***P.* 'Bredon'** (illus. p.247). Strong-growing, evergreen regal geranium. H 18in (45cm), S to 12in (30cm). Has large maroon flowers.
***P.* 'Brookside Primrose'** (illus. p.246). Dwarf zonal geranium. H 4–5in (10–12cm), S 3–4in (7–10cm). Bears double, pale pink flowers. Leaves have a butterfly mark in the center of each leaf. Is good as a pot plant or for bedding.
***P.* 'Butterfly Lorelei'** (illus. p.246). Fancy-leaved, zonal geranium. H 10–12in (25–30cm), S 6–8in (15–20cm). Has butterfly-shaped leaves and double, pale salmon-pink flowers. Is suitable as a pot plant in a greenhouse.
***P.* 'Caligula'** (illus. p.247). Evergreen, miniature zonal geranium. H 6 8in (15–20cm), S 4in (10cm). Has small, double crimson flowers and tiny, dark green leaves. Good on a windowsill.
***P.* 'Capen'** (illus. p.247). Bushy zonal geranium. H 15–18in (38–45cm), S 6–8in (15–20cm). Bears coral-pink, semi-double flowers. Is good as a pot plant.
P. capitatum (illus. p.247). Evergreen scented-leaved geranium. H 12–24in (30–60cm), S 12in (30cm). Has mauve flowers and irregularly 3-lobed leaves that smell faintly of roses. Is mainly used to produce geranium oil for the perfume industry, but it may be grown as a pot plant.
P. carnosum. Deciduous, shrubby geranium (unclassified), with thick, succulent stems and a woody, swollen, tuberlike rootstock. H and S 12in (30cm). Has long, gray-green leaves with triangular, deeply lobed leaflets. Produces branched, umbel-like flower heads with white or greenish yellow flowers, the upper petals streaked red and shorter than the green sepals.
***P.* 'Cherry Blossom'** (illus. p.246). Vigorous, evergreen zonal geranium. H and S to 18in (45cm). Semi-double flowers are mauve-pink with white centers.
***P.* 'Chew Magna'.** Evergreen regal geranium. H 12–18in (30–45cm), S to 12in (30cm). Each petal of the pale pink flowers has a wine red blaze.
***P.* 'Clorinda'** (illus. p.246). Vigorous, scented-leaved geranium. H 18–20in (45–50cm), S 8–10in (20–25cm). Leaves smell of cedar and are 3-lobed. Bears large, single, rose-pink flowers and is excellent in a large pot. Suitable for a greenhouse or patio.
***P. crispum* 'Variegatum'** (illus. p.247). Evergreen, upright scented-leaved geranium. H to 3ft (1m), S 1–1½ft (30–45cm). Has gold-variegated leaves and small, pale lilac flowers. Foliage tends to become creamy white in winter.
***P.* 'Dale Queen'** (illus. p.246). Evergreen, bushy zonal geranium. H 9–12in (23–30cm), S 9in (23cm). Single flowers are delicate salmon-pink. Is particularly suitable for a pot.
***P.* 'Dolly Varden'** (illus. p.247). Evergreen zonal geranium. H 12in (30cm), S 9in (23cm). Green leaves have handsome purple-brown, white, and crimson markings. Single scarlet flowers are insignificant.
***P.* 'Emma Hössle'.** See *P.* 'Frau Emma Hössle'.
***P.* 'Fair Ellen'** (illus. p.246). Compact scented-leaved geranium. H and S 12in (30cm). Has dark green leaves and pale pink flowers marked with red.
***P.* 'Flower of Spring'** (Silver-leaved geranium; illus. p.247). Vigorous, evergreen zonal geranium. H 24in (60cm), S 12in (30cm). Has green-and-white leaves and single red flowers.
***P.* x *fragrans*.** See *P.* 'Fragrans'.
***P.* 'Fragrans'**, syn. *P.* x *fragrans*, *P.* Fragrans Group (illus. p.246). Evergreen, very bushy scented-leaved geranium. H and S 12in (30cm). Rounded, shallowly lobed, gray-green leaves smell strongly of pine. Bears small white flowers.
***P.* Fragrans Group.** See *P.* 'Fragrans'.
***P.* 'Fraiche Beauté'**, syn. *P.* 'Fraicher Beauty' (illus. p.246). Evergreen zonal geranium. H 12in (30cm),S 9in (23cm). Flowers are fully double and perfectly formed with delicate coloring: white with a thin red edge to each petal. Is excellent as a pot plant.
***P.* 'Fraicher Beauty'.** See *P.* 'Fraiche Beauté'.
***P.* 'Francis Parrett'** (illus. p.246). Evergreen, short-jointed zonal geranium. H 6–8in (15–20cm), S 4in (10cm). Bears fully double, purplish mauve flowers and small green leaves. Is good for a windowsill.
***P.* 'Frau Emma Hössle**, syn. *P.* 'Emma

Hössle'. Evergreen, dwarf zonal geranium. H 8–10in (20–25cm), S 6in (15cm). Bears large, fully double, mauve-pink flowers. Is useful for a window box.
***P.* 'Friesdorf'** (illus. p.247). Evergreen zonal geranium. H 10in (25cm), S 6in (15cm). Has dark green foliage and narrow-petaled, single, orange-scarlet flowers. Is good for a window box or planted in a large group.
***P.* 'Golden Lilac Mist'** (illus. p.246). Bushy zonal geranium. H 10–12in (25–30cm), S 6–8in (15–20cm). Leaves are gold marked with bronze. Bears double, lavender-pink flowers. Is a good window-box plant.
***P.* 'Gustav Emich'** (illus. p.247). Vigorous, evergreen, zonal geranium. H and S to 24in (60cm). Semi-double flowers are vivid scarlet.
***P.* 'Irene'** (illus. p.247). Evergreen zonal geranium. H 18in (45cm), S 9–12in (23–30cm). Bears large, semi-double, light crimson blooms.
***P.* 'Ivalo'** (illus. p.246). Evergreen, bushy, short-jointed zonal geranium. H 9–12in (23–30cm), S 9in (23cm). Large, semi-double flowers are pale pink with crimson-dotted white centers.
***P.* 'Lachsball'** (illus. p.246). Vigorous zonal geranium. H 18–20in (45–50cm), S 6–8in (15–20cm). Bears semi-double, salmon-pink flowers with a scarlet eye. Is good for summer bedding.
***P.* 'Lachskönigin'** (illus. p.246). Evergreen, trailing, brittle-jointed geranium. H and S to 24in (60cm). Has fleshy leaves with pointed lobes, and semi-double, deep rosy pink flowers. Good in a hanging basket or window box.
***P.* 'L'Elégante'** (illus. p.247). Evergreen, trailing ivy-leaved geranium. H and S to 24in (60cm). Foliage is variegated with creamy white margins, sometimes turning pink at the edges; semi-double flowers are pale mauve. Is best grown in a hanging basket.
***P.* 'Leslie Judd'** (illus. p.246). Vigorous, evergreen, bushy regal geranium. H 1–1½ft (30–45cm), S to 12in (30cm). Flowers are soft salmon-pink with a central red blotch. Pinch out growing tips before flowering to control shape.
***P.* 'Mabel Grey'** (illus. p.247). Evergreen scented-leaved geranium. H 18–24in (45–60cm), S 1–1½ft (30–45cm). Has diamond-shaped, rough-textured, toothed, strongly lemon-scented leaves, with 5–7 pointed lobes, and mauve flowers.
***P.* 'Madame Fournier'** (illus. p.247). Evergreen, short-jointed zonal geranium. H 6–8in (15–20cm), S 4in (10cm). Small, single scarlet flowers contrast well with almost black leaves. Is useful for a pot or as a summer bedding plant.
***P.* 'Manx Maid'** (illus. p.246). Evergreen regal geranium. H 12–15in (30–38cm), S 10in (25cm). Flowers and leaves are small for regal type. Pink flowers are veined and blotched with burgundy.
***P.* 'Mauritania'** (illus. p.246). Evergreen zonal geranium. H 12in (30cm), S 9in (23cm). Single white flowers are ringed toward centers with pale salmon-pink.
***P.* 'Mini Cascade'** (illus. p.247). Evergreen, trailing, short-jointed ivy-leaved geranium. H and S 1–1½ft (30–45cm). Bears many single red flowers. Regular deadheading is essential for continuous display.
***P.* 'Mr. Everaarts'** (illus. p.246). Bushy dwarf zonal geranium. H 6–8in (15–20cm), S 4–5in (10–12cm). Bears double, bright pink flowers. Is good in a window box.
***P.* 'Mr. Henry Cox'**, syn. *P.* 'Mrs. Henry Cox' (illus. p.246). Evergreen zonal geranium. H 12in (30cm), S 6in (15cm). Midgreen leaves are marked with red, yellow, and purple-brown. Flowers are single and pink.
***P.* 'Mrs. Henry Cox'.** See *P.* 'Mr. Henry Cox'.
***P.* 'Mrs. Pollock'** (illus. p.247). Evergreen zonal geranium. H 12in (30cm), S 6in (15cm). Each golden leaf has a gray-green butterfly mark in center, with a bronze zone running through it. Bears small, single, orange-red flowers.
***P.* 'Mrs. Quilter'** (illus. p.247). Evergreen zonal geranium. H 12in (30cm), S 9in (23cm). Has yellow leaves with wide, chestnut brown zones and single pink flowers.
***P.* Multibloom Series** (illus. p.328). Seed-raised, single-flowered zonal geranium. H 10–12in (25–30cm), S 12in (30cm). Abundant flowers in shades of white, pink, and red, some with white eyes, are borne in clusters. Early flowering over a long period. Is tolerant of wet conditions.
***P.* 'Orange Ricard'** (illus. p.247). Vigorous, robust, evergreen zonal geranium. H 18–24in (45–60cm), S 12in (30cm). Produces masses of large, semi-double orange blooms.
***P.* Orbit Series.** Group of slow-growing, evergreen, bushy zonal geraniums grown as annuals. H and S 12–24in (30–60cm). Has rounded, lobed, bronze- or red-zoned, midgreen leaves and large, domed, single flower heads in mixed or separate colors, including shades of white, pink, red, and orange (salmon, illus. p.321).
***P.* 'Paton's Unique'** (illus. p.247). Vigorous unique geranium with pungent-smelling leaves. H 15–18in (38–45cm), S 6–8in (15–20cm). Flowers are single red or pale pink, each with a small white eye.
***P.* 'Paul Humphries'** (illus. p.247). Evergreen, bushy, compact zonal geranium. H 12in (30cm), S 9in (23cm). Has fully double, deep wine red flowers. Is good as a pot plant.
P. peltatum. Evergreen, trailing, brittle-jointed geranium from which ivy-leaved cultivars have been derived. H and S to 5ft (1.5m). Has fleshy leaves with pointed lobes and produces single mauve or white flowers. Cultivars are good in hanging baskets and window boxes.
***P.* 'Polka'** (illus. p.247). Vigorous unique geranium. H 18–20in (45–50cm), S 8–10in (20–25cm). Flowers are semi-double. Upper petals are orange-red, blotched and feathered deep purple; lower ones are salmon-orange.
***P.* 'Prince of Orange'** (illus. p.247). Scented-leaved geranium. H 10–12in (25–30cm), S 6–8in (15–20cm). Small, rounded leaves smell of orange. Bears single mauve flowers. Is good as a pot plant indoors.
***P.* 'Purple Emperor'** (illus. p.246). Evergreen regal geranium. H 18in (45cm), S 12in (30cm). Pink-mauve flowers have a deeper, central coloration. Flowers well into autumn.
***P.* 'Purple Unique'** (illus. p.247). Vigorous, evergreen, upright, shrubby unique geranium. H and S 3ft (1m) or more. Rounded, large-lobed leaves are very aromatic. Has single, open trumpet-shaped, light purple flowers. Does well when trained against a sunny wall.
***P.* 'Purple Wonder'** (illus. p.247). Vigorous zonal geranium. H 15–18in (38–45cm), S 8–10in (20–25cm). Bears semi-double, cerise-purple flowers. Is good as a pot plant in the greenhouse or in the garden.
***P.* 'Rica'** (illus. p.246). Bushy zonal geranium. H 12–15in (30–38cm), S 6–8in (15–20cm). Flowers are semi-double and deep rose-pink, each with a large white eye. Is good in a window box or as a greenhouse pot plant.
***P.* 'Robe'** (illus. p.247). Vigorous zonal geranium. H 15–18in (38–45cm), S 6–8in (15–20cm). Bears semi-double, cerise-crimson flowers. Is suitable as a pot plant in a greenhouse, or as a bedding plant.
***P.* 'Rollisson's Unique'** (illus. p.247). Evergreen, shrubby geranium (unique). H 24in (60cm) or more, S 12in (30cm). Has oval, notched, pungent leaves and small, single, open trumpet-shaped, wine red flowers with purple veins.
***P.* 'Rouletta'** (illus. p.247). Vigorous, evergreen, trailing ivy-leaved geranium. H and S 2–3ft (60cm–1m). Bears semi-double, red-and-white flowers. To control shape, growing tips should be pinched out regularly.
***P.* 'Royal Oak'** (illus. p.247). Evergreen, bushy, compact scented-leaved geranium. H 15in (38cm), S 12in (30cm). Oaklike, slightly sticky leaves have a spicy fragrance and are dark green with central brown markings. Flowers are small and mauve-pink.
***P.* 'Schöne Helena'** (illus. p.246). Evergreen zonal geranium. H 1–1½ft (30–45cm), S 9in (23cm). Produces masses of large, semi-double, salmon-pink blooms.
***P.* Sprinter Series.** Group of slow-growing, evergreen, branching, bushy zonal geraniums grown as annuals. H and S 12–24in (30–60cm). Has rounded, lobed, light to midgreen leaves. Bears large, domed, single flower heads in shades of red. Is very free-flowering.
'Tavira' (illus. p.247). Evergreen, trailing, brittle-jointed geranium. H and S 12–16in (30–40cm). Has fleshy leaves, with pointed lobes, and single, soft cerise-red flowers. Good in a hanging basket or window box.
***P.* 'The Boar'** (illus. p.246). Evergreen, trailing geranium (species). H and S to 24in (60cm). Has unusual, 5-lobed, notched leaves, each with a central, dark brown blotch, and long-stemmed, single, salmon-pink flowers. Is useful for a hanging basket.
***P.* 'Timothy Clifford'** (illus. p.246). Evergreen, short-jointed zonal geranium. H 6–8in (15–20cm), S 4in (10cm). Has dark green leaves and fully double, salmon-pink flowers. Good on a windowsill.
***P.* 'Tip Top Duet'** (illus. p.247). Evergreen, bushy, free-branching regal geranium. H 12–15in (30–38cm), S 10in (25cm). Leaves and blooms are small for regal type. Bears pink-veined white flowers; uppermost petals have dark burgundy blotches.
P. tomentosum (Peppermint geranium; illus. p.247). Evergreen, bushy scented-leaved geranium. H 12–24in (30–60cm), S 3ft (1m). Large, rounded, shallowly lobed, velvety, gray-green leaves have a strong peppermint aroma. Bears clusters of small white flowers. Growing tips should be pinched out to control spread. Dislikes full sun.
***P.* Video Series.** Group of slow-growing, evergreen, branching, bushy zonal geraniums grown as annuals. H and S 12–24in (30–60cm). Has rounded, lobed, bronze-zoned, deep green leaves and large, domed, single flower heads in white and shades of pink or red.
***P.* 'Voodoo'** (illus. p.247). Unique geranium. H 20–24in (50–60cm), S 8–10in (20–25cm). Flowers are single and pale burgundy with a purple-black blaze on each petal. Suitable as a greenhouse pot plant.

PELLAEA

ADIANTACEAE

Genus of deciduous, semi-evergreen or evergreen ferns. Grow in semi-shade and gritty, moist but well-drained soil. Remove fading fronds regularly. Propagate by spores in summer.
P. atropurpurea (Purple rock brake, Purple-stemmed cliff brake). Semi-evergreen or evergreen fern. H and S 12in (30cm). Small, narrowly lance-shaped, divided fronds have oblong, blunt pinnae and are dark green with a purplish tinge. Z8–10 H10–8.
P. rotundifolia (Button fern). Evergreen fern. H and S 6in (15cm). Small, narrowly lance-shaped, divided fronds are dark green and have rounded pinnae. Z8–10 H10–8.

Pellionia. Reclassified as *Elatostema.*
Peltiphyllum. Reclassified as *Darmera.*

PENNISETUM

GRAMINEAE/POACEAE

See also GRASSES, BAMBOOS, RUSHES, and SEDGES.
P. alopecuroides, syn. *P. compressum* (Chinese fountain grass). Tuft-forming,

herbaceous, perennial grass. H 3ft (1m), S 18in (45cm). Has narrow, mid-green leaves; leaf sheaths each have a hairy tip. In late summer bears arching, cylindrical panicles with decorative purple bristles that last well into winter. Z6–9 H9-6.
P. compressum. See *P. alopecuroides.*
P. longistylum. See *P. villosum.*
P. rueppellii. See *P. setaceum.*
P. setaceum, syn. *P. rueppellii* (African fountain grass). Tuft-forming, herbaceous, perennial grass. H 3ft (1m), S 18in (45cm). Has very rough, midgreen leaves and stems. In summer bears dense, cylindrical panicles of copper-red spikelets, with decorative, bearded bristles, that last well into winter. Z8–11 H12–8.
P. villosum, syn. *P. longistylum*, illus. p.307.

PENSTEMON

SCROPHULARIACEAE

Genus of annuals, perennials, subshrubs and shrubs, most of which are semi-evergreen or evergreen. Prefers full sun and fertile, well-drained soil. Propagate species by seed in autumn or spring or by softwood or semi-ripe cuttings of non-flowering shoots in midsummer, cultivars by cuttings only. See also feature panel p.248.
***P.* 'Alice Hindley'** (illus. p.248). Large-leaved, semi-evergreen perennial. H 36in (90cm), S 18in (45cm). Bears tubular to bell-shaped, pale lilac-blue flowers, white inside, tinged mauve-pink outside, from midsummer to early or midautumn. Leaves are linear to lance-shaped and midgreen. Z7-10 H10–7.
***P.* 'Andenken an Friedrich Hahn'**, syn. *P.* 'Garnet' (illus. p.248). H 2–2½ft (60–75cm), S 2ft (60cm). Vigorous, semi-evergreeen, bushy perennial. Bears sprays of tubular, deep wine red flowers from midsummer to autumn. Has narrow, fresh green leaves. Z7-10 H10–7.
***P.* 'Apple Blossom'** (illus. p.248). Semi-evergreen, bushy perennial. H and S 24in (60cm). Carries sprays of small, tubular, pale pink flowers from midsummer onward above narrow, fresh green foliage. Z7-10 H10–7.
P. barbatus, syn. *Chelone barbata*. Semi-evergreen, rosette-forming perennial. H 3ft (1m), S 1ft (30cm). From midsummer to early autumn bears racemes of slightly nodding, tubular, 2-lipped, rose-red flowers. Flower stems rise from rosettes of oblong to oval, midgreen leaves.
***P.* 'Barbara Barker'.** See *P.* 'Beech Park'.
***P.* 'Beech Park'**, syn. *P.* 'Barbara Barker' (illus. p.248). Semi-evergreen perennial. H and S 24in (60cm). Bears bright pink and white flowers. Leaves are linear and light green. Z7-11 H12–3.
***P.* 'Burford Seedling'.** See *P.* 'Burgundy'.
***P.* 'Burford White'.** See *P.* 'White Bedder'.
***P.* 'Burgundy'**, syn. *P.* 'Burford Seedling' (illus. p.248). Robust, semi-evergreen perennial. H 4ft (1.2m), S 2ft (60cm). Produces purplish red flowers with white throats streaked dark red. Leaves are linear and light green. Z7–11 H12–3.
P. campanulatus, syn. *P. pulchellus*. Semi-evergreen, upright perennial. H 12–24in (30–60cm), S 12in (30cm). Long racemes of bell-shaped, dark purple, violet, or occasionally white flowers appear in early summer above lance-shaped, toothed, mid-green leaves. Z7–10 H12–3.
P. cardwellii (illus. p.248). Spreading, sometimes stem-rooting, evergreen subshrub. H and S 12–20in (30–50cm). In early summer, produces racemelike panicles of slender, tubular to funnel-shaped, deep purple flowers. Leaves are elliptic, finely toothed, and midgreen. Z6–9 H9–6.
***P.* 'Chester Scarlet'** (illus. p.248). Semi-evergreen perennial. H and S 36in (90cm). Large, bright red flowers are borne above narrowly lance-shaped, light green leaves. Z7-10 H10–7.
P. confertus. Semi-evergreen, neat, clump-forming perennial. H 18in (45cm), S 12in (30cm). Bears spikes of tubular, creamy yellow flowers above long, lance-shaped, midgreen leaves in early summer. Z7-10 H10–7.
***P.* 'Countess of Dalkeith'** (illus. p.248). Erect, semi-evergreen perennial. H 3ft (1m), S 2ft (60cm). Produces large, deep purple flowers, each with a pure white throat. Leaves are linear and light green. Z7-10 H10–7.
P. davidsonii. Evergreen, prostrate shrub. H 3in (8cm), occasionally more, S 6in (15cm) or more. In late spring and early summer, funnel-shaped violet to ruby red flowers with protruding lips develop from leaf axils. Leaves are small, oval to rounded, and leathery. Trim after flowering. Z5–9 H9–5. subsp. ***menziesii*** see *P. menziesii.*
P. diffusus. See *P. serrulatus.*
***P.* 'Evelyn'** (illus. p.248). Semi-evergreen, bushy perennial. H and S 18in (45cm). Racemes of small, tubular pink flowers open from mid-summer onward. Has broadly lance-shaped, midgreen leaves. Z7–10 H12–3.
***P.* 'Firebird'.** See *P.* 'Schoenholzeri'.
P. fruticosus. Evergreen, upright, woody-based subshrub. H and S 6–12in (15–30cm). Has lance-shaped to oval, toothed leaves and, in early summer, funnel-shaped, lipped, lavender-blue flowers. Is suitable for a rock garden. Trim back after flowering. Z4–9 H9-1. subsp. ***scouleri*** (syn. *P. scouleri*) has pale to deep purple flowers. subsp. ***scouleri* f. *albus*** (syn. *P. scouleri* f. *albus*; illus. p.248) has white flowers.
***P.* 'Garnet'.** See *P.* 'Andenken an Friedrich Hahn'.
P. hartwegii. Semi-evergreen, erect perennial. H 24in (60cm) or more, S 12in (30cm). Bears sprays of slightly pendent, tubular to bell-shaped scarlet flowers from mid- to late summer. Lance-shaped leaves are midgreen. Z4–9 H9–1.
P. heterophyllus (Foothill penstemon) (illus. p.248). Evergreen subshrub. H and S 12–20in (30–50cm). In summer, produces racemes of tubular to funnel-shaped, pinkish blue flowers with blue or lilac lobes. Leaves are linear to lance-shaped, entire, and mid-green or bluish green. Z7–10 H10–7. **'True Blue'** has pale green leaves and pure blue flowers, borne on short side-shoots. Trim back after flowering. Good in a rock garden.
P. hirsutus. Short-lived, evergreen, open subshrub. H 2–3ft (60cm–1m), S 1–2ft (30–60cm). In summer produces hairy, tubular, lipped, purple- or blue-flushed white flowers. Leaves are oval and dark green. Is suitable for a rock garden. Z3–9 H9–1. var. ***pygmaeus*** illus. p.380.
P. isophyllus illus. p.163.
***P.* 'Maurice Gibbs'** (illus. p.248). Semi-evergreen perennial. H 3ft (90cm), S 2ft (60cm). Bears claret red flowers with white throats. Has lance-shaped, light green leaves. Z9–11 H12–3.
P. menziesii, syn. *P. davidsonii* subsp. *menziesii.* Evergreen, prostrate shrub. H 2in (5cm), S 8in (20cm). In late spring and early summer bears funnel-shaped, lavender-blue flowers. Has small, rounded, toothed leaves. Z6–9 H9–6.
P. newberryi (Mountain pride). Evergreen, mat-forming shrub. H 6–8in (15–20cm), S 12in (30cm). Branches are covered in small, oval, leathery, dark green leaves. Bears short sprays of tubular, lipped, deep rose-pink flowers in early summer. Trim back after flowering. Is good for a rock garden. Z7–10 H10–7. f. ***humilior*** illus. p.354.
***P.* 'Pennington Gem'** (illus. p.248). Vigorous, semi-evergreen perennial. H 3ft (1m), S 18in (45cm). Bears sprays of tubular pink flowers from midsummer to autumn. Leaves are narrow and fresh green. Z6–9 H9–6.
P. pinifolius illus. p.354. **'Mersea Yellow'** is an evergreen, bushy subshrub, H 4–8in (10–20cm), S 10in (25cm), with branched stems clothed in fine, dark green leaves. In summer, very narrow, tubular, bright deep yellow flowers are borne in loose, terminal spikes. Z4–10 H10–1.
P. procerus. Upright, semi-evergreen perennial. H 20in (50cm), S 8in (20cm). Leaves are oblong to lance-shaped. Produces slim spikes of funnel-shaped, blue-purple flowers in summer. Is suitable for a rock garden. Z4–10 H10–1.
P. pulchellus. See *P. campanulatus.*
***P.* 'Royal White'.** See *P.* 'White Bedder'.
***P.* 'Rubicundus'** (illus. p.248). Erect, semi-evergreen perennial. H 4ft (1.2m), S 2ft (60cm). Bears very large, bright red flowers each with a white throat. Leaves are linear and light green. Z6–9 H9–6.
P. rupicola. Evergreen, prostrate shrub. H 2in (5cm), S 6in (15cm). Has rounded to oval, fleshy, blue-gray leaves and, in summer, variable, funnel-shaped, pale to deep pink flowers. Is best grown in a rock garden. Seed may not come true. Z4–9 H9–1.
***P.* 'Schoenholzeri'**, syn. *P.* 'Firebird' (illus. p.248). Vigorous, semi-evergreen, upright perennial. H 3ft (1m), S 1–1½ft (30–45cm). Produces racemes of trumpet-shaped, brilliant scarlet flowers from midsummer to autumn. Lance-shaped to narrowly oval leaves are midgreen. Z6–9 H9–6.
P. scouleri. See *P. fruticosus* subsp. *scouleri.* f. ***albus*** see *P. fruticosus* subsp. *scouleri* f. *albus.*
P. serrulatus, syn. *P. diffusus*, illus. p.355.
***P.* 'Six Hills'.** Evergreen, prostrate shrub. H 2in (5cm), S 6in (15cm). Has rounded, fleshy, gray-green leaves. In summer carries funnel-shaped, cool lilac flowers at stem tips. Is suitable for a rock garden. Z4-10 H10–1.
***P.* 'Snow Storm'.** See *P.* 'White Bedder'.
***P.* 'Sour Grapes'** (illus. p.248). Semi-evergreen perennial. H 36in (90cm), S 24in (60cm). Light green leaves are narrowly lance-shaped. Bears deep purple-blue flowers suffused violet. Z7–10 H10–7.
***P.* 'Stapleford Gem'** (illus. p.248). Large-leaved, semi-evergreen perennial. H to 24in (60cm), S 18in (45cm). Bears large, tubular to bell-shaped, lilac-purple flowers from midsummer to early or midautumn; upper lips are pale pink-lilac; lower lips and throats are white with purple lines. Leaves are linear to lance-shaped and midgreen. Z6–9 H9–6.
***P.* 'White Bedder'**, syn. *P.* 'Burford White', *P.* 'Royal White', *P.* 'Snow Storm' (illus p.248). Semi-evergreen, free-flowering perennial. H 28in (70cm), S 24in (60cm). Has white flowers with dark anthers and linear, fresh green leaves. Z7–10 H10–7.

PENTACHONDRA

EPACRIDACEAE

Genus of evergreen, spreading shrubs with heathlike leaves. Needs full light and gritty, moist, peaty soil. Is difficult to grow, especially in hot, dry areas. Propagate by rooted offsets in spring, by semi-ripe cuttings in summer or by seed in autumn.
P. pumila. Evergreen, mat-forming, dense shrub. H 1¼–4in (3–10cm), S 8in (20cm) or more. Has oblong to narrowly oval, purplish green leaves. Small, tubular white flowers with reflexed lobes open in early summer, followed (though rarely in cultivation) by small, spherical orange fruits. Z7–9 H9–7.

Pentapterygium. Reclassified as *Agapetes.*

PENTAS

RUBIACEAE

Genus of mainly evergreen perennials

and shrubs grown for their flowers. Needs full light or partial shade and fertile, well-drained soil. Water freely when in full growth, moderately at other times. May be hard pruned in winter. Propagate by softwood cuttings in summer or by seed in spring. Is prone to whitefly.
P. carnea. See *P. lanceolata*.
P. lanceolata, syn. *P. carnea*, illus. p.163.

PEPEROMIA

PIPERACEAE

Genus of annuals and evergreen perennials grown for their foliage. Grow in full light or partial shade, ideally in a peat-based soil mix. Do not overwater. Propagate by division, by seed, or by leaf or stem cuttings in spring or summer.
P. argyreia, syn. *P. sandersii* (Watermelon plant). Evergreen, bushy, compact perennial. H and S 8in (20cm). Has red-stalked, oval, fleshy, dark green leaves, to 4in (10cm) or more long, striped with broad bands of silver. Flowers are insignificant. Z14–15 H12-10.
P. caperata illus. p.300.
P. clusiifolia (Baby rubber plant). Evergreen perennial with branching, sometimes prostrate, reddish green stems. H to 8in (20cm), S 10in (25cm). Narrowly oval, fleshy leaves, 3–6in (8–16cm) long, are dark green, edged with red. Flowers are insignificant. Z14–15 H12-10.Leaves of **'Variegata'** have cream-and-red margins.
P. glabella illus. p.305.
P. griseoargentea, syn. *P. hederifolia* (Ivy peperomia, Silver-leaf peperomia). Evergreen, bushy perennial. H to 6in (15cm), S 8in (20cm). Oval, fleshy leaves, 2in (5cm) or more long, each have a heart-shaped base, a quilted green surface, and a silvery sheen. Flowers are insignificant. Z14–15 H12-10.
P. hederifolia. See *P. griseoargentea*.
P. magnoliifolia. See *P. obtusifolia*.
P. marmorata illus. p.304.
P. metallica. Evergreen perennial with erect, branching, reddish green stems. H and S to 6in (15cm). Narrowly oval, dark green leaves, to 1in (2.5cm) long, have a metallic sheen, and wide, pale midribs above, reddish green veins below. Flowers are insignificant. Z14–15 H12-10.
P. nummulariifolia. See *P. rotundifolia*.
P. obtusifolia, syn. *P. magnoliifolia* (Pepper face) Evergreen perennial with leathery, dull green leaves. H and S 10in (25cm). Bears spikes of white flowers. Z14–15 H12-10. **'Green and Gold'** has green leaves with golden yellow margins. **'Variegata'** illus. p.305.
P. rotundifolia, syn. *P. nummulariifolia*. Evergreen, creeping perennial. H 2–3in (5–8cm), S 12in (30cm) or more. Very slender stems produce tiny, rounded, fleshy, bright green leaves, ½in (1cm) wide. Flowers are insignificant. Is useful for a hanging basket. Z14–15 H12-10.
P. rubella. Evergreen perennial with erect, branching, red stems. H and S 6in (15cm). Leaves, in whorls of 4, are ½in (1cm) long, narrowly oval, fleshy, and dark green above, crimson below. Flowers are insignificant. Z14–15 H12-10.
P. sandersii. See *P. argyreia*.
P. scandens (Cupid peperomia). Evergreen, climbing or trailing perennial with pinkish green stems. H and S to 3ft (1m). Oval, pointed, fleshy leaves, to 2in (5cm) or more long, are waxy and bright green. Flowers are insignificant. Z14–15 H12-10.

PERESKIA

CACTACEAE

Genus of deciduous cacti, some of which are climbing, with fleshy leaves and woody, green, then brown stems. Is considered the most primitive genus of the *Cactaceae*, producing true leaves unlike most members of the family. Needs sun and well-drained soil. Water moderately in summer. Propagate by stem cuttings in spring or summer.
P. aculeata illus. p.457. **'Godseffiana'** (syn. *P.a.* var. *godseffiana*) is a fast-growing, deciduous, erect, then climbing cactus. H to 30ft (10m), S 15ft (5m). Broadly oval, slightly fleshy, orange-brown leaves, usually purplish beneath and 3½in (9cm) long, mature to glossy, green. Short flower stems, carrying roselike, single, orange-centered cream flowers, 2in (5cm) across, appear in autumn on plants over 3ft (1m) high. Cut back hard to main stems in autumn. Z12–15 H12-10.
P. grandifolia, syn. *Rhodocactus grandifolius*, illus. p.458.

PERICALLIS

ASTERACEAE/COMPOSITAE

Genus of perennials and subshrubs, sometimes grown as annuals, especially for their daisylike flower heads. Requires sun or partial shade and fertile, well-drained soil. Propagate by seed sown from spring to midsummer.
P. x hybrida, syn. *Cineraria cruentus* of gardens, *C.* x *hybridus*, *Senecio* x *hybridus* (Cineraria). H 18–24in (45–60cm), S 10–24in (25–60cm). Slow-growing, evergreen, mound- or dome-shaped perennial. Cultivars are grown as biennials. All have oval, serrated, mid- to deep green leaves. Large, daisylike, single, semi-double, or double flower heads, in shades of blue, red, pink, or white, sometimes bicolored, are produced in winter or spring. Z12–13 H7–1. **'Brilliant'** has large flower heads in a mixture of white, blue, deep red, copper, and rose pink, plus bicolors. **'Royalty'** is late-flowering, with flower heads in sky blue, cherry red, lilac with a white eye, and bicolors. **'Spring Glory'** illus. p.332. **'Star Wars'**, H 6in (15cm), S 8in (20cm), is compact, with flower heads in a mixture of white, blue, rose pink, carmine, and purple; ideal for small containers.

PERILLA

LABIATAE/LAMIACEAE

Genus of annuals grown for their foliage. Grow in sun and in fertile, well-drained soil. Pinch out growing tips of young plants to encourage a bushy habit. Propagate by seed sown under cover in early spring.
P. frutescens. Moderately fast-growing, upright, bushy annual. H 24in (60cm), S 12in (30cm). Has oval, serrated, aromatic, reddish purple leaves. In summer produces spikes of very small, tubular white flowers. H12–1.

PERISTROPHE

ACANTHACEAE

Genus of mainly evergreen perennials and subshrubs grown usually for their flowers. Grow in sun or partial shade and in well-drained soil; do not overwater in winter. Propagate by stem cuttings in spring or summer.
P. angustifolia. See *P. hyssopifolia*.
P. hyssopifolia, syn. *P. angustifolia*. Evergreen, bushy perennial. H to 2ft (60cm), S 3–4ft (1–1.2m). Broadly lance-shaped leaves, with long-pointed tips, are 3in (8cm) long. Small clusters of tubular, deep rose-pink flowers are borne in winter. **'Aureovariegata'** illus. p.267. Z14–15 H12-1.

Pernettya mucronata. See *Gaultheria mucronata*.
Pernettya prostrata. See *Gaultheria myrsinoides*.
Pernettya pumila. See *Gaultheria pumila*.
Pernettya tasmanica. See *Gaultheria tasmanica*.

PEROVSKIA

LABIATAE/LAMIACEAE

Genus of deciduous subshrubs grown for their aromatic, gray-green foliage and blue flowers. Needs full sun and very well-drained soil. Cut plants back hard, almost to base, in spring, as new growth starts. Propagate by softwood cuttings in late spring.
P. atriplicifolia. Deciduous, upright subshrub. H 4ft (1.2m), S 3ft (1m). Gray-white stems bear narrowly oval, coarsely toothed leaves. Bears 2-lipped, violet-blue flowers in long, slender spikes from late summer to midautumn. Z6–9 H9–6.
P. 'Blue Spire' illus. p.168.
P. 'Hybrida'. Deciduous, upright subshrub. H 3ft (1m), S 30in (75cm). Has oval, deeply lobed and toothed leaves and, from late summer to mid-autumn, tall spires of 2-lipped, deep lavender-blue flowers. Z6–9 H9–6.

PERSICARIA

Knotweed

POLYGONACEAE

Genus of annuals, sometimes invasive perennials and rarely evergreen, semi-evergreen or deciduous subshrubs grown for their autumn leaf color. Has spikes or panicles of small, usually long-lasting white, pink, or red flowers. Needs sun or partial shade and moist soil. Propagate by seed in spring. Divide perennials in spring or autumn. Contact with all parts may irritate skin; the sap may cause mild stomach upset if ingested.
P. affinis, syn. *Polygonum affine*. Mat-forming, evergreen perennial. H 6–12in (15–30cm), S 12in (30cm) or more. Thick stems bear small, lance-shaped, glossy green leaves that turn red-bronze in winter. From midsummer to midautumn carries dense spikes of small, funnel-shaped, rose-red flowers, fading to pale pink. Is good on a bank or in a rock garden. Z3–8 H8–1. **'Darjeeling Red'**, H 8–10in (20–25cm), has long spikes of deep red flowers. **'Donald Lowndes'** illus. p.376.
P. amplexicaulis, syn. *Polygonum amplexicaule*. Clump-forming, leafy perennial. H and S 4ft (1.2m). Bears profuse spikes of small, rich red flowers in summer-autumn. Has oval to heart-shaped, midgreen leaves. Z3–8 H8–1. **'Firetail'** illus. p.249.
P. bistorta, syn. *Polygonum bistorta* (Bistort). **'Superba'** illus. p.243.
P. campanulata, syn. *Polygonum campanulatum*, illus. p.259.
P. capitata, syn. *Polygonum capitatum*. Compact, spreading perennial. H 2in (5cm), S 6–8in (15–20cm). Small, oval leaves are green with darker marks. Small, spherical heads of pink flowers are borne in summer. Is suitable for a rock garden or bank.
P. macrophylla, syn. *P. sphaerostachya*, *Polygonum macrophyllum*, *P. sphaerostachyum*, illus. p.279.
P. milletii, syn. *Polygonum milletii*. Compact perennial. H and S 24in (60cm). Produces slender spikes of rich crimson flowers from midsummer to early autumn. Narrow, lance-shaped leaves are midgreen.
P. sphaerostachya. See *P. macrophylla*.
P. vacciniifolia, syn. *Polygonum vacciniifolium*, illus. p.387.
***P. virginiana* 'Painter's Palette'**, syn. *Polygonum virginianum* 'Painter's Palette', *Tovara virginiana* 'Painter's Palette', illus. p.290.

PETASITES

ASTERACEAE/COMPOSITAE

Genus of invasive perennials grown for their usually large leaves and value as a groundcover. Tolerates sun or shade and prefers moist but well-drained soil. Propagate by division in spring or autumn.
P. fragrans (Winter heliotrope). Spreading, invasive perennial. H 9–12in (23–30cm), S 4ft (1.2m). Has rounded to heart-shaped, dark green leaves. Small, vanilla-scented, daisy-like, pinkish white flower heads are produced in late winter before foliage. Z7–9 H9–7.
P. japonicus illus. p.274.

PETREA

VERBENACEAE

Genus of evergreen shrubs and woody-stemmed, twining climbers grown for their flowers. Needs full light and fertile, well-drained soil. Water regularly, less when not in full growth. Provide support. Thin out and spur back crowded growth in spring. Propagate by semi-ripe cuttings in summer. Mealy bug and whitefly may cause problems.
P. volubilis illus. p.206.

PETROCOSMEA

GESNERIACEAE

Genus of evergreen, rhizomatous perennials. Requires shade and well-drained, peaty soil. Propagate by seed in early spring or by leaf cuttings in early summer.
P. kerrii illus. p.374.

PETRORHAGIA

CARYOPHYLLACEAE

Genus of annuals and perennials grown for their flowers. Is suitable for rock gardens and banks. Prefers sun and well-drained, sandy soil. Propagate by seed in autumn. Self-seeds readily.
P. saxifraga, syn. *Tunica saxifraga* (Tunic flower), illus. p.375. **'Rosette'** is a mat-forming perennial. H 4in (10cm), S 6in (15cm). Has tufts of grasslike leaves. In summer, slender stems carry a profusion of cup-shaped, double white to pale pink flowers, sometimes veined deeper pink. Z5–7 H7–5.

PETUNIA

SOLANACEAE

Genus of annuals and perennials, almost always grown as annuals, with showy, colorful flowers. Grow in a sunny position that is sheltered from wind and in fertile, well-drained soil. Deadhead regularly. Propagate by seed sown under cover in autumn or midspring. May suffer from viruses, including cucumber mosaic and tomato spotted wilt.

The many cultivars that have been produced are moderately fast-growing, branching, bushy plants, H 6–12in (15–30cm), S 12in (30cm), with oval, mid to deep green leaves, usually 2–5in (5–12cm) long. In summer-autumn, they produce flared, trumpet-shaped, single or double flowers in a wide range of colors (available in mixtures or singly), including blue, violet, purple, red, pink, and white. Some have dark veining, central white stars, halos (throats in contrasting colors), or picotee margins.

Petunias are generally hardy in Z11 H12–1, although protection may extend cold hardiness to Zone 8 for some.

The cultivars are divided into 2 groups, Grandiflora and Multiflora petunias.
Grandiflora petunias have very large flowers, 3–4in (8–10cm) wide, but they are easily damaged by rain and, where summer rains are frequent, are best grown in sheltered hanging baskets and containers.
Multiflora petunias are bushier than the Grandiflora petunias, and produce smaller flowers, 2in (5cm) wide, in greater quantity. They tend to be more resistant to rain damage and are excellent for summer bedding or for a mixed border.

***P.* Aladdin Series.** Grandiflora petunias, illus. p.322.
***P.* Carpet Series.** Multiflora petunias, illus. p.328.
***P.* Cascade Series.** Grandiflora petunias. H 8–12in (20–30cm), S 12–36in (30–90cm). Trailing stems produce flowers in a wide range of colors.
***P.* 'Cherry Tart'.** Multiflora petunia. H 6–12in (15–30cm), S 12–24in (30–60cm). Bears double, deep pink-and-white flowers.
***P.* 'Colour Parade'.** Grandiflora petunia. H 8–12in (20–30cm), S 12–36in (30–90cm). Has a wide color range of flowers with ruffled petals.
***P.* Daddy Series.** Grandiflora petunias. H to 14in (35cm), S 12–36in (30–90cm). Bear large, heavily veined flowers in pastel to deep pink, salmon-pink, purple, or lavender-blue. **'Sugar Daddy'** illus p.331.
***P.* Flash Series.** Compact, Grandiflora petunias. H 9–16in (23–40cm), S 12–36in (30–90cm). Produce flowers in a range of bright colors, including bicolors.
***P.* 'Gypsy'.** Multiflora petunia. H 6–12in (15–30cm), S 12–24in (30–60cm). Has salmon-red flowers.
***P.* Jamboree Series.** Multiflora petunias. H 6–12in (15–30cm), S 12–36in (30–90cm). Produce pendulous stems bearing flowers in a range of colors.
***P.* 'Magic Cherry'.** Compact, Grandiflora petunia. H 8–12in (20–30cm), S 12–24in (30–60cm). Has cherry-red flowers.
***P.* 'Mirage Velvet'.** Multiflora petunia, illus. p.326.
***P.* Pearl Series.** Dwarf, Multiflora petunias. H 6–8in (15–20cm), S 8–20in (20–50cm). Bear small flowers in a wide range of colors.
***P.* Picotee Ruffled Series.** Multiflora petunias. H 6–12in (15–30cm), S 12–36in (30–90cm). Bear ruffled flowers, edged with white, in a range of colors.
***P.* Picotee Series.** Grandiflora petunias, illus. p.328. **'Picotee Rose'** illus. p.326.
***P.* Plum Crazy Series.** Multiflora petunias. H 6–8in (15–20cm), S 12–36in (30–90cm). Produce flowers that have contrasting veins and throats. Colors available include white with yellow throat and veins, and shades of violet, pink, and magenta, all with darker throats and veins.
***P.* Primetime Series.** Multiflora petunias, illus. p.323.
***P.* 'Razzle Dazzle'.** Grandiflora petunia. H 8–12in (20–30cm), S 12–36in (30–90cm). Has flowers in various colors, striped with white.
***P.* Recoverer Series.** Grandiflora petunias, illus. p.318.
***P.* 'Red Satin'.** Multiflora petunia. H 6–12in (15–30cm), S 12–24in (30–60cm). Has brilliant scarlet flowers.
***P.* Resisto Series.** Multiflora petunias, [blue] illus. p.332; [rose-pink] illus. p.325.
***P.* Surfinia Series 'Surfinia Purple'** (illus. p.55). Vigorous Grandiflora petunia. H 9–16in (23–40cm), S 12–36in (30–90cm). Bears masses of magenta flowers with purple veining. Has good wet-weather tolerance.

PHACELIA

HYDROPHYLLACEAE

Genus of annuals, biennials, and perennials. Grow in sun and in fertile, well-drained soil. Tall species may need support. Propagate by seed sown outdoors in spring or early autumn. Contact with foliage may aggravate skin allergies.
P. campanularia illus. p.334.
P. tanacetifolia. Moderately fast-growing, upright annual. H 24in (60cm) or more, S 12in (30cm). Has feathery, deep green leaves. In summer, bears spikes of bell-shaped, lavender-blue flowers. Z5–10 H9–1.

PHAEDRANASSA

AMARYLLIDACEAE

Genus of bulbs with tubular, often pendent flowers. Needs full sun or partial shade and fairly rich, well-drained soil. Apply high-potassium fertilizer in summer. Reduce watering in winter. Propagate by seed or offsets in spring.
P. carmioli illus. p.400.

Phaedranthus buccinatorius. See *Distictis buccinatoria*.
Phaiophleps biflora. See *Olsynium biflorum*.

PHAIUS

See also ORCHIDS.
P. tankervilleae (illus. p.297). Semi-evergreen, terrestrial orchid. H 30in (75cm). Tall spikes of flowers, 3½in (9cm) across, brown within, silvery gray outside and each with a long, red-marked pink lip, open in early summer. Leaves are broadly oval, ribbed and 24in (60cm) long. Provide semi-shade in summer. Z12–15 H12–6.

PHALAENOPSIS

See also ORCHIDS.
***P.* Allegria** (illus. p.296). Evergreen, epiphytic orchid for a warm greenhouse. H 6in (15cm). Carries sprays of white flowers, to 5in (12cm) across; flowering season varies. Broadly oval, fleshy leaves are 6in (15cm) long. Needs shade in summer. Z14-15 H12–6.
P. cornu-cervi (illus. p.298). Evergreen, epiphytic orchid for a warm greenhouse. H 6in (15cm). Yellowish green flowers, 2in (5cm) across, with brown marks, are borne successively, either singly or in pairs, in summer. Has broadly oval leaves, 4in (10cm) long. Needs shade in summer. Z14-15 H12–6.
***P.* Lady Jersey x Lippeglut** (illus. p.297). Evergreen, epiphytic orchid for a warm greenhouse. H 6in (15cm). Tall, pendent spikes of pink flowers, 3½in (9cm) across, appear at varying times of year. Broadly oval leaves are 4in (10cm) long. Requires shade in summer. Z14-15 H12–6.
***P.* Lundy** (illus. p.298). Evergreen, epiphytic orchid for a warm greenhouse. H 6in (15cm). Has sprays of yellow flowers, 3in (8cm) across, with red-stripes; flowering season varies. Broadly oval leaves are 9in (23cm) long. Grow in shade in summer. Z14-15 H12–6.

PHALARIS

GRAMINEAE/POACEAE

See also GRASSES, BAMBOOS, RUSHES, and SEDGES.
P. arundinacea var. ***picta***, syn. *P.a.* 'Picta', illus. p.306. **'Picta'** see *P.a.* var. *picta*.

Phanerophlebia fortunei. See *Cyrtomium fortunei*.
Pharbitis. Reclassified as *Ipomoea*.
Phaseolus caracalla. See *Vigna caracalla*.

PHEGOPTERIS

THELYPTERIDACEAE

Genus of deciduous ferns. Grow in semi-shade and in organic, moist but well-drained soil. Propagate by division in spring or by spores in summer.
P. connectilis, syn. *Thelypteris phegopteris* (Beech fern). Deciduous fern. H 9in (23cm), S 12in (30cm). Broadly lance-shaped, midgreen fronds, each consisting of tiny, triangular pinnae on wiry stalks, arise from a creeping rootstock. Is useful as a groundcover. Z4–6 H6–1.

PHELLODENDRON

RUTACEAE

Genus of deciduous trees grown for their foliage, which colors well in autumn. Male and female flowers are produced on different plants.
Young growth is susceptible to damage by late frosts. Needs full sun and fertile, well-drained soil. Propagate by softwood cuttings in summer, by seed in autumn or by root cuttings in late winter.
P. amurense (Amur cork tree). Deciduous, spreading tree. H 40ft (12m), S 50ft (15m). Has corky, dark bark when old. Aromatic leaves, each with 5 to 11 oblong leaflets, are glossy, dark green, becoming yellow in autumn. Tiny green flowers in early summer are

followed by small, persistent, rounded black fruits that smell of resin. Z4–7 H8–5.
P. chinense illus. p.81.

PHILADELPHUS

HYDRANGEACEAE/PHILADELPHACEAE

Genus of deciduous, mainly summer-flowering shrubs grown for their usually fragrant flowers. Needs sun and fertile, well-drained soil. After flowering, cut some older shoots back to young growths, leaving young shoots to flower the following year. Propagate by softwood cuttings in summer. May become infested with aphids.
***P.* 'Beauclerk'** illus. p.135.
***P.* 'Belle Etoile'** illus. p.136.
***P.* 'Boule d'Argent'** illus. p.137.
P. coronarius (Mock orange). **'Aureus'** is a deciduous, upright shrub. H 8ft (2.5m), S 5ft (1.5m). Clusters of very fragrant, 4-petaled, creamy white flowers are produced in late spring and early summer. Oval, golden yellow young leaves turn yellow-green in summer. Protect from full sun. Z4–7 H7–1. **'Variegatus'** illus. p.139.
***P.* 'Buckley's Quill'.** Upright deciduous shrub. H 6ft (2m) S 4ft (1.2m). Semi-double to double fragrant white flowers with about 30 narrow quill-like petals, divided at their tips, appear in early summer. Leaves are midgreen and slightly toothed. Z5–8 H8–5.
***P.* 'Dame Blanche'** illus. p.137.
P. delavayi. Deciduous, upright shrub. H 10ft (3m), S 8ft (2.5m). Dense clusters of very fragrant, 4-petaled white flowers, with sometimes purple-flushed green sepals, open from early to midsummer. Leaves are dark green, oval, and toothed. Z6–9 H9–6. f. ***melanocalyx*** (syn. *P. purpurascens*) illus. p.139.
P.* x *lemoinei. See *P.* 'Lemoinei'.
***P.* 'Lemoinei'**, syn. *P.* x *lemoinei*, illus. p.138.
***P.* 'Manteau d'Hermine'** illus. p.158.
P. purpurascens. See *P. delavayi* f. *melanocalyx*.
***P.* 'Snowbelle'.** Semi-dwarf, deciduous shrub with dark green, narrow foliage. H and S 4ft (1.2m). The fragrant white flowers have 8–15 rounded petals in a compact inflorescence. Z5–8 H8–5.
***P.* 'Virginal'.** Vigorous, deciduous, upright shrub. H 10ft (3m), S 8ft (2.5m). Has oval, dark green leaves. Produces masses of large, very fragrant, double or semi-double, pure white flowers in loose racemes from early to midsummer. Z5–8 H8–5.

PHILESIA

LILIACEAE/PHILESIACEAE

Genus of one species of evergreen shrub grown for its showy flowers. Thrives only in mild, moist areas. Needs semi-shade and organic, moist, acidic soil. Benefits from an annual dressing of leaf mold. Propagate by semi-ripe cuttings in summer or by suckers in autumn.
P. magellanica. Evergreen, erect shrub. H 3ft (1m), S 6ft (2m). Bears trumpet-shaped, waxy, crimson-pink flowers, in leaf axils, from midsummer to late autumn. Narrowly oblong, dark green leaves are bluish white beneath.

PHILLYREA

OLEACEAE

Genus of evergreen shrubs and trees, with inconspicuous flowers, grown for their foliage. Does best in full sun and in fertile, well-drained soil. To restrict growth, cut back in spring. Propagate by semi-ripe cuttings in summer.
P. angustifolia. Evergreen, bushy, dense shrub. H and S 10ft (3m). Leaves are narrowly oblong and dark green. Small, fragrant, 4-lobed, greenish white flowers in late spring and early summer are followed by spherical, blue-black fruits. Z7–9 H9–7.
P. decora. See *Osmanthus decorus.*
P. latifolia. Evergreen, rounded shrub or tree. H and S 25ft (8m). Has oval, glossy, dark green leaves. Bears tiny, fragrant, 4-lobed, greenish white flowers from late spring to early summer, then spherical, blue-black fruits. Z7–9 H9–7.

PHILODENDRON

ARACEAE

Genus of evergreen shrubs and woody-based, root climbers grown for their handsome leaves. Intermittently bears insignificant flowers. Needs partial shade and organic, well-drained soil. Water moderately, sparingly in cold weather. Provide support. Young stem tips may be removed to promote branching. Propagate by leaf-bud or stem-tip cuttings in summer. All parts may cause severe discomfort if ingested; contact with sap may irritate skin.
P. auritum of gardens. See *Syngonium auritum.*
P. bipinnatifidum, syn. *P. selloum* (Tree philodendron; illus. p.152). Treelike shrub with a single, erect stem and very long-stalked leaves. Z14-15 H12–4.
***P.* 'Burgundy'.** Slow-growing, evergreen, woody-based, root climber. H 6ft (2m) or more. Leaves are narrowly oblong, red-flushed, deep green above, wine red beneath, and up to 12in (30cm) long. Z14-15 H12–1.
P. cordatum (Heart leaf). Moderately vigorous, evergreen, woody-based, root climber. H 10ft (3m) or more. Has heart-shaped, lustrous, rich green leaves to 18in (45cm) long. Z11–12 H12–1.
P. domesticum, syn. *P. hastatum* of gardens (Elephant's ear, Spade leaf). Fairly slow-growing, evergreen, woody-based, root climber. H 6–10ft (2–3m). Lustrous, bright green leaves, 12–16in (30–40cm) long, are arrow-shaped on young plants and later have prominent, basal lobes. Z14-15 H12–1.
P. erubescens (Blushing philodendron). Evergreen, erect, woody-based, root climber. H to 10ft (3m). Oval to triangular leaves, 6–10in (15–25cm) long, have long red stalks and are dark green with a lustrous coppery flush. Z14-15 H12–1.
P. hastatum of gardens. See *P. domesticum*.
P. laciniatum. See *P. pedatum*.
P. melanochrysum illus. p.220.
P. pedatum, syn. *P. laciniatum*. Slow-growing, evergreen, woody-based, root climber. H 6–10ft (2–3m). Has oval, lustrous, deep green leaves, 12–32in (30–80cm) long, cut into 5 or 7 prominent lobes. Z14-15 H12–1.
P. pinnatifidum. Evergreen, erect, robust, unbranched shrub. H to 10ft (3m), S 3–6ft (1–2m). Glossy, deep green leaves are broadly oval in outline, 16–24in (40–60cm) long and divided into 15 or more fingerlike lobes. Z14-15 H12–1.
P. sagittatum. See *P. sagittifolium*.
P. sagittifolium, syn. *P. sagittatum*. Slow-growing, evergreen, woody-based, root climber. H 6–10ft (2–3m). Oval leaves with basal lobes are up to 16–24in (40–60cm) long and glossy, bright green. Z14-15 H12–1.
P. scandens illus. p.220.
P. selloum. See *P. bipinnatifidum*.
P. trifoliatum. See *Syngonium auritum.*

PHLEBODIUM

POLYPODIACEAE

Genus of evergreen or semi-evergreen ferns. Needs full light or semi-shade and organic, moist but well-drained soil. Remove fading fronds regularly. Propagate by division in spring or by spores in summer.
P. aureum, syn. *Polypodium aureum*, illus. p.311. **'Mandaianum'** illus. p.310.

PHLOMIS

LABIATAE/LAMIACEAE

Genus of evergreen, summer-flowering shrubs and perennials grown for their conspicuous, hooded flowers, which are borne in dense whorls, and for their foliage. Prefers full sun and well-drained soil. Propagate by seed in autumn; increase shrubs from softwood cuttings in summer and perennials by division in spring.
P. cashmeriana. Evergreen, upright shrub. H 24in (60cm), S 18in (45cm). Produces masses of 2-lipped, pale lilac flowers in summer. Narrowly oval, mid-green leaves have woolly white undersides. Z8–9 H9–8.
P. chrysophylla. Evergreen, rounded, stiffly branched shrub. H and S 3ft (1m). Bears 2-lipped, golden yellow flowers in early summer. Oval leaves are gray-green when young, becoming golden green. Z9–10H10–9.
P. fruticosa illus. p.170.
P. italica illus. p.162.
P. longifolia var. ***bailanica.*** Evergreen, bushy shrub. H 4ft (1.2m), S 3ft (1m). Leaves are oblong to heart-shaped, deeply veined, and bright green. Has 2-lipped, deep yellow flowers from early to midsummer. Z8–9 H9–8.
P. russeliana illus. p.255.

PHLOX

POLEMONIACEAE

Genus of mainly late spring- or summer-flowering annuals and perennials, some of which are semi-evergreen or evergreen, grown for their terminal panicles or profusion of brightly colored flowers. Does best in sun or semi-shade and in fertile, moist but well-drained soil; some species prefer acidic soil; in light, dry soils is better grown in partial shade. Trim back rock garden species after flowering. Propagate rock garden species and hybrids by cuttings from non-flowering shoots in spring or summer; species by seed in autumn or spring; *P. maculata*, *P. paniculata,* and their cultivars also by division in early spring or by root cuttings in winter; and annuals by seed in spring. *P. maculata*, *P. paniculata,* and their cultivars are susceptible to nematodes and mildew. See also feature panel p.242.
P. adsurgens. Evergreen, mat-forming, prostrate perennial. H 4in (10cm), S 12in (30cm). Woody-based stems are clothed in oval, light to midgreen leaves. In summer produces terminal clusters of short-stemmed, saucer-shaped purple, pink, or white flowers with overlapping petals. Is good for a rock garden. Prefers partial shade and gritty, peaty, acidic soil. Z4–8 H8–1. **'Wagon Wheel'** illus. p.376.
***P. amoena* 'Variegata'.** See *P.* x *procumbens* 'Variegata'.
P. bifida illus. p.381.
P. caespitosa. Evergreen, mound-forming, compact perennial. H 3in (8cm), S 5in (12cm). Leaves are narrow and needlelike. Solitary almost stemless, saucer-shaped lilac or white flowers are borne in summer. Good in a rock garden or trough. Needs sun and very well-drained soil. Z4–8 H8–1.
***P.* 'Camla'** illus. p.379.
***P.* 'Chatahoochee'.** See *P. divaricata* subsp. *laphamii* 'Chatahoochee'.
P. divaricata. Semi-evergreen, creeping perennial. H 12in (30cm) or more, S 8in (20cm). In early summer, upright stems carry saucer-shaped, lavender-blue flowers in loose clusters. Leaves are oval. Good in a rock garden. Prefers semi-shade and moist but well-drained, peaty soil. Z4–8 H8–1. subsp. ***laphamii*** illus. p.356. subsp. ***laphamii* 'Chatahoochee'** (syn. *P.* 'Chatahoochee') illus. p.356.
***P. douglasii* 'Boothman's Variety'** illus. p.380. **'Crackerjack'** illus. p.379. **'May Snow'** is an evergreen, mound-forming perennial. H 3in (8cm), S 8in (20cm). Masses of saucer-shaped white flowers are carried in early summer. Leaves are lance-shaped and midgreen. Is suitable for a rock garden, wall, or bank. Vigorous, compact **'Red Admiral'**, H 6in (15cm), has crimson flowers. Both Z5–7 H7–5.
P. drummondii (Annual phlox). **'African Sunset'** illus. p.327. **Beauty Series** is a group of moderately fast-growing, compact, upright annuals.

H 6in (15cm), S 4in (10cm). Has lance-shaped, pale green leaves and, from summer to early autumn, heads of star-shaped flowers in many colors, including red, pink, blue, purple, and white. **'Carnival'** has larger flowers with contrasting centers. **'Chanal'** illus. p.326. **'Petticoat'** has bicolored flowers. **'Sternenzauber'** (syn. *P.d.* 'Twinkle') illus. p.326. **'Twinkle'** see *P.d.* 'Sternenzauber'. All H12–1.
***P.* 'Emerald Cushion'** illus. p.381.
P. hoodii. Evergreen, compact, prostrate perennial. H 2in (5cm), S 4in (10cm). Solitary, flat white flowers open in early summer above fine, needlelike, hairy leaves. Good in a rock garden. Needs sun and very well-drained soil.
P. maculata. Erect perennial. H 3ft (1m), S 1½ft (45cm). In summer produces cylindrical panicles of tubular, 5-lobed, mauve-pink flowers above oval, midgreen leaves. Z5–8 H8–1. **'Alpha'** (illus. p.242) has rose-pink flowers. **'Omega'** (illus. p.242) has white flowers, each with a lilac eye.
P. paniculata. Upright perennial, seldom grown, since it has been almost completely replaced in gardens by its more colorful cultivars. H 4ft (1.2m), S 2ft (60cm). Tubular, 5-lobed flowers are borne in conical heads above oval, midgreen leaves in late summer. Z4–8 H8–1. **'Aida'** is purple-red, each flower with a purple eye. Flowers of **'Amethyst'** (illus. p.242) are pale lilac with paler-edged petals. **'Balmoral'** (illus. p.242) has large, rosy-mauve flowers. **'Brigadier'** (illus. p.242) has deep orange-red flowers. **'Bright Eyes'** has pale pink flowers, each with a red eye. **'Eva Cullum'** (illus. p.242) has clear pink flowers with magenta eyes. **'Eventide'** (illus. p.242) produces lavender-blue flowers. **'Fujiyama'** (illus. p.242) has star-shaped white flowers. Flowers of **'Graf Zeppelin'** (illus. p.242) are white with red centers. **'Hampton Court'** (illus. p.242) is a mauve-blue cultivar, with dark green foliage. **'Harlequin'** (illus. p.242) has reddish purple flowers. Leaves are variegated ivory-white. **'Le Mahdi'** (illus. p.242) has deep purple flowers. **'Mia Ruys'** (illus. p.242), H 18in (45cm), has large white flowers and is shorter than most other cultivars. **'Mother of Pearl'** (illus. p.242) has white flowers tinted pink. **'Norah Leigh'** (illus. p.242) has pale lilac flowers and ivory-variegated leaves. **'Prince of Orange'** (illus. p.242) is orange-red. **'Russian Violet'** is of open habit and has pale lilac-blue flowers. Flowers of **'Sandringham'** (illus. p.242) have widely spaced petals and are pink with darker centers. **'Sir John Falstaff'** has large, deep salmon flowers, each with a cherry red eye. **'White Admiral'** (illus. p.242) bears pure white flowers. Those of **'Windsor'** (illus. p.242) are carmine-rose with red eyes.
***P.* x *procumbens* 'Millstream'.** Evergreen, prostrate perennial. H to 6in (15cm), S 12in (30cm). Has narrowly oval, glossy, green leaves. In early summer produces small, saucer-shaped, deep lavender-pink flowers with white eyes. Is suitable for a rock garden. Z3–8 H8–1. **'Variegata'** (syn. *P. amoena* 'Variegata'), H 1in (2.5cm), S 10in (25cm), has white-margined leaves and bright cerise-pink flowers.
P. stolonifera (Creeping phlox). Evergreen, prostrate, spreading perennial. H 4–6in (10–15cm), S 12in (30cm) or more. Has small, saucer-shaped, pale blue flowers in early summer. Leaves are oblong to oval. Prefers moist, peaty, acidic soil; is good for a rock garden. Z4–8 H8–1. **'Ariane'** illus. p.373. **'Blue Ridge'** has masses of lavender-blue flowers.
P. subulata. Evergreen, mound-forming perennial. H 4in (10cm), S 8in (20cm). Bears fine, needlelike leaves. Masses of star-shaped white, pink, or mauve flowers appear in early summer. Is good for a sunny rock garden. Z3–8 H8–1. **'Marjorie'** illus. p.378.

PHOENIX

ARECACEAE/PALMAE

Genus of evergreen palms grown for their overall appearance and their edible fruits. Grow in full light, though tolerates partial shade, in any fertile, well-drained soil. Water potted specimens moderately, less during winter. Propagate by seed in spring at not less than 75°F (24°C). Spider mite may be a nuisance.
P. canariensis (Canary Island date palm). Evergreen, upright palm with a robust trunk. H 60ft (18m) or more, S 30ft (10m) or more. Feather-shaped, arching leaves, each to 15ft (5m) long, are divided into narrowly lance-shaped, leathery, bright green leaflets. Bears large, pendent clusters of tiny, yellowish brown flowers that on mature specimens are followed by shortly oblong yellow to red fruits in autumn-winter. Z11-12 H12–10.
P. roebelenii (Miniature date palm, Pygmy date palm). Evergreen palm with a slender trunk. H 6–12ft (2–4m), S 3–6ft (1–2m). Has feather-shaped, arching, glossy, dark green leaves, 3–4ft (1–1.2m) long, and, in summer, large panicles of tiny yellow flowers. Egg-shaped black fruits are borne in pendent clusters, 18in (45cm) long, in autumn. Z11–12 H12–10.

PHORMIUM

New Zealand flax

AGAVACEAE/PHORMIACEAE

Genus of evergreen perennials grown for their bold, sword-shaped leaves. Requires sun and moist but well-drained soil. Propagate by division or seed in spring.
***P.* 'Bronze Baby'** illus. p.302.
P. colensoi. See *P. cookianum.*
P. cookianum, syn. *P. colensoi* (Mountain flax). Evergreen, upright perennial. H 3–6ft (1–2m), S 1ft (30cm). Has tufts of sword-shaped, dark green leaves. Panicles of tubular, pale yellowish green flowers are borne in summer. Z9–11 H12–1. subsp. ***hookeri* 'Tricolor'** has leaves striped vertically with red, yellow, and green. **'Variegatum'** has cream-striped leaves.
***P.* 'Dazzler'** illus. p.264.
P. tenax. Evergreen, upright perennial. H 10ft (3m), S 3–6ft (1–2m). Has tufts of sword-shaped, stiff, dark green leaves. Panicles of tubular, dull red flowers are produced on short, slightly glaucous green stems in summer. Thrives by the sea. Z9–11 H12–6. **'Aurora'** has leaves vertically striped with red, bronze, salmon-pink, and yellow. **Purpureum Group** illus. p.232. **'Veitchianum'** (syn. *P.t.* 'Veitchii') bears broad, creamy white-striped leaves. **'Veitchii'** see *P.t.* 'Veitchianum'.

PHOTINIA,

syn. STRANVAESIA

ROSACEAE

Genus of evergreen or deciduous shrubs and trees, with small white flowers, grown for their foliage and, in the case of deciduous species, for their autumn color and fruits. Protect evergreen species from strong, cold winds. Requires sun or semi-shade and fertile, well-drained soil; some species prefer acidic soil. Propagate evergreen and deciduous species by semi-ripe cuttings in summer, deciduous species also by seed in autumn.
P. arbutifolia, syn. *Heteromeles arbutifolia* (Christmas berry, Toyon). Evergreen, bushy, spreading shrub or tree. H 20ft (6m), S 25ft (8m). Has oblong, sharply toothed, leathery, glossy, dark green leaves. Broad, flat heads of small, 5-petaled white flowers, produced in late summer, are succeeded by large clusters of rounded red fruits. Z9–10.
P. davidiana illus. p.94.
P.* x *fraseri. Group of evergreen, hybrid shrubs. Has good resistance to damage by late frosts. Leaves are bold and oblong. Young growths are attractive over a long period. Z8–9 H9-8. **'Birmingham'** illus. p.117. **'Red Robin'** is upright and dense. H 20ft (6m), S 12ft (4m). Glossy, dark green leaves are brilliant red when young. Bears 5-petaled flowers in late spring.
P. nussia. Evergreen, spreading tree. H and S 20ft (6m). Produces oblong, leathery, glossy, dark green leaves and saucer-shaped, 5-petaled white flowers in midsummer, followed by rounded, orange-red fruits.
P. serratifolia, syn. *P. serrulata.* Evergreen, upright shrub or bushy-headed tree. H 30ft (10m), S 25ft (8m). Oblong, often sharply toothed leaves are red when young, maturing to glossy, dark green. Small, 5-petaled flowers from mid- to late spring are sometimes followed by spherical red fruits. Young growth may be damaged by late frosts. Z9–10 H10–9.
P. serrulata. See *P. serratifolia.*
P. villosa. Deciduous, upright shrub or spreading tree. H and S 15ft (5m). Oval, dark green leaves, bronze-margined when young, become brilliant orange-red in autumn. Clusters of 5-petaled flowers, produced in late spring, are followed by spherical red fruits. Prefers acidic soil. Z4–9 H9–1.

PHRAGMIPEDIUM

See also ORCHIDS.
P. caudatum. Evergreen, epiphytic orchid for an intermediate greenhouse. H 9in (23cm). In summer produces sprays of flowers with light green and tan sepals and pouches and drooping, ribbonlike yellow and brownish crimson petals, to 12in (30cm) long. Has narrowly oval leaves, 12in (30cm) long. Needs shade in summer. Z14–15 H12–10.

PHUOPSIS

RUBIACEAE

Genus of one species of mat-forming, summer-flowering perennial grown for its small, pungent, tubular flowers. Is good as a groundcover, especially on banks and in rock gardens. Needs sun and well-drained soil. Propagate by division in spring, by semi-ripe cuttings in summer, or by seed in autumn.
P. stylosa, syn. *Crucianella stylosa*, illus. p.352.

PHYGELIUS

SCROPHULARIACEAE

Genus of evergreen or semi-evergreen shrubs and subshrubs grown for their showy, tubular flowers. Grows best if planted in a sheltered position; will attain a considerably greater height when grown against a south- or west-facing wall. Needs sun and fertile, well-drained but not too dry soil. Where marginally hardy it loses leaves or has shoots cut to ground by cold. Cut back to just above ground level in spring, or, if plants have woody bases, prune to live wood. Propagate by softwood cuttings in summer.
P. aequalis illus. p.166. **'Yellow Trumpet'** illus. p.169.
***P. capensis* 'Coccineus'.** Evergreen or semi-evergreen, upright subshrub. H 5ft (1.5m), S 6ft (2m). Tubular, curved, bright orange-red flowers, each with a red mouth and a yellow throat, are produced from midsummer to early autumn in tall, slender spires amid triangular, dark green leaves. Z8–9 H9–8.
***P.* x *rectus* 'Winchester Fanfare'.** Evergreen or semi-evergreen, upright subshrub. H 5ft (1.5m), S 6ft (2m). Has pendulous, tubular, dusky, reddish pink flowers, each with scarlet lobes and a yellow throat, from midsummer to early autumn, and triangular, dark green leaves. Z8–9 H9–8.

Phyllanthus nivosus. See *Breynia disticha.*
Phyllitis scolopendrium. See *Asplenium scolopendrium.*
***Phyllitis scolopendrium* 'Marginatum'.** See *Asplenium scolopendrium* Marginatum Group.

PHYLLOCLADUS

PHYLLOCLADACEAE/PODOCARPACEAE

See also CONIFERS.
P. aspleniifolius (Tasman celery pine). Slow-growing, upright conifer. H 15–30ft (5–10m), S 10–15ft (3–5m). Instead of true leaves has flattened, leaflike shoots known as phylloclades; these are dull dark green and resemble celery leaves in outline. Produces inedible, white-coated nuts with fleshy red bases.
P. trichomanoides illus. p.106.

PHYLLODOCE

ERICACEAE

Genus of evergreen shrubs grown for their heathlike leaves and attractive flowers. Needs semi-shade and moist, peaty, acidic soil. Propagate by semi-ripe cuttings in late summer or by seed in spring.
P. caerulea, syn. *P. taxifolia*, illus. p.348.
P. empetriformis illus. p.348.
***P. x intermedia* 'Drummondii'** illus. p.347. **'Fred Stoker'** is an evergreen, upright shrub. H and S 9in (23cm). Has narrow, glossy, green leaves. From late spring to early summer carries terminal clusters of pitcher-shaped, bright reddish purple flowers on slender red stalks. Z3–7 H7–1.
P. nipponica. Evergreen, upright shrub. H 4–8in (10–20cm), S 4–6in (10–15cm). Freely branched stems bear fine, linear leaves and, in late spring and summer, stalked, bell-shaped white flowers from their tips. Z3–7 H7–1.
P. taxifolia. See *P. caerulea*.

PHYLLOSTACHYS

GRAMINEAE/POACEAE

See also GRASSES, BAMBOOS, RUSHES, and SEDGES.
P. aurea (Fishpole bamboo, Golden bamboo). Evergreen, clump-forming bamboo. H 20–25ft (6–8m), S indefinite. Erect, grooved stems have cup-shaped swellings beneath most nodes, which, toward the base, are often close together and distorted. Bears midgreen leaves. Flowers are unimportant; they are rarely produced. Z7–11 H12–7.
P. aureosulcata (Golden-groove bamboo). Evergreen, clump-forming bamboo. H 20–25ft (6–8m), S indefinite. Bears striped sheaths and yellow grooves on rough, brownish green stems. Midgreen leaves are up to 6in (15cm) long; flowers are unimportant because they are so rarely produced. Z5–11 H12–3.
P. bambusoides illus. p.308.
P. flexuosa illus. p.308.
***P.* 'Henonis'.** See *P. nigra* var. *henonis*.
P. nigra (Black bamboo). Evergreen, clump-forming bamboo. H 20–25ft (6–8m), S indefinite. Grooved, greenish brown stems turn black in thier second season of growth. Almost unmarked culm sheaths bear bristled auricles and midgreen leaves. Flowers are unimportant because they are so rarely produced. Z7–11 H12–4. var. ***henonis*** (syn. *P.* 'Henonis') illus. p.308.
P. viridiglaucescens illus. p.309.

PHYSALIS

Chinese lantern

SOLANACEAE

Genus of summer-flowering perennials and annuals grown mainly for their decorative, lanternlike calyces and fruits, produced in autumn. Grows in sun or shade and in well-drained soil. Propagate by division or softwood cuttings in spring, annuals by seed in spring or autumn. All parts of *P. alkekengi*, except the fully ripe fruit, may cause mild stomach upset if ingested; contact with foliage may irritate skin.
P. alkekengi (Bladder cherry, Winter cherry). Spreading invasive, perennial. H 18in (45cm), S 24in (60cm). Inconspicuous, nodding, star-shaped white flowers in summer are followed, in autumn, by rounded, bright orange-red fruits surrounded by inflated orange calyces. Leaves are midgreen and oval. Z3–9 H8–1.

PHYSOCARPUS

ROSACEAE

Genus of deciduous, mainly summer-flowering shrubs grown for their foliage and flowers. Requires sun and fertile, not too dry soil. Prefers acidic soil and does not grow well on shallow, alkaline soil. Thin established plants occasionally by cutting some older shoots back to ground level after flowering. Propagate by softwood cuttings in summer.
P. opulifolius (Ninebark). Deciduous, arching, dense shrub. H 10ft (3m), S 15ft (5m). Has peeling bark and broadly oval, toothed and lobed, midgreen leaves. Clusters of tiny, sometimes pink-tinged white flowers are borne in early summer. Z3–7 H7–1. **'Dart's Gold'** illus. p.146.

PHYSOPLEXIS

CAMPANULACEAE

Genus of one species of tufted perennial grown for its flowers. Is good grown on tufa and in rock gardens, troughs, and alpine houses. Needs sun and very well-drained, alkaline soil but should face away from midday sun. Keep fairly dry in winter. Propagate by seed in autumn or by softwood cuttings in early summer. Is susceptible to slug damage.
P. comosa, syn. *Phyteuma comosum*, illus. p.380.

PHYSOSTEGIA

Obedient plant

LABIATAE/LAMIACEAE

Genus of summer- to early autumn-flowering perennials. Needs sun and fertile, moist but well-drained soil. Propagate by division in spring.
P. virginiana. Erect perennial. H 3ft (1m), S 2ft (60cm). In late summer produces spikes of hooded, 2-lipped, rose-purple flowers with hinged stalks that allow flowers to remain in position once moved. Has lance-shaped, toothed, midgreen leaves. Z4–8 H8–1. subsp. ***speciosa* 'Variegata'** see *P.v.* 'Variegata'. **'Summer Snow'** has pure white flowers. **'Variegata'** (syn. *P.v.* subsp. *speciosa* 'Variegata') illus. p.244. **'Vivid'** illus. p.279.

PHYTEUMA

Horned rampion

CAMPANULACEAE

Genus of early- to midsummer-flowering perennials that are useful for rock gardens. Needs sun and well-drained soil. Propagate by seed in autumn.
P. comosum. See *Physoplexis comosa*.
P. scheuchzeri illus. p.357.

PHYTOLACCA

PHYTOLACCACEAE

Genus of perennials and evergreen shrubs and trees grown for their overall appearance and decorative but poisonous fruits. Tolerates sun or shade and requires fertile, moist soil. Propagate by seed in autumn or spring. All parts may cause severe discomfort if ingested; the fruit of *P. americana* may be lethal if eaten. Contact with the sap may irritate skin.
P. americana, syn. *P. decandra* (Red-ink plant, Virginia pokeweed). Upright, spreading perennial. H and S 4–5ft (1.2–1.5m). Oval to lance-shaped, midgreen leaves are tinged purple in autumn. Shallowly cup-shaped, sometimes pink-flushed, white-and-green flowers, borne in terminal racemes in summer, are followed by poisonous, rounded, fleshy, blackish purple berries. Z5–9 H9–5.
P. clavigera. See *P. polyandra*.
P. decandra. See *P. americana*.
P. polyandra, syn. *P. clavigera*. Thick, upright perennial. H and S 4ft (1.2m). Has brilliant crimson stems and oval to lance-shaped, midgreen leaves that turn yellow in autumn. In summer bears clusters of shallowly cup-shaped pink flowers followed by poisonous, blackish purple berries.

PICEA

Spruce

PINACEAE

Genus of conifers with needlelike leaves set on a pronounced peg on the shoots and arranged spirally. Cones are pendulous and ripen in their first autumn; scales are woody and flexible. See also CONIFERS.
P. abies (Common spruce, Norway spruce; illus. p.104). Fast-growing conifer, narrowly conical when young, broader with age. H 70–100ft (20–30m), S 15–22ft (5–7m). Has needlelike, dark green leaves and bears pendulous cones. Z3–8 H8–1. **'Clanbrassiliana'**, H 15ft (5m), S 10–15ft (3–5m), is slow-growing, rounded, and spreading. **'Gregoryana'** (illus. p.111), H and S 2ft (60cm), is slow-growing, with a dense, globose form. **'Inversa'**, H 15–30ft (5–10m), S 6ft (2m), has an erect leader, but pendent side branches. **'Little Gem'**, H and S 12–20in (30–50cm), has a nest-shaped, central depression caused by spreading branches. **'Nidiformis'**, H 3ft (1m), S 3–6ft (1–2m), is larger and faster-growing. **'Ohlendorffii'** (illus. p.110), H and S 3ft (1m), is slow-growing, initially rounded, becoming conical with age. **'Reflexa'** (illus. p.110), H 1ft (30cm), S 15ft (5m), is prostrate and ground-hugging, but itmay be trained up a stake to form a mound of weeping foliage.
P. breweriana illus. p.105.
P. engelmannii illus. p.105.
P. glauca (White spruce). Narrowly conical conifer. H 30–50ft (10–15m), S 12–15ft (4–5m). Glaucous shoots produce blue-green leaves. Ovoid, light brown cones fall after ripening. Z2–7 H7–2. var. ***albertiana* 'Conica'** (syn. *P.g.* 'Albertiana Conica'; illus. p.111), H 6–15ft (2–5m), S 3–6ft (1–2m), is of neat, pyramidal habit and slow-growing, with longer leaves and smaller cones. Z2–6 H6–1. **'Albertiana Conica'** see *P.g.* var. *albertiana* 'Conica'. **'Coerulea'** illus. p.105. **'Echiniformis'**, H 20in (50cm), S 36in (90cm), is a dwarf, flat-topped, rounded form. Z3–6 H6–1.
P. likiangensis (Lijiang spruce). Upright conifer. H 50ft (15m), S 15–30ft (5–10m). Bluish white leaves are well-spaced. Cones, 8–15cm (3–6in) long, are cylindrical, females bright red when young, ripening to purple, males pink.
P. mariana (Black spruce). Conical conifer, whose lowest branches often layer naturally, forming a ring of stems around the parent plant. H 30–50ft (10–15m), S 10ft (3m). Leaves are bluish green or bluish white. Oval cones are dark gray-brown. Z3–6 H6–1. **'Doumetii'** illus. p.108. **'Nana'** (illus. p.110), H 20in (50cm), S 20–32in (50–80cm), is a neat shrub with blue-gray foliage. Z2–6 H6–1.
***P. x mariorika* 'Gnom'**, syn. *P. omorika* 'Gnom' is a shrublike conifer with pendent branches arching at tips. H to 5ft (1.5m), S 3–6ft (1–2m). Dark green leaves are white beneath. Z5–8 H8–5.
P. morrisonicola illus. p.107.
P. omorika illus. p.103. **'Gnom'** see *P. x mariorika* 'Gnom'. **'Nana'**, H and S 3ft (1m), is a slow-growing, rounded or oval cultivar. Z3–7 H7–1.
P. orientalis (Caucasian spruce, Oriental spruce). Columnar, dense conifer. H 70ft (20m), S 15ft (5m). Has glossy, deep green leaves and ovoid to conical cones, 2½–4in (6–10cm) long, dark purple, ripening to brown, the males brick red in spring. Z5–8 H8–5. **'Aurea'** has golden, young foliage in spring, later turning green. **'Skylands'** illus. p.104.
P. pungens (Colorado spruce). Columnar conifer. H 50ft (15m), S 15ft

(5m). Has scaly gray bark and very sharp, thick, grayish green or bright blue leaves. Cylindrical, light brown cones have papery scales. Z3–8 H8–1. **'Hoopsii'**, H 30–50ft (10–15m), has silvery blue foliage. **'Koster'** illus. p.105. **'Montgomery'** (illus. p.110), H and S 3ft (1m), is dwarf, compact, spreading or conical, with gray-blue leaves.
P. sitchensis (Sitka spruce). Very vigorous, broadly conical conifer. H 100–160ft (30–50m) in damp locations, 50–70ft (15–20m) in dry situations, S 20–30ft (6–10m). Bark scales on old trees. Has prickly, bright deep green leaves and cylindrical, papery, pale brown or whitish cones, 2–4in (5–10cm) long. Is good on an exposed or poor site. Z7–8 H8–7.
P. smithiana (Morinda spruce, West Himalayan spruce). Slow-growing conifer, conical when young, columnar with horizontal branches and weeping shoots when mature. H 80–100ft (25–30m), S 20ft (6m). Has dark green leaves and produces cylindrical, bright brown cones, 4–8in (10–20cm) long. Z7–8 H8–1.

PICRASMA

SIMAROUBACEAE

Genus of deciduous trees grown for their brilliant autumn color. Produces insignificant flowers in late spring. Requires sun or semi-shade and fertile, well-drained soil. Propagate by seed in autumn.
P. ailanthoides. See *P. quassioides*.
P. quassioides, syn. *P. ailanthoides*, illus. p.97.

PIERIS

ERICACEAE

Genus of evergreen shrubs grown for their foliage and small, profuse, urn-shaped flowers. Needs a sheltered site in semi-shade or shade and in moist, peaty, acidic soil. *P. floribunda*, however, grows well in any acidic soil. Young shoots are sometimes frost-killed in spring and should be cut back as soon as possible. Deadheading after flowering improves growth. Propagate by soft tip or semi-ripe cuttings in summer. Leaves may cause severe discomfort if ingested.
***P.* 'Bert Chandler'.** Evergreen, bushy shrub. H 6ft (2m), S 5ft (1.5m). Lance-shaped leaves are bright pink when young, becoming creamy yellow, then white and finally dark green. Produces white flowers only very rarely. Likes an open position. Z7–9 H9–7.
P. floribunda illus. p.127.
***P.* 'Forest Flame'.** Evergreen, upright shrub. H 12ft (4m), S 6ft (2m). Narrowly oval, glossy leaves are brilliant red when young, then turn pink, cream, and finally dark green. White flowers are borne with the young leaves from mid- to late spring. Z6–9 H9–6.
P. formosa. Evergreen, bushy, dense shrub. H and S 12ft (4m). Large, oblong, glossy, dark green leaves are bronze when young. Bears large clusters of white flowers from mid- to late spring. Z7–9 H9–7. var. ***forrestii*** **'Wakehurst'** illus. p.142. **'Henry Price'** has deep-veined leaves that are bronze-red when young.
P. japonica illus. p.116. **'Daisen'** is an evergreen, rounded, dense shrub. H and S 10ft (3m). Oval, bronze leaves mature to glossy, dark green. Bears drooping clusters of red-budded, deep pink flowers in spring. Z6–8 H8-6. **'Dorothy Wyckoff'** has deep crimson buds, opening to pink blooms; foliage is bronze in winter. Z6–8 H8–4. Young foliage of **'Mountain Fire'** is brilliant red. Z5–9 H9-1. **'Scarlett O'Hara'** illus. p.127. **Taiwanensis Group** (syn. *P. taiwanensis*), S 15ft (5m), has narrow leaves that are bronze-red when young. Bears clusters of white flowers in early and midspring. Z3–6 H6–1. **'Variegata'** is slow-growing, with small leaves edged with white. Z6–8 H8–4.
P. nana, syn. *Arcterica nana*. Evergreen, prostrate, dwarf shrub. H 1–2in (2.5–5cm), S 4–6in (10–15cm). Has tiny, oval, leathery, dark green leaves, usually in whorls of 3, on fine stems that root readily. In early spring bears small, terminal clusters of white flowers with green or red calyces. Is excellent in a rock garden. Z3–6 H6–1.
P. taiwanensis. See *P. japonica* Taiwanensis Group.

PILEA

URTICACEAE

Genus of bushy or trailing annuals and evergreen perennials grown for their ornamental foliage. Grow in any well-drained soil out of direct sunlight and drafts; do not overwater in winter. Pinch out tips in growing season to avoid straggly plants. Propagate perennials by stem cuttings in spring or summer, annuals by seed in spring or autumn. Spider mite may be a problem.
P. cadierei illus. p.300.
P. involucrata, syn. *P. mollis* (Friendship plant). Evergreen, bushy perennial. H 6in (15cm), S 12in (30cm). Oval to rounded leaves, to 2in (5cm) long, have corrugated surfaces and are bronze above, reddish green below; leaves are green when grown in shade. Z14–15 H12–1.
P. mollis. See *P. involucrata*.
P. nummulariifolia illus. p.305.

PILEOSTEGIA

HYDRANGEACEAE

Genus of evergreen, woody-stemmed, root climbers. Grows in sun or shade and in any well-drained soil; is useful for planting against a north wall. Prune in spring, if required. Propagate by semi-ripe cuttings in summer.
P. viburnoides, syn. *Schizophragma viburnoides*, illus. p.208.

PILOSOCEREUS

CACTACEAE

Genus of columnar, summer-flowering cacti with wool-like spines in flowering zones at crowns. Some species are included in *Cephalocereus*. Needs full sun and very well-drained soil. Propagate by seed or stem cuttings in spring or summer.
P. leucocephalus. See *P. palmeri*.
P. palmeri, syn. *P. leucocephalus*, illus. p.458.

PIMELEA

THYMELAEACEAE

Genus of evergreen shrubs grown for their flowers and overall appearance. Needs full sun and well-drained, neutral to acidic soil. Water potted plants moderately, less when temperatures are low. Needs good winter light and ventilation in northern temperate greenhouses. Propagate by seed in spring or by semi-ripe cuttings in late summer.
P. ferruginea illus. p.162.

PINGUICULA

LENTIBULARIACEAE

Genus of summer-flowering perennials with sticky leaves that trap insects and digest them for food. Is useful in pots under cover among plants at risk from aphids. Needs sun and wet soil. Propagate by division in early spring or by seed in autumn.
P. caudata. See *P. moranensis* var. *caudata*.
P. grandiflora illus. p.382.
P. moranensis var. ***caudata***, syn. *P. caudata*. Basal-rosetted perennial. H 5–6in (12–15cm), S 2in (5cm). Leaves are narrowly oval and dull green with inrolled purplish margins. In summer, 5-petaled, deep carmine flowers are produced on long stems. Z13–15 H12–10.

PINUS

Pine

PINACEAE

Genus of small to large conifers with spirally arranged leaves in bundles, usually of 2, 3, or 5 needles. Cones ripen over 2 years and are small in the first year. See also CONIFERS.
P. aristata illus. p.108.
P. armandii (Armand pine, David's pine). Conical, open conifer. H 30–50ft (10–15m), S 15–25ft (5–8m). Has pendent, glaucous blue leaves and conical green cones, 3–10in (8–25cm) long, ripening to brown. Z6–8 H8–6.
P. banksiana illus. p.107.
P. bungeana illus. p.108.
P. cembra illus. p.106.
P. cembroides illus. p.109.
P. chylla. See *P. wallichiana*.
P. contorta illus. p.107. var. ***latifolia*** illus. p.106. **'Spaan's Dwarf'** is a conical, open, dwarf conifer with short, stiffly erect shoots. H and S 30in (75cm). Has bright green leaves in 2s. Z6–8 H8–6.
P. coulteri illus. p.102.
P. densiflora (Japanese red pine). Flat-topped conifer. H 50ft (15m), S 15–22ft (5–7m). Has scaling, reddish brown bark, bright green leaves, and conical yellow or pale brown cones. Z4–7 H7–1. **'Alice Verkade'**, H and S 30in (75cm), is a diminutive, rounded form with fresh green leaves. **'Tagyosho'** see *P.d.* 'Umbraculifera'. **'Umbraculifera'** (syn. *P.d.* 'Tagyosho'), H 12ft (4m), S 20ft (6m), is a slow-growing, rounded or umbrella-shaped form.
P. excelsa. See *P. wallichiana*.
P. griffithii. See *P. wallichiana*.
P. halepensis illus. p.107.
P. heldreichii, syn. *P.h.* var. *leucodermis*, *P. leucodermis*, illus. p.104. **'Compact Gem'** (syn. *P.h.* var. *leucodermis* 'Compact Gem') is a broadly conical, dense, dwarf conifer. H and S 10–12in (25–30cm). Has very dark green leaves in 2s. Grows only 1in (2.5cm) a year. Z6–8 H8–6. var. ***leucodermis*** see *P. heldreichii*. **'Smidtii'** (syn *P.h.* var. *leucodermis* 'Schmidtii'; illus. p.111) is a dwarf form with an ovoid habit and sharp, dark green leaves. Z4–8 H8–1.
P.* x *holfordiana illus. p.101.
P. insignis. See *P. radiata*.
P. jeffreyi illus. p.103.
P. leucodermis. See *P. heldreichii*.
P. mugo (Dwarf pine, Mountain pine, Swiss mountain pine). Spreading, shrubby conifer. H 10–15ft (3–5m), S 15–25ft (5–8m). Has bright to dark green leaves in 2s and ovoid, brown cones. Z3–7 H7–1. **'Gnom'**, H and S to 6ft (2m), and **'Mops'**, H 3ft (1m), S 6ft (2m), are rounded cultivars.
P. muricata illus. p.103.
P. nigra (Black pine). Upright, later spreading conifer, generally grown in one of the following forms. Z5–8 H8–4. **'Hornibrookiana'**, H 5–6ft (1.5–2m), S 6ft (2m), is shrubby with thick, spreading or erect branches and dark green leaves in 2s. subsp. ***laricio*** (syn. *P.n.* var. *maritima*; Corsican pine), H 80–100ft (25–30m), S 25ft (8m), is fast-growing and narrowly conical with an open crown; bears gray-green leaves in 2s, and ovoid to conical, yellow- or pale gray-brown cones. var. ***maritima*** see *P.n.* subsp. *laricio*. subsp. ***nigra*** illus. p.104.
P. parviflora illus. p.105. **'Adcock's Dwarf'** is a slow-growing, rounded, dense, dwarf conifer. H 6–10ft (2–3m), S 5–6ft (1.5–2m). Bears gray-green leaves in 5s. Z6–9 H9–6.
P. peuce illus. p.101.
P. pinaster illus. p.103.
P. pinea illus. p.109.
P. ponderosa illus. p.103.
P. pumila (Dwarf Siberian pine). Spreading, shrubby conifer. H 6–10ft (2–3m), S 10–15ft (3–5m). Has bright blue-green leaves in 5s. Ovoid cones are violet-purple, ripening to red-brown or yellow-brown, the males bright red-purple in spring. Z3–6 H7–1. **'Globe'**, H and S 1½–3ft (50cm–1m), is a rounded cultivar with blue foliage.
P. radiata, syn. *P. insignis*, illus. p.104.

P. resinosa (Red pine). Conical tree with ascendant branches. H 50–80ft (15–25m) S 20–25ft (6-8m). Young shoots are orange-brown and have pairs of long needles. The older branches have flaking red bark. Good on poor, sandy, or gravelly soils. Z3–7 H7–1.
P. rigida illus. p.106.
P. strobus illus. p.102. **'Radiata'** (syn. *P.s.* f. *nana*, *P.s.* 'Nana') is a rounded, dwarf conifer with an open, sparse, whorled crown. H 3–6ft (1–2m), S 6–10ft (2–3m). Gray bark is smooth at first, later fissured. Bears gray-green leaves in 5s. Z4–9 H9-1.
P. sylvestris (Scots pine). Conifer, upright and with whorled branches when young, that develops a spreading, rounded crown with age. H 50–80ft (15–25m), S 25–30ft (8–10m). Bark is flaking and red-brown on upper trunk, fissured and purple-gray at base. Has blue-green leaves in 2s and conical, green cones that ripen to pale gray- or red-brown. Z3–7 H7–1. **'Aurea'** (illus. p.111), H 30ft (10m), S 12ft (4m), has golden yellow leaves in winter-spring, otherwise blue-green. **'Beuvronensis'**, H and S 3ft (1m), is a rounded shrub. **'Doone Valley'** (illus. p.110), H and S 3ft (1m), is an upright, irregularly shaped shrub. f. ***fastigiata*** see *P.s.* 'Fastigiata'. **'Fastigiata'** (syn. *P.s.* f. *fastigiata*) illus. p.108. **'Gold Coin'** (illus. p.111), H and S 6ft (2m), is a dwarf version of *P.s.* 'Aurea'. **'Nana'** see *P.s.* 'Watereri'. **'Watereri'** (syn. *P.s.* 'Nana'; illus. p.110), H and S 20in (50cm), is a very dense cultivar with widely spaced leaves.
P. thunbergii illus. p.106.
P. virginiana illus. p.107.
P. wallichiana, syn. *P. chylla*, *P. excelsa*, *P. griffithii*, illus. p.103.

PIPTANTHUS

LEGUMINOSAE/PAPILIONACEAE

Genus of deciduous or semi-evergreen shrubs grown for their foliage and flowers. Requires sun and fertile, well-drained soil. In spring cut some older shoots back to ground level and prune any cold-damaged shoots back to healthy wood. Propagate by seed in autumn.
P. laburnifolius. See *P. nepalensis.*
P. nepalensis, syn. *P. laburnifolius*, illus. p.146.

PISONIA

NYCTAGINACEAE

Genus of evergreen shrubs and trees grown for their foliage and overall appearance. Needs full light or partial shade and organic, well-drained soil. Water containerized specimens freely when in full growth, moderately at other times. Pruning is tolerated if required. Propagate by seed in spring or by semi-ripe cuttings in summer.
P. brunoniana. See *P. umbellifera.*
P. umbellifera, syn. *Heimerliodendron brunonianum*, *P. brunoniana* (Bird-catcher tree, Para para). Evergreen, rounded large shrub or small tree. H and S 10–20ft (3–6m). Bears oval, leathery, lustrous leaves. In spring, produces clusters of tiny green or pink flowers, followed by 5-winged, sticky, brownish fruits. Z13–15 H12–10.

PISTACIA

ANACARDIACEAE

Genus of evergreen or deciduous trees grown for their foliage and overall appearance. Requires full light and free-draining, even dry soil. Water containerized plants moderately when in full growth, sparingly at other times. Pruning is tolerated if necessary. Propagate by seed in spring or by semi-ripe cuttings in summer.
P. lentiscus (Mastic tree). Evergreen, irregularly rounded shrub or tree. H 15ft (5m), S to 10ft (3m). Bears leaves that are divided into 2–5 pairs of oval, leathery, glossy leaflets. Produces auxillary clusters of insignificant flowers from spring to early summer that develop into globose red then black fruits in autumn. Z9–11 H12–9.
P. terebinthus (Cyprus turpentine, Terebinth tree). Deciduous, rounded to ovoid tree. H 20–28ft (6–9m), S 10–20ft (3–6m). Leaves have 5–9 oval, usually lustrous, rich green leaflets. Axillary clusters of small flowers borne in spring and early summer develop into tiny, globular to ovoid red then purple-brown fruits in autumn. Z9–10 H12–9.

PISTIA

ARACEAE

Genus of one species of deciduous, perennial, floating water plant grown for its foliage. In water above 66–70°F (19–21°C) is evergreen. Is suitable for tropical aquariums and frost-free pools. Grows in sun or semi-shade. Remove fading foliage and thin plants out as necessary. Propagate by separating plantlets in summer.
P. stratiotes illus. p.449.

PITTOSPORUM

PITTOSPORACEAE

Genus of evergreen trees and shrubs grown for their ornamental foliage and fragrant flowers. Where marginally hardy, grow against a south- or west-facing wall. *P. crassifolium* and *P. ralphii* make wind-resistant hedges in mild coastal areas; like forms with variegated or purple leaves, they prefer sun. Others will grow in sun or semi-shade. All need well-drained soil. Propagate *P. dallii* by budding in summer, other species by seed in autumn or spring or by semi-ripe cuttings in summer; selected forms by semi-ripe cuttings only in summer.
P. crassifolium (Karo). Evergreen, bushy-headed, dense tree or shrub. H 15ft (5m), S 10ft (3m). Has oblong, dark green leaves, gray- felted beneath. Clusters of small, fragrant, star-shaped, dark reddish purple flowers are borne in spring. Z9–11 H12–10. **'Variegatum'** illus. p.99.
P. dallii illus. p.100.
P. eugenioides. Evergreen, columnar tree. H 30ft (10m), S 15ft (5m). Narrowly oval, wavy-edged leaves are glossy, dark green. Honey-scented, star-shaped, pale yellow flowers are produced in spring. Z9–11 H12–10. **'Variegatum'** illus. p.99.
***P.* 'Garnettii'** illus. p.126.
P. ralphii. Evergreen, bushy-headed tree or shrub. H 12ft (4m), S 10ft (3m). Large leaves are oblong, leathery and gray-green, very hairy beneath. Produces small, fragrant, star-shaped, dark red flowers in spring. Z9–10 H10–9.
P. tenuifolium illus. p.127. **'Margaret Turnbull'** is an evergreen, compact shrub. H 6ft (1.8m), S 3ft (1m). Has dark green leaves centrally splashed golden yellow. Z9–10 H10–9. **'Tom Thumb'** illus. p.177.
P. tobira (Japanese pittosporum, Mock orange). Evergreen, bushy-headed, dense tree or shrub. H 20ft (6m), S 12ft (4m). Has oblong to oval, glossy, dark green leaves. Very fragrant, star-shaped white flowers, opening in late spring, later become creamy yellow. Z9–10 H10–9.
P. undulatum (Victorian box). Evergreen, broadly conical tree. H 40ft (12m), S 25ft (8m). Has long, narrowly oval, pointed, wavy-edged, dark green leaves. Fragrant, star-shaped white flowers are borne in late spring and early summer, followed by rounded orange fruits. Z9–10 H10–9.

PITYROGRAMMA

ADIANTACEAE/PTERIDACEAE

Genus of semi-evergreen or evergreen ferns, suitable for hanging baskets. Needs semi-shade and organic, moist but well-drained soil. Remove fading fronds regularly. Water carefully to avoid spoiling farina (mealy coating) on fronds. Propagate by spores in late summer.
P. triangularis. Semi-evergreen or evergreen fern. H and S 18in (45cm). Has broadly triangular, delicately divided, midgreen fronds with orange or creamy white farina. Z10–11 H12–9.

Plagiorhegma dubia. See *Jeffersonia dubia.*

PLANTAGO

PLANTAGINACEAE

Genus of summer-flowering annuals, biennials, and evergreen perennials and shrubs. Many species are weeds, but a few are grown for their foliage and architectural value. Needs full sun and well-drained soil. Water potted plants moderately, sparingly in winter. Propagate by seed or division in spring.
P. nivalis (illus. p.391) has lance-shaped, silky-hairy, silver-green leaves and tiny, gray-brown flowers. Z6–7 H7–6.

PLATANUS

Plane, Sycamore

PLATANACEAE

Genus of deciduous trees grown for their habit, foliage and flaking bark. Flowers are inconspicuous. Spherical fruit clusters hang from shoots in autumn. Needs full sun and deep, fertile, well-drained soil. Propagate species by seed in autumn, *P.* x *hispanica* by hardwood cuttings in early winter. All the following are susceptible to the fungal disease anthracnose. Contact with the basal tufts of hair on the fruits may irritate the skin and respiratory system.
P.* x *acerifolia. See *P.* x *hispanica.*
P.* x *hispanica, syn. *P.* x *acerifolia*, illus. p.67. **'Suttneri'** is a vigorous, deciduous, spreading tree. H 70ft (20m), S 50ft (15m). Has flaking bark and large, palmate, 5-lobed, sharply toothed, bright green leaves that are blotched with creamy white. Z5–8 H8–5.
P. occidentalis (Buttonwood, Sycamore). Open crowned, vigorous deciduous tree. H 80ft (25m) S 70ft (20m). Has three-lobed leaves up to 8in (20cm) long and attractive, flaking cream and brown bark. Brown globular fruits persist through winter. Z5–8 H8–5.

PLATYCARYA

JUGLANDACEAE

Genus of one species of deciduous tree grown for its foliage and catkins. Requires full sun and fertile, well-drained soil. Propagate by seed in autumn.
P. strobilacea. Deciduous, spreading tree. H and S 30ft (10m). Has ashlike, bright green leaves with 5–15 leaflets. Upright green catkins are borne from mid- to late summer; males are slender and cylindrical, often drooping at tips, females are conelike, become brown, and persist through winter. Z6–9 H9–6.

PLATYCERIUM

Stag's-horn fern

POLYPODIACEAE

Genus of evergreen, epiphytic ferns best grown in hanging baskets or fastened to and suspended from pieces of wood. Produces 2 kinds of fronds: permanent, broad, sterile "nest" leaves forming the main part of the plant, and strap-shaped, usually partly bifurcated, arching fertile fronds. Thrives in warm, humid conditions in semi-shade and needs fibrous, peaty potting mix with very little soil. Propagate by detaching buds in spring or summer and planting in soil mix, or by spores in summer or early autumn.
P. alcicorne of gardens**.** See *P. bifurcatum.*
P. bifurcatum, syn. *P. alcicorne* of gardens, illus. p.310.

Platycladus. Reclassified as *Thuja.*

PLATYCODON
Balloon flower

CAMPANULACEAE

Genus of one species of perennial grown for its flowers in summer. Needs sun and light, sandy soil. Propagate by basal cuttings of non-flowering shoots in summer, preferably with a piece of root attached, or by seed in autumn.
P. grandiflorus illus. p.284. var. ***mariesii*** (syn. *P.g.* 'Mariesii') is a neat, clump-forming perennial. H and S 1–1½ft (30–45cm). In midsummer produces solitary terminal, large, balloonlike flower buds opening to bell-shaped blue or purplish blue flowers. Has oval, sharply toothed, bluish green leaves. Z3–8 H8–1. **'Mariesii'** see *P.g.* var. *mariesii.*

PLATYSTEMON

PAPAVERACEAE

Genus of one species of summer-flowering annual. Grow in sun and in fertile, well-drained soil. Propagate by seed sown outdoors in spring or early autumn.
P. californicus illus. p.335.

PLECTRANTHUS

LABIATAE/LAMIACEAE

Genus of evergreen, trailing, or bushy perennials grown for their foliage. Is easy to grow if kept moist in partial shade or bright light. Cut back stem tips in growing season if plants become too straggly. Propagate by stem cuttings or division in spring or summer.
P. australis of gardens. See *P. verticillatus.*
***P. coleoides* 'Variegatus'** of gardens. See *P. madagascariensis* 'Variegated Mintleaf'.
***P. forsteri* 'Marginatus'**, illus. p.264.
P. madagascarienis (Mintleaf) Creeping perennial. H 12in (30cm), S indefinite. Has rounded, scalloped, fleshy leaves. Bears 2-lipped, lavender-blue or white flowers, often dotted with red. H12–1.**'Variegated Mintleaf'** (syn. *P. coleoides* 'Variegatus' of gardens) has variegated white leaves.
P. oertendahlii (Prostrate coleus, Swedish ivy). Evergreen, prostrate perennial. H to 6in (15cm), S indefinite. Rounded, scalloped, dark green leaves are reddish green below with white veins above. Racemes of tubular white or pale mauve flowers are produced at irregular intervals throughout the year. Z11–12 H12–1.
P. thyrsoideus, syn. *Coleus thyrsoideus.* Fast-growing, bushy perennial, often grown as an annual. H to 3ft (1m), S 2ft (60cm). Has heart-shaped, serrated, midgreen leaves. Bears spikes of tubular, bright blue flowers at various times of the year. Z11–12 H12–1.
P. verticillatus, syn. *P. australis* of gardens (Swedish ivy). Evergreen, trailing perennial with square stems. H to 6in (15cm), S indefinite. Has rounded, waxy, glossy green leaves with scalloped edges. Racemes of tubular white or pale mauve flowers are produced intermittently through the year. H12–1.

PLEIOBLASTUS

GRAMINEAE/POACEAE

See also GRASSES, BAMBOOS, RUSHES, and SEDGES.
P. auricomus, syn. *Arundinaria auricoma, A. viridistriata, P. viridistriatus*, illus. p.309.
P. variegatus, syn. *Arundinaria fortunei, A. variegata*, illus. p.306.
P. viridistriatus. See *P. auricomus.*

PLEIONE

See also ORCHIDS.
P. bulbocodioides (illus. p.297). Deciduous, terrestrial orchid. H 8in (20cm). In spring, usually before solitary leaf appears, bears pink, rose, or magenta flowers, 2–5in (5–12cm) across, with darker purple marks on lips. Leaf is narrowly lance-shaped, 5½in (14cm) long. Is often difficult to flower: regular fertilixing helps increase pseudobulbs to flowering size. Z12–15 H12–10.
P. x confusa. Deciduous, terrestrial orchid. H 6in (15cm). Canary-yellow flowers, 2–3in (5–8cm) across, with brown or purple blotches on lips, appear singly in spring, before foliage. Has lance-shaped leaves, 4–7in (10–18cm) long. Does best in an alpine house. Needs semi-shade. Z9–10 H12–10.
P. hookeriana. Deciduous, terrestrial orchid. H 3–6in (8–15cm). Lilac-pink, rose or white flowers, 2–3in (5–7cm) across, each with a brown- or purplish-spotted lip, are borne singly in spring with lance-shaped leaves, 2–8in (5–20cm) long. Cultivate as for *P.* x *confusa*. Z9–10 H12–10.
P. humilis. Deciduous, terrestrial orchid. H 2–3in (5–8cm). In winter, before foliage appears, white flowers, 3–3½in (7–9cm) across, each with a crimson-spotted lip, are borne singly or in pairs. Lance-shaped leaves are 7–10in (18–25cm) long. Cultivate as for *P.* x *confusa*. Z9–10 H12–10.
P. praecox. Deciduous, terrestrial orchid. H 3–5in (8–13cm). Flowers, to 3in (8cm) across, appear in pairs in autumn, after foliage. They are white to pinkish purple or lilac-purple, with violet marks. Leaves are oblong to lance-shaped and 6–10in (15–25cm) long. Cultivate as for *P.* x *confusa*. Z9–10 H12–10.

PLEIOSPILOS

AIZOACEAE

Genus of clump-forming succulents with almost stemless rosettes bearing up to 4 pairs of fleshy, erect leaves, like pieces of granite, each with a flat upper surface and each pair united at the base. Flowers are daisylike. Individual species are very similar, and many are difficult to identify. Needs sun and well-drained soil. Propagate by seed or division in spring or summer.
P. bolusii illus. p.479.
P. compactus illus. p.478.

PLEUROTHALLIS

See also ORCHIDS.
P. grobyi. Evergreen, epiphytic orchid for a cool greenhouse. H 1in (2.5cm). In summer produces sprays of minute, white flowers, ⅛in (0.25cm) long. Leaves are oval, fleshy. and ¼in (0.5cm) long. Provide shade in summer.

PLUMBAGO

PLUMBAGINACEAE

Genus of annuals, evergreen or semi-evergreen shrubs, perennials, and woody-stemmed, scrambling climbers grown for their phloxlike flowers. Grow in full light or semi-shade and in fertile, well-drained soil. Water regularly, less when not in full growth. Tie stems to supports. Thin out or spur back all previous year's growth in early spring. Propagate by semi-ripe cuttings in summer. Whitefly may be a problem.
P. auriculata, syn. *P. capensis*, illus. p.215.
P. capensis. See *P. auriculata.*
P. indica, syn. *P. rosea.* Evergreen or semi-evergreen, spreading shrub or semi-climber. H 6ft (2m), S 3–6ft (1–2m). Leaves are oval to elliptic and midgreen. Has terminal racemes of phloxlike red or pink flowers, 1in (2.5cm) long. These are produced in summer, if hard pruned annually in spring, or from late winter onward, if left unpruned and trained as a climber.
P. rosea. See *P. indica.*

PLUMERIA
Frangipani

APOCYNACEAE

Genus of mainly deciduous, fleshy-branched shrubs and trees grown for their flowers in summer-autumn. Requires full sun and freely draining soil. Water potted specimens moderately while in growth, and keep dry in winter when leafless. Stem tips may be cut out to induce branching. Propagate by seed or leafless stem-tip cuttings in late spring. Spider mite may be a nuisance. The milky sap may cause mild stomach upset if ingested.
P. acuminata. See *P. rubra* var. *acutifolia.*
P. acutifolia. See *P. rubra* var. *acutifolia.*
P. alba (West Indian jasmine). Deciduous, rounded, sparingly branched tree. H to 20ft (6m), S to 12ft (4m). Leaves are lance-shaped and slender-pointed, to 12in (30cm) long. Terminal clusters of fragrant, yellow-eyed white flowers, each with 5 spreading petals and a tubular base, appear in summer. Z11–12 H12–10.
P. rubra illus. p.96. var. ***acutifolia*** (syn. *P. acuminata, P. acutifolia*) is a deciduous, spreading, sparsely branched tree or shrub. H and S 12ft (4m) or more. Produces fragrant, yellow-centered white flowers, with 5 spreading petals, in summer-autumn. Leaves are lance-shaped to oval and 8–12in (20–30cm) long. Z14–15 H12–10.

PODOCARPUS

PODOCARPACEAE

See also CONIFERS.
P. alpinus (Tasmanian podocarp). Rounded, spreading, shrubby conifer. H 6ft (2m), S 10–15ft (3–5m). Has linear, dull green leaves and rounded, egg-shaped, fleshy, bright red fruits. Z7–10 H10–7.
P. andinus. See *Prumnopitys andina.*
P. macrophyllus (Kusamaki). Erect conifer. H 30ft (10m), S 10–15ft (3–5m). Long, linear leaves are bright green above, glaucous beneath. Z7–11 H12–7.
P. nivalis (Alpine totara; illus. p.110). Rounded, spreading, shrubby conifer. H 6ft (2m), S 10–15ft (3–5m). Is very similar to *P. alpinus* but bears longer, broader, more rigid leaves. Z7–9 H12–7.
P. salignus illus. p.106.

PODOPHYLLUM

BERBERIDACEAE

Genus of spring-flowering, rhizomatous perennials. Young leaves may be damaged by frost. Does best in semi-shade and moist, peaty soil. Propagate by division in spring or by seed in autumn. All parts are highly toxic if ingested.
P. emodi. See *P. hexandrum.*
P. hexandrum, syn. *P. emodi*, illus. p.268.
P. peltatum (May apple). Vigorous, spreading, rhizomatous perennial. H 1–1½ft (30–45cm), S 12in (30cm). Palmate, sometimes brown-mottled, light green leaves with 3–5 deep lobes push up through soil, looking like closed umbrellas, and are followed in spring by nodding, cup-shaped white flowers. Produces large, fleshy, plum-like, glossy, deep rose-pink fruits in autumn. Z3–9 H8–2.

Poinciana gilliesii. See *Caesalpinia gilliesii.*
Poinciana pulcherrima. See *Caesalpinia pulcherrima.*

POLEMONIUM
Jacob's ladder

POLEMONIACEAE

Genus of late spring- or summer-flowering annuals and perennials, some perennials tending to be short-lived. Prefers sun and fertile, well-drained soil. Propagate by division in spring or by seed in autumn.
P. caeruleum illus. p.285.
P. carneum illus. p.283.
P. foliosissimum. Vigorous, clump-forming perennial. H 30in (75cm), S 24in (60cm). Terminal clusters of cup-shaped lilac flowers with yellow stamens are borne in summer above

oblong to lance-shaped, midgreen leaves, each composed of numerous, small leaflets. Z4–8 H8–1.
P. pulcherrimum illus. p.284.

POLIANTHES

AGAVACEAE

Genus of tuberous perennials grown for their fragrant flowers in summer. Needs a sheltered site in full sun and well-drained soil. Water well in spring-summer; give liquid fertilizer every 2 weeks when in growth. Dry off after leaves die down in winter. Propagate by seed or offsets in spring.
P. geminiflora, syn. *Bravoa geminiflora*, illus. p.423.
P. tuberosa (Tuberose). Summer-flowering, tuberous perennial. H 24–36in (60–90cm), S 4–6in (10–15cm). Has a basal cluster of strap-shaped, erect leaves; flower stem also bears leaves on lower part. Produces a spike of funnel-shaped, single white flowers with 6 spreading petals. A double form is also available. Z7–11 H11–7.

POLYGALA

POLYGALACEAE

Genus of annuals and evergreen perennials, shrubs, and trees grown mainly for their pealike flowers. Needs full light or partial shade and moist but sharply drained soil. Water potted specimens freely when in full growth, moderately at other times. Lanky stems may be cut back hard in late winter. Propagate by seed in spring or by semi-ripe cuttings in late summer. Is susceptible to whitefly.
P. calcarea illus. p.384. **'Bulley's Form'** illus. p.384.
P. chamaebuxus illus. p.385. var. ***grandiflora*** (syn. *P.c.* var. *purpurea*, *P.c.* var. *rhodoptera*) illus. p.368. var. ***purpurea*** see *P.c.* var. *grandiflora*. var. ***rhodoptera*** see *P.c.* var. *grandiflora*.
P.* x *dalmaisiana, syn. *P. myrtifolia* var. *grandiflora* of gardens, illus. p.167.
P. myrtifolia var. ***grandiflora*** of gardens. See *P.* x *dalmaisiana.*
P. vayredae. Evergreen, mat-forming shrub. H 2–4in (5–10cm), S 8–12in (20–30cm). Slender, prostrate stems bear small, linear leaves. Pealike, reddish purple flowers, each with a yellow lip, are produced in late spring and early summer. Good in a rock garden or alpine house. Z7–9 H9–7.

POLYGONATUM

Solomon's seal

CONVALLARIACEAE/LILIACEAE

Genus of spring- or early summer-flowering, rhizomatous perennials. Requires a cool, shady situation and fertile, well-drained soil. Propagate by division in early spring or by seed in autumn. All parts may cause mild stomach upset if ingested.
P. biflorum, syn. *P. canaliculatum*, *P. commutatum*, *P. giganteum* (Great Solomon's seal). Arching, rhizomatous perennial. H 5ft (1.5m) or more, S 2ft (60cm). Bears oval to oblong, midgreen leaves. Pendent clusters of bell-shaped white flowers are borne in leaf axils during late spring. Z3–7 H9–1.
P. canaliculatum. See *P. biflorum*.
P. commutatum. See *P. biflorum.*
P. giganteum. See *P. biflorum.*
P. hirtum, syn. *P. latifolium*. Upright, then arching, rhizomatous perennial. H 3ft (1m), S 1ft (30cm). Clusters of 2–5 drooping, tubular, green-tipped white flowers open in late spring. Undersides of stems, leaf stalks, and oval to lance-shaped, midgreen leaves are hairy. Z5–8 H8–5.
P. hookeri illus. p.367.
P.* x *hybridum illus. p.238.
P. latifolium. See *P. hirtum.*
P. multiflorum. Arching, leafy perennial with fleshy rhizomes. H 3ft (1m), S 1ft (30cm). Bears clusters of 2–6 pendent, tubular, green-tipped white flowers in late spring, then spherical black fruit. Has oval to lance-shaped, midgreen leaves. Z4–8 H8–1. **'Flore Pleno'** has double flowers. **'Striatum'** (syn. *P.m.* 'Variegatum'), H 2ft (60cm), has leaves with creamy white stripes. **'Variegatum'** see *P.m.* 'Striatum'.
P. odoratum (Angled Solomon's seal). Arching, rhizomatous perennial. H 24in (60cm), S 12in (30cm). Produces pairs of fragrant, tubular to bell-shaped, green-tipped white flowers in late spring. Oval to lance-shaped leaves are midgreen. Z3–8 H9–1.
P. verticillatum (Whorled Solomon's seal). Upright, rhizomatous perennial. H 4ft (1.2m), S 1½ft (45cm). Bears whorls of stalkless, lance-shaped, midgreen leaves. In early summer produces narrowly bell-shaped, greenish white flowers. Z5–8 H8–5.

Polygonum affine. See *Persicaria affinis.*
Polygonum amplexicaule. See *Persicaria amplexicaulis.*
Polygonum aubertii. See *Fallopia aubertii.*
Polygonum baldschuanicum. See *Fallopia baldschuanica.*
Polygonum bistorta. See *Persicaria bistorta.*
Polygonum campanulatum. See *Persicaria campanulata.*
Polygonum capitatum. See *Persicaria capitata.*
Polygonum macrophyllum. See *Persicaria macrophylla.*
Polygonum milletii. See *Persicaria milletii.*
Polygonum sphaerostachyum. See *Persicaria macrophylla.*
Polygonum vacciniifolium. See *Persicaria vacciniifolia.*
***Polygonum virginianum* 'Painter's Palette'.** See *Persicaria virginiana* 'Painter's Palette'.

POLYPODIUM

POLYPODIACEAE

Genus of deciduous, semi-evergreen or evergreen ferns grown for their sculptural fronds. Grow in semi-shade and fibrous, moist but well-drained soil. Propagate by division in spring or by spores in late summer.
P. aureum. See *Phlebodium aureum.*
P. australe. See *P. cambricum.*
P. cambricum, syn. *P. australe*, *P. vulgare* subsp. *serratum* (Southern polypody, Wintergreen fern). Deciduous, creeping fern. H 6–24in (15–60cm), S indefinite. Has broadly lance-shaped to broadly triangular-ovate, divided, midgreen fronds, to 24in (60cm) long, with linear or oblong pinnae that often have toothed margins. New fronds appear in late summer and die back by early summer. Sori are conspicuously yellow in winter. Z6–8 H8–6.
P. glycyrrhiza illus. p.310.
P. scouleri illus. p.311.
P. vulgare illus. p.313. **'Cornubiense'** illus. p.312. **'Cristatum'** is an evergreen, creeping fern. H and S 10–12in (25–30cm). Narrowly lance-shaped, divided, midgreen fronds, with semi-pendulous, terminal crests, grow from creeping rhizomes covered with coppery brown scales. Z6–8 H8–6. subsp. ***serratum*** see *P. cambricum.*

POLYSCIAS

ARALIACEAE

Genus of evergreen trees and shrubs grown for their foliage. Sometimes has insignificant flowers in summer, but only on large, mature specimens. Needs partial shade and organic, well-drained soil. Water containerized plants freely when in full growth, moderately at other times. Straggly stems may be cut out in spring. Propagate by seed in spring or by stem-tip or leafless stem-section cuttings in summer. Spider mite may be troublesome.
P. filicifolia illus. p.152. **'Marginata'** is an evergreen, erect, sparsely branched shrub. H 6ft (2m) or more, S 3ft (1m) or more. Has 1ft (30cm) long leaves with many small, oval to lance-shaped, serrated, bright green leaflets with white edges. Z14–15 H12–1.
P. guilfoylei (Wild coffee). Slow-growing, evergreen, rounded tree. H 10–25ft (3–8m), S to 6ft (2m) or more. Leaves are 10–16in (25–40cm) long and divided into oval to rounded, serrated, deep green leaflets. Z14–15 H12–1. **'Victoriae'** illus. p.126.

POLYSTICHUM

DRYOPTERIDACEAE

Genus of evergreen, semi-evergreen or deciduous ferns. Does best in semi-shade and moist but well-drained soil enriched with fibrous organic matter. Remove faded fronds regularly. Propagate species by division in spring or by spores in summer, selected forms by division in spring.
P. acrostichoides (Christmas fern). Evergreen fern. H 24in (60cm), S 18in (45cm). Slender, lance-shaped, deep green fronds have small, hollylike pinnae. Is excellent for cutting. Z3–8 H8–1.
P. aculeatum (Hard shield fern, Prickly shield fern). Semi-evergreen fern. H 24in (60cm), S 30in (75cm). Broadly lance-shaped, yellowish green then deep green fronds, with oblong to oval, spiny-edged, glossy pinnae, are produced on stems often covered in brown scales. Z3–8 H8–1. **'Pulcherrimum'** illus. p.310.
P. braunii. Evergreen or semi-evergreen fern. H and S 18–30in (45–75cm). Produces a rosette of spreading to arching, lance-shaped, divided, dark green fronds, to 2ft (60cm) long. Young fronds are densely covered with orange-brown scales when unfurling in spring. Z3–8 H8–1.
P. munitum illus. p.310.
P. polyblepharum. Evergreen fern. H 24–32in (60–80cm), S 36in (90cm). Produces "shuttlecocks" of spreading, lance-shaped, divided, shiny, dark green fronds, 12–32in (30–80cm) long, covered with golden hairs when they unfurl. Pinnae lobes are oblong-ovate and have spiny-toothed margins. Z6–8 H8–5.
P. rigens. Evergreen fern. H 16in (40cm), S 24in (60cm). Has "shuttlecocks" of narrowly ovate-oblong, divided, leathery, harsh-textured, dull green fronds, 1–1½ft (30–45cm) long. Broad, lance-shaped pinnae are divided into ovate, spiny-toothed lobes. Fronds are yellowish green in spring. Z6–9 H9–6.
P. setiferum (Soft shield fern). **'Divisilobum'** see *P.s.* Divisilobum Group. **Divisilobum Group** (syn. *P.s.* 'Divisilobum') illus. p.311. **Plumosodivisilobum Group** illus. p.313.
P. tsussimense. Semi-evergreen fern. H 12in (30cm), S 9in (23cm). Has broadly lance-shaped, dull green fronds divided into oblong, finely spiny-edged pinnae. Is suitable for an alpine house. Z6–9 H9–5.

PONCIRUS

RUTACEAE

Genus of one species of very spiny, deciduous shrub or small tree grown for its foliage, showy flowers, and orangelike fruits. Is very effective as a protective hedge. Needs sun and fertile, well-drained soil. Cut out dead wood in spring, and trim hedges in early summer. Propagate by semi-ripe cuttings in summer or by seed when ripe, in autumn.
P. trifoliata (Hardy orange, trifoliate orange). Deciduous, bushy shrub or tree. H and S 15ft (5m). Thick, spiny green shoots bear dark green leaves each composed of 3 oval leaflets. Fragrant white flowers, with 4 or 5 large petals, borne in late spring and often again in autumn, are followed by

rounded, ¾–1¼in (2–3cm) wide fruits. Z5–9 H9–5.

PONTEDERIA

PONTEDERIACEAE

Genus of deciduous, perennial, marginal water plants grown for their foliage and flower spikes. Needs full sun and up to 9in (23cm) depth of water. Remove fading flowers regularly. Propagate in spring by division or seed.
P. cordata illus. p.448.

POPULUS

Poplar

SALICACEAE

Genus of deciduous trees grown for their habit, foliage, and very fast growth. Has catkins in late winter or spring. Female trees produce copious amounts of fluffy white seeds. Prefers full sun and needs deep, fertile, moist but well-drained soil; resents dry soil, apart from *P. alba*, which thrives in coastal gardens. Extensive root systems can undermine foundations and so make poplars unsuitable for planting close to buildings, particularly on clay soil. Propagate by hardwood cuttings in winter. Is susceptible to bacterial canker and fungal diseases.
P. alba illus. p.64. Is much confused with the commoner *P. canescens*. f. ***pyramidalis*** (syn. *P.a.* 'Pyramidalis') is a vigorous, deciduous, upright tree. H 70ft (20m), S 15ft (5m). Broadly oval, wavy-margined or lobed, dark green leaves,white beneath, turn yellow in autumn. Z4–9 H9–1. **'Pyramidalis'** see *P.a.* f. *pyramidalis*. **'Raket'** (syn. *P.a.* 'Rocket') illus. p.69. **'Richardii'**, H 50ft (15m), S 40ft (12m), has leaves golden yellow above. **'Rocket'** see *P.a.* 'Raket'.
P. balsamifera (Balsam poplar, Tacamahac). Fast-growing, deciduous, upright tree. H 30m (100ft), S 25ft (8m). Oval, glossy, dark green leaves, whitish beneath, have a strong fragrance of balsam when young. Z5–9 H9–5.
P. x berolinensis (Berlin poplar). Deciduous, columnar tree. H 80ft (25m), S 25ft (8m). Has broadly oval, bright green leaves with white undersides. Z2–8 H8–1.
P. x canadensis (Canadian poplar). **'Eugenei'** (Carolina poplar) is a deciduous, columnar tree. H 100ft (30m), S 40ft (12m). Has broadly oval bronze young leaves, maturing to dark green, and red catkins in spring. Z5–9 H9–5. **'Robusta'** illus. p.65. **'Serotina de Selys'** (syn. *P. x c.* 'Serotina Erecta') illus. p.66.
P. x candicans, syn. *P. gileadensis*, *P. x jackii* 'Gileadensis' (Balm of Gilead, Ontario poplar). Very fast-growing, deciduous, conical tree. H 80ft (25m), S 30ft (10m). Oval leaves are dark green and, when young, balsam-scented. Is very susceptible to canker. Z4–9 H9–1. **'Aurora'**, H 50ft (15m) or more, S 20ft (6m), has leaves that are heavily but irregularly blotched with creamy white.
P. x canescens illus. p.65. **'Tower'.** A very narrow selection. H 65ft (20m) S 12ft (4m). It is canker resistant, does not sucker, and sets very little seed. Z4–9 H9–1.
P. deltoides (Cottonwood, Eastern cottonwood, Necklace poplar). Very fast-growing, deciduous, spreading tree. H 100ft (30m), S 70ft (20m). Has lush growth of broadly oval, glossy, bright green leaves. Z3–9 H9–1.
P. gileadensis. See *P. candicans*.
***P. x jackii* 'Gileadensis'.** See *P. x candicans*.
P. lasiocarpa (Chinese necklace poplar). Very fast-growing, deciduous, spreading tree. H 50ft (15m), S 40ft (12m). Has thick shoots and very large, heart-shaped, midgreen leaves with red veins, on long red stalks. Bears thick, drooping yellow catkins in spring. Z6–9 H9–6.
P. maximowiczii illus. p.64.
P. nigra (Black poplar). Fast-growing, deciduous, spreading tree. H 80ft (25m), S 70ft (20m). Has dark bark. Diamond-shaped bronze young leaves turn bright green then yellow in autumn. Male trees bear red catkins in midspring. Z3–9 H9–1. **'Italica'** illus. p.66. **'Thevestina'** (Theves' poplar). Similar to *P. n.* 'Italica' but with a whitish bark and less prone to disease. Z2–9 H9–1.
***P.* 'Northwest'.** A fast growing hybrid that forms a large tree at maturity. H 100ft (30m) S 70ft (20m). It is resistant to many of the diseases that attack poplars. Z3–9 H9–1.
P. szechuanica. Very fast-growing, deciduous, conical tree. H 80ft (25m), S 30ft (10m). Has flaking, pinkish gray bark and large, heart-shaped, dark green leaves. Z4–9 H9–1.
P. tremula (Aspen). Vigorous, deciduous, spreading tree. H 50ft (15m), S 30ft (10m). Rounded leaves are bronze-red when young, gray-green when mature, and yellow in autumn. Flattened stalks make foliage tremble and rattle in wind. Z2–8 H8–1. **'Erecta'**, S 15ft (5m), has an upright habit. **'Pendula'** illus. p.79.
P. tremuloides (American aspen, Quaking aspen). Very fast-growing, deciduous, spreading tree. H 50ft (15m) or more, S 30ft (10m). Has rounded, finely toothed, glossy, dark green leaves that flutter in the wind and turn yellow in autumn. Z1–8 H8–1.
P. trichocarpa (Black cottonwood, Western balsam poplar). Very fast-growing, deciduous, conical tree. H 100ft (30m) or more, S 30ft (10m). Bears dense growth of oval, glossy, dark green leaves with green-veined white undersides, strongly balsam-scented when young. Foliage turns yellow in autumn. Z4–9 H9–1.

PORTULACA

PORTULACACEAE

Genus of fleshy annuals and perennials with flowers that open in sun and close in shade. Needs full light and any well-drained soil. Propagate by seed sown under cover in early spring, or outdoors in late spring. Is prone to aphid attack.
P. grandiflora (Sun plant). Slow-growing, partially prostrate annual. H 6–8in (15–20cm), S 6in (15cm). Has lance-shaped, succulent, bright green leaves. In summer and early autumn bears shallowly bowl-shaped flowers, 1in (2.5cm) wide and with conspicuous stamens, in shades of yellow, red, orange, pink, or white. Z9–11 H12–1. **Minilaca Hybrids** have a double-flowered cultivar. **Sundance Hybrids** illus. p.326. **Sundial Series** has double flowers in a broad color range. Bred for longer flowering in poor conditions and cooler climates.

PORTULACARIA

PORTULACACEAE

Genus of one species of evergreen or semi-evergreen, succulent-leaved shrub grown for its foliage and overall appearance. Needs full sun and well-drained soil. Water potted plants moderately when in full growth, sparingly at other times. Propagate by semi-ripe cuttings in summer.
P. afra illus. p.153. **'Foliisvariegatus'** (syn. *P.a.* 'Variegatus') is an evergreen or semi-evergreen, erect shrub with more or less horizontal branches. H and S 6–10ft (2–3m). Has oval to rounded, fleshy, cream-edged, bright green leaves. From late spring to summer, bears tiny, star-shaped, pale pink flowers in small clusters. Z13–15 H12–10. **'Variegatus'** see *P.a.* 'Foliisvariegatus'.

POTAMOGETON

POTAMOGETONACEAE

Genus of deciduous, perennial, submerged water plants grown for their foliage. Is suitable for cold-water pools and aquariums. Prefers sun. Remove fading foliage and thin plants as necessary. Propagate by stem cuttings in spring or summer.
P. crispus illus. p.448.
P. pectinatus (Fennel-leaved pondweed). Deciduous, perennial, submerged water plant. S 10ft (3m). Has very narrow, linear green to brownish green leaves, and produces inconspicuous flowers in summer. Is suitable for a medium to large pond.

POTENTILLA

ROSACEAE

Genus of perennials and deciduous shrubs grown for their clusters of small, flattish to saucer-shaped flowers and for their foliage. Tall species – particularly the shrubs – are useful in borders. Dwarf potentillas are good for rock gardens. Does best in full sun, but flower color is better on orange-, red- and pink-flowered cultivars if they are shaded from hot sun. Needs well-drained soil. Propagate perennial species by seed in autumn or by division in spring or autumn; selected forms by division only in spring or autumn. Shrubby species may be raised by seed in autumn or by softwood or greenwood cuttings in summer, selected forms by softwood or greenwood cuttings during summer.
***P.* 'Abbotswood'.** See *P. fruticosa* 'Abbotswood'.
P. alba illus. p.373.
P. arbuscula. See *P. fruticosa* var. *arbuscula*.
P. argyrophylla. See *P. atrosanguinea* var. *argyrophylla*.
P. atrosanguinea illus. p.283. var. ***argyrophylla*** (syn. *P. argyrophylla*) is a clump-forming perennial. H 18in (45cm), S 24in (60cm). Saucer-shaped yellow or yellow-orange flowers are produced in profusion from early to late summer above strawberry-like silvery leaves. Z5–8 H8–5.
P. aurea illus. p.386.
***P.* 'Beesii'.** See *P. fruticosa* 'Beesii'.
P. crantzii (Alpine cinquefoil). Upright perennial with a thick, woody rootstock. H and S 4–8in (10–20cm). Produces wedge-shaped, 5-lobed leaves and, in spring, flattish yellow flowers with orange centers. Good in a rock garden. Z5–8 H8–5.
P. davurica var. ***mandschurica*** of gardens. See *P. fruticosa* 'Manchu'.
***P.* 'Daydawn'.** See *P. fruticosa* 'Daydawn'.
***P.* 'Elizabeth'.** See *P. fruticosa* 'Elizabeth'.
P. eriocarpa illus. p.385.
***P.* 'Etna'.** Clump-forming perennial. H 30in (75cm), S 18in (45cm). In midsummer produces saucer-shaped, maroon flowers above strawberry-like, dark green leaves. Z5–8 H8–5.
P. fruticosa. Deciduous, bushy, dense shrub. H 3ft (1m), S 5ft (1.5m). From late spring to late summer produces saucer-shaped, bright yellow flowers. Dark green leaves have 5 narrowly oblong leaflets. Z3–7 H7–1. **'Abbotswood'** (syn. *P.* 'Abbotswood') illus. p.158. var. ***arbuscula*** (syn. *P. arbuscula*), S 4ft (1.2m), bears golden yellow flowers amid gray-green to silver-gray leaves. **'Beesii'** (syn. *P.* 'Beesii', *P.* 'Nana Argentea'), H 30in (75cm), S 3ft (1m), is slow-growing and compact. Has golden yellow flowers and silver leaves. **'Daydawn'** (syn. *P.* 'Daydawn') illus. p.161. **'Elizabeth'** (syn. *P.* 'Elizabeth') illus. p.169. **'Farrer's White'** illus. p.159. **'Friedrichsenii'** illus. p.169. **'Gold Drop'** (syn. *P. parvifolia* 'Gold Drop'), H and S 4ft (1.2m), bears a mass of golden yellow flowers amid bright green leaves. Z2–7 H7–1. **'Goldfinger'** (syn. *P.* 'Goldfinger') bears large, rich yellow flowers in profusion. **'Jackman's Variety'** (syn. *P.* 'Jackman's Variety'), H 4ft (1.2m), has large, bright yellow flowers. **'Maanelys'** (syn. *P.* 'Maanelys', *P.* 'Manelys', *P.* 'Moonlight'), H 4ft (1.2m), S 6ft (2m), has soft yellow flowers and gray-green foliage. **'Manchu'** (syn. *P. davurica* var. *mandschurica* of gardens, *P.* 'Manchu') illus. p.158. **'Red Ace'** (syn. *P.* 'Red Ace') illus. p.166. **'Royal Flush'** (syn. *P.* 'Royal Flush'), H 18in (45cm), S 30in

(75cm), produces midgreen leaves and sometimes semi-double, yellow-stamened, rich pink flowers, fading to white in full sun. **'Sunset'** (syn. *P.* 'Sunset') illus. p.171. **'Tangerine'** (syn. *P.* 'Tangerine'), H 4ft (1.2m), bears yellow flowers, flushed with pale orange-red, amid midgreen leaves. **'Vilmoriniana'** (syn. *P.* 'Vilmoriniana') illus. p.169.
***P.* 'Gibson's Scarlet'.** Clump-forming perennial. H and S 18in (45cm). Bears saucer-shaped, brilliant scarlet flowers from mid- to late summer. Dark green leaves are strawberry-like.
***P.* 'Gloire de Nancy'**, syn. *P.* 'Glory of Nancy'. Clump-forming perennial. H and S 18in (45cm). Very large, saucer-shaped, semi-double orange and coppery red flowers appear throughout summer. Has strawberry-like, dark green leaves.
***P.* 'Glory of Nancy'.** See *P.* 'Gloire de Nancy'.
***P.* 'Goldfinger'.** See *P. fruticosa* 'Goldfinger'.
***P.* 'Jackman's Variety'.** See *P. fruticosa* 'Jackman's Variety'.
***P.* 'Maanelys'.** See *P. fruticosa* 'Maanelys'.
***P.* 'Manchu'.** See *P. fruticosa* 'Manchu'.
***P.* 'Manelys'.** See *P. fruticosa* 'Maanelys'.
P. megalantha illus. p.292.
***P.* 'Monsieur Rouillard'.** Clump-forming perennial. H and S 18in (45cm). Bears saucer-shaped, double, blood red flowers in summer above strawberry-like, dark green leaves.
***P.* 'Moonlight'.** See *P. fruticosa* 'Maanelys'.
***P.* 'Nana Argentea'.** See *P. fruticosa* 'Beesii'.
***P. nepalensis* 'Miss Willmott'** illus. p.282.
P. nitida. Dense, mat-forming perennial. H 1–2in (2.5–5cm), S 8in (20cm). Has rounded, 3-lobed silver leaves. Flower stems each carry 1–2 rose-pink flowers with dark centers in early summer. Is often shy-flowering. Good in a rock garden or trough.
***P. parvifolia* 'Gold Drop'.** See *P. fruticosa* 'Gold Drop'.
P. recta. Clump-forming, hairy perennial. H 24in (60cm), S 18in (45cm). From early to late summer bears pale yellow flowers. **'Macrantha'** see *P.r.* 'Warrenii'. **'Warrenii'** (syn. *P.r.* 'Macrantha') illus. p.291.
***P.* 'Red Ace'.** See *P. fruticosa* 'Red Ace'.
***P.* 'Royal Flush'.** See *P. fruticosa* 'Royal Flush'.
***P.* 'Sunset'.** See *P. fruticosa* 'Sunset'.
***P.* 'Tangerine'.** See *P. fruticosa* 'Tangerine'.
P.* x *tonguei. Mat-forming perennial. H 2in (5cm), S 10in (25cm). Has rounded, 3–5 lobed green leaves. Prostrate branches bear flattish, orange-yellow flowers with red centers during summer. Is good in a a rock garden.
***P.* 'Vilmoriniana'.** See *P. fruticosa* 'Vilmoriniana'.
***P.* 'William Rollison'.** Clump-forming perennial. H and S 18in (45cm). From mid- to late summer bears saucer-shaped, semi-double, scarlet-suffused, deep orange flowers with yellow centers. Has dark green leaves. Z4–7 H7–1.
***P.* 'Yellow Queen'** illus. p.292

Pothos. Reclassified as *Epipremnum.*

x POTINARA

See also ORCHIDS.
x *P.* Cherub 'Spring Daffodil' (illus. p.299). Evergreen, epiphytic orchid for an intermediate greenhouse. H 6in (15cm). Sprays of yellow flowers, 2in (5cm) across, open in spring. Broadly oval, rigid leaves are 4in (10cm) long. Provide good light in summer. Z14–15 H12–6.

PRATIA

CAMPANULACEAE

Genus of evergreen, mat-forming perennials with small leaves, grown for their mass of star-shaped flowers; is suitable for rock gardens. Sometimes included in *Lobelia.* Some species may be invasive. Prefers shade and moist soil. Propagate by division or seed in autumn.
P. angulata. Evergreen, creeping perennial. H ½in (1cm), S indefinite. Bears small, broadly oval, dark green leaves. Star-shaped white flowers with 5 unevenly spaced petals are carried in leaf axils in late spring and are followed by globose, purplish red fruits in autumn. Z6–10 H10–6.
P. pedunculata illus. p.383. **'County Park'** is a vigorous, evergreen, creeping perennial. H ½in (1cm), S indefinite. Has small, rounded to oval leaves and, in summer, a profusion of star-shaped, rich violet-blue flowers. Makes a good groundcover. Z5–7 H7–5.

PRIMULA

Primrose

PRIMULACEAE

Genus of mainly herbaceous perennials, some woody-based and evergreen. All have leaves in basal rosettes and tubular, bell-shaped, or flat flowers. In some primroses, the flower stems, leaves, sepals and, occasionally, sections of the petals are covered with a waxy powder known as farina. There are primroses suitable for almost every type of site: the border, scree garden, rock garden, bog garden, pond margin, greenhouse, and alpine house. Some may be difficult to grow, since they dislike winter damp or summer heat. Repot pot-grown plants annually. Neaten fading foliage and deadhead as flowering ceases. Propagate species by seed when fresh or in spring; increase selected forms when dormant, either by division in autumn-spring, or by root cuttings in winter. Auricula primroses should be propagated by offsets in early spring or early autumn. Border cultivars may be prone to slug damage in damp situations and to attack by root aphids when grown in very dry conditions or in pots.

Primroses are divided into many different horticultural groups, of which the following are in common use. See also feature panel pp.272–3.

Auricula primroses
These are evergreen primulas, derived from hybrids between *P. auricula* and *P. hirsuta*, producing flat, smooth flowers carried in an umbel on a stem above the foliage. There are 3 main sub-groups: alpine, border, and show.
Alpine Auricula Group. In these, the color of the flower center is strikingly different from that of the petals. They may be either light-centered (white or pale in the center) or gold-centered (yellow or gold in the center). There is no farina on either leaves or flowers. Grow in an alpine house or rock garden.
Show Auricula Group has flowers with a distinct circle of white meal or "paste" in the center. Some are self-colored, with one color, which may be red, yellow, blue, or violet, from the central paste to the petal margins; edged cultivars have a black ring surrounding the central paste, feathering out to an often green, gray, or white margin; in fancy cultivars the paste is surrounded by a color other than black, with a green, gray, or white margin. Show Auriculas have white farina on their foliage (except those with green-edged flowers), on their flower eyes, and, sometimes, on their petal margins. Grow under cover to protect the flowers from rain.
Border Auricula Group has generally robust, garden Auricula primroses, which are often very fragrant. Some have farina on flower stems and leaves. Grow in a mixed or herbaceous border.

Candelabra primroses
These are robust, herbaceous perennials with tubular, flat-faced flowers borne in tiered whorls up tall, sturdy stems. Some are deciduous, dying back to basal buds; others are semi-evergreen, dying back to reduced rosettes. Grow in moist shade or woodland, especially by streams.

Primrose-Polyanthus primroses
A diverse group of evergreen, semi-evergreen, or deciduous perennial hybrids, derived from *P. vulgaris*, crossed with *P. veris*, *P. juliae,* and other species. They are divided into two main groups.
Primrose Group Most produce solitary flowers among the leaves. Are mainly grown as herbaceous perennials, flowering in spring, or as biennial, greenhouse container plants flowering in winter-spring.
Polyanthus Group Produce flowers in long-stalked umbels. Usually grown as biennials for bedding, sown in summer to flower in winter and the following spring, or under cover as winter- and spring-flowering container plants.

Cultivation
Primroses have varying cultivation requirements. For ease of reference, these have been grouped as follows:
1 – Full sun or partial shade, in moist, but well-drained, organic soil.
2 – Partial shade, in deep, organic, moist, neutral to acidic soil.
3 – Deep or partial shade, in peaty, gritty, moist but sharply drained, acidic soil. Protect from excessive winter wet.
4 – Under cover in an alpine house or frame. Avoid wetting foliage of mealy species and hybrids.
5 – Full sun with some midday shade, or partial shade, in moist but sharply drained, gritty, organic, slightly alkaline soil.
6 – In a cool or temperate greenhouse, or as a houseplant, in bright, filtered light.

***P.* 'Adrian'** (illus. p.273). Alpine Auricula primrose. H and S 4in (10cm). Produces flat, light to dark blue flowers, with light centers and paler margins, in mid- to late spring. Leaves are oval to rounded and midgreen. Is useful for exhibition. Cultivation group 1 or 4. Z4–8 H8–1.
P. allionii (illus. p.272). Rosette-forming, evergreen perennial. H 3–4in (7–10cm), S 8in (20cm). Better grown in an alpine house. Tubular rose, mauve, or white flowers cover a tight cushion of oval, midgreen leaves in spring. Cultivation group 4. Z4–8 H8–1.
P. alpicola. Compact, rosette-forming perennial. H 20in (50cm), S 12in (30cm). Produces terminal clusters of pendent, bell-shaped yellow to white or purple flowers on slender stems in early summer. Midgreen leaves are oval to lance-shaped. Cultivation group 2. Z4–8 H8–1. var. ***alpicola*** (syn. *P.a.* var. *luna*; illus. p.273) has soft sulfur yellow flowers. var. ***luna*** see *P.a.* var. *alpicola*.
P. aurantiaca. Small, rosette-forming Candelabra primrose. H 12in (30cm), S 16in (40cm). Tubular, reddish orange flowers are borne in early summer. Has long, broadly oval to lance-shaped, coarse, midgreen leaves. Cultivation group 2. Z5–8 H8–1.
P. aureata (illus. p.273). Rosette-forming, evergreen perennial. H 6in (15cm), S 8in (20cm). Produces small umbels of flat cream to yellow flowers in spring. In summer, oval, toothed, midgreen leaves have striking purple-red midribs; in winter, leaves form tight buds covered with whitish farina. Cultivation group 3 or 4. Z4–8 H8–1.
P. auricula. Rosette-forming, evergreen, sometimes white-mealy perennial. H 8in (20cm), S 10in (25cm). Bears fragrant, flat yellow flowers in large umbels in spring. Oval, soft, pale green to gray-green leaves are densely covered with white farina. Cultivation group 1, 4 or 5. Z3–8 H8–1.
P. bhutanica (illus. p.273). Rosette-forming perennial. H 6in (15cm), S 8in (20cm). Often short-lived. In spring produces neat umbels of tubular, pale purplish blue flowers, each with a white or creamy white eye, close to oval to

PRIMULA

lance-shaped, crinkled, midgreen leaves. Cultivation group 3. Z4–8 H8–1.
P. 'Blairside Yellow' (illus. p.273). Compact, border Auricula primrose. H 4in (10cm), S 8in (20cm). In early spring, bell-shaped, golden yellow flowers nestle in a rosette of tiny, rounded to oval, pale green leaves. Cultivation group 2 or 5. Z4–8 H8–1.
P. 'Blossom' (illus. p.273). Vigorous, alpine Auricula primrose. H and S 4in (10cm). Flat, deep crimson to bright red flowers with golden centers are borne profusely in spring. Has oval, dark green leaves. Is suitable for exhibition. Cultivation group 1 or 4. Z4–8 H8–1.
P. bulleyana (illus. p.273). Rosette-forming, semi-evergreen, Candelabra primrose. H and S 24in (60cm). Tubular, deep orange flowers appear in early summer. Leaves are oval to lance-shaped, toothed and dark green. Cultivation group 2. Z5–8 H8–5.
P. chionantha **subsp. *melanops*.** See *P. melanops*.
P. 'Chloë' (illus. p.273). Green-edged, show Auricula primrose. H and S 4in (10cm). In late spring produces flat, dark-green-edged flowers with a black body color and brilliant white paste centers. Oval leaves are dark green and have no farina. Is good for exhibition. Cultivation group 4. Z5–8 H8–5.
P. chungensis (illus. p.273). Vigorous, rosette-forming Candelabra primrose. H 32in (80cm), S 24in (60cm). In summer bears tiered whorls of tubular orange flowers among oval to lance-shaped, midgreen leaves. Cultivation group 2. Z5–8 H8–5.
P. clarkei (illus. p.272). Small, rosette-forming perennial. H 3in (7cm), S 6in (15cm). In spring has flat, rose-pink flowers with yellow eyes, just above a clump of rounded to oval, pale green leaves. Cultivation group 2 or 4. Divide in late winter. Z6–8 H8–6.
P. clusiana (illus. p.272). Small, rosette-forming, evergreen perennial. H 3in (8cm), S 6in (15cm). In spring bears umbels of tubular, rose-pink flowers with white eyes. Leaves are oval, glossy and midgreen. Cultivation group 4 or 5. Z5–8 H8–5.
P. 'Craddock White' (illus. p.272). Rosette-forming, deciduous or semi-evergreen, Primrose Group primrose. H to 5in (12cm), S 10in (25cm). Fragrant, upward-facing, flat white flowers with yellow eyes are borne in spring just above long, oval, red-veined, dark green leaves. Cultivation group 1 or 2. Z4–8 H8–1.
P. 'David Green'. Rosette-forming, Primrose Group primrose. H 4in (10cm), S 6–8in (15–20cm). In spring produces flat, bright crimson-purple flowers amid oval, coarse, midgreen leaves. Cultivation group 1 or 2.
P. denticulata (Drumstick primrose; illus. p.273). Robust, rosette-forming perennial. H and S 18in (45cm). From early to midspring, dense, rounded heads of flat lilac, purple, or pink flowers are borne on tops of thick stems. Midgreen leaves are broadly lance-shaped and toothed. Cultivation group 1 or 2. var. ***alba*** (illus. p.272) has white flowers. Z2–8 H8–1.
P. 'Dreamer' illus. p. 328; cultivation group 6.
P. edgeworthii. See *P. nana*.
P. elatior (Oxlip; illus. p.273). Variable, rosette-forming, evergreen or semi-evergreen perennial. H 12in (30cm), S 10in (25cm). Umbels of small, fragrant, tubular yellow flowers appear in spring, above neat, oval to lance-shaped, toothed, midgreen leaves. Cultivation group 1 or 2. Z4–8 H8–1.
P. 'E.R. Janes'. Vigorous, rosette-forming, semi-evergreen, Primrose Group primrose. H 4–6in (10–15cm), S 12–16in (30–40cm). Flat, pale rose-pink flowers flushed with orange are borne in spring amid broadly oval, toothed, midgreen leaves. Cultivation group 1 or 2. Z5–8 H8–5.
P. farinosa (Bird's-eye primrose; illus. p.272). Rosette-forming perennial. H and S 10in (25cm). In spring, umbels of tubular, lilac-pink, occasionally white flowers are borne on short, thick stems. Oval, toothed, midgreen leaves are densely covered with white farina. Cultivation group 2 or 4. Z4–8 H8–1.
P. flaccida, syn. *P. nutans* of gardens (illus. p.273). Lax, rosette-forming, short-lived perennial. H 20in (50cm), S 12in (30cm). In early summer, each thick stem produces a conical head of pendent, bell-shaped lavender or violet flowers above narrowly oval, pale to midgreen leaves. Cultivation group 3 or 4. Z4–8 H8–1.
P. florindae (Giant cowslip; illus. p.273). Bold, rosette-forming perennial. H 4ft (1.2m), S 3ft (1m). In summer, large heads of pendent, bell-shaped, sulfur yellow flowers appear above broadly lance-shaped, toothed, midgreen leaves. Cultivation group 1 or 2. Z3–8 H8–1.
P. forrestii (illus. p.273). Rosette-forming, evergreen perennial. H 24in (60cm), S 18in (45cm). Dense umbels of flat yellow flowers with orange eyes are borne in late spring or early summer. Has oval, toothed, dark green leaves. Cultivation group 4 or 5. Z6–8 H8–6.
P. frondosa (illus. p.272). Compact, rosette-forming perennial. H 6in (15cm), S 10in (25cm). In spring bears umbels of flat, yellow-eyed, lilac-rose to reddish purple flowers on short stems above neat, oval, midgreen leaves, densely covered with white farina. Cultivation group 2 or 4. Z4–8 H8–1.
P. 'Garryarde Guinevere'. Vigorous, rosette-forming, evergreen Polyanthus Group primrose. H 5in (12cm), S 10in (25cm). Flat, purplish pink flowers with yellow eyes are produced in spring among oval, toothed, bronze-green leaves. Cultivation group 2. Z5–8 H8–5.
P. Gold Laced Group (illus. p.273). Erect, semi-evergreen or evergreen, Polyanthus Group primroses. H 10in (25cm), S 12in (30cm). Produces flat flowers in a variety of colors with gold-laced margins, from mid- to late spring. Leaves are oval and midgreen, sometimes tinged red. Raise annually by seed. Cultivation group 2 or 4.
P. gracilipes (illus. p.272). Rosette-forming, evergreen or semi-evergreen perennial. H 4in (10cm), S 8in (20cm). Tubular, purplish pink flowers with greenish yellow eyes are borne singly in spring or early summer among oval, wavy, toothed, midgreen leaves. Cultivation group 3 or 4. Z5–8 H8–5.
P. 'Harlow Car'. Rosette-forming Alpine Auricula. H 4–6in (10–15cm), S 6–8in (15–20cm). In spring produces flat white flowers on short stems above oval, soft, midgreen leaves. Cultivation group 1 or 4. Z3–8 H8–1.
P. helodoxa. See *P. prolifera*.
P. hirsuta, syn. *P. rubra* (illus. p.272). Rosette-forming, evergreen perennial. H 4in (10cm), S 10in (25cm). Produces small umbels of flat rose or lilac flowers in spring. Has small, rounded to oval, sticky, midgreen leaves. Cultivation group 1, 2, or 4. Z3–8 H8–1.
P. 'Inverewe' (illus. p.273). Vigorous, rosette-forming, semi-evergreen, Candelabra primrose. H 30in (75cm), S 24in (60cm). Tubular, bright orange-red flowers are produced in summer on stems coated with white farina. Has oval to lance-shaped, toothed, coarse, midgreen leaves. Cultivation group 2. Z4–8 H8–1.
P. ioessa. Rosette-forming perennial. H and S 12in (30cm). Clustered heads of funnel-shaped pink, pinkish mauve, or sometimes white flowers are borne in spring/early summer above oval to lance-shaped, toothed, midgreen leaves. Cultivation group 2, 3, or 4. Z5–8 H8–5.
P. 'Janet' (illus. p.272). Vigorous, rosette-forming evergreen perennial. H 6–8in (15–20cm), S 6in (15cm). In spring, clusters of outward-facing, flat, purplish pink flowers are produced above a rosette of oval to rounded, soft, midgreen leaves. Cultivation group 1 or 4. Propagate by offsets after flowering. Z3–8 H8–1.
P. 'Janie Hill' (illus. p.273). Rosette-forming, alpine Auricula. H 4in (10cm), S 6in (15cm). Flat, dark to golden brown flowers with golden centers open in mid- to late spring. Has oval, midgreen leaves. Is useful for exhibition. Cultivation group 4 or 5. Z3–8 H8–1.
P. japonica. Robust, rosette-forming, Candelabra primrose. H and S 18in (45cm). In early summer produces tubular, deep red flowers on thick stems above oval to lance-shaped, toothed, coarse, pale green leaves. Cultivation group 2. Z4–8 H8–1. **'Miller's Crimson'** (illus. p.272) has intense crimson flowers. **'Postford White'** (illus. p.272) bears white flowers.
P. × kewensis (illus. p.273). Rosette-forming, evergreen perennial. H 18in (45cm), S 8in (20cm). Produces whorls of fragrant, tubular, bright yellow flowers in winter and early spring. Oval to lance-shaped, toothed, pale green leaves are covered with white farina. Cultivation group 6. Z9–11 H6–1.
P. 'Linda Pope' (illus. p.273). Vigorous, rosette-forming, evergreen or semi-evergreen perennial. H 6in (15cm), S 12in (30cm). In spring bears flat, mauve-blue flowers on short stems above oval, toothed, midgreen leaves covered with white farina. Cultivation group 4 or 5. Z4–8 H8–1.
P. malacoides (single, double, illus. p.272). Erect, rosette-forming, evergreen perennial, usually grown as an annual. H 1–1½ft (30–45cm), S 8in (20cm). Dense whorls of small, flat, single or double pink, purplish pink, or white flowers open in winter-spring. Leaves are oval, hairy, soft, and pale green. Cultivation group 6. Z8–10 H10–8.
P. 'Margaret Martin' (illus. p.273). Rosette-forming, show Auricula primrose. H 4in (10cm), S 6in (15cm). Bears flat, gray-edged flowers with a black body color and white centers in mid- to late spring. Has spoon-shaped, gray-green leaves covered with white farina. Is excellent for exhibition. Cultivation group 4. Z4–8 H8–1.
P. marginata (illus. p.273). Rosette-forming, evergreen or semi-evergreen perennial. H 6in (15cm), S 12in (30cm). In spring, clusters of funnel-shaped, blue-lilac flowers appear above oval, toothed, midgreen leaves densely covered with white farina. Cultivation group 4 or 5. Z3–8 H8–1. **'Prichard's Variety'** (illus. p.273) has lilac-purple flowers with white eyes.
P. 'Mark' (illus. p.273). Vigorous, alpine Auricula primrose. H and S 4in (10cm). Produces flat pink flowers with light yellow centers in spring. Leaves are oval and vibrant green. Is a leading exhibition cultivar. Cultivation group 4. Z4–8 H8–1.
P. melanops, syn. *P. chionantha* subsp. *melanops* (illus. p.272). Rosette-forming perennial. H 14in (35cm), S 20in (50cm). In summer has umbels of pendent, narrowly funnel-shaped, deep violet-purple flowers with black eyes above long, strap-shaped, midgreen leaves. Cultivation group 2 or 4. Z4–8 H8–1.
P. modesta. Rosette-forming perennial. H and S 8in (20cm). Dense heads of small, tubular, pinkish purple flowers appear on short stems in spring. Rounded to oval, midgreen leaves are covered with yellow farina. Cultivation group 1 or 4. Z4–8 H8–1. var. ***fauriae*** (illus. p.272), H and S 2in (5cm), produces yellow-eyed, pinkish purple flowers and leaves covered with white farina.
P. 'Moonstone' (illus. p.273). Rosette-forming, border Auricula primrose. H 5in (12cm), S 6in (15cm). Rounded, double, whitish- or greenish yellow flowers are produced in profusion in spring. Leaves are oval and midgreen. Preferably, grow under cover. Cultivation group 4 or 5. Z4–8 H8–1.
P. 'Mrs. J.H. Wilson' (illus. p.272). Rosette-forming, alpine Auricula primrose. H and S 4–6in (10–15cm). Bears small umbels of flat, white-centered purple flowers in spring. Oval leaves are grayish green. Cultivation group 1 or 4. Z4–8 H8–1.

P. nana, syn. *P. edgeworthii* (illus. p.272). Rosette-forming perennial. H 4in (10cm), S 6in (15cm). Flat, pale mauve flowers with white eyes appear singly among oval, toothed, pale green leaves in spring. Cultivation group 3 or 4. Z4–8 H8–1.
P. nutans of gardens. See *P. flaccida*.
P. obconica. Erect, rosette-forming, evergreen perennial, usually grown as an annual. H 9–16in (23–40cm), S 10in (25cm). Flat purple, lilac, or white flowers with yellow eyes are borne in dense umbels during winter-spring. Leaves are oval, toothed, hairy, and pale green. Cultivation group 6. Z10–12 H6–1.
***P.* 'Orb'.** Neat, show Auricula primrose. H and S 4in (10cm). Flat, dark-green-edged flowers, each with a black body color and a central zone of white paste, are produced from mid- to late spring. Spoon-shaped, dark green leaves lack farina. Cultivation group 4.
***P.* Pacific Series** (Polyanthus). Polyanthus Group primrose illus. p.339, (dwarf) illus. p 328; cultivation group 1, 2, 4, or 6.
P. palinuri (illus. p.273). Rosette-forming, evergreen perennial. H and S 12in (30cm). One-sided clusters of semi-pendent, narrowly funnel-shaped yellow flowers appear on thick stems in early summer. Has rounded to oval, lightly toothed, thick-textured, powdered green leaves. Cultivation group 1 or 4; requires full sun. Z6-8 H8–1.
P. petiolaris (illus. p.272). Rosette-forming, evergreen perennial. H 4in (10cm), S 8in (20cm). Tubular, purplish pink flowers with toothed petals are borne singly in spring. Has small, oval, toothed, midgreen leaves. Cultivation group 3 or 4. Z4–8 H8–1.
P. polyneura (illus. p.272). Rosette-forming perennial. H and S 18in (45cm). Dense heads of tubular, pale rose, rich rose, or purple-rose flowers are produced in late spring or early summer. Rounded to oval, shallowly lobed, downy, soft leaves are midgreen. Cultivation group 2. Z3–8 H8–1.
P. prolifera, syn *P. helodoxa* (illus. p.273). Rosette-forming, evergreen, Candelabra primrose. H and S 24in (60cm). Bell-shaped yellow flowers are borne in summer. Leaves are oval, toothed, and pale green. Cultivation group 2. Z4–8 H8–1.
P. pulverulenta (illus. p.272). Rosette-forming, Candelabra primrose. H 36in (90cm), S 24in (60cm). In early summer bears tubular, deep red flowers with purple-red eyes on stems covered with white farina. Has broadly lance-shaped, toothed, coarse, midgreen leaves. Cultivation group 2. Z4–8 H8–1. **'Bartley'** (illus. p.272) has pink flowers.
P. reidii. Robust, rosette-forming perennial. H 2–6in (5–15cm), S 4–6in (10–15cm). Produces dense clusters of bell-shaped, pure white flowers on slender stems in early summer. Has oval, hairy, pale green leaves. Cultivation group 3 or 4. Z5–8 H8–5. var. ***williamsii*** (illus. p.273) is more robust and has purplish blue to pale blue flowers.
P. rosea (illus. p.272). Rosette-forming perennial. H and S 8in (20cm). In early spring bears small clusters of flat, glowing rose-pink flowers on short stems among oval to lance-shaped, midgreen leaves, often bronze-flushed when young. Cultivation group 2. Z3–8 H8–1.
***P.* 'Royal Velvet'.** Vigorous, rosette-forming, border Auricula primrose. H and S 6–8in (15–20cm). Flat, velvety, blue-tinged maroon flowers, with frilled petals and large, creamy yellow centers, are produced in spring. Has large, spoon-shaped, pale green leaves. Cultivation group 2 or 5.
P. rubra. See *P. hirsuta*.
P. x scapeosa (illus. p.272). Vigorous, rosette-forming perennial. H 4in (10cm), S 10in (25cm). Clusters of outward-facing, flat, mauve-pink flowers in early spring are initially hidden by broadly oval, sharply toothed, midgreen leaves covered at first with slight farina; later, flower stem elongates above leaves. Cultivation group 3 or 4. Z2–8 H8–1.
P. secundiflora (illus. p.272). Rosette-forming, evergreen or semi-evergreen perennial. H 24–36in (60–90cm), S 24in (60cm). Has clusters of pendent, funnel-shaped, reddish purple flowers in summer above lance-shaped, toothed leaves. Cultivation group 2. Z4–8 H8–1.
P. sieboldii (illus. p.272). Rosette-forming perennial. H 12in (30cm), S 18in (45cm). Umbels of flat white, pink, or purple flowers, with white eyes, open above oval, round-toothed, downy, soft, pale green leaves in early summer. Cultivation group 2. Z4–8 H8–1. **'Sumina'** bears large, wisteria blue flowers. **'Wine Lady'** (illus. p.272) has white flowers strongly suffused with purplish red.
P. sikkimensis (illus. p.273). Rosette-forming perennial. H 24–36in (60–90cm), S 24in (60cm). Pendent clusters of funnel-shaped,yellow flowers are borne in summer. Has rounded to oval, toothed, pale green leaves. Cultivation group 2. Z4–8 H8–1.
P. sinensis (illus. p.272). Erect, rosette-forming, evergreen perennial. H and S 6–8in (15–20cm). Flat purple, purple-rose, pink, or white flowers with yellow eyes are produced in neat whorls in winter-spring. Leaves are oval, toothed, hairy, and midgreen. Cultivation group 6. Z7–8 H8–7.
P. sonchifolia (illus. p.272). Rosette-forming, deciduous perennial. H 2in (5cm), S 12in (30cm). Produces dense umbels of tubular, blue-purple flowers with white eyes and yellow margins in spring. Leaves are oval to lance-shaped, toothed, and midgreen. Cultivation group 3 or 4. Z5–8 H8–5.
***P.* Super Giants Series.** Rosette-forming Polyanthus Group primroses, usually grown as biennials. H and S 6–8in (15–20cm). Produce large, fragrant, flat flowers in a wide range of colors in spring (blue, illus. p.332). Cultivation group 1 or 2. Z6–8 H8–1.
***P.* 'Tawny Port'.** Very dwarf, rosette-forming, evergreen or semi-evergreen, Polyanthus Group primrose. H 4–6in (10–15cm), S 6–8in (15–20cm). Bears flat, port wine-colored flowers on short stems in spring. Rounded to oval, toothed leaves are reddish green. Cultivation group 1, 2 or 4. Z3–8 H8–1.
P. veris (Cowslip; illus. p.273). Very variable, rosette-forming, evergreen or semi-evergreen perennial. H and S 10in (25cm). Tight clusters of fragrant, tubular yellow flowers are produced on thick stems in spring. Leaves are oval to lance-shaped, toothed and midgreen. Cultivation group 1 or 2. Z3–8 H8–1.
P. verticillata (illus. p.273). Rosette-forming perennial. H 8–10in (20–25cm), S 6–8in (15–20cm). Fragrant, bell-shaped yellow flowers are borne in whorls in spring. Has oval, toothed, midgreen leaves. Cultivation group 4 or 6. Z3–8 H8–1.
P. vialii (illus. p.272). Rosette-forming, often short-lived perennial. H 12–24in (30–60cm), S 12in (30cm). Dense, conical spikes of tubular, bluish purple-and-red flowers are produced in late spring. Has lance-shaped, toothed, soft, midgreen leaves. Cultivation group 1 or 2. Z5–8 H8–5.
P. vulgaris (Primrose; illus. p.273). Rosette-forming, evergreen or semi-evergreen perennial. H 8in (20cm), S 14in (35cm). Flat, soft yellow flowers, with darker eyes, are borne singly among oval to lance-shaped, toothed, bright green leaves in spring. Cultivation group 2. Z4–8 H8–1. **'Alba Plena'** has doubl white flowers. **'Gigha White'** (illus. p.272) is very floriferous and has yellow-eyed white flowers. subsp. ***sibthorpii*** (illus. p.272) has pink or purplish pink flowers.
***P.* 'Wanda'.** Very vigorous, long-flowering, rosette-forming, evergreen or semi-evergreen perennial. H 4–6in (10–15cm), S 12–16in (30–40cm). In spring, produces clusters of flat, crimson-purple flowers singly amid oval, toothed, purplish green foliage. Cultivation group 1 or 2. Thrives well in both sun and shade.
P. warshenewskiana (illus. p.272). Rosette-forming perennial. H 3in (7cm), S 6in (15cm). Tiny, flat, white-eyed, bright pink flowers sit just above spoon-shaped, dark green leaves in early spring. Cultivation group 2 or 4. Divide clumps regularly in late winter before flowering. Z4–8 H8–1.

PRINSEPIA

ROSACEAE

Genus of deciduous, usually spiny, spring- and early summer-flowering shrubs grown for their habit, flowers, and fruits. Needs sun and any not too dry soil. Propagate by softwood cuttings in summer or by seed in autumn.
P. sinensis (Cherry prinsepia). Spreading deciduous shrub with spiny, light gray branches. H 6ft (2m) S 10ft (3m). Clusters of up to 8 bright yellow flowers open in spring and become red to purple edible fruit. Makes a good hedge. Z3–7 H7–1.
P. uniflora illus. p.137.

PROBOSCIDEA

MARTYNIACEAE/PEDALIACEAE

Genus of annuals and perennials. Grow in a sunny, sheltered position and in fertile, well-drained soil. Propagate by seed sown under cover in early spring.
P. fragrans. Moderately fast-growing, upright annual. H 24in (60cm), S 12in (30cm). Has rounded, serrated, or lobed leaves. Fragrant, bell-shaped, crimson-purple flowers, to 2in (5cm) long, appear in summer-autumn, followed by rounded, horned brown fruits, 3–4in (8–10cm) long, which, if gathered young, may be pickled and eaten. Z8–9 H9–7.
P. jussieui. See *P. louisianica*.
P. louisianica, syn. *Martynia louisianica*, *P. jussieui*, *P. proboscidea* (Common devil's claw, Common unicorn plant, Ram's horn). Erect to spreading annual. Has rounded to ovate, unlobed leaves. In summer, bears funnel-shaped, fragrant, reddish purple to purple flowers, followed by narrow, crested fruit, to 2½in (6cm) long, with beaklike projections. Z7–9 H9–7.
P. proboscidea. See *P. louisianica*.

PROSTANTHERA

Mint bush

LABIATAE/LAMIACEAE

Genus of evergreen shrubs grown for their flowers and mint-scented foliage. Requires full light or partial shade and fertile, well-drained soil. Water containerized specimens freely when in full growth, moderately at other times. Leggy stems may be cut back after flowering. Propagate by seed in spring or by semi-ripe cuttings in late summer.
P. ovalifolia illus. p.145.
P. rotundifolia illus. p.145.

PROTEA

PROTEACEAE

Genus of evergreen shrubs and trees grown mainly for their colorful bracted flower heads. Difficult to grow. Requires full light and well-drained, neutral to acidic soil, low in phosphates and nitrates. Water containerized specimens moderately, less when not in full growth. Plants under cover must have plenty of ventilation throughout the year. Prune, if necessary, in early spring. Propagate by seed in spring or by semi-ripe cuttings in summer.
P. barbigera. See *P. magnifica*.
P. cynaroides illus. p.161.
P. magnifica, syn. *P. barbigera*. Evergreen, rounded to spreading shrub. H and S 3ft (1m). Has oblong to elliptic, leathery, mid- to grayish green leaves. Spherical flower heads, 6–8in (15–20cm) wide, with petal-like pink, red, yellow, or white bracts, appear in spring-summer. Z9–10 H10–9.
P. mellifera. See *P. repens*.
P. neriifolia illus. p.140.
P. repens, syn. *P. mellifera* (Sugar

bush). Evergreen, ovoid to rounded shrub. H and S 6–10ft (2–3m). Midgreen leaves are narrowly oblong to elliptic and tinted blue-gray. In spring-summer produces cup-shaped, 5in (13cm) long flower heads, with petal-like pink, red, or white bracts. Z9–10 H10–9.

PRUMNOPITYS

PODOCARPACEAE

See also CONIFERS.
P. andina, syn. *Podocarpus andinus* (Plum yew, Plum-fruited yew). Conifer with a domed crown on several stems. H 50ft (15m), S 25ft (8m). Has smooth, gray-brown bark, needlelike, flattened, bluish green leaves, and edible, yellowish white fruits like small plums.

PRUNELLA
Self-heal

LABIATAE/LAMIACEAE

Genus of semi-evergreen perennials with spreading mats of leaves from which arise short, stubby flower spikes in midsummer. Good in rock gardens. Grows well in sun or shade and in moist but well-drained soil. Propagate by division in spring.
P. grandiflora, syn. *P.* x *webbiana* (Large self-heal) illus. p.382. **'Loveliness'** illus. p.381. **'Pink Loveliness'** bears soft pink flowers in terminal spikes in summer. Makes a good groundcover but may be invasive. Cut off old flower stems before they produce seed. **'White Loveliness'** has white flowers. Both Z5–8 H8–5.
***P.* x *webbiana*.** See *P. grandiflora*.

PRUNUS
Cherry

ROSACEAE

Genus of deciduous or evergreen shrubs and trees. The trees are grown mainly for their single (5-petaled) to double flowers and autumn color; the shrubs for their autumn color, bark, flowers, or fruits. All have oval to oblong leaves. Evergreen species tolerate sun or shade; deciduous species prefer full sun. All may be grown in any but waterlogged soil. Trim deciduous hedges after flowering, evergreen ones in early or midspring. Propagate deciduous species by seed in autumn, deciduous hybrids and selected forms by softwood cuttings in summer. Increase evergreens by semi-ripe cuttings in summer. Foliage may be attacked by aphids, caterpillars, and the fungal diseases. Flowering cherries are prone to a fungus that causes "witches' brooms" (abnormal, crowded shoots). Certain *Prunus* species and cultivars, notably cultivars of the almond (*P. dulcis*) and the peach (*P. persica*), are grown for their edible fruits. Leaves and fruits of most other species may cause severe discomfort if ingested.
***P.* 'Accolade'** illus. p.88.
***P.* 'Amanogawa'.** Deciduous, upright tree. H 30ft (10m), S 12ft (4m). Bears fragrant, semi-double, pale pink flowers in late spring. Oblong to oval, taper-pointed, dark green leaves turn orange and red in autumn. Z6-8 H8–6.
***P.* x *amygdalopersica* 'Pollardii'.** Deciduous, spreading tree. H and S 7m (22ft). Large, 5-petaled, bright pink flowers open from early to midspring, before oval, glossy, midgreen leaves emerge. Green then brown fruits are like almonds in shape and taste. Z6–8 H8–6
P. avium illus. p.71. **'Plena'** illus. p.76.
***P.* x *blireana*.** Deciduous, spreading shrub or small tree. H and S 12ft (4m). Bears double, pink flowers in mid-spring and has oval purple leaves. Z5–8 H8–5.
P. campanulata (Bell-flowered cherry, Taiwan cherry). Deciduous, spreading tree. H and S 25ft (8m). Shallowly bell-shaped, deep rose-red flowers are produced from early to midspring, before or with oval, taper-pointed, dark green leaves. Fruits are small, rounded, and reddish. Z7–8 H8–7.
P. cerasifera (Cherry plum, Myrobalan). **'Nigra'** illus. p.91. **'Pissardii'** is a deciduous, round-headed tree. H and S 30ft (10m). Small, 5-petaled, pale pink flowers open from early to midspring and are often followed by edible, plumlike red fruits. Has oval red young leaves turning deeper red, then purple. May be used for hedging. Z4–8 H8–1.
***P.* 'Cheal's Weeping'.** See *P.* 'Kiku-shidare-zakura'.
P.* x *cistena illus. p.154.
P. davidiana (David's peach). Deciduous, spreading tree. H and S 25ft (8m). Saucer-shaped, 5-petaled white or pale pink flowers are carried on slender shoots in late winter and early spring but are susceptible to late frosts. Leaves are narrowly oval and dark green. Fruits are rounded and reddish. Z4–8 H8–1.
P. dulcis (Almond). **'Roseoplena'** is a deciduous, spreading tree. H and S 25ft (8m). Bears double pink flowers in late winter and early spring, before oblong, pointed, toothed, dark green leaves. Z5–8 H8–5.
***P. glandulosa* 'Alba Plena'** illus. p.153. **'Rosea Plena'** see *P.g.* 'Sinensis'. **'Sinensis'** (syn. *P.g.* 'Rosea Plena') is a deciduous, rounded, open shrub. H and S 5ft (1.5m). Produces double, bright rose-pink flowers in late spring and oval, midgreen leaves. Flowers best when grown against a south- or west-facing wall. Cut back young shoots to within a few buds of old wood after flowering. Z5–8 H8–3.
***P.* 'Hally Jolivette'.** Deciduous, rounded, compact tree. H and S 15ft (5m). Double white flowers open from pink buds in midspring. Leaves are oval and dark green. Z6–8 H8–3.
***P.* x *hillieri* 'Spire'.** See *P.* 'Spire'.
***P.* 'Hokusai'**, syn. *P.* 'Uzuzakura', illus. p.87.
P. incisa (Fuji cherry) illus. p.86. **'February Pink'** is a deciduous, spreading tree. H and S 25ft (8m). Oval, sharply toothed, dark green leaves are reddish when young, orange-red in autumn. During mild winter periods bears 5-petaled, pale pink flowers. Has tiny, rounded, reddish fruits. Z6–8 H8–6.
P. jamasakura, syn. *P. serrulata* var. *spontanea*, illus. p.76.
***P.* 'Kanzan'** illus. p.77.
***P.* 'Kiku-shidare-zakura'**, syn. *P.* 'Cheal's Weeping', illus. p.88.
***P.* 'Kursar'.** Deciduous, spreading tree. H and S 25ft (8m). Bears masses of small, 5-petaled, deep pink flowers in early spring. Oval, dark green leaves turn brilliant orange in autumn. Z6–8 H8–6.
P. laurocerasus (Cherry laurel, Laurel). Evergreen, dense, bushy shrub becoming spreading and open. H 20ft (6m), S 30ft (10m). Has long spikes of small, single white flowers from mid- to late spring, large, oblong, glossy, bright green leaves and cherry-shaped red then black fruits. Restrict growth by cutting back hard in spring. Z6–9 H9–6. **'Otto Luyken'** illus. p.154. **'Schipkaensis'**, H 6ft (2m), S 10ft (3m), is of elegant, spreading habit, with narrow leaves and freely borne flowers in upright spikes. **'Zabeliana'** illus. p.154.
P. lusitanica (Laurel, Portugal laurel). Evergreen, bushy, dense shrub or spreading tree. H and S 20–30ft (6–10m). Reddish purple shoots bear oval, glossy, dark green leaves. Slender spikes of small, fragrant, 5-petaled white flowers appear in early summer, followed by egg-shaped, fleshy, deep purple fruits. Restrict growth by pruning hard in spring. Z7–9 H9–4. subsp. ***azorica*** illus. p.126. **'Variegata'** illus. p.126.
P. maackii illus. p.84.
P. mahaleb illus. p.76.
***P.* 'Mount Fuji'.** See *P.* 'Shirotae'.
P. mume (Japanese apricot). **'Beni-chidori'** (syn. *P.m.* 'Beni-shidon', *P.m.* 'Beni-shidori') illus. p.130. **'Omoi-no-mama'** (syn. *P.m.* 'Omoi-no-wac') illus. p.130. **'Pendula'** is a deciduous, weeping tree with slender, arching branches. H and S 20ft (6m). Fragrant, 5-petaled, pink flowers appear in late winter or early spring, before broadly oval, bright green leaves and are sometimes succeeded by edible, apricot-like yellow fruits. Z6–8 H8–6.
***P.* 'Okame'.** Deciduous, bushy-headed tree. H 30ft (10m), S 25ft (8m). Bears masses of 5-petaled, carmine-pink flowers in early spring. Oval, sharply toothed, dark green leaves turn orange-red in autumn. Z5–8 H8–5.
P. padus (Bird cherry) illus. p.76. **'Colorata'** is a deciduous, spreading tree, conical when young. H 50ft (15m), S 30ft (10m). Produces pendent racemes of fragrant, cup-shaped, 5-petaled pink flowers in late spring, followed by small, pea-shaped black fruits. Oval, reddish purple young leaves mature to dark green and then turn red or yellow in autumn. Z4–8 H8–1.**'Grandiflora'** see *P.p.* 'Watereri'. **'Plena'** has long-lasting, double flowers and no fruits. **'Watereri'** (syn. *P.p.* 'Grandiflora') bears long racemes of flowers from mid- to late spring.
***P.* 'Pandora'** illus. p.87.
***P. pendula* 'Pendula Rubra'.** See *P.* x *subhirtella* 'Pendula Rubra'. **'Stellata'** see *P.* x *subhirtella* 'Stellata'.
P. pensylvanica (Pin cherry). Deciduous, spreading tree. H 50ft (15m), S 30ft (10m). Has peeling, red-banded bark and oval, taper-pointed, bright green leaves. Produces clusters of small, star-shaped, 5-petaled white flowers from mid- to late spring, followed by small, pea-shaped red fruits. Z6–8 H8–6.
P. persica (Peach). **'Klara Meyer'** is a deciduous, spreading tree. H 15ft (5m), S 20ft (6m). Bears double, bright pink flowers in midspring. Has slender, lance-shaped, bright green leaves. Is susceptible to the fungal disease peach leaf curl. Z4–8 H8–1. **'Prince Charming'** illus. p.88.
***P.* 'Pink Perfection'** illus. p.87.
***P* 'Pink Star'.** See *P. subhirtella* 'Stellata'.
P. sargentii illus. p.87.
P. serotina illus. p.65.
***P. serrula*.** Deciduous, round-headed tree. H and S 30ft (10m). Has gleaming, coppery red bark that peels. In late spring bears small, 5-petaled white flowers amid oval, tapering, toothed, dark green leaves that turn yellow in autumn. Fruits are tiny, rounded, and reddish brown. Z6–8 H8–6.
***P. serrulata* var. *spontanea*.** See *P. jamasakura*.
***P.* 'Shirofugen'** illus. p.87.
***P.* 'Shirotae'**, syn. *P.* 'Mount Fuji', illus. p.86.
***P.* 'Shogetsu'**, syn. *P.* 'Shimidsu', illus. p.86.
P. spinosa (Blackthorn, Sloe). **'Purpurea'** illus. p.122.
***P.* 'Spire'**, syn. *P.* x *hillieri* 'Spire', illus. p.87.
P.* x *subhirtella (Higan cherry, Rosebud cherry). Deciduous, spreading tree. H and S 25ft (8m). From early to mid-spring, a profusion of small, 5-petaled, pale pink flowers appear before oval, taper-pointed, dark green leaves that turn yellow in autumn. Has small, rounded, reddish brown fruits. Z6–8 H8–6. **'Autumnalis'** has semi-double white flowers, pink in bud, during mild periods in winter. **'Pendula Rubra'** (syn. *P. pendula* 'Pendula Rubra') illus. p.88. **'Stellata'** (syn. *P. pendula* 'Stellata', *P.* 'Pink Star') illus. p.87.
***P.* 'Taihaku'** illus. p.86.
P. tenella illus. p.155. **'Fire Hill'** is a deciduous, bushy shrub with upright, then spreading branches. H and S 6ft (2m). Narrowly oval, glossy, dark green leaves are a foil for small, almondlike, single, very deep pink flowers borne profusely from mid- to late spring, followed by small, almondlike fruits. Z6–8 H8–6.
P. tomentosa (Downy cherry). Deciduous, bushy, dense shrub. H 5ft (1.5m), S 6ft (2m). Has small, 5-petaled, pale pink flowers from early to midspring before oval, downy, dark green leaves appear. Fruits are

spherical and bright red. Z2–7 H7–1.
***P.* 'Trailblazer'.** Deciduous, spreading tree. H and S 15ft (5m). Bears 5-petaled white flowers from early to midspring, sometimes followed by edible, plumlike red fruits. Oval, light green young leaves mature to deep red-purple. Z6–8 H8–6.
***P. triloba* 'Multiplex'.** Deciduous, bushy, spreading tree or shrub. H and S 12ft (4m). Double pink flowers are borne in midspring. Has oval, dark green leaves, often 3-lobed, that turn yellow in autumn. Often does best against a sunny wall. Cut back young shoots to within a few buds of old wood after flowering. Z6–8 H8–6.
***P.* 'Ukon'** illus. p.86.
***P.* 'Uzuzakura'.** See *P.* 'Hokusai'.
P. virginiana (Virginian bird cherry). **'Shubert'** is a deciduous, conical tree. H 30ft (10m), S 25ft (8m). Produces dense spikes of small, star-shaped white flowers from mid- to late spring, followed by dark purple-red fruits. Has oval, pale green young leaves that turn deep reddish purple in summer. Z3–8 H8–1.
***P.* 'Yae-murasaki'** illus. p.88.
P.* x *yedoensis illus. p.87.

PSEUDERANTHEMUM

ACANTHACEAE

Genus of evergreen perennials and shrubs grown mainly for their foliage. Requires partial shade and fertile, well-drained soil. Water potted plants freely when in full growth, moderately at other times. Tip prune young plants to promote a bushy habit. Cut leggy plants back hard in spring. Propagate annually or biennially as a pot plant by greenwood cuttings in spring or summer. Whitefly may sometimes attack.
P. atropurpureum, syn. *Eranthemum atropurpureum*. Evergreen, erect shrub. H 3–4ft (1–1.2m), S 1–2ft (30–60cm). Has oval, strongly purple-flushed leaves and, mainly in summer, short spikes of tubular, purple-marked white flowers. Z13-15 H12–1.

PSEUDOCYDONIA

ROSACEAE

Genus of one species of deciduous or semi-evergreen, spring-flowering tree grown for its bark, flowers, and fruits. Where marginally hardy, it is best grown against a south- or west-facing wall. Requires full sun. Needs well-drained soil. Propagate by seed in autumn.
P. sinensis, syn. *Cydonia sinensis*. Deciduous or semi-evergreen, spreading tree. H and S 20ft (6m). Has decorative, flaking bark. Shallowly cup-shaped pink flowers, borne from mid- to late spring, are followed by large, egg-shaped, yellow fruits. Oval, finely toothed leaves are dark green. Z6–8 H8–4.

Pseudofumaria lutea. See *Corydalis lutea.*
Pseudofumaria ochroleuca. See *Corydalis ochroleuca.*
Pseudogynoxys chenopodioides. See *Senecio confusus.*

PSEUDOLARIX

PINACEAE

See also CONIFERS.
P. amabilis, syn. *P. kaempferi*, illus. p.107.
P. kaempferi. See *P. amabilis*.

Pseudolobivia aurea. See *Echinopsis aurea.*
Pseudomuscari azureum. See *Muscari azureum.*

PSEUDOPANAX, syn. NEOPANAX, NOTHOPANAX

ARALIACEAE

Genus of evergreen trees and shrubs grown for their unusual foliage and fruits. Is excellent for landscaping and may also be grown in large containers. Insignificant flowers are produced in summer. Grows in sun or semi-shade and in fertile, well-drained soil. Propagate by semi-ripe cuttings in summer or by seed in autumn or spring.
P. arboreus (Five fingers). Evergreen, round-headed, thick-branched tree. H 20ft (6m), S 12ft (4m). Large, glossy, dark green leaves are divided into 5 or 7 oblong leaflets. Produces tiny, honey-scented green flowers in summer, followed by rounded, purplish black fruits on female plants. Z10–11 H12–7.
P. crassifolius (Lancewood). Evergreen tree, unbranched for many years, then becoming round-headed. H 20ft (6m), S 6ft (2m). Dark green leaves are extremely variable in shape on young trees but eventually become long, narrow, rigid, and downward-pointing on older specimens. Female plants produce small, rounded black fruits. Z8–10 H10–8.
P. ferox illus. p.92.
P. laetus. Evergreen, round-headed, thick-branched tree or shrub. H and S 10ft (3m). Has large, long-stalked, leathery leaves composed of 5 or 7 oblong, dark green leaflets, to 12in (30cm) long. Bears tiny, greenish purple flowers, to 8in (20cm) across, in summer, followed by rounded, purplish black fruits on female plants in autumn.

PSEUDOSASA

GRAMINEAE/POACEAE

See also GRASSES, BAMBOOS, RUSHES, and SEDGES.
P. japonica, syn. *Arundinaria japonica*, illus. p.308.

PSEUDOTSUGA

PINACEAE

See also CONIFERS.
P. douglasii. See *P. menziesii.*
P. menziesii, syn. *P. douglasii*, *P. taxifolia* (Douglas fir). Fast-growing, conical conifer. H 80ft (25m), S 25–40ft (8–12m). Has thick, corky, fissured, gray-brown bark. Spirally arranged, aromatic, needlelike, slightly flattened leaves, which develop from sharply pointed buds, are dark green with white bands beneath. Elliptic cones, 3–4in (8–10cm) long, with projecting bracts, are dull brown. Z5–7 H7–5. **'Fletcheri'**, H 10ft (3m), S 6–10ft (2–3m), makes a flat-topped shrub. **'Fretsii'** (illus. p.110), H 20ft (6m) or more, S 3–4m (10–12ft), is slow-growing, with very short, dull green leaves. var. ***glauca*** illus. p.102. **'Oudemansii'** (illus. p.111) is very slow-growing, with ascending branches and short, glossy leaves, dark green all over.
P. taxifolia. See *P. menziesii.*

PSEUDOWINTERA

WINTERACEAE

Genus of evergreen shrubs and trees grown for their foliage. Needs full light or partial shade and organic, well-drained but moisture-retentive soil, ideally neutral to acidic. Water containerized plants freely when in full growth, only moderately at other times. Pruning is tolerated if needed. Propagate by semi-ripe cuttings taken in summer or by seed when ripe in autumn, or in spring.
P. axillaris, syn. *Drimys axillaris* (Heropito, Pepper-tree). Evergreen, rounded shrub or tree. H and S 10–25ft (3–8m). Has oval, lustrous, midgreen leaves, blue-gray beneath. Tiny, star-shaped, greenish yellow flowers appear in spring-summer, followed by bright red fruits. Z9–10 H10–9.
P. colorata, syn. *Drimys colorata*. Evergreen, bushy, spreading shrub. H 3ft (1m), S 5ft (1.5m). Has oval, leathery, pale yellow-green leaves, to 3in (8cm) long, blotched with pink and narrowly edged with deep red-purple; undersides are bluish white. Clusters of 2–5 small, star-shaped, greenish yellow flowers appear in midspring. Z9–10 H10–9.

PSYCHOPSIS

See also ORCHIDS.
P. papilio, syn. *Oncidium papilio* (Butterfly orchid; illus. p.299). Evergreen, epiphytic orchid for a warm greenhouse. H 6in (15cm). In summer, rich yellow-marked, orange-brown flowers, 3in (8cm) long, are borne singly and in succession on tops of stems. Has oval, semi-rigid, mottled leaves, 4–6in (10–15cm) long. Grow in good light in summer. Z14–15 H12–6.

PSYLLIOSTACHYS
Statice

PLUMBAGINACEAE

Genus of annuals, perennials, and evergreen subshrubs grown for cut flowers and for drying. Is suitable for coastal areas. Grow in sun and fertile, well-drained soil. If required for drying, cut flowers before they are fully open. Cut down dead stems of perennials in autumn. Propagate by seed sown under cover in early spring; perennials and subshrubs may also be increased by softwood cuttings in spring. Botrytis and powdery mildew may be troublesome.
P. suworowii, syn. *Limonium suworowii*, *Statice suworowii*, illus. p.330.

PTELEA

RUTACEAE

Genus of deciduous trees and shrubs grown for their foliage and fruits. Requires sun and fertile soil. Propagate species by softwood cuttings in summer or by seed in autumn, selected forms by softwood cuttings only in summer.
P. trifoliata (Hop tree). Deciduous, bushy, spreading tree or shrub. H and S 22ft (7m). Produces aromatic, dark green leaves with 3 narrowly oval leaflets. Clusters of small, star-shaped green flowers from early to midsummer are succeeded by clusters of winged, pale green fruits. Z5–9 H9–5. **'Aurea'** illus. p.145.

PTERIS

ADIANTACEAE/PTERIDACEAE

Genus of deciduous, semi-evergreen or evergreen ferns. Tolerates sun or shade. Grow in moist, peaty soil. Remove faded fronds regularly. Propagate by division in spring or by spores in summer.
P. cretica (Cretan brake). Evergreen or semi-evergreen fern. H 18in (45cm), S 12in (30cm). Produces triangular to broadly oval, divided, pale green fronds that have fingerlike pinnae. Z12–15 h12–10. var. ***albolineata*** see *P.c.* 'Albolineata'. **'Albolineata'** (syn. *P.c.* var. *albolineata*) has pale green fronds centrally variegated with creamy white. Variegated **'Mayi'**, H 12in (30cm), has crested frond tips. **'Wimsettii'** (illus p.311) is compact, with the margins of the pinnae deeply and irregularly lobed.
P. ensiformis (Snow brake). Deciduous or semi-evergreen fern. H 12in (30cm), S 9in (23cm). Dark green fronds, often grayish white around the midribs, are coarsely divided into finger-shaped pinnae. Z10–11 H12–10.**'Arguta'**, H 18in (45cm), has deeper green fronds with central, silver-white marks.

PTEROCARYA
Wing nut

JUGLANDACEAE

Genus of deciduous trees grown for their foliage and catkins. Needs full sun and any deep, moist but well-drained soil. Suckers should be removed regularly. Propagate by softwood cuttings in summer or by suckers or seed, when ripe, in autumn.
P. fraxinifolia (Caucasian wing nut). Deciduous, spreading tree. H 80ft (25m), S 70ft (20m). Large, ashlike, glossy, dark green leaves turn yellow in autumn. Long green catkins are borne in summer, the females developing

winged green then brown fruits. Z6–9 H9–6.
P.* x *rehderiana illus. p.69.
P. stenoptera (Chinese wing nut). Deciduous, spreading tree. H 70ft (20m), S 50ft (15m). Ashlike, bright green leaves, each with a winged stalk, turn yellow in autumn. Produces long green catkins in summer, the females developing winged, pink-tinged green fruits. Z7–9 H9–7.

PTEROCEPHALUS

DIPSACACEAE

Genus of compact, summer-flowering annuals, perennials, and semi-evergreen subshrubs grown for their scabiosa-like flower heads and feathery seed heads. Is useful for rock gardens. Requires sun and well-drained soil. Propagate by softwood or semi-ripe cuttings in summer or by seed in autumn. Self-seeds moderately.
P. parnassi. See *P. perennis.*
P. perennis, syn. *P. parnassi*, illus. p.380.

PTEROSTYRAX

STYRACACEAE

Genus of deciduous trees and shrubs grown for their foliage and fragrant flowers. Requires sun or semi-shade and deep, well-drained, neutral to acidic soil. Propagate by softwood or semi-ripe cuttings in summer or by seed in autumn.
P. hispida (Epaulette tree). Deciduous, spreading tree or shrub with aromatic gray bark. H 50ft (15m), S 40ft (12m). Has oblong to oval, midgreen leaves, 8in (20cm) long. Bears large, drooping panicles of small, bell-shaped white flowers from early to midsummer. Z5–8 H8–5.

Ptilotrichum spinosum. See *Alyssum spinosum.*

PUERARIA

LEGUMINOSAE/PAPILIONACEAE

Genus of deciduous, woody-stemmed or herbaceous, twining climbers. Grow in full sun and in any well-drained soil. Propagate by seed in spring.
P. hirsuta. See *P. lobata.*
P. lobata, syn. *P. hirsuta*, *P. montana* var. *lobata*, *P. thunbergiana* (Kudzu vine). Deciduous, invasive, woody-stemmed, twining climber with hairy stems. H to 15ft (5m) or to 100ft (30m) in the wild. Leaves have 3 broadly oval leaflets. In summer produces racemes, to 12in (30cm) long, of small, scented, sweet-pealike, reddish purple flowers, followed by long, slender, hairy pods, 2½–3in (6–8cm) long. Z7–9 H9–3.
P. montana var. ***lobata.*** See *P. lobata.*
P. thunbergiana. See *P. lobata.*

PULMONARIA

Lungwort

BORAGINACEAE

Genus of mainly spring-flowering perennials, some of which are semi-evergreen with small, overwintering rosettes of leaves. Prefers shade; grows in any moist but well-drained soil. Propagate by division in spring or autumn.
P. angustifolia. Clump-forming, usually deciduous perennial. H 9in (23cm), S 8–12in (20–30cm) or more. Has lance-shaped, unspotted, midgreen leaves, 16in (40cm) long. In early spring produces heads of tubular, 5-lobed, boragelike, sometimes pink-tinged, deep blue flowers. Z2–7 H8–1.
P. longifolia. Clump-forming, deciduous perennial. H 12in (30cm), S 18in (45cm). Bears very narrowly lance-shaped, dark green leaves, to 18in (45cm), spotted with silvery white. Heads of tubular, 5-lobed, boragelike, vivid blue flowers appear in late spring. Z3–8 H8–4.
***P.* 'Mawson's Blue'** illus. p.271.
***P. officinalis* 'Sissinghurst White'**, syn. *P. saccharata* 'Sissinghurst White', illus. p.267.
P. rubra. Semi-evergreen, clump-forming perennial. H 12in (30cm), S 24in (60cm). Has oval, velvety, mid-green leaves. Heads of tubular, 5-lobed, boragelike, brick red flowers open from late winter to early spring. Z5–8 H8–3.
P. saccharata illus. p.271.
'Sissinghurst White' see *P. officinalis* 'Sissinghurst White'.

PULSATILLA

RANUNCULACEAE

Genus of perennials, some of which are evergreen, grown for their large, feathery leaves, their upright or pendent, bell- or cup-shaped flowers, covered in fine hairs, and feathery seed heads. Has fibrous, woody rootstocks. Leaves increase in size after flowering time. Suitable for large rock gardens. Needs full sun and organic, well-drained soil. Resents disturbance to roots. Propagate by root cuttings in winter or by seed when fresh. All parts of the plant may cause mild stomach upset if ingested, and, in rare instances, contact with the sap may irritate skin.
P. alpina illus. p.346. subsp. ***apiifolia*** (syn. *P.a.* subsp. *sulphurea*) is a clump-forming perennial. H 6–12in (15–30cm), S to 4in (10cm). Has feathery, soft green leaves. Bears upright, bell shaped, soft pale yellow flowers in spring, followed by feathery silvery seed heads. Z5–7 H7–5. subsp. ***sulphurea*** see *P.a.* subsp. *apiifolia*.
P. halleri illus. p.348. subsp. ***grandis*** (syn. *P. vulgaris* subsp. *grandis*) is a clump-forming perennial. H and S 6–9in (15–23cm). In spring, before feathery, light green leaves appear, bears large, upright, shallowly bell-shaped, lavender-blue flowers, 2in (5cm) wide, with bright yellow centers. Flower stems rapidly elongate as feathery silvery seed heads mature. Z5–7 H7–5.
P. occidentalis. Clump-forming perennial. H 8in (20cm), S 6in (15cm). In late spring to early summer, solitary nodding buds develop into erect, goblet-shaped white flowers, stained blue-violet at base outside and sometimes flushed pink, followed by feathery silvery seed heads. Bears feathery leaves. Difficult to grow and flower well at low altitudes. Z5–7 H7–5.
P. vernalis illus. p.363. ***P. vulgaris*** illus. p.348. subsp. ***grandis*** see *P. halleri* subsp. *grandis.*

PUNICA

Pomegranate

LYTHRACEAE/PUNICACEAE

Genus of deciduous, summer-flowering shrubs and trees grown for their bright red flowers and yellow to orange-red fruits that ripen and become edible only in warm climates. Needs a sheltered, sunny position and well-drained soil. Propagate by seed in spring or by semi-ripe cuttings in summer.
P. granatum. Deciduous, rounded shrub or tree. H and S 6–25ft (2–8m). Has narrowly oblong leaves and, in summer, funnel-shaped, bright red flowers with crumpled petals. Fruits are spherical and deep yellow to orange. May be grown in a southern or eastern exposure, either free-standing or, where marginally hardy, against a wall. Z7–10 H12–1.
var. ***nana*** illus. p.355.

PUSCHKINIA

LILIACEAE

Genus of dwarf, *Scilla*-like bulbs grown for their early spring flowers. Needs sun or partial shade and organic soil that has grit or sand added to ensure good drainage. Plant in autumn. Dies down in summer. Propagate by offsets in late summer or by seed in autumn.
P. libanotica. See *P. scilloides* var. *libanotica.*
P. scilloides var. ***libanotica***, syn. *P. libanotica*, illus. p.432. **'Alba'** illus. p.426.

PUYA

BROMELIACEAE

Genus of evergreen, rosette-forming perennials and shrubs grown for their overall appearance. Requires full light and well-drained soil. Water moderately during the growing season, sparingly at other times. Propagate by seed or offsets in spring.
P. alpestris (illus. p.265). Evergreen perennial with thick, branched, prostrate stems. H to 6ft (2m), S 10ft (3m). Linear, tapering, arching, bright green leaves are fleshy, with hooked, spiny teeth along the edges and dense white scales beneath. Tubular, deep metallic blue flowers aging to purple-red are borne in stiff, erect panicles and are produced in early summer. Z9–15 H12–1.
P. chilensis (illus. p.265). Evergreen, upright perennial with a short, woody stem. H and S to 6ft (2m). Stem is crowned by a dense rosette of linear, tapering, arching, fleshy, gray-green leaves with margins of hooked, spiny teeth. Bears tubular, metallic- or greenish yellow flowers in erect, branched panicles in summer. Z9–15 H12–1.

PYCNOSTACHYS

LABIATAE/LAMIACEAE

Genus of bushy perennials grown for their whorled clusters of flowers. Grow in bright light and in fertile, well-drained soil. Propagate by stem cuttings in early summer.
P. dawei illus. p.233.
P. urticifolia. Strong-growing, erect perennial with square stems. H 3–6ft (1–2m), S 8–24in (20–60cm). Has oval, toothed, hairy, midgreen leaves. Bears whorls of small, tubular, bright blue flowers in racemes in winter.

PYRACANTHA

Firethorn

ROSACEAE

Genus of evergreen, spiny, summer-flowering shrubs grown for their foliage, flowers and fruits. Requires a sheltered site in sun or semi-shade and fertile soil. To produce a compact habit on a plant grown against a wall, train and cut back long shoots after flowering. Propagate by semi-ripe cuttings in summer. Susceptible to scab and fireblight. The seeds may cause mild stomach upset if ingested.
P. angustifolia. Evergreen, bushy, dense shrub. H and S 10ft (3m). Has narrowly oblong leaves, dark green above, gray beneath. Bears clusters of small, 5-petaled white flowers in early summer, followed by spherical, orange-yellow fruits, ⅜in (8mm) across, in autumn. Z4–8 H12–1.
P. atalantioides. Vigorous, evergreen shrub, part upright, part arching. H 15ft (5m), S 12ft (4m). Oblong leaves are glossy and dark green. Large clusters of small, 5-petaled white flowers in early summer are followed by spherical red fruits in early autumn. Z6–9 H9–6. **'Aurea'** illus. p.124.
P. coccinea. Evergreen, dense, bushy shrub. H and S 12ft (4m). Dense clusters of small, 5-petaled white flowers open amid oval, dark green leaves in early summer and are succeeded by spherical, bright red fruits. Z6–9 H9–6. **'Lalandei'** has larger leaves and larger, orange-red fruits.
***P.* 'Golden Charmer'** illus. p.149.
***P.* 'Golden Dome'** illus. p.149.
***P.* 'Mohave'.** Vigorous, evergreen, bushy shrub. H 12ft (4m), S 15ft (5m). Produces clusters of small, 5-petaled white flowers in early summer, then spherical, orange-red fruits. Leaves are broadly oval and dark green. Is disease-resistant. Z6–9 H9–6.
***P.* 'Orange Glow'.** Evergreen, upright, dense shrub. H 15ft (5m), S 10ft (3m). Has oblong, glossy, dark green leaves. Clusters of small, 5-petaled white flowers in early

summer are followed by spherical orange fruits. Z7–9 H9–7.
P. rogersiana. Evergreen, upright, then arching shrub. H and S 10ft (3m). Leaves are narrowly oblong, glossy, and bright green. Produces clusters of small, 5-petaled white flowers in early summer, followed by round, orange-red or yellow fruits. Z8–9 H9–8.
***P.* x *watereri*,** syn. *P.* 'Waterer's Orange', illus. p.136.
***P.* 'Waterer's Orange'.** See *P.* x *watereri.*

Pyrethropsis hosmariense. See *Rhodanthemum hosmariense.*
***Pyrethrum* 'Brenda'.** See *Tanacetum coccineum* 'Brenda'.
Pyrethrum coccineum. See *Tanacetum coccineum.*
Pyrethrum parthenium. See *Tanacetum parthenium.*
Pyrethrum roseum. See *Tanacetum coccineum.*

PYROLA
Wintergreen

PYROLACEAE

Genus of evergreen, spreading, spring- and summer-flowering perennials. Needs partial shade, cool conditions, and well-drained, peaty, acidic soil; grows best in light woodlands. Resents disturbance. Propagate by seed in autumn or spring or by division in spring.
P. asarifolia. Evergreen, rosette-forming perennial. H 6–10in (15–25cm), S 6in (15cm) or more. Has kidney-shaped, leathery, glossy, light green leaves. Bears open tubular, pale to deep pink flowers in spring. Z5–8 H8–5.
P. rotundifolia (Round-leaved wintergreen, Wild lily-of-the-valley). Creeping, evergreen, rosette-forming perennial. H 9in (23cm), S 12in (30cm). Produces rounded, leathery, glossy, midgreen leaves and, in late spring and early summer, sprays of fragrant white flowers that resemble lily-of-the-valley. Z5–8 H8–5.

PYROSTEGIA

BIGNONIACEAE

Genus of evergreen, woody-stemmed, tendril climbers grown for their flowers. Needs full light and fertile, well-drained soil. Water regularly, less in winter. Provide support. Thin stems after flowering. Propagate by semi-ripe cuttings or layering in summer.
P. ignea. See *P. venusta.*
***P. venusta*,** syn. *P. ignea*, illus. p.218.

PYRUS
Pear

ROSACEAE

Genus of deciduous, spring-flowering trees grown for their habit, foliage, flowers, and edible fruits (pears). Does best in full sun and needs well-drained soil. Propagate species by seed in autumn, cultivars by budding in summer or by grafting in winter. Many species are susceptible to fireblight, scab, and pear decline.
P. amygdaliformis. Deciduous, spreading tree. H 30ft (10m), S 25ft (8m). Lance-shaped leaves are gray when young, maturing to glossy, dark green. Clusters of 5-petaled white flowers are produced in midspring and are followed by small brownish fruits. Z7–9 H9–7.
P. calleryana (Callery pear). Deciduous, broadly conical tree. H and S to 50ft (15m). Oval, glossy, dark green leaves often turn red in autumn. Bears 5-petaled white flowers from mid- to late spring and small brownish fruits. Z5–8 H8–3. **'Bradford'**, S 30ft (10m), is resistant to fireblight. **'Chanticleer'** illus. p.76.
P. communis (Common pear). **'Beech Hill'** is a deciduous, narrowly conical tree. H 30ft (10m), S 22ft (7m). Oval, glossy, dark green leaves often turn orange and red in autumn. From mid- to late spring produces 5-petaled white flowers as the leaves emerge, followed by small brownish fruits. Z5–9 H9–5.
P. elaeagrifolia. Deciduous, spreading, thorny tree. H and S 25ft (8m). Has lance-shaped, gray-green leaves. Produces loose clusters of 5-petaled, creamy white flowers in midspring, followed by small, pear-shaped brownish fruits. Z5–9 H9–5.
P. salicifolia. Deciduous, mound-shaped tree with slightly drooping branches. H 15–25ft (5–8m), S 12ft (4m). White flowers with 5 petals open as lance-shaped gray leaves emerge in midspring. Fruits are small and brownish. Z5–9 H9–5. **'Pendula'** illus. p.91.
P. ussuriensis (Chinese pear). A broadly conical, deciduous tree with dark green leaves that turn yellow to orange in autumn. H 40ft (12m) S 25ft (8m). White flowers in small upright racemes open in spring and become small almost spherical green fruits. Z4–9 H9–1.

Q

Quamoclit coccinea. See *Ipomoea coccinea.*
Quamoclit lobata. See *Ipomoea lobata.*
Quamoclit pennata. See *Ipomoea quamoclit.*

QUERCUS
Oak

FAGACEAE

Genus of deciduous or evergreen trees and shrubs grown for their habit, foliage, and, in some deciduous species, autumn color. Produces insignificant flowers from late spring to early summer, followed by egg-shaped to rounded brown fruits (acorns). Does best in sun or semi-shade and in deep, well-drained soil. Except where stated otherwise, will tolerate limestone. Propagate species by seed in autumn, selected forms and hybrids by grafting in late winter. May be affected, though not usually seriously, by mildew, various galls, and oak wilt.
Q. acutissima (Sawtooth oak). Deciduous, round-headed tree. H and S 50ft (15m). Has chestnutlike, glossy, dark green leaves, edged with bristle-tipped teeth, that last until late in the year. Z5–8 H8–3.
Q. aegilops. See *Q. macrolepis.*
Q. agrifolia illus. p.85.
Q. alba illus. p.71.
Q. aliena (Oriental white oak). Deciduous, spreading tree. H 50ft (15m), S 40ft (12m). Has large, oblong, prominently toothed, glossy, dark green leaves. Z6–9 H9–6.
Q. bicolor (Swamp white oak). Deciduous spreading tree H 70ft (20m), S 50ft (15m). Has glossy, dark green, shallowly lobed leaves that turn orange to red in autumn. Bark is gray-brown and peels in flakes. Z4–8 H8–1.
Q. canariensis illus. p.66.
Q. castaneifolia illus. p.68.
Q. cerris (Turkey oak). Fast-growing, deciduous, spreading tree of stately habit. H 100ft (30m), S 80ft (25m). Oblong, glossy, dark green leaves are deeply lobed. Thrives on shallow, alkaline soil. Z7–9 H9–7. **'Argenteo-variegata'** (syn. *Q.c.* 'Variegata') illus. p.78.
Q. coccifera (Kermes oak). Evergreen, bushy, compact tree or shrub. H and S 15ft (5m). Hollylike leaves are glossy, dark green, and rigid with spiny margins. Z7–9 H9–7.
Q. coccinea illus. p.70. **'Splendens'** is a deciduous, round-headed tree. H 70ft (20m), S 50ft (15m). Has oblong, glossy, midgreen leaves, with deep, toothlike lobes, that turn deep scarlet in autumn. Prefers acidic soil. Z5–9 H9–5.
Q. dentata (Daimio oak). Deciduous, spreading, thick-branched tree of rugged habit. H 50ft (15m), S 30ft (10m). Has oval, lobed, dark green leaves, 12in (30cm) or more long. Prefers acidic soil. Z6–8 H8–6.
Q. ellipsoidalis illus. p.70.
Q. frainetto illus. p.69.
Q. garryana illus. p.80.
Q.* x *heterophylla illus. p.82.
Q.* x *hispanica 'Lucombeana', syn. *Q.* x *lucombeana* 'William Lucombe', illus. p.73.
Q. ilex (Holm oak). Evergreen, round-headed tree. H 80ft (25m), S 70ft (20m). Glossy, dark green leaves are silvery gray when young and very variably shaped but are most often oval. Excellent for an exposed, coastal position. Z4–8 H9–2.
Q. imbricaria (Shingle oak). Deciduous, spreading tree. H 70ft (20m), S 50ft (15m). Bears long, narrow leaves that are yellowish when young, dark green in summer, and yellowish brown in autumn. Z5–8 H8–4.
Q. ithaburensis subsp. ***macrolepis.*** See *Q. macrolepis.*
Q. laurifolia illus. p.69.
***Q.* x *lucombeana* 'William Lucombe'.** See *Q.* x *hispanica* 'Lucombeana'.
Q. macranthera illus. p.66.
Q. macrocarpa illus. p.80.
***Q. macrolepis*,** syn. *Q. aegilops*, *Q. ithaburensis* subsp. *macrolepis*, illus. p.80.
Q. marilandica illus. p.80.
Q. mongolica var. ***grosseserrata.*** Deciduous, spreading tree. H 70ft (20m), S 50ft (15m). Has large, oblong, lobed, dark green leaves with prominent, triangular teeth. Z5–9 H9–5.
Q. muehlenbergii illus. p.67.
Q. myrsinifolia illus. p.84.
Q. nigra illus. p.68.
Q. palustris illus. p.69.
Q. petraea (Durmast oak, Sessile oak). Deciduous, spreading tree. H 100ft (30m), S 80ft (25m). Has oblong, lobed, leathery, dark green leaves with yellow stalks. Z5–8 H8–5. **'Columna'** illus. p.68.
Q. phellos illus. p.71.
Q. prinus (Chestnut oak, basket oak). Deciduous, rounded tree. H and S 60ft (18m). The shiny, dark green leaves are gray-woolly beneath and turn yellow in autumn. Z4–8 H8–3.
Q. robur (English oak, Pedunculate oak). Deciduous, spreading, rugged tree. H and S 80ft (25m). Bears oblong, wavy, lobed, dark green leaves. Z5–8 H8–3. **'Concordia'**, H 30ft (10m), is slow-growing and has golden yellow young foliage that becomes yellowish green in midsummer. f. ***fastigiata*** illus. p.66.
Q. rubra illus. p.69. **'Aurea'** illus. p.80.
Q. suber illus. p.73.
Q.* x *turneri illus. p.73.
Q. velutina (Black oak). Fast-growing, deciduous, spreading tree. H 100ft (30m), S 80ft (25m). Large, oblong, lobed, glossy, dark green leaves turn reddish brown in autumn. Z4–8 H8–1.

QUISQUALIS

COMBRETACEAE

Genus of evergreen or deciduous, scandent shrubs and twining climbers grown for their flowers. Provide organic, moist but well-drained soil and full light or semi-shade. Water freely when in full growth, less in cold weather. Stems need support. Thin out crowded growth in spring. Propagate by seed in spring or by semi-ripe cuttings in summer.
Q. indica illus. p.211.

R

RAMONDA

GESNERIACEAE

Genus of evergreen perennials grown for their rosettes of rounded, crinkled, hairy leaves and for their flowers. Is useful for rock gardens. Prefers shade and moist soil. Water plants well if they curl in a dry spell. Propagate by rooting offsets in early summer or by leaf cuttings or seed in early autumn.

R. myconi, syn. *R. pyrenaica*, illus. p.382.

R. nathaliae. Evergreen, basal-rosetted perennial. H and S 4in (10cm). Has small, pale green leaves and, in late spring and early summer, bears umbels of small, outward-facing, flattish white or lavender flowers with yellow anthers. Z6–7 H7–6.

R. pyrenaica. See *R. myconi.*

R. serbica. Evergreen, basal-rosetted perennial. H and S 4in (10cm). Is similar to *R. nathaliae* but has cup-shaped, lilac-blue flowers and dark violet-blue anthers. Z6–7 H7–6.

RANUNCULUS

Buttercup

RANUNCULACEAE

Genus of annuals, aquatics, and perennials, some of which are evergreen or semi-evergreen, grown mainly for their flowers. Many species grow from a thickened rootstock or a cluster of tubers. Some are invasive. Grows in sun or shade and in moist but well-drained soil. Propagate by seed when fresh or by division in spring or autumn. Contact with the sap may irritate skin.

R. aconitifolius and **'Flore Pleno'** illus. p.233.

R. acris (Meadow buttercup). **'Flore Pleno'** illus. p.292.

R. alpestris illus. p.363.

R. amplexicaulis. Upright perennial. H 10in (25cm), S 4in (10cm). Has narrowly oval, blue-gray leaves. In early summer produces clusters of shallowly cup-shaped white flowers with yellow anthers. Needs organic soil. Z4–8 H8–1.

R. aquatilis (Water crowfoot). Aquatic annual or usually evergreen perennial. H ½in (1cm), S indefinite. Submerged, branched, slender stems bear dark green leaves having many threadlike segments; the floating leaves are kidney-shaped to rounded and deeply divided into 3–7 lobes. In midsummer, produces solitary, bowl- or saucer-shaped, white-based yellow flowers, ½in (1cm) across, on the surface. Z5–8 H8–5.

R. asiaticus [red form] illus. p.421, [yellow form] illus. p.423.

R. bulbosus **'Speciosus Plenus'** of gardens. See *R. constantinopolitanus* 'Plenus'.

R. bullatus. Clump-forming perennial with thick, fibrous roots. H 2–3in (5–8cm), S 3–4in (8–10cm). Produces fragrant, shallowly cup-shaped, bright yellow flowers in autumn above neat mounds of foliage. Oblong to oval green leaves have sharply toothed tips and are puckered. Good in an alpine house or rock garden. Z7–9 H9–7.

R. calandrinioides illus. p.360.

R. constantinopolitanus **'Plenus'**, syn. *R. bulbosus* 'Speciosus Plenus' of gardens, *R. gouanii* 'Plenus', *R. speciosus* 'Plenus', illus. p.292.

R. crenatus. Semi-evergreen, rosetted perennial with thick, fibrous roots. H and S 4in (10cm). Produces rounded, toothed, green leaves and, in summer, short stems bearing 1 or 2 shallowly cup-shaped white flowers just above the foliage. May also be propagated by removing a flower stem at its first joint in summer; rosettes will form and may then be rooted. Rarely sets seed in cultivation. Good in an alpine house or rock garden.

R. ficaria (Lesser celandine). **'Albus'** illus. p.363. **'Aurantiacus'** illus. p.373. **'Brazen Hussy'** is a mat-forming, tuberous perennial. H 2in (5cm), S to 8in (20cm). Is grown for its heart-shaped, purple-bronze leaves produced in spring. Shallowly cup-shaped, glossy, sulfur yellow flowers with bronze reverses appear in early spring. All *R. ficaria* forms die down in late spring. May spread rapidly; is good for a wild garden. Z4–8 H8–1 **'Flore Pleno'** illus. p.372.

R. glacialis. Hummock-forming perennial with fibrous roots. H 2–10in (5–25cm), S 2in (5cm) or more. Bears rounded, deeply lobed, glossy, dark green leaves and, in late spring and early summer, clusters of shallowly cup-shaped white or pink flowers. Is very difficult to grow at low altitudes. Good in a scree or alpine house. Prefers organic, moist, acidic soil that is drier in winter. Z3–5 H5–1.

R. gouanii **'Plenus'.** See *R. constantinopolitanus* 'Plenus'.

R. gramineus illus. p.359.

R. lingua illus. p.451. **'Grandiflorus'** is a deciduous, perennial, marginal water plant. H 3ft (1m), S 1ft (30cm). Has thick, pinkish green stems, lance-shaped, glaucous leaves, and, in late spring, racemes of large, saucer-shaped, yellow flowers. Z4–9 H9–1.

R. lyallii (Giant buttercup). Evergreen, thick, upright, tufted perennial. H and S 12in (30cm) or more. Has rounded, leathery, dark green leaves, each 6in (15cm) or more across, and, in summer, bears panicles of large, shallowly cup-shaped white flowers. Is very difficult to flower in hot, dry climates. Is suitable for an alpine house. Rarely sets seed in cultivation. Z4–9 H9–1.

R. montanus **'Molten Gold'.** Clump-forming, compact perennial. H 6in (15cm), S 4in (10cm). Leaves are rounded and 3-lobed. Flower stems each produce a shallowly cup-shaped, shiny, bright golden yellow flower in early summer. Is useful for a sunny rock garden. Z5–8 H8–5.

R. speciosus **'Plenus'.** See *R. constantinopolitanus* 'Plenus'.

RANZANIA

BERBERIDACEAE

Genus of one species of perennial grown for its unusual appearance as well as its flowers. Is ideal for woodland gardens. Prefers shade or semi-shade and organic, moist soil. Propagate by division in spring or by seed in autumn.

R. japonica. Upright perennial. H 18in (45cm), S 12in (30cm). Produces 3-parted, fresh green leaves and, in early summer, small clusters of nodding, shallowly cup-shaped, pale mauve flowers. Z4–8 H8–1.

RAOULIA

ASTERACEAE/COMPOSITAE

Genus of evergreen, mat-forming perennials grown for their foliage. Some species are suitable for alpine houses, others for rock gardens. Needs sun or semi-shade and gritty, moist but well-drained, peaty soil. Propagate by seed when fresh or by division in spring.

R. australis illus. p.390.

R. eximia. Evergreen, cushion-forming perennial. H 1in (2.5cm), S 2in (5cm). Has oblong to oval, overlapping, woolly gray leaves and, in late spring-summer, small, rounded heads of yellowish white flowers. Good in an alpine house. Prefers some shade. Z7–8 H8–7.

R. haastii illus. p.391.

R. hookeri var. ***albo-sericea*** illus. p.389.

R. leontopodium. See *Leucogenes leontopodium.*

RAVENALA

STRELITZIACEAE

Genus of one species of evergreen, palmlike tree grown for its foliage and overall appearance. Is related to *Strelitzia*. Requires full light and organic, well-drained soil. Water potted specimens freely in summer, less in winter or when temperatures are low. Propagate by seed in spring. Spider mite may be troublesome.

R. madagascariensis (Traveler's tree). Evergreen, upright, fan-shaped tree. H and S to 30ft (10m). Has bananalike, long-stalked leaves, each 10–20ft (3–6m) long, with expanded stalk bases. Groups of boat-shaped spathes with 6-parted white flowers emerge from leaf axils in summer. Z11 H12–1.

REBUTIA

CACTACEAE

Genus of mostly clump-forming, spherical to columnar cacti. Produces flowers in profusion from plant bases, usually 2–3 years after raising from seed. Much-ribbed, tuberculate green stems have short spines. A few species are sometimes included in *Aylostera.* Requires a position in sun or partial shade and well-drained soil. Is easy to grow. Propagate by seed in spring or summer.

R. arenacea, syn. *Sulcorebutia arenacea*, illus. p.480.

R. aureiflora illus. p.480.

R. fiebrigii, syn. *R. muscula*, illus. p.480.

R. krainziana illus. p.474.

R. minuscula, syn. *R. violaciflora*, illus. p.472

R. muscula. See *R. fiebrigii.*

R. neocumingii, syn. *Weingartia neocumingii*. Spherical cactus. H and S 4in (10cm). Stem is tuberculate and green. Areoles bear dense clusters of yellow spines, ⅝in (1.5cm) long, some thicker than others, and several cup-shaped, dark yellow flowers, 1¼in (3cm) long, in spring. Z12–15 H12–10.

R. pygmaea, syn. *Lobivia pygmaea*. Clump-forming, columnar cactus. H 2in (5cm), S 4in (10cm). Very short, comblike spines are pressed against gray- to purple-green stem. Trumpet-shaped pink to salmon or rose-purple flowers, to ¾in (2cm) across, appear in spring. Prefers a sunny position. Z12–15 H12–10.

R. rauschii, syn. *Sulcorebutia rauschii*. Flattened spherical cactus. H 2in (5cm), S 4in (10cm). Gray-green stem bears very short, comblike, golden or black spines. Bears flattish, 1¼in (3cm) wide, deep purple flowers in spring. Grows better when grafted. Z12–15 H12–10.

R. senilis. Clump-forming cactus. H 2in (5cm), S 6in (15cm). Has soft, white spines, 1¼in (3cm) long, matted around a 2in (5cm) wide stem. In spring bears trumpet-shaped red, yellow, pink, or orange flowers, 2in (5cm) across. Prefers a sunny site. Z12–15 H12–10.

R. spegazziniana illus. p.475.

R. tiraquensis, syn. *Sulcorebutia tiraquensis*, illus. p.474.

R. violaciflora. See *R. minuscula.*

REHDERODENDRON

STYRACACEAE

Genus of deciduous, spring-flowering trees grown for their flowers and fruits. Needs sun or semi-shade, some shelter, and fertile, moist, but well-drained, acidic soil. Propagate by semi-ripe cuttings in summer or by seed in autumn.

R. macrocarpum. Deciduous, spreading tree. H 30ft (10m), S 22ft (7m). Young shoots are red. Pendent clusters of lemon-scented, cup-shaped, pink-tinged white flowers are borne amid oblong, taper-pointed, red-stalked, glossy, dark green leaves in late spring. Bears cylindrical, woody red then brown fruits in autumn. Z8–10 H10–8.

REHMANNIA

SCROPHULARIACEAE

Genus of spring- and summer-flowering perennials. Needs a warm, sunny position and light soil. Propagate by seed in autumn or spring or by root cuttings in winter.

R. angulata of gardens. See *R. elata.*

R. elata, syn. *R. angulata* of gardens, illus. p.244.
R. glutinosa. Rosette-forming perennial. H 12in (30cm), S 10in (25cm). Tubular pink, red-brown, or yellow flowers with purple veins are borne on leafy shoots in late spring and early summer. Leaves are oval to lance-shaped, toothed, hairy, and light green. Z9–11 H12–9.

REINWARDTIA

LINACEAE

Genus of evergreen subshrubs grown for their flowers. Needs full light or partial shade and fertile, well-drained soil. Water freely when growing, moderately at other times. Tip prune young plants to promote branching; cut back hard after flowering. Raise softwood cuttings annually in late spring. Spider mite may cause problems.
R. indica, syn. *R. trigyna*, illus. p.170.
R. trigyna. See *R. indica*.

RESEDA

Mignonette

RESEDACEAE

Genus of annuals and biennials with flowers that attract bees and that are also suitable for cutting. Grow in a sunny position and in any fertile, well-drained soil. Deadheading regularly ensures a prolonged flowering period. Propagate by sowing seed outdoors in spring or early autumn.
R. odorata illus. p.319.

Retama monosperma. See *Genista monosperma*.
Reynoutria. Reclassified as *Fallopia*.

RHAMNUS

Buckthorn

RHAMNACEAE

Genus of deciduous or evergreen shrubs and trees, with inconspicuous flowers, grown mainly for their foliage and fruits. Requires sun or semi-shade and fertile soil. Propagate deciduous species by seed in autumn, evergreen species by semi-ripe cuttings in summer. All parts may cause severe discomfort if ingested.
R. alaternus (Italian buckthorn). **'Argenteovariegata'** is an evergreen, bushy shrub. H and S 10ft (3m). Has oval, leathery, glossy, gray-green leaves edged with creamy white. Tiny, yellowish green flowers are produced from early to midsummer and followed by spherical red then black fruits. Z7–9 H9–7.
R. frangula (Alder buckthorn). Deciduous, spreading, open shrub. H and S 15ft (5m). Has oval, glossy, dark green leaves that turn red in autumn. Small green flowers in summer are followed by spherical red fruit that turn black. Z3–8 H8–1. **'Asplenifolia'** has leaves that are elongated and irregularly scalloped.

RHAPHIOLEPIS

ROSACEAE

Genus of evergreen shrubs grown for their flowers and foliage. Needs sun and fertile, well-drained soil. Propagate by semi-ripe cuttings in late summer.
***R.* x *delacourii* 'Coates' Crimson'.** Evergreen, rounded shrub. H 6ft (2m), S 8ft (2.5m). Clusters of fragrant, star-shaped, deep pink flowers, produced in spring or summer, are set off by the oval, leathery, dark green leaves. Z8–10 H10–8.
R. indica (Indian hawthorn). Evergreen, bushy shrub. H 5ft (1.5m), S 6ft (2m). Clusters of fragrant, star-shaped white flowers, flushed with pink, are borne in spring or early summer amid narrowly lance-shaped, glossy, dark green leaves. Z8–11 H9–3.
R. japonica. See *R. umbellata*.
R. ovata. See *R. umbellata*.
R. umbellata, syn. *R. japonica*, *R. ovata*, illus. p.160.

RHAPIS

ARECACEAE/PALMAE

Genus of evergreen fan palms grown for their foliage and overall appearance. May have tiny yellow flowers in summer. Needs partial shade and organic, well-drained soil. Water containerized specimens freely when growing, moderately at other times. Propagate by seed, suckers, or division in spring. Is susceptible to spider mite.
R. excelsa, syn. *R. flabelliformis*, illus. p.152.
R. flabelliformis. See *R. excelsa*.

Rhazya orientalis. See *Amsonia orientalis*.

RHEUM

Rhubarb

POLYGONACEAE

Genus of perennials grown for their foliage and striking overall appearance. Includes the edible rhubarb and various ornamental plants. Some species are extremely large and require plenty of space. Prefers sun or semi-shade and deep, rich, well-drained soil. Propagate by division in spring or by seed in autumn. Leaves may cause severe discomfort if ingested.
R. nobile. Clump-forming perennial. H 5ft (1.5m), S 3ft (1m). Leaves are oblong to oval, leathery, basal, midgreen, 2ft (60cm) long. In late summer produces long stems and conical spikes of large, overlapping, pale cream bracts hiding nonshowy flowers. Z6–9 H9–6.
R. palmatum. Clump-forming perennial. H and S 6ft (2m). Has 2–2½ft (60–75cm) long, rounded, 5-lobed, midgreen leaves. In early summer produces broad panicles of small, creamy white flowers. Z5–9 H9–5. **'Atrosanguineum'** illus. p.227.

Rhipsalidopsis gaertneri. See *Hatiora gaertneri*.

RHIPSALIS

Mistletoe cactus

CACTACEAE

Genus of epiphytic cacti with usually pendent, variously formed stems. Flowers are followed by spherical, translucent berries. Needs partial shade and rich, well-drained soil. Prefers 80% relative humidity – higher than for most cacti. Give only occasional, very light watering in winter. Propagate by seed or stem cuttings in spring or summer.
R. capilliformis. Pendent cactus. H 3ft (1m), S 20in (50cm). Has freely branching, cylindrical green stems and, in winter-spring, short, funnel-shaped white flowers, to ½in (1cm), with recurved tips, then white berries. Z13–15 H12-10.
R. cereuscula illus. p.461.
R. clavata. See *Hatiora clavata*.
R. crispata. Bushy then pendent cactus. H 3ft (1m), S indefinite. Has leaflike, elliptic to oblong, pale green stem segments, to 5in (12cm) long, with undulating edges that produce short, funnel-shaped, cream or pale yellow flowers, to ½in (1cm) across, with recurved tips, in winter-spring, then white berries. Z13–15 H12-10.
R. floccosa, syn. *R. tucumanensis*, illus. p.461.
R. paradoxa (Chain cactus). Bushy then pendent cactus. H 3ft (1m), S indefinite. Triangular green stems have segments alternately set at different angles. Short, funnel-shaped white flowers, ¾in (2cm) across, with recurved tips, appear from stem edges in winter-spring and are followed by red berries. Z13–15 H12-10.
R. salicornioides. See *Hatiora salicornioides*.
R. tucumanensis. See *R. floccosa*.
R. warmingiana. See *Lepismium warmingianum*.

RHODANTHE, syn. ACROCLINIUM

Strawflower

ASTERACEAE/COMPOSITAE

Genus of drought-tolerant annuals, perennials, and subshrubs grown for their daisylike, papery flower heads excellent for cutting and drying. Grow in sun and in poor, very well-drained soil. Propagate by seed sown outdoors in midspring. Aphids may attack.
R. chlorocephala subsp. ***rosea***, syn. *Acroclinium roseum*, *Helipterum roseum*, illus. p.321.
R. manglesii, syn. *Helipterum manglesii*, illus. p.321.

RHODANTHEMUM

ASTERACEAE/COMPOSITAE

Genus of mat-forming, often rhizomatous perennials and subshrubs grown for their solitary, large, daisylike white flower heads, surrounded by prominent, usually green bracts. Needs full sun and moderately fertile, very well-drained soil. Propagate by seed in spring or by softwood cuttings in summer.
R. hosmariense, syn. *Chrysanthemum hosmariense*, *Pyrethropsis hosmariense*, illus. p.346.

RHODIOLA

CRASSULACEAE

Genus of perennials, some dioecious, with thick, fleshy rhizomes producing scaly brown basal leaves and stiffly erect stems that bear triangular-oval to lance-shaped, fleshy, gray-green leaves. Star-shaped flowers have prominent stamens and may be unisexual or bisexual. Grow in full sun and moderately fertile soil. Propagate by seed in spring or autumn, divide rhizomes in spring or early summer, or take leaf cuttings in summer.
R. heterodonta, syn. *Sedum heterodontum*, *S. rosea* var. *heterodontum*, illus. p.293.
R. rosea, syn. *Sedum rosea* (Roseroot). Clump-forming perennial. H and S 12in (30cm). Stems are clothed with oval to inversely lance-shaped, toothed, fleshy, glaucous leaves and, in late spring or early summer, bear dense, terminal heads of pink buds that open to small, star-shaped, greenish-, yellowish- or purplish white flowers.

Rhodocactus grandifolius. See *Pereskia grandifolia*.

RHODOCHITON

SCROPHULARIACEAE

Genus of one species of evergreen, leaf-stalk climber grown for its unusual flowers. Does best when grown as an annual. May be planted against fences and trellises or used as groundcover. Grow in sun and in any well-drained soil. Propagate by seed in early spring.
R. atrosanguineus, syn. *R. volubilis*, illus. p.211.
R. volubilis. See *R. atrosanguineus*.

RHODODENDRON

Azalea, Rhododendron

ERICACEAE

Genus of evergreen, semi-evergreen, or deciduous shrubs, ranging from a dwarf habit to a treelike stature, grown mainly for beauty of flower. Most prefer dappled shade, but a considerable number tolerates full sun, especially in cooler climates. Needs neutral to acidic soil – ideally, organic and well-drained. Shallow planting is essential, since plants are surface-rooting. Deadhead spent flowers, wherever practical, to encourage energy into growth rather than seed production. Propagate by layering or semi-ripe cuttings in late summer. Yellowing leaves are usually caused by poor drainage, excessively deep planting, or lime in soil. Weevils and powdery mildew may also cause problems. The nectar of some rhododendron flowers may cause severe discomfort if ingested. See also feature panel pp.132-4.

Rhododendrons and **azaleas**
The genus *Rhododendron* includes not only evergreen, large-leaved, and frequently large-flowered species and hybrids, but also dwarf, smaller-leaved shrubs, both evergreen and deciduous, with few-flowered clusters of usually small blooms. "Azalea" is the common name given to the deciduous species and hybrids as well as to a group of compact, evergreen shrubs derived mainly from Japanese species. They are valued for their mass of small, colorful blooms produced in late spring. Many of the evergreen azaleas (sometimes known as Belgian azaleas) may also be grown as house plants. Botanically, however, all are classified as *Rhododendron*. The flowers are usually single but may be semi-double or double, including hose-in-hose (one flower tube inside the other). Unless otherwise stated below, flowers are single and leaves are mid- to dark green and oval.
R. albrechtii. Deciduous, upright, bushy azalea. H to 10ft (3m), S 6ft (2m). Has spoon-shaped leaves clustered at branch tips and, in spring, loose clusters of 3–5 bell-shaped, green-spotted purple or pink flowers. Z6–8 H8–6.
***R.* 'America'.** Sprawling, evergreen rhododendron. H 5ft (1.5m), S 6ft (2m). Leaves are broadly oval. Produces compact clusters of bell-shaped, dark red flowers in spring. Z5–9 H9–5.
***R.* 'Angelo'.** Evergreen, bushy rhododendron. H and S to 12ft (4m). Has bold foliage and large, fragrant, bell-shaped white flowers in midsummer. Good in light woodland. Z7–9 H9–7.
***R.* 'Anna H. Hall'.** Small, bushy, evergreen rhododendron. H 3ft (1m), S 4ft (1.2m). Narrow leaves with a brown indumentum on the new foliage. Flowers are in clusters of about 15 blooms with bright pink buds that open white in midspring. Z5–8 H8–5.
***R.* 'Apricot Surprise'.** Deciduous bushy azalea. H and S 4–5ft (1.2–1.5m). Apricot flowers with a yellow throat are produced in early summer. Foliage turns a coppery shade in autumn. Z5–8 H8–5.
R. arboreum (illus. p.133). Evergreen, treelike rhododendron. H to 40ft (12m), S 10ft (3m). Undersides of broadly lance-shaped leaves are silver, fawn, or cinnamon. In spring has dense clusters of bell-shaped flowers in colors ranging from red (in the most tender form) through pink to white. Z7–9 H9–7.
R. argyrophyllum (illus. p.132). Evergreen, spreading rhododendron. H and S to 15ft (5m). Oblong leaves are silvery white on undersides. Loose bunches of bell-shaped, rich pink flowers, sometimes with deeper colored spots, are borne in spring. Is ideal for a light woodland. Z7–9 H9–7.
R. augustinii (illus. p.133). Evergreen, bushy rhododendron. H and S to 12ft (4m). Has lance-shaped to oblong, light green leaves and, in spring, bears an abundance of multi-stemmed, widely funnel-shaped, pale to deep blue or lavender flowers. Z6–9 H9–6.
R. auriculatum (illus. p.132). Evergreen, bushy, widely branching rhododendron. H and S to 6m (20ft). Has large, oblong, hairy leaves with distinct, earlike lobes at their base. In late summer bears loose bunches of 7–15 large, heavily scented, tubular to funnel-shaped white flowers. Is best in light woodland. Z6–11 H12–6.
***R.* 'Azuma-kagami'** (illus. p.132). Evergreen, compact azalea. H and S 4ft (1.2m). Bears many small, hose-in-hose, deep pink flowers in midspring. Is best in semi-shade. Z7–9 H9–7.
***R.* 'Beauty of Littleworth'** (illus. p.132). Evergreen, open, shrubby rhododendron. H and S 12ft (4m). . Bears huge, conical bunches of scented, funnel-shaped, crimson-spotted white flowers in late spring. Z7–9 H9–7.
***R.* 'Belle Heller'.** A vigorous, evergreen rhododendron. H and S 5ft (1.5m). Has dense, conical clusters of white flowers with a gold flare. Does well in sun and may rebloom in autumn in mild regions.
***R.* 'Besse Howells'.** Compact, evergreen rhododendron. H and S 4ft (1.2m). Has ruffled burgundy red flowers with a darker blotch in globe-shaped clusters in early summer.
***R.* 'Blue Diamond'.** Evergreen, upright rhododendron. H and S to 5ft (1.5m). Small, neat leaves contrast with funnel-shaped, bright blue flowers borne in mid- to late spring. Likes full sun. Z6–9 H9–1.
***R.* 'Blue Ensign'.** Medium-sized, evergreen rhododendron. H 4ft (1.2m), S 5ft (1.5m). Has pale lavender flowers with a prominent darker blotch in rounded clusters of 15 blooms in early summer.
***R.* 'Blue Peter'** (illus. p.133). Evergreen, bushy rhododendron. H and S to 12ft (4m). In early summer produces bold, open funnel-shaped, two-tone lavender-purple flowers with frilled petal edges. Z6–9 H9–6.
R. calendulaceum (Flame azalea). Deciduous, bushy azalea. H and S 6–10ft (2–3m). In early summer bears funnel-shaped scarlet, yellow, or orange flowers in bunches of 5–7. Z5–8 H9–4.
R. calophytum (illus. p.132). Evergreen, widely-branched rhododendron. H and S to 20ft (6m). Produces large, lance-shaped leaves and, in early spring, huge bunches of bell-shaped white or pale pink flowers with crimson spots. Z6–9 H9–6.
R. calostrotum (illus. p.133). Evergreen, compact rhododendron. H and S to 3ft (1m). Has attractive, blue-green leaves and, in late spring, saucer-shaped purple or scarlet flowers in clusters of 2–5. Z7–9 H9–7.
***R.* 'Catawbiense Album'.** Evergreen, rounded rhododendron. H and S to 10ft (3m). Bears glossy leaves and, in early summer, dense, rounded bunches of bell-shaped white flowers. Z4–8 H8–1.
***R.* 'Catawbiense Boursault'.** Evergreen, rounded rhododendron. H and S to 10ft (3m). Has glossy leaves. Dense, rounded bunches of bell-shaped, lilac-purple blooms are borne in early summer. Z4–8 H8–1.
***R.* 'Chionoides'.** Dense, evergreen rhododendron with narrow foliage. H 4ft (1.2m), S 5ft (1.5m). Flowers are in dome-shaped clusters, white with a yellow eye. Z5–9 H9–4.
***R.* 'Cilpinense'**, syn. *R.* x *cilpinense*. Semi-evergreen, compact rhododendron. H and S to 5ft (1.5m). Leaves are dark green and glossy. Bears masses of large, bell-shaped, blush-pink flowers, flushed deeper in bud, in early spring. Z8–9 H9–8.
R. cinnabarinum (illus. p.133). Evergreen, upright rhododendron. H and S 5–12ft (1.5–4m). Has blue-green leaves with small scales. Narrowly tubular, waxy orange to red flowers are borne in loose, drooping bunches in late spring. Z8–9 H9–8. subsp. ***xanthocodon*** (syn. *R. xanthocodon*; illus. p.133) is of open, upright habit. H and S 5–12ft (1.5–4m). Aromatic leaves are blue-green when young, maturing to midgreen. Produces loose clusters of bell-shaped, waxy yellow flowers during late spring.
***R.* 'Coccineum Speciosum'.** Deciduous, bushy azalea. H and S 1.5–2.5m (5–8ft). Produces open funnel-shaped, brilliant rich orange-red blooms in early summer. Broadly lance-shaped leaves provide good autumn color. Z9–10 H10–9.
***R.* 'Corneille'** (illus. p.132). Deciduous, bushy azalea. H and S 5–8ft (1.5–2.5m). In early summer produces fragrant, honeysuckle-like cream flowers flushed pink outside. Has attractive autumn foliage. Z5–8 H8–5.
***R.* 'Crest'**, syn. *R.* 'Hawk Crest' (illus. p.134). Evergreen rhododendron of open habit. H and S 5–12ft (1.5–4m). Has broadly lance-shaped leaves. Bell-shaped flowers are borne in loose, flat-topped bunches, and are apricot in bud, opening to clear sulfur yellow in late spring. Z7–9 H9–7.
***R.* 'Curlew'** (illus. p.134). Evergreen rhododendron of compact, spreading habit. H and S 1ft (30cm). Produces dull green leaves and, in late spring, relatively large, open funnel-shaped yellow flowers. Z7–9 H9–7.
***R.* 'Cynthia'** (illus. p.133). Vigorous, evergreen, dome-shaped rhododendron. H and S to 20ft (6m). Bears conical bunches of bell-shaped, magenta-purple flowers, marked blackish red within, in late spring. Is excellent for sun or shade. Z6–9 H9–6.
R. dauricum. Evergreen, upright rhododendron. H and S to 5ft (1.5m). Produces funnel-shaped, vivid purple flowers in loose clusters throughout winter. Green leaves turn purple-brown in cold weather. Z4–8 H8–1.
R. davidsonianum (illus. p.133). Deciduous, upright rhododendron. H 5–12ft (1.5–4m). Aromatic leaves are lance-shaped to oblong. In late spring has clusters of funnel-shaped flowers, ranging from pale pink to medium lilac-mauve. Z7–9 H9–7.
R. decorum. Evergreen, bushy rhododendron. H and S 12ft (4m). Oblong to lance-shaped leaves are mid-green above, paler beneath. Large, fragrant, funnel-shaped white or shell pink flowers, green- or pink-spotted within, are produced in early summer. Z7–9 H9–7.
R. discolor. See *R. fortunei* subsp. *discolor*.
***R.* 'Dora Amateis'.** Evergreen, compact rhododendron. H and S 2ft (60cm). Leaves are slender, glossy, and pointed. Masses of broadly funnel-shaped white flowers tinged with pink and marked with green appear in late spring. Is sun tolerant. Z5–8 H8–1.
***R.* 'Elizabeth'** (illus. p.133). Evergreen, dome-shaped rhododendron. H and S to 5ft (1.5m). Leaves are oblong. Has large, trumpet-shaped, brilliant red flowers in late spring. Good in sun or partial shade. Z7–9 H9–7.
***R.* 'Elizabeth Lockhart'.** Evergreen, dome-shaped rhododendron. H and S 2ft (60cm). Produces shiny, purple-green leaves that become darker in winter. Bell-shaped, deep pink flowers are carried in spring. Z7–9 H9–7.
***R.* 'English Roseum'.** Evergreen, vigorous, bushy rhododendron. H and S to 8ft (2.5m). Handsome leaves are dark green, paler beneath. Bears compact bunches of funnel-shaped, lilac-rose flowers in late spring.
***R.* 'Fabia'** (illus. p134). Evergreen, dome-shaped rhododendron. H and S 6ft (2m). Leaves are lance-shaped. Loose, flat clusters of funnel-shaped, orange-tinted scarlet flowers are produced in early summer. Z8–9 H9–8.
***R.* 'Fastuosum Flore Pleno'.** Evergreen, dome-shaped rhododendron. H and S 5–12ft (1.5–4m). In early summer produces loose bunches of funnel-shaped, double, rich mauve flowers with red-brown marks and wavy edges. Z5–8 H8–5.
R. fictolacteum. See *R. rex* subsp. *fictolacteum*.
***R.* 'Fireball'.** Mounded deciduous azalea with coppery red young foliage. H and S 3ft (1m). Blooms in early summer with deep orange-red flowers. Z5–9 H9–3.
***R.* 'Firefly'.** See *R.* 'Hexe'.
R. fortunei subsp. ***discolor***, syn. *R. discolor*. Evergreen, treelike rhododendron. H and S to 25ft (8m). Leaves are oblong to oval. Bears fragrant, funnel-shaped pink flowers that give a magnificent display in midsummer. Is ideal in a light woodland. Z5–9 H9–5.
***R.* 'Freya'** (illus. p.134). Deciduous azalea of compact, shrubby habit. H and S 5ft (1.5m). Fragrant, funnel-shaped, pink-flushed, orange-salmon flowers appear from late spring to early summer. Z5–8 H8–5.
***R.* 'Frome'** (illus. p.134). Deciduous azalea of shrubby habit. H and S to 5ft (1.5m). In spring bears trumpet-shaped, saffron yellow flowers, overlaid red in throats; petals are frilled and wavy-margined. Z5–8 H8–5.
R. fulvum (illus. p.132). Evergreen,

RHODODENDRON

bushy rhododendron. H and S 5–12ft (1.5–4m). Oblong to oval, polished, deep green leaves are brown-felted beneath. In early spring has loose bunches of bell-shaped, red-blotched pink flowers that fade to white. Z7–9 H9–7.

***R.* 'George Reynolds'** (illus. p.134). Deciduous, bushy azalea. H and S to 6ft (2m). Large, funnel-shaped yellow flowers, flushed pink in bud, are borne with or before the leaves in spring. Z5–8 H8–5.

***R.* 'Gibraltar'.** Vigorous, deciduous azalea. Grows well in full sun. H and S 5ft (1.5m). Dark orange buds open to give flame-orange flowers with a yellow flare and frilled petals. Z5–8 H8–5.

***R.* 'Gloria Mundi'** (illus. p.134). Deciduous, twiggy azalea. H and S to 6ft (2m). Produces fragrant, honeysuckle-like, yellow-flared orange flowers with frilled margins in early summer. Z5–8 H8–5.

***R.* 'Glory of Littleworth'** (illus. p.134). Evergreen or semi-evergreen, bushy hybrid between a rhododendron and an azalea. H and S 5ft (1.5m). Compact bunches of fragrant, bell-shaped, orange-marked, creamy white flowers are borne abundantly in late spring and early summer. Is not easy to cultivate. Z7–9 H9–7.

***R.* 'Golden Lights'.** Upright, deciduous azalea. H and S 6ft (2m). Has fragrant gold to bright yellow flowers in midspring. Z3–6 H6–1.

***R.* 'Gomer Waterer'.** Evergreen, compact rhododendron. H and S 5–12ft (1.5–4m). Leaves are curved back at margins. Bell-shaped flowers, borne in dense bunches in early summer, are white flushed mauve, each with a basal mustard blotch. Likes sun or partial shade. Z5–8 H8–1.

***R.* 'Hatsugiri'** (illus. p.133). Evergreen, compact azalea. H and S 2ft (60cm). Has small, but very numerous, funnel-shaped, bright crimson-purple flowers in spring. Flowers very reliably. Z7–9 H9–7.

***R.* 'Hawk Crest'.** See *R.* 'Crest'.

***R.* 'Hinode-giri'** (illus. p.133). Evergreen, compact azalea. H and S 5ft (1.5m). Funnel-shaped, bright crimson flowers are small but produced in abundance in late spring. Likes sun or light shade. Z6–9 H9–6.

***R.* 'Hinomayo'** (illus. p.133). Evergreen, compact azalea. H and S 5ft (1.5m). Small, funnel-shaped, clear pink flowers are produced in great abundance in spring. Likes sun or light shade. Z7–9 H9–7.

R. hippophaeoides (illus. p.133). Evergreen, erect rhododendron. H and S 5ft (1.5m). Narrowly lance-shaped, aromatic leaves are gray-green. Has small, funnel-shaped lavender or lilac flowers in spring. Tolerates wet but not stagnant soil. Z5–8 H8–5.

***R.* 'Homebush'** (illus. p.133). Deciduous, compact azalea. H and S 5ft (1.5m). In late spring bears tight, rounded heads of trumpet-shaped, semi-double, rose-purple flowers with paler shading. Z5–8 H8–5.

***R.* 'Hotei'.** Evergreen, rhododendron of neat, compact habit. H and S 5–8ft (1.5–2.5m). Has excellent foliage. Large, funnel-shaped, deep yellow flowers are freely produced in late spring. Z7–9 H9–7.

R. impeditum. Slow-growing, evergreen rhododendron. H and S to 2ft (60cm). Aromatic leaves are gray-green.Funnel-shaped, purplish blue flowers appear in spring. Is ideal for a rock garden. Z5–8 H8–1.

***R.* 'Irohayama'** (illus. p.133). Evergreen, compact azalea. H and S to 5ft (1.5m). Has abundant, small, funnel-shaped white flowers with pale lavender margins and faint brown eyes in spring. Does well in light shade. Z7–9 H9–7.

***R.* 'John Cairns'** (illus. p.133). Evergreen, upright, compact azalea. H and S 5–6ft (1.5–2m). Bears abundant funnel-shaped, orange-red flowers in spring. Grows reliably and consistently in sun or semi-shade. Z6–9 H9–6.

R. kaempferi (illus. p.133). Semi-evergreen, erect, loosely branched azalea. H and S 5–8ft (1.5–2.5m). Leaves are lance-shaped. Has an abundance of funnel-shaped flowers in various shades of orange or red in late spring and early summer. Z6–9 H9–6.

***R.* 'Kilimanjaro'.** Evergreen, bushy rhododendron. H and S 5–12ft (1.5–4m). Bears broadly lance-shaped leaves. Produces large, rounded bunches of funnel- to bell-shaped, wavy-edged, maroon-red flowers spotted chocolate within in late spring and early summer. Z7–9 H9–7.

***R.* 'Kirin'** (illus. p.132). Evergreen, compact azalea. H and S to 5ft (1.5m). In spring has numerous hose-in-hose flowers that are deep rose shaded delicate silvery rose. Z7–9 H9–7.

R. kiusianum. Semi-evergreen azalea of compact habit. H and S to 2ft (60cm). Leaves are narrowly oval. Produces clusters of 2–5 funnel-shaped flowers, usually lilac-rose or mauve-purple, in late spring. Prefers full sun. Z7–9 H9–7.

***R.* 'Klondyke'.** Mounded, deciduous azalea that grows best in full sun. H and S 6ft (2m). Young foliage has a copper tint, and buds are flushed red. Flowers are orange-gold with a red reverse and in large clusters. Z5–8 H8–4.

***R.* 'Lady Clementine Mitford'.** Evergreen, rounded, dense rhododendron. H and S 12ft (4m). Has broadly oval, glossy, dark green leaves that are silvery when young and, in late spring and early summer, bold bunches of tubular- to bell-shaped flowers, peach-pink fading to white in the center, with V-shaped pink, green, and brown marks within. Z7–9 H9–7.

***R.* 'Lees Dark Purple'.** An open, rounded, evergreen rhododendron with slightly wavy foliage. H 6ft (2m), S 5ft (1.5m). Flowers are royal purple with brownish markings inside, in dense rounded clusters. May rebloom in autumn in warmer climates. Z5–7 H7–5.

***R.* 'Loderi King George'.** Large, evergreen rhododendron of open habit. H and S 12ft (4m). Has large leaves. In late spring and early summer, pale pink buds open to huge clusters of funnel-shaped, fragrant, pure white flowers, 3½–4½in (9–11cm) long, with subtle green marks in the throats. Z7–9 H9–7.

R. lutescens (illus. p.133). Semi-evergreen, upright rhododendron. H and S 5–10ft (1.5–3m). Has oval to lance-shaped leaves that are bronze-red when young. In early spring bears funnel-shaped, primrose yellow flowers. Elegant and delicate, it is effective in a light woodland. Z7–9 H9–7.

R. luteum (illus. p.134). Open deciduous azalea. H and S 5–8ft (1.5–2.5m). Leaves are oblong to lance-shaped. Has very fragrant, bold yellow, funnel-shaped blooms in spring. Autumn foliage is rich and colorful. Z7–9 H9–7.

R. macabeanum (illus. p.134). Evergreen, treelike rhododendron. H and S up to 45ft (13.5m). Has bold, broadly oval leaves, dark green above, gray-felted beneath, and, in early spring, large bunches of bell-shaped, yellow flowers, blotched purple within. Z8–11 H12–10.

***R.* 'May Day'** (illus. p.133). Evergreen, spreading rhododendron. H and S to 5ft (1.5m). Leaves are fresh green above, whitish-felted beneath. Has masses of loose bunches of long-lasting, funnel-shaped scarlet flowers in late spring; petal-like calyces match the flower color. Z7–9 H9–7.

***R.* 'Medway'** (illus. p.134). Deciduous, bushy, open azalea. H and S 5–8ft (1.5–2.5m). In late spring has large, trumpet-shaped, pale pink flowers with darker edges and orange-flashed throats; petal edges are frilled. Z5–8 H8–5.

***R.* 'Moonshine Crescent'** (illus. p.134). Evergreen, rounded to upright rhododendron. H 6–8ft (2–2.5m), S 6ft (2m). In late spring produces compact clusters of bell-shaped yellow flowers. Leaves are oblong to oval and dark green. Z6–8 H8–6.

R. moupinense. Evergreen, rounded, compact rhododendron. H and S to 5ft (1.5m). Produces funnel-shaped, pink blooms in loose bunches in late winter and early spring. Leaves are glossy, dark green above, paler beneath. Is best grown in a sheltered situation to reduce risk of frosted flowers. Z7–9 H9–7.

***R.* 'Mrs G.W. Leak'** (illus. p.132). Evergreen, upright, compact rhododendron. H and S 12ft (4m). In late spring bears compact, conical bunches of funnel-shaped pink flowers with black-brown and crimson marks within. Z7–9 H9–7.

R. nakaharae. Evergreen, mound-forming azalea. H and S 2ft (60cm). Shoots and oblong to oval leaves are densely hairy. Funnel-shaped, dark brick red flowers are borne in small clusters. Is valuable for midsummer flowering and is ideal for a rock garden. Z5–8 H8–5.

***R.* 'Nancy Waterer'.** Deciduous, twiggy azalea. H and S 5–8ft (1.5–2.5m). Has large, long-tubed and honeysuckle-like, brilliant golden yellow flowers in early summer. Is ideal in a light woodland or full sun. Z5–8 H8–5.

***R.* 'Narcissiflorum'** (illus. p.134). Vigorous, deciduous, compact azalea. H and S 5–8ft (1.5–2.5m). Sweetly scented, hose-in-hose, pale yellow flowers, darker outside and in center, are borne in late spring or early summer. Autumn foliage is bronze. Z5–8 H8–5.

***R.* Nobleanum Group** (illus. p.132). Evergreen, upright shrub or treelike rhododendron. H and S to 15ft (5m). Bears large, compact bunches of broadly funnel-shaped, rose-red, pink, or white flowers in winter or early spring. Will flower for long periods in mild weather; is best in a sheltered position. Z7–9 H9–7.

***R.* 'Norma'.** Vigorous, deciduous, compact azalea. H and S to 5ft (1.5m). Bears masses of hose-in-hose, rose-red flowers with a salmon glow in spring. Grows well in sun or light shade. Z6–9 H9–6.

***R.* Northern Lights Group.** A strain of deciduous azaleas that form upright, rounded shrubs. H 5ft (1.5m), S 4ft (1.2m). Have dense clusters of funnel-shaped flowers in pastel colors. Z3–7 H7–1.

***R.* 'Nova Zembla'.** Vigorous, evergreen, upright rhododendron. H and S 5–12ft (1.5–4m). Has funnel-shaped, dark red flowers in closely set bunches from late spring to early summer. Z5–8 H8–1.

R. occidentale (illus. p.132). Bushy, deciduous, azalea. H and S 5–8ft (1.5–2.5m). Glossy leaves turn yellow or orange in autumn. Bears fragrant, funnel-shaped white or pale pink flowers, each with a basal, yellow-orange blotch, in early to midsummer. Z7–9 H9–7.

***R.* 'Olga Mezzit'.** Spreading, evergreen, small-leaved rhododendron. H 4ft (1.2m), S 5–6ft (1.5–2m). Has small clusters of pinkish purple flowers in early summer. Foliage turns light red in cold weather. Z4–8 H8–1.

R. orbiculare (illus. p.132). Evergreen rhododendron of compact habit. H and S to 10ft (3m). Produces rounded, bright green leaves. Bell-shaped, rose-pink flowers are borne in loose bunches in late spring. Z7–9 H9–7.

***R.* 'Orchid Lights'.** Upright, deciduous azalea. H 6ft (2m) S 5ft (1.5m). Has tubular orchid-pink flowers in dense clusters in early summer. Z3–7 H7–1.

R. oreotrephes (illus. p.133). Deciduous, upright shrub or treelike rhododendron. H and S to 15ft (5m). Has attractive, scaly, gray-green foliage. In spring bears loose bunches of 3–10 broadly funnel-shaped flowers, usually mauve or purple but variable, often with crimson spots. Z7–9 H9–7.

***R.* 'Palestrina'** (illus. p.132). Evergreen or semi-evergreen, compact, free-flowering azalea. H and S to 4ft (1.2m). Has large, open funnel-shaped white flowers with faint green marks in late spring. Grows well in light shade. Z5–8 H8–3.

***R.* 'Percy Wiseman'** (illus. p.132). Evergreen rhododendron with a domed, compact habit. H and S to 6ft (2m). In late spring produces open funnel-shaped, peach-yellow flowers that fade to white. Z6–9 H9–6.
***R.* 'Peter John Mezitt'**, syn. *R.* 'P.J.M.' Evergreen, compact rhododendron. H and S up to 5ft (1.5m). Aromatic leaves are small, dark green in summer and bronze-purple in winter. Bears frost-resistant, funnel-shaped, lavender-pink flowers in early spring. Is good in full sun. Z4–8 H8–1.
***R.* 'Pink Pearl'** (illus. p.133). Vigorous, evergreen, upright, open rhododendron. H and S 12ft (4m) or more. Tall bunches of open funnel-shaped pink flowers give a spectacular display in late spring. Z7–9 H9–7.
***R.* 'P.J.M.'** See *R.* 'Peter John Mezitt'.
***R.* 'President Roosevelt'** (illus. p133). Slow-growing, evergreen, open, weakly branched rhododendron. H and S to 6ft (2m). Leaves are yellow-variegated but have a tendency to revert to plain green. Open bell-shaped, pale pink flowers, lighter toward centers and frilled at margins, appear from mid- to late spring. Z7–9 H9–7.
***R.* 'Purple Gem'.** Rounded, dwarf, evergreen rhododendron with new foliage tinged blue. H 2ft (60cm), S 4ft (1.2m). Has small clusters of open funnel-shaped, light purple flowers. Good on a rock garden. Z5–8 H8–5.
***R.* 'Purple Splendour'.** Evergreen, bushy rhododendron. H and S to 10ft (3m). Has well-formed bunches of open funnel-shaped, rich royal purple flowers, with prominent black marks in throats, in late spring or early summer. Z6–9 H9–6.
***R.* 'Queen Elizabeth II'** (illus. p.133). Evergreen, bushy rhododendron. H and S 5–12ft (1.5–4m). Bears funnel-shaped, greenish yellow flowers in loose bunches in late spring. Leaves are narrowly oval or lance-shaped, glossy and midgreen above, paler beneath. Z7–9 H9–7.
R. racemosum (illus. p.132). Evergreen, upright, stiffly branched rhododendron. H and S to 8ft (2.5m). Has clusters of widely funnel-shaped, bright pink flowers carried along the stems in spring. Small, broadly oval, aromatic leaves are dull green above, gray-green below. Z6 9 H9 6.
***R.* 'Ramapo'.** Similar to 'Purple Gem' but slightly smaller. H 18in (45cm), S 4ft (1.2m). New foliage is a blue-gray turning a metallic blue in winter. Flowers are violet-purple. It does best in sun. Z4–8 H8–1.
R. rex. Vigorous, evergreen, upright shrub or treelike rhododendron. H and S 12ft (4m) or more. Leaves are pale buff-felted beneath. Pink or white flowers each have a crimson blotch and a spotted throat. Z8–10 H10–8. subsp. ***fictolacteum*** (syn. *R. fictolacteum*; illus. p.132), H to 45ft (13.5m), has large leaves, green above, brown-felted beneath. Bears bunches of bell-shaped white flowers in spring, each with a maroon blotch and often a spotted throat. Z8–11 H12–8.
***R.* 'Rosalind'** (illus. p.133). Vigorous, evergreen rhododendron of open-branched habit. H and S 12ft (4m). Leaves are dull green. Bears broadly funnel-shaped pink flowers in loose bunches in spring. Z7–9 H9–7.
***R.* 'Roseum Elegans'.** Vigorous, evergreen, rounded rhododendron. H and S 8ft (2.5m) or more. Foliage is bold and glossy, deep green. In early summer, bears rounded bunches of broadly funnel-shaped, reddish purple flowers, each marked with yellow-brown. Z5–9 H9–4.
***R.* 'Scarlet Wonder'.** Small, compact evergreen rhododendron. H 2ft (60cm), S 4ft (1.2m). Has loose clusters of ruby red, trumpet-shaped flowers with frilly margins. Z5–8 H8–1.
R. schlippenbachii (illus. p.132). Deciduous, rounded, open azalea. H and S 8ft (2.5m). Spoon-shaped leaves are in whorls at branch ends. Bears loose bunches of 3–6 saucer-shaped pink flowers in midspring. Good in a light woodland. Z5–8 H8–5.
***R.* 'Scintillation'.** Vigorous, evergreen rhododendron, with long, shiny, waxy foliage. H 5ft (1.5m), S 6ft (2m). Has large clusters of scented, pastel pink flowers with golden bronze marking in the throat. Z5–9 H9–5.
***R.* 'Seta'** (illus. p.132). Evergreen, erect rhododendron. H 5ft (1.5m), S 3–5ft (1–1.5m). In early spring bears loose bunches of tubular, shiny, vivid pink-and-white-striped flowers fading to white at bases. Z7–9 H9–7.
***R.* 'Seven Stars'** (illus. p.132). Vigorous, evergreen, upright, dense rhododendron. H and S 6–10ft (2–3m). Has yellowish green foliage and, in spring, masses of bunches of large, bell-shaped, wavy-margined white flowers, flushed with appleblossom pink, pink in bud. Z7–9 H9–7.
***R.* 'Silver Moon'** (illus. p.132). Evergreen azalea of broad, spreading habit. H and S 5–8ft (1.5–2.5m). Funnel-shaped white flowers, with pale green-blotched throats and frilled petal edges, appear in spring. Grows best in partial shade. Z7–9 H9–7.
R. souliei (illus. p.132). Evergreen, open rhododendron. H and S 5–12ft (1.5–4m). Has rounded leaves and, in late spring, saucer-shaped, soft pink flowers. Grows best in areas of low rainfall. Z7–9 H9–7.
***R.* 'Spek's Orange'.** Deciduous, bushy azalea. H and S to 8ft (2.5m). In late spring carries bold bunches of large, slender-tubed blooms that are bright reddish orange with greenish marks within. Z5–8 H8–5.
***R.* 'Spicy Lights'.** Upright, deciduous azalea. H 5ft (1.5m), S 4ft (1.2m). Has loose clusters of orange-red flowers in early summer. Z4–7 H7–1.
***R.* 'Strawberry Ice'** (illus. p.132). Deciduous, bushy azalea. H and S 5–8ft (1.5–2.5m). Bears trumpet-shaped flowers, deep pink in bud, opening flesh pink and mottled deeper pink at petal edges with deep yellow-marked throats, in late spring. Z4–8 H8–1.
***R.* 'Surprise'.** Evergreen, dense azalea. H and S to 5ft (1.5m). Has abundant, small, funnel-shaped, light orange-red flowers in midspring. Looks effective when mass planted and is ideal in light shade or full sun. Z7–9 H9–7.
***R.* 'Susan'** (illus. p.133). Close-growing, evergreen rhododendron. H and S 5–12ft (1.5–4m). Handsome foliage is glossy, dark green. In spring bears large bunches of open funnel-shaped flowers in 2 shades of blue-mauve, spotted purple within. Z6–9 H9–6.
R. sutchuenense (illus. p.132). Evergreen, spreading shrub or treelike rhododendron. H and S to 5m (16ft). Has large leaves and, in early spring, large bunches of broadly funnel-shaped pink flowers, spotted deeper within. Good in a light woodland. Z6–9 H9–6.
***R.* 'Temple Belle'.** Evergreen rhododendron of neat, compact habit. H and S 5–8ft (1.5–2.5m). Loose bunches of bell-shaped, clear pink flowers are produced in spring. Rounded leaves are dark green above, gray-green beneath. Z8–9 H9–8.
R. thomsonii (illus. p.133). Evergreen, rounded rhododendron of open habit. H and S to 18ft (5.5m). Leaves are waxy, dark green above, whiter beneath. Peeling, fawn-colored bark contrasts well with bell-shaped, waxy red flowers in spring. Z8–12 H12–10.
***R.* 'Vulcan'.** An evergreen rhododendron with pointed leaves that makes a rounded plant. H and S 5ft (1.5m). Bright red flowers with wavy margins are in dome-shaped clusters in early summer. Z5–8 H8–5.
***R.* 'Vuyk's Scarlet'** (illus. p.133). Evergreen, compact azalea. H and S to 2ft (60cm). In spring bears an abundance of relatively large, open funnel-shaped, brilliant red flowers with wavy petals that completely cover the glossy foliage. Z6–9 H9–5.
R. wardii (illus. p.133). Evergreen, compact rhododendron. H and S 5–12ft (1.5–4m). Leaves are rounded. In late spring bears loose bunches of saucer-shaped, clear yellow flowers with basal crimson blotches. Z7–9 H9–7.
***R.* 'White Lights'.** Hardy, deciduous azalea forming a mounded bush. H 5ft (1.5m), S 4ft (1.2m). Fragrant flowers are very pale pink to white with a yellow center. Z3–8 H8–1.
R. williamsianum (illus. p.132). Evergreen rhododendron of compact, spreading habit. H and S 5ft (1.5m). Young leaves are bronze, maturing to midgreen. Has loosely clustered, bell-shaped pink flowers in spring. Is ideal for a small garden. Z7–9 H9–7.
***R.* 'Woodcock'.** Evergreen, compact, spreading rhododendron. H and S 5–8ft (1.5–2.5m). Has semi-glossy, dark green leaves and, in spring, masses of loose bunches of funnel-shaped, rose-red flowers. Z7–9 H9–7.
R. xanthocodon. See *R. cinnabarinum* subsp. *xanthocodon.*
R. yakushimanum (illus. p.132). Evergreen, dome-shaped rhododendron of neat, compact habit. H 3ft (1m), S 5ft (1.5m). Leaves are broadly oval, silvery at first, maturing to deepest green, and brown-felted beneath. In late spring has open funnel-shaped pink flowers that fade to near white and are flecked green within. Z5–9 H9–5.
***R.* 'Yellow Hammer'** (illus. p.134). Evergreen, erect, bushy rhododendron. H and S to 6ft (2m). Bears abundant clusters of tubular, bright yellow flowers in spring; frequently flowers again in autumn. Z6–9 H9–6.
R. yunnanense (illus. p.132). Semi-evergreen, open rhododendron. H and S 5–12ft (1.5–4m). Has aromatic, gray-green leaves and masses of butterfly-like, pale pink or white flowers with blotched throats in spring. Z6–9 H9–6.

RHODOHYPOXIS

HYPOXIDACEAE

Genus of dwarf, spring- to summer-flowering, tuberous perennials grown for their pink, red, or white flowers, each consisting of 6 petals that meet at the center, so the flower has no eye. Needs full sun, sandy, peaty soil, plenty of moisture in summer, and to be kept fairly dry while dormant. Propagate in spring by seed or offsets.
***R.* 'Albrighton'** illus. p.380.
R. baurii. Spring- and early summer-flowering, tuberous perennial. H 2–4in (5–10cm), S 1–2in (2.5–5cm). Has an erect, basal tuft of narrowly lance-shaped, hairy leaves. Bears a succession of erect, flattish white, pale pink, or red flowers, ¾in (2cm) across, on slender stems. Z9-10 H10–9. var. ***platypetala*** has 1in (2.5cm) wide, white or very pale pink flowers.
***R.* 'Douglas'** illus. p.380.
***R.* 'Margaret Rose'** illus. p.376.

RHODOLEIA

HAMAMELIDACEAE

Genus of evergreen, mainly spring-flowering trees grown for their foliage and flowers. Needs full light or partial shade and organic, well-drained, neutral to acidic soil. Water potted specimens freely and sparingly when not in full growth. Tolerates pruning if necessary. Propagate by semi-ripe cuttings in summer or by seed when ripe, in autumn or in spring.
R. championii. Evergreen, bushy tree. H and S 12–25ft (4–8m). Elliptic to oval, bright green leaves, each to 3½in (9cm) long, are borne near the shoot tips. Clusters of tiny flowers, surrounded by petal-like pink bracts, appear in spring. Z11 H12–10.

RHODOPHIALA

AMARYLLIDACEAE

Genus of bulbs grown for their large, funnel-shaped flowers. Needs full sun or partial shade and well-drained soil. Keep dormant bulbs dry in winter. Propagate by seed in spring or by offsets in spring (for summer-flowering species).

R. advena, syn. *Hippeastrum advenum*, illus. p.421.

RHODOTHAMNUS

ERICACEAE

Genus of one species of evergreen, semi-prostrate, open shrub grown for its flowers. Is suitable for rock gardens. Needs sun and organic, well-drained, acidic soil. Propagate by seed in spring or by semi-ripe cuttings in summer.
R. chamaecistus illus. p.352.

RHODOTYPOS

ROSACEAE

Genus of one species of deciduous shrub grown for its flowers. Needs sun or semi-shade and moist but well-drained, fertile soil. On established plants, cut some older shoots back or to ground level after flowering,. Propagate by softwood cuttings in summer or by seed in autumn.
R. kerrioides. See *R. scandens.*
R. scandens, syn. *R. kerrioides*, illus. p.158.

Rhoeo discolor. See *Tradescantia spathacea.*
Rhoeo spathacea. See *Tradescantia spathacea.*

RHOICISSUS

VITACEAE

Genus of evergreen, tendril climbers grown for their handsome foliage. Bears inconspicuous flowers intermittently during the year. Grow in any fertile, well-drained soil with light shade in summer. Water regularly, less in cold weather. Provide support. Remove crowded stems when necessary or in early spring. Propagate by seed in spring or by semi-ripe cuttings in summer.
R. capensis (Cape grape). Vigorous, evergreen, tendril climber. H and S to 15ft (5m). Rounded, toothed, lustrous, mid- to deep green leaves, to 8in (20cm) wide, have deeply rounded, heart-shaped bases. Z11 H12–10.
R. rhombifolia. See *Cissus rhombifolia.*
R. rhomboidea. See *Cissus rhombifolia.*

RHOMBOPHYLLUM

AIZOACEAE

Genus of mat-forming succulents with dense, basal rosettes of linear or semi-cylindrical leaves, each expanded toward the middle or tip; leaf tip is reflexed or incurved. Needs sun and very well-drained soil. Propagate by seed or stem cuttings in spring or summer.
R. rhomboideum illus. p.478.

RHUS

Sumac

ANACARDIACEAE

Genus of deciduous trees, shrubs, and scrambling climbers grown for their divided, ashlike foliage, autumn color, and, in some species, showy fruit clusters. Requires sun and well-drained soil. Propagate by semi-ripe cuttings in summer, by seed in autumn, or by root cuttings in winter. May be attacked by coral spot fungus. All parts of *R. verniciflua* are highly toxic if ingested; contact with its foliage, and that of a number of related species, including *R. succedanea*, may aggravate skin allergies.
R. aromatica (Fragrant sumac). Deciduous, bushy shrub. H 3ft (1m), S 5ft (1.5m). Deep green leaves, each composed of 3 oval leaflets, turn orange or reddish purple in autumn. Tiny yellow flowers are borne in mid-spring before foliage, followed by spherical red fruits. Z2–8 H8–1.
R. copallina (Dwarf sumac). Deciduous, upright shrub. H and S 3–5ft (1–1.5m), or more. Has glossy, dark green leaves, with numerous lance-shaped leaflets, that turn red-purple in autumn. Minute, greenish yellow flowers, borne in dense clusters from mid to late summer, develop into narrowly egg-shaped, bright red fruits. Z5–9 H9–4.
R. cotinoides. See *Cotinus obovatus.*
R. cotinus. See *Cotinus coggygria.*
R. glabra illus. p.143.
R. hirta. See. *R. typhina* **'Laciniata'** see. *R. typhina* 'Dissecta'.
R. potaninii. Deciduous, round-headed tree. H 40ft (12m), S 25ft (8m). Has large, dark green leaves with usually 7–11 oval leaflets that turn red in autumn. In summer produces dense clusters of tiny, yellow-green flowers. Female flower clusters develop into tiny, spherical black or brownish fruits. Z5–9 H9–5.
R. succedanea, syn. *Toxicodendron succedaneum* (Wax tree). Deciduous, spreading tree. H and S 30ft (10m). Large, glossy, dark green leaves, each made up of 9–15 oval leaflets, turn red in autumn. Has dense clusters of tiny, yellow-green flowers in summer. Female flowers develop into tiny, spherical black or brownish fruits. Z5–8 H8–5.
R. trichocarpa illus. p.95.
R. typhina, syn. *R. hirta* (Staghorn sumac). Deciduous, spreading, suckering, open shrub or tree. H 15ft (5m), S 20ft (6m). Velvety shoots are clothed in dark green leaves with oblong leaflets. Produces minute, greenish white flowers from mid- to late summer. Leaves become brilliant orange-red in autumn, accompanying clusters of spherical, deep red fruits on female plants. Z3–8 H8–1. **'Dissecta'** (syn. *R. hirta* 'Laciniata', *R.t.* 'Laciniata' of gardens), illus. p.124. **'Laciniata'** of gardens see *R.t.* 'Dissecta'.
R. verniciflua, syn. *Toxicodendron verniciflaum* (Varnish tree). Deciduous, spreading tree. H 50ft (15m), S 30ft (10m). Large, glossy, bright green leaves with 7–13 oval leaflets redden in autumn. Bears dense clusters of tiny, yellow-green flowers in summer, followed by berrylike, brownish yellow fruits. Contact with the sap may severely irritate the skin. Z6–9 H9–6.

Rhynchelytrum repens. See *Melinis repens.*
Rhynchelytrum roseum. See *Melinis repens.*

RIBES

Currant

GROSSULARIACEAE/SAXIFRAGACEAE

Genus of deciduous or evergreen, mainly spring-flowering shrubs grown for their edible fruits (currants and gooseberries) or their flowers. Needs full sun and well-drained, fertile soil, but *R. laurifolium* tolerates shade. After flowering cut out some older shoots and, in winter or early spring, prune straggly old plants hard. Propagate deciduous species by hardwood cuttings in winter, evergreens by semi-ripe cuttings in summer. Aphids attack young foliage.
R. alpinum (Alpine currant). Deciduous, mounded shrub often used for hedges. H 2ft (60cm), S 3ft (1m). Erect racemes of bell-shaped yellow flowers appear in spring, with male and female flowers on separate plants. Female plants have dark red, spherical fruit in late summer. Z2–6 H6–1.
R. aureum of gardens. See *R. odoratum.*
R. laurifolium illus. p.175.
R. odoratum, syn. *R. aureum* of gardens (Buffalo currant). Deciduous, upright shrub. H and S 6ft (2m). Clusters of clove-scented, tubular, golden yellow flowers are borne from mid- to late spring, followed by rounded, purple fruits. Rounded, 3-lobed, bright green leaves turn red and purple in autumn. Z5–8 H8–5.
R. sanguineum (Flowering currant). **'Brocklebankii'** illus. p.155. **'King Edward VII'** is a deciduous, upright, compact shrub. H and S 6ft (2m). Small, tubular, deep reddish pink flowers are freely borne amid rounded, 3–5-lobed, aromatic, dark green leaves from mid- to late spring and are sometimes succeeded by spherical black fruits with a white bloom. Is useful for hedging. Z6–8 H8–6. **'Pulborough Scarlet'** illus. p.130. **'Tydeman's White'**, H and S 8ft (2.5m), is less compact, with white flowers.
R. speciosum (Fuchsia-flowered currant). Deciduous, bushy, spiny shrub. H and S 6ft (2m). Slender, drooping, tubular red flowers with long red stamens open mid- to late spring. Fruits are spherical and red. Has red young shoots and oval, 3–5-lobed, glossy, bright green leaves. Attractive trained on a wall. Z7–9 H9–7.

RICHEA

EPACRIDACEAE

Genus of evergreen, summer-flowering shrubs grown for their foliage and densely clustered flowers. Needs sun or semi-shade and moist, peaty, neutral to acidic soil. Propagate by semi-ripe cuttings in summer or by seed in autumn.
R. scoparia. Evergreen, upright shrub. H and S 6ft (2m). Shoots are covered with narrowly lance-shaped, sharp-pointed, dark green leaves. Bears dense, upright spikes of small, egg-shaped pink, white, orange, or maroon flowers in early summer. Z9–10 H10–9.

RICINUS

EUPHORBIACEAE

Genus of one species of fast-growing, evergreen, treelike shrub grown for its foliage. In cool climates is grown as an annual. Needs sun and fertile to rich, well-drained soil. May require support in exposed areas. Propagate by seed sown under cover in early spring. All parts of *R. communis*, particularly the seeds, are highly toxic if ingested; contact with the foliage may aggravate skin allergies.
R. communis illus. p.335. **'Impala'** illus. p.330.

ROBINIA

LEGUMINOSAE/PAPILIONACEAE

Genus of deciduous, mainly summer-flowering trees and shrubs grown for their foliage and clusters of pealike flowers. Is useful for poor, dry soil. Needs a sunny position. Grows in any but waterlogged soil. Branches are brittle and may be damaged by strong winds. Propagate by seed or suckers in autumn or by root cuttings in winter. All parts may cause severe discomfort if ingested. Borers may be a problem.
R. x ambigua **'Decaisneana'.** Deciduous, spreading tree. H 50ft (15m), S 30ft (10m). Dark green leaves have numerous oval leaflets. Long, hanging clusters of pealike pink flowers are borne in early summer. Z4–11 H12–1.
R. hispida illus. p.141. var. ***kelseyi*** (syn. *R. kelseyi*) is a deciduous, spreading, open shrub. H 8ft (2.5m), S 12ft (4m). Clusters of pealike, rose-pink flowers open in late spring or early summer, followed by pendent red seed pods. Dark green leaves consist of 9 or 11 oval leaflets. Z6–11 H12–6.
R. kelseyi. See *R. hispida* var. *kelseyi.*
R. pseudoacacia (False acacia, Locust). Fast-growing, deciduous, spreading tree. H 80ft (25m), S 50ft (15m). Dark green leaves consist of 11–23 oval leaflets. Dense, drooping clusters of fragrant, pealike white flowers are borne in late spring and early summer. Z4–9 H9–3. **'Frisia'** illus. p.81. **'Umbraculifera'** (Mophead black locust), H and S 20ft (6m), rarely produces a rounded, dense flower head. Z4–9 H9–1.

Rochea coccinea. See *Crassula coccinea.*

RODGERSIA

SAXIFRAGACEAE

Genus of summer-flowering, rhizomatous perennials. Is ideal for pondsides. Grows in sun or semi-shade and in soil that is moist; requires shelter from strong winds, which may damage foliage. Propagate by division in spring or by seed in autumn.

R. aesculifolia illus. p.241.

***R. pinnata* 'Superba'.** Clump-forming, rhizomatous perennial. H 3–4ft (1–1.2m), S 2½ft (75cm). Leaves are bronze-tinged, emerald green, with 5–9 narrowly oval leaflets. Long, much-branched, dense panicles of star-shaped, bright pink flowers appear in midsummer. Z3–7 H7–1.

R. podophylla illus. p.240.

R. sambucifolia illus. p.240.

ROMNEYA

Tree poppy

PAPAVERACEAE

Genus of summer-flowering, woody-based perennials and deciduous sub-shrubs. Requires a warm, sunny position and deep, well-drained soil. Is difficult to establish, resents being moved, and, where marginally hardy, roots will need protection in winter. Once established, may spread rapidly. Propagate by softwood cuttings of basal shoots in early spring, by seed in autumn (transplanting seedlings without disturbing rootballs) or by root cuttings in winter.

R. coulteri illus. p.226.

***R.* 'White Cloud'.** Vigorous, bushy, woody-based perennial. H and S 3ft (1m). Throughout summer produces large, slightly fragrant, shallowly cup-shaped white flowers with prominent golden stamens. Leaves are oval, deeply lobed, and gray. Z8–10 H9–2.

ROMULEA

IRIDACEAE

Genus of crocuslike corms grown for their funnel-shaped flowers. Needs full light and well-drained, sandy soil. Water freely during the growing period. Most species die down in summer and then need warmth and dryness. *R. macowanii*, however, is dormant in winter. Propagate by seed in autumn, or in spring for *R. macowanii*.

R. bulbocodioides of gardens. See *R. flava*.

R. bulbocodium illus. p.431.

R. flava, syn. *R. bulbocodioides* of gardens. Early spring-flowering corm. H to 4in (10cm), S 1–2in (2.5–5cm). Has a threadlike, erect, basal leaf and 1–5 upright, widely funnel-shaped, usually yellow flowers, ¾–1½in (2–4cm) across, with deeper yellow centers.

R. longituba. See *R. macowanii* var. *alticola*.

R. macowanii var. ***alticola***, syn. *R. longituba*. Summer-flowering corm. H and S ½–¾in (1–2cm). Leaves are threadlike, erect, and basal. Produces 1–3 upright, yellow flowers, each 1¼in (3cm) across, expanding to become a wide funnel shape. Z8–10 H10–8.

R. sabulosa. Early spring-flowering corm. H 2–6in (5–15cm), S 1–2in (2.5–5cm). Forms threadlike, erect, basal leaves. Stems bear 1–4 upward-facing, funnel-shaped, black-centered, bright red flowers that open flattish, to 1½–2in (4–5cm) across, in the sun. Z9–10 H10–9.

RONDELETIA

RUBIACEAE

Genus of evergreen, mainly summer-flowering trees and shrubs grown primarily for their flowers. Requires full light or partial shade and fertile, well-drained soil. Water containerized specimens freely when in full growth, moderately at other times. Stems may be shortened in early spring if necessary. Propagate by seed in spring or by semi-ripe cuttings in summer.

R. amoena. Evergreen, rounded shrub. H and S 6–12ft (2–4m). Oval, dark green leaves have dense brown down on undersides. Produces dense clusters of tubular, 4- or 5-lobed pink flowers in summer. Z11 H12–10.

Rooksbya euphorbioides. See *Neobuxbaumia euphorbioides*.

ROSA

Rose

ROSACEAE

Genus of deciduous or semi-evergreen, open shrubs and scrambling climbers grown for their profusion of flowers, often fragrant, and sometimes for their fruits (rose hips). Leaves are divided into usually 5 or 7 oval leaflets, with rounded or pointed tips, that are sometimes toothed. Stems usually bear thorns, or prickles. Most of the bush and climbing roses grow well in Z5–9 H9–5 (unless otherwise stated) but are often grown in colder zones and protected for the winter by mounding, deep planting, or burying. Prefers an open, sunny site and requires fertile, moist but well-drained soil. Avoid planting in an area where roses have been grown in recent years, since problems due to harmful organisms may occur: either exchange the soil, which may be used satisfactorily elsewhere, or choose another site for the new rose. To obtain blooms of high quality, fertilize in late winter or early spring with a balanced fertilizer and apply a mulch. In spring and summer fertilize regularly at 3-weekly intervals. Remove spent flower heads from plants that are remontant ("rising up again"; other terms used are repeat- or perpetual-flowering). May be trimmed for neatness in early winter.

To improve health, flower quality, and shape of bush, prune in the dormant season or, preferably, in spring, before young shoots develop from dormant growth buds: remove dead, damaged, and dying wood; lightly trim old garden and groundcover roses (see below); remove two-thirds of previous summer's growth of modern bush, (including miniature) roses. Correct treatment of modern shrub and climbing roses, ramblers, and species roses depends on the individual variety, but in general they should be pruned only lightly. Propagate by budding in summer or by hardwood cuttings in autumn. All roses are prone to attack by various pests and diseases, including aphids, mites, Japanese beetle, black-spot, powdery mildew, and rust.

Roses are officially classified in three groups, each consisting of different types. Flowers occur in a variety of forms (illustrated and described on p.184) and are single (4–7 petals), semi-double (8–14 petals), double (15–30 petals) or fully double (over 30 petals). Roses are illustrated on pp.180–99.

Species roses

Species, or wild, roses and **species hybrids** that share most of the characteristics of the parent species. Includes shrubs and climbing roses. Produces usually single flowers mainly in summer, borne generally in one flush, followed by red or black hips in autumn.

Old Garden roses

Alba – large, freely branching shrubs with clusters of, usually, 5–7 semi-double to double flowers in mid-summer. Has abundant, grayish green leaves. Is very hardy and is good for borders and as specimen plants.

Bourbon – open, remontant shrubs that may be trained to climb. Produces usually fully double flowers, borne commonly in 3s, in summer-autumn. Is suitable for borders and for training over fences, walls, and pillars.

China – remontant shrubs that produce single to double flowers, borne singly or in clusters of 2–13, in summer-autumn. Has pointed, shiny leaflets. Often benefits from a sheltered position. Is suitable for borders and walls.

Damask – open shrubs with usually very fragrant, semi- to fully double flowers, borne singly or in loose clusters of 5–7 mainly in summer. Is suitable for borders.

Gallica – shrubs of fairly dense, free-branching growth. Leaves are dull green. Produces single to fully double, richly colored flowers, often in clusters of 3, in summer. Is suitable for borders and as hedging.

Hybrid Perpetual – vigorous, free-branching, remontant shrubs that bear fully double flowers, held singly or in 3s, in summer-autumn. Leaves are usually olive green. Is suitable for beds and borders.

Moss – often lax shrubs with a furry, mosslike growth on stems and calyces. Leaves are usually dark green. Has double to fully double flowers in summer.

Noisette – remontant climbing roses that bear clusters of up to 9 usually double flowers, with a slight spicy fragrance, in summer-autumn. Has generally smooth stems and glossy leaves. Suitable for a wall.

Portland – upright, remontant shrubs with semi-double to double flowers, held singly or in 3s, in summer-autumn. Good in beds and borders.

Provence (Centifolia) – lax, thorny shrubs that produce scented, usually double to fully double flowers, borne singly or in 3s, in summer. Leaves are often dark green. Suitable for borders.

Sempervirens – semi-evergreen climbing roses with shiny, light green leaves and, in late summer, numerous semi- to fully double flowers. Is ideal for naturalizing or for growing on fences and pergolas.

Tea – remontant shrubs and climbing roses that produce spicy-scented, slender-stemmed, pointed, semi- to fully double flowers, borne singly or in 3s, in summer-autumn. Leaves are shiny and pale green. Often benefits from a sheltered position. Is suitable for beds and borders.

Modern roses

Shrub – a diverse group of modern roses, most of which are remontant, that grow larger (mostly H 3–6ft (1–2m)) than most bush roses. Has single to fully double flowers, singly or in sprays, in summer and/or autumn. Is suitable for beds and borders and for growing as specimen plants.

Large-flowered bush (Hybrid Tea) – remontant shrubs with mostly pointed, double flowers, 3in (8cm) or more across, borne singly or in 3s, in summer-autumn. Is excellent for beds, borders, hedges. and cutting.

Cluster-flowered bush (Floribunda) – remontant shrubs that produce sprays of usually 3–25 single to fully double flowers in summer-autumn. Is excellent for beds, borders, and hedges.

Dwarf cluster-flowered bush (Patio) – neat, remontant shrubs, H 15–24in (38–60cm), S 12–24in (30–60cm), that bear sprays of generally 3–11 single to double flowers in summer-autumn. Is ideal for beds, borders, and hedges and for growing in containers.

Miniature bush – remontant shrubs, H to 18in (45cm), S to 16in (40cm), with sprays of usually 3–11 tiny, single to fully double flowers in summer-autumn. Has tiny leaves. Is suitable for rock gardens, small spaces, and for growing in containers.

Polyantha – tough, compact, remontant shrubs with sprays of usually 7–15 small, 5-petaled, single to double flowers in summer-autumn. Is suitable for beds.

Groundcover – trailing and spreading roses, many of which are remontant, with single to fully double flowers, borne mostly in clusters of 3–11, in summer and/or autumn. Is suitable for beds, banks, and walls.

Climbing – vigorous climbing roses, some of which are remontant, with stiff stems and single to fully double flowers borne singly or in clusters from late spring to autumn. Suitable to train over

walls, fences, and pergolas.
Rambler – vigorous climbing roses with lax stems. Has clusters of 3–21 single to fully double flowers, mainly in summer. Suitable for training over walls, fences, pergolas, and trees.

***R.* 'Adelaide Hoodless'.** Vigorous, arching shrub rose. H 3ft (1m), S 2ft (60cm). Has large clusters of up to 35 semi-double red flowers, often in two flushes. Prune off first crop of fruit to promote second blooming. Z2–9 H9–1.
***R.* 'Agnes'.** An upright, *R. rugosa* hybrid shrub rose. H. 6ft (2m), S 4ft (1.2m). Has dark green leaves on very thorny canes. Cupped, scented, double, butter yellow flowers open in late spring. Occasionally reblooms. Z2–7 H7–1.
***R.* 'Aimée Vibert'**, syn. *R.* 'Bouquet de la Mariée'. Noisette climbing rose with long, smooth stems. H 15ft (5m), S 10ft (3m). Bears clusters of lightly scented, cupped, fully double, blush pink to white flowers, 3in (8cm) across, in summer-autumn. Leaves are glossy and dark green. Z6–9 H9–6.
***R.* 'Alba Semiplena'**, syn. *R.* x *alba* 'Semiplena'.Vigorous, bushy Alba rose. H 6ft (2m), S 5ft (1.5m). Bears sweetly scented, flat, semi-double white flowers, 3in (8cm) across, in midsummer. Has grayish green leaves. Suitable for a hedge. Z3–9 H9–1.
***R.* 'Albéric Barbier'** illus. p.196.
***R.* 'Albertine'** illus. p.197.
***R.* ALEC'S RED ('Cored')** illus. p.192.
***R.* ALEXANDER ('Harlex')**, syn. *R.* 'Alexandra', illus. p.192.
***R.* 'Alexander Mackenzie'.** Upright, vigorous shrub rose with excellent mildew and blackspot resistance. H 6ft (2m), S 4.5ft (1.5m). Has deep red, cup-shaped flowers with 40–50 petals in clusters of 10–12. Recurrent blooming. Z3–9 H9–1.
***R.* 'Alfred de Dalmas'.** See *R.* 'Mousseline'.
***R.* 'Alister Stella Gray'**, syn. *R.* 'Golden Rambler'. Noisette climbing rose with long, vigorous, upright stems. H 15ft (5m), S 10ft (3m). Bears clusters of musk-scented, quartered, fully double, yolk yellow flowers, 2½in (6cm) across, in summer-autumn. Has glossy, midgreen leaves. Z6–9 H9–6.
***R.* 'Aloha'** illus. p.198.
***R.* 'Alpine Sunset'** illus. p.190.
***R.* AMBER QUEEN ('Harroony')** illus. p.193.
***R.* 'American Pillar'.** Vigorous rambler rose of lax growth. H to 15ft (5m), S 12ft (4m). Large clusters of cupped, single, carmine-red flowers with white eyes are borne freely in midsummer. Leathery foliage is glossy and midgreen. Z5–9 H9–5.
***R.* 'Amruda'.** See *R.* RED ACE.
***R.* 'Andeli'.** See *R.* DOUBLE DELIGHT.
***R.* ANGELA RIPPON ('Ocarina')**, syn. *R.* 'Ocaru', illus. p.195.
***R.* 'Angelita'.** See *R.* 'Snowball'.
***R.* ANISLEY DICKSON ('Dickimono')**, syn. *R.* 'Dicky', *R.* 'Münchner Kindl', illus. p.191.
***R.* ANNA FORD ('Harpiccolo')** illus. p.191.
***R.* 'ANNE HARKNESS' ('Harkaramel')** illus. p.194.
***R.* 'Apothecary's Rose'.** See *R. gallica* var. *officinalis*.
***R.* 'Arthur Bell'.** Upright, cluster-flowered bush rose. H 3ft (1m), S 2ft (60cm). Clusters of fragrant, cupped, double yellow flowers, 3in (8cm) across, are borne in summer-autumn. Foliage is bright green.
***R.* 'Assemblage des Beautés'**, syn. *R.* 'Rouge Eblouissante'. Upright, dense Gallica rose. H 4ft (1.2m), S 3ft (1m). In summer bears faintly scented, rounded, fully double, green-eyed cerise to crimson-purple flowers, 3in (8cm) across. Has rich green leaves. Z6–10 H10–1.
***R.* 'Ausmary'.** See *R.* MARY ROSE.
***R.* 'Ausmas'.** See *R.* GRAHAM THOMAS.
***R.* 'Austance'.** See *R.* CONSTANCE SPRY.
***R.* 'Baby Carnival'.** See *R.* BABY MASQUERADE.
***R.* BABY MASQUERADE ('Tanba')**, syn. 'Baby Carnival', illus. p.195.
R. banksiae, syn. *R.b.* var. *normalis* (Banksian rose). Climbing species rose. H and S 30ft (10m). Dense clusters of fragrant, flat, single white flowers, 1in (2.5cm) across, are borne on slender, thornless, light green stems in late spring. Leaves are small and pale green. Z8–9 H9–8. **'Lutea'** (syn. *R.b.* var. *lutea*) illus. p.199.
***R.* 'Beauty of Glazenwood'.** See *R.* x *odorata* 'Pseudindica'.
***R.* 'Belle Courtisanne'.** See *R.* 'Königin von Dänemark'.
***R.* 'Belle de Crécy'** illus. p.188.
***R.* 'Belle de Londres'.** See *R.* 'Compassion'.
***R.* 'Bizarre Triomphant'.** See *R.* 'Charles de Mills'.
***R.* 'Blanc Double de Coubert'.** Dense spreading shrub rose, a *R. rugosa* hybrid. H 5ft (1.5m), S 4ft (1.2m). Has semi-double, fragrant white flowers with prominent yellow stamens from spring to autumn. Z3–9 H9–1.
***R.* 'Blanche Moreau'.** Moss rose of rather lax growth. H 5ft (1.5m), S 4ft (1.2m). Fragrant, cupped, fully double, white flowers, 4in (10cm) across, with brownish mossing, appear in summer. Has dull green leaves. Z8–9 H9–1.
***R.* 'Blaze'.** Vigorous climbing rose. H and S 8ft (2.5m). Large semi-double bright red flowers are borne from late spring to early autumn. Z5–11 H11–5.
***R.* 'Blessings'** illus. p.190.
***R.* BLUE MOON ('Tannacht')**, syn. *R.* 'Mainzer Fastnacht', *R.* 'Sissi'. Large-flowered bush rose of open habit. H 3ft (1m), S 2ft (60cm). Sweetly scented, pointed, fully double lilac flowers, 4in (10cm) across, are borne in summer-autumn. Leaves are large and dark green.
***R.* 'Blue Rambler'.** See *R.* 'Veilchenblau'.
***R.* 'Blush Noisette'.** See *R.* 'Noisette Carnée'.
***R.* BONICA ('Meidomonac')**, syn. *R.* 'Bonica '82', illus. p186.
***R.* 'Boule de Neige'** illus. p.184.
***R.* 'Bouquet de la Mariée'.** See *R.* 'Aimée Vibert'.
***R.* 'Brass Ring'.** See *R.* PEEK-A-BOO.
***R.* BREATH OF LIFE ('Harquanne')** illus. p.197.
***R.* BRIGHT SMILE ('Dicdance')** illus. p.193.
***R.* 'Buff Beauty'.** Rounded shrub rose. H and S 4ft (1.2m). Slightly fragrant, cupped, fully double, apricot-buff flowers, 3½in (9cm) across, are borne freely in summer, sparsely in autumn. Has plentiful, glossy, dark green leaves. Z6–10 H10–6.
***R.* 'Canary Bird'.** See *R. xanthina* 'Canary Bird'.
***R.* 'Capitaine John Ingram'.** Vigorous, bushy Moss rose. H and S 4ft (1.2m). In summer bears fragrant, cupped, fully double, rich maroon-crimson flowers, 3in (8cm) across; petals are paler on reverses. Foliage is dark green. Z4–9 H9–1.
***R.* 'Cardinal de Richelieu'** illus. p.188.
***R.* CARDINAL HUME ('Harregale')** illus. p.188.
***R.* CASINO ('Macca')**, syn. *R.* 'Gerbe d'Or', illus. p.199.
***R.* 'Cécile Brünner'**, syn. *R.* 'Mignon'. Upright, spindly China rose with fairly smooth stems. H 30in (75cm), S 24in (60cm). Produces slightly scented, urn-shaped, fully double, light pink flowers, 1½in (4cm) across, in summer-autumn. Small, dark green leaves are sparse. Z5–9 H9–1.
***R.* 'Céleste'**, syn. *R.* 'Celestial', illus. p.185.
***R.* 'Celestial'.** See *R.* 'Céleste'.
***R.* x *centifolia* 'Cristata'**, syn. *R.* 'Chapeau de Napoléon', *R.* 'Cristata' (Crested moss). Bushy, lanky Provence rose. H 5ft (1.5m), S 4ft (1.2m). In summer, very fragrant, cupped, fully double pink flowers, 3½in (9cm) across and with tufted sepals, are borne on nodding stems amid dull green foliage. May be grown on a support. **'Muscosa'** (Common moss, Old pink moss) is a vigorous, lax Moss rose. H 5ft (1.5m), S 4ft (1.2m). Bears fragrant, rounded to cupped, fully double, mossed pink flowers, 3in (8cm) across, in summer. Leaves are matte, dull green. Best with support. Both Z4–9 H9–1.
***R.* CHAMPAGNE COCKTAIL ('Horflash')** illus. p.192.
***R.* 'Champlain'.** Free-flowering shrub rose that makes a good informal hedge. H and S 3ft (1m). Has velvety red, slightly fragrant, double flowers. Good resistance to mildew. Z3–9 H9–1.
***R.* 'Chapeau de Napoléon'.** See *R.* x *centifolia* 'Cristata'.
***R.* 'Chaplin's Pink Companion'** illus. p.197.
***R.* 'Charles Albanel'.** A low, spreading shrub rose that makes a good ground-cover. H 18in (45cm), S 3ft (1m). Medium red, fragrant flowers freely produced in spring and then sporadically through the summer. Excellent blackspot and mildew resistance. Z2–9 H9–1.
***R.* 'Charles de Mills'**, syn. *R.* 'Bizarre Triomphant'. Upright, arching Gallica rose with fairly smooth stems. H 4ft (1.2m), S 3ft (1m). Very fragrant, quartered-rosette, fully double, crimson-purple flowers, 4in (10cm) across, appear in summer. Leaves are plentiful and midgreen. May be grown on a support. Z3–9 H9–1.
***R.* 'Chewarvel'.** See *R.* LAURA FORD.
***R. chinensis* var. *minima*.** See *R.* 'Rouletii'. **'Mutabilis'** see *R.* x *odorata* 'Mutabilis'.
***R.* CITY GIRL ('Harzorba')** illus. p.198.
***R.* CITY OF LONDON ('Harukfore')**. Rounded, cluster-flowered bush rose. H 3ft (1m), S 2½ft (75cm). In summer-autumn, bears dainty sprays of sweet-smelling, urn-shaped, double, blush pink flowers, 3in (8cm) across, amid bright green foliage.
***R.* CLARISSA ('Harprocrustes')**. Upright, cluster-flowered bush rose. H 30in (75cm), S 18in (45cm). Dense sprays of slightly scented, urn-shaped, fully double apricot flowers, 2in (5cm) across, appear in summer-autumn. Has many small, glossy leaves. Makes a good, narrow hedge.
***R.* 'Cocabest'.** See *R.* WEE JOCK.
***R.* 'Cocdestin'.** See *R.* REMEMBER ME.
***R.* COLIBRE '79 ('Meidanover')** illus. p.196.
***R.* 'Commandant Beaurepaire'**, syn. *R.* 'Panachée d'Angers'. Vigorous, spreading Bourbon rose. H and S 4ft (1.2m). Fragrant, cupped, double flowers, 4in (10cm) across, are borne in summer-autumn. They are blush pink, splashed with mauve, purple, crimson, and scarlet. Light green leaflets have wavy margins. Z6–9 H9–1.
***R.* 'Compassion'**, syn. *R.* 'Belle de Londres', illus. p198.
***R.* 'Complicata'** illus. p.186.
***R.* 'Comte de Chambord'.** See *R.* 'Madame Knorr'.
***R.* CONGRATULATIONS ('Korlift')**, syn. *R.* 'Sylvia'. Upright, vigorous, large-flowered bush rose. H 4ft (1.2m), S 3ft (1m). Produces neat, urn-shaped, fully double, deep rose pink flowers, 4½in (11cm) across, on long stems in summer-autumn. Leaves are large and dark green. Makes a tall hedge.
***R.* 'Conrad Ferdinand Meyer'** illus. p185.
***R.* CONSTANCE SPRY ('Austance')** illus. p.186.
***R.* 'Cored'.** See *R.* ALEC'S RED.
***R.* 'Cristata'.** See *R.* x *centifolia* 'Cristata'.
***R.* 'Cuisse de Nymphe'.** See *R.* 'Great Maiden's Blush'.
***R.* 'Cuthbert Grant'.** A vigorous semi-upright shrub rose. H 3ft (1m), S 2ft (60cm). Strongly fragrant, crimson red, semi-double flowers about 4in (10cm) across are produced in two flushes. Plants have excellent resistance to mildew and blackspot. Z3–9 H9–1.
***R.* 'Danse du Feu'**, syn. *R.* 'Spectacular', illus. p.198.
***R.* 'David Thompson'.** A *R. rugosa* hybrid shrub rose. H and S 4ft (1.2m). Free flowering, with 3in (7cm) medium red blooms. It does not set fruit. Highly

resistant to blackspot and mildew. Z2–9 H9–1.
***R.* 'Dicdance'.** See *R.* BRIGHT SMILE.
***R.* 'Dicdivine'.** See *R.* POT O' GOLD.
***R.* 'Dicgrow'.** See *R.* PEEK-A-BOO.
***R.* 'Dicinfra'.** See *R.* DISCO DANCER.
***R.* 'Dicjana'.** See *R.* ELINA.
***R.* 'Dicjem'.** See *R.* FREEDOM.
***R.* 'Dicjubell'.** See *R.* LOVELY LADY.
***R.* 'Dickimono'.** See *R.* ANISLEY DICKSON.
***R.* 'Dicky'.** See *R.* ANISLEY DICKSON.
***R.* 'Diclittle'.** See *R.* LITTLE WOMAN.
***R.* 'Diclulu'.** See *R.* GENTLE TOUCH.
***R.* 'Dicmagic'.** See *R.* SWEET MAGIC.
***R.* DISCO DANCER ('Dicinfra').** Dense, rounded, cluster-flowered bush rose. H 30in (75cm), S 24in (60cm). Bears dense sprays of slightly fragrant, cupped, double, bright orange-red flowers, 2½in (6cm) across, in summer-autumn, amid a mass of glossy foliage.
***R.* 'Don Juan',** syn. 'Malandrone'. Branching, upright climbing rose. H 10ft (3m), S 6ft (2m). Very fragrant, fully double, dark red cupped flowers in clusters repeated throughout the summer. Z5–9 H9–1.
***R.* 'Doris Tysterman'** illus. p.194.
***R.* 'Dortmund'** illus. p.198.
***R.* DOUBLE DELIGHT ('Andeli')** illus. p.191.
***R.* 'Double Velvet'.** See *R.* 'Tuscany Superb'.
***R.* 'Doux Parfum'.** See *R.* L'AIMANT.
***R.* DRUMMER BOY ('Harvacity').** Dwarf cluster-flowered bush rose of bushy, spreading habit. H and S 20in (50cm). Faintly scented, cupped, double, bright crimson flowers, 2in (5cm) across, appear in dense sprays amid a mass of small, dark green leaves in summer-autumn. Makes a good low hedge.
***R.* DUBLIN BAY ('Macdub')** illus. p.198.
***R.* 'Duchesse d'Istrie'.** See *R.* 'William Lobb'.
***R.* 'Duftzauber '84'.** See *R.* ROYAL WILLIAM.
***R.* 'Du Maître d'Ecole'.** Bushy, spreading Gallica rose. H 4ft (1.2m), S 3ft (1m). Bears fragrant, quartered-rosette, fully double, carmine to light pink flowers, 4in (10cm) across, in summer. Foliage is dull green.
***R.* 'Dupontii',** syn. *R. moschata* var. *nivea*, illus. p.185.
R. ecae illus. p.188.
***R. eglanteria*.** See *R. rubiginosa*.
***R.* ELINA ('Dicjana'),** syn. *R.* 'Peaudouce'. Vigorous, shrubby, large-flowered bush rose. H 3½ft (1.1m), S 2½ft (75cm). Lightly scented, rounded, fully double, ivory-white flowers, 6in (15cm) across, with lemon yellow centers, are borne freely in summer-autumn. Has abundant reddish foliage. Z4–11 H12–1.
***R.* 'Elizabeth Harkness'** illus. p.189.
***R.* 'Emily Gray'** illus. p199.
***R.* 'Empereur du Maroc'** illus. p.188.
***R.* ESCAPADE ('Harpade')** illus. p.191.
***R.* 'Fantin-Latour'** illus. p.185.
***R.* FASCINATION ('Poulmax'),** syn. *R.* 'Fredensborg'. Vigorous, cluster-flowered bush rose. H 3ft (1m), S 2ft (60cm). In summer-autumn bears clusters of fragrant, rounded, double, shrimp pink blooms amid dark green, glossy foliage. Is good for beds and hedges. Z4–11 H12–1.
***R.* 'Felicia'** illus. p.185.
***R.* 'Félicité Parmentier'.** Vigorous, compact, upright Alba rose. H 4ft (1.2m), S 3ft (1m). Fragrant, cupped to flat, fully double, pale flesh pink flowers, 2½in (6cm) across, are borne in midsummer. Has abundant, grayish green leaves. Makes a good hedge. Z3–9 H9–3.
***R.* 'Félicité Perpétue'** illus. p.196.
***R. filipes* 'Kiftsgate'** illus. p.196.
***R.* 'Fire Princess'** illus. p.195.
***R.* 'F.J.Grootendorst'.** Very vigorous and spiny shrub rose. H 4ft (1.2m), S 3ft (1m). Has small crimson, double, very fragrant flowers all summer. Good orange fruit persist into winter.
***R. foetida* 'Persiana',** syn. *R.* 'Persian Yellow', illus. p.188.
***R.* 'Fortune's Double Yellow'.** See *R.* x *odorata* 'Pseudindica'.
***R.* FRAGRANT CLOUD ('Tanellis').** Bushy, dense, large-flowered bush rose. H 30in (75cm), S 24in (60cm). Very fragrant, rounded, double, dusky scarlet flowers, 5in (12cm) across, are borne freely in summer-autumn. Has plentiful, dark green foliage. Z4–11 H12–1.
***R.* 'Fragrant Delight'.** Bushy, cluster-flowered bush rose of uneven habit. H 3ft (1m), S 2½ft (75cm). Produces an abundance of reddish green foliage, amid which clusters of fragrant, urn-shaped, double, salmon pink flowers, 3in (8cm) across, are borne freely in summer-autumn.
***R.* 'Frau Dagmar Hartopp'.** See *R.* 'Fru Dagmar Hastrup'.
***R.* 'Fredensborg'.** See *R.* FASCINATION.
***R.* FREEDOM ('Dicjem')** illus. p.193.
***R.* 'Friesia'.** See *R.* 'Korresia'.
***R.* 'Fru Dagmar Hastrup',** syn. 'Frau Dagmar Hartopp'. A spreading *R. rugosa* hybrid. H 3ft (1m), S 4ft (1.2m). Single, clove-scented, light pink flowers with cream stamens in spring and sporadically until autumn. Produces large crops of crimson hips that persist well. Z2–9 H9–1.
***R.* 'Frühlingsmorgen',** syn. *R.* 'Spring Morning'. Open, free-branching shrub rose. H 6ft (2m), S 5ft (1.5m). Foliage is grayish green. In late spring produces hay scented, cupped, single pink flowers, 5in (12cm) across, with a primrose center and reddish stamens. Z4–9 H9–4.
***R. gallica* var. *officinalis*,** syn. *R.* 'Apothecary's Rose', *R. officinalis* (Red rose of Lancaster). Bushy species rose of neat habit. H to 32in (80cm), S 36in (1m). In summer bears flat, semi-double, pinkish red flowers, 3in (8cm) across, with a moderate scent. Z3–9 H9–1. **'Versicolor'** illus. p.187.
***R.* 'Gaumo'.** See *R.* ROSE GAUJARD.
***R.* GENTLE TOUCH ('Diclulu').** Upright, dwarf cluster-flowered bush rose. H 20in (50cm), S 12in (30cm). Bears sprays of faintly scented, urn-shaped, semi-double, pale salmon-pink flowers, 2in (5cm) across, in summer-autumn. Leaves are small and dark green. Is good as a low hedge.
***R.* 'Geranium'.** See *R. moyesii* 'Geranium'.
***R.* 'Gerbe d'Or'.** See *R.* 'Casino'.
***R.* 'Gioia'.** See *R.* 'Peace'.
***R.* 'Gipsy Boy'.** See *R.* 'Zigeunerknabe'.
***R. glauca*,** syn. *R. rubrifolia*, illus. p.186.
***R.* 'Glenfiddich'** illus. p.193.
***R.* 'Gloire de Dijon'** illus. p.196.
***R.* 'Gloire des Mousseux'.** Vigorous, bushy Moss rose. H 4ft (1.2m), S 3ft (1m). Has plentiful, light green foliage. In summer bears fragrant, cupped, fully double flowers, 6in (15cm) across. These are bright pink, paling to blush pink, with light green mossing. Z5–9 H9–1.
***R.* 'Gloria Dei'.** See *R.* 'Peace'.
***R.* 'Gold of Ophir'.** See *R.* x *odorata* 'Pseudindica'.
***R.* GOLDEN PENNY ('Rugul'),** syn. *R.* 'Guletta', *R.* 'Tapis Jaune', illus. p.192.
***R.* 'Golden Rambler'.** See *R.* 'Alister Stella Gray'.
***R.* 'Golden Showers'** illus. p.199.
***R.* 'Golden Sunblaze'.** See *R.* 'Rise 'n' Shine'.
***R.* 'Golden Wings'.** Bushy, spreading shrub rose. H 3½ft (1.1m), S 4½ft (1.35m). Bears fragrant, cupped, single, pale yellow flowers, 5in (12cm) across, amid light green foliage, in summer-autumn. Good for a hedge. Z4–9 H9–1.
***R.* 'Goldfinch'.** Vigorous, arching rambler rose. H 9ft (2.7m), S 6ft (2m). In summer produces lightly scented, rosette, double, yolk yellow flowers, 1½in (4cm) across, that fade to white. Has plentiful, bright light green leaves. Z5–9 H9–5.
***R.* 'Goldsmith'.** See *R.* SIMBA.
***R.* GRAHAM THOMAS ('Ausmas')** illus. p.189.
***R.* 'Grandpa Dickson',** syn. *R.* 'Irish Gold', illus. p.193.
***R.* 'Great Maiden's Blush',** syn. *R.* 'Cuisse de Nymphe', *R.* 'La Séduisante', illus. p.185.
***R.* GROUSE ('Korimro')** illus. p.189.
***R.* 'Guinée'** illus. p.199.
***R.* 'Guletta'.** See *R.* GOLDEN PENNY.
***R.* HANDEL ('Macha')** illus. p.197.
***R.* HANNAH GORDON ('Korweiso').** Bushy, open, cluster-flowered bush rose. H 30in (75cm), S 2ft (60cm). Sprays of slightly fragrant, cupped, double, blush pink flowers, 3in (8cm) across, margined with reddish pink, appear in summer-autumn. Leaves are dark green. Z4–11 H12–1.
***R.* 'Hansa'.** A very free-flowering *R. rugosa* hybrid. H 4ft (1.2m), S 3ft (1m). Highly fragrant, double reddish purple flowers with fringed petals produced all summer long. One of the best and most floriferous *rugosa* hybrids. Z3–9 H9–1.
***R.* x *harisonii* 'Harison's Yellow'.** (Yellow rose of Texas). Upright, spiny rose that makes a good hedge. H 6ft (2m), S 4ft (1.2m). Has cupped, semi-double, bright yellow flowers in spring and blackish red hips. Z3–9 H9–1.
***R.* 'Harkaramel'.** See *R.* ANNE HARKNESS.
***R.* 'Harkuly'.** See *R.* MARGARET MERRIL.
***R.* 'Harlex'.** See *R.* ALEXANDER.
***R.* 'Harmantelle'.** See *R.* MOUNTBATTEN.
***R.* 'Harpade'.** See *R.* ESCAPADE.
***R.* 'Harpiccolo'.** See *R.* ANNA FORD.
***R.* 'Harprocrustes'.** See *R.* CLARISSA.
***R.* 'Harquanne'.** See *R.* BREATH OF LIFE.
***R.* 'Harqueterwife'.** See *R.* PAUL SHIRVILLE.
***R.* 'Harregale'.** See *R.* CARDINAL HUME.
***R.* 'Harroony'.** See *R.* AMBER QUEEN.
***R.* 'Harrowbond'.** See *R.* ROSEMARY HARKNESS.
***R.* 'Harsherry'.** See *R.* SHEILA'S PERFUME.
***R.* 'Harukfore'.** See *R.* CITY OF LONDON.
***R.* 'Harwanna'.** See *R.* JACQUELINE DU PRÉ.
***R.* 'Harwanted'.** See *R.* MANY HAPPY RETURNS.
***R.* 'Haryup'.** See *R.* HIGH HOPES.
***R.* 'Harzorba'.** See *R.* CITY GIRL.
***R.* 'Heartthrob'.** See *R.* 'Paul Shirville'.
***R.* 'Heideröslein'.** See *R.* 'Nozomi'.
***R.* 'Henri Martin',** syn. *R.* 'Red Moss', illus. p.187.
***R.* 'Henry Hudson'.** Semi-dwarf, disease resistant shrub rose. H 2ft (60cm), S 3ft (1m). Fragrant flowers are white with a tinge of pink and produced all summer. Z2–9 H9–1.
***R.* 'Henry Kelsey'.** A repeat-flowering climbing rose. H 8ft (2.5m), S 5ft (1.5m). Flowers are medium red with a spicy fragrance and produced in clusters of 5–18 blooms. Good mildew resistance. Z3–9 H9–1.
***R.* HIGH HOPES ('Haryup')** illus. p.198.
***R.* 'Honorine de Brabant'.** Vigorous, bushy, sprawling Bourbon rose. H and S 6ft (2m). Fragrant, quartered, double flowers, 4in (10cm) across, in lilac-pink marked with light purple and crimson, are produced in summer-autumn. Has plentiful, light green foliage. Z5–9 H9–5.
***R.* 'Horflash'.** See *R.* CHAMPAGNE COCKTAIL.
***R.* 'Hula Girl'** illus. p.195.
***R.* ICEBERG ('Korbin'),** syn. *R.* 'Schneewittchen', illus. p.189.
***R.* 'Iced Ginger'** illus. p.190.
***R.* INGRID BERGMAN ('Poulman').** Upright, branching, large-flowered bush rose. H 30in (75cm), S 24in (60cm). Bears slightly scented, urn-shaped, double, dark red flowers, 4½in (11cm) across, in summer-autumn. Has leathery, semi-glossy, dark green foliage.
***R.* 'Interall'.** See *R.* ROSY CUSHION.
***R.* INVINCIBLE ('Runatru').** Upright, cluster-flowered bush rose. H 3ft (1m), S 2ft (60cm). Faintly scented, cupped, fully double, bright crimson flowers, 3½in (9cm) across, appear in open clusters in summer-autumn. Leaves are semi-glossy.
***R.* 'Irish Gold'.** See *R.* 'Grandpa Dickson'.

***R.* 'Ispahan'**, syn. *R.* 'Pompon des Princes', *R.* 'Rose d'Isfahan'. Vigorous, bushy, dense Damask rose. H 5ft (1.5m), S 4ft (1.2m). Produces fragrant, cupped, double, clear pink flowers, 3in (8cm) across, amid grayish green foliage throughout summer and autumn. Z4–9 H9–1.
***R.* Jacqueline du Pré ('Harwanna')**. Vigorous, arching shrub rose. H 6ft (2m), S 5ft (1.5m). In summer-autumn bears musk-scented, cupped, double, ivory-white flowers, 4in (10cm) across, with scalloped petals and red stamens. Has abundant, glossy leaves. Z5–9 H9–5.
***R.* 'Jens Munk'.** A vigorous, spiny shrub rose with good disease resistance. H 6ft (2m), S 5ft (1.5m). Semi-double, fragrant pink flowers bloom in summer, and showy orange hips that last into winter. Z2–8 H8–1.
***R.* 'John Cabot'.** Vigorous shrub rose. H 5ft (1.5m), S 4ft (1.2m). Has yellow-green leaves and, in summer-autumn, clusters of fragrant, cupped, double magenta flowers, 2½in (6cm) across. May be grown as a climber or hedge. Z3–9 H9–1.
***R.* 'John Davies'.** A free-flowering climbing rose. H 8ft (2.5m), S 4ft (1.2m). Has clusters of up to 18 medium pink flower with a spicy perfume that open from buds like a miniature hybrid tea rose. Excellent disease resistance. Foliage turns a yellow to orange in autumn. Z3–9 H9–1.
***R.* 'John Franklin'.** A bushy, upright shrub rose. H and S 4ft (1.2m). Medium red flowers with fringed petals are borne from spring to autumn in large clusters. Z3–9 H9–1..
***R.* 'J.P.Connell'.** A vigorous, upright shrub rose with good resistance to mildew and blackspot. H 15ft (5m), S 4ft (1.2m). Semi-double flowers open yellow and fade to a cream but with prominent yellow stamens. Flowers best on established plants.
***R.* 'Julia's Rose'.** Spindly, branching, large-flowered bush rose. H 30in (75cm), S 18in (45cm). In summer-autumn produces faintly scented, urn-shaped, double, brownish pink to buff flowers, 4in (10cm) across. Foliage is reddish green. Is good for flower arrangements. Z5–9 H9–1.
***R.* 'Just Joey'** illus. p.194.
***R.* 'Karl Forster'.** Bushy shrub rose with light green foliage. H 5ft (1.5m), S 4ft (1.2m). Very showy large double white flowers with golden stamens when fully open. Blooms well later in summer. Z4–9 H9–1.
***R.* 'Kathleen Harrop'.** Arching, lax Bourbon rose. H 8ft (2.5m), S 6ft (2m). Fragrant, double, cupped, pale pink flowers, 3in (8cm) across, are borne in summer-autumn. Plentiful, dark green foliage is susceptible to mildew. May be grown as a climber or hedge. Z6 9 H9 6.
***R.* Keepsake ('Kormalda')** illus. p.191.
***R.* 'Königin von Dänemark'**, syn. *R.* 'Belle Courtisanne', illus. p.186.
***R.* 'Königliche Hoheit'.** See *R.* 'Royal Highness'.
***R.* 'Korbelma'.** See *R.* Simba.
***R.* 'Korbin'.** See *R.* Iceberg.
***R.* 'Korblue'.** See *R.* Shocking Blue.
***R.* 'Korimro'.** See *R.* Grouse.
***R.* 'Korlift'.** See *R.* Congratulations.
***R.* 'Kormalda'.** See *R.* Keepsake.
***R.* 'Korpeahn'.** See *R.* The Times Rose.
***R.* 'Korresia'**, syn. *R.* 'Friesia', illus. p.193.
***R.* 'Korweiso'.** See *R.* Hannah Gordon.
***R.* 'Korzaun'.** See *R.* Royal William.
***R.* 'La Séduisante'.** See *R.* 'Great Maiden's Blush'.
***R.* 'Lanken'.** See *R.* Felicity Kendal.
***R.* Laura Ford ('Chewarvel')** illus. p.199.
***R.* 'Leggab'.** See *R.* Pearl Drift.
***R.* 'Legnews'.** See *R.* News.
***R.* 'Lenip'.** See *R.* Pascali.
***R.* Little Woman ('Diclittle').** Upright, dwarf cluster-flowered bush rose. H 20in (50cm), S 40cm (16in). In summer-autumn bears sprays of faintly fragrant, urn-shaped, double, salmon-pink flowers, 2in (5cm) across. Has small, dark green leaves. Is suitable for a narrow hedge.
***R.* 'Louise Odier'**, syn. *R.* 'Madame de Stella'. Elegant, upright Bourbon rose. H 6ft (2m), S 4ft (1.2m). Has light grayish green foliage and fragrant, cupped, fully double, warm rose pink flowers, 5in (12cm) across, borne in summer-autumn. Z3–9 H9–1.
***R.* 'Louis Jolliet'.** Disease resistant climbing rose with a trailing habit. H 6ft (2m), S 4ft (1.2m). Pink flowers in small clusters are produced continuously from June to September.
***R.* Lovely Lady ('Dicjubell')** illus. p.190.
***R.* 'Macangeli'.** See *R.* Snowball.
***R.* 'Macar'.** See *R.* Piccadilly.
***R.* 'Macca'.** See *R.* Casino.
***R.* 'Maccarpe'.** See *R.* Snow Carpet.
***R.* 'Macdub'.** See *R.* Dublin Bay.
***R.* 'Macha'.** See *R.* Handel.
***R.* 'Macrexy'.** See *R.* Sexy Rexy.
R. macrophylla. Vigorous species rose. H 12ft (4m), S 10ft (3m). Bears moderately fragrant, flat, single red flowers, 2in (5cm) across, in summer, followed by flask-shaped, red hips. Has red stems and large, midgreen leaves. Z5–9 H9–1.
***R.* 'Mactru'.** See *R.* Trumpeter.
***R.* 'Madame Alfred Carrière'** illus. p.196.
***R.* 'Madame A. Meilland'.** See *R.* Peace.
***R.* 'Madame de Stella'.** See *R.* 'Louise Odier'.
***R.* 'Madame Ernest Calvat'.** Vigorous, arching Bourbon rose. H 6–10ft (2–3m), S 6ft (2m). Fragrant, cupped to quartered-rosette, fully double, rose pink flowers, 6in (15cm) across, are borne freely in summer-autumn. Has plentiful, large leaves. Z6–9 H9–1.
***R.* 'Madame Grégoire Staechelin'**, syn. *R.* 'Spanish Beauty', illus. p.197.
***R.* 'Madame Hardy'** illus. p.184.
***R.* 'Madame Hébert'.** See *R.* 'Président de Sèze'.
***R.* 'Madame Isaac Pereire'** illus. p.187.
***R.* 'Madame Pierre Oger'.** Lax Bourbon rose. H 6ft (2m), S 4ft (1.2m). In summer-autumn, slender stems carry sweetly scented, cupped or bowl-shaped, double, pink flowers, 3in (8cm) across, with rose-lilac tints. Has light green leaves. Grows well on a pillar. Z6–9.
***R.* Magic Carousel ('Moorcar').** Bushy, miniature bush rose. H 16in (40cm), S 12in (30cm). Slightly scented, rosette, fully double, yellow-and-red flowers, 1½in (4cm) across, with petals arranged in diminishing circles, appear in summer-autumn. Has small, glossy leaves.
***R.* 'Maigold'** illus. p.199.
***R.* 'Mainzer Fastnacht'.** See *R.* Blue Moon.
***R.* 'Malandrone'.** See *R.* 'Don Juan'.
***R.* Many Happy Returns ('Harwanted')**, syn. *R.* 'Prima'. Bushy, spreading shrub rose. H 3ft (1m), S 4ft (1.2m). In summer-autumn bears lightly fragrant, cupped, double, blush pink flowers, 4in (10cm) across, freely amid glossy, dark green leaves. Z6–9 H9–1.
***R.* 'Maréchal Davoust'.** Vigorous, bushy Moss rose. H 5ft (1.5m), S 4ft (1.2m). In summer bears moderately fragrant, cupped, fully double, deep reddish pink to purple flowers, 4in (10cm) across, with a green eye and brownish mossing. Leaves are dull green and lance-shaped. Z5–9 H9–1.
***R.* 'Maréchal Niel'.** Vigorous, spreading Noisette or Tea climbing rose. H 10ft (3m), S 6ft (2m). Drooping stems carry rich green foliage and moderately scented, pointed, fully double, clear yellow flowers, 4in (10cm) across, in summer-autumn. Z7–9 H9–7.
***R.* Margaret Merril ('Harkuly')** illus. p.189.
***R.* 'Marguerite Hilling'**, syn. *R.* 'Pink Nevada', illus. p.186.
***R.* Mary Rose ('Ausmary').** Bushy, spreading shrub rose. H and S 4ft (1.2m). Produces moderately fragrant, cupped, fully double, rose pink flowers, 3½in (9cm) across, in summer-autumn. Has plentiful leaves. Z6–9 H9–6.
***R.* 'Meidanover'.** See *R.* Colibre '79.
***R.* 'Meidomonac'.** See *R.* Bonica.
***R.* 'Meijikitar'.** See *R.* Orange Sunblaze.
***R.* 'Mermaid'** illus. p.199.
***R.* 'Mignon'.** See *R.* 'Cécile Brünner'.
***R.* 'Moorcar'.** See *R.* Magic Carousel.
***R.* 'Morden Amorette'.** Compact, repeat blooming shrub rose. H 0.5m (18in), S 3ft (1m). Fully double rose carmine flowers have up to 30 rolled petals. Deadheading promotes continuous blooms. Good disease resistance. Z3–9 H9–1.
***R.* 'Morden Blush'.** Variable, dwarf, shrub rose. H 18–36in (0.5–1m), S 18in (0.5m). Flowers from June until hard frost with double, flat blooms that are pink in cool weather and white in hot. Good disease resistance. Z2–9 H9–1.
***R.* 'Morden Centennial'.** Repeat-blooming dwarf shrub rose. H 3ft (1m), S 2ft (60cm). Fragrant, double, light pink flowers with about 40 petals are borne in small clusters. Z2–9 H9–1.
***R.* 'Morning Jewel'.** Free-branching climbing rose. H 8ft (2.5m), S 2.2m (7ft). Has plentiful, glossy foliage and cupped, double, bright pink flowers, 3½in (9cm) across, freely borne, usually in clusters, in summer-autumn. May be pruned to a shrub. Z5–9 H9–1.
***R.* 'Morsherry.** See *R.* Sheri Anne.
***R. moschata* var. *nivea*.** See *R.* 'Dupontii'.
***R.* Mountbatten ('Harmantelle')** illus. p.193.
***R.* 'Mousseline'**, syn. *R.* 'Alfred de Dalmas'. Bushy Moss rose with twiggy growth. H and S 3ft (1m). Mainly in summer bears pleasantly scented, cupped, fully double, blush pink flowers, 3in (8cm) across, with little mossing. Has matte green leaves. Z6–9 H9–1.
R. moyesii. Vigorous, arching species rose. H 12ft (4m), S 10ft (3m). In summer, faintly scented, flat, single, dusky scarlet flowers, 2in (5cm) across, with yellow stamens, are borne close to branches. Produces long red hips in autumn. Sparse, small, dark green leaves are composed of 7–13 leaflets. Z4–9 H9–3.**'Geranium'** (syn. *R.* 'Geranium') illus. p.187.
***R.* 'Mrs John Laing'** illus. p.187.
***R.* 'Münchner Kindl'.** See *R.* Anisley Dickson.
***R.* 'National Trust'.** Compact, large-flowered bush rose. H 30in (75cm), S 24in (60cm). Slightly scented, urn-shaped, fully double, scarlet-crimson flowers, 4in (10cm) across, are borne freely in summer-autumn. Produces plentiful, dark green foliage. Makes a good, low hedge.
***R.* 'Nevada'** illus. p.185.
***R.* 'New Dawn'** illus. p.197.
***R.* 'Noisette Carnée'**, syn. *R.* 'Blush Noisette'. Noisette climbing rose of branching habit and lax growth. H 6–12ft (2–4m), S 6–8ft (2–2.5m). In summer-autumn, smooth stems bear clusters of spice-scented, cupped, double, blush-pink flowers, 1½in (4cm) across. Has matte foliage. May be grown as a shrub. Z6–9.
***R.* 'Nozomi'**, syn. *R.* 'Heideröslein', illus. p.189.
***R.* 'Nuits de Young'**, syn. *R.* 'Old Black'. Erect Moss rose with wiry stems. H 4ft (1.2m), S 3ft (1m). Bears in summer, slightly scented, double, flat, dark maroon-purple flowers, 2in (5cm) across, with brownish mossing. Leaves are small and dark green. Z4–9 H9–1.
***R.* 'Ocarina'.** See *R.* Angela Rippon.
***R.* 'Ocaru'.** See *R.* Angela Rippon.
***R.* x *odorata* 'Mutabilis'**, syn. *R. chinensis* 'Mutabilis', illus. p.187. **'Pallida'** illus. p.187. **'Pseudindica'** (syn. *R.* 'Beauty of Glazenwood', *R.* 'Fortune's Double Yellow', *R.* 'Gold of Ophir', *R.* 'San Rafael Rose') is a lax climbing rose of restrained growth. H 8ft (2.5m), S 5ft (1.5m). In summer

bears small clusters of scented, pointed to cupped, semi-double, copper-suffused yellow flowers, 2in (5cm) across. Leaves are glossy, light green. Prune very lightly. Z8–9 H9–8.
R. officinalis. See *R. gallica* var. *officinalis*.
***R.* 'Old Black'.** See *R.* 'Nuits de Young'.
***R.* 'Omar Khayyám'.** Dense, prickly Damask rose. H and S 3ft (1m). Fragrant, quartered-rosette, fully double, light pink flowers, 3in (8cm) across, are borne amid downy grayish foliage in summer. Z5–9 H9–1.
***R. omeiensis* f. *pteracantha*.** See *R. sericea* subsp. *omeiensis* f. *pteracantha*.
***R.* 'Opa Potschke'.** See *R.* 'Precious Platinum'.
***R.* 'Ophelia'.** Upright, open, large-flowered bush rose. H 3ft (1m), S 2ft (60cm). In summer-autumn produces sweetly fragrant, urn-shaped, double, creamy blush pink flowers, 4in (10cm) across, singly or in clusters. Dark green foliage is sparse.
***R.* Orange Sunblaze ('Meijikitar')**, syn. *R.* 'Sunblaze', illus. p.196.
***R.* 'Panachée d'Angers'.** See *R.* 'Commandant Beaurepaire'.
***R.* Pascali ('Lenip').** Upright, large-flowered bush rose. H 3ft (1m), S 2ft (60cm). Bears faintly scented, neat, urn-shaped, fully double white flowers, 3½in (9cm) across, in summer-autumn. Has deep green leaves. Z4–11 H12–1.
***R.* Paul Shirville ('Harqueterwife')**, syn. *R.* 'Heartthrob', illus. p.191.
***R.* 'Paul Transon'.** Vigorous, rather lax rambler rose. H 12ft (4m), S 5ft (1.5m). In summer bears slightly fragrant, flat, double, faintly coppery, salmon-pink flowers, 3in (8cm) across, with pleated petals. Plentiful foliage is glossy, dark green. Z5–9 H9–1.
***R.* 'Paul's Himalayan Musk'**, syn. *R.* 'Paul's Himalayan Musk Rambler'. Very vigorous climbing rose. H and S 30ft (10m). Large clusters of slightly fragrant, rosette, double, blush pink flowers, 1½in (4cm) across, are freely borne in late summer. Has thorny, trailing shoots and drooping leaves. Is suitable for growing up a tree or in a wild garden. Z6–9 H9–6.
***R.* 'Paul's Himalayan Musk Rambler'.** See *R.* 'Paul's Himalayan Musk'.
***R.* 'Paul's Lemon Pillar'** illus. p.196.
***R.* Peace ('Madame A. Meilland')**, syn. *R.* 'Gioia', *R.* 'Gloria Dei', illus. p.192.
***R.* Pearl Drift ('Leggab')** illus. p.185.
***R.* 'Peaudouce'.** See *R.* Elina.
***R.* Peek-a-boo ('Dicgrow')**, syn. *R.* 'Brass Ring', illus. p.190.
***R.* 'Penelope'** illus. p.184.
***R.* 'Perle d'Or'.** China rose that forms a twiggy, leafy, small shrub. H 2½ft (75cm), S 2ft (60cm). Small, slightly scented, urn-shaped, fully double, honey-pink flowers, 1½in (4cm) across, are borne in summer-autumn. Leaves have pointed, glossy leaflets. Z4-11 H12–1.
***R.* 'Persian Yellow'.** See *R. foetida* 'Persiana'.
***R.* Petit Four ('Interfour').** Compact, dwarf cluster-flowered bush rose. H and S 40cm (16in). In summer-autumn, bears dense clusters of slightly fragrant, flat, wide-opening, semi-double, pink-and-white flowers, 1½in (4cm) across, amid plentiful midgreen foliage.
***R.* Piccadilly ('Macar')** illus. p.194.
R. pimpinellifolia, syn. *R. spinosissima* (Burnet rose, Scotch rose). **'Plena'** illus. p.184.
***R.* Pink Bells ('Poulbells')** illus. p.190.
***R.* 'Pink Grootendorst'** illus. p.186.
***R.* 'Pink Nevada'.** See *R.* 'Marguerite Hilling'.
***R.* 'Pink Parfait'.** Bushy, cluster-flowered bush rose. H 2½ft (75cm), S 2ft (60cm). In summer-autumn, slightly fragrant, urn-shaped, double flowers, 3½in (9cm) across, in shades of light pink, are produced freely. Has plentiful foliage. Z4–11 H12–4.
***R.* 'Pink Perpétué'** illus. p.197.
***R.* 'Pompon de Paris'.** See *R.* 'Rouletii'.
***R.* 'Pompon des Princes'.** See *R.* 'Ispahan'.
***R.* Pot o' Gold ('Dicdivine')** illus. p.194.
***R.* 'Poulbells'.** See *R.* Pink Bells.
***R.* 'Poulcov'.** See *R.* Kent.
***R.* 'Poulman'.** See *R.* Ingrid Bergman.
***R.* 'Poulmax'.** See *R.* Fascination.
***R.* 'Poumidor'.** See *R.* Troika.
***R.* 'Prairie Dawn'.** An upright shrub rose with spiny canes that is good for hedging. H 5ft (1.5m), S 3ft (1m). Has fully double, medium pink blooms, with a good fragrance and disease resistance. Z3–9 H9–1.
***R.* 'Precious Platinum'**, syn. *R.* 'Opa Potschke', illus. p.192.
***R.* 'Président de Sèze'**, syn. *R.* 'Madame Hébert'. Vigorous, rather open Gallica rose. H and S 4ft (1.2m). Bears fragrant, quartered-rosette, fully double, magenta-pink to pale lilac-pink flowers, 4in (10cm) across, in summer. Z3–9 H9–1.
***R.* 'Prima'.** See *R.* 'Many Happy Returns'.
R. primula illus. p.188.
***R.* Princess Michael of Kent ('Harlightly').** Neat, compact, cluster-flowered bush rose. H 24in (60cm), S 20in (50cm). In summer-autumn produces pleasantly scented, rounded, fully double yellow flowers,3½in (9cm) across, singly or in clusters. Leaves are glossy, bright green, and very healthy. Makes a good low hedge.
***R.* 'Queen Elizabeth'**, syn. *R.* 'The Queen Elizabeth', illus. p.190.
***R.* 'Queen of the Violets'.** See *R.* 'Reine des Violettes'.
***R.* 'Rambling Rector'** illus. p.198.
***R.* 'Ramona'**, syn. *R.* 'Red Cherokee'. Rather stiff, open climbing rose. H 9ft (2.7m), S 10ft (3m). Fragrant, flat, single, carmine-red flowers, 4in (10cm) across, with a grayish red reverse and gold stamens, appear mainly in summer, a few later. Has sparse foliage. Z7–9 H9–1.
***R.* Red Ace ('Amruda')** illus. p.195.
***R.* 'Red Cherokee'.** See *R.* 'Ramona'.
***R.* 'Red Moss'.** See *R.* 'Henri Martin'.
***R.* 'Reine des Violettes'**, syn. *R.* 'Queen of the Violets'. Spreading, vigorous Hybrid Perpetual rose. H and S 6ft (2m). Has grayish-toned leaves and fragrant, quartered-rosette, fully double violet to purple flowers, 3in (8cm) across, in summer-autumn. May be grown on a support. Z5–9 H9–5.
***R.* 'Reine Victoria'** illus. p.186.
***R.* Remember Me ('Cocdestin')** illus. p.194.
***R.* 'Rise 'n' Shine'**, syn. *R.* 'Golden Sunblaze', illus. p.196.
***R.* 'Robert le Diable'.** Lax, bushy Provence rose. H and S 3ft (1m). In summer bears slightly scented, pompon, double flowers, 3in (8cm) across, in mixed bright and dull purple. Has narrowly oval, dark green leaves. Is best trailing over a low support. Z4–9 H9–1.
***R.* 'Rose d'Isfahan'.** See *R.* 'Ispahan'.
***R.* Rose Gaujard ('Gaumo').** Upright, strong, large-flowered bush rose. H 3½ft (1.1m), S 2½ft (75cm). Has plentiful glossy foliage. Bears slightly scented, urn-shaped, double, cherry red and blush pink flowers, 4in (10cm) across, freely in summer-autumn.
***R.* Rosemary Harkness ('Harrowbond')** illus. p190.
***R.* 'Roseraie de l'Haÿ'** illus. p.187.
***R.* Rosy Cushion ('Interall')** illus. p.186.
***R.* 'Rosy Mantle'** illus. p.197.
***R.* 'Rouge Eblouissante'.** See *R.* 'Assemblage des Beautés'.
***R.* 'Rouletii'**, syn. *R. chinensis* var. *minima*, *R.* 'Pompon de Paris'. Compact miniature China rose with thin stems. H and S 8in (20cm). Has midgreen leaves consisting of many lance-shaped leaflets, and freely produces cupped, double, deep pink flowers, ¾in (2cm) across, from summer to autumn. Z5–9 H9–5.
***R.* 'Royal Dane'.** See *R.* Troika.
***R.* 'Royal Highness'**, syn. *R.* 'Königliche Hoheit'. Upright, large-flowered bush rose. H 3½ft (1.1m), S 2ft (60cm). In summer-autumn, firm stems bear leathery, dark green foliage and large, fragrant, pointed, fully double, pearl pink flowers, 5in (12cm) across.
***R.* Royal William ('Korzaun')**, syn. *R.* 'Duftzauber '84', illus. p.192.
R. rubiginosa, syn. *R. eglanteria*, illus. p.185.
R. rubrifolia. See *R. glauca*.
R. rugosa illus. p.187. var. ***alba*** is a dense, vigorous, species hybrid rose. H and S 3–6ft (1–2m). Bears a succession of fragrant, cupped, single, white flowers, 3½in (9cm) across, in summer-autumn. They are followed by large, tomato-shaped hips. Abundant foliage is leathery, wrinkled, and glossy. Z2–9 H9–1.
***R.* 'Rugul'.** See *R.* Golden Penny.
***R.* 'Runatru'.** See *R.* Invincible.
***R.* 'Saint Nicholas'.** Vigorous, erect Damask rose. H and S 4ft (1.2m). In summer bears lightly scented, cupped, semi-double, rose-pink flowers, 5in (12cm) across, with golden stamens, followed by red hips in autumn. Has plentiful, dark green foliage. Z6–9 H9–1.
***R.* 'San Rafael Rose'.** See *R.* x *odorata* 'Pseudindica'.
***R.* 'Schneewittchen'.** See *R.* Iceberg.
R. sericea subsp. ***omeiensis*** f. ***pteracantha***, syn. *R. omeiensis* f. *pteracantha* (Winged thorn rose). Stiff, upright, vigorous species rose. H 8ft (2.5m), S 7ft (2.2m). Has small, fernlike, light green leaves and large red prickles on young stems. In summer, solitary, flat white flowers, 1–2½in (2.5–6cm) across, are borne briefly along the stems. Z6–9 H9–5.
***R.* Sexy Rexy ('Macrexy')** illus. p.190.
***R.* Sheila Macqueen ('Harwotnext').** Narrow, upright, cluster-flowered bush rose. H 30in (75cm), S 18in (45cm). In summer-autumn produces dense clusters of peppery-scented, cupped, double green flowers, 2½in (6cm) across, tinged apricot-pink. Has leathery leaves.
***R.* Sheila's Perfume ('Harsherry').** Upright, cluster-flowered bush rose. H 2½ft (75cm), S 2ft (60cm). Has glossy, reddish foliage. Fragrant, urn-shaped, double, red-and-yellow flowers, 3½in (9cm) across, are produced singly or in clusters in summer-autumn.
***R.* Sheri Anne ('Morsherry')** illus. p.195.
***R.* Shocking Blue ('Korblue').** Bushy, cluster-flowered bush rose. H 2½ft (75cm), S 2ft (60cm). Bears, in summer-autumn, fragrant, pointed, well-formed, fully double, purple flowers, 4in (10cm) across, singly or in clusters. Foliage is dark green.
***R.* 'Silver Jubilee'** illus. p.191.
***R.* Simba ('Korbelma')**, syn. *R.* 'Goldsmith', illus. p.193.
***R.* 'Sissi'.** See *R.* Blue Moon.
***R.* Snow Carpet ('Maccarpe').** Prostrate, creeping, miniature bush rose. H 6in (15cm), S 20in (50cm). Has many small glossy leaves and pompon, fully double white flowers, 1¼in (3cm) across, in summer, a few in autumn. Makes a good, compact groundcover.
***R.* Snowball ('Macangeli')**, syn. *R.* 'Angelita', illus. p.195.
***R.* 'Southampton'**, syn. *R.* 'Susan Ann', illus. p.194.
***R.* 'Souvenir d'Alphonse Lavallée'.** Vigorous, sprawling Hybrid Perpetual rose. H 7ft (2.2m), S 6ft (2m). Fragrant, cupped, double, burgundy-red to maroon-purple flowers, 4in (10cm) across, are borne in summer-autumn. Leaves are small and midgreen. Is best grown on a light support. Z6–9 H9–6.
***R.* 'Souvenir de la Malmaison'.** Dense, spreading Bourbon rose. H and S 5ft (1.5m). Bears spice-scented, quartered-rosette, fully double, blush pink to white flowers, 5in (12cm) across, in summer-autumn. Has large, dark green leaves. Z6–9 H9–6.
***R.* 'Spanish Beauty'.** See *R.* 'Madame Grégoire Staechelin'.

***R.* 'Spectacular'.** See *R.* 'Danse du Feu'.
R. spinosissima. See *R. pimpinellifolia.*
***R.* 'Spring Morning'.** See *R.* 'Frühlingsmorgen'.
***R.* 'Stacey Sue'** illus. p.195.
***R.* 'Sunblaze'.** See *R.* ORANGE SUNBLAZE.
***R.* SUNSET BOULEVARD ('Harbabble').** Upright cluster-flowered bush rose. H 3ft (1m), S 2ft (60cm). Bears open sprays of lightly scented, pointed to cupped, double, salmon-pink flowers, 3½in (9cm) across, in summer-autumn on glossy-foliaged plants. Is excellent for beds and cutting.
***R.* 'Susan Ann'.** See *R.* 'Southampton'.
***R.* 'Swan Lake'.** A vigorous climbing rose with an upright habit. H 8ft (2.5m), S 6ft (2m). Pointed buds open to give fully double white flowers with a pale pink flush in the center.
***R.* SWEET DREAM ('Fryminicot').** Compact, dwarf cluster-flowered bush rose. H 16in (40cm), S 14in (35cm). Clusters of slightly scented, pompon, fully double, peach-apricot flowers, 2½in (6cm) across, appear in summer-autumn. Leaves are small. Z3–9 H9–1.
***R.* SWEET MAGIC ('Dicmagic')** illus. p.194.
***R.* 'Sylvia'.** See *R.* CONGRATULATIONS.
***R.* 'Sympathie'** illus. p.198.
***R.* 'Tanba'.** See *R.* BABY MASQUERADE.
***R.* 'Tanellis'.** See *R.* FRAGRANT CLOUD.
***R.* 'Tanky'.** See *R.* WHISKY MAC.
***R.* 'Tannacht'.** See *R.* BLUE MOON.
***R.* 'Tapis d'Orient'.** See *R.* 'Yesterday'.
***R.* 'Tapis Jaune'.** See *R.* GOLDEN PENNY.
***R.* 'The Fairy'** illus. p.189.
***R.* 'The Queen Elizabeth'.** See *R.* 'Queen Elizabeth'.
***R.* 'Thérèse Bugnet'.** A hybrid *rugosa* rose that does not have the typical rough foliage. H and S 6ft (2m). Double fragrant flowers open a dark pink and fade with age. Blooms from June to frost, and the red canes are attractive in winter. Z3–9 H9–1.
***R.* THE TIMES ROSE ('Korpeahn')** illus. p.192.
***R.* 'Tour de Malakoff'** illus. p.188.
***R.* 'Tricolore de Flandre'.** Vigorous, upright Gallica rose. H and S 3ft (1m). Fragrant, pompon, fully double, blush pink flowers, 2½in (6cm) across, striped with pink and purple, open in summer. Has dull green leaves. Z3–9 H9–1.
***R.* TROIKA ('Poumidor'),** syn. *R.* 'Royal Dane', illus. p.194.
***R.* TRUMPETER ('Mactru')** illus. p.191.
***R.* 'Tuscany Superb'**, syn. *R.* 'Double Velvet'. Vigorous, upright Gallica rose. H 3½ft (1.1m), S 1m (3ft). In summer, produces, slightly scented, cupped to flat, double flowers, 2in (5cm) across, deep crimson-maroon, aging to purple, with gold stamens. Leaves are dark green. Z3–9 H9–1.
***R.* 'Variegata di Bologna'.** Upright, arching Bourbon rose. H 6ft (2m), S 4½ft (1.4m). Has small leaves and, in summer-autumn, fragrant, quartered-rosette, fully double flowers, 3in (8cm) across, in blush pink striped with rose-purple. Needs fertile soil and is prone to blackspot. Z6–9 H9–6.
***R.* 'Veilchenblau'**, syn. *R.* 'Blue Rambler', illus. p.199
***R.* 'Wedding Day'.** Rampant climbing rose. H 25ft (8m), S 12ft (4m). Produces large clusters of fruity-scented, flat, single, creamy white flowers, 1in (2.5cm) across, that mature to blush pink, in late summer. Is suitable for growing up a tree or in a wild garden. Z5–9 H9–1.
***R.* WEE JOCK ('Cocabest')** illus. p.192.
***R.* WHISKY MAC ('Tanky').** Neat, upright, large-flowered bush rose. H 2½ft (75cm), S 2ft (60cm). Fragrant, rounded, fully double amber flowers, 3½in (9cm) across, appear freely in summer-autumn. Reddish foliage is prone to mildew.
***R.* 'White Cockade'.** Slow-growing, bushy, upright, large-flowered climber. H 6–10ft (2–3m), S 5ft (1.5m). Bears slightly fragrant, rounded, well-formed, fully double white flowers, 3½in (9cm) across, in summer-autumn. May be pruned and grown as a shrub.
***R.* 'William Baffin'.** A tall, upright climbing rose. H 10ft (3m), S 4ft (1.2m). Clusters of up to 30 slightly fragrant, medium red flowers appear from June to September. Highly resistant to blackspot and mildew. Z2–9 H9–1.
***R.* 'William Lobb'**, syn. *R.* 'Duchesse d'Istrie', illus. p.188.
***R.* 'Winnipeg Parks'.** A recurrent-blooming dwarf shrub rose that makes a good container plant. H and S 15–40in (40–70cm). Plants form dense bushes with slightly fragrant medium red blooms in small clusters. Foliage is shiny, dark green and turns red in autumn. Z2–9 H9–1.
***R. xanthina* 'Canary Bird'**, syn. *R.* 'Canary Bird', illus. p.189.
***R.* 'Yesterday'**, syn. *R.* 'Tapis d'Orient'. Bushy, arching Polyantha bush rose. H and S 30in (75cm), or more if lightly pruned. Fragrant, rosette, semi-double, lilac-pink flowers, 1in (2.5cm) across, are borne, mainly in clusters, from summer through to early winter. Produces small, dark green leaves. Makes a hedge.
***R.* 'Yvonne Rabier'.** Dense, bushy Polyantha bush rose. H 18in (45cm), S 40cm (16in). Plentiful leaves are bright green. Bears moderately scented, rounded, double, creamy white flowers, 2in (5cm) across, in summer-autumn.
***R.* 'Zéphirine Drouhin'** illus. p.197.
***R.* 'Zigeunerknabe'**, syn. *R.* 'Gipsy Boy'. Vigorous, thorny Bourbon rose of lanky habit. H and S 6ft (2m). Faintly scented, cupped to flat, double, purplish crimson flowers, 3in (8cm) across, are borne in summer. Leaves are dark green. Z6–9 H9–6.
***R.* 'Zonta Rose'.** See *R.* PRINCESS ALICE.

ROSCOEA

ZINGIBERACEAE

Genus of late summer- and early autumn-flowering, tuberous perennials, related to ginger, grown for their orchidlike flowers. Good in open borders, rock gardens, and woodland gardens. Grows in sun or partial shade and in cool, well-drained organic soil that must be kept moist in summer. Dies down in winter, when a top dressing of leaf mold or well-rotted compost is beneficial. Propagate by division in spring or by seed, exposed to frost for best germination, in autumn or winter.
R. cautleyoides illus. p.436.
R. humeana illus. p.436.
R. procera. See *R. purpurea.*
R. purpurea, syn. *R. procera.* Summer-flowering, tuberous perennial. H 8–12in (20–30cm), S 6–8in (15–20cm). Lance-shaped, erect leaves are long-pointed and wrap around each other at base to form a false stem. Has long-tubed purple flowers, each with a hooded, upper petal, wide-lobed, lower lip and 2 narrower petals.

ROSMARINUS

LABIATAE/LAMIACEAE

Genus of evergreen shrubs grown for their flowers and aromatic foliage, or as a culinary herb. At limits of hardiness grow against a south- or west-facing wall. Requires sun and well-drained soil. Cut back frost-damaged plants to healthy wood in spring; straggly old plants may be cut back hard at same time. After flowering, trim hedges. Propagate by semi-ripe cuttings in summer.
R. lavandulaceus of gardens. See *R. officinalis* 'Prostratus'.
R. officinalis (Rosemary) illus. p.167. **'Miss Jessopp's Upright'** is an evergreen, compact, upright shrub. H and S 6ft (2m). From mid- to late spring and sometimes again in autumn bears small, 2-lipped blue flowers amid narrowly oblong, aromatic, dark green leaves. Is good when grown for hedging. Z7–11 H12–7. **'Prostratus'** (syn. *R. lavandulaceus* of gardens), H 6in (15cm), is prostrate and among the least hardy fors. Z8–10 H12–2. **'Severn Sea'**, H 3ft (1m), is arching, with bright blue flowers.

ROSSIOGLOSSUM

See also ORCHIDS.
R. grande, syn. *Odontoglossum grande* (illus. p.297). Evergreen, epiphytic orchid for a cool greenhouse. H 6in (15cm). Spikes of rich yellow flowers, to 6in (15cm) across and heavily marked chestnut brown, are produced in autumn. Has broadly oval, stiff leaves, 6in (15cm) long. Provide shade in summer and keep very dry in winter. Z14–15 H12–6.

ROTHMANNIA

RUBIACEAE

Genus of evergreen, summer-flowering shrubs and trees grown for their flowers. Is related to *Gardenia*. Needs a position in full light or partial shade and organic, well-drained, neutral to acidic soil. Water potted plants freely when in full growth, moderately at other times. Propagate by seed in spring or by semi-ripe cuttings in summer.
R. capensis, syn. *Gardenia capensis*, *G. rothmannia*. Evergreen, ovoid shrub or tree. H 20ft (6m) or more, S 10ft (3m) or more. Leaves are oval, lustrous, and rich green. Has fragrant, tubular flowers, each with 5 arching, white to creamy yellow petal lobes and a purple-dotted throat, in summer. Z13–15 H12-10.

ROYSTONEA

Royal palm

ARECACEAE/PALMAE

Genus of evergreen palms grown for their majestic appearance. Produces racemes of insignificant flowers in summer. Needs full light or partial shade and fertile, well-drained but moisture-retentive soil. Water potted plants freely when in full growth, less at other times, especially when temperatures are low. Propagate by seed in spring at not less than 81°F (27°C). Spider mite may be a problem.
R. regia (Cuban royal palm). Evergreen palm with upright stem, sometimes thickened about the middle. H 70ft (20m) or more, S to 20ft (6m). Leaves are feather-shaped, 10ft (3m) long, upright at first, later arching and pendent, and are divided into narrowly oblong, leathery, bright green leaflets. Z11–12 H12-10.

RUBUS

Blackberry, Bramble

ROSACEAE

Genus of deciduous, semi-evergreen or evergreen shrubs and woody-stemmed, scrambling climbers. Some species are cultivated solely for their edible fruits, including raspberries and blackberries. Those described here are grown mainly for their foliage, flowers, or ornamental, often prickly stems, though some may also bear edible fruits. Deciduous species grown for their winter stems prefer full sun; other deciduous species need sun or semi-shade; evergreens and semi-evergreens tolerate sun or shade. All *Rubus* require fertile, well-drained soil. Cut old stems of *R. biflorus*, *R. cockburnianus*, and *R. thibetanus* to ground after fruiting. Propagate by seed or cuttings (semi-ripe for evergreens, softwood or hardwood for deciduous species) in summer or winter. *R. odoratus* may be increased by division, and *R.* 'Benenden' and *R. ulmifolius* 'Bellidiflorus' by layering in spring.

***R.* 'Benenden'**, syn. *R.* 'Tridel', illus. p.136.
R. biflorus illus. p.149.
R. cockburnianus. Deciduous, arching shrub. H and S 8ft (2.5m). Prickly shoots are brilliant blue-white in winter. Dark green leaves, white beneath, each have usually 9 oval leaflets. Bears panicles of 5-petaled purple flowers in early summer, followed by unpalatable, spherical black fruits. Z6–8 H8–6.
R. henryi var. ***bambusarum.*** Fast-growing, vigorous, evergreen, woody-stemmed, scrambling climber grown mainly for its attractive foliage. H to 20ft (6m). Leaves have 3 broadly oval leaflets, white-felted beneath. Tiny pink flowers are borne in small clusters in summer. Z5–9 H9–5.
R. odoratus (Flowering raspberry, Thimbleberry). Vigorous, deciduous, upright, thicket-forming shrub. H and S 8ft (2.5m). Thornless, peeling shoots bear large, velvety, dark green leaves, each with 5 broadly triangular lobes. Large, fragrant, 5-petaled, rose pink flowers appear from early summer to early autumn and are sometimes followed by unpalatable, flattened red fruits. Z3–7 H7–1.
R. thibetanus illus. p.149.
R. tricolor. Evergreen shrub with both prostrate and arching shoots covered in red bristles. H 2ft (60cm), S 6ft (2m). Oval, toothed, glossy, dark green leaves set off cup-shaped, 5-petaled white flowers borne in midsummer. Has edible, raspberry-like red fruits. Makes a good groundcover. Z7–9 H9–7.
***R.* 'Tridel'.** See *R.* 'Benenden'.
***R. ulmifolius* 'Bellidiflorus'.** Vigorous, deciduous or semi-evergreen, arching shrub. H 8ft (2.5m), S 12ft (4m). Prickly stems bear dark green leaves, with 3 or 5 oval leaflets, and, in mid- to late summer, large panicles of daisylike, double pink flowers. Z6–9 H9–6.

RUDBECKIA
Coneflower

ASTERACEAE/COMPOSITAE

Genus of annuals, biennials and perennials grown for their flowers. Thrives in sun or shade and well-drained or moist soil. Propagate by division in spring or by seed in autumn or spring.
R. fulgida (Black-eyed Susan). var. ***deamii*** is an erect perennial. H 3ft (1m), S 2ft (60cm) or more. In late summer and autumn produces daisylike yellow flower heads with central black cones. Has narrowly lance-shaped, midgreen leaves. Prefers moist soil. Z4–9 H9–1.var. ***sullivantii* 'Goldsturm'** illus. p.256.
***R.* 'Goldquelle'** illus. p.229.
***R.* 'Herbstsonne'** illus. p.232.
R. hirta. Moderately fast-growing, upright, branching, short-lived perennial grown as an annual. H 1–3ft (30cm–1m), S 1–1½ft (30–45cm). Has lance-shaped, midgreen leaves and, in summer-autumn, large, daisylike, deep yellow flower heads with conical purple centers. Needs sun and well-drained soil. Z3–7 H7–1. **'Goldilocks'** illus. p.340. **'Irish Eyes'**, H to 2½ft (75cm), has yellow flower heads with bright green centers. **'Marmalade'** and **'Rustic Dwarfs'** illus. p.340.
***R. laciniata* 'Golden Glow'.** Erect perennial. H 6–7ft (2–2.2m), S 2–3ft (60cm–1m). Bears daisylike, double, golden yellow flower heads with green centers in late summer and autumn. Midgreen leaves are divided into lance-shaped leaflets, themselves further cut. Prefers well-drained soil. Z3–9 H9–1.
R. purpurea. See *Echinacea purpurea.*

RUELLIA

ACANTHACEAE

Genus of perennials and evergreen subshrubs and shrubs with showy flowers. Grow in partial shade and moist but well-drained soil. Propagate by stem cuttings or seed in spring.
R. amoena. See *R. graecizans.*
R. devosiana illus. p.277.
R. graecizans, syn. *R. amoena*, illus. p.249.

RUSCHIA

AIZOACEAE

Genus of mostly small, tufted succulents and evergreen shrubs with leaves united up to one-third of their lengths around stems or with very short sheaths. Needs sun and well-drained soil. Propagate by seed or stem cuttings in spring or summer.
R. acuminata. Evergreen, erect, succulent shrub. H 8in (20cm), S 20in (50cm). Has woody stems as well as non-woody, bluish green stems with darker dots. Produces solid, 3-angled, 1¼in (3cm) long leaves, each with a blunt keel and a short sheath. Daisy-like, white to pale pink flowers, 1¼in (3cm) across, appear in summer. Z13–15 H12-10.
R. crassa. Evergreen, erect, succulent shrub. H and S 20in (50cm). Bears solid, 3-angled, bluish green leaves, ¾in (2cm) long, with short white hairs; the undersides are keeled, each with a single tooth. Has 1in (2.5cm) wide, daisylike white flowers in summer. Z13–15 H12-10.
R. macowanii. Erect then spreading succulent. H 6in (15cm), S 3ft (1m). Has solid, slightly keeled, 3-angled, bluish green leaves, to 1¼in (3cm) long. In summer carries masses of daisylike, bright pink flowers, 1¼in (3cm) across, with darker stripes. Z13–15 H12-10.

RUSCUS

RUSCACEAE/LILIACEAE

Genus of evergreen, clump-forming, spring-flowering shrubs grown for their foliage and fruits. The apparent leaves are actually flattened shoots, on which flowers and fruits are borne. Usually, separate male and female plants are required for fruiting. Is particularly useful for dry, shady sites. Tolerates sun or shade and any soil other than waterlogged. Cut back dead shoots to base in spring. Propagate by division in spring. The berries of *R. aculeatus* may cause mild stomach upset if ingested.
R. aculeatus (Butcher's broom). Evergreen, erect, thicket-forming shrub. H 2½ft (75cm), S 3ft (1m). Spine-tipped "leaves" are glossy and dark green. Tiny, star-shaped green flowers in spring are succeeded by large, spherical, bright red fruits. Z7–9 H9–7.
R. hypoglossum illus. p.176.

RUSSELIA

SCROPHULARIACEAE

Genus of evergreen shrubs and subshrubs with showy flowers. Needs sun or partial shade. Requires organic, light, well-drained soil. Propagate by stem cuttings or division in spring.
R. equisetiformis, syn. *R. juncea*, illus. p.250.
R. juncea. See *R. equisetiformis.*

RUTA
Rue

RUTACEAE

Genus of evergreen, summer-flowering subshrubs, with deeply divided, aromatic leaves, grown for their foliage and flowers and used as a medicinal herb. Requires a sunny position and well-drained soil. Cut back to old wood in spring to keep compact. Propagate by semi-ripe cuttings in summer. All parts may cause severe discomfort if eaten; the foliage may cause severe photo-dermatitis on contact, especially on sunny, humid days.
R. graveolens (Common rue). **'Jackman's Blue'** illus. p.177.

SABAL

ARECACEAE/PALMAE

Genus of evergreen fan palms grown for their foliage and overall appearance. Prefers full sun and fertile, well-drained soil. Water moderately, less when not in full growth. Propagate by seed in spring. Spider mite may be troublesome.
S. minor illus. p.176.

SAGINA

CARYOPHYLLACEAE

Genus of mat-forming annuals and evergreen perennials grown for their foliage. Is suitable for banks and in paving. Some species may be very invasive. Prefers sun and gritty, moist soil; dislikes hot, dry conditions. Propagate by division in spring, by seed in autumn, or, for *S. boydii*, by tip cuttings in summer. Aphids and spider mite may cause problems.
S. boydii illus. p.390.

SAGITTARIA
Arrowhead

ALISMATACEAE

Genus of deciduous, perennial, submerged and marginal water plants grown for their foliage and flowers. Some species are suitable for ponds, others for aquariums. All require full sun. Remove fading foliage as necessary. Propagate by division in spring or summer or by breaking off turions (scaly young shoots) in spring.
S. japonica. See *S. sagittifolia* 'Flore Pleno'.
S. latifolia illus. p.446.
S. sagittifolia (Common arrowhead). Deciduous, perennial, marginal water plant. H 18in (45cm), S 12in (30cm). Upright, midgreen leaves are acutely arrow-shaped. In summer produces 3-petaled white flowers with dark purple centers. May be grown in up to 9in (23cm) depth of water. Z5–11 H12–3. **'Flore Pleno'** (syn. *S. japonica*; Japanese arrowhead) has double flowers.

SAINTPAULIA
African violet

GESNERIACEAE

Genus of evergreen, rosette-forming perennials grown (mostly as house plants)for their showy flowers. Needs a constant temperature, a humid atmosphere, partial shade, and fertile soil. Propagate by leaf cuttings in summer. Whitefly and mealy bug may cause problems with indoor plants.

African violet cultivars

There are over 2,000 cultivars, mainly derived from *S. ionantha*, with star- or bell-shaped white, pink, red, blue, violet, and bi- or multi-colored flowers borne throughout the year. They may be single, semi-double, or fully double. Petal edges may be ruffled, rounded, frilled, or fringed. The broadly ovate to oval leaves are usually mid- or dark green and may be feathered, flecked, or otherwise variegated white, pink, or cream. See also feature panel p.302.

Cultivars are divided into 5 groups, according to rosette size. The measurement given below is the diameter of the rosette; the spread of each cultivar is the same as this.
Micro-miniature – less than 3in (8cm);
Miniature – 3–6in (8–16cm);
Semi-miniature – 6–8in (16–21cm);
Standard – 8–16in (21–40cm) ;
Large – over 16in (40cm).

All of the following African violets are H12–10.

***S.* 'Bright Eyes'** (illus. p.302). Standard Group. H to 6in (15cm). Has dark green leaves and single, deep violet-blue flowers with yellow centers.
***S.* 'Chantabent'.** Semi-miniature Group. H 4–6in (10–15cm). Has dark green leaves with deep red undersides and bears large, single, violet-blue flowers.

***S.* 'Colorado'** (illus. p.302). Standard Group. H 6–8in (15–20cm). Bears dark green leaves and frilled, single magenta flowers.
***S.* 'Delft'** (illus. p.302). Standard Group. H to 6in (15cm). Leaves are dark green, and flowers are semi-double and violet-blue.
***S.* 'Dorothy'.** Standard Group. H to 6in (15cm). Has long-stalked, light green leaves and bears large, single, rich pink flowers with frilled white margins.
***S.* 'Garden News'** (illus. p.302). Standard Group. H to 6in (15cm). Has bright green leaves and double, pure white flowers.
***S.* 'Ice Maiden'** (illus. p.302). Standard Group. H to 6in (15cm). Bears single white flowers with purple-blue markings.
S. ionantha. Evergreen, stemless, rosette-forming perennial, often forming clumps. H to 4in (10cm), S 10in (25cm). Almost rounded, scalloped, long-stalked, fleshy, usually hairy leaves, to 3in (8cm) long, are midgreen above and often reddish green below. Loose clusters of 2–8 tubular, 5-lobed, violet-blue flowers, to 1in (2.5cm) across, are produced on stems held above leaves and appear year-round.
***S.* 'Pip Squeek'** (illus. p.302). Micro-miniature Group. H to 3in (8cm). Has oval, unscalloped, deep green leaves, ½–¾in (1–2cm) long, and bell-shaped, pale pink flowers, ½in (1cm) wide.
***S.* 'Porcelain'** (illus. p.302). Standard Group. H to 6in (15cm). Bears semi-double white flowers with purple-blue edges.
***S.* 'Rococo Anna'**, syn. *S.* 'Rococo Pink' (illus. p.302). Standard Group. H to 6in (15cm). Bears double, iridescent pink flowers.
***S.* 'Starry Trail'** (illus. p.302). Standard Group. H to 6in (15cm). Has dark green leaves and narrow-petaled, semi-double to double white flowers, sometimes flushed pale pink.
***S.* 'Zoja'** (illus. p.302). Standard Group. H to 6in (15cm). Produces large, single to semi-double, purple-blue flowers with a bold white line at the margin of each petal.

SALIX

Willow

SALICACEAE

Genus of deciduous trees and shrubs grown for their habit, foliage, catkins, and, in some cases, colorful winter shoots. Male catkins are more striking than female; each plant usually bears catkins of only one sex. Most prefer full sun. Most species grow well in any but very dry soil; *S. caprea*, *S. purpurea*, and their variants also thrive in dry soil. Plants grown for their colorful winter shoots should be cut back hard in early spring, every 1–3 years. Propagate by semi-ripe cuttings in summer or by hardwood cuttings in winter. Fungal diseases may cause canker, particularly in *S. babylonica* and *S.* x *sepulcralis* var. *chrysocoma*. Willows may become infested with such pests as caterpillars, aphids, and gall mites.
S. aegyptiaca (Musk willow). Vigorous, deciduous, bushy shrub or tree. H 12ft (4m), S 15ft (5m). Gray catkins that turn to yellow appear on bare, thick shoots in late winter or early spring, before large, narrowly oval, deep green leaves. Z5–8 H8–5.
S. alba (White willow). f. ***argentea*** see *S.a.* var. *sericea*. **'Britzensis'** see *S.a.* var. *vitellina* 'Britzensis'. var. ***caerulea*** (Cricket-bat willow) is a very fast-growing, deciduous, conical tree with upright branches. H 80ft (25m), S 30ft (10m). Has long, narrowly lance-shaped, deep bluish green leaves and, in early spring, small, pendent, yellowish green catkins. Z4–9 H9–1. **'Chermesina'** see *S.a.* var. *vitellina* 'Chermesina'. **'Sericea'** see *S.a.* var. *sericea*. var. ***sericea*** (syn. *S.a.* f. *argentea*, *S.a.* 'Sericea'; Silver willow), H 50ft (15m), S 25ft (8m), is a spreading tree that is conical when young and has bright silver-gray leaves. **'Tristis'** (syn. *S. vitellina* 'Pendula') has a more weeping habit and produces only female catkins. **'Tristis'** of gardens see *S.* x *sepulcralis* var. *chrysocoma*. var. ***vitellina*** illus. p.74. var. ***vitellina* 'Britzensis'** (syn. *S.a.* 'Britzensis'), which has green leaves and bright orange-red, young shoots, is usually cut back to near ground level to provide winter color. var. ***vitellina* 'Chermesina'** (syn. *S.a.* 'Chermesina') has carmine-red, young winter shoots.
S. apoda illus. p.363.
S. arbuscula (Mountain willow). Deciduous, spreading shrub. H and S 2ft (60cm) or more. In spring, dark brown stems produce narrowly oval, toothed leaves and white-haired, sometimes red-tinged yellow catkins. Good in a rock garden. Z3–9 H9–1.
S. babylonica (Weeping willow). Deciduous, weeping tree with slender, pendent shoots that reach almost to the ground. H and S 40ft (12m). Bears narrowly lance-shaped, long-pointed leaves. Has yellowish green catkins in early spring. Is susceptible to canker and has been largely replaced in cultivation by *S.* x *sepulcralis* var. *chrysocoma*. Z6–9 H9–1. var. ***pekinensis* 'Tortuosa'** (syn. *S. matsudana* 'Tortuosa') illus. p.85.
S. bockii. Deciduous, bushy shrub. H and S 8ft (2.5m). Has slender, upright, gray-hairy shoots and oblong, glossy, bright green leaves with silky-hairy undersides. Usually female in cultivation; bears green catkins in early and midautumn. Z4–7 H7–1.
S.* x *boydii illus. p.361.
S. caprea (Goat willow, Pussy willow). Deciduous, bushy shrub or tree. H 30ft (10m), S 25ft (8m). Oval leaves are dark green above, gray beneath. Catkins are borne in spring before foliage emerges: females are silky and gray, males are gray with yellow anthers. Z6–8 H8–6. **'Kilmarnock'** (Kilmarnock willow), H 5–6ft (1.5–2m), S 6ft (2m), is dense-headed and weeping. From early to mid-spring produces gray catkins that later become yellow.
***S.* 'Chrysocoma'.** See *S.* x *sepulcralis* var. *chrysocoma*.
S. daphnoides illus. p.74.
S. elaeagnos (Hoary willow). Deciduous, upright, dense shrub. H 10ft (3m), S 15ft (5m). In spring, long shoots bear slender yellow catkins as leaves appear. These are narrowly oblong and dark green, with white undersides, and turn yellow in autumn. Z4–7 H7–1.
S. fargesii, syn. *S. moupinensis* of gardens. Deciduous, upright, open shrub. H and S 10ft (3m). Has purplish red winter shoots and buds. Slender, erect green catkins are carried in spring at the same time as bold, oblong, glossy, dark green leaves. Z5–8 H8–5.
S. fragilis (Crack willow). Deciduous tree with a broad, bushy head. H 50ft (15m), S 40–45ft (12–15m). Has long, narrow, pointed, glossy, bright green leaves. Catkins, borne in early spring, are yellow on male plants, green on females. Z4–7 H7–1.
S. gracilistyla. Deciduous, bushy shrub. H 10ft (3m), S 12ft (4m). Large, silky gray catkins with red then bright yellow anthers are produced from early to midspring and are followed by lance-shaped, silky gray, young leaves that mature to bright, glossy green. Z5–8 H8–5. **'Melanostachys'** (syn. *S.* 'Melanostachys'; Black willow) bears almost black catkins with red anthers in early spring, before bright green leaves emerge.
***S. hastata* 'Wehrhahnii'** illus. p.153.
S. helvetica illus. p.349.
S. herbacea (Dwarf willow, Least willow). Deciduous, creeping shrub. H 1in (2.5cm), S 8in (20cm) or more. Has small, rounded to oval leaves and, in spring, small, yellow or yellowish green catkins are produced. Is good for a rock garden. Needs moist soil.
S. irrorata. Deciduous, upright shrub. H 10ft (3m), S 15ft (5m). Purple young shoots are white-bloomed in winter. Catkins with red then yellow anthers appear from early to midspring before narrowly oblong, glossy, bright green leaves emerge. Z5–9 H9–5.
S. lanata illus. p.156. **'Stuartii'** see *S.* 'Stuartii'.
S. lindleyana. Deciduous, creeping, mat-forming shrub with long, creeping stems. H ¾–1¼in (2–3cm), S 16in (40cm) or more. Small, narrowly oval to linear, pale green leaves are densely set on short branchlets that produce brownish pink catkins, ½in (1cm) long, in spring. Good in a rock garden or bank. Needs partial shade and damp soil. Is often confused with the very similar *S. furcata* (syn. *S. fruticulosa*, *S. hylematica*), which is more lax, with spreading, sometimes erect stems. Z7–8 H8–7.
S. magnifica. Deciduous, upright shrub. H 15ft (5m), S 10ft (3m). Produces very long, slender green catkins on thick red shoots in spring, as large, magnolia-like, blue-green leaves emerge. Z7–8 H8–7.
***S. matsudana* 'Tortuosa'.** See *S. babylonica* var. *pekinensis* 'Tortuosa'.
***S.* 'Melanostachys'.** See *S. gracilistyla* 'Melanostachys'.
S. moupinensis of gardens. See *S. fargesii*.
S. pentandra (Bay willow, Laurel willow). Deciduous, large shrub, then small tree with broad, bushy head. H and S 30ft (10m). Oval, glossy green leaves are blue-white beneath. Catkins – males bright yellow, females gray-green – open in early summer when the tree is in full leaf. Z5–9 H9–1.
S. purpurea (Purple osier). Deciduous, bushy, spreading shrub. H and S 15ft (5m). Gray male catkins, with yellow anthers, and insignificant female catkins are both borne on slender, often purple shoots in spring, before narrowly oblong, deep green leaves emerge. Z4–7 H7–1. **'Nana'** (syn. *S.p.* f. *gracilis*, *S.p.* 'Gracilis'), H and S 1.5m (5ft), is dense, with silver-gray leaves; is good as a hedge.
S. repens illus. p.156.
S. reticulata illus. p.370.
***S.* x *rubens* 'Basfordiana'.** Deciduous, spreading tree. H 50ft (15m), S 30ft (10m). Has bright orange-yellow young shoots in winter and long, narrow leaves, gray-green when young, becoming glossy, bright green in summer. Yellowish green catkins appear in early spring. Z5–7 H7–5.
***S. sachalinensis* 'Sekka'.** See *S. udensis* 'Sekka'.
S.* x *sepulcralis var. ***chrysocoma***, syn. *S. alba* 'Tristis' of gardens, *S.* 'Chrysocoma', illus. p.74.
***S.* 'Stuartii'**, syn. *S. lanata* 'Stuartii'. Slow-growing, deciduous, spreading shrub. H 3ft (1m), S 6ft (2m). Has yellow winter shoots. Thick, gray-green catkins open from orange buds in spring, as oval, woolly gray leaves emerge. Z5–9 H9–5.
***S. udensis* 'Sekka'**, syn. *S. sachalinensis* 'Sekka'. Deciduous, spreading shrub. H 15ft (5m), S 30ft (10m). Has flattened shoots that are red in winter and lance-shaped, glossy, bright green leaves. Silver catkins are produced in early spring. Z4–7 H7–1.
***S. vitellina* 'Pendula'.** See *S. alba* 'Tristis'.

SALPIGLOSSIS

SOLANACEAE

Genus of annuals and biennials. Usually only annuals are cultivated, either for color in borders or as greenhouse plants. Grow in sun and in rich, well-drained soil. Stems need support. Deadhead regularly. Propagate by seed sown under cover in early spring, or in early autumn for winter flowering indoors. Aphids may be troublesome.
***S. sinuata* Bolero Hybrids.** Group of moderately fast-growing, branching, upright annuals. H 2ft (60cm), S 1ft (30cm). Has lance-shaped, pale green leaves. Outward-facing, widely flared,

trumpet-shaped, conspicuously veined flowers, 2in (5cm) across, appear in summer and early autumn. Is available in a mixture of rich colors. H12–1. **Casino Series** illus. p.329. **'Friendship'** has upward-facing flowers in a range of colors. H12–1.

SALVIA
Sage

LABIATAE/LAMIACEAE

Genus of annuals, biennials, perennials, and evergreen or semi-evergreen shrubs and subshrubs grown for their tubular, 2-lipped, often brightly colored flowers and aromatic foliage. Leaves of some species may be used for flavoring foods. Needs sun and fertile, well-drained soil. Propagate perennials by division in spring, and perennials, shrubs, and subshrubs by softwood cuttings in midsummer. Sow seed of annuals under cover in early spring and of species outdoors in midspring.

S. blepharophylla. Spreading, rhizomatous perennial. H and S 18in (45cm). Has oval, glossy, dark green leaves and slender racemes of bright red flowers with maroon calyces in summer-autumn. Z8–10 H10–8.

S. bulleyana. Rosette-forming perennial. H and S 24in (60cm). Racemes of nettle-like yellow flowers with maroon lips are borne in summer above a basal mass of broadly oval, coarse, prominently veined, dark green leaves. Z7–9 H9–7.

S. farinacea **f.** ***alba.*** Moderately fast-growing, upright perennial grown as an annual. H 3ft (1m), S 1ft (30cm). Has lance-shaped, midgreen leaves. Spikes of white flowers are produced in summer. Z8–11 H12–1. **'Strata'** has blue and white flowers. **'Victoria'** illus. p.332. Dwarf forms are also available.

S. fulgens illus. p.166.

S. grahamii. See *S. microphylla* var. *microphylla*.

S. greggii. Evergreen, erect subshrub. H to 3ft (1m), S to 2ft (60cm). Leaves are narrowly oblong and matte, deep green. Has terminal racemes of bright red-purple flowers in autumn. Z7–9 H9–4.

S. haematodes. See *S. pratensis* Haematodes Group.

S. horminum. See *S. viridis*.

S. involucrata. Bushy, woody-based perennial. H 2–2½ft (60–75cm) or more, S 3ft (1m). Has oval, midgreen leaves and, in late summer and autumn, racemes of large, rose-crimson flowers. Z11–15 H12–10. **'Bethellii'** illus. p.231.

S. jurisicii. Rosette-forming perennial. H 18in (45cm), S 12in (30cm). Stems are clothed with midgreen leaves, divided into 4–6 pairs of linear leaflets. In early summer produces racemes of inverted, violet-blue flowers.

S. leucantha (Mexican bush sage). Evergreen, erect, well-branched shrub. H and S to 2ft (60cm) or more. Narrowly lance-shaped, finely wrinkled leaves are deep green above, white-downy beneath. In summer-autumn produces terminal spikes of hairy white flowers, each from a woolly violet calyx. Z9–11 H12–4.

S. microphylla var. ***microphylla***, syn. *S. grahamii*. Evergreen, erect, well-branched shrub. H and S 3–4ft (1–1.2m). Has oval to elliptic, mid- to deep green leaves. Racemes of dark crimson flowers, aging to purple and with purple-tinted calyces, appear in late summer and autumn. Z12–15 H12–10. var. ***neurepia*** illus. p.166.

S. nemorosa, syn. *S. virgata* var. *nemorosa*. Neat, clump-forming perennial. H 3ft (1m), S 1½ft (45cm). Has narrowly oval, rough, midgreen leaves and, in summer, branching racemes densely set with violet-blue flowers. Z5–9 H9–5. **'East Friesland'** see *S.n.* 'Ostfriesland'. **'Lubecca'**, H 1½ft (45cm), is a dwarf form. **'Ostfriesland'** (syn. *S.n.* 'East Friesland'), H 2½ft (75cm), is smaller.

S. officinalis (Sage). **'Icterina'** illus. p.177. **'Purpurascens'** is an evergreen or semi-evergreen, bushy shrub. H 2ft (60cm), S 3ft (1m). Oblong, gray-green leaves are used as a culinary herb and are purple-flushed when young. Racemes of blue-purple flowers are produced in summer. Z4–10 H10–1.

S. patens **'Cambridge Blue'** illus. p.287.

S. pratensis **Haematodes Group**, syn. *S. haematodes*. Short-lived, rosette-forming perennial. H 3ft (1m), S 1½ft (45cm). In early summer produces panicles massed with lavender-blue flowers above large, broadly oval, wavy-edged, toothed, rough, dark green leaves. Z7–10 H10–7.

S. sclarea var. ***turkestanica*** illus. p.330.

S. splendens. Slow-growing, bushy perennial or evergreen subshrub grown as an annual. H to 12in (30cm), S 8–12in (20–30cm). Has oval, serrated, fresh green leaves, and dense racemes of scarlet flowers in summer and early autumn. Z11–12 H12–1. **'Blaze of Fire'** has brilliant scarlet flowers. **Cleopatra Series** (salmon, illus. p.321; violet, illus. p.331) are available in mixed or single colors. **'Rambo'**, H to 24in (60cm), is very tall, vigorous, and bushy, with dark green leaves and scarlet flowers. **'Red Riches'** (syn. *S.s.* 'Ryco'), S 12–16in (30–40cm) has dark green leaves and scarlet flowers. **'Ryco'** see *S.s.* 'Red Riches'. **'Scarlet King'** illus. p.328. **Sizzler Series** illus p.327.

S. x ***superba.*** Clump-forming, erect, branched perennial. H 24–36in (60–90cm), S 18–24in (45–60cm). Leaves are lance-shaped to oblong, scalloped and midgreen, slightly hairy beneath. Slender, terminal racemes of bright violet or purple flowers, to ½in (1.5cm) long, are produced from midsummer to early autumn. Z5–9 H9–5. **'Mainacht'** (syn. *S.* x *s.* 'May Night') illus. p.252.

S. uliginosa (Bog sage). Graceful, upright, branching perennial. H 6ft (2m), S 1½ft (45cm). Has oblong to lance-shaped, saw-edged, midgreen leaves and, in autumn, long racemes with whorls of bright blue flowers. Prefers moist soil. Z8–11 H12–7.

S. virgata var. ***nemorosa.*** See *S. nemorosa*.

S. viridis, syn. *S. horminum*, illus. p.331. **'Bouquet'** (syn. *S.v.* 'Monarch Bouquet') is a moderately fast-growing, upright, branching annual with oval to oblong leaves. H 18–20in (45–50cm), S 9in (23cm). Tubular, lipped flowers, with blue, rose-pink, white, deep carmine-pink, or purple bracts, are carried in spikes at tops of stems in summer and early autumn; also available as single colors. Z11–15 H12-10. Bracts of **Claryssa Series** are in a wide range of brilliant colors, including white, pink, purple, and blue. **'Monarch Bouquet'** see *S.v.* 'Bouquet'. **'Oxford Blue'**, H 12in (30cm), has violet-blue bracts.

SALVINIA

SALVINIACEAE

Genus of deciduous, perennial, floating water ferns, evergreen in tropical conditions and aquariums. Does best in warm water, with plenty of light. Remove fading foliage, and thin plants when crowded. Propagate by dividing young plants in summer.

S. auriculata illus. p.449.

S. natans. Deciduous, perennial, floating water plant. S indefinite. Oval, elongated, midgreen leaves are borne on branching stems. Tolerates colder conditions than other species and is often used in a cold-water aquarium.

SAMBUCUS
Elder, Elderberry

CAPRIFOLIACEAE

Genus of perennials, deciduous shrubs and trees grown for their foliage, flowers, and fruits. Needs sun and fertile, moist soil. For best foliage effect, either cut all shoots to ground in winter or prune out old shoots and reduce length of young shoots by half. Propagate species by softwood cuttings in summer, by seed in autumn, or by hardwood cuttings in winter, some forms by cuttings only. All parts may cause severe discomfort if ingested, although fruits are safe when cooked; contact with the leaves may irritate skin.

S. canadensis (American elder). **'Aurea'** is a deciduous, upright shrub. H and S 12ft (4m). Has large, golden yellow leaves, each with usually 7 oblong leaflets. In midsummer bears large, domed heads of small, star-shaped, creamy white flowers, then spherical red fruits. Z4–9 H9–1.

S. nigra (European elder). **'Aurea'** (Golden European elder) is a deciduous, bushy shrub. H and S 20ft (6m). Has thick, corky shoots and golden yellow leaves of usually 5 oval leaflets. Flattened heads of fragrant, star-shaped, creamy white flowers in early summer are followed by spherical black fruits. Dark green foliage of **'Guincho Purple'** matures to deep blackish purple. Bears purple-stalked flowers, pink in bud and opening to white within, pink outside. Both Z6–8 H8–6.

S. racemosa (Red-berried elder). Deciduous, bushy shrub. H and S 10ft (3m). Midgreen leaves each have usually 5 oval leaflets. Star-shaped, creamy yellow flowers, borne in dense, conical clusters in midspring, are succeeded by spherical red fruits. Z3–7 H7–1. **'Plumosa'** has leaves with finely cut leaflets, as does **'Plumosa Aurea'**, but those of the latter are bronze when young, maturing to golden yellow. **'Sutherland Gold'** retains its golden yellow color throughout the summer.

SANCHEZIA

ACANTHACEAE

Genus of evergreen, mainly summer-flowering perennials, shrubs and scrambling climbers grown for their flowers and foliage. Requires full light or partial shade and fertile, well-drained soil. Water potted plants freely when in full growth, less at other times. Tip prune young plants to promote a branching habit. Propagate by greenwood cuttings in spring or summer. Is prone to whitefly and soft scale.

S. nobilis of gardens. See *S. speciosa*.

S. speciosa, syn. *S. nobilis* of gardens, illus. p.177.

SANDERSONIA

COLCHICACEAE/LILIACEAE

Genus of one species of deciduous, tuberous climber with urn-shaped flowers in summer. Needs a sheltered, sunny site and well-drained soil. Provide support. Lift tubers for winter. Propagate in spring by seed or by naturally divided tubers.

S. aurantiaca illus. p.423.

SANGUINARIA
Bloodroot

PAPAVERACEAE

Genus of one species of spring-flowering, rhizomatous perennial. Grow in sun or semi-shade and in organic, moist but well-drained soil. Propagate by division of rhizomes in summer or by seed in autumn.

S. canadensis illus. p.363. **'Plena'** (syn. *S.c.* 'Flore Pleno') is a clump-forming, rhizomatous perennial with fleshy, underground stems that exude red sap when cut. H 6in (15cm), S 12–18in (30–45cm). Short-lived, rounded, fully double white flowers emerge in spring followed by large, rounded to heart-shaped, scalloped, gray-green leaves with glaucous undersides. Z3–9 H9–1.

SANGUISORBA
Burnet

ROSACEAE

Genus of perennials grown for their bottlebrush-like flower spikes. Requires sun and moist soil. Propagate by division in spring or by seed in autumn.

S. canadensis illus. p.226.

S. obtusa. Clump-forming perennial.

H 3–4ft (1–1.2m), S 2ft (60cm). Arching stems bear spikes of rose-crimson flowers in midsummer. Pairs of oval leaflets are pale green above, blue-green beneath. Z4–7 H8–3.
S. officinalis (Great burnet). **'Rubra'** is a clump-forming perennial. H 4ft (1.2m), S 2ft (60cm). Produces small spikes of red-brown flowers in late summer above a mass of midgreen leaves, divided into oval leaflets. Z3–8 H8–1.

SANSEVIERIA

AGAVACEAE/DRACAENACEAE

Genus of evergreen, rhizomatous perennials grown for their rosettes of stiff, fleshy leaves. Tolerates sun and shade and is easy to grow in most soil conditions if not overwatered. Propagate by leaf cuttings or division in summer.
S. cylindrica. Evergreen, stemless, rhizomatous perennial. H 1½–4ft (45cm–1.2m), S 4in (10cm). Has a rosette of 3–4 cylindrical, stiff, fleshy, erect leaves, to 4ft (1.2m) long, in dark green with paler horizontal bands. Racemes of small, tubular, 6-lobed pink or white flowers are occasionally produced.
S. trifasciata (Mother-in-law's tongue). Evergreen, stemless, rhizomatous perennial. H 1½–4ft (45cm–1.2m), S 4in (10cm). Has a rosette of about 5 lance-shaped, pointed, stiff, fleshy, erect leaves, to 4ft (1.2m) long, banded horizontally with pale green and yellow. Occasionally carries racemes of tubular, 6-lobed green flowers. Z14–15 H12–1. **'Golden Hahnii'** illus. p.305. **'Hahnii'** illus. p.303. **'Laurentii'** illus. p.267.

SANTOLINA

ASTERACEAE/COMPOSITAE

Genus of evergreen, summer-flowering shrubs grown for their aromatic foliage and their buttonlike flower heads, each on a long stem. Needs sun and not too rich, well-drained soil. Cut off old flower heads and reduce long shoots in autumn. Cut straggly, old plants back hard each spring. Propagate by semi-ripe cuttings in summer.
S. chamaecyparissus, syn. *S. incana* (Lavender cotton). Evergreen, rounded, dense shrub. H 2½ft (75cm), S 3ft (1m). Shoots are covered with woolly white growth; narrowly oblong, finely toothed leaves are also white. Bright yellow flower heads are borne in mid- and late summer.
S. incana. See *S. chamaecyparissus*.
S. neapolitana. See *S. pinnata* subsp. *neapolitana*.
S. pinnata. Evergreen shrub, mainly grown as subsp. ***neapolitana*** (syn. *S. neapolitana*), which is of rounded and bushy habit. H 2½ft (75cm), S 3ft (1m). Slender flower stems bear a head of lemon yellow flowers in midsummer, among feathery, deeply cut, gray-green foliage. Z9–11 H12–9. subsp. ***neapolitana*** **'Sulphurea'** illus. p.169.
S. rosmarinifolia, syn. *S. virens* (Holy flax). Evergreen, bushy, dense shrub. H 2ft (60cm), S 3ft (1m). Has finely cut, bright green leaves. Each slender stem produces a head of bright yellow flowers in midsummer. Z6–9 H9–6. **'Primrose Gem'** has pale yellow flower heads.
S. virens. See *S. rosmarinifolia*.

SANVITALIA

ASTERACEAE/COMPOSITAE

Genus of perennials and annuals. Grow in sun and in fertile, well-drained soil. Propagate by seed sown outdoors in spring or early autumn.
S. procumbens illus. p.336. **'Mandarin Orange'** illus. p.341.

SAPONARIA

Soapwort

CARYOPHYLLACEAE

Genus of summer-flowering annuals and perennials grown for their flowers. Is good for rock gardens, screes, and banks. Needs sun and well-drained soil. Propagate by seed in spring or autumn or by softwood cuttings in early summer.
***S.* 'Bressingham'**, syn. *S.* 'Bressingham Hybrid'. Loose, mat-forming perennial. H 3in (8cm), S 4in (10cm). Has small, narrowly oval leaves. Flattish, deep vibrant pink flowers are produced in clustered heads in summer. Is good for a trough. Z4–8 H8–1.
S. caespitosa illus. p.378.
S. ocymoides illus. p.378.
S. officinalis **'Rubra Plena'** (Double soapwort). Upright perennial. H to 3ft (1m), S 1ft (30cm). Has oval, rough, midgreen leaves on erect stems. Clusters of ragged, double red flowers are produced from leaf axils on upper part of flower stems in summer. Z3–9 H9–1.
S.* x *olivana illus. p.376.

SARCOCOCCA

Christmas box, Sweet box

BUXACEAE

Genus of evergreen shrubs grown for their foliage, fragrant, winter flowers, and spherical fruits. Flowers are tiny – the only conspicuous part being the anthers. Grows in sun or shade and in fertile, not too dry soil. Propagate by semi-ripe cuttings in summer or by seed in autumn.
S. confusa. Evergreen, bushy, dense shrub. H and S 3ft (1m). Leaves are small, oval, taper-pointed, glossy, and dark green. Has tiny white flowers in winter, then black fruits. Z6–9 H9–6.
S. hookeriana. Evergreen, upright, dense, suckering shrub. H 5ft (1.5m), S 6ft (2m). Forms clumps of narrowly oblong, pointed, dark green leaves. Has tiny white flowers in the leaf axils during winter. Fruits are black. Z6–9 H9–6. var. ***digyna*** illus. p.174. var. ***humilis*** see *S. humilis*.
S. humilis, syn. *S. hookeriana* var. *humilis*, illus. p.174.
S. ruscifolia. Evergreen, upright, arching shrub. H and S 3ft (1m). Has oval, glossy, dark green leaves and, in winter, creamy white flowers then red fruits. Z8–9 H9–7. var. ***chinensis*** has narrower leaves.

SARRACENIA

Pitcher plant

SARRACENIACEAE

Genus of insectivorous perennials, some of which are evergreen, with pitchers formed from modified leaves with hooded tops. Grow in sun or partial shade and in peat. Keep very wet, except in winter, when drier conditions are needed. Propagate by seed in spring.
S. flava illus. p.290.
S. purpurea (Common pitcher plant, Huntsman's cup). Evergreen, erect to semi-prostrate, rosette-forming perennial. H 12in (30cm), S 12–15in (30–38cm). Inflated, green pitchers, to 6in (15cm) long, are tinged and veined purplish red. In spring, 5-petaled purple flowers, 2in (5cm) or more wide, are carried well above pitchers. Z2–9 H9–1.

SASA

GRAMINEAE/POACEAE

See also GRASSES, BAMBOOS, RUSHES, and SEDGES.
S. albomarginata. See *S. veitchii*.
S. palmata. Evergreen, spreading bamboo. H 6ft (2m), S indefinite. A fine foliage plant, it produces very broad, rich green leaves, to 16in (40cm) long. Hollow, purple-streaked stems have one branch at each node. Flower spikes are unimportant. Z7–11 H12–7.
S. veitchii, syn. *S. albomarginata*, illus. p.306.

SASSAFRAS

LAURACEAE

Genus of deciduous trees, with inconspicuous flowers, grown for their aromatic foliage. Needs sun or light shade and deep, fertile, well-drained, preferably acidic soil. Propagate by seed or suckers in autumn or by root cuttings in winter.
S. albidum illus. p.68.

SATUREJA

LABIATAE/LAMIACEAE

Genus of summer-flowering annuals, semi-evergreen perennials, and subshrubs grown for their highly aromatic leaves and attractive flowers. Is useful for rock gardens and dry banks. Needs sun and well-drained soil. Propagate by seed in winter or spring or by softwood cuttings in summer.
S. montana (Winter savory). Semi-evergreen, upright perennial or subshrub. H 12in (30cm), S 8in (20cm) or more. Leaves are linear to oval, aromatic, and green or grayish green. Carries loose whorls of tubular, 2-lipped lavender flowers in summer. Z5–8 H12–1. **'Prostrate White'**, H 3–6in (7–15cm), has a prostrate habit and produces white flowers.

SAUROMATUM

ARACEAE

Genus of spring-flowering, tuberous perennials with tubular spathes that expand into waved, twisted blades. Tubers will flower without soil or moisture and before leaves appear. Needs a sheltered, semi-shaded position and organic, well-drained soil. Water well in summer. Dry off or lift when dormant in winter. Propagate by offsets in spring.
S. guttatum. See *S. venosum*.
S. venosum, syn. *S. guttatum*, illus. p.413.

SAURURUS

SAURURACEAE

Genus of deciduous, perennial, bog and marginal water plants grown for their foliage. Prefers full sun but tolerates some shade. Remove faded leaves and divide plants as required to maintain vigor. Propagate by division in spring.
S. cernuus illus. p.447.

SAXEGOTHAEA

PODOCARPACEAE

See also CONIFERS.
S. conspicua (Prince Albert's yew). Conifer that is conical in mild areas, more bushy in colder areas. H 15–50ft (5–15m), S 12–15ft (4–5m). Needle-like, flattened, dark green leaves are produced in whorls at ends of shoots. Bears globose, fleshy, glaucous green cones. Z8–10 H10–8.

SAXIFRAGA

Saxifrage

SAXIFRAGACEAE

Genus of often rosetted perennials, most of which are evergreen or semi-evergreen, grown for their flowers and attractive foliage. Is excellent in rock gardens, raised beds, and alpine houses. Propagate by seed in autumn or by rooted offsets in winter.
For cultivation, saxifrages may be grouped as follows:

1 – Needs protection from midday sun and moist soil.
2 – Needs semi-shaded, well-drained soil. Is good among rocks and screes.
3 – Thrives in well-drained rock pockets, troughs, and alpine-house pans, shaded from midday sun. Must never be dry at roots. Most form tight cushions and flower in early spring, flower stems being barely visible above leaves.
4 – Needs full sun and well-drained, alkaline soil. Good in rock pockets. Most have hard leaves encrusted in lime.

S. aizoides. Evergreen perennial forming a loose mat. H 6in (15cm), S 12in

(30cm) or more. Has small, narrowly oval, fleshy, shiny green leaves and, in spring-summer, terminal racemes of star-shaped, bright yellow or orange flowers, often spotted red, on 3in (8cm) stems. Cult. group 1. Z1–6 H6–1.
S. aizoon. See *S. paniculata.*
***S.* x *anglica* 'Cranbourne'**, syn. *S.* 'Cranbourne'. Evergreen, cushion-forming perennial. H and S 12cm (5in). In early spring produces solitary, cup-shaped, bright purplish lilac flowers on short stems just above tight rosettes of linear green leaves. Flower stems are longer if plant is grown in an alpine house. Cultivation group 3. Z7–9 H9–7.
***S.* x *apiculata* 'Gregor Mendel'**, syn. *S.* 'Gregor Mendel', illus. p.371; Cultivation group 2.
***S.* 'Arco'.** See. *S.* x *arco-valleyi* 'Arco'.
***S.* x *arco-valleyi* 'Arco'**, syn. *S.* 'Arco'. Evergreen perennial forming a tight cushion. H and S 4in (10cm). In early spring produces upturned, cup-shaped to flattish, pale lilac flowers almost resting on tight rosettes of oblong to linear leaves. Cult. group 3. Z6–8 H8–6.
***S.* 'Aretiastrum'.** See *S.* 'Valerie Finnis'.
***S.* 'Bob Hawkins'.** Evergreen perennial with a loose rosette of leaves. H 1–2in (2.5–5cm), S 6in (15cm). Carries small, upturned, rounded, greenish white flowers in summer on 2in (5cm) stems. Oval green leaves are white-splashed. Cult. grp. 1. Z6–8 H8–6.
***S.* x *boydii* 'Hindhead Seedling'** illus. p.371; cultivation group 2.
***S.* 'Brookside'.** See *S. burseriana* 'Brookside'.
S. brunoniana. See *S. brunonis.*
S. brunonis, syn. *S. brunoniana.* Semi-evergreen, rosetted perennial. H 4in (10cm), S 8in (20cm). Small, soft green rosettes of lance-shaped, rigid leaves produce masses of long, threadlike red runners. Many of the rosettes die down to large terminal buds in winter. Short racemes of 5-petaled, spreading, pale yellow flowers are produced in late spring and summer on 2–3in (5–8cm) stems. Difficult; cult. grp. 1. Z6–8 H8–6.
S. burseriana illus. p.363. **'Brookside'** (syn. *S.* 'Brookside') is a slow-growing, evergreen perennial forming a hard cushion. H 1–2in (2.5–5cm), S to 4in (10cm). Has broadly linear, spiky, gray-green leaves. In early spring bears upturned, rounded, shallowly cup-shaped, bright yellow flowers on short red stems. Flowers of **'Crenata'** (syn. *S.* 'Crenata') have fringed white petals and red sepals. **'Gloria'** (syn. *S.* 'Gloria') has dark reddish brown stems, each bearing 1 or 2 flowers, with red sepals and white petals, in late spring. Cultivation group 3. All Z6–8 H8–6.
S. callosa, syn. *S. lingulata.* Evergreen, tightly rosetted perennial. H 10in (25cm), S to 8in (20cm). Bears long, linear, stiff, lime-encrusted leaves and, in early summer, upright then arching panicles of star-shaped white flowers with red-spotted petals. Rosettes die after flowering; new ones are produced annually from short stolons. Cultivation group 4. Z7–8 H8–7.
S. cochlearis. Evergreen, rosetted perennial. H 8in (20cm), S 10in (25cm). Has spoon-shaped green leaves with white-encrusted edges. Produces loose panicles of rounded white flowers, often with red-spotted petals, in early summer. Z7–8 H8–7. **'Minor'**, H and S 5in (12cm), has smaller leaf rosettes and loose panicles of red-spotted white flowers on red stems. Is ideal for a trough. Cult. grp. 4.
S. cortusifolia var. ***fortunei.*** See *S. fortunei.*
S. cotyledon illus. p.352; cultivation group 2.
***S.* 'Cranbourne'.** See *S.* x *anglica* 'Cranbourne'.
***S.* 'Crenata'.** See *S. burseriana* 'Crenata'.
S. cuneifolia illus. p.351; cultivation group 1.
***S.* 'Elizabethae'**, syn. *S.* x *elizabethae,* illus. p.371; cultivation group 2.
S. exarata subsp. ***moschata***, syn. *S. moschata.* Evergreen perennial forming a loose to tight hummock. H and S 4in (10cm). Rosettes consist of small, lance-shaped, sometimes 3-toothed, green leaves. Bears 2–5 star-shaped, creamy white or dull yellow flowers on slender stems in summer. Z5–7 H7–5. **'Cloth of Gold'** illus. p.391. Cultivation group 1.
S. ferdinandi-coburgi. Evergreen, cushion-forming perennial. H and S 6in (15cm). Forms rosettes of linear, spiny, glaucous green leaves and, in early spring, bears racemes of open cup-shaped, rich yellow flowers on stems 1–4in (3–10cm) long. Cultivation group 3.
S. fortunei, syn. *S. cortusifolia* var. *fortunei.* Semi-evergreen or herbaceous, clump-forming perennial. H and S 12in (30cm). Has rounded, 5- or 7-lobed, fleshy green or brownish green leaves, red beneath. In autumn produces panicles of tiny white flowers, with 4 equal-sized petals and one elongated petal, on upright stems. Propagate by division in spring. Z6–8 H8–6.**'Rubrifolia'** has dark red flower stems and dark reddish green leaves with beet red undersides. Cult. grp. 1.
S. frederici-augustii subsp. ***grisebachii* 'Wisley Variety'**, syn. *S. grisebachii* 'Wisley Variety', illus. p.367; cultivation group 4.
S.* x *geum illus. p.347; cultivation group 1.
***S.* 'Gloria'.** See *S. burseriana* 'Gloria'.
S. granulata (Fair maids of France, Meadow saxifrage) illus. p.346. **'Plena'** is a clump-forming perennial. H 9–15in (23–38cm), S to 6in (15cm) or more. Loses its kidney-shaped, glossy, pale to midgreen leaves soon after flowering. Has a loose panicle of large, rounded, double white flowers in late spring or early summer. Bulbils or resting buds form at base of foliage. Cultivation group 1. Z7–8 H8–7.
***S.* 'Gregor Mendel'.** See *S.* x *apiculata* 'Gregor Mendel'.
***S. grisebachii* 'Wisley Variety'.** See *S. frederici-augustii* subsp. *grisebachii* 'Wisley Variety'.
S. hirsuta illus. p.347; cultivation group 1.
***S.* 'Irvingii'.** See *S.* x *irvingii* 'Walter Irving'.
***S.* x *irvingii* 'Jenkinsiae'**, syn. *S.* 'Jenkinsiae', illus. p.365; cultivation group 2. **'Walter Irving'** (syn. *S.* 'Irvingii') is a very slow-growing, evergreen, hard-domed perennial. H ¾in (2cm), S 3in (8cm). Bears minute leaves in rosettes. Stemless, cup-shaped, lilac-pink flowers open in early spring. Cultivation group 3. Z6–7 H7–6.
***S.* 'Jenkinsiae'.** See *S.* x *irvingii* 'Jenkinsiae'.
S. lingulata. See *S. callosa.*
S. longifolia. Rosetted perennial. H 24in (60cm), S 8–10in (20–25cm). Has long, narrow, lime-encrusted leaves forming attractive rosettes that, after 3–4 years, develop long, arching, conical to cylindrical panicles bearing numerous rounded, 5-petaled white flowers in late spring and summer. Rosettes die after flowering, and no daughter rosettes are formed, so propagate by seed in spring or autumn. In cultivation, hybridizes readily with other related species. Cultivation group 4. Z6–7 H7–6.
S. moschata. See *S. exarata* subsp. *moschata.*
S. oppositifolia illus. p.366. **'Ruth Draper'** is an evergreen, loose mat-forming perennial. H 1–2in (2.5–5cm), S 6in (15cm). Has small, opposite, oblong to oval, white-flecked, dark green leaves closely set along prostrate stems. Large, cup-shaped, deep purple-pink flowers appear in early spring just above foliage. Prefers peaty soil. Cultivation group 1. Z1–7 H7–1.
S. paniculata, syn. *S. aizoon.* Evergreen, tightly rosetted perennial. H 6–12in (15–30cm), S 8in (20cm). In summer produces loose panicles of rounded, usually white flowers, with or without purplish red spots, on upright stems above rosettes of oblong to oval, lime-encrusted leaves. Is very variable in size. Pale yellow or pale pink forms also occur. Cult. grp. 4. Z2–6 H6–1.
S.* x *primulaize, syn. *S.* 'Primulaize'. Evergreen, loosely rosetted perennial. H and S 6in (15cm). In summer, branched flower stems, 2–3in (5–8cm) long, produce star shaped, salmon pink flowers. Leaves are tiny, narrowly oval, slightly indented, and fleshy. Cultivation group 1. Z6–7 H7–6.
S. sancta illus. p.371; cultivation group 2.
S. sarmentosa. See *S. stolonifera.*
S. scardica illus. p.362; cultivation group 3.
S. sempervivum illus. p.367; cultivation group 3.
***S.* 'Southside Seedling'** illus. p.352; cultivation group 4.
S. stolonifera, syn. *S. sarmentosa* (Mother of thousands). Evergreen, prostrate perennial with runners. H 6in (15cm) or more, S 12in (30cm) or more. Has large, rounded, shallowly lobed, hairy, silver-veined, olive green leaves that are reddish purple beneath. Loose panicles of tiny, mothlike white flowers, each with 4 equal-sized petals and one elongated petal, appear in summer on slender, upright stems. Makes a good ground-cover. Z7–9 H9–5. **'Tricolor'** (syn. *S.* 'Tricolor'; Strawberry geranium) has green-and-red leaves with silver marks. Cultivation group 1.
S. stribrnyi illus. p.368; cultivation group 3.
***S.* 'Tricolor'.** See *S. stolonifera* 'Tricolor'.
***S.* 'Tumbling Waters'** illus. p.347; cultivation group 4.
S.* x *urbium (London pride). Evergreen, rosetted, spreading perennial. H 12in (30cm), S indefinite. Has spoon-shaped, toothed, leathery green leaves. Flower stems bear tiny, star-shaped, at times pink-flushed, white flowers with red spots in summer. Is useful as a ground-cover. Cultivation group 1. Z6–7 H7–6.
***S.* 'Valerie Finnis'**, syn. *S.* 'Aretiastrum'. Evergreen, hard cushion-forming perennial. H and S 4in (10cm). Short red stems carry upturned, cup-shaped, sulfur yellow flowers above tight rosettes of oval green leaves in spring. Cultivation group 3. Z7–10 H10–7.

SCABIOSA
Scabious

DIPSACACEAE

Genus of annuals and perennials, some of which are evergreen, with flower heads that are good for cutting. Prefers sun and fertile, well-drained, alkaline soil. Propagate annuals by seed in spring and perennials by cuttings of young, basal growths in summer, by seed in autumn, or by division in early spring.
S. arvensis. See *Knautia arvensis.*
S. atropurpurea (Sweet scabious). Moderately fast-growing, upright, bushy annual. H to 3ft (1m), S 8–12in (20–30cm). Has lance-shaped, lobed, midgreen leaves. Domed heads of scented, pincushion-like, deep crimson flower heads, 2in (5cm) wide, are produced on wiry stems in summer and early autumn. Tall forms, H 3ft (1m), and dwarf, H 18in (45cm), are available with flower heads in shades of blue, purple, red, pink, or white. Z4–11 H8–3.
***S. caucasica.* 'Clive Greaves'** illus. p.285. **'Floral Queen'** is a clump-forming perennial. H and S 24in (60cm). Large, frilled, violet-blue flower heads with pincushion-like centers are produced throughout summer. Light green leaves are lance-shaped at base of plant and segmented on stems. **'Miss Willmott'** has creamy white flowers. Both Z4–9 H9–1.
S. columbaria var. ***ochroleuca.*** See *S. ochroleuca.*
S. graminifolia. Evergreen, clump-forming perennial, often with a woody base. H and S 6–10in (15–25cm). Has tufts of narrow, grasslike, pointed, silver-haired leaves. In summer

produces stiff stems with spherical, bluish violet to lilac flower heads like pincushions. Resents disturbance. Good in a rock garden. Z5–7 H7–5.
S. lucida illus. p.355.
S. ochroleuca, syn. *S. columbaria* var. *ochroleuca*. Clump-forming perennial. H and S 3ft (1m). In late summer, branching stems carry many heads of frilled, sulfur yellow flower heads with pincushion-like centers. Has narrowly oval, toothed, gray-green leaves. Z4–9 H9–1.
S. rumelica. See *Knautia macedonica*.

SCADOXUS

AMARYLLIDACEAE

Genus of bulbs with dense, mainly spherical umbels of red flowers. Requires partial shade and organic, well-drained soil. Reduce watering in winter, when not in active growth. Propagate by seed or offsets in spring.
S. multiflorus, syn. *Haemanthus multiflorus*. Summer-flowering bulb. H to 28in (70cm), S 12–18in (30–45cm). Has broadly lance-shaped, semi-erect, basal leaves. Produces a spherical umbel, 4–6in (10–15cm) wide, of up to 200 narrow-petaled flowers. Z14–15 H12–10. subsp. ***katherinae*** (syn. *Haemanthus katherinae*) illus. p.401.
S. puniceus, syn. *Haemanthus magnificus*, *H. natalensis*, *H. puniceus* (Royal paintbrush). Spring- and summer-flowering bulb. H 12–16in (30–40cm), S 12–18in (30–45cm). Has elliptic, semi-erect leaves in a basal cluster. Leaf bases are joined, forming a false stem. Flower stem bears up to 100 tubular, orange-red flowers in a conical umbel surrounded by a whorl of red bracts.

SCAEVOLA

Blue fan flower

GOODENIACEAE

Genus of summer flowering perennials grown for their arching stems, with spoon-shaped toothed leaves. Grow in full sun or very light shade and well-drained soil, rich in organic matter. Will tolerate sandy soils as long as they are kept moist. Propagate by cuttings in early spring.
S. aemula. Tender perennial, usually grown as an annual from cuttings. H and S 18in (45cm). Pale blue flowers have all the petals on one side, giving a fanlike effect. Z11–12 H12–1. **'Blue Wonder'** is more trailing with lilac-blue flowers from early summer to fall. H 6in (15cm), S 4ft (1.2m). Good for baskets, window boxes, and planters.

SCHEFFLERA,
syn. BRASSAIA, HEPTAPLEURUM

ARALIACEAE

Genus of evergreen shrubs and trees grown mainly for their handsome foliage. Grows in any fertile, well-drained but moisture-retentive soil and in full light or partial shade. Water potted specimens freely when in full growth, moderately at other times. Pruning is tolerated if needed. Propagate by air-layering in spring, by semi-ripe cuttings in summer, or by seed as soon as ripe in late summer.
S. actinophylla illus. p.84.
S. arboricola. Evergreen, erect, well-branched shrub or tree. H 6–15ft (2–5m), S 3–10ft (1–3m). Leaves each have 7–16 oval, stalked, glossy, deep green leaflets. Mature plants carry small, spherical heads of tiny green flowers in spring-summer. Z11–12 H12–1.
S. digitata. Evergreen, rounded to ovoid shrub or bushy tree. H and S 10–25ft (3–8m). Leaves are hand-shaped, with 5–10 oval, glossy, rich green leaflets. Has tiny greenish flowers in large, terminal panicles in spring and tiny, globular, dark violet fruits in autumn. Z11–12 H12–1.
S. elegantissima, syn. *Aralia elegantissima*, *Dizygotheca elegantissima*, illus. p.127.

SCHIMA

THEACEAE

Genus of one species of very variable, evergreen tree or shrub grown for its foliage and flowers. Prefers organic, well-drained, neutral to acidic soil and sun or partial shade. Water potted plants freely in full growth, moderately at other times. Pruning is tolerated if necessary. Propagate by seed as soon as ripe or by semi-ripe cuttings in summer.
S. wallichii. Robust, evergreen, ovoid tree or shrub. H 80–100ft (25–30m), S 40ft (12m) or more. Elliptic to oblong, red-veined, dark green leaves are 10–18cm (4–7in) long, red-flushed beneath. In late summer has solitary fragrant, cup-shaped white flowers, 1½in (4cm) wide, red-flushed in bud. Z9–10 H10–9

SCHINUS

ANACARDIACEAE

Genus of evergreen shrubs and trees grown mainly for their foliage and for shade. Grows in any freely draining soil and in full light. Water potted specimens moderately, hardly at all in winter. Propagate by seed in spring or by semi-ripe cuttings in summer.
S. molle (Californian pepper-tree, Peruvian mastic tree, Peruvian pepper-tree). Fast-growing, evergreen, weeping tree. H and S to 25ft (8m). Fernlike leaves are divided into many narrowly lance-shaped, glossy, rich green leaflets. Has open clusters of tiny yellow flowers from late winter to summer, followed by pea-sized, pink-red fruits. Z8–11 H12–8.
S. terebinthifolius. Evergreen shrub or tree, usually of bushy, spreading habit. H 10ft (3m) or more, S 6–10ft (2–3m) or more. Leaves have 3–13 oval, mid- to deep green leaflets. Tiny white flowers are borne in clusters in summer-autumn, followed by pea-sized red fruits, but only if plants of both sexes are grown close together. Z9–11 H12–9.

SCHISANDRA

SCHISANDRACEAE

Genus of deciduous, woody-stemmed, twining climbers. Male and female flowers are borne on separate plants, so grow plants of both sexes if fruits are desired. Is useful for growing against shady walls and training up pillars and fences. Grow in sun or partial shade and rich, well-drained soil. Propagate by greenwood or semi-ripe cuttings in summer.
S. grandiflora var. ***rubriflora.*** See *S. rubriflora*.
S. henryi. Deciduous, woody-stemmed, twining climber, with stems that are angled and winged when young. H 10–12ft (3–4m). Glossy green leaves are oval or heart-shaped. Small, cup-shaped white flowers appear in spring. Pendent spikes, 2–3in (5–7cm) long, of spherical, fleshy, red fruits are borne in late summer on female plants.
S. rubriflora, syn. *S. grandiflora* var. *rubriflora*, illus. p.211.

SCHIZANTHUS

Butterfly flower, Poor man's orchid

SOLANACEAE

Genus of annuals grown for their showy flowers. Makes excellent pot plants. Grow in a sunny, sheltered position and in fertile, well-drained soil. Pinch out growing tips of young plants to ensure a bushy habit. Propagate by seed sown under cover in early spring for summer-autumn flowers and in late summer for plants to flower in pots in late winter or spring. Is prone to damage by aphids.
***S.* 'Hit Parade'** illus. p.322.
S. pinnatus illus. p.330.
***S.* 'Star Parade'.** Compact annual with a distinctive pyramidal habit. H 8–10in (20–25cm), S 9–12in (23–30cm). Has almost fernlike, light green leaves. From spring to autumn, bears tubular, then flared, 2-lipped white, yellow, pink, purple, or red flowers. Z12–15 H8–1.

Schizocentron elegans. See *Heterocentron elegans*.

SCHIZOPETALON

BRASSICACEAE/CRUCIFERAE

Genus of annuals. Grow in sun and in well-drained, fertile soil. Propagate by seed sown under cover in spring.
S. walkeri. Moderately fast-growing, upright, slightly branching annual. H 18in (45cm), S 8in (20cm). Has deeply divided, midgreen leaves and, in summer, almond-scented white flowers with deeply cut petals. H8–1.

SCHIZOPHRAGMA

HYDRANGEACEAE

Genus of deciduous, woody-stemmed, root climbers useful for training up large trees. Flowers best in sun, but will grow against a north-facing wall. Needs well-drained soil. Tie young plants to supports. Propagate by seed in spring or by greenwood or semi-ripe cuttings in summer.
S. hydrangeoides (Japanese hydrangea vine). Deciduous, woody-stemmed, root climber. H to 40ft (12m). Broadly oval leaves are 4–6in (10–15cm) long. Small white or creamy white flowers, in flat heads 8–10in (20–25cm) across, are produced on pendent side-branches in summer; these are surrounded by marginal sterile flowers, which each have an oval or heart-shaped, pale yellow sepal, ¾–1½in (2–4cm) long. Z6–9 H9–6.
S. integrifolium illus. p.208.
S. viburnoides. See *Pileostegia viburnoides*.

SCHIZOSTYLIS

Kaffir lily

IRIDACEAE

Genus of rhizomatous perennials with flowers that are excellent for cutting. Requires sun and fertile, moist soil. Divide in spring every few years to avoid congestion.
***S. coccinea* 'Major'**, syn. *S.c.* 'Grandiflora', illus. p.294. **'Mrs. Hegarty'** is a vigorous, clump-forming, rhizomatous perennial. H 24in (60cm), S 9–12in (23–30cm). In midautumn produces spikes of shallowly cup-shaped, pale pink flowers above tufts of grasslike, midgreen leaves. **'Sunrise'** illus. p.294. **'Viscountess Byng'** has pink flowers that last until late autumn.
All Z7–9 H9–7.

SCHLUMBERGERA

Holiday cactus

CACTACEAE

Genus of bushy cacti with erect, then pendent stems and flattened, oblong stem segments with indented notches at margins – toothlike in some species. Stem tips produce flowers with prominent stigmas and stamens and with petals of different lengths set in 2 rows. In the wild, it often grows over mossy rocks, rooting at ends of stem segments. Needs partial shade and rich, well-drained soil. Propagate by stem cuttings in spring or early summer.
S. bridgesii. See *S.* x *buckleyi*.
***S.* 'Bristol Beauty'** illus. p.475.
S.* x *buckleyi, syn. *S. bridgesii* (Christmas cactus). Erect then pendent cactus. H 6in (15cm), S 3ft (1m). Has glossy, green stem segments and produces red-violet flowers in midwinter. Z11–12 H12–1.
***S.* 'Gold Charm'** illus. p.472.
S. truncata, syn. *Zygocactus truncatus*, illus. p.473.
***S.* 'Wintermärchen'.** Erect, then

pendent cactus. H 6in (15cm), S 12in (30cm). Has glossy green stem segments. In early autumn bears white flowers that become pink and white in winter. Z13-15 H12–10.
***S.* 'Zara'.** Erect then pendent cactus. H 6in (15cm), S 12in (30cm). Has glossy green stem segments. Bears deep orange-red flowers in early autumn and winter. Z13-15 H12–10.

SCHOENOPLECTUS

CYPERACEAE

See also GRASSES, BAMBOOS, RUSHES, and SEDGES.
***S. lacustris* subsp. *tabernaemontani* 'Zebrinus'**, syn. *Scirpus lacustris* var. *tabernaemontani* 'Zebrinus', *Scirpus tabernaemontani* 'Zebrinus', illus. p.306.

SCHWANTESIA

AIZOACEAE

Genus of cushion-forming succulents with stemless rosettes of unequal-sized pairs of keeled leaves and daisylike yellow flowers. Needs full sun and well-drained soil. Propagate by seed or stem cuttings in spring or summer.
S. ruedebuschii illus. p.478.

SCIADOPITYS

SCIADOPITYACEAE

See also CONIFERS.
S. verticillata illus. p.106.

SCILLA

HYACINTHACEAE/LILIACEAE

Genus of mainly spring- and summer-flowering bulbs with leaves in basal clusters and spikes of small, often blue flowers. Needs sun or partial shade and well-drained soil. Propagate by division in late summer or by seed in autumn.
S. adlamii. See *Ledebouria cooperi*.
S. bifolia. Early spring-flowering bulb. H 2–6in (5–15cm), S 1–2in (2.5–5cm). Has 2 narrowly strap-shaped, semi-erect, basal leaves that widen toward the tips. Stem produces one-sided spike of up to 20 star-shaped, purple-blue, pink, or white flowers. Z3–8 H8–1.
S. campanulata. See *Hyacinthoides hispanica*.
S. chinensis. See *S. scilloides*.
S. cooperi. See *Ledebouria cooperi*.
S. hispanica. See *Hyacinthoides hispanica*.
S. italica. See *Hyacinthoides italica*.
S. japonica. See *S. scilloides*.
S. litardierei, syn. *S. pratensis*. Clump-forming, early summer-flowering bulb. H 4–10in (10–25cm), S 2–3in (5–8cm). Bears up to 5 strap-shaped, semi-erect, basal leaves. Stem bears a dense spike of flat, star-shaped, violet flowers, ½–⅝in (1–1.5cm) across. Z6–9 H9–6
S. mischtschenkoana, syn. *S. tubergeniana*, *S.* 'Tubergeniana', illus. p.432.
S. natalensis. Clump-forming, summer-flowering bulb. H 12–18in (30–45cm), S 6–8in (15–20cm). Lance-shaped, semi-erect, basal leaves lengthen after flowering. Has a long spike of up to 100 flattish blue flowers, each ⅝–¾in (1.5–2cm) across.
S. non-scripta. See *Hyacinthoides non-scripta*.
S. nutans. See *Hyacinthoides non-scripta*.
S. peruviana illus. p.436.
S. pratensis. See *S. litardierei*.
S. scilloides, syn. *S. chinensis*, *S. japonica*, illus. p.424.
S. siberica (Siberian squill). **'Atrocoerulea'** illus. p.432.
S. socialis. See *Ledebouria socialis*.
S. tubergeniana. See *S. mischtschenkoana*.
***S.* 'Tubergeniana'.** See *S. mischtschenkoana*.
S. violacea. See *Ledebouria socialis*.

***Scindapsus aureus* 'Marble Queen'.** See *Epipremnum aureum* 'Marble Queen'.
***Scindapsus pictus* 'Argyraeus'.** See *Epipremnum pictum* 'Argyraeum'.

SCIRPOIDES

CYPERACEAE

See also GRASSES, BAMBOOS, RUSHES, and SEDGES.
S. holoschoenus, syn. *Scirpus holoschoenus* (Round-headed club-rush). **'Variegatus'** is an evergreen, tuft-forming, perennial rush. H 3ft (1m), S 1½ft (45cm). Rounded, leafless green stems are striped horizontally with cream and bear long-stalked, dense, spherical heads of egg-shaped, awned brown spikelets, produced from mid-summer to early autumn. Z6–9 H9–6.

Scirpus holoschoenus. See *Scirpoides holoschoenus*.
***Scirpus lacustris* 'Spiralis'.** See *Juncus effusus* 'Spiralis'.
***Scirpus lacustris* subsp. *tabernaemontani* 'Zebrinus'.** See *Schoenoplectus lacustris* subsp. *tabernaemontani* 'Zebrinus'.
Scirpus setaceus. See *Isolepsis setaceus*.
***Scirpus tabernaemontani* 'Zebrinus'.** See *Schoenoplectus lacustris* subsp. *tabernaemontani* 'Zebrinus'.

SCLEROCACTUS

CACTACEAE

Genus of cacti grown for their depressed-spherical to club-shaped or columnar stems, each with a long, fleshy tap root and deeply notched or warty ribs. Needs full sun with some midday shade and very well-drained soil. May rot if over-watered. Propagate by seed in spring.
S. scheeri, syn. *Ancistrocactus megarhizus*, *A. scheeri*, *Echinocactus scheeri*, illus. p.477.
S. uncinatus, syn. *Ancistrocactus uncinatus*, *Echinocactus uncinatus*, *Glandulicactus uncinatus*, *Hamatocactus uncinatus*. Globose to columnar cactus. H 8in (20cm), S 4in (10cm). Stem is blue-green. Areoles each produce 1–4 very long, hooked reddish spines and 15–18 straight ones. Has cup-shaped, brown-green or reddish flowers, ¾in (2cm) across, in spring. Z13-15 H12–10.

SCOLIOPUS

LILIACEAE/TRILLIACEAE

Genus of one species of spring-flowering perennial. Is usually grown in alpine houses, where its neat habit and curious flowers, which arise directly from buds on the rootstock early in the season, may be better appreciated. Is also suitable for rock gardens. Requires sun or partial shade and moist but well-drained soil. Propagate by seed when fresh, in summer or autumn.
S. bigelowii, syn. *S. bigelovii*, illus. p.364.

Scolopendrium vulgare. See *Asplenium scolopendrium*.

SCOPOLIA

SOLANACEAE

Genus of spring-flowering perennials. Prefers shade and fertile, very well-drained soil. Propagate by division in spring or by seed in autumn. All parts are highly toxic if ingested.
S. carniolica illus. p.271.

SCROPHULARIA

Figwort

SCROPHULARIACEAE

Genus of perennials and subshrubs, some of which are semi-evergreen or evergreen. Most species are weeds, but some are grown for their variegated foliage. Does best in semi-shade and moist soil. Propagate by division in spring or by softwood cuttings in summer.
***S. aquatica* 'Variegata'.** See *S. auriculata* 'Variegata'.
***S. auriculata* 'Variegata'**, syn. *S. aquatica* 'Variegata' (Water figwort). Evergreen, clump-forming perennial. H 24in (60cm), S 12in (30cm) or more. Has attractive, oval, toothed, dark green leaves with cream marks. Remove spikes of insignificant maroon flowers, borne in summer. Z5–9 H9–5.

SCUTELLARIA

Skullcap

LABIATAE/LAMIACEAE

Genus of rhizomatous perennials grown for their summer flowers. Needs sun and well-drained soil. Propagate by softwood cuttings in summer or by seed in autumn.
S. indica. Upright, rhizomatous perennial. H 6–12in (15–30cm), S 4in (10cm) or more. Leaves are oval, toothed and hairy. Has dense racemes of long-tubed, 2-lipped, slate blue, occasionally white flowers in summer. Good in a rock garden. Z6–8 H8–6.
S. orientalis illus. p.385.
S. scordiifolia. Mat-forming, rhizomatous perennial. H and S 6in (15cm) or more. Bears narrowly oval, wrinkled leaves. In summer-autumn has racemes of tubular, hooded purple flowers, each with a white-streaked lip. Divide in spring. Z5–8 H8–5.

SEDUM

Stonecrop

CRASSULACEAE

Genus of often fleshy or succulent annuals, evergreen biennials, mostly evergreen or semi-evergreen perennials, and evergreen shrubs and subshrubs, suitable for rock gardens and borders. Needs sun. Does best in fertile, well-drained soil. Propagate perennials, subshrubs, and shrubs by division or by softwood cuttings of non-flowering shoots from spring to midsummer or by seed in autumn or spring. Propagate annuals and biennials by seed sown under cover in early spring or outdoors in midspring. All parts may cause mild stomach upset if ingested; contact with the sap may irritate skin.
S. acre illus. p.384. **'Aureum'** illus. p.385.
S. aizoon. Evergreen, erect perennial. H and S 18in (45cm). Midgreen leaves are oblong to lance-shaped, fleshy, and toothed. In summer bears flat heads of star-shaped yellow flowers. Z3–8 H8–1. **'Aurantiacum'** illus. p.293.
S. anacampseros, syn. *Hylotelephium anacampseros*. Semi-evergreen, trailing perennial with overwintering foliage rosettes. H 4in (10cm), S 10in (25cm) or more. Prostrate, loosely rosetted brown stems bear oblong to oval, fleshy, glaucous green leaves. Dense, sub-globose, terminal heads of small, cup-shaped, purplish pink flowers appear in summer.
S. caeruleum illus. p.333.
S. cauticola, syn. *Hylotelephium cauticola*. Trailing, shallow-rooted perennial with stolons. H 2in (5cm), S 8in (20cm). Has oval to oblong, stalked, fleshy, blue-green leaves on procumbent, purplish red stems. Bears leafy, branched, flattish heads of star-shaped, pale purplish pink flowers in early autumn. Cut back old stems in winter.
S. ewersii, syn. *Hylotelephium ewersii*. Trailing perennial. H 2in (5cm), S 6in (15cm). Is similar to *S. cauticola* but has more rounded, stem-clasping leaves, often tinted red, and dense, rounded flower heads.
S. heterodontum. See *Rhodiola heterodonta*.
S. kamtschaticum. Semi-evergreen, prostrate perennial with overwintering foliage rosettes. H 2–3in (5–8cm), S 8in (20cm). Bears narrowly oval, toothed, fleshy, midgreen leaves. Spreading, terminal clusters of star-shaped, orange-flushed yellow flowers appear in summer-autumn. Z3–8 H8–1. **'Variegatum'** illus. p.391.
S. lydium illus. p.388.
S. morganianum (Burro's tail, Donkey-

tail). Evergreen, prostrate succulent perennial. H 12in (30cm) or more, S indefinite. Stems are clothed in oblong to lance-shaped, almost cylindrical, fleshy, waxy white leaves. Has terminal clusters of star-shaped, rose pink flowers in summer. Z11–12 H12–1.
S. obtusatum illus. p.388.
S. palmeri. Evergreen, clump-forming perennial. H 8in (20cm), S 12in (30cm). Bears sprays of star-shaped yellow or orange flowers in early summer above oblong-oval to spoon-shaped, fleshy, gray-green leaves.
S. populifolium, syn. *Hylotelephium populifolium*. Semi-evergreen, bushy perennial. H 12–18in (30–45cm), S 12in (30cm). Terminal clusters of hawthorn-scented, star-shaped, pale pink or white flowers are borne in late summer. Has broadly oval, irregularly toothed, fleshy, midgreen leaves.
S. reflexum. See *S. rupestre*.
S. rosea. See *Rhodiola rosea*. var. ***heterodontum*** see *R. heterodonta*.
S. rupestre, syn. *S. reflexum*, illus. p.359.
S. sempervivoides. Evergreen, basal-rosetted biennial. H 3–4in (8–10cm), S 2in (5cm). Has rosettes that are similar to those of *Sempervivum*; oval to strap-shaped, leathery, glaucous green leaves are strongly marked red-purple. Produces domed heads of star-shaped scarlet flowers in summer. Dislikes winter wet. Is good for an alpine house. Z9–10 H10–9.
***S. sieboldii* 'Mediovariegatum'**, *S.s.* 'Variegatum'. Evergreen, spreading, tuberous perennial with long, tapering taproots. H 4in (10cm), S 8in (20cm) or more. Rounded, fleshy, blue-green leaves, splashed cream and occasionally red-edged, appear in whorls of 3. Bears open, terminal heads of star-shaped pink flowers in late summer. Z6–9 H9–6.
S. spathulifolium illus. p.389. **'Cape Blanco'** (syn. *S.s.* 'Cappa Blanca') illus. p.391.
S. spectabile, syn. *Hylotelephium spectabile* (Ice-plant). Clump-forming perennial. H and S 18in (45cm). Has oval, indented, fleshy, gray-green leaves, above which flat heads of small, star-shaped pink flowers that attract butterflies are borne in late summer. Z4–9 H9–1. **'Brilliant'** illus. p.294.
S. spurium. Semi-evergreen, mat-forming, creeping perennial. H 4in (10cm) or more, S indefinite. Oblong to oval, toothed leaves are borne along hairy stems. Large, slightly rounded heads of small, star-shaped flowers are borne in summer. Flower color varies from deep purple to white. Z4–9 H9–1.
S. tatarinowii, syn. *Hylotelephium tatarinowii*. Arching, spreading, tuberous perennial. H 4in (10cm), S 8in (20cm). Rounded, terminal heads of star-shaped, pink-flushed white flowers appear in late summer above small, oval, toothed, green leaves borne along purplish stems. Good in an alpine house.

SELAGINELLA

SELAGINELLACEAE

Genus of evergreen, mosslike perennials grown for their foliage. Prefers semi-shade and needs moist but well-drained, peaty soil. Remove faded foliage regularly. Propagate from pieces with roots attached that have been broken off plant in any season.
S. kraussiana illus. p.312.
'Aurea' is an evergreen, mosslike perennial. H ½in (1cm), S indefinite. Spreading, filigreed, bright yellowish green fronds are much-branched, denser toward the growing tips and easily root on the soil surface.
'Variegata' has foliage splashed with creamy yellow. Both Z6–9 H–5.
S. lepidophylla (Resurrection plant, Rose of Jericho). Evergreen, mosslike perennial. H and S 4in (10cm). Bluntly rounded, emerald green fronds aging red-brown or gray-green are produced in dense tufts. On drying, fronds curl inward into a tight ball; they unfold when placed in water. Z8–10 H10–8.
S. martensii illus. p.311.

SELENICEREUS

CACTACEAE

Genus of summer-flowering cacti with climbing, 4–10-ribbed green stems to ¾in (2cm) across. Nocturnal, funnel-shaped flowers eventually open flat. Needs sun or partial shade and rich, well-drained soil. Propagate by seed or stem cuttings in spring or summer.
S. grandiflorus illus. p.456.

SELINUM

APIACEAE/UMBELLIFERAE

Genus of summer-flowering perennials ideal for informal gardens and backs of borders. Prefers sun but will grow in semi-shade, and any well-drained soil. Once established, roots resent disturbance. Propagate by seed when fresh, in summer or autumn.
S. tenuifolium. See *S. wallichianum*.
S. wallichianum, syn *S. tenuifolium*. Upright, architectural perennial. H 5ft (1.5m), S 2ft (60cm). In summer produces small, star-shaped white flowers borne in large, flat heads, one above another. Has very finely divided, midgreen leaves. Z4–7.

SEMELE

LILIACEAE/RUSCACEAE

Genus of one species of evergreen, twining climber. Male and female flowers are produced on the same plant. Needs partial shade and prefers rich, well-drained soil. Propagate by division or seed in spring.
S. androgyna (Climbing butcher's broom). Evergreen climber, twining in upper part, branched and bearing oval cladodes, 2–4in (5–10cm) long. H to 22ft (7m). Star-shaped cream flowers appear in early summer in notches on cladode margins, followed by orange-red berries. Z9–10 H10–9.

SEMIAQUILEGIA

RANUNCULACEAE

Genus of perennials grown for their flowers. These differ from those of *Aquilegia*, with which it is sometimes included, by having no spurs. Is good in rock gardens. Requires sun and moist but well-drained soil. Propagate by seed in autumn.
S. ecalcarata illus. p.355.

SEMIARUNDINARIA

GRAMINEAE/POACEAE

See also GRASSES, BAMBOOS, RUSHES, and SEDGES.
S. fastuosa, syn. *Arundinaria fastuosa*, illus. p.308.

SEMPERVIVUM

Houseleek

CRASSULACEAE

Genus of evergreen perennials that spread by short stolons and are grown for their symmetrical rosettes of oval to strap-shaped, pointed, fleshy leaves. Makes ground-hugging mats suitable for rock gardens, screes, walls, banks, and alpine houses. Flowers are star-shaped with 8–16 spreading petals. Needs sun and gritty soil. Takes several years to reach flowering size. Rosettes die after flowering but leave numerous offsets. Propagate by offsets in summer.
S. arachnoideum illus. p.389.
S. ciliosum illus. p.389.
***S.* 'Commander Hay'.** Evergreen, basal-rosetted perennial. H 6in (15cm), S to 12in (30cm). Grown for its very large, dark red rosettes to 4in (10cm) across. Bears terminal clusters of dull greenish red flowers in summer. Z7–10 H10–7.
S. giuseppii illus. p.391.
S. grandiflorum. Evergreen, basal-rosetted perennial. H 4in (10cm), S to 8in (20cm). Variable, densely haired, red-tinted, dark green rosettes exude a goatlike smell when crushed. Produces loose, terminal clusters of yellow-green flowers, stained purple in centers, on long flower stems in summer. Prefers organic, acidic soil. Z6–9 H9–6.
S. hirtum. See *Jovibarba hirta*.
S. montanum illus. p.390.
S. soboliferum. See *Jovibarba sobolifera*.
S. tectorum illus. p.389.

SENECIO

ASTERACEAE/COMPOSITAE

Genus of annuals, succulent and non-succulent perennials, and evergreen shrubs, subshrubs, and twining climbers grown for their foliage and usually daisylike flower heads. Some shrubby species are now referred to the genus *Brachyglottis*. Shrubs are excellent for coastal gardens. Most prefer full sun and well-drained soil (although *S. articulatus* and *S. rowleyanus* tolerate partial shade and need very well-drained soil). Propagate shrubs and climbers by semi-ripe cuttings in summer, annuals by seed in spring, perennials by division in spring (*S. articulatus* and *S. rowleyanus* by seed or stem cuttings in spring or summer). All parts may cause severe discomfort if ingested.
S. articulatus, syn. *Kleinia articulata* (Candle plant). Deciduous, spreading succulent. H 2ft (60cm), S indefinite. Branching, gray-marked blue stems have weak joints. Bears rounded to oval, 3–5-lobed, gray leaves and flattish heads of small, cup-shaped yellow flowers from spring to autumn. Offsets freely from stolons. Z131–15 H12–10. **'Variegatus'** illus. p.462.
S. cineraria, syn. *S. maritimus*. Moderately fast-growing, evergreen, bushy subshrub, often grown as an annual. H and S 1ft (30cm). Has long, oval, very deeply lobed, hairy, silver-gray leaves. Rounded yellow flower heads appear in summer but are best removed. Z8–11 H12–1. **'Cirrus'** (illus. p.37) has elliptic, finely toothed or lobed, silvery green to white leaves. **'Silver Dust'** illus. p.334.
***S. clivorum* 'Desdemona'.** See *Ligularia dentata* 'Desdemona'.
S. compactus. See *Brachyglottis compacta*.
S. confusus, syn. *Pseudogynoxys chenopodioides*, illus. p.217.
***S.* Dunedin Hybrids.** See *Brachyglottis* Dunedin Hybrids.
S. elegans. Moderately fast-growing, upright annual. H 18in (45cm), S 6in (15cm). Has oval, deeply lobed, deep green leaves. Daisylike purple flower heads appear on branching stems in summer. H8–1.
S. grandifolius, syn. *Telanthophora grandiflora*. Evergreen, erect, robust-stemmed shrub. H 10–15ft (3–5m), S 6–10ft (2–3m). Has oval, toothed, boldly veined leaves, 8–18in (20–45cm) long, glossy, rich green above, red-brown-haired beneath. Carries terminal clusters, 12in (30cm) wide, of small, daisylike yellow flower heads in winter-spring. Z12–15 H12–1.
S. greyi of gardens. See *Brachyglottis* Dunedin Hybrids.
S.* x *hybridus. See *Pericallis* x *hybrida*.
S. laxifolius. See *Brachyglottis laxifolia*.
S. laxifolius of gardens. See *Brachyglottis* Dunedin Hybrids.
S. macroglossus (Natal ivy, Wax vine). Evergreen, woody-stemmed, twining climber. H 10ft (3m). Leaves are sharply triangular, fleshy-textured, and glossy. Loose clusters of daisylike flower heads, each with a few white ray petals and a central yellow disk, are borne mainly in winter. Z12–15 H12–10. **'Variegatus'** illus. p.219.
S. maritimus. See *S. cineraria*.
S. mikanioides, syn. *Delairea odorata* (German ivy). Evergreen, semi-woody, twining climber. H 6–10ft (2–3m). Has fleshy leaves with 5–7 broad, pointed, radiating lobes. Mature plants carry large clusters of small yellow flower heads in autumn-winter.
S. monroi. See *Brachyglottis monroi*.
S. przewalskii. See *Ligularia przewalskii*.

S. pulcher illus. p.294.
S. reinholdii. See *Brachyglottis rotundifolia*.
S. rotundifolius. See *Brachyglottis rotundifolia*.
S. rowleyanus illus. p.462.
S. smithii. Bushy perennial. H 3–4ft (1–1.2m), S 2½–3ft (75cm–1m). Woolly stems are clothed with long, oval, toothed, leathery, dark green leaves. Daisylike white flower heads with yellow centers are borne in terminal clusters, up to 6in (15cm) across, in early summer. Likes boggy conditions. Z6–8 H8–6.
***S.* 'Spring Glory'.** See *Pericallis* x *hybrida* 'Spring Glory'.
***S.* 'Sunshine'.** See *Brachyglottis* Dunedin Hybrids 'Sunshine'.
S. tamoides. Evergreen, woody-stemmed, twining climber. H 15ft (5m) or more. Has ivy-shaped, light green leaves. In autumn-winter bears yellow flower heads that are daisylike, but with only a few ray petals. Z6–8 H8–6.

SENNA

CAESALPINIACEAE/LEGUMINOSAE

Genus of evergreen trees, shrubs, and perennials grown for their pealike flowers. Requires full sun and moist but well-drained soil. Propagate by seed sown in spring, or by semi-ripe cuttings in summer. Divide perennials in spring.
S. artemisioides, syn. *Cassia artemisioides* (Silver cassia, Wormwood cassia). Evergreen, erect to spreading, wiry shrub. H and S 3–6ft (1–2m). Leaves each have 6–8 linear leaflets covered with silky, white down. Axillary spikes of cup-shaped yellow flowers appear from winter to early summer.
S. corymbosa, syn. *Cassia corymbosa*, illus. p.147.
S. didymobotrya, syn. *Cassia didymobotrya*, illus. p.147.
S.* x *floribunda, syn. *Cassia corymbosa* var. *plurijuga* of gardens, *C.* x *floribunda*. Vigorous, evergreen or deciduous, rounded shrub with robust stems. H and S 5–6ft (1.5–2m). Bright green leaves consist of 4–6 oval leaflets. Carries very large clusters of bowl-shaped, rich yellow flowers in late summer.
S. siamea, syn. *Cassia siamea*. Fast-growing, evergreen, rounded tree. H and S 25–30ft (8–10m) or more. Leaves, 6–12in (15–30cm) long, have 7–12 pairs of elliptic leaflets. Large terminal panicles of small, cup-shaped, bright yellow flowers are borne in spring, followed by flat, dark brown pods to 9in (23cm) long.

SEQUOIA

TAXODIACEAE

See also CONIFERS.
S. sempervirens (Coast redwood, Redwood). Very vigorous, columnar to conical conifer with horizontal branches. H 70–100ft (20–30m), S 15–25ft (5–8m), although one specimen – which is believed to be the tallest tree in the world – has reached 375ft (112m). Has thick, soft, fibrous, red-brown bark and needlelike, flattened, pale green leaves, spirally arranged on shoots. Produces rounded to cylindrical cones, initially green, ripening to dark brown. Will regrow if cut back. Where hardy, cold winters kill foliage but without affecting the tree. Z8–9 H9–8.

SEQUOIADENDRON

TAXODIACEAE

See also CONIFERS.
S. giganteum illus. p.102. **'Pendulum'** is a weeping conifer. H 30ft (10m), S 6ft (2m) or more. Bark is thick, soft, fibrous, and red-brown. Has spiraled, needlelike, incurved, gray-green leaves that darken and become glossy. Z6–9 H9–4.

SERAPIAS

See also ORCHIDS.
S. cordigera. Deciduous, terrestrial orchid. H 16in (40cm). Spikes of reddish or dark purple flowers, 1½in (4cm) long, are borne in spring. Has lance-shaped, red-spotted leaves, 6in (15cm) long. Grow in semi-shade.

SERENOA

ARECACEAE/PALMAE

Genus of one species of evergreen fan palm grown for its foliage. Requires full light or partial shade and well-drained soil. Water potted plants moderately during growing season, less at other times. Propagate by seed or suckers in spring. Spider mite may be troublesome.
S. repens (Saw palmetto, Scrub palmetto). Evergreen, rhizomatous fan palm, usually stemless. H 2–3ft (60cm–1m), S 6ft (2m) or more. Palmate leaves, 18–30in (45–75cm) wide, are gray to blue-green, and each divided into 6–20 strap-shaped lobes. Clusters of tiny, fragrant cream flowers are hidden among leaves in summer, followed by egg-shaped, purple-black fruits. Z9–11 H12–9.

SERISSA

RUBIACEAE

Genus of one species of evergreen shrub grown for its overall appearance. Needs sun or partial shade and fertile, well-drained soil. Water containerized specimens moderately, less when not in growth. May be trimmed after flowering. Propagate by semi-ripe cuttings in summer.
S. foetida, syn. *S. japonica*. Evergreen, spreading to rounded, freely branching shrub. H to 2ft (60cm), S 2–3ft (60cm–1m). Tiny, oval leaves are lustrous and deep green. Small, funnel-shaped, 4- or 5-lobed white flowers are produced from spring to autumn. Z11–15 H12–10.
S. japonica. See *S. foetida*.

SERRATULA

ASTERACEAE/COMPOSITAE

Genus of perennials grown for their thistlelike flower heads. Requires sun and well-drained soil. Propagate by seed or by division in spring.
S. seoanei, syn. *S. shawii*. Upright, compact perennial. H 9in (23cm), S 5–6in (12–15cm). Stems bear feathery, finely cut leaves and, in autumn, terminal panicles of small, thistlelike purple flower heads. Is useful for a rock garden.
S. shawii. See *S. seoanei*.

SESLERIA

GRAMINEAE/POACEAE

See also GRASSES, BAMBOOS, RUSHES, and SEDGES.
S. heufleriana (Balkan blue grass). Evergreen, tuft-forming, perennial grass. H 20in (50cm), S 12–18in (30–45cm). Bears rich green leaves, glaucous beneath, and, in spring, compact panicles of purple spikelets. Z5–8 H8–5.

SETARIA

GRAMINEAE/POACEAE

See also GRASSES, BAMBOOS, RUSHES, and SEDGES.
S. italica (Foxtail millet, Italian millet). Moderately fast-growing, annual grass with thick stems. H 5ft (1.5m), S to 3ft (1m). Has lance-shaped, midgreen leaves, to 1½ft (45cm) long, and loose panicles of white, cream, yellow, red, brown, or black flowers in summer-autumn. Z9–10 H10–9.

Setcreasea purpurea. See *Tradescantia pallida* 'Purpurea'.

SHEPHERDIA

ELAEAGNACEAE

Genus of deciduous or evergreen shrubs grown for their foliage and fruits. Separate male and female plants are needed in order to obtain fruits. Requires sun and well-drained soil. Propagate by softwood cuttings in summer or by seed in autumn.
S. argentea (Buffalo berry). Deciduous, bushy, often treelike shrub. H and S 12ft (4m). Bears tiny, inconspicuous yellow flowers amid oblong silvery leaves in spring, followed by small, egg-shaped, bright red fruits. Z3–6 H6–1.

SHIBATAEA

GRAMINEAE/POACEAE

See also GRASSES, BAMBOOS, RUSHES, and SEDGES.
S. kumasasa illus. p.308.

SHORTIA

DIAPENSIACEAE

Genus of evergreen, spring-flowering perennials with leaves that often turn red in autumn-winter. Buds may be frosted in areas without snow cover. Difficult to grow in hot, dry climates. Needs shade or semi-shade and well-drained, peaty, sandy, acidic soil. Propagate by runners in summer or by seed when available.
S. galacifolia illus. p.364.
S. soldanelloides illus. p.366. var. ***ilicifolia*** is an evergreen, mat-forming perennial. H 2–4in (5–10cm), S 4–6in (10–15cm). Has rounded, toothed leaves. In late spring each flower stem carries 4–6 small, pendent, bell-shaped flowers with fringed edges and rose pink centers shading to white. Flowers of var. ***magna*** are rose pink throughout. Both Z6–8 H8–5.
***S. uniflora* 'Grandiflora'.** Vigorous, evergreen, mat-forming perennial with a few rooted runners. H 3in (8cm), S 8in (20cm). Leaves are rounded, toothed, leathery, and glossy. Flower stems bear cup-shaped, 2in (5cm) wide, white-pink flowers with serrated petals in spring. Z5–8 H8–5.

SIBIRAEA

ROSACEAE

Genus of deciduous shrubs grown for their foliage and flowers. Needs sunny, well-drained soil. Established plants benefit from having old or weak shoots cut to base after flowering. Propagate by softwood cuttings in summer.
S. altaiensis, syn. *S. laevigata*. Deciduous, spreading, open shrub. H 3ft (1m), S 5ft (1.5m). Has narrowly oblong, blue-green leaves and, in late spring and early summer, dense, terminal clusters of tiny, star-shaped white flowers. Z6–8 H8–6.
S. laevigata. See *S. altaiensis*.

SIDALCEA

MALVACEAE

Genus of summer-flowering perennials grown for their hollyhock-like flowers. Needs sun and well-drained soil. Propagate by division in spring.
***S.* 'Loveliness'.** Upright perennial. H 3ft (1m), S 1½ft (45cm). Has buttercup-like, divided leaves with narrowly oblong segments. In summer bears racemes of shallowly cup-shaped, shell pink flowers. Z9–10 H10–9.
***S.* 'Oberon'** illus. p.243.
***S.* 'Puck'.** Upright perennial. H 2ft (60cm), S 1½ft (45cm). Has buttercup like, divided leaves with narrowly oblong segments. In summer bears racemes of shallowly cup-shaped, deep pink flowers. Z6–8 H8–6.
***S.* 'Sussex Beauty'.** Upright perennial. H 4ft (1.2m), S 1½ft (45cm). Has buttercup-like, divided leaves with narrowly oblong segments and, in summer, shallowly cup-shaped, deep rose pink flowers. Z6–8 H8–6.

SIDERITIS

LABIATAE/LAMIACEAE

Genus of evergreen perennials, sub-shrubs, and shrubs grown mainly for their foliage. Needs full light and well-drained soil. Water containerized plants

moderately, less when temper-atures are low. Remove spent flower spikes after flowering. Propagate by seed in spring or by semi-ripe cuttings in summer.
S. candicans. Evergreen, erect, well-branched shrub. H to 2½ft (75cm), S to 2ft (60cm). Lance-shaped to narrowly oval or triangular leaves bear dense white wool. Produces leafy, terminal spikes of tubular, pale yellow-and-light-brown or orange-red flowers in summer. Z9–10 H10–9.

SILENE
Campion, Catchfly

CARYOPHYLLACEAE

Genus of annuals and perennials, some of which are evergreen, grown for their masses of 5-petaled flowers. Needs sun and fertile, well-drained soil. Propagate by softwood cuttings in spring or by seed in spring or early autumn.
S. acaulis illus. p.365.
S. alpestris, syn. *Heliosperma alpestris*, illus. p.373.
***S. armeria* 'Electra'** illus. p.323.
S. coeli-rosa, syn. *Agrostemma coelirosa, Lychnis coeli-rosa, Viscaria elegans*, illus. p.320. **'Rose Angel'** illus. p.325.
S. elisabethae. Basal-rosetted perennial. H 4in (10cm), S 8in (20cm). Has rosettes of strap-shaped, midgreen leaves. In summer, stems bear large, often solitary, deep rose-red flowers with green centers. Is suitable for a rock garden. Z7–9 H9–7.
S. hookeri. Short-lived, trailing, prostrate, late summer-deciduous perennial with a long, slender taproot. H 2in (5cm), S 8in (20cm). Slender stems bear oval gray leaves and, in late summer, soft pink, salmon, or orange flowers deeply cleft to base. Z5–8 H8–5.
***S. maritima* 'Flore Pleno'.** See *S. uniflora* 'Robin Whitebreast'.
S. pendula (Nodding catchfly). Moderately fast-growing, bushy annual. H and S 6–8in (15–20cm). Has oval, hairy, midgreen leaves and, in summer and early autumn, clusters of light pink flowers.
S. schafta illus. p.379.
***S. uniflora* 'Robin Whitebreast'**, syn. *S. maritima* 'Flore Pleno', *S.u.* 'Flore Pleno', *S. vulgaris* subsp. *maritima* 'Flore Pleno' (Double sea campion). Lax perennial with deep, wandering roots. H and S 8in (20cm). Leaves are lance-shaped and gray-green. Has pomponlike, double white flowers on branched stems in summer. Z3–7 H7–1.
***S. vulgaris* subsp. *maritima* 'Flore Pleno'.** See *S. uniflora* 'Robin Whitebreast'.

SILPHIUM

ASTERACEAE/COMPOSITAE

Genus of fairly coarse, summer-flowering perennials. Does best in sun or semi-shade and in moist but well-drained soil. Propagate by division in spring or by seed when fresh, in autumn.
S. laciniatum (Compass plant). Clump-forming perennial. H 6ft (2m), S 2ft (60cm). Midgreen leaves, composed of opposite pairs of oblong to lance-shaped leaflets, face north and south wherever the plant is grown, hence the common name. Large clusters of slightly pendent, daisylike yellow flower heads are borne in late summer. Z5–9 H9–5.

SILYBUM

ASTERACEAE/COMPOSITAE

Genus of thistlelike biennials grown for their spectacular foliage. Grow in sun and in any well-drained soil. Propagate by seed in late spring or early summer. Is prone to slug and snail damage.
S. marianum illus. p.322.

Sinarundinaria jaunsarensis. See *Yushania anceps*.
Sinarundinaria murieliae. See *Fargesia murieliae*.
Sinarundinaria nitida. See *Fargesia nitida*.

SINNINGIA

GESNERIACEAE

Genus of usually summer-flowering, tuberous perennials and deciduous subshrubs with showy flowers. Grow in bright light but not direct sun. Prefers a humid atmosphere and moist but not water-logged, peaty soil. When leaves die down after flowering, allow tubers to dry out; then store in a frost-free area. Propagate in spring by seed or in late spring or summer by stem cuttings or by dividing tubers into sections, each with a young shoot.
S. barbata. Bushy, tuberous perennial with square red stems. H and S 2ft (60cm) or more. Broadly lance-shaped leaves, to 6in (15cm) long, are glossy, midgreen above, reddish green beneath. In summer has 5-lobed, pouched white flowers, 1½in (4cm) long. Z14–15 H12–10.
S. concinna. Rosetted perennial with very small tubers. H and S to 6in (15cm). Oval to almost round, scalloped, velvety, red-veined, midgreen leaves, ¾in (2cm) long, are red below. Trumpet-shaped, bicolored purple and white flowers to ¾in (2cm) long are produced continuously. Z14–15 H12–10.
***S.* 'Etoile du Feu'.** Short-stemmed, rosetted, tuberous perennial. H 12in (30cm), S 16in (40cm) or more. Has oval, velvety leaves, 8–9½in (20–24cm) long. Upright, trumpet-shaped, carmine-red flowers appear in summer. Z14–15 H12–10.
***S.* 'Mont Blanc'.** Short-stemmed, rosetted, tuberous perennial. H 12in (30cm), S 16in (40cm) or more. Oval, velvety, midgreen leaves are 8–9½in (20–24cm) long. In summer bears upright, trumpet-shaped, pure white flowers. Z14–15 H12–10.
***S.* 'Red Flicker'** illus. p.282.
S. speciosa, syn. *Gloxinia speciosa* (Gloxinia). Short-stemmed, rosetted, tuberous perennial. H and S to 1ft (30cm). Oval, velvety, green leaves are 8in (20cm) long. Nodding, funnel-shaped, fleshy violet, red, or white flowers, to 2in (5cm) long and pouched on lower sides, are produced in summer. Is a parent of many named hybrids, of which a selection is included above and below.
***S.* 'Switzerland'** illus. p.282.
***S.* 'Waterloo'.** Short-stemmed, rosetted, tuberous perennial. H 12in (30cm), S 16in (40cm) or more. Has oval, velvety leaves, 8–9½in (20–24cm) long. Upright, trumpet-shaped, bright scarlet flowers open in summer. Z14–15 H12–10.

SINOFRANCHETIA

LARDIZABALACEAE

Genus of one species of deciduous, twining climber grown mainly for its handsome leaves. Is suitable for covering buildings and growing up large trees. Male and female flowers are produced on separate plants. Grow in semi-shade and in any well-drained soil. Propagate by semi-ripe cuttings in summer.
S. chinensis. Deciduous, twining climber. H to 50ft (15m). Mid- to dark green leaves have 3 oblong to oval leaflets, each 5–15cm (2–6in) long. In late spring has small, dull white flowers in pendent racemes, to 4in (10cm) long. Pale purple berries follow in summer. Z7–10 H10–7.

SINOJACKIA

STYRACACEAE

Genus of deciduous shrubs and trees grown for their flowers. Requires a sheltered position in sun or partial shade and fertile, organic, moist, acidic soil. Propagate by softwood cuttings in summer.
S. rehderiana. Deciduous, bushy shrub or spreading tree. H and S 20ft (6m). Nodding, saucer-shaped white flowers, each with a central cluster of yellow anthers, appear in late spring and early summer. Oval leaves are dark green. Z6–10 H10–6.

SINOWILSONIA

HAMAMELIDACEAE

Genus of one species of deciduous tree grown for its foliage and catkins. Requires sun or semi-shade and fertile, moist but well-drained soil. Propagate by seed in autumn.
S. henryi. Deciduous, spreading, sometimes shrubby tree. H and S 25ft (8m). Has oval, toothed, glossy, bright green leaves, and long, pendent green catkins in late spring. Z6–9 H9–6.

Siphonosmanthus delavayi. See *Osmanthus delavayi*.

SISYRINCHIUM

IRIDACEAE

Genus of annuals and perennials, some of which are semi-evergreen. Prefers sun (but tolerates partial shade) and well-drained or moist soil. Propagate by division in early spring or by seed in spring or autumn.
S. angustifolium. See *S. graminoides*.
S. bellum of gardens. See *S. idahoense*.
S. bermudiana. See *S. graminoides*.
S. brachypus. See *S. californicum*.
S. californicum (Golden-eyed grass). Semi-evergreen, upright perennial. H 12–24in (30–60cm), S 12in (30cm). Has grasslike tufts of basal, light green leaves. For a long period in spring-summer produces flattish, bright yellow flowers, with slightly darker veins, on winged stems. Outer leaves may die off and turn black in autumn. Dwarf forms are known as *S. brachypus*. Prefers moist soil. Z8–9 H9–7.
S. douglasii. See *Olsynium douglasii*.
S. graminoides, syn. *S. angustifolium, S. bermudiana*, illus. p.356.
S. grandiflorum. See *Olsynium douglasii*.
S. idahoense, syn. *S. bellum* of gardens, illus. p.383.
S. odoratissimum. See *Olsynium biflorum*.
S. striatum illus. p.290. **'Aunt May'** (syn. *S.s.* 'Variegatum') is a semi-evergreen, upright perennial. H 18–24in (45–60cm), S 12in (30cm). Produces tufts of long, narrow, cream-striped, grayish green leaves. Slender spikes of trumpet-shaped, purple-striped, straw yellow flowers are borne in summer. Z7–8 H8–7.

SKIMMIA

RUTACEAE

Genus of evergreen shrubs and trees grown for their spring flowers, aromatic foliage and their fruits. Except with *S. japonica* subsp. *reevesiana*, separate male and female plants are needed in order to obtain fruits. Needs shade or semi-shade and fertile, moist soil. Poor soil or too much sun may cause chlorosis. Propagate by semi-ripe cuttings in late summer or by seed in autumn. The fruits may cause mild stomach upset if ingested.
S. anquetilia. Evergreen, bushy, open shrub. H 4ft (1.2m), S 6ft (2m). Produces small clusters of tiny yellow flowers from mid- to late spring, then spherical scarlet fruits. Leaves are oblong to oval, pointed, strongly aromatic, and dark green. Z7–9 H9–7.
S.* x *foremanii of gardens. See *S. japonica* 'Veitchii'.
S. japonica illus. p.175. **'Fructo Albo'** (female) illus. p.173. subsp. ***reevesiana* 'Robert Fortune'** (syn. *S. reevesiana*; hermaphrodite) and **'Rubella'** (male) illus. p.174. **'Veitchii'** (syn. *S.* x *foremanii* of gardens) is a vigorous, evergreen, upright, dense, female shrub. H and S 5ft (1.5m). Broadly oval leaves are rich green. In mid- and late spring bears dense clusters of small, star-shaped white flowers, followed by large, spherical, bright red fruits. Z7–9 H9–7.
S. reevesiana. See *S. japonica* subsp. *reevesiana* 'Robert Fortune'.

SMILACINA

CONVALLARIACEAE/LILIACEAE

Genus of perennials grown for their graceful appearance. Prefers semi-shade and organic, moist, neutral to acidic soil. Propagate by division in spring or by seed in autumn.
S. racemosa illus. p.233.

SMILAX

LILIACEAE/SMILACACEAE

Genus of deciduous or evergreen, woody-stemmed or herbaceous, scrambling climbers with tubers or rhizomes. Male and female flowers are borne on separate plants. Grow in any well-drained soil, in sun or semi-shade. Propagate by division or seed in spring or by semi-ripe cuttings in summer.
S. china. Deciduous, woody-based, scrambling climber with straggling, sometimes spiny stems. H to 15ft (5m). Leaves are broadly oval to rounded. Umbels of yellow-green flowers are produced in spring; tiny red berries appear in autumn. Z7–10 H10–7.

SMITHIANTHA

GESNERIACEAE

Genus of bushy, erect perennials with tuberlike rhizomes, grown for their flowers and foliage. Grow in organic, well-drained soil and in bright light but out of direct sun. Reduce watering after flowering and water sparingly in winter. Propagate by division of rhizomes in early spring.
S. cinnabarina (Temple bells). Robust, erect, rhizomatous perennial. H and S to 2ft (60cm). Broadly oval to almost rounded, toothed leaves, to 6in (15cm) long, are dark green with dark red hairs. Bell-shaped, orange-red flowers lined with pale yellow are produced in summer-autumn. Z14–15 H12–10.
***S.* 'Orange King'** illus. p.283.
S. zebrina. Bushy, rhizomatous perennial with velvety-haired stems. H and S to 3ft (1m). Oval, toothed, hairy leaves, to 7in (18cm) long, are deep green marked with reddish brown. In summer produces tubular flowers, scarlet above, yellow below, spotted red inside and with orange-yellow lobes. Z14–15 H12–10.

SMYRNIUM

APIACEAE/UMBELLIFERAE

Genus of biennials grown for their flowers. Grow in sun and in fertile, well-drained soil. Propagate by seed sown outdoors in autumn or spring.
S. perfoliatum illus. p.335.

SOLANDRA

SOLANACEAE

Genus of evergreen, woody-stemmed, scrambling climbers grown for their large, trumpet-shaped flowers. Needs full light and fertile, well-drained soil. Water freely when in full growth. Tie to supports. Thin out crowded stems after flowering. Propagate by semi-ripe cuttings in summer.
S. maxima illus. p.206.

SOLANUM

SOLANACEAE

Genus of annuals, perennials (some of which are evergreen), and evergreen, semi-evergreen, or deciduous subshrubs, shrubs (occasionally scandent), and woody-stemmed, scrambling or leaf-stalk climbers, grown for their flowers and ornamental fruits. Requires full sun and fertile, well-drained soil. Water regularly but sparingly in winter. Support scrambling climbers. Thin out and spur back crowded growth of climbers in spring. Propagate by seed in spring or by semi-ripe cuttings in summer. Spider mite, whitefly, and aphids may cause problems. All parts of most species, especially the fruits of *S. capsicastrum* and *S. pseudocapsicum*, can cause severe discomfort if ingested.
S. capsicastrum (Winter cherry). Fairly slow-growing, evergreen, bushy subshrub grown as an annual. H and S 1–1½ft (30–45cm). Has lance-shaped, deep green leaves. In summer bears small, star-shaped white flowers, followed by egg-shaped, pointed, orange-red or scarlet fruits, at least ½in (1cm) in diameter, which are at their best in winter. Z13–15 H12–10.
***S. crispum* 'Glasnevin'** illus. p.214.
S. jasminoides (Potato vine). Semi-evergreen, woody-stemmed, scrambling climber. H to 20ft (6m). Oval to lance-shaped leaves may be lobed or have leaflets at base. Small, 5-petaled, pale gray-blue flowers are produced in summer-autumn; tiny purple berries appear in autumn. Z9–11 H12–3. **'Album'** illus. p.207.
S. pseudocapsicum (Jerusalem cherry). Fairly slow-growing, evergreen, bushy shrub, usually grown as an annual. H and S to 4ft (1.2m). Has oval or lance-shaped, bright green leaves. Small, star-shaped white flowers appear in summer and are followed by spherical scarlet fruits. Z11–12 H12–6. Has several smaller selections: **'Balloon'** illus. p.341; **'Fancy'**, H 1ft (30cm), with scarlet fruits; **'Red Giant'** illus. p.341; and **'Snowfire'**, H 1ft (30cm), with white fruits that later turn red. All Z12-14 H12–1.
S. rantonnetii, syn. *Lycianthes rantonnetii* (Blue potato bush). **'Royal Robe'** illus. p.145.
S. seaforthianum illus. p.206.
S. wendlandii illus. p.214.

SOLDANELLA

Snowbell

PRIMULACEAE

Genus of evergreen perennials grown for their early spring flowers. Is good for rock gardens, troughs, and alpine houses. Flower buds are set in autumn and may be destroyed by cold if there is no snow cover. Requires partial shade and organic, well-drained, peaty soil. Propagate by seed in spring or by division in late summer. Slugs may attack flower buds.
S. alpina illus. p.368.
S. minima (Least snowbell). Evergreen, prostrate perennial. H 1in (2.5cm), S 4in (10cm). Forms a mat of minute, rounded leaves on soil surface. In early spring produces solitary, almost stemless, bell-shaped, pale lavender-blue or white flowers with fringed mouths. Z4–7 H7–1.
S. montana (Mountain tassel). Evergreen, mound-forming perennial. H 4in (10cm), S 6in (15cm). In early spring produces tall flower stems carrying long, pendent, bell-shaped, lavender-blue flowers with fringed mouths. Leaves are rounded and leathery. Z4–7 H7–1.
S. villosa illus. p.368.

SOLEIROLIA

Baby's tears, Mind-your-own-business, Mother of thousands

URTICACEAE

Genus of one species of (usually evergreen) prostrate perennial that forms a dense carpet of foliage. Tolerates sun or shade, and prefers moist soil. Propagate by division from spring to midsummer.
S. soleirolii, syn. *Helxine soleirolii*, illus. p.304.

SOLENOSTEMON

Painted nettle

LABIATAE/LAMIACEAE

Genus of evergreen, bushy, subshrubby perennials grown for their colorful leaves and flowers. Makes excellent pot plants. Grow in sun or partial shade and in fertile, well-drained soil, choosing a sheltered position. Water freely in summer, less at other times. Pinch out growing shoots of young plants to encourage a bushy habit. Propagate by seed sown under cover in spring or by softwood cuttings in spring or summer. Mealy bugs and whitefly may cause problems.
S. scutellarioides, syn. *Coleus blumei* var. *verschaffeltii*, illus. p.324. **'Brightness'** illus. p.329. **'Fashion Parade'** is a fast-growing, bushy perennial grown as an annual. H to 18in (45cm), S 12in (30cm) or more. Has multicolored, serrated leaves of various shapes, from oval and unlobed to deeply lobed. Spikes of tiny blue flowers are produced in summer and are best removed. **'Scarlet Poncho'**, with a pendulous habit and oval, serrated, bright red leaves, and **Wizard Series**, also with oval, serrated leaves, but in a very wide range of leaf colors, are both dwarf forms, H 12in (30cm). All Z11–12 H12–1.

SOLIDAGO

Goldenrod

ASTERACEAE/COMPOSITAE

Genus of summer- and autumn-flowering perennials, some species of which are vigorous, coarse plants that tend to crowd out others in borders. Most tolerate sun or shade and any well-drained soil. Propagate by division in spring. Occasionally self-seeds.
***S.* 'Golden Wings'.** Upright perennial. H 5ft (1.5m), S 3ft (1m). Bears large, feathery panicles of small, bright yellow flower heads in early autumn. Has lance-shaped, toothed, slightly hairy, midgreen leaves. Z5–9 H9–5.
***S.* 'Goldenmosa'** illus. p.255.
***S.* 'Laurin'** illus. p.256.
S. virgaurea subsp. ***minuta***, syn. *S.v.* subsp. *alpestris*. Mound-forming perennial. H and S 4in (10cm). Has small, lance-shaped, green leaves and, in autumn, neat spikes of small yellow flower heads. Is suitable for a rock garden, trough, or alpine house. Needs shade and moist soil. Z5–9 H9–5.

x SOLIDASTER

ASTERACEAE/COMPOSITAE

Hybrid genus (*Solidago* x *Aster*) of one summer-flowering perennial. Grows in sun or shade and in any fertile soil. Propagate by division in spring.
x *S. hybridus.* See x *S. luteus*.
x *S. luteus*, syn. x *S. hybridus*, illus. p.291.

SOLLYA

Bluebell creeper

PITTOSPORACEAE

Genus of evergreen, woody-based, twining climbers grown for their attractive flowers. Grow in sun and well-drained soil. Propagate by seed in spring orby softwood or greenwood cuttings in summer.
S. heterophylla illus. p.206.

SONERILA

MELASTOMATACEAE

Genus of evergreen, bushy perennials and shrubs grown for their foliage and flowers. Prefers a humid atmosphere in semi-shade and peaty soil. Propagate by tip cuttings in spring.
S. margaritacea. Evergreen, bushy, semi-prostrate perennial. H and S 8–10in (20–25cm). Red stems produce oval, dark green leaves, 2–3in (5–8cm) long, reddish below, silver-patterned above. Has racemes of 3-petaled, rose-pink flowers in summer. Z15 H12–10. **'Argentea'** has more silvery leaves with green veins; **'Hendersonii'** is more compact with white-spotted leaves.

SOPHORA

LEGUMINOSAE/PAPILIONACEAE

Genus of deciduous or semi-evergreen trees and shrubs grown for their habit, foliage, and flowers. Requires full sun (*S. microphylla* and *S. tetraptera* often benefit from being grown against a south- or west-facing wall) and fertile, well-drained soil. Propagate by seed in autumn; semi-evergreens may also be raised from softwood cuttings in summer.

S. davidii, syn. *S. viciifolia*, illus. p.145.
S. japonica (Pagoda tree). Deciduous, spreading tree. H and S 70ft (20m). Dark green leaves consist of 9–15 oval leaflets. On mature trees, long clusters of pealike, creamy white flowers appear in late summer and early autumn. Z5–9 H9–1. **'Pendula'**, H and S 10ft (3m), has long, hanging shoots clothed with dark green foliage. Z5–9 H9–5. **'Violacea'** illus. p.71.
S. microphylla, syn. *Edwardsia microphylla*. Semi-evergreen, spreading tree. H and S 25ft (8m). Dark green leaves are composed of numerous tiny, oblong leaflets. Produces clusters of pealike, deep yellow flowers in late spring. Z8–10 H10–8.
S. tetraptera illus. p.89.
S. viciifolia. See *S. davidii*.

x SOPHROLAELIO-CATTLEYA

See also ORCHIDS.
x ***S.* Hazel Boyd 'Apricot Glow'** (illus. p.299). Evergreen, epiphytic orchid for an intermediate greenhouse. H 4in (10cm). In spring and early summer produces small heads of apricot-orange flowers, 3½in (9cm) across, with crimson marks on lips. Has oval, rigid leaves, 4in (10cm) long. Grow in good light in summer. Z14–15 H12-10.
x ***S.* Trizac 'Purple Emperor'** (illus. p.297). Evergreen, epiphytic orchid for an intermediate greenhouse. H 4in (10cm). In spring, has crimson-lipped, pinkish purple flowers, 2½in (6cm) across, in small heads. Has oval, rigid leaves, 4in (10cm) long. Provide good light in summer. Z14–15 H12-10.

SORBARIA

ROSACEAE

Genus of deciduous, summer-flowering shrubs grown for their foliage and large panicles of small white flowers. Prefers sun and deep, fertile, moist soil. In winter cut out some older stems on mature plants and prune back remaining shoots to growing points. Remove suckers at base to prevent *Sorbaria* from spreading too widely. Propagate by softwood cuttings in summer, by division in autumn or by root cuttings in late winter.
S. aitchisonii. See *S. tomentosa* var. *angustifolia*.
S. arborea. See *S. kirilowii*.
S. kirilowii, syn. *S. arborea*, *Spiraea arborea*. Vigorous, deciduous, arching shrub. H and S 20ft (6m). Leaves are composed of 13–17 lance-shaped, taper-pointed, deep green leaflets. Nodding panicles of star-shaped, white flowers are produced in mid- and late summer. Z5–9 H9–5.
S. sorbifolia, syn. *Spiraea sorbifolia*, illus. p.137.
S. tomentosa var. ***angustifolia***, syn. *S. aitchisonii*, *Spiraea aitchisonii*. Deciduous, arching shrub. H and S 10ft (3m). Shoots are red when young. Leaves have 11–23 narrowly lance-shaped, taper-pointed, dark green leaflets. Upright panicles of star-shaped white flowers are produced from mid- to late summer. Z8–11 H12–8.

SORBUS

ROSACEAE

Genus of deciduous trees and shrubs grown for their foliage, small, 5-petaled flowers, attractive fruits, and, in some species, autumn color. Leaves may be whole or divided into leaflets. Needs sun or semi-shade and fertile, well-drained but moist soil. Species with leaves composed of leaflets do not grow well in very dry soil. Propagate by softwood cuttings or budding in summer, by seed in autumn, or by grafting in winter. Is susceptible to fireblight. Raw fruit may cause mild stomach upset if ingested.
S. alnifolia (Korean mountain ash). Deciduous, conical, then spreading tree. H 50ft (15m), S 25ft (8m). Oval, toothed, bright green leaves turn orange and red in autumn. Has small white flowers in late spring, then egg-shaped, orange-red fruits. Z3–6 H8–1.
S. americana (American mountain ash). Deciduous, round-headed tree. H 30ft (10m), S 22ft (7m). Light green leaves, divided into 11–17 narrowly oval leaflets, usually color well in autumn. Bears small white flowers in early summer, then rounded, bright red fruits, ripening in early autumn. Z3–8 H8–1.
S. aria (Whitebeam). Deciduous, spreading tree. H 50ft (15m), S 30ft (10m). Oval, toothed leaves are silver-gray when young, maturing to dark green above, white-felted beneath. Clusters of small white flowers in late spring are followed by rounded, brown-speckled, deep red fruits. Z4–5 H8–6. **'Chrysophylla'**, H 30ft (10m), S 22ft (7m), bears golden yellow young leaves. **'Decaisneana'** see *S.a.* 'Majestica'. **'Lutescens'** illus. p.78. **'Majestica'** (syn. *S.a.* 'Decaisneana') has larger leaves, white-haired when young, and larger fruits. Z4–7 H7–1.
S. aucuparia (European mountain ash, Rowan) illus. p.81. **'Fastigiata'** (syn. *S. scopulina* of gardens) is a deciduous, dense, conical tree with upright branches. H 25ft (8m), S 15ft (5m). Bears divided, dark green leaves, and clusters of small white flowers in late spring or early summer followed by large, dark red fruits, ½in (1cm) across. **'Fructu Luteo'** is a spreading tree, H 50ft (15m), S 25ft (8m). Leaves consist of 13–15 narrowly oval, midgreen leaflets that turn yellow or red in autumn. Bears orange-yellow fruits. Fruits of **'Rossica Major'** (syn. *S.a.* 'Rossica') are large and deep red. **'Sheerwater Seedling'**, S 12ft (4m), has a narrow, upright habit. All cultivars Z4–7 H7–1.
S. cashmiriana illus. p.93.
S. commixta, syn. *S. discolor* of gardens, illus. p.81. **'Embley'** is a vigorous, deciduous, elegant tree with steeply ascending branches. H 40ft (12m), S 28ft (9m). Glossy, deep green leaves, each with 13–17 slender, lance-shaped leaflets, turn orange and red in late autumn. Bears small white flowers in late spring, and rounded, bright red fruits in autumn. Z6–8 H8–6.
S. cuspidata. See *S. vestita*.
S. decora. Deciduous, spreading, sometimes shrubby tree. H 30ft (10m), S 25ft (8m). Leaves are composed of oblong, blue-green leaflets. Small white flowers in late spring are succeeded by rounded, orange-red fruits. Z3–8 H8–1.
S. discolor of gardens. See *S. commixta*.
S. esserteauana. Deciduous, spreading tree. H and S 30ft (10m). Dark green leaves with broadly oblong leaflets redden in autumn. Has small white flowers in late spring, followed by large clusters of rounded, bright red, sometimes orange-yellow fruits. Z6–8 H8–6.
S. hupehensis (Hupeh mountain ash). Deciduous, spreading tree. H 40ft (12m), S 25ft (8m). Leaves have 9–17 oblong, blue-green leaflets that turn orange-red in late autumn. Small white flowers in late spring are followed by clusters of rounded, pink-tinged white fruits. Z3–8 H8–1. **'Rosea'** (syn. *S.h.* var. *obtusa*) illus. p.81.
S. insignis. Deciduous, spreading tree. H 25ft (8m), S 20ft (6m). Leaves consist of usually 9–21 large, oblong, glossy, dark green leaflets. Large clusters of small, creamy white flowers in late spring are followed by rounded pink fruits that become white in winter. Z8–10 H10–8.
S. intermedia (Swedish whitebeam). Deciduous, broad-headed, dense tree. H and S 40ft (12m). Has broadly oval, deeply lobed, dark green leaves. Carries clusters of small white flowers in late spring, succeeded by rounded red fruits. Z5–8 H8–3.
***S.* 'Joseph Rock'** illus. p.82.
S.* x *kewensis, syn. *S. pohuashanensis* of gardens. Deciduous, spreading tree. H 30ft (10m), S 25ft (8m). Dark green leaves are divided into 11–15 oblong leaflets. Has small white flowers in late spring, followed by dense clusters of rounded red fruits. Z6–8 H8–6.
S. latifolia. Deciduous, spreading tree. H 40ft (12m), S 30ft (10m). Has peeling bark and broadly oval, sharply lobed, glossy, dark green leaves. Small white flowers in late spring are succeeded by rounded, brownish red fruits. Z6–8 H8–5.
***S.* 'Mitchellii'.** See *S. thibetica* 'John Mitchell'.
S. pohuashanensis of gardens. See *S.* x *kewensis*.
S. prattii. Deciduous, spreading tree. H and S 20ft (6m). Dark green leaves are divided into 21–9 oblong, sharply toothed leaflets. Produces small white flowers in late spring, followed by rounded white fruits. Z6–8 H8–6.
S. reducta illus. p.360.
S. sargentiana (Sargent's mountain ash). Deciduous, sparsely branched, spreading tree. H and S 20ft (6m). Has thick shoots and large, midgreen leaves, consisting of 7–11 oblong leaflets, that turn brilliant red in autumn. Small white flowers in late spring are succeeded by rounded red fruits. Z5–7 H7–5.
S. scalaris. Deciduous, spreading, graceful tree. H and S 30ft (10m). Produces leaves with 21–33 narrowly oblong, glossy, deep green leaflets that become deep red and purple in autumn. Produces small white flowers in late spring, followed by rounded red fruits in large, dense clusters. Z6–8 H8–6.
S. scopulina of gardens. See *S. aucuparia* 'Fastigiata'.
S. thibetica. Deciduous, conical tree. H 70ft (20m), S 50ft (15m). Large, broadly oval, dark green leaves are silvery white when young and remain so on undersides. Heads of small white flowers in late spring are followed by rounded brown fruits. Z5–7 H7–5. **'John Mitchell'** (syn. *S.* 'Mitchellii') illus. p.79.
S.* x *thuringiaca. Deciduous, broadly conical, compact tree. H 40ft (12m), S 25ft (8m). Oval, dark green leaves are deeply lobed and have basal leaflets. Small white flowers appear in late spring, followed by rounded, bright red fruits. **'Fastigiata'** has upright branches and a broad, oval, dense crown. Both Z5–8 H8–5.
S. vestita. syn. *S. cuspidata*, illus. p.78.
S. vilmorinii illus. p.94.
***S.* 'Wilfred Fox'.** Deciduous tree, upright when young, later with a dense, oval head. H 50ft (15m), S 30ft (10m). Has broadly oval, glossy, dark green leaves and small white flowers in late spring, followed by rounded, orange-brown fruits. Z5–7 H7–5.

SPARAXIS

Harlequin flower

IRIDACEAE

Genus of spring- and early summer-flowering corms grown for their very gaudy flowers. Needs a sunny, well-drained site. Plant in autumn. Dry off corms after flowering. Propagate by offsets in late summer or by seed in autumn.
S. elegans, syn. *Streptanthera cuprea*, *S. elegans*. Spring-flowering corm. H 4–10in (10–25cm), S 3–5in (8–12cm). Has lance-shaped leaves in an erect, basal fan. Stem produces a loose spike of 1–5 flattish orange or white blooms, each 1¼–1½in (3–4cm) wide and with a yellow center surrounded by a purple-black band.
S. fragrans subsp. ***grandiflora***, syn. *S. grandiflora*. Spring-flowering corm. H 6–16in (15–40cm), S 3–5in (8–12cm). Has sword-shaped leaves in an erect, basal fan. Stem bears a loose spike of up to 5 flattish, yellow tubed, deep purple flowers, each 1½–2in (4–5cm) across.
S. grandiflora. See *S. fragrans* subsp. *grandiflora*.
S. tricolor illus. p.430.

SPARGANIUM
Bur reed

SPARGANIACEAE/TYPHACEAE

Genus of deciduous or semi-evergreen, perennial, marginal water plants grown for their foliage. Tolerates deep shade and cold water. Remove faded foliage and cut plants back regularly to control growth. Propagate by seed or division in spring.
S. erectum, syn. *S. ramosum*, illus. p.449.
S. minimum. See *S. natans*.
S. natans, syn. *S. minimum* (Least bur reed). Vigorous, deciduous or semi-evergreen, perennial, marginal water plant. H 1–3ft (30cm–1m), S 1ft (30cm). Midgreen leaves are grasslike, some erect, some floating. In summer has insignificant, brownish green flowers in the form of burrs. Z5–9 H9–1.
S. ramosum. See *S. erectum*.

Sparmannia. Reclassified as *Sparrmannia*.

SPARRMANNIA,
syn. SPARMANNIA

TILIACEAE

Genus of evergreen trees and shrubs grown for their flowers and foliage. Prefers full light and fertile, well-drained soil. Water freely when in full growth, moderately at other times. Flowered stems may be cut back after flowering to promote a more compact habit. Propagate by greenwood cuttings in late spring. Is prone to whitefly.
S. africana illus. p.118.

SPARTINA

GRAMINEAE/POACEAE

See also GRASSES, BAMBOOS, RUSHES, and SEDGES.
***S. pectinata* 'Aureomarginata'**, syn. *S.p.* 'Aureovariegata', illus. p.309.

SPARTIUM

LEGUMINOSAE/PAPILIONACEAE

Genus of one species of deciduous, almost leafless shrub grown for its green shoots and showy flowers. Needs sun and not too rich, well-drained soil. To maintain a compact habit, trim in early spring. Propagate by seed in autumn.
S. junceum illus. p.147.

SPATHIPHYLLUM

ARACEAE

Genus of evergreen perennials, with rhizomes, grown for their foliage and flowers. Prefers a humid atmosphere, organic, moist soil, and partial shade. Propagate by division in spring or summer. All parts of the plants may cause mild stomach upset if ingested; contact with the sap may irritate skin.
***S.* 'Clevelandii'.** See *S. wallisii* 'Clevelandii'.
S. floribundum. Evergreen, tufted, short-stemmed perennial. H and S to 1ft (30cm). Has clusters of lance-shaped, long-pointed, long-stalked, glossy, dark green leaves, to 6in (15cm) long. Intermittently, bears narrowly oval white spathes, to 3in (8cm) long, each enclosing a green-and-white spadix. Z14–15 H12–1.
***S.* 'Mauna Loa'** illus. p.299.
S. wallisii illus. p.300. **'Clevelandii'** (syn. *S.* 'Clevelandii') is an evergreen, tufted perennial. H and S to 2ft (60cm). Has broadly lance-shaped, semi-erect, glossy, midgreen leaves, 1ft (30cm) or more long. Intermittently bears oval white spathes, each 6in (15cm) long with a central green line, that surround fragrant white spadices. Z14–15 H12–1.

SPATHODEA

BIGNONIACEAE

Genus of evergreen trees grown for their flowers, mainly from autumn to spring, and for their overall appearance. Needs full light and fertile, well-drained but moisture-retentive soil. Container-grown and immature plants seldom bear flowers. Propagate by seed in spring or by semi-ripe cuttings in summer.
S. campanulata illus. p.71.

SPHAERALCEA

MALVACEAE

Genus of perennials and deciduous subshrubs that are evergreen in warm climates. Requires a warm, sunny situation and fertile, well-drained soil. Propagate by seed or division in spring or by softwood cuttings in midsummer.
S. ambigua illus. p.258.
S. munroana. Branching, woody-based perennial. H and S 18in (45cm). Broadly funnel-shaped, brilliant coral-pink flowers are borne singly in leaf axils from summer until first frosts. Has oval, round-toothed, hairy, midgreen leaves. Z4–10 H12–8.

Sphaeropteris. Reclassified as *Cyathea*.
Spiloxene capensis. See *Hypoxis capensis*.

SPIRAEA

ROSACEAE

Genus of deciduous or semi-evergreen shrubs grown for their mass of small flowers and, in some species, their foliage. Requires sun and fertile, well-drained but not overly dry soil. On species and cultivars that flower on the current year's growth – *S.* x *billiardii*, *S. douglasii*, and *S. japonica* and its cultivars – cut back young stems and remove very old ones in early spring. On species that flower on old wood, cut out older shoots in early spring, leaving young shoots to flower that year. Propagate *S. douglasii* by division between late autumn and early spring, and other species and cultivars by softwood cuttings in summer.
S. aitchisonii. See *Sorbaria tomentosa* var. *angustifolia*.
S. arborea. See *Sorbaria kirilowii*.
***S.* 'Arguta'** (Bridal wreath, Foam of May). Deciduous, arching, dense shrub. H and S 8ft (2.5m). Produces clusters of 5-petaled white flowers from mid- to late spring. Leaves are narrowly oblong and bright green. Z5–8 H8–5.
S. aruncus. See *Aruncus dioicus*.
S.* x *billiardii. Deciduous, upright, dense shrub. H and S 8ft (2.5m). Has oval, finely toothed, dark green leaves and dense panicles of 5-petaled pink flowers in summer. Z4–8 H8-1. **'Triumphans'** has large, broadly conical panicles of bright purplish pink flowers.
S. canescens illus. p.136.
S. douglasii. Vigorous, deciduous, upright shrub. H and S 6ft (2m). Dense, narrow panicles of 5-petaled, purplish pink flowers are borne from early to midsummer among oblong, midgreen leaves with gray-white undersides. Z5–8 H8–5. Leaves of subsp. ***menziesii***, H 3ft (1m), are green on both sides.
***S. japonica* 'Anthony Waterer'**, **'Goldflame'** and **'Little Princess'** illus. p.163.
S. nipponica. Deciduous, arching shrub. H and S 8ft (2.5m). Bears dense clusters of 5-petaled white flowers in early summer. Thick reddish shoots carry small, rounded, dark green leaves. Z4–8 H8–1. **'Halward's Silver'**, H and S 1m (3ft), is slow-growing, very dense, and flowers profusely. **'Snowmound'** (syn. *S.n.* var. *tosaensis* of gardens) illus. p.139.
S. prunifolia. Deciduous, arching, graceful shrub. H and S 6ft (2m). In mid- and late spring has clusters of rosettelike, double white flowers amid rounded to oblong, bright green leaves, coloring to bronze-yellow in autumn. Z5–8 H8–5.
***S.* 'Snow White'**, syn. *S. trichocarpa* 'Snow White'. Deciduous, arching shrub. H and S 6ft (2m). Leaves are oblong and midgreen. Dense clusters of 5-petaled white flowers are borne in late spring and early summer. Z5–8 H8–5.
S. sorbifolia. See *Sorbaria sorbifolia*.
S. thunbergii. Deciduous or semi-evergreen, arching, dense shrub. H 5ft (1.5m), S 6ft (2m). Small clusters of 5-petaled white flowers are borne from early to midspring. Has narrowly oblong, pale green leaves. Z5–8 H8–5.
***S. trichocarpa* 'Snow White'.** See *S.* 'Snow White'.
S. trilobata. Deciduous, arching, graceful shrub. H 3ft (1m), S 5ft (1.5m). In early summer bears 5-petaled white flowers in clusters along slender shoots. Has rounded, shallowly lobed, toothed, blue-green leaves. Z3–7 H7–1.
S. ulmaria. See *Filipendula ulmaria*.
S.* x *vanhouttei illus. p.154.
S. veitchii. Vigorous, deciduous, upright shrub. H and S 10ft (3m). Has arching red branches and oblong, dark green leaves. Produces heads of 5-petaled white flowers from early to midsummer. Z4–7 H7-1.

SPIRANTHES

See also ORCHIDS.
S. cernua (illus. p.296). Deciduous, terrestrial orchid. H 20in (50cm). Spikes of delicate, white flowers, ½in (1cm) long, with pale yellow centers, appear in autumn. Has narrowly lance-shaped leaves, 2–5in (5–12cm) long. Requires semi-shade in summer. Z4–8 H8–4.

SPREKELIA

AMARYLLIDACEAE

Genus of one species of bulb grown for its showy red flowers in spring. Needs an open, sunny site and well-drained soil. Keep dry in winter; start into growth by watering in spring. Propagate by offsets in early autumn.
S. formosissima illus. p.413.

STACHYS

LABIATAE/LAMIACEAE

Genus of late spring- or summer-flowering perennials, shrubs, and sub-shrubs, some of which are evergreen. Grows in any well-drained soil, tolerating even poor soil. Species mentioned below prefer an open, sunny position; others are woodland plants and grow better in semi-shade. Propagate by division in spring.
S. byzantina, syn. *S. lanata*, *S. olympica*, illus. p.304. **'Primrose Heron'** illus. p.291. **'Silver Carpet'** is an evergreen, mat-forming perennial. H 6in (15cm), S 24in (60cm). Has oval, woolly gray leaves. Rarely produces flowers. Makes an excellent front-of-the-border or groundcover plant. Z4–8 H8–1.
S. coccinea. Clump-forming perennial. H 24in (60cm), S 18in (45cm). Has oval, midgreen leaves with a pronounced network of veins. From early to late summer, spikes of small, hooded, bright scarlet flowers protruding from purple calyces arise from leaf axils. Z4–8 H8–1.
S. lanata. See *S. byzantina*.
S. macrantha. Clump-forming perennial. H and S 12in (30cm). Has heart-shaped, crinkled, round-toothed, soft green leaves. Whorls of large, hooded, rose-purple flowers are produced in summer. Z7–9 H9–7. **'Superba'** illus. p.285.
S. officinalis, syn. *Betonica officinalis* (Betony). Mat-forming perennial. H 18–24in (45–60cm), S 12–18in (30–45cm). Bears whorls of hooded, tubular purple, pink, or white flowers on sturdy stems, arising in summer from mats of oval to oblong, round-toothed, midgreen leaves. Z5–8 H8–4. **'Rosea'** has flowers of clearer pink.
S. olympica. See *S. byzantina*.

STACHYURUS

STACHYURACEAE

Genus of deciduous shrubs grown for

their flowers, which are borne before the leaves. Flower spikes, formed in autumn, are harmed by hard frosts. Requires a position in sun or semi-shade, and fertile, moist but well-drained, not too heavy soil, preferably peaty and acidic. Does well when trained against a south- or west-facing wall. Propagate by softwood cuttings in summer.
S. chinensis. Deciduous, spreading, open shrub. H 6ft (2m), S 12ft (4m). Pendent spikes of small, bell-shaped, pale yellow flowers open in late winter and early spring. Leaves are oval and deep green. Z8–9 H9–8.
S. praecox illus. p.150. **'Magpie'** is a deciduous, spreading, open shrub, less vigorous than the species. H 5ft (1.5m), S 6ft (2m). Has arching, red-purple shoots and oval, tapered, gray-green leaves edged with creamy white. Bell-shaped, pale yellow flowers are borne in late winter and early spring. Z7–9 H9–7.

STANHOPEA

See also ORCHIDS.
S. tigrina. Evergreen, epiphytic orchid for a cool greenhouse. H 9in (23cm). Pendent spikes of fragrant, waxy, rich yellow and maroon flowers, 6in (15cm) across, with red-spotted white lips, are produced in summer. Has broadly oval, ribbed leaves, 12in (30cm) long. Is best grown in a hanging, slatted basket. Provide semi-shade in summer. Z13-15 H12–10.

STAPELIA

ASCLEPIADACEAE

Genus of clump-forming succulents with erect, 4-angled stems. Stem edges are often indented and may bear small leaves that drop after only a few weeks. Flowers are often foul-smelling. Needs a site in sun or partial shade, with well-drained soil. Propagate by seed or stem cuttings in spring or summer.
S. europaea. See *Caralluma europaea*.
S. flavirostris. See *S. grandiflora*.
S. gigantea illus. p.476.
S. grandiflora, syn. *S. flavirostris*, illus. p.476.
S. variegata. See *Orbea variegata*.

STAPHYLEA

Bladder nut

STAPHYLEACEAE

Genus of deciduous, spring-flowering shrubs and trees grown for their flowers and bladderlike fruits. Requires sun or semi-shade and fertile, moist soil. Propagate species by softwood or greenwood cuttings in summer or by seed in autumn, and selected forms by softwood or greenwood cuttings in summer.
S. colchica. Deciduous, upright shrub. H and S 11ft (3.5m). Erect panicles of bell-shaped white flowers are borne in late spring and are followed by inflated, greenish white fruits. Bright green leaves each consist of 3–5 oval leaflets. Z6–9 H9–6.
***S. holocarpa* 'Rosea'** illus. p.117.
S. pinnata illus. p.116.
S. trifoliata (American bladdernut). Upright, deciduous, suckering shrub. H 15ft (5m), S 8ft (2.5m). Leaves have three sharply pointed leaflets and are softly hairy beneath. Greenish white flowers in spring produce inflated fruit with loose seeds that rattle in the wind. Does well in part shade. Z3–8 H8–1.

Statice. Reclassified as *Limonium* except for:
S. suworowii for which see *Psylliostachys suworowii*.

STAUNTONIA

LARDIZABALACEAE

Genus of evergreen, woody-stemmed, twining climbers. Male and female flowers are produced on separate plants. Grow in any well-drained soil and in sun or semi-shade. To keep under control, prune in early spring. Propagate by seed in spring or by stem cuttings in summer or autumn.
S. hexaphylla. Evergreen, woody-stemmed, twining climber. H to 30ft (10m) or more. Leaves have 3–7 oval leaflets, each 2–5in (5–13cm) long. In spring has racemes of small, fragrant, cup-shaped, pale violet flowers, followed by egg-shaped, edible, fleshy purple fruits, 1–2in (2.5–5cm) long, on female plants if pollinated by a nearby male. Z9–10 H10–9.

STENANTHIUM

LILIACEAE/MELANTHIACEAE

Genus of attractive but seldom cultivated summer-flowering bulbs. Needs an open, sunny position in any well-drained soil. Grow in a sheltered site in light soil that does not dry out excessively. Propagate by seed in autumn or by division in spring.
S. gramineum. Summer-flowering bulb. H to 5ft (1.5m), S 1½–2ft (45–60cm). Has long, narrowly strap-shaped, semi-erect, basal leaves. Stem produces a dense, branched, often arching spike of fragrant, star-shaped white or green flowers, each ½–⅝in (1–1.5cm) across. Z7–9 H9–7.

STENOCACTUS, syn. ECHINOFOSSULOCACTUS

CACTACEAE

Genus of spherical cacti with spiny green stems that have very narrow, wavy ribs. Needs a sunny position and well-drained soil. Propagate by seed in spring or summer.
S. coptonogonus illus. p.476.
S. lamellosus. Spherical cactus. H and S 3in (8cm). Green stem has 30–35 ribs. Funnel-shaped, flesh-colored or red flowers, ½–1¼in (1–3cm) across, are produced from crown in spring. Has flattened upper radial spines, shorter, more rounded lower ones, and longer, rounded central spines with darker tips. Z12–15 H12–10.
S. obvallatus, syn. *Echinofossulatus pentacanthus*, *E. violaciflorus*, illus. p.472.

STENOCARPUS

PROTEACEAE

Genus of evergreen, summer- and autumn-flowering trees grown for their flowers and foliage. Needs full light and fertile, well-drained soil. Water containerized plants moderately, less in winter. Pruning is rarely necessary. Propagate by seed in spring or by semi-ripe cuttings in summer.
S. sinuatus (Australian firewheel tree). Slow-growing, evergreen, upright tree. H 40ft (12m) or more, S 15ft (5m). Has lustrous, deep green leaves, each 5–10in (12–25cm) long, lance-shaped and entire or with pairs of oblong lobes. Bottle-shaped, bright scarlet flowers, clustered like the spokes of a wheel, are produced from late summer to autumn. Z11 H12–10.

STENOCEREUS

CACTACEAE

Genus of treelike or shrubby cacti with prominently ribbed stems often densely spined. Needs full sun and very well-drained soil. Propagate by seed in spring or stem cuttings in summer.
S. marginatus. See *Pachycereus marginatus*.
S. thurberi, syn. *Lemaireocereus thurberi*. Columnar cactus, branching from low down. H to 22ft (7m), S 3ft (1m). Has 5- or 6-ribbed, glossy, dark green stems with very short-spined areoles set in close rows down each rib. Produces funnel-shaped purple or pink flowers with red sepals in summer. Z14–15 H12–10.

Stenolobium stans. See *Tecoma stans*.

STENOMESSON

AMARYLLIDACEAE

Genus of bulbs grown for their long, often pendent, tubular flowers. Needs an open, sunny site and well-drained soil. Propagate by offsets in autumn.
S. incarnatum. See *S. variegatum*.
S. miniatum, syn. *Urceolina peruviana*, illus. p.419.
S. variegatum, syn. *S. incarnatum*, illus. p.419.

STENOTAPHRUM

GRAMINEAE/POACEAE

See also GRASSES, BAMBOOS, RUSHES, and SEDGES.
S. secundatum (St. Augustine grass) **'Variegatum'** is an evergreen, spreading, rhizomatous, perennial grass. H 6in (15cm), S indefinite. Leaves are midgreen with cream stripes and last well into winter. Has erect racemes of brownish green spikelets in summer. In warm climates is used for lawns. Z9–11 H12–9.

STEPHANANDRA

ROSACEAE

Genus of deciduous, summer-flowering shrubs grown for their habit, foliage, autumn color, and winter shoots. Needs sun or semi-shade and fertile, not too dry soil. On established plants cut out some older shoots after flowering. Propagate by softwood cuttings in summer or by division in autumn.
S. incisa. Deciduous, arching shrub. H 5ft (1.5m), S 10ft (3m). Oval, deeply lobed and toothed, bright green leaves turn orange-yellow in autumn and stems become rich brown in winter. Produces crowded panicles of tiny, star-shaped, greenish white flowers in early summer. Z3–8 H8–4. **'Crispa'**, H 2ft (60cm), has wavy-edged and more deeply lobed leaves.
S. tanakae illus. p.140.

STEPHANOTIS

ASCLEPIADACEAE

Genus of evergreen, woody-stemmed, twining climbers grown for their scented, waxy flowers. Provide organic, well-drained soil and partial shade in summer. Water moderately, less in cold weather. Provide stems with support. Shorten overly long or crowded stems in spring. Propagate by seed in spring or by semi-ripe cuttings in summer.
S. floribunda illus. p.204.

Sterculia acerifolia. See *Brachychiton acerifolius*.
Sterculia diversifolia. See *Brachychiton populneus*.
Sterculia platanifolia. See *Firmiana simplex*.

STERNBERGIA

AMARYLLIDACEAE

Genus of spring- or autumn-flowering bulbs grown for their large, crocuslike flowers. Benefits from a hot, sunny site and any well-drained, heavy or light soil that dries out in summer, when bulbs die down and need warmth and dryness. Leave undisturbed to form clumps. Propagate by division in spring or autumn.
S. candida illus. p.426.
S. clusiana. Autumn-flowering bulb. H to ¾in (2cm), S 3–4in (8–10cm). Strap-shaped, semi-erect, basal, grayish green leaves, often twisted lengthwise, appear after flowering. Stems carry erect, goblet-shaped yellow or greenish yellow flowers, 1½–3in (4–8cm) long. Z7–10 H10–7.
S. lutea illus. p.439.
S. sicula. Autumn-flowering bulb. H 1–3in (2.5–7cm), S 2–3in (5–8cm). Narrowly strap-shaped, semi-erect, basal, deep green leaves, each with a central, paler green stripe, appear with flowers. Each stem bears a funnel-shaped, bright yellow flower, ¾–1½in (2–4cm) long. Z6–9 H9–6.

STETSONIA

CACTACEAE

Genus of one species of treelike cactus with a thick trunk. Nocturnal, funnel-shaped flowers are 6in (15cm) long. Needs a sunny, well-drained position. Propagate by seed in spring or summer.
S. coryne illus. p.457.

STEWARTIA,
syn. STUARTIA

THEACEAE

Genus of deciduous trees and shrubs grown for their flowers, autumn color, and usually peeling bark. Needs a sunny position, but preferably with roots in shade, and shelter from strong winds. Requires fertile, moist but well-drained, neutral to acidic soil. Resents being transplanted. Propagate by softwood cuttings in summer or by seed in autumn.
S. malacodendron. Deciduous, spreading tree or shrub. H 12ft (4m), S 10ft (3m). Roselike, purple-stamened white flowers, some-times purple-streaked, are borne in midsummer amid oval, dark green leaves. Z7–9 H9–6.
S. monadelpha illus. p.82.
S. pseudocamellia illus. p.78.
S. sinensis. Deciduous, spreading tree. H 40ft (12m), S 22ft (7m). Has peeling bark and oval, bright green leaves that turn brilliant red in autumn. Fragrant, roselike white flowers are produced in midsummer. Z5–8 H8–5.

STIGMAPHYLLON

MALPIGHIACEAE

Genus of evergreen, woody-stemmed, twining climbers grown for their flowers. Fertile, well-drained soil is needed with partial shade in summer. Water freely when in full growth, less in low temperatures. Provide stems with support. Thin out crowded stems in spring. Propagate by semi-ripe cuttings in summer.
S. ciliatum illus. p.216.

STIPA

GRAMINEAE/POACEAE

See also GRASSES, BAMBOOS, RUSHES, and SEDGES.
S. arundinacea (Pheasant grass). Evergreen, tuft-forming, perennial grass. H 5ft (1.5m), S 4ft (1.2m). Brownish green leaves, 12in (30cm) long, turn soft orange in late summer. Has pendent, open panicles of purplish green flower spikes in autumn. Z8–15 H12–1.
S. calamagrostis, syn. *Achnatherum calamagrostis*. Evergreen, tuft-forming, perennial grass. H 3ft (1m), S 1½ft (45cm). Leaves are bluish green and inrolled. In summer bears decorative, large, loose panicles of sandy brown spikelets that dry and last well into winter.
S. gigantea illus. p.307.

STOKESIA

ASTERACEAE/COMPOSITAE

Genus of one species of evergreen, summer-flowering perennial. Requires sun or semi-shade and fertile, well-drained soil. Propagate by division in spring or by seed in autumn.
S. laevis illus. p.285. **'Blue Star'** is an evergreen, basal-rosetted perennial. H and S 12–18in (30–45cm). Bears cornflower-like, deep blue flower heads singly at stem tips in summer. Has rosettes of narrowly lance-shaped, dark green leaves. Z5–9 H9–5.

STOMATIUM

AIZOACEAE

Genus of mat-forming succulents with short stems, each bearing 4–6 pairs of solid, 3-angled or semi-cylindrical leaves, often with toothed edges and incurved tips. Needs sun and well-drained soil. Propagate by seed or stem cuttings in spring or summer.
S. agninum. Mat-forming succulent. H 2in (5cm), S 3ft (1m) or more. Has solid, 3-angled or semi-cylindrical, soft gray-green leaves, 1½–2in (4–5cm) long, often without teeth. In summer, fragrant, daisylike yellow flowers, ¾–2in (2–5cm) across, open in evening. Z13-15 H12-10.
S. patulum. Mat-forming succulent. H 1¼in (3cm), S 3ft (1m). Has semi-cylindrical, gray-green leaves, each ¾in (2cm) long, with rough dots and 2–9 toothlike tubercles on upper surface. Bears ¾in (2cm) wide, fragrant, daisylike, pale yellow flowers in evening in summer. Z13-15 H12-10.

Strangweja spicata. See *Bellevalia hyacinthoides*.
Stranvaesia. Reclassified as *Photinia*.

STRATIOTES

HYDROCHARITACEAE

Genus of semi-evergreen, perennial, submerged, free-floating water plants grown for their foliage. Requires sun. Grows in any depth of cool water. Propagate by separating young plants from runners in summer.
S. aloides illus. p.447.

STRELITZIA
Bird-of-paradise flower

MUSACEAE/STRELITZIACEAE

Genus of large, evergreen, tufted, clump-forming, palmlike perennials grown for their showy flowers. Grow in fertile, well-drained soil and in bright light shaded from direct sun in summer. Reduce watering in low temperatures. Propagate by seed or division of suckers in spring.
S. nicolai illus. p.232.
S. reginae illus. p.267.

Streptanthera cuprea. See *Sparaxis elegans*.
Streptanthera elegans. See *Sparaxis elegans*.

STREPTOCARPUS

GESNERIACEAE

Genus of perennials, some of which are evergreen, with showy flowers. Grow in a humid atmosphere in organic, moist soil and in bright light away from direct sunlight. Avoid wetting leaves when watering; water less during cold periods. Propagate by seed, if available, in spring, by division after flowering, or by tip cuttings from bushy species or leaf cuttings from stemless species in spring or summer.
S. caulescens illus. p.276.
***S.* 'Constant Nymph'** illus. p.303.
***S.* 'Nicola'** illus. p.301.
S. rexii (Cape primrose). Stemless perennial. H to 10in (25cm), S to 20in (50cm). Has a rosette of strap-shaped, wrinkled, green leaves. Stems, 6in (15cm) or more long, bear loose clusters of funnel-shaped, pale blue or mauve flowers, 2in (5cm) long and with darker lines, intermittently at any time of year. Z13–15 H12–10.
S. saxorum illus. p.284.

STREPTOSOLEN

SOLANACEAE

Genus of one species of evergreen or semi-evergreen, loosely scrambling shrub grown for its flowers. Requires full sun and organic, well-drained soil. Water freely when in full growth, less at other times. After flowering or in spring, remove flowered shoots and tie in new growths. Propagate by softwood or semi-ripe cuttings in summer.
S. jamesonii illus. p.220.

STROBILANTHES

ACANTHACEAE

Genus of perennials and evergreen subshrubs grown for their flowers. Grow in semi-shade in fertile, well-drained soil. Propagate by seed, basal stem cuttings, or division in spring.
S. atropurpureus illus. p.263.

STROMANTHE

MARANTACEAE

Genus of evergreen, creeping perennials grown mainly for their foliage. Prefers high humidity and partial shade. Grow in open soil or soil mx, use soft water if possible, and do not allow to dry out completely. Propagate by division in spring.
S. sanguinea. Strong-growing, evergreen, creeping perennial. H and S to 5ft (1.5m). Lance-shaped leaves, to 18in (45cm) long, are glossy green above with paler midribs, reddish below. Bears panicles of small, 3 petaled white flowers in axils of showy, bright red bracts, usually in spring but also in summer-autumn. Z13–15 H12-10.

STROMBOCACTUS

CACTACEAE

Genus of extremely slow-growing, hemispherical to cylindrical cacti. Takes 5 years from seed to reach ½in (1cm) high. Funnel-shaped flowers are 1½in (4cm) across. Needs sun and very well-drained soil. Is difficult to grow and very susceptible to overwatering. Propagate by seed or grafting in spring or summer.
S. disciformis illus. p.470.

STRONGYLODON

LEGUMINOSAE/PAPILIONACEAE

Genus of evergreen, woody-stemmed, twining climbers grown for their large, clawlike flowers. Needs organic, moist but well-drained soil and partial shade in summer. Water freely when in full growth, less at other times. Provide support. If necessary, thin crowded stems in spring. Propagate by seed or stem cuttings in summer or by layering in spring.
S. macrobotrys illus. p.206.

Stuartia. Reclassified as *Stewartia*.

STYLIDIUM

STYLIDIACEAE

Genus of perennials, with grasslike leaves, grown for their unusual flowers that have fused, "triggered" stamens adapted for pollination by insects. Grow in fertile soil and in bright light. Propagate by division or seed in spring.
S. graminifolium (Trigger plant). Rosetted perennial. H and S to 6in (15cm) or more. Grasslike, stiff, dark green leaves with toothed margins rise from ground level. Bears tiny, pale pinkish mauve flowers in narrow spikes, 12in (30cm) or more long, in summer. Z13-15 H12-10.

STYLOPHORUM

PAPAVERACEAE

Genus of spring-flowering perennials with large, deeply lobed leaves, nearly all as basal rosettes. Needs semi-shade and organic, moist, peaty soil. Propagate by division in spring or by seed in autumn.
S. diphyllum illus. p.350.

STYRAX

STYRACACEAE

Genus of deciduous, summer-flowering trees and shrubs grown for their foliage and flowers. Prefers a sheltered position in sun or semi-shade and moist, neutral to acidic soil. Propagate by softwood cuttings in summer or by seed in autumn.
S. japonicus illus. p.77.
S. obassia (Fragrant snowbell). Deciduous, spreading tree. H 40ft (12m), S 22ft (7m). Bears long, spreading clusters of fragrant, bell- to

funnel-shaped white flowers in early summer. Has broad, rounded, deep green leaves. Z6–8 H8–6.
S. officinalis illus. p.118.
S. wilsonii illus. p.138.

Sulcorebutia arenacea. See *Rebutia arenacea.*
Sulcorebutia rauschii. See *Rebutia rauschii.*
Sulcorebutia tiraquensis. See *Rebutia tiraquensis.*

SUTERA

SCROPHULARIACEAE

Genus of annuals, perennials, and evergreen shrubs used for summer bedding. Needs a position in sun and in well-drained soil. Propagate by seed or division in spring or by softwood cuttings in summer.
S. cordata (*Bacopa* of gardens). Spreading perennial usually treated as an annual. H 6in (15cm), S 18in (45cm). Has toothed, dark green leaves and small white or pink flowers, freely produced. Grows best if shaded during the heat of the day. Do not allow to dry out. Z11–12 H12–10.
S. grandiflora. (Purple glory plant). Much-branched, subshrubby perennial. H 3ft (1m), S 12–18in (30–45cm). Has oval to oblong, round-toothed leaves. Tubular, 5-lobed, frilled, deep purple flowers are produced from midsummer to autumn. Z12-15 H12–10.

SUTHERLANDIA

LEGUMINOSAE/PAPILIONACEAE

Genus of evergreen shrubs grown for their flowers and fruits. Requires full light and fertile, well-drained soil. Water containerized specimens freely when in full growth, moderately at other times. Remove old, twiggy stems at ground level in late winter. Propagate by seed in spring. Spider mite may be troublesome.
S. frutescens illus. p.165.

SWAINSONA

LEGUMINOSAE/PAPILIONACEAE

Genus of annuals, evergreen perennials, subshrubs and shrubs grown for their flowers. Needs full light or partial shade and organic, well-drained soil. Water freely when in active growth, moderately at other times. Propagate by seed in spring or by semi-ripe cuttings in summer.
S. galegifolia (Darling pea). Evergreen, sprawling subshrub. H 2–4ft (60cm–1.2m), S 1–2ft (30–60cm). Leaves have 11–25 narrowly oval, mid- to deep green leaflets. Bears pealike red, pink, purple, blue, or yellow flowers in late spring and summer. Remove old, flowered shoots in late winter. Z13-15 H12–10.

SYAGRUS

Queen palm

ARECACEAE/PALMAE

Genus of one species of evergreen palm grown for its majestic appearance. Requires full light or partial shade and organic, well-drained soil. Water containerized specimens moderately, less when temperatures are low. Propagate by seed in spring at not less than 75°F (24°C). Spider mite may be a nuisance.
S. romanzoffiana illus. p.73.

SYCOPSIS

HAMAMELIDACEAE

Genus of evergreen trees and shrubs grown for their foliage and flowers. Needs a sheltered position in sun or semi-shade and fertile, not too dry, peaty soil. Propagate by semi-ripe cuttings in summer.
S. sinensis. Evergreen, upright shrub. H 15ft (5m), S 12ft (4m). Leaves are oval, glossy, and dark green. Flowers lack petals but have showy, dense clusters of red-tinged yellow anthers in late winter or early spring. Z11 H12–10.

SYMPHORICARPOS

CAPRIFOLIACEAE

Genus of deciduous shrubs, with inconspicuous, bell-shaped flowers, grown mainly for their clusters of showy, long-persistent fruits. Requires sun or semi-shade and fertile soil. Propagate by softwood cuttings in summer or by division in autumn. Fruits may cause mild stomach upset if ingested; contact with them may irritate skin.
S. albus (Snowberry). var. ***laevigatus*** is a vigorous, deciduous, dense shrub, part upright, part arching. H and S 6ft (2m). Large, marblelike white fruits follow pink flowers borne in summer. Rounded leaves are dark green. Z3–7 H7–1.
S. x ***chenaultii* 'Hancock'.** Deciduous, procumbent, dense shrub. H 3ft (1m), S 10ft (3m). Has oval, bronze leaves maturing to bright green. White flowers appear from early to midsummer. Small, spherical, deep lilac-pink fruits are sparsely borne. Makes an excellent groundcover. Z4–7 H7–1.
S. orbiculatus (Coralberry, Indian currant). Deciduous, bushy, dense shrub. H and S 6ft (2m). White or pink flowers in late summer and early autumn, then spherical, deep purplish red fruits. Oval leaves are dark green. Z2–7 H7–1. **'Foliis Variegatis'** (syn. *S.o.* 'Variegatus') illus. p.168.

SYMPHYANDRA

CAMPANULACEAE

Genus of short-lived, summer-flowering perennials, best grown as biennials. Good in large rock gardens and bases of banks. Needs sun and well-drained soil. Propagate by seed in autumn. Self-seeds readily.
S. armena. Upright or spreading perennial. H 1–2ft (30–60cm), S 1ft (30cm). Panicles of upright, bell-shaped blue or white flowers appear in summer. Leaves are oval, irregularly toothed, hairy, and midgreen. Z7–9 H9–7.
S. pendula. Arching perennial. H 1–2ft (30–60cm), S 1ft (30cm). Produces panicles of pendent, bell-shaped, cream flowers in summer. Has oval, hairy, pale green leaves. Becomes woody at base with age. Z6–9 H9–6.
S. wanneri illus. p.357.

SYMPHYTUM

Comfrey

BORAGINACEAE

Genus of vigorous, coarse perennials, often best grown in wild gardens. Prefers sun or semi-shade and moist soil. Propagate by division in spring or by seed in autumn; usually self-seeds. Propagate named cultivars by division only. Roots and leaves may cause severe discomfort if ingested; contact with foliage may irritate skin.
S. caucasicum illus. p.238.
***S.* 'Goldsmith'**, syn. *S. ibericum* 'Jubilee', *S. ibericum* 'Variegatum', *S.* 'Jubilee'. Clump-forming perennial. H and S 12in (30cm). Has ovate, hairy, dark green leaves with gold and cream markings. Bears pale blue flowers tinged cream or pink in spring. Z5–9 H9–5.
S. grandiflorum of gardens. See *S. ibericum.*
***S.* 'Hidcote Blue'.** Clump-forming perennial. H 20in (50cm), S 24in (60cm). Is similar to *S. ibericum* but has pale blue flowers. Z4–7.
S. ibericum, syn. *S. grandiflorum* of gardens. Clump-forming perennial. H 10in (25cm), S 24in (60cm). Has lance-shaped, hairy, rich green leaves. Bears one-sided racemes of tubular creamy flowers in spring. Makes a good groundcover. Z3–9 H9–1.
'Jubilee' see *S.* 'Goldsmith'.
'Variegatum' see *S.* 'Goldsmith'.
***S.* 'Jubilee'.** See *S.* 'Goldsmith'.
S. x ***uplandicum*** (Russian comfrey). **'Variegatum'** illus. p.238.

SYMPLOCOS

SYMPLOCACEAE

Genus of evergreen or deciduous trees and shrubs, of which only the species described is in general cultivation. This is grown for its flowers and fruits. Fruits are most prolific when several plants are grown together. Needs full sun and fertile, moist but well-drained soil. Propagate by seed in autumn.
S. paniculata illus. p.138.

SYNADENIUM

EUPHORBIACEAE

Genus of evergreen, semi-succulent shrubs grown for their foliage. Requires full light and fertile, freely draining soil. Water containerized plants moderately, less in winter. Prune in late winter if necessary. Propagate by seed in spring or by softwood cuttings in summer. All parts are highly toxic if ingested; sap may irritate skin.
S. compactum var. ***rubrum***, syn. *S. grantii* 'Rubrum'. Evergreen, erect, robust-stemmed shrub. H 10–12ft (3–4m), S 6ft (2m) or more. Has very small red flowers in autumn, largely concealed by lance-shaped to oval, glossy, purplish green leaves, red-purple beneath. Z13-15 H12–10.
***S. grantii* 'Rubrum'.** See *S. compactum* var. *rubrum.*

SYNGONIUM

ARACEAE

Genus of evergreen, woody-stemmed, root climbers grown for their ornamental foliage. Flowers are seldom produced in cultivation. Needs partial shade and organic, well-drained soil. Water moderately, less in low temperatures. Provide support, ideally with moss poles. Remove young stem tips to promote branching. Propagate by leaf-bud or stem-tip cuttings in summer. All parts may cause mild stomach upset if ingested; contact with the sap may irritate skin.
S. auritum, syn. *Philodendron auritum* of gardens, *P. trifoliatum* (Five fingers). Fairly slow-growing, evergreen, woody-stemmed, root climber. H 3–6ft (1–2m). Has glossy, rich green leaves divided into 3, sometimes 5 oval leaflets, the central one the largest. Z14–15 H12–10.
S. erythrophyllum. Slow-growing, evergreen, root climber with slender, woody stems. H 3ft (1m) or more. Young plants have arrowhead-shaped leaves flushed purple beneath. Leaves on mature plants have 3 lobes or leaflets and thicker, longer stems. Z14–15 H12–10.
S. hoffmannii. Moderately vigorous, evergreen, woody-stemmed, root climber. H 6–10ft (2–3m). Young plants have arrowhead-shaped leaves; mature ones have leaves divided into 3 gray-green leaflets with silvery white veins. Z14–15 H12–10.
S. podophyllum, syn. *Nephthytis triphylla* of gardens, illus. p.220. **'Trileaf Wonder'** illus. p.219.

SYNTHYRIS

SCROPHULARIACEAE

Genus of evergreen or deciduous, spring-flowering perennials with gently spreading, rhizomatous rootstocks. Is useful for rock gardens. Prefers partial shade and moist soil. Propagate in late spring by seed or division.
S. reniformis. Evergreen, clump-forming perennial. H 3–4in (8–10cm), S 6in (15cm). Has kidney-shaped to rounded, toothed, dark green leaves and, in spring, short, dense racemes of small, bell-shaped blue flowers. Z7-9 H9–7.
S. stellata illus. p.369.

SYRINGA

Lilac

OLEACEAE

Genus of deciduous shrubs and trees grown for their dense panicles of small, tubular flowers, usually quite fragrant. Needs sun and deep, fertile, well-drained, preferably alkaline soil. Try to obtain plants on their own roots, since grafted plants usually sucker freely. Remove flower heads from newly planted lilacs, and deadhead for the first few years. Cut out weak shoots in winter and, to maintain shape, prune after flowering. Straggly old plants may be cut back hard in winter, but the next season's flowers will then be lost. Propagate by softwood cuttings in summer. Leaf miners, borers, leaf spot, mildew, and blight may be troublesome. See also feature panel p.120

***S.* 'Belle de Nancy'.** See *S. vulgaris* 'Belle de Nancy'.

***S.* 'Blue Hyacinth'.** See *S.* x *hyacinthiflora* 'Blue Hyacinth'.

***S.* 'Charles Joly'.** See *S. vulgaris* 'Charles Joly'.

S.* x *chinensis (Rouen lilac). Deciduous, arching shrub. H and S 12ft (4m). Bears large, arching panicles of fragrant, tubular, single, lilac-purple flowers in late spring. Oval leaves are dark green. Z3–8 H8-1. **'Alba'** (illus. p.120) has white flowers.

***S.* 'Clarke's Giant'.** See *S.* x *hyacinthiflora* 'Clarke's Giant'.

***S.* 'Congo'.** See *S. vulgaris* 'Congo'.

***S.* 'Cora Brandt'.** See *S.* x *hyacinthiflora* 'Cora Brandt'.

***S.* 'Decaisne'.** See *S. vulgaris* 'Decaisne'.

S. emodi (Himalayan lilac). Vigorous, deciduous, upright shrub. H 15ft (5m), S 12ft (4m). Bears unpleasantly scented, tubular, single, very pale lilac flowers in large, upright panicles in early summer. Has large, oval, dark green leaves. Z7–8 H8–7.

***S.* 'Esther Staley'.** See *S.* x *hyacinthiflora* 'Esther Staley'.

***S.* 'Fountain'.** Vigorous, deciduous, arching, open shrub. H 12ft (4m), S 15ft (5m). Large, nodding panicles of fragrant, tubular, single, deep pink flowers open above large, oval, dark green leaves in early summer. Z7–8 H8–7.

***S.* x *hyacinthiflora* 'Blue Hyacinth'**, syn. *S.* 'Blue Hyacinth' (illus. p.120). Deciduous, bushy shrub, upright when young, later spreading. H and S 10ft (3m). Bears large, loose panicles of fragrant, single, pale lilac-blue flowers from midspring to early summer and has broadly heart-shaped, midgreen leaves. Vigorous **'Clarke's Giant'** (syn. *S.* 'Clarke's Giant'; illus p.120), H and S 15ft (5m), has lavender flowers, mauve-pink within, opening from mauve-pink buds from mid- to late spring. Has dark green leaves. **'Cora Brandt'** (syn. *S.* 'Cora Brandt'; illus. p.120) produces double, white flowers in large open panicles. **'Esther Staley'** (syn. *S.* 'Esther Staley'; illus. p.120) is vigorous, with broadly conical panicles of red buds opening to lilac-pink flowers. All Z3–7 H7–1.

S. **'James Macfarlane'.** See *S. prestoniae* 'James Macfarlane'.

***S.* 'Jan van Tol'.** See *S. vulgaris* 'Jan van Tol'.

***S.* x *josiflexa* 'Royalty'**, syn. *S.* 'Royalty'. Deciduous, upright, then arching shrub. H 12ft (4m), S 15ft (5m). Large panicles of fragrant, tubular, single, bright purple flowers are borne above oval, dark green leaves in late spring and early summer. Z4–7 H7–1.

***S.* 'Katherine Havemeyer'.** See *S. vulgaris* 'Katherine Havemeyer'.

***S.* 'Madame Antoine Buchner'.** See *S. vulgaris* 'Madame Antoine Buchner'.

***S.* 'Madame F. Morel'.** See *S. vulgaris* 'Madame F. Morel'.

***S.* 'Madame Florent Stepman'.** See *S. vulgaris* 'Madame Florent Stepman'.

***S.* 'Madame Lemoine'.** See *S. vulgaris* 'Madame Lemoine'.

***S.* 'Maréchal Foch'.** See *S. vulgaris* 'Maréchal Foch'.

***S.* 'Masséna'.** See *S. vulgaris* 'Masséna'.

***S.* 'Maud Notcutt'.** See *S. vulgaris* 'Maud Notcutt'.

***S. meyeri* 'Palibin'**, syn. *S. palibianina* of gardens, *S. velutina* of gardens (illus. p.120). Slow-growing, deciduous, bushy, dense shrub. H and S 5ft (1.5m). Produces dense panicles of fragrant, tubular, single, lilac-pink flowers in late spring and early summer. Has small, oval deep green leaves. Z4–7 H7–1.

***S.* 'Michel Buchner'.** See *S. vulgaris* 'Michel Buchner'.

S. microphylla. See *S. pubescens* subsp. *microphylla.*

***S.* 'Minuet'.** Deciduous, upright, bushy shrub. H 8ft (2.5m), S 6ft (2m). Dense panicles of small, very fragrant, pale pink flowers open from magenta-pink buds in early summer. Very free flowering, even when young, on a rounded bush. Z4–7 H7–1.

***S.* 'Monge'.** See *S. vulgaris* 'Monge'.

***S.* 'Mrs. Edward Harding'.** See *S. vulgaris* 'Mrs. Edward Harding'.

S. palibiniana of gardens. See *S. meyeri* 'Palibin'.

S. patula 'Miss Kim'. See *S.pubescens.* ssp. *patula* 'Miss Kim'.

***S.* 'Paul Thirion'.** See *S. vulgaris* 'Paul Thirion'.

S.* x *persica (Persian lilac; illus. p.120). Deciduous, bushy, dense shrub. H and S 6ft (2m). Produces small, dense panicles of fragrant purple flowers in late spring. Leaves are narrow, pointed, and dark green. Z3–7 H7–1.

***S.* 'Président Grévy'.** See *S. vulgaris* 'Président Grévy'.

***S.* x *prestoniae* 'James Macfarlane'**, syn. *S.* 'J. Macfarlane'. Vigorous, deciduous, upright shrub. H and S 12ft (4m). Has large, nodding panicles of fragrant, tubular, single, salmon-pink flowers, paler within, in early summer, and large, oval, dark green leaves. Z2–7 H7–1.

***S.* 'Primrose'.** See *S. vulgaris* 'Primrose'.

S. pubescens subsp. ***microphylla***, syn. *S. microphylla*. Deciduous, bushy shrub. H and S 6ft (2m). Small panicles of very fragrant, tubular, single pink flowers appear in early summer (and often again in autumn) amid oval, mid-green leaves. Z5–8 H8–3. **'Superba'** illus. p.120. ssp. ***patula*** 'Miss Kim' (syn. *S. patula* 'Miss Kim'). Deciduous, mounded shrub with purple new shoots and foliage that often turns purple in fall. H 8ft (2.5m), S 10ft (3m). Pale lilac-blue flowers are in erect panicles in early summer. Z3–8 H8–1.

S. reticulata. (Japanese tree lilac) Deciduous, broadly conical tree or shrub. H 30ft (10m), S 20ft (6m). Large panicles of fragrant, tubular, single, creamy white flowers open above oval, taper-pointed, bright green leaves from early to midsummer. Z3–8 H8–3. **'Ivory Silk'** is smaller. H 12ft (4m), S 6ft (2m). It is usually grown as a tree and flowers freely when young. Z4–8 H8–1.

***S.* 'Souvenir de Louis Spaeth'.** See *S. vulgaris* 'Andenken an Ludwig Spaeth'.

S. velutina of gardens. See *S. meyeri* 'Palibin'.

***S. vulgaris* 'Agincourt Beauty'** bears short panicles of large, dark purple, single flowers with cupped petals. **'Andenken an Ludwig Spaeth'** (syn. *S.* 'Souvenir de Louis Spaeth'). Deciduous, upright, then spreading shrub. H and S 15ft (5m). Long, slender panicles of fragrant, tubular, single, deep purplish red flowers are borne profusely above heart-shaped, dark green leaves in late spring. 'Beauty of Moscow'. See 'Krasavitsa Moskvy'. **'Belle de Nancy'** (syn. *S.* 'Belle de Nancy') has large, dense panicles of double, mauve-pink flowers opening from purple-red buds. **'Charles Joly'** (syn. *S.* 'Charles Joly'; illus. p.120), H and S 10ft (3m), carries deep purple-red flowers from mid-spring to early summer. **'Congo'** (syn. *S.* 'Congo'; illus. p.120) bears large panicles of single, deep lilac-purple flowers, purplish red in bud, in spring. **'Decaisne'** (syn. *S.* 'Decaisne'; illus. p.120) is compact, with masses of single, dark blue flowers that are shaded purple, and midgreen leaves. **'Jan van Tol'** (syn. *S.* 'Jan van Tol'; illus. p.120) bears long, semi-pendent panicles of single, narrow-petaled, pure white flowers. **'Katherine Havemeyer'** (syn. *S.* 'Katherine Havemeyer') has double, lavender-purple then lavender-pink flowers in dense, conical panicles. **'Krasavitsa Moskvy'** (syn. 'Beauty of Moscow') has dense panicles of double creamy white flowers that open from lavender-tinted buds. **'Madame Antoine Buchner'** (syn. *S.* 'Madame Antoine Buchner'; illus. p.120) carries long, narrow panicles of deep purple-red buds that open to double, pinkish mauve flowers, fading with age. **'Madame F. Morel'** (syn. *S.* 'Madame F. Morel'; illus. p.120) produces large panicles of single, light violet-purple flowers that are purple in bud. **'Madame Florent Stepman'** (syn. *S.* 'Madame Florent Stepman'; illus. p.120) bears large panicles of single white flowers. **'Madame Lemoine'** (syn. *S.* 'Madame Lemoine'; illus. p.120) bears compact panicles of large, double white flowers. **'Maréchal Foch'** (syn. *S.* 'Maréchal Foch'; illus. p.120) has broad, open panicles of very large, single, carmine-pink flowers. **'Masséna'** (syn. *S.* 'Masséna'; illus. p.120). bears loose panicles of large, deep red-purple flowers. **'Maud Notcutt'** (syn. *S.* 'Maud Notcutt') produces large panicles of single, pure white flowers. **'Michel Buchner'** (syn. *S.* 'Michel Buchner'; illus. p.120) has large panicles of double, pink-lilac flowers, each with a white eye. **'Monge'** (syn. *S.* 'Monge'; illus. p.120) produces masses of very large, single, deep purple-red flowers. **'Mrs. Edward Harding'** (syn. *S.* 'Mrs. Edward Harding'; illus. p.120) has large panicles of double or semi-double, purple-red flowers that fade to pink. **'Paul Thirion'** (syn. *S.* 'Paul Thirion'; illus. p.120) carries double lilac-pink flowers that open from deep purple-red buds. **'Président Grévy'** (syn. *S.* 'Président Grévy'; illus. p.120) bears very large panicles of double, lilac-blue flowers that open from red-violet buds. **'Primrose'** (syn. *S.* 'Primrose'; illus. p.120) produces small, dense panicles of pale yellow flowers. **'Sensation'** has slightly open clusters of single, deep purple flowers, with each petal edged in white. All Z4–8 H8–1.

S. yunnanensis (illus. p.120). Deciduous, upright shrub. H 10ft (3m), S to 10ft (3m). In early summer, large, oval, pointed, dark green leaves set off slender panicles of 4-petaled, pale pink or white flowers. Z6–7 H7–6.

SYZYGIUM

MYRTACEAE

Genus of evergreen shrubs and trees grown for their overall appearance. Prefers full light (but tolerates some shade) and fertile, well-drained soil. Water containerized plants freely when in full growth, moderately at other times. Is very tolerant of pruning, but is best grown naturally. Propagate by seed in spring or semi-ripe cuttings in summer.

S. paniculatum, syn. *Eugenia australis* of gardens, *E. paniculata*, illus. p.81.

T

TABEBUIA

BIGNONIACEAE

Genus of deciduous or evergreen, mainly spring-flowering trees grown for their flowers and for shade. Requires full light and fertile, well-drained but not dry soil. Pot-grown plants are unlikely to flower. Pruning, other than shaping while young in autumn, is not needed. Propagate by seed or air-layering in spring or by semi-ripe cuttings in summer.

T. chrysotricha illus. 97.

T. donnell-smithii. See *Cybistax donnell-smithii.*

T. pentaphylla of gardens. See *T. rosea.*

T. rosea, syn. *T. pentaphylla* of gardens (Pink trumpet tree). Fast-growing, evergreen, rounded tree, deciduous in cool climates. H and S 50ft (15m) or more. Leaves have 5 oval leaflets. Produces trumpet-shaped rose- to lavender-pink or white flowers, with yellow throats, in terminal clusters in spring. Z14–15 H12–10.

TACCA

TACCACEAE

Genus of perennials with rhizomes, grown for their curious flowers. Needs a fairly humid atmosphere, partial shade, and peaty soil. Water sparingly during resting period in winter. Propagate by division or seed, if available, in spring.

T. chantrierei (Bat flower, Cat's whiskers). Clump-forming, rhizomatous perennial. H and S 1ft (30cm). Narrowly oblong, stalked, arching leaves are 1½ft (45cm) or more long. In summer produces flower umbels with green or purplish bracts on stems up to 2ft (60cm) long. Individual flowers are nodding, bell-shaped, 6-petaled, and green, turning purple with long, pendent maroon to purple threads. Z14–15 H12–10.

T. leontopetaloides (East Indian arrowroot, South Sea arrowroot). Clump-forming, rhizomatous perennial. H and S 1½ft (45cm). Green leaves, to 3ft (1m) long, are deeply 3-lobed, each lobe also divided, on stalks to over 3ft (1m). In summer, on stems up to 3ft (1m) long, flower umbels are produced with 4–12 purple or brown bracts and 20–40 small, 6-petaled yellow or purplish green flowers, with long purple to brown threads. Rhizomes yield edible starch. Z14–15 H12–10.

Tacitus bellus. See *Graptopetalum bellum.*

Tacsonia mollissima. See *Passiflora mollissima.*

Tacsonia van-volxemii. See *Passiflora antioquiensis.*

TAGETES

ASTERACEAE/COMPOSITAE

Genus of annuals that flower continuously throughout summer and until the autumn frosts. Is useful as bedding plants and for edging. Grow in sun and in fertile, well-drained soil. Deadhead to ensure a long flowering period. Propagate by seed sown under cover in midspring. Is prone to slugs, snails, mites, and botrytis. The African marigolds are excellent for formal bedding, whereas the French, Afro-French, and Signet marigolds are more suitable for the edge of a mixed border. All are good in containers and provide long-lasting cut flowers. Contact with the foliage may aggravate skin allergies. Four main hybrid groups are in cultivation.

African marigolds (African Group) Compact annuals derived from *T. erecta*, with angular, hairless stems and pinnate, sparsely glandular leaves, 2–4in (5–10cm) long, each with 11–17 narrowly lance-shaped, pointed, sharply toothed leaflets, to 2in (5cm) long. Large, densely double, pompon-like, terminal flower heads, usually to 5in (12cm) across, each with 5–8 or more ray florets and numerous orange to yellow disk florets, are produced from late spring to autumn. S to 18in (45cm).

French marigolds (French Group) Compact annuals derived from *T. patula*, with hairless, purple-tinged stems and pinnate leaves, to 4in (10cm) long, with lance-shaped to narrowly lance-shaped, toothed leaflets, to 1¼in (3cm) long. Solitary, usually double flower heads, typically to 2in (5cm) across, with few to many red-brown, yellow, orange, or bi-colored raybflorets and usually several disk florets, are borne singly or in cymelike inflorescences from late spring to autumn. S to 12in (30cm).

Afro-French marigolds (Afro-French Group) Bushy annuals derived from crosses of *T. erecta* and *T. patula*, with angular to rounded stems, branched and sometimes stained purple, and pinnate leaves, 2–5in (5–13cm) long, with lance-shaped leaflets, to 2in (5cm) long. Numerous small, single or double yellow or orange flower heads, usually 1–2½in (2.5–6cm) across, often marked red-brown, are borne singly or in cymelike inflorescences from late spring to autumn. S 12–16in (30–40cm).

Signet marigolds (Signet Group) Upright annuals derived from *T. tenuifolia*, with cylindrical, simple or many-branched stems and pinnate leaves, 2–5in (5–13cm) long, with narrowly lance-shaped, toothed leaflets, to ¾in (2cm) long. Many single flower heads, usually to 1in (2.5cm) across, with yellow or orange florets (few ray florets and several disk florets), are borne in cymelike inflorescences from late spring to autumn. S to 16in (40cm).

All of the following marigolds grow well in H12–1.

***T.* Antigua Series.** African marigolds. H to 12in (30cm). Bear orange, lemon yellow, golden yellow, or primrose yellow flower heads from late spring to early autumn.

***T.* Beaux Series.** Afro-French marigolds. H 14in (35cm). Bear double flower heads of rich golden yellow, orange with a red splash, or copper-red from late spring to early autumn.

***T.* Bonanza Series.** French marigolds. H 12in (30cm). In summer, they have double flower heads in deep orange-mahogany with gold margins, golden orange-mahogany, or orange-yellow-mahogany.

***T.* Boy Series** illus. p.340.

***T.* 'Cinnabar'** illus. p.329.

***T.* Disco Series.** French marigolds. H 8–10in (20–25cm). Single, weather-resistant flower heads in a range of colors, including yellow, golden yellow with mahogany markings, golden red, and red-orange, are borne from late spring to early autumn.

T. erecta (African marigold, Aztec marigold). Fast-growing, upright, bushy annual. H 1–3ft (30cm–1m), S 1–1½ft (30–45cm). Has very deeply divided, aromatic, glossy, deep green leaves. Daisylike, double flower heads, 2in (5cm) wide, are carried in summer and early autumn.

***T.* Gem Series.** Signet marigolds. H to 9in (23cm). Produce flower heads in lemon yellow, deep orange, or bright orange with darker markings. **'Lemon Gem'** has lemon yellow flower heads. **'Tangerine Gem'** illus. p.340.

***T.* 'Gold Coins'** illus. p.336.

***T.* 'Honeycomb'.** French marigold. H 10in (25cm). Produces crested, double, yellow- and reddish orange flower heads.

***T.* Lady Series.** African marigolds. H 16–18in (40–45cm). Produce orange, primrose yellow, yellow, or golden yellow flower heads from late spring to early autumn.

***T.* Marvel Series.** Compact African marigolds. H 18in (45cm). Produce densely double flower heads in gold, orange, yellow, lemon yellow, or in a formula mixture of colors, from late spring to early autumn.

***T.* Mischief Series.** French marigolds. H to 12in (30cm) or more. Have single flower heads in mahogany-red, yellow, or golden yellow, with some bicolors, from late spring to early autumn.

***T.* 'Naughty Marietta'** illus. p.338.

***T.* 'Orange Winner'** illus. p.340.

T. patula (French marigold). Fast-growing, bushy annual. H and S to 1ft (30cm). Has deeply divided, aromatic, deep green leaves. Single or carnation-like, double flower heads, in shades of yellow, orange, red, or mahogany, are borne in summer and early autumn.

***T.* Safari Series 'Safari Tangerine'** (illus. p.43). French marigolds. H 8–10in (20–25cm). Has double, broad-petaled, rich tangerine-orange flower heads from late spring to early autumn.

***T.* Solar Series** illus. p.338.

***T.* 'Vanilla'.** African marigold. H to 14in (35cm). Has creamy white flower heads from late spring to early autumn.

***T.* Voyager Series.** Compact African marigolds. H 12–14in (30–35cm). Large, yellow or orange flower heads, to 4in (10cm) across, are borne from late spring to early autumn.

***T.* Zenith Series.** Afro-French marigolds. H 12in (30cm). Have flower heads in yellow, golden yellow, lemon yellow, red, or orange, from late spring to early autumn.

Talbotia elegans. See *Vellozia elegans.*

TALINUM

PORTULACACEAE

Genus of summer-flowering perennials, some of which are evergreen, grown for their flowers and succulent foliage. Is useful for rock gardens, troughs, and alpine houses and as pot plants. Needs sun and gritty, not too dry, well-drained soil. Propagate by seed in autumn.

T. okanoganense. Cushion- or mat-forming, prostrate perennial. H to 1½in (4cm), S to 4in (10cm). Succulent stems produce tufts of cylindrical, succulent, grayish green leaves and, in summer, bear tiny, cup-shaped white flowers. Is excellent for cultivating in a trough or alpine house. Z6–8 H8–6.

TAMARINDUS

CAESALPINIACEAE/LEGUMINOSAE

Genus of one species of evergreen tree grown for its edible fruits and overall appearance as well as for shade. Needs full light and well-drained soil. Propagate by seed or air-layering in spring.

T. indica (Tamarind). Slow-growing, evergreen, rounded tree. H and S to 80ft (25m). Leaves have 10–15 pairs of oblong to elliptic, bright green leaflets. Produces profuse racemes of asymmetric, 5-petaled, pale yellow flowers veined red in summer, then long brownish pods containing edible but acidic pulp. Z5–9 H9–5.

TAMARIX

Tamarisk

TAMARICACEAE

Genus of deciduous or evergreen shrubs and trees grown for their foliage, habit, and abundant racemes of small flowers. Thrives in exposed, coastal positions. Requires sun and fertile, well-drained soil. Restrict growth by cutting back in spring; trim hedges at the same time. Propagate by semi-ripe cuttings in summer or by hardwood cuttings in winter.

T. parviflora. Deciduous spreading shrub. H 15ft (5m), S 20ft (6m). Has arching purple shoots with small pointed leaves, and 4-petaled pale pink flowers borne on arching racemes in late spring. Z5–8 H8–3.

T. pentandra. See *T. ramosissima.*

T. ramosissima, syn. *T. pentandra*, illus. p.121.

TANACETUM

ASTERACEAE/COMPOSITAE

Genus of perennials, some of which are evergreen, often with aromatic foliage, grown for their daisylike flower heads. Grow in sun and in fertile, well-drained soil. Propagate by division in spring. Contact with the foliage may aggravate skin allergies.

T. argenteum, syn. *Achillea argentea*, illus. p.360.

T. coccineum, syn. *Chrysanthemum coccineum*, *Pyrethrum coccineum*,

Pyrethrum roseum (Pyrethrum). **'Brenda'** (syn. *Pyrethrum* 'Brenda') illus. p.238. **'Eileen May Robinson'** is an upright perennial. H to 30in (75cm), S 18in (45cm). Has slightly aromatic, feathery, recurved leaves, 2in (5cm) long. In summer bears strong-stemmed pink flower heads, 2in (5cm) wide, with yellow centers. Is useful for cut flowers. **'James Kelway'** has deep crimson flower heads aging to pink. Both Z5–9 H9–5.
T. densum subsp. ***amani***, syn. *Chrysanthemum densum*, illus. p.361.
T. haradjanii, syn. *Chrysanthemum haradjanii*. Evergreen, mat-forming, woody-based perennial with a taproot. H and S 9–15in (23–38cm). Has broadly lance-shaped, much-divided, silvery gray leaves and, in summer terminal clusters of bright yellow flower heads. Is useful for a rock garden or alpine house.
T. parthenium, syn. *Chrysanthemum parthenium*, *Pyrethrum parthenium*, illus. p.319. **'Aureum'** is a short-lived, bushy perennial grown as an annual. H and S 8–18in (20–45cm). Has oval, lobed, aromatic, green-gold leaves and, in summer and early autumn, daisylike white flower heads. Z4–9 H9–1.

TANAKAEA

SAXIFRAGACEAE

Genus of one species of evergreen, spreading perennial grown for its foliage and flowers. Is suitable for rock gardens. Needs partial shade and well-drained, peaty, sandy soil. Propagate by runners in spring.
T. radicans. Evergreen, dense, basal-rosetted perennial. H 2½–3in (6–8cm), S 8in (20cm). Leaves are narrowly oval to heart-shaped, leathery, and mid- to dark green. Bears small panicles of tiny, outward-facing, star-shaped white flowers in late spring. Z6–8 H8–6.

TAPEINOCHILOS

COSTACEAE/ZINGIBERACEAE

Genus of mostly evergreen perennials grown for their colorful, leaflike bracts. Needs high humidity, partial shade, and organic soil. Is not easy to grow successfully in pots. Propagate by division in spring. Spider mite may be a problem with pot-grown plants.
T. ananassae. Evergreen, tufted perennial. H to 6ft (2m), S 2½ft (75cm). Non-flowering stems are erect and unbranched, with narrowly oval, long-pointed leaves, to 6in (15cm) long. Flowering stems are leafless, to over 3ft (1m) long, and, in summer, bear ovoid, dense spikes, 6in (15cm) or more long, of small, tubular yellow flowers. Showy, recurved, hard scarlet bracts enclose and almost hide flowers. Z15 H12–10.

TAXODIUM

TAXODIACEAE

See also CONIFERS.
T. distichum illus. p.104.

TAXUS

TAXACEAE

All parts (but not the seed coating) are highly toxic if ingested. See also CONIFERS.
T. baccata (Yew). Slow-growing conifer with a broadly conical, later domed crown. H 30–50ft (10–15m), S 15–30ft (5–10m). Needlelike, flattened leaves are dark green. Female plants bear cup-shaped, fleshy, bright red fruits; only the red part, not the seed, is edible. Will regrow if cut back. The following forms are H 20–30ft (6–10m), S 15–25ft (5–8m) unless otherwise stated. Z7–8 H8–7.
'Adpressa' is a shrubby, female form with short, broad leaves. **Aurea Group** (syn. *T.b.* 'Aurea'; illus. p.111) has golden yellow foliage. **'Dovastoniana'** is spreading, with weeping branchlets. **'Dovastonii Aurea'** (illus. p.111) is similar to *T.b.* 'Dovastoniana' but has golden shoots and yellow-margined leaves. **'Fastigiata'**, H 30–50ft (10–15m), S 12–15ft (4–5m), has erect branches and dark green foliage that stands out all around shoots.
'Fastigiata Aurea' is similar to *T.b.* 'Fastigiata' but has gold-variegated leaves. **'Repandens'**, H 2ft (60cm), S 15ft (5m), is a spreading form. **'Semperaurea'**, H 10ft (3m), S 15ft (5m), has ascending branches with dense, golden foliage.
T. cuspidata illus. p.109. **'Aurescens'** is a spreading, bushy, dwarf conifer. H 1ft (30cm), S 3ft (1m). Needlelike, flattened leaves are deep golden yellow in their first year and mature to dark green. Z4–7 H7–1. **'Capitata'**, H 30ft (10m), S 6ft (2m), is upright in habit. **'Densa'**, H 4ft (1.2m), S 20ft (6m), is a female form with short, erect shoots. Both Z5–7 H7–5.
T. x media. Dense conifer that is very variably shaped. H and S 10–20ft (3–6m). Has needlelike, flattened leaves, spreading on either side of olive green shoots. Leaves are stiff, broad, and widen abruptly at the base. Fruits are similar to those of *T. baccata*. Z5–7 H7–5. **'Brownii'**, H 8ft (2.5m), S 11ft (3.5m), is a dense, globose form with dark green foliage. **'Densiformis'**, H 6–10ft (2–3m), is dense and rounded, with masses of shoots that have bright green leaves. **'Hicksii'**, H to 20ft (6m), is columnar and has ascending branches. Male and female forms exist. **'Hillii'**, H and S 10ft (3m), is a broadly conical to rounded, dense bush with glossy green leaves. **'Wardii'**, H 6ft (2m), S 20ft (6m), is a flat, globose, female form.

TECOMA,
syn. TECOMARIA

BIGNONIACEAE

Genus of mainly evergreen shrubs and trees grown for their flowers from spring to autumn. Prefers moist but well-drained soil and full light. Water potted specimens moderately, and sparingly in winter. May be pruned annually after flowering to maintain as a shrub. Propagate by seed in spring or by semi-ripe cuttings in summer. Spider mite may be troublesome.
T. australis. See *Pandorea pandorana*.
T. capensis, syn. *Bignonia capensis* (Cape honeysuckle). Evergreen, scrambling climber, shrublike when young. H 6–10ft (2–3m). Leaves have 5–9 rounded, serrated, glossy, dark green leaflets. Tubular, orange-red flowers are carried in short spikes mainly in spring-summer. Z12–15 H12–10. **'Aurea'** (syn. *Tecomaria capensis* 'Aurea') illus. p.206.
T. grandiflora. See *Campsis grandiflora*.
T. radicans. See *Campsis radicans*.
T. ricasoliana. See *Podranea ricasoliana*.
T. stans, syn. *Bignonia stans*, *Stenolobium stans*, illus. p.96.

TECOMANTHE

BIGNONIACEAE

Genus of evergreen, twining climbers grown for their flowers. Provide organic, well-drained soil and light shade in summer. Water freely when in full growth, less at other times. Provide stems with support. If necessary, thin out crowded stems in spring. Propagate by seed in spring or by semi-ripe cuttings in summer.
T. speciosa. Strong-growing, evergreen, twining climber. H to 30ft (10m) or more. Has leaves of 3 or 5 oval leaflets. Bears dense clusters of foxglovelike, fleshy-textured cream flowers, tinged with green, in autumn. Z14–15 H12-10.

Tecomaria. Reclassified as *Tecoma*.

TECOPHILAEA

LILIACEAE/TECOPHILAEACEAE

Genus of spring-flowering corms, rare in cultivation and extinct in the wild, grown for their beautiful flowers. Usually grown in a cold greenhouse or cold frame. Requires sun and well-drained soil. Water in winter and spring. Keep corms dry, but not sunbaked, from early summer to autumn, then replant. Propagate in autumn by seed or offsets.
T. cyanocrocus illus. p.433.
var. ***leichtlinii*** (syn. *T.c.* 'Leichtlinii') illus. p.432.

TELEKIA

ASTERACEAE/COMPOSITAE

Genus of summer-flowering perennials grown for their bold foliage and large flower heads. Grows in sun or shade and in moist soil. Propagate by division in spring or by seed in autumn.
T. speciosa, syn. *Buphthalmum speciosum*. Upright, spreading perennial. H 4–5ft (1.2–1.5m), S 3–4ft (1–1.2m). Midgreen leaves are heart-shaped at base of plant, oval on stems. In late summer, branched stems bear large, daisylike, rich gold flower heads. Is ideal for a pondside or woodland. Z5–8 H8–5.

Telesonix jamesii. See *Boykinia jamesii*.

TELLIMA

SAXIFRAGACEAE

Genus of one species of semi-evergreen, late spring-flowering perennial. Makes a good groundcover and is ideal for cool, semi-shaded woodland gardens and beneath shrubs in sunny borders. Grows in any well-drained soil. Propagate by division in spring or by seed in autumn.
T. grandiflora (Fringecups). Semi-evergreen, clump-forming perennial. H and S 24in (60cm). Has heart-shaped, toothed, hairy, purple-tinted, bright green leaves. Bears racemes of small, bell-shaped, fringed cream flowers, well above foliage, in late spring. Z4–8 H8–1. **Rubra Group** (syn. *T.g.*'Purpurea') illus. p.302.

TELOPEA

PROTEACEAE

Genus of evergreen trees and shrubs grown mainly for their flower heads. Requires full sun or semi-shade and organic, moist but well-drained, neutral to acidic soil. Water containerized plants freely when in full growth, moderately at other times. Propagate by seed in spring or by layering in winter.
T. speciosissima illus. p.142.
T. truncata illus. p.131.

TEMPLETONIA

LEGUMINOSAE/PAPILIONACEAE

Genus of evergreen shrubs grown for their flowers. Prefers full light and freely draining, alkaline soil. Water potted specimens moderately, less in winter. Propagate by seed in spring or by semi-ripe cuttings in summer.
T. retusa (Coral bush). Evergreen, erect, irregularly branched shrub. H 6ft (2m), S 3–5ft (1–1.5m). Has oval to elliptic, leathery, bluish green leaves. Pealike red flowers, sometimes pink or cream, appear in spring-summer. Z14–15 H12–10.

TERMINALIA

COMBRETACEAE

Genus of evergreen trees and shrubs grown for their overall appearance, edible seeds (nuts), and for shade. Requires full light and well-drained soil. Water potted specimens moderately, scarcely at all when temperatures are low. Pruning is seldom necessary. Propagate by seed in spring.
T. catappa (Indian almond, Tropical almond). Evergreen, rounded tree. H and S 50ft (15m) or more. Has broadly oval, lustrous green leaves at stem tips. Small, greenish white flowers appear in spring, followed by

flattened ovoid, keeled green to red fruits, each with an edible seed. Z14–15 H12–10.

TERNSTROEMIA

THEACEAE

Genus of evergreen trees and shrubs grown for their overall appearance. Requires full sun or semi-shade and organic, well-drained, neutral to acidic soil. Water containerized specimens copiously when in full growth, moderately at other times. Prune in spring if necessary. Propagate by seed when ripe or in spring or by semi-ripe cuttings in late summer.

T. gymnanthera, syn. *T. japonica*. Evergreen, rounded, dense shrub. H and S 6ft (2m). Oval leaves are lustrous, mid- to deep green. In summer, pendent, 5-petaled white flowers are borne singly from leaf axils. Pea-sized, berrylike, bright red fruits appear in autumn. Z8–10 H10–8. Leaves of **'Variegata'** are white-bordered with a pink tinge.

T. japonica. See *T. gymnathera*.

Testudinaria elephantipes. See *Dioscorea elephantipes*.

TETRACENTRON

TETRACENTRACEAE

Genus of one species of deciduous tree grown for its foliage and catkins. Needs sun or partial shade and fertile, well-drained soil. Propagate by seed in autumn.

T. sinense. Deciduous, spreading tree of graceful habit. H and S 30ft (10m) or more. Bears oval, finely toothed, dark green leaves and long, slender yellow catkins in early summer. Z6–8 H8–6.

TETRADIUM,
syn. EUODIA, EVODIA

RUTACEAE

Genus of deciduous trees grown for their foliage, late flowers, and fruits. Needs full sun and fertile, well-drained soil. Propagate by softwood cuttings in summer, by seed in autumn, or by root cuttings in late winter.

T. daniellii, syn. *Euodia hupehensis*. Deciduous, spreading tree. H and S 50ft (15m). Ashlike, dark green leaves with 5–11 oval to oblong leaflets turn yellow in autumn. Has small, fragrant, 5-petaled white flower clusters in early autumn, then beaked red fruits. Z5–8 H8–5.

TETRANEMA

SCROPHULARIACEAE

Genus of perennials grown for their flowers. Grow in a light position, shaded from direct sunlight, and in well-drained soil; avoid waterlogging and an excessively humid atmosphere. Propagate by division, or seed if available, in spring.

T. mexicanum. See *T. roseum*.

T. roseum, syn. *T. mexicanum*, illus. p.303.

TETRAPANAX

ARALIACEAE

Genus of one species of evergreen, summer- to autumn-flowering shrub grown for its foliage. Requires full sun or partial shade and organic, moist but well-drained soil. Water containerized specimens freely, less in winter. Leggy stems may be cut back to near ground level in winter. Propagate by suckers or seed in early spring.

T. papyrifer, syn. *Fatsia papyrifera*, illus. p.126.

TETRASTIGMA

VITACEAE

Genus of evergreen, woody-stemmed, tendril climbers grown for their handsome leaves. Grow in any fertile, well-drained soil, with shade in summer. Water freely while in active growth, less in low temperatures. Provide stems with support; cut out crowded stems in spring. Propagate by layering in spring or by semi-ripe cuttings in summer.

T. voinierianum, syn. *Cissus voinieriana*, illus. p.220.

TEUCRIUM

LABIATAE/LAMIACEAE

Genus of evergreen or deciduous shrubs, subshrubs, and perennials grown for their flowers, foliage (sometimes aromatic), or habit. Needs full sun and well-drained soil. Propagate shrubs and subshrubs by softwood or semi-ripe cuttings in summer, perennials by seed or division in spring.

T. aroanium. Evergreen, procumbent, much-branched subshrub. H 1in (2.5cm), S 4–6in (10–15cm). Has white-haired twigs and oblong to oval, slightly hairy leaves that are densely hairy below, and, in summer, whorls of small, tubular, 2-lipped purple flowers. Is good for a trough. Z7–10 H10–7.

T. fruticans (Shrubby germander, Tree germander). **'Azureum'** is an evergreen, arching shrub. H 6ft (2m), S 12ft (4m). Has oval, aromatic, gray-green leaves, white beneath. Bears tubular, 2-lipped, deep blue flowers with prominent stamens in summer. Cut out dead wood in spring. Z8–9 H9–8.

T. polium illus. p.379.

THALIA

MARANTACEAE

Genus of deciduous, perennial, marginal water plants grown for their foliage and flowers. Needs an open, sunny position in up to 18in (45cm) depth of water. Some species tolerate cool water. Remove fading foliage regularly. Propagate in spring by division or seed.

T. dealbata. Deciduous, perennial, marginal water plant. H 5ft (1.5m). S 2ft (60cm). Oval, long-stalked, blue-green leaves have a mealy white covering. Spikes of narrowly tubular violet flowers in summer are followed by decorative seed heads. Tolerates cool water. Z6–11 H12–6.

T. geniculata. Deciduous, perennial, marginal water plant. H 6ft (2m), S 2ft (60cm). Has oval, long-stalked, blue-green leaves and, in summer, spikes of narrowly tubular violet flowers. Needs warm water.

THALICTRUM
Meadow rue

RANUNCULACEAE

Genus of perennials grown for their divided foliage and fluffy flower heads. Flowers lack petals, but each has prominent tufts of stamens and 4 or 5 sepals, which rapidly fall. Does well at edges of woodland gardens. Tall species and cultivars make excellent foils in borders for perennials with bolder leaves and flowers. Requires sun or light shade. Grows in any well-drained soil, although some species prefer cool, moist conditions. Propagate by seed when fresh in autumn, or by division in spring.

T. aquilegiifolium illus. p.251. **'White Cloud'** illus. p.240.

T. chelidonii. Clump-forming perennial. H 3–5ft (1–1.5m), S 2ft (60cm). Has finely divided, midgreen leaves and, in summer, produces panicles of fluffy, 4- or 5-sepaled mauve flowers. Prefers cool soil that does not dry out. Z5–9 H9–5.

T. delavayi, syn. *T. dipterocarpum* of gardens. Elegant, clump-forming perennial. H 5–6ft (1.5–2m), S 2ft (60cm). Has much-divided, midgreen leaves, above which large panicles of nodding lilac flowers with 4 or 5 sepals and prominent yellow stamens appear from mid- to late summer. Z4–7 H7–1. **Hewitt's Double'** has double flowers. Z6–8 H8–4.

T. diffusiflorum. Clump-forming perennial. H 3ft (1m), S 1–2ft (30–60cm). Has much-divided, basal, midgreen leaves. Slender stems produce large sprays of delicate, drooping mauve flowers in summer. Prefers cool, moist soil. Z5–9 H9–5.

T. dipterocarpum of gardens. See *T. delavayi*.

T. flavum. Clump-forming perennial. H 4–5ft (1.2m–1.5m), S 2ft (60cm). Has much-divided, glaucous blue-green leaves and, from mid- to late summer, clusters of fluffy, pale yellow flowers on slender stems. Z3–10 H10–9. **'Illuminator'** is a pale yellow cultivar with bright green foliage.

T. kiusianum. Mat-forming perennial with short runners. H 3in (8cm), S 6in (15cm) or more. Has small, fernlike, 3-lobed leaves and, throughout summer, loose clusters of small, light purple flowers. Is excellent in a rock garden, trough, or alpine house. Is difficult to grow in hot, dry areas. Prefers shade and moist, sandy, peaty soil. Z4–8 H8–1.

T. lucidum illus. p.254.

T. orientale. Spreading perennial with short runners. H 6in (15cm), S 8in (20cm). Leaves are fernlike with oval to rounded, lobed leaflets. Bears small, saucer-shaped, blue-mauve to violet flowers with yellow stamens and large sepals in late spring. Z5-9 H9–1.

Thamnocalamus falconeri. See *Himalayacalamus falconeri*.

Thamnocalamus murieliae. See *Fargesia murieliae*.

Thamnocalamus spathaceus of gardens. See *Fargesia murieliae*.

THELOCACTUS

CACTACEAE

Genus of spherical to columnar cacti with ribbed or tuberculate stems. Elongated areoles in crowns produce funnel-shaped flowers. Requires sun and well-drained soil. Propagate by seed in spring or summer.

T. bicolor illus. p.472.

T. leucacanthus. Clump-forming cactus. H 4in (10cm), S 12in (30cm). Spherical to columnar, dark green stem has 8–13 tuberculate ribs. Areoles each bear up to 20 short golden spines and yellow flowers, 2in (5cm) across, in summer. Z12–15 H12–10.

T. macdowellii, syn. *Echinomastus macdowellii*. Also sometimes included in *Neolloydia*. Spherical cactus. H and S 6in (15cm). Has a tuberculate, dark green stem densely covered with white spines to 1¼in (3cm) long. Violet-red flowers, 1½in (4cm) across, appear in spring-summer. Z12–15 H12–10.

T. setispinus, syn. *Ferocactus setispinus*, *Hamatocactus setispinus*, illus. p.467.

THELYPTERIS

THELYPTERIDACEAE

Genus of deciduous ferns. Tolerates sun or semi-shade. Grow in moist or very moist soil. Remove fading fronds regularly. Propagate by division in spring.

T. oreopteris. See *Oreopteris limbosperma*.

T. palustris illus. p.312.

T. phegopteris. See *Phegopteris connectilis*.

THERMOPSIS

LEGUMINOSAE/PAPILIONACEAE

Genus of summer-flowering perennials. Prefers sun and rich, light soil. Propagate by division in spring or by seed in autumn.

T. caroliniana. See *T. villosa*.

T. montana. See *T. rhombifolia*.

T. rhombifolia, syn. *T. montana*, illus. p.256.

T. villosa, syn. *T. caroliniana*. Straggling perennial. H 3ft (1m) or more, S 2ft (60cm). Bears racemes of pealike yellow flowers in late summer.

Glaucous leaves are divided into 3 oval leaflets. Z4–8 H9–1.

THESPESIA

MALVACEAE

Genus of evergreen perennials, shrubs and trees grown for their flowers. Needs full light and well-drained soil. Water containerized plants freely when in full growth, less at other times. Prune in early spring to maintain as a shrub. Propagate by seed in spring or by semi-ripe cuttings in summer. Whitefly and spider mite may be a nuisance.

T. populnea (Mahoe, Portia oil nut). Evergreen tree, bushy when young, thinning with age. H 40ft (12m) or more, S 10–20ft (3–6m). Leaves are heart-shaped. Intermittently, or all year round if warm enough, produces cup-shaped yellow flowers, each with a maroon eye, that age to purple. Grows well by the sea. Z14–15 H12-10.

THEVETIA

APOCYNACEAE

Genus of evergreen shrubs and trees grown for their flowers from winter to summer. Is related to *Frangipani.* Has poisonous, milky sap. Needs full light and well-drained soil. Water containerized specimens moderately, less in winter. Young stems may be tip pruned in winter to promote branching. Propagate by seed in spring or by semi-ripe cuttings in summer. The seeds are highly toxic if ingested.

T. neriifolia. See *T. peruviana.*

T. peruviana, syn. *T. neriifolia*, illus. p.93.

THLADIANTHA

CUCURBITACEAE

Genus of herbaceous or deciduous, tendril climbers grown for their bell-shaped yellow flowers and oval to heart-shaped, midgreen leaves. Requires a sheltered position in full sun and fertile, well-drained soil. Propagate by seed sown under cover in spring or by division in early spring.

T. dubia illus. p.216.

THLASPI

BRASSICACEAE/CRUCIFERAE

Genus of annuals and perennials, some of which are evergreen, grown for their flowers. Small plants may flower themselves to death, so remove buds for 2 years to encourage a large plant. Is difficult to grow at low altitudes and may require frequent renewal from seed. Is good for screes and troughs. Needs sun and moist but well-drained soil. Propagate by seed in autumn.

T. alpestre **of gardens.** See *T. alpinium.*

T. alpinum, syn. *T. alpestre* of gardens (Alpine penny-cress). Evergreen, mat-forming perennial. H 2in (5cm), S 4in (10cm). Has small, oval, midgreen leaves. Produces racemes of small, 4-petaled white flowers in spring. Z6–9 H9–6.

T. bulbosum. Clump-forming, tuberous perennial. H 3in (8cm), S 6–8in (15–20cm). Bears broadly oval, glaucous leaves and, in summer, racemes of 4-petaled, dark violet flowers. Good in a rock garden. Z8–10 H10–8.

T. cepaeifolium subsp. ***rotundifolium***, syn. *T. rotundifolium*, illus. p.365.

T. macrophyllum. See *Pachyphragma macrophyllum.*

T. rotundifolium. See *T. cepaeifolium* subsp. *rotundifolium*.

THUJA,
syn. PLATYCLADUS

CUPRESSACEAE

Contact with the foliage may aggravate skin allergies. See also CONIFERS.

T. koraiensis (Korean arborvitae). Upright conifer, sometimes sprawling and shrubby. H 10–30ft (3–10m), S 10–15ft (3–5m). Scalelike foliage is bright green or yellow-green above, glaucous silver beneath, and smells of almonds when crushed. Contact with the foliage may aggravate skin allergies. Z5–7 H7–5.

T. occidentalis (American arborvitae, Eastern white cedar, White cedar). Slow-growing conifer with a narrow crown. H 50ft (15m), S 10–15ft (3–5m). Has orange-brown bark and flat sprays of scalelike, yellowish green leaves, pale or grayish green beneath, smelling of apples when crushed. Ovoid cones are yellow-green, ripening to brown. Z2–7 H7–1. **'Caespitosa'** (illus. p.110). H 12in (30cm), S 16in (40cm), is a cushion-shaped, dwarf cultivar. **'Fastigiata'**, H to 50ft (15m), S to 15ft (5m), is broadly columnar, with erect, spreading branches and light green leaves. **'Filiformis'** (illus. p.111), H 5ft (1.5m), S 5–6ft (1.5–2m), forms a mound with pendent, whiplike shoots. **'Hetz Midget'**, H and S 20in (50cm), growing only 1in (2.5cm) each year, is a globose, dwarf form with blue-green foliage. **'Holmstrup'**, H 10–12ft (3–4m), S 3ft (1m), is slow-growing, dense, and conical, with rich green foliage. **'Little Champion'**, H and S 20in (50cm) or more, is a globose, dwarf form, conical when young, with foliage turning brown in winter. **'Lutea Nana'**, H 6ft (2m), S 3–6ft (1–2m), is a dwarf form with golden yellow foliage. **'Rheingold'**, H 10–12ft (3–4m), S 6–12ft (2–4m), is slow-growing, with golden yellow foliage that becomes bronze in winter. **'Smaragd'**, H 6–8ft (2–2.5m), S 2–2½ft (60–75cm), is slow-growing and conical, with erect sprays of bright green leaves. **'Spiralis'**, H 30–50ft (10–15m), S 6–10ft (2–3m), produces foliage in twisted, fernlike sprays. **'Woodwardii'**, H 8ft (2.5m), S to 15ft (5m), is very slow-growing and globose, with midgreen foliage.

T. orientalis, syn. *Biota orientalis* (Biota, Chinese arborvitae). Conifer with an irregularly rounded crown. H 30–50ft (10–15m), S 15ft (5m). Has fibrous bark and flattened, vertical sprays of scalelike, scentless, dark green leaves. Egg-shaped cones are glaucous gray. Z6–9 H9–6. **'Aurea Nana'** (illus. p.111), H and S 24in (60cm), is a dwarf cultivar with yellow-green foliage that turns bronze in winter. **'Semperaurea'** (illus. p.111), H 10ft (3m), S 6ft (2m), is compact, with golden leaves.

T. plicata (Western red cedar). Fast-growing, conical conifer that has large, curving branches low down. H 70–100ft (20–30m), S 15–25ft (5–8m), greater if lower branches self-layer. Has red-brown bark, scalelike, glossy, dark green leaves, which have a pineapple aroma when crushed, and erect, ovoid green cones, ripening to brown. Z6–8 H8–6. **'Atrovirens'** has darker green foliage. **'Aurea'** has golden yellow foliage. **'Collyer's Gold'** (illus. p.111), H to 6ft (2m), S 3ft (1m), is a dwarf form with yellow young foliage turning light green. **'Cuprea'**, H 3ft (1m), S 2½–3ft (75cm–1m), is a conical shrub with copper- to bronze-yellow leaves. **'Hillieri'** (illus. p.111), H and S to 3ft (1m), is a slow-growing, dense, rounded, dwarf shrub with mosslike, rich green foliage. **'Stoneham Gold'** (illus. p.111), H 3–6ft (1–2m), S 3ft (1m), is a conical, dwarf form with bright gold foliage. **'Zebrina'**, H 50ft (15m), has leaves banded with yellowish white.

THUJOPSIS

CUPRESSACEAE

See also CONIFERS.

T. dolabrata (Hiba). Conical or bushy conifer with a mass of stems. H 30–70ft (10–20m), S 25–30ft (8–10m). Produces heavy, flat sprays of scalelike leaves, glossy, bright green above, silvery white beneath. Small, rounded cones are blue-gray. Z5–7 H7–5. **'Variegata'** illus. p.109.

THUNBERGIA

ACANTHACEAE

Genus of annual or mainly evergreen, perennial, twining climbers, perennials and shrubs grown for their flowers. Any fertile, well-drained soil is suitable, with full sun or light shade in summer. Water freely when in full growth, less at other times. Requires support. Thin out crowded stems in early spring. Propagate by seed in spring or by softwood or semi-ripe cuttings in summer.

T. alata illus. p.216.

T. coccinea. Evergreen, woody-stemmed, perennial, twining climber with narrowly oval leaves. H 20ft (6m) or more. Pendent racemes of tubular scarlet flowers are produced in winter-spring. Z14–15 H12-10.

T. gibsonii. See *T. gregorii.*

T. grandiflora (Blue trumpet vine). Evergreen, woody-stemmed, perennial, twining climber. H 20–30ft (6–10m). Oval leaves, 4–8in (10–20cm) long, have a few toothlike lobes. In summer has trumpet-shaped, pale to deep violet-blue flowers. Z14–15 H12–10.

T. gregorii, syn. *T. gibsonii*, illus. p.217.

T. mysorensis illus. p.207.

THYMUS
Thyme

LABIATAE/LAMIACEAE

Genus of evergreen, mat-forming and dome-shaped shrubs, subshrubs, and woody-based perennials with aromatic leaves. Is useful for growing on banks and in rock gardens, troughs, and paving. Requires sun and moist but well-drained soil. Propagate by softwood or semi-ripe cuttings in summer.

T. azoricus. See *T. caespititius.*

T. caespititius, syn. *T. azoricus*, *T. micans*, illus. p.375.

T. carnosus, syn. *T. nitidus* of gardens. Evergreen, spreading shrub. H and S 8in (20cm). Has tiny, narrowly oval, aromatic leaves. Erect flowering stems bear whorls of small, 2-lipped white flowers in summer. Needs a sheltered position. Z5–9 H9–5.

***T.* x *citriodorus* 'Aureus'.** Evergreen, spreading shrub. H 4in (10cm), S 4–10in (10–25cm). Tiny, rounded to oval, golden yellow leaves are very fragrant when crushed. Produces terminal clusters of small, 2-lipped lilac flowers in summer. Cut back in spring. Z6–9 H9–6. **'Silver Queen'** bears silvery white foliage.

T. herba-barona illus. p.381.

T. leucotrichus illus. p.381.

T. micans. See *T. caespititius.*

T. nitidus **of gardens.** See *T. carnosus.*

***T.* 'Porlock'.** Evergreen, dome-shaped perennial. H 3in (8cm), S 8in (20cm). Thin stems are covered in small, rounded to oval, very aromatic, glossy green leaves. In summer produces clusters of small, 2-lipped pink flowers.

T. pseudolanuginosus. Evergreen, prostrate shrub. H 1–2in (2.5–5cm), S 8in (20cm) or more. Has dense mats of very hairy stems bearing tiny, aromatic gray leaves. Produces 2-lipped, pinkish lilac flowers in leaf axils in summer. Z4–9 H9–1.

T. serpyllum. Evergreen, mat-forming subshrub. H 10in (25cm), S 18in (45cm). Finely hairy, trailing stems bear linear to elliptic to oval, midgreen leaves. Whorls of two-lipped purple flowers are borne in summer. Z4–9 H9–1. **'Annie Hall'**, H 2in (5cm), S 8in (20cm), has pale purple-pink flowers and light green leaves. **'Elfin'**, H 2in (5cm), S 4in (10cm), produces emerald green leaves in dense hummocks; occasionally bears purple flowers.

TIARELLA
Foamflower

SAXIFRAGACEAE

Genus of perennials, some evergreen, that spread by runners. Excellent as a groundcover. Tolerates deep shade and prefers moist but well-drained soil. Propagate by division in spring.

T. cordifolia illus. p.347. var. ***collina*** see *T. wherryi*.
T. wherryi, syn. *T. cordifolia* var. *collina*. Slow-growing, clump-forming perennial. H 4in (10cm), S 6in (15cm). Triangular, lobed, hairy, basal green leaves are stained dark red, with heart-shaped bases. Bears racemes of tiny, star-shaped, soft pink or white flowers from late spring to early summer. Z3–7 H7–1.

TIBOUCHINA

MELASTOMATACEAE

Genus of evergreen perennials, subshrubs, shrubs, and scandent climbers grown for their flowers and leaves. Prefers full sun and fertile, well-drained, neutral to acidic soil. Water potted specimens freely when in full growth, moderately at other times. Cut back flowered stems, each to 2 pairs of buds, in spring. Tip prune young plants to promote branching. Propagate by greenwood or semi-ripe cuttings in late spring or summer.
T. semidecandra of gardens. See *T. urvilleana*.
T. urvilleana, syn. *T. semidecandra* of gardens, illus. p.122.

TIGRIDIA

IRIDACEAE

Genus of summer-flowering bulbs grown for their highly colorful but short-lived flowers, rather irislike in shape, with 3 large, outer petals. Needs sun and well-drained soil, with ample water in summer. Plant in spring. Lift in autumn; then partially dry bulbs and store in peat or sand at 46–54°F (8–12°C). Propagate by seed in spring.
T. pavonia illus. p.423.

TILIA

Lime, Linden

TILIACEAE

Genus of deciduous trees grown for their small, fragrant, cup-shaped flowers and stately habit. Flowers attract bees but are toxic to them in some cases. Requires sun or semi-shade and fertile, well-drained soil. Propagate species by seed in autumn, selected forms and hybrids by grafting in late summer. Except for *T.* x *euchlora*, trees are usually attacked by aphids, which cover growth and ground beneath with sticky honeydew. The nectar of *T.* 'Petiolaris' and *T. tomentosa* and may be toxic, especially to bumblebees.
T. americana (American linden, Basswood). Deciduous, spreading tree. H 80ft (25m), S 40ft (12m). Has large, rounded, sharply toothed, glossy, dark green leaves. Small, yellowish white flowers appear in summer. Z2–8 H8–1.
T. cordata (Small-leaved linden). Deciduous, spreading tree. H 100ft (30m), S 40ft (12m). In midsummer has small, glossy, dark green leaves and small, yellowish white flowers. Z3–8 H8–1. **'Greenspire'**, S 25ft (8m), is very vigorous and pyramidal in habit, even when young. **'Rancho'** illus. p.80. Both 4–8 H8–1.
T.* x *euchlora (Crimean linden). Deciduous, spreading tree with lower branches that droop with age. H 70ft (20m), S 30ft (10m). Rounded, very glossy, deep green leaves turn yellow in autumn. Bears small, yellowish white flowers, toxic to bees, in summer. Is relatively pest-free. Z3–7 H7–1.
T.* x *europaea, syn. *T.* x *vulgaris*. (European linden). Vigorous, deciduous, spreading tree. H 120ft (35m), S 50ft (15m). Has rounded, dark green leaves. Small, yellowish white flowers, toxic to bees, appear in summer. Periodically remove shoots from burrs at base. Z4–7 H7-1.
T. henryana. Deciduous, spreading tree. H and S 30ft (10m). Broadly heart-shaped, glossy, bright green leaves, fringed with long teeth, are often tinged red when young. Has masses of small, creamy white flowers in autumn. Z6–8 H8–6.
T. mongolica (Mongolian linden). Deciduous, spreading, graceful tree. H 50ft (15m), S 40ft (12m). Young shoots are red. Heart-shaped, coarsely toothed, glossy, dark green leaves turn yellow in autumn. Small, yellowish white flowers appear in summer. Z3–7 H7–1.
T. oliveri illus. p.67.
T. petiolaris. See *T.* 'Petiolaris'.
***T.* 'Petiolaris'**, syn. *T. petiolaris*, illus. p.68.
T. platyphyllos (Large-leaved linden). Deciduous, spreading tree. H 100ft (30m), S 70ft (20m). Has rounded, dark green leaves and small, dull yellowish white flowers in midsummer. Z2–6 H6–1. **'Prince's Street'** is upright, with bright red shoots in winter. Z5–8 H8–5.
T. tomentosa (European white linden, Silver linden). Deciduous, spreading tree. H 80ft (25m), S 70ft (20m). Leaves are large, rounded, sharply toothed, dark green above and white beneath. Very fragrant, small, dull white flowers, toxic to bees, are borne in late summer. Z6–9.
T.* x *vulgaris. See. *T.* x *europaea*.

TILLANDSIA

BROMELIACEAE

Genus of evergreen, epiphytic perennials, often rosette-forming, some with branching stems and spirally arranged leaves, all grown for their flowers or overall appearance. Requires semi-shade. Provide a rooting medium of equal parts organic soil and either sphagnum moss or bark or plastic chips used for orchid culture. May also be grown on slabs of bark or sections of trees. Using soft water, water moderately in summer, sparingly at other times; spray plants grown on bark or tree sections with water several times a week from midspring to mid-autumn. Propagate by offsets or division in spring.
T. argentea (illus. p.265). Evergreen, basal-rosetted, epiphytic perennial. H and S 4–6in (10–15cm). Very narrow, almost threadlike leaves covered with white scales are produced in dense, near-spherical rosettes, each with a fleshy, bulblike base. In summer, small, loose racemes of tubular red flowers are produced. Z13–15 H12–1.
T. caput-medusae (illus. p.265). Evergreen, basal-rosetted, epiphytic perennial. H and S 6in (15cm) or more. Linear, channeled, twisted and rolled, incurved leaves covered in gray scales develop in loose rosettes that have hollow, bulblike bases. In summer, spikes of tubular, violet-blue flowers appear above foliage. Z13–15 H12–1.
T. cyanea (illus. p.265). Evergreen, basal-rosetted, epiphytic perennial. H and S 10in (25cm). Forms dense rosettes of linear, pointed, channeled, arching, usually deep green leaves. In summer, broadly oval, bladelike spikes of pansy-shaped, deep purple-blue flowers, emerging from pink or red bracts, are produced among foliage. Z13–15 H12–1.
T. fasciculata (illus. p.265). Evergreen, basal-rosetted, epiphytic perennial. H and S 12in (30cm) or more. Has dense rosettes of narrowly triangular, tapering, arching, midgreen leaves. In summer, flat spikes of tubular, purple-blue flowers emerge from red or reddish yellow bracts, just above leaf tips. Bracts require strong light to develop reddish tones. Z13–15 H12–1.
T. ionantha (Sky plant). Evergreen, clump-forming, basal-rosetted, epiphytic perennial. H and S 5in (12cm). Linear, incurved, arching leaves covered in gray scales are produced in dense rosettes; the inner leaves turn red at flowering time. Spikes of tubular, violet-blue flowers, emerging in summer from narrow white bracts, are borne just above foliage. Z13–15 H12–1.
T. lindenii (Blue-flowered torch; illus. p.265). Evergreen, basal-rosetted, epiphytic perennial. H and S 16in (40cm). Linear, pointed, channeled, arching, midgreen leaves with red-brown lines form dense rosettes. In summer, produces bladelike spikes of widely pansy-shaped, deep blue flowers, emerging from sometimes pink-tinted green bracts, which are borne just above leaves. Z13–15 H12–1.
T. recurvata. Evergreen, basal-rosetted, epiphytic perennial. H and S 4–8in (10–20cm). Has long, loose, stemlike rosettes of linear, arching to recurved leaves densely covered in silvery gray scales. In summer produces short, dense spikes of small, tubular, pale blue or pale green flowers that appear above the leaves. Z13–15 H12–1.
T. stricta (illus. p.265). Evergreen, clump-forming, basal-rosetted, epiphytic perennial. H and S 8–12in (20–30cm). Narrowly triangular, tapering, arching, midgreen leaves, usually with gray scales, are produced in dense rosettes. Large, tubular blue flowers emerge from drooping, conelike spikes of bright red bracts, usually in summer. Z13–15 H12–1.
T. usneoides (Spanish moss; illus. p.265). Evergreen, pendent, epiphytic perennial. H 3ft (1m) or more, S 4–8in (10–20cm). Slender, branched, drooping stems bear linear, incurved leaves densely covered in silvery white scales. Inconspicuous, tubular, greenish yellow or pale blue flowers, hidden among foliage, are produced in summer. Z9–15 H12–1.

TIPUANA

LEGUMINOSAE/PAPILIONACEAE

Genus of one species of evergreen, spring-flowering tree grown for its flowers and overall appearance when mature and for shade. In certain conditions may be deciduous. Requires full light and fertile, well-drained soil. Container-grown plants will not produce flowers. Young specimens may be pruned in winter. Propagate by seed in spring.
T. speciosa. See *T. tipu*.
T. tipu, syn. *T. speciosa* (Pride of Bolivia, Tipa tree, Tipu tree). Fast-growing, mainly evergreen, bushy tree. H 30ft (10m), S 25–30ft (8–10m). Bears leaves, 10in (25cm) long, with 11–25 oval leaflets. Produces pealike, orange-yellow flowers, 1¼in (3cm) wide, in spring, followed by short, woody, winged brownish pods in autumn-winter. Z13–15 H12–10.

TITANOPSIS

AIZOACEAE

Genus of basal-rosetted succulents eventually forming small, dense clumps. Produces 6–8 opposite pairs of fleshy, triangular leaves, ¾–1¼in (2–3cm) long, narrow at stems and expanding to straight tips. Requires a position in sun and well-drained soil. Propagate by seed in spring or summer.
T. calcarea illus. p.479.
T. schwantesii. Clump-forming succulent. H 1¼in (3cm), S 4in (10cm). Has a basal rosette of triangular, gray-blue leaves, covered with small, wartlike, yellow-brown tubercles. Carries daisylike, light yellow flowers, ¾in (2cm) wide, in summer-autumn. Z13–15 H12-10.

TITHONIA

ASTERACEAE/COMPOSITAE

Genus of annuals. Grow in sun and in fertile, well-drained soil. Provide support and deadhead regularly. Propagate by seed sown under cover in late winter or early spring.
T. rotundifolia (Mexican sunflower). **'Torch'** illus. p.340.

TOLMIEA

SAXIFRAGACEAE

Genus of one species of perennial that is sometimes semi-evergreen and is grown as a groundcover. Is suitable for cool woodland gardens. Prefers a position in shade and requires well-drained, neutral to acidic soil. Propagate by division in spring or by seed in autumn.

T. menziesii (Pick-a-back-plant, Youth-on-age). Mat-forming perennial, sometimes semi-evergreen. H 18–24in (45–60cm), S 12in (30cm) or more. Young plantlets develop where ivy-shaped, midgreen leaves join stem. Produces spikes of tiny, nodding, tubular to bell-shaped green and chocolate brown flowers, which appear in spring. Z6–9 H9–6.

TOLPIS

ASTERACEAE/COMPOSITAE

Genus of summer-flowering annuals and perennials. Grow in sun and in fertile, well-drained soil. Propagate by seed sown outdoors in spring.

T. barbata. Moderately fast-growing, upright, branching annual. H 1½–2ft (45–60cm), S 1ft (30cm). Has lance-shaped, serrated, midgreen leaves. Daisylike, bright yellow flower heads, 1in (2.5cm) or more wide, with maroon centers, are produced in summer. H9–1.

TOONA

MELIACEAE

Genus of deciduous trees grown for their foliage, autumn color, and flowers. Prefers full sun; requires fertile, well-drained soil. Propagate by seed in autumn, root cuttings in winter.

T. sinensis, syn. *Cedrela sinensis*, illus. p.79.

TORENIA

SCROPHULARIACEAE

Genus of annuals and perennials. Grow in semi-shade and in a sheltered position in fertile, well-drained soil. Pinch out growing shoots of young plants to encourage a busy habit. Propagate by seed sown under cover in early spring.

T. fournieri illus. p.333.

TORREYA

TAXACEAE

See also CONIFERS.

T. californica illus. p.107.

***Tovara virginiana* 'Painter's Palette'.** See *Persicaria virginiana* 'Painter's Palette'.

TOWNSENDIA

ASTERACEAE/COMPOSITAE

Genus of evergreen, short-lived perennials and biennials grown for their daisylike flower heads. Good in alpine houses; dislikes winter wet. Needs sun and moist soil. Propagate by seed in autumn.

T. grandiflora illus. p.383.

T. parryi. Evergreen, basal-rosetted, short-lived perennial. H 3–6in (7–15cm), S 2in (5cm). In late spring produces daisylike lavender or violet-blue flower heads with bright yellow centers above spoon-shaped leaves. Z4-7 H7–1.

Toxicodendron succedaneum. See *Rhus succedanea*.

Toxicodendron vernicifluum. See *Rhus verniciflua*.

TRACHELIUM,
syn. DIOSPHAERA

CAMPANULACEAE

Genus of small perennials, useful for rock gardens and mixed borders. Some are good in alpine houses. Protect under cover in winter, since they resent damp conditions. Grow in a sunny, sheltered position and in fertile, very well-drained soil (*T. asperuloides* prefers lime-rich soil). Propagate by seed in early or midspring or by softwood cuttings in spring.

T. asperuloides, syn. *Diosphaera asperuloides*, illus. p.383.

T. caeruleum illus. p.330.

TRACHELOSPERMUM

APOCYNACEAE

Genus of evergreen, woody-stemmed, twining climbers with stems that exude milky sap when cut. Grow in any well-drained soil and in sun or semi-shade. Propagate by seed in spring, by layering in summer, or by semi-ripe cuttings in late summer or autumn.

T. asiaticum. Evergreen, woody-stemmed, much-branched, twining climber. H to 20ft (6m). Bears oval, glossy, dark green leaves that are 1in (2.5cm) long. Scented, tubular cream flowers with expanded mouths, that age to yellow, are produced in summer. Pairs of long, slender pods, 5–9in (12–22cm) long, contain silky seeds. Z7–11 H12–7.

T. jasminoides illus. p.207.

TRACHYCARPUS

ARECACEAE/PALMAE

Genus of evergreen, summer-flowering palms grown for their habit, foliage, and flowers. Requires full sun and does best in a position sheltered from strong, cold winds, especially when young. Needs fertile, well-drained soil. Propagate by seed in autumn or spring.

T. fortunei illus. p.84.

TRACHYMENE

APIACEAE/UMBELLIFERAE

Genus of summer-flowering annuals. Grow in a sunny, sheltered position and in fertile, well-drained soil. Support with sticks. Propagate by seed sown under cover in early spring.

T. coerulea, syn. *Didiscus coeruleus* (Blue lace flower). Moderately fast-growing, upright, branching annual. H 18in (45cm), S 8in (20cm). Has deeply divided, pale green leaves. Spherical heads, to 2in (5cm) wide, of tiny blue flowers are produced in summer. Flowers are excellent for cutting. H12–6.

TRADESCANTIA
Spiderwort

COMMELINACEAE

Genus of perennials, some of which are evergreen, grown for their flowers or ornamental foliage. Grow in fertile, moist to dry soil and in sun or partial shade. Cut back or repropagate trailing species when they become straggly. Propagate hardy species by division; tender species by tip cuttings in spring, summer, or autumn. Contact with the foliage may irritate skin.

T. albiflora. See *T. fluminensis*.

***T.* Andersoniana Group 'J.C. Weguelin'**, syn. *T.* 'J.C. Weguelin'. Clump-forming perennial. H to 2ft (60cm), S 1½ft (45cm). Has narrowly lance-shaped, fleshy, green leaves, 6–12in (15–30cm) long. In summer produces clusters of 3-petaled, lavender-blue flowers, 1in (2.5cm) or more wide, surrounded by 2 leaflike bracts. Z5–9 H9–5. **'Osprey'** (syn. *T.* 'Osprey') illus. p.276. **'Purple Dome'** (syn. *T.* 'Purple Dome') illus. p.284.

T. blossfeldiana. See *T. cerinthoides*.

T. cerinthoides, syn. *T. blossfeldiana*. Evergreen, creeping perennial. H 2in (5cm), S indefinite. Narrowly oval, fleshy, stem-clasping leaves, to 4in (10cm) long, are glossy, dark green above and purple with long white hairs below. Inter-mittently produces clusters of tiny pink flowers with white centers, surrounded by 2 leaflike bracts. Z14–15 H12-10. Leaves of **'Variegata'** have longitudinal cream stripes.

T. fluminensis, syn. *T. albiflora* (Inch plant, Wandering Jew). Evergreen perennial with trailing, rooting stems. H 2in (5cm), S to 24in (60cm) or more. Oval, fleshy leaves, 1½in (4cm) long, that clasp the stem, are glossy and green above, sometimes tinged purple below. Intermittently has clusters of tiny white flowers enclosed in 2 leaflike bracts. Z13–15 H12–1. **'Albovittata'** and **'Variegata'** illus. p.300.

***T.* 'J.C. Weguelin'.** See *T.* Andersoniana Group 'J.C. Weguelin'.

T. navicularis. See *Callisia navicularis*.

***T.* 'Osprey'.** See *T.* Andersoniana Group 'Osprey'.

***T. pallida* 'Purpurea'**, syn. *T.p.* 'Purple Heart', *Setcreasea purpurea*, illus. p.303.

T. pexata. See *T. sillamontana*.

***T.* 'Purple Dome'.** See *T.* Andersoniana Group 'Purple Dome'.

T. purpusii. See *T. zebrina* 'Purpusii'.

T. sillamontana, syn. *T. pexata*, *T. velutina*, illus. p.303.

T. spathacea, syn. *Rhoeo discolor*, *R. spathacea* (Boat lily, Moses-in-the-cradle). Evergreen, clump-forming perennial. H 20in (50cm), S 10in (25cm). Rosette of lance-shaped, fleshy leaves, to 12in (30cm) long, is green above, purple below. Bears small white flowers, enclosed in boat-shaped, leaflike bracts, year-round. Z11–12 H12–1. **'Vittata'** has leaves striped longitudinally with pale yellow.

T. velutina. See *T. sillamontana*.

T. zebrina, syn. *Zebrina pendula*, illus. p.301. **'Purpusii'** (syn. *T. purpusii*) is a strong-growing, evergreen, trailing or mat-forming perennial. H 4in (10cm), S indefinite. Has elliptic, purple-tinged, bluish green leaves and tiny, shallowly cup-shaped pink flowers. **'Quadricolor'** has leaves striped green, pink, red, and white. Both Z14–15 H12–1.

TRAPA

TRAPACEAE

Genus of deciduous, perennial and annual, floating water plants grown for their foliage and flowers. Requires sun. Propagate in spring from seed gathered in autumn and stored in water or damp moss.

T. natans illus. p.449.

Trichocereus bridgesii. See *Echinopsis lageniformis*.

Trichocereus candicans. See *Echinopsis candicans*.

Trichocereus spachianus. See *Echinopsis spachiana*.

TRICHODIADEMA

AIZOACEAE

Genus of bushy succulents with woody or tuberous roots and cylindrical to semi-cylindrical leaves. Needs sun and well-drained soil. Propagate by seed or stem cuttings in spring or summer.

T. densum. Tufted succulent. H 4in (10cm), S 8in (20cm). Cylindrical, pale green leaves are each ½–¾in (1–2cm) long and tipped with clusters of white bristles. Roots and prostrate green stem are both fleshy and form caudex. Stem tip has daisylike cerise flowers, 1¼in (3cm) across, in summer. Z13–15 H12–1.

T. mirabile illus. p.469.

TRICHOSANTHES

CUCURBITACEAE

Genus of annual and evergreen, perennial, tendril climbers grown for their fruits and overall appearance. Needs full sun or partial shade and organic soil. Water freely in growing season, less in cool weather. Provide support. Propagate by seed in spring at not less than 70°F (21°C).

T. anguina. See *T. cucumerina* var. *anguina*.

T. cucumerina* var. *anguina, syn. *T. anguina* (Snake gourd). Erect to spreading, annual, tendril climber. H 10–15ft (3–5m). Has broadly oval to almost triangular, sometimes shallowly 3- to 5-lobed, mid- to pale green leaves, to 8in (20cm) long. In summer produces 5-petaled white flowers, 1–2in (2.5–5cm) across, with heavily fringed petals; females are solitary, the males in racemes. Cylindrical fruits, 2ft (60cm) or rarely to 6ft (2m) long, often twisted or coiled, are green-and-white striped and ripen to dull orange. Z14-15 H12-10.

Trichosma suavis. See *Eria coronaria.*
Tricuspidaria lanceolata. See *Crinodendron hookerianum.*

TRICYRTIS
Toad lily

CONVALLARIACEAE/LILIACEAE

Genus of late summer- and autumn-flowering, rhizomatous perennials. Grows in sun or, in warmer areas, in partial shade. Needs organic, moist soil. Propagate by division in spring or by seed in autumn.

T. formosana, syn. *T. stolonifera*, illus. p.259.

T. hirta. Upright, rhizomatous perennial. H 1–3ft (30cm–1m), S 1½ft (45cm). In late summer and early autumn, clusters of large, open bell-shaped, white-spotted purple flowers appear from axils of uppermost leaves. Leaves are narrowly oval, hairy, and dark green and clasp stems. Z4–9 H9–1. var. ***alba*** illus. p.294.

T. macrantha. Upright, rhizomatous perennial. H and S 24in (60cm). In early autumn has loose sheaves of open bell-shaped, deep primrose yellow flowers, spotted light chocolate, at tips of arching stems, and small, oval, dark green leaves. Z8–9 H9–8.

T. stolonifera. See *T. formosana.*

TRIFOLIUM
Clover

LEGUMINOSAE/PAPILIONACEAE

Genus of annuals, biennials and perennials, some of which are semi-evergreen, with round, usually 3-lobed leaves and heads of pealike flowers. Some species are useful in rock gardens or on banks, others in agriculture. Many are invasive. Needs sun and well-drained soil. Propagate by division in spring or by seed in autumn. Self-seeds readily.

T. repens **'Purpurascens'** illus. p.388.

TRILLIUM
Trinity flower, Wood lily, Wakerubin

LILIACEAE/TRILLIACEAE

Genus of perennials with petals, sepals, and leaves that are all borne in whorls of 3. Is excellent for woodland gardens. Enjoys partial shade and fertile, moist but well-drained, neutral to acidic soil. Propagate by division after foliage has died down in summer or by seed in autumn.

T. cernuum illus. p.267.

T. chloropetalum illus. p.268.

T. erectum illus. p.269.

T. grandiflorum illus. p.268. **'Flore Pleno'** is a clump-forming perennial. H 15in (38cm), S 12in (30cm). Large, double, pure white flowers are borne singly in spring, turning pink with age. Has large, broadly oval, dark green leaves. Z4–7 H7–3.

T. nivale (Dwarf white wood lily, Snow trillium). Early spring-flowering, rhizomatous perennial. H 3in (7cm), S 4in (10cm). Whorls of 3 oval leaves emerge at same time as outward-facing, slightly nodding white flowers, each with 3 narrowly oval petals. Thrives in a trough or alpine house. Is difficult to grow. Z5–8 H8–5.

T. ovatum illus. p.268.

T. rivale illus. p.365.

T. sessile illus. p.269.

T. undulatum (Painted trillium, Painted wood lily). Clump-forming perennial. H 4–8in (10–20cm), S 6–8in (15–20cm). Open funnel-shaped flowers with red-bordered green sepals and 3 white or pink petals, each with a basal carmine stripe, are borne singly in spring, above broadly oval, basal, blue-green leaves. Z4–8 H8–1.

TRIPETALEIA

ERICACEAE

Genus of one species of deciduous shrub grown for its flowers; is now often included in *Elliottia*. Needs semi-shade and moist, peaty, neutral to acidic soil. Propagate by softwood cuttings in summer or by seed in autumn.

T. paniculata, syn. *Elliottia paniculata*. Deciduous, upright shrub. H and S 5ft (1.5m). Bears upright panicles of pink-tinged white flowers, each with 3 (or 4 or 5) narrow petals, from midsummer to early autumn. Lance-shaped, dark green leaves persist well into autumn. Z6–9 H9–6

TRIPTERYGIUM

CELASTRACEAE

Genus of deciduous, twining or scrambling climbers grown for their foliage and fruits. Grow in any fertile, well-drained soil and in full sun or light shade. Water freely while in full growth, less in low temperatures. Provide stems with support. Thin out crowded stems in winter or early spring. Propagate by seed when ripe or in spring or by semi-ripe cuttings in summer.

T. regelii. Deciduous, thin-stemmed, twining or scrambling climber. H 30ft (10m). Leaves are oval and usually rich green. In late summer produces clusters, 8–10in (20–25cm) long, of small, off-white flowers, followed by 3-winged, pale green fruits. Z5–8 H8–5.

Tristania conferta. See *Lophostemon confertus.*

TRITELEIA

ALLIACEAE/LILIACEAE

Genus of late spring- and early summer-flowering corms with wiry stems carrying *Allium*-like umbels of funnel-shaped flowers. Long, narrow leaves usually die away by flowering time. Needs an open but sheltered, sunny situation and well-drained soil that dries out to some extent in summer. Dies down in mid- to late summer until winter or spring; plant during dormancy in early autumn. Propagate by seed or offsets in autumn.

T. hyacinthina, syn. *Brodiaea hyacinthina*, *B. lactea*, illus. p.419.

T. ixioides, syn. *Brodiaea ixioides*, *B. lutea*. Early summer-flowering corm. H to 20in (50cm), S 3–4in (8–10cm). Bears semi-erect, basal leaves. Stem has a loose umbel, to 5in (12cm) across, of yellow flowers; petals each have a purple-stripe. Z7–13 H12–7.

T. laxa, syn. *Brodiaea laxa*, illus. p.422.

T. peduncularis, syn. *Brodiaea peduncularis*. Early summer-flowering corm. H 4–16in (10–40cm), S 4–6in (10–15cm). Bears semi-erect, basal leaves. Stem has a loose umbel, to 14in (35cm) across, of white flowers, each ⅝–1¼in (1.5–3cm) long, faintly tinged blue. Z7–13 H12–7.

TRITONIA

IRIDACEAE

Genus of corms, with flattish fans of sword-shaped, erect leaves, grown for their spikes of colorful flowers. Needs a sunny, sheltered site and well-drained soil. Plant corms in autumn (*T. disticha* subsp. *rubrolucens* in spring). Dry off once leaves start dying back in summer (winter for *T. disticha* subsp. *rubrolucens*). Propagate by seed in autumn or by offsets at replanting time.

T. crocata, syn. *T. hyalina*. Spring-flowering corm. H 6–14in (15–35cm), S 2–3in (5–8cm). Has erect, basal leaves. Each wiry stem has a loose spike of up to 10 widely cup-shaped, orange or pink flowers, 1½–2in (4–5cm) across, with transparent margins. Z8–10 H10–8.

T. disticha subsp. ***rubrolucens***, syn. *T. rosea*, *T. rubrolucens*, illus. p.420.

T. hyalina. See *T. crocata*.

T. rosea. See *T. disticha* subsp. *rubrolucens*.

T. rubrolucens. See *T. disticha* subsp. *rubrolucens*.

TROCHOCARPA

EPACRIDACEAE

Genus of evergreen shrubs grown for their nodding flower spikes. Needs sun and moist but well-drained, peaty, sandy soil. Propagate by semi-ripe cuttings in summer.

T. thymifolia. Slow-growing, evergreen, erect shrub. H 12in (30cm), S to 8in (20cm). Stems are covered in minute, thymelike leaves. Carries 1½in (4cm) long spikes of tiny, bell-shaped pink flowers in summer-autumn. Good in an alpine house.

TROCHODENDRON

TROCHODENDRACEAE

Genus of one species of evergreen tree grown for its foliage and flowers. Needs shelter from strong, cold winds. Tolerates a sunny or shady position and requires moist but well-drained soil; dislikes very dry or very shallow, alkaline soil. Propagate by semi-ripe cuttings in summer or by seed in autumn.

T. aralioides illus. p.84.

TROLLIUS
Globeflower

RANUNCULACEAE

Genus of spring- or summer-flowering perennials that thrive beside ponds and streams. Tolerates sun or shade. Propagate by division in early autumn or by seed in summer or autumn.

T. × ***cultorum*** **'Alabaster'** illus. p.274. **'Earliest of All'** is a clump-forming perennial. H 24in (60cm), S 18in (45cm). Globular, butter yellow flowers are borne singly in spring above rounded, deeply divided, midgreen leaves. **'Goldquelle'** has large, rich orange flowers. **'Orange Princess'**, H 30in (75cm), S 18in (45cm), bears orange-gold flowers. All Z5–8 H8–5.

T. europaeus illus. p.275. **'Canary Bird'** is a clump-forming perennial. H 24in (60cm), S 18in (45cm). In spring bears globular, canary yellow flowers above rounded, deeply divided, mid-green leaves. Z5–8 H8–5.

T. pumilus illus. p.373.

T. yunnanensis. Clump-forming perennial. H 2ft (60cm), S 1ft (30cm). Has broadly oval leaves with 3–5 deep lobes. Produces buttercup-like, bright yellow flowers in late spring or summer. Z5-8 H8–5.

TROPAEOLUM
Nasturtium

TROPAEOLACEAE

Genus of annuals, perennials, and herbaceous, twining climbers grown for their brightly colored flowers. Most species prefer sun and well-drained soil. Propagate by seed, tubers, or basal stem cuttings in spring. Aphids and caterpillars of cabbage white butterfly and its relatives may cause problems.

T. **Alaska Series** illus. p.339.

T. azureum. Herbaceous, leaf-stalk climber with small tubers. H to 4ft (1.2m). Leaves, to 2in (5cm) across, have 5 narrow lobes. Small, purple-blue flowers with notched petals open in late summer. Z11–12 H12–1.

T. canariense. See *T. peregrinum.*

T. **'Empress of India'.** Fast-growing, bushy annual. H 12in (24cm), S 18in (45cm). Has rounded, purple-green leaves. Trumpet-shaped, spurred, semi-double, rich scarlet flowers, 2in (5cm) wide, are borne from early summer to early autumn. Z11–12 H12–1.

T. **Gleam Series.** Fast-growing, semi-trailing annual. H 16in (40cm), S 24in (60cm). Have rounded, midgreen leaves. From early summer to early autumn, bears trumpet-shaped, spurred, semi-double flowers, 2in (5cm) wide, in single colors or in a mixture that includes scarlet, yellow, and orange and pastel shades. Z11–12 H12–1.

T. **Jewel Series** illus. p.341.

T. majus. Fast growing, bushy annual. H 3–10ft (1–3m), S 5–15ft (1.5–5m). Has rounded to kidney-shaped, wavy-margined, pale green leaves. From summer to autumn bears long-spurred red, orange, or yellow flowers, 2–2½in

(5–6cm) wide. Many cultivars often attributed to *T. majus* (and with similar characteristics to that species) are of hybrid origin. They are described in this book under their cultivar names. Z11–12 H12–1.
***T.* 'Peach Melba'.** Fast-growing, bushy annual. H to 18in (45cm), S 12in (30cm). Bears rounded, midgreen leaves. Trumpet-shaped, spurred, pale yellow flowers, 2in (5cm) wide and blotched with scarlet, are produced from early summer to early autumn. Z11–12 H12–1.
T. peregrinum, syn. *T. canariense* (Canary creeper). Herbaceous, leaf-stalk climber. H to 6ft (2m). Gray-green leaves have 5 broad lobes. Small, bright yellow flowers, the 2 upper petals much larger and fringed, are borne from summer until first frosts. In cold areas is grown as an annual. Z11–12 H12–1.
T. polyphyllum illus. p.293.
T. speciosum illus. p.210.
T. tricolor. See *T. tricolorum*.
T. tricolorum, syn. *T. tricolor*, illus. p.205.
T. tuberosum illus. p.218. var. ***lineamaculatum* 'Ken Aslet'** illus. p.216.
***T.* Whirlybird Series'.** Fast-growing, bushy annual. H 10in (25cm), S 14in (35cm). Have rounded, midgreen leaves. Trumpet-shaped, spurred, single to semi-double flowers, 2in (5cm) wide, are borne in a mixture or in single colors from early summer to early autumn. Z11–12 H12–1.

TSUGA

PINACEAE

See also CONIFERS.
T. canadensis illus. p.107. **'Aurea'** (illus. p.111) is a broadly conical conifer, often with several stems. H 15ft (5m) or more, S 6–10ft (2–3m). Shoots are gray with spirally arranged, needlelike, flattened leaves, golden yellow when young, ageing to green in second year, those along top inverted to show silver bands. Has ovoid, light brown cones. **'Bennett'**, H 3–6ft (1–2m), S 6ft (2m), is a compact, dwarf form with arching branches and a nest-shaped, central depression. **'Pendula'** (syn. *T.c. f. pendula)* has weeping branches that may be trained to create a domed mound, H and S 10–15ft (3–5m), or left to spread at ground level, H 20in (50cm), S 6–15ft (2–5m). All Z4–8 H8–1.
T. caroliniana (Carolina hemlock). Conifer with a conical or ovoid crown. H 30–50ft (10–15m), S 15–25ft (5–8m). Red-brown shoots produce spirally set, needlelike, flattened, glossy, dark green leaves. Bears ovoid green cones, ripening to brown. Z3–8 H7–3.
T. diversifolia (Japanese hemlock, Northern Japanese hemlock). Conifer with a broad, dense crown. H 30–50ft (10–15m), S 25–40ft (8–12m). Has orange shoots and needlelike, flattened, glossy, deep green leaves, banded with white beneath, that are spirally set. Ovoid cones are dark brown. Z6–8 H8–6.
T. heterophylla (Western hemlock). Vigorous, conical conifer with drooping branchlets. H 70–100ft (20–30m), S 25–30ft (8–10m). Gray shoots bear spirally set, needlelike, flattened, dark green leaves with silvery bands beneath. Bears ovoid, pale green cones that ripen to dark brown. Z6–8 H8–6.
T. mertensiana (Mountain hemlock). Narrowly conical conifer with short, horizontal branches. H 25–50ft (8–15m), S 10–20ft (3–6m). Red-brown shoots bear needlelike, flattened, glaucous blue-green or gray-green leaves, spirally arranged. Cones are cylindrical and yellow-green to purple, ripening to dark brown. Z6–8 H8–6. **'Glauca'** illus. p.105.
T. sieboldii (Japanese hemlock, Southern Japanese hemlock). Broadly conical conifer. H 50ft (15m), S 25–30ft (8–10m). Has glossy buff shoots that bear needlelike, flattened, lustrous, dark green leaves, set spirally. Cones are ovoid and dark brown. Z6–8 H8–6.

TSUSIOPHYLLUM

ERICACEAE

Genus of one species of semi-evergreen shrub grown for its flowers. Suitable for rock gardens. Requires shade and well-drained, peaty, sandy soil. Propagate by softwood cuttings in spring or early summer or by seed in autumn or spring.
T. tanakae. Semi-evergreen, spreading shrub. H 6in (15cm) or more, S 10in (25cm). Twiggy, branched stems bear tiny, narrowly oval, hairy leaves. In early summer produces small, tubular white or pinkish white flowers at stem tips. Z6–8 H8–6.

TUBERARIA

CISTACEAE

Genus of annuals. Grow in sun and in any very well-drained soil. Propagate by seed in spring.
T. guttata, syn. *Helianthemum guttatum*. Moderately fast-growing, upright, branching annual. H and S 4–12in (10–30cm). Has lance-shaped, hairy, midgreen leaves and, in summer, yellow flowers, sometimes red-spotted at base of petals, that look like small, single roses. H9–1.

TULBAGHIA

ALLIACEAE/LILIACEAE

Genus of semi-evergreen perennials. Needs full sun and well-drained soil. Propagate by division or seed in spring.
T. natalensis. Semi-evergreen, clump-forming perennial. H 5in (12cm), S 4in (10cm). In midsummer, umbels of delicately fragrant, tubular, yellow-centered white flowers with spreading petal lobes open above fine, grasslike, midgreen foliage. Z7–9 H9–7.
T. violacea illus. p.283.

TULIPA

Tulip

LILIACEAE

Genus of mainly spring-flowering bulbs grown for their bright, upward-facing flowers. Each bulb bears a few linear to lance-shaped, green or gray-green leaves on the stem. Flowers bear 6 usually pointed petals (botanically known as perianth segments) and 6 stamens, singly, unless otherwise stated below. Each plant has a spread of up to 8in (20cm). Requires a sunny position with well-drained soil and appreciates a summer baking; in cool, wet areas, bulbs may be lifted when the leaves have died down, then stored in a dry place for replanting in autumn. Propagate by division of bulbs in autumn or for species by seed in spring or autumn. If ingested, all parts may cause mild stomach upset, and contact with any part may aggravate skin allergies.

Tulips grow well in Z3–8 H8–1.

Horticulturally, tulips are grouped into the following divisions. See also feature panel pp.410–12.

Div.1 Single early – has cup-shaped, single flowers, often opening wide in sun, from early to midspring.
Div.2 Double early – double flowers open wide, appear in early and mid-spring, and are long-lasting.
Div.3 Triumph – sturdy stems bear rather conical, single flowers, opening to a more rounded shape, in mid- and late spring.
Div.4 Darwin hybrids – large, single flowers of variable shape are borne on strong stems from mid- to late spring.
Div.5 Single late – single flowers, variable in shape but often ovoid or squarish and usually with pointed petals, appear in late spring and very early summer.
Div.6 Lily-flowered – strong stems bear narrow-waisted, single flowers, with long, pointed petals often reflexed at tips, in late spring.
Div.7 Fringed – flowers are similar to those in Div.6 but have fringed petals.
Div.8 Viridiflora – variably shaped, single flowers, with partly greenish petals, are borne in late spring.
Div.9 Rembrandt – consists mostly ofvery old cultivars, similar to Div.6, but has colors "broken" into striped or feathered patterns owing to virus. Flowers in late spring.
Div.10 Parrot – large, single flowers of variable shape, with petals frilled or fringed and usually twisted, appear in late spring.
Div.11 Double late (peony-flowered) – double flowers are usually bowl-shaped and appear in late spring.
Div.12 Kaufmanniana hybrids – single flowers are usually bicolored, open flat in sun, and are borne in early spring. Leaves are usually mottled or striped.
Div.13 Fosteriana hybrids – has large, single flowers that open wide in sun from early to midspring. Leaves are often mottled or striped.
Div.14 Greigii hybrids – large, single flowers appear in mid- and late spring. Leaves are generally wavy-edged and always mottled or striped.
Div.15 Miscellaneous – a miscellaneous category of other species and their varieties and hybrids. Flowers appear in spring and early summer.

T. acuminata (Horned tulip; illus. p.411). Div.15. Midspring-flowering bulb. H 12–18in (30–45cm). Flowers are 3–5in (7–13cm) long, with long-pointed, tapered, pale red or yellow petals, often tinged with red or green outside.
***T.* 'Ad Rem'** (illus. p.411). Div.4. Mid- to late spring-flowering bulb. H 24in (60cm). Flowers are scarlet with black bases and yellow edges. Anthers are yellow.
T. aitchisonii. See *T. clusiana*.
***T.* 'Ancilla'**, Div.12. Early spring-flowering bulb. H 6in (15cm). Flowers are pink and reddish outside, white inside, each with a central, red ring.
***T.* 'Angélique'** (illus. p.410), Div.11. Late spring-flowering bulb. H 16in (40cm). Delicately scented, double, pale pink flowers deepen with age. Each petal has paler streaks and a lighter edge. Is good for bedding.
***T.* 'Apeldoorn's Elite'** (illus. p.411), Div.4. Mid- to late spring-flowering bulb. H 24in (60cm). Has buttercup yellow flowers feathered with cherry red and with yellowish green bases.
***T.* 'Apricot Beauty'** (illus. p.412), Div.1. Early spring-flowering bulb. H 16in (40cm). Flowers are salmon-pink faintly tinged with red.
***T.* 'Artist'** (illus. p.412), Div.8. Late spring-flowering bulb. H 18in (45cm). Flowers are salmon-pink and purple outside, sometimes marked with green, and deep salmon-pink and green inside.
***T.* 'Attila'** (illus. p.411), Div.3. Mid-spring-flowering bulb. H 16in (40cm). Strong stems carry long-lasting pink flowers. Is good for bedding.
T. aucheriana, Div.15. Early spring-flowering bulb. H to 8in (20cm). Has gray-green leaves. Yellow-centered pink flowers, ¾–2in (2–5cm) long, each tapered at the base, have oval petals.
T. australis. See *T. sylvestris*.
T. bakeri. See *T. saxatilis*.
***T.* 'Balalaika'** (illus. p.411), Div.5. Late spring-flowering bulb. H 20in (50cm). Bright red flowers each have a yellow base and black stamens.
***T.* 'Ballade'** (illus. p.410), Div.6. Late spring-flowering bulb. H 20in (50cm). Reddish magenta flowers with a white-edged yellow base have long petals that are edged with white.
T. batalinii (illus. p.412), Div.15. Early spring-flowering bulb. H 4–12in (10–30cm). Is often included under *T. linifolia*. Leaves are gray-green. Flowers, ¾–2½in (2–6cm) long, have broadly oval petals and are bowl-shaped at the base. Pale yellow petals are darker yellow or brown at bases

inside. Several cultivars are hybrids between *T. batalinii* and *T. linifolia*. These include **'Apricot Jewel'** with flowers that are orange-red outside, yellow inside; **'Bright Gem'**, which has yellow flowers flushed with orange; and **'Bronze Charm'**, which bears yellow flowers with bronze feathering.

***T.* 'Bellona'** (illus. p.412), Div.1. Early spring-flowering bulb. H 12in (30cm). Fragrant flowers are deep golden yellow. Is good for bedding and forcing.

T. biflora, syn. *T. polychroma* (illus. p.410), Div.15. Early spring-flowering bulb. H 2–4in (5–10cm). Has gray-green leaves. Stem bears 1–5 fragrant, yellow-centered white flowers, ⅝–1½in (1.5–3.5cm) long and tapered at the bases. Narrowly oval petals are flushed outside with greenish gray or greenish pink. Good in a rock garden.

***T.* 'Bing Crosby'** (illus. p.411), Div.3. Mid- to late spring-flowering bulb. H 20in (50cm). Has glowing scarlet flowers.

***T.* 'Bird of Paradise'** (illus. p.411), Div.10. Late spring-flowering bulb. H 18in (45cm). Produces cardinal red flowers that are edged with orange and have bright yellow bases. Anthers are purple.

***T.* 'Blue Parrot'** (illus. p.412), Div.10. Late spring-flowering bulb. H 24in (60cm). Very large, bright violet flowers, sometimes bronze outside, are borne on strong stems.

***T.* 'Burgundy Lace'**, Div.7. Late spring-flowering bulb. H 24in (60cm). Flowers are wine red, each petal with a fringed edge.

***T.* 'Candela'** (illus. p.412), Div.13. Early to midspring-flowering bulb. H 12in (30cm). Large flowers are yellow with black anthers, and long-lasting.

***T.* 'Cape Cod'** (illus. p.412), Div.14. Mid- to late spring-flowering bulb. H 18in (45cm). Gray-green leaves have reddish stripes. Yellowish bronze flowers each have a black-and-red base; petals are edged with yellow outside.

***T.* 'Carnaval de Nice'** (illus. p.410), Div.11. Late spring-flowering bulb. H 16in (40cm). Double flowers are white, feathered with deep red.

***T.* 'China Pink'** (illus. p.410), Div.6. Late spring-flowering bulb. H 22in (55cm). Flowers are pink, each with a white base, and have slightly reflexed petals.

***T.* 'Chopin'**, Div.12. Early spring-flowering bulb. H 8in (20cm). Has brown- mottled, gray-green leaves. Lemon yellow flowers have black bases.

T. chrysantha. See *Tulipa clusiana* var. *chrysantha*.

***T.* 'Clara Butt'**, Div.5. Late spring-flowering bulb. H 24in (60cm). Flowers are salmon-pink. Is particularly good for bedding.

T. clusiana, syn. *T. aitchisonii* (Lady tulip; illus. p.411), Div.15. Midspring-flowering bulb. H to 12in (30cm). Has gray-green leaves. Each stem bears 1 or 2 flowers, ¾–2½in (2–6.5cm) long, that are bowl-shaped at the base. Narrowly oval white petals are purple or crimson at base inside, striped deep pink outside. Stamens are purple. Flowers of var. ***chrysantha*** (syn. *T. chrysantha*; illus. p.412) are yellow, flushed red or brown outside, with yellow stamens, var. ***stellata*** has white flowers with yellow bases and yellow stamens.

***T.* 'Couleur Cardinal'.** Div.3. Mid-spring-flowering bulb. H 14in (35cm). Plum-purple flowers are dark crimson-scarlet inside.

T. dasystemon of gardens. See *T. tarda*.

***T.* 'Dawnglow'**, Div.4. Mid- to late-spring-flowering bulb. H 24in (60cm). Pale apricot flowers are flushed with deep pink outside and are deep yellow inside. Has purple anthers.

***T.* 'Diana'** (illus. p.410), Div.1. Early spring-flowering bulb. H 11in (28cm). Large, pure white flowers are carried on strong stems.

***T.* 'Dillenburg'** (illus. p.412), Div.5. Late spring-flowering bulb. H 26in (65cm). Flowers are brick-orange and are good for bedding.

***T.* 'Don Quichotte'** (illus. p.410), Div.3. Midspring-flowering bulb. H 16in (40cm). Purple-pink flowers are long-lasting.

***T.* 'Dreamboat'** (illus. p.412), Div.14. Mid- to late spring-flowering bulb. H 10in (25cm). Produces gray-green leaves with brown stripes. Urn-shaped, red-tinged, amber-yellow flowers have greenish bronze bases with red blotches.

***T.* 'Dreaming Maid'** (illus. p.412), Div.3. Mid- to late spring-flowering bulb. H 22in (55cm). Flowers have violet petals edged with white.

***T.* 'Dreamland'** (illus. p.411), Div.5. Late spring-flowering bulb. H 24in (60cm). Flowers are red with white bases and yellow anthers.

T. eichleri. See *T. undulatifolia*.

***T.* 'Estella Rijnveld'** (illus. p.411), Div.10. Late spring-flowering bulb. H 24in (60cm). Large flowers are red, streaked with white and green.

***T.* 'Fancy Frills'** (illus. p.410), Div.10. Late spring-flowering bulb. H 20in (50cm). Fringed, ivory-white petals are striped and edged with pink outside; inside, base is rose-pink. Anthers are pale yellow.

T. fosteriana, Div.15. Early spring-flowering bulb. H 8–18in (20–45cm). Has a downy stem and gray-green leaves, downy above. Flowers 1¾–4in (4.5–10cm) long, are bowl-shaped at the base with narrowly oval, bright red petals, and each has a purplish black center inside, ringed with yellow.

***T.* 'Fringed Beauty'** (illus. p.411), Div.7. Early to midspring-flowering bulb. H 13in (32cm). Fringed petals are bright red with yellow edges. Is excellent for forcing.

***T.* 'Fringed Elegance'**, Div.7. Late spring-flowering bulb. H 20in (50cm). Has pale yellow flowers dotted with pink outside; inside, bases have bronze-green blotches. Each petal has a yellow fringe. Anthers are purple.

***T.* 'Gala Beauty'**, Div.9. Late spring-flowering bulb. H 24in (60cm). Yellow flowers are streaked with crimson.

***T.* 'Garden Party'** (illus. p.411), Div.3. Mid- to late spring-flowering bulb. H 16–18in (40–45cm). Produces white flowers; petals are edged with deep pink outside and inside are streaked with deep pink.

***T.* 'Glück'** (illus. p.411), Div.12. Early spring-flowering bulb. H 6in (15cm). Has reddish brown-mottled, gray-green leaves. Petals are red edged with yellow outside, and yellow inside, each with a darker base.

***T.* 'Golden Apeldoorn'**(illus. p.412) , Div.4. Mid- to late spring-flowering bulb. H 50–60cm (20–24in). Golden yellow flowers each have a black base and black stamens.

***T.* 'Golden Artist'** (illus. p.412), Div.8. Late spring-flowering bulb. H 18in (45cm). Flowers are bright golden yellow.

***T.* 'Gordon Cooper'** (illus. p.411), Div.4. Mid- to late spring-flowering bulb. H 24in (60cm). Petals are deep pink outside, edged with red; inside they are red with blue-and-yellow bases. Has black anthers.

***T.* 'Greenland'.** See *T.* 'Groenland'.

T. greigii, Div.15. Early spring-flowering bulb. H 8–18in (20–45cm). Has downy stems. Leaves are streaked or mottled with red or purple. Cup-shaped flowers, 1¼–4in (3–10cm) long, with broadly oval red or yellow petals, have yellow-ringed black centers.

***T.* 'Greuze'** (illus. p.412), Div.5. Late spring-flowering bulb. H 26in (65cm). Flowers are dark violet-purple and are good for bedding.

***T.* 'Groenland'**, syn. *T.* 'Greenland' (illus. p.410), Div.8. Late spring-flowering bulb. H 20in (50cm). Bears flowers with green petals that are edged with rose-pink. Is a good bedding tulip.

T. hageri (illus. p.411), Div.15. Mid-spring-flowering bulb. H 4–12in (10–30cm). Stem has 1–4 flowers, 1½–2½in (3–6cm) long, tapered at the base and with oval, dull red petals tinged with green outside.

***T.* 'Heart's Delight'**, Div.12. Early spring-flowering bulb. H 8–10in (20–25cm). Has green leaves striped red-brown. Bears deep pinkish red flowers edged with pale pink, and pale pink inside with red-blotched yellow bases.

***T.* 'Hollywood'**, Div.8. Late spring-flowering bulb. H 12in (30cm). Red flowers, tinged and streaked with green, have yellow bases. Is good for bedding.

T. humilis (illus. p.412), Div.15. Early spring-flowering bulb. A variable species, often considered to include *T. aucheriana*, *T. pulchella,* and *T. violacea*. H to 8in (20cm). Has gray-green leaves. Stem bears usually 1, sometimes 2 or 3 pinkish magenta flowers, ¾–2in (2–5cm) long, tapered at the base and with a yellow center inside. Petals are oval. Is suitable for a rock garden.

***T.* 'Jack Laan'**, Div.9. Late spring-flowering bulb. H 24in (60cm). Purple flowers are shaded with brown and feathered with white and yellow.

***T.* 'Juan'** (illus. p.411), Div.13. Early to midspring-flowering bulb. H 14in (35cm). Flowers are deep orange overlaid with scarlet. Leaves are marked with reddish brown.

T. kaufmanniana (Waterlily tulip; illus. p.412), Div.15. Early spring-flowering bulb. H 4–14in (10–35cm). Leaves are gray-green. Stem has 1–5 often scented flowers, 1½–4in (3–10cm) long and bowl-shaped at the base. Narrowly oval petals are usually either cream or yellow, flushed with pink or gray-green outside; centers are often a different color. Pink, orange, or red forms occasionally occur.

***T.* 'Keizerskroon'** (illus. p.411), Div.1. Early spring-flowering bulb. H 14in (35cm). Flowers have crimson-scarlet petals with broad, bright yellow margins. Is a good, reliable bedding tulip.

***T.* 'Kingsblood'** (illus. p.411), Div.5. Late spring-flowering bulb. H 24in (60cm). Cherry red flowers are edged with scarlet.

T. linifolia (illus. p.411), Div.15. Early spring-flowering bulb. H 4–12in (10–30cm). A variable species, often considered to include *T. batalinii* and *T. maximowiczii*. Has gray-green leaves. Red flowers, ¾–2½in (2–6cm) long, are bowl-shaped at the base and inside have blackish purple centers that are usually ringed with cream or yellow. Petals are broadly oval.

***T.* 'Lustige Witwe'**, syn. *T.* 'Merry Widow'(illus. p.411), Div.3. Mid- to late spring-flowering bulb. Flowers have deep glowing red petals edged with white.

***T.* 'Madame Lefèber'**, syn. *T.* 'Red Emperor' (illus. p.411), Div.13. Early to midspring-flowering bulb. H 14–16in (35–40cm). Produces very large, brilliant red flowers.

***T.* 'Maja'** (illus. p.412), Div.7. Late spring-flowering bulb. H 20in (50cm). Produces egg-shaped, pale yellow flowers with fringed petals that are bronze-yellow at the base. Anthers are yellow.

***T.* 'Margot Fonteyn'** (illus. p.411), Div.3. Mid- to late spring-flowering bulb. H 16–18in (40–45cm). Flowers have yellow-edged, bright red petals, each with a yellow base inside. Anthers are black.

T. marjollettii (illus. p.411), Div.15. Midspring-flowering bulb. H 16–20in (40–50cm). Produces flowers, 1½–2½in (4–6cm) long and bowl-shaped at the base, with broadly oval, creamy white petals edged and marked with deep pink.

T. maximowiczii, Div.15. Early spring-flowering bulb. H 4–12in (10–30cm). Has gray-green leaves. Bright red flowers, ¾–2½in (2–6cm) long, with broadly oval petals, have white-bordered black centers and are bowl-shaped at the base.

***T.* 'Menton'** (illus. p.410), Div.5. Late spring-flowering bulb. H 24in (60cm). Flowers have rose-pink petals that are edged with light orange, and bright yellow and white bases. Anthers are yellow.

***T.* 'Merry Widow'.** See *T.* 'Lustige Witwe'.

***T.* 'Monte Carlo'**, Div.2. Early spring-flowering bulb. H 16in (40cm). Has double yellow flowers with sparse red streaks.
***T.* 'New Design'** (illus. p.410), Div.3. Midspring-flowering bulb. H 16in (40cm). Flowers have yellow petals that fade to pinkish white and are edged with red outside and marked with apricot inside. Leaves have pinkish white margins.
***T.* 'Orange Emperor'**, Div.13. Early to midspring-flowering bulb. H 16in (40cm). Flowers are bright orange, each with a yellow base inside, and have black anthers.
***T.* 'Orange Triumph'**, Div.11. Late spring-flowering bulb. H 20in (50cm). Has double, soft orange-red flowers flushed with brown; each petal has a yellow margin.
***T.* 'Oranje Nassau'** (illus. p.411), Div.2. Early spring-flowering bulb. H 10–12in (25–30cm). Has double, blood red flowers flushed fiery orange-red. Is good for forcing.
***T.* 'Oratorio'**, Div.14. Mid- to late spring-flowering bulb. H 8in (20cm). Has reddish brown-mottled, gray-green leaves. Broadly urn-shaped flowers are rose-pink outside, apricot-pink inside with black bases.
T. orphanidea (illus. p.412), Div.15. Midspring-flowering bulb. H 4–12in (10–30cm). Green leaves often have reddish margins. Stem has 1–4 flowers, 1¼–2½in (3–6cm) long and tapered at the base. Oval petals are orange-brown, tinged outside with green and often purple.
***T.* 'Page Polka'** (illus. p.410), Div.3. Midspring-flowering bulb. Large, deep red flowers have white bases and are striped with white. Anthers are yellow.
***T.* 'Palestrina'**, Div.5. Late spring-flowering bulb. H 18in (45cm). Petals of large, salmon-pink flowers are green outside.
***T.* 'Peach Blossom'**, Div.2. Early spring-flowering bulb. H 10–12in (25–30cm). Produces double, silvery pink flowers flushed with deep pink.
***T.* 'Peer Gynt'** (illus. p.411), Div.3. Mid- to late spring-flowering bulb. H 20in (50cm). Flowers have fuchsia-red petals with purple edges and white bases spotted with yellow. Anthers are purplish gray.
***T.* 'Plaisir'** (illus. p.411), Div.14. Mid to late spring-flowering bulb. H 6–8in (15–20cm). Has gray-green leaves mottled with red-brown. Bears broadly urn-shaped, deep pinkish red flowers with petals edged pale yellow and with black-and-yellow bases.
T. polychroma. See *T. biflora*.
***T. praestans* 'Fusilier'**, Div.15. Early spring-flowering bulb. H 4–18in (10–45cm). Has a minutely downy stem and downy, gray-green leaves. Stem bears 3–5 flowers that are 2¼–2½in (5.5–6.5cm) long and bowl-shaped at the base. Oval petals are orange-scarlet. **'Unicum'** (illus. p.411) has leaves that are edged with pale yellow. Flowers have bright red petals with yellow bases and blue-black anthers. **'Van Tubergen's Variety'** (illus. p.412) produces 2–5 flowers per stem that are often yellow at the base; it increases very freely.
***T.* 'Prinses Irene'** (illus. p.412), Div.1. Early spring-flowering bulb. H 12–14in (30–35cm). Produces orange flowers streaked with purple.
T. pulchella, Div.15. Early spring-flowering bulb. H to 8in (20cm). Has gray-green leaves. Flowers, ¾–2in (2–5cm) long and tapered at the base, have oval purple petals and yellow or bluish black centers inside. Is useful for a rock garden.
***T.* 'Purissima'**, syn. *T.* 'White Emperor' (illus. p.410), Div.13. Early to midspring-flowering bulb. H 14–16in (35–40cm). Flowers are pure white.
***T.* 'Queen of Night'** (illus. p.412), Div.5. Late spring-flowering bulb. H 24in (60cm). The darkest of all tulips has long-lasting, very dark maroon-black flowers on sturdy stems. Useful for bedding.
***T.* 'Red Emperor'.** See *T.* 'Madame Lefèber'.
***T.* 'Red Parrot'** (illus. p.411), Div.10. Late spring-flowering bulb. H 24in (60cm). Large, raspberry red flowers are carried on strong stems.
***T.* 'Red Riding Hood'** (illus. p.411), Div.14. Late spring-flowering bulb. H 8in (20cm). Produces vivid, black-based scarlet flowers amid spreading, dark green leaves that are mottled brownish purple.
T. saxatilis, syn. *T. bakeri* (illus. p.410), Div.15. Early spring-flowering bulb. H 6–18in (15–45cm). Has shiny green leaves. Stem produces 1–4 scented flowers, 1½–2¼in (4–5.5cm) long and tapered at the base. Oval pink to lilac petals are yellow at the base inside.
***T.* 'Shakespeare'** (illus. p.412), Div.12. Early spring-flowering bulb. H 5–6in (12–15cm). Petals are deep red, edged with salmon outside, and salmon flushed red with a yellow base inside.
T. sprengeri (illus. p.411), Div.15. Late spring- and early summer-flowering bulb. H 12–18in (30–45cm). Flowers are 1¾–2½in (4.5–6.5cm) long and tapered at the base. Bears narrowly oval, orange-red petals, the outer 3 with buff-yellow backs. Is the latest-flowering tulip. Increases very rapidly.
***T.* 'Spring Green'** (illus. p.410), Div.8. Late spring-flowering bulb. H 14–15in (35–38cm). Has white flowers feathered with green. Anthers are pale green.
T. sylvestris, syn. *T. australis* (illus. p.412), Div.15. Early spring-flowering bulb. H 4–18in (10–45cm). Yellow flowers, usually borne singly, are 1½–2½in (3.5–6.5cm) long and tapered at the base. Narrowly oval petals are often tinged with green outside.
T. tarda, syn. *T. dasystemon* of gardens (illus. p.412), Div.15. Early spring-flowering bulb. H to 6in (15cm). Has glossy, green leaves. Flowers, 4–6 per stem, are 1¼–1½in (3–4cm) long and tapered at the base. Oval white petals have yellow lower halves inside and are tinged with green and sometimes red outside. Good in a rock garden or raised bed.
***T.* 'Toronto'**, Div.14. Mid- to late spring-flowering bulb. H 12in (30cm). Has mottled leaves and 2 or 3 long-lasting flowers per stem. Open, broadly cup-shaped flowers have pointed, bright red petals each with a brownish green-yellow base inside. Anthers are bronze.
T. turkestanica (illus. p.410), Div.15. Early spring-flowering bulb. H 4–12in (10–30cm). Has a hairy stem and gray-green leaves. Unpleasant-smelling flowers, up to 12 per stem, are ⅝–1½in (1.5–3.5cm) long and tapered at the base. Oval white petals are flushed green or pink outside; flowers have yellow or orange centers inside.
***T.* 'Uncle Tom'** (illus. p.411), Div.11. Late spring-flowering bulb. H 20in (50cm). Double flowers are maroon.
T. undulatifolia, syn. *T. eichleri* (illus. p.411), Div.15. Early to midspring-flowering bulb. H 6–20in (15–50cm). Has a downy stem and gray-green leaves. Flowers, 1¼–3in (3–8cm) long, are bowl-shaped at the base. Narrowly oval red or orange-red petals each have a pale red or buff back and a yellow-bordered, dark green or black blotch at the base inside.
***T.* 'Union Jack'** (illus. p.411), Div.5. Late spring-flowering bulb. H 24in (60cm). Ivory-white petals, marked with deep pinkish red flames, have blue-edged white bases.
T. urumiensis (illus. p.412), Div.15. Early spring-flowering bulb. H 10–20cm (4–8in). Stem is mostly below soil level. Leaves are green or grayish green. Bears 1 or 2 flowers, each 1½in (4cm) long and tapered at the base. Narrowly oval yellow petals are flushed mauve or red-brown outside. Is useful for a rock garden.
T. violacea (illus. p.412), Div.15. Early spring-flowering bulb. H to 8in (20cm). Has gray-green leaves. Violet-pink flowers, ¾–2in (2–5cm) long, are tapered at the base and have yellow or bluish black centers inside. Petals are oval. Good in a rock garden or raised bed.
***T.* 'West Point'** (illus. p.412), Div.6. Late spring-flowering bulb. H 20in (50cm). Primrose yellow flowers have long-pointed, recurved petals.
***T.* 'White Dream'** (illus. p.410), Div.3. Mid- to late spring-flowering bulb. H 16–18in (40–45cm). Flowers are white with yellow anthers.
***T.* 'White Emperor'.** See *T.* 'Purissima'.
***T.* 'White Parrot'** (illus. p.410), Div.10. Late spring-flowering bulb. H 22in (55cm). Large flowers have ruffled white petals flecked green near the base. Is good for cutting.
***T.* 'White Triumphator'** (illus. p.410), Div.6. Late spring-flowering bulb. H 26–28in (65–70cm). White flowers have elegantly reflexed petals.
T. whittallii (illus. p.412), Div.15. Mid-spring-flowering bulb. H 12–14in (30–35cm). Stem produces 1–4 flowers, 1¼–2½in (3–6cm) long and tapered at the base. Oval petals are bright brownish orange.
***T.* 'Yokohama'** (illus. p.412), Div.1. Early to midspring-flowering bulb. H 14in (35cm). Pointed flowers are deep yellow.

Tunica saxifraga. See *Petrorhagia saxifraga*.

TURRAEA

MELIACEAE

Genus of evergreen trees and shrubs grown for their flowers and foliage. Prefers full sun. Needs fertile, well-drained soil. Water freely in full growth, less at other times. Young plants may need growing point removed to promote branching. Prune after flowering if necessary. Propagate by seed in spring or by semi-ripe cuttings in summer.
T. obtusifolia illus. p.172.

TWEEDIA

ASCLEPIADACEAE

Genus of herbaceous, twining climbers; only one species is in general cultivation. In cool climates may be grown as an annual. Grow in sun and in well-drained soil. Pinch out tips of shoots to encourage branching. Propagate by seed in spring.
T. caerulea, syn. *Oxypetalum caeruleum*, illus. p.215

TYLECODON

CRASSULACEAE

Genus of deciduous, bushy, winter-growing, succulent shrubs with very swollen stems. Likes sun and very well-drained soil. Propagate by seed or stem cuttings in summer. The leaves of *T. papillaris* subsp. *wallichii* are highly toxic if ingested.
T. paniculatus, syn. *Cotyledon paniculata* (Butter tree). Deciduous, bushy, succulent shrub. H and S 6ft (2m). Swollen stem and branches have papery yellow coverings. Leaves are oblong to oval, fleshy, and bright green. In summer produces clusters of tubular, green-striped red flowers at stem tips. Z12–15 H12–10.
T. papillaris* subsp. *wallichii, syn. *T. wallichii*, *Cotyledon wallichii*. Deciduous, bushy, succulent shrub. H and S 1ft (30cm). Has 1¼in (3cm) thick stems with cylindrical, grooved-topped, green leaves at tips. After leaf fall, stems are neatly covered in raised leaf bases. Bears tubular, yellow-green flowers, ¾in (2cm) long, in autumn. Z12–15 H12–10.
T. reticulatus, syn. *Cotyledon reticulata*, illus. p.465.
T. wallichii. See *T. papillaris* subsp. *wallichii*.

TYPHA

TYPHACEAE

Genus of deciduous, perennial, marginal water plants grown for their decorative, cylindrical seed heads. Grows in sun or shade. Propagate in

spring by seed or division.
T. latifolia illus. p.448. **'Variegata'** is a deciduous, perennial marginal water plant. H 3–4ft (90cm–1.2m), S indefinite. Strap-shaped, midgreen leaves have longitudinal cream stripes. Spikes of beige flowers in late summer are followed by decorative, cylindrical, dark brown seed heads. Z2–11 H12–1.
T. minima illus. p.449.

U

UGNI

MYRTACEAE

Genus of densely leafy, evergreen shrubs or trees. *U. molinae*, the only species usually cultivated, is valued for its foliage, flowers, and fruit. Needs full sun or partial shade and moist but well-drained soil. Propagate by semi-ripe cuttings in late summer.
U. molinae, syn. *Eugenia ugni*, *Myrtus ugni*. Evergreen, upright, densely branched shrub. H 5ft (1.5m), S 3ft (1m). Glossy, dark green leaves are oval. Has fragrant, slightly nodding, cup-shaped, white/pink-tinted flowers in late spring, then aromatic, edible, spherical, dark red fruits. Z9–10 H10–9.

ULEX

LEGUMINOSAE/PAPILIONACEAE/

Genus of leafless, or almost leafless, shrubs that appear evergreen as a result of their year-round green shoots and spines. Is grown for its flowers in spring. Needs full sun, and prefers poor, well-drained, acidic soil. Trim each year after flowering to maintain compact habit. Straggly old plants may be cut back hard in spring. Propagate by seed in autumn. The seeds may cause mild stomach upset if ingested.
U. europaeus illus. p.157.
'Flore Pleno' is a leafless, or almost leafless, bushy shrub. H 3ft (1m), S 4ft (1.2m). In spring bears masses of fragrant, pealike, double yellow flowers on leafless, dark green shoots. Z6–8 H8–6.

ULMUS

Elm

ULMACEAE

Genus of deciduous or, rarely, semi-evergreen trees and shrubs, often large and stately, grown for their foliage and habit. Inconspicuous flowers appear in spring. Requires full sun and fertile, well-drained soil. Propagate by softwood cuttings in summer or by seed or suckers in autumn. Is susceptible to Dutch elm disease, which is quickly fatal, although *U. parvifolia* and *U. pumila* appear more resistant than other species and hybrids.
U. americana (American elm, White elm). Deciduous, spreading tree. H and S 100ft (30m). Has gray bark and drooping branchlets. Large, oval, dark green leaves are sharply toothed and rough-textured. Z3–9 H9–1.
U. angustifolia. See *U. minor* subsp. *angustifolia*. var. ***cornubiensis*** see *U. minor* 'Cornubiensis'.
***U.* 'Camperdownii'**. See *U. glabra* 'Camperdownii'.
U. carpinifolia. See *U. minor*.
***U.* 'Dicksonii'**. See *U. minor* 'Dicksonii'.
U. glabra (Wych elm). Deciduous, spreading tree. H 100ft (30m), S 80ft (25m). Has broadly oval, toothed, very rough, dark green leaves, often slightly lobed at tips. From mid- to late spring bears clusters of winged green fruits on bare branches. Z3–9 H8–2.
'Camperdownii' (syn. *U.* 'Camperdownii') illus. p.92.
'Exoniensis' (Exeter elm), H 50ft (15m), S 15ft (5m), is narrow with upright branches when young, later becoming more spreading. Z5-7 H7–5.
U. × hollandica (Dutch elm). Vigorous, deciduous tree with a short trunk and spreading to arching branches. H 100ft (30m), S 80ft (25m). Has oval, toothed, glossy, dark green leaves. Is very susceptible to Dutch elm disease.
'Jacqueline Hillier', H and S 6ft (2m), is slow-growing and suitable for hedging. Small leaves, rough-textured and sharply toothed, form 2 rows on each shoot; they persist into early winter.
'Vegeta' (Huntingdon elm), H 120ft (35m), has upright, central branches and pendent, outer shoots. Broadly oval leaves turn yellow in autumn. All Z5–7 H7–5.
U. minor, syn. *U. carpinifolia* (Smooth-leaved elm). Deciduous, spreading tree with arching branches and pendent shoots. H 100ft (30m), S 70ft (20m). Small, oval, toothed, glossy, bright green leaves turn yellow in autumn. subsp. ***angustifolia*** (syn. *U. angustifolia*; Goodyer's elm) has a rounded canopy and elliptic to oval, double-toothed, mid- to dark green leaves, paler beneath. **'Cornubiensis'** (syn. *U. angustifolia* var. *cornubiensis*; Cornish elm), S 50ft (15m), is conical when young and with a vase-shaped head when mature. **'Dicksonii'** (syn. *U.m.* 'Sarniensis Aurea', *U.* 'Dicksonii', *U.* 'Wheatleyi Aurea') illus. p.81.
'Sarniensis' (Jersey elm, Wheatley elm), S 30ft (10m), is a conical, dense tree with upright branches. Small, broadly oval leaves are midgreen.
'Sarniensis Aurea' see *U.m.* 'Dicksonii'. All Z5–8 H8–5.
U. parvifolia (Chinese elm). Deciduous or semi-evergreen, rounded tree. H and S 50ft (15m). Small, oval, glossy, dark green leaves last well into winter or, in mild areas, may persist until fresh growth appears. Z5–9 H9–5.
U. procera (English elm). Vigorous, deciduous, spreading tree with a bushy, dense, dome-shaped head. H 120ft (35m), S 50ft (15m). Broadly oval, toothed, rough, dark green leaves turn yellow in autumn. Z5–8 H8–1.
U. pumila (Siberian elm). Deciduous, spreading, sometimes shrubby tree. H 50ft (15m), S 40ft (12m). Has oval, toothed, dark green leaves. Has some resistance to Dutch elm disease, but seedlings may be susceptible in hot summers. Z3–9 H9–1.
***U.* 'Wheatleyi Aurea'.** See *U. minor* 'Dicksonii'.

UMBELLULARIA

Headache tree

LAURACEAE

Genus of evergreen, spring-flowering trees grown for their aromatic foliage, although the scent of the crushed leaves may induce headaches and nausea in some people. Requires shelter from strong, cold winds when young. Needs sun and fertile, moist but well-drained soil. Propagate by seed in autumn.
U. californica illus. p.74.

Urceolina peruviana. See *Stenomesson miniatum*.

URGINEA

HYACINTHACEAE/LILIACEAE

Genus of late summer- or early autumn-flowering bulbs, growing on or near soil surface, with spear-shaped flower spikes up to 5ft (1.5m) high. Needs sun and well-drained soil that dries out while bulbs are dormant in summer. Plant in mid- to late summer. Water until leaves die down. Propagate by seed in autumn or by offsets in late summer.
U. maritima (Crusaders' spears, Sea onion, Sea squill). Late summer- or early autumn-flowering bulb. H 5ft (1.5m), S 1–1½ft (30–45cm). Broadly sword-shaped, erect, basal leaves appear in autumn after a long spike of star-shaped white flowers, each ½–⅝in (1–1.5cm) across, has developed. Z10-11 H12–10

URSINIA

ASTERACEAE/COMPOSITAE

Genus of annuals, evergreen perennials and subshrubs grown mainly for their flower heads usually in summer, a few species for their foliage. Needs full light and well-drained soil. Water potted plants moderately, less when not in full growth. Requires good ventilation if grown under cover. Propagate by seed or greenwood cuttings in spring. Aphids may attack.
U. anthemoides illus. p.338.
U. chrysanthemoides. Evergreen, bushy perennial. H and S 2ft (60cm) or more. Narrowly oval, feathery, strongly scented green leaves are 2in (5cm) long. Has small, long-stalked, daisylike yellow flower heads, sometimes coppery below, in summer. Z13–15 H12–10.
U. sericea. Evergreen, bushy subshrub. H and S 10–18in (25–45cm). Leaves are cut into an elegant filigree of very slender, silver-haired segments. Daisy-like yellow flower heads, 1½in (4cm) across, in summer. Grown mainly grown for its foliage. Z13-15 H12-10.

UTRICULARIA

LENTIBULARIACEAE

Genus of deciduous or evergreen, perennial, carnivorous water plants with bladderlike, modified leaves that trap and digest insects. Most species in cultivation are free-floating. Some species are suitable only for tropical aquar-iums; those grown in outdoor ponds require full sun. Thin out plants that are overcrowded or become laden with algae. Propagate by division of floating foliage in spring or summer.
U. exoleta. See *U. gibba*.
U. gibba, syn. *U. exoleta*. Deciduous, perennial, free-floating water plant. S 6in (15cm). Slender stems carry finely divided, midgreen leaves on which small bladders develop. Pouched, bright yellow flowers are borne in summer. Is evergreen in very warm water; suitable only for a tropical aquarium. Z12-15 H12-10.
U. vulgaris. Deciduous, perennial, free-floating water plant. S 12in (30cm). Much-divided, bronze-green leaves studded with small bladders are produced on slender stems. Bears pouched, bright yellow flowers in summer. May be grown in a pond or cold-water aquarium. Z12-15 H12-10.

UVULARIA

CONVALLARIACEAE/LILIACEAE

Genus of spring-flowering perennials that thrive in moist woodlands. Requires semi-shade and prefers moist but well-drained, peaty soil. Propagate in early spring, before flowering, by division.
U. grandiflora illus. p.274.
U. perfoliata. Clump-forming perennial. H 18in (45cm), S 12in (30cm). In spring, clusters of pendent, bell-shaped, pale yellow flowers with twisted petals appear on numerous slender stems above stem-clasping, narrowly oval, midgreen leaves. Z4–9 H9–1.

VACCINIUM

ERICACEAE

Genus of deciduous or evergreen subshrubs, shrubs, and trees grown for their foliage, their autumn color (on deciduous species), their flowers, and their fruits, which are often edible. Requires a position in sun or semi-shade and moist but well-drained, peaty or sandy, acidic soil. Propagate by semi-ripe cuttings in summer or by seed in autumn.
V. angustifolium. var. ***laevifolium*** illus. p.172.

V. arctostaphylos (Caucasian whortleberry). Deciduous, upright shrub. H 10ft (3m), S 6ft (2m). Has red-brown young shoots and oval, dark green leaves that mature to red and purple in autumn. Bell-shaped white flowers tinged with red are produced in spreading racemes in early summer, followed by spherical, purplish black fruits. Z6–8 H8–6.
V. corymbosum (Highbush blueberry) illus. p.160. **'Pioneer'** illus. p.173.
V. glaucoalbum illus. p.176.
V. myrtillus (Bilberry, Whortleberry). Deciduous, usually prostrate shrub. H 6in (15cm) or more, S 12in (30cm) or more. Bears small, heart-shaped, leathery, bright green leaves. Produces pendent, bell-shaped, pale pink flowers in early summer; these are followed by edible, round, blue-black fruits. Z5–7 H7–5.
V. nummularia. Evergreen, prostrate shrub. H 4in (10cm), S 8in (20cm). Slender stems covered in red-brown bristles bear oval, wrinkled, bright green leaves with red-brown bristles at their margins. Produces small racemes of bell-shaped white to deep pink flowers at stem tips in early summer, followed by small, round black fruits. Suitable for growing in a rock garden. Needs semi-shade. May also be propagated by division in spring. Z7–9 H9–7.
V. parvifolium illus. p.173.
V. vitis-idaea (Cowberry). Vigorous, evergreen, prostrate shrub, spreading by underground runners. H ¾–10in (2–25cm), S indefinite. Forms hummocks of oval, hard, leathery leaves. Bell-shaped white to pink flowers are borne in nodding racemes from early summer to autumn, followed by bright red fruits in autumn-winter. May also be propagated by division in spring. Z2–6 H6–1. subsp. ***minus*** (syn. *V.v.-i.* 'Minus') illus. p.366.

VALERIANA
Valerian

VALERIANACEAE

Genus of summer-flowering perennials that are suitable for growing in borders and rock gardens. Requires a position in sun and well-drained soil. Propagate by division in autumn, but *V. officinalis* is best propagated by seed in spring.
V. officinalis illus. p.241.
***V. phu* 'Aurea'** illus. p.274.

VALLEA

ELAEOCARPACEAE

Genus of one species of evergreen shrub grown for its overall appearance. Prefers a position in full sun and organic, well-drained soil. Containerized plants should be watered freely during the growing season, moderately at other times. Messy growth may be cut out in early spring. Propagate by seed in spring or by semi-ripe cuttings in summer. Spider mite may be a nuisance.
V. stipularis. Evergreen, erect, then loose and spreading shrub. H and S 6–15ft (2–5m). Leaves are lance-shaped to rounded and lobed, deep green above, gray beneath. Small, cup-shaped flowers, each with 5 deep pink petals that have 3 lobes, are borne in small terminal and lateral clusters in spring-summer. Z9–10 H10–9.

VALLISNERIA

HYDROCHARITACEAE

Genus of evergreen, perennial, submerged water plants grown for their foliage. Is suitable for pools and aquariums. Requires sun or semi-shade and deep, clear water. Remove fading foliage, and thin overcrowded plants as required. Propagate by division in spring or summer.
V. americana, syn. *V. gigantea.* Vigorous, evergreen, perennial, submerged water plant. S indefinite. Quickly grows to form colonies of long, strap-shaped, midgreen leaves. Produces insignificant greenish flowers all year.
V. gigantea. See *V. americana.*
V. spiralis (Eel grass, Tape grass). Vigorous, evergreen, perennial, submerged water plant. S indefinite. Forms a mass of long, strap-shaped, midgreen leaves, but on a smaller scale than *V. americana.* Insignificant greenish flowers are borne year-round.

Vallota speciosa. See *Cyrtanthus elatus.*

VANCOUVERIA

BERBERIDACEAE

Genus of perennials, some of which are evergreen, suitable as a groundcover. Prefers cool, partially shaded positions and moist, peaty soil. Propagate by division in spring.
V. chrysantha. Evergreen, sprawling perennial. H 12in (30cm), S indefinite. Oval, dark green leaves borne on flower stems are divided into rounded diamond-shaped leaflets with thickened, undulating margins. Loose sprays of small, bell-shaped yellow flowers are borne in spring. Z6–8 H8–6.
V. hexandra illus. p.347.

VANDA

See also ORCHIDS.
***V.* Rothschildiana** (illus. p.298). Evergreen, epiphytic orchid for a cool or intermediate greenhouse. H 24in (60cm). Sprays of dark-veined, violet-blue flowers, 4in (10cm) across, are borne twice a year in varying seasons. Has narrowly oval, rigid leaves, 4–5in (10–12cm) long. Grow in a hanging basket and provide good light in summer. Z15 H12-10.

VELLOZIA

VELLOZIACEAE

Genus of evergreen perennials and shrubs grown for their showy flowers. Grow in full sun and moderately fertile, sharply drained soil. Propagate by seed or division in spring.
V. elegans, syn. *Barbacenia elegans, Talbotia elegans.* Evergreen, mat-forming perennial with slightly woody stems. H to 6in (15cm), S 6–12in (15–30cm). Lance-shaped, leathery, dark green leaves, to 8in (20cm) long, each has a V-shaped keel. In late spring bears solitary small, star-shaped white flowers on slender stems above leaves. Z14–15 H12–10.

VELTHEIMIA

HYACINTHACEAE/LILIACEAE

Genus of winter-flowering bulbs with dense spikes of pendent, tubular flowers and rosettes of basal leaves. Requires good light (to keep foliage compact and to develop flower colors fully) and well-drained soil. Plant in autumn with tips above soil surface. Reduce watering in summer. Propagate by seed or offsets in autumn.
V. bracteata, syn. *V. capensis* of gardens, *V. undulata, V. viridifolia,* illus. p.425.
V. capensis, syn. *V. glauca, V. viridifolia* of gardens. Winter-flowering bulb. H 12–18in (30–45cm), S 8–12in (20–30cm). Has a basal rosette of lance-shaped leaves, usually with very wavy edges. Stem produces a dense spike of pink or red flowers, each ¾–1¼in (2–3cm) long. Z12–15 H12-10.
V. capensis of gardens. See *V. bracteata.*
V. glauca. See *V. capensis.*
V. undulata. See *V. bracteata.*
V. viridifolia. See *V. bracteata.*
V. viridifolia of gardens. See *V. capensis.*

x ***Venidioarctotis.*** Reclassified as *Arctotis*, also as *Arctotis* Harlequin Hybrids.

VERATRUM

LILIACEAE/MELANTHIACEAE

Genus of perennials, with poisonous black rhizomes, ideal for woodland gardens. Requires semi-shade and fertile, moist soil. Propagate by division or seed in autumn. All parts are highly toxic if ingested. Contact with the foliage may irritate the skin.
V. album (White false hellebore). Clump-forming perennial. H 6ft (2m), S 2ft (60cm). Basal leaves are pleated, oval, and dark green. Stems bear dense, terminal panicles of saucer-shaped, yellowish white flowers in summer. Z12–15 H12–10.
V. nigrum illus. p.228.

VERBASCUM
Mullein

SCROPHULARIACEAE

Genus of mainly summer-flowering perennials, some of which are semi-evergreen or evergreen, and evergreen biennials and shrubs. Tolerates shade but prefers an open, sunny site and well-drained soil. Propagate species by seed in spring or late summer or by root cuttings in winter, selected forms by root cuttings only. Some species self seed freely.
V. bombyciferum. Evergreen, erect biennial. H 4–6ft (1.2–2m), S 2ft (60cm). Oval leaves and stems are covered with silver hairs. Produces upright racemes densely set with 5-lobed yellow flowers in summer. Z5–9 H9–2.
V. chaixii. Erect perennial, covered with silvery hairs. H 3ft (1m), S 2ft (60cm). Has oval, toothed, rough, nettlelike leaves. Produces slender spires of 5-lobed yellow (sometimes white) flowers with purple stamens in summer. Z5–9 H9–5.
***V.* 'Cotswold Queen'.** Short-lived, rosette-forming perennial. H 3–4ft (1–1.2m), S 1–2ft (30–60cm). Throughout summer, branched racemes of 5-lobed, apricot-buff flowers are borne on stems that arise from oval, midgreen leaves. Z5–9 H9–5.
V. densiflorum, syn. *V. thapsiforme.* Fairly slow-growing, semi-evergreen, upright perennial. H 4–5ft (1.2–1.5m), S 2ft (60cm). Has a rosette of large, oval, crinkled, hairy, midgreen leaves. Hairy stems each produce a bold spike of flattish, 5-lobed yellow flowers in summer. Z5–9 H9–5.
V. dumulosum illus. p.359.
***V.* 'Gainsborough'** illus. p.254.
***V.* 'Letitia'** illus. p.358.
V. lychnitis (White mullein). Slow-growing, evergreen, upright, branching biennial. H 2–3ft (60cm–1m), S 2ft (60cm). Has lance-shaped, dark gray-green leaves. Flattish, 5-lobed white flowers are borne on branching stems in summer. Z5–8 H8–5.
V. nigrum illus. p.256.
V. olympicum illus. p.229.
***V.* 'Pink Domino'.** Short-lived, rosette-forming perennial. H 4ft (1.2m), S 1–2ft (30–60cm). Produces branched racemes of 5-lobed, rose pink flowers throughout summer above oval, midgreen leaves. Z5–9 H9–1.
V. thapsiforme. See *V. densiflorum.*

VERBENA

VERBENACEAE

Genus of summer- and autumn-flowering biennials and perennials, some of which are semi-evergreen. Prefers sun and well-drained soil. Propagate by stem cuttings in late summer or autumn or by seed in autumn or spring.
V. alpina of gardens. See *V.* x *maonettii.*
V. bonariensis, syn. *V. patagonica,* illus. p.228.
V. chamaedrifolia. See *V. peruviana.*
V. chamaedrioides. See *V. peruviana.*
***V.* x *hybrida* Derby Series.** Erect, bushy perennial grown as an annual. H 10in (25cm), S 12in (30cm). Has oval, serrated, mid- to deep green leaves. Clusters of small, tubular, lobed flowers, in a wide color range including red, pink, blue, mauve, and white,

appear in summer and early autumn. Cultivars of **Novalis Series** are erect and bushy, with flowers in rose pink, deep blue, pinkish red, and scarlet, as well as single colors of bright scarlet, white, or rose-pink. **'Peaches and Cream'** is spreading and branching and produces pastel orange-pink flowers, maturing to apricot-yellow and eventually creamy yellow. **Romance Series** cultivars are erect and bushy, and has flowers in deep wine red, intense scarlet, carmine-rose-red, and blue-purple as well as single colors of white, bright scarlet, dark rose, or lavender-pink. All Z9–11 H12–1.
Sandy Series illus. p.328.
'Showtime' illus. p.326.
V.* x *maonettii, syn. *V. alpina* of gardens, *V. tenera* var. *maonetti*. Spreading perennial with a slightly woody base. H 3in (8cm), S 6in (15cm). Has oblong to oval leaves, deeply cut into linear, toothed, mid-green segments and, in summer, terminal clusters of small, tubular, reddish violet flowers with white-edged lobes. Z7–9 H9–7.
V. patagonica. See *V. bonariensis*.
V. peruviana, syn. *V. chamaedrifolia, V. chamaedrioides*. Semi-evergreen, prostrate perennial. H to 3in (8cm), S 3ft (1m). Heads of small, tubular, brilliant scarlet flowers with spreading petal lobes are produced from early summer to early autumn. Oval, toothed leaves are midgreen. Prefers to grow in dry soil that is not too rich. Z9–11 H12–9
V. rigida, syn. *V. venosa*, illus. p.284.
***V.* 'Sissinghurst'** illus. p.282.
V. tenera var. ***maonettii.*** See *V.* x *maonettii*.
V. venosa. See *V. rigida*.

VERONICA

SCROPHULARIACEAE

Genus of perennials and subshrubs, some of which are semi-evergreen or evergreen, grown for their usually blue flowers. Some need sun and well-drained soil, others prefer a moist site in sun or partial shade. Propagate by division in spring or autumn, by softwood or semi-ripe cuttings in summer, or by seed in autumn.
V. austriaca. Mat-forming or upright perennial. H and S 10–20in (25–50cm). Leaves are very variable: from broadly oval to narrowly oblong, and from entire to deeply cut and fernlike. Short, dense or lax racemes of small, saucer-shaped, bright blue flowers appear in early summer. Good in a rock garden or bank. Z4–8 H8–2. subsp. ***teucrium*** (syn. *V. teucrium*) illus. p.358. subsp. ***teucrium* 'Royal Blue'** has deep royal-blue flowers. Propagate by division in spring or by softwood cuttings in summer.
V. cinerea. Spreading, much-branched, woody-based perennial. H 6in (15cm), S 12in (30cm). Has small, linear, occasionally oval, hairy, silvery white leaves. Trailing flower stems bear saucer-shaped, deep blue to purplish blue flowers with white eyes in early summer. Is suitable for a sunny rock garden. Z5–8 H8–5.
V. exaltata. See *V. longifolia*.
V. fruticans (Rock speedwell). Deciduous, upright to procumbent subshrub. H 6in (15cm), S 12in (30cm). Leaves are oval and green. Spikes of saucer-shaped, bright blue flowers, each with a red eye, are borne in summer. Is suitable for a rock garden. Z5–8 H8–5.
V. gentianoides illus. p.287.
V. incana. See *V. spicata* subsp. *incana*.
V. longifolia, syn. *V. exaltata*. Variable, upright perennial. H 3–4ft (1–1.2m), S 1ft (30cm) or more. In late summer and early autumn, long, terminal racemes of star-shaped, lilac-blue flowers are borne on stems clothed with whorls of narrowly oval to lance-shaped, toothed, midgreen leaves. Z4–8 H8–1.
V. pectinata. Dense, mat-forming perennial that is sometimes semi-erect. H and S 8in (20cm). Has small, narrowly oval, hairy leaves and bears loose sprays of saucer-shaped, soft blue to blue-violet flowers in summer. Good for a rock garden or bank. Z2–7 H7–1. **'Rosea'**, H 3in (8cm), has rose-lilac flowers. Z3–7 H7–1.
V. peduncularis illus. p.287.
V. perfoliata. See *Parahebe perfoliata*.
V. prostrata, syn. *V. rupestris*, illus. p.357. **'Kapitan'** and **'Trehane'** illus. p.357. **'Spode Blue'** is a dense, mat-forming perennial. H to 12in (30cm), S indefinite. Upright spikes of small, saucer-shaped, china blue flowers appear in early summer. Leaves are narrowly oval and toothed. Z5–8 H8–5.
V. rupestris. See *V. prostrata*.
V. spicata (Spiked speedwell). Clump-forming perennial. H 12–24in (30–60cm), S 18in (45cm). Spikes of small, star-shaped, bright blue flowers are borne in summer above narrowly oval, toothed, midgreen leaves. Z3–8 H8–1. subsp. ***incana*** (syn. *V. incana*) illus. p.287. **'Romiley Purple'** illus. p.251.
V. teucrium. See *V. austriaca* subsp. *teucrium*.
V. virginica. See *Veronicastrum virginicum*. f. ***alba*** see *Veronicastrum virginicum* f. *album*.

VERONICASTRUM

SCROPHULARIACEAE

Genus of evergreen perennials grown for their elegant leaves and flowers. Requires a position in sun and moist soil. Propagate by division in spring or autumn, by softwood or semi-ripe cuttings in summer, or by seed in autumn.
V. virginicum, syn. *Veronica virginica*. (Culver's root). Upright perennial. H 4ft (1.2m), S 1½ft (45cm). In late summer, racemes of small, star-shaped, purple-blue or pink flowers crown stems clothed with whorls of narrowly lance-shaped, dark green leaves. Z3–8 H8–1. f. ***album*** (syn. *Veronica virginica* f. *alba)* illus. p.241.

VESTIA

SOLANACEAE

Genus of one species of evergreen shrub grown for its flowers and foliage. At the limits of hardiness is often cut to ground level and is best grown against a south-facing wall. Requires sun and fertile, well-drained soil. Propagate by semi-ripe cuttings in summer or by seed in autumn or spring.
V. foetida, syn. *V. lycioides*. Evergreen, upright shrub. H 6ft (2m), S 5ft (1.5m). Oblong, glossy, dark green leaves have an unpleasant scent. Has pendent, tubular, pale yellow flowers from mid-spring to midsummer. Z8–10 H10–8.
V. lycioides. See *V. foetida*.

VIBURNUM

CAPRIFOLIACEAE

Genus of deciduous, semi-evergreen or evergreen shrubs and trees grown for their foliage, autumn color (in many deciduous species), flowers, and, often, fruits. Fruiting is generally most prolific when several plants of different clones are planted together. Grow in sun or semi-shade and in deep, fertile, not too dry soil. To thin out overgrown plants cut out some older shoots after flowering. Propagate by cuttings (softwood for deciduous species, semi-ripe for evergreens) in summer or by seed in autumn. The fruits of viburnums may cause mild stomach upset if ingested.
V. acerifolium illus. p.161.
V. betulifolium illus. p.148.
***V.* x *bodnantense* 'Dawn'** illus. p.150. **'Deben'** is a deciduous, upright shrub. H 10ft (3m), S 6ft (2m). Oval, toothed, dark green leaves are bronze when young. Clusters of fragrant, tubular white flowers, tinted with pale pink, open during mild periods from late autumn through to early spring. B7–8 H8–7.
V.* x *burkwoodii. Semi-evergreen, bushy, open shrub. H and S 8ft (2.5m). Rounded heads of fragrant, tubular pink then white flowers are borne amid oval, glossy, dark green leaves from mid- to late spring. Z5–8 H8–1. **'Anne Russell'**, H and S 5ft (1.5m), is deciduous and has very fragrant white flowers. **'Park Farm Hybrid'** bears very fragrant white flowers that are slightly pink in bud, and older leaves turn bright red in autumn. Both Z4–8 H8–1.
V.* x *carlcephalum illus. p.117.
V. carlesii illus. p.154. **'Diana'** is a deciduous, bushy, dense shrub. H and S 6ft (2m). Broadly oval leaves are bronze when young and turn purple-red in autumn. From mid- to late spring bears rounded heads of red buds that open to very fragrant, tubular pink flowers fading to white. Z5–8 H8–5.
***V.* 'Cayuga'.** Upright, slightly spreading, deciduous shrub. H 5ft (1.5m), S 4ft (1.2m). Has scalloped, dark green leaves that turn a dull orange tone in autumn. In spring, pink buds open to fragrant white flowers with the outer ones flushed pink. Fruit change through green, red, and finally black. Z4–7 H7–1.
V. dentatum (Arrow-wood). An upright, deciduous shrub with arching branches and straight stems. H and S 10ft (3m). Small white flowers are borne in dense, flattened corymbs and give rise to blue-black fruit. The coarsely toothed dark green leaves turn orange to red in autumn. Z3–8 H8–1.
V. dilatatum. Deciduous, upright shrub. H 10ft (3m), S 6ft (2m). Oval, sharply toothed, dark green leaves sometimes redden in autumn. Flat heads of small, star-shaped white flowers in late spring and early summer are succeeded by showy, egg-shaped, bright red fruits. Z5–8 H8–5. **'Catskill'** illus. p.139.
V. farreri, syn. *V. fragrans*, illus. p.147. **'Candidissimum'** is a deciduous, upright shrub. H 10ft (3m), S 6ft (2m). Oval, toothed, dark green leaves are pale green when young. Produces clusters of fragrant, tubular, pure white flowers in late autumn and during mild periods in winter and early spring. Z6–8 H8–6.
V. foetens, syn. *V. grandiflorum* f. *foetens*, illus. p.149.
V. fragrans. See *V. farreri*.
V. grandiflorum. Deciduous, upright, open shrub. H and S 6ft (2m). Stiff branches bear oblong, dark green leaves that become deep purple in autumn. Dense clusters of fragrant, tubular, white-and-pink flowers open from deep pink buds from midwinter to early spring. Z6–8 H8–6. f. ***foetens*** *see V. foetens*.
V.* x *juddii illus. p.154.
V. lantana (Wayfaring tree). Vigorous, deciduous, upright shrub. H 15ft (5m), S 12ft (4m). Has broadly oval, gray-green leaves that redden in autumn, flattened heads of small, 5-lobed white flowers in late spring and early summer, then egg-shaped red fruits that ripen to black. Z4–8 H8–1.
V. lentago (Nannyberry). Vigorous, deciduous, upright shrub. H 12ft (4m), S 10ft (3m). Oval, glossy, dark green leaves turn red and purple in autumn. Bears flattened heads of small, fragrant, star-shaped white flowers in late spring and early summer, then egg-shaped, blue-black fruits. Z2–8 H8–1.
***V.* 'Oneida'.** A broadly upright deciduous shrub. H. 10ft (3m), S 8ft (2.5m). Thin, almost circular, dark green, toothed leaves turn yellow to orange-red in autumn. Flat heads of white flowers in lacecap heads appear in spring and through the summer and turn into glossy red berries that persist into winter. Z5–7 H7–5.
V. opulus (Guelder rose). Vigorous, deciduous, bushy shrub. H and S 12ft (4m). Bears broadly oval, lobed, deep green leaves that redden in autumn and, in late spring and early summer, flattened, lacecap heads of white flowers. Produces large bunches of spherical, bright red fruits. Z3–8 H8–1. **'Compactum'** illus. p.172. **'Roseum'** (European snowball). Has large globular heads of sterile flowers. Is very prone to aphid damage.

V. plicatum (Japanese snowball tree). Deciduous, bushy, spreading shrub. H 10ft (3m), S 12ft (4m). Leaves are oval, toothed, deeply veined, and dark green, turning reddish purple in autumn. Dense, rounded heads of large, sterile, flattish white flowers are borne along branches in late spring and early summer. Z4–8 H8–1. **'Mariesii'** illus. p.116. **'Nanum Semperflorens'** (syn. *V.p.* 'Watanabe', *V.p.* 'Watanabei', *V. watanabei*), H 6ft (2m), S 5ft (1.5m), is slow-growing, conical, and dense. Produces small flower heads from late spring until early autumn. Z6–8 H8–6. **'Pink Beauty'** illus. p.130. f. ***tomentosum*** has tiered branches, flattish, lacecap flower heads and red fruits, ripening to black. **'Summer Snowflake'** has tiered branches and lacecap flower heads in late spring and through the summer. Autumn foliage is purple-tinted. Z5–8 H8–1. **'Watanabe'** see *V.p.* 'Nanum Semperflorens'. **'Watanabei'** see *V.p.* 'Nanum Semperflorens'.

V.* x *pragense. See *V.* 'Pragense'.

***V.* 'Pragense'**, syn. *V.* x *pragense*, illus. p.139.

***V. rhytidophylloides* 'Alleghany'.** Forms a dense, rounded evergreen shrub. H and S 10ft (3m). The dark green, leathery foliage turns a dull purple in autumn and may be deciduous above the snow at the limits of hardiness. Domed heads of creamy white flowers appear in late spring and give rise to bright red fruit that turn black. Z5–8 H8–5.

V. rhytidophyllum illus. p.118.

V. sargentii. Deciduous, bushy shrub. H and S 10ft (3m). Maplelike, midgreen foliage often changes to yellow or red in autumn. Broad, flattish, lacecap heads of white flowers in late spring are followed by spherical, bright red fruits. Z4–7 H7–1. **'Onondaga'**, S 6ft (2m), has bronze-red young leaves, becoming deep green, then bronze-red again in autumn. Flower buds are pink.

V. sieboldii. Deciduous, rounded, dense shrub. H 12ft (4m), S 20ft (6m). Has large, oblong to oval, glossy, bright green leaves. Rounded heads of tubular, creamy white flowers are borne in late spring, followed by egg-shaped, red-stalked red fruits that ripen to black. Z5–8 H8–5.

V. tinus (Laurustinus) illus. p.149. **'Gwenllian'** has pale pink flowers and fruits very freely. Z8–10H10–8.

V. trilobum (American cranberry bush, Highbush cranberry). An upright, slender deciduous shrub with maplelike leaves that turn reddish in autumn. H 15ft (5m), S 10ft (3m). In spring, has flattened lacecap heads of white flowers. Bright red berries persist into winter. Z2–7 H7–1. **'Alfredo'** is only half this height with brighter autumn color. **'Wentworth'** has orange-red autumn color and yellow-red fruits that ripen later.

V. watanabei. See *V. plicatum* 'Nanum Semperflorens'.

VIGNA

LEGUMINOSAE/PAPILIONACEAE

Genus of evergreen, annual and perennial, erect or scrambling and twining climbers grown mainly as crop plants for their leaves, pods and seeds. Provide full light and organic, well-drained soil. Water freely when in full growth, sparingly at other times. Stems require support. Thin crowded stems or cut back hard in spring. Propagate by seed in autumn or spring.

V. caracalla, syn. *Phaseolus caracalla* (Snail flower). Evergreen, perennial, fast-growing, twining climber. H 10–15ft (3–5m). Leaves consist of 3 oval leaflets. From summer to early autumn carries pealike, purple-marked cream flowers that turn orange-yellow. H12–10.

Villarsia nymphoides. See *Nymphoides peltata.*

VINCA
Periwinkle

APOCYNACEAE

Genus of evergreen, trailing subshrubs and perennials grown for their foliage and flowers. Flowers are tubular with 5 spreading lobes. Is useful as a groundcover in shade but flowers more freely given some sun. Grows in any soil that is not too dry. Propagate by semi-ripe cuttings in summer or by division from autumn to spring. All parts may cause mild stomach upset if ingested.

V. difformis. Evergreen, prostrate subshrub. H 12in (30cm), S indefinite. Slender, trailing stems bear oval, glossy, dark green leaves. Erect flower stems produce pale blue flowers in late autumn and early winter. Z8–9 H9–8.

V. major (Greater periwinkle, Quater). Evergreen, prostrate, arching subshrub. H 18in (45cm), S indefinite. Leaves are broadly oval, glossy, and dark green. Large, bright blue flowers are produced from late spring to early autumn. Z7–9 H9–7. subsp. ***hirsuta*** see *V.m.* var. *oxyloba*. var. ***oxyloba*** (syn. *V.m.* subsp. *hirsuta*) has leaves, leaf stalks and calyces edged with long hairs. **'Variegata'** illus. p.175.

V. minor (Lesser periwinkle) illus. p.176. **'Alba Variegata'** is an evergreen, prostrate subshrub. H 6in (15cm), S indefinite. Forms extensive mats of small, oval, glossy, dark green leaves edged with pale yellow, above which white flowers are carried from midspring to early summer then intermittently into autumn. **'Bowles' Blue'** see *V.m.* 'La Grave'. **'Bowles' White'** bears large white flowers that are pinkish white in bud. **'Gertrude Jekyll'** is of dense growth and produces a profusion of small white flowers. Flowers of **'La Grave'** (syn. *V.m.* 'Bowles' Blue') are large and lavender-blue. All Z4–9 H9–1.

V. rosea. See *Catharanthus roseus.*

VIOLA
Violet

VIOLACEAE

Genus of annuals, perennials, some of which are semi-evergreen, and deciduous subshrubs grown for their distinctive flowers. Annuals are suitable as summer bedding; perennials and subshrubs are good in rock gardens, screes, and alpine houses. Grow in sun or shade and well-drained but moisture-retentive soil unless otherwise stated; a few species prefer acidic soil. Propagate annuals by seed sown according to flowering season, perennials and subshrubs by softwood cuttings in spring unless otherwise stated. Species may also be propagated by seed in spring or autumn.

V. aetolica illus. 371.

V. biflora (Twin-flowered violet). Creeping, rhizomatous perennial. H 2–6in (5–15cm), S 6in (15cm). Flat-faced, deep lemon yellow flowers veined dark brown are borne singly or in pairs on upright stems in summer. Leaves are kidney-shaped and midgreen. Needs shade. May also be propagated by division. Z4–8 H8-1.

V. calcarata illus. p.368.

V. cazorlensis. Tufted, woody-based perennial. H to 2in (5cm), S to 3in (8cm). Has small, linear to lance-shaped leaves and in late spring carries small, flat-faced, long-spurred, deep pink flowers, singly on short stems. Good in an alpine house. Difficult to grow. Z8–10 H10–8.

V. cenisia. Spreading perennial with runners. H 3in (7cm), S 4in (10cm). Small, flat-faced, bright violet flowers, each with a deep purple line radiating from the center, are produced on very short stems in summer. Has a deep taproot and tiny, heart-shaped or oblong, dark green leaves. Good in a scree. Propagate by division in spring. Z8-10 H10–8.

V. cornuta illus. p.349.

V. cucullata. See *V. obliqua.*

V. elatior. Upright, little-branched perennial. H 8–12in (20–30cm), S 6in (15cm). Leaves are broadly lance-shaped and toothed. Produces flat-faced, pale blue flowers with white centers in early summer. Prefers semi-shade and moist soil. Propagate in spring by division. Z5–8 H8–5.

V. glabella. Clump-forming perennial with a scaly, horizontal rootstock. H 4in (10cm), S 8in (20cm). Produces flat-faced, bright yellow flowers with purplish-veined lower petals in late spring above toothed, heart-shaped, bright green leaves. Needs shade. Propagate by division in spring. Z5–8 H8–5.

V. gracilis. Mat-forming perennial. H 5in (12cm), S 6in (15cm) or more. Flat-faced, yellow-centered, violet-blue or sometimes yellow flowers are produced in summer. Has small, dissected leaves with linear or oblong segments. Needs sun.

***V.* 'Haslemere'.** See *V.* 'Nellie Britton'.

V. hederacea, syn. *Erpetion reniforme, V. reniforme* (Australian violet, Ivy-leaved violet). Evergreen, creeping, mat-forming perennial. H 1–2in (2.5–5cm), S indefinite. Has tiny, rounded leaves and bears purple or white flowers on short stems in summer. Good in an alpine house. Prefers semi-shade. Propagate by division in spring. Z8–9 H9–8.

***V.* 'Huntercombe Purple'** illus. p.382.

***V.* 'Irish Molly'.** Evergreen, clump-forming, short-lived perennial. H 4in (10cm), S 6–8in (15–20cm). Has broadly oval, dissected leaves and, in summer, a succession of flat-faced, old gold flowers with brown centers. Needs sun. Z5–7 H7–5.

***V.* 'Jackanapes'** illus. p.372.

***V. labradorica* 'Purpurea'.** See *V. riviniana* 'Purpurea'.

V. lutea (Mountain pansy). Mat-forming, rhizomatous perennial. H 4in (10cm), S 6in (15cm). Has small, oval to lance-shaped leaves. Flat-faced yellow, violet, or bicolored flowers are produced in spring and summer. Z4–8 H8–1.

***V.* 'Nellie Britton'**, syn. *V.* 'Haslemere', illus. p.381.

V. obliqua, syn. *V. cucullata*. Variable, spreading perennial with fleshy rhizomes. H 2in (5cm), S 4–6in (10–15cm). Has kidney-shaped, toothed, midgreen leaves. In late spring produces flat-faced, blue-violet, sometimes white or pale blue flowers. Propagate in spring by division. Self seeds freely. Z4–9 H9–7.

V. odorata (Sweet violet). Semi-evergreen, spreading, rhizomatous perennial. H 3in (7cm), S6in (15cm) or more. Leaves are heart-shaped and toothed. Long stems each carry a fragrant, flat-faced violet or white flower from late winter to early spring. Is useful in a wild garden. Self seeds prolifically. May also be propagated by division. Z6–8 H8–6.

V. palmata. Spreading perennial. H 4in (10cm), S 6in (15cm). Has short-stemmed, flat-faced, pale violet flowers in late spring and deeply dissected leaves. Prefers dry, well-drained soil. Self seeds readily. Z8–9 H9–8.

V. pedata illus. p.369. var. ***bicolor*** is a clump-forming perennial with a thick rootstock. H 2in (5cm), S 3in (8cm). Flat-faced, velvety purple or white flowers are borne singly on slender stems in late spring and early summer. Leaves are finely divided into 5–7 or more, narrow, toothed segments. Good in an alpine house. May be difficult to grow; needs peaty, sandy soil. Z4–8 H8–1.

V. reniforme. See *V. hederacea.*

***V. riviniana* 'Purpurea'**, syn. *V. labradorica* 'Purpurea', illus. p.369.

V. tricolor illus. p.369. **'Bowles' Black'** illus. p.370.

V.* x *wittrockiana (Pansy). Group of slow- to moderately fast-growing, mainly bushy perennials usually grown as annuals or biennials. H 6–8in (15–20cm), S 8in (20cm). Has oval, often serrated, midgreen leaves. Flattish, 5-petaled flowers, 1–4in (2.5–10cm) across, in a very wide color range, appear throughout summer or in winter-spring. Z6–9 H9–1. The following are among those available:

'Baby Lucia' (summer-flowering) has small, deep blue flowers.

Clear Crystals Series (summer-flowering) is in a wide range of clear colors (yellow, illus. p.337).

'Clear Sky Primrose' (winter- to spring-flowering) illus p.336.

Crystal Bowl Series (summer-flowering) is in a range of colors (yellow, illus. p.337).

Floral Dance Series (winter-flowering) has a wide range of colors (mixed, illus. p.329; white, illus. p.319).

Forerunner Series (winter- to spring-flowering) illus. p.338.

Imperial Series 'Imperial Frosty Rose' (summer-flowering) illus. p.327.

Imperial Series 'Orange Prince' (summer-flowering) has orange flowers with black blotches.

Imperial Series 'Sky Blue' (summer-flowering) has sky blue flowers, each with a deeper-colored blotch.

Joker Series (summer-flowering) illus. p.332.

'Majestic Giants' (summer-flowering) has large flowers in a wide color range.

Princess Series (spring- to summer-flowering) are neat in habit and produce small flowers in blue, cream, bicolored purple and white, dark purple, or yellow.

'Silver Princess' (summer-flowering) has white flowers, each with a deep pink blotch.

'Super Chalon Giants' (summer- to autumn-flowering) illus. p.336.

'True Blue' (winter- to summer-flowering) illus p.333.

Ultima Series (winter- to spring-flowering) has medium-sized flowers in a very broad range of colors, including bicolors.

Universal Series (winter- to spring-flowering) produces flowers in an extensive range of separate colors (apricot, illus. p.339) as well as in a mixture of colors.

VIRGILIA

LEGUMINOSAE/PAPILIONACEAE

Genus of short-lived, evergreen shrubs and trees grown for their flowers which are borne in spring and summer. Prefers a position in full light and well-drained soil. Water pot-grown plants freely when in full growth, less at other times. Pruning is usually not required. Propagate in spring by seed, ideally soaked in warm water for 24 hours before sowing.

V. capensis. See *V. oroboides.*

V. oroboides, syn. *V. capensis*. Fast-growing, evergreen, rounded shrub or tree. H and S 20–30ft (6–10m). Has leaves of 11–21 oblong leaflets. Racemes of fragrant, pealike, bright mauve-pink flowers, sometimes pink, crimson, or white, are produced in late spring and summer, usually in great profusion. Z10-11 H12–10.

Viscaria alpina. See *Lychnis alpina*.
Viscaria elegans. See *Silene coeli-rosa.*

VITALIANA

PRIMULACEAE

Genus of one species of evergreen, spring-flowering perennial grown for its flowers. Is often included in *Douglasia* and is useful for rock gardens, screes, and alpine houses. Requires sun and moist but well-drained soil. Propagate by softwood cuttings in summer or by seed in autumn.

V. primuliflora, syn. *Douglasia vitaliana*, illus. p.372.

VITEX

VERBENACEAE

Genus of evergreen or deciduous trees and shrubs grown for their flowers. At limits of hardiness grow against a south- or west-facing wall. Needs full sun and well-drained soil. Propagate by semi-ripe cuttings in summer or by seed in autumn or spring.

V. agnus-castus (Chaste tree). Deciduous, spreading, open, aromatic shrub. H and S 8ft (2.5m). Upright panicles of fragrant, tubular, violet-blue flowers appear in early and midautumn. Dark green leaves are each divided into 5 or 7 long, narrowly lance-shaped leaflets. Z6–9 H9–6.

V. negundo. Deciduous, bushy shrub. H and S 10ft (3m). Midgreen leaves are each composed of 3–7 narrowly oval, sharply toothed leaflets. Produces loose panicles of small, tubular, violet-blue flowers from late summer through to early autumn. Z6–9 H9–6.

VITIS

Grape

VITACEAE

Genus of deciduous, woody-stemmed, tendril climbers grown for their foliage and fruits (grapes), which are produced in bunches. Prefers fertile, well-drained, alkaline soil and sun or semi-shade. Propagate by hardwood cuttings in late autumn.

V. aconitifolia. See *Ampelopsis aconitifolia.*

V. amurensis (Amur grape). Vigorous, deciduous, woody-stemmed, tendril climber. H 20ft (6m). Bears dark green, 3- or 5-lobed leaves, 5–12in (12–30cm) long, that mature to red and purple in autumn. Produces inconspicuous flowers throughout the summer, followed in late summer and autumn, by tiny black fruits. Z4–9 H9–1.

***V.* 'Brant'.** Deciduous, woody-stemmed, tendril climber. H to 22ft (7m) or more. Bears leaves that are lobed, toothed, 4–9in (10–22cm) long and bright green. In autumn they mature to brown-red, except for the veins. Produces inconspicuous flowers in summer, followed by green or purple fruits. Z5–9 H9–5.

V. coignetiae illus. p.218.

V. davidii. Deciduous, woody-stemmed, tendril climber; young stems are densely covered with short prickles. H to 25ft (8m) or more. Heart-shaped leaves, 4–10in (10–25cm) long, are blue- or gray-green beneath, turning scarlet in autumn. Insignificant greenish flowers in summer are followed by small black fruits. Z7-10 H10–7.

V. henryana. See *Parthenocissus henryana.*

V. heterophylla. See *Ampelopsis brevipedunculata* var. *maximowiczii.*

V. quinquefolia. See *Parthenocissus quinquefolia.*

V. striata. See *Cissus striata.*

V thomsonii. See *Parthenocissus thomsonii.*

V. vinifera. (Grape vine) **'Purpurea'** illus. p.218.

VRIESEA

BROMELIACEAE

Genus of evergreen, rosette-forming, epiphytic perennials grown for their flowers and overall appearance. Needs a position in semi-shade and a rooting medium of equal parts organic soil and either sphagnum moss or bark or plastic chips used for orchid culture. Using soft water, water moderately when in growth, sparingly at other times, and from midspring to mid-autumn keep rosette centers filled with water. Propagate plants by offsets or seed in spring.

V. fenestralis. Evergreen, epiphytic perennial with dense, funnel-shaped rosettes. H and S 12–16in (30–40cm). Pale green leaves with dark lines and cross-bands are very broadly strap-shaped and arching or rolled under at tips. In summer, flat racemes of tubular, yellowish green flowers with green bracts are carried above the foliage. Z14-15 H12-10.

V. fosteriana. Evergreen, epiphytic perennial with dense, funnel-shaped rosettes. H and S 24in (60cm) or more. Has broadly strap-shaped, arching, yellowish- to deep green leaves cross-banded with reddish-brown, particularly beneath. In summer-autumn, flat spikes of tubular, pale yellow or greenish yellow flowers with brownish red tips are produced well above the foliage. Z14-15 H12-10.

V. hieroglyphica (King of the bromeliads). Evergreen, epiphytic perennial with dense, funnel-shaped rosettes. H and S 2–3ft (60cm–1m). Produces very broadly strap-shaped, arching, yellowish green leaves cross-banded and checkered with dark brownish green. In summer bears panicles of tubular yellow flowers well above the leaves. Z11–12 H12–1.

V. platynema. Evergreen, basal-rosetted, epiphytic perennial. H and S 24in (60cm). Broadly strap-shaped, mid- to light green leaves with purple tips form dense rosettes. In summer flat racemes of tubular, green-and-yellow flowers with red or yellow bracts are produced. Z14-15 H12-1.

V. psittacina. Evergreen, spreading, basal-rosetted, epiphytic perennial. H and S 16–24in (40–60cm). Has dense rosettes of strap-shaped, arching, pale green leaves. Flat spikes of tubular yellow flowers with green tips, emerging from red-and-yellow or red-and-green bracts, are borne above foliage in summer-autumn. Z14-15 H12-1.

V. splendens (Flaming sword; illus. p.265). Evergreen, basal-rosetted, epiphytic perennial. H and S 12in (30cm). Has dense rosettes of strap-shaped, arching, olive green leaves with purple to reddish brown cross-bands. Bears flat, sword-shaped racemes of tubular yellow flowers between bright red bracts in summer and autumn. Z14–15 H12–1.

x VUYLSTEKEARA

See also ORCHIDS.

x *V. cambria* 'Lensing's Favorite' (illus. p.297). Evergreen, epiphytic orchid for a cool greenhouse. H 9in (23cm). Has narrowly oval leaves, 4–6in (10–15cm) long. Bears long sprays of wine red flowers, 4in (10cm) across, heavily marked with white; flowering season varies. Needs shade in summer. Z14–15 H12–6.

WACHENDORFIA

HAEMODORACEAE

Genus of summer-flowering perennials with deep roots Requires full sun and moist soil. Propagate by division in spring or by seed in autumn or spring.

W. thyrsiflora. Clump-forming perennial. H 5–6ft (1.5–2m), S 1½ft (45cm). Shallowly cup-shaped yellow to orange flowers are produced in dense panicles in early summer. Midgreen leaves are narrowly sword-shaped, pleated, and rather coarse. Z9-10 H10–9.

WAHLENBERGIA

CAMPANULACEAE

Genus of summer-flowering annuals, biennials and short-lived perennials grown for their bell-shaped flowers. Is useful for alpine houses. Needs a sheltered site, partial shade, and well-drained, peaty, sandy soil. Propagate by seed in autumn.

W. albomarginata (New Zealand bluebell). Basal-rosetted, rhizomatous perennial. H and S 6in (15cm) or more. Slender stems each carry a bell-shaped, clear blue flower that opens flat in summer. Has narrowly elliptic to oval, midgreen leaves in tufts. Is good in a rock garden. Z6–7 H7–6

W. congesta, syn. *W. saxicola* var. *congesta*. Mat-forming, creeping, rhizomatous perennial. H 3in (7cm), S 4in (10cm). Has small, rounded or

spoon-shaped, midgreen leaves and, in summer, bell-shaped, lavender-blue or white flowers held singly on wiry stems. Z8–10 H10–8.
W. saxicola var. ***congesta***. See *W. congesta*.
W. serpyllifolia. See *Edraianthus serpyllifolius*.

WALDSTEINIA

ROSACEAE

Genus of semi-evergreen, creeping perennials with runners. Makes a good groundcover. Needs sun and well-drained soil. Propagate by division in early spring.
W. ternata, syn. *W. trifolia*, illus. p.385.
W. trifolia. See *W. ternata*.

WASHINGTONIA

ARECACEAE/PALMAE

Genus of evergreen palms grown for their stately appearance. Grows in fertile, well-drained soil and in full sun. Water containerized specimens freely in summer, moderately at other times. Remove skirt of persistent dead leaves regularly, sincethey are a fire risk. Propagate by seed in spring at not less than 275°F (4°C). Spider mite may be a nuisance.
W. filifera (Desert fan palm). Fast-growing, evergreen palm. H and S to 80ft (25m). Has fan-shaped, long-stalked, gray-green leaves, each lobe with a filamentous tip. Long-stalked clusters of tiny, creamy white flowers are borne in summer and berrylike black fruits in winter. Z8-11 H12–8.
W. robusta illus. p.73.

WATSONIA

IRIDACEAE

Genus of clump-forming corms, *Gladiolus*-like in overall appearance, although flowers are more tubular. Requires an open, sunny position and light, well-drained soil. Plant in autumn, 4–6in (10–15cm) deep; protect with straw or similar loose, dry during the first winter, especially where marginally hardy. Feed with slow-acting fertilizer, such as bonemeal, in summer. Corms are best left undisturbed to form clumps. Propagate by seed in autumn.
W. beatricis. See *W. pillansii*.
W. borbonica, syn. *W. pyramidata*, illus. p.400.
W. fourcadei. Clump-forming, summer-flowering corm. H to 5ft (1.5m), S 1–1½ft (30–45cm). Sword-shaped, erect leaves are mostly basal. Has a dense spike of tubular, salmon-red flowers, each 3–3½in (8–9cm) long and with 6 lobes. Z9–10 H10–9.
W. merianiae. Clump-forming, summer-flowering corm. H to 1m (3ft), S 1–1½ft (30–45cm). Has sword-shaped, erect leaves both on stem and at base. Stem carries a loose spike of tubular, pinkish red flowers, each 2–2½in (5–6cm) long and with 6 spreading lobes. Z9–10 H10–9.
W. pillansii, syn. *W. beatricis*, illus. p.400.
W. pyramidata. See *W. borbonica*.

Wattakaka sinensis. See *Dregea sinensis*.

WEIGELA

CAPRIFOLIACEAE

Genus of deciduous shrubs grown for their showy, funnel-shaped flowers. Prefers sunny, fertile soil. To maintain vigor, prune out a few older branches to ground level after flowering each year. Straggly old plants may be pruned hard in spring (though this will lose one season's flowers). Propagate by softwood cuttings in summer.
***W.* 'Bristol Ruby'.** Vigorous, deciduous, upright shrub. H 8ft (2.5m), S 6ft (2m). Deep red flowers open from darker buds amid oval, toothed, midgreen leaves in late spring and early summer. Z4–9 H9–1.
***W.* 'Eva Rathke'.** Deciduous, upright, dense shrub. H and S 5ft (1.5m). Has oval, toothed, dark green leaves. Broad-mouthed crimson flowers open from darker buds from late spring to early summer. Z5–9 H9–5.
W. florida. Deciduous, arching shrub. H and S 8ft (2.5m). Bears deep pink flowers, pale pink to white inside, in late spring and early summer. Oval, toothed leaves are midgreen. Z5–8 H8–4.
'Foliis Purpureis' illus. p.163.
'Variegata' illus. p.160.
***W.* 'Minuet'.** Compact, dwarf, spreading, deciduous shrub. H 30in (75cm), S 4ft (1.2m). Purple-tinged foliage and slightly fragrant, bell-shaped pink blooms that are darker outside and have a yellow throat. Z3–7 H7–1.
***W.* 'Red Prince'.** Upright, deciduous shrub. H 6ft (2m), S 4ft (1.2m). The bright red, non-fading flowers are borne in early summer with repeat blooms in late summer. Z4–8 H8–1.
***W.* 'Tango'.** Deciduous, compact shrub with purple-tinged foliage. H 24in (60cm), S 30in (75cm). In late spring and early summer has bell-shaped red flowers with yellow throats. Z4–7 H7–1.

Weingartia neocumingii. See *Rebutia neocumingii*.

WEINMANNIA

CUNONIACEAE

Genus of evergreen trees and shrubs grown for their foliage, flowers, and overall appearance. Requires a position in partial shade or full light and organic, well-drained but not dry soil, ideally neutral to acidic. Water containerized plants freely when in full growth, moderately at other times. Pruning is tolerated if needed. Propagate by seed in spring or by semi-ripe cuttings in summer.
W. trichosperma. Evergreen, ovoid to round-headed tree. H 40ft (12m) or more, S 25–30ft (8–10m). Glossy, rich green leaves have 9–19 oval, boldly toothed leaflets borne on a winged midrib. Spikes of tiny, fragrant white flowers with pink stamens are produced in early summer.

WELDENIA

COMMELINACEAE

Genus of one species of summer-flowering, tuberous perennial grown for its flowers. Needs sun and gritty, well-drained soil. Keep dry from autumn until growth restarts in late winter. Is suitable for growing in alpine houses. Propagate by root cuttings in winter or by division in early spring.
W. candida illus. p.362.

WELWITSCHIA

WELWITSCHIACEAE

Genus of one species of evergreen, desert-growing perennial with a deep taproot. Has only 2 leaves, which lie on the ground and grow continuously from the base for up to 100 years. Requires sun and sharply drained soil. Requires desert conditions: may succeed in a mixture of stone chips and leaf mold, in a length of drainpipe to take its long tap- root. Propagate by seed when ripe.
W. bainesii. See *W. mirabilis*.
W. mirabilis, syn. *W. bainesii*, illus. p.304.

WESTRINGIA

LABIATAE/LAMIACEAE

Genus of evergreen shrubs grown for their flowers and overall appearance. Requires full light and well-drained soil. Water containerized specimens moderately, less when not in full growth. Propagate by seed in spring or by semi-ripe cuttings in late summer.
W. fruticosa, syn. *W. rosmariniformis*, illus. p.158.
W. rosmariniformis. See *W. fruticosa*.

WIGANDIA

HYDROPHYLLACEAE

Genus of evergreen perennials and shrubs grown for their flowers and foliage. Needs full light and moist but well-drained soil. Water potted plants freely when in full growth, moderately at other times. Cut down flowered stems in spring to prevent plants becoming straggly. Propagate by seed or softwood cuttings in spring. Whitefly is sometimes troublesome. Contact with foliage may aggravate skin allergies.
W. caracasana. Evergreen, erect, sparsely branched shrub. H 6–10ft (2–3m), S 3–6ft (1–2m). Produces oval, wavy-edged, toothed, deep green leaves, 18in (45cm) long and covered with white hairs beneath. Carries 5-petaled, violet-purple flowers in large, terminal clusters from spring through to autumn. Is often grown annually from seed purely for its handsome leaves. Z13-15 H12-

Wigginsia vorwerkiana. See *Parodia erinacea*.
Wilcoxia albiflora. See *Echinocereus leucanthus*.
Wilcoxia schmollii. See *Echinocereus schmollii*.

x WILSONARA

See also ORCHIDS.
x *W.* Hambuhren Stern 'Cheam' (illus. p.297). Evergreen, epiphytic orchid for a cool greenhouse. H 9in (23cm). Narrowly oval leaves are 4in (10cm) long. Bears spikes of deep reddish brown flowers, 3½in (9cm) across, each with a yellow lip; flowering season varies. Requires shade in summer. Z14-15 H12–6.

Wintera aromatica. See *Drimys winteri*.

WISTERIA

LEGUMINOSAE/PAPILIONACEAE

Genus of deciduous, woody-stemmed, twining climbers grown for their spectacular flowers and suitable for walls and pergolas and for growing against buildings and trees. Grows in sun and in fertile, well-drained soil. Prune after flowering and again in late winter. Propagate by bench grafting in winter or by seed in autumn or spring. Plants produced from seed may not flower until some years old and often have poor flowers. All parts may cause severe discomfort if ingested.
W. brachybotrys f. ***alba.*** See *W.b.* 'Shiro Kapitan'. **'Shiro Kapitan'** (syn. *W.b. f. alba, W. venusta, W.v. 'Alba Plena'*; Silky wisteria) is a deciduous, woody-stemmed, twining climber. H to 28ft (9m) or more. Leaves are 8–14in (20–35cm) long, each with 9–13 oval leaflets. Produces 4–6in (10–15cm) long racemes of scented, pealike white flowers, each with a yellow blotch at base of upper petal, in early summer; sometimes flowers again sparsely in autumn. Z5–9 H9–5.
W. chinensis. See *W. sinensis*.
W. floribunda (Japanese wisteria). **'Alba'** (syn. *W.f.* 'Shiro Noda') illus. p.207. **'Black Dragon'** see *W.f.* 'Royal Purple'. **'Lawrence'** has blue flowers in early summer. **'Macrobotrys'** (syn. *W.f.* 'Multijuga') is a deciduous, woody-stemmed, twining climber. H to 28ft (9m). Leaves, 10–14in (25–35cm) long, have 11–19 oval leaflets. Scented, pealike lilac flowers flushed darker and carried in racemes 3–4ft (1–1.2m) long are produced in early summer and may produce oblong, velvety pods in late summer and autumn. **'Multijuga'** see *W.f.* 'Macrobotrys'. **'Royal Purple'** (syn. *W.f.* 'Black Dragon') has double, deep purple flowers, carried in racemes, 5–10in (12–25cm) long, produced in early summer; sometimes flowers again sparsely in autumn. **'Shiro Noda'** see *W.f.* 'Alba'. All Z5–9 H9–5.

W.* x *formosa illus. p.215.
W. sinensis, syn. *W. chinensis*, illus. p.215. **'Alba'** illus. p.207. **'Prolific'**, H to 100ft (30m), is vigorous, with masses of single, lilac or pale violet flowers in longer racemes. Z6–8 H8–6.
W. venusta. See *W. brachybotrys* 'Shiro Kapitan'. **'Alba Plena'** see *W. brachybotrys* 'Shiro Kapitan'

WOLFFIA
Duckweed

LEMNACEAE

Genus of semi-evergreen, perennial, floating water plants grown for their curiosity value as the smallest known flowering plants. Is ideal for cold-water aquariums. Needs a sunny position. Remove excess plantlets as required. Propagate by redistribution of plantlets as required.
W. arrhiza (Least duckweed). Semi-evergreen, perennial, floating water plant. S 1/32in (1mm). Leaves are rounded and midgreen. Insignificant greenish flowers appear year-round. Z8–10 H10–8.

WOODSIA

DRYOPTERIDACEAE

Genus of deciduous ferns suitable for rock gardens and alpine houses. Tolerates sun or semi-shade. May be difficult to cultivate: soil must provide constant moisture and also be quick-draining, and crowns of plants must sit above soil to avoid rotting. Propagate by division in early spring.
W. polystichoides (Holly-fern woodsia). Deciduous, tufted fern. H 4–12in (10–30cm), S 8–16in (20–40cm). In early spring has lance-shaped, divided, pale green fronds, to 14in (35cm) long, softly hairy on both surfaces and scaly beneath; each is composed of 15–30 pairs of narrowly sickle-shaped or oblong pinnae with slightly toothed margins. May be damaged by late frosts. Z4–8 H8–1.

WOODWARDIA

BLECHNACEAE

Genus of evergreen or deciduous ferns. Prefers semi-shade and fibrous, moist, peaty soil. Remove faded fronds regularly. Propagate by division in spring.
W. radicans (Chain fern). Vigorous, evergreen, spreading fern. H 4ft (1.2m), S 2ft (60cm). Large, broadly lance-shaped, coarsely divided, arching fronds with narrowly oval pinnae are midgreen. Z8–9 H9–8.
W. unigemmata (Asian chain fern). Evergreen fern very similar to *W. radicans*. H 3ft (1m), S 10ft (3m). New foliage emerges brilliant red and fades to brown and then green. Z8–9 H9–8.

WORSLEYA
Blue amaryllis

AMARYLLIDACEAE

Genus of one species of evergreen, winter-flowering bulb, with a neck up to 2½ft (75cm) high crowned by a tuft of leaves and a 8–12in (20–30cm) leafless flower stem. Needs full sun and well-drained soil, or a potting mix consisting of osmunda fiber, perlite or bark chips, and some leaf mold. Soil should never dry out. Propagate by seed in spring.
W. procera. See *W. rayneri*.
W. rayneri, syn. *Hippeastrum procerum*, *W. procera*. Evergreen, winter-flowering bulb. H 3–4ft (1–1.2m), S 1½–2ft (45–60cm). Bears long, strap-shaped, strongly curved leaves and up to 14 funnel-shaped, lilac-blue flowers, 6in (15cm) long, with wavy-edged petals. Z14-15 H12-10.

WULFENIA

SCROPHULARIACEAE

Genus of evergreen, summer-flowering perennials with rough-textured leaves. Is suitable for alpine house, since it dislikes winter wet. Needs full sun and well-drained soil. Propagate by division in spring or by seed in autumn.
W. amherstiana illus. p.356.
W. carinthiaca. Evergreen, basal-rosetted perennial. H and S 10in (25cm). Has oblong to oval, toothed, dark green leaves, hairy beneath. The top quarter of each flower stem is covered in a dense spike of small, tubular, violet-blue flowers in summer. Z5–9 H9–1.

XANTHOCERAS

SAPINDACEAE

Genus of one species of deciduous, spring- to summer-flowering shrub or tree grown for its foliage and flowers. Requires sun and fertile, well-drained soil. Propagate by seed in autumn or by root cuttings or suckers in late winter.
X. sorbifolium illus. p.118.

XANTHOPHTHALMUM

ASTERACEAE/COMPOSITAE

Genus of annuals grown for their daisy-like flower heads. Prefers full sun and well-drained soil. Propagate by seed in spring.
X. coronarium, syn. *Chrysanthemum coronarium*. Fast-growing, upright, branching annual. H 1–3ft (30cm–90cm), S 15in (38cm). Has feathery, divided, light green leaves. In summer bears single or semi-double, daisylike yellow or yellow-and-white flower heads to 2in (5cm) across.
X. segetum, syn. *Chrysanthemum segetum*, illus. p.337.

XANTHORHIZA

RANUNCULACEAE

Genus of one species of deciduous, spring-flowering shrub grown for its foliage and flowers. Prefers shade or semi-shade and moist soil. Propagate by division in autumn.
X. apiifolia. See *X. simplicissima*.
X. simplicissima, syn. *X. apiifolia* (Yellow-root). Deciduous, upright shrub that spreads by underground stems. H 2ft (60cm), S 5ft (1.5m). Bright green leaves, each consisting of usually 5 oval to lance-shaped, sharply toothed leaflets, turn bronze or purple in autumn. Bears nodding panicles of tiny, star-shaped purple flowers from early to midspring as foliage emerges. Z3–9 H9–1.

XANTHORRHOEA
Blackboy, Grass tree

XANTHORRHOEACEAE

Genus of evergreen, long-lived perennials grown mainly as foliage plants. Needs full sun, well-drained soil, and a fairly dry atmosphere. Propagate by basal offsets or seed in spring.
X. australis. Evergreen perennial with a thick, dark trunk. H 2–4ft (60cm–1.2m), S 4–5ft (1.2–1.5m). Very narrow, arching, flattened, silvery green leaves, 2ft (60cm) or more long, 1/16in (2mm) wide, spread from top of the trunk. In summer may produce small, fragrant, 6-petaled white flowers in dense, candlelike spikes, 2ft (60cm) or more long, on stems of similar length.

XANTHOSOMA

ARACEAE

Genus of perennials with underground tubers or thick stems above ground, grown mainly for their attractive foliage. Many species are cultivated in the tropics for their edible, starchy tubers. Requires a position in partial shade and rich, moist soil. The atmosphere should be kept moist at all times. Propagate by division; alternatively take stem cuttings in spring or summer.
X. sagittifolium illus. p.266.
X. violaceum. Stemless perennial with large, underground tubers and leaves rising from ground level. H and S 4ft (1.2m). Purplish leaf stalks, to over 2ft (60cm) long, carry broadly arrow-shaped leaf blades, 28in (70cm) long, dark green with purple midribs and veins. Intermittently bears greenish purple spathes, yellower within, surrounding a brownish spadix. Z11 H12–10.

XERANTHEMUM
Immortelle

ASTERACEAE/COMPOSITAE

Genus of summer-flowering annuals. Grow in sun and in fertile, very well-drained soil. Propagate by seed sown outdoors in spring.
X. annuum. Fairly fast-growing, upright annual with branching flower heads. H 2ft (60cm), S 1½ft (45cm). Has lance-shaped silvery leaves. Daisylike, papery purple flower heads are produced in summer. Double forms are available in shades of pink, mauve, purple, or white (illus. p.325). H9–1.

XERONEMA

AGAVACEAE/PHORMIACEAE

Genus of evergreen, robust, tufted perennials, with short, creeping rootstocks, grown for their flowers. Grow in sun or partial shade and in organic, well-drained soil. Propagate by seed or division in spring.
X. callistemon. Evergreen, irislike, clump-forming perennial. H 2–3ft (60cm–1m), S indefinite. Erect, folded leaves, 2–3ft (60cm–1m) long, are very narrow and hard-textured. In summer, short-stalked, 6-petaled red flowers, to 1¼in (3cm) wide, are borne on one-sided racemes, 6–12in (15–30cm) long. Z13-15 H12-10.

XEROPHYLLUM

LILIACEAE/MELANTHIACEAE

Genus of elegant, summer-flowering, rhizomatous perennials. Prefers full sun and moist, peaty soil. May be difficult to cultivate. Propagate by seed in autumn.
X. tenax. Clump-forming perennial. H 3–4ft (1–1.2m), S 1–2ft (30–60cm). Star-shaped white flowers with violet anthers are borne in dense, terminal racemes in summer. Basal leaves are linear and midgreen. Z5–8 H8–5.

YUCCA,
syn. HESPEROYUCCA

AGAVACEAE

Genus of evergreen shrubs and trees grown for the architectural value of their bold, sword-shaped, clustered leaves and their showy panicles of usually white flowers. Makes excellent container-grown plants. Requires a position in full sun and well-drained soil. Water containerized specimens moderately except when they are not in full growth, when watering should be reduced. Regularly remove spent flowering stems. Propagate in spring: frost-tender species by seed or suckers, hardier species by root cuttings or division.
Y. aloifolia illus. p.153.
***Y. elephantipes* 'Variegata'** (illus. p.47). Evergreen, large, upright shrub or small tree. H to 30ft (10m), S 15–25ft (5–8m). Several to many sparsely branched trunks arise near ground level. Leaves are narrowly lance-shaped, stiffly leathery, light to midgreen, and creamy white at the margins. On mature plants, pendent, hemispherical white to cream flowers

are borne in dense, erect panicles from summer to autumn. Z11–12 H12–10.
Y. filamentosa (Adam's needle). Clump-forming, evergreen, basal-rosetted shrub. H 6ft (2m), S 5ft (1.5m). From mid- through to late summer produces tall panicles of pendulous, tulip-shaped white flowers that rise up through low-growing tufts of sword-shaped, deep green leaves, each edged with white threads. Z4–11 H12–5. **'Golden Sword'** has foliage with a central yellow band.
***Y. filifera* 'Ivory'.** See *Y. flaccida* 'Ivory'.
***Y. flaccida* 'Ivory'**, syn. *Y. filifera* 'Ivory', illus. p.160.
Y. glauca (Spanish bayonet). Evergreen, rosette-forming shrub with sharply tipped, narrow leaves up to 2ft (60cm) long. H and S 4ft (1.2m). When established will send up 3ft (1m) tall spikes of creamy white, waxy bell-like flowers in summer. Z5–10 H10–5.
Y. gloriosa (Spanish dagger) illus. p.137. **'Nobilis'** is an evergreen shrub. H and S 6ft (2m). Stem is thick and usually unbranched and crowned with a large tuft of long, sword-shaped, sharply pointed, blue-green leaves, the outer ones semi-pendent. Pendulous, tulip-shaped, red-backed white flowers are borne in long, erect panicles from midsummer to early autumn. Z7–10 H10–7.
Y. parviflora. See *Hesperaloe parviflora.*
Y. whipplei illus. p.160.

YUSHANIA

GRAMINEAE/POACEAE

See also GRASSES, BAMBOOS, RUSHES, and SEDGES.
Y. anceps, syn. *Arundinaria anceps, A. jaunsarensis, Sinarundinaria jaunsarensis*, illus. p.308.

Z

ZALUZIANSKYA

SCROPHULARIACEAE

Genus of sticky, low-growing annuals and evergreen perennials and subshrubs grown for their spikes of very fragrant, tubular flowers with spreading petals. Needs full sun and moist but sharply drained, organic soil. Propagate by stem-tip cuttings regularly in summer, since plants are short-lived.
Z. ovata. Clump-forming, evergreen perennial. H to 10in (25cm), S to 24in (60cm). Branching, brittle stems bear ovate, toothed, sticky, gray-green leaves. Produces crimson-backed white flowers over a long period in summer. Z9–10 H10–9

ZANTEDESCHIA

ARACEAE

Genus of summer-flowering, tuberous perennials, usually remaining evergreen in a warm climate, grown for their erect, funnel-shaped spathes, each of which encloses a club-shaped spadix. Requires a position in full sun or partial shade and well-drained soil. *Z. aethiopica*, however, will also grow in 6–12in (15–30cm) of water and therefore is suitable as a marginal water plant. Propagate by offsets in winter. All parts of the plant may cause mild stomach upset if ingested, and contact with the sap may irritate the skin.
Z. aethiopica (Calla lily). **'Crowborough'** illus. p.397. **'Green Goddess'** illus. p.397.
Z. albomaculata, syn. *Z. melanoleuca*. Summer-flowering, tuberous perennial. H 12–16in (30–40cm), S 12in (30cm). Bears arrow-shaped, semi-erect, basal leaves with transparent spots. Produces a yellow spadix inside a white spathe, 5–8in (12–20cm) long, shading to green at the base and with a deep purple blotch inside. Z11–12 H12–7.
***Z.* 'Black-eyed Beauty'.** Summer-flowering, tuberous perennial. H 12–16in (30–40cm), S 6in (15cm). Broadly heart-shaped, semi-erect, mid- to dark green, basal leaves are heavily white spotted. Each flower stem has a golden yellow spadix, surrounded by a cream spathe, 6in (15cm) long, with a central black mark in the throat. Z8–10 H10–4.
***Z.* 'Black Magic'.** Summer-flowering, tuberous perennial. H 30in (75cm), S 8in (20cm). Broadly heart-shaped, semi-erect, mid- to dark green, basal leaves are heavily mottled with white. Each flower stem produces a golden yellow spadix surrounded by a black-throated yellow spathe, 6in (15cm) long. Z8–10 H10–4.
Z. elliottiana illus. p.402.
Z. melanoleuca. See *Z. albomaculata.*
Z. rehmannii (Pink calla lily). Summer-flowering, tuberous perennial. H 16in (40cm), S 12in (30cm). Basal leaves are arrow-shaped, semi-erect, green, and generally without marks. Each flower stem produces a yellow spadix surrounded by a reddish pink spathe, 7–3in (8cm) long and narrowly tubular at the base. Z8–10 H10–4.

ZANTHOXYLUM

RUTACEAE

Genus of deciduous or evergreen, spiny shrubs and trees grown for their aromatic foliage, fruits, and habit. Requires a position in sun or semi-shade and in fertile soil. Propagate by seed in autumn or by root cuttings in late winter.
Z. piperitum illus. p.145.
Z. simulans illus. p.148.

ZAUSCHNERIA

ONAGRACEAE

Genus of subshrubby, evergreen or deciduous perennials grown for their mass of flowers. Requires a sunny position and well-drained soil. Propagate by seed or division in spring or by taking side-shoot cuttings in summer.
Z. californica, syn. *Epilobium californicum.* Clump-forming, woody-based, evergreen or semi-evergreen perennial. H and S 18in (45cm). Terminal clusters of tubular, bright scarlet flowers borne on slender stems are produced in late summer and early autumn. Bears lance-shaped, rich green leaves. Z8–11 H12–8. subsp. ***cana*** (syn. *Epilobium canum, Z. cana)*, H 12in (30cm) is deciduous and produces linear gray leaves and fuchsialike, brilliant scarlet flowers. Subsp. ***cana* 'Dublin'** (syn. *Z.c.* 'Glasnevin') illus. p.355. **'Glasnevin'** see *Z.c.* subsp. *cana* 'Dublin'.
Z. cana. See *Z. californica* subsp. *cana*.
Z. septentrionalis, syn. *Epilobium septentrionale.* Mat-forming, non-woody, deciduous perennial. H 4–8in (10–20cm), S to 8in (20cm). Terminal clusters of numerous, short-stalked, tubular scarlet flowers are produced in late summer. Has oval to lance-shaped, gray to gray-green leaves.

ZEA

Corn, Maize

GRAMINEAE/POACEAE

See also GRASSES, BAMBOOS, RUSHES, and SEDGES.
Z. mays (Ornamental maize, Sweet corn). **'Gracillima Variegata'** illus. p.320. **'Harlequin'** is a fairly fast-growing, upright annual. H 3–6ft (1–2m), S 2ft (60cm). Lance-shaped leaves are 2ft (60cm) long and striped with green, red, and white. Feathery, silky flower heads, 6in (15cm) long and borne on long stems are produced in midsummer, followed by large, cylindrical, green-sheathed yellow seed heads, known as ears, with deep red kernels. **'Strawberry Corn'**, H 4ft (1.2m), produces seed heads with small, yellow to burgundy red kernels, enclosed within yellow-green spathe-bracts (husks). Both H12–1.

Zebrina pendula. See *Tradescantia zebrina.*

ZELKOVA

ULMACEAE

Genus of deciduous trees grown mainly for their foliage and habit and are best when planted as isolated specimens. Produces insignificant flowers in spring. Does best in full sun and requires deep, fertile, moist but well-drained soil. Propagate by seed in autumn.
Z. abelicea, syn. *Z. cretica.* Deciduous, bushy-headed, spreading tree. H 15ft (5m), S 22ft (7m). Produces small leaves that are oval, prominently toothed, and glossy, dark green. Z8–9 H9–8.
Z. carpinifolia (Caucasian elm). Deciduous tree with a short, thick trunk from which many upright branches arise to make an oval, dense crown. H 100ft (30m), S 80ft (25m). Produces oval, sharply toothed, dark green leaves turning to orange-brown in autumn. Z5–9 H9–5.
Z. cretica. See *Z. abelicea.*
Z. serrata illus. p.71.

ZENOBIA

ERICACEAE

Genus of one species of deciduous or semi-evergreen, summer-flowering shrub grown for its flowers. Requires semi-shade and moist, peaty, acidic soil. Prune out older, weaker shoots after flowering to maintain vigor. Propagate by semi-ripe cuttings in summer.
Z. pulverulenta illus. p.138.

ZEPHYRANTHES

Rain lily, Windflower

AMARYLLIDACEAE

Genus of clump-forming bulbs with an erect, crocuslike flower on each stem. Needs a sheltered, sunny site and open, well-drained but moist soil. Container-grown bulbs need a dryish warm period after foliage dies down in summer, followed by copious amounts of water to stimulate flowering. Propagate by seed in autumn or in spring.
Z. atamasco (Atamasco lily). Clump-forming, early summer-flowering bulb. H 6–10in (15–25cm), S 3–4in (8–10cm). Basal leaves are very narrow, grasslike, and semi-erect. Each stem produces a widely funnel-shaped, purple-tinged white flower, opening to 4in (10cm) wide, in spring or summer. Z7–10 H12–10.
Z. candida illus. p.437.
Z. carinata. See *Z. grandiflora.*
Z. citrina. Clump-forming, autumn-flowering bulb. H 4–6in (10–15cm), S 2–3in (5–8cm). Has rushlike, erect, basal green leaves. Stems produce funnel-shaped, bright yellow flowers, opening to 1½–2in (4–5cm) wide, in autumn. Z7–10 h10–7.
Z. grandiflora, syn. *Z. carinata, Z. rosea* of gardens, illus. p.424.
Z. robusta. See *Habranthus robustus.*
Z. rosea. Clump-forming, autumn-flowering bulb. H 6–8in (15–20cm), S 3–4in (8–10cm). Has semi-erect, grasslike, basal green leaves. Stems produce short-tubed, funnel-shaped pink flowers. Z7–10 H12–10.
Z. rosea of gardens. See *Z. grandiflora.*

ZIGADENUS

LILIACEAE/MELANTHIACEAE

Genus of summer-flowering bulbs with spikes of star-shaped, 6-petaled flowers. It requires a position in sun or

partial shade and well-drained soil. Water copiously in spring and summer when in growth; less at other times. Remains dormant in winter. Propagate by division in early spring or by seed in autumn or spring. All parts are highly toxic if ingested.
Z. elegans. Clump-forming, summer-flowering bulb. H 12–20in (30–50cm), S 4–6in (10–15cm). Bears long, narrowly strap-shaped, semi-erect, basal leaves. Every stem produces a spike of greenish white flowers, each ½in (1cm) wide and with a yellowish green nectary near the base of every petal. Z5–9 H9–5.
Z. fremontii illus. p.420.
Z. nuttallii. Clump-forming, summer-flowering bulb. H 12–24in (30–60cm), S 3in (8cm). Narrowly strap-shaped, semi-erect, basal leaves are mid- to dark green. Produces dense spikes of numerous, tiny, creamy yellow flowers, each ¼–⅜in (6–8mm) across. Z6–9 H9–6.

ZINNIA

ASTERACEAE/COMPOSITAE

Genus of annuals with large, dahlialike flower heads that are excellent for cutting. Requires a position in sun and in fertile, well-drained soil. Dead flower heads should be removed regularly to promote flowering. Propagate by seed sown under cover in early spring.
***Z. angustifolia* 'Orange Star'.** See *Z. haageana* 'Orange Star'. **'Persian Carpet'** see *Z. haageana* 'Persian Carpet'.
Z. elegans. Moderately fast-growing, upright, sturdy annual. H 2–2½ft (60–75cm), S 1ft (30cm). Bears oval to lance-shaped leaves that are pale or midgreen. Dahlialike purple flower heads, over 2in (5cm) wide, are produced in summer and early autumn. Hybrids of *Z. elegans* are available in shades of yellow, red, pink, purple, cream, or white. All H12–1.
'Belvedere' illus. p.338.
Cactus-flowered Group, H 24–36in (60–90cm), have large, semi-double flower heads, similar to those of cactus dahlias, with long, narrow, quilled petals in a broad range of colors.
Dreamland Series, H 8–10in (20–25cm), are compact and good for growing in containers or for bedding.
'Envy' illus. p.335.
Hobgoblin Series, H to 18in (45cm), produce sturdy, bushy plants with small, single, weather-resistant flower heads in a broad range of colors.
Peter Pan Series, H 8in (20cm), are very dwarf, with double flower heads in a wide range of colors.
Ruffles Series (mixed) illus. p.329, (scarlet) illus. p.328.
Short Stuff Series, H 10in (25cm), are dwarf, with double flower heads in a broad range of colors.
Small World Series, H to 18in (45cm), are dwarf and produce long-lasting, double flower heads in an extensive range of colors, including pale pink.
'State Fair', H to 30in (75cm), is vigorous and produces large, double lavender, rose-pink, orange, purple, or scarlet flower heads.
Thumbelina Series illus. p.322.
***Z. haageana* 'Classic'.** See *Z.h.* 'Orange Star'. **'Orange Star'** (syn. *Z. angustifolia* 'Orange Star', *Z. haageana* 'Classic') illus p.341.
'Persian Carpet' (syn. *Z. angustifolia* 'Persian Carpet') is a moderately fast-growing, upright, dwarf annual. H 15in (38cm), S 12in (30cm). Pale-green leaves are lance-shaped and hairy. Small, weather-resistant, dahlialike, double flower heads, opening to over 1in (2.5cm) wide, are produced through the summer in a range of colors. H12-1.

ZIZANIA

GRAMINEAE/POACEAE

See also GRASSES, BAMBOOS, RUSHES, and SEDGES.
Z. aquatica (Canada wild rice). Annual, grasslike, marginal water plant. H 10ft (3m), S 18in (45cm). Has grass-like, midgreen leaves and, in summer, grasslike, pale green flowers followed by ricelike seeds that attract waterfowl. Needs sun; suitable for up to 9in (23cm) deep water. Propagate from seed stored damp and sown in spring. Z3–9 H9–1.

Zygocactus truncatus. See *Schlumbergera truncata.*

ZYGOPETALUM

See also ORCHIDS.
Z. mackaii, syn. *Z. mackayi* (illus. p.298). Evergreen, epiphytic orchid for growing in a cool or intermediate greenhouse. H 12in (30cm). In autumn produces long sprays of fragrant, brown-blotched green flowers, 3in (8cm) across, with reddish indigo veins and white lips. Ribbed leaves are narrowly oval and 12in (30cm) long. Requires semi-shade in summer.
Z. mackayi. See *Z. mackaii.*
***Z.* Perrenoudii** (illus. p.298). Evergreen, epiphytic orchid for a cool or intermediate greenhouse. H 12in (30cm). Spikes of fragrant, violet-purple-lipped, dark brown flowers, 3in (8cm) across, are produced in winter. Has narrowly oval, ribbed leaves, 12in (30cm) long. Requires a position in semi-shade in summer. Z14–15 H12–6.

INDEX OF COMMON NAMES

B

D

E

F

G

H

I

J

K

L

M

N

O

P

Q

R

S

T

U

Z

Glossary of Terms

Terms printed in *italics* refer to other glossary entries.

Acidic [of soil]. With a *pH* value of less than 7; see also *alkaline* and *neutral*.
Adventitious [of roots]. Arising directly from a stem or leaf.
Aerial root. See *root*.
Air-layering. A method of propagation by which a portion of stem is induced to root by enclosing it in a suitable medium such as damp moss and securing it with plastic wrap or similar material; roots will form if the moss is kept moist.
Alkaline [of soil]. With a *pH* value of more than 7; some plants will not tolerate alkaline soils and must be grown in *neutral* or *acidic* soil.
Alpine house. A minimally heated greenhouse, used for the cultivation of mainly alpine and bulbous plants, that provides greater ventilation and usually more light than a conventional greenhouse.
Alternate [of leaves]. Borne singly at each *node*, on either side of a stem.
Annual. A plant that completes its life cycle, from germination through to flowering and seeding and then death, in one growing season.
Anther. The part of a *stamen* that produces pollen; it is usually borne on a *filament*.
Apex. The tip or growing point of an organ such as a leaf or shoot.
Areole. A modified, cushionlike *tubercle*, peculiar to the family Cactaceae, that bears hairs, spines, leaves, side branches, and/or flowers.
Asclepiad. A member of the family Asclepiadaceae, e.g. *Asclepias*, *Hoya*, *Stephanotis*.
Auricle. An earlike lobe such as is sometimes found at the base of a leaf.
Awn. A stiff, bristlelike projection commonly found on grass seeds and *spikelets*.
Axil. The angle between a leaf and stem where an axillary bud develops.
Bedding plant. A plant that is mass-planted to provide a temporary display.
Biennial. A plant that flowers, seeds, and dies in the second season after germination, producing only stems, roots, and leaves in the first season.
Blade. The flattened and often broad part of a leaf.
Bloom. 1. A flower or blossom. 2. A fine, waxy, whitish or bluish white coating on stems, leaves, or fruits.
Bog garden. An area where the soil is kept permanently damp but not waterlogged.
Bolt. To produce flowers and seed prematurely, particularly in the case of vegetables such as lettuce and beet.
Bonsai. A method of producing dwarf trees or shrubs by special techniques that include pruning roots, pinching out shoots, removing growth buds, and training branches and stems.
Bract. A modified leaf at the base of a flower or flower cluster. Bracts may resemble normal leaves or be reduced and scalelike in appearance; they are often large and brightly colored.
Bud. A rudimentary or condensed shoot containing embryonic leaves or flowers.
Bulb. A storage organ consisting mainly of fleshy scales and swollen, modified leaf bases on a much reduced stem. Bulbs usually, but not always, grow underground.
Bulbil. A small, *bulb*-like organ, often borne in a leaf *axil*, occasionally in a *flower head*; it may be used for propagation.
Bulblet. A small *bulb* produced at the base of a mature one.
Burr. 1. A prickly or spiny *fruit*, or aggregate of fruits. 2. A woody outgrowth on the stems of certain trees.
Cactus (pl. cacti). A member of the family Cactaceae, often *succulent* and spiny.
Calyx (pl. calyces). The outer part of a flower, usually small and green but sometimes showy and brightly colored, that encloses the petals in bud and is formed from the *sepals*.
Capsule. A dry *fruit* that splits open when ripe to release its seeds.
Carpel. The female portion of a flower, or part of it, consisting of an *ovary*, *stigma* and *style*.
Catkin. A flower cluster, normally pendulous. Flowers lack petals, are often stalkless, are surrounded by scale-like *bracts*, and are usually unisexual (male or female only).
Caudex (pl. caudices). The stem base of a woody plant such as a *palm* or tree fern.
Cladode. A stem, often flattened, with the function and appearance of a leaf.
Claw. The narrow, basal portion of petals in some genera, e.g. *Dianthus*.
Climber. A plant that climbs using other plants or objects as a support: a **leaf-stalk** climber by coiling its leaf stalks around supports; a **root** climber by producing aerial, supporting roots; a **self-clinging** climber by means of suckering pads; a **tendril** climber by coiling its tendrils; a **twining** climber by coiling stems. **Scandent**, **scrambling**, and **trailing climbers** produce long stems that grow over plants or other supports; they attach themselves only loosely, if at all.
Clone. A group of genetically identical plants, propagated vegetatively.
Compound. Made up of several or many parts, e.g. a leaf divided into 2 or more *leaflets*.
Cone. The clustered flowers or woody, seed-bearing structures of a conifer.
Coppice. To cut back to near ground level each year in order to produce vigorous, ornamental shoots, as is done with some *Cornus* and *Eucalyptus*.
Cordon. A trained plant restricted in growth to one main stem, occasionally 2–4 stems.
Corm. A *bulb*-like, underground storage organ consisting mainly of a swollen stem base and often surrounded by a papery tunic.
Cormlet. A small *corm* arising at the base of a mature one.
Corolla. The part of a flower formed by the petals.
Corona (crown). A petal-like outgrowth sometimes borne on the *corolla*, e.g. the trumpet or cup of a *Narcissus*.
Corymb. A racemose flower cluster in which the inner flower stalks are shorter than the outer, resulting in a rounded or flat-topped head.
Cotyledon. See *seed leaf*.
Creeper. A plant that grows close to the ground, usually rooting as it spreads.
Crisped. Minutely wavy-edged.
Crown. 1. The part of the plant at or just below the soil surface from which new shoots are produced and to which they die back in autumn. 2. The upper, branched part of a tree above the *bole*. 3. A *corona*.
Culm. The usually hollow stem of a grass or bamboo.
Cutting. A section of a plant that is removed and used for propagation. The various types of cutting are: **basal** – taken from the base of a plant (usually *herbaceous*) as it begins to produce growth in spring; **greenwood** – made from the tip of young growth; **hardwood** – mature wood taken at the end of the growing season; **leaf** – a detached leaf or part of a leaf; **root** – part of a semi-mature or mature root; **semi-ripe** – half-ripened wood taken during the growing season; **softwood** – young growth taken at the beginning of the growing season; **stem** – a greenwood, hardwood, semi-ripe or softwood cutting; **tip** – a greenwood cutting.
Cyme. A flower cluster in which each growing point terminates in a flower.
Deadhead. To remove spent flower heads so as to promote further growth or flowering, prevent seeding, or improve appearance.
Deciduous. Losing its leaves annually at the end of the growing season; **semi-deciduous** plants lose only some leaves.
Decumbent. Growing close to the ground but ascending at the tips.
Dentate. With toothed margins.
Dieback. Death of the tips of shoots due to frost or disease.
Dioecious. Bearing male and female flowers on separate plants.
Disbud. To remove surplus buds to promote larger flowers or fruits.
Disk floret, disk flower. A small and often individually inconspicuous, usually tubular flower, one of many that make up the central portion of a composite flower head such as a daisy.
Division. A method of propagation by which a clump is divided into several parts during dormancy.
Elliptic [of leaves]. Broadening in the center and narrowing towards each end.
Entire [of leaves]. With untoothed margins.
Epiphyte. A plant that in nature grows on the surface of another without being parasitic.
Evergreen. Retaining its leaves at the end of the growing season, although losing some older leaves regularly throughout the year; **semi-evergreen** plants retain only some leaves or lose older leaves only when the new growth is produced.
F1 hybrid. The first generation derived from crossing 2 distinct plants, usually when the parents are pure-bred lines and the offspring are vigorous. Seed from F1 hybrids does not come *true*.
Fall. An outer *perianth segment* of an iris, which projects outward or downward from the inner segments.
Fan palm. A *palm* with *palmate* rather than *pinnate* leaves.
Farina. A powdery, white, sometimes yellowish deposit naturally occurring on some leaves and flowers.
Fibrous root. A fine, young root, usually one of many.
Filament. The stalk of an *anther*.
Floret. A single flower in a head of many flowers.
Flower. The basic flower forms are: **single**, with one row of usually 4–6 *petals*; **semi-double**, with more petals, usually in 2 rows; **double**, with many petals in several rows and few or no *stamens*; **fully double**, usually rounded in shape, with densely packed petals and the stamens absent or obscured.
Flower head. A mass of small *flowers* or *florets* that together appear as one flower, e.g. a daisy.
Force. To induce artificially the early production of growth, flowers, or *fruits*.
Frond. The leaflike organ of a fern. Some ferns produce both barren and fertile fronds, the fertile fronds bearing *spores*.
Fruit. The structure in plants that bears one or more ripe seeds, e.g. a berry or nut.
Glabrous. Not hairy.
Glaucous. Bluish white, bluish green or bluish gray.
Globose. Spherical.
Glochid. One of the barbed bristles or hairs, usually small, borne on a cactus *areole*.
Grafting. A method of propagation by which an artificial union is made between different parts of individual plants; usually the *shoot* (scion) of one is grafted onto the *rootstock* (stock) of another.
Heel. The small portion of old wood that is retained at the base of a cutting when it is removed from the stem.
Herbaceous. Dying down at the end of the growing season.
Hose-in-hose [of flowers]. With one *corolla* borne inside another, forming a double or semi-double *flower*.
Inflorescence. A cluster of flowers with a distinct arrangement, e.g. *corymb*, *cyme*, *panicle*, *raceme*, *spike*, *umbel*.
Insectivorous plant. A plant that traps and digests insects and other small animals to supplement its nutrient intake.
Key. A winged seed such as is produced by maples (*Acer*)
Lateral. A side growth that arises from the side of a shoot or root.
Layering. A method of propagation by which a stem is induced to root by being pegged down into the soil while it is still attached to the parent plant. See also *air-layering*.
Leaflet. The subdivision of a compound leaf.
Lenticel. A small, usually corky area on a stem or other part of a plant, which acts as a breathing pore.
Lime. Compounds of calcium; the amount of lime in soil determines whether it is *alkaline*, *neutral,* or *acidic*.
Linear [of leaves]. Very narrow with parallel sides.

Lip. A lobe consisting of 2 or more flat or sometimes pouched *perianth segments*.
Loam. Well-structured, fertile soil that is moisture-retentive but free-draining.
Marginal water plant. A plant that grows partially submerged in shallow water or in moist soil at the edge of a pond.
Midrib. The main, central vein of a leaf or the central stalk to which the *leaflets* of a *pinnate* leaf are attached.
Monocarpic. Flowering and fruiting only once before dying; such plants may take several years to reach flowering size.
Mulch. A layer of organic matter applied to the soil over or around a plant to conserve moisture, protect the roots from heaving, reduce the growth of weeds, and enrich the soil.
Naturalize. To establish and grow as if in the wild.
Nectar. A sweet, sugary liquid secreted by the **nectary** – glandular tissue usually found in the flower but sometimes found on the leaves or stems.
Neutral [of soil]. With a *pH* value of 7, the point at which soil is neither *acidic* nor *alkaline*.
Node. The point on a stem from which a leaf or leaves arise.
Offset. A small plant that arises by natural vegetative reproduction, usually at the base of the mother plant.
Opposite [of leaves]. Borne 2 to each *node*, one opposite the other.
Ovary. The part of the female portion of the flower, containing embryonic seeds, that will eventually form the *fruit*.
Palm. An evergreen *tree* or *shrub*-like plant, normally single-stemmed, with *palmate* or *pinnate* leaves usually in terminal rosettes; strictly a member of the family Palmae.
Palmate. Lobed in the fashion of a hand, strictly with 5 lobes arising from the same point.
Pan. A shallow, free-draining pot in which alpine plants or bulbs are grown.
Panicle. A branched *raceme*.
Papilla (pl. papillae). A minute protuberance or glandlike structure.
Pea-like [of flowers]. Of the same structure as a pea flower.
Pedicel. The stalk of an individual flower.
Peduncle. The stalk of a flower cluster.
Peltate [of leaves]. Shield-shaped, with the stalk inserted toward or at the centre of the blade and not at the margin.
Perennial. Living for at least 3 seasons. In this book the term when used as a noun, and unless qualified, denotes an *herbaceous* perennial. A woody-based perennial dies down only partially, leaving a woody stem at the base.
Perianth. The outer parts of the flower consisting of the *calyx* and the *corolla*. The term is often used when the calyx and the corolla are very similar in form.
Perianth segment. One portion of the *perianth*, resembling a *petal* and sometimes known as a tepal.
Petal. One portion of the often showy and colored part of the *corolla*. In some families, e.g. Liliaceae, the *perianth segments* are petal-like and referred to horticulturally as petals.
Petaloid. Like a petal.
Petiole. The stalk of a *leaf*.
pH. The scale by which the acidity or alkalinity of soil is measured. See also *acid*, *alkaline*, *neutral*.
Phyllode. A flattened leaf stalk, which functions as and resembles a leaf.
Pinch out. To remove the growing tips of a plant to induce the production of side-shoots.
Pinna (pl. pinnae). The primary division of a *pinnate* leaf. The fertile pinnae of ferns produce *spores*; vegetative pinnae do not.
Pinnate [of leaves]. Compound, with *leaflets* arranged on opposite sides of a central stalk.
Pistil. The female part of a flower consisting of the *ovary*, *stigma*, and *style*.
Pollard [of a tree]. To cut back to its main branches in order to restrict growth.
Pollination. The transfer of pollen from the *anthers* to the *stigma* of the same or different flowers, resulting in the fertilization of the embryonic seeds in the *ovary*.
Procumbent. Prostrate, creeping along the ground.
Raceme. An unbranched flower cluster with several or many stalked flowers borne singly along a main axis, the youngest at the apex.
Ray floret, ray flower. One of the flowers, usually with strap-shaped petals, that together form the outer ring of flowers in a composite *flower head* such as a daisy.
Ray petal. The petal or fused petals, often showy, of a ray *floret*.
Recurved. Curved backward.
Reflexed. Bent sharply backward.
Revert. To return to its original state, as when a plain green leaf is produced on a variegated plant.
Rhizome. An underground, creeping stem that acts as a storage organ and bears leafy shoots.
Root. The part of a plant, normally underground, that functions as anchorage and through which water and nutrients are absorbed. An **aerial root** emerges from the stem at some distance above the soil level.
Rootball. The roots and accompanying soil or soil mix visible when a plant is lifted.
Rootstock. A well-rooted plant onto which a scion is grafted; see *grafting*.
Rosette. A group of leaves radiating from approximately the same point, often borne at ground level at the base of a very short stem.
Runner. A horizontally spreading, usually slender stem that forms roots at each node, often confused with *stolon*.
Scale. 1. A reduced or modified leaf. 2. Part of a conifer *cone*.
Scandent. See *climber*.
Scarify. To scar the coat of a seed by abrasion in order to speed water intake and hence germination.
Scion. See *grafting*.
Scree. An area composed of a deep layer of stone chips mixed with a small amount of soil. It provides extremely sharp drainage for plants that resent moisture at their base.
Seed head. Any usually dry *fruit* that contains ripe seeds.
Seed leaf/leaves (cotyledon[s]). The first leaf, pair of leaves, or occasionally group of leaves produced by a seed as it germinates.
Self-seed. To produce seedlings around the parent plant.
Sepal. Part of a *calyx*, usually insignificant but sometimes showy.
Series. The name applied to a group of similar but not identical plants, usually annuals, linked by one or more common features.
Sessile. Without a stalk.
Sheath. A cylindrical structure that surrounds or encircles, partially or fully, another plant organ such as a stem.
Shoot. The aerial part of a plant which bears leaves. A **side-shoot** arises from the side of a main shoot.
Shrub. A plant with *woody stems*, usually well-branched from or near the base.
Shy-flowering. Reluctant to flower; producing few flowers.
Simple [of leaves]. Not divided into leaflets.
Soft-stemmed. The opposite of *woody-stemmed*.
Spadix (pl. spadices). A *spike*-like flower cluster that is usually fleshy and bears numerous small flowers. Spadices are characteristic of the family Araceae, e.g. *Arisaema*.
Spathe. A large *bract*, or sometimes two, frequently colored and showy, that surrounds a *spadix* (as in *Arisaema*) or an individual flower bud (as in *Narcissus*).
Sphagnum. Mosses common to bogs; their moisture-retentive character makes them ideal components of some growing media.
Spike. A racemose flower cluster with several or many unstalked flowers borne along a common axis.
Spikelet. 1. The flowering unit of grasses consisting of one or several flowers with basal *bracts*. 2. A small *spike*, part of a branched flower cluster.
Spore. The minute reproductive structure of flowerless plants, e.g. ferns, fungi and mosses.
Sporangium (pl. sporangia). A body that produces *spores*.
Sport. A mutation, caused by an accidental or induced change in the genetic makeup of a plant, which gives rise to a shoot with different characteristics to those of the parent plant.
Spur. 1. A hollow projection from a petal, often producing *nectar*. 2. A short stem bearing a group of flower buds, such as is found on apple and pear trees.
Spur back. To cut back side-shoots to within 2 or 3 buds of the main shoot.
Stamen. The *anther* and *filament*.
Standard. 1. A *tree* or *shrub* with a clear length of bare stem below the first branches. Certain shrubs, e.g. roses and fuchsias, may be trained to form standards. 2. One of the 3 inner and often erect *perianth segments* of the iris flower. 3. The larger, usually upright back petal of a flower in the family Leguminosae, e.g. *Lathyrus*.
Stapeliad. A member of the genus *Stapelia* and closely related genera of the family Asclepiadaceae.
Stem segment. A portion of a jointed stem between 2 *nodes*, most frequently occurring in cacti.
Sterile. Infertile, not bearing *spores*, pollen, seeds etc.
Stigma. The part of the female portion of the flower, borne at the tip of the *style*, that receives pollen.
Stipule. A small scale- or leaflike appendage, usually one of a pair, mostly borne at a *node* or below a leaf stalk.
Stock. See *rootstock*.
Stolon. A horizontally spreading or arching stem, usually above ground, which roots at its tip to produce a new plant.
Stop. To remove certain growing points of a plant to control growth or the size and number of flowers.
Stratify. To break the dormancy of some seeds by exposing them to a period of cold.
Style. The part of the flower on which the *stigma* is borne.
Sub-globose. Almost spherical.
Subshrub. A plant that is woody at the base, although the terminal shoots die back in winter.
Succulent. A plant with thick, fleshy leaves and/or stems; in this book, it is evergreen unless otherwise stated.
Sucker. A shoot that arises from below ground level, directly from the *root* or *rootstock*.
Summer-deciduous. Losing its leaves naturally in summer.
Taproot. The main, downward-growing root of a plant; it is also applied generally to any strong, downward-growing root.
Tendril. A threadlike structure, used to provide support; see also *climber*.
Tooth. A small, marginal, often pointed lobe on a leaf, *calyx* or *corolla*.
Tepal. See *perianth segment*.
Tree. A woody plant usually having a well-defined trunk or stem with a head of branches above.
Trifoliate. With 3 leaves; loosely, with 3 *leaflets*.
Trifoliolate. With 3 *leaflets*.
True [of seedlings]. Retaining the distinctive characteristics of the parent when raised from seed.
Tuber. A thickened, usually underground, storage organ derived from a stem or root.
Tubercle. A small, rounded protuberance; see also *areole*.
Turion. 1. A bud on a *rhizome*. 2. A fleshy, overwintering bud found on certain water plants.
Umbel. A usually flat-topped or rounded flower cluster in which the individual flower stalks arise from a central point. In a compound umbel, each primary stalk ends in an umbel.
Upright [of habit]. With vertical or semi-vertical main branches.
Water bud. See *turion*.
Whorl. The arrangement of 3 or more organs arising from the same point.
Winged [of seeds or fruits]. Having a marginal flange or membrane.
Woody-stemmed. With a stem composed of woody fibers and therefore persistent, as opposed to soft-stemmed and *herbaceous*. A **semi-woody stem** contains some softer tissue and may be only partially persistent.
x The sign used to denote a hybrid plant derived from the crossing of two or more botanically distinct plants.
+ The sign used to denote a graft hybrid; see *grafting*.

Acknowledgments

1	4	7	10
2	5	8	11
3	6	9	12

The publisher would like to thank the following for their kind permission to reproduce their photographs. Most of the photographs are found in The Plant Catalog and are referenced by two numbers: the page number is given first, followed by the specific number or numbers of the photographs separated by hyphens. The photograph number is determined by the position of the photograph's caption according to one of two page grids. The twelve grid is shown alongside. The same numbering principle has been used for photographs in the feature panels, with numbers from 1 to 42; illustrations elsewhere in the book use the key: A=above; B=below; C=center; L=left; R=right; T=top.

Alpine Garden Society Slide Library 288/41, 334/5, 348/4–9, 354/3, 356/11, 362/3, 364/10, 373/9, 375/12, 378/6, 379/5, 383/5, 388/3, 396/10, 400/3, 428/13, 429/2–26, 435/1, 436/9
Jacques Amand Ltd/John Amand 236/5–26, 289/42, 431/24
Aylett Nurseries 406/7
A–Z Botanical Collection 144/26, 175/9, 196/6, 199/10, 218/11, 234/35, 242/35, 282/7, 347/6, 374/2, 404/31, 447/2–10, 448/6; Malcolm Richards 13/Row4/1; A. Young 13/Row5/2
Gillian Beckett 119/1, 123/2–3, 132/21, 140/5, 145/1, 150/5, 154/4, 155/7, 157/12, 168/12, 171/1, 174/11, 219/6, 250/4, 251/4, 254/12, 256/1, 264/1, 273/12, 290/5, 292/3, 311/4, 313/10, 320/1, 348/5, 354/11, 356/12, 360/2, 361/1, 363/1, 367/11, 368/12, 373/1, 374/8–9, 377/6, 378/1, 381/10, 383/2, 385/3, 389/1, 402/9, 405/5–33, 412/3–6, 413/3–6, 414/10, 415/3, 417/21–38, 421/3, 423/6, 431/37, 432/2–3, 433/8, 434/1, 435/7, 439/9–10, 440/3–7, 446/6, 448/7–9
Kenneth A. Beckett 77/4, 206/3, 366/2, 368/4
Biofotos/Heather Angel 205/8, 448/12
Patrick Booth/John Thirkell 230/26–37–38
Ann & Roger Bowden 288/35, 289/15
Christopher Brickell 89/4, 100/1, 131/2–4, 132/17, 133/4–25, 134/6, 135/1, 142/12, 147/4, 148/1–5, 165/22, 205/4
Pat Brindley 136/4, 208/12, 210/7, 215/4, 235/5, 237/20, 242/26, 248/30, 295/19, 313/4, 320/2, 321/8, 322/11, 324/8–12, 325/1, 326/10, 328/1–12, 329/1, 331/6, 332/3–4, 333/9, 336/4, 341/6, 399/5, 410/23, 411/8–41, 412/13–17–27–31, 429/7–29–37, 448/8
British Iris Society 235/2–14–20
Jonathan Buckley 129/2
Brinsley Burbridge 209/12
Ray Cobb 429/9
Eric Crichton 65/5, 70/4, 71/2, 93/1, 97/3, 99/10, 143/3, 157/9, 168/4, 177/11, 208/10, 215/1, 231/3, 234/7–15–29, 238/3, 243/1, 255/1–10, 282/10, 313/9, 320/10, 324/7, 338/7, 349/9, 354/10, 355/1, 357/9, 358/3, 369/1, 375/3, 379/1, 382/9, 383/3, 387/3, 396/7, 407/9, 410/17, 419/11, 420/1, 429/31, 450/31
Philip Damp 406/33
Kate Donald 416/21–28
Alan M. Edwards 418/2, 428/17
Raymond Evison 212/27–31–32–39, 213/12–13–14–15–17–18–33–35–41
John Fielding 37/BR, 40/BL, 48/TL, 50/TL, 51/TR, 53/TR
Valerie Finnis 354/7
Ron & Christine Foord 272/11
Maureen Foster 235/13
John Galbally 281/10
Garden Picture Library Brian Carter 44/TR; Eric Crichton 442&443; Geoff Dann 44/CR; Ron Evans 112&113, 342&343; John Glover 180&181, 222&223, 248/37, 253/10, 317/BC, 344/TC; Neil Holmes 204/6, 206/4, 237/19; Mayer/Le Scanff 445/BR; Jerry Pavia 314&315, 344&345/T, 452&453; Morley Read 43/TR; Howard Rice 331/12, 395/L; JS Sira 39/BR, 45/TL, 183/TL; Ron Sutherland 345/BL; Brigitte Thomas 40&41/T; Steven Wooster 182/CL, 200&201, 202/BL
John Glover 131/3, 134/27, 158/8, 242/42, 249/9, 286/1, 441/3
Derek Gould 116/11, 124/11, 134/4, 135/4, 144/40, 150/6, 153/6, 157/10, 170/2, 205/10, 208/7, 218/6, 233/7, 236/21, 240/4, 241/3–6–8, 249/1, 253/12, 258/11, 268/12, 272/34, 277/6, 279/8, 290/3, 334/11, 347/2, 359/7, 386/7, 390/4, 397/7, 412/11, 415/8, 427/3, 447/7
Diana Grenfell 257/6–10, 289/18
Christopher Grey–Wilson 10/BL
Peter Harkness 198/3–4
Jerry Harpur 55/BL, 55/TR
The Heather Society Slide Library 13/Row5/3, 178/12
Terry Hewitt 456/9, 472/2, 474/2, 480/1
D. Hewlett 407/23
Muriel Hodgeman 353/11, 359/10, 383/12, 385/1
Hortico 418/15
International Flower Bulb Centre 399/7, 431/35
Mike Ireland 367/2, 374/3, 377/7, 429/4–38
Brita Johansson 179/22
Roy Lancaster 11/C–CR
Andrew Lawson 2, 36/C, 38/T, 49/B, 57/T, 60&61, 114/BR, 182&183/B, 205/9, 324/1, 392&393, 404/11–16, 405/3–30
Sidney Linnegar 234/4 (G.E. Cassidy)–11 (R. Henley)–31 (R. Henley)–37 (G.E. Cassidy), 235/3–34 (G.E. Cassidy)– 40 (G.E. Cassidy)
Brian Mathew 402/3, 414/11, 419/1–4, 421/9, 423/11, 424/3, 426/9, 434/11
S. & O. Mathews 151/7
Dr E. Charles Nelson 13/Row2/2–Row3/1
Oxford Scientific Films/Fredrik Ehrenstrom 449/11
Photos Horticultural 105/3, 204/3, 231/12, 234/10, 237/1, 242/18–21, 277/3, 329/3, 335/5, 405/11, 424/2
Plant Pictures Worldwide 339/2
Collection & Photo Riviere (France, 26 Drôme) 236/19, 237/23–36
Howard Rice 14&15, 34&35, 206/5, 444&445/B
Royal Botanic Gardens, Kew 11/TR
Royal Horticultural Society, Lindley Library 11BL Curtis's Botanical Magazine (CBM), cliv (1928), T.9241; 417 CBM, vii (1794), T.252
A.D. Schilling 83/10, 90/11, 132/4, 166/8, 169/9
Harry Smith Collection 13/Row1/1, 65/6, 69/3–12, 70/1, 71/4–10, 72/7–10, 75/7–22–36, 80/4–11(inset), 81/3, 82/6–8, 83/9, 89/6, 91/1–6, 92/3–12, 93/2–6–7–9, 95/8, 97/4–6, 102/1, 104/3–12, 106/9, 108/8–12, 109/6, 111/33, 116/7, 117/1–6, 118/11, 119/4, 121/11, 123/1, 124/1–7, 125/6, 126/9, 129/26–32, 130/12, 131/5–11, 132/20–22–27–32–35, 133/16, 134/16, 135/2, 141/4, 142/7, 143/5, 145/9, 146/7, 147/2–5–12, 148/10, 149/2, 150/1, 151/11, 154/7, 155/3–6, 158/12, 159/25, 160/6, 164/24–36, 165/12, 167/8–10, 170/10, 171/3, 172/6, 173/5–6–12, 177/7, 196/8, 199/1–2–3, 204/10, 206/7, 207/3, 208/1–9, 209/3–9, 210/1–5–6, 211/2–3–7, 214/2–3–4, 217/2–12, 218/8–10, 219/2–3, 220/12, 221/26, 226/3, 228/9, 230/19–35–40, 231/9, 232/1–5, 235/4–23, 236/15, 237/17–18–37, 238/10, 242/13–19–29, 244/11, 248/33–40, 254/6, 257/16, 258/9, 263/9–10, 266/1, 268/8, 269/7, 270/1–4, 271/8, 273/1–4–18, 275/12, 278/6, 282/1–9, 283/12, 286/4, 287/6, 288/26–38, 293/6–10, 295/19, 319/10–12, 320/4, 321/4–9, 327/1, 329/11, 330/4, 331/3–4–5–7, 332/12, 334/3–4–6–7, 338/10, 339/4–8–9, 340/9, 341/4–8–9, 347/1–5, 349/2–10, 351/9, 352/6, 356/9, 357/6, 360/1–4–7, 361/4, 364/5–12, 365/9, 366/11, 368/10, 369/9–11, 371/6–7–8–10, 373/2, 375/5–9, 380/12, 381/5, 383/1–7, 386/8–9, 387/8–12, 388/4, 391/6, 397/4, 398/2, 399/14–26–32–37, 400/1–2, 401/12, 402/5, 403/12, 404/12–15–17–18–19, 405/10–12–19–40, 408/1–6, 409/6, 411/32, 412/5–38, 413/12, 414/6, 415/6, 420/7, 421/6, 422/7–9, 423/1, 424/9, 425/1–11, 426/7, 427/12, 428/16–28–30–42, 429/8–16–34, 430/10, 432/1–4–11, 434/9, 435/3, 436/1–7–10, 437/11, 438/1–4, 439/4, 440/2–11, 441/4–7–10, 447/3–4–12, 449/7–10, 450/11, 467/7, 475/10
Suttons Seeds 327/4
Thompson & Morgan 333/12, 335/6, 336/1
Unwin Seeds Ltd 322/12, 326/9, 328/9, 331/9, 332/1, 336/3, 340/3
Van Staaveren Aalsmeer BV 425/12
W.B. Wade 260/6–13–29–30–33–38, 261/ 6–13–16–18–21–22– 27–28
Jack Wemyss–Cooke 273/13–14–35
John Wright 164/3, 165/10.

Jacket: **Jerry Harpur** front BR.

Picture research Andrew Brown, Susan Mennel
Picture research for the second edition Anna Lord

The publishers would like to thank all those who generously assisted the photographers and provided plants for photography, in particular the curators, directors, and staff of the following organizations and those private individuals listed below. Special thanks are due to those at the Royal Botanic Gardens, Kew, and the Royal Horticultural Society's Garden, Wisley, for their invaluable assistance and support.

African Violet Centre, Terrington St Clement, Norfolk; Ken Akers, Great Saling, Essex; Jacques Amand Ltd, Clamphill, Middx; Anmore Exotics, Havant, Hants; David Austin Roses, Albrighton, Shrops; Avon Bulbs, Bradford-on-Avon, Wilts; Ayletts Nurseries, St Albans, Herts; Steven Bailey Ltd, Sway, Hants; Bill Baker, Tidmarsh, Berks; Batsford Arboretum, Moreton-in-Marsh, Glos; Booker Seeds, Sleaford, Lincs; Rupert Bowlby, Reigate, Surrey; Bressingham Gardens, Diss, Norfolk; Roy Brooks, Newent, Glos; British Orchid Growers' Association; Broadleigh Gardens, Somerset; Burford House Gardens, Tenbury Wells, Shrops; Cambridge Bulbs, Newton, Cambs; Nola Carr, Sydney, Australia; Beth Chatto Gardens, Colchester, Essex; Chelsea Physic Garden, London; Colegrave Seeds, Banbury, Oxon; County Park Nurseries, Hornchurch, Essex; Jill Cowley, Chelmsford, Essex; Mrs Anne Dexter, Oxford; Edrom Nurseries, Coldingham, Berwicks; Dr Jack Elliott, Ashford, Kent; Joe Elliott, Broadwell, Glos; Erdigg (National Trust), Clwyd, Wales; Fibrex Nurseries, Pebworth, Warwicks; Fisk's Clematis Nursery, Westleton, Suffolk; Mr & Mrs Thomas Gibson, Westwell, Oxon; Glasgow Botanic Garden, Glasgow; 'Glazenwood', Braintree, Essex.

R. Harkness & Co. Ltd, Hitchin, Herts; Harry Hay, Lower Kingswood, Surrey; Hazeldene Nurseries, East Farleigh, Kent; Hidcote Manor (National Trust), Chipping Camden, Glos; Hillier Gardens and Arboretum, Romsey, Hants; Hillier Nurseries (Winchester) Ltd, Romsey, Hants; Holly Gate Cactus Nursery, Ashington, Sussex; Hopleys Plants, Much Hadham, Herts; Huntingdon Botanical Gardens, San Marino, California; W.E.Th. Ingwersen Ltd, East Grinstead, Sussex; the late Clive Innes; Kelways Nurseries, Langport, Somerset; Kiftsgate Court Gardens, Chipping Camden, Glos; Lechlade Fuchsia Centre, Lechlade, Glos; The Living Desert, Palm Desert, California; Robin Loder, Leonardslee, Sussex; Los Angeles State and County Arboreta and Botanical Gardens, Los Angeles, California; Lotusland Foundation, Santa Barbara, California; McBeans Orchids, Lewes, Sussex; Merrist Wood Agricultural College, Worplesdon, Surrey; Mrs J.F. Phillips, Westwell, Oxon; Mr & Mrs Richard Purdon, Ramsden, Oxon; Ramparts Nurseries, Colchester, Essex; Ratcliffe Orchids, Didcot, Oxon; Mrs Joyce Robinson, Denmans, Fontwell, Sussex; Peter Q. Rose, Castle Cary, Somerset; Royal Botanic Garden, Edinburgh; Royal Botanic Gardens, Kew, Surrey; Royal Botanic Gardens, Sydney, Australia; Royal National Rose Society, St Albans, Herts; Royal Horticultural Society's Garden, Wisley, Surrey.

Santa Barbara Botanic Garden, Santa Barbara, California; Savill Garden, Windsor, Berks; Mr & Mrs K. Schoenenberger, Shipton-under-Wychwood, Oxon; Mrs Martin Simmons, Burghclere, Berks; Dr James Smart, Barnstaple, Devon; Arthur Smith, Wigston, Leics; P.J. Smith, Ashington, Sussex; Springfields Gardens, Spalding, Lincs; Staite & Sons, Evesham, Worcs; Stapeley Water Gardens, Nantwich, Cheshire; Strybing Arboreta Society of Golden Gate Park, San Francisco, California; David Stuart, Dunbar, East Lothian; Suffolk Herbs, Sudbury, Suffolk; University Botanic Garden, Cambridge; University of British Columbia Botanical Garden, Vancouver; University of California Arboretum, Davis, California; University of California Arboretum, Santa Cruz, California; University of California Botanical Garden, Berkeley, California; University of California Botanical Gardens, Los Angeles, California; University of Reading Botanic Garden, Reading, Berks; Unwins Seeds Ltd, Histon, Cambridge; Jack Vass, Haywards Heath, Sussex; Rosemary Verey, Barnsley, Glos; Vesutor Air Plants, Ashington, Sussex; Wakehurst Place (Royal Botanic Gardens, Kew), Ardingly, Sussex; Primrose Warburg, Oxford; Waterperry Gardens, Wheatley, Oxon; Westonbirt Arboretum, Westonbirt, Glos; Woolman's Nurseries, Dorridge, West Midlands; Wyld Court Orchids, Newbury, Berks; Eric Young Orchid Foundation, Jersey, Channel Islands.

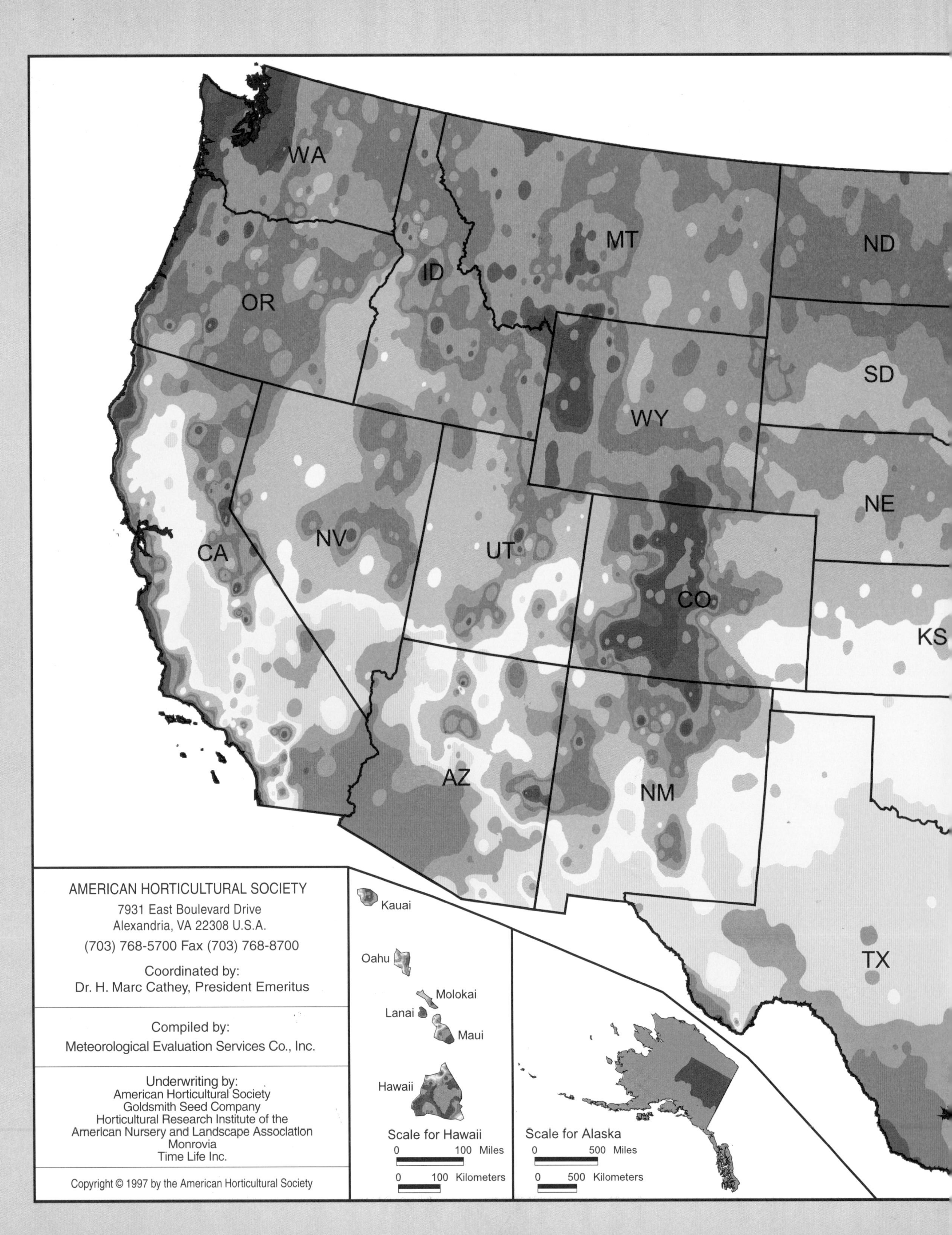

AMERICAN HORTICULTURAL SOCIETY
7931 East Boulevard Drive
Alexandria, VA 22308 U.S.A.
(703) 768-5700 Fax (703) 768-8700

Coordinated by:
Dr. H. Marc Cathey, President Emeritus

Compiled by:
Meteorological Evaluation Services Co., Inc.

Underwriting by:
American Horticultural Society
Goldsmith Seed Company
Horticultural Research Institute of the
American Nursery and Landscape Association
Monrovia
Time Life Inc.